THE ANNUAL DIRECTORY OF

American and Canadian Bed & Breakfasts

1996 Edition

Tracey Menges, *Compiler*

RUTLEDGE HILL PRESS
NASHVILLE, TENNESSEE

Published in Nashville, Tennessee, by Rutledge Hill Press, Inc., 211 Seventh Avenue North, Nashville, Tennessee 37219. Distributed in Canada by H. B. Fenn and Company, Ltd., 1090 Lorimar Drive, Mississauga, Ontario L5S 1R7. Distributed in the United Kingdom by Verulam Publishing, Ltd., 152a Park Street Lane, Park Street, St. Albans, Hertfordshire AL2 2AU.

Cover design and book design by Harriette Bateman

ISBN 1-55853-367-2; ISSN 1081-34545

Printed in the United States of America.

1 2 3 4 5 6—98 97 96 95

Contents

Introduction

The 1996 edition of *The Annual Directory of American and Canadian Bed & Breakfasts* is one of the most comprehensive directories available today. Whether planning your honeymoon, a family vacation or reunion, or a business trip (many bed and breakfasts provide conference facilities), you will find what you are looking for at a bed and breakfast. From a restored sea captain's home in Maine to an antebellum plantation in Mississippi. From an adobe hideaway in Santa Fe to a working farm in Iowa. From a lavish Victorian in San Francisco to a rustic cabin near the glaciers in Alaska. They are all here just waiting to be discovered.

Once you know your destination, look for it, or one close by, to see what accommodations are available. Each state has a general map with city locations to help you plan your trip efficiently. There are listings for all 50 states, Canada, Puerto Rico, and the Virgin Islands. Don't be surprised to find a listing in the remote spot you thought only you knew about. Even if your favorite hideaway isn't listed, you're sure to discover a new one.

How to Use This Guide

The sample listing below is typical of the entries in this directory. Each bed and breakfast is listed alphabetically by city and establishment name. The description provides an overview of the bed and breakfast and may include nearby activities and attractions. *Please note that the descriptions have been provided by the hosts. The publisher has not visited these bed and breakfasts and is not responsible for inaccuracies.*

Following the description are notes that have been designed for easy reference. Looking at the sample, a quick glance tells you that this bed and breakfast

GREAT TOWN _____

Favorite Bed and Breakfast

123 Main Street, 12345
(800) 555-1234

This quaint bed and breakfast is surrounded by five acres of award-winning landscaping and gardens. There are four guest rooms, each individually decorated with antiques.

It is close to antique shops, restaurants, and outdoor activities. Breakfast includes homemade specialties and is served in the formal dining room at guests' leisure. Minimum stay of two nights.

Hosts: Sue and Jim Smith
Rooms: 4 (2 PB; 2 SB) $65-80
Full Breakfast
Credit Cards: A, B
Notes: 2, 5, 8, 10, 11, 12, 13

has four guest rooms, two with private baths (PB) and two that share a bath (SB). The rates are for two people sharing one room. Tax may or may not be included. The specifics of "Credit Cards" and "Notes" are listed at the bottom of each page. For example, the letter A means that MasterCard is accepted. The number 10 means that tennis is available on the premises or within 10 to 15 miles.

In many cases, a bed and breakfast is listed with a reservation service that represents several houses in one area. This service is responsible for bookings and can answer other questions you may have. They also inspect each listing and can help you choose the best place for your needs.

Before You Arrive

Now that you have chosen the bed and breakfast that interests you, there are some things you need to find out. You should always make reservations in advance, and while you are doing so you should ask about the local taxes. City taxes can be an unwelcome surprise. Make sure there are accommodations for your children. If you have dietary needs or prefer nonsmoking rooms, find out if these requirements can be met. Ask about check-in times and cancellation policies. Get specific directions. Most bed and breakfasts are readily accessible, but many are a little out of the way.

When You Arrive

In many instances you are visiting someone's home. Be respectful of their property, their schedules, and their requests. Don't smoke if they ask you not to, and don't show up with pets without prior arrangement. Be tidy in shared bathrooms, and be prompt. Most places have small staffs or may be run single-handedly and cannot easily adjust to surprises.

With a little effort and a sense of adventure you will learn firsthand the advantages of bed and breakfast travel. You will rediscover hospitality in a time when kindness seems to have been pushed aside. With the help of this directory, you will find accommodations that are just as exciting as your traveling plans.

We would like to hear from you about any experiences you have had or any inns you wish to recommend. Please write us at the following address:

> The Annual Directory of American and
> Canadian Bed & Breakfasts
> 211 Seventh Avenue North
> Nashville, Tennessee 37219

this elegant contemporary home offers a breathtaking panoramic vista of the river and Wilson and Wheeler dams. Guests can have breakfast on the deck and watch sailboats, barges, and even beavers on the river. Enjoy the hammock and swing and late afternoon refreshments. The home was architecturally designed and professionally decorated, blending antiques with contemporary furnishings. Fresh flowers a specialty. Room with private bath, $75. Suite with kitchen and private entrance, $85.

Riverview Bed and Breakfast

Route 7, Box 123G, 35630
(205) 757-8667

The banks of the beautiful Tennessee River between Wilson and Wheeler dams offer a spectacular view. Recently constructed contemporary home was architecturally designed and professionally decorated to blend with the surrounding wooded area and lake view. Guest rooms have decks and patios, offering panoramic views of sailboats a few feet away. Smoking restricted. Not suitable for children.

Hosts: Edith and Buddy Meeks
Rooms: 2 (PB) $75-95
Full Breakfast
Credit Cards: A, B
Notes: 2, 5, 10, 12, 14

GENEVA

Live Oaks of Geneva

307 South Academy Street, 36340
(334) 684-2489

Beautifully restored 1918 home one block from downtown in southeast Alabama, this bed and breakfast offers comfortable bedrooms, private baths, and TVs. Enjoy the large porch, sunroom, and living room as a family member. A guest entrance allows

Live Oaks of Geneva

visitors to come and go as they wish. Smoking is restricted to the porch. No pets in bedrooms.

Hosts: Horace and Pamela Newman
Rooms: 3 (PB) $40
Continental Breakfast
Credit Cards: None
Notes: 2, 5, 8, 12

GREENSBORO

Blue Shadows Bed and Breakfast Guest Home

Rural Route 2, Box 432, 36744
(205) 624-3637

Country setting on 320 acres offers elegant accommodations. Enjoy the nature trail, private fish pond, bird sanctuary, and formal garden. Afternoon tea and sherry served by request. Nearby attractions include historic sites, Marion Military Institute, Judson College, University of Alabama, Tuscaloosa Indian Mounds, antique shops, and beautiful churches. Come and enjoy Southern hospitality! Reservations a must! Limited smoking allowed.

Hosts: Janet and Thaddeus May
Suite: 1 (SB) $65
Continental Breakfast
Credit Cards: None
Notes: 2, 5, 8, 9

7 No smoking; 8 Children welcome; 9 Social drinking allowed; 10 Tennis nearby; 11 Swimming nearby; 12 Golf nearby; 13 Skiing nearby; 14 May be booked through a travel agent.

JEMISON

Horse Shoe Bunk House

356 County Road 164, 35085
(205) 646-4109

This three-bedroom home is right off I-65 between Birmingham and Montgomery, in the peach country of central Alabama. Decor is cowboy, Indian, and Oriental (in one bedroom). Pet the horses, fish in the lake, or just relax. Full country breakfast is served. No pets. Christian atmosphere. Children over 15 welcome.

Host: Kay Red Horse
Rooms: 3 (1 PB; 2 SB) $45-50
Full Breakfast
Credit Cards: None
Notes: 2, 3, 4, 5, 7, 14

MENTONE

Madaperca Bed and Breakfast

5024 AL Highway 117, 35984
(205) 634-4792

Madaperca is a mountain stone estate developed from an original log cabin built in 1916. All driveways, walkways, patios, fences, and buildings were finished in local Lookout Mountain stone from 1946 to 1952. Most of the furnishings are original to the home and date to the early 1930s. Madaperca is a riverside retreat where guests can step back in time while still enjoying modern conveniences. Sleep to the sound of rippling water as the purest stream in Alabama (Little River) passes over a mountain-stone dam as it flows its way to DeSoto Falls. Awake to the smell of a country breakfast like Grandma used to make. Canoe on the premises, hike in the park, or sightsee at the canyon or the caves.

Hosts: Don and Yvonne Brock
Rooms: 3 (PB) $60-75
Full Breakfast
Credit Cards: None
Notes: 2, 5, 7, 8, 10, 11, 12, 13

Mentone Inn

P.O. Box 290, 35984
(205) 634-4836; (800) 455-7470 (reservations)

Nestled majestically atop Lookout Mountain, this inn was built during the height of the Roaring Twenties. The beaded, hand-polished wood paneling and gracious porch reflect the spirit of that bold era. Enjoy full service dining for breakfast, lunch, and dinner at Catherine's Wild Flower, a restaurant within the Mentone Inn. Nearby activities include rafting, canoeing, fishing, swimming, golfing, hiking, biking, horseback riding, rock climbing, and skiing. Mentone Inn offers peace and relaxation.

Hosts: Frances and Karl Waller
Rooms: 12 (PB) $59.95-125
Full Breakfast
Credit Cards: A, B, C
Notes: 2, 3, 4, 5, 8, 11, 12, 13

MOBILE

Malaga Inn

359 Church Street, 36602
(334) 438-4701; (800) 235-1586

The Malaga Inn, in the historic district of downtown, is the only hotel of its kind in the state. Originally the two townhouses were built in 1862 by two brothers-in-law when the Civil War was going well for the South. The two homes have been lovingly restored around a quiet patio garden. All rooms are furnished with a great deal of individuality, reminiscent of the finest Southern tradition. The friendly and courteous attention afforded to each guest, the convenient location next to the Civic Auditorium, and all the historic sites of Mobile have attracted those who relish the inn's Old Town atmosphere for many years. Restaurant, lounge, and pool on the premises. Breakfast is not included in the rates.

Host: Julie Beem
Rooms: 40 (PB) $69-79
No Breakfast
Credit Cards: A, B, C, D
Notes: 2, 3, 4, 5, 7, 8, 9, 11, 12, 14

NOTES: Credit cards accepted: A MasterCard; B Visa; C American Express; D Discover; E Diners Club; F Other; 2 Personal checks accepted; 3 Lunch available; 4 Dinner available; 5 Open all year; 6 Pets welcome;

Portman House Inn

1615 Government Street, 36606
(334) 471-1703; (800) 471-1701 (reservations)
FAX (334) 471-1214

Portman House is in the heart of Mobile's National Historic District and offers luxurious accommodations and apartments for descriminating guests. Portman House is in the middle of everything that makes Mobile wonderful. Close to museums, hospitals, and shopping; part of the Azalea Trail Festival; and is the gateway to the world's most beautiful beaches on the Florida and Alabama Gulf Coast. Amenities include fully equipped kitchens, Jacuzzis, and working fireplaces in most accommodations; cable TV, private on-site parking, concierge service, garden picnic area, individual climate control, and private telephones.

Rooms: 8 (PB) $85-120
Continental Breakfast
Credit Cards: A, B, C, D, E, F
Notes: 2, 5, 6, 7, 8, 9, 10, 11, 12, 13, 14

MONTGOMERY

The Lattice Inn Bed and Breakfast

1414 South Hull Street, 36104
(334) 832-9931; (800) 525-0652
FAX (334) 264-0075

The Lattice Inn

The Lattice Inn is Montgomery's quiet way to relax in Southern comfort. In the historic garden district, this turn-of-the-century home, built in 1906, has been lovingly restored to provide a wonderful and comfortable retreat for today's traveler. The shady front porch has just enough lattice to provide privacy while reading or lounging on its swing. The pool and decks in the back yard provide restful places to unwind. Smoking is allowed outside only.

Host: Michael Pierce
Rooms: 5 (PB) $55-70
Full Breakfast
Credit Cards: A, B, C, D
Notes: 2, 5, 9, 10, 11, 12, 14

Red Bluff Cottage

Red Bluff Cottage

551 Clay Street, P.O. Box 1026, 36101
(334) 264-0056; FAX (334) 262-1872

The Waldos built Red Bluff Cottage in 1987 high above the Alabama River in the historic Cottage Hill District. A raised cottage, all guest rooms are on the ground floor, with easy access to off-street parking, gazebo, and fenced play yard. Upstairs, guests will enjoy pleasantly light and airy public rooms, including dining, living, music (piano and harpsichord), and sitting (TV) rooms. A deep porch overlooks downtown, the state capitol, and the river plain.

Hosts: Ann and Mark Waldo
Rooms: 4 (PB) $65
Full Breakfast
Credit Cards: A, B, C, D
Notes: 2, 5, 7, 8, 9, 14

7 No smoking; 8 Children welcome; 9 Social drinking allowed; 10 Tennis nearby; 11 Swimming nearby; 12 Golf nearby; 13 Skiing nearby; 14 May be booked through a travel agent.

NAUVOO

The William Cook House

William Cook Parkway, 35578
(334) 272-1972; (205) 697-5792

Scottish-immigrant, coal-mining pioneers built this home, circa 1900, in the heart of the Alabama Highlands' booming coal-mining district. Furnished with original heirloom pieces, it is on the Alabama Register of Historic Places and convenient to other tourist attractions. Comfortable rooms, circular porches, and Continental breakfast. Victorian atmosphere adds to the romance of the home. Prefer nonsmoking guests.

Hosts: Jean Dillon and Frances Vance
Rooms: 2 (SB) $45-55
Continental Breakfast
Credit Cards: None
Notes: 2

SELMA

Grace Hall
Bed and Breakfast Inn

506 Lauderdale Street, 36701
(334) 875-5744; (334) 875-9967

This antebellum mansion, circa 1857, is on the National Register of Historic Places. Restoration certified by the Department of the Interior. The Evans, Baker, and Jones families have occupied this home for the

Grace Hall

past 110 years. There are many original antiques to view while taking a tour; admission is $5 for adults, $3 for students, no charge for children under six. Group rates for the tour are available. Dinner and lunch available for parties of ten or more. Smoking outside only. Pets welcome by prior arrangements. May be booked through travel agent by prior arrangement. Children over five welcome.

Hosts: Joey and Coy Dillon
Rooms: 6 (PB) $80-110
Full Breakfast
Credit Cards: A, B, C, D
Notes: 2, 5, 9, 10, 11, 12

TALLADEGA

The Governor's House

500 Meadowlake Lane, 35160
(205) 763-2186

The Governor's House, built in 1850 by a former governor of Alabama, is on a knoll overlooking Logan Martin Lake and part of a polled Hereford cattle farm. It was moved to the farm and furnished with antiques from the hosts' families. There is a Horse Barn Galleries Antique shop and a wicker-furnished broad front porch. Come enjoy quiet, peaceful country living at its best. Just two miles south of Exit 165 on I-20 in Lincoln. A delicious full breakfast is served in the dining room or on the front porch. Air-conditioned. Ceiling fans throughout. Twin, double, and queen-size beds available. Plexi-paved, lighted tennis courts are available on premises, as well as professional lessons. Guests may enjoy bass and bream fishing in stocked pond, picnicking, hiking over pastures, or seasonal patio boat rides on the lake. Reduced rates for use of entire house. Smoking outside only. Children over 12 welcome.

Hosts: Mary Sue and Ralph Gaines
Rooms: 3 (1 PB; 2 SB) $70-80
Full Breakfast
Credit Cards: None
Notes: 2, 3, 4, 5, 9, 12

NOTES: Credit cards accepted: A MasterCard; B Visa; C American Express; D Discover; E Diners Club;
F Other; 2 Personal checks accepted; 3 Lunch available; 4 Dinner available; 5 Open all year; 6 Pets welcome;

TROY

The House of Dunn's Bed and Breakfast Inn

204 South Brundidge Street, 36081
(334) 566-9414

The House of Dunn's is a great way to get in touch with what southerners call "down-home" experiences. The house itself was built in the late 1800s and has 16-foot ceilings and large, cozy, comfortable rooms. Homemade goodies and coffee or tea await guests upon their arrival. Each room has a private bath. Some rooms have plush sofas, and one has a claw-foot tub. Remote-controlled cable TVs are in each room. A full breakfast is served with homemade buttermilk biscuits. Lunch and dinner available upon request. An additional $10 charge for each additional person.

Hosts: Gardner and Ramona Dunn
Rooms: 4 (PB) $50
Full Breakfast
Credit Cards: A, B, D
Notes: 2, 5, 7, 8, 14

WINFIELD

White Oaks Inn

Route 5, Box 32, 35594
(205) 487-4115; (800) 482-4115

White Oaks Inn is a restored 1918 family home built by the Pearce family. The inside has been completely renovated to include a private bath for each guest room. All rooms have TVs and telephones. A large-screen TV and VCR are available in the den for movies and sporting events. A pool and hot tub are available for guests. The large front porch with swing and rockers invites guests to relax. Five cabins are also available. Located in a dry county; no alcoholic beverages permitted. Children in cabins only.

Hosts: Linda and Roger Sanders
Rooms: 5 (PB) $60
Cabins: 2 $50-60
Credit Cards: A, B, C, D
Notes: 2, 5, 7, 10, 11

7 No smoking; 8 Children welcome; 9 Social drinking allowed; 10 Tennis nearby; 11 Swimming nearby; 12 Golf nearby; 13 Skiing nearby; 14 May be booked through a travel agent.

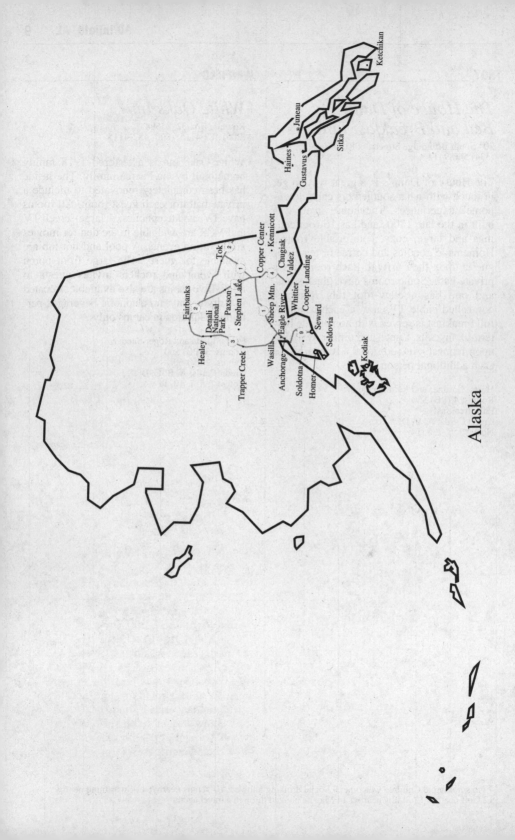

Alaska

Alaska

A Homestay at Homesteads

Box 771283, Eagle River, 99577
(907) 272-8644; FAX (907) 274-8644

A1. The crossroads of life in a residential area is within walking distance to town, coastal trail access for skiing in the winter, and biking, skating, and walking in the summer. Hosts are a professional family. Nonsmoking. Private and shared baths. Full breakfast. $65-90.

A2. The owners have converted an apartment complex to accommodate folks who like the freedom of their own kitchen. Studio, one- and two-bedroom suites in the heart of downtown are available, depending on the season and space desired. $80-140.

A3. In downtown Anchorage, this home is open year round. A big breakfast is served in the common room. Honeymoon suite is available with mountain views. $85-115.

A4. Just at the tree line with a great trail across the creek lies this delightful home. In the winter ski from the porch. In the summer climb the mountains surrounding this unique getaway. A wood stove provides the warmth. Homemade quilts. No smoking. Full breakfast. $65-95.

A5. In the great Alaskan outdoors (what the Alaskans call the "bush") guests are just 30 minutes from downtown Anchorage.

A6. This bed and breakfast on wheels takes guests to the best sightseeing, fishing, and trails for hiking and biking. Guests' meals are provided. Guests stay in the mobile home, while the hosts "tent out" at night. Call or FAX for rates. Include dates preferred.

A7. This home has a perfect private executive suite overlooking Ship Creek and downtown Anchorage. Two bedrooms, full gourmet kitchen, telephone, and sitting room with balcony are available. Continental breakfast. Weekly and monthly rates available upon request. $125.

Alaskan Frontier Gardens Bed and Breakfast

P.O. Box 241881, 99524-1881
(907) 345-6556; FAX (907) 562-2923

Alaskan estate nestles in the trees on a scenic three-acre wilderness site of lawn and landscaped gardens in Anchorage's peaceful hillside area near the Chugach State Park, 10 minutes from the airport and 20 minutes from downtown. Spacious and luxurious suites with multiperson Jacuzzi, sauna, and fireplace. Great for honeymooners. Thirty-year resident offers a museum-like environment with Alaskan hospitality and exceptional comfort. Year-round service, phone in each room, cable TV, laundry facilities, gourmet breakfast.

Host: Rita Gittins
Rooms: 5 (2 PB; 3 SB) $100-175
Full Breakfast
Credit Cards: A, B, C
Notes: 2, 5, 7, 8, 9, 10, 11, 12, 13, 14

NOTES: Credit cards: A MasterCard; B Visa; C American Express; D Discover; E Diners Club; F Other; 2 Personal checks accepted; 3 Lunch available; 4 Dinner available; 5 Open all year; 6 Pets welcome; 7 No smoking; 8 Children welcome; 9 Social drinking allowed; 10 Tennis nearby; 11 Swimming nearby; 12 Golf nearby; 13 Skiing nearby; 14 May be booked through a travel agent.

Arctic Loon Bed and Breakfast

P.O. Box 110333, 99511
(907) 345-4935

Elegant accommodations in this exquisite 6,500-square-foot Scandinavian home in the hillside area of south Anchorage afford breathtaking, spectacular views of Mount McKinley and Anchorage Bowl. An eight-person Jacuzzi, sauna, and rosewood grand piano provide relaxation after a full gourmet breakfast. Fully licensed, this bed and breakfast has a quiet mountain setting near golf course, zoo, and Chugach State Park hiking trails.

Hosts: Janie and Lee Johnson
Rooms: 3 (1 PB; 2 SB) $75-90
Full Breakfast
Credit Cards: A, B
Notes: 2, 5, 7, 8, 9, 10, 11, 12, 13, 14

Coastal Trail Bed and Breakfast

3100 Iliamna Drive, 99517
(907) 243-5809

Coastal Trail Bed and Breakfast invites guests to a comfortable Alaskan homestay. The three-room suite is furnished for comfort and includes telephone, TV, and VCR. Enjoy the outdoor hot tub. Be amazed at the beauty and rarity of flowers in the gardens. Hunting and fishing tips are provided by traditional Alaskan hosts. In the center of a gracious neighborhood, Coastal Trail adjoins an urban walking trail where guests may enjoy wildflowers, migratory birds, whales, and views of Denali. Full breakfast served.

Hosts: Sherry and Derek Tomlinson
Suite: 1 (PB) $75
Full Breakfast
Cards: None
Notes: 2, 5, 7, 8, 10, 13, 14

CHUGIAK

Birch Trails Bed and Breakfast

22719 Robinson Road, 99567
(907) 688-5713

Birch Trails is a warm, comfortable, secluded home, tastefully decorated with antiques and traditional Alaskan artwork. The lower level of the hosts' home has been dedicated to the guests—from a private entrance and game and exercise area, to a living area with Alaskan library, VCR, TV, and a complimentary stocked kitchenette. Join Tom and Angie for a complete Alaskan gourmet breakfast and gaze through the many windows at a spectacular mountain panorama.

Hosts: Tom and Angie Hamill
Rooms: 2 (SB) $75
Full Breakfast
Credit Cards: None
Notes: 2, 3, 4, 5, 7, 8, 9, 10, 11, 13, 14

Peters Creek Inn

22635 Davidson Road, P.O. Box 671487, 99567
(907) 688-2776; (800) 680-2776
FAX (907) 688-5031

A rural, wooded setting that suggests remoteness, yet possesses metropolitan convenience. Choose from the five Alaskan themed rooms, each with a private bath. Beverage service available 24 hours. A barbecue is available for the one that didn't get

Peters Creek Inn

away. Walk along the creek's edge or through the woods to see picturesque mountains and Cook Inlet. Nordic ski trails abound in the winter.

Hosts: Martha and Burl Rogers
Rooms: 5 (PB) $65-75
Full Breakfast
Credit Cards: A, B
Notes: 3, 4, 5, 6, 8, 9, 10, 11, 12, 13, 14

COOPER LANDING

Gwin's Lodge, Inc.
Mile Post 52–Sterling Highway, HC 64, Box 50, 99572
(907) 595-1266; FAX (907) 595-1681

Gwin's Lodge is nestled in the beautiful Chugach Mountains surrounded by the Chugach National Forest and the Kenai National Wildlife Refuge. Six modern log cabins are available. Each of the carpeted cabins features two double beds and private bath with shower. Roll away beds are also available. Recreational vehicle parking and camping available. The Kenai Peninsula offers visitors a wide assortment of activities. Gift and outdoor equipment store on the premises, as well as a restaurant and bar. Rates are increased $5 per child over the age of three. In-state personal checks accepted only.

Hosts: The Siter Family
Rooms: 8 (6PB) $88
Full Breakfast
Credit Cards: A, B, D
Notes: 3, 4, 8, 9, 12, 14

A Homestay at Homesteads
Box 771283, Eagle River, 99577
(907) 272-8644; FAX (907) 274-8644

CL. Need one huge room? This one comes with two queen-size beds, one twin, and lots of floor mats. Fishing parties, hikers, and families all love to stay here. Private. Transportation available, but not included. $150.

CL1. This inn is rustic and was founded in an original log house that still has the best restaurant around. The cabins have two double beds and private baths. The rug is warm, and the place is open year-round. Also, one has a kitchenette. Meals available, but not included. From $65.

Red Salmon Guest House
Mile 48.2 Sterling Highway, P.O. Box 725, 99572
(907) 595-1 RED

On the banks of a wild and curving salmon river, the Upper Kenai, these rooms and Alaskan cabins have spectacular views. Go world-class fishing or scenic river rafting right from the Guest House, take a wonderful day hike to nearby Exit Glacier and the Russian River Falls, or relax on the deck and watch the water peacefully roll by while moose visit, eagles fish, and sheep graze on the mountain. An Alaskan breakfast is often the highlight as guests gather together in the beautiful dining room overlooking the river.

Hosts: Patti and George Heim
Rooms: 7 (5 PB; 2 SB) $79-199
Full Breakfast
Credit Cards: A, B
Notes: 2, 3, 4, 7, 9, 12, 14

COPPER CENTER

A Homestay at Homesteads
Box 771283, Eagle River, 99577
(907) 272-8644; FAX (907) 274-8644

CC1. This homey and historic place is in the original dog team and carriage stop—a two-story building. Some of the rooms are still slightly warped, but the hosts are upgrading the baths and rooms more each year. Travelers come from miles around for "out to dine" in the formal dining room. Meals available, but not included. Some private baths, some shared. Rest overnight and enjoy it during the day. $55-75.

7 No smoking; 8 Children welcome; 9 Social drinking allowed; 10 Tennis nearby; 11 Swimming nearby; 12 Golf nearby; 13 Skiing nearby; 14 May be booked through a travel agent.

DENALI NATIONAL PARK (HEALEY)_____

A Homestay at Homesteads
Box 771283, Eagle River, 99577
(907) 272-8644; FAX (907) 274-8644

D1. How about a nice hot tub at the end of the day? The hosts do not serve breakfast but do offer guests a spectacular view in individual log cabins on the side of the mountain above the hustle and bustle of the tourists. Private baths. Walk to the best restaurants. $115-145.

D2. These cabins fit many budgets, from the central bath and shower units to full family cabins with private baths. Right on the park's highway, guests have access to marvelous wooded pathways between the cabins. No breakfast served, but the shuttle will take guests to the park's entrance or to good restaurants. $90-145.

D3. How about a tent with breakfast? This experience provides outdoor variety for folks who want to hike, pan for gold, and enjoy stories around the fire at night. Rates include transportation and tour through the park. $175.

D3a. A short drive toward Fairbanks from the Denali Park entrance brings visitors to the tiny town of Healey and out of the tourist traffic. An original carriage and dog team stop, this old hotel with wood floors is all charm and an inexpensive stopover. Some rooms have shared baths. Wonderful restaurant next door. Smoking and non-smoking areas. $60-120.

Kantishna Roadhouse
P.O. Box 130, 99755
(907) 683-1475; (800) 942-7420

Kantishna Roadhouse is a modern, full-service lodge with all the amenities guests would expect from a first-class wilderness resort. Packages include transportation to and from Kantishna, three home-cooked meals a day, and a wide range of activities. Open June 5 through September 10.

Host: Roberta Koppenberg
Cabins: 27 (PB)
Full Breakfast
Credit Cards: A, B
Notes: 2, 8, 9, 14

EAGLE RIVER (PETERS CREEK)_____

A Homestay at Homesteads
Box 771283, Eagle River, 99577
(907) 272-8644; FAX (907) 274-8644

ER1. Surrounded by wilderness guests can ski from the porch or hike across the creek on the wilderness trail. Wonderful wood stove and fireplace encourage guests to relax in Alaskan style. Enjoy the lifestyle here, seven tree-lined miles up the dirt road with two glaciers "back valley" and Denali framed in the window "down valley." Nonsmoking. Full Alaskan-style breakfast at Heaven Crest. $65-90.

ER2. The hosts built their own home in this wilderness-surrounded area. Their big dogs get first choice on the davenport, but guests may join the hosts at the cooking bar for great food and shared stories. Birders will enjoy the activity both summer and winter. Smoking permitted. Double with private bath and a complete, immaculate Airstream trailer for families available. Full breakfast is served, of course, at the Birdhouse. $65-120.

ER3. Here at Chickadee, there is a new all-glass addition to the living room, so guests can watch it snow in the winter and all the birds can see inside. This family is 4H- and homemaker-minded. The hosts have built their own home in the high wilderness area. Only eight miles from the main highway, guests return for the same reason Alaskans stay here. The hosts love to cook full breakfasts. Private entrance to the suite of rooms downstairs with a private patio. $80-120.

ER4. This spacious home is furnished with beautiful Victorian antiques. A delicious hearty Alaskan breakfast is served. Peters Creek is 17 short miles from downtown Anchorage. Explore the forest and the king salmon that spawn in the creek. Physically challenged design. $75-95.

ER5. Guests enjoy fabulous creek in the middle of town. Two bedrooms with shared or private bath and a huge family room. Exercise equipment and mobile phone for adults and a garden for kids. Open year-round. Gourmet breakfast. $65-85.

FAIRBANKS

The Blue Goose Bed and Breakfast
4466 Dartmouth, 99709
(907) 479-6973; (800) 478-6973 (Alaska only)
FAX (907) 457-6973

The Blue Goose Bed and Breakfast, a tri-level home, is near the university and the airport. Furnished with antiques, quilts, and old treasures, all of the rooms have ceiling fans and "blue" goose down comforters. A full breakfast is served with the specialty blue-ribbon Alaska rhubarb pie baked each morning. "Alaska is a special place and we want our guests to leave with that feeling."

Hosts: Susan and Ken Bisse
Rooms: 3 (1 PB; 2 SB) $45-75
Full Breakfast
Credit Cards: A, B, C, D, E
Notes: 2, 5, 7, 8, 9, 14

A Homestay at Homesteads
Box 771283, Eagle River, 99577
(907) 272-8644; FAX (907) 274-8644

F1. Nestled in the hills of the town, this secluded neighborhood is the perfect area to watch birds and take walks on dirt roads. The hosts catch and release birds as a banding unit for birding count. Berries growing almost wild in the garden make this a special place for special people. Private bath. Full breakfast upstairs with hosts. Nonsmoking. $65-90.

7 Gables Inn

7 Gables Inn
P.O. Box 80488, 99708
(907) 479-0751

Historically, Alaska's 7 Gables Inn was a fraternity house within walking distance to the UAF campus, yet near the river and airport. This spacious 10,000-square-foot Tudor-style home features a floral solarium, antique stained glass in the foyer with an indoor waterfall, cathedral ceilings, a wedding chapel, wine cellar, and rooms with dormers. A gourmet breakfast is served daily. Other amenities include cable TV and telephone in each room, laundry facilities, Jacuzzis, bikes, and canoes.

Hosts: Paul and Leicha Welton
Rooms: 12 (PB) $50-120
Full Breakfast
Credit Cards: A, B, C, D, E
Notes: 2, 5, 7, 8, 9, 11, 12, 13, 14

GUSTAVUS (GLACIER BAY)

Glacier Bay Country Inn
P.O. Box 5-AD, 99826
(907) 697-2288; FAX (907) 697-2289
Winter: P.O. Box 2557, Saint George, UT 84771
(801) 673-8480; FAX (801) 673-8481

7 No smoking; 8 Children welcome; 9 Social drinking allowed; 10 Tennis nearby; 11 Swimming nearby; 12 Golf nearby; 13 Skiing nearby; 14 May be booked through a travel agent.

Peaceful storybook accommodations away from the crowds in a wilderness setting come with cozy comforters and warm flannel sheets. Superb dining features local seafood, garden-fresh produce, home-baked breads, and spectacular desserts. Enjoy fishing, whale watching, sightseeing, hiking, bird watching, photography, and Glacier Bay boat and plane tours. Rates include three meals, airport transfers, and use of bicycles. A second inn, the Whalesong Lodge, offers bed and breakfast rooms, condominium rentals, and full meal packages as well.

Hosts: Al and Annie Unrein
Rooms: 9 (8 PB; 1 SB) $149-238
Full Breakfast
Credit Cards: None
Notes: 2, 3, 4, 7, 8, 9, 14

Good River Bed and Breakfast

P.O. Box 37C, 99826
(907) 697-2241 (phone and FAX)

Spectacular Glacier Bay with its sixteen tidewater glaciers, whales, fishing, kayaking, nature walks, and wilderness is a great place to stay. Elegant log house, comfy beds, handmade quilts, fresh bread, and reasonable rates. Also rustic log cabin available. Free bikes to explore unique town. Come and see.

Host: Sandy Burd
Rooms: 5 (S2B) $50-75
Full Breakfast
Credit Cards: None
Notes: 2, 8, 14

Gustavus Inn

Box 60, 99826
(907) 697-2254; FAX (907) 697-2255

Glacier Bay's historic homestead, newly renovated, full-service inn accommodates 26. Family-style meals, seafood, garden produce, wild edibles. Boat tours of Glacier Bay, charter fishing, and air transportation from Juneau arranged. Kayaking and hiking nearby. Bikes and airport transfers

Gustavus Inn

included in the daily rates. Lunch and dinner included. American Plan only. Closed September 20 through May 1.

Hosts: David and Jo Ann Lesh
Rooms: 13 (11 PB; 2 SB) $130
Full Breakfast
Credit Cards: A, B, C
Notes: 2, 3, 4, 7, 8, 9, 14

A Puffin's Bed and Breakfast Lodge

1/4 Mile Logging Road, Box 3, 99826
(907) 697-2260

Guests stay in their own modern cottage on a five-acre, partially wooded homestead carpeted in wildflowers and berries. Full country breakfast served in new picturesque lodge with private meeting room. Covered picnic area with barbeque and coin-operated laundry available. Lunch and dinner available within walking distance. Special diets accommodated. Hike beaches or bicycle miles of country roads. See marine life from a charter cruiser or kayak. Courtesy transportation: Glacier Bay tours and travel services available. Special rates for children and senior citizens. Closed September 30 through May 1. Travel service open year-round. Limited smoking allowed. Social drinking allowed in cabins only.

Hosts: Chuck and Sandy Schroth
Cottages: 5 (PB) $50-100
Full Breakfast
Credit Cards: A, B
Notes: 6, 8, 14

NOTES: Credit cards accepted: A MasterCard; B Visa; C American Express; D Discover; E Diners Club; F Other; 2 Personal checks accepted; 3 Lunch available; 4 Dinner available; 5 Open all year; 6 Pets welcome;

HAINES

A Homestay at Homesteads

Box 771283, Eagle River, 99577
(907) 272-8644; FAX (907) 274-8644

H1. The flower box is always full. Hosts have one room to share with travelers. If traveling on the ferry, better call early as all the rooms in town are full. A nice place to visit. Breakfast is served. $65.

HOMER

A Homestay at Homesteads

Box 771283, Eagle River, 99577
(907) 272-8644; FAX (907) 274-8644

H1. This two-story contemporary beach house with all-glass on the ocean side is like no other. Because of the elegant floors and rugs, guests are asked to leave their shoes at the door. Private and shared baths available. Gourmet cooking is the hosts' specialty. $70-120.

H2A. This is the oldest and the only place to stay at the end of the Homer split. Walk from here to catch fishing charters, day boat tours, or fish from the beach while watching the boats come and go. Rooms have private baths. Breakfast is not served. When making reservations, please specify smoking or nonsmoking. $75-140.

H2B. Enjoy the hot tub at the end of the day after hiking, fishing, or sightseeing. All this and a great breakfast, too. Nonsmoking. $65-95.

H3. Join all of the guests for a huge, home-made, typically Alaskan, breakfast at the glass-rimmed dining area. These hosts were the first to entertain bed and breakfast guests, and years later they would not change their hospitality for anything. Enjoy cozy rooms in the house or family spaces in the "out" buildings. Everyone joins for breakfast. The hosts can get guests the best in fishing, touring boats, and travel! Guests do need transportation to get to this hilltop home with a panoramic view. $75-90.

Brass Ring Bed and Breakfast

P.O. Box 2090, 99603
(907) 235-5450; FAX (907) 235-5451

This Alaskan log home is in the heart of Homer, within walking distance of shops and restaurants. Quiet atmosphere. Private cottage with spectacular mountain view also available. Full hot breakfast is served from 7 to 9 A.M. Fishing and sightseeing. Children over six welcome.

Hosts: Vicki and Dave Van Liere
Rooms: 6 (1 PB; 5 SB) $65-80
Full Breakfast
Credit Cards: A, B
Notes: 2, 7, 14

JUNEAU

A Homestay at Homesteads

Box 771283, Eagle River, 99577
(907) 272-8644; FAX (907) 274-8644

J1. These hosts have the view and know the ferry is a long way out of town. If guests need a rental car, they arrange it, and if guests want to be picked up they can do that, too! Breakfast is included (most of the time). The inn is booked to assist the legislature when in session; otherwise they will welcome guests. Laundry, cooking, sauna, and picnic area. Nonsmoking. $65-85.

Alaska Wolf House

P.O. Box 21321, 99802
(907) 586-2422 (phone and FAX)

Alaska Wolf House is a lovely 4,000-square-foot cedar-log home one mile from downtown Juneau. Built on the forested

7 No smoking; 8 Children welcome; 9 Social drinking allowed; 10 Tennis nearby; 11 Swimming nearby; 12 Golf nearby; 13 Skiing nearby; 14 May be booked through a travel agent.

side of Mount Juneau, with black bear in the back yard, the house features a southern exposure for enjoying sunrises and sunsets over Gastineau Channel and moonrises over the statuesque mountains of Douglas Island. A delicious breakfast is served in the Glassroom. Alaska Wolf House is decorated with antiques and art. Choose from Jack London, John Muir, Botkin-Russian rooms, and Scot's Lair and Texas suites with kitchens.

Hosts: Philip and Cloris Dennis
Rooms: 5 (1 PB; 4 SB) $70-95
Full Breakfast
Credit Cards: A, B
Notes: 2, 5, 7, 8, 9, 10, 11, 12, 13, 14

The Lost Chord

2200 Fritz Cove Road, 99801
(907) 789-7296

The hosts' music business has expanded to become a homey bed and breakfast on an exquisite private beach. Breakfast is with the proprietors, who have been in Alaska since 1946. In the country 12 miles from Juneau; a car is suggested. Pets welcome by prior arrangements.

Hosts: Jesse and Ellen Jones
Rooms: 4 (1 PB; 3 SB) $55.50-94.35
Full Breakfast
Credit Cards: None
Notes: 2, 5, 7, 8, 9, 10, 11, 12, 13, 14

Mt. Juneau Inn

1801 Old Glacier Highway, 99801
(907) 463-5855; FAX (907) 463-5423

Mt. Juneau Inn is surrounded by gardens with native-carved totems and views of the mountains and channel. The inn offers seven country-style rooms and a comfortably furnished one bedroom apartment, all decorated with Alaska photographs and native art. Amenities include bountiful home-cooked breakfast, evening snacks, robes, slippers, guest kitchen, laundry and freezer facilities, bicycles, and outdoor gear. On city, ferry, and airport buslines.

Hosts: Phil and Karen Greeney
Rooms: 8 (2 PB; 6 SB) $65-110
Full Breakfast
Credit Cards: A, B, D
Notes: 2, 5, 7, 8, 9, 11, 13, 14

Pearson's Pond Luxury Inn

Pearson's Pond Luxury Inn

4541 Sawa Circle, 99801-8723
(907) 789-3772; FAX (907) 789-6722

Relax in style at this welcome retreat tucked in the forest amid spectacular scenery and abundant wildlife. Soothe cares in a steaming spa on the banks of a natural pond left by the retreating Mendenhall Glacier nearby. Enjoy every imaginable amenity in guests' own private studio with decks leading to the hot tub. Guest suites are on a separate floor from the hosts to ensure guests' privacy. Kitchenettes, barbecue, freezer, rowboat, poles, and bikes. Guests will be away from the crowds, yet close to major attractions. Open year-round. Ski packages, weekly and monthly rates during October through April. Be sure to book far in advance for summer visits. Guests say it's the highest combination of beauty, comfort, privacy, and warmth. AAA-rated three diamonds, ABBA-rated three crowns; excellence awards from both AAA and the ABBA.

NOTES: Credit cards accepted: A MasterCard; B Visa; C American Express; D Discover; E Diners Club; F Other; 2 Personal checks accepted; 3 Lunch available; 4 Dinner available; 5 Open all year; 6 Pets welcome;

Hosts: Steve and Diane Pearson
Rooms: 2 (SB) $69-149
Suite: 1 (PB)
Continental Breakfast
Credit Cards: A, B, C, E
Notes: 2, 5, 7, 8, 9, 10, 11, 12, 13, 14

KENAI-SOLDATNA

A Homestay at Homesteads

Box 771283, Eagle River, 99577
(907) 272-8644; FAX (907) 274-8644

KS1. Enjoy the turn of the tide on this island. This bed and breakfast is more than breakfast as guests will fly in from Kenai in a small plane that lands there at low tide. Guests are welcomed to explore this spot where Captain Cook anchored. If guest are so inclined, the hosts' commercially set net site needs crew, too. Rates included meals. Guests pay plane direct (est. $380 round trip). Rates are $135 per person for cabin, $125 for bunkhouse.

KENNICOTT

A Homestay at Homesteads

Box 771283, Eagle River, 99577
(907) 272-8644; FAX (907) 274-8644

When the old hotel burned to the ground, the hosts took the original plans (updating the baths) and built a new "old" hotel. This newly made antique is just waiting for adventurous souls to enjoy the gourmet dining and tales of the mining days. Share baths as in the olden times. Day rates vary with the size of the traveling group, but calculate $115 per person with meals. Overnight with no meals also available. Plan to spend at least two nights; the hosts and the area are worth it. Most people drive in, but guests may fly in (weather permitting). Public transportation available from Valdez and Anchorage.

KETCHIKAN

A Homestay at Homesteads

Box 771283, Eagle River, 99577
(907) 272-8644; FAX (907) 274-8644

K. On the only road north of the ferry terminal, guests will need a car (rentals available) to find this secluded beach-side home in Ward Cove. Join the hosts with the wilderness all around and the lapping waters that put guests to sleep. Nonsmoking. $75-85.

Captain's Quarters

325 Lund Street, 99901
(907) 225-4912

New construction on a historic hillside within walking distance of downtown Ketchikan has private entrance, bath, TV, and phones. Spectacular view of busy waterfront and Alaskan wilderness. Continental breakfast includes home-baked pastry served in a common area.

Hosts: Marv and Dorothy Wendeborn
Rooms: 3 (PB) $75
Continental Breakfast
Credit Cards: A, B, C
Notes: 2, 5, 7, 9

KODIAK

A Homestay at Homesteads

Box 771283, Eagle River, 99577
(907) 272-8644; FAX (907) 274-8644

KA1. Guests will need a good set of legs, a bicycle, or a rental car for this place just outside of town. This oceanside bed and breakfast is the place to relax, enjoy the very way of life for which guests came to Kodiak to enjoy. No smoking. $65-95.

KA2. Enjoy the country flavor of this bed and breakfast right in the middle of a wonderful coastal town. Hosts enjoy visitors

7 No smoking; 8 Children welcome; 9 Social drinking allowed; 10 Tennis nearby; 11 Swimming nearby;
12 Golf nearby; 13 Skiing nearby; 14 May be booked through a travel agent.

and plan great breakfasts to share with them. Hosts can help guests in planning where to visit and how to get there. $65-95.

Kodiak Bed and Breakfast

308 Cope Street, 99616
(907) 486-5367; FAX (907) 486-6567

Visitors enjoy a spectacular view of Kodiak's busy fishing fleet in a location just above the boat harbor. Mary's home is easy walking distance from a historic Russian church, art galleries, Baronof Museum, air charters, and downtown restaurants. Enjoy this fishing city with its Russian heritage, stunning beaches, cliffs, and abundant fish and bird life. Fresh local fish is often a breakfast option.

Host: Mary A. Monroe
Rooms: 11 (3 PB; 8 SB) $60-72
Full Breakfast
Credit Cards: A, B, C
Notes: 2, 5, 6, 7, 8, 9, 14

PAXSON (DENALI HIGHWAY)

A Homestay at Homesteads

Box 771283, Eagle River, 99577
(907) 272-8644; FAX (907) 274-8644

McClaren River in the heart of the Denali Highway (just a two and one-half hour drive from Denali Park) produces fishing, hiking, wilderness skiing, hunting, and a wonderful old lodge. Some cozy rooms upstairs and some cabins outside are available. Come linger with the year-round pioneering owners. Full breakfast included. Other meals available. Specify smoking or nonsmoking rooms. $40-90.

SELDOVIA

A Homestay at Homesteads

Box 771283, Eagle River, 99577
(907) 272-8644; FAX (907) 274-8644

SL1. Come dance with the eagles at this lodge over the water where the tides march in and out. The hosts have kayaks to rent, as well as bikes, a nice cozy hot tub (most of the time), and rooms inside the house as well as the self-contained cabin by the hot tub. Flexible and fun-loving hosts. Closed for the winter so as not to freeze the pipes, but the inn plans to be open May 15 through September 15. From $50.

SEWARD

A Homestay at Homesteads

Box 771283, Eagle River, 99577
(907) 272-8644; FAX (907) 274-8644

S1. Guests' very own log cabin is nestled in the trees next to a rushing salmon spawning stream. Fresh pastries, fruit, and juice are delivered to the door. Lounge in bed and watch the wilderness from the picture windows. So the pipes do not freeze in the winter, there is a year-round heated central bath and shower. There are camping spots available, too. Creekside is a treat worth waiting for. Families are welcome. Just off the highway on the road to Exit Glacier. $65-130.

S2. These hosts have a big family and an even bigger white house just across the creek on the way into Seward. Guest rooms are separate, nonsmoking with shared or private baths. In the guest space is a nice kitchen stocked with breakfast goodies to share with the other guests. Visit winter or summer. $65-90.

S3. If guests like their mornings calm, they will enjoy a full breakfast with these hosts in their typical two-story split-level home. Within walking distance to town and the boat harbor, guests can catch the tours into the Kenai Fjords National Park. Close to the train, and the bus will let guests off at the corner. $65-85.

NOTES: Credit cards accepted: A MasterCard; B Visa; C American Express; D Discover; E Diners Club; F Other; 2 Personal checks accepted; 3 Lunch available; 4 Dinner available; 5 Open all year; 6 Pets welcome;

S4. Smell the fresh cinnamon buns upon awakening in the morning. Enjoy sitting with other guests at the formal dining room table. Just out of town and down the lane enough to know where the real Alaskans live, breathe, and enjoy life. $65-85.

S5. Guests have their own spacious rooms and common room next to the hosts' log home. Rushing streams on both sides of the property hum in the night. $75-95.

SHEEP MOUNTAIN

A Homestay at Homesteads

Box 771283, Eagle River, 99577
(907) 272-8644; FAX (907) 274-8644

SM. Make these log cabins home. Most have private baths. Dorm rooms are available with central bath. Finest meals around with homemade pastries and pies available, but not included. $75-90.

SITKA

A Homestay at Homesteads

Box 771283, Eagle River, 99577
(907) 272-8644; FAX (907) 274-8644

ST1. After stepping off the ferry, walk right across the street and up the hill to this home. The rooms have the finest views around. The hosts have been here for years and love to talk about their adventures. Breakfast is included. Shared bath. $55.

SOLDOTNA

Posey's Kenai River Hideaway Bed and Breakfast Lodge

P.O. Box 4094-ABB, 99669
(907) 262-7430; FAX (907) 262-7430

Posey's Kenai River Hideaway

On the bank of the Kenai River with its world-record king salmon guests enjoy good, wholesome breakfast served before fishing. Hosts will arrange guided salmon or halibut charter, also fly-out fishing or sightseeing trips. After catching fish, relax on the sun deck built out over the river and swap fish stories. Hosts will freeze and pack fish for the return trip home. Seasonal rates available.

Hosts: Ray and June Posey
Rooms: 10 (3 PB; 7 SB) $110-130
Full Breakfast
Credit Cards: A, B
Notes: 2, 5, 9, 12, 13, 14

STEPHEN LAKE

A Homestay at Homesteads

Box 771283, Eagle River, 99577
(907) 272-8644; FAX (907) 274-8644

SL. The hosts will pick up guests in their plane and fly them to the dock in front of the main house. Great fishing in the stream nearby. The hosts love to cook gourmet meals; all meals are included. Because of the flight time, guests stay for an unforgettable experience for two or more nights (three or more days). Non-hunting or non-fishing guests may receive reduced rates. Fly-out cabins available; hosts will bring meals out to guests. Call for rates.

7 No smoking; 8 Children welcome; 9 Social drinking allowed; 10 Tennis nearby; 11 Swimming nearby; 12 Golf nearby; 13 Skiing nearby; 14 May be booked through a travel agent.

TRAPPER CREEK _____

McKinley Foothills Bed and Breakfast

P.O. Box 13089, 99683
(907) 733-1454; FAX (907) 733-1454

Great view of Mount McKinley. Secluded, rustic, and comfortable log cabins completely furnished with kitchenettes and accommodations for four people. Home-cooked meals features omelets and sourdough waffles. Special meals available with notice prior to arrival. King salmon fishing, snowmobiling, cross-country skiing, and dog mushing available. Children under eight free. No smoking indoors.

Hosts: Bob and Vilma Anderson
Rooms: 3 (PB and SB) $75-85
Full Breakfast
Cards: A, B, C
Notes: 3, 4, 5, 6, 8, 13, 14

VALDEZ_____

A Homestay at Homesteads

Box 771283, Eagle River, 99577
(907) 272-8644; FAX (907) 274-8644

V1. If guests want the best of all bed and breakfasts, it is right here! Since the hosts have enjoyed travelers in their home for years, they decided to add on just the right rooms for guests. Private or shared baths. Taking the ferry? It is always early or late, so the hosts will keep the coffee pot hot! Full breakfast. $60-80.

V2. Down-home style Continental breakfast is served so guests can take advantage of whatever their next adventure brings. The hosts' cocker will greet guests, yet prefers not to have other four-footed competition as guests. No smoking. Three rooms share two baths. $60-80.

V3. Guests cannot put a boat next to the house, but this inn is within walking distance of the water! Hosts can tell guests the best hiking spots and boating trips to take. Shared baths. Breakfast is served. $75-90.

V4. If guests have a family looking for the perfect stop, the hosts have the right rooms with double and bunk beds. What a joy to find a fun family stop that loves and welcomes well-behaved kids as well as their parents. Need a hickory stick? The hosts might be able to find that, too. Families and large groups are welcomed. From $85.

Alaska Flower Forget-Me-Not Bed and Breakfast

P.O. Box 1153, 99686
(907) 835-2717

Prince William Sound hospitality at its best! Guests will enjoy their visit as they relax in one of the luxurious guest rooms with panoramic views of the Chugach Mountains. A nutritious complimentary breakfast is served from 6:00 to 8:00 A.M. Walk to nearby cruise ships, the ferry, and the downtown area. Tour nearby glaciers, the Alyeska Pipeline terminal, and pristine waters and mountains.

Host: Betty Schackne
Rooms: 4 (1 PB; 3 SB) $65-80
Continental Breakfast
Credit Cards: None
Notes: 2, 5, 7, 8, 9, 13, 14

Best of All Bed and Breakfast

1104 Mineral Creek Drive, Box 1578, 99686
(907) 835-4524

Each room of this private home with Asian Alaskan Decor has its own personality with TV/VCR and a beautiful view of the moun-

---

NOTES: Credit cards accepted: A MasterCard; B Visa; C American Express; D Discover; E Diners Club;
F Other; 2 Personal checks accepted; 3 Lunch available; 4 Dinner available; 5 Open all year; 6 Pets welcome;

tains from every window. Special breakfasts are served. Convenient to downtown, ferry, restaurants, and bike and hiking trails. Smoking outside please.

Hosts: Barry and Sue Kennedy
Rooms: 3 (1 PB; 2 SB) $60-85
Full and Continental Breakfasts
Credit Cards: None
Notes: 5, 8, 10, 11, 13, 14

WASILLA

Yukon Don's

1830 East Parks Highway, Suite 386, 99654 (mail)
2221 Yukon Circle, 99654
(907) 376-7422; (800) 478-7472

When traveling in Alaska, guests do not want to miss staying at Yukon Don's. All rooms are decorated with authentic Alaskana. Stay in the Iditarod, Fishing, Denali, and Hunting rooms, or in the Matanuska suite. Guests are pampered by relaxing in the Alaska room, complete with Alaskan historic library, video library, pool table, cable TV, and gift bar. The all-glass-view room on the second floor offers the grandest view in the Matanuska Valley. Hosts also offer telephones in each room. Enjoy Yukon Don's own expanded

Continental breakfast bar, sauna, and exercise room. Alaska's Award Winning Bed and Breakfast Inn. Alaska's Family Business of the Year, 1994. Top 50 Inns in America, 1991. American Bed and Breakfast Association Award of Excellence. Wasilla's Official Bed and Breakfast Accommodation.

Host: Yukon Don and Kristan Tanner
Rooms: 6 (2 PB; 4 SB) $75-115
Continental Breakfast
Credit Cards: A, B, C
Notes: 2, 5, 7, 8, 9, 10, 11, 12, 13, 14

WHITTIER

A Homestay at Homesteads

Box 771283, Eagle River, 99577
(907) 272-8644; FAX (907) 274-8644

Guests have a world-class view of the spectacular fjord at this warm water port where two-thirds of the population live in the high-rise built for troops during World War II. The ferry leaves from the docks below. Enjoy plenty of winter skiing, summer hiking, and kayaking. Hosts' small boat will carry guests to wilderness fishing and glacier and shrimping areas. Nonsmoking. Boat not included. $40-90.

7 No smoking; 8 Children welcome; 9 Social drinking allowed; 10 Tennis nearby; 11 Swimming nearby; 12 Golf nearby; 13 Skiing nearby; 14 May be booked through a travel agent.

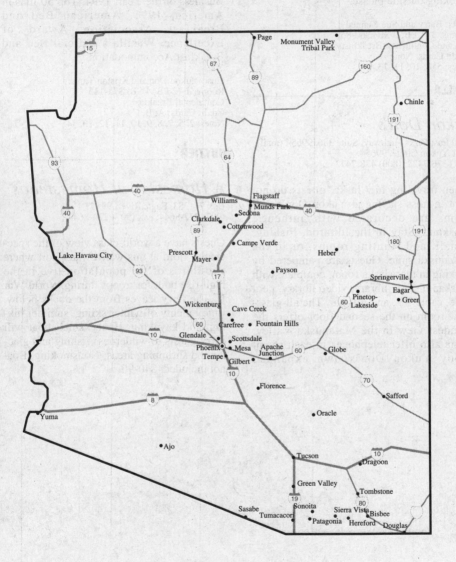

Arizona

Arizona

AJO

Bed and Breakfast Inn Arizona

8900 East Via Linda, Suite 101, Scottsdale, 85258
(602) 860-9338 (phone and FAX)

AJ001. This stately guest house from the mid-1920s has been totally renovated and is now peaceful and relaxing. Close to Organ Pipe Cactus National Monument. Spectacular desert scenes. Call for rates.

AJ101. The old mine manager's home, built at the turn of the century, has been completely renovated in styles of the period. Breakfast is lavish. There is a guest library, sunroom, small gift shop, and a spa. Golf course nearby. All rooms have private baths; only one room allows smoking. No pets or children. Modest to deluxe rates.

Mi Casa Su Casa

P.O. Box 950, Tempe, 85280-0950
(602) 990-0682; (800) 456-0682 (reservations only)

291. Near Organ Pipe Cactus National Monument and 50 minutes from Mexico. Originally built in 1925 to accommodate visiting company officials for Phelps Dodge, this inn has six guest rooms, queen-size and twin beds, five private baths, a reputation for warm hospitality, and excellent breakfasts. The furnishings reflect the rich traditions of Arizona. Children welcome. No smoking. Roll away bed available for an extra ten-dollar charge. $69.

APACHE JUNCTION

Bed and Breakfast Inn Arizona

8900 East Via Linda, Suite 101, Scottsdale, 85258
(602) 860-9338 (phone and FAX)

AJ102. A ranch family used this guest ranch as the main headquarters for their cattle operation in the White Mountains. These are hospitable country folk who have been written about as far away as Europe, and they know how to provide true hospitality. Individual cabins with private baths. Enjoy breakfast in the main house. Gift shop full of Western goodies. Horseback riding can be arranged nearby. Smoking permitted. Superior rates.

AJ104. Experience the Sonoran Desert at its finest, yet stay within an easy drive of the amenities of the Phoenix metro area in this rugged native stone and siding second-floor guest house. The Majestic Mountain Room has a queen-size bed and queen-size Hide-a-bed, private bath, picture window, sitting area, and TV. The Valley View Room has a queen-size bed and a trundle (makes into double or twin beds), private bath, and deck. Both rooms have small refrigerators, microwave ovens, and coffee makers. No children. Rugged terrain and

---

NOTES: Credit cards: A MasterCard; B Visa; C American Express; D Discover; E Diners Club; F Other;
2 Personal checks accepted; 3 Lunch available; 4 Dinner available; 5 Open all year; 6 Pets welcome;
7 No smoking; 8 Children welcome; 9 Social drinking allowed; 10 Tennis nearby; 11 Swimming nearby;
12 Golf nearby; 13 Skiing nearby; 14 May be booked through a travel agent.

stairs not suitable for handicapped. Deluxe rates include Continental breakfast.

Mi Casa Su Casa

P.O. Box 950, Tempe, 85280-0950
(602) 990-0682; (800) 456-0682 (reservations only)

306. On the Western face of the world famous Superstition Mountains, this five-acre Flatiron Ranch blends a secluded desert mountain retreat with the exciting diversity of recreational activities. One room has a queen-size bed, a queen-size Hide-a-bed, microwave, small refrigerator, coffee service, and a bath with shower ensuite. The second room has a queen-size bed, two twin-size beds, and a bath with shower ensuite. Continental plus breakfast. No smoking. No pets. Children over 12 welcome. Ten dollars for additional person. $71.

BISBEE

Bed and Breakfast Inn Arizona

8900 East Via Linda, Suite 101, Scottsdale, 85258
(602) 860-9338 (phone and FAX)

BE001. Beautifully appointed mansion has linens, lace, crystal chandeliers, canopied beds, and fireplaces. Call for rates.

BE002. Spanish-style original mining company VIP guest house. Grandly spacious rooms with antique furnishings. Leaded-, beveled-glass windows. Call for rates.

BE005. In the center of Bisbee atop Castle Rock, a 1906 restored mansion with exceptional views. A relaxing and inspiring atmosphere. Handicapped accessible. All amenities. Call for rates.

BE106. The delightful host couple is steeped in the lore and tradition of the area and welcomes guests as family. Breakfasts, usually served in the sunroom, feature delicious fresh breads and goodies of choice. The spacious home, built in 1912, faces a park with tennis and golf only a few steps away. TV and library. All fully restored bedrooms are upstairs. Two rooms have private baths, and two share a bath. Deluxe and modest rates. No children or pets; there is a friendly resident cat.

The Inn at Castle Rock

112 Tombstone Canyon Road, P.O. Box 1161, 85603
(520) 432-4449; (520) 432-7195; (800) 566-4449

An old Victorian miner's boarding house in central historic Bisbee features antiques, original art, gardens, and two parlors. Each of the rooms and suites has its own unique decor, original art, and bath. Top floor is a parlor, and the first floor has the Indian Spring. Breakfast includes a healthy fare of fresh fruit, juices, homemade muffins, coffees, and teas. Bisbee has a rich history and is elevated 5,300 feet into the Mule Mountains. Near wild country and nature conservancy areas.

Host: Jim Babcock
Rooms: 16 (PB) $50-60
Full Breakfast
Credit Cards: A, B
Notes: 2, 5, 7, 8, 11

Mi Casa Su Casa

P.O. Box 950, Tempe, 85280-0950
(602) 990-0682; (800) 456-0682 (reservations only)

255. A first glimpse of historic Bisbee seems to turn the clock back a century. Cradled in a valley in the Mule Mountains 90 miles from Tucson is this 1920s 5,000-square-foot two-story Mediterranean-style home. The host couple are Bisbee natives and extend a casual Western welcome to

---

NOTES: Credit cards accepted: A MasterCard; B Visa; C American Express; D Discover; E Diners Club; F Other; 2 Personal checks accepted; 3 Lunch available; 4 Dinner available; 5 Open all year; 6 Pets welcome;

guests. All guest rooms are on the second floor. Room one has a queen-size bed and private bath. Room two has a queen-size waterbed and private bath. Room three has a king-size bed or twin beds. Room four has a double bed. Rooms three and four have balconies and share a hall bath. Full breakfast. Children welcome. Resident cat. Smoking allowed outside. Visa and MasterCard accepted. $40-60.

2552. Newly restored and decorated home built around the turn of the century is in the Warren area. Step back in time while enjoying the art collection and antiques. All guest rooms are on the second floor. The master guest room has a queen-size bed, private bath, and a two-night minimum stay. Two other guest rooms have queen-size beds and share a bath. A family room with TV, VCR, many books, and a sunroom decorated in antique wicker and green plants are available for relaxing and reading. Full breakfast. No children. Resident dog and cat. Smoking outside. $55-65.

2553. This bed and breakfast inn, built in 1906 by a mining company, is a fine example of Craftsman architecture. It offers the privacy of eight suites and rooms furnished in antiques, private baths, and claw-foot tubs. Most baths have showers. Kitchens are stocked, and freshly baked muffins are delivered each day. Original billiard room has pool table and TV. Guest patio has a barbecue area. Air-conditioned. Two-night minimum stay. Nonsmoking. Fifteen dollars for additional person. $75-125.

Old Pueblo Homestays

P.O. Box 13603, Tucson, 85732
(800) 333-9 RSO

Park Place Bed and Breakfast. No visit to Arizona is complete without seeing the historical old mining town of Bisbee, some 25 miles from Tombstone. Cool in the summer and far enough south to have mild winters. Park Place is a 1920s well-cared-for two-story Mediterranean-style home with spacious bedrooms, balconies, terraces, library, and sunroom. Two guest rooms have queen-size beds and adjoining baths. Two other bedrooms share hall bathroom. Minimum stay is two nights. $40-70.

School House Inn

818 Tombstone Canyon, P.O. Box 32, 85603
(520) 432-2996; (800) 537-4333

An old schoolhouse built in 1918 and converted into lovely large rooms and suites with 12-foot ceilings and private baths. High up Tombstone Canyon, the 5,600-foot elevation provides spectacular scenery, clean air, and a relaxing retreat. A full breakfast is served on the shaded patio or in the spacious family room. The inn is close to mine tours, art galleries, antique shops, hiking, bird watching, and much more.

Hosts: Marc and Shirl Negus
Rooms: 9 (PB) $45-65
Full Breakfast
Credit Cards: A, B, C, D, E
Notes: 2, 5, 11, 12

CAMP VERDE

Mi Casa Su Casa

P.O. Box 950, Tempe, 85280-0950
(602) 990-0682; (800) 456-0682 (reservations only)

360. Built in 1915, this ranch house is a double-wall adobe two-story house that served as the homestead for one of northern Arizona's most prosperous cattle ranches. The house includes an artist's studio, exotic and domestic birds and animals, views of mountains surrounding the valley, and is less than one hour from spectacular red rock formations, conifer forests, Indian ruins, golf courses, a ghost town, and an old military fort. The first floor has two guest rooms with shared bath. The second floor suite

7 No smoking; 8 Children welcome; 9 Social drinking allowed; 10 Tennis nearby; 11 Swimming nearby; 12 Golf nearby; 13 Skiing nearby; 14 May be booked through a travel agent.

includes the entire upper floor and sleeps six comfortably. Guests welcome to use the living/dining room, kitchen, or to stroll around the farm. Full breakfast. No smoking. No pets. Children nine and over welcome. $50-75.

CAREFREE

Bed and Breakfast Inn Arizona

8900 East Via Linda, Suite 101, Scottsdale, 85258
(602) 860-9338 (phone and FAX)

CF 190. Relax in own private casita with views that are breathtaking. Fireplace, queen-size bed makes this desert oasis pure rejuvenation. Modest to deluxe rates.

CF 192. Farm animals, horses, and wildlife greet guests at this charming desert oasis. Privacy abounds as nature takes over. Modest to deluxe rates.

SD 142. Surrounded by the tranquil beauty of the desert, this deluxe retreat boasts four individual private casitas. A pool and jacuzzi are nestled into the mountain. After the sumptuous breakfast, guests can go hiking or mountain biking. Private cook-to-order dinners are available. This executive retreat is available for exclusive use. Modest to deluxe rates.

Old Pueblo Homestays

P.O. Box 13603, Tucson, 85732
(800) 333-9RSO

Desert Farren Hacienda. A deluxe private executive retreat on 20 plus private acres is surrounded by the Tonto National Forest. There are four spacious guest rooms with queen-size beds and private baths. Guest accommodations include large, comfortable fireplace rooms, stereo with CD, cassette, AM/FM, color remote control TV, VCR,

daily paper, iron and ironing board, hair dryers, complimentary laundry service, and full concierge services. Pool and spa on premises. A heart healthy breakfast is served in the scenic courtyard, weather permitting. Afternoon munchies and evening dinner are available. Only 45 minutes from Sky Harbor Airport and the heart of Scottsdale. Golf, horseback riding, hiking, mountain bike riding, jeep tours, and fine dinner are nearby. Smoking outside only. No pets. Inquire about children being welcome. Weekly rates available upon request. Additional charge for extra people. $78-149.

CAVE CREEK

Mi Casa Su Casa

P.O. Box 950, Tempe, 85280-0950
(602) 990-0682; (800) 456-0682 (reservations only)

233. Spacious, comfortable ranch-style home rests on ten acres of virgin desert adjacent to state land and the scenic foothills. Hike and become surrounded by the lush and undisturbed wonders of the Sonoran Desert. Enjoy the panoramic view of sunrises and midnight constellations from the deck. This ranch is ideal for the scenic Prescott/Jerome/Sedona day-trip loop. Private guest wing has guest room with queen-size bed, TV, sitting/game room, private bath with shower, and private entrance. Main kitchen privileges. Continental breakfast. Smoking outside. Children are welcome. Horses boarded. $65.

286. Large rustic home on five acres. Guest accommodations are in one section of the house. Large suite has own living room, TV, large bedroom with queen-size bed, double bed, twin bed, and connecting full bath. The second bedroom is smaller and has a double bed and a hall bath. The apartment has a private entrance, bath, kitchenette, and two rooms each with a double

NOTES: Credit cards accepted: A MasterCard; B Visa; C American Express; D Discover; E Diners Club; F Other; 2 Personal checks accepted; 3 Lunch available; 4 Dinner available; 5 Open all year; 6 Pets welcome;

bed. Pool available. Cookouts, barbecues, and hay rides available by appointment. Continental breakfast weekdays, and full breakfast on weekends. Resident dog. Smoking outside only. Ten-dollar charge for well-behaved children over ten years of age. $40-65.

394. This hillside home with fantastic views offers a separate but attached 650 square foot guest apartment. Private entrance, living room, king- and queen-size beds, full bath, gas fireplace, cable TV, VCR, private telephone, fully equipped kitchen with microwave and full-size refrigerator. The kitchen is stocked with breakfast items and snacks. Mexican tiled sunroom and an elevated porch with barbecue grill. Restaurants, shopping, and golf nearby. No smoking. No pets. Children 12 and over welcome. $110.

CHINLE

Bed and Breakfast
Inn Arizona
8900 East Via Linda, Suite 101, Scottsdale, 85258
(602) 860-9338 (phone and FAX)

CN002. Historic lodge in spectacular, scenic Navajo land near Canyon de Chelly National Monument. Charming restaurant inside original 1896 trading post. Private baths. Call for rates.

CLARKDALE

Mi Casa Su Casa
P.O. Box 950, Tempe, 85280-0950
(602) 990-0682; (800) 456-0682 (reservations only)

145. Ideal for all who love and appreciate nature. All accommodations have Arizona country decor. A separate guest house is nestled under majestic old cottonwood trees. It has a queen-size bed, private bath with shower. The country condo is separate but attached to the main house. It has a private entrance, porch, bedroom with queen-size bed, an extra-large double shower, and a full kitchen with microwave oven. There is a comfortable sofa in the living/dining room where a third person could sleep. There is also a guest room in the main house which has a private entrance, a double bed, and private hall bath. Full breakfast. Children are welcome. Smoking outside. Guest pet with permission. $65-75.

COTTONWOOD

Bed and Breakfast
Inn Arizona
8900 East Via Linda, Suite 101, Scottsdale, 85258
(602) 860-9338 (phone and FAX)

CW103. This rustic cottage is a romantic hideaway for two, complete with queen-size bed, private bath, country decor, and outside hot tub. This hostess enjoys serving sun-ripened fruit (in season) from her organic garden with a country breakfast. In the main house is an additional bedroom with queen-size bed, private hall bath, and a second bedroom for children. Only ten minutes from Clarkdale train. Outside dog and cat. Modest to deluxe rates.

CW104. Magnificent views of Mingus Mountain, the Verde Valley, the red rocks of Sedona, and on clear days, the San Francisco Peaks. This friendly host couple makes sure guests are comfortable, and they serve a wonderful country-style full breakfast. Spa and a choice of the Sunrise Room, with queen-size bed, private hall bath, TV in room; or the Guest House, with queen-size bed, private, connecting bath, wood-burning stove, and kitchenette, decorated in Early American style. Dogs and cats on premises. Children over five are welcome. Modest to deluxe rates.

7 No smoking; 8 Children welcome; 9 Social drinking allowed; 10 Tennis nearby; 11 Swimming nearby; 12 Golf nearby; 13 Skiing nearby; 14 May be booked through a travel agent.

DOUGLAS

Mi Casa Su Casa

P.O. Box 950, Tempe, 85280-0950
(602) 990-0682; (800) 456-0682 (reservations
only)

1628. This ranch is on the northeastern slope of the Chiricahua Mountains near many historic sites, museums, and old Mexico. Daily trail rides are available for four to 20 people, and the ranch can supply pack animals for heavy packs. One- or two-room bunk houses have baths; an apartment includes a kitchenette and private patio. Camper and trailer hook-ups are nearby. A swimming pool and a three-acre catfish pond are on the premises. Rates include room, three daily meals, and horseback riding. $85-160.

DRAGOON

Mi Casa Su Casa

P.O. Box 950, Tempe, 85280-0950
(602) 990-0682; (800) 456-0682 (reservations
only)

307. This bed and breakfast offers spectacular views and the opportunity to enjoy country living. Both the main house and the separate guest house are rammed earth, passive solar structures. The guest house has two bedrooms, one with a queen-size bed and the other with twin beds. The hall bath with shower is shared. Guest rooms have electric heaters and electric blankets. The sitting area is warmed by a potbellied stove, and the small kitchen has a coffee maker, sink, microwave oven, toaster oven, electric skillet, and small refrigerator. Private sun deck and gas grill available. Children over 12 are welcome. Full breakfast. Smoking is allowed outside only. A spa is available in the main house. $50-55.

EAGAR

Bed and Breakfast Inn Arizona

8900 East Via Linda, Suite 101, Scottsdale, 85258
(602) 860-9338 (phone and FAX)

EA101. Step back into time in this wonderfully restored historic landmark home from the early 1900s, built in the Colonial Revival style. Four luxurious rooms, each with private bath, plus a deluxe breakfast, make this a quaint getaway worth the trip in winter for skiing, or summertime to escape the desert heat. Three rooms with double beds, one suite with a double bed in one room, and twin in the other. The guest parlor has an old-fashioned soda fountain. Swimming and tennis nearby. Deluxe rates.

FLAGSTAFF

Arizona Mountain Inn

685 Lake Mary Road, 86001
(602) 774-8959

The Old English Tudor-style inn and cottages are about three miles from Flagstaff. There are 13 wooded acres surrounded by national forest. The rooms are decorated in antiques, crystal, and lace in a beautiful mix of European charm and classic Southwestern elegance.

Hosts: The Wanek family
Rooms: 3 (PB) $70-100
Continental Breakfast
Credit Cards: A, B, D
Notes: 2, 5, 7, 9, 12, 13

Bed and Breakfast Inn Arizona

8900 East Via Linda, Suite 101, Scottsdale, 85258
(602) 860-9338 (phone and FAX)

FS001. Premier, extreme trilevel contemporary amongst the pines. Quiet, close to

---

NOTES: Credit cards accepted: A MasterCard; B Visa; C American Express; D Discover; E Diners Club;
F Other; 2 Personal checks accepted; 3 Lunch available; 4 Dinner available; 5 Open all year; 6 Pets welcome;

downtown and park. Views of the San Francisco peaks. Full breakfast served. Call for rates.

FS003. The charming, quaint, and comfortable ambience here is unsurpassed. Previously a stately family residence. Full breakfast. Call for rates.

FS112. Three cozy little cottages in the heart of old Flagstaff are the ultimate for privacy. The hostess will greet guests and show them to a private two-bedroom cottage and leave the first morning's breakfast for guests to self-cater. Built in the 1920s, the cottages have been furnished in the spirit of those times. Laundry facilities, TV, and telephone. Playground nearby—great for families. No pets. Some traffic noise can be heard in two of the cottages on the road to the canyon. Superior rates.

Birch Tree Inn

824 West Birch Avenue, 86001
(520) 774-1042

The Birch Tree Inn, circa 1917, offers guests comfortable surroundings amidst authentic period furnishings in one of the city's finest historic old homes. The parlor offers guests a place to read, converse, or relax in front of a roaring fire. Each bedroom features its own comfortable atmosphere: antiques, heirlooms, Southwestern or wicker, with specially chosen linens and wall coverings to add the perfect finishing touches. Off-street parking. A full breakfast is prepared and served in the sunny dining room or outside on the veranda, while early morning coffee is served in the upstairs hall. Afternoon refreshments are served in the parlor. "A wonderfully relaxing time to meet other interesting guests or plan the evening."

Hosts: Sandy and Ed Znetko;
   Donna and Rodger Pettinger
Rooms: 5 (3 PB; 2 SB) $50-80

Full Breakfast
Credit Cards: A, B, C
Notes: 2, 5, 7, 9, 10, 12, 13

Comfi Cottages of Flagstaff

1612 North Aztec Street, 86001
(520) 774-0731

In historic downtown Flagstaff, the cottages are beautifully decorated and furnished with antique pieces having a touch of the Southwest. These one-, two-, and three- bedroom cottages are equipped with everything guests need for comfortable daily living. The guests' choice of breakfast foods are placed in the refrigerator to be prepared at their leisure. All cottages have a picnic table, lawn chairs, and barbecue grills; some have fireplaces. Guests may borrow bicycles to explore historic Flagstaff or ride the urban trail. Inquire about bringing pets.

Hosts: Pat and Ed Wiebe
Cottages: 5 (PB and SB) $65-195
Full Breakfast
Credit Cards: A, B
Notes: 2, 5, 7, 8, 9, 10, 11, 12, 13, 14

Dierker House

423 West Cherry Street, 86001
(520) 774-3249

Charming old house with spacious antique-filled rooms, private entrance, sitting room, and guest kitchen. An excellent breakfast is served at 8:00 A.M. in the downstairs dining room; Continental breakfast for late risers.

Host: Dorothea Dierker
Rooms: 3 (SB) $45
Full and Continental Breakfasts
Credit Cards: None
Notes: 2, 5, 7, 9, 10, 11, 12, 13

The Inn at 410

410 North Leroux Street, 86001
(800) 774-2008

The Inn at 410 offers guests four seasons of hospitality in a charming 1907 home. Elegantly furnished with antiques, this inn

7 No smoking; 8 Children welcome; 9 Social drinking allowed; 10 Tennis nearby; 11 Swimming nearby; 12 Golf nearby; 13 Skiing nearby; 14 May be booked through a travel agent.

The Inn at 410

has stained glass and touches of the Southwest. Eight distinctive suites, each with its own private bath, mini-fridge and coffee maker; some with fireplace and/or Jacuzzi tub. Each guest is pampered with a personal touch that includes oven-fresh cookies, healthy breakfasts, and recommendations about day trips to the Grand Canyon, Indian ruins, hiking, or skiing.

Hosts: Howard and Sally Krueger
Rooms: 8 (PB) $100-150
Full Breakfast
Credit Cards: A, B, C
Notes: 2, 5, 7, 8, 9, 12, 13, 14

Mi Casa Su Casa

P.O. Box 950, Tempe, 85280-0950
(602) 990-0682; (800) 456-0682 (reservations
  only)

100. Very nice split-level house built in 1967 on a sloping mountain lot in a pretty residential neighborhood. The guest rooms are on the first level, several steps down from the front door. The host couple live on the second floor. Both guest rooms have king-size beds. Full hall bath. Recreation room has cable TV, VCR, refrigerator, fireplace, and a double sofa bed. Only one party accepted at a time. Great for families. Crib available. Full breakfast. Resident dog. Smoking allowed outside. Infants stay at no charge. Five dollars for children under five years of age and $10 for children over five. Forty-five dollars for additional adults. $65.

247. Contemporary, trilevel home in the forest has multiple spacious decks, views, and extra-large rooms with tongue-in-groove wood ceilings. The house is decorated with Grand Canyon and Navajo art. Host couple and son live on second and third levels. The guest area on the first level has a private entrance, king-size bed, double-size futon, small flip chair, playpen, and private full hall bath. Also on the first level is a very large family room with a wet bar, microwave, small refrigerator, TV/VCR, private telephone, and a wood-burning stove. Full breakfast. Resident dog and cat. Smoking allowed outside only. Perfect for families. Five dollars for children under five years of age and $10 for children over five. Infants free. Fifteen dollars for additional adult. $75.

259. First a private home, then a fraternity house, this historic two-story house built in 1917 is now a bed and breakfast inn. Two couples are the innkeepers. Five guest rooms on the second floor. The Pella Room and the Wicker Room have queen-size beds and share a hall bath. Carol's Room has a queen-size bed with a private bath. The large Southwest Room has a king-size bed and large private bath. Full breakfast. Resident dog. Children ten and older are welcome. Smoking allowed outside. Free Amtrak pick-up. $55-80.

364. Private home has spacious suite, private entrance, deck, and one small guest room. Chemically and environmentally sensitive surroundings feature ionizing air cleaners, natural non-perfumed soaps and non-toxic cleansers, unscented toilet paper and facial tissue, non-toxic paints, tile floors, and linens washed with biodegradable detergent. Suite has bedroom with king-size bed, living room, TV, twin beds, kitchen, and private bath. The second room has a double bed and shares a hall bath. Continental-plus breakfast. Children over nine welcome. No pets. No smoking. Open

NOTES: Credit cards accepted: A MasterCard; B Visa; C American Express; D Discover; E Diners Club; F Other; 2 Personal checks accepted; 3 Lunch available; 4 Dinner available; 5 Open all year; 6 Pets welcome;

May 1 through November 1. A two-night minimum preferred. $65-95.

Old Pueblo Homestays

P.O. Box 13603, Tucson, 85732
(800) 333-9 RSO

Hakatai House Bed and Breakfast. In northern Arizona about 75 miles from the Grand Canyon, this bed and breakfast is close to ski areas, Sunset Crater, and other points of interest. This three-story home has a large king-size bedroom with private bath. The first-floor family room has a double futon and a twin bed. There is also a wet bar, microwave, TV, VCR, and fireplace for guests' convenience. Select breakfast from a menu. Two resident outside cats and a dog. Five dollars each child under five and $10 for children over five. $75.

FLORENCE

Mi Casa Su Casa

P.O. Box 950, Tempe, 85280-0950
(602) 990-0682; (800) 456-0682 (reservations only)

393. Recently renovated to its original charm, guests will feel at ease at this 1930s adobe guest ranch on 16 acres. Six guest rooms with air conditioning, private entrances, private baths, and TVs. Three rooms have queen-size beds, one with a double bed and a twin bed, and another room has twin beds or can be made into a king-size bed. The suite has a full kitchen, and a sitting room with a queen-size sofa bed. Pool. Barbecue area. Continental breakfast buffet with daily rates only. Pets welcome with prior approval. Children welcome. Weekly and monthly rates available. $59.

Old Pueblo Homestays

P.O. Box 13603, Tucson, 85732
(800) 333-9 RSO

Inn at Rancho Sonora. An original 1930's adobe guest ranch with locally handcrafted beds. Rancho Sonora is an ideal setting for a special event or just relaxing by the pool with cabana or in the bricked courtyard enclosed by a stuccoed adobe wall featuring a magnificent fountain with landscaping. TV, individual heating and air conditioning. A complete Continental breakfast is served in the country style dining room or outside on the patio. Smoking outside. Inquire about pets being welcome. Children welcome. $60-120.

FOUNTAIN HILLS

Bed and Breakfast Inn Arizona

8900 East Via Linda, Suite 101, Scottsdale, 85258
(602) 860-9338 (phone and FAX)

FH106. Just minutes from Scottsdale, Saguaro Lake, and some of the finest golf in the Phoenix area. Lovely guest suite with private entrance, spa, and sitting room. A queen-size bed, private bath, and sitting room Hide-a-bed, all done in Southwestern style, has an uninterrupted view of the mountains and desert sunrise. Join the family for a full breakfast. Visit Out of Africa, a nearby wildlife park. Because of the pool, only children ten and older are welcome. No smokers. Superior rates.

FH107. A stunning multilevel private home bed and breakfast built into the side of a small canyon with private entrances for each room. Charming, professional hosts serve full breakfasts in the main part of the house, or a Continental breakfast can be delivered to the suites. Explore the Verde River or laze around the pool in the sunshine. The Linger Longer suite is a charmingly eclectic mix of Victorian and Southwestern, with a queen-size bed, private bath, and an efficiency kitchen. Second room has twin beds, private hall bath. Both rooms have French doors opening onto a lovely patio overlooking the pool. Dog in residence. Children are welcome by prior arrangement. Modest to deluxe rates.

Mi Casa Su Casa

P.O. Box 950, Tempe, 85280-0950
(602) 990-0682; (800) 456-0682 (reservations only)

407. This trilevel contemporary home built in 1986 offers panoramic views of the desert, surrounding mountains, and the world's tallest fountain. It offers a great room with fireplace, cable TV, and VCR. A sitting room for reading or relaxing leads outdoors to a heated spa. One guest room has a queen-size bed. The other guest room has an antique full-size bed. Shared full hall bath. Guests are welcome to use the two mountain bikes. Scottsdale and Mesa are nearby. Full breakfast. No pets. No children. $75.

409. An elegant and beautiful home built on a hill with 50 to 80 miles of panoramic mountain views. Pleasant and simple European decor throughout. The house is air-conditioned. The master suite has a king-size bed, patio door, TV, walk-in closet, and large luxurious bath with extra-large shower, whirlpool tub, and chaise. The second room has a queen-size bed, shared connecting full bath with third room that has twin beds. The fourth room has twin beds, full private bath, and walk-in closet. Continental plus breakfast. No smoking. No pets. No children. $65-175.

GILBERT

Mi Casa Su Casa

P.O. Box 950, Tempe, 85280-0950
(602) 990-0682; (800) 456-0682 (reservations only)

417. Guests will enjoy a new community built around a small lake. Guest room has a queen-size bed and full private hall bath. Guests are welcome to use the living room for reading, the TV in the family room, or the pool. Continental plus breakfast on weekdays, and full breakfast on weekends. Air conditioning. Smoking restricted. No pets. No children. $60.

GLENDALE

Mi Casa Su Casa

P.O. Box 950, Tempe, 85280-0950
(602) 990-0682; (800) 456-0682 (reservations only)

411. Spanish-style home on golf course has air conditioning, shared bath, and two rooms with queen-size beds. Guests welcome to use the cable TV in the family room or read in the living room. Complimentary refreshments. Full breakfast. Small outside dog in residence. Public transportation and large shopping mall nearby. Smoking restricted. No pets. No children. $75

GLOBE

Bed and Breakfast Inn Arizona

8900 East Via Linda, Suite 101, Scottsdale, 85258
(602) 860-9338 (phone and FAX)

GL101. A wonderful modern guest house on a working horse farm (horses are not for hire). The kitchen window overlooks Besh Ba Gowah Archaeological Park, a partially reconstructed Salado Indian ruin, and Pinal Mountains. Two bedrooms, one with queen-size bed and private bath (shower only); and one with two twin beds or king-size bed with private bath (shower and tub). Self-catered Continental breakfast. Children over 12 welcome. Deluxe rates.

NOTES: Credit cards accepted: A MasterCard; B Visa; C American Express; D Discover; E Diners Club; F Other; 2 Personal checks accepted; 3 Lunch available; 4 Dinner available; 5 Open all year; 6 Pets welcome;

Mi Casa Su Casa

P.O. Box 950, Tempe, 85280-0950
(602) 990-0682; (800) 456-0682 (reservations
only)

302. Handsome, brick, ranch-style home
has separate guest house with a large living
room/full kitchen and two guest rooms,
each with private bath. Room one has a
queen-size bed, and room two has twin
beds. The hostess raises Paso Fino horses
and the host is an attorney and a volunteer
firefighter. Their seven-acre horse farm is
at the edge of town with a panoramic view
of the nearby Pinal Mountains and is near a
famous archeological site. The breakfast is
self-catering as the kitchen is stocked with
breakfast items. Two-night minimum.
Children 12 and older are welcome.
Smoking allowed outside. $65.

GREEN VALLEY

Old Pueblo Homestays

P.O. Box 13603, Tucson, 85732
(800) 333-9RSO

The 1490 Ranch Bed and Breakfast. A
charming three-bedroom Western stucco
and masonry home filled with antique furniture has two bedrooms sharing a hall bath.
TV, radio, and telephone. Full or Continental breakfast is served. Madera Canyon,
Titan Historic Missile Site, Tubac Country
Club, and several golf courses are nearby.
On premises is a dog and cat inside at night
only. No smoking. No pets. Children over
10 welcome. Two-night minimum. A roll
away bed is also available at an additional
cost. $45-65.

GREER

Bed and Breakfast
Inn Arizona

8900 East Via Linda, Suite 101, Scottsdale, 85258
(602) 860-9338 (phone and FAX)

GR001. Southwestern hospitality in a 100-
year-old farmhouse is nestled in remote
mountain valley. Special homemade breakfast offerings. Selected full housekeeping
cabins also available. Call for rates.

Mi Casa Su Casa

P.O. Box 950, Tempe, 85280-0950
(602) 990-0682; (800) 456-0682 (reservations
only)

303. Meadowview is a ten-room house that
combines the feel of a traditional log cabin
with modern convenience and luxury. The
master suite on the first floor includes a
queen-size bed, fireplace, and full bath with
Jacuzzi tub. Private entrance to large front
deck with a view of beautiful Greer Valley.
A second bedroom is on the second floor
and has a king-size bed, two trundle twin
beds, and a private hall bath. Continental
breakfast. Children eight and older are welcome. Smoking allowed outside. Extra
charge for each additional guest in room
two. $55-75.

Ramsey Canyon Inn

HEREFORD

Ramsey Canyon Inn

31 Ramsey Canyon Road, 85615
(520) 378-3010

Capture the romantic spirit of simple country living with a warmth and graciousness

---

that is traditionally Arizona. In the Huachuca Mountains at an elevation of 5,400 feet, Ramsey Canyon is truly a hummingbird haven, with 15 species on record. Nestled by a winding mountain stream and surrounded by syca-more, maple, juniper, oak, and pine trees, wildlife is abundant. The average summer temperature is 75 degrees. One-bedroom cottages are also available. Come and discover the rich history of Cochise County. Limited smoking.

Hosts: Ronald and Shirlene DeSantis
Rooms: 6 (PB) $90-105
Cottages: 2
Full Breakfast
Credit Cards: F
Notes: 2, 5, 9, 10, 11, 12

LAKE HAVASU CITY

Bed and Breakfast Inn Arizona

8900 East Via Linda, Suite 101, Scottsdale, 85258
(602) 860-9338 (phone and FAX)

LH001. Friendly resort inn, lake view rooms, suites, fireplaces, pool, and Jacuzzi. Call for rates.

LAKESIDE

Bartram's Bed and Breakfast

Route 1, Box 1014, 85929
(602) 367-1408

Bartram's

Bartram's can be found at the edge of the Apache Indian reservation in a lovely, quiet setting surrounded by two acres of maintained yard. Guests enjoy a wonderful country setting about a mile from town and great restaurants, antique stores, shopping, and a variety of activities, such as horseback riding, golf, hiking, fishing, and more. A full seven-course breakfast is served in a dining room with a large bay window and a great view. Picnic lunches are available at additional cost. Inquire about accommodations for pets.

Hosts: Petie and Ray Bartram
Rooms: 5 (PB) $85
Full Breakfast
Credit Cards: None
Notes: 2, 5, 7, 8, 9, 10, 11, 12, 13, 14

MAYER

Bed and Breakfast Inn Arizona

8900 East Via Linda, Suite 101, Scottsdale, 85258
(602) 860-9338 (phone and FAX)

MA001. Victorian setting in old mining town. Pool, Jacuzzi, private entrance. Close to Prescott, Sedona, Verde Valley, and Jerome areas. Call for rates.

MESA

Bed and Breakfast Inn Arizona

8900 East Via Linda, Suite 101, Scottsdale, 85258
(602) 860-9338 (phone and FAX)

ME103. This delightful Mediterranean-style guest house has a queen-size bed, private entrance, pool, and lakeside frontage in the midst of citrus trees and flowers. Small refrigerator, microwave oven, coffee maker, electric skillet, and private bath. Gazebo next to lake for eating or relaxing. Weekdays, Continental breakfast; weekends, full breakfast. Ideal for family, with

NOTES: Credit cards accepted: A MasterCard; B Visa; C American Express; D Discover; E Diners Club;
F Other; 2 Personal checks accepted; 3 Lunch available; 4 Dinner available; 5 Open all year; 6 Pets welcome;

the best of both privacy and a bed and breakfast host. Children are welcome. Deluxe rates.

ME104. A fantastic adult community with a homey atmosphere, this bustling retirement resort boasts everything for the visitor, with breakfast plus the choice of second meal daily in their restaurant, cable TV, 24-hour staffing, crafts, game and exercise rooms, heated pool and spa, and even an in-house parlor. Fully furnished apartments available by the day, week, or month include a living room, bedroom, bath, and furnished kitchen. The younger crowd is welcome for shorter visits. Superior rates.

Mi Casa Su Casa

P.O. Box 950, Tempe, 85280-0950
(602) 990-0682; (800) 456-0682 (reservations only)

001. Country living in the city places guests only twenty minutes from Tempe and Scottsdale. These two accommodations are nestled in a large citrus grove. The guest room in the main house offers a room with twin beds, cable TV, private hall bath, and full breakfast. The self-contained guest cottage, built in 1975 to match the handsome main house, has a living room with TV and phone, complete kitchen, bedroom with queen-size bed, dressing room, full bath, and enclosed garage. No children. No resident pets. No smoking. Special weekly and monthly rates available. Ten dollar charge for each additional guests. $115.

002. Friendly, busy host couple welcome guests to their casual, happy home. Their very large, contemporary Spanish home on one acre is close to shopping, golf, and spring baseball training. Guest suite has private entrance, living room with double bed, double Hide-a-Bed, private bath, dining area, sink, refrigerator, and TV. Casual breakfasts might include homemade

breads, jams, and fresh eggs produced on the premises. Pool. Resident dog. Handicapped facilities possible. Children over nine are welcome. Smoking outside. Ten dollars extra for children. $45.

220. Friendly, caring Scandinavian host couple from Minnesota welcome guests to a spacious Spanish-style home. In a quiet, handsome neighborhood, it is one mile to the golf course, three miles to baseball spring training, and an easy drive to the Superstition Mountains and Apache Trail. Decor is traditional with Scandinavian touch. Room one has a queen-size bed, room two has a double bed; they share a hall bath. Only one party accepted at a time. Laundry facilities are available. Continental-plus breakfast. Children 12 and older are welcome. No smoking. Weekly rates are available. $40-50.

230. Outgoing hostess of Irish background enjoys bed and breakfast guests. She has a small three-bedroom, two-bath home. Friendly, accommodating atmosphere. Near golf courses, two miles from the Chicago Cubs spring training, 15 miles to Indian reservation and gambling. Near public transportation. Master bedroom has queen-size bed and private bath. A smaller guest room has twin beds and a shared bath. Guests are welcome to use family room with TV and fireplace. Full breakfast. Kitchen privileges. Children under 12 are welcome. No resident pets. Small guest pet possible. Smoking allowed outside. $40-55.

236. This spacious stucco Mediterranean-looking home has beautiful landscaping and a view of the Superstition Mountains. The hostess, an outstanding cook, enjoys fixing gourmet breakfasts and evening snacks. Three guest rooms are available in private guest wing that has one bath. Only one party at a time. Room one has a king-size bed, room two has a queen-size bed,

7 No smoking; 8 Children welcome; 9 Social drinking allowed; 10 Tennis nearby; 11 Swimming nearby; 12 Golf nearby; 13 Skiing nearby; 14 May be booked through a travel agent.

and room three has one twin bed. Guests are welcome to use the family room with stereo and fireplace or living room that has cable TV and VCR. Pool. Small resident dog. Smoking allowed outside. Fifteen dollars extra for children over ten. $65.

358. In east Mesa, near Apache Junction, the Superstition Mountains, and the Apache Trail, is this contemporary home on an acre of land. Two guest rooms have queen-size beds and share a hall bath. Guests are welcome to swim in the solar-heated swimming pool or to relax by the living room fireplace. Full breakfast. Children are welcome. Pre-arranged baby-sitting available. Resident cat. Smoking allowed outside. Special rates for long stays. $45-55.

381. Large, handsome home is in quiet residential neighborhood on a cul-de-sac in citrus growing area. Guest suite is very private. The guest room has a king-size bed. The private full bath in hall has two sinks. The guest sitting area has a TV and double sofa bed for a third person. Crib available. Infants only. No pets. No smoking. $70.

MONUMENT VALLEY TRIBAL PARK

Bed and Breakfast Inn Arizona

8900 East Via Linda, Suite 101, Scottsdale, 85258
(602) 860-9338 (phone and FAX)

MV001. Lodge and trading post open since 1924. Adjacent to Navajo tribal park, motor inn-type accommodations, attractively furnished, Southwestern-style rooms, panoramic views, some on hillside level with balconies and patios. Indoor heated pool. Call for rates.

MR001. Discover the Navajo Nation. Southwestern/Navajo-style rooms with TV,

private bath, and restaurant with traditional Navajo dishes and Southwestern-style foods. Personalized tours of Navajo Nation available. Call for rates.

MUNDS PARK

Mi Casa Su Casa

P.O. Box 950, Tempe, 85280-0950
(602) 990-0682; (800) 456-0682 (reservations only)

342. Sociable couple have a two-story country cottage in a heavily wooded area. Built in the 1960s, the house is in a country club area 17 miles south of Flagstaff, which offers an 18-hole golf course, tennis, heated pool, bingo, and bridge. The second floor has two bedrooms that share a full hall bath. Room one has a king-size bed, and room two has twin beds. Only one party accepted at a time. Guests are welcome to use the living room, which has cable TV. The couple has a suite on the first floor. Full healthy breakfasts. Resident dog. No smoking. No children. Open May 15 through September 15. $65.

ORACLE

Bed and Breakfast Inn Arizona

8900 East Via Linda, Suite 101, Scottsdale, 85258
(602) 860-9338 (phone and FAX)

OR001. Spanish-style hideaway has private entrances off the courtyard. Spacious rooms with fireplaces and private baths. Close to prehistoric cliff dwellings and Biosphere 2. Call for rates.

OR101. An original homestead ranch with three separate cottages, plus a romantic suite in the main house. Guests enjoy breakfast with the gracious hosts in the spacious country kitchen of the 100-year-old ranch house. The Hill House has three bedrooms, living room, fully equipped kitchen, bath with antique tub/shower, and porch. The Guest House is an adobe with queen-size bedroom/sitting room, private bath, and a screened sleeping porch. The Forman's House is secluded, with two bedrooms, a full kitchen, private bath, and screened porch. The Trowbridge Suite, in the main house, is a romantic hideaway with a queen-size bed, fireplace, sitting area, private bath, rose arbor entrance, and private patio. Children welcome. Deluxe rates.

Mi Casa Su Casa

P.O. Box 950, Tempe, 85280-0950
(602) 990-0682; (800) 456-0682 (reservations only)

376. Near Biosphere 2, this home in a country-desert setting has four guest rooms, all with private baths and private entrances onto a courtyard. Guests enjoy the distant mountain views and the hiking. Near Catalina Park, 35 minutes from Tucson, eight miles to Peppersauce Canyon, 30 minutes to Aravaipa Canyon. Two queen-size beds, one double bed, and one pair of twin beds. No resident pets. Children over 12 are welcome. Ten dollars for third person in same room. Weekly and monthly rates available. Rates with a Continental breakfast are $55. Rates with a full breakfast are $60.

Old Pueblo Homestays

P.O. Box 13603, Tucson, 85732
(800) 333-9 RSO

Villa Cardinale. A Spanish hideaway with red-tile roofs and courtyard with fountain is just 35 minutes from Tucson but a world away from the city's fast pace. Catalina Mountain country with spectacular views and clear, starry nights. Spacious rooms, private entrance, fireplace, baths. A full country breakfast is included as part of every stay. Minimum stay is two nights. Children over 16. $55.

PAGE

Bed and Breakfast Inn Arizona

8900 East Via Linda, Suite 101, Scottsdale, 85258
(602) 860-9338 (phone and FAX)

PG001. This full-service miniresort features Southwestern Indian-designed architecture. Private bath and bedrooms with two double beds or king-size beds. Pool. Call for rates.

PG002. Lodge overlooking spectacular lake. Pool, restaurants, and TV available. Housekeeping units. Call for rates.

PG103. Home with a modern setting. Hosts are outdoor enthusiasts and river-raft runners. Landscaped patio and garden. Private entrance, bath. Breakfast. Call for rates.

Mi Casa Su Casa

P.O. Box 950, Tempe, 85280-0950
(602) 990-0682; (800) 456-0682 (reservations only)

359. Spacious home on edge of Page has sunken courtyard and formal garden. Homes here are ranchette style on lots no smaller than two acres. The large guest room has air conditioning, queen-size bed, cable TV, walk-in closet, sink, telephone, and Southwest decor. There is one folding cot available. Private full hall bath. The breakfast possibilities include Western specialties, or a buffet is set, depending upon the scheduled river trips. The hosts enjoy activities in the many nearby national parks, reading, theater, and gardening. Resident cats. Smoking allowed outside. Third person an additional five dollars. $65.

365. This two-story home overlooks the shear sandstone of the Vermillion Cliffs beyond a wide expanse of open desert, the

7 No smoking; 8 Children welcome; 9 Social drinking allowed; 10 Tennis nearby; 11 Swimming nearby; 12 Golf nearby; 13 Skiing nearby; 14 May be booked through a travel agent.

blue waters of Lake Powell, and the impressive face of Glen Canyon Dam. The large guest room has a queen-size bed, sitting area, private bath, and private upstairs balcony. Double air mattress available. Continental plus breakfast. Smoking restricted. No pets. For each additional person an extra five dollars. $75.

Old Pueblo Homestays

P.O. Box 13603, Tucson, 85732
(800) 333-9 RSO

A Place Above the Cliff. In northern Arizona, this two-story home has a large room on the second floor with French doors leading to a balcony overlooking Lake Powell. The room has a queen-size bed and private bath with marble shower. An air bed is available for children. Continental breakfast is served. A grand piano and cable TV are available. Smoking allowed outside only. No pets. $75.

PATAGONIA

Bed and Breakfast Inn Arizona

8900 East Via Linda, Suite 101, Scottsdale, 85258
(602) 860-9338 (phone and FAX)

PA001. Turn-of-the-century Adobe miners' apartments has private entrances. Full breakfast, beautiful sunsets, and scenery. Call for rates.

PA002. Guest house has private and relaxing atmosphere. Close to the Mexican border. Patio, fireplace, private baths. Full breakfast. Golf, hiking, and shopping close by. Call for rates.

PA003. In town and within walking distance of all activities. Full breakfast. Close to San Rafael Mountains, ghost towns, and silver mines. Call for rates.

Mi Casa Su Casa

P.O. Box 950, Tempe, 85280-0950
(602) 990-0682; (800) 456-0682 (reservations only)

356. Hostess and son welcome guests to historic adobe home on the square one block from the town square. The home is decorated with original artwork by area artists. Suite one has a bedroom with twin beds, sitting room with twin beds, and connecting private bath. Suite two is decorated with period antiques, has a bedroom with a queen-size bed, a sitting room with twin beds, and a connecting private bath. Suite three has a bedroom with a queen-size bed, a sitting room with one twin bed and a wood-burning stove, and a private bath. Resident dog. Full breakfast. Smoking restricted. No pets. $65.

363. Originally built in the 1930s, this cottage is a frame house in the bungalow style, much like an English cottage. There are many trees, flowers, and vines. The interior is light and airy with antique and contemporary furnishings. The adobe is a small house next door to the cottage. The cottage has a living room, full kitchen, two bedrooms, each with a double bed, a full hall bath, and private patio. The adobe has a private entrance from the porch into the king-size bedroom. Attached to the bedroom is a smaller bedroom with one single bed and then a full bath. There is also a small living room and full kitchen. The front room in the adobe has a private entrance and a small craft-gallery. Bicycles are available for guest use. Kitchens are stocked with breakfast supplies. Additional persons are $20 each. Smoking restricted. No pets. Children 12 and over welcome. $75.

1624. Warm host couple have separate guest cottage in a pretty flower garden. Room one has a king-size bed and private bath. Room two has a queen-size bed and private bath. Many guests ask for recipes after having the full breakfast here, which is served in the main house. Up to two children over eight are welcome if family takes whole house. Handicapped accessible. Resident cat. Smoking allowed outside only. $60-80.

Old Pueblo Homestays

P.O. Box 13603, Tucson, 35732
(800) 333-9 RSO

The Duquesne House. On the original main street of Patagonia, this turn-of-the-century adobe structure was originally built as miners' apartments when it was a thriving mountain town. Sixty miles south of Tucson and 20 miles east of Nogales near the US Border, Patagonia is known for its scenic beauty and diversity of birds and plant life. Each accommodation has a private entrance and consists of a sitting room with a twin bed, a bedroom and private bath with two twin/queen-size beds. Full breakfast. Smoking permitted outside only. No pets. Fifteen dollars for den with twin bed. $65.

PAYSON

Bed and Breakfast Inn Arizona

8900 East Via Linda, Suite 101, Scottsdale, 85258
(602) 860-9338 (phone and FAX)

PA25. Breathtaking views of the mountains and forest exist from everywhere on this working ranch. Barnyard pets and a stall for overnight accommodations for guests' horse make this the perfect getaway for pure relaxation. Hiking and horseback riding are nearby to work off the full gourmet breakfast. Afterwards enjoy a relaxing dip in the hot tub on the deck. Modest to deluxe rates.

PY001. Ranch with lodge rooms and cabins has pool, sauna, fireplaces, stables, lounge and restaurant. Just off the banks of the Tonto Creek "Zane Grey Territory." Call for rates.

PY002. Beautiful quality lodging has bedrooms with queen- or king-size beds and Jacuzzi suites. Call for rates.

PY103. This treetop hideaway in Payson is ideal for a family escape from the desert heat—or a fast weekend getaway. It is a little guest house, completely equipped with full kitchen, TV in living room with single sofa sleeper, and a bedroom with a private bath. This hospitable family will leave breakfast fixings the night before, so guests can eat at leisure in the morning. Children are welcome. Hosts have ten-year-old and toddler boys, an eight-year-old girl, a dog, chickens, and a guinea pig. A comfy, homey, down-home host family will make guests comfortable, yet offer the privacy of a separate guest house. Deluxe rates.

Mi Casa Su Casa

P.O. Box 950, Tempe, 85280-0950
(602) 990-0682; (800) 456-0682 (reservations only)

47. Three miles south of Payson, a very large A-frame house adjoins the national forest. Queen-size bedroom with trundle beds and private full bath has a large balcony which overlooks the living room. Easy drive to Mogollon Rim, Zane Grey's cabin, and Tonto Natural Bridge. Continental breakfast. Two-night minimum stay is required. No smoking. No alcoholic beverages allowed. $45-50.

---

7 No smoking; 8 Children welcome; 9 Social drinking allowed; 10 Tennis nearby; 11 Swimming nearby; 12 Golf nearby; 13 Skiing nearby; 14 May be booked through a travel agent.

PHOENIX

Bed and Breakfast Inn Arizona

8900 East Via Linda, Suite 101, Scottsdale, 85258
(602) 860-9338 (phone and FAX)

PX003. Superb location at the base of Camelback Mountain, this former estate has magnificent grounds and gardens. Swimming pools, tennis, and golf amid date palms. Call for rates.

PX008. In the prestigious Arcadia area of Phoenix, close to the valley's finest shops and restaurants, this three-acre adobe estate, circa 1900s features period furnishings and decorator designed for comfort. The main courtyard features a firepit, bird aviary, and tranquil Mexican fountain. The palm tree-lined swimming pool, Jacuzzi, and sauna are highlighted among the sprawling lawns, citrus trees, and palm grove. Fashioned after the world's finest five-star resorts with one exception...only seven guest suites. Casual comfort with a touch of class, where guests preserve their privacy. Modest to deluxe rates.

PX105. Minutes from the downtown area, this Spanish-style home is a beautifully preserved tribute to a bygone era. Built in 1937, it is decorated with English antiques, with beamed living room ceiling and arched doorways lending quaint charm. Warm, friendly hosts like to cater to their guests. Room has queen-size bed, English lace curtains, and a view of the garden, yard, and gazebo. Private hall bath with shower. Extra room with single-size bed. Traditional full American breakfast, which can be prepared to accommodate dietary needs. No children; no pets. Modest to deluxe rates.

PX108. Gracious second-generation bed and breakfast hostess will make sure of guests' comfort in this quiet stucco home in a peaceful Phoenix neighborhood. Pool and patio where one can watch the hummingbirds feed, nice views of Camelback Mountain, and very convenient to Sky Harbor, downtown, and Scottsdale. It's a real bargain! Bedroom with one queen-size bed, private bath, telephone, and TV. Delicious full breakfast. Children over eight are welcome. Modest rates.

PX111. An airily decorated guest house in the heart of north central Phoenix is on an expansive old homesite, where guests will be served a gourmet breakfast in the summerhouse. Two double beds, bath, living room, and kitchen make this second-story bed and breakfast a perfect stopover for comfort. With pool and patio, citrus trees, large lawn, off-street parking, guests will have easy access to all parts of the city. Professional hosts and their children will make any stay a comfortable one. Children over five welcome. Deluxe rates.

PX115. Don't be fooled by the quiet, plain exterior of this tract home—inside, it is a never-never-land filled with stained glass and antiques. Warm, gracious hostess is a tour guide at the Phoenix Art Museum and a gourmet chef; host creates stained-glass windows. Breakfast of choice. Back yard has gazebo, open-pit fireplace, and Jacuzzi—an oasis in the midst of the urban crush. Double bedroom with private bath down the hall. Child with a single parent welcome. Deluxe rates.

PX116. A quiet townhome guest room at the top of a spiral staircase, with queen-size bed and private hall bath, is convenient to the airport, downtown, and Scottsdale. Retired librarian hostess and artist husband are world travelers and assure guests a warm welcome. Join them at a delicious full breakfast, then relax by the pool or on the patio. Ideal for the business traveler. Lovely Burmese cat in residence. Children over ten welcome. Modest to deluxe rates.

NOTES: Credit cards accepted: A MasterCard; B Visa; C American Express; D Discover; E Diners Club; F Other; 2 Personal checks accepted; 3 Lunch available; 4 Dinner available; 5 Open all year; 6 Pets welcome;

PX124. This lovely condominium is hosted by a professional artist/decorator who has filled the house with an eclectic mixture of antiques and art pieces. Room with twin beds, private bath, and a small "Arcadia" garden, plus a Continental breakfast with the hosts, makes this the perfect base for business or pleasure in the center of the city. Only a mile to the Arizona Center. No children. Deluxe rates.

PX125. Quiet, immaculate home with retired host couple who welcome guests. Hostess bakes homemade cinnamon and pecan rolls, bread, and jams with full breakfast. Close to Metro Center, Western International University, Sun City, and easy access to I-17 to travel south to the airport and Tucson, and north to Sedona and the Grand Canyon. Hosts will be very helpful in orienting guests to the area. One bedroom with twin beds, one with double bed, share a hall bath with each other. Sunny yard with fountain. Modest rates.

PX134. Near the interstate, Metro Center, and North Mountain Park, this suite with private entrance, kitchenette, private bath, king-size bed or twin beds is a real find for the bed and breakfast guest. The hosts are avid hikers and bikers and know all about the great places to see in Arizona. Plus, they will take guests on overnight jaunts in their motor home to those hidden back roads or day trips to the Superstition Mountains, etc. It is perfect for a longer stay, too, with a bus line nearby. Full breakfast weekends; fixings left in the kitchen weekdays. Modest rates.

PX136. Numerous awards winner! Casual, but sophisticated luxury casita townhouse bed and breakfast has Southwestern decorations and design. Private petite patio, queen-size bed, private bath, TV, VCR, telephone, and FAX. Hearty Southwestern breakfast, country club privileges. On the golf course; pool, health club, tennis, and more! Call for rates.

PX139. If visitors want a sophisticated getaway in the heart of uptown, this luxury home is perfect. Savor a Continental breakfast in the privacy of one's own suite, join the host and hostess on the sunny back deck, enjoy the Jacuzzi, or relax next to the fireplace inside. The Library Suite has a four-poster king-size bed, private connecting bath, and private deck entrance. The library has a desk and a sofa sleeper for a third person. The Victorian Suite has a sitting room and private bath. Private entrances and private baths in the remaining three suites. Deluxe and superior rates.

PX141. Featuring 35 individual casitas, these accommodations range from single bedrooms to villas with full kitchens that can sleep up to eight. All are decorated in classic Spanish/Mexican style for privacy and pleasure. Nestled on six acres of beautifully landscaped desert, amenities include a pool, Jacuzzis, tennis courts, and handcrafted details throughout that reflect the old Phoenix of days gone by. Although breakfast is not included, most rooms have kitchenettes, and a restaurant is being restored on the property. There are plenty of nearby eateries. Children are welcome. Smoking allowed. Deluxe to superior rates.

PX142. In the Biltmore area of Phoenix, this home has magnificent gardens and a pool, and it blends into the impeccably kept gardens creating an island of serenity. Join the hosts for a full breakfast, then relax in the lovely surroundings. There are four suites all with private entrances, mini-refrigerators, microwave ovens, TVs, and private baths. No children, please; the pool and fountain are not child-proof. Superior rates.

7 No smoking; 8 Children welcome; 9 Social drinking allowed; 10 Tennis nearby; 11 Swimming nearby; 12 Golf nearby; 13 Skiing nearby; 14 May be booked through a travel agent.

PX143. Historic inn with guest house built of adobe and other natural, local materials has private entrances, pool. Full breakfast. Nestled near the solitude of the Squaw Peak Mountain Preserve. Call for rates.

PX145. Romantic timbered and gabled English Tudor built in 1934 in prestigious North Central Phoenix is filled with beautiful Victorian antiques and period furniture and is warmly decorated with forest greens and deep roses. The gracious main house gathering rooms, formal living room, dining room and breakfast room, expansive lawns and gardens, patios and gazebo spa are all available to guests. Modest to deluxe rates.

The Cottage

311 East Rose Lane, 85012
(602) 266-3114; FAX (602) 277-0429

The Cottage is a two-story guest house on an acre of land close to the downtown Phoenix area. The Heard Museum, The Phoenix Suns arena, Symphony Hall, and the Jerberger Theatre are nearby. The Cottage is an airy, sun-filled guest house with a living room of white wicker furniture, a bedroom with two double beds, a bathroom with an old claw-footed tub and a handheld shower. A spacious kitchen provides a coffee maker, toaster oven, microwave, and full refrigerator. The guest house overlooks the swimming pool on one side and an acre of manicured lawn with grapefruit, orange, lemon, and pecan trees. Seasonal rates. Skiing two hours north.

Hosts: Vickie and Winston McKellar
Rooms: 1 (PB) $75
Continental Breakfast
Credit Cards: None
Notes: 7, 9, 11, 12

Desert Farren "Privar" Hacienda Inn

P.O. Box 5550, Carefree, 85377
(602) 488-1110; FAX (602) 488-1500

The air is clear, the sky is blue, and Saguaro cactus dot the landscape. The large, comfortable fireplace rooms, which invite conversation or a quiet retreat, are furnished in mission style oak with burnt adobe walls, accented by oak ceilings, and highlighted by effective lighting and southwestern rugs. Guest amenities include stereo with CD, cassette, AM/FM, color remote control TV, VCR, daily newspaper, table/board games and a library. The healthy breakfast menu is lowfat with low or zero cholesterol. Natural ingredients are used in all recipes and served at the guests' convenience. Host is prepared to assist guests with full concierge services, and the latest on golf, tennis, hiking, biking, and horseback riding. Lunch is available by advance arrangements.

Host: Darrell Trapp
Rooms: 6 (PB) $66-149
Continental Breakfast
Credit Cards: A, B, C
Notes: 2, 4, 5, 9, 10, 11, 12, 14

The International Bed & Breakfast Club, Inc.

504 Amherst Street, Buffalo, NY 14207
(800) 723-4262; FAX (716) 873-4462

AZ3868PP. A deluxe private resort offers country club privileges, such as golf, tennis, and Olympic pool. Guests are greeted with casual Western comfort, class, and privacy. Six rooms with private baths. Full breakfast. $49-122.

Maricopa Manor

15 West Pasadena Avenue, 85013
(602) 274-6302

Five luxury suites, spacious public rooms, patios, decks, and the gazebo spa offer an intimate Old World atmosphere in an elegant urban setting. Maricopa Manor is in the heart of the Valley of the Sun, convenient to shops, restaurants, museums, churches, and civic and government centers. The Spanish-style manor house, built in 1928, houses beautiful art, antiques, and a warm Southwestern hospitality. Advance reservations required.

Hosts: Mary Ellen and Paul Kelley
Suites: 5 (PB) $79-129
Continental Breakfast
Credit Cards: A, B, C, D
Notes: 2, 5, 7, 8, 9, 10, 11, 12, 14

Mi Casa Su Casa

P.O. Box 950, Tempe, 85280-0950
(602) 990-0682; (800) 456-0682 (reservations
  only)

82. Handsome, large home near Biltmore has an extra-large yard with a pool. Separate guest wing has a large bedroom with a king-size bed, private bath with a shower, sitting and writing area, and a private entrance. A full breakfast is served. Minimum stay is three nights. $85.

155. In the historic district of Phoenix, this Spanish-style home was built circa 1930 and has been renovated and furnished in 1930s style. Beamed living room ceilings and arched doorways lend quaint charm. The guest room, overlooking the garden and gazebo, has a private hall bath, a queen-size bed, and lace curtains from England. Full breakfast. Minimum stay is two nights. $60-70.

165. Spanish-style house in a residential neighborhood sits at the foot of a mountain. Ten minutes from downtown and 20 minutes from downtown Scottsdale. Large bedroom has extra-long twin beds or king-size bed, bath with Roman tub and shower, small refrigerator, microwave oven, TV, telephone, dressing room, and sitting area with a private entrance. Continental breakfast. Minimum stay is three nights. $75.

268. Gracious hostess welcomes guests to a very large Southwestern stucco ranch-style home. This house was built beside a golf course in a handsome neighborhood with large trees. One guest room has a queen-size bed and full hall bath; another guest room has twin beds, TV, and shares the full hall bath. Only one party is accepted at a time. Guests are welcome to use the large living room with fireplace, cable TV, VCR, or pool. Full breakfast. Smoking allowed outside. No resident pets. Ten dollar charge for children between ten and 16. Those 16 and older pay full rate. $70.

270. Traditional ranch home with 3,200-square feet is in the "green belt" of central Phoenix. Private guest wing has two large guest rooms with king-size beds, TVs, and telephones. One guest room has a connecting bath with a shower, and the other guest room has a private, full hall bath. Hostess is professional cake decorator; host is in food sales business. Full breakfast on weekends. Continental on weekdays. $75.

282. This 1955 ranch-style home is in a beautiful older neighborhood with large, mature trees. Near a mall, public transportation, and the freeway. Photographic exhibit is in the sunroom. The guest room has a queen-size bed with private hall bath. It has a private entrance opening to the patio and pool. Hosts are knowledgeable about their city and state. Resident dog. Full, heart-healthy breakfasts. $50-55.

293. In a quiet upscale neighborhood with beautiful landscaping, large shade trees, flowering bushes, pool, and magnificent view of Camelback Mountain, this guest house provides in-town convenience in a quiet setting. Private entrance, private parking, private telephone line with answering machine, TV, VCR, fireplace. Air conditioning. Twin or king-size beds in bedroom. Breakfast items furnished for first morning. Cat in residence. No pets. Children over 12 welcome. $85.

7 No smoking; 8 Children welcome; 9 Social drinking allowed; 10 Tennis nearby; 11 Swimming nearby; 12 Golf nearby; 13 Skiing nearby; 14 May be booked through a travel agent.

Mi Casa Su Casa (continued)

313. Recently remodeled home has patio, swimming pool, view of Camelback Mountain, and is twenty minutes from downtown Phoenix, Scottsdale, and the airport. Enthusiastic, friendly host couple receives happy evaluations from their guests. They enjoy classical music, travel, and the Phoenix Suns. Hosts have been Arizona residents for over 40 years—giving suggestions about places to visit. Award-winning Southwestern-design guest room has a queen-size bed, TV, phone, and connecting bath with shower. Full breakfast featuring home-baked bread. No resident pets. Smoking allowed outside only. Two-night minimum stay preferred. $45-50.

315. Contemporary two-story townhouse in a small complex in a citrus grove is near Camelback Mountain, twenty minutes from downtown Phoenix, Scottsdale, or airport. Near public transportation. Guests write glowing evaluations about their visits. The host couple has lived worldwide and enjoys talking with guests. Guest room is up a spiral staircase onto second floor and has a pleasant Southwestern decor, queen-size bed, private bath, phone, and TV. The pool is next door. Two nights preferred. Full breakfast. No smoking. Resident cat. $65.

319. Helpful, warm-hearted host couple has a large architect-designed home, built in 1987 in a very nice neighborhood. Spanish-style with stucco exterior and a tile roof. There are two large rooms and bath over the two-car garage. One room is used for storage; the other is the guest room. It has a queen-size bed, TV, private entrance with exterior stairs, private hall bath, and telephone. Pool. Continental plus self-serve breakfast. Two-night minimum. Crib and portable crib available. No smoking. Children up to age six only, and they stay free of charge. Weekly and no-breakfast rates are available. $55-65.

338. Guests will enjoy the acre of flowering shrubs, palm, citrus, and pomegranate. The main house was built in 1924, and the guest cottage was built in the 1950s. The second-story "cottage" offers a kitchenette, a bedroom with two double beds, a living room with TV, a private bath with claw-foot tub, and a porch with a view of the pool. Ten minutes from the Heard Museum, twenty minutes from the airport, and two blocks from Central Avenue. Breakfast is self-catering. Smoking allowed outside only. Children over six who can swim are welcome. Special rates for longer stays. $75.

341. Retired, friendly host couple were farmers in the Midwest. Active in the Mennonite church, they enjoy hiking, bowling, and spectator sports. Modest home in residential neighborhood. Room one has a double bed, TV, and shares a full hall bath with room two, which has twin beds and TV. Near public transportation. Full breakfast with homemade breads and pecan rolls is served in the dining room or on the patio in pretty back yard. No resident pets. Children are welcome. No smoking. Weekly stay receives a ten-percent discount. $35-45.

352. Handsome two-story home near the Hilton Pointe Tapatio. Sociable host couple enjoys horseback riding, hiking, hunting, and fishing. Room one on the first floor has a queen-size bed and private hall bath. Room two on the second floor has a queen-size bed and private hall bath and balcony. Queen-size sofa bed is also available on the second floor. Heated pool, tennis, golf course, and stables are nearby. Spanish spoken. Continental breakfast weekdays, full breakfast on weekends. Children nine and older are welcome. Smoking allowed

---

NOTES: Credit cards accepted: A MasterCard; B Visa; C American Express; D Discover; E Diners Club; F Other; 2 Personal checks accepted; 3 Lunch available; 4 Dinner available; 5 Open all year; 6 Pets welcome;

outside. Two-night minimum. Ten-dollar charge per child. $65.

368. Rambling brick four-bedroom, three-bath home is surrounded by mature trees filled with birds in a quiet, convenient neighborhood near Phoenix College and one block from the Phoenix College Library. Handsome, contemporary decor with fireplaces, fine art, wide assortment of books, magazines, and travel guides. Guests welcome in large living room and covered patio, front and back lawns. Walk to bike paths, tennis, park, golf, shopping, and churches or temple. Guest room one has a king-size or twin beds. Second room is Southwestern with twin beds. Rooms share spacious bath with shower. Cable TV and VCR. Distilled water. A computer, printer, and modem available. Grapefruit tree on property provides fresh fruit or marmalade for homemade bread. Resident cat and dog. Minimum stay is two nights. Special weekly rates available. $45-60.

385. Pretty, spacious, and comfortable ranch-style house built in 1959 in very quiet, up-scale neighborhood "near everything." Many birds in vicinity, near Camelback Mountain. Some antiques, eclectic decor. Air-conditioned. Room one has a king-size bed and shares the full bath with room two which has twin beds. Only one party accepted at a time. A real find for the bed and breakfast traveler, guests are welcome to use the pool table in the family room, the TV in the den with fireplace, or the large covered patio. Fenced, unheated diving pool in the nice back yard. No resident pets. Minimum stay is two nights. Special rates for children. $75.

391. A vine-covered historic house and guest house that is on one acre of verdant land that has many fruit trees, including pomegranate, fig, tangerine, lime, grapefruit, and five varieties of orange trees.

Guest cottage has private entrance, individually controlled air conditioning and heat. Large bedroom/sitting room has one queen-size bed and a twin bed. Cable TV, stereo, VCR, library of tapes, house telephone, coffee pot, small microwave, and compact refrigerator. There is a dressing room and bath with shower. Light kitchen and laundry privileges in main house. There is a second guest room in the main house with a double bed, private hall bath with shower and whirlpool tub. Complimentary refreshments. Computer available. Twenty minutes from downtown Phoenix, Scottsdale, or the airport. Restaurants, fine shopping, golf, and tennis are nearby. Full breakfast. Dog, cat, and lop-eared rabbit in residence. Smoking restricted. Children ten and over and infants welcome. Pets welcome with prior arrangements. $55-75.

392. Pleasant one-story, Spanish-style home built in 1970 has a desert front yard, and a back yard with citrus trees, a patio with fountain, beehive fireplace, and a barbecue. Air conditioning and own heating. Small apartment has private entrance, bedroom/sitting room, efficiency kitchen, bath with shower ensuite. The twin beds or king-size bed folds up into the wall during the day. TV, radio, telephone. During the week, food is furnished for guests to prepare. Full breakfast is served on weekends. Smoking restricted. No pets. Special rates available for extended stay. $50.

399. From a unique natural desert area within Phoenix, guests look to the west of this house at Shadow Mountain in a mountain preserve, and to the east at a panoramic view of Paradise Valley, Scottsdale, and beyond. The Preserve has many hiking trails and wildlife. Convenient to shopping and golf, there are many fine restaurants nearby. The apartment is attached but separate from the house with a private entrance, living room with TV, bedroom with queen-size bed, bath with shower, and full

7 No smoking; 8 Children welcome; 9 Social drinking allowed; 10 Tennis nearby; 11 Swimming nearby; 12 Golf nearby; 13 Skiing nearby; 14 May be booked through a travel agent.

kitchen. There are two covered patios and a pool. A light breakfast is served the first two mornings, and after that, the refrigerator will be stocked for self-catering. Cat in residence. Smoking restricted. No pets. Inquire about children. $75.

Old Pueblo Homestays

P.O. Box 13603, Tucson, 85732
(800) 333-9 RSO

The Tudor House Bed and Breakfast. In the prestigious North Central Phoenix, this English Tudor style manor built in 1934 is filled with beautiful Victorian antiques and period furniture with five elegantly furnished bedrooms. This desert oasis is surrounded by acres of lush green lawns, fruit orchards, rose garden, patios, and gazebo spa. A full country breakfast is served sitdown style in the delightful dining and breakfast rooms. On premises is one outside dog. Smoking outside only. No pets. No children. $98-115.

PINETOP-LAKESIDE

Bed and Breakfast Inn Arizona

8900 East Via Linda, Suite 101, Scottsdale, 85258
(602) 860-9338 (phone and FAX)

PT103. This little log home in the pines, done in rustic frontier style, is a wonderful escape into the White Mountains during the summer. There are two bedrooms. The Indian Room Suite has an antique double bed in one room and two studio beds in the adjoining room. The Cowboy Room has handmade log twin beds. Both share a hall bath. Feast on a full country breakfast and enjoy afternoon tea on the old log porch. Children over 12 are welcome. Available Memorial Day through Labor Day.

PT104. A deluxe getaway in the Mogollon Rim country, this executive retreat boasts five self-contained cabins, tennis courts, sauna, private lakes, a gazebo, fitness center, and peace and quiet! Each cabin has a fully stocked kitchen with staples (coffee, tea, sugar) and cookware provided, but guests bring their own goodies. Breakfast is not provided. The Cheyenne Cabin has three bedrooms; the Santa Fe has two bedrooms; the Honeymoon has one bedroom; the Barn has two bedrooms; and the Pueblo Lodge can accommodate up to 14 people. Minimum two-night stay. Children welcome. No pets. Superior rates.

PRESCOTT

Bed and Breakfast Inn Arizona

8900 East Via Linda, Suite 101, Scottsdale, 85258
(602) 860-9338 (phone and FAX)

PR001. Nestled amid shade trees in the center of the Mount Vernon historic district, Arizona's largest Victorian neighborhood. Various deluxe accommodations offered. Full breakfast and afternoon refreshments. Call for rates.

PR002. Secluded country elegance overlooking the creek and mountains. Private baths, hot tubs, and decks. A big farm-fresh breakfast is served. Close to city amenities. Call for rates.

PR104. This meticulously restored lodging house is near the courthouse square. Original oak planking is refinished, and walls are covered with period wallpapers. Bedrooms with twin or queen-size beds, private baths, and ceiling fans. Continental breakfast is served. Smoking permitted. One- or two-room suites available. This facility is suitable for large parties, such as weddings. Deluxe to superior rates.

PR106. A stunning, modern, but very comfortable home built on, and actually into, a mountain above Prescott. The twin or king-size master bedroom has a private bath, floor-to-ceiling windows with a breathtaking view of Prescott and the fabulous rock hillside. A second bedroom (not available separately) has a queen-size bed and shares bath with suite. Watch the wildlife while eating a lavish breakfast on the second-floor deck. Hostess is a superb cook and can cook for special diets if asked. Resident dog. Children eight or older are welcome. Deluxe rates.

PR109. A lovely, completely renovated old home dating from the turn of the century. There are four beautifully decorated rooms with private baths, afternoon refreshments, and full or Continental breakfast. The elegant downstairs Terrace Suite has a queen-size bed, sofa bed in sitting room, bath, and private covered terrace; enough room for two couples. All other rooms are upstairs. The Pine View Suite has a queen-size bed, bath, fireplace, and sofa sleeper. The Garden Room has a queen-size bed, bath, and wicker furnishings. The Coventry Room has twin beds, private hall bath, and lovely views of the mountains. Children over ten welcome. Superior rates.

Hassayampa Inn

122 East Gurley Street, 86301
(520) 778-9434; (800) 322-1927

Nestled in the pines of mile-high Prescott is the majestic Hassayampa Inn. Locally known as "Prescott's Grand Hotel," the inn offers 68 graciously appointed rooms, and a full-service restaurant and lounge. Built in 1927 and completely renovated in 1985, the lobby is acknowledged as one of the most beautiful in Arizona. Featuring tile floors, Oriental rugs, oversize easy chairs, and potted palms, the focal point, however, is the beamed ceiling decorated with Spanish and Indian motifs. The renowned Peacock Room serves breakfast, lunch, and dinner and boasts a combination of tapestry

Hassayampa Inn

print booths and etched Deco-style glass with ambience and Prescott's finest cuisine. Overnight rooms include daily breakfast and an evening cocktail.

Hosts: Bill and Georgia Teich
Rooms: 68 (PB) $89-175
Full Breakfast
Credit Cards: A, B, C, D, E
Notes: 2, 3, 4, 5, 8, 10, 11, 12, 14

Lynx Creek Farm Bed and Breakfast

P.O. Box 4301, 86302
(602) 778-9573

Secluded country hilltop setting with great views overlooking Lynx Creek has spacious suites in separate guest house filled with antiques and country decor. Organic garden and orchard supply fresh fruit, produce, and homemade apple cider for full gourmet breakfasts. Hot tub, cold pool, croquet, volleyball, horseshoes, gold-panning, big swing, animals, and exotic birds. Light cocktails and hors d'oeuvres each evening. Also available for weddings and cooking classes. Voted "Best Bed and Breakfast in Arizona" by the *Arizona Republic* newspaper in November 1994. Smoking restricted.

Hosts: Greg and Wendy Temple
Rooms: 6 (PB) $75-140
Full Breakfast
Credit Cards: A, B, C, D
Notes: 2, 5, 6, 8, 9, 10, 11, 12, 14

7 No smoking; 8 Children welcome; 9 Social drinking allowed; 10 Tennis nearby; 11 Swimming nearby; 12 Golf nearby; 13 Skiing nearby; 14 May be booked through a travel agent.

Mi Casa Su Casa

P.O. Box 950, Tempe, 85280-0950
(602) 990-0682; (800) 456-0682 (reservations only)

1063. Join the host couple on the veranda of a magnificently restored turreted Queen Anne Victorian in Arizona's first capital. A short walk to the courthouse, museums, galleries, restaurants, and antiquing. The two-bedroom Ivy Suite on the first floor has a private bath. Three guest rooms are on the second floor. The Tea Rose has a queen-size bed and private bath in the hall. The Princess Victoria has a queen-size bed, a view of the southern mountains, and a private bath with an 1800s bathhouse-style copper tub. The Queen Anne Suite has a king-size bed, turret sitting room, white wicker, and a private bath. Rates include afternoon refreshments and a full breakfast. Resident dog. Smoking allowed outside. Visa and MasterCard accepted. $75-120.

1064. A wonderfully romantic bed and breakfast has rural luxury and scenic views on a 25-acre, wooded, hilly property. The two guest cottages each have two suites featuring antiques or western decor and king- or queen-size beds. The cottages can accommodate up to 12 guests. Amenities include decks, spa, hiking, volleyball, and exotic birds in the large main house. Families welcome. Children enjoy seeing the farm animals. Full country breakfasts are served in the main house. Smoking outside. Fifteen dollars for additional adult. Ten dollars for children. $85-130.

1065. Contemporary redwood home with open floor plan and three decks is in a setting of granite boulders, rolling hills, and forests. Easy drive to various local activities and recreation. One guest room has a king-size bed or twins beds with a private bath, a microwave oven, and an adjacent covered patio. Another room has a queen-size bed and is ideal for a third or fourth party sharing a bath with the other guest room. Full breakfast. $60-70.

1067. In historic downtown, a hostess and her son welcome guests to a two-story bed and breakfast inn built in 1906. On the first floor, the two-room Terrace Suite has a bedroom with private deck. Upstairs, there are three guest rooms. The two-room Pine View Suite has a bedroom with a king-size bed, sitting room with queen-size sofa bed, and fireplace. The Garden Room has a queen-size bed and private bath. The Coventry has twin beds and private bath in the hall. Full breakfast and afternoon refreshments are served. Available for seminars, meetings, and weddings. Smoking allowed outside only. Well-behaved children are welcome. $80-120.

1068. Within walking distance to downtown Prescott and minutes away from hiking, lakes, and national forest land, this delightful Craftsman bungalow has an atmosphere of a small European country inn featuring turn-of-the-century woods in paneling and floors. Guest rooms are decorated in European country styles. Guests are welcome in the great room with fireplace, library, and antique grand piano. The Tuscany room has an Italian country flavor, featuring twelve windows looking out on the lawn, garden pond, and evergreen trees. Amenities incluse queen-size bed, queen-size sofa bed, sitting area, and private bath. A touch of French countryside with provincial floral fabrics is featured in the Provence room which has rich wood paneling, beamed ceilings, and French doors. Queen-size bed, sitting area, private bath. Smoking outside. No pets. Credit cards accepted. Full breakfast. $70-90.

Mt. Vernon Inn

204 North Mt. Vernon Avenue, 86301
(520) 778-0886

Step back in time at this inn nestled among towering shade trees in the midst of Arizona's largest Victorian neighborhood. Guests will delight in the climate with occasional snow in mild winters, colorful wild-

---

NOTES: Credit cards accepted: A MasterCard; B Visa; C American Express; D Discover; E Diners Club;
F Other; 2 Personal checks accepted; 3 Lunch available; 4 Dinner available; 5 Open all year; 6 Pets welcome;

Mt. Vernon Inn

flowers and greenery in the spring, brisk breezes and comfortable nights in summer, and fall foliage of gold and maroon. Guests may enjoy a host of outdoor sports, relax in front of the sitting room fire with a fine collection of old movies and a VCR, or linger on the Greek Revival porch in the warm weather. Start the day with freshly baked muffins, homemade granola, and light, healthy specialties.

Hosts: John and Sybil Nelson
Rooms: 7 (PB) $90-110
Full Breakfast
Credit Cards: A, B, C, D
Notes: 2, 5, 7, 8, 9, 10, 12, 14

SAFFORD

Bed and Breakfast Inn Arizona

8900 East Via Linda, Suite 101, Scottsdale, 85258
(602) 860-9338 (phone and FAX)

SA001. Western Colonial Revival-style architecture in a rural setting. Spectacular scenery, hot springs, fishing, and hiking are found nearby. Full breakfast. Call for rates.

Mi Casa Su Casa

P.O. Box 950, Tempe, 85280-0950
(602) 990-0682; (800) 456-0682 (reservations only)

322. Western Colonial-style brick house built in 1890 has wide verandas that run across the front of the house. Three large, old-fashioned guest rooms all share a large hall bath. One room has a double bed, a twin bed, and an old-fashioned pedestal sink. Another room has a double bed, dressing room, and a large window that overlooks two old, large pecan trees. A third room has an antique armoire, double bed, French doors to the balcony, and two 12-foot pocket doors to the sitting room. A guest cottage is also available. Full breakfast is served. No smoking. Visa and MasterCard. $70.

SASABE

Mi Casa Su Casa

P.O. Box 950, Tempe, 85280-0950
(602) 990-0682; (800) 456-0682 (reservations only)

1627. Reaching 3,800-feet high in the Sonoran Desert, this fascinating 250-year-old ranch is one of the last great Spanish haciendas still standing in the United States. There are 16 full modernized guest rooms, each with its own private bath and fireplace. Heated pool, spa, hot tub, variety of recreational activities on site, including horseback riding. Three meals are served a day. Horseback riding packages. $90-115.

SCOTTSDALE

Bed and Breakfast Inn Arizona

8900 East Via Linda, Suite 101, Scottsdale, 85258
(602) 860-9338 (phone and FAX)

SD002. This elegant inn features luxurious suites, original artwork, antiques, and Southwestern Santa Fe decor. Fireplaces and balconies. Continental breakfast is served. Call for rates.

---

7 No smoking; 8 Children welcome; 9 Social drinking allowed; 10 Tennis nearby; 11 Swimming nearby; 12 Golf nearby; 13 Skiing nearby; 14 May be booked through a travel agent.

Bed and Breakfast Inn Arizona (continued)

SD003. These designer-decorated casitas and luxury villas are nestled in the foothills of the Sonoran Desert. Featuring gourmet dining, romantic lounge, and fitness center. Call for rates.

SD106. Attached guest house with kitchenette, private entrance, king-size bed, private bath, and French doors opening onto a patio. Pool and citrus trees. Pool can be heated except in January and February. TV and his-and-her golf clubs available. The hosts have tickets for guests to watch the Giants baseball team train. Near downtown Scottsdale. Breakfast is served only on the first day. Deluxe rates.

SD107. Very friendly Scottsdale home where host and hostess always get rave reviews. Interesting couple has traveled widely and knows how bed and breakfast is supposed to be done. Full breakfast served. Light, airy ambience in king-size bed master suite with private bath. Has pool, bicycle, and golf clubs. Seven golf courses are only five minutes away. Deluxe rates.

SD127. Trilevel Scottsdale townhouse with swimming pool is in walking distance from Fashion Square and art galleries. Hostess will prepare anything guests want for breakfast, within reason. Cool, lower-level studio with sitting area, king-size or twin beds, small refrigerator, cable TV, and stereo. Sitting area with couch, a small table where snacks, coffee, and the like may be enjoyed. Private bath with shower. Refreshments before bed, if guests wish. Hide-a-Bed for third person available. Private carport parking. Modest to deluxe rates.

SD132. Just for the larger party or longer stay, this set of suites in the heart of downtown Scottsdale offers classic resort amenities: heated pools, Jacuzzis, tennis, gas-fired grills, and putting green. The Arizona Canal provides jogging out the back door, and there are sun decks, horseshoes, and croquet. Each spacious suite has two bedrooms with twin, double, or queen-size bed available, two baths, living room, fully appointed kitchen, cable TV, and telephone. Guests are on their own for breakfast. Children are welcome; cribs available. No pets. Superior rates.

SD134. This guest house has two suites, both with spectacular views from poolside. Relax on guest patio at the Camelback Suite with sweeping Camelback Mountain views. The suite also has a fireplace and feather king-size bed. The Papago Suite offers Southwestern decor and spectacular pool views. Modest to deluxe rates.

SD135. This beautiful adobe-style guest house boasts privacy, elegance, and quiet surroundings, yet is within walking distance of more than a dozen restaurants and the most exclusive shopping in Scottsdale. Charming hostess puts first-day Continental breakfast fixings in guests' kitchen. Relax on the queen-size bed or in the sitting area, enjoy the stereo, and wake to fresh coffee in the morning. Queen-size sofa bed in same room for additional guest. Dog in main residence. Deluxe rates.

SD136. A quiet home just south of McCormick Ranch is a real find for the bed and breakfast traveler. Artist hostess is antique collector and has a house full of lovely pieces. Master bedroom with queen-size bed is decorated in 1820s country antiques, has connecting private bath with shower. Family room with TV, pool and patio, and bikes available. Hostess prepares

NOTES: Credit cards accepted: A MasterCard; B Visa; C American Express; D Discover; E Diners Club; F Other; 2 Personal checks accepted; 3 Lunch available; 4 Dinner available; 5 Open all year; 6 Pets welcome;

guests' choice of breakfast. Children 12 and over welcome. Resident cat. Modest rates.

SD137. A modest rock-walled guest house faces the pool in this northern-area bed and breakfast, only 15 minutes to Westworld (horseworld) and the Mayo Clinic, a satellite facility of the clinic in Minnesota. King-size or twin beds, private bath, and complete kitchen make it the ideal haven for quiet relaxation. Continental breakfast self-catered with goodies left by the hostess. Private guest parking, private entrance, kitchen, TV, and patio. A short drive to shopping, restaurants, and golf. The pool is unfenced; no children or pets. Deluxe rates.

SD139. Lovely home on quiet street is convenient to downtown Scottsdale with all its art galleries, wonderful restaurants, and shopping. The hostess serves a full breakfast while guests enjoy the scenery of the lovely pool and private back yard. The guest bedroom has a double bed with private adjoining bath with tub and shower. Second bedroom for additional guests in same party has private hall bath. Outdoor hot tub must be reserved in advance. Older teens and adults only; cat and dog in residence. Modest to deluxe rates.

SD140. Private garden and patio greets guests as they enter this very private guest house with pool. Close to the Borgata. Modest to deluxe rates.

Inn at the Citadel

8700 East Pinnacle Peak Road, 85255
(602) 585-6133; (800) 927-8367

Enjoy the splendor of the Sonoran Desert's enchantment. Private, intimate suites are appointed with antiques and original artwork. Fireplaces, terraces, and spectacular views are woven together into a tapestry of unequaled ambience. Fine dining, shopping, and salons await at the Citadel. A deluxe Continental breakfast is served. Pets welcome by prior arrangements. Summer rates available upon request.

Rooms: 11 (PB) $225-265
Continental Breakfast
Credit Cards: A, B, C, E
Notes: 2, 3, 4, 5, 7, 8, 9, 10, 11, 12, 14

Mi Casa Su Casa

P.O. Box 950, Tempe, 85280-0950
(602) 990-0682; (800) 456-0682 (reservations only)

134. *Hafod-y-Gwynt* means "shelter from the wind" in Welsh. This is the place to experience quiet desert living. On ten acres with mountains in every direction, the 600-square-foot guest apartment with private entrance is connected to the main house in a remote, scenic area. Air-conditioned. Comfortable 20' x 20' combined living room and bedroom with twin beds, TV, and traditional decor. Bathroom has shower. fully equipped kitchen stocked for first few days' breakfasts. Resident pets include horses, dogs, and one cat. Closed May 15 through October 15. Three-night minimum stay is required. $65.

227. Luxurious, spacious home designed by an architect is on two desert-landscaped acres with panoramic views of the McDowell Mountains. Comfortable, contemporary furnishings complement the New Mexico-style home. Conveniently near Carefree, Taliesin West, Mayo Clinic (Arizona facility), Rawhide, fine dining, and several golf courses. Sociable hostess is gourmet cook; host is excellent golfer. Guest room has a pair of twin beds with handmade quilts, TV, private, full hall bath, private exit to the pool, patio, and parking areas. Full gourmet breakfast. No smoking. Minimum stay is two nights. $55-65.

7 No smoking; 8 Children welcome; 9 Social drinking allowed; 10 Tennis nearby; 11 Swimming nearby; 12 Golf nearby; 13 Skiing nearby; 14 May be booked through a travel agent.

Bed and Breakfast
Inn Arizona
(continued)

245. Attractive ranch-style house is on one acre of tall palms, pines, and native plants. Lush resort landscaping surrounds the pool. Large, private guest suite includes a sitting room, office area with a FAX, private bath with a shower, and smaller second bedroom with a twin bed. Private tennis/health club facilities accessible for a small extra fee. Breakfast and complimentary refreshments are served. $65-75.

278. In a handsome neighborhood on an acre in north central Scottsdale is a charming guest house with a bedroom/living room with queen-size bed, sofa bed, fully-equipped kitchen, full bath, and contemporary furnishings. Arcadia doors lead to pool. Guests enjoy jogging or hiking along the nearby scenic canal. Walk to Hilton Village, public transportation. For short stays, breakfast items are stocked in the kitchen. For longer stays, self-catering. Smoking allowed outside only. Laundry facilities available. Children six and older who can swim are welcome. Two-night minimum stay is required. Ten dollars for each additional guest. $75.

301. Stone-front cozy guest cottage built in 1985 is opposite the main house with the pool in between. Full kitchen, private bath with shower, white tile floors, contemporary furniture, and well-maintained yard with flowering bushes. Twin beds or king-size bed and TV. Kitchen stocked with breakfast items first morning. Self-catering. Phone, water purifier, and air purifier. Near shopping centers and aquatic center. No smoking. Weekly, monthly, and summer rates are available. $79.

327. A luxurious 7,500-square-foot contemporary adobe home with panoramic mountain views in a quiet desert setting. The owner has spared no expense with this beautiful home and two guest casitas. Green lawns and palm trees surround the pool area. There is also a tiled, outdoor spa and private tennis court. Guest casita one has a bedroom with a king-size bed, a living room with TV and kiva fireplace, private bath, and kitchen. Guest casita two has a bedroom with a king-size bed, a living room with big screen TV and kiva fireplace, private bath, kitchen, and a sauna. The main house has two bedrooms, each with a queen-size bed and private bath. Full breakfast. No resident pets. Smoking allowed outside. One child ten or older is welcome in main house. Two-night minimum stay is required. $150-175.

331. Handsome home with Southwestern decor in upscale area. Quiet, but close to shopping and restaurants. Near tennis courts, canal bank for jogging. Sociable couple enjoy the outdoors. Host knows Arizona well as he has explored little-known back roads and canyons. Hostess is a potter, using Native American methods of collecting clay and firing. The guest room has a queen-size bed and private bath. Guests are welcome to use large living room with TV. Host couple area is at opposite end of house. Full, healthy breakfasts. Resident dog. No smoking. No children. Open October 15 through May 1. $85.

347. On a beautiful lake and golf course in well-maintained McCormick Ranch, this stucco home with red tile roof was built in 1977 with many windows looking out to the lake. Very large master guest room has lake view, four-poster queen-size bed with luxurious linens, private bath, walk-in closet, private entrance, cable TV, CD player, stereo, and telephone. Paddle boat available. Full breakfast. No resident pets. Smoking allowed outside. Minimum two nights. Ten percent discount for seniors staying a week. $125.

348. A homey, quiet, and comfortable bed and breakfast for guests who appreciate

NOTES: Credit cards accepted: A MasterCard; B Visa; C American Express; D Discover; E Diners Club; F Other; 2 Personal checks accepted; 3 Lunch available; 4 Dinner available; 5 Open all year; 6 Pets welcome;

American country antiques. The hostess is an artist who always has great guest reviews. The guest room has a queen-size bed and private, full hall bath. Guests are welcome to use the family room with TV. Pool and laundry facilities are available. Hostess prepares guests' choice of breakfast. Friendly cat. Smoking allowed outside only. Children over 11 welcome. $45-55.

379. Hostess from New Zealand welcomes guests to the tranquil atmosphere and hospitality of this home in a quiet neighborhood. near famous Camelback Mountain. This "home away from home" is convenient to downtown where art galleries, theaters, wonderful restaurants, and shopping abound. Breakfast is served in the lovely dining room overlooking the pool and yard. Enjoy waffles with strawberry sauce, delicious muffins and breads and/or cereals, omelets, fresh fruit, and natural health foods, all lovingly prepared. Room one has a double bed with private adjoining bath that includes a tub and shower. Room two has one twin bed with a private hall bath. Please reserve outdoor hot tub in advance for heating. Quiet surroundings make this a delightful break from the busy Scottsdale scene. Resident cat and dog. Two night minimum. $45-55.

380. Four-level condominium with white interior is in a very nice complex one mile from Scottsdale Fashion Square. Room one has sitting area and private bath. Room two has a shared full bath. Community pool is heated except December through February. Full breakfast served. Two-night stay preferred. Children over nine. No pets. Outside smoking. $65-75.

389. Handsome home in the very nice residential area of McCormick Ranch overlooks a beautiful man-made lake. The three-room suite is totally private, having a door between it and the living room. The bedroom has a queen-size bed and very large closet. Full bath ensuite with a pretty

atrium. The separate sitting room has a TV and a view of a garden out of the windows. Guests welcome in large living room, charming enclosed garden with attractive plantings. Restaurants and golf course are nearby. Cat in residence. Smoking is restricted. No pets. No children. Full breakfast. Two-night stay preferred. $110.

395. Extra large ranch-style home on a large lot is in a quiet neighborhood and has a desert front yard, green back yard, and extra large pleasant patio with a fountain surrounded by green plants. Amenities include air conditioning and own heat controls. Newly added L-shaped guest wing has modern, comfortable decor and feels spacious. Private entrance. Queen-size bed. Comfortable sofa and occasional chairs, TV, private telephone, kitchen with refrigerator, microwave, and hot plate. Cabinet for hanging clothes (no closet). AKC Maltese dogs in main part of house only. Smoking restricted. Pets welcome with prior permission. Ten minutes from downtown Scottsdale, twenty minutes from downtown Tempe. Two-night stay preferred. Monthly rate available. $75.

398. Near the heart of Scottsdale, this bed and breakfast is in a condominium complex. Nearby are good restaurants, a popular high end mall, Scottsdale Stadium, Civic Center, and Old Town Scottsdale. Pool. Air conditioning. Guest room has a king-size bed, double sofa bed and chairs, TV, telephone, table and chairs, walk-in closet. Private bathroom with shower. Private garage parking with normal entry through the garage level. No pets. Inquire about children. Continental breakfast. Two-night stay preferred; if staying only one night there is an additional $10 charge. $75-90.

401. Charming hostess welcomes guests to a luxurious home built in 1983 in a traditional, large ranch house style. Chemically

7 No smoking; 8 Children welcome; 9 Social drinking allowed; 10 Tennis nearby; 11 Swimming nearby; 12 Golf nearby; 13 Skiing nearby; 14 May be booked through a travel agent.

Bed and Breakfast Inn Arizona (continued)

free environment. Exterior features Southwestern flora. Next to national preserve with unobstructed views of the McDowell Mountains, Red Rock Mountain, and Saddleback Mountain. Two miles from Mayo Clinic (Arizona facility). Air conditioning. The very private extra large guest room has king-size bed, satellite TV, sitting area, dressing room, telephone, full bath. Crib available. Light kitchen privileges. Outside barbecue. Dog in residence. Spanish and Dutch spoken. Smoking outside. Pets welcome with prior arrangements. Children welcome. Full breakfast. Two-night stay preferred. Additional $10 charge for extra person. $125.

406. Luxurious 1990 Santa Barbara type home in the McDowell Mountain foothills is in the upscale Pinnacle Peak area, minutes from the Princess Hotel, home of the Phoenix Open golf tournament, Pinnacle Peak Patio, world-famous restaurant, Rawhide (Wrangler Jeans Rodeo), Westworld (Arabian Horse shows, Barrett-Jackson Antique Auto sales), Mayo Clinic (Arizona facility), Carefree, and Frank Lloyd Wright's Taliesen West. Air conditioning. The Mexican Suite is in a private area in the home, has a queen-size bed, private hall bath, TV, VCR, telephone. The Wicker Room has a double bed and shares the hall bath. Only one party accepted at a time. Guests have use of a separate family room and access to a computer and copier upon request. Smoking restricted. No pets. Two-night stay preferred. Continental plus breakfast. $85.

410. Two-story Southwest Spanish-style home built in 1995 is in the upscale Pinnacle Peak area. The decor is eclectic; a few antiques are mixed with Spanish and contemporary furniture. Air conditioning. Master bedroom on the first floor has a king-size bed, private full bath, cable TV, exit to patio and nearby heated community swimming pool and spa. On the second floor are two guest rooms that each have cable TV and share a full hall bath. One room has a queen-size bed and the other has twin beds. Spanish spoken. Smoking restricted. No pets. No children. Full breakfast with "Picnic breakfasts" available at an additional charge. Two-night stay preferred. $65-85.

416. This bed and breakfast is for those guests who appreciate quiet luxury in a beautiful older area with big trees near the excellent shopping and dining Scottsdale offers. Flowering oleander bushes line the large circular drive that has in its center tall, lacy desert trees. The new, very private cottage has its own patio and sitting area. Air conditioning. King-size bed, full kitchen and dining area, bath with extra large shower, closet with stacked washer and dryer, cable TV, VCR, and movies. Pool. Spanish spoken. Smoking restricted. No pets. No children. Continental plus breakfast. Two-night stay preferred. $125.

Old Pueblo Homestays

P.O. Box 13603, Tucson, 85732
(800) 333-9RSO

Briarwood Bed and Breakfast. In the North Scottsdale Valley of the Sun Area. This lovely home has a stucco and stone front guest cottage near a large pool. The cottage has one bedroom with king-size bed and shower bath, a full facility kitchen, TV, telephone, and own temperature control. A self-serve Continental plus breakfast is provided on short term stays. On premises is a small miniature poodle. Special summer rates available upon request. No smoking. No pets. Inquire about children. $80.

SEDONA

Bed and Breakfast at Saddle Rock Ranch

P.O. Box 10095, 86339
(520) 282-7640; FAX (520) 282-6829

History, romance, antiques, and elegance combine in this Old West movie estate. The three-acre hillside aerie. Fabulous views. The quiet, romantic rooms feature wood-burning fireplaces, and canopied beds. Private baths with huge, fluffy towels, terry robes, and luxurious toiletries. Scrumptious breakfasts, saucer-size cookies, and after-noon snacks beside the pool or parlor fire-place. Whirlpool spa. Views. Gardens. Wildlife. Bird watching. Hiking. Jeep tours.

Hosts: Fran and Dan Bruno
Rooms: 3 (PB) $105-135
Full Breakfast
Credit Cards: None
Notes: 2, 5, 7, 9, 10, 11, 12, 13

Bed and Breakfast Inn Arizona

8900 East Via Linda, Suite 101, Scottsdale, 85258
(602) 860-9338 (phone and FAX)

SE001. Charming cottages along the banks of Oak Creek. Quiet, soothing atmosphere. Full breakfast. Call for rates.

SE002. This elegant French-style country inn is a retreat to the understated luxury and tranquility of genteel country life. Full breakfast. Call for rates.

SE003. This bed and breakfast has quiet and relaxing, award-winning architecture. Overlooks waterfalls. Beautiful antique fur-nishings. Scrumptious breakfast creations. Call for rates.

SE005. Old West ambience. Western movie location. Jacuzzi, fireplaces. Full breakfast and snacks. Call for rates.

SE006. Cabins amid the pines in Oak Creek Canyon. Magnificent scenery. Hiking and fishing. Call for rates.

SE007. Farmhouse nestled in the pines between the Sedona red rocks and Wild Horse Mesa. Bridle paths, hiking. Horse accommodations available. Full breakfast. Call for rates.

SE008. These deluxe cabins amid a lush forest setting feature private decks and kitchens. Magnificent scenery of the Oak Creek Canyon area. Call for rates.

SE009. Bed and breakfast near Red Rock Crossing. Swimming, hiking, and fishing. Breakfast included. Call for rates.

SE010. Elegant and rustic bed and break-fast. Handicapped accessible. Full breakfast and evening refreshments are served. Call for rates.

SE012. This modern Sedona bed and breakfast features a hot tub and an outdoor barbecue. Gourmet breakfast is served. Quiet and casual atmosphere. Call for rates.

SE013. This rambling country inn with magnificent red rock views features a pri-vate deck. Full breakfast. Call for rates.

SE014. This cozy inn with country French antique decor features private entrances for the guest rooms and a convenient location. Call for rates.

7 No smoking; 8 Children welcome; 9 Social drinking allowed; 10 Tennis nearby; 11 Swimming nearby; 12 Golf nearby; 13 Skiing nearby; 14 May be booked through a travel agent.

Bed and Breakfast Inn Arizona (continued)

SE015. Unique and elegant. Pool, spa, and private balconies with dramatic views of red rock country. Gourmet breakfast is served. Call for rates.

SE114. An artists' and photographers' favorite! Half-century-old historic ranch estate has magnificent red rock views and beautiful gardens with spa and pool. Hostess serves a lavish Continental breakfast. Late afternoon refreshments are served, and a homemade goody is provided with turndown. View Suite has superb views, a canopied queen-size bed, rock fireplace, dressing room, and private bath. Rose Garden Room has king-size or twin beds, marble-topped nightstands, cozy rock fireplace, private bath, and French doors opening onto a walled rose garden. Special occasion packages available. Two small resident dogs. Two-night minimum stay is required. Superior rates.

SE120. If one is looking for luxury in a commercial-style bed and breakfast, look no further than this exquisite ten-room gem between Sedona and Oak Creek. This Spanish-style home has private connecting bath with whirlpool tubs, private balconies or patios, and unrestricted views of the red rocks in each room. The gracious hosts provide a full breakfast, then treat guests to late afternoon refreshments by the pool. Can accommodate small parties. Special honeymoon packages. No pets. Children over ten welcome. No smoking. Superior rates.

SE121. Extraordinary bed and breakfast. A haven for relaxation, hospitality, and fantastic red rock views. Hearty Southwestern breakfast. Call for rates.

SE122. Ranch-style setting. Superb views. Queen-size beds, sitting rooms with fireplaces, and private baths. At the base of Castle Rock. Convenient location to golf, shops, and restaurants.

Briar Patch Inn

H-C 30, Box 1002, 86336
(602) 282-2342

Nestled in Oak Creek Canyon on nine lush creekside acres, this oasis is described by guests as a paradise. Summer mornings guests can breakfast by the creek with Bach and Mozart played by resident musicians. In the winter, cozy up to a favorite fireplace with a good book. Handcrafted cabins, Southwestern furnishings, and Native American crafts create relaxing and memorable moments. Discover Sedona's unique beauty: Indian ruins, hiking, galleries, and vortex energy. Close to the Grand Canyon and Navajo and Hopi Indians. A real gem! No smoking in cabins.

Hosts: JoAnn and Ike Olson
Rooms: 16 (PB) $135-215
Full Breakfast
Credit Cards: A, B
Notes: 2, 5, 8, 9, 11, 12, 14

Canyon Villa Bed and Breakfast Inn

125 Canyon Circle Drive, 86351
(520) 284-1226; (800) 453-1166

Nestled among the red rocks of Sedona, this AAA four-diamond award bed and breakfast offers 11 luxurious guest rooms with fantastic views and relaxing whirlpool tubs. Enjoy the gourmet breakfasts, fireplaces, and heated pool.

Hosts: Chuck and Marion Yadon
Rooms: 11 (PB) $125-205
Full Breakfast
Credit Cards: A, B
Notes: 2, 5, 7, 9, 10, 11, 12, 14

NOTES: Credit cards accepted: A MasterCard; B Visa; C American Express; D Discover; E Diners Club;
F Other; 2 Personal checks accepted; 3 Lunch available; 4 Dinner available; 5 Open all year; 6 Pets welcome;

The Canyon Wren—Cabins for Two

Star Route 3, Box 1140, 86336
(520) 282-6900; (800) 437-WREN (9736)

Six miles north of Sedona, four cabins are set against the parklike frame of red rock cliffs and green canyon landscape. Specializing in one to two adults only for private retreats or romantic getaways, the cabins offer kitchens, fireplaces, and whirlpool bathtubs. No TVs or phones will disturb you. Barbecue grills with charcoal provided. Continental plus breakfast. Away from bustle of Sedona, yet close enough to enjoy town benefits. Personal, friendly service. Non-smoking property inside and outside. Creek swimming, hiking, and fishing are a stone's throw away.

Hosts: Milena Pfeifer and Mike Smith
Cabins: 4 (PB) $125-135
Continental Breakfast
Credit Cards: A, B
Notes: 2, 5, 7, 9, 10, 11, 12, 13

Casa Sedona

Casa Sedona

55 Hozoni Drive, 86336
(602) 282-2938; (800) 525-3756

Casa Sedona offers fabulous red rock views from each of its 15 terraced guest rooms. Individually appointed to please and pamper guests, the rooms are spacious, luxurious, and include private baths, spa tubs, and a delightful fireplace. Guests are served a hearty Southwestern breakfast in a smoke-free environment (inside and out).

On an acre of wooded grounds, Casa Sedona offers a tranquil, serene experience.

Hosts: Lori and Misty Zitko; Dick Curtis
Rooms: 15 (PB) $105-165
Full Breakfast
Credit Cards: A, B, D
Notes: 2, 5, 7, 9, 10, 11, 12, 13, 14

The Cozy Cactus

80 Canyon Circle Drive, 86351-8678
(520) 284-0082; (800) 788-2082

Cozy Cactus Bed and Breakfast is at the foot of Castle Rock between Sedona's red rock cliffs and Wild Horse Mesa. Cozy Cactus is a ranch-style home comfortably furnished with family heirlooms and theatrical memorabilia. Each room has a private bath, and each pair of bedrooms shares a sitting room with a fireplace. Breakfasts are served in the great room. Guests have direct access into Coconino National Forest for hiking, bird watching, and photography.

Hosts: Bob and Lynne Gillman
Rooms: 5 (PB) $90-110
Full Breakfast
Credit Cards: A, B, C, D
Notes: 2, 5, 8, 9, 10, 11, 12, 13, 14

The Graham Bed and Breakfast Inn

150 Canyon Circle Drive, 86351
(602) 284-1425; (800) 228-1425
FAX (602) 284-0767

The Graham Inn is an impressive, contemporary Southwest inn with huge windows providing views of Sedona's famous red rock formations. Six guest rooms with private bath, TV, VCR, and balconies with red rock views. Some rooms have fireplaces and whirlpool tubs. Enjoy wonderful breakfasts, afternoon refreshments, pool, and Jacuzzi. Innkeepers give orientation program after breakfast.

Hosts: Roger and Carol Redenbaugh
Rooms: 6 (PB) $99-209
Full Breakfast
Cards: A, B, D
Notes: 2, 5, 7, 8, 9, 10, 11, 12, 14

7 No smoking; 8 Children welcome; 9 Social drinking allowed; 10 Tennis nearby; 11 Swimming nearby; 12 Golf nearby; 13 Skiing nearby; 14 May be booked through a travel agent.

Mi Casa Su Casa

P.O. Box 950, Tempe, 85280-0950
(602) 990-0682; (800) 456-0682 (reservations
    only)

309. Experience the ever-changing red rock
vistas that surround this five-bedroom inn.
Built in 1983, the inn is a triplex ranch-
style house at the foot of Castle Rock. All
bedrooms have large windows, queen-size
beds, private baths, and their own unique
furnishings and artwork. Each pair of bedrooms shares a sitting room featuring a
fireplace and small kitchen. The fifth bedroom is in the main part of the triplex and
has a private bath. Full breakfasts served in
the great room at a large knotty pine table
with view. Two small resident dogs.
School-age children are welcome. Smoking
allowed outside. Handicapped accessible.
$80-110.

357. The hostess invites guests into her
large one-story home where she has a suite
on one side of the house. The Honeymoon
Suite is entered from the living room and
has a king-size bed; windows have a view
of the red rocks, patio, and gardens; flagstone floor and private bath with a
whirlpool tub. Entered from a hall near the
front door are two guest rooms. Room two
is decorated with Native American and
Mexican arts and crafts and has a queen-
size bed and connecting bath. Room three
has king-size or twin beds, a small private
balcony, family heirlooms, and a full hall
bath. A full breakfast features gourmet
recipes. Children ten and older are welcome. Smoking allowed outside. $115-150.

375. Contemporary stucco and tile home
nestled into a rock slope. Built in 1993, it is
in a peaceful, residential neighborhood
with breathtaking views of the red rocks.
Separate apartment with private entrance,
deck, and sitting room. The bedroom, with
its glorious views, has a queen-size bed and
a lounging sofa. Featuring a kitchenette,

full private bath, cable TV, and telephone.
Two-night minimum stay. No children. No
pets. No smoking. $75.

Old Pueblo Homestays

P.O. Box 13603, Tucson, 85732
(800) 333-9RSO

Casa Sedona, A Bed and Breakfast. A
serene respite offering fabulous red rock
views from each of its eleven terraced guest
rooms individually appointed to please and
pamper guests. The rooms are spacious,
luxurious, and include private bath, spa
tubs, and a delightful fireplace. A hearty
Southwestern breakfast is served in a total
smoke-free environment in the privacy of
guests' room, the dining room next to the
kitchen, or outdoors on either of two patios.
Open year-round. Golf and tennis packages
available. No smoking. Pets welcome. Children over 10 welcome. $95-150.

Rose Tree Inn

376 Cedar Street, 86336
(602) 282-2065

"The best kept secret in Sedona" describes
the three small, quaint, private, and quiet

units with fully furnished kitchenettes. Beautiful property in a lovely English garden environment is within walking distance of Old Town. One hundred miles north of Phoenix; two and one-half hours to the Grand Canyon. Reservations a must.

Host: Rachel Gillespie
Rooms: 4 (PB) $82-116
Coffee and Tea in room
Credit Cards: A, B
Notes: 2, 5, 9, 10, 12, 14

Territorial House

Territorial House: An Old West Bed and Breakfast

65 Piki Drive, 86336
(520) 204-2737; (800) 801-2737
FAX (520) 204-2230

The Territorial House, built of native stone and cedar, is nestled among cottonwood, juniper, and pine trees. Each unique room is comfortably decorated with a theme depicting Sedona's territorial history. Guests enjoy western hospitality as they relax around the large native-stone fireplace, watch numerous birds from the veranda, soak in the hot tub, or just rest in the peaceful, serene setting. Rooms available with fireplaces, balcony, deck, whirlpool tub, and TV. Full gourmet breakfasts are served in the saltillo-tiled dining room. Late afternoon snacks are available after a full day of exploring Sedona's Red Rock Country.

Hosts: John and Linda Steele
Rooms: 4 (PB) $90-140

Full Breakfast
Credit Cards: A, B, C
Notes: 2, 5, 7, 8, 9, 10, 11, 12, 13, 14

A Touch of Sedona Bed and Breakfast

595 Jordan Road, 86336
(602) 282-6462; FAX (602) 282-1534

In historic uptown, this California ranch-style inn is within easy walking distance of shops, galleries, restaurants, the Sedona Art Center, and playhouse. The eclectic elegance features stained glass, antiques, and contemporary furnishings and art. Beautiful red rock views and sensational stargazing from the deck. Private baths. Generous hospitality, multi-course gourmet breakfasts with home-baked goodies. Quiet, residential area is also near forest service trails. Smoke-free environment. No pets. AAA three-diamond rating. ABBA three-crown rating.

Hosts: Bill and Sharon Larsen
Rooms: 5 (PB) $85-135
Full Breakfast
Credit Cards: A, B, D
Notes: 5, 9, 10, 11, 12, 14

SIERRA VISTA

Mi Casa Su Casa

P.O. Box 950, Tempe, 85280-0950
(602) 990-0682; (800) 456-0682 (reservations only)

362. Enjoy Southeast Arizona's high desert country with mild temperatures year-round and an area rich in history and legend. Surrounded by rolling hills, this handsome two-story house and separate but attached guest cottage "casita" are on the historic San Pedro River. Many guests enjoy walking to the nearby river that has towering cottonwood trees along its banks and bird watching in the San Pedro Riparian National Conservation Area. The casita is across the patio from the main house. This large spacious room is complete with its own private entrance, queen-size bed, bathroom,

7 No smoking; 8 Children welcome; 9 Social drinking allowed; 10 Tennis nearby; 11 Swimming nearby; 12 Golf nearby; 13 Skiing nearby; 14 May be booked through a travel agent.

microwave, refrigerator. The second floor guest room in the main house has a queen-size bed and private hall bath. There is a shaded garden courtyard with a Mexican fountain surrounded by flowers and plants. Within the walled patio area is a hot tub and swimming pool to use in season. Guests are welcome to use the common room in the main house where there is a TV and regulation size pool table. Dog in residence. Two-night minimum stay. Smoking restricted. No pets. Children over 12 welcome. Continental plus breakfast during the week and a full breakfast on weekends. $55-75.

Old Pueblo Homestays

P.O. Box 13603, Tucson, 85732
(800) 333-9 RSO

San Pedro Bed and Breakfast. This secluded two-story ranch house with a separate guest casita is in a quiet, rural area on five acres surrounded by rolling hills and towering cottonwood trees. Perfect setting for bird watching, hiking, or sightseeing. The guest house has a private entrance, queen-size bed, bath with shower only, microwave, and refrigerator. The common room provides a TV/VCR, pool table, card table, and small library. Shaded garden courtyard, walled patio area, pool, and spa. Southwestern breakfast. Minimum two nights. No pets. Children over 12 welcome. No smoking inside. Seven dollars each additional person. $60-65.

SONOITA

Bed and Breakfast Inn Arizona

8900 East Via Linda, Suite 101, Scottsdale, 85258
(602) 860-9338 (phone and FAX)

SN001. Luxurious accommodation on a working cattle ranch. In a land of beautiful views. Pool, tennis court. Continental breakfast. Call for rates.

Mi Casa Su Casa

P.O. Box 950, Tempe, 85280-0950
(602) 990-0682; (800) 456-0682 (reservations only)

1623. This working ranch offers luxury accommodations in Arizona's high grass country. There are facilities for 16 people in both the main house and guest house, and sizes of beds range from king-size to twin. For those wanting more privacy, the entire house can be rented. Ranch is next to the National Forest, foothills, and Santa Rita Mountains. Guests are not waited on hand and foot, because the hosts believe that most people want privacy, seclusion, and the freedom to choose their own meal-times. Kitchen privileges, partial maid service, bed linens, pool, and tennis court are all available. Self-serve Continental breakfast. Minimum stay is two nights. $75-300.

SPRINGERVILLE

Mi Casa Su Casa

P.O. Box 950, Tempe, 85280-0950
(602) 990-0682; (800) 456-0682 (reservations only)

325. Carefully restored Colonial Revival home circa 1910 allows a visitor to step back in time. Enjoy antiques such as an original soda fountain, two old, operable jukeboxes, and Coca-Cola signs. Four bedrooms with private baths are furnished with antiques, handmade quilts, and goosedown pillows. Full breakfast is served with antique crystal, china, and table linens. Smoking outside only. $65-75.

TEMPE

Bed and Breakfast Inn Arizona

8900 East Via Linda, Suite 101, Scottsdale, 85258
(602) 860-9338 (phone and FAX)

NOTES: Credit cards accepted: A MasterCard; B Visa; C American Express; D Discover; E Diners Club; F Other; 2 Personal checks accepted; 3 Lunch available; 4 Dinner available; 5 Open all year; 6 Pets welcome;

TE104. This gentle, old home is in the heart of Tempe, close to the airport and ASU. The hosts have created a new addition to their 50-year-old home with guests' comfort in mind. Twin or king-size beds, private entrance, and private, connecting bath available. There is also a sitting area with sofa bed for extra guest. French door opens onto a patio. Citrus trees on the property mean fresh juice in season with gourmet breakfast. Library wall, TV, small refrigerator, and microwave oven available. Sweet, old dog in house. Infants or children over seven welcome. Deluxe rates.

Mi Casa Su Casa

P.O. Box 950, 85280-0950
(602) 990-0682; (800) 456-0682 (reservations only)

314. This bed and breakfast is in an older, quiet, well-kept neighborhood two blocks from ASU and downtown Tempe. The main house was built in 1939 and is typical of the "cottage" architecture of that time. A new 475-square-foot addition with a private entrance onto the patio blends well with the old house. This area consists of large, open space with sitting room/bedroom with TV, VCR, microwave, and small refrigerator. The private bath has a whirlpool tub. King-size bed and queen-size sofa bed. Resident outside dog who is willing to share fenced area with a guest dog. Smoking allowed outside. Infants are welcome; Port-a-crib available. Minimum stay is two nights. Ten dollars each for third and fourth persons. $65.

412. Casual comfort is found at this bed and breakfast, a Japanese-style home that brings the "outdoors in" with a 350 square-foot garden enclosed in the center of the house. The garden has a waterfall, an aviary with Lady Goulding finches, and a spa that is available to guests. One mile from downtown Tempe and ASU and two miles from the football stadium. There is one large bedroom with a queen-size bed, a sitting room with a double sofa bed, TV, a desk, and telephone. An outdoor pool is solar heated and is above 70 degrees March through October. Crib available. Smoking restricted. No pets. Full breakfast. $75.

413. A four-bedroom and two-bath house built in 1967, this bed and breakfast is a ranch-style home in a mature, quiet neighborhood with a delightful host couple. The front yard is desert landscaped and the back yard is in grass with a large diving pool and many mature citrus trees. Air-conditioned. Room one is extra large and has a queen-size bed, TV, telephone, exercise equipment, and hall bath. Room two has a double bed, telephone, and shared hall bath. Guests are welcome in the family room that has cable TV and a fireplace. Dog in residence. Smoking restricted. Inquire about children welcome. Continental plus breakfast on weekdays and full breakfast on weekends. $55-65.

Valley O' the Sun Bed and Breakfast

P.O. Box 2214, 85252
(602) 941-1281; (800) 689-1281

In the college district of Tempe but still close enough to Scottsdale to enjoy the glamour of its shops, restaurants, and theaters, Valley O' the Sun Bed and Breakfast offers clean, comfortable rooms at reasonable and affordable rates.

Host: Kathleen Curtis
Rooms: 3 (1 PB; 2 SB) $35-40
Continental Breakfast
Credit Cards: None
Notes: 5, 9, 10, 11, 12, 13, 14

TOMBSTONE

Bed and Breakfast Inn Arizona

8900 East Via Linda, Suite 101, Scottsdale, 85258
(602) 860-9338 (phone and FAX)

7 No smoking; 8 Children welcome; 9 Social drinking allowed; 10 Tennis nearby; 11 Swimming nearby; 12 Golf nearby; 13 Skiing nearby; 14 May be booked through a travel agent.

TM102. This 1880 Adobe house is in the heart of Old Tombstone. Rooms furnished with antiques and collectibles. Hearty breakfast in country kitchen. Call for rates.

Mi Casa Su Casa

P.O. Box 950, Tempe, 85280-0950
(602) 990-0682; (800) 456-0682 (reservations only)

330. Personable, friendly host couple have carefully restored these historic buildings built around 1880. There are two white stucco buildings: the main house and the "miner's cabin." The hardwood floors have been refinished and each room is decorated in a simple, authentic 1890 western motif. The parlor is furnished in Victorian style and has a baby grand piano and a TV. There are six guest rooms in the main house, each with a private entrance. The seventh room is in the miner's cabin. Most rooms have private baths. A full breakfast is served in a large dining room. Inquire about children welcome. No resident pets. Smoking allowed outside. $55-70.

Old Pueblo Homestays

P.O. Box 13603, Tucson, 85732
(800) 333-9RS0

Buford House Bed and Breakfast. Listed on the National Historic Register of Homes, this 1880 adobe home was built originally as a boarding house. Rooms upstairs are furnished with antiques of various themes, with private and shared baths. The downstairs guest room has private entrance and private bath. The common room is filled with antiques and memorabilia and has puzzles, games, and books for guests' enjoyment. A full breakfast is either served in the dining room or on the Territorial style porch. A barbecue area is an added feature for the convenience of the guests. Walking distance to town. Smoking outside only. No pets. Children over six welcome. $65-85.

Priscilla's Bed and Breakfast. This is Tombstone's only remaining two-story clapboard country Victorian house. Built in 1904 and immaculately restored, the house has all the original wood and still has some of the original gas lighting fixtures as well as a large oak staircase. The three rooms upstairs are tastefully decorated to fit the era reminiscent of grandma's house. The Primrose, Violet, and Rose rooms have double beds, sinks, and vanities. Breakfast is served on a lace-covered oak table, and home-baked breads complete the atmosphere of earlier days. Across the street is Arizona's first Protestant church, built in 1876. Smoking is limited. $35-55.

Tombstone Boarding House. Two 1880 adobe houses are surrounded by an 1880-style picket fence. The first house, built by the town's first banker, was remodeled and enlarged in early 1930. The second house was the original Barrows House where legend has it that in the 1880s the notorious Buckskin Frank Leslie roomed. In the 1930s renowned artist H.E. Wenck built a studio addition with a large picture window and a spectacular view of the surrounding mountains and Sheep's Head. A hearty breakfast is served in a sunny, antique-filled country kitchen. Each of six rooms furnished with antiques features a private entrance and bath. Children are welcome. Smoking permitted outside only. $45-75.

TUCSON

Bed and Breakfast Inn Arizona

8900 East Via Linda, Suite 101, Scottsdale, 85258
(602) 860-9338 (phone and FAX)

TU002. This ranch inn sits on the slopes of the Tucson Mountains near extensive natural desert grounds and 30 acres of pristine chaparral country. Fantastic amenities including pool and spa. Close to all attractions. Continental breakfast. Call for rates.

TU003. Adobe home in the quiet central foothills of Tucson has private entrances, Jacuzzi, and Continental breakfast. Great mountain views. Call for rates.

TU004. Unique inn with massive beams. Great for nature lovers. Kitchens, patios, and pools. Close to Arizona-Sonora Desert Museum and Old Tucson. Call for rates.

TU006. This Southwestern hacienda features privacy, scenery, and solitude. Pool, courtyard with fountain, and beautiful views. Full breakfast is served.

TU007. In quiet residential neighborhood encompassing Santa Fe-style decor, this bed and breakfast was built in 1930 as Clark Gable's getaway home. Features king-size beds, spa, and a Continental breakfast. Call for rates.

TU010. Unique territorial inn has innkeeper and host who is a retired travel agent with extensive knowledge of who, what, when, and where. Walking distance to shopping, museums, etc. Gourmet breakfast. Call for rates.

TU011. Elegant inn built in the 1902s is in the heart of the city. Walking distance to University of Arizona and University Hospital. Call for rates.

TU102. Luxurious, contemporary 1,100-square-foot guest house has solar-heated pool, patio, and gorgeous views of the Santa Catalina Mountains. Near golf course. Full kitchen, breakfast bar, stone fireplace, king-size bed, one twin bed, TV, and own telephone. Private bath and entrance. Garage

space for guest vehicle. Wheelchair accommodations. Full breakfast served on weekends by Swedish hostess. Hostess works outside the home, so weekday breakfast fixings are left in guest kitchen. Cat in residence. Deluxe to superior rates.

TU109. Enjoy the mountain views while soaking in the Jacuzzi or pool; these can be heated for additional charge. Two suites available and may be used together for large party. One suite has washer/dryer, and kitchen stocked with groceries for guests to fix their own breakfast. Private entrance, hall bath with shower. Bedroom with king-size bed, twin bed in the Arizona Room, and queen-size Hide-a-Bed in living room. Children over 16 accepted in this suite with parents. Smoking is allowed in this suite. The second suite has Continental breakfast. Private entrance, two bedrooms with double beds, hall bath with tub and shower. No smoking in this suite. Resident dog and cat; guest pets are welcome. Deluxe rates.

TU114. This small ranch high in the Sonoran Desert foothills above the city is a bird watcher's paradise, and home to fowl, horses, well-behaved dogs, and peaceful cats. Enjoy a full ranch breakfast on the patio with fountain and birds. Private guest room with Ben Franklin stove, private bathroom (shower), and patio. Sleeping accommodations include a queen-size bed, two twins, and a single roll away if needed for children. Crib also available. Color TV, radio, tape player, phone, snack refrigerator, books, and games. Jacuzzi and pool. Children are welcome. Deluxe rates.

TU119. A Southwestern-style home in downtown Tucson has a choice of three rooms: the Cabana, which has a double bed and private bath; the Studio, which is a private apartment with double bed and complete kitchen; and the Governor's Room,

7 No smoking; 8 Children welcome; 9 Social drinking allowed; 10 Tennis nearby; 11 Swimming nearby; 12 Golf nearby; 13 Skiing nearby; 14 May be booked through a travel agent.

Bed and Breakfast Inn Arizona (continued)

which has a queen-size antique bed, private bath, and sitting area with fireplace. Pool and patio. Full breakfast, racquet club privileges, and a sophisticated, warm atmosphere make this well worth the rates. Dog and cats in residence. Superior rates.

TU120. This fascinating rammed-earth pueblo-style home with a stupendous view of the Santa Catalina Mountains in the northern part of the city is hosted by a tour guide. Grandmother's heirloom guest room has a queen-size bed, private hall bath, and guests are welcome to the great room with TV and VCR. Second bedroom is available for additional guests in same party, but they will need to share hall bath with first bedroom. Redwood deck for relaxing and watching the wildlife, and a hot tub will complete the stay. If guests cannot escape work, there is a desk and telephone available. Continental breakfast. Two small dogs. No children. Deluxe rates; weekly rates for longer stays.

TU121. Tucson's premier corporate retreat is nestled on over four acres against the Santa Catalina Mountains. Each room reflects host's favorite international hotels. Heated pool, patio, magnificent views, and polished, professional service make this a most sophisticated, yet comfortably intimate bed and breakfast. Full breakfast. Each room has a private bath, TV, VCR, phone, terry-cloth robes, and all the amenities one would expect in a world-class bed and breakfast. The Oriental Room has a queen-size bed, private Jacuzzi, and Oriental furnishings. The Regent has a queen-size bed and French doors that open onto the patio. The Four Seasons has a queen-size canopied bed and warm mahogany furnishings. The Cannaught has Chippendale furniture and a decorative non-working fireplace. Closely supervised children welcome. Minimum two-night stay is required. Superior rates.

TU122. This private home is a real classic in the Craftsman tradition. The sparkling hostess presides over a full breakfast. There is a guest parlor with TV and VCR. Pool and patio in the back. Off-street parking available. The home is decorated with antique furnishings. The Amethyst Room has an antique queen-size bed, the original Victorian wallpaper, and a private hall bath with original claw-foot tub. The Saguaro Room is decorated with a lodgepole queen-size bed, armoire, table and chairs, cozy fireplace, and private bath. The Spanish Room has a queen-size bed and private bath. The Rose Quartz Room has one twin and one double bed, a private bath, and French doors that open onto the living room area (some traffic noise in this room). No children. Deluxe to superior rates.

TU123. Privacy, magnificent views, pool, patio, and desert surroundings highlight this delightful Southwestern-style guest house. Two bedrooms (only one guest party at a time), full kitchen and bath, have private entrance into a finely detailed, handcrafted guest house complete with handpainted Mexican tiles and custom Southwestern cabinetry. The Catalina Room has a queen-size bed, desk, sitting area; the Patio Room has twins, rustic rawhide table and chairs, and French doors onto the patio. Telephones, TV, and VCR are all in the guest house, and the hostess leaves full breakfast fixings for guests to self-cater when they feel like getting up. Bikes available for the adventurous. No children under five. Dog and cats in main house. Two-night minimum stay. Superior rates.

NOTES: Credit cards accepted: A MasterCard; B Visa; C American Express; D Discover; E Diners Club; F Other; 2 Personal checks accepted; 3 Lunch available; 4 Dinner available; 5 Open all year; 6 Pets welcome;

Car-Mar's Southwest Bed and Breakfast

6766 West Oklahoma, 85746
(520) 578-1730

Southwestern by design, close to popular attractions such as Arizona Sonora Desert Museum and Old Tucson movie studios. Each room is uniquely decorated with lodgepole and saguaro rib furniture. Hot tub under the stars, poolside refreshments and luxurious robes may be relished during guests' stay. Fresh-baked treats at turn down. Full, scrumptious breakfast served in dining room or garden by request. "Super Summer" special in effect May 15 through August 31. (Buy two nights, get the third consecutive night free.)

Host: Carole Martinez
Rooms: 4 (2 PB; 2 SB) $65-125
Full Breakfast
Credit Cards: A, B
Notes: 2, 5, 7, 9, 10, 11, 12, 14

Casa Alegre Bed and Breakfast Inn

316 East Speedway, 85705
(520) 628-1800

This distinguished 1915 home is between the University of Arizona and downtown Tucson. A scrumptious full breakfast is served in the formal dining room or poolside on the serene patio. Casa Alegre allows easy access to Tucson's many historic, cultural, and recreational attractions, state and national parks, as well as great shopping and fantastic eateries.

Host: Phyllis Florek
Rooms: 4 (PB) $70-95
Full Breakfast
Credit Cards: A, B, D
Notes: 2, 5, 7, 9, 10, 11, 12, 14

Casa Tierra Adobe Bed and Breakfast Inn

11155 West Calle Pima, 85743
(520) 578-3058

Casa Tierra is on five acres of beautiful Sonoran desert 30 minutes west of Tucson. This secluded area has hundreds of saguaro cactus, spectacular mountain views, and brilliant sunsets. The rustic adobe house features entryways with vaulted brick ceilings, an interior arched courtyard, Mexican furnishings, and a Jacuzzi overlooking the desert. Great hiking and bird watching. Near Arizona-Sonora Desert Museum, Saguaro National Park, and Old Tucson.

Hosts: Karen and Lyle Hymer-Thompson
Rooms: 3 (PB) $85-95
Full Breakfast
Credit Cards: None
Notes: 2, 7, 8, 9

Catalina Park Inn

309 East First Street, 85705
(520) 792-4541; (800) 792-4885
FAX (520) 792-0838

Overlooking Catalina Park, this historic residence affords guests an environment of understated elegance. All rooms are handsomely furnished with antiques. Some have private porches. All have a private bath. Perfect for a romantic getaway, honeymoon, or just for a chance to relax. A sumptuous extended Continental breakfast is included. Enjoy our lush Mediterranean garden. Superb location in the West University Historic District, just blocks from the University of Arizona and Fourth Avenue's eclectic shops and restaurants. Minimum stay requirements during some periods. Limited smoking allowed. Children over 10 welcome.

Hosts: Mark Hall and Paul Richard
Rooms: 4 (PB) $67.50-115
Continental Breakfast
Cards: A, B
Notes: 2, 5, 9, 10, 11, 12, 13, 14

June's Bed and Breakfast

3212 West Holladay Street, 85746
(520) 578-0857

7 No smoking; 8 Children welcome; 9 Social drinking allowed; 10 Tennis nearby; 11 Swimming nearby; 12 Golf nearby; 13 Skiing nearby; 14 May be booked through a travel agent.

This Tucson Mountain hideaway features a magnificent view and a friendly hostess who is an artist.

Host: June Henderson
Rooms: 3 (1 PB; 2 SB) $45-55
Continental Breakfast
Credit Cards: None
Notes: 2, 5, 9, 10, 11, 12, 13

The Lodge on the Desert

306 North Alvernon Way, P.O. Box 42500, 85711
(520) 325-3366; (800) 456-5634
FAX (520) 327-5834

A small resort hotel providing the finest in food and accommodations, the Lodge has been under the same family ownership for more than 50 years. Close to golf, tennis, and shopping. One-half hour from Arizona-Sonora Desert Museum, Old Tucson movie location, Coronado National Forest. Three miles from the University of Arizona. Inquire about arrangements for pets. Pool on the premises.

Host: Schuyler W. Lininger
Rooms: 40 (PB) $58-177
Continental Breakfast
Credit Cards: A, B, C, D, E
Notes: 2, 3, 4, 5, 8, 9, 10, 11, 12, 13, 14

Mi Casa Su Casa

P.O. Box 950, Tempe, 85280-0950
(602) 990-0682; (800) 456-0682 (reservations only)

038. Townhouse in a quiet area with attractive desert trees, plants, and mountain and city views is near La Paloma, Sabino Canyon. Guest room has a king-size bed, TV, and private bath. Pool adjacent to the house is available during the summer and a nearby pool is heated in the winter. Near tennis courts and resort golf courses. Continental plus breakfast. No resident pets. Smoking allowed outside. No children. Two-night minimum. $55-60.

142. Guests describe this architect-designed 1,100-square-foot guest cottage as a home away from home. Next to 127 acres of natural desert, it is near the Catalina Mountain Foothills and Sabino Canyon. The guest house has a patio, comfortable living room with a double sofa bed, TV, and private phone. There is a full kitchen, washer and dryer, and dining area. The bedroom has twin beds and connecting bath. The kitchen is stocked for short stays. For longer stays, breakfast is not included. Smoking allowed outside. Children over eight who are swimmers welcome. Fifteen dollars for third person. Special weekly and monthly rates. Three-night minimum stay is required. $115.

175. Built in 1886 amid other historic mansions, this inn has been featured in books and articles. The charming Carriage House has a living room/kitchen, bedroom with queen-size bed, and private bath. In the main house, the Gate House suite has a living room/bedroom with a queen-size bed, Pullman kitchen, private bath, and private entrance. The Victorian Suite has a bedroom with queen-size bed, private bath, and a large sitting room. The Quilt Room has a double bed and private bath. Full gourmet breakfasts. Smoking allowed outside. No resident pets. Children age 15 and older are welcome. Two-night minimum stay with exception of the Carriage House, which has a three-night minimum stay. $85-120.

212. Attached but separate architect-designed, very large, charming guest cottage with private patio is in the Catalina Mountain Foothills. Many windows look out on the beautiful pool and yard. The furnishings include contemporary furniture with Southwestern and Scandinavian accents. Living room/bedroom has fireplace, king-size bed, one twin bed, full kitchen, and large private bath. For short stays, the kitchen is stocked, and guests serve themselves during the week. Full breakfasts are served on the weekends. Well-behaved children who can swim are

NOTES: Credit cards accepted: A MasterCard; B Visa; C American Express; D Discover; E Diners Club; F Other; 2 Personal checks accepted; 3 Lunch available; 4 Dinner available; 5 Open all year; 6 Pets welcome;

welcome. Three-night minimum. Resident dog in main house. Smoking allowed outside. Monthly rate available. Weekly rates do not include breakfast. $85.

223. Imagine being able to ski on Mount Lemmon in the morning and sun by the pool in the afternoon! Tranquil home and separate guest house have panoramic view of the city and the mountains surrounding Tucson. Two guest rooms in main house have private baths and TVs. One has a queen-size bed, the other has a pair of extra-long twin beds. Guests are welcome to use large living room. The three-room guest cottage has a living room with queen-size sofa bed, TV, fireplace, bedroom with queen-size bed, hall bath, full kitchen, and private courtyard. Full breakfast is served in the main house. Two small resident dogs. Smoking allowed outside. No children. Three-night minimum stay in guest cottage. $95-140.

243. Brick house built in 1947 has an eclectic, comfortable decor and is in a quiet neighborhood about two miles from University of Arizona and three miles from downtown business district. Room one has a king-size bed, private bath, and private entrance. Room two has a queen-size bed and a shared hall bath. Continental plus breakfast served. Infants welcome. Pets welcome with prior approval. Resident cats live in hosts' area. Outside smoking only. $45-65.

276. An adobe bed and breakfast with central courtyard and rustic charm reminiscent of haciendas found in central Mexico. Join the hosts in their serene desert living, bird watching, and hiking. The three guest rooms have queen-size beds, private baths, private entrances, and patios. Two nights preferred. Full breakfast is served. Resident dogs and cats. Smoking allowed outside only. Children are welcome. Roll away and crib available for $10. $75-85.

277. Handsome two-level home in the Catalina Foothills in a quiet neighborhood, has a view of majestic mountains above and a birds' eye view of the Tucson Valley below. Near Sabino Canyon with its spectacular mountain tram tour, and twenty minutes from downtown Tucson. House is air-conditioned. The four guest rooms are decorated with American antiques and Southwestern furnishings, and they have their own private entrance, coming in from the pool/patio area, into a large guest living room and dining room area. There is a private telephone for guests. Available are a large refrigerator and ice maker, sink, microwave, toaster, coffee maker, and dishes. There is a TV, VCR., fireplace, and small library with books and brochures. Room one has a queen-size bed, and room two has extra-long twin beds with a bath in between them. Rooms three and four each have a queen-size bed and private bath. Smoking restricted. No pets. Children over eight who can swim welcome. Breakfast is self-catering. Available on monthly basis only. Call for rates.

280. This charming hostess welcomes guests to her Santa Fe-style patio home, built in 1993, in a quiet north central area. Guests enjoy beautiful, unobstructed views of the mountains. Landscaped back yard with desert plantings and access to community pool. Room one has twin beds, private hall bath, and private patio. The master bedroom with a queen-size bed, connecting private bath, and private patio is available for two-week or longer stays. Guests are welcome to enjoy the living room with fireplace. Laundry privileges. Enclosed garage. Full breakfast served. Smoking allowed outside. Children over three are welcome. $45-60.

304. Luxury townhouse in a beautifully landscaped green area near malls, theaters, good restaurants, and 20 minutes from the university. One very large room has a king-size bed, TV, phone, and a connecting full

Mi Casa Su Casa
(continued)

bath. Heated pool, spa, and tennis court are in complex. Complimentary refreshments and Continental breakfast. No resident pets. No smoking allowed. Three-night minimum stay. $90.

310. Panoramic view of the ever-changing Catalina Mountains in a quiet country setting. Many articles have been written about this spacious, passive-solar environmentally designed Santa Fe-style home. All homes in the area are on one- or two-acre lots, so guests might see roadrunners, hummingbirds, or quail. Golf and tennis nearby. Room one has a queen-size bed. Room two has twin beds or king-size bed. Full hall bath is private to guests. The master bedroom has a view, fireplace, queen-size bed, and private bath. Spa. Continental breakfast. Two small, resident dogs. Smoking allowed outside. No children. $65-85.

316. Warm, outgoing hostess welcomes guests to a delightfully restored two-story home built around 1900 in a quiet, well-kept neighborhood near the University of Arizona. On the first floor, room one has a queen-size bed, sitting area, and a private bath. Room two on the second floor has a canopied double bed and shares the hall bath. Light kitchen privileges available. Near public transportation. Continental plus breakfast is served. No resident pets. Children welcome. $55-65.

326. Host couple welcomes guests to their large stucco home built in 1990 in a resort community north of the Catalina foothills. The back yard adjoins state open range, which is nice for hiking and bird watching. Twenty-four miles from downtown Tucson. Available are a club house with its own restaurant, tennis courts, 18-hole golf course, two heated swimming pools, driving range, and health club with spa. Guests have private use of the living room with fireplace, dining room, and den. Room one has a king-size bed or twin beds and a private full bath. Room two has a queen-size sofa bed for additional members of the party and shares the hall bath. Full breakfast is served. No resident pets. Children welcome. Guest pets welcome by arrangement. Smoking permitted. Weekly rates are available. Closed May 1 through October 1. $65-75.

343. Near the University of Arizona is a 1915 Craftsman-style bungalow with mahogany and leaded glass, built-in cabinetry, and hardwood floors. The hostess enjoys helping guests discover the special offerings of the region. The four guest rooms have private baths and their decor reflects facets of Tucson's history. One guest room has twin beds. Tasty, full breakfasts. Restful patio and pool. No resident pets. Children ten and older are welcome. Smoking allowed outside. Discount rates June 1 through September 1. $65-80.

351. Enjoy the unobstructed spectacular views of the Saguaro National Monument East and a sweeping valley going up to the mountains. Near the airport and downtown Tucson. Separate but attached apartment has a private entrance, living room with trundle beds that can be made into two single beds or a king-size bed, TV, and VCR. Bedroom with queen-size bed has a full bath. In the large main house, the guest room has a queen-size bed and private hall bath. Apartment has enclosed patio with spa. For short stays, the kitchen is stocked. For longer stays, self-catering. Children over nine welcome. Smoking allowed outside. Resident cat and dog. French spoken. Apartment rented by the month. $55-75.

354. At the northeastern edge of Tucson is a mini-ranch of five acres with wonderful

NOTES: Credit cards accepted: A MasterCard; B Visa; C American Express; D Discover; E Diners Club; F Other; 2 Personal checks accepted; 3 Lunch available; 4 Dinner available; 5 Open all year; 6 Pets welcome;

views of the Catalina Mountains. The main house and guest area are separated by a patio. Nearby are the Coronado and the Saguaro national forests. Guest area has a private entrance, queen-size bed, two single (trundle) beds, private bath, refrigerator, TV, library of bird and western lore, private patio, pool, and spa. Full ranch breakfast. Children two and older welcome. Smoking allowed outside. Ten dollars additional for children. $65.

355. Guests are welcome to use common room with cable TV, VCR, and fireplace. Light kitchen privileges, grill, outside spa, laundry facilities, and cordless telephones in rooms. Roll away and cot available for small additional fee. The Quail's Nest Honeymoon Suite has views, private porch, queen-size bed, TV, fireplace, and private bath with double whirlpool tub. The Cactus Wren has views, double bed, private bath with whirlpool tub, and TV. Continental plus and full breakfasts. Well-behaved children are welcome. Smoking allowed outside only. Resident pets. Handicapped accessible. Two-night minimum. $75-95.

361. Host couple welcomes guests to this luxury, contemporary home with 80-mile views in northeast Tucson. The area offers the quiet of the desert, but is convenient to all of Tucson's cultural activities and superb restaurants. Inside, guests will find terra cotta tiles, Oriental rugs, fresh flowers, and a sense of serenity. Private guest suite has a bedroom with queen-size bed, spacious private bath, separate reading room with sofa, desert library, TV, and telephone. Full breakfast. No resident pets. No children. No smoking. $95.

367. Quiet neighborhood is within walking distance of park mall, restaurants, theaters. Charming hostess has home with antiques, very nice decor. Two guest rooms both have double beds, one with bath with

shower ensuite, the other with shared full hall bath. Guests welcome to watch cable TV in den or use the living room or back yard. Dog and cat in residence. Hostess offers choice of breakfasts. Public transportation nearby. Two-nights minimum stay. No smoking. No pets. Children over 12 welcome. $55.

371. Secluded desert setting is on over three acres of native plants and trees with panoramic mountain views of the Catalinas and Rincons. Private guest wing has two bedrooms, a sitting room with TV, telephone, and a utility room with washer and dryer. Both rooms have queen-size beds and private baths. Exercise room and pool available. Traditional breakfasts are featured, as well as low-fat, gluten-free, and vegetarian diets. Children over six welcome. No pets. Smoking allowed outside only. $65-75.

372. This beautiful, spacious adobe-style home in fashionable north Tucson offers mountain views and an overview of Tucson. Large room has a king-size bed, plus a sofa that converts to a double bed. Large bath with walk-in closet. Sliding glass doors lead to garden and pool. Continental plus breakfast provided. Two-night stay preferred. Children over ten welcome. No pets. Smoking allowed outside only. $75.

378. This home is decorated in an eclectic style, incorporating African carvings and art, American Indian arts and crafts, an art collection, and antique china—reflecting years of world travel. Private, newly remodeled guest area has two rooms. Room one has a double pull-down bed. Room two is a sitting room that has two trundle beds. There is a shared bath. Private entrance with small garden, private telephone, and laundry facilities available. Room three is very large with a queen-size bed, library, and private hall bath. Full breakfast is

Mi Casa Su Casa
(continued)

served. Well-behaved children welcome. Resident cat. Small pet with prior approval. No smoking. $65-75.

403. The small size of this new contemporary Southwestern home lends itself to personal attention and expertise from hostess. Air-conditioned. Room one has a queen-size bed and private full bath. Room two is an overflow room with one twin bed and shared bath. Gourmet breakfasts. Enclosed outdoor patio with mountain views. Guests welcome to use TV and VCR in living room. Access to house laundry facilities, Ping Pong table. Airport pick-up available at additional cost. Smoking outside. No pets. No children. $30-70.

404. Handsome Southwestern-style home on four acres has beautiful flowers in season and attached but separate apartment. Two beds with baths ensuite available. Antiques, many works of art. Home is air-conditioned. Apartment has private entrance, living room with TV, queen-size sofa bed and fireplace, bath with shower, kitchen with full-sized stove and oven, double sink, microwave, and large refrigerator. The second bedroom has a queen-size bed, TV, full bath ensuite, antiques. Unheated pool, fountain, barbecue. Laundry facilities. French spoken. Dog in residence. Two nights stay preferred. No smoking. No pets. Children over 16 welcome. Continental plus breakfast. $85-125.

414. This Santa Fe-style house built in 1994 has beehive fireplaces, vigas, and Mexican saltillo tile floors. In a small residential community in the northern foothills of the Santa Catalina Mountains, it is beautifully decorated with a mix of American country antiques, a delightful rustic birdhouse collection, and Southwestern decor.

From the patio and yard, guests will enjoy magnificent mountain views, sunsets, and star-gazing at its best. Air-conditioned. Room one has a king-size bed, full bath ensuite, and TV. Room two has a queen-size bed, private full hall bath, and TV. Two-night stay preferred. No smoking. No pets. No children. Full breakfast. $80.

415. In the country on 16 acres near the Saguaro National Monument East, this home is a large adobe structure built around an interior courtyard in the Spanish style. With an unobstructed view of the Rincon Mountains, its restful environment is appealing to nature lovers. Both guest rooms have an informal Southwestern country flavor, ornate antique heating stoves, a sofa bed, and private entrances. Two-room suite has a queen-size bed, living room, kitchenette, and shared hall bath, and evaporative cooling. Another spacious room offers a king-size bed, sitting area, small kitchenette, private bath, and private porch. Air-conditioned. TV and VCR. Outside cats in residence. Minimum stay of two nights preferred. Smoking outside. No pets. Children welcome. Handicapped possible. Continental plus breakfast. An additional $15 for each extra guest. $75.

419. Built in 1974, this is a luxurious Spanish-style hacienda nestled on over six acres in the Tucson Mountains high above the city. The main house offers views from all directions. There is a courtyard facing its own mountain, pool, and heated spa. Guests are welcome in the large Arizona room with a baby grand piano and a large fireplace. The separate apartment has air conditioning, a living/dining room, fireplace, full kitchen, TV, and VCR. The two bedrooms each have a queen-size bed and a full bath. In the main house are three suites. One suite has a Southwestern flair, a king-size bed, large living room, fireplace, Jacuzzi for two, cable TV, and refrigerator. Another suite has a queen-size bed and bath ensuite with shower. Third suite has

NOTES: Credit cards accepted: A MasterCard; B Visa; C American Express; D Discover; E Diners Club; F Other; 2 Personal checks accepted; 3 Lunch available; 4 Dinner available; 5 Open all year; 6 Pets welcome;

twin-size beds and a full bath ensuite. Cats in main house. Smoking restricted. Inquire about pets and children. Self-catered Continental plus breakfast. $65-175.

1625. Here at this guest and working ranch, some activities include cookouts, rodeos, team-roping, and steer wrestling. Riding instruction is also available. The heated pool and the indoor redwood hot tub are also popular with guests. Children will enjoy the petting zoo. Rates include all meals, hayrides, and all ranch activities. All rooms have private baths, and most rooms have double beds. Deluxe suites have a fireplace, whirlpool tub, king-size bed, roll away bed available. Laundry facilities. Families are welcome. No smoking in dining room. Free airport transportation. Closed May 1 through October 1. Four-night minimum. Children under two stay at no charge. Seventy-nine dollars for third person in room. $125-134.

Natural Bed and Breakfast

3150 East Presidio Road, 85716
(520) 881-4582

At Natural Bed and Breakfast, the word "natural" is true in all senses of the word. Attention is paid to a natural, non-toxic, and non-allergenic environment. For example, this home is water cooled rather than air-conditioned, and only natural foods are served. Shoes are not worn inside. The natural home environment is very nurturing. Professional massage is available. Guests are invited to share the large, homey living room with fireplace.

Host: Marc Habermon
Rooms: 3 (2 PB; 1 SB) $55-65
Full Breakfast
Credit Cards: None
Notes: 2, 3, 4, 5, 7, 8, 9, 10, 11, 12, 13, 14

Old Pueblo Homestays

P.O. Box 13603, 85732
(800) 333-9 RSO

Adobe House. This home is in the foothills between the Santa Catalina Mountains and midtown Tucson. Private bath and sitting room with TV and radio. Outside is a covered porch complete with swing and a patio. Beautiful mountain views can be enjoyed during the day. Continental breakfast served outside, weather permitting, including freshly squeezed juice. Minimum stay is two nights. No children. Smoking outside only. $60.

El Adobe Ranch Bed and Breakfast. Nestled deep in the Tucson Mountains within walking distance of the scenic Saguaro National Monument West, an area known for its magnificent saguaro, cacti, spectacular mountains and inspiring desert landscapes, this ranch is just 20 minutes from downtown Tucson. El Adobe Ranch offers three private adobe casitas with Southwestern furnishings, complete kitchens, high-beam ceilings, fireplace in both the living room and bedroom, twin sofa beds in the living room, cozy patios, gardens, and flagstone floors. The refrigerator is stocked with ingredients for a Continental breakfast. Outdoors is a wedding gazebo, ramada, barbecue area, hiking and walking trails, and horse facilities. Eighteen miles from Tucson International Airport. Greek is spoken. Smoking permitted outside only. Pets welcome by prior arrangements. Children welcome. $175.

The Adobe Rose Inn. This adobe home is filled with antiques, stained glass, tile, attractive gardens, patios, and pool. Near the pool is a separate guest house with a queen-size bed and sitting room, also a separate suite with a kitchenette and king-size bed. In the main house are three bedrooms with private baths. Two bedrooms have fireplaces. This comfortable home surrounded by a six-foot wall is in a quiet neighborhood east of the University of Arizona. The hostess takes pride in her

7 No smoking; 8 Children welcome; 9 Social drinking allowed; 10 Tennis nearby; 11 Swimming nearby; 12 Golf nearby; 13 Skiing nearby; 14 May be booked through a travel agent.

Old Pueblo Homestays (continued)

gourmet breakfast. Minimum stay of two nights. Smoking permitted outside only. Pets welcome. Children under one year old and over 12 welcome. $105.03-126.93.

The Antik House Bed and Breakfast. This lovely territorial home in northeast Tucson reflects the travels of the hosts in the Orient and in Europe. Enjoy mountain views with pool-side full or Continental breakfast. One room with king-size bed overlooking pool/patio area with radio, color TV, and private bath and entrance. Other room with twin beds, radio, and shared hall bath. Close to a bus stop, Sabino Canyon, Restaurant Row, shopping, and hiking. Bicycles available. Hosts have two small poodles. Two-night minimum. Smoking outside only. Children over 12 welcome. No pets. $55-65.

The Birdhouse Hollow Bed and Breakfast. A Santa Fe style home in a small residential community in the foothills of the Catalina Mountains has beehive fireplaces, vigas, and Mexican Saltillo tile accents a touch of elegant Southwestern decor. A delightful rustic birdhouse collection stands out against primitive antiques. From the secluded patio and yard the guest will enjoy magnificent mountain views and amazing sunsets. Evenings will bring star gazing at its best. This comfortable home has central air conditioning, one king-size bed with private bath, and a queen-size bed with hall bath. Families with children are welcome and baby-sitting is provided for a fee. A Continental plus breakfast is served. Minutes away from shops and fine dining, as well as other points of interest. No smoking. No pets. $75-80.

Bonnie's Bed and Breakfast. A large ranch decorated in traditional and romantic

style offers a three-room suite and a fully furnished guest cottage. The suite has a queen-size bed, private bath and entrance, and close parking. The one-room guest cottage has a double bed, twin beds, and a kitchenette. A full breakfast is served in front of the fireplace, in the back yard, or in guests' room. Within walking distance of a mall, church, library, business district, and restaurants. Christian videos, books, and tapes available. Children and pets welcome in cottage only for a five-dollar charge. No single men accepted. Smoking outside only. $75.

Bridle Way Bed and Breakfast. This one-story Ranch style home has tile floors, large Arizona room or great room with guest kitchen facilities, desert landscaping, patio, spa, and pool. There are four bedrooms. Two bedrooms have private baths and private entrances. The other two rooms share a bath. A Continental breakfast is served in the great room. Two-night stay minimum. $60-80.

Car-Mar's Southwest. Attractive bed and breakfast is in a quiet country setting with courtyards and pathways accentuated by native desert landscaping and wildlife feeders. There are four suites uniquely and romantically inspired by the rustic charm of lodgepole and saguaro rib furniture. Perfect setting for weddings and parties. Pool, spa, TV/VCR, refrigerator, microwave, and barbecue patio. Full breakfast. Smoking outside only. Inquire about children. No pets. $65-125.

Casa Adobes Bed and Breakfast. Separate adobe guest cottage with a carport opens into a back yard pool area. The living room with dining area is furnished with Southwestern and modern leather. Also a sofa couch opens into a queen-size Hide-a-Bed, full kitchen, bedroom with king-size bed, and a private full bath. Color TV, telephone, laundry facilities are also available. Also available is poolside studio efficiency apartment with Saltillo tile flooring, a small stove and oven, refrigerator, color TV, telephone, queen-size Hide-a-Bed, and shower only. Outside, well-trained-friendly dog and cats. Weekly and monthly stays only. Smoking outside. No pets. Children over 12 welcome. $150-450.

Casa Alegre. A 1915 Craftsman bungalow between the University of Arizona and downtown Tucson has four guest rooms in the main house each with private baths and decorated in a different influence of Tucson's past. The Arizona room with TV/VCR opens onto the serene patio and swimming pool area. Also next door is the Buchanan House Suite. Two bedrooms sleep four. Share kitchen and dining room and living room with host. A scrumptious full breakfast is served either in sun room, dining room, or outside on the patio where guests enjoy watching birds who inhabit the area. Nearby are golf, tennis, mountain and desert attractions, cultural and sports events as well as the University of Arizona, Fourth Avenue business and eateries, Tucson Convention Center and much more. Smoking permitted outside only. No pets allowed. Inquire about children being welcome. $85-130.

Casa Tierra. This is an all adobe house featuring more than 50 arches and interior courtyard. There are three rooms with private baths and queen-size beds. All guests have access to a small refrigerator, barbecue, and microwave oven. Each room has its own private entrance and private patio that overlook the desert landscape. In addition, each room opens into the common courtyard, where guests can socialize and enjoy each other's company. Enjoy relaxing in the spa under the desert sky. The area is great for hiking and bird watching. Mornings begin with fresh ground coffee, a variety of teas, and a full breakfast includ-

ing home-baked goods. Guests may join the hosts in the family dining room or may dine in the privacy of guests' room or patio. Two resident cats, two dogs, and one tortoise live on premises outside. Minimum of two-nights stay required. Smoking permitted on own private patio only. No pets allowed. Inquire about children being welcome. $75-85.

La Casita. Townhouse set in lush desert growth area. Hostess is a former travel agent. One room with a king-size waterbed and private bath. Pool adjacent to the house for enjoyment in the hot summer, and another pool is heated during the winter. Jacuzzi is heated year-round. Continental breakfast. Near La Paloma, Vantana Canyons, and resort golf courses. Minimum stay is two nights. $55-65.

Catalina Park Inn. This 1927 historic residence is a two story stucco/brick building. There is a suite and two bedrooms, all with private baths. A Continental breakfast and newspaper is delivered to door. Each room features a color remote TV, telephone, bathrobes, hair dryer, full-length mirror, down comforters and pillows, fresh flowers, iron and ironing board, and air conditioning. Relax in the expansive living room or the intimate study. Within walking distance of the University of Arizona, the Fourth Avenue Arts District, and many fine restaurants. Two-night stay minimum during some periods. Smoking outside only. No pets. Children over 10 welcome. Fifteen dollars for each extra person. $90-130.

The Cat and Whistle Bed and Breakfast. A brick home built in a quiet Eastside neighborhood is decorated in a southwestern style incorporating the owners' collection of African and American Indian carvings and art accumulated from her world travels. Suite of rooms has a comfortable double off-the-wall bed. In the sitting room

7 No smoking; 8 Children welcome; 9 Social drinking allowed; 10 Tennis nearby; 11 Swimming nearby; 12 Golf nearby; 13 Skiing nearby; 14 May be booked through a travel agent.

Old Pueblo Homestays (continued)

is a trundle bed for children. The suite has its own separate air-conditioner, private bath, and entrance. In the residence, which is cooled by an evaporative cooler, there is a queen-size bed and private bath. A Continental plus breakfast is served. Walking distance of bus stop and plenty of excellent restaurants. No smoking. No pets. Children over four welcome. Ten dollars extra for each additional bed. Higher rates during Gem and Mineral Show. $65.

Cloud House. Southwestern Territorial home is nestled in the Catalina foothills above the city. A blend of Southwestern furnishings tastefully decorate the two bedrooms. TV and VCR in the family room. The stereo is by the fireplace in the living room. The Quails Nest Master Honeymoon Suite includes private porch, queen-size bed, down comforter, and fireplace. The Cactus Wren Bedroom has city lights and double bed with Jacuzzi tub. Guests can enjoy their breakfast in the dining room or privately in their own quarters. A Continental plus breakfast served weekdays; full breakfast served weekends. No smoking. Children are welcome. Friendly dog and cat. $75-95.

The Cove. This family hacienda was built in 1955 around a lovely courtyard, in a quiet neighborhood, northeast of downtown business district near the University of Arizona Medical Center. Four rooms with king-size beds and three rooms with queen-size beds, all have private baths. The rooms surround a great room for guests to lounge and watch TV. Also there is a small refrigerator, microwave, etc. for guests' use. Relax outside in an enclosed garden courtyard. A Continental plus breakfast is provided. Close to a bus stop with easy access to the Convention Center the Downtown

Arts District, Tucson Art Museum, shops, and restaurants. Two-night minimum stay. Smoking outside. No pets. Inquire about children being welcome. $65-80.

Coyote Bunkhouse Bed and Breakfast. This Southwestern style home with high ceilings, tile floors, large Arizona room or great room has filled with African and Southwestern art, a fireplace, large dining and kitchen area also with a fireplace, two large charming guest rooms each with private entrance, and large shared bathroom with a spacious shower. Floral walkways, desert landscaping, and large guest patio permit guests to enjoy abundant views, wildlife, sunrises, or city lights. One bedroom has a king-size bed and handbasin. The other room has a queen-size bed. Both have coffee makers. TV is available on request subject to the viewing of what is on satellite reception in the great room. Cross the courtyard to enjoy a Continental plus breakfast served before a crackling fire. Fresh ground coffee, homemade muffins, etc. This bed and breakfast is on 10 acres in the heart of the Tucson Mountains on the edge of the Saguaro National Park West, 30 minutes from downtown Tucson. Minimum of two-nights stay required. Smoking permitted outside only. No pets. Inquire about children being welcome. $75.

The Desert Yankee-Too. This home has a suite with kitchenette, private entrance, king-size bed, and private shower bath. The circular drive provides adequate parking in a quiet neighborhood. Relax outside in an enclosed garden with well-established cactus and desert plants. Continental plus breakfast. Close to bus stop with easy access to the Convention Center and downtown shopping, the downtown arts district, Tucson Art Museum, shops, and restaurants. Two-night minimum. Smoking allowed outside only. Children and pets are welcome. $55-65.

NOTES: Credit cards accepted: A MasterCard; B Visa; C American Express; D Discover; E Diners Club; F Other; 2 Personal checks accepted; 3 Lunch available; 4 Dinner available; 5 Open all year; 6 Pets welcome;

Double K Ranch. Bird watcher's paradise! Private guest facility has Ben Franklin stove, private shower, and patio. Color TV, radio, tape player, telephone, Western books, and games. Jacuzzi and pool available. Experience splendid bird watching, explore ancient Hohokam sites on private trail, or venture off on nearby national forest trails. The ranch is home to many animals. Tennis is five minutes away, and bicycles are available to guests. Children are welcome. $55-65.

Elizabeth's Bed and Breakfast. This modest, attractively decorated home with an Arizona room for relaxing with a book is within walking distance of a bus stop, regional park, golf course, and driving range. The guest bedroom has a queen-size bed, large closet and dresser space, TV, radio, and telephone. Limited kitchen and laundry privileges. Continental breakfast. No children. No pets. Smoking outside only. Two-night minimum. Five-dollar charge for full breakfast. $45-55.

The Elysian Grove Market Bed and Breakfast. Built in the 1920s as a corner market in one of Tucson's historic barrios, this adobe building is filled with antiques and folk art. The great room has a fireplace, books, music, etc. There are two guest rooms with double beds that share a tiled bath. There is also a lower-level room. Guests may relax outside in an enclosed garden with desert plants. Continental breakfast is served. Close to the downtown art district, Tucson Art Museum, shops, restaurants, and the Convention Center. Children welcome. No pets. Smoking allowed outside only. $55-75.

Ford's Bed and Breakfast. A warm welcome awaits guests at this nonsmoking, air-conditioned home in a residential cul-de-sac on Tucson's northeastern side. Guests enjoy a bird's-eye view of the mountains from their own private patio. Suite consists of two bedrooms, small sitting room with TV, refrigerator, private bath, and separate entrance. Continental plus breakfast served. Visit Saguaro Monument East, Sabino Canyon, Colossal Cave, and scenic drives. Minimum stay is two nights. Children over 12 are welcome. $40-50.

Fort Escalante. A mile from Saguaro National Monument, this French Chateau-styled home offers guests a breathtaking, unobstructed view of the beautiful Sonoran Desert. Guest quarters feature a furnished living room with a TV, satellite, VCR, radio, telephone, full bath, separate bedroom with a double bed, and a sofa that will turn into a king-size bed or twin beds. Also available in the main house is a bedroom decorated in blue with a king-size bed. Smoking limited to the patio. No pets. Children over 12 are welcome. $50-70.

The Gable House. The picturesque style of Santa Fe Pueblo Indians with Mexican influence is found throughout this home, which was built in 1930. Clark Gable lived in this house in the early 1940s. Air conditioning. Southwestern decor throughout. Hostess is a licensed massage therapist; massage is available on the premises. Continental plus breakfast is served in the dining room or on the patio. Hosts are vegetarians, but try to accommodate guests. There are three guest rooms: one room has shared bath and a TV; the second has shared bath, TV, and VCR; and the third has a private bath, fireplace, and TV. All rooms have telephone service. No smoking allowed. Children ten and older are welcome. $55-85.

Hacienda Del Desierto. An adobe hideaway providing the flavor of old Mexico is not far from the modern city limits. Its restful environment is perfect for the independent traveler, especially nature lovers. The

7 No smoking; 8 Children welcome; 9 Social drinking allowed; 10 Tennis nearby; 11 Swimming nearby; 12 Golf nearby; 13 Skiing nearby; 14 May be booked through a travel agent.

Old Pueblo Homestays (continued)

living room boasts a piano and large fireplace. Both guest rooms have an informal country Southwestern flavor, ornate antique heating stoves, a Hide-a-Bed or day bed which sleeps two, and private entrances. The two room suite, by the interior Spanish courtyard and garden with fountain, offers a queen-size bed, living room, kitchenette, and shared hall bath. Another spacious room offers a king-size bed, sitting area, small kitchenette, private bath, and private porch. TV and VCR are available. An inviting Continental plus breakfast is served on the patio or looking out onto it. Three resident cats, mostly outside and never in guest rooms. Complimentary refreshments are provided upon arrival. Smoking permitted outside. No pets. Children welcome. Fifteen dollars for each additional guest. $75.

Horizons Bed and Breakfast. This elegant modern Western adobe home is on three and one-half acres on the edge of the Coronado National Forest and the Catalina Mountains. The private guest suite has two rooms with queen-size bed and couch, writing alcove, and private bath. A full breakfast is served on the upper pool patio or in the dining room; special diets are accommodated cheerfully. Enjoy evening tea or coffee in front of a fire. Children welcome. No pets. Two resident mini-Dachshunds. No smoking. Fifteen dollars each additional person. $95.

Jane Cooper House. This historic, fashionable two-story fired red brick building with its second-story balcony built in 1905 has four bedrooms, each furnished with country antiques. There are three rooms upstairs. The first is an apartment which incldes a double bed, a queen-size canopied bed, private bath, and kitchenette. The sec-

ond room has a sitting room with twin bed and shares a bath with the third room which has a king-size bed and balcony. Downstairs is a queen-size suite with private bath. A full breakfast is served in either the sunny dining room or outside in the garden; guests may also have breakfast served in their room. Relax in the shade of the garden or in the private hot tub. A certified massage therapist may be requested. Smoking permitted outside only. Children are welcome. $55-75.

June's Bed and Breakfast. This home offers a relaxed, friendly atmosphere. Three rooms have shared bath. Queen-size bedroom has private bath. Hostess sets out a very special Continental breakfast. Easy access to desert and mountain trails, community center, downtown Tucson, and the University of Arizona. Share family room, TV, and pool. Minimum stay is two nights. Children over 12 welcome. $45-55.

Katy's Hacienda. Charming home is filled with antiques. Colorful, restful back yard. A choice breakfast is served. Within walking distance of Park Mall, theaters, and many fine restaurants. Close to bus line. One room with private bath. Resident dog. Minimum stay is two nights. Children over 12 welcome. $45-55.

Lantana Place Bed and Breakfast. A comfortable townhouse in the Catalina foothills is near the Swan/Sunrise area of central Tucson. This modern, traditional air-conditioned townhouse filled with books, art, and music has a patio that gives guests a light airy spacious feeling. Nearby is the clubhouse with community pools and spa. There is one guest bedroom with a new queen-size sofa bed, and private bath, TV, radio, and telephone. Also a utility room with washer and dryer is available for guest use. A Continental breakfast is served. Minimum stay of two nights.

Smoking permitted outside. No pets. Children over four welcome. $60.

Melissa's Desert Classic. A three-story home loaded with antiques, tile floors, attractive desert landscaping, patio, spa, and pool. There is a separate guest house with two bedrooms, large living room, and full kitchen. On the top floor of the main house is a bedroom suite with king-size bed and private bath. A queen-size bedroom with large private bath is on the lower level. There are also two rooms that share a bath. Enjoy the large great room with cable TV. Full breakfast. Inquire about children. No pets. Smoking outside only. Two-night minimum. $40-75.

Mountain Views Bed and Breakfast. This spacious territorial adobe home is on a little over three acres with unobstructed scenic views of the Catalina Mountains. Each of the guest quarters in a dedicated wing has a queen-size bed, private bath, sitting room with TV, writing desk, and reading material. A utility room with washer and dryer is available for guest use. Breakfast menu will cater to low-cholesterol, low fat, gluten-free diets, but not exclusively. Picnic lunches available on order, and quiet romantic dinners are available on special request. Children welcome. Pets welcome. No smoking. $65-75.

Las Naranjas. Restored Spanish Colonial, circa 1900, is in the West University area close to Fourth Avenue and city bus lines. The Rebecca Room and the Canopy Room feature exquisite antiques and private baths. Enjoy the working fireplace, covered front porch, breakfast room with large bay window, laundry and kitchen facilities, and Edgar, the bed and breakfast cat. Continental breakfast features lots of homemade goodies, and the hostess stocks a cookie jar full of homemade chocolate

chip cookies. Smoking allowed; children and some pets allowed. $50-65.

Paz Entera: Bed, Breakfast, and Beyond. A secluded two-story adobe and rock ranch house built in 1937 has hardwood floors and a spectacular view of 30 acres. Enjoy the library, piano, fireplace, TV, and telephone. Guest casitas and bunk houses, large patio, pool, Jacuzzi, hammocks, and hiking and walking trails. Meeting rooms, indoor and outdoor locations for weddings, reunions, workshops, barbecues, etc. Continental breakfast buffet is served. Arrangements for group-event lunch and dinner may be made. Two-night minimum. Children over ten are welcome. No pets. Smoking outside only. Ten dollars additional for an extra child. $90-135.

Pine Grove Bed and Breakfast. A large Southwestern hacienda in the foothills of the Santa Catalina Mountains is two miles from city limits. One room on one wing of the main house offers a queen-size bed with private bath. Adjacent on the same wing is a completely furnished queen-size suite with adjoining bath and a living room with gas fireplace, a queen-size sofa bed and TV, full kitchen, and laundry facilities. Both units can be combined or separate and open into a backyard with pool, fountain, and large garden area which is often used for weddings. The front entrance is beautifully landscaped offering spectacular mountain views. A Continental breakfast is served on short term stays. Share the desert plants, flowers, birds, animals, and hiking along with gorgeous sunsets and city lights at dusk. Minimum two night stay required. No smoking. No pets. Children over 10 welcome. $85-115.

El Presidio Bed and Breakfast. This bed and breakfast is in the historical district and featured in the book *Desert Southwest* and many magazines. Owners meticulously

7 No smoking; 8 Children welcome; 9 Social drinking allowed; 10 Tennis nearby; 11 Swimming nearby; 12 Golf nearby; 13 Skiing nearby; 14 May be booked through a travel agent.

Old Pueblo Homestays (continued)

restored house and gardens. Accommodations include the Carriage House Suite with queen-size bed, bath with shower, kitchenette stocked with complimentary beverages and fruit, living room with period antiques, and private entrance; the Gatehouse Suite with combined sitting/bedroom, wicker queen-size bed, French country decor, stocked kitchenette, full private bath, and private entrance; and the Victorian Suite has bedroom with queen-size bed, full private bath and connecting sitting room with antique wicker. Full breakfast, bicycles, and daily newspapers. Close to restaurants, museums, art galleries, shopping, and University of Arizona. TVs and telephone in each accommodation. Minimum of two-night stay required. No smoking allowed. No pets allowed. Inquire about children being welcome. $58-105.

Quail's Vista. Panoramic view of the Catalina Mountains gives guests in this Santa Fe-style, rammed-earth solar structure the feeling of true desert living. Guest room has a queen-sized bed with private full hall bath. Swim-stream spa, and hostess' membership at private country club with golf, tennis, and aerobics available to guests. Continental breakfast is served. Resident dog. Smoking allowed outside only. No pets or children. $65-85.

Rimrock West. A Southwestern hacienda of two talented artists is on 20 acres in the foothills of the Santa Catalina Mountains two miles from city limits. Two rooms in one wing of the main house with private baths open onto a courtyard with fountain. On another wing is a two-room suite. Separate adobe guest house near pool area has living room, full kitchen, bedroom. Breakfast is informal and plentiful, includ-

ing freshly baked muffins and interesting conversation. Minimum stay is two nights. $90-130.

Roadrunner. Stay in a home with a spectacular view of the mountains. A low patio wall affords a striking view of the city while guests eat. The great room provides reading material, TV, and piano for guests' use. All rooms are light and cheerful, tastefully furnished with cherry and walnut antiques and Oriental rugs. Telephone in each room. TV upon request. Private baths, two with a Jacuzzi. Full gourmet breakfast with a special of cracked broiled wholewheat served with delicious desert honey and syrup. Five rooms are available. Smoking outside only. Pets welcome. Children over 12 welcome. $60-90.

Shadow Mountain Ranch Bed and Breakfast. A luxurious Spanish Hacienda nestled on six-and-one half acres in the Tucson Mountains high above the city is a paradise in the desert. A nature and wildlife lover's dream location, close to Saguaro National Monument West, Sanctuary Cove, hiking, and walking trails. There is a beautifully landscaped courtyard facing its own mountain. A unique pool and heated spa. This spectacular residence has a sunken Arizona room with fireplace and baby grand piano. There are suites available in the main house and also a cozy guest apartment with private entrance and patio. Private baths. A Continental breakfast is served. A horse corral is available for guests' horses. Twenty-six miles from the Tucson International Airport. Smoking permitted outside only. No pets. Inquire about children being welcome. $65-175.

The Swedish Guest House. *Välkommen!* Guests will feel this is their "home away from home." This bed and breakfast in the beginning of the Catalina foothills offers 1,100 square feet of total comfort and elegance with one king-size bed and one twin bed and an open, light, and airy great room and luxurious bathroom. Swedish and Southwestern touches throughout. Amenities include solar-heated swimming pool, beautiful stone fireplace, phone (private line), cable TV, radio, and private patio. Totally self-contained. Heating and air conditioning. Wheelchair accessible. Full breakfasts served on weekends. Weekdays, breakfasts are self-catered with necessary nutrients provided. Minimum two-night stay. Smoking permitted outside. No pets. Children over 12 welcome. $85.

The Tillinghast Place. In a world-class resort community known as Saddlebrooke this inn has a clubhouse with a restaurant, tennis courts, 18-hole golf course, two swimming pools (heated), driving range, practice putting green, and health club. Guests may hike in the desert or just sit in the back yard with a beautiful view of the Catalina Mountains and observe the wildlife. Guests have private use of the living room with fireplace, dining room, and den. Private bath. Only one couple with children or two couples traveling together. $40-75.

Timrod. Desert living at its best describes this beautiful home set in a lovely rural area with mountain vistas. A self-contained four-room suite has private bath, full kitchen, separate entrance. Hostess stocks refrigerator with breakfast foods. Second suite two bedrooms and bath. Pool can be heated at additional charge. Pottery lessons available by hostess. Resident dog. Minimum stay is two nights. Children over 15 welcome. $60-80.

View Point. This lovely two-level home in the Catalina foothills has four large bedrooms and a beautiful blend of antique and Southwestern furniture. Large bedrooms surround inviting great room opening onto

a solar pool. Refrigerator, microwave oven, toaster, coffee maker, TV, VCR, fireplace, and small library available. Convenient to everything. Continental to a full breakfast served in the dining room or on the poolside patio. Private entrance into great room. No smoking. Children over 16 are welcome. $55-70.

Villa Fiori Bed and Breakfast. This quiet home is within a walled and gated one-acre area with large trees and mature landscaping. Terraces run along three sides of the villa, which was built in the 18th century. Two queen-size bedrooms feature step down Roman private baths, TV, VCR, telephone and private entrances. Also on premises is a walled pool house area with heated pool. A Continental breakfast is served. Minutes to Sabino Canyon, Tanque Verde area "Restaurant Row," entertainment, shopping, and sports. Hosts have two small Shelties. Minimum two-night stay. Smoking permitted outside. Inquire about pets being welcome. Children welcome. $70-75.

The Villa Talia Bed and Breakfast. Beautiful ironwork secures this ranch home on a secluded acre surrounded by citrus, pines, and desert trees in the northwest area in what was formerly an orange grove estate. Property is bordered by twenty acres of unspoiled desert full of abundant wildlife and many birds. Watch the sunsets from the porch swing. Lounge by the architect-designed pool or relax in the heated spa. A Continental plus breakfast on the patio or pool area if desired. Other amenities include a queen-size bed, private shower/bath, radio, and refrigerator. Also available for guests' use is a barbecue, cable TV, evening newspaper, gym facilities by special arrangement, and a piano for guests' pleasure. Only 15 minutes from the University of Arizona, UA Medical School, and downtown Tucson. Shopping, fine dining, and hiking trails within five minutes.

7 No smoking; 8 Children welcome; 9 Social drinking allowed; 10 Tennis nearby; 11 Swimming nearby; 12 Golf nearby; 13 Skiing nearby; 14 May be booked through a travel agent.

On premises are two dachshunds and a cat. Smoking outside only. No pets or children allowed. $85.

Peppertree Bed and Breakfast Inn

724 East University Boulevard, 85719
(520) 622-7167; (800) 348-5768

A 1905 Victorian Territorial house just two blocks west of the main gates of the University of Arizona is furnished with family antiques and is within easy walking distance of the university, museums, shops, restaurants, theaters, and downtown. There are three guest rooms with private baths, and two two-bedroom guest houses. Each guest house contains a living room, dining room, full kitchen with washer/dryer, and private patio. They are ideal for families or couples traveling together. The hostess is a published cookbook author and is renowned for her gourmet breakfasts.

Host: Marjorie Martin
Rooms: 5 (1 PB; 4 SB) $65-80
Full Breakfast
Credit Cards: A, B, D
Notes: 2, 5, 7, 8, 9, 10, 11, 12, 13

La Posada Del Valle

1640 North Campbell Avenue, 85719
(520) 795-3840 (phone and FAX)

An elegant 1920s inn nestled in the heart of the city has five guest rooms with private baths and outside entrances. Mature orange trees perfume the air as guests enjoy a gourmet breakfast and sip tea each afternoon on the patio overlooking the garden. Full breakfast served weekends only. Children over eight welcome.

Hosts: Tom and Karin Dennen
Rooms: 5 (PB) $90-125
Full and Continental Breakfasts
Credit Cards: A, B
Notes: 2, 5, 7, 9, 10, 11, 12, 13, 14

El Presidio

El Presidio Bed and Breakfast

297 North Main Street, 85701
(520) 623-6151

A Victorian adobe, this inn is a splendid example of American-Territorial style and is listed on the National Register of Historic Places. Close to downtown and within walking distance of the best restaurants, museums, and shopping. Guests enjoy true Southwestern charm in spacious suites, two with kitchens that open onto large courtyards and gardens, fountains, and lush floral displays. A tranquil oasis with the ambience of Old Mexico. Three-star rating from Mobil and AAA.

Host: Patti Toci
Rooms: 3 (PB) $85-110
Full Breakfast
Credit Cards: None
Notes: 2, 5, 7, 9, 10, 11, 12, 14

The Swedish Guest House Bed and Breakfast

9411 West Calle Dadivoso, 85704
(520) 742-6490

At the beginning of the Catalina Foothills, this spacious guest house offers 1,100-square-foot quarters. Amenities include fireplace, telephone with private number, TV, radio, air conditioning, parking in garage, own patio overlooking the swimming pool. Plush bathroom has bathtub and an extra large shower. Nearby are golf courses, hiking, horseback riding. Eighteen minutes from the University of Arizona. Hosts are transplanted Swedes from Stockholm and Tucson residents since 1977. Smoking outside only. Weekly rates available. Full breakfast served on weekends only. Self-serve during the week. Closed July. *Välkommen!*

Hosts: Lars and Florence Ejrup
Guest house: 1 (PB) $85
Full Breakfast
Credit Cards: None
Notes: 9, 11, 14

TUMACACORI

Old Pueblo Homestays

P.O. Box 13603, Tucson, 85732
(800) 333-9 RSO

The Old Mission Store. The building was constructed in the late 1920s and served as a grocery store, post office, and gathering place until the 1960s. It is adjacent to the Demano Gallery, featuring work by local and regional artists. Guests are near the ruins of an old Spanish Colonial Mission and the Tumacacori National Historical Park, three miles south of Tubac and 21 miles north of U.S. border at Nogales, Arizona. The south wing consists of a breakfast/sitting room, bedroom with twin beds, private bath, additional sleeping room, and private entrance and patio. Resident feline named Buddy. No smoking. Children are welcome. $60.

WICKENBURG

Mi Casa Su Casa

P.O. Box 950, Tempe, 85280-0950
(602) 990-0682; (800) 456-0682 (reservations only)

1626. Homesteaded at the turn of the century and a guest ranch since 1926, this working ranch is listed on both the state and national historic registers. The handmade adobe buildings are snuggled close by the Hassayampa River, and the food is worth a letter home. Three meals a day are includ-ed, and guests can choose from a variety of lodging choices. Horseback riding and heated pool. Two-night minimum stay is required. Visa and MasterCard accepted. $95-355.

WILLIAMS

Bed and Breakfast Inn Arizona

8900 East Via Linda, Suite 101, Scottsdale, 85258
(602) 860-9338 (phone and FAX)

WM002. Convenient and charming setting in small Arizona town serves a Continental breakfast. Grand Canyon National Park and Grand Canyon Restored Historic R.R. Excursion are only a whistle away! Queen-size and double beds, private baths. Call for rates.

WM003. This log bed and breakfast deluxe home has private baths, cozy beds, daily hospitality hour, and breakfast. Gateway to the Grand Canyon. Call for rates.

The Johnstonian Bed and Breakfast

321 West Sheridan Avenue, 86046
(520) 635-2178

As guests cross the threshold of this century-old, two-story Victorian home, the hosts will welcome them into a relaxed family atmosphere in keeping with the same spirit of hospitality that pervaded the Victorian era. Guests' senses will transport them to the turn-of-the-century when they see the quaint rooms furnished with antiques and smell fresh bread baking. Enjoy breakfast in the dining room at the round oak table. Smoking permitted on porch.

Hosts: Bill and Pidge Johnston
Rooms: 4 (1 PB; 3 SB) $50-65
Full Breakfast
Credit Cards: None
Notes: 2, 5, 8, 9, 10, 12, 13, 14

7 No smoking; 8 Children welcome; 9 Social drinking allowed; 10 Tennis nearby; 11 Swimming nearby; 12 Golf nearby; 13 Skiing nearby; 14 May be booked through a travel agent.

Mi Casa Su Casa

P.O. Box 950, Tempe, 85280-0950
(602) 990-0682; (800) 456-0682 (reservations
   only)

1631. This two-story inn is convenient to
the center of Williams, two blocks from the
Grand Canyon Railroad Station. Each of
the nine rooms is decorated differently.
Continental plus breakfast. $45-75.

Old Pueblo Homestays

P.O. Box 13603, Tucson, 85732
(800) 333-9RSO

Terry Ranch Bed and Breakfast. This
ranch is in Northern Arizona, a short drive
to the Grand Canyon, Oak Creek Canyon.
Close to ski areas, Sunset and Meteor
Craters, Lowell Observatory, and other
points of interest. This two-story log home
features four elegantly furnished first-floor
rooms, with antique and king-size beds.
Each room named for the brides who lived
at Terry Ranch in Utah during the 1800s.
Wash off the trail dust in own private claw-
foot tub. A full breakfast is served at 8 A.M.,
in the private dining room only, then off to
ride the steam train to the Grand Canyon, or
visit other points of interest. Handicapped
accessible. Smoking permitted outside only.
No pets. Children welcome. $85-105.

YUMA

Mi Casa Su Casa

P.O. Box 950, Tempe, 85280-0950
(602) 990-0682; (800) 456-0682 (reservations
   only)

110. This handsome adobe home is on large
lot in quiet older neighborhood. Eclectic,
charming interior. Guest room has fine
antiques, double bed, and private hall bath.
Full attractive breakfasts served on fine
china and table linens. Sociable hostess is a
native of Yuma. Smokers are welcome.
Pool. $50-55.

Arkansas

CROSSETT

The Trieschmann House Bed and Breakfast

707 Cedar, 71635
(501) 364-7592; (800) TRIESCH

Built in 1903 for an official of the Crossett Company, this lovely bed and breakfast is nine miles from the Felsenthal Refuge for good fishing and hunting. Front porch with wicker swing and furniture; common room with a wood-burning stove, cable TV, and games. Full breakfast is served in the kitchen, and the home is furnished with furniture from the past. The hosts invite guests to travel back in time with them.

Hosts: Pat and Herman Owens
Rooms: 3 (1 PB; 2 SB) $50-60
Full Breakfast
Credit Cards: A, B, C
Notes: 2, 5, 7, 8, 10, 12, 14

EUREKA SPRINGS

Arbour Glen Bed and Breakfast Victorian Inn

7 Lema, 72632
(501) 253-9010; (800) 515-GLEN

Circa 1896, this inn on Eureka Springs historic district loop and trolley route is only a five-minute walk from downtown shops and cafes. Completely renovated with guests' comfort in mind, the Arbour Glen still retains its Victorian charm, elegance, and romance. On the veranda guests may relax and enjoy the picturesque setting of the tree-covered hollow for an unforgettable experience. Hosts offer Jacuzzis for two, antique furnishings, private baths, color cable TV, full gourmet breakfasts, smoke-free suites, and a nature trail.

Rooms: 3 (PB) $75-125
Full Breakfast
Credit Cards: A, B
Notes: 2, 5, 7, 9, 11, 14

Arsenic and Old Lace

Arsenic and Old Lace

60 Hillside Avenue, 72632
(501) 253-5454; (800) 243-LACE
FAX (501) 253-2246

An elegant and luxurious Queen Anne Victorian mansion, complete with wraparound verandas and tower, has antiques and original pieces of art. Enjoy the Jacuzzis, fireplaces, TV/VCRs, and fresh flowers. A full gourmet breakfast is served in the morning room overlooking the English perennial garden. Ideal location on a trolley stop in the historic district, the inn is within easy access of all major tourist attractions.

Hosts: Gary and Phyllis Jones
Rooms: 5 (PB) $90-150

7 No smoking; 8 Children welcome; 9 Social drinking allowed; 10 Tennis nearby; 11 Swimming nearby; 12 Golf nearby; 13 Skiing nearby; 14 May be booked through a travel agent.

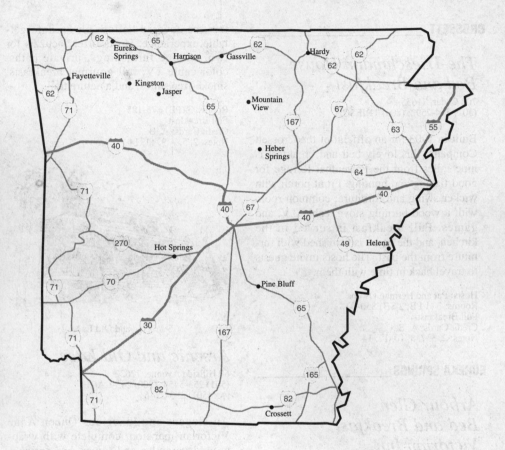

Arkansas

Full Breakfast
Credit Cards: A, B, C, D
Notes: 2, 5, 7, 9, 10, 11, 12, 14

Bonnybrooke Farm Atop Misty Mountain

Route 2, Box 335A, 72632
(501) 253-6903

If guests' hearts are in the country—or long
to be—the hosts invite them to come share
in the sweet quiet and serenity that awaits
them in their home away from home. Five
cottages are distinctly different in their
tempting pleasures: fireplace and Jacuzzi
for two, full glass fronts, mountaintop
views, shower under the stars in the glass
shower, wicker porch swing in front of the
fireplace, and a water fall Jacuzzi. Guests
are gonna love it! In order to preserve privacy, the location is not made public and is
given to registered guests only.

Hosts: Bonny and Josh
Cottages: 5 (PB) $95-125
Credit Cards: None
Notes: 2, 5, 7, 9, 11, 13, 14

Bridgeford House Bed and Breakfast

263 Spring Street, 72632
(501) 253-7853

Nestled in the heart of Eureka Springs' historic residential district, Bridgeford House
is an 1884 Victorian delight. Outside are
shady porches that invite guests to pull up a
chair and watch the world go by on Spring
Street. Each room has a private entrance,
antique furnishings, and private bath. Fresh
coffee in the suite, a selection of fine teas,
color TV, air conditioning, and a mouth-
watering breakfast are available.

Hosts: Michael and Denise McDonald
Rooms: 4 (PB) $85-95
Full Breakfast
Credit Cards: A, B
Notes: 2, 5, 8, 9, 10, 11, 12, 14

Brownstone Inn

Brownstone Inn, Inc.

75 Hillside, 72632
(501) 253-7505

The inn was built in 1895 and for 70 years
served as the site for the Ozarka Water
Company, which bottled the healing
waters from Eureka's springs. The two-
story limestone structure maintains the
original façade while the interior has been
converted and offers two large suites opening onto a second floor wood deck. Two
smaller units open onto a brick parquet
patio overlooking the floral garden. Each
is uniquely finished in Victorian decor
with many antiques, private entrance, private bath, queen-size bed, cable TV, ceiling fans, and independently controlled central heat and air conditioning. Ample off-
street parking. Enjoy a basket delivered to
one's door before breakfast with gourmet
coffee, tea, or juice. Historic train depot
nearby. The trolley stops at the depot,
offering easy access to shopping and
attractions. Limited smoking allowed.

Hosts: Marvin and Donna Shepard
Rooms: 4 (PB) $80-105
Full Breakfast
Credit Cards: A, B
Notes: 2, 9, 14

NOTES: Credit cards: A MasterCard; B Visa; C American Express; D Discover; E Diners Club; F Other;
2 Personal checks accepted; 3 Lunch available; 4 Dinner available; 5 Open all year; 6 Pets welcome;
7 No smoking; 8 Children welcome; 9 Social drinking allowed; 10 Tennis nearby; 11 Swimming nearby;
12 Golf nearby; 13 Skiing nearby; 14 May be booked through a travel agent.

Crescent Cottage Inn

Crescent Cottage Inn

211 Spring Street, 72632
(501) 253-6022

Premier-class 1881 Victorian "painted lady" is on the national register and was built for the first governor of Arkansas after the Civil War. Oldest, most historic and photographed bed and breakfast has beautiful gardens and panoramic views. Walk to town and trolley stop. Queen-size beds, some private double Jacuzzis, private baths, verandas, and antiques. Newly redecorated. Featured in magazines and books. Great breakfasts! Area known for wonderful music, arts, crafts, lakes, forests, and Passion play. AAA rated three diamonds and Mobil quality rated. No smoking indoors. Children over 12 welcome. Also available on the WWW at URL:http://fohnix. metronet.com/cimarron/.

Hosts: Ralph and Phyllis Becker
Rooms: 4 (PB) $75-115
Full Breakfast
Credit Cards: A, B, D
Notes: 2, 5, 9, 10, 11, 14

Dairy Hollow House

515 Spring Street, 72632
(501) 253-7444; (800) 562-8650

Welcome to Dairy Hollow House, a tiny, irresistible country inn and restaurant nestled in a serene, wooded valley. Just one mile from historic downtown, there are two houses, each with the prettiest rooms and suites imaginable. Waiting for guests are fireplaces, landscaped hot tub, fresh flowers, regional antiques, and Ozark wildflower soaps. Three-time Uncle Ben's "Best Inn of the Year" winner. Rated by AAA as a three diamond inn. Home of *Dairy Hollow House Soup and Bread: A Country Inn Cookbook*. The restaurant serves a *prix fixe* "Nouveau 'Zarks Haute Country Cuisine" dinner Thursday through Monday nights at 7:00 P.M. Hosts are members of BBAA and PAII.

Hosts: Crescent Dragonwagon and Ned Shank
Rooms: 6 (PB) $125-165
Full Breakfast
Credit Cards: A, B, C, D, E
Notes: 2, 4, 5, 7, 8, 9, 10, 11, 12, 14

Dr. R. G. Floyd House

246 Spring Street, 72632
(501) 253-7525

This 1892 authentically restored Queen Anne is surrounded by award winning terraced gardens in a wooded area. Eureka's finest home is on the historic loop within easy walking distance of the galleries, shops, and restaurants. All rooms are appointed with Victorian wall and ceiling papers, carpeting, beautiful woodwork, period antiques, and meticulous attention to detail. Guest quarters include a two-bedroom suite. Each day begins with a gourmet breakfast served in the privacy of guest's room or on the veranda. Smoking permitted outside only.

Hosts: Georgia Rubley and Bill Rubley
Rooms: 2 (PB) $90-155
Cottage: 1 (PB)
Full Breakfast
Credit Cards: A, B, D
Notes: 2, 5, 9, 11, 12

Enchanted Cottages

18 Nut Street, 72632
(501) 253-6790; (800) 862-2788

In a secluded parklike setting in the historic district, Enchanted Cottages are romantic

NOTES: Credit cards accepted: A MasterCard; B Visa; C American Express; D Discover; E Diners Club; F Other; 2 Personal checks accepted; 3 Lunch available; 4 Dinner available; 5 Open all year; 6 Pets welcome;

and private. Just two-and-a-half blocks to shops and restaurants. These storybook cottages are surrounded by woods frequently visited by a neighborhood family of deer. Each cottage has either an indoor Jacuzzi for two or a private outdoor hot tub. Accommodations include king- or queen-size beds, antique furnishings, cable TV, kitchens, and patios with grills. Special honeymoon and anniversary packages!

Hosts: Barbara Kellogg and David Pettit
Rooms: 3 (PB) $75-129
Continental Breakfast
Credit Cards: A, B
Notes: 2, 5, 7, 9, 14

Evening Shade Inn

Route 1, Box 446, Highway 62 East, 72632
(501) 253-6264; (800) 992-1224 (reservations)

Relax in elegantly decorated luxury rooms in the tranquil mountain woodlands, or sit on the porch and enjoy the view and wildlife. New Honeymoon Cottage with wood-burning fireplace, huge Jacuzzi, king-size bed, private bath, and cable TV with HBO. Private balcony deck overlooking the woods with romantic swing on it. Breakfast served in rooms at guests' leisure. Near the center of Eureka Springs' exciting attractions, but secluded and quiet with ample parking. Telephones in rooms. On trolley route. Daily maid service.

Hosts: Ed and Shirley Nussbaum
Rooms: 5 (PB) $100-150
Continental Breakfast
Credit Cards: A, B, D
Notes: 2, 5, 7, 9, 12, 14

The Gardener's Cottage

11 Singleton, 72632
(501) 253-9111; (800) 833-3394

Tucked away in a wooded area in the historic district, this private cottage features charming country decor with romantic touches and a Jacuzzi for two. This cozy retreat with beamed cathedral ceiling, skylights, full kitchen, TV, ceiling fan, and air

conditioning is within walking distance of the galleries and cafes. Guests can relax on the spacious porch with its swing and hammock while listening to the bubbling stream just yards away. Discounts for five days or more. Open April through November. Breakfast is not included, but can be prearranged for $12 when space is available at Singleton House.

Host: Barbara Gavron
Cottage: 1 (PB) $95-125
No Breakfast
Credit Cards: A, B, C, D
Notes: 2, 7, 9, 11, 12, 14

Harvest House

104 Wall Street, 72632
(501) 253-9363

This turn-of-the-century Victorian house is filled with lovely antiques, collectibles, and family favorites. The guest rooms have private entrances and private baths. In the historic district of Eureka Springs, Harvest House is a step off the beaten path yet close to the bustle of downtown. A full breakfast is served in the dining room or, weather permitting, in the screened-in gazebo overlooking pine and oak trees. Bill is a native Arkansan and knows all the hidden treasures of the area. Patt is the shopper with a particular interest in antiques and the local attractions.

Hosts: Bill and Patt Carmichael
Rooms: 4 (PB) $75-110
Full Breakfast
Credit Cards: A, B, D
Notes: 2, 5, 6, 7, 9

Heart of the Hills Inn

5 Summit Street, 72632
(501) 253-7468; (800) 253-7468

This historic home was built in the 1800s and offers three rooms with air conditioning, refrigerator, and TV. Rooms have private baths or tubs with showers, and one suite has a two-person Jacuzzi with shower. There is also a completely equipped cottage with deck overlooking the woods. Eureka

7 No smoking; 8 Children welcome; 9 Social drinking allowed; 10 Tennis nearby; 11 Swimming nearby; 12 Golf nearby; 13 Skiing nearby; 14 May be booked through a travel agent.

Springs is noted for its Passion play and its many restaurants, fine museums, and trolley system.

Rooms: 3 (PB) $69-119
Cottage: 1 (PB)
Full Breakfast
Credit Cards: A, B
Notes: 2, 8, 9, 10, 11, 13, 14

The Heartstone Inn

The Heartstone Inn and Cottages

35 Kings Highway, 72632
(501) 253-8916

In the historic district, this Victorian house combines nostalgic charm with complete 20th-century convenience. Guest rooms are inviting with antiques, fresh flowers, beautiful linens, private entrances, bath, cable TV, and air conditioning. The adjacent Victoria house has ten-foot ceilings, fireplace, and two large bedrooms, or choose the cozy Country Cottage for two. Relax on the verandas or in the gazebo surrounded by flowers and shade trees. Experience the treat of a revitalizing, therapeutic massage. Stroll down tree-lined streets to parks, shops, and restaurants. Mobil, AAA, and ABBA approved. Minimum-stay requirements for weekends and holidays. Closed during Christmas.

Hosts: Iris and Bill Simantel
Rooms: 10 (PB) $67-118
Cottages: 2 (PB)
Full Breakfast
Credit Cards: A, B, C, D
Notes: 2, 7, 9, 11, 12, 14

The Inn at Rose Hall

56 Hillside, P.O. Box 386, 72632
(501) 253-5405; (800) 828-4255

Hospitality begins here with romantic elegance and gracious service. Perfect for Victorian weddings, receptions, and romantic honeymoons. Enjoy every private amenity, including Jacuzzis and showers for two, Victorian gazebo, secluded garden and courtyard, windows of stained glass, dramatic tower, and fireplaces. The Inn at Rose Hall is for guests who wish to experience the ambience of luxury.

Host: Sandy Latimer
Rooms: 5 (PB) $110-150
Full Breakfast
Credit Cards: A, B, C, D, E
Notes: 2, 5, 7, 9, 11, 12, 14

Ozark Mountain Country Bed and Breakfast

P.O. Box 295, Branson, MO, 65616
(417) 334-4720; (800) 695-1546

A305. This Victorian inn is in the historic district. Each room is filled with antiques and collectibles. One block to shops. Special breakfast with hot entrees and homemade goodies served in dining area or on balcony overlooking garden. One suite has kitchen, private baths, and double or twin beds. The other guest room has a whirlpool for two and double bed. Additional $10 for extra child and $15 for extra adult. $69-90.

A315. Luxury Victorian inn has seven antique-filled suites with private baths. TV/VCR, refrigerator, microwave, fireplaces, individually controlled heat and air conditioning. Whirlpool for two. Continental breakfast basket delivered to suite. Smoking on decks only. Open year-round. Winter rates available. $125-145.

A319. This classic home in the historic distric was built in 1908 and has been lovingly restored. Amenities include central heat and air conditioning and gourmet breakfast. One luxurious three-room suite has queen-size bed and full kitchen. A second suite has a private entrance, living room, kitchen, TV, queen-size bedroom, and whirlpool bath. There are three upstairs guest rooms. One room has queen-size bed and private bath with shower. The other two rooms have queen-size and twin-size beds and share a hall bath. Complete kitchen for guests. Resident cat. Smoking permitted on decks. No pets. $79-119.

A320. Guests can feel like they are in the country and actually be in town. A cottage has French-country decor, queen-size bed, and Jacuzzi. One suite has queen-size bedroom, sitting room with Murphy bed, whirlpool, and private entrance. Garden pond and walking trail available. $95-115.

Ridgeway House Bed and Breakfast

28 Ridgeway, 72632
(501) 253-6618; (800) 477-6618

Gracious southern hospitality makes this lovely, immaculately restored bed and breakfast in the historic district the perfect place to have that much needed "getaway," or to celebrate that special occasion. Built in 1908 by W. O. Perkins, the inn has large porches and decks, robes in each room, high ceilings, and guest kitchens, and other amenities. Excellent location, quiet street within walking distance of downtown. Jacuzzi suites available. Smoking allowed on porches and decks. Children welcome in the suites.

Hosts: Becky and "Sony" Taylor
Rooms: 5 (3 PB; 2 SB) $79-139
Full Breakfast
Credit Cards: A, B, D
Notes: 2, 5, 9, 14

Scandia Bed and Breakfast Inn

33 Avo, Highway 62 West, 72632
(501) 253-8922; (800) 523-8922

The Scandia Inn has charming 1940s era guest cottages that combine privacy with the traditional services of a fine bed and breakfast inn. Set in the pines overlooking Johnson Springs Hollow, it is five blocks from downtown, and serviced by two trolley routes. Each of the seven cottages has its own bright and airy style with luxurious linens and amenities. The romantic Honeymoon Suite includes an oversized bath with a Jacuzzi for two. A year-round favorite is the Dogwood Deck that includes a hot tub spa and gazebo, is the perfect place to relax after a busy day of sightseeing. Breakfast is served in the main house where only the finest ingredients are accompanied by interesting fresh roasted and ground coffees. Guest privileges include championship golf, lighted tennis, and swimming. Water skiing is nearby.

Hosts: Cynthia Barnes and Marty Lavine
Rooms: 7 (PB) $69-119
Full Breakfast
Credit Cards: A, B, D
Notes: 2, 5, 8, 9, 10, 11, 12, 14

Singleton House Bed and Breakfast

11 Singleton Street, 72632
(501) 253-9111; (800) 833-3394

This country Victorian home in the historic district is an old-fashioned place with a touch of magic. Each guest room is whim-

Singleton House

sically decorated with a delightful collection of antiques and folk art. Breakfast is served on the balcony overlooking the fantasy wildflower garden below, with its goldfish pond and curious birdhouse collection. Guests park and walk a scenic, wooded pathway to Eureka's shops and cafes. Innkeeper apprenticeship program available. A honeymoon cottage with a Jacuzzi is available without breakfast at a separate location.

Host: Barbara Gavron
Rooms: 5 (PB) $65-95
Cottage: 1 (PB) $95
Full Breakfast
Credit Cards: A, B, C, D
Notes: 2, 5, 7, 8, 9, 11, 12, 14

Sunnyside Bed and Breakfast Inn

5 Ridgeway, 72632
(501) 253-6638; (800) 554-9499

Lovingly restored, circa 1880 Victorian home in the historic district is beautifully appointed, with air-conditioned rooms. Quiet and restful surroundings are smoke and alcohol free. Honeymoon suite has a Jacuzzi. View the wilderness from the deck. Walking distance to downtown.

Host: Gladys Rose Foris
Rooms: 5 (PB) $80-125
Full Breakfast
Credit Cards: None
Notes: 2, 5, 8, 14

FAYETTEVILLE

Eton House

1485 Eton, 72703
(501) 443-7517; (800) 452-8959

This buff-brick ranch-style home has a cathedral ceiling and is furnished in delicate pastels, Victorian wicker, and more staid European pieces. Guests are welcome to relax in the living room by a cozy fireplace during winter months, but the screened-in

patio overlooking a parklike setting is a spring and summer delight. A gazebo can be used for weddings, and the church minister is only a few yards away. Walton Arts Center, donated by the late Sam Walton of Wal-Mart fame, is just three miles away. The area is rich in arts, crafts, and southern hospitality. Fayetteville is the home of the University of Arkansas. Personal checks accepted at least two weeks in advance. Smoking in designated areas only.

Host: Patricia Parks
Rooms: 3 (PB) $49
Continental Breakfast
Credit Cards: A, B
Notes: 5, 9, 10, 11, 12, 14

Hill Avenue Bed and Breakfast

131 South Hill Avenue, 72701
(501) 444-0865

In a residential neighborhood, this home is near the University of Arkansas, Walton Arts Center, and the town square. Guests will find immaculate and comfortable accommodations. A hearty country breakfast is served in the dining room or on the large porch.

Hosts: Dale and Cecelia Thompson
Room: 1 (PB) $40
Suite: $60
Full Breakfast
Credit Cards: None
Notes: 5, 7

GASSVILLE

Lithia Springs Lodge

Route 1, Box 77-A, Highway 126, 72365
(501) 435-6100

A lovingly restored former lodge with an additional gift shop, featuring many of the host's own handcrafts. A full breakfast is served on the large screened front porch or in the dining room. On 39 acres of meadows and woods, it reflects the original char-

---

NOTES: Credit cards accepted: A MasterCard; B Visa; C American Express; D Discover; E Diners Club; F Other; 2 Personal checks accepted; 3 Lunch available; 4 Dinner available; 5 Open all year; 6 Pets welcome;

acter of the lodge. World-class fishing can be found in the nearby White and Buffalo rivers, with canoeing, hiking, and boating in or near Bull Shoals or Norfork Lake.

Hosts: Paul and Reita Johnson
Rooms: 5 (3 PB; 2 SB) $50-55
Full Breakfast
Credit Cards: A, B
Notes: 2, 5, 7, 10, 11, 12, 14

HARDY

Olde Stonehouse Bed and Breakfast Inn

511 Main Street, 72542
(501) 856-2983; (800) 514-2983
FAX (501) 856-4036

Native Arkansas stone house with large porches lined with jumbo rocking chairs is comfortably furnished with antiques and features zoned heat and air, ceiling fans, queen-size beds, and private baths. One block from Spring River and the shops of old Hardy town. Country music theaters, golf courses, horseback riding, canoeing, and fishing nearby. Local attractions include Mammoth Spring State Park, Grand Gulf, Evening Shade, and Arkansas Traveller Theater. Two-room "special occasion" suites are in a separate 1905 cottage. Smoking permitted on porches. Mystery weekends and other packages available. Approved by AAA, BBAA, and ABBA.

Host: Peggy Johnson
Rooms: 9 (PB) $55-85
Full Breakfast
Credit Cards: A, B, C, D
Notes: 2, 3, 5, 9, 10, 11, 12, 14

Ozark Mountain Country Bed and Breakfast

P.O. Box 295, Branson, MO, 65616
(417) 334-4720; (800) 695-1546

A312. This bed and breakfast is a refurbished native stone inn on Main Street in the historic district on the Arkansas River. Six guest rooms with antiques have private baths. Hearty breakfast like Grandma used to make. Open year-round. $59-69.

HARRISON

Ozark Mountain Country Bed and Breakfast

P.O. Box 295, Branson, MO, 65616
(417) 334-4720; (800) 695-1546

A311. This bed and breakfast is between Harrison and Branson with a million dollar view from three directions. Three guest rooms are available. One has two double beds, another has a double bed, and the final guest room has a day bed. Private entrance, sitting area, and TV. Shared baths. Children welcome. $45-50.

A314. This uniquely restored Victorian home is decorated with antiques and stained glass. Four guest rooms include two with private baths and two that share a bath. Big screen TV in sitting area. Cottage has equipped kitchenette, queen-size bed, and TV. Full breakfast. Open year-round. Children over 12 welcome. No smoking. Seasonal discount November through March. $58-75.

HELENA

Foxglove

229 Beech Street, 72342
(501) 338-9391

On a ridge overlooking historic Helena and the Mississippi River, stunning antiques abound in this nationally registered inn. Parqueted floors, quarter swan oak woodwork, stained glass, and six original fireplaces are complimented by private marble baths, whirlpool tubs, phones, cable, fax, air conditioning, and other modern conveniences. Points of interest include Delta

7 No smoking; 8 Children welcome; 9 Social drinking allowed; 10 Tennis nearby; 11 Swimming nearby; 12 Golf nearby; 13 Skiing nearby; 14 May be booked through a travel agent.

Cultural Center, Confederate Cemetery, antique shops, and a casino, all within five minutes' travel. Complimentary wine and beverages available in the evening. Inquire about accommodations for children over 12.

Host: John Butkiewicz
Rooms: 10 (9 PB; 1 SB) $69-109
Continental Breakfast
Credit Cards: A, B, C
Notes: 2, 5, 7, 9, 14

Vintage Comfort Inn

HOT SPRINGS NATIONAL PARK

The Gables Inn

318 Quapaw Avenue, 71901
(501) 623-7576; (800) 625-7576

This 1905 Victorian bed and breakfast with some of the original chandeliers, stained-glass windows, wood floors, and woodwork is in President Clinton's boyhood hometown, where visitors can still experience the luxury of hot mineral springs baths and massages in historic bath houses. Walk downtown to art galleries, shops, and restaurants, or relax on the spacious porch. All guest rooms have private baths and handmade quilts. A full breakfast is served in the turn-of-the-century dining room. Children over 10 welcome.

Hosts: Shirley and Larry Robins
Rooms: 4 (PB) $55-75
Full Breakfast
Credit Cards: A, B, C
Notes: 2, 5, 7, 9, 11, 12, 14

Vintage Comfort Bed and Breakfast Inn

303 Quapaw, 71901
(501) 623-3258

Vintage Comfort Bed and Breakfast is an elegant, two-story Victorian home with warmth, graciousness, and comfort as its key ingredients. A delicious full breakfast is served, and guests are pampered with old-fashioned hospitality. Within easy walking distance of Hot Springs Bathhouse

Row, art galleries, restaurants, shops, and Hot Springs National Park. Children over five welcome.

Host: Helen R. Bartlett
Rooms: 4 (PB) $60-85
Full Breakfast
Credit Cards: A, B, C, E
Notes: 2, 5, 9, 10, 11, 12, 14

Wildwood 1884 Bed and Breakfast

808 Park Avenue, 71901
(501) 624-4267

Peach and ivory Victorian mansion on one acre of grounds has a carriage turnaround in the front. Beautiful cherry, walnut, and mahogany woodworks are all made of Arkansas native trees. Original stained glass windows and gas chandeliers. Visiting Wildwood 1884 is like stepping back somewhere in time. Listed on the National Register of Historic Places.

Hosts: Randy and Karen Duncan
Rooms: 5 (PB) $85-95
Full Breakfast
Credit Cards: A, B, D
Notes: 2, 5, 10, 11, 12, 14

JASPER

Brambly Hedge Cottage

HCR 31, Box 39, 72641
(501) 446-5849; (800) BRAMBLY

Breakfast above the clouds at this mountain-top home right on Scenic Highway 7. Gorgeous view "clear to Missouri" overlooks Buffalo River Valley. Guests enjoy country French-Victorian elegance in the rugged Ozarks. "Absolutely charming," says *National Geographic Traveller*. Thick-walled living room is a homestead log cabin. Bodywork relaxations available. Minutes from Buffalo National River float trips, hiking trails, and craft shops; short distance to Eureka Springs; Branson, Missouri; major lakes. Less than five miles south of Jasper.

Host: Jacquelyn Smyers
Rooms: 3 (PB) $65-75
Full Breakfast
Credit Cards: None
Notes: 2, 5, 7, 9, 14

KINGSTON

Ozark Mountain Country Bed and Breakfast

P.O. Box 295, Branson, MO, 65616
(417) 334-4720; (800) 695-1546

A308. This contemporary bed and breakfast overlooks mountains and has easy access to famous Buffalo River. Guests enjoy spacious deck, hot tub, and antiques. Three guest rooms are available. Country breakfast. $55.

MOUNTAIN VIEW

Wildflower Bed and Breakfast

On the Square, P.O. Box 72, 72560-0072
(501) 269-4383; (800) 591-4879 (reservations)

The Wildflower Bed and Breakfast is on the historic courthouse square, where local musicians gather to play old-time music. These affordable European-style accom-modations are in a restored 1918 Craftsman-style inn listed on the National Register of Historic Places. Attractive without being pretentious, the rooms include handmade curtains, dust ruffles, original dressers, and iron bedsteads. The home of the award-winning HearthStone Bakery also boasts a modest bookshop. Guests are urged to come with an appetite for relaxation, entertainment, conversation, and good food.

Hosts: Todd and Andrea Budy
Rooms: 8 (6 PB; 2 SB) $41-70
Continental Breakfast
Credit Cards: A, B, C, D
Notes: 2, 3, 7, 8, 10, 11, 12

PINE BLUFF

Margland II, III, and IV Bed and Breakfast Inns

703 West Second Street, 71601
(501) 536-6000; (800) 545-5383

Southern hospitality as it was meant to be—each suite is carefully furnished for the perfect combination of atmosphere and comfort. Guests may savor breakfast in the garden or in the formal dining room and have access to cable TV, private baths, VCRs, FAX, and Jacuzzis. Twin, full, or queen-size beds; conference rooms; exercise room. Margland II is handicapped accessible. All buildings are equipped with sprinkler fire protection system. Lunch and dinner reservations are required for groups of eight or more.

Host: Wanda Bateman
Rooms: 17 (PB) $65-95
Full Breakfast
Credit Cards: A, B, C, D, E
Notes: 2, 5, 7, 8, 9, 10, 11, 12, 14

7 No smoking; 8 Children welcome; 9 Social drinking allowed; 10 Tennis nearby; 11 Swimming nearby; 12 Golf nearby; 13 Skiing nearby; 14 May be booked through a travel agent.

California

California

Silver Spur Bed and Breakfast

44625 Silver Spur Trail, 93601
(209) 683-2896

The Silver Spur Bed and Breakfast is nestled in the Sierra Nevadas of California, just off historic Highway 49. Key to the California Gold Country and the south and west gates of famed Yosemite National Park, it is only minutes from many outdoor sports. It features beautiful clean rooms with private baths and entrances and comfortable beds and is tastefully decorated in American Southwest. Outdoor rest and dining areas boast outstanding Sierra views. A Continental breakfast is served daily. Come enjoy Yosemite, and be treated to old-fashioned hospitality and great value.

Hosts: Patty and Bryan Hays
Rooms: 2 (PB) $45-60
Continental Breakfast
Credit Cards: A, B, D
Notes: 2, 5, 7, 8, 9, 10, 11, 12, 13, 14

ALAMEDA

Garratt Mansion

900 Union Street, 94501
(510) 521-4779

This 1893 Victorian makes time stand still on the tranquil island of Alameda. Only 15 miles to Berkeley or downtown San Francisco. The hosts will help maximize vacation plans or leave guests alone to regroup. Rooms are large and comfortable, and breakfasts are nutritious and filling.

Hosts: Royce and Betty Gladden
Rooms: 7 (5 PB; 2 SB) $75-125
Full Breakfast
Credit Cards: A, B, C, E
Notes: 2, 5, 7, 8, 11, 12, 14

ALBION

Albion River Inn

P.O. Box 100, 95410
(707) 937-1919

This romantic inn and restaurant offers beauty, serenity, and luxury in New England-style cottages with garden entrances, cliff top ocean views, wood-burning fireplaces, decks, Jacuzzis, and double tubs. Each room is individually decorated. Complimentary wine, morning newspaper, fresh coffee, and delicious full breakfast. The celebrated coastal cuisine of Chef Stephen Smith is served nightly in the restaurant, paired with the award-winning wine list and entertainment on weekends. Weddings are welcomed!

Hosts: Flurry Healy and Peter Wells
Rooms: 20 (PB) $160-250
Full Breakfast
Credit Cards: A, B, C
Notes: 2, 4, 5, 8, 9, 10, 11, 12

Fensalden Inn

P.O. Box 99, 95410
(707) 937-4042; (800) 959-3850

This restored 1860s stagecoach way station has antique furnishings, and several units have fireplaces. Quiet country setting with pastoral and ocean views. Enjoy strolling country lanes where grazing deer share the crisp morning air, or the evening panorama of the setting sun over a crimson-stained ocean. Minimum-stay requirements weekends and holidays.

Hosts: Frances and Scott Brazil
Rooms: 8 (PB) $85-130
Full Breakfast
Credit Cards: A, B
Notes: 2, 5, 7, 9, 10, 11, 12, 14

ANAHEIM

Bed and Breakfast California

P.O. Box 282910, San Francisco, 94128-2910
(415) 696-1690; (800) 872-4500
FAX (415) 696-1699

7-4. Kids are really welcome in this lovely older home near Disneyland. There are three guest rooms; one has a fireplace and a balcony, and another one has a TV and small refrigerator. All have private baths. The hostess is a weaver and doll collector. Full breakfast is served. Special rates for four people. $55.

7-5. The guest wing of this spacious house in Anaheim has room for the entire family, with a living room with a fireplace, balcony, kitchen, and private bath. Living room couch converts to a bed for the kids. Two downstairs guest rooms share a bath. Enjoy the spa and patio, as well as the full country breakfast. Pets welcome. Affordable rates. $60.

Country Comfort Bed and Breakfast. Guests are treated with country-style hospitality at this homestead in a quiet residential area. King- and queen-size rooms are available. A full breakfast is included, often featuring stuffed French toast and other specialties. Amenities include pool with cover, cable TV, VCR, private atrium, and

fireplace. Handicapped accessible. Disneyland and Anaheim Convention Center are seven miles away. Anaheim Stadium, home of the baseball Angels, is only four miles away. $50-60.

Southern Comfort Bed and Breakfast. Decorated in country antiques, this bed and breakfast is in a quiet residential neighborhood, ideal for the single business travelers and also for large families. Only five minutes from Disneyland and the Anaheim Convention Center and freeway, guests will be close to all Southern California attractions. "Grandma's Suite" includes a queen-size bed, living room (with queen-size sofa bed), fireplace, full bath, balcony, and kitchenette. Two double rooms on the ground floor are handicapped accessible and share a bath. Patio, barbecue, and Jacuzzi available. Full farm-style breakfast served. $50-60.

Eye Openers Bed and Breakfast Reservations

P.O. Box 694, Altadena, 91003-0694
(213) 684-4428; (818) 797-2055
FAX (818) 798-3640

AN-A91. Beautiful restored and decorated 1910 Princess Anne Victorian, now a friendly bed and breakfast, is surrounded by lovely gardens and is in a residential area convenient to most Orange County attractions with local bus service. Hearty breakfast and afternoon refreshments. No smoking. Nine guest rooms with private and shared baths. $65-120.

AN-P3. This bed and breakfast, with its country kitchen and full breakfast, offers comfort, convenience, economy, and good location near restaurants and public transportation. Bicycles, hot tub, and complimentary transport to Disneyland are avail-

NOTES: Credit cards accepted: A MasterCard; B Visa; C American Express; D Discover; E Diners Club; F Other; 2 Personal checks accepted; 3 Lunch available; 4 Dinner available; 5 Open all year; 6 Pets welcome;

able. Children welcome. Two guest rooms with private and shared baths. $40-60.

GG-04. Convenient to Orange County attractions, this home features large comfortable rooms, full breakfast, and TV room with fireplace. Four guest rooms with private and shared baths. $45-55.

OR-C3. Enjoy a delicious country-style breakfast in this contemporary wood-and-glass bed and breakfast. Relax in the pool, Jacuzzi, living room, or interesting family room. Convenient to Disneyland, Anaheim Convention Center, and Stadium. Handicapped accessible with adaptive equipment. No smoking. Three guest rooms available. $60-65.

SA-W1. This 1930s Renaissance cottage with antiques and country French decor features one guest room with French doors that open onto a deck overlooking a garden and pond. Choice of breakfast. It has a queen-size bed and private bath. Near South Coast Plaza, Orange County Airport, and major freeways. No smoking. $65-75.

ANGWIN

Forest Manor

415 Cold Springs Road, 94508
(707) 965-3538; (800) 788-0364

Secluded 20-acre English Tudor estate tucked among forest vineyards in famous Napa wine country. Described as "one of the most romantic country inns. A small exclusive resort." Fireplaces, verandas, 53-foot pool, spas, spacious suites (one with Jacuzzi), refrigerators, coffee makers, home-baked breakfast. Close to more than 200 wineries, ballooning, hot springs, and a lake. No smoking inside.

Hosts: Harold and Corlene Lambeth
Rooms: 3 (PB) $110-239

Full Breakfast
Credit Cards: A, B
Notes: 2, 5, 9, 10, 11, 14

APTOS

Apple Lane Inn

6265 Soquel Drive, 95003-3117
(408) 475-6868

Apple Lane Inn is a historic Victorian farmhouse restored to the charm and tranquility of an earlier age. It is just south of Santa Cruz on two and one-half acres of grounds, with gardens, a romantic gazebo, and fields. Explore the many miles of beaches within walking distance. Golf, hiking, fishing, shopping, and dining are all nearby.

Hosts: Doug and Diana Groom
Rooms: 5 (PB) $70-175
Full Breakfast
Credit Cards: A, B, D
Notes: 2, 5, 7, 8, 9, 10, 11, 12, 14

Bayview Hotel

8041 Soquel Drive, 95003
(800) 4-BAYVIEW; FAX (408) 688-5128

The Bayview Hotel is proud to be the oldest operating inn on the Monterey Bay. This elegant Victorian-Italianate structure was built in 1878 by Joseph Arano who imported fine furniture for his "grand hotel." Guest rooms are comfortably furnished and decorated in the style Mr. Arano originally planned. All rooms have private baths, some have fireplaces and extra-large soaking tubs. Some of the original furniture is still at the inn and many photographs tell of times past. One of the Bayview's contemporary amenities is the Veranda, a four-star restaurant serving the finest regional American cuisine.

Host: Gwen Burkard
Rooms: 11 (PB) $90-150
Full Breakfast
Credit Cards: A, B, C
Notes: 2, 3, 4, 5, 7, 9, 10, 11, 12, 14

7 No smoking; 8 Children welcome; 9 Social drinking allowed; 10 Tennis nearby; 11 Swimming nearby; 12 Golf nearby; 13 Skiing nearby; 14 May be booked through a travel agent.

Mangels House

Mangels House

570 Aptos Creek Road, Box 302, 95001
(408) 688-7982

A large southern Colonial on four acres of
lawn and orchard, and bounded by a
10,000-acre redwood forest, is less than a
mile from the beach. The five large, airy
rooms are eclectic in decor and European
in feel, reflecting the owners' background.
Closed December 24 through 26. Inquire
first regarding pets. Limited smoking
allowed. Children over 10 welcome.

Hosts: Jacqueline and Ronald Fisher
Rooms: 5 (PB) $105-135
Full Breakfast
Credit Cards: A, B, C
Notes: 2, 5, 9, 10, 11, 12, 14

ARNOLD

Lodge at Manuel Mill

1573 White Pines Road, 95223
(209) 795-2622

A unique Sierra bed and breakfast resort on
the banks of a historic millpond has guest
rooms decorated with country elegance and
enhanced with antiques and wood-burning
stoves. Guests enjoy spacious lodge and
expansive decks. The Stanislas National
Forest provides nature walks and hiking
trails.

Hosts: Mac and Andy Brown
Rooms: 5 (PB) $90-120
Full Breakfast
Credit Cards: A, B
Notes: 2, 5, 7, 9, 10, 11, 12, 13, 14

ARROYO GRANDE

Arroyo Village Inn

407 El Camino Real, 93420
(805) 489-5926

Romantic, award-winning English country-
style inn offering a delightful blend of yesterday's charm and hospitality with today's
comforts and conveniences. Spacious suites
are decorated with Laura Ashley prints and
antiques with private baths, window seats,
and balconies. In the heart of California's
Central Coast, halfway between Los
Angeles and San Francisco. Near beaches,
wineries, mineral spas, San Luis Obispo;
less than one hour to Hearst Castle. "The
best kept secret on the Central Coast," says
the *Los Angeles Times.*

Host: Gina Glass
Rooms: 7 (PB) $95-195
Full Breakfast
Credit Cards: A, B, C, D, E
Notes: 2, 5, 7, 8, 9, 10, 11, 12, 14

Bed and Breakfast California

P.O. Box 282910, San Francisco, 94128-2910
(415) 696-1690; (800) 872-4500
FAX (415) 696-1699

Arroyo Village Inn. Award-winning Victorian built in 1988 has seven garden-theme
suites decorated in Laura Ashley prints and
antiques with such amenities as window
seats, skylights, balconies, and air conditioning. Full breakfast and evening cordials
available. A special section of the *Los
Angeles Times* has featured many rave
reviews. Near beaches, Hearst Castle,
wineries, and mineral springs. Horseback
riding on the beach. $85-175.

NOTES: Credit cards accepted: A MasterCard; B Visa; C American Express; D Discover; E Diners Club;
F Other; 2 Personal checks accepted; 3 Lunch available; 4 Dinner available; 5 Open all year; 6 Pets welcome;

AUBURN

Power's Mansion Inn

164 Cleveland Avenue, 95603
(916) 885-1166; FAX (916) 885-1386

This magnificent mansion was built from a gold fortune in the late 1800s. It has easy access to I-80 and off-street parking. Close to gold country, antiquing, water sports, hiking, horseback riding, skiing, ballooning, and restaurants.

Owners: Arno and Jean Lejnieks
Innkeepers: Tony and Tina Verhaart
Rooms: 11 (PB) $69-149
Full Breakfast
Credit Cards: A, B, C
Notes: 2, 5, 7, 8, 9, 10, 11, 12, 13, 14

Power's Mansion Inn

AVALON

Gull House

344 Whittley Avenue, Box 1381, 90704
(310) 510-2547; FAX (310) 510-9569

Honeymooners and those celebrating anniversaries will enjoy this AAA-approved contemporary house with swimming pool, spa, barbecue, gas log fireplaces, morning room with refrigerator, and color TV. Close to bay beaches and all water activities. Deposit or full payment in advance reserves taxi pickup and return. Ask about the guest rooms. Two-night minimum stay is required. Ten percent commission if booked through a travel agent.

Hosts: Bob and Hattie Michalis
Suites: 2 (PB) $110-145

Continental Breakfast
Credit Cards: None
Notes: 2, 7, 8, 10, 11, 12, 13, 14

Zane Grey Pueblo

199 Chimes Tower Road, P.O. Box 216, 90704
(310) 510-0966

Zane Grey's home built in 1926. A Hopi Indian-style pueblo on a bluff overlooking the breathtaking ocean view. Quietest hotel in town. Each room is different, and all are named after Zane Grey's novels, which are available for guests to borrow from the office. No TVs or telephones in rooms. The living room does have cable TV, a grand piano, a fireplace, and a deck that overlooks the ocean. There is also a pool in the shape of an arrowhead. Complimentary pickup at the boat dock on arrival and to and from the hotel six times a day.

Host: Karen Baker
Rooms: 17 (PB) $55-125
Continental Breakfast
Credit Cards: A, B, C
Notes: 2, 5, 8, 9, 10, 11, 12, 14

BAYWOOD

Baywood Bed and Breakfast Inn

1370 2nd Street, Baywood Park, 93402
(805) 528-8888

The Baywood Bed and Breakfast is on Morro Bay on the central California coastline, 12 miles west of San Luis Obispo in a small neighborhood on a tiny peninsula. The inn is close to kayaking, golf, hiking, bicycling, and picnicking. Beautiful Montano De Oro State Park and Hearst Castle are minutes away. The inn features 15 highly decorated theme suites. All have lovely bay views, cozy seating areas, wood-burning fireplaces, and private baths. Guests are treated to afternoon wine and cheese, room tours, and breakfast in bed.

Hosts: Edie Havard; Pat and Alex Benson
Rooms: 15 (PB) $90-160

7 No smoking; 8 Children welcome; 9 Social drinking allowed; 10 Tennis nearby; 11 Swimming nearby; 12 Golf nearby; 13 Skiing nearby; 14 May be booked through a travel agent.

Full Breakfast
Credit Cards: A, B
Notes: 2, 3, 4, 5, 7, 8, 9, 11, 12, 14

BENICIA

Union Hotel and Gardens

401 First Street, 94510
(707) 746-0100; (800) 544-2278 (CA only)

Built in 1882 and active as a 20-room bordello until the early 1950s, the Union Hotel was completely renovated in 1981 into a 12-room hotel and bed and breakfast. Each of the 12 rooms is decorated with a theme and named accordingly. Each room has a queen- or king-size bed, individual temperature controls, Jacuzzi, and TV. The superb stained-glass picture windows in the bar and dining room are worth a trip on their own. Award-winning restaurant on premises. Brunch served on Saturday and Sunday. No smoking is permitted in the lounge or restaurant. Twenty minutes from the wine country, 45 minutes from San Francisco, and 20 minutes from the ferry to Fisherman's Wharf.

Host: William Berg
Rooms: 12 (PB) $79-140
Continental Breakfast
Credit Cards: A, B, C, D, E
Notes: 3, 4, 5, 9, 14

BERKELEY

Eye Openers Bed and Breakfast Reservations

P.O. Box 694, Altadena, 91003-0694
(213) 684-4428; (818) 797-2055;
FAX (818) 798-3640

BE-H51. This 1904 Craftsman-style inn is close to the university campus, restaurants, hiking, and public transportation. Relax in the parlors or patio areas on the lovely grounds. Five guest rooms with private baths and king- or queen-size or twin beds. No smoking. Continental plus breakfast. $60-100.

Gramma's Rose Garden Inn

2740 Telegraph Avenue, 94705
(510) 549-2145; FAX (510) 549-1085

Two turn-of-the-century Tudor-style mansions, garden, cottage, and carriage houses are set amid English country gardens. Some rooms furnished with antiques; many have fireplaces, decks, porches, and/or views. Near the university, shops, parks, and museums. Restaurant on premises is open for dinner. Also serves Sunday brunch.

Host: Kathy Kuttner
Rooms: 40 (PB) $85-145
Continental Breakfast
Credit Cards: A, B, C, D, E
Notes: 2, 5, 7, 11, 14

BEVERLY HILLS

Bed and Breakfast California

P.O. Box 282910, San Francisco, 94128-2910
(415) 696-1690; (800) 872-4500
FAX (415) 696-1699

Century City Condo. Walking distance from the upscale Century City Mall, this top-floor luxury apartment is close to Beverly Hills and Westwood. Two guest rooms have private baths: one with twin beds and the other with a king-size bed and private patio. Includes underground parking, Jacuzzi, sauna, and a Continental plus breakfast. Families and long-term visitors welcome. $55-85.

Heart of Beverly Hills. This luxury condo includes a comfortable, spacious separate suite with twin beds and a private bath. Residential neighborhood is quiet, close to shopping and business district in Beverly Hills, and only a few steps from public transportation. The hostess lives in a separate wing of the home and serves a Continental plus breakfast. Handicapped accessible. $50-55.

NOTES: Credit cards accepted: A MasterCard; B Visa; C American Express; D Discover; E Diners Club; F Other; 2 Personal checks accepted; 3 Lunch available; 4 Dinner available; 5 Open all year; 6 Pets welcome;

Full View of the Griffith Park Observatory. This designer home was built in the 1940s with an eye for blending with the impressive natural environment. Guests have an entire spacious suite to themselves: bedroom, living room (replete with the owner's fine art and ceramics collection), full bath, and kitchenette. $100.

Eye Openers Bed and Breakfast Reservations

P.O. Box 694, Altadena, 91003-0694
(213) 684-4428; (818) 797-2055
FAX (818) 798-3640

BH-N1. In the heart of Beverly Hills, guest cottage in garden area of host home offers privacy and comfort. Cottage has twin beds, private bath, microwave, refrigerator, and choice of Continental or full breakfast. Public transportation available. $50-55.

BH-W2. Charming canyon cottage behind the Beverly Hills Hotel provides a large suite and smaller guest room with private baths. One has king-size bed, the other has a queen-size bed. Convenient to UCLA, Hollywood, and Studio City. Host is biographer, theatre critic, and UCLA instructor. No smoking. Three-night minimum stay. $65-85.

BIG BEAR

Bed and Breakfast California

P.O. Box 282910, San Francisco, 94128-2910
(415) 696-1690; (800) 872-4500
FAX (415) 696-1699

The Old Hayloft. A model railroader's dream! In the midst of the mountains, guests will be pampered in this historic residence built in 1922 as a general store and post office. A "G" scale train serves a Continental plus breakfast in the guests' room.

There are trains in every room so guests can enjoy the collection of 100 1/10-scale locomotives, or guests may bring their own to use on the tracks. There is a heated indoor Jacuzzi and fully equipped family room with mini-theater and arcade. $75.

Festive Big Bear Victorian. On the southern shore of Big Bear Lake, this four-room Victorian focuses on beautiful surroundings and creature comforts. Rooms are large and well decorated, and all have private baths. Breakfast in the sunny dining room features "exclusive culinary creations." Afternoons feature teatime or a wine and cheese fest. $90-150.

BIG BEAR LAKE

Truffles Bed and Breakfast

43591 Bow Canyon Drive, 92315
(909) 585-2772

Gracious hospitality in peaceful surroundings describes this country manor home in a mountain resort with lake, golf, and ski facilities nearby. Attention to detail is evident with five individually appointed bedrooms with private baths and featherbeds, full breakfast, afternoon appetizers, and truffles on bedtime pillows. This spacious facility is traditionally furnished and includes large comfortable gathering room

Truffles

---

7 No smoking; 8 Children welcome; 9 Social drinking allowed; 10 Tennis nearby; 11 Swimming nearby; 12 Golf nearby; 13 Skiing nearby; 14 May be booked through a travel agent.

with piano, TV, video library, and fireplace. Large outside decks also available.

Hosts: Marilyn Kane and Carol Bracey
Rooms: 5 (PB) $110-140
Full Breakfast
Credit Cards: A, B
Notes: 2, 5, 7, 9, 12, 13, 14

BIG SUR

Ventana Inn

Highway 1, 93920
(408) 667-2331; (800) 628-6500

Deluxe romantic inn on 243 acres above Pacific, 35 miles from Monterey airport. Decorator-designed accommodations in 12 buildings with king- or queen-size bed, terrace, air conditioning, and telephone; most with fireplace, some with wet bar and hot tub. All with TVs and VCRs. Three townhouse suites. Wheelchair accessibility. Complimentary Continental breakfast and afternoon wine and cheese are served. Highly regarded restaurant and fireside lounge. Two heated pools, sauna, massage, two Japanese hot baths, horseback riding, and hiking. Country store and gallery. Beach nearby. Smoking on a limited basis.

Host: R.E. Bussinger
Rooms: 60 (PB) $175-890
Continental Breakfast
Credit Cards: A, B, C, D, E
Notes: 2, 3, 4, 5, 9, 11, 14

BOLINAS (MARIN COUNTY)

Bed and Breakfast California

P.O. Box 282910, San Francisco, 94128-2910
(415) 696-1690; (800) 872-4500
FAX (415) 696-1699

This cabin is on a spit of land surrounded by Bolinas Bay. Point Reyes National Park is on one side; Stinson Beach and Mount Tamalpais on the other side. Two bedrooms, a living room, a full kitchen, and a bathroom. The cabin is well stocked, including charcoal for the barbecue. $125.

BOONVILLE

Anderson Creek Inn

12050 Anderson Valley Way, P.O. Box 217, 95415
(707) 895-3091; (800) LLAMA-02

Elegant and secluded, this spacious inn is on 16 lovely acres with views from every room. Guests are treated to wine and appetizers in the evenings, and a full gourmet breakfast served in the dining room, the patio, or in a basket brought to the room. Lazy days can be spent walking the grounds, visiting the animals, or lounging around the Olympic size pool. Wine tasting, shopping, restaurants, hiking, and the Mendocino Coast are just minutes away.

Notes: Rob and Nancy Graham
Rooms: 5 (PB) $110-165
Full Breakfast
Credit Cards: A, B
Notes: 2, 5, 7, 9, 10, 11, 12

BORREGO SPRINGS (DEATH VALLEY)

Bed and Breakfast California

P.O. Box 282910, San Francisco, 94128-2910
(415) 696-1690; (800) 872-4500
FAX (415) 696-1699

Watch the wildflowers bloom at this perfectly restored desert resort. All rooms have private baths, TVs, and a panoramic view of the valley. Sun yourself at the pool or take advantage of the many hiking trails and canyons. Grounds include indoor and outdoor restaurant areas at reasonable prices. Affordable to luxury rates.

BRENTWOOD

Bed and Breakfast California

P.O. Box 282910, San Francisco, 94128-2910
(415) 696-1690; (800) 872-4500
FAX (415) 696-1699

NOTES: Credit cards accepted: A MasterCard; B Visa; C American Express; D Discover; E Diners Club; F Other; 2 Personal checks accepted; 3 Lunch available; 4 Dinner available; 5 Open all year; 6 Pets welcome;

Stretch Out in Delta Country. Set among two acres of fruit and nut trees, this private cottage is only an hour east of San Francisco in the Sacramento River Delta. Air-conditioned accommodations include queen-size bed, private bath, and private entrance, as well as pool, spa, gardens, and gazebo. The bountiful breakfast includes homegrown produce and fresh gourmet coffee. Close to Mount Diablo, Black Diamond Mines Regional Park, Contra Loma Lake, and several U-Pick fruit farms. $65.

BRIDGEPORT

The Cain House

340 Main Street, 93517
(619) 932-7040; (800) 433-CAIN

In a small valley with a view of the rugged eastern Sierras, the Cain House has blended European elegance with a western atmosphere. Every amenity has been provided, including wine and cheese in the evenings. After breakfast, the pristine beauty of the valley, lakes, and streams await for a day of hiking, boating, fishing, hunting, and cross-country skiing. Three-diamond AAA and Mobil approved.

Hosts: Chris and Marachal Gohlich
Rooms: 7 (PB) $80-135
Full Breakfast
Credit Cards: A, B, C
Notes: 2, 9, 10

BURBANK

Bed and Breakfast California

P.O. Box 282910, San Francisco, 94128-2910
(415) 696-1690; (800) 872-4500
FAX (415) 696-1699

Burbank Bungalow. This charming cottage has pool, patio, barbecue, and wet bar all opening to a lush, landscaped yard. Accommodations include trundle beds and a private bath. The host is a minister, just in case you want to tie the knot. Handicapped accessible. $60.

BURLINGAME

Burlingame Bed and Breakfast

1021 Balboa Avenue, 94010
(415) 344-5815

Boating, swimming, fishing (bay and ocean), running, golf, hiking, art, entertainment, sports. Near Stanford, other colleges, and transportation.

Hosts: Joe and Elnora Fernandez
Room: 1 (PB) $40-50
Continental Breakfast
Credit Cards: None
Notes: 2, 5, 7, 8, 10, 11, 12

CALISTOGA

Bed and Breakfast California

P.O. Box 282910, San Francisco, 94128-2910
(415) 696-1690; (800) 872-4500
FAX (415) 696-1699

Country Inn at Calistoga. An intimate retreat tucked away in a small canyon, the hostess, Scarlet, has three exquisitely appointed suites set in the quiet mood of green lawns and tall pines overlooking the vineyards. All have private entrances, private baths, queen-size beds, air conditioning, microwaves, small refrigerators, and spacious lawns for play. One suite has a fireplace and two have fold-out couches in separate rooms for children. Enjoy the delicious breakfast poolside under the apple trees or in a cozy sitting room. Children welcome at no charge. $95-150.

Wisteria Cottage. This rural 1930s farmhouse has three suites with fireplaces, kitchens, and redwood decks. The "family cottage" can accommodate up to six. It has a refrigerator stocked with goodies and French doors that open onto the vineyards. The bed and breakfast is in the country, just outside Calistoga. Enjoy breakfast under a 150-year-old oak tree. Antique furnishings, including an iron-and-brass bed, remind guests of the slower pace of Old California. Call for rates.

Calistoga Wayside Inn

1523 Foothill Boulevard, 94515
(707) 942-0645; (800) 845-3632
FAX (707) 942-4169

This 1920s Spanish-style home in Napa Valley has a park-like setting of fountains and gardens. Full breakfast is served in the dining room or on the lower patio. King- and queen-size beds and private baths available. Near hiking, golf, tennis, shopping, wineries, restaurants, glider and balloon rides. Complimentary wine and cheese. In-week specials. Walking distance from town. Gift certificates available.

Hosts: Pat O'Neil and Carmine Scelzi
Rooms: 3 (PB) $110-140
Full Breakfast
Credit Cards: A, B, C
Notes: 2, 5, 7, 8, 9, 10, 11, 12, 14

Christopher's Inn

1010 Foothill Boulevard, 94515
(707) 942-5755

An architect created this country inn with exceptional landscaped grounds close to the center of historic Calistoga. Elegant formality and privacy with English country ambience is created with fine antiques and Laura Ashley matching comforters, balloon drapes, wallpaper, and fluffy pillow covers. Play croquet beneath ancient cedar trees. Step across the road to a romantic spa that creates the ultimate bath experience, especially for couples. Then return to the guest room, private bath, secret gardens, fresh flowers, and breakfast in bed while snuggling by a cozy, private fireplace. Children welcome by prior arrangements only. May be booked by a travel agent for weekday stays.

Hosts: Christopher and Adele Layton
Rooms: 10 (PB) $120-170
Continental Breakfast
Credit Cards: A, B, C
Notes: 2, 5, 7, 9, 10, 11, 12

"Culvers," A Country Inn

1805 Foothill Boulevard, 94515
(707) 942-4535

A lovely Victorian residence built in 1875, filled with antiques and offering a full country breakfast. Jacuzzi and seasonal pool. Within minutes of wineries, mud baths, and downtown Calistoga. Lovely view of St. Helena mountain range from the veranda. Sherry and hors d'oeuvres are offered in the afternoon, with an afternoon beverage and baked treats offered upon arrival. Closed December through January, and Thanksgiving and New Year's. Reservations held for seven days on credit card, with payment by personal or traveler's check. Children 16 and older welcome.

Hosts: Meg and Tony Wheatley
Rooms: 4 (SB) $128.80-140
Full Breakfast
Credit Cards: None
Notes: 2, 7, 9, 10, 11, 12, 14

The Elms
Bed and Breakfast Inn

1300 Cedar Street, 94515
(707) 942-9476; (800) 235-4316

This 1871 French three-story Victorian is one-half block from town next to a park on the Napa River. It is very quiet and peaceful, yet within walking distance of restaurants, spas, gliders, bike rentals, golf, and tennis. The rooms are very romantic—decorated with antiques. All have private baths, coffee makers, bathrobes, chocolates, and port for after dinner. The feather beds are piled high with pillows and down comforters. Some rooms have fireplaces, TV, and spa tubs. A huge gourmet breakfast is served, and wine and cheese are served in the afternoon.

Host: Stephen and Karla Wyle
Rooms: 7 (PB) $100-170
Full Breakfast
Credit Cards: A, B
Notes: 2, 5, 7, 11, 12, 14

Eye Openers Bed and Breakfast Reservations

P.O. Box 694, Altadena, 91003-0694
(213) 684-4428; (818) 797-2055
FAX (818) 798-3640

CA-S31. Very close to Napa Valley wineries, 1900 country farmhouse on several acres offers quiet and comfort. Each accommodation has a private entrance. Full breakfast and afternoon refreshments are served in room, suite, or on the tree-shaded pool deck. One guest room and two suites have private baths and queen-size beds. No smoking. $95-150.

CA-S91. Uniquely decorated rooms, some with fireplaces and whirlpool tubs, and a pool fed by the inn's own hot springs are some of the special offerings at this wine country estate. A Continental plus breakfast and afternoon refreshments are provided. Nine guest rooms with private baths and king- or queen-size beds. No smoking. $125-210.

Foothill House

3037 Foothill Boulevard, 94515
(707) 942-6933; (800) 942-6933

"The most romantic inn of the Napa Valley," according to the *Chicago Tribune* travel editor. In a country setting, Foothill House offers spacious suites individually decorated with antiques, each with private bath and entrance, fireplace, and small refrigerator. Two suites offer Jacuzzi tubs. Complimentary wine and hors d'oeuvres each evening, and free turndown service. Private elegant cottage also available.

Hosts: Doris and Gus Beckert
Rooms: 3 (PB) $135-250
Full Breakfast
Credit Cards: A, B, C, D
Notes: 2, 5, 7, 9, 10, 11, 12, 14

Foothill House

Hillcrest

3225 Lake County Highway, 94515
(707) 942-6334

Breathtaking view of Napa Valley countryside. Hiking, swimming, and fishing on 40 acres. Family-owned since 1860. Hilltop modern country home decorated with heirlooms from family mansion. Rooms have balconies. Fireplace and grand piano, rare art work, silver, crystal, china, and Oriental rugs. Family photo albums date back to 1870s. Breakfast is served weekends on a 12-foot antique table fit for a king. Outdoor spa and large pool.

Host: Debbie O'Gorman
Rooms: 4 (1 PB; 3 SB) $45-90
Continental Breakfast
Credit Cards: None
Notes: 2, 5, 6, 9, 10, 11, 12, 14

The Pink Mansion

1415 Foothill Boulevard, 94515
(707) 942-0558

A 120-year-old Victorian in the heart of the Napa Valley wine country. Within biking distance of several wineries; walking distance to Calistoga's many spas and restaurants. Fully air-conditioned; complimentary wine and cheese. Each room has a

7 No smoking; 8 Children welcome; 9 Social drinking allowed; 10 Tennis nearby; 11 Swimming nearby; 12 Golf nearby; 13 Skiing nearby; 14 May be booked through a travel agent.

wonderful view and private bath. Two-night minimum stay required for weekends and holidays.

Hosts: Leslie Sakai and Toppa Epps
Rooms: 5 (PB) $85-175
Full Breakfast
Credit Cards: A, B,
Notes: 2, 5, 6, 7, 8, 9, 10, 11, 12, 14

Quail Mountain Inn

Quail Mountain Bed and Breakfast Inn

4455 North St. Helena Highway, 94515
(707) 942-0316

Quail Mountain is a secluded luxury bed and breakfast on 26 beautiful wooded acres. There are a vineyard and a fruit orchard on the property. Three guest rooms, each with king-size bed, private bath, and private deck. Complimentary wine and full breakfast. Close to Napa Valley wineries and restaurants. A two-night minimum stay is required on all weekends and holidays.

Hosts: Don and Alma Swiers
Rooms: 3 (PB) $100-125
Full Breakfast
Credit Cards: A, B
Notes: 2, 5, 7, 9, 10, 11, 12, 14

Trailside Inn

4201 Silverado Trail, 94515
(707) 942-4106

A charming 1930s farmhouse in the country with three very private suites. Each suite has its own entrance, porch or deck, bedroom, bath, fireplace, and air conditioning. Fresh home-baked breads provided in guests' fully equipped kitchen.

Hosts: Randy and Lani Gray
Suites: 3 (PB) $95-120
Continental Breakfast
Credit Cards: A, B, C, D
Notes: 2, 5, 7, 8, 9, 10, 11, 12, 14

Washington Street Lodging

1605 Washington Street, 94515
(707) 942-6968

Washington Street Lodging offers private cottages in a secluded river setting. Two cottages with bedroom, living room, and full kitchen. Three cottages have mini-kitchen and private decks. The decor is country comfortable. A Continental breakfast is placed in the room for guests to enjoy at their leisure, and downtown spas, shopping, and more than 20 great restaurants are within walking distance. Wineries are a five-minute drive away.

Hosts: Diane Byrne and Joan Ranieri
Rooms: 5 (PB) $90
Continental Breakfast
Credit Cards: None
Notes: 2, 5, 6, 7, 8, 9, 10, 11, 12, 14

Zinfandel House

1253 Summit Drive, 94515
(707) 942-0733

Zinfandel House is in a wooded setting on a western hillside with a spectacular view of the famous Napa Valley vineyards. Halfway between St. Helena and Calistoga. Choose from three tastefully decorated rooms with a private or shared bath. Breakfast is served on the deck or in the solarium.

Hosts: Bette and George Starke
Rooms: 3 (PB or SB) $75-100
Full Breakfast
Credit Cards: None
Notes: 2, 5, 7, 9, 10, 11, 12

NOTES: Credit cards accepted: A MasterCard; B Visa; C American Express; D Discover; E Diners Club; F Other; 2 Personal checks accepted; 3 Lunch available; 4 Dinner available; 5 Open all year; 6 Pets welcome;

CAMARILLO

Bed and Breakfast California

P.O. Box 282910, San Francisco, 94128-2910
(415) 696-1690; (800) 872-4500
FAX (415) 696-1699

Richard in Ojai. This homey bed and breakfast is nestled among the oaks outside of town, with the mountains as a picturesque backdrop. Drink fresh orange juice from the orchard while sitting on the side patio near the fountain. Features three sunny guest rooms sharing a bath, with plantation-style decor and mahogany furnishings. Very, very peaceful. $75

CAMBRIA

Bed and Breakfast California

P.O. Box 282910, San Francisco, 94128-2910
(415) 696-1690; (800) 872-4500
FAX (415) 696-1699

Watch the ocean from the hot tub. The entire lower level of this luxury home in Cambria is designed for bed and breakfast pampering. There is a bedroom with queen-size bed, living room with fireplace, stereo and TV systems, dining area, fully equipped kitchen (including goodies!), and two decks—both with ocean view and one with guests' own hot tub. British hostess bakes fresh scones as part of every gourmet breakfast. Walking distance to town. There is even a secret, private entrance. $110.

A Summer Place. From this wooded coastal site, guests can peek at the ocean through the pines. It's quiet and uncrowded, a perfect setting for this Cape Cod house and the hosts' warm bed and breakfast hospitality. Don and Desi's special touches give the interior a special warm feeling. At the top of the stairs, bedrooms with sloped ceilings await guests. Gathering around the living room fireplace is popular on chilly evenings. Casual hosts welcome guests to enjoy their home and their own. $75.

Eye Openers Bed and Breakfast Reservations

P.O. Box 694, Altadena, 91003-0694
(213) 684-4428; (818) 797-2055
FAX (818) 798-3640

CA-B1. Charming couple host an elegant bed and breakfast with a relaxed atmosphere near Hearst Castle and mid-coast beaches. First floor is guests' domain with large bedroom/sitting room in English Country decor. Private bath and twin or king-size bed. No smoking. $90.

CA-B71. Contemporary oceanfront bed and breakfast inn on the beach has antique furnishings, ocean views, and outdoor decks. Continental breakfast. No smoking. Seven guest rooms. Private bath. $120-150.

CA-D2. Friendly, comfortable bed and breakfast in wooded area offers a peek at the ocean and quiet surroundings. Two guest rooms with double and twin beds. Private bath. No smoking. Full breakfast. $35-60.

CA-061. Each of the six guest rooms in this 1873 Greek Revival-style historic inn is decorated differently, but all have antiques from the 1800s. Full breakfast. No smoking. Six guest rooms. Private bath. $85-125.

CA-P31. Just south of Hearst Castle at the ocean, this bed and breakfast features rooms with fireplaces, private patios, and bath ensuite. A full breakfast is served with

7 No smoking; 8 Children welcome; 9 Social drinking allowed; 10 Tennis nearby; 11 Swimming nearby; 12 Golf nearby; 13 Skiing nearby; 14 May be booked through a travel agent.

an ocean view. No smoking. Three guest rooms. Private bath. $85.

The Pickford House Bed and Breakfast

2555 Macleod Way, 93428
(805) 927-8619

Only eight miles from Hearst Castle, Pickford House is decorated with antiques reminiscent of the golden age of film. Eight rooms have king- or queen-size beds, private baths, fireplaces, and a view of the mountains. Parlor with an 1860 bar is used for wine and tea bread at 5:00 P.M. TV in rooms. All have claw-foot tubs and showers in rooms. Enjoy wine tasting nearby or rock collecting on the beach. Twenty dollars for each additional person.

Host: Anna Larsen
Rooms: 8 (PB) $89-130
Full Breakfast
Credit Cards: A, B
Notes: 2, 5, 7, 8, 9, 10, 11, 12, 14

The Squibb House

4063 Burton Drive, 93428
(805) 927-9600

In the heart of Cambria, within steps of galleries, shops, and fine restaurants, there is a place suspended in time. Step through the Squibb House gate and into a century past. Restored to re-create the charm of the late 1800s, the Squibb House recalls a simpler time. Relax in the main parlor, stroll the garden path, or rock on the porch as the world goes by.

Owner: Bruce Black
Hosts: Martha, Linda, Christy, and Barbara
Rooms: 5 (PB) $95-125
Continental Breakfast
Credit Cards: A, B
Notes: 2, 5, 7, 9, 12, 14

CARLSBAD

Pelican Cove Inn

320 Walnut Avenue, 92008
(619) 434-5995

Pelican Cove Inn features two rooms with spa tubs, feather beds, fireplaces, private entries, private baths, lovely antiques, a sun deck, balconies, and a gazebo. Walk to the beach and restaurants. Palomar Airport and Amtrak pickup. Beach chairs, towels, picnic baskets available. Beautiful gardens. Two-night minimum stay is required for weekends and holidays.

Hosts: Kris and Nancy Nayudu
Rooms: 8 (PB) $85-175
Full Breakfast
Credit Cards: A, B, C
Notes: 2, 5, 7, 8, 10, 11, 12, 14

CARMEL

Bed and Breakfast California

P.O. Box 282910, San Francisco, 94128-2910
(415) 696-1690; (800) 872-4500
FAX (415) 696-1699

Carmel Ocean View. These hosts have one room with double bed and shared bath, partial ocean view at a great Carmel location, and they will also make their whole house available (two bedrooms, two baths) by the week. Complete ocean view with a fully equipped kitchen. Breakfast is full and the hosts allow full use of the house— even their bicycles! Rates available for the whole house. $70.

Bed and Breakfast International

P.O. Box 282910, San Francisco, 94128-2910
(415) 696-1690; (800) 872-4500
FAX (415) 696-1699

203. Large contemporary home has several decks and is surrounded by hills. Ten minutes from Carmel. There is a studio guest house with a queen-size lodgepole pine bed, wood-burning fireplace, and private entrance. There is a hot tub on one of the decks for guests to use. Breakfast is brought to the guest house by the host. $98.

207. Contemporary townhouse with fine art and tasteful furnishings on the east side of Highway 1, five minutes from Carmel Beach. The guest room is large and has a queen-size bed and private bath. There is a pool available for guests' use. $78.

Bed and Breakfast San Francisco

P.O. Box 420009, San Francisco, 94142
(415) 931-3083; FAX (415) 921-BBSF (2273)

20. Guests enjoy a glass of wine in front of a roaring fire as they watch the sunset over the Pacific Ocean. The view is magnificent! The hosts, two well-known and successful artists, offer two comfortable rooms with a third should the need arise. They feature private baths and TVs in each room. The area offers a wealth of things to do, from enjoying a walk along the ocean to playing golf at the world-famous Pebble Beach Golf Club. Carmel, Monterey, restaurants, shops, and galleries are just a short distance away. Full breakfast. $100.

21. Nestled on a hilltop with panoramic views overlooking the Monterey Peninsula is a private cottage with deck and hot tub. The trees and skylight create a tree house feeling. The decor is Southwest with a big pine bed, wood-burning stove, sitting area, and a large private bath. Surroundings are very romantic. Restaurants, art galleries, and the famous Monterey coast are only a few minutes away. World-famous Pebble Beach and its golf courses are also close. Enjoy the gorgeous 17-mile drive through Pacific Grove, Pebble Beach, and Carmel. Full breakfast. $105-115.

Carriage House Inn

Junipero between 7th and 8th, 93921
(800) 433-4732

Fresh flowers and country inn flavor. Continental breakfast and newspaper delivered to the room each morning. Wood-burning fireplaces, down comforters. Spacious rooms, many with open-beam ceilings and sunken tubs. Wine and hors d'oeuvres each evening in the library. Carmel's AAA four-diamond inn. A romantic getaway! Two-night minimum stay required for weekends and holidays.

Host: Raul Lopez
Rooms: 13 (PB) $145-250
Continental Breakfast
Credit Cards: All Major
Notes: 2, 5, 9, 11, 12, 14

Eye Openers Bed and Breakfast Reservations

P.O. Box 694, Altadena, 91003-0694
(213) 684-4428; (818) 797-2055
FAX (818) 798-3640

CA-251. This country inn offers 25 large, nicely decorated guest rooms with fireplace, full breakfast, afternoon and evening refreshments. Convenient to all Carmel area attractions. No smoking. Private bath. $105-180.

CA-V11I. Fireplaces and mini-refrigerators in all rooms in a lovely English Tudor-style inn built around a courtyard. Eleven guest rooms and suites with king-, queen-size, or double beds; private baths. Walking distance to beaches. Some suites have kitchenettes. A Continental breakfast is served. $80-145.

CA-D12I. Rustic bed and breakfast near Carmel shops offers twelve rooms and suites with fireplaces. Queen-, king-size, or twin beds and private baths. Continental breakfast. $80-135.

Holiday House

P.O. Box 782, Camino Real at 7th Avenue, 93921
(408) 624-6267

Built in 1905, this comfortable inn is a brown-shingled house on a hillside amid a

7 No smoking; 8 Children welcome; 9 Social drinking allowed; 10 Tennis nearby; 11 Swimming nearby; 12 Golf nearby; 13 Skiing nearby; 14 May be booked through a travel agent.

colorful, well-maintained garden. Six quaint rooms, four with private baths, offer refuge and relaxation. All rooms are furnished with antiques, complimenting the slanted ceilings and dormer windows looking out onto ocean or garden. A full breakfast is served buffet-style daily. Three blocks to beach and one block off Carmel's main street. A cozy getaway right in the heart of charming Carmel.

Hosts: Dieter and Ruth Back
Rooms: 6 (4 PB; 2 SB) $100-125
Full Breakfast
Credit Cards: A, B
Notes: 2, 5, 9, 10, 11, 12

Monte Verde Inn

Ocean Avenue and Monte Verde, P.O. Box 394, 93921
(408) 624-6046; (800) 328-7707

A charming country inn nestled in the heart of Carmel is surrounded by beautiful gardens. The inn has ten rooms, all with unique private baths and king- or queen-size beds. Some rooms have spectacular ocean views, some have wood-burning fireplaces. Only three short blocks to the shimmering Pacific Ocean.

Hosts: Ernest and Wella Aylaian
Rooms: 10 (PB) $95-155
Continental Breakfast
Credit Cards: A, B, C
Notes: 2, 5, 7, 8, 9, 10, 11, 12, 14

The Sandpiper Inn-at-the-Beach

2408 Bay View Avenue, 93923
(408) 624-6433; (800) 633-6433
FAX (408) 624-5964

Within sight and sound of beautiful Carmel Beach. Quiet comfort and luxury in a relaxed atmosphere. Rooms and cottages are filled with antiques and fresh flowers; all have private baths. Some have glorious ocean views, others have fireplaces. Buffet breakfast and complimentary afternoon beverages are served in the comfortable

lounge. Perfect for celebrating anniversaries and special occasions.

Hosts: Graeme and Irene Mackenzie; Kevin Roberts
Rooms: 16 (PB) $95-190
Continental Breakfast
Credit Cards: A, B, C
Notes: 2, 5, 9, 10, 11, 12, 14

Sea View Inn

P.O. Box 4138, 93921
(408) 624-8778

The Sea View Inn, a simple country Victorian, has been welcoming guests for more than 70 years. A quiet, cozy bed and breakfast, the Sea View has eight individually decorated rooms, six with private baths. Near the village and the beach, the Sea View provides a welcoming retreat. A generous Continental breakfast and afternoon tea are complimentary.

Host: Diane Hydorn
Rooms: 8 (6 PB; 2 SB) $85-120
Continental Breakfast
Credit Cards: A, B
Notes: 2, 5, 7, 9, 10, 11, 12

The Stonehouse Inn

P.O. Box 2517, 93921
(408) 624-4569; (800) 748-6618

Built in 1906, this truly lovely stone house is historic, romantic, and close to all of the shops. Guests can hear and see the ocean from upstairs rooms. Experience this luxurious country house in a quiet neighborhood setting. Each room is decorated in soft colors, featuring antiques, cozy quilts, fresh flowers, assorted pillows. There is a sunroom, dining room, front porch, patio, and many gardens. Children over 12 welcome.

Host: Ad Navailles
Rooms: 6 (S3B) $90-149
Full Breakfast
Credit Cards: A, B, C
Notes: 2, 5, 7, 9, 10, 11, 12, 14

Vagabond's House Inn

P.O. Box 2747, 93921
(408) 624-7738; (800) 262-1262 (US reservations);
  (800) 221-1262 (CA reservations)

In the heart of the village, this inn surrounds a Carmel-stone courtyard dominated by large oak trees, plants, ferns, and flowers in profusion. The 11 unique guest rooms are appointed with a combination of collectibles and antiques in a mixture of European elegance and country tradition. Limited smoking allowed.

Hosts: Honey Spence and Jewell Brown
Rooms: 11 (PB) $85-145
Continental Breakfast
Credit Cards: A, B, C
Notes: 2, 5, 6, 9, 10, 11, 12, 14

CARPINTERIA

Carpinteria Beach Condo

1825 Cravens Lane, 93013
(805) 684-1579

In a lush flower-growing valley and across the street from "the world's safest beach." Unit has mountain view. Tropical island decor has a sunset wall mural, fully furnished kitchen, queen-size bed, and color cable TV. Pool, spa, and gas barbecue on complex. Self-catering with beverage provided and fruit from host's ranch. Sleeps four. Eleven miles south of Santa Barbara. Hosts available for tennis, bridge, or tour of their semitropical fruit ranch.

Hosts: Bev and Don Schroeder
Suite: 1 (PB) $60-65

Continental Breakfast
Credit Cards: None
Notes: 2, 5, 7, 8, 9, 10, 11, 12

D&B Schroeder Ranch Bed and Breakfast

1825 Cravens Lane, 93013
(805) 684-1579

Nestled in the foothills of Carpinteria one mile from Highway 101 with an ocean view, the Schroeder ranch produces avocados and semitropical fruit. The guest accommodation has a separate entrance, queen-size bed, color TV, small refrigerator, and private bath. There are decks for viewing the Pacific Ocean, Channel Islands, and gorgeous sunsets. Guests may enjoy strolling around the ten acres, discovering fruit trees and a year-round creek. There is a spa in a lush tropical setting to soothe weary travelers. The "world's safest beach' is two miles away. Santa Barbara is twelve miles away. The hosts are ready for a bridge game or tennis.

Hosts: Bev and Don Schroeder
Room: 1 (PB) $60-65
Full Breakfast
Credit Cards: None
Notes: 2, 5, 7, 9, 10, 11

CATALINA

Bed and Breakfast California

P.O. Box 282910, San Francisco, 94128-2910
(415) 696-1690; (800) 872-4500
FAX (415) 696-1699

Canyon Resort on Catalina. This elegant resort "on the island" is in a quaint canyon overlooking Avalon. Rooms include king- or queen-sized beds, private baths, TVs, and phones. Heated pool, Jacuzzi, and sauna. Hosts provide complimentary shuttles to and from town. Accommodations do not include breakfast. Special midweek rates. $55-135.

7 No smoking; 8 Children welcome; 9 Social drinking allowed; 10 Tennis nearby; 11 Swimming nearby; 12 Golf nearby; 13 Skiing nearby; 14 May be booked through a travel agent.

CATALINA ISLAND

Bed and Breakfast California

P.O. Box 282910, San Francisco, 94128-2910
(415) 696-1690; (800) 872-4500
FAX (415) 696-1699

Inn by the Sea in Avalon. Old fashioned with modern conveniences, king- and queen-size beds have fireplaces and spa in some rooms. Romantic honeymoon packages and weddings (the host is a licensed minister) are also available. Complimentary muffins, juice, and coffee. $75-125.

Rooms with a View. This affordable spot on the hill has 20 rooms, all with private baths, many with whirlpool tubs and ocean views. Accommodations are motel-style, not fancy, but include Continental breakfast. $65-85.

Historic Old Hotel. This 22-bedroom inn was the original home of Zane Grey was converted to a hotel in the 1950s. High on a hill, it has an incredible view of the mountain and the bay. Each room is unique, mostly done in Western style with interesting art and a library of all Zane Grey's books. Facilities include a mountaintop pool, living room, and social area, where a Continental breakfast is served. $75-95.

CLAREMONT (PASADENA)

Bed and Breakfast California

P.O. Box 282910, San Francisco, 94128-2910
(415) 696-1690; (800) 872-4500
FAX (415) 696-1699

Family Home in Claremont. Close to the colleges and the mountains, this sprawling ranch-style home features two guest rooms, one with private bath and one that shares with the family kids. Guests' children are welcome. A pool, a fenced yard, and lots of toys are available. A fresh, healthy breakfast served daily. $50-60.

CLEAR LAKE

Muktip Manor

12540 Lakeshore Drive, 95422
(707) 994-9571

Suite consisting of one bedroom, bath, kitchenette, sitting room, TV, and deck. Private beach on the largest lake in California, with canoes and bicycles available. Several golf courses are in the county. Hiking, biking, and rock hounding. One hundred ten miles north of San Francisco, near five wineries.

Hosts: Jerry and Nadine Schiffman
Room: 1 (PB) $65
Full Breakfast
Credit Cards: None
Notes: 2, 5, 6, 9, 10, 11, 12

CLOVERDALE

Ye Olde' Shelford House

29955 River Road, 95425
(707) 894-5956; (800) 833-6479

This country Victorian in the wine country is just like Grandma's house, with six beautifully decorated rooms, private baths, homemade quilts, family antiques, full delicious breakfasts, flowers, dolls, hot tub, and pool. For an extra charge, take Grandpa's 1929 Model A wine tour that concludes with a picnic lunch.

Host: Sheila Haverson
Rooms: 6 (PB) $90-115
Full Breakfast
Credit Cards: A, B
Notes: 2, 5, 7, 9, 11, 12, 14

COLUMBIA

Columbia City Hotel

Box 1870, 95310
(209) 532-1479

NOTES: Credit cards accepted: A MasterCard; B Visa; C American Express; D Discover; E Diners Club; F Other; 2 Personal checks accepted; 3 Lunch available; 4 Dinner available; 5 Open all year; 6 Pets welcome;

In the heart of a historic gold rush town that is preserved and protected by the state of California, this impeccable inn is surrounded by relics of the past. All rooms have been restored to reflect the 1850s. Downstairs, the highly acclaimed restaurant and always inviting What Cheer Saloon provide a haven for travelers seeking comfort and gracious hospitality. All rooms have half-baths; hall showers. Closed Christmas Eve and Christmas Day.

Host: Tom Bender
Rooms: 10 (PB) $70-95
Continental Breakfast
Credit Cards: A, B, C, D
Notes: 2, 4, 7, 8, 9, 10, 11, 12, 13, 14

Fallon Hotel

Washington Street, 95310
(209) 532-1470

Since 1857, the historic Fallon Hotel has provided a home away from home to countless visitors. Authentically restored to its Victorian grandeur, most of the furnishings are original to the inn. Several rooms have private balconies, and all rooms have half-baths. Baskets of toiletries, robes, and slippers are provided for the showers off the hallway. One handicapped room available. In the heart of a state-restored gold rush town. Adjacent to the Fallon Theatre, which provides year-round productions. Call or write for price information.

Host: Tom Bender
Rooms: 14 (SB) $55-95
Continental Breakfast
Credit Cards: A, B, C, D
Notes: 2, 5, 7, 8, 9, 10, 11, 12, 13, 14

CORONA

Bed and Breakfast California

P.O. Box 282910, San Francisco, 94128-2910
(415) 696-1690; (800) 872-4500
FAX (415) 696-1699

The Smith House. This sunny, colorful house is only a mile from the resort at Glean Ivy Hot Springs. The guest suite features a bedroom, sitting room, and private bath. The deck includes a koi pond, and the dining area holds a view of the entire valley. The sitting room can also sleep a child or two. Full breakfast. $85.

CRESTLINE

Bed and Breakfast California

P.O. Box 282910, San Francisco, 94128-2910
(415) 696-1690; (800) 872-4500
FAX (415) 696-1699

A Quaint and Historic Resort in the Forest. On an acre of wooded forest, this lodge offers individually decorated cabin suites. Enjoy a living room with fireplace, color TV with HBO, and fully equipped kitchen with coffee maker and complimentary coffee. Celebrate the four seasons with access to a beach with water slide, boating, sailing, windsurfing, fishing, hiking, and downhill and cross-country skiing. Nearby picturesque village offers antique shops, movies, and fine restaurants. $77-97.

Eye Openers Bed and Breakfast Reservations

P.O. Box 694, Altadena, 91003-0694
(213) 684-4428; (818) 797-2055
FAX (818) 798-3640

CE-O2. Model train enthusiasts will enjoy their stay at this unique bed and breakfast, a former 1922 saloon whose decor now features model trains. Breakfast is brought by a model train. Guests enjoy their stay in the mountains with lakes, hiking, boating, fishing, and skiing nearby. Two guest rooms with queen-size beds and private or shared bath. No smoking. $125-150.

7 No smoking; 8 Children welcome; 9 Social drinking allowed; 10 Tennis nearby; 11 Swimming nearby; 12 Golf nearby; 13 Skiing nearby; 14 May be booked through a travel agent.

CUPERTINO

Eye Openers
Bed and Breakfast
Reservations

P.O. Box 694, Altadena, 91003-0694
(213) 684-4428; (818) 797-2055
FAX (818) 798-3640

CU-M2. Townhouse with pool and within commuting distance to San Jose, Stanford, and San Francisco. Two guest rooms have Country English decor. Choice of breakfast and other amenities. Private or shared baths. No smoking. $40-50.

DAVENPORT

New Davenport
Bed and Breakfast

31 Davenport Avenue, 95017
(408) 425-1818; (408) 426-4122

Halfway between Carmel-Monterey and San Francisco, on Coast Highway 1. Small, rural, coastal town noted for whale watching, wind surfing, Ano Nuevo Elephant Seal State Reserve, hiking, bicycling, and beach access. Wonderful restaurant and gift store with unusual treasures and jewelry.

Hosts: Bruce and Marcia McDougal
Rooms: 12 (PB) $70-120
Full Breakfast
Credit Cards: A, B, C
Notes: 2, 3, 4, 5, 7, 8, 9, 11

DAVIS

University Inn
Bed and Breakfast

340 A Street, 95616
(916) 756-8648; (800) 756-8648

Adjacent to the University of California-Davis, this country inn offers a charming escape from a busy college town in a homelike setting. Each room has a private bath, telephone, refrigerator, cable TV, and microwave oven. There are complimentary chocolates, beverages, and flowers. A generous Continental plus breakfast is served. Inquire to see what type of pets accepted. Limited smoking allowed.

Hosts: Lynda and Ross Yancher
Rooms: 4 (PB) $55
Continental Breakfast
Credit Cards: A, B, C, D, E, F
Notes: 2, 5, 8, 9, 10, 11, 12, 14

DEATH VALLEY

Bed and Breakfast
California

P.O. Box 282910, San Francisco, 94128-2910
(415) 696-1690; (800) 872-4500
FAX (415) 696-1699

Death Valley Oasis. This inn and ranch resort stand as an oasis deep in the desert. Accommodations are elegant and formal, but the environment is simple and serene with Date palms, flower gardens, and classic Spanish architecture. Tennis, swimming, biking, dancing, volleyball, carriage rides, and even a video arcade. $70-195.

DEL MAR

The Blue Door

13707 Durango Drive, 92014
(619) 755-3819

Enjoy New England charm in a quiet Southern California setting. Lower-level two-room suite with king-size bed, private bath, and cozy sitting room opening onto bougainvillaea-splashed patio with open vista of Torrey Pines Reserve Canyon. Only 20 miles north of San Diego. Creative full breakfast. Children over 16 welcome.

Hosts: Bob and Anna Belle Schock
Suite: 1 (PB) $60-70
Full Breakfast
Credit Cards: None
Notes: 2, 5, 7, 9, 10, 11, 12

NOTES: Credit cards accepted: A MasterCard; B Visa; C American Express; D Discover; E Diners Club;
F Other; 2 Personal checks accepted; 3 Lunch available; 4 Dinner available; 5 Open all year; 6 Pets welcome;

Eye Openers
Bed and Breakfast
Reservations

P.O. Box 694, Altadena, 91003-0694
(213) 684-4428; (818) 797-2055
FAX (818) 798-3640

DM-R101. Romantic getaway in a lovely seaside village just north of San Diego offers a choice of ten rooms, many with an ocean view and one with a fireplace. Enjoy a Continental plus breakfast, afternoon refreshments, a walk on the beach, or a trip to the racetrack or nearby renowned flower-growing areas. Private and shared bath. $85-150.

Gull's Nest

P.O. Box 1056, 92014
(619) 259-4863

Gull's Nest rustic hideaway is a contemporary wood home surrounded by pines with a beautiful ocean and bird sanctuary view from two upper decks. There is a third deck on the studio apartment. Home is decorated with many paintings, mosaics, and wood carvings. Fifteen minutes from La Jolla and five minutes from Del Mar. Close to I-5, and just 20 minutes from the San Diego Zoo and airport. Children over five welcome.

Hosts: Michael and Constance Segel
Rooms: 2 (PB) $75-95
Full Breakfast
Credit Cards: None
Notes: 2, 5, 7, 9, 10, 11, 12

DESERT HOT SPRINGS

Bed and Breakfast
California

P.O. Box 282910, San Francisco, 94128-2910
(415) 696-1690; (800) 872-4500
FAX (415) 696-1699

Oasis at the Hot Springs. This peaceful, sunny house was designed to welcome visitors. Three guest rooms have queen-size beds; one has private bath and two share. Owners are a skilled woodworker and a gourmet cook. Breakfast is served poolside. $55-75.

Travellers Repose

66920 First Street, P.O. Box 655, 92240
(619) 329-9584

Bay windows, gingerbread trim, and stained glass decorate this two-story Victorian home. The interior is color coordinated throughout, blending natural woods and wallpapers. The three individually decorated bedrooms are spacious and all have queen-size beds. Guests enjoy the view of desert floor and mountains rising to 11,000 feet. Amenities include a patio, gardens, and spa. Desert Hot Springs is famous for its natural hot mineral waters. Palm Springs is only minutes away, with its museums, shopping, famous restaurants, celebrities, golf tournaments, tennis tournaments, theaters, and stage shows.

Hosts: Marian Relkoff
Rooms: 3 (1 PB; 2 SB) $55-75
Continental Breakfast
Credit Cards: None
Notes: 2, 7, 9, 10, 11, 12, 14

DULZURA

Brookside Farm
Bed and Breakfast Inn

1373 Marron Valley Road, 91917
(619) 468-3043

A country farmhouse furnished with collectibles, handmade quilts, and stained glass. Tree-shaded terraces by a stream, farm animals, gardens, hot tub in the grape arbor. Perfect for country walks. Close to Tecate, Mexico, and 35 minutes from San Diego. Two-night minimum stay required for holidays and some rooms.

Hosts: Edd and Sally Guishard
Rooms: 10 (PB) $55-115

7 No smoking; 8 Children welcome; 9 Social drinking allowed; 10 Tennis nearby; 11 Swimming nearby; 12 Golf nearby; 13 Skiing nearby; 14 May be booked through a travel agent.

Full Breakfast
Credit Cards: A, B, C, D
Notes: 2, 4, 5, 7, 9, 12, 14

ELK

Griffin House at Greenwood Cove

5910 South Highway 1, P.O. Box 172, 95432
(707) 877-3422

The seven cottages and main house (now Bridget Dolan's Pub) were built between 1890 and 1920; three of the cozy, informal cottages have spectacular views of Greenwood Cove, while the other four are nestled in a peaceful garden setting. All cottages have wood-burning stoves and private baths. A hearty breakfast is delivered to each door between 8:30 and 9:00 A.M. The Pub serves dinner seasonally.

Host: Leslie Griffin Lawson
Rooms: 7 (PB) $75-150
Full Breakfast
Credit Cards: A, B
Notes: 2, 7, 8, 9, 10, 11, 12, 14

Sandpiper House Inn

5520 South Highway One, Box 149, 95432
(707) 877-3587

Built in 1916 on the bluffs of the rugged Mendocino Coast, this inn boasts rich redwood paneling and beamed ceilings in the living and dining rooms. It is tastefully furnished in the style of a European country inn and offers stunning ocean views over perennial gardens and private beach access. The guest rooms are all beautifully appointed with antiques and comfortable, traditional furnishings.

Hosts: Clair and Richard Melrose
Rooms: 5 (PB) $110-215
Full Breakfast
Credit Cards: A, B, C, D
Notes: 2, 5, 7, 9, 10, 12

ENCINITAS

Bed and Breakfast California

P.O. Box 282910, San Francisco, 94128-2910
(415) 696-1690; (800) 872-4500
fax (415) 696-1699

At Home in Encinitas. A quick walk from Moonlight Beach, this quaint bed and breakfast is decorated in Southwestern style. Each of the five rooms has a private entrance and a private bath. Two rooms have sitting areas, fireplaces, kitchenettes, decks, and hot tubs have oceanview. Encinitas is a short trip from Del Mar, La Jolla, and downtown San Diego. $75-150.

Eye Openers Bed and Breakfast Reservations

P.O. Box 694, Altadena, 91003-0694
(213) 684-4428; (818) 797-2055
FAX (818) 798-3640

EN-S4I. In renowned flower-growing area in Southern California, this family-run bed and breakfast with ocean views, Southwestern decor, and a relaxed atmosphere has large rooms, an apartment, and penthouse with Jacuzzi. They have queen- or king-size beds and private baths. Continental plus breakfast and afternoon refreshments are served. Walking distance to the ocean. No smoking. $75-150.

SeaBreeze Bed and Breakfast

121 North Vulcan Avenue, 92024
(619) 944-0318

Encinitas's first bed and breakfast. A true find, squeaky clean. "An absolute treasure," said KABC talk radio. Features in this contemporary two-story oceanview home are three bedrooms all with private baths, downstairs that has common sitting room with a fireplace and kitchenette, done in southwest custom-designed handcrafted furnishings and decor. A new addition to the inn is the penthouse, a true "boudoir," with a king-size bed, cable TV and VCR, whirlpool tub and shower, plus an eight-foot spa on an oceanview balcony. Also, an upstairs one-bedroom apartment with fireplace, kitchen, and double soaking tub equipped with bubble bath and champagne. There is a lovely sun deck in the front yard with a waterfall and fish pond. Intimate wedding grotto available. Make reservations early.

Host: Kirsten Richter
Rooms: 5 (PB) $75-150
Continental Breakfast
Credit Cards: A, B, D
Notes: 2, 5, 8, 9, 10, 11, 12, 14

ESCONDIDO

Eye Openers Bed and Breakfast Reservations

P.O. Box 694, Altadena, 91003-0694
(213) 684-4428; (818) 797-2055
FAX (818) 798-3640

ES-W51. Enjoy hiking or jogging on the 48 acres of this country bed and breakfast near San Diego's Wild Animal Park. Convenient to sightseeing in San Diego and wineries in Southern California and many local recreational areas. A full breakfast and afternoon refreshments are included. Five guest rooms have queen-size beds and private or shared baths. No smoking. $88-128.

EUREKA

"An Elegant Victorian Mansion"

1406 C Street, 95501
(707) 444-3144; (707) 442-5594

An award-winning 1888 National Historic Landmark featuring spectacular Ginger-

"An Elegant Victorian Mansion"

bread exteriors, opulent Victorian interiors, antique furnishings, and an acclaimed French-gourmet breakfast. Eureka's most prestigious and luxurious bed and breakfast experience—exclusively for the non-smoker. Breathtakingly authentic, with all the nostalgic trimmings of a century ago, this meticulously restored Victorian masterpiece offers both history and hospitality, combined with romance and pampering. Enjoy the regal splendor of this spectacular state historic site, and indulge in four-star luxury. Eureka's only AAA officially appointed and recommended bed and breakfast has also been rated by inn-goers statewide as the "Best Bed & Breakfast in California." With "The most stunningly spectacular interiors in the state," World Traveler magazine calls it "The best lodging value in California." Complimentary horseless-carriage ride, bicycles, sauna, and security parking. Ocean views, beaches, Redwood National Park, antique shops, and factory-outlet shopping nearby.

Hosts: Doug and Lily Vieyra
Rooms: 4 (2 PB; 2 SB) $75-145
Full Breakfast
Credit Cards: A, B
Notes: 5, 7, 9, 10, 11, 12, 13, 14

Bed and Breakfast California

P.O. Box 282910, San Francisco, 94128-2910
(415) 696-1690; (800) 872-4500
FAX (415) 696-1699

Weaver's Studio in Eureka. Play croquet at this studio home built in 1883. Amenities include a Japanese garden, fresh gourmet food, antique spinning wheels, and a soaking tub in room. Three rooms, two of which share a bath, are available. The hosts have a full weaving studio in the house and love to show guests around. Call for rates.

Eye Openers
Bed and Breakfast
Reservations

P.O. Box 694, Altadena, 91003-0694
(213) 684-4428; (818) 797-2055
FAX (818) 798-3640

WE-4SI. This 1883 Victorian offers old-fashioned hospitality, wonderful gardens, and features a studio of a fiber artist. Full breakfast is served. Four guest rooms have king- or queen-size, or twin beds. Private and shared baths. No smoking. $55-110.

EU-C30I. These charming 1981 and 1986 re-creations of 1880 Victorian mansions offer superb hospitality and excellent full breakfasts. This seaport town offers many recreational activities, including fishing, hiking, golf, biking, and museums. One site has seven guest rooms and the other has 23 guest rooms with private and shared baths. King- or queen-size or double beds available. No smoking. $80-350.

Heuer's Victorian Inn

1302 E Street, 95501
(707) 442-7334

This Queen Anne Victorian was built in 1893 and restored to its present splendor in 1980. Just like being transported back in time to an earlier era. For that quiet, relaxing time, it's a must.

Hosts: Charles and Ausbern Heuer
Rooms: 3 (1 PB; 2 SB) $75
Continental Breakfast
Credit Cards: A, B, C, D, E, F
Notes: 2, 5, 7, 9, 10, 12

Old Town
Bed and Breakfast Inn

1521 Third Street, 95501
(707) 445-3951; (800) 331-5098
FAX (707) 445-8346

The uniquely Victorian seaport of Eureka is the setting for this 1871 Greek Revival Italianate two-story Victorian. A short stroll to Humboldt Bay brings nostalgic memories of the great fleets of sailing ships that once carried loads of redwood lumber to San Francisco and the world and brought the bounty of the fishing fleets home. Only two blocks from lumber baron William Carson's famous mansion. Teak hot tub, evening tea, and homemade cookies. Bring cameras and appetites. Single and corporate rates available. Children over 10 welcome.

Hosts: Leigh and Diane Benson
Rooms: 6 (4 PB; 2 SB) $75-150
Full Breakfast
Credit Cards: A, B, C, D, E, F
Notes: 2, 7, 9, 10, 11, 12, 14

Upstairs at the Waterfront

102 F Street, 95501
(707) 443-9190

Upstairs at the Waterfront, offering a beautiful bay view, was built in 1892 and restored in 1992. The upstairs, a brothel in the 1950s, has been completely rebuilt as a 1,500-square-foot salon that is rented as a two-bedroom, two-bath bed and breakfast. The space is ideal for two couples traveling together or can be completely private for two separate parties. The downstairs Cafe Waterfront offers a friendly relaxed atmosphere and some of the best food in Humboldt County. Breakfast is served downstairs.

Host: Diane Smith
Rooms: 2 (PB) $75-250
Full Breakfast
Credit Cards: A, B
Notes: 2, 3, 4, 5, 7, 9, 12

NOTES: Credit cards accepted: A MasterCard; B Visa; C American Express; D Discover; E Diners Club; F Other; 2 Personal checks accepted; 3 Lunch available; 4 Dinner available; 5 Open all year; 6 Pets welcome;

A Weaver's Inn

1440 B Street, 95501
(707) 443-8119

A Weaver's Inn, the home and studio of a fiber artist and her husband, is a stately Queen Anne Colonial Revival house built in 1883 and remodeled in 1907. Placed in a spacious fenced garden, it is airy and light, but cozy and warm when veiled by wisps of fog. Visit the studio, try the spinning wheel before the fire, or weave on the antique loom before having refreshments.

Hosts: Bob and Dorothy Swendeman
Rooms: 4 (2 PB; 2 SB) $65-110
Full Breakfast
Credit Cards: A, B, C, D
Notes: 2, 5, 6, 8, 9, 14

FERNDALE

The Gingerbread Mansion

400 Berding Street, P.O. Box 40, 95536
(707) 786-4000

The Gingerbread Mansion Inn is well known as one of America's most photographed homes. Its striking Victorian architecture trimmed with gingerbread, its colorful peach and yellow paint, and its surrounding English gardens all make the Gingerbread Mansion a photographer's delight. It is an understatement to say that the interiors are also spectacular. Rated four diamonds by AAA. Rates are subject to change.

Hosts: Ken and Sandie Torbert
Rooms: 6 (PB) $130-380
Suites: 5 (PB)
Full Breakfast
Credit Cards: A, B, C
Notes: 2, 5, 7, 9, 10, 12, 14

Shaw House
Bed and Breakfast Inn

703 Main Street, P.O. Box 1125, 95536
(707) 786-9958; FAX (707) 786-9958

An 1854 carpenter Gothic built by the founders of Ferndale, Shaw House is on an acre in a tranquil parklike estate with Victorian gardens. Guests can enjoy the gazebo, bicycles, and croquet. Coffee or tea at check-in and before a full breakfast in the morning. The hosts also offer umbrellas, robes, slippers, and much more. Within walking distance of shops and restaurants, and a half hour from the Avenue of the Giants. Three-crown rating from ABBA, and three-star rating from Northern California Best Places.

Hosts: Norma and Ben Bessingpas
Rooms: 6 (PB) $75-135
Full Breakfast
Credit Cards: A, B, C
Notes: 2, 5, 7, 9, 12, 14

FISH CAMP

Scotty's Bed and Breakfast

1223 Hwy 41, P.O. Box 82, 93623
(209) 683-6936

Guests will enjoy a cozy room with a private entrance and bath, full or queen-size bed, river rock fireplace, microwave, Continental breakfast, beautiful yard, barbecue, creekside view, fishing, golf, skiing, historical train ride, back country hiking, biking, and stables. All of this and more is only two miles from Yosemite National Park.

Host: Scott B. Sanders
Rooms: 2 (1 PB; 1 SB) $55-75
Continental Breakfast
Credit Cards: None
Notes: 5, 8, 9, 10, 11, 12, 13

FORT BRAGG

Avalon House

561 Stewart Street, 95437
(707) 964-5555; (800) 964-5556

A 1905 Craftsman house, built completely of redwood and extensively remodeled in 1988, Avalon House is furnished with a mix of antiques and willow furniture. The emphasis here is on luxury and comfort: fireplaces, whirlpool tubs, down comforters and pillows, good bedside lights, as well as mood lights to create a romantic ambience. The inn is in a quiet residential area three blocks from the Pacific Ocean and one block from Highway 1. The Skunk Train Depot is two blocks away.

Host: Anne Sorrells
Rooms: 6 (PB) $70-135
Full Breakfast
Credit Cards: A, B, C, D
Notes: 2, 5, 7, 8, 9, 14

Bed and Breakfast California

P.O. Box 282910, San Francisco, 94128-2910
(415) 696-1690; (800) 872-4500
FAX (415) 696-1699

Huckleberry House. Four suites are available, three designed for families of up to four people, with queen-size beds, lofts, and lots of gardens and hiking trails. Guests enjoy a full, fresh breakfast and are just a short walk from the ocean. $95-120.

Eye Openers Bed and Breakfast Reservations

P.O. Box 694, Altadena, 91003-0694
(213) 684-4428; (818) 797-2055
FAX (818) 798-3640

FB-G14I. Landmark redwood building has 14 guest rooms, all with private baths. King, queen, double, and twin beds are available. Near scenic railway, state parks, beaches, fishing, and hiking, and within walking distance to shops and galleries. Full breakfast. No smoking. $75-170.

Glass Beach Bed and Breakfast Inn

726 North Main Street, 95437
(707) 964-6774

Gracious 1920 Craftsman-style home. cozy rooms all with private baths, some with fireplaces. Wonderful country-style breakfast is prepared to order. Melt one's cares away in the private spa. Beaches, shops, restaurants, museum, and the famous Shunk Train are nearby.

Host: Nancy Cardenas
Rooms: 9 (PB) $80-125
Full Breakfast
Credit Cards: A, B, D
Notes: 2, 5, 8, 9, 10, 11, 12, 14

Grey Whale Inn

615 North Main Street, 95437
(707) 964-0640; (800) 382-7244 (reservations)

Handsome four-story Mendocino Coast landmark since 1915. Cozy rooms to expansive suites, all private baths. Ocean, garden, or hill and city views. Some have fireplaces and/or TVs; one has whirlpool tub; all have telephones. Recreation area: pool table, books, fireside lounge, and TV theater. Conference room seats 16 people. Friendly, helpful staff. Buffet breakfast features Colette's Blue-ribbon coffeecakes. Relaxed seaside charm, five blocks from beach. Celebrate a special occasion at the fabled Mendocino Coast! Mobil three-star rating. ABBA three crowns. Limited facilities for children.

Host: Colette Bailey
Rooms: 14 (PB) $80-150
Full Breakfast
Credit Cards: A, B, C, D, F
Notes: 2, 5, 7, 9, 10, 11, 12, 14

Pudding Creek Inn

700 North Main Street, 95437
(707) 964-9529; (800) 227-9529

These two Victorian homes were built in 1884 by a Russian count and are connected by a lush enclosed garden. All rooms are comfortably decorated in Victorian style. All have private baths; some have fireplaces. Exceptional accommodations include personal service, hospitality, and

Pudding Creek Inn

special emphasis on privacy. Within walking distance of Glass Beach, Pudding Creek, and downtown shops and restaurants. Guest house museum and Skunk Train Depot are nearby.

Hosts: Garry and Carole Anloff
Rooms: 10 (PB) $65-140
Full Breakfast
Credit Cards: A, B, C, D
Notes: 2, 5, 7, 8, 9, 10, 11, 12, 14

FREMONT

Lord Bradley's Inn

43344 Mission Boulevard, 94539
(415) 490-0520

This Victorian is nestled below Mission Peak, adjacent to the Mission San Jose. Numerous olive trees on the property were planted by the Ohlone Indians. Common

room, garden, patio. Parking in rear. Take the bus or Bay Area Rapid Transit to San Francisco for a day.

Hosts: Keith and Anne Bradley Medeiros
Rooms: 8 (PB) $65-75
Continental Breakfast
Credit Cards: A, B, D
Notes: 2, 5, 7, 9, 10, 12, 14

GARDEN VALLEY

Mountainside Bed and Breakfast

5821 Spanish Flat Road, 95633
(800) 237-0832

Between Placerville and Georgetown, this old country home is in the center of 80 acres with a 180-degree view. Three guest rooms have private baths and a large attic with bath and deck can sleep eight. A full country breakfast is served in the dining room or sunny breakfast room. Guests can enjoy the cozy parlor with fireplace and piano or spa after a day of rafting, hiking, or fishing. Limited smoking allowed.

Hosts: Paul and Mary Ellen Mello
Rooms: 4 (PB) $70-80
Full Breakfast
Credit Cards: A, B
Notes: 2, 5, 9, 10, 11, 14

GEORGETOWN

Bed and Breakfast California

P.O. Box 282910, San Francisco, 94128-2910
(415) 696-1690; (800) 872-4500
FAX (415) 696-1699

The Dees' House. This bed and breakfast is on 18 acres of forested land between Placerville and Auburn, only an hour northeast of Sacramento. The hosts have three guest rooms, one of which is a full suite, including a kitchen. The atmosphere is extremely friendly. A full country breakfast is served. $60-80.

7 No smoking; 8 Children welcome; 9 Social drinking allowed; 10 Tennis nearby; 11 Swimming nearby; 12 Golf nearby; 13 Skiing nearby; 14 May be booked through a travel agent.

GEYSERVILLE

Campbell Ranch Inn

1475 Canyon Road, 95441
(707) 857-3476

A thirty-five-acre country setting in the heart of Sonoma County wine country. Spectacular view, beautiful gardens, tennis court, swimming pool, hot tub, and bicycles. Five spacious rooms, one with fireplace. All rooms have private baths, king-size beds, balconies, fresh flowers, and fruit. Air-conditioned. Refreshments and homemade evening dessert. Full breakfast served on the terrace. Teenagers welcome. Color brochure available. Minimum-stay requirements for weekends.

Hosts: Mary Jane and Jerry Campbell
Rooms: 5 (PB) $100-165
Full Breakfast
Credit Cards: A, B, C
Notes: 2, 5, 7, 9, 10, 11, 12, 14

Isis Oasis Lodge

20889 Geyserville Avenue, 95441
(707) 857-3524

A classic lodge of 12 rooms, lounge with fireplace, meeting room, and game area. A pool spa and sauna in a secluded garden. Acres of land with exotic birds and animals to play with. A honeymoon cottage with fireplace and private hot tub. The Retreat House, Vineyard House, and Tower House in addition to yurts, a tipi, and a wine barrel room give guests a variety of options. Wine and country breakfasts. Group rates.

Hosts: Loreon Vigne and Paul Ramses
Rooms: 23 (7 PB; 16 SB) $55-130
Full Breakfast
Credit Cards: A, B, C
Notes: 2, 3, 4, 5, 6, 7, 8, 9, 10, 11, 12

GLEN ELLEN

Bed and Breakfast California

P.O. Box 282910, San Francisco, 94128-2910
(415) 696-1690; (800) 872-4500
FAX (415) 696-1699

Secluded Country Bed and Breakfast. This bed and breakfast is only a mile from the little village of Glen Ellen, on an acre of parklike secluded gardens. The huge guest suite has a bedroom with a brass bed, sitting room with fireplace, cathedral ceilings, cable TV, private bath, and a refrigerator stocked with wine and goodies. Breakfast is served by the pool, on the deck, or in the room. $85.

GROVELAND

Berkshire Inn

19950 Highway 120, P.O. Box 207, 95321
(209) 962-6744

This beautiful 12,000-square-foot house sits on 20 acres of pine- and oak-covered mountains. Massive open beam construction, loungers, breakfast area, and breathtaking views create a warm and cozy environment. Offering large bedrooms, all with private baths, private entrances, queen-size beds, and wooden decks. An extended Continental breakfast is served. Just minutes away from Yosemite National Park. Near boating, water and snow skiing, white-water rafting, golf courses, and historical towns and landmarks. No smoking in rooms.

Hosts: Carl, Dody, Kim, Mike, and Christopher Yates
Rooms: 10 (PB) $79
Continental Breakfast
Credit Cards: A, B, D
Notes: 2, 5, 8, 9, 10, 11, 12, 13, 14

The Groveland Hotel

18767 Main Street, P.O. Box 289, 95321
(209) 962-4000; (800) 273-3314
fax (209) 962-6674

Yosemite National Park is 23 miles away, on Highway 120. The two buildings, an 1849 adobe and a 1914 frame building, have been completely restored. They house 14 guest rooms, a California seasonal fresh gourmet restaurant, and a conference room. Furnishings are European antiques and down comforters. Each room has terry-cloth robes, upscale linens, and very Victorian decor. There are also three suites with fireplaces and Jacuzzis. The courtyard is a garden setting for weddings, parties, and outdoor dining. Golf, tennis, swimming, fishing, hiking, skiing, and world-class white-water rafting are minutes away. The conference room is available for meetings of up to 25 people. Complimentary wine is served in the evenings.

Hosts: Peggy and Grover Mosley
Rooms: 17 (PB) $85-165
Continental Breakfast
Credit Cards: A, B, C, D, E
Notes: 2, 4, 5, 6, 7, 8, 9, 10, 11, 12, 13, 14

GUALALA

North Coast Country Inn
34591 South Highway 1, 95445
(707) 884-4537; (800) 959-4537

A cluster of rustic redwood buildings with ocean views. Rooms feature queen-size beds, fireplaces, kitchenettes, private baths, decks, and private entries. The inn has a hot tub and gazebo. Full breakfast is served in guest rooms. Golf, hiking, horseback riding, fishing, and beaches are nearby. Minimum stay requirements for weekends and holidays.

Hosts: Loren and Nancy Flanagan
Rooms: 4 (PB) $148.50
Full Breakfast
Credit Cards: A, B, C
Notes: 2, 5, 7, 9, 10, 11, 12, 14

GUERNEVILLE

Bed and Breakfast International
P.O. Box 282910, San Francisco, 94128-2910
(415) 696-1690; (800) 872-4500
FAX (415) 696-1699

304. A vacation home in one of Northern California's most beautiful wine country areas. Very peaceful atmosphere, high quality decor, fireplace, and hot tub. Sleeps six. Walk to the Russian River. $125.

Ridenhour Ranch House Inn
12850 River Road, 95446
(707) 887-1033

A 1906 inn on two and one-quarter acres of trees, gardens, and meadow in the Russian River area of Northern California. Each room is decorated in country English and American antiques, quilts, plants, and fresh flowers. The area has many restaurants, and dinner can be arranged at the inn.

Hosts: Diane and Fritz Rechberger
Rooms: 8 (PB) $95-130
Full Breakfast
Credit Cards: A, B, C
Notes: 2, 4, 5, 7 12, 14

Santa Nella House
Pocket Creek Canyon, 12130 Highway 16, 95446
(707) 869-9488

Santa Nella is nestled in a redwood forest where quiet and beauty prevail. Enjoy a short walk to the Russian River and Korbel Champagne Cellars when the summer bridge is in. The house is a bucolic Country Victorian, circa 1870, with a grand wrap-around veranda and restored turn-of-the-century guest rooms—all with wood-burning fireplaces. A well-stocked library is available and a large country kitchen with wood-burning stove and a bay window, as well as a parlor/music room, provide a pleasant atmosphere for friendly conversation. Large country breakfasts consisting of fresh fruits, juices, freshly ground and brewed coffee, various egg dishes, waffles, and homemade cakes are served in the dining room or on the veranda and gazebo on warm mornings.

Hosts: Ed and Joyce Ferrington
Rooms: 4 (PB) $90-100
Full Breakfast
Credit Cards: A, B, C
Notes: 2, 9, 10, 12, 14

7 No smoking; 8 Children welcome; 9 Social drinking allowed; 10 Tennis nearby; 11 Swimming nearby; 12 Golf nearby; 13 Skiing nearby; 14 May be booked through a travel agent.

HALF MOON BAY

Bed and Breakfast California

P.O. Box 282910, San Francisco, 94128-2910
(415) 696-1690; (800) 872-4500
FAX (415) 696-1699

Old Time Inn in Half Moon Bay. A beautifully restored, charming 1899 Queen Anne Victorian, this inn offers guest rooms named for familiar herbs. All of the rooms are unique, with lovely antiques, stuffed animals, fresh flowers, and private baths. Cozy fireplaces and whirlpool baths are in most of the rooms. Full breakfasts are served each morning in the parlor, with a background of classical music. Located on historic Main Street, the inn is near shops, restaurants, and galleries. Call for rates.

Old Thyme Inn

779 Main Street, 94019
(415) 726-1616

This lovingly restored 1899 Queen Anne Victorian is on historic Main Street in Old Town. Seven unique rooms with lovely antiques, whimsical stuffed bears, fresh flowers, cozy fireplaces, and/or luxurious whirlpool tubs, and some rooms have TVs. Private suite has TV, VCR, stereo, and refrigerator. Delicious breakfasts are served in the parlor. Walking distance to beaches, art galleries, local shops, and gourmet restaurants. Local activities include hiking, bird watching, surfing, golf, horseback riding, and whale watching.

Hosts: George and Marcia Dempsey
Rooms: 7 (PB) $65-210
Full Breakfast
Credit Cards: A, B
Notes: 2, 5, 7, 8, 9, 10, 11, 12, 14

Zaballa House

324 Main Street, 94019
(415) 726-9123

The first house built in Half Moon Bay (1859), standing at the entrance to historic Main Street, has been carefully restored into a bed and breakfast. The inn is set in a garden across the street from shopping and two fine restaurants. Guests enjoy the Victorian decor in rooms with high ceilings and antiques, some with double-wide whirlpool tubs and fireplaces. The friendly innkeeper provides drinks in the evening and a wonderful breakfast in the morning.

Host: Kerry Pendergast
Rooms: 9 (PB) $65-165
Full Breakfast
Credit Cards: A, B, C, D
Notes: 2, 5, 6, 7, 9, 10, 12, 14

HANFORD

The Irwin Street Inn

522 North Irwin Street, 93230
(209) 583-8000; FAX (209) 583-8793

Charming Victorian-style inn is furnished with antiques and stained glass. Each individually decorated room has a private bath, telephone, and cable television. The beautiful grounds offer the perfect atmosphere for a leisurely stroll or quiet relaxation. A Continental breakfast is included, and the restaurant on premises serves breakfast and lunch daily and dinner on Friday and Saturday nights. Close to shops, parks, and Hanford's restored historic district. Inquire about pets.

Rooms: 30 (PB) $69-99
Continental Breakfast
Credit Cards: A, B, C, D, E
Notes: 5, 7, 8, 11, 12, 14

HAWTHORNE

Bed and Breakfast California

P.O. Box 282910, San Francisco, 94128-2910
(415) 696-1690; (800) 872-4500
FAX (415) 696-1699

Hosts Will Pick You Up! This contemporary home in Hawthorne has two guest rooms. One is a master bedroom with pri-

NOTES: Credit cards accepted: A MasterCard; B Visa; C American Express; D Discover; E Diners Club;
F Other; 2 Personal checks accepted; 3 Lunch available; 4 Dinner available; 5 Open all year; 6 Pets welcome;

vate bath and a television. Other bedroom has a television and shares a bath with the hostess. Guests have access to the washer and dryer, a microwave oven, a refrigerator, and even exercise equipment. The hostess is bilingual. She serves a full breakfast and will even pick guests up at the airport if asked. $50-60.

HEALDSBURG

Bed and Breakfast California

P.O. Box 282910, San Francisco, 94128-2910
(415) 696-1690; (800) 872-4500
FAX (415) 696-1699

Wine Country Comfort. This little bed and breakfast was built in 1908 and is typical of fine Victorian architecture. Each of the three rooms has been upgraded with a private bath, skylights, deep pastel colors, stained-glass windows, and private decks. Hosts serve a full, homemade breakfast. Amenities include a sauna, table tennis, and bicycles. $90-110.

Bubble Bath Tubs. This 1908 Victorian home offers three individually decorated guest rooms, all with private baths. Roof windows and skylights, large deep bubble-bath tubs, views of neighboring Geyser Peak, and a pool and spa are just some of the amenities. The hosts serve a full breakfast in the dining room or, weather permitting, in the garden. $85-115.

In the Town of Healdsburg. This 1912 Queen Anne Victorian has an intimate, cozy feeling, within walking distance of historic downtown Healdsburg. Six guest rooms have private and semiprivate baths (three with claw-foot tubs), two guest parlors, a wonderful wraparound veranda, and a sumptuous country breakfast. Mid-week rates are available. $70-125.

Bed and Breakfast San Francisco

P.O. Box 420009, San Francisco, 94142
(415) 931-3083; FAX (415) 921-BBSF (2273)

23. Jane's place is just minutes from some of California's finest wineries, close to the Russian River beaches and resorts, and only one half-hour from the Pacific Coast. Three quaintly furnished rooms overlook vineyards. All the bedrooms have private baths. Some mornings, while guests enjoy a home-cooked breakfast, wild turkeys have been known to entertain. $85.

24. A wonderful bed and breakfast hideaway near the center of town. The owners grow their own grapes and bottle their own wines. The beautiful accommodation has a private entrance and a private bath. Full breakfast is served. Guests may also enjoy a deck and hot tub. $100-125.

Calderwood: A Victorian Inn

25 West Grant Street, P.O. Box 967, 95448
(707) 431-1110; (800) 600-5444

A beautifully restored Queen Anne Victorian built in 1902 is furnished with the innkeeper's personal collection. Relax in the parlor, on the front porch, or in the garden. Enjoy afternoon refreshments. Full breakfast served in the dining room at 9 A.M. Rooms have queen-size beds and are air-conditioned. Wineries, unique restaurants, antique stores, and biking nearby. Two-night minimum stay on weekends. Holidays may require three nights. Reservation deposit required. Minimum seven-day cancellation notice.

Hosts: Christine and Robert Maxwell
Rooms: 6 (PB) $95-185
Full Breakfast
Credit Cards: None
Notes: 2, 5, 7, 10, 11, 12, 14

---

7 No smoking; 8 Children welcome; 9 Social drinking allowed; 10 Tennis nearby; 11 Swimming nearby; 12 Golf nearby; 13 Skiing nearby; 14 May be booked through a travel agent.

Eye Openers Bed and Breakfast Reservations

P.O. Box 694, Altadena, 91003-0694
(213) 684-4428; (818) 797-2055
FAX (818) 798-3640

HE-F2. This 70-acre grape ranch in Sonoma County's spectacular Dry Creek Valley is a family-run bed and breakfast. Enjoy charming antique-decorated guest rooms, tranquil vineyard setting and walks, swimming pool, garden terrace, and wildlife pond. Two guest rooms have queen-size beds and private baths. A full breakfast is served. No smoking. $90.

Healdsburg Inn on the Plaza

110 Matheson Street, P.O. Box 1196, 95448
(707) 433-6991

This 1900 brick Victorian, formerly a Wells Fargo stagecoach express station, has been restored and is now elegantly furnished as a bed and breakfast. Features include bay windows with a view of the Plaza, fireplaces, and central heat/air. Solarium for afternoon snacks, popcorn, wine, music. Coffee and cookies available all day. Champagne breakfasts on weekends. TV, VCR, telephone, and gift certificates. Family owned and operated; close to everything. Midweek and winter rates are discounted 20 to 30 percent.

Hosts: Genny Jenkins and LeRoy Steck
Rooms: 10 (PB) $145-195
Full Breakfast
Credit Cards: A, B
Notes: 2, 5, 7, 9, 10, 11, 12

Madrona Manor, A Country Inn

1001 Westside Road, 95448
(707) 433-4231; (800) 258-4003
FAX (707) 433-0703

This 21-room inn in a national historic district is distinguished by its sense of homey elegance that combines the graciousness one might feel at a friend's home with luxurious European amenities: thick terrycloth robes, an expansive breakfast buffet, stately furniture, elegant decor. Nationally acclaimed restaurant. Inquire about limitations on pets and children.

Hosts: John and Carol Muir
Rooms: 21 (PB) $140-235
Full Breakfast
Credit Cards: A, B, C, D, E
Notes: 2, 4, 5, 10, 11, 12, 14

The Raford House

10630 Wohler Road, 95448
(707) 887-9573

This charming 1880s Victorian summer house overlooks award-winning vineyards and is listed as a Sonoma County historical landmark. Surrounding the inn are towering palm trees and old-fashioned flower gardens. The seven guest rooms are furnished with turn-of-the-century antiques. A full breakfast is served in the dining room. The sunroom and front porch entice guests to the splendid view and complimentary wine and hors d'oeuvres in the evening. Near many fine wineries, restaurants, historical points of interest, the Russian River, and the rugged Northern California coast.

Hosts: Carole and Jack Vore
Rooms: 7 (5 PB; 2 SB) $95-140
Full Breakfast
Credit Cards: A, B, C, D
Notes: 2, 5, 9, 10, 11, 12, 14

HOLLYWOOD

Bed and Breakfast California

P.O. Box 282910, San Francisco, 94128-2910
(415) 696-1690; (800) 872-4500
FAX (415) 696-1699

Cottages around the pool in West Hollywood. The owner of this inn has bought all the little houses in the neighborhood to set up housekeeping for singles and couples in this great midcity location. Rooms range from studios with shared kitchens and baths to whole apartments. Continental breakfast is served by the pool. $65-120.

Eye Openers Bed and Breakfast Reservations

P.O. Box 694, Altadena, 91003-0694
(213) 684-4428; (818) 797-2055
FAX (818) 798-3640

HH-G1. Savor a panoramic view of the Los Angeles basin from this Hollywood Hills bed and breakfast. One guest room with king-size or twin beds and private bath. Ten minutes from Westwood or Beverly Hills. A full breakfast is served. No smoking. $75-90.

HO-N1. Historic West Hollywood neighborhood is the setting for very private self-hosted one-bedroom guest house with kitchen, living room, private bath, double bed, and pool. Central to most tourist attractions, and good public transportation is available. No smoking. $90–100.

HH-C1. Enjoy a quiet canyon view from this Hollywood Hills private guest house with fireplace, kitchen, private bath, and terrace. King-size or twin beds. Extended Continental breakfast. No smoking. $85.

LA-G2. This 1910 California bungalow on a quiet palm-lined street close to Hollywood's well-known attractions offers two second-floor guest rooms, one with a sun deck overlooking the spacious garden. Well-traveled hosts speak several languages. Continental breakfast. Good public transportation. Resident dog and cat. No smoking. Private bath. $40–45.

Hollywood, California Bed and Breakfast

1616 North Sierra Bonita Avenue, 90046
(213) 876-5715; FAX (213) 851-6243

This 1910 Californian bungalow is on a palm-lined street in Hollywood convenient to public transportation and many tourist attractions. Two upstairs guest rooms, one has private sundeck, bathtub with shower, coffee maker, and sitting area. Both rooms have private bath, refrigerator, color cable TV, queen-size beds, and air conditioning. Hosts speak French, German, Russian, Hebrew, Spanish, and Italian and welcome overseas guests. Hosts offer tour of Hollywood and great restaurant and sightseeing recommendations. Families welcome. Universal Studios, Hollywood Bowl, Chinese Theatre, and other Hollywood attractions nearby.

Hosts: Avik and Elaine Gilboa
Rooms: 2 (PB) $40-50
Continental Breakfast
Credit Cards: None
Notes: 2, 4, 6, 8, 9, 10, 11, 12, 14

HOMEWOOD (LAKE TAHOE)

Tahoma Meadows Bed and Breakfast

P.O. Box 810, 96141
(916) 525-1553

Scattered among the huge Sugar Pine trees on the west shores of Lake Tahoe is Tahoma Meadows. The historic and charming little red cabins are newly and uniquely decorated with rustic elegance and all have private baths. Outdoor activities include hiking, swimming, fishing, mountain biking, skiing, and cross-country skiing. Casinos are 30 minutes away. A wonderful full breakfast is served every morning in the main lodge. Pets welcome in one room.

Hosts: Bill and Missy Sandeman
Rooms: 9 (PB) $65-75
Full Breakfast
Credit Cards: A, B
Notes: 2, 5, 7, 8, 9, 11, 12, 13, 14

7 No smoking; 8 Children welcome; 9 Social drinking allowed; 10 Tennis nearby; 11 Swimming nearby; 12 Golf nearby; 13 Skiing nearby; 14 May be booked through a travel agent.

HUNTINGTON BEACH

Bed and Breakfast California

P.O. Box 282910, San Francisco, 94128-2910
(415) 696-1690; (800) 872-4500
FAX (415) 696-1699

Convenient to Huntington Beach. About a mile from the beach, this trilevel condo has two guest rooms decorated with antiques. Private baths available. The hostess tailors breakfast to individual guests, and encourages them to use the pool and spa. $65.

IDYLLWILD

The Pine Cove Inn

23481 Highway 243, P.O. Box 2181, 92549
(909) 659-5033

The Pine Cove Inn is on three acres of wooded property three miles north of town. Nine separate units all have private bath and private entrance. Some have wood-burning fireplaces, and six have glorious views of Mount San Jacinto and Mount Tahquitz.

Hosts: Bob Bollmann and Michelle Johanson
Rooms: 9 (PB) $70-90
Full Breakfast
Credit Cards: A, B
Notes: 2, 5, 8, 9, 14

Wilkum Inn

26770 Highway 243, P.O. Box 1115, 92549
(909) 659-4087; (800) 659-4086

Sheltered by pines and cedars, this two-story shingle-style inn offers that "at home" feeling. Warm hospitality and innkeepers' attention to detail are enhanced by hand-made quilts and family antiques, as comfort combines with nostalgia in an ambience of yesteryear. Enjoy the pine-forested mountain village with unique shops, excellent restaurants, and fine and performing arts. Create memories hiking under clear skies or just by relaxing in front of the fireplace with a good book.

Wilkum Inn

Hosts: Annamae Chambers and Barbara Jones
Rooms: 4 (2 PB; 2 SB) $75-95
Continental Breakfast
Credit Cards: None
Notes: 2, 5, 9, 14

INVERNESS

Bed and Breakfast California

P.O. Box 282910, San Francisco, 94128-2910
(415) 696-1690; (800) 872-4500
FAX (415) 696-1699

These hosts have thought of everything for the perfect rural vacation. This farmhouse has a bedroom, loft, living room, fireplace, fully equipped kitchen, bath, private garden (with a pond), kids' playhouse and swing, deck-top hot tub (with oceanview), barnyard animals, TV, stereo, VCR (with movies), library, typewriter, guitar, and teddy bears. $125.

Cottage Overlooks Forested Canyon. Complete privacy nestled in a magnificent stand of 200-foot-tall Douglas firs provides the setting for luxurious cottage with cathedral ceilings. Living room, bedroom, and bath can be separated by a six-foot wide barn door in order to accommodate two couples. A fully-stocked kitchen with breakfast supplies, snacks, and beverages. $125.

NOTES: Credit cards accepted: A MasterCard; B Visa; C American Express; D Discover; E Diners Club; F Other; 2 Personal checks accepted; 3 Lunch available; 4 Dinner available; 5 Open all year; 6 Pets welcome;

Fairwinds Farm Bed and Breakfast Cottage

82 Drake's Summit, P.O. Box 581, 94937
(415) 663-9454

Atop Inverness Ridge overlooking 75,000 acres of national seashore with direct access. Only visible light is the lighthouse on Farallon Islands. Over 100-square-foot private cottage, fully equipped kitchen, full bath, fireplace (wood) furnace, TV, stereo, VCR (400-plus movies), guitar, library, binoculars, beach umbrella, toys, separate playhouse, barnyard animals, garden with ponds, waterfalls, giant swing. Hot tub with oceanview. Homemade evening desserts. Queen-size bed, two doubles, crib, and two futons. The ultimate secluded getaway!

Cottage: 1 (PB) $137.50
Full Breakfast
Credit Cards: None
Notes: 2, 5, 7, 8, 9, 10, 11, 12

IONE

The Heirloom

214 Shakeley Lane, 95640
(209) 274-4468

Travel down a country lane into a romantic English garden where a petite Colonial mansion (circa 1863) is shaded by century-old trees and scented by magnolias and gardenias. Fireplaces and balconies. Breakfast has a French flair. Enjoy gracious

The Heirloom

hospitality. Closed Thanksgiving, Christmas Eve, and Christmas Day. Children over ten accepted.

Hosts: Patricia Cross and Melisande Hubbs
Rooms: 6 (4 PB; 2 SB) $60-92
Full Breakfast
Credit Cards: A, B, C
Notes: 2, 7, 9, 11, 12, 14

ISLETON

Delta Daze Inn

20 Main Street, P.O. Box 607, 95641
(916) 777-INNS

This historic bed and breakfast offers relaxation with fun. Boat and bus tours, free bikes, or just sitting by the river are all part of the Delta experience. After guests have browsed through the boutiques and art galleries, relax in the parlor, or have a Delta Delite from the old-fashioned ice cream parlor while listening to music from the 1920s on a hand-crank Grafanola. It's all part of living, Delta style.

Host: Shirley Russell
Rooms: 12 (PB) $90-125
Full Breakfast
Credit Cards: A, B
Notes: 2, 5, 7, 8, 9, 11, 12, 13, 14

JACKSON

Eye Openers Bed and Breakfast Reservations

P.O. Box 694, Altadena, 91003-0694
(213) 684-4428; (818) 797-2055
FAX (818) 798-3640

JA-C5I. This 1872 Victorian inn, with a lovely rose garden and spa, is within walking distance to the historic area of this gold rush town. Near wineries. Five guest rooms have king, queen, or double beds and private or shared baths. A full breakfast and afternoon refreshments are served. Other gold rush towns nearby. No smoking. $90-130.

7 No smoking; 8 Children welcome; 9 Social drinking allowed; 10 Tennis nearby; 11 Swimming nearby; 12 Golf nearby; 13 Skiing nearby; 14 May be booked through a travel agent.

Gate House Inn

1330 Jackson Gate Road, 95642
(209) 223-3500; (800) 841-1072
FAX (209) 223-1299

Charming turn-of-the-century Victorian in
the country on an acre of garden property
with a swimming pool. Rooms are decorated with Victorian and country furnishings
and feature an angel theme. One has a fireplace, and the private cottage has a wood
stove. Walk to fine restaurants and historic
sites. Three-star Mobil rating. Angel gift
shop on the premises. Children over 12
accepted.

Hosts: Keith and Gail Sweet
Rooms: 5 (PB) $85-120
Full Breakfast
Credit Cards: A, B, C, D
Notes: 2, 5, 8, 9, 10, 11, 12, 14

The Wedgewood

11941 Narcissus Road, 95642
(209) 296-4300; (800) 933-4393

Charming Victorian replica tucked away on
wooded acreage. Antique decor, afternoon
refreshments, porch swing, balcony, wood-
burning stoves, full gourmet breakfast. In
the heart of the gold country, close to
excellent dining, shopping, and sightseeing.
Gazebo and terraced English gardens.
Mobil travel guide three stars. AAA three
diamonds. Smoking allowed outside only.
Children over 12 accepted. Limited smoking allowed.

Hosts: Vic and Jeannine Beltz
Rooms: 6 (PB) $85-140
Full Breakfast
Credit Cards: A, B, C, D
Notes: 2, 5, 9, 12, 13, 14

JAMESTOWN

The National Hotel

77 Main Street, P.O. Box 502, 95327
(209) 984-3446

The historic National Hotel bed and breakfast, an 11-room gold rush hotel built in

1859. Fully restored, with an outstanding
restaurant and the original saloon. Classic
cuisine and gracious service are only part
of the charm. Pets and children welcome
by prior arrangements only. Limited smoking allowed.

Hosts: Stephen and Pamela Willey
Rooms: 11 (5 PB; 6 SB) $65-80
Continental Breakfast
Credit Cards: A, B, C, D, E
Notes: 2, 3, 4, 5, 9, 10, 11, 12, 13, 14

Royal Hotel

18239 Main Street, P.O. Box 219, 95327
(714) 835-8787

Gold rush Victorian theme, English
antiques, axminster carpeting, honeymoon
cottage in second oldest gold mining town
in the West. Nostalgic items and book shop
specializing in Coca-Cola, WWI, WWII,
Hollywood, transportation, and Western
America. Two-story, on one-half acre, four
cottages, and four-unit miner's shack. Main
building built in 1922. Impeccably clean.
Town of 1,200 people and one long block of
restaurants, antique shops, and memorabilia.

Hosts: Joyce and Don Chitty
Rooms: 19 (10 PB; 9 SB) $37.50-85
Continental Breakfast
Credit Cards: A, B, C
Notes: 5, 7, 8, 9, 12, 13, 14

JENNER

Bed and Breakfast California

P.O. Box 282910, San Francisco, 94128-2910
(415) 696-1690; (800) 872-4500
FAX (415) 696-1699

Bountiful Buffet in Jenner. Jenner is a little town just north of Point Reyes. Guests
may rent one of the 11 rooms or a whole
beachfront house. The inn has some of the
furnishings of the house's original owners
from the 1890s. Try snuggling down on a
Chesterfield in the main room with a good
book. Full breakfast is provided. House
rentals include linens and firewood but no

breakfast. Groups as large as ten may be accommodated. Call for rates.

JOSHUA TREE

Bed and Breakfast California

P.O. Box 282910, San Francisco, 94128-2910
(415) 696-1690; (800) 872-4500
FAX (415) 696-1699

Joshua Tree Inn. The Joshua Tree Inn, has ten rooms, arranged courtyard-style around abundant gardens and a lovely sparkling pool. $95-175.

JULIAN

Bed and Breakfast California

P.O. Box 282910, San Francisco, 94128-2910
(415) 696-1690; (800) 872-4500
FAX (415) 696-1699

Getaway with a Shoji Gazebo Spa. Guests enjoy a relaxed country experience on three acres of private parklike grounds. Apple and pear orchards can be found amidst nearby pastoral oak and pine-covered hills. Wine tasting at the Menghini Winery, unlimited hiking trails, horse and carriage rides, bicycle tours, boating, and fishing available. Choose either a hideaway cottage with full kitchen and windowed Swedish wood stove, or a wing of the main house with a private entry through French doors and a private garden-patio and stone fireplace. Full breakfast. $100-120.

Greenridge Ranch. Two cottages are available on a real cattle ranch in Julian. One cabin is a studio featuring a bed/living room, kitchen, and bathroom; the other has separate bedroom, living room with TV, kitchen, and bath. Hosts provide a free breakfast at a nearby "apple pie" restaurant. $85-95.

Horseman's Cabin. A very nice private cottage, one mile from the historic mining town of Julian is on a mini horse ranch with an abundant supply of apple trees from which guests may pick fruit during the season. Accommodations include two bedrooms, full bath, complete kitchen, TV, VCR, barbecue on private patio, horseshoe pit, gazebo, and wood for stove. Guest horses are welcome. There are miles of hiking and riding trails through the Cuyamaca State Park. Continental breakfast; nice family atmosphere. $95.

Julian White House. This intimate, petite Colonial mansion sits among tree-lined country roads just a few miles from town. Four guest rooms are appointed with antiques, each with private bath. The honeymoon suite is spacious with mountain views, a claw-foot slipper tub, and white canopied bed. Full breakfast served in the dining room or in room upon request. Freshly baked cookies are a terrific tuck-in treat. $90-135.

Butterfield Bed and Breakfast

2284 Sunset Drive, Box 1115, 92036
(619) 765-2179; (800) 379-4262

This five-room inn, all with private baths, is in the historic mountain community of Julian. Guests are pampered in romantic suites with fireplaces, gourmet breakfasts, candlelight dinners, and afternoon tea parties. The garden gazebo provides a beautiful setting for afternoon weddings. Terraces with waterfalls and fountains let guests relax in this serene setting. Teddy bear teas and holidays are a specialty at Butterfield's. Hiking and biking trails nearby.

Hosts: Ray and Mary Trimmins
Rooms: 5 (PB) $89-135
Full Breakfast
Credit Cards: A, B, D
Notes: 2, 3, 4, 5, 7, 8, 9, 12, 14

7 No smoking; 8 Children welcome; 9 Social drinking allowed; 10 Tennis nearby; 11 Swimming nearby; 12 Golf nearby; 13 Skiing nearby; 14 May be booked through a travel agent.

KERNVILLE

Bed and Breakfast California

P.O. Box 282910, San Francisco, 94128-2910
(415) 696-1690; (800) 872-4500
FAX (415) 696-1699

At the Colorado River. Old-fashioned hospitality and great river views are this inn's claim to fame. Reasonably priced rooms include private bath, king- or queen-size brass beds, fireplaces, and whirlpool tubs. Full breakfast and afternoon snacks help prepare you for days of white-water rafting, kayaking, fishing, and hiking. And don't forget Kernville's antique shops. Moderate rates.

Historic restoration at the Kern. This amazing house was first built in Kernville in 1878 but fell into decline and disuse for over 100 years. Hosts lovingly dismantled, moved, and reconstructed it in 1989. Four rooms, two with private bath, two shared, all with down comforters and antique furnishings. Take a deep bath in the claw-foot tub, try the player piano, doze by the fire, browse in the library, or hike or raft in the Kern River Valley. Call for rates.

Kern River Inn Bed and Breakfast

119 Kern River Drive, P.O. Box 1725, 93238
(619) 376-6750; (800) 986-4382

A charming country riverfront bed and breakfast on the wild and scenic Kern River in the quaint little town of Kernville within Sequoia National Forest and the southern Sierra Mountains. Six individually decorated theme rooms reflect the charm of the Kern River Valley. All have river views, private baths, and either king- or queen-size brass beds. Some rooms feature fireplaces or whirlpool tubs. Full breakfasts feature egg entrees, giant cinnamon rolls or fruit muffins, homemade granola, fresh fruit and a variety of beverages. Walk to restaurants, parks, museums, and antique shops. For the adventuresome, the Kern River offers white-water rafting, kayaking, and fishing. Hiking and biking trails nearby offer a chance to explore the surrounding mountains and view beautiful vistas, giant redwood trees, spring wildflowers, and fall foliage. Golf and skiing nearby. Winter rates and gift certificates available.

Hosts: Jack and Carita
Rooms: 6 (PB) $89-99
Full Breakfast
Credit Cards: A, B
Notes: 2, 5, 7, 8, 9, 10, 11, 12, 13

LAGUNA BEACH

Bed and Breakfast California

P.O. Box 282910, San Francisco, 94128-2910
(415) 696-1690; (800) 872-4500
FAX (415) 696-1699

Laguna Pacifica. This custom-built suite on the cliffs of Laguna Beach has a bedroom, sitting area, minikitchen, private bath, and an incredible view. The sitting room has a sofa bed facing guests' own very large, private sun deck. A refrigerator of goodies is provided. $95.

The Carriage House

1322 Catalina Street, 92651
(714) 494-8945

The Carriage House features all private suites with living room, bedroom, bath, and some kitchen facilities. Two-bedroom suites available. All surround a courtyard of plants and flowers, two blocks from the ocean. Close to art galleries, restaurants, and shops. Minimum-stay requirements for weekends and holidays.

Hosts: Vern, Dee, and Tom Taylor
Suites: 6 (PB) $95-150
Continental Breakfast
Credit Cards: None
Notes: 2, 5, 6, 7, 8, 9, 10, 11, 12, 14

Eiler's Inn
Bed and Breakfast
741 South Coast Highway, 92651
(714) 494-3004

In the heart of Laguna, just a few steps from the Pacific Ocean. Tennis, shops, and restaurants are within walking distance. The inn offers elegant yet casual sophistication, with all rooms furnished in antiques, ocean views from the sun deck, fireplaces, and flower-scented brick courtyard with bubbling fountain.

Hosts: Henk and Annette Wirtz
Rooms: 12 (PB) $100-175
Full Breakfast
Credit Cards: A, B, C, D
Notes: 2, 5, 9, 10, 11, 12, 14

Eye Openers
Bed and Breakfast
Reservations
P.O. Box 694, Altadena, 91003-0694
(213) 684-4428; (818) 797-2055
FAX (818) 798-3640

LA-C6I. This New Orleans-style Colonial inn with central courtyard and subtropical plants is two blocks from the beach. It is in the heart of the village and within walking distance to shops and galleries. A Continental plus breakfast is served in the dining room or courtyard. The six guest rooms have private baths and queen-size beds. $95-150.

LA-J1. Sitting room, bedroom, private bath, private entrance, and large deck with panoramic ocean views make up this suite. Sitting room has a refrigerator, microwave, TV, and VCR. Full breakfast served. Walk to the beach. No smoking. $95.

LG-B2. Hilltop bed and breakfast has an ocean view. European hostess can accommodate up to eight guests. Full or Continental breakfast is served. Resident dog. Two guest rooms. Private and shared baths available. No smoking. $60-70.

LG-B3. Spacious bed and breakfast with ocean view in the hills above Pacific Coast Highway. Full breakfast. $65-75.

LG-C201. Charming Spanish-style bed and breakfast inn with unique guest rooms and suites provides a generous buffet breakfast and evening refreshments in the library or poolside. Nineteen guest rooms and one cottage. Private bath. $95-155.

LG-E121. Rooms in lovely Continental-style bed and breakfast in the heart of Laguna are set around a courtyard. Guests may enjoy breakfast and lounging near the fountain, flowers, and tables. The beach is just outside the back gate. No smoking. Eleven guest rooms and one suite. Private bath. $100-165.

LA JOLLA

Bed and Breakfast
California
P.O. Box 282910, San Francisco, 94128-2910
(415) 696-1690; (800) 872-4500
FAX (415) 696-1699

This Mediterranean-style home is set in an exclusive area with a stunning view of the Pacific. Hosts have two rooms, both with twin-size or a king-size bed and private bath. Hosts are an architect and a retired teacher who also collect modern art. Full breakfast on the terrace by the pool. $85.

Prospect Park. Elegant 22-room inn is at the heart of old La Jolla, surrounded by unique shops, art galleries, and fine restaurants. Many rooms have oceanviews. All have queen-size beds, cable TV, private baths, and air conditioning. Continental breakfast and the daily news are served on the deck or in the room. $90-125.

7 No smoking; 8 Children welcome; 9 Social drinking allowed; 10 Tennis nearby; 11 Swimming nearby; 12 Golf nearby; 13 Skiing nearby; 14 May be booked through a travel agent.

The Bed and Breakfast Inn at La Jolla

7753 Draper Avenue, 92037
(619) 456-2066

Offering deluxe accommodations in 16 charmingly decorated rooms, the Bed and Breakfast Inn at La Jolla is listed as Historical Site 179 on the San Diego registry. Fireplaces and ocean views are featured in many rooms, and every bedroom offers either a queen-size bed, a pair of twin beds, or one king-size bed. Fresh fruit, sherry, fresh flowers, and terry-cloth robes await in each guest room. Savor a large breakfast in the dining room, on the patio, the sun deck, or the bedroom. A picnic basket to add the finishing touch to the day is also available.

Rooms: 16 (15-PB; 1-SB) $85-225
Full Breakfast
Credit Cards: A, B,
Notes: 2, 5, 7, 9, 10, 11, 14

Eye Openers Bed and Breakfast Reservations

P.O. Box 694, Altadena, 91003-0694
(213) 684-4428; (818) 797-2055
FAX (818) 798-3640

LJ-S2. Tastefully decorated contemporary bed and breakfast designed by the architect/host in La Jolla features views of San Diego and beaches from the pool and Jacuzzi. Two guest rooms feature king-size or twin beds with private baths and private entrances. A full breakfast is served. No smoking. $65-75.

LAKE ARROWHEAD

Bed and Breakfast California

P.O. Box 282910, San Francisco, 94128-2910
(415) 696-1690; (800) 872-4500
FAX (415) 696-1699

At Home in Blue Jay. Blue Jay is a little town on the west shore of Lake Arrowhead,

surrounded by natural beauty. Four guest rooms (one a full suite with fireplace, refrigerator, and private deck) have private baths and are decorated with art and handicrafts. Guests may start the day with a gourmet breakfast on the huge upstairs deck, go for an afternoon skate at the nearby rink, or come home for snacks in front of the roaring Hunt Room fireplace. $90-150.

Skylights in Skyforest. Twenty-four skylights open to the trees in this romantic hideaway five minutes from Lake Arrowhead. Five intimate rooms are designed to emphasize nature and warmth. Enjoy full breakfast in the dining room and wine and hors d'oeuvres around the fireplace in the evening. $75-125.

The Carriage House Bed and Breakfast

472 Emerald Drive, P.O. Box 982, 92352
(909) 336-1400; (800) 526-5070

New England-style house hidden in the woods, with views of Lake Arrowhead. Country decor, with feather beds and down comforters. Three rooms, each with private bath. Beverages and snacks in afternoon. Large sunroom and deck. Close to lake and wonderful walking trails. Returning guests rave about the warmth and hospitality of the hosts and the great breakfasts. May be booked through a travel agent Monday through Thursday only.

Hosts: Lee and Johan Karstens
Rooms: 3 (PB) $95-120
Full Breakfast
Credit Cards: A, B, D
Notes: 2, 5, 7, 9, 11, 13

Eagle's Landing

12406 Cedarwood, 92317
P.O. Box 1510, Blue Jay, 92317 (mail)
(909) 336-2642

The interesting Mountain Gothic architecture, tower, stained glass, 26-foot ceilings, and walls of glass with grand views of

Lake Arrowhead make Eagle's Landing a landmark; but the warmth, fun, and hospitality of the hosts are what guests return for. The three beautiful rooms are decorated with art, antiques, and crafts collected from around the world. The suite is cabin-like and done in Early California style.

Host: Dorothy Stone
Rooms: 4 (PB) $95-195
Full Breakfast
Credit Cards: A, B, D
Notes: 2, 5, 9, 10, 11, 13, 14

Storybook Inn

28717 Highway 18, P.O. Box 362, Skyforest, 92385
(909) 336-1483

Nine elegantly decorated rooms, all with baths, some with fireplaces, and glass porches in the suites. A separate rustic three-bedroom, two-bath cabin with stone fireplace. The inn has a spectacular 100-mile view. Full home-cooked breakfast is served in the guest room on white wicker trays with Bavarian china, silverplate, and crystal or in the elegant dining room with its fantastic view and fine furnishings. A nightly social hour includes complimentary wines and hors d'oeuvres. Hot chocolate chip cookies are served before bed with liquors. Conference room, wedding gazebo, nearby hiking trails, and private picnics. Inquire about lunch and dinner availability.

Hosts: Kathleen and John Wooley
Rooms: 9 plus cabin (PB) $79-200
Full Breakfast
Credit Cards: A, B, C, D
Notes: 2, 5, 8, 9, 10, 11, 12, 13, 14

LAKEPORT

Forbestown Inn

825 Forbes Street, 95453
(707) 263-7858

The peace, solitude, and charm of Forbestown Inn will please the senses.

Built in 1869 when Lakeport was known as Forbestown, it is furnished with unique American oak antiques. Enjoy the beautiful gardens, swimming pool, and outdoor spa. Full, hearty breakfast; afternoon tea; baked goods; or wine, cheese, and crackers. The inn is one block from Clear Lake, boating, Jet Ski, water skiing, parasailing, bicycling, fishing, wineries, antique hunting, gold mines, geothermal steam wells.

Hosts: Nancy and Jack Dunne
Rooms: 4 (1 PB; 3 SB) $75-110
Full Breakfast
Credit Cards: A, B, C
Notes: 2, 5, 7, 9, 10, 11, 12, 14

LAKE TAHOE

Bed and Breakfast California

P.O. Box 282910, San Francisco, 94128-2910
(415) 696-1690; (800) 872-4500
FAX (415) 696-1699

Country Inn in Tahoe. On the west shore of the lake, this 1930s inn features a gourmet quality breakfast, a restaurant and bar for other meals, a huge stone fireplace, bed and breakfast rooms, and five cottages nestled in the pine trees. Take a quick hike to Sugar Pine State Park or drive to Emerald Bay. Guests are welcome to use the pool, spa, horseshoes, and Ping Pong tables. Bike paths and discount lift tickets are available, and the inn will tailor food and recreational activities to parties' needs. Kids and pets welcome. $80-125.

Old-World Charm. Each of the five upstairs rooms in this European-style guest house opens onto a balcony, offering views of the surrounding Sierra Nevadas. A lake with private beach, swimming pool, golf, water sports, and hiking, plus skiing in the winter at Diamond Peak, Mount Rose, and Heavenly Valley make this a year-round getaway. A full breakfast is served in a cozy dining room. A casino is only minutes away. $65-100.

7 No smoking; 8 Children welcome; 9 Social drinking allowed; 10 Tennis nearby; 11 Swimming nearby; 12 Golf nearby; 13 Skiing nearby; 14 May be booked through a travel agent.

Serene Cottages. Pine trees and serenity surround guests at this historic lodge on the west shore of Lake Tahoe. The Fireplace Room and Studio accommodate two people; the Cottage and Family Suites are best for three or four. Features include a hearty breakfast, Scandinavian sauna, and one of the nicest beaches on the lake. The main house is always open for games, piano playing, or lounging by the fire. Call for rates.

Eye Openers
Bed and Breakfast
Reservations

P.O. Box 694, Altadena, 91003-0694
(213) 684-4428; (818) 797-2055
FAX (818) 798-3640

LT-C3. This lakefront 1928 Tahoe-style stone house bed and breakfast has contemporary decor with antique accents. Continental or full breakfast. Three rooms and a suite. Private bath. No smoking. $100-115.

LT-C71. This 1938 Old Tahoe-style with European pine furniture offers cottage suites and large rooms, full breakfast, afternoon refreshments, private beach with a dock, and winter ski packages. Private bath. No smoking. $100-160.

LT-R41. This lakefront bed and breakfast is decorated with Laura Ashley fabrics, has pine walls and a lake view. Full breakfast. Four guest rooms. Private and shared baths. $100-200.

LARKSPUR

Bed and Breakfast
San Francisco

P.O. Box 420009, San Francisco, 94142
(415) 931-3083; FAX (415) 921-BBSF (2273)

18. The quaint town of Larkspur is nestled beneath Mount Tamalpais. Guests enjoy an entire floor with living room (complete with grand piano), two bedrooms, bath, a wonderful private patio, and swimming pool. Marin County offers a wealth of wonderful things to do, from shopping in the small town of Sausalito, to hiking and biking Mount Tamalpais. Muir Woods, Stenson Beach and the rugged California coast are just a short drive away. Full breakfast served. $85-115.

LITTLE RIVER

Glendeven Inn and Gallery

8221 North Highway 1, 95456
(707) 937-0083; (800) 822-4536

Glendeven is a small country inn pivoting around a handsome New England-style farmhouse. The restored haybarn, adjacent water tower, Stevenscroft addition, and tended gardens all invite peacefulness and relaxation. The two and one-half acre rural setting is set back on a headland meadow with views of Little River Bay. The village of Mendocino is just a mile-and-a-half to the north. The rooms are light, spacious and decorated with fine-crafted antiques and well-chosen contemporary art. All accommodations include private baths and most have fireplaces.

Hosts: Virginia Ebner, Danny Nelson, Michael
  Sumja and Jean Selk
Rooms: 10 (PB) $90-200
Continental Breakfast
Credit Cards: A, B, C
Notes: 2, 5, 7, 9, 12, 14

S.S. SeaFoam Lodge

6751 North Coast Highway 1, 95436
P.O. Box 68, Mendocino, 95460 (mailing)
(707) 937-1827; (707) 937-1022

S.S. SeaFoam Lodge has panoramic oceanviews, breathtaking coastal sunsets, and a hillside with six acres of coastal gardens.

All rooms provide private decks with oceanviews. A short walk to Buckhorn Cove and tide pools.

Rooms: 24 (PB) $85-150
Continental Breakfast
Credit Cards: A, B
Notes: 2, 5, 6, 8, 12, 14

LONG BEACH

Bed and Breakfast California

P.O. Box 282910, San Francisco, 94128-2910
(415) 696-1690; (800) 872-4500
FAX (415) 696-1699

Bluff Park Bed and Breakfast. This perfectly restored 1912 Craftsman home has two big guest rooms and one smaller one: perfect for a family. On a quiet residential street, just two blocks from the beach. Antique furnishings are simple and serene. Breakfast is sumptuous on weekends, self-serve during the week. $65.

The Painted Lady. Deep pastels swathe this 1903 home on a hill in Long Beach. Two guest rooms (one with kids' beds, and toys!) share one and a half baths, a large wooden deck, a hot tub and old-fashioned garden—and it's all less than a mile from the airport or the beach. Full breakfast. $55.

Eye Openers Bed and Breakfast Reservations

P.O. Box 694, Altadena, 91003-0694
(213) 684-4428; (818) 797-2055
FAX (818) 798-3640

LB-L5I. Former mayor's home is now a bed and breakfast inn with spacious rooms. Convenient for the tourist or business traveler. A full breakfast is served in the dining room or on porch-patios. The five guest rooms have private baths and queen or twin beds. No smoking. $95.

LB-M1. This bed and breakfast is three short blocks from the beach, with a second-floor guest room and suite with kitchen. Continental breakfast. Weekly rates available. Private bath. $50-75.

Lord Mayor's Inn Bed and Breakfast

435 Cedar Avenue, 90802
(310) 436-0324

This elegantly restored 1904 home of the first mayor of Long Beach invites guests to enjoy the ambience of years gone by. Recipient of awards in 1991 for restoration and beautification, the inn's rooms have ten-foot ceilings and are all tastefully decorated with period antiques. Each unique bedroom has a private bath and access to a large sun deck. A full breakfast is prepared by the hosts and served in the dining room or on the deck overlooking the garden area. Convenient to beaches, the convention center, civic center, and theaters. Limited smoking allowed.

Hosts: Laura and Reuben Brasser
Rooms: 5 (PB) $85-105
Full Breakfast
Credit Cards: A, B, C, D
Notes: 2, 5, 8, 10, 11, 12, 14

LOS ALAMOS

The Union Hotel and Victorian Mansion

362 Bell Street, P.O. Box 616, 93440
(800) 230-2744

The mansion has six elaborately furnished fantasy rooms. Guests can choose from the world of make-believe in the 1950s, Gypsy, Roman, Egyptian, French, or Pirate themes. Each room has a hot tub, a hidden TV, a bathroom, a fireplace, and champagne. Breakfast is served in the room. The 1880 Union Hotel is an original Wells Fargo Stagecoach stop filled with beautiful period antiques. Full-service dining and saloon are

7 No smoking; 8 Children welcome; 9 Social drinking allowed; 10 Tennis nearby; 11 Swimming nearby; 12 Golf nearby; 13 Skiing nearby; 14 May be booked through a travel agent.

available. The grounds have the largest living maze west of the Mississippi.

Hosts: Bill and Vivian Bubbel
Rooms: 20 (9 PB; 11 SB) $60-220
Full Breakfast
Credit Cards: A, B, C, D
Notes: 4, 5, 9, 10, 11, 12, 14

LOS ANGELES

Bed and Breakfast California

P.O. Box 282910, San Francisco, 94128-2910
(415) 696-1690; (800) 872-4500
FAX (415) 696-1699

3-5. This retired couple lives in a quiet neighborhood and have two guest rooms and one bath in an upstairs suite. Toys, crib, and TV. Guests can walk to Universal Studios. Affordable rates. $60.

Art Nouveau in Old LA. This 1930s custom home is on manicured grounds in prestigious Hancock Park. Elegant guest suite has sitting area, queen-size bed, and huge, original tile bath. Full breakfast in the formal dining room on weekends; Continental on weekdays. Very, very beautiful architecture. $85.

California Classic Near Sunset Boulevard. This stunning California Spanish mansion is on a residential street one block from Sunset Boulevard and has four guest rooms, two with private bath and two sharing a bath. Phones and TVs available. Amenities include terraced garden, gazebo, hot tub, and gated parking. The host is a gourmet chef and can provide meals in addition to the full breakfast upon arrangement. $55-75.

Country in the City. Just a few minutes from the airport, this condo is shared with the interior decorator hostess. The bedroom has a private bath and is appointed with bent-willow furniture and country charm. The hostess can pick up guests at the airport and help with other arrangements. Full breakfast. $60-70.

Country Manor in Westwood. This elegant mansion was built when Los Angeles still had rolling hills and UCLA was a budding university. Just a block from Wilshire Boulevard and a mile from the campus, two bedrooms are impeccably decorated, including the original hand-painted bathroom tile. Full breakfast in the dining room or in the country gardens. $65.

Gail's and Carol's Houses. At the edge of elegant Hancock Park, these side-by-side houses have a total of three guest rooms: one with a queen-size bed, private bath, and balcony; the other with a queen-size bed, and twin beds, sharing a bath. Both are sunny, artfully decorated, and perfect for working or "touristing" in Los Angeles. Fresh, healthy breakfasts. $65-75.

Historic Ambiance. Close to the USC campus, this 1910 Craftsman historic registry home has two upstairs guest rooms, with a bath between them. There's a shaded porch in front, a sunny deck in the rear, and a smaller sun porch off one guest room. Close to the freeways and Music Center, and very close to the Convention Center. $50-60.

Moon Villa in Washington Heights. Enjoy 360-degree views from the multi-level deck/patio of this spacious hillside house. The Western Room can accommodate a family of four; the others come with sunken double tubs. Start the day with a full gourmet breakfast and then enjoy the attractions of Los Angeles, Pasadena, and the San Gabriel Mountains. $65-75.

NOTES: Credit cards accepted: A MasterCard; B Visa; C American Express; D Discover; E Diners Club; F Other; 2 Personal checks accepted; 3 Lunch available; 4 Dinner available; 5 Open all year; 6 Pets welcome;

Terraced Mansion High in the Hills. The TV-producer hosts of this incredible home make their three-room guest suite available to visitors. There's a queen-size bed in the bedroom, a full office or sitting room, and an elegant bath. Suite opens on to the guests' own deck, with a panoramic view of the city. Fresh Continental breakfast is served in the hilltop garden gazebo or in guests' room. $120.

California Home Hospitality

P.O. Box 66662, 90066
(310) 390-1526 (phone and FAX)

This hilltop home enjoys a spectacular view of the Santa Monica Mountains and the entire northern portion of the city, including Beverly Hills, Westwood, and Century City. The city lights in the evening are lovely. Guests are just 15 minutes from the beach at Santa Monica and adjacent to Marina del Rey Yacht Harbor and Santa Monica Municipal Airport. Hostess stresses comfort, cleanliness, secure surroundings, and lots of TLC! For enthusiastic sight-seers, a rental car is suggested, although public transportation is within walking distance.

Host: Helen Hause
Room: 1 (PB) $45
Full Breakfast
Credit Cards: None
Notes: 2, 5, 7, 9, 10, 11, 12

Eye Openers Bed and Breakfast Reservations

P.O. Box 694, Altadena, 91003-0694
(213) 684-4428; (818) 797-2055
FAX (818) 798-3640

LA-B1. Five minutes from the Marina and LAX and walking distance to parks, tennis courts, golf, and restaurants, this cozy bed and breakfast is also near public transportation. Continental breakfast. No smoking. One guest room. Shared bath. $35-45.

LA-B4. At the foot of the Hollywood Hills near West Hollywood restaurants and attractions, this Mediterranean-style house with a music room, interesting artifacts, and antiques offers four guest rooms with queen-size, double, or twin beds and private or shared baths. Amenities include a full breakfast, patio areas, hot tub, and off-street parking. Good public transportation is available. No smoking. $50-70.

LA-C2. Beautifully restored Craftsman-style house on the National Register of Historic Places is close to USC and civic and convention centers. Two comfortable guest rooms, lovely gardens, and patio are available for guests to enjoy. No smoking. Shared and private baths. $45-50.

LA-D1. Spacious apartment with elegant hospitality, interesting artifacts, and a location near most West Side destinations makes this a good bed and breakfast at a modest price. Swimming pool and hot tub available. Continental breakfast. No smoking allowed. Two guest rooms. Private baths. $50-75.

HA-D2. Convenient to L.A. International Airport, this comfortable, homey bed and breakfast with two spacious guest rooms has full exercise equipment room and hearty American breakfast. Hosts speak Spanish. No smoking. Private and shared baths. $40-45.

LA-P1. Walk to Westwood and UCLA from this attractive Wilshire Boulevard bed and breakfast. Enjoy an ample Continental breakfast on the balcony prepared by French-speaking host. No smoking. Good public transportation nearby. One guest room with private bath. $60.

LA-S1. This convenient and spacious 800-square-foot, three-room apartment with

7 No smoking; 8 Children welcome; 9 Social drinking allowed; 10 Tennis nearby; 11 Swimming nearby; 12 Golf nearby; 13 Skiing nearby; 14 May be booked through a travel agent.

patios is a good location for vacationing sightseers, business people, and people interested in relocating to the Los Angeles area. Breakfast is self-catered. Weekly rates are available. No smoking. $65-75.

LA-S3. Two-story, Art Deco-style, architect-designed bed and breakfast nestled in the beautiful Los Feliz Hills of near Griffith Park and the Greek Theatre. Offering a quiet, comfortable setting convenient to fine restaurants, entertainment, and tourist attractions. Two guest rooms with private bath. Public transportation available. $60-65.

LA-S51. This antique-decorated, restored 1908 Craftsman home provides the setting and mood of an earlier era. Features a marvelous full gourmet breakfast and evening refreshments. Convenient to the University of Southern California, Civic Center, Hollywood, and tourist attractions. Five guest rooms. Shared and private baths. $75-150.

LA-S1B. Very private suite in the Hollywood Hills with grand views of Los Angeles offers a large living room with kitchen area. Guest suite has a double bed and private bath. No smoking. $100-135.

WLA-C2. French country decor and collectibles throughout this lovely, spacious apartment hosted by interior decorator. Two guest rooms with queen-size or twin beds and private baths. Convenient to LAX, beach cities, freeways, and many tourist attractions. Enjoy an extended Continental breakfast on balcony. Garage parking. No smoking. $50-60.

WW-P2. English country decor fills this lovely home within walking distance of UCLA. Two guest rooms have queen-size or twin beds with private or shared baths.

Continental-plus breakfast served. Good public transportation available. Resident dogs. No smoking. $62-70.

LOWER LAKE

Big Canyon Inn
P.O. Box 1311, 95457
(707) 928-5631; (707) 928-4892

Secluded and peaceful home is on a hilly 12 acres of pines and oaks beneath Cobb Mountain. Guests stay in a bedroom suite with private porch and entrance, private bath and kitchenette. The suite is cozy in winter with its own wood stove and comfortable in summer with air conditioning.

Hosts: John and Helen Wiegand
Rooms: 2 (PB) $65
Continental Breakfast
Cards: F
Notes: 2, 5, 7, 8, 9, 10, 11, 12, 14

LUCERNE

Kristalberg Bed and Breakfast
P.O. Box 1629, 95458
(707) 274-8009

Romantic hideaway and eagle's nest high over Clear Lake is one-half mile off Highway 20. Guests will enjoy the tranquil, country setting and antique furnishings. The congenial host is trilingual. Friendly dog in residence. Full gourmet breakfast is served in formal dining room. Amenities include deluxe suite with whirlpool tub. Great hiking and biking, antique shops, wineries, and good restaurants are nearby. Complimentary refreshments. Discounts for extended stays.

Host: Merv Myers
Rooms: 3 (2 PB; 1 SB) $60-150
Full Breakfast
Credit Cards: A, B, C, D
Notes: 2, 3, 4, 5, 6, 7, 8, 9, 10, 11, 14

NOTES: Credit cards accepted: A MasterCard; B Visa; C American Express; D Discover; E Diners Club; F Other; 2 Personal checks accepted; 3 Lunch available; 4 Dinner available; 5 Open all year; 6 Pets welcome;

MALIBU

Bed and Breakfast California

P.O. Box 282910, San Francisco, 94128-2910
(415) 696-1690; (800) 872-4500
FAX (415) 696-1699

Cliffside in North Malibu. Romantic 4,500-square-foot Country English estate is on a bluff overlooking the Pacific. The Cliffside is decorated with antiques and Oriental rugs. Guests have use of a steam room and hot tub with views of the ocean and Point Dume. Expect a full vegetarian breakfast and tea or wine upon arrival. The perfect place for serene beach walks, examining tide pools, or hiking to Point Dume to watch porpoises and whales (seasonally). Smoking permitted outside. Massage and yoga available for additional charge. $80-130.

Pirate's Cove Guest. This charming cottage retreat has views through the canyon to the ocean, a full bedroom, a living room with a futon-couch, kitchen thoughtfully stocked with all the necessities, full bath, and private deck. Close to hiking, Pirate's Cove, upscale Malibu dining spots. $75.

Topanga Canyon Hideaway. This amazing estate has been a boys' school, a convent, and a brothel. Now it is owned by a gentleman who spent years restoring its original handcrafted character. Two guest rooms look out to the pool and over an acre of gardens. One room is huge, all white and round, with historic chandelier and massive marble bath fixtures. The Tower Room is shaped like an octagon and features an antique double bed that looks like a throne. Truly hidden in the hills. $100-125.

Casa Larronde

Box 86, 90265
(213) 456-9333

This is the area of the "famous," so the locals call this beach "Millionaires' Row." The Ocean Suite has 40 feet of windows adjoining its deck. Features include TV, telephone, fireplace, kitchenette, ceiling fan over a king-size bed, floor-to-ceiling three-way mirrors in the dressing room, and a large bathroom with twin basins. Cocktails are offered in the evening, and a full American breakfast is served leisurely in the morning. Closed July through mid-October. Inquire about arrangements for children.

Host: Charlou Larronde
Rooms: 2 (PB) $110-125
Full Breakfast
Credit Cards: None
Notes: 2, 7, 9, 10, 11, 12

Malibu Country Inn

6506 Westward Beach Road, 90265
(310) 457-9622; (800) FUN-N-SURF

In this enchanting country inn nestled on a bluff above one of the world's most beautiful beaches, guests will find intimate accommodations in the midst of a private, three-acre, lush garden setting. Each room is provided with a thoughtful array of amenities: refrigerator, coffee maker, remote control television, telephone, private patio, and snack basket. A heated swimming pool overlooks both the ocean and mountains. Complimentary Continental breakfast is served; full breakfast is available at an additional cost. Paradise awaits guests!

Hosts: Charity Dailey
Rooms: 16 (PB) $95-175
Continental Breakfast
Credit Cards: A, B, C, E
Notes: 3, 5, 6, 8, 9, 10, 11, 12, 14

MAMMOTH

Bed and Breakfast California

P.O. Box 282910, San Francisco, 94128-2910
(415) 696-1690; (800) 872-4500
FAX (415) 696-1699

7 No smoking; 8 Children welcome; 9 Social drinking allowed; 10 Tennis nearby; 11 Swimming nearby; 12 Golf nearby; 13 Skiing nearby; 14 May be booked through a travel agent.

Family Ski Packages. Snuggle up in this 19-room inn or in one of the two-bedroom apartments. The hostess can arrange great ski packages and also offers a hot tub, a big social room, and an early evening appetizer party. Full breakfast and low rates—even lower in the summer. $60-85.

Luxurious Mountain Retreat. Enjoy the Emperor's Room, with antique Chinese bed, or the Tribal Room, filled with artifacts of the Paiute and Shoshone Tribes that once populated these mountains. This special home has a billiard room (with fireplace and a bar), where afternoon snacks are served, and a mud room with lockers for guests' vacation gear. All rooms have private baths. Full breakfast. $125-175.

Rainbow in the High Sierras. Nestled against the colorful granite spires, 7,000 feet high, this rustic bed and breakfast is surrounded by meadows and babbling brooks. Three large rooms are decorated with antiques and down comforters. Two have Jacuzzi tubs, the other a skylight through which guests can watch the stars. Full breakfast is served on the deck, weather permitting, along with afternoon snacks. Dog, cat, chickens, ducks, and horses are in residence. $85-95.

Vintage Mammoth Chalet. Enjoy elegant accommodations, warm personal service, and breathtaking views at this private mountain home. The hostess serves breakfast each morning and beverages and cheese in the evening. Two guest rooms overlook magnificent century-old Jeffrey pines or a view of the beautiful White Mountains. Ski lifts are only a five-minute drive. $85-125.

MANHATTAN BEACH

Bed and Breakfast California

P.O. Box 282910, San Francisco, 94128-2910
(415) 696-1690; (800) 872-4500
FAX (415) 696-1699

Old California. This early 1900s home was built by the owners' grandfather, only a block from the ocean. The guest room has a double bed and private bath. Enjoy the hot tub, two large sun decks (one private), and a terrific oceanview. Take a short stroll to restaurants, shops, and the waves of the Pacific. $65.

Eye Openers Bed and Breakfast Reservations

P.O. Box 694, Altadena, 91003-0694
(213) 684-4428; (818) 797-2055
FAX (818) 798-3640

MB-C2. Walk to the beach, shops, and restaurants from this restored beach bungalow. Ocean view from upstairs guest room. Continental breakfast and other amenities available. No smoking. Two guest rooms. Private and shared bath. $50-75.

MB-L2. Beachfront Bed and Breakfast is the entire first floor of this lovely home on the Strand. Private entrance, living/dining room area with fireplace, wet bar, and guest parking are some of the amenities offered. Continental breakfast. No smoking. Two guest rooms available. Private bath. $75-85.

MARINA DEL REY

Bed and Breakfast California

P.O. Box 282910, San Francisco, 94128-2910
(415) 696-1690; (800) 872-4500
FAX (415) 696-1699

Gloria's Place. A luxury condo with a guest room has a queen-size bed, private bath, and its own entry. Facilities include pool, exercise room, spa, and gardens. Ten minutes to the airport, one-half mile to the beach. $65.

NOTES: Credit cards accepted: A MasterCard; B Visa; C American Express; D Discover; E Diners Club; F Other; 2 Personal checks accepted; 3 Lunch available; 4 Dinner available; 5 Open all year; 6 Pets welcome;

Eye Openers
Bed and Breakfast
Reservations

P.O. Box 694, Altadena, 91003-0694
(213) 684-4428; (818) 797-2055
FAX (818) 798-3640

MR-M40I. French country decor is featured in this large bed and breakfast inn close to the beach, good restaurants, and shopping. Forty guest rooms have queen-size or twin beds and private baths. A Continental breakfast is served. No smoking. $70-125.

PL-D2. Set on a hillside near the beach, this three-story tudor-style bed and breakfast offers the first story as guest quarters with two bedrooms, living room and patio. Gourmet, Continental, or full breakfast served. No smoking. Private bath. $60-80.

MARIPOSA

Bed and Breakfast California

P.O. Box 282910, San Francisco, 94128-2910
(415) 696-1690; (800) 872-4500
FAX (415) 696-1699

Historic Ranch in Mariposa. Built in 1858 as the original stagecoach stop in Yosemite, this bed and breakfast combines European and country flavor under a blanket of twinkling stars. It is surrounded by rolling meadows, a creek (with an old-fashioned water wheel), and glorious natural habitat. Four guest rooms and one cottage feature claw-foot tubs, fireplaces, and brass beds. Hosts serve afternoon drinks and hors d'oeuvres. Full country breakfast. $85-100.

Eye Openers
Bed and Breakfast
Reservations

P.O. Box 694, Altadena, 91003-0694
(213) 684-4428; (818) 797-2055
FAX (818) 798-3640

MA-L3I. This contemporary bed and breakfast on an old stagecoach route, hosted by long-time residents, is on four acres and offers gold panning and hiking on the inn's property. Three guest rooms have queen-size beds and private baths. Mini refrigerator, TV, VCR, and many other amenities are available. The inn is near museums, wineries, and Yosemite National Park. Handicapped accessible. Continental breakfast. $80-100.

MA-O6I. Early American Colonial-style inn is in this gold rush town near museums, recreational areas, and Yosemite National Park. Six guest rooms with king- or queen-size or twin beds and private baths. Full breakfast. No smoking. $65-85.

Little Valley Inn
at the Creek

3483 Brooks Road, 95338
(800) 889-5444; FAX (209) 742-5099

This special place to stay near Yosemite National Park in California Gold Country has spacious, modern rooms with private baths, decks, and entrances. A country setting with huge oaks, pines, historic Indian grinding stones, and beautiful flowing creeks includes nature walks and picnic areas. Free goldpanning lessons available. Several restaurants and convenience stores nearby.

Hosts: Robert and Kay Hewitt
Rooms: 3 (PB) $80-100
Full Breakfast
Credit Cards: A, B, C
Notes: 5, 8, 9, 11, 12, 13, 14

Oak Meadows, too.

5263 Highway 140N, Box 619, 95338
(209) 742-6161

In a historic gold rush town, this bed and breakfast has turn-of-the-century charm and New England architecture. Guest rooms are decorated with handmade quilts,

7 No smoking; 8 Children welcome; 9 Social drinking allowed; 10 Tennis nearby; 11 Swimming nearby; 12 Golf nearby; 13 Skiing nearby; 14 May be booked through a travel agent.

wallpaper, and brass headboards. Close to Yosemite and Home of the California State Mining and Mineral Museum.

Hosts: Frank Ross and Karen Black
Rooms: 6 (PB) $59-89
Continental Breakfast
Credit Cards: A, B
Notes: 2, 5, 7, 14

The Pelennor

3871 Highway 49 South, 95338
(209) 966-2832

Country atmosphere about 45 minutes from Yosemite National Park. Four guest rooms, featuring twin, double, and queen-size beds. After a day of sightseeing, guests may want to take a few laps in the pool, unwind in the spa, enjoy the available games, relax in the sauna, and listen to an occasional tune played on the bagpipes. Smoking permitted outside.

Hosts: Dick and Gwen Foster
Rooms: 4 (SB) $45
Full Breakfast
Credit Cards: None
Notes: 2, 5, 6, 8, 9, 11

MCCLOUD

McCloud Guest House

606 West Colombero Drive, P.O. Box 1510, 96057
(916) 964-3160

Built in 1907, this beautiful old country home is nestled among stately oaks and lofty pines on the lower slopes of majestic Mount Shasta. On the first floor is one of

McCloud Guest House

Siskiyou County's finer dining establishments. The second floor has a large parlor surrounded by five guest rooms, each individually decorated. Two-night minimum stay required for some holidays.

Hosts: Bill and Patti Leigh; Dennis and Pat Abreu
Rooms: 5 (PB) $75-90
Continental Breakfast
Credit Cards: A, B
Notes: 4, 5, 7, 11, 12, 13

McCloud Hotel

McCloud Hotel: A Bed and Breakfast Hotel

408 Main Street, 96057
(800) 964-2823

Experience historic hospitality and stay in meticulously restored and enlarged guest rooms, each with its own private bath. Large luxurious suites with whirlpool tubs. Wonderful lobby and fireplace. Reasonable prices include Continental plus breakfast and afternoon tea and scones. Many recreational choices in all seasons at the foot of Mount Shasta. From I-95 to Mount Shasta, travel east for nine miles on Highway 89 to McCloud. Follow signs to historical district.

Hosts: Lee and Marilyn Ogden
Rooms: 18 (PB) $68-130
Continental Breakfast
Credit Cards: A, B
Notes: 2, 3, 4, 5, 7, 12, 13

MENDOCINO

Agate Cove Inn

11201 Lansing Street, Box 1150, 95460
(707) 937-0551; (800) 527-3111

NOTES: Credit cards accepted: A MasterCard; B Visa; C American Express; D Discover; E Diners Club; F Other; 2 Personal checks accepted; 3 Lunch available; 4 Dinner available; 5 Open all year; 6 Pets welcome;

Agate Cove Inn is on an ocean bluff with dramatic views of the Pacific and rugged coastline. There are individual cottages, each with an oceanview, a Franklin fireplace, and a private bath. Full country breakfast served in the main 1860s farmhouse. Hiking, golf, and tennis close by.

Hosts: Scott and Betsy Buckwald
Rooms: 10 (PB) $129-189
Full Breakfast
Credit Cards: A, B
Notes: 2, 5, 7, 9, 10, 12

Bed and Breakfast California

P.O. Box 282910, San Francisco, 94128-2910
(415) 696-1690; (800) 872-4500
FAX (415) 696-1699

16-7. These hosts raised a total of 12 children in this Victorian home before taking in bed and breakfast guests. Four guest rooms, all with private baths. The house has plenty of activities for kids and includes all the necessities a parent could ask for. Kids stay free in parents' room. Breakfast is not included. Affordable rates.

At Jughandle Beach. Offering views of the ocean and the country, this classic little bed and breakfast inn is run by devoted owner-occupants who take satisfaction in making a stay memorable. There are four bedrooms, all with private baths and full breakfast, two with oceanviews. In the little town of Fort Bragg, near Mendocino. Try whale watching from December through March, or charter a boat at Noyo Harbor. Hiking, beachcombing, riding, canoeing, cycling, or just relaxing to the sound of the ocean are all here for guests. $70-100.

Avalon House. This perfectly upgraded Craftsman-style mansion is on the coast in Fort Bragg. Rooms are artfully decorated and range from the simple to the opulent, with fireplaces, oceanviews, and whirlpool tubs. All have supportive mattresses, down comforters, and individual temperature control. Enjoy this haven for serious romantics. Mid-week rates are available. $105-125.

Brewery Gulch Inn

9350 Coast Highway 1, 95460
(707) 937-4752

An authentic country bed and breakfast farm on the rugged coast, just one mile from the village of Mendocino. The lovely old white farmhouse is furnished in the Victorian style with queen-size beds, homemade quilts, and down pillows. Each guest room window provides views of the gardens and meadows beyond.

Hosts: Linda and Bill Howarth
Rooms: 5 (3 PB; 2 SB) $75-130
Full Breakfast
Credit Cards: A, B
Notes: 2, 5, 7, 10, 11, 12

Captain's Cove Inn

P.O. Box 803, 95460
(707) 937-5150; (800) 780-7905

This oceanfront bed and breakfast is on Main Street in the village, two blocks from all activity, yet still very secluded with private parking and private path to the beach. The rooms have a front porch, a private deck, and a great view. Enjoy a full breakfast in the oceanfront dining room.

Hosts: Bob and Linda Blum
Rooms: 5 (PB) $145-185
Full Breakfast
Credit Cards: A, B
Notes: 2, 5, 7, 9, 11, 12, 14

Eye Openers Bed and Breakfast Reservations

P.O. Box 694, Altadena, 91003-0694
(213) 684-4428; (818) 797-2055
FAX (818) 798-3640

ME-M12I. This 1882 New England-style Victorian bed and breakfast is in the village

7 No smoking; 8 Children welcome; 9 Social drinking allowed; 10 Tennis nearby; 11 Swimming nearby; 12 Golf nearby; 13 Skiing nearby; 14 May be booked through a travel agent.

conveniently near shops, hiking trails, fishing, and golf. Twelve guest rooms with queen-size and double beds, private baths, and some with fireplaces. Full breakfast. No smoking. $75-190.

The Headlands Inn

Box 132, 95460
(707) 937-4431; (800) 354-4431

The Headlands Inn is an 1868 Victorian, within Mendocino village on California's scenic north coast minutes from redwoods and wineries. Full gourmet breakfasts are served in the room. All rooms have wood-burning fireplaces and private baths. Two rooms have spectacular ocean views overlooking an English-style garden. King- or queen-size feather beds, parlor, and many antiques. Afternoon tea service with mineral waters, cookies, and mixed nuts. Minimum-stay requirements for weekends and holidays.

The Headlands Inn

Hosts: Sharon and David Hyman
Rooms: 7 (PB) $95-189
Full Breakfast
Credit Cards: A, B
Notes: 2, 5, 7, 10, 11, 12, 14

John Dougherty House

571 Ukiah Street, P.O. Box 817, 95460
(707) 937-5266

Historic John Dougherty House was built in 1867 and is one of the oldest houses in Mendocino. On land bordered by Ukiah and Albion streets, the inn has some of the best ocean and bay views in the historic village; steps away from great restaurants and shopping, but years removed from 20th-century reality. The main house is furnished with period country antiques taking guests back to 1867. Enjoy quiet, peaceful nights seldom experienced in today's urban living.

Hosts: David and Marion Wells
Rooms: 6 (PB) $95-165
Full Breakfast
Credit Cards: A, B, D
Notes: 2, 5, 7, 10, 11, 12, 14

Joshua Grindle Inn

44800 Little Lake Road, P.O. Box 647, 95460
(707) 937-4143; (800) GRINDLE

On two acres in a historic village overlooking the ocean, the Joshua Grindle Inn is a short walk to the beach, art center, shops, and fine restaurants. Stay in the lovely two-story Victorian farmhouse, a New England-style cottage, or a three-story water tower. Six rooms have fireplaces; all have private baths, antiques, and comfortable reading areas. Enjoy a full breakfast served around a ten-foot 1830s harvest table.

Hosts: Jim and Arlene Moorehead
Rooms: 10 (PB) $90-160
Full Breakfast
Credit Cards: A, B, C
Notes: 2, 5, 7, 9, 10, 11, 12

NOTES: Credit cards accepted: A MasterCard; B Visa; C American Express; D Discover; E Diners Club; F Other; 2 Personal checks accepted; 3 Lunch available; 4 Dinner available; 5 Open all year; 6 Pets welcome;

Mendocino Farmhouse

Mendocino Farmhouse

Box 247, 95460
(707) 937-0241; FAX (707) 937-2932

Mendocino Farmhouse is a small bed and breakfast with all the comforts of home, surrounded by redwood forest, beautiful gardens, a pond, and meadow. Choose from comfortable rooms decorated with country antiques for a quiet night's rest and enjoy a farmhouse breakfast in the morning. Midweek discounts available. Children welcome by prior arrangements.

Hosts: Margie and Bud Kamb
Rooms: 5 (PB) $85-115
Full Breakfast
Credit Cards: A, B
Notes: 2, 5, 10, 11, 12

Mendocino Village Inn

44860 Main Street, P.O. Box 626, 95460
(707) 937-0246; (800) 882-7029

Guests' home on the north coast, complete with lush gardens, frog ponds, fireplaces, and water tower suite. This 1882 Queen Anne Victorian offers hearty breakfasts, beach trails, and good company. Coastal whimsy, quiet merriment, and repose. Minimum-stay requirements for weekends

and some holidays. No smoking indoors. Children ten and older are welcome. No third party reservations are welcome.

Hosts: Bill and Kathleen Erwin
Rooms: 13 (11 PB; 2 SB) $65-190
Full Breakfast
Credit Cards: None
Notes: 2, 5, 9, 10, 11, 12

Stevenswood Lodge

P.O. Box 170, 95460
(707) 937-2810; (800) 421-2810

Distinctive contemporary suites, all hand-crafted, on Mendocino's spectacular coast. Virgin "old-growth" setting off shoreline Highway 1, with beach access and forest trails. Hosts serve a three-course gourmet breakfast. Ocean views, fireplaces, stocked refrigerators, 33-channel remote-control TV, executive conference room, VCR, and art gallery. AAA four-diamond rated.

Hosts: Robert and Vera Zimmer
Room: 1 (PB) $95-115
Suites: 9 (PB) $120-195
Full Breakfast
Credit Cards: A, B, C, D
Notes: 2, 5, 8, 9, 10, 11, 12, 14

Whitegate Inn

499 Howard Street, P.O. Box 150, 95460
(707) 937-4892; (800) 531-7282

Everything travelers look for in a bed and breakfast experience: antiques, fireplaces, ocean views, and private baths. Elegant 1880 Victorian, in the center of the historic preservation village of Mendocino. Shops, galleries, and nationally acclaimed restaurants are just steps away. A perfect setting for romance, weddings, or just a little rest and relaxation.

Hosts: Carol and George Bechtloff
Rooms: 6 (PB) $95-165
Full Breakfast
Credit Cards: A, B, D
Notes: 2, 5, 7, 8, 9, 10, 11, 12

7 No smoking; 8 Children welcome; 9 Social drinking allowed; 10 Tennis nearby; 11 Swimming nearby; 12 Golf nearby; 13 Skiing nearby; 14 May be booked through a travel agent.

MILL VALLEY

Mountain Home Inn

810 Panoramic Highway, 94941
(415) 381-9000

A romantic country inn high atop Mount Tamalpais, offering spectacular views of the Marin Hills and San Francisco Bay. Ten guest rooms, some offer Jacuzzi baths, private decks, and fireplaces. Just outside the front door is Mount Tamalpais State Park, offering miles of hiking trails. Muir Woods National Monument, Muir Beach, and Stinson Beach are a short drive away, with downtown San Francisco only 25 minutes away. Restaurant on premises. Limited smoking allowed.

Rooms: 10 (PB) $131-239
Full Breakfast
Credit Cards: A, B
Notes: 2, 3, 4, 5, 8, 9, 10, 11, 12, 14

MISSION VIEJO

Bed and Breakfast California

P.O. Box 282910, San Francisco, 94128-2910
(415) 696-1690; (800) 872-4500
FAX (415) 696-1699

Harvey House. This private home has many wonderful amenities. The Emerald Room has a private bath and balcony. The home includes a spa and pool table. Full breakfast is served on antique dishes. $60.

MONTARA

The Goose and Turrets

835 George Street, Box 937, 94037
(415) 728-5451

A quiet, historic bed and breakfast catering to readers, nature lovers, pilots—and enthusiastic eaters who appreciate afternoon tea and four-course breakfasts. Only 30 minutes from San Francisco airport and 5 minutes from the beach, this makes a convenient headquarters for visits to San Francisco, Berkeley, Silicon Valley, Monterey, and Carmel. Nearby are tidepools, wetland preserves, elephant seals, whale watching trips, aerotours, fishing, and horseback riding, as well as restaurants, shops, and galleries. French spoken.

Hosts: Raymond and Emily Hoche-Mong
Rooms: 5 (PB) $85-110
Full Breakfast
Credit Cards: A, B, C, D
Notes: 2, 5, 7, 8, 9, 10, 11, 12, 14

MONTEREY

Bed and Breakfast California

P.O. Box 282910, San Francisco, 94128-2910
(415) 696-1690; (800) 872-4500
FAX (415) 696-1699

Carmel-3. Easy family travel. This 19-room inn has rooms with fireplaces, living room suites, and two-bedroom units, and it is in the heart of Monterey. There is a heated pool. Continental breakfast is served. There is no charge for a child in adult's room. $95-175.

Beauty, Whimsy, and Charm. One of the best bed and breakfasts in town, this perfect antique inn sits high on a hill, four blocks above Cannery Row and the aquarium. All five rooms are decorated with fine art and unusual furniture, hand-sewn linens, and goose-down comforters. Relax on the sun porch overlooking Fern Falls, and breakfast by the fireplace or in bed. Perfect for a honeymoon or special romantic retreat. $105-175.

Bed and Breakfast International

P.O. Box 282910, San Francisco, 94128-2910
(415) 696-1690; (800) 872-4500
FAX (415) 696-1699

204. Two homes on the southern end of Monterey, all modestly priced. Two have views of the bay. There are six rooms that offer twin, queen-size, and double beds. All have shared baths. Excellent breakfasts are prepared by experienced hosts. $50-60.

Del Monte Beach Inn

1110 Del Monte Avenue, 93940
(408) 649-4410; FAX (408) 375-3818

The only one of its kind on the Monterey Peninsula, the Del Monte Beach Inn offers guests all of the charm and comfort of a quaint European bed and breakfast at comfortably affordable rates in an ideal location. Walk across the boulevard to the beach and the biking and walking trail. Only minutes from Fisherman's Wharf, Cannery Row, historic Monterey, and the Aquarium.

Host: Kathy Pedulla
Rooms: 18 (2 PB; 16 SB) $35-75
Continental Breakfast
Credit Cards: A, B, C, D
Notes: 2, 5, 7, 8, 9, 10, 11, 12, 14

The Jabberwock

598 Laine Street, 93940
(408) 372-4777

Alice's Wonderland just four blocks above Cannery Row and Monterey Bay Aquarium. The Jabberwock has one-half acre of lush gardens and waterfalls overlooking the bay. Each room has down pillows and comforters. hors d'oeuvres at 5:00 P.M. and cookies and milk at bedtime.

Hosts: Jim and Barbara Allen
Rooms: 7 (3 PB; 4 S2B) $100-180
Full Breakfast
Credit Cards: A, B
Notes: 2, 5, 7, 8, 9, 10, 11, 12, 14

MONTE RIO

Huckleberry Springs Country Inn and Spa

8105 Old Beedle Road, P.O. Box 400, 95462
(800) 822-2683

On 56 acres of redwoods in the heart of the Russian River region offering private cottage accommodations in an intimate and peaceful setting. Four modern cottages offer guests amenities, including VCR, stereo, coffee makers, hair dryers, sitting areas, queen-size beds, and wood-burning stoves. The lodge boasts dramatic views from its mountaintop location. There is also a swimming pool and Japanese-style spa. Massage is available. Full breakfast is served each morning and a four-course gourmet dinner is available on Wednesdays and Saturdays. Canoeing the Russian River, wine tasting, and exploring the Sonoma coast are favorite activities of guests.

Host: Suzanne Greene
Rooms: 4 (PB) $145
Full Breakfast
Credit Cards: A, B, C
Notes: 2, 4, 7, 10, 11, 12

MORAGA

Hallman Bed and Breakfast

309 Constance Place, 94556
(415) 376-4318

Bed and breakfast on a quiet cul-de-sac in the beautiful Moraga Valley. Bed down in one of the tastefully appointed rooms; one in the Victorian manor and the second as contemporary as California itself. Awake refreshed with breakfast on the delightful terrace or comfortable dining room. Take off and "do" San Francisco or any other bay area attractions. Return in time for a refreshing dip in the pool or a relaxing time in the Jacuzzi spa, which is available May through September. There are many fine restaurants nearby for an enjoyable dinner. There are two guest rooms available, each with a comfortable queen-size bed. Shared bath. Both rooms are used only when guests are in the same party.

Hosts: Frank and Virginia Hallman
Rooms: 2 (SB) $60
Full Breakfast
Credit Cards: None
Notes: 2, 5, 8, 9, 11

7 No smoking; 8 Children welcome; 9 Social drinking allowed; 10 Tennis nearby; 11 Swimming nearby; 12 Golf nearby; 13 Skiing nearby; 14 May be booked through a travel agent.

MORRO BAY

Bed and Breakfast California

P.O. Box 282910, San Francisco, 94128-2910
(415) 696-1690; (800) 872-4500
FAX (415) 696-1699

The Howell House. This incredible mansion on the coast has a guest suite with bedroom, full private bath, oceanview deck, and a full English-style pub sitting room. Coffee service is delivered by dumbwaiter, and a refrigerator is available. The Scottish hostess makes a great, gracious breakfast. $100-120.

Ocean and Bay Views. One block away from the Embarcadero and the Bay, this new house has large rooms with queen-size beds, private baths, and platform rockers. Guests are 30 miles from Hearst Castle. Continental plus breakfast. Very relaxing and a great view. $75-95.

MOUNT SHASTA

Eye Openers Bed and Breakfast Reservations

P.O. Box 694, Altadena, 91003-0694
(213) 684-4428; (818) 797-2055
FAX (818) 798-3640

MS-M9I. This 1923 two-story ranch house is near fishing, hiking, boating, and skiing areas. Full breakfast and afternoon refreshments served. Hot tub. Nine guest rooms with queen-size and twin beds and private and shared baths. No smoking. $70-85.

MS-W2I. Small ranch in a mountain sanctuary near skiing, boating, fishing, golf, and hiking. Enjoy a wonderful full breakfast, large deck with spectacular views, ranch animals, and walking trails. Two guest

rooms with king- and queen-size beds and private baths. No smoking. $65-80.

Mount Shasta Ranch

1008 W. A. Barr Road, 96067
(916) 926-3870

This Northern California historic two-story ranch house offers affordable elegance. There are four spacious guest rooms in the main house, each with private bath. Carriage house accommodations include five rooms. Two-bedroom vacation cottage available year-round. Guests are invited to enjoy the rec room with Ping Pong, pool table, and piano. Relax in the Hot-Spring spa. Close to lake, town, and ski slopes. Full country-style breakfasts each morning.

Hosts: Bill and Mary Larsen
Rooms: 9 (4 PB; 5 SB) $55-95
Cottage: 1
Full Breakfast
Credit Cards: A, B, C, D
Notes: 2, 5, 7, 8, 9, 10, 11, 12, 13, 14

MUIR BEACH

Bed and Breakfast San Francisco

P.O. Box 420009, San Francisco, 94142
(415) 931-3083; FAX (415) 921-BBSF (2273)

19. A lovely bedroom suite with private entrance, fireplace, and private bath that overlooks the Pacific Ocean. Muir Beach is a quiet community on Highway 1 north of San Francisco not to far from Stenson Beach. It's a place for thos who really want to get away. Full breakfast served. $100.

MURPHYS

Dunbar House, 1880

271 Jones Street, 95247
(209) 728-2897

Explore gold country during the day and enjoy a glass of lemonade or local wine on the wide porches in the afternoon. Inviting fireplaces and down comforters in antique-filled rooms. The Cedar Room has a two-person whirlpool bath. All rooms have TVs, VCRs, and a classic video library. Breakfast may be served in the room, in the dining room, or out in the century-old gardens. Two-night minimum stay required for weekends. Children over 10 welcome.

Hosts: Bob and Barbara Costa
Rooms: 4 (PB) $105-145
Full Breakfast
Credit Cards: A, B, C
Notes: 2, 5, 7, 9, 10, 11, 12, 13, 14

NAPA

Arbor Guest House

1436 G Street, 94559
(707) 252-8144; (800) 707-8144

This gracious 1906 Colonial transition home and carriage house are furnished with antiques and separated by trumpet vine-covered arbor. Bask in the spa tubs in the Winter Haven or Autumn Harvest rooms while enjoying the warmth of a crackling fire. Rose's Bower provides an intimate getaway with fireplace. Afternoon refreshments and delicious full breakfasts are served by thoughtful host/owners fireside or in the garden. Near wineries, gourmet restaurants, Wine Train, ballooning, golf, and shopping. All rooms feature private baths and queen-size beds.

Hosts: Bruce and Rosemary Logan
Rooms: 5 (PB) $85-165
Full Breakfast
Credit Cards: A, B, C
Notes: 2, 5, 8, 9, 10, 12, 14

Beazley House

1910 First Street, 94559
(707) 257-1649

Guests sense the hospitality as they stroll the walk past verdant lawns and bright flowers. The landmark 1902 mansion is a chocolate brown masterpiece. Visitors feel instantly welcome as they are greeted by a smiling innkeeper. The view from each room reveals beautiful gardens. And all rooms have a private bath; some have a private spa and a fireplace. Napa's first bed and breakfast and still its best!

Hosts: Carol and Jim Beazley
Rooms: 11 (PB) $105-185
Full Breakfast
Credit Cards: A, B, C
Notes: 2, 5, 9, 10, 11, 12, 14

Bed and Breakfast California

P.O. Box 282910, San Francisco, 94128-2910
(415) 696-1690; (800) 872-4500
FAX (415) 696-1699

Blue Violet Mansion. This romantic Queen Anne Victorian mansion in historic Old Town Napa features large sunny rooms and a full country breakfast. Accommodations include king- and queen-size beds with private baths, most with fireplaces and whirlpool spas or balconies. Wine is served at check-in. Scrumptious late-night desserts and beverages are available. In-room massages, candlelight dinners by arrangement, hot-air ballon rides, and golf packages make this a Disneyland for grownups. $110-185.

Euro-Spa on Pine Street. Enjoy this wine country retreat with European ambience in a comfortable, relaxed setting. Just a short walk to quaint shops and restaurants, this resort and spa offers individual theme decor with private baths. Mineral pool, and hot whirlpool, massages, facials, wraps, and more are available. $135-195.

Take the Wine Train. This perfect little bed and breakfast is in the heart of Napa. Built in 1906, there are three guest rooms in the main house, and two in the carriage house. Rooms feature Victorian garden wall-coverings and oak and wicker furnishings; several have wood-burning fireplaces and private decks. Full breakfast and complimentary afternoon refreshments in the garden. $100-125.

7 No smoking; 8 Children welcome; 9 Social drinking allowed; 10 Tennis nearby; 11 Swimming nearby; 12 Golf nearby; 13 Skiing nearby; 14 May be booked through a travel agent.

Bed and Breakfast International

P.O. Box 282910, San Francisco, 94128-2910
(415) 696-1690; (800) 872-4500
FAX (415) 696-1699

303. Guests cannot go wrong when choosing this location. The fabulous architecture in the 101-year-old home is modeled after an English country estate. Great hosts, antiques galore, and one of the best prices in the wine country. $99-169.

The Blue Violet Mansion

443 Brown Street, 94559-3348
(707) 253-BLUE (2583)

An 1886 Queen Anne Victorian mansion on one acre, this inn is listed on the National Register of Historic Places. King- and queen-size beds. Two rooms with balcony and five with fireplaces; three with spas. Antique furnishings and Oriental carpets. Complimentary use of bicycles and kites. Picnic baskets. Candlelight champagne breakfast, dinner, and massage services are available in guests' room. Evening wine service and late-night desserts. Full breakfast served in the dining room. In historic Old Town near shops, Napa Wine Train, hot air balloons, and wine tastings.

Hosts: Bob and Kathy Morris
Rooms: 10 (PB) $95-195
Suite: 1
Full Breakfast
Credit Cards: A, B, C, E, F
Notes: 2, 3, 4, 5, 7, 8, 9, 10, 11, 12, 14

Cedar Gables Inn

486 Coombs Street, 94559
(707) 224-7969

In Old Town Napa, this 100-year-old home is styled after English country manors of the 16th century. Antique furnishings are throughout the house. Some rooms have fireplaces and whirlpool tubs. Huge family room with large fireplace and big-screen TV is also available for guests. Minutes from wineries, restaurants, and the Napa Valley Wine Train.

Hosts: Margaret and Craig Sansdell
Rooms: 6 (PB) $89-159
Full Breakfast
Credit Cards: A, B, C
Notes: 2, 5, 7, 9, 12, 14

Churchill Manor Bed and Breakfast Inn

485 Brown Street, 94559
(707) 253-7733

A magnificent 1889 mansion resting on an acre of beautiful gardens, Churchill Manor is listed on the National Register of Historic Places. Elegant parlors boast carved-wood ceilings and columns, leaded-glass windows, Oriental rugs, brass and crystal chandeliers, four fireplaces, and a grand piano. Ten guest rooms are individually decorated with gorgeous antiques. Guests enjoy afternoon fresh-baked cookies and lemonade, two hours of evening wines and cheeses, and a delicious full gourmet breakfast served in a mosaic-floored sunroom. Complimentary tandem bicycles and croquet.

Host: Joanna Guidotti and Brian Jensen
Rooms: 10 (PB) $75-145
Full Breakfast
Credit Cards: A, B, C, D
Notes: 2, 5, 7, 9, 10, 11, 12, 14

Eye Openers Bed and Breakfast Reservations

P.O. Box 694, Altadena, 91003-0694
(213) 684-4428; (818) 797-2055
FAX (818) 798-3640

NA-B11. This 1902 Napa landmark is a striking, elegant mansion on one-half acres of lawns and gardens. Eleven guest rooms are individually decorated with antiques and have queen-size beds and private baths. The Carriage House hosts five large rooms with private spas and fireplaces. A full buffet breakfast is served. No smoking. $105-190.

NA-C91. Bed and breakfast in the heart of wine country is offered in the 1889 mansion that has been designated a national historic landmark. Each guest room is individually decorated. Enjoy an extended Continental breakfast, and relax on the veranda with evening refreshments. No smoking. Nine guest rooms. Private bath. $75-160.

Hennessey House

1727 Main Street, 94559
(707) 226-3774; FAX (707) 226-2975

This 1889 Queen Anne Victorian is in downtown Napa, the gateway to the historic wine country. Listed on the National Register of Historic Places, the main house and carriage house are decorated with antique furnishings. Private baths are available. Selected rooms have fireplaces and whirlpool tubs. Guests may relax in the gardens. Full breakfast is served in the dining room, which features a beautiful, hand-painted, stamped, tin ceiling. Complimentary sherry. Weekend wine and hors d'oeuvres. Wine Train packages and golf packages can be arranged.

Hosts: Lauriann Delay and Andrea LaMar
Rooms: 10 (PB) $80-155
Full Breakfast
Credit Cards: A, B, C, D
Notes: 2, 5, 7, 9, 12, 14

The International Bed and Breakfast Club, Inc.

504 Amherst Street, Buffalo, NY 14207
(800) 723-4262; FAX (716) 873-4462

CA1444PP. This beautiful Queen Anne Victorian home was built in 1899 for Harry and Madaline Johnston and was given to them as a wedding gift. The Johnstons were prominent Napa residents and contributed much to Napa's history. The inn is on one of the nicest, quiet, tree-lined streets in the historical section of town and is within walking distance to downtown, several restaurants, and just four blocks east of Highway 29 that traverses the Napa Valley. Some of the area attractions include golf, biking, horseback riding, hot air ballooning, gliders, the Napa Valley Wine Train, fine dining, and world-famous wineries. Upon arrival at the inn, afternoon refreshments and evening desserts are available. Coffee is ready by 8 a.m., and a full breakfast is served at 9 a.m. in the dining room. Six guest rooms with private baths. $120-170.

CA2583PP. This elegant 1886 Queen Anne home, in the historic district of Napa, was built for Emanuel Manasse, an executive at the Sawyer Tannery. His innovative leather tanning techniques are still in use today. Evidence of his craft remains in the embossed leather wainscoting adorning the main foyer. The mansion has been lovingly restored and offers a blend of quiet country living and Victorian elegance to ensure visits are pleasurable experiences. Relax in the Victorian ambience of the parlors, outside in the garden gazebo, or on the veranda or shaded deck. Nine rooms with private baths. Gourmet breakfast. $115-195.

Napa Inn

1137 Warren Street, 94559
(707) 257-1444; (800) 435-1144

The Napa Inn is a beautiful Queen Anne Victorian on a quiet, tree-lined street in the historic section of the town of Napa. Furnished with turn-of-the-century antiques, the inn features six guest rooms, a large parlor, and formal dining room. Each spacious bedroom has its own private bath, and two suites feature fireplaces. The inn is convenient to the Napa, Sonoma, and Carneros wine regions. Also many other

7 No smoking; 8 Children welcome; 9 Social drinking allowed; 10 Tennis nearby; 11 Swimming nearby; 12 Golf nearby; 13 Skiing nearby; 14 May be booked through a travel agent.

activities: hot air ballooning, gliding, biking, hiking, golf, tennis, many fine restaurants, and the Napa Valley Wine Train. Closed Christmas Day.

Hosts: Ann and Denny Mahoney
Rooms: 6 (PB) $120-170
Full Breakfast
Credit Cards: A, B
Notes: 2, 5, 7, 10, 12, 14

Oak Knoll Inn

2200 East Oak Knoll Avenue, Napa Valley, 94558
(707) 255-2200

Tall French windows, rustic stone walls, and vaulted ceilings distinguish the four spacious guest rooms at this luxurious inn, set well off the bustle of the main roads and surrounded by 600 acres of Chardonnay vineyards. The rooms have king-size brass beds, marble fireplaces, private baths, and sitting areas with overstuffed chairs and sofas. A full breakfast is served at guests' leisure in the room, dining room, or on the veranda surrounding the heated pool, spa, and magnificent views.

Hosts: Barbara Passino and John Kuhlmann
Rooms: 4 (PB) $175-250
Full Breakfast
Credit Cards: A, B
Notes: 2, 5, 7, 10, 11, 12, 14

The Old World Inn

1301 Jefferson Street, 94559
(707) 257-0112

For a holiday of romance and plentiful gourmet delights, plan a stay at this charming Victorian inn. Relax in the outdoor spa or choose a room with a sunken spa tub. Guests are pampered with home-baked treats throughout their stay: savor afternoon tea and cookies when one arrives, unwind during the wine and cheese social, treat oneself to a chocolate lover's dessert buffet before retiring, and awaken to a gourmet breakfast.

Host: Diane Dumaine
Rooms: 8 (PB) $110-145

Full Breakfast
Credit Cards: A, B, C, D
Notes: 2, 5, 7, 9, 12, 14

La Residence Country Inn

4066 St. Helena Highway, 94558
(707) 253-0337

Accommodations, most with fireplaces, are in two structures: a Gothic Revival home, decorated in traditional American antiques, and the "French barn," decorated with European pine antiques. Two acres of grounds with hot tub and a heated swimming pool are surrounded by a gazebo and trellis. Wine is served each evening.

Hosts: David Jackson and Craig Calussen
Rooms: 20 (18 PB; 2 SB) $85-190
Full Breakfast
Credit Cards: A, B, E
Notes: 5, 7, 8, 9, 10, 11, 12, 14

NAPA VALLEY

Bartels Ranch and Country Inn

1200 Conn Valley Road, St. Helena, 94574
(707) 963-4001; FAX (707) 963-5100

In the heart of world-famous Napa Valley wine country, this peaceful, romantic 60-acre country estate overlooks a valley, oak-covered hillsides, and estate vineyards. All just six minutes east of St. Helena's finest wineries, restaurants, and shopping. Listed in "Best Places to Stay in California." Guests may choose from three uniquely decorated rooms with special views. Accommodations offer amenities including fireplaces, music, movies, in-room coffee makers, robes, bubble bath, and bedside reading. Hike or bike to lakeside picnics and private estate wineries. Library and sunken living room with baby grand piano. Massive beams and glass walls enclose entertainment room with billiards, Ping Pong, English darts, chess, and fireside sherry. Candlelight breakfast served until noon in formal dining room or landscaped terraces. Telephone, FAX, and refrigerators available. Antiques, fine art galleries, wineries, horseback riding, golf, tennis, hot-air ballooning, gliders, and spas nearby. Limousine, helicopter, and shuttle available. Friendly staff and personalized wine itineraries are a well-known house specialty. Awarded 1994 AAA Award of Excellence by ABBA. Lunch and dinner catered. Limited smoking allowed.

Host: Jami Bartels
Rooms: 4 (PB) $115-315
Full Breakfast
Credit Cards: A, B, C, D, E, F
Notes: 2, 5, 9, 10, 11, 12, 14

Bed and Breakfast San Francisco

P.O. Box 420009, San Francisco, 94142
(415) 931-3083; FAX (415) 921-BBSF (2273)

25. Enjoy California's famous wine region. The hosts have just completed building a gorgeous custom designed home in the heart of the Napa Valley. The guest room has its own entrance, patio, queen-size bed, private bath, and refrigerator. From the patio the view is overlooking the new stable and horses. All the famous wineries are nearby as well as a wealth of excellent restaurants. Full breakfast served. $100.

NEVADA CITY _____

Bed and Breakfast California

P.O. Box 282910, San Francisco, 94128-2910
(415) 696-1690; (800) 872-4500
FAX (415) 696-1699

The Parsonage. In the historic district of Nevada City, history comes alive in this 125-year-old home. Cozy guest rooms, all with private baths, share a parlor lovingly furnished with the innkeeper's family antiques. Enjoy full breakfast on the veranda or in the formal dining room. Call for rates.

Emma Nevada House

528 East Broad Street, 95959
(916) 265-4415; (800) 916-EMMA

Opera star Emma Nevada would be proud of the inn that bears her name. This elegantly restored and decorated 1856 home sparkles from an abundance of antique windows, one of many architectural details. Beautiful guest rooms offer fluffy down comforters and Jacuzzi or claw-foot tubs. Spacious living areas and porches allow guests to relax or observe horse-drawn buggies touring the Victorian neighborhood. A gourmet breakfast is served overlooking the forest-like setting behind the inn.

Host: Ruth Ann Riese
Rooms: 6 (PB) $100-150
Full Breakfast
Credit Cards: A, B, C, D
Notes: 2, 5, 7, 9, 10, 11, 12, 13, 14

The Parsonage Bed and Breakfast

427 Broad Street, 95959
(916) 265-9478

This home, dating back to 1865, offers six guest rooms with private baths. Each guest room honors a California pioneer ancestor of the owner. The entire home is furnished with family antiques that date back to the 1850s. A Continental breakfast, including fresh baked muffins and croissants, homemade jam, yogurt, fresh fruit, juice, and coffee, is served at a table with line-dried and hand-pressed linens. In every way, the hosts like to transport their guests back 100 years to a gentler era where people cared about each other. A Sunday brunch is also served. Inquire to see if children are welcome.

Host: Deborah Dane
Rooms: 6 (PB) $65-120
Continental Breakfast
Credit Cards: A, B
Notes: 2, 5, 7, 9, 10, 11, 12, 13, 14

7 No smoking; 8 Children welcome; 9 Social drinking allowed; 10 Tennis nearby; 11 Swimming nearby; 12 Golf nearby; 13 Skiing nearby; 14 May be booked through a travel agent.

The Red Castle Historic Lodgings
109 Prospect Street, 95959
(916) 265-5135

An incomparable 1860 Gothic Revival four-story brick mansion acclaimed for its "strong sense of time and place, is one of ten top Historic Country Inns" (*US Air*) and "celebrated nationally as setting the standard for bed and breakfast inns" (*LA Times*). Crowning forested Prospect Hill with unsurpassed views from encircling verandas, picturesque terraced gardens, and winding footpaths to town, the inn "would top my list of places to stay; nothing else quite compares with it" (*Gourmet*).

Hosts: Conley and Mary Louise Weaver
Rooms: 7 (PB) $70-125
Full Breakfast
Credit Cards: A, B
Notes: 2, 4, 5, 7, 9, 10, 11, 12, 13, 14

NEWPORT BEACH

Bed and Breakfast California
P.O. Box 282910, San Francisco, 94128-2910
(415) 696-1690; (800) 872-4500
FAX (415) 696-1699

At the Fun Zone. This landmark 1924 inn is at the tip of the Balboa Peninsula in Newport Beach. There is a pool, hot tub, many rooms with oceanview, and ample Continental breakfast. Kids welcome. The beach, carnival rides, and a fresh fish dinner are nearby. $95-125.

Lido Island Waterfront. The architect-owners of this beautiful home love to take visitors out on their boat. They have two guest suites, one with an incredible oceanview and both with queen-size bed and private bath. Breakfast is fresh and bountiful. Beautiful setting and Lido Island is convenient to restaurants, shops, and attractions. $90-115.

On Newport Peninsula. This charming home in a quiet neighborhood on the Balboa Peninsula of Newport Beach features stained glass, used bricks, and natural wood surroundings. Upstairs loft room has a queen-size bed, private bath, and access to a large sun deck with ocean and beach views. Downstairs brass bedroom offers a double bed and large private bath. Just steps from the beach and bay. Bicycles and beach chairs are available. Full breakfast. $85.

Doryman's Oceanfront Inn
2102 West Oceanfront, 92663
(714) 675-7300

Romance, luxury, resounding Victorian elegance await guests at this exquisite waterfront inn. Enjoy spectacular Pacific sunsets, sip champagne on the oceanfront sundeck. Enjoy a soak in one of the sunk-in Italian marble Jacuzzi tubs or nestle in a guest room in front of a crackling fireplace. Disneyland and other activities are within 15 minutes; Los Angeles and Beverly Hills are within 40 minutes. All rooms feature beautiful canopied and wood beds, French Country-style antiques, and oceanviews. Breakfast can be served in the guests' room or in the breakfast parlor or on the sun deck. Complimentary champagne for special occasions.

Rooms: 10 (PB) $135-275
Continental Breakfast
Credit Cards: A, B, C
Notes: 2, 3, 4, 5, 8, 9, 10, 11, 12, 13, 14

Eye Openers Bed and Breakfast Reservations
P.O. Box 694, Altadena, 91003-0694
(213) 684-4428; (818) 797-2055
FAX (818) 798-3640

NP-D2. Crow's nest with 360-degree view tops this trilevel beach home. The third level is a large guest deck with barbecue and refrigerator. Stained glass is featured throughout the house. Perfect for beach and

NOTES: Credit cards accepted: A MasterCard; B Visa; C American Express; D Discover; E Diners Club;
F Other; 2 Personal checks accepted; 3 Lunch available; 4 Dinner available; 5 Open all year; 6 Pets welcome;

bay activities; bicycle and beach chairs available. Full or Continental breakfast and afternoon refreshments. Two guest rooms. Private baths. $50-75.

NP-D101. A very special beachfront bed and breakfast inn has spacious antique-filled guest rooms, each with its own fireplace and some with oceanviews and Jacuzzis. Delicious full breakfast is served in the room, on the patio, or in the parlor. Ten guest rooms. Private baths. $135-275.

NP-W2. Stunning, well-decorated bed and breakfast on the water's edge has two guest rooms, private baths, a guest den with retractable roof, lounge chairs, refrigerator, and grassy yard for sunbathing. Take the shuttle or bike to unique shops and restaurants. Continental breakfast. Minimum stay is two nights. Resident dog. $80-85.

Little Inn on the Bay

617 Lido Park Drive, 92663
(714) 673-8800; (800) 438-4466

This 30-room Cape Cod-style bed and breakfast is on the waterfront and boasts spectacular Pacific Ocean. Enjoy complimentary wine and cheese and hot cocoa and Danish butter cookies before bed. Nestled snuggly between the ocean and the bay, the views are breathtaking. Shopping and fine dining are in walking distance. Complimentary bicycles are available.

Hosts: Laura Ann Laing and Hond Laing
Rooms: 30 (PB) $75-200
Continental Breakfast
Credit Cards: A, B, C
Notes: 2, 3, 4, 5, 7, 8, 9, 10, 11, 12, 13, 14

NICE

Featherbed Railroad Company

2870 Lakeshore Boulevard, P.O. Box 4016, 95464
(707) 274-4434; (800) 966-6322

Nine lovingly refurbished theme cabooses reflect the Casablanca Orient Express. Most have Jacuzzi tubs for two. All have small refrigerators, cable TV (some with VCRs). Small sitting areas, coffee pot, assorted complimentary beverages, private pool, and spa are available. Full breakfast. Year-round fishing boat and Jet Ski rental available. Enjoy serene country setting.

Hosts: Len and Lorraine Bassignani
Rooms: 9 (PB) $90-140
Full Breakfast
Credit Cards: A, B, C, D
Notes: 2, 5, 7, 8, 9, 10, 11, 12, 14

NIPOMO

Bed and Breakfast California

P.O. Box 282910, San Francisco, 94128-2910
(415) 696-1690; (800) 872-4500
FAX (415) 696-1699

Turn of the Century Inn. This little inn features original woodwork, stained glass, hand-carved furniture, attentive hosts, and a full gourmet breakfast. All four rooms have private baths. Enjoy charming accommodations at reasonable rates. $70-95.

Kaleidoscope Inn Bed and Breakfast

130 East Dana Street, P.O. Box 1297, 93444
(805) 929-5444

This 1886 Victorian is furnished with antiques and offers beautiful gardens, delicious full breakfasts, a Jacuzzi in one bath, and a king-size bed in one guest room. Halfway between Los Angeles and San Francisco, this bed and breakfast is near local attractions, golf, beach, lakes, hot springs, great dining, theater, horseback riding, and wind surfing. The owner loves to spoil guests.

Host: Patty Linane
Rooms: 3 (PB) $80
Full Breakfast
Credit Cards: A, B, C
Notes: 2, 5, 7, 9, 10, 11, 12, 14

NIPTON

Hotel Nipton

72 Nipton Road, 92364
(619) 856-2335

Hotel Nipton, originally built in 1904, was restored in 1986. In the Mojave National Preserve, United State's newest park, 65 miles southwest of Las Vegas between the Grand Canyon and Death Valley. Enjoy the beautiful panoramic views of Ivanpah Valley and New York Mountains. Outside Jacuzzi for star gazing. Only bed and breakfast in this historic mining town with a population of 60.

Hosts: Jerry and Roxanne Freeman
Rooms: 4 (SB) $54.50
Continental Breakfast
Credit Cards: A, B, E, F
Notes: 2, 5, 7, 8, 9, 11, 12, 14

NORTH HOLLYWOOD

Bed and Breakfast California

P.O. Box 282910, San Francisco, 94128-2910
(415) 696-1690; (800) 872-4500
FAX (415) 696-1699

Mediterranean Warmth. This sunny North Hollywood home is drenched with art and color. The guest room has twin beds and a private bath. A Continental breakfast is served poolside in a walled garden.

Guests are within walking distance to shops, public transportation, a large variety of restaurants, and are near studios and Burbank Airport. $55-60.

Touch of Mexico. This Southwest-style home in Toluca Lake features two guest rooms, each with private bath, TV, and private entrances opening to the deck, pool, and spa. One room has a full line of baby equipment. $85.

European Ambience in Studio City. This cozy condo feels like it's in the country, but it's just two blocks from famed Ventura Boulevard and just a few miles from the studios. Guest quarters include a bedroom, bathroom, and living room that are draped in warmth, color, and texture. Gourmet breakfast available. $85.

OAKHURST

Chateau du Sureau

P.O. Box 577, 48688 Victoria Lane, 93644
(209) 683-6860

On the rim of Yosemite National Park commanding extraordinary views of the Sierra Nevada sits this seven and one-half acre French-country estate. An enchanting, authentic European castle, the hotel offers nine exquisite guest rooms, all lovingly

Chateau du Sureau

decorated with period antiques, king-size canopied beds, wood-burning fireplaces, CD and stereo systems, and gorgeous baths with lots of hand-painted French tile and deep Roman tubs large enough for two. A sumptuous full breakfast is served by warm and friendly personnel in the breakfast room, starting the day with a smile. On the grounds, pathways meander through wildflower gardens, a European pool, and an outdoor chess and checkers court.

Host: Erna Kubin-Clanin
Rooms: 9 (PB) $260-360
Full Breakfast
Credit Cards: A, B, C
Notes: 2, 3, 4, 7, 10, 11, 12, 13, 14

OCCIDENTAL

The Inn at Occidental

3657 Church Street, 95465
(707) 874-1047; (800) 522-6324 (reservations)
FAX (707) 874-1078

In a charming village near the spectacular Sonoma coast and wine country, The Inn at Occidental is a completely renovated 1877 Victorian with European ambience. With antique furnishings and goose-down comforters, each room features original art, antiques, fresh flowers, and a private bath. Amenities include a courtyard garden, fireplaces, afternoon refreshments, and sumptuous breakfast. Two-night minimum stay required for weekends and holidays. Children over 10 welcome.

Rooms: 8 (PB) $95-195
Full Breakfast
Credit Cards: A, B, C, D
Notes: 2, 5, 7, 9, 10, 11, 12, 14

OLEMA

Point Reyes Seashore Lodge

10021 Highway 1, P.O. Box 39, 94950
(415) 663-9000; (800) 404-5634;
FAX (415) 663-9030

A re-creation of a turn-of-the-century lodge offers 18 rooms, three suites, and a freestanding cottage. Many rooms have whirlpool tubs and fireplaces. Borders the Point Reyes National Seashore Park, making for a great base for hiking and biking, whale watching and bird watching.

Hosts: Jean and Scott Taylor
Rooms: 22 (PB) $75-250
Continental Breakfast
Credit Cards: A, B, C, D
Notes: 2, 5, 7, 8, 9, 10, 11, 12, 14

ORANGE

Bed and Breakfast California

P.O. Box 282910, San Francisco, 94128-2910
(415) 696-1690; (800) 872-4500
FAX (415) 696-1699

Historic Estate. This estate was built in 1890 and remodeled in 1917 in the early Revival style with a few of the original Victorian architectural features remaining. It is within walking distance of the historic Old Towne Plaza district. The Ukrainian hosts serve a full breakfast, afternoon tea, and hors d'oeuvres in the evening. Three spacious guest rooms are available with private access to the sun deck and guest library/sitting room with fireplace, cable TV, books, and games. $65-100.

Country Comfort Bed and Breakfast

5104 East Valencia Drive, 92669
(714) 532-2802

In a quiet residential area, this house has been furnished with comfort and pleasure in mind. It is handicapped accessible with adaptive equipment available. Amenities include a swimming pool, big screen cable TV and VCR, atrium, fireplace, piano, and Jacuzzi. Breakfast often features delicious Scotch eggs, stuffed French toast, hash,

7 No smoking; 8 Children welcome; 9 Social drinking allowed; 10 Tennis nearby; 11 Swimming nearby; 12 Golf nearby; 13 Skiing nearby; 14 May be booked through a travel agent.

fruits and assorted beverages. Vegetarian selections are also available. Six miles to Disneyland and Knott's Berry Farm. Smoking in designated areas only.

Hosts: Geri Lopker and Joanne Angell
Rooms: 3 (2 PB; 1 SB) $60-65
Full Breakfast
Credit Cards: None
Notes: 2, 5, 8, 9, 10, 11, 12, 14

ORLAND

The Inn at Shallow Creek Farm

4712 Road DD, 95963
(916) 865-4093; (800) 865-4093

A gracious two-story farmhouse offering spacious rooms furnished with antiques—a blend of nostalgia and comfortable country living. Three miles off I-5. The inn is surrounded by an orange grove. Breakfast features old-fashioned baked goods and fruits and juices from the family orchard.

Hosts: Kurt and Mary Glaeseman
Rooms: 4 (2 PB; 2 SB) $55-75
Full Breakfast
Credit Cards: A, B
Notes: 2, 5, 7, 9, 11, 12, 14

OROVILLE

Jean's Riverside Bed and Breakfast

45 Cabana Drive, P.O. Box 2334, 95965
(916) 533-1413

Romantic getaway located on old Wells Fargo route along the banks of Feather River with individualized rooms and suites, some with private Jacuzzis, Franklin fireplaces, and window walls. Also available is a parlor with gold quartz fireplace and antique amusements. Fishing, swimming, gold panning, bird watching, badminton, and croquet are all on the property. Quaint shops with antiques and local handcrafts, excellent restaurants, Oroville Dam and

Lake, fish hatchery, historic sites, hiking, and scenic drives are nearby.

Host: Jean Pratt
Rooms: 15 (PB) $55-125
Full Breakfast
Credit Cards: A, B, C, E
Notes: 2, 5, 9, 10, 11, 12, 14

PACIFIC GROVE

Eye Openers Bed and Breakfast Reservations

P.O. Box 694, Altadena, 91003-0694
(213) 684-4428; (818) 797-2055
FAX (818) 798-3640

PG-C20I. This century-old Victorian boarding house is now a refurbished award-winning bed and breakfast inn. Beautifully decorated rooms, delicious breakfast, and afternoon refreshments. All private baths. $80-185.

PG-G08I. This 1884 Victorian with ocean-view has been renovated and opened its doors in 1990 to become a Pacific Grove bed and breakfast inn close to the beach. Each room is uniquely decorated and features views or sundecks. Delicious full breakfast and afternoon refreshments are provided. No smoking allowed. Private bath. $110-150.

PG-G11I. This 1888 Queen Anne-style mansion-by-the-sea has a panoramic view of Monterey Bay. Delicious breakfast and afternoon refreshments. Shared and private baths. $100-160.

PG-G21I. Beautifully preserved 1887 Victorian on the National Register of Historic Places can now be enjoyed as a bed and breakfast inn. Wonderful breakfast, afternoon hors d'oeuvres, and wine or tea served. $85-185.

Gosby House Inn

643 Lighthouse Avenue, 93950
(408) 375-1284

The Gosby House Inn sits in teh heart of the quaint town of Pacific Grove. Its magnificent Queen Anne Victorian architecture will enchant guests, as will its individually decorated sleeping rooms, antique doll collection, and gracious staff. A bountiful breakfst is served, along with afternoon wine and hors d'oeuvres. Fluffy robes, complimentary beverages, and a heaping cookie jar.

Host: Suzi Russ; innkeeper
Rooms: 22 (20 PB; 2 SB) $85-150
Full Breakfast
Credit Cards: A, B, C
Notes: 2, 5, 8, 9, 10, 11, 12, 14

Green Gables Inn

104 Fifth Street, 93950
(408) 375-2095; (800) 722-1774

A magnificent Victorian mansion just steps from the water. Each room has a spectacular view of the water. The 11 guest rooms are furnished with antiques; many have fireplaces and are immaculately maintained. A gourmet breakfast is served each morning and may be ordered in the guests' room. Afternoon tea is served in the parlor at 4:30 P.M. Complimentary morning paper, turndown service, hot and cold beverages and concierge all provided. The Green Gables Inn makes sure any special occasion is celebrated in style.

Hosts: Roger and Sally Post; Tess Desmond
   Arthur, innkeeper
Rooms: 11 (7 PB; 4 SB) $100-160
Full Breakfast
Credit Cards: A, B, C
Notes: 2, 5, 7, 8, 9, 10, 11, 12, 14

The Old St. Angela Inn

321 Central Avenue, 93950
(408) 372-3246; (800) 748-6306

The Old St. Angela's Inn began as a country home in 1910, converted to a rectory and then a convent in 1920, and is now a cozy bed and breakfast inn overlooking the natural beauty of the Monterey Bay. Within this historic Cape Cod home are rooms of distinctive individuality and warmth to provide guests with comfort and serenity. Country pine furniture, little teddy bears, and other pleasant surroundings provide a relaxing, informal, and home-away-from-home atmosphere. Mingle with fellow guests by the fireplace in the living room and enjoy an afternoon wine, tea, or coffee and cookies. Relax in the garden patio amidst beautiful flowers, butterflies, and sunshine. Just 100 yards from the water and only minutes from excellent restaurants and shopping areas, and other activities.

Host: Kathy Pedullà
Rooms: 8 (5 PB; 3 SB) $90-150
Full Breakfast
Credit Cards: A, B, C
Notes: 5, 9, 10, 11, 12, 14

PACIFIC PALISADES

Bed and Breakfast California

P.O. Box 282910, San Francisco, 94128-2910
(415) 696-1690; (800) 872-4500
FAX (415) 696-1699

Ellen's Bed and Breakfast. Between Santa Monica and Malibu is this quiet condominium. It has a bedroom with two beds and private bath. Accommodations include pool, sun deck, Jacuzzi, sauna, and a fully equipped exercise room. Tennis courts, picnic areas, and a playground are within walking distance. Hostess is the president of a nonprofit organization helping worldwide environmental efforts, and her home is adjacent to Will Rogers Historic Park and the J. Paul Getty Museum. $55.

Jane's House is a sprawling home in luxurious Pacific Palisades with five guest rooms, three with private baths, several with views of the garden and pool. One Victorian-style suite has a perfect kid-sized attic room. Breakfast is full of fresh, homegrown fruit. On the bluffs not far from the ocean. $50-65.

Eye Openers Bed and Breakfast Reservations

P.O. Box 694, Altadena, 91003-0694
(213) 684-4428; (818) 797-2055
FAX (818) 798-3640

PP-H1. Large, sunny condominium one-half mile from the ocean offers a good location, friendly hospitality, and pool. The guest room has twin beds and private bath. Continental breakfast. No smoking. Resident cat. $50-55.

PALM DESERT

Bed and Breakfast California

P.O. Box 282910, San Francisco, 94128-2910
(415) 696-1690; (800) 872-4500
FAX (415) 696-1699

Blue Desert Skies. In the heart of Palm Desert, Tres Palmas features lovely rooms uniquely decorated in the Southwestern style. Indulge in specialty coffees and teas as part of a special Continental breakfast in the dining room, around the pool, or in the privacy of the room. Hosts of this cozy bed and breakfast offer individual attention as they help make stays a pleasant experience. $90-135.

Eye Openers Bed and Breakfast Reservations

P.O. Box 694, Altadena, 91003-0694
(213) 684-4428; (818) 797-2055
FAX (818) 798-3640

PD-B4. New contemporary-style bed and breakfast features Southwestern decor, a

welcome, delightful atmosphere, many amenities, pool, and spa. Four guest rooms have queen- or king-size beds with private baths. An extended Continental breakfast is served, and refreshments are available during the day. It is walking distance to El Paseo with its boutiques, galleries, and restaurants and to other entertainment areas. No smoking. $90-140.

Tres Palmas Bed and Breakfast

73135 Tumbleweed Lane, 92260
(619) 773-9858

Tres Palmas is only one block south of El Paseo, the "Rodeo Drive of the Desert," where guests will find boutiques, art galleries, and fine restaurants. Guests can choose to stay "home" to relax and enjoy the desert sun in and around the pool and spa. The guest rooms feature queen- or king-size beds, climate controls, and TVs and are uniquely decorated in Southwestern style. Lemonade and iced tea are always available. Snacks are provided in the late afternoons. Rated A plus by ABBA and three diamond by AAA.

Hosts: Terry and Karen Bennett
Rooms: 4 (PB) $100-160
Continental Breakfast
Credit Cards: A, B
Notes: 2, 5, 7, 9, 10, 11, 12, 14

PALM SPRINGS

Bed and Breakfast California

P.O. Box 282910, San Francisco, 94128-2910
(415) 696-1690; (800) 872-4500
FAX (415) 696-1699

Desert Tranquillity. This 1930s desert garden retreat has been lovingly restored to more than its former grandeur. Forty rooms, suites, and bungalows (many with full kitchens) are scattered across landscaped acres with full mountain views. There are

NOTES: Credit cards accepted: A MasterCard; B Visa; C American Express; D Discover; E Diners Club; F Other; 2 Personal checks accepted; 3 Lunch available; 4 Dinner available; 5 Open all year; 6 Pets welcome;

more than a dozen pools, spas, patios, and gardens. No two rooms are alike. Continental breakfast available, including fresh citrus from the gardens from November to May. Reduced summer rates. Just a short walk to Palm Springs Village. $65-175.

Family Water Resort. Find homelike comfort here in a choice of 110 two-bedroom, two-bath villas on a private 27-acre resort. Choose from four styles of condos, with sleeping accommodations for two to six or two to eight people. Accommodations include private patios with gas barbecues, fully equipped kitchens, "California" breakfast, eight swimming pools, nine hot spas, and five tennis courts. Complimentary water park tickets. Bicycle, VCR, and video rentals available. Low group rates available. $99-159.

Moroccan Oasis in the Desert. Originally built as a Mecca for Hollywood literati, this 12-room villa is walking distance from Palm Springs restaurants and galleries. The host is an architectural preservationist who seeks to share "the vanishing concept of European service and hospitality." All rooms and suites have private baths; and include Continental breakfast. $95-150.

Casa Cody
Bed and Breakfast
Country Inn

175 South Cahuilla, 92262
(619) 320-9346

Romantic, historic hideaway in the heart of Palm Springs village. Beautifully redecorated in Santa Fe decor, with kitchens, wood-burning fireplaces, patios, two pools, and a spa. Close to the Desert Museum, Heritage Center, and Moorten Botanical Gardens. Nearby hiking in Indian canyons, horseback riding, tennis, golf. Polo, ballooning, helicopter, and desert Jeep tours.

Near celebrity homes, date gardens, and Joshua Tree National Monument.

Hosts: Therese Hayes and Frank Tysen
Rooms: 17 (PB) $69-185
Continental Breakfast
Credit Cards: A, B, C, D, E
Notes: 2, 5, 6, 8, 9, 10, 11, 12, 13, 14

Casa de los Niños d'Amor

P.O. Box 8453, 92263
(619) 323-4733; FAX (619) 323-0203

Built in 1934 in the heart of Palm Springs, the hacienda-style Casa de los Niños d'Amor offers privacy and tranquillity in truly elegant ambience. Restaurants, entertainment, and fine shops are within walking distance. Choice of a suite with king-size poster bed, fireplace, and bathroom with sunken Roman tub or a twin double studio with private bath. Two-night stay minimum. Wine and cheese are served at sunset. Enjoy solar-heated swimming pool, exhilarating view of Mount San Jacinto, central heating and air conditioning, and cable TV. French, German, and Italian spoken. Continental plus breakfast served.

Hosts: Gabriella and Otto Liebeskind
Rooms: 2 (PB) $65-149
Continental Breakfast
Credit Cards: None
Notes: 5, 7, 9, 10, 11, 12, 13, 14

Eye Openers
Bed and Breakfast
Reservations

P.O. Box 694, Altadena, 91003-0694
(213) 684-4428; (818) 797-2055
FAX (818) 798-3640

PA-C3. This Japanese-style inn and decor create a relaxed bed and breakfast stay. Shoji windows open to the pool. Three guest rooms have queen-size or twin futons with private baths. Shiatsu massage, kimonos, and additional amenities available. Choice of American or Japanese breakfast. No smoking. $55-75.

7 No smoking; 8 Children welcome; 9 Social drinking allowed; 10 Tennis nearby; 11 Swimming nearby; 12 Golf nearby; 13 Skiing nearby; 14 May be booked through a travel agent.

PS-H3. This former home of a glamorous 1930-40s movie star is now a unique bed and breakfast with a suite and two additional guest rooms. King- or queen-size beds and private baths. Wonderfully decorated with period pieces and appointed antiques, this bed and breakfast has warm and gracious hospitality. Full breakfast served by the pool, patios, or dining room. No smoking. $60-100.

PALO ALTO

Adella Villa

P.O. Box 4528, 94309
(415) 321-5195; FAX (415) 325-5121

Exclusive luxury villa on a secluded acre. Electronic gates, pool, fountains, and barbecue. The 4,000-square-foot residence has five bedrooms, five private baths (two with Jacuzzi tubs), and a grand piano in the music foyer. Breakfast is cooked to order. Complimentary sherry and white wine are served. Bicycles are available. Thirty minutes from San Francisco. No smoking indoors.

Host: Tricia Young
Rooms: 5 (PB) $95-110
Full Breakfast
Credit Cards: A, B, C, E
Notes: 2, 5, 9, 10, 11, 12, 14

Eye Openers Bed and Breakfast Reservations

P.O. Box 694, Altadena, 91003-0694
(213) 684-4428; (818) 797-2055
FAX (818) 798-3640

PA-C14I. This 1896 Victorian bed and breakfast is walking distance of Stanford University and downtown Palo Alto. Near public transportation to San Jose and San Francisco. Fourteen guest rooms with king- or queen-size, or double beds and private and shared baths. No smoking. $60-100.

ST-Y4. This 1920 vintage house on a one-acre estate, 30 miles south of San Francisco near the Stanford college community, offer privacy and tranquility in a parklike setting. Amenities include solar heated pool, bicycles, afternoon refreshments, and superb hospitality. Four guest rooms with king- and queen-size beds and private baths. No smoking. $95-105.

Hotel California

2431 Ash Street, 94306
(415) 322-7666

A unique bed and breakfast inn ideal for visiting professionals, out-of-town guests, and many foreign academic visitors. One of the most reasonably priced places to stay. Twenty comfortable rooms, each with private bathroom, attractively furnished with turn-of-the-century pieces. A great and convenient place to stay when visiting Stanford University or "Silicon Valley." Close to shops. Breakfast is served downstairs in the bakery.

Hosts: Andy and Michelle Hite
Rooms: 20 (PB) $55-63
Continental Breakfast
Credit Cards: A, B, C, D, E, F
Notes: 5, 7, 14

The Victorian on Lytton

555 Lytton Avenue, 94301
(415) 322-8555

Special amenities include down comforters, Battenberg lace canopies, botanical prints, Blue Willow china, and claw-foot tubs. Wander through the English country garden with over 900 perennial plants. Five king-size and five queen-size beds available. Relax in the parlor with a picture book or novel and a cup of tea while listening to classical music.

Hosts: Maxwell and Susan Hall
Rooms: 10 (PB) $98-175
Continental Breakfast
Credit Cards: A, B, C
Notes: 2, 5, 7, 9, 10, 11, 12

NOTES: Credit cards accepted: A MasterCard; B Visa; C American Express; D Discover; E Diners Club; F Other; 2 Personal checks accepted; 3 Lunch available; 4 Dinner available; 5 Open all year; 6 Pets welcome;

PALOS VERDES

Bed and Breakfast California

P.O. Box 282910, San Francisco, 94128-2910
(415) 696-1690; (800) 872-4500
FAX (415) 696-1699

View of the Ocean. Sprawling over the hillside, this house in colorful Palos Verdes offers three rooms with private baths. One room has a crib. Try a visit to the tidepools a few blocks from the door. Special rates for four people. $60.

Eye Openers Bed and Breakfast Reservations

P.O. Box 694, Altadena, 91003-0694
(213) 684-4428; (818) 797-2055
FAX (818) 798-3640

PV-B2. Ocean breezes, a panoramic view of the Pacific, and private beach facilities are offered by this homey bed and breakfast with two guest rooms and a private bath. Extended Continental breakfasts are served in the dining area or on the deck by well-traveled host. No smoking. $55-60.

PASADENA

Bed and Breakfast California

P.O. Box 282910, San Francisco, 94128-2910
(415) 696-1690; (800) 872-4500
FAX (415) 696-1699

Private Apartment near Pasadena. This cute South Pasadena duplex sits on a woodsy, quiet hill near the middle of town. There are twin beds in the bedroom, a queen-size sofa bed in the living room, and full kitchen and bath. The host lives next door and brings Continental breakfast each morning. $85.

Three-story Victorian Mansion. Wake up to the smell of fresh-baked bread as part of a full breakfast on weekends. Enjoy hearty Continental breakfast during the week. Elegantly restored Victorian house on a half-acre corner lot features a romantic suite and two warmly decorated guest rooms, each with private bath. Conveniently near Old Town Pasadena, museums, and the renowned Huntington Library. $100-150.

Rancho Cucamonga Victorian. Seven miles from Ontario Airport, this 1904 Queen Anne mansion features magnificent stained glass, hand-carved decor, and landscaped gardens. Choose from seven guest rooms, four with private bath, one with private courtyard and whirlpool. Full breakfast on weekends, Continental on weekdays. $75-155.

Eye Openers Bed and Breakfast Reservations

P.O. Box 694, Altadena, 91003-0694
(213) 684-4428; (818) 797-2055
FAX (818) 798-3640

AL-C2. A special 1926 French Normandy farmhouse in a lovely neighborhood has two-story living room and open-hearth fireplace. Enjoy an elegant Continental breakfast in the garden patio or dining room. Good hiking trails, museums, and libraries nearby. Short drive to Los Angeles. No smoking. Two guest rooms. Private and shared baths. $55.

AL-J1. This pool house with a small kitchen, queen-size sofa bed, twin bed, and private bath offers privacy and comfort on a cul-de-sac across from golf course. Good local hiking, but only 15- to 20-minute drive to LA Civic Center or to Hollywood. Continental breakfast is served. No smoking. $45-55.

7 No smoking; 8 Children welcome; 9 Social drinking allowed; 10 Tennis nearby; 11 Swimming nearby; 12 Golf nearby; 13 Skiing nearby; 14 May be booked through a travel agent.

Eye Openers
Bed and Breakfast
Reservations
(continued)

AL-L1. Pool house bed and breakfast hosted by multi-lingual hosts is near the mountains and hiking trails but close to Old Town and Los Angeles tourist attractions. It has twin beds and private bath. Continental breakfast. No smoking. $50-55.

AL-M2. Large Mediterranean-style home with mountain views offers two large guest rooms with twin or king-size beds and private baths. Beautiful neighborhood with good hiking areas, yet seven minutes to Old Town and 20 minutes to Los Angeles. Resident dog and cat. No smoking. $50-55.

AL-R2. Large, contemporary home with Old World wine cellar has Angeles National Forest as its back yard. Enjoy a Continental or full breakfast on the deck overlooking pool and view of the valley. Host teaches wine classes and is a gourmet cook. No smoking. Two guest rooms. Private baths. Wine dinners and wine tastings available upon request. $55-60.

AL-S1. This large, well-landscaped yard in a quiet residential community is a wonderful retreat at the end of the day. A delicious Continental breakfast is served. No smoking. One guest room. Private bath. $50-55.

AL-W2. Cape Code-style bed and breakfast appointed with early American antiques is on one of Altadena's loveliest streets is hosted by horse enthusiasts. Two guest rooms have twin or double beds and private baths. Large yard with pool. Continental breakfast. No smoking. Resident dogs. $50-55.

AR-P2. Horseracing and garden enthusiasts will be close to Santa Anita Racetrack and the Los Angeles County Arboretum while enjoying the hospitality at this large, well-decorated, contemporary home. Enjoy a Continental breakfast by the pool or in the family room. Two guest rooms. Private and shared baths. $45-50.

AR-W2. This home sits on a quiet cul-de-sac near the Santa Anita Racetrack, Los Angeles County Arboretum, Huntington Library, golf courses, and the beautiful San Gabriel Mountains. Host loves to garden, hike, and travel. Enjoy a Continental breakfast on the pool patio. No smoking. Two guest rooms with private and shared baths. $35-45.

PA-A2. Pasadena neighborhood known for its spacious homes, large lawns, and yards is the setting for this bed and breakfast offering warm hospitality and Continental breakfast. Two guest rooms have twin or double beds and private baths. No smoking. Resident cats. $45-50.

PA-C1. Walking distance to Convention Center, Old Town, and museums, uniquely decorated condominium offers privacy and wonderful sitting areas. Full breakfast on week ends. Garage parking. One guest room has twin beds and private bath. No smoking. $55-60.

PA-H1. Near the historic Huntington Hotel, now the Ritz-Carlton, this contemporary bed and breakfast is hosted by a retired school administrator. Enjoy the lovely garden room, where an ample Continental breakfast is served. Convenient to all local tourist attractions. Resident cat. No smoking. One guest room with private bath. $50-55.

PA-L1. Dramatic contemporary bed and breakfast within walking distance of the Rose Bowl offers a quiet setting near most tourist attractions. The guest room has

NOTES: Credit cards accepted: A MasterCard; B Visa; C American Express; D Discover; E Diners Club; F Other; 2 Personal checks accepted; 3 Lunch available; 4 Dinner available; 5 Open all year; 6 Pets welcome;

queen-size bed and a private bath. Continental breakfast is served in the dining area or pool side. No smoking. $85.

PA-O1. In renowned residential area known as Bungalow Heaven, this comfortable bed and breakfast offers friendly hospitality, Continental breakfast, and an interesting host who works in the movie industry. The guest room has a double bed and private bath. No smoking. $45-50.

PA-P2A. Sprawling ranch-style house in Colonial style has a large living room and book-lined library, both with a fireplace. A full scrumptious breakfast is served on the sunny patio or formal dining room. Host is concert pianist, organist, and harpsichordist. Close to Los Angeles and most tourist attractions. No smoking. Two guest rooms. Private and shared baths. $65.

PA-P2B. This craftsman-style house near Orange Grove's historic millionaire's row offers gracious surroundings and friendly well-traveled hosts. Guest room has king-size beds private bath. Walk to Old Town, restaurants, and museums. Continental breakfast. No smoking. $75.

PA-R3. Short walk to Pasadena Civic and Convention Center, this bed and breakfast is an older, well-kept California bungalow with first-floor guest accommodations, as well as a separate, private apartment. Hosts who enjoy travel have lived abroad and speak Swedish. Continental or full breakfast. No smoking. Private and shared baths. $35-75.

PA-S9. Gracious hosts interested in art offer very private guest quarters, which make up the entire first floor of this contemporary hillside home, with guest living room and patio. Garden and pool lend an Oriental atmosphere, and a delicious full

breakfast served along with a view of the city make this bed and breakfast a special place for guests to stay. No smoking. Two guest rooms; shared bath. $65-75.

PA-W2. Half-timbered Tudor-style home was designed and built by the host, who is a magician, yoga enthusiast, and vegetarian gourmet cook. Lovely community with good hiking is close to museums and tourist attractions. No smoking. One guest room with private bath. $55-60.

SM-S1. Very private guest house set in nicely landscaped yard of quiet, lovely neighborhood near the Huntington Library. Small kitchen, trundle beds, and private bath. No smoking. Special weekly and monthly rates available. $50-60.

SP-A4I. This 1895 Victorian farmhouse has been refurbished and decorated to recall the heritage of the home and city. Full breakfast and afternoon refreshments. Four guest rooms with double, queen- or king-size beds and private baths. No smoking. $90-100.

SP-B3I. Restored elegant Victorian on the National Register of Historic Places close to Old Town, museums, and restaurants. Host offers gracious hospitality, lovely grounds, and a full breakfast served in the dining room or patio areas. Three guest rooms have queen-size beds and private baths. No smoking. $100-150.

SP-P1. A 400-square-foot redwood guest house shares patio and Jacuzzi with host's home, which faces Arroyo Seco natural recreation area. Horse stable, par three golf course, racquetball, and tennis courts are within walking distance. Cottage has cooking facilities and TV. Twelve-minute drive to Los Angeles. No smoking. Private bath. $55-75.

7 No smoking; 8 Children welcome; 9 Social drinking allowed; 10 Tennis nearby; 11 Swimming nearby; 12 Golf nearby; 13 Skiing nearby; 14 May be booked through a travel agent.

PASO ROBLES

Gillie Archer Inn

1433 Oak Street, 93446
(805) 238-0879

The Inn is a 1917 Transitional Craftsman decorated with antiques as a romantic getaway for the wine country. The Inn has two working fireplaces, air conditioning, a gazebo with stained glass, a fountain, and beautiful organic gardens. There are 30 wineries, soon to be five golf courses, and an Amtrak stop in Paso Robles. The Inn is 30 minutes from the ocean, yet it retains the warmth and friendliness of small-town America. In the morning homemade breads and pastries, fresh juice, and fresh fruit from the twice weekly farmers' market are enjoyed to the sounds of classical music. The inn is halfway between San Francisco and Los Angeles on Highway 101. Children over 12 welcome.

Host: Kathleen Stratton-Haas
Rooms: 5 (2 PB; 3 SB) $85-125
Continental Breakfast
Credit Cards: A, B, C
Notes: 5, 7, 9, 10, 12, 14

PETALUMA

Cavanagh Inn

10 Keller Street, 94952
(707) 765-4657

Step back into the romantic past and enjoy the warmth and charm of Petaluma's first bed and breakfast. Appreciate the rare redwood heart paneling in both the 1902 Georgian Revival home and the 1912 California Craftsman cottage. The beautiful garden includes roses, oranges, and fruits. Guests may help themselves to the always full cookie jar. Local wines are served in the evening. Cavanagh Inn is in the historic downtown area and within walking distance of restaurants, shops, and the riverfront. San Francisco is 42 miles south across the Golden Gate Bridge.

Host: Ray and Jeanne Farris
Rooms: 7 (5 PB; 2 SB) $65-105
Full Breakfast
Credit Cards: A, B, C
Notes: 2, 5, 7, 10, 11, 12, 14

PLACERVILLE

Bed and Breakfast California

P.O. Box 282910, San Francisco, 94128-2910
(415) 696-1690; (800) 872-4500
FAX (415) 696-1699

A. Watch white-water rafting from the deck of this contemporary inn on the American River. Three guest rooms and one suite, most with private baths. Hot tub. Other outside adventures include fishing, swimming, gold panning, and searching for antiques in nearby Placerville. A full breakfast is served on the deck or beside the fireplace. $75-95.

The Chichester-McKee House

The Chichester–McKee House

800 Spring Street, 95667
(916) 626-1882; (800) 831-4008

This elegant 1892 home was built by lumber baron D. W. Chichester. Enjoy fireplaces, fretwork, stained glass, antiques, and relaxing hospitality. A "special" full

NOTES: Credit cards accepted: A MasterCard; B Visa; C American Express; D Discover; E Diners Club;
F Other; 2 Personal checks accepted; 3 Lunch available; 4 Dinner available; 5 Open all year; 6 Pets welcome;

breakfast is served in the dining room, and three air-conditioned guest rooms with private baths and robes are available. Downtown near Apple Hill and Gold Discovery Site.

Hosts: Doreen and Bill Thornhill
Rooms: 3 (PB) $75-85
Full Breakfast
Credit Cards: A, B, C, D
Notes: 2, 5, 7, 8, 9, 10, 11, 12, 13, 14

POINT REYES STATION

Bed and Breakfast California

P.O. Box 282910, San Francisco, 94128-2910
(415) 696-1690; (800) 872-4500
FAX (415) 696-1699

A. Gather breakfast eggs and pick flowers at this mystical cottage in Point Reyes. The house is stocked with breakfast goodies, beds for four, and a crib. Five minutes from the center of town, guests can walk through rolling meadows and the owners' "help yourself" garden of flowers, vegetables, herbs, fruit trees, and chickens. The library is full of books, and the woodshed is full of wood. Call for rates.

Carriage House. These two cottages are adjacent to the Point Reyes National Seashore, one hour north of San Francisco and one hour south of the wine country. Built in the 1920s and recently remodeled, the cottages have private entrances, bedrooms with queen-size beds, living rooms with fireplaces, queen-size sleeping couches, and additional daybeds. Full baths, complete kitchens, TV, and an outdoor barbecue are all surrounded by seashore gardens. Crib or child care available. Enjoy more than 100 miles of nearby trails for hiking, bicycling, horseback riding, bird watching, beachcombing, and whale watching. $120.

The Country House. This three-bedroom, two-bath inn, in the picturesque Point Reyes Station, features a huge country kitchen fireplace. All linens, dishes, cooking utensils, and firewood are provided. An acre of orchards and gardens overlook Inverness Ridge. Full breakfast. $100-125.

The Country House

P.O. Box 98, 94956
(415) 663-1627

California ranch house on an acre overlooking Point Reyes Station has a private suite with fireplace, queen-size bed, and private bath. Antiques, beautiful views, apple orchard, and cottage flower garden. Walk to village; easy drive to Point Reyes National Seashore. Minimum-stay requirements for holidays and weekends. Deposit required. Entire house suitable for vacation rentals for conferences or families.

Host: Ewell H. McIsaac
Suite: 1 (PB) From $89
Credit Cards: None
Notes: 2, 5, 8, 9, 11, 14

Ferrandos Hideaway

12010 Highway 1, 94956
(415) 663-1966; (800) 337-2636
FAX (415) 663-1825

Rich and homey bed and breakfast one mile north of Point Reyes Station. Two private cottages with fully equipped kitchens. Three rooms in main house. Hot tub, private baths, wood-burning stoves, vegetable garden, chickens. Close to Point Reyes National Seashore, hiking, biking, birding, horseback riding, whale watching, and miles of sandy beaches.

Hosts: Greg and Doris Ferrando
Rooms: 3 (PB) $95-250
Cottage: 2
Full Breakfast
Credit Cards: None
Notes: 2, 5, 7, 8, 9, 11, 12, 14

7 No smoking; 8 Children welcome; 9 Social drinking allowed; 10 Tennis nearby; 11 Swimming nearby; 12 Golf nearby; 13 Skiing nearby; 14 May be booked through a travel agent.

Holly Tree Inn and Cottages

3 Silverhills Road, P.O. Box 642, 94956
(415) 663-1554; FAX (415) 663-8566

This inn's setting is a 19-acre valley of lawns, herbs, and wooded hillsides with a gazebo and garden hot tub. Spacious living and dining rooms decorated in flowery prints and antiques have vast couches, French doors, and fireplaces. Two cottages, the Sea Star Cottage on Tomales Bay and Vision Cottage in the bishop pine forest, each have queen-size beds, hot tub, and fireplace. The Cottage-in-the-Woods is a magical two-room getaway, with fireplace and claw-foot soaking tub. Outstanding breakfasts, afternoon tea.

Hosts: Diane and Tom Balogh
Rooms: 4 (PB) $110-225
Cottages: 3 (PB)
Full Breakfast
Credit Cards: A, B, C
Notes: 2, 5, 7, 8, 9, 11, 12, 14

Marsh Cottage Bed and Breakfast

Box 1121, 94956
(415) 669-7168

The privacy of a peaceful bayside retreat near Inverness and the spectacular Point Reyes National Seashore. Exceptional location and views, tasteful interior, fireplace, fully equipped kitchen, complete bath. Breakfast provided in the cottage. Ideal for romantics and naturalists. Hiking nearby. Two-night minimum stay required for weekends and holidays

Host: Wendy Schwartz
Room: 1 (PB) $95-110
Full Breakfast
Credit Cards: None
Notes: 2, 5, 7, 8, 9, 11

Terri's Homestay

P.O. Box 113, 94956
(415) 663-1289; (800) 969-1289

High atop the Inverness Ridge this sunny, secluded trailside bed and breakfast offers magnificent views. Private bath, entrance, and deck. Natural fiber bedding and colorful central-American decor. Step outside and enjoy the extensive network of Point Reyes National Seashore Trails. Relax in the ozone-purified hot tub that uses 95 percent less chlorine. Health-oriented, supportive staff also provides professional massage, which couples can receive simultaneously. Approximately an hour-and-a-half's drive north of San Francisco; detailed map provided with reservation. Continental plus breakfast. Outdoor pets welcome.

Hosts: Terri Elaine
Rooms: 2 (PB) $95-115
Continental Breakfast
Credit Cards: A, B, C
Notes: 2, 5, 7, 8, 9, 11

QUINCY

The Feather Bed

542 Jackson Street, P.O. Box 3200, 95971
(916) 283-0102; (800) 696-8624

The Feather Bed is a country Victorian, circa 1893, in a small community in the high Sierras. All seven guest rooms have private baths, queen-size beds, and private entrances. An abundant country breakfast is served each morning in the charming dining room and, during the summer months, on the Victorian patio. Guests can enjoy hiking, swimming, picnicking, and other outdoor activities nearby. Enjoy a stroll through historic downtown Quincy, dine in one of the fine restaurants, or relax on the old-fashioned veranda.

Hosts: Bob and Jan Janowski
Rooms: 7 (PB) $75-120
Full Breakfast
Credit Cards: A, B, C, D, E
Notes: 2, 5, 7, 9, 10, 11, 12, 14

RAMONA

Bed and Breakfast California

P.O. Box 282910, San Francisco, 94128-2910
(415) 696-1690; (800) 872-4500
FAX (415) 696-1699

NOTES: Credit cards accepted: A MasterCard; B Visa; C American Express; D Discover; E Diners Club; F Other; 2 Personal checks accepted; 3 Lunch available; 4 Dinner available; 5 Open all year; 6 Pets welcome;

Sunset Balcony and Breakfast. High in the hills above Lake Southerland, this elegant log cabin bed and breakfast has three guest rooms that share a bath and one honeymoon suite with king-size bed, cathedral ceilings, fireplace, oversized sunken tub, and lakeview balcony. Surrounded by gardens and hiking trails, guests are just a few miles from the quaint country town of Ramona. Enjoy fancy desserts by the fireplace and full breakfast. Try a day trip to Julian, which is only 16 scenic miles away. Call for rates.

REDDING

Bed and Breakfast California

P.O. Box 282910, San Francisco, 94128-2910
(415) 696-1690; (800) 872-4500
FAX (415) 696-1699

Hands-on Ranching. This circa 1914 unique guest ranch will allow guests to experience as much as they wish of the family farm of yesterday. Programs include livestock caretaking, calf roping, children's nature lessons and crafts, harvesting crops, processing butter and cheese, and milking and herding cows. Relax like a cowhand with wagon and buggy rides, swimming, hiking, barbecues, and campfire fun. One price pays for three farm-and-ranch-style meals and lodging in private rooms and baths furnished with country charm. $75-100.

Palisades Paradise Bed and Breakfast

1200 Palisades Avenue, 96003
(916) 223-5305; (800) 382-4649

Guests will love the breathtaking view of the Sacramento River, the city, and surrounding mountains from this beautiful contemporary home with its spa, fireplace,

Palisades Paradise

wide-screen TV, VCR, and homelike atmosphere. Palisades Paradise is a serene setting for a quiet hideaway, yet one mile from shopping and I-5, with water skiing and river rafting nearby. Inspected, rated, and approved by the ABBA. Full breakfast is served only on the weekends. Limited smoking allowed.

Host: Gail Goetz
Rooms: 2 (SB) $55-85
Continental and Full Breakfasts
Credit Cards: A, B, C
Notes: 2, 5, 9, 10, 11, 12, 13, 14

REDLANDS

Morey Mansion Bed and Breakfast Inn

190 Terracina Boulevard, 92373
(909) 793-7970

Built in 1890 by David Morey, a retired shipbuilder, this Queen Anne Victorian with a Russian dome is a landmark in historical Redlands. There are five guest rooms available, four with a private bath, and a Continental breakfast is served in the morning. The downstairs area, as well as the veranda and lawn, are available for weddings, receptions, and teas.

Host: Dolly Wimer
Rooms: 5 (3 PB; 2 SB) $109-185
Continental Breakfast
Credit Cards: A, B, C, D, F
Notes: 2, 5, 7, 8, 9, 10, 11, 12, 13, 14

7 No smoking; 8 Children welcome; 9 Social drinking allowed; 10 Tennis nearby; 11 Swimming nearby; 12 Golf nearby; 13 Skiing nearby; 14 May be booked through a travel agent.

REDONDO BEACH _____

Bed and Breakfast California

P.O. Box 282910, San Francisco, 94128-2910
(415) 696-1690; (800) 872-4500
FAX (415) 696-1699

Eagan House. Hosts have remodeled their home to include a guest suite with private bath. Quiet, residential neighborhood, close to LA International Airport but not far from the beach or tourist attractions. Hosts are both teachers and serve full breakfast on weekends and, in the summer, guests may have breakfast served at the Jacuzzi on their deck. $60-70.

Eye Openers Bed and Breakfast Reservations

P.O. Box 694, Altadena, 91003-0694
(213) 684-4428; (818) 797-2055
FAX (818) 798-3640

RE-E2. Walk to Redondo Beach from this cozy, comfortable bed and breakfast in quiet, residential neighborhood. Sunny guest room has private entrance, double bed, private bath, deck, and hot tub. Continental plus breakfast. $65-75.

Ocean Breeze Bed and Breakfast

122 South Juanita Avenue, 90277
(310) 316-5123

Near the beach, between Los Angeles and Long Beach, close to freeways. Private entry, spa bathtub, and hospital beds with plush mattress covers. Remote TV, microwave oven, refrigerator, toaster, and coffee maker in large luxurious rooms. Additional room with twin beds. Special rates for two or more nights and for seniors. Children over twelve welcome.

Hosts: Norris and Betty Binding
Rooms: 2 (PB) $40-55
Continental Breakfast

Credit Cards: None
Notes: 2, 5, 7, 9, 10, 11, 12

REEDLEY _____

The Fairweather Inn Bed and Breakfast

259 South Reed Avenue, 93654
(209) 638-1918

This Craftsman home was built in 1914 and has 3,500 square feet. It was refurbished over a period of four years to bring it back to the early 1900s. The inn has been beautifully restored and decorated. All furniture, light fixtures, tubs, sinks, etchings, etc., have been collected all over the country. This charming early California home will make guests feel like the clock has been turned back to an earlier era.

Host: Vi Demyan
Rooms: 4 (2 PB; 2 SB) $75-85
Full Breakfast
Credit Cards: A, B, C
Notes: 5, 7, 11, 12, 13, 14

RUNNING SPRINGS _____

Bed and Breakfast California

P.O. Box 282910, San Francisco, 94128-2910
(415) 696-1690; (800) 872-4500
FAX (415) 696-1699

Running Springs Hideaway. In the middle of the San Bernadino Mountains, this country bed and breakfast was originally part of a sawmill. Open for winter skiing and summer sunning, two guest rooms feature antique furnishings and quilts. Enjoy a full breakfast served by the fireplace or on the deck. Enjoy wine and cheese in the afternoon, brandy in the evening, and maybe a song from the host. $95-125.

RUTHERFORD _____

Rancho Caymus

1140 Rutherford Road, P.O. Box 78, 94573
(707) 963-1777; (800) 845-1777
FAX (707) 963-5387

NOTES: Credit cards accepted: A MasterCard; B Visa; C American Express; D Discover; E Diners Club; F Other; 2 Personal checks accepted; 3 Lunch available; 4 Dinner available; 5 Open all year; 6 Pets welcome;

Rancho Caymus, an early California Hacienda-style inn has 26 handcrafted guest rooms that surround an award-winning garden courtyard. All the rooms are suites featuring a sitting area, queen-size bed, wetbar, refrigerator, and private bath. Most have a wood-burning fireplace and a private patio, while a few of the rooms also have Jacuzzi tubs. The inn is in the town of Rutherford, the heart of the Napa Valley, minutes away from five dozen wineries and numerous gourmet restaurants.

Host: Otto Komes
Rooms: 26 (PB) $120-295
Continental Breakfast
Credit Cards: A, B, C
Notes: 5, 14

SACRAMENTO

Abigail's Bed and Breakfast
2120 G Street, 95816
(916) 441-5007; (800) 858-1568

Sacramento's loveliest bed and breakfast has quiet elegance and old Sacramento charm in a historic district. Guests are within walking distance to restaurants and the state capitol. Award-winning breakfasts, large airy rooms with king- or queen-size beds, private baths. One bathroom has a whirlpool tub. Hot tub in secluded garden. Telephones, a refrigerator, and TV available. Knowledgeable innkeepers. Resident cats.

Hosts: Susanne and Ken Ventura
Rooms: 5 (PB) $95-155
Full Breakfast
Credit Cards: A, B, C, D, E
Notes: 2, 5, 7, 9, 10, 11, 12, 14

Bed and Breakfast California
P.O. Box 282910, San Francisco, 94128-2910
(415) 696-1690; (800) 872-4500
FAX (415) 696-1699

Circa 1899 at the Capitol. Six blocks from the capitol building, this turn-of-the-

century Colonial has nine rooms, all with phones and TVs. Three have fireplaces and spas. Full breakfast served in the garden. Ambience is truly old California. $90-135.

Elegant Amber House. These two houses, a 1905 Craftsman and a 1913 Mediterranean, are seven blocks from the state capitol. They have a total of eight rooms, four with whirlpool baths for two. The accommodations include full breakfast, phones, color TVs, and VCRs. $95-110.

Bed and Breakfast International
P.O. Box 282910, San Francisco, 94128-2910
(415) 696-1690; (800) 872-4500
FAX (415) 696-1699

402. Historic Victorian home close to the capitol, Old Town, museums, and restaurants. It is on the Sacramento Old House Tour and is furnished with antiques. There is an upstairs sitting room with a fireplace. One guest room with private bath; one with shared bath. $65-85.

Eye Openers Bed and Breakfast Reservations
P.O. Box 694, Altadena, 91003-0694
(213) 684-4428; (818) 797-2055
FAX (818) 798-3640

SA-A5I. In the historic district, this 1912 Colonial Revival offers spacious, airy rooms with appointed antiques. Walk to the capitol or restaurants, relax in the hot tub, enjoy gourmet full breakfasts and afternoon refreshments. Five guest rooms have private baths and king- or queen-size beds. No smoking. $95-135.

SA-A9I. Just eight blocks from the capitol, this inn is on a quiet tree-lined street of historic homes. Cozy rooms or elegant suites have private baths, double, king- or queen-size beds. Full breakfast and afternoon refreshments help guests relax after a day of business or sightseeing. No smoking allowed. $85-195.

SA-I7I. The 1936 grand mansion is the former home of an ambassador to the United States and is across from Southside Park in the state capitol area. Seven guest rooms have private baths. Amenities include a full breakfast, hot tub room, and guest kitchenette. No smoking. $70-185.

Hartley House
Bed and Breakfast Inn

700 22nd Street, 95816
(916) 447-7829; (800) 831-5806
FAX (916) 447-1820

A stunning turn-of-the-century mansion, surrounded by majestic elms and stately old homes of historic Boulevard Park in midtown. Offering exquisitely appointed rooms, the inn is near the capitol, Old Town, the convention center, the city's finest restaurants, and coffee and dessert cafes. Step back in time and ride a horse and carriage to a restaurant and back to the inn. The host also has a cookie jar filled with freshly baked cookies!

Host: Randy Hartley
Rooms: 5 (PB) $95-145
Full Breakfast
Credit Cards: A, B, C, D, E, F
Notes: 2, 5, 7, 9, 10, 11, 12, 13, 14

ST. HELENA

Bed and Breakfast
California

P.O. Box 282910, San Francisco, 94128-2910
(415) 696-1690; (800) 872-4500
FAX (415) 696-1699

Cottage on a Winery. Be the personal guests of winery owners in this guest house in St. Helena. Accommodations include

beautifully decorated bed, bath, and living rooms with a refrigerator, a potbelly stove, and a sofa bed for a third or fourth person. The hosts give tours of their estate and bring breakfast to the door each morning. The guest house is deep in the vineyards, overlooking all of Napa Valley. $125.

Bartels Ranch and Country Inn

Bartels Ranch and
Country Inn

1200 Conn Valley Road, 94574
(707) 963-4001; FAX (707) 963-5100

In the heart of world-famous Napa Valley wine country, this peaceful, romantic 60-acre country estate overlooks a valley, oak-covered hillsides and estate vineyards. All just six minutes east of St. Helena's finest wineries, restaurants, and shopping. Listed in "Best Places to Stay in California." Guests may choose from three uniquely decorated rooms with special views. Accommodations offer amenities including fireplaces, music, movies, in-room coffee makers, robes, bubble bath, and bedside reading. Hike or bike to lakeside picnics and private estate wineries. Library and sunken living room with baby grand piano. Massive beams and glass walls enclose entertainment room with billiards, Ping Pong, English darts, chess, and fireside sherry. Candlelight breakfast served until noon in formal dining room or landscaped terraces. Telephone, FAX, and refrigerators available. Antiques, fine art galleries, wineries, horseback riding, golf, tennis, hot-air ballooning, gliders, and spas nearby.

Limousine, helicopter, and shuttle available. Friendly staff and personalized wine itineraries are a well-known house specialty. Awarded 1994 AAA Award of Excellence by ABBA. Lunch and dinner catered. Limited smoking allowed.

Host: Jami Bartels
Rooms: 4 (PB) $115-315
Full Breakfast
Credit Cards: A, B, C, D, E, F
Notes: 2, 5, 9, 10, 11, 12, 14

Cinnamon Bear Bed and Breakfast

1407 Kearney Street, 94574
(707) 963-4653

This classic Arts and Craft house, built in 1910, is furnished in that style with lots of bears. Guests are close to downtown shops and restaurants. Air-conditioned. Afternoon socializing with snacks, beverages, TV, telephone. Family-owned and operated. Midweek and winter discounts available.

Host: Genny Jenkins
Rooms: 3 (PB) $145-155
Full Breakfast
Credit Cards: A, B
Notes: 2, 5, 7, 8, 9, 10, 11, 12

Deer Run Inn

3995 Spring Mountain Road, 94574
(707) 963-3794; (800) 843-3408
FAX (707) 963-9026

Old World hospitality awaits guests at Deer Run Inn tucked away in the forest on Spring Mountain Road in the wine country of Napa Valley. A cedar-shingled bungalow on four lush acres, lovingly restored, offers comfort, friendly ambience, and gracious personal service. Rooms are decorated with family antiques and heirlooms, fireplaces, private baths, down quilts, evening brandy, mints, and robes.

Hosts: Tom and Carol Wilson
Rooms: 4 (PB) $125-155
Full Breakfast
Credit Cards: A, B, C
Notes: 2, 5, 7, 9, 10, 11, 12, 14

Eye Openers Bed and Breakfast Reservations

P.O. Box 694, Altadena, 91003-0694
(213) 684-4428; (818) 797-2055
FAX (818) 798-3640

SH-D3I. Secluded in a forest above vineyards, yet near town, this small bed and breakfast offers a peaceful, rustic retreat. Guest room has private entrance and fireplace. Carriage Room, studio, and two-room cottage are decorated with antiques and very private. Queen- or king-size beds and private baths. A full breakfast is served. No smoking. $125-140.

SH-C3I. This 1904 Craftsman-style inn with 1920 vintage furnishings is within walking distance to shopping areas and restaurants. Three spacious, comfortable rooms have queen-size beds and private baths. Full breakfasts and afternoon refreshments are provided. Self-hosted cottages also available just outside town. No smoking. $115-155.

SH-W20I. This New England-style inn offers large, comfortable rooms and elegant hospitality. There are 20 guest rooms and suites, many with a fireplace, whirlpool, patio, balcony, and beautiful views. Queen-size and double beds. Private baths. Continental plus buffet breakfast is served. No smoking. $140-210.

La Fleur Bed and Breakfast Inn

1475 Inglewood Avenue, 94574
(707) 963-0233 (phone and FAX)

A charming 1882 Queen Anne Victorian nestled in the heart of Napa Valley is on a quiet country lane. The guest rooms are custom decorated and beautifully appointed, featuring spectacular views, private baths,

7 No smoking; 8 Children welcome; 9 Social drinking allowed; 10 Tennis nearby; 11 Swimming nearby; 12 Golf nearby; 13 Skiing nearby; 14 May be booked through a travel agent.

and queen-size beds. Some rooms have balconies and fireplaces. A breakfast of gourmet delights is served in the solarium overlooking St. Helena's beautiful vineyards. Join the hosts for a private tour of the award-winning Villa Helena Winery.

Host: Ms. Kay Murphy
Rooms: 4 (PB) $125-150
Full Breakfast
Credit Cards: None
Notes: 2, 5, 7, 9, 10, 11, 12, 14

Hilltop House Bed and Breakfast

9550 St. Helena Road, P.O. Box 726, 94574
(707) 944-0880

Poised at the very top of a ridge that separates the famous wine regions of Napa and Sonoma, Hilltop House is a country retreat with all the comforts of home and a view that must be seen to be believed. The hosts built this contemporary home with this mountain panorama in mind, and the vast deck allows guests to enjoy it at leisure with a glass of wine in the afternoon, with breakfast in the morning, or with a long soak in the hot tub. From this vantage point sunrises and sunsets are simply amazing. Guests will cherish the natural setting, caring hospitality, and prize location.

Host: Annette Gevarter
Rooms: 4 (PB) $115-175
Full Breakfast
Credit Cards: A, B, C
Notes: 2, 5, 7, 8, 9, 10, 11, 12, 14

Shady Oaks Country Inn

399 Zinfandel Lane, 94574
(707) 963-1190

Secluded and romantic on two acres, nestled among the finest wineries and restaurants in Napa Valley. Wine and cheese are served each evening, and the full champagne breakfast is known as "the best in the valley." The inn's reputation has been built on warm, sincere hospitality with all comforts in mind. Each immaculate room is spacious and furnished with antiques; ele-

gant ambience and country tranquility. Off-season and midweek rates available.

Hosts: John and Lisa Wild-Runnells
Rooms: 4 (PB) $125-165
Full Breakfast
Credit Cards: None
Notes: 2, 5, 7, 9, 10, 11, 12, 14

Villa St. Helena

2727 Sulphur Springs Avenue, 94574
(707) 963-2514

This secluded hilltop Mediterranean villa combines quiet, country elegance with panoramic views of Napa Valley. Romantic antique-filled rooms, private baths, entrances, and fireplaces in some. A private world on a wooded 20-acre estate; walking trails, spacious courtyard, cozy library. World-class wine tasting, dining, and shopping nearby. Convenient to tennis and golf. Complimentary wine and an exclusive Continental breakfast.

Rooms: 3 (PB) $145-245
Continental Breakfast
Credit Cards: A, B
Notes: 2, 5, 9, 10, 11, 12, 14

SAN ANDREAS

Robin's Nest

247 West Saint Charles Street, P.O. Box 1408, 95249
(209) 754-1076

Robin's Nest

NOTES: Credit cards accepted: A MasterCard; B Visa; C American Express; D Discover; E Diners Club; F Other; 2 Personal checks accepted; 3 Lunch available; 4 Dinner available; 5 Open all year; 6 Pets welcome;

This Victorian, built in 1895, retains its dramatic character and Old World charm with modern conveniences. The inn is on an acre of grass and fruit trees. Nearby activities include California Caverns, art and antique shops, Big Trees State Park, wine tasting, boating, fishing, water-skiing, and cross-country skiing.

Hosts: George and Carolee Jones
Rooms: 9 (7 PB; 2 SB) $55-95
Full Breakfast
Credit Cards: A, B, C
Notes: 2, 5, 8, 10, 11, 12, 13, 14

SAN ANSELMO

Bed and Breakfast California

P.O. Box 282910, San Francisco, 94128-2910
(415) 696-1690; (800) 872-4500
FAX (415) 696-1699

Rustic Charm in Old Marin. Only 14 miles from the Golden Gate Bridge, this private guest suite is full of natural old wood, Oriental rugs, and hand-crafted furniture, including a curved redwood sleeping alcove. French doors lead to private deck, with sunlight filtering through a canopy of fruit trees. Surrounded by hiking trails, guests are within walking distance of fine restaurants and shops. Full breakfast served. Both the wine country and Point Reyes National Seashore only an hour away. $85.

SAN CLEMENTE

Bed and Breakfast California

P.O. Box 282910, San Francisco, 94128-2910
(415) 696-1690; (800) 872-4500
FAX (415) 696-1699

Casa Tropicana. Lovingly built by owner-operators, this perfect little bed and breakfast looks out on the ocean and the San Clemente pier. Seven rooms have tropical,

jungle, or country French motifs. All rooms have oceanviews. Several have Jacuzzis and fireplaces. Hosts serve an elegant full breakfast on guests' very own private deck. $120-325.

Casa de Flores Bed and Breakfast

184 Avenue La Cuesta, 92672
(714) 498-1344

San Clemente's best-kept secret. Midway between Los Angeles and San Diego sits this beautiful 5,500-square-foot Spanish home, offering two two-room suites and a spectacular view of the ocean and Dana Point Harbor. One suite features a fireplace in the bedroom and a spa in its own private enclosed patio; the other has a double sofa bed in the sitting room for two additional people at an extra charge. Both suites offer TV/VCRs and in-room coffee. Beach chairs and towels, more than 500 videos, pool table, washer, dryer, and iron available. Complimentary beverages. Turndown service. Beautiful beaches and fine restaurants within one mile. Inspected and approved by the Automobile Club of Southern California. Two-night minimum stay required for holidays and weekends. Limited smoking allowed.

Hosts: Marilee and Robert Arsenault
Suites: 2 (PB) $75-100
Full Breakfast
Credit Cards: None
Notes: 2, 5, 8, 9, 10, 11, 12, 14

SAN DIEGO

The Balboa Park Inn

3402 Park Boulevard, 92103
(619) 298-0823; (800) 938-8181
FAX (619) 294-8070

One of San Diego's most romantic settings—a guest house in the heart of the city. The affordable difference is a suite for the price of a room. Within easy walking

---

7 No smoking; 8 Children welcome; 9 Social drinking allowed; 10 Tennis nearby; 11 Swimming nearby; 12 Golf nearby; 13 Skiing nearby; 14 May be booked through a travel agent.

The Balboa Park Inn

distance of the San Diego Zoo, Old Globe Theatre, museums, and restaurants, and only ten minutes to the beach.

Host: Ed Wilcox
Suites: 26 (PB) $80-190
Continental Breakfast
Credit Cards: A, B, C, D, E, F
Notes: 5, 7, 8, 9, 10, 11, 12, 14

Bears at the Beach Bed and Breakfast in Pacific Beach

1047 Grand Avenue, 92109
(619) 272-2578

Bears at the Beach offers the enchantment of San Diego in a casual beach setting. The Pacific Ocean is two blocks away and Mission Bay is three blocks. Walk to restaurants and nightlife. Walk, bike, or skate along. Visit SeaWorld, the world-famous San Diego Zoo, and Balboa Park. Amenities include in-room cable TV, ceiling fans, private patio, ocean breezes, and perpetual sunshine. If private bath is desired, only one room will be rented; otherwise, the large, full bath is shared by two rooms. Smoking allowed on patio only. Children over ten welcome.

Hosts: Doña Denson
Rooms: 2 (PB/SB) $65-95
Full Breakfast
Credit Cards: None
Notes: 2, 5, 9, 10, 11, 12, 14

Bed and Breakfast International

P.O. Box 282910, San Francisco, 94128-2910
(415) 696-1690; (800) 872-4500
FAX (415) 696-1699

503. San Diego does not get any better than this. A gorgeous plantation-style home with oceanviews from the pool and spa. Lots of art, work, European decor, and hospitality. Classy and inviting. $75-85.

Banker's Hill Victorian. Guests are within walking distance to the San Diego Zoo and Balboa Park. The main house and guest cottage comprise eight bedrooms. The rooms are appointed in furnishings of the 1880s, with lush tropical grounds surrounding the property. A full breakfast is served in the dining room. Relax in the garden or on the front porch and enjoy a peaceful moment in the sunshine. $50-85.

Blom House. This charming cottage in a quiet residential neighborhood is on a bluff less than 10 minutes from downtown, the beach, and all local tourist attractions. The 65-foot deck features a spa and a superb view of Hotel Circle below. All accommodations have 14-foot ceilings, antique furnishings, color TV/VCR, phones, refrigerators with complimentary wine and cheese, and bathrobes. A four-course cooked breakfast, limited kitchen privileges, and two-for-one dining coupons to various restaurants are included. $75-110.

Carole's Bed and Breakfast. This friendly congenial home is close to all major attractions. One and one-half mile from the downtown area and the San Diego Zoo, this house, built in 1904 by the mayor of San Diego, is decorated with family antiques and handmade quilts. Atmosphere is cozy, with five bedrooms sharing three baths. Breakfast is bountiful. Big swimming pool. $65-85.

NOTES: Credit cards accepted: A MasterCard; B Visa; C American Express; D Discover; E Diners Club; F Other; 2 Personal checks accepted; 3 Lunch available; 4 Dinner available; 5 Open all year; 6 Pets welcome;

Bed and Breakfast California

P.O. Box 282910, San Francisco, 94128-2910
(415) 696-1690; (800) 872-4500
FAX (415) 696-1699

This classic Victorian in a private park in Old San Diego is a perfectly restored mansion with seven guest rooms and a huge family cottage. Four rooms share baths; the rest are private. The cottage has two bedrooms, one with a king-size four-poster bed, the other with twins. Also a wonderful marble bath with double sunken tub. Hosts provide elegant afternoon snacks and a full buffet breakfast. Definitely the best in San Diego! $90-225.

Blom House Bed and Breakfast

1372 Minden Drive, 92111
(619) 467-0890

Blom House is a charming cottage in a quiet residential neighborhood less than ten minutes from downtown, the zoo, airport, beach, and all local tourist attractions. The 65-foot deck features a spa and a superb view of Hotel Circle lights and the I-163 and I-8 interchange below. All accommodations have 14-foot ceilings, antique furnishings, TV, VCR, air conditioning, phones, refrigerators with complimentary wine and cheese, bathrobes, and private baths. A two-bedroom suite with private bath is also available for families or two couples. Guest lounge offers after-dinner drinks, cookies, and a video library.

Hosts: Bette and John Blom
Rooms: 3 (PB) $59-80
Full Breakfast
Credit Cards: None
Notes: 2, 5, 7, 8, 9, 10, 11, 12, 14

Carole's Bed and Breakfast Inn

3227 Grim Avenue, 92104
(619) 280-5258

Historic 1904 two-story Craftsman home built by the city's mayor is furnished with antiques and a piano; a rose garden is on the grounds. Swimming pool, hot tub, and gas barbecue. Less than one mile to zoo. Close to all major attractions. Continental plus breakfast is served in guest room or dining area. Refreshments served in the evening. Dinner is available, but not included in the rate. Smoking allowed outside. Senior rates are available. Reservation deposit is required. Travelers checks are accepted.

Hosts: Carole Dugdale and Michael O'Brien
Rooms: 6 (2 PB; 4 SB) $65-85
Continental Breakfast
Credit Cards: A, B, C, D
Notes: 3, 4, 5, 9, 10, 11, 12, 14

The Cottage

The Cottage

3829 Albatross Street, P.O. Box 3292, 92103
(619) 299-1564

Between the zoo and SeaWorld, The Cottage is a quiet retreat in the heart of a downtown residential neighborhood. The turn-of-the-century furnishings throughout evoke visions of a bygone era. Each morning guests will be served a breakfast of freshly baked bread, juice, and beverage.

Hosts: Robert and Carol Emerick
Rooms: 2 (PB) $55-95
Continental Breakfast
Credit Cards: A, B, C
Notes: 2, 5, 7, 8, 9, 10, 11, 12, 14

7 No smoking; 8 Children welcome; 9 Social drinking allowed; 10 Tennis nearby; 11 Swimming nearby; 12 Golf nearby; 13 Skiing nearby; 14 May be booked through a travel agent.

Eye Openers Bed and Breakfast Reservations

P.O. Box 694, Altadena, 91003-0694
(213) 684-4428; (818) 797-2055
FAX (818) 798-3640

FA-B2. Large country French chateau is nestled on a working avocado ranch. Relax and unwind poolside in a peaceful hilltop setting. Antiques are throughout this lovely bed and breakfast, and the guest room overlooks the garden. Full breakfast. Wineries, antique shops, and golf courses are nearby. Resident cats and dogs. No smoking. Guest rooms with private bath. $75.

SD-B2. Pacific beach bed and breakfast is a short walk to the ocean or to Mission Bay. The two guest rooms have queen-size and double beds with a shared bath. Enjoy the relaxed beach atmosphere and the homemade full breakfast served in the dining room or on the private, walled patio. No smoking. $65-85.

SD-B4. Ten minutes from downtown, beaches, and local tourist attractions. Relax and enjoy views from the 75-foot deck with spa. Four guest rooms have twin, queen- or king-size beds and private baths. Robes, minirefrigerator, TV, and VCR are provided, as well as a gourmet breakfast and afternoon refreshments. No smoking allowed. $75-95.

SD-E1. Separate guest house with turn-of-the-century furnishings assures privacy in central San Diego and offers a bedroom, sitting room with wood-burning stove, and dining area where a delicious Continental breakfast is served. Additional guest room with private entrance is available. Private bath. $55-75.

SD-E21. Newly built bed and breakfast less than a block from the beach offers friendly hospitality and a wonderful convenient location. Cape Cod-style architecture. An extended Continental breakfast is served. Seven guest rooms offer queen-size beds and private baths. No smoking. $85.

SD-H61. This trilevel bed and breakfast inn has a harbor and garden view. Near Balboa Park, Sea World, and the zoo. Continental breakfast. All six guest rooms have private baths. $65-95.

SD-H91. This 1889 Victorian antique-furnished bed and breakfast inn is in a restored village convenient to tourist attractions. Full breakfast, candlelight dinners, and special amenities available. No smoking. Nine guest rooms. Private baths. $85-225.

SD-Y1. Pacific beach cottage includes pool and garden. It has a double bed and private bath. Walk to tourist attractions along Mission Bay. Public transportation available. Continental breakfast. No smoking. Weekly rates available. $75.

Harbor Hill Guest House

2330 Albatross Street, 92101
(619) 233-0638

Overlooking the San Diego Harbor is the ideal location for business, weekend getaways, honeymoons, and family reunions. Accommodates 16 adults. The Carriage House is a separate hideaway for two. Private baths. Continental breakfast. Each level has a semiprivate entry. A kitchen is on each level.

Rooms: 5 (PB) $65-90
Continental Breakfast
Credit Cards: A, B
Notes: 2, 5, 8, 9, 12, 14

Vera's Cozy Corner

2810 Albatross Street, 92103
(619) 296-1938

This crisp white Colonial with black shutters sits in a quiet cul-de-sac overlooking

NOTES: Credit cards accepted: A MasterCard; B Visa; C American Express; D Discover; E Diners Club;
F Other; 2 Personal checks accepted; 3 Lunch available; 4 Dinner available; 5 Open all year; 6 Pets welcome;

San Diego Bay. Comfortable guest quarters consist of a separate cottage with private entrance across a flower-filled patio. The hostess offers freshly squeezed orange juice from her own fruit trees in season as a prelude to breakfast, which is served in the dining room. The house is convenient to local shops and restaurants, beaches, and is one mile from the San Diego Zoo.

Host: Vera V. Warden
Room: 1 (PB) $45-50
Continental Breakfast
Credit Cards: None
Notes: 2, 5, 7, 9, 10, 11, 12, 14

SAN FRANCISCO

Albion House Inn

135 Gough Street, 94102
(415) 621-0896

The Albion House is an elegant bed and breakfast in the Performing Arts District. Each room is individually furnished with antiques and fresh flowers. The central living room accommodates a 15-foot beamed ceiling, grand piano, and lounge area with marble fireplace. Enjoy complimentary brandy and pleasurable walks to the opera, symphony, ballet, and numerous shops and restaurants. Just minutes away from Union Square, Fisherman's Wharf, and Golden Gate Park by public transportation.

Hosts: Aziz and Regina Bouagon
Rooms: 9 (7 PB; 2 SB) $85-195
Full Breakfast
Credit Cards: A, B, C, D
Notes: 2, 5, 8, 9, 10, 11, 12, 14

Art Center and Bed and Breakfast Suites, Wamsley

1902 Filbert Street, 94123
(415) 567-1526; (800) 821-3877

The best residential area—Marina, Cow Hollow—where history stands still. Just a 20-minute walk to Fisherman's Wharf. A French New Orleans inn with privacy, kitchens, canopied queen-size beds, fire-places, and whirlpool suite. Shopping on Union Street and jogging at the marina. Day tours of Northern California's charms, nearby theater, music, cruising, and dancing on the bay—all within easy reach. Business travelers and families welcome. Commercial discounts, art classes, and gallery.

Hosts: George and Helvi Wamsley
Rooms: 5 (PB) $75-120
Continental Breakfast
Credit Cards: A, B, C, D, E, F
Notes: 2, 5, 7, 8, 9, 10, 12, 14

Bed and Breakfast California

P.O. Box 282910, San Francisco, 94128-2910
(415) 696-1690; (800) 872-4500
FAX (415) 696-1699

14-1. Walk to Golden Gate Park from this three-story Victorian that is geared toward traveling families. Two guest rooms share one bath on each floor. Full breakfast is provided, and guests are welcome to use the kitchen, fireplace, and even the playpen. Host's teenage daughter is willing to baby-sit. Family rates are available.

A. This hostess offers two guest rooms, one with twins and the other with a queen-size bed. Bath between the two is shared. On Knob Hill, Chinatown is only three blocks away. $75.

C. This classic inn, a "painted lady," was one of San Francisco's original golden-era mansions. Built in 1878, it has quaint rooms with shared baths, more spacious ones with private baths, and several elegant suites that can sleep up to five. Afternoon goodies and full buffet breakfast are provided. Parking is available. Guests will enjoy the bonus—big, old-fashioned hot tub in the garden. $70-175.

D. This fairy-tale Victorian has just one elegant suite: bedroom with brass bed and

7 No smoking; 8 Children welcome; 9 Social drinking allowed; 10 Tennis nearby; 11 Swimming nearby; 12 Golf nearby; 13 Skiing nearby; 14 May be booked through a travel agent.

Bed and Breakfast California (continued)

down comforter, sitting room with kitchenette, and a private bath. Popcorn, drinks, and fresh flowers abound. A different gourmet breakfast is served every morning. Hosts are there to pamper. $85.

1906 Earthquake Survivor. Respectfully restored transitional Victorian mansion provides gracious, Oriental-influenced rooms and suites. Enjoy Continental breakfast privately or with other guests in the morning room. Afternoon tea or wine. This inn is in tree-shaded Alamo Square. The hosts are quite knowledgeable of San Francisco and the Bay area and will gladly assist with restaurant, theater, and entertainment information. $70-175.

Victorians Everywhere. Another stately, antique-accented Victorian, this bed and breakfast offers three rooms with shared baths. One room has a king-size bed, a second a double bed, and the third has twin beds. Guests are in "the Avenues" and very convenient to Fisherman's Wharf and Union Square. Breakfast is served in the glass-sided solarium or wonderful, overgrown garden. $75.

Victorian near Golden Gate. This great old home just north of the park has three guest rooms, all with double beds and one with private bath. The hostess serves a full breakfast and specializes in turning visitors into friends. The kitchen is filled with sunshine and flowers and veggies from the garden. $60-75.

"Herb'N Inn." This "urban inn" has five rooms named after the herbs in the garden. Decorated with eccentricity and charm, four rooms share two baths and one has its own private bath. Full breakfast served. Parking is included. This 100-plus-year-old inn is in the Haight-Ashbury area. Innkeepers have restored it lovingly with hardwood floors and hanging quilts. They also operate a private tour company for visitors who want to see the bay or just need a convenient lift to town. $65-75.

Little Cottage on a Hill. Hidden on a forested hill close to Golden Gate Park, this cute cottage has twin beds, a fireplace, kitchen, bath, and a beautiful full view of the city. Enjoy a self-serve breakfast and total privacy. $80.

Near Union Square. With all the charm of a small European hotel, this original 1909 inn offers spacious, beautifully decorated rooms with remodeled bathrooms and friendly service. Guests are just minutes from square shopping, Chinatown, historic cable cars, and the financial district. Some very low cost rooms with shared baths available. Continental breakfast. $65-85.

Bed and Breakfast International

P.O. Box 282910, 94128-2910
(415) 696-1690; (800) 872-4500
FAX (415) 696-1699

101. Location, location, location. This charming bed and breakfast in a Victorian home is a stone's throw from cable cars, Fisherman's Wharf, Ghiradelli Square, North Beach, and the bay. $65-125.

102. Second-floor home in a modernized Victorian building near the North Beach area on Telegraph Hill. Walking distance to Fisherman's Wharf and many restaurants. Cable car is three blocks away. Two rooms share a bath. $55-68.

103. Three-story turn-of-the-century home that has been pictured in *Sunset* magazine. Favorite spot for many returning guests. Only 15 minutes from Union Square and an equal distance to Ocean Beach. Within walking distance to Golden Gate Park, the Presidio, and the many shops and restaurants on Clement Street. One room with sitting area and private bath. Two rooms with shared bath. $60-70.

105. This 1876 Victorian is "eccentrically, eclectically, and very tastefully decorated." This home is truly San Francisco and is close to shops and restaurants in popular Pacific Heights. There is a guest room with private bath, minikitchen, and sitting room. In the back garden, a guest cottage affords privacy and opens onto the patio. $85-95.

106. Combine elegance, location, lots of space, and a view of the bay in the heart of the city in this Russian Hill 1908 Italianate Victorian. Two bedrooms, a sunroom, living room with fireplace, and fully equipped kitchen. $125-175.

107. Four homes all built around the 1920s furnished with antiques and near many interesting shops and restaurants on Haight Street. All homes have back decks. About 15 minutes from downtown and walking distance to Golden Gate Park. Ten rooms with all types of bed sizes. All have shared baths. $53-75.

108. This place has everything. Location: guests are right at the bottom of the crooked part of Lombard Street. Charm: this is a 1903 Edwardian with wonderful views. Hospitality: the charming host is also a gourmet cook. Three guest rooms all have private baths. $105-145.

109. This quintessential 1896 Victorian in Pacific Heights has been lovingly restored and is close to downtown and within walking distance to shops and restaurants on popular Fillmore Street. High quality antiques and linens are used in three guest rooms. One guest room has a private bath and the other two guest rooms share a bath. $78-98.

110. Did you see *Mrs. Doubtfire*? This bed and breakfast is less than a block away from the movie site and offers bay views. An old English beach house offers two rooms. Both have private baths and are very spacious. $95-105.

Bed and Breakfast San Francisco

P.O. Box 420009, 94142
(415) 931-3083; FAX (415) 921-BBSF (2273)

1. Enjoy a new addition to a charming old San Francisco home. If guests prefer privacy, this nonhosted private cottage will be most enjoyable. The large bedroom with double bed has a view of North Beach. Excellent Italian restaurants are in the neighborhood. Fisherman's Wharf and Chinatown are a short walk away. Double sofa bed and a crib are available. Full breakfast. Additional charge for children. $125.

2. A wonderful San Francisco neighborhood has excellent local shops and restaurants on 24th Street. Liz's bed and breakfast is on the J-Church Street car line only 20 minutes from downtown. This lovely, warm home has comfortable bedroom has a double bed. One wonderful cat on the premises. Shared bath. Full breakfast. $60.

3. A cozy country-style bed and breakfast in the heart of San Francisco has four guest rooms that are comfortably furnished in

7 No smoking; 8 Children welcome; 9 Social drinking allowed; 10 Tennis nearby; 11 Swimming nearby; 12 Golf nearby; 13 Skiing nearby; 14 May be booked through a travel agent.

Bed and Breakfast
San Francisco
(continued)

country antiques and brass beds. The house is at the end of a quiet street, away from the city noise. There is a small patio with trees and birds for the guests to enjoy. A full breakfast is served in the sunny kitchen each morning, and complimentary wine is always available. Four guest rooms share two full baths. $65.

4. In one of the most photographed areas of San Francisco, the historic district of Alamo Square, the bed and breakfast is close to the Civic Center, Opera House, Davies Symphony Hall, Union Square, and all of the sights that make the city famous. Most of the guest rooms feature fireplaces, and private baths have been tastefully decorated to show the charm of old San Francisco homes. One room features an antique Chinese wedding bed. A sumptuous full breakfast is served every morning with sunshine (the city's famous fog permitting). In the evening guests can help themselves to wine, relax in the hot tub, and perhaps enjoy a surprise visit from "Nosey," the neighborhood resident raccoon. Two-bedroom family apartment with fireplace and kitchen is also available. $65-125.

5. In one of San Francisco's most beautiful neighborhoods, Jay's place is atop the Broadway tunnel. Walk down the steps to North Beach Italian restaurants, Fisherman's Wharf, and Chinatown. Cable cars are only one block away. This exclusive, quiet location offers San Francisco sights just minutes away. Jay's one bed and breakfast guest room is traditionally furnished and has a private bath. Full breakfast. $95.

6. A beautifully restored 1880s Victorian is just a few blocks from Golden Gate Park. Three guest rooms are furnished in family

antiques. The Asian Art Museum, Steinhart Aquarium, the Japanese Tea Garden, jogging, and bike trails are at hand in the park. Full breakfast. $85.

7. Originally built in 1895 as a candy store, Cathy's bed and breakfast is a beautifully renovated Victorian at the top of Ashbury Terrace. She offers a beautiful main-floor apartment furnished in heirloom antiques and a Scandinavian motif. The living room has a garden view. Accommodations include queen-size bed, full kitchen, and large bath. Close to the city center, Golden Gate Park, and UC Medical Center. Full breakfast. $100.

8. The Richmond district offers a wealth of wonderful things to do from bike riding and walking trails to excellent restaurants. Its ethnic diversity makes it one of San Francisco's most interesting neighborhoods. The host offers one guest room with queen-size bed, TV and VCR, and private bath. The living room has a fireplace and oceanview. The world famous Cliff House restaurant, Seal Rocks, and Ocean Beach are just a few blocks away. Transportation to downtown is excellent. Union Square is 15 minutes away by express bus. Full breakfast. $75.

9. One of San Francisco's famous Victorians featured in the book *Painted Ladies* is in the heart of North Beach and close to great restaurants and quaint coffee houses. Fisherman's Wharf and Chinatown are a short walk away. The host offers a charming two-bedroom apartment filled with family antiques. Accommodations include private entrance, living room with fireplace, full bath, and kitchen. Upstairs are two more charming antique-filled guest rooms. The view is great. Full breakfast. $65-125.

10. A million-dollar panoramic view of San Francisco Bay and the Golden Gate Bridge

NOTES: Credit cards accepted: A MasterCard; B Visa; C American Express; D Discover; E Diners Club; F Other; 2 Personal checks accepted; 3 Lunch available; 4 Dinner available; 5 Open all year; 6 Pets welcome;

plays host to this upscale Presidio Heights bed and breakfast. This prestigious area offers a wealth of wonderful restaurants, interesting walks and the historic Presidio. Two rooms are available. One is very large with a queen-size bed, private bath, and a private balcony. The other has a double bed and private bath. Full breakfast. $75-125.

11. A scenic location in San Francisco with a panoramic view. Three guest rooms, each facing west, provide a lovely sunset view overlooking the Glen Canyon Park with its beautiful eucalyptus grove. Mount David-son (the highest point in the city) towers majestically over the canyon in full view of each guest room. Room choices include twin beds, a queen-size bed, or a large family room accommodating up to four persons. Each room is equipped with a TV. The spacious family room also has a sitting area and a piano. Two bathrooms are available. Guests have ample on-street parking in a quiet neighborhood. Public transportation is nearby. Full breakfast. $65.

12. High atop charming Russian Hill, a two-bedroom Victorian apartment has a spectacular view of the bay. A great place for two couples or a family includes a living room, sunny solarium, a full kitchen, and bath. One bedroom has a double bed, the other a queen-size bed. A futon is also available. The living room has TV, fireplace, and phone. The area is great for walking. Cable cars are on the corner, and the wharf is just a short distance away. Special rates for stays over seven days. Full breakfast. $125.

13. A wonderful, charming, recently reno-vated Victorian bed and breakfast. Three guest rooms, two with bay views. At the bottom of world-famous, crooked Lombard Street, guests are within walking distance of Fisherman's Wharf, North Beach restaurants, and cable cars. Excellent parking. All rooms have private baths. Full breakfast. $85-125.

14. One of San Francisco's most enjoyable neighborhoods, Noe Valley is a local treasure of restaurants and shops. This beauti-fully renovated charming San Francisco home offers a bed and breakfast suite. Private entrance, king-size bed, and full kitchen. Full breakfast. Transportation to the center of downtown (15 minutes away) is excellent. $75.

15. In the exclusive St. Francis woods area of San Francisco, a large Spanish-style home offers three luxurious guest rooms plus a family suite. All rooms have private baths. The garden surrounds an enclosed pool and pool house. The pool house has a shower and sauna as well as a living room. Full breakfast. $95-125.

16. On a quiet street atop a hill in the Dolores Heights area, guest room has a private entrance off a deck with a beautiful view of the city and the Bay Bridge. Immaculately decorated. Queen-size bed and private bath. Full breakfast. $95.

Brady Acres

649 Jones Street, 94102
(415) 929-8033; (800) 6 BRADY 6 (627-2396)
FAX (415) 441-8033

Small hotel in theater district three blocks northwest of Union Square. Close to shopping and cable car. Fully accessorized with kitchen ware, all rooms have wet bar with microwave, refrigerator, coffee maker, and toaster. Six very sunny rooms with bay windows are decorated with antiques. All rooms are fully furnished and have private baths with tub and shower. All have private-line telephone with answering machine, color TV, and cassette player. Laundry facilities available. Weekly rates are also available.

Host: Deborah Brady
Rooms: 25 (PB) $60-75
Continental Breakfast
Credit Cards: A, B, F
Notes: 2, 5, 8, 11, 14

7 No smoking; 8 Children welcome; 9 Social drinking allowed; 10 Tennis nearby; 11 Swimming nearby; 12 Golf nearby; 13 Skiing nearby; 14 May be booked through a travel agent.

The Cartwright Hotel

524 Sutter Street, 94102
(415) 421-2865; (800) 227-3844;
FAX (415) 398-6345

The newly renovated Cartwright Hotel proudly features complimentary morning coffee and afternoon tea and cakes in the elegant library. Deluxe accommodations include rooms featuring authentic antiques and plush terry robes in every room. In the heart of Union Square, San Francisco's shopping district, guests are just steps from Chinatown, the theaters, and cable cars. Smoking and nonsmoking rooms available.

Host: Lisa Fong, general manager
Rooms: 114 (PB) $139-179
Continental Breakfast
Credit Cards: A, B, C, D, E, F
Notes: 2, 5, 8, 9, 10, 11, 12, 14

Casa Arguello

Casa Arguello

225 Arguello Boulevard, 94118
(415) 752-9482

Built in the 1920s, Casa Arguello combines antique furniture with a modern flair to make the guests' stay both beautiful and comfortable. A Continental plus breakfast is served in an elegant dining room among visitors from all over the globe. Quaint shops on nearby Sacramento Street and Laurel Village make shopping a breeze, or take a ten-minute bus ride to Union Square. Golden Gate Park, the Presidio, and fine restaurants are within walking distance. Call for rates.

Hosts: Emma Baires and Marina McKenzie
Rooms: 4 (2 PB; 2 SB)
Continental Breakfast
Credit Cards: None
Notes: 2, 5, 7, 11, 12

Country Cottage Bed and Breakfast

5 Dolores Terrace, 94110
(415) 479-1913; (800) 452-8249
FAX (415) 921-2273

A cozy country-style bed and breakfast in the heart of San Francisco. The four guest rooms are comfortably furnished with antiques and brass beds. The house is at the end of a quiet street, away from the city noise. There is a small patio with trees and birds. A full breakfast is served in the sunny kitchen.

Hosts: Susan and Richard Kreibich
Rooms: 4 (S2B) $65
Full Breakfast
Credit Cards: A, B, C
Notes: 2, 5, 7, 8, 9, 10, 11, 12, 14

Dockside Boat and Bed

Pier 39, 94133
(415) 392-5526
77 Jack London Square, Oakland, 94607
(510) 444-5858

Spend a romantic evening on a yacht! Luxurious private yachts for overnight dockside accommodations allow fantasy to become reality. The boats range in size from 35 to 68 feet in length, and several are available for charter with a captain. Romantic candlelight catered dinners add to the fantasy of living the life of the "rich and famous."

Host: Rob Harris
Yachts: 10 (PB) $95-275
Continental Breakfast
Credit Cards: A, B, C
Notes: 2, 4, 5, 8, 9, 14

NOTES: Credit cards accepted: A MasterCard; B Visa; C American Express; D Discover; E Diners Club; F Other; 2 Personal checks accepted; 3 Lunch available; 4 Dinner available; 5 Open all year; 6 Pets welcome;

Eye Openers
Bed and Breakfast
Reservations

P.O. Box 694, Altadena, 91003-0694
(213) 684-4428; (818) 797-2055
FAX (818) 798-3640

SF-A3. Victorian with Old World decor offers friendly hospitality and excellent location in the Marina District. Good public transportation. Continental breakfast. Three guest rooms. Shared baths. $75-85.

SF-B1. Unique small cottage to the rear of the host home atop one of San Francisco's highest points near Golden Gate Park. Fireplace and kitchen. Continental breakfast is self-catered. Car essential. Minimum stay is three nights. Private bath. $75-85.

SF-K51. This Victorian bed and breakfast features three guest rooms with fireplace, Jacuzzi, and full breakfast. Excellent location with good transportation to all tourist attractions and business meetings. Five guest rooms. Private and shared baths available. $75-125.

SF-L1. This convenient Victorian condo is well decorated with period pieces and offers privacy in lovely surroundings. Continental breakfast. Self-hosted apartment. No smoking. $125.

SF-M1. Upstairs guest room in a well-maintained garden apartment is in a quiet neighborhood three miles from Golden Gate Park, five miles from downtown, and provides a Continental-plus breakfast. No smoking. One guest room with shared bath. $40-45.

SF-M301. This four-story Victorian hotel, now a Marina District bed and breakfast inn, features four-poster beds and modern amenities. Continental breakfast is served. Thirty guest rooms. Private baths. $65-85.

SF-P261. Two unique bed and breakfast inns, one French Country and the other formal English, are two blocks from Union Square and offer beautifully appointed rooms, hospitality, afternoon refreshments, and wonderful breakfast. Twenty-six guest rooms. Private bath. $110-250.

SF-P3. Hilltop home in Diamond Heights area has glorious view of the bay and city from the two-story living room. Enjoy a full breakfast in the Scandinavian dining area. Each of three guest rooms has a balcony. Two baths. $40-50.

SF-G23I. This 1913 turn-of-the-century Edwardian family-run bed and breakfast with antique furnishings is two blocks from Union Square and the cable cars. Continental breakfast served. Twenty-three guest rooms with private and shared baths available. $60-90.

The Golden Gate Hotel

775 Bush Street, 94108
(415) 392-3702; (800) 835-1118

The ambience, location, and price make the Golden Gate Hotel an extraordinary find in the heart of San Francisco. Dedicated to a high standard of quality and personal attention, the hosts keep fresh flowers in all the rooms. The Continental breakfast includes fresh croissants and the city's strongest coffee. Personal checks and pets welcome by prior arrangements.

Hosts: John and Renate Kenaston
Rooms: 23 (14 PB; 9 SB) $59-99
Continental Breakfast
Credit Cards: A, B, C, E, F
Notes: 8, 9, 10, 11, 12, 14

The Grove Inn

890 Grove Street, 94117
(415) 929-0780; (800) 829-0780

The Grove Inn is a charming, intimate, and affordable Victorian bed and breakfast.

7 No smoking; 8 Children welcome; 9 Social drinking allowed; 10 Tennis nearby; 11 Swimming nearby; 12 Golf nearby; 13 Skiing nearby; 14 May be booked through a travel agent.

The Grove Inn

Close to public transportation. The owners and managers are always available for information, help in renting cars, booking shuttles to the airport, and city tours. Free parking. Closed December.

Hosts: Klaus and Rosetta Zimmermann
Rooms: 18 (14 PB; 4 SB) $50-80
Continental Breakfast
Credit Cards: A, B, C
Notes: 2, 5, 7, 8, 9, 10, 11, 12, 14

The Inn at Union Square

440 Post Street, 94102
(415) 397-3510; (800) 288-4346

An elegant, small European-style hotel in the heart of San Francisco's financial, theater, and shopping districts. Each floor has an intimate lobby and fireplace where guests enjoy complimentary Continental breakfast in the morning, afternoon tea, and wine and hors d'oeuvres in the evening. Rooms are individually decorated with beautiful fabrics and comfortable Georgian furniture, and soft terry-cloth robes are provided. Penthouse accommodations include a cozy sauna, whirlpool bath, fireplace, and wet bar. Personalized service and attention to detail.

Host: Mr. Brooks Bayly
Rooms: 30 (PB) $130-300
Penthouse: 1 (PB) $300
Continental Breakfast
Credit Cards: A, B, C, E
Notes: 2, 3, 4, 5, 7, 8, 9, 14

The Inn San Francisco

943 South Van Ness Avenue, 94110
(415) 641-0188; (800) 359-0913
FAX (415) 641-1701

Authentic historic Italianate Victorian mansion, circa 1872. Ornate woodwork, Oriental carpets, marble fireplaces, and lovely antiques are combined with modern hotel conveniences. Full buffet breakfast provided. Relax in the redwood hot tub in the garden or reserve a room with a private spa tub—the perfect romantic escape! Two-night minimum stay may be required for weekends and holidays. Limited smoking permitted.

Hosts: Marty Neely and Connie Wu
Rooms: 22 (17 PB; 5 SB) $75-195
Full Breakfast
Credit Cards: A, B, C, D
Notes: 2, 5, 8, 12, 14

Jackson Court

2198 Jackson Street, 94115
(415) 929-7670; (800) 872-4500
FAX (415) 929-1405

Jackson Court is a magnificent brownstone mansion built in the late 19th century. It is in Pacific Heights, one of the finest residential neighborhoods. Tastefully decorated in antique and contemporary furnishings, Jackson Court is in the tradition of old San Francisco—simple elegance. All of the rooms have private baths, private phone lines, cable TV, and two of the rooms have wood-burning fireplaces. Refreshments are served in the late afternoon before a hand-carved stone fireplace in the entrance living room. A Continental plus breakfast is served.

Host: Pat Cremier
Rooms: 10 (PB) $113-160
Continental Breakfast
Cards: A, B, C
Notes: 5, 7, 9, 10, 12, 14

Mansions Hotel

2220 Sacramento, 94115
(415) 929-9444; (800) 826-9398;
FAX (415) 567-9391

NOTES: Credit cards accepted: A MasterCard; B Visa; C American Express; D Discover; E Diners Club; F Other; 2 Personal checks accepted; 3 Lunch available; 4 Dinner available; 5 Open all year; 6 Pets welcome;

The Mansions Hotel is made up of two historic mansions connected by an interior corridor. Rates include a sumptuous breakfast, flowers in guest's room, nightly magic performances, billiard room, sculpture gardens, and much more. The Mansions houses one of San Francisco's most important restaurants. Two blocks from chic Fillmore Street with its boutiques and restaurants. In the middle of everything but really a million miles away.

Host: Robert C. Pritikin
Rooms: 21 (PB) $129-350
Full Breakfast
Credit Cards: A, B, C, D, E
Notes: 2, 4, 5, 6, 8, 9, 10, 14

The Monte Cristo

600 Presidio Avenue, 94115
(415) 931-1875; FAX (415) 931-6005

The elegantly restored Monte Cristo was originally built in 1875 as a saloon and hotel. It has served as a bordello, a refuge after the 1906 earthquake, and a speakeasy. Only two blocks from Victorian shops, restaurants, and antique stores on Sacramento Street; ten minutes to any other point in the city. Buffet breakfast served. Two-night minimum stay required for weekends and holidays.

Host: George
Rooms: 14 (11 PB; 3 SB) $63-108
Continental Breakfast
Credit Cards: A, B, C, D, E
Notes: 5, 7, 8, 14

No Name Victorian Bed and Breakfast

847 Fillmore Street, 94117
(415) 479-1913; (800) 452-8249
FAX (415) 921-2273

This bed and breakfast is in one of the city's most photographed areas, the historic district of Alamo Square. Close to the civic center, opera house, Davies Symphony Hall, Union Square, and all the sights that make the city famous. Three of the guest rooms have fireplaces. In the evening,

guests can help themselves to wine and relaxation in the hot tub, where many a guest has had a surprise visit from the neighborhood resident, Nosey the raccoon.

Hosts: Susan and Richard Kreibich
Rooms: 5 (3 PB; 2 SB) $75-125
Credit Cards: A, B, C
Notes: 2, 5, 7, 8, 9, 10, 11, 12, 14

Petite Auberge

863 Bush Street, 94108
(415) 928-6000

A French Country inn in the heart of San Francisco. Each room is individually decorated; many have fireplaces. Guests enjoy a full buffet breakfast, afternoon wine and hors d'oeuvres, valet parking, fresh fruit, and homemade cookies. Truly romantic.

Host: Celeste Lytle
Rooms: 26 (PB) $110-220
Full Breakfast
Credit Cards: A, B, C
Notes: 2, 5, 7, 8, 9, 10, 12, 14

Pied-A-Terre

2443 Fillmore Street #277, 94115
(415) 929-8033; (800) 6 BRADY 6 (627-2396)
FAX (415) 441-8033

Two luxury apartments, each with two bedrooms, kitchen, dining room, and fireplaces, are fully furnished and accessorized with a mixture of antiques and modern furnishings, a garden, laundry facilities, color TV, cable, and VCR. Quiet elegance in historic Pacific Heights neighborhood is one block from famous Upper Fillmore shopping district. Near shops, restaurants, and movies.

Host: Deborah Brady
Flats: 2 (PB) $150-200
Continental Breakfast
Credit Cards: A, B, F
Notes: 2, 5, 8, 10, 11

The Queen Anne Hotel

1590 Sutter Street, 94109
(415) 441-2828

This 1890 landmark has been beautifully restored with 49 individually designed

7 No smoking; 8 Children welcome; 9 Social drinking allowed; 10 Tennis nearby; 11 Swimming nearby; 12 Golf nearby; 13 Skiing nearby; 14 May be booked through a travel agent.

rooms and suites, many of which include bay windows, fireplaces, and turn-of-the-century antiques. The Queen Anne Hotel is on the corner of Sutter and Octavia streets in lower Pacific Heights. Easy access to downtown, civic center, and Fisherman's Wharf. Complimentary Continental breakfast, morning limousine to downtown (weekdays), and nightly tea and sherry are only a few of the amenities provided.

Host: Steven L. Bobb
Rooms: 49 (PB) $99-275
Continental Breakfast
Credit Cards: A, B, C, D, E
Notes: 2, 5, 8, 14

Red Victorian Bed and Breakfast Inn

1665 Haight Street, 94117
(415) 861-7264; (415) 864-1978
FAX (415) 863-3293

Built at the turn of the century as a country resort hotel serving nearby Golden Gate Park, the Red Victorian enjoys an international clientele of globally minded people. From the aquarium bathroom to the Redwood Forest Room to the Peace Gallery where breakfast is served among Transformational paintings, the Red Victorian exudes color and joy.

Host: Sami Sunchild
Rooms: 18 (4 PB; 14 SB) $55-100
Continental Breakfast
Credit Cards: A, B, C
Notes: 5, 7, 14

The Union Street Inn

2229 Union Street, 94123
(415) 346-0424; FAX (415) 922-8046

In the heart of San Francisco's most fascinating shopping and dining area, the Union Street Inn and its delightful English garden offer an elegant, tranquil haven. Experience warm European hospitality in this charming Edwardian inn. All rooms feature antique furnishings, down comforters, fresh flowers, and fruit. Breakfast is a superb culinary treat. Smoking outside only.

Host: Jane Bertorelli
Rooms: 6 (PB) $125-225
Full Breakfast
Credit Cards: A, B, C
Notes: 2, 5, 8, 9, 14

Victorian Inn on the Park

301 Lyon Street, 94117
(415) 931-1830; (800) 435-1967

Queen Anne Victorian near Golden Gate Park and decorated with Victorian antiques. Many rooms have fireplaces, and the Belvedere Room features a private balcony overlooking the park. The inn features fireplaces, dining room with oak paneling, and a parlor with fireplace. Complimentary wine served nightly; fresh breads baked daily. Parking available.

Hosts: Lisa and William Benau
Rooms: 12 (PB) $99-164
Continental Breakfast
Credit Cards: A, B, C, D, E
Notes: 2, 5, 8, 9, 10, 11, 12, 14

The Washington Square Inn

1660 Stockton Street, 94114
(415) 981-4220; (800) 388-0220
FAX (415) 397-7242

The Washington Square Inn is in the heart of San Francisco's historic North Beach area just one block from Telegraph Hill. Continental breakfast, afternoon tea, wine and hors d'oeuvres are served. With only 15 rooms, the inn is special for those who care about quiet and comfort with dashes of elegance. The staff has time to concentrate on the guests' individual needs and wants.

Host: Brooks Bayly
Rooms: 15 (10 PB; 5 SB) $85-180
Continental Breakfast
Credit Cards: A, B, C, E, F
Notes: 2, 5, 7, 8, 9, 14

White Swan Inn

845 Bush Street, 94108
(415) 775-1755

In the heart of San Francisco, a bit of London resides. Each oversize guest room

NOTES: Credit cards accepted: A MasterCard; B Visa; C American Express; D Discover; E Diners Club; F Other; 2 Personal checks accepted; 3 Lunch available; 4 Dinner available; 5 Open all year; 6 Pets welcome;

has a fireplace, wet bar, sitting area, color TV, radio, bathrobes, fresh fruit, and soft drinks. Enjoy a full breakfast, afternoon wine and hors d'oeuvres, newspaper, valet parking, concierge, laundry, FAX machine, living room, library, and gracious service.

Host: Celeste Lytle
Rooms: 26 (PB) $145-250
Full Breakfast
Credit Cards: A, B, C
Notes: 2, 5, 7, 8, 9, 10, 12, 14

SAN GREGORIO

Bed and Breakfast California

P.O. Box 282910, San Francisco, 94128-2910
(415) 696-1690; (800) 872-4500
FAX (415) 696-1699

Country Retreat in San Gregorio. Guests are ten miles south of Half Moon Bay and 45 minutes from San Francisco International Airport. Designed in Spanish Mission-style, the inn was once the country estate for the San Gregorio Ranch and is filled with redwood beams, handmade terra cotta tile, carved oak furniture, and claw-foot tubs. Breakfast includes Swedish egg cake with wild blackberry sauce. Guests are welcome to sun on the deck overlooking the hills and the creek, hike through the orchard, or play badminton, volleyball, horseshoes, or croquet. Rooms are warm, woodsy, spacious; have several have fireplaces and all have private baths. Call for rates.

Rancho San Gregorio

5086 San Gregorio Road, P.O. Box 21, 94074
(415) 747-0810

Five miles inland from the Pacific off Highway 1 in a rural valley, Rancho San Gregorio welcomes travelers to share relaxed hospitality. This country getaway has 15 acres, an old barn, creek, gardens, decks, and gazebo. Full country breakfast features home-grown specialties. Only

forty-five minutes from San Francisco, Santa Cruz, and the bay area. Limited smoking allowed.

Hosts: Bud and Lee Raynor
Rooms: 4 (PB) $75-105
Suite: $145
Full Breakfast
Credit Cards: A, B, C, D
Notes: 2, 5, 8, 9, 11, 12, 14

The Hensley House

SAN JOSE

The Hensley House

456 North Third Street, 95112
(408) 298-3537

Three-story Queen Anne with square witches cap tower, 40-foot living room with hand-painted beam ceilings and walls, ten-foot fireplace, antique crystal and brass chandeliers, and hand-painted and gilded walls and ceilings. Queen-size beds with down comforters, European feather beds, TV, VCR, telephones, and air conditioning. Two rooms have whirlpool baths, while one room features a fireplace and bar. Gourmet breakfasts are served in the dining room or on the patio. Lunch and dinner are available upon request. Refreshments are served in the afternoon. Downtown historical district nearby, with restaurants, museums, and theaters also close.

Innkeeper: Sharon Layne and Bill Priest
Rooms: 5 (PB) $82.50-174.50
Full Breakfast
Credit Cards: A, B, C, D
Notes: 2, 5, 7, 9, 10, 11, 12, 14

7 No smoking; 8 Children welcome; 9 Social drinking allowed; 10 Tennis nearby; 11 Swimming nearby; 12 Golf nearby; 13 Skiing nearby; 14 May be booked through a travel agent.

SAN JUAN CAPISTRANO _____

Eye Openers Bed and Breakfast Reservations

P.O. Box 694, Altadena, 91003-0694
(213) 684-4428; (818) 797-2055
FAX (818) 798-3640

SJ-V2. Set in the heart of historic San Juan, across from the train station and near the Mission, restaurants, and shopping, new Western-style bed and breakfast with Victorian decor and appointed antiques offers friendly hospitality, a full breakfast, and a great location. Use the bicycles to visit nearby beaches and marina. Two guest rooms with double beds and shared bath. No smoking. Call for rates.

SAN LUIS OBISPO (ARROYO GRANDE)_____

Eye Openers Bed and Breakfast Reservations

P.O. Box 694, Altadena, 91003-0694
(213) 684-4428; (818) 797-2055
FAX (818) 798-3640

LO-03. This well-traveled, multilingual host offers comfortable accommodations. Living room has a view of Morro Rock. A delicious breakfast is served. No smoking. Two guest rooms. Private baths. $40-50.

PB-S301. Contemporary inn on the beach in the midst of 23 miles of unspoiled sand and surf. Continental breakfast delivered to the guest room. Twenty-five guest rooms. Private bath. $75-165.

SL-G9I. One block from the 1772 San Luis Mission, this restored 1887 Italianate Queen Anne home is near shops and restaurants. Spacious rooms, some with gas fireplace and whirlpool tub, individually decorated. A full breakfast and afternoon refreshments are served in the dining room or patio areas. Eleven guest rooms and four suites. Private baths. No smoking. $90-160.

Garden Street Inn

1212 Garden Street, 93401
(805) 545-9802

In a celebrated California community, the grace and simplicity of yesteryear prevail at this 1887 Italianate Queen Anne home. Classic Victorian decor in nine guest rooms and four suites appointed with antiques, fireplaces, Jacuzzis, and historic, cultural, and personal memorabilia. Homemade full breakfast, spacious outside decks, and well-stocked library. One block from a 1772 mission and the old-fashioned downtown. Close to Hearst Castle, Pismo Beach, Morro Bay, and Cambria.

Hosts: Dan and Kathy Smith
Rooms: 9 (PB) $90-160
Suites: 4
Full Breakfast
Credit Cards: A, B, C
Notes: 2, 5, 9, 10, 11, 12, 14

SAN LUIS OBISPO _____

Heritage Inn

978 Olive Street, 90242
(805) 544-7440

Seven guest rooms in a private home include three with private bath/shower and four rooms that share two bathrooms with antique claw-foot tubs. Bubble bath is provided. Antique furnishings, fireplaces in rooms with shared bath, fireplaces in parlor and breakfast rooms, window seats, balconies, and lovely views. Creekside garden has cats, ducks, and deer. Full breakfast. Wine and cheese in the evenings. Walking distance to 1770s mission, quaint downtown, restaurants, and pubs. Near beaches, mountains, and Hearst Castle.

Host: Georgia Adrian
Rooms: 7 (3 PB; 4 S2B) $75-120

NOTES: Credit cards accepted: A MasterCard; B Visa; C American Express; D Discover; E Diners Club; F Other; 2 Personal checks accepted; 3 Lunch available; 4 Dinner available; 5 Open all year; 6 Pets welcome;

Full Breakfast
Credit Cards: A, B, C
Notes: 2, 5, 7, 8, 9, 10, 11, 12

SAN MATEO

Bed and Breakfast California

P.O. Box 282910, San Francisco, 94128-2910
(415) 696-1690; (800) 872-4500
FAX (415) 696-1699

Feel Right at Home. Built in 1907, this Craftsman-style private home invites guests to enjoy an elegant breakfast with freshly baked bread. The Brooks family offers rooms with private or shared bath. $75.

The Palm House

1216 Palm Avenue, 94402
(415) 573-7256

Built in 1907, this Craftsman-style home is in a quiet residential area within walking distance of public transportation, restaurants, and shops. San Francisco International Airport is eight miles to the north. Stanford University to the south and the Pacific Ocean to the west are each 30 minutes by car. The Palm House is one block east of Highway 82 between 12th and 13th Avenues.

Hosts: Alan and Marian Brooks
Rooms: 3 (1 PB; 2 SB) $65-70
Continental Breakfast
Credit Cards: F
Notes: 2, 5, 8, 9, 10, 14

SANTA ANA

Bed and Breakfast California

P.O. Box 282910, San Francisco, 94128-2910
(415) 696-1690; (800) 872-4500
FAX (415) 696-1699

Built in the early 1920s, this registered historic home has been decorated for beauty and romance. One private guest suite features queen-size bed, private bath, French doors to the deck, garden, and Koi pond. A wonderful full gourmet breakfast is served in the guest room or on the deck. Host is an artist with an eye for sunshine and perfection. $75.

SANTA BARBARA

Bath Street Inn

1720 Bath Street, 93101
(805) 682-9680; (800) 788-2284

An 1890 Queen Anne Victorian in the heart of historic Santa Barbara. Scenic downtown is within walking distance. Rooms have views, balconies, and private baths, and two feature fireplaces and Jacuzzis. Breakfast is served in the dining room or in the garden; evening wine and afternoon tea.

Host: Susan Brown
Rooms: 12 (PB) $75-175
Full Breakfast
Credit Cards: A, B, C
Notes: 2, 5, 8, 9, 10, 11, 12, 14

The Bayberry Inn Bed and Breakfast

111 West Valerio Street, 93101
(805) 682-3199

A bit of paradise. The Bayberry Inn has been warmly welcoming guests since 1981. A quiet haven from the excitement and bustle of the West Coast's most popular resort city. The Bayberry Inn is the perfect departure point for a tour to the wine country, a sunny day at the beach, or a walking tour of the unique shops that have made this town a shopping mecca.

Host: Bharti Singh
Rooms: 8 (PB) $85-135
Full Breakfast
Credit Cards: A, B, C, D
Notes: 2, 5, 6, 7, 8, 9, 10, 11, 12, 14

7 No smoking; 8 Children welcome; 9 Social drinking allowed; 10 Tennis nearby; 11 Swimming nearby; 12 Golf nearby; 13 Skiing nearby; 14 May be booked through a travel agent.

Bed and Breakfast California

P.O. Box 282910, San Francisco, 94128-2910
(415) 696-1690; (800) 872-4500
FAX (415) 696-1699

A. Nestled in a garden, these delightful little cottages offer sunny rooms decorated in deep pastels with whimsical antiques. Most rooms have private baths, several have claw-foot tubs, fireplaces, sitting rooms, and private decks. Fresh-baked breakfast. $85-175.

Heart of Santa Barbara. This inn offers the traditional warmth and hospitality of a European bed and breakfast close to the heart of Santa Barbara. Eight guest rooms are individually decorated, each with private bath. Amenities include wine and cheese in the afternoon and an elegant buffet in the morning. $95-155.

Lloyd House. Only three blocks from State Street, the upstairs of this old home is available as a complete bed and breakfast apartment. Guests have a living room, bedroom with queen-size bed, full bath, full kitchen, full deck facing the ocean and the city, and private entrance. Big TV is in the living room with a queen-size futon couch for another couple or the kids. Continental breakfast. $90-125.

Private Condo near the Beach. Just ten miles south of Santa Barbara, this one-bedroom condo in Carpenteria has a queen-size bed plus a sofa bed that folds out into two singles. Spectacular sandy beach is right across the street. Condo features full kitchen, pool and spa, and cable TV. Breakfast is "self-catered." Coffee, tea, cocoa, and fruit from the ranch is provided. Guests are welcome to make as many meals as they wish. Visit the hosts' avocado and lemon ranch or play tennis at the nearby polo and racquet club. $75.

Riviera Rendezvous. This Santa Barbara mid-twenties estate sits on a hilltop in the middle of town. The guest room has a private entrance and the intimacy of a cottage. Cozy guest suite has a private bathroom, artwork, and its own romantic patio overlooking terraced gardens. Full gourmet or Continental breakfasts are served with a spectacular view of the city and harbor. Off-street parking. $95-120.

Whole House at the Beach. This gorgeous classic Spanish home with lush gardens is only a half-block away from the pristine white sands of East Beach. This private 1500-square-foot nonsmoking rental has two bedrooms, one with a queen-size bed and the other with two double beds, two bathrooms, a sunken living room with a brick fireplace, dining room, and spacious kitchen with French windows. Amenities include laundry facilities, daily maid service, color TVs, outdoor fireplace, and barbecue. Affiliated with the Cabrillo Inn at the beach, guests may enjoy those facilities, including two pools, two large sun decks, and Continental breakfast in their ocean-view lounge. $225.

Casa Del Mar Inn

18 Bath Street, 93101
(805) 963-4418; (800) 433-3097
FAX (805) 966-4240

A unique Mediterranean-style inn less than a block from the beach and harbor in Santa Barbara. Walk to all beach activities, sailing, shopping and fine restaurants. Lush gardens year-round. Twenty rooms offer a variety of accommodation options ranging from one- or two-bedroom bungalow-style family suites with full kitchens and fireplaces to cozy rooms with one king- or queen-size bed. One room is newly remodeled for full handicapped access. All rooms feature private baths, telephones, and color remote-control TV. Amenities include a garden, courtyard spa and sun deck, buffet-

NOTES: Credit cards accepted: A MasterCard; B Visa; C American Express; D Discover; E Diners Club;
F Other; 2 Personal checks accepted; 3 Lunch available; 4 Dinner available; 5 Open all year; 6 Pets welcome;

style breakfast, evening wine and cheese social hour, and kind attention from caring innkeepers and staff. A best value at a prime location. Some smoking rooms are available.

Hosts: Mike and Becky Montgomery
Rooms: 20 (PB) $59-199
Continental Breakfast
Credit Cards: A, B, C, D, E
Notes: 2, 5, 6, 8, 9, 10, 11, 12, 14

Cheshire Cat Inn

36 West Valerio Street, 93101
(805) 569-1610; FAX (805) 682-1876

Victorian elegance in a Southern California seaside village. The Cheshire Cat is near theaters, restaurants, and shops. Decorated exclusively in Laura Ashley papers and linens, the sunny guest rooms have private baths; some with fireplaces, spas, and balconies. Collectibles, English antiques, and fresh flowers enhance any stay in beautiful Santa Barbara. Special midweek rates are available.

Hosts: Christine Dunstan and Jenny Martin
Rooms: 14 (PB) $89-249
Full Breakfast
Credit Cards: A, B
Notes: 2, 7, 10, 11, 12, 14

Cliff Drive Guest House— An Oceanview Bed and Breakfast

1405 Cliff Drive, 93109
(805) 963-3525

A 1940s Spanish hacienda with a red tile roof. Three blocks from an accessible secluded beach, one can enjoy a full oceanview. The two-thirds acre is studded with giant oaks and artful landscaping. A deluxe Continental breakfast, served in a picnic basket, may be taken to the gazebo, dining room, oceanview porch, or roof-top deck. Enjoy the charming ambience of Santa Barbara in the nearby wooded ocean trails or while relaxing in the spa.

Hosts: Bob and Phyllis Adams
Rooms: 2 (SB) $85
Continental Breakfast
Credit Cards: A, B
Notes: 2, 5, 7, 8, 9, 10, 11, 12

Eye Openers Bed and Breakfast Reservations

P.O. Box 694, Altadena, 91003-0694
(213) 684-4428; (818) 797-2055
FAX (818) 798-3640

SB-B1. Hosts designed this home in the hills above Santa Barbara. The setting brings guests close to nature, but the center of town is a 10-minute drive away. The guest room has a queen-size bed and private bath. Full breakfast. No smoking. $85.

SB-C2. This Victorian home is in a lovely residential community of Santa Barbara, within walking distance from shops and restaurants. Two suites with Victorian decor have kitchens. Deluxe suite has fireplace and deck with a Western sunrise, unique to Santa Barbara. Self-hosted Continental breakfast. Queen-size beds and private baths. No smoking. $100-120.

SB-C110. Luxurious Victorian inn with a wide choice of uniquely decorated guest rooms is convenient and offers an excellent breakfast. No smoking. Eleven rooms. Private bath. $110-250.

SB-O61. Delicious, elegant breakfasts, comfortable rooms, and friendly hospitality can be found at this convenient inn near beaches and mission. This 1904 Craftsman-style bungalow has individually decorated rooms, several with private decks. Beach towels and chairs provided. Six rooms with private baths. Full breakfast. $105-175.

SB-R1. This architect-designed contemporary home is nestled among oaks near Santa Barbara Mission and five minutes to

7 No smoking; 8 Children welcome; 9 Social drinking allowed; 10 Tennis nearby; 11 Swimming nearby; 12 Golf nearby; 13 Skiing nearby; 14 May be booked through a travel agent.

the beach and shopping. Choice of full or Continental breakfast. One room. Private bath. No smoking. $45-55.

SB-S8. Convenient and filled with country charm, this inn's beautiful grounds provide a feeling of seclusion. Delicious full breakfast and evening refreshments. Bicycles available. No smoking. Eight rooms. Private and shared bath. $95-155.

Glenborough Inn

1327 Bath Street, 93101
(805) 966-0589

Experience the ultimate in romance. Full gourmet breakfast served to guests' room, parlor fireside, or in the lush gardens. Elegant fireplace suites. Secluded spa for private use. Evening social hour including hors d'oeuvres and late night desserts and beverages. Stocked guest refrigerator. Two bicycles. Walk three blocks to fine shops, restaurants, and theaters. Regular electric shuttle bus to and from the beach daily.

Hosts: Michael, Steve, and Ken
Rooms: 11 (5 PB; 6 SB) $95-225
Full Breakfast
Credit Cards: A, B, C, D, E
Notes: 2, 5, 7, 9, 10, 11, 12, 14

Long's Seaview Bed and Breakfast

317 Piedmont Road, 93105
(805) 687-2947

Relax and recharge in this lovely ranchstyle home overlooking the ocean and Channel Islands. Prestigious, quiet neighborhood. Gardens and family orchard. Huge patio offers fantastic views. Large bedroom with king-size bed, private bath, and private entrance. Carefully prepared breakfast featuring the bed and breakfast's own fresh fruits. Local information and maps. Warm hospitality.

Host: LaVerne Long
Room: 1 (PB) $75-79

Full Breakfast
Credit Cards: None
Notes: 2, 7, 9, 10, 11, 12

Ocean View House

312 Salida del Sol, P.O. Box 3373, 93105-3373
(805) 966-6659

Enjoy the comfort of a private home in a quiet neighborhood. Guests can walk to the ocean, to the church, or to a shopping center. The civic center and tourist attractions are within three miles. A Continental breakfast is served on a patio while viewing sailboats and Channel Islands. A two-room suite with an antique room, queen-size bed, TV, bathroom with a shower, adjoining is a paneled den with double bed divan, TV, and sliding glass door providing a private entrance. children are delighted with a back yard with many fruit trees. For guest's convenience there is a telephone and refrigerator. Smoking on the patio only. Reservations held only a week without deposit. Two-day minimum stay.

Host: Carolyn Canfield
Rooms: 2 (PB) $60
Continental Breakfast
Credit Cards: F
Notes: 2, 5, 6, 7, 8, 9, 10, 11, 12, 14

The Old Yacht Club Inn

431 Corona Del Mar Drive, 93103
(805) 962-1277; (800) 549-1676 (CA)
(800) 676-1676 (US)

The Old Yacht Club Inn has nine guest rooms in two houses: a 1912 California Craftsman and a 1920s Early Californiastyle building. The inn opened as Santa Barbara's first bed and breakfast in 1980 and is now world-renowned for its hospitality and warmth in comfortable surroundings and for its fine food. Within a block of the beach, the inn is close to tennis, swimming, boating, fishing, and golf. Evening wine, bikes, and beach chairs included. Dinner is available Saturdays.

Hosts: Nancy Donaldson, Lu Caruso, Sandy Hunt
Rooms: 9 (PB) $90-150

NOTES: Credit cards accepted: A MasterCard; B Visa; C American Express; D Discover; E Diners Club; F Other; 2 Personal checks accepted; 3 Lunch available; 4 Dinner available; 5 Open all year; 6 Pets welcome;

Full Breakfast
Credit Cards: A, B, C, D
Notes: 2, 4, 5, 7, 8, 9, 10, 11, 12, 14

The Olive House

1604 Olive Street, 93101
(805) 962-4902; (800) 786-6422
FAX (805) 899-2754

Enjoy the quiet comfort and gracious hospitality of an owner-occupied, lovingly restored 1904 Craftsman-style house in a quiet residential neighborhood near the Mission and downtown. Ocean and mountain views, terraced garden, large sun deck, and off-street parking. Gracious living room replete with redwood paneling, bay windows, fireplace, and studio grand piano. Private decks and hot tubs. A delicious breakfast is served in the large, sunny dining room. Afternoon wine, evening tea, sherry, and treats.

Host: Lois Gregg
Rooms: 6 (PB) $105-175
Full Breakfast
Credit Cards: A, B, C, D
Notes: 2, 5, 7, 9, 10, 11, 12, 14

Secret Garden Inn and Cottages (formerly Blue Quail Inn)

1908 Bath Street, 93101
(805) 687-2300; (800) 676-1622
FAX (805) 687-4576

Relax and enjoy the quiet garden that surrounds the main house and cottages. Linger over a delicious full breakfast, including home-baked goods, served on the patio or in the main house dining room. Take the inn's bicycles for a day of adventure, then return for afternoon wine and light hors d'oeuvres. Sip hot spiced apple cider in the evening before enjoying a restful sleep in a cottage, suite, or guest room. Near town and beaches.

Host: Jack C. Greenwald
Rooms: 9 (PB) $95-165
Full Breakfast
Credit Cards: A, B, C
Notes: 2, 5, 7, 9, 10, 11, 12, 14

Simpson House Inn

121 East Arrellaga, 93101
(805) 963-7067; (800) 676-1280

Beautifully restored 1874 Victorian estate secluded on an acre of English gardens. Only a five-minute walk to historic downtown, restaurants, and shopping. Cottages, suites, and rooms elegantly furnished with antiques and Oriental rugs feature private patios with fountains, fireplaces, and Jacuzzis. Rates include afternoon beverages, evening wine, bicycles, and croquet. Minimum-stay requirements for weekends and holidays.

Hosts: Gillean Wilson, Glyn and Linda Davies
Rooms: 14 (PB) $105-275
Full Breakfast
Credit Cards: A, B, C, D
Notes: 2, 5, 7, 9, 10, 11, 12, 14

The Upham Hotel and Garden Cottages

1404 De la Vina Street, 93101
(800) 727-0876

Established 1871, this beautifully restored Victorian hotel is on an acre of gardens. Guest rooms and suites feature period furnishings and antiques. Continental breakfast and afternoon wine and cheese. Walk to museums, galleries, historic attractions, shops, and restaurants downtown.

Host: Jan Martin Winn
Rooms: 49 (PB) $120-350
Continental Breakfast
Credit Cards: A, B, C, D, E, F
Notes: 3, 4, 5, 7, 8, 9, 10, 11, 12, 14

SANTA CRUZ

Babbling Brook Inn

1025 Laurel Street, 95060
(408) 427-2437; (800) 866-1131
FAX (408) 427-2457

Waterfalls and a meandering brook are in the gardens of this 12-room inn with French decor. Each room has a private bath, telephone, TV, fireplace, private

7 No smoking; 8 Children welcome; 9 Social drinking allowed; 10 Tennis nearby; 11 Swimming nearby; 12 Golf nearby; 13 Skiing nearby; 14 May be booked through a travel agent.

The Babbling Brook Inn

deck, and private entrance. Two have deep soaking bathtubs, while two feature bathtubs "for two." Walk to beaches, the boardwalk, a garden mall, or tennis. Full breakfast and complimentary wine and cheese. Romantic garden gazebo available for weddings. Historic water tower. Two-night minimum stay required for weekends. May be booked through travel agent with a ten percent commission.

Host: Helen King
Rooms: 12 (PB) $165
Full Breakfast
Credit Cards: A, B, C, D, E, F
Notes: 2, 5, 8, 9, 10, 11, 12, 14

Bed and Breakfast California

P.O. Box 282910, San Francisco, 94128-2910
(415) 696-1690; (800) 872-4500
FAX (415) 696-1699

New Davenport Bed and Breakfast. This friendly inn is on the coast just north of Santa Cruz, halfway between Carmel and San Francisco, in a village noted for whale watching, windsurfing, hiking, biking, and the Año Nuevo Seal Reserve. Accommodations include a visit to pottery studios and a gift shop filled with unusual treasures and jewelry. Continental plus breakfast is served in the sitting room on weekends;

weekdays join the hosts for breakfast in their restaurant. Low winter rates available. $75-125.

Private Home Bed and Breakfast among the Redwoods. At the base of the Santa Cruz mountains, this home features three rooms, two with private baths and entrances and one with a fireplace. Each room is uniquely decorated with prized antiques and collectibles, a TV, and a lovely deck for relaxing and enjoying fresh fruit drinks, champagne, and hors d'oeuvres. Breakfast is whatever guests want. Feel free to picnic in beautiful redwood grove. Santa Cruz and Monterey are a short, scenic drive away. $65-75.

Santa Cruz-1. Majesty on the cliffs. Santa Cruz is the home of this beautiful mansion overlooking the ocean. Eight rooms, mostly with semi-private bath, are filled with unusual antiques and artwork. Guests can busy themselves by the great room fireplace, visit the Boardwalk, or walk through the redwoods.

Santa Cruz-2. Vacation home in the redwoods. This 1,600-square-foot home was built to blend with the breathtaking natural environment, just ten minutes from the Santa Cruz beaches. Two bedrooms, both with private bath and spa robes, a fully equipped kitchen, cable TV, VCR, stone fireplace, and redwood deck with hot tub— even a piano. The hosts stock the refrigerator with a sumptuous full breakfast, and a welcoming bottle of wine. $125.

Serene Retreat in the Redwood Forest Inn. This secluded and private inn is beside a babbling creek and has access to whale watching, wine tasting, antique shopping, hiking, bicycling, the Santa Cruz Beach, and the Redwood State Parks. Relax in the cozy sitting room with a wet bar, stereo,

VCR, and games. Rooms are large and comfortable with queen-size beds, feather comforters, and a private deck overlooking the creek. Full country-style breakfast. Herb tea, cookies, fruit, and popcorn are always available. $75-110.

Victorian Farmhouse. Restored to the charm of an earlier age, this small inn has five beautifully furnished rooms, all with private baths. Full country breakfast is served in the parlor. There is always something to do: player piano, darts, cards, table games, horseshoes, and croquet. Explore nearby beaches, wineries, redwood parks, or Monterey Bay; or just relax with the quiet country feeling in the Victorian gazebo perched amid lawns and flowering gardens. $85-135.

Bed and Breakfast San Francisco

P.O. Box 420009, San Francisco, 94142
(415) 931-3083; FAX (415) 921-BBSF (2273)

22. A fantasy in the forest. One romantic room, with a solarium feel, looks out into the forest. It has a queen-size bed, private bath, fireplace, TV, and VCR. The second guest room is fixed up like an old-fashioned barn loft or chicken coop. It's filled with country antiques, a queen-size bed, private bath, fireplace, TV, and VCR. In the evening, ice cream treats are served in the soda fountain room downstairs. There are ten forest-filled acres to hike and explore, two ponds, and an outside fireplace pit. Santa Cruz is nine miles south and Bonnie Doon Beach is just a five-minute drive down the mountain. Full breakfast served. $100-125.

Chateau Victorian, A Bed and Breakfast Inn

118 First Street, 95060
(408) 458-9458

Chateau Victorian was built in the 1880s as a family home. Only one block from the beach and Monterey Bay. The house was opened in June 1983 as an elegant bed and breakfast inn. Each room has a private bath, fireplace, queen-size bed, carpeting, and individual heating system. Expanded Continental breakfast served. Each room is furnished in Victorian style. Within walking distance of downtown, the municipal wharf, the Boardwalk amusement park, and fine dining

Hostess: Alice June
Rooms: 7 (PB) $110-140
Continental Breakfast
Credit Cards: A, B, C
Notes: 2, 5, 7, 9, 10, 11, 12

Chateau Victorian

Downeyland Bed and Breakfast

4205 Vine Hill Lane, 95065
(408) 425-8065

Redwoods surrounding Downeyland provide serenity, yet it is a short distance from Santa Cruz and Monterey Bay. The charming house is filled with antiques, a parlor for gatherings. The large Rose Camilla Room has a classical queen-size bed, fireplace, TV, and its own entrance. The Sweetheart Room, a Victorian cottage bedroom has a double bed, TV. The Redwood suite has twin beds, small sitting room, private bath and entrance, and TV. The party may use drop-arm couch in sitting room.

Breakfast, which includes the hosts' famous banana-nut, persimmon, and cinnamon breads, can be served on the attractive porch while wild birds, deer, and cottontails entertain. The redwood grove has picnic tables. Lounge furniture is available. Guests are given personal instructions on how to reach local culinary and sightseeing locations. Lunch is available picnic style for additional charge and with prior arrangement. Inquire about children being welcome.

Hosts: Leah and Jim Downey
Rooms: 3 (PB) $65-85
Suite: $108
Full Breakfast
Credit Cards: None
Notes: 2, 5, 9, 10, 11, 12

Eye Openers Bed and Breakfast Reservations

P.O. Box 694, Altadena, 91003-0694
(213) 684-4428; (818) 797-2055
FAX (818) 798-3640

SC-B12I. This restored 1909 country bed and breakfast is set in a landscape featuring water. Enjoy the relaxing sounds in a room with a whirlpool or fireplace. A full breakfast and afternoon refreshments are provided. Twelve guest rooms have king- or queen-size beds and private baths. No smoking. $85-150.

Jasmine Cottage

731 Riverside Avenue, 95060
(408) 429-1415

Charming home with all amenities and fresh foods cooked to individual taste. Double bed and private bath. Deposit required to confirm booking.

Host: Dorothy Allen
Room: 1 (PB) $45-65
Full Breakfast
Credit Cards: A, B
Notes: 2, 5, 7, 9, 10

Pleasure Point Bed and Breakfast

2-3665 East Cliff Drive, 95062
(408) 475-4657

This beachfront home overlooks the beautiful Monterey Bay. Guest rooms have oceanviews, private baths, whirlpool tubs, and fireplaces. Forty-foot motor yacht for fishing or cruising daily. Within walking distance of Capitola Beach and three miles to the Santa Cruz Beach boardwalk. Innkeepers love to share their inn with guests.

Hosts: Margaret and Sal Margo
Rooms: 4 (PB) $100-135
Continental Breakfast
Credit Cards: A, B
Notes: 2, 5, 7, 8, 10, 11, 12, 14

SANTA MONICA

Bed and Breakfast California

P.O. Box 282910, San Francisco, 94128-2910
(415) 696-1690; (800) 872-4500
FAX (415) 696-1699

Creekside in Santa Monica. Creekside hideaway cottage near Will Rogers Park in Brentwood has guest house with private entrance, one large room with queen-size bed, a second room with a kitchenette, and a third smaller room with a futon for extra guests. Hosts live next door and serve fresh fruit juice, muffins, and beverages on the patio. A private room in the main house has a king-size bed and a bath is also available. Call for rates.

Elegant Beach Inn. This perfectly restored Santa Monica mansion has 14 guest rooms, all with private bath and phones. Features include oceanviews, a hilltop spa, Continental breakfast, and afternoon goodies. Guests are a short stroll from the beach. Handicapped accessible. Call for rates.

NOTES: Credit cards accepted: A MasterCard; B Visa; C American Express; D Discover; E Diners Club; F Other; 2 Personal checks accepted; 3 Lunch available; 4 Dinner available; 5 Open all year; 6 Pets welcome;

Channel Road Inn

219 West Channel Road, 90402
(310) 459-1920

Elegant inn one block from the beach in Santa Monica. "One of the most romantic places in Los Angeles," says *LA* magazine. Views and bicycles. Guests are two miles from the J. Paul Getty Museum. No smoking inside.

Hosts: Kathy Jensen and Susan Zolla
Rooms: 14 (PB) $85-225
Full Breakfast
Credit Cards: A, B, C
Notes: 2, 5, 8, 9, 10, 11, 12, 14

Eye Openers Bed and Breakfast Reservations

P.O. Box 694, Altadena, 91003-0694
(213) 684-4428; (818) 797-2055
FAX (818) 798-3640

SM-C14I. Near Santa Monica Canyon and the beach, this 1910 shingle-clad Colonial Revival inn offers gracious hospitality and an excellent location. It has 14 guest rooms with double, queen- or king-size beds and private baths. Some of the amenities provided are a spa, bicycles, and a full breakfast. No smoking. $95-200.

SM-M2. Redwood country-style bed and breakfast nestled in wooded, historic Rustic Canyon on a private road by a natural stream is private and quiet. The two-bedroom guest house with kitchen is minutes from the Getty Museum, Santa Monica Mountains, and beaches. Guests are within walking distance of public parks, tennis courts, and nature trails. Continental plus breakfast. Two additional guest rooms, one with private entrance, are in the main house. Queen-size beds and private baths. No smoking. $75-150.

VE-V101. This turn-of-the-century beach estate is now a lovely bed and breakfast inn. Guest rooms and suites individually decorated with antiques and hand-detailed furnishings. Large Continental breakfast and evening refreshments are served. Ten guest rooms have shared and private baths. No smoking. $90-150.

SANTA PAULA

Bed and Breakfast California

P.O. Box 282910, San Francisco, 94128-2910
(415) 696-1690; (800) 872-4500
FAX (415) 696-1699

Cen Coast-3. House Beautiful in Santa Paula. Once home to the town doctor and his (abundant) family, this stately Spanish mansion has four guest rooms, all with private bath. Well-kept gardens surround the heated pool. Breakfast is ample, decor is soothing and tasteful, and the little town of Santa Paula is perfect for a stroll. $95-125.

SANTA ROSA

The Gables Inn

4257 Petaluma Hill Inn, 95404
(707) 585-7777

A beautifully restored Victorian mansion sits grandly on three and one-half acres in the center of Sonoma wine country. Elegant guest rooms feature fluffy goose-down comforters, antiques, and private bathrooms. A separate cozy creekside cottage features a whirlpool tub for two. Sumptuous four-course gourmet breakfast available. Easy access to 140 premium wineries, the giant redwoods, the Russian River Resort, the craggy north coastline, and just one hour north of San Francisco.

Hosts: Mike and Judy Ogne
Rooms: 8 (PB) $95-175
Full Breakfast
Credit Cards: A, B, C, D
Notes: 2, 5, 7, 9, 10, 11, 12, 14

7 No smoking; 8 Children welcome; 9 Social drinking allowed; 10 Tennis nearby; 11 Swimming nearby; 12 Golf nearby; 13 Skiing nearby; 14 May be booked through a travel agent.

Melitta Station Inn

5850 Melita Road, 95409
(707) 538-7712

An 1880 converted railroad station with six rooms of antiques and country collectibles. On a country lane with a faraway feeling though only minutes from fine wineries and restaurants. Full breakfast and afternoon refreshments. An "out of the ordinary accommodation" as mentioned in the *Los Angeles Times*.

Hosts: Diane Crandon and Vic Amstadter
Rooms: 6 (4 PB; 2 SB) $75-90
Full Breakfast
Credit Cards: A, B
Notes: 2, 5, 7, 9, 10, 12, 14

Vintners Inn

4350 Barnes Road, 95403
(707) 575-7350; (800) 421-2584

Amid a 50-acre vineyard in the Sonoma wine country, this four-diamond, 44-room, European-style inn features antique furnishings, modern private baths, fireplaces if desired, balconies or patios, vineyard and plaza views, along with a complimentary breakfast. Beautiful sun deck and Jacuzzi. Also the home of the nationally acclaimed John Ash & Co. Restaurant.

Hosts: John and Cindy Duffy
Rooms: 44 (PB) $127.44-199.80
Continental Breakfast
Credit Cards: A, B, C, E
Notes: 3, 4, 5, 8, 9, 10, 11, 12, 14

SAUSALITO

Bed and Breakfast International

P.O. Box 282910, San Francisco, 94128-2910
(415) 696-1690; (800) 872-4500
FAX (415) 696-1699

108. For a unique stay try this private houseboat in Sausalito. This "floating home" is a charming Japanese design with panoramic views of the bay. A perfect way to unwind and relax. The houseboat will delight guests with its extensive collection of exotic artifacts and carpets from the Orient. Two outdoor decks. $135.

Bed and Breakfast San Francisco

P.O. Box 420009, San Francisco, 94142
(415) 931-3083; FAX (415) 921-BBSF (2273)

17. The Marin County picturesque village of Sausalito offers wonderful restaurants, quaint shops, and a romantic view of San Francisco. Stay aboard a houseboat, a permanently moored home on the bay. There are decks on three sides, living room with fireplace, king-size bed in the bedroom, full kitchen, and a full bath. The home is non-hosted but all breakfast items are supplied. Enjoy the view as the city lights come on and the sun slips behind Mount Tamalpais. Full breakfast. $125.

Eye Openers Bed and Breakfast Reservations

P.O. Box 694, Altadena, 91003-0694
(213) 684-4428; (818) 797-2055
FAX (818) 798-3640

SA-C35I. This 1885 Victorian-style inn with restaurant can be found in the hills. There are 35 guest rooms with private baths, king- or queen-size beds, and some with fireplaces. A Continental breakfast is served. No smoking. $105-225.

SEAL BEACH

Eye Openers Bed and Breakfast Reservations

P.O. Box 694, Altadena, 91003-0694
(213) 684-4428; (818) 797-2055
FAX (818) 798-3640

SB-B2. Large villa on the sand with colorful gardens beach-side beckons guests to indulge in water sports, sun on the dunes,

NOTES: Credit cards accepted: A MasterCard; B Visa; C American Express; D Discover; E Diners Club; F Other; 2 Personal checks accepted; 3 Lunch available; 4 Dinner available; 5 Open all year; 6 Pets welcome;

or relax on an enclosed balcony with an oceanview. Indoor Jacuzzi. Continental-plus breakfast. Two guest rooms. Private bath. No smoking. $95.

SB-S241. A bed and breakfast inn with the look and ambience of an elegant European inn is surrounded by lovely gardens. Inn has a brick courtyard, pool, library, and a gracious dining room for large Continental breakfasts and evening refreshments. Twenty-four guest rooms all have individual decor and private baths. This lovely, quiet beach community is a well-kept secret. $110-225.

Seal Beach
Inn and Gardens

212 Fifth Street, 90740
(310) 493-2416

Chosen as one of the top 12 inns by *Country Inn* magazine. An elegant country inn by the sea, with a classic French Mediterranean appearance. The accommodations are appointed in handsome antique furnishings. Many have sitting areas and kitchens. The inn is surrounded by lush, colorful, gardens, French sculpture, fountains, and ancient garden art. An Old World-style bed and breakfast, but far more than that. This is a full-service country inn with all the conveniences, activities, and amenities of a fine hotel. Water-skiing nearby.

Host: Marjorie Bettenhausen
Rooms: 23 (PB) $118-185
Full Breakfast
Credit Cards: A, B, C, D, E
Notes: 5, 7, 8, 10, 11, 12, 13, 14

SEBASTOPOL

Bed and Breakfast
California

P.O. Box 282910, San Francisco, 94128-2910
(415) 696-1690; (800) 872-4500
FAX (415) 696-1699

Intimate Historic Inn. This landmark inn was built in 1872 and is an elegant oasis of apple orchards, old redwoods, and lush gardens. Four lovingly detailed rooms are furnished with antiques. All rooms have queen-size beds and veranda, and two of the rooms share a bath. A suite with wood-burning fireplace offers a delightful hideaway for all seasons. Enjoy wisteria arbor, heated pool, 1890 Chickering piano, wood-fired stove, and easy chairs. Nearby are vineyards, historical sites, hot springs spas, antique browsing, golf courses, canoeing, kayaking, hiking, country roads, four-star restaurants, and hot air ballooning. Continental breakfast in dining room or room. $85-110.

SEQUOIA NATIONAL PARK

Bed and Breakfast
California

P.O. Box 282910, San Francisco, 94128-2910
(415) 696-1690; (800) 872-4500
FAX (415) 696-1699

A. At the foot of Sequoia National Park is a classic country bed and breakfast with nine guest rooms, four in the main house and three suites in the garden. All rooms have private bath and several include sitting areas and claw-foot tubs. Friendly hosts serve a full country breakfast in the dining room. $70-85.

B. This family cottage in the little town of Three Rivers was built by an architect for beauty and efficiency. It has a bedroom, living room, bath, full kitchen, and redwood deck. The splendor of the wilderness surrounds this cottage. Moderate rates.

Eye Openers
Bed and Breakfast
Reservations

P.O. Box 694, Altadena, 91003-0694
(213) 684-4428; (818) 797-2055
FAX (818) 798-3640

7 No smoking; 8 Children welcome; 9 Social drinking allowed; 10 Tennis nearby; 11 Swimming nearby; 12 Golf nearby; 13 Skiing nearby; 14 May be booked through a travel agent.

LE-L9I. Family-run inn near entrance to Sequoia National Park offers gorgeous scenery and friendly hospitality. Ten guest rooms have queen- or king-size beds and private or shared baths. Full breakfast. No smoking. $55-95.

TR-R1. Sequoia National Park is very near this lovely, quiet, rural community. Self-contained cottage adjacent to hosts' home offers fireplace, queen-size bed, and private bath. Continental breakfast. No smoking allowed. $75.

TR-C1. Enjoy an architect-designed cottage with kitchen facilities. Beautiful views of the mountains. Near the entrance to Sequoia National Park. Hot tub available. Private bath. No smoking. $75.

Lemon Cove Bed and Breakfast

33038 Highway 198, Lemoncove, 93244
(800) 240-1466

Near the Sequoia National Park, the Lemon Cove Bed and Breakfast is nestled in the Sierra foothills, just one mile below Lake Kaweah. A bridal suite with fireplace, whirlpool bath, and balcony is one of nine romantic rooms tastefully decorated with antiques and quilts. Off-street parking. Evening refreshments served.

Hosts: Pat and Kay Bonette
Rooms: 9 (7 PB; 2 SB) $55-89
Full Breakfast
Credit Cards: A, B, C, D
Notes: 2, 5, 7, 8, 9, 11, 12, 14

SKYFOREST

Bed and Breakfast California

P.O. Box 282910, San Francisco, 94128-2910
(415) 696-1690; (800) 872-4500
FAX (415) 696-1699

Graystone. This quaint country French chateau has four bedrooms, each with a private bath. The master suite has a king-size bed, fireplace, and two-person Jacuzzi. The fireplace and bookshelves in the parlor, which is 200 years old, were imported from a chateau in France. Full breakfast served in the morning, and wine and cheese in the afternoon. $95-125.

SOLANO BEACH

Bed and Breakfast California

P.O. Box 282910, San Francisco, 94128-2910
(415) 696-1690; (800) 872-4500
FAX (415) 696-1699

Spectacular Ocean Bluff View. A large two-bedroom, two-and-one-half bath condominium is in a beautifully landscaped complex on a bluff overlooking the ocean (beach access) with a 180-degree ocean-view from the private deck. Near Del Mar Racetrack and Fairgrounds. Guests have unlimited use of facilities, including swimming pools and tennis. Fully equipped kitchen, washer and dryer, free local calls, two cable color TVs and VCR are also available. $75-150.

SOLVANG

The Alisal Guest Ranch and Resort

1054 Alisal Road, 93463
(805) 688-6411; (800) 425-4725
FAX (805) 688-2510

Enjoy a journey back to the Old West. Tucked away amidst 10,000 acres of picturesque countryside, the Alisal is California's only full-service guest ranch. The rustic charm of a historic cattle ranch combines with first-class accommodations, fine conference facilities, horseback riding, golf, tennis, boating, and fishing on private lake.

NOTES: Credit cards accepted: A MasterCard; B Visa; C American Express; D Discover; E Diners Club;
F Other; 2 Personal checks accepted; 3 Lunch available; 4 Dinner available; 5 Open all year; 6 Pets welcome;

A one-of-a kind getaway and meeting destination offers 73 cottages with fireplaces. Amenities include two championship golf courses, one hundred-acre private lake, supervised activities for children, 6,000-square feet of meeting space, theme parties and western barbecues, and group rodeos and cattle drives. Modified American Plan.

Host: David S. Lautensack, general manager
Rooms: 73 (PB) $295-380
Full Breakfast
Credit Cards: A, B, C
Notes: 2, 3, 4, 5, 8, 9, 10, 11, 12, 14

Bed and Breakfast California

P.O. Box 282910, San Francisco, 94128-2910
(415) 696-1690; (800) 872-4500
FAX (415) 696-1699

Charming Cannon Home. This lovely nonsmoking home has a guest room with a queen-size bed. The hostess serves afternoon wine or cider. Children over six are welcome. Continental breakfast served. Guests may sit and relax on the screened porch in good weather. Just a short walk to the little Danish town of Solvang. $85.

Storybook Inn. Just a short walk from the middle of town, this exquisite seven-room inn features four-poster beds, window seats, and Jacuzzi tubs for two. Each room is decorated with unique colors and antiques to follow the theme of a different Hans Christian Andersen story. Enjoy gourmet breakfast, afternoon goodies, and a big parlor for socializing or watching TV throughout the day. Call for rates.

Eye Openers Bed and Breakfast Reservations

P.O. Box 694, Altadena, 91003-0694
(213) 684-4428; (818) 797-2055
FAX (818) 798-3640

SO-S9I. This English Tudor is decorated with Hans Christian Andersen story themes and antique furnishings. Many rooms have fireplaces, and several whirlpool tubs. Nine guest rooms with queen-size beds and private baths available. A full breakfast is served in the dining room. No smoking. $90-180.

SO-C1. In the rolling hills above Solvang, this spacious home is on one acre. Lovely guest room with queen-size bed and large bath ensuite. Relax in the living room or on the screened patio. Walk a mile into town or bicycle or drive to nearby Lake Cachuma and Santa Ynez wineries. Horseback riding, golf, and boating are all nearby. Pet dog in residence. $85.

SONOMA

Bed and Breakfast California

P.O. Box 282910, San Francisco, 94128-2910
(415) 696-1690; (800) 872-4500
FAX (415) 696-1699

Indulge in the peace of a private cottage close to this small town. Artist hosts have decorated these distinctive suites with their original art. Enjoy a Continental breakfast in the shadow of a lilac-lined drive leading to a vineyard or mountain view. All rooms feature deluxe queen-size beds, patios, and full baths. Call for rates.

Bed and Breakfast International

P.O. Box 282910, San Francisco, 94128-2910
(415) 696-1690; (800) 872-4500
FAX (415) 696-1699

301. In the heart of Sonoma, within walking distance to the plaza and wineries, is an old stonecutter's cottage. It has a king/twin bed with bath and large deck. There is a

Franklin stove in the cottage. In a garden setting surrounded by countryside studded with giant oaks. Breakfast is served in the main house. $125.

302. Contemporary, Colonial-style, two-story home in the Sonoma Valley wine country. Surrounded by 17 acres, it has views of rolling hills and Mount St. Helena, yet is only three miles from downtown Healdsburg. Guest quarters are in a separate building from the main house and are furnished in antiques, quilts, and Oriental rugs. Both rooms have double beds and private baths. Breakfast is in main house. $80.

Eye Openers Bed and Breakfast Reservations

P.O. Box 694, Altadena, 91003-0694
(213) 684-4428; (818) 797-2055
FAX (818) 798-3640

HE-C91. This 1869 Italianate Victorian townhouse on one-half acre has landscaped grounds with pool and large antique-filled guest rooms Breakfast with fresh baked breads and afternoon refreshments are served. Nine guest rooms. Shared and private baths. $75-135.

HE-G71. This 1902 Queen Anne Victorian offers an elegant return to a bygone era. Upstairs rooms have roof windows and view of the lovely grounds. Full country breakfast. Seven guest rooms. Private bath. No smoking. $85-130.

Sonoma Chalet

18935 5th Street West, 95476
(707) 938-3129

In the beautiful Valley of the Moon, this inn is surrounded by early California history. Visit the wineries and enjoy the rich colorful vineyards and natural beauty of Sonoma Valley. The chalet has overnight accommodations in a wonderful country farm setting. The Swiss-style farmhouse and country cottages are on three beautiful acres just minutes away from some of the valley's most celebrated wineries. Listed as one of the "Best places to kiss in the bay area." No smoking inside.

Host: Joe Leese
Rooms: 7 (5 PB; 2 SB) $75-135
Continental Breakfast
Credit Cards: A, B, C
Notes: 2, 5, 8, 9, 10, 11, 12, 14

Sonoma Hotel

110 West Spain Street, 95476
(707) 996-2996; (800) 468-6016
FAX (707) 996-7014

This beautiful vintage hotel offers accommodations and dining to the discriminating seeker of relaxation and respite from the urban hustle. To spend an evening here is to step back into a romantic period of history. Each antique bedroom evokes a distinct feel of early California; the emphasis on comfort is European. On a tree-lined plaza, it is within walking distance of famous wineries, beautiful picnic spots, distinctive art galleries, unique shops, and historic landmarks. Guests receive wine on arrival.

Hosts: John and Dorene Musilli
Rooms: 17 (5 PB; 12 SB) $75-130
Continental Breakfast
Credit Cards: A, B, C,
Notes: 2, 3, 4, 5, 7, 8, 9, 10, 11, 12, 14

Sparrows' Nest Inn

424 Denmark Street, 95476
(707) 996-3750; FAX (707) 938-5023

This charming private cottage one mile from the historic town square of Sonoma has an English country style that is tidy and comfortable. Surrounded by flower gardens, the romantic one-bedroom cottage includes a small kitchen, living room, private bathroom, cable TV, and telephone. Pets are welcome by prior arrangement.

Hosts: Thomas and Kathleen Anderson
Rooms: 1 (PB) $85-105
Full Breakfast
Credit Cards: A, B, C, D
Notes: 2, 5, 7, 8, 10, 11, 12

Victorian Garden Inn

316 East Napa Street, 95476
(707) 996-5339; (800) 543-5339

Nestled beside Nathanson Creek on an acre of beautiful gardens with private patios and winding paths, this lovely and historic (1870) farmhouse is just one-and-a-half blocks from Sonoma's historic plaza and the Sebastiani Winery. The comfortable and artfully decorated rooms, furnished with antiques, are designed for comfort and have a view of the gardens and secluded swimming pool. A gourmet California breakfast is served in the cheerful dining room, on the patios, or in rooms as requested. Concierge services are provided for the ultimate romantic experience in this sophisticated and gracious environment.

Host: Donna Lewis
Rooms: 4 (3 PB; 1 SB) $79-139
Continental Breakfast
Credit Cards: A, B, C
Notes: 2, 5, 7, 9, 10, 11, 12, 14

Bed and Breakfast California

P.O. Box 282910, San Francisco, 94128-2910
(415) 696-1690; (800) 872-4500
FAX (415) 696-1699

17-2. Play with the llamas at this creekside guest ranch in the country. Features hot tub and sauna, music room/library with lots of kids' games, and gracious Southern hospitality. Moderate rates.

Gold Rush Town. This homey 1886 Victorian bed and breakfast is close to Columbia State Historic Park, "Railtown

1897," snow and water skiing, fishing, hunting, horseback riding, and gold panning. Theater and ski packages are available. The inn is on Gold Street in historic Sonora. There are five guest rooms, all with wraparound porches and a hearty full breakfast. $75.

SOQUEL

Blue Spruce Inn

2815 Main Street, 95073
(408) 464-1137; (800) 559-1137
FAX (408) 475-0608

Spa tubs, fireplaces, and quiet gardens foster relaxation for guests. The Blue Spruce is four miles south of Santa Cruz, one mile inland from Capitola Beach—an ideal location for a romantic getaway, special celebration, business travel, or a special business meeting. Hike in the redwoods. Bike through country fields. Walk to fine dining. Relax in the outdoor hot tub. Professional, personal attention is the hallmark of this inn. Visit soon!

Hosts: Pat and Tom O'Brien
Rooms: 6 (PB) $85-135
Full Breakfast
Credit Cards: A, B, C, D
Notes: 2, 5, 7, 9, 10, 11, 12, 14

SOUTH PASADENA

Bissell House

201 Orange Grove Avenue, 91030
(818) 441-3535; (800) 441-3531
FAX (818) 441-3671

Now a recognized historic landmark that was built in 1887, the Bissell House is an elegant Victorian bed and breakfast offering quiet and intimate accommodations. It is on the southern west anchor of Pasadena's Millionaires Row and just a whisper's distance from Old Town Pasadena, Wrigley Mansion, the Rose Bowl, Norton Simon Museum, Pacific Asian Museum, Gamble

7 No smoking; 8 Children welcome; 9 Social drinking allowed; 10 Tennis nearby; 11 Swimming nearby; 12 Golf nearby; 13 Skiing nearby; 14 May be booked through a travel agent.

Bissell House

House, and the Huntington Library. Twelve minutes and one hundred years from downtown Los Angeles, the Bissell House offers convenience and pleasure to the business and vacation traveler alike. Continental breakfast is served weekdays with a ten percent discount. Smoking outside only. Inquire about accommodations for children. Skiing is within 30 miles. Two-night minimum stay on weekends if Saturday is included.

Hosts: Russ and Leonore Butcher
Rooms: 3 (PB) $90-150
Full and Continental Breakfast
Credit Cards: A, B, C
Notes: 2, 5, 9, 10, 11, 12, 4

SPRINGVILLE

Annie's Bed and Breakfast

33024 Globe Drive, 93265
(209) 539-3827

On five acres in the beautiful Sierra foothills, this inn is beautifully furnished with antiques, feather beds, and handmade quilts. Full country breakfast is prepared on an antique wood cookstove. The host has a custom saddle shop and horse training facility on the property. Close to redwoods, golf, tennis, fishing, hiking, and boating. Enjoy a great place to relax and enjoy the peace and quiet of country life. Members of CABBI and PAII.

Hosts: John and Annie Bozanich
Rooms: 3 (PB) $85
Full Breakfast
Credit Cards: A, B, C, E
Notes: 2, 3, 4, 5, 7, 9, 10, 11, 12, 14

SUMMERLAND

Summerland Inn

2161 Ortega Hill Road, P.O. Box 1209, 93067
(805) 969-5225

The Summerland Inn, "where New England meets the Pacific," is a delightful bed and breakfast with 11 rooms, private baths, telephones, TV, and breakfast served in guests' room. Summerland has its own beach a short walk from the inn, antique and gift shops, and places to eat.

Host: James R. Farned
Rooms: 11 (PB) $55-140
Continental Breakfast
Credit Cards: A, B, C, D, E
Notes: 2, 5, 7, 8, 14

SUNSET BEACH

Bed and Breakfast California

P.O. Box 282910, San Francisco, 94128-2910
(415) 696-1690; (800) 872-4500
FAX (415) 696-1699

Walk to Sunset Beach. This quaint little bed and breakfast is just a half-block from the water's edge in the romantic town of Sunset Beach. Rooms all have private baths and cozy, country decor. Continental breakfast served. $65-85.

SUSANVILLE

Roseberry House

609 North Street, 96130
(916) 257-5675

The Roseberry House is just two blocks from Main Street in historic uptown Susanville. It was built in 1902 by Thomas Roseberry, a California assemblyman, for his wife. The area affords a variety of recreational activities. Hiking and biking trails are nearby; deer and bird watching is excellent. Famous Eagle Lake trout are only minutes away. Cross-country skiing and

NOTES: Credit cards accepted: A MasterCard; B Visa; C American Express; D Discover; E Diners Club; F Other; 2 Personal checks accepted; 3 Lunch available; 4 Dinner available; 5 Open all year; 6 Pets welcome;

snowmobiling are favorite wintertime pursuits. The Roseberry House lives up to its name with roses in profusion in carpets, wallpapers, and vases. It features an unusual collection of antiques, with each guest room distinctly different. Early morning coffee is served in the upstairs hall. Enjoy a tastefully prepared full breakfast in the formal dining room. Fresh breads and fruits are served, along with other specialties. Smoking is permitted only on the porch or the upstairs balcony.

Rooms: 4 (PB) $55-80
Full Breakfast
Credit Cards: A, B, C
Notes: 2, 5, 10, 11, 12

TAHOE CITY

Chaney House

4725 West Lake Boulevard, P.O. Box 7852, 96145
(916) 525-7333

Built on the Lake Tahoe shore by Italian stonemasons, Chaney House has an almost medieval quality with its dramatic arched windows, 18-inch-thick stone walls, and enormous fireplace. The private beach and pier beckon guests. Bicycling, hiking, boating, fishing, and 19 ski areas are close at hand. Scrumptious breakfasts are served on the patio overlooking the lake on mild days. Children over 12 welcome. May be booked through a travel agent midweek and during the off-season.

Hosts: Gary and Lori Chaney
Rooms: 4 (PB) $100-115

Chaney House

Full Breakfast
Credit Cards: None
Notes: 2, 5, 7, 9, 10, 11, 12, 13

The Cottage Inn at Lake Tahoe

1690 West Lake Boulevard, P.O. Box 66, 96145
(916) 581-4073; FAX (916) 581-0226

The Cottage Inn bed and breakfast is nestled among the pines just steps from Lake Tahoe. It's a storybook collection of newly decorated knotty pine cottages with fireplaces, televisions, lake views, beach access, sauna, free ski shuttles, and full breakfast. A crackling fire, homemade cookies, and fresh popcorn are always waiting for you in our homey lodge. The Cottage Inn is on the west shore of Lake Tahoe near Tahoe City and several major ski areas.

Hosts: Linda Keller
Rooms: 14 (PB) $100-165
Full Breakfast
Credit Cards: A, B
Notes: 2, 5, 7, 10, 11, 12, 13, 14

Mayfield House

236 Grove Street, P.O. Box 5999, 96145
(916) 583-1001

Snug and cozy 1930s Tahoe home, one-half block from the beach. Premium skiing within five miles. Full breakfast. Homemade baked goods. Within walking distance of shops and restaurants in Tahoe City. Off-street parking.

Hosts: Cynthia and Bruce Knauss
Rooms: 6 (SB) $90-160
Full Breakfast
Credit Cards: A, B, C
Notes: 2, 5, 7, 9, 10, 11, 12, 13, 14

TEHACHAPI

Bed and Breakfast California

P.O. Box 282910, San Francisco, 94128-2910
(415) 696-1690; (800) 872-4500
FAX (415) 696-1699

7 No smoking; 8 Children welcome; 9 Social drinking allowed; 10 Tennis nearby; 11 Swimming nearby; 12 Golf nearby; 13 Skiing nearby; 14 May be booked through a travel agent.

Family-Style Cowboy Ranch. This 31,000-acre cattle ranch is deep in the Tehachapi Mountains and has been owned by the same family sine 1863. Accommodations include 12 guest rooms, all with private bath and three meals a day. Horseback riding, biking, tennis, fishing, swimming, and supervised kid's activities promise the perfect year-round hideaway—below the winter snow but above the summer heat. $100-125.

TEMECULA

Eye Openers Bed and Breakfast Reservations

P.O. Box 694, Altadena, 91003-0694
(213) 684-4428; (818) 797-2055
FAX (818) 798-3640

TE-L61. In Southern California's wine country, this lovely bed and breakfast has six uniquely decorated guest rooms. Full country breakfast. No smoking. Private bath. $95-125.

Loma Vista Bed and Breakfast

33350 La Serena Way, 92591
(909) 676-7047

Loma Vista

Loma Vista, in the heart of Temecula's wine country, is convenient to any spot in Southern California. This beautiful new Mission-style home is surrounded by citrus groves and premium vineyards. All six rooms have private baths; most have balconies. A full champagne breakfast is served. Closed Thanksgiving, Christmas, New Year's days.

Hosts: Betty and Dick Ryan
Rooms: 6 (PB) $95-125
Full Breakfast
Credit Cards: A, B, D
Notes: 2, 7, 9, 10, 11, 12, 14

TEMPLETON

Bed and Breakfast California

P.O. Box 282910, San Francisco, 94128-2910
(415) 696-1690; (800) 872-4500
FAX (415) 696-1699

In the Little Town of Templeton. Just north of San Luis Obispo on Highway 101, this quaint little town takes guests back 100 years. The Country Inn is perfectly restored, including parlor and veranda. Four guest rooms in pastel colors, two with private baths and two that share, are available. Low mid-week rates are available. $75-85.

THOUSAND OAKS

Bed and Breakfast California

P.O. Box 282910, San Francisco, 94128-2910
(415) 696-1690; (800) 872-4500
FAX (415) 696-1699

Decorator Perfect. Overlooking a regional park with hiking trails in Thousand Oaks, this beautifully decorated house features a patio with pool and spa, fireplace, and lovely views. Upstairs guest room has twin beds, a private bath, balcony. Den can accommodate extra guest. Cars are essential in this area. School-age children are welcome. $65.

NOTES: Credit cards accepted: A MasterCard; B Visa; C American Express; D Discover; E Diners Club;
F Other; 2 Personal checks accepted; 3 Lunch available; 4 Dinner available; 5 Open all year; 6 Pets welcome;

TORRANCE

Bed and Breakfast California

P.O. Box 282910, San Francisco, 94128-2910
(415) 696-1690; (800) 872-4500
FAX (415) 696-1699

Lovely ranch-style home is about a mile from the beach. This home features two guest rooms, both with private bath. One room has a queen-size bed and a twin bed; the other has a queen-size bed, a kitchenette, and sliding doors to the deck and garden. Hostess loves to visit and makes whatever you want for breakfast! Close to both LA International Airport and the southern beaches. $55-65.

TRINIDAD

Bed and Breakfast California

P.O. Box 282910, San Francisco, 94128-2910
(415) 696-1690; (800) 872-4500
FAX (415) 696-1699

Guests can watch the waves from the hot tub, while the kids are out berry-picking at this perfect family vacation spot. Hosts designed this bed and breakfast retreat for family fun and comfort. Breakfast is big and nutritious; town is nearby and full of activity; and scenic trails to tide pools are at the doorstep. The kids are provided with an enclosed playground, playhouse, barnyard animals, and storytelling. Need a night out? Childcare is available, too. Call for rates.

The Lost Whale Bed and Breakfast

3452 Patrick's Point Drive, 95570
(707) 677-3425

Unique bed and breakfast on four wooded acres with a private beach and trail. Wake to barking sea lions and a spectacular oceanview. Amenities include outdoor hot tub, afternoon tea, private baths, and queen-size beds. Fifteen minutes from Eureka airport and the largest redwood forests in the world. Enjoy the gardens, decks, and gourmet breakfast.

Hosts: Lee Miller and Susanne Lakin
Rooms: 8 (PB) $95-140
Full Breakfast
Credit Cards: A, B, C, D
Notes: 2, 5, 7, 8, 12, 11, 13, 14

Trinidad Bay

Trinidad Bay Bed and Breakfast

560 Edwards Street, P.O. Box 849, 95570
(707) 677-0840

A Cape Cod-style home overlooking beautiful Trinidad Bay. The inn offers spectacular views of the rugged coastline and fishing harbor from two suites, one with a fireplace, and two upstairs bedrooms, all with private baths. Surrounded by beaches, trails, and redwood parks. Within walking distance of restaurants and shops. The suites enjoy breakfast delivered. The other two rooms enjoy breakfast at a family-style table.

Hosts: Paul and Carol Kirk
Rooms: (PB) $105-155
Continental Breakfast
Credit Cards: A, B
Notes: 2, 7, 8, 9, 10, 12

7 No smoking; 8 Children welcome; 9 Social drinking allowed; 10 Tennis nearby; 11 Swimming nearby; 12 Golf nearby; 13 Skiing nearby; 14 May be booked through a travel agent.

TRUCKEE

The Truckee Hotel

10007 Bridge Street, 96161
(800) 659-6921

This circa 1873 Victorian bed and breakfast
is in Truckee's historical district. Begin the
day with an expanded Continental breakfast, and enjoy the sights and activities that
this beautiful Sierra location offers. In-
house dining at The Passage offers fine
wine and cuisine. Relax fireside in the parlor before turning in for the night.
Shopping and dining are moments from the
inn, and Amtrak is close by. Come for a
visit by train. Call for brochure.

Host: Rachelle L. Pellissier
Rooms: 36 (8 PB; 28 SB) $60-115
Continental Breakfast
Credit Cards: A, B, C
Notes: 2, 5, 7, 8, 11, 12, 13

TWENTYNINE PALMS

Bed and Breakfast California

P.O. Box 282910, San Francisco, 94128-2910
(415) 696-1690; (800) 872-4500
FAX (415) 696-1699

Homestead Inn. The Homestead is a classic 1920s-style adobe, cool in summer and
cozy in winter. Three rooms are available.
The inn boasts the third oldest bathtub in the
county. The atmosphere is gracious, serene,
and very, very homey. Full breakfast.
Evening hors d'oeuvres. Hot tub and
gazebo. Gift shop. $75-150.

Roughly Manor. A warm, elegant surprise
in the middle of the desert. An enormous
Cape Cod-style mansion with five bedrooms. Most rooms have queen-size beds;
several have fireplaces. Enjoy a full breakfast in the huge, flower bedecked dining
room, and afternoon wine and goodies.
Warm antiques, floral quilts and wallpaper,
original tubs and tile, art and sunshine provide ambience. $70-125.

UKIAH

Bed and Breakfast California

P.O. Box 282910, San Francisco, 94128-2910
(415) 696-1690; (800) 872-4500
FAX (415) 696-1699

16-8. The champagne baths are the center
of attention at this parklike resort at the
foot of the Mendocino Hills. Twelve individually decorated rooms with private
baths date from the 1860s. The two free-
standing cottages, complete with modern
kitchens, were built in 1854. Abundant
wildlife in the 700 acres of woods, meadows, streams, and falls that surround the
ranch. Sailing, windsurfing, Jet Skiing, and
salmon fishing are all within easy reach,
and naturally carbonated hot tubs are at the
doorstep. Moderate to luxury rates.

Eye Openers Bed and Breakfast Reservations

P.O. Box 694, Altadena, 91003-0694
(213) 684-4428; (818) 797-2055
FAX (818) 798-3640

UK-V12I. This 1854 California historic
landmark, once a favorite retreat of writers
and United States presidents, still features
warm, naturally carbonated mineral baths.
The bed and breakfast is on 700 acres and
features an Olympic-size pool, large
Jacuzzi, indoor and outdoor mineral tubs,
and massages. There are 12 guest rooms
and two cottages with private baths and
queen-size or twin beds. Hike or bike on the
property. Many recreational opportunities
are at nearby coast. An expanded Continental breakfast. No smoking. $125-160.

Oak Knoll Bed and Breakfast

858 Sanel Drive, 95482
(707) 462-8322

A large redwood contemporary home has
spectacular views of hills, valleys, vine-

NOTES: Credit cards accepted: A MasterCard; B Visa; C American Express; D Discover; E Diners Club;
F Other; 2 Personal checks accepted; 3 Lunch available; 4 Dinner available; 5 Open all year; 6 Pets welcome;

yards, and sheep. Guests enjoy a spacious deck and lovely Oriental furnishings and chandeliers. Two rooms are available with shared bath, adjacent sitting room, TV, and movies on a 40-inch screen in the family room. Full breakfast in the dining room or on the deck in summer. Hiking, golf, and boating are nearby.

Host: Shirley Wadley
Rooms: 2 (SB) $80
Full Breakfast
Credit Cards: None
Notes: 2, 5, 7, 9, 10, 11, 12, 14

Vichy Springs Resort and Inn

2605 Vichy Springs Road, 95482
(707) 462-9515

Vichy Springs Resort, a delightful two-hour drive north of San Francisco, 12 rooms and two self-contained cottages that have been renovated and individually decorated. Nearby are 14 tubs built in 1860 and used by the rich and famous in California's history. Vichy features naturally sparkling 90-degree mineral baths, a communal 104-degree pool, Olympic-size pool, 700 private acres with a waterfall, trails and roads for hiking, jogging, picnicking, and mountain bicycling, and Swedish massage, reflexology, and herbal facials. Relax!

Hosts: Gilbert and Marjorie Ashoff
Rooms: 14 (PB) $89-165
Full Breakfast
Credit Cards: A, B, C, D, E, F
Notes: 2, 3, 4, 5, 7, 8, 9, 10, 11, 12, 14

UNIVERSAL CITY

Bed and Breakfast California

P.O. Box 282910, San Francisco, 94128-2910
(415) 696-1690; (800) 872-4500
FAX (415) 696-1699

Designer House in the Valley. This house was built with a private wing for the in-laws. Full bedroom, living room, bath, and kitchenette available. The living room has a

view of the valley: Griffith Park on one side and Universal Studios on the other. The local scenery is full of blooming cactus and succulents. Breakfast is self-serve in room or feel free to eat by the pool. $120.

VALLEY FORD

Eye Openers Bed and Breakfast Reservations

P.O. Box 694, Altadena, 91003-0694
(213) 684-4428; (818) 797-2055
FAX (818) 798-3640

VF-141. This 1870 Victorian farmhouse, with library and wood-burning stove in the parlor, is set on lovely surroundings. Four guest rooms have private and shared baths and queen-size or double beds. Enjoy a Continental plus breakfast and afternoon refreshments. Excellent hiking, biking, and touring areas nearby. No smoking. $60-85.

VAN NUYS

Bed and Breakfast California

P.O. Box 282910, San Francisco, 94128-2910
(415) 696-1690; (800) 872-4500
FAX (415) 696-1699

Guest Suite with Kitchenette. Enjoy the tranquility of this house with two guest wings, both with kitchenettes. Pool, sports equipment, and bikes are available. Upstairs suite has a king-size bed with balcony and private bath. Downstairs has a queen-size bedroom and dual twin bedrooms that share a bath. $60-75.

VENICE

Bed and Breakfast California

P.O. Box 282910, San Francisco, 94128-2910
(415) 696-1690; (800) 872-4500
FAX (415) 696-1699

---

7 No smoking; 8 Children welcome; 9 Social drinking allowed; 10 Tennis nearby; 11 Swimming nearby; 12 Golf nearby; 13 Skiing nearby; 14 May be booked through a travel agent.

Craftsman Mansion at Venice Beach.
Beautiful turn-of-the-century home just
steps from the beach has five rooms with
private baths. Four rooms share two baths.
One suite has a fireplace and oceanview;
another has a private Jacuzzi tub. Large
breakfast served in sunny living room.
Close to restaurants, cafes, shopping, bike
paths, and people watching. $90-150.

The Venice Beach House
Bed and Breakfast

15 Thirtieth Avenue, 90401
(310) 823-1966; FAX (310) 823-1842

In 1911 Abbot Kinney, the founder of
Venice, and his family built this home, just
steps from the beach and all that makes
Venice unlike anywhere in the world. The
nine guest room house is decorated with
dark oak antiques, hardwood floors, and a
large living room with a real wood-burning
fireplace. All five of the suites have king-
size beds and private baths. There are also
four rooms sharing two baths; all quaintly
decorated. Breakfast includes homemade
breads, muffins, granola, quiches, freshly
squeezed juice, seasonal fruits, freshly
brewed coffee and a fine selection of teas,
served in the sunny French windowed
alcove overlooking the beautiful front lawn
and garden. There are also homemade cookies and hot and iced tea all afternoon.

Host: Leslie Smith
Rooms: 9 (5 PB; 4 S2B) $80-150
Full and Continental Breakfast
Credit Cards: A, B, C
Notes: 5, 7, 8, 9, 10, 11, 12, 13, 14

VENTURA

Bed and Breakfast
California

P.O. Box 282910, San Francisco, 94128-2910
(415) 696-1690; (800) 872-4500
FAX (415) 696-1699

3-14. This four-acre ranch in Camarillo has
stables, fruit trees, a spa, and hiking trails.

The two guest wings have a total of five
rooms which are perfect for a large family.
Only half an hour to Santa Barbara. $65.

Bella Maggiore Inn

67 South California Street, 93001
(805) 652-0277

This 1920s northern Italian-style inn was
designed by A. C. Martin, architect of the
Los Angeles City Hall. The home is in the
old business district near Mission San
Buenaventura. Full breakfast served in the
dining room or courtyard. Appetizers with
beverages served in the afternoon.
Telephone, TV in all rooms. Whirlpool, fireplace, and air conditioning in some rooms.

Hosts: Thomas Wood
Rooms: 24 (PB) $75-150
Full Breakfast
Cards: A, B, C, D, E
Notes: 3, 4, 5, 7, 8, 9, 11, 12, 14

Eye Openers
Bed and Breakfast
Reservations

P.O. Box 694, Altadena, 91003-0694
(213) 684-4428; (818) 797-2055
FAX (818) 798-3640

VE-B171. Three blocks from the beach,
this inn with Mediterranean decor offers
comfort and convenience. Full breakfast
and afternoon refreshments. Seventeen
rooms. Private bath. $75-150.

VE-M5I. Bavarian-style hospitality is featured at this lovely bed and breakfast near
the beach. Five guest rooms have queen- or
king-size beds and private baths. Walking
or biking distance from shops, restaurants,
and attractions. Short commute to Santa
Barbara, Ojai, and Santa Ynez Valley. Full
breakfast. No smoking. $100-155.

La Mer Bed and Breakfast

411 Poli Street, 93001
(805) 643-3600; FAX (805) 653-7329

NOTES: Credit cards accepted: A MasterCard; B Visa; C American Express; D Discover; E Diners Club;
F Other; 2 Personal checks accepted; 3 Lunch available; 4 Dinner available; 5 Open all year; 6 Pets welcome;

Built in 1890, this is a romantic European getaway in a Victorian Cape Cod home. A historic landmark nestled on a green hillside overlooking the spectacular California coastline has distinctive guest rooms, all with private entrances and baths. Each is a European adventure, furnished in European antiques to capture the feeling of a specific country. Bavarian buffet-style breakfast and complimentary refreshments; midweek packages; antique horse carriage rides, etc. AAA and Mobil approved.

Host: Gisela Flender Baida
Rooms: 5 (PB) $80-155
Full Breakfast
Credit Cards: B, C
Notes: 2, 5, 7, 9, 10, 11, 12, 14

WESTPORT

Howard Creek Ranch

Box 121, 95488
(707) 964-6725

A historic 1867 farm on 40 acres, only 100 yards from the beach. A rural retreat adjoining wilderness. Suite and cabins; views of ocean, mountains, creek, or gardens; fireplace/wood stoves; period furnishings; hot tub, sauna, ornamental spring-fed pool, and horseback riding nearby. Gift certificates available. Inquire about pets and children. Limited smoking permitted.

Hosts: Charles (Sunny) and Sally Grigg
Rooms: 10 (8 PB; 2 SB) $55-145
Full Breakfast
Credit Cards: A, B, C
Notes: 2, 5, 9, 11

YOSEMITE

Bed and Breakfast California

P.O. Box 282910, San Francisco, 94128-2910
(415) 696-1690; (800) 872-4500
FAX (415) 696-1699

Restful Nest. A little corner of paradise on 11 acres of land has stunning surroundings.

Three large suites and a guest house for four, all with private baths, private entrances, TV/VCR, refrigerator, and microwave. Full Canadian breakfast. Enjoy fishing in the pond or swimming in the pool. Barbecue area can accommodate ten people at a time. Forty-five minutes from Yosemite, ten minutes from beautiful Mariposa. Hosts speak French. $75-95.

Eye Openers Bed and Breakfast Reservations

P.O. Box 694, Altadena, 91003-0694
(213) 684-4428; (818) 797-2055
FAX (818) 798-3640

YO-P3I. Halfway between Yosemite Valley and Wawona is this beautiful, new bed and breakfast with uniquely decorated rooms, each with fireplace and one with Jacuzzi for two. The three guest rooms have double, queen-, and king-size beds and private baths. Outdoor decks offer serenity, views, and a hot tub. Full breakfast. No smoking. $100-150.

YO-W2I. In Yosemite at 6,400 feet, 14 miles from Yosemite Valley, this contemporary bed and breakfast offers a unique Yosemite holiday. The wooded area has excellent hiking trails. A suite and guest room with private baths are available. A full breakfast is served. Closed December through February. $68-88.

Lee's Middle Fork Resort

11399 Cherry Oil Road, 95321
(209) 962-7408; (800) 626-7408
FAX (209) 962-7400

Lee's Middle Fork Resort in on Highway 120, just 150 miles from San Francisco and 11 miles from the Big Oak Flat entrance to Yosemite National Park, the most direct route into the park and the most scenic. For anglers, the Middle Fork of the Tuolumne

7 No smoking; 8 Children welcome; 9 Social drinking allowed; 10 Tennis nearby; 11 Swimming nearby; 12 Golf nearby; 13 Skiing nearby; 14 May be booked through a travel agent.

River is well-stocked with pan-size trout, and the river flows right through the resort. Other nearby activities include white-water rafting on the Tuolumne, hiking, swimming, and panning for gold, and in the winter downhill skiing. Continental breakfast in summers only.

Hosts: Lee and Nita Hilarides
Rooms: 20 (PB) $49-135
Continental Breakfast
Credit Cards: A, B, C, D, E, F
Notes: 5, 8, 11, 12, 13, 14

YOUNTVILLE

Eye Openers Bed and Breakfast Reservations

P.O. Box 694, Altadena, 91003-0694
(213) 684-4428; (818) 797-2055
FAX (818) 798-3640

YO-M13I. Newly renovated 100-year-old inn with French country decor in the heart of the Napa Valley serves a full breakfast. Thirteen guest rooms with queen- or king-size beds and private baths. Relax at the pool and Jacuzzi. Good restaurants nearby. No smoking. $110-190.

YO-V8OI. Each spacious room at this large, new bed and breakfast inn has a fireplace and tub with Jacuzzi jets. All-year round heated pool, Jacuzzi, and tennis courts are on the property and a health club is within walking distance. Eighty guest rooms, all with private baths and king- or queen-size beds are available. Continental plus champagne breakfast. Wineries are nearby, and limousine service is available. $135-215.

Maison Fleurie

6529 Yount Street, 94599
(707) 944-2056; (800) 788-0369
FAX (707) 944-9342

A 100-year-old French country inn, the Maison Fleurie features 13 guest rooms in the three vine-covered buildings. The Old Bakery features four spacious king-size rooms with fireplaces and small patio. Guests enjoy vineyard views, large pool, and outdoor spa. Full breakfast, wine, hors d'oeuvres.

Hosts: Roger and Sally Post; Roger Asbill, innkeeper
Rooms: 13 (PB) $110-190
Full Breakfast
Credit Cards: A, B, C
Notes: 2, 5, 7, 8, 11, 12, 14

Vintage Inn

6541 Washington Street, 94599
(800) 351-1133

Vintage Inn in Napa Valley is a contemporary luxury country inn on a historic 23-acre winery estate in the walking town of Yountville. Centered amidst some of Napa Valley's finest vineyards, guests enjoy a unique resort atmosphere with pool, spa, tennis, cycling, and hot air ballooning. A California champagne buffet breakfast of pastries, assorted fruits, cheeses, yogurt, and cereals is included with each guest stay. Superb accommodations for year-round comfort, featuring wood-burning fireplaces, whirlpool baths, compact refrigerators, and many other extras.

Host: Nancy M. Lochmann
Rooms: 80 (PB) $136-216
Continental Breakfast
Credit Cards: A, B, C, D, E, F
Notes: 2, 3, 4, 5, 6, 7, 8, 9, 10, 11, 12, 14

YUBA CITY

Harkey House Bed and Breakfast

212 C Street, 95991
(916) 674-1942

An 1874 Victorian Gothic with queen-size beds, fireplaces, TV/VCR/CD players, and telephones. Breakfast is served in the dining room or on the patio. Spa, basketball court, chess, game table, and library. Air-conditioned. Original art work, piano, and

NOTES: Credit cards accepted: A MasterCard; B Visa; C American Express; D Discover; E Diners Club; F Other; 2 Personal checks accepted; 3 Lunch available; 4 Dinner available; 5 Open all year; 6 Pets welcome;

fountains. Near museums, hiking, and fishing. Fresh flowers and down comforters. Complimentary beverage and popcorn. A romantic getaway! Reservation deposit required. Five-day cancellation notice required. Ten dollar cancellation fee. Call for business rates.

Hosts: Bob and Lee Jones
Rooms: 4 (PB) $75-100
Full Breakfast
Credit Cards: A, B, C
Notes: 2, 5, 7, 8, 9, 10, 11, 12, 13, 14

ZEPHYR COVE

Bed and Breakfast International

P.O. Box 282910, San Francisco, 94128-2910
(415) 696-1690; (800) 872-4500
FAX (415) 696-1699

401. Large, attractive alpine-style house with views of Zephyr Cove is near the South Shore of Lake Tahoe. Hosts are extremely accommodating, and it has been said that the breakfasts are wonderful. $75.

7 No smoking; 8 Children welcome; 9 Social drinking allowed; 10 Tennis nearby; 11 Swimming nearby; 12 Golf nearby; 13 Skiing nearby; 14 May be booked through a travel agent.

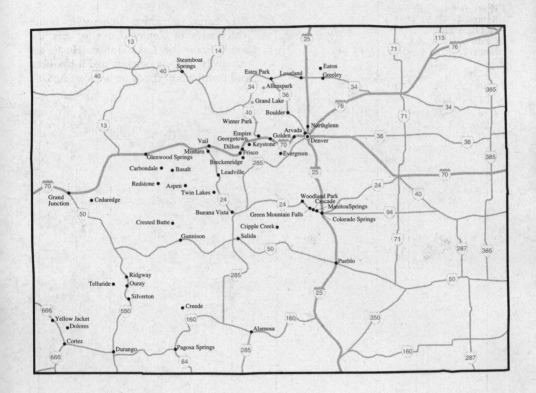

Colorado

Colorado

ALAMOSA

Cottonwood Inn
Bed and Breakfast
and Gallery

123 San Juan Avenue, 81101
(719) 589-3882

Lovely turn-of-the-century Craftsman-style inn is decorated with antiques and local artwork. Packages available with the Cumbres Toltec Railway and golf courses. Near the Great Sand Dunes, wildlife refuges, Adams State College, cross-country skiing, and the Rio Grande. Delicious breakfasts featuring freshly ground coffee, homemade baked goods, and fresh fruit. Famous for green chili strata.

Hosts: Julie Mordecai and George Sellman
Rooms: 7 (4 PB, 3 SB) $58-85
Full Breakfast
Credit Cards: A, B, C, D, E
Notes: 2, 5, 7, 8, 9, 10, 11, 12, 14

ALLENSPARK

Allenspark Lodge

184 Main, P.O. Box 247, 80510
(303) 747-2552; (800) 206-2552

A 1933 three-story, hand-hewn log lodge with a great room, game and reception room, hot tub, and the Wilderquest Room, with a selection of beverages and hors d'oeuvres. Fourteen rooms, some with private bath and deep bear-claw tubs, three cabins. Horseback riding available. Minutes from Rocky Mountain National Park. Three housekeeping cabins are also available. Children over 14 welcome.

Hosts: Mike and Becky Osmun
Rooms: 12 (5 PB; 7 SB) $45-90
Continental Breakfast
Credit Cards: A, B
Notes: 2, 3, 4, 5, 7, 10, 11, 12, 13, 14

ARVADA

Bed and Breakfast Agency
of Colorado at Vail

P.O. 491, Vail, 81658
(970) 949-1212; (800) 748-2666

ARV 201. For European hospitality and a relaxing blend of country comfort, come to this romantic retreat on ten acres, with fishing pond, swimming pool, and hot tubs. Only 15 miles from Denver. Enjoy many activities, full breakfast, and afternoon kaffeeklatsch. Five rooms are offered with private baths. No smoking. No pets. $50-100.

ASPEN

Bed and Breakfast Agency
of Colorado at Vail

P.O. 491, Vail, 81658
(970) 949-1212; (800) 748-2666

Aspen 101. Welcome to the historic Alpine Lodge, originally built in 1890 to house a successful miner and his family. Enjoy European hospitality, gourmet meals, and a cozy Bavarian setting within walking distance of the center of town. Stay in one of

---

NOTES: Credit cards: A MasterCard; B Visa; C American Express; D Discover; E Diners Club; F Other; 2 Personal checks accepted; 3 Lunch available; 4 Dinner available; 5 Open all year; 6 Pets welcome; 7 No smoking; 8 Children welcome; 9 Social drinking allowed; 10 Tennis nearby; 11 Swimming nearby; 12 Golf nearby; 13 Skiing nearby; 14 May be booked through a travel agent.

Bed and Breakfast Agency of Colorado at Vail (continued)

the charming cabins with kitchenette, in the main lodge with private bath, or in one of the rooms with a private European bath. A Continental breakfast is included in summer, and full breakfasts and dinners are available in winter (for a small additional charge). From goosedown comforters to personal home-cooked dinners, the warmth and charm of this inn is something to remember. No smoking. No pets. $59-99.

Aspen 102. Enjoy Aspen, Glenwood Springs, and the beautiful Crystal Valley in this spacious chalet-style home, featuring vaulted ceilings throughout. The 1950s ski-lodge decor of the very large Aspen Suite or the Victorian elegance of the Sonoma Room with its romantic four-poster bed are ideal for getaways. The Santa Fe Room is alive with the warmth of the Southwest. All rooms adjoin the library sitting room on the balcony. The Kuauai Room features atmosphere and a two-person Jacuzzi. Full breakfasts. No smoking. $70-90.

Aspen 103. Experience European charm in the heart of the Rockies. Thirty distinctive rooms and one suite feature private baths, telephones, and cable TV; most have mountain views. Lodge amenities include Jacuzzi and sauna, heated pool (summers only), daily housekeeping, complimentary breakfast buffet, and aprés ski appetizers and drinks (winter only). Choose between rustic-traditional rooms in the main lodge, or deluxe-contemporary rooms. Enjoy two fireplace areas, barbecue/patio area, and year-round hospitality and comfort. Airport transportation and free shuttle downtown (one quarter mile). $50-175.

Aspen 104. High in the mountains, where the roar of the creek below and the rustle of

the towering pines soothes the spirit, is a small country inn called the Heatherbed. For over 30 years it has welcomed mountain travelers with its sunny pine, bright copper, fresh wildflowers, and friendly faces. Although it's only two miles from one of the most exciting resorts in the world, this inn's loyal following comes not from its sophistication, but from its European tradition of Alpine hospitality, where the guests are a part of the family. Fifteen rooms with private baths are either creekside or mountainside. Breakfast, hot tub, and pool (seasonal) are just a few of the amenities offered. $75-155.

Aspen 106. Wake up to panoramic views of Mount Sopris and the Elk Mountain Range on 70 private acres in scenic Snowmass Valley. Enjoy a Continental breakfast on the deck overlooking a beautiful mountain fishing stream, just 20 minutes from Aspen. Two rooms and one small apartment. Enjoy the patio outdoor hot tub. No smoking. No pets. $70-100.

Aspen 107. This European cottage with quiet location is 25 minutes from downtown Aspen. Each of the four guest rooms has spectacular views of Mount Sopris. Country decor with antiques adorn each room. There is an outdoor hot tub. Full breakfast is provided. No smoking. No pets. $60-95.

Aspen 108. Hot tub under a star-filled sky warms guests after a long day on the slopes. Hosts are restaurateurs who serve a hearty breakfast. Five minutes to Snowmass Mountain and 15 minutes to downtown Aspen. On bus route. No smoking. $65-85.

Aspen 110 For the feel of being in the mountains with a great view, this is it! A former home that has been renovated into four units, this apartment was the family's

patio overlooking Aspen highlands and Maroon Bells. Within walking distance of downtown Aspen, these rooms offer plenty of privacy with a lock-off master bedroom suite and a sunken Japanese tub in the bathroom. A warm, comfortable stay. $65-75.

Aspen 111. Offering comfortable accommodations with a delicious and healthy breakfast, beautiful mountain views, all in a most convenient location. This bed and breakfast is in a family home, complete with fireplace, TV, VCR, Jacuzzi, and resident golden retrievers. It's on a sunny hillside at the base of Snowmass Ski resort on the free bus route. Two rooms are offered with private baths. Rates reflect on room selection, number of guests, and time of year. $50-200.

Boomerang Lodge

500 West Hopkins, 81611
(970) 925-3416; (800) 992-8852

This unique ski lodge in the quiet West End is within walking distance to downtown or the music festival. All guest rooms and fireplace apartments have a sunny patio or balcony, thanks to the handsome design influenced by the owner-architect's teacher, Frank Lloyd Wright. Thoughtful touches include pool, whirlpool, and sauna. Additional winter amenities include afternoon tea and town courtesy van. Discover why devoted guests return to Boomerang.

Hosts: Charles and Fonda Paterson
Rooms: 35 (PB) $99-180
Continental Breakfast
Credit Cards: A, B, C, E
Notes: 2, 5, 7, 8, 9, 10, 11, 12, 13, 14

Crestahaus Lodge

1301 East Cooper Avenue, 81611
(970) 925-7081; (800) 344-3853

Experience European charm in the heart of the Rockies. Thirty-one distinctive rooms including one suite feature private baths,

telephones, cable TV, and many have mountain views. Lodge amenities include Jacuzzi and sauna, heated pool (open summers only), daily housekeeping, complimentary breakfast buffet, après ski appetizers, and drinks (winter only). Choose between rustic-traditional rooms in the main lodge, or deluxe-contemporary rooms. Enjoy two fireplace areas, barbecue/patio area, and year-round hospitality and comfort. Aspen airport transportation and free shuttle downtown (one-quarter mile). No smoking in common rooms.

Host: Melinda Goldrich
Rooms: 31 (PB) $50-175
Continental Breakfast
Credit Cards: A, B, E
Notes: 2, 5, 6, 8, 9, 10, 11, 12, 13, 14

Little Red Ski Haus

118 East Cooper Street, 81611
(970) 925-3333

Charming 108-year-old Victorian is in the middle of Aspen. Guests can travel the world just sitting in the living room. The house is very popular with Australians. Exceptionally clean and friendly. Full breakfast served in winter, Continental in summer. Closed April 10 through May 31.

Hosts: Marge Babcock and Derek Brown
Rooms: 20 (PB/SB) $23-60
Full and Continental Breakfast
Credit Cards: A, B
Notes: 4, 8, 9, 10, 11, 12, 13, 14

Sardy House Hotel and Restaurant

128 East Main Street, 81611
(970) 920-2525; (800) 321-3457;
FAX (970) 920-4478

One of Aspen's finest Victorians, built in 1892, is now a beautifully restored 20 room luxury hotel. Our rooms are graciously decorated with cherrywood beds and armoires, feather comforters, whirlpool baths, and robes. Amenities include full breakfast, concierge, room service, heated pool, spa,

7 No smoking; 8 Children welcome; 9 Social drinking allowed; 10 Tennis nearby; 11 Swimming nearby; 12 Golf nearby; 13 Skiing nearby; 14 May be booked through a travel agent.

sauna, bar, gourmet restaurant, and twice-daily maid service. Awarded Mobil Travel Guide's four star: "Outstanding...worth a special trip."

Host: Jayne Poss
Room: 20 (PB) $169-699
Full Breakfast
Credit Cards: A, B, C, E
Notes: 2, 4, 5, 7, 8, 9, 10, 11, 12, 13, 14

Snow Queen Victorian Lodge Bed and Breakfast

124 East Cooper Street, 81611
(970) 925-8455; (970) 925-6971

This quaint, family-operated Victorian ski lodge was built in the 1880s. The charming parlor has a fireplace and color TV for guests. There is a variety of rooms with private baths, plus two kitchen units. The lodge is in town, within walking distance of restaurants, shops, and the ski area. A nice outdoor hot tub is available. Special lower rates are available during off-season and summer visits. Closed April 15 through May 15.

Hosts: Norma Dolle and Larry Ledingham
Rooms: 5 (PB) $65-138
Continental Breakfast
Credit Cards: A, B, C
Notes: 2, 8, 9, 10, 11, 12, 13, 14

BASALT

Altamira Ranch Bed and Breakfast

23484 Highway 82, 81621
(303) 927-3309

Beautiful ranch 15 minutes from Aspen on the Roaring Fork River, a gold medal trout stream. Enjoy quiet, peaceful country atmosphere adjacent to all the mountain activities, including skiing, hiking, river sports, and famous Glenwood Hot Springs. There is an antique shop on the premises of the inn. Guests can come enjoy a special

home away from home. Children over six are welcome.

Host: Martha Waterman
Rooms: 2 (SB) $50-75
Full Breakfast
Credit Cards: A, B
Notes: 2, 5, 9, 13, 14

Shenandoah Inn

600 Frying Pan Road, Box 578, 81621
(303) 927-4991

Contemporary western Colorado bed and breakfast is on two riverfront acres on the Frying Pan River, one of North America's premier trout streams, in the heart of the White River National Forest. The inn is only twenty minutes from Aspen and Glenwood Hot Springs; year-round access to the best of Colorado's numerous outdoor activities. Enjoy the riverside hot tub, the warm, friendly atmosphere, and the exceptional cuisine.

Hosts: Bob and Terri Ziets
Rooms: 4 (2SB; 2 PB) $70-90
Full Gourmet Breakfast
Credit Cards: None
Notes: 2, 5, 9, 10, 12, 13, 14

BOULDER

Bed and Breakfast Agency of Colorado at Vail

P.O. 491, Vail, 81658
(970) 949-1212; (800) 748-2666

BLD 301. There is a bright sunny feeling in this home, which has been decorated with a Southwestern contemporary flair. The second floor is just for guests; the bedrooms have a great view of the mountains, and guests can relax in the private sitting room. The hostess, a Colorado native who also designed the home, serves a Continental breakfast. A lovely garden is available for warm weather enjoyment. Only one block from bus. No smoking allowed. $50-60.

NOTES: Credit cards accepted: A MasterCard; B Visa; C American Express; D Discover; E Diners Club; F Other; 2 Personal checks accepted; 3 Lunch available; 4 Dinner available; 5 Open all year; 6 Pets welcome;

Bed and Breakfast at Sunset House

1740 Sunset Boulevard, 80304
(303) 444-0801

Two rooms offered with shared bath and a private entrance. The family room has a cozy fireplace, small library, and a TV. Outside patios overlook the city to the south and the Flatirons to the west. Bicycles are available for guests to use on Boulder's nearby bike paths. The Pearl Street Mall is a ten-minute walk away. Taikoo, a Shih Tzu mix, is the resident dog. Sunset House provides a nonsmoking environment.

Hosts: Phyllis and Roger Olson
Rooms: 2 (SB) $80
Full Breakfast
Credit Cards: None
Notes: 2, 5, 9

The Boulder Victoria Historic Bed and Breakfast

1305 Pine Street, 80302
(303) 938-1300

Downtown Boulder's exquisitely renovated Victorian inn offers seven unique guest rooms that feature antique furniture, private baths, telephone, and TV. Enjoy tea and scones in the elegant parlor, luxuriate in a private steam shower, or enjoy breakfast in the bay-windowed dining room. Soak in Boulder's sun on the spacious patio. Convenient to downtown, campus, and mountain activities.

Hosts: Kristen Peterson and Zoe Kircos
Rooms: 7 (PB) $114-164
Continental Breakfast
Credit Cards: A, B, C
Notes: 2, 5, 7, 9, 10, 11, 12, 13, 14

Briar Rose Bed and Breakfast

2151 Arapahoe Avenue, 80302
(303) 442-3007

Patterned after an English country cottage, the Briar Rose offers nine unique guest rooms conveniently in mid town Boulder. Breakfast of homemade granola, yogurt and fruit, croissants, homemade muffins or nut bread, fresh orange juice, coffee, and tea is included. Afternoon tea and cookies. Rooms feel just as comfortable as Grandma's house and are equipped with both private telephones and private baths.

Hosts: Bob and Margaret Weisenbach
Rooms: 9 (PB) $99-135
Continental Breakfast
Credit Cards: A, B, C
Notes: 2, 5, 7, 9, 10, 11, 12, 13, 14

Briar Rose

The House on 21st Street

2222-21st, 80302
(303) 443-4604 (phone and FAX)

This beautiful, light, airy home in one of Boulder's oldest, central neighborhoods has nine-foot ceilings downstairs and cathedral ceilings upstairs, embracing the outdoors and framing views of the Flatirons and surrounding mountains with its large windows and French doors. Designed by one of Boulder's best contractors, the House on 21st Street is a new Victorian home. Two beautiful bedrooms accommodate the special occasion, business trip, or romantic getaway. The larger bedroom affords mountain views and a large balcony that captures the morning and evening sun. Enjoy a delicious, nourishing breakfast and sip the morning coffee or tea in the flower filled courtyard. Upon request, professional massage, facials, local health club facilities, catered meals, or the use of the bicycles. Mountains, ski areas, lakes, golf courses, and the Rocky Mountain National Park are all nearby.

Host: Donne Ruiz
Rooms: 2 (1 PB; 1 SB) $70-85
Continental Breakfast
Credit Cards: None
Notes: 2, 5, 7, 9, 10, 11, 12, 13, 14

BRECKENRIDGE

Allaire Timbers Inn

9511 Highway 9, South Main Street, 80424
(970) 453-7530; (800) 624-4904

This award-winning mountain inn combines contemporary Southwestern and rustic log furnishings in a newly constructed log setting. Guest rooms have private bath and deck with mountain views. Suites offer private fireplace and hot tub. Great room with fireplace, sunroom, loft, and outdoor spa all have spectacular views of the Colorado Rockies. Hearty breakfast and afternoon happy hour included daily. Wheelchair accessible. In Breckenridge, Colorado's oldest Victorian mountain town, offering an abundance of year-round activities. Nonsmoking inn.

Hosts: Jack and Kathy Gumph
Rooms: 10 (PB) $115-250
Full Breakfast
Credit Cards: A, B, C, D
Notes: 2, 5, 7, 9, 10, 11, 12, 13, 14

Bed and Breakfast Agency of Colorado at Vail

P.O. 491, Vail, 81658
(970) 949-1212; (800) 748-2666

BRECK 401. Cozy 1886 Victorian in Historic District with three beautiful turn-of-the-century rooms. A full breakfast, freshly ground coffee, and afternoon refreshments in a friendly environment. All attractions within walking distance. Common room with mountain view has a home-away-from-home feel. $80-95.

BRECK 402. This inn, housed in an 1880 building, is only two blocks from Main Street in the National Historic District of the town. The inn offers a variety of accommodations: a suite, rooms with private baths, or dorm facilities with shared baths. A hot tub and parlor with open-hearth fireplace are on the property. Breakfasts include sourdough French toast, eggs, and buttermilk pancakes. Ski and golf packages available. $75-95.

BRECK 403. Two blocks from downtown shops and restaurants on the free shuttle bus during ski season, this inn offers free parking and ski storage. In the historic section of this Victorian mining town, this inn offers guests comfortable accommodations and use of a central living room with TV, games, books, and fireplace. Summer activities include hiking, backpacking, bicycling, four-wheeling, sailing, horseback riding, golf, and rafting. If meeting people and spending time with travelers who want a true bed and breakfast experience is appealing, guests will enjoy staying at this inn. $69-98.

BRECK 404. This lovely, contemporary cedar home sits in a large, peaceful forest one and one-half miles south of the Breckenridge ski area. With a private entrance, guests have a large sitting room with a full-size pool table, color TV, and wood-burning stove. Full breakfast on weekends; Continental on weekdays.

NOTES: Credit cards accepted: A MasterCard; B Visa; C American Express; D Discover; E Diners Club; F Other; 2 Personal checks accepted; 3 Lunch available; 4 Dinner available; 5 Open all year; 6 Pets welcome;

Cross-country skiing available from the front door in winter; hiking trails to lakes in summer. No smoking. $95.

BRECK 405. Enter through the private entrance reserved for guests and enjoy a beautiful mountain view. Handpainted chairs and knickknacks, stenciled ducks, and bears decorate the home and breakfast nook. A kitchenette with microwave and refrigerator is available. Two suites with private bath are offered. Outside hot tub. Full breakfast served. Smoking permitted unless other guests object. $59-98.

BRECK 406. Upscale luxury Victorian Inn, with spectacular mountain views of the ski area from balconies off each of the four guest rooms with Jacuzzi tubs. Complimentary sherry in the rooms. Full hearty breakfast; afternoon tea or wine and cheese. No smoking. $99-199.

Cotten House

102 South French Street, P.O. Box 387, 80424
(970) 453-5509

In the heart of beautiful historic Breckenridge, the Cotten House is a restored 1886 Victorian with a full view of the ten-mile range. Three clean, fully decorated rooms with flowers await guests. A hearty seven-day menu breakfast and after-

Cotten House

noon refreshments are served. Winter activities are available at the front door on the free bus. Evening activities and restaurants are two blocks away. Spring, summer, and fall events, and sports make this area unforgettable. AAA approved.

Hosts: Pete and Georgette Contos
Rooms: 3 (1 PB; 2 SB) $50-90
Full Breakfast
Credit Cards: None
Notes: 2, 5, 7, 8, 9, 10, 11, 12, 13

Muggins Gulch Inn

4023 Tiger Road
P.O. Box 3756, 80424
(303) 453-7414

The inn is a unique post and beam lodge on 160 secluded acres surrounded by the Arapaho National Forest. Hiking and biking on the Colorado Trail from the doorstep. Golf is four miles away; snowmobiling, skiing, and the excitement of Breckenridge are just minutes away. Two charming rooms with private baths. Two spacious suites. Enjoy the great room with huge fireplace and gourmet breakfast and afternoon snack in skylighted garden room with exquisite views.

Hosts: Bethanne and Tom Hossley
Rooms: 4 (PB) $65-195
Full Breakfast
Cards: A, B
Notes: 2, 5, 7, 9, 12, 13, 14

Swan Mountain Inn

16172 Highway 9, 80424; P.O. Box 2900, Dillon,
80435 (mailing)
(800) 578-3687

The Swan Mountain Inn strives to combine a warm, cozy environment with luxury and pampering to give its guests the perfect Colorado getaway. Enjoy exceptional fireside dining for breakfast and dinner, a full-service bar, private and starlit hot tubs, TV/VCR, movies, and beautiful decor. The location is less than ten minutes to four of the hottest Colorado ski areas and golf

7 No smoking; 8 Children welcome; 9 Social drinking allowed; 10 Tennis nearby; 11 Swimming nearby; 12 Golf nearby; 13 Skiing nearby; 14 May be booked through a travel agent.

courses. On the bike path, next to the Blue River and Lake Dillon. No pets. Children welcome. No smoking. Lunch available in the summer.

Rooms: 4 (3 PB; 1 SB) $40-135
Full Breakfast
Cards: A, B, D
Notes: 2, 4, 5, 7, 8, 9, 10, 11, 12, 13, 14

Williams House, Circa 1885, and Victorian Cottage, Circa 1880

303 North Main Street, P.O. Box 2454, 80424
(970) 453-2975; (800) 795-2975

Enjoy this romantic in-town getaway. Beautifully restored mining home and Victorian cottage are furnished in fine antiques. Bedrooms are decorated in period furnishings and fine linens. Private baths. In the main house, parlors graced with mantled fireplaces welcome guests. The adjacent Victorian cottage for two has a large Jacuzzi, shower for two, mantled fireplace, separate sitting room with TV, VCR, stereo and kitchenette. A hearty miner's breakfast is served during the ski season and a lighter full breakfast at other times. Afternoon refreshments. Guests may soothe body and soul in the large outdoor hot tub with spectacular mountain views. In historic district, on trolley route, near bike path, town amenities, and other outdoor activities.

Hosts: Fred Kinat and Diane Jaynes
Rooms: 5 (PB) $79-140
Cottage: 1 (PB) $165-200
Full Breakfast
Credit Cards: C
Notes: 2, 3, 5, 7, 9, 10, 11, 12, 13, 14

BUENA VISTA

Bed and Breakfast Agency of Colorado at Vail

P.O. 491, Vail, 81658
(970) 949-1212; (800) 748-2666

BV 401. This original 1890 boarding house has been totally refurbished by its new owners and offers four rooms and a cabin. Decorated with country furnishings and antiques. Wake up and enjoy a full breakfast. Cakes and goodies are offered throughout the day, with a variety of teas and coffees. Satellite TV, video library, and three common areas for relaxing. No smoking. No pets. $75-95.

Trout City Inn

P.O. Box 431, 81211
(719) 495-0348

Historic railway station on Trout Creek Pass in national forest has Victorian decor and antiques in depot rooms—plus elegant private Pullman car and Drover's caboose. Enjoy its own railroad, trout stream, beaver ponds, and gold mine, with grand view of canyon and Collegiate peaks. White-water rafting, horseback riding, mountain hiking and climbing, mountain bike trails are just minutes away—plus great eating and shopping in historic Buena Vista. Trophy trout fishing in river and lakes, ghost towns, caves, Jeep tours, melodrama, antique shops all nearby.

Hosts: Juel and Irene Kjeldsen
Rooms: 4 (PB) $32-40
Full Breakfast
Credit Cards: A, B
Notes: 2, 8, 9, 10, 11, 12, 14

CARBONDALE

The Ambiance Inn

66 North 2nd Street, 81623
(303) 963-3597

Enjoy Aspen, Glenwood Springs, and the beautiful Crystal Valley from this spacious chalet-style home featuring vaulted ceilings throughout. The 1950s ski lodge decor of the very large Aspen Suite or the Victorian elegance of the Sonoma Room featuring a romantic four-poster bed are ideal for getaways. The Santa Fe Room is alive with the warmth of the Southwest. The Kauai Room features special atmosphere and a two-person Jacuzzi. All rooms adjoin the library-sitting room. Inquire about accommodations for children.

Hosts: Norma and Robert Morris
Rooms: 4 (PB) $60-80
Full Breakfast
Credit Cards: A, B, C
Notes: 2, 3, 5, 7, 9, 10, 11, 12, 13, 14

CASCADE

Black Bear Inn of Pikes Peak

5250 Pikes Peak Highway, 80809
(719) 684-0151

The Black Bear Inn is a newly constructed, nine-room mountain inn in the Colorado mountains. Ten acres of privacy go hand in hand with the beautiful forested mountain views seen from every window in the inn. The hot tub in a forest setting will take guest's cares away. Minutes from Colorado Springs and many well-known tourist attractions. Hiking and biking trails leave right from the inn.

Hosts: Kevin and Christi Heidenreich
Rooms: 9 (PB) $70-85
Full Breakfast
Credit Cards: None
Notes: 2, 5, 7, 8, 9, 11, 12, 13, 14

CEDAREDGE

Cedars' Edge Llamas Bed and Breakfast

2169 Highway 65, 81413
(970) 856-6836

Beautiful cedar home is nestled high on the southern slope of Grand Mesa. This peaceful llama farm features a spectacular 100-mile view and a quiet, restful atmosphere. Rooms are filled with handmade country decor, quilts, and plants. Breakfast on the private deck or in the sunroom. Cottage features very private honeymoon suite with double tub. Close to hiking, fishing, skiing, and much more.

Hosts: Ray and Gail Record
Rooms: 4 (PB) $50-75
Full Breakfast
Credit Cards: A, B
Notes: 2, 5, 7, 8, 9, 10, 12, 14

Holden House

COLORADO SPRINGS

Holden House—1902 Bed and Breakfast Inn

1102 West Pikes Peak Avenue, 80904
(719) 471-3980

A 1902 storybook Victorian, a 1906 carriage house, and adjacent 1898 Victorian are filled with antiques and heirlooms. Immaculate accommodations in a residential area near historic district and central to the Pikes Peak region. Enjoy the parlor, living room with fireplace, or veranda with mountain views. Guest rooms boast queen-size beds, down pillows, and private baths. Honeymoon suites with tubs for two, fireplaces, and more! Complimentary refreshments. Friendly resident cats named Muffin and Mingtoy. Experience the romance of the past with the comforts of today. AAA and Mobil approved. One room is handicapped accessible. Minimum-stay requirements for holidays, special events, and during high season.

Hosts: Sallie and Welling Clark
Rooms: 2 (PB) $75
Suites: 4 (PB) $100-110
Full Breakfast
Credit Cards: A, B, C, D, E
Notes: 2, 5, 7, 9, 10, 11, 12, 14

7 No smoking; 8 Children welcome; 9 Social drinking allowed; 10 Tennis nearby; 11 Swimming nearby; 12 Golf nearby; 13 Skiing nearby; 14 May be booked through a travel agent.

The Painted Lady
Bed and Breakfast Inn

1318 West Colorado Avenue, 80904
(719) 473-3165

This restored 1894 Victorian home is complete with gingerbread trim, wraparound porches, coach lights, and wonderful mountain views. Inside, guest rooms feature lace curtains and period furnishings. The suite includes a claw-foot tub for two. Common rooms are bright and inviting. A hearty breakfast is served. Convenient to Pike's Peak, shopping, and historic Old Colorado City. Skiing only two hours away. Resident cat on hand to greet you. No guest pets. Children over eight welcome.

Hosts: Valerie and Zan Maslowski
Rooms: 2 (PB) $65-115
Suite: 1 (PB)
Full Breakfast
Cards: A, B, D
Notes: 2, 5, 7, 9, 10, 11, 12, 14

CREEDE

Creede Hotel

Box 284, 81130
(719) 658-2608

The hotel is a landmark in Creede, dating back to the wild days of the silver boom. Four rooms, all with private baths, have been individually restored; two family units in adjacent building. The hotel dining room is open to the public and is noted for its delicious food. Guests love Creede and the hotel.

Hosts: Cathy and Rich Ormsby
Rooms: 6 (PB) $59-79
Full Breakfast
Credit Cards: A, B, D
Notes: 2, 3, 4, 9

CRESTED BUTTE

The Alpine Lace
Bed and Breakfast

726 Maroon, P.O.Box 2183, 81224
(970) 349-9857

The Alpine Lace Bed and Breakfast is a romantic getaway, located in the historic town of Crested Butte, high in the Colorado Rockies. Built in the style of a Swiss chalet, the informal elegance is evident throughout. Each room has a private bath and a balcony. Enjoy the living room with stone fireplace and sunroom with Jacuzzi. The full gourmet breakfasts are a highlight, served on china with crystal each morning. Fresh baked goodies and beverages are available to guests throughout the day. Inquire about minimum night stay.

Hosts: Ward and Loree Weisman
Rooms: 3 (PB) $85-145
Full Breakfast
Credit Cards: A, B, D
Notes: 2, 7, 9, 10, 12, 13, 14

Bed and Breakfast Agency
of Colorado at Vail

P.O. 491, Vail, 81658
(970) 949-1212; (800) 748-2666

CB 1. An inviting inn where the charm of the past and the amenities of the present can be found features 17 rooms, each with private bath, pine bed, armoire, and warm down comforters. The views from these rooms of the surrounding mountains are spectacular. Enjoy the deluxe Continental breakfast by the fireplace in the spacious great room, stroll on the second-floor sun deck, or relax in the Jacuzzi. For guests requiring special assistance, all ADA requirements are met and elevator service is available to all rooms. No smoking allowed. $89-129.

The Elizabeth Anne
Bed and Breakfast

703 Maroon Avenue, P.O. Box 1051, 81224
(970) 349-0147

The Elizabeth Anne is a modern Victorian home which reflects the warmth and charm of Crested Butte's mining past. It is tastefully appointed with Queen Anne furniture and accessories of the period. We feature four spacious bedrooms each decorated with period furnishings and wallpaper. Each has a private bath and cable TV. Each day enjoy our sumptuous breakfasts, afternoon refreshments in the parlor, and a soothing soak in the hot tub. Convenient to restaurants, shopping, and shuttle bus. Rates do not include tax. Inquire to see if children are welcome.

Hosts: Carl and Judy Jones
Rooms: 4 (PB) $69-99
Full Breakfast
Credit Cards: A, B, C
Notes: 2, 7, 9, 10, 11, 12, 13, 14

Purple Mountain Lodge

Box 897, 81224
(303) 349-5888

Guests enjoy sharing their adventures and discussing plans in the living room by a fire in the massive stone fireplace. If conversation slows, cable TV is available. The spa in the sunroom offers welcome relief to tired muscles. Crested Butte is 8,885 feet above sea level in an open valley surrounded by the Elk Mountains. It has many trails and roads to explore by foot, mountain bike, horseback, or four-wheel-drive automobile. The nearby mountain lakes and streams provide canoeing, kayaking, rafting, and fishing.

Hosts: Walter and Sherron Green
Rooms: 5 (3 PB; 2 SB) $55-90
Full Breakfast
Credit Cards: A, B, C, D
Notes: 2, 5, 6, 7, 8, 9, 10, 12, 13, 14

CRIPPLE CREEK

Bed and Breakfast Agency of Colorado at Vail

P.O. 491, Vail, 81658
(970) 949-1212; (800) 748-2666

CC 315. Host has completely renovated this 1900 former hospital to create an award-winning building with 18 guest rooms. Outside, relax in the gazebo hot tub; watch the world (and the gamblers) go by from either of two enclosed porches. On-site amenities include a beauty parlor, game room, playground, and campground. There are many casinos within walking distance. $49-99.

Imperial Hotel and Casino

123 North Third Street, 80813
(719) 689-2713; (719) 689-7777; (800) 235-2922
FAX (719) 689-0416

The Imperial offers the unique combination of comfortable accommodations, excellent cuisine, limited-stakes gaming, and fine entertainment under one roof. The Imperial players have been performing superior melodrama in the Gold Bar Room Theater for almost 50 years. Just one hour's drive from Colorado Springs through breathtaking mountain scenery, Cripple Creek features museums, historic sites, gold mine tours, and exceptional Victorian architecture. Complimentary wine, cheese, and fruit basket for special occasions. Two suites available. In-state personal checks accepted.

Rooms: 29 (12 1/2 PB; 16 SB) $65-145
Suites: 2
Full Breakfast
Credit Cards: A, B, C, D
Notes: 3, 4, 5, 8, 9, 14

CORTEZ

Bed and Breakfast Agency of Colorado at Vail

P.O. 491, Vail, 81658
(970) 949-1212; (800) 748-2666

CTZ 86. This gateway to the San Juan Mountains is 20 minutes from Mesa Verde and 40 miles from Durango. Built on a lake in 1983, it features five bedrooms, two overlooking the lake. Offers a full breakfast and afternoon refreshments. Hot tub. No smoking. $60-90.

7 No smoking; 8 Children welcome; 9 Social drinking allowed; 10 Tennis nearby; 11 Swimming nearby; 12 Golf nearby; 13 Skiing nearby; 14 May be booked through a travel agent.

DENVER

Bed and Breakfast Agency of Colorado at Vail

P.O. 491, Vail, 81658
(970) 949-1212; (800) 748-2666

DEN 96. A charming guest house rests in the middle of a ten-acre forest, with 60-foot oaks and maples all around. Balconies on the front and back provide a perfect spot for breakfast or afternoon tea. Five bed-rooms each have private baths; four have wood-burning fireplaces. Full breakfasts. Guests are welcome to use the kitchen and laundry facilities. No smoking. No pets. $65-95.

Castle Marne

1572 Race Street, 80206
(303) 331-0621; (800) 92 MARNE

Come, fall under the spell of one of Denver's grandest historic mansions. Built in 1889, the Marne is on both the local and national historic registers. Guest's stay is a unique experience in pampered luxury. Three rooms with private balconies and hot tubs for two. Two rooms with Jacuzzi tubs for two. Minutes from the finest cultural, shopping, sightseeing attractions, and the

Castle Marne

convention center. Ask about the candle-light dinners.

Hosts: The Peiker Family
Rooms: 9 (PB) $85-190
Full Breakfast
Credit Cards: A, B, C, D, E
Notes: 2, 3, 4, 5, 7, 9, 10, 11, 12, 13, 14

Haus Berlin

Haus Berlin

1651 Emerson Street, 80218
(303) 837-9527; (800) 659-0253

Haus Berlin, a newly renovated Victorian townhouse in a historic district, is on a quiet tree-lined street just minutes from downtown Denver. Three bedrooms and one suite have either queen- or king-size beds. All the bed and bath linens are supe-rior 100-percent cotton and the decor is a beautiful eclectic mix of the old and the new. Come and enjoy. Hosts are urban, friendly, and comfortable, just like their guests. A gourmet breakfast is served.

Hosts: Christiana and Dennis Brown
Rooms: 4 (PB) $85-120

NOTES: Credit cards accepted: A MasterCard; B Visa; C American Express; D Discover; E Diners Club; F Other; 2 Personal checks accepted; 3 Lunch available; 4 Dinner available; 5 Open all year; 6 Pets welcome;

Continental Breakfast
Credit Cards: A, B, C
Notes: 2, 5, 7, 9, 10, 12, 13, 14

The Queen Anne Bed and Breakfast Inn

2147 Tremont Place, 80205
(303) 296-6666; (800) 432-INNS (out of state)
FAX (303) 296-2151

Experience history, elegance, and warm hospitality in side-by-side Victorians facing a park on a quiet street that is within walking distance of downtown Denver's pedestrian mall, state capitol, shops, museums, restaurants, theaters, convention center, and businesses. Enjoy a full breakfast, period furnishings, private baths, chamber music, fresh flowers, telephones, and off-street parking. Choose from 14 individually decorated rooms, including four "gallery suites" dedicated to artists Remington, Rockwell, Audubon, and Calder. The inn has been named among the ten most romantic across the country, the ten best nationally, Best of Denver, and is AAA and Mobil rated.

Host: Tom King
Rooms: 14 (PB) $75-155
Full Breakfast
Credit Cards: A, B, C, D, E
Notes: 2, 5, 7, 9, 10, 12, 14

Victoria Oaks Inn

1575 Race Street, 80206
(303) 355-1818

The warmth and hospitality of Victoria Oaks Inn is apparent the moment guests enter this historic restored 1896 mansion. Elegant original oak woodwork, tile fireplaces, and dramatic hanging staircase replete with ornate brass chandelier set the mood for a delightful visit.

Hosts: Clyde and Rie
Rooms: 9 (1 PB; 8 SB) $55-85
Continental Breakfast
Credit Cards: A, B, C, E, F
Notes: 2, 5, 8, 9, 10, 11, 12, 14

DILLON

Bed and Breakfast Agency of Colorado at Vail

P.O. 491, Vail, 81658
(970) 949-1212; (800) 748-2666

DILL 73. This quiet home provides comfortable and economical accommodations convenient to an area full of activity. It offers four large bedroom suites, with private bath, daily maid service, TV, telephone, laundry facilities, and storage space for skis. Swimming, Jacuzzi, and sauna are available, as is parking. Continental plus breakfast includes homemade coffeecakes, bagels, fruits, yogurt, coffee, tea, espresso, or cappuccino. No smoking and no pets. $45-100.

DILL 74. This large, warm, and comfortable home, decorated with antiques, offers a choice of double, twin, or bunk rooms. Good food and company abound. Home away from home. Outside hot tub. $45-85.

Paradox Lodge

35 Montezuma Road, 80435
(970) 468-9445

Paradox Lodge is a secluded 37-acre Alpine location surrounded by Arapahoe National Forest providing picturesque views of mountain peaks and forests along the Continental Divide. Guests may have a choice of a comfortable, completely furnished cabin that can sleep five or a room for two in the main lodge. A wood-fired outdoor hot tub is available for guest use.

Hosts: George and Connie O' Bleness
Rooms: 7 (3 PB; 4 SB) $55-120
Continental Breakfast
Credit Cards: A, B, C, D, E
Notes: 2, 5, 7, 8, 10, 11, 12, 13, 14

7 No smoking; 8 Children welcome; 9 Social drinking allowed; 10 Tennis nearby; 11 Swimming nearby; 12 Golf nearby; 13 Skiing nearby; 14 May be booked through a travel agent.

DOLORES

Historic Rio Grande Southern Hotel

101 South 5th Street, P.O. Box 516, 81323
(303) 882-7527

This historic railroad hotel was built in 1893. On the town square, it is within walking distance to the Dolores River and McFee Reservoir. Within driving distance are Mesa Verde National Park, Anasazi Heritage Center, and Crow Canyon. Golfing, fishing, skiing, hunting, backpacking, and bicycling are available in the area. Ski Telluride half-price program available. Open year-round. There is a suite available as well. Full service restaurant.

Hosts: Cathy and Fred Green
Rooms: 9 (3 PB; 6 SB) $45-120
Full Breakfast
Credit Cards: A, B
Notes: 2, 3, 4, 5, 7, 8, 9, 10, 11, 12, 13, 14

Mountain View Bed and Breakfast

28050 County Road P, 81323
(303) 882-7861

Mountain View is in the "four corners area," and is one mile from the gateway to the San Juan Skyway, a nationally designated 238-mile scenic loop, and 12 miles from the entrance to Mesa Verde National Park. Mountain View includes 22 acres with walking trails, cottonwood-lined stream, and canyon. The west slope of the San Juan Mountains is at an elevation of 6,500 feet overlooking the beautiful Montezuma Valley.

Hosts: Brenda and Cecil Dunn
Rooms: 8 (PB) $49-59
Full Breakfast
Credit Cards: A, B
Notes: 2, 5, 7, 8, 11, 12, 13, 14

DURANGO

Bed and Breakfast Agency of Colorado at Vail

P.O. Box 491, Vail, 81658
(970) 949-1212; (800) 748-2666

DUR 115. Nestled below rocky bluffs, there's a spectacular view of the San Juan Mountains from this spacious ranch home. Enjoy the sound of the Animas River flowing or the sight of abundant wildlife from the deck. The bed and breakfast has spacious common areas and private baths, serves full hearty breakfasts, and is central to many area attractions. $77-90.

DUR 116. The most unique feature of this bed and breakfast is the gorgeous view of the only waterfall in the Animas Valley. Sit, relax, and enjoy the roar in the spring and the gentle ripple in the summer. This bed and breakfast is on two acres featuring apple, apricot, pear, and cherry orchards. The guest deck faces the red cliffs and enables guests to view the Narrow Gauge train. Two large rooms are offered with a deluxe Continental breakfast. A Jacuzzi is also provided for guests' relaxation. Open May 1 through October 31. $75-85.

Country Sunshine Bed and Breakfast

35130 North Highway 550, 81301
(970) 247-2853; (800) 383-2853
FAX (970) 247-1203

Ranch-style house on three wooded acres is a spacious home with seven guest rooms with private baths, large leisure room with fireplace, and large outdoor spa. Wildlife and views are abundant. Unique, full breakfast with variety of refreshments always available. Purgatory ski area, Mesa Verde National Park, Durango/Silverton Narrow Gauge Railroad are nearby. Great family getaway with casual atmosphere.

NOTES: Credit cards accepted: A MasterCard; B Visa; C American Express; D Discover; E Diners Club; F Other; 2 Personal checks accepted; 3 Lunch available; 4 Dinner available; 5 Open all year; 6 Pets welcome;

Hosts: Beanie and Gary Archie
Rooms: 7 (PB) $75-85
Full Breakfast
Credit Cards: A, B, C, D, E
Notes: 2, 5, 7, 8, 9, 10, 11, 12, 13, 14

The Leland House Bed and Breakfast Suites Hotel

721 East Second Avenue, 81301
(970) 385-1920; (800) 664-1920;
FAX (970) 385-1967

Lovingly restored 1920s brick Craftsman-style apartment house has six rooms that are actually three-room suites: kitchen, living room, and bedroom with private bath. Breakfast served in the Victorian cottage restaurant next door. Rooms are decorated with Southwestern and Western Victoriana antiques.

Hosts: Diane, Kirk, and Kara Komick
Rooms: 10 (PB)
Full Breakfast
Cards: A, B
Notes: 3, 4, 5, 7, 8, 9, 12, 13, 14

The Leland House

Logwood Bed and Breakfast

35060 US Highway 550 North, 81301
(970) 259-4396

Luxurious red cedar log home is a well designed bed and breakfast lodge. View the beauty of the upper Animas River and mountains through the guest rooms' large windows. Every room has its own private bath. Suite with fireplace. Lounge on the 700-square-foot deck or the yard hammock, fish on the river while enjoying the views, or walk through the five acres of property while deer and bird watching. Full country breakfasts and evening award-winning desserts are served. Children over eight are welcome.

Hosts: Debby and Greg Verheyden
Rooms: 6 (PB) $65-125
Suite: 1
Full Breakfast
Credit Cards: A, B
Notes: 2, 5, 7, 9, 12, 13, 14

River House

River House Bed and Breakfast

495 Animas View Drive, 81301
(303) 247-4775; (800) 544-0009

River House is a large, sprawling, Southwestern home facing the Animas River. Guests eat in a large atrium filled with plants, a fountain, and eight skylights. Antiques, art, and artifacts from around the world decorate the seven bedrooms, snooker, and music room. Enjoy a soak in the hot tub before a relaxing massage or retiring to the living room to watch a favorite video on the large screen TV, and enjoy the warmth of the fire in the beautiful stone and brass fireplace. Comfort, casualness, and fun are themes.

Host: Crystal Carroll; Kate and Lars Enggren
Rooms: 7 (PB) $70-95
Full Breakfast
Credit Cards: A, B, C, D
Notes: 2, 3, 4, 5, 7, 8, 9, 10, 11, 12, 13, 14

7 No smoking; 8 Children welcome; 9 Social drinking allowed; 10 Tennis nearby; 11 Swimming nearby; 12 Golf nearby; 13 Skiing nearby; 14 May be booked through a travel agent.

Rochester Hotel

726 East Second Avenue, 81301
(970) 385-1920; (800) 664-1920;
FAX (970) 385-1967

Luxury accommodations in the Wild West!
Western movies, made in the four-corners
area, were the inspiration for the decor in
this newly renovated 1890s hotel. Tall ceilings, wide hallways, and a beautifully landscaped courtyard add to the elegance.
Cowboy Victoriana furnishings and antique
accessories make the Rochester unique.
Full gourmet breakfast provided. Children
over 12 welcome.

Hosts: Diane Komick and son Kirk
Rooms: 15 (PB) $112-185
Full Breakfast
Cards: A, B
Notes: 2, 3, 4, 5, 7, 9, 12, 13, 14

The Victorian Veranda

Scrubby Oaks
Bed and Breakfast Inn

P.O. Box 1047, 81302
(970) 247-2176

On ten acres overlooking the spectacular
Animas Valley and surrounding mountains.
Three miles from downtown Durango.
Rooms are spacious and furnished with
antiques, art works, and good books.
Beautiful gardens and patios frame the inn
outside, with large sitting areas inside for
guest use.

Host: Mary Ann Craig
Rooms: 7 (3 PB; 4 S2B) $65-75
Full Breakfast
Credit Cards: None
Notes: 2, 8, 9, 10, 11, 12, 14

EATON

The Victorian Veranda
Bed and Breakfast

515 Cheyenne Avenue, 80615
(970) 454-3890

This very beautiful and comfortable two-
story Queen Anne 100-year-old home has a

view of the Rockies from the wraparound
porch. The rates are low because the bed
and breakfast is 50 miles from the tourist
areas. Just one hour drive from Denver,
Estes Park, and Cheyenne, Wyoming. The
guests can enjoy bicycles built for two,
player piano, and a beautiful yard. Guests
can cook out on a gas grill or in the fire pit.
Smoking is allowed on the veranda only.
Skiing is 50 miles away.

Host: Nadine White
Rooms: 3 (1 PB; 2 SB) $45-60
Full Breakfast
Credit Cards: None
Notes: 2, 5, 8, 9, 10, 12, 14

EMPIRE

The International
Bed and Breakfast

504 Amherst Street, Buffalo, NY 14207
(800) 723-4262; FAX (716) 873-4462

CO2003PP. A Victorian cottage built in
1881, offers a rustic atmosphere and old
mountain charm and is in a picturesque star-
shaped valley of the majestic Rock Mountains, 42 miles west of Denver. Six major
ski areas within 15 to 45 minutes. Miles of

NOTES: Credit cards accepted: A MasterCard; B Visa; C American Express; D Discover; E Diners Club;
F Other; 2 Personal checks accepted; 3 Lunch available; 4 Dinner available; 5 Open all year; 6 Pets welcome;

backcountry trails and bowls await the cross-country skier in the bed and breakfast's backyard. Summer fun includes white-water rafting, hiking, mountain biking, and train rides. Open all year. Outdoor hot tub. Complimentary cross-country ski gear and mountian bikes. Three guest rooms with private and shared baths. Afternoon tea and homemade cookies. No smoking. Full breakfast. $49-69.

ESTES PARK

Aspen Lodge at Estes Park

6120 Highway 7, 80517
(970) 586-8133; (800) 332-MTNS

This magnificent 3,000-acre, year-round ranch resort celebrates Colorado's largest log lodge and cozy cabins with fantastic food, and recreation. Enjoy the incredible views and wildlife of the surrounding Rocky Mountain National Park, plus a multitude of activities. Enjoy the Sports Center, nearby golf, an exciting children's program, as well as extensive winter activities, including snowmobiling and cross-country skiing. Advanced open-country horseback riding on 36,000 acres that will stir the soul. No pets.

Hosts: Tom and Jill Hall
Rooms: 59 (PB) $99 ($240 including meals)
Full and Continental Breakfast
Cards: A, B, C, D, E
Notes: 2, 3, 4, 5, 7, 8, 9, 10, 11, 12, 13, 14

Big Horn Guest House

P.O. Box 4486, 80517
(970) 586-4175; (800) 734-0473

Big Horn Guest House is a lovely, intimate hideaway. Enjoy the gracious hospitality and warmth that abounds in this 1923 home, decorated with antiques that add to the relaxing and traditional atmosphere. Home-baked treats and goodies await, along with a scrumptious, full Rocky Mountain breakfast (special diets are honored with advance notice) in the sunny breakfast area overlook-

ing natural rock outcroppings. Each guest room has its own TV. Relax in the comfortable living room with its wood-burning fireplace, TV, and VCR, or just sit back and read or enjoy music. Some guests may even thrill to the sight of elk and deer that frequent the yard and neighborhood. Close to horseback riding, open air concerts, trolley tours, and the various other activities Estes Park has to offer. Cross-country skiing is nearby.

Host: Calla Ferrari Haack
Rooms: 2 (SB) $60-75
Full Breakfast
Credit Cards: A, B
Notes: 2, 5, 7, 10, 11, 12, 14

Eagle Cliff Bed and Breakfast

2383 Highway 66, Box 4312, 80517
(303) 586-5425

A warm and friendly facility is nestled in ponderosa pines at the base of Eagle Cliff Mountain. Relax in the comfort of soft colors native to Southwestern decor, combined with the beautiful woods used in American antiques, to create warmth and hospitality. Enjoy the enticing aromas of a hearty country breakfast served in our bright and sunny breakfast nook Tender homemade breads and rolls and fresh fruit each morning. The abundant breakfast and "never empty" cookie jar keep guests ready for a full day of activities in the heart of Colorado's most spectacular landscapes.

Hosts: Nancy and Mike Conrin
Rooms: 3 (PB) $80-95
Full Breakfast
Credit Cards: None
Notes: 2, 5, 8, 9, 10, 11, 12

EVERGREEN

The Inn at Soda Creek

32163 Soda Creek Drive, 80439
(800) 670-3798

The Inn at Soda Creek is 30 miles west of Denver, almost halfway between Denver

7 No smoking; 8 Children welcome; 9 Social drinking allowed; 10 Tennis nearby; 11 Swimming nearby; 12 Golf nearby; 13 Skiing nearby; 14 May be booked through a travel agent.

and the Continental Divide and less than one hour from the finest skiing in the world. Amenities of the inn include commercial steam room, dry sauna, hot tub, exercise room, and hiking area. Four guest rooms with beautiful decor. Private and shared baths. No children. No pets. Smoking outside only.

Host: Cyndi Gilliland
Rooms: 5 (3 PB; 2 SB) $75-120
Full Breakfast
Cards: A, B
Notes: 2, 5, 10, 11, 12, 13, 14

FRISCO

Bed and Breakfast Agency of Colorado at Vail

P.O. 491, Vail, 81658
(970) 949-1212; (800) 748-2666

FRIS 111. This Frisco country house welcomes guests with a beautiful mountain view from the large open living room and wraparound deck. The two bedrooms and bath downstairs can form a suite. A third bedroom upstairs has one double bed and one twin, with a private half-bath. The hot tub is on the outside deck; inside, there's a huge moss-rock fireplace. Full and hearty country breakfast. $59-89.

FRIS 112. This home in a quiet neighborhood offers a one-bedroom suite with private entrance and bath. It accommodates up to four people with pull-out bed, sitting room, TV, refrigerator, and laundry facilities. The entire floor is reserved for guests, although the hosts enjoy visiting and are happy to let visitors cuddle up to their wood-burning stove. Breakfast is served enuite or in the main living room. Hosts have lived in the area for more than 20 years. $45-95.

FRIS 113. This home in Summit County, just one-half block west of the Frisco Elementary School, is close to six downhill ski areas, cross-country skiing, bike paths, hiking, fishing, and sailing. All units are nonsmoking and have private baths. Homemade jams and goodies are offered for breakfast before a hard day on the slopes or hiking. Outside hot tub. $49-99.

Frisco Lodge

321 Main Street, P.O. Box 1325, 80443
(303) 668-0195; (800) 279-6000

The Frisco Lodge, built in 1885, is the longest ongoing lodging facility in Summit County. It was a stagecoach stop as well as a facility serving train passengers on the D&RGW Railroad. The lodge is convenient to all the finer shops and restaurants in town and offers outdoor hot tub, ski and bicycle tuning, storage room, free movies, and telephones. Great location near the extensive 50-plus mile paved bike path network. Central to all the Summit ski areas.

Host: Susan Wentworth
Rooms: 18 (10 PB; 8 SB) $30-90
Full Breakfast
Credit Cards: A, B, C, D
Notes: 2, 5, 7, 8, 9, 10, 11, 12, 13, 14

Galena Street Mountain Inn

106 Galena Street, P.O. Box 417, 80443
(303) 668-3224; (800) 248-9138

Galena Street Mountain Inn

A wonderful combination of old world charm and mid-western comfort reminiscent of the Arts and Crafts movement of the 1920s, the Galena Street Mountain Inn is simplicity at its most luxurious. Striking Neo-mission style furnishing, down comforters, and window seats with stunning mountain views enhance each of the inn's 14 rooms. Amenities include gourmet breakfast, private baths, phones, cable TV, hot tub, sun deck, private porches, meeting rooms, complimentary beverages, and home-baked treats. Full breakfast is served in the winter, and a Continental breakfast is served in the summer.

Host: Brenda McDonnell
Rooms: 14 (PB) $79-150
Full and Continental Breakfast
Credit Cards: A, B, C, D, E
Notes: 2, 5, 7, 9, 10, 11, 12, 13, 14

The Lark Mountain Inn

109 Granite, P.O. Box 1646, 80443
(303) 668-5327

One block off Frisco's Main Street, in the historical section, this recently renovated log cabin offers seven comfortable guest rooms. The Lark's accommodations feature rooms with shared and private baths, queen-size beds, or two double beds, down comforters, robes, a warm intimate fireplace, and an outdoor hot tub. The wood beamed dining and living area features a TV/VCR, books, periodicals, games, antiques, and overstuffed couches. Children over six welcome.

Hosts: Louise and Roberto Moreno
Rooms: 6 (S4B) $65-150
Full Breakfast
Credit Cards: A, B
Notes: 2, 5, 7, 9, 10, 11, 12, 13, 14

MarDei's Mountain Retreat

221 South 4th Avenue, 80443
(303) 668-5337

MarDei's chalet architecture is influenced by and features European design interior. Guest rooms have twin, queen-, and king-size beds with down comforters. Hot tub and fireplaces available, and the inn is in the center of four ski areas. Bicycle trails, rafting, fishing, and sailing are also nearby. European breakfast.

Hosts: Michael and Amy Wolach
Rooms: 5 (2 PB; 3 SB) $35-100
Full Breakfast
Credit Cards: None
Notes: 2, 5, 7, 8, 9, 13

GEORGETOWN

Creekside Bed and Breakfast Inn

610 Seventh Street, Box 917, 80444
(303) 569-2664; (800) 484-9493-5896

Creekside Bed and Breakfast is in the Victorian Historic District of Georgetown. A spectacular view surrounds the inn. Antiques and a magnificent glass collection grace each room with warmth and charm from the past. Listen to the gentle symphony of the creek or lounge on the deck to capture the beauty that awaits. Near most major ski and tourist areas. Fishing, seasonal hunting, boating, hiking, biking, horseback riding, carriage rides, historical museums, and Georgetown Loop Railroad nearby. The International airport is an hour and a half away, and Denver is 42 miles away. Inquire about accommodations for children.

Host: Carol A. Curran
Rooms: 4 (PB) $65-85
Full Breakfast
Credit Cards: A, B, D
Notes: 2, 5, 7, 10, 12, 13, 14

Hillside House

1034 Main Street, P.O. Box 266, 80444
(800) 490-9012

High in the Colorado Rockies in the beautifully restored Victorian mining town of Georgetown, guests will find the Hillside House bed and breakfast. Enjoy the warmth of cathedral-planked floors and stained glass windows. Sit on the veranda in the evening and drink in the beauty of the majestic mountains. Choose the warm, cozy Rose Room overlooking the flower-filled garden and nearby mountains, or the Columbine suite with dormered ceiling, beautiful woodwork, and four-poster queen-size bed.

Hosts: Ken and Marge Acker
Rooms: 2 (PB) $60-75
Full Breakfast
Credit Cards: B
Notes: 2, 5, 7, 8, 9, 13, 14

KIP on the Creek

1205 Rose Street, 80444
(800) 821-6545

On the banks of Clear Creek, in historic Georgetown, less than an hour's drive from Denver, this inn offers old-fashioned hospitality with hearty breakfasts and modern amenities. Decorated in antique oak and wicker, it exemplifies country teddy-bear warmth and charm. Indoor hot tub. The Stratford room has a private sauna.

Hosts: Sue and Terry Yordt
Rooms: 3 (PB) $64-85
Full Breakfast
Credit Cards: A, B
Notes: 2, 5, 7, 9, 13

GLENWOOD SPRINGS

Back In Time

927 Cooper, 81601
(303) 945-6183

A wonderful 1903 Victorian lovingly restored by owners. The spacious home is filled with antiques, family quilts, and clocks. Two bedrooms filled with antiques, down comforters, and quilts are available. A full breakfast is served in the dining room. Enjoy skiing in the winter, swimming and rafting in the summer. Within walking distance to shopping, dining, and the world's largest hot springs. Forty miles from Aspen.

Hosts: June and Ron Robinson
Rooms: 2 (PB) $55
Full Breakfast
Cards: A, B
Notes: 2, 5, 7, 10, 11, 12, 13, 14

GOLDEN

Antique Rose Bed and Breakfast

1422 Washington Avenue, 80401
(303) 277-1893

The Antique Rose, a renovated 1880s Queen Anne Victorian home, features four tastefully appointed guest rooms, two with private baths, two with private whirlpool baths. Rates include a full, formal American-style breakfast. Room occupancy is limited to two people; however, adjoining rooms can be booked to accommodate larger parties. Just 13 miles west of Denver near the Coors Brewery and the Colorado School of Mines. Within easy access to major highways into the mountains and the gaming casinos of Blackhawk and Central City. Brochure available.

Innkeeper: Sharon Bennetts
Rooms: 4 (PB) $75-115
Full Breakfast
Credit Cards: A, B, C
Notes: 2, 5, 7, 8, 9, 10, 11, 12, 13, 14

Bed and Breakfast Agency of Colorado at Vail

P.O. 491, Vail, 81658
(970) 949-1212; (800) 748-2666

GOLD 18. Enjoy elegant executive suites or champagne honeymoon weekends in these cozy country rooms. Fifteen minutes from downtown shops, and 20 minutes from casino, opera, and hot jazz. Fabulous full breakfasts include filet mignon and eggs Benedict. Horseback riding with lessons is also available on-site. The suite has private entrance, deck, balcony, and sunken tub. Guests will leave this property wanting to return soon. $45-150.

NOTES: Credit cards accepted: A MasterCard; B Visa; C American Express; D Discover; E Diners Club; F Other; 2 Personal checks accepted; 3 Lunch available; 4 Dinner available; 5 Open all year; 6 Pets welcome;

The Dove Inn
711 14th Street, 80401-1906
(303) 278-2209; FAX (303) 278-4029

Charming Victorian inn is in the foothills
of west Denver, yet has the small-town
atmosphere of Golden. Close to Coors
tours and Rocky Mountain National Park;
one hour to ski areas. No unmarried couples, please. Inquire about children being
welcome.

Hosts: Sue and Guy Beals
Rooms: 6 (4 PB; 2 SB) $48-77
Full Breakfast
Credit Cards: A, B, C, E
Notes: 2, 5, 10, 11, 12, 13, 14

GRAND JUNCTION

Bed and Breakfast Agency of Colorado at Vail
P.O. 491, Vail, 81658
(970) 949-1212; (800) 748-2666

GL 96. On the canal to Grand Lake, these
unhosted cabins offer the guest relaxation at
its finest. Cabins with simple decor begin
with one room and private baths. One
medium-size bedroom has private bath,
deck, kitchenette, and fireplace. Large two-
bedroom has bath, fireplace, deck, and
kitchenette. $45-75.

The Cider House Bed and Breakfast
1126 Grand Avenue, 81501
(303) 242-9087

The Cider House Bed and Breakfast is at
home in a 1907 frame house refurbished
and decorated with wallpaper and lace.
Antiques and French doors carry out the
Victorian theme. The guest rooms are
queen-size, well-lighted, and quiet. A full
breakfast is served in the formal dining
room. The hostess enjoys entertaining and
welcomes the opportunity to make the
guests' travel experiences memorable.

Host: Helen Mills
Rooms: 4 (1 PB; 3 SB) $38-45
Full Breakfast
Credit Cards: A, B, C
Notes: 2, 3, 4, 5, 7, 8, 9, 10, 11, 12, 13, 14

Junction Country Inn Bed and Breakfast
861 Grand Avenue, 81501
(303) 241-2817

The elegance of a turn-of-the-century show
house, mixed with the comforts of home,
awaits guests at Junction Country Inn. Four
beautifully decorated rooms, have both private and shared baths. Hosts will gladly
help with trip-planning. A delicious full
breakfast and afternoon snack are served in
the parlor and dining room. No pets.

Hosts: The Bloom Family
Rooms: 4 (2 PB; 2 SB) $35-69
Full Breakfast
Cards: A, B, C
Notes: 2, 5, 7, 8, 9, 10, 11, 12, 13, 14

GRAND LAKE

Bed and Breakfast Agency of Colorado at Vail
P.O. 491, Vail, 81658
(970) 949-1212; (800) 748-2666

GL96. These unhosted cabins on the canal
to Grand Lake offer the guest relaxation at
its finest. Cabins with simple decor include
one room with private bath; medium-size
bedroom with bath, deck, kitchenette, fireplace; large two-bedroom with bath, fireplace, deck, and kitchenette. $45-75.

GREELEY

Bed and Breakfast Agency of Colorado at Vail
P.O. 491, Vail, 81658
(970) 949-1212; (800) 748-2666

7 No smoking; 8 Children welcome; 9 Social drinking allowed; 10 Tennis nearby; 11 Swimming nearby;
12 Golf nearby; 13 Skiing nearby; 14 May be booked through a travel agent.

GREE 43. Enjoy the comfort and charm of this recently renovated 100-year-old Victorian, once the home of one of Greeley's pioneers. Two rooms, both decorated with antiques, are available with queen-size beds, private baths, and many amenities for the business traveler. Full gourmet breakfast. No pets. Smoking on the back porch only. Children over ten welcome. $59-87.

GREEN MOUNTAIN FALLS

Outlook Lodge

P.O. Box 5, 6975 Howard Street, 80819
(719) 684-2303

Built in 1889 as the parsonage for the church in the Wildwood, Outlook Lodge sits nestled in the pines of the scenic mountain town of Green Mountain Falls. Nearby hiking to the town's two waterfalls, close to horseback riding, fishing, swimming, and tennis. Short drive to Colorado Springs and its attractions. Lodge furnished with period antiques as well as local art. Large veranda. Delicious full gourmet breakfast. Open year-round. BBIC approved.

Hosts: Hayley and Patrick Moran
Rooms: 7 (PB) $60-85
Full Breakfast
Credit Cards: A, B, D
Notes: 2, 5, 7, 8, 9, 10, 11, 12, 14

GUNNISON

Mary Lawrence Inn

601 North Taylor Street, 81230
(970) 641-3343

Make this Victorian home the center of excursions through Gunnison country. The mountains, rivers, and lakes are extraordinary. Golf, swimming, rafting are accessible. The inn is furnished with antiques and collectibles. Breakfasts are bountiful and imaginative. Special fly fishing weekends.

Great ski package offered for Crested Butte skiing. Children over six welcome.

Host: Pat and Jim Kennedy
Rooms: 3 (PB) $69
Suites: 2 (PB) $85
Full Breakfast
Credit Cards: A, B
Notes: 2, 5, 7, 9, 10, 11, 12, 13, 14

KEYSTONE

Ski Tip Lodge

Keystone Resort, Box 38, 80435
(800) 222-0188

The transition from a mid-1800s stage stop to the quaint bed and breakfast inn of today has been gracefully done. Reminiscent of an old Swiss hostel, window boxes spill their bounty of flowers in summer. During the winter months, the beaver pond freezes and the sloping lawns are softly blanketed with snow. The ski slopes are visible from the front room. Each room is simply furnished in a rustic style, many with authentic antiques. A retreat for the body and soul, there are no television sets or telephones in the lodge. Rooms with or without bath are available to accommodate a variety of groups. Full breakfast is served in the winter and a Continental breakfast is served in the summer.

Hosts: Erin Clark and Audrey Aylor-Voeks
Rooms: 11 (9 PB; 2 SB) $74-198
Full and Continental Breakfast
Credit Cards: A, B, C, D, E
Notes: 4, 5, 7, 8, 10, 11, 12, 13, 14

LEADVILLE

The Apple Blossom Inn

120 West 4th Street, 80461
(800) 982-9279

This elegant and comfortable vintage 1879 banker's home contains beautiful stained-glass windows, majestic Victorian fireplaces, gorgeous hardwood floors, and impressive brass and four-poster feather beds. In Colorado's largest historical district and he inn is close to shopping, dining, and museums. Leadville is Colorado's highest incorporated city at 10,500 feet. Enjoy delicious full breakfast and complimentary afternoon snacks as well as lemonade and hot teas.

Host: Maggie Senn
Rooms: 8 (3 PB; 4 SB) $59-79
Full Breakfast
Credit Cards: A, B, C
Notes: 2, 3, 5, 7, 8, 9, 10, 11, 12, 13, 14

Bed and Breakfast Agency of Colorado at Vail

P.O. 491, Vail, 81658
(970) 949-1212; (800) 748-2666

LEAD 651. Originally built in 1879, this former banker's home features beautiful stained-glass windows, Victorian fireplaces, and hardwood floors. Eight rooms are available, with luscious brass and four-poster feather beds. It is in a historic district. Suite with kitchenette is also available. Delicious breakfasts. $55-115.

LEAD 652. In the city with the highest elevation in the United States at 10,430 feet, this gracious Victorian inn was built at the turn of the century using the lumber from the famous Leadville Ice Palace. Each romantic guest room, elegantly decorated with antiques and quilts, has an exquisite bath. Begin the day with a delicious gourmet breakfast served in this historic inn. $79-109.

Historic Delaware Hotel

700 Harrison Avenue, 80461
(719) 486-1418; (800) 748-2004

Enjoy the ambience of this historic hotel, circa 1886. Each of the 36 rooms features antique furnishings and heirloom-style bedspreads. Each room features a private bath and TV. A Jacuzzi, Callaway's Restaurant,

Historic Delaware Hotel

and Victorian lobby and lounge are also available for guests to enjoy.

Rooms: 36 (PB) $65-100
Full Breakfast
Credit Cards: A, B, C, D, E
Notes: 2, 3, 4, 5, 7, 8, 9, 10, 11, 12, 13, 14

The Ice Palace Inn and Antiques

813 Spruce Street, 80461
(719) 486-8272

This gracious Victorian inn was built at the turn of the century, using the lumber from the famous Leadville Ice Palace. Romantic guest rooms, elegantly decorated with antiques and quilts, each with an exquisite private bath, are named after the original rooms of the Ice Palace. Begin the day with a delicious gourmet breakfast served in this historic inn.

Hosts: Giles and Kami Kolakowski
Rooms: 3 (PB) $79-119
Full Breakfast
Credit Cards: None
Notes: 2, 5, 7, 8, 9, 10, 11, 12, 13, 14

Wood Haven Manor

809 Spruce, P.O. Box 1291, 80461
(719) 486-0109; (800) 748-2570

History and romance await guests in these two beautifully restored Victorian homes completely furnished with lovely antiques and collectibles. These turn-of-the-century

7 No smoking; 8 Children welcome; 9 Social drinking allowed; 10 Tennis nearby; 11 Swimming nearby; 12 Golf nearby; 13 Skiing nearby; 14 May be booked through a travel agent.

homes are on Leadville's historic Banker's Row. The eight rooms are a charming blend of nostalgia and modern amenities with private baths and suites with whirlpool or antebellum four-poster canopied beds. Warm hospitality, delicious breakfast, afternoon treats, and cozy atmosphere create a memorable experience.

Hosts: Bobby and Jolene Wood
Rooms: 7 (PB) $59-99
Full Breakfast
Credit Cards: A, B, C, D
Notes: 2, 5, 7, 8, 9, 10, 11, 12, 13, 14

Wood Haven Manor

LOVELAND

The Lovelander Bed and Breakfast Inn

217 West 4th Street, 80537
(303) 669-0798

Nestled against the Rocky Mountain foothills, minutes from Rocky Mountain National Park, The Lovelander is a rambling Victorian-style inn. Its beauty and elegance are characteristic of the turn of the century, when the home was built. Near restaurants, shops, museums, and art galleries, the Lovelander is a haven for business and recreational travelers and romantics. Meeting and reception facilities are available. Children over ten welcome.

Hosts: Marilyn and Bob Wiltgen
Rooms: 11 (PB) $79-125
Full Breakfast
Credit Cards: A, B, C, D
Notes: 2, 5, 9, 10, 11, 12, 14

MANITOU SPRINGS

Gray's Avenue Hotel

711 Manitou Avenue, 80829
(719) 685-1277

This bed and breakfast is in the Manitou Springs Historic Preservation District. It was built in 1886 and opened as the Avenue Hotel, one of the original seven hotels in this resort town. Within minutes of most tourist attractions and easy walking distance of many shops and restaurants. Children must be over ten, please. One suite is available in addition to the regular guest rooms.

Hosts: Tom and Lee Gray
Rooms: 9 (3 PB; 6 SB) $40-65
Full Breakfast
Credit Cards: A, B, C
Notes: 2, 5, 7, 10, 11, 12, 14

Victoria's Keep A Bed and Breakfast Inn

202 Ruxton Avenue, 80829
(719) 685-5354; (800) 905-KEEP

Victoria's Keep, an antique, gourmet inn, was built in 1892. The inn is housed in a fully restored Queen Anne Victorian home complete with nine stained-glass windows, period wall coverings and wainscoting, a wraparound porch, and a turret. Each of the 18 rooms is decorated with period antiques. The five guest rooms all have queen-size

NOTES: Credit cards accepted: A MasterCard; B Visa; C American Express; D Discover; E Diners Club; F Other; 2 Personal checks accepted; 3 Lunch available; 4 Dinner available; 5 Open all year; 6 Pets welcome;

beds, fireplaces, and private baths, one with Jacuzzi tub. Twenty-four-hour beverages, spa, bicycles, and wine are also offered. Personal checks accepted with prior notice.

Hosts: Marvin and Vicki Keith
Rooms: 4 (PB) $65-120
Full Breakfast
Credit Cards: A, B, C, D
Notes: 5, 7, 9, 10, 11, 12, 13, 14

MINTURN

Eagle River Inn

145 North Main Street, Box 100, 81645
(970) 827-5761; (800) 344-1750

This lovely 12-room inn is decorated in the Southwestern style. Enjoy a gourmet breakfast in the sunny breakfast room; in the evenings, relax in front of the fireplace while enjoying wine and appetizers, or experience the outdoor hot tub overlooking the Eagle River. Seven miles from Vail and Beaver Creek ski resorts. Seven-night minimum stay required during Christmas. Closed during May. Children over 12 are welcome.

Hosts: Patty Bidez and Richard Galloway
Rooms: 12 (PB) $95-200
Full Breakfast
Credit Cards: A, B, C
Notes: 2, 9, 10, 11, 12, 13, 14

NORTHGLENN

Country Gardens Bed and Breakfast

1619 East 136th Avenue, P.O. Box 33765, 80233
(303) 451-1724; (800) 475-1724

This 1979 country Victorian home on four acres of gardens, trees, and lawn areas features a wraparound porch with swing and lots of wicker. Enjoy the mountain view from the large gazebo or relaxing hot tub. All rooms and common areas furnished with family antiques and treasures. Only 25 minutes to downtown Denver attractions.

Just 20 minutes to the mountains and Boulder. The large suite with whirlpool bath is the perfect place for a romantic getaway. Children 12 and over welcome.

Hosts: Arlie and Donna Munsie
Rooms: 4 (PB) $60-95
Full Breakfast
Credit Cards: A, B
Notes: 2, 5, 7, 9, 10, 11, 12, 14

OURAY

Bed and Breakfast Agency of Colorado at Vail

P.O. 491, Vail, 81658
(970) 949-1212; (800) 748-2666

OUR 19. Nestled 7,800 feet high in the San Juan mountains, this 1890 manor house offers polished Victorian charm in a quiet setting, one block from Ouray's unique shops and restaurants. Relax in the natural hot springs pool. Off-roading tours, hiking, backpacking, cross-country skiing, skating, and ice climbing are all nearby. Parlor with TV and fireplace; balcony, patio, croquet courts, and manicured grounds. Buffet-style Continental breakfast. Outdoor hot tub. In winter, half-price tickets to Telluride ski mountain. $75-85.

Main Street Bed and Breakfast

322 Main Street, P.O. Box 641, 81427
(303) 325-4871

Two superbly renovated, turn-of-the-century residences offer three suites, three rooms, and a two-story cottage. All accommodations have private baths, queen-size beds, and cable TV. Five of the units have decks with spectacular views of the San Juan Mountains. Three units have fully equipped modern kitchens. Guests who stay in rooms without kitchens are served a full breakfast on antique china. Guests who

7 No smoking; 8 Children welcome; 9 Social drinking allowed; 10 Tennis nearby; 11 Swimming nearby; 12 Golf nearby; 13 Skiing nearby; 14 May be booked through a travel agent.

stay in kitchen suites are provided with supplies for a hearty breakfast.

Hosts: Lee and Kathy Bates
Rooms: 7 (PB) $68-100
Full Breakfast
Credit Cards: A, B
Notes: 2, 7, 8, 9, 10, 11

St. Elmo Hotel

426 Main Street, P.O. Box 667, 81427
(303) 325-4951

Listed on the National Register of Historic Places and established in 1898 as a miners' hotel, St. Elmo's is now fully renovated with stained glass, antiques, polished wood, and brass trim throughout. An outdoor hot tub and aspen-lined sauna are available, as well as a cozy parlor and a breakfast room.

Hosts: Sandy and Dan Lingenfelter
Rooms: 9 (PB) $60-98
Full Breakfast
Credit Cards: A, B, C, D
Notes: 4, 5, 7, 8, 9, 10, 11, 12, 13, 14

PAGOSA SPRINGS

Echo Manor Inn

3366 Highway 84, 81147
(303) 264-5646; (800) 628-5004

Beautiful country Dutch Tudor manor with towers, turrets, and gables, set in the majestic San Juan Mountains and described by many as a "fairy tale castle." This lovely bed and breakfast offers a honeymoon suite, country breakfast, hot tub, horseback riding, rafting, snowmobiling, fishing, hunting, and boating. Across the street is beautiful Echo Lake. Guests are invited to enjoy cozy wood stoves and fireplaces. Children over ten welcome.

Hosts: Maureen and John Widmer
Rooms: 9 (6 PB; 3 SB) $65-150
Suite: 1
Full Breakfast
Credit Cards: A, B
Notes: 2, 5, 7, 9, 10, 11, 12, 13, 14

Royal Pine Inn

56 Talisman 4002, 81147
(303) 731-4179

This inn is designed in the old Tudor fashion and offers five bedrooms, three with private baths. Two bedrooms share an extra large full bath with a half-bath across the hall. Bedrooms are large and spacious and decorated in Laura Ashley-style. All rooms have their own TV and breathtaking views. The hosts serve a full breakfast of waffles, French toast, and eggs to order, with freshly baked pastries, jams, fresh fruit, and cold cereal. Limited smoking permitted.

Hosts: Kathy and Roy
Rooms: 5 (3 PB; 2 SB) $49-65
Full Breakfast
Credit Cards: A, B
Notes: 5, 8, 10, 11, 12, 13

Royal Pine Inn

PUEBLO

Abriendo Inn

300 West Abriendo Avenue, 81004
(719) 544-2703

A classic bed and breakfast on the National Register of Historic Places, in the heart of Pueblo and one mile off the interstate. Bask in the comfort, style, and luxury of the past in rooms delightfully decorated with antiques, crocheted bedspreads, and brass and four-poster beds. Restaurants, shops,

Abriendo Inn

galleries, golf, tennis, and other attractions are all within five minutes of the inn. Children over seven welcome.

Host: Kerrelyn Trent
Rooms: 10 (PB) $56-89
Full Breakfast
Credit Cards: A, B, C, E
Notes: 2, 5, 7, 9, 10, 11, 12, 13, 14

REDSTONE

Cleveholm Manor: The "Historic" Redstone Castle

0058 Redstone Boulevard, 81623
(303) 963-3463; (800) 643-4837

Cleveholm Manor is a majestic 42-room manor built at the turn of the century by coal and steel baron John Cleveland Osgood. The finest quality craftsmanship, furnishings, and decoration lend charm and grace to transport a guest back in time to an era of solitude and serenity. Cleveholm operates today as a bed and breakfast mountain inn, and as a host for special events, retreats, weddings, concerts, conferences, and elegant dinners most Friday and Saturday evenings. Limited smoking allowed.

Hosts: Rose Marie Johnson and Cyd Lange
Rooms: 16 (8 PB; 8 SB) $95-180
Continental Breakfast
Credit Cards: A, B, C
Notes: 2, 4, 5, 6, 8, 9, 14

RIDGWAY

Chipeta Sun Lodge Bed and Breakfast

304 South Lena, P.O. Box 2013, 81432
(970) 626-3737; (800) 633-5868

New classy solar adobe bed and breakfast has exquisite Southwestern design and decor. The most picturesque region of Colorado is close to historic Ouray and Telluride. Restaurants, shops, and hot springs nearby. Unique sunny rooms have many special details; hearty breakfast in two-story Solarium, stone fireplace in Great Room, and hot tub in the Tower. Spectacular views. Mountain activities abound so plan on several days to enjoy it all.

Hosts: Lyle and Shari Braund
Rooms: 12 (PB) $65-105
Full Breakfast
Credit Cards: A, B, C, D
Notes: 2, 5, 7, 9, 10, 11, 12, 13, 14

SALIDA

Poor Farm Country Inn

8495 CR 160, 81201
(719) 539-3818

Historic Victorian home decorated in antiques is surrounded by beautiful mountains on the Arkansas River. Seven rooms and co-ed dorm have cozy atmosphere. Excellent fishing is just steps away. A pleasant, cozy interlude that guests will long remember. Rest and relaxation is the speciality. Limited smoking allowed.

Rooms: 7 (3 PB; 4 SB) $45-55
Full Breakfast
Credit Cards: A, B
Notes: 2, 5, 8, 9, 10, 11, 12, 13, 14

The Tudor Rose

6720 Paradise Road, P.O. Box 89, 81201
(719) 539-2002; (800) 379-0889

Stately country manor, high on a piñon hill overlooking the Arkansas River valley, is built on 37 acres of an 1890s homestead. Six distinctive rooms, including the Henry Tudor suite with its private Jacuzzi tub room, highlight the inn. A formal Queen Anne living room, relaxing Wolf's den, deck with sunken spa, exercise room, and a full heart breakfast are complimentary. Facilities include a barn, fenced paddocks, access to thousands of federal acres and outdoor dog accommodations.

Hosts: Jon and Terre´ Terrell
Rooms: 6 (1 PB; 5 SB) $50-105
Full Breakfast
Credit Cards: A, B, C
Notes: 2, 3, 5, 6, 7, 8, 9, 11, 12, 13, 14

SILVERTON

Alma House

220 East 10th Street, P.O. Box 359, 81433
(303) 387-5336

A totally restored European-style hotel with Victorian decor. Step back in time and experience the gracious charm of yesteryear. Superb cuisine served in Christine's fine-dining restaurant. Enjoy fine wines and relax in the splendor of a time gone by. Room service is available. Continental breakfast is served.

Host: Christine Alicia Payne
Rooms: 10 (2 PB; 8 SB) $55-85
Continental Breakfast
Cards: A, B, C, D
Notes: 3, 4, 5, 6, 8, 9, 10, 13, 14

Wyman Hotel and Inn

1371 Greene Street, P.O. Box 780, 81433
(970) 387-5372; (800) 609-7845
FAX (970) 387-5745

The Inn was built in 1902 and totally restored in 1987. The rooms are antique to modern, all with telephones, TV/VCRs, bathrooms, ceiling fans, and European down comforters for those crisp mountain nights. All hot water baseboard heat adds to the comfort. Over 400 free videos for the guests' viewing pleasure. At 9,318 feet ele-

vation, the inn offers spectacular views of the San Juan mountains which surround this nationally registered historic town. AAA and Mobil rated. Seasonal rates.

Rooms: 19 (PB) $68-78
Continental Breakfast
Credit Cards: A, B, C, D
Notes: 2, 5, 6, 7, 8, 10, 11, 12, 13, 14

STEAMBOAT SPRINGS

Bed and Breakfast Agency of Colorado at Vail

P.O. 491, Vail, 81658
(970) 949-1212; (800) 748-2666

STBT 34. Simply decorated and affordable, this is a great place for skiers seeking comfortable accommodations. It is within walking distance of downtown shops and restaurants and three miles from the ski area. Amenities include in-room TV, whirlpool, a fully stocked library, bumper pool, and movies. $89-95.

STBT 35. In the heart of downtown, restaurants, shops, and mineral springs are within walking distance. Each room has unique decor. Telephone, TV with HBO. Kids stay FREE. Continental breakfast. $60-119.

STBT 36. A cheerful greeting, great background music, guest rooms so comfortable guests won't want to leave, a crackling fire all contribute to the relaxing atmosphere topped off by personal touches from the hosts. Built with logs from the town mill and bricks from the old flour mill this was a former college president's residence until it became a bed and breakfast in 1993. Full gourmet breakfasts, four rooms are offered, one a suite. $89-125.

STBT 37. This four-bedroom traditional Southwestern home offers gracious bed and breakfast accommodations in the historic

NOTES: Credit cards accepted: A MasterCard; B Visa; C American Express; D Discover; E Diners Club; F Other; 2 Personal checks accepted; 3 Lunch available; 4 Dinner available; 5 Open all year; 6 Pets welcome;

Western town. Full buffet breakfast is served including the famous Smoothies. Relax in the inviting greenhouse/sunroom overlooking the pond after a busy day of skiing or summer activities. $85.

The Log Cabin

47890 County Road 129, 80487
(970) 879-5837

The spectacular Elk River Valley is the rural ranch setting for this small guest cabin, uniquely constructed of whole logs and river rock. Its queen-size bed, large shower, wood stove, library, microwave, and mini-refrigerator ensure comfort and privacy for two. Full breakfast served in main house. The hosts are knowledgeable about nearby national forest trails and familiar with the Steamboat ski area.

Hosts: Ann and Bill Root
Cabins: 1 (PB) $63-75
Full Breakfast
Credit Cards: None
Notes: 2, 5, 7, 9, 10, 11, 12, 13, 14

Steamboat Valley Guest House

1245 Crawford Avenue, P.O. Box 773815, 80477
(970) 870-9017; (800) 530-3866
FAX (970) 879-0361

On spacious grounds, this western log house has spectacular views of skiing and Old Town. Family treasures and antiques accent log walls and lovely wallpapers. English and Scandinavian decor include lace at every window. Great room features a fireplace and grand piano. Seasonal outdoor hot tub. Easy walk to restaurants, shops, bike path, river activities, and historic sites. Covered parking. Ski area is easily reached by town bus.

Hosts: George and Alice Lund
Rooms: 4 (PB) $70-150
Full Breakfast
Credit Cards: A, B, C, D, E
Notes: 2, 5, 7, 11, 12, 13, 14

TELLURIDE

Alpine Inn Bed and Breakfast

440 West Colorado Avenue, P.O. Box 2398, 81435
(970) 728-6282; (800) 707-3344

Enjoy the charm and spectacular views at this restored Victorian inn in the historic district of Telluride. The inn is within walking distance of ski lifts, hiking trails, and festivals. Each room captures a Victorian serenity with antiques and soft colors. Enjoy breakfast with views from the sunroom or sun deck. Relax on the porch by the wildflower garden, read a good book by the fire, or enjoy sunset views from the hot tub.

Hosts: Denise and John Weaver
Rooms: 8 (6 PB; 2 SB) $65-220
Full Breakfast
Credit Cards: A, B
Notes: 2, 5, 7, 9, 10, 11, 12, 13, 14

Bear Creek Bed and Breakfast

221 East Colorado, P.O. Box 1797, 81435
(303) 728-6681; (800) 338-7064

This charming European-style bed and breakfast is on Telluride's historic Main Street. Guests are only steps away from dining, shopping, hiking, ski slopes, Town Park, and summer festivals. Private telephones and cable TV with HBO. Complimentary après-ski. Other amenities include a central fireplace, sauna, steam room, and a roof deck with its stunning 360-degree view of the mountains. Children ten and over welcome.

Hosts: Tom and Colleen Whiteman
Rooms: 10 (PB) $65-155
Full Breakfast
Credit Cards: A, B
Notes: 5, 7, 9, 10, 11, 12, 13, 14

7 No smoking; 8 Children welcome; 9 Social drinking allowed; 10 Tennis nearby; 11 Swimming nearby; 12 Golf nearby; 13 Skiing nearby; 14 May be booked through a travel agent.

Johnstone Inn

Johnstone Inn

403 West Colorado, Box 546, 81435
(970) 728-3316; (800) 752-1901

A true, 100-year-old restored Victorian boarding house is in the center of Telluride and the spectacular San Juan Mountains. Rooms are warm and romantic with Victorian marble and brass private baths. Full breakfast is served. Winter season includes après-ski refreshments. A sitting room with fireplace and outdoor hot tub complete the amenities. Nordic and alpine skiing, hiking, Jeep tours, and loafing are within walking distance of the inn.

Hosts: Bill Schiffbauer
Rooms: 8 (PB) $80-140
Full Breakfast
Credit Cards: A, B, C
Notes: 2, 5, 7, 9, 10, 12, 13, 14

New Sheridan Hotel

231 West Colorado Avenue, 81435
(970) 728-4351; (800) 200-1891

The New Sheridan Hotel has been welcoming guests to Telluride since 1891. Each of its 38 rooms and suites is immaculately restored to reflect the Victorian elegance of the period combined with the relaxed comfort of an alpine lodge. Enjoy a hearty country breakfast each morning and wine and hors d'oeuvres in the afternoon. Complimentary morning paper, turndown service, and terry robes provided. Fitness room available. Seasonal rates.

Hosts: Roger and Sall Post; Tom Taylor, innkeeper
Rooms: 38 (PB) $65-295
Full Breakfast
Credit Cards: A, B, C
Notes: 2, 7, 8, 9, 13

San Sophia

330 West Pacific Avenue, P.O. Box 1825, 81435
(800) 537-4781

Elegant, luxurious accommodations for the discriminating traveler. Indoor and outdoor dining areas, huge bathtubs for two, brass beds, handmade quilts, and a dramatic view of the surrounding 13,000-foot mountains. Common areas include an observatory, library, and gazebo with Jacuzzi. "One of the most luxurious and romantic inns in America," according to *Inside America*. Complimentary refreshments each afternoon. Closed April 10 through May 14 and October 20 through November 24.

Hosts: Dianne and Gary Eschman
Rooms: 16 (PB) $95-250
Full Breakfast
Credit Cards: A, B, C
Notes: 2, 7, 9, 10, 11, 12, 13, 14

San Sophia

NOTES: Credit cards accepted: A MasterCard; B Visa; C American Express; D Discover; E Diners Club; F Other; 2 Personal checks accepted; 3 Lunch available; 4 Dinner available; 5 Open all year; 6 Pets welcome;

TWIN LAKES

Twin Lakes Mountain Retreat
129 Lang, Box 175, 81251
(719) 486-2593

This clean and relaxing country inn is tucked away in one of Colorado's last unspoiled high mountain valleys. Come see the real Colorado and experience bright sunny mornings, delicious country breakfasts, unlimited activities, homemade bakery goods with quiet relaxing evenings in front of the fire. The inn sits at the base of Colorado's highest peak and across from the breathtaking beauty of Twin Lakes. All of these features combine to make a visit to Twin Lakes Mountain Retreat truly unforgettable. Dinner available by prior arrangement only.

Hosts: Roger and Denny Miller
Rooms: 5 (3 PB; 2 SB) $69-73
Full Breakfast
Credit Cards: A, B
Notes: 2, 7, 9, 10, 11, 12, 13, 14

VAIL

Bed and Breakfast Agency of Colorado at Vail
P.O. 491, 81658
(970) 949-1212; (800) 748-2666

Alpen Haus. This Austrian-flavored home is one bus stop from Vail village on the golf course. Great views from each bedroom, one overlooking the Gore Range and Vail Village; the other looks out on tall pines and aspens. Common gathering room available for après-ski with TV, VCR, and library. Kitchenette with microwave oven and refrigerator. No smoking. $105-115.

Alpine Creek. This beautiful house is on Alpine, just minutes from downtown. Two rooms with private baths are offered in this home. Elegantly decorated with European flair. Guests wake up to the rip-pling sound of the creek and the smell of fresh-brewed coffee. A delicious breakfast starts off each day of winter skiing or summer recreation. $85-125.

Aspen Haus. If guests would like to be pampered, then this is the house. Set on a hillside, surrounded by trees, the guest suite has a delightful, homey feeling with a great view. There is a TV, telephone, and large couch to snuggle into and relax. The bath is in the suite for extra privacy. Breakfast is served upstairs in the European decorated home. High ceilings and wonderful German artifacts grace the sunny kitchen area. The hosts offer a ski locker in town at the base of the the mountain, as well as an athletic club membership, discounted parking tickets, and ski tickets (limited availability). Wine and cheese is served each afternoon. $125.

Bagels n' Grits. This self-contained apartment is perfect for parties of four or more. A fully stocked kitchen, fireplace, TV/VCR, and ski storage are available. The creekside property is less than five minutes from downtown Vail on the FREE bus service. Call for rates.

Base Cabin. This single-family home is hidden away creekside only minutes from Beaver Creek. The owner, who built this log house, is a world-traveled climber, adventurer, and Himalayan guide. The artifacts collected from his travels make the home seem like a minimuseum, and of course there is a great story behind each item. Sherpa, the resident cocker spaniel and master of mischief, is always eager to greet guests and discuss his toys. Base Camp is a little off the beaten path but well worth the effort. No place else in the valley offers privacy like this. Guests will love it if they do not mind the short drive and would like to save some money. No smoking and no pets. $50-85.

Bed and Breakfast Agency of Colorado at Vail (continued)

BB Inn. This inn is everything guests would expect from a Rocky Mountain getaway. On Gore Creek, this handcrafted log inn with an enormous main room has a cozy fire, great views, and warmth beyond compare. Breakfast features baked breads, rolls, muffins, fruits in season, and a daily gourmet creation. Aprés ski snacks and appetizers are also served daily. $80-175.

Bluebird. This wonderful mountain home offers warmth and charm to all guests who stay here. The hostess offers quaint rooms, each with its own decor. Additional children are welcome in the room or on the futon for an extra $10-15. Microwave oven and refrigerator are available for guests to use. Views of Vail and surrounding mountains are spectacular. In summer, relax on the outside sunny deck while feasting on breakfast. Bus stops at the end of the street, and free shuttle to downtown. $80-95.

Chalet Chamonix. If privacy is needed in a bed and breakfast, then this self-contained apartment suite will meet that need. The small, intimate property has kitchenette, private bath, living room, TV, and private entrance. A Continental breakfast is served each day. On the free bus route; however, hosts suggest that guests use their cars because it is a bit of a walk to the bus stop. No smoking and no pets. $85-125.

Colorado Comfort. For peace and quiet, only minutes from the active world, this inn is the place. Guest suite has a private entrance, TV, fireplace, fully stocked kitchenette, spectacular views, and gracious hosts. Breakfast is prepared and offered early, so rise and enjoy the splendor of the Vail Valley year-round. The outside patio is on the golf course for long leisurely summer breakfasts or cross-country ski jaunts in the winter. A deluxe accommodation for golfers or skiers. $95-155.

Creekside Retreat. This comfortable suite features a bedroom, private bath, kitchenette, living room, and dining area. A spacious, sunny, high-vaulted room has a private entrance and offers privacy to those guests who prefer to be separate from hosts. Hosts live in next-door unit and provide breakfast each morning. Relax at own pace each day with the TV and VCR or hop on the free shuttle to Vail for skiing and recreation. This home is perfect for couple wanting space, quality, and a kitchen for additional meals. $125-150.

Dave's Domain. On Vail's free bus shuttle, this self-contained apartment is perfect for two traveling couples or a family of four. Full kitchen, private entrance, TV, small living room. Host lives upstairs. Five minutes from downtown Vail and close to shopping and skiing. $90-125.

Elk View. This gorgeous townhome nestled on the hillside of Beaver Creek boasts five levels with a breathtaking view of Beaver Creek Mountain. Beautifully decorated, each room has a charm of its own, and the house is impeccably furnished. In summer, breakfast can be enjoyed on one of the three outside decks, and in the winter, after a long day of skiing, relax in the outside hot tub. This property is perfect for honeymoon couples and guests wanting to relax with the locals. $85.

Fairway House. This beautiful rustic mountain home lies very close to the ski mountain. The guest room is cozy, with a stucco fireplace and magnificent view of Gore Range. Adjoining living room with fireplace, TV, VCR, wet bar, library, pool table. Two blocks from free bus route. Continental breakfast. $100-125.

NOTES: Credit cards accepted: A MasterCard; B Visa; C American Express; D Discover; E Diners Club; F Other; 2 Personal checks accepted; 3 Lunch available; 4 Dinner available; 5 Open all year; 6 Pets welcome;

Family Home. This young family's cozy home is set up with other young families in mind. The hosts have playpens and toys with many additions so that children are very welcome. A full breakfast is served. There is a membership to a health club with a pool, weights, tennis, and exercise equipment. A TV, VCR, radio, and queen-size sofa bed will enhance guests' stay. Please contact the office for more details. $75-95.

Heather Inn. Just east of downtown Vail, this one-bedroom property with private entrance is like walking into the past. Decorated with a 100-year-old Queen Anne four-poster bed and various antiques and quilts, its comfort and warmth are unending. Guest room is spacious, with an Empire chair and dresser that converts to a desk. Breakfast is served in the dining room overlooking the stream and beaver-pond. Resident dog. No smoking. $65-125.

Hilltop. This townhouse features impeccably decorated rooms with wonderful views from each. Nestled in the trees on a hillside, it is less than ten minutes from downtown. Exercise equipment and a large steamroom are available. Full breakfasts feature fresh homemade breads. $65-125.

Just Relax. If relaxing in a private apartment sounds appealing, then this home is perfect. Joint entry leads to newly renovated garden-level unit, with private bedroom and bath, living room with fireplace, TV, and pullout couch, and fully stocked kitchenette. This unit is perfect for a small family or two couples traveling together. Go cross-country skiing on the golf course in winter, snowshoe just off the deck, or downhill ski at Vail or Beaver Creek, minutes away. Continental plus breakfast is provided in the morning. $75-150.

Kay's Corner. This new home, nestled in a corner lot, offers a great view and sereni-ty. Bedroom is spacious with TV, refrigerator, and a great view. Host is a ski instructor. Continental breakfast. $80-95.

Lover's Haven. Few bed and breakfasts in America or the Vail area can offer the serenity and mountain views guests experience here. This beautiful Southwestern adobe home makes guests feel like they are in Santa Fe. The decor is impeccable, breakfasts are superb and served in a glassed-in room overlooking the Vail Valley, and terry robes are offered should guests forget their own robes. The hostess is supreme in hosting people—this is a bed and breakfast guests will not forget. Smoking permitted on the patios only. $100-125.

Matterhorn. TVs in rooms, telephone nearby, snow tires suggested for driveway. Enjoy a hearty breakfast with a magnificent view of the Gore Valley. A European family (all speak German—daughter is bilingual) offers a comfortable, cozy home. Box lunch is provided for early rising convention attendants. Great for single travelers. $60-75.

Mountain Chalet. Ski out the front door to cross-country terrain, or just walk on the Vail Golf Course in summer. This beautiful Bavarian mountain chalet is wonderfully decorated with antiques. Large moss-rock fireplace and sitting room with TV and stereo. On bus route. Full breakfast. Rate includes two rooms. $185.

Mountain Hideaway. Bring bathing suits to soothe weary bones in the hot tub while sipping a glass of wine or cappuccino while enjoying après-ski refreshments. On a wooded lot overlooking a creek, this spacious mountain home beckons travelers. Newly renovated with high vaulted ceilings and a beautiful glassed-in kitchen nook, guests will find countless hours of relaxation here. Close to the village on the free

7 No smoking; 8 Children welcome; 9 Social drinking allowed; 10 Tennis nearby; 11 Swimming nearby; 12 Golf nearby; 13 Skiing nearby; 14 May be booked through a travel agent.

Bed and Breakfast Agency of Colorado at Vail (continued)

bus route, the host family's hospitality is incomparable. Discounted Vail parking is available. $90-125.

Mountain Retreat. If guest is looking for an out-of-the-way spectacular home with an unsurpassed view, this bed and breakfast will meet those needs. Travelers will need a car to get there, because it is not on any of the bus routes, but once they arrive, they will never want to leave. The hostess pampers every need with breakfast served on fine china and crystal. A hot tub room is available while enjoying the views of Beaver Creek and Arrowhead mountains. Guest room is impeccably decorated and offers another great view. $100-125.

Mountain Top. If guest is wanting peace and quiet, close enough but far enough away as only eight minutes to the downtown Vail area, this is the perfect place. A two bedroom apartment decorated with mountain flair, fabulous views, fireplace, private entrance, full kitchen, and on-sight hosts that love to entertain. Summer or winter guests will feel at peace visiting this bed and breakfast. $99.

Outdoorsman. Overlooking a lake and the majestic mountains, this beautifully appointed condo is decorated with an abundance of antiques and special color blends. Full breakfast. No smoking. $65-75.

Powder Stash. Even though this property is in a condo unit, it offers all the amenities of being in a private home and then some. There is a pool and Jacuzzi on-site and a balcony off the living room with a magnificent view of Beaver Creek. The hosts are avid skiers and can describe the

mountain well, and in summer they know as much about activities as a concierge. Guests will love the hospitality from this couple. The kitchen is available for additional meals. $50-89.

Snowed Inn. For affordable luxury, this home on an 18-hole golf course welcomes guests summer or winter. It is perfect for golfers, and in the winter, cross-country skiing is right out the back door. The guest rooms have a sitting room with TV, refrigerator, microwave, and dry bar right outside the door. Guests look forward to returning each season to sample the hospitality that reigns in this comfortably formal home. Breakfasts are unbeatable! Beaver Creek and Arrowhead Mountains are minutes away. $100-125.

Sportsman's Haven. Surrounded by pine trees and nestled on a creek, this home is a warm, spacious mountain home that beckons guests to snuggle in during the winter, or lounge on the sunny, private sun decks in summer. The hosts offer a ski home with two rooms. One is bright and cheery with pine trees outside every window, and the downstairs room has a private bath with a sauna and offers an adjoining family room with TV, pool table, shuffleboard, and fireplace. The home is within easy walking distance to the free bus. Discounted parking tickets available if guests should decide to drive. $79-95.

Streamside. This townhouse is conveniently just a few minutes west of Vail Village. The bus stop is only a few steps away so guests do not even need a car. The hosts are a young couple and avid skiers, and are eager to share their life in Vail with guests. On cold afternoons, visitors can look forward to a warm or cold après-ski drink, hot microwave popcorn, or stored drinks in the refrigerator. Upstairs, relax by the fire in the main living room to watch TV or read a

NOTES: Credit cards accepted: A MasterCard; B Visa; C American Express; D Discover; E Diners Club; F Other; 2 Personal checks accepted; 3 Lunch available; 4 Dinner available; 5 Open all year; 6 Pets welcome;

book. Perfect for two couples traveling together or a young family. $70-85.

Summer's End. Perched on a 9,000 foot hillside conveniently just minutes from Beaver Creek; guests will be enchanted with amazing views. Laura Ashley, Ralph Lauren, and Waverly textiles comfortably decorate this home where a fire is stoked nearly every evening. A breakfast buffet is served daily. Picnic lunches tucked into backpacks are always available with advance notice. Three rooms are offered with private baths. $79-99.

Sweet Surrender. This beautiful new home has picturesque mountain views of the Vail Valley. Begin the morning with a warm fireside breakfast while viewing the ski conditions. After a day of skiing, enjoy warm refreshments on a sunny deck or just relax by the fire while watching big screen TV. All rooms have a TV and relaxing sound system. Baths are decorated in specially selected Italian tiles. The hosts have enjoyed sports in the valley for more than 14 years. In summer, golf is only minutes away, as is hiking and mountain biking. $95-125.

Taste of Vermont. The hosts, who have been in Vail business for many years as a local restaurateur and ski instructor, opened this newly built spacious home to guests. For a taste of New England charm, the suites boast a logged frame, tweed sheets, private bath, TV, and a view of the mountains that is incomparable. Each morning breakfast is served in the great room with homemade delight. Each afternoon enjoy self-serve hot chocolate and après ski refreshments. This welcoming home has a large living room where guests may enjoy conversation with the hosts. The suite is a perfect room to snuggle while relaxing. Great views from each room help to understand how special it is living in the mountains. $100-125.

Village Artist. This inn is on the free bus route, central to the heart of Vail. Within walking distance of the village, slopes, Vail's nightlife, Vista Bahn, and Lionshead Gondola. Share the living area, TV, fireplace, and kitchen with hostess. Full or Continental breakfast. $75.

Whiskey Hill. If a quiet, secluded, romantic bed and breakfast room is desired, it can be found here at Whiskey Hill. The guest room on a private floor has a rock fireplace and private bath and entrance. Near shops, restaurants, and close to Beaver Creek. Continental breakfast. No smoking. $80.

Zimmerfret. This hostess has a knack for entertaining. The home is nestled among beautiful aspen and pine trees and welcomes any guest year-round. Cross-country skiing is moments away, as is Vail Mountain. On the FREE bus route. Great morning breakfasts are offered with a European flair. $90-95.

Intermountain Bed and Breakfast

2754 Basingdale Boulevard, 81657
(970) 476-4935; FAX (970) 476-7926

This contemporary home is two miles from the ski lifts on a free shuttle bus route. Rooms have cable TV and refrigerators stocked with complimentary beverages. Breakfast includes home-baked pastries, fresh fruit, cereal, yogurt, and freshly squeezed orange juice. Enjoy an espresso or cappuccino on the garden patio. An award-winning fly fishing creek and paved recreation path are just a short walk away, and a cozy hot tub is on the secluded patio.

Hosts: Kay and Sepp Cheney
Rooms: 2 (PB) $50-125
Continental Breakfast
Credit Cards: None
Notes: 2, 5, 7, 10, 12, 13, 14

7 No smoking; 8 Children welcome; 9 Social drinking allowed; 10 Tennis nearby; 11 Swimming nearby; 12 Golf nearby; 13 Skiing nearby; 14 May be booked through a travel agent.

WINTER PARK

Alpen Rose Bed and Breakfast

244 Forest Trail, P.O. Box 769, 80482
(303) 726-5039

This inn is surrounded by aspen and pine trees and has a spectacular view of the front range. In a sporting paradise, two miles from nation's fifth largest ski area and 40 minutes from Rocky Mountain National Park, the Alpen Rose reflects the owners' love of Austria and feels like an Austrian chalet. Five rooms with Austrian furnishings, down puffs, and handmade quilts make guests feel at home. A memorable breakfast with Austrian specialties awaits in the morning; crackling fire, hot tea, and cookies beckon travelers home after an enjoyable day in the Rockies.

Hosts: Robin and Rupert Sommerauer
Rooms: 5 (PB) $67-115
Full Breakfast
Credit Cards: A, B, C, D
Notes: 2, 5, 7, 9, 10, 11, 12, 13, 14

AngelMark Bed and Breakfast

50 Little Pierre Avenue, P.O. Box 161, 80482
(970) 726-5354; (800) 424-2158

A beautiful mountain home in a forest setting provides guests with a safe, quiet stay. African or cowboy collections decorate the roomy Safari and Winchester suites with kitchenette and fireplace. Enjoy the hot tub, sun deck, and picnic area. Gourmet breakfasts are served, as well as complimentary hors d'oeuvres. The area offers all the amenities of a small winter/summer mountain resort town. Top-of-the-line accommodations and hospitality.

Hosts: Bob and Jeanenne Temple
Rooms: 2 (PB) $90-105
Full Breakfast
Credit Cards: A, B, C, D
Notes: 2, 5, 9, 10, 11, 12, 13

Engelmann Pines Bed and Breakfast

P.O. Box 1305, 80482
(970) 726-4632

Engelmann Pines is a contemporary mountain home furnished with European and American antiques, Oriental rugs, and art. Beds have European down comforters and handmade quilts. This spacious home provides a TV room, reading room, sitting room with piano, and kitchen for guests' use. The hosts serve a full gourmet breakfast, including Swiss specialties. The home is nestled among the pines, high in the Rocky Mountains, close to Winter Park Ski Resort, Pole Creek Golf Course, and Rocky Mountain National Park.

Hosts: Margaret and Heinz Engle
Rooms: 7 (5 PB; 2 SB) $55-115
Full Breakfast
Credit Cards: A, B, C, D
Notes: 2, 5, 7, 8, 9, 10, 11, 12, 13, 14

WOODLAND PARK

Pikes Peak Paradise

236 Pinecrest Road, 80863
(719) 687-6656; (800) 728-8282;
FAX (719) 687-9008

This mountainside home in national forest land has a spectacular view of Pikes Peak. Imagine a suite with hot tub, fireplace, wet bar, love seat, private deck, and gourmet breakfast. That's Pikes Peak Paradise! Very romantic and secluded, but close to shopping, hiking, gambling, mountain biking, cross-country skiing, fishing, boating, and natural wonders! Do it all from a suite in this "Southern Mansion"!

Host: Priscilla Arthur
Rooms: 5 (PB) $110-195
Full Breakfast
Credit Cards: A, B, C, D
Notes: 2, 4, 5, 7, 9, 13, 14

NOTES: Credit cards accepted: A MasterCard; B Visa; C American Express; D Discover; E Diners Club;
F Other; 2 Personal checks accepted; 3 Lunch available; 4 Dinner available; 5 Open all year; 6 Pets welcome;

Woodland Inn Bed and Breakfast

159 Trull Road, 80863-9027
(719) 687-8209; (800) 226-9565
FAX (719) 687-3112

Come to a cozy country inn in the heart of the Rocky Mountains where guests enjoy a relaxing home-like atmosphere and fantastic views. Peacefully secluded on 12 private acres of woodlands, the inn is convenient to a variety of attractions in the Pikes Peak region. The hosts will prepare a picnic lunch for a day of hiking, biking, or skiing, or guests may join the hosts in a morning of hot air ballooning. Reduced rate for singles available.

Hosts: Frank and Nancy O'Neil
Rooms: 4 (1 PB; 3 SB) $55-75
Full Breakfast
Credit Cards: A, B
Notes: 2, 5, 6, 7, 8, 9, 12, 13, 14

YELLOW JACKET

Wilson's Pinto Bean Farm

House No. 21434, Road 16, Box 252, 81335
(303) 562-4476

The Wilson's farm is in Montezuma County, 40 miles from the Four Corners where the four western states join. Accommodations include three rooms with double beds and shared baths. Waving wheat, fragrant alfalfa, pinto beans, and mountains are visible in every direction. The farmhouse sits among elm trees, with orchards and gardens around. There are farm animals to enjoy, home-cooked meals, eggs to hunt, and fruits to pick in season. Children of all ages can see the delights of farm animals and country living.

Hosts: Arthur and Esther M. Wilson
Rooms: 3 (SB) $50
Full Breakfast
Credit Cards: B
Notes: 2, 3, 4, 6, 8, 9, 11

7 No smoking; 8 Children welcome; 9 Social drinking allowed; 10 Tennis nearby; 11 Swimming nearby; 12 Golf nearby; 13 Skiing nearby; 14 May be booked through a travel agent.

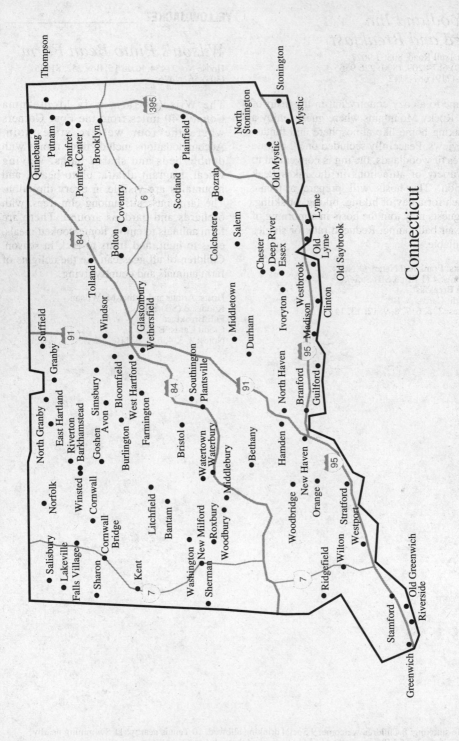

Connecticut

Connecticut

AVON

Nutmeg Bed and Breakfast Agency

P.O. Box 1117, West Hartford, 06107-1117
(203) 236-6698; (800) 727-7542
FAX (203) 232-7680

414. This bright, spacious contemporary has a solarium, deck, and lovely grounds including a Japanese garden with a pond and a waterfall. One room has a cathedral ceiling and skylight; adjacent studio. Six languages spoken here. Continental breakfast and afternoon tea served. Children welcome; baby-sitting is available. No smoking allowed.

BANTAM

Nutmeg Bed and Breakfast Agency

P.O. Box 1117, West Hartford, 06107-1117
(203) 236-6698; (800) 727-7542
FAX (203) 232-7680

319. Deer Island Guest house on Bantam Lake with a lake view in back, front on road; rustic but comfortable. One bedroom with three twin beds, fireplace, chairs, table for dining in a completely equipped kitchen, bath with a shower; kitchen stocked for breakfast; canoe rentals and restaurant nearby. Continental breakfast; children allowed; no smoking; no pets in the guest house.

BARKHAMSTED

Covered Bridge

P.O. Box 447, Norfolk, 06058
(203) 542-5944

Rustic Victorian lake lodge features fireside concerts on the antique grand piano, wraparound porch with a commanding view of woods, and crystal clear lake. Feel free to borrow the canoe, relax on the private beach, or enjoy a country walk. Three guest rooms, one with balcony overlooking the lake, share a bath-and-a-half. $80-95.

BETHANY

Bed and Breakfast, Ltd.

P.O. Box 216, New Haven, 06513
(203) 469-3260

This Normandy French manor house, that is architecturally fascinating, has a woodsy setting in horse country, yet is close to Yale. Interesting furnishings. Gregarious hosts. Reservations hours 5:00 until 9:00 P.M. only September through July. Phones available anytime July and August. $85-95.

BLOOMFIELD

Nutmeg Bed and Breakfast Agency

P.O. Box 1117, West Hartford, 06107-1117
(203) 236-6698; (800) 727-7542
FAX (203) 232-7680

450. Hospitality rules here, with a den, refrigerator, and ice. Four guest rooms with

NOTES: Credit cards: A MasterCard; B Visa; C American Express; D Discover; E Diners Club; F Other;
2 Personal checks accepted; 3 Lunch available; 4 Dinner available; 5 Open all year; 6 Pets welcome;
7 No smoking; 8 Children welcome; 9 Social drinking allowed; 10 Tennis nearby; 11 Swimming nearby;
12 Golf nearby; 13 Skiing nearby; 14 May be booked through a travel agent.

private and shared baths. One has connecting playroom with TV and telephone. Convenient to West Hartford and Hartford, and across the road from Penwood State Forest for walking, jogging, or cross-country skiing. Full breakfast served. Children are welcome.

BOLTON

Jared Cone House

25 Hebron Road, 06043
(203) 643-8538

Enjoy the charm of this historic home. Spacious bedroom accommodations on the second floor with queen-size bed, fireplaces, and scenic views of the countryside. A full breakfast is served featuring homemade maple syrup. Antiques, hiking, canoeing are nearby. Game room above the post and beam barn.

Hosts: Jeff and Cinde Smith
Rooms: 3 (1 PB; 2 SB) $60-70
Full Breakfast
Credit Cards: None
Notes: 2, 5, 7, 8, 10, 11, 12

BOZRAH

Covered Bridge

P.O. Box 44, Norfolk, 06058
(203) 542-5944

Circa 1790 farmhouse is set in a vineyard, offering a very special getaway. The four guest rooms all offer private baths, fireplaces, TV, and telephones. A full breakfast is served. $125.

Nutmeg Bed and Breakfast Agency

P.O. Box 1117, West Hartford, 06107-1117
(203) 236-6698; (800) 727-7542
FAX (203) 232-7680

505. Gambral Home circa 1790. Lovely country setting; host grows berries and makes wine; the berries are served in the

mouth-watering country breakfast. Twenty minutes from Mystic and Ledyard. The four guest rooms have private baths, TVs, phones, gas fireplaces, beautiful furnishings, ceiling fans; one bath has jet tub. Breakfast is served in glass-enclosed sunroom and guests have use of several sitting rooms. Guest room wing has its own private entrance. No children, no smoking.

BRANFORD

Bed and Breakfast, Ltd.

P.O. Box 216, New Haven, 06513
(203) 469-3260

1. Elegant, artfully decorated home near the water has artist in residence. "Storybook" double canopied bed with private bath. Antique filled, near great restaurants and Yale. Very dramatic. $65-85.

BRISTOL

Bed and Breakfast, Ltd.

P.O. Box 216, New Haven, 06513
(203) 469-3260

3. A 1930s, 30-room mansion on two-and-one-half acres. Eclectic furnishings. Five suites with private baths. Near the New England Carousel Museum. Great breakfasts. $95-105.

Chimney Crest Manor

5 Founders Drive, 06010
(203) 582-4219

Experience quiet elegance in this splendid 32-room Tudor mansion. Chimney Crest was built in 1930 in the Federal Hill historic district, just minutes away from the Litchfield Hills, where guests will find antiques, wineries, parks, museums, and restaurants. Stay in the spacious suites for pleasure or on business. Guests are treated with warm, attentive hospitality set in the splendor and style of a bygone era. Listed

---

NOTES: Credit cards accepted: A MasterCard; B Visa; C American Express; D Discover; E Diners Club; F Other; 2 Personal checks accepted; 3 Lunch available; 4 Dinner available; 5 Open all year; 6 Pets welcome;

on the National Register of Historic Homes. Mobil Travel Guide three-star rated.

Hosts: Dan and Cynthia Cimadamore
Suites: 5 (PB) $65-135
Full Breakfast
Credit Cards: A, B, C, D
Notes: 5, 7, 10, 11, 12, 13, 14

Nutmeg Bed and Breakfast Agency

P.O. Box 1117, West Hartford, 06107-1117
(203) 236-6698; (800) 727-7542
FAX (203) 232-7680

411. Bright and spacious English Tudor mansion has a grand foyer, large den, elegant formal dining room, sunroom, and back patio overlooking Farmington Valley and the fountains in the large yard. The ballroom suite contains a large living room with double sofa bed, a full eat-in kitchen, bedroom with double bed, and bath. Also five suites on second floor, including one with two bedrooms and a kitchen. All rooms have ceiling fans and TVs. Full breakfast. Designated smoking area. Children welcome.

433. Visitors to Bristol's clock museum and history lovers will especially enjoy a stay in the Dutch Colonial home of the city historian. Large lawns and gardens surround this home in a residential area. One guest room with private bath. Full breakfast served. No smoking.

BROOKLYN

Bed and Breakfast, Ltd.

P.O. Box 216, New Haven, 06513
(203) 469-3260

2. This 1760s Georgian Colonial, with its nine fireplaces, is on 14 acres. Guests have use of the library. There are three guest rooms. One guest room has a bedroom, a

sitting room, a single sofa bed, and a private entrance. Another guest room has a double bed. The third guest room has twin beds. Two roll away beds available. Twenty minutes to Mystic. $70-100.

BURLINGTON

Nutmeg Bed and Breakfast Agency

P.O. Box 1117, West Hartford, 06107-1117
(203) 236-6698; (800) 727-7542
FAX (203) 232-7680

412. Ten-room Dutch Colonial built around 1930, surrounded by 12 acres of woods crisscrossed with marked paths. First floor guest room with double brass bed and private bath; second floor room with twin beds, private bath. Full breakfast. No children, no smoking.

478. This ranch-style home has a screened porch, pool, and lovely gardens. There is a room with a queen-size bed, private bath, living room, porch, and deck for guests' use. Convenient to Avon Old Farms, Miss Porter's, and the University of Connecticut Medical Center. Full breakfast. No children. No smoking. Dog on premises.

CHESTER

Inn at Chester

318 West Main Street, 06412
(203) 526-9541; (800) 949-STAY
FAX (203) 526-4387

Nestled in the Connecticut River valley, the inn is on 12 wooded acres. A full-service inn offers fine dining, a tavern, game room, exercise room, sauna, bikes, and tennis. All the rooms are decorated with Eldred Wheller reproductions. Two rooms have fireplaces. Each room has telephones, TV, air conditioning, and private bath. The post and beam dining room was voted best new

7 No smoking; 8 Children welcome; 9 Social drinking allowed; 10 Tennis nearby; 11 Swimming nearby; 12 Golf nearby; 13 Skiing nearby; 14 May be booked through a travel agent.

restaurant in 1992 in Connecticut and has continued to win awards for its dining.

Host: Deborah Moore
Rooms: 42 (PB) $98-205
Continental Breakfast
Credit Cards: A, B, C
Notes: 2, 3, 4, 5, 6, 8, 10, 11, 12, 13, 14

CLINTON

Captain Dibbell House

21 Commerce Street, 06413
(203) 669-1646

This 1866 Victorian, on a historic residential street, is two blocks from the harbor and has a century-old, wisteria-covered iron truss bridge. Rooms are furnished with a comfortable mix of heirlooms, antiques, auction finds, and a growing collection of original art by New England artists. Bicycles are available. The inn is closed January through March. Children over 14 are welcome.

Hosts: Helen and Ellis Adams
Rooms: 4 (PB) $80-95
Full Breakfast
Credit Cards: A, B, C, D
Notes: 2, 7, 9, 10, 11, 12, 13, 14

COLCHESTER

Bed and Breakfast, Ltd.

P.O. Box 216, New Haven, 06153
(203) 469-3260

6. This 1776 Federal house is on a historical green. It has seven fireplaces and museum-quality antique furnishings. There are four completed bed and breakfast rooms with newly refurbished private baths. The Goodspeed Opera House is 15 minutes away. $75-100.

CORNWALL

Cornwall Inn

Route 7, 06754
(800) 786-6884

Nestled in the northwest hills of Connecticut, an inn for all seasons. Antique-decorated inn rooms and country motel-type rooms all have private baths. Enjoy the pool and patio in the summer or the roaring fireplace in the dining room in the winter.

Hosts: Lois and Emily
Rooms: 12 (11 PB; 1 SB) $50-115
Full Breakfast
Credit Cards: A, B, C, D
Notes: 2, 3, 4, 5, 6, 7, 8, 9, 11, 12, 13, 14

Covered Bridge

P.O. Box 447, Norfolk, 06058
(203) 542-5944

1C. An 1808 Colonial farmhouse set on 20 acres adjoining Mohawk State Forest. The guest living room has a large old Colonial fireplace and wood stove. Breakfast is served in the country kitchen, or on the terrace in summer. Three bedrooms decorated in period antiques with shared full and half-baths. $85.

2C. Enjoy warm, quiet hospitality at this custom-designed stone home set on a 64-acre private estate with breathtaking views of the countryside. Hearty full breakfasts are served before the library fireplace or on the terrace. All of the rooms are decorated in antiques. Two guest rooms with private baths. $112.

CORNWALL BRIDGE

Nutmeg Bed and Breakfast Agency

P.O. Box 1117, West Hartford, 06107-1117
(203) 236-6698; (800) 727-7542
FAX (203) 232-7680

344. Recently renovated small inn/motel has five rooms on the second floor of inn; three rooms have private baths, two share and are rented to families or to couples traveling together; also second-floor sitting

room with TV, books, and games. Motel rooms have queen- or king-size beds (some have two queen-size beds), private baths, and TV. Full breakfast included; inn also has restaurant (serving lunch and dinner) and a bar. Children allowed (five and under stay free); smoking allowed; dog and cat on premises; pets accepted. Check-in 2:00 P.M.; check-out 11:00 A.M.

COVENTRY

Bed and Breakfast, Ltd.

P.O. Box 216, New Haven, 06513
(203) 469-3260

5. This Colonial Cape-style farmhouse, circa 1731, has 11 rooms decorated with a mixture of antique and traditional furnishings. Fireplace in common room and front parlor. In-ground pool, hot tub in solarium, hammocks, picnic area, and hiking. Three horses on premises. $60-80.

Nutmeg Bed and Breakfast Agency

P.O. Box 1117, West Hartford, 06107-1117
(203) 236-6698; (800) 727-7542
FAX (203) 232-7680

457. This Colonial was built in 1731 and operated as a tavern until 1823. It was used as part of the underground railroad stops for slaves in the mid-1800s. The two guest rooms have queen-size canopied beds, working fireplaces, and a feather mattress for winter warmth. One has a private bath, the other a shared. There is also a cottage with private entrance, queen-size sofa bed, private bath, fireplace, and small kitchen. Hostess will prepare a hearth-cooked dinner with advance notice. Full country breakfast on weekends; Continental weekdays. Children ten and over welcome. No smoking. Cat in residence.

458. Pink-towered Victorian with a well-traveled hostess who collects antique toys has a shop and museum. Bed and breakfast dining area has picture windows and skylights; solarium has potted plants. House is air-conditioned; two guest rooms have private baths, one has a queen-size bed, and the other a pair of twin beds; both have access to large, guest balcony overlooking the garden. Another room with twin beds shares a bath with hosts. Full breakfast; children allowed; no smoking; no pets.

463. Fully modernized Colonial home built in 1731 on three and one-quarter acres with a pool, Jacuzzi, maple trees with hammocks, and three fireplaces. Four guest rooms with double beds share one upstairs and one downstairs bath. Roll away available. Full breakfast. Infants and over five allowed. No smoking. Dog in residence.

DEEP RIVER

Riverwind Inn

209 Main Street, 06417
(203) 526-2014

With its eight wonderfully appointed guest rooms, rambling common areas, and informal country atmosphere, Riverwind is more than just a place to stay; it's a destination. Relax, step back in time, and enjoy a stay amid an enchanting collection of New England and Southern country antiques. Each morning starts with the inn's complimentary Southern buffet breakfast.

Hosts: Barbara Barlow and Bob Bucknall
Rooms: 8 (PB) $90-155
Full Breakfast
Credit Cards: A, B, C
Notes: 2, 5, 9, 10, 11, 12, 14

DURHAM

Bed and Breakfast, Ltd.

P.O. Box 216, New Haven, 06513
(203) 469-3260

---

7 No smoking; 8 Children welcome; 9 Social drinking allowed; 10 Tennis nearby; 11 Swimming nearby; 12 Golf nearby; 13 Skiing nearby; 14 May be booked through a travel agent.

4. Charming Center Hall Colonial. Two rooms with a sitting room. In-ground pool. Crib available. Very historic town near Wesleyan. $75.

Nutmeg Bed and Breakfast Agency

P.O. Box 1117, West Hartford, 06107-1117
(203) 236-6698; (800) 727-7542
FAX (203) 232-7680

509. Georgian Colonial built in 1740 with museum-quality restoration. Furnished with antiques. Two second-floor guest rooms with private baths, one room with twin beds, and one pencil post double canopied rope bed. Both rooms have beautiful non-working fireplaces. Continental breakfast; no smoking. Charming cat on the premises.

EAST HARTLAND

Nutmeg Bed and Breakfast Agency

P.O. Box 1117, West Hartford, 06107-1117
(203) 236-6698; (800) 727-7542
FAX (203) 232-7680

480. Guest house adjacent to Colonial farmhouse built in 1700s. Private entrance to sitting room with working fireplace, double Murphy bed, complete kitchen, full bath, and beautiful setting with horses, stone fences, and hills beyond. Full breakfast served in antique-filled main dining room or in guest house. Only 20 minutes to the airport; hiking, skiing, biking, fishing minutes away. Children allowed. No smoking. No pets in guest house.

ESSEX

Bed and Breakfast, Ltd.

P.O. Box 216, New Haven, 06513
(203) 469-3260

8. Cedar-shingle Bermuda style home on river with dock. Eclectic furnishings. Suite available. Antique dealer hostess. Minutes to Main Street. $85-125.

Nutmeg Bed and Breakfast Agency

P.O. Box 1117, West Hartford, 06107-1117
(203) 236-6698; (800) 727-7542
FAX (203) 232-7680

508. If guests are boating enthusiasts, this entertaining hostess, whose family shares the passion, would love to trade some sailing stories. This special home, right on the bank of the Connecticut River, is convenient to many attractions of the area, 20 miles from Mystic, and close to Hammonasset public beach in Madison. Theaters and fine restaurants are nearby. Two rooms, one with a double bed and one with twins, have private baths. Full breakfast can be served on the glass porch overlooking the river. Children welcome.

FALLS VILLAGE

Nutmeg Bed and Breakfast Agency

P.O. Box 1117, West Hartford, 06107-1117
(203) 236-6698; (800) 727-7542
FAX (203) 232-7680

307. This elegant Dutch Colonial, circa 1700, is in the northwest corner of the state and is on the Housatonic River. The house offers three guest rooms. One has a king-size bed, fireplace, and private bath. The second room has a double bed with private bath. The third room has twin beds and a shared bath. This bed and breakfast is on 40 acres. A great getaway with many walking trails. Full breakfast served on weekends. Children are welcome. No smoking allowed.

NOTES: Credit cards accepted: A MasterCard; B Visa; C American Express; D Discover; E Diners Club; F Other; 2 Personal checks accepted; 3 Lunch available; 4 Dinner available; 5 Open all year; 6 Pets welcome;

FARMINGTON

Nutmeg Bed and Breakfast Agency

P.O. Box 1117, West Hartford, 06107-1117
(203) 236-6698; (800) 727-7542
FAX (203) 232-7680

402. Small inn has traditional country furnishings. Rooms have double, queen-, and king-size beds with private baths, TV, VCR, and telephones. Children under 12 stay free in same room. Continental breakfast served.

406. This elegant estate is now a gracious small inn with beautifully landscaped grounds, pool, tennis court, conference room, and lounge. There are seven rooms with TVs, telephones, and private baths. A short drive from Hartford. Perfect for the business traveler. Continental breakfast. Children welcome.

415. This is a luxurious new inn with suites complete with kitchens, fireplaces, and bathrooms with all the amenities. Enjoy complimentary racquet club privileges with pools and tennis courts. Continental breakfast. Children welcome.

The Farmington Inn

827 Farmington Avenue, 06032
(203) 667-2821; (800) 648-9804

In the heart of the unspoiled and scenic Farmington River Valley, one mile off Exit 39, I-84 at Routes 4 and 10. Seventy-two charming guest rooms and suites blending antique furnishings, original paintings, and fresh flowers in a setting with historic homes, museums, and prep schools. Exceptional complimentary breakfast and daily newspapers. Unique meeting facilities. Deluxe amenities. Four-star restaurant. Golfing, tennis, canoeing, antiquing, fishing, sun-bathing, beach, ballooning, and hiking all nearby.

Rooms: 72 (PB) $89-109
Continental Breakfast
Credit Cards: A, B, C, D, E, F
Notes: 2, 3, 4, 5, 6, 7, 8, 10, 11, 12, 13, 14

GLASTONBURY

Butternut Farm

1654 Main Street, 06033
(860) 633-7197

An 18th-century architectural jewel is furnished in museum-quality period antiques. Estate setting has ancient trees, herb gardens, prize dairy goats, barnyard chickens, pigeons, and a goose. Three Abyssinians inhabit the main house. Ten minutes from Hartford. All of Connecticut is within 90 minutes. Two rooms, two suites, and one apartment.

Host: Don Reid
Rooms: 5 (PB) $68-88
Full Breakfast
Credit Cards: C
Notes: 2, 5, 7, 8, 9, 10, 11, 12, 13

GOSHEN

Bed and Breakfast, Ltd.

P.O. Box 216, New Haven, 06513
(203) 469-3260

9. Federal style home, circa 1809, is filled with antiques. Four guest rooms with feather beds. Air conditioning. Full breakfast. American and English museum-quality pieces. Six miles from Litchfield. $75-125.

Covered Bridge

P.O. Box 447, Norfolk, 06058
(203) 542-5944

1GCT. An 1809 Federal Colonial set on 24 acres has been beautifully restored and decorated with antiques. The couple and their two young children welcome other families to enjoy the special atmosphere at their bed and breakfast. A full breakfast is served in the elegant dining room. There are two guest rooms, one with a fireplace and one with a Jacuzzi. Both rooms have private baths. $100-150.

GRANBY

Nutmeg Bed and Breakfast Agency

P.O. Box 1117, West Hartford, 06107-1117
(203) 236-6698; (800) 727-7542
FAX (203) 232-7680

442. There is a sophisticated country atmosphere to this stone house. The separate guest wing includes a sitting room with TV, and two guest rooms with private baths. Convenient to Bradley International Airport, state parks, historic Old Newgate Prison, and local attractions. Guests enjoy wine, cheese, and crackers in the afternoon, and a Continental breakfast is served. Horses can be boarded for a nominal fee. Children welcome. No smoking.

GREENWICH

Bed and Breakfast, Ltd.

P.O. Box 216, New Haven, 06513
(203) 469-3260

11. Delightful Cape-style home on water has modern decor. Near golf course. Fireplace in living room. Very eclectic. Double room with love seat, TV, and VCR. $75-85.

The Stanton House Inn

76 Maple Avenue, 06830
(203) 869-2110; (203) 869-4262
FAX (203) 629-8116

The Stanton House Inn is a converted mansion that is now a bed and breakfast inn, in the prestigious village of Greenwich. The Stanton House Inn offers elegant surroundings, comfortable rooms and a satisfying Continental breakfast at rate competitive with commercial motels and hotels in the area. The rooms are bright and cheery, decorated primarily with Laura Ashley-style fabrics, period antiques, and reproductions. Closed Christmas week.

Hosts: Tog and Doreen Pearson
Rooms: 24 (22 PB; 2 SB) $70-135
Continental Breakfast
Credit Cards: A, B, C, D
Notes: 7, 9, 10, 11, 14

GUILFORD

Bed and Breakfast, Ltd.

P.O. Box 216, New Haven, 06513
(203) 469-3260

10. Newer home near village green has suite available. Pet dog allowed. Pool. Deck available. $70-85.

12. Federal-style home, circa 1825, is one and one-half miles to village green. Two double rooms. Antique filled. Bright, cheerful, and interesting hosts. $75.

Nutmeg Bed and Breakfast Agency

P.O. Box 1117, West Hartford, 06107-1117
(203) 236-6698; (800) 727-7542
FAX (203) 232-7680

503. Contemporary home in wooded setting bordering Neck River and State Forest is on three acres. Suite has double bed and private bath with shower, kitchenette, and sitting area. Sliding glass doors open to lower level garden. (Can be used in good weather as private entrance.) Room has TV and separate phone line. On the upper level is a room with a double bed and private bath. Full breakfast. Children welcome. No smoking.

NOTES: Credit cards accepted: A MasterCard; B Visa; C American Express; D Discover; E Diners Club; F Other; 2 Personal checks accepted; 3 Lunch available; 4 Dinner available; 5 Open all year; 6 Pets welcome;

510. A contemporary home with lovely grounds awaits the guest who wishes to be near the coast line. The two rooms have private baths—one has a king-size bed and the other has twin beds. There is also a private sitting room for guests. Enjoy a short walk to the village green, Colonial churches, and shops. Full breakfast. Children welcome. Smoking in designated areas.

518. This cottage has a private entrance, gardens, and lovely grounds. In the cottage guests will find a small sitting room and small dining room with refrigerator and microwave. The bedroom has a king-size bed with a private bath. The sitting room can accommodate a third person in a pull-out bed. Continental breakfast is served in the cottage. Children welcome. No smoking allowed.

HAMDEN

Nutmeg Bed and Breakfast Agency

P.O. Box 1117, West Hartford, 06107-1117
(203) 236-6698; (800) 727-7542
FAX (203) 232-7680

207. A pool and lovely deck add to the enjoyment of this comfortable home. Right outside New Haven, this house has one guest room with shared bath, perfect for the single traveler. Continental breakfast. No smoking.

IVORYTON

The Copper Beech Inn

46 Main Street, 06442
(203) 767-0330

Gracious gardens and rustic woodlands set the stage for this handsome inn. A gallery offers antique Oriental porcelain, and the dining room is noted for fine country French cuisine. Breakfast includes fresh fruit,

The Copper Beech Inn

homemade pastries, breads, cereal, juice, tea, and coffee. Beautiful countryside, quaint villages, museums, antique shops, theater, and water sports distinguish the area. Two-night minimum stay for weekends and holidays. Closed Mondays, Christmas, and New Year's Day. Children over eight welcome.

Hosts: Eldon and Sally Senner
Rooms: 13 (PB) $117.60-184.80
Continental Breakfast
Credit Cards: A, B, C, E
Notes: 2, 4, 5, 7, 9, 10, 11, 12

KENT

Covered Bridge

P.O. Box 447, Norfolk, 06058
(203) 542-5944

1K. Charming 18th-century house is one of the oldest in Kent, and is a splendid example of Federal architecture and decor. Living room with fireplace is available for guests; upstairs suite has an ornately carved four-poster canopied bed and private bath. Continental breakfast. $85-120.

2K. This 1860 Colonial set on two acres is close to Kent Falls. The owner, who also has an antique shop on the grounds, has decorated all of the rooms with period furniture. There is a living room and a den with a fireplace and TV. Continental breakfast. Three guest rooms with shared and private baths. $85-95.

7 No smoking; 8 Children welcome; 9 Social drinking allowed; 10 Tennis nearby; 11 Swimming nearby; 12 Golf nearby; 13 Skiing nearby; 14 May be booked through a travel agent.

Nutmeg Bed and Breakfast Agency

P.O. Box 1117, West Hartford, 06107-1117
(203) 236-6698; (800) 727-7542
FAX (203) 232-7680

306. This 1790s farmhouse is in the middle of 200 acres of fields and woods. The furnishings are a blend of antique and contemporary. The two first-floor rooms, one double and one queen-size, have private baths. The two rooms on the second floor share a bath—one is a double, the other a single. Continental breakfast; children over three welcome. Several cats in residence.

322. Friendliness awaits guests at this 1860s Colonial bed and breakfast home. Unwind in the romantic Rose Stenciled Room with beamed ceiling or the Country Blue Room with carved Victorian headboard, both with private baths. There is an adjacent cottage with a sitting area, a queen-size room, a private bath, and kitchen. Relax by the fireplace in the cozy den or walk the lovely grounds and view St. John's Ledges. After a Continental breakfast in the charming dining room, visit the antique shop. Near hiking, skiing, canoeing, museums, and fine restaurants. Children over 12 welcome. No smoking.

303. Enjoy the fall foliage in this lovely Colonial, circa 1790. Guests are offered a suite that has a kitchen, living room, private bath, and air conditioning. There is a pull-out bed in the suite's sitting room for extra family members. Two additional guest rooms share a bath. One has a king-size bed, one has a single bed. Both have ceiling fans. Continental breakfast served in the guest's room. Children welcome. No smoking. Dogs and cat on premises.

LAKEVILLE

Covered Bridge

P.O. Box 447, Norfolk, 06058
(203) 542-5944

1LCT. Victorian home within walking distance of the center offers a living room with a fireplace and a music room with a piano. A full breakfast is served in the dining room. There are four guest rooms, all with antique bed and two with private baths. $85-110.

Nutmeg Bed and Breakfast Agency

P.O. Box 1117, West Hartford, 06107-1117
(203) 236-6698; (800) 727-7542
FAX (203) 232-7680

328. Set along a lovely lake, this 15-room turn-of-the-century bed and breakfast is filled with antiques and charm. Guests may choose guest rooms with a sleigh or a spool bed, each with its own private bath. After a sumptuous Continental breakfast, enjoy some of the area's many attractions: Lime Rock Park, Music Mountain, and Mohawk Ski Area. Children over eight are welcome. No smoking.

331. Dutch Colonial home on eight scenic acres overlooks banks of a trout stream. One room with king-size or twin beds, one with single, one with double. All have shared baths. A twin-bedded room can have private bath. Breakfast is served on enclosed porch overlooking waterfall. Five minutes to Lime Rock, two miles to Salisbury or Hotchkiss Schools. Continental breakfast. Children one and over welcome. No smoking allowed. Cats in residence.

LITCHFIELD

Covered Bridge

P.O. Box 447, Norfolk, 06058
(203) 542-5944

Pre-Revolutionary War Colonial home is set on more than 200 acres. In summer, guests can enjoy a full breakfast overlooking a wooded brook. There are three guest rooms: one on the first floor with a queen-

NOTES: Credit cards accepted: A MasterCard; B Visa; C American Express; D Discover; E Diners Club; F Other; 2 Personal checks accepted; 3 Lunch available; 4 Dinner available; 5 Open all year; 6 Pets welcome;

size bed and private bath, and two king-size bedrooms on the second floor with a bath between the rooms. $95.

Nutmeg Bed and Breakfast Agency

P.O. Box 1117, West Hartford, 06107-1117
(203) 236-6698; (800) 727-7542
FAX (203) 232-7680

333. On a quiet country road outside the historic village of Litchfield, this bed and breakfast features one guest room with queen-size bed and private bath. The house is a pre-Revolutionary Colonial, shaded by century-old sugar maples. Horses and sheep graze in the pasture. Guests may enjoy a delicious full breakfast on the stone terrace or the covered porch in warm weather where they can overlook a view of the wooded brook. Children over 12 are welcome.

Tollgate Hill Inn and Restaurant

Route 202 and Tollgate Road, P.O. Box 1339,
   06759
(203) 567-4545; FAX (203) 567-8397

This 1745 inn is listed on the National Register of Historic Places and has 20 guest rooms. Air-conditioned. Private baths. Direct dial telephones. Cable TV. Half of the rooms have wood-burning fireplaces. Excellent restaurant on premises. Seasonal and corporate rates are available upon request.

Host: Frederick J. Zivic
Rooms: 20 (PB) $110-175
Continental Breakfast
Credit Cards: None
Notes: 2, 3, 4, 5, 6, 8, 9, 10, 11, 12, 13, 14

LYME

Bed and Breakfast, Ltd.

P.O. Box 216, New Haven, 06513
(203) 469-3260

13. Country house, circa 1760, was once owned by Broadway actor. Georgian entry, stone terraces, reflecting pool. Three elegant double rooms with private baths. Cozy library for reading and relaxing. Afternoon tea. $85-110.

Covered Bridge

P.O. Box 447, Norfolk, 06058
(203) 542-5944

1LY. A 1765 Colonial set on four acres is surrounded by stone walls, gardens, and terraces. Relax in the living room with fireplace and the original beehive oven or choose a book from the library. Full breakfast served. Four guest rooms with private bath. $95-110.

2LY. European charm and antiques make this Colonial set on 14 acres a very special retreat. A full breakfast is served in the elegant dining room or in the sitting room that has a wood-burning stove and a lovely view of the grounds. Several pieces of furniture have been hand-painted by the hostess, reflecting her Swiss heritage. The three queen-bedded guest rooms, each with a private bath, have gorgeous handmade quilts. $95-110.

Nutmeg Bed and Breakfast Agency

P.O. Box 1117, West Hartford, 06107-1117
(203) 236-6698; (800) 727-7542
FAX (203) 232-7680

512. This new center-chimney Colonial is on several acres of woods and has its own walking trail and horseshoe court. Two guest rooms with private baths are accented by family pieces and European furnishings. Convenient to the Old Lyme Art Center, all the shoreline attractions, and many restaurants. Full breakfast served. No smoking allowed.

7 No smoking; 8 Children welcome; 9 Social drinking allowed; 10 Tennis nearby; 11 Swimming nearby;
12 Golf nearby; 13 Skiing nearby; 14 May be booked through a travel agent.

MADISON

Madison Beach Hotel

94 West Wharf Road, 06443
(203) 245-1404

Built in the early 1800s, the Madison Beach Hotel is nestled on a private beach on Long Island Sound, and it is distinctly Victorian in style and decor. Many rooms have private balconies overlooking the water. Antique oak bureaus, wainscoting, wicker, and rattan furniture, along with old-fashioned wallpaper, complete the Victorian feeling. The hotel's restaurant serves lunch and dinner. Closed January and February.

Hosts: Betty and Henry Cooney; Roben and Kathy
  Bagdasarian
Rooms: 35 (PB) $70-195
Continental Breakfast
Credit Cards: A, B, C, D, E
Notes: 2, 3, 4, 7, 8, 9, 10, 11, 14

Nutmeg Bed and Breakfast Agency

P.O. Box 1117, West Hartford, 06107-1117
(203) 236-6698; (800) 727-7542
FAX (203) 232-7680

520. Lovely center-chimney Colonial about 20-years-old, large living room for guests, lovely dining room, pool, comfortably large eat-in kitchen, fireplace in family room, pool, patio for breakfast on nice days; about five minutes from beach. Two second-floor guest rooms share bath; one has double-spool bed, wicker chaise, chest, large closet, shuttered windows overlooking pool; one has twin beds, bedroom chair, chest, large closet. Continental breakfast. No children. No smoking. No resident pets.

525. This lovely raised ranch is on a quiet street several blocks from the coastline and some very fine beaches. The private lower level has a queen-size bed, fireplace, several couches, a private bath, and TV/VCR. There is also a small single room for a third person. Full breakfast. Children are welcome. No smoking allowed.

MIDDLEBURY

Bed and Breakfast, Ltd.

P.O. Box 216, New Haven, 06513
(203) 469-3260

14. New England-style home is large and spacious. Bright and sunny. Living room for guests and formal dining room. Near great antique shops. Full breakfast. $65-75.

New Hampshire Bed and Breakfast

128 South Hoop Pole Road, Guilford, 06437
(203) 457-0042; (800) 582-0853

CT-1133. This gracious 1923 Colonial home is on lovely grounds, and lightly shaded by ancient oaks and maples. Guests enjoy a parlor with fireplace, and a formal dining room where a full, hearty breakfast is served. Four spacious guest rooms with shared or private baths are furnished with a flourish of English country or romantic decor. State parks, museums, theater, concerts, and historical sites are nearby. Golf, tennis, fishing, and hiking trails are also nearby. One resident cat. No smoking. No pets. $70-90.

Tucker Hill Inn

96 Tucker Hill Road, 06762
(203) 758-8334

Tucker Hill Inn is a large center hall Colonial just down from the village green in Middlebury. It was built around 1920 and was a restaurant and catering house for almost 40 years. The period rooms are spacious. Nearby are antiques, country drives, music and theater, golf, tennis, water sports, fishing, hiking, and cross-country skiing. Closed Christmas Day.

Hosts: Richard and Susan Cabelenski
Rooms: 4 (2 PB; 2 SB) $60-100

Full Breakfast
Credit Cards: A, B, C
Notes: 2, 7, 8, 9, 10, 11, 12, 14

MIDDLETOWN

Bed and Breakfast, Ltd.
P.O. Box 216, New Haven, 06513
(203) 469-3260

15. White Colonial, circa 1922, is loaded with charm and panache. Furnished mostly with antiques. Three lovely double rooms with ceiling fans. Deck with barbecue. Tennis two blocks away. Five minutes to Wesleyan University. $45-55.

MYSTIC

Bed and Breakfast, Ltd.
P.O. Box 216, New Haven, 06513
(203) 469-3260

16. A 1790s era home surrounded by lush greenery and flower gardens has fireplace in living room, dining room, and TV room. Four rooms and one suite. Warm hospitality. One and one-half miles to downtown Mystic. $85-125.

Comolli's House
36 Bruggeman Place, 06355
(203) 536-8723

Ideal for vacationers touring historic Mystic or the business person who desires a homey respite while traveling. This immaculate home, on a quiet hill overlooking the Mystic Seaport complex, is convenient to Olde Mistick Village and the aquarium. Sightseeing, sporting activities, shopping, and restaurant information is provided by the hosts. Off-season rates are available.

Host: Dorothy M. Comolli
Rooms: 2 (PB) $65-95
Continental Breakfast
Credit Cards: F
Notes: 5, 7

Covered Bridge
P.O. Box 447, Norfolk, 06058
(203) 542-5944

1MYCT. This restored 150-year-old Victorian farmhouse is on two acres of lovely, landscaped grounds with old stone walls, fruit trees, and an outdoor eating area for the enjoyment of guests. A full breakfast is served in the dining room and a Scottish tea is served in the afternoon. There are six guest rooms, one with fireplace and all with private baths.$85-120.

2MYCT. An 1840s Greek Revival just outside the center of town is beautifully decorated with antiques and offers four exquisitely decorated guest rooms: one with a fireplace and another with a Jacuzzi. A delicious full breakfast is served in the dining room. $95-145.

Nutmeg Bed and Breakfast Agency
P.O. Box 1117, West Hartford, 06107-1117
(203) 236-6698; (800) 727-7542
FAX (203) 232-7680

513. Built in 1837, this large farmhouse is surrounded by fruit trees and strawberry beds. Five guest rooms have private baths; two have fireplaces. There is also a spacious dining room and a warm family room. The home-cooked breakfast with specialty muffins is amply satisfying. Full breakfast. Children welcome. Cat and dog in residence. No smoking.

Steamboat Inn
73 Steamboat Wharf, 06355
(203) 536-8300; (800) 364-6100

On the river, this romantic and luxurious inn is quiet and elegant in the heart of downtown Mystic. Ten beautiful rooms, all with antique and custom furnishings, TV, telephones, and individually controlled heat

7 No smoking; 8 Children welcome; 9 Social drinking allowed; 10 Tennis nearby; 11 Swimming nearby; 12 Golf nearby; 13 Skiing nearby; 14 May be booked through a travel agent.

and air conditioning. Six rooms feature wood-burning fireplaces, along with four dock-level semi-suites with double whirlpools. A Continental breakfast is included, featuring pastries and muffins daily. Many shops, restaurants, and boats within walking distance.

Host: Diana Stadtmiller
Rooms: 10 (PB) $95-250
Continental Breakfast
Credit Cards: A, B, C
Notes: 2, 5, 7, 8, 10, 11, 12, 14

NEW HAVEN

Bed and Breakfast, Ltd.

P.O. Box 216, 06513
(203) 469-3260

Bed and Breakfast, Ltd. offers over 125 listings of bed and breakfasts throughout Connecticut from elegantly simple to simply elegant. The emphasis is on variety of accommodations, gracious hospitality, and very affordable rates. In operation for the 14th year, the service features Victorian, Federal, Greek Revival, Tudor, Italianate, and comtemporary style homes in every price range. Deluxe and suite rates are slightly higher. Children are welcome at some establishments.

Host: Jack Argenio
Rooms: 125 plus (80 PB; 45 SB) $55-95
Full and Continental Breakfasts
Credit Cards: A, B, F
Notes: 2, 5, 7, 9, 10, 11, 12, 13

Bed and Breakfast, Ltd.

P.O. Box 216, 06513
(203) 469-3260

17. Charming 1912 Colonial in lovely, safe residential neighborhood is spacious and beautifully furnished. Color TV in room. Many family heirlooms. $50-75.

18. Elegant English Tudor has great sunroom, screened porch, and warm, cozy, country furnishings. The three Laura Ash-ley-styled rooms have both private and shared baths. $65-75.

19. Historic Italianate is on the National Register of Historic Places and house tours. Antique filled showplace. Four room suite with kitchen, breakfast room, living room, and Victorian bedroom. Private entrance. Color TV, stereo, and telephone. Five minutes to Yale. $95-125.

New Hampshire Bed and Breakfast

128 South Hoop Pole Road, Guilford, 06437
(203) 457-0042; (800) 582-0853

CT-1130. Two miles from Yale University and in a beautiful residential neighborhood of the Westville section of New Haven sits this majestic English Tudor bed and breakfast home. Choose from three guest rooms, a living room, den, porch, and gardens to relax in. Activities at Yale Bowl, the Volvo tennis court, summer concert center, Schubert Theatre, art and history museums, Little Italy, and numerous fine restaurants and shops are all minutes away. Full breakfast. No smoking. $65.

Nutmeg Bed and Breakfast Agency

P.O. Box 1117, West Hartford, 06107-1117
(203) 236-6698; (800) 727-7542
FAX (203) 232-7680

203. The home, near Yale, was built in 1920 and has beamed ceilings. The host has traveled extensively and many of the furnishings are from far-off lands. Two guest rooms with a shared bath on each floor. Continental breakfast. Children welcome. No smoking.

205. This turn-of-the-century, grand, gracious large home is in a special residential area. Formal dining room and lovely gardens await visitors. The third floor has a

NOTES: Credit cards accepted: A MasterCard; B Visa; C American Express; D Discover; E Diners Club; F Other; 2 Personal checks accepted; 3 Lunch available; 4 Dinner available; 5 Open all year; 6 Pets welcome;

room with an antique brass queen-size bed with a walk-through full bath shared with a room with two double beds. On the second floor, one room has twin beds with a full private bath and may be used with a room with a single bed. Also there is a lovely suite with a queen-size bed and private bath with a tub. The shower is down the hall. First and second floors are air-conditioned and the third floor has a large fan. Continental breakfast. Children welcome. No smoking.

208. Catch a game at the Yale Bowl or the bus downtown from this bed and breakfast in the Westville section. This English Tudor has guest rooms with double beds and shared bath. Guests help themselves to Continental breakfast. Children welcome. Smoking restricted. Dog in residence.

210. Walk to Yale from this gracious Victorian home set in the residential section of New Haven. A newly decorated third-floor suite consists of a bedroom with a large private bath and a smaller bedroom. A guest room is also available on the second floor. Continental breakfast. Children welcome. Cats in residence.

215. This home near Yale is a 1910 Dutch Colonial with a private garden and deck. Two guest rooms are on the second floor. One has a double bed and the other has twin beds; both share a bath. Baby equipment available. The house is just over one block from the bus. Continental breakfast; infants welcome. No smoking allowed. Dog in residence.

NEW MILFORD

Covered Bridge

P.O. Box 447, Norfolk, 06058
(203) 542-5944

1NM. Vista for viewing, woods for walking, hills for cross-country skiing, streams

for fishing, flower gardens, and a pool are some of the attractions of this sprawling estate three miles outside of town. First-floor guest room with private bath and an upstairs guest room. $60-95.

Nutmeg Bed and Breakfast Agency

P.O. Box 1117, West Hartford, 06107-1117
(203) 236-6698; (800) 727-7542
FAX (203) 232-7680

A charming home built with wood from a reverse wood tobacco barn, this bed and breakfast is delightfully landscaped with a pool. First floor room with separate entrance to deck has twins or king-size bed and private bath. Second floor room has twin beds and shared bath. One small bedroom on second floor is suitable for a child. Continental breakfast includes home-grown berries, homemade jams, popovers, and muffins prepared by a former chef. Children welcome. Smoking in designated area only. Dog in residence.

NORFOLK

Covered Bridge

P.O. Box 44, 06058
(203) 542-5944

2N. Romantic 1880 Victorian on 11 acres of woods, gardens, and a brook is just steps from the village green. A full breakfast is served on one one of the lovely porches, in the dining room, or in one of the four enchanting guest rooms. All have private baths, two with Jacuzzis. $110-140.

Greenwoods Gate Bed and Breakfast Inn

105 Greenwoods Road East, 06058
(203) 542-5439

Warm hospitality greets guests in this beautifully restored 1797 Colonial home. Small and elegant with four exquisitely appointed guest suites, each has private bath and one has a Jacuzzi. Fine antiques, fireplaces, and sumptuous breakfasts indulge guests. *Yankee* magazine calls this "New England's most romantic Bed and Breakfast." *Country Inns Bed and Breakfast* magazine calls it "A Connecticut Jewel." Join in on the new Deanne Raymond renowned romantic cooking classes; call for details. Afternoon tea; early evening refreshments served. Children over 12 welcome.

Hosts: George and Marian Schumaker
Suites: 4 (PB) $170-225
Full Breakfast
Credit Cards: None
Notes: 2, 5, 7, 9, 10, 11, 12, 13, 14

Manor House

Maple Avenue, P.O. Box 447, 06058
(203) 542-5690

Victorian elegance awaits guests at this historic Tudor/Bavarian estate. Antique decorated guest rooms; several with fireplaces, canopies, balconies, a two-person Jacuzzi, and a two-person soaking tub offer a romantic retreat. Enjoy a sumptuous breakfast in the Tiffany-windowed dining rooms or treat yourself to breakfast in bed. Designated Connecticut's Most Romantic Hideaway and included in *Fifty Best Bed and Breakfast's in the USA*. Children over 12 welcome.

Hosts: Hank and Diane Tremblay
Rooms: 9 (PB) $95-190
Full Breakfast
Credit Cards: A, B, C, D
Notes: 2, 5, 7, 9, 10, 11, 12, 13, 14

Manor House

Mountain View Inn

Mountain View Inn

67 Litchfield Road, Route 272, 06058-0467
(203) 542-5595

A lovingly restored 1875 Victorian country inn in timeless Norfolk. Norfolk is in the Northwestern corner of Connecticut with its village green, bell towers, and postcard landscapes. Seven antique-filled guest rooms offer an intimate setting for romantic weekends. A full, hearty American breakfast is offered daily. Candlelight fireside or open-air dining is available on weekends. Private facilities for weddings and parties. Children over ten welcome.

Host: Michele Sloane
Rooms: 7 (6 PB; 1 SB) $65-125
Full Breakfast
Credit Cards: A, B, D
Notes: 2, 5, 9, 10, 11, 12, 13, 14

Nutmeg Bed and Breakfast Agency

P.O. Box 1117, West Hartford, 06107-1117
(203) 236-6698; (800) 727-7542
FAX (203) 232-7680

317. Lovingly restored Victorian has common room with original Tiffany windows, grand foyer, and huge fieldstone fireplace. Eight guest rooms with double, queen- or king-size beds and private baths. Full breakfast. Children over 12. Smoking in designated area only. One cat in residence.

NOTES: Credit cards accepted: A MasterCard; B Visa; C American Express; D Discover; E Diners Club; F Other; 2 Personal checks accepted; 3 Lunch available; 4 Dinner available; 5 Open all year; 6 Pets welcome;

336. This 1898 house on main street of town features handmade rugs and comfortable furnishings. Opposite Norfolk Chamber Music Festival and near three state parks for hiking and cross-country skiing. Four guest rooms share two full baths. Full breakfast. Children welcome. No smoking. Cat in residence.

Weaver's House

58 Greenwoods Road West, 06058
(203) 542-5108; (800) 283-1551

Turn-of-the-century home on Main Street overlooks the estate of the Norfolk Chamber Music Festival. Host couple offers simple hospitality. Guest rooms are enhanced with handwoven curtains and rag rugs made by the hostess. Full breakfast features home baking and good coffee. Tanglewood is nearby, Music Mountain, Lime Rock Park, skiing, antiquing, swimming, boating, fine dining, and more. German spoken.

Hosts: Arnold and Judy Tsukroff
Rooms: 4 (SB) $43-48
Full Breakfast
Credit Cards: A, B, C
Notes: 2, 5, 7, 9, 11, 13, 14

NORTH GRANBY

Nutmeg Bed and Breakfast Agency

P.O. Box 1117, West Hartford, 06107-1117
(203) 236-6698; (800) 727-7542
FAX (203) 232-7680

401. A contemporary home on five acres sits near a three-quarter-acre pond. There are many hiking trails, and three bridges span the stream. A guest suite has a bedroom with a queen-size bed, sitting area, private bath with sauna, wood-burning stove, and a deck. The other room has a double Hide-a-Bed and private bath. Continental breakfast. Children welcome. Cat in residence.

NORTH HAVEN

Nutmeg Bed and Breakfast Agency

P.O. Box 1117, West Hartford, 06107-1117
(203) 236-6698; (800) 727-7542
FAX (203) 232-7680

202. This 50-year-old English Tudor home is ten minutes out of the city of New Haven and one block from public transportation. There are three second floor guest rooms. One has a double waterbed, one has a single bed, and the third room has twin beds. All rooms share a half-bath on that floor with a full bath on the first floor. Full breakfast. Children welcome. No smoking.

NORTH STONINGTON

Bed and Breakfast, Ltd.

P.O. Box 216, New Haven, 06513
(203) 469-3260

20. An 1861 renovated Victorian home has very formal American and English antiques—all for sale. An English breakfast is served on the covered porch. Patio for guests' use. TV. Fresh flowers in season. Sherry. Ample parking. $95-125.

Covered Bridge

P.O. Box 447, Norfolk, 06058
(203) 542-5944

1NS. Two 1861 and 1820 Victorian houses are linked by a courtyard and set in a charming, historic seacoast town close to Mystic. The hosts furnished their home in the Georgian manner with formal antique furniture and accessories, many of which are offered for sale. The four guest rooms in the 1861 house have four-poster canopied beds. A full English breakfast is served. $90-185.

7 No smoking; 8 Children welcome; 9 Social drinking allowed; 10 Tennis nearby; 11 Swimming nearby; 12 Golf nearby; 13 Skiing nearby; 14 May be booked through a travel agent.

Nutmeg Bed and Breakfast Agency

P.O. Box 1117, West Hartford, 06107-1117
(203) 236-6698; (800) 727-7542
FAX (203) 232-7680

506. This beautiful Victorian, built in 1861, has a covered porch and lovely flower and herb gardens. The rooms are beautifully furnished, and a gourmet breakfast is served in the elegant dining room with silver and china. There are four guest rooms; two with private baths, and some with four-poster canopied beds. Mystic Seaport just ten minutes away; Rhode Island beaches are close by, as are Stonington Village and local vineyards. Full breakfast served. No smoking.

511. A 1742 Colonial home on 150-acre horse farm has beautiful pasture views of southeast Connecticut. Enjoy Mystic and Foxwoods Casino. Two guest rooms have queen-size beds and the third room has a king-size or twin beds. All have private baths. Full breakfast. Children welcome. No smoking. Dogs and horses on premises.

OLD GREENWICH

Nutmeg Bed and Breakfast Agency

P.O. Box 1117, West Hartford, 06107-1117
(203) 236-6698; (800) 727-7542
FAX (203) 232-7680

120. On Long Meadow Creek, an open, airy beach house with a dock on the tidal inlet off Greenwich Cove is within walking distance to the village and train to New York City, and about a mile off I-95. First floor room with queen-size sofa bed (open when guests arrive), wicker sofa, TV, private bath with shower. Full breakfast. Ask about children. No smoking. Resident cats.

Old Lyme Inn

OLD LYME

Old Lyme Inn

85 Lyme Street, P.O. Box 787, 06371
(860) 434-2600; (800) 434-5352
FAX (860) 434-5352

Outside, wildflowers bloom all summer; inside, fireplaces burn all winter, beckoning guests to enjoy the romance and charm of this 13-room Victorian country inn with an award-winning, three-star *New York Times* dining room. Within easy reach of the state's attractions, it is tucked away in an old New England art colony. Closed first two weeks in January. Nonsmoking rooms available.

Host: Diana Field Atwood
Manager: Debbie Capone
Rooms: 13 (PB) $99-158
Continental Breakfast
Credit Cards: A, B, C, D, E
Notes: 2, 3, 4, 6, 8, 9, 10, 11, 12, 14

OLD MYSTIC

Covered Bridge

P.O. Box 447, Norfolk, 06058
(203) 542-5944

1OMCT. This 1800s Colonial village setting offers a quiet retreat only minutes from the center of Mystic. There is a pleasant living room with a fireplace and a large dining room where a full breakfast is served. There are four guest rooms in the main house, three with fireplaces, and four guest rooms in the carriage house, two with whirlpool tubs. All rooms have queen-size beds and private baths. $98-135.

NOTES: Credit cards accepted: A MasterCard; B Visa; C American Express; D Discover; E Diners Club; F Other; 2 Personal checks accepted; 3 Lunch available; 4 Dinner available; 5 Open all year; 6 Pets welcome;

The Old Mystic Inn

52 Main Street, P.O. Box 634, 06372
(203) 572-9422

Nestled at the head of the Mystic River this
1794 Colonial provides warmth, comfort,
and genuine hospitality. Enjoy the lawns
and gardens in summer; warm inviting fireplaces in winter. Guests choose from eight
rooms in the inn or carriage house. All have
queen-size beds, private baths, air conditioning, and sitting areas. Rooms vary with
choice of canopied beds, whirlpool tubs, or
fireplaces. A full country breakfast is served
each morning by candlelight in the sunny
breakfast room. An international community of guests enjoy complimentary wine
and cheese Saturday evenings. A pleasant,
memorable experience for guests of all
ages.

Hosts: Mary and Peter Knight
Rooms: 8 (PB) $95-135
Full Breakfast
Credit Cards: A, B, C
Notes: 2, 5, 7, 8, 10, 11, 12, 14

Deacon Timothy Pratt

fee, tea, and snacks always available. Walk
to shops, restaurants, movie theaters, town
green activities, Hart House museum, and
Saybrook Point at the mouth of Connecticut
River. Wonderful area for walking, biking,
boating, beaches.

Hosts: Dale and Shelley Nobile
Rooms: 2 (PB) $75-90
Full Breakfast
Credit Cards: None
Notes: 2, 5, 7, 8, 9, 10, 11, 12, 13

ORANGE

Bed and Breakfast, Ltd.

P.O. Box 216, New Haven, 06513
(203) 469-3260

21. A 1725 white Colonial on a ten-acre
working farm is furnished mostly with
antiques, three rooms with glorious decors.
Near Yale. Great breakfast. Beach pass.
$65-75.

The Old Mystic Inn

OLD SAYBROOK

Deacon Timothy Pratt Bed and Breakfast

325 Main Street, 06475
(203) 395-1229

Step back in time and enjoy the splendor of
yesteryear in this circa 1746 center-chimney
Colonial in the heart of the historic district.
Guest rooms are romantically furnished in
period style with private baths and fireplaces. Full country breakfast, gourmet cof-

Nutmeg Bed and Breakfast Agency

P.O. Box 1117, West Hartford, 06107-1117
(203) 236-6698; (800) 727-7542
FAX (203) 232-7680

206. This bright Colonial farmhouse was
built in 1725 and has been in the same family for 11 generations. It remains a working
dairy farm and there is always fresh milk.
There are two second floor guest rooms
which share a bath. One room has a double

7 No smoking; 8 Children welcome; 9 Social drinking allowed; 10 Tennis nearby; 11 Swimming nearby;
12 Golf nearby; 13 Skiing nearby; 14 May be booked through a travel agent.

bed, the other twin beds. Continental breakfast. Children welcome. No smoking. Dog, cows, and horses on premises.

French Renaissance House

PLAINFIELD

French Renaissance House

550 Norwich Road, 06374
(203) 564-3277

This lovely historic home, built in 1871 by a wealthy Victorian gentleman, is one of the finest examples of French Renaissance Second Empire architecture in Connecticut. It is near Plainfield Greyhound Park, within reasonable driving distance of Mystic Seaport, Hartford, Providence, Newport, and Sturbridge Village, Massachusetts. Near Foxwood Indian Casino. Winter rates are available.

Host: Lucile Melber
Rooms: 4 (1 PB; 3 S2B) $55
Full Breakfast
Credit Cards: A, B, C, E
Notes: 2, 5, 7, 8, 9, 10, 11, 12

PLANTSVILLE

Bed and Breakfast, Ltd.

P.O. Box 216, New Haven, 06513
(203) 469-3260

22. A 1730 red Colonial on one acre has 12 rooms, antiques, and collectible furnishings. Two rooms done with flair and elegance.

Large fireplace. In-ground pool. Several decks, picnic grill, and complimentary cordials. $65-75.

Nutmeg Bed and Breakfast Agency

P.O. Box 1117, West Hartford, 06107-1117
(203) 236-6698; (800) 727-7542
FAX (203) 232-7680

465. This 11-room central-chimney Colonial circa 1740 is on a beautifully landscaped acre with a pool and surrounded by centuries-old maple trees. There are four fireplaces and a Dutch oven in the great room. One guest room has a king-size bed and a private bath; another has queen-size bed, private bath, and working fireplace. Both rooms are air-conditioned. Full breakfast is served. Children are allowed; smoking is restricted; cat and dog on the premises.

POMFRET

Covered Bridge

P.O. Box 447, Norfolk, 06058
(203) 542-5944

Set on more than six acres, this 18-room Victorian cottage offers a very secluded country getaway. All of the common rooms and guest rooms are exquisitely decorated with Oriental rugs and antiques. There is a large living room with a fireplace and a very elegant dining room. There are two guest rooms with private baths and a two-bedroom suite with a bath. Several rooms also have fireplaces. A full breakfast and afternoon tea are served. $75-110.

POMFRET CENTER

Nutmeg Bed and Breakfast Agency

P.O. Box 1117, West Hartford, 06107-1117
(203) 236-6698; (800) 727-7542
FAX (203) 232-7680

NOTES: Credit cards accepted: A MasterCard; B Visa; C American Express; D Discover; E Diners Club; F Other; 2 Personal checks accepted; 3 Lunch available; 4 Dinner available; 5 Open all year; 6 Pets welcome;

413. 1730 Cape secluded in middle of 23 acres has ideal country setting with birds galore and abundant wildlife. Two guest rooms with double beds and antique furnishings share a bath. Convenient to Pomfret and Rectory Schools. Full breakfast. Children welcome. No smoking. One dog and two cats on premises.

421. This Victorian sits on six acres with flower and vegetable gardens. The formal dining room and sitting room have fireplaces. There are two queen-size rooms with private baths, and a twin- and queen-size room with a shared bath. Full breakfast. No smoking. Children welcome. Dog in residence.

PUTNAM

The Felshaw Tavern

Five Mile River Road, 06260
(203) 928-3467

Built as a tavern in 1742, this noble white center-chimney Colonial served the Revolutionary militiamen, notably Israel Putnam of Bunker Hill fame. In 1982, its present owners opened it as a bed and breakfast. Convenient to Boston, Hartford, Providence, and Worcester, it is three and one-half hours from New York. Two guest rooms furnished in antiques offer private baths and working fireplaces. Quiet rural setting on three acres.

Hosts: Herb and Terry Kinsman
Rooms: 2 (PB) $80
Full Breakfast
Credit Cards: F
Notes: 2, 5, 6, 7, 8, 9, 11, 12, 14

Nutmeg Bed and Breakfast Agency

P.O. Box 1117, West Hartford, 06107-1117
(203) 236-6698; (800) 727-7542
FAX (203) 232-7680

424. A 1742 two-story tavern has an oak-paneled den and antique furnishings in the guest rooms. Each room has a private bath, working fireplace, and queen-size bed. There is a smaller room with a double bed for a child. Continental breakfast. Children welcome. No smoking.

QUINEBAUG

Captain Parker's Inn at Quinebaug

32 Walker Road, 06262
(203) 935-5219; (800) 707-7303

Captain Parker's Inn at Quinebaug is a new bed and breakfast in the quiet northeastern corner of Connecticut. The home features beautiful varied hardwoods throughout. Although the ocean is about an hour away, the decor portrays a nautical theme. This fine house with Victorian flair and an elegant atmosphere lends itself to romantic getaways and small weddings. Each guest room features a different hardwood flooring and trim, and most have a bathroom ensuite. The more-than-ample common areas include a library with a wood stove, a large foyer with a baby grand piano, a relaxing entertainment room, a formal dining room with a fireplace, and a pretty, hospitable kitchen. No smoking permitted inside.

Host: David J. Parker
Rooms: 6 (PB)
Full Breakfast

RIDGEFIELD

Nutmeg Bed and Breakfast Agency

P.O. Box 1117, West Hartford, 06107-1117
(203) 236-6698; (800) 727-7542
FAX (203) 232-7680

304. Originally a private boys' school, this home sits on a hilltop overlooking five pastoral acres with a magnificent view and is only one hour from Manhattan. It has a private suite with a large sitting room with fireplace, a king-size bed in the bedroom, and a private bath. French doors separate the main house from the guest suite. Continental breakfast. Smoking permitted.

West Lane Inn

22 West Lane, Route 35, 06877
(203) 438-7323

The West Lane Inn offers Colonial elegance in overnight accommodations. Special attention is paid to detail and the individual. Also close to shopping, museums, and points of interest.

Host: M.M. Mayer
Rooms: 20 (PB) $120-165
Continental Breakfast
Credit Cards: A, B, C, E
Notes: 5, 8, 10, 11, 12, 13, 14

RIVERSIDE

Nutmeg Bed and Breakfast Agency

P.O. Box 1117, West Hartford, 06107-1117
(203) 236-6698; (800) 727-7542
FAX (203) 232-7680

105. These active hosts have decided to share this lovely country-style Cape home. Guest room has private bath. New York City is only one hour away. Full breakfast. Children welcome. No smoking.

RIVERTON

Nutmeg Bed and Breakfast Agency

P.O. Box 1117, West Hartford, 06107-1117
(203) 236-6698; (800) 727-7542
FAX (203) 232-7680

305. Close to Lime Rock Park and many of the private schools, this log home is secluded on five acres. Superb place for

cross-country skiing, hiking, and stream fishing. The guest rooms have private baths and one room has a queen-size bed; the other has a king-size bed. The former innkeepers will also prepare a hearty dinner for overnight guests with prior arrangements. Children welcome. Full breakfast is served. Smoking in designated area. Cat in residence.

ROXBURY

Nutmeg Bed and Breakfast Agency

P.O. Box 1117, West Hartford, 06107-1117
(203) 236-6698; (800) 727-7542
FAX (203) 232-7680

301. The main house was built in 1970. There is a private guest wing with its own entrance. The guest wing is one large room with a queen-size canopied water bed with a feather mattress with a sitting area on the backside of the room. The sitting area has a double pull-out bed to accommodate children. Guests may use the main house to relax in front of the wood-burning stove. Full breakfast. Children welcome. No smoking. Pets on premises.

SALEM

New Hampshire Bed and Breakfast

128 South Hoop Pole Road, Guilford, 06437
(203) 457-0042; (800) 582-0853

CT-1100. This 200-year-old central chimney Colonial sits on a hilltop with views of surrounding pastures, stone walls, and gardens. Enjoy the farm setting complete with horses and chickens. Six guest rooms, private or shared baths, and sitting rooms with fireplaces are available. Hiking and biking abound. Mystic, Norwich, Ledyard, the coast, and the Cillete Castle are all nearby. No smoking allowed. No pets. Children over 12 are welcome. $65-95.

NOTES: Credit cards accepted: A MasterCard; B Visa; C American Express; D Discover; E Diners Club; F Other; 2 Personal checks accepted; 3 Lunch available; 4 Dinner available; 5 Open all year; 6 Pets welcome;

Nutmeg Bed and Breakfast Agency

P.O. Box 1117, West Hartford, 06107-1117
(203) 236-6698; (800) 727-7542
FAX (203) 232-7680

524. A center chimney Colonial built over 200 years ago has a pastoral view. Close to Mystic Seaport, Foxwoods Casino, the Connecticut shoreline and Rhode Island beaches. Six guest rooms, one with private bath and fireplace. Continental breakfast. Children over 12 welcome. No smoking. Dogs, cats, and horses on premises.

SALISBURY

Covered Bridge

P.O. Box 447, Norfolk, 06058
(203) 542-5944

1S. This 1810 Colonial is set on two private, landscaped acres in the center of town. Large living room with a fireplace and a study with a TV for guests. A full breakfast is served. Two guest rooms. $95.

Nutmeg Bed and Breakfast Agency

P.O. Box 1117, West Hartford, 06107-1117
(203) 236-6698; (800) 727-7542
FAX (203) 232-7680

337. This 1813 Colonial is in the historic district of Salisbury, one of Connecticut's most charming villages. Two guest rooms with private baths. Breakfast in the dining room or on the stone terrace. Walk to fine restaurants, shops, and antiques. Convenient to Lime Rock. Children welcome. No smoking. Pets on premises.

SCOTLAND

Nutmeg Bed and Breakfast Agency

P.O. Box 1117, West Hartford, 06107-1117
(203) 236-6698; (800) 727-7542
FAX (203) 232-7680

454. A 1797 Colonial-style country inn with a large sitting room for guests, keeping room, and kitchen for breakfast. Also a TV room with fireplace, double bedroom, and queen-size bedroom with fireplace. Both share a bath. Full breakfast. Children over ten allowed. No smoking allowed. Cat on premises.

SHARON

Covered Bridge

P.O. Box 447, Norfolk, 06058
(203) 542-5944

1SH. Beautifully nestled in a secluded setting, this lovely contemporary home is decorated throughout with antiques. Guests are welcome to enjoy the large living room, sun porch, and deck. Within walking distance of the village green and the Sharon Playhouse. Reserve a suite or just ask for the bedroom. $85-125.

2SH. An 1890 Colonial on the main street in Sharon is set on beautifully landscaped grounds. There is a large living room and sun porch for guests. A large lake is nearby for swimming, and several areas for skiing in the winter. Four guest rooms with private baths; two with microwave and refrigerator. Full breakfast. $95-105.

SHERMAN

Barnes Hill Farm Bed and Breakfast

29 Route 37 East, 06784
(203) 354-4404; FAX (203) 350-6151

The Barnes Hill Farm, circa 1835, historic Colonial farmhouse, delights guests with the charm of the 1800s but with every convenience of today. All rooms are decorated and furnished with antiques and special country accents. There is plenty to do in all seasons. Available activities include both

---

7 No smoking; 8 Children welcome; 9 Social drinking allowed; 10 Tennis nearby; 11 Swimming nearby; 12 Golf nearby; 13 Skiing nearby; 14 May be booked through a travel agent.

downhill and cross-country skiing, antiquing, hiking, horseback riding, tennis, boating, fishing, and swimming. If guests are in the mood for a quiet relaxing visit, the scenery is spectacular and there are acres and acres of fields to walk. The outside Jacuzzi is open all year. All rooms have private baths, air conditioning, and swimming pool available in the summer.

Hosts: Richard and Sallee Johnson
Rooms: 4 (PB) $75-95
Full Breakfast
Credit Cards: A, B
Notes: 2, 5, 7, 8, 9, 10, 11, 12, 13

Covered Bridge

P.O. Box 447, Norfolk, 06058
(203) 542-5944

1SHR. Circa 1835, this restored bed and breakfast was a rest stop for travelers throughout the 1800s. There is a pleasant living room for guests' use and a Jacuzzi on the deck overlooking the secluded grounds. Acres of woods and fields for hiking or cross-country skiing. Three guest rooms have their own private baths and a two-bedroom suite has a bath. Full breakfast served. $85-95.

Nutmeg Bed and Breakfast Agency

P.O. Box 1117, West Hartford, 06107-1117
(203) 236-6698; (800) 727-7542
FAX (203) 232-7680

321. This superbly restored 1835 Colonial farmhouse has three air-conditioned guest rooms which are furnished with antiques and have private baths. A king-size and a twin bedroom share a bath. After a full country breakfast, guests are invited to enjoy the outdoor Jacuzzi, game room, or sitting room with TV. One mile from Candlewood Lake, boating, fishing, swimming, and cross-country skiing nearby. Children over ten are welcome. No smoking. Dog and cat in residence.

SIMSBURY

Merrywood Bed and Breakfast

100 Hartford Road (Route 185), 06070
(203) 651-1785; FAX (203) 651-8273

On five acres in the woods providing a quiet and private surrounding, guests can stroll the grounds, visit the greenhouse, or use the porch, living room with fireplace, and small library. The inn is a Colonial Revival with three large guest rooms. Two are single rooms and the third is a two-room suite with sitting room and personal sauna. They are furnished with period antiques and have either king- or queen-size beds, private baths, cable TV, VCR, telephone, and air conditioning. Dinner available for overnight guests only.

Hosts: Michael and Gerlinde Marti
Rooms: 3 (PB) $95-135
Full Breakfast
Credit Cards: A, B, C, D, E
Notes: 2, 5, 7, 10, 11, 12, 13, 14

Nutmeg Bed and Breakfast Agency

P.O. Box 1117, West Hartford, 06107-1117
(203) 236-6698; (800) 727-7542
FAX (203) 232-7680

425. Small inn listed on the National Register of Historic Places has rooms with private baths, TV, phone, and amenities. Full service dining room. Wedding and banquet facilities. Country Continental breakfast. Children welcome. Smoking allowed.

Simsbury 1820 House

731 Hopmeadow Street, 06070
(203) 658-7658

Elegant country inn and restaurant featuring 34 luxurious guest rooms with private baths, is antique-furnished with modern amenities of today. Highly acclaimed restaurant offers lunch, dinner, and Sunday brunch. Seasonal fireplaces and outdoor dining on scenic veranda. Country Continental breakfast served in dining room each morning. Seasonal discounts available.

Host: Wayne Bursey
Rooms: 34 (PB) $95-140
Suite: 1 (PB) $140
Continental Breakfast
Credit Cards: A, B, C, D, E, F
Notes: 2, 3, 4, 5, 8, 9, 10, 11, 12, 13, 14

SOUTHINGTON

Nutmeg Bed and Breakfast Agency

P.O. Box 1117, West Hartford, 06107-1117
(203) 236-6698; (800) 727-7542
FAX (203) 232-7680

461. A two-story Colonial-style farmhouse has a large wraparound pillared veranda, 70 acres of grounds with a fish pond, pine grove, and rolling hills. Traditional furnishings in two upstairs bedrooms, each with double beds and shared full bath at the end of the hall. Full Continental or low-calorie breakfast, also special diets are accommodated if necessary. Long term preferred. Children allowed.

STAMFORD

Nutmeg Bed and Breakfast Agency

P.O. Box 1117, West Hartford, 06107-1117
(203) 236-6698; (800) 727-7542
FAX (203) 232-7680

116. This Nantucket Colonial has a water view on a sandy beach. Breakfast is served on the sun porch. One guest room has built-in twin beds, while one has a single bed and both share a bath. The third room has a queen-size bed and private bath. Full breakfast; children welcome. No smoking.

117. This 1960s ranch-style inn has a cozy family room with fireplace, a country kitchen, and a screened porch. The first-floor bedroom trundle bed can be single or double. Private bath and TV. Continental breakfast. No children. No smoking allowed. One dog on premises.

STONINGTON

Covered Bridge

P.O. Box 44, Norfolk, 06058
(203) 542-5944

This 1890s home and cottage are set in historic village only a block from the harbor. The cottage has a sitting and dining area with a woodstove, four-poster queen-size bed, and its own terrace. $120

STRATFORD

Bed and Breakfast, Ltd.

P.O. Box 216, New Haven, 06513
(203) 469-3260

24. Fabulous Colonial farmhouse with barn has decorator furnishings throughout. Gorgeous wallpaper, fireplace in family room, and beautiful grounds. Full breakfast. Close to Westport and antique shops. Gregarious hosts. $85-95.

SUFFIELD

Nutmeg Bed and Breakfast Agency

P.O. Box 1117, West Hartford, 06107-1117
(203) 236-6698; (800) 727-7542
FAX (203) 232-7680

474. An 1825 Federal Colonial near the town green on Main Street is a five-minute walk to the grocery, library, pharmacy, movies, and restaurants. There is a choice of a bedroom with attached bath with tub and shower, double four-poster bed, chest,

7 No smoking; 8 Children welcome; 9 Social drinking allowed; 10 Tennis nearby; 11 Swimming nearby; 12 Golf nearby; 13 Skiing nearby; 14 May be booked through a travel agent.

easy chair, and a large built-in closet, or a bedroom not attached to bath with old Victorian double bed, princess dresser, easy chair, bookcase, two closets, and sink. Will rent either room but not both; guests have use of living room, dining room, kitchen, and yard. There is a TV with HBO in one room. It is ten minutes to Bradley; host will provide transportation to and from airport with advance notice. Long term only. No children. No smoking. No resident pets.

THOMPSON

Lord Thompson Manor

Route 200, P.O. Box 428, 06277
(203) 923-3886

Set on 62 acres, Lord Thompson Manor, once a private estate, offers eight guest rooms, four of which are luxury suites, each with an inviting fireplace and private bath. For romance, Lord Thompson Manor offers guests private candlelight dining, gourmet picnic basket dinners, and romantic candlelight bubble baths. Explore the grounds and gardens landscaped by the renowned Frederick Law Olmstead. For breakfast, enjoy fresh-squeezed orange juice, freshly ground coffee, fresh fruit, waffles, pancakes, and sausages.

Rooms: 8 (4 PB; 4 SB) $75-120
Full Breakfast
Credit Cards: A, B
Notes: 2, 3, 4, 5, 8, 9, 10, 11, 12, 13, 14

Nutmeg Bed and Breakfast Agency

P.O. Box 1117, West Hartford, 06107-1117
(203) 236-6698; (800) 727-7542
FAX (203) 232-7680

468. A new post-and-beam two-story home in a wooded area with lake frontage, three acres, a picnic and swimming area, is within walking distance to convenience store and antique furnishings. The inn offers cable TV, VCR, and telephone. One dou-

ble-size bedroom and one with twin beds share a bath and large sitting room, and each has a private entrance. Queen-size Hide-a-Bed in the sitting room. Roll aways and a refrigerator available to guests. Convenient to Sturbridge Village, Woodstock Fair, Thompson Raceway. Pets welcome. Full breakfast. Children welcome. No smoking. Resident dogs.

470. Lovely Cape-style house was built in 1780, fully modernized with "touch of Ireland" decor throughout. Completely separate guest quarters overlooking back patio have queen-size bed and private bath, TV, telephone; second upstairs studio has whirlpool tub in shared bath (this room perfect for children); third queen-size bed room has half-bath and shares Jacuzzi bath with second room if that room is booked. Charming sitting room and dining room for guests, but most prefer breakfast in the family dining room or the sun porch overlooking the back patio and gardens. Full breakfast served. Children ten and over welcome. No smoking.

TOLLAND

The Tolland Inn

63 Tolland Green, 06084-0717
(203) 872-0800

Built in 1800, the inn stands on Tolland's historic village green, less than one mile north of I-84 Exit 68. Seven guest rooms

The Tolland Inn

are decorated with antiques and furniture made by the host. Two suites have queen-size canopied beds, one with fireplace, one with kitchen and sitting room. The first floor room has a queen-size canopied bed, fireplace, and a sunken hot tub. Three beautiful common rooms and a fireplace complete the picture. Convenient to Brimfield Fair, Old Sturbridge, and the University of Connecticut.

Hosts: Susan and Stephen Beeching
Rooms: 7 (PB) $56-78.40
Suites: $78.40-134.40
Full Breakfast
Credit Cards: A, B, C, D, E
Notes: 2, 5, 7, 9, 10, 11, 12, 14

WASHINGTON

Covered Bridge
P.O. Box 447, Norfolk, 06058
(203) 542-5944

1WACT. A guest cottage overlooking rolling lawns, fields, woodlands, and a small pond has a sitting room, spacious bedroom, separate sleeping alcove, and private bath. Continental plus breakfast. $110-125.

WATERBURY

Covered Bridge
P.O. Box 447, Norfolk, 06058
(203) 542-5944

1WAT. An 1888 Victorian house on the National Register of Historic Places is set on an acre in a historic district. There are several common rooms, including an antique-decorated living room with a fireplace. All guest rooms are decorated with antiques. Full breakfast and high tea are served. $75-150.

WATERTOWN

The Clarks
97 Scott Avenue, 06795
(203) 274-4866

The Clarks is a 1939 Cape-style home three blocks from Taft Preparatory School and convenient for travelers on Routes 8 and 84. Two guest rooms, one with a double bed and one with twin beds, have ceiling fans. Guests are welcome to use the entire house, including porches, barbecue grill, and laundry facilities. The hosts are active in Lions Club, community, and church, and provide a warm family atmosphere. Closed February and March.

Hosts: Richard and Barbara Clark
Rooms: 2 (SB) $40-45
Continental Breakfast
Credit Cards: None
Notes: 7, 8, 9

WESTBROOK

Binder's Farm
593 Essex Road, 06498
(203) 399-6407

Since 1928, three generations of Binders have lived on and worked this land. Now the hosts offer their home to share with vacationers and travelers from all over the globe. The 1820 home was built by a sea captain at a time when everyone was a farmer. The hosts still grow corn and pumpkins. Have eggs from the farm, homemade jams and jellies, and fresh baked breads for breakfast. One mile from I-95; close to town beach and convenient to many local attractions. There is a fourth room available for families.

Hosts: Ed and Anna Binder
Rooms: 3 (PB) $95
Full Breakfast
Credit Cards: None
Notes: 2, 8, 9, 11

Talcott House Bed and Breakfast
161 Seaside Avenue, P.O. Box 1016, 06498
(203) 399-5020

The host invites guests to join her at Talcott House, a beautifully restored 1890 home on

7 No smoking; 8 Children welcome; 9 Social drinking allowed; 10 Tennis nearby; 11 Swimming nearby; 12 Golf nearby; 13 Skiing nearby; 14 May be booked through a travel agent.

Long Island Sound. Comfort is assured in any of the four spacious oceanfront suites, one with its own veranda. All have private baths, and each is decorated to reflect the warmth and tradition of the house. An efficiency apartment is also available. Cozy fireplaces encourage relaxation in the living room. Enjoy the adjacent beaches for a refreshing swim or a walk at sunset. Relax and enjoy the scenic water views from the spacious lawn. For boating enthusiasts, Pilots Point Marina is just a short half-mile walk away.

Host: Cathy
Rooms: 4 (PB) $125-135
Full Breakfast
Credit Cards: A, B
Notes: 2, 7, 9, 10, 11, 12

Welcome Inn Bed and Breakfast

433 Essex Road, 06498
(203) 399-2500

Originally a strawberry farm, the Welcome Inn was built around 1897 and retains its country charm. It is convenient to everything the Connecticut River Valley and seashore have to offer. There are three lovely guest rooms. The house and rooms are decorated with antiques, fine reproductions, lace, and family heirlooms. A complimentary full breakfast is served from 8:00 A.M. to 9:30 A.M. daily with delicious homemade goodies and special coffee. Relax in the parlor with a crackling fire, a glass of sherry and a good book, or in the garden (weather permitting). Hosts can assist guests with arranging restaurant reservations, tours, and other activities. Lunch and dinner are available through prior arrangements. Children over 11 are welcome.

Hosts: Alison and Robert Bambino
Rooms: 3 (SB) $85-110
Full Breakfast
Credit Cards: None
Notes: 2, 11, 12

WEST HARTFORD

Nutmeg Bed and Breakfast Agency

P.O. Box 1117, 06127-1117
(203) 236-6698; (800) 727-7542
FAX (203) 232-7680

405. Colonial-style home has large living room, formal dining room, and two guest rooms on second floor. One has queen-size bed, one has twins; both are nicely decorated. Queen room has private bath; twin has shared bath. Continental breakfast. Children welcome. No smoking.

441. The single-story home is furnished with a blend of modern, traditional, and antique. One guest room with TV has twin or king-size bed and private bath. Continental breakfast. Hungarian spoken. Children welcome. No smoking.

455. This center hall colonial has a year-round sunroom. On the bus line and within walking distance of the University of Connecticut, West Hartford branch, and St. Joseph's College. Small child in house. Second floor bedroom with double bed and bath shared with the family. Long term preferred. Continental breakfast. Children allowed. No smoking. No pets.

WESTPORT

Nutmeg Bed and Breakfast Agency

P.O. Box 1117, West Hartford, 06107-1117
(203) 236-6698; (800) 727-7542
FAX (203) 232-7680

104. Georgian Colonial with pool has second floor guest room with twins or king-size bed, wicker furnishings, private bath with shower. Convenient to railroad station. Full breakfast. Children welcome. No smoking. Dog in residence.

NOTES: Credit cards accepted: A MasterCard; B Visa; C American Express; D Discover; E Diners Club; F Other; 2 Personal checks accepted; 3 Lunch available; 4 Dinner available; 5 Open all year; 6 Pets welcome;

111. Breathtaking setting overlooking Long Island Sound, this home combines rural beauty with metropolitan sophistication. Guest wing is private with its own sitting room, fireplace, and entrance. Three guest rooms with private and shared bath. Enjoy the beach during summer. Continental breakfast. Children welcome. No smoking allowed. $60.

114. A large Colonial surrounded by many old trees on a hilly, wooded acre just outside of town. The original part of the house was built in 1740; guest quarters with separate entrance, bedroom with separate sitting room, double bed, a Hide-a-Bed in sitting room. Full private bath; parking in front lot. Pool and spa for guests; dog pen available. Continental breakfast. Children allowed. No smoking. Dogs on premises.

WETHERSFIELD

Nutmeg Bed and Breakfast Agency

P.O. Box 1117, West Hartford, 06107-1117
(203) 236-6698; (800) 727-7542
FAX (203) 232-7680

408. Nestled in the historic village of Old Wethersfield, this classic Greek Revival brick house has been lovingly restored to provide a warm and gracious New England welcome to all travelers. Built in 1830, it boasts five airy guest rooms furnished with period antiques. Three rooms have private baths; two rooms share a bath. Fresh flowers, cozy living room and parlor; afternoon tea and elegant full breakfast. Children over 11 welcome.

429. This attractive Colonial home is rich in the history of the town. The hostess, a member of the historical society, offers one guest room with private bath. A small room suitable for a child available. Close to a park and safe for walking. Full breakfast. Children welcome. Smoking restricted.

WILTON

Nutmeg Bed and Breakfast Agency

P.O. Box 1117, West Hartford, 06107-1117
(203) 236-6698; (800) 727-7542
FAX (203) 232-7680

119. Contemporary cottage with Oriental architectural accents beside a rushing stream and two small waterfalls. The guest room has a living room/bedroom with two glass walls overlooking the stream and two pull-out queen-size beds. The kitchen has a deck beside the waterfall. Private bath in cottage; guests have use of the heated spa/sunroom. Full breakfast. Children allowed. Smoking allowed. No resident pets. Dogs welcome.

WINDSOR

Covered Bridge

P.O. Box 447, Norfolk, 06058
(203) 542-5944

1WINCT. This 1860 Queen Anne Victorian rests in Connecticut's oldest town, and is furnished with exquisite period antiques and William Morris wallpapers. Guests are welcome to relax in the living room or music room with a grand piano and a century-old music box. The three guest rooms, one with a fireplace, have private baths. $75-100.

Nutmeg Bed and Breakfast Agency

P.O. Box 1117, West Hartford, 06107-1117
(203) 236-6698; (800) 727-7542
FAX (203) 232-7680

469. Charming Victorian home dating to 1860s, renovated with an addition in 1890. Lovely antique furniture, large front porch, three second floor bedrooms, two with extra-long double beds, one with extra-long twin beds, with private baths. Convenient to airport, University of Hartford, and Loomis Chaffee. Full breakfast. Children over 12. No smoking. Dog on premises.

WINSTED

Nutmeg Bed and Breakfast Agency

P.O. Box 1117, West Hartford, 06107-1117
(203) 236-6698; (800) 727-7542
FAX (203) 232-7680

326. French Provincial style home featuring unique oak carvings, oak paneling, and lovely open staircase. All rooms are air-conditioned. Second floor sitting room with cable TV, fully-equipped kitchen for guest snacks. All six guest rooms have either double, twin, or king-size beds and share two baths. Continental breakfast. Children welcome. Designated smoking area.

WOODBRIDGE

Nutmeg Bed and Breakfast Agency

P.O. Box 1117, West Hartford, 06107-1117
(203) 236-6698; (800) 727-7542
FAX (203) 232-7680

201. Convenient to New Haven, this bilevel contemporary home is on two acres. Guests may enjoy a suite with a sliding glass door to the patio. The bedroom has a double bed, TV, a sitting room with a fireplace and a small kitchen. Ideal for a long stay. Continental breakfast. No smoking.

WOODBURY

Covered Bridge

P.O. Box 447, Norfolk, 06058
(203) 542-5944

1WOCT. This 1789 Colonial set on four acres, is in a town which has been described as the Antique Capital of Connecticut. Many of the original features of the house, such as the large covered porch, wide oak floorboards, and fireplaces, have been preserved. A grand living room with a fireplace and a library are available for guest use. A full country breakfast is served in the dining room or on the south porch. There are five lovely bedrooms and suites. $80-100.

Curtis House

506 Main Street, 06798
(203) 263-2101

Connecticut's oldest inn has been in operation since 1754 in this quaint New England town famous for antique shops. The inn features canopied beds and a popular restaurant serving regional American fare, amply portioned and moderately priced. Closed Christmas Day and Monday lunch.

Host: The Hardisty family
Rooms: 18 (12 PB; 6 SB) $30-70
Continental Breakfast
Credit Cards: A, B
Notes: 2, 3, 4, 9, 10, 11, 12, 13, 14

Merryvale Bed and Breakfast

1204 Main Street, South, 06798
(203) 266-0880; FAX (203) 263-4479

A historic house, lovingly restored with a craftman's attention to detail, has guest rooms as pretty as a Victorian valentine and as comfortable as an easy chair. Guests awake to a home-cooked breakfast with time to truly enjoy it. Cold nights promise a roaring fire in the hearth and summer days invite a ramble on the lawns.

Hosts: Gary Nurnberger and Pat Ubaldi Nurnberger
Rooms: 4 (PB) $99-115
Full Breakfast
Credit Cards: A, B, C
Notes: 2, 3, 5, 7, 8, 9, 10, 11, 12, 13

Nutmeg Bed and Breakfast Agency

P.O. Box 1117, West Hartford, 06107-1117
(203) 236-6698; (800) 727-7542
FAX (203) 232-7680

345. This 1789 Colonial on three acres is carefully restored and tastefully furnished with antiques. Two guest rooms have double beds and shared bath; combined they make a suite. Remaining three guest rooms all have private baths. They have either twin, king-, or queen-size beds. Full breakfast. Children five and over welcome. No smoking allowed. Resident cat on the premises.

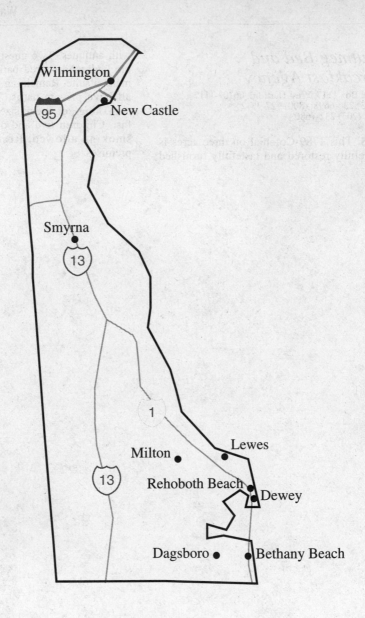

Delaware

Delaware

BETHANY BEACH

The Addy Sea

P.O. Box 275, 19930
(302) 539-3707

In beautiful Bethany Beach, the Addy Sea is nestled on the oceanfront. This charming and elegant Victorian mansion is decorated with antique furnishings set against period wall coverings, crystal chandeliers, original woodwork, and classic tin ceilings. At the Addy Sea, guests can step back into the Victorian era when time was taken to enjoy the art of conversation, a promenade on the boardwalk, or a quiet spell in a rocking chair overlooking the Atlantic Ocean.

Hosts: Leroy, Jeff, and Sherene Gravatte
Rooms: 14 (41/2 PB; 10 SB) $100-140
Continental Breakfast
Credit Cards: A, B
Notes: 2, 7, 8, 9, 10, 11, 12

DAGSBORO

Amanda's Bed and Breakfast Reservation Service

428 Park Avenue, Baltimore, MD, 21217-4230
(410) 225-0001; (800) 899-7533
FAX (410) 728-8957

248. This bed and breakfast is the oldest house in Dagsboro and is about 20 minutes from the Delaware beaches. Pool on premises. Three rooms each with a private bath. Continental breakfast. $65-75.

DEWEY

Barry's Gull Cottage

116 Chesapeake Street, Dewey Beach, 19971
(302) 227-7000 (May to October); (302) 227-0547

A "very special place" for those who want to get away, Gull Cottage, decorated in wicker and offering modern conveniences, centers around pampering its guests. The ocean is one block away and the bay is within walking distance. Guests can plan the day while enjoying a healthy gourmet breakfast overlooking the lake. Nearby shopping includes numerous factory outlets and antique malls, as well as dining, ranging from French cuisine to the Eastern Seaboard's finest seafood. Fresh fruits and vegetables abound in nearby orchards and farmers' markets. Afternoon tea, hot tub by candlelight, and free parking are among the many amenities. Minimum-stay requirements for weekends and holidays. Reservations are required. Weekday package discounts.

Innkeepers: Bob and Vivian Barry
Rooms: 3 (1 PB; 2 SB) $85-125
Full Breakfast
Credit Cards: None
Note: 2, 7, 9, 10, 11, 12

LEWES

Savannah Inn Bed and Breakfast

30 Savannah Road, 19958
(302) 645-5592

NOTES: Credit cards: A MasterCard; B Visa; C American Express; D Discover; E Diners Club; F Other; 2 Personal checks accepted; 3 Lunch available; 4 Dinner available; 5 Open all year; 6 Pets welcome; 7 No smoking; 8 Children welcome; 9 Social drinking allowed; 10 Tennis nearby; 11 Swimming nearby; 12 Golf nearby; 13 Skiing nearby; 14 May be booked through a travel agent.

This inn is in a quaint village near ocean and bay beaches, state park, and resorts. Casual, comfortable bedrooms with fans, books, piano, back yard, airy porch, and delicious vegetarian breakfast create an atmosphere for a relaxing stay. Hosts enjoy nature, outdoor sports, and gardening. Resident cat. Room sinks (lavatories) available. Other bath facilities are shared. Minimum stay is two nights on weekends. Weekly discount for extended stays. Breakfast served Memorial Day through September 30. Rooms available off-season with reduced rates; no breakfast. Smoking in rooms only, not in common areas.

Hosts: Dick and Susan Stafursky
Rooms: 7 (SB) $40-65
Continental Breakfast
Credit Cards: None
Notes: 2, 8, 9, 10, 11

MILTON

The International Bed and Breakfast

504 Amherst Street, Buffalo, NY 14207
(800) 723-4262; FAX (716) 873-4462

DE8325PP. Welcome to a tranquil corner of southern Delaware, in the heart of the countryside on five acres near historic Lewes, the first town in the first state. There are two guest rooms each with a large private bath. A spa room, with an oversized Jacuzzi, cedar walls and ceiling, woodstove, and skylight lookout over the countryside through two large sliding glass doors. The grounds are being developed into an herb, vegetable, and fruit garden. A traditional English breakfast including seasonal fresh fruit. Vegetarians and those who have menu-specific requests welcome. $90-115.

NEW CASTLE

Armitage Inn

2 The Strand, 19720
(302) 328-6618

Built in 1732, the Armitage Inn is on the banks of the Delaware River. Elegantly furnished, air-conditioned guest rooms, all with private baths, and most with whirlpool tubs, overlook the picturesque vistas of the grand Delaware River, the acres of parkland surrounding the inn, and a peaceful walled garden. The gourmet-buffet breakfast is served in the grand dining room or in the garden. The inn is in the heart of this historic town that was established in 1651 and functions today as a living museum, with buildings dating back to its founding years. New Castle is in the heart of the Brandywine Valley with its numerous museums and attractions. Children over 12 welcome.

Hosts: Stephen and Rina Marks
Rooms: 5 (PB) $95-135
Full Breakfast
Credit Cards: None
Notes: 2, 5, 7, 10, 14

William Penn Guest House

206 Delaware Street, 19720
(302) 328-7736

Choose one of four guest rooms in this beautifully restored 1682 guest house in the center of historic New Castle, 20 minutes from museum and public gardens. Children over 12 welcome.

Hosts: Richard and Irma Burwell
Rooms: 4 (SB) $50-75
Continental Breakfast
Credit Cards: None
Notes: 2, 5, 9, 10

REHOBOTH BEACH

The Royal Rose Inn Bed and Breakfast

41 Baltimore Avenue, 19971
(302) 226-2535

A charming and relaxing 1920s beach cottage, this bed and breakfast is tastefully furnished with antiques and a romantic rose theme. A scrumptious breakfast of homemade bread, muffins, egg dishes, and much

NOTES: Credit cards accepted: A MasterCard; B Visa; C American Express; D Discover; E Diners Club;
F Other; 2 Personal checks accepted; 3 Lunch available; 4 Dinner available; 5 Open all year; 6 Pets welcome;

The Royal Rose Inn

more is served on a large, screened porch. Air-conditioned bedrooms, guest refrigerator, and off-street parking are real pluses for guests. One and a half blocks from the Atlantic Ocean and boardwalk. Midweek special; weekend packages; gift certificates. Open May through October.

Hosts: Kenny and Cindy Vincent
Rooms: 7 (3 PB; 4 SB) $35-115
Continental Breakfast
Credit Cards: None
Notes: 2, 9, 10, 11, 12

Tembo Bed and Breakfast

100 Laurel Street, 19971
(302) 227-3360

Only 750 feet from the beach in a quiet, residential area, Tembo offers a casual atmosphere with warm hospitality. Relax among Early American furnishings, antiques, oil paintings, waterfowl carvings, and Gerry's elephant collection. The air-conditioned bedrooms offer firm beds. Minimum-stay requirements for weekends and holidays. Inquire about pets being welcome. Children over 12 welcome.

Hosts: Don and Gerry Cooper
Rooms: 6 (1 PB; 5 SB) $60-125

Continental Breakfast
Credit Cards: None
Notes: 2, 5, 7, 9, 10, 11, 12

SMYRNA

The Main Stay

41 South Main Street, 19977
(302) 653-4293

This early 1800s white clapboard Colonial townhouse is in the heart of the downtown historic area. It is furnished with Oriental rugs and antique furniture and is accented with needlework and handmade quilts. Each bedroom has twin beds and shares a bath. A hearty gourmet breakfast may include homemade muffins, bread, scones, or hot cakes. Closed May 1 through November 1.

Host: Phyllis E. Howarth
Rooms: 3 (SB) $50
Full Breakfast
Credit Cards: None
Notes: 7, 8, 9, 10, 11, 12

WILMINGTON

The Boulevard Bed and Breakfast

1909 Baynardx Boulevard, 19802
(302) 656-9700

This beautifully restored city mansion was originally built in 1913. Impressive foyer and magnificent staircase lead to a landing complete with window seat and leaded-glass windows flanked by 15-foot columns. Breakfast is served on the screened porch. Close to the business district and area attractions.

Hosts: Charles and Judy Powell
Rooms: 6 (4 PB; 2 SB) $60-75
Full Breakfast
Credit Cards: A, B, C
Notes: 2, 5, 7, 8, 9, 10, 12

7 No smoking; 8 Children welcome; 9 Social drinking allowed; 10 Tennis nearby; 11 Swimming nearby; 12 Golf nearby; 13 Skiing nearby; 14 May be booked through a travel agent.

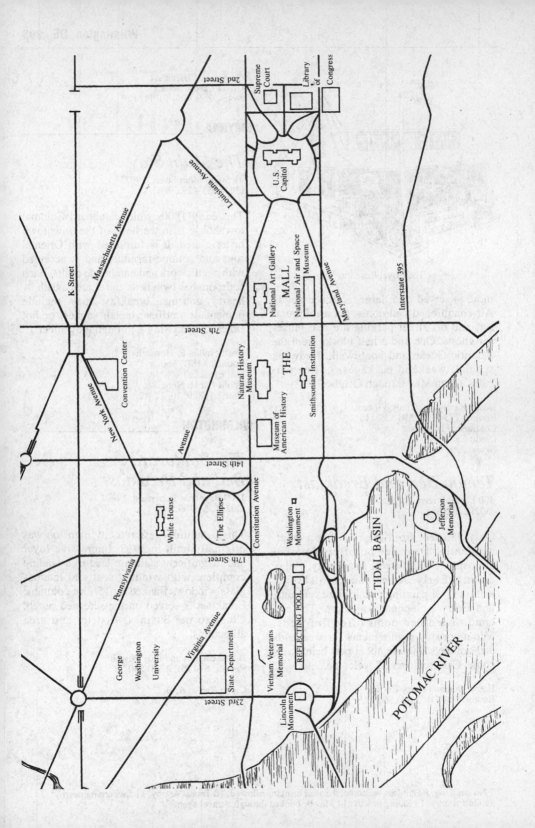

District of Columbia

Amanda's Regional Reservation Service for Bed and Breakfast

1428 Park Avenue, Baltimore, MD 21217
(410) 225-0001; (800) 899-7533
FAX (410) 728-8957

194. Subtle sunrises to fiery sunsets, the view is spectacular. On the water in Edgewater, just minutes from downtown Annapolis. Pool with hot tub, boat dock, and waterfront balcony. Two cats also reside here. King- and queen-size bedrooms. Private bath. $65-80.

227. A lovely home near Dupont Circle Metro on a tree-lined street. Leave the car at home. Convenient to area restaurants and shops. Relax in the garden after sightseeing downtown. Uniquely furnished. Continental breakfast. $71.50.

228. European-style row houses form a group of comfortable, affordable bed and breakfasts. Walk to Metro, shops, and restaurants. Also near the Shorham, Hilton and Sheraton Hotels. Private and shared baths. $45-95.

230. Two small inns in the Adams Morgan area of District of Columbia are near the zoo. Each room with private bath. One art deco, the other Jeffersonian. Rooms and suites available. Space for a small meeting. TV and dial direct telephones. About eight blocks to Dupont Circle Metro. Continental breakfast. $79-150.

Adams Inn

Adams Inn

1744 Lanier Place, NW, 20009
(202) 745-3600

Convenient, comfortable, home-style atmosphere in a neighborhood with over 40 ethnic restaurants to choose from. Near the bus lines, shopping, Metro, museums, government buildings, and convention sites. Economical for the tourist and business traveler. Both private and shared bathrooms are available.

Hosts: Gene and Nancy Thompson; Anne Owens
Rooms: 25 (12 PB; 13 SB) $55-95
Continental Breakfast
Credit Cards: A, B, C, D, E
Notes: 2, 5, 7, 8, 14

NOTES: Credit cards: A MasterCard; B Visa; C American Express; D Discover; E Diners Club; F Other;
2 Personal checks accepted; 3 Lunch available; 4 Dinner available; 5 Open all year; 6 Pets welcome;
7 No smoking; 8 Children welcome; 9 Social drinking allowed; 10 Tennis nearby; 11 Swimming nearby;
12 Golf nearby; 13 Skiing nearby; 14 May be booked through a travel agent.

Bed and Breakfast Accommodations, Ltd.

P.O. Box 12011, 20005
(202) 328-3510; FAX (202) 332-3885

101. Dupont Circle is the setting for this spacious modern townhouse. The Metro is only one and one-half blocks away. Accommodations include a room with a double bed, a private bath with tub and shower, color TV, stereo, and telephone. Off-street parking. No smoking. $75.

104. This three-story home built in 1927 is in one of the oldest and most exclusive neighborhoods in Bethesda, Maryland. Decorated with a mix of antiques and reproductions, the second floor features a room with a double bed and a room with twin beds that share a hall bath. The third floor offers a room with a double bed and private hall bath with tub only. A large comfortable den on the second floor with color TV, telephone, and exercise machine is available for guests' use. Convenient to NIH, and a ten- to fifteen-minute walk to Bethesda Metro. Free street parking. No smoking. Resident cat. $65.

107. Right in the heart of Georgetown, this is a relatively new townhouse. The guest room features a queen-size bed and private bath. Guests also have access to a den with a color TV and a small kitchenette. One-half block to major bus line. Street parking with permit. No smoking. $75.

108. This turn-of-the-century three-story bayfront was completely renovated from 1990 to 1992. It boasts central air conditioning, fireplaces, books, and plants galore. Hosts offer two large guest rooms with private baths, ceiling fans, king-size beds, comfortable chairs, and televisions. Guests are also invited to enjoy the living room, library, and back patio. This is a nonsmoking household. $90-110.

111. On General's Row, a row of townhouses constructed in the late 1880s, this house is just three blocks from Dupont Circle, second only to Georgetown as a neighborhood for the trendy. Dupont Circle offers good restaurants, boutiques, and theaters, and the Dupont Circle Metro is three blocks away. Four guest rooms have either double or a pair of twin beds, and both shared and private baths are available. The hostess is an artist with an MA from the University of Alabama. There is a resident cat. $60-75.

124. Designed and built in 1912 by William Phelan, this large Chevy Chase, District of Columbia home is only one block from Connecticut Avenue. Accommodations include the Green Room, with a double bed, private hall bath, ceiling fan, and color TV. The other room features a queen-size bed, private bath with dual pedestal sink, claw-foot tub, color TV, and telephone. Ten-minute walk to Friendship Heights Metro. Resident cat. Street parking. No smoking allowed. $65-75.

125. This Victorian townhouse was built in 1990 and is filled with an eclectic mix of period pieces, Oriental, and contemporary art. Four gracefully appointed bedrooms share two baths on the second floor. A third-floor suite adjoins a private bath and can accommodate up to four people. In the heart of the city, this home is one mile north of the White House and six blocks from Dupont Circle Metro stop on the red line. No smoking. No children. $65-75.

126. This house is a Georgian-style brick Colonial with a slate roof. On a wide, tree-lined avenue in a residential neighborhood, Tenley Circle is between Georgetown and Chevy Chase, Maryland. Guests have easy access to downtown business areas and major bus routes and are within two blocks of many restaurants, shops, movie theaters,

NOTES: Credit cards accepted: A MasterCard; B Visa; C American Express; D Discover; E Diners Club; F Other; 2 Personal checks accepted; 3 Lunch available; 4 Dinner available; 5 Open all year; 6 Pets welcome;

tennis courts, and an indoor pool. Two large guest rooms each have a private bath with a tiled shower. Dog and cat in residence. Guest pets and smoking are not permitted. $70-80.

128. This un-hosted one bedroom apartment is just two blocks from Dupont Circle. It is tastefully decorated and offers a queen-size bed, full bath with tub and shower, fully-equipped kitchen, living room with sleeper-sofa, TV, stereo, VCR, and telephone. No parking. No smoking. Monthly rates available. $80.

129. This red brick, former schoolhouse, circa 1880, was converted about four years ago into condominiums. It features enormous windows and 15-foot ceilings and is four and one-half blocks from Union Station. The guest room was designed by the hostess, an avid collector of antiques. It has an Old World-style bed built into an existing alcove, and an entertainment center and appliances are all operated by remote control so that a tired guest can prop himself against a pillow and never have to move. Walking distance to charming cafes and restaurants that line Massachusetts Avenue. $60, single only.

132. Designed in the style of a classic 18th-century manor, this award-winning inn is in historic Old Town Alexandria. The decor includes fine Federal Period reproductions, including four-poster beds and decorative fireplaces. Forty-five rooms include some suites. Weekend packages include breakfast and parking. $160-295.

133. This beautifully restored Victorian home was built in 1859. The house is full of lovely antiques, including antique beds in the guest rooms, and features a lovely garden area with Koi pond and fountain, which has been the site of several weddings. One guest room has a white iron and brass queen-size bed, antique armoire, ceiling fan, stained-glass window, dressing room, and private bath with a large walk-in double shower. The other guest room has a large Victorian double bed and antique furnishings, including handmade rugs from North Carolina. The room is decorated in Laura Ashley wallpaper, linens, and fabrics, and has its own private attached bath. $85-100.

137. Seven blocks behind the Capitol, guests are within walking distance to the Supreme Court and Library of Congress and have a ten-minute walk to both Eastern Market Metro and Union Station. This house, built in 1902, has been restored to its present condition by the owner, a fashion designer whose renovations have been featured in *Better Homes and Gardens* and the *Washington Post*. Two guest rooms are available, each with queen-size beds, color TV, telephone, and shared bath. $65-75.

139. This spacious five-bedroom house was designed by famed Washington architect Harry Wardman, who developed this elegant, tree-lined district adjacent to Rock Creek Park. One guest room has twin beds, a sitting room, and a private bath. The second guest room has a twin bed and shared bath. There is an enclosed garden in the back where parking is available. $60-75.

146. Built in 1926, this semi-detached residence is part of the larger three-story rowhouse developments of beautiful North Cleveland Park in northwest Washington, yet is still quaint like Georgetown. On a tree-lined street, the house is recessed from the road. The guest rooms are on the second floor. The Green room can either have twin beds or a sumptuous king-size bed, and includes a comfortable loveseat, an antique writing table, extra large closet, and a shared bath with shower/tub. The Mauve

7 No smoking; 8 Children welcome; 9 Social drinking allowed; 10 Tennis nearby; 11 Swimming nearby; 12 Golf nearby; 13 Skiing nearby; 14 May be booked through a travel agent.

Bed and Breakfast Accommodations, Ltd. (continued)

Room is furnished with a king-size bed, dressing room/office, television, and private bath with shower. Private telephone line and TV/VCR. Airport/station pick-up or drop-offs can be arranged.

154. This house was originally built in the late 19th century and was completely renovated in 1977 and 1978. In the Foggy Bottom-West End section, the home has a Victorian facade although the interior is sleek and contemporary. There is one guest room with twin beds and a private bath. Access to a great room with fireplace, color TV, and telephone. One and one-half blocks to Foggy Bottom Metro. Resident cat. No smoking. $75-85.

155. A 19th-century inn is in historic Virginia just 45 minutes from downtown and has been lovingly restored as a beautiful, cozy bed and breakfast. There are 14 unique rooms furnished with antiques and reproductions, and each is named for a noteworthy Virginian. The dining room was inspired by Belvoir, the home of William Fairfax. Lovely gardens designed to reflect the era when the inn was constructed have been added to both the front and back of the building. Full breakfast and high tea are both served. $130-250.

158. A three-story brick townhouse at Tiber Island is right in the heart of the city on Washington's waterfront. Guests have an easy stroll to the Smithsonian Institute, the Jefferson Memorial, and the Tidal Basin. Accommodations include a queen-size bed, private hall bath, and music/video room. $85.

168. This exceptional Victorian bay-front was built in 1881 and has been featured on the Capitol Hill House Tour. Guests are just five blocks from the Capitol, the Library of Congress, Supreme Court, and the Mall. The Blue/Orange Metro line is less than a ten-minute walk. The guest suite has a private bath, sitting room, queen-size reproduction of a Victorian iron bed, color TV, VCR, and telephone. Outside smoking only. $80.

170. The house is a beautifully restored Victorian retaining most of the original architectural details. It faces Pennsylvania Avenue and is furnished with American antiques throughout. Guests are invited to use the Florida room where breakfast is served, as well as the Florentine room and garden. There are two large guest rooms sharing a bath, one with a period antique double bed and one with a queen-size bed. $65-80.

175. This beautiful old Federal front row-house built in 1885, just twenty years after the Civil War, is furnished with lovely pieces from the 1930s and 1940s which gives guests the feeling of grandmother's house. There are two bedrooms with private baths. The living room features a working fireplace and guests are invited to use the beautiful French Quarter-style patio and enjoy the fountains and fish pond, directly off the living room. Off-street parking is available. No smoking in the house. $70-90.

190. A spacious two-bedroom English basement apartment is decorated with original art, new European-style modern furnishings, and a fully-equipped kitchen with dishwasher and disposal. There is a private patio entrance to the living room, security doors at the front and rear, and windows throughout. Other amenities include color

NOTES: Credit cards accepted: A MasterCard; B Visa; C American Express; D Discover; E Diners Club; F Other; 2 Personal checks accepted; 3 Lunch available; 4 Dinner available; 5 Open all year; 6 Pets welcome;

TV, stereo/radio/cassette sound system, and central heat and air. There is a fireplace in the living room, but it can only be used by special arrangement with the owner. $80-115.

200. Each of the 54 guest rooms and suites are unique. Many contain historical features. Each guest room is individually decorated with original art work and authentic period furnishings complimented by custom design and hand-crafted pieces. Guest room features include maid service twice a day, including turn-down service; convenient in-room bar and refreshments; baths with marble vanities and personal toiletries; many rooms with bay windows and some with porches; individually controlled heating and air conditioning; telephones, computer access data ports; color TV and in-room movies; and AM/FM radios. Valet parking is available. Special weekly rates. $135-185.

The Bed and Breakfast League, Ltd/Sweet Dreams and Toast, Inc.

P.O. Box 9490, 20016
(202) 363-7767

196. The Park House is a late Victorian house overlooking Folger Park, three blocks from the U.S. Capitol and the Capitol South Metro stop. The master bedroom has king-size bed, sitting area with TV, desk, telephone, and private bath. Two other bedrooms, each with one queen-size bed, TV, and telephone, share a bath. Guests are invited to use the living room with wet bar. On-street parking available with a guest parking permit. Credit cards and personal check accepted. Open year-round. No smoking. Social drinking allowed. Full breakfast. $65-100.

296. The Madison House is across the street from the Madison Building of the Library of Congress and one block from the Capitol South Metro stop. Built in 1850 and retaining the original woodwork and mantels, it is elegantly decorated with antiques and reproductions, Oriental rugs, and Waterford chandeliers. One guest suite has two bedrooms with twin-size beds or a queen-size bed, sitting room, and bath. The master suite has a bedroom with a king-size bed and double private bath with Jacuzzi and sauna. The first floor suite has a bedroom with a queen-size bed, living room with double bed, full kitchen, and bath. Breakfast is served in the dining room in front of the fireplace. Off-street parking is available. Credit cards and personal checks accepted. Open year-round. No smoking. Children welcome. Social drinking allowed. Full breakfast. $75-140.

396. This charming turn-of-the-century Victorian was lovingly restored in 1988. It is decorated with period furnishings, beautiful wallpaper, linens, and antique fixtures. Four guest rooms with queen-size beds share two baths. The fifth guest room, that can accommodate four people, has a private bath. Relax in the parlor, in the library, or on the deck. A five-minute walk takes guests to all the restaurants and shops of DuPont Circle and Adams-Morgan and a ten-minute walk takes them to the DuPont Circle Metro stop. Credit cards and personal checks accepted. Open year-round. No smoking. Social drinking allowed. Continental breakfast. $70-115.

796. Georgetown is the oldest section of the city, home to some of the city's best restaurants, and renowned for its world-class shopping. After a full day of touring, return to this quiet, secluded suite and relax in the sitting room before walking out for dinner.

---

7 No smoking; 8 Children welcome; 9 Social drinking allowed; 10 Tennis nearby; 11 Swimming nearby; 12 Golf nearby; 13 Skiing nearby; 14 May be booked through a travel agent.

Bed and Breakfast Accommodations, Ltd. (continued)

In addition to the sitting room with a TV, there is a wet bar, bedroom with queen-size bed, and a private bath. All the shops and restaurants are within easy walking distance, as are Georgetown University and Dumbartown Oaks. Credit cards and personal checks accepted. Open year-round. No smoking. Social drinking allowed. Continental breakfast. $75-85.

896. This unhosted apartment is part of a turn-of-the-century home on one of the prettiest blocks in the Capitol Hill Historic District. It is three blocks from the Eastern Market Metro stop, two blocks from the oldest farmers' market in the city, and eight blocks east of the U.S. Capitol. The apartment has a bedroom with a queen-size bed, private bath, large closet, living room with a queen-size pull-out bed, and a kitchen with a washer and dryer. The kitchen is stocked for a Continental breakfast, and there is off-street parking. Credit cards and personal checks accepted. Open year-round. No smoking. Children welcome. Social drinking. $80-90.

996. Just ten minutes from Georgetown and five minutes from American University and the Potomac River is this handsome house built on a hillside in one of the most beautiful parts of Washington. One guest room has a queen-size bed and private bath; the second has twin-size beds and private bath. Guests also have the use of the den and wet bar. Parking is on-street and easy. The hosts, an artist and a defense policy analyst, serve a much-admired breakfast and often ferry their guests to the Metro stops close by. Credit cards and personal checks accepted. Open year-round. No smoking. Social drinking allowed. Continental breakfast. $70-80.

1096. This handsome Victorian townhouse is on Capitol Hill, a ten- or fifteen-minute walk to the U.S. Capitol, Supreme Court, and Union Station Metro. The interior of the house has been completely renovated and retains its antique charm enhanced by the original brick walls and new skylights. It is furnished with family antiques and mementoes from the host's travels while in the Peace Corps. The guest accommodations are a bedroom with double bed, adjoining bedroom with twin-size beds and private bath. There are delightful cats in residence. Credit cards and personal checks accepted. Open year-round. No smoking. Social drinking allowed. Continental breakfast. $60-80.

1196. The Magnolia House suite on Capitol Hill is two blocks from the Capitol South Metro stop and the Library of Congress and three blocks from the U.S. Capitol. Furnished with one-of-a-kind furniture and art by Washington artists, the suite contains a living room, breakfast nook, kitchenette, sleeping area with queen-size bed, and private bath. A private telephone with answering machine and color TV are included. Credit cards and personal checks accepted. Open year-round. No smoking. Children welcome. Social drinking allowed. Continental breakfast. Call for rates.

1296. This completely furnished, full daylight, English basement apartment on Capitol Hill draws guests back again and again because the hosts have thought of everything their guests might need, including superb hospitality. The suite includes a private entrance, living/dining room, complete kitchen, bedroom with double bed, private bath, laundry facilities, color cable TV, and private telephone line. The Eastern Market Metro stop is a ten-minute walk away, and the U.S. Capitol is eleven blocks away. Credit cards and personal checks accepted. Open year-round. No smoking allowed.

NOTES: Credit cards accepted: A MasterCard; B Visa; C American Express; D Discover; E Diners Club; F Other; 2 Personal checks accepted; 3 Lunch available; 4 Dinner available; 5 Open all year; 6 Pets welcome;

Social drinking allowed. Continental breakfast served. Call for rates.

1396. This light and sunny English basement apartment is the complete first floor of a 103-year-old Victorian house in the well-established Lincoln Park section of Capitol Hill. From the private entrance, guests walk into a bay-front living/dining room, then go on to a complete kitchen, den with color cable TV and telephone, bedroom with queen-size bed, and modern bath. There is off-street parking for one car. The suite is a ten-minute walk from Eastern Market Metro stop, a ten- or twenty-minute walk to restaurants, shops, the U.S. Capitol and Library of Congress. Credit cards and personal checks accepted. Open year-round. No smoking. Social drinking allowed. Continental breakfast. $85-95.

1496. This completely restored three-story Victorian townhouse built in 1895 is set back from the brick sidewalk on a wide, pretty avenue on Capitol Hill just one block from the Eastern Market Metro stop. There are two guest rooms, one with a double bed and one with a twin bed; each has a private bath. Guests are also welcome to enjoy the living room, den, garden, and three gorgeous and rare Birman cats. Restaurants, the U.S. Capitol, and Library of Congress are five to fifteen minutes away. Credit cards and personal checks accepted. Open year-round. No smoking. Social drinking allowed. Continental breakfast. $75-85.

1596. This turn-of-the-century townhouse is a one-minute walk away from the DuPont Circle Metro stop and a number of restaurants, but the street is secluded and quiet. The spacious rooms have high ceilings and wonderful furnishings, many from the Far East. The guest bedroom has double bed, stereo, TV, telephone, and private bath. The first floor apartment can accommodate four people and has a living/dining room, bedroom, kitchen, and private bath. There is off-street parking. Credit cards and personal checks accepted. Open year-round. No smoking. Social drinking allowed. Continental breakfast. $80-100.

1696. This 110-year-old brick townhouse is a two-minute walk from DuPont Circle, its Metro stop, and many restaurants. The large rooms have high ceilings, the original fireplaces, gas lamps, and beautiful antique furniture and rugs. The ten guest rooms have twin or queen-size beds, and two share a bath. Some of the baths have Jacuzzi tubs. Credit cards and personal checks accepted. Open year-round. No smoking. Social drinking allowed. Continental breakfast. $80-225.

1796. The Swann bed and breakfast appeals to travelers who appreciate Far Eastern and American Victorian furniture and art and the friendly hospitality of a well-traveled, very interesting hostess. A five- or ten-minute walk to a major convention hotel, numerous restaurants, art galleries, and the DuPont Circle Metro stop. Three guest rooms share one bath. Credit cards and personal checks accepted. Open year-round. No smoking. Social drinking allowed. Continental breakfast. $50-60.

1896. This elegant Georgian home, built in 1910, is a ten-minute walk to DuPont Circle and the Metro stop and a five- or fifteen-minute walk to all the restaurants, shops, and galleries of DuPont Circle and Adams-Morgan. The high-ceilinged rooms offer a perfect backdrop for the hosts' antique furniture, porcelain objects, and Oriental rugs. Four guest rooms with queen-size or twin beds share two baths and a third-floor deck. Credit cards and personal checks accepted. Open year-round. No smoking. Social drinking allowed. Continental breakfast. $70-85.

7 No smoking; 8 Children welcome; 9 Social drinking allowed; 10 Tennis nearby; 11 Swimming nearby; 12 Golf nearby; 13 Skiing nearby; 14 May be booked through a travel agent.

Bed and Breakfast Accommodations, Ltd. (continued)

1996. This Cape Cod-style home is in Cleveland Park, the most beautiful and sought after historic district in the city. Filled with family antiques, this light, airy home offers quiet and tranquility close to downtown. The Metro stop and several blocks of shops and restaurants are a ten- or fifteen-minute walk from the house. The master bedroom has a queen-size bed and private bath. Two other rooms have one twin bed each and share a hall bath. Two wonderful dogs will help make guests welcome. Credit cards and personal checks accepted. Open year-round. No smoking. Social drinking allowed. Continental breakfast. $75-85.

2096. This Victorian home in Cleveland Park was built as a summer home in the late 1800s and later converted to year-round use. The very large house has wraparound porches, high ceilings, beautiful wood paneling, and antique furniture. Breakfast is often served in the breakfast room which looks into large, mature trees. One guest bedroom has an antique double sleigh bed and private bath; the second guest room has an antique 3/4 double bed and shared bath. There is off-street parking, and the Cleveland Park Metro stop is an eight-minute walk away. Credit cards and personal checks accepted. Open year-round. No smoking. Children welcome. Social drinking allowed. Continental breakfast. $65-80.

2196. Sitting on the back porch or in the library of this large rambling Victorian home in Cleveland Park, looking into the enormous trees surrounding the house, it's hard to believe it is a ten-minute walk from the Cleveland Park Metro stop and a number of restaurants and a five-minute Metro ride to downtown. The house is furnished with handsome English and American antiques, as is the guest bedroom with an extra large double bed and private bath. Off-street parking is available. Credit cards and personal checks accepted. Open year-round. No smoking. Social drinking allowed. Continental breakfast. $70-85.

2296. This comfortable 1930s Cleveland Park home sits on a hill on a secluded street and looks down into the neighboring gardens. A quiet, tranquil place, it is a ten-minute walk to the Cleveland Park Metro stop and the restaurants on Connecticut Avenue. The warm, friendly hostess offers one guest room with a queen-size and a twin bed and private bath, and a second guest room with a double bed and private bath. There is easy, safe on-street parking. Credit cards and personal checks accepted. Open year-round. No smoking. Children welcome. Social drinking allowed. Continental breakfast. $65-80.

2396. This English Tudor-style home is in North Cleveland Park near the new Embassy District, one of the best close-in sections of the city and an eight-minute walk to the Van Ness Metro stop. The house and guest rooms are full of fine 18th- and 19th-century furniture and Oriental rugs. Two delightful dogs provide warm hospitality and many laughs. There are three guest bedrooms with twin, queen, or double beds, TVs, and telephones, that can accommodate a party of six. Secure off-street parking is available, and there are numerous restaurants within walking distance of the house. Credit cards and personal checks accepted. Open year-round. No smoking. Social drinking allowed. Continental breakfast. $50-85.

Capitol Hill Guest House

101 Fifth Street Northeast, 20002
(202) 547-1050

The Capitol Hill Guest House is a 19th-century Queen Anne-style row house only three blocks behind the U.S. Supreme Court on historic Capitol Hill. There are ten moderately priced rooms with the flavor of a bygone era when all visitors to the nation's capital stayed in the many guest houses that dotted Capitol Hill.

Host: Antonio Cintra
Rooms: 10 (2 PB; 8 SB) $45-100
Continental Breakfast
Credit Cards: A, B, C, D
Notes: 5, 7, 9, 11, 14

The Dupont at the Circle

1606 19th Street Northwest, 20009
(202) 332-5251; FAX (202) 408-8308

Discover a completely restored Victorian townhouse combining the charm of yesteryear with the convenience of today. Original gas lamps, pocket doors, ornate moldings, elegant fireplaces, tasteful furnishings, and luxurious marble bathrooms with Jacuzzis all provide the perfect splendor for guests' stay. Dupont Circle abounds with many fine restaurants of all types and price ranges. Coffee houses, delis, boutique shops, movie theaters, art galleries, the White House, the Washington Monument and the Metrorail are all close-by. Children over 14 welcome.

Hosts: Anexora and Alan Skvirsky
Rooms: 6 (PB) $95-125
Continental Breakfast
Credit Cards: A, B, C
Notes: 5, 7, 9, 10, 11, 14

Henley Park Hotel

926 Massachusetts Avenue, Northwest, 20001
(202) 638-5200; FAX (202) 638-6740

This intimate 96-room luxury property reminiscent of a traditional European country inn specializes in personalized services, such as mini-bars, and 24-hour room service. The restaurant offers award-winning cuisine, and has been named in the top five most romantic restaurants, with its sun-filled atrium. Marley's lounge offers live jazz. The Wilkes Room has a traditional tea with scones and Devonshire cream in a cozy atmosphere of

fresh flowers and a fireplace. Near Union Station, the Capitol, Smithsonian museums, and the Metro.

General Manager: Ruedi Bertschinger
Rooms: 96 (PB) $185-350
Continental Breakfast
Credit Cards: A, B, C, D, E
Notes: 2, 3, 4, 5, 7, 8, 9, 12, 14

Kalorama Guest House at Kalorama Park

1854 Mintwood Place Northwest, 20009
(202) 667-6369

A charming Victorian inn in a quiet downtown residential neighborhood is only a short stroll to the underground Metro and a potpourri of ethnic restaurants and shops. Enjoy the hospitality of the innkeepers, a complimentary continental breakfast, and evening apéritif. Just ten minutes from the mall, White House, and most attractions. Economical rates bring guests back again and again.

Hosts: Tami, Jim, and Carlotta
Rooms: 30 (12 PB; 18 SB) $45-95
Continental Breakfast
Credit Cards: A, B, C, E
Notes: 2, 5, 7, 8, 9, 14

Kalorama Guest House at Woodley Park

2700 Cathedral Avenue Northwest, 20008
(202) 328-0860

This turn-of-the-century Victorian townhouse offers guests a downtown residential home away from home. Decorated in period antiques, the guest house is a short walk to the underground Metro, restaurants, and shops. Only ten minutes from the Smithsonian and the White House, yet offering guests the relaxation and hospitality of a country inn. Enjoy a complimentary Continental breakfast and evening aperitif.

Hosts: Michael and MaryAnne
Rooms: 19 (12 PB; 7 SB) $40-85
Continental Breakfast
Credit Cards: A, B, C, E
Notes: 2, 5, 7, 8, 9, 14

7 No smoking; 8 Children welcome; 9 Social drinking allowed; 10 Tennis nearby; 11 Swimming nearby; 12 Golf nearby; 13 Skiing nearby; 14 May be booked through a travel agent.

Morrison–Clark Inn

Massachusetts and 11th Street Northwest, 20001
(202) 898-1200

The restored Morrison-Clark Inn preserves the elegance of Victorian design and creates the feel of an elegant turn-of-the-century Washington home. The guest rooms and suites are individually decorated with authentic period furnishings. Breakfast, lunch, and dinner are served in the restaurant, one of the best in Washington. The inn is just six blocks from the White House near downtown shopping, Chinatown, and the convention center. Weekend rates are available. Nonsmoking rooms available.

Host: Donald Schoen
Rooms: 54 (PB) $99-195
Continental Breakfast
Credit Cards: A, B, C, D, E
Notes: 2, 3, 4, 5, 8, 9, 10, 11, 12, 14

The Reeds

P.O. Box 12011, 20005
(202) 328-3510

A 100-year-old Victorian mansion has been carefully and extensively restored and has original wood paneling, stained glass, chandeliers, and porch. Each room has a color TV and telephone; laundry facilities are available. Adjoins Logan Circle Historic District, with excellent transportation and easy parking. This beautiful home was selected as a part of the "Christmas at the Smithsonian" festivities, and was featured in the *Washington Post* in December when it was decorated for Christmas. Ten blocks from the White House. The hosts speak English and French. Personal checks accepted two weeks prior to arrival.

Hosts: Charles and Jackie Reed
Rooms: 6 (SB) $55-82.50
Continental Breakfast
Credit Cards: A, B, C, E
Notes: 5, 7, 8, 9, 14

Florida

Amelia Island Williams House

AMELIA ISLAND

Amelia Island Williams House

103 South 9th Street, 32034
(904) 277-2328

This 1856 antebellum mansion is listed on the National Register of Historic Places. It features four exquisite guest chambers with art and antiques that date back to the 1500s, including a robe that belonged to the Last Emperor of China, a carpet that belonged to Napoleon III, and a vase owned by Empress Eugenie. The mahogony and cherry grand staircase is lined with five stained-glass windows. It was featured as "Inn of the Month" in the June 1995 issue of *Country Inns* magazine, called "Florida's most exquisite bed and breakfast," and featured on *Inn Country USA* (PBS). Guests may relax on the 240 feet of Southern-style verandas, in the formal English gardens, or in the informal fountainhead courtyard.

Hosts: Dick Flitz and Chris Carter
Rooms: 4 (PB) $95-135
Full Breakfast
Credit Cards: A, B
Notes: 2, 5, 7, 9, 10, 11, 12, 14

Elizabeth Pointe Lodge

98 South Fletcher Avenue, 32034
(904) 277-4851

This seaside lodge of an 1890s Nantucket shingle-style architecture has large porches that overlook the ocean. Enjoy great room with fireplace and library, oversize tubs, remote color cable TV, fresh flowers, and newspaper delivered to room. Wine at 6:00 P.M. Homemade snack and desserts always available. Rock on the porch with a glass of lemonade. Baby-sitting, laundry room service, and concierge assistance. Historic seaport of Fernandina nearby. Bikes available for touring the island.

Hosts: David and Susan Caples
Rooms: 25 (PB) $95-175
Full Breakfast
Credit Cards: A, B, C, D
Notes: 2, 3, 4, 5, 7, 8, 10, 11, 12, 14

Elizabeth Pointe Lodge

The Fairbanks House

227 South Seventh Street, 32034
(904) 277-0500; (800) 261-4838

The Fairbanks House is an Italianate villa, built in 1885 and listed on the National

---

7 No smoking; 8 Children welcome; 9 Social drinking allowed; 10 Tennis nearby; 11 Swimming nearby; 12 Golf nearby; 13 Skiing nearby; 14 May be booked through a travel agent.

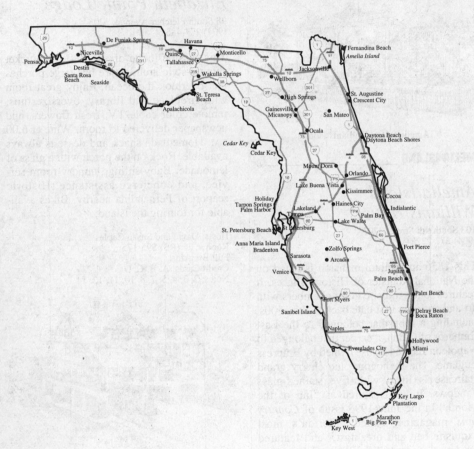

Florida

The Fairbanks House

Register of Historic Places. It has ten rooms, suites, or cottages, all with private baths, telephones, and TVs. Four-poster king, queen, or twin beds are available with claw-foot tubs, showers, or Jacuzzis. The Fairbanks House has been completely restored. Furnishings are done in antiques, period-pieces, and Oriental rugs. Enjoy the piazzas, swimming pool, and beautiful gardens. A gourmet breakfast and complimentary afternoon refreshments are included in rates.

Hosts: Mary and Nelson Smelker
Rooms: 8 (PB) $85-150
Full Breakfast
Credit Cards: A, B, C, D
Notes: 2, 5, 7, 8, 9, 10, 11, 12, 14

ANNA MARIA ISLAND

Harrington House Beachfront Bed and Breakfast

5626 Gulf Drive, Holmes Beach, 34217
(813) 778-5444

The charm of old Florida architecture and the casual elegance of beachfront living are beautifully combined at the Harrington House, a one-of-a-kind bed and breakfast guest house on Anna Maria Island. Built in 1925, this lovingly restored home has seven charming bedrooms, each with private bath. Most rooms have French doors leading to balconies overlooking the pool, the beach, and the blue-green Gulf of Mexico. Guests are served a full breakfast in the dining room as they enjoy stimulating conversation with other guests. Relax by the pool, take a moonlit stroll on the beach, or listen to the surf. AAA rated; Mobil Guide rated; ABBA rated.

Hosts: Frank and Jo Adele Davis
Rooms: 7 (PB) $89-189
Full Breakfast
Credit Cards: A, B, C
Notes: 2, 5, 9, 11, 14

APALACHICOLA

Bed and Breakfast Scenic Florida

P.O. Box 3385, Tallahassee, 23215-3385
(904) 386-8196

16. This Southern plantation home was built in 1838. Today with careful renovation complete, the home is, once more, grandly inviting and comfortable, and the grounds are lush with gardens, shaded walkways, and complete with swimming pool. Sitting areas, gas log fireplaces, designer bed and bath linens, and special amenities to pamper guests are common to both individually decorated rooms. One guest chamber has a canopied king-size bed, and the bath has a combination tub and shower with jets for a relaxing soak. The other guest chamber has a queen-size four-poster bed, and the bath has a modern walk-in shower. Guests can enjoy a view of the river from the upstairs porch, or unwind with a book in the first-floor library. TV is provided in guest rooms and in the library. Fine coffees and homemade treats begin the morning in guests' rooms followed by a full breakfast served in the formal dining room. Late afternoon refreshments are also complimentary. Shops, galleries, cafes, and fine dining are all within walking distance. The

NOTES: Credit cards: A MasterCard; B Visa; C American Express; D Discover; E Diners Club; F Other;
2 Personal checks accepted; 3 Lunch available; 4 Dinner available; 5 Open all year; 6 Pets welcome;
7 No smoking; 8 Children welcome; 9 Social drinking allowed; 10 Tennis nearby; 11 Swimming nearby;
12 Golf nearby; 13 Skiing nearby; 14 May be booked through a travel agent.

Apalachicola National Forest, Torreya State Park, and island beaches offer additional outdoor recreation. No smoking. No children allowed. $150.

ARCADIA

Bed and Breakfast Scenic Florida

P.O. Box 3385, Tallahassee, 32315-3385
(904) 386-8196

FL46. Built in the 1890s, this Southern Double Porch Colonial home has a 1914 addition. Public rooms include the formal dining room and parlor. Upstairs porches are furnished with wicker and overlook the grounds. Guests may choose from three second-floor rooms with double beds, fireplaces, shared or private baths, including a claw-foot tub and shower. The home is also centrally heated and air-conditioned. Breakfast includes homemade muffins and is served in the formal dining room from 8:00 to 10:00 A.M. No smoking. $60-75.

BIG PINE KEY

The Barnacle

Route 1, Box 780A, 33043
(305) 872-3298

Enjoy the ambience of a homestay bed and breakfast with every amenity. A unique experience on the ocean, surrounded by

The Barnacle

lush, verdant foliage, where guests can enjoy peace and quiet, yet they are only 30 miles from the attractions of Key West.

Hosts: Wood and Joan Cornell
Rooms: 4 (PB) $75-110
Full Breakfast
Credit Cards: None
Notes: 2, 5, 9, 11

Canal Cottage

P.O. Box 430266, 33043-0266
(305) 872-3881

Relax in the private apartment of this quaint, natural-wood stilt home. Nestled in the treetops, cooled by island breezes and Bahama fans. Enjoy the bicycles, cable TV, gas grill, and fully furnished kitchen. Private club privileges for pool, tennis, and racquetball. Weekly discounts.

Hosts: Dean and Patti Nickless
Rooms: 2 (PB) $85
Continental Breakfast
Credit Cards: None
Notes: 2, 5, 8, 9, 10, 11, 14

Deer Run

Long Beach Road, Box 431, 33043
(305) 872-2015; (305) 872-2800

Deer Run is a Florida Cracker-style house nestled among lush native trees on the ocean. Breakfast is served on the large veranda overlooking the ocean. Dive at Looe Key National Marine Sanctuary, fish the Gulf Stream, or lie on the beach. A nature lover's paradise and a bird watcher's heaven. Two-night minimum stay required.

Host: Sue Abbott
Rooms: 2 (PB) $85-110
Full Breakfast
Credit Cards: None
Notes: 2, 5, 7, 9, 10, 11, 12

BOCA RATON

Bed and Breakfast Company

P.O. Box 262, South Miami, 33243
(305) 661-3270; FAX (305) 661-3270

NOTES: Credit cards accepted: A MasterCard; B Visa; C American Express; D Discover; E Diners Club; F Other; 2 Personal checks accepted; 3 Lunch available; 4 Dinner available; 5 Open all year; 6 Pets welcome;

BR064. This conventional suburban ranch home in Boca Raton offers a variety of personal touches that reflect the hosts' interests in needlework, gardening, and flowers. In a pleasant neighborhood, near ten golf courses, two miles to a large mall, and seven miles to the beach. Two comfortable bed and breakfast rooms available with double bed and shared bath. Very hospitable hosts. $40.

BRADENTON

Bed and Breakfast Company

P.O. Box 262, South Miami, 33243
(305) 661-3270; FAX (305) 661-3270

BB275. Renovated Victorian home built in the late 1800s was moved by barge in 1946 along the Manatee River to its present location, across the street from the gulf beach. Interesting antique furnishings in the guest room and one-bedroom apartment. A delightful, low key, restful spot for the tourist or professional who wants to relax. Gracious hostess serves speciality breakfast favorites. $60-75.

CEDAR KEY

Bed and Breakfast Scenic Florida

P.O. Box 3385, Tallahassee, 32315-3385
(904) 386-8196

FL48. Dating to 1859, this home is listed on the National Register of Historic Places. Public rooms include lounges and second-floor porch with paddle fans and eclectic furnishings. No TVs or room telephones intrude. Ten guest bedrooms are upstairs and have a mix of private in-suite baths, private hall baths, and shared baths. Rooms have ceiling fans and window air conditioners. Guests have access to cozy bar and gourmet dinners served in the dining room or adjoining porch. A full American breakfast is available from 8:00-11:00 A.M. No children. No smoking. $75-85.

The Island Hotel

P.O. Box 460, 32625
(904) 543-5111

A pre-Civil War building with Jamaican-style architecture is rustic and authentic, with much of the original structure. On the National Register of Historic Places. Gourmet seafood dining room, serving local Cedar Key specialties. Like stepping back in time, with muraled walls, paddle fans, French doors, and a wide wraparound porch which catches gulf breezes. A cozy lounge bar completes a perfect place to get away from it all. No smoking in bedrooms. Inquire about children being welcome.

Hosts: Tom and Alison Sanders
Rooms: 10 (6 PB; 4 S2B) $75-95
Full Breakfast
Credit Cards: A, B, C
Notes: 2, 4, 5, 9, 10, 11, 12, 14

COCOA

FMH Bed and Breakfast

809 Clearlake Road, 32922
(407) 632-7060

The hosts welcome guests to their modern modular private homes. Enjoy a private kitchen, bath, two bedrooms, living room, patio, etc. Walk to shopping centers. Public golf courses and recreation, fishing, etc., are within five miles; Space Center is within 15 miles; and beaches are within ten miles. Disney World, MGM, Epcot, Universal Studio, and Sea World are within a one-hour drive. $5 per additional person.

Hosts: Bill and Joyce Frey
Rooms: 5 (PB) $35
Continental Breakfast
Credit Cards: None
Notes: 5, 8

---

7 No smoking; 8 Children welcome; 9 Social drinking allowed; 10 Tennis nearby; 11 Swimming nearby; 12 Golf nearby; 13 Skiing nearby; 14 May be booked through a travel agent.

CRESCENT CITY

Bed and Breakfast Scenic Florida

P.O. Box 3385, Tallahassee, 32315-3385
(904) 386-8196

FL 26. Within easy driving distance of Atlantic beaches, this 1892 Steamboat Gothic home is shaded by moss-draped oaks. All rooms and suites are on the second floor, have private baths, and are air-conditioned. Most have TVs. Choices include three rooms with double beds, two suites with queen-size beds, and a third suite that is large and modern. A full gourmet breakfast is served in the full service restaurant. Lunch and dinner are also available, and diners come from surrounding communities. No children. No smoking. $50-125.

Sprague House Inn and Restaurant

125 Central Avenue, 32012
(904) 698-2430

This 103-year-old inn, with wraparound porches and a view of Crescent Lake, is in a quiet fishing town. Each room has a private bath and sitting room, with two newly renovated deluxe suites. A full gourmet breakfast is served in the award-winning restaurant. Relax among the shady oaks while the hosts prepare gourmet meals and desserts.

Hosts: Terry and Vena Moyer
Rooms: 6 (PB) $50-125
Full Breakfast
Credit Cards: A, B
Notes: 3, 4, 5, 7, 9, 10

DAYTONA BEACH

Bed and Breakfast Company

P.O. Box 262, South Miami, 33243
(305) 661-3270; FAX (305) 661-3270

DB263. This two-story suburban home is on a new golf course development just off I-4. The guest bedroom has a queen-size bed; private bath is on the second floor. The retired hosts are gracious and hospitable. $40.

The Villa Bed and Breakfast

801 North Peninsula Drive, 32118
(904) 248-2020

Enjoy elegant accommodations in a historic Spanish mansion on more than one and one-quarter acres of land in the heart of Daytona Beach. Decorated with fine antiques, this lovely inn has richly detailed public areas, a formal living room, dining and breakfast rooms, and a library/entertainment room. Enjoy the private, walled flower gardens, the pool, and the sunning area. Guests are within walking distance of Daytona's famous beach, restaurants, shopping, nightlife, and the famous Boardwalk and Arcade area. Inquire about accommodations for children.

Host: Jim Camp
Rooms: 4 (PB) $65-170
Continental Breakfast
Credit Cards: A, B, C
Notes: 5, 10, 11, 12, 13, 14

DAYTONA BEACH SHORES

Bed and Breakfast Company

P.O. Box 262, South Miami, 33243
(305) 661-3270; FAX (305) 661-3270

DB323. Super luxury in a townhouse development on A1A across from the ocean. All appointments throughout guest room and home are top quality, harmonious, and comfortable. King-size bed in guest room with double convertible in den for third person. Par-three golf course, tennis, pool, fitness equipment available at no cost. Walk to restaurants, shops, and public transportation to mall, race track, etc. Children over eight are welcome. $75.

NOTES: Credit cards accepted: A MasterCard; B Visa; C American Express; D Discover; E Diners Club; F Other; 2 Personal checks accepted; 3 Lunch available; 4 Dinner available; 5 Open all year; 6 Pets welcome;

DE FUNIAK SPRINGS

Bed and Breakfast Scenic Florida

P.O. Box 3385, Tallahassee, 32315-3385
(904) 386-8196

FL14. This Queen Anne Victorian home was the residence of Florida Governor Sidney J. Catts and dates back to the 1880s. Porches provide a place to relax, and the atmosphere reflects the era. A third-floor common room provides TV, VCR, and reading alcove. A collectible shop is also on the third floor. Three guest rooms are available. Guests may choose a full-size bed with large private bath, a full-size bed with hot tub, or king-size bed with claw-foot tub and shower. All rooms have ceiling fans and carpeting. Wake-up coffee or tea precedes a full breakfast in the formal dining room that includes special offerings. No children. No smoking. $75.

DELRAY BEACH

Bed and Breakfast Company

P.O. Box 262, South Miami, 33243
(305) 661-3270; FAX (305) 661-3270

DB39601. Cruise and snooze, or a bedroom for landlubbers in this bed and breakfast waterway home. The 44-foot sloop can sleep ten, has two baths, and is completely entertainment equipped. Special Snooze and Cruise packages include wine and hors d'oeuvres, dessert with champagne, dinner aboard, overnight stay and breakfast. Bedroom also available in lovely ranch home. $40-250.

DESTIN

Henderson Park Inn— A Beachside Bed and Breakfast

2700 Highway 98E-Beach Route, 32541
(800) 336-4853

Destin's first and only beachside bed and breakfast combines the charm of a Queen Anne-style inn with the amenities of a modern resort. The perfect place for couples and romantics; rooms are decorated with cozy impressionistic themes, antique hand-crafted reproductions, high ceilings, some rooms have fireplaces and four-poster canopied beds, fine linens, and private balconies and baths, some of which have Jacuzzis. Villas are perfect for families up to six. Southern beachside breakfast, beach service, maid service, turndown service, evening social receptions, heated pool, veranda, palm grove, and restaurant. Dedicated conference/meeting facilities for up to 60.

Host: Susie Nunnelley
Rooms: 20 (PB) $54-210
Villas: 18
Full Breakfast
Credit Cards: A, B, C, D
Notes: 2, 3, 4, 5, 8, 9, 10, 11, 12, 14

EVERGLADES CITY

The Ivey House Bed and Breakfast

107 Camellia Street, P.O. Box 5038, 33929
(813) 695-3299; FAX (813) 695-4155

This quaint bed and breakfast is for those who want to explore the Everglades National Park without leaving the comforts of home. There are ten air-conditioned rooms with shared bathrooms, and a large living room including an Everglades-area library. Smoking and drinking are allowed only on the outside porches. Guided adventures including canoeing, kayaking, biking, hiking, and sea shelling are provided daily. Also available are canoe, kayak, and bicycle rentals (bikes are complimentary for guests).

Hosts: Catlin McLeod and Lee Lambert
Rooms: 11 (1 PB; 10 SB) $40-50
Full Breakfast
Credit Cards: A, B
Notes: 2, 3, 4, 8, 10, 11, 14

7 No smoking; 8 Children welcome; 9 Social drinking allowed; 10 Tennis nearby; 11 Swimming nearby; 12 Golf nearby; 13 Skiing nearby; 14 May be booked through a travel agent.

The Bailey House

FERNANDINA BEACH (AMELIA ISLAND) ___

The Bailey House

P.O. Box 805, 32034
(904) 261-5390

Completed in 1895, this fine old home is an outstanding example of the Queen Anne style. The owners have filled the home with a vast collection of carefully chosen period antiques collected across the nation. The large, comfortable, and elegant guest rooms are furnished with authentic antique furniture and decorator pieces, yet offer the modern conveniences of a private bath. For guests, a complimentary expanded Continental breakfast is served each morning in the main dining room. The Bailey House has central heat and air for year-round comfort. Near Fort Clinch State Park, horseback riding, and beautiful beaches. In consideration of all guests, the hosts must say no to pets and children under ten years of age. Come enjoy the charm and history of this beautiful turn-of-the-century home and relax in the ambience of a bygone era. Children over eight are welcome.

Host: Thomas W. Bishop, Jr.
Rooms: 5 (PB) $85-115
Continental Breakfast
Credit Cards: A, B, C
Notes: 2, 5, 7, 8, 11, 12, 14

Bed and Breakfast Company

P.O. Box 262, South Miami, 33243
(305) 661-3270; FAX (305) 661-3270

FB210. This two-story frame beach house is across the road from the ocean. Two suites: one with full kitchen, TV, and video collection; the other has a sitting room, microwave, and refrigerator. An outstanding collection of books, magazines, and adult activity items available. $65-75.

FORT MYERS _____

Bed and Breakfast Company

P.O. Box 262, South Miami, 33243
(305) 661-3270; FAX (305) 661-3270

FM301-01. Hostess has lovingly and painstakingly restored three small one- and two-bedroom homes with living room, kitchen, baths, etc., in quasi-historical area just off Route 441 near the downtown area. A real bargain awaits couples or a family. Hostess is a school teacher who enjoys this additional activity and can direct guests to all of the sites in and around the city proper and neighboring beaches. $45.

Embe's Hobby House

5570-4 Woodrace Court, 33907
(941) 936-6378

Large mini suite and private bath in a modern townhouse is close to Sanibel and Captiva Islands, the beaches, and Edison home. Cats in residence, but not permitted in the guest quarters.

Host: Embe Burdick
Rooms: 1 (PB) $75
Continental Breakfast
Credit Cards: None
Notes: 2, 5, 7, 9, 10, 11, 12, 14

FORT PIERCE _____

Bed and Breakfast Company

P.O. Box 262, South Miami, 33243
(305) 661-3270; FAX (305) 661-3270

NOTES: Credit cards accepted: A MasterCard; B Visa; C American Express; D Discover; E Diners Club;
F Other; 2 Personal checks accepted; 3 Lunch available; 4 Dinner available; 5 Open all year; 6 Pets welcome;

FP33901. Guests fish for grouper and trout off the bank of the river when they stay in this 80-year-old duplex along the Intracoastal Waterway. Lots of antiques, collectibles, and excellent art collection. The home sits atop a small hill with a lovely view of the river. Three bedrooms with private baths. Outside cat. Smoking outside. $45.

GAINESVILLE

Bed and Breakfast Scenic Florida

P.O. Box 3385, Tallahassee, 32315-3385
(940) 386-8196

FL20. The historic district is home to this 1885 French Second Empire Victorian guest house. All six guest rooms have gas fireplaces, ceiling fans, and are decorated in period pieces. Guests have a choice of rooms on two stories. Accommodations include double bed and day bed, queen-size bed, double iron bed, a four-poster queen-size bed, a bridal chamber with a canopied double bed, and a suite with a queen-size bed. Baths are private, some with claw-foot tub and shower. A breakfast of specialties is served in the dining room. No children. No smoking. $60-90.

HAINES CITY

Holly Garden Inn

106 First Street South, 33844
(813) 421-9867

This romantic bed and breakfast is in a historic small town in the heart of central Florida's citrus groves. The 1924 home has been lovingly restored to recapture the grand elegance of the Old South. Just 20 miles from Walt Disney World and most central Florida attractions, it is a perfect spot for that romantic getaway, family vacation, wedding, or small meeting. Escape to a special place where the flag still waves and classic Southern hospitality

is a way of life. Lunches are served Monday through Friday.

Hosts: Camilla and Wesley Donnelly
Rooms: 5 (4 PB; 1 SB) $79-89
Full Breakfast
Credit Cards: A, B, C
Notes: 2, 5, 7, 8, 9, 10, 12, 14

HAVANA

Gaver's Bed and Breakfast

301 East Sixth Avenue, 32333
(904) 539-5611

This bed and breakfast, found on a quiet residential street two blocks from the center of town, is a likely stop for collectors. At last count, Havana had 30 antique shops plus many related businesses. Tallahassee, the state capital and home of Florida State University, is only 15 minutes away by car. Gaver's restored 1907 frame house has a large screened porch. Guests are welcome to watch cable TV in the common area. For breakfast, the hosts will design a menu to suit guests' preferences.

Hosts: Shirley and Bruce Gaver
Rooms: 2 (PB) $65-75
Full Breakfast
Credit Cards: None
Notes: 2, 5, 7, 9, 12

HIGH SPRINGS

Bed and Breakfast Scenic Florida

P.O. Box 3385, Tallahassee, 32315-3385
(940) 386-8196

FL21. This two-story Victorian home was built in 1906. Guests may enjoy the common areas, including the formal parlor, glassed sunroom with TV and stereo, deck, gazebo, and porches. Three guest rooms have double beds and a large shared bath with claw-foot tub and shower. Instructional packages for scuba diving are available, and gear may be stored securely on the grounds. Breakfast is served buffet style. No children. No smoking. $70-85.

7 No smoking; 8 Children welcome; 9 Social drinking allowed; 10 Tennis nearby; 11 Swimming nearby; 12 Golf nearby; 13 Skiing nearby; 14 May be booked through a travel agent.

FL 36. A deep, shady porch distinguishes this 1917 Craftsman bungalow. Guests may enjoy the front parlor or the game room. A canoe and bicycles are also available. Accommodations include a guest room with an antique iron double bed and three suites with queen-size, king-size, and double beds. Twin beds may be requested, and a day bed accommodates a third person. A modern bath is available, as well as period claw-foot tubs and a tin tub. A buffet breakfast is served indoors or on the porch. No smoking. $69-79.

HOLIDAY

Oakridge House

P.O. Box 3773, 34690-0773
(813) 372-8444; (800) 554-0085

Spacious country home in picturesque setting on one and one-half acres of attractively landscaped grounds. The bedrooms are newly decorated with handmade quilts, ceiling fans, and Early American heirlooms. Guests are welcome to enjoy the screened patio with 20' x 40' pool or relax in the comfortable TV room or parlor. Shopping and gulf are minutes away. Breakfast, evening meal, and personal laundry service are complimentary.

Host: Karen Pflanzer
Rooms: 2 (SB) $35-55
Full Breakfast
Credit Cards: None
Notes: 2, 5, 7, 8, 9, 10, 11, 12

HOLLYWOOD

The International Bed & Breakfast Club, Inc.

504 Amherst Street, Buffalo, NY 14207
(800) 723-4262; FAX (716) 873-4462

FL7168PP. Stunning contemporary with Oriental decor has easy access and easy living in this one-story ranch home. Two bedrooms with shared bath. Full breakfast served. Tropical garden and in-ground swimming pool. Fifteen minutes from shopping center and Fort Lauderdale airport; ten minutes from beach. Renting by the week only. Open November through May. Smoking permitted. $65-70.

INDIALANTIC

Bed and Breakfast Company

P.O. Box 262, South Miami, 33243
(305) 661-3270; FAX (305) 661-3270

IN340. This ranch-style home is only one and one-half blocks from the beach in Indianlantic, a quiet community bordering the ocean just east of Melborne. Thirty miles from the Space Center and about two hours from Orlando. Three miles to downtown Melbourne with its restaurants, stores, and antique shops. Two roomy, comfortable bedrooms (queen-size and double beds) share a bath. There is a queen-size convertible available in the study. $40-45.

JACKSONVILLE

Bed and Breakfast Scenic Florida

P.O. Box 3385, Tallahassee, 32315-3385
(904) 386-8196

FL 29. This Prairie-style home built in 1914 is in Jacksonville's Riverside area, which is part of the National Historic District. It is just minutes from the convention center and a few steps from the St. Johns riverbank. Guests may enjoy two distinct living areas, one with TV and comfortable couches, and three porches. Two upstairs rooms have queen-size beds and may connect for family use. A large bath has both walk-in shower and deep pedestal tub. A full Continental breakfast with homemade breads may be served in the dining room, on the porch, or in the guest's room. No children. No smoking. $60.

NOTES: Credit cards accepted: A MasterCard; B Visa; C American Express; D Discover; E Diners Club; F Other; 2 Personal checks accepted; 3 Lunch available; 4 Dinner available; 5 Open all year; 6 Pets welcome;

Club Continental Suites

2143 Astor Street, P.O. Box 7059, Orange Park,
  32073
(904) 264-6070; (800) 877-6070

The Club Continental Suites is a
Mediterranean-style inn overlooking the
broad St. Johns River, featuring romantic
Continental dining with "old Florida
charm." The Club, built in 1923 as the
Palmolive family estate, now hosts 22
riverview suites with expansive grounds,
giant live oaks, lush gardens, seven tennis
courts, three pools, and a pre-Civil War
Riverhouse Pub with live entertainment.
Sunday brunch available. Lunch and dinner
available Tuesday through Friday. Inquire
about what type of pets welcome.

Hosts: Caleb Massee and Karrie Massee
Rooms: 22 (PB) $60-140
Continental Breakfast
Credit Cards: A, B, C
Notes: 5, 8, 9, 10, 11, 12, 14

House on Cherry Street

1844 Cherry Street, 32205
(904) 384-1999; FAX (904) 981-2998

Historic restored home on the St. Johns
River near downtown Jacksonville, features
antiques, elegant breakfasts, wine, snacks,
and bicycles for guest use. Children over
nine welcome.

Host: Carol Anderson
Rooms: 4 (PB) $77.75-88.99
Full Breakfast
Credit Cards: A, B
Notes: 2, 5, 9, 10, 12, 14

JUPITER

Innisfail

134 Timber Lane, 33458
(407) 744-5905

A contemporary ranch framed by palm trees
is the home gallery of the Van Noorden
sculptors. While guests don't have to be art
lovers to visit, it helps to be a pet lover, as
the four-footed family consists of three dogs
and two cats. Enjoy a relaxing poolside
Continental breakfast before exploring the
lovely beaches of Jupiter and the many sights
and activities of the Palm Beach area.

Host: Katherine Van Noorden
Room: 1 (PB) $50-60
Continental Breakfast
Credit Cards: None
Notes: 2, 4, 5, 6, 7, 8, 9, 10, 11, 12

KEY LARGO

Bed and Breakfast Company

P.O. Box 262, South Miami, 33243
(305) 661-3270; FAX (305) 661-3270

LK260. Romantic one-bedroom apartment
that opens onto a sand beach, the ocean, and
a pool. Also a protected patio and grassy
area for lounging. An L-shaped area where
bedrooms are closed off from sitting area.
Hosts live on the second level and have a
child and two dogs. Lovely breeze.
Continental breakfast supplies are left in the
kitchen. $125.

KEY WEST

Andrew's Inn

Zero Walton Lane, 33040
(305) 294-7730

Central Old Town Key West and down a
shaded lane off Duval Street. Each queen-
size or king-size deluxe room is distinctive
and beautiful. All have private entrances,
full bath, remote control TV, air conditioning, and telephone. Guests will be served a
full breakfast each morning, and cocktails
are on the house. Overlooking the
Hemingway estate.

Hosts: Tim Gatewood and Andrew Cleveland
Rooms: 9 (PB) $98-148
Full Breakfast
Credit Cards: A, B, C, D
Notes: 2, 5, 9, 10, 11, 12, 14

---

7 No smoking; 8 Children welcome; 9 Social drinking allowed; 10 Tennis nearby; 11 Swimming nearby;
12 Golf nearby; 13 Skiing nearby; 14 May be booked through a travel agent.

The Banyan Resort

323 Whitehead Street, 33040
(800) 225-0639; FAX (305) 294-1107

A lush Caribbean estate on half a block in
the heart of Old Town Key West. Extensive
botanical gardens, fruit trees, two swimming pools, Jacuzzi, and Tiki bar. Thirty-
eight modern suites with all amenities in
eight elegant Victorian homes, of which
five are on the National Register of
Historic Places. Kitchen in each room.
Coffee by the pool. Weekly rates available.
No pets.

Host: Martin J. Bettercourt
Rooms: 38 (PB) $115-265
Credit Cards: A, B, C, D
Notes: 3, 5, 9, 10, 11, 12, 14

Bed and Breakfast Company

P.O. Box 262, South Miami, 33243
(305) 661-3270; FAX (305) 661-3270

KW42. The hostess is a well-known artist
who graciously opens her home to guests from
October through April. The two bedrooms and
baths have designer touches that help make a
visit memorable. Delightful patio with colorful
plants and tropical foliage adjoins the kitchen.
Walk to the center of the village for unique
shopping, attractions, historic sites, beaches,
and an unbelievable choice of restaurants. Do
not miss a ride on the Conch Tour Train or Old
Town Trolly. $80.

Chelsea House

707 Truman Avenue, 33040
(305) 296-2211; (800) 845-8859

Beautifully restored Victorian mansion. All
rooms have been tastefully appointed with
period pieces and Caribbean ambience.
Breakfast is served poolside, with cooking
facilities available. Off-street parking. Easy
walking to all attractions in Old Town Key
West. It's truly paradise!

Hosts: Jim, Gary, and Robb
Rooms: 14 (PB) $78-148

Continental Breakfast
Credit Cards: A, B, D
Notes: 5, 9, 10, 11, 12, 14

The Curry Mansion

511 Caroline Street, 33040
(305) 294-5349; (800) 253-3466
FAX (305) 294-4093

The Victorian Masterpiece Museum, now a
guest house, is on the National Register of
Historic Places and has been voted Key
West's Best. Romantic, air-conditioned
rooms with private baths, fans, and handmade quilts are available. Breakfast and
daily cocktail party available. Swim at the
pool or private beach club. Downtown walk
to everything. Available for weddings, parties, and meetings. Small animals welcome.
Inquire to see if children are welcome.

Hosts: Albert and Edith Amsterdam
Rooms: 28 (PB) $125-200
Continental Breakfast
Credit Cards: A, B, C, D, E, F
Notes: 2, 5, 10, 11, 12, 14

Duval House

815 Duval Street, 33040
(305) 294-1666; (800) 22 DUVAL

This beautifully restored, century-old
Victorian house has a special charm and
deluxe amenities. Enjoy the large swimming pool and quiet tropical gardens. Walk
to any one of the many nearby restaurants

Duval House

and attractions. AAA and Mobil Travel Guide approved.

Host: Richard Kamradt
Rooms: 28 (25 PB; 3 SB) $80-195
Continental Breakfast
Credit Cards: A, B, C, D, E
Notes: 5, 7, 9, 10, 11, 12, 14

Eden House

1015 Fleming Street, 33040
(800) 533-KEYS

A charming 1924 Art Deco hotel in Key West. Features air conditioning, pool, Caribbean Jacuzzi, garden cafe, and a tropical garden. Come experience the feeling of Old Key West. Wicker furniture, balconies, private parking lot, and complimentary happy hour. Call for rates. Please inquire first regarding pets.

Host: Stephen Clement
Rooms: 42 (22 PB; 20 SB)
No Breakfast
Credit Cards: A, B
Notes: 3, 4, 5, 6, 8, 9, 10, 11, 12

Garden House of Key West

329 Elizabeth Street, 33040
(305) 296-5368; (800) 695-6453
FAX (305) 292-1160

In the historic district and within walking distance of everything. Tropical gardens, spa with waterfall, and sun decks. Rooms are air-conditioned with both private and shared bath. Complimentary Continental buffet breakfast and wine hour daily under the covered patio.

Hosts: John and Helene Montagu
Rooms: 10 (8 PB; 2 SB) $66-125
Continental Breakfast
Credit Cards: A, B, C, D
Notes: 5, 6, 7, 8, 9, 10, 11, 12, 14

Heron House

512 Simonton Street, 33040
(305) 294-9227

Heron House is not for those who wish to spend the night, but, rather, for those who

Heron House

have the time to enjoy. Heron House is Key West's perfect getaway. With a labor of love and the freedom to create from the heart, local artists have painstakingly hand-crafted Heron House for over ten years. Relax in the comfort and warmth of natural oak, redwood, and cedar adorning the walls of guest rooms. Enjoy the coolness of Italian tile and marble under one's feet. Rest on huge oak beds as the morning sunlight filters through hand-crafted stained-glass transoms heralding the new day. Step outside the room and listen to the tree frogs in the evening. Smell the orchid flowers in the trees, and watch the stars from our "moon" deck. And all this peace in the very center of historic Key West. Personal checks accepted for deposit only.

Host: Fred Geibelt
Rooms: 21 (PB) $105.45-249.75
Continental Breakfast
Credit Cards: A, B, C
Notes: 5, 7, 9, 10, 11, 12, 14

The Island City House Hotel

411 William Street, 33040
(305) 294-5702; (800) 634-8230

The Island City House Hotel is three historic Victorian guest houses offering 24 one- and two-bedroom suites with tropical gardens and red brick walkways winding throughout. Enjoy a complimentary breakfast buffet of fruits, breads, and coffee on a secluded patio,

7 No smoking; 8 Children welcome; 9 Social drinking allowed; 10 Tennis nearby; 11 Swimming nearby; 12 Golf nearby; 13 Skiing nearby; 14 May be booked through a travel agent.

or relax on the deck in our crystalline pool and Jacuzzi in this lush tropical paradise.

Hosts: Stanley and Janet Corneal
Rooms: 24 (PB) $95-210
Continental Breakfast
Credit Cards: A, B, D, E, F
Notes: 5, 8, 9, 10, 11, 12, 14

Key West Bed and Breakfast: The Popular House

415 William, 33040
(305) 296-7274; (800) 438-6155

A classically restored turn-of-the-century three-story Victorian was built by Bahamian shipbuilders on a quiet tree-shaded street. The house is decorated in a Caribbean style. Four porches, sun deck, tropical gardens, Jacuzzi, and sauna for immediate relaxation. In the heart of the historic preservation district and within walking distance of many restaurants, beaches, and shops.

Host: Jody Carlson
Rooms: 8 (4 PB; 4 SB) $59-200
Continental Breakfast
Credit Cards: A, B, C, D, E
Notes: 2, 5, 7, 9, 10, 11, 12, 14

Merlinn Guest House

811 Simonton Street, 33040
(305) 296-3336

Lush tropical gardens, decks, and pool in the heart of Old Town. Freshly baked

Merlinn Guest House

breakfast served among exotic birds in the secluded garden. Evening get-together. Eighteen rooms and apartments with private baths, TV, and air conditioning. Also wheelchair accessible unit with private garden. The staff can arrange a day on the water—snorkeling, fishing, sailing, or playing. Guests never want to leave! Three-night minimum stay during holidays. Personal checks accepted for deposit.

Host: Pat Hoffman
Rooms: 18 (PB) $67.50-150
Full Breakfast
Credit Cards: A, B, C, D
Notes: 5, 6, 7, 8, 9, 11, 14

Nassau House

1016 Fleming Street, 33040
(305) 296-8513; (800) 296-8513

In Old Town Key West, Nassau House is a century old Conch house, completely renovated in 1994, offering charming rooms and suites. All rooms feature private baths, air conditioning, cable TV, phones, clock radios, comfortable king- and queen-size beds, and wicker and antique furnishings. The Treetop Suites feature living rooms and kitchens. The house boasts a large and airy front porch with wicker rocking chairs, and a lush tropical garden with lagoon-style pool/Jacuzzi nestled into the foliage. A trilevel deck accessible from several rooms overlooks the pool area. The shops and excitement of Duval Street, the Mallory Square Sunset Celebration, and beaches are all within walking distance. Bicycle rental available on the property. Minimum stay during holidays.

Hosts: Damon Leard and Bob Tracy
Rooms: 7 (PB) $69-149
Continental Breakfast
Credit Cards: A, B, C
Notes: 5, 6, 9, 10, 11, 12, 14

Papa's Hideaway

309 Louisa, 33040
(305) 294-7709

Enjoy a secluded private getaway in lush tropical gardens. Lounge in a studio apartment with private bath, patio, kitchenette, air conditioning, and color cable TV. Or choose the quaint two-bedroom, two-bath cottage with living and dining rooms, kitchen, wraparound porches, and private sun deck. Complimentary Continental breakfast is served by the heated pool and Jacuzzi daily. One block off the main street, guests are within walking or biking distance to beaches, clubs, theaters, and restaurants.

Hosts: Pat McGee and Ellen Nowlin
Rooms: 5 (PB) $65-200
Continental Breakfast
Credit Cards: A, B, C, D, E
Notes: 5, 9, 10, 11, 12, 14

Seascape

420 Olivia Street, 33040
(305) 296-7776; (800) 765-6438

Listed on the National Register of Historic Places, this inn has a heated pool-spa nestled under crimson bougainvillea, a tropical garden, and fabulous sun decks. All rooms feature private baths, air conditioning, Bahama fan, cable TV, and a queen-size bed. Complimentary Continental breakfast and wine hour (in-season). In the heart of Old Town. Minutes from the Atlantic Ocean and the Gulf of Mexico. Steps away from the finest shops and eating and drinking establishments. "Sparkling"—*New York Times*.

Host: Alan Melnick
Rooms: 5 (PB) $69-114
Continental Breakfast
Credit Cards: A, B, C, D
Notes: 5, 9, 10, 11, 12, 14

Treetop Inn Historic Bed and Breakfast

806 Truman Avenue, 33040
(305) 293-0712; (800) 926-0712
FAX 294-3668

Built in 1902, Treetop Inn has been restored (1993) to provide modern comforts in a 1900s setting. It received the 1994 Key West Chamber of Commerce's Business for

Beauty award. In central Old Town, Treetop Inn is within walking distance of numerous beaches, restaurants, and shops. Breakfast is provided on the pool deck amid lush tropical gardens. The hosts are knowledgeable about all Key West activities. The spacious rooms are graciously furnished and include cable TV, air conditioning, and telephones.

Hosts: Sue and Fred Leake
Rooms: 3 (1 PB; 2 SB) $78-148
Full Breakfast
Credit Cards: A, B, D
Notes: 5, 7, 9, 10, 11, 12

The Watson House

525 Simonton Street, 33040
(305) 294-6712; (800) 621-9405

The Watson House, circa 1860, is a distinctively furnished small guest house in the historic preservation district. Received 1987 award for excellence in rehabilitation from Historical Florida Keys Preservation Board. Heated swimming pool, heated Jacuzzi, patio, decks, and gardens. All units have their own distinct style, private baths, color TV, air conditioning, and telephone; larger suites have fully equipped kitchens. Privacy prevails; adults only; no pets. Brochure available.

Hosts: Joe Beres and Ed Czaplicki
Suites: 3 (PB) $95-360
Continental Breakfast
Credit Cards: A, B, C
Notes: 5, 7, 9, 10, 11, 12, 14

Whispers Bed and Breakfast Inn

409 William Street, 33040
(305) 294-5969; (800) 856-SHHH

The owner-managers take great pride in the service, hospitality, and the romance of their historic 1866 inn. Each room is unique and appointed with antiques. Included in the room rate is a full gourmet breakfast served in the tropical gardens and membership at a local beach club and health spa. Limited smoking permitted. Inquire about children.

Host: John Marburg
Rooms: 7 (5 PB; 2SB) $69-175
Full Breakfast
Credit Cards: A, B, C, D
Notes: 2, 5, 7, 9, 10, 11, 12

The Wicker Guest House: An Island Bed and Breakfast

913 Duval Street, 33040
(305) 296-4275; (800) 880-4275
FAX (305) 294-7240

On the colorful Duval Street in the heart of the historic district, a complex of new and restored houses offers guests a variety of accommodations from inexpensive shared bathrooms to luxurious fully equipped studio apartments. Spacious tropical garden has pool. Breakfast is served poolside. Friendly, helpful staff. Families welcome.

Hosts: Mark and Libby Curtis
Rooms: 21 (11 PB; 10 SB) $45-145
Continental Breakfast
Credit Cards: A, B, C, D, E
Notes: 5, 8, 9, 10, 11, 12, 14

KISSIMMEE

The Unicorn Inn

8 South Orlando Avenue, 34741
(407) 846-1200

The Unicorn Inn

The Unicorn Inn is in the historic district of downtown in a secure location offering peace and tranquility and a slower lifestyle. The Inn is only 300 yards from Lake Tohopekaliga, where guests can bass fish or hire a boat. Golf courses nearby. Twenty to 30 minutes to area attractions such as the Disney Sea World and Epcot Center. Twenty-five minutes from Orlando Airport. This 1901 Colonial house has been tastefully remodeled with antique pottery and prints. All rooms have private baths, air conditioning, and TVs. All rooms are individually decorated and wallpapered. Kitchen facilities available. British owned and operated with an all-British breakfast menu. Guests receive a homey welcome at all times. Walk to shops and restaurants. AAA approved.

Hosts: Fran and Don Williamson
Rooms: 6 (PB) $55-65
Full Breakfast
Credit Cards: A, B, C, D, E
Notes: 2, 5, 7, 8, 14

LAKE BUENA VISTA

Bed and Breakfast Scenic Florida

P.O. Box 3385, Tallahassee, 32315-3385
(904) 386-8196

FL42. Within minutes of the heart of Disney World, this home is on a secluded 20-acre parcel of land. Completed in 1990, the home has been designed to offer comfort to single travelers and families. Four guest rooms are available. Amenities include a private entrance to the grounds, convenient parking, private baths with combination tub and shower, ceiling fans, TV, telephone, and central heat and air conditioning. Choices include queen- and king-size beds with space for a crib. The great room is a gathering place for guests. An extended, self-service Continental breakfast is available. Children are welcome. No smoking allowed. $79.

LAKELAND

Bed and Breakfast Scenic Florida

P.O. Box 3385
Tallahassee, FL 32315-3385
(904) 386-8196

FL43. This fully restored country inn is a blend of Victorian and Colonial Revival architecture, and it is listed on the National Register of Historic Places. Four rooms with common parlors have twin, double, or queen-size beds. Privacy screens complement claw-foot tubs and furnishings reflect Oriental, French, and Queen Anne decor. TV is available. Evening wine and cheese or desserts are served in the formal parlor. Breakfast features Southern breads and other specialties; at lunch the tearoom opens to the public with a full menu. No smoking. $95.

Chalet Suzanne Country Inn

LAKE WALES

Chalet Suzanne Country Inn and Restaurant

3800 Chalet Suzanne Drive, 33853-7060
(813) 676-6011; (800) 433-6011

Discover Europe in the heart of Florida. This historic country inn is on 70 acres surrounded by orange groves. It has 30 charming guest rooms with private baths; award-winning dining overlooking Lake Suzanne. It is just 45 minutes southwest of the Orlando area.

Hosts: Carl and Vita Hinshaw
Rooms: 30 (PB) $125-185
Full Breakfast
Credit Cards: A, B, C, D, E
Notes: 2, 3, 4, 5, 6, 8, 9, 10, 11, 12, 14

MARATHON

Hopp-Inn Guest House

500 Sombrero Beach Road, 33050
(305) 743-4118; (908) 223-5979 (June 1 through October 1); FAX (305) 743-3750

In the heart of the Florida Keys. Every room has a water view. Families welcome in villas. Closed June 1 through October 1.

Host: The Hopp family
Rooms: 5 (PB) $50-150
Villas: 4 (PB)
Full Breakfast
Credit Cards: A, B
Notes: 10, 11, 12

Latigo Bed and Breakfast Cruise

1021 11th Street, Ocean, 33050
(305) 289-1066 (phone/FAX)

On this 56-foot luxury yacht with three private staterooms guests begin their experience on a sunset cruise, sipping champagne with a variety of hors d'oeuvres, followed by a first-class gourmet dinner. Champagne, wine, and beer are complimentary. The yacht is anchored overnight nestled behind a cluster of islands offering complete privacy. The following morning after breakfast, guests may snorkel over the beautiful coral reef or swim before returning dockside. Extended cruises are also available to

Latigo

7 No smoking; 8 Children welcome; 9 Social drinking allowed; 10 Tennis nearby; 11 Swimming nearby; 12 Golf nearby; 13 Skiing nearby; 14 May be booked through a travel agent.

Key West, Dry Tortugas, Bahamas. Fishing, diving, water-skiing are available. Rate includes two meals, lodging, sunset and snorkel cruises.

Hosts: Ken and Valerie Waine
Rooms: 3 (1 PB; 2 SB) $149 (per person)
Full or Continental Breakfast
Credit Cards: A, B
Notes: 2, 3, 5, 8, 9, 10, 11, 13, 14

MIAMI

Bed and Breakfast Company

P.O. Box 262, South Miami, 33243
(305) 661-3270; FAX (305) 661-3270

MI08. Spacious ranch home is in prestigious residential area of Key Biscayne. There is a private entrance to two bedrooms that open onto the screened pool area. Walk or bike to beautiful sand beach. The Seaquarium, Ocean World, and state park are nearby, with other Miami attractions just across the causeway. $45-80.

MI14. Exclusive residential area near Kings Bay Country Club and Biscayne Bay is about ten miles south of the downtown area. Charming home with two private-bath bedrooms; screened pool area. These delightful hosts enjoy entertaining guests. $40.

MI018. Casual, comfortable, and exceptionally attractive small home is designed to integrate the garden areas into the living space. Excellent location, close to shops, restaurants, entertainment, and local transportation, including metrorail. Near Coral Gables and University of Miami. Shared bath. Single only. $38.

MI034. Spend memorable days in a Miami Beach mansion on a private residential island in Biscayne Bay. Furnishings reflect the Old World charm of this Danish family. They are expert sailors and love travel and the arts. Host is a harbor pilot; hostess, a nurse. Swim in an ecologically balanced pool—no chemicals, only fish and plants, and luxuriate in the hot tub. Three rooms with private baths. Children welcome. $80.

MI058. This large ranch home is one mile west of the renowned Dadeland Mall; one-half mile from the metrorail, bus, other shops, and restaurants. A traditional home, attractively furnished. Bed and breakfast room is large, with king-size bed, and private bath with tub and shower. Hospitable, charming hosts. $40.

MI077. Nestled in a large, deep lot with many trees and plants is this ranch home in South Miami. Comfortably furnished with traditional and antique pieces, accessorized with interesting collectibles from the hostess's extensive travels. Walk to the University of Miami, metrorail, shops, restaurant, and movies. Bus is a half block away. High-rise bed, private bath adjoining in hall. Single occupancy only. $40.

MI219. Luxury home on the shore of the Intracoastal Waterway is near Bal Harbor and the exclusive shops and the ocean. Enjoy the pool and hot tub. Three bedrooms with private baths, two rooms with water view. Hosts are retired executives who enjoy travel, golf, and gourmet cooking. Children welcome. $60-75.

MI244. Perfect spot for exploring all the facets of Miami Beach's "South Beach Art Deco District," from the ocean and beach itself to the many restaurants, sidewalk cafes, trendy shops, historic architecture, and more! This studio efficiency has a view of the ocean, and has two double beds that fold into the wall, thus providing ample living space. Full kitchen, eating area, and bath. Unhosted. Parking on city block one and one-half blocks away. $85-95.

NOTES: Credit cards accepted: A MasterCard; B Visa; C American Express; D Discover; E Diners Club;
F Other; 2 Personal checks accepted; 3 Lunch available; 4 Dinner available; 5 Open all year; 6 Pets welcome;

MI246. Ultra luxury, private one-bedroom apartment is in a spectacular tropical setting in Coconut Grove! Within a lush walled estate also containing main house. Grounds are beautifully landscaped with specimen tropical plantings, splashy colored bromeliads, and natural pool with fountain. Apartment completely equipped for a permanent home with full kitchen, cable TV, VCR, phone—all the creature comforts. Double bed. Sofa can be used for additional guest. $100.

MI293. A unique experience is guaranteed by this bed and breakfast. A 36-foot luxury trawler yacht with all the comforts and conveniences of home. Sleeps six. Has two staterooms, two full baths, TV with VCR, stereo, completely equipped kitchen. Basically a charter boat, with most business in the afternoon; available for bed and breakfast in the evenings and when not booked for a charter. Also featuring a Cruise and Snooze option. This includes a one hour cruise on the intracoastal, dinner aboard ship, and bed and breakfast. $95-250.

MI316. This exceptional pool home in Coral Gables on a large corner lot has an adjoining cabana with a private garden entrance available for bed and breakfast guests. It opens onto a beautiful garden and pool area. Comfortable and airy, with king-size bed, private bath, and refrigerator. Close to metrorail, shops, and restaurants. Hosts are antique dealers. $80.

MI371. Lovely luxury cottage on Coconut Grove private one-acre estate has electronically controlled security. Mansion listed in historic registry. Walk five blocks to Coconut Grove Village with its trendy sidewalk cafes, restaurants, boutiques, and shops. Fireplace, efficiency kitchen, antique furniture, and elegant accessories.

Opens to private covered patio and large pool. Queen-size bed. Suite with twin beds is also available in the main house. $125.

MB40501. Very large efficiency apartment in Miami Beach's Art Deco area. Balcony with fantastic view of the ocean. Full kitchen, two double beds, luxury condo with all the amenities. Unit is just below the penthouse. Convenient walk to convention center and sidewalk cafes. $135.

MI28501. Charming two-room suite with sleeper sofa in sitting room and an extra bedroom if desired. In choice area of the Grove, near Vizcaya and the bay. Fifteen-minute walk to the village; fifteen-minute drive to downtown, port, or airport. Double bed in suite bedroom, private entry, large bath with stall shower. A small cottage with stall shower suitable for single is also available. Beautifully landscaped grounds with fruit trees and hibiscus. $45-75.

Miami River Inn

118 Southwest South River Drive, 33130
(305) 325-0045; (800) HOTEL 89
FAX (305) 325-9227

Built between 1906 and 1910, the Miami River Inn boasts four wooden cottages surrounding a pool and Jacuzzi in a lush tropical garden. The inn consists of 40 rooms, each individually decorated with antique furnishings, featuring cable TV, touch-tone telephones, central air/heat, and private bathrooms. A quick walk to downtown offers shopping, dining, museums, and galleries. Office services available free to business travelers. Beaches, airport, and Port of Miami are a short drive.

Hosts: Jane Caporelli and Sallye Jude
Rooms: 40 (38 PB; 2 SB) $69-125
Continental Breakfast
Credit Cards: A, B, C, D, E, F
Notes: 2, 5, 7, 8, 9, 10, 11, 12, 14

7 No smoking; 8 Children welcome; 9 Social drinking allowed; 10 Tennis nearby; 11 Swimming nearby; 12 Golf nearby; 13 Skiing nearby; 14 May be booked through a travel agent.

Redland's Bed and Breakfast

19521 SW 128 C, 33177
((305)238-5285

The romantic tropical guest house is 750 square feet with a fully furnished kitchen, living room, bedroom, and private bath. It sleeps four (two private) and has private entrance, TV, air conditioning, pool, and Jacuzzi. Self-catered breakfast can be enjoyed poolside or at the garden gazebo. Bicycles also available for the nearby bike trails. Near Miami's farming community, 25 minutes from Florida Keys and Miami International Airport.

Hosts: Marianne and Tim Hamilton
Rooms: 1 (PB) $65
Continental Breakfast
Notes: 2, 5, 7, 8, 9, 10, 11, 12

MICANOPY

Bed and Breakfast Scenic Florida

P.O. Box 3385, Tallahassee, 32315-3385
(940) 386-8196

FL18. This Classical Revival mansion was built over the original 1845 structure and reflects the wealth of the family in 1915. Ten rooms and suites and the first-floor parlor are available. Private baths, large windows, ceiling fans, and period decor are common to all rooms. Choices include a canopied king-size bed, cast-iron double bed, a brass and copper double bed, and a queen-size bed. Baths include both modern and period facilities. One suite has a Jacuzzi, and a restored cottage offers added privacy and a kitchenette. Guests may choose an early, full Continental breakfast or a formal, seated breakfast at 9:00 A.M. No smoking. $60-140.

FL25. Open porches and stained glass make this new structure reminiscent of yesteryear. Five guest rooms and suites with private baths and TVs are available. Choices include queen-size beds, four-poster beds, and a king-size water bed. Baths may be modern or period with claw-foot tub. Stained glass art classes are available. The full breakfast may be hearty Southern or gourmet and is served in the dining room. Room service is also available. No smoking. $75-125.

Herlong Mansion

402 Northeast Cholokka Boulevard
P.O. Box 667, 32667
(904) 466-3322

"Micanopy is the prettiest town in Florida. The Herlong Mansion is its crown jewel"— *Florida Trend*, November 1989. The brick Greek Revival structure has four Corinthian columns, ten fireplaces, six different types of wood, and is decorated in period antiques. Built in 1845 and 1910, the three-story house has 11 bedrooms, all with private baths, on two acres with moss-draped oaks, pecans, dogwoods, and magnolias.

Host: H. C. (Sony) Howard, Jr.
Rooms: 12 (PB) $50-150
Full Breakfast
Credit Cards: A, B
Notes: 2, 5, 8, 9, 14

Herlong Mansion

Shady Oak Bed and Breakfast

203 Cholokka Boulevard, 32667
(904) 466-3476

The Shady Oak stands majestically in the center of historic downtown. A marvelous canopy of old live oaks, quiet shaded streets, and store fronts offer visitors a memorable connection to Florida's past. This three-story 19th-century-style mansion features beautifully spacious suites and porches, Jacuzzi, Florida room, and widow's walk. A delicious country breakfast is served on weekdays, and a fabulous gourmet breakfast is served on weekends. Local activities include antiquing, bicycling, canoeing, bird watching, and much more. "Playfully elegant accommodations, where stained glass, antiques, and innkeeping go together as kindly as warm hugs with old friends."

Host: Frank James
Rooms: 5 (PB) $75-125
Full Breakfast
Credit Cards: A, B, D
Notes: 2, 3, 4, 5, 7, 8, 9, 14

MONTICELLO

Bed and Breakfast Scenic Florida

P.O. Box 3385, Tallahassee, 32315-3385
(940) 386-8196

FL47. Old live oak trees surround this stately Classical Revival home, which was built in 1836. It is listed on the National Register of Historic Places and is the oldest home in the county. The formal parlor, glassed sunrooms, and an open porch are all public areas. Four guest bedrooms are individually heated and air-conditioned and have private baths. Two rooms have antique canopy beds, one double and one queen-size. Other rooms have four-poster double beds. Telephone and TV are available. Breakfast is casual and served in the sunroom. Weekday fare is deluxe Continental; weekend meal is expanded with traditional items. No smoking allowed. $70-90.

The Emerald Hill Inn

MOUNT DORA

The Emerald Hill Inn

27751 Lake Jem Road, 32757
(904) 383-2777; FAX (904) 383-6701

Tucked away on a secluded country road is a serene, sprawling 1941 lakefront estate on two acres with tall oaks and broad, sweeping lawn. Spectacular sunsets make this a place to rediscover romance. Resembling a lodge, the living room is stunning with a majestic coquina rock fireplace, wood cathedral ceiling, polished oak floors, and spacious designer rooms. Ten minutes to Mount Dora antique shops, restaurants, festivals. Forty-five minutes to Orlando/Disney World. AAA three diamond rating. Continental plus breakfast. Inquire about children being welcome.

Hosts: Michael and Diane Wiseman
Rooms: 4 (2 PB; 2 SB) $75-115
Continental Breakfast
Credit Cards: A, B
Notes: 5, 7, 9, 12, 14

Farnsworth House Bed and Breakfast

1029 East 5th Avenue, 32757
(904) 735-1894

On one and one-half acres in the historic town of Mount Dora with its many boutiques and antique shops, this home was

7 No smoking; 8 Children welcome; 9 Social drinking allowed; 10 Tennis nearby; 11 Swimming nearby; 12 Golf nearby; 13 Skiing nearby; 14 May be booked through a travel agent.

built in 1886 with three suites and two efficiencies each decorated in a unique theme with private baths and kitchens. Guests can enjoy the large screened porch, living and dining room, and hot tub enclosed within a screened gazebo. Twenty-five miles northwest of Orlando.

Hosts: Dick and Sandy Shelton
Rooms: 5 (PB) $75-95
Credit Cards: A, B
Notes: 2, 5, 9, 10, 11, 12, 13, 14

NAPLES

Bed and Breakfast Company

P.O. Box 262, South Miami, 33243
(305) 661-3270; FAX (305) 661-3270

NA067. Comfort and convenience describe this home just two blocks from Vanderbilt Beach, in the shadow of the classy Ritz-Carlton Hotel. This two bedroom cottage-type home is in a small development of modest one-story homes. The bedroom is cozy; some antiques decorate the home. Hosts are hospitable professionals, gracious, and helpful. Home is about nine miles north of city center. $45.

NICEVILLE

The International Bed and Breakfast Club, Inc.

504 Amherst Street, Buffalo, NY 14207
(800) 723-4262; FAX (716) 873-4462

FL5644PP. The Bluewater Bay resort offers Northwest Florida's number-one-ranked golf course says *Golfweek*; one of the top 50 tennis resorts says *Tennis* magazine; and one of America's top ten vacation resorts says *Family Circle*. Easy drive from Atlanta, Nashville, New Orleans, and Dallas. Private bayside beach, casual and fine dining, and a natural deep-water marina with four swimming pools. Park areas, nature and biking trails are also available.

Residence provides suite with private bath. Full breakfast served. $85.

OCALA

Bed and Breakfast Scenic Florida

P.O. Box 3385, Tallahassee, 32315-3385
(904) 386-8196

FL34. Built as a family home in 1888, this three-story Queen Anne Victorian inn is one of *Southern Living* magazine's six best bed and breakfast inns. Seven rooms and suites are individually decorated. Choices include twin, double, queen-size, and king-size beds. Some are canopied, iron, or four-poster beds. Baths include both modern facilities and period claw-foot tubs. A full breakfast is a gourmet affair with special items. No children. No smoking. $105-135.

FL35. A bed and breakfast oasis just minutes from I-75 in a pastoral, horse-country setting has six spacious bed/sitting rooms with private entrances off a central courtyard. Common to all rooms are a wood-burning fireplace, TV, individual climate control, and bath with both a walk-in shower and Jacuzzi tub. Unusual touches such as Palladian windows, handcrafted furniture, and the use of native Florida wood and stone make these rooms especially inviting. Each room decor represents an era of Florida history. Two rooms have two double beds; another two rooms have queen-size canopied beds; a fifth room has a king-size four-poster bed; and the sixth room has a king-size lattice bed. A gazebo in the courtyard and the screened-in pool area are relaxing and meeting places for guests. Breakfast is served in the main house at tables overlooking the green fields. Rainbow Springs State Park is nearby, and the hosts can also arrange riding at a local stable for a close-up look at Florida's

Thoroughbred horse country. No smoking. No children. Handicapped accessible. $74.

Seven Sisters Inn

820 Southeast Fort King Street, 34471
(904) 867-1170; FAX (904) 732-7764

The Seven Sisters Inn is an elegant yet cozy retreat recently rated as one of the top ten restorations in the United States. This *Country Inns* magazine award winner is nestled in the heart of the historic district and Thoroughbred horse country. Eight beautifully appointed Victorian rooms each have a private bath, some with deep soaking tubs or Jacuzzi. Amenities include full gourmet breakfast, murder mystery weekends, weekend candlelight dinners, romantic rendezvous packages, family Swedish dinners, and gourmet picnic dinners on weekends. Close to famous Silver Springs glass-bottom boats, horse farm tours, unique antique shops, and the unspoiled Ocala National Forest. The inn has been featured in *Southern Living* magazine, *Country Inns*, *Conde Nast Traveler*, *National Geographic*, Mobil Travel and Fodor's guides. Canoe, hiking, golf, and antique packages available. Romantic getaways. Pet sitter is available. Inquire about children being welcome.

Hosts: Ken Oden and Bonnie Morehardt
Rooms: 8 (PB) $105-165
Full Breakfast
Credit Cards: A, B, C, D, E
Notes: 2, 3, 4 , 5, 6, 7, 9, 11, 12, 14

ORLANDO

The Courtyard at Lake Lucerne

211 North Lucerne Circle East, 32801
(407) 648-5188; (800) 444-5289

Victorian and Art Deco elegance describe this site in a tropical setting in the heart of downtown Orlando. Three separate buildings, each with its own distinctive style, sur-

The Courtyard at Lake Lucerne

rounding a luxuriously landscaped brick courtyard with fountains. Complimentary bottle of wine on arrival and expanded Continental breakfast each morning. Award-winning renovation in beautiful surroundings, convenient to everything the area has to offer. One house is nonsmoking.

Hosts: Charles Meiner, Sam and Eleanor Meiner, and Paula Bowers
Rooms: 22 (PB) $65-150
Continental Breakfast
Credit Cards: A, B, C, E
Notes: 5, 8, 9, 10, 11, 12, 13, 14

The International Bed and Breakfast Club, Inc.

504 Amherst Street, Buffalo, NY 14207
(800) 723-4262; FAX (716) 873-4462

FL4830PP. This country estate is nestled in "Disney's backyard." Each of four guest rooms is furnished with a queen-size brass bed or king-size four-poster, with private bath, outside entrance, TV, telephone, and air conditioning. Pool and Jacuzzi are also available. Continental breakfast. $65-75.

Perri House Bed and Breakfast Inn

10417 State Road 535, 32836
(407) 876-4830; (800) 780-4830
FAX (407) 876-0241

Perri House is a quiet, private, secluded country estate conveniently in the back yard of the Walt Disney World resort area. Because of its outstanding location, Disney Village is only three minutes away, and

7 No smoking; 8 Children welcome; 9 Social drinking allowed; 10 Tennis nearby; 11 Swimming nearby; 12 Golf nearby; 13 Skiing nearby; 14 May be booked through a travel agent.

EPCOT is only five minutes away. An upscale Continental breakfast awaits each morning to start the day. The hosts offer a unique blend of cordial hospitality, comfort, and friendship to all their guests.

Hosts: Nick and Angi Perretti
Rooms: 6 (PB) $69-89
Continental Breakfast
Credit Cards: A, B, C, D
Notes: 5, 7, 8, 9, 10, 11, 12, 14

PALM BAY

Casa Del Sol

Country Estates, 232 Rheine Road Northwest, 32907
(407) 728-4676

This award-winning home is on Florida's central east coast. Breakfast is served on the lanai, with breathtaking foliage. From here see a spaceship launched. Enjoy the luxury of a Roman tub. Minutes away from the space pad, all Disney attractions, and the Marlins' winter quarters. Closed April 16 through November 7.

Host: Stanley Finkelstein
Rooms: 3 (1 PB; 2 SB) $55-125
Full Breakfast
Credit Cards: None
Notes: 2, 6, 8, 9, 10, 11, 12, 13, 14

Casa Del Sol

PALM BEACH

Bed and Breakfast Company

P.O. Box 262, South Miami, 33243
(305) 661-3270; FAX (305) 661-3270

MI369. Luxurious contemporary estate is on the intracoastal in Palm Beach Gardens. Common areas include a sunken living room with stone fireplace; a den with TV, VCR, and fireplace; sunken dining room; second-floor central foyer and balcony; pool; patio with Jacuzzi; deck with boat slips; and beautiful landscaped grounds. Four rooms are available for bed and breakfast with private entrances and baths, and small refrigerator. Full-size double beds in three rooms, king-size bed in fourth bedroom. There are also two staterooms available on a yacht. $80-100.

Palm Beach Historic Inn

365 South County Road, 33480
(407) 832-4009

A historic landmark building, beautifully restored to preserve its original integrity and stately elegance, has every modern convenience. Four suites and nine guest rooms, tastefully and individually appointed, private baths and showers, air conditioning, cable TV and telephones. Guests will be served a complimentary deluxe Continental breakfast in their rooms. Walk one block to the beach and two blocks to the world-famous Worth Avenue shopping. Perfect for weekend getaways, family vacations, relaxing retreats, business trips, and romantic weekends. ABBA "A" rating for excellence.

Innkeeper: Melissa J. Laitman
Rooms: 9 (PB) $75-150
Suites: 4 (PB) $125-250
Continental Breakfast
Credit Cards: A, B, C, D, E
Notes: 2, 5, 8, 10, 11, 12, 14

Palm Beach Polo Bed and Breakfast

1120 Royal Palm Beach Boulevard #384, 33411
(407) 798-4072; (800) 344-0335
FAX (407) 791-4424

Rooms all have large king-size beds, large closets, and privacy. Three common baths are available for guests. A workout room

NOTES: Credit cards accepted: A MasterCard; B Visa; C American Express; D Discover; E Diners Club; F Other; 2 Personal checks accepted; 3 Lunch available; 4 Dinner available; 5 Open all year; 6 Pets welcome;

with Stair Masters, free weights, and multiple workout equipment typify this living arrangement. A fresh-water pool with sparkling water is double enclosed by a privacy fence that makes this property exclusive, intimate, and private. So work out, swim, live in a nice home close to horse country and polo grounds, and be just minutes from Palm Beach nightlife. Go out, scuba dive, entertain oneself, eat alligator at a local restaurant two minutes away (bring an out-of-state license plate for a free pitcher of beer there), hit the beach, the nightlife, take a boat ride, go out for a horse ride, watch a polo match or the greyhounds, then come back to tranquility and quiet in a suburban/rural tropical private home with a nightly dip in the pool. Guests need to inquire to see if their pets and children are welcome, and if lunch is available. Water-skiing is nearby.

Rooms: 3 (3 SB) $29-79
Continental Breakfast
Credit Cards: C, D
Notes: 2, 5, 7, 9, 10, 11, 12, 13

PALM HARBOR

Bed and Breakfast of Tampa Bay

126 Old Oak Circle, 34683
(813) 785-2342

An Art Deco look invites guests to enjoy paintings, artifacts, and statues from all over the world. Two miles from the Suncoast white sand beaches, golf, tennis, boating, and fishing are all a short distance away. Ninety miles to Disney World and Seaworld. Busch Gardens, Adventureland, Dali Museum, and historic Tarpon Springs are all within a day's visit. Bus lines, shopping malls, ice skating, and fine restaurants nearby. AAA building for travel assistance within walking distance. A Jacuzzi and swimming pool are available for guests to use, and color TV and telephone are in every room.

Hosts: Vivian and David Grimm
Rooms: 4 (2 PB; 2 SB) $45-75

Full Breakfast
Credit Cards: None
Notes: 2, 5, 8, 9, 11, 12

PENSACOLA

Bed and Breakfast Scenic Florida

P.O. Box 3385, Tallahassee, 32315-3385
(904)386-8196

FL39. This Victorian residence was built in 1904 and is within the sixteen-block historic district. Recent renovation in the 1980s has preserved the original gas lighting and the beauty of the wood staircase and floors. The first-floor parlor, dining room, and glassed side porch are available for business or social functions. Amenities include TV, VCR with large tape selection, coffee maker, small refrigerator, and private phone. Guests are treated to breakfast, lunch, or dinner (their choice) at the famous landmark, the Hopkins Boarding House, where Southern home-cooked meals have been served family style since 1948. The spacious guest suite has a queen-size bed tucked into an alcove and a Pauley Island hammock for relaxing. The bath is modern with a walk-in shower. No smoking. $70.

PLANTATION

Bed and Breakfast Company

P.O. Box 262, South Miami, 33243
(305) 661-3270; FAX (305) 661-3270

PL068. In Plantation (west of I-95, eight miles from the ocean), this bed and breakfast is in an upscale community of ranch-style homes. Bed and breakfast room with two single beds and private hall bath. Furnishings are attractive, comfortable, and conventional. Community is north of Nova University. Lots of tennis available (home is across the street from a community pool and tennis court). $40.

7 No smoking; 8 Children welcome; 9 Social drinking allowed; 10 Tennis nearby; 11 Swimming nearby; 12 Golf nearby; 13 Skiing nearby; 14 May be booked through a travel agent.

QUINCY

Bed and Breakfast Scenic Florida

P.O. Box 3385, Tallahassee, 32315-3385
(940) 386-8196

FL23. This Classic Revival Raised cottage was built in 1843. A major renovation in 1990 resulted in five rooms on two levels. Guests may choose two double beds, individual double beds, or one king-size bed. All have private baths, including some with claw-foot tub and shower. All rooms have TV and telephone with a laundry, small kitchen, and refrigerator available for guests' use. An extended Continental breakfast is served in the upstairs parlor, and trays permit guests to return to their rooms if they prefer. No smoking. $69.90.

ST. AUGUSTINE

Carriage Way Bed and Breakfast

70 Cuna Street, 32084
(904) 829-2467; FAX (904) 826-1461

A beautifully restored 1883 Victorian home in the heart of the historic district is within walking distance of the waterfront, shops, restaurants, and historic sites. Rooms are decorated with antiques and reproductions. Private baths have showers or antique

Carriage Way

claw-foot tubs with showers. The atmosphere is leisurely and casual. Complimentary beverages, newspaper, cookies, and full gourmet breakfast. Roses, fruit and cheese tray, gourmet picnic lunch, carriage rides, and breakfast in bed are available as "special touches." Selected one of the 125 facilities in "Best Places to Stay in Florida."

Hosts: Bill and Diane Johnson
Rooms: 9 (PB) $59-115
Full Breakfast
Credit Cards: A, B, C, D
Notes: 2, 5, 9, 10, 11, 12, 14

Casablanca Inn on the Bay in Old St. Augustine

24 Avenida Menendez, 32084
(800) 826-2626

Casablanca Inn features elegant suites and rooms with fine antiques, panoramic bayfront views, private entrances and baths, some with Jacuzzis. A hearty full breakfast is served on the grand front porches overlooking the bay. Wines and sweets are included. Bicycles available. In historic district; restaurants, shopping, and all historic points are within walking distance. "What divine decadence!"—*Frommer's Travel Guide.* "St. Augustine's loveliest...spit and polish elegant."—*Gulf Shore Life.*

Hosts: Tom and Janet Murray
Full Breakfast
Rooms: 12 (PB) $59-155
Credit Cards: A, B, C, D
Notes: 2, 5, 7, 9, 10, 11, 12, 14

Casa de la Paz

22 Avenida Menendez, 32084
(904) 829-2915

Mediterranean-style inn with elegant furnishings and imported fine linens overlooks the Matanzas Bay in the historic district. From the guest rooms or from a second-story veranda, enjoy a view of Matanzas Bay. From the veranda an open stairway leads to a beautiful walled gar-

NOTES: Credit cards accepted: A MasterCard; B Visa; C American Express; D Discover; E Diners Club; F Other; 2 Personal checks accepted; 3 Lunch available; 4 Dinner available; 5 Open all year; 6 Pets welcome;

den courtyard. The inn is central to all historic sites, fine restaurants, and miles of ocean beaches. Complimentary sherry; full breakfast available. Rated three diamonds by AAA.

Host: Jan Maki
Rooms: 6 (PB) $65-125
Full Breakfast
Credit Cards: A, B, C
Notes: 2, 5, 7, 9, 10, 11, 12, 14

Casa de Solana

Casa de Solana Bed and Breakfast Inn

21 Aviles Street, 32084-4441
(904) 824-3555

A lovingly renovated Colonial home is in the heart of St. Augustine's historical area within walking distance of restaurants, museums, and quaint shops. There are four antique-filled guest accommodations. All are suites; some have fireplaces, others have balconies that overlook the beautiful garden, and others have a breathtaking view of the Matanzas Bay. All have private baths. Tariff includes a full breakfast served in the formal guest dining room, cable TV, chocolates, decanter of sherry, and the use of bicycles for touring the ever-inviting St. Augustine.

Host: Fayé Lang-McMurry
Rooms: 4 (PB) $125
Full Breakfast
Credit Cards: A, B, C, D
Notes: 2, 5, 7, 9, 10, 11, 12, 14

Castle Garden

15 Shenandoah Street, 32084
(904) 829-3839

Stay at a castle and be treated like royalty! Relax and enjoy the peace and quiet of royal treatment at this newly restored 100-year-old castle of Moorish Revival design, where the only sound to hear is the occasional roar of a cannon shot from the old fort 200 yards to the south, the creak of the original solid wood floor, or the chirping of birds. The unusual coquina stone exterior is interesting to see, while the interior of this former Warden Castle carriage house has been completely renovated and features two romantic honeymoon suites with sunken bedrooms, in-room Jacuzzis, and cathedral ceilings. Amenities include complimentary wine, chocolates, bikes, and fenced parking. There are also many unique specialty gift baskets.

Hosts: Bruce Kloeckner and Kim Van Kooten
Rooms: 6 (PB) $65-150
Full Breakfast
Credit Cards: A, B, C, D
Notes: 2, 5, 7, 8, 10, 11, 12, 14

The Cedar House Inn

79 Cedar Street, 32084
(904) 829-0079; (800) CEDAR-INN

Capture romantic moments at this 1893 Victorian home in the heart of the ancient city. Escape into an antique-filled bedroom with private bath and claw-foot tub or enjoy the grand parlor with its fireplace, player piano, and antique Victrola. Elegant full breakfast, complimentary beverages, evening snack, convenient on-premises parking, Jacuzzi spa, and bicycles. Walk to all historic sites. Easy drive to I-95, Atlantic Ocean beaches, tennis, and golf.

Hosts: Nina and Russ Thomas
Rooms: 6 (PB) $59-150
Full Breakfast
Credit Cards: A, B, D
Notes: 2, 4, 5, 7, 9, 10, 11, 12, 14

7 No smoking; 8 Children welcome; 9 Social drinking allowed; 10 Tennis nearby; 11 Swimming nearby; 12 Golf nearby; 13 Skiing nearby; 14 May be booked through a travel agent.

The Kenwood Inn

The Kenwood Inn

38 Marine Street, 32084
(904) 824-2116

Local maps and early records show the inn was built between 1865 and 1885 and was functioning as a private boarding house as early as 1886. In the historic district, the inn is within walking distance of many fine restaurants and all historic sights. One block from the Intracoastal Waterway, with its passing fishing trawlers, yachts at anchor, and the classic Bridge of Lions. Beautiful ocean beaches are just across the bridge.

Hosts: Mark Kerrianne and Caitlin Constant
Rooms: 14 (PB) $75-135
Continental Breakfast
Credit Cards: A, B, D
Notes: 2, 5, 7, 9, 10, 11, 12

Old City House Inn and Restaurant

115 Cordova Street, 32084
(904) 826-0113

In the heart of town, within walking distance of all the sites sits the Old City House, a classic example of St. Augustine Colonial Revival architecture. Restored in 1990, the premises include five bed and breakfast rooms and a full-service award-winning restaurant. It commands a view of some of the most beautiful historic architecture in northeastern Florida. Enjoy

wine on the veranda in the afternoons. Queen-size beds, private baths, cable TV, air conditioning, private entrances, and a full breakfast. Special weekday rates are available.

Hosts: John and Darcy Compton
Rooms: 5 (PB) $60-105
Full Breakfast
Credit Cards: A, B, C, D, E
Notes: 2, 3, 4, 5, 8, 9, 10, 11, 12

Old Powder House Inn

38 Cordova Street, 32084
(904) 824-4149; (800) 447-4149

High ceilings, wraparound verandas, and elaborate woodwork distinguish this Victorian home built in 1899 on the site of an 18th-century Spanish powder magazine. Cordova Street is in the heart of the historic area with horse and buggies going right past the house. Restaurants, antique stores, and quaint shops are within easy walking distance. Full gourmet breakfast, tea and pastries in the afternoon, and sparkling juice, wine, and hors d'oeuvres each day. Bicycles and tandems. In-ground Jacuzzi and parking on the premises.

Hosts: Al and Eunice Howes
Rooms: 9 (PB) $55-115
Full Breakfast
Credit Cards: A, B, D
Notes: 2, 5, 9, 10, 11, 12, 14

Penny Farthing Inn

83 Cedar Street, 32084
(904) 824-2100

In the heart of the ancient city is this 1890s inn offering three elegant bedrooms and a two-room honeymoom suite decorated with antiques, queen-size beds, private baths, and porches. Full breakfast. Special weekday rates. Bicycling weekend packages.

Hosts: Pam and Walt James
Rooms: 4 (PB) $85-135
Full Breakfast
Credit Cards: A, B
Notes: 5, 7, 9, 11, 12

NOTES: Credit cards accepted: A MasterCard; B Visa; C American Express; D Discover; E Diners Club;
F Other; 2 Personal checks accepted; 3 Lunch available; 4 Dinner available; 5 Open all year; 6 Pets welcome;

St. Francis Inn

279 St. George Street, 32084
(904) 824-6068; (800) 824-6062

The St. Francis Inn, in the historic district of St. Augustine, was built as a private home for a Spanish soldier in 1791. Originally known as the Garcia-Dummett House, it began operating as an inn in 1845. It is a Spanish Colonial structure with a private courtyard, fireplaces, balconies furnished with rocking chairs, and the modern addition of a swimming pool. The inn has a wide variety of accommodations ranging from single rooms, to two- and three-room suites, to an entire cottage. The warmth and peacefulness of the inn itself, its location, and the kind of guests it attracts are all strong assets. Inquire about accommodations for children.

Hosts: Stan and Regina Reynolds
Rooms: 14 (PB) $58-125
Continental Breakfast
Credit Cards: A, B
Notes: 2, 5, 7, 9, 10 ,11, 12, 14

St. Francis Inn

Victorian House Bed and Breakfast

11 Cadiz Street, 32084
(904) 824-5214

In the heart of the historic district, the Victorian House was built in 1897 and has been restored and furnished in period antiques. Enjoy canopied beds, handwoven coverlets, quilts, stenciled walls, and hand-hooked rugs on heart pine floors. Featured in *Country Home*, *Better Homes and Gardens*, *Southern Homes*, *Country Almanac*, and *Innsider* magazines. Guests are within walking distance of fine restaurants, the waterfront, shops, museums, and the plaza. Limited parking available, inquire about off-street parking. Weekly and monthly rates are available upon request. Inquire about accommodations for children.

Host: Daisy Morden
Room: 8 (PB) $60-95
Continental Breakfast
Credit Cards: A, B, C
Notes: 2

Westcott House

146 Avenida Menendez, 32084
(904) 824-4301

One of St. Augustine's most elegant guest houses overlooking Matanzas Bay. Circa 1890, restored in 1983, in the historic area and within walking distance to historic sites. All rooms have private baths, king-size beds, cable TV, private telephone, and are furnished in antiques. Year-round climate control. Complimentary bottle of wine upon arrival. One-half block from the city's yacht pier.

Hosts: Sherry and David Dennison
Rooms: 8 (PB) $95-150
Continental Breakfast
Credit Cards: A, B
Notes: 2, 5, 8, 9, 10, 11, 12, 14

ST. PETERSBURG

Bayboro House Bed and Breakfast

1719 Beach Drive Southeast, 33701
(813) 823-4955

Turn-of-the-century Queen Anne home furnished in antiques. Old-fashioned porch swing to enjoy sea gulls and sailboats on Old Tampa Bay. Minutes from the Dali

7 No smoking; 8 Children welcome; 9 Social drinking allowed; 10 Tennis nearby; 11 Swimming nearby; 12 Golf nearby; 13 Skiing nearby; 14 May be booked through a travel agent.

Museum, Pier, Suncoast Dome, Bayfront Center, and Al Lange Stadium. Many fine restaurants in the area. Personal suite available on request. Historic designated. AAA rated three diamond. Smoking on the veranda only.

Hosts: Gordon and Antonia Powers
Rooms: 4 (PB) $95-145
Continental Breakfast
Credit Cards: A, B
Notes: 2, 5, 9, 10, 11, 12, 14

Beach Haven Villas

4980 Gulf Boulevard, 33706
(813) 367-8642

Directly on the sparkling Gulf of Mexico, Beach Haven harkens back to the days when much of Florida offered vacationers colorful Art Deco-style motels. Still in pink, Beach Haven retains its charming personality, while providing updated interiors and furnishings. Close to shopping, dining, and entertainment. Add the peaceful setting, a gulf-front pool, and a sandy beachfront setting and guests will know why Beach Haven is so popular. Non-smoking units available.

Hosts: Jone and Millard Gamble
Rooms: 18 (PB)
Continental Breakfast
Credit Cards: A, B
Notes: 5, 8, 10, 11, 12, 14

Bed and Breakfast Scenic Florida

P.O. Box 3385, Tallahassee, 32315-3385
(904) 386-8196

FL45. Located downtown, this 1904 Southern home is near Busch Gardens and Weeki Wachee. Guests enjoy mingling in the first-floor sitting room with fireplace and piano or on the porch and patio. Five guest rooms and a separate carriage house room have private baths, ceiling fans, and sitting areas. Choices include one room with twin beds and five with queen-size beds, all with central heat and air conditioning. A substantial English breakfast that features Welsh cakes and home fries is served from 8:00-9:30 A.M. in twin dining rooms. No children. No smoking. $60-65.

Mansion House

105 5th Avenue Northeast, 33701
(813) 821-9391

Charming turn-of-the-century Southern home was recently renovated. Wood floors, stained glass, fireplace, sitting porches, and soft furnishings add to the relaxing ambience. Hearty breakfast served with Welsh hospitality. Walking distance to marina, pier, museums, restaurants, theaters, beach, pool, tennis, sailing, and other Bay Shore amenities.

Hosts: Suzanne and Alan Lucas
Rooms: 6 (PB) From $60
Full Breakfast
Credit Cards: A, B, C, D
Notes: 2, 5, 7, 9, 10, 11, 12, 14

Mansion House

ST. PETERSBURG BEACH

Island's End Resort

1 Pass-A-Grille Way, 33706
(813) 360-5023; FAX (813) 367-7890

At the southernmost tip of St. Petersburg Beach, Island's End is a combination of the charming ambience of sand, sea, and sky creating a unique atmosphere of rustic charm among gray weathered cottages and natural wooded walkways. Experience the brilliant sunrises in the east while sipping freshly squeezed orange juice in the gazebo. Later in the day enjoy the spectacular sunsets so famous along the Florida Suncoast. All cottages have modern kitchens and bathrooms (some with Jacuzzis). Furnishings are contemporary and extremely comfortable. Quality accommodations that enhance the ever-changing beauty and diversity of the waterfront are at the guests' disposal.

Hosts: Jone and Millard Gamble
Rooms: 6 (PB) $61-160
Continental Breakfast
Credit Cards: A, B
Notes: 2, 5, 8, 9, 10, 11, 12

ST. TERESA BEACH

Bed and Breakfast Scenic Florida

P.O. Box 3385, Tallahassee, 32315-3385
(940) 386-8196

FL32. This two-story beach house was built in the early 1980s. The location is ideal for shelling, sunning, and swimming at the beach. The common parlor has TV, VCR, a fireplace, and wicker furnishings. Three bedrooms are available. One has a double bed, ceiling fan, and a bath with shower. Two other rooms have double beds and a shared bath with combination tub and shower. A Southern breakfast is served in the common room. No children. No smoking allowed. $75.

SANIBEL ISLAND

Sanibel's Seaside Inn

541 East Gulf Drive, 33957
(813) 472-1400; (800) 831-7384 (reservations)

Sanibel's Seaside Inn, a cozy beachfront inn that exudes old Florida charm, offers newly renovated studios, one-bedroom cottages and apartments, and a three-bedroom suite. Guests will enjoy such complimentary amenities as a heated pool, shuffleboard, bicycles, library of videos and books, a daily Continental breakfast, and outdoor barbecue grills.

Host: Jack Reed
Rooms: 32 (PB) $124-239
Continental Breakfast
Credit Cards: A, B, C, D, E, F
Notes: 2, 5, 8, 9, 10, 11, 12, 14

Song of the Sea

Song of the Sea

863 East Gulf Drive, 33957
(813) 472-2220; (800) 231-1045 (reservations)

Song of the Sea, Sanibel Island's romantic European-style seaside inn, features luxurious studios and one-bedroom apartments, each with a fully equipped kitchen, microwave, color cable TV, and private terrace. Guests enjoy complimentary wine and fresh flowers upon arrival, a heated gulfside pool and whirlpool, pristine white beach, library of books and videos, bicycles, daily newspaper, and Continental breakfast al fresco.

Host: Linda Logan
Rooms: 30 (PB) $144-299
Continental Breakfast
Credit Cards: A, B, C, D, E, F
Notes: 2, 5, 8, 9, 10, 11, 12, 14

7 No smoking; 8 Children welcome; 9 Social drinking allowed; 10 Tennis nearby; 11 Swimming nearby; 12 Golf nearby; 13 Skiing nearby; 14 May be booked through a travel agent.

SAN MATEO

Bed and Breakfast Scenic Florida

P.O. Box 3385, Tallahassee, 32315-3385
(904) 386-8196

FL44. This three-story 1889 Victorian home is less than an hour from Atlantic beaches. Public rooms include the parlor with TV, music and game room, and a formal dining room. One two-bedroom suite and four guest rooms are on the second floor. The suite features queen-size beds and a private bath with claw-foot tub and shower. The other rooms offer double, queen-, and king-size beds with modern or period baths. A full gourmet breakfast is served and features homemade breads. $45-100.

SANTA ROSA BEACH

Bed and Breakfast Scenic Florida

P.O. Box 3385, Tallahassee, 32315-3385
(904) 386-8196

FL38. This antebellum plantation-style home was built in 1990 as a bed and breakfast. It is just steps from the beach and has a deep, wide porch where guests can relax on wicker furniture. The home is fully heated and air-conditioned. The guest parlor provides a TV, stereo, ice maker, and fireplace. Four guest rooms and a carriage house have private entrances and private baths with tub and shower combinations. Guests may choose rooms with queen-size or double four-poster beds or the carriage house, which has a king-size bed and queen-size sleeper. A dining area includes a microwave, toaster, coffee maker, small refrigerator, glassware, and dishes. A TV is also provided. Breakfast is served in the formal dining room and features a variety of unique items. No smoking. Special rates December through February. $83-105.

SARASOTA

Crescent House Bed and Breakfast

459 Beach Road, 34242
(941) 346-0857

Enjoy this gracious, comfortable home with its antique charm. Guests have four bedrooms to choose from, each with its own personality and charm. Color TV with cable is in every room. A Continental breakfast is served each morning between 8:00 a.m. and 9:00 a.m. Relax or sunbathe in the privacy of the spacious wooden deck. Directly across the street is the beautiful beach on the Gulf of Mexico. Rentals of sailboards, sailboats, or bicycles are available in Siesta Village, or take time to enjoy the public beach and its many facilities, all within walking distance.

Rooms: 4 (2 PB; 2 SB) $60-110
Continental Breakfast
Credit Cards: None
Notes: 2, 5, 8, 9, 10, 11, 12, 13, 14

SEASIDE

Josephine's French Country Inn at Seaside

101 Seaside Avenue, P.O. Box 4767, 32459
(904) 231-1940; FAX (904) 231-2446

Guests can enjoy a striking view of the Gulf of Mexico from this Victorian mansion in the heart of the award-winning beach community of Seaside. Amenities include a private beach, tennis, pools, biking, and shopping. Surrounded by nature's splendor, enjoy extraordinary accommodations and dining. Named one of the top 12 inns in America.

Hosts: Bruce, Judy, Jody, and Sean
Rooms: 11 (PB) $120-215
Full Breakfast
Credit Cards: A, B
Notes: 2, 4, 5, 7, 8, 9, 10, 11, 12, 13, 14

NOTES: Credit cards accepted: A MasterCard; B Visa; C American Express; D Discover; E Diners Club; F Other; 2 Personal checks accepted; 3 Lunch available; 4 Dinner available; 5 Open all year; 6 Pets welcome;

TALLAHASSEE

Bed and Breakfast Scenic Florida

P.O. Box 3385, 32315-3385
(904) 386-8196

FL17. This Federal-style two-story brick home sits among stately oaks in a quiet residential area, near the downtown capital complex, restaurants, and shops. Two guest rooms have private baths; one has a queen-size bed and a twin bed in an adjoining room. A casual first-floor sitting room has a TV for guests' use. A cozy breakfast for two may be served, or a larger group may use the formal dining room. A fresh fruit platter, quality breads, jams, and beverages are served. Business meetings and social events can be arranged. Wine and flowers are available for special occasions. No smoking. $75-90

Governors Inn

209 South Adams Street, 32301
(904) 681-6855

The Governors Inn combines original woodwork, exposed beams, and brilliant skylights to create a French country environment. The 41 guest rooms and suites are furnished with antique armoires and English pub tables. No two rooms are alike. Some have French four-poster beds and framed prints. Others have loft bed-

Governors Inn

rooms and fireplaces, spiral staircases, and clerestory windows. The Spessard Holland suite has a wet bar and vaulted ceilings. Conferences for up to 75 people can be arranged. One half-block from the state capitol.

Rooms: 41 (PB) $99-229
Continental Breakfast
Credit Cards: A, B, C, D, E
Notes: 5, 7, 8, 9, 12, 14

TAMPA

Gram's Place Bed and Breakfast Guest House

3109 North Ola, 33603
(813) 221-0596; (813) 292-1415 (pager)

Named in honor of legendary singer/songwriter Gram Parsons, Gram's Place is a relaxing, eclectic Key West-style bed and breakfast, reminiscent of the music and times of the 1960s and 1970s, as well as of all eras. Two cottage houses were built in 1945. Three rooms have shared bath (European style with sinks in rooms), and three rooms have private baths with queen-size canopied beds and hardwood floors. Each house has full kitchen and dining area. A very safe mixed neighborhood two miles northwest of downtown Tampa and historic Ybor City is well-lighted on an off-street for secure parking. Amenities include oversized Jacuzzi, waterfall, sun deck, courtyard with BYOB bar, outside shower/toilet facilities, and ice maker. Telephone, cable TV, and HBO.

Host: Mark Holland
Rooms: 7 (4 PB; 3 SB) $45-75
Continental Breakfast
Credit Cards: A, B, C
Notes: 3, 4, 5, 8, 9, 14

Hyde Park Inn

404 West Kennedy Boulevard, 33606
(813) 254-5834 (phone and FAX); (800) 347-5834

Enjoy Tampa's only Victorian bed and breakfast hotel since 1908 in historic Hyde

7 No smoking; 8 Children welcome; 9 Social drinking allowed; 10 Tennis nearby; 11 Swimming nearby; 12 Golf nearby; 13 Skiing nearby; 14 May be booked through a travel agent.

Park. Furnishings are period antiques with warm Southern style. Gourmet breakfast is served daily, and two fine European restaurants are adjacent. Parks, museums, superb shopping, and theaters are within walking distance.

Host: George Bailey
Rooms: 38 (9 PB; 29 SB) $55-115
Full Breakfast
Credit Cards: A, B
Notes: 5, 8, 9, 10, 11, 12

TARPON SPRINGS

East Lake Bed and Breakfast

421 Old East Lake Road, 34689
(813) 937-5487

Private home on two and one-half acres, on a quiet road along Lake Tarpon. Bedroom and adjoining private bath are at the front of the house, away from the family quarters. Twenty-four-hour access. Room has color TV and telephone. The hosts are retired business people who enjoy new friends and are well informed about the area. A full home-cooked breakfast is served. Limited smoking allowed.

Hosts: Marie and Dick Fiorito
Room: 1 (PB) $35-40
Full Breakfast
Credit Cards: None
Notes: 2, 5, 9, 10, 11, 12

Inn on the Bayou

P.O. Box 1545, 34688
(813) 942-4468

Guests will stay in a beautiful, modern, contemporary home on a quiet bayou. Fish for a big old red, or watch blue herons and pelicans in a bird sanctuary behind the inn. Enjoy a swim in the solar-heated pool or relax in a whirlpool spa. Just minutes to a white-sand beach and breathtaking sunsets. Take a stroll through the famous sponge docks or go antiquing on Main Street. Busch Gardens and Adventure Island are all

close by. Private tours with transportation are available.

Hosts: Al and Chris Stark
Rooms: 3 (PB & SB) $45-60
Continental Breakfast
Credit Cards: None
Notes: 2, 5, 7, 8, 9, 11, 12

Spring Bayou

Spring Bayou Bed and Breakfast

32 West Tarpon Avenue, 34689
(813) 938-9333

A large elegant home built in 1905 is in the center of the historical district. Enjoy the beautiful Spring Bayou, downtown antique shops, and area attractions of a small Greek village. Excellent restaurants are nearby, and guests have a short drive to the beach. Well-appointed rooms have antique furnishings and modern conveniences, and guests enjoy spacious wraparound front porch.

Host: Sharon Birk
Rooms: 5 (3 PB; 2 SB) $80-110
Continental Breakfast
Credit Cards: None
Notes: 2, 5, 7, 10, 11, 12

VENICE

The Banyan House

519 South Harbor Drive, 34285
(813) 484-1385

Experience the Old World charm of one of Venice's historic Mediterranean homes,

NOTES: Credit cards accepted: A MasterCard; B Visa; C American Express; D Discover; E Diners Club; F Other; 2 Personal checks accepted; 3 Lunch available; 4 Dinner available; 5 Open all year; 6 Pets welcome;

circa 1926, on Florida's Gulf Coast. Fully equipped efficiencies are tastefully decorated, each with its own character. Large shaded courtyard with pool and Jacuzzi. Close to beaches, restaurants, golf, and fishing. Complimentary bicycles. Nonsmoking. Children over 12 welcome.

Hosts: Chuck and Susan McCormick
Rooms: 9 (7 PB; 2 SB) $59-99
Continental Breakfast
Credit Cards: None
Notes: 2, 5, 7, 9, 10, 11, 12

WAKULLA SPRINGS

Wakulla Springs Lodge
One Spring Drive, 32305
(904) 224-5950

Wakulla Springs Lodge is a 27-room lodge, built in 1937 with imported marble, rare Spanish tile, and paint and wrought-iron work by artisans—a most unique retreat. Standing today as it did then, changed only for improvements in modern conveniences and fire safety, the Wakulla Springs Lodge attracts guests worldwide and guarantees the need for return visits to all who venture just 15 miles south of Florida's capitol in Tallahassee. Full restaurant, snack bar, and gift shop in lobby. On the National Register of Historic Places. In Edward Ball Wakulla Springs State Park. Glass-bottom and riverboat cruises. Open year-round.

Hosts: William Roberts, General Manager
Rooms: 27 (PB) $60-85
Full Breakfast
Credit Cards: A, B
Notes: 2, 3, 4, 5, 8, 9, 11, 14

Wakulla Springs, FL

WELLBORN

1909 McLeran House
12408 County Road 137, 32094
(904) 963-4603

A beautifully restored two-story Victorian home on five landscaped acres features a lovely garden area with gazebo, garden swing, deck area, goldfish pond, and an abundance of trees and shrubs. Guests enjoy a large, comfortable room with minirefrigerator and cable TV. The private bath features a claw-foot tub with shower. Enjoy the many antiques throughout the house, relax in the garden, stroll the grounds, or visit the "collectibles" shop in the old barn. Additional charge for extra people.

Hosts: Bob and Mary Ryals
Rooms: 2 (1 PB; 1 SB) $60
Continental Breakfast
Credit Cards: None
Notes: 2, 5, 7, 9, 10, 11, 12

WEST PALM BEACH

West Palm Beach Bed and Breakfast
419 32nd Street, 33407
(407) 848-4064; (800) 736-4064
FAX (407) 848-2422

A cozy Key West-style cottage built in the 1930s has all of today's conveniences: private baths, air conditioning, paddle fans, and cable TV. The hosts have retained the charm of old Florida with white wicker furniture in a colorful Caribbean decor; sun by the lush tropical pool, ride complimentary bicycles, or just relax! In the Old Northwood Historic District, just one block from the waterway, and minutes to the tropical waters of the Atlantic or Palm Beach.

Host: Dennis Keimel
Rooms: 3 (PB) $55-115
Continental Breakfast
Credit Cards: A, B, C, E
Notes: 2, 5, 7, 9, 10, 11, 12, 14

7 No smoking; 8 Children welcome; 9 Social drinking allowed; 10 Tennis nearby; 11 Swimming nearby; 12 Golf nearby; 13 Skiing nearby; 14 May be booked through a travel agent.

ZOLFO SPRINGS

Double M Ranch Bed and Breakfast

Route 1, P.O. Box 292, 33890
(813) 735-0266 (after 6:00 P.M.)

The Mathenys welcome guests to this 4,500-acre working cattle and citrus ranch in the heart of agricultural Florida. There are numerous recreational opportunities nearby, including fishing, golf, canoeing, and a state park. Sporting clays course on the ranch. Accommodations include approximately 1,000 square feet of space and a private entrance. A ranch tour is an option most guests enjoy taking. If guests want to see a part of Florida most tourists miss, come out to the ranch! Two-night minimum stay required.

Hosts: Mary Jane and Charles Matheny
Rooms: 2 (1 PB; 1 SB) $65
Continental Breakfast
Credit Cards: None
Notes: 2, 5, 7, 9, 11, 12, 14

Georgia

ALPHARETTA

Bed and Breakfast Atlanta

1801 Piedmont Avenue, Suite 208, 30324
(404) 875-0525; (800) 96PEACH
FAX (404) 875-9672

Rates not applicable during the summer of 1996 due to the Olympic summer games.

0-10. Thirty-minute drive to Atlanta and convenient to all Northern Georgia Mountain attractions. This lakeview manor in a beautiful residential development is a recently built European-style home with comfortable areas for relaxation, both in- and outdoors. The large guest room has a queen-size bed, full private bath, TV, phone, and individually controlled heat and air conditioning. Delicious Southern-style breakfasts, complimentary late-night dessert and many other amenities. Non-smokers, please. $80.

AMERICUS

The Pathway Inn

501 South Lee Street, 31709
(912) 928-2078; (800) 889-1466

This inn is in the heart of the extensive historic district where guests may walk to restaurants and shops. Five guest rooms have private baths; some have whirlpools. Cable TV and telephones in each room. Enjoy sumptuous breakfast and evening wine and refreshments on the 1906 veranda. Home of Habitat for Humanity. Antique shops nearby. President Carter's home is nine miles away, and guests can visit there to hear him teach Sunday school. Georgia Veteran State Park is 15 miles away. Inquire about accommodations available for pets.

Hosts: Sheila and David Judah
Rooms: 5 (PB) $60-107
Full Breakfast
Credit Cards: A, B, C, D
Notes: 2, 5, 9, 12, 14

ANDERSONVILLE

A Place Away Cottage

110 Oglethorpe Street, 31711
(912) 924-1004; (912) 924-2558

Country-style guest cottage with polished pine floors, private baths, TV, coffee maker, and small refrigerator in each room; front porch with rocking chairs; and back deck overlooking yard with barbecue grills and picnic tables. Common room with round pine table is where breakfast is served.

Hosts: Peggy and Fred Sheppard
Rooms: 2 (PB) $45-50
Continental Breakfast
Credit Cards: None
Notes: 2, 5, 7, 8, 9, 10

ATHENS

The Nicholson House

6295 Jefferson Road, 30607
(706) 353-2200

The casual elegance of the Nicholson House sets it apart from the rest. Built in 1820, this historic inn is nestled among six wooded acres of rolling hills, streams, and nature trails. Three miles from downtown Athens, home of the University of Georgia, we offer

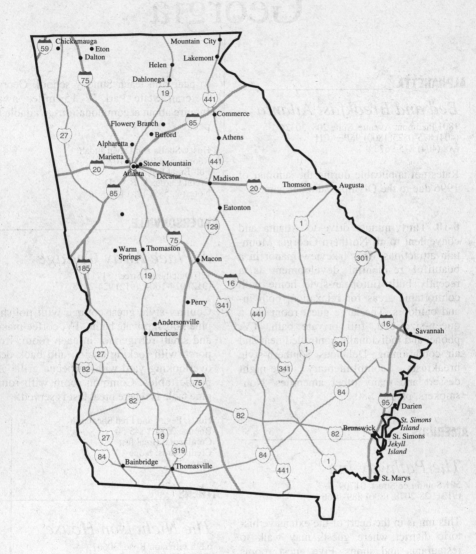

Georgia

five spacious rooms, each with private bath, television, and telephone. The warmth of antiques, Persian rugs, and rich jewel tones reflect the professionally appointed decor. A full, healthy breakfast is served.

Host: Lynda Kelley
Rooms: 5 (PB) $75 per room per night
Full Breakfast
Credit Cards: A, B, C, D
Notes: 5, 7, 9, 10, 12, 14

ATLANTA

Buckhead Bed and Breakfast Inn

70 Lenox Pointe, NE, 30324
(404) 237-9209; (800) 224-8797

A new, gracious Southern inn offering 19 rooms appointed with four-poster beds, French writing desks, and antique furniture. In the heart of Buckhead, with immediate access to Atlanta's finest restaurants and shopping districts. From a Continental breakfst with the morning paper to an evening cocktail in the private lounge with wood-burning fireplace, guests' are promised warm hospitality. The staff will make reservations from golf to dinner (local menus available).

Host: Mr. Jerry H. Cates
Rooms: 19 (PB) $72-92
Continental Breakfast
Credit Cards: A, B
Notes: 2, 5, 8, 9, 10, 12, 14

Bed and Breakfast Atlanta

1801 Piedmont Avenue, Suite 208, 30324
(404) 875-0525; (800) 96PEACH
FAX (404) 875-9672

Rates not applicable during the summer of 1996 due to the Olympic summer games.

A1. This early 1900s neighborhood is on the historic register and has special appeal for walkers and joggers. Nearby are the Woodruff Arts Center, High Museum, Botanical Gardens, Piedmont Park, and Colony Square with many appealing restaurants and shops. Public transit is excellent. Host couple resides in Dutch Colonial home with private cottage in rear. Bright, cheery, spacious unit has bedroom alcove with double bed and desk. The living-dining space has a double sleep sofa, chair, and breakfast table. New full bath and galley kitchen. Cable TV and telephone available. Self-catered breakfast. No smoking. $88-100.

A2. This bed and breakfast in Midtown, two to three miles to downtown, has excellent public transportation in a historic neighborhood of winding streets and parks. Private entry guest unit offers a bedroom with twin beds, adjacent sitting room with cable TV, private shower-only bath, and special amenities for minor cooking such as a small refrigerator, coffee maker, toaster oven, and a microwave oven. Breakfast provisions are stocked for self-catering. Host welcomes nonsmokers. $68-80.

A3. A Georgian-style brick building in Midtown (Ansley Park) offers one bed and breakfast room in a large second-floor owner-occupied apartment. Small, attractive room has twin beds, telephone, TV, and private bath off the hall. A small sitting room and den with a single bed are available for parties traveling together with a willingness to share the bath. Computer available. Nonsmokers only. Continental breakfast. $52-60.

A4. In one of the few contemporary residences in this interesting close-in historic area. Guest suite has a private entrance, living room, kitchen, bedroom, full bath, separate heating and air conditioning system, private telephone line, stereo, and cable TV. FAX is available. Kitchen has a refrigerator stocked for self-catered breakfast,

Bed and Breakfast Atlanta (continued)

microwave oven, toaster, coffee maker, etc. Within walking distance to Woodruff Art Center or the Botanical Gardens. $72-88.

A5. This bed and breakfast is a few miles from downtown. Excellent public transportation. Architecturally interesting home built about 1910; neighborhood is on the National Register of Historic Places. There are two large guest rooms with a shared full bath. One bedroom offers a king-size bed and sitting area. The other room has twin beds. Interesting mixture of contemporary and antique furniture. Continental-plus breakfast is served in glassed breakfast area which features beautiful outdoor viewing and bird watching. Hosts readily share their love of Atlanta and a vast well of information about the city. Nonsmokers only. Both rooms are used only with party traveling together. $80.

B1. Secluded privacy in the Cottage, a guest house in Buckhead, one of Atlanta's loveliest residential areas. Expansive guest house, nestled behind large residence on four acres, offers two spacious bedrooms, full bath, living room, dining area with adjacent deck, and a small, well-equipped kitchen. Breakfast provisions are stocked daily for self-catering. Washer/dryer, private phone line, TV, VCR, central heating and air system, pool, and croquet. $120-180.

B2. Charming, newly renovated two-story brick traditional home offers delightful vistas of lush green trees, beautifully landscaped yard, and a golf course across the street. Two upstairs bedrooms are offered with one full bath. Both rooms are used only when party is traveling together. King room has a small refrigerator and large desk. Upstairs is private to guests.

Continental breakfast served. Cat on premises. $68-80.

B3. Rambling Cape Cod-style home is in a beautiful residential area near Peachtree Road. Private entry to the guest room is through a welcoming patio next to the swimming pool. Upstairs room has dormer windows which look out over lush greenery and lovely homes. Traditional furnishings include twin beds, chairs, and a round table suitable for breakfast in the room if desired. Breakfast is also served in a downstairs dining area or on the patio. Nonsmokers preferred. $60-68.

D1. An intimate bed and breakfast just a few blocks off the square in Decatur, the house was built in 1937. There are two bedrooms for guests. The gourmet breakfasts include homemade breads, muffins, fresh fruit or fruit smoothies, freshly ground coffee, imported tea, and sweet, dark honey gathered from hives in the lower garden. There is a hot tub and a nearby pool available to guests. The city of Decatur is one of Atlanta's most historic and well maintained neighborhoods. It is less than six miles from downtown Atlanta and three miles from Emory University, the CDC, and the American Cancer Society. $60-72.

D3. A cream-colored Victorian brick house with convenient access to MARTA public transportation. Enter the private-entry suite from a large front porch with rocking chairs. Suite offers an elegant library and sitting room with fireplace, large bedroom with antique double bed and adjoining new stall-shower bath. There is also a second-floor bedroom with private bath. Full or Continental breakfast served in formal dining room, contemporary kitchen, or on the rear deck overlooking garden, pool, and hot tub. Bicycles are available. Smoking allowed in outdoor areas only. Resident dogs and cats. $80-120.

NOTES: Credit cards accepted: A MasterCard; B Visa; C American Express; D Discover; E Diners Club; F Other; 2 Personal checks accepted; 3 Lunch available; 4 Dinner available; 5 Open all year; 6 Pets welcome;

E1. This traditional two-story house with swimming pool is on 12 beautiful wooded acres in Druid Hills. Two guest rooms, each with queen-size bed, share one bath. One room has handmade quilts and an antique doll collection. The other provides a wonderful view of the pool, woods, and flowers. An expanded Continental breakfast is served in the charming downstairs dining room. One of the hosts builds beautiful reproduction furniture; an impressive silver chest in the front entry is evidence of his skill. $60-72.

E2. Lovely 1930s brick bungalow houses a bed and breakfast that is in walking distance to Emory University. Excellent public transportation for downtown meetings as well. This bright, cheerful room has an antique double bed; adjacent den with TV is private to guests. The full bath and dressing area have been totally renovated. Gracious Continental breakfast is served each morning in a large, modern kitchen with views of the lovely patio on the rear of the house and numerous birdfeeders. Nonsmokers only. $60-72.

E3. This very special private guest cottage in Druid Hills includes a living room with a love seat that opens into a twin bed, fully equipped kitchen, bedroom with full-size brass bed, and bath. Furnishings are overstuffed vintage, with beautiful linens, down comforters, and ample breakfast provisions for self-catering. Hosts share their enthusiasm for Atlanta's sights. No smoking. Weekly and monthly rates upon request. $100-140.

E-8. Two very beautiful private entry rooms are available in this stunning renovation of an older home in Druid Hills. Proximity to Fernbank, Virginia-Highland, Emory University, Decatur, or downtown makes this an appealing choice for business or tourist travel. One guest room has twin-size beds and the other a queen-size bed. Baths adjoin each room–one is a full bath and one is shower only. Both open to terraces viewing landscaped grounds. A small built-in area between the two rooms is stocked and effectively equipped for self-catered breakfasts. $80-92.

I1. Small inn overlooks Springvale Park in the historic Victorian neighborhood, Inman Park. Two guest rooms, each with double bed and private bath, are offered. In addition, the Garden Suite is a private apartment on the terrace level with its own entrance, lawn, and parking. The suite has a living room with sleep sofa, bedroom with queen-size bed, full bath, and a totally equipped kitchen. Cable TV, washer/dryer, and private phone are included. Garden Suite guests may enjoy breakfast in the upstairs dining room or self-cater. Weekly and monthly rates available. Two resident cats. No smoking. $60-100.

I3. This Santa Fe suite is a private full upstairs living unit in a private residence in the Victorian neighborhood on Inman Park. The guest suite has been carefully and lovingly put together. Huge bedroom with queen-size bed; sitting area with sofa and TV is spacious, comfortable, and filled with natural light. Totally new bath adjoins bedroom, has stall shower, dressing room, and washer-dryer. Small, well-equipped kitchen is stocked with breakfast provisions for self-catering. There is a separate breakfast area with seating for four and a small office with desk and workspace for the business traveler. Cat in residence downstairs only. Secured parking and excellent public transit are available. Nonsmokers please. Weekly and monthly rates can be quoted. $88-100.

K1. Fully renovated, spacious 1960s brick ranch-style home offers one sunny antique-furnished double with adjoining bath and

7 No smoking; 8 Children welcome; 9 Social drinking allowed; 10 Tennis nearby; 11 Swimming nearby; 12 Golf nearby; 13 Skiing nearby; 14 May be booked through a travel agent.

Bed and Breakfast Atlanta (continued)

one spacious and bright twin-bed room with private bath adjacent. A single-bed studio room with full view of the patio and garden is sometimes available. Host couple serves nutritious breakfasts featuring home-baked breads, and lively hospitality complete the picture as a bed and breakfast winner. Within walking distance of Emory University. Kosher dietary laws observed. Excellent access to public transportation. No smoking. $68-80.

M1. A 60-year-old Colonial brick home in Morningside. Excellent public transportation. Walk to shops, restaurants and points of interest. Spacious, light-filled bedroom on the second floor has queen-size brass bed and adjoining shower-only bath. Third-floor guest suite affords total privacy with a large living room with cable TV, bedroom with queen-size bed, and adjoining bath with shower. Guests enjoy sitting areas downstairs and a lovely rear terrace over-looking walled yard. The smell of fresh baking completes the picture. Continental or full breakfast. No smoking. Resident dog and cat. $72-88.

M2. Private entry apartment in 1920s neighborhood called Morningside offers easy access to downtown, Midtown, Emory University, CDC, and Virginia-Highland. This immaculately kept second-floor guest suite offers a bedroom with queen-size bed, spacious living room, well-equipped kitchen, and full bath. A second guest room with an antique sleigh bed across the hall from the suite is used only when needed by the same party. Beautiful, eclectic furnishings. Individual heating, air conditioning, TV, and telephone. Host sets in provisions for self-catered breakfast. $80-160.

O3. Large, quiet apartment near Perimeter Center offers a private entrance with off-street parking and a patio overlooking wooded area. This luxury, contemporary one-bedroom unit has 1,100-square feet. The bedroom has a queen-size bed and full bath. Spacious living and dining area has queen-size sleep sofa, love seat, and table and chairs. Kitchen is totally equipped. Cable TV, washer/dryer, and telephone are available. Ample provisions for self-catered breakfast and wonderful guidance for local attractions provided. $80-100.

V1. Private garden cottage behind large home is in Virginia-Highland. This neighborhood allows walks to unique shops, diverse entertainment, and wonderful restaurants. Bed and breakfast offers a living room with sofa, TV, table and chairs, bedroom with double iron bed, bath, and well-equipped kitchen. Guests also enjoy small rear patio. Private telephone line and provisions for self-serve catered breakfast. No smoking. $68-76.

V-2. Quiet, private cottage offers comfort and convenience. Atkins Park, a small neighborhood listed on the National Register of Historic Places, is part of Virginia-Highland. The cozy accommodation has a bedroom with single and trundle bed, adjoining bath with shower, full kitchen, air conditioning, and a color TV. A beautiful verdant landscaped garden with native Georgia shrubs is adjacent to the cottage and provides an inviting retreat for relaxation or outdoor breakfasts. Breakfast provisions are provided, but breakfast is self-catered. Proximity to downtown and excellent public transportation make this ideal for downtown meetings as well as tourism. $64-72.

V-3. Walk to shops, restaurants, and galleries nearby or access downtown meetings in minutes by transit or car. Built in 1913,

this Craftsman home has been totally renovated to provide elegance and sophistication as an intimate, carefully tended bed
and breakfast inn. The Rose Room features
a hand-painted four-poster queen-size bed,
private bath, and a gas log fireplace. The
English Suite has a hand-carved four-poster
queen-size bed, working fireplace, adjoining living room-dining area with queen-
size sofa bed, private bath with two-person
whirlpool and steam bath and shower, and
private walled deck. The Ivy Cottage is a
completely detached second-story unit that
features a bedroom with a king-size bed,
full bath, a private balcony, and a separate
living room with queen-size sofa bed.
Extensive amenities include a fully
equipped kitchen, as well as a washer and
dryer. $85-155.

Beverly Hills Inn

Beverly Hills Inn

65 Sheridan Drive, 30305
(404) 233-8520

A charming city retreat one-half block from
public transportation, one and one-half
miles from Lenox Square, and five minutes
from the Atlanta Historical Society. Full
kitchens, library, free parking, color TV,
and Continental breakfast.

Host: Mit Amin
Rooms: 18 (PB) $80-160
Continental Breakfast
Credit Cards: A, B, C, E, F
Notes: 2, 5, 6, 8

Enchanted Forest Bed and Breakfast

955 Canter Road NE, 30324
(404) 262-9753

Guests are just steps from shopping, restaurants and rail transportation. Nestled deep
within two wooded acres. Rooms are spacious and comfortable. Glass enclosed living and dining rooms bring nature indoors.
Get cozy by the fireplace, breakfast outdoors under the forest canopy, or watch
wildlife from the bridge overlooking the
stream. Deluxe breakfast including delicious homemade banana bread and
gourmet coffees. If not for the ultraconve-
nient city locale, guests would think they
were in the country. Children welcome.

Host: Linda A. Verrill
Rooms: 2 (SB) $60-90
Continental Breakfast
Credit Cards: A,B
Notes: 2, 5, 7, 8, 9

Inman Park Bed and Breakfast

100 Waverly Way NE, 30307
(404) 688-9498

The honeymoon cottage of Robert Woodruff,
Atlanta's famous anonymous donor and soft-
drink magnate, is a totally restored Victorian
in historic Inman Park. One block from the
subway station, close to dining. Its 12-foot
ceilings, heart-pine woodwork, fireplaces,
antiques, screened porch, and private garden
are to enjoy. Personal checks accepted for
deposit only.

Host: Eleanor Matthews
Rooms: 3 (PB) $70-90
Continental Breakfast
Credit Cards: A, B, C
Notes: 5, 7, 8, 9, 10, 11, 12, 14

King-Keith House

889 Edgewood Avenue NE, 30307
(404) 688-7330

This 1890 Queen Anne Victorian home is
in a National Register of Historic Places

7 No smoking; 8 Children welcome; 9 Social drinking allowed; 10 Tennis nearby; 11 Swimming nearby;
12 Golf nearby; 13 Skiing nearby; 14 May be booked through a travel agent.

neighborhood. Ideal for walking and jogging, this home is close to Atlanta's most popular in-town shopping, restaurant, and theater districts. Two miles to downtown Atlanta. Two-and-a-half blocks to MARTA (subway) with direct connections to the airport as well as all sporting and cultural events. Unusually spacious guest rooms, with high ceilings, filled with antiques. Private upstairs balcony. One of Atlanta's most photographed historical homes.

Hosts: Jan and Windell Keith
Rooms: 3 (2 PB; 1 SB) $75-95
Continental Breakfast
Credit Cards: A, B, C
Notes: 2, 5, 7, 8, 9, 10, 12, 14

Oakwood House
Bed and Breakfast

951 Edgewood Avenue NE, 30307
(404) 521-9320

Oakwood House is a classic 1911 home in historic Inman Park just outside downtown Atlanta. Guests will find original woodwork, stained glass, front porch swing, and hundreds of books. The hosts live next door, offering traditional hospitality and privacy. Whirlpool and family suites. A short walk to Little Five Points for ethnic dining, theater, and shopping. The Carter Presidential Library and Martin Luther King Historic District are nearby. Walk to the subway for downtown's Underground, World Congress Center, and CNN. Continental-plus breakfast. Freshly baked muffins and a bottomless cookie jar. All the comforts of a home—only better. Olympics rental agent. No smoking indoors.

Hosts: Robert and Judy Hotchkiss
Rooms: 5 (PB) $65-175
Continental Breakfast
Credit Cards: A, B, C
Notes: 2, 5, 8, 9, 12, 14

Shellmont
Bed and Breakfast Lodge

821 Piedmont Avenue NE, 30308
(404) 872-9290; FAX (404) 872-5379

Impeccably restored 1891 mansion is in midtown—Atlanta's theater, restaurant, and cultural district. Independently listed on the National Register of Historic Places and designated, a City of Atlanta Landmark Building, the lodge is a virtual treasure chest of stained, leaded, and beveled glass, intricately carved woodwork, and hand-painted stenciling. Wicker-laden verandas overlook Victorian fish pond and gardens. Legally licensed since 1984. AAA-rated three diamonds. Member of Independent Innkeepers Association.

Hosts: Ed and Debbie McCord
Rooms: 5 (PB) $89-109
Full Breakfast
Credit Cards: A, B, C, E
Notes: 2, 5, 7

AUGUSTA

Into the Woods
Bed and Breakfast

176 Longhorn Road, Hephzibah, 30815
(706) 554-1400

This house was built in the late 1800s and completely restored and furnished with antiques of the period. Relax in the Victorian parlor, step out onto one of the porches, or pull up a rocker and have a cookie from the kitchen. All of the guest rooms have good firm beds. Guests can take

Into the Woods

NOTES: Credit cards accepted: A MasterCard; B Visa; C American Express; D Discover; E Diners Club; F Other; 2 Personal checks accepted; 3 Lunch available; 4 Dinner available; 5 Open all year; 6 Pets welcome;

a short drive to Augusta for a lovely walk on the Riverwalk along the Savannah River, or visit the restaurants and shops. Enjoy breakfast in the sunny dining room after a good night's rest.

Hosts: Mr. and Mrs. Robert L. Risser
Rooms: 4 (2 PB; 2 SB) $55-75
Full Breakfast
Credit Cards: A, B, D
Notes: 2, 5, 7, 8, 12

Oglethorpe Inn

Oglethorpe Inn

836 Greene Street, 30901
(706) 724-9774

Named after Augusta's founder, General James Oglethorpe, Oglethorpe Inn is Augusta's only historic bed and breakfast. Shaded by 100-year-old magnolias, it is in the very heart of the central business district. It is within walking distance of Augusta's new Riverwalk, the Civic Center, and other historic sites. All rooms have been carefully renovated to include all of the modern conveniences the lodging guest requires. Some with fireplaces and whirlpool tubs.

Host: Fran Upton
Rooms: 19 (PB) $85-125
Full Breakfast
Credit Cards: A, B, C, D, E
Notes: 2, 5, 7, 8, 9, 12, 14

The Perrin Guest House Inn

208 LaFayette Drive, 30909
(706) 731-0920; FAX (706) 731-9009

The Perrin Place is an old cotton plantation established in 1863. The plantation has long since become the site for the Augusta National, home of the Masters, while the three acres of the homeplace remain a little spot of magnolia heaven surrounded by shopping, golfing, and fine dining. The guest house has beautifully redecorated bedrooms that feature fireplaces, Jacuzzis, antiques, and comforters. Enjoy the private fireplaces in spacious accommodations; share the pleasure of a front porch rocker, the comfort of a cozy parlor, or the cool of a scuppernong arbor with other guests. Weddings, receptions, and other social functions, treasured events when held at the Perrin Inn. Available by reservation only.

Hosts: Ed and Audrey Peel
Rooms: 10 (PB) $72-155
Continental Breakfast
Credit Cards: A, B, C
Notes: 2, 5, 7, 9, 10, 11, 12, 13, 14

BAINBRIDGE

Bed and Breakfast Scenic Florida

P.O. Box 3385, Tallahassee, FL 32315-3385
(940) 386-8196

FL41. Built in the mid-1800s, this Southern Colonial home was restored in the 1980s. Guests are only 45 minutes north of Tallahassee and have local access to Lake Seminole. Modern amenities include full baths, central heat and air conditioning, room telephones, and a pool and gazebo. The parlor and second-floor gallery and library serve as common room for guests. Three individually decorated guest rooms are available. Guests may choose queen-size four-poster bed with private shower and bath or twin beds and antique double bed that share a large bath with walk-in shower. Continental breakfast with fine

7 No smoking; 8 Children welcome; 9 Social drinking allowed; 10 Tennis nearby; 11 Swimming nearby; 12 Golf nearby; 13 Skiing nearby; 14 May be booked through a travel agent.

specialty breads is served in the large formal dining room or at poolside. No children and no smoking allowed. $40-45.

BRUNSWICK

Brunswick Manor

825 Egmont Street, 31520
(912) 265-6889

Enjoy gracious hospitality in a coastal Deep South setting. Experience this concept of bed and breakfast accommodations with canopied beds, megathick towels, robes, designer linens, and a wraparound veranda with antique wicker swing. Hot tub found on private, trellised patio. Savor a full gourmet breakfast served in the formal dining room and afternoon tea. Captain charters aboard *Alamar* and *China Doll* also available.

Hosts: Claudia and Harry Tzucanow
Rooms: 8 (5 PB; 3 SB) $55-85
Full Breakfast
Credit Cards: A, B
Notes: 5, 7, 9, 10, 11, 12

BUFORD

Bed and Breakfast Atlanta

1801 Piedmont Avenue, Suite 208, 30324
(404) 875-0525; (800) 96PEACH
FAX (404) 875-9672

Rates not applicable during the summer of 1996 due to the Olympic summer games..

O-11. A luxurious private entry apartment has wood-burning fireplace and a Jacuzzi bath on beautiful Lake Lanier, only 50 miles from downtown Atlanta. This modern 2000-square-foot private entry, two-bedroom unit can accommodate up to four people. One bedroom has a firm queen-size four-poster bed, the other has an antique double bed. The beautiful birchwood kitchen is equipped with every convenience including a washer/dryer and even a wine rack. The spacious, tiled bath includes Jacuzzi tub as well as a stall shower. Enjoy this lakefront hideaway, the wood-burning fireplace, the 31-inch cable TV, hiking, golfing, and more for the midweek or weekend getaway or to celebrate that special occasion. Gracious Continental breakfast will be stocked for self-catering. Handicapped accessible. Nonsmoking. Weekly and monthly rates quoted upon request. $120-180.

CHICKAMAUGA

Gordon-Lee Mansion Bed and Breakfast Inn

217 Cove Road, 30707
(706) 375-4728; (800) 487-4728

Circa 1847. Step back in time and enjoy this beautifully restored antebellum plantation house, set on seven acres with formal gardens and furnished with museum-quality period antiques in the atmosphere of early Southern aristocracy. Used as a Union headquarters and hospital. Near the Chickamauga Battlefield and 15 miles from Chattanooga, Tennessee. Continental plus breakfast served in the elegant dining room. Civil War artifacts museum. Private baths. National Register of Historic Places.

Host: Richard Barclift
Rooms: 5 (PB) $70-100
Continental Breakfast
Credit Cards: A, B
Notes: 2, 5, 7, 9, 10, 12, 14

COMMERCE

The Pittman House

81 Homer Road, 30529
(706) 335-3823

This house is a grand 1890 Colonial completely furnished with period antiques. Wraparound porch just waiting to be rocked on. In the northeastern Georgia foothills near many interesting places. One

NOTES: Credit cards accepted: A MasterCard; B Visa; C American Express; D Discover; E Diners Club;
F Other; 2 Personal checks accepted; 3 Lunch available; 4 Dinner available; 5 Open all year; 6 Pets welcome;

hour northeast of Atlanta just off I-85. Tennis, golf, discount shopping mall, fishing, antiquing, and watersports all nearby.

Hosts: Tom and Dot Tomberlin
Rooms: 4 (2 PB; 2 SB) $55-65
Full Breakfast
Credit Cards: A, B
Notes: 2, 5, 7, 10, 11, 12, 13, 14

DAHLONEGA

Mountain Top Lodge at Dahlonega
Route 7, Box 150, 30533
(706) 864-5257

Share the magic of a secluded bed and breakfast inn surrounded by towering trees and spectacular views. Enjoy antique-filled rooms, cathedral ceiling, great room, spacious decks, and heated outdoor spa; some rooms have fireplaces, whirlpool tubs, and porches. Deluxe room accommodations also available. Generous country breakfast with homemade biscuits. Two-night minimum stay required for holidays and weekends during the fall season. Children over 12 welcome.

Host: Karen Lewan
Rooms: 13 (PB) $61.05-137.50
Full Breakfast
Credit Cards: A, B, C
Notes: 2, 5, 9, 12, 14

Worley Homestead Inn
410 West Main Street, 30533
(706) 864-7002

Step back into the past when staying at this restored 1845 ancestral home. Only two blocks from Dahlonega's famous Courthouse Square, the inn is across from the gold-topped steeple of North Georgia College, site of the U.S. Mint when Dahlonega was the gold center of the United States. Member of National Trust for Historic Preservation. Rates are subject to change during holidays and special events.

Hosts: Bill and Mary Scott
Rooms: 8 (PB) $65-75
Full Breakfast
Credit Cards: A, B, C, D
Notes: 2, 5, 7, 9, 12

DALTON

The Holly Tree House
217 West Cuyler Street, 30720
(706) 278-6620; FAX (706) 278-1851

Lovely restored home circa 1924 in historical district of noteworthy Civil War and Cherokee Indian area. Convenient to many points of interest, the home is furnished in antiques and collectibles from around the world. Each spacious room has a private bath, TV, and VCR. A video library is available for guests' use. A three-course breakfast is served of carefully prepared specialities. Before retiring, cordials are available. The home is 100 miles north of Atlanta and 30 miles south of Chattanooga.

Host: Doris FioRito
Rooms: 4 (PB) $85
Full Breakfast
Credit Cards: A, B, C, D
Notes: 2, 5, 7, 9, 12

DARIEN

Open Gates Bed and Breakfast
Vernon Square National Historic District, 31305
(912) 437-6985

Explore untrammeled barrier islands and the Altamaha River Delta via a scenic byway one and one-half miles east of I-95. Open Gates was an 1876 timber baron's home; it has been featured on the cover of *Southern Homes,* in *Georgia Off the Beaten Path, Fodor's: Bed and Breakfasts,* and *Country Inns.* Family heirlooms, a superb library of coastal material, locally produced caviar, and hostess knowledgeable about Georgia's second oldest town and environment enhance guests' stay. Ecological and historical tours. Bicycles and canoeing.

7 No smoking; 8 Children welcome; 9 Social drinking allowed; 10 Tennis nearby; 11 Swimming nearby; 12 Golf nearby; 13 Skiing nearby; 14 May be booked through a travel agent.

Open Gates

Sailing school nearby. Bird watching groups. Limited smoking allowed.

Host: Carolyn Hodges
Rooms: 4 (2 PB; 2 SB) $52.80-58.30
Full Breakfast
Credit Cards: None
Notes: 2, 5, 9, 11, 14

DECATUR

Bed and Breakfast Atlanta

1801 Piedmont Avenue, Suite 208, 30324
(404) 875-0525; (800) 96PEACH
FAX (404) 875-9672

Rates not applicable during the summer of 1996 due to the Olympic summer games..

D-2. Only 20 minutes by car from Atlanta's World Congress Center is a quintessentially English-style homestay bed and breakfast in the heart of Decatur. A full English breakfast (on weekends), as well as afternoon tea with freshly baked scones or Irish soda bread, is the standard fare. The single suite accommodation has a bedroom, study, full bath, and a private garden entry. An antique candlestick queen-size four-poster bed, a working fireplace, a queen-size sleeper-sofa, desk, cable TV, and a VCR with collection of British tapes in the study add to guests privacy and comfort. Sleeps up to four guests. Public transportation accessible. Nonsmoking, please. $72-88.

D-5. Only six miles east of downtown Atlanta or one-half mile walk from the Decatur MARTA station, this fully renovated 1940s Cape Cod-style bungalow offers visitors a delightful respite from the pursuit of business or pleasure. A second floor suite, queen-size bed, with sitting room, and full bath overlooks the swimming pool from its own very large deck. Furnishings reflect the taste and interests of a well-traveled host, who has sailed the east coast of Africa from Durban to the Red Sea, builds architectural scale models, and speaks fluent Dutch. Continental or full English breakfast may be shared in the family dining room, or eaten on the private deck. The suite is accessed via an outside stairway. Three docile cats assist in extending Southern hospitality to nonsmoking guests. Long-term rates can be quoted upon request. $72-88.

ETON

Ivy Inn

245 Fifth Avenue, E., P.O. Box 406, 30742
(706) 517-0526; (800) 201-5477

This inn reminds its guests of those restful, secure nights at Grandmother's or a favorite aunt's country home. A casual air with rocking chair porches is waiting for weary travelers. The Ivy Inn has bicycles for guests' use. Horseback riding and stables are next door; white-water rafting is only 45 minutes away. Smoking is limited to front porch and grounds. Twelve miles from carpet capital of the world; three miles from crafts and antique shops.

Hosts: Gene and Juanita Twiggs
Rooms: 3 (PB) $87
Full Breakfast
Credit Cards: A, B, C, D
Notes: 2, 5, 8, 11, 13

EATONTON

The Crockett House

671 Madison Road, 31024
(706) 485-2248

Nearly a century of good living has given the Crockett House a mellow ambience. A stately and gracious turn-of-the-century Victorian home on Georgia's historic Antebellum Trail offers a warm welcome and comfortable accommodations year-round. Just minutes from Lake Oconee, Georgia's second largest lake, and surrounded by Oconee National Forest. The large, cozy bedrooms are thoughtfully decorated with antiques, heart-of-pine floors, 12-foot ceilings, fireplaces, and private baths. Rates include a full breakfast with lots of homemade goodies. Smoking is limited to outside porch and balcony.

Hosts: Christa and Peter Crockett
Rooms: 6 (PB) $55-75
Full Breakfast
Credit Cards: A, B, C
Notes: 2, 3, 4, 5, 8, 9, 10, 11, 12, 14

The Crockett House

FLOWERY BRANCH

Whitworth Inn

6593 McEver Road, 30542
(404) 967-2386

Contemporary country inn on five wooded acres offers relaxing atmosphere, 11 uniquely decorated guest rooms, and two guest living rooms with TVs. Full country breakfast served in large sunlit dining room. Meeting and party space available.

Thirty minutes northeast of Atlanta at Lake Lanier. Nearby attractions and activities include boating, golf, beaches, and water parks. Close to Road Atlanta and Chateau Elan Winery and Golf Course. Easily accessible from major interstates. Three-diamond AAA rating.

Hosts: Ken and Chris Jonick
Rooms: 10 (PB) $55-125
Full Breakfast
Credit Cards: A, B, C
Notes: 2, 5, 7, 8, 10, 11, 12, 14

HELEN

Chattahoochee Ridge Lodge and Cabins

P.O. Box 175, 30545
(706) 878-3144; (800) 476-8331

Perched on a wooded ridge a mile from Alpine Helen, each new unit has cable TV, air conditioning, refrigerator, coffee maker, free phone, and large Jacuzzi. Some have a full kitchen, extra bedroom, and fireplace. There is also a gas grill on the back deck. Hosts are "earth friendly" with double insulation and back-up solar heating. Everything guests need is furnished and on the premises, including hosts who can fill guests in on attractions. Chalets in the woods are also available; please inquire.

Hosts: Bob and Mary Swift
Rooms: 5 (PB) $45-70
Continental Breakfast
Credit Cards: A, B, C, D
Notes: 2, 5, 8, 9, 10, 11, 12

Habersham Hollow Bed and Breakfast and Cabins

Route 6, Box 6208, Clarkesville, 30523
(706) 754-5147

This elegant country home is nestled in the northeast Georgia mountains. Five minutes from Alpine Helen. Spacious rooms; a suite with a fireplace, sitting room, and its own

7 No smoking; 8 Children welcome; 9 Social drinking allowed; 10 Tennis nearby; 11 Swimming nearby; 12 Golf nearby; 13 Skiing nearby; 14 May be booked through a travel agent.

covered porch. King-size beds, terry robes, and TV are all included. Relaxed, casual, and friendly atmosphere. Cozy cabins with fireplaces on the grounds where well-behaved pets are welcome.

Hosts: C. J. and Maryann Gibbons
Rooms: 4 (PB) $85
Full Breakfast
Credit Cards: A, B
Notes: 2, 5, 9, 10, 11, 12, 13

LAKEMONT

Lake Rabun Hotel

Lake Rabun Road, P.O. Box 10, 30552-0010
(404) 782-4946

An original mountain inn built in 1922 is a Rabun County landmark. Antique mountain furnishings, rustic, charming; huge fieldstone fireplace in downstairs great room. Has 16 rooms, private and shared baths. Honeymoon Room with fireplace upstairs. Third-generation guests now visit.

Hosts: Rosa and Bill Pettys
Rooms: 16 (2 PB; 14 SB) $60-70
Continental Breakfast
Credit Cards: A, B, D
Notes: 2, 7, 8, 9, 10, 11, 12, 13, 14

MACON

1842 Inn

353 College, 31201
(912) 741-1842; (800) 336-1842 (reservations)

Four-diamond-award winner for seven consecutive years. Elegant antebellum Greek Revival Tara in heart of beautiful historic district. In-room complimentary breakfast, evening hors d'oeuvres and light piano music, plus concierge turndown service. Restaurant and museum houses within walking distance. Exit 52, I-75, five blocks.

Hosts: Phillip Jenkins and Richard Meils
Rooms: 21 (PB) $95-135
Continental Breakfast
Credit Cards: A, B, C
Notes: 2, 5, 7, 9, 10, 11, 12, 14

MADISON

The Brady Inn

250 North Second Street, 30650
(706) 342-4400

Two Victorian cottages linked together by an extended porch filled with rockers welcome guests to this bed and breakfast. All rooms have private baths, heart-pine floors, and antiques. Come enjoy Southern hospitality and see "the town Sherman refused to burn."

Hosts: C.G. and L.J. Rasch
Rooms: 6 (PB) $50-70
Full Breakfast
Credit Cards: A, B, C
Notes: 2, 3, 4, 5, 6, 8, 9, 10, 11, 12

MARIETTA

Bed and Breakfast Atlanta

1801 Piedmont Avenue, Suite 208, 30324
(404) 875-0525; (800) 96PEACH
FAX (404) 875-9672

Rates not applicable during the summer of 1996 due to the Olympic summer games..

O4. This French Regency-style Victorian house in Marietta, circa 1872, was saved from demolition in 1990 and restored by the current owners. There are front and rear porches where breakfast is served when the weather permits, as well as a downstairs sitting room. Gourmet breakfast is served in the dining room, with careful attention given to low-fat ingredients and special dietary needs. Four guest rooms are available, one with king-size bed and three with queen-size beds, all with private baths. $76-120.

MOUNTAIN CITY

The York House

P.O. Box 126, 30562
(800) 231-YORK; 706-746-2068

NOTES: Credit cards accepted: A MasterCard; B Visa; C American Express; D Discover; E Diners Club; F Other; 2 Personal checks accepted; 3 Lunch available; 4 Dinner available; 5 Open all year; 6 Pets welcome;

A lovely 1896 bed and breakfast inn with a country flair is listed on the National Register of Historic Places. It is nestled among the beautiful north Georgia mountains and is close to recreational activities. Completely renovated, the 13 guest rooms are decorated with period antiques and offer private baths and cable TV. Guests begin their day with a full Continental breakfast served in their rooms on a silver tray. Between Clayton and Dillard one-quarter mile off Highway 441 on the York House Road.

Hosts: Ben Collins and Joey Barnes
Rooms: 13 (PB) $74-89
Continental Breakfast
Credit Cards: A, B, C
Notes: 2, 5, 7, 8, 9, 10, 11, 12, 13, 14

PERRY

Swift Street Inn

1204 Swift Street, 31069
(912) 988-4477

Step back 137 years to a time of Southern charm, romance, and luxury. A gourmet breakfast, deluxe service, and spacious guest rooms, each with its own unique character and all filled with antiques, await. Come experience the elegance and warm feeling of a small inn in a growing Southern town. The hosts take pride in making guests' stay restful, pleasant, and memorable.

Hosts: Dennis and Carolyn Lovejoy
Rooms: 4 (PB) $65-85
Full Breakfast
Credit Cards: A, B, C
Notes: 2, 4, 5, 6, 7, 9, 10, 11, 12, 14

ST. MARYS

Goodbread House

209 Osborne Street, 31558
(912) 882-7490

The Goodbread House is a carefully restored Victorian home. The high ceilings, fireplaces, wide pine floors, and original wood trim add to its ambience. Each antique-filled bedroom has its own fireplace and private bath, as well as ceiling fans and air conditioning. The ferry to Cumberland Island National Seashore is only a block away. Restaurants within walking distance. Smoking in designated areas only.

Hosts: Betty and George Krauss
Rooms: 4 (PB) $55-65
Full Breakfast
Credit Cards: None
Notes: 2, 5, 9, 11, 12, 14

Riverview Hotel

105 Osborne Street, 31558
(912) 882-3242

Built in 1916, the Riverview Hotel rests on the banks of the St. Marys River, near the ferry to Cumberland Island. The hotel boasts a sitting room and a veranda, complete with rocking chairs and a swing, and 18 guest rooms with private baths, air conditioning, and cable TV. St. Marys offers self-guided tours of the historic district, including a pavilion on the waterfront, shops, art galleries, and beautiful pre-Civil War Oak Grove Cemetery. Crooked River State Park and Kings Bay Naval Submarine Base are minutes away. Within an hour's drive are the Okefenokee Swamp and Georgia's Golden Isles, and within two hours are historic Savannah to the north and St. Augustine to the south. Seagle's Restaurant and Lounge, in the Riverview Hotel, is open every day with moderate prices. Seagle's also packs picnic lunches and has a banquet room with seating for up to 30.

Hosts: Jerry and Gaila Brandon
Rooms: 18 (PB) $48-65
Continental Breakfast
Credit Cards: A, B, C, D, E
Notes: 2, 3, 4, 5, 8, 9, 10, 12, 14

ST. SIMONS

Little St. Simons Island

P.O. Box 21078ABB, 31522
(912) 638-7472; FAX (912) 634-1811
E-mail 76465.431 @ Compuserve.com

7 No smoking; 8 Children welcome; 9 Social drinking allowed; 10 Tennis nearby; 11 Swimming nearby; 12 Golf nearby; 13 Skiing nearby; 14 May be booked through a travel agent.

Privately owned, 10,000-acre barrier island retreat has seven miles of pristine beaches. Comfortable accommodations, bountiful regional meals with hors d'oeuvres and wine, horseback riding, fishing, boating, canoeing, bird watching, and naturalist expeditions. Orvis endorsed lodge with fly fishing instruction and excursions. Limited boat docking also available. A unique experience in an unspoiled, natural environment. Day trips and full island rentals available. Open February through November. Limited smoking. Inquire about accommodations for children.

Host: Debbie McIntyre
Rooms: 11 (PB) $275-500 FAP
Full Breakfast
Credit Cards: A, B
Notes: 2, 3, 4, 5, 9, 11, 14

SAVANNAH

Ballastone Inn and Townhouse

14 East Oglethorpe Avenue, 31401
(912) 236-1484; (800) 822-4553
FAX (912) 236-4626

A beautifully restored Victorian mansion dating from 1838 in the heart of the city's historic district, the Ballastone Inn is the epitome of gracious Southern hospitality.

Ballastone Inn

The guest rooms reflect a distinct Victorian flavor. Added touches include flowers and fresh fruit, terry-cloth robes, fireplace, TV with VCR, and some Jacuzzis. There is a beautifully landscaped courtyard and a full-service bar. In the mornings, a Continental breakfast is served in guests' room, the parlor, or the courtyard. Sherry, coffee or tea, fruit, and pastries are available in the front parlor. Nightly turndown service includes robes, chocolates, and brandy. The inn is recommended by the *New York Times*, *Brides*, *Glamour*, *Atlantic*, and *Gourmet* magazines.

Hosts: Richard Carlson and Tim Hargus
Rooms: 22 (PB) $95-200
Continental Breakfast
Credit Cards: A, B, C
Notes: 2, 5, 6, 9, 10, 11, 12, 14

East Bay Inn

225 East Bay Street, 31401
(912) 238-1225; (800) 500-1225
FAX (912) 232-2709

The East Bay Inn has 28 charming guest rooms that invite guests to relax and enjoy Savannah. Walk to historic house museums and through the beautiful city squares. Return for evening wine and cheese and dine at Skyler's restaurant. All rooms are furnished with reproduction furniture in an 18th-century style, and have private baths. Enjoy deluxe Continental breakfast each morning, and turndown service with chocolates at night. Higher rates apply for special events. Pets welcome on a limited basis. Nonsmoking rooms available.

Host: Jean Ryerson, innkeeper
Rooms: 28 (PB) $89-119
Continental Breakfast
Credit Cards: A, B, C, D, E
Notes: 3, 4, 5, 8, 9, 10, 11, 12, 14

Foley House Inn

14 West Hull Street, 31401
(912) 232-6622; (800) 647-3708
FAX (912) 231-1218

On the beautiful Chippewa Square, in the heart of the historic landmark district, this wonderful 1896 inn awaits its guests. The individually decorated rooms offer four-poster rice beds, Oriental rugs, and English antique furnishings. Most of the rooms have fireplaces, some have Jacuzzi baths, and all have cable TV. After a full day exploring the historic city of Savannah, return to the inn for tea, cordials, and snacks. An extensive film library is available if guests want to curl up and relax. If guests want more activity, the innkeepers can make arrangements for tennis and golf.

Hosts: Inge Svensson Moore and Mark Moore
Rooms: 19 (PB) $85-190
Continental Breakfast
Credit Cards: A, B, C
Notes: 2, 5, 8, 9, 10, 12, 14

The Forsyth Park Inn

The Forsyth Park Inn

102 West Hall Street, 31401
(912) 233-6800

Circa 1893 Queen Anne Victorian mansion with 16-foot ceilings and 14-foot doors. Ornate woodwork, floors, stairways, fireplaces, antiques, whirlpool baths, and courtyard cottage. Faces a 25-acre park in large historic district. Complimentary wine, social hour; fine dining, tours, museum homes, river cruises, and beaches nearby. Personal checks accepted in advance.

Hosts: Virginia and Hal Sullivan
Rooms: 10 (PB) $95-175
Continental Breakfast
Credit Cards: A, B, C, D
Notes: 5, 8, 9, 10, 11, 12, 14

Habersham at York Inn

130 Habersham Street, 31401
(912) 234-2499

Here, gentle manners still prevail. Habersham at York Inn is on the garden floor of a handsomely restored Italianate residence constructed in 1884 on the northeast corner of Columbia Square. Features a bubbling fountain, fragrant gardens, and a private entrance to bed and breakfast. Fresh flowers, turndown service, and surprise snack. Convenient walk to excellent restaurants. Complimentary wine/champagne for special occasions. Intimate setting, a great place for anniversaries and honeymoons. Continental-plus breakfast, served in room, lounge, or garden, includes freshly squeezed orange juice and fresh breads.

Host: M. B. Rossini
Rooms: 2 (PB) $135
Continental Breakfast
Credit Cards: A, B
Notes: 2, 5, 8, 9, 10, 11, 12, 14

The Jesse Mount House

209 West Jones Street, 31401
(912) 236-1774

An 1854 Greek Revival townhouse has four luxurious suites. All have gas log fireplaces, canopied beds, and private baths, some with whirlpools. The house is furnished with many rare antiques and an eclectic art collection. Access to a private courtyard with fountains. Garden suite features a full kitchen. Complimentary turndown service, wine, and sweets. Bicycles available.

Host: Sue Dron
Suites: 4 (PB) $125-155
Full Breakfast
Credit Cards: A, B, C, D
Notes: 5, 8, 9, 14

Joan's on Jones Bed and Breakfast

17 West Jones Street, 31401
(912) 234-3863; (800) 407-3863

7 No smoking; 8 Children welcome; 9 Social drinking allowed; 10 Tennis nearby; 11 Swimming nearby; 12 Golf nearby; 13 Skiing nearby; 14 May be booked through a travel agent.

Joan's on Jones

In the heart of the historic district, two charming bed and breakfast suites distinguish the garden level of this three-story Victorian private home. Each suite has private entry, off-street parking, bedroom, sitting room, kitchen, bath, private telephone, and cable TV. Note the original heart-pine floors, period furnishings, and Savannah gray brick walls. Innkeepers Joan and Gary Levy, former restaurateurs, live upstairs and invite guests on a tour of their home if they are staying two nights or more. Pets welcome by arrangement only.

Host: Joan Levy
Suites: 2 (PB) $95-110
Continental Breakfast
Credit Cards: None
Notes: 2, 6, 7, 8, 9, 10, 11, 12, 14

Lion's Head Inn

120 East Gaston Street, 31401
(912) 232-4580; (800) 355-LION

A stately 19th-century home is in a quiet neighborhood just north of picturesque Forsyth Park. This lovely 9,200-square-foot mansion is filled with fine Empire antiques. Each guest room is exquisitely appointed with four-poster beds, private baths, period furnishings, fireplaces, TVs, and telephones. Each morning enjoy a deluxe Continental breakfast, and in the evening enjoy wine and cheese on the sweeping veranda overlooking the marbled courtyard.

Host: Christy Dell'Orco
Rooms: 6 (PB) $75-150
Continental Breakfast
Credit Cards: A, B, C
Notes: 2, 5, 7, 8, 9, 10, 11, 12, 14

Olde Harbour Inn

508 East Factor's Walk, 31401
(912) 234-4100; (800) 553-6533
FAX (912) 233-5979

Overlooking the Savannah River, the Olde Harbour Inn offers 24 guest suites. All suites have a full kitchen and private bath. Rooms are decorated in 18th-century style, and range in size from studio suites to two bedrooms with loft. Within walking distance to Savannah's beautiful city squares and historic homes. Return to the Grand Salon for wine and cheese reception in the evening, and retire to find the guest room "turned down" and an ice cream treat in the guest freezer. Higher rates apply for special events.

Rooms: 24 (PB) $105-155
Continental Breakfast
Credit Cards: A, B, C, D, E
Notes: 5, 6, 8, 9, 10, 11, 12, 14

Presidents' Quarters (A Premier Historic Inn)

225 East President Street, 31401
(912) 233-1600; (800) 233-1776
FAX (912) 238-0849

Four-diamond award-winning inn in the heart of historic district offers suites with TVs and VCRs, Jacuzzis, fireplaces, balconies overlooking secluded courtyard. Private parking. Physically challenged facilities available. Daily amenities include full afternoon tea and nightly turndown with cordial; fruit and wine in suite upon arrival. Continental-plus breakfast. An inn fit for a president.

General Manager/Innkeeper: Muril Broy
Rooms: 16 (PB) $107-167
Continental Breakfast
Credit Cards: A, B, C, D, E
Notes: 2, 5, 7, 8, 9, 10, 11, 12, 14

Remshart-Brooks House

106 West Jones Street, 31401
(912) 234-6928

Enjoy casual Southern hospitality at this historic Savannah home built in 1853. The guest accommodations are furnished with comfortable country antiques. Share the garden for a Continental breakfast. Private off-street covered parking is free. Rates slightly higher for three to four persons staying in the suite.

Host: Anne E. Barnett
Suite: 1 (PB) $75 plus tax
Continental Breakfast
Credit Cards: None
Notes: 2, 5, 9, 10, 11, 12

Remshart-Brooks House

R.S.V.P. Savannah: Bed and Breakfast Reservation Service

9489 Whitfield Avenue, Box 49, Savannah, GA
31406
(912) 232-7789; (800) 729-7787

All accommodations are in historic homes or old cotton warehouses. All are within walking distance to major museums, parks, shops, churchs, restaurants, and waterfront areas in historic Savannah, Tybee Island, and Brunswick, Georgia, and Charleston and Beaufort, South Carolina. Sonja, the agent, has been in every room in each inn and will help with accommodations, send a map leading guests to the door of the inn, and information on tours, restaurants, etc. There are 15 hosted private homes, 20 bed and breakfast inns, and eight unhosted accommodations. Discounts for children under 12 vary from host to host. Many provide sleeper-sofa or cots. Discount for seven days or more. Agent: Sonja Lazzaro. $60-285.

SENOIA

Culpepper House

35 Broad Street, 30276
(404) 599-8182

Step back 120 years to casual Victorian elegance at the Culpepper House. Share a special evening in a four-poster canopied bed next to a fireplace, with sounds of the night coming through the window. Wake to a gourmet breakfast, then take a tandem bike ride through the historic town, visit area shops and picturesque countryside, or just sit on the porch and rock. Only 30 minutes from Atlanta.

Hosts: Maggie Armstrong and Barb Storm
Rooms: 3 (1 PB; 2 SB) $75
Full Breakfast
Credit Cards: A, B, C
Notes: 2, 5, 9, 10, 11, 12

7 No smoking; 8 Children welcome; 9 Social drinking allowed; 10 Tennis nearby; 11 Swimming nearby; 12 Golf nearby; 13 Skiing nearby; 14 May be booked through a travel agent.

The Veranda

The Veranda

252 Seavy Street, P.O. Box 177, 30276-0177
(404) 599-3905; FAX (404) 599-0806

Guests stay in beautifully restored spacious Victorian rooms in a 1907 hotel on the National Register of Historic Places. Just 30 miles south of Atlanta airport. Freshly prepared Southern gourmet meals by reservation. Unusual gift shop featuring kaleidoscopes. Memorabilia and 1930 Wurlitzer player piano pipe organ. One room has a whirlpool bath; all have private baths and air conditioning.

Hosts: Jan and Bobby Boal
Rooms: 9 (PB) $100-125
Full Breakfast
Credit Cards: A, B, C
Notes: 2, 3, 4, 5, 7, 8, 10, 12, 14

STONE MOUNTAIN

Bed and Breakfast Atlanta

1801 Piedmont Avenue, Suite 208, 30324
(404) 875-0525; (800) 96PEACH
FAX (404) 875-9672

Rates not applicable during the summer of 1996 due to the Olympic summer games..

O2. This authentic 1830s white two-story farmhouse in Stone Mountain was moved and carefully reassembled on this site in 1984. The house has porches on all sides. In the main house there is a terrace room with a private entry, king-size poster bed, antique furniture, a fireplace, and a large

full bath. The carriage house has a suite with a large living room, dining room with a wet bar, undercounter refrigerator, and microwave, and a large screen TV. The bedroom features a king-size canopied bed and more interesting antiques. The private bath has a shower only. There is a queen-size sleep sofa in the living room, and a Port-a-crib is available. $72-92.

THOMASTON

Woodall House

324 West Main Street, 30286
(706) 647-7044

The interior "gingerbread" is original in this restored Victorian home built by the county physician at the turn of the century. Private baths with individual air conditioning and cable TV. One-half block from beautiful old courthouse square, ten miles from Flint River, 40 miles from Roosevelt's Little White House and Andersonville Confederate Cemetery, and 60 miles from Plains, Georgia, home of former President Jimmy Carter. Only 50 miles from Atlanta, Columbus, and Macon. "Home away from home" is the management philosophy. Smoking allowed outside.

Hosts: Bill and Charlene Woodall
Rooms: 3 (PB) $50
Full Breakfast
Credit Cards: None
Notes: 2, 5, 8, 9, 10, 11, 12

THOMASVILLE

Evans House
Bed and Breakfast

725 South Hansell Street, 31792
(912) 226-1343; (800) 344-4717
FAX (912) 226-0653

In the Parkfront Historical District, this restored Victorian home is directly across from the 27-acre Paradise Park near fine downtown antique shops and dining.

Featuring four guest rooms with private baths. Full breakfast served in the country kitchen. Bikes and many other amenities.

Hosts: Lee and John Puskar
Rooms: 4 (PB) $65-115
Full Breakfast
Credit Cards: None
Notes: 2, 5, 7, 8, 9, 12, 14

Quail Country Bed and Breakfast, Ltd.

1104 Old Monticello Road, 31792
(912) 226-7218; (912) 226-6882

1. This quaint Williamsburg-style guest house is next to the pool. Twin beds, private bath, dressing room, and full kitchen. The 18th-century garden overlooks other dependencies. Children welcome. $50.

2. Surrounded by natural woodland of oaks and pines, this charming country French Provincial house is near shopping center and restaurants. Excellent area for walking and bird watching. $40.

3. In a lovely residential area, this second-story garage apartment overlooks a beautiful swimming pool. Two bedrooms, bath, equipped kitchen, and living area. Crib available. The owner is an antique car enthusiast. $50.

4. Built in 1900 in pecan groves, this Neo-classical-style house features porches with large columns on three sides of the house. Each bedroom has its own bath and fireplace. The floors throughout the house are heart pine, and the rooms are furnished with antiques. $40.

5. Twenty-five-year-old bungalow in a lovely residential neighborhood has a bedroom with twin beds and private bath. $40.

THOMSON

Four Chimneys

2316 Wire Road Southeast, 30824
(706) 597-0220

Early 1800s plantation-plain-styled country house has original hand-planed pine board floors, walls, and ceilings. Furnished with antiques and reproductions; all guest rooms have fireplaces and four-posters. Beautiful grounds with Colonial-style herb and flower garden. Equestrian events, golf, and antique shops are nearby. Easy access to I-20 and Augusta. Two miles to town and restaurants. Higher rates for special events.

Hosts: Maggie and Ralph Zieger
Rooms: 4 (2 PB; 2 SB) $40-50
Continental Breakfast
Credit Cards: A, B
Notes: 2, 5, 9, 10, 12

WARM SPRINGS

Hotel Warm Springs Bed and Breakfast

P.O. Box 351, 17 Broad Street, 31830
(706) 655-2114; (800) 366-7616

Relive history and the Roosevelt era. Visit this 1907 hotel, ice cream parlor, and gift shops. Authentically restored, beautifully decorated with Roosevelt furniture and family antiques. Featured are cable TV, the ultimate honeymoon suite with heart tub, and king-size bed, social hour, and individual heat and air conditioning. Nestled in quaint Warm Springs Village—a shopper's paradise. Home of FDR's Little White House, 14 miles from Callaway Gardens, and one hour south of Atlanta.

Hosts: Lee and Geraldine Thompson
Rooms: 11 (PB) $60-160
Suites: 3
Full Breakfast
Credit Cards: A, B, C, D
Notes: 2, 5, 7, 8, 12, 14

Hawaii

Kauai

Princeville, Kalihiwai
Hanalei Kilauea
Anahola
Kapaa
Waifua
Wailua
Koloa
Waimea Poipu
Kalaheo

Oahu

Kaneohe
Kailua
Lanikai
Hawaii Kai
Aiea
Pearl City
Honolulu

Molokai

Kaunakakai

Lanai

Lanai City

Maui

Haiku
Hana
Wailuku Paia Kula
Kihei
Lahaina

Hawaii

Hawi
Honokaa
Kamuela
Hilo
Keaau
Pahoa
Volcano
Holualoa
Honaunau-Kona
Naalehu
Kailua Kona
Kealakekua
Captain Cook
Honaunau-Kona
Honolulu

Hawaii

HAWAII—CAPTAIN COOK

Aloha Bed and Breakfast

85-4577 Mamalahoa Highway 8E, 96704
(808) 328-9726; (808) 326-2272; (800) 328-9726
(800) 395-2272; FAX (808) 326-9492

Formerly Adrienne's Bed and Breakfast, this lovely custom cedar home has an unobstructed view of the ocean from the hot tub on the lanai where a Continental breakfast is served. All rooms king- or queen-size beds with private baths, entrances, TV, VCR (over 1,000 movies), and refrigerator. Ed and Grace, the hosts, share information on restaurants, snorkel and swimming places, and hiking trails. Flashlights, ice chests, boogie boards, and snorkel gear are available. Near beautiful beaches and Place of Refuge.

Hosts: Ed and Grace Kobus
Rooms: 4 (PB) $50-80
Continental Breakfast
Credit Cards: None
Notes: 2, 5, 7, 8, 9, 10, 11, 12, 13, 14

Bed and Breakfast Hawaii

P.O. Box 449, Kapaa, 96746
(808) 822-7771; (800) 733-1632

H-31. Nestled in the heart of Kona's coffee country, this bed and breakfast features a 550-square-foot unit with separate entrance and lanai, fully equipped kitchen with microwave, washer and dryer, queen-size bed, cable TV, covered parking, and twin-size sleeper-sofa plus private master bath. The windows frame 30 miles of striking shoreline, mountain, and sunset views. Outside smoking only. Children welcome. Three-night minimum. $10 for each extra guest. $75.

The Rainbow Plantation

P.O. Box 122, 96704
(808) 323-2393; FAX (808) 323-9445

Relax at Rainbow Plantation. Explore the peaceful surroundings. Stroll under the shade of the enchanted macadamia forest, among coffee trees, tropical plants, and flowers. Listen to the birds and gentle breezes. Join the hosts in their oceanview sunset hour. Just seven miles south of Kona, near Kealakekua Bay, a marine sanctuary. Private entrances. TV. Refrigerators. *On parle français, wir sprechen Deutsch.*

Hosts: Marianna and Keiner Schrepfer
Rooms: 3 (PB) $65-95
Continental Breakfast
Credit Cards: A, B, C
Notes: 2, 5, 6, 8, 9, 11, 14

HAWAII—GOLD COAST

A-1 Pacific-Hawaii Bed and Breakfast and Vacation Rental Reservation Agency

P.O. Box 1468, Kapaau, 96755-9998
(800) 999-6026; (800) 277-0509
FAX (808) 261-6573 or (808) 889-0500

At the northern tip of the Kohala Gold Coast, this estate is within a prestigious gated community, just 25 minutes north of the world-class resorts of Mauna Kea and Mauna Lani. Unobstructed oceanview with large lanai, patio, pool with slide. Guest suite has private entrance, two bedrooms with private baths, one with a two king-size beds and the other with a king-size bed, kitchen, and a small living room with TV. Horseback riding, tennis, golf, deep-sea

NOTES: Credit cards: A MasterCard; B Visa; C American Express; D Discover; E Diners Club; F Other; 2 Personal checks accepted; 3 Lunch available; 4 Dinner available; 5 Open all year; 6 Pets welcome; 7 No smoking; 8 Children welcome; 9 Social drinking allowed; 10 Tennis nearby; 11 Swimming nearby; 12 Golf nearby; 13 Skiing nearby; 14 May be booked through a travel agent.

fishing, hiking, skiing, and swimming. Full breakfast. Three-night minimum stay in high season. Additional charge of $10 for children. $95 for second room. $178.48.

HAWAII—HAWI

Bed and Breakfast Hawaii

P.O. Box 449, Kapaa, 96746
(808) 822-7771; (800) 733-1632
FAX (808) 822-2723

H63. This host home is three miles from Hawi on a gentle slope of the Kohala Mountains. Unobstructed view of the ocean and across Alenuihaha channel to the Haleakala peak on Maui. Secluded, quiet, and relaxing. Private access, living room area, kitchenette, and bedroom with queen-size bed and private bath. Two-night minimum. $65.

Bed and Breakfast Honolulu (Statewide)

3242 Kaohinani Drive, Honolulu, 96817
(808) 595-7533; (800) 288-4666
FAX (808) 595-2030

CHAPD. Private downstairs unit at the tip of the Big Island in the old Hawaiian town of Hawaii. Private entrance and bath, refrigerator, coffee maker, TV, and twin beds. A swimming beach is three miles away. Hike to the king's birthplace or a sacred Heiau. Children over 12 welcome. $50.

HAWAII—HILO

Bed and Breakfast Hawaii

P.O. Box 449, Kapaa, 96746
(808) 822-7771; (800) 733-1632
FAX (808) 822-2723

H1. A large Hawaiian-style house about two miles north of Hilo overlooking Hilo Bay. There are two bedrooms available to guests, each with a pair of twin beds, one converts to a king-size bed, if desired. Beautifully landscaped yard with pool. $55.

H2. Hale Paliku, which means "house against the cliff," is the name of this 1930s home. Three blocks from downtown Hilo. Guests share the TV, tape deck, microwave, and refrigerator. Two rooms with shared bath, one with oceanview and private balcony. Each room has down pillows, comforters, shuttered windows, and a table for two. Hosts live downstairs. $55-65.

H3. Large, modern, Hawaiian-style home surrounded by nearly four acres of parklike setting on an oceanfront bluff. Spectacular view of Wailea Bay. A tennis court and a municipal beach park are within walking distance, and the world-famous Akaka Falls is a short drive away. The spacious one-bedroom apartment includes bedroom, bath, fully equipped kitchenette, and living room with cable TV, radio, piano, and day beds. Children over eight welcome. $75.

H5. This beautiful Hilo home offesr three exceptional rooms along with a common area for lounging. Two bedrooms offer views of the ocean and Hilo and one bedroom looks out to one of the many garden areas. All rooms have a private entrance. Three-night minimum. No smoking. $75-80.

H7. On a bluff overlooking the ocean, this home offers an oceanfront pool with Jacuzzi and a view of a popular surfing beach. Large, covered decks face the ocean just two miles from downtown Hilo but quiet and private. Three guest rooms with private baths are separated by a family room with TV, VCR, and a private entrance to the pool. The master suite is sometimes available. Minimum stay is three nights. $95-120.

H8. Paradise Place is one-half mile from the ocean. Accommodations are downstairs with a private entrance and consist of a two-room suite with a double bed in the bedroom, sofa sleeper in the living room, and private bath with a shower. This area also

NOTES: Credit cards accepted: A MasterCard; B Visa; C American Express; D Discover; E Diners Club; F Other; 2 Personal checks accepted; 3 Lunch available; 4 Dinner available; 5 Open all year; 6 Pets welcome;

has a TV with VCR, microwave, small refrigerator.Explore fresh lava flows and Volcano National Park. Seventh night is free. $65.

H33. A rain forest retreat just south of Hilo is adjacent to an orchid nursery. The hostess tends the orchids and boards horses on her property. A private studio complete with a king-size bed, private bath, and light cooking appliances. Hot tub. Only 30 minutes from Hilo and Volcano National Park. $65-90

Bed and Breakfast Honolulu (Statewide)

3242 Kaohinani Drive, Honolulu, 96817
(808) 595-7533; (800) 288-4666
FAX (808) 595-2030

KEGLS. A five-minute walk to the center of Hilo, this home offers two guest rooms that share a bath. Living room has TV, microwave, refrigerator, and ocean-mountain view. Smoking outside. Children over 12. $60.

LANNA. Two miles out of Hilo on a cliff overlooking Hilo Bay, this home has a private yard with a lovely pool. Two bedrooms available. A full bath and a half-bath are reserved for guests. Charming tea house on the grounds. Children welcomed. $60.

Bjornen

111 Honolii Pali, 96720
(808) 935-6330

A beautiful four-star bed and breakfast on the bluff facing the ocean, surfing beach, and Hilo Bay. Two miles from downtown Hilo, yet quiet and private. Swimming pool and hot tub, large deck, and bar room. All rooms face the ocean and have private baths and cable TV. Two miles from Rainbow Falls and Botanical Gardens; nine miles from Akaka Falls and 30 miles from the

volcanoes and Waipo Valley. Excellent restaurants nearby. Guest cottage with kitchen facilities is also available. Limited smoking. Inquire about accommodations for children.

Hosts: Evonne Bjornen and Paul Tallett
Rooms: 5 (PB) $85-105
Full Breakfast
Credit Cards: None
Notes: 2, 5, 9, 11, 12, 14

Go Native · · Hawaii

P.O.Box 11418, 65 Halaulani Place, Hilo, 96721
(808) 935-4178; (800) 925-9065
FAX (808) 935-4178

Hale Paliku. "House against the cliff" is a 1930s kamaaina home just three blocks from the downtown area. Spectacular view of the Pacific at Hilo Bay. Explore historic old Hilo, starting at the Lyman Museum two blocks away. A short stroll to shops, restaurants, art galleries, and Kalakaua Park, and a short drive to gorgeous waterfalls and the scenic Hamakua coastline. House is 45 minutes away from Volcanoes National Park. Two guest rooms, one mountainside and one oceanside, contain down pillows, comforters, Laura Ashley prints, and "happi coats" (bathrobes). $55-100.

Keoni's Macadamia Nut House is on the lower slopes of Mauna Kea, only five miles from downtown Hilo. The home was built in 1993 and has two bedrooms, two private baths, private lanai, queen-size bed, TV, ceiling fan, and refrigerator. Private entrances. Volcanoes National Park is 35 miles away. $80.

Pi´ihonua. This private guest studio is just five minutes above downtown Hilo. Self-contained kitchenette, bath, cable TV, VCR, stereo and air conditioning. Continental breakfast. Minutes from Rainbow Falls, Lyman House Museum, and Hilo Farmer's Market. Children are welcome. Weekly rates available. Additional charge for extra person. No smoking. $65.

---

7 No smoking; 8 Children welcome; 9 Social drinking allowed; 10 Tennis nearby; 11 Swimming nearby; 12 Golf nearby; 13 Skiing nearby; 14 May be booked through a travel agent.

HAWAII—HOLUALOA

Bed and Breakfast Above the Kona Coast

P.O. Box 197, 96725
(808) 322-3295

A newly built house on seven and one-half acres is designed with the guests' needs in mind. A large lanai encircles the main house where guests can have breakfast while enjoying the expansive view of the ocean. A grass courtyard separates the main house from the guest buildings. Each room has a private entrance, TV, queen-size bed, full bath, and angled high windows that act as skylights. Relax in the hot tub under an umbrella of stars.

Host: John and Rosanne Lyle
Rooms: $65
Continental Breakfast
Credit Cards: None
Notes: 2, 5, 7, 8, 9, 10, 11, 12, 14

HAWAII—HONAUNAU

Bed and Breakfast Honolulu (Statewide)

3242 Kaohinani Drive, Honolulu, 96817
(808) 595-7533; (800) 288-4666
FAX (808) 595-2030

DEFAC. This Kona-style home is on the slopes above the City of Refuge. King-size bed, bath, and refrigerator are in the separate guest quarters on the ground level. Breakfast is served on the lanai with a panoramic view of the ocean. Enjoy the cool, quiet, private half-acre of gardens. $65.

RITZA. This lovely home is on the slopes above the City of Refuge in Hanaunau. View the ocean from the dining lanai and the hot tub. Hosts offer four rooms, two on the garden level with TV, VCR, refrigerator, microwave, and private bath and entrance. The room on the main level has a queen-size bed and shares a bath with the loft room. $50.

HAWAII—HONAUNAU-KONA

The Dragonfly Ranch: Tropical Fantasy Lodging

P.O. Box 675, 96726
(808) 328-9570; (800) 487-2159

The Dragonfly Ranch is on the Big Island's sunny Kona Coast near playful dolphins and magical snorkeling. This peaceful country estate offers tropical fantasy lodging with the elegant simplicity of openness and privacy in a lush jungle setting. Each unique suite has an oceanview, private outdoor shower and indoor bathroom, cable TV/VCR, and food preparation areas. Ideal for reunions, weddings, and romantic honeymoons. Smoking outside only.

Hosts: Barbara Moore-Link and David Link
Rooms: 5 (3 PB; 2 SB) $60-160
Continental Breakfast
Credit Cards: A, B
Notes: 2, 5, 8, 9, 10, 11, 12, 13, 14

HAWAII—HONOKAA

Bed and Breakfast Hawaii

P.O. Box 449, Kapaa, 96746
(808) 822-7771; (800) 733-1632
FAX (808) 822-2723

H11. With oceanviews on three sides, this estate is built on an ocean point just outside Honokaa. The main house has three guest accommodations: a large suite with fireplace, bedroom, private lanai, and private bath; a queen room with private bath, 12-foot ceilings, and tongue-and-groove woodwork. Two cottages also available. Lighted tennis courts, gazebo, macadamia orchard, fruit trees, and lush tropical flowers throughout the estate. $75-200.

H21. Unique, cozy cottage surrounded by lush foliage above the city of Kailua Kona. Fully equipped kitchen. TV, VCR, and telephone. The bedroom has a queen-size bed and a spectacular view of the Kona coastline. Awaken each morning to the songs of

NOTES: Credit cards accepted: A MasterCard; B Visa; C American Express; D Discover; E Diners Club; F Other; 2 Personal checks accepted; 3 Lunch available; 4 Dinner available; 5 Open all year; 6 Pets welcome;

the cardinals and smaller birds. Enjoy the hot tub while viewing a beautiful Kona sunset. Two-night minimum. Outside smoking only. $60.

HAWAII—HONOLULU

Aston Waikiki Beachside Hotel

2452 Kalakaua Avenue, 96815
(808) 931-2100; (800) 922-7866 (reservations)
FAX (808) 931-2129

An elegant boutique hotel with a prestigious address overlooking famous Waikiki Beach features 18th-century European and Asian artwork, antiques, and elaborate reproductions. Special touches include imported French-milled toiletries, English goose down pillows, and a seashell in a silk purse left with a welcome note on the eve of arrival complement the friendly and enthusiastic Hawaiian hospitality. Unique to Waikiki, the charm of a quaint country inn combined with the sophistication and service of a fine hotel. Inquire about accommodations for children.

Hosts: Donna Wheeler, general manager
  Shirley Tsukano, director of sales
Rooms: 79 (PB) $175-365
Continental Breakfast
Credit Cards: A, B, C, D, E, F
Notes: 2, 5, 9, 10, 11, 12, 14

HAWAII—KAILUA-KONA

Adrienne's Casa Del Sol Bed and Breakfast Inn

77-6335 Alii Drive, 96740
(808) 326-CASA (2272); (800) 395-2272
FAX (808) 326-9492

This beautiful Mediterranean-style home has wrought iron throughout, sweeping arched private oceanview lanais from every room and suite. Breakfast buffet is served poolside or by oceanview spa. A personal chef is available for lunch and dinner. All rooms have king- or queen-size beds; suites have full kitchens, living rooms, dining rooms, private bath, telephone with voice mail and modem connection, and private entrances. Less than five minutes to world-class golf, tennis, skin diving, fishing charter (best marlin tournaments), surfing, snorkeling, beaches, restaurants, and shopping. Between Kailua-Kona and resort community of Keauhou in the heart of the resort community.

Hosts: Adrienne and Reginald Batty
Rooms: 2 (PB)
Suites: 2
Continental Breakfast
Credit Cards: A, B
Notes: 2, 5, 7, 8, 9, 10, 11, 12, 13, 14

Anne's Three Bears' Bed and Breakfast

72-1001 Puukala Street, 96740
(808) 325-7563; (800) 765-0480

Comfortable, friendly accommodations and a spectacular oceanview of the Kona coastline. This beautiful cedar home is close to Kailua town and the many beaches on the Kona Coast. Breakfast is served on the lanai, and complimentary beach chairs, coolers, and boogie boards are provided. The hosts also have a free reservation service specializing in bed and breakfast accommodations on all Hawaiian islands. German is spoken.

Hosts: Anne, Art and Nanette Stockel
Rooms: 2 (PB) $59-75
Full Breakfast
Credit Cards: A, B
Notes: 2, 5, 8, 9, 10, 11, 12, 14

Bed and Breakfast Hawaii

P.O. Box 449, Kapaa, 96746
(808) 822-7771; (800) 733-1632
FAX (808) 822-2723

H10. A spacious home surrounded by tropical foliage. A five-minute drive from the ocean. The downstairs accommodation includes a private lanai with an oceanview and a separate entrance through glass doors to the bedroom. Mini-refrigerator, microwave, TV, and telephone. Continental breakfast. No smoking. Two-night minimum stay. $70.

7 No smoking; 8 Children welcome; 9 Social drinking allowed; 10 Tennis nearby; 11 Swimming nearby; 12 Golf nearby; 13 Skiing nearby; 14 May be booked through a travel agent.

Bed and Breakfast Hawaii (continued)

H23. Magnificent panoramic view from this hillside home. Choose between the Hula Room, with queen-size bed and large, private lanai, and the Garden Room, with two twin beds. Both have TV, microwave, and refrigerator. Smoking outside only. $65-75.

H26. A peaceful hillside on Hualalai Mountain overlooking the Kona coast. This lovely 2,500-square-foot home is meticulously furnished. Guest quarters are on the first level and have two bedrooms with one bath and a kitchen and living area. Large deck for guests' exclusive use. Breakfast fixings provided. Three-night minimum stay. $65-75.

H32A. This luxurious, comfortable oceanfront home is on the beach in Kona. Two rooms available: one is oceanfront with a queen-size bed, and the other is oceanview with a queen-size bed. Both have full private baths and TV. No smoking. $95-115.

H34. This beautiful new home is 12 minutes from the airport and 15 minutes from Kailua Village in the cool Kaloko Mauka area. An attractive separate apartment at garden level with two bedrooms, bath, sitting room with TV, and limited cooking facilities. After a busy day of sports, shopping, or sightseeing, rest on the lanai high above the Kona Coast and enjoy the magnificent sunset. Resident dog, cats, and llamas. Two-night minimum. No smoking. $85.

H44. Charming cottage very near Kailua Bay and village.Private courtyard with a lovely garden view. The one-bedroom cottage offers a queen-size bed and private bath, TV, VCR, and stereo. The kitchenette offers a full refrigerator, microwave, coffee pot, toaster oven, and blender. Great for a small family. Hosts have two children and welcome families with

children. Beach equipment is available, and tennis courts are close by. Two-night minimum stay. Special weekly rates. $65.

H46. Elegant, brand new, with an oceanview and separate from the main house. One bedroom with a queen-size bed and full bathroom, plus a sitting area with TV. A dining area with a refrigerator and wet bar. Private deck. No smoking. Two-night minimum stay. $80.

H50. This bed and breakfast has a private entrance on the lower level of this beautiful, brand-new, two-story Art Deco home. Choice of two large bedrooms, with access to the gardens that offer a beautiful oceanview. Family room furnished with a piano, pool, Ping-Pong tables, and big-screen TV. Great for two couples traveling together. $50-80.

H50C. Minutes from Kailua-Kona, this "Hawaiian Hut" offers a separate studio with a queen-size bed, private bath with shower, refrigerator, and private lanai with magnificent ocean and sunset views. Breakfast at the main house each morning. No smoking. Three-night minimum stay. Weekly rates available. $95.

H59. On a three-acre estate overlooking the coastline just above Kona Village, these accommodations are self-contained and private. A separate apartment features one bedroom with a queen-size bed, living room with a fold-out sofa, private bath, kitchen, TV, private entrance, and lanai with barbecue. A queen-size futon is also available. The building is designed like a dome with open beam ceilings. Smoking outside only. $80-95.

H70. On the west side of the Big Island and 18 miles south of Kailua Kona, this is a garden-level accommodation at a host home with a private entrance. Unobstructed

NOTES: Credit cards accepted: A MasterCard; B Visa; C American Express; D Discover; E Diners Club; F Other; 2 Personal checks accepted; 3 Lunch available; 4 Dinner available; 5 Open all year; 6 Pets welcome;

oceanview. The bedroom has a king-size bed, private bath, refrigerator, coffee pot, microwave, and TV. Continental breakfast. Only five minutes from the beaches and the best snorkeling and swimming on the island. Three-night minimum stay. $50-70.

H71. This home is just six miles from the airport and three miles from the beach and offers beautiful oceanviews. A private suite, decorated with antique oak furniture throughout, offers a queen-size bed and large, private bath with shower. Kitchenette is available, including a microwave and refrigerator. Sitting area with TV, lanai, washer-dryer, and a lap pool with cabana and waterfall. Continental breakfast . Outside smoking only. Minimum stay is two nights. $75-85.

H72. A large, private studio is on a hillside in a quiet, residential neighborhood. The bedroom has a queen-size bed. A double futon is also available. Full kitchen and private bath. Outside covered lanai with barbecue, TV, and phone. Children welcome. Smoking outside only. Two-night minimum stay. $55-65.

H73. A one-bedroom apartment on the ground floor of a host home. Queen-size bed plus a double futon for a third person. Kitchenette includes refrigerator and microwave. Private bath. From the lanai guests may barbecue and enjoy an oceanview and the fabulous sunsets of Kona. Smoking outside only. Children ten years and older. $65-70.

Go Native •• Hawaii

P.O.Box 11418, 65 Halaulani Place, Hilo, 96721
(808) 935-4178; (800) 925-9065
FAX (808) 935-4178

Hale Kipa 'O Pele. The tropical estate and plantation-style home are distinctly unique. A majestic volcanic dome graces the entrance drive. The house surrounds an open-air atrium with cascading lava rock waterfalls into a koi pond. The atrium's tiled walkway provides a private entrance to each room/suite. Each room has its own private bath. Continental breakfast. Guests enjoy year-round tour and sport activities, or walk along the scenic shores and quaint village-style shops of old Kona town. $75-115.

Hale Malia A spacious, modern home built in the old plantation-style. Choose the oceanfront bedroom or the partial oceanview and enjoy a private bath and a queen-size bed, TV, and lots of charm. Two miles south of picturesque Kailua-Kona on the ocean and just minutes from scuba diving, snorkeling, fishing, kayaking, golf, tennis, and biking. Kilauea, erupting continuously since 1983, is a major attraction. $95-115

Luna Kai. Choice accommodations in either a self-contained cottage or delightful studio. The cottage is nestled in a tropical garden and has a king-size bed, private bath, and outside lanai. A studio is below the main house. Continental breakfast. Open lanai with a 180° view of Kailua Bay and the Kona coastline. $80.

Puanani Bed and Breakfast. Nestled in a quiet hillside on a cul-de-sac, these three-room private suites provide spectacular views of the Pacific. The grounds are beautiful with indigenous landscaping to encourage bird watching. Amenities include antiques, private entrance, queen-size bed, large sitting room, kitchenette, and lanai. Enjoy an exercise-weight room, a 40-foot lap pool with waterfalls, and a fish pond with water lilies and hyacinths. $70-85.

Hale Maluhia
Bed and Breakfast

76-770 Hualalai Road, 96740
(800) 559-6627; (808) 329-5573
FAX (808) 326-5487

Gracious up-country plantation living in the heart of the Kona Recreational Paradise. In

7 No smoking; 8 Children welcome; 9 Social drinking allowed; 10 Tennis nearby; 11 Swimming nearby; 12 Golf nearby; 13 Skiing nearby; 14 May be booked through a travel agent.

beautiful Holualoa coffee land. Large rooms, private baths, good beds, and spa. Old Hawaii living with native woods, open beam ceilings, koa cabinets, big lanais, four common areas, and a stream with waterfalls and lily ponds. Two and one-half miles from the Kailua-Kona Village; easy airport access. Cable TV/VCR with movie library. Beach and snorkeling equipment. Wheelchair friendly. Inquire about pets.

Hosts: Ken and Ann Smith
Rooms: 5 (PB) $55-85
Cottages: 2 (PB) $110-135
Full Breakfast
Credit Cards: A, B, C, D
Notes: 2, 5, 7, 8, 9, 10, 11, 12, 13, 14

HAWAII—KAMUELA

Bed and Breakfast Hawaii

P.O. Box 449, Kapaa, 96746
(808) 822-7771; (800) 733-1632
FAX (808) 822-2723

H41. In the historic area of North Kohala about seven miles from lush Pololu Valley and the rugged coastline of beautiful Hawai. This modified A-frame home is set back from the road and includes a self-contained studio under the main house with a separate entrance, limited kitchenette, private bath, and double bed. No smoking. Two-night minimum stay. $50.

H62. Part of a beautiful Swiss chalet-style home just three and one-half miles from Kamuela and only 12 minutes from Hapuna Beach. A two-bedroom apartment with a queen-size bed, full bath, and living room with a fireplace, TV, and telephone. Views of Mauna Kea and the ocean from the private sun deck. $65-75.

H67. Charming Victorian home with breathtaking sunset and mountain vistas. Mauna Kea, Mauna Loa, and Mount Hualalai visable from the wraparound lanais. Soak in the hot tub underneath the stars or enjoy the beaches of the Kohala

Coast just a short drive away. One room with a queen-size bed and private bath with shower; the other with a queen-size bed and shared full bath. No smoking. Two-night minimum stay. $75-95.

Bed and Breakfast Honolulu (Statewide)

3242 Kaohinani Drive, Honolulu, 96817
(808) 595-7533; (800) 288-4666
FAX (808) 595-2030

BATEG. Parker ranch country. This Hawaiian missionary-style home is by a quiet, meandering stream. Guest quarters contain bedroom, living room, light cooking facilities, and a full bath. Guests have a 360° view of famous Mauna Kea and Mauna Loa Mountains and the blue Pacific. $75.

DICKD. This lovely home is a three-mile country drive from Waimea. Two beautiful guest rooms (queen and double) and a suite with private entrance and antique twin beds. No children. Smoking outside only. $65.

MITCD. On Kalaki Road, this beautiful two-story Swiss chalet borders the ranch lands of Mauna Kea. Two-bedroom unit is on the first floor with private entrance, fireplace, kitchen, and full bath. Three miles from Kamuela town center and 14 miles from the island's best white-sand beaches and Waipio Valley. Two-night minimum. Smoking outside only. $60.

Go Native • • Hawaii

65 Halaulani Place, P.O.Box 11418, Hilo, 96721
(808) 935-4178; (800) 662-8483

Kamuela's Mauna Kea View. Private suites with panoramic views of Parker Ranch and majestic Mauna Kea. Suites modeled after Swiss chalets are minutes from restaurants, shopping, and the Big Island's best beaches. Private entrances, two bedrooms, cozy fireplaces, relaxing sun decks, and colorful gardens. Close to

NOTES: Credit cards accepted: A MasterCard; B Visa; C American Express; D Discover; E Diners Club;
F Other; 2 Personal checks accepted; 3 Lunch available; 4 Dinner available; 5 Open all year; 6 Pets welcome;

hiking, horseback riding, golf, tennis, skiing, and more. $55-65

Kamuela Inn

P.O. Box 1994, 96743
(808) 885-4243; FAX (808) 885-8857

Comfortable, cozy rooms and suites with private baths, with or without kitchenettes, all with cable TV. Continental breakfast served in a sunny lanai each morning. In a quiet, peaceful setting near shops, parks, museums, and restaurants. Hawaii's white sand beaches, golf, and valley and mountain tours are only minutes away.

Host: Carolyn Cascavilla
Rooms: 31 (PB) $54-165
Continental Breakfast
Credit Cards: A, B, C, D, E, F
Notes: 2, 5, 7, 8, 10, 11, 12, 13, 14

HAWAII—KAPAA

A-1 Pacific-Hawaii Bed and Breakfast and Vacation Rental Reservation Agency

P.O. Box 1468, 96755-9998
(800) 999-6026; (800) 277-0509
FAX (808) 261-6573 or (808) 889-0500

The island of Hawaii, known as the "Big Island," is one of the most unique ecosystems in the world. This reservation service has about 100 listings of accommodations, cottages, or homes in all areas of this beautiful island. From $65 to $180 for bed and breakfast accommodations or cottages or up to $450 per day for an entire home. Contact: Doris Epp-Reichert.

HAWAII—KEAAU

Bed and Breakfast Hawaii

P.O. Box 449, Kapaa, 96746
(808) 822-7771; (800) 733-1632
FAX (808) 822-2723

H69. Twenty minutes from the Hilo airport, this accommodation is for those who want to

vacation in rural Hawaii. Great for hiking and biking, only 15 minutes from beaches, shopping, restaurants, volcanoes, and golf courses. Guest rooms have private entrances and baths. A covered porch area with refrigerator, microwave, and barbecue. Two-night minimum stay. Outside smoking only. $40.

Bed and Breakfast Honolulu (Statewide)

3242 Kaohinani Drive, Honolulu, 96817
(808) 595-7533; (800) 288-4666
FAX (808) 595-2030

MERCE. Two guest rooms with private baths in a pretty country setting five minutes outside Keaau and 20-minutes from Hilo. Spacious living room and lovely views. Full breakfast. No small children. Hosts speak French and some Italian. $50.

Na Hala O Ke Kai (The Hala Trees by the Sea)

HCR 2 Box 9591, 96749
(808) 966-4384

Aloha! This beautiful oceanfront home is furnished with antiques and family heirlooms. The bed and breakfast lodging is downstairs, with direct access to the shoreline, pounding surf, and black lava cliffs. Studio apartment with private entrance and bath, efficiency kitchen, and dining and sitting areas. Enjoy a gourmet breakfast on the deck overlooking the coastline while watching for dolphins, turtles, and whales.

Hosts: Pedar and Eileen Wold and
    Randi Wold-Brennon
Room: 1 (PB) $75
Continental Breakfast
Credit Cards: None
Notes: 2, 5, 8, 9, 11, 12, 14

Ohia Cottage

HCR 2, Box 9591, 96749
(808) 966-4384

This charming plantation-style cottage was built in the 1930s and is on the National

---

7 No smoking; 8 Children welcome; 9 Social drinking allowed; 10 Tennis nearby; 11 Swimming nearby; 12 Golf nearby; 13 Skiing nearby; 14 May be booked through a travel agent.

Register of Historic Places. The ideal get-away for families. Furnished for comfort, Ohia Cottage has three bedrooms, shared bath, full kitchen, fireplace, and wheelchair-accessible. Just a half-mile from Hawaii Volcanoes National Park, guests may explore the unbelievable beauty of the world's most active volcano. Golf courses are less than 30 minutes away.

Hosts: Pedar and Eileen Wold and
  Randi Wold-Brennon
Rooms: 3 (SB) $75
Continental Breakfast
Credit Cards: None
Notes: 2, 5, 8, 9, 12, 14

HAWAII—KEALAKEKUA

Bed and Breakfast Hawaii

P.O. Box 449, Kapaa, 96746
(808) 822-7771; (800) 733-1632
FAX (808) 822-2723

H38. This is an unusual and beautifully designed home with hardwood floors, decks, and lots of windows with screens. This two-story home is just 200 yards from Napoopoo Bay, a great area for swimming and snorkeling. Downstairs, two separate bedrooms with private baths and queen-size beds share a sitting room with a covered deck that views the ocean. $80.

Bed and Breakfast Honolulu (Statewide)

3242 Kaohinani Drive, Honolulu, 96817
(808) 595-7533; (800) 288-4666
FAX (808) 595-2030

BOONW. This home is on an expanse of emerald lawn with palms and exotic fruit trees. It is fenced along the road with head-high poinsettias and is surrounded by a wall of banana trees among groves of coffee and macadamias. Enjoy the pool, tennis, or beaches. Three rooms share a bath. Continental breakfast. Resident dog. $65.

OBERJ. Near the Captain Cook Monument, a room with a queen-size bed and private bath

and entrance. Great ocean and mountain views. The beach is nearby. Adjacent sitting room with a refrigerator, toaster oven, and lanai. Continental breakfast. Smoking is allowed on the lanai only. Children are welcome. Two-night minimum stay. $75.

Merryman's Bed and Breakfast

P.O. Box 474, 96750
(808) 323-2276; (800) 545-4390
FAX (808) 323-3749

Enjoy all the Kona Coast has to offer from this peaceful dream home with outdoor Jacuzzi set on a breezy hillside in the coffee farm country of Kealakekua–Captain Cook area. Charming oceanview bed and breakfast in Kaelakekua, minutes from snorkeling. Immaculate, spacious rooms furnished with antiques and fresh flowers. Hawaiian breakfast of fresh fruits, chef's special, and Kona coffee served each morning. Snorkel gear provided. Smoking outdoors only.

Hosts: Penny and Don Merryman
Rooms: 4 (2 PB; 2 SB) $75-95
Full Breakfast
Credit Cards: A, B, D
Notes: 2, 5, 9, 11, 12, 14

HAWAII—KEHENA BEACH

Kalani Honua by the Sea

Rural Route 2, Box 4500, 96778
(808) 965-7828; (800) 800-6886

Experience the only coastal lodging within Hawaii's largest conservation area. Kalani Honua, meaning "Harmony of Heaven and Earth," is the ideal location for culture and relaxation. Private cottages with oceanviews. Three gourmet meals served each day. Take an ongoing class. Enjoy a massage or relax at the spa. Many natural wonders nearby, including a black-sand beach, warm springs, and Volcanoes National Park. Limited smoking.

Hosts: Richard Koob and Dottie Kaiser
Rooms: 30 (11 PB; 19 SB) $52-97
Full Breakfast
Credit Cards: A, B, C, E, F
Notes: 3, 4, 5, 8, 9 10, 11, 14

HAWAII—KONA

Bed and Breakfast Honolulu (Statewide)

3242 Kaohinani Drive, Honolulu, 96817
(808) 595-7533; (800) 288-4666
FAX (808) 595-2030

FREIS. Beautiful new two-story home overlooking the ocean with three large guest rooms (queen, king, and twin beds). King room has a private bath. Queen and twin rooms share a bath. Family room is furnished with a piano, pool table, Ping-Pong, big screen TV, wet bar, and refrigerator for drinks or snacks. Great for couples traveling together. No smoking. No children. $55.

HAWAII—NAALEHU

Bed and Breakfast Hawaii

P.O. Box 449, Kapaa, 96746
(808) 822-7771; (800) 733-1632
FAX (808) 822-2723

H55. In the southernmost community in the United States. Sixty-four miles from Hilo, 56 miles from Kona, Naalehu offers exploration of the site of the first Polynesian landings on the island, spectacular views of the cliffs and shoreline, and green sea turtles in Punalu'u State Park. A 50-year-old plantation house. Full breakfast served. Queen-size and double beds; private and shared baths. $45-65.

HAWAII—PAHOA

Bed and Breakfast Hawaii

P.O. Box 449, Kapaa, 96746
(808) 822-7771; (800) 733-1632
FAX (808) 822-2723

H64. A private cottage attached to the main house by a breezeway. In Pahoa just 25 minutes from Hilo and 30 minutes to Volcano. The cottage has a private entrance from the lanai, a queen-size bed, and full private bath. A full kitchen allows for light cooking. TV, VCR, washer-dryer, above-ground pool, and a barbecue are also available. Two-night minimum. An additional $15 for third person. $60.

HAWAII—PAPAIKOU

Bed and Breakfast Honolulu (Statewide)

3242 Kaohinani Drive, Honolulu, 96817
(808) 595-7533; (800) 288-4666
FAX (808) 595-2030

MILLS. Large cedar home with four guest rooms just outside Hilo is within walking distance to shops and cafes. One room has a private bath. All guest rooms have private lanais. Common room has a TV, fireplace, and piano. Hearty breakfast served. Smoking outside. Children over 11. $60.

HAWAII—VOLCANO

Bed and Breakfast Hawaii

P.O. Box 449, Kapaa, 96746
(808) 822-7771; (800) 733-1632
FAX (808) 822-2723

H18. This cottage in Volcano Village is a charming, cozy plantation-style cottage surrounded by giant cedars, native koa and ohia trees, and hapu'u ferns. The perfect place for a quiet vacation. Ideal for families or golf weekends, the cottage includes three bedrooms, two double rooms and one single room. Shared bath, fully equipped kitchen, fireplace, cable TV, and a ramp entrance. Continental breakfast . Can be rented by the room (shared bath) or the entire cottage for up to five guests. Two-night minimum. Children welcome. No smoking. $55-150.

H51. Just two miles from Volcanoes National Park. Helpful hosts offer a king-size bedroom with its own entrance and private bath and a futon for a third person. Great breakfasts are served every morning. $70.

H51A. Also available in H51 are three cottages. Guests check in with hosts and receive keys. The refrigerator and kitchen are stocked with breakfast foods ample for a week's stay. Choose from three cottages. All are plush and beautifully furnished with fireplaces, TV, VCR, and stereo. $85-125.

Bed and Breakfast Honolulu (Statewide)

3242 Kaohinani Drive, Honolulu, 96817
(808) 595-7533; (800) 288-4666
FAX (808) 595-2030

COLEP. Two rooms are offered with a shared bath, one with a double bed and one with a pair of twins. Restaurants and convenience stores nearby. Kitchen is available to guests. Continental breakfast. Smoking outside only. $55.

MORSG. This historic home, circa 1889, is on a seven-acre estate. The drive is the original road from Volcano to Hilo. Volcanoes National Park (and eruptions), golf, hiking, museum, art, and helicopter tours are nearby. Rooms on each of the three floors have queen and single beds. All baths are shared. A cottage is available with three rooms, private entrance, and lanai. The studio has a fully equipped kitchen, TV, and telephone. Children and smokers welcome. Resident dog. $45.

Chalet Kilauea— The Inn at Volcano

P.O. Box 998, 96785
(808) 967-7786; (800) 937-7786)
FAX (808) 967-8660

This inn at 3,500 feet amid the lush splendor of a tropical rain forest is near Volcanoes National Park. Choose from superior theme rooms and suites including the Treehouse Suite and separate spacious vacation homes. Awaken to a candlelit, two-course full gourmet breakfast featuring international and local cuisine. Enjoy afternoon tea in the living room filled with stunning and fascinating art from around the world or outside on the huge covered veranda with its own fountain. All units have private entrance and private bath, some feature marble Jacuzzi tubs. Other features include fireplaces, outside Jacuzzi, TV, VCR, and a video, music, and book library. Exquisitely tasteful and reassuringly comfortable.

Hosts: Lisha and Brian Crawford
Rooms: 11 (PB) $75-225
Full Breakfast
Credit Cards: A, B, C, D, F
Notes: 2, 5, 7, 8, 9, 11, 12, 14

Kilauea Lodge

P.O. Box 116, 96785
(808) 967-7366; FAX (808) 967-7367

Charming mountain lodge one mile from Volcanoes National Park. Full service dining room with excellent wine list. Full breakfast readies guests for an active day of hiking and viewing the wonders of Pele, the volcano goddess. Private baths. Six rooms have fireplaces. Common area.

Rooms: 12 (PB) $90-125
Full Breakfast
Credit Cards: A, B
Notes: 2, 4, 5, 8, 9, 12

Volcano Bed and Breakfast

P.O. Box 998, 96785
(808) 967-7779; (800) 736-7140
FAX (808) 967-8660

Volcano Bed and Breakfast offers a peaceful setting and safe haven that draws visitors from all over the world. All five rooms in the three-story turn-of-the-century home look out onto tree ferns, fragrant ginger, and native ohia forest. Various activities nearby include golf, black-sand beaches, and Volcanoes National Park's hiking trails and spectacular lava flows. Private cottage also available.

Host: Saul Rollason and Henry Haan
Rooms: 5 (SB) $55-95
Full Breakfast
Credit Cards: A, B, C, D, F
Notes: 2, 5, 7, 8, 9, 10, 11, 12, 14

NOTES: Credit cards accepted: A MasterCard; B Visa; C American Express; D Discover; E Diners Club; F Other; 2 Personal checks accepted; 3 Lunch available; 4 Dinner available; 5 Open all year; 6 Pets welcome;

KAUAI—ANAHOLA

Bed and Breakfast Hawaii

P.O. Box 449, Kapaa, 96746
(808) 822-7771; (800) 733-1632
FAX (808) 822-2723

K67. Beautiful tropical surroundings at Anahola Beach. Enjoy beautiful views and beach atmosphere in this bright studio with private yard and entrance, full bath, and breakfast facilities. The home is across the street from a beach great for swimming, snorkeling, boogie boarding, and wind surfing. Convenient to all Kauai attractions. Tropical Continental breakfast fixings are provided. A two-night minimum stay is required. $75.

K87. A very secluded and private 15-acre estate just a few hundred feet from the ocean in the quiet rural area of Anahola. The guest accommodation is separate from the main home. Unobstructed view of the Anahola Mountains, partial oceanview, total privacy, and quiet. The studio has a queen-size futon plus an additional single bed, private bath with indoor/outdoor shower, full kitchen, washer-dryer, TV, VCR, and barbecue. Smoking allowed outside only. Two-night minimum stay required. Weekly rates are available. $90.

Bed and Breakfast Honolulu (Statewide)

3242 Kaohinani Drive, Honolulu, 96817
(808) 595-7533; (800) 288-4666
FAX (808) 595-2030

SKAGJ. On the beach for a peaceful vacation or a romantic honeymoon! Private studio with TV, laundry facilities, and ready for light cooking. Continental breakfast fixings are provided. The beach is reef-protected for swimming. $75.

Mahina Kai

P.O. Box 699, 96703
(808) 822-9451

Asian Pacific beach villa overlooking Anahola Bay Lagoon pool, hot tub, waterfall in lush tropical gardens on almost two acres of land. Japanese-style house with shoji screen doors, blue cobalt tile roof. Three guest rooms with private bath and lanais opening to a living room and library. One two-bedroom apartment with private bath and efficiency kitchen sleeping six in ancient Heian temple ruins on property. Snorkeling gear, beach towels, and umbrellas included.

Host: Trudy Comba
Rooms: 3 (PB) $115-150
Continental Breakfast
Credit Cards: None
Notes: 2, 3, 4, 5, 7, 9, 10, 11, 12, 14

KAUAI—HANALEI

Bed and Breakfast Hawaii

P.O. Box 449, Kapaa, 96746
(808) 822-7771; (800) 733-1632
FAX (808) 822-2723

K21. Beach house on Anini Beach, halfway between Kilauea and Hanalei. The guest room has a double bed and shared bath. Large covered porch for relaxing and viewing the sunsets of the North Shore. Two-night minimum stay. $50.

K45. This bed and breakfast accommodation is 100 yards from gorgeous Hanalei Bay. Perfect for hiking, watersports, sightseeing, golf, sunbathing, or just long walks in a quaint, unpretentious town. Sunsets from the lanai are breathtaking. A two-story home with 1,000 square feet of deck surrounding the second floor and providing a partial oceanview and a mountain view of waterfalls. Continental breakfast. $65-85.

K83. This Hanalei cottage is just two blocks from Hanalei Bay and Hanalei Town and can sleep four comfortably. The bedroom has twin beds that convert to king-size and a queen-size sofa bed in the living area. Private bath, complete kitchen, washer-dryer,

7 No smoking; 8 Children welcome; 9 Social drinking allowed; 10 Tennis nearby; 11 Swimming nearby; 12 Golf nearby; 13 Skiing nearby; 14 May be booked through a travel agent.

and private lanai. Light breakfast fixings are available in the cottage. Three-night minimum. Outside smoking only. $85.

Bed and Breakfast Honolulu (Statewide)

3242 Kaohinani Drive, Honolulu, 96817
(808) 595-7533; (800) 288-4666
FAX (808) 595-2030

BARNC. This lovely home has three units. One guest room has a private bath and queen bed. The downstairs one-bedroom apartment with light cooking facilities, TV, private patio, and garden with ocean view. The third-floor unit sleeps four. View Hanalei Bay. Living room TV. The beach is 100 yards away. Children over 12 welcome. Three-night minimum stay. $55-100.

Go Native • • Hawaii

65 Halaulani Place, P.O. Box 11418, Hilo, 96721
(808) 935-4178; (800) 662-8483

Bed, Breakfast, and Beach. This three-story house is stylish and tastefully designed with a lanai surrounding the second floor. Two rooms, one studio, one apartment, and one honeymoon suite are available. All have queen-size beds, private baths, and kitchen access. Guests may boat, canoe, wind-surf, swim, snorkel, hike, picnic, or fish in the town of Hanalei. Within walking distance of markets, restaurants, shopping, and local art displays. Continental breakfast. Inquire about accommodations for children. Smoking outside only. $60-80.

KAUAI—KALAHEO

Bed and Breakfast Hawaii

P.O. Box 449, Kapaa, 96746
(808) 822-7771; (800) 733-1632
FAX (808) 822-2723

K19. Three bedrooms open onto a swimming pool flanked by flowering hibiscus, garde-

nias, and bougainvillaeas in this home in the hills of South Kauai. A second-story wooden porch overlooks sugar cane fields, jungle, and the National Botanical Gardens. It is only a 7- to 20-minute drive to beaches. All rooms have private baths. One room is handicapped accessible. No smoking. $55-75.

K27. In quaint, quiet old Kalaheo town, this is a modern, executive-style home overlooking Poipu with distant mountain and ocean-views and several rooms for guests, including two master suites. Makai offers a large room with king-size bed and private bath with Jacuzzi. Mauka suite offers a queen-size bed with private bath. Also, two bedrooms, one with a double bed and the other with twin beds, share a bath with tub and shower plus additional shower. Two-night minimum. Children over 16 are welcome. No smoking allowed in bedrooms. $50-85.

K85. Mango Hills Cottage is on two and one-half acres in Kalaheo overlooking the ocean and many acres of coffee fields. The living room has a pull-out queen-size sofa bed, cable TV. Full kitchen with counter seating. The bedroom has a mountain view and a queen-size bed with adjoining bath. Pool. Four-night minimum stay. $85.

Bed and Breakfast Honolulu (Statewide)

3242 Kaohinani Drive, Honolulu, 96817
(808) 595-7533; (800) 288-4666
FAX (808) 595-2030

GROWR. Self-contained cottages minutes away from major attractions in the countryside of Kaleheo on the garden island of Kauai. Antique stained-glass leaded windows and all the comforts of home. Fully furnished, complete kitchens, TVs, and daily linen service. Ten minutes to Kukuiolono Golf Course. $55.

NOTES: Credit cards accepted: A MasterCard; B Visa; C American Express; D Discover; E Diners Club;
F Other; 2 Personal checks accepted; 3 Lunch available; 4 Dinner available; 5 Open all year; 6 Pets welcome;

Go Native ·· Hawaii

P.O.Box 11418, 65 Halaulani Place, Hilo, 96721
(808) 935-4178; (800) 925-9065
FAX (808) 935-4178

South Shore Vista. Ten minutes from the Poipu Beach resort area and ten minutes from beaches to the west. Accommodations include a bedroom with queen-size bed, private full bath, living area, and kitchenette. Beautifully decorated, this one-bedroom ohana has an oceanview and looks out toward the spectacular mountain scenery of Kauai's sunny south shore. Sleeps up to four. Children over four welcome. $75.

KAUAI-KALIHIWAI

Bed and Breakfast Hawaii

P.O. Box 449, Kapaa, 96746
(808) 822-7771; (800) 733-1632
FAX (808) 822-2723

K34. In Kalihiwai Valley, this relaxing home is only minutes away from Princeville. Private entrance, a fully equipped kitchen, two queen-size beds, a private shower, washer and dryer, and TV. The perfect setting for a North shore stay. Threenight minimum. No smoking. $75.

KAUAI—KAPAA

Bed and Breakfast Hawaii

P.O. Box 449, Kapaa, 96746
(808) 822-7771; (800) 733-1632
FAX (808) 822-2723

K1. A secluded oceanfront home on beautiful Anahola Bay has a large studio apartment detached from the main house. Queen-size bed and private bath with a garden shower, cable TV, and a kitchenette. Breakfast fixings provided for the first three days. Occasionally a honeymoon room with a deep Jacuzzi is available. Enjoy the oceanfront amenities and privacy. Three-day minimum stay. Weekly rates. $95-125

K3A. Cloud Nine Holiday is a spacious apartment with a private entrance. Cable TV, a microwave, a small refrigerator, and breakfast fixings. The lanai overlooks a beautifully landscaped "bird of paradise" tropical garden perfect for romantic sunrise or sunset strolls. Near the beach and public tennis court. No smoking. $60-100.

K6. These three fresh and comfortable accommodations overlook a horse pasture skirted by Opaekaa Stream. Waterfalls are often visible in the distance from the lanai. Private entrances to all suites decorated in wicker and rattan. All rooms feature kingor queen-size beds, kitchen areas, and private baths. Smoking outside only. $60-100.

K10. In the foothills of Kaua'i's beautiful Mount Waialeale, the hosts offer two bed and breakfast units surrounded by a threeacre working tropical flower farm. Hal'Akahi is a spacious two-room unit on the ground floor with a private entrance and a screened porch. It features a king-size bed, private bath with shower and deep bath tub for soaking, and a kitchenette. An additional twin bed is available for a third guest. The Hale 'Elua unit is a ground-floor studio featuring a queen-size bed, private bath with shower, and a full-size kitchen. The sitting area has a queen-size futon. Each unit has TV and laundry facilities. Only minutes from the beach. No smoking. Two-night minimum. An additional $20 for extra guests. $70-75.

K16. Three rooms on the coconut coast of Kauai, just two blocks inland from the beach. Two rooms in the main house have private baths. A third room is separate from the main house. Enjoy breakfast with the hosts or selfcater. No smoking in rooms. $55.

K40. "On the Beach..." is set on the golden shores of Waipouli. As guests enter their rooms, they will step into a gentle blend of Hawaiian, Asian, and European artifacts

7 No smoking; 8 Children welcome; 9 Social drinking allowed; 10 Tennis nearby; 11 Swimming nearby; 12 Golf nearby; 13 Skiing nearby; 14 May be booked through a travel agent.

Bed and Breakfast Hawaii (continued)

and antiquities. The studio unit has a separate entrance, complete private bath, and a kitchenette with a full-sized refrigerator and small appliances. Enjoy the comfort of a queen-size bed, a ceiling fan, and cable TV with HBO and Showtime. Continental breakfast items will be supplied. Smoking allowed outside only. $70.

K78. This one-bedroom condo with ocean-view is not really a bed and breakfast, but breakfast can be arranged easily. Queen-size bed and private bath, plus the living room can sleep two more on the double Murphy bed. Full kitchen and private lanai with an oceanview, and the beach is only a few steps away. Pool, Jacuzzi. Restaurants and shops are within walking distance. Weekly rates available. Minimum stay is three nights. $85.

K82. A two-story house on a mountainview plateau property. One unit has a queen-size bed, private bath, living area with queen-size sofa bed, TV, wet bar, refrigerator, and microwave. Another larger unit includes a bedroom with a pair of twin beds, spacious living area with a queen-size sofa bed, large private bath, TV, wet bar, refrigerator, and microwave. Each area has its own lanai and entrance. Enjoy the gazebo with sauna and Jacuzzi. $75-105.

Bed and Breakfast Honolulu (Statewide)

3242 Kaohinani Drive, Honolulu, 96817
(808) 595-7533; (800) 288-4666
FAX (808) 595-2030

LOWYT. This private mountain bed and breakfast is behind Sleeping Giant Mountain on a lovely landscaped half-acre. The rooms have private baths with tubs and showers. Continental breakfast served. Well-lit off-street parking and five minutes to Wailua Bay. $55.

SMITR. Above Opaekaa Fall, this home is in the restored Wailua Homestead area and offers two guest rooms. One room has a king-size bed, and the other room has a queen-size and twin beds. Both have private baths. The mountain and valley views from the porch are breathtaking. Two one-bedroom condos on the beach also available. Enjoy the sounds of the Pacific from the lanais adjoining the condos and the bedrooms have queen-size beds. Smoking outside only. $60.

Go Native •• Hawaii

65 Halaulani Place, P.O.Box 11418, Hilo, 96721
(808) 935-4178; (800) 925-9065
FAX (808) 935-4178

Winters Guest House. This guest house sits behind the hosts' home with a view of Queen's Acres and Sleeping Giant. One bedroom has king-size or twin beds, an over-sized bath, queen-size Hide-a-bed in the great room, and a sleeping loft for two additional guests. Other amenities include a combination tub/shower, color TV with cable, and full kitchen help. Continental breakfast. $80.

Winters Mac Nut Farm and Inn. This two-bedroom accommodation is in a tranquil country setting with beautiful mountain views, including Mount Waialeale and Sleeping Giant. Beaches, golf, tennis, shopping, and dining are three miles away. Accommodations include king-size bed, queen-size bed, cable TV, refrigerator, and shared bath with ceramic tub and shower. Continental breakfast. Rooms are rented to single party of two couples or family. $50.

Kay Barker's Bed and Breakfast

P.O. Box 740, 96746
(808) 822-3073; (800) 835-2845

The home is in a lovely garden setting, in a quiet rural area, with pastoral and mountain views. There is a large living room, TV room, extensive library, and lanai for guests to enjoy. Brochures are available.

NOTES: Credit cards accepted: A MasterCard; B Visa; C American Express; D Discover; E Diners Club; F Other; 2 Personal checks accepted; 3 Lunch available; 4 Dinner available; 5 Open all year; 6 Pets welcome;

Host: Gordon Barker
Rooms: 5 (PB) $49.05-76.30
Continental Breakfast
Credit Cards: A, B, D
Notes: 2, 5, 8, 9, 10, 11, 12, 14

KAUAI—KILAUEA

Bed and Breakfast Hawaii

P.O. Box 449, Kapaa, 96746
(808) 822-7771; (800) 733-1632
FAX (808) 822-2723

K31. A private guest house is the perfect setting for getting away from it all. Accommodations include a light cooking area, full bath, queen-size bed, and a sitting area. Overlooking the beautiful Kilauea River and "Rainbow Valley," named for the brilliant rainbows that stretch from the lush recesses of the valley floor to the ocean. A private hiking trail leads to a secluded, semiprivate beach. The main house has a pool available to guests. $115.

KAUAI—KOLOA

Bed and Breakfast Hawaii

P.O. Box 449, Kapaa, 96746
(808) 822-7771; (800) 733-1632
FAX (808) 822-2723

K51-KOLOA. This private guest cottage is in the hills of Omao on the south shore just minutes away from sunny Poipu and some of the most magnificent beaches in the world. The secluded lanai enjoys views of the majestic mountains and ocean. The cottage offers a large bedroom with queen-size bed, private bath (shower only), sitting room that includes TV/VCR, and a full kitchen. Guests have a choice of breakfasts or no breakfast at a reduced rate. Smoking outside only. An additional $15 for extra guests. $75.

K61. On the sunny south shore this bed and breakfast offers a charming, self-contained guest house with a panoramic scene of coffee and sugarcane fields. The carpeted

unit has a private entrance and is furnished with a queen-size bed, private bath with shower, kitchenette, cable TV, and VCR. Breakfast is served on the covered lanai. Enjoy the outdoor spa in a garden setting. Laundry facilities also available. No smoking. Three-night minimum. $85.

K88. The sunny shore of Kauai is perfect for this host and hostess who operate a scuba and snorkel charter. A cozy studio with a private entrance and decorated with a Hawaiian flair is perfect for a couple or young family. King-size bed and a full-size Hide-a-bed. Private bathroom, dining area, living room with TV and telephone, and complete kitchenette. A large deck has mountain and distant ocean-views. Two-night minimum. Smoking outside only. $65.

Bed and Breakfast Honolulu (Statewide)

3242 Kaohinani Drive, Honolulu, 96817
(808) 595-7533; (800) 288-4666
FAX (808) 595-2030

BOULS. Only four miles from sunny Poipu, this 500-square-foot one-bedroom apartment has beamed ceilings and a deck with ocean and mountain views. The bedroom has a queen-size bed, and the living room has a queen-size Hide-a-Bed. Light cooking and a TV. $60.

NAKAS. This accommodation is between the two ends of the island for easy sightseeing. The host offers a guest room with twin beds, private bath, and entrance. Small refrigerator, TV, private patio in a tropical setting. Sandy beaches are an easy 15- to 20-minute walk. Two-night minimum. Cat that stays outside on premises. Continental breakfast. $50.

Island Home

1707 Kelaukia Street, 96756
(808) 742-2839; (800) 555-3881

7 No smoking; 8 Children welcome; 9 Social drinking allowed; 10 Tennis nearby; 11 Swimming nearby; 12 Golf nearby; 13 Skiing nearby; 14 May be booked through a travel agent.

Enjoy Kauai's sunny south shore at Island Home in Poipuu Kai Resort. Minutes from great snorkeling and swimming beaches, turtle watching, restaurants, and the beautiful Hyatt Regency. Tropical breakfasts are served. The units offer private entrances, lanai or deck, TVs, VCRs, compact refrigerators, microwaves, coffee pot, beach and picnic gear with laundry facilities available. Queen- or king-size beds. Three-night minimum.

Hosts: Michael and Gail Beeson
Rooms: 2 (PB) $65-75
Continental Breakfast
Credit Cards: None
Notes: 5, 7, 9, 10, 11, 12, 14

KAUAI—LAWAI

Bed and Breakfast Honolulu (Statewide)

3242 Kaohinani Drive, Honolulu, 96817
(808) 595-7533; (800) 288-4666
FAX (808) 595-2030

SEYME. Perched high in the hills of southern Kauai, this hillside inn is an oasis of pampered comfort and privacy. Three guest rooms and a studio apartment overlook a pool deck. Continental breakfast. Poipu beaches are only ten minutes away. Five minutes to golf course, boutiques, and restaurants. Rental cars, helicopter tours, and horseback riding nearby. One room is handicapped accessible. $65.

KAUAI—NORTH SHORE

A-1 Pacific-Hawaii Bed and Breakfast and Vacation Rental Reservation Agency

P.O. Box 1468, Kapaau, 96755-9998
(800) 999-6026; (800) 277-0509
FAX (808) 261-6573 or (808) 889-0500

Carl. A perfect honeymoon accommodation on a private residential estate. This 500-square-foot, one-bedroom guest house has a panoramic view of Tiver Valley rainbows and mountains. Lap pool right outside the door. Fully equipped kitchen, queen-size bed behind sliding glass shoji doors and a sitting area with a double fold-out couch. Decorated in tropical-style teak wood furnishings. Walk down a trail from this property to a beautiful secluded, crescent-shaped white-sand beach. $132.20.

Bed and Breakfast Hawaii

P.O. Box 449, Kapaa, 96746
(808) 822-7771; (800) 733-1632
FAX (808) 822-2723

K01. This suite is surrounded by what the hosts call "real Hawaii." The river that adjoins the property has been beautifully landscaped with its own waterfalls and is perfect for swimming. Two outdoor hot tubs, eight-person Jacuzzi, and massage are also available to guests. The accommodation is a private guest house with a loft bed, kitchen, and queen-size brass bed on the main level. Living area has a VCR and stereo CD-cassette player. Indoor and outdoor showers also available. $105-130.

K39A. On the north shore of Kauai in Kalahiwai, hosts offer a room with a private entrance and adjoining bath. This home adjoins a 600-acre guava orchard. The accommodations are elegant, large, soundproofed, and include a king-size bed, double-head tiled shower, TV, VCR, and a bay window that overlooks the grounds. No smoking. Minimum three-night stay. $90.

K45. This accommodation is perfect for guests who enjoy hiking, water sports, sightseeing, golf, sunbathing, or long walks in a quiet unpretentious Hawaiian-style town. The house is a stylish two-story home on grounds abundant with coconut, plumeria, and papaya trees, and the views from the deck and the lanai are breathtaking. The rooms feature queen-size beds and private baths. Continental breakfast. $65-85.

NOTES: Credit cards accepted: A MasterCard; B Visa; C American Express; D Discover; E Diners Club; F Other; 2 Personal checks accepted; 3 Lunch available; 4 Dinner available; 5 Open all year; 6 Pets welcome;

K56. This guest house is tucked away on the North Shore with a private studio that includes a living room, downstairs bedroom with a queen-size bed, an additional queen-size bed in the upstairs loft, kitchenette, and private bath with shower. A high-beamed ceiling with fans and wood floors offer the best of island-style living. Children over ten are welcome and laundry facilities are available. Outside smoking. Two-night minimum. Weekly rates available. $85.

K64. This private, handcrafted redwood cottage is carefully and comfortably equipped with a kitchenette, a private full bath, queen-size bed in the bedroom, and a living room with a large futon couch. French doors open to deck that offers distant mountain, ocean and sunset views. The surrounding area contains thoroughbred horse farms and organic fruit, flower, and vegetable farms. No smoking inside. Children welcome. $85.

K74. A slightly rustic accommodation on a working farm. The guest area includes a bedroom, efficiency kitchen, and private bath. Comfortable king-size bed and double sofa bed furnish the room. The grounds have a pineapple patch and orchid greenhouse. Children welcome. $80.

KAUAI—POIPU

Bed and Breakfast Hawaii

P.O. Box 449, Kapaa, 96746
(808) 822-7771; (800) 733-1632
FAX (808) 822-2723

K22. This plantation house offers two lovely rooms with private baths. Relax in the screened-in lanai or in the common living room. Continental breakfast . Two-night minimum stay is preferred. Smoking outside. $70-75.

K24. Poipu Plantation is not really a bed and breakfast accommodation because as many as 20 people can be accommodated in the small inn. Nine rooms feature a variety of bed sizes, face the garden or ocean, and have their own telephone lines. Two units are two-bedroom, two-bath suites. A barbecue, sunning area, and laundry facilities are available. $85-125.

K29. Brand-new one-bedroom apartment overlooking the shore of Kauai is just minutes from the beach and in O'mao. The apartment is upstairs through a private entrance and has a kitchen, telephone, cable TV, queen-size bed in the bedroom, private bath, and sofa bed in the living room. Guests can enjoy oceanview from their private deck. Smoking outside only. Minimum stay is three nights. $60.

K38. Each guest room in this house has been designed and decorated with comfort and beauty in mind. Just two blocks from the beaches and golf courses in Poipu, each room has a private entrance, TV, VCR, refrigerator, and microwave. One room has a king-size bed and private bath with stall shower, and the other has a queen-size bed, private bath with shower and tub, and a sitting room. Guests have swimming pool and tennis court privileges in Poipu Kai. Two-night minimum. No smoking. $65-75.

Go Native • • Hawaii

65 Halaulani Place, P.O.Box 11418, Hilo, 96721
(808) 935-4178; (800) 925-9065
FAX (808) 935-4178

This large home on Kaui offers two accommodations. One has a sitting room, bedroom with queen-size bed, and bath. The other has a bedroom with king-size bed, lanai, and bath. Both have private entrances, TVs, VCRs, microwaves, and compact refrigerators. Hosts provide beach mats, beach towels, and coolers. Laundry facilities are available.No smoking allowed in house. No children allowed. $65-75.

Gloria's Spouting Horn Bed and Breakfast

4464 Lawai Beach Road, 96756
(808) 742-6995

Oceanfront rooms are just steps away from the surf and a secluded beach. This beach house is nestled between the sea and acres of sugarcane. Walk to the Spouting Horn, the legendary blowhole a few steps away, or to Poipu Beach, where swimming and snorkeling are at their best year-round. Rooms feature Japanese-style deep soaking tubs, wet bars, and surfside lanais.

Hosts: Bob and Gloria Merkle
Rooms: 3 (PB) $125-150
Continental Breakfast
Credit Cards: A, B
Notes: 2, 5, 7, 9, 10, 11, 12, 14

KAUAI—PRINCEVILLE

Bed and Breakfast Hawaii

P.O. Box 449, Kapaa, 96746
(808) 822-7771; (800) 733-1632
FAX (808) 822-2723

K66. The Princeville area is known for its magnificent views, and this host home is on the famous golf course with distant ocean and mountain views all around. Just one mile from the Princeville Hotel, the host offers a studio on the ground floor of her two-story home. The bedroom has a king-size bed. Additional futons are available. Private bath with tub and shower and kitchenette for light cooking. Three French doors lead to the outside lanai area. Perfect for a honeymoon couple or a small family. Two-night minimum. No smoking. $80.

Go Native •• Hawaii

65 Halaulani Place, P.O.Box 11418, Hilo, 96721
(808) 935-4178; (800) 925-9065
FAX (808) 935-4178

Hale Ho'o Maha. This bed and breakfast's name means "House of Rest." It is on Kauai's famous North shore, it is a five-minute drive from Lauai's most beautiful beaches and rivers. Panoramic view of the Kalalau mountain range and ocean can be seen from every window of the house. Guest accommodations include the Pineapple Room, with private entrance and private bath and king-sized bed, and the Mango Room with a shared bath, cable TV, and double bed. $55-80.

Hale 'Aha—Bed and Breakfast in Paradise

Box 3370, 96722
(808) 826-6733; (800) 826-6733

Hale 'Aha opened in 1990 in peaceful Princeville Resort on 480 feet of PGA golf course, overlooking the ocean and majestic mountains of Kauai. Walk down the secret trails to secluded beaches, or drive to quaint Hanalei, where *South Pacific* was filmed. The famous Napoli Coast is known to hikers all over the world. Canoe rivers, helicopters, and boat trips. Snorkel, swim, or stroll miles of beautiful beaches. Three-night minimums. Continental plus breakfast.

Hosts: Herb and Ruth Bockelman
Rooms: 4 (PB) $85-210
Continental Breakfast
Credit Cards: A, B
Notes: 2, 5, 7, 9, 10, 11, 12, 14

KAUAI—WAILUA

Bed and Breakfast Hawaii

P.O. Box 449, Kapaa, 96746
(808) 822-7771; (800) 733-1632
FAX (808) 822-2723

K5B. Makana Inn offers two separate units. A one-bedroom guest cottage with private bath and light cooking facilities has a private lanai overlooking Mount Waialeale and green pastures. The apartment is downstairs in the main house and has a bedroom, sitting area, private bath, and kitchenette. Continental breakfast. Three miles from beach, golf, tennis, shopping, and dining. Two-night minimum stay. $95.

K8. This luxurious tropical garden home in Wailua on Kaumo'o Ridge overlooks the Wailua River Gorge. Three bed and breakfast rooms are offered, two with a queen-size bed and shared bath. Connecting doors can open up the rooms for couples traveling together. The third room is furnished with a king-size bamboo sleigh bed, dressing room, and private bath. A private apartment is also available with a queen-size bed and queen-size futon, kitchenette, dining area, full bath, and cable TV. Breakfast is not included in the apartment. Enjoy the lounge equipped with a large-screen stereo cable TV, CD collection, or share a special evening of entertainment in the state-of-the-art screening room. Relax in the garden hot tub. Outside smoking only. Two-night minimum in bed and breakfast room, three-night minimum in the apartment. $80-90.

K14. This accommodation, tucked in the mountains above the town of Kapaa, overlooks the Wailua River. Japanese-style home offers two bed and breakfast rooms. The garden view room offers a queen-size bed and large private bath. Glass doors lead to a multilevel deck with pool and hot tub. The master bedroom offers a queen-size bed and private full bath featuring dual showers. This room faces the deck and opens up to the pool. Futons may be provided for children ten years or older. Three-night minimum. No smoking. $70-85.

K30. The Fern Grotto Inn is on the only private property in the middle of the Wailua River State Park. Breakfast is served on elegant English china in the plantation dining room with its many windows providing a view of the Wailua River. Three bedrooms with queen-size beds and goose down pillows. Elegant adjoining private bath. $70-100.

K47. A spectacular view of the ocean, Sleeping Giant, and Mount Waialeale can be seen from this bilevel cottage that sleeps up to six people. The bedroom has a queen-size bed, and the living room has a queen-size sofa. A private bath, living room, large screened-in lanai, and loft complete the accommodations. Children welcome. Three-night minimum stay. $80.

K50. A contemporary tropical elegant residence in Wailua Hui Hoani, the most desirable and sacred area of ancient Kauai. The view of the Wailua River from cliffside is gorgeous and Mount Waialeale provides a mystical backdrop. Opaekaa Falls and the Sleeping Giant (Nonou Forest Reserve) are opposite. Two bright, comfortable rooms are available, both with ceiling fans, garden views, and spacious tiled baths. One room has a queen-size bed and the other twin beds. A kitchenette is downstairs. Three-night minimum. No smoking. $65-75.

K63. A private, cool, mountain bed and breakfast nestled behind Sleeping Giant Mountain. Enjoy the cozy and comfortable recreation room with a fully equipped kitchen plus a fireplace. Three bedrooms have private adjoining baths. Continental breakfast. Laundry service available. On Kauai with a scenic drive past Opaeka'a Falls and only five minutes from Wailua Bay. $50-55.

KAUAI—WAIMEA

Bed and Breakfast Hawaii

P.O. Box 449, Kapaa, 96746
(808) 822-7771; (800) 733-1632
FAX (808) 822-2723

K42. In the heart of old Waimea and within walking distance of the pier, restaurants, and shops, this home is perfect for those who want to hike the Waimea Canyon and explore Kokee State Park. There is a private entrance into the cozy bedroom, sitting area, and light cooking area. Private bath. Three-night minimum stay. $60.

7 No smoking; 8 Children welcome; 9 Social drinking allowed; 10 Tennis nearby; 11 Swimming nearby; 12 Golf nearby; 13 Skiing nearby; 14 May be booked through a travel agent.

LANAI—LANAI CITY

Bed and Breakfast Hawaii

P.O. Box 449, Kapaa, 96746
(808) 822-7771; (800) 733-1632
FAX (808) 822-2723

L1. Two of the bedrooms in this retired nurse's home are available for guests who are visiting the beautiful, small, and fairly remote island of Lanai. One of the guest rooms has a double and single bed, and the other guest room has a queen-size bed. Both hostess and guests share a full and a half-bath. $60-75.

Bed and Breakfast Honolulu (Statewide)

3242 Kaohinani Drive, Honolulu, 96817
(808) 595-7533; (800) 288-4666
FAX (808) 595-2030

GRAHLU. Two bedrooms are available for guests in this modest but very comfortable home. A full bath and a half-bath are shared. The hostess is a long-time resident of Lanai. $65.

KAUAI—LAWAI

Bed and Breakfast Honolulu (Statewide)

3242 Kaohinani Drive, Honolulu, 96817
(808) 595-7533; (800) 288-4666
FAX (808) 595-2030

SEYME. Perched high in the hills of southern Kauai, this hillside inn is an oasis of pampered comfort and privacy. Three guest rooms and a studio apartment overlook a pool deck. Continental breakfast served. Poipu beaches are only ten minutes away. Five minutes to golf course, boutiques, and restaurants. Rental cars, helicopter tours, and horseback riding are all available nearby. One guest room is handicapped accessible. $65.

MAUI—HANA

Hana Plantation Houses

P.O. Box 249, 96713
(808) 248-7049; (800) 228-HANA
FAX (808) 248-8240

Discover Hana, the other Maui, with waterfalls, secluded beaches, and hiking in bamboo jungles just steps from the tropical and beachfront cottages. Exotic black-sand beaches, and natural sparkling pools once known only to Hawaiian royalty. Many of the homes have spas, TVs, and kitchens. A cafe is in the botanical gardens.

Hosts: Blair Shurtleff and Tom Nunn
Rooms: 18 (PB) $60-185
Full and Continental Breakfasts
Credit Cards: A, B, C
Notes: 2, 3, 5, 7, 8, 9, 10, 11, 14

Kaia Ranch Bed and Breakfast

P.O. Box 404, 96713
(808) 248-7725

In a tropical, botanical 27-acre garden setting. Two studios with queen-size beds and kitchens. Quiet and relaxing atmosphere. There is also a chalet on the Big Island of Hawaii near Volcano National Park. Three rooms with queen-size and twin beds, and shared sitting room/kitchen. Two-night minimum stay. Host resides nearby. No alcohol.

Host: JoLoyce Kaia
Rooms: 5 (PB) $50-75
Continental Breakfast
Notes: 2, 5, 7, 11, 12, 14

MAUI—HAIKU

A-1 Pacific-Hawaii Bed and Breakfast and Vacation Rental Reservation Agency

P.O. Box 1468, Kapaau, 96755-9998
(800) 999-6026; (800) 277-0509
FAX (808) 261-6573 or (808) 889-0500

NOTES: Credit cards accepted: A MasterCard; B Visa; C American Express; D Discover; E Diners Club; F Other; 2 Personal checks accepted; 3 Lunch available; 4 Dinner available; 5 Open all year; 6 Pets welcome;

Sto. This "Look Out House" has a spacious first floor guest suite with two private entrances. King-size bed in the large bedroom with spectacular views. On one side the bedroom opens to a large covered deck, and on the other side there is a kitchenette which opens out through French doors to another private deck. $104.66.

Bed and Breakfast Hawaii

P.O. Box 449, Kapaa, 96746
(808) 822-7771; (800) 733-1632
FAX (808) 822-2723

M7. This two-bedroom studio is on a quiet, secluded two-acre horse ranch among tropical flower gardens and banana orchards where vistas of Mount Haleakala and the ocean await. One queen-size bed and one double bed, kitchen, dining, and living room. The living area has TV/VCR, and stereo. Guests have use of the washer-dryer. Three-night minimum. Children welcome. No smoking. $70-80.

M66. Two accommodations on Huelo Point in upcountry Maui.Spectacular views, privacy, and natural beauty. At the main house, a suite with a private entrance has a large bedroom with a queen-size bed. The bedroom and the kitchenette open onto a large covered deck. Private bath. Upstairs is a large bedroom and study area. Downstairs a full kitchen plus sitting room and solarium with a deck extending into the garden. Private bath. A pull-out sofa is downstairs for a second couple. Two-night minimum. Children in cottage only. No smoking. $95-125.

Bed and Breakfast Honolulu (Statewide)

3242 Kaohinani Drive, Honolulu, 96817
(808) 595-7533; (800) 288-4666
FAX (808) 595-2030

FOXF. In the quiet country hillside at the base of Mount Haleakala, this 100-year-old Hawaiian plantation house was recently renovated with antiques. Four guest rooms have private baths. Continental breakfast. The beach is two miles away, and the airport is 12 miles away. $80.

HOPKJ. Enjoy a panoramic view of Mount Haleakala and the ocean from two secluded acres. Two guest rooms with private entrance and bath: one with a king-size bed; one with twins. Eight minutes to windsurfing and beaches. $55.

Halfway to Hana House

P.O. Box 675, 96708
(808) 572-1176; FAX (808) 572-3609

A truly delightful bed and breakfast with exquisite ocean and mountain views, Halfway to Hana House is peaceful and quiet. The clean, airy studio has a separate entrance, spacious private bath, and covered patio. Its mini-kitchen has a microwave, hot plate, toaster oven, coffee maker, and refrigerator. The exotic tropical breakfast is served outdoors in a colorful, breezy setting of bamboo and palms overlooking the sea. Off the beaten path and on the way to Hana, in the proximity of freshwater pools and waterfalls, this is a memorable hideaway. Continental plus breakfast.

Host: Gail Pickholz
Room: 1 (PB) $60-85
Continental Breakfast
Credit Cards: None
Notes: 5, 7, 8, 9, 10, 11, 12, 14

MAUI—KIHEI

Affordable Accommodations Maui

2825 Kauhale Street, 96753
(808) 879-7865; (808) 874-0831 (phone and FAX)

Listing bed and breakfast accommodations throughout Maui and the outer islands. Some bed and breakfasts may include pools and/or

7 No smoking; 8 Children welcome; 9 Social drinking allowed; 10 Tennis nearby; 11 Swimming nearby; 12 Golf nearby; 13 Skiing nearby; 14 May be booked through a travel agent.

Jacuzzis. The available listings include guest rooms, studios, and cottages.

Accommodations: 50 plus
Rates: $50-150
Continental Breakfast
Credit Cards: None
Notes: 2, 5

Bed and Breakfast Hawaii

P.O. Box 449, Kapaa, 96746
(808) 822-7771; (800) 733-1632
FAX (808) 822-2723

M16. This large home on the edge of Ulapalakua Ranch is totally surrounded by decks. Breakfast is served on the upper deck, which provides a great place to whale-watch, and accommodations include two bedrooms decorated with Japanese antique furnishings. Both share a bath. A studio with a kitchenette, private entrance, and private bath and a cottage with one bedroom offer more room and privacy for families. $65-85.

M17. Tennis buffs could not ask for a better place to vacation than sunny Kihei, with courts available right outside their door. The accommodation is a full apartment with one bedroom, private bath, kitchenette, living/dining room, cable TV. The home has an oceanview and is a short drive to beaches, golf, and restaurants. Three-night minimum stay. $65-100.

M22. This hideaway sits at the top of a hill overlooking the beautiful south beaches of Maui. Two accommodations are available. The Pink Shell Room is spacious with a king-size bed and private bath across the hall. Air conditioned, ceiling fans, telephone, and TV. The Blue Ocean Room offers a private entrance, queen-size bed, private bath, private lanai, phone, TV, and ceiling fans. Continental breakfast is served on the lana. Guests are welcome to use the large Ohana room including kitchen area, dining, and living room. Two-night minimum. No smoking allowed. $55.

M24. In sunny Kihei on a half-acre in Maui Meadows, pick fruit from trees outside the door or swim in the black-bottom pool surrounded by tropical flowers. The accommodation is on the ground floor and has a private entrance and lanai area. The bedroom has a queen-size bed. An additional queen-size sofa bed is in the living room. A fully equipped kitchen, washer-dryer, TV, VCR, stereo, and hot tub make this a great vacation spot for short or long stays. Three-night minimum. Children over 12. Outside smoking only. $55-65.

M28. Luxuriate in the privacy of one of three guest rooms in this large home. One accommodation is a suite with two bedrooms, queen-size beds, minikitchen, and one and one-half baths. A third bedroom has a king-size bed that can convert to twins, a loft bed, private entrance, and private bath. Three-night minimum. $85-110.

M32. This beautiful home offers a bedroom with a private bath and private entrance. The room has a queen-size bed and TV. Another single bedroom is next door. The hostess loves to treat her guests to delicious breakfast treats. Three-night minimum stay. $55.

M32A. A large garden-level apartment with fully equipped kitchen and two bedrooms with one bath. Ideal for a small family. The hostess serves breakfast on the lanai upstairs. One-week minimum stay. $80.

M35. Two bed and breakfast rooms in a large plantation-style home and a private one-bedroom studio just two blocks from the beach. One bedroom is furnished with a queen-size bed and shares a bath with the host. Large decks offer mountain and ocean views. The studio is 500-square feet with a private yard and patio. The unit has a queen-size bed and well-equipped kitchen as well as a gas grill. Washer-dryer. Children are wel-

NOTES: Credit cards accepted: A MasterCard; B Visa; C American Express; D Discover; E Diners Club;
F Other; 2 Personal checks accepted; 3 Lunch available; 4 Dinner available; 5 Open all year; 6 Pets welcome;

come in the studio. No smoking. Three-night minimum. Host offers 10 percent off weekly stay. Additional $10 for third person. $60-90.

M38. This accommodation offers two bedrooms on the second level of an oceanfront home. Each bedroom has a private entrance, private bath, small refrigerator, TV, and a queen-size bed. Breakfast is served downstairs, and guest rooms share a covered deck that overlooks the ocean and islands of Kahoolawe and Molokini. Three-night minimum. No smoking. Children over 12. Resident dog. $70.

M75. This 350-square-foot studio is just one mile from the ocean and 12 miles from the airport. Oceanview, pool, hot tub, and kitchenette that includes a refrigerator and microwave. Private entrance, private bath with shower, and king-size bed. Three-night minimum. No smoking. $75.

M58. Just one block from the ocean in Kihei, the hosts offer two accommodations convenient to shopping, restaurants, and some of the best swimming beaches on Maui. The master suite has a queen-size bed, additional double sofa bed, private bath. Small refrigerator, TV. French doors lead onto a screened lanai where breakfast is served each morning. The studio offers a large comfortable room with a private entrance, queen-size bed, additional double sofa bed, private bath, kitchenette, and TV. No smoking. Two-night minimum. Additional $15 for third person. $60-65.

Bed and Breakfast Honolulu (Statewide)
3242 Kaohinani Drive, Honolulu, 96817
(808) 595-7533; (800) 288-4666
FAX (808) 595-2030

HURLD. Two offerings. The first is a guest room for two people with one queen and one twin bed, private entrance, and private bath. Breakfast is served to this unit. The other, the Ohana suite, is a self-contained unit with a queen-size bed in the bedroom and a queen-size sofa sleeper in the living room. Ideal for a small family. Private entrance and bath. Full kitchen. Breakfast is not served to the suite. Minutes drive to swimming beach. $60.

Go Native •• Hawaii
65 Halaulani Place, P.O.Box 11418, Hilo, 96721
(808) 935-4178; (800) 925-9065;
FAX (808) 935-4178

Whale Watch House. This Hawaiian pole house is on a hill at the edge of Ulapalakua Ranch. Five minutes from the beach and resort areas of Wailea and Kihei. Four units, including two guest rooms with private baths. Private garden-level "Ohana" studio has private entrance, queen-size beds, refrigerator, cable TV, access to a poolside deck, separate kitchen, living area, bath, king-size bed, and oceanviews. A thatched room cottage is an ideal honeymoon hideaway with private entrance, separate kitchen, living area, queen-size bed, Hide-a-Bed, bath, and poolside deck. Access to a natural swimming pool with waterfall. $65-85.

Jasmine House
883 Kupulau Drive, 96753
(808) 875-0400; (800) 604-4BED
FAX (808) 875-7324

In one of the finest residential areas, this bed and breakfast feels like a fine European inn. It is 800 feet above sea level and overlooks 2,000-square miles of the Pacific Ocean, ancient volcanic mountains, and other islands. Rooms range from tastefully decorated bed and bath to a lavish 700-square-foot suite.

Hosts: Art and Pat Pryor
Rooms: 6 (PB) $110-225
Continental Breakfast
Credit Cards: A, B, D
Notes: 2, 5, 9, 11, 12, 14

---

7 No smoking; 8 Children welcome; 9 Social drinking allowed; 10 Tennis nearby; 11 Swimming nearby; 12 Golf nearby; 13 Skiing nearby; 14 May be booked through a travel agent.

MAUI—KULA

Bed and Breakfast Hawaii

P.O. Box 449, Kapaa, 96746
(808) 822-7771; (800) 733-1632
FAX (808) 822-2723

M50. On Mount Haleakala at 3,000 feet this home offers two bed and breakfast rooms surrounded by ranchland with a sweeping view of the mountains, sea, and sunsets. Both accommodations offer private entrances. An upstairs studio has a queen-size bed, private bath, and an additional single bed for a third person. Breakfast fixings provided. The ground-floor apartment is adequate for a party of four with a queen-size bed plus additional Hide-a-Bed, private bath, and full kitchen. Laundry available for both units. No smoking, please. Additional $10 for extra guests. $95-105.

M52. A lovely home with two guest rooms in Kula. The master bedroom has a private bath. The second room shares the bath in the hall. Lovely landscaping and large decks with magnificent views. Breakfast is served in the dining area. $60.

M53. Enjoy an elegant and comfortable stay on the slopes of the dormant volcano, Haleakala. Two separate bedrooms with private baths and separate entrances. About 30 minutes by car to the beaches and 40 minutes to the airport, this is truly a quiet, relaxing place to enjoy Maui. Three-night minimum stay. $60-65.

Bed and Breakfast Honolulu (Statewide)

3242 Kaohinani Drive, Honolulu, 96817
(808) 595-7533; (800) 288-4666
FAX (808) 595-2030

GERRS. One of the top bed and breakfasts in the state, this host offers several accommodations in an inn-style. The plantation home has six bedrooms with private baths.

The Bunkhouse is a U-shaped building with five small apartments, all of which have kitchens and one has a fireplace. The Lahaina cottage is a honeymoon suite. It has an old wood-burning stove, complete kitchen, king-size bed, a lanai running along three sides, and a large red bathtub with oceanviews. $75.

KAUAS. This host offers a large, beautiful suite on an upper floor with a private deck and private bath (full shower, no tub). Continental breakfast. Great oceanviews and views of West Maui Mountains from all windows of room including view of Haleakala. $75.

Kula View Bed and Breakfast

140 Holopuni Road, P.O. Box 322, 96790
(808) 878-6736

Glorious sunrise and sunsets, sweeping ocean, mountain and garden views from every guest rooms. Raised 2,000 feet above sea level on the slopes of the dormant volcano, Haleakala. Kula View is surrounded by two acres of lush greenery, fruits, flowers, banana and coffee trees, and yet is close to the Kahului airport, shopping centers, hiking parks, and beaches. The upper-level suite has a private entrance, deck, and private bath luxuriously appointed with a queen-size bed, reading area, wicker breakfast nook, and minirefrigerator. Kula View offers personal old-fashioned Maui up-country-style hospitality. Two-night minimum stay.

Host: Susan Kauai
Room: 1 (PB) $85
Continental Breakfast
Credit Cards: None
Notes: 2, 5, 9, 11, 12, 14

MAUI—LAHAINA

Bed and Breakfast Hawaii

P.O. Box 449, Kapaa, 96746
(808) 822-7771; (800) 733-1632
FAX (808) 822-2723

NOTES: Credit cards accepted: A MasterCard; B Visa; C American Express; D Discover; E Diners Club;
F Other; 2 Personal checks accepted; 3 Lunch available; 4 Dinner available; 5 Open all year; 6 Pets welcome;

M2. A new ocean-front room has a private entrance and features a queen-size bed, private bath, TV, private lanai, and small refrigerator. Great snorkeling and beautiful swimming beaches are just minutes away. Shopping and dining are minutes away in Lahaina and Kaanapali. Two-night minimum. No smoking. $70.

M2A. An attached cottage, Ohana House, is just 50 feet from the ocean. The cottage has a kitchenette and private bath and entrance. The refrigerator is stocked with fresh fruit and juice. Two-night minimum. $90.

M5. This guest house is a private home where every guest room offers optimum privacy with TV, refrigerator, ceiling fan, and air conditioning. All rooms have private baths, and one includes a Jacuzzi tub. The shared family room has a VCR, and the living room has a 350-gallon marine aquarium. A short walk to shops and restaurants as well as the beach, or relax beside the pool. $75-95.

M15. Just minutes from Lahaina, Kaanapali, and Kapalua, this two-story home offers three private rooms and baths plus full use of the main living areas, screened lanais, and gourmet kitchen. Enjoy the outstanding views of the ocean and islands of Lanai and Molokai, or take a short stroll to a nice sandy beach. Bedrooms are air-conditioned and have TV. Guests also have use of a lap pool. No smoking. $75-95.

M44. An exclusive hideaway for the discerning visitor in Lahaina, the gem of the West Side of Maui, with a large selection of shops, restaurants, and a mecca of art galleries. An elegant private home furnished in exquisite taste with artistic appointed details. Light and airy one-bedroom apartment offers spacious living-dining room, queen-size bed plus queen-size Hide-a-Bed, TV, VCR, fully equipped kitchen, and sliding glass door leading to pool and garden. A

studio offers a queen-size bed, TV/VCR, fully equipped kitchenette, private entrance and bath, and a private landscaped courtyard. Two-night minimum. Children 12 and over. Outside smoking only. $95-125.

M78. Just two blocks from the beach in Lahaina, two accommodations are available to visitors to the Valley Isle. A garden studio sits on a quarter-acre lot with a private deck and oceanview. The bedroom has a queen-size bed. An additional queen-size sofa sleeper is in the sitting area with TV. A private bath and kitchenette are also available. Perfect for a small family or three traveling together. The studio is air-conditioned and hosts offer laundry facilities. Hosts also offer a bed and breakfast room. The bedroom has a queen-size bed and private bath and guests are treated to a Continental breakfast in the morning. Two-night minimum for bed and breakfast room. Three-night minimum for studio. No smoking. $50-95.

Bed and Breakfast Honolulu (Statewide)

3242 Kaohinani Drive, Honolulu, 96817
(808) 595-7533; (800) 288-4666
FAX (808) 595-2030

SWANT. A cottage, three guest rooms, and a family suite. Most offer private entrance, bath, TV, refrigerator, air conditioning, and lanai. One has a Jacuzzi. Decked pool. Beach park is two blocks away. Continental breakfast. $90.

Go Native •• Hawaii

65 Halaulani Place, P.O.Box 11418, Hilo, 96721
(808) 935-4178; (800) 925-9065;
FAX (808) 935-4178

Blue Horizons. A new inn, one block from the ocean between Kaanapali and Kapalua. Accommodations include three suites with living rooms, private kitchens, and baths. Two guest rooms are also available. TV and air conditioning are included. A common

7 No smoking; 8 Children welcome; 9 Social drinking allowed; 10 Tennis nearby; 11 Swimming nearby; 12 Golf nearby; 13 Skiing nearby; 14 May be booked through a travel agent.

living room and gourmet guest kitchen serve all guests. Pool, barbecue, and washer-dryer. $75-95.

Lahaina Guest House. In the heart of Lahaina, one block from the beach, an elegant tropical-style home with delightful, easy-living appointments. Offers four personalized guest rooms, all with private baths and Jacuzzis, a spacious family room, and a relaxing living room. Full use of kitchenette. Continental breakfast. $95.

Laha 'Ole. A wonderful oceanfront home in Lahaina at the water's edge. One bedroom delightfully appointed with a queen-size day bed, TV, private bath, and oceanview. Accommodates two. Within walking distance of shops, restaurants, and entertainment. Continental breakfast. $65.

Lahaina Inn

127 Lahajnaluna Road, 96761-1502
(800) 669-3444; FAX (808) 667-9480

Twelve intimate, individually decorated, antique-filled rooms in the heart of Old Lahaina. "One of the best country inns"— *Glamour.* "One of the ten most romantic country inns"—*American Historic Inns.* Home of David Paul's Lahaina Grill, which has been rated "Best Maui Restaurant" in 1994 and 1995. Call for a free brochure.

Host: Ken Eisley
Rooms: 12 (PB) $89-129
Continental Breakfast
Credit Cards: A, B, C, D
Notes: 2, 4, 5, 9, 10, 11, 12, 14

Old Lahaina House

P.O. Box 10355, 96761
(808) 667-4663; (800) 847-0761
FAX (808) 667-5615

This convenient, relaxing place from which to visit Maui allows guests to enjoy the romantic, secluded ambience of a private pool in a tropical courtyard. Only steps from a serene beach and convenient walking distance to dining and shopping in historic Lahaina Town, a culturally rich and diverse old whaling town. Old Lahaina House is a home away from home, a special retreat, an intimate piece of paradise! No smoking in rooms.

Hosts: John and Sherry Barbier
Rooms: 4 (2 PB; 2 SB) $60-95
Continental Breakfast
Credit Cards: A, B, C
Notes: 5, , 8, 9, 10, 11, 12, 14

MAUI—MAUI MEADOWS

Bed and Breakfast Honolulu (Statewide)

3242 Kaohinani Drive, Honolulu, 96817
(808) 595-7533; (800) 288-4666
FAX (808) 595-2030

FEKEJ. This large studio with private entrance and bath has light cooking facilities. Just six blocks to the beach. Full breakfast served. Ocean view and wheelchair accessible. $65.

LOWRP. This hostess offers a studio with a queen-size bed, a cottage with a queen-size bed in the loft, and a Hide-a-Bed in the living room. Two rooms in the home share a bath. A five-minute drive to the beach and a pool on site. Breakfast is provided in the bed and breakfast room, and studio and cottage have light cooking facilities. $65.

SVENK. Above Wailea, this home offers three private rooms, each with TV, private entrance, and private bath. One mile from the beach, but with ocean and mountain views. Breakfast is served on the large lanai overlooking the ocean. The host also has a two-bedroom separate cottage. Each room has two twins to make into a king. The living room has a queen-size pull-out sofa. The cottage has a view from each room and a full kitchen. Children welcome. The host has cats and a dog. $55.

MAUI—PAIA

Bed and Breakfast Hawaii

P.O. Box 449, Kapaa, 96746
(808) 822-7771; (800) 733-1632
FAX (808) 822-2723

M1. Million-dollar views of west Maui, the ocean, and two islands surround this house perched on top of a dormant volcano. The large studio has its own entrance, queen-size bed, wicker furniture, private bath, and minikitchen. No smoking. Minimum two-night stay. $75.

M4A. This charming inn was built in 1850 for Maui's first doctor. Newly refurbished, it sits among pineapple fields and pine trees. Just 700 feet above sea level and down the road from Hookipa Beach, this bed and breakfast includes full breakfast, twin or queen-size beds, and private baths in all rooms. $85.

M12. Right on the beach and convenient for sightseeing, this large plantation-style home is in an exclusive neighborhood adjacent to the Maui Country Club. It offers a large guest room with a private bath. A short walk leads to a stretch of white, sandy beach. No smoking inside. $70.

Go Native •• Hawaii

65 Halaulani Place, P.O.Box 11418, Hilo, 96721
(808) 935-4178; (800) 925-9065;
FAX (808) 935-4178

Huelo Point Flower Farm. A two-acre stunning oceanfront estate set high on the edge of a cliff overlooking Waipio Bay on Maui's rugged north shore. Only 30 minutes from Kahului, this breathtaking site offers a marvelous gazebo, queen-size futon, wicker furnishings, TV, small refrigerator, hot plate, and many other amenities. The cliffside views from the outside hot tub are unforgettable. $95.

MAUI—UPCOUNTRY

A-1 Pacific-Hawaii Bed and Breakfast and Vacation Rental Reservation Agency

P.O. Box 1468, Kapaau, 96755-9998
(800) 999-6026; (800) 277-0509
FAX (808) 261-6573 or (808) 889-0500

Rob. Several plantation-style one-bedroom cottages on a seven-acre private estate with an unobstructed oceanview. Advance reservations are necessary. All units have a full kitchen, living room, king-size beds, TV, VCR, and telephone. Special atmosphere and privacy for a honeymoon visit to Maui. $88.14.

Bed and Breakfast Hawaii

P.O. Box 449, Kapaa, 96746
(808) 822-7771; (800) 733-1632
FAX (808) 822-2723

M9. A delightful bed and breakfast with an oceanview setting, this studio is in a quiet, private setting. The accommodation offers a separate entrance and is furnished with rattan furniture, a double bed, private bath, ceramic tile floors, and a minikitchen with a microwave, toaster, coffee maker, and refrigerator. $70.

M15. For the free-spirited, this glass gazebo is perched on the cliff overlooking Waipio Bay on Huelo Point. Fully carpeted with a futon on the floor; nicely appointed with a stereo, small refrigerator, and coffee maker. The half-bath is hidden behind all-glass sliding doors. The hot/cold shower is outside in the newly landscaped gardens, and the large cement patio includes a hot tub shared with the hosts who live in the main house. Hosts rent the entire home when they are away. Three-night minimum stay. $95.

M26. Named Halemanu, which is Hawaiian for birdhouse, this home is perched 3,500 feet above the town of Kula and provides an awesome view of the island of Maui. The home is new and has lots of windows and decks. The guest room has its own private deck, private full bath, and queen-size bed. Breakfast is served on the deck or in the dining area. $75.

M55. Real island-style living can be enjoyed while staying here, just five minutes from Hookipa, the windsurfing beach of Maui. Overlooking pineapple fields, this studio has a separate entrance and sun deck with tropical flowers and fruit trees. The artwork was done by a famous Maui artist. Three-night minimum stay. $65.

MAUI—WAILUKU

Bed and Breakfast Hawaii

P.O. Box 449, Kapaa, 96746
(808) 822-7771; (800) 733-1632
FAX (808) 822-2723

M14. This comfortable home is only a few minutes from the Kahului airport. Two bedrooms, each with private entrance and shared bath. Outdoor patio is shared and includes a pool. No children. No smoking. Two-night minimum stay. $60.

M41. A modern-style home close to the ocean and airport. The main-floor bedroom has a separate deck with oceanviews and Haleakala. King-size bed and private spa, bath, and shower. Continental breakfast. Close to golf course, and tee times are available with a two-day notice. Two-night minimum. $45-55.

MOLOKAI—KAMALO

Bed and Breakfast Honolulu (Statewide)

3242 Kaohinani Drive, Honolulu, 96817
(808) 595-7533; (800) 288-4666
FAX (808) 595-2030

FOSTG. A lovely five-acre lime orchard and tropical garden plantation offers two guest rooms in the main home. The smaller guest room has two twin waterbeds and shares a bath with the larger guest room, which has two twin beds and a microwave oven, refrigerator, coffee maker, and sitting room. Two cats and three dogs live on the property—not in guests' quarters. One-nighters are welcome. A private studio cottage with twin beds is also available for guests. $55-75.

MOLOKAI—KAUNAKAKAI

Bed and Breakfast Hawaii

P.O. Box 449, Kapaa, 96746
(808) 822-7771; (800) 733-1632
FAX (808) 822-2723

MO2. Across the road from Father Damien's historic St. Joseph Church stands Kamalo Plantation, a five-acre tropical garden and lime orchard at the foot of Mount Kamakou. Ancient stone ruins beside the plantation offer a unique sense of peace and tranquility. Stay at the country cottage with a fully equipped kitchen or in the main house with two rooms and a shared bath. Three-night minimum stay required. No smoking allowed. $65-75.

Go Native • • Hawaii

65 Halaulani Place, P.O.Box 11418, Hilo, 96721
(808) 935-4178; (800) 925-9065;
FAX (808) 935-4178

Kamalo Plantation. A quaint, cozy cottage with accommodations on the grounds of the main house. Only ten miles east of Kaunakakai and across from the Father Damien Church. Lovely setting with mountains in the background and a cascading waterfall. Features studio accommodations with cooking facilities, twin beds, bath, and self-catered Continental breakfast. Two adults maximum. A three-night minimum stay is required. $70.

NOTES: Credit cards accepted: A MasterCard; B Visa; C American Express; D Discover; E Diners Club; F Other; 2 Personal checks accepted; 3 Lunch available; 4 Dinner available; 5 Open all year; 6 Pets welcome;

OAHU—AIEA

A-1 Pacific-Hawaii Bed and Breakfast and Vacation Rental Reservation Agency

P.O. Box 1468, 96755-9998
(800) 999-6026; (800) 277-0509
FAX (808) 261-6573 or (808) 889-0500

The island of Hawaii known as the "Big Island," is one of the most unique ecosystems in the world. This reservation service has about 100 listings of accommodations, cottages, or homes in all areas of this beautiful island. From $65 to $125 for bed and breakfast accommodations or cottages or up to $450 per day for an entire home. Contact: Doris Epp-Reichert.

Pearl Harbor View/ Pacific—Hawaii B&B

99-442 Kekoa Place, 96701
(808) 486-8838; (808) 487-1228
(808) 486-3187; (800) 999-6026
FAX (808) 261-6573 or (808) 487-1228

Home away from home. Convenient location. Complete two-bedroom upstairs apartment with kitchen and living room. View of Pearl Harbor and a yard full of orchids and tropical flower and fruit trees. Beautifully furnished with Oriental antiques. King-size and single beds. Cable TV, phone, and more. Best value for the money. Five-day minimum. Also a reservation service for more than 400 bed and breakfasts across the islands of Hawaii. Monthly rates available.

Host: Doris Epp-Reichert
Suite: 1 (PB) $65
No breakfast
Credit Cards: A, B
Notes: 2, 5, 6, 7, 8, 9, 11, 12, 14

OAHU—HAWAII KAI

Bed and Breakfast Hawaii

P.O. Box 449, Kapaa, 96746
(808) 822-7771; (800) 733-1632
FAX (808) 822-2723

O19. The hosts, mother and daughter, are from England and combine Old World charm with New World Aloha to make sure their guests have a good time. In this home there is a spacious, airy bedroom with private bath, TV, and sliding door leading to the swimming pool.No smoking. Two-night minimum stay. $60.

Bed and Breakfast Honolulu (Statewide)

3242 Kaohinani Drive, Honolulu, 96817
(808) 595-7533; (800) 288-4666
FAX (808) 595-2030

ABEB. The hosts have two guest rooms, one with private bath, TV, and refrigerator. The other has a TV and shared bath. A Continental breakfast is served. Seven-minute drive to swimming beaches and Hanauma Bay. Enjoy the pool or shop in the on-premises gallery of items collected from around the world. No smoking. Adults only. Two-night minimum stay. $60.

CRIPJ. Sitting high on Mariner's Ridge, this host has two units in her large home for travelers. Enjoy the two lanais for an ocean-view breakfast. One room has a twin bed and the other has a queen-size bed. A loft with a twin and double bed is used in conjunction with one of the rooms for overflow—ideal for families. Shared bath. Enjoy TV in the game room. Smoking only on the lanai. Children welcome. The host has two dogs and a cat mostly outside. English and French spoken. $55.

OAHU—HONOLULU

Bed and Breakfast Hawaii

P.O. Box 449, Kapaa, 96746
(808) 822-7771; (800) 733-1632
FAX (808) 822-2723

O22. Outstanding views characterize this home on the edge of the beach and near local tourist attractions. Two upstairs suites with private baths and lanai. The Mauka Suite has an antique bed and a view of Diamond Head. The Makai Suite has two double beds and a view of the garden. $75-100.

O53. Built on a hillside about one-fifth of a mile from the University of Hawaii at Manoa, this home has two comfortable rooms for guests. Sit on the large deck and enjoy the city's skyline and the ocean below. One room has a queen-size bed and a private bath with a shower. The other room has extra-long twin beds, a private half-bath, and a shared shower. Smoking allowed outside only. Children over ten years old are welcome. Minimum three-night stay. $55-65.

Bed and Breakfast Honolulu (Statewide)

3242 Kaohinani Drive, Honolulu, 96817
(808) 595-7533; (800) 288-4666
FAX (808) 595-2030

NEESB. This home is only about two miles from Pearl Harbor and the *U.S.S. Arizona* Memorial. Two rooms are available for guests. Kitchen privileges, laundry facilities, and TV. Children and smokers are accepted. $45.

The Manoa Valley Inn

2001 Vancouver Drive, 96822
(808) 947-6019; (800) 535-0085

An intimate country inn in lush Manoa Valley two miles from Waikiki Beach. Furnished in antiques, each room is decorated to enhance its charm and personality. Continental breakfast buffet; fruits and cheese served evenings on the shady veranda. Call for rates.

Host: Lisa Hookano-Holly
Rooms: 8 (SB)
Continental Breakfast
Credit Cards: A, B, C, D, E
Notes: 2, 5, 9, 10, 11, 12, 14

OAHU—KAAAWA

Bed and Breakfast Honolulu (Statewide)

3242 Kaohinani Drive, Honolulu, 96817
(808) 595-7533; (800) 288-4666
FAX (808) 595-2030

PARRB. This oceanfront home offers two bedrooms with queen and twin beds, two bathrooms, and a queen-size sofa sleeper. Fully equipped kitchen, cable TV, telephone, and washer-dryer are some of the amenities. Towels and linen provided. Good restaurants and shopping within short driving distance. Three-night minimum stay. Security deposit required. $110.

FRASJ. In a rural area on the north shore and windward Oahu, two units nestled against the Ko'olau Mountains are a three-minute walk to the beach, shopping, or post office. Private baths, full cooking facilities, and ocean views. Host stocks the kitchen for a plentiful breakfast. The upstairs unit has a private deck and an oceanview. $75.

OAHU—KAILUA

A-1 Pacific-Hawaii Bed and Breakfast and Vacation Rental Reservation Agency

P.O. Box 1468, 96755-9998
(800) 999-6026; (800) 277-0509
FAX (808) 261-6573 or (808) 889-0500

Shan. One short block to beautiful white-sand beach of Kailua. New and tastefully decorated guest unit built above the garage of the family residence. Open beam ceilings, air-conditioned with living room, bedroom, and kitchenette. King-size bed and queen-size sofa bed. Toaster oven, refrigerator, hot plate, and electric skillet. TV and telephone. Two lanais. Perfect and convenient for a small family. Children additional $10 each. $99.15.

NOTES: Credit cards accepted: A MasterCard; B Visa; C American Express; D Discover; E Diners Club;
F Other; 2 Personal checks accepted; 3 Lunch available; 4 Dinner available; 5 Open all year; 6 Pets welcome;

Kny. In beautiful Kailua, 100 yards from gorgeous Kailua Beach, a four-mile stretch of white sand and ideal swimming, wind surfing, and boogie boarding beach. Just 20 minutes from Honolulu and Waikiki. Residential community offers good restaurants, shopping, and theaters. Two guest units in this freestanding guest home. The upper bedroom features beautiful koa wood cabinets, a U-shaped bar, and marble bathroom. Very large lanai to enjoy the ocean breeze just 100 feet away. Queen-size bed and sonfle bed. Full kitchen. Open, airy floor plan. Very romantic. First-floor unit is a one-room studio with private entrance and bath. $93.64-165.26.

All Islands Bed and Breakfast

823 Kainui Drive, 96734-2025
(808) 263-2342; (800) 542-0344
FAX (808) 263-0308

Experience the real Hawaii! More than 500 private accommodations on all Hawaiian islands. Rooms in private homes $55-65 average. Studios in private homes $65-75. Ohana cottages $75-85. Excellent rental car and inter-island air rates. Free brochure.

Rooms: 1,000 (900 PB; 100 SB) $45-260
Continental Breakfast
Cards: A, B, C
Notes: 2, 5, 7, 8, 9, 10, 11, 12, 14

Bed and Breakfast Hawaii

P.O. Box 449, Kapaa, 96746
(808) 822-7771; (800) 733-1632
FAX (808) 822-2723

O8A. Within walking distance of Kailua Beach on the canal, this studio apartment is perfect for longer stays. The bedroom area has a queen-size bed. A kitchenette allows light cooking. The bathroom has a two-person Jacuzzi. Pool. Five-night minimum stay. Special weekly rates. $65.

O12. Lounge by the pool and enjoy a leisurely breakfast or sit in the hot tub after a day of sightseeing. One mile from Kailua Beach, this home offers two rooms with a shared bath. One room has a double bed, and the other has a twin bed. One-night stays have an extra $5 surcharge. $55.

O16. A gracious home on a private access road one-half block from a safe swimming beach. Two large bedrooms with adjoining bath. Ideal for couples traveling together. Two covered lanais surrounded by tropical foliage. A separate refrigerator for guests. Shopping center and restaurants within walking distance. Adults only. $65.

O25. Ka Hale La'i means "House of Peacefulness" in Hawaiian and this delightful home is just that. Two rooms, each with a queen-size bed, private bath, and air conditioning. The main bedroom has sliding glass doors opening onto a covered lanai area by the pool, cable TV, and a bathroom with a sunken shower. The second bedroom is only used when two couples are traveling together. Two miles from Kailua Beach, a very pretty, safe beach for swimming and a popular spot for windsurfing. Snorkel to Flat Island to turtle watch. Golf courses are close by. A very loving golden Labrador retriever lives here. No smoking. Adults only. Two-night minimum. $65-120.

O31. An elegant oceanfront home with a large pool and Jacuzzi. The home is spacious and has comfortable areas for relaxing after a day of sightseeing. Bedrooms have private bath and private entrance from the pool-courtyard area. Continental breakfast is served. $120.

O42. A block away from Kailua Beach, two newly remodeled bedrooms available with private baths, TV, microwave, and refrigerator, plus use of the pool. Three-night minimum stay. $55-65.

O57. Within walking distance from Kailua Beach, this two-bedroom apartment on the

7 No smoking; 8 Children welcome; 9 Social drinking allowed; 10 Tennis nearby; 11 Swimming nearby; 12 Golf nearby; 13 Skiing nearby; 14 May be booked through a travel agent.

ground level of a two-story home has two bedrooms, a private bath, and complete kitchenette. Living room has TV, rattan furniture, and sliding glass doors to the patio and fenced yard. Perfect for a family of four. Smoking outside. $75; $100 for four.

O63. This complete studio cottage is separate from the main house and one block from Kailua Beach. It is well kept and nicely furnished with tropical rattan. The cottage sits on the edge of the pool near an attractive gazebo. Queen-size bed, full bath, TV, table and chairs, light cooking area, and telephone. Smokers accepted. No children. Minimum three-night stay. $70.

Bed and Breakfast Honolulu (Statewide)

3242 Kaohinani Drive, Honolulu, 96817
(808) 595-7533; (800) 288-4666
FAX (808) 595-2030

ISAAC. Two hundred yards from the ocean, this accommodation has two bedrooms. One room has a pair of twin beds that can be made into a king, and the other room has a king-size bed. Both rooms have private entrances, private bath, microwave, coffee maker, and small refrigerator. Use the pool. Breakfast is provided for the first three days of stay. No children under 16. $55.

NOELW. Two studio units on the lake. The larger unit has a king-size bed, TV, telephone, full bath with tub-shower, private entrance, lanai, light cooking, air conditioning, and Continental breakfast. The other unit has a queen-size bed, TV, telephone, private entrance, access to lanai, light cooking, and garden view. $50.

PRICS. Beautiful windward home; casual host. Two rooms with queen-size beds, TV, and refrigerator. For larger parties a small twin room can be used. Guest rooms share a

bath. Walk to the beach (five minutes). Swim in the pool. Enjoy the serenity of the view. Stroll to the boat dock on the quiet canal running just beyond the landscaped lawn. Continental breakfast served. Children over nine and swimmers are welcome. Resident cats. $55.

WOODL. This single-family home has two guest rooms. Bed and breakfast guests share a bath. Limited kitchen and refrigerator privileges. Continental breakfast. Car not essential—bus is close by. $45.

Go Native •• Hawaii

65 Halaulani Place, P.O.Box 11418, Hilo, 96721
(808) 935-4178; (800) 925-9065;
FAX (808) 935-4178

Kailua Bed and Breakfast. This accommodation is a garden level, two-bedroom facility four blocks from Kailua Beach. Complete kitchen, outside lanai with grill, TV, telephone, and washer-dryer. A queen-size bed, twin beds, and one bath are available. Continental breakfast supplies are provided. Additional charge for extra person(s). No smoking. $75-100.

Papaya Paradise

395 Auwinala Road, 96734
(808) 261-0316

Private, quiet, tropical, and near all attractions. Enjoy the pool. Relax in the Jacuzzi. Stroll Kailua Beach. Savor breakfast on the lanai surrounded by Hawaiian plants, trees, and flowers with Mount Olomana in the background. Rooms with private bath, private entry, refrigerator, air conditioning, and TV. Tennis, golf, and all kinds of water sports nearby. Just 20 miles from Waikiki and the Honolulu airport. Minimum three-night stay.

Hosts: Bob and Jeanette Martz
Rooms: 2 (PB) $65-75
Continental Breakfast
Credit Cards: None
Notes: 2, 5, 8, 9, 10, 11, 12

OAHU—KANEOHE

Bed and Breakfast Hawaii

P.O. Box 449, Kapaa, 96746
(808) 822-7771; (800) 733-1632
FAX (808) 822-2723

O56. A luxuriously furnished private home with beautiful views of Kanehoe Bay from the living room, dining room, and pool area. Two bedrooms, each with a private bath. One room has twin beds with a bath across the hall, and the other room has a double bed and has an adjoining bath. Tea is served in the late afternoon. $55-60.

O64. The home stands at the end of a private road and near the ocean with two guest rooms with a casual atmosphere. These accommodations have private baths and separate entrances. The larger suite has a bedroom with king-size bed and an additional sitting room with sofa, dinette, TV, and light kitchen. The other room offers a queen-size bed and a small refrigerator. Outside smoking. Three-night minimum. Additional $25 for each additional guest. $60-65.

Bed and Breakfast Honolulu (Statewide)

3242 Kaohinani Drive, Honolulu, 96817
(808) 595-7533; (800) 288-4666
FAX (808) 595-2030

MUNRD. This bed and breakfast overlooks Kanehoe Bay and the historic Heeia fish pond on windward Oahu. Continental breakfast served. One room has a double bed, and the other room has a pair of twins. Both have private baths. $60.

PICOD. Two guest rooms. The king room has a private bath, private entrance, adjacent sitting room with futon sofa, and small dinette with microwave oven, coffee maker, refrigerator, and TV. The queen room has a private bath, private entrance, and small dinette with coffee maker, toaster oven, and refrigerator. Close to the village shopping center, supermarket, cinema, and restaurants. Two miles to one of the loveliest beaches on the island. Fifteen miles from the airport. $55.

RAYB. Beautiful, quiet Japanese-Hawaiian home with pool. Two guest rooms with king-size beds and private garden baths with dressing rooms. Refrigerator by the pool cabana. Two miles to beach, shopping, and cafes. Adults only. Smoking outside. Cheese and wine served poolside 5-6 P.M. Resident cats. $65.

Go Native • • Hawaii

65 Halaulani Place, P.O.Box 11418, Hilo, 96721
(808) 935-4178; (800) 925-9065;
FAX (808) 935-4178

Windward. A spacious and delightful tropical home with Continental ambience. In the bedroom community of Kaneohe, it offers two guest bedrooms with private baths. Beautifully furnished with antiques. Pool. The library overlooks Kaneohe Bay and ancient Heeia fish pond. Continental breakfast and afternoon tea are served. $55-60.

OAHU—LANIKA

Bed and Breakfast Hawaii

P.O. Box 449, Kapaa, 96746
(808) 822-7771; (800) 733-1632
FAX (808) 822-2723

O35. Lanikai Beach is one of the most photographed beaches in Hawaii. Not only is the view magnificent, this beach is great for swimming. Two rooms 20 feet from the ocean. One bedroom offers a queen-size bed with private bath and the other a smaller room with a double bed and shared bath. Guests may use the kitchen for light food preparation and a refrigerator is available. Three-night minimum. No smoking. $60-75.

7 No smoking; 8 Children welcome; 9 Social drinking allowed; 10 Tennis nearby; 11 Swimming nearby; 12 Golf nearby; 13 Skiing nearby; 14 May be booked through a travel agent.

OAHU—MANOA

Bed and Breakfast Honolulu (Statewide)

3242 Kaohinani Drive, Honolulu, 96817
(808) 595-7533; (800) 288-4666
FAX (808) 595-2030

CADEM. Host offers master bedroom with private bath, queen bed, and TV. Beautiful view of Diamond Head from the sun deck. Second room has twin beds and a half-bath with shared shower. Continental breakfast. Resident cat. No smoking. Children welcome. $65.

OAHU—PEARL CITY

Bed and Breakfast Hawaii

P.O. Box 449, Kapaa, 96746
(808) 822-7771; (800) 733-1632
FAX (808) 822-2723

O1A. Eight miles from Honolulu International Airport, this home is near the Pearl City Golf Course. The guest room is a garden-level apartment with a separate entrance and private bath. A large pool is just outside the door. Three-night minimum. $65.

OAHU—WAIALUA

Bed and Breakfast Honolulu (Statewide)

3242 Kaohinani Drive, Honolulu, 96817
(808) 595-7533; (800) 288-4666
FAX (808) 595-2030

RICHN. Two large guest rooms. The master bedroom has a queen-size bed, air conditioning, and TV. The other room has twin beds and shared bath. Continental breakfast is served. Five-minute drive to North Shore's famous beaches; 40 minutes to the airport. $55.

OAHU—WAIKIKI

Bed and Breakfast Honolulu (Statewide)

3242 Kaohinani Drive, Honolulu, 96817
(808) 595-7533; (800) 288-4666
FAX (808) 595-2030

SHEAR. Two blocks to beach, this tasteful condo has two guest rooms. The master bedroom has king-size bed and private bath. The other room has a king or two twin beds and a shared bath. Continental breakfast. An easy walk to shopping, restaurants, shows, and local tour agencies. $45.

Idaho

Idaho Heritage Inn

BOISE

Idaho Heritage Inn

109 West Idaho, 83702
(208) 342-8066

This inn was a former governor's mansion and home to the late Senator Frank Church. In the historic Warm Springs District, the inn enjoys the convenience of natural geothermal water. The inn is surrounded by other distinguished turn-of-the-century homes, and is also within walking distance of downtown, beautiful parks, museums, and Boise's famous Greenbelt River walkway. All rooms have been comfortably and charmingly appointed with private baths, period furniture, and crisp linens.

Hosts: Phyllis and Tom Lupher
Rooms: 6 (PB) $59-89
Full Breakfast
Credit Cards: A, B, C, D
Notes: 2, 5, 7, 9, 10, 11, 12, 13, 14

COEUR D'ALENE

Bed and Breakfast Western Adventure

P.O. Box 4308, Bozeman, MT, 59772
(406) 585-0557; FAX (406) 585-2869

510. This stately three-story 1908 mansion is on the National Register of Historic Places. Some say it was a bordello during the 1930s. The third floor with its gracefully arched half-moon windows, once a dance hall, now has three bedrooms. There are a total of nine bedrooms, seven with private baths, decorated with antiques and down comforters from Ireland. Hand-stenciled walls, strategic wallpaper, light and airy rooms, and sheer white curtains are accented by winding mahogany staircases and arched passageways throughout the house. Year-round outdoor spa, air conditioning, suites, and skiing nearby. Full breakfast. Low seasonal discounts. No smoking. No pets. $55-95.

520. This charming Victorian home, in historic Fort Sherman, is within walking distance of the lake, park, downtown, and North Idaho College. The spacious common area is comfortably furnished with plants, overstuffed chairs, and an antique parlor furnace. There are three attractively decorated bedrooms, all with queen-size beds (one has an additional eaves and room with a double feather bed). Two rooms with sinks share a large bath. The exquisite honeymoon suite has its own large private bath with claw-foot tub and shower. Large hot tub and sauna room opens onto a deck. Rooms have cable TVs and VCRs. Water sports on Lake Coeur d'Alene. Downhill skiing is one hour's drive. A ten-minute walk from Coeur d'Alene's restaurants, boutiques, and lake attractions. Winter discounts. Cat and dog in residence. Full breakfast. No smoking. Children over 12 welcome. $90-125.

7 No smoking; 8 Children welcome; 9 Social drinking allowed; 10 Tennis nearby; 11 Swimming nearby; 12 Golf nearby; 13 Skiing nearby; 14 May be booked through a travel agent.

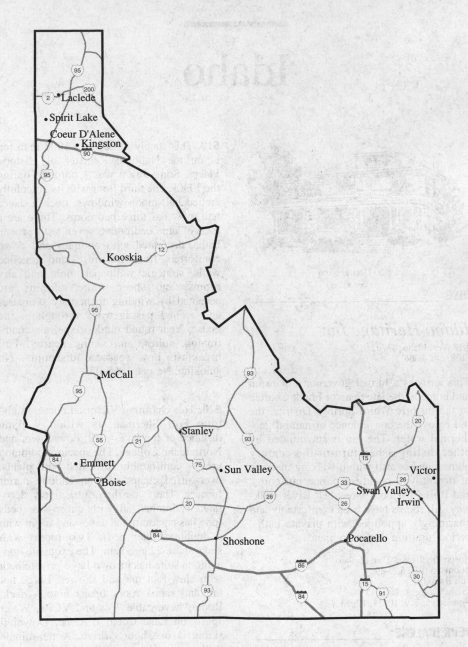

95
2　Laclede
200
• Spirit Lake
Coeur D'Alene
• Kingston
90
95

12
• Kooskia

95

• McCall
93

Stanley
55　21
93
75
• Sun Valley
84
20
• Emmett
• Boise
33
26
26
20

84
Shoshone
86
84
93

15
91

20
15
• Victor
26
Swan Valley
Irwin
• Pocatello
30

Idaho

Berry Patch Inn

Berry Patch Inn Bed and Breakfast

North 1150 Four Winds Road, 83814
(208) 765-4994; FAX (800) 664-2668

Nationally acclaimed and featured by Nordstrom stores. Private elegant mountaintop chalet, backed to pristine forest. Only three and one-half miles to dining and shopping. Lakes, golf, and skiing. Heart-healthy delicious, full breakfast with berry conserve from the garden. Down comforters for sweet sleep. Tea, fruit, and wine complimentary. Gift certificates. Adults only. Honeymoons. On CompuServe and Internet. Air-conditioned. Parking for boat trailers and RVs.

Hosts: Lee M. and Bob D. Ray
Rooms: 3 (1 PB; 2 SB) $89-135
Full Breakfast
Credit Cards: A, B
Notes: 2, 5, 7, 11, 12, 13, 14

The Country Ranch

1495 South Greenferry Road, 83814
(208) 664-1189 (phone and FAX)

Nature in all its magnificence provides an idyllic setting for The Country Ranch. A special romantic destination. Lovely air-conditioned suites, with queen-size poster beds, sitting areas, and private baths, overlook 29 acres. A gourmet breakfast is served in guests' suite, windowed dining room, outdoor deck, or glass-enclosed morning room. Nearby, visit Lake Coeur d'Alene, Schweitzer, or Silver Mountain. Enjoy wine and classical music in the evening. Thirty miles east of Spokane, Washington. Inquire about pets.

Hosts: Ann and Harry Holmberg
Rooms: 2 (PB) $85-95
Full Breakfast
Credit Cards: A, B
Notes: 2, 4, 5, 7, 9, 10, 12, 13

Greenbriar Inn

315 Wallace, 83814
(208) 667-9660

Built in 1908, the Greenbriar is Coeur d'Alene's only nationally registered inn. Just four blocks from downtown and five blocks from the lake, the Greenbriar reflects the residential charm of years gone by.

Greenbriar Inn

NOTES: Credit cards: A MasterCard; B Visa; C American Express; D Discover; E Diners Club; F Other; 2 Personal checks accepted; 3 Lunch available; 4 Dinner available; 5 Open all year; 6 Pets welcome; 7 No smoking; 8 Children welcome; 9 Social drinking allowed; 10 Tennis nearby; 11 Swimming nearby; 12 Golf nearby; 13 Skiing nearby; 14 May be booked through a travel agent.

Surrounded by 40-foot-high maples, guests enjoy the spa outside, the wine and tea hour late in the afternoon, and a famous three-course gourmet breakfast in the morning.

Host: Kris McIlvenna
Rooms: 9 (6 PB; 3 SB) $55-105
Full Breakfast
Credit Cards: A, B, C, D
Notes: 2, 4, 5, 8, 9, 10, 11, 12, 13, 14

Gregory's McFarland House Bed and Breakfast

601 Foster Avenue, 83814
(208) 667-1232

Surrender to the elegance of this award-winning historical home, circa 1905. Breakfast is gourmet to the last crumb, and the cookie jar is always full. Guests will find an ideal blending of beauty, comfort, and clean surroundings. Jerry Hulse of the *Los Angeles Times* says, "Entering Gregory's McFarland House is like stepping back 100 years to an unhurried time when four-posters were in fashion, and lace curtains fluttered at the windows." Private baths and air conditioning. Weddings. Resident minister and professional photographer available.

Hosts: Winifred, Carol, and Stephen
Rooms: 5 (PB) $75-120
Full Breakfast
Credit Cards: A, B
Notes: 2, 5, 10, 11, 12, 13, 14

Katie's Wild Rose Inn

E. 5150 Coeur d' Alene Lake Drive, 83814
(208) 765-WISH (9474)

Katie's welcomes all who enjoy a cozy, warm atmosphere. The house is decorated country cottage-style, offering four guest rooms. The suite includes a view of the lake, large spa bathtub, and queen-size bed. Three and one-half miles east of Coeur d'Alene, it is on the Centennial Trail for hikers and bicyclists. Relax and enjoy the library, TV, or a game of pool. Weddings are a specialty.

Katie's Wild Rose Inn

Hosts: Lee and Joisse Knowles
Rooms: 4 (2 PB; 2 SB) $55-95
Full Breakfast
Credit Cards: A, B
Notes: 2, 5, 7, 9, 10, 11, 12, 13

EMMETT

Frozen Dog Digs

4325 Frozen Dog Road, 83617
(208) 365-7372

Frozen Dog Digs is as unique as its name. Nestled in the foothills and surrounded by fruit orchards, the Digs offers a panoramic view of the Emmett Valley. Sunsets viewed from the romantic gazebo are an artist's dream. The owner designed and built amenities including a racquetball court, chip-and-putt golf greens, landscaped gardens with secluded spa, and sports bar. For the adventuresome, world-famous recreational areas and white-water rapids are within an echo and beckon.

Host: Jon Elsberry
Rooms: 4 (2 PB; 2 SB) $59-99
Full Breakfast
Credit Cards: A, B, D
Notes: 2, 5, 7, 9, 10, 11, 12, 13

IRWIN

Swan Valley Bed and Breakfast

535 Swan Lane, P.O. Box 115, 83428
(800) 241-SWAN; (208) 483-4663

NOTES: Credit cards accepted: A MasterCard; B Visa; C American Express; D Discover; E Diners Club; F Other; 2 Personal checks accepted; 3 Lunch available; 4 Dinner available; 5 Open all year; 6 Pets welcome;

In scenic Swan Valley, Idaho, on the bank of the beautiful south fork of the Snake River, guests can enjoy world-famous trout fishing, bicycle riding, hiking, floating, snow skiing, and much more. Only 55 minutes from Jackson Hole, Wyoming, or Idaho Falls. Spacious accommodations offer private baths, riverviews, a comfortable common area, and a spa overlooking the river. Outside smoking only.

Rooms: 5 (PB) $65-125
Full Breakfast
Cards: A, B, C, D
Notes: 2, 5, 7, 8, 9, 11, 12, 13, 14

KINGSTON

Kingston 5 Ranch Bed and Breakfast

42297 Silver Valley Road, P.O. Box 130, 83839
(208) 682-4862

The Kingston 5 Ranch is located in the heart of the Coeur d'Alene Mountains. The luxurious suite offers spectacular sweeping views of the surrounding mountains and valley. This 4500-square-foot home offers guests many relaxing options including in-room fireplace and bath with jetted tub; separate TV and music room and library; and outdoor hot tub. Ski Silver Mountain. Float the CDA river, swim, fish, canoe, play golf and tennis. Major factory outlets nearby. Hike, mountain bike, or ride horseback right from the bed and breakfast. Can accommodate horses. Pets are able to be accommodated one mile from the bed and breakfast.

Hosts: Walt and Pat Gentry
Rooms: 2 (PB) $85-125
Full Breakfast
Credit Cards: None
Notes: 2, 3, 4, 5, 7, 9, 10, 11, 12, 13, 14

KOOSKIA

Three Rivers Bed and Breakfast

HC 75 Box 61, Highway 12, 83539
(208) 926-4430

In the heart of the Idaho wilderness these bed and breakfast cabins sit high on the hill in privacy. A log cabin, a grand open beam A-fame, and the view is spectacular. Each one has a fireplace, a Jacuzzi, and an antique brass bed in a mountain paradise.

Hosts: Mike and Marie Smith
Rooms: 15 (PB) $45-97.50
Full Breakfast
Credit Cards: A, B, C, D, E
Note: 2, 3, 4, 5, 6, 9, 11

River Birch Farm

LACLEDE

River Birch Farm

P.O. Box 0280, 83841
(208) 263-3705; (800) 700-3705

Imagine gazing from the parlor windows of a large turn-of-the-century home, and visualize a panoramic view of a wide river surrounded by meadows, forests, and mountains. Experience a fun-filled summer holiday swimming and canoeing from the dock facilities. Relax in the Jacuzzi. Capture the rich history of the area during a colorful autumn weekend. Spend a quiet winter evening relaxing by the fireplace after skiing. Look for spring wildflowers during a leisurely vacation. Come stay for any occasion and enjoy the scenic serenity, friendly people, and special hospitality of northern Idaho.

Hosts: Charlie and Barbro Johnson
Rooms: 6 (1PB; 5 SB) $75-130
Full Breakfast
Credit Cards: A, B
Notes: 2, 5, 9, 10, 11, 12, 13, 14

7 No smoking; 8 Children welcome; 9 Social drinking allowed; 10 Tennis nearby; 11 Swimming nearby; 12 Golf nearby; 13 Skiing nearby; 14 May be booked through a travel agent.

MCCALL

Northwest Passage

201 Rio Vista Boulevard, P.O. Box 4208, 83638
(208) 634-5349; (800) 597-6658

Originally built in 1938 for the crew of the film *Northwest Passage* starring Spencer Tracy, this beautiful pine lodge is nestled in tall ponderosa pines. Six guest rooms with private baths and a guest apartment that sleeps up to 12 with a kitchen, fireplace, and TV. Area activities: water sports on Payette Lake, fishing, snowmobiling, skiing, hunting, golf, tennis, mountain biking, and hiking. Groups of up to 22 welcome!

Hosts: Steve and Barbara Schott
Rooms: 6 (PB) $70-80
Apartment: 1 $150
Full Breakfast
Credit Cards: A, B, D
Notes: 2, 5, 6, 7, 8, 9, 10, 11, 12, 13, 14

POCATELLO

Bed and Breakfast Western Adventure

P.O. Box 4308, Bozeman, MT, 59772
(406) 585-0557; FAX (406) 585-2869

527. In an expansive yard with large trees and carefully-tended gardens sits a handsome gemstone brick ranch-style home. Guests can relax and roam the grounds of this quiet country setting where children are welcome. A swing set and tree house are in the large yard. Two attractively furnished rooms that share a bath are available for guests; the larger room has a queen-size bed and can accommodate children, the other has twin beds. Skiing, hiking, and fishing are nearby. Yellowstone National Park is about two hours from the western entrance. Ski in winter; rodeos and activities in summer. See "Old Town" Pocatello and Fort Hall Replica and Museum with zoo of Idaho wildlife including buffalo and coyote. A sports arena at Idaho State University sponsors rodeos, musical groups, expos, and great football. Full breakfast. No smoking. No pets. $40-50.

SHOSHONE

Governors Mansion Bed and Breakfast Inn

315 South Greenwood, P.O. Box 326, 83352
(208) 886-2858

First occupied in 1906, the Governor's Mansion was built by the Gooding family. It was owned by Thomas Gooding, older brother of Frank Gooding, once Governor of Idaho. Come to a small-town atmosphere 55 miles from Sun Valley and near many Idaho attractions, including Shoshone Falls and the Craters of the Moon. Hosts offer a friendly, home-like atmosphere and breakfast to guest's order. Air-conditioned.

Host: Edith Collins
Rooms: 7 (2 PB; 5 SB) $45-65
Full Breakfast
Credit Cards: None
Notes: 2, 5, 6, 8, 9, 11, 13

SPIRIT LAKE

Fireside Lodge

P.O. Box 445, 83869
(208) 623-2871

The Fireside Lodge, built in 1907, was one of the first buildings on Spirit Lake. The lodge is right on the banks of Spirit Lake with a great northwestern view which includes wildlife on certain days and great fishing; guests can use a canoe. The upstairs rooms are decorated in country-Victorian with lots of unique visiting and resting areas. A restaurant and gift shoppe are on the main floor with unusual decor and unique dinner music. Guests will enjoy the warm atmosphere.

Hosts: Rod and Nancy Erickson
Rooms: 4 (SB) $45-50
Full Breakfast
Credit Cards: A, B
Notes: 2, 3, 4, 7, 11, 12, 13

NOTES: Credit cards accepted: A MasterCard; B Visa; C American Express; D Discover; E Diners Club; F Other; 2 Personal checks accepted; 3 Lunch available; 4 Dinner available; 5 Open all year; 6 Pets welcome;

Idaho Rocky Mountain Ranch

STANLEY

Idaho Rocky Mountain Ranch

HC 64, Box 9934, 83278
(208) 774-3544

One of Idaho's oldest and finest guest ranches, offering comfortably decorated lodge and cabin accommodations. Beautiful mountain vistas from the front porch. Delightful meals served by a friendly staff. Hiking, fishing, horseback riding, mountain biking, rafting, cross-country skiing, wildlife viewing, and much more, both on and off the ranch. Fifty miles north of Sun Valley in the Sawtooth National Recreation Area and on Highway 75. Brochure available; weekly rates available. Closed April 1 through May 31 and September 30 through November 25.

Hosts: Bill and Jeana Leavell
Rooms: 21 (PB) $92-204
Credit Cards: A, B, D
Notes: 2, 3, 4, 7, 8, 9, 11, 13

SUN VALLEY (KETCHUM)

The Idaho Country Inn

134 Latigo Lane, P.O. Box 2355, 83353
(208) 726-1019

The Idaho Country Inn is on a lofty knoll halfway between Ketchum and Sun Valley. Designed with a love of Idaho, the inn features ten spacious guest rooms, each named and decorated with a different Idaho theme. The large living room with river-rock fireplace gives spacious yet cozy ambience. Breakfast served each morning includes "something healthy" and "something decadent." Each room has a spectacular view, and the view from the large outdoor hot tub is breathtaking. ABBA four-crown rating.

Rooms: 10 (PB) $85-185
Full Breakfast
Credit Cards: A, B, C
Notes: 5, 7, 8, 9, 10, 12, 13, 14

Pinnacle Inn at the Mountain

100 Picabo Street, P.O. Box 2559, 83353
(800) 255-3391

Just steps away from the ski lifts the Pinnacle Inn has captured the style, elegance, and superb service of world-famous Sun Valley. Guests can enjoy rooms with refrigerators and VCRs or request a suite complete with a kitchen, fireplace, separate bedrooms, extra bathrooms, and relaxing Jacuzzi tubs.

Hosts: Andrea and James Gibson
Rooms: 9 (11 PB) $60-590
Continental Breakfast
Credit Cards: A, B, C
Notes: 2, 3, 5, 7, 8, 9, 10, 11, 12, 13, 14

SWAN VALLEY

Bed and Breakfast Western Adventure

P.O. Box 4308, Bozeman, MT, 59772
(406) 585-0557; FAX (406) 585-2869

516. This expansive country-style two-story log home with a wraparound deck is nestled among towering cottonwood trees on the bank of the beautiful Snake River. Outdoor enthusiasts will enjoy the relaxed setting of this lovely inn. Many activities can be arranged by the hosts. The four guest rooms, each with private bath, are all tastefully decorated with quilts and collectibles and have their own entrance that opens onto a large deck overlooking the river. A common area with comfortable chairs, reading material, and telephone is available at any time. Guests are welcome downstairs to enjoy the big screen TV and fireplace. Flowers in room, private entrance, hot tub, and big screen TV. Hostess can pack a lunch, arrange a rafting and/or fishing trip with advance notice. Full breakfast. Dog in residence. No smoking. No pets. $85.

VICTOR

Moose Creek Ranch

Box 350, 215 East Moose Creek Road, 83455
(208) 787-2784; (800) 676-0075
FAX (208) 787-2284

Come and enjoy the natural wonders of Teton-Yellowstone Country from the secluded comfort of the Moose Creek Ranch. A traditional Dude Ranch in the summer, only 35 minutes from either Teton Village or Grand Targhee ski resorts and Nordic skiing right out the cabin door. Full sit-down breakfast. Hot tub and sauna, and use of the lodge for fireplace viewing (no television).

Hosts: Kelly and Roxann Van Orden
Rooms: 9 (PB)
Credit Cards: A, B, C, D
Notes: 2, 3, 4, 7, 8, 9, 13, 14

Illinois

Victorian Rose Garden

ALGONQUIN

Victorian Rose Garden Bed and Breakfast

314 Washington Street, 60102
(847) 854-9667; FAX (847) 854-3236

Built in 1886, the Victorian Rose Garden invites guests to come and relax on its wraparound porch and enjoy the garden. Rooms are decorated with a mix of antiques and much loved furniture. Play the baby grand piano or Baldwin organ, or just relax by the fireplace. The area provides golfing, antiquing, bike trail, acclaimed restaurants, and is only one hour from Chicago. Closed over Christmas.

Hosts: Don and Sherry Brewer
Rooms: 5 (3 PB; 2 SB) $55-135
Full Breakfast
Credit Cards: A, B, C
Notes: 2, 7, 12

ATWOOD

Harshbarger Homestead

Rural Route 1, Box 110, 61913
(217) 578-2265

A casual, quiet, and comfortable country home amid central Illinois Prairie. Ten miles from Illinois' largest Amish community. Many craft and antique shops. Visitors will enjoy beautiful herb and flower gardens, interesting coveys of collectibles throughout the house, and a 150-year-old log cabin displaying antiques with family history. Special playroom and sleeping quarters for children. Fun for all ages. Special event: Women's Retreat in January and February only. Special rates.

Host: Shirley Harshbarger
Rooms: 3 (S2B) $55
Full and Continental Breakfast
Credit Cards: F
Notes: 2, 8, 9

BELLEVILLE

Victory Inn Bed and Breakfast

712 South Jackson Street, 62220
(618) 277-1538; FAX (618) 277-1576

The stately home, built in 1877, offers an inviting picture from first sight. Guests often feel transformed back in time while sipping tea in the dining room or sharing experiences in the parlor. Modern conveniences are also present including a whirlpool tub, private telephones, fax, computer, electronic entry, and modem access.

Hosts: Tom and Jo Brannan
Rooms: 4 (2 PB; 2 SB) $50-85
Continental Breakfast
Credit Cards: A, B, C, D, E
Notes: 2, 5, 7, 9, 10, 12, 14

7 No smoking; 8 Children welcome; 9 Social drinking allowed; 10 Tennis nearby; 11 Swimming nearby; 12 Golf nearby; 13 Skiing nearby; 14 May be booked through a travel agent.

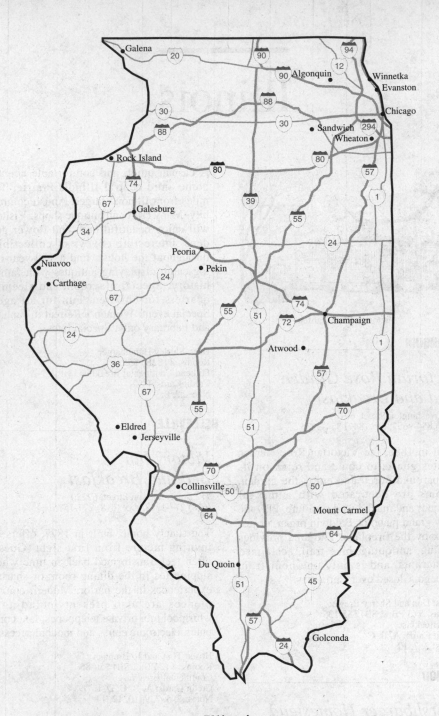

Illinois

CARTHAGE

The Wright Farmhouse

2146 East US Hwy 136, 62321
(217) 357-2421

Comfortable, quiet rooms with period furnishings in a restored 19th-century home on a working farm. Country charm plus private baths, air conditioning, and private guest entrance. Nearby attractions include historic town square and courthouse and the scenic Mississippi River.

Hosts: John and Connie Wright
Rooms: 4 (PB) $31.80-58.30
Continental Breakfast
Credit Cards: A, B
Notes: 7, 8, 9, 10, 11, 12

CHAMPAIGN

The Golds
Bed and Breakfast

2065 County Road 525 East, 61821
(217) 586-4345

Restored 1874 farmhouse with antique furnishings, just off I-74 west of Champaign, surrounded by farm fields. Antique shopping, golf, university, and parks nearby. Continental breakfast includes homemade coffeecake, muffins, jam, fresh fruit, and

The Golds

juice. Enjoy a cool beverage on the deck. The hosts will strive to make the stay an enjoyable bed and breakfast experience. Call or write for a descriptive brochure.

Hosts: Rita and Bob Gold
Rooms: 3 (P1/2B; SB) $45
Continental Breakfast
Credit Cards: None
Notes: 2, 5, 7, 9, 11, 12, 14

Grandma Joan's Homestay

2204 Brett Drive, 61821
(217) 356-5828

This comfortable, contemporary home features two fireplaces, multilevel decks, Jacuzzi, screened-in porch, and collection of modern and folk art. Grandma pampers guests with cookies and milk at bedtime and a healthy breakfast in the morning. Ten minutes from the University of Illinois. Closed December 20 through January 10. Let this be a home away from home.

Host: Joan Erickson
Rooms: 3 (1 PB; 2 SB) $50-70
Full Breakfast
Credit Cards: None
Notes: 2, 9, 10, 11, 12

CHICAGO

Amber Creek's
Chicago Connection

1260 North Dearborn, Chicago
Mailing: P.O. Box 5, Galena, 61036
(815) 777-9320

Charming apartment on Chicago's Gold Coast in a quiet, secure building only one-half block from the Ambassador Hotel. Tastefully decorated, spacious living room with nice views, including lake. Full kitchen and bath. Romantic bedroom with king-size bed, down quilts, and extra pillows. Linens and towels provided. Walk to lake, Water Tower, and Michigan Avenue shopping. Half block to airport limousine

NOTES: Credit cards: A MasterCard; B Visa; C American Express; D Discover; E Diners Club; F Other;
2 Personal checks accepted; 3 Lunch available; 4 Dinner available; 5 Open all year; 6 Pets welcome;
7 No smoking; 8 Children welcome; 9 Social drinking allowed; 10 Tennis nearby; 11 Swimming nearby;
12 Golf nearby; 13 Skiing nearby; 14 May be booked through a travel agent.

and public transportation. Parking garage next door. Ideal for one couple. Queen-size futon provides sleeping for additional guests.

Host: Kate Freeman
Apartment: 1 (PB) $75-125
Continental Breakfast
Credit Cards: A, B, C, D
Notes: 2, 3, 4, 5, 8, 9, 11, 14

Bed and Breakfast/ Chicago, Inc.

P.O. Box 14088, 60614-0088
(312) 951-0085; FAX (312) 649-9243

2. This historic Kenwood home was recently restored by the architect/owner and her co-host who is a public TV producer. Its Prairie-style architecture is wonderfully harmonized with antique furniture for an Old World European charm. $75-85.

3. This self-contained one-bedroom garden apartment is in a renovated frame building. Recently decorated, it is furnished with a four-poster queen-size bed and sleeper sofa and offers kitchen and private bath. There is a lovely garden for guests to sit in and have breakfast, weather permitting. The host family lives upstairs; he is a TV reporter and she owns Bed and Breakfast/Chicago, Inc. Air conditioning and TV. $95-125.

4. This spacious, self-contained, one-bedroom apartment is in a vintage high-rise building in the north part of the Gold Coast. King-size bed, full bath, living room, and kitchen. Within walking distance of the Magnificent Mile. Café in the building. Air-conditioned. TV. $95-125.

8. This renovated Victorian brick home offers several possibilities. There is a queen-size guest room with a private adjoining bath available in the apartment of the owner. Another area is a one-bedroom

unit with a queen-size bed (a twin bed can be added), a sleeper-sofa in the living room, a Jacuzzi, and a kitchenette. Also in the home, a self-contained two-bedroom apartment has a queen-size bed in one bedroom and a king or set of twin beds in the other, depending on preference. There is a full kitchen and a shower, but no tub, in this apartment. Guest room, $75-85; one-bedroom apartment, $95-105; two-bedroom apartment, $125-150.

9. This self-contained one-bedroom garden apartment has been recently decorated and offers a queen-size bed, bath, full kitchen, and a living room. Air conditioning and TV. Just a short walk to the metro and many fine restaurants. No smoking. $95.

29. This high-rise apartment offers a guest room in the spacious condominium of a real estate professional. The guest room in this stylish, contemporary home is furnished with a double bed and has a private bath. Air conditioning and TV. $75-85.

30. This Victorian home on Chicago's Near North side has a private one-bedroom apartment on the third floor and a guest room on the second floor. The home has original woodwork. Four blocks from Michigan Avenue and close to downtown. Parking is available. $85-125.

33. This is a warm, one-bedroom apartment featuring wood floors, a working fireplace, interesting artwork, and pleasant outdoor space for guest use. Full kitchen, queen-size bed, and a sleeper-sofa in the living room. Four blocks to the elevated train. The hosts who live upstairs are an architect and a graphic designer. $95-125.

40. This exquisite two-bedroom, one-bath apartment in a small Victorian building has a wood-burning fireplace in the living

NOTES: Credit cards accepted: A MasterCard; B Visa; C American Express; D Discover; E Diners Club; F Other; 2 Personal checks accepted; 3 Lunch available; 4 Dinner available; 5 Open all year; 6 Pets welcome;

room. The unit has double bed in each bedroom and a trundle in the living room. The style is "Ralph Laurenish" with period antiques. The unit has a new kitchen and bath. $95-150.

64. This Victorian mansion in prime Lincoln Park has been rehabbed to maintain the original feeling, but has been opened up to make the space feel more contemporary. The lovely home is furnished with antiques, wicker furniture, etc. It offers two guest rooms with private baths. One room has a private entrance. $75-85.

71. This beautifully rehabbed Victorian Queen Anne, built in the late 1800s, offers charm, original woodwork, hardwood floors, two fireplaces, and at the same time provides the best in modern comforts. The guest room offers a double bed, private hall bath, and sitting area. Air conditioning and TV. No smoking. $85.

Annie's. This comfortable, completely furnished studio apartment has a fully equipped kitchen, queen-size bed, private bath, and private entrance. Close to some of Chicago's best restaurants, live theater, and fine shopping. Air conditioned. TV. $85.

City View Inn. This lovely 22-room property was originally a private club. On the 40th floor of a building in the financial district, all rooms have king-size beds, marble baths, and gorgeous views. Included in the rate is use of the first-class health club in the building. Parking and Continental breakfast. $135-185.

Gold Coast Guest House. The hostess welcomes guests to this charming, newly rehabbed four-room guest house just blocks west of Michigan Avenue. Each guest room has an attached bath. Three rooms have queen-size beds and the other has twin-size beds. There is a lovely garden where the Continental breakfast will be served, weather permitting. There are spiral staircases between levels. $85-135.

Maud Travels. This single-family home has just been redone. The host, who has traveled extensively and loves staying in bed and breakfasts, lives in a coach house behind this accommodation. Three guest rooms with private baths offered. Breakfast is self-serve from the kitchen. This is an ideal arrangement for groups traveling together or visitors in Chicago for an extended time who want to settle in and feel they have found a home away from home. Air conditioning and TV. Weekly and monthly rates are available. $65-85.

The Heritage Bed and Breakfast Registry

758 Wacker Drive, Suite 3600, 60601
(312) 857-0800; FAX (312) 857-0805

H600. This unhosted downtown accommodation is in the same building and one floor above accommodation H667. It is a self-catering studio apartment with a kitchen, private bath, and a day bed that is used as a couch by day, and is equipped with a trundle bed that can either be one king-size bed or two twin beds by night. Children welcome. Continental breakfast. Handicapped accessible. Within blocks of public transportation and nightlife. $95.

H601. Close to downtown in the old town neighborhood, this hosted accommodation offers a great location in the windy city. The home has contemporary furnishings along with some antiques and family heirlooms. The two guest rooms each have a sleigh bed and share a bathroom with a Jacuzzi tub. There is a fireplace in the living room. Continental breakfast served. Within blocks of public transportation and nightlife. Air-conditioned. $75.

7 No smoking; 8 Children welcome; 9 Social drinking allowed; 10 Tennis nearby; 11 Swimming nearby; 12 Golf nearby; 13 Skiing nearby; 14 May be booked through a travel agent.

The Heritage Bed and Breakfast Registry (continued)

H606. The unhosted house is decorated in a blend of antique and collector pieces. The guest bedroom is a large addition to the house with floor-to-ceiling windows overlooking a private yard full of trees and flowers. The room has a queen-size bed as well as a queen-size sofa/sleeper which enables the room to accommodate up to four people. The room also has its own bathroom, kitchenette, private patio, TV, and telephone. Continental breakfast. Children welcome. Within blocks of public transportation. Air-conditioned. An additional $10 for each extra person. $55.

H609. This unhosted downtown self-catered studio suite is just steps away from Chicago's Michigan Avenue shopping district. The tastefully decorated suite offers a queen-size bed as well as Prairie-style sofa/futon that can sleep a third and fourth person. It also boasts a state-of-the-art TV/VCR/stereo system and telephone. There is a full kitchen and a balcony that offers a beautiful view of downtown. Included with this accommodation is access to the building's rooftop swimming pool, exercise room, and sundeck. Indoor parking and laundry facilities are also available for an additional charge. Continental breakfast. Within blocks of public transportation and nightlife. Air-conditioned. Additional $25 for extra persons. $95.

H650. Originally built as a carriage house, this accommodation has been transformed into a very contemporary setting due to the imagination of its host. Two guest rooms offer the choice of a queen-size bed or twin beds, private baths, and TV. The house, which was designed entirely by the host, is sunny and spacious. A wall of floor-to-ceiling windows in the large living room leads to a lush garden/patio, a wonderful place for breakfast in the summertime. The house has an open, airy feeling due to its unique cathedral ceiling and skylights throughout. Within blocks of public transportation, downtown, and nightlife. Air-conditioned. No smoking. Continental breakfast. $75.

H652. A passion for the arts and travel is evident in this accommodation. The guest room is decorated with a light Victorian flavor using soft colors for the walls and fabrics, and a beautiful iron headboard as its focal point. It is on the first floor and includes a bathroom with a Jacuzzi tub and an adjacent sitting room with cable TV, VCR, and telephone. The sitting room has sleeper-sofa that can accommodate two extra people. Air-conditioned. Within blocks of public transportation, downtown, and the nightlife. No smoking. Continental breakfast. Rates are slightly higher with each additional person. $85.

H654. This accommodation offers a bit of history along with guest's stay. The mansion is over 100 years' old and is on a street along with several other mansions, some on the National Register of Historic Places. The interior of the house has a strong European influence due both to the home's beautifully restored architectural features and the host's collection of European antiques and furnishings. Guest rooms range in size and price. They offer both private and shared baths. The entire home is graced with original woodwork, fixtures, and fireplaces, all lovingly restored. Pets in residence. Air-conditioned. Within blocks of public transportation. Other languages spoken. No smoking. Continental breakfast. $85.

H656. Guests are encouraged to make themselves at home in this delightful unhosted one-bedroom apartment. This accommodation is close to area shops, restaurants, and public transportation. The

NOTES: Credit cards accepted: A MasterCard; B Visa; C American Express; D Discover; E Diners Club; F Other; 2 Personal checks accepted; 3 Lunch available; 4 Dinner available; 5 Open all year; 6 Pets welcome;

living room has a wood-burning fireplace, TV, telephone, and a sleeper-sofa that can accommodate up to two extra people. The bedroom gets its warm feeling from the exposed brick walls and a decor reminiscent of Laura Ashley. There is also a kitchen that makes being away from home a little easier. Children welcome. Bicycle available. Continental breakfast. An additional $25 for each extra person. $85.

H657. This accommodation affords travelers to Chicago an ideal place to make themselves at home, as well as plenty of space in which to do so. It is an unhosted two-bedroom apartment on the tenth floor of a modern high-rise, and in the very heart of the Gold Coast. Each of the bedrooms has a full-size bed as well as its own bathroom. There is a full kitchen and dining area as well as a cozy living room. The entire apartment is furnished in a contemporary style, and is available as a one or two bedroom facility. It is ideal for two couples traveling together, or two business people. Children welcome. Within blocks of public transportation, downtown, and the nightlife. Air-conditioned. TV and telephone. Parking available. Continental breakfast. Rates are slightly higher with each additional person. $135.

H661. With all the comforts of home, this host offers guests a cozy visit to Chicago. The accommodation is blocks from Lincoln Avenue, within walking distance of the restaurants, shops, and the bus. The home is on a quiet street with ample parking and is decorated with original art throughout. The guest room has a brass bed and an antique armoire and the bathroom is directly across the hall. Telephone. No smoking. Dog on premises. Children welcome. Continental breakfast. $55.

H662. The home is in a charming old building on a tree-lined street, and is decorated with a blend of old and new furnishings accented by the building's original woodwork, and a working fireplace in the living room. The guest bedroom is in the front of the house and has a comfortable sleeper-sofa, as well as a desk for both day and night use and telephone. The close proximity to the lake, entertainment, and public transportation makes this an ideal setting. No smoking. Continental breakfast. $70.

H667. Soaring high atop Chicago's skyline, this unhosted accommodation exemplifies city living. The guest suite is an entire one-bedroom apartment with private bath on the 21st floor of a downtown high-rise and is complete with a full kitchen and dinette area. There is a queen-size bed in the bedroom as well as a queen-size sofa/sleeper in the living room, thus accommodating up to four people. The entire apartment is decorated in a clean, contemporary look and affords a beautiful view of Chicago's downtown area. It is ideally suited to people visiting Chicago on business or people with extended stays. Within blocks of public transportation and night life. Air-conditioned. TV and telephone in room. Parking available. Continental breakfast. Additional $25 for third and fourth persons. $115.

H668. The accommodation is unhosted and can be used as either a one- or two-bedroom suite according to guest's needs. Includes a full kitchen, TV, telephone, and private bath. It is decorated in a comfortable contemporary style, accented with interesting antiques such as school art table. Children welcome. No smoking. Close to public transportation, downtown, and the night life. Air-conditioned. Continental breakfast. $85-125.

H673. This hosted accommodation offers a delightful blend of Old World charm, exotic travel destinations, and just a touch of the contemporary. The house is a rowhouse, circa 1880, in the Old Town's historic district. The generous use of rich wood throughout provides the perfect setting for its country European decor. The guest room offers a queen-size bed, sleeper-sofa with a Sealey mattress that makes it ideal for day as well as evening use. There is a wood-burning fireplace in the TV room as well as a telephone and private entrance to the street. There is also a twin bed available for a third person. A beautiful flower garden in the backyard offers just a touch of New Orleans flavor in the summertime. Dog on premises. No smoking. Private bath. Within blocks of public transportation, downtown, and the night life. Continental breakfast. An additional $25 for extra guests. $85.

H674. This one-bedroom apartment is a delightful home away from home in an urban setting. Its decor represents its occupant's eclectic interests. Glass doors lead to the bedroom. Amenities include private bath, TV, and telephone.There is a tiny balcony off of the kitchen and a piano in the living room. Children welcome. Within blocks of public transportation and night life. Continental breakfast. $75.

H675. Just doors away from host 673, this accommodation offers a similar rowhouse with contemporary decor. The guest room reflects a Euro-style with walls lined with bookshelves, lending clean lines to the room. The bed is a sleeper-sofa which is ideal for day use. There is a private bath as well as a private entrance to the street. The rest of the house is decorated in the same light, contemporary Euro-style graced with original art created by noted Chicago artists. Amenities include TV, telephone, fireplace, and air conditioning. Dog on premises. Within blocks of public transportation, downtown, and the night life. Continental breakfast. $85.

Hyde Park House

5210 South Kenwood Avenue, 60615
(312) 363-4595

This is a Victorian house with a veranda, porch swing, rear deck, two grand pianos, and attic greenhouse. Near the University of Chicago, the Museum of Science and Industry, and 15 minutes from downtown by bus along the Lake Michigan shore, seven minutes from McCormick Convention Center. Also within walking distance are excellent sushi, Thai, Cantonese, Greek, Italian, and Continental restaurants, gift shops, and art galleries.

Host: Irene Custer
Rooms: 3 (1 PB; 2 SB) $55-70
Continental Breakfast
Credit Cards: None
Notes: 2, 5, 6, 8, 9, 10, 11, 12, 14

COLLINSVILLE

Maggie's Bed and Breakfast

2102 North Keebler, 62234
(618) 344-8283

A turn-of-the-century boarding house now filled with antiques and collectibles from all over the world. Maggie's has five guest rooms and offers robes and slippers for guests. All natural breakfast with home-made jellies and jams and organically grown fruits and vegetables. Inquire about accommodations for children.

Host: Maggie Leyda
Rooms: 5 (4 PB; 1 SB) $35-70
Full Breakfast
Credit Cards: None
Notes: 2, 5, 6, 7, 9, 12, 14

DU QUOIN

Francie's Bed and Breakfast Inn

104 South Line Street, 62832
(618) 542-6686

A quiet getaway in a restored 1908 orphanage. Four lovely air-conditioned guest rooms (two of which are suites) with a full breakfast served on the balcony, to the guest room, or in the dining room. Perfect accommodations for group seminars or retreats. Meeting rooms and meals available for 15 to 60 persons. Hosts will arrange a murder mystery weekend for a group or five couples. Call for information or reservations.

Hosts: Tom and Francie Morgan
Rooms: 4 (PB) $60-80
Full Breakfast
Credit Cards: A, B
Notes: 2, 5, 7, 9, 10, 11, 12

ELDRED

Bluffdale Vacation Farm

Rural Route 1, 62027
(217) 983-2854

This new hideaway cottage in the woods is cozy and secluded. Its lovely accommodations include a wood-burning rock fireplace, inside and outside private whirlpool spas, a cathedral ceiling with native log rafters and beams, and wide plank floors. On the side of the bluffs, it has a large deck with sheltering trees growing through it and a magnificent view of the Illinois River Valley. An adjoining bedroom with private bath can sleep up to four children. Guest house rooms also available.

Hosts: Bill and Lindy Hobson
Rooms: 9 (PB) $62-80
Full Breakfast
Credit Cards: None
Notes: 2, 3, 4, 8, 9, 11, 12, 14

EVANSTON

The Heritage Bed and Breakfast Registry

758 Wacker Drive, Suite 3600, 60601
(312) 857-0800; FAX (312) 857-0805

H620. This is ideal for people visiting any of the universities or those who want a smaller town feeling while visiting Chicago. The accommodation lies about four blocks from Lake Michigan, two blocks from the elevated train, Northwestern University, and Kendall College. The two guest rooms have a wonderfully stately feel to their decor and can accommodate one king-size or two twin-size beds. The host provides such niceties as bathrobes and fresh scones. No smoking. Continental breakfast. $65-75.

The Margarita European Inn

1566 Oak Avenue, 60201
(708) 869-2273

Originally a women's private club, this Georgian mansion north of Chicago has been reopened as a charming bed and breakfast inn with an Italian ristorante. Choose from 34 individually appointed guest rooms, half with newly decorated private baths. Relax in the spacious parlor which features a molded fireplace and floor-to-ceiling arched windows. A rooftop garden, paneled library, and party rooms are also available. Continental breakfast includes muffins, pastries, and fresh fruit. Lunch and dinner are available in the restaurant. Facilities for weddings and meetings are available.

Hosts: Barbara and Tim Gorham, Owners; Judith Baker, Innkeeper
Rooms: 34 (PB)
Continental Breakfast
Credit Cards: A, B, C
Notes: 2, 3, 4, 5, 8, 9, 10, 11, 12, 14

GALENA

Avery Guest House

606 South Prospect Street, 61036
(815) 777-3883

This pre-Civil War home, within Galena's historic district, is a short walk from antique shops and historic buildings. Enjoy the scenic view from the porch swing. Breakfast is served in the sunny dining room with a bay window overlooking the Galena River valley. Two-night minimum stay required for weekends and holidays.

Hosts: Flo and Roger Jensen
Rooms: 4 (S2B) $65-75
Full Breakfast
Credit Cards: A, B, D
Notes: 2, 5, 7, 9, 10, 11, 12, 13

Belle Aire Mansion Guest House

11410 Route 20 West, 61036
(815) 777-0893

Belle Aire Mansion is a pre-Civil War home set on 11 beautiful acres just minutes from Galena. Three of the rooms feature gas fireplaces, and one suite has a double whirlpool. Two-night minimum stay for weekends is required. Closed Christmas. Guests say, "It's just like visiting friends." The hosts say, "Welcome home—to our home."

Hosts: Jan and Lorraine Svec
Rooms: 5 (PB) $70.85-147.15
Full Breakfast
Credit Cards: A, B, D
Notes: 2, 7, 8, 9, 11, 12, 13

Belle Aire Mansion

Brierwreath Manor Bed and Breakfast

216 North Bench Street, 61036
(815) 777-0608

Brierwreath Manor

Circa 1884 Queen Anne house with wrap-around porch only one short block from historic Main Street. Cable TV, early morning coffee buffet, and full breakfast are only a few of the comforts guests will experience. The manor has three large suites with sitting rooms, gas log fireplaces, and private baths. Each room is furnished with an eclectic blend of antiques and modern comforts. Special packages available.

Hosts: Mike and Lyn Cook
Suites: 3 (PB) $85-95
Full Breakfast
Credit Cards: None
Notes: 2, 5, 7, 9, 11, 12, 13

Eagle's Nest

410 South High Street, 61036
(815) 777-9320

Charming 1842 Federal brick cottage tucked into a wooded hillside in the historic district, within walking distance of shops and restaurants. Faithfully restored and furnished with period antiques. Living room with fireplace, master bedroom with queen-size bed, second bedroom with double bed. Fully equipped kitchen, bath with shower and double whirlpool, TV, stereo, deck, and grill. Linens and towels provided. Perfect for history and antique buffs. Ideal for one couple; will accommodate two couples or a small family.

NOTES: Credit cards accepted: A MasterCard; B Visa; C American Express; D Discover; E Diners Club; F Other; 2 Personal checks accepted; 3 Lunch available; 4 Dinner available; 5 Open all year; 6 Pets welcome;

Host: Kate Freeman
Room: 1 (PB)
Continental Breakfast
Credit Card: A, B, C, D, E
Notes: 2, 3, 4, 5, 6,, 8, 9, 10, 11, 12, 13, 14

Grandview Guest Home

113 South Prospect Street, 61036
(815) 777-1387; (800) 373-0732

A 125-year-old brick traditional on Quality Hill, overlooking the city and countryside. Victorian furnishings. The full breakfast features home-baked goods and European coffees. Two blocks from Main Street shops, museums, and restaurants.

Hosts: Harry and Marjorie Dugan
Rooms: 3 (1 PB; 2 SB) $65-80
Full Breakfast
Credit Cards: A, B, C, D
Notes: 2, 5, 8, 9, 10, 11, 12, 13

Park Avenue Guest House

208 Park Avenue, 61036
(815) 777-1075; (800) 359-0743

An 1893 Queen Anne "painted lady," with wraparound screened porch and shaded garden with gazebo. Original woodwork, queen-size beds, and antique furniture. Central air conditioning. In-room fireplaces. Second parlor has cable TV. Walk to town; ample parking. Continental plus breakfast.

Host: Sharon Fallbacher
Rooms: 4 (PB) $65-105
Continental Breakfast
Credit Cards: A, B, D
Notes: 2, 5, 7, 9, 10, 11, 12, 13

Pine Hollow Inn

4700 North Council Hill, 61036
(815) 777-1071

On a 120-acre Christmas tree farm one mile north of Galena. "Helping make it one of the best are spacious rooms with fireplaces, skylights, private baths, and whirlpools, plus some superb scenery." Rooms at the inn are very large. Each is

appointed with beautiful country furnishings. One of the unique qualities of the area is the peaceful solitude that is especially nice when enjoyed from the large porch surrounding the house.

Hosts: Larry and Sally Priske
Rooms: 5 (PB) $75-110
Continental Breakfast
Credit Cards: A, B, D
Notes: 2, 5, 7, 9, 10, 11, 12, 13, 14

Queen Anne Guest House

200 Park Avenue, 61036
(815) 777-3849

Restored 1891 Queen Anne Victorian nestled in a quiet residential neighborhood of historic Galena. Four romantically furnished rooms with private baths, claw-foot tubs, ceiling fans, twin-, queen- and king-size beds, antiques, and period furnishings. Library, double parlors, wraparound porch, and delicious breakfasts. A short stroll to antique shopping, museums, and fine restaurants in historic downtown district. Minutes to skiing, golf, riverboat excursions, and casino boats. Listed in AAA and Mobil.

Hosts: Frank Checchin and Diane Thompson
Rooms: 4 (PB) $75-95
Continental Breakfast
Credit Cards: A, B, D
Notes: 2, 5, 7, 9, 10, 11, 12, 13

Queen Anne Guest House

7 No smoking; 8 Children welcome; 9 Social drinking allowed; 10 Tennis nearby; 11 Swimming nearby; 12 Golf nearby; 13 Skiing nearby; 14 May be booked through a travel agent.

GALESBURG

Seacord House Bed and Breakfast

624 North Cherry Street, 61401-2731
(309) 342-4107

This 1890s Eastlake Victorian is lovingly furnished in period decor with family antiques. Enjoy a landmark house filled with traditional comfort, hospitality, and charm. Guests may use the parlors for conversation or reading, or relax on the patio. Books and games are always on hand. The inn is close to Knox College, the Sandburg Birthplace, Bishop Hill, and Spoon River Country. The Continental plus breakfast includes special recipe muffins or waffles made from scratch daily. Inspected and approved by the Illinois Bed and Breakfast Association.

Hosts: Gwen and Lyle Johnson
Rooms: 3 (SB) $40
Continental Breakfast
Credit Cards: A, B, D
Notes: 2, 5, 7, 9

GOLCONDA

Marilee's Guest House

Washington and Monroe Streets, P.O. Box 627, 62938
(618) 683-2751; (800) 582-2563

Attractive bungalow, warmly furnished, comfortable; telephone, air conditioners, TV, refrigerator, snacks, wood-burning fireplace, and spacious rooms with open-beam ceilings. Near the beautiful Ohio River, two blocks from the marina at Smithland Pool. The deer capital of Illinois, near the Shawnee National Forest. Deer hunting, bass fishing, wild turkey, and quail country. Children welcome.

Host: Marilee Joiner
Rooms: 3 (1 PB; 2 SB) $45
Full Breakfast
Credit Cards: None
Notes: 2, 4, 5, 8, 9, 10, 11, 12, 13

GURNEE

Sweet Basil Hill Farm Bed and Breakfast Inn

15937 West Washington Street, 60031
(708) 244-3333; (708) 263-6693

Sitting atop a hill on seven and one-half wooded acres, this inn is midway between Chicago and Milwaukee. Sheep and llamas, paths, gardens, hammock, and a lawn swing all offer a more restful pace. The common room, with English pine antiques and fireplace, makes a cozy winter retreat. Full breakfast, beverages, and snacks served in the knotty pine breakfast room. Featured in the August 1991 *Country Home* magazine, April 1993 *Country Inns,* and *The Romance of Country Inns* by Gail Greco. Private telephones, TV, VCR, video library, and individual air conditioning in all rooms.

Hosts: Teri and Bob Jones
Rooms: 3 (PB) $85-150
Guesthouse: 1 (PB)
Full Breakfast
Credit Cards: A, B, D, E, F
Notes: 2, 5, 7, 8, 9, 10, 11, 12, 13, 14

JERSEYVILLE

The Homeridge Bed and Breakfast

1470 North State Street, 62052
(618) 498-3442

Beautiful, warm, brick Italianate Victorian private home, circa 1867, on 18 acres in comfortable country atmosphere. Drive through stately iron gates and pine tree-lined driveway to the 14-room historic estate of Senator Theodore Chapman. Beautiful, expansive pillared front porch. Handcarved stairway to spacious guest rooms and third floor. Large swimming pool. Central air conditioning. Between Springfield, Illinois, and St. Louis, Missouri.

Hosts: Sue and Howard Landon
Rooms: 4 (PB) $65

NOTES: Credit cards accepted: A MasterCard; B Visa; C American Express; D Discover; E Diners Club; F Other; 2 Personal checks accepted; 3 Lunch available; 4 Dinner available; 5 Open all year; 6 Pets welcome;

Full Breakfast
Credit Cards: A, B
Notes: 2, 5, 7, 10, 11, 12

MOUNT CARMEL

The Poor Farm Bed and Breakfast

Poor Farm Road, 62863-9803
(800) 646-FARM (3276); FAX (618) 262-8199

From 1857 to 1949, the Poor Farm served as a home for the homeless. Today, it is home for the traveler who enjoys a warm, friendly atmosphere, authentic country charm, and an abundance of local history. A gracious glimpse of yesteryear awaits the guests as they enter the 35-room stately brick structure. Enjoy luxury in one of the four-room suites or spacious double rooms, all with private baths. Within walking distance are golf, tennis, swimming, and two parks with fishing. In three minutes guests can be on the banks of the historic Wabash River, and in the spectacular Beall Woods Nature Preserve in 15 minutes. Historic old New Harmony, Indiana, and riverboat gaming in Evansville, Indiana, are 45 minutes away. Come enjoy!

Hosts: Liz and John Stelzer
Rooms: 5 (PB) $50-95
Credit Cards: A, B, C, D
Notes: 2, 5, 8, 9, 10, 11, 12, 14

Prairie Path Guest House

1002 Lowden Road, 61053
(815) 244-3462

This Victorian home, built in 1876, sits at the edge of historic Mount Carroll. Country and Victorian rooms are available where guests are treated to warm hospitality and a full country breakfast of eggs, bacon, homemade breads with homemade jams and jellies, fresh fruit, or French toast, or waffles with ham, and other specialities. Make this a home away from home. Private

Prairie Path Guest House

and shared baths are available, and the house has central air conditioning. There is a unique quilt and antique shop on the premises with old-fashioned ambience! Full advance deposit is required or credit cards may be used to guarantee a reservation.

Rooms: 3 (1 PB; 2 SB) $60-70
Full Breakfast
Credit Cards: A, B
Notes: 2, 5, 7, 9, 10, 11, 12, 13

NAUVOO

Mississippi Memories

Rural Route 1, Box 291, 62354
(217) 453-2771

Gracious lodging on the Mississippi riverbank. Elegantly served full homemade breakfasts; quiet wooded setting. Five minutes from restored Mormon city, "the

Mississippi Memories

7 No smoking; 8 Children welcome; 9 Social drinking allowed; 10 Tennis nearby; 11 Swimming nearby; 12 Golf nearby; 13 Skiing nearby; 14 May be booked through a travel agent.

Williamsburg of the Midwest." From two decks watch spectacular sunsets, abundant wildlife, and barges drifting by. Excellent geode hunting. Air conditioning, two fireplaces, two pianos, and fruit and flowers in rooms. Triple A rated three stars.

Hosts: Marge and Dean Starr
Rooms: 5 (3 PB; 2 SB) $45
Full Breakfast
Credit Cards: A, B
Notes: 2, 5, 7, 11, 12

PEKIN

Herget House: An Edwardian Inn

420 Washington Street, 61554
(309) 353-4025

Listed on the National Register of Historic Places, this Classical Revival home was built in 1912 during the Edwardian Era. It has elegant architectural detail and provides deluxe accommodations for both business and vacation travelers. Each of the bedrooms is furnished to a standard of luxury not found since the turn of the century.

Host: Rick Walsh
Rooms: 5 (3 PB; 2 SB) $85-100
Full Breakfast
Credit Cards: None
Notes: 2, 5, 7, 11, 12

PEORIA (MOSSVILLE)

Old Church House Inn Bed and Breakfast

1416 East Mossville Road, 61552
(309) 579-2300

Come take sanctuary from the cares of life in this 1869 renovated "one-room country church," where sleeping is encouraged! Nestled in central Illinois, guests delight in the plush warmth of a Victorian era where attention to detail radiates. Stroll through colorful flower gardens, capture memories by the fireplace, and sink into queen-size featherbeds for a restful night's sleep. Continental plus breakfast is served. Cross-country skiing.

Hosts: Dean and Holly Ramseyer
Rooms: 2 (1 PB or 2 SB) $69-99
Continental Breakfast
Credit Cards: A, B
Notes: 2, 3, 5, 7, 10, 11, 12, 13

ROCK ISLAND

Bed and Breakfasts of the QCA Room Availability Cooperative

P.O. Box 3464, 61201
(319) 322-5055

This owners' association has information on 12 bed and breakfasts on both sides of the Mississippi River in the Iowa and Illinois Quad Cities. This includes Davenport, Iowa, Rock Island, and the surrounding areas. Selections range from modern to historic, rural to city, and even a train caboose. Cruise the river, sample the local festivals and museums, ride the bike trails, or run the Bix 7 Race. Come savor the midwestern hospitality and variety. $40-135.

The Potter House

1906 7th Avenue, 61201
(309) 788-1906; (800) 747-0339

Enjoy a full breakfast in a 1907 solarium with arched windows framed by columns and a marble-tile floor. On the national register and in a historic neighborhood. Outstanding architectural features include stained glass, leather wall covering, six fireplaces, and grand staircase. Amenities include refreshments, in-room cable TV, and telephones. Walk to casino boat, dinner theater, and restaurants. Five-room historic guest cottage sleeps four in two bedrooms and has complete kitchen facilities. AAA three diamond rating.

Hosts: Gary and Nancy Pheiffer
Rooms: 5 (PB) $70-100

NOTES: Credit cards accepted: A MasterCard; B Visa; C American Express; D Discover; E Diners Club; F Other; 2 Personal checks accepted; 3 Lunch available; 4 Dinner available; 5 Open all year; 6 Pets welcome;

Cottage: 1
Full Breakfast
Credit Cards: A, B, C, D, E
Notes: 2, 5, 7, 9, 10, 11, 12, 13, 14

Top o' the Morning

1505 19th Avenue, 61201
(309) 786-3513

Sam and Peggy welcome guests to this brick mansion on the bluffs overlooking the Mississippi River. Fantastic view day or night. Three-acre wooded estate with winding drive, orchard, and gardens. Air-conditioned bedrooms, whirlpool tub, and natural fireplaces.

Hosts: Sam and Peggy Doak
Rooms: 3 (PB) $40-100
Full Breakfast
Credit Cards: None
Notes: 2, 5, 7, 8, 9, 10, 11, 12, 13

Victorian Inn Bed and Breakfast

702 20th Street, 61201
(309) 788-7068

Light from the windows of the stained-glass tower welcomes guests to Victorian Inn Bed and Breakfast. In the Broadway historic area near riverboat gambling and festival attractions. Antiques adorn the five spacious guest rooms with private baths. Close to Augustana College. Built with Old World charm in 1888. Step back in time to gracious living in this home listed on the National Register of Historic Places. Smoking permitted in designated areas.

Hosts: David and Barbara Parker
Rooms: 5 (PB) $55-75
Full Breakfast
Credit Cards: A, B
Notes: 2, 5, 8, 9, 10, 11, 12, 13, 14

SANDWICH

The Swanders' Inn

824 South Main Street, 60548
(815) 786-2335

The Swanders' Inn is open year-round to accommodate both the professional traveler as well as the tourist. Off-street parking is provided, and downtown Sandwich is within walking distance of restaurants, retail shops, antique stores, and the opera house. Also in close proximity is the fairgrounds, as well as golf courses and state parks. Four spacious guest rooms are available. A country-fresh breakfast is provided on weekends, and Continental breakfast is served on weekdays.

Hosts: John and Sharon Swander
Rooms: 4 (2 PB; 2 SB) $45-55
Full and Continental Breakfast
Credit Cards: None
Notes: 2, 5, 7, 9, 12, 14

WHEATON

The Wheaton Inn

301 West Roosevelt Road, 60187
(708) 690-2600; (800) 447-4667
FAX (708) 690-2623

The Wheaton Inn was built in 1987 to reflect America's Colonial Williamsburg. Offering 16 individually decorated guest rooms, all with private baths, several with Jacuzzi tubs and gas fireplaces. A homemade full country breakfast wakes guests in the morning, complimentary wine buffet soothes the afternoon, and freshly baked cookies with milk are offered before retiring. Biking, shopping, golf, and restaurants nearby. Only 25 miles west of Chicago. Romantic getaways.

Host: Debbie Castiglia
Rooms: 16 (PB) $99-195
Full Breakfast
Credit Cards: A, B, C, D, E
Notes: 2, 5, 8, 9, 10, 11, 12, 14

WINNETKA (CHICAGO)

Chateau des Fleurs

552 Ridge Road, 60093
(708) 256-7272

7 No smoking; 8 Children welcome; 9 Social drinking allowed; 10 Tennis nearby; 11 Swimming nearby; 12 Golf nearby; 13 Skiing nearby; 14 May be booked through a travel agent.

Chateau des Fleurs

Chateau des Fleurs is an elegant respite from the world that welcomes guests with light, beauty, warmth, and lovely views of magnificent trees, gardens, and a swim-ming pool. A French country home filled with antiques, four fireplaces, 50-inch TV, and a grand piano. By a private road for jogging or walking; only four blocks from shops and restaurants and a 30-minute train ride to Chicago's Loop. Ten minutes from Northwestern University. There is a FAX machine and each room has a private tele-phone line. Minimum stay of two nights. Children over 11 are welcome.

Host: Sally H. Ward
Rooms: 3 (PB) $95
Full Breakfast
Credit Cards: None
Notes: 2, 9, 10, 11, 12, 13, 14

Indiana

ANGOLA

Sycamore Hill Bed and Breakfast

1245 Golden Lake Road, 46703
(219) 665-2690

This two-story Colonial, pillared home was built in 1963 by master craftsmen. Tucked away amid 26 acres of rolling hills and woods. Great for bird watching. Shady back yard with two picnic tables at guests' disposal. Sumptuous breakfast. Gas grill in the back yard. Six minutes from Pokagon State Park beaches, nature trails, canoeing, and golfing.

Host: Betsey Goranson
Rooms: 4 (1 PB; 3 SB) $40-60
Full Breakfast
Credit Cards: A, B
Notes: 2, 5, 7, 8, 10, 11, 12, 13

BLOOMINGTON

Scholars Inn

801 North College Avenue, 47404
(812) 332-1892

The Scholars Inn is a restored, elegant brick mansion blending the past with the present for a warm and comfortable atmosphere. This 100-year-old styled mansion includes the finest in amenities. Five bedrooms have either king- or queen-size beds with pillow top mattresses. Private baths, two bathrooms feature Jacuzzi-style tubs.

Host: Nickky Jackson
Rooms: 5 (PB) $69-135
Continental Breakfast
Credit Cards: A, B, C
Notes: 2, 5, 6, 7, 9, 10, 11, 12, 13

BRISTOL

Tyler's Place Bed and Breakfast

19562 State Road 120, 19562
(219) 848-7145

Tyler's Place is in the heart of the Amish country, on a 27-hole golf course, with four rooms available. Guests can relax on the deck enjoying the outdoor water garden and the warm Hoosier hospitality. Full breakfast served. A back road tour to some outstanding Amish homes and stores is available. Three miles from I-80/90 Toll Road.

Host: Esther Tyler
Rooms: 4 (1 PB; 3 SB) $45-65
Full Breakfast
Credit Cards: A, B
Notes: 2, 5, 7, 8, 10, 11, 12, 13

CHESTERTON

Gray Goose Inn

350 Indian Boundary Road, 46304
(219) 926-5781; (800) 521-5127

Gray Goose Inn

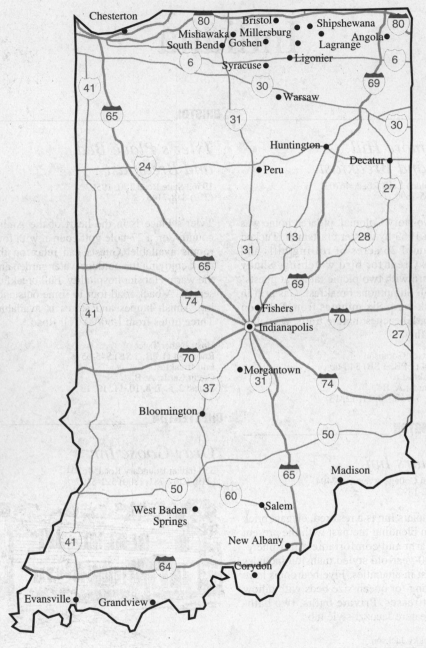

Middlebury

Chesterton

Bristol
Shipshewana
80
80

Mishawaka
Millersburg
Angola

South Bend
Goshen
Lagrange

41
6
Syracuse
Ligonier
6

30
69

65
31
30

24
Huntington

Peru
Decatur

27

13
28

31

65

69

74
Fishers

70

41
Indianapolis
27

70

Morgantown
31
74

37
Bloomington

50

65
Madison

50

West Baden
Salem
Springs
60

New Albany

41
Corydon

64

Evansville
Grandview

Indiana

English-style country house on 100 wooded acres overlooks a private lake. Walking trails, paddleboat. Minutes from Dunes State and National Lake Shore parks; 50 minutes from Chicago. Featured in *Country Inns*, 1994. Children over 12 welcome.

Hosts: Tim Wilk and Chuck Ramsey
Rooms: 8 (PB) $80-135
Full Breakfast
Credit Cards: A, B, C, D
Notes: 2, 5, 7, 9, 10, 11, 12, 13, 14

Indian Oak Resort and Spa

558 Indian Boundary Road, 46304
(219) 926-2200; (800) 552-4232

Nestled among tall oaks on private Lake Chubb, and forty-five minutes from Chicago, guests are just off the intersection of Interstate 94 and 49, close to Lake Michigan, Indian Dunes State Park, and Indiana National Lakeshore Park. Exceptional restaurants, hiking trails, dramatic sunsets, exquisite gardens, and more. Lovely woodside and lake-side rooms, professionally licensed full-service salon, fitness center with pool and whirlpool, live entertainment and comedy club. Meeting and conference space available.

Host: Catherine Chubb
Rooms: 100 (PB) $70-150
Continental Breakfast
Credit Cards: A, B, C, D, E
Notes: 2, 3, 4, 5, 7, 8, 9, 10, 11, 12, 13, 14

CORYDON

Kintner House Inn

101 South Capitol Avenue, 47112
(812) 738-2020

Completely restored inn, circa 1873, is a national historical landmark, with 15 rooms, each with private bath, telephone, color cable TV, five rooms with fireplaces, and seven rooms with VCRs, furnished in Victorian and country antiques. Serves full breakfast. Unique shops, fine restaurants,

antique malls, historic sites, museums, art glass factory, and excursion train all within walking distance of the inn. Sports available. Rated AAA and Mobil. A hideaway for romantics.

Host: Mary Jane Bridgwater
Rooms: 15 (PB) $39-89
Full Breakfast
Credit Cards: A, B, C, D, E
Notes: 2, 5, 7, 8, 9, 10, 11, 12, 14

DECATUR

Cragwood Inn Bed and Breakfast

303 North Second, 46733
(219) 728-2000

Cragwood Inn is a beautiful Queen Anne home with magnificent woodwork and beveled, leaded glass windows. Four porches. Four fireplaces. Original light fixtures. Wonderful flower gardens. Innovative weekends.

Hosts: George and Nancy Craig
Rooms: 4 (2 PB; 2 SB) $55-65
Full Breakfast
Credit Cards: A, B
Notes: 2, 5, 7, 9, 10, 11, 12, 14

EVANSVILLE

The River's Inn

414 Southeast Riverside Drive, 47713
(812) 428-7777; (800) 797-7990

A delightful 19th-century guest house tastefully restored with period antiques. The flower-bordered balconies overlook the Ohio River in downtown Evansville. A full breakfast offers gourmet dining freshly prepared each morning and served in the formal dining room in view of the Victorian garden. The guest rooms feature beds constructed in the 1800s with complementary pieces, Oriental rugs, lace, and fine linens. Bridal chamber available. Airport service, fax and copier service,

NOTES: Credit cards: A MasterCard; B Visa; C American Express; D Discover; E Diners Club; F Other; 2 Personal checks accepted; 3 Lunch available; 4 Dinner available; 5 Open all year; 6 Pets welcome; 7 No smoking; 8 Children welcome; 9 Social drinking allowed; 10 Tennis nearby; 11 Swimming nearby; 12 Golf nearby; 13 Skiing nearby; 14 May be booked through a travel agent.

private entrance, and off-street parking. Across the street from the museum in the historic district.

Hosts: Marsha and Allan Trockman
Rooms: 5 (PB) $75-135
Full Breakfast
Credit Cards: A, B, C
Notes: 2, 5, 7, 10, 14

FISHERS

The Frederick-Talbott Inn

13805 Allisonville Road, 46038
(317) 578-3600; (800) 566-2337

The Frederick-Talbott Inn consists of 11 individually styled guest rooms; each has a large private bath and television. A sumptuous full breakfast for two is included in the room rate. The inn exudes the luxury and comfort once reserved for a less hectic time. Tastefully appointed in 19th-century antiques, the establishment is a reflection of the innkeepers' gracious hospitality. The inn is six miles from Indianapolis, across the street from Conner Prairie Living History Museum.

Hosts: Susan Muller and Ann Irvine
Rooms: 11 (PB) $89-150
Full Breakfast
Credit Cards: A, B, C, D
Notes: 2, 5, 6, 8, 9, 12, 14

GOSHEN

The Checkerberry Inn

62644 County Road 37, 46526
(219) 642-4445

At the Checkerberry Inn, in the heart of northern Indiana Amish country, guests will find a unique atmosphere, different from anywhere else in the Midwest. Each individually decorated room has a breathtaking view of the unspoiled countryside. Outdoor pool, tennis court, and croquet green. Cycling, jogging, and walking area. Shopping and golf within ten to 15 minutes. Award-winning restaurant. Closed January.

Hosts: John and Susan Graff
Rooms: 14 (PB) $140-325
Continental Breakfast
Credit Cards: A, B, C
Notes: 2, 3, 4, 6, 7, 8, 9, 10, 11, 12, 14

Timberidge Bed and Breakfast

16801 State Road #4, 46526
(219) 533-7133

This Austrian Chalet white pine log home is nestled in the beauty of the quiet woods, just two miles from Goshen and near many points of interest. Sharing this serene setting, the hosts welcome guests to a gracious suite with a private bath and entrance. A Victorian bedroom set and other antique and other country furnishings make this hideaway comfortably elegant. Guests join the hosts in their large-windowed great room for breakfast.

Hosts: Edward and Donita Brookmyer
Master suite: 1 (PB) $60-80
Continental Breakfast
Credit Cards: None
Notes: 2, 5, 7, 5, 10, 11, 12, 13

Timberidge

GRANDVIEW

The River Belle

P.O. Box 669, 47615
(812) 649-2500; (800) 877-5165

Come to the River Belle for a little bit of Southern charm in southern Indiana on the

Jo Ann Ash

The River Belle

Ohio River. Guests may choose from one of three accommodations: an 1866 white-painted brick Steamboat-style, an 1890 red-brick Italianate, or the "little house under the pecan tree"—an 1860 cottage with full kitchen. Guests may choose to walk along the river or sit quietly and watch the white squirrels play among the magnolias, pecan trees, and azaleas. Within 20 miles of the Lincoln Boyhood National Memorial, Lincoln State Park, Lincoln drama, and Holiday World—the nation's oldest amusement park.

Hosts: Don and Pat Phillips
Rooms: 6 (2 PB; 4 SB) $45-65
Continental Breakfast
Credit Cards: A, B
Notes: 2, 5, 7, 8

HUNTINGTON

Purviance House

326 South Jefferson, 46750
(219) 356-9215; (219) 356-4218

Majestic Greek Revival-Italianate was built in 1859 and is listed on the National Register of Historic Places. Lovingly restored and decorated with period furnishings. Features include ornate plaster designs, solid cherry winding stairway, parquet floors, and four fireplaces with unique designs. In a safe, secure community near downtown, off-street parking and air conditioning are some amenities along with complimentary snacks and beverages.

Hosts: Robert and Jean Gernand
Rooms: 5 (2 PB; 3 SB) $45-65
Full Breakfast
Credit Cards: A, B, D
Notes: 2, 5, 7, 9, 10, 11, 12, 14

INDIANAPOLIS

Boone Docks on the River

7159 Edgewater Place, 46240
(317) 257-3671

A 1920s English Tudor home on the White River, just north of Broad Ripple Village, Boone Docks is a resort-like setting overlooking the river. Enjoy the comforts and charm of the River Room Suite, gracefully decorated in blue, white eyelet, and lace. A hearty breakfast is enjoyed seasonally in the sunroom or on the deck. Convenient to dining, entertainment, shopping, museums, antiquing, and many downtown attractions.

Hosts: Lynne and Mike Boone
Room: 1 (PB) $65
Full Breakfast
Credit Cards: C
Notes: 2, 5, 7, 8, 10, 11, 12

LAGRANGE

The 1886 Inn

212 Factory Street, 46761
(219) 463-4227

The 1866 Inn bed and breakfast is filled with historical charm and elegance and glows with old-fashioned beauty in every room. Finest lodging yet affordable, this inn is ten minutes from Shipshewana Flea Market. Continental plus breakfast served.

Hosts: Duane and Gloria Billman
Rooms: 3 (PB) $89
Continental Breakfast
Credit Cards: A, B
Notes: 2, 7, 10, 12

7 No smoking; 8 Children welcome; 9 Social drinking allowed; 10 Tennis nearby; 11 Swimming nearby; 12 Golf nearby; 13 Skiing nearby; 14 May be booked through a travel agent.

Solomon Mier Manor

LIGONIER

Solomon Mier Manor

508 South Cavin Street, 46767
(219) 894-3668

This Italian/Queen Anne Renaissance home was built in 1899. It has four guest rooms completely furnished in antique furniture of the period. Each room has its own private bath. This home is on the edge of Ligonier's business district, which is in an area that has been placed on the National Register of Historic Places. It contains some of the grandest architecture to be seen. It is minutes away from the Shipshewana flea market, Nappanee Amish Acres, Auburn-Cord Dusenburg Museum, Das Essenhause at Middlebury, and much more. Air conditioning. Additional $25 per extra person in room.

Hosts: Ron and Doris Blue
Rooms: 4 (PB) $55
Continental Breakfast
Credit Cards: A, B
Notes: 2, 5, 7, 12

MADISON

Main Street Bed and Breakfast

739 West Main Street, 47250
(812) 265-3539; (800) 362-6246

Graceful, classic, Revival home built circa 1843. Offering three tastefully decorated

guest rooms, all with private baths. Elegant atmosphere, yet relaxed and friendly. Within the historic district of Madison. A gentle walk to shops, restaurants, and the Ohio River. A perfect base for sampling southern Indiana and refreshing one's soul.

Hosts: Mark and Mary Balph
Rooms: 3 (PB) $85-135
Full Breakfast
Credit Cards: A, B
Notes: 2, 5, 9, 10, 11, 12, 13, 14

Schussler House Bed and Breakfast

514 Jefferson Street, 47250
(812) 273-2068; (800) 392-1931

Experience the quiet elegance of a circa 1849 Federal Greek Revival home tastefully combined with today's modern amenities. Madison's historic district, antique shops, restaurants, historic sites, and the Ohio River are within a pleasant walk. This gracious home offers spacious rooms decorated with antiques and reproductions and carefully selected fabrics and wall coverings. A sumptuous breakfast in the sun-filled dining room is a relaxing beginning to the day.

Hosts: Jill and Bill Gilbert
Rooms: 3 (PB) $90
Full Breakfast
Credit Cards: A, B, D
Notes: 2, 5, 7, 10, 11, 12, 13, 14

MIDDLEBURY

Bee Hive Bed and Breakfast

Box 1191, 46540
(219) 825-5023

Come home to the farm. Enjoy country life, snuggle under a handmade quilt, and wake to the smell of freshly baked muffins. In the heart of Amish country. Enjoy the shops, flea markets, and antique stores in the area. Right off the Indiana Turnpike. Guest cottage available.

Hosts: Herb and Treva Swarm
Rooms: 4 (1 PB; 3 SB) $52-68

NOTES: Credit cards accepted: A MasterCard; B Visa; C American Express; D Discover; E Diners Club; F Other; 2 Personal checks accepted; 3 Lunch available; 4 Dinner available; 5 Open all year; 6 Pets welcome;

Full Breakfast
Credit Cards: A, B
Notes: 2, 5, 7, 8, 10, 12, 13

Empty Nest Bed and Breakfast

13347 C.R. 12, 46540
(219) 825-1042

Four-level contemporary home is on a hillside overlooking two ponds—home to swans, geese, and ducks—gentle hills, woods, and flowered fields. Antique and craft gift shops, Shipshewana's famous 1,000 stall flea market and antique auction, Amish country, museums, parks, rivers, lakes, Goshen College, and Notre Dame are all nearby. Hosts will entertain guests with selections on the grand piano and can cook up a hearty breakfast. Secluded outdoor swimming pool. Guest rooms are newly furnished, including queen-size beds. Air-conditioned.

Hosts: Sherry and Tim Bryant
Rooms: 3 (1 PB; 2 SB) $60-70
Full Breakfast
Credit Cards: A, B
Notes: 2, 5, 9, 10, 11, 12, 13

Varns Guest House

205 South Main Street, P.O. Box 125, 46540
(219) 825-9666; (800) 398-5424

Varns Guest House

A circa 1898 house built by the innkeeper's great-grandparents, this home has been in the Varns family for over 100 years. Recently restored, it is in the heart of Amish country just three miles south of the Indiana toll road's Middlebury exit. There are five air-conditioned guest rooms, each with private bath and individually decorated and named after the hosts' ancestors. Relax on the wraparound porch or snuggle before a wood-burning fireplace in the parlor during cold weather. Area attractions include giant Shipshewana flea market, Amish communities, fine shops, and restaurants. Continental plus breakfast served.

Hosts: Carl and Diane Eash
Rooms: 5 (PB) $69
Continental Breakfast
Credit Cards: A, B, D
Notes: 2, 5, 7, 8, 9, 10, 11, 12, 14

MILLERSBURG

The Big House in the Little Woods

4245 South 1000 West, 46543
(219) 593-9076

Newly built 3500-square foot Colonial-style home in a quiet country setting is in the heart of a large Amish community. Three spacious guest rooms have TVs, some antique furniture, hand-made quilts, and air conditioning. Take a stroll down the quiet country road or relax in a guest room, living room, or in the quiet woods and watch for birds or woodland animals. Only nine miles to Shipshewana. Inquire about the accommodations available for children. Golf, swimming, and tennis are only ten miles away.

Hosts: Sarah and Jacob Stoltzfus
Rooms: 3 (PB) $60-70
Full Breakfast
Credit Cards: None
Notes: 2, 5, 7, 10, 11, 12

7 No smoking; 8 Children welcome; 9 Social drinking allowed; 10 Tennis nearby; 11 Swimming nearby; 12 Golf nearby; 13 Skiing nearby; 14 May be booked through a travel agent.

MISHAWAKA

The Beiger Mansion Inn Fables Gallery, Inc.

317 Lincoln Way East, 46544
(219) 256-0365; (800) 437-0131
FAX (219) 259-2622

The 22,000-square-foot inn offers gracious accommodations for travelers who appreciate its blend of historic and cultural personality. The romance and nostalgia of the mansion appeal to travelers, whether on holiday or business trip. Listed on the National Register of Historic Places. Close to South Bend and Notre Dame. Gift and art gallery on main level. Gourmet dining Friday and Saturday evenings; lunch Tuesday.

Hosts: Ron Montandon and Phil Robinson
Rooms: 7 (PB) $65-195
Full Breakfast
Credit Cards: A, B, C, D, E, F
Notes: 2, 5, 7, 9, 10, 11, 12, 14

MORGANTOWN

The Rock House

380 West Washington Street, P.O. Box 10, 46160
(812) 597-5100

Circa 1894, this unique landmark of Morgan County has delighted its guests with an exterior festooned with rocks, geodes, shells, and many other family souvenirs. Inside guests will find a homey atmosphere and antique furnishings. The hosts will gladly direct guests to such local attractions as Brown County State Park, Little Nashville Opry, Ski World, and the artist colony of Nashville, which hosts more than 200 shops just minutes from The Rock House. Lunch and dinner available by reservation only.

Rooms: 6 (PB) $75.90
Full Breakfast
Credit Cards: A, B, C, D
Notes: 2, 5, 7, 10, 11, 12, 13, 14

NEW ALBANY

Honeymoon Mansion

1014 East Main Street, 47150
(800) 759-7270

Honeymoon Mansion is a lovely Victorian antebellum home. It was built in 1850 and is a national historic landmark. The beautiful interior combined with Southern charm lets guests enjoy the serenity and romance of yesteryear. Six beautiful bedrooms, each with a lovely bath, await guests' enjoyment. Three suites have large marble Jacuzzis with eight-foot high marble columns. One suite has a fireplace and private entrance. The Ohio River can be seen from the penthouse suite. Ten minutes from Louisville. Smoking restricted.

Hosts: Franklin and Beverly Dennis
Rooms: 6 (PB) $68-135
Full Breakfast
Credit Cards: F
Notes: 2, 5, 9, 10, 11, 12, 13, 14

PERU

Rosewood Mansion Inn

54 North Hood, 46970
(317) 472-7151

Step back in time. The Rosewood Mansion is a beautiful Victorian home in the heart of Peru, a town rich in railroad and circus history. Built in 1872, it showcases an open grand staircase of tiger oak, beautiful stained-glass windows, gorgeous natural woodwork, large windows and bays overlooking beautiful grounds, an oak-paneled library, and antique furnishings. Enjoy the quiet, comfortable elegance, warm hospitality, and delicious breakfasts.

Hosts: Lynn and David Hausner
Rooms: 8 (PB) $70-85
Full Breakfast
Credit Cards: A, B, C, D
Notes: 2, 5, 7, 8, 9, 10, 11, 12, 14

NOTES: Credit cards accepted: A MasterCard; B Visa; C American Express; D Discover; E Diners Club; F Other; 2 Personal checks accepted; 3 Lunch available; 4 Dinner available; 5 Open all year; 6 Pets welcome;

SALEM

Lanning House and 1920 Annex

206 East Poplar Street, 47167
(812) 883-3484

This 1873 house and the 1920 Annex are 45 minutes from Louisville, Kentucky. They are a part of the John Hay Center, which included a museum and pioneer village. Hay was Lincoln's secretary and later secretary of state under Presidents William McKinley and Theodore Roosevelt. Genealogical researchers appreciate the museum library and the help the local people give them. Hikers and spelunkers like the Knobstone trails at Delany Park or caving at Spring Mill State Park.

Host: Mrs. Jeannette Hart
Rooms: 7 (4PB; 3SB) $30-60
Full Breakfast
Credit Cards: None
Notes: 2, 5, 7, 8, 10, 11, 12, 13

SHIPSHEWANA

Morton Street Bed and Breakfast

140 Morton Street, P.O. Box 775, 46565
(219) 768-4391; (800) 447-6475

In the heart of Amish country, guests will find themselves within walking distance of all kinds of shops and the famous Shipshewana flea market. Special winter and weekend rates available. Full breakfast Monday through Saturday, Continental breakfast on Sunday, and lunch and dinner available at the restaurant next door. Inquire about arrangements for children.

Hosts: Joel and Kim Mishler and Esther Mishler
Rooms: 10 (PB)
Full and Continental Breakfasts
Credit Cards: A, B, D
Notes: 2, 5, 7, 8, 12, 13, 14

SOUTH BEND

The Book Inn

508 West Washington Street, 46601
(219) 288-1990

Second Empire home in downtown South Bend. Designers' showcase—every room beautifully decorated. Fresh flowers, silver, fine china, and candlelight. The hosts emphasize service for the business person as well as leisured guests. The inn also houses a quality used bookstore, and guest rooms include the Louisa May Alcott, Jane Austen, and Charlotte Brontë rooms. Corporate rates available.

Hosts: Peggy and John Livingston
Rooms: 5 (PB) $65-80
Continental Breakfast
Credit Cards: A, B, C
Notes: 2, 5, 7, 9, 10, 11, 12, 14

Queen Anne Inn

Queen Anne Inn

420 West Washington Street, 46601
(219) 234-5959; (800) 582-2379

The Queen Anne Inn, an 1893 Victorian home listed on the historic register, is famous for the Frank Lloyd Wright bookcases and leaded glass. Antiques are used throughout the house. The inn is three blocks from downtown South Bend, near Notre Dame and Oliver House Museum. Relax and step back into the past.

Hosts: Bob and Pauline Medhurst
Rooms: 5 (PB) $65-100
Full Breakfast
Credit Cards: A, B, C
Notes: 2, 5, 7, 8, 10, 11, 12, 13, 14

7 No smoking; 8 Children welcome; 9 Social drinking allowed; 10 Tennis nearby; 11 Swimming nearby;
12 Golf nearby; 13 Skiing nearby; 14 May be booked through a travel agent.

Anchor Inn

SYRACUSE

Anchor Inn
Bed and Breakfast

11007 North State Road 13, 46567
(219) 457-4714

Anchor Inn is a turn-of-the-century, two-story home filled with period furniture and antiques. Features of the home include claw-foot tub, pier mirror, transomed doorways, hardwood floors, and a large, inviting front porch that overlooks the greens of an 18-hole public golf course. Halfway between South Bend and Fort Wayne in Indiana's lake region and directly across the highway from Lake Wawasee (Indiana's largest natural lake). Nearby attractions include the Amish communities of Nappanee and Shipshewana, several antique shops, flea markets, two live theater groups, stern-wheeler paddleboat rides, 101 lakes in Kosciusko County, and a 3,400-acre game preserve. Air-conditioned.

Hosts: Robert and Jean Kennedy
Rooms: 8 (5 PB; 3 SB) $50-65
Full Breakfast
Credit Cards: A, B, D
Notes: 2, 5, 7, 11, 12

WARSAW

Candlelight Inn

503 East Ft. Wayne, 46580
(219) 267-2906; (800) 352-0640

The Candlelight Inn is in a small town where guests can enjoy two lakes within walking distance as well as one of Indiana's finest gardens down the block. The inn is decorated in warm Victorian style with antiques, comfortable beds, and private baths in each room. Warm cookies, a turned-down bed, and soft, glowing candles await guests as they return to their rooms each night. Breakfast is served in the dining room in elegant fashion with delicious homemade creations. The inn serves the visitor on vacation or corporate guests. Telephones and TV in each room, along with a fax for the business traveler.

Hosts: Bill and Debi Hambright
Rooms: 10 (PB) $69-130
Full Breakfast
Credit Cards: A, B, C
Notes: 2, 5, 9, 10, 11, 12, 14

White Hill Manor

2513 East Center Street, 46580
(219) 269-6933; FAX (219) 268-2260

The White Hill Manor is a restored English Tudor mansion with eight elegant bedrooms, private baths, phones, desks, TVs, air conditioning, and conference room. Luxurious suite with double Jacuzzi bath. Full breakfast. Adjacent to Wagon Wheel Theatre, lake recreation, and antique shops. Historically renovated in 1988. Direct access to US 30.

Manager: Gladys Deloe
Rooms: 7 (PB) $80-110
Suite: 1 (PB) $99-120
Credit Cards: A, B, C, D
Notes: 2, 5, 7, 8, 10, 11, 12

WEST BADEN SPRINGS

E. B. Rhodes House
Bed and Breakfast

Box 7, 47469
(812) 936-7378

A spacious first edition home, built in 1901 with beautiful hand-carved woodwork and

---

NOTES: Credit cards accepted: A MasterCard; B Visa; C American Express; D Discover; E Diners Club;
F Other; 2 Personal checks accepted; 3 Lunch available; 4 Dinner available; 5 Open all year; 6 Pets welcome;

stained-glass windows. Two large porches complete with rockers for guests to enjoy southern Indiana vistas and just plain relaxing. Entertainment for all seasons and tastes includes gracious dining, historical tours, steam locomotive rides, antiquing, museums, and theater. For the more adventurous there is water or snow skiing, nearby state parks, and caving. Smoking restricted.

Hosts: Frank and Marlene Sipes; Tom
   and Tina Hilgediek
Rooms: 2 (PB) $35-45
Full Breakfast
Credit Cards: A B
Notes: 2, 5, 8, 10, 11, 12, 13

7 No smoking; 8 Children welcome; 9 Social drinking allowed; 10 Tennis nearby; 11 Swimming nearby; 12 Golf nearby; 13 Skiing nearby; 14 May be booked through a travel agent.

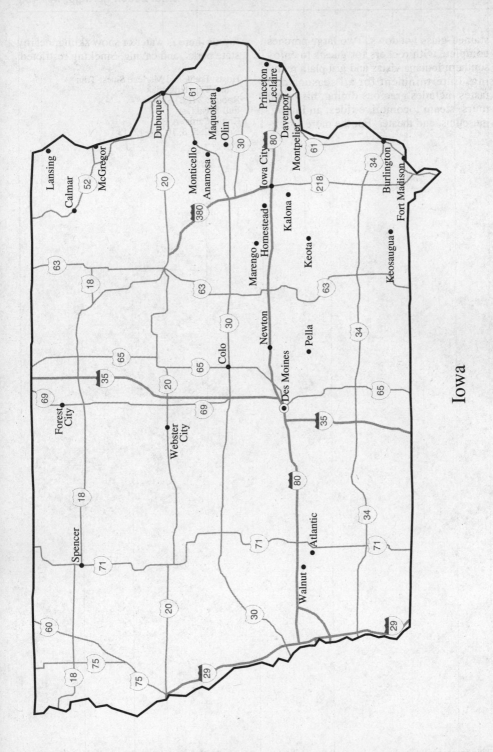

Iowa

The Shaw House

ANAMOSA

The Shaw House

509 South Oak, 52205
(319) 462-4485

Enjoy a relaxing step back in time in this three-story, 1866 Italianate mansion on a hilltop overlooking scenery immortalized in the paintings of native son Grant Wood. Special rooms include porch with panoramic countryside view, two-room tower suite, and ballroom. The mansion is on a 45-acre farm within easy walking distance of town. State park, antique shops, and canoeing are nearby.

Hosts: Connie and Andy McKean
Rooms: 4 (3 PB; 1 SB) $45-75
Full Breakfast
Credit Cards: None
Notes: 2, 3, 4, 5, 7, 8, 9, 10, 11, 12, 13, 14

ATLANTIC

Chestnut Charm Bed and Breakfast

1409 Chestnut Street, 50022
(712) 243-5652

An enchanting 1898 Victorian historic mansion with serene surroundings. Experience beauty, pleasure, and fantasy with someone special or enjoy a wonderful respite in a busy travel schedule. Relax and enjoy the tranquility! Elegant guest rooms with private baths. Exquisite gourmet meals with advance reservations. Awaken to the aroma of gourmet coffee and home baking. Experience gracious Iowa hospitality. Short drive to the famous bridges of Madison County. Air-conditioned. One suite is also available.

Host: Barbara Stensvad
Rooms: 5 (PB) $65-95
Full Breakfast
Credit Cards: A, B
Notes: 2, 5, 7, 10, 11, 12, 14

BURLINGTON

The Schramm House Bed and Breakfast

616 Columbia Street, 52601
(319) 754-0373

Step into the past when entering this restored 1870s Victorian in the heart of the historical district. High ceilings, parquet floors, wainscoting, original oak

---

NOTES: Credit cards: A MasterCard; B Visa; C American Express; D Discover; E Diners Club; F Other;
2 Personal checks accepted; 3 Lunch available; 4 Dinner available; 5 Open all year; 6 Pets welcome;
7 No smoking; 8 Children welcome; 9 Social drinking allowed; 10 Tennis nearby; 11 Swimming nearby;
12 Golf nearby; 13 Skiing nearby; 14 May be booked through a travel agent.

woodwork, and antique furnishings create the mood of an era past. Experience Burlington hospitality while having lemonade on the porch or tea by the fire with the gracious hosts. Walk to the Mississippi River, restaurants, and antique shops. An architectural masterpiece awaits guests in the City of Steeples. Smoking restricted.

Hosts: Sandy and Bruce Morrison
Rooms: 2 (PB) $65-75
Full Breakfast
Credit Cards: A, B
Notes: 2, 5, 9, 10, 11, 12

CALMAR

Calmar Guesthouse

103 West North Street, 52132
(319) 562-3851

Newly remodeled Victorian home in northeast Iowa with many antiques, near Luther College and the newly accredited NICC (Northeast Iowa Community College, formerly Northeast Iowa Technical Institute). Close to world-famous Bily Clocks in Spillville, Niagara Cave, Lake Meye. Air-conditioned. Wake up to a fresh country breakfast. Good variety of restaurants in the area. Bike trail one block away. Smoking restricted.

Hosts: Lucille Kruse
Rooms: 5 (1 PB; 4 SB) $45-50
Full Breakfast
Credit Cards: A, B
Notes: 2, 5, 8, 9, 10, 11, 12, 13

COLO

Martha's Vineyard Bed and Breakfast

620 West Street, 50056
(515) 377-2586

This bed and breakfast is a working farm on the edge of town just 15 minutes east of US 35 on Highway 30. This 1920 fourth-generation family home has been lovingly restored and is furnished with

antiques and collectibles throughout. Homemade and homegrown food is served. A wildlife area and an old-fashioned flower garden add quiet beauty. Open May through October. The hostess is a retired home economics teacher. Just like a visit to Grandma's house.

Hosts: Norb and Martha Kash
Rooms: 2 (PB) $45-50
Full Breakfast
Credit Cards: None
Notes: 2, 7, 8, 9, 10, 11, 12, 14

DAVENPORT

Bed and Breakfasts of the QCA Room Availability Cooperative

P.O. Box 3464, Rock Island, IL, 61201
(319) 322-5055

This owners association has information on 12 bed and breakfasts on both sides of the Mississippi River in the Iowa and Illinois Quad Cities. This includes Davenport; Rock Island, Illinois; and the surrounding areas. Selections range from modern to historic, rural to urban, and even a train caboose. Cruise the river, sample the local festivals and museums, ride the bike trails, or run the Bix 7 Race. Come savor Midwestern hospitality and variety. $40-135.

Fulton's Landing Guest House

1206 East River Drive, 52803
(319) 322-4069

The old Fulton mansion is a large Italianate stone residence built in 1871 by Ambrose Cowperthwaite Fulton. Listed on the National Register of Historic Places, the home offers a majestic view of the Mississippi River and is only minutes away from all area attractions. Five bedrooms are available for guests. A full breakfast is served in the dining room. Two large

NOTES: Credit cards accepted: A MasterCard; B Visa; C American Express; D Discover; E Diners Club; F Other; 2 Personal checks accepted; 3 Lunch available; 4 Dinner available; 5 Open all year; 6 Pets welcome;

Fulton's Landing Guest House

porches overlook the river, one on the main floor, and the other on the second floor with easy access from all the bedrooms. On Route 67 near downtown Davenport.

Hosts: Pat and Bill Schmidt
Rooms: 5 (3 PB; 2 SB) $55-100
Full Breakfast
Credit Cards: A, B, C
Notes: 2, 5, 8, 9, 12

DES MOINES

Carter House Inn

640 20th Street, 50314
(515) 288-7850

Built in the late 1870s, this Italianate was moved from its original site in 1988 to save it from demolition. In the Sherman Hill historic district, this bed and breakfast features original stenciling and faux marble fireplaces. Guest rooms have private or shared baths with claw-foot tubs. Breakfast is served in the formal dining room.

Host: Penny Schlitz
Rooms: 4 (2 PB; 2 SB) $50-60
Full Breakfast
Credit Cards: A, B
Notes: 2, 4, 5, 7, 12, 14

Ellendale Bed and Breakfast

5340 Ashworth Road, 50266 (W.D.M.)
(515) 225-2219

Ellendale combines Old World Scandinavian decor and hospitality with established old farmstead setting and gardens. A short distance from I-80 and I-35, Ellendale is conveniently near Living History Farms, historic and creatively restored Valley Junction (Iowa's antique capital), and a major mall. Des Moines offers many cultural events, beautiful parks and churches, botanical art, and historical centers. Three-room suite plus fireplace and garden room.

Hosts: Ellen and Dale Jackson
Rooms: 2 (PB) $60-70
Full Breakfast
Credit Cards: None
Notes: 2, 5, 7, 8, 10, 11, 12

DUBUQUE

Juniper Hill Farm

15325 Budd Road, 52002
(319) 582-4405; (800) 572-1449
FAX (319) 583-6607

Beautiful country setting on 40 acres of woods with walking trails and a stocked pond. Adjacent to Sundown Ski Area (the only bed and breakfast in Iowa where guests can ski to the front door); ride to Heritage Bicycle Trail. Comfortably and restfully appointed with country atmosphere and some antiques. All rooms have private baths, one with whirlpool, and all rooms have access to an eight-foot outdoor hot tub.

Hosts: Ruth and Bill McEllhiney
Rooms: 3 (PB) $70-140
Full Breakfast
Credit Cards: A, B, D
Notes: 2, 5, 7, 8, 9, 12, 13, 14

The Mandolin Inn

199 Loras Boulevard, 52001
(319) 556-0069; (800) 524-7996 (reservations)

7 No smoking; 8 Children welcome; 9 Social drinking allowed; 10 Tennis nearby; 11 Swimming nearby; 12 Golf nearby; 13 Skiing nearby; 14 May be booked through a travel agent.

The Mandolin Inn

A 1908 Queen Anne Victorian that considers the comfort and pleasure of its guests to be its most important responsibility. A three-course breakfast is served in an oak dining room with a fantasy forest oil painting. Bed chambers have fabulously comfortable queen-size beds with down comforters and period antiques. During the summer the veranda is filled with wicker furniture.

Host: Jan Oswald
Rooms: 8 (4 PB; 4 SB) $65-110
Full Breakfast
Credit Cards: A, B, C, D
Notes: 2, 5, 7, 8, 9, 10, 11, 12, 13, 14

The Richards House Bed and Breakfast

1492 Locust Street, 52001
(319) 557-1492

Relax in this 1883 stick-style Victorian mansion with original interior, over 80 stained-glass windows, eight working fireplaces, embossed wall coverings, period furnishings, eight varieties of varnished woodwork, and more. Most rooms include working fireplaces, concealed TVs, and telephones. A full breakfast is served in the formal dining room. Easy access with plenty of parking.

Host: Michelle Delaney
Rooms: 5 (4 PB; 1 SB) $40-85
Full Breakfast
Credit Cards: A, B, C, D, E
Notes: 2, 5, 8, 9, 10, 11, 12, 13, 14

FOREST CITY

1897 Victorian House Bed and Breakfast and Antiques

306 South Clark, 50436
(515) 582-3613

The 1897 house is a Queen Anne Victorian style, furnished in period furniture, much of which is for sale. The aroma of coffee and a four-course breakfast awaken guests each morning. House is available for weddings, showers, dinners, teas, and weekend retreats. Antique shop. Air conditioned.

Hosts: Richard and Doris Johnson
Rooms: 5 (PB) $60-80
Full Breakfast
Credit Cards: A, B
Notes: 2, 5, 7, 11, 12, 14

FORT MADISON

Kingsley Inn

707 Avenue H on Highway 61, 52627
(319) 372-7074; (800) 441-2327

Yesterday's charm and today's luxury describe this historic Victorian inn on the Mississippi River. Enjoy lunch and dinner at Alpha's, the unique in-house theme restaurant. Walk to the faithfully restored 1808 Old Fort Madison, Train Depot

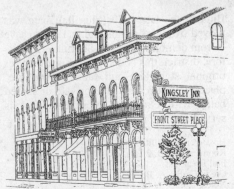

Kingsley Inn

Museum, Steam Engine, unique shops, the Flood Museum, the Riverboat Casino, and galleries. Stately 19th-century residential district is nearby, and guests are a ten-minute drive to historic Nauvoo, Illinois, which has been called the "Williamsburg of the Midwest," with 40 restored 1840s shops and homes. Rooms have private baths, some have whirlpools. cable TV, air conditioning, telephones, sprinklers, and alarms. Elevator and fax machine available.

Host: Myrna Reinhard
Rooms: 14 (PB) $70-115
Continental Breakfast
Credit Cards: A, B, C, D, E
Notes: 2, 3, 4, 5, 7, 9, 14

HOMESTEAD (AMANA COLONIES)

Die Heimat Country Inn

Main Street, Homestead, 52236
(319) 622-3937

Die Heimat, German for "the home place," is a century-old 1854 historic inn with 19 rooms, all furnished with Amana walnut and cherry furniture, private baths, TVs, and air conditioning. Colony heirlooms are found throughout the inn. Some rooms have Amana walnut canopied beds. Nature trail, golf course, wineries, woolen mills, and restaurants are all nearby. Murder mystery evenings available. Cash, traveler's checks, or personal checks preferred. Cross-country skiing.

Hosts: Warren and Jacki Lock
Rooms: 19 (PB) $42.95-65.95
Full Breakfast
Credit Cards: A, B, D
Notes: 2, 5, 6, 8, 9, 10, 11, 12, 13 (cross-country)

IOWA CITY

Bella Vista Place
Bed and Breakfast

2 Bella Vista, 52245
(319) 338-4129

The hostess has furnished this lovely 1920s home with antiques and artifacts she acquired on travels in Europe and Latin America. Downtown Iowa City and the University of Iowa are within walking distance. The Hoover Library, Amana Colonies, and the Amish center of Kalona are all nearby. Breakfast consisting of coffee, tea, juice, fresh fruit, croissants, muffins, bagels, and eggs is served in the dining room's unique antique setting. Tennis courts and a pool are nearby in city park. One mile south of I-80 at exit 244.

Host: Daissy P. Owen
Rooms: 3 (1 PB; 2 SB) $55-65
Full Breakfast
Credit Cards: None
Notes: 2, 5, 7, 8, 9, 10, 11, 12, 14

The Golden Haug

517 East Washington Street, 52240
(319) 338-6452

Elegance and whimsy decorate this 1920 arts and crafts house. Guests can retreat to one of four suites with in-room private bath or enjoy camaraderie of other guests. A full breakfast is served family-style. Relax on the porch swing, munch on sweets from the candy bowl, soak in the whirlpool or birthday bath, and enjoy tasty evening dessert in air-conditioned comfort. In the heart of Iowa City within a couple of blocks of the University of Iowa, eateries, and shopping.

Hosts: Nila Haug and Dennis Nowotny
Suites: 4 (PB) $68-95
Full Breakfast
Credit Cards: None
Notes: 2, 5, 8, 9, 10, 11, 12, 14

Haverkamps' Linn
Street Homestay

619 North Linn Street, 52245
(319) 337-4363

A large and comfortable 1908 Edwardian-style home filled with antiques and collectibles. Wonderful front porch with

---

7 No smoking; 8 Children welcome; 9 Social drinking allowed; 10 Tennis nearby; 11 Swimming nearby; 12 Golf nearby; 13 Skiing nearby; 14 May be booked through a travel agent.

old-fashioned swing. Walking distance to University of Iowa campus and the downtown area. Only a short drive to the Amana Villages, Kalona, Hoover Museum in West Branch, and Cedar Rapids. One mile south of I-80 at exit 244.

Hosts: Clarence and Dorothy Haverkamp
Rooms: 3 (SB) $35-45
Full Breakfast
Credit Cards: None
Notes: 2, 5, 7, 8, 9, 10, 11, 12, 13, 14

KALONA

Raspberry Patch

2325 Highway 1 SW, 52247
(319) 683-2403

A country bed and breakfast near the Mennonite and Amish settlement of Kalona that is noted for its Old World methods of living and farming, quilts, crafts, historic village, antiques, bakery, and homemade noodles. Scrumptious homemade applesauce, raspberry treats, and sourdough bread will tempt guests' palates. Enjoy the birds and flowers, play horseshoes, or watch TV. Swing set and sandbox available. University of Iowa with its hospitals and clinics is nearby.

Hosts: Emery and Helen Kleinschmidt
Rooms: 2 (SB) $40-50
Full Breakfast
Credit Cards: None
Notes: 2, 7, 8, 9, 11, 12

KEOSAUQUA

Mason House Inn of Bentonsport

Route 2, Box 237, 52565
(800) 592-3133

The Mason House Inn was built in 1846, the year Iowa became a state, by Mormon craftsmen making their famous trek to Utah. It is the oldest steamboat river inn still serving overnight guests in the Mid-

Mason House Inn

west. The inn has the only fold-down copper bathtub in the state. Oral tradition has it that John C. Frémont, Abraham Lincoln, and Mark Twain slept here. The entire village is on the National Register of Historic Places. Guests will find a full cookie-jar in every room. AAA approved.

Hosts: Sheral and William McDermet III
Rooms: 9 (5 PB; 4 SB) $49-74
Full Breakfast
Credit Cards: A, B
Notes: 2, 3, 4, 5, 7, 8, 9, 11, 12

KEOTA

Elmhurst

1994 Keokuk Washington Road, 52248
(515) 636-3001

This 1905 Victorian mansion was built with no expense spared by Thomas Singmaster. The family was the world's largest importer of draft horses. The mansion retains much of its original grandeur: prismed stained-glass and curved windows, circular solarium, parquet floors, beamed ceilings, Italian marble fireplace mantels, third floor ballroom, beveled plate-glass windows, two grand stairways, leather wall coverings, and much more. The house is filled with history and antiques. Golf course, swimming, and 14-mile nature trail nearby. Closed January and February. Smoking restricted.

Host: Marjie Schantz-Koehler
Rooms: 5 (SB) $42
Full Breakfast
Credit Cards: None
Notes: 2, 3, 4, 9, 10, 11, 12

NOTES: Credit cards accepted: A MasterCard; B Visa; C American Express; D Discover; E Diners Club; F Other; 2 Personal checks accepted; 3 Lunch available; 4 Dinner available; 5 Open all year; 6 Pets welcome;

LANSING

FitzGerald's Inn
Bed and Breakfast

160 North 3rd Street, 52151
(319) 538-4872

This antique-filled Victorian home, circa 1863, is in scenic northeast Iowa. Five bedrooms and four baths (one large suite) available. Spacious grounds rise to a bluff-top screened gazebo overlooking the Mississippi River at one of its most beautiful stretches. A delicious full breakfast is served each morning featuring home-baked goods, fresh fruit, and various breakfast items. Whole house rental available.

Hosts: Marie and Jeff FitzGerald
Rooms: 5 (3 PB; 2 SB) $60-75
Full Breakfast
Credit Cards: None
Notes: 2, 5, 7, 8, 9, 10, 11, 12, 13, 14

LECLAIRE

Monarch Bed and Breakfast
Inn and McCaffrey House
Bed and Breakfast

303 South Second Street, 52753
(319) 289-3011; (800) 772-7724

The Monarch Bed and Breakfast Inn, circa 1850, and the McCaffrey House Bed and Breakfast (circa 1870) are working together to provide guests with ideal settings for relaxation, meetings, and retreats. Wooden floors, high ceilings, and antique furniture help the home retain its original charm while air conditioning, enclosed porches, open decks, and off-street parking provide modern-day comforts. Magnificent Mississippi River views, river cruises, antique shopping, and Buffalo Bill Museum all await guests in LeClaire.

Hosts: David and Emilie Oltman; Jean Duncan
Rooms: 7 (4 PB; 3 SB) $40-55

Full and Continental Breakfasts
Credit Cards: None
Notes: 2, 5, 7, 8, 12, 14

MAQUOKETA

Squiers Manor
Bed and Breakfast

418 West Pleasant, 52060
(319) 652-6961

Awaken to the aroma of homemade goodies and elegant entrees in this historic Queen Anne brick mansion, circa 1882, with period furnishings. Eight elegant guest rooms including three suites, single and double whirlpools. Candlelight evening dessert. Crackling fireplaces. All this in a quiet, romantic, and friendly atmosphere.

Hosts: Virl and Kathy Banowetz
Rooms: 8 (PB) $75-195
Full Breakfast
Credit Cards: A, B, C
Notes: 2, 5, 8, 9, 10, 11, 12, 13, 14

MARENGO

Loy's Farm
Bed and Breakfast

2077 KK Avenue, 52301
(319) 642-7787

In the heartland of Iowa, this corn and hog farm has a recreation room and outdoor enjoyment with play equipment for all ages. Full breakfast with homemade products. Close to Amana Colonies, Iowa City, and Cedar Rapids. Designer outlet mall and golf courses nearby. Close to I-80. Farm tour and hunting. Three miles off I-80, exit 216N. Inquire about accommodations for pets.

Hosts: Loy and Robert Walker
Rooms: 3 (1 PB; 1 SB) $50-60
Full Breakfast
Credit Cards: None
Notes: 2, 4, 5, 8, 9, 10, 11, 12, 14

7 No smoking; 8 Children welcome; 9 Social drinking allowed; 10 Tennis nearby; 11 Swimming nearby; 12 Golf nearby; 13 Skiing nearby; 14 May be booked through a travel agent.

McGREGOR

River's Edge Bed and Breakfast

112 Main Street, 52157
(319) 873-3501

McGregor's premiere waterfront location. Cozy comfortable rooms overlooking the Mississippi River. Fully equipped kitchen and dining room for guest use. Each guest room has a private bath and cable TV. Spacious family room, patio, screened porch, and a second-level deck. Central air. Unique antique shopping, quaint restaurants, riverboat gambling, and various recreational activities can be found in this area. Come for a special getaway.

Host: Rita Lange
Rooms: 3 (PB) $50
Continental Breakfast
Credit Cards: A, B
Notes: 2, 5, 8, 9, 10, 11, 12, 13

MONTPELIER

Varners' Caboose Bed and Breakfast

204 East 2nd, P.O. Box 10, 52759
(319) 381-3652

Stay in a real Rock Island Lines caboose. Set on its own track behind the hosts' house, the caboose is a self-contained unit, with bath, shower, and complete kitchen. It sleeps four, with a queen-size bed and two twins in the cupola. There is color TV, central air and heat, plus plenty of off-street parking. A fully prepared country breakfast is left in the caboose kitchen to be enjoyed by guests whenever they choose. On Route 22, halfway between Davenport and Muscatine.

Hosts: Bob and Nancy Varner
Room: 1 (PB) $55
Full Breakfast
Credit Cards: None
Notes: 2, 5, 6, 7, 8, 9

MONTICELLO

The Blue Inn

250 North Main, 52310
(319) 465-6116

The Blue Inn and adjoining restaurant, The Blue Chip, create quite the fortuitous pair. There are 11 regular rooms with queen-size beds, two chairs, a vanity separate from the bathroom, a table, and a 20-inch color, remote controlled TV. One executive suite includes a queen-size canopied bed, a sitting area with a couch and two cozy chairs, and a large table, along with all of the other features in the standard rooms. The restaurant offers over 75 items to choose from. Skiing is 30 miles away.

Hosts: Bobby Tuetken
Rooms: 12 (PB) $38.95
Continental Breakfast
Credit Cards: A, B, C, D
Notes: 2, 3, 4, 5, 6, 7, 9, 10, 11, 12, 14

NEWTON

La Corsette Maison Inn

629 First Avenue East, 50208
(515) 792-6833

This opulent, mission-style mansion built in 1909 by Iowa state senator August Bergman maintains the charm of its original oak woodwork, art nouveau stained- glass windows, brass light fixtures, and even some original furnishings. Despite the addition of contemporary comforts, the bed chambers' original features have been retained—the beveled glass windows in the penthouse and the French country decor in the renovated servant's quarters. Downfilled pillows and comforters. Enjoy Kay's special hot spiced wine in front of one of three fireplaces. Be prepared for a delectable breakfast served in the gracious tradition of La Corsette. Pets and children welcomed by prior arrangements only.

NOTES: Credit cards accepted: A MasterCard; B Visa; C American Express; D Discover; E Diners Club; F Other; 2 Personal checks accepted; 3 Lunch available; 4 Dinner available; 5 Open all year; 6 Pets welcome;

Host: Kay Owen
Rooms: 9 (PB) $70-185
Full Breakfast
Credit Cards: A, B, C
Notes: 2, 4, 6, 7, 9, 10, 11, 12, 13, 14

PELLA

Avongloren (Sunset View)

984 198th Place, 50219-7845
(515) 628-1578

This bed and breakfast is in a quiet area on the southwest edge of Pella near the new golf course, Red Rock Lake, and on the bike trail. Amenities include central air, a room with fireplace, and a TV. True to Dutch heritage it has live plants in the home and flowers outside. A back deck for guests' use has a lovely view. A home away from home. A sumptuous Dutch breakfast is served.

Hosts: Henry and Luella Bandstra
Rooms: 3 (3 S1B) $45-55
Full Breakfast
Credit Cards: None
Notes: 2, 5, 7, 12

PRINCETON

The Woodlands

P.O. Box 127, 52768
(319) 289-3177; (319) 289-4661

A secluded woodland escape that can be as private or social as guests wish. The Wood-

The Woodlands

lands bed and breakfast is nestled among pines on 26 acres of forest and meadows in a private wildlife refuge. Guests delight in an elegant breakfast by the swimming pool or by a cozy fireplace while viewing the outdoor wildlife activity. Boating and fishing on the Mississippi River, cross-country skiing, golfing, and hiking are available. A short drive to the Quad City metropolitan area, shopping, art galleries, museums, theater, restaurants, and sporting events. Smoking restricted.

Hosts: Betsy Wallace and E. Lindebraekke
Rooms: 3 (2 PB; 1 SB) $75-115
Full Breakfast
Credit Cards: None
Notes: 2, 3, 4, 5, 8, 9, 10, 11, 12, 13, 14

SPENCER

Hannah Marie Country Inn

4070 Highway 71, 51301
(712) 262-1286; (800) 792-1286
FAX (712) 262-3294

Two lovingly restored farm homes offer a hearty gourmet breakfast. Guests are pampered with private baths, air conditioning, softened water, double whirlpools, or clawfoot tubs. Lunch available Wednesday through Saturday. Iowa Great Lakes 20 miles away. Large herb garden and croquet court. Closed December through April.

Host: Mary Nichols
Rooms: 5 (PB) $50-87
Full Breakfast
Credit Cards: A, B, C, D
Notes: 2, 4, 6, 7, 8, 10, 11, 12, 14

WALNUT

Antique City Inn Bed and Breakfast

P.O. Box 584, 400 Antique City Drive, 51577
(712) 784-3722

This 1911 Victorian home has a wraparound porch, beautiful woodwork, French doors, butler pantry, and dumbwaiter ice

7 No smoking; 8 Children welcome; 9 Social drinking allowed; 10 Tennis nearby; 11 Swimming nearby; 12 Golf nearby; 13 Skiing nearby; 14 May be booked through a travel agent.

box. One block from antique shops with 250 antique dealers, turn-of-the-century brick streets, storefronts, globed street lights, historical museum, and a restored opera house. Home of a country music museum and Iowa's Country Music Hall of Fame. Children over 12 welcome.

Host: Sylvia Reddie
Rooms: 5 (1 PB; 4 SB) $40
Full Breakfast
Credit Cards: A, B
Notes: 2, 3, 4, 5, 7, 9, 14

WEBSTER CITY

Centennial Farm Bed and Breakfast

1091 220th Street, Rural Route 2, 50595-7571
(515) 832-3050

Built in 1869, parts of the original homestead and barns have been incorporated into the air-conditioned farmhouse, which is among fields of corn and soybeans. The hosts are fourth-generation farmers here, and Tom was born in the downstairs bedroom. Guests can see the farm operation and Tom's 1929 Model A Ford pickup. Close to golf, tennis, swimming, antiques, parks, and fine dining. Just 22 miles west of I-35 at exit 142 or 144.

Hosts: Tom and Shirley Yungclas
Rooms: 2 (SB) $35
Full Breakfast
Credit Cards: None
Notes: 2, 5, 8, 9, 10, 11, 12

Kansas

Balfours' House

ABILENE

Balfours' House

940 1900 Avenue, 67410
(913) 263-4262

Modern, cottage-style home set on a hillside, on just over two acres. Guests have a private entrance into the family room, which includes a fireplace, piano, and TV. The main attraction is a hexagonal recreation room with a swimming pool, spa, and dressing area with shower. The hosts will gladly direct guests to the Eisenhower Museum, Greyhound Hall of Fame, and old historic mansions. A separate bungalow is also available.

Hosts: Gil and Marie Balfour
Suites: 2 (PB) $65
Full Breakfast
Credit Cards: A, B, C
Notes: 2, 5, 6, 7, 8, 9, 11

Windmill Inn

1787 Rain Road, Chapman, 67431
(913) 263-8755

Windmill Inn is a Prairie-style, four-square home built in 1917. Surrounded by acres of farm ground and nestled near historic Abilene, this bed and breakfast inn re-creates the charm of a bygone era. Special attention has been given to every detail of the restoration, down to the beautiful oak woodwork and brilliant stained and beveled glass in the common areas. The wraparound front porch lures guests to enjoy the sights and sounds of country life while relaxing in a porch swing or rocking chair, or enjoy the stars while basking in the therapeutic spa. Children over eight are welcome.

Hosts: Deb and Tim Sanders
Rooms: 4 (PB) $55-75
Full Breakfast
Credit Cards: A, B, D
Notes: 2, 4, 5, 9, 10, 11, 12, 14

COTTONWOOD FALLS

1874 Stonehouse on Mulberry Hill

Rural Route 1, Box 67A, 66845
(316) 273-8481 (phone and FAX)

Relax at the old stone house or explore the 120 acres that have old stone fences, a river

1874 Stonehouse

7 No smoking; 8 Children welcome; 9 Social drinking allowed; 10 Tennis nearby; 11 Swimming nearby; 12 Golf nearby; 13 Skiing nearby; 14 May be booked through a travel agent.

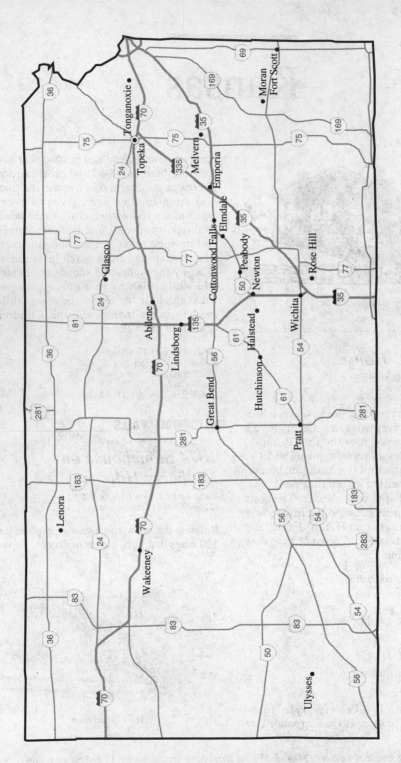

Kansas

valley that crosses the property, over 10 acres of woods, a pond, ruins of an old stone barn and corral, an abandoned railway right-of-way, and a decrepit "hired hands place." A haven for bird watchers, cyclists, hikers, naturalists, antiquers, historians, photographers, equestrains, hunters, and fishermen. Take a romantic break in the quiet and beauty of the Kansas Flint Hills. Three lovely rooms on the second floor. Private baths. Two common rooms with a stone fireplace offer peace and quiet.

Hosts: Dan and Carrie Riggs
Rooms: 3 (PB) $75
Full Breakfast
Credit Cards: None
Notes: 2, 5, 6, 7, 8, 12

ELMDALE

Clover Cliff Ranch Bed and Breakfast

Rural Route 30-1, 66850
(316) 273-6698; (800) 457-7406

The Clover Cliff is a 4,000 acre ranch nestled in the heart of the Flint Hills. The property is listed in the National Register of Historic Places. The main house was established in 1860 and is an imposing limestone mansion furnished with antiques. A full country breakfast is served at the main house on the veranda. Two guest houses are available and are the perfect setting for a family reunion or a corporate retreat.

Hosts: Jim and Joan Donahue
Rooms: 4 (2 PB; 2 SB) $85-115
Full Breakfast
Credit Cards: None
Notes: 2, 5, 7, 8, 9

EMPORIA

Plumb House Bed and Breakfast

628 Exchange Street, 66801
(316) 342-6881

Step back in time for a restful stay in the restored Victorian home of early day Emporians, George and Ellen Plumb. Experience the elegance of pocket doors, beveled glass windows, lace curtains, and antique furnishings, combined with 1990s convenience. Guests will awaken to the smell of fresh bread and home cooking! Morning coffee or afternoon tea may be taken on the balcony, or front porch, or in the garden.

Host: Barbara Stoecklein
Rooms: 5 (3 PB; 2 SB) $55-75
Full Breakfast
Credit Cards: A, B, C
Notes: 2, 5, 8, 9, 10, 11, 12

The White Rose Inn

901 Merchant Street, 66801
(316) 343-6336

The stay at The White Rose Inn begins with afternoon tea; the table is full of sumptuous treats. Retire to a private suite that has its own private bath and sitting room. In the morning, the smell of fresh baked biscuits, coffee cakes, or muffins will entice guests to the dining room or guests may have their breakfast in bed for a special romantic treat. The elegant Victorian home is the perfect setting for romantic getaways and civilized business travel.

Hosts: Samuel and Lisa Tosti
Rooms: 4 (PB) $50-75
Full Breakfast
Credit Cards: A, B, C, D, E
Notes: 2, 3, 4, 5, 7, 8, 9, 10, 11, 12, 14

FORT SCOTT

The Chenault Mansion

820 South National Avenue, 66701
(316) 223-6800

At the gracious home built by Edwin Chenault, little has changed since 1887. Take a step back in the time when graciousness was routine. Visit in the Victorian parlor, sleep in a period room, and

---

NOTES: Credit cards: A MasterCard; B Visa; C American Express; D Discover; E Diners Club; F Other; 2 Personal checks accepted; 3 Lunch available; 4 Dinner available; 5 Open all year; 6 Pets welcome; 7 No smoking; 8 Children welcome; 9 Social drinking allowed; 10 Tennis nearby; 11 Swimming nearby; 12 Golf nearby; 13 Skiing nearby; 14 May be booked through a travel agent.

enjoy a full breakfast under one of the crystal chandeliers. The elegant interior features curved glass windows, stained and leaded glass, ornate cherry, gum, ash, and oak woodwork, pocket doors, and fireplaces. The home is furnished with antiques, as well as a large china and glass collection. All rooms include private baths, queen-size beds, and central air conditioning for guests' comfort. Hospitality is not just the hosts' business, it's their way of life. Dinner available by reservations. Smoking restricted.

Hosts: Bob and Elizabeth Schafer
Rooms: 5 (PB) $70-85
Full Breakfast
Credit Cards: A, B, D
Notes: 2, 5, 8, 9, 10, 11, 12, 14

The Courtland Bed and Breakfast Inn

121 East 1st Street, 66701
(316) 223-0098; (800) 882-4 BED

The Courtland Bed and Breakfast Inn is truly a unique place in historic downtown Fort Scott. Built in 1906 as a railroad hotel, the Courtland has been lovingly restored and includes a cafe, lounge, gift shop, and banquet facilities. The Courtland offers an ideal location for those who truly want to explore this charming town. The Fort, Dolly the Trolley, gift and antique shops, and Main Street are all within walking distance. Friday and Saturday night specials and corporate rates available.

Hosts: Barbara Kelly and Darcy Heiser-Beck
Rooms: 15 (PB) $55-85
Full Breakfast
Credit Cards: A, B, C, D
Notes: 2, 3, 4, 5, 9

The Lyons' House for Bed and Breakfast

742 South National, 66701
(800) 78 GUEST

Fort Scott's landmark Victorian mansion, circa 1876, offers a prestigious location for special and business entertaining as well as bed and breakfast. Four guest rooms are arranged in two spacious suites decorated with antiques and collectibles from around the world. Full breakfast served in the formal dining room that reflects the Southern hospitality of the innkeeper. Private parties include Mystery in a Parlor and tea parties in the Victorian manner.

Hosts: Pat and Larry Lyons
Rooms: 4 (2 PB; 2 SB) $60-65
Full Breakfast
Credit Cards: None
Notes: 2, 5, 7, 8, 9, 10, 11, 12

GLASCO

Rustic Remembrances

Route 1, Box 68, 67445
(913) 546-2552

Rustic Remembrances is a warm, quiet, relaxing country home in north central Kansas in the heart of wheat country. Enjoy the collection of antiques, read a good book from the library, or go for a quiet walk. The home is close to Cloud Country Stained Glass Tour, a buffalo ranch, historic Brown Grand Theatre, and plenty of opportunities for hunting and fishing.

Hosts: Larry and Madonna Sorell
Rooms: 3 (SB) $45-65
Full Breakfast
Credit Cards: None
Notes: 2, 4, 5, 7

GREAT BEND

Peaceful Acres Bed and Breakfast

Route 5, Box 153, 67530
(316) 793-7527

This sprawling farmhouse has a working windmill, small livestock, chickens, and guineas. Five miles from Great Bend and close to Cheyenne Bottoms and Quivira Wet Lands, Fort Larned, Pawnee Rock, Wilson Lake, Lake Kanopolis, and Santa

NOTES: Credit cards accepted: A MasterCard; B Visa; C American Express; D Discover; E Diners Club; F Other; 2 Personal checks accepted; 3 Lunch available; 4 Dinner available; 5 Open all year; 6 Pets welcome;

Fe Trail. Enjoy hospitality and the quiet of the country in this farmhouse furnished with some antiques. Homegrown and homemade foods. Full country breakfast is served. Kitchen available.

Hosts: Dale and Doris Nitzel
Rooms: 2-3 (SB) $30
Full Breakfast
Credit Cards: None
Notes: 2, 5, 6, 7, 8, 10, 11, 12, 14

HALSTEAD

Heritage Inn

300 Main Street, 67056
(316) 835-2118

Heritage Inn is an extraordinary 1922 bed and breakfast inn in the heart of Kansas. The moment guests step through the doors of the Heritage Inn, they will feel the comfort and relaxed charm of the 1920s, but will enjoy the convenience of the 1990s.

Hosts: Jim and Gery Hartong
Rooms: 7 (PB) $29
Continental Breakfast
Credit Cards: A, B
Notes: 2, 5, 8, 9, 10, 11, 12

HUTCHINSON

The Rose Garden

3815 East 56th, 67502
(316) 663-5317

This ranch home across the street from Sandhill State Park offers peace and quiet, yet is close to places of interest in Hutchinson. Kansas Cosmosphere, state fairgrounds, and the softball complex are within a couple of miles. Summer months guests can enjoy the patio of roses and sip iced tea. Winter takes the guests inside to a pool table and TV room to relax with hot chocolate.

Hosts: Barbara and Bruce Moots
Rooms: 2 (PB) $55
Full Breakfast
Credit Cards: None
Notes: 2, 5, 7, 10, 11, 12

LENORA

Barbeau House

210 East Washington Avenue, 67645
(913) 567-4886

This Queen Anne Victorian, circa 1899, has been restored to a new reign as a "painted lady" of the plains. Delightful features of the house are a massive handworked oak staircase, exquisite etched glass exterior doors, and elegant light fixtures. The fireplace and a working player piano reflect the elegance of the period. Hosts' collection of trains and pocket watches will also intrigue the guests. Full French breakfast. Open May through September.

Hosts: Brad and Lea Hall
Rooms: 4 (1 PB; 3 SB) $40-50
Full Breakfast
Credit Cards: None
Notes: 2, 3, 4, 7, 8, 9

LINDSBORG

Swedish Country Inn

112 West Lincoln Street, 67456
(913) 227-2985; (800) 231-0266 out of state

Lindsborg is a lovely Swedish community in the center of Kansas. The inn is furnished with Swedish pine furniture, and all of the beds have hand-quilted quilts. A delicious full Scandinavian breakfast is served, and all rooms have private bath and TV. No smoking or guest pets

Swedish Country Inn

7 No smoking; 8 Children welcome; 9 Social drinking allowed; 10 Tennis nearby; 11 Swimming nearby; 12 Golf nearby; 13 Skiing nearby; 14 May be booked through a travel agent.

allowed. Near Bethany College, where Handel's *Messiah* is performed on Palm and Easter Sundays.

Hosts: Gene and Helen Van Amburg
Rooms: 19 (PB) $45-75
Full Breakfast
Credit Cards: A, B, D
Notes: 2, 5, 8, 10, 11, 12

MELVERN

Schoolhouse Inn

106 East Beck, 66510
(913) 549-3473

Built in 1870 as Melvern's first school-house, this two-story limestone structure sits on an acre-and-a-half lot with shade trees. The guest rooms are furnished with antique and contemporary furnishings. The inn is away from busy streets, making it an ideal place for a weekend getaway. A full breakfast is served at a large dining table. Three miles from Melvern Lake where guests can enjoy all types of water sports.

Hosts: Rudy and Alice White
Rooms: 4 (2 PB; 2 SB) $50-60
Full Breakfast
Credit Cards: A, B
Notes: 2, 5, 7, 8, 11

MORAN

Hedgeapple Acres Bed and Breakfast, Inc.

Rural Route 2, Box 27, 66755
(316) 237-4646

Enjoy the personal touches and quiet country surroundings strolling through the beautiful grounds and resting comfortably for the night in one of the well appointed guest rooms. Meeting rooms for business meetings, seminars, weddings, receptions, and family reunions. Supper included. Handicapped accessible.

Hosts: Jack and Ann Donaldson
Rooms: 6 (PB) $58-65
Full Breakfast

Credit Cards: A, B, C, D
Notes: 2, 3, 4, 5, 7, 8, 9, 12

NEWTON

Hawk House Bed and Breakfast

307 West Broadway, 67114
(316) 283-2045; (800) 500-2045

In the heart of wheat country. A three-story Victorian home with massive oak staircase and spacious common rooms accented by oak floors and stained glass. Each guest room is fully furnished with antiques, linens, and appointments. Guests are surrounded with elegance and hospitality. Air conditioning.

Hosts: Lon and Carol Buller
Rooms: 4 (1 PB; 3 SB) $50-60
Full Breakfast
Credit Cards: A, B
Notes: 2, 5, 7, 8, 9, 10, 11, 12, 14

PEABODY

Jones Sheep Farm Bed and Breakfast

Rural Route 2, Box 185, 66866
(316) 983-2815

Enjoy a turn-of-the-century home in a pastoral setting. On a working sheep farm "at the end of the road," the house is furnished in 1930s style (no telephone or TV). Quiet

Jones Sheep Farm

and private. A wonderful historic small town is nearby. The full country breakfast features fresh farm produce.

Hosts: Gary and Marilyn Jones
Rooms: 2 (SB) $45
Full Breakfast
Credit Cards: None
Notes: 2, 5, 6, 7, 10, 11, 12

PRATT

Pratt Guest House Bed and Breakfast Inn

105 North Iuka Street, P.O. Box 326, 67124
(316) 672-1200

Listed on the National Register of Historic Places, the Pratt Guest House offers luxury accommodations in a historic setting. Magnificent quarter-sawn oak cabinetry and staircase, leaded glass, period antiques, and a hearty morning meal combine to create an atmosphere of comfort, romance, and pampering. Near national and state wildlife areas. An ideal spot for world-class bird watching or bicycle riding along rural roads. Area antique stores and auction houses beckon. Inquire about accommodations for children.

Host: Marguerite Flanagan
Rooms: 5 (PB) $45-90
Full Breakfast
Credit Cards: A, B
Notes: 2, 5, 7, 9

ROSE HILL

Queen Anne's Lace Bed and Breakfast

15335 SW Queen Anne's Lace, 67133
(316) 733-4075

The Queen Anne's Lace Bed and Breakfast is southeast of Wichita. Accommodations in one of two tastefully furnished rooms include a full-size bed, private bath, and tea and cookies upon arrival; the common area/den provides a TV, VCR, and a fire-place, as well as a walkout entry to the large patio with a picnic table and a hot tub. Full country breakfast served. Queen Anne's Lace Bed and Breakfast is convenient to the many antique markets and most local aircraft factories. It is perfect as a weekend getaway. Sorry, not wheelchair accessible. A deposit of $25 required to hold reservation. Children over three welcome.

Hosts: Bob and Jackie Collison
Rooms: 2 (PB) $50
Full Breakfast
Credit Cards: None
Notes: 2, 5, 7, 9, 12

TONGANOXIE

Almeda's Bed and Breakfast Inn

220 South Main Street, 66086
(913) 845-2295

In a picturesque small town designated a historic site in 1983, the inn dates back to World War I. Sip a cup of coffee at the stone bar once used as a bus stop in 1930. In fact, this room was the inspiration for the play *Bus Stop*. Close driving distance to Kansas City International Airport, Kansas City Country Club Plaza, the Renaissance Festival, the "Sandstone" Amphitheater, Woodlands Racetrack, the National Agriculture Hall of Fame, the University of Kansas, Weston and Snow Creek skiing, Topeka State Capitol, and antique shops.

Hosts: Almeda and Richard Tinberg
Rooms: 7 (PB and SB) $40-65
Continental Breakfast
Credit Cards: None
Notes: 2, 5, 7, 9, 11, 12

TOPEKA

Heritage House

3535 Southwest 6th Street, 66606
(913) 233-3800

A charming country inn, listed on the National Register of Historic Places, near

---

7 No smoking; 8 Children welcome; 9 Social drinking allowed; 10 Tennis nearby; 11 Swimming nearby; 12 Golf nearby; 13 Skiing nearby; 14 May be booked through a travel agent.

the zoo, park, and museum. Twelve taste-ful, designer-decorated rooms with private baths, telephones, and TVs. The sunroom-dining room is well known for its outstanding Continental cuisine.

Host: Chad Marsh
Rooms: 12 (PB) $60-145
Full Breakfast
Credit Cards: A, B, C, D, E
Notes: 2, 3, 4, 5, 7, 8, 9, 10, 11, 12, 14

ULYSSES

Fort's Cedar View

1675 West Patterson, 67880
(316) 356-2570

Fort's Cedar View is in the heart of the world's largest natural-gas field. It is on the Santa Fe Trail, eight miles north of famed Wagon Bed Springs, the first source of water after crossing the Cimarron River west of Dodge City, which is 80 miles northeast.

Host: Lynda Fort
Rooms: 5 (2 PB; 3 SB) $35-55
Full Breakfast
Credit Cards: None
Notes: 2, 5, 7, 10, 11, 12

WAKEENEY

Thistle Hill
Bed and Breakfast

Route 1, Box 93, 67672
(913) 743-2644

A comfortable, secluded cedar farm home situated midway between Kansas City and Denver along I-70. Experience farm life and visit Castle Rock. Self-guided wild-flower walks through a 60-acre prairie restoration project. Enjoy a hearty country breakfast by the fireplace or on the summer porch overlooking the herb garden. Inquire about accommodations for pets. Smoking restricted.

Hosts: Dave and Mary Hendricks
Rooms: 4 (3 PB; 1 SB) $55-65
Full Breakfast
Credit Cards: A, B
Notes: 2, 5, 8, 9, 10, 11, 12, 14

The Castle Inn Riverside

WICHITA

The Castle Inn Riverside

1155 North River Boulevard, 67203
(316) 263-9300

Listed on the State and National Register of Historic Places. The Castle is of Richard-sonian Romanesque architectural style. Fourteen uniquely appointed rooms with baths and fireplaces. Five sitting areas, gift shop, coffee bar, seminar rooms with business amenities, and exercise facility. Amenities include gourmet breakfast, wine and cheese, dessert and coffee, and more. The hosts tailor their services to meet guests' individual needs and will go out of their way to make any occasion special. Smoking outside only.

Hosts: Terry and Paula Lowry
Rooms: 14 (PB) $125-225
Full and Continental Breakfast
Credit Cards: A, B, C, D
Notes: 2, 5, 9, 10, 12, 14

Inn at the Park

3751 East Douglas, 67218
(316) 652-0500; (800) 258-1951

Elegant Old World charm and comfort in a completely renovated mansion. Twelve distinctive suites, ten in the main house and two in the carriage house. Some of the amenities include fireplaces, whirlpool bath, private courtyard, hot tub, and many spacious three-room suites. A preferred hideaway among people looking for a romantic retreat or convenient base of operation for corporate guests. The Inn at the Park was named one of the top ten outstanding new inns in the country by *Inn Review* newsletter in 1989. Limited smoking allowed.

Host: Michelle Hickman
Rooms: 12 (PB) $75-135
Continental Breakfast
Credit Cards: A, B, C, D
Notes: 2, 3, 4, 5, 8, 9, 10, 14

7 No smoking; 8 Children welcome; 9 Social drinking allowed; 10 Tennis nearby; 11 Swimming nearby; 12 Golf nearby; 13 Skiing nearby; 14 May be booked through a travel agent.

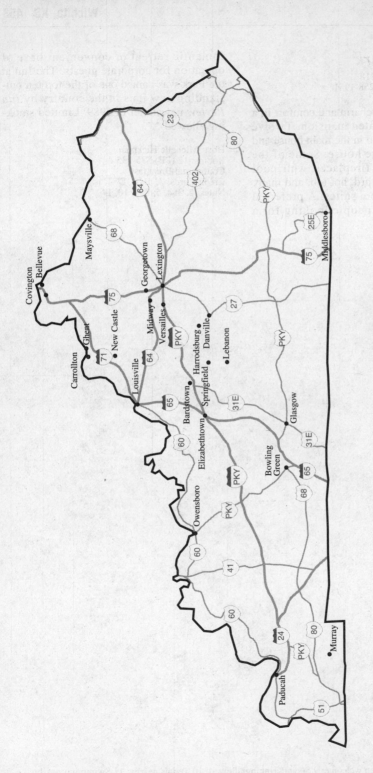

Kentucky

Kentucky

BARDSTOWN

Amber Le Ann
Bed and Breakfast

209 East Stephen Foster Avenue, 40004
(502) 349-0014; (800) 828-3330

Charm and relaxed comfort in a unique
Victorian setting. Elegant guest rooms
and beautiful decor await guests in this
newly remodeled home. King-size beds
and private baths. In the center of town
within walking distance of most attractions. Full breakfast and evening desserts
provided. Listed with AAA. Children
over 12 welcome.

Host: Jan Taylor
Rooms: 5 (PB) $85-125
Full Breakfast
Credit Cards: A, B, C, D
Notes: 2, 5, 7, 9, 10, 12, 14

Beautiful Dreamer
Bed and Breakfast

440 East Stephen Foster Avenue, 40004
(502) 348-4004

Antiques and cherry furniture compliment
this newly built Federal designed home that
overlooks historic My Old Kentucky
Home. The Beautiful Dreamer Room has a
double Jacuzzi. The Captain's Room has a
single Jacuzzi and fireplace. The Stephen
Foster Room is handicapped accessible. All
rooms are air-conditioned, have queen-size
beds, and include a hearty breakfast.
Within walking distance of *The Stephen
Foster Story.*

Host: Lynell Ginter
Rooms: 3 (PB) $69-99
Full Breakfast
Credit Cards: A, B
Notes: 5, 7, 12

Jailer's Inn

Jailer's Inn

111 West Stephen Foster Avenue, 40004
(502) 348-5551

In 1819, Jailer's Inn was originally constructed for use as a jail. In 1874 it was
turned into the jailer's residence. This complex was the oldest operating jail in the
Commonwealth of Kentucky until 1987.
Large rooms, completely renovated and
furnished with heirlooms and antiques. One
room resembles a cell, with two of the
original bunk beds plus a waterbed; decorated in prison black and white. One room
has a Jacuzzi. A Continental plus breakfast
is served. Closed January. Call for rates.

Hosts: Challen and Fran McCoy
Rooms: 6 (PB)
Continental Breakfast
Credit Cards: A, B, C, D
Notes: 2, 8, 9, 10, 11, 12, 14

NOTES: Credit cards: A MasterCard; B Visa; C American Express; D Discover; E Diners Club; F Other;
2 Personal checks accepted; 3 Lunch available; 4 Dinner available; 5 Open all year; 6 Pets welcome;
7 No smoking; 8 Children welcome; 9 Social drinking allowed; 10 Tennis nearby; 11 Swimming nearby;
12 Golf nearby; 13 Skiing nearby; 14 May be booked through a travel agent.

The Mansion Bed and Breakfast

1003 North 3rd Street, 40004
(502) 348-2586; (800) 399-2586

A beautiful Greek Revival mansion built in 1851 and is on the National Register of Historic Places. On more than three acres of land with magnificent trees and plantings, it reminds one of more genteel times. The Mansion is on the site where the first Confederate flag, the Stars and Bars, was raised in Kentucky for the first time. The rooms feature period antiques, hand-crocheted bedspreads, dust ruffles, and shams. Continental plus breakfast. Smoking restricted. Children over ten welcome.

Host: Joseph D. Downs
Rooms: 8 (PB) $75-85
Continental Breakfast
Credit Cards: A, B, C, D
Notes: 2, 5, 9, 10, 11, 12, 14

BELLEVUE

Weller Haus Bed and Breakfast

319 Poplar Street, 41073
(606) 431-6829; (800) 431-4287

Savor the casual elegance of an era past in these historic preservation awarded 1880's Victorian Gothic homes. The inn is five minutes from downtown Cincinnati, Ohio, antique-appointed, and offers a sumptuous candlelit breakfast. Other amenities include a Jacuzzi suite for two, private English garden, ivy-covered gathering kitchen. Ohio riverboat row with its attractions and dining spots is within walking distance. Smoking in restricted areas only. Inquire about accommodations for children.

Hosts: Mary and Vernon Weller
Rooms: 5 (PB) $72-125
Full Breakfast
Credit Cards: A, B
Notes: 2, 5, 9, 10, 11, 12, 13, 14

BOWLING GREEN

Walnut Lawn Bed and Breakfast

1800 Morgantown Road, 42101
(502) 781-7255

This is a restored Victorian house, part of which was built in 1805. It is furnished with family antiques of the period. On a farm three miles from the center of Bowling Green and just off Green River Parkway and I-65. The place has been in the family for 125 years. Walnut Lawn requires reservations and serves a Continental breakfast.

Host: George Anna McKenzie
Rooms: 4 (3 PB; 1 SB) $65
Continental Breakfast
Credit Cards: None
Notes: 2, 5, 7, 9

CARROLLTON

Baker House Bed and Breakfast

406 Highland Avenue, 41008
(502) 732-4210

Upon entering this large Victorian home, listed on the National Historic Register, one gets the feeling of having stepped back to the 1800s. The original oil lamp chandeliers, hand-carved cherry staircase, ornate fireplaces, and period antiques embellish the ornate house. The day begins with coffee or tea room service, followed by an elegant breakfast served in the candlelit dining room. Four miles off of I-71 midway between Cincinnati and Louisville, across the Ohio River from Madison, Indiana.

Host: Maggie Klein
Rooms: 4 (3 PB; 1 SB) $68
Full Breakfast
Credit Cards: A, B, C
Notes: 2, 5, 8, 9, 12, 13

NOTES: Credit cards accepted: A MasterCard; B Visa; C American Express; D Discover; E Diners Club; F Other; 2 Personal checks accepted; 3 Lunch available; 4 Dinner available; 5 Open all year; 6 Pets welcome;

COVINGTON

Amos Shinkle Townhouse Bed and Breakfast

215 Garrard Street, 41011
(606) 431-2118; (800) 972-7012

This restored mansion, circa 1854, has won several preservation awards. It features a Greco-Italianate façade with a cast-iron filigree porch. Inside the decor includes lavish crown moldings, 16-foot ceilings, Italianate mantels on the fireplaces, and Rococo Revival chandeliers (Carnelius-Baker). Guest rooms have either four-poster or massive Victorian-style beds and period furnishings. Here Southern hospitality is at its finest. Just a 15-minute walk to downtown Cincinnati, Ohio.

Hosts: Harry (Don) Nash and Bernie Moorman
Rooms: 7 (PB) $73-130
Full Breakfast
Credit Cards: A, B, C, D, E
Notes: 2, 5, 8, 9, 14

DAISY HILL

Bluegrass Bed and Breakfast

Route 1, Box 263, Versailles, 40383
(606) 873-3208

This stately brick home and extensive tree-shaded grounds and horse farm have been in the owner's family since 1812. It's a glorious combination of antique furnishings and modern luxuries. A large downstairs bedroom with elegantly canopied double bed and private bath opens onto a brick courtyard and lawn. A large upstairs bedroom with a king-size bed and private bath overlooks the grounds including the family cemetery dating from 1810. Another room sharing a bath is available for family groups. Air-conditioned. $90.

DANVILLE

Bluegrass Bed and Breakfast

Route 1, Box 263, Versailles, 40383
(606) 873-3208

From its wraparound front porch to its spacious screened back porch overlooking the tree-shaded lawn, this home offers turn-of-the-century charm and comfort. The upstairs guest suite has two larger corner bedrooms and one bath. Choose between a twin or double bedded room. Both rooms are rented only when families or friends want to share the bath. Continental breakfast is served in the dining room, or, weather willing, on the screened porch. Air-conditioned. $64.

ELIZABETHTOWN

The Olde Bethlehem Academy Inn

7051 St. John's Road, 42701
(502) 862-9003; (800) 662-5670

Built in 1818 for the family of Gov. John LaRue Helm, the property was acquired in 1830 and converted to a girls' academy by the Sister of Loretto. Each room is furnished with antiques, reproduction pieces, and a private bath. The decorations and beautiful grounds are matched by the quality of the food service and the gracious dining areas. The mural of Moses and the Pharaoh in the chapel is truly a work of art. A true testament to the 19th century, the Olde Bethlehem Academy Inn invites guests to step back in time and enjoy the artifacts that remain from its significantly rich past.

Hosts: The Taylor family
Rooms: 6 (PB) $75-95
Full Breakfast
Credit Cards: A, B, C
Notes: 2, 3, 4, 5, 6, 7, 8, 9, 10, 11, 12

7 No smoking; 8 Children welcome; 9 Social drinking allowed; 10 Tennis nearby; 11 Swimming nearby; 12 Golf nearby; 13 Skiing nearby; 14 May be booked through a travel agent.

Blackridge Hall

GEORGETOWN

Blackridge Hall

4055 Paris Pike, 40324
(502) 863-2069; (800) 768-9308

Blackridge Hall is a luxurious Southern Georgian-style mansion on five acres in Bluegrass horse country. There are five guest rooms containing antique and reproduction furnishings. Two master suites have Jacuzzi tubs, while all baths are private. A full gourmet breakfast is served in the dining room or on the veranda. A cozy guest kitchenette is available with snacks and soft drinks. Minutes to Lexington, Horse Park, Keeneland and Red Mile Racetracks, University of Kentucky, Toyota Motor Corp. Tours, and historic Georgetown antique shops.

Hosts: Jim D. Black, proprietor
Rooms: 5 (PB) $89-159
Full Breakfast
Credit Cards: A, B, C, D
Notes: 2, 5, 7, 9, 10, 11, 12, 14

Bluegrass Bed and Breakfast

Route 1, Box 263, Versailles, 40383
(606) 873-3208

Log House. This is a once-in-a-lifetime experience. A genuine log cabin from the days when Kentucky was the frontier. Handsomely restored and transformed into comfortable quarters that retain the charm. Two bedrooms, one very large, living room with stone fireplace, fully equipped kitchen large enough to eat it. Even a front porch for sitting and rocking. Twenty minutes from Lexington, 25 minutes from Keeneland Racecourse, and 15 minutes from the Kentucky Horse Park. Complete privacy. Air-conditioned. $75 for two; $105 for four.

Log Cabin Bed and Breakfast

350 North Broadway, 40324
(502) 863-3514

Enjoy this Kentucky log cabin, circa 1809, with its shake roof, chinked logs, and period furnishings. Completely private. Two bedrooms, fireplace, and fully equipped kitchen. Only five miles to Kentucky Horse Park and 12 miles north of Lexington.

Hosts: Clay and Janis McKnight
Cabin: (PB) $75
Continental Breakfast
Credit Cards: None
Notes: 2, 5, 6, 8, 9, 10, 11, 12

GHENT

Ghent House Bed and Breakfast

411 Main Street (US 42), P.O. Box 478, 41045
(502) 347-5807 (weekends)

Ghent House is a gracious reminder of the antebellum days of the "Old South." Federal-style with a beautiful fantail window, two slave walls, rose and English gardens, gazebo, crystal chandeliers, fireplaces, and whirlpool. Ghent House has a spectacular view of the Ohio River halfway between Cincinnati and Louisville, and one can almost visualize the steamboats. Go back in time and stay at the Ghent House. Come as a guest—leave as a friend.

Hosts: Wayne and Diane Young
Rooms: 3 (PB) $60-90
Full Breakfast

NOTES: Credit cards accepted: A MasterCard; B Visa; C American Express; D Discover; E Diners Club; F Other; 2 Personal checks accepted; 3 Lunch available; 4 Dinner available; 5 Open all year; 6 Pets welcome;

Credit Cards: A, B, C
Notes: 2, 5, 8, 9, 10, 11, 12, 13, 14

GLASGOW

Four Seasons Country Inn

4107 Scottsville Road, 42141
(502) 678-1000

Charming Victorian-style inn built in 1989.
Most rooms have queen-size, four-poster
beds, private baths, remote-equipped TVs
with cable. Continental breakfast served in
inviting lobby with wood-burning fireplace. Some rooms open out to spacious
deck or large front porch. Swimming pool.
Near Mammoth Cave National Park and
Barren River Lake State Park.

Host: Charles Smith
Rooms: 17 (PB) $56-62

Four Seasons Country Inn

Continental Breakfast
Credit Cards: A, B, C, D, E
Notes: 5, 7, 8, 9, 10, 11, 12, 13, 14

HARRODSBURG

Bauer Haus Bed and Breakfast

362 North College Street, 40330
(606) 734-6289

Savor the craftsmanship of the past in this
1880s Victorian home listed on the National
Register of Historic Places and designated a
Kentucky landmark. Nestle in the sitting
room, sip tea or coffee in the dining room,
repose in the parlor, or ascend the staircase
to a private room for a relaxing visit. In

Kentucky's oldest settlement, Bauer Haus is
within walking distance of Old Fort Harrod
State Park and historic Harrodsburg.

Hosts: Dick and Marian Bauer
Rooms: 4 (2 PB; 2 SB) $55-65
Full Breakfast
Credit Cards: None
Notes: 2, 5, 7, 9, 12, 14

Inn at Shaker Village of Pleasant Hill

3500 Lexington Road, 40330
(606) 734-5411

The Shaker Village of Pleasant Hill offers a
one-of-a-kind guest experience. Its 80 guest
rooms in buildings where Shakers once lived
and worked are simply and beautifully furnished with Shaker-crafted furniture. This
national historic landmark sets on 2,700
acres of rolling bluegrass farmland. The village offers tours, daily exhibitions of Shaker
crafts, and hearty country dining. Riverboat
excursions from April through October.

Host: Ted Burunoff
Rooms: 80 (PB) $55-100
Full and Continental Breakfast
Credit Cards: A, B
Notes: 2, 3, 4, 5, 8, 9, 11, 12, 14

LAND O' GOSHEN (LOUISVILLE)

Bluegrass Bed and Breakfast

Route 1, Box 263, Versailles, 40383
(606) 873-3208

1. For anyone who has never stayed in a
country bed and breakfast with 18 rooms and
breakfast eggs fresh from the henhouse, here
is the chance. The grounds include stone
walls, a pond, flower and vegetable gardens,
iron gates and a boxwood *allée*. Two rooms
are available, one with a double bed and one
with a twin bed. Both have fireplaces, private
baths, and are furnished with antiques. This
whole house illustrates a way of life virtually
unknown in today's world. A stay here is not

7 No smoking; 8 Children welcome; 9 Social drinking allowed; 10 Tennis nearby; 11 Swimming nearby;
12 Golf nearby; 13 Skiing nearby; 14 May be booked through a travel agent.

to be missed. Air-conditioned. Resident dogs and cats. $80.

2. The Magnolia Place is in old Louisville. Ten minutes from Churchill Downs, five minutes from Shakespeare-in-the-Park, and close to University of Louisville and hospitals. This attractive house has four rooms, two with double beds and two with twin beds. $85.

LEXINGTON

Bluegrass Bed and Breakfast

Route 1, Box 263, Versailles, 40383
(606) 873-3208

This lovely inn-townhouse is so surrounded by woods that guests scarcely realize there are neighbors. Contemporary in style, its spacious feeling derives from its two-storied living room and generous use of glass. The guest room has twin mahogany four-posters and attached private bath. Also a king-size bedroom with a private bath. Fully air-conditioned. $58.

Gratz Park Inn

120 West Second Street, 40507
(606) 231-1777; (800) 227-4362

Gratz Park Inn is in downtown Lexington in a historical district. The building is on the National Register of Historic Places. Each room is unique with fine antique reproduction furniture and four-poster beds. The inn offers a complimentary breakfast and limousine service in the evenings to downtown restaurants, as well as airport transportation. Turndown service includes fresh flowers and home-baked cookies each evening. *USA Today* is delivered right to guests' room door.

Rooms: 44 (PB) $95-250
Continental Breakfast
Credit Cards: A, B, C, D, E
Notes: 3, 4, 5, 7, 8, 9, 10, 11, 12, 14

LOUISVILLE

Inn at the Park

1332 South Fourth Street, 40208
(502) 637-6930

This Victorian mansion was built in 1886, as a premier example of Richardsonian Romanesque architecture. The inn is elegantly furnished in Victorian antiques and antique reproductions. Very spacious with 14-foot ceilings, eight fireplaces, picturesque porches overlooking Central Park, and rich hardwood floors. Many guests are awestruck upon their first entrance into the foyer—the grand, sweeping staircase is magnificent! Appropriate for special occasions and the very particular guest. Enjoy cocktails on any of five porches, or an evening stroll in the park. Personal attention from the innkeepers and an excellent full breakfast make guests' visit complete.

Hosts: John and Sandra Mullins
Rooms: 6 (4 PB; 2 SB) $70-119
Full Breakfast
Credit Cards: A, B, C
Notes: 2, 5, 7, 9, 10, 11, 12, 14

Kentucky Homes Bed and Breakfast Inc.

1219 South Fourth Avenue, 40203
(502) 635-7341

A reservation service for Louisville and Kentucky offers approximately 45 rooms with private baths, priced from $55-85.

Full and Continental Breakfast
Credit Cards: A, B, C
Notes: 2, 5, 8, 10, 12

Old Louisville Inn

1359 South Third Street, 40208
(502) 635-1574; FAX (502) 637-5892

Wake up to the aroma of freshly baked popovers and muffins when staying in one of the 11 guest rooms or the two-bedroom suite with living room and private bath.

NOTES: Credit cards accepted: A MasterCard; B Visa; C American Express; D Discover; E Diners Club; F Other; 2 Personal checks accepted; 3 Lunch available; 4 Dinner available; 5 Open all year; 6 Pets welcome;

Old Louisville Inn

Centrally situated between downtown and the airport. Stay for a romantic getaway or relax on a business trip with the special packages and consider this inn home away from home.

Host: Marianne Lesher
Rooms: 13 (8 PB; 3 SB) $65-195
Continental Breakfast
Credit Cards: A, B
Notes: 2, 5, 8, 9, 10, 12, 14

The Red Room Bed and Breakfast

(502) 458-7197

Spacious condo just five minutes from mid-city. Tree-lined street in an older established neighborhood. One block from Bardstown Road and its wall-to-wall antique shops and restaurants. Queen-size and twin bedrooms with private baths. Smokers welcome.

Rooms: 2 (PB) $50-60
Full Breakfast
Credit Cards: None
Notes: 2, 5, 9

The Victorian Secret Bed and Breakfast

1132 South First Street, 40203
(502) 581-1914

In historic old Louisville guests will find a three-story brick mansion appropriately named the Victorian Secret Bed and

Breakfast. Its 14 rooms offer spacious accommodations, high ceilings, 11 fireplaces, and original woodwork. Recently restored to its former elegance, the 110-year-old structure provides a peaceful setting for enjoying period furnishings and antiques.

Hosts: Nan and Steve Roosa
Rooms: 3 (1 PB; 2 SB) $53-78
Continental Breakfast
Credit Cards: None
Notes: 5, 8, 9, 10, 11, 12, 13, 14

Welcome House Bed and Breakfast

1613 Forrest Hill Drive, 40205
(502) 452-6629

Gracious Colonial home in a lovely suburban neighborhood offers two queen-size, two double, and two single bedrooms with three baths. Off the beaten path, but convenient to antique shops, shopping malls, and the expressways. Great for reunions and conventions. Close to fairgrounds.

Host: Jo DuBose Boone
Rooms: 5 (3 PB; 2 SB) $50-65
Full Breakfast
Credit Cards: None
Notes: 2, 5, 8, 9, 10, 11, 12, 13, 14

MAYSVILLE

Bluegrass Bed and Breakfast

Route 1, Box 263, Versailles, 40383
(606) 873-3208

One of the most beautiful stretches of the Ohio River is at Maysville with its bridge and graceful bend in the river. Guests have spectacular, unobstructed views of it from the fourth (top) floor of a classic 1920s apartment house. A large corner guest room has a double bed, an alcove with daybed, and private bath (tub, no shower). Weather permitting, enjoy the Continental breakfast on the veranda that runs almost the length of the building. Elevator; air-conditioned.

7 No smoking; 8 Children welcome; 9 Social drinking allowed; 10 Tennis nearby; 11 Swimming nearby; 12 Golf nearby; 13 Skiing nearby; 14 May be booked through a travel agent.

Additional double bedroom with bath is available. One hour from Cincinnati. $60.

The RidgeRunner

MIDDLESBORO

The RidgeRunner Bed and Breakfast

208 Arthur Heights, 40965
(606) 248-4299

This 1891 Victorian home is furnished with authentic antiques and nestled in the Cumberland Gap Mountains. A picturesque view is enjoyed from the 60-foot front porch, welcoming guests with rocking chairs, swings, and hammocks. Guests are treated like special people, in a relaxed, peaceful atmosphere. Five minutes from Cumberland Gap National Park, 12 minutes from Pine Mountain State Park, 50 miles from Knoxville, Tennessee. Interesting history and hosts await.

Hosts: Sue Richards and Irma Gall
Rooms: 4 (2PB; 2SB) $55-65
Full Breakfast
Credit Cards: None
Notes: 2, 5, 7, 9, 10, 12

MIDWAY

Bluegrass Bed and Breakfast

Route 1, Box 263, Versailles, 40383
(606) 873-3208

Holly Hill. Holly Hill is a small country inn on a hill just outside downtown Midway, close enough to the antique shops yet with enough privacy for overnight guests to stroll the grounds. The inn has become a favorite dining place for travelers and natives alike. Two rooms. $54.

Scottwood. An Early American jewel. Step back in time in this 1795 brick house on a lazy bend of the Elkhorn. Restored and furnished to absolute perfection, Scottwood will touch guests' hearts if they love the beauty of the past. Choose a north wing room with a fireplace and private bath or the queen-size pencil post room. Both open onto a sitting room with fireplace and games table. There is also a sunlit guest cottage with deck overlooking the creek. No smoking. $90.

MURRAY

Diuguid House Bed and Breakfast

603 Main Street, 42071
(502) 753-5470

This beautiful home, listed on the National Register of Historic Places, features a sweeping oak staircase, comfortable and spacious rooms, and a generous guest lounge area. This bed and breakfast is in town near the university, lake area, and many antique shops. Full breakfast is included in the reasonable rates, and the area has the reputation for being a top rated retirement area.

Hosts: Karen and George Chapman
Rooms: 3 (SB) $40
Full Breakfast
Credit Cards: A, B, E
Notes: 2, 5, 7, 8, 10, 12, 14

NEW CASTLE

The Oldham House

111 South Main Street, P.O. Box 628, 40050
(502) 845-0103

NOTES: Credit cards accepted: A MasterCard; B Visa; C American Express; D Discover; E Diners Club; F Other; 2 Personal checks accepted; 3 Lunch available; 4 Dinner available; 5 Open all year; 6 Pets welcome;

The Oldham House, circa 1820, is a Federal period structure between the Bluegrass region of Kentucky and the Ohio River, amid rolling hills and spacious farms, convenient to Louisville, Lexington, and Cincinnati. This marvelous home features country, primitive, and period antiques and accessories, most of which are available for purchase. Horse farms abound; Keeneland and Churchill Downs, scenic Ohio River towns, golfing, and antiquing await guests nearby. Children over 12 welcome.

Hosts: Emmy and Alan Blincoe
Rooms: 2 (PB) $70-75
Full Breakfast
Credit Cards: A, B
Notes: 2, 5, 7, 9, 12, 13

OWENSBORO

Trail's End

5931 Highway 56, 42301
(502) 771-5590; fax (502) 771-4723

A condo cottage with three bedrooms—double, side-by-side twin, and three bunk beds. Kitchen is fully equipped with stocked refrigerator of breakfast fixings. Furnished with antiques, there are laundry facilities, a patio with a lovely view, and stables for lessons or trail riding nearby. On Highway 45 ten minutes north of Owensboro and three miles west of Rockport, Indiana. A bed and breakfast country cottage with a queen-sized bed and four bunk beds in three bedrooms is three miles west of Owensboro on Highway 56. Guests may enjoy indoor/outdoor tennis, Nautilus fitness, and a sauna. A country-style breakfast is served at the indoor tennis club on the property. Summer pool and a large fireplace in the winter add charm to the accommodations. The cottages are air-conditioned. A two-bedroom trailer with two beds is also available. Weekly rates available for all accommodations.

Host: Joan G. Ramey
Condo: 1 (PB) $75
Cottage: 1 (PB) $50
Trailer: 1 (PB) $35

Full Breakfast
Credit Cards: A, B
Notes: 2, 5, 6, 7, 8, 9, 10, 11, 12

PADUCAH

Ehrhardt's Bed and Breakfast

285 Springwell Lane, 42001
(502) 554-0644

This brick Colonial home is just one mile off I-24, a highway noted for its lovely scenery. The hosts strive to make guests feel at home in antique-filled bedrooms and a cozy den with a fireplace. Nearby are the beautiful Kentucky and Barkley lakes and the famous Land Between the Lakes area.

Hosts: Eileen and Phil Ehrhardt
Rooms: 3 (SB) $40-45
Full Breakfast
Credit Cards: None
Notes: 2, 5, 11, 12

The 1857's Bed and Breakfast

P.O. Box 7771
127 Market House Square, 42002-7771
(502) 444-3960; (800) 264-5607

This three-story brick building, listed on the National Register of Historic Places, has a warm, friendly Victorian atmosphere. The first floor houses Cynthia's Ristorante; the second floor houses two guest rooms; and the third floor houses the family room and game room with hot tub and billiards table. This home is in the downtown historic district, with antique stores, carriage rides, quilt museum, restaurants, and the Market House Cultural Center within walking distance. The entire second floor with private bath may be booked for $85; two-night minimum stay.

Hosts: Deborah and Steve Bohnert
Rooms: 3 (SB) $65-85
Continental Breakfast
Credit Cards: A, B
Notes: 2, 5, 8, 9, 10, 11, 12, 13, 14

7 No smoking; 8 Children welcome; 9 Social drinking allowed; 10 Tennis nearby; 11 Swimming nearby; 12 Golf nearby; 13 Skiing nearby; 14 May be booked through a travel agent.

Paducah Harbor Plaza

Paducah Harbor Plaza Bed and Breakfast

201 Broadway, 42001
(502) 442-2698; (800) 719-7799

A warm, friendly atmosphere in the restored turn-of-the-century, five-story bed and breakfast overlooking the Ohio River in downtown Paducah. Antiques abound, and the family antique quilt collection complements the New Quilters Museum built by the American Quilters Society, one block from the bed and breakfast. Paducah is known as "Quilt City, USA." Museum, shops, and antique stores are accessible via a brick promenade along the river. Nostalgia is created with songs of the past played on a 1911 player piano. Sing-alongs are encouraged by Beverly.

Hosts: Beverly McKinley
Rooms: 4 (SB) $65-125
Continental Breakfast
Credit Cards: A, B, C
Notes: 2, 5, 8, 9, 11, 12, 13, 14

SPRINGFIELD

Glenmar Plantation Bed and Breakfast

2444 Valley Hill Road, 40069
(606) 284-7791; (800) 828-3330

Relax in a romantic setting on this 1785 250-acre horse farm. On the National Register of Historic Places. Recipient of the Kentucky Commemorative Historic Farm Award. Guests may stroll along walking trails, go riding, walking, cycling. Antiques and historic buildings including slave quarters and oldest buildings in Kentucky. There are animals including horses, llamas, cattle, and sheep.

Host: Kenny Mandell
Rooms: 8 (6 PB; 2 SB) $75-150
Full Breakfast
Credit Cards: A, B, C, D
Notes: 2, 3, 4, 5, 7, 8, 9, 10, 11, 12, 14

Maple Hill Manor

2941 Perryville Road, 40069
(606) 336-3075

Under construction for three years, this 14-room antebellum mansion, circa 1851, is listed on the National Register of Historic Places. On 14 tranquil acres in the Bluegrass region. The honeymoon hideaway has a canopy bed and Jacuzzi. One hour from Louisville and Lexington, close to the Stephen Foster Home and Perryville Battlefield. Complimentary dessert and beverages served in the evenings. Brochure available.

Hosts: Kay and Bob Carroll
Rooms: 7 (PB) $65-85
Full Breakfast
Credit Cards: A, B
Notes: 2, 5, 7, 8, 9, 10, 12, 14

VERSAILLES

Bluegrass Bed and Breakfast

Route 1, Box 263, 40383
(606) 873-3208

The Caboose. For the railroad buff, a red wooded caboose transplanted from the B&O Railroad is on a farm just outside Versailles. Guests have four bunk beds along the sides for daytime seating, or may climb up to sit in

NOTES: Credit cards accepted: A MasterCard; B Visa; C American Express; D Discover; E Diners Club; F Other; 2 Personal checks accepted; 3 Lunch available; 4 Dinner available; 5 Open all year; 6 Pets welcome;

the cupola where the conductor and flagman kept watch over the train. Amenities are as on a small boat; mini-refrigerator, two-burner hotplate, coffee maker, two-piece bath, and space heater. Outside are cold showers, yard chairs, picnic table, and croquet set. Air-conditioned. No TV. $100.

Peacham. Nine fireplaces typify the charm of this house built in 1829 from brick fired on the farm. Set amid ancient trees on a knoll one-half mile from the highway, this home is a quiet oasis bordered by horse farms. One second-floor room has twin beds and private bath. Very private first-floor suite; living room, bedroom with queen-size canopied bed, air conditioning, and private bath. No smoking. $60-75.

Polly Place. An artist's dream studio; beautiful, comfortable, yet with touches of whimsy. First level is one great room oriented around a huge fireplace. Above are open balconied bedrooms and bath with Jacuzzi. Studio rests on a shaded knoll on a 200-acre farm. Sleeps four comfortably. Guests have the entire house. Two-night minimum stay. $100-170.

Springdale. Nestled on a grassy slope above a stone springhouse, this fine old home is the perfect setting for those who want to experience quiet country living. The original dwelling, built about 1800, forms the nucleus of the airy brick home shaded by old trees. One air-conditioned bedroom has double bed and private bath. Another room is available for additional family or friends. Crib available. No smoking. $64.

Versailles II. The newest "old" house is on a tree-lined street of beautiful old homes. Built in 1980, this brick Colonial has the charm and character of a truly old home, including the antique furnishings, while offering modern amenities and comfort. The two guest rooms are upstairs, each with

a full bath (tub with shower). The front room has twin tester beds. The other room overlooks a terrace and garden, and has a four-poster bed. Air-conditioned. $65.

Welcome Hall. Built in 1792 when Kentucky was still the westernmost segment of Virginia, this handsome stone house and its grounds are a prime example of that period's self-sufficient country estate. Now devoted to blooded horses, as well as general farming, it provides a unique experience to its guests. Newly restored and air-conditioned two-room cabin has a double four-poster. Light breakfast. Two-night minimum stay. $100.

Shepherd Place

US 60 and Heritage Road, 40383
(606) 873-7843

Marlin and Sylvia invite guests to share their pre-Civil War home, built between 1820 and 1850. The house has windows that go all the way to the floor, crown moldings, hardwood floors, and large rooms with private baths, as well as a parlor and front porch swing for relaxation. Stroll up to the barn and meet the resident ewes, or ride through the bluegrass horse farms. Horseback riding nearby.

Hosts: Marlin and Sylvia Yawn
Rooms: 2 (PB) $65
Full Breakfast
Credit Cards: A, B
Notes: 2, 5, 7, 9, 12

Shepherd Place

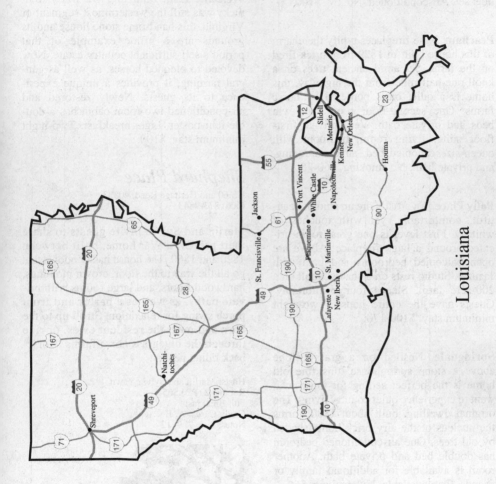

Louisiana

Louisiana

HOUMA

New Orleans Bed and Breakfast

P.O. Box 8163, New Orleans, 70182
(504) 838-0071; FAX (504) 838-0140

Acadian Country. Here are several marvelous hosts who share their charming modern homes, food, and stories with guests. Full breakfast. $55-60.

JACKSON

Milbank

3045 Bank Street, 70748
(504) 634-5901

Built in 1836, Milbank is a romantic antebellum mansion with irresistible charm. Come and spend quiet time in this small historic town. Sleep in a queen-size canopied mallard bed. Museum, winery, churches, houses, golf, and walking tour.

Milbank

Hosts: Paul and Margurite Carter
Rooms: 3 (PB) $75
Suite: 1 (SB) $125
Full Breakfast
Credit Cards: A, B, D
Notes: 2, 5, 7, 8, 9, 12

KENNER (NEW ORLEANS)

Seven Oaks Plantation

2600 Gay Lynn Drive, 70065
(504) 888-8649

This 10,000-square-foot West Indies-style home overlooking the lake is convenient to the airport and is 20 minutes from the New Orleans French Quarter. Guest rooms open into a large living room and into 12-foot galleries. A full plantation breakfast is served and the entire home can be toured. Antiques and Mardi Gras memorabilia are found throughout. Seven Oaks offers Southern hospitality and will make guests' visits full of warm, pleasant memories.

Hosts: Kay and Henry Andressen
Rooms: 2 (PB) $95-115
Full and Continental Breakfast
Credit Cards: A, B, C
Notes: 2, 5, 7, 9, 12, 14

LAFAYETTE

Alida's A Bed and Breakfast

2631 SE Evangeline Throughway, 70508-2168
(318) 264-1191; (800) 9 CAJUN 7 (922-5867)

In the heart of "Cajun Country," Alida's is characterized by the gracious hospitality of its innkeepers. After completing a three-and-a-half-year restoration of this

NOTES: Credit cards: A MasterCard; B Visa; C American Express; D Discover; E Diners Club; F Other;
2 Personal checks accepted; 3 Lunch available; 4 Dinner available; 5 Open all year; 6 Pets welcome;
7 No smoking; 8 Children welcome; 9 Social drinking allowed; 10 Tennis nearby; 11 Swimming nearby;
12 Golf nearby; 13 Skiing nearby; 14 May be booked through a travel agent.

turn-of-the-century Victorian cottage, the hosts opened their home to the weary traveler. They give generously of themselves, making every guest feel comfortable, at ease, and at home. Fresh cut flowers and wonderful aromas from the kitchen give the feeling of visiting grandma's house. At the end of the day, guests can slip into one of the huge antique claw-foot tubs, sip a glass of wine in the parlor, or just relax on one of the swings on the front porch or rear patio. Smoking outside only.

Hosts: Tanya and Douglas Greenwald
Rooms: 4 (PB) $75-150
Full Breakfast
Credit Cards: A, B, C, D
Notes: 2, 3, 4, 5, 9, 10, 12, 14

New Orleans Bed and Breakfast

P.O. Box 8163, New Orleans, 70182
(504) 838-0071; FAX (504) 838-0140

Acadian City. Stay in a turn-of-the-century home. Listen to stories the hosts tell of the families whose lives revolved around this home. Choose any one of the four memento filled rooms and imagine life there 90 years ago. Enjoy a full breakfast and afternoon refreshments. $100-125.

METAIRIE

New Orleans Bed and Breakfast

P.O. Box 8163, 70182
(504) 838-0071; FAX (504) 838-0140

LK1. A West Indies-style plantation home built from remains of a long-ago plantation mansion and filled with antiques, Mardi Gras mementoes, and giant Audubon prints. Two bedrooms, private baths, and breezeway on the second floor. On the levee, guests can jog, ride bikes, or stroll hand-in-hand. A full plantation breakfast is served in the family dining room. Near the airport, 25 minutes by car to the French Quarter. $95-125.

Madewood Plantation House

NAPOLEONVILLE

Madewood Plantation House

4250 Highway 308, 70390
(504) 369-7151

A national historic landmark, Madewood is a stately Greek Revival mansion on Bayou Lafourche about 75 miles from New Orleans' French Quarter. Set on 20 acres in front of a working sugar cane plantation, Madewood is furnished with antiques. Bedrooms have canopied beds. Guests dine by candlelight, family-style, after a wine and cheese party in the library. Featured in *Vogue*, *Country Home*, *Country Inns*, *Innsider*, the *Los Angeles Times*, BBC radio, and many more. In cottage, Continental breakfast; in mansion, full breakfast, and dinner for two.

Hosts: Keith and Millie Marshall; Dave D'Aunoy
Rooms: 9 (PB) $175
Full Breakfast
Credit Cards: A, B, C, D
Closed major holidays
Notes: 2, 4, 5, 8, 9, 14

NATCHITOCHES

Breazeale House Bed and Breakfast

926 Washington Street, 71457
(318) 352-5630; (800) 352-5631

Built for Congressman Phanor Breazeale in the late 1800s, Breazeale house is within walking distance of the historic downtown district. This Victorian house features 11 fireplaces, 12-foot ceilings, nine stained-glass windows, a set of servants' stairs, three balconies, eight bedrooms, and three floors with over 6,000 square feet of living space. President Taft slept here, and this house can be seen in *Steel Magnolias*.

Hosts: Willa and Jack Freeman
Rooms: 5 (2 PB; 3 SB) $50-75
Full Breakfast
Credit Cards: A, B, C
Notes: 2, 5, 7, 8, 9, 11, 14

Cane River House

910 Washington Street, 71457
(318) 352-5912

Cane River House is in the Natchitoches historic district, close to shops and restaurants and convenient to plantations and Kisatchie National Forest. This stunning, spacious craftsman bungalow was built in 1923. The interior boasts original heart pine woodwork. The rooms are decorated in arts and crafts furniture and other period antiques. The Guest House, at the rear of the property, is set among lush banana trees. A gourmet breakfast, including fresh ground coffee, is served in the dining room.

Hosts: Alan and Janny Pezaro
Rooms: 3 (PB) $65-90
Full Breakfast
Credit Cards: A, B, D
Notes: 2, 5, 7, 9, 10, 12, 14

Fleur de Lis
Bed and Breakfast Inn

336 Second Street, 71457
(318) 352-6621; (800) 489-6621

This grand old Victorian house is in the oldest settlement in the Louisiana Purchase and is listed on the National Register of Historic Places. Guests at the inn may expect a warm welcome, a room tastefully decorated with king- or queen-size beds, private baths, make-up vanities, sitting area, as well as the many amenities one expects

in a friend's home. Delicious full breakfast with rich Louisiana coffee and orange juice.

Hosts: Tom and Harriette Palmer
Rooms: 5 (PB) $65
Full Breakfast
Credit Cards: A, B, C
Notes: 2, 5, 7, 8, 9, 10, 11, 12, 14

Fleur de Lis

Martin's Roost

1735 1/2 Washington Street, 71457
(318) 352-9215

Comfortable contemporary home with country atmosphere. Patios, pool, and deck with panoramic view of former Red River roadbed. Arts, crafts, plantation doll houses, and needlework. Home of background props filmed in *Steel Magnolias*. Gourmet breakfast; dinner du jour. Certified tour guide to enchanting history of oldest settlement in Louisiana Purchase.

Hosts: Ronald and Vicki Martin
Rooms: 2 (PB) $65
Full Breakfast
Credit Cards: None
Notes: 2, 3, 4, 5, 9, 11, 12, 14

NEW IBERIA

The Inn at leRosier

314 East Main Street, 70560
(318) 367-5306

LeRosier, an 1870 country inn complete with rose gardens and gourmet breakfast, is a perfect getaway for romantics. There

7 No smoking; 8 Children welcome; 9 Social drinking allowed; 10 Tennis nearby; 11 Swimming nearby; 12 Golf nearby; 13 Skiing nearby; 14 May be booked through a travel agent.

are four guest rooms furnished with lovely antiques and elegant appointments. Each room has its own stocked refrigerator, bath, telephone, and television. Cozy parlors, fireplaces, world-class dining, and personal service at acclaimed leRosier restaurant. In historic district New Iberia across from Shadows-on-the-Teche, a National Trust owned property. Completely smoke-free environment.

Hosts: L. Hallman and Mary Beth Woods
Rooms: 4 (PB) $100
Full Breakfast
Credit Cards: A, B, C
Notes: 2, 3, 4, 5, 7, 9, 14

New Orleans Bed and Breakfast

P.O. Box 8163, New Orleans, 70182
(504) 838-0071

Country Estate. A modern plantation mansion with all the beauty, comfort, serenity, and interest one could wish for. "Enchanting…flowers, trees, pond, peacocks and swans….A personification of luxury!" Enjoy the pool, gym, steam room, billiard room in this most luxurious home. Deluxe $85-95.

NEW ORLEANS

Beau Séjour Bed and Breakfast

1930 Napoleon Avenue, 70115
(504) 897-3746

This turn-of-the-century mansion is uptown on the Mardi Gras parade route and near the historic streetcar that carries guests to the French Quarter, convention center, Superdome, aquarium, and universities. Beau Séjour boasts a casual, tropical atmosphere with spacious rooms, queen-size beds, and antiques, embodying the charm and ambience of old New Orleans.

Hosts: Gilles and Kim Gagnon
Rooms: 5 (PB) $85-125
Continental Breakfast

Credit Cards: None
Notes: 2, 5, 8, 9, 10, 11, 12

Bed and Breakfast Inc.

1021 Moss Street, Box 52257, 70152-2257
(504) 488-4640; (800) 729-4640
FAX (504) 488-4639

Architectural Gem. Remaining true to the original design of this wonderful guest cottage has been of primary concern to the owners. They have overseen the renovation project from top to bottom, paying careful attention not to disturb the historic detail of this building. Thick exposed brick walls and three brick fireplaces, used in the 1830s as the kitchen facilities for the main house, reflect the authenticity of this historic restoration. Uniquely designed private baths adjoin each of the two cozy bedrooms. Self-serve Continental breakfast is provided for leisurely enjoyment. $75-150.

Bayou St. John Home. This home is of the "box step cottage" design that is typical of the architectural style of this area. Its street is named after scenic Bayou St. John which passes close by. Set in a charming neighborhood of historic properties, several small French cafes, specialty coffee shop, and gourmet grocery-deli are just a stroll away. Along the banks of Bayou St. John is City Park, the home of the New Orleans Museum of Art set amongst giant oaks in one of America's largest metropolitan parks. Friendly hosts are both nurses and enjoy collecting everything from Mardi Gras memorabilia to antique match books. Ask them for unique and out-of-the-way restaurant suggestions. Dining out is one of their fondest passions. Bus to the French Quarter and downtown where convention centers are nearby in under 15 minutes (five minutes by car). Continental breakfast.

Bourbon Street Suite. Guests enjoy this private, first-floor suite opening onto world-famous Bourbon Street. The host is a

New Orleans native and shares his vast knowledge of the special spots not to miss. One bedroom; private bath; Continental breakfast. $75-100.

Creole Cottage. This quaint Creole cottage was built in 1902. The home is minutes away from major New Orleans attractions. The historic Saint Charles Avenue streetcar line makes the famous restaurants, jazz clubs, art galleries, and antique shops accessible. Two bedrooms; Continental breakfast provided on silver service. $50-70.

Dauphine Street Suite. In the heart of the residential part of the French Quarter, this guest suite is nestled in the courtyard of an 1840s Creole cottage. The second-story suite is off the charming brick courtyard and has a private entrance, horse-hair double bed, and bath. Self-serve Continental breakfast is provided. $75-100.

Designer Guest Cottage. Originally the studio of a famous Southern sculptor, the cottage displays his artistic creativity while preserving its historic past. A short streetcar ride to galleries, antiques, restaurants, and the French Quarter. One bedroom with private bath; Continental breakfast served. $95-135.

Desmond Place. This Mediterranean Villa-style home with blue tile roof and terrazzo entryway typifies 1940s New Orleans. In a quiet neighborhood and surrounded by live oak trees, the home is furnished with antiques and artifacts collected by the hosts. Relax after a day of sightseeing or conventions in the inviting pool and patio area. The hosts enjoy dining out, so ask them for out-of-the-way and unique restaurant suggestions. A traditional bed and breakfast, hosts offer two guest bedrooms, each with its own private bath. The French Quarter, Garden District, and Uptown are only minutes away by car or taxi. Off-street parking available. Continental breakfast.

Desoto Suite. Built in the 1880s, this raised Victorian home displays the architectural charm so typical of New Orleans cottages. Set in an area of ongoing restorations, several small French restaurants, a specialty coffee shop, and a gourmet grocery-deli are just a stroll away. Along the banks of Bayou St. John is City Park, one of America's largest metropolitan parks and the home of the New Orleans Museum of Art. From this home, the bus takes guests to the French Quarter and downtown to conventions in under 15 minutes (five minutes by car). The host, whose private living quarters are also in the same house, is warm and welcoming. A New Orleans native, he gladly shares his extensive knowledge of the city. Feel free to ask for restaurant and tour suggestions. Guest suite is spacious with separate entrance, living room-bedroom, bath, and kitchenette. Self-serve Continental breakfast.

Galleried Home. Historians delight in this French Plantation-style home with its lovely antiques. The guest suite is just off the host's living room and opens onto the front balcony. The suite offers a sitting room, bedroom with four-poster double bed, and bath. The garden below provides a tropical setting. Continental breakfast. $95-110.

Garden District Building. Right on the streetcar line, a fun ride to downtown and the French Quarter is less than 15 minutes. Guests will be sharing the host's lovely condominium and will have access to the swimming pool. One bedroom with private bath; Continental breakfast. $50-70.

Garden District Guest Suite. Three lovely antique twin beds grace a nicely decorated suite. Comfortably spacious with a living room and kitchen. Enjoy the special flavors of New Orleans-style cooking at the nearby famous bistros. Two bedrooms with private bath; Continental breakfast supplies provided. $50-80.

7 No smoking; 8 Children welcome; 9 Social drinking allowed; 10 Tennis nearby; 11 Swimming nearby; 12 Golf nearby; 13 Skiing nearby; 14 May be booked through a travel agent.

Bed and Breakfast Inc. (continued)

Greek Revival Home. Nestled in a historic community just across the Mississippi River from the French Quarter, this imposing Greek Revival home offers guests a private apartment overlooking the swimming pool. Walk or drive to the free ferry for a brief romantic ride. One bedroom available with private bath; Continental breakfast is provided. $50-80.

Guest Atelier. In the heart of the French Quarter's antique and art gallery district, this guest suite features natural brick walls and original artworks. A narrow staircase leads guests to a cozy third floor studio apartment, whose windows overlook a walkway famous for fencing masters of the past. Guests enjoy strolling to well-known restaurants and jazz clubs and to nearby downtown convention centers. A minibus and riverfront antique streetcar are available for those who prefer to ride. The personable owner of the property, an artist, is just downstairs. The apartment has a bedroom with sitting area, kitchenette, and private bath.

Guest Suite in Greek Revival Cottage. Greek Revival cottage offers a well-appointed guest apartment with its own private entrance overlooking the swimming pool. Hosts have tastefully decorated their home. The streetcar ride to downtown is just ten minutes. A short walk takes guests to other attractions. One bedroom with private bath; Continental breakfast. $50-90.

Home Near Audubon Park. Guests can ride the streetcar to the interesting Riverbend with specialty shops and to French coffee houses, art galleries, antiques, famous restaurants, music clubs, and more. This 1950s brick home is set in a lovely historic neighborhood. One bedroom with hall bath; Continental breakfast. $35-50.

La Maison Marigny. In the French Quarter, this petite bed and breakfast inn was just completely renovated down to window dressings and dust ruffles. Each of the three guest rooms has a private entrance and modern bath. Enjoy a Continental breakfast downstairs or outside in the traditional walled garden and patio. $75-100.

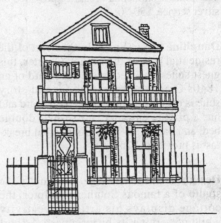

La Maison Marigny

The Lanaux House. The historic Lanaux House was constructed in 1879 and has been restored by the hostess. A private entrance leads to the second-floor guest suite. Guests enjoy their own lovely living room, bedroom with antique brass double bed, bath, and kitchenette. Self-serve Continental breakfast. $100-150.

La Petite Suite. This stylish guest suite, in the courtyard of an 1850s Creole cottage, offers the romance and history that is the ambience of New Orleans. The second-floor suite has a private entrance off the charmingly landscaped courtyard area. Once inside, guests enjoy the comfort of a four-poster bed, bath, and kitchenette. Continental breakfast. $75-100.

Le Garçoniere Guest Suite. A charming couple welcomes guests to their historic home in the French Quarter. Antique shops, restaurants, and jazz clubs are just a short walk from this quiet neighborhood. The private, two-story guest cottage overlooks the tropical courtyard with a balcony and full kitchen. Experience the streetcar along the Mississippi River. Continental breakfast. $75-100.

Mallard Suite. This historic Italianate-style home was constructed in 1879. It is a favorite background for movies filmed in New Orleans. The extensive restoration of the home includes the return of original pieces and warrants the high regard it receives. Guests are invited to a tour of the home. The second-floor guest suite is a spacious sitting room and bedroom combination. It is graced with authentic antique pieces including Morris Henry Hobbs etchings, Royal Bokara Oriental rugs, and early Victorian rosewood bed in the style of Mallard circa 1840. At their leisure, guests enjoy Continental breakfast in privacy of their own suite.

The Orleans Cottage. In the French Quarter area, this 1890s historic Victorian cottage was recently renovated. One bedroom with private bath; Continental breakfast is provided. $75-110.

Prytania Street Suite. The designer of this 19th-century home modeled it after an Austrian manse. Guests enjoy a lovely apartment that includes two bedrooms, full kitchen, and one and one-half baths. Just one block from the St. Charles Avenue streetcar line, this suite is convenient to all. Continental breakfast. $75-125.

Quaint Guest Cottages. A special place filled with romance and decorated with antiques and architectural details, the cot-

Quaint Guest Cottages

tages look onto a patio and antique swing. The streetcar is downtown at the French Quarter in just 15 minutes. Guests enjoy antiques, famous bistros, and music nearby. Two cottages with private baths; Continental breakfast. $60-125.

Queen Anne Victorian Home. Recently renovated, this home, with its original artwork and fabric-dressed walls, shows the special touches of the hostess, an interior designer. The Garden District mansions of the past are just steps away, as are restaurants, antiques, and art galleries. Three bedrooms with shared hall bath; Continental breakfast. $45-70.

St. Charles Avenue Home. Hosts love sharing their enthusiasm for New Orleans in a historic, homespun setting. Walking distance to the interesting Riverbend area with its specialty shops, coffee houses, and popular restaurants. The host was born in this house that boasts some of the original antiques. Two bedrooms with hall bath; Continental breakfast. $50-60.

7 No smoking; 8 Children welcome; 9 Social drinking allowed; 10 Tennis nearby; 11 Swimming nearby; 12 Golf nearby; 13 Skiing nearby; 14 May be booked through a travel agent.

Bed and Breakfast Inc. (continued)

University Area Home. A welcoming couple provides a comfortable, homey flavor in this raised cottage. University campuses, restaurants, specialty shops, and music clubs are nearby. A pleasurable 40-minute streetcar ride will take guests downtown. One bedroom with private bath; Continental breakfast. $30-70.

The Uptown Home. Guests enjoy this residential neighborhood, with its shady trees and historic homes. Close to universities, restaurants, antique shops, art galleries, and the streetcar line, which can take guests to many attractions. Each of the three bedrooms has a double bed and shared bath. Great for the budget-minded. Continental breakfast. $40-60.

Vendome Place. In a quiet neighborhood and surrounded by live oak trees, this home offers two beautifully decorated private entrance rooms, each with newly renovated private bath. Guests love to relax after a day of sightseeing or conventions in the inviting pool and patio area. Charming hosts love to give tour and restaurant suggestions. The French Quarter, Garden district, and Uptown are only minutes away by car or taxi. Off-street parking available. Continental breakfast.

Victorian Cottage. The host has lovingly restored this home. It offers peaceful, intimate guest rooms, comfortably furnished, and has a private bath and private entrance onto the patio. Nearby is the old French Market and Mississippi River Walk. Continental breakfast is served on the patio, which has a wet bar. $55-70.

Victorian Manse. An authentic bejeweled crown and scepter, recalling Mardi Gras balls of the past, rest regally on the front parlor mantel of this beautifully restored 100-year-old Victorian home. Just around the corner from charming boutiques, delightful restaurants, and French coffee houses in the hub of the established Historic Uptown District. Designer-decorated guest bedroom and bath are on the second floor. Continental breakfast is served in the country kitchen. $60-70.

The Columns Hotel

3811 St. Charles Avenue, 70115
(504) 899-9308

One of the stateliest remaining examples of turn-of-the-century Louisiana architecture, the Columns Hotel offers a return to former elegance. Despite its elegance, the Columns is affordable and comfortable. Its 19 rooms range from very simple to very grand. Each features some small delight for the experienced traveler: unique fireplace, armoires, and claw-foot tubs. Sunday brunch and private parties are hosted here where guests can expect impeccable service. Creole dishes served *lagniappe* during happy hour 5 P.M. to 7 P.M. daily. Convenient to many restaurants, the French Quarter, Audubon Park, the universities, and the casino. Listed on the National Register of Historic Places. Featured in *Good Housekeeping, Elle,* the *New York Times, Esquire,* on *Good Morning America,* and others.

Hosts: Claire and Jacques Creppel
Rooms: 19 (10 PB; 9 SB) $60-150
Continental Breakfast
Credit Cards: A, B, C
Notes: 5, 6, 8, 9, 10, 11, 12, 14

The Cornstalk Hotel

915 Royal Street, 70116
(504) 523-1515

This early 1800s home is central to the sights, sounds, gourmet foods, and night life of old New Orleans. In perhaps the most distinctive and most photographed of

The Cornstalk Hotel

the small inns of the French Quarter, guests will have a unique experience of Victorian charm in the Vieux Carré. Glowing crystal chandeliers, antique furnishings, stained-glass windows, fireplaces, Oriental rugs, canopy beds, and complimentary morning newspaper set the mood of quiet comfort during any stay.

Hosts: David and Debi Spencer
Rooms: 14 (PB) $75-150
Continental Breakfast
Credit Cards: A, B, C
Notes: 5, 9

French Quarter Guest House

623 Ursuline Avenue, 70116
(504) 529-5489; FAX (504) 529-1902

Nine luxurious rooms provide a quiet romantic and charming retreat, located in the preferred upper part of the French Quarter. Walking distance to all major sightseeing attractions. Continental breakfast provided across the street.

Rooms: 9 (PB) $59-175
Continental Breakfast
Credit Cards: A, B, C, D
Notes: 2, 5, 7, 8, 9, 14

The Glimmer Inn

1631 Seventh Street, 70115
(504) 897-1895

This restored 1891 Victorian home features 12-foot cove ceilings, Cypress woodwork, side and front galleries, wraparound porch, and enclosed brick patio. Across the street from the Garden District, just a half block to St. Charles streetcar, and easy access to French Quarter and Audubon Park and Zoo. A private carriage house is also available. All rooms are air-conditioned. Continental plus breakfast served.

Hosts: Sharon Agiewich and Cathy Andros
Rooms: 6 (1 PB; 5 SB) $55-85
Continental Breakfast
Credit Cards: None
Notes: 5, 9, 10, 12, 14

The Historic French Market Inn

501 Rue Decatur, 70730
(504) 561-5621; (800) 548-5148;
FAX (504) 566-0160

In the heart of the French Quarter, walking distance to all major attractions, this historic inn, renowned for its relaxing ambience and Southern hospitality, offers 60 romantic rooms and suites centered around a beautifully landscaped courtyard. Complimentary Continental breakfast, evening cocktail, and hot tub-pool.

Rooms: 60 (PB) $79-250
Continental Breakfast
Credit Cards: A, B, C, D, E
Notes: 2, 5, 7, 8, 9, 14

Hotel Ste. Helene

508 Chartres, 70130
(504) 522-5014; (800) 348-3888

Hotel Ste. Helene's traditional setting is New Orleans. Courtyards and gardens create a romantic and relaxing atmosphere. The 26 guest rooms feature 18th-century antiques. Join the hosts in the breakfast room overlooking the pool or have breakfast brought

7 No smoking; 8 Children welcome; 9 Social drinking allowed; 10 Tennis nearby; 11 Swimming nearby; 12 Golf nearby; 13 Skiing nearby; 14 May be booked through a travel agent.

to guest room door. Enjoy champagne during happy hour. Jackson Square and the mighty Mississippi are a few steps away. Seasonal rates available.

Rooms: 26 (PB) $130-225
Continental Breakfast
Credit Cards: A, B, C, D, E, F
Notes: 2, 5, 8, 9, 11, 14

Hotel St. Pierre

911 Burgundy Street, 70116
(504) 524-4401; (800) 535-7785

Hotel St. Pierre embodies the architecture and ambience of the 18th-century French Quarter. The 75 guest rooms and suites are set among courtyards and swimming pools. Each morning, complimentary coffee and doughnuts await guests in the Louis Armstrong breakfast room. Two blocks off Bourbon Street and all that jazz!

Host: James Millican
Rooms: 75 (PB) $89-129
Continental Breakfast
Credit Cards: A, B, C, D, E
Notes: 5, 6, 8, 9, 10, 11, 12, 14

Lafitte Guest House

1003 Bourbon Street, 70116
(504) 581-2678; (800) 331-7971

This elegant French manor house, in the heart of the French Quarter, is meticulously restored to its original splendor and furnished in fine antiques and reproductions. Every modern convenience, including air conditioning, is provided for guests' comfort. Complimentary Continental breakfast, wine- and hors d'oeuvres at cocktail hour, and on-site parking.

Host: Dr. Robert Guyton
Rooms: 14 (PB) $79-165
Continental Breakfast
Credit Cards: A, B, C, D
Notes: 5, 14

Lamothe House

621 Esplanade Avenue, 70116
(504) 947-1161; (504) 943-6536; (800) 367-5858

Elegantly restored Victorian mansion. All rooms have private baths, color TV, telephones, and air conditioning. Some have high ceilings. Jackson Square, French Market, many jazz clubs, and fine restaurants just a stroll away.

Rooms: 20 (PB) $99-150
Continental Breakfast
Credit Cards: A, B, C
Notes: 5, 8, 9, 10, 12, 14

Macarty Park Guest House/Historic Homes

3820 Burgundy Street, 70117-5708
(504) 943-4994; (800) 521-2790

Feel right at home in this century-old classic Victorian guest house and cottages just five minutes from the French Quarter. Step out of your room into lush tropical gardens and jump into the sparkling swimming pool. Our rooms are tastefully decorated in antique, reproduction, or contemporary furnishings, each with private bath, TV, telephone, and air conditioning. Free parking. Continental breakfast.

Host: John Maher
Rooms: 9 (PB) $45-160
Continental Breakfast
Credit Cards: A, B, C
Notes: 5, 9, 11, 14

La Maison

608-10 Kerlerec Street, 70116
(504) 271-0228 (phone and FAX) ; (800) 307-7179

Built in 1805 by Bernard De Marigny in the historical area called Faubourg Marigny.

La Maison

The Faubourg Marigny is an area of architectural significance with the Creole Cottage as the most predominant form of early development. All suites include private baths, parlor with color TV and phone, and bedroom. Special events rates are given upon request. Cancellation policy is seven days' advance notice.

Host: Alma F. Hulin
Suites: 8 (PB) $85-165
Continental Breakfast
Credit Cards: None
Notes: 2, 5, 7

Mazant Guest House

906 Mazant Street, 70117
(504) 944-2662

In the shade of a magnificent magnolia, the Mazant Guest House combines the Old-World charm of a European-style pension with typical Southern hospitality. This 19th-century home features comfortable rooms accented by antique and period furnishings, an equipped eat-in kitchen, and TV lounge. Off-street parking is free. With city buses within two blocks, and a super staff, the Mazant Guest House continues to delight visitors from around the world.

Rooms: 11 (5 PB; 6 SB) $35-50
Continental Breakfast
Credit Cards: None
Notes: 5, 6, 8, 9, 12

Mechling's 1860's Mansion

2023 Esplanade Avenue, 70116
(504) 943-4131

This 1860s historical mansion is on beautiful Esplanade Avenue. Come and experience the Victorian era and all the elegance and comforts of a grand mansion. Guests are just a stroll away from the French Quarter and City Park. Spacious, beautifully decorated rooms with private baths. Complimentary breakfasts and airport pickups. Afternoon tea is served in parlor, veranda, or dining room. Public transportation right outside the door. Guests' comfort is the hosts' pleasure.

Hosts: Claudine, Keith, Kelly, and Taina Mechling
Rooms: 6 (PB) $95-155
Full Breakfast
Credit Cards: A, B, C
Notes: 2, 5, 7, 9, 12, 14

Melrose Mansion

937 Esplanade Avenue, 70116
(504) 944-2255

The Melrose is an 1884 Victorian mansion that has been completely restored to perfection. This opulent, galleried mansion features eight antique-filled guest rooms with luxurious private baths, spacious heated pool and tropical patio, whirlpools, and wet bars with refrigerators in the rooms. Complimentary airport pick-up and delivery with house limousine, open bar at cocktail hour, and a full Creole breakfast. New Orleans grandeur at its very finest.

Hosts: Melvin and Rosemary Jones
Rooms: 8 (PB) $225-425
Full Breakfast
Credit Cards: A, B, C, D
Notes: 2, 5, 9, 11, 14

New Orleans Bed and Breakfast

P.O. Box 8163, 70182
(504) 838-0071; FAX (504) 943-3417

A1. In a typical uptown New Orleans bungalow, the guests have spacious quarters upstairs; bright, airy, newly redone; queen-size bed in bedroom and queen-size sofa bed in living room. Spacious for two, but adequate for four. $95.

A2. A stately Spanish home off St. Charles Avenue; has two bedrooms and two baths; spacious living, dining, kitchen area; self-serve Continental breakfast and pool. $100.

A3. On the third floor in a newly renovated Victorian home, the hosts have created an

7 No smoking; 8 Children welcome; 9 Social drinking allowed; 10 Tennis nearby; 11 Swimming nearby; 12 Golf nearby; 13 Skiing nearby; 14 May be booked through a travel agent.

New Orleans Bed and Breakfast (continued)

airy haven for their guests' pleasure. A double bed and private bath accommodate two. A Continental breakfast is served downstairs or on a tray by room. $85.

A4. A short distance from French Quarter and downtown, one block from the street-car; a late 1800 house, newly renovated, has two bedrooms with shared bath. The guests are welcome into the comfortable living-dining area. A Continental breakfast is provided for guest convenience. $75.

BD1. Very friendly hosts have converted a commercial building into a comfortable, attractive home and offer two guest rooms with bath in between. Two other smaller rooms with double beds share a hall bath. Off-street parking is available. No smoking; no small children. $40-50.

CP1. In the historic district of the city and to the rear of an 1890 Creole cottage is a spacious efficiency apartment with double bed, double sofa bed, private bath, kitchenette, and private entrance. Walking distance to the Museum of Art, St. Louis Cemetery, plantation homes, and the beautiful 150-year-old oaks in City Park. Continental breakfast. $55-70.

CP2. A comfortable one-bedroom apartment, completely private with twin beds and a fully furnished kitchen. A double sofa bed is in living room. Walk to activities in City Park or catch a bus to the French Quarter. No smoking; Continental breakfast. $55-70.

GE1. On this tree-shaded boulevard, one large brick house has three bedrooms. The master bedroom is done in rose and black,

has five tall windows, king-size bed, and private bath. Two other rooms share a bath. Continental breakfast. $55-75.

GE2. A pretty garage apartment has double bed and a trundle bed in the living area; kitchen, bath, and loads of off-street parking. Continental breakfast. $55-70.

LV1. One large, friendly home has two upstairs bedrooms with common den and independent bath. Great for family or two couples. Continental breakfast. $55-70.

LV2. In a delightful lake-view subdivision, a cozy bungalow offers one bedroom with twin beds and private bath, private entrance, and off-street parking. The guests will find a restful den and lovely back yard garden. Continental breakfast. $55-70.

UP2. This friendly, relaxed home has a cozy patio, spacious bedrooms, some with private baths, and double or queen-size beds. Guests have full use of the kitchen facilities. The hostess is a licensed tour guide and speaks both Spanish and French. Continental breakfast is served. $40-70.

UP4. One moderately priced, luxurious home is near first-class restaurants. One bedroom with private bath. Hostess loves to travel. Continental breakfast. From $75.

UP6. In a lovely uptown home with serene atmosphere is a large two-bedroom and bath suite, one with king-size bed and the other with a queen-size bed. Deluxe antiques, private entrance. Just steps away from St. Charles Avenue streetcar. Continental breakfast. $75.

UP10. This renovated historic uptown residence was once a plantation home. It consists of five bedrooms, each with a private

NOTES: Credit cards accepted: A MasterCard; B Visa; C American Express; D Discover; E Diners Club; F Other; 2 Personal checks accepted; 3 Lunch available; 4 Dinner available; 5 Open all year; 6 Pets welcome;

bath. Built in 1840, the house is furnished with antiques or reproductions of antiques, and all bedrooms have queen-size beds except one, which has a double Edwardian bed. Situated near the streetcar line and many fine restaurants. Continental breakfast. $95 plus.

UP11. Guests in this historic 1840 home enjoy a suite which has a sitting room overlooking the pool, a spacious bedroom with a king-size bed, two marble bathrooms, and a wet bar. The sitting area is furnished with a day bed which accommodates two singles or another couple. $95.

UP11A. Adjoining this property is another newly restored small home. Here are two bedrooms, each with a private bath and a common sitting room. Suitable for two congenial couples or a family. Continental breakfast is served in the dining room of the main house or on the veranda. $65.

UP12. Near the historic streetcar line, a cozy guest house is often available for the enjoyment of the guests. There is a living room, kitchen-dining area, bedroom with queen-size bed, and bath. Breakfast is in the refrigerator for guests' convenience. $85-95.

UP13. In a varied 1800 neighborhood shaded by ancient oaks is a restored camelback double—a lovely single home to a professional couple. Here the guest has traditional well-appointed bedroom and bath. Breakfast is served in the room. There is off-street parking, a patio, and living room for the guests' enjoyment. $85-95.

UP14. Near Audubon Park and the University area, a delightful hostess shares her home with our guests. The guest room has either two twin beds or one king-size bed, and a private bath. A Continental breakfast is served. $65-75.

New Orleans First Bed and Breakfast

3660 Gentilly Boulevard, 70122
(504) 947-3401; (504) 838-0071;
FAX (504) 838-0140

Live oak trees shade this quiet family-oriented area. Two cross-town buses offer easy transport to popular areas. New Orleans First Bed and Breakfast offers a large master bedroom with king-size bed and a private bath, and two double bed bedrooms with a shared bath. Continental breakfast served in the dining room. Off-street parking. Discount coupons for many activities are available. Please inquire regarding restrictions on personal checks, pets, and children.

Innkeeper: Sarah Margaret Brown
Rooms: 3 (1 PB; 2 SB) $55-125
Continental Breakfast
Credit Cards: A, B, C, D
Notes: 5, 7, 9, 12, 14

New Orleans Guest House

1118 Ursulines Street, 70116
(504) 566-1177; (800) 562-1177

An 1848 Creole cottage with lush courtyard where a complimentary Continental breakfast is served each morning. Private baths, free parking, tastefully decorated with antiques or contemporary furnishings, air conditioning, telephones, and TV. Three blocks to famous Bourbon Street.

Hosts: Ray and Alvin
Rooms: 14 (PB) $69-89
Continental Breakfast
Credit Cards: A, B, C
Notes: 5, 7

Nicolas M. Benachi House—"Rendezvous des Chasseurs"

2257 Bayou Road, 70119
(504) 525-7040; (800) 308-7040

The quintessential charm of 19th-century New Orleans awaits guests in this graceful

7 No smoking; 8 Children welcome; 9 Social drinking allowed; 10 Tennis nearby; 11 Swimming nearby; 12 Golf nearby; 13 Skiing nearby; 14 May be booked through a travel agent.

Nicolas M. Benachi House

Southern mansion. It has been lovingly restored and furnished. Gardens and fountains, oaks and sycamores, and parlors and grand dining room—all in period antiques. Walk to the French Quarter, City Park, and gourmet restaurants. Three-room suite with sitting room and shared bath; other private rooms and baths. Continental plus breakfast. Gracious hospitality. Secure parking.

Hosts: James G. Derbes and Cecilia J. Rau
Rooms: 4 (2 PB; 2 SB) $85-130
Continental Breakfast
Credit Cards: A, B, C, D
Notes: 2, 7, 9, 10, 12, 14

Nine-O-Five Royal Hotel

905 Royal Street, 70116
(504) 523-0219

Quaint European style hotel located in the heart of the French Quarter. One of the first smaller hotels in the French Quarter. Built in the 1890s, the Nine-O-Five has a courtyard and balconies overlooking the Southern charm and hospitality of Royal Street. Period furnishings, high ceilings and kitchenettes in all rooms.

Rooms and Suites: 10 (PB) $65-120
Credit Cards: A, B
Notes: 5, 8

The Prytania Inn

1415 Prytania Street, 70130
(504) 566-1515

Restored to its pre-Civil War glory and situated in the historic district, the inn received the 1984 Commission Award. Tender care; full gourmet breakfast. Patio, slave quarters, 18 rooms with private baths, and most with kitchen facilities or microwave and refrigerators. Five minutes to the French Quarter and one-block walk to St. Charles Avenue and the streetcar. Free parking. Hosts speak German.

Hosts: Sally and Peter Schreiber
Rooms: 18 (PB) $35-55
Full Breakfast
Credit Cards: A, B, C, D, E, F
Notes: 5, 6, 7, 8

The Robert Gordy House

2630 Bell Street, 70119
(504) 486-9424

This 1880s Italianate cottage was the home of Robert Gordy. His work hangs in the house and his studio is open to guests, as is the rest of the house. Translucent window treatments, bright millwork, and 14-foot ceilings give the house a light, airy feeling. Nearby City Park features golf courses, an art museum, a historic carousel, and many other attractions. The excitement of the French Quarter is five minutes away by bus or cab. Rates are subject to change during special events.

Host: Stewart Walker
Rooms: 3 (1 PB; 2 SB) $75-95
Continental Breakfast
Credit Cards: None
Notes: 5, 6, 7, 8, 9, 10, 12, 14

Rue Dumaine

731 Dumaine Street, 70116
(504) 581-2802

Guests' private entranceway leads through a lush, secluded patio to a hideaway in the heart of the bustling French Quarter. Built in 1824, these completely renovated slave quarters have every amenity, including central air and heat, ceiling fans, working fireplace, balcony, private bath, telephones, intercom, and kitchenette with microwave and refrigerator. Have a great time on Bourbon Street just one-half block away and yet sleep soundly in the quiet of an exclusive retreat. Twin beds only.

Host: Clydia Davenport
Room: 1 (PB) $90-150
Continental Breakfast
Credit Cards: D
Notes: 2, 5, 7, 9, 14

St. Charles Guest House Bed and Breakfast

1748 Prytania, 70130
(504) 523-6556

A simple, cozy, and affordable European-style pension operating in the lower Garden District for over 40 years. On streetcar line. Minutes to downtown and all attractions. Complimentary Continental breakfast, pool, and decks enjoyable almost year-round. Favored by writers, artists, performers, and world travelers; over 4,000 guests per year. Charming, eclectic, uniquely "Old New Orleans," low tech, and relaxing, from backpacker rooms at $30 to antiques and queen-size beds at $85. Historic district. In guidebooks worldwide. Personal checks accepted in advance.

Hosts: Joanne and Dennis Hilton
Rooms: 38 (26 PB; 12 SB) $30-85
Continental Breakfast
Credit Cards: A, B, C
Notes: 5, 7, 8, 9

St. Charles Guest House

Soniat House

1133 Chartres Street, 70116
(504) 522-0570; (800) 544-8808
FAX (504) 522-7208

Hidden in a quiet residential section of New Orleans' French Quarter, Soniat House was built in 1829 as a town home for the large family of Joseph Soniat Dufossat, a wealthy plantation owner. Typical of the period, the Creole house incorporates classic Greek Revival details. A wide carriageway entrance leads to a quiet and beautiful courtyard; galleries are framed by lace ironwork, and open spiral stairs lead to the two upper floors. All rooms are tastefully furnished with fine antiques, hand-carved bedsteads, and the work of contemporary New Orleans artists. The Soniat House was recognized as the French Quarter's best restoration on the 50th anniversary of the Vieux Carré Commission. Supplemental charge of $6 per person for Continental breakfast.

Hosts: Rodney and Frances Smith
Rooms: 31 (PB) $135-550
Continental Breakfast
Credit Cards: A, B, C
Notes: 5, 14

Terrell House Mansion

1441 Magazine Street, 70130
(504) 524-9859; (800) 878-9859

Terrell House was built in the Classical Revival style in 1858 by Richard Terrell as his family residence. The main mansion rooms are the original bedrooms of the house and feature balconies, galleries, and authentic furnishings and overlook the courtyard. Original carriage house has been converted to four guest rooms, each furnished with period antiques and all open onto or overlook the courtyard. The house contains Oriental rugs, marble mantels, gold-leaf mirrors. Gaslite era chandeliers and lamps grace every room along with Mardi Gras memorabilia to recreate the ambience of old New Orleans.

Hosts: Bobby and Cindy Hogan
Rooms: 10 (PB) $85-150
Full Breakfast
Credit Cards: A, B, C, D
Notes: 2, 4, 5, 7, 8, 9, 10, 11, 12, 14

7 No smoking; 8 Children welcome; 9 Social drinking allowed; 10 Tennis nearby; 11 Swimming nearby; 12 Golf nearby; 13 Skiing nearby; 14 May be booked through a travel agent.

PLAQUEMINE

Old Turnerville Bed and Breakfast

23230 Nadler Street, 70764
(504) 687-5337; (504) 687-6029

Antique-furnished guest bedroom with private bath in Miss Louise's house, a century-old raised cottage in Old Turnerville, an 1800s village on the Mississippi. Beautiful wide front gallery with relaxing swing and rockers. Separate guest cottage also available. Continental breakfast. Tour of two Old Turnerville house museums includes tariff. Antique shop. In the heart of plantation country. Twenty miles south of Baton Rouge.

Host: Brenda Bourgoyne Blanchard
Room: 1 (PB) $65
Cottage: 1 (PB) $85
Continental Breakfast
Credit Cards: A, B
Notes: 2, 5, 8, 9

PORT VINCENT

Tree House in the Park

16520 Airport Road, Prairieville, 70769
(504) 622-3885; (800) LE CABIN

A Cajun cabin inn with two bed and breakfast accommodations and a bridal suite, each with a private entrance off the front porch, private bath, and queen-size waterbed. Private hot tub on sun deck, and pool on lower deck (heated May through October). Boat slip, fishing dock, and double kayak float trip on Amite River. Four acres of ponds, bridges, cypress trees, ducks, and geese. Complimentary supper on arrival. Very peaceful.

Host: Fran Schmieder
Rooms: 2 (PB) $110-150
Full Breakfast
Credit Cards: A, B, C, D
Notes: 2, 4, 5, 9, 11, 14

ST. FRANCISVILLE

Barrow House Inn

9779 Royal Street, Box 700, 70775-0700
(504) 635-4791

Sip wine and relax in a wicker rocker on the front porch while enjoying the ambience of a quiet neighborhood of antebellum homes. Guest rooms are all furnished in beautiful antiques from 1840 to 1870. Delicious gourmet candlelight dinners are available upon request, and a cassette walking tour of the historic district is included for guests. Closed December 23 through Christmas Day.

Hosts: Shirley Dittloff and Chris Dennis
Rooms: 5 (PB) $85-95
Suites: 3 (PB) $115-135
Full or Continental Breakfast
Credit Cards: A, B
Notes: 2, 4, 5, 8, 9, 12, 14

Green Springs Plantation Bed and Breakfast

7463 Tunica Trace, 70775
(800) 457-4978

Sprawling country estate in Tunica Hills nature area. Peaceful garden setting with butterflies, flowers, birds, creek, natural spring, and Indian mound. Gracious Southern home of area native. Spacious, beautifully decorated rooms with queen-size or twin beds and private baths. Antique furnishings, and modern plumbing. A delicious hot plantation breakfast is cooked by the creator of "spinach Madeline." Near antebellum homes, Civil War battlefield, antique shops, Mississippi River ferry, and golf course. Biking and hiking are also available.

Hosts: Madeline and Ivan Nevill
Rooms: 3 (PB) $85
Full Breakfast
Credit Cards: A, B
Notes: 2, 5, 7, 8, 9, 12, 14

NOTES: Credit cards accepted: A MasterCard; B Visa; C American Express; D Discover; E Diners Club; F Other; 2 Personal checks accepted; 3 Lunch available; 4 Dinner available; 5 Open all year; 6 Pets welcome;

ST. MARTINVILLE

Old Castillo Bed and Breakfast

220 Evangeline Boulevard, 70582
(318) 394-4010; (800) 621-3017
FAX (318) 394-7983

Almost beneath the moss-draped branches of the legendary Evangeline Oak, the Greek Revival structure of the Old Castillo Hotel, circa 1830, rises from the banks of the historic Bayou Teche. Now both tourists and area residents can step back in time to share the warmth of Acadian culture and cuisine. Cherish time spent leisurely beside the slow moving waters of Bayou Teche. Listed on the National Register of Historic Buildings since 1979. Limited smoking permitted. Inquire about accommodations for children.

Hosts: Peggy and Shawn Hulin
Rooms: 5 (PB) $50-80
Full Breakfast
Credit Cards: A, B, C
Notes: 3, 4, 5, 9, 14

SHREVEPORT

Fairfield Place Bed and Breakfast

2221 Fairfield Avenue, 71104
(318) 222-0048

Built before the turn of the century, Fairfield Place has been beautifully restored to bring guests all the charm of a bygone era, as well as being convenient to downtown, I-20, the medical centers, Louisiana Downs, and Riverboat casinos. Within walking distance of fine restaurants and unique shops. Breakfast includes rich Cajun coffee and freshly baked croissants, served in the privacy of guests' rooms, the balcony, porch, or courtyard.

Host: Jane Lipscomb
Rooms: 9 (PB) $95-135
Full Breakfast
Credit Cards: A, B, C
Notes: 2, 5, 9, 10, 11, 12

SLIDELL

Salmen-Fritchie House Bed and Breakfast

127 Cleveland Avenue, 70458
(504) 643-1405; (800) 235-4168

Built before the turn of the century by one of the founders of this city, this Victorian mansion is listed on the National Register of Historic Places. Just 30 minutes from New Orleans' famous French Quarter. Beautiful grounds have 300-year-old trees. Several bedrooms have fireplaces. All have private baths, telephones, and TVs. Beautiful period antique furnishings with huge poster beds. A cottage that sleeps two to four people have living room/kitchen combination, bedroom with marble Jacuzzi for two, a courtyard and screened porch, and laundry facilities. Children over ten welcome.

Hosts: Sharon and Homer Fritchie
Rooms: 5 (PB) $85-95
Full Breakfast
Credit Cards: A, B, C
Notes: 2, 5, 7, 9, 10, 12, 13, 14

WHITE CASTLE

Nottoway Plantation Inn and Restaurant

P.O. Box 160, Louisiana Highway 1, 70788
(504) 545-2730

Nottoway, circa 1859, is a Greek Revival and Italianate mansion built for a wealthy sugarcane planter just before the Civil War. The home is beside the Mississippi River and surrounded by large oak and pecan trees. Rooms are also available in a restored 150-year-old overseer's cottage.

Hosts: Cindy Hidalgo and Faye Russell
Rooms: 13 (PB) $125-250
Full Breakfast
Credit Cards: A, B, C, D
Notes: 2, 3, 4, 5, 8, 9, 10, 11, 12, 14

---

7 No smoking; 8 Children welcome; 9 Social drinking allowed; 10 Tennis nearby; 11 Swimming nearby; 12 Golf nearby; 13 Skiing nearby; 14 May be booked through a travel agent.

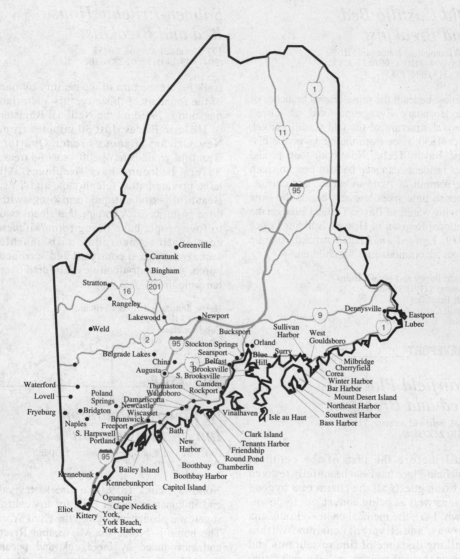

Maine

Maine

AUGUSTA

Maple Hill Farm
Bed and Breakfast Inn

Outlet Road, Rural Route 1, Box 1145, 04347
(207) 622-2708; (800) 622-2708
FAX (207) 622-0655

Quiet, relaxed elegance, away from all traffic on more than 60 acres of unspoiled rural beauty. Central to Maine's lake regions, mountains, and coast. Close to the national historic district offering unique shopping, dining, and antiques. Hearty custom-cooked country breakfast served. Rooms are tastefully furnished with antiques and overlook rolling meadows, woods, and gardens; private suite with Jacuzzi available. Experience the freedom of open skies and country solitude for an intimate weekend, or as an alternative to everyday business accommodations, just minutes from the Maine Turnpike.

Host: Scott Cowger
Rooms: 7 (4 PB; 3 SB) $55-90
Full Breakfast
Credit Cards: A, B, C, D, E
Notes: 2, 5, 7, 8, 9, 11, 12, 13, 14

BAILEY ISLAND

Captain York House
Bed and Breakfast

Route 24, P.O. Box 32, 04003
(207) 833-6224

Enjoy true island atmosphere on scenic Bailey Island, an unspoiled fishing village

Captain York House

accessible by car over the only cribstone bridge in the world. Near Brunswick, Freeport, and Portland. Former sea captain's home tastefully restored to original charm, furnished with antiques. Informal, friendly atmosphere and ocean views from every room. From the deck, enjoy sights of local lobstermen hauling traps and sunsets to remember. Nearby fine dining/summer nature cruise. Oceanview apartment rental also available.

Hosts: Charles and Ingrid Di Vita
Rooms: 4 (2 PB; 2 SB) $64-84
Full Breakfast
Credit Cards: None
Notes: 2, 5, 7, 9, 11, 14

BAR HARBOR

Black Friar Inn

10 Summer Street, 04609
(207) 288-5091

This comfortably restored and rebuilt Victorian house with antiques is on a quiet side street. Six guest rooms with queen-size beds

NOTES: Credit cards: A MasterCard; B Visa; C American Express; D Discover; E Diners Club; F Other;
2 Personal checks accepted; 3 Lunch available; 4 Dinner available; 5 Open all year; 6 Pets welcome;
7 No smoking; 8 Children welcome; 9 Social drinking allowed; 10 Tennis nearby; 11 Swimming nearby;
12 Golf nearby; 13 Skiing nearby; 14 May be booked through a travel agent.

and private baths. A suite with king-size bed, private bath, fireplace, and day bed. Rates include delicious full breakfast, late afternoon refreshments, and rainy day teas. Easy access to Acadia National Park. Short walk to waterfront, shops, and restaurants. Ample parking. Two-night minimum July 1 through mid-October. Sorry, no cots or roll away beds; the six guest rooms can accommodate one or two people only. Children over 11 welcome.

Hosts: Perry and Sharon Risley and Falke
Rooms: 6 (PB) $85-135
Suite: 1 (PB)
Full Breakfast
Credit Cards: A, B
Notes: 2, 5, 7, 9, 10, 12

Breakwater-1904

45 Hancock Street, 04609
(207) 288-2313; (800) 238-6309

Indulge in the luxury of Breakwater-1904, an English Tudor estate on the shores of Frenchman's Bay in Bar Harbor, Maine. Six grand individually appointed bed chambers with fireplaces and private baths await guests' arrival. Relax on the veranda with afternoon tea or evening refreshments and watch the yachts sail by. Listed on the National Register of Historic Places. Full breakfast is included. Nonsmoking bed and breakfast, not appropriate for young children or pets. Inquire about off-season rates. Cross-country skiing nearby.

Rooms: 6 (PB) $180-310
Full Breakfast
Credit Cards: A, B, C
Notes: 2, 7, 9, 10, 11, 12, 13, 14

Castlemaine Inn

39 Holland Avenue, 04609
(207) 288-4563; (800) 338-4563

Castlemaine Inn is nestled on a quiet side street in the village of Bar Harbor, which is surrounded by the magnificent Acadia National Park. The rooms are well appointed, with canopied beds and fireplaces. A delightful Continental buffet-style breakfast is served. Open May through October. Children over 13 are welcome.

Hosts: Terence O'Connell and Norah O'Brien
Rooms: 13 (PB) $98-168
Continental Breakfast
Credit Cards: A, B
Notes: 2, 9, 10, 11, 12

Graycote Inn

40 Holland Avenue, 04609
(207) 288-3044

For a truly romantic getaway, this painstakingly restored 1881 Country Victorian, on a peaceful one-acre village lot, has extra large rooms or suites—all with private baths, some with fireplaces, sun porches or balconies. Sleep beneath a cloud of lace and cutwork canopy in king- or queen-size beds. Wake to the aroma of fresh baked muffins and fresh ground coffee as prelude to a sumptuous full breakfast served on the sun soaked breakfast porch with tables for two. Relax in the casual atmosphere of the front porch sipping lemonade or in the comfortable parlor before a warm cozy fire. Park free and walk to town.

Hosts: Joe and Judy Losquadro
Rooms: 12 (PB) $95-145
Full Breakfast
Credit Cards: A, B, D
Notes: 2, 3, 7, 9, 10, 12

Hearthside

7 High Street, 04609
(207) 288-4533

Built at the turn of the century as the residence for Dr. George Hagerthy, Hearthside is now a cozy and comfortable bed and breakfast. Hearthside is on a quiet side street in Bar Harbor. All of the rooms have queen-size beds and private baths; some have private porches, whirlpool tubs, or working fireplaces. Some rooms have air conditioning. Each morning a lavish breakfast buffet is served, and lemonade and homemade cookies are offered each afternoon. Off-season rates and spring packages are available.

NOTES: Credit cards accepted: A MasterCard; B Visa; C American Express; D Discover; E Diners Club; F Other; 2 Personal checks accepted; 3 Lunch available; 4 Dinner available; 5 Open all year; 6 Pets welcome;

Hearthside

Hosts: Susan and Barry Schwartz
Rooms: 9 (PB) $85-125
Full Breakfast
Credit Cards: A, B, D
Notes: 2, 5, 7, 9, 10, 11, 12

Holbrook House Inn

74 Mount Desert Street, 04609
(207) 288-4970; (800) 695-1120

Holbrook House offers a splendid opportunity to relax amid the charm and ambience of Bar Harbor's "golden years." Holbrook House was one of the first cottages to provide lodging for wealthy Easterners who had discovered the beauty of Mount Desert Island in the late 1800s. Spared from the devastating fire of 1947 by a providential change in the wind, the inn remains a symbol of the hospitality which has been the hallmark of Bar Harbor for over 100 years. A visit to the Holbrook is a delightful Victorian fantasy with today's comfort and convenience.

Hosts: Jack and Jeani Ochtera
Rooms: 12 (PB) $75-145
Full Breakfast
Credit Cards: A, B
Notes: 2, 7, 10, 11

The Inn at Bay Ledge

1385 Sand Point Road, 04609
(207) 288-4204 (phone and FAX)

Amidst towering pines, the Inn at Bay Ledge literally clings to the cliffs of Mount Desert Island, which is locally and aptly referred to as "the Eden of New England." The many tiered decks which overlook the spectacular coastline are extremely inviting and guests may enjoy a swim in the heated pool, relax in the Jacuzzi, or simply enjoy a walk on the private beach. The elegant bedrooms complement the style of the inn that was built in the early 1900s and possesses an upscale country ambience. Beautifully decorated with antiques, all rooms are unique with views of Frenchman's Bay and nearby mountains. King-and queen-size canopied and antique four-poster beds are covered with designer linens, down quilts, and feather beds. The cottages offer extra privacy and more country style in heavy woods a few steps away from the main inn. Each morning a lavish full breakfast is served either on the deck overlooking Frenchman's Bay or before a roaring fire. Unique in character, size, location, and privacy. The Inn at Bay Ledge offers its guests the finest blend of luxury and Maine rustic living.

Hosts: Jack and Jeani Ochtera
Rooms: 10 (PB) $75-235
Full Breakfast
Credit Cards: A, B
Notes: 2, 7, 10, 11

The Kedge
Bed and Breakfast

112 West Street, 04609
(207) 288-5180; (800) 597-8306

The Kedge, built in 1870, has a peaceful beauty that is full of light and comfortable elegance. In town across the street from Frenchman Bay, this bed and breakfast rests on a double lot and has beautiful gardens. The dream room is 18 by 22 feet, has a king-size brass bed, fireplace, and whirlpool tub. In the historical district. Smoke free. Full breakfast. AAA. Children seven and older welcome.

Hosts: Leo and Cheryl Higgins
Rooms: 5 (PB) $55-150
Full Breakfast
Credit Cards: A, B, C, D
Notes: 2, 5, 7, 9, 10, 11, 12, 13, 14

7 No smoking; 8 Children welcome; 9 Social drinking allowed; 10 Tennis nearby; 11 Swimming nearby;
12 Golf nearby; 13 Skiing nearby; 14 May be booked through a travel agent.

Long Pond Inn

Box 120, Mount Desert, 04660
(207) 244-5854

In historic Somesville, the heart of Mount
Desert Island, offering a peaceful retreat
within fifteen minutes of all island activities. The inn offers warmth and hospitality
that reflects an admired tradition associated with New England inns. The inn was
built with dismantled vintage materials
from summer estates, country stores,
hotels, and cottages. Four guest bedrooms
are uniquely furnished featuring a cozy
two-room suite with king-size bed, private
deck, bath, and Jacuzzi tub. There are also
three rooms with queen-sized beds, private
baths, and one additional Jacuzzi. The stay
includes a hearty Continental breakfast of
fresh seasonal fruit and homemade
muffins. After breakfast take a stroll in the
gardens or paddle one of the rental canoes
on Long Pond.

Hosts: Brian and Lois Hamor
Rooms: 7 (PB) $75-125
Continental Breakfast
Credit Cards: A, B
Notes: 2, 9, 10, 11, 12

Manor House Inn

106 West Street, 04609
(207) 288-3759; (800) 437-0088

This beautiful 1887 Victorian summer cottage is listed on the National Register of
Historic Places. Near Acadia National Park.
Within walking distance of downtown Bar
Harbor and waterfront. Enjoy the acre of
landscaped grounds and gardens. Minimum
stay July, August, and holidays is two
nights. Closed November through mid-
April. Children over eight welcome.

Host: Mac Noyes
Rooms: 14 (PB) $55-165
Full Breakfast
Credit Cards: A, B
Notes: 2, 7, 8, 9, 10, 11, 12

Mansion at the Atlantic Oakes by-the-Sea

P.O. Box 3, 04609
(800) 33-MAINE; FAX (207) 288-8402

Restored in 1993, "this oceanfront cottage"
on the grounds of the Atlantic Oakes Resort
offers the ambience of an elegant inn, full
resort amenities, the convenience of a bed
and breakfast, stone-walled gardens, splendid oceanviews, plus tennis and swimming.
Nine lovely guest rooms: two suites, private
baths, king- or queen-size beds. Continental
plus breakfast is served in high season.
Minutes to Acadia National Park and
Downtown Bar Harbor.

Rooms: 9 (PB) $55-195
Continental Breakfast
Credit Cards: A, B, C
Notes: 2, 7, 10, 11, 12, 13, 14

The Maples Inn

16 Roberts Avenue, 04609
(207) 288-3443

Built in early 1900, the Maples Inn originally
housed the wealthy summer visitors to
Mount Desert Island. It is on a quiet, residential, tree-lined street. Guests will be away
from the traffic of Bar Harbor, yet

The Maples Inn

within walking distance of attractive boutiques, intimate restaurants, and the surrounding sea. For the perfect romantic getaway, reserve the White Birch Suite, complete with a blue and white tiled fireplace. Palates will be treated to host's personal breakfast recipes, some of which have been featured in *Bon Appétit* and *Gourmet* magazines. Enjoy the beauty of Acadia National Park and Mount Desert Island year-round.

Host: Susan Sinclair
Rooms: 6 (PB) $60-145
Full Breakfast
Credit Cards: A, B, D
Notes: 2, 5, 7, 9, 10, 11, 12,13

Mira Monte Inn and Suites

69 Mount Desert Street, 04609
(800) 553-5109; FAX (207) 288-3115

Quiet two-acre landscaped village estate with exquisite gardens and paved terraces. This 1864 Victorian has balconies, bay windows, fireplaces, pleasant common rooms, and a library. Rooms are furnished in antiques with either a king- or queen-size bed, private baths, whirlpools, and all rooms have cable TV, telephones, and air conditioning. In a separate building on the property are two suites. Each suite has a parlor with fireplace, kitchenette unit, bedroom with a lace canopy queen-size bed, two-person whirlpool, and a private deck overlooking the grounds. Spring, fall, and honeymoon packages available. One two-bedroom housekeeping suite for weekly rental.

Host: Marian Burns
Rooms: 12 (PB) and 3 suites (PB) $115-180
Full Breakfast
Credit Cards: A, B, C, D
Notes: 2, 9, 10, 12, 14

Pachelbel Inn

20 Roberts Avenue, 04609
(207) 288-9655

Join Russell and Helene Fye, along with their children Russ and Samantha, in this comfortable Victorian home. Central to

Pachelbel Inn

town. Easy walking to shops, restaurants, and the harbor. Five-minute drive to the Blue Nose Ferry Terminal and one mile to Acadia National Park. Smoking on front porch only. People remember the Fyes for their great breakfasts and warm hospitality. All children are welcome. Seasonal rates are available.

Hosts: Russ and Helene Fye
Rooms: 6 (4 PB; 2 SB) $85-110
Full Breakfast
Credit Cards: A, B
Notes: 2, 5, 8, 10, 11, 12, 13

The Ridgeway Inn

11 High Street, 04609
(207) 288-9682

Built at the turn-of-the-century, today the Ridgeway Inn offers warm hospitality in a comfortable atmosphere. Set in a quiet in-town location, the inn is just a short walk from the many shops, restaurants, the harbor, and Acadia National Park. The aged stone walls, bright flower lined yard, and porch with ornamental wrought iron furniture invites guests inside. Hardwood floors with scattered rugs, fireplaces with ornate mantels, lace curtains set in bay windows, and a sprinkling of antiques including a

7 No smoking; 8 Children welcome; 9 Social drinking allowed; 10 Tennis nearby; 11 Swimming nearby;
12 Golf nearby; 13 Skiing nearby; 14 May be booked through a travel agent.

working pump organ provide an intimate and visually pleasing atmosphere. Open year-round with seasonal rates.

Host: Lucie Rioux Hollfelder
Rooms: 5 (PB) $100-150
Full Breakfast
Credit Cards: A, B
Notes: 2, 5, 7, 9, 10, 11, 12, 13

Stratford House Inn

45 Mount Desert Street, 04609
(207) 288-5189

Stratford House Inn features English Tudor architecture with a likeness to Queen Elizabeth's summer home. Beautiful bedrooms, each with its own individual decor. Easy walk to stores, restaurants, or the waterfront. Acadia National Park is nearby with beautiful scenery and activities for everyone. Minimum stay on weekends and holidays is two nights. Closed November through May.

Hosts: Barbara and Norman Moulton
Rooms: 10 (8 PB; 2 SB) $75-150
Continental Breakfast
Credit Cards: A, B
Notes: 2, 8, 9, 10, 11, 12

Stratford House Inn

Thornhedge Inn

47 Mount Desert Street, 04609
(207) 288-5398; (800) 580-0800

Built in 1900 by the publisher of *Little Women*, this Queen Anne-styled shingled cottage is in the historic corridor district, one block from the main restaurant and shopping area. There are 13 spacious guest rooms. There are also many common areas including a dining room with original furnishings, three parlor areas with fireplaces, and a spacious porch with wicker furniture. All rooms provide a private bath, color cable TV, and most have a queen-size bed. Some rooms also have a fireplace with Sterno logs. Continental breakfast of homemade breads and muffins, orange juice, and coffee or tea is served each morning. Seasonal May 15 through October 15.

Host: Elinor G. Geel
Rooms: 13 (PB) $80-140
Continental Breakfast
Credit Cards: A, B, C
Notes: 2, 7, 9, 10, 11, 12

The Tides

119 West Street, 04609
(207) 288-4968

Oceanfront estate in the historic district of Bar Harbor. Elegant Greek Revival architecture featuring expansive wraparound veranda with fireplace and filled with wicker furniture; a great spot to enjoy breakfast while watching the boating activities. The Tides offers two-room suites, each with queen-size bed, private bath, and full oceanfront views. Private parlors have cable TV. Some suites have working fireplaces. Within walking distance of leisure activities, restaurants, and shops. Very close to Acadia National Park entrance. Cross-country skiing nearby.

Host: Margaret Eden
Rooms: 3 (PB) $175-255
Full Breakfast
Credit Cards: A, B
Notes: 2, 7, 9, 10, 11, 12, 13, 14

Willows at Atlantic Oakes-by-the-Sea

119 Eden Street, P.O. Box 3, 04609
(800) 33MAINE

The Willows, circa 1913, is on the grounds of Atlantic Oakes-by-the-Sea and was

Willows at Atlantic Oakes-By-The-Sea

named after the willow trees on the entrance drive. There are nine guest rooms. All rooms on the ocean side have oceanviews and balconies. Rooms two and three connect via the bath and are rented to one party. Four rooms have king-size beds and the other three rooms each have double beds. Continental plus breakfast served in the mansion in season. There is an apartment and penthouse separate from the bed and breakfast available. Not suitable for children. Seasonal rates available.

Rooms: 9 (7 PB; 2 SB) $55-230
Continental Breakfast
Credit Cards: None
Notes: 7, 10, 11

Bed and Breakfast Inns of New England

128 S. Hoop Pole Road, Guilford, CT, 06437
(203) 457-0042; (800) 582-0853

ME-853. Once a sea captain's home during Colonial times, this bed and breakfast offers six guest rooms, two with private baths, a large sitting room with TV, large deck with oceanviews, and a large screened porch with hammock, a relaxing swing chair, and the best spot to view the unforgettable sunsets. Decor of nautical accents and comfortable furnishings. Walk on nature trails; climb nearby mountains; and fish, swim, or canoe in the lakes. No smoking. Children ten and older are welcome. Resident cat; no guest pets. Two-night minimum stay between July and

September. Fifteen dollars for third person. $65-95.

BASS HARBOR

Pointy Head Inn
Route 102A, 04653
(207) 244-7261

Relax on the quiet side of Mount Desert Island near Acadia National Park in an old sea captain's home. On the shore of a picturesque harbor where schooners anchor overnight. Haven for photographers and artists. Minutes to lighthouse, trails, restaurants, stores. Children over ten welcome.

Hosts: Doris and Warren Townsend
Rooms: 6 (2 PB; 4 SB) $60-85
Full Breakfast
Credit Cards: None
Notes: 2, 7, 9, 10, 11, 12, 14

BATH

Bed and Breakfast Inns of New England

128 S. Hoop Pole Road, Guilford, CT, 06437
(203) 457-0042; (800) 582-0853

ME818. A small, charming bed and breakfast home within walking distance of the Maritime Museum, antique shops, and the town of Bath. Two guest rooms—both share a bath—are very large and well-furnished. Enjoy a Continental plus breakfast, air conditioning, a nice living room with TV and VCR, games, a grand piano, and a library. No smoking. One resident dog with lots of Teddy bears. No guest pets, please. Children over 12 welcome. $53-60.

Fairhaven Inn at Bath
North Bath Road, Rural Route 2, Box 85, 04530
(207) 443-4391

Where eagles soar, birds sing, and tidal river meets meadow. This comfortable, quiet 1790 Colonial is renowned for its

7 No smoking; 8 Children welcome; 9 Social drinking allowed; 10 Tennis nearby; 11 Swimming nearby;
12 Golf nearby; 13 Skiing nearby; 14 May be booked through a travel agent.

breakfast, and is the perfect midcoast base from which to enjoy all that Maine's coast has to offer. Hiking and cross-country skiing on property. Beaches and Maritime Museum nearby. Inquire about accommodations for pets. Smoking restricted.

Hosts: Susie and Dave Reed
Rooms: 8 (PB and SB) $65-80
Full Breakfast
Credit Cards: A, B
Notes: 2, 5, 8, 9, 10, 11, 12, 13, 14

Glad II

60 Pearl Street, 04530
(207) 443-1191

A comfortable Victorian home, circa 1851, near the center of town and convenient to Maritime Museum, beaches, Freeport shopping, L. L. Bean, and Boothbay Harbor. The host and her four-legged concierge, Nicholas, love to welcome new friends. Two-night minimum stay weekends and holidays.

Host: Gladys Lansky
Rooms: 2 (SB) $50 plus tax
Continental Breakfast
Credit Cards: A, B, C
Notes: 2, 7, 9, 10, 11, 12, 13, 14

BELFAST

Bed and Breakfast Inns of New England

128 S. Hoop Pole Road, Guilford, CT, 06437
(203) 457-0042; (800) 582-0853

ME-840. This Greek Revival house was built around 1845 during Belfast's period of great architectural activity. Guests are welcome to use the beautiful formal living room with ornate tiled fireplace. Three large bedrooms with pine floors and a variety of bed sizes are available. All bedrooms have private baths. There is a screened and glassed-in porch overlooking a garden where breakfast is usually served. Complimentary afternoon wine is served in the living room. No pets. Children over ten welcome. No smoking. $50-60.

The Jeweled Turret Inn

16 Pearl Street, 04915
(207) 338-2304; (800) 696-2304 (in state)

Step back into a time when lace, elegant furnishings, and afternoon tea were everyday necessities. The inn is named for the grand staircase that winds up the turret, lighted by stained- and leaded-glass panels with jewel-like embellishments. Lots of woodwork, fireplaces, public rooms, and two verandas available for relaxation. Mornings welcome visitors with gourmet breakfasts, and afternoon tea is available in the dining room or, during summer, on the veranda. In the historic district; shops, restaurants, and waterfront close by. Smoking restricted.

Hosts: Carl and Cathy Heffentrager
Rooms: 7 (PB) $65-95
Full Breakfast
Credit Cards: A, B
Notes: 2, 5, 9, 10, 11, 12, 13, 14

The Jeweled Turret Inn

The Thomas Pitcher House

5 Franklin Street, 04915
(207) 338-6454

Thomas Pitcher built this handsome in-town Victorian in 1873. An airy Italian ceramic tile foyer provides access to the common areas. Large bay windows and marble fireplace accent the bright and inviting parlor. Hearty breakfasts are served in the large Chippendale dining room. Guest rooms and common areas feature original Victorian architecture and offer a blend of antiques and reproduction pieces. Convenient to Acadia National Park and other mid-coast Maine attractions.

Hosts: Fran and Ron Kresge
Rooms: 4 (PB) $60-80
Full Breakfast
Credit Cards: None
Notes: 2, 5, 7, 9, 10, 11, 12, 13, 14

BELGRADE LAKES

Wings Hill

Route 27, P.O. Box 386, 04918
(800) 50 WINGS

A 200-year-old farm house that has been dramatically renovated and restored. Decorated with art, quilts, Oriental objects, and antiques. Quiet adult atmosphere. Ideal site to tour the middle of the state. Mountains, lakes, and the coast nearby. Large beautiful rooms with private baths. Water, loons, and summer breezes.

Hosts: Dick Hofmann
Rooms: 8 (PB) $95
Full Breakfast
Credit Cards: A, B
Notes: 2, 5, 7, 8, 9, 11, 12, 13, 14

BETHEL

The Douglass Place

162 Mayville Road, 04217
(207) 824-2229

This four-season, 19th-century, Early American/Victorian home is between two major ski areas and the White Mountains of New Hampshire. Marvelous area for antiquing, summer sports, and hiking. Gardens and gazebo in summer; game room, cozy fireplace in winter. Two-night minimum stay required for weekends and holidays. Closed Christmas and for two weeks in April.

Hosts: Dana and Barbara Douglass
Rooms: 4 (SB) $58.85

Continental Breakfast
Credit Cards: C
Notes: 2, 8, 9, 10, 11, 12, 13

Sudbury Inn

Box 369, Main Street, 04217
(800) 395-7837; (207) 824-2174

A three-story historic inn less than six miles from Sunday River ski area. Full breakfast and dinner are served in the fine dining restaurant, with casual dining and live entertainment in the world famous Suds Pub. Area attractions include White Mountain National Forest, Grafton Notch State Park, an 18-hole golf course, hiking, biking, canoeing, swimming, and shopping.

Host: John E. Martin
Rooms: 18 (PB) $60-100
Full Breakfast
Credit Cards: A, B, C
Notes: 2, 4, 5, 6, 7, 8, 10, 11, 12, 13, 14

BINGHAM

Mrs. G's Bed and Breakfast

Meadow Street, P.O. Box 389, 04920
(207) 672-4034

Four-bedroom old Victorian home has rocking chairs on the front porch. Loft with nine beds for groups. Walking distance to town and tennis court. White-water rafting on the Kennebec and Dead Rivers. Scenic drive 165 miles north on 201 to Quebec. Quiet, restful town with beautiful waterfalls. Beautiful foliage in fall.

Hosts: Frances Gibson
Rooms: 4 (SB) $60
Full Breakfast
Credit Cards: None
Notes: 2, 8, 9, 10, 11, 14

BLUE HILL

Mountain Road House

Mountain Road, Rural Route 1, Box 2040, 04614
(207) 374-2794

7 No smoking; 8 Children welcome; 9 Social drinking allowed; 10 Tennis nearby; 11 Swimming nearby; 12 Golf nearby; 13 Skiing nearby; 14 May be booked through a travel agent.

Mountain Road House

This 1894 farmhouse is on the only road that traverses the face of Blue Hill Mountain. It offers views of the bay while only one mile from the village. Choose twin, double, or queen-size bedrooms; each with private bath. Early bird coffee and tea available at 7:00 A.M., then breakfast with hot entree, fresh fruit, and muffins. Enjoy antiquing, galleries, bookstores, musical events, fine dining, coastal vistas and villages, and, of course, Acadia National Park.

Hosts: Carol and John McCulloch
Rooms: 3 (PB) $55-85
Full Breakfast
Credit Cards: A, B
Notes: 2, 5, 7, 8, 14

BOOTHBAY

Kenniston Hill Inn

Route 27, P.O. Box 125, 04537
(207) 633-2159; (800) 992-2915

Kenniston Hill Inn

Step back two centuries in time at Kenniston Hill Inn, a 1786 Colonial home with seven working fireplaces and ten rooms, each with private bath. A delicious full breakfast is included. On four beautiful acres, the inn is the oldest in Boothbay. Open all year.

Hosts: David and Susan Straight
Rooms: 10 (PB) $65-110
Full Breakfast
Credit Cards: A, B
Notes: 2, 5, 7, 9, 10, 11, 12, 14

BOOTHBAY HARBOR

Anchor Watch Bed and Breakfast

3 Eames Road, 04538
(207) 633-7565

Islands, fir trees, and lobster boats provide the setting for this cozy bed and breakfast on the prettiest shore of the harbor. Country quilts and stenciling set the style inside. Breakfast features a baked cheese omelet or baked orange French toast. Enjoy a table for two or sit with others at an oceanview window. The lawn slopes down to water and ends with a private pier and float. Five-minute walk to shops, boat trips, Monhegan ferry, and fine dining. One hour to beaches, lighthouse museums, and Freeport shopping. It is lovely here in all seasons. Open year-round.

Hosts: Diane and Bob Campbell
Rooms: 4 (PB) $65-105
Full Breakfast
Credit Cards: A, B
Notes: 2, 5, 7, 9, 10, 11, 12, 14

The Atlantic Ark Inn

64 Atlantic Avenue, 04538
(207) 633-5690

An intimate bed and breakfast inn, offering lovely views of the harbor and only a five-minute stroll to town over a historic footbridge. This 100-year-old Maine

NOTES: Credit cards accepted: A MasterCard; B Visa; C American Express; D Discover; E Diners Club; F Other; 2 Personal checks accepted; 3 Lunch available; 4 Dinner available; 5 Open all year; 6 Pets welcome;

home has been lovingly restored and tastefully furnished with antiques and Oriental rugs. Guest rooms are adorned with fresh flowers, floor-length drapes, queen-size poster beds, and private baths, including one with double Jacuzzi and another with Greek tub. Each morning celebrate the day with a beautiful breakfast of gourmet coffees, fresh fruits, home-baked breads, and always an interesting main entree prepared with the freshest and purist of ingredients. Recommended by the late Stephen Birnbaum in *Good Housekeeping* magazine as one of the best places to stay in Boothbay Harbor. Inquire about accommodations for children.

Host: Donna Piggott
Rooms: 6 (PB) $70-159
Full Breakfast
Credit Cards: A, B, C
Notes: 2, 7, 9, 10, 11, 12, 14

Bed and Breakfast Inns of New England

128 S. Hoop Pole Road, Guilford, CT, 06437
(203) 457-0042; (800) 582-0853

ME807. A two-minute stroll from the village in beautiful Boothbay Harbor lies this lovely 1879 Victorian. Enjoy five charmingly decorated guest rooms with shared or private baths. Three rooms with magnificent harbor views. Enjoy dinner theater and entertainment, boat tours, sailing, fishing trips, clambakes, an aquarium, museums, and weekly concerts on the library lawn. Continental plus breakfast. $75-95.

ME813. Beautiful waterfront bed and breakfast is in this exciting seacoast town. In this Victorian inn guests may enjoy any of twelve guest rooms, all with private baths, decks or patios, and a guest parlor with fireplace and shelves full with books. Continental plus breakfast. No smoking. No pets. $85-125.

Bed and Breakfast Marblehead and North Shore

P.O. Box 35, Newtonville, MA, 02160
(617) 964-1606; (800) 832-2632
FAX (617) 332-8572

Gull and Gardens B&B. This cozy 1850 New England Cape home, surrounded by perennial gardens, is a short walk from the shops and restaurants of the Harbor. The master guest room has a full, detached private bath, with the option of king-size or two single beds. A two-room guest suite has double beds and shared bath, perfect for families or small groups; a single room in the suite may be taken at private-bath rates. A fabulous full breakfast is served daily. No smoking. Children over 16 welcome. Open year-round. $65-85.

Five Gables Inn

P.O. Box 75, Murray Hill Road
East Boothbay, 04544
(207) 633-4551; (800) 451-5048

Five Gables Inn is a completely restored Victorian, circa 1865, on Linekin Bay. All rooms have an ocean view and five have fireplaces. A gourmet breakfast is served in the large common room or on the spacious wraparound veranda. Minimum stay requirements for weekends and holidays. Closed November 16 through May 15. Children over 12 welcome.

Hosts: Ellen and Paul Morissette
Rooms: 15 (PB) $80-140
Full Breakfast
Credit Cards: A, B
Notes: 2, 9, 10, 11, 12

Harbour Towne Inn on the Waterfront

71 Townsend Avenue, 04538
(207) 633-4300; (800) 722-4240

7 No smoking; 8 Children welcome; 9 Social drinking allowed; 10 Tennis nearby; 11 Swimming nearby; 12 Golf nearby; 13 Skiing nearby; 14 May be booked through a travel agent.

"The Finest Bed and Breakfast on the Waterfront." A short stroll from the historic coastal village, with scenic harbor views and outside decks in a quiet location on Boothbay Harbor, the boating capital of New England. All rooms have private baths in this refurbished Victorian townhouse that has been updated in traditional style. Also available is a luxury penthouse that will sleep six in absolute privacy. Walk to fascinating shops, art galleries, restaurants, churches, library, dinner theaters, boat trips, and fishing. One-to two-hour drive to skiing. Reservations recommended. Special off-season getaway packages. Inquire about accommodations for children.

Host: George Thomas
Rooms: 12 (PB) $59-225
Continental Breakfast
Credit Cards: A, B, C, D
Notes: 2, 5, 7, 9, 10, 11, 12, 13, 14

The Howard House

buffet breakfast. Shopping, sightseeing, boating, island clam bakes, seal and whale watches, and fine restaurants are nearby. AAA three diamond and *Mobil Travel Guide* approved. Smoking restricted.

Hosts: The Farrins
Rooms: 15 (PB) $58-83
Full Breakfast
Credit Cards: None
Notes: 2, 8, 9, 10, 11, 12, 14

BRIDGTON

Harbour Towne Inn

The Howard House Motel Bed and Breakfast

Route 27, 04538
(207) 633-3933; (207) 633-6244

Unique chalet design on 20 wooded acres, quiet setting, beautiful flowers. Each spacious, sparkling clean room features glass patio door with private balcony, cable TV, and full private bath. Delicious, healthful

The Noble House Bed and Breakfast

37 Highland Road, P.O. Box 180, 04009
(207) 647-3733

Romantic turn-of-the-century manor, set amid stately old oaks and towering pines. Secluded lake frontage on scenic Highland Lake. Barbecue, canoe, foot-pedal boat, and hammock for guests' use. Experience Shaker village, antique and craft shops, museums, and chamber music festival in summer. Cross-country and downhill skiing close at hand in winter. One hour inland from Portland, and one hour from the White Mountains. Sumptuous full breakfast. Whirlpool baths and family suites. Smoking restricted. Open November through June by advance reservation only.

Hosts: Jane and Dick Starets
Rooms: 8 (5 PB; 3 SB) $70-115
Full Breakfast
Credit Cards: A, B, C
Notes: 2, 8, 9, 10, 11, 12, 13, 14

BROOKSVILLE

Oakland House's Shore Oaks Seaside Inn

Herrick Road, Rural Route 1, Box 400, 04617
(207) 359-8521; (800) 359-RELAX

A "youngster" on Oakland House's secluded Bicentennial Farm, this Craftsman circa 1907 has antiques, living room with stone fireplace, library, dining room, porch, gazebo/deck. Dirt roads, loons, seals, blueberries, and pine. Relax or dream. Breakfast, dinner (in season), dock, rowboats, firewood, salt- and freshwater beaches, grand vistas. Picturesque ventures to nearby Bar Harbor, Acadia National Park, Stonington, Blue Hill, Isle au Haut, and the "Mailboat."

Hosts: Jim and Sally Littlefield
Rooms: 10 (7 PB; 3 SB)
Full or Continental Breakfast
Credit Cards: None
Notes: 2, 3, 7, 8, 9, 11, 12, 14

BRUNSWICK

Bethel Point Bed and Breakfast

Rural Route 5, Bethel Point Road, Box 2387, 04011
(207) 725-1115

Peaceful oceanside comfort in 150-year-old home. Perfect view of ocean birds, seals, and lobster boats. Opportunities for ocean swimming and shoreline walks to explore the local coast. An easy drive to points of

Bethel Point

interest such as Bowdoin College, Popham Beach, L. L. Bean, and local restaurants featuring seafood specialties.

Hosts: Peter and Betsy Packard
Rooms: 3 (SB) $70-100
Full Breakfast
Credit Cards: A, B
Notes: 2, 5, 7, 8, 9, 11, 13

Brunswick Bed and Breakfast

165 Park Row, 04011
(800) 299-4914

The Brunswick Bed and Breakfast is a Greek Revival house overlooking the town green. On the main level, the twin front parlors offer guests the inviting warmth of two fireplaces for wintertime comfort or the wraparound front porch for summer leisure. The guest rooms are decorated with antique furnishings, unique accessories, and quilts. Within walking distance of local restaurants, museums, and shops. Convenient, allowing guests to easily explore midcoast Maine harbors and coastline.

Hosts: Mercie and Steve Normand
Rooms: 6 (4 PB; 2 SB) $69-89
Full Breakfast
Credit Cards: A, B
Notes: 2, 5, 7, 8, 9, 10, 12

The Samuel Newman House

7 South Street, 04011
(207) 729-6959

Adjoining the Bowdoin College campus, this handsome Federal house was built in 1821 and is comfortably furnished with antiques. Hearty Continental breakfast includes freshly baked muffins/pastry and homemade granola. Brunswick is a culturally rich college town just ten minutes north of Freeport, and 20 minutes from Portland.

Host: Guenter Rose
Rooms: 7 (SB) $50-75
Continental Breakfast
Credit Cards: A, B
Notes: 2, 7, 8, 9, 11, 12

7 No smoking; 8 Children welcome; 9 Social drinking allowed; 10 Tennis nearby; 11 Swimming nearby; 12 Golf nearby; 13 Skiing nearby; 14 May be booked through a travel agent.

BUCKSPORT

The River Inn
Bed and Breakfast

210 Main Street, P.O. Box 1657, 04416-1657
(207) 469-3783

Spacious old sea captain's home on the Penobscot River in historic Bucksport. Conveniently at the northern tip of Penobscot Bay, Bucksport offers easy access to east and west bay tour areas. Antiquing, auctions, crafts, fishing, golf, water, and winter sports are available. Public boat launch is nearby, as are mooring rentals. Large deck offers panoramic river views, and a rare player grand piano will interest guests. Breakfast features fruit plates (in season). Please make reservations for pets. Children over 12. No smokers accepted.

Hosts: The Stone Family
Rooms: 4 (2 PB; 2 SB) $40-60
Full Breakfast
Credit Cards: None
Notes: 2, 5, 9, 10, 11, 12, 13, 14

CAMDEN

Abigail's Bed and
Breakfast Inn

8 High Street, 04843
(207) 236-2501, (800) 292-2501

Abigail's

This Greek Revival home built in 1847 is completely furnished in antiques. Rooms have queen-size poster beds, sitting areas with good reading lights, fluffy robes, full bath, and crisp linens. Guests meet for breakfast in the sunny dining room and enjoy a varying menu of fresh juices, fruit, souffles, quiches, waffles, scones, muffins, or coffee cakes. Walk to harbor, shops, restaurants, and galleries.

Hosts: Donna and Ed Misner
Rooms: 4 (PB) $65-125
Suites: 2
Full Breakfast
Credit Cards: A, B
Notes: 2, 5, 7, 8, 9, 10, 11, 12, 13, 14

Bed and Breakfast
Inns of New England

128 S. Hoop Pole Road, Guilford, CT, 06437
(203) 457-0042; (800) 582-0853

ME835. This early Colonial home in Camden's historic district is five minutes from the famous harbor with its galleries, restaurants, and unique shops. Choose from eight guest rooms with shared or private baths. Enjoy the guest parlor that has a fireplace or the deck. No smoking. No pets. Children over ten welcome. Full breakfast. $65-95.

Camden Harbour Inn

83 Bayview Street, 04843
(207) 236-4200; (800) 236-4266

This historic inn dates back to 1874 when travelers on steamships visited en route to Bangor from Boston. Perched high on a hill, within a five-minute walk the village center, the inn offers expansive views of the harbor, bay, and mountains from its wraparound porch, 22 guest rooms, and restaurant. A Victorian parlor, fireplaces, private decks, and patios add to the ambience. Cetacea, the inn's restaurant, serves distinctive regional and classic dishes in a relaxed and romantic candlelit dining room. Seasonal packages available. Full country breakfast served May through November.

NOTES: Credit cards accepted: A MasterCard; B Visa; C American Express; D Discover; E Diners Club;
F Other; 2 Personal checks accepted; 3 Lunch available; 4 Dinner available; 5 Open all year; 6 Pets welcome;

Camden Harbour Inn

Continental breakfast, December through April. No smoking in the dining room. Children over 12 welcome.

Hosts: Sal Vella and Patti Babij
Rooms: 22 (PB) $95-225
Full or Continental Breakfast
Credit Cards: A, B, C, D
Notes: 2, 4, 5, 9, 10, 11, 12, 13, 14

Castleview by the Sea

59 High Street, 04843
(207) 236-2344; (800) 272-VIEW (8439)

Spectacular glass-walled rooms overlooking Camden's only two castles and the sea, right from your bed! Count the stars across the bay and wake up to inspiring Maine views found nowhere else. Bright and airy charm of classical 1856 cape architecture, wide pumpkin-pine floors, beamed ceilings, claw-foot tubs, skylights, ceiling fans, and stained glass. Five-minute walk to harbor. Video and reading libraries. Healthy breakfast.

Host: Bill Butler
Rooms: 4 (PB) $95-130
Full or Continental Breakfast
Credit Cards: A, B
Notes: 2, 5, 6, 7, 8, 9, 10, 11, 12, 13, 14

The Elms Bed and Breakfast

84 Elm Street, Route 1, 04843
(207) 236-6250; (800) 755-ELMS (3567)
FAX (207) 236-7330

The Elms is a restored circa 1806 Colonial that recaptures the rich heritage of Early America. While it looks stately and elegant, guests will soon sense its casual warmth. Experience the innkeepers' love for lighthouses and the sea through extensive artwork, books, and collectibles. Walk to the harbor, shops, galleries, and restaurants, or hike the many trails of Mount Battie for spectacular views of the bay. Visit the Elms and leave with a feeling of having just visited friends. Children over 12 welcome.

Hosts: Ted and Jo Panayotoff
Rooms: 6 (4 PB; 2 SB) $60-100
Full and Continental Breakfast
Credit Cards: A, B
Notes: 2, 5, 7, 9, 10, 11, 12, 13

Hawthorn Inn Bed and Breakfast

9 High Street, 04843
(207) 236-8842

This elegant, turreted Victorian mansion overlooks the Camden harbor with spacious grounds, bright and airy rooms, large deck, lovely antiques throughout, full buffet breakfast, and friendly innkeepers. A three-minute stroll through the back garden to town amphitheater and harbor park. Near shops and restaurants. Carriage house rooms have full harbor views, private decks, double Jacuzzis, fireplaces, and VCRs. Recommended by *Yankee, Glamour,* and *Outside* magazines. Featured in *Minneapolis Star Tribune* and *Chicago Tribune.* Children over 12 welcome.

Hosts: Abigail and Ken Stern
Rooms: 10 (PB) $75-185
Full Breakfast
Credit Cards: A, B, C
Notes: 2, 5, 7, 9, 10, 11, 12, 13, 14

A Little Dream

66 High Street, 04843
(207) 236-8742

Sweet dreams and little luxuries abound in this lovely white Victorian with wraparound

7 No smoking; 8 Children welcome; 9 Social drinking allowed; 10 Tennis nearby; 11 Swimming nearby; 12 Golf nearby; 13 Skiing nearby; 14 May be booked through a travel agent.

porch. Noted for its lovely breakfast, beautiful rooms, and charming atmosphere. A Little Dream's English country-Victorian decor has been featured in *Country Inns* magazine, and in *Glamour*, "40 Best Getaways Across the Country." In the historic district just a few minutes from shops and harbor, it is listed on the National Register of Historic Places. Rooms have either a private deck, view, or fireplace. All have special touches such as imported soaps and chocolates, and a hostess who will do her very best to please.

Hosts: Joanna Ball and Bill Fontana
Rooms: 5 (PB) $95-139
Full Breakfast
Credit Cards: A, B, C
Notes: 2, 5, 7, 10, 11, 12, 13

Maine Stay

22 High Street, 04843
(207) 236-9636

A comfortable bed, a hearty breakfast, and three friendly innkeepers will be found in this 1802 Colonial home in Camden's historic district. Take a short walk to the harbor, shops, restaurants, and state park. Recommended by the *Bangor Daily News*, *Miami Herald*, *Boston Globe*, *Harper's Bazaar*, *Country Inns, Glamour,* and *Country Living* magazines. Children over eight welcome.

Hosts: Peter and Donny Smith; Diana Robson
Rooms: 8 (4 PB; 4 SB) $75-115
Full Breakfast
Credit Cards: A, B, C
Notes: 2, 5, 7 9, 10, 11, 12, 13, 14

The Owl and Turtle Harbor View Guest Rooms

8 Bayview, 04843
(207) 236-9014

Three lovely rooms with balconies immediately overlook Camden's inner harbor. Same building houses The Owl and Turtle Bookshop, one of Maine's finest. Surrounded with fine restaurants and shops.

Beautiful walks nearby. Air conditioning, TV, telephone, and private parking. A Continental breakfast is served to guests' rooms on a tray.

Hosts: The Conrad Family
Rooms: 3 (PB) $75-85
Continental Breakfast
Credit Cards: A, B
Notes: 2, 5, 7, 8, 10, 11, 12, 13, 14

The Swan House

49 Mountain Street, 04843
(207) 236-8275; (800) 207-8275

This fine Victorian home dates from 1870 and has been renovated to offer six spacious guest rooms—all with private baths. Some offer private sitting areas as well. A creative and generous full breakfast is served each morning on the sun porch. Landscaped grounds and a gazebo are available for guests to relax and enjoy. A hiking trail leading to Camden Hills State Park starts right behind the inn. Off busy Route 1, Swan House is a short walk to Camden's beautiful harbor, shops, and restaurants. Seasonal rates.

Hosts: Lyn and Ken Kohl
Rooms: 6 (PB) $65-120
Full Breakfast
Credit Cards: A, B
Notes: 2, 5, 8, 9, 10, 11, 12, 13, 14

The Swan House

The Victorian

The Victorian
Bed and Breakfast

Seaview Road, P.O. Box 258, Lincolnville, 04849
(207) 236-3785; (800) 382-9817

An 1881 Victorian restored to its original charm has spacious rooms, queen-size beds, private baths, waterviews, and fireplaces. Decorated in Period decor provides a quiet atmosphere in a unique country setting. Relax on the beautiful porch and enjoy spectacular views of the gardens, the ocean, and the islands off the coast. Wake up to a full country breakfast to start off the day. Off Route 1 and 300 feet from the shore. Only five minutes from downtown Camden.

Hosts: Ray and Marie Donner
Rooms: 6 (PB) $75-135
Full Breakfast
Credit Cards: A, B
Notes: 2, 4, 5, 7, 9, 10, 11, 12, 13, 14

Windward House

6 High Street, 04843
(207) 236-9656

A historic 1854 Greek Revival on stately High Street above picturesque Camden Harbor. Seven tastefully appointed guest rooms are furnished with period antiques and have private baths. Several common rooms, gardens, full gourmet breakfast. Only a short walk to shops, restaurants, and the harbor. Children over 12 welcome.

Hosts: Jon and Mary Davis
Rooms: 7 (PB) $65-135
Full Breakfast
Credit Cards: A, B, C
Notes: 2, 7, 9, 10, 11, 12, 13

CAPE NEDDICK

Ye Olde Perkins Place

749 Shore Road, 03902
(207) 361-1119

Ye Olde Perkins Place is a charming pre-Revolutionary Colonial home and attached guest house with oceanview. Just a short walk to a picturesque pebble beach and cove for sunbathing and swimming. Close to gift shops, restaurants, and boating at Perkins Cove and Marginal Way, a one-and-a-half-mile ocean walk. Golf ten miles away. Quiet, peaceful atmosphere. Open late June to Labor Day. Personal checks accepted for deposit.

Hosts: Prim and Dick Winkler
Rooms: 6 (SB) $55-65
Continental Breakfast
Credit Cards: None
Notes: 2, 9, 10, 11, 12

CAPITOL ISLAND

Albonegon Inn

04538
(207) 633-2521

Perched on the rocks of a private island four miles from Boothbay Harbor, the Albonegon offers spectacular views of outer islands, wildlife, and boating traffic. Built in the 1880s, the inn is one of the last original Maine Island stays. It is simple and charming—a great place to relax and unwind.

Hosts: Kim and Bob Peckham
Rooms: 14 (3 PB; 11 SB) $70-120
Continental Breakfast
Credit Cards: None
Notes: 2, 7, 10, 11

CARATUNK

The Sterling Inn

Route 201, P.O. Box 21
c/o New England Whitewater Center, 04925
(800) 766-7238; FAX (207) 672-4375

7 No smoking; 8 Children welcome; 9 Social drinking allowed; 10 Tennis nearby; 11 Swimming nearby; 12 Golf nearby; 13 Skiing nearby; 14 May be booked through a travel agent.

The historic Sterling Inn, in the Upper Kennebec Valley region of Maine, is a place where guests can enjoy a quiet, relaxing stay any time of the year. The cozy country atmosphere of the inn, with its hardwood floors, wood stoves, down comforters, and sitting rooms recalls the slower paced days of a Maine sporting lodge at the turn-of-the-century. The large wraparound porch is a perfect spot in the warmer months to enjoy a good book or to gather with friends. Golf is 45 minutes away. Downhill skiing is an hour and fifteen minutes away. Cross-country skiing on site.

Host: Matthew A. Polstein
Rooms: 17 (PB) $45-75
Full Breakfast
Credit Cards: A, B, C, D
Notes: 2, 4, 5, 7, 8, 9, 11, 14

CHAMBERLAIN

Ocean Reefs on Long Cove

Route 32, 04541-3530
(207) 677-2386

Watch the waves break over the reefs, lobstermen hauling in traps, or the shoreline between tides. Hike or bicycle on the roads along the rocky coast. Pemaquid Beach, Pemaquid Lighthouse, Fort William Henry, and the boat to Monhegan Island are all within five miles. Two-night minimum stay required during July and August. Closed September 30 through Memorial Day.

Rooms: 4 (PB) $66
Continental Breakfast
Credit Cards: None
Notes: 2, 7, 9, 10, 11, 12

CHERRYFIELD

Ricker House

Park Street, Box 256, 04622
(207) 546-2780

Selected as one of the top 50 inns in America. Comfortable 1802 Federal Colonial,

Ricker House

on the National Register of Historic Places, borders the Narraguagus River and offers guests a central place for enjoying the many wonderful activities in Down East Maine including scenic coastal area, swimming, canoeing, hiking, and fishing. Inquire about accommodations for pets. Cross-country skiing nearby.

Hosts: William and Jean Conway
Rooms: 3 (SB) $48.15-53.50
Full Breakfast
Credit Cards: None
Notes: 2, 7, 9, 10, 11, 12, 13

CHINA

Loon's Call Inn

Fire Road #28, Route 202 & 9
Lakeview Drive, 04926
(207) 968-2025

The Loon's Call Inn rests on the shore of beautiful China Lake. The private guest wing features two lovely, spacious rooms with private baths each with Jacuzzi tubs, wonderful lake views, a kitchenette, fireplace, and quiet sitting area. The grounds are spectacular with many water sights. Great fishing, swimming, and boating. Docking facilities available. Delicious full breakfast and meals are served. Convenient to all central Maine attractions.

Hosts: Gary and Tera Coull and family
Rooms: 2 (PB) $75-99
Full Breakfast
Credit Cards: A, B
Notes: 2, 3, 4, 5, 7, 8, 9, 10, 11, 12, 13, 14

NOTES: Credit cards accepted: A MasterCard; B Visa; C American Express; D Discover; E Diners Club;
F Other; 2 Personal checks accepted; 3 Lunch available; 4 Dinner available; 5 Open all year; 6 Pets welcome;

CLARK ISLAND

Craignair Inn

533 Clark Island Road, 04859
(207) 594-7644; FAX (207) 596-7124

Built in 1929 to house the stonecutters from the nearby quarries, this gracious and cheery inn overlooks the water and off-shore islands, clam flats, tidal pools, and lobster boats. Ten miles from Rockland, the Monhegan ferry, and Owls Head Light. Swim before dinner in the nearby deepwater quarry pool, or explore miles of coastal trails leading from the inn. Dinner served Monday through Saturday.

Hosts: Norman and Theresa Smith
Rooms: 24 (8 PB; 16 SB) $64-93
Full Breakfast
Credit Cards: A, B, C, E
Notes: 2, 6, 7, 8, 11, 12, 14

COREA

The Black Duck on Corea Harbor

Crowley Island Road, P.O. Box 39, 04624
(207) 963-2689

This restored 1890s house, filled with art and antiques overlooks Down East Lobster Harbor and open ocean in a tranquil fishing village. Explore the 12 acres and discover hidden salt marshes and a private bay. Curl up in front of a fireplace to read or find a sunny rock outcrop and watch the gulls soar overhead, and maybe spot a bald eagle. Rooms and cottages furnished in antiques of various periods. Children under one and over eight are welcome. Low-fat, but elegant breakfast in the antique- and art-filled dining room.

Hosts: Barry Canner and Robert Travers
Rooms: 5 (3 PB; 2 SB) $60-90
Suite: 1 (PB) $125
Full Breakfast
Credit Cards: None
Notes: 2, 5, 7, 9, 11, 12, 14

DAMARISCOTTA

Brannon-Bunker Inn

HCR 64, Box 045X, 04543
(207) 563-5941

Intimate, relaxed, country bed and breakfast in an 1820 Cape, 1880 converted barn, and 1900 carriage house. Seven rooms furnished in themes reflecting the charm of yesterday with the comforts of today. Ten minutes to lighthouse, fort, beach, antiques, and craft shopping. Antique shop on the premises.

Hosts: Jeanne and Joe Hovance
Rooms: 7 (5 PB; 2 SB) $58.85-69.55
Continental Breakfast
Credit Cards: A, B, C
Notes: 2, 5, 7, 8, 9, 10, 11, 12, 13, 14

The Down Easter Inn

Bristol Road, Route 129/130, 04543
(207) 563-5332

A unique example of Greek Revival architecture, the Down Easter Inn is one mile from downtown Damariscotta, in the heart of the rocky coast of Maine. The inn is fronted by a two-story porch with magnificent Corinthian columns. It is minutes from swimming, fishing, boating, and golf. Listed on the National Register of Historic Places, it features 22 rooms with private baths and TVs. Complimentary Continental breakfast served from 8:00 to 10:00 A.M.

Hosts: Robert and Mary Colquhoun
Rooms: 22 (PB) $65-85
Continental Breakfast
Credit Cards: A, B
Notes: 2, 7, 8, 9

Mill Pond Inn

50 Main Street, Nobleboro, 04555
(207) 563-8014

Whimsical and cozy, this bed and breakfast in a 1780 home offers an excellent atmosphere to view the wonders of Maine's wildlife. The breakfast room has a view of the pond, complete with loons, otters, beavers, herons, resident bald eagles, and breathtaking Maine wildflowers. The complimentary canoes can be paddled from the pond in the back yard directly into Damariscotta Lake (15.5 miles long), to within 20 feet of a bald eagle's nest! Two mountain bikes are available for guest use, or take a dip in the pond. The host is also a registered Maine guide, and guided fishing trips are another added feature to this lovely inn. Nestled in the little 1800s village of Damariscotta Mills this inn offers guests a unique experience. Boothbay Harbor, Camden Hills, Pemaquid Lighthouse, Bath-Brunswick area, and the rugged coast of midcoast Maine await.

Hosts: Bobby and Sherry Whear
Rooms: 6 (PB) $75
Full Breakfast
Credit Cards: None
Notes: 2, 5, 7, 8, 9, 10, 11, 12

DENNYSVILLE

Lincoln House Country Inn

Routes 1 and 86, 04628
(207) 726-3953

The centerpiece of northeastern coastal Maine. Two lovingly restored Colonials on 100 acres bordering beautiful Cobscook Bay. Eagles, osprey, and seals can be seen from the front door; whale watching, island hopping from nearby Eastport. Excellent hiking, choice accommodations, and unusual hospitality. Rates include breakfast and dinner. Children over ten welcome.

Lincoln House Country Inn

Hosts: Mary and Jerry Haggerty
Rooms: 10 (6 PB; 4 SB) $160–180 MAP
Full Breakfast
Credit Cards: A, B, C
Notes: 2, 4, 9, 10, 11, 12, 13, 14

EASTPORT

The Milliken House

29 Washington Street, 04631
(207) 853-2955

Large, gracious 1846 Victorian home just two blocks up from Eastport's waterfront historic district will delight Victoriana buffs with its ornately carved, marbletopped furniture and knickknacks. Breakfasts are sumptuous and as elegant as the heavy carved dining room furniture from which they are served. Eastport is a small 19th-century island city on Moose Island, connected by causeway to the mainland. Whale watching excursions available. Ferry to Canada. Limited smoking allowed.

Host: Joyce Weber
Rooms: 5 (SB) $60
Full Breakfast
Credit Cards: A, B, C
Notes: 2, 5, 6, 8, 9, 10, 11, 12, 14

Todd House

1 Capen Avenue, Todd's Head, 04631
(207) 853-2328

Originally built as a half Cape and later enlarged to a full Cape during the Revolutionary War, the Todd House has a unique history. On August 8, 1801, Eastern Lodge Number 7 of the Masonic Order was instituted in it, and during the 1860s it was used as a barracks for soldiers manning the mud battery on the Head. The house has a mammoth center chimney and a unique "good morning" staircase. It has spectacular oceanviews. Continental plus breakfast served.

Host: Ruth McInnis
Rooms: 6 (2 PB; 4 SB) $45-80
Continental Breakfast
Credit Cards: A, B
Notes: 2, 5, 6, 7, 8, 9

Weston House

26 Boynton Street, 04631
(207) 853-2907; (800) 853-2907

This imposing 1810 Federal-style house overlooks Passamaquoddy Bay across to Campobello Island. Listed on the National Register of Historic Places; in a lovely Down East coastal village. Grounds include a lawn suitable for croquet and a flower garden for quiet relaxation. Picnic lunches available.

Hosts: Jett and John Peterson
Rooms: $58.85-74.90
Full Breakfast
Credit Cards: None
Notes: 2, 3, 4, 5, 9, 10

ELIOT (KITTERY)

The Farmstead Bed and Breakfast

379 Goodwin Road, 03903
(207) 439-5033; (207) 748-3145

Come and step back in time and enjoy the hospitality that Farmstead offers its guests. Awake to the aroma of coffee, bacon, sausage, and blueberry pancakes on the griddle. Inspect the 1704 Cape and the "new" floor built in 1896. Explore the two and one-half acres, swing under the pear tree, or have an early morning cup of coffee on the glider after a quiet restful night. All rooms have private bath, mini-refrigerator, and microwave oven. Picnic facilities and gas grill available.

Hosts: Col. and Mrs. John Lippincott
Rooms: 7 (PB) $54
Full Breakfast
Credit Cards: A, B
Notes: 2, 5, 6, 7, 8, 9, 10, 12, 14

High Meadows Bed and Breakfast

Route 101, 03903
(207) 439-0590

High Meadows, on a hill four and one-half miles from US 1 and I-95, has been in oper-

ation as a bed and breakfast since 1982. The original Colonial structure, circa 1736, houses five guest rooms, a large den, porch, and patio for guests' use. Outlet shopping malls are close by, sandy beaches, and harbor cruising. Wines and iced tea are served in the afternoon. Open April through October. Smoking restricted. Children over 12 are welcome.

Host: Elaine Raymond
Rooms: 5 (PB)
Full Breakfast
Credit Cards: A, B
Notes: 2, 9, 11, 12

The Bagley House

FREEPORT

The Bagley House

Route 139, 04222
(207) 865-6566; (800) 765-1776

Peace, tranquility, and history abound in this magnificent 1772 country home. Six acres of fields and woods invite nature lovers, hikers, berry pickers, and cross-country skiers. The kitchen's hand-hewn beams and enormous free-standing fireplace with beehive oven inspire mouth-watering breakfasts. A warm welcome awaits guests.

Hosts: Suzanne O'Connor and Susan Backhouse
Rooms: 5 (PB) $80-100
Full Breakfast
Credit Cards: A, B, C, D
Notes: 2, 5, 8, 9, 10, 11, 12, 13, 14

7 No smoking; 8 Children welcome; 9 Social drinking allowed; 10 Tennis nearby; 11 Swimming nearby;
12 Golf nearby; 13 Skiing nearby; 14 May be booked through a travel agent.

Bayberry
Bed and Breakfast

8 Maple Avenue, 04032
(207) 865-1868; (207) 865-6021

The Bayberry Bed and Breakfast is in the village district, one block north of L. L. Bean and all the fine shops and restaurants. The Bayberry has been recently restored preserving the early charm of the 1853 Federal home. All rooms have private baths and are tastefully decorated. Choose between king-, queen-size, double, or twin beds. A delicious full breakfast, prepared with fresh local produce, is served daily in the dining room. Relax in the bright and sunny sitting room with TV, VCR, books, games, or good conversation. Several telephones in the hall and guest rooms are available for free local or long distance calls. Freeport has a beautiful coastline with spectacular view, harbor cruises, sailing, fishing, golfing, hiking, etc. Ample parking in front of inn.

Hosts: The Frank Family
Rooms: 5 (PB) $55-95
Full Breakfast
Credit Cards: A, B
Notes: 2, 5, 7, 8, 9, 10, 11, 12, 13, 14

Bed and Breakfast
Inns of New England

128 S. Hoop Pole Road, Guilford, CT, 06437
(203) 457-0042; (800) 582-0853

ME811. Magnificent 1772 country home just ten minutes from downtown Freeport on six lovely acres of fields and woods. Five guest rooms, all private bath, each furnished with antiques, feature hand-sewn quilts, and stencilled rugs. Full breakfast is served at an antique baker's table in front of the huge brick fireplace, wide pine floors, hand-hewn beams, and a beehive oven. No smoking. Resident dog. No guest pets. Children of all ages welcome. $85-100.

ME812. Lovely 1779 ship captain's home whose friend, Mark Twain, spent many a visit. Only a three-minute walk to L. L. Bean and more than 120 factory outlets. Relax on the two acres of flower gardens and lawns. Enjoy the porch or lawn swings. Seven guest rooms with private bath. Enjoy a full country breakfast. No smoking. Children 12 and over welcome. Resident cat. No guest pets. $58-85.

Brewster House
Bed and Breakfast

180 Main Street, 04032
(207) 865-4121; (800) 865-0822

Brewster House is a newly renovated 1888 Queen Anne home. Each room is quiet, comfortable, furnished with antiques, and has a full-size private bath. Guests enjoy a delicious full breakfast including home-baked muffins and breads and a variety of main dishes. Just two blocks from L. L. Bean. Park in the lot and walk to Freeport's many outlets, shops, and restaurants. AAA rated three diamond. Children eight and over welcome.

Hosts: Matthew and Amy Cartmell
Rooms: 5 (PB) $70-105
Full Breakfast
Credit Cards: A, B, D
Notes: 2, 5, 7, 9, 10, 11, 12, 13, 14

Captain Josiah
Mitchell House

188 Main Street, 04032
(207) 865-3289

Famous, historic ship captain's home, circa 1779. The 1866 miraculous survival-at-sea story of Captain Mitchell of the ship *Hornet*

NOTES: Credit cards accepted: A MasterCard; B Visa; C American Express; D Discover; E Diners Club; F Other; 2 Personal checks accepted; 3 Lunch available; 4 Dinner available; 5 Open all year; 6 Pets welcome;

is a classic. Mark Twain, then a young newspaperman, wrote about it. Restored more than 25 years ago by the present owners, the house is filled with antiques. Beautiful grounds and only a five-minute walk to L. L. Bean. Fourteenth year as an inn. Off-season rates available.

Hosts: Alan and Loretta Bradley
Rooms: 6 (PB) $78-85
Full Breakfast
Credit Cards: A, B
Notes: 2, 5, 7, 11, 12, 13, 14

Country at Heart Bed and Breakfast

37 Bow Street, 04032
(207) 865-0512

Enjoy staying in a cozy 1870 country home with handmade crafts, antiques, and reproduction furnishings. Choose one of the country-decorated rooms, the Shaker Quilt or Teddy Bear. A full breakfast is served on an eight-foot oak dining table. After breakfast, browse through Primitive Pastimes, a shop with rug hooking supplies and crafts. Park and walk to more than 100 outlet stores, restaurants, and L. L. Bean just two blocks away.

Hosts: Robert and Kim Dubay
Rooms: 3 (PB) $65-85
Full Breakfast
Credit Cards: None
Notes: 2, 5, 7, 8, 9, 12, 14

Country at Heart

Harraseeket Inn

162 Main Street, 04032
(207) 865-9377; (800) 342-6423
FAX (207) 865-1684

An elegant 54-room country inn two blocks north of L. L. Bean in the village of Freeport. Antiques, 23 fireplaces, Jacuzzi tubs, air conditioning, cable TV, lovely gardens, and two restaurants. Steps from 110 upscale factory outlets; three miles from waterfront. Afternoon tea included. AAA four diamond rating.

Hosts: The Gray Family
Rooms: 54 (PB) $95-225
Full Breakfast
Credit Cards: A, B, C, D, E
Notes: 3, 4, 5, 8, 9, 11, 12, 14

Holbrook Inn

7 Holbrook Street, 04032
(207) 865-6693

The Holbrook Inn has queen-size beds and private baths. A hearty Maine breakfast is served in this 120-year-old Victorian home. Each room is decorated with antiques and hosts' personal touch. Each room has air conditioning and cable TV. Ample parking and excellent "home base" for day trips.

Hosts: The Routhier Family
Rooms: 4 (PB) $75
Full Breakfast
Credit Cards: A, B
Notes: 2, 5, 7, 8, 9, 11, 12, 14

181 Main Street Bed and Breakfast

181 Main Street, 04032
(207) 865-1226

Comfortably elegant, antique-filled 1840 Cape. Just a five-minute walk to L. L. Bean and Freeport's luxury outlets. Hosts provide a renowned breakfast, New England hospitality, and information on all that Maine has to offer—on and off the beaten path. In-ground pool; ample parking. Featured in

7 No smoking; 8 Children welcome; 9 Social drinking allowed; 10 Tennis nearby; 11 Swimming nearby; 12 Golf nearby; 13 Skiing nearby; 14 May be booked through a travel agent.

Country Home magazine, and ABBA and AAA approved.

Rooms: 7 (PB) $75-95
Full Breakfast
Credit Cards: A, B
Notes: 2, 5, 7, 9, 10, 11, 12, 13

White Cedar Inn

178 Main Street, 04032
(207) 865-9099

Historic Victorian home stands just two blocks north of L. L. Bean. Spacious and cozy rooms are antique furnished with private baths. Full country breakfast served in the sunroom overlooking beautifully landscaped grounds. Air-conditioned. AAA inspected.

Hosts: Phil and Carla Kerber
Rooms: 6 (PB) $75-95
Full Breakfast
Credit Cards: A, B, C
Notes: 5, 7, 9, 10, 12, 13

White Cedar Inn

FRIENDSHIP

The Outsiders' Inn
Bed and Breakfast

Box 521A, Corner of Routes 97 and 220, 04547
(207) 832-5197

The Outsiders' Inn is in the center of the village of Friendship, a short walk from the harbor, the home of historic Friendship Sloops and scores of lobster boats. This inn

features five comfortable guest rooms with double beds; private and semiprivate baths. Efficiency cottage also available. Full breakfasts served daily. Sea kayak rentals and guided tours available. Friendship Sloop charters and dinners are also available by prior arrangement. Country furnishings, delicious food, friendly folks. Come enjoy midcoast Maine.

Hosts: Debbie and Bill Michaud
Rooms: 5 (1 PB; 4 SB) $50-65
Full Breakfast
Credit Cards: A, B
Notes: 2, 5, 7, 8, 9, 11

FRYEBURG

Admiral Peary House

9 Elm Street, 04037
(207) 935-3365; (800) 237-8080

This home was once the residence of Arctic explorer Admiral Robert E. Peary. It has been lovingly restored for guests' comfort, with air-conditioned rooms and private bathrooms, country breakfast, and billiards. The clay tennis court is framed by spacious lawns and perennial gardens. Use one of the bicycles to explore the village and nearby sights. Spend a few hours or a day canoeing and swimming the Saco River. Top it off with a leisurely soak in the outdoor spa. "We look forward to your visit and hope you'll enjoy the admiral's home as much as we do," say the hosts. Inquire about accomodations for children.

Hosts: Ed and Nancy Greenberg
Rooms: 4 (PB) $70-108
Full Breakfast
Credit Cards: A, B
Notes: 2, 5, 7, 9, 10, 11, 12, 13, 14

GREENVILLE

Greenville Inn

P.O. Box 1194, Norris Street, 04441
(207) 695-2206

This 1895 Victorian lumber baron's mansion is on a hill overlooking Moosehead

Greenville Inn

Lake and Squaw Mountain. A large, leaded-glass window decorated with a painted spruce tree is the focal point at the landing of the stairway. Gas lights, embossed wall coverings, carved fireplace mantels, and cherry and oak paneling grace the inn. In the elegantly appointed dining rooms, diners may savor fresh Maine seafood, glazed roast duckling, grilled chops, or steaks. Whether relaxing by a cozy fire or sipping cocktails on the veranda at sunset, the evening hours are most enjoyable.

Hosts: The Schnetzers
Rooms: 9 (7 PB; 2 SB) $75-95
Continental Breakfast
Credit Cards: A, B, D
Notes: 2, 4, 5, 8, 9, 10, 11, 12, 13

The Sawyer House

P.O. Box 521, Lakeview Street, 04441
(207) 695-2369

The Sawyer House bed and breakfast overlooks Moosehead Lake, just a short walk to shops, restaurants, and local attractions. Relax in the restored steamship captain's home, circa 1849. All rooms have king- or queen-size beds and private baths. Enjoy the view of Moosehead Lake from one of the outside porches, or relax in the parlor with cable TV.

Hosts: Pat and Hans Zieten
Rooms: 3 (PB) $60-70
Full Breakfast
Credit Cards: A, B, D
Notes: 2, 5, 9, 10, 11, 12, 13

HARRISON

Bed and Breakfast Inns of New England

128 S. Hoop Pole Road, Guilford, CT, 06437
(203) 457-0042; (800) 582-0853

ME812. Enjoy panoramic views overlooking Long Lake from this 1867 restored homestead. Fifty-five miles of sparkling lakes are available for year-round enjoyment. Guests enjoy the large living room with TV, VCR, and fireplace. Five guest rooms with shared or private baths, some with four-poster canopied beds. No smoking. One resident dog. No guest pets. $55-85.

ISLE AU HAUT

The Keepers House

P.O. Box 26, 04645
(207) 367-2261

Remote island lighthouse station in the undeveloped wilderness area of Acadia National Park. Guests arrive on the mail boat from Stonington. No telephones, cars, TV, or crowds. Osprey, seal, deer, rugged trails, spectacular scenery, seclusion, and inspiration. Minimum stay July-August: two nights. Closed November 1-April 30. Rates include three elegant meals and bikes.

Hosts: Jeff and Judi Burke
Rooms: 5(SB) $250
Credit Cards: None
Notes: 2, 3, 4, 7, 8, 9, 11

KENNEBUNK

Arundel Meadows Inn

P.O. Box 1129, 04043-1129
(207) 985-3770

This 165-year-old farmhouse, two miles north on Route 1 from the center of town, combines the charm of antiques and art with the comfort of seven individually decorated

7 No smoking; 8 Children welcome; 9 Social drinking allowed; 10 Tennis nearby; 11 Swimming nearby; 12 Golf nearby; 13 Skiing nearby; 14 May be booked through a travel agent.

Arundel Meadows Inn

bedrooms with sitting areas. Two of the rooms are suites, three have fireplaces, some have cable TV, and all have private bathrooms and summer air conditioning. Full homemade breakfasts and afternoon teas are prepared by co-owner Mark Bachelder, a professionally trained chef.

Hosts: Mark Bachelder and Murray Yaeger
Rooms: 7 (PB) $75-125
Full Breakfast
Credit Cards: A, B
Notes: 2, 5, 7, 9, 11, 12, 14

Bed and Breakfast Inns of New England

128 S. Hoop Pole Road, Guilford, CT, 06437
(203) 457-0042; (800) 582-0853

ME-810. Step back in time to this 1756 farmhouse set on six acres of rolling hills. Common rooms, including a Colonial kitchen, are furnished with period antiques, stenciled walls, pumpkin pine floors, and six fireplaces. Continental breakfast is served on the sun porch each morning. Three rooms with double beds are available, two include private baths, and one has a fireplace. Resident pets, but no guest pets. Children over 14 are welcome. No smoking allowed. $80.

English Meadows Inn

141 Port Road, 04043
(207) 967-5766

English Meadows is an 1860 Victorian farmhouse that has been operating as an inn for more than 80 years. Within a five- or ten-minute stroll past interesting shops and galleries to the village of Kennebunkport, English Meadows offers its guests a peaceful taste of country living and the many unique attractions of the area. Antique appointed guest rooms, deliciously full breakfasts, and convivial hosts add further pleasure for visitors at this wonderful inn. Children over nine welcome.

Host: Charlie Doane
Rooms: 13 (11 PB; 2 SB) $75-98
Full Breakfast
Credit Cards: A, B
Notes: 2, 5, 10, 11, 12

Sundial Inn

P.O. Box 1147, 48 Beach Avenue, 04043
(207) 967-3850

Unique oceanfront inn furnished with turn-of-the-century Victorian antiques. Each of the 34 guest rooms has a private bath, color TV, telephone, and air conditioning. Several rooms also offer ocean views and whirlpool baths. Visit Kennebunkport's art galleries and studios, museums, and gift shops. Go whale watching, deep-sea fishing, or hiking at the nearby wildlife refuge and estuary. Golf and tennis are nearby. Continental breakfast features muffins and coffeecakes. Handicapped accessible.

Hosts: Larry and Pat Kenny
Rooms: 34 (PB) $60-148
Continental Breakfast
Credit Cards: A, B, C, E
Notes: 5, 7, 9, 10, 11, 12

KENNEBUNKPORT

Captain Fairfield Inn

Pleasant and Green Streets, P.O. Box 1308, 04046
(207) 967-4454; (800) 322-1928

A gracious 1813 sea captain's mansion in Kennebunkport's historic district, only steps to the village green and harbor. A delightful walk to sandy beaches, Dock Square Marina, shops, and excellent restaurants. On the corner of Pleasant and Green streets. Gracious and elegant, the bedrooms are beautifully decorated with antiques and period furnishings that lend an atmosphere of tranquility and charm. Several bedrooms have fireplaces, and guests are welcome to relax in the living room, study, or enjoy the tree-shaded grounds and gardens. Guests will awaken to birdsong, fresh sea air, and the aroma of gourmet coffee. Come and enjoy a refreshing, comfortable, and memorable stay. Children over six welcome.

Hosts: Bonnie and Dennis Tallagnon
Rooms: 9 (PB) $85-160
Full Breakfast
Credit Cards: A, B, C, D, E
Notes: 2, 5, 7, 9, 10, 11, 12, 14

The Captain Lord Mansion

P.O. Box 800, 04046
(207) 967-3141

The Captain Lord Mansion is an intimate 16-room luxury country inn, at the head of a sweeping lawn, overlooking the Kennebunk River. The inn is famous for its warm, friendly hospitality, attention to cleanliness, and hearty breakfasts served family-style in the big country kitchen.

Hosts: Bev Davis and Rick Litchfield
Rooms: 16 (PB)
Full Breakfast
Credit Cards: A, B, D
Notes: 2, 5, 7, 8, 9, 10, 11, 12, 14

The Captain Lord Mansion

Charrid House

2 Arlington Avenue, 04046
(207) 967-5695

Built in 1887, this charming cedar-shingled home started life as a gambling casino for the Kennebunkport River Club. It went through incarnations as a tennis clubhouse and a single-family home before becoming Charrid House in 1986. The Charrid House is one block from the stunning scenery of Ocean Avenue and the Colony Beach on a residential street. Several restaurants and shops are within walking distance and the village itself is one mile south.

Host: Ann M. Dubay
Rooms: 2 (2 S1B) $60
Full Breakfast
Credit Cards: F
Notes: 2, 7, 8, 10, 11, 12

Cove House

11 South Maine Street, 04046
(207) 967-3704

This cozy bed and breakfast is an Early Colonial home in a quiet residential area on a cove with views of the water from the yard. Decorated with antiques and a collection of Flow Blue, it offers charm with authentic bed and breakfast hospitality. A hearty breakfast is served each morning in the dining room. A short walk from the village and beach. An additional $15 for third person.

Hosts: The Jones Family (Kathy, Bob, and Barry)
Rooms: 3 (PB) $75-85
Full Breakfast
Credit Cards: A, B
Notes: 2, 5, 7, 8, 9, 10, 11, 12, 14

The Green Heron Inn

126 Ocean Avenue, P.O. Box 2578, 04046
(207) 967-3315

This ten-room bed and breakfast inn offers the best breakfast in town, according to local folks. Each guest room and cottage is air-conditioned, has a private bath, TV, and telephone for outgoing calls. The rooms are attractive, clean, and bright and filled with the spirit of a friendlier, simpler time. Breakfast is included in the guest rates. Within walking distance of both the village and the shore. Seasonal rates are

7 No smoking; 8 Children welcome; 9 Social drinking allowed; 10 Tennis nearby; 11 Swimming nearby; 12 Golf nearby; 13 Skiing nearby; 14 May be booked through a travel agent.

available. Closed in the month of January. Inquire about accommodations for pets.

Owners: Charles and Elizabeth Reid
Host: Carol Stahe, manager
Rooms: 10 (PB) $65-128
Full Breakfast
Credit Cards: None
Notes: 2, 8, 9, 10, 11, 12

The Inn on South Street

South Street, P.O. Box 478A, 04046
(207) 967-5151

Now approaching its 200th birthday, this stately Greek Revival house is in the historic district. There are three beautifully decorated guest rooms and one luxury suite. Private baths, fireplaces, a common room, afternoon refreshments, and early morning coffee. A sumptuous breakfast is served in the large country kitchen with views of the river and ocean. On a quiet street within walking distance of restaurants, shops, and the water.

Hosts: Jacques and Eva Downs
Rooms: 3 (PB) $85-185
Suite: 1 (PB)
Full Breakfast
Credit Cards: A, B
Notes: 2, 7, 10, 11, 12, 13, 14

The Inn on South Street

Kylemere House 1818 "Crosstrees"

South Street, Box 1333, 04046-1333
(207) 967-2780

Tucked into a quiet corner of Kennebunkport's historic district is this beautifully restored, 1818 Federal-style inn on the National Register of Historic Places. Surrounded by spacious, shaded grounds, lovely perennial gardens, and a sparkling pond, guests come to relax and feel refreshed. Inside are four guest rooms decorated individually with antiques and period furniture, private baths, one with fireplace, and queen, king, or twin beds. Guests enjoy early morning coffee and afternoon refreshments in the guest parlor or on the porch. A delicious breakfast is served in the dining room overlooking the gardens. A quiet haven just a short walk from shops, galleries, marinas, restaurants, and the ocean. Closed mid-December through April. Children over 12 welcome.

Hosts: Ruth and Helen Toohey
Rooms: 4 (PB) $85-135
Full Breakfast
Credit Cards: A, B
Notes: 2, 9, 10, 11, 12, 14

Maine Stay Inn and Cottages

Box 500 A, 04046
(207) 967-2117; (800) 950-2117

Elegant rooms and delightful cottages in the quiet historic district surroundings of Kennebunkport. Complimentary breakfast, afternoon tea, New England desserts. Color cable TV, private baths, and fireplaces. Easy walking distance to restaurants, galleries, shops, and harbor. One mile to beach and golf.

Hosts: Lindsay and Carol Copeland
Rooms: 17 (PB) $85-120
Full Breakfast
Credit Cards: A, B, C, D
Notes: 5, 8, 9, 10, 11, 12, 14

Old Fort Inn and Resort

Box M-30, 04046
(207) 967-5353; (800) 828-FORT
FAX (207) 967-4547

Discover the hospitality of a luxurious New England inn that combines all of yesterday's

Old Fort Inn

charm with today's conveniences—from the daily buffet breakfast to the comfort and privacy of antique-appointed rooms. Includes pool, tennis court, TV, telephones, air conditioning, and a charming antique shop, all in a secluded setting. AAA rated four diamonds. Closed mid-December through mid-April.

Hosts: David and Sheila Aldrich
Rooms: 16 (PB) $125-240
Full Breakfast
Credit Cards: A, B, C, D
Notes: 2, 9, 10, 11, 12, 14

White Barn Inn

Beach Street, P.O. Box 560C, 04046
(207) 967-2321; FAX (207) 967-1100

This 1850s farmhouse and its signature white barn have been transformed into a sophisticated inn and award-winning restaurant. Twenty-four elegant accommodations all with private baths and lovely antiques, many with whirlpool baths and fireplaces. A five-minute walk to the beach or to downtown Kennebunkport. Member Relais and Chateaux. AAA five-diamond dining. Selected among the top 12 inns for the year 1992.

Hosts: Mr. Laurie Bongiorno and Ms. Laurie Cameron
Rooms: 24 (PB) $140-275
Continental Breakfast
Credit Cards: A, B, C
Notes: 2, 4, 5, 7, 9, 10, 11, 12, 13, 14

KITTERY

Bed and Breakfast Inns of New England

128 S. Hoop Pole Road, Guilford, CT, 06437
(203) 457-0042; (800) 582-0853

ME805. A romantic ambience and elegant antique furnishings await guests at this 1890 Princess Anne Victorian bed and breakfast. Enjoy a full breakfast of gourmet coffees, omelets, and pastries in the garden or on the sun deck. Eight guest rooms are available with double and queen-size beds, shared and private baths. Resident pets, and guest pets are welcome. Children are welcome. No smoking. $60-125.

Enchanted Nights Bed and Breakfast

29 Wentworth Street, Route 103, 03904
(207) 439-1489

An 1890 Princess Anne Gothic Victorian between Boston and Portland. Three minutes to dining and dancing in Portsmouth, historic homes, scenic ocean drives, and the renowned Kittery outlet malls. Convenient day trips to neighboring resorts. For the romantic at heart who delight in the subtle elegance of yesteryear; for those who are soothed by the whimsical charm of a French country inn. Gourmet coffee, omelets, and pastries. Enjoy the suites with whirlpool for two. Cable TV and air conditioning. Pets welcome with restrictions.

Hosts: Nancy Bogenberger and Peter Lamandia
Rooms: 6 (PB) $42-135
Full Breakfast
Credit Cards: A, B, C, D
Notes: 2, 5, 6, 7, 8, 9, 10, 11, 12, 14

LAKEWOOD

Bed and Breakfast Inns of New England

128 S. Hoop Pole Road, Guilford, CT, 06437
(203) 457-0042; (800) 582-0853

7 No smoking; 8 Children welcome; 9 Social drinking allowed; 10 Tennis nearby; 11 Swimming nearby; 12 Golf nearby; 13 Skiing nearby; 14 May be booked through a travel agent.

ME814. This Victorian lakefront inn was built in the early 1900s by a playwright. Enjoy the oldest summer theater in the nation. Five spacious guest rooms, with shared or private baths, and a guest parlor with TV and fireplace. In the summertime swim, fish, golf, play tennis, or enjoy the theater—all are within easy walking distance. During the winter, enjoy miles of finely groomed snowmobile trails. Children welcome, but no infants please. $50-85.

LOVELL

Stone Wall Bed and Breakfast

Rural Route 1, Box 26, 04051
(207) 925-1080; (800) 413-1080

This early 1800s New England farmhouse is a short walk from Lovell village and offers panoramic views of Mount Washington and the Western Maine mountains. All the guest rooms and suites are comfortably furnished with antiques and provide inviting queen-size beds, private baths with Jacuzzis, and mountain views. Enjoy the area's many outdoor activities, view the fall foliage, or simply enjoy the view from the screened porch.

Hosts: Cathy Beals and Susan Peterson
Rooms: 4 (PB) $100-125
Full Breakfast
Credit Cards: A, B
Notes: 2, 5, 7, 9, 10, 11, 12, 13

LUBEC

Bed and Breakfast Inns of New England

128 S. Hoop Pole Road, Guilford, CT, 06437
(203) 457-0042; (800) 582-0853

ME875. Enjoy any of the four area lighthouses when staying at this early American bed and breakfast home. Guests can actually walk out on the ocean floor during low tide, to the one on Campobello Island. Enjoy the eternal beauty of Quaddy Head State Park—the Easterly most point in the United States. Go clam digging and steam them on outdoor barbecues. Visit the home of FDR on Campobello Island. Guest rooms with private or shared baths. No smoking. No pets. $55-85.

Breakers by the Bay

37 Washington, 04652
(207) 733-2487

One of the oldest houses in the 200-year-old town of Lubec, a small fishing village. Three blocks to Campobello Island, the home of Franklin D. Roosevelt. All rooms have refrigerators, TVs, hand-crocheted tablecloths, hand-quilted bedspreads, and private decks for viewing the bay. All rooms that share a bath have their own washstands.

Host: E. M. Elg
Rooms: 5 (4 PB; 1 SB) $64.20
Full Breakfast
Credit Cards: None
Notes: 7, 12, 14

MILBRIDGE

Bed and Breakfast Inns of New England

128 S. Hoop Pole Road, Guilford, CT, 06437
(203) 457-0042; (800) 582-0853

ME-855. This large Victorian has outstanding views of the bay and Narraguagus River. Common rooms include a sitting room, formal living room, dining room, and sun porch. This bed and breakfast is in a rural village with restaurants, light shopping, and an inexpensive movie theater a short walk from the doorstep. Full breakfast includes a bottomless cup of coffee or tea. Five guest rooms with a variety of bed sizes; shared and private baths are available. Children over 12 are welcome. No pets. Smoking outside only. $45-55.

NOTES: Credit cards accepted: A MasterCard; B Visa; C American Express; D Discover; E Diners Club; F Other; 2 Personal checks accepted; 3 Lunch available; 4 Dinner available; 5 Open all year; 6 Pets welcome;

MOUNT DESERT

Reibers' Bed and Breakfast

P.O. Box 163, 04660
(207) 244-3047

Handsome Colonial homestead on four acres with tidal creek and meadow is on outskirts of historic village on scenic Mount Desert Island. A short drive to Bar Harbor and Acadia National Park. Full breakfast served with home-baked breads. Screened porch in summer and snapping fires in winter. Nonsmokers are preferred. Cross-country skiing nearby.

Hosts: Gail and David Reiber
Rooms: 2 (1 PB; 1 SB) $65-75
Full Breakfast
Credit Cards: A, B
Notes: 2, 5, 7, 8, 9, 10, 11, 12, 13

MacDonald's Bed and Breakfast

P.O. Box 52, 04660
(207) 244-3316

This 1850 home, listed in the National Register of Historic Places, offers the pleasure of village living without summer crowds. In Somesville, Mount Desert Island's first permanent settlement. Surrounded by Acadia National Park and eight miles from Bar Harbor. Mountain and waterviews from all rooms. Full breakfast features fresh fruit, homemade breads, muffins, blueberry pancakes, and crêpes. Cross-country skiing nearby. Children over five welcome.

Hosts: Stan and Binnie MacDonald
Rooms: 3 (PB) $50-75
Full Breakfast
Credit Cards: A, B
Notes: 2, 5, 7, 9, 11, 12, 13

NAPLES

The Augustus Bove House

Rural Route 1, Box 501, 04055
(207) 693-6365

Guests are always welcome at the historic 1850 hotel. Originally known as Hotel Naples, it is restored for comfort and a relaxed atmosphere at affordable prices. Guest rooms have elegant yet homey furnishings, some with views of Long Lake. An easy walk to the water, shops, and recreation in a four-season area. Open all year, with off-season and midweek discounts. Air conditioning, TV, and VCR. Coffee or tea anytime. AAA approved. Inquire about availability of dinner.

Hosts: David and Arlene Stetson
Rooms: 11 (7 PB; 2+2 SB) $49-95
Full Breakfast
Credit Cards: A, B, C, D
Notes: 2, 5, 6, 7, 8, 9, 10, 11, 12, 13, 14

Inn at Long Lake

P.O. Box 806, 04055
(207) 693-6226

Enjoy romantic elegance and turn-of-the-century charm at the Inn at Long Lake, nestled amid the pines and waterways of the beautiful Sebago Lakes region. The inn has 16 restored rooms with TVs, air conditioners, and private baths. One minute's walk from the Naples Causeway. Four-season activities and fine dining nearby. This three-diamond AAA facility is worth the trip. Midweek discounts available. Named one of the top ten bed and breakfasts in the United States in a video competition by Innovations, Inc. of Cranford, New Jersey.

Hosts: Maynard and Irene Hincks
Rooms: 16 (PB) $59-120
Continental Breakfast
Credit Cards: A, B, C, D
Notes: 2, 5, 7, 8, 9, 10, 11, 12, 13, 14

Inn at Long Lake

---

7 No smoking; 8 Children welcome; 9 Social drinking allowed; 10 Tennis nearby; 11 Swimming nearby; 12 Golf nearby; 13 Skiing nearby; 14 May be booked through a travel agent.

Lamb's Mill Inn

Lamb's Mill Inn

Lamb's Mill Road, Box 676, 04055
(207) 693-6253

A charming country inn in the foothills of Maine's western mountain and lake region. Romantic country atmosphere on 20 acres of fields and woods. Five rooms with private baths and a full country breakfast. Hot tub available. Near lakes, antique shops, skiing, and canoeing.

Hosts: Laurel Tinkham and Sandra Long
Rooms: 5 (PB) $75-85
Full Breakfast
Credit Cards: A, B
Notes: 2, 5, 7, 8, 9, 10, 11, 12, 13, 14

NEWCASTLE

The Newcastle Inn

River Road, 04553
(800) 832-8669; (207) 563-5685

A country inn of distinction on the Damariscotta River. All 15 rooms have private baths, most have river views, and some have canopied beds and fireplaces. Enjoy the changing tide while sitting on the glassed and screened sun porch. In the dining room, elegant four-star candlelight dinners and multi-course breakfasts are served. Featured in *Food and Wine*.

Hosts: Ted and Chris Sprague
Rooms: 15 (PB) $60-150
Full Breakfast
Credit Cards: A, B, D
Notes: 2, 4, 5, 7, 10, 11, 12, 13, 14

NEW HARBOR

Gosnold Arms

HC 61, Box 161, Route 32, 04554
(207) 677-3727

On the harbor, the Gosnold Arms Inn and cottages, all with private baths, most with water view. A glassed-in dining room overlooking the water is open for breakfast and dinner. The Gosnold wharf and moorings accommodate cruising boats. Within a ten-mile radius are lakes, beaches, lobster pounds, historic sites, boat trips, golf, antiques, shops, and restaurants.

Host: The Phinney Family
Rooms: 26 (PB) $79-124
Full Breakfast
Credit Cards: A, B
Notes: 2, 4, 8, 9, 11, 12

NEWPORT

Lake Sebasticook Bed and Breakfast

P.O. Box 502, 8 Sebasticook Avenue, 04953
(207) 368-5507

Take a step back in history in this 1903 Victorian home on a quiet street. Relax on the second-floor sun porch or comfortable wraparound porch and enjoy the sounds of ducks and loons on Lake Sebasticook. Take a short walk to the lake park, or play tennis at the city park a block away. In the morning, savor a full country breakfast including homemade breads. Closed from November to May 1.

Hosts: Bob and Trudy Zothner
Rooms: 3 (SB) $55
Full Breakfast
Credit Cards: C
Notes: 2, 10, 11

NORTHEAST HARBOR

Harbourside Inn

Northeast Harbor, 04662
(207) 276-3272

Peace and quiet, flower gardens at the edge of the forest, and woodland trails into Acadia National Park add to the delights of this genuine 1888 country inn. Spacious rooms and suites, all with private baths,

NOTES: Credit cards accepted: A MasterCard; B Visa; C American Express; D Discover; E Diners Club;
F Other; 2 Personal checks accepted; 3 Lunch available; 4 Dinner available; 5 Open all year; 6 Pets welcome;

many with king- or queen-size beds. Beautiful antiques, working fireplaces in all first- and second-floor rooms. Guests can walk or drive into nearby Acadia National Park. Sailing, deep-sea fishing, and carriage rides in the park. Reservations accepted for two nights or more.

Hosts: The Sweet Family
Rooms: 11 (PB) $85-210
Suites: 3 (PB)
Continental Breakfast
Credit Cards: None
Notes: 2, 7, 10, 11, 12

Harbourside Inn

OGUNQUIT

The Beachmere Inn

Box 2340, 03907
(207) 646-2021; (800) 336-3983
FAX (207) 646-2231

A Victorian inn owned by the Merrill family since 1937, the Beachmere was built at the turn of the century and features accommodations with kitchenettes; most with decks, some with working fireplaces. Rooms overlook the Little Beach, manicured lawns, and gardens to the Marginal Way. Close to trolley route and village activities. Open April to mid-December. Off-season packages. AAA and Mobil Travel Guide approved. Smoking restricted.

Host: Louesa Mace
Rooms: 44 (PB) $50-180
Continental Breakfast
Credit Cards: A, B, C, D, E
Notes: 2, 8, 9, 10, 11, 12, 14

Hartwell House

118 Shore Road, P.O. Box 393, 03907
(207) 646-7210; (800) 235-8883

In the tradition of fine European country inns, Hartwell House offers rooms and suites elegantly furnished with Early American and English antiques. A full gourmet breakfast is served daily. Perkins Cove, fine restaurants, shops, the fabulous Ogunquit Beach, and the Marginal Way are all within walking distance. Seasonal package arrangements. Minimum one- to three-night stay weekends and holidays. Conference facility that hold up to 65 people and an Executive Board Room that seats 18 available year-round.

Hosts: Jim and Trisha Hartwell;
    William and Anne Mozingo
Rooms: 16 (PB) $80-175
Full Breakfast
Credit Cards: A, B, C, D
Notes: 2, 5, 7, 9, 10, 11, 12, 13, 14

Holiday Guest House

P.O. Box 2247, 03907
(207) 646-5582

Fully restored 1814 Colonial close to beaches, restaurants, antique shops, outlets, and nature trails. Guest accommodations have private baths and refrigerators.

Hosts: Lou and Rose LePage
Rooms: 2 (PB) $35-65
Continental Breakfast
Credit Cards: A, B, C, D
Notes: 2, 5, 8, 9, 10, 11, 12, 14

Puffin Inn

233 U.S. Route 1, P.O. Box 2232, 03907
(207) 646-5496

Puffin Inn is in a small, picturesque village by the sea. The inn, an old sea captain's house, exudes a special warmth and charm of days gone by. Each of the ten rooms has heat, air conditioning, private bath, and refrigerator. A generous homemade breakfast is served each morning on the enclosed porch. Relax and enjoy fresh sea breezes on

7 No smoking; 8 Children welcome; 9 Social drinking allowed; 10 Tennis nearby; 11 Swimming nearby;
12 Golf nearby; 13 Skiing nearby; 14 May be booked through a travel agent.

the open veranda or in the back yard. Five-minute walk to center of village, shops, art galleries, and restaurants. Ten-minute walk to three miles of pristine white sand beach. Open March through November. Personal checks accepted in advance.

Hosts: Maurice and Lee Williams
Rooms: 10 (PB) $60-90
Continental Breakfast
Credit Cards: A, B
Notes: 7, 8, 10, 11, 12

The Trellis House

2 Beachmere Place, P.O. Box 2229, 03907
(207) 646-7909

A turn-of-the-century beach house, completely restored and appointed with an eclectic blend of antiques. All rooms have private baths. Breakfast consists of fresh fruits, muffins and breads, juices, coffee, tea, and special entree. The Trellis House is just a short walk to all that is special in Ogunquit. Cross-country skiing nearby.

Hosts: Pat and Jerry Houlihan
Rooms: 4 (PB) $75-100
Full Breakfast
Credit Cards: A, B, D
Notes: 2, 5, 7, 9, 10, 11, 12, 13

ORLAND

Alamoosook Lodge

P.O. Box 16, 04472
(207) 469-6393; FAX (207) 469-2528

Welcome to the lodge and the marvelous views of the lake. Enjoy freshwater swimming, canoeing, and fishing. Listen and watch for loons. Experience fall foliage transformed into a blaze of reflecting colors. The winters are magical with skating, cross-country skiing, and cozy warmth. Start the day with a sumptuous breakfast, stroll along the water, browse through the gardens, bask in the sun, and soak up the view. The six cheerful rooms with private baths are nonsmoking. Convenient to Bar Harbor, Blue Hill, Castine, and Deer Isle. Three miles off Route 1.

Hosts: Jan and Doug Gibson
Rooms: 6 (PB) $65-73
Full Breakfast
Credit Cards: A, B, C
Notes: 2, 5, 7, 8, 9, 11, 12

The Sign of the Amiable Pig

The Sign of the Amiable Pig

P.O. Box 237, Route 175, 04472-0232
(207) 469-2561

The Sign of the Amiable Pig is in Orland Village just off Route 1. The house, named for the delightful weathervane which tops the garage, was built in the 18th century. Furnished with interesting antiques and Oriental rugs, the house has six working fireplaces, including the large cooking fireplace with its built-in bake oven in the keeping room. Full breakfast is served in either the dining room or the keeping room. Skiing in Camden or Acadia.

Hosts: Charlotte and Wes Pipher
Rooms: 3 (1 PB; 2 SB) $55
Full Breakfast
Credit Cards: None
Notes: 2, 5, 7, 8, 9, 10, 11, 12, 13

POLAND SPRINGS

Poland Spring Inn Bed and Breakfast

Route 26, 04274
(207) 998-4351

In 1790 the Ricker family established a stage coach stop on this site. It was to become the most famous resort in America. Twenty rooms with private baths, fireplaces, electric heat, and air conditioning. A world-class golf course is just a few steps from the inn. Most of the food comes from local farms and dairies; everything is fresh and delicious. They have never heard of diets, cholesterol, or vegetarians. Guests need to bring their own towels, soap, and room cups or glasses. Social activities include concerts, swimming, shuffleboard, horseshoes, croquet, putting green, grass tennis courts, game rooms, around-the-world shopping, private library, fishing pond, and more. No telephones in the rooms. Children over 16 welcome.

Host: Mel Robbins
Rooms: 20 (PB) $79
Full Breakfast
Credit Cards: A, B, C, D
Notes: 3, 4, 9, 10, 11, 12

PORTLAND

Andrews Lodging Bed and Breakfast

417 Auburn Street, 04103
(207) 797-9157

On over an acre of beautifully landscaped grounds on the outskirts of the city of Portland, this 250-year-old Colonial home has been completely renovated for year-round comfort. Hosts offer modern baths, one with whirlpool, a completely applianced guest kitchen, a library, and a solarium overlooking beautiful gardens or pristine snow in the winter. Guests can expect refreshments in the refrigerator, turndown service, and warm hospitality. Close to ocean, lakes, golf, skiing, and the mountains. ABBA rated two and one-half crowns in 1994. Inquire about accommodations for children.

Hosts: Elizabeth and Douglas Andrews
Rooms: 6 (1 PB; 5 SB) $65-125
Continental Breakfast
Credit Cards: A, B, C
Notes: 2, 5, 6, 7, 9, 12, 14

Inn on Carleton

46 Carleton Street, 04102
(207) 775-1910; (800) 639-1779

Inn on Carleton, a graciously restored 1869 Victorian townhouse in Portland's historic West End, is on a quiet, tree-lined street in a unique residential district. It is a short walk to the Portland Museum of Art and the Performing Arts Center. Casco Bay's Calendar Islands, the international ferry to Nova Scotia, and the Old Port with its cobbled streets, colorful shops, and fine restaurants. Smoking restricted. Air conditioning.

Hosts: Philip and Sue Cox
Rooms: 7 (4 PB; 3 SB) $55-105
Full Breakfast
Credit Cards: A, B, D
Notes: 2, 5, 8, 9, 10, 11, 12, 13, 14

West End Inn

146 Pine Street, 04102
(207) 772-1377

A very special place where the elegance and charm of yesteryear has been preserved and blended with the amenities and convenience of today. All rooms are uniquely decorated and provide private baths, cable TV, and telephone access. Breakfast is cooked to order and reflects the quality of this establishment. The staff creates an atmosphere of relaxation and enjoyment throughout the guests' stay and are quick to assist with travel tips or dinner reservations.

Host: John Leonard
Rooms: 5 (PB) $75-149
Full Breakfast
Credit Cards: A, B, C
Notes: 2, 5, 7, 8, 10, 12, 13, 14

RANGELEY

Northwoods

P.O. Box 79, Main Street, 04970
(207) 864-2440

A historic 1912 home of rare charm and easy elegance, Northwoods is in Rangeley Village. Features spacious rooms, a lakefront

7 No smoking; 8 Children welcome; 9 Social drinking allowed; 10 Tennis nearby; 11 Swimming nearby; 12 Golf nearby; 13 Skiing nearby; 14 May be booked through a travel agent.

porch, expansive grounds, and private boat dock, Northwoods provides superb accommodations. Golf, tennis, hiking, water sports, and skiing are a few of the many activities offered by the region. Inquire about accommodations for children.

Hosts: Carol and Robert Scofield
Rooms: 4 (3 PB; 1 SB) $60-75
Full Breakfast
Credit Cards: A, B
Notes: 2, 5, 7, 9, 10, 11, 12, 13, 14

ROCKPORT

Bed and Breakfast Marblehead and North Shore

P.O. Box 35, Newtonville, 02160
(617) 964-1606; (800) 832-2632
FAX (617) 332-8572

Harbor House Bed and Breakfast. This exquisite bed and breakfast overlooks Rockport Harbor, just a few miles south of Camden. It has two private balconies and a large deck, offering spectacular views of the harbor and Camden Hills. Three sun-filled guest rooms are available, some with private baths, some with skylights, fireplaces, and Jacuzzi. All open onto balconies or terraces on the harbor. Private pier where the host's 30-foot sloop awaits charter by day or week. Resident cats. Open June through November. Two-night minimum on weekends. Children over 12 are welcome. Smoking restricted.Full breakfast. $100-185.

ROUND POND

The Briar Rose

Route 32, P.O. Box 27, 04564
(207) 529-5478

Escape to an unspoiled fishing village close to the Pemaquid Lighthouse, beaches, Monhegan Island boat service, and other recreational facilities. The 150-year-old home faces Round Pond Harbor and offers large, airy rooms filled with comfortable antique furnishings and collectibles. Relax in the gardens, enjoy walks in the village, visit local antique shops, country stores, studios, and galleries. Older children welcome; reservations recommended.

Hosts: Anita and Fred Palsgrove
Rooms: 3 (PB) $55-75
Full Breakfast
Credit Cards: None
Notes: 2, 5, 7, 9, 11, 12

SEARSPORT

Brass Lantern Inn

81 West Main Street, P.O. Box 407, 04974
(207) 548-0150; (800) 691-0150

Nestled at the edge of the woods, this gracious Victorian inn, circa 1850, overlooks Penobscot Bay. All of the comfortable guest rooms have private baths. Enjoy a hearty breakfast with friendly hospitality. On the National Register of Historic Places. "Open all year, the Brass Lantern will be lit in welcome!"

Hosts: Pat Gatto; Dan and Lee Anne Lee
Rooms: 4 (PB) $50-75
Continental Breakfast
Credit Cards: A, B
Notes: 2, 5, 7, 8, 10, 11, 12, 14

Homeport Inn

Box 647, East Main Street, Route 1, 04974
(207) 548-2259; (800) 742-5814

Homeport, listed on the National Register of Historic Places, is a fine example of a New England sea captain's mansion on beautiful landscaped grounds, with flower gardens and pond that extend to the ocean. This elegant home is furnished with family heirlooms and antiques. There are ten guest rooms, six with private baths. A Victorian cottage is also available. A visit offers a rare opportunity to vacation or be an overnight guest in a warm, homey, hospitable atmosphere without the customary traveler's commercialism. Limited smoking permitted.

Hosts: Edith and George Johnson
Rooms: 10 (6 PB; 4 SB) $55-75
Cottage: $500
Full Breakfast
Credit Cards: A, B, C, D, F
Notes: 2, 5, 8, 9, 10, 11, 12, 13, 14

Thurston House Bed and Breakfast Inn

8 Elm Street, P.O. Box 686, 04974
(207) 548-2213; (800) 240-2213

Beautiful circa 1830 Colonial home with well and carriage house. Built as a parsonage for Stephen Thurston, uncle of Winslow Homer who visited often. Now guests can visit in a casual environment. Quiet village setting is steps away from Penobscot Marine Museum, beach park on Penobscot Bay, restaurants, tavern, galleries, and antiques. Relax in one of four beautiful guest rooms, and enjoy the "forget about lunch" breakfasts.

Hosts: Carl and Beverly Eppig
Rooms: 4 (2 PB; 2 SB) $50-65
Full Breakfast
Credit Cards: A, B
Notes: 2, 5, 7, 8, 9, 10, 11, 12, 13, 14

The Victorian Inn

35 West Main Street, P.O. Box 807, 04974
(800) 943-0044

Step back to an earlier era in the splendor of this Victorian sea captain's mansion. All original features including five fireplaces, double parlors, ceiling medallions, and light fixtures have been preserved. Rooms are spacious with king-size, double, or twin beds. A large suite is available for families. A full breakfast is served in the formal dining room with a fire in the hearth on cold mornings.

Hosts: Ed and Judie Upham
Rooms: 3 (2 PB; 1 SB) $50-80
Full Breakfast
Credit Cards: A, B
Notes: 2, 5, 7, 8

Watchtide

190 West Main Street, 04974
(207) 548-6575; (800) 698-6575

Watchtide is a wondrous, New England-style Cape circa 1795 with a barn attached. Watch ships sail by on the Penobscot Bay while enjoying a full gourmet breakfast served on the wicker-furnished magnificent sun porch. Established as the College Club Inn in 1917 and serving such notables as Eleanor and Franklin Roosevelt. Enjoy birds and wildlife, artwork, antique furnishings, sweeping lawns and gardens, and the Angels to Antiques shoppe. The hosts love to spoil their guests with special treats and treatment. Mid-coast with exceptional antiquing, museums, parks, historical sites, and accessible to most everything. Dinner available off-season.

Hosts: Nancy-Linn and Jack Elliott
Rooms: 4 (2 PB; 2 SB) $55-85
Full Breakfast
Credit Cards: None
Notes: 2, 5, 9, 11, 12, 13, 14

SOUTH BROOKSVILLE

Buck's Harbor Inn

Steamboat Wharf Road, P.O. Box 268, 04617
(207) 326-8660; FAX (207) 326-0730

Charming country inn on Buck's Harbor, Penobscot Bay, a famed yachting and boating center. Halfway between Acadia National Park/Bar Harbor and Camden. Historic Deer Isle, Castine, and Blue Hill are just a short drive away. Seasonal restaurant (The Landing) next door. Remote, beautiful, comfortable, Brooksville is just the way Maine should be experienced.

Hosts: Peter and Ann Ebeling
Rooms: 6 (SB) $60
Full Breakfast
Credit Cards: A, B
Notes: 2, 5, 7, 8, 9, 10, 11, 12

7 No smoking; 8 Children welcome; 9 Social drinking allowed; 10 Tennis nearby; 11 Swimming nearby; 12 Golf nearby; 13 Skiing nearby; 14 May be booked through a travel agent.

SOUTH HARPSWELL

Harpswell Inn

141 Lookout Point Road, 04079
(800) 843-5509

Waterfront, historical 1761 Harpswell Inn at Lookout Point dominates a knoll overlooking a quaint cove that serves as a snug harbor for lobster boats. Enjoy fabulous sunsets, countless islands, swimming, boating, fishing, or just relaxing by the ocean. Freeport shopping, Popham Beach, Maine Maritime Museum, Bowdoin College, and Maine Music Theater are all less than 30 minutes away. Thirteen rooms in the inn with breakfast and two luxury suites without breakfast.

Hosts: Susan and Bill Menz
Rooms: 15 (6 PB; 9 SB) $58-150
Full Breakfast
Credit Cards: A, B
Notes: 2, 5, 7, 9, 10, 11, 12, 14

SOUTHWEST HARBOR

Harbour Cottage Inn

P.O. Box 258, 04679-0258
(207) 244-5738

This elegant but informal inn is in the heart of Acadia National Park. Private baths offer either whirlpools or steam showers and hair dryers. Harbor-facing guest rooms have individual heat and ceiling fans.

Harbour Cottage Inn

Hikers, bikers, boaters, skiers, and tourists are welcome to enjoy the warm, friendly hospitality. Closed during November.

Hosts: Ann and Mike Pedreschi
Rooms: 8 (PB) $60-135
Full Breakfast
Credit Cards: A, B, C, D
Notes: 2, 7, 9, 10, 11, 12, 13, 14

The Island House

Box 1006, 04679
(207) 244-5180

Relax in a gracious, restful seacoast home on the quiet side of the island. Island House favorites such as blueberry coffeecake and sausage/cheese casserole are served for breakfast. Charming, private loft apartment available. Acadia National Park is just a five-minute drive away. The house is across the street from the harbor with swimming, sailing, biking, and hiking nearby. Inquire about accommodations for children. Cross-country skiing nearby.

Hosts: Charles and Ann Bradford
Rooms: 5 (1 PB; 4 SB) $55-100
Full Breakfast
Credit Cards: A, B
Notes: 2, 5, 7, 9, 10, 11, 12, 13, 14

Island Watch Bed and Breakfast

Freeman Ridge Road, P.O. Box 1359, 04679
(207) 244-7229

Overlooking the harbors of Mount Desert Island and the village of Southwest Harbor, Island Watch sits atop Freeman Ridge on the quiet side of the island. The finest panoramic views, privacy, and comfort. Walk to Acadia National Park and the fishing village of Southwest Harbor. Private baths, and a smoke-free environment. Full breakfasts served in dining room or glass-enclosed garden room. Children over 12 welcome.

Host: Maxine M. Clark
Rooms: 6 (PB) $75
Full Breakfast

NOTES: Credit cards accepted: A MasterCard; B Visa; C American Express; D Discover; E Diners Club; F Other; 2 Personal checks accepted; 3 Lunch available; 4 Dinner available; 5 Open all year; 6 Pets welcome;

Credit Cards: F (travelers checks)
Notes: 2, 7, 9, 10, 11, 12

The Kingsleigh Inn

373 Main Street, Box 1426, 04679
(207) 244-5302

In the heart of Acadia National Park overlooking the picturesque harbor is a romantic, intimate inn that will surround guests with charm the moment they walk through the door. Many rooms enjoy spectacular harbor views, and all are tastefully decorated. Children over 12 welcome. Cross-country skiing nearby.

Hosts: Tom and Nancy Cervelli
Rooms: 8 (PB) $55-165
Full Breakfast
Credit Cards: A, B, D
Notes: 2, 5, 7, 9, 11, 12

The Lambs Ear Inn

The Lambs Ear Inn

Clark Point Road, P.O. Box 30, 04679
(207) 244-9828

The inn is a stately old Maine house, circa 1857. Comfortable and serene, with a sparkling harbor view. Have sweet dreams on comfortable beds with crisp, fresh linens. Start the day with a memorable breakfast. Spend pleasant days here filled with salt air and sunshine. Please visit this special village in the heart of Mount Desert Island surrounded by Acadia National Park. Open year-round by reservation only. Children over eight welcome. Social drinking allowed in guest rooms.

Hosts: Elizabeth Hoke
Rooms: 6 (PB) $75-125
Full Breakfast
Credit Cards: A, B
Notes: 2, 7, 10, 11, 12, 14

STOCKTON SPRINGS

The Hichborn Inn

Church Street, P.O. Box 115, 04981
(207) 567-4183

This romantic Victorian inn is listed on the National Register of Historic Places. Quiet area just off Route 1. Period furnishings, beds appointed with fine linens and down comforters, sumptuous full breakfasts, which may feature crêpes made with the inn's own raspberries. Penobscot Marine Museum, numerous antique shops, and fine dining nearby. Advance reservations recommended.

Hosts: Nancy and Bruce Suppes
Rooms: 4 (2 PB; 2 SB) $55-80
Full Breakfast
Credit Cards: None
Notes: 2, 5, 7, 11, 14

Whistlestop by the Bay

Rural Free Delivery 1, Box 639
Maple Street, 04981
(207) 567-3726

Beautiful oceanviews and seclusion await guests in this comfortable New England home. Two large rooms, one with twin beds, the other with a double bed. Awake to a delicious full breakfast. The hosts enjoy hiking, running, art, and music and are eager to help guests enjoy coastal Maine. The inn is midway between Camden and Acadia National Park, only one-half mile from Route 1.

Hosts: David and Katherine Christie-Wilson
Rooms: 2 (SB) $50-70
Full Breakfast
Credit Cards: A, B
Notes: 2, 5, 7, 8, 9, 11

7 No smoking; 8 Children welcome; 9 Social drinking allowed; 10 Tennis nearby; 11 Swimming nearby;
12 Golf nearby; 13 Skiing nearby; 14 May be booked through a travel agent.

STRATTON

The Widow's Walk

171 Main Street, P.O. Box 150, 04982
(207) 246-6901; (800) 943-6995

The Steamboat Gothic architecture of this Victorian home led to a listing in the National Register of Historic Places. Nearby Bigelow Mountain, the Appalachian Trail, and Flagstaff Lake present many opportunities for boating, fishing, and hiking. In the winter, Sugarloaf USA, Maine's largest ski resort, offers both alpine and cross-country skiing, as well as dogsled rides. Dogs and cats in residence. Inquire about accomodations for children.

Hosts: Mary and Jerry Hopson
Rooms: 6 (SB) $30-46
Full Breakfast
Credit Cards: A, B
Notes: 2, 5, 7, 9, 11, 12, 13

SULLIVAN HARBOR

Islandview Inn

Route 1, HCR 32, Box 24, 04664
(207) 422-3031

Turn-of-the-century summer cottage is just off Route 1, 15 minutes from Ellsworth and 35 minutes from Bar Harbor. Choose from seven guest rooms, five with private bath. Each room features original furniture, detailed restoration work, and picturesque views of Frenchman's Bay and Mount Desert Island. Private beach, sailing, canoe, and dinghy available. Smoking restricted.

Host: Evelyn Joost
Rooms: 7 (5 PB; 2 SB) $50-85
Full Breakfast
Credit Cards: A, B, D
Notes: 2, 9, 11, 12

SURRY

The Surry Inn

P.O. Box 25, 04684
(207) 667-5091; (800) 742-3414

Two gracious buildings on sprawling grounds provide warmth, comfort, and exceptional dining. The main house, built in 1834, served as lodging for stage and steamship passengers in the last century. The expansive grounds have shore walks and a beach with the warmest saltwater bathing in the area. There are croquet, horseshoes, a canoe, and a rowboat. Midway between Mount Desert Island and lovely Deer Island. Smoking restricted. Children over five welcome.

Host: Peter Krinsky
Rooms: 13 (11 PB; 2 SB) $48-72
Full Breakfast
Credit Cards: A, B
Notes: 2, 4, 5, 9, 10, 11, 12, 13, 14

TENANTS HARBOR

The East Wind Inn

P.O. Box 149, 04860
(207) 372-6366; (800) 241-VIEW

This authentic country inn at water's edge is owned and operated by a native of Tenants Harbor. Life slows to a comfortable pace in this tiny seaside village, and the natural harmony is evident inside the inn as well. Antique-filled guest rooms and a dining room that serves New England country cooking offer spectacular views of the harbor. Bookshelves, rich with Maine stories, and a staff that is genuinely friendly will make guests feel like they have found a safe haven. The inn and Meeting House with conference facilities are available year-round. Call before bringing pets.

Host: Tim Watts
Rooms: 26 (12 PB; 14 SB) $64-150
Full and Continental Breakfast
Credit Cards: A, B, C, D
Notes: 2, 4, 8, 9, 10, 11, 12, 13, 14

THOMASTON

Cap'n Frost's Bed and Breakfast

241 West Main Street, 04861
(207) 354-8217

This 1840 Cape Cod cottage is furnished with country antiques, some for sale. If travelers are visiting the midcoast area, this is a comfortable overnight stay, close to Monhegan Island and a two-hour drive to Acadia National Park. Reservations are helpful.

Hosts: Arlene and Harold Frost
Rooms: 3 (1 PB; 2 SB) $40
Full Breakfast
Credit Cards: None
Notes: 2, 7, 9, 11

VINALHAVEN

Bed and Breakfast Inns of New England

128 S. Hoop Pole Road, Guilford, CT, 06437
(203) 457-0042; (800) 582-0853

ME-830. Stay at this comfortable, affordable bed and breakfast in a fishing village by Carver's Harbor. Explore uncrowded woodlands, visit seaside nature preserves and parks, and feast on Maine's freshest seafood caught daily in the surrounding waters. Each morning starts with a Continental breakfast, and guests can prepare a picnic in the guest kitchen for the day's adventures. Available are six guest rooms, all with shared baths. Children over ten are welcome. Resident dog, no guest pets. No smoking. $50-80.

Fox Island Inn

Carver Street, P.O. Box 451, 04863
(207) 863-2122

Discover the unspoiled coastal Maine island of Vinalhaven. This comfortable, affordable bed and breakfast is in the quaint fishing village nestled around picturesque Carver's Harbor. Enjoy swimming in the abandoned granite quarries and exploring seaside nature preserves by foot or bicycle. State-operated car ferry from Rockland runs six times daily. Island activities include flea markets, church suppers, and wonderful local restaurants.

Host: Gail Reinertsen
Rooms: 6 (SB) $40-60
Continental Breakfast
Credit Cards: None
Notes: 2, 7, 9, 11

WALDOBORO

Bed and Breakfast Inns of New England

128 S. Hoop Pole Road, Guilford, CT, 06437
(203) 457-0042; (800) 582-0853

ME-815. This lovely 1830 inn is handsomely decorated with Victorian furnishings. There is a sun deck and shade garden with a hammock. The inn features a delicious full breakfast, and tea or sherry is served each afternoon. Five guest rooms include a variety of bed sizes, along with shared and private baths. Children over 12 are welcome. No guest pets. Smoking limited. $60-80.

ME-816. Built in 1905, this Victorian bed and breakfast features classic woodwork, tin ceilings, two fireplaces, and a large screened porch. Explore the flower and vegetable gardens or the gallery and gift shop in the barn. Coffee, tea, or hot chocolate is brought to guests' rooms and a full breakfast is served in the dining room. Special diets can be accommodated. Four guest rooms are available with shared and private baths, with a variety of bed sizes. Children welcome. No guest pets. No smoking. $55-65.

Broad Bay Inn and Gallery Bed and Breakfast

Box 607, 1014 Main Street, 04572
(207) 832-6668; (800) 736-6769

Lovingly restored 1830 inn, handsomely appointed with Victorian furnishings, canopied beds, paintings, art and theatrical library, and foreign films. Breakfast banquet feasts and afternoon tea or sherry on the deck. Established art gallery in the barn.

7 No smoking; 8 Children welcome; 9 Social drinking allowed; 10 Tennis nearby; 11 Swimming nearby; 12 Golf nearby; 13 Skiing nearby; 14 May be booked through a travel agent.

Broad Bay Inn

Walk down to the river, to tennis, the theater, and antique shops. A short drive to the lighthouse, Audubon sanctuary, and fishing villages. Send for a free brochure. Children over ten welcome.

Hosts: Jim and Libby Hopkins
Rooms: 5 (S3B) $45-75
Full Breakfast
Credit Cards: A, B
Closed January
Notes: 2, 4, 5, 7, 9, 10, 11, 12, 13, 14

The Roaring Lion

995 East Main Street, P.O. Box 756, 04572
(207) 832-4038

A 1905 Victorian home with tin ceilings; elegant woodwork throughout. The Roaring Lion accommodates special diets and serves miso soup, sourdough bread, homemade jams and jellies. Hosts are well traveled and lived for two years in West Africa. Their interests include books, gardening, art, and cooking. Gallery and gift shop on premises.

Hosts: Bill and Robin Branigan
Rooms: 4 (1 PB; 3 SB) $58.85-69.55
Full Breakfast
Credit Cards: None
Notes: 2, 5, 8, 10, 11, 12, 13, 14

WATERFORD

Kedarburn Inn

Route 35, P.O. Box 61, 04088
(207) 583-6182

In historic Waterford Village, a place to step back in time while enjoying the comforts of today. Charming bedrooms decorated with warm country touches, and handmade quilts by the hostess will add pleasure to guests' visit. Each day will start with a hearty breakfast. In the evening guests can relax and enjoy an elegant dinner.

Hosts: Margaret and Derek Gibson
Rooms: 6 (4 PB; 2 SB) $69-88
Full Breakfast
Credit Cards: A, B, C
Notes: 2, 4, 5, 6, 8, 9, 11, 12, 13, 14

The Parsonage House Bed and Breakfast

Rice Road, P.O. Box 116, 04088
(207) 583-4115

The Parsonage House, built in 1870 for the Waterford Church, overlooks Waterford Village, Keoka Lake, and Mount Tirem. In a four-season area, the area provides many opportunities for outdoor enthusiasts. The Parsonage is a haven of peace and quiet. Double guest rooms or private suite available. A full breakfast is served on the screened porch or in the large farm kitchen beside a glowing wood stove.

Hosts: Joseph and Gail St. Hilaire
Rooms: 3 (1 PB; 2 SB) $55-80
Full Breakfast
Credit Cards: None
Notes: 2, 3, 5, 7, 8, 11, 12, 13

The Waterford Inne

Box 149, Chadbourne Road, 04088
(207) 583-4037

Escape to country quiet in an inn offering the elegance of a fine country home. Ten uniquely decorated guest rooms and carefully furnished common rooms provide a fine setting for four-star dining in historic Waterford. Near mountains and coastline; water and woodland activities nearby. Closed April. Call before bringing pets.

Hosts: Barbara and Rosalie Vanderzanden
Rooms: 10 (7 PB; 3 SB) $75-100
Full Breakfast
Credit Cards: C
Notes: 2, 4, 8, 9, 10, 11, 12, 13

NOTES: Credit cards accepted: A MasterCard; B Visa; C American Express; D Discover; E Diners Club; F Other; 2 Personal checks accepted; 3 Lunch available; 4 Dinner available; 5 Open all year; 6 Pets welcome;

WELD

Kawanhee Inn
Lakeside Lodge

Webb Lake, Mt. Blue, Box 119, Weld, 04285
(207) 585-2000
7 High Street, Farmington, 04938–in winter

Kawanhee Inn is on Webb Lake. "Webb Beach, one of the top ten beaches of New England," says *U.S. Air* magazine, May 1994. Early morning excursions by canoe will allow guests to see moose feeding by the water's edge and the sun rising over the western mountains. Have breakfast before climbing Tumbledown Mountain or going gold panning in the Swift River. Bring a mountain bike, tennis rackets, or golfing equipment for a game at nearby course. Before dinner on the screened porches, swim the private, sandy beach. Seasonal May 15 to October 15.

Host: Martha Strunk
Rooms: 9 (5 PB; 4 SB) $60-85
Continental Breakfast
Credit Cards: A, B
Notes: 4, 7, 8, 9, 10, 11, 12, 14

WEST GOULDSBORO

Bed and Breakfast
Inn of New England

128 South Hoop Pole Road, Guilford, CT 06437
(203) 457-0042; (800) 582-0853

ME850. A traditional Victorian bed and breakfast, with water on three sides of the grounds. The three and one-half mile freshwater pond behind the bed and breakfast is great for swimming. There are also a mill stream on the side and a tidal salt water pool out front. Enjoy the lovely water views or the dairy goats and farm animals in the pasture. Resident cat and dog. No guest pets please. No smoking. Six guest rooms have shared or private baths. No toddlers please. $59-79.

Sunset House
Bed and Breakfast

Route 186, 04607
(800) 233-7156

This late Victorian home offers guests a choice of six spacious bedrooms spread over three floors with a selection of ocean and freshwater views. The second floor has three bedrooms with private baths. The third floor includes three bedrooms with shared bath and optional kitchen. Perfect accommodations for reunions and traveling couples. A full country breakfast is served.

Hosts: Carl and Kathy Johnson
Rooms: 6 (3 PB; 3 SB) $69-79
Full Breakfast
Credit Cards: A, B, C, D
Notes: 2, 5, 7, 9, 11, 12, 13

WINTER HARBOR

Main Stay Inn

P.O. Box 459, 04693
(207) 963-5561

Restored Victorian home overlooks Henry's Cove. Housekeeping units with fireplaces. Walk to restaurants and post office. A quiet village within a mile of Acadia. Guest may enjoy hiking, biking, and local activities.

Hosts: Pearl and Roger Barto
Rooms: 3 plus 2 units (PB) $45
Credit Cards: A, B
Notes: 2, 5, 8, 9, 11, 12

WISCASSET

The Squire Tarbox Inn

Rural Route 2, Box 620, 04578
(207) 882-7693

Clean, casual, comfortable, and all country, this is a historic Colonial farmhouse on a back road near midcoast Maine harbors, beaches, antique shops, museums, and lobster shacks. The inn offers a proper balance

7 No smoking; 8 Children welcome; 9 Social drinking allowed; 10 Tennis nearby; 11 Swimming nearby; 12 Golf nearby; 13 Skiing nearby; 14 May be booked through a travel agent.

The Squire Tarbox Inn

of history, quiet country, good food, and relaxation. Serves a delicious fresh goat cheese by the fire before dinner. Known primarily for rural privacy and five-course dinners. Children over 14 welcome.

Hosts: Karen and Bill Mitman
Rooms: 11 (PB) $85-166
Full Breakfast
Credit Cards: A, B, C, D
Notes: 2, 4, 7, 9, 14

YORK

The Cape Neddick House

1300 Route 1, P.O. Box 70, Cape Neddick, 03902
(207) 363-2500

In the historic coastal community of York, this 1800s Victorian farmhouse is central to beaches, boutiques, antique shops, wildlife sanctuaries, boat cruises, factory outlets, and historical and cultural opportunities. Sleeping on antique high-back beds, snuggled under handmade quilts, guests are assured of pleasant dreams. No alarm clock needed, as the fragrant smells of cinnamon popovers, apple almond tortes, or ham and apple biscuits drift by, gently waking guests. Reason enough to return time and again. All private baths. Two-room suite with fireplace available. Inquire about availability of dinner. Smoking restricted. Cross-country skiing nearby.

Hosts: John and Dianne Goodwin
Rooms: 5 (PB) $65-90

Full Breakfast
Credit Cards: None
Notes: 2, 5, 9, 10, 11, 12, 13

YORK BEACH

Red Shutters

7 Cross Street, P.O. Box 1281, 03910-1281
(207) 363-6292; (800) 890-9766

Red Shutters, a cozy bed and breakfast for nonsmokers, is in a quiet, residential neighborhood and is a five-minute walk to the ocean beach, shops, and restaurants. Three comfortably furnished guest rooms offer guests a refreshing night's rest. Homemade breakfast includes hot-from-the-oven muffins, fresh seasonal fruit, granola, assorted juices, and hot beverages. Hosts are happy to accommodate special dietary needs and food allergies. Within a short drive to historic sites, outlet shopping, antique shops, and Maine's scenic villages and rocky coastline. Open mid-June through Labor Day.

Hosts: Gil and Evelyn Billings
Rooms: 3 (1 PB; 2 SB) $55-65
Continental Breakfast
Credit Cards: A, B
Notes: 2, 7, 9, 11

Homestead Inn Bed and Breakfast

5 Long Beach Avenue (Route 1A), 03910
(207) 363-8952

NOTES: Credit cards accepted: A MasterCard; B Visa; C American Express; D Discover; E Diners Club; F Other; 2 Personal checks accepted; 3 Lunch available; 4 Dinner available; 5 Open all year; 6 Pets welcome;

A converted 1905 summer boarding house, the inn is at Short Sands Beach. Individually decorated rooms have ocean views. Walk to beach, enjoy sunsets, or visit local Nubble Lighthouse. Historic landmarks; fine restaurants. Relax, be pampered, and let the seashore entertain. Continental plus breakfast.

Hosts: Dan and Danielle Duffy
Rooms: 4 (S2B) $49-59
Continental Breakfast
Credit Cards: None
Notes: 2, 7, 9, 10, 11, 12

YORK HARBOR

Bell Buoy Bed and Breakfast

570 York Street, 03911
(207) 363-7264

At the Bell Buoy, there are no strangers, only friends who have not met. Open year-round and minutes from US 95, Route 1, and the Kittery outlet malls. We are a short walk to sandy beaches, or guests may relax on our large porch or in the guests-only living room with fireplace. A full home-made breakfast will be served in the dining room or on the porch, as desired.

Hosts: Wes and Kathie Cook
Rooms: 3 (1 PB; 2 SB) $60-85
Full Breakfast
Credit Cards: None
Notes: 2, 5, 7, 9, 11, 12

Dockside Guest Quarters

Harris Island Road, P.O. Box 205, York, 03909
(207) 363-2868

The Dockside Guest Quarters is a small resort on a private peninsula in York Harbor. Panorama of ocean and harbor activities. Spacious grounds with privacy and relaxing atmosphere. Beaches, outlet shopping, and numerous scenic walks close by. Accommodations are in a seacoast inn and multi-unit cottages. Full service marina, wedding facilities, and restaurant on site. Packages and off-season rates are available. Open year-round.

Host: The Lusty Family
Rooms: 21 (19 PB; 2 SB) $60-145
Continental Breakfast
Credit Cards: A, B
Notes: 2, 3, 4, 5, 8, 9, 10, 11, 12, 14

Dockside Guest Quarters

York Harbor Inn

Box 573, Route 1A, 03911
(207) 363-5119; (800) 343-3869

Coastal country inn overlooks beautiful York Harbor in an exclusive residential neighborhood. There are 35 air-conditioned rooms with antiques, ocean views, and seven working fireplaces; and some rooms have Jacuzzi spas and oceanview decks. Fine dining year-round. An English pub on the premises with entertainment. The beach is within walking distance; and boating, fishing, antique shops are all nearby.

Hosts: Joe, Jean, Garry, and Nancy Dominguez
Rooms: 35 (PB) $79-139
Continental Breakfast
Credit Cards: A, B, C, E, F
Notes: 2, 3, 4, 5, 8, 9, 10, 11, 12, 14

7 No smoking; 8 Children welcome; 9 Social drinking allowed; 10 Tennis nearby; 11 Swimming nearby; 12 Golf nearby; 13 Skiing nearby; 14 May be booked through a travel agent.

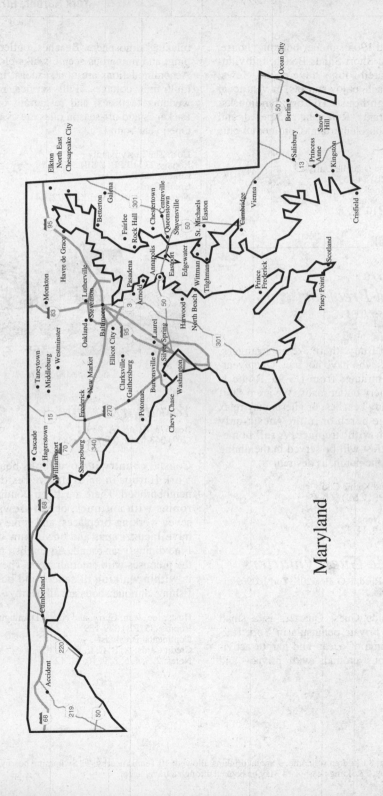

Maryland

Elkton
North East
Chesapeake City

Ocean City

50

Berlin

Snow Hill

Salisbury

13

Princess Anne

Kingston

Cristfield

Galena
301
Betterton
Chestertown
Centreville
Fairlee
Centreville
Queenstown
Rock Hall
Stevensville
Havre de Grace
50
St. Michaels
Cambridge
Easton
Vienna

Monkton
Lutherville
Pasadena
Annapolis
Eastport
Stevenson
Arnold
Edgewater
Wittman
Prince
Frederick
83
Baltimore
3
50
Tilghman
Westminster
Oakland
95
Harwood
Scotland
Taneytown
Ellicott City
Laurel
North Beach
Piney Point
Middleburg
New Market
Clarksville
Silver Spring
301
Gaithersburg
Burtonsville
Frederick
270
Cascade
15
Potomac
Chevy Chase
Washington
Hagerstown
70
Williamsport
340
Sharpsburg
68

Cumberland

68
220
Accident

68
219
50

Maryland

ACCIDENT

Amanda's
Bed and Breakfast

1428 Park Avenue, Baltimore, 21217-4230
(410) 225-0001; (800) 899-7533
FAX (410) 728-8957

329. A country farmhouse near Deep Creek Lake with year-round recreational activities; ski in the winter, water sports in the summer, beautiful fall colors, and scenic trails. Horseback riding nearby. Four rooms: two have private baths. Full breakfast. $65-85.

ANNAPOLIS

Amanda's
Bed and Breakfast

1428 Park Avenue, Baltimore, 21217-4230
(410) 225-0001; (800) 899-7533
FAX (410) 728-8957

112. Among beautiful trees on the cove of Severn River, this charming 1850 barn has been renovated with a taste of country, including antiques and old quilts. Historic Annapolis, U.S. Naval Academy, and sailing schools are all nearby. Convenient snack bar. Children welcome. Continental breakfast or farm breakfast. One queen-size bed with private half-bath; one double bed with private half-bath and deck. $70.

124. Quiet Annapolis suburb near Quiet Waters Park, just four miles from historic Annapolis. Two rooms, each with a private bath. Full breakfast. $75-85.

139. Choose from four historic locations in downtown Annapolis that accurately reflect early architecture. Some include dining rooms, taverns, and conference space. Continental breakfast. $85-250.

141. Nestled between the U.S. Naval Academy and St. John's College, this beautifully decorated historic district townhouse features a private apartment suite that has a fireplace and ivy-covered courtyard. Another suite occupies the entire third floor of the main house. Continental breakfast. Two-night minimum. $120-140.

163. This ten-room bed and breakfast is on the main street in downtown Annapolis, just steps away from the docks, shops, and historic buildings. All rooms have private baths. As the inn is above a famous deli, breakfast may be chosen from a special menu. Full breakfast. $65-85.

182. This beautiful, modern condo on the water looks out onto a marina. Just 15 minutes (three miles) from downtown historic Annapolis. Continental breakfast. One queen-size bed. Private bath. $85.

218. Two older homes and a newer addition are in the heart of the historic district of Annapolis. There are a total of 20 guest

NOTES: Credit cards: A MasterCard; B Visa; C American Express; D Discover; E Diners Club; F Other; 2 Personal checks accepted; 3 Lunch available; 4 Dinner available; 5 Open all year; 6 Pets welcome; 7 No smoking; 8 Children welcome; 9 Social drinking allowed; 10 Tennis nearby; 11 Swimming nearby; 12 Golf nearby; 13 Skiing nearby; 14 May be booked through a travel agent.

Amanda's
Bed and Breakfast
(continued)

rooms. Parlors, dining and meeting rooms are all lovingly furnished with beautiful antiques. $72-120.

234. An unusual octagon-shaped house on a wooded lot overlooking the South River. Newly created suite with water view, private bath, and sitting area. A fireplace for cool weather enjoyment. Breakfast options available. $125.

258. A luxury 55-foot motor yacht on a lovely creek has every amenity. Put worries to rest in the lounging area that adjoins the master stateroom. A spacious aft deck and fly bridge are also included for your enjoyment. Historic Annapolis city docks and restaurants are just minutes away with the help of a water taxi. Private bath. Continental breakfast. $175.

295. Lighthouse replica, built by the water with a beautiful view of the bay. Unique and private. Each of the three rooms has a private bath. Parking and Continental breakfast. A view to be enjoyed. $85-95.

306. A former corner store, now decorated with a European country flavor. Walk to everything in Annapolis: restaurants, historic sites, naval academy, and shops. Four rooms, two with private baths. Full breakfast. $75-95.

316. Nestled in the woods on the water about five minutes from downtown Annapolis. A charming cottage with one room and private bath. Double hammock by the water. Full breakfast. $100.

322. Downtown Annapolis within walking distance to historic sites, shops, restaurants, and Naval Academy. Lovely antiques; newly decorated. One room with private bath; and one suite with private bath. Full breakfast. $95-150.

334. Just north of the city in a quiet wooded area. A ranch-style home built by the owners. Inside some furniture made by the "men" of the family. A private entrance wing with queen-size bed and sitting area overlooking dogwood garden. Walking trail just behind the house. Full breakfast. $75-85.

355. Only ten minutes from downtown Annapolis. Enjoy the water and a pool at this small, comfortable cottage set off from the main house. Private entrance. Double bed. Three rooms in main house available for a family. Full breakfast. $85-100.

366. A private space with a large room, sitting area, kitchenette, double bed, and bath. Just steps from the water and minutes from downtown Annapolis. Very quiet and peaceful. Self-catered breakfast provided. $85.

373. Just steps from the Naval Academy gates, downtown shops, docks, and historic places throughout town. Four rooms, each with a private bath. Continental breakfast. $95-115.

American Heritage
Bed and Breakfast

108 Charles Road, 21401
(410) 280-1620

This charming century-old home is filled with family heirlooms and antiques, some dating back to the Civil War, for guests to enjoy. Graciously appointed rooms and attention to detail offer travelers, honeymoon couples, and family guests a pleasurable respite. Air conditioning and ceiling fans throughout. Wake to the aromas of a hearty breakfast served elegantly to pamper. Therapeutic massage offered by appointment on premises. Easy walking distance to attractions. Gift certificates available.

Hosts: Bob and Adria Smith
Rooms: 2 (PB) $90-100
Full Breakfast
Credit Cards: None
Notes: 2, 5, 7, 9, 14

The Barn on Howard's Cove

500 Wilson Road, 21401
(410) 266-6840

A restored 1850s barn on a secluded cove off the Severn River, two miles from the center of this historic state capital, sailing center of the United States, and home of the U.S. Naval Academy. Convenient to Baltimore and Washington, D.C. Beautiful gardens, rural setting. Country decor with antiques, Noah's Ark collection, and handmade quilts. One room has a deck and a loft. Breakfast is served in the flower-filled solarium or on the large deck overlooking the river.

Hosts: Dr. and Mrs. Graham Gutsche
Rooms: 2 (P1/2B, SFB) $70
Full Breakfast
Credit Cards: None
Notes: 2, 5, 8, 10, 11, 12, 14

Bed and Breakfast of Maryland/Traveller in Maryland, Inc.

P.O. Box 2277, 21494-2277
(410) 269-6232; FAX (410) 263-4841

107. This Victorian Italianate villa, circa 1864, is a charming piece of architecture nestled in the central historic district. At the entry a circular staircase flows up to the second-floor guest room area. Furnished with period antiques, some reproductions, and numerous objets d'art. There are three guest rooms. One with a queen-size bed, fireplace, and private bath. The second has a double bed, TV, telephone, and private hall bath with shower and separate Jacuzzi. The third has a single bed and may be used with either room for an additional person. Resident cats in owners' private wing only. No smoking. Full breakfast. $50-95.

109. This turn-of-the-century home is on Spa Creek and convenient to all attractions in the historic district. It is filled with antiques and family heirlooms. There is a second-floor sun porch, nice yard, and a terrace where guests can watch the sailboats quietly slip by. Four guest rooms that have private or shared baths. No smoking. Full breakfast. $60-70.

111. This charming, old home, dating from the 1690s and early 1700s, is one of Annapolis' two oldest residences. It is a registered historic landmark still occupied by descendants of the original owners. In the historic district and furnished in elements of the original Colonial structure. There are three guest rooms. One with a double bed, fireplace, and private bath. The second has a double bed, and shares a bath with the third room with twin beds. Resident cat and dog. No smoking. Continental breakfast. $65-95.

113. This two-story waterfront home has prominent views of the South River, and is a ten-minute drive to the historic district. Family room contains TV, fireplace, and large windows that offer guests the world outside. The rear yard has a tiled patio with a panoramic view. There are three guest rooms with double or king-size beds and private baths. Resident cat. Restricted smoking. Full breakfast. $65-75.

7 No smoking; 8 Children welcome; 9 Social drinking allowed; 10 Tennis nearby; 11 Swimming nearby; 12 Golf nearby; 13 Skiing nearby; 14 May be booked through a travel agent.

Bed and Breakfast of Maryland/Traveller in Maryland, Inc. (continued)

119. This restored horse barn, circa 1860, is nestled on a secluded cove off the Severn River. Plank flooring, working fireplace, handmade quilts, farm tools, workpieces, and open views of the woodlands and water grace this home. The two guest rooms, with double or king-size beds, have private half-baths and share a shower-tub room that connects to each half-bath. No smoking. Full breakfast. $55-75.

121. This unhosted, three-story, 1900s home is in the historic district. The first floor has a living room with queen sofa bed and center dining room with large rear kitchen. Rear brick patio surrounded by a ten-foot high brick wall adds privacy. Second floor has two bedrooms with double beds. One with sitting area and full bath. Second room contains half-bath. Resident dog. No smoking. Three-night minimum stay. $275.

123. This contemporary townhome is on the fringe of the historic district overlooking Spa Creek. With eclectic furnishings, it has a nice water view from the dining and living rooms. The two guest rooms have waterfront balconies, one with double and one with twin beds. They share a hall bath. Central air conditioning. Restricted smoking area. Continental breakfast. $60-65.

127. This Victorian bed and breakfast is in the historic district three blocks from the city waterfront and walking distance to fine restaurants, shopping, the historic sites, and the U.S. Naval Academy. Furnished with antiques and family collectibles. Rear yard with brick patio. The guest suite has a queen-size bed, separate living room with TV, and private bath. Air conditioning. No smoking. Continental breakfast. $90.

129. This Georgian-Revival brick home furnished in family collectibles is in the historic district and within three blocks of the waterfront. The owner-operator, Naval Academy graduate and retired Naval officer, has hosted Academy guests over the years. The first guest room has a double bed and private hall bath. The second has king-size or twin beds, fireplace, and private bath. The third has a double bed, two trundle beds, and private bath. Can easily accommodate a family. Garden patio provides a relaxing sit on seasonal days where a full breakfast is served. Smoking restricted. Children welcome. Fifteen dollars for each extra person. $75-85.

139. A recently renovated 70-year-old corner store features three guest rooms that combine yesteryear (original tin ceiling and oak counter) with contemporary conveniences (in-room coffee makers, TVs). Decorated in west coast pastels, turn-of-the-century furnishings with art accents from Europe and South America. The three guest rooms have double, queen- or king-size beds and private baths. Two-minute walk from city dock and Naval Academy. Off-street parking at modest cost. Continental plus breakfast served. No smoking allowed. $75-95.

141. This contemporary, waterfront home is within a swift five to eight minutes of the historic district by auto. Covered waterview deck and small dock facility on the property. This converted fishing bungalow is furnished with a comfortable country decor and feel. The upstairs guest room has a queen-size bed and private hall bath. The second is a ground-floor accommodation with private entrance, living room with working fireplace, bedroom with queen-size bed, private bath, a butler's kitchen with microwave, no stove. Cats in residence in the main house. No smoking. Full breakfast. $65-90.

NOTES: Credit cards accepted: A MasterCard; B Visa; C American Express; D Discover; E Diners Club; F Other; 2 Personal checks accepted; 3 Lunch available; 4 Dinner available; 5 Open all year; 6 Pets welcome;

147. This elegant brick townhouse features eclectic decor with a flair including antiques, contemporary pieces, and a collection of Oriental pieces that cover the mirror-finished antique softwood floors. Accommodations include two entire floor suites. One guest suite is a completely private garden apartment with separate entrance offering full kitchen, sitting area with fireplace, TV, VCR, telephone, double bed, and private bath. The second suite is on the third floor with sitting room, TV, VCR, double bed, and private bath. Convenient to the U.S. Naval Academy and St. Johns College. A "breakfast-out" option is available. Continental breakfast served. No smoking allowed. $140-160.

149. This restored four-square home built in 1908 is in the historic district of Annapolis and offers its guest a combination of Victorian elegance and quiet splendor. The inn is carefully furnished in genuine antiques and period reproductions. There are five distinctively appointed guest rooms with queen-size beds. Shared and private baths. A well-behaved dog is in residence. Air-conditioned. No smoking. Full buffet breakfast. $75-150.

151. This restored pre-revolutionary Georgian Colonial was built in 1747 as a forensic club by William Paca and associates and is also on the National Register of Historic Places. Amble out the back door to Main Street shopping and restaurants, the city waterfront, and the Naval Academy. Three guest rooms are beautifully decorated with period Colonial reproductions, antiques, museum prints, and floral arrangements. All have private baths and queen- or king-size beds. Cat in residence (Muffin). No smoking. Continental breakfast. $100.

153. This historic district home is decorated with Colonial and English flair, including antiques and fishnet canopied beds. Oriental and braided rugs adorn pine floors. Special touches such as baskets filled with toiletries and bathrobes are provided. Three guest rooms with twin, double, or queen-size canopied bed share a hall bath with shower. No smoking. At breakfast time, serve yourself from the Sheraton sideboard laden with seasonal morning fare. $60-80.

155. A Victorian historic district home, circa 1858, blended with the comforts of Laura Ashley decor, working fireplaces, antiques, and crafted quilts. Seven guest rooms have queen- or king-size beds and private baths. Two-room suite has a queen-size bed and private bath with whirlpool and cable. One-half block from the Naval Academy and the waterfront area. TV. No smoking. Continental breakfast. $70-120.

Chez Amis
Bed and Breakfast

85 East Street, 21401
(410) 263-6631

Renovated 70-year-old corner store offers four guest rooms combining yesteryear ambience with today's conveniences—air conditioning, TVs, and beverage centers. The 19th-century American antiques, original oak store counter, tin ceilings, and Georgia pine floors blend with European and country decor. In historic district one block from city dock, state capitol, and the U.S. Naval Academy. Enjoy romance and warm

hospitality in America's sailing capital at "The House of Friends."

Hosts: Don and Mickie Deline
Rooms: 4 (2PB, 2SB) $75-95
Full Breakfast
Credit Cards: A, B
Notes: 2, 5, 7, 14

College House Suites

One College Avenue, 21401-1603
(410) 263-6124

This elegant brick townhouse, nestled between the U.S. Naval Academy and St. John's College, features two suites: the Annapolitan Suite has a fireplace and private entrance through the ivy-covered courtyard; the Colonial Suite has superb Oriental rugs, antiques, and views of Naval Academy grounds. Fresh flowers, bathrobes, toiletries, fruit baskets, and special chocolates enhance the romantic atmosphere. A "breakfast-out" option is available at a $20 rate reduction. AAA approved. Three Star Award. Two-night minimum stay.

Hosts: Don and Jo Anne Wolfrey
Suites: 2 (PB) $160
Continental Breakfast
Credit Cards: A, B
Notes: 5, 7, 9, 14

Hunter House Bed and Breakfast

154 Prince George Street, 21401
(410) 626-1268; (800) 871-1268

Nineteenth-century, three-story townhouse is on a quiet, tree-lined residential street in historic downtown Annapolis. Just around the corner from all kinds of boats in city dock and the U.S. Naval Academy. Full breakfast, often with homemade Irish soda bread. Guests welcome to relax in the living room or the private garden. One guest room and one suite. The suite has one bedroom and one sitting room with sleep sofa.

Hosts: Ed and Johnell Hunter
Rooms: 2 (2 SB) $75-85

Full Breakfast
Credit Cards: None
Notes: 2, 5, 8

The International Bed & Breakfast Club, Inc.

504 Amherst Street, Buffalo, NY 14207
(800) 723-4262; FAX (716) 873-4462

MD6631PP. In the historic district of Annapolis. Renovated 70-year-old home which had been the site of a corner store; architecturally interesting because of the building's unusual wedge shape and its positioning at the convergence of two streets. Perfect for events at the U.S. Naval Academy and boat shows in "America's Sailing Capital." Guests enjoy the host hospitality, convenient central location, and charming decor. Three guest rooms with private or shared baths. Children welcome. No smoking. Continental plus breakfast. $75-90.

Jonas Green House Bed and Breakfast

124 Charles Street, 21401
(410) 263-5892

Charming old home, dating from the 1690s and early 1700s, one of Annapolis' two oldest residences. Home of Jonas Green, colonial printer and patriot, from 1738 until his death in 1767, continuously occupied by his family ever since (current owner is Jonas's five-greats grandson). Furnished with attractive antiques and maintained in tradition of simple charm. In the middle of the historic district, five- or ten-minute walk from all of Annapolis' historic attractions, fine restaurants, shops, and the Naval Academy.

Hosts: Dede and Randy Brown
Rooms: 3 (1PB; 2SB) $65-95
Continental Breakfast
Credit Cards: A, B, C
Notes: 2, 5, 6, 7, 8, 9, 11, 12, 14

NOTES: Credit cards accepted: A MasterCard; B Visa; C American Express; D Discover; E Diners Club; F Other; 2 Personal checks accepted; 3 Lunch available; 4 Dinner available; 5 Open all year; 6 Pets welcome;

Reynolds Tavern

7 Church Circle, P.O. Box 748, 21404
(410) 626-0380; FAX (410) 626-0381

This authentically restored 18th-century tavern (circa 1747) sits quietly in the heart of the nation's largest historic district. The tavern offers four spacious lodging rooms with full private baths, beautiful antique furnishings, separate sitting rooms in three suites, individual heating, and air conditioning. Enjoy the creative menu that is served daily in the tavern's highly rated dining room. Light fare and spirits are also available in the friendly Colonial pub. A shady garden cafe and terrace also await guests.

Hosts: Sandy and Ramsay Stallman
Rooms: 4 (PB) $90-125
Continental Breakfast
Credit Cards: A, B, C
Notes: 2, 3, 4, 5, 7, 9, 14

ARNOLD

Bed and Breakfast of Maryland/Traveller in Maryland, Inc.

P.O. Box 2277, Annapolis, 21494-2277
(410) 269-6232; FAX (410) 263-4841

125. This lovely, professionally decorated, two-story home has been elegantly furnished in antiques and beautiful accessories. Only a ten-minute drive from Annapolis and the historic district. This home offers a large, formal living room, family room, screened porch, and in-ground swimming pool. The first guest room has a king-size bed and private bath. The second guest room has a double bed and private hall bath. The third has a single bed and may be shared with the second guest room. Central air conditioning. No smoking allowed. Full breakfast served. $50-80.

BALTIMORE

Abacrombie Badger Bed and Breakfast

58 West Biddle Street, 21201
(410) 244-7227; FAX (410) 244-8415

Elegant lodgings in the heart of Baltimore's cultural center has twelve beautifully decorated rooms in the 162-year-old mansion of Major Thomas Biddle, all with private baths and private telephones. *Tasso Tana* (The Badgery) restaurant and bar on premises. Free parking, Continental breakfast, cable TV. Next door to Meyerhoff Symphony Hall. Walk to the opera, Antique Row, University of Baltimore, and Light Rail. Near the Inner Harbor, art galleries, University of Maryland, and Maryland Institute College of Art.

Hosts: Paul Bragaw and Collin Clarke
Rooms: 12 (PB) $99-129
Continental Breakfast
Credit Cards: A, B, C
Notes: 2, 3, 4, 5, 7, 9, 14

Amanda's Bed and Breakfast

1428 Park Avenue, 21217-4230
(410) 225-0001; (800) 899-7533
FAX (410) 728-8957

101. Spacious four-story townhouse, circa 1870, in historic downtown neighborhood of Bolton Hill. Twelve-foot ceilings, crown moldings, six marble mantels, and other original architectural features. Three large rooms with private baths. Ride the Light Rail to Camden Yards and the Inner Harbor. Walk to the Myerhoff Symphony Hall, Lyric Theater, or the Maryland Institute College of Art. Continental breakfast. $85.

102. A four-story row house in historic Mount Vernon neighborhood has a king-size bed and private bath. Ride the new

7 No smoking; 8 Children welcome; 9 Social drinking allowed; 10 Tennis nearby; 11 Swimming nearby;
12 Golf nearby; 13 Skiing nearby; 14 May be booked through a travel agent.

Amanda's
Bed and Breakfast
(continued)

Light Rail to Oriole Park at Camden Yards and Inner Harbor. Only minutes away from the Inner Harbor, shopping, and restaurants. Continental breakfast. $65-75.

109. A colorful 18th-century community, Fell's Point is the location for this wonderfully renovated urban inn at the water's edge. All rooms feature private baths and are individually designed and decorated with antiques and period reproductions. Other attractions include an English pub and elegant dining room. $85-up.

110. Tudor-style guest house, near Johns Hopkins University Homewood campus, is just minutes from the Inner Harbor, convention center, and stadium. The neighborhood is bordered by two parks and a lake. Biking, fitness track, and public golf course are all within walking distance. One queen-size. Private bath. Full breakfast. $75.

111. Federal-style townhouse offers two delightful guest rooms and is within walking distance of Inner Harbor. Convention center, other meeting centers, financial district, sports arena, Harbor Place, galleries, museums, theaters, and restaurants are all nearby. One double; one twin. Shared baths. $50-60.

117. Restored 18th-century townhouse in historic Fell's Point, a waterfront community with unique shops and restaurants. Inner Harbor is just one mile away either by walking, water taxi, or trolley. Three doubles. Private baths. Continental breakfast. $85-95.

119. Elegant Victorian mansion is decorated with imported antiques and is in the historic Mount Vernon area near Antique

Row. All 15 guest rooms/suites have kitchenettes, private baths, and meeting facilities. Ride the Light Rail to Camden Yards and Inner Harbor or walk to the harbor just ten blocks away. Fine dining is nearby. Continental breakfast. $85-105.

131. Downtown historic neighborhood townhouse is furnished with antiques and is on a quiet street facing a park. Public transportation, cultural center, and churches are all nearby. The guest room is a large king-size suite with all the amenities and with private kitchenette. Swimming pool privileges. $85.

186. Restored Victorian townhouse nestled in the Union Square historic district and just minutes away from the Inner Harbor, convention center, and the new sports complex in Camden Station. The rooms, with double beds and private baths, are decorated with period furnishings. Full breakfast. $80-120.

190. Charmingly historic, intimate waterfront retreat is in Fell's Point. This bed and breakfast is listed on the National Register of Historic Places. Includes English garden, marina, and period furnishings. Restaurants and shops are within walking distance and a water taxi is available from May to October. Smoke-free. Continental breakfast. All rooms have private baths, some have a water view. $110-150.

195. An attractive Federal Hill row house, just one and one-half blocks from the science center and Inner Harbor, within walking distance to sites, attractions, restaurants, and shopping. Water taxi is available for rides around harbor. The guest room has a queen-size bed, private bath, and is bright and airy. Great breakfast. $85.

201. Waterfront Manor house built in 1900 with large light-filled room; antiques and collectibles. Docking privileges, swimming

NOTES: Credit cards accepted: A MasterCard; B Visa; C American Express; D Discover; E Diners Club; F Other; 2 Personal checks accepted; 3 Lunch available; 4 Dinner available; 5 Open all year; 6 Pets welcome;

pool, excellent seafood restaurants, and quiet setting. Master suite has fireplace and Jacuzzi. Full breakfast. $75-125.

225. In Charles Village near Johns Hopkins University. The decor spans a century of styles, from the Victorian to the contemporary. All rooms have brass fixtures, English soaps, amenities, hair dryers, alarm clocks, air conditioning, and color TVs. Double beds; private baths. Continental breakfast served to room. $69-129.

226. Built in 1897, the official guest house of the city of Baltimore is comprised of three townhouses in historic Mount Vernon. Guests are treated to personalized service, private baths, ornate and unusual decor. Great location with guest parking. Continental breakfast. $100-125.

236. Enjoy a relaxing time by the fireplace in the guest parlor, walk to the Inner Harbor, snooze in queen-size bed with private bath, and start the day with a satisfying breakfast. A sunny Federal Hill row house, open spiral staircase. $110.

265. This Federal-style townhouse was built in 1982. Features include three stories, patio, garden in back, fireplace in den and living room. Two rooms with double beds. A springer spaniel, Rocky, loves people. Continental breakfast is served in the dining room. $65-75.

312. Restored carriage house in historic Charles Village. Near Johns Hopkins University and convenient to the Inner Harbor. Parking on premises. King-size or double bed, bath, washer/dryer. Self-catered breakfast. $100.

330. Historic Bolton Hill just two blocks from the Light Rail to Camden Yards or the Inner Harbor. Primarily a residential neighborhood with tree-lined streets, marble

steps, and large, early 19th-century row houses. One room with private bath with Jacuzzi tub. $95.

346. Federal Hill, a residential and commercial area on the south side of the Inner Harbor. Walk to the many activities, restaurants, and shops at the harbor. Also walk to Oriole Park at Camden Yards. Private little house with two bedrooms. Self-catered breakfast. $125-165.

Bed and Breakfast of Maryland/Traveller in Maryland, Inc.

P.O. Box 2277, Annapolis, 21494-2277
(410) 269-6232; FAX (410) 263-4841

157. Experience the charm and character of these recently restored and renovated two-hundred-year-old townhomes a half-block off the waterfront of historic Fell's Point. Great care went into preserving much of the original woodwork and fireplace mantels. Eleven original fireplaces, one of which is in the large bathroom on the third floor. Walking distance to several restaurants and pubs. Main house features two guest rooms: one has a fireplace, double rope bed, and private bath; the other has twin beds and a private bath. A third guest room is on the second floor of the annex with a double bed and private bath. The fourth accommodation is a two-room suite with sitting area, fireplace, bedroom with double bed and private bath. Private patios are to the rear of each townhouse. No smoking. Continental breakfast. $80-95.

159. A Federal-period townhouse built in 1830, which later took on an Italianate appearance with the addition of a fourth floor and additional cornice work to the exterior during the Victorian period. On the first floor there is a sitting room with grand piano, comfortable chairs, sofa, and fireplace. Two guest rooms with double beds and a shared hall bath. The dining room

7 No smoking; 8 Children welcome; 9 Social drinking allowed; 10 Tennis nearby; 11 Swimming nearby; 12 Golf nearby; 13 Skiing nearby; 14 May be booked through a travel agent.

features a banquet table, circa 1790, with 12 matching chairs, where a full sumptuous breakfast is served daily. No smoking. $75.

161. This small urban inn is an exciting combination of European charm of the bed and breakfast and the warm hospitality of the American country inn. Walking distance of "Antique" and "Boutique" rows, which are continuous avenues of antique shops and galleries. Surrounding the inn are the Meyerhoff Symphony Hall, the 1904 Lyric Opera House, Maryland Institute College of Art, the Theatre Project, and the School of Performing Arts. On-site bar and restaurant. Fifteen guest accommodations have private baths and are tastefully decorated with rich Baltimorean artwork, antique furniture, brass beds, and fresh flowers. Restricted smoking area. Continental breakfast. $90-140.

Betsy's Bed and Breakfast

1428 Park Avenue, 21217-4230
(410) 383-1274; (800) 899-7533

This four-story "petite" estate in downtown Bolton Hill is on a tree-lined street with white marble steps and brass rails. This spacious home features a hallway laid in alternating strips of oak and walnut, ceiling medallions, six marble mantels, and a center staircase that rises to meet a skylight. The expansive walls are hung with handsome brass rubbings and family heirloom quilts. Guests may relax in a hot tub shaded by a large pin oak tree in season.

Host: Betsy Grater
Rooms: 3 (PB) $85
Full Breakfast
Credit Cards: A, B, C, D
Notes: 2, 5, 7, 8, 9, 10, 11, 14

Celie's Waterfront Bed and Breakfast

Historic Fell's Point, 1714 Thames Street, 21231
(410) 522-2323; (800) 432-0184
FAX (410) 522-2324

On Baltimore Harbor. Ideal for business or pleasure. Seven air-conditioned guest rooms, one wheelchair accessible, others also accessible to a private garden and harbor view roof deck. Some with whirlpools, fireplaces, private balconies, and harbor views, in a relaxed atmosphere. Private telephones, fax, and TV. Marina close by. Minutes to Harbor Place, central business district, and Orioles Stadium by water taxi.

Host: Celie Ives
Rooms: 7 (PB) $100-160
Continental Breakfast
Credit Cards: A, B, C, D
Notes: 2, 5, 7, 9, 14

Mr. Mole Bed and Breakfast

1601 Bolton Street, 21217
(410) 728-1179

"Maryland's only four-star award winning bed and breakfast." (1995 *Mobil Travel Guide*). Decorated like a designers' showcase home. Amid quiet, tree-lined streets on historic Bolton Hill, two miles north of Inner Harbor. This 1870 row house has 14-foot ceilings, some two-bedroom suites. Private telephone and bath, garage parking (with automatic garage door opener), large Continental breakfast included. Near symphony, opera, museums, art galleries, Antique Row, universities, and Orioles Park. Member of the Maryland B&B Association. AAA approved.

Hosts: Collin Clarke and Paul Bragaw
Rooms: 5 (PB) $95-125
Continental Breakfast
Credit Cards: A, B, C, D
Notes: 2, 5, 7, 9, 14

The Paulus Gasthaus

2406 Kentucky Avenue, 21213
410-467-1688

Guests have described the Paulus Gasthaus as the best little bed and breakfast within the eastern American corridor. This European Tudor home is four and a half miles from Inner Harbor, very close to Johns Hopkins, theaters, and best seafood restaurants. Convenient to all major highways. Lovely residential neighborhood. The hosts offer quality accommodations and full American or German breakfast. Fluent German and some French spoken. Lots of *gemüetlichkeit* (personal service). Within walking distance to public golf, tennis courts, and fitness trails.

Hosts: Lucie and Ed Paulus
Rooms: 2 (1 PB; 2 SB) $75
Full Breakfast
Credit Cards: A, B, C
Notes: 2, 5, 7, 9, 10, 12, 14

Twin Gates
Bed and Breakfast Inn

308 Morris Avenue, Lutherville, 21093
(301) 252-3131; (800) 635-0370

A peaceful Victorian mansion and gardens, just minutes from Baltimore's attractions: the National Aquarium, Harbor Place, and Maryland hunt country. Friendly hosts, wine and cheese, and gourmet breakfasts. Two-night minimum stay weekends and holidays.

Hosts: Gwen and Bob Vaughan
Rooms: 6 (PB) $95-145
Full Breakfast
Credit Cards: A, B, C
Notes: 2, 5, 7, 9, 10, 14

Twin Gates

BERLIN

Amanda's
Bed and Breakfast

1428 Park Avenue, Baltimore, 21217-4230
(410) 225-0001; (800) 899-7533
FAX (410) 728-8957

164. Spacious grounds, quiet peaceful setting near great restaurants and the ocean. Beautifully restored early 19th-century Victorian with wraparound porch. All rooms are decorated with quality antiques. Honeymoon suite with Jacuzzi. Full breakfast. $125-150.

Atlantic Hotel

Atlantic Hotel
Inn and Restaurant

2 North Main Street, 21811
(410) 641-3589; (800) 814-7672

Restored Victorian hotel with 16 period-furnished rooms. A national register building in the historic district. Elegant dining and piano lounge on the premises. Eight miles west of Ocean City and Assateague Island National Seashore. Walk to nearby antique shops, gallery, and museum.

Rooms: 16 (PB) $65-135
Continental Breakfast
Credit Cards: A, B, C
Notes: 2, 3, 4, 5, 8, 9, 10, 11, 12

7 No smoking; 8 Children welcome; 9 Social drinking allowed; 10 Tennis nearby; 11 Swimming nearby; 12 Golf nearby; 13 Skiing nearby; 14 May be booked through a travel agent.

Bed and Breakfast of Maryland/Traveller in Maryland, Inc.

P.O. Box 2277, Annapolis, 21494-2277
(410) 269-6232; FAX (410) 263-4841

171. This faithfully restored 1895 Victorian inn was placed on the National Register of Historic Places in 1980. Carefully restored to its former elegance and grandeur, it is in the center of Berlin's historic district; eight miles from Ocean City and Assateague National Seashore. All 16 guest rooms have private bath, air conditioning, and direct dial telephones. Each room is unique and furnished with antiques. Smoking is restricted. Continental breakfast. $60-108.

Merry Sherwood Plantation

8909 Worchester Highway, 21811
(410) 641-2112; (800) 660-0358

Merry Sherwood Plantation, circa 1859, was listed on the National Register of Historic Places in 1991. A wonderful blend of Greek Revival, Classic Italianate, and Gothic architecture, this elegant 27-room mansion has nine Victorian-style fireplaces, private baths, ballroom, 19 acres of 19th-century lush private gardens, and authentic period antiques. Convenient to Ocean City and many historic and resort attractions. Full gourmet breakfast included. Smoking restricted.

Host: Kirk Burbage
Rooms: 8 (6 PB; 2 SB)

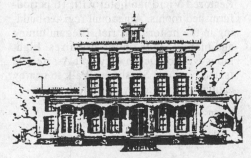
Merry Sherwood Plantation

Full Breakfast
Credit Cards: A, B
Notes: 2, 5, 10, 11, 12, 14

BETTERTON

Amanda's Bed and Breakfast

1428 Park Avenue, Baltimore, 21217-4230
(410) 225-0001; (800) 899-7533
FAX (410) 728-8957

162. The mouth of the Sassafras River and the headwaters of the Chesapeake Bay open up to this restored 1904 Victorian inn in the resort town of Betterton. In the heart of goose and duck hunting country, this inn is one block from the beach, biking, boating, and wildlife refuges. Full breakfast. Seven rooms, private and shared baths. $60-85.

Lantern Inn

115 Ericsson Avenue, P.O. Box 25, 21610
(410) 348-5809; (800) 499-7265

This restored 1904 inn is in a quiet town on Maryland's Eastern Shore. One and one-half blocks to a nice sand beach on the Chesapeake Bay. Near historic Chestertown, hiking trails, and three wildlife refuges. Miles of excellent biking roads, with detailed maps provided. Antiquing and good seafood restaurants abound. No smoking in guest rooms. Children over 12 welcome.

Hosts: Ken and Ann Washburn
Rooms: 13 (4 PB; 9 SB) $68-85
Full Breakfast
Credit Cards: A, B
Notes: 2, 5, 9, 10, 11

BURTONSVILLE

Bed and Breakfast of Maryland/Traveller in Maryland, Inc.

P.O. Box 2277, Annapolis, 21494-2277
(410) 269-6232; FAX (410) 263-4841

NOTES: Credit cards accepted: A MasterCard; B Visa; C American Express; D Discover; E Diners Club;
F Other; 2 Personal checks accepted; 3 Lunch available; 4 Dinner available; 5 Open all year; 6 Pets welcome;

204. The contemporary charm of this guest house features an airy living-dining area highlighted by a yellow pine interior, cathedral ceilings, and an expansive picture window offering an uninterrupted view of the natural surroundings. Guests can enjoy sunny mornings on the outdoor deck, afternoon tea in the greenhouse, or cool nights by the fireplace. Come enjoy life on a working horse farm and equestrian center, tour the 18th-century log cabin with herb and flower gardens, stroll along the miles of wooded trails bordering the Rocky Gorge reservoir, and get a glimpse of the deer, waterfowl, and other natural wildlife occupying more than 1,000 acres of adjacent wooded watershed. The two guest rooms have private baths and are furnished with a unique sleep system that allows guests to achieve their own comfort level by adjusting the firmness of the mattress. No smoking. Full breakfast. $75-105.

CAMBRIDGE

Bed and Breakfast of Maryland/Traveller in Maryland, Inc.

P.O. Box 2277, Annapolis, 21494-2277
(410) 269-6232; FAX (410) 263-4841

175. The "Cottage" is a gracious suite in a garden setting, with a spacious living and dining room with a view of its own fountain. Complete kitchen, fully equipped. Bedroom has either twin or king-size bed, and the sitting room has a queen-size sofa sleeper. TV, telephone, and air conditioning provided. The "Carriage House" is in a country setting, with fully equipped kitchen, bedroom with twin canopied beds, a spacious living room with double sleeper-sofa, TV, telephone, and air conditioning. Relax after a fun-filled day of exploring the local byways on the patio under great old trees overlooking the broad sweep of gardens. Easy access to the ocean and other interesting attractions such as antique shopping, biking, fishing, hunting, bird watching, and Blackwater National Wildlife Refuge. No smoking. Stocked Continental breakfast. $75-85.

Sarke Plantation Inn

Sarke Plantation Inn

6033 Todd Point Road, 21613
(410) 228-7020; (800) 814-7020

An Eastern Shore waterfront property of 27 country acres with a spacious house that is furnished tastefully with many antiques. There is a large pool room with a regulation table, and the living room has a large fireplace, a good stereo system, and a grand piano for guests' enjoyment. Closed New Year's Eve. Children over ten welcome.

Host: Genevieve Finley
Rooms: 5 (3 PB; 2 SB) $50-90
Continental Breakfast
Credit Cards: A, B, C
Notes: 2, 5, 6, 9, 11

CASCADE

Amanda's Bed and Breakfast

1428 Park Avenue, Baltimore, 21217-4230
(410) 225-0001; (800) 899-7533
FAX (410) 728-8957

261. Visit the Blue Ridge Summit and Cascade, the undiscovered summer hideaway. Explore Gettysburg or Frederick, ski, or hike. This elegant 1900 manor house on the Mason-Dixon line offers gracious old-fashioned porches, luxury, and beauty. Four rooms available. Fireplace. Jacuzzi. $95-125.

7 No smoking; 8 Children welcome; 9 Social drinking allowed; 10 Tennis nearby; 11 Swimming nearby; 12 Golf nearby; 13 Skiing nearby; 14 May be booked through a travel agent.

CENTREVILLE

Amanda's
Bed and Breakfast

1428 Park Avenue, Baltimore, 21217-4230
(410) 225-0001; (800) 899-7533
FAX (410) 728-8957

280. Formerly a school for males only built in 1804 and now a bed and breakfast with antiques. The new owners are refurbishing and adding personal touches. Two rooms each have a king-size bed and private bath. Near Chestertown and the scenic Eastern Shore. $68.

CHESAPEAKE CITY

Bed and Breakfast
of Maryland/Traveller
in Maryland, Inc.

P.O. Box 2277, Annapolis, 21494-2277
(410) 269-6232; FAX (410) 263-4841

190. Relax on three porches or meet other guests in two comfortable parlors of this Georgian-style inn. The inn was built in 1844 and was occupied by renowned author Jack Hunter during the period in which he wrote his famous book *The Blue Max*, the story of the highest honor in the German air force. Six comfortably furnished guest accommodations with private baths. Families welcome. No smoking. No pets. Continental breakfast. $65-85.

Guesthouses, Inc.

P.O. Box 2137, West Chester, PA 19380
(215) 692-4575

Two Rivers Farm. On the scenic point of land where two rivers join the Chesapeake Bay stands a majestic, newly restored historic stone river house, circa 1840, welcoming visitors by land or by sea. There is a wide veranda surrounding three sides, making a perfect place for a relaxing afternoon refreshment while gazing across the broad sweeping lawns. The first floor reception rooms are very large and grandly furnished; light streams in from floor-to-ceiling windows illuminating the beautiful and interesting collections of equine objets d'art. The air-conditioned guest rooms with views are on the second and third floors. Appropriately furnished and decorated to its place and time, guests will find comfort in the large sunny rooms with a choice of either queen- or king-size or twin beds. For guests who want to be alone, the Jacuzzi Suite provides complete privacy with its separate entrance and complete list of amenities including kitchenette and entertainment center. Dining "at home" can be arranged for parties of ten or more. A full country breakfast is served in the formal dining room. Outdoor pool is available for guests in season. $85-170.

CHESTERTOWN

Amanda's
Bed and Breakfast

1428 Park Avenue, Baltimore, 21217-4230
(410) 225-0001; (800) 899-7533
FAX (410) 728-8957

136. The inn sits on the Chester River, four miles below town. The original part of the house was built in the 1830s and was completely renovated prior to its opening as an inn in 1985. Five acres of waterfront make up the grounds, and a marina offers deep-water slips. Five rooms, all with private baths, are available. Continental breakfast served. $85-115.

204. This Victorian inn was built in 1877 and is in the heart of town. Restored to its original charm, the dining room and double parlor feature plaster moldings. Walk to historic Washington College and shops. Five rooms, all with private baths, are available. Continental breakfast. $75-135.

205. Lovely brick Georgian manor house sitting at the mouth of the Fairlee Creek and the Chesapeake Bay outside of Chestertown. Twelve acres of landscaped grounds. Golfing, swimming, and tennis accessible. Small conferences. Eleven rooms, each with a private bath. $80-165.

Bed and Breakfast of Maryland/Traveller in Maryland, Inc.

P.O. Box 2277, Annapolis, 21494-2277
(410) 269-6232; FAX (410) 263-4841

192. Built in 1877, this beautifully restored inn is one of the finest Victorian houses in Chestertown. Only a short walk to the historic Washington College and the shops of High Street. All seven guest rooms are decorated in period furnishings and have private baths. Restricted smoking area. Continental breakfast. $50-110.

The Imperial Hotel

208 High Street, 21620
(410) 778-5000; FAX (410) 778-9662

This Victorian hotel has interiors so elegant, hosts so charming, and regional American dining so very special that people drive from Wilmington and Philadelphia just for lunch; it's also a great weekend getaway in a well-preserved Colonial-era Chesapeake Bayport town. The Imperial Hotel has an award-winning wine list and sinfully delicious desserts.

Hosts: Robert and Barbara LaVelle
Rooms: 13 (PB) $95-300
Continental Breakfast
Credit Cards: A, B, C, D
Notes: 2, 3, 4, 5, 6, 7, 8, 9, 10, 11, 12, 14

The River Inn at Rolph's Wharf

1008 Rolph's Wharf Road, 21620
(410) 778-6347; (800) 894-6347

The River Inn is an 1830s Victorian inn on the scenic Chester River, just three miles south of Chestertown, Maryland. All guest rooms have private baths and a view of the river. Light breakfast is served with fresh squeezed orange juice, and a restaurant is on premises for lunch or dinner. A boat ramp, ice, bait, and a pool are also available. The view is terrific!

Rooms: 6 (PB), $65-115
Continental Breakfast
Credit Cards: A, B, C, D
Notes: 2, 3, 4, 5, 7, 8, 9

CHEVY CHASE

Chevy Chase Bed and Breakfast

6815 Connecticut Avenue, 20815
(301) 656-5867 (phone and FAX)

Enjoy gracious hospitality and the convenience of being close to the sights of Washington, D.C., and conferences in Bethesda, in a charming beamed-ceiling, turn-of-the-century house and garden in historic Chevy Chase. Furnished with rare tapestries, Oriental rugs, and native crafts from around the world. Special breakfasts of European hot breads, jams, cheeses, fresh fruits, and a special blend of Louisiana coffee.

Host: S. C. Gotbaum
Rooms: 2 (PB) $70
Full Breakfast
Credit Cards: None
Notes: 2, 5, 7, 8, 10, 11, 12, 14

CLARKSVILLE

Amanda's Bed and Breakfast

1428 Park Avenue, Baltimore, 21217-4230
(410) 225-0001; (800) 899-7533
FAX (410) 728-8957

350. A renovated antique shop in an old barn. Pleasantly created space with sitting and eating area with kitchenette. Separate

7 No smoking; 8 Children welcome; 9 Social drinking allowed; 10 Tennis nearby; 11 Swimming nearby; 12 Golf nearby; 13 Skiing nearby; 14 May be booked through a travel agent.

bedroom and bath. Plank floors and beamed ceilings. Double bed. Furnished with country antiques. Scenic trails and picnic by pond. $125.

The Beeches
Bed and Breakfast

11746 Route 108, 21029
(410) 531-5332; FAX (410) 531-5650

The Beeches is the contemporary home of two designers, nestled in three wooded acres. Accommodations include a suite with private bath and sitting room; and two rooms, shared bath, and sitting room. Welcome beverage offered in the sunroom where gourmet breakfasts are served. The Beeches also extends corporate amenities to the business traveler. Come and relax in nature's beauty. Five minutes to Columbia, ten minutes to historic Ellicott City, thirty minutes to Baltimore and historic Annapolis, forty minutes to District of Columbia.

Hosts: Carolyn and Warren Langston
Rooms: 3 (1 PB; 2 SB) $85-100
Full Breakfast
Credit Cards: A, B, C
Notes: 2, 5, 7, 9, 10, 12, 14

CRISFIELD

Amanda's
Bed and Breakfast

1428 Park Avenue, Baltimore, 21217-4230
(410) 225-0001; (800) 899-7533
FAX (410) 728-8957

290. Lovingly restored and decorated with antiques, this Queen Anne-style home has grandeur and charm. In town, walk to docks and touring boats. Four rooms, each with a private bath. $85.

CUMBERLAND

Inn at Walnut Bottom

120 Greene Street, 21502
(301) 777-0003; (800) 286-9718

Inn at Walnut Bottom

Traditional country inn bed and breakfast in the city of Cumberland, Maryland. Twelve guest rooms and family suites, two parlors, gift shop, private parking. Eighteen fifteen and 1890 buildings beautifully refurbished. Private telephones and color TVs in guest rooms. Full breakfast served with overnight lodging. The Oxford House Restaurant serves traditional and gourmet food to inn guests and the public daily. Walk to the Scenic Railroad, the historic district, and live theater. Bicycle rentals for nearby C&O Canal Towpath.

Host: Sharon Ennis Kazary
Rooms: 12 (8 PB; 4 SB) $65-90
Suites $99-130
Full Breakfast
Credit Cards: A, B, C, D
Notes: 3, 4, 5, 7, 8, 11, 12, 13, 14

EASTON

Amanda's
Bed and Breakfast

1428 Park Avenue, Baltimore, 21217-4230
(410) 225-0001; (800) 899-7533
FAX (410) 728-8957

118. This charming 1890 Victorian bed and breakfast is registered in the historic section of Easton, the colonial capital of Maryland's Eastern Shore. Within walking distance of historical points of interest, restaurants, and antique shops, this inn has a wraparound porch and offers seven guest rooms, all with private baths. Continental breakfast. $75-110.

NOTES: Credit cards accepted: A MasterCard; B Visa; C American Express; D Discover; E Diners Club; F Other; 2 Personal checks accepted; 3 Lunch available; 4 Dinner available; 5 Open all year; 6 Pets welcome;

235. A lovely 60-acre estate with a large Georgian plantation home built in 1760 on the water. Several original dependency buildings are also on the property. A romantic getaway. Great for weddings, small conferences, or retreats. Dock, pool, chipping course, croquet, and walking trails. Each room is a complete suite. Full breakfast served. $295.

380. A cottage on the water in Easton has a beautiful view from private deck. Separate from main house, with equipped kitchen, bath, sitting area with pull-out sofa, and bedroom. TV. Air-conditioned. Continental breakfast. $85-125.

Bed and Breakfast of Maryland/Traveller in Maryland, Inc.

P.O. Box 2277, Annapolis, 21494-2277
(410) 269-6232; FAX (410) 263-4841

177. The roots of this urban inn go back over 265 years when the Talbot County Courthouse was moved here from Oxford. In 1891, a new frame inn was erected on the site of the present-day establishment. The inn met its fate by fire in 1947. But, like the phoenix, a new inn took flight. In 1948 the inn reopened to a reception of over 4,000 persons. Today, as in the early 1700s, hospitality lives once again. There are 114 beautifully decorated guest accommodations and suites with private baths, TV, and telephone. Full service restaurant and professional staff await. Restricted smoking area. Continental breakfast. $114-295.

179. This charming Victorian home is registered in the historic section of Easton, colonial capital of Maryland's Eastern Shore. Built circa 1890, the inn has a high octagonal tower, a hipped roof with dormers and a southern wraparound porch for a relaxing afternoon or evening rest. All

seven guest accommodations are spacious and bright. Each accommodation is equipped with air conditioning, ceiling fans, and a choice of private or shared bath. Resident cat. No smoking allowed. Continental breakfast. $70-110.

The Bishop's House Bed and Breakfast

214 Goldsborough Street, P.O. Box 2217, 21601
(410) 820-7290 (phone and FAX); (800) 223-7290

Restored historic district circa 1880 in-town Victorian. Romantically furnished in period style. Accommodations include air conditioning, whirlpool tubs, working fireplaces, private off-street parking, secured overnight storage for bicycles, route maps for cycling, and sumptuous breakfasts. Within three blocks of boutiques, antique shops, and restaurants and within ten miles of historic Oxford and St. Michaels. Small business group retreats, planning sessions, or private social functions welcome.

Hosts: Diane M. Laird-Ippolito and
  John B. Ippolito
Rooms: 6 (4 PB; 2 SB) $75-110
Full Breakfast
Credit Cards: None
Notes: 2, 5, 10, 12, 14

EASTPORT

Bed and Breakfast of Maryland/Traveller in Maryland, Inc.

P.O. Box 2277, Annapolis, 21494-2277
(410) 269-6232; FAX (410) 263-4841

133. This contemporary townhouse offers uncomplicated and comfortable furnishings. Walking distance to several sailing schools and historic district. Ground transportation may be by water taxi to and from the city dock. One guest room with twin beds and private hall bath. Dog in residence. No smoking. Continental breakfast. $55-60.

EDGEWATER

Bed and Breakfast of Maryland/Traveller in Maryland, Inc.

P.O. Box 2277, Annapolis, 21494-2277
(410) 269-6232; FAX (410) 263-4841

145. Untroubled lifestyle and tranquility abound in this contemporary home nestled on the banks of Church Creek, a small tributary of the South River. The beautiful gardens are landscaped for seclusion. Two waterview bedrooms with queen-size beds have a private or shared bath. There is a separate living room with TV, VCR, and telephone, making the entire level private to the guest. An upper-level family room and a deck are also available for guests to use. Outdoor cat. No smoking allowed. Full breakfast served. $75.

ELKTON

The Garden Cottage

234 Blair Shore Road, 21921
(410) 398-5566

In a setting with an early plantation house, including a 400-year-old sycamore, the Garden Cottage nestles at the edge of a meadow flanked by herb gardens and an old barn with gift shop. It has a sitting room with working fireplace, bedroom, and bath. Freshly ground coffee and herbal teas are offered with the full country breakfast. Longwood Gardens and Winterthur Museum are 50 minutes away. Historic Chesapeake City is only seven minutes away. An additional $25 charge for a third person in the room.

Hosts: Bill and Ann Stubbs
Cottage: 1 (PB) $85
Full Breakfast
Credit Cards: A, B
Notes: 2, 5, 8, 9, 12. 14

ELLICOTT CITY

Bed and Breakfast of Maryland/Traveller in Maryland, Inc.

P.O. Box 2277, Annapolis, 21494-2277
(410) 269-6232; FAX (410) 263-4841

170. This stately Federal-period stone farmhouse is on two acres with a pond near the historic mill town of Ellicott City. Continuing the tradition of a lighted candle in each window, indicating the availability of rooms, the candles remain lighted as a nostalgic reminder of the inn's past. In the winter months, a fire in the parlor fireplace or the fireplace in the adjoining music room may encourage guests to linger over a game of chess or checkers. Four guest accomodations with double and queen-size beds. Two have private baths, and the two remaining rooms share a hall bath. No smoking allowed. Continental breakfast served. $70-90.

The Wayside Inn Bed and Breakfast

4344 Columbia Road, 21042
(410) 461-4636

The inn is a 150-year-old restored stone farmhouse on two acres with spacious grounds and a pond. Rooms are furnished with antiques, family heirlooms, and reproductions. The smaller rooms have working fireplaces. An enclosed porch overlooking a pond is open spring through fall. As on-premise innkeepers, the hosts' goal is to make their guests' visit a memorable experience with plenty of personal attention. Gourmet breakfast.

Hosts: Margo and John Osantowski
Rooms: 4 (2 PB; 2 SB) $70-90
Continental Breakfast
Credit Cards: A, B, C
Notes: 2, 5, 7, 14

NOTES: Credit cards accepted: A MasterCard; B Visa; C American Express; D Discover; E Diners Club; F Other; 2 Personal checks accepted; 3 Lunch available; 4 Dinner available; 5 Open all year; 6 Pets welcome;

FAIRLEE

Bed and Breakfast of Maryland/Traveller in Maryland, Inc.

P.O. Box 2277, Annapolis, 21494-2277
(410) 269-6232; FAX (410) 263-4841

186. This historic Georgian waterfront manor is on the Chesapeake Bay. A regal 25-room mansion featuring a spectacular view and 12 acres of luxurious lawns and gardens. A private footpath leads to a quaint, sunny beach with gazebo. Guests have use of a swimming pool, tennis courts, nine-hole golf course, and yacht charter service. Nine guest rooms or suites are well-decorated, spacious, and bright with private baths. No smoking. Continental breakfast. $85-165.

FREDERICK

Amanda's Bed and Breakfast

1428 Park Avenue, Baltimore, 21217-4230
(410) 225-0001; (800) 899-7533
FAX (410) 728-8957

106. This inn's 26-acre grounds include a picturesque garden and henhouse. Each room offers a delightful 19th-century ambience, and all rooms have private baths and air conditioning. A stone fireplace, stained-glass windows, and skylights highlight the keeping room where guests can relax. Four rooms, all of which have private baths, are available. Continental breakfast. $95.

Middle Plantation Inn

9549 Liberty Road, 21701
(301) 898-7128

A rustic bed and breakfast built of stone and log. Drive through horse country to the village of Mount Pleasant. Several miles east of Frederick, on 26 acres. Each room has furnishings of antiques with private bath, air conditioning, and TV. Nearby are antique shops, museums, and many historic attractions. Children over 14 welcome.

Hosts: Shirley and Dwight Mullican
Rooms: 4 (PB) $85-95
Continental Breakfast
Credit Cards: A, B
Notes: 2, 5, 7, 8, 9, 10, 11, 12, 14

Turning Point Inn

Turning Point Inn

3406 Urbana Pike, 21701
(301) 874-2421

Turning Point Inn is a 1910 Edwardian estate home with Georgian features. Less than an hour from Washington, D.C., Baltimore, Gettysburg, and Antietam, this inn is nice for getaway weekends of sightseeing, shopping, antiquing, hiking, or exploring historic towns and battlefields. Limited smoking allowed.

Host: Charlie Seymour
Rooms: 5 (PB) $75-85
Cottages: 2 (PB) $100-150
Full Breakfast
Credit Cards: A, B, D
Notes: 2, 3, 4, 5, 8, 9, 14

7 No smoking; 8 Children welcome; 9 Social drinking allowed; 10 Tennis nearby; 11 Swimming nearby; 12 Golf nearby; 13 Skiing nearby; 14 May be booked through a travel agent.

GAITHERSBURG _____

Amanda's
Bed and Breakfast

1428 Park Avenue, Baltimore, 21217-4230
(410) 225-0001; (800) 899-7533
FAX (410) 728-8957

120. This is a comfortable luxury home in a planned community, with ample parking, a large screened-in porch, close proximity to restaurants and Washington, D.C. Two rooms, both with private baths, are available for guests. Full breakfast. $65-100.

Bed and Breakfast
of Maryland/Traveller
in Maryland, Inc.

P.O. Box 2277, Annapolis, 21494-2277
(410) 269-6232; FAX (410) 263-4841

198. This two-story, red brick, contemporary, private homestay is furnished with family pieces and has the comfort of the guest in mind. Restaurants, shopping, recreation, and the community lake are nearby. Residential streets provide quiet walks around the lake. Two beautifully furnished guest rooms extend a feeling of warmth and homeyness and share a private hall bath. No smoking. Full breakfast. $55.

Gaithersburg Hospitality
Bed and Breakfast

18908 Chimney Place, 20879
(301) 977-7377

In Montgomery Village near restaurants, shopping, and recreation, this luxury home is in a residential neighborhood, offers all amenities, and is a 30-minute ride to Washington, D.C. via the car or Metro. It is conveniently near I-270 for a drive north to Harpers Ferry, Gettysburg, and Antietam. Hosts delight in catering to travel needs with home cooking and spacious cozy comfort.

Hosts: Joe and Suzanne Danilowicz
Doubles: (PB) $55
Singles: (PB) $45
Full Breakfast
Credit Cards: None
Notes: 2, 7, 8, 10, 11, 12, 14

GALENA _____

Rosehill Farm
Bed and Breakfast

13842 Gregg Neck Road, 21635
(410) 648-5334

On 100 scenic acres, Rosehill Farm is close to marinas, excellent restaurants, and historic towns (Chestertown, Easton, and St. Michaels). On the grounds is a working greenhouse which grows miniature roses and ivy topiary. Wildlife abounds with guests frequently seeing fox, deer, geese, ducks, and blue heron, among others. Children two and older are welcome. Dog runs available. Guests will experience a thoroughly relaxing visit.

Host: Marie Jolly
Rooms: 3 (PB) $60-70
Continental Breakfast
Credit Cards: None
Notes: 2, 5, 7, 10, 11, 14

GLEN ARM _____

Amanda's
Bed and Breakfast

1428 Park Avenue, Baltimore, 21217-4230
(410) 225-0001; (800) 899-7533
FAX (410) 728-8957

372. Williamsburg-style home on tree-filled acreage in Hunt country. Furnished with antiques and period pieces as well as items from around the world. Quiet neighborhood convenient to Hunt Valley area. Queen four-poster bed and private bath. $85.

HAGERSTOWN

Amanda's Bed and Breakfast

1428 Park Avenue, Baltimore, 21217-4230
(410) 225-0001; (800) 899-7533
FAX (410) 728-8957

156. An 1890 Queen Anne Victorian on a tree-lined street of grand old homes. Furnished in antiques that provide a tranquil setting. Three rooms each have private baths. Full breakfast. $95.

Beaver Creek House

Beaver Creek House Bed and Breakfast

20432 Beaver Creek Road, 21740
(301) 797-4764

A turn-of-the-century country home filled with family antiques and memorabilia. Five central air-conditioned guest rooms. A full country breakfast is served on the screened porch or in the elegantly decorated dining room. The parlor with fireplace is the setting for afternoon tea. A sitting room has reading material of local interest. Guests can enjoy a country garden with fish pond and fountain. Visiting historic sites, hiking, biking, skiing, golf, and antiquing are popular recreational pursuits.

Hosts: Don and Shirley Day
Rooms: 5 (PB) $75-90
Full Breakfast
Credit Cards: A, B, C, D
Notes: 2, 5, 7, 9, 10, 11, 12, 13, 14

Blue Ridge Bed and Breakfast

Route 2, Box 3895, Berryville, VA 22611
(703) 955-1246

A. Large 1890 Victorian filled with beautiful antiques. A culinary delight. Close to downtown shopping. Corporate rates and packages available. $65-75.

B. Turn-of-the-century farmhouse filled with antiques and collectibles in the middle of 125 acres, 40 of which are woods. Hosts speak Spanish, German, and Italian. Close to I-70 and I-81, Antietam battlefield, C&O Canal, Crystal Grottoes Caverns, Potomac River, outlet stores, and antique shops. Children are always welcome. $40-68.

Lewrene Farm Bed and Breakfast

9738 Downsville Pike, 21740
(301) 582-1735

Spacious Colonial country farmhome near I-70 and I-81. Large living room, fireplace, piano, and antique family heirlooms. Deluxe bedrooms with canopied poster beds and other antique beds. Bedside snacks, shared and private baths, one of which has a whirlpool. Full breakfast. Home away from home for tourists, business people, families. Children welcome. Peacocks, old-fashioned swing, and a gazebo. Quilts for sale. Antietam

Lewrene Farm

7 No smoking; 8 Children welcome; 9 Social drinking allowed; 10 Tennis nearby; 11 Swimming nearby; 12 Golf nearby; 13 Skiing nearby; 14 May be booked through a travel agent.

battlefield, Harpers Ferry, C&O Canal, and antique malls nearby. Seventy miles to Washington and Baltimore.

Hosts: Lewis and Irene Lehman
Rooms: 5 (2 PB; 3 SB) $50-90
Full Breakfast
Credit Cards: A, B
Notes: 2, 5, 7, 8, 10, 11, 12, 13

Sunday's

Sunday's
Bed and Breakfast

39 Broadway, 21740
(800) 221-4828

In historic Hagerstown, this romantic 1890 Queen Anne Victorian is distinctively furnished with antiques. Guests may want to explore the national historic parks of Antietam, Harpers Ferry, and the C&O Canal. Antique shops, museums, golfing, fishing, skiing, and shopping outlets are all nearby. Full breakfast, afternoon tea and desserts, evening wine and cheese, late-night cordial and truffle, fruit basket, and more await guests.

Host: Bob Ferrino
Rooms: 3 (PB) $95
Full Breakfast
Credit Cards: None
Notes: 2, 3, 4, 5, 7, 8, 9, 10, 11, 12, 13, 14

The Wingrove Manor Inn
Bed and Breakfast

635 Oak Hill Avenue, 21740
(301) 797-7769

This beautifully restored bed and breakfast, on a street lined with Victorian mansions, is decorated with magnificent turn-of-the-century craftsmanship, marble fireplaces, winding staircase, Queen Anne furniture, Oriental rugs, crystal chandeliers, and white towering columns all reflecting the home's Victorian lineage. The Canopy Room, a suite, has a queen-size bed, marble fireplace, TV, VCR, telephone, private entrance, and private bath with a Jacuzzi. The second floor has three spacious guest rooms, all with private baths, double thick towels, fragrant sprays and oils, sweet soaps, queen-size beds, TV, VCR, and a telephone to serve the business travelers. Evening turn-down service with chocolates on the pillow. Continental plus breakfast is served in the dining room or on the southern porch. Host tries to accommodate any special dietary needs or restrictions guest may have.

Host: Winnie Price
Rooms: 4 (PB) $88-125
Continental Breakfast
Credit Cards: A, B
Notes: 2, 5, 7, 9, 10, 12, 13

HARWOOD

Amanda's
Bed and Breakfast

1428 Park Avenue, Baltimore, 21217-4230
(410) 225-0001; (800) 899-7533
FAX (410) 728-8957

158. This guest room has a balcony that overlooks a working farm. Ample parking area for a boat trailer or camper. Two rooms share a bath. Just twenty minutes from Annapolis. Continental breakfast. $75.

NOTES: Credit cards accepted: A MasterCard; B Visa; C American Express; D Discover; E Diners Club; F Other; 2 Personal checks accepted; 3 Lunch available; 4 Dinner available; 5 Open all year; 6 Pets welcome;

HAVRE DE GRACE

Amanda's Bed and Breakfast

1428 Park Avenue, Baltimore, 21217-4230
(410) 225-0001; (800) 899-7533
FAX (410) 728-8957

302. Explore historic Havre de Grace, the upper Chesapeake Bay region, while spending nights in a turn-of-the-century Victorian house, little changed from its original construction. Visit the Concord Point Lighthouse, a decoy museum, canal museum, and a state park; enjoy local seafood and the bay. A newly renovated cottage, queen-size bed, TV/VCR, kitchenette, antiques, Jacuzzi, and fireplace is available for $125. $65-85.

Spencer Silver Mansion

200 South Union Avenue, 21078
(410) 939-1097

Built in 1896 the Spencer Silver Mansion has been restored to its turn-of-the-century elegance. The five guest rooms are furnished with Victorian antiques and are quite spacious. The Carriage House suite features a fireplace and whirlpool bath. The parlors and dining room feature stained glass, oak floors, and fabulous woodwork.

The lavish full breakfast is served at the guest's convenience. In the historic district, just two blocks from the water. Near shops and restaurants. The inn is just two miles off I-95.

Hosts: Carol and Jim Nemeth
Rooms: 5 (3 PB; 2 SB) $65-120
Full Breakfast
Credit Cards: A, B, C
Notes: 2, 5, 7, 8, 9, 10, 11, 12, 14

Vandiver Inn

301 South Union Avenue, 21078
(800) 245-1655

Turn-of-the-century charm and Victorian hospitality await the visitor to the unprecedented Vandiver Inn, historic Havre de Grace's finest guest inn. Enjoy tastefully appointed rooms, fireplaces, and culinary delights all designed to reward the overnight guest or hungry traveler. Journey back to the heyday of gracious Maryland living, Chesapeake Bay style, when visiting the Vandiver Inn. The inn is surrounded by historic sites, museums, and four full-service marinas. Inquire about availability for dinner.

Host: Mary McKee
Rooms: 8 (PB) $65-95
Full Breakfast
Credit Cards: A, B, C
Notes: 2, 5, 9, 12, 14

Spencer Silver Mansion

7 No smoking; 8 Children welcome; 9 Social drinking allowed; 10 Tennis nearby; 11 Swimming nearby; 12 Golf nearby; 13 Skiing nearby; 14 May be booked through a travel agent.

KENT ISLAND

Amanda's
Bed and Breakfast

1428 Park Avenue, Baltimore, 21217-4230
(410) 225-0001; (800) 899-7533
FAX (410) 728-8957

376. This newly constructed Victorian on the water on the most northern point of Kent island has a stunning, breathtaking view of the bay. A hot tub built into the side of a cliff overlooks the water. Guest may enjoy a pool, decks, and many excellent seafood restaurants nearby on the island. Continental breakfast. $85-180.

KINGSTON

Bed and Breakfast
of Maryland/Traveller
in Maryland, Inc.

P.O. Box 2277, Annapolis, 21494-2277
(410) 269-6232; FAX (410) 263-4841

194. This inn, is on five waterfront acres and nestled on a sweeping bend of the Chester River, boasts a deep water marina. The original part of the house was built in the 1830s and was completely renovated prior to the inn's opening. The inn offers swimming pool and family restaurant featuring fine Eastern Shore food. All six guest accommodations are furnished in the classic style of the house and equipped with private baths. Restricted smoking area. Continental breakfast. $65-115.

LAUREL

Amanda's
Bed and Breakfast

1428 Park Avenue, Baltimore, MD, 21217-4230
(410) 225-0001; (800) 899-7533
FAX (410) 728-8957

217. Peaceful country setting. This 18th-century manor house is listed on the National Register of Historic Places. Ideal place to experience the flavor of the Eastern Shore. Full breakfast. $65-85.

LUTHERVILLE

Amanda's
Bed and Breakfast

1428 Park Avenue, Baltimore, MD, 21217-4230
(410) 225-0001; (800) 899-7533
FAX (410) 728-8957

128. Serene elegance surrounds this romantic Victorian mansion. There are five rooms decorated in a different theme from the owner's favorite places. Charming and spacious with a lavish breakfast. Private baths. Full breakfast. Ride the Light Rail to Oriole Park and Inner Harbor. $85-135.

Bed and Breakfast
of Maryland/Traveller
in Maryland, Inc.

P.O. Box 2277, Annapolis, 21494-2277
(410) 269-6232; FAX (410) 263-4841

167. A beautifully appointed Victorian home framed by twin gates and a curved driveway. Furnished with whimsical touches throughout, with cozy nooks and corners in the downstairs living rooms, the wide front porch, the lovely gazebo and flower gardens, or the third-floor library. Upon entering the center hall, guests are greeted by the sights and sounds of "coming home": soft music, fresh flowers, and the smell of muffins baking. Fireplaces are frequently going, either in the living room or in the cozy greeting room next to the dining room. A wide staircase leads to the seven gracious guest rooms with private or shared baths. Each is decorated in a unique style, from the California Suite and Cape May Room to the Maryland Hunt and Pride of Baltimore Rooms. No smoking. Full breakfast. $75-125.

NOTES: Credit cards accepted: A MasterCard; B Visa; C American Express; D Discover; E Diners Club; F Other; 2 Personal checks accepted; 3 Lunch available; 4 Dinner available; 5 Open all year; 6 Pets welcome;

MIDDLEBURG

Amanda's Bed and Breakfast

1428 Park Avenue, Baltimore, MD, 21217-4230
(410) 225-0001; (800) 899-7533
FAX (410) 728-8957

297. A country inn with afternoon tea, full country breakfast, and free use of nearby athletic club. Each room has a private bath and color TV. Two rooms feature a large Jacuzzi tub. Spacious for many special events. $95-155.

Bowling Brook Country Inn

Bowling Brook Country Inn

6000 Middleburg Road, 21757
(410) 848-0353

Steeped in the rich tradition of horse racing, Bowling Brook Country Inn represents the modern evolution of a farmhouse built in 1837. All bedrooms include a private bath and color TV, and several rooms feature a large Jacuzzi and king-size canopied bed. Enjoy the amenities of graceful country living—stroll leisurely through the expansive grounds, partake of afternoon tea, wine, and cheese, and simply gaze at the scenery while taking in the country air.

Hosts: Dave and Ginna Welsh
Rooms: 5 (PB) $95-155
Full Breakfast
Credit Cards: A, B, C
Notes: 2, 4, 5, 8, 9, 12, 13

MONKTON

Amanda's Bed and Breakfast

1428 Park Avenue, Baltimore, MD, 21217-4230
(410) 225-0001; (800) 899-7533
FAX (410) 728-8957

209. Warm hospitality and exceptional accommodations are offered on this working farm. Pond with fishing privileges (catch and throw back), bicycling and hiking trails, and tubing on Gunpowder River. Near North Central Railroad, Ladew Gardens, and Amish Country. One room is offered to guests, and it features a private bath and fireplace. Continental or full breakfast. $85.

NEW MARKET

National Pike Inn

9 West Main Street, Box 299, 21774
(301) 865-5055

The National Pike Inn offers five guest rooms, each air-conditioned and decorated in a different theme. Private baths are available, and the large Federal sitting room is available for all guests to use. The private enclosed courtyard is perfect for a quiet retreat outdoors. New Market, founded in 1793, offers more than 30 specialized antique shops, all in historic homes along Main Street. An old-fashioned general store

National Pike Inn

7 No smoking; 8 Children welcome; 9 Social drinking allowed; 10 Tennis nearby; 11 Swimming nearby; 12 Golf nearby; 13 Skiing nearby; 14 May be booked through a travel agent.

is everyone's favorite, and Mealey's, a well-known restaurant, is a few steps away. Open year-round by reservation. Social drinking permitted but BYOB. Inquire about accommodations for children. Cross-country skiing is seven miles away.

Hosts: Tom and Terry Rimel
Rooms: 5 (3 PB; 2 SB) $75-125
Full Breakfast
Credit Cards: A, B
Notes: 2, 7, 10, 12, 13

NORTH BEACH

Amanda's Bed and Breakfast

1428 Park Avenue, Baltimore, MD, 21217-4230
(410) 225-0001; (800) 899-7533
FAX (410) 728-8957

356. Calvert Country offers the pleasures of southern Maryland in an original guest house built in 1903. Eight guest rooms. Near a sandy beach and water activities. Mostly private baths. $65-85.

NORTH EAST

The Mill House Bed and Breakfast

102 Mill Lane, 21901
(410) 287-3532

This circa 1710 mill house is completely furnished with antiques. The extensive grounds include mill ruins, a tidal marsh with a variety of wildflowers, and a lawn down to the North East Creek. North East has antique and specialty shops and good restaurants. Boating and golf are nearby. After a restful night in a canopied bed, let a full breakfast with homemade hot breads get the day off to a good start. Open March 1st through December 1st.

Hosts: Lucia and Nick Demond
Rooms: 2 (SB) $65-75
Full Breakfast
Credit Cards: A, B
Notes: 2, 7, 12, 14

Guesthouses, Inc.

P.O. Box 2137, West Chester, 19380
(610) 692-4575

705. This 1710 miller's house sits on a couple of grassy acres at the mouth of the North East River, in the little waterfront village at the north end of the Chesapeake Bay. The house is architecturally and historically very important; Henry Francis Pierre duPont took the living room wainscoting for his own bedroom at Winterthur. The main house and its original rooms, all elegantly furnished with 18th-century antiques, are for guests exclusively. The two guest bedrooms are on the second floor with a bath in the hall. Full breakfast served in the formal dining room using the family's antique silver, crystal, and porcelain. Within walking distance are several antique shops, a bay museum, and restaurants. $75-150

OAKLAND

Amanda's Bed and Breakfast

1428 Park Avenue, Baltimore, MD, 21217-4230
(410) 225-0001; (800) 899-7533
FAX (410) 728-8957

157. Recreation land! Water, ice, and snow for year-round fun. Colonial Revival with a large lawn and mature trees in a historic district. Four rooms. Fireside breakfast in dining room. Relax after sporting day in cozy TV room. $55-80.

The Oak and Apple Bed and Breakfast

208 North Second Street, 21550
(301) 334-9265

Built circa 1915, this restored Colonial Revival sits on a beautiful, large lawn with mature trees and includes a large, columned front porch, enclosed sun porch, parlor with fireplace, and cozy gathering room with TV. Awake to a fresh Continental breakfast served fireside in the dining room or on the sun porch. The quaint town of Oakland offers a wonderful small-town atmosphere; and deep creek Lake, Wisp Ski Resort, and state parks with hiking, fishing, swimming, boating, and skiing are nearby.

Hosts: Jana and Ed Kight
Rooms: 5 (3 PB; 2 SB) $60-85
Continental Breakfast
Credit Cards: A, B
Notes: 2, 5, 9, 10, 11, 12, 13, 14

OCEAN CITY

Amanda's
Bed and Breakfast

1428 Park Avenue, Baltimore, MD, 21217-4230
(410) 225-0001; (800) 899-7533
FAX (410) 728-8957

170. In old Ocean City near the boardwalk and beach. A 14-room bed and breakfast, originally a rooming house for young women. Current owners are local natives and new caring and decorating are a plus. Some private baths. Enjoy good weather off-season. Near Fifth and Boardwalk in the older section of Ocean City. Parking available. In-season and off-season rates available. $60-110.

PASADENA

Amanda's
Bed and Breakfast

1428 Park Avenue, Baltimore, MD, 21217-4230
(410) 225-0001; (800) 899-7533
FAX (410) 728-8957

231. A lovely setting on the water, this waterfront community called Sunset Knoll is on one and one-half acres on the Magothy River about 15 minutes from downtown Annapolis. Quiet and convenient to Annapolis, Washington, D.C., or Baltimore. Two rooms, one double, one queen, and private baths are available for guests. Full breakfast. $85.

PINEY POINT

Amanda's
Bed and Breakfast

1428 Park Avenue, Baltimore, MD, 21217-4230
(410) 225-0001; (800) 899-7533
FAX (410) 728-8957

199. On the Potomac River with sandy beach in front. A gazebo on the beach has a lovely view of the water, passing boats, and birds. Quiet and peaceful. A 20-minute drive to St. Marys or Solomons Island. Private bath. Piney Point Lighthouse open to the public. This lighthouse is one of eleven that formerly guided mariners on the Potomac and is currently one of four left in existence along the river. $75-85.

POTOMAC

Amanda's
Bed and Breakfast

1428 Park Avenue, Baltimore, MD, 21217-4230
(410) 225-0001; (800) 899-7533
FAX (410) 728-8957

198. This forested, single-family home is complimented by Early American furnishings. In Maryland's suburbs of Washington, D.C. Two rooms, with private baths, are available. Continental breakfast. $65-75.

PRINCE FREDERICK

Amanda's
Bed and Breakfast

1428 Park Avenue, Baltimore, MD, 21217-4230
(410) 225-0001; (800) 899-7533
FAX (410) 728-8957

153. This century-old farmhouse with a wraparound porch is in a country setting of fields, woods, and a view of the river. The private suite for guests includes a parlor and separate entrance. Near Chesapeake Bay, Broomes Island, and Cypress Swamp. Full breakfast. $90.

7 No smoking; 8 Children welcome; 9 Social drinking allowed; 10 Tennis nearby; 11 Swimming nearby; 12 Golf nearby; 13 Skiing nearby; 14 May be booked through a travel agent.

PRINCESS ANNE

Amanda's Bed and Breakfast

1428 Park Avenue, Baltimore, MD, 21217-4230
(410) 225-0001; (800) 899-7533
FAX (410) 728-8957

188. This authentically restored Federal-style home is on the national Register of Historic Places and is on a 160-acre farm near the ocean and bay. A popular activity for guests is crabbing and oystering along a mile-long shoreline on the Manokin River, and shallow draft boats are welcome. Four rooms, plus two cottages, are available. Private baths. Full breakfast. $95-135.

QUEENSTOWN

Bed and Breakfast of Maryland/Traveller in Maryland, Inc.

P.O. Box 2277, Annapolis, 21494-2277
(410) 269-6232; FAX (410) 263-4841

173. On Main Street in a quaint waterfront historic village, with easy accessibility to Annapolis, Washington, Baltimore, Easton, Chestertown, and other areas of the Western and Eastern Shores. Each of the four rooms is comfortably and tastefully decorated, and has a private bath. Large family room is a spacious gathering place for guests to "unwind" and meet new acquaintances. No smoking. No pets. Continental breakfast. $65.

ROCK HALL

Bed and Breakfast of Maryland/Traveller in Maryland, Inc.

P.O. Box 2277, Annapolis, 21494-2277
(410) 269-6232; FAX (410) 263-4841

188. This gracious waterfront manor is reminiscent of yesteryear with a huge stone fireplace, and beautiful wood floors and cabinetry. This inn is only minutes away from Rock Hall, one of the last refuges of Maryland's famous watermen, on 201 acres of prime waterfront property. Five guest rooms with private baths. Central heat and air conditioning, expansive porches, and pleasant company. No smoking. No pets. Continental breakfast. $75-145.

The Inn at Osprey

20786 Rock Hall Avenue, 21661
(410) 639-2194; FAX (410) 639-7716

Enjoy a relaxing visit on the Eastern Shore of Maryland at this inn on scenic Swan Creek. Choose from five spacious guest rooms, each with private bath. In addition, there are two suites: Escapade, with marble bathroom and Jacuzzi tub, and Bolero, with a cozy fireplace. Elegant gourmet restaurant and bar. Osprey is on 30 acres with pleasant surroundings, a swimming pool, and picnic areas. Bicycles are available. Close to Chestertown and approximately one and one-half hours from Philadelphia, Baltimore, and Washington. Inquire about accommodations for children.

Rooms: 7 (PB) $110-150
Continental Breakfast
Credit Cards: A, B
Notes: 2, 4, 5, 7, 9, 10, 11, 12

ST. MICHAELS

Amanda's Bed and Breakfast

1428 Park Avenue, Baltimore, MD, 21217-4230
(410) 225-0001; (800) 899-7533
FAX (410) 728-8957

245. This historic house, dating back to 1805 with period furnishings, working fireplaces, and four-poster canopied beds, is in a historic waterman's village on the Eastern Shore of the Chesapeake Bay. Within walk-

NOTES: Credit cards accepted: A MasterCard; B Visa; C American Express; D Discover; E Diners Club;
F Other; 2 Personal checks accepted; 3 Lunch available; 4 Dinner available; 5 Open all year; 6 Pets welcome;

ing distance of shops, restaurants, and the museum, this inn offers seven rooms and one cottage with private and shared baths. Continental breakfast. $65-105.

351. Late 1880s Colonial home near all of the water activities in St. Michaels. Romantic setting with Jacuzzis and fireplaces. Afternoon tea weekends. Full breakfast. Special three-night package Sunday through Thursday. Walk to shops, restaurants, and the water. $130-190.

Bed and Breakfast of Maryland/Traveller in Maryland, Inc.

P.O. Box 2277, Annapolis, 21494-2277
(410) 269-6232; FAX (410) 263-4841

182. At this elegant waterfront inn, built just after the War of 1812, English and American antiques are elegantly offset by the understated, classic Laura Ashley fabrics and wallpapers. Luxury that is comfortable and cozy. In addition to pleasant little surprises everywhere, guests will naturally find fresh flowers, fruit, and mineral water in their room. All 19 guest rooms and suites have private baths, telephone, cable TV, air conditioning, and daily newspaper. Afternoon high tea and full American breakfast. $195-450.

184. Enjoy lodging and breakfast in this Eastern Shore inn. In historic St. Michaels, just off the main street within walking distance of all the shops, restaurants, harbor, and Maritime Museum. This Georgian home, built in 1805 by shipwright and soldier Col. Joseph Kemp, offers period furnishing, working fireplaces, and balcony. There are six guest rooms in the main house with shared or private baths, and a cottage behind the main house with double bed and full bath. No smoking. No pets. Continental breakfast. $55-95.

Chesapeake Wood Duck Inn

Gibsontown Road, P.O. Box 202
Tilghman Island, 21671
(410) 886-2070; (800) 956-2070

"Southern hospitality on the Chesapeake Bay" is not merely a marketing theme, but a way of life of owners/innkeepers, Dave and Stephanie. Eighteen ninety Victorian, graciously restored, overlooks Dogwood Harbor, home of the last fleet of antique skipjack sailing vessels in North America. According to TVs *Travel, Travel,* "The charming Victorian Wood Duck Inn, is a destination in itself. Guests enjoy the quiet ambience of yesteryear." Impeccably appointed with period furnishings, Oriental rugs, original art, luxurious linens, and fresh flowers. On Maryland's Eastern Shore and the Chesapeake Bay, in a quaint fishing village offering spectacular scenery, serenity, and a forgotten way of life. Within walking distance of restaurants, shops, and water activities. Bikes available.

Hosts: Stephanie and Dave Feith
Rooms: 6 (PB) $115-125
Full Breakfast
Credit Cards: A, B
Notes: 2, 5, 7, 9, 10, 11, 12, 14

The Inn at Christmas Farm

8873 Tilghman Island Road, Wittman, 21676
(410) 745-5312; FAX (410) 745-5618

Welcome, *bienvenue.* This waterfront farm near St. Michaels offers a unique combination of solitude at the water's edge, broad lawns, meticulously restored suites (including Christmas Cottage with Jacuzzi) while fine restaurants, antiques, and historic towns are but minutes away. Enjoy gourmet breakfasts, including French apple cake hot from the oven, while watching peacocks, waterfowl, sheep, and the tiny horse, James, meander nearby. Walk along the creek or simply spend a lazy afternoon "pondside" with its magnificent views of marsh, field, and farm. Children over 12 welcome.

7 No smoking; 8 Children welcome; 9 Social drinking allowed; 10 Tennis nearby; 11 Swimming nearby; 12 Golf nearby; 13 Skiing nearby; 14 May be booked through a travel agent.

Hosts: David and Beatrice Lee
Rooms: 5 (4 PB; 1 SB) $125-165
Continental Breakfast
Credit Cards: A, B
Notes: 2, 3, 4, 5, 9, 10, 11, 12, 14

Kemp House Inn

412 Talbot Street, P.O. Box 638, 21663-0638
(410) 745-2243

Built in 1807 by Colonel Joseph Kemp, this superbly crafted home is one of a small collection of large Federal period brick structures in St. Michaels. Elegant Federal details are evident throughout the house. Each of the rooms is tastefully furnished with period decor. Cozy antique four-poster rope beds with patchwork quilts, down pillows, wingback sitting chairs, and Queen Anne tables grace each room. Old-fashioned nightshirts, low-light sconces, candles, and working fireplaces create an ambience of the early 19th century.

Hosts: Diane and Steve Cooper
Rooms: 8 (6 PB; 2 SB) $65-105
Continental Breakfast
Credit Cards: A, B, D
Notes: 2, 5, 7, 8, 9, 10, 11, 12, 14

Parsonage Inn

210 North Talbot Street, Route 33, 21663
(410) 745-5519; (800) 394-5519

Late Victorian bed and breakfast, circa 1883, lavishly restored in 1985 with seven guest rooms, private baths, king- or queen-size brass beds with Laura Ashley linens. Parlor and dining room in European tradition. Gourmet restaurant receiving rave reviews next door. Two blocks to Chesapeake Maritime Museum, shops, and harbor. Ten percent off midweek for AARP or retired officers. ABBA approved; Mobil three-star award winner.

Host: Anthony Deyesu
Rooms: 8 (PB) $80-130
Full Breakfast
Credit Cards: A, B
Notes: 2, 5, 8, 9, 10, 12

Wades Point Inn on the Bay

P.O. Box 7, 21663
(410) 745-2500

On the Eastern Shore of Chesapeake Bay, this historic country inn is ideal for those seeking country serenity and bay splendor. The main house, circa 1819, was built by a noted shipwright. From 1890 to the present the inn has provided a peaceful setting for relaxation and recreation such as fishing, crabbing, and a one-mile nature and jogging trail on 120 acres. Chesapeake Bay Maritime Museum, cruises, sailing charters, fine shops, and restaurants are nearby.

Hosts: Betsy and John Feiler
Rooms: 24 (14 PB; 10 SB) $75-173
Continental Breakfast
Credit Cards: A, B
Notes: 2, 7, 8, 9, 10, 11, 12

SALISBURY

Amanda's Bed and Breakfast

1428 Park Avenue, Baltimore, MD, 21217-4230
(410) 225-0001; (800) 899-7533
FAX (410) 728-8957

358. This country bed and breakfast is just five miles south of Salisbury on a small bass pond. Go fishing and paddling. Three rooms. Public golf nearby. One black Lab and two cats also reside on premises. Shared bath. $65.

SCOTLAND

St. Michael's Manor Bed and Breakfast

Box 17A, Route 5, 20687
(301) 872-4025

The land belongs to St. Michael's Manor (1805) and was originally patented to Leonard Calvert in 1637. The house, on

NOTES: Credit cards accepted: A MasterCard; B Visa; C American Express; D Discover; E Diners Club; F Other; 2 Personal checks accepted; 3 Lunch available; 4 Dinner available; 5 Open all year; 6 Pets welcome;

Long Neck Creek, is furnished with antiques. Boating, canoeing, a swimming pool, bikes, and wine-tasting are available. Near Point Lookout State Park, Civil War monuments, and historic St. Mary's City. Limited smoking permitted. Inquire about accommodations for children.

Hosts: Joseph and Nancy Dick
Rooms: 4 (SB) $45-70
Full Breakfast
Credit Cards: None
Notes: 2, 5, 9, 10, 11, 12

SHARPSBURG

Amanda's
Bed and Breakfast

1428 Park Avenue, Baltimore, MD, 21217-4230
(410) 225-0001; (800) 899-7533
FAX (410) 728-8957

268. This inn sits amidst the hallowed ground of the Civil War's Antietam battlefield. Furnishings of Victorian vintage define a gentler way of life, and the pastoral surroundings of the misty Blue Ridge Mountains can be seen from a wraparound porch. Four rooms have private baths. Continental breakfast. $95-105.

SILVER SPRING

Amanda's
Bed and Breakfast

1428 Park Avenue, Baltimore, MD, 21217-4230
(410) 225-0001; (800) 899-7533
FAX (410) 728-8957

325. Easy commute to Washington. Wooded park setting in an older residential neighborhood. Tudor-style home with European antiques. Walk to local restaurants. One suite with queen-size bed and private bath. One twin bedroom. Continental breakfast. $70-85.

Bed and Breakfast
of Maryland/Traveller
in Maryland, Inc.

P.O. Box 2277, Annapolis, 21494-2277
(410) 269-6232; FAX (410) 263-4841

200. This English Tudor home is built of brick with a steep slate roof. It sits alone on one acre of landscaped gardens, including two patios that overlook the creek and woods below. The home is secluded among 50-foot beech and oak trees with a sweeping view of Sligo Creek. Two guest rooms are furnished in lovely antiques and family collectibles. One has a private bath; the other has a shared hall bath. No smoking or pets. Continental breakfast. $55-75.

202. This homestay is new Victorian-style, with wraparound porches and decks for sitting or sunning. Backed by a wooded area, the location is so secluded that it is sometimes difficult to realize that Washington, D.C. lies only a short distance away. Two comfortably furnished guest rooms with private or shared bath arrangement. Dogs in residence. No smoking allowed. Full breakfast served. $65.

Park Crest House

8101 Park Crest Drive, 20910
(301) 588-2845

This English Tudor house is set in the woods of Sligo Creek Parkway. Park Crest House is one and one-half miles from Silver Spring and Takoma Metro stations, and three minutes from a bus stop. A Continental plus breakfast of homemade bread, fresh fruits, and granola is served in the gardens, weather permitting. Chintzes, Oriental carpets, and European antiques create an atmosphere of elegance. The Emery suite has a queen-size bed, color TV, air conditioning, private garden, private bath and showers, and private telephone line. Two other rooms also available that share a bath.

Hosts: Lowel and Rosemary Peterson
Rooms: 3 (1 PB; 2 SB) $60-75
Continental Breakfast
Credit Cards: None
Notes: 2, 5, 6, 7, 8, 9, 10, 11, 12

SNOW HILL

Chanceford Hall
Bed and Breakfast Inn

209 West Federal Street, 21863
(410) 632-2231

A 1759 Eastern Shore mansion impeccably restored. Listed in Smithsonian's *Guide to Historic America*. Listed on the National Register of Historic Places. All private baths, canopied beds, and Oriental rugs throughout. Ten working fireplaces, centrally air-conditioned. Dinner by prior arrangement. Full breakfast served in formal dining room. Lap pool and bicycles. Ocean beaches 20 miles away. Canoe the famous Pocomoke River two blocks away. Complimentary wine and hors d'oeuvres. "When guests require the finest."

Hosts: Michael and Thelma C. Driscoll
Rooms: 5 (PB) $110-130
Full Breakfast
Credit Cards: None
Notes: 2, 5, 9, 10, 11, 12

River House Inn

201 East Market Street, 21863
(410) 632-2722

Casual yet elegant retreat in historic waterfront village. Acres of lawns and gardens back up to the wild and scenic Pocomoke River. Queen-size beds, fireplaces, ceiling fans, and antiques. Main house built in 1860, Little House in 1835, and River Cottage in 1900. Enjoy canoeing, cycling, bird watching, beaches, and the historic district. Golf, canoeing, and cycling packages are available.

River House Inn

Hosts: Larry and Susanne Knudsen
Rooms: 9 (PB) $89-130
Full Breakfast
Credit Cards: A, B, C
Notes: 2, 4, 5, 7, 8, 9, 10, 11, 12, 14

SOLOMONS

Solomons Victorian Inn

125 Charles Street, P.O. Box 759, 20688
(410) 326-4811

Be romanced by the Chesapeake with its unsurpassed harbor views from this Queen Anne Victorian. Greet the morning sunshine on the porch while enjoying a sumptuous breakfast. Take a stroll along the riverwalk, through the quaint fishing village of Solomons, to the many fine shops and restaurants. Experience local lore at the maritime museum. Enjoy an afternoon cruise. End the day on the lush grounds of the inn, watching the boats drop anchor in the setting sun.

Hosts: Helen and Richard Bauer
Rooms: 6 (PB) $80-140
Full Breakfast
Credit Cards: A, B
Notes: 2, 5, 7, 9, 10, 11, 12

STEVENSON

Amanda's
Bed and Breakfast

1428 Park Avenue, Baltimore, MD, 21217-4230
(410) 225-0001; (800) 899-7533
FAX (410) 728-8957

NOTES: Credit cards accepted: A MasterCard; B Visa; C American Express; D Discover; E Diners Club;
F Other; 2 Personal checks accepted; 3 Lunch available; 4 Dinner available; 5 Open all year; 6 Pets welcome;

115. Historic 45-acre estate offers elegant living. Nineteen hundreds-style fireplaces, whirlpool tub, gourmet breakfast, swimming pool, tennis, woodland trails and streams, and flower and herb gardens make this majestic estate a special place to stay. Five guest rooms, all with private baths and some with fireplaces. A full breakfast is served. $90-150.

Bed and Breakfast of Maryland/Traveller in Maryland, Inc.

P.O. Box 2277, Annapolis, 21494-2277
(410) 269-6232; FAX (410) 263-4841

165. A majestic estate, quietly nestled on 45 acres in Maryland's splendid Green Spring Valley, provides an elegant lifestyle portrayed in the early 1900s. Guests will enjoy suites with fireplaces, private baths (some with Jacuzzi), expansive porches, pool, and tennis court. Woodland trails, streams, flower and herb gardens abound on this estate. Abundant history is associated with this house through its builder Alexander J. Cassatt, owner of the Pennsylvania Railroad and brother of Mary Cassat, the American impressionist. Later, it was owned by the Brewster family, descendants of Benjamin Franklin and important in government. In the 1950s it became the Koinonia Foundation, a predecessor of the Peace Corps. Four guest suites with double or king-size beds with private baths. Some suites have separate living room and porches. Nonsmoking. Dog in residence. Full gourmet breakfast. $90-125.

STEVENSVILLE

Amanda's Bed and Breakfast

1428 Park Avenue, Baltimore, MD, 21217-4230
(410) 225-0001; (800) 899-7533
FAX (410) 728-8957

180. This historic manor is on Kent Island on the Eastern Shore side of the Bay Bridge. This grand mansion, circa 1820, is on the Maryland historic register. The inn is surrounded by 226 acres of land and is one and one-half miles from the waterfront. The Victorian decor will make any stay here memorable. Restaurant has a four-star rating. Continental breakfast. $109-149.

TANEYTOWN

Amanda's Bed and Breakfast

1428 Park Avenue, Baltimore, MD, 21217-4230
(410) 225-0001; (800) 899-7533
FAX (410) 728-8957

161. This restored 1844 mansion sits on 24 acres with clay tennis courts, croquet, gardens, a view of the Catoctin Mountains, and gourmet dinners provided with reservations. Winner of "Baltimore's Most Romantic Getaway," this inn offers eight rooms, all with private baths, fireplaces, and Jacuzzis. Excellent dining facilities. Full breakfast. $150-275.

Bed and Breakfast of Maryland/Traveller in Maryland, Inc.

P.O. Box 2277, Annapolis, 21494-2277
(410) 269-6232; FAX (410) 263-4841

168. A Georgian-style country house with a Victorian-style addition. A hideaway guest house on a large working farm, placed in the serene Piedmont countryside of Maryland is a remarkable getaway. The property is part of a 3,000-acre tract of land called Runnymeade. Enlarged, patented prior to the American Revolution by Dr. Upton Scott, whose home on Shipwright Street in Annapolis is still a landmark. Enjoy the living room setting with a large fireplace, a dining room, and a wraparound porch with rocking chairs overlooking Bear Branch. Each air-conditioned bedroom has a pleasant view of lawns, pastures, creeks, or woods. One suite has a private screened porch. A hundred yards across the wide and shaded lawn lies the guest house with two large bedrooms, a living room, and a kitchenette. Guest house is air-conditioned. No smoking. Full Maryland breakfast. $55-100.

TILGHMAN

Black Walnut Point Inn

Black Walnut Road, P.O. Box 308, 21671
(410) 886-2452

Black Walnut Point Inn is on 57 acres surrounded by water. Some amenities include bayside hammocks, pool, tennis court, rocking chairs, and bicycles. Guests enjoy comfort, privacy, peace, and quiet. The island's most romantic bed and breakfast with Key West sunsets.

Rooms: 7 (PB) $110-160
Continental Breakfast
Credit Cards: A, B
Notes: 2, 5, 7, 9, 10, 11, 12

VIENNA

Amanda's Bed and Breakfast

1428 Park Avenue, Baltimore, MD, 21217-4230
(410) 225-0001; (800) 899-7533
FAX (410) 728-8957

149. On the Nanticoke River in historic Vienna, this authentic Colonial tavern has been carefully restored. This original tavern house shares much of the history of the town, as it was built in 1706. Public tennis courts, boat ramp, and the Blackwater Wildlife Refuge are nearby. Four rooms with private and shared bath and fireplace are available for guests. Continental breakfast. $65-75.

Bed and Breakfast of Maryland/Traveller in Maryland, Inc.

P.O. Box 2277, Annapolis, 21494-2277
(410) 269-6232; FAX (410) 263-4841

196. This early Victorian structure was built in 1861 on the banks of the Nanticoke River. Known locally as the "Brick House," being the first home to be built of brick in Vienna. The inn still maintains its original character having twelve-foot ceilings, cornices, medallions, working fireplaces, a beautiful three-story spiral staircase, and many windows and doorways accented with wood paneling. All eight guest rooms are furnished in a manner that befits this great home and have shared and private baths. Restricted smoking area. Outdoor cat. Continental breakfast. $75-85.

The Tavern House

Box 98, 21869
(301) 376-3347

A Colonial tavern on the Nanticoke River featuring the simple elegance of Colonial living and special breakfasts that are a social occasion. A glimpse into Michener's Chesapeake for those who love Colonial homes, the peace of a small town, or watching osprey in flight. Children over 12 are welcome.

Hosts: Harvey and Elise Altergott
Rooms: 4 (SB) $60-70
Full Breakfast
Credit Cards: A, B
Notes: 2, 5, 10, 12

WESTMINSTER

Amanda's Bed and Breakfast

1428 Park Avenue, Baltimore, MD, 21217-4230
(410) 225-0001; (800) 899-7533
FAX (410) 728-8957

219. This Victorian inn is a former schoolhouse 45 minutes from northwest Balti-

NOTES: Credit cards accepted: A MasterCard; B Visa; C American Express; D Discover; E Diners Club;
F Other; 2 Personal checks accepted; 3 Lunch available; 4 Dinner available; 5 Open all year; 6 Pets welcome;

more. All guest rooms have queen-size beds and Jacuzzis. Hearty breakfast buffet and an athletic club available to guests, which includes swimming, jogging, racquetball, and weight machines. Historic Union Hills Homestead and museums are all nearby. $110-155.

Bed and Breakfast of Maryland/ Traveller in Maryland, Inc.

P.O. Box 2277, Annapolis, 21494-2277
(410) 269-6232; FAX (410) 263-4841

208. At the turn of the century this inn was a schoolhouse for children of all ages. Today it has been transformed into one of the most elegant getaway destinations in the region. Furnished in collectibles and antiques, the ambience is truly unique. The thirteen guest rooms have queen-size beds and private baths with Jacuzzis. The use of the on-site, state-of-the-art athletic facility adjacent to the inn is included. The inn also offers a fine dining restaurant for its guests. Smoking restricted. Continental breakfast. $105-155.

WILLIAMSPORT

Bed and Breakfast of Maryland/ Traveller in Maryland, Inc.

P.O. Box 2277, Annapolis, 21494-2277
(410) 269-6232; FAX (410) 263-4841

206. This diverse homestay is a recently built log house set on 120 acres of farm and woodland with comfortable and cozy eclectic country furnishings. The totally unique aspect of this farm is its collection of wolves, both full blood and wolf-hybrids; hence the name "Wolf's End Farm." Guests will be serenaded by the wolves' unique howling. Each of the two guest rooms have a private bath and furnishings that allow for comfort. No smoking. Full breakfast. $80-100.

WITTMAN

Bed and Breakfast of Maryland/ Traveller in Maryland, Inc.

P.O. Box 2277, Annapolis, 21494-2277
(410) 269-6232; FAX (410) 263-4841

180. A 50-acre waterfront farm, circa 1800, offers the ultimate in peace and privacy. A comfortably restored Bay hundred farmhouse and St. James Church (a property saved through historic preservation by the owners) offers the ambience and serenity of a waterman's retreat. Waterfowl and wildlife abound. Antiquing, boating, biking, bird watching, fine restaurants, and museums are but minutes away. All three guest accommodations are suites with private baths. An array of main house pets (cats and dog) and yard livestock (peacocks, goats). No smoking. Continental breakfast. $135.

7 No smoking; 8 Children welcome; 9 Social drinking allowed; 10 Tennis nearby; 11 Swimming nearby; 12 Golf nearby; 13 Skiing nearby; 14 May be booked through a travel agent.

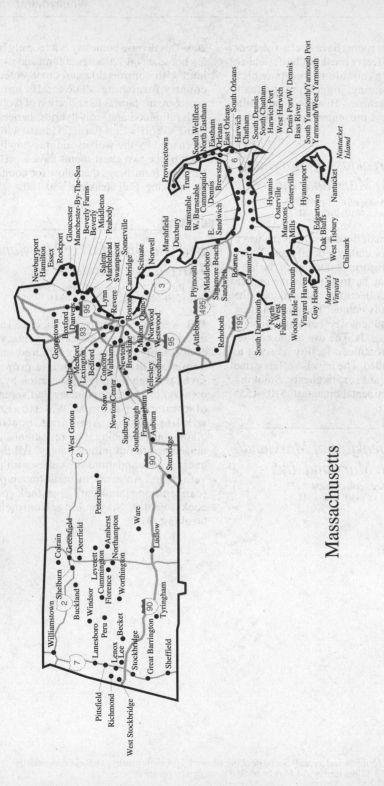

Massachusetts

Newburyport
Hamilton
Essex
Rockport
Gloucester
Manchester-By-The-Sea
Beverly Farms
Beverly
Middleton
Peabody
Salem
Marblehead
Swampscott
Somerville
Cambridge
Lynn
Revere
Boston
Quincy
Milton
Norwood
Westwood
Wellesley
Needham
Newton
Brookline
Waltham
Concord
Newton Center
Bedford
Lexington
Lowell
Medford
Stow
Georgetown
Boxford
Danvers

95
93
95
3
495
195

Scituate
Norwell
Marshfield
Duxbury
Plymouth
Middleboro
Sagamore Beach
Sandwich
Bourne
Cataumet
North & West Falmouth
Woods Hole
Falmouth
Vinyard Haven
Gay Head
West Tisbury
Chilmark

Martha's Vinyard

Barnstable
W. Barnstable
Cummaquid
E. Dennis
Brewster
Sandwich

Provincetown
Truro
South Wellfleet
North Eastham
Eastham
Orleans
East Orleans
Chatham

6

Harwich
South Orleans
South Dennis
West Harwich
Harwich Port
South Chatham
Denis Port/W. Dennis
Bass River
South Yarmouth/Yarmouth Port
Yarmouth/West Yarmouth

Hyannis
Osterville
Centerville
Marstons Mills
Hyannisport

Edgartown
Oak Bluffs
Nantucket

Nantucket Island

Attleboro
Rehoboth
South Dartmouth

Sudbury
Southborough
Framingham
Auburn
Sturbridge
West Groton

2
90

Petersham
Ware
Ludlow

Shelburn
Colrain
Greenfield
Deerfield
Leverett
Cummington
Amherst
Florence
Northampton
Worthington
Windsor
Peru
Becket
Tyringham

2
90

Williamstown
Lanesboro
Lenox
Lee
Stockbridge
Great Barrington
Sheffield
Pittsfield
Richmond
West Stockbridge

7

Buckland

Massachusetts

AMHERST

Allen House Victorian Bed and Breakfast Inn

599 Main Street, 01002
(413) 253-5000

This authentic 1886 Queen Anne-style Victorian features spacious bed chambers with private baths and air conditioning. Period antiques, decor, art, and wall coverings are historically and accurately featured. In the heart of Amherst on three scenic acres and within walking distance of the Emily Dickinson House. Amherst College, the University of Massachusetts, fine galleries, museums, theaters, shops, and restaurants are nearby. Free busing throughout the five college area. A full formal breakfast is served. Brochure available. Winner of the 1991 Historic Commission Award. Rated excellent by ABBA. Three diamond

Allen House

AAA/Mobil approved. Smoking restricted. Children over nine welcome.

Hosts: Alan and Ann Zieminski
Rooms: 5 (PB) $45-115
Full Breakfast
Credit Cards: A, B, C, D, E
Notes: 2, 5, 9, 10, 11, 12, 13

American Country Collection

1353 Union Street, Schectady, NY 12054
(518) 439-7001; (518) 439-4301

120. This convenient in-town Victorian with wraparound veranda for outdoor relaxation is on a quiet tree-lined street within walking distance to the college, university, and downtown. The first-floor suite is actually a self-contained flat with bath and full kitchen with eating area. New second-floor guest quarters contain two bedrooms, shared bath plus kitchen and eating area. Smoking outside only. Children welcome. $70-90.

ATTLEBORO

Anna's Victorian Connection

5 Fowler Avenue, Newport, RI 02840
(401) 849-2489

0012. A casual country interior welcomes guests to this excellent example of Greek Revival architecture. A great getaway for the business or vacation traveler, the inn offers 16 guest rooms with shared or private baths. A hearty breakfast buffet is served daily, and a full tea is served several times a week. The Carriage House is available for

NOTES: Credit cards: A MasterCard; B Visa; C American Express; D Discover; E Diners Club; F Other;
2 Personal checks accepted; 3 Lunch available; 4 Dinner available; 5 Open all year; 6 Pets welcome;
7 No smoking; 8 Children welcome; 9 Social drinking allowed; 10 Tennis nearby; 11 Swimming nearby;
12 Golf nearby; 13 Skiing nearby; 14 May be booked through a travel agent.

conferences, seminars, or special gatherings; lunch, dinner, and special parties can be arranged. Just off I-95 between Boston and Providence, the inn is on the commuter-rail line to Boston and convenient to Great Woods, Cape Cod, and Foxboro Stadium. $42-72.

AUBURN

Captain Samuel Eddy House

609 Oxford Street South, 01501
(508) 832-7282

The center chimney Colonial home, circa 1765, has been restored and handsomely decorated in period style by the owners. In addition to the large keeping room where guests gather for breakfast, there are three common areas for guests to relax. Each parlor has a fireplace, and the plant-filled sunroom allows guests to enjoy the country setting with views of Eddy Pond, the surrounding woods, and gardens. Children over five are welcome.

Hosts: Diedre and Michael Meddaugh
Rooms: 5 (PB) $65-85
Full Breakfast
Credit Cards: None
Notes: 2, 5, 7, 9, 12, 14

BARNSTABLE (CAPE COD)

Ashley Manor

Box 856, 3660 Old Kings Highway, 02630
(508) 362-8044

Ashley Manor is a very special place, a gracious 1699 mansion on a two-acre estate in Cape Cod's historic district. Romantic rooms and suites feature private baths and fireplaces. Elegant public rooms with antiques and Oriental rugs. Delicious full breakfast in formal dining room or on terrace overlooking park-like grounds and new tennis court. Walk to the beach and village. Prices subject to change. Children over 14 welcome.

Ashley Manor

Hosts: Donald and Fay Bain
Rooms: 6 (PB) $115-175
Full Breakfast
Credit Cards: A, B, C
Notes: 2, 5, 9, 10, 11, 12, 14

Bed and Breakfast Cape Cod

P.O. Box 341, West Hyannisport, 02672-0341
(508) 775-2772; FAX (508) 775-2884

2. This 1864 sea captain's house is complete with wide board floors, glimpses of Cape Cod Bay, and a gracious rural setting. Two bedrooms are used for one party of guests, assuring a private bath. A child's room with a crib is available in an adjoining guest room. Enjoy a full breakfast on the terrace or in the dining room. Whale watch boats, the harbor, and fine restaurants are one-half mile away. Three miles to Hyannis and the ferry to Nantucket or Martha's Vineyard. $75-85.

4. Built in 1754 it was operated as a tavern for many years. The restoration several years ago has been marvelous. Wide board floors and lovely antiques add to the charm of bedrooms with fireplaces and private baths. Listed in the National Register of Historic Places, this bed and breakfast has all the charm of yesteryear and the plus of a fine inn. The Continental breakfast is served in the dining room before a large fireplace. Walk to the shops in the village or the harbor from which the whale watch ships depart. Four miles to Hyannis and ferry to Nantucket. No smoking. Children over 14 welcome. $75-85.

35. Not many bed and breakfast travelers have a chance to stay in a house built in 1635. This charming old building was part of the Cape Cod designer's tour of homes in 1989. The owner has two bedrooms used for bed and breakfast, with a king-size bed in one room and a pair of twins in the other. The two rooms are let out to one party at a time, thereby assuring a private bath. The grounds are like a rural wooded setting with great trails for walking. A parlor is available on the first floor for guests to use. $70.

Bed and Breakfast Greater Boston and Cape Cod

P.O. Box 35, Newtonville, 02160
(617) 964-1606; (800) 832-2632
FAX (617) 332-8572

Olde Kings Highway Tavern. Built in 1754 and now fully restored, invites guests to take a step back into history. The four guest rooms are decorated in period antiques; each has a fireplace and a private bath. A hearty Continental breakfast with home-baked breads and pastries is included. Many activities are a short walk away, including fishing, boating, whale watching, golf, and antiquing. The ferries to Martha's Vineyard and Nantucket are just ten minutes away in Hyannis. Children over 12 welcome. No smoking. $85-100.

Sea Captains Guest House. This gracious Greek Revival-style home is in Cobb's Hill and is listed on the National Register of Historic Places. The guest suite includes one guest room with a double iron bed, an adjoining nursery with a crib and changing table, and the other guest room with an antique sleigh bed. The suite shares a large,

modern bath, and is rented to family groups or just one room at a time. In addition to the suite, guests may have use of the front porch, brick terrace, gated yard, front parlor, and sitting room (both with working fireplaces). A full country breakfast and late afternoon refreshment are included. Baby-sitting can be arranged. Guests are within walking distance to Millway Beach, the whale watching boats, charter fishing vessels, a great ice cream shop, several museums, and restaurants. Seasonal rates available. Twenty-five dollars for child in second room or nursery. $75-150.

Beechwood

2839 Main Street, 02630
(508) 362-6618; (800) 609-6618

This romantic Victorian inn has six large guest rooms, some with fireplaces or water views. All rooms are furnished with beautiful period antiques and have private baths. Gourmet breakfasts are served in the paneled dining room, and afternoon tea by the parlor fireplace in winter. In summer iced tea and lemonade are served on the veranda that overlooks one and one-half acres of beautifully landscaped lawns and gardens.

Hosts: Debbie and Ken Traugot
Rooms: 6 (PB) $115-150
Full Breakfast
Credit Cards: A, B, C
Notes: 2, 5, 9, 10, 11, 12, 14

Beechwood

The Anchorage

BASS RIVER

The Anchorage

122 South Shore Drive, 02664
(508) 398-8265

The Anchorage is an ideal place to spend a holiday if people enjoy Cape Cod's broad, sandy beaches and warm water. The ocean is just a few steps away. There are theaters, restaurants, hiking, fishing, boating, and all activities to complete your holiday. "Join us for a quiet, relaxing visit where the gentle sea breezes help to leave all your cares behind."

Host: Ruth T. Masciarotte
Rooms: 3 (PB) $31-50
Continental Breakfast
Credit Cards: None
Notes: 2, 5, 9, 10, 11,12

BECKET

Covered Bridge

P.O. Box 447A, Norfolk, CT 06058
(203) 542-5944

1BMA. This totally restored 1790 tavern and stagecoach stop is furnished with beautiful antiques and is set on 12 acres. The original ballroom is now a sitting room for guests. There are five guest rooms, all with their own private baths, and many of the bedrooms have hand stenciling. A delicious full breakfast is served in the dining room. $70-95.

BEDFORD

Bed and Breakfast Folks

48 Springs Road, 01730
(617) 275-9025

Bed and Breakfast Folks offers tourists, business travelers, relocating personnel, or anyone visiting this area an opportunity to experience the warmth and friendliness of a private New England home. Choose from historic, contemporary, or farmhomes. Learn about the charm and history of New England and experience true hospitality. Near Concord, Lexington, and Boston. Close to lake region, skiing, fall foliage, and much more. $40.

BEVERLY

Bed and Breakfast Marblehead and North Shore

P.O. Box 35, Newtonville, 02160
(617) 964-1606; (800) 832-2632
FAX (617) 332-8572

Beverly Farms Bed and Breakfast. Enjoy the warmth and charm of an authentic antique Colonial home, dating back to 1839. Three guest bedrooms share a bath, as well as a downstairs common room, half-bath, and an outside deck and back yard. A gourmet Continental breakfast and an afternoon tea are complimentary. This accommodation is within walking distance of town, commuter-rail train to Boston and other parts of the North Shore, including an oceanside beach. No smoking. Children over 12 welcome. $65-75.

Lady Slippers. A charming Dutch Colonial home offering wonderful views from its location opposite a small park and sandy beach. Guests may relax in the sitting room or on the screened porch. Two guest rooms have double beds (one with ocean views) and shared bath. Two guest rooms have twin beds with private/shared bath. Guests are close to the commuter rail line for easy transportation to Boston and other areas of the North Shore. This is a nonsmoking accommodation. Children are welcome. Continental plus breakfast. Special rates for long-term guests. $40-75.

Next Door Inn. A beautifully decorated, cozy, Colonial-style home offers guests use of kitchen facilities, color TV in living room, enclosed sun porch, telephone, and off-street parking. There are three attractive guest rooms: a room with a queen-size bed and private bath, another room with a double bed and a fireplace, and a third room with a double and twins. (Second and third rooms share a bath.) In hot weather, common areas have air conditioning, and the guest rooms have fans. Continental breakfast. No smoking. Whole house available for groups of nine or less. $65-75.

Bunny's Bed and Breakfast

17 Kernwood Heights, 01915
(508) 922-2392

Victorian-style bed and breakfast with three bedrooms; one with a fireplace. Cozy living room also has a fireplace. Formal dining room. Made-from-scratch muffins are served every morning. Travelers' checks accepted. Two miles from Salem; restaurants within half a mile. Off-street parking available. Train is within walking distance. Continental plus breakfast served.

Hosts: Bunny and Joe Stacey
Rooms: 3 (1 PB; 2 SB) $55-85
Continental Breakfast
Credit Cards: F
Notes: 2, 5, 7, 8, 9, 11

BEVERLY FARMS

Jon Larcom House

28 Hart Street, 01915
(508) 922-6074

Charming old Colonial with beams, Indian shutters, and fireplaces on the historic and picturesque North Shore. Three bedrooms are available, two with fireplaces, shared and private baths. Within walking distance of the village, train, and lovely beaches. Gourmet Continental breakfast and afternoon tea (weekends only) are served in this smoke-free home. Children over 12 are welcome.

Hosts: Steve and Peg Powers
Rooms: 3 (1 PB; 2 SB) $65-85
Continental Breakfast
Credit Cards: None
Notes: 2, 5, 7, 10, 11, 12, 13

Jon Larcom House

BOSTON

Beacon Hill Bed and Breakfast

27 Brimmer Street, 02108
(617) 523-7376

An 1869 spacious Victorian townhouse overlooking Charles River with large bed-sitting rooms, TV, and air conditioning within an elegant historic neighborhood of brick sidewalks, gas lamps, and tree-lined streets. Boston's best location—two blocks from "Cheers," easy walk to Boston Common, Freedom Trail connecting historic sites, Quincy Market, Filene's Basement, convention center, subway, downtown, public garages, restaurants,

7 No smoking; 8 Children welcome; 9 Social drinking allowed; 10 Tennis nearby; 11 Swimming nearby; 12 Golf nearby; 13 Skiing nearby; 14 May be booked through a travel agent.

Beacon Hill

and shops. Elevator for luggage. Personal checks accepted for deposit.

Host: Susan Butterworth
Rooms: 3 (PB) $125-150
Full Breakfast
Credit Cards: None
Notes: 5, 8, 9, 14

A Bed & Breakfast Agency of Boston and Boston Harbor Bed and Breakfast

47 Commercial Wharf, 02110
(617) 720-3540; (800) 248-9262
0 800 89 5128 (free phone from U.K.)

Downtown Boston's largest selection of guest rooms in historic bed and breakfast homes including Federal and Victorian townhouses and beautifully restored 1840s waterfront lofts. Also a lovely selection of furnished private studio, or one- and two-bedroom condominiums that are great for families. Exclusive locations include waterfront, Faneuil Hall and Quincy Market, North End, Back Bay, Beacon Hill, Copley Square, Cambridge, Cape Cod, and the Islands. Yachts and houseboats also are available. $65-120.

Bed and Breakfast Associates Bay Colony, Ltd.

P.O. Box 57166, Babson Park, 02157-0166
(617) 449-5302; (800) 347-5088
FAX (617) 449-5958

M101. The best view in Boston! This stunning condo overlooks Boston's popular harbor front area from its 30th-floor perch. Watch the sailboards in the harbor or peer down at Quincy Market and Faneuil Hall and the famous clock tower. One attractive guest room with a twin-king option, contemporary furnishing, and private bath. $125.

M104. Those seeking the charm of an old European hotel will enjoy staying in this prestigious private club with its elegant drawing room and small, gracious dining room. Convenient to Newbury Street shops, historic sites, and the Hynes Convention Center. Four guest rooms, two with private baths. Continental breakfast served. Elevator service. Children are welcome. $66-107.

M131. In Boston's prestigious Beacon Hill and adjacent to the historic Massachusetts State House, this inn is a loving restoration of two attached 1830s townhouses. The fine period furnishings include four-poster and canopied beds, decorative fireplaces, and reproduction desks. New private baths throughout, and guests are always welcome to use the kitchen, the dining room, and the parlors. $89-109.

M136. This handsome 46-room mansion at the foot of Beacon Hill is within walking distance of many Boston attractions. Modern amenities have been incorporated into this careful restoration, and rooms include telephone lines, private baths, color TVs, individual climate controls, and some kitchenettes. Elevator and handicapped access is available. The gracious double parlor with working fireplace and period

NOTES: Credit cards accepted: A MasterCard; B Visa; C American Express; D Discover; E Diners Club;
F Other; 2 Personal checks accepted; 3 Lunch available; 4 Dinner available; 5 Open all year; 6 Pets welcome;

furnishings serves as the lobby, and reproduction furnishings create a warm, elegant atmosphere. Continental breakfast. Laundry and valet. $85-140.

M137. Boston has only one Newbury Street, and it is *the* street for art galleries, designer clothing boutiques, and fine window shopping. This 32-room Newbury Street Inn puts all of this at the doorstep. Opened in 1991, this property is restored and offers warm, comfortable rooms with 19th-century reproductions. The front patio is a perfect spot for people-watching; breakfast is served here when the weather permits. Selectively priced rooms available on all four floors. Reserved parking available in the rear for $10 per day. Two blocks to Copley Square and Hynes Convention Center. $95-155.

M138. In Copley Square, this 64-room inn offers modern business amenities, a gracious lobby, and the best location in the city. All rooms have private bath, queen-size or twin beds, TV, telephone, and individual climate control. Discount on-site parking. $95-110.

M142. Stay in a true Back Bay mansion! This opulent home defines luxury and in-town convenience. Just two blocks from the renowned shops and cafes of Newbury Street, this bed and breakfast features two lavish guest rooms and a breakfast buffet station. Queen-size canopied beds. In-hall baths are each shared with one tenant. $98.

M143. Atop Beacon Hill, this romantic penthouse studio apartment with its beamed cathedral ceiling has an enchanting decor. In summer, enjoy the marvelous view of Boston from the private balcony with its intricate iron railing and working fountain. In winter, the large fireplace warms guests as they settle in to enjoy the cozy atmosphere. Only three blocks from Charles Street's fine restaurants, antiques, and art. $125-150.

M144. This 1940s New York-style apartment building offers one guest room with queen-size bed and private bath for double occupancy, and overlooks Boston's Public Gardens. This immaculate, attractive apartment features both great location and grand views. $99.

M229. Two blocks from Symphony Hall, this pretty Victorian townhouse offers several pleasant guest rooms and suites, some with private baths, some that share a bath with one other room. King-size, double, and twin beds. Suite $156. $88.

M230. On a quiet street of gracious brownstones in Boston's Back Bay, near the Hynes Convention Center, this friendly family offers one very special guest room with queen-size bed, private deck, and private bath ensuite. Completely restored and tastefully decorated. $90.

M240. Lovely Victorian townhouse in the Back Bay just steps from the Prudential Center and Copley Place. This warm and hospitable couple offers their guests full use of their second floor with two charming guest rooms and a bath. They also offer a garden-level efficiency with a new kitchenette and private bath. Children welcome. Continental breakfast served. No smoking allowed. $65-80.

M300. Appleton is one of Boston's prettiest residential streets, and it is just two blocks from the Back Bay station in historic Copley Square. The hostess is delighted to offer her beautifully decorated and quiet third-floor guest room with queen-size bed, new private bath, TV, and telephone. $98.

7 No smoking; 8 Children welcome; 9 Social drinking allowed; 10 Tennis nearby; 11 Swimming nearby; 12 Golf nearby; 13 Skiing nearby; 14 May be booked through a travel agent.

Bed and Breakfast Associates Bay Colony, Ltd. (continued)

M301. Near Copley Square, in Boston's End, this pretty Victorian brownstone has been restored with great care and attention to detail and is decorated with lovely antiques. Two third-floor guest rooms, one with a carved king-size and the other with a four-poster canopy queen-size bed, share a bath. Parking available for $10. $80.

M302. A fully furnished one-bedroom apartment with private roof deck in Boston's South End, convenient to Copley Square. Cozy and comfortable, this fourth-floor unit has one bedroom with queen-size bed, living room with sleep-sofa, fully equipped kitchen, dining area, and bath. Weekly and monthly rates available. $75.

M303. This bed and breakfast host couple offers a wealth of knowledge about Boston along with their kind attention to guest needs. Each of the two guest rooms reflects splendid taste and attention to detail. Near Copley Square, their brownstone townhouse is convenient to Boston's tourist and convention centers. $80.

M304. A furnished one-bedroom apartment with free underground parking is a rarity in central Boston. This contemporary unit is in a converted church building which was recently transformed into stylish condos. Elevator to third floor, queen-size bed, private bath, living-dining room, and fully equipped kitchen. $85.

M306. In a 19th-century townhouse three blocks from Copley Square, guests enjoy the privacy and convenience of this newly decorated studio apartment with a Murphy double bed, futon couch, cooking nook, and private bath. $85.

M308. This 500-square-foot, garden-level suite in a renovated brownstone townhouse is just three blocks from the Boston Common and Copley Square. Guests enjoy a large, brick-walled bedroom with queen-size and twin beds, sitting room, private bath and patio, color TV, stereo, refrigerator, and a laundry. Continental breakfast. Children over 13 welcome. Off-season monthly rates available. $78.

M309. Enjoy privacy in this newly renovated Victorian townhouse on a lovely South End street, three blocks from the Boston Common. This attractive third-floor room offers private bath ensuite, color TV, and twin beds. Kitchenette with breakfast foods provided. $72

M314. Attention to detail and gracious hospitality are the hallmark of this bed and breakfast. Selected as one of the 100 best bed and breakfasts in the country, this 1863 townhouse is set in the historic district right next to Boston's famed Copley Square. Each impeccable guest room offers unique decorative features that include wide-pine floors, bow windows, marble fireplaces, queen-size brass beds, Chinese rugs, and private baths. Sumptuous breakfast served in the penthouse dining room. $97-135.

M323. This well-kept and appealing 1869 brick townhouse, near the Hynes Convention Center, features two nicely decorated second-floor guest rooms; one includes a queen-size bed, "decorative" fireplace, delightful antiques, and a bay window breakfast spot. Shared bath. Parking is available on request at $10 per day. $75.

M326. This stunning architectural delight is the result of a complete restoration of a once traditional South End townhouse. Bring the camera to show the folks back home the results of this collaborative effort by Boston's best artisans. The guest suite features double brass bed, designer bath, elegant foyer and private sitting room. $97.

M356. For extended stays, ask about this one-bedroom apartment with a new eat-in kitchenette, queen-size bed, living room with sleeper-sofa, color TV, and private bath in an 1857 townhouse on a quiet street in the South End. Clean and well maintained. $1,300 per month. $80 per night.

M359. This comfortable Victorian townhouse is near Copley Square and the Hynes Convention Center in Boston's South End. The host has thoughtfully furnished two guest rooms which share one full and one half-bath. The studio room has a private attached kitchen and a double bed. The sunrise room has a twins-king option. $75.

M362. This private-entry suite offers a comfortable home away from home in central Boston near Tremont Street's "restaurant row." The spacious two-room suite with eleven-foot ceilings includes a kitchenette, a private bath, twin beds (or king), and a spacious living room with a large bay window. $110.

M416. In historic Charlestown, one block from the famed Freedom Trail, this 1846 townhouse has been wonderfully restored and attractively furnished with lovely antiques. Two spacious guest rooms, each with private bath. $65-75.

M482. In historic Charlestown, on Boston's famed Freedom Trail, guests enjoy a second-floor suite with deck overlooking gardens and private entrance in this 1847 Greek Revival townhouse. The traditionally furnished guest room has queen-size bed and private bath. A queen-size sleeper-sofa is also available in the attached sitting room. $85.

M510. A wonderful 12-room Victorian in the Jamaica Pond area near the Farber, Children's, and Brigham hospitals. Very large third-floor guest room provides privacy, and its furnishings include a desk and a sofa. A private bath and a full private kitchen adjoin. Ten minutes drive to downtown Boston. Self-serve Continental breakfast. No smoking. Monthly rates available. $78.

Bed and Breakfast Greater Boston and Cape Cod
P.O. Box 35, Newtonville, 02160
(617) 964-1606; (800) 832-2632
FAX (617) 322-8572

Bed and Breakfast Afloat. This completely refurbished yacht in Boston's waterfront district sleeps two to four and offers a galley kitchen stocked with breakfast food, living room with double futon bed, air conditioning, color TV, and a separate bedroom with double bed and private bath. By prior arrangement, hosts will cater private boatside parties or dinners. Available May 1 through October 15. $120-190.

The Garden Bed and Breakfast. A perfect place to experience Boston. This Victorian brick row house, built in 1860, is in the largest historic Victorian neighborhood in the United States. The accommodation has a separate private entrance leading to a double parlor; the bedroom has a king-size bed (or two singles), TV, VCR, and air conditioning. There are also a fully equipped efficiency kitchen and a shower bath. No breakfast is provided, but the host will stock the cupboard and refrigerator. Weekly and extended rates. No smoking allowed. $100-125.

The South End Guest House. Formerly the parlor room of a brick row house in the 1860s, this charming guest room has its own private bath and beautiful, decorative marble fireplace. Lace curtains grace the long parlor room windows that look out on to a quiet one-way street. The room is tastefully decorated and has a double bed, TV, and air conditioning. Just outside the guest room is a cozy sitting area with couch and working fireplace. Guests will enjoy a delicious Continental breakfast. A short walk through lovely tree-lined streets to public transportation and major tourist attractions in Boston, including the Hynes Convention Center, Prudential Center, Copley Square, the Boston Symphony, Fenway Park, South End Medical Centers, and area universities. $85.

Bed and Breakfast/ Inns of New England

128 South Hoop Pole Road, Guilford, CT 06437
(203) 457-0042; (800) 582-0853

MA-1007. Built in 1894 by a prosperous Boston leather merchant, this late Victorian house was later converted to a retirement home, which it was for more than 70 years. The current owners extensively refurbished the house when they bought it. Spacious rooms, gleaming woodwork, and sparkling stained-glass windows give the house its character. Guests are invited to enjoy the parlor, oak-paneled sitting room with TV, sunny dining room, and breakfast kitchen. A substantial "help yourself" breakfast is provided each morning, and guests are welcome to use the kitchen for snacks or light meals. Six comfortable guest rooms, all with stained-glass windows. Two rooms have private baths; the other four rooms share two additional bathrooms. $60-90.

Chandler Inn

26 Chandler at Berkeley, 02116
(617) 482-3450; (800) 842-3450

Boston's best value! On the edge of the historic Back Bay and within walking distance to Newbury Street, Copley Place, shopping, theaters, and restaurants. All rooms have a private bath, TV, direct-dial telephone, and air conditioning.

Host: Peter Kirk
Rooms: 56 (PB) $69-89
Continental Breakfast
Credit Cards: A, B, C, D, E
Notes: 5, 8, 9, 14

82 Chandler Street Bed and Breakfast

82 Chandler Street, 02116
(617) 482-0408

This 1863 red brick row house is downtown in a historic residential neighborhood, just off famous Copley Square. nearby Hynes Convention Center, public gardens, Freedom Trail, Quincy Market, and the Back Bay subway and Amtrack station. Each room, with private bath and queen-size bed, is beautifully decorated and finely furnished. Telephones and air conditioning in every room. "82" is appreciated for its quiet residential downtown neighborhood, personal hospitality, and

82 Chandler Street

delicious family-style breakfasts, that are served in the sun-filled penthouse kitchen. Dining, theater, and shopping are all within easy walking distance, so a car is not needed to enjoy a stay here.

Hosts: Denis F. Coté and Dominic C. Beraldi
Rooms: 5 (PB) $95-125
Full Breakfast
Credit Cards: None
Notes: 2, 5, 7, 9, 14

Greater Boston Hospitality

P.O. Box 1142, Brookline, 02146
(617) 277-5430

07. Walk up an eliptical staircase for two flights, passing a stunning pewter chandelier to be greeted by charming hosts. This 1880 Victorian townhouse has French Chateauesque turrets, white walls, great wooden floors, and high ceilings with a 30-foot indoor cupola. Working fireplace in the living room for the winter, and in the summer guests may enjoy coffee in an attractive tiered side yard. Central air conditioning. Queen-size bed, private bath, and excellent Continental breakfast. Thank you for not smoking. Children over ten welcome. Parking possibilities, one block to the "T," and a second bedroom possibility. Unobtrusive very fat tabby in resident. $80.

12. Stunning unhosted apartment in 19th-century chocolate factory, completely rehabbed in 1982, is minutes to the waterfront and North End, wonderful restaurants and Quincy Market. There is a living room with dining area, well-stocked kitchen, bedroom with king-size bed, and modern bathroom. Several garages for cars nearby. Central air conditioning, elevated building, washer and dryer available. No pets. No smoking. Adults only. Many amenities. $120.

18. Renovated and refurbished, this 1880 Victorian townhouse has a queen-size bedroom, private bath, and air conditioning.

Gleaming pine floors and white interiors make this bed and breakfast airy, light, and restful. The hostess is a personnel manager and speaks French. Breakfast and plenty of on-street parking in this interesting Boston area. $70.

21. In the Back Bay area, a classic 1890 brownstone is in one of Boston's finest residential areas, minutes from the Public Garden, fine shops, and scores of elegant restaurants. Guests occupy one of four large, understated rooms with 18th-century mahogany furniture, and dark mahogany floors, some appointed with Oriental rugs. Two rooms have twin beds, each with private adjoining bathroom. Two rooms have king-size beds, each with private adjoining bath. Grand piano, TV, air conditioning, and use of other rooms. Continental breakfast and lunch and dinner available by reservation. Many amenities. Smoking restricted. Parking possibilities. Older children welcome. $95.

22. An elegant turn-of-the-century brownstone in Boston's Back Bay area includes two private single rooms with shared bath. High ceilings, nice appointments in prime location. Lunch and dinner available by reservation. Parking extra. Continental breakfast. Adults only. $62 per person.

23. This chic, elevated, New York-style building in Boston's most exclusive area overlooking the Public Garden is minutes from the Ritz, the State House, Cheers, and the Boston Common. The host offers a queen-size room with full, private bath amid splendid antiques. Ample Continental breakfast. Walk everywhere from this excellent downtown site. $90.

26. Modeled after a small European inn, these two renovated townhouses comprise an intimate fifteen-room bed and breakfast

7 No smoking; 8 Children welcome; 9 Social drinking allowed; 10 Tennis nearby; 11 Swimming nearby;
12 Golf nearby; 13 Skiing nearby; 14 May be booked through a travel agent.

Greater Boston Hospitality (continued)

in the heart of Boston's Back Bay area, minutes from the Prudential Center, Copley Square, and the Christian Science Center. Continental breakfast and refreshments and hors d'oeuvres on the outdoor deck or in the living room. Central air conditioning, private telephones, and color TVs. Limited smoking permitted. Adults only. Garage close by. Some parking available. Fifteen well-appointed single, twin, double and queen-size bedded rooms with private and shared baths. $62-89.

28. Distinctive red brick townhouses include studio and one-bedroom apartments. Fully decorated and furnished in Queen Anne style, guests will have complete kitchen and dining facilities, private bath, and all household necessities—linen and maid service, local telephone, and cable TV. Bedrooms have double and queen-size beds, with some double and queen-size Hide-a-Beds in the living room. Some parking spaces. $65-110.

29. Gorgeous 1790 townhouse in this famous historic district offers separate bed and breakfast floor with double-bed bedroom, bathroom, dining room, modern kitchen, living room, and connecting roof deck that is ablaze with flowers and blue spruce. Breakfast is either served or stocked in the guest kitchen. No parking, but garages close by. This elegant home is owned by a prominent European hostess. No smoking. $95.

33. Up three flights of stairs to "Sarah's Loft," guests will have a queen-size bedroom with private bath as well as a private dining and sitting area. This 100-year-old white stucco home has been completely renovated into a spacious, modern, airy accommodation with stunning oak floors and skylights. There is also a crib and extra queen-size futon sofa bed. Air conditioning and ceiling fans. Thank you for not smoking. Children welcome. Parking included. Breakfast is included as well as guests' own microwave, refrigerator, flatware, and dishes. $70-85.

36. Convenient for driving in or out of Boston, very near public transportation, this fine, older brick Colonial offers two lovely guest rooms on separate bed and breakfast floor. Adjoining den for guests' use and patio off each bedroom. Guests share modern full bath with stall shower. Two beautiful guest rooms, one with twin beds and the other with queen-size bed. Color TV in each room. Piano. Excellent breakfasts. Five-minute walk to subway. Prestige neighborhood. No children. No smoking. Parking included. $63.

37. This unusual five-star bed and breakfast is in a converted Georgian carriage house, formerly part of a larger estate, on a cul-de-sac in an outstanding neighborhood, close to the museum and medical area. Set in among gracious older homes, this home offers a twin or queen-size guest room with private bath and guest sitting room on a completely separate level. Glass doors open from bedroom to a large tree-enclosed patio where breakfast is sometimes served in the summer. Many amenities. Parking included, or short walk to express carline to center of the city. No smoking. Adults only. $82.

40. London hostess offers a very large, outstanding, white Colonial surrounded by more than one acre of beautiful grounds covered with hemlocks, white pines, locust, and maple trees. There are two large rooms with shared bath: one with a queen-size bed and the other with twin beds. Parking close to the "T." Piano. Children over eight welcome. Full breakfast. No smoking. $62-79.

47. Eclectic, 40-year-old center entrance Colonial in a quiet, residential neighborhood, minutes to the Longwood Medical area and the Museum of Fine Arts. Three guest rooms are decorated with original paintings. One is a large bedroom with a king-size bed and private adjoining bath. Another has twin beds with a shared bath. A third room with single bed is also available. Parking included and close to public transportation. Adults and children welcome. $45-60.

125. For the guest desiring a larger inn, this 64-room inn traditionally furnished with handsome appointments, is in the prestigious Back Bay/Copley Square area, only a ten-minute walk to the Hynes Convention Center and Boston Common. All rooms have color TV, individually controlled heat and air conditioning units, and private baths. There are queen-size and twin beds available as well as several living rooms, a library, a skylit atrium, and a fitness center for guests' use. A parking garage is adjacent to the inn. Many amenities. $90.

181. Stunning 1867 townhouse has two large bed and breakfast rooms that share one and one-half baths. One has an antique double bed and adjoining kitchenette, and it overlooks a great weeping cherry tree. A second room has twin beds. Cable TV and telephone in each bedroom. Many amenities. Wonderful art and greenery. Nearby garages and some on-street parking. Breakfast served in dining room or on a tray. Twenty dollars for each extra persons in room. $75.

218. Spacious 1860 brownstone home is across from Bullfinch-designed city park and is owned by school administrator. Five bedrooms, most with 14-1/2-inch ceilings, each with queen- or king-size beds, shared baths. Self-serve, excellent Continental plus breakfast. Interesting art work in an unusual home. Black-and-white TVs in each room. Many fireplaces. Adults only. Limited on-street parking. Smoking restricted. $120.

Host Homes of Boston

P.O. Box 117, 02168
(617) 244-1308; FAX (617) 244-5156

Architect's Home. Early Victorian-era townhouse with contemporary furnishings on a quiet street. Bright and private fourth-floor guest room with queen-size bed and roof deck with skyline view. Private bath. Walk to Park Plaza Hotel, restaurants, theaters, Copley Square, and the convention center. No smoking. $75.

Around the Corner. This 1826 Federal townhouse has exceptional decor. Guest suite has two small single bedrooms, sitting room, TV, and bath. Single guest room with bath on lower level. Near State House, Massachusetts General Hospital, major hotels, MIT, Harvard, and restaurants. No smoking. $85-136.

Bailey's Copley. This typical 1840 Federal townhouse has two guest parlors, a private patio, and a cozy atmosphere. Three guest rooms on the second and third floors (king-size or twin beds) share two baths. Self-serve breakfast 7:30-10:00 A.M. Resident dogs. Walk to Boston Common, Copley Square, Hynes Convention Center, Amtrak, and subway. Air-conditioned. $75-93.

Near Faneuil Hall. Boston's past and present meet in this colorful Faneuil Hall and Quincy Market area. Host's fifth- and sixth-floor walk-up has brick and beam decor and balcony. Spacious guest room with double bed, skylights, and private bath. Subway two blocks away. Walk to harbor hotels, Freedom Trail, financial center, and restaurants. Air-conditioned. No smoking. $81.

7 No smoking; 8 Children welcome; 9 Social drinking allowed; 10 Tennis nearby; 11 Swimming nearby; 12 Golf nearby; 13 Skiing nearby; 14 May be booked through a travel agent.

Host Homes of Boston (continued)

The Nocturne. This 1867 Victorian home in a quiet historic neighborhood has a roof deck and greenhouse. Two third-floor guest rooms (twin beds, or king-size and double with kitchen) with air conditioning and cable TV. Roll away available. Walk to fine restaurants, Back Bay shops, Copley Square, convention center, Amtrak, and subway. No smoking allowed. Children welcome. $75.

On the Avenue. Boston Common, Copley Place, convention hotels, and the subway are steps away from 19th-century ambience in private professional club. Dining room; guest parlor. Three spacious doubles have twin beds, telephone, and private bath. Four small singles (one twin bed) share two baths. Roll away: $20. Air conditioning, TV, elevator. $105.

On the Hill. This brick Federal townhouse (1790) on the Hill's loveliest street offers exceptional third-floor quarters—living room, bedroom, modern bath, kitchen, and dining room where breakfast is served. Near Freedom Trail, hotels, State House. Air conditioning; no smoking allowed; TV. $115.

On the Park. This 1865 Victorian bowfront in a historic district features antiques and authentic decor. Two fourth-floor guest rooms (king-size and twin beds, or two twins) share a bath. Resident dogs. Four blocks to Copley Square, Hynes Convention Center, Back Bay Orange Line, and Amtrak. No smoking. $75.

Popham House. This elegant 1940 New York-style brick townhouse overlooks the Public Gardens. Host's second-floor home, replete with traditional antiques, has one guest room with queen-size bed and private bath. TV in parlor. Steps from major hotels, theaters, restaurants, convention center, and subway. Air-conditioned. $108.

Proper Bostonian. Business people like this 1872 townhouse with authentic decor. Spacious third-floor guest room has twin beds, sitting area, and small stocked kitchen where guests make their own breakfast. Another twin room often available, if same party. Busy hosts offer privacy in best area. Four blocks to Copley Square and Hynes Convention Center. Near Boston Common. Air conditioning; private bath; TV. $90.

Victorian Bowfront. Brick townhouse, circa 1869, in historic neighborhood boasts the era's high ceilings, carved wood detail, and marble fireplaces. Two second-floor guest rooms with queen-size beds that share a bath. City room has TV. Country room has striking wall mural and basin. Breakfast is served in rooms. Resident dog and cat. Central location. Walk three blocks to convention center and subway. No smoking. Air-conditioned. $75.

Oasis Guest House

22 Edgerly Road, 02115
(617) 267-2262; FAX (617) 267-1920

Two renovated Back Bay townhouses with color TV, telephones, central air, and private baths. Within walking distance of restaurants, museums, and points of interest. This is a great in-town location near the Hynes Convention Center. Enjoy the outside decks. Parking. Fine lodging accommodations in the heart of the city for a price much less than at major hotels. Thirteen seasons of mostly repeat and referrals. Call, fax, or write for more information.

Rooms: 16 (11 PB; 5 SB) $60-82
Continental Breakfast
Credit Cards: A, B, C
Notes: 5, 7, 9, 14

NOTES: Credit cards accepted: A MasterCard; B Visa; C American Express; D Discover; E Diners Club; F Other; 2 Personal checks accepted; 3 Lunch available; 4 Dinner available; 5 Open all year; 6 Pets welcome;

BOURNE

Golden Slumber Accommodations

640 Revere Beach Boulevard, Revere, 02151
(800) 892-3231; (617) 289-1053

103. Charming contemporary Colonial nestled in a country setting features traditional decor and antique furnishings. Beautifully appointed guest rooms feature twin, double, or queen-size beds and private or shared baths. Enjoy the scrumptious Dutch-inspired full breakfast served in the formal dining room, or a romantic breakfast in bed with fine linen and silver service. Piano, Jacuzzi, fireplace, and laundry facilities. Near island ferries, historic attractions, and private beaches. A rare find with many delightful suprises! $75-95.

BOXFORD

Bed and Breakfast Marblehead and North Shore

P.O. Box 35, Newtonville, 02160
(617) 964-1606; (800) 832-2632
FAX (617) 332-8572

Day's End. A beautiful architect-designed contemporary home in a country setting on 30 acres with swimming pool. The three guest rooms can be rented individually or as a separate entrance suite. In addition to the efficiency kitchenette and sitting room, the first-floor living room has facilities for entertaining, available for a fee. Children welcome. Weekly and monthly rates available. Executive homestays available. Open year-round. Continental breakfast. No smoking. $55-75.

BREWSTER (CAPE COD)

Bed and Breakfast Cape Cod

P.O. Box 341, West Hyannisport, 02672-0341
(508) 775-2772; FAX (508) 775-2884

17. Along the banks of Cape Cod Bay in historic Brewster is this 1750 sea captain's house. Six hundred yards from the house is a public beach where swimming and fishing are available. A Continental breakfast is served each morning on the patio, which has a beautifal ocean view. Double or twin beds available. Golf, Nickerson State Park, and the village are all less than one mile away. $65.

28. This Cape Cod-style house was built in 1739. Today, this lovely old house retains its original appearance and is very well maintained. In a remote area, the variety of birds and plants offer a natural wonderland for sitting or walking in the woods. A two-room suite with a sitting room, double bed, and private full bath is available, and a second guest room on the second floor is also available with a double bed and private bath. A delicious Continental breakfast is served. $85.

33. Perched on a cliff 50 feet above the waters of a beautiful freshwater pond sits a ranch home with two private bath-bedroom suites. On the ground floor, a room with a king-size bed, large sitting area, and a lake view is also available. The hosts serve a Continental breakfast in a lovely, bright dining room, and guests are encouraged to use the parlor. Bring a swimsuit and fishing pole and be prepared to relax in this private setting on the beach. $80.

41. In an antique village, this lovely home was rebuilt in 1973 and has all amenities, including air conditioning, TV, and traditional decor. A large second-floor private bath- bedroom has a king-size bed, and four other rooms with either double or queen-size beds are also available. A short walk takes guests to shops, bay beaches, and other points of interest. A delicious big gourmet breakfast is served each morning. $70-135.

7 No smoking; 8 Children welcome; 9 Social drinking allowed; 10 Tennis nearby; 11 Swimming nearby; 12 Golf nearby; 13 Skiing nearby; 14 May be booked through a travel agent.

The Bramble Inn and Restaurant

2019 Main Street, 02631
(508) 896-7644

Three antique buildings in the heart of the historic district lovingly restored to reflect a bygone era. All 13 rooms have private baths and air conditioning. Chef-owned nationally acclaimed restaurant with five intimate dining rooms, candle-light, antiques, and fresh flowers. *Prix fixe* four-course dinners by reservation. House specialties include rack of lamb and native seafoods presented with an innovative air. "Best of 1990"—*Travel and Leisure* magazine. Children seven and older welcome.

Hosts: Cliff and Ruth Manchester
Rooms: 13 (PB) $75-125
Full Breakfast
Credit Cards: A, B, C, D
Notes: 2, 4, 7, 9, 10, 11, 12, 14

Brewster Farmhouse Inn

716 Main Street, 02631
(508) 896-3910; (800) 892-3910
FAX (508) 896-4232

Understated elegance and unsurpassed service and amenities. Impeccably furnished gathering room with fireplace, full gourmet breakfasts, creative afternoon teas, heated pool, spa, gardens, and orchard. A country-like setting, yet only a short walk to the

Brewster Farmhouse Inn

beach. Evening turndown with chocolates and sherry. Cozy terry-cloth robes, oversize towels, hair dryers, and fine toiletries. All rooms (some with fireplaces) feature king- or queen-size beds, air conditioning, and TV with HBO.

Rooms: 5 (4 PB; 1 SB) $70-150
Full Breakfast
Credit Cards: A, B, C, D, E
Notes: 2, 7, 9, 10, 11, 12, 14

High Brewster

964 Satucket Road, 02631
(508) 896-3636; (800) 203-2634

A charming farmhouse, built in 1738, the four cottages, and the main house are on three and a half acres overlooking Lower Mill Pond. The main inn has two rooms; the accommodations vary in the cottages. High Brewster is a very tranquil and relaxed setting where people come to escape a fast-paced lifestyle. The restaurant is one of the area's finest. Guests enjoy American cuisine served in one of three cozy dining rooms. Perfect for a romantic getaway.

Rooms: 8 (PB) $80-190
Continental Breakfast
Credit Cards: A, B, C
Notes: 2, 4, 5, 6, 8, 9, 10, 11, 12, 14

Isaiah Clark House

1187 Main Street, 02631
(508) 896-2223; (800) 822-4001

Built in 1780, this inn was once the mansion of a famous sea captain and is set on five acres of landscaped gardens. All guests enjoy a full American breakfast served on a deck overlooking the gardens. Many guest rooms have working fireplaces. All rooms are air-conditioned. Special welcome for honeymooners. Smoking restricted.

Host: Richard E. Griffin
Rooms: 7 (PB) $95-120
Full Breakfast
Credit Cards: A, B, C
Notes: 5, 8, 9, 10, 11, 12, 14

Old Sea Pines Inn

Old Sea Pines Inn

2553 Main Street, 02631
(508) 896-6114

Lovely turn-of-the-century mansion, once the Sea Pines School of Charm and Personality for Young Women, now a newly renovated and redecorated country inn. Furnished with antiques, some of the rooms have working fireplaces. On three and one-half acres of land, with a wraparound porch looking out over the lawn, trees, and flowers. Complimentary beverage on arrival. Dinner theater on Sunday evening, June, July, and August. Children over eight welcome.

Hosts: Stephen and Michele Rowan
Rooms: 16 (PB) $45-95
Full Breakfast
Credit Cards: A, B, C, D, E
Notes: 2, 4, 5, 8, 9, 10, 11, 12, 14

Orleans Bed and Breakfast Associates

P.O. Box 1312, Orleans, 02653
(508) 255-3824; (800) 541-6226

Stonybrook. A pre-1776 restored Colonial house in a storybook setting next to the old grist mill and famous Stony Brook Herring Run. Private entrance to upstairs large double room with fireplace, sitting room, small modern kitchenette, and private bath. The suite has a TV and air conditioning. An attractive sitting area outside overlooks the mill pond. $60.

BROOKLINE

Beacon Inn

1087 and 1750 Beacon Street, 02146
(617) 566-0088

These turn-of-the-century townhouses have been converted into two of Brookline's most charming guest houses. The original woodwork is reminiscent of their 19th-century construction, and the lobby fireplaces offer a friendly welcome to travelers. Large, comfortably furnished, sunny rooms provide pleasant accommodations at a reasonable price. The Beacon Inn is minutes away from downtown Boston. The area offers a wide variety of restaurants, shops, museums, theaters, and other attractions.

Hosts: Colleen and Karl Carrigan
Rooms: 24 (15 PB; 9 SB) $59-99
Continental Breakfast
Credit Cards: A, B, C
Notes: 5, 7, 8, 9, 14

Bed and Breakfast Associates Bay Colony, Ltd.

P.O. Box 57166, Babson Park, Boston, 02157-0166
(617) 449-5302; (800) 347-5088
FAX (617) 449-5958

M610. This quiet Brookline Hills neighborhood is convenient to the Longwood Medical area as well as the "T" to central

Bed and Breakfast Associates Bay Colony, Ltd. (continued)

Boston. The guest suite is a large room featuring a fully stocked kitchenette, private bath, dining table, and sofa. Continental breakfast; children welcome; no smoking allowed. $75.

M641. Once part of the Underground Railroad, this 18th-century farm cottage in Brookline Village is steeped in history and is surrounded by imposing mansions on a quiet street near the Longwood Medical area. Three guest rooms with shared bath all feature antique furnishings. Guests have a choice between double, queen-size, or twin beds. $68.

M644. Close to the medical center (Children's Hospital, Harvard Medical School, Dana-Farber Cancer), this lovingly restored and authentically furnished Victorian home offers exceptional guest privacy. On the third floor, the main guest room is furnished with carved antique twin beds. Lace accents add to the charm. An auxiliary single room is available for parties of three. Driveway parking. $75.

M661. On Beacon Street, between Boston University and Boston College, this historic townhouse dates back to 1894. Fully restored and tastefully furnished with antiques, the guest room has a bird's-eye-maple four-poster bed and a twin bed, with a private bath in the hall. Free driveway parking. $78.

Bed and Breakfast Greater Boston and Cape Cod

P.O. Box 35, Newtonville, 02160
(617) 964-1606; (800) 832-2632
FAX (617) 322-8572

The Old Manse. This bed and breakfast offers guests a private hall bath and two single beds in a charming six-room apartment decorated with fine art and African artifacts collected by the hostess during her two-year stay in West Africa. Guests are welcome to use the living room, dining room, and eat-in kitchen. A roll away cot and cradle are available for an extra guest or infant. Continental breakfast. No smoking. $65-85.

Beech Tree Inn

83 Longwood Avenue, 02146
(617) 277-1620; (800) 544-9660

The Beech Tree Inn is a turn-of-the-century Victorian private home that has been converted to a bed and breakfast. Each room is individually decorated, some with fireplaces, and they vary in size and decor. A Continental breakfast is served, and a fully equipped kitchen is available. The inn is within walking distance of many shops, restaurants, and world-renowned medical centers; and internationally famous academic institutions are only a few blocks away. The nearby subway will take visitors into downtown Boston in 12 minutes. A pleasant interlude for a night, a weekend, or even a week.

Hosts: Kathrine Anderson and Bette Allen
Rooms: 9 (4 PB; 5 SB) $49.36-76.79
Continental Breakfast
Credit Cards: None
Notes: 2, 5, 6, 7, 8

The Bertram Inn

92 Sewall Avenue, 02146
(617) 566-2234; (800) 295-3822
FAX (617) 277-1887

Come home to Victorian elegance. The Bertram Inn offers the comfort of a quiet neighborhood and is only ten minutes from downtown Boston by trolley. Additionally, fine shops and restaurants are a short walk. The 12-room inn, built in 1907, has been restored to its original splendor using

NOTES: Credit cards accepted: A MasterCard; B Visa; C American Express; D Discover; E Diners Club;
F Other; 2 Personal checks accepted; 3 Lunch available; 4 Dinner available; 5 Open all year; 6 Pets welcome;

period antiques, fine wallpaper, and draperies. Some rooms have working fireplaces and all have TVs and telephones. A hearty Continental breakfast is served daily. Parking included.

Host: Bryan Austin
Rooms: 12 (9PB; 3 SB) $59-154
Continental Breakfast
Credit Cards: A, B
Notes: 2, 5, 6, 7, 9

Greater Boston Hospitality

P.O. Box 1142, 02146
(617) 277-5430

Hundreds of accommodations in outstanding Georgian, Federal, Victorian, and Colonial homes, condos, and inns in the greater Boston area. All include breakfast, many include parking, and others are on excellent transport system. Many are minutes from colleges, medical area, museum, and Freedom Trail. Visit Boston as a native while staying at Greater Boston Hospitality. Write or call today for free brochure.

Manager: Kelly Simpson
Rooms: 125 (100 PB; 25 SB) $47-75
Full and Continental Breakfast
Credit Cards: A, B
Notes: 2, 3, 5, 8, 10, 11, 12, 14

Host Homes of Boston

P.O. Box 117, 02168
(617) 244-1308; FAX (617) 244-5156

Heath House. Country atmosphere close to city in classic Colonial on rolling lawn. English hostess offers two second-floor guest rooms (queen with air conditioning and twins). Children welcome. Near Pine Manor, Boston College, and Longwood medical area. Boston five miles. Green Line-D one-half mile. No smoking. $75.

Sarah's Loft. Bright and spacious third-floor suite with private entrance. Guest quarters include two queen bedrooms. Also, a large living area with skylights, stereo, dining table (where breakfast is served), refrigerator, microwave, and extra sofa bed. Children are welcome. Green Line-C and village two blocks. Fenway Park, Boston one mile. Air conditioning; crib; private bath; TV; no smoking. $75.

Studio Apartment. Colonial home (1620 Salem house replica) on quiet cul-de-sac offers above-ground basement room with double bed, sofa, galley kitchen, patio, and private entrance. Choice of breakfast on tray or self-serve. Five blocks to Green Line-C. Ten minutes to Copley Square. TV; air conditioning; no smoking allowed; private bath. $75.

BROOKLINE HILLS

Host Homes of Boston

P.O. Box 117, 02168
(617) 244-1308; FAX (617) 244-5156

The Tree House. Meg's modern townhouse with traditional decor has a sweeping view from the glass-walled living room and deck. Two second-floor guest rooms (double and twins). Also, in season, a king room with air conditioning and private bath. Two Siamese cats. Near Back Bay, Boston

7 No smoking; 8 Children welcome; 9 Social drinking allowed; 10 Tennis nearby; 11 Swimming nearby; 12 Golf nearby; 13 Skiing nearby; 14 May be booked through a travel agent.

College, and Boston University. Ten minutes to Hynes Convention Center via Green Line-C and D three blocks. Private bath and TV. No smoking allowed. $61-75.

BUCKLAND

1797 House

Upper Street-Charlemont Road, 01338
(413) 625-2975

This 18th-century home is in a peaceful, rural area, yet is convenient to many attractions and all points in New England. Large rooms, private baths, down quilts, and a lovely screened porch ensure comfort. Experience a modicum of civilization in an increasingly uncivilized world. Closed in December.

Host: Janet Turley
Rooms: 3 (PB) $60-75
Full Breakfast
Credit Cards: None
Notes: 2, 7, 10, 11, 12, 13

CAMBRIDGE

Bed and Breakfast Associates Bay Colony, Ltd.

P.O. Box 57166, Babson Park, Boston, 02157-0166
(617) 449-5302; (800) 347-5088
FAX (617) 449-5958

M804. Near Harvard Yard, this impeccable Philadelphia-style Victorian, circa 1890, is on a quiet street among the finest homes in Cambridge. The two-room suite features a spacious sitting room with sleeper-sofa, fireplace, writing table, TV, and balcony. Continental breakfast; children welcome; no smoking. $85.

M806. Walk to MIT or pick up the subway to Harvard from this immaculate home. The hostess, who lives nearby, maintains the two guest rooms, one with queen-size bed and the other with single bed. Kitchen, dining area, and spacious living room with fireplace for bed and breakfast guests. Additional futon available. The whole house can be rented for $146. Or the rooms can be rented individually for $78.

M830. On a quiet street near Harvard Law School just north of Harvard Square, this delightful Queen Anne Victorian has two gracious guest rooms, one queen-size and one double, with private baths. Hosts have preserved authentic Victorian details throughout the home. Limited parking. $85.

M875. A large home set in a quiet neighborhood adjacent to jogging paths. Just a 20-minute walk from Harvard Square, this home features skylights, sliding doors to deck, many plants, antiques, playroom, and a fenced yard. Three guest rooms with private baths. Full and imaginative breakfast; children welcome. Family and monthly rates available. $55

M885. This congenial hostess, a Boston attorney, shares her cozy Greek Revival home, circa 1853, just outside Harvard Square. The decor is accented by a refreshing mix of country antiques and the quiet urban neighborhood provides a convenient setting for activities in Boston or Cambridge. Three guest rooms share two full baths. Full breakfast upon request; children welcome; no smoking. Family and monthly rates available. $55-72

M888. Bright, cheerful, and convenient to Harvard Square. This bed and breakfast home has three guest rooms, a guest parlor, and dining room. The third-floor suite has skylights, private bath, twin-king option, and space for queen-size futon for children. Second floor rooms have queen-size beds and share a bath. Free parking on street. $70-75.

NOTES: Credit cards accepted: A MasterCard; B Visa; C American Express; D Discover; E Diners Club; F Other; 2 Personal checks accepted; 3 Lunch available; 4 Dinner available; 5 Open all year; 6 Pets welcome;

M900. This fine bed and breakfast inn is in a Harvard Square neighborhood. The recently completed historic restoration has produced 18 guest rooms with private baths and tasteful decor. Romantics enjoy the second-floor suite with fireplace. Limited reserved parking available. $95-135.

M930. A spectacular decorator-furnished bed and breakfast inn in North Cambridge. Each room has a built-in vanity with sink and color TV. Full breakfast is served in the formal Victorian dining room, and guests are invited to relax in one of the gracious parlors. A lovely carriage house and a nearby guest house have also been restored and are offered as bed and breakfast accommodations. Private baths; children over six welcome; smoking allowed on porch only. $119-169.

Bed and Breakfast Greater Boston and Cape Cod

P.O. Box 35, Newtonville, 02160
(617) 964-1606; (800) 832-2632
FAX (617) 322-8521

Prospect Place. An Italianate style attached single family residence built in 1866. Prospect Place was originally owned by the Merrill-Ackers family for more than 100 years. The host family purchased the home in 1994, beginning an extensive period restoration. Great care has been taken to tastefully integrate reconstruction to maintain the original spaces and design. Period details abound, from classic archways and marble fireplaces, to the elegant Victorian dining room and graceful winding staircase. Two guest rooms, double and two singles, share a bath. The third, double, has a private bath. A delicious breakfast is included. Conveniently in the center of Cambridge, only a short walk from MIT, Harvard Square, and public transportation to Boston. No smoking. Families with children welcome. $60-95.

Bed and Breakfast, Ltd.

P.O. Box 216, New Haven, CT 06513
(203) 469-3260

7. This lovely apartment is convenient to MIT. Decorated with antiques and Persian carpets. Living room with fireplace and a miniature museum. $60-75.

Greater Boston Hospitality

P.O. Box 1142, Brookline, 02146
(617) 277-5430

27. This 1890 Cambridge Colonial has been completely renovated. Enjoy a room with double bed, skylights, and private bath in this dramatic, yet comfortable home. Interesting and affordable accommodations in an excellent mid-Cambridge location. Two unobtrusive cats on the premises. Breakfast and parking included. $75.

42. Two bed and breakfast rooms in this 1890 late Colonial home have three working fireplaces in prime Harvard Square area. Two large rooms have twin beds pushed together and shared bath. A third room has a double bed with private bath. A family-style, full breakfast and use of whole house, including a piano, are available. Children welcome. Folding bed, playpen, and extra mattress. $65-80.

43. An attractive Victorian guest house right next to Harvard Square has friendly and knowledgeable hosts. Built in 1894, the house has five guest rooms, each with either a double or queen-size bed and private bath. Parking is included. Continental breakfast, air conditioning, and also convenient to the subway. $77.

49. This 1857 Victorian offers three bed and breakfast rooms. A charming queen-size bed with private bath and unusual antiques, overlooks a small, city garden. Another room, the library, has twin beds and overlooks a cityscape. The bath is shared. The cozy third room has a single bed. Enjoy an excellent homemade breakfast served on an 18th-century table in an unusual kitchen overlooking a splendid Italianate garden. Children over eight welcome. $70-95.

Host Homes of Boston

P.O. Box 117, Boston, 02168
(617) 244-1308; FAX (617) 244-5156

Blue Hawthorne. This 100-year-old Victorian home off Brattle Street is a quiet oasis near bustling Harvard Square. The host offers two first-floor guest rooms (queen and twins) with private baths, telephone, and TV. Shady side garden. Three blocks to the square, Red Line, Charles Hotel, restaurants, and shops. Air conditioning; TV; no smoking. $81.

Cambridge Suite. This large home, circa 1855, is on a quiet road only three blocks from bustling Harvard Square. The first-floor guest suite has a queen bedroom and sitting room with sofa and desk. Breakfast served in the dining room. Near William James Hall and law school. Red Line three blocks. Air conditioning. No smoking. $95.

The Missing Bell. Antiques, extraordinary detailed woodwork in this large Victorian, circa 1883, on a quiet street. Young, welcoming hosts offer two spacious second-floor guest rooms with private baths; one with a queen-size bed and the other with a double bed. Air conditioning. Fireplace in the dining room. Parlor for guests. Restaurants, shops, Harvard and Porter Squares, and subway are all nearby. No smoking. On-street parking. $85.

Near Harvard Square. Just a seven-minute walk to the square, Harvard Yard, Brattle Street, and Red Line. Quiet. Shady location. European decor. Coffee ground

fresh for breakfast. Private first-floor guest room with double bed. Air conditioning; TV; shared bath. $75.

True Victorian. Host's Victorian jewel sits on a quiet hill near Massachusetts Avenue between Harvard and Porter squares. Three second-floor guest rooms—two with double bed, TV, and desk; king room. Guest rooms are air-conditioned. Only two rooms booked at a time. Shared family bath. Hearty breakfast in sunny kitchen, often self-serve on weekdays. Red Line and train at Porter Square three blocks. TV; no smoking. $68.

The Missing Bell

16 Sacramento Street, 02138
(617) 876-0987

This 1883 Queen Anne Victorian is exceptionally beautiful with its unusual hand-carved woodwork, stained-glass windows, and elegant spaces. The spacious guest rooms, carefully furnished with antiques, have private baths, comfortable beds, and air conditioning. Breakfast often gets rave reviews. Served in the dining room, it includes hot-from-the-oven baked goods, a special fruit dish, and freshly ground coffee. Close to Harvard; six blocks to subway at Harvard Square.

Hosts: Kristin Quinlan and J. P. Massar
Rooms: 2 (PB) $85
Continental Breakfast
Credit Cards: A, B
Notes: 2, 5, 7, 9

CAPE COD

Bed and Breakfast Greater Boston and Cape Cod

P.O. Box 35, Newtonville, 02160
(617) 964-1606; (800) 832-2632
FAX (617) 964-1606

Great Pond House. A beautiful contemporary home in a secluded area on the shores of Great Pond. Only a few miles from the beaches of the bay and ocean. Whale watching and charter fishing are available from nearby harbors. The large master guest room has a private bath, queen-size bed, and color TV. A second large guest room has a waterview, two twin beds, and private hall bath. Guests are invited to relax in the living room, sit on the deck, or simply enjoy the lovely gardens and grounds around the house. Continental plus breakfast. No smoking allowed. Open May through September. $85.

The Inn on the Beach. This 1880 Victorian inn offers magnificent views of Cape Cod Bay. "The Mansion" has seven beautifully decorated, sun-filled rooms, all with private baths. Some rooms have private balconies. "The Cottage" has two suites with outdoor, beach-side patios. One suite has separate bedroom, eat-in galley kitchen, and sitting room. "The Guest House" is a Cape Cod-style home that has five suites perfect for short or longer stays. All offer waterviews; some have kitchens. A generous Continental breakfast is included for guests at "The Mansion," served in the waterfront dining room, front veranda, sun parlor, or gazebo, weather permitting. In cooler weather, enjoy a cozy respite by the fire. The Mansion, Guest House, and Cottage may be rented for meetings, weddings, and special occasions. Open year-round. Children welcome in Guest House and Cottage. $75-150.

CATAUMET

Bed and Breakfast Cape Cod
P.O. Box 341, West Hyannisport, 02672-0341
(508) 775-2772; FAX (508) 775-2884

46. Cataumet is a quiet rural village at the western edge of Cape Cod. Buzzards Bay, a mile from the house, has fine warm-water swimming in the summer and fine beaches. The Edwardian-style home, built in 1910, has two guest rooms with queen-size beds

and private baths. The full Continental breakfast is served in the dining room or on the deck overlooking the grounds. The ferry to Martha's Vineyard is 20 minutes away. This quiet family setting is ideal for relaxing in a special Cape Cod setting. No smoking. $75-95.

CENTERVILLE

Adam's Terrace Gardens Inn
539 Main Street, 02632
(508) 775-4707

A quaint old sea captain's home is surrounded by beautiful gardens. Excellent for touring all parts of the enchanting Cape, islands, Nantucket, and Martha's Vineyard. Within walking distance to church, library, and world-famous Craigville Beach.

Host: Louise Pritchard
Rooms: 8 (5 PB; 3 SB) $65-95
Full Breakfast
Credit Cards: A, B, C
Notes: 2, 5, 7, 8, 11, 12

Adam's Terrace Gardens Inn

Bed and Breakfast Cape Cod
P.O. Box 341, West Hyannisport, 02672-0341
(508) 775-2772; FAX (508) 775-2884

43. This quiet bed and breakfast overlooks Lake Wequaquet, the largest freshwater lake on Cape Cod. The second floor has

Bed and Breakfast Cape Cod (continued)

been set aside for guests, featuring two rooms that share a bath. A first-floor room offers a king-size bed and a private bath. Continental breakfast. $55-65.

63. On the banks of a beautiful freshwater lake amid a grove of trees and with fresh breezes stands a 140-year-old contemporary home offering a suite. It is never booked to more than one party at a time in either a room with a queen-size bed or a room with twin beds. The living room has TV and VCR and a wonderful lakeview. Swim, fish, and relax on the dock, all outside guests' private deck. Within minutes of wonderful shops, fine restaurants, and the ferry to either Martha's Vineyard or Nantucket. A great honeymooners' hideaway. No smoking. Children over 12 welcome. $60-125.

67. This is a comfortable bed and breakfast host home overlooking beautiful Lake Wequaquet. Beautifully landscaped grounds and lake waterviews are part of the natural appeal of this accommodation. Room one, on the first floor, has a private bath and king-size bed. Room two is a small room with a twin bed and a shared bath. A Continental plus breakfast is served from 8 to 10 A.M. in the dining area. Enjoy freshwater swimming in the nearby lake and visit Hyannis—the population center of the Cape, just a short drive away. $65.

82. Lake Wequaquet is the largest freshwater lake on Cape Cod. Nestled along the banks of the lake is this expanded home featuring two bedrooms that share a bath. The guest rooms have either a king-size or a double bed. Great swimming, fishing, or simply sitting on the banks of the lake are but some of the pleasures here. The great restaurants, shops, and the ferry to either

Martha's Vineyard or Nantucket are four miles away. Continental breakfast is served daily. A great spot for a family of up to four persons. No smoking. $60.

Bed and Breakfast/ Inns of New England

128 South Hoop Pole Road, Guilford, CT 06437
(203) 457-0042; (800) 582-0853

MA-1045. This inn offers the warmth and luxury of a Victorian home in the romantic ambience of an earlier time. Guest rooms have hardwood floors of cherry, maple, and oak, Oriental carpets, and antiques. Privacy is assured, for this 100-year-old home was designed so that no two guest rooms share the same wall. Five suites with private bath (two more with a shared bath), fireplaces, cathedral ceilings, roof deck, and a private library make this inn unique. Garden cottage with queen-size bed, wraparound porch, and private bath also available. $95-135.

Copper Beech Inn

497 Main Street, 02632
(508) 771-5488

Built in 1830 by an intercoastal ship captain, this charmingly restored house is now on the National Register of Historic Places. It

Copper Beech Inn

stands amid tall trees, including the largest European beech tree on Cape Cod. Interior features include a parlor and a common room for guest use. Walk to Craigville Beach, one of the ten best beaches in the United States. Hyannis, the population center of the Cape, where the ferry to Nantucket and Martha's Vineyard is boarded, is four miles away. Air-conditioned. Two-night minimum stay is required for May 25 through October 10. Smoking limited.

Host: Joyce Diehl
Rooms: 3 (PB) $90
Full Breakfast
Credit Cards: A, B, D
Notes: 2, 5, 9, 10, 11, 12

The Old Hundred House

1211 Craigville Beach Road, 02632
(508) 775-6166

An old sea captain's home in a quiet coun-try village. Within easy travel of many points of interest, shops, restaurants, churches, etc. Two- to three-minute walk from one of the best beaches on the Cape. Rooms are nicely furnished, airy, and sunny. The great veranda is very popular and gets a constant southwest breeze, keep-ing it cool.

Hosts: Jack and Marina Downes
Rooms: 7 (SB) $45-58
Continental Breakfast
Notes: 2, 7, 8, 9, 10, 11, 12

CHARLESTOWN (BOSTON)

Bed and Breakfast Associates Bay Colony, Ltd.

P.O. Box 57166, Babson Park, Boston, 02157-0166
(617) 449-5302; (800) 347-5088
FAX (617) 449-5958

M466. This ground-level apartment offers privacy and space in an 1870s Victorian townhouse near the base of the famed Bunker Hill Monument. The private entry suite features an antique double bed, a Pull-man kitchen, a small living room with

sleeper-sofa, TV, and private bath. Weekly rates offered. $88.

CHATHAM

Bed and Breakfast Associates Bay Colony, Ltd.

P.O. Box 57166, Babson Park, Boston, 02157-0166
(617) 449-5302; (800) 347-5088
FAX (617) 449-5958

CC475. The hostess invites guests to share this sprawling Cape-style home with its Early American decor. This wooded setting is perfect for country walks. Nearby is the village of Chatham, renowned for its trea-sure trove of galleries, shops, ice cream par-lors, and restaurants in a gracious, old-fashioned, seaside setting. Three guest rooms, some with private baths. Continental breakfast; children welcome; no smoking. $68-83.

Bed and Breakfast Cape Cod

P.O. Box 341, West Hyannisport, 02672-0341
(508) 775-2772; FAX (508) 775-2884

12. This reproduction of an Early American Cape Cod home offers a first-floor room with a private bath, double bed; the second floor offers two rooms with double beds. (These rooms are never rented separately, so they share a "private" bath.) Continental breakfast. A short walk to the village, fish pier, and the beach. $65.

42. Built in 1973, this Cape Cod-style house has a large second-floor bedroom with extra long double bed and private bath for guests. The house is in an area occupied by many birds and natural wildlife. The hosts offer a Continental plus breakfast each morning served in the dining area or on the deck. Relax here or walk to all village locations including the beach, shops, restaurants, summer theater, and band concerts in the park in the summer. $65.

7 No smoking; 8 Children welcome; 9 Social drinking allowed; 10 Tennis nearby; 11 Swimming nearby; 12 Golf nearby; 13 Skiing nearby; 14 May be booked through a travel agent.

Bed and Breakfast Cape Cod (continued)

62. This spacious Colonial designed home built in 1946 is in one of the most prestigious parts of the village of Chatham. The house has three private baths, air-conditioned bedrooms, all of which are tastefully done and very comfortable. Breakfast is served in a sunny, bright summer room overlooking the two reflecting pools. Lovely grounds add to the charm of the house and complete a wonderful accommodation. One-half mile away are the beaches, lighthouse, fine restaurants, and much more. No smoking. No children. $95-150.

65. This Cape Cod-style home built more than 40 years ago was expanded in 1987 and now is a spacious, convenient, and beautifully maintained home. It is only a few hundred yards from Oyster Pond, an ocean inlet, and only one mile from popular Hardings Beach on the Atlantic Ocean. The guest rooms on the second floor are always rented to one party at a time ensuring privacy and an accommodation that will comfortably suit four persons. Air-conditioned and with glimpses of the ocean, it is a quiet and relaxing environment. No smoking. No children. $70-85.

66. Hardings Beach, a popular ocean setting, is a five-minute walk from this Cape Cod-style house. Two bedrooms have either king-size or twin beds and private baths. The Continental plus breakfast is served in the dining room. The comfortable guest sitting room has a TV and VCR. The guest bedrooms are air-conditioned. The decor is traditional. This lovely clean home is ideal for quiet relaxing in one of the most popular areas. No smoking. No children under nine. $80.

76. The village of Chatham offers something for everyone. This home, in a quiet residential area, has three guest rooms with private baths. Living room with TV as well as a deck that is great for relaxing after a day at the beach or shopping in the village. Immaculate and beautifully decorated. Continental breakfast served. $65-70.

Bed and Breakfast Greater Boston and Cape Cod

P.O. Box 35, Newtonville, 02160
(617) 964-1606; (800) 832-2632
FAX (617) 322-8572

Classic Cape. Privacy and charm at this classic Cape Cod-style home, close to some of the area's most beautiful beaches and rugged shoreline. Guest accommodation has a separate entrance leading up to a large, sunny room with a double and twins, plus a full private bath. Downstairs there is a guest sitting room with fireplace. A delicious and generous Continental breakfast is served. No smoking; open year-round. Two-night minimum stay. Infants and children over 12 are welcome. $75-85.

The Bradford Inn and Motel

26 Cross Street, P.O. Box 750, 02633
(508) 945-1030; (800) CHATHAM (242-8420)

The Bradford Inn and Motel is a unique complex of 25 rooms in the quaint seaside village of Chatham. Rooms have king- and queen-size canopied beds. There are eleven fireplaces, cable TV, telephones, and air conditioning. It is within the historic district, a short stroll from charming shops, theaters, concerts, restaurants, beach, golf, and tennis. Yet the accommodations are in a secluded area away from the hustle of the village proper. Outdoor heated pool. Full beverage license.

Hosts: William and Audrey Gray
Rooms: 25 (PB) $80-175
Full Breakfast
Credit Cards: A, B, C, D
Notes: 2, 3, 5, 7, 8, 9, 10, 11, 12, 14

NOTES: Credit cards accepted: A MasterCard; B Visa; C American Express; D Discover; E Diners Club; F Other; 2 Personal checks accepted; 3 Lunch available; 4 Dinner available; 5 Open all year; 6 Pets welcome;

Carriage House Inn

407 Old Harbor Road, 02633
(508) 945-4688

A small, cozy bed and breakfast with splendid breakfasts! Charming antique home tastefully restored, furnished with antiques and family pieces. Six light and airy bedrooms with queen-size beds and private baths; air-conditioned; three carriage house rooms have working fireplaces. Fireplaced living room with piano, farmer's porch, deck, and spacious grounds are all available for guests' enjoyment. Home-baked Continental plus breakfast. Guest pantry stocked with beverages and homemade cookies. Easy walk to village and fish pier. Bicycles and beach towels available. Friendly golden retriever, Sadie, in residence. Come relax awhile with these hosts!

Hosts: Pam and Tom Patton
Rooms: 6 (PB) $75-150
Continental Breakfast
Credit Cards: A, B, C
Notes: 2, 5, 7, 9, 10, 11,12, 14

Cranberry Inn at Chatham

359 Main Street, 02633
(508) 945-9232; (800) 332-4667
FAX (508) 945-3769

Chatham's oldest inn has been completely renovated. Conveniently in the heart of the historic village district within steps of shopping, dining, and beautiful beaches. Each of the 18 guest rooms is individually appointed and furnished with antiques and reproductions. All private baths. Rooms with fireplaces, balconies, and wet bars available. Spacious, deluxe suite available with fireplace and loft. Homemade breakfast including hot selections is served daily. Hospitable hosts and staff. There is also a pub with fireplace.

Hosts: Ray and Brenda Raffurty
Rooms: 18 (PB) $79-205
Full Breakfast
Credit Cards: A, B, C
Notes: 2, 5, 7, 9, 10, 11, 12, 14

The Cyrus Kent House

The Cyrus Kent House Inn

63 Cross Street, 02633
(800) 338-5368

Comfortably elegant, the inn is an award-winning restoration of a 19th-century sea captain's mansion. Rooms are large, bright, and airy, furnished with antiques. Private baths, telephone, and TV. On a quiet lane in the quaint seaside village of Chatham, a historic district. Excellent restaurants and beaches are within steps. Children over ten are welcome.

Host: Sharon Mitchell Swan
Rooms: 10 (PB) $75-165
Continental Breakfast
Credit Cards: A, B
Notes: 2, 5, 7, 9, 10, 11, 12, 14

CHILMARK (MARTHA'S VINEYARD)

Breakfast at Tiasquam

Rural Route 1, Box 296, 02535
(508) 645-3685

Breakfast at Tiasquam is set among the farms, ponds, woodlands, and rolling pastures of Martha's Vineyard, on the peak of a hill, well off the beaten path. Just minutes away is Lucy Vincent, one of the most beautiful beaches on the entire East Coast. A delicious full country breakfast is served. A beautifully decorated and smoke-free

Breakfast at Tiasquam

house with attention paid to craftsmanship, privacy, comfort, and quiet. Breakfast at Tiasquam will make every stay on Martha's Vineyard truly unforgettable.

Host: Ron Crowe
Rooms: 8 (2 PB; 6 SB) $70-195
Full Breakfast
Credit Cards: None
Notes: 2, 5, 7, 8, 9, 10, 11, 12

COLRAIN

Bed and Breakfast Inns of New England

128 South Hoop Pole Road, Guilford, CT 06437
(203) 457-0042; (800) 582-0853

MA1014. Guests love this 160-acre working farm in the hills of northwestern Massachusetts. A 19th-century farmhouse offers comfortable lodgings with private or shared baths. Explore woodland trails, sweeping pastures, and panoramic views that wind through some of the most beautiful hill country in New England. Dotting the landscape are longwool sheep, graceful llamas, gentle Norwegian Fjord horses, cows, and goats. For those guests who wish to experience farm life firsthand, there are a variety of activities for all levels of interest and skill. Box stalls are available, by prior reservation, for guests' horses. Enjoy the many area attractions including the fine dining, arts, and entertainment available in the Berkshires and southern Vermont. No smoking. $55-75.

Covered Bridge

P.O. Box 447, Norfolk, CT 06058
(203) 542-5944

1COMA. This 160-acre working farm is in the hills of northwestern Massachusetts and offers a charming 19th-century farmhouse with unusual timber frame construction and exposed beams. There are four guest rooms; one has a whirlpool bathtub. Horsedrawn rides and llama hikes are a special additional feature available at this secluded getaway. A breakfast buffet is offered daily. $55-75.

CONCORD

Bed and Breakfast Greater Boston and Cape Cod

P.O. Box 35, Newtonville, 02160
(617) 964-1606; (800) 832-2632
FAX (617) 332-8572

1775 Colonial Inn. Just 20 miles west of Boston with easy access to main highways, this meticulously restored Colonial inn offers five guest rooms, all with private baths, color TV, air conditioning, and telephones. Hearty Continental buffet breakfast is served in the mornings, and afternoon tea or sherry is served by the fireplace in the 200-year-old sitting room. Fitness club facilities only a short walk from the inn. $85-95.

Bed and Breakfast/ Inns of New England

128 South Hoop Pole Road, Guilford, CT 06437
(203) 457-0042; (800) 582-0853

MA-1009. This 1775 center-chimney Colonial has hand-hewn beams, gunstock posts, handsome six-over-six windows, and 18th-century paneling or molding. Guest rooms have double and queen-size beds; all have private bathrooms, direct-dial telephone, color TV, and individual climate control.

NOTES: Credit cards accepted: A MasterCard; B Visa; C American Express; D Discover; E Diners Club; F Other; 2 Personal checks accepted; 3 Lunch available; 4 Dinner available; 5 Open all year; 6 Pets welcome;

The inn is two miles from Walden Pond and within a one-minute walk from the Concord Fitness Center, where visitors can stretch, swim, and sauna as a guest of the inn. No smoking. No pets. $85-95.

Colonel Roger Brown

1694 Main Street, 01742
(508) 369-9119; (800) 292-1369

This 1775 Colonial home is on the historic register and close to the Concord and Lexington historic districts, 15 miles west of Boston and Cambridge. Five rooms with air conditioning, private baths, color TV, and telephones. Continental plus breakfast and complimentary beverages at all times. Complimentary use of Concord Fitness Club adjacent to inn. Comfortable and cozy atmosphere. Inquire about accommodations for children.

Host: Lauri Berlied
Rooms: 5 (PB) $75-90
Continental Breakfast
Credit Cards: A, B, C, E
Notes: 2, 5, 7, 9, 10, 11, 12, 13, 14

Greater Boston Hospitality

P.O. Box 1142, Brookline, 02146
(617) 277-5430

44. This center entrance Colonial was built in 1775 by a minuteman when the British arrived in Concord. Hand-hewn beams, gunstock posts, six-over-six windows and raised paneling and molding were lovingly restored in 1879 and 1986. Today it is a five-bedroom inn, each with private bath. Guests enjoy quiet reading or conversation in front of a roaring fire in a 200-year-old sitting room. For more strenuous activity, guests may walk to a private fitness club where guests have a complimentary membership. There is an excellent, bountiful Continental breakfast. Each room has direct-dial telephone, color TV, and is air-conditioned. Children are considered on an individual basis. No smoking. Ample parking. $75-100.

Hawthorne Inn

462 Lexington Road, 01742
(508) 369-5610; FAX (508) 287-4949

Built circa 1870 on land once owned by Emerson, Hawthorne, and the Alcotts. Alongside the "battle road" of 1775 and within walking distance of authors' homes, battle sites, and Walden Pond. Furnished with antiques, handmade quilts, original artwork, Japanese prints, and sculpture.

Hosts: G. Burch and M. Mudry
Rooms: 7 (PB) $75-160
Continental Breakfast
Credit Cards: A, B, C, D
Notes: 2, 5, 8, 9, 10, 11, 12, 13, 14

CUMMAQUID

The Acworth Inn

4352 Old Kings Highway, P.O. Box 256, 02637
(508) 362-3330; (800) 362-6363

The Acworth Inn sits among the trees along the Old Kings Highway that winds through the historic, unspoiled north side of Cape Cod. Close to the renowned and quaint Barnstable Village, the Acworth Inn offers guests an opportunity to experience the gracious lifestyle of a bygone era. Built in 1860, the inn is a classic Cape house, completely renovated and outfitted with charming hand-painted pieces and colorful fabrics. From its central location, day trips to all points on the Cape,

The Acworth Inn

7 No smoking; 8 Children welcome; 9 Social drinking allowed; 10 Tennis nearby; 11 Swimming nearby; 12 Golf nearby; 13 Skiing nearby; 14 May be booked through a travel agent.

Martha's Vineyard, and Nantucket are easily accomplished.

Hosts: Jack and Cheryl Ferrell
Rooms: 6 (PB) $65-95
Continental Breakfast
Credit Cards: A, B, C, D
Notes: 2, 5, 7, 9, 10, 11, 12

Bed and Breakfast Associates Bay Colony, Ltd.

P.O. Box 57166, Babson Park, Boston, 02157-0166
(617) 449-5302; (800) 347-5088
FAX (617) 449-5958

CC220. Mid-Cape Barnstable County. On the North Shore of Cape Cod in the oldest historical district in the USA, this quaint Cape-style home has three spotless guest rooms (twin and queen-size), each with private bath. Full breakfast. Walk to Barnstable Harbor or Cape Cod Bay, or just relax on two and one-half acres of private grounds. Fine art galleries and restaurants nearby. $80-90.

Bed and Breakfast Cape Cod

P.O. Box 341, West Hyannisport, 02672-0341
(508) 775-2772; FAX (508) 775-2884

61. Just east of Barnstable, this house built in 1950 is a typical Cape Cod-style home with several acres of manicured grounds. Three guest rooms with private baths available. Hostess serves a full country breakfast with a Scandinavian flair. Hyannis and the ferry to Nantucket or Martha's Vineyard are four miles away. No smoking. No children. $65-90.

CUMMINGTON

Cumworth Farm

472 West Cummington Road, 01026
(413) 634-5529

A 200-year-old house with a sugar house and blueberry and raspberry fields on the premises. Pick berries in season. The farm

raises sheep and is close to Tanglewood, Smith College, the William Cullen Bryant Homestead, cross-country skiing, and hiking trails. Hot tub.

Hosts: Ed and Mary McColgan
Rooms: 6 (SB) $60
Full Breakfast
Credit Cards: None
Notes: 2, 5, 8, 9, 10, 11, 12, 13

DANVERS

Bed and Breakfast Marblehead and North Shore

P.O. Box 35, Newtonville, 02160
(617) 964-1606; (800) 832-2632
FAX (617) 332-8572

The Antique Sleigh Bed and Breakfast. A beautiful 1854 Colonial home on the National Register of Historic Places in an area originally known as "Olde Salem Village." Near Route 95, in the Salem and Marblehead area with easy access to Boston and the North Shore. Kid-friendly and family-friendly accommodations. Antiques and collectibles throughout, but many children can also touch and enjoy. Four beautiful rooms with shared baths. Roll aways are available at an additional cost. All rooms are air-conditioned and have color cable TV. Common room with TV and fireplace and full-sized swimming pool out back. No smoking. Children welcome. $75-85.

Greater Boston Hospitality

P.O. Box 1142, Brookline, 02146
(617) 277-5430

112. This 1854 historic home is close to all the North Shore attractions. TVs and air-conditioned. Two fireplaces in the house. Interesting antiques. Guests may enjoy the family room or swim in a beautifully landscaped, private swimming pool. Enjoy a full breakfast in lovely, old dining room. There are two queen-size bedrooms that share a bath. One bedroom has a single bed as well.

Also available are two cots, crib, and Port-a-crib. Parking included. Twenty dollars for extra person. $70.

DEERFIELD

Bed and Breakfast Inns of New England

128 South Hoop Pole Road, Guilford, CT 06437
(203) 457-0042; (800) 582-0853

MA1015. This architecturally intriguing multi-gabled early American home is near the historic district of Deerfield and adjacent to a historic battle site of 1675. Period antiques fill the guest porch, elegant dining room, and guest parlor. Choose from three guest rooms with shared or private baths and air conditioning. A special full breakfast is included. No pets. Children 12 and over are welcome. No smoking. $80-90.

DENNIS

Captain Nickerson Inn

333 Main Street, 02660
(508) 398-5966; (800) 282-1619

Delightful Victorian sea captain's home built in 1828 was changed to its present Queen Anne style in 1879. Comfortable front porch is lined with white wicker rockers and tables. There are five guest rooms decorated with period four-poster or white iron queen-size beds and Oriental or hand-woven rugs. Three rooms offer private baths and two rooms share a bath. The fireplaced living room is comfortable yet lovely and has a cable TV, VCR, and stained-glass windows. The dining room is also fireplaced and has a stained-glass picture window. The inn is on a bike path and offers bicycles to guests for a small fee. Popular board games are available for guests' use, as are a limited selection of video movies. The Cape Cod 20 plus-mile bike Rail Trail is only one-half mile from the inn. Area attractions include golf courses, beaches,

paddle boats, horseback riding, museums, Cape Playhouse, fishing, craft and antique shops, and a local church that houses the oldest working pipe organ in this country. Children of all ages are welcome. Smoking is restricted to the front porch.

Hosts: Pat and Dave York
Rooms: 5 (3 PB; 2 SB) $55-85
Full Breakfast
Credit Cards: A, B, D
Notes: 2, 5, 8, 9, 10, 11, 12, 14

The Four Chimneys Inn

The Four Chimneys Inn

946 Main Street, 02638
(508) 385-6317

Newly restored, spacious 1881 Victorian home with lovely gardens on Historic Route 6A. Across from Scargo Lake, it's a short walk to Cape Cod Bay beaches, the Cape Playhouse, art museum, restaurants, auctions, concerts, and shops. Golf, tennis, and bike trails within two miles. Central to all of Cape Cod. Closed November through March. Children over eight are welcome.

Hosts: Russell and Kathy Tomasetti
Rooms: 8 (PB) $75-105
Continental Breakfast
Credit Cards: A, B, C, D
Notes: 2, 7, 9, 10, 11, 12, 14

Isaiah Hall Bed and Breakfast Inn

P.O. Box 1007, 152 Whig Street, 02638
(508) 385-9928; (800) 736-0160

Enjoy country ambience and hospitality in the heart of Cape Cod. This lovely 1857 farmhouse is tucked away on a quiet historic sidestreet. Within walking distance of

7 No smoking; 8 Children welcome; 9 Social drinking allowed; 10 Tennis nearby; 11 Swimming nearby; 12 Golf nearby; 13 Skiing nearby; 14 May be booked through a travel agent.

the beach and village shops, restaurants, museums, cinema, and playhouse. Nearby bike trails, tennis, and golf. Comfortably appointed with antiques and Orientals. Excellent central location for day trips. Continental plus breakfast is served. Closed mid-October through April 1. Children over seven are welcome.

Host: Marie Brophy
Rooms: 11 (10 PB; 1 SB) $59-112
Continental Breakfast
Credit Cards: A, B, C
Notes: 2, 7, 9, 10, 11, 12, 14

DENNIS PORT

"By the Sea" Guests

8 Inman Road Ext & Chase Avenue
P.O. Box 507, 02639-0006
(508) 398-8685; (800) 447-9202
FAX (508) 398-0334

A delightful oceanfront bed and breakfast on its own spacious private beach. Warm, relaxing atmosphere. Comfortable rooms with private baths, color TVs, and refrigerators. Most rooms with oceanfront and seaviews. A Continental plus breakfast is included and served on 100-foot glass-screened enclosed veranda overlooking Nantucket Sound. Oversized living room with fireplace and color cable TV. Newly renovated. Conference and meeting rooms available. Restaurant on premises.

Hosts: The Kossifos Family
Rooms: 12 (PB) $65-125
Continental Breakfast
Credit Cards: A, B, C, E, F
Notes: 8, 9, 10, 11, 12, 14

The Rose Petal
Bed and Breakfast

152 Sea Street, Box 974, 02639
(508) 398-8470

A picturesque traditional New England home complete with picket fence invites guests to share this historic 1872 residence in a delightful seaside resort neighborhood.

The Rose Petal

Stroll past century-old homes to a sandy beach. Home-baked pastries highlight a full breakfast. A comfortable parlor offers TV, piano, and reading. Enjoy queen-size brass beds, antiques, hand-stitched quilts, and spacious and bright baths. Convenient to all Cape Cod's attractions. Air-conditioned rooms. AAA rated three diamonds. ABBA rated three crowns. Two-night minimum stay on holidays.

Hosts: Dan and Gayle Kelly
Rooms: 3 (2 PB; 1 SB) $50-89
Full Breakfast
Credit Cards: A, B, C
Notes: 2, 5, 7, 8, 9, 10, 11, 12, 14

DUXBURY (PLYMOUTH)

Bed and Breakfast/
Inns of New England

128 South Hoop Pole Road, Guilford, CT 06437
(203) 457-0042; (800) 582-0853

MA 1030. This bed and breakfast home is set in a quiet, wooded area. Enjoy the full breakfast on the deck, in the garden, or on the screened porch. The town, on Duxbury Bay, offers many examples of old homes dating from 1637 to 1870. The hosts provide a self-guided written tour of historic Duxbury and shuttle service to the beach. Great restaurants and beach only one mile away. Tennis courts are across the street. Three guest rooms, shared bath, central air, and fresh flowers in each guest room. Two-

NOTES: Credit cards accepted: A MasterCard; B Visa; C American Express; D Discover; E Diners Club; F Other; 2 Personal checks accepted; 3 Lunch available; 4 Dinner available; 5 Open all year; 6 Pets welcome;

night minimum during holidays. Children 13 and older are welcome. No smoking and no guest pets. $60-75.

EASTHAM

Bed and Breakfast Cape Cod

P.O. Box 341, West Hyannisport, 02672-0341
(508) 775-2772; FAX (508) 775-2884

54. This Cape Cod-style house built in 1972 stands along the banks of one of Cape Cod's many freshwater lakes. Pure drinking water to swim or fish in is 50 feet from the deck on the back of the house. The ocean beach is three miles away. Two bedrooms with either queen-size or double bed and private baths are available. A Continental breakfast is served from 8 to 10 A.M. The Cape Cod bike trails are a couple of blocks away from this quiet residential setting. No smoking. No children. $75.

72. This 60-year-old beach home is in the heart of what is now Cape Cod National Seashore Park. Enter from a private entrance to a living room with TV, library, and sitting area. Two bedrooms, one with a queen-size bed and one with a pair of twin beds, share the suite's bath. Casual, eclectic decor adds to the relaxed style of this popular beach setting. Continental breakfast from 7:30 to 9:30 A.M. Oceanview. No smoking. $120.

84. Standing in the midst of a grove of tall pines is a 1983 contemporary home built by the owners. There is a ground-floor suite with a king-size bed and a private bath with shower. The sitting area has a TV and sliders to a private porch. The private entrance makes this a quiet place for visitors. The Cape Cod Bike Trail is 100 yards from the house. Continental breakfast. No smoking allowed. $65.

85. Built in 1868 in the Fort Hill section of the village of Eastham, this house was restored within the past five years. It is now a wonderful bed and breakfast offering oceanviews, nature trails, and elegance in the accommodation. Two guest rooms with private baths are suites that have been beautifully decorated keeping the antique feel with the modern amenities that many seek. A great Continental plus breakfast is available each morning. Plan early; the season is from mid-June through August. A wonderful place to see and enjoy the ocean. No smoking. No children. $90-110.

Bed and Breakfast/ Inns of New England

128 South Hoop Pole Road, Guilford, CT 06437
(203) 457-0042; (800) 582-0853

MA 1050. A traditional two-story home in the secluded area on the shore of Great Pond. There is a 1927 Chickering Grand Piano in the music room. The large master bedroom and bath on the second floor has a queen-size bed and color TV. A second large bedroom with pond view has twin beds. A private bathroom is directly across from the bedroom. A Continental breakfast is served on the deck or in the dining room. No children; no smoking; no pets. $75-80.

Orleans Bed and Breakfast Associates

P.O. Box 1312, Orleans, 02653
(508) 255-3824; (800) 541-6226

The Aerie. This light-filled, attractive suite has a high outlook over the marsh with unimpeded view of Cape Cod Bay. Guests' own garage, entrance, king-size bed, private bath, refrigerator, and sitting area with TV. In addition, guests have a deck on which to sit and observe the spectacular sunsets. Breakfast is served in the main house. This is an interesting musical household. Private tennis courts nearby. $100.

---

7 No smoking; 8 Children welcome; 9 Social drinking allowed; 10 Tennis nearby; 11 Swimming nearby; 12 Golf nearby; 13 Skiing nearby; 14 May be booked through a travel agent.

Orleans Bed and Breakfast Associates (continued)

Bayside Path. An attractive, comfortable home in a wonderful location. Walk five minutes to beautiful private beach and scenic views of Cape Cod Bay. Home is nestled in secluded setting. Quiet bedrooms on first floor, one queen-size and one with twin beds, share modern bath. Comfortably furnished adjacent guest living room offers cable TV and VCR. Sunny deck overlooking woods for breakfast. Popular walking and biking area. $70.

Bread and Roses. Cozy, sunlit, modern suite. Two bedrooms with skylights, one double and one twin, separated by reading area with color TV. Bath has stall shower. Access to clean, freshwater pond for swimming and canoeing. Breakfast served in dining area or on sunny deck off music room. Artistic, musical hosts. Ideal for those traveling with children. $65.

Ocean Walk. A wooded path winds past the Three Sisters lighthouses and leads from this comfortable house to the Nauset Light Beach only two-tenths of a mile away. There is a large separate living room for guests with a fireplace, big windows, and deep couches to invite relaxed reading or TV watching. A queen bedroom includes a guest refrigerator and a private bath with an extra-large tub and shower. Hosts leave early to work with the Dolphin Fleet, so a nice Continental breakfast is laid out for guests to enjoy in privacy. $80.

Soft Winds. Staying here is like having a private, comfortable apartment. Guest wing with living room, kitchen, bath, bedroom, and personal deck. Cable TV with HBO. Continental breakfast foods on hand. On a bike path, convenient to beaches and ponds. $90.

Spindrift. Delightful wing of old house just five-minute walk to Coast Guard Beach. Near bike path. Private entrance into library-sitting room with windows facing ocean. Queen or twin room with private bath. Patio. Interesting hosts offer privacy or great hospitality as guests wish. Breakfast served on dishes made by the host, a potter who maintains a shop in Orleans. $120.

Sylvanus Knowles House. Magnificent views of Nauset Marsh and leisurely walks on historic Fort Hill surround this impeccably restored 1838 Greek Revival farmhouse. The original house contains two guest rooms furnished with fine antiques. One romantic suite has a private library and sitting room, bedroom with lace-canopied bed, and elegant bathroom featuring an oversized tub and window seat. Upstairs, a quaint, airy double room has its own private bath, hall, and dressing room. Breakfast served in elegant dining room. $90-110.

Tory Hill. An old Cape house with a private entrance into separate guest wing. Twin sitting room with vanity and refrigerator. Full private bath. Guests are invited to share the adjoining family room and lovely patio with hosts. Owners have a specialized antique business in an adjacent barn, and everything reflects their lively interest. Walk to the ice cream parlor from here! Three-fourths of a mile to Bay Beach and two miles to the ocean. $75.

Windmill View. An adult-sized dollhouse just perfect for two or with one small child ($20 extra), with separate entrance and parking space. Exceptionally gracious, hospitable hosts will serve breakfast in the house or on the sunny patio. A spacious double bedroom with TV plus single convertible couch. Fully equipped eat-in kitchen and full bath (as well as warm-water

NOTES: Credit cards accepted: A MasterCard; B Visa; C American Express; D Discover; E Diners Club; F Other; 2 Personal checks accepted; 3 Lunch available; 4 Dinner available; 5 Open all year; 6 Pets welcome;

outside shower). This little house sits in a uniquely landscaped garden with grassy lawn and a path leading to Long Pond for freshwater bathing. A short walk to convenience store and library. Close to National Seashore Visitors Center. $80.

The Over Look Inn

The Over Look Inn Cape Cod

3085 County Road, Route 6, 02642
(508) 255-1886

Victorian mansion across from Cape Cod National Seashore offering Scottish hospitality. Antique-filled guest rooms, all with private baths, and the garden room with working fireplace and porch. Victorian parlor for afternoon tea. Winston Churchill library, Hemingway billiard room, and Edward Hopper dining room where a full leisurely breakfast is served each morning. Excellent biking and wildlife sanctuary nearby.

Hosts: The Aitchison Family
Rooms: 10 (PB) $95-125
Full Breakfast
Credit Cards: A, B, C, D, E
Notes: 2, 5, 8, 9, 10, 11, 12, 14

The Whalewalk Inn

220 Bridge Road, 02642
(508) 255-0617

The gracious, welcoming hosts of this inn promise guests an unspoiled environment

on outer Cape Cod—one of the country's most beautiful areas. On a back road, the site consists of three acres. Only minutes by car or bike to beaches, bike trails, or Orleans Village. This 1830s home has been authentically restored and creatively decorated with handsome antiques. The seven guest rooms and five large suites with full kitchens are furnished with a mix of country antiques, fine linens, and local art. All rooms have private baths; some suites have fireplaces. Breakfast and afternoon hors d'oeuvres are served.

Hosts: Carolyn and Richard Smith
Rooms: 12 (PB) $95-175
Full Breakfast
Credit Cards: A, B
Notes: 2, 7, 9, 10, 11, 12, 14

EAST ORLEANS

Bed and Breakfast Cape Cod

P.O. Box 341, West Hyannisport, 02672-0341
(508) 775-2772; FAX (508) 775-2884

11. This Cape Cod house was built in 1928 and expanded in 1990, adding a lovely ground-floor suite. It offers a private entrance, a large living room with a twin pull-out, a dining area, and a fully equipped kitchen. The bedroom has a queen-size bed and private bath with shower. Very convenient to the village and only a mile from Nauset Beach, one of the best beaches on the East Coast. The hostess provides a Continental breakfast each morning. An ideal private accommodation for up to four persons. $100.

25. This Cape Cod-style house offers a second-floor suite with a pair of twin beds that convert to king-size, private bath, and a separate sitting room with studio couch and twin pull-out. The village is one mile away, and the host will pick up and drop off guests at Nauset Beach. Continental breakfast. No smoking. $65.

7 No smoking; 8 Children welcome; 9 Social drinking allowed; 10 Tennis nearby; 11 Swimming nearby; 12 Golf nearby; 13 Skiing nearby; 14 May be booked through a travel agent.

73. This very special Colonial-style house offers one suite. The honeymoon suite offers queen-size bed, Jacuzzi for two, skylights, private entrance, and Victorian decor. Full breakfast is served each morning. Harbor is one hundred yards away. Children over seven. $150.

Bed and Breakfast/ Inns of New England

128 South Hoop Pole Road, Guilford, CT 06437
(203) 457-0042; (800) 582-0853

MA 1048. Built over 170 years ago, this inn is a restored sea captain's home that offers travelers the charm of old-style New England lodging with all the conveniences the modern guest has learned to expect. Enjoy the Continental breakfast that includes homemade breads. Each of 19 guest rooms is individually decorated in nautical style with Colonial color schemes and antiques. Some rooms have ocean views, and the master suite has a working fireplace. Enjoy the beautiful sand-duned Nauset Beach. Swimming and tennis on premises. Children over 12 welcome. Limited smoking. No guest pets. $50-100.

The Farmhouse

163 Beach Road, Orleans, 02653
(508) 255-6654

This 19th-century farmhouse has been carefully restored and furnished to provide a unique blend of country life in a seashore

The Farmhouse

setting. Short walk to Nauset Beach, close to sailing, golf, tennis, bike trails, theater, fishing, shopping, museums, and surfing. Some oceanview rooms. Breakfast is served on an oceanview deck. Licensed establishment. Limited smoking allowed. Children six and over welcome.

Hosts: The Standishes
Rooms: 8 (PB) $42-95
Continental Breakfast
Credit Cards: A, B
Notes: 2, 5, 9, 10, 11, 12, 14

Nauset House Inn

143 Beach Road, Box 774, 02643
(508) 255-2195

The Nauset House Inn is a place where the gentle amenities of life are still observed, a place where sea and shore, orchard and field all combine to create a perfect setting for tranquil relaxation. The Nauset House Inn is ideally near one of the world's great ocean beaches, yet is close to antique and craft shops, restaurants, art galleries, scenic paths, and remote places for sunning, swimming, and picnicking. Continental breakfast available for lesser rate. Closed November 1 through March 31.

Hosts: Diane and Al Johnson, Cindy and
    John Vessella
Rooms: 14 (8 PB; 6 SB) $75-115
Full Breakfast
Credit Cards: A, B
Notes: 2, 7, 9, 10, 11, 12

Orleans Bed and Breakfast Associates

P.O. Box 1312, Orleans, 02653
(508) 255-3824; (800) 541-6226

Kadee's Gray Elephant. Brightly painted wicker, lace, and patchwork quilts set the theme of six charming studios in the heart of East Orleans, one mile to Nauset Beach. Guests are welcome to a queen-size bed, fully equipped kitchen, air conditioning, bath, telephone, and cable TV. Thoroughly romantic and private. $110-120.

Kadee's Seaside. This waterfront suite has a spectacular view of East Orleans Marina and sits beside the salt water leading to Pleasant Bay, private beaches, and the Atlantic. Wraparound veranda is graced with wicker, flowers, and porch swing for guests to enjoy the comings and goings of boats, both motor and sail. Two private entrances to guest suite that is cooled with a ceiling fan, floor to ceiling windows, or air conditioning. Comfort abounds with a queen-size bed, private bath, TV, telephone, beverage refrigerator, and coffee maker. Chilly?...a fireplace too. Continental breakfast. $160.

The Lyttle House. A sunny new apartment with separate entrance. Living room with single sofa-sleeper, cable TV, phone. Nice dining area and full kitchen stocked for breakfast. A separate queen bedroom and modern bath with shower. Private deck. Children welcome ($20 extra per child; crib provided). Excellent location for biking to Nauset Beach. $100.

The Red Geranium. From the moment guests step into this lovely country Cape, they will feel the warmth of home. Comfortable bedrooms decorated with heirloom treasures, double or twin beds. Large bath and cozy sitting room. Guest wing with separate entrance, living room, complete kitchen, and romantic bedroom with queen-size bed and private bath. All guest rooms have individually controlled air conditioning and cable TV. Breakfast is served buffet-style in a beautifully appointed Colonial dining room in the Main House. A bike ride to Nauset Beach, walk to East Orleans village and fine dining. $78-110.

Seasounds. This spectacular contemporary home, within the sound of the surf, is a short walk to the Atlantic Ocean. King-size master suite has bath with Jacuzzi ensuite and a private deck. A second, queen-size

bedroom also has a private bath. Hosts are expert gardeners and the lovely shaded grounds display their talents. $90-110.

The Parsonage Inn

The Parsonage Inn

202 Main Street, P.O. Box 1501, 02643
(508) 255-8217

Originally a parsonage, circa 1770, this full Cape home is now a cozy, romantic inn only one and one-half miles from one of Cape Cod's most beautiful beaches, Nauset Beach. All eight rooms are uniquely decorated with country antiques, quilts, and stenciling and each has a private bath. A bountiful breakfast is served either in the dining room or under sunny skies on the patio. Continental plus breakfast. Appetizers are served in the evening in the parlor where guests can mingle while perusing menus of the many fine restaurants. Children over six are welcome.

Hosts: Ian and Elizabeth Browne
Rooms: 8 (PB) $75-105
Continental Breakfast
Credit Cards: A, B, C
Notes: 2, 5, 9, 10, 11, 12, 14

Ship's Knees Inn

186 Beach Road, P.O. Box 756, 02643
(508) 255-1312

A 170-year-old restored sea captain's home; rooms individually appointed with their own Colonial color schemes and authentic antiques. Only a three-minute walk to popular sand-duned Nauset Beach. Swimming pool and tennis on premises. Also available three miles away, overlooking Orleans Cove, are an efficiency and two heated cottages. Children over 12 are welcome.

Rooms: 22 (8 PB; 14 SB) $45-100
Continental Breakfast
Credit Cards: A, B
Notes: 2, 5, 7, 9, 10, 11, 12, 14

EAST SANDWICH

Spring Garden

578 Route 6A, P.O. Box 867, 02537
(508) 888-0710

Charming country inn. Tranquil, panoramic views of salt marsh and Tidal Creek from deck or patio. Color cable TV, air conditioning, room telephones, refrigerators, efficiencies, one suite, pool, or walk to private beach. Free generous Continental breakfast. All guest rooms are individually decorated with pillow shams, comforters, dust ruffles, and decorator sheets. Beamed ceilings. Central to entire Cape, Boston, and Newport.

Hosts: Marvin and Judith Gluckman
Rooms: 11 (PB) $39-65
Continental Breakfast
Credit Cards: A, B, C, D
Notes: 2, 8, 10, 11, 12

EDGARTOWN (MARTHA'S VINEYARD)

The Arbor

222 Upper Main Street, P.O. Box 1228, 02539
(508) 627-8137

This turn-of-the-century home was originally built on the adjoining island of Chappaquiddick and moved by barge to its present location. A short stroll to village shops, fine restaurants, and the bustling activity of Edgartown Harbor, The Arbor is filled with the fragrance of fresh flowers. Peggy will gladly direct visitors to the walking trails, unspoiled beaches, fishing, and all the delights of Martha's Vineyard.

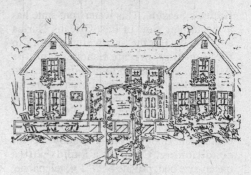

The Arbor

Host: Peggy Hall
Rooms: 10 (8 PB; 2 SB) $65-135
Continental Breakfast
Credit Cards: A, B, F
Notes: 2, 7, 9, 10, 11, 12, 14

Bed and Breakfast Nantucket/ Martha's Vineyard

P.O. Box 341, West Hyannisport, 02672-0341
(508) 775-2772; FAX (508) 775-2884

204. This 1840s sea captain's house offers 11 rooms with private baths, some with fireplaces. The decor is Victorian. Transportation to the beach is right outside the door, and a short walk takes guests to the village shops and restaurants. Continental breakfast. Children over 11 welcome. $110-185.

Captain Dexter House of Edgartown

35 Pease's Point Way, P.O. Box 2798, 02539
(508) 627-7289

This historic inn offers both charm and hospitality. Enjoy beautiful gardens. Savor a home-baked Continental breakfast and evening apéritif. Relax in a four-poster, lace-canopied bed in a room with a working fireplace. Stroll to the harbor, town, and restaurants. Bicycle or walk to the beach. Let the innkeepers make a vacation special! Continental plus breakfast.

Hosts: Rick and Birdie
Rooms: 11 (PB) $65-190

NOTES: Credit cards accepted: A MasterCard; B Visa; C American Express; D Discover; E Diners Club; F Other; 2 Personal checks accepted; 3 Lunch available; 4 Dinner available; 5 Open all year; 6 Pets welcome;

Continental Breakfast
Credit Cards: A, B, C, E
Notes: 2, 8, 9, 10, 11, 12, 14

The Charlotte Inn

27 South Summer Street, 02539
(508) 627-4751

Fine English antiques and fireplaces in a
romantic garden setting with private courtyards and porches. Has 24 impeccably
maintained and individually decorated
guest rooms. Attention to detail is the Charlotte Inn's trademark. Walking distance to
shops, beaches, tennis, and sailing. Excellent French restaurant called l'Étoile in the
inn. Serves dinner and Sunday brunch.
Member of Relais and Chateaux. Voted one
of two Country House Hotels of the year—
Andrew Harper's Hideaway Report.

Hosts: Gery and Paula Conover
Rooms: 25 (PB) $125-650
Full or Continental Breakfast
Credit Cards: A, B, C
Notes: 2, 4, 5, 9, 10, 11, 12

Colonial Inn of Martha's Vineyard

38 North Water Street, P.O. Box 68, 02539
(508) 627-4711; (800) 627-4701

In the heart of historic Edgartown overlooking the harbor, sits the Colonial Inn. It
offers 42 newly renovated and lovingly
refurbished rooms, all with heat, air conditioning, color TV, telephone, and private
bath. Continental breakfast is served daily
in the solarium and garden courtyard.
Affordable luxury. Closed January
through March.

Host: Linda Malcouronne
Rooms: 42 (PB) $65-213
Continental Breakfast
Credit Cards: A, B, C
Notes: 2, 3, 4, 8, 9, 10, 11, 12, 14

The Edgartown Inn

56 North Water Street, 02539
(508) 627-4794

Historic inn built in 1798 as the home for
whaling Captain Worth. Early guests
included Daniel Webster, Nathaniel
Hawthorne, and Charles Summer. Later,
John Kennedy stayed here as a young senator. Completely restored over the last 150
years, today it is filled with antiques. Convenient to beaches, harbor, and restaurants. Famous for breakfast, including
homemade breads and cakes.

Hosts: Liliane and Earle Radford
Rooms: 20 (16 PB; 4 SB) $85-180
Full and Continental Breakfast
Credit Cards: None
Notes: 2, 7, 9, 10, 11, 12, 14

Point Way Inn

Box 5255, 02539
(508) 627-8633

This delightful country inn provides a
warm, relaxed retreat with working fireplaces in its 11 guest rooms. Tea and scones
are provided in the winter; in the summer,
lemonade and oatmeal cookies are served in
the gazebo overlooking the croquet court
and gardens. Complimentary courtesy car
available. Minimum stay holidays is two
nights. Seasonal rates available.

Hosts: Linda and Ben Smith
Rooms: 15 (PB) $125-250
Continental Breakfast
Credit Cards: A, B, C
Notes: 2, 5, 8, 9, 10, 11, 12, 14

7 No smoking; 8 Children welcome; 9 Social drinking allowed; 10 Tennis nearby; 11 Swimming nearby;
12 Golf nearby; 13 Skiing nearby; 14 May be booked through a travel agent.

The Shiretown Inn on the Island of Martha's Vineyard

21 North Water Street, P.O. Box 921, 02539
(800) 541-0090

Shiretown Inn, which is listed in the National Register of Historic Places, is composed of two 1700s Captain's houses, carriage houses, cottage, restaurant, and pub. Some rooms and suites have cable TV, air conditioning, telephones, canopied beds, harbor views, garden views, and decks. On North Water Street in the center of Edgartown one block from the Chappaquiddick Ferry, Town Wharf, and Harbor, it is a short stroll to shops, galleries, and lovely public beaches.

Host: Sonya Lima
Rooms: 34 (PB) $59-259
Continental Breakfast
Credit Cards: A, B, D
Notes: 2, 4, 7, 8, 9, 10, 11, 12, 14

EGREMONT

American Country Collection

1353 Union Street, Schnectady, NY 12054
(518) 439-7001; FAX 9518) 439-4301

138. This 1700s Victorian rural farm is on 500 acres of rolling hills, woods, and fields. It is furnished with antiques and Oriental rugs. There are four guest rooms, two with private baths. Tanglewood, Norman Rockwell Museum, Berkshire Festival, and skiing are all within 15 minutes. There is an in-ground pool available for guest use. Full breakfast. Smoking outdoors. Resident dog. Children over ten welcome. $74-94.

ESSEX

Bed and Breakfast Marblehead and North Shore

P.O. Box 35, Newtonville, 02160
(617) 964-1606; (800) 832-2632
FAX (617) 332-8572

Essex River Inn. An 1830 Federal-style house built by shipwrights. Six guest rooms have private baths, individual heat and air conditioning, TV, and telephones; three have working fireplaces. One suite sleeps four and has a fireplace and balcony; a penthouse suite has a private deck and kitchenette. A delicious full breakfast is included and may be served "in bed" on request. Restricted smoking. $79-129.

FALMOUTH

Bed and Breakfast Associates Bay Colony, Ltd.

P.O. Box 57166, Babson Park, Boston, 02157-0166
(617) 449-5302; (800) 347-5088
FAX (617) 449-5958

CC129. Antique house circa 1820 with lovely period furnishings and three guest rooms with private baths. On the village green, just two blocks from the shuttle bus to the ferry to Martha's Vineyard. $90.

Bed and Breakfast Cape Cod

P.O. Box 341, West Hyannisport, 02672-0341
(508) 775-2772; FAX (508) 775-2884

10. This beachfront ranch-style house faces a beautiful saltwater inlet that offers private beach, quiet walks, fishing from the host's property, sailing, and clamming. Two rooms with double beds have private baths and are furnished with antiques. Full country breakfast. Children over 12. $85.

38. Built in 1880, this home on the road to Woods Hole has been restored comfortably, offering four guest rooms with private baths. Guests will enjoy a full breakfast served in the dining room, and a nice parlor for reading or relaxing is also available. The village shops in Falmouth are a mile away, and the ferry is one and one-half miles. No smoking. Children over seven are welcome. $65-85.

NOTES: Credit cards accepted: A MasterCard; B Visa; C American Express; D Discover; E Diners Club; F Other; 2 Personal checks accepted; 3 Lunch available; 4 Dinner available; 5 Open all year; 6 Pets welcome;

42. This gracious Federal Colonial home built in 1822 is on the beautiful village green in Falmouth. Through the years this prominent home has been photographed many times as a reflection of architecture and picturesque New England. Restored some years ago by the hostess, the home now offers two bedrooms with private baths, air conditioning, and canopied four-poster beds. A full breakfast is served. Walk to the bus to Martha's Vineyard ferry or stroll across the green to shops and fine restaurants. $80-90.

The Elms

495 Route 28A, P.O. Box 895, 02574
(508) 540-7232

Charming Victorian, built in the early 1800s, features nine beautifully appointed bedrooms, seven private baths, and antique decor throughout. A full Continental breakfast is served. Tour the manicured grounds to survey the flower and herb gardens or relax in the gazebo. In the historic district, walk to restaurants, antique shops, and one-half mile to the ocean.

Hosts: Betty and Joe Mazzucchelli
Rooms: 9 (7 PB; 2 SB) $65-85
Continental Breakfast
Credit Cards: A, B, C
Notes: 2, 5, 7, 9, 10, 11, 12

Golden Slumber Accommodations

640 Revere Beach Boulevard, Revere, 02151
(800) 892-3231; (617) 289-1053

124. This enchanting Cape boasts charming European country decor. The bright and spacious rooms each feature full or single beds, antiques, cable television, and private bath. There is also a suite available. The large deck and outdoor grill are employable in season. A generous full breakfast featuring homemade delicacies is served in the spacious kitchen. In close proximity to Woods Hole and island ferries, as well as

the best in fine dining and shopping. Come enjoy Falmouth's best-kept lodging secret! $65-100.

Grafton Inn

Grafton Inn

261 Grand Avenue South, 02540
(508) 540-8688; (800) 642-4069
FAX (508) 540-1861

Oceanfront Victorian inn with miles of beautiful beach and breathtaking views of Martha's Vineyard. Sumptuous breakfasts are served on a lovely enclosed porch. Comfortable air-conditioned rooms furnished with period antiques and thoughtful amenities. Bicycles are available, as is ample parking. Short walk to restaurant, shops, and ferry. AAA, Mobil rated.

Hosts: Liz and Rudy Cvitan
Rooms: 11 (PB) $75-145
Full Breakfast
Credit Cards: A, B, C
Notes: 2, 5, 7, 9, 10, 11, 12, 14

The Inn at One Main Street

One Main Street, 02540
(508) 540-7469

This elegant 1892 Victorian is in Falmouth's historic district, where the roads to Woods Hole begin. The inn is within walking distance to beaches, bike path, restaurants, shops, and ferry shuttle. Enjoy a romantic getaway in one of six freshly decorated rooms, all with private baths. Whatever wishes guests may have, the hosts will do their very best to ensure an

7 No smoking; 8 Children welcome; 9 Social drinking allowed; 10 Tennis nearby; 11 Swimming nearby; 12 Golf nearby; 13 Skiing nearby; 14 May be booked through a travel agent.

enjoyable stay and send guests home feeling fully refreshed.

Hosts: Karen Hart and Mari Zylinski
Rooms: 6 (PB) $75-105
Full Breakfast
Credit Cards: A, B, C
Notes: 2, 5, 10, 11, 12

Inn on the Sound

313 Grand Avenue, 02540
(508) 457-9666

Oceanfront bed and breakfast with ten spacious guest rooms, most with spectacular ocean views, all with private baths, and several with fireplaces. Full gourmet breakfast served each morning with homemade pastries and coffeecakes, fresh fruit, juices, and specialty entrees. Minutes' walk to beach and to Martha's Vineyard Island ferry. Near museums and galleries, shops, and restaurants, bike path, golf, and tennis Day trips: whale watching, Plymouth Rock, and Woods Hole Oceanographic Institute.

Hosts: Renée Ross and David Ross
Rooms: 10 (PB) $95-140
Full Breakfast
Credit Cards: A, B, C, D
Notes: 2, 5, 9, 10, 11, 12, 14

The Moorings Lodge

207 Grand Avenue South, 02540
(508) 540-2370

Enjoy homemade breads for buffet breakfast served on a large glassed-in porch with lovely ocean view. This charming old sea captain's home with spacious, airy rooms overlooks Vineyard Sound and Martha's Vineyard Island. Just opposite a safe and clean family beach and within a short walking distance of good restaurants and the island ferry. Delicious breakfast served. Smoking is restricted.

Hosts: Ernie and Shirley Benard
Rooms: 8 (PB) $75-95
Full Breakfast
Credit Cards: A, B
Notes: 2, 9, 10, 11, 12

Mostly Hall

Mostly Hall Bed and Breakfast Inn

27 Main Street, 02540
(508) 548-3786; (800) 682-0565

Romantic 1849 Southern plantation-style Cape Cod home with wraparound veranda and widow's walk. Set back from the road on an acre of beautiful gardens with a gazebo. Close to restaurants, shops, beaches, and island ferries. Spacious corner rooms with queen-size canopied beds, central air conditioning, gourmet breakfast, bicycles, and private baths. Minimum stay Memorial Day through Columbus Day is two nights. Closed January through mid-February.

Hosts: Caroline and Jim Lloyd
Rooms: 6 (PB) $85-125
Full Breakfast
Credit Cards: A, B, C, D
Notes: 2, 7, 9, 10, 11, 12

The Palmer House Inn

81 Palmer Avenue, 02540-2857
(508) 548-1230; (800) 472-2632
FAX (508) 540-1878

Turn-of-the-century Victorian bed and breakfast in the historic district. Antique furnishings return guests to the romance of a bygone era. Full gourmet breakfast featuring pain perdu, Belgian waffles, and Finnish pancakes. Close to island ferries, beaches, and shops. Bicycles available. Personal

NOTES: Credit cards accepted: A MasterCard; B Visa; C American Express; D Discover; E Diners Club; F Other; 2 Personal checks accepted; 3 Lunch available; 4 Dinner available; 5 Open all year; 6 Pets welcome;

checks accepted for deposits only. Children over ten welcome.

Hosts: Ken and Joanne Baker
Rooms: 13 (PB) $65-165
Full Breakfast
Credit Cards: A, B, C, D, E
Notes: 5, 7, 9, 10, 11, 12, 14

Village Green Inn

40 West Main Street, 02540
(508) 548-5621

Gracious old Victorian, ideally located on historic village green. Walk to fine shops and restaurants, bike to beaches, tennis, and the picturesque bike path to Woods Hole. Enjoy 19th-century charm and warm hospitality in elegant surroundings. Four lovely guest rooms and one romantic suite all have private baths. Also offer bicycles, seasonal beverages, working fireplaces, and beach passes. Open March through December.

Hosts: Diane and Don Crosby
Rooms: 5 (PB) $85-120
Full Breakfast
Credit Cards: A, B, C
Notes: 2, 7, 9, 10, 11, 12

Village Green Inn

FLORENCE

Lupine House

185 North Main Street
P.O. Box 60483, 01060-0483
(413) 586-9766; (800) 890-9766

Lupine House, a newly remodeled turn-of-the-century home at the gateway to the Berkshires, offers three tastefully decorated

guestrooms, with private baths. "Look Park's" walking and biking trails are just up the street; the bike trail abuts the property. Breakfast includes assorted fresh breads, fruit, homemade granola, juices, and hot beverages. Food allergies and special dietary needs are easily accommodated. Within a short drive are Smith, Amherst, Hampshire, and Mount Holyoke colleges, University of Massachusetts, Deerfield Academy, and the Williston Northampton School. Open mid-September through mid-June.

Hosts: Gil and Evelyn Billings
Rooms: 3 (PB) $70
Continental Breakfast
Credit Cards: A, B
Notes: 2, 9

FRAMINGHAM

Bed and Breakfast Associates Bay Colony, Ltd.

P.O. Box 57166, Babson Park, Boston, 02157-0166
(617) 449-5302; (800) 347-5088
FAX (617) 449-5958

CW625. This is an idyllic country setting at the end of a private road, yet a short walk to Framingham Centre shops and public transportation. The home was once a barn. The contemporary restoration was completed just over 20 years ago but the weathered siding has the rich hues of age. Exit the first-floor suite via French doors to acres of open land. The guest room has a cathedral ceiling and an attached sitting area. Full breakfast; children welcome. Monthly rates available. $68-78.

GAY HEAD

Duck Inn

Off State Road, RFD 160, 02535
(508) 645-9018

A 200-year-old, five-bedroom farmhouse on eight and one-half acres just a short walk to the beach. Ocean views in most rooms.

7 No smoking; 8 Children welcome; 9 Social drinking allowed; 10 Tennis nearby; 11 Swimming nearby; 12 Golf nearby; 13 Skiing nearby; 14 May be booked through a travel agent.

Watch the sun set over the cliffs and ocean. Fireplaces, decks, piano, hot tub, masseuse, and gourmet health breakfasts. Casual and eclectic antique setting. Open year-round with off-season rates.

Host: Elise LeBovit
Rooms: 5 (1 PB; 4 SB) $65-175
Full Breakfast
Credit Cards: A, B
Notes: 2, 5, 6, 8, 9, 11, 14

GEORGETOWN

Bed and Breakfast Marblehead and North Shore

P.O. Box 35, Newtonville, 02160
(617) 964-1606; (800) 832-2632;
FAX (617) 332-8572

The Georgetown Country Manor. A beautiful contemporary Colonial home only 40 minutes from Boston and 15 minutes from historic Newburyport. There is an exercise room with complete Nautilus station and computerized bicycle. All rooms have private bath, telephones, and TV. The master suite has king-size bed with private ensuite Jacuzzi bath. Guests may relax in the front sitting room with fireplace and grand piano. Outside guests may wander through the gardens and enjoy the swimming pool and heated spa. Guests are offered the option of dinner with menu and prices posted daily. Continental plus breakfast. No smoking. Special-occasion packages can be arranged at an additional cost. $100-125.

GLOUCESTER

Bed and Breakfast Associates Bay Colony, Ltd.

P.O. Box 57166, Babson Park, Boston, 02157-0166
(617) 449-5302; (800) 347-5088
FAX (617) 449-5958

NS505. Originally an 1898 Victorian "cottage," this splendid seaside retreat has been completely updated and redecorated.

It is on the banks of the Annisquam River, and guests may enjoy watching passing boats from each of the guest rooms, the inviting decks, or the gardens below. There is also a private swimming beach. These three beautifully decorated rooms share two full baths. Continental breakfast; children over 12 welcome. $65-75; family rates available.

Bed and Breakfast Cape Cod

P.O. Box 341, West Hyannisport, 02672-0341
(508) 775-2772; FAX (508) 775-2884

30. This 1899 restoration is the perfect place to watch ships sail by. Decorated with both Victorian and traditional themes, this home offers four carpeted guest rooms that have twin, double, or queen-size beds and share two full baths. All have a view of the water, and each morning a Continental breakfast is served in the dining area or on the 100-foot wraparound porch. $65-75.

Bed and Breakfast Marblehead and North Shore

P.O. Box 35, Newtonville, 02160
(617) 964-1606; (800) 832-2632
FAX (617) 332-8572

Oceanfront Cottage. Small one-bedroom oceanfront cottage in spectacular location, with lawn sloping down to rocky shoreline. Small kitchen, living room, and private bath with shower only. Full breakfast in refrigerator which guests prepare themselves. Children welcome. Smoking permitted. No pets. Open mid-May through September. Two-night minimum stay. Weekly rates available. $90.

Riverview Bed and Breakfast. An exquisite turn-of-the-century restored waterfront home with 100-foot wraparound porch perched high above the Annisquam River. Each of the beautifully decorated guest rooms share two full baths. Two front rooms have private decks. The back room has a queen-size brass bed, sink, and water view. The terraced grounds and gardens lead to a private pier. Guests may relax in the sitting room with TV or check out the local restaurant menus and tourist information. Restricted smoking. Continental breakfast. $65-85.

Greater Boston Hospitality

P.O. Box 1142, Brookline, 02146
(617) 277-5430

111. This 1889 waterfront bed and breakfast home is less than an hour out of Boston. Boasting a private beach on a warm, calm ocean riverway that is great for swimming, and Laura Ashley decorated bedrooms all with water views, this bed and breakfast is an outstanding value. Gloucester abounds with things to do and see: eight minutes to the marina to catch the whale watch; surrounded by art colonies, unique shops and galleries, fascinating museums, and scrumptious fresh seafood restaurants. Four large bedrooms, two with private decks, and two baths. Parking and breakfast included. Cot available for an additional $15. $75.

GREAT BARRINGTON

American Country Collection

1353 Union Street, Schnectady, NY, 12054
(518) 439-7001; FAX (518) 439-4301

221. This Victorian in the historic district was built in the 1890s. Near southern Berkshire County attractions, Tanglewood, Norman Rockwell Museum, and ski areas of Butternut, Catamount, Brodie, and Jimminy. With a combination of contemporary and antique furnishings, this location features three double rooms, all with private baths. A full breakfast and afternoon tea are served. Special seasonal rates are also available. $60-90.

Baldwin Hill Farm Bed and Breakfast

121 Baldwin Hill Road N/S, 01230
(413) 528-4092

A Victorian farm homestead atop Baldwin Hill has 450 acres, barns, orchards, and fields. Spectacular panoramic 360-degree views of the Berkshires. Country breakfasts from menu. Fieldstone fireplace, living rooms, screened porch, pool, gardens. Walks, hiking, biking, and cross-country trails. Near concerts, theater, museums, dance, galleries, historic places, and alpine skiing. Shops, antiques, and fine restaurants nearby, with Appalachian trail botanical and natural preserves. Elegant family antiques and friendly atmosphere. Two rooms have vanity sinks. Children over ten welcome.

Hosts: Richard and Priscilla Burdsall
Rooms: 4 (2 PB; 2 SB) $70-94
Full Breakfast
Credit Cards: A, B
Notes: 2, 5, 7, 9, 10, 11, 12, 13, 14

Bed and Breakfast Inns of New England

128 South Hoop Pole Road, Guilford, CT 06437
(203) 457-0042; (800) 582-0853

MA 1020. A circa 1800 farmhouse built by the Indians early in the last century. It has been added to over the years until it assumed its present rambling shape. There are five brightly furnished guest rooms, each with its own private bath. Bathrobes are found in the bedroom closets for the guests to use. All bedrooms are air-conditioned and equipped with telephones and clock radios. $85-100.

Covered Bridge

P. O. Box 447A, Norfolk, CT 06058
(203) 542-5944

1GBMA. Charming Victorian farmhouse in a rural setting. A full breakfast is served in the dining room. There are three large

7 No smoking; 8 Children welcome; 9 Social drinking allowed; 10 Tennis nearby; 11 Swimming nearby; 12 Golf nearby; 13 Skiing nearby; 14 May be booked through a travel agent.

rooms, each with private bath, cable TV, and air conditioning. Two of the rooms have queen-size beds, and one has twins. A barn on the grounds has also been converted into a two-bedroom cottage. $85-110.

2GBMA. This charming cottage bed and breakfast is within walking distance of the center of town in a very pleasant residential area. The cottage, with a Scandinavian decor, offers a full kitchen and bath, dining and sitting area with a woodstove, and an antique double bed. $125-150.

Littlejohn Manor Bed and Breakfast

1 Newsboy Monument Lane, 01230
(413) 528-2882

Victorian charm recaptured in this uniquely personable home. Antiques grace four warmly furnished, air-conditioned guest rooms—one with fireplace. Guest parlor with color TV and fireplace. Full English breakfast and afternoon tea with scones and shortbread included if reserved by noon. Set on spacious, landscaped grounds with extensive herb and flower beds. Scenic views. Close to major ski areas and Berkshire attractions. Children over 12 are welcome. Limited smoking.

Hosts: Herbert Littlejohn Jr. and Paul A. DuFour
Rooms: 4 (SB) $60-90
Full Breakfast
Credit Cards: None
Notes: 2, 5, 9, 10, 11, 12, 13

Nutmeg Bed and Breakfast Agency

P.O. Box 1117, West Hartford, CT 06107
(203) 236-6698

332. This 100-year-old Victorian with porch, deck, and hot tub has one first-floor room with double bed and private bath; two second-floor rooms with double beds which share a bath; and two other second-floor rooms with private baths. There are sitting areas in all rooms, TV in two of the rooms. Continental breakfast. No children. Smoking permitted. Two dogs on premises.

Seekonk Pines Inn

142 Seekonk Cross Road, 01230
(413) 528-4192; (800) 292-4192

This restored 1830s homestead, set amid lovely flower and vegetable gardens, offers a large guest living room with a fireplace and grand piano. A full country breakfast is different every day, and special diets can be accommodated. Convenient to Tanglewood and other cultural events, museums, shops, golf, and hiking. Features antique quilts, stenciling, original artwork, gardens, picnic tables, in-ground pool, and guest pantry. Featured in the *Boston Globe, Philadelphia Inquirer, Los Angeles Times,* and the August 1992 issue of *Country Inns* magazine.

Hosts: Linda and Chris Best
Rooms: 6 (PB) $70-110
Full Breakfast
Credit Cards: A, B
Notes: 2, 5, 7, 8, 9, 10, 11, 12, 13

The Turning Point Inn

3 Lake Buel Road, 01230
(413) 528-4777

An 18th-century former stagecoach inn. Full, delicious breakfast. Featured in the *New York Times, Boston Globe,* and *Los Angeles Times.* Adjacent to Butternut Ski Basin; near Tanglewood and all Berkshire attractions. Hiking and cross-country ski trails. Sitting rooms with fireplaces, piano, cable TV. Groups and families welcome.

Hosts: The Yosts
Rooms: 8 (6 PB; 2 SB) $80-100
Full Breakfast
Credit Cards: A, B, C
Notes: 2, 5, 7, 8, 9, 10, 11, 12, 13, 14

NOTES: Credit cards accepted: A MasterCard; B Visa; C American Express; D Discover; E Diners Club; F Other; 2 Personal checks accepted; 3 Lunch available; 4 Dinner available; 5 Open all year; 6 Pets welcome;

GREENFIELD (COLRAIN)

The Brandt House

29 Highland Avenue, 01301-3605
(413) 774-3329; (800) 235-3329; (413) 772-2908

High on a hill just five minutes from historic Deerfield, and a five-minute walk to town, this 16-room estate offers privacy, elegance, and comfort. Private baths, wraparound porches, a clay tennis court, fireplaces, pool table, feather beds, antiques, glowing hardwood floors, fresh flowers, and cozy bathrobes await guests. A sumptuous home-cooked breakfast is included. Call to see if pets are welcome.

Owner/Innkeeper: Phoebe Compton
Rooms: 7 (PB) $50-135
Credit Cards: A, B
Notes: 2, 5, 7, 8, 9, 10, 11, 12, 13, 14

Hitchcock House

15 Congress Street, 01301
(413) 774-7452

This 1881 Victorian house was built by Edward P. Hitchock and designed by F. C. Currier, a renowned Springfield architect. Surrounded by well-known schools and colleges. Just minutes away from historic Deerfield, tennis courts, golf courses, woodsy hiking trails, the town center, and several places of worship. Skiing of all kinds and white-water rafting are all nearby. The rooms are complimented with antique furnishings, country quilts, and accessories. Reduced rates for weekdays with Continental breakfast, for stays of more than three days, and for off-season dates. Suites and rooms with or without private bath are available. Children over six are welcome.

Hosts: Betty and Peter Gott
Rooms: 5 (2PB; 3SB) $60-100
Full Breakfast (weekends)
Continental Breakfast (weekdays)
Credit Cards: A, B C
Notes: 2, 5, 7, 9, 10, 11, 12, 13, 14

HAMILTON

Bed and Breakfast Marblehead and North Shore

P.O. Box 35, Newtonville, 02160
(617) 964-1606; (800) 832-2632
FAX (617) 332-8572

The Country Mannor Inn. This is an exceptional bed and breakfast on 30 acres of land, with eight guest rooms, most of which have private baths. The house is a country Colonial built in 1790 and expanded over the years. There are 12 working fireplaces throughout, as well as several sitting rooms and porches available for guest use. There are beautiful views, wonderful gardens, and a river flowing through the property. Hosts are seasoned bicyclists who will be happy to map out interesting routes throughout the area for guests. Wonderful breakfast. Children are welcome. No smoking. $70-125.

The Elms. Surrounded by tall elm trees, this bed and breakfast offers cozy guest accommodations with the feel of home. Two guest rooms with double and twin beds share a bath and sitting room. Guests may also enjoy daytime use of the downstairs living room, dining area, patio, and gardens. Just a short walk to the commuter-rail line into Boston, and close to the many tourist attractions on the North Shore. A delicious breakfast includes homemade jellies and jams. Children over 12 are welcome. No smoking. $10 additional charge for private bath when available. $60-75.

Host Homes of Boston

P.O. Box 117, Boston, 02168
(617) 244-1308; FAX (617) 244-5156

Miles River Country Inn. A 200-year-old estate in Cape Ann's horse country near Crane's Beach. The inn is a 24-room vintage Colonial on 30 acres of varied gardens,

---

7 No smoking; 8 Children welcome; 9 Social drinking allowed; 10 Tennis nearby; 11 Swimming nearby; 12 Golf nearby; 13 Skiing nearby; 14 May be booked through a travel agent.

woods, and wetlands. Eight guest rooms include a suite with twins and a double, and two queens with private baths. Hosts produce eggs, fruit, and honey for breakfast. Thirty minutes from Boston. Resident dogs. $65-90.

HARWICH

Bed and Breakfast Cape Cod

P.O. Box 341, West Hyannisport, 02672-0341
(508) 775-2772; FAX (508) 775-2884

7. This Cape-style home is 100 yards from a freshwater pond and offers two bedrooms, one with a double bed and the other, a pair of twins. The bath is shared, and a full breakfast served in the dining room features home-baked specialties. The pond is available for swimming or fishing, and the beach is close to this pleasant accommodation. No smoking. Children over eight. $68.

47. This Cape-style host home is in a quiet residential section near two freshwater lakes. The house has two guest rooms with either a king-size bed or two twins. A great breakfast is available each morning. It is convenient with easy access to other parts of the Cape, including the beaches on either Cape Cod Bay or Nantucket Sound. This very clean and well-maintained home is excellent for a family or group of up to four people. $65.

Bed and Breakfast Inns of New England

128 South Hoop Pole Road, Guilford, CT 06437
(203) 457-0042; (800) 582-0853

MA-1047. Set on one and one-half acres with flower and vegetable gardens, the main house was built in 1835. A contemporary wing has since been added. Upstairs there are twin beds with a shared bath. Down-

stairs there is a king-size bed with private bath and entrance. This room boasts five windows and is especially delightful in the summer. An extra-small room with a twin bed for a third guest is available, with a shared bath. A Continental breakfast is served each morning. No children; no smoking; resident cat. $30-60.

HARWICH PORT (CAPE COD)

Bed and Breakfast Associates Bay Colony, Ltd.

P.O. Box 57166, Babson Park, Boston, 02157-0166
(617) 449-5302; (800) 347-5088
FAX (617) 449-5958

CC365. This eight-bedroom inn sits just footsteps from the famed sandy beaches of the Cape's South Shore. Guests are delighted by the facilities, which include elegant guest rooms with private baths, welcoming common rooms, and romantic decor. Full breakfast provided. $75-155.

CC370. White wicker rocking chairs and hanging geraniums on the wraparound porch beckon guests to this Victorian home one-third mile from the sandy beach. There are five guest rooms with brass beds, fine period furnishings, and pleasing pastel wallpapers. Shops and restaurants are within easy walking distance. Continental breakfast; family and monthly rates are available. $95.

CC371. These hosts offer excellent family accommodations in the relaxed atmosphere of this guest house. All rooms are thoughtfully furnished, spacious, and breezy. A Continental breakfast is served in the dining room, while an outdoor pool awaits just beyond. The beach is less than one-half mile. Children welcome. $95.

NOTES: Credit cards accepted: A MasterCard; B Visa; C American Express; D Discover; E Diners Club;
F Other; 2 Personal checks accepted; 3 Lunch available; 4 Dinner available; 5 Open all year; 6 Pets welcome;

Bed and Breakfast Greater Boston and Cape Cod

P.O. Box 35, Newtonville, 02160
(617) 964-1606; (800) 832-2632
FAX (617) 332-8572

Inn by the Sea. This elegant bed and breakfast inn is only a short walk from a private, sandy beach on Nantucket Sound. Each of the inn rooms offers private bath and king-size, queen-size, or twin beds. Some rooms are air-conditioned; several have fireplaces. Two units have separate entrances. There is also a cozy cottage with a fireplace. Full breakfast. The host can also accommodate guests celebrating special occasions with romantic packages, which include champagne, long-stem roses, chocolates, fresh fruit, etc. The inn is open year-round. Children over 12 are welcome. Some smoking rooms are available. Seasonal rates available. $95-195.

Cape Cod

P.O. Box 341, West Hyannisport, 02672-0341
(508) 775-2772; FAX (508) 775-2884

13. This Dutch-style Colonial has served as a small inn for 30 years and is on a private beach on the Nantucket Sound. The house features a large sun porch, living room with fireplace, and a large dining area. A variety of rooms, all of which offer private baths and have queen- and king-size beds, are available. Two apartments with separate entrances are also available. Children over 11 welcome. $105-165.

56. This restored 1860s country Victorian home is very close to Bank Street Beach, village shops, fine restaurants, and two public golf courses. There are two bedrooms available with a shared bath, one with twin beds and the other with a double bed. Ideal private quarters for a couple with two children or two couples traveling together. There are also a guest room with a

king-size bed and private bath, and a carriage house efficiency with private bath. Fresh fruit, hot breads, brewed coffee or tea, and cereals included. $65-100.

Cape Cod Claddagh Country Inn

77 Main Street, P.O. Box 667, 02671-0667
(508) 432-9628; (800) 356-9628(reservations)

Irish hospitality in a Victorian ambience. Reminiscent of an Irish manor. Eight private suites with air conditioning, TV, and refrigerators. Set on two acres with a pool, Irish art gallery, fine dining courtyard restaurant with homemade fare at fair prices, and Irish pub. Relaxed, friendly atmosphere, comfortable antiques, and designer linens. Perfect location for day trips anywhere on the Cape, islands, Plymouth, and Boston. Limited smoking allowed.

Hosts: Jack and Eileen Connell
Rooms: 8 (PB) $75-120
Full Breakfast
Credit Cards: A, B
Notes: 2, 3, 4, 8, 9, 10, 11, 12, 14

Captain's Quarters

85 Bank Street, 02642
(800) 992-6550

A romantic 1850s Victorian with a classic wraparound porch, nostalgic gingerbread trim, and a graceful curving front stairway. Guest rooms have private baths, queen-size brass beds with eyelet lace-trimmed sheets, lace curtains, and comfortable reading chairs. Just a three-minute walk into town and a five-minute walk to an ocean beach. Experience Cape Cod in a relaxed and friendly atmosphere.

Hosts: Ed and Susan Kenney
Rooms: 5 (PB) $65-95
Continental Breakfast
Credit Cards: A, B, C, D
Notes: 2, 5, 7, 9, 10, 11, 12, 14

7 No smoking; 8 Children welcome; 9 Social drinking allowed; 10 Tennis nearby; 11 Swimming nearby; 12 Golf nearby; 13 Skiing nearby; 14 May be booked through a travel agent.

Country Inn

86 Sisson Road, 02646
(508) 432-2769; (800) 231-1722

An inn of New England tradition set on six country acres. Newly restored guest rooms with color TVs, air conditioning, and romantic bedding offer a perfect setting for a getaway or vacation. Some rooms offer fireplaces. Cozy fireside dining in the fall and winter, and a varied menu features the freshest of native seafood and the finest of meats and poultry. Tennis courts, an in-ground swimming pool, and private beach. Parking provided free of charge at our other facility, Sea Shell Motel, directly on the ocean. Smoking is limited. Children welcome in some rooms.

Hosts: The Dings family
Rooms: 7 (PB) $75-125
Continental Breakfast
Credit Cards: A, B, C
Notes: 2, 4, 5, 9, 10, 11, 12

Country Inn

HYANNIS

The Inn on Sea Street

358 Sea Street, 02601
(508) 775-8030

This elegant 1849 Victorian inn, with ten romantic rooms, plus a carriage house, is just steps from the beach. Features

The Inn on Sea Street

antiques, Persian rugs, and canopied beds in this unpretentious, hospitable atmosphere, where no detail has been overlooked in assuring comfort. Refrigerator and telephone available for guests' use. Full gourmet breakfast of fresh fruit and home-baked delights served at individual tables set with the hosts' finest silver, china, crystal, and fresh flowers. One-night stays are welcome.

Hosts: Lois M. Nelson and J. B. Whitehead
Rooms: 10 (8 PB; 2 SB) $70-110
Full Breakfast
Credit Cards: A, B, C, D
Notes: 2, 7, 9, 10, 11, 12, 14

Sea Breeze Inn

397 Sea Street, 02601
(508) 771-7213

Sea Breeze is a Victorian bed and breakfast close to ferries and the islands. Canopied beds, air conditioning, private baths, and an expanded breakfast of delicious muffins, bagels, and fruit. The beach is just a three-minute walk away. Restaurants and theaters are just a five-minute drive away. Personal checks accepted for deposit. There is a 10 percent commission added to your charge when booked through a travel agent.

Hosts: Martin and Patricia Battle
Rooms: 14 (PB) $55-120
Continental Breakfast
Credit Cards: A, B, C, D
Notes: 5, 7, 8, 9, 10, 11, 12

NOTES: Credit cards accepted: A MasterCard; B Visa; C American Express; D Discover; E Diners Club; F Other; 2 Personal checks accepted; 3 Lunch available; 4 Dinner available; 5 Open all year; 6 Pets welcome;

HYANNISPORT

Bed and Breakfast Cape Cod

P.O. Box 341, West Hyannisport, 02672-0341
(508) 775-2772; FAX (508) 775-2884

32. This 200-year-old Colonial-style house is one mile from the center of town, five blocks from the Kennedy compound, two blocks from the ferry to Martha's Vineyard or Nantucket, and less than a mile away from great beaches. One bedroom with a double bed shares a tub and shower with a bedroom that has a pair of twin beds. A Continental breakfast is served each morning, and guests are welcome to use the parlor for relaxing. Children over 12. $60.

The Simmons Homestead Inn

288 Scudder Avenue, 02647
(508) 778-4999; (800) 637-1649
FAX (508) 790-1342

This sea captain's estate was built in 1820 and was made into a great bed and breakfast inn in 1988. Beautiful and fun-filled rooms, private baths, fireplaces, full breakfasts, wine hours, and much more make this one of the very best inns on Cape Cod. Within a mile of town, beaches, and the harbor, the inn is in quiet Hyannis Port.

Host: Bill Putman
Rooms: 10 (PB) $100-130
Full Breakfast
Credit Cards: A, B, C, D
Notes: 2, 5, 8, 9, 10, 11, 12, 14

JAMAICA PLAIN (BOSTON)

Bed and Breakfast Associates Bay Colony, Ltd.

P.O. Box 57166, Babson Park, Boston, 02157-0166
(617) 449-5302; (800) 347-5088
FAX (617) 449-5958

M484. Contemporary home is decorated with artifacts and collectibles from around the world. This circa 1909 converted carriage house on a quiet street near Jamaica Pond has a pleasant guests room with a queen-size bed and a private bath in the hall. Walk to bus or trolley. Free off-street parking. $75.

LANESBORO

The Tuckered Turkey

30 Old Cheshire Road, 01237
(413) 442-0260

Country Colonial with fabulous views of the Berkshire hills is central to all cultural attractions in Lenox, Williamstown, minutes to Mount Greylock, Berkshire Mall, and 20 minutes to new Mass Moca, a contemporary art museum. No smoking. Midweek and weekly specials. Country charm.

Hosts: Daniel and Marianne Sullivan
Rooms: 3 (SB) $35-85
Continental Breakfast
Credit Cards: None
Notes: 2, 5, 7, 8, 9, 10, 11, 12, 13, 14

LEE

Applegate

279 West Park Street, 01238
(413) 243-4451

A circular driveway leads to this pillared Georgian Colonial home set on six peaceful acres. Applegate is special in every way with canopied beds, antiques, fireplaces, pool, and manicured gardens. Its mood is warm, hospitable, and relaxed. Enjoy complimentary wine and cheese in the living room, complete with a baby grand piano. Candlelight breakfast is served. New TV room with VCR, and a small video library. Near Norman Rockwell museum and Tanglewood in the heart of the Berkshires. Children over 12 are welcome. Limited smoking.

Hosts: Nancy Begbie-Cannata and Richard Cannata
Rooms: 6 (PB) $85-225
Continental Breakfast
Credit Cards: A, B
Notes: 2, 5, 9, 10, 11, 12, 13

7 No smoking; 8 Children welcome; 9 Social drinking allowed; 10 Tennis nearby; 11 Swimming nearby; 12 Golf nearby; 13 Skiing nearby; 14 May be booked through a travel agent.

Chambéry Inn

199 Main Street, 01238
(413) 243-2221; (800) 537-4321
FAX (413) 243-3600

Restful, romantic, and rejuvenating; this schoolhouse teaches guests the three "Rs" of travel. Come visit Berkshires' 1885 petite chateau. Built as the country's first parochial school, the inn serves as one of the most spectacular examples of purist restoration. All 400- to 500-square-foot suites are individually decorated with soothing tapestries, fabrics, and colors. Standard features include 13-foot ceilings, eight-foot windows, sitting areas with fireplace, full sparkling and new private baths with whirlpool, air conditioning, decks, phones, and color TV. Choose a king-size canopied or two queen-size beds. Room-delivered breakfast included. Hospitality and facilities—par excellence!

Hosts: Marilyn Kelly and Joseph Toole
Rooms: 8 (PB) $55-195
Continental Breakfast
Credit Cards: A, B, C, D
Notes: 2, 3, 4, 5, 7, 9, 10, 11, 12, 13

Haus Andreas

85 Stockbridge Road, 01238
(413) 243-3298; (800) 664-0880
FAX (413) 243-1360

Historic, country estate offering the charm of yesterday and the amenities of today. Set on 40 acres of lawn and fields yet near all Berkshire attractions (Tanglewood, etc). King- or queen-size beds in all suites, fireplaces in four bedrooms, heated pool, tennis court, bicycles, and golf course nearby. Children over ten welcome.

Hosts: Sally and Ben Schenck
Rooms: 10 (PB) $60-250
Full Breakfast
Credit Cards: A, B, C
Notes: 2, 5, 9, 10, 11, 12, 13, 14

LENOX

American Country Collection

1353 Union Street, Schnectady, NY 12054
(518) 439-7001; FAX (518) 439-4301

154. A Berkshire tradition since 1780, this gracious country home has 18 guest rooms: seven with jet tubs and private porches, eight with fireplaces, five with air conditioning, and all with private baths. Rooms are cozy and comfortable. The 72-foot swimming pool is available for guest use. A full breakfast is served daily. Children over 12 welcome; smoking permitted. $80-195.

Apple Tree Inn

334 West Street, 01240
(413) 637-1447

The Apple Tree Inn, on 22 hilltop acres, is directly across the road from the Tanglewood festival. The Apple Tree is a cultural haven during spring and summer and a cozy retreat through the chill of fall. Stay in this 100 plus-year-old main house, which features country bedrooms, some with fireplaces, most with private baths, and all air-conditioned. Relax in the parlor or stroll in the apple orchard. Guests can enjoy both excellent cuisine and a panoramic view of the surrounding hills in the circular dining room. Continental breakfast included in rates, but guests are offered a full breakfast at an extra price. Tennis and swimming are both on property.

Hosts: Greg and Aurora Smith
Rooms: 35 (33 PB; 2 SB) $95-300
Continental Breakfast
Credit Cards: A, B, C, D
Notes: 2, 4, 9, 10, 11, 12, 13

NOTES: Credit cards accepted: A MasterCard; B Visa; C American Express; D Discover; E Diners Club;
F Other; 2 Personal checks accepted; 3 Lunch available; 4 Dinner available; 5 Open all year; 6 Pets welcome;

Bed and Breakfast Inns of New England

128 South Hoop Pole Road, Guilford, CT 06437
(203) 457-0042; (800) 582-0853

MA1025. This lovely bed and breakfast home is three miles from Tanglewood. Guests can enjoy nearby restaurants, unique shops, galleries, Jacob's Pillow, Hancock Village, summer stock theater, a Norman Rockwell gallery, Shaker Village, and all other intriguing Berkshire attractions. Chose from three guest rooms with shared baths, a sun porch, den, and dining room with a woodstove where a hearty light breakfast is served. No smoking. No pets. $90.

Birchwood Inn

7 Hubbard Street, 01240
(413) 637-2600; (800) 524-1646

Drive through the village of Lenox, and at the top of the hill stands the historic Birchwood Inn. The first town meeting was held here in 1767. Elegant and beautifully restored, the inn is known for its hospitality throughout the region. Enjoy antiques, fireplaces, library, and wonderful porch. Cultural activities include the Boston Symphony at Tanglewood and performing arts. There is marvelous fall foliage, hiking, and biking. Full breakfast with international specialities daily.

Hosts: Joan, Dick, and Dan Toner
Rooms: 12 (10 PB; 2 SB) $60-199
Full Breakfast
Credit Cards: A, B, C, D, E
Notes: 2, 5, 7, 9, 10, 11, 12, 13

Blantyre

16 Blantyre Road, P.O. Box 995, 01240
(413) 637-3556 (mid-May to early November)
(413) 298-3806

A gracious country house/hotel surrounded by 85 acres of grounds. The hotel has a European atmosphere and exceptional cuisine. Offers tennis, croquet, and swimming as its leisure activities.

Host: Roderick Anderson
Rooms: 23 (PB) $220-550
Full or Continental Breakfast
Credit Cards: A, B, C, E
Notes: 2, 3, 4, 10, 11, 12, 14

Brook Farm Inn

15 Hawthorne Street, 01240
(413) 637-3013

There is poetry here. A lovely century-old Victorian home, nestled in a wooded glen amid gardens and a pool. There is a large library with fireplace, and several guest rooms feature fireplaces and canopied or brass beds. Poetry readings with tea and scones are offered each Saturday. Near Tanglewood, theater, ballet, and museums. Enjoy hiking, biking, and wonderful fall foliage. In winter, cross-country and downhill skiing are close by. Relax and enjoy. Children over 15 welcome. Limited smoking.

Hosts: Joe and Anne Miller
Rooms: 12 (PB) $65-170
Continental Breakfast
Credit Cards: A, B, D
Notes: 2, 5, 9, 10, 11, 12, 13

Brook Farm Inn

Covered Bridge

P.O. Box 447, Norfolk, CT 06058
(203) 542-5944

1LEMA. Nestled in a pine grove and set on one and one-half acres, this 22-year-old home offers a restful retreat from all of the Berkshire activities. There is a sitting room with a fireplace and two first-floor guest rooms that share a bath. A Continental breakfast is served. $75-85.

The Gables Inn

The Gables Inn

103 Walker Street, 01240
(413) 637-3416

Former home of novelist Edith Wharton. Queen Anne-style with period furnishings, pool, tennis, fireplaces, and theme rooms.

Host: Frank Newton
Rooms: 18 (PB) $60-195
Continental Breakfast
Credit Cards: A, B, D
Notes: 2, 5, 10, 11, 12, 13

Garden Gables Inn

141 Main Street, P.O. Box 52, 01240
(413) 637-0193; FAX (413) 637-4554

A charming 19-room, 200-year-old gabled inn in the historic center of Lenox on five wooded acres dotted with gardens, maples, and fruit trees. A 72-foot outdoor swimming pool, fireplaces, and Jacuzzi. Minutes

from Tanglewood and other attractions. Good skiing in winter. In-room phones. Breakfast included.

Hosts: Mario and Lynn Mekinda
Rooms: 14 (PB) $70-200
Full Breakfast
Credit Cards: A, B, C, D
Notes: 2, 5, 9, 10, 11, 12, 13

The Kemble Inn

2 Kemble Street, 01240
(800) 353-4113

Nestled in the beautiful Berkshire Hills and perched on the edge of historic Lenox village stands The Kemble Inn. With its distant, panoramic mountain views to the west and its spacious Georgian elegance, the Kemble Inn has 12 large rooms and central air. Each room has a private bath, color TV, and a telephone, and some rooms have a fireplace. Seasonal attractions include Jacob's Pillow Dance Festival, The Berkshire Theatre Festival, Tanglewood, and the Chesterwood and Norman Rockwell museums in the summer. Leaf foliage, and Art and crafts festivals in the fall. In the winter there are holiday celebrations, outlet shopping, and cross-country and downhill skiing. Children over 12 welcome. BYOB. Cross-country skiing nearby.

Hosts: Richard and Linda Reardon
Rooms: 12 (PB) $75-275
Continental Breakfast
Credit Cards: A, B, C, D, E
Notes: 2, 5, 7, 10, 11, 12, 13, 14

Summer Hill Farm

950 East Street, 01240
(413) 442-2057

Comfortable 200-year-old farmhouse and converted barn guest cottage on 20-acre horse farm are tastefully furnished with genuine English antiques and Oriental rugs. The satisfying country breakfast is served in the dining room or on the sun porch looking out over the gardens and view. The atmosphere is peaceful, relaxed, friendly, and

Summer Hill Farm

unpretentious. Close to Tanglewood, Jacob's Pillow Dance Festival, museums, galleries, theaters, Hancock Shaker Village, good restaurants, and shops.

Hosts: Michael and Sonya Chassell Wessel
Rooms: 7 (PB) $55-160
Full or Continental Breakfast
Credit Cards: None
Notes: 2, 5, 7, 8, 10, 11, 12, 13, 14

Underledge Inn

106 Cliffwood Street, 01240
(413) 637-0236

Enjoy this country mansion, which can be found on four private acres in the Berkshires, home of Tanglewood Music Festival as well as the Norman Rockwell museum. Spend time pursuing many other cultural attractions, shopping, hiking, or skiing. At day's end, relaxing in elegant parlor bedrooms with Victorian appointments, fireplaces, and lovely views completes the experience of a bygone era. Seasonal rates available.

Hosts: Marcie and Cheryl Lanoue
Rooms: 8 (PB) $60-205
Continental Breakfast
Credit Cards: A, B, C
Notes: 7, 9, 10, 11, 12, 13, 14

Whistler's Inn

5 Greenwood Street, 01240
(413) 637-0975; FAX (413) 637-2190

An English Tudor mansion built in 1820 in the heart of the Berkshire hills near Tanglewood takes you into a period of Old World charm and relaxation. Across from the famous Church on the Hill and Kennedy Park, Whistler's Inn is just two blocks to the center of Lenox and to some of the finest restaurants and shops in the Berkshires. The Whistler's Inn captures the warmth and elegance of a bygone era. Each room is individually furnished with antiques (some with fireplaces) and all have private baths. Featured in *Fodor's Bed & Breakfast Country Inns & Other Weekend Pleasures–New England, New York* magazine, "Great Escapes," *National Geographic Traveler,* and *Ladies Home Journal.*

Rooms: 14 (PB) $70-200
Full Breakfast
Credit Cards: A, B, C, D
Notes: 2, 5, 7, 8, 9, 10, 11, 12, 13, 14

Whistler's Inn

LEVERETT

Hannah Dudley House

114 Dudleyville Road, 01054
(413) 367-2323

This elegant country inn is on 110 tranquil, rural acres and is the ideal getaway. The 200-year-old house has been romantically restored with spacious guest rooms, private baths, fireplaces throughout, and attention to detail. Each room is meticulously and individually decorated with its own theme and comfortably furnished in Colonial style. Three common rooms, two patios, and an array of benches and hammocks

7 No smoking; 8 Children welcome; 9 Social drinking allowed; 10 Tennis nearby; 11 Swimming nearby; 12 Golf nearby; 13 Skiing nearby; 14 May be booked through a travel agent.

offer a variety of relaxation options both inside and out. The inn's intimate setting also includes a swimming pool, hiking trails, scenic picnic spots, ponds, and special places just waiting to be discovered. The extensive grounds are ideal for weddings, receptions, anniversaries, business meetings, or other group gatherings, as well as quiet retreats for two. Please inquire about availability of lunch and dinner. Children over ten welcome.

Hosts: Erni and Daryl Johnson
Rooms: 4 (PB) $125-185
Full Breakfast
Credit Cards: A, B
Notes: 2, 5, 7, 9, 11, 12, 13

LEXINGTON

Bed and Breakfast Inns of New England

128 South Hoop Pole Road, Guilford, CT 06437
(203) 457-0042; (800) 582-0853

MA1008. Originally built in 1909, this Colonial was rebuilt by Bob Villa of *This Old House.* Enjoy Early American antiques among the luxury and conveniences of its superb restoration. All four guest rooms have private bath and one has Jacuzzi tub. No smoking. Families welcome. Guest pets accepted with prior arrangements. Full breakfast. $70-80.

LOWELL

Bed and Breakfast Associates Bay Colony, Ltd.

P.O. Box 57166, Babson Park, Boston, 02157-0166
(617) 449-5302; (800) 347-5008
FAX (617) 449-5958

CN300. This beautiful Victorian home with its wraparound porch and stained glass is meticulously maintained and is graced by many authentic architectural details and tasteful period furnishings. Two guest rooms on the second floor share a bath. Continental plus breakfast. Children welcome. No smoking. Family rates available. $65.

LUDLOW

Misty Meadows, Ltd.

467 Fuller Street, 01056
(413) 583-8103

One of Ludlow's oldest, this 200-year-old house has 85 acres on which to wander. A country scenic atmosphere on a working farm that raises "Scottish Highlanders." A scenic patio overlooks the Minechaug mountain range. Screened cabana with in-ground pool. Brook fishing nearby. An area with a lot of history and many historical sites less than one-half hour away.

Host: Donnabelle Haluch
Rooms: 2 (SB) $30-50
Continental Breakfast
Credit Cards: None
Notes: 2, 5, 8, 9, 10, 11, 12, 13

LYNN

Diamond District Bed and Breakfast

142 Ocean Street, 01902-2007
(617) 599-4470; (800) 666-3076
FAX (617) 599-4470

This 17-room architect-designed clapboard mansion was built in 1911. The mansion features a gracious foyer, a grand staircase

Diamond District

winding up the three floors, a spacious fireplace in the living room finished in Mexican mahogany and with an oceanview, French doors leading to an adjacent large veranda that overlooks the gardens and ocean, and a banquet-size dining room. Antiques and Oriental rugs fill the house. Other furnishings include an 1895 rosewood Knabe concert grand piano, custom Chippendale dining room table and chairs. Bedrooms offer a custom 1870s Victorian bed and twin beds. Each room boasts the elegance of yesteryear. Inquire about accommodations for pets.

Hosts: Sandra and Jerry Caron
Rooms: 8 (4 PB; 4 SB) $58-105
Full Breakfast
Credit Cards: A, B, C, D, E
Notes: 2, 5, 7, 11, 12, 14

MANCHESTER-BY-THE-SEA

Bed and Breakfast Associates Bay Colony, Ltd.

P.O. Box 57166, Babson Park, Boston, 02157-0166
(617) 449-5302; (800) 347-5088
FAX (617) 449-5958

NS311. This Georgian Colonial reproduction was built in 1929 and boasts a glorious fourth generation English country garden with fish pond and gazebo that has been selected to be featured in *Better Homes and Gardens*. A beautiful English-style decorated home just one-quarter mile from the harbor. The guest room has a double brass bed and shares a bath. $68.

MARBLEHEAD

Bed and Breakfast Associates Bay Colony, Ltd.

P.O. Box 57166, Babson Park, Boston, 02157-0166
(617) 449-5302; (800) 347-5088
FAX (617) 449-5958

NS261. Just two blocks to beaches, antique shops, and restaurants, this restored Federal home offers beamed cathedral ceilings and a cozy, charming decor. Two guest rooms on the second floor share a bath. Continental breakfast; children welcome; no smoking. $75-80.

NS262. This friendly couple offers two guest rooms in their charming multilevel hillside home. Both rooms overlook Marblehead Harbor. Two guest rooms share a bath. Generous Continental breakfast; children welcome. Family rates available. $68.

Bed and Breakfast Marblehead and North Shore

P.O. Box 35, Newtonville, 02160
(617) 964-1606; (800) 832-2632
FAX (617) 332-8572

Marblehead Victorian. This gracious 1890 Victorian home features three guest rooms, with choice of twin, double, or queen-size beds. All rooms share a full bath in the hall and a half-bath downstairs. A separate-entrance guest suite sleeps three people comfortably and has a private bath, TV, and refrigerator. Breakfast, featuring home-baked bread and muffins, is served in breakfast room or country gardens out back. Close to beaches. Recreation room includes pool table. Smoking outside only. Children welcome; portable crib or adult-size cot available for extra fee. Resident dog. Weekly rates available. $75-115.

Oceanside Tudor. This gracious Victorian Tudor-style inn offers spectacular oceanviews from most guest rooms and common areas. All guest rooms are beautifully decorated with king- or queen-size beds, and all have private baths. Two rooms feature working fireplaces. A gourmet Continental breakfast is provided in the common rooms that have panoramic oceanviews. In cooler weather, guests may relax in front of the fireplace after a day of sightseeing. In warmer weather, the outside courtyard, gardens, and walkways add to the numerous amenities this inn offers. Early risers can view the sunrise over the ocean. Seasonal rates available. No smoking. $139-189.

The Village Nook. A cozy 19th-century bed and breakfast accommodation offering the warmth and comfort of home. Within walking distance to the quaint shops, wonderful restaurants, galleries, and world-renowned harbor of Old Town Marblehead. Accommodations include pretty guest rooms, one queen-size bed and two twin beds, which share a bath. Guests may enjoy the use of the downstairs living room, deck, and hot tub. No smoking. Children are welcome. $75.

The Harbor Light Inn

58 Washington Street, 01945
(617) 631-2186

Premier inn one block from the harbor with rooms featuring air conditioning, TV, private baths, and working fireplaces. Two rooms have double Jacuzzis and sun decks. Beautiful 18th-century period mahogany furniture. Recent acquisition of an adjacent Federalist manor provides more room and amenities, including a conference room and swimming pool.

The Harbor Light Inn

Hosts: Peter and Suzanne Conway
Rooms: 20 (PB) $85-150
Suites: (PB) $160-195
Continental Breakfast
Credit Cards: A, B, C
Notes: 2, 5, 8, 9, 10, 11, 12

Harborside House

Harborside House

23 Gregory Street, 01945
(617) 631-1032

This handsome 1850 home in the historic district overlooks Marblehead Harbor. Enjoy water views from a fireplaced parlor, period dining room, third-story sun deck, and summer breakfast porch where guests may sample home-baked breads and muffins. Walk to historic sights, excellent restaurants, and unique shops. Hostess is a professional dressmaker and nationally ranked competitive swimmer. Enjoy quiet comfort and convenience. Children over ten welcome.

Host: Susan Livingston
Rooms: 2 (SB) $65-75
Continental Breakfast
Credit Cards: None
Notes: 2, 5, 7, 10, 11, 14

The Nesting Place

16 Village Street, 01945
(617) 631-6655; (617) 586-5889

This charming 19th-century home is in historic Marblehead and within walking distance of the renowned harbor, beaches, historic homes, galleries, eateries, shops, and famous parks. A relaxing, refreshing

NOTES: Credit cards accepted: A MasterCard; B Visa; C American Express; D Discover; E Diners Club; F Other; 2 Personal checks accepted; 3 Lunch available; 4 Dinner available; 5 Open all year; 6 Pets welcome;

home away from home. Two comfortably furnished guest rooms feature a healthful breakfast, outdoor hot tub, and a smoke-free environment. One-half hour from Boston, or one hour from New Hampshire. Day trips by car or bicycle are possible. Seasonal rates available.

Host: Louise Hirshberg
Rooms: 2 (SB) $55-65
Continental Breakfast
Credit Cards: A, B
Notes: 2, 5, 6, 7, 8, 9, 10, 11

Pleasant Manor Inn

264 Pleasant Street, 01945
(617) 631-5843

Pleasant Manor, a fine example of classic Victorian architecture, was built in 1872 and has been a charming inn since 1923. On the bus line 14 miles north of Boston and two miles from Salem. Beaches, restaurants, shops, and historic points of interest are easily accessible from this convenient location. Some features include private baths, TVs, VCRs, air conditioning, tennis court, off-street parking, and immaculate accommodations. Welcome to one of the most beautiful towns in the country.

Hosts: Takami and Richard Phelan
Rooms: 12 (PB) $65-75
Continental Breakfast
Credit Cards: None
Notes: 2, 5, 7, 8, 9, 10, 11, 14

Spray Cliff on the Ocean

25 Spray Avenue, 01945
(617) 631-6789; (800) 626-1530
FAX (617) 639-4563

A marvelous Old English Tudor mansion set high above the Atlantic with views that extend forever. Six guest rooms with private baths, some with fireplaces, most with oceanviews. Continental breakfast. Steps from a sandy beach.

Hosts: Roger and Sally Plauche
Rooms: 7 (PB) $150-200
Continental Breakfast
Credit Cards: A, B, C
Notes: 2, 5, 7, 9, 10, 11, 12, 14

Stillpoint

27 Gregory Street, 01945
(617) 631-1667; (800) 882-3891

Nicely appointed 1840s home is open all year, graciously landscaped, and filled with antiques, fireplace, piano, books, no TV, and quiet, refreshing ambience. Three spacious bedrooms share two full baths (the option of a private bath is available) and a deliciously healthy breakfast of fresh fruits, cereals, yogurt, and quality breads and muffins is served in the morning on the deck overlooking Marblehead Harbor in good weather. Within walking distance to shops, restaurants, beaches, and public transportation. Twenty miles north of Boston, near Logan airport, and an hour south of Maine-New Hampshire border. Trips to Concord, Lexington, Sturbridge Village, antique stores, and New Hampshire ski slopes are feasible. Children over ten welcome.

Host: Sarah Lincoln-Harrison
Rooms: 3 (1 PB; 2SB) $70-80
Continental Breakfast
Credit Cards: A, B
Notes: 2, 5, 7, 9, 10, 11, 14

Stillpoint

MARSHFIELD

Bed and Breakfast Associates Bay Colony, Ltd.

P.O. Box 57166, Babson Park, Boston, 02157-0166
(617) 449-5302; (800) 347-5088
FAX (617) 449-5958

SS350. What enthusiasm and hospitality this retired couple brings to hosting! Their New

---

7 No smoking; 8 Children welcome; 9 Social drinking allowed; 10 Tennis nearby; 11 Swimming nearby; 12 Golf nearby; 13 Skiing nearby; 14 May be booked through a travel agent.

England farm-style home is one block from Marshfield Beach. Built in 1875, it is furnished with warmth and charm; guests will find this bed and breakfast a welcoming retreat. Three guest rooms with private baths. Full breakfast served. Children are welcome. No smoking allowed. Family rates available. $60-75.

Bed and Breakfast Cape Cod

P.O. Box 341, West Hyannisport, 02672-0341
(508) 775-2772; FAX (508) 775-2884

77. This two-story home facing the water has two rooms for bed and breakfast, one with a double bed and the other with a pair of twin beds. The bath is shared, and the breakfast is Continental, served between 8:00 and 9:30 A.M. The inn is convenient to the bus to Boston. Children over 12 are welcome. $65.

MARSTONS MILLS

Bed and Breakfast Cape Cod

P.O. Box 341, West Hyannisport, 02672-0341
(508) 775-2772; FAX (508) 775-2884

34. Built in 1986 in a quiet residential neighborhood, this ranch-style house has all the extras one could ask for. One room has queen-size bed, private deck, and private entrance, and another room has a queen-size bed and private bath. The beach is two miles away and the ferry to Martha's Vineyard or Nantucket is three miles away. Children over 12 welcome. No smoking allowed. $75-85.

58. Built in 1790, this beautiful Colonial-style inn sits on three acres of rolling hillside and overlooks a freshwater pond. A working fireplace and country furnishings create a warm, comfortable atmosphere in the first-floor parlor, and a porch with white wicker furniture and fresh floral arrangements looks out onto a swimming pool. A

small suite, a carriage house, and three guest rooms offer special appeal. Children over 12. $65-135.

MEDFORD

Bed and Breakfast Associates Bay Colony, Ltd.

P.O. Box 57166, Babson Park,Boston 02157-0166
(617) 449-5302; (800) 347-5088
FAX (617) 449-5958

IN205. This host couple offers two beautiful properties in Medford's finest neighborhood of stately homes near Tufts University. Fully restored and attractively furnished, the guest rooms offer all bed sizes and most share baths with one other room. A three-room family suite has a private bath and balcony with view of Boston. $68-150.

MIDDLEBORO

On Cranberry Pond Bed and Breakfast

43 Fuller Street, 02346
(508) 946-0768

Snuggled away among the hills and bogs of northeastern Middleboro is a haven from the daily routine that offers a restful, cozy, country escape with all the modern amenities and more. Three working fireplaces, two common rooms, flower room, corporate meeting room, and dining room. Bass fishing, canoeing, mountain biking, and lots of walking trails are nearby. Thirty minutes from Plymouth, 45 minutes from Boston, Fall River, and New Bedford, and 40 minutes to Cape Cod.

Hosts: Jeannie and Tim LaBossiere
Rooms: 5 (3 PB; 2 SB) $85-105
Full and Continental Breakfast
Credit Cards: A, B
Notes: 2, 5, 7, 9, 10, 11, 12, 14

NOTES: Credit cards accepted: A MasterCard; B Visa; C American Express; D Discover; E Diners Club;
F Other; 2 Personal checks accepted; 3 Lunch available; 4 Dinner available; 5 Open all year; 6 Pets welcome;

MIDDLETON

Bed and Breakfast Marblehead and North Shore

P.O. Box 35, Newtonville, 02160
(617) 964-1606; (800) 832-2632
FAX (617) 332-8572

The Blue Door Bed and Breakfast. This beautiful bed and breakfast accommodation is at the Salem/Marblehead area just 35 minutes north of Boston. It is a ten-room historic home on two acres of land, dating back to the 1690s and restored to include some surprising 20th-century amenities. There are four working fireplaces. The two guest rooms are decorated with period furniture using a specific theme. The 20s Room has a whirlpool private bath and The Victorian Room has a fireplace and private bath. A single room off of The 20s Room"offers a suite with private bath for groups of three. Guest rooms have TVs and air conditioning. Guests may stroll the grounds that offer a goldfish pond, Victorian-style gazebo, lovely perennial gardens, a horseshoe pitching range, and bocce court. Rates include Continental breakfast, served on the enclosed porch overlooking the surrounding gardens and grounds, weather permitting. The host offers romantic dinners for two, arranged by appointment. No smoking. Open year-round. $125-155.

MILTON

Host Homes of Boston

P.O. Box 117, Boston, 02168
(617) 244-1308; FAX (617) 244-5156

Historic Country Home. This 1780 country home restored by architect/owners blends heirlooms and modern amenities for a special stay. Second-floor guest room offers a pair of twin beds, and the grounds offer a swimming pool and a barn. Near I-93, Route 128, and I-95. $68.

NANTUCKET

Bed and Breakfast Inns of New England

128 South Hoop Pole Road, Guilford, CT 06437
(203) 457-0042; (800) 582-0853

MA1090. This authentic, historic home, has been newly renovated to offer guest rooms with canopied beds, harbor views, and lots of charm. A home-baked Continental breakfast is included. Enjoy the spacious gardens on premises, or take a two-minute stroll to the wharf or the whaling museum. Browse in the many shops around town. Gentle ocean breezes, cobblestone streets, endless moors, and beaches await guests. All ages welcome. Family suites available. Seasonal rates available. $50-195.

The Carlisle House Inn

26 North Water Street, 02554
(508) 228-0720

Built in 1765, the Carlisle House has been a quality inn for more than 100 years. Just off the center of town, the inn has been carefully restored. Hand-stenciled wallpapers,

The Carlisle House Inn

7 No smoking; 8 Children welcome; 9 Social drinking allowed; 10 Tennis nearby; 11 Swimming nearby; 12 Golf nearby; 13 Skiing nearby; 14 May be booked through a travel agent.

working fireplaces, inlaid pine paneling, wide-board floor, and rich Oriental carpets. Minimum stay of two nights. Seasonal rates available.

Hosts: Peter and Suzanne Conway
Rooms: 14 (8 PB; 6 SB) $60-165
Continental Breakfast
Credit Cards: A, B, C
Notes: 2, 7, 9, 10, 11, 12

The Carriage House

Five Ray's Court, 02554
(508) 228-0326

Established in 1974, The Carriage House bed and breakfast is lovingly cared for by Jeanne McHugh and son, Haziel. Originally serving as a carriage house for a whaling mansion in the mid-1800s, it is just a half block behind Main Street on one of the prettiest lanes in town. Convenient to museums, shops, restaurants, and all the activities of town, yet blissfully quiet and removed from them. The Carriage House is quality-rated in the AAA and Mobil travel guides. It has been written about in many travel publications including *Yankee Travel Guide*, *National Geographic*, and the *International Herald Tribune*.

Hosts: Jeanne McHugh and son
Rooms: 7 (PB) $65-150
Continental Breakfast
Credit Cards: None
Notes: 2, 5, 8, 9, 10, 11, 12, 14

Cobblestone Inn

5 Ash Street, 02554
(508) 228-1987

On a cobbled side street two blocks from Steamship Wharf, the Cobblestone Inn was built in 1725 and later expanded to a five-bedroom guest house. The weathered shingle building survived the Great Fire of 1846 and now displays such original features as four fireplaces, wide floorboards, and curved corner support posts from the frame of a ship. Most of the rooms are large, with period decorations; some have fireplaces and canopied beds, and all have their own private baths. One room has a beautiful view of the harbor.

Host: Robin Hammer-Yankow
Rooms: 5 (PB) $100-150
Continental Breakfast
Credit Cards: A, B
Notes: 2, 5, 7, 8, 9, 10, 11, 12, 14

The Fairway

9 Fair Street, 02554
(508) 228-9467

Enjoy complete privacy or become "part of the family." This stately home in the historic core district is run by a Nantucket native. It has a large yard, many antiques, and offers a homemade Continental breakfast in the formal dining room. A private latticed porch allows guests to watch the world go by.

Host: Lee Holmes
Rooms: 2 (PB) $125
Continental Breakfast
Credit Cards: A, B
Notes: 2, 9, 10, 11, 12

House of Seven Gables

32 Cliff Road, 02554
(508) 228-4706

In the historic district of Nantucket. A Continental breakfast is served in the room. Most rooms in this 100-year-old Victorian have a view of Nantucket Sound.

Host: Suzanne Walton
Rooms: 10 (8 PB; 2 SB) $60-150
Continental Breakfast
Credit Cards: A, B, C
Notes: 2, 5, 7, 10, 11, 12

Hussey House–1795

15 North Water Street, 02554
(508) 228-0747

The 1795 home of captain Uriel Hussey has five rooms with private baths, antiques, fireplaces, Oriental rugs, and fresh flowers. Beautiful garden is on the grounds.

Hosts: The Johnson family
Rooms: 6 (PB) $95-150
Continental Breakfast

Credit Cards: None
Notes: 2, 8, 9, 10, 11, 12, 14

The Martin House Inn

61 Centre Street, P.O. Box 743, 02554
(508) 228-0678

In a stately 1803 mariner's home in the
Nantucket historic district, a romantic
sojourn awaits guests. A glowing fire in the
spacious living room-dining room is the
perfect place to read and relax. Large, airy
guest rooms with authentic period pieces
and four-poster beds and a lovely yard and
veranda for peaceful, summer afternoons
make sure guests have a memorable stay. A
large breakfast featuring homemade breads
and muffins, fresh fruits, and granola is
served in the dining room. Working fireplaces in three rooms.

Hosts: Ceci and Channing Moore
Rooms: 13 (9 PB; 4 SB) $85-145
Continental Breakfast
Credit Cards: A, B, C
Notes: 2, 5, 7, 8, 9 10, 11, 12

76 Main Street

76 Main Street, 02554
(508) 228-2533

All the quiet and subtle beauty of Nantucket
is here for guests to explore in comfort from
this 1883 Victorian home in the historic district on elm-shaded and cobblestoned Main
Street. The host is dedicated to guests'
enjoyment of the island and looks forward
to accommodating their needs. All rooms
are nonsmoking.

Host: Shirley Peters
Rooms: 18 (PB) $125-145
Continental Breakfast
Credit Cards: A, B, C, D
Notes: 2, 8, 9, 10, 11, 12, 14

Stumble Inne

109 Orange Street, 02554
(508) 228-4482; FAX (508) 228-4752

The Stumble Inne and Starbuck House are
on historic Orange Street, a pleasant ten-
minute walk to Main Street town center for
shops and restaurants. The Stumble Inne
has seven double and queen-size rooms, all
with cable TV, and most with bar refrigerators. Some rooms are air-conditioned. The
Starbuck House, right across the street, has
six double rooms. All rooms in both buildings feature period antiques and Laura
Ashley decor.

Hosts: Mary Kay and Mal Condon
Rooms: 13 (11 PB; 2 SB) $65-190
Continental Breakfast
Credit Cards: A, B, C
Notes: 2, 8, 9, 10, 11, 12, 14

Tuckernuck Inn

60 Unions Street, 02554
(508) 228-4886; (800) 228-4886

Tuckernuck Inn is named for the small island
just one mile off Nantucket's westernmost

Tuckernuck Inn

7 No smoking; 8 Children welcome; 9 Social drinking allowed; 10 Tennis nearby; 11 Swimming nearby; 12
Golf nearby; 13 Skiing nearby; 14 May be booked through a travel agent.

tip. Tuckernuck is an Indian word meaning "a loaf of bread." The inn is Colonial in decor and quite comfortable. Amenities include a large back lawn for relaxing and a rooftop widow's walk deck overlooking Nantucket Harbor. Fine dining is offered May through October at the in-house restaurant, American Bounty. Personal attention for each guest is the primary objective, and many of the guests return year after year. Tuckernuck Inn is recommended by AAA and *Mobil Travel Guide*. Continental breakfast is served November through April; full breakfast is served May through October.

Hosts: Ken and Phyllis Parker
Rooms: 16 (PB) $80-145
Suites: 2 (PB) $125-220
Full and Continental Breakfast
Credit Cards: A, B, C
Notes: 4, 5, 7, 8, 9, 10, 11, 12, 14

The Woodbox Inn

29 Fair Street, 02554
(508) 228-0587

Nantucket's oldest inn, built in 1709, is one-and-a-half blocks from the center of town. The Woodbox offers three queen-size rooms and six suites with working fireplaces, all with private bath. A full breakfast is available along with candlelight gourmet dinners. Voted Nantucket's Most Romantic Dining Room and also rated Nantucket's Finest Dining. Closed mid-October through June 1.

Host: Dexter Tutein
Rooms: 9 (PB) $125-200
Full Breakfast
Credit Cards: None
Notes: 2, 4, 7, 8, 9, 10, 11, 12

NANTUCKET ISLAND

Folger Hotel

P.O. Box 628, 89 Easton Street, 02554
(508) 228-0313

A family resort in a quiet neighborhood, a five-minute walk from downtown, and a short distance to the beaches. The hotel is surrounded with wide verandas which overlook the landscaped grounds and water gardens. A full breakfast is included with the room (in-season), served in the Whale Restaurant. Nonsmoking rooms available.

Hosts: Bob and Barbara Bowman
Rooms: 60 (40 PB; 20 SB) $80-140
Full Breakfast
Credit Cards: A, B, C, D
Notes: 2, 4, 8, 9, 10, 11, 12, 14

NEEDHAM

Bed and Breakfast Associates Bay Colony, Ltd.

P.O. Box 57166, Babson Park, Boston, 02157-0166
(617) 449-5302; (800) 347-5088
FAX (617) 449-5958

IW630. This sweet little Cape-style home epitomizes New England suburban serenity. Convenient to commuter railway, or Boston is only 20 minutes by car. Two guest rooms (large room with double bed or smaller room with twin beds) share a bath on the second floor. Host quarters are on the first floor. Driveway parking. $45-55.

IW638. A delightful multilevel Colonial home with a tasteful and appealing decor. Three guest rooms on the third floor with designer bath. This is a delightful neighborhood! 25 minutes west of downtown Boston. Family rates available. $85.

Bed and Breakfast Greater Boston and Cape Cod

P.O. Box 35, Newtonville, 02160
(617) 964-1606; (800) 832-2632
FAX (617) 332-8572

South Court Bed and Breakfast. A multilevel contemporary Colonial, beautifully designed and decorated by the host, in a lovely suburb west of Boston, just minutes from Route 128. Peaceful surroundings.

Within walking distance to many shops and fine restaurants. Close to a number of local area colleges and the commuter rail into Boston. Three guest accommodations include a king-size bedroom with skylight and two rooms with two single beds. An oversized private bath is just adjacent to the guest rooms and a half-bath is on the lower level. Guests may relax in the beautiful sitting room with fireplace or on the outside deck, weather permitting. This accommodation is centrally air-conditioned for guests' comfort. A delicious, generous Continental breakfast is included. No smoking. Children welcome. $65-100.

Greater Boston Hospitality

P.O. Box 1142, Brookline, 02146
(617) 277-5430

101. Beautiful 66-year-old Royal Barry Wills home is full of nooks and crannies. Close to Wellesley, Babson, and Mount Ida colleges, Glover Hospital, and the Route 128 Industrial Park. Charming hosts offer three guest rooms, one with a queen-size bed, one with a double bed, and one with twin beds, that share one and one-half baths. Parking included, but close to public transportation. Enjoy full, outstanding, authentic New England breakfasts in lovely dining room or on the sun deck. Guest den. Well-informed hostess. No smoking. Children over 12 welcome. Twenty dollars extra for twin bed in room. $65.

Host Homes of Boston

P.O. Box 117, Boston, 02168
(617) 244-1308; FAX (617) 244-5156

The Thistle Bed and Breakfast. Typical, cozy Cape Cod on a quiet street has a fireplaced living room for guests and two second-floor guest rooms with doubles or twins and private and shared baths. A few blocks from Route 128/I-95, and guests can walk to the train. $61-68.

NEWBURYPORT

Bed and Breakfast Inns of New England

128 South Hoop Pole Road, Guilford, CT 06437
(203) 457-0042; (800) 582-0853

MA-1000. Built in 1806 by Captain William Hoyt, this estate typifies the three-story square style of the Federal period. Among its many fine architectural features are cornices, mantles, balustrades, and a graceful hanging staircase. There are summer and winter porches, a formal front parlor, and library. Many special events are offered throughout the year, including weekend murder mysteries, fashion shows, weddings, and corporate conferences. Just a five-minute walk from downtown Newburyport, a seaport area. There are nine guest rooms on the inn's three floors, all furnished in antiques and some with canopied beds. Children 12 and older welcome. $60-77.

Bed and Breakfast Marblehead and North Shore

P.O. Box 35, Newtonville, 02160
(617) 964-1606; (800) 832-2632
FAX (617) 332-8572

The Homestead. This is a charming ten-room 1813 Federalist-style home, with wonderful antiques and period furnishings. There are ten fireplaces throughout the house. Guest rooms have double and single beds. Host prefers to offer private bath for one room or shared bath for guests traveling together. Guests have use of the downstairs living room area and back screened porch. Host is very actively involved in the nearby Parker River National Wildlife Refuge and donates a portion of her bed and breakfast income to benefit conservation. Hikers, bikers, history buffs, and nature lovers will appreciate the host's knowledge of the local and regional area attractions. A Continental

7 No smoking; 8 Children welcome; 9 Social drinking allowed; 10 Tennis nearby; 11 Swimming nearby; 12 Golf nearby; 13 Skiing nearby; 14 May be booked through a travel agent.

breakfast, featuring fresh orange juice, fresh ground coffee, and home-baked goodies is included. No smoking. $70-80.

The Windsor House

The Windsor House in Newburyport

38 Federal Street, 01950
(508) 462-3778

Built as a wedding present, this eighteenth-century Federal mansion offers a rare blend of Yankee hospitality and the English tradition of bed and breakfast. Designed as a residence/ship's chandlery, the inn's spacious rooms recall the spirit of an English country house. In a historic seaport near a wildlife refuge. Whale watching, museums, theater, and antiques. Rates include afternoon tea, English-cooked breakfast, tax, and service.

Hosts: Judith and John Harris
Rooms: 6 (3 PB; 3 SB) $75-125
Full Breakfast
Credit Cards: A, B, C, D
Notes: 2, 5, 6, 7, 8, 10, 11, 12, 13, 14

NEWTON

Bed and Breakfast Associates Bay Colony, Ltd.

P.O. Box 57166, Babson Park, Boston, 02157-0166
(617) 449-5302; (800) 347-5088
FAX (617) 449-5958

IW255. This stately Victorian in a neighborhood of grand 19th-century homes has a private two-room guest suite with light cooking, a charming sitting room, and a dazzling new private bath. Leave the car in the driveway and walk to the express bus for a ten-minute trip to central Boston. Amenities include cable TV, VCR, telephone, a small refrigerator, microwave, built-in sandwich bar, and a Victorian desk and sofa. Ten to twenty minutes west of Boston. $89.

IW265. The host, a lovely lady, will proudly show guests the distinctive interior and spectacular landscaping of the ranch-style home that her architect husband designed. Large windows afford delightful views of the seasonal splendor. This is one of Boston's best suburban neighborhoods. One guest room with private bath and a single den rented with guest room. Full breakfast; children over ten welcome; no smoking. $80.

Bed and Breakfast Greater Boston and Cape Cod

P.O. Box 35, Newtonville, 02160
(617) 964-1606; (800) 832-2632
FAX (617) 332-8572

Crescent Avenue. In a lovely suburb just west of Boston, with easy access by car and public transportation to Boston and Cambridge. Large, gracious, 12-room Greek Revival home has lovely gardens and an in-ground pool. Beautifully decorated. Two guest rooms with private baths, separate entrance, and parking. Generous Continental breakfast is served in the dining room or on the screened porch. Kitchen area available for guest use. Cat and dog in residence, but they are kept away from guest traffic. No smoking. $75-100.

The Suite at Chestnut Hill. This gorgeous furnished efficiency, in a neighborhood of

---

very beautiful homes, offers easy access by public transportation to Boston and Cambridge. Efficiency has a kitchen area, full bath, color TV, telephone, air conditioning, separate dining and sitting areas, and a queen-size bed. Self-catered breakfast provided. $90.

Greater Boston Hospitality

P.O. Box 1142, Brookline, 02146
(617) 277-5430

31. Guests will enter from a driveway through to own entrance to a hideaway all their own in the separate wing of a spacious 1876 antique Revival home. Large room with cathedral ceiling has queen-size bed, two studio beds, dining area, private bath, skylight, TV, refrigerator, microwave, and other amenities. Parking, but very close to subway. No smoking. $80.

107. Double four-poster mahogany bed with private bath and many antiques in small, but very comfortable room on second floor of a wonderful 115-year-old country home. This home is owned by a delightful couple with one son and a great dog. Continental breakfast is provided in room for guests to eat at their leisure. Plenty of parking, but minutes to the subway. No smoking. $78.

108. Excellent suburban bed and breakfast. This restful, well-maintained, custom-built home offers guests a room that has a double bed and private bath. Attentive, pleasant, retired hostess offers a full breakfast, served in dining room or glassed-in porch in the summer, and makes homemade peach preserves. Air-conditioned. Parking included. No smoking. Thirty dollars extra for cot. $78.

Host Homes of Boston

P.O. Box 117, Boston, 02168
(617) 244-1308; FAX (617) 244-5156

Alderwood. Guests migrate to the gourmet kitchen in this 1930 Colonial. Second-floor guest room has twin beds. "Pumpkin" the cat lives here. Children welcome. Quiet road near Boston College law campus. One mile to Green Line-D. Ten-minute drive to Boston. Private bath; TV. $68.

Briarwood. This historic district landmark home (1875) combines Early American antiques with modern amenities. Exceptional guest wing with private entrance and bath, featuring queen-size bed, two twins that double as sofas, skylights, air conditioning, TV, an alcove with dining table, picture window, and light-cooking facilities. Guests prepare own breakfast, food provided. Near restaurants and elegant mall, four blocks to public transit (Green Line-D), one block to Boston College. Boston, three miles. No smoking. $85.

The Evergreens. Older Colonial is filled with host's pottery and Mexican art collection. Two second-floor guest rooms share bath. Cozy screened porch. Five-minute walk to Boston College or Green Line-B to Boston University, Back Bay, and downtown. Air conditioning. Shared bath. $64.

Rockledge. Stately 1882 Victorian in prime location. Cordial hosts offer bright, spacious rooms, antiques, trees, and gardens. Three second-floor guest rooms, but only two booked at a time. Ceiling fans. Second-floor guest parlor. Resident cat. Two blocks to lake, village, and subway. Older children welcome. Shared or private bath. TV. No smoking. $64-75.

Upper Falls Aerie. Victorian farmhouse, circa 1904, perched on a hill in quiet neighborhood. Terraced side lawn and patio face woods. Small second floor guest room with double bed and private bath has sunset view. Resident cat. Walk to local

---

7 No smoking; 8 Children welcome; 9 Social drinking allowed; 10 Tennis nearby; 11 Swimming nearby; 12 Golf nearby; 13 Skiing nearby; 14 May be booked through a travel agent.

restaurants and antique supermarket. Boston is 15 minutes away. Close to subway, Routes 95 and 9, Boston College, and Wellesley College. Parking included. No smoking allowed. $68.

NEWTON CENTER

Bed and Breakfast Associates Bay Colony, Ltd.

P.O. Box 57166, Babson Park,Boston 02157-0166
(617) 449-5302; (800) 347-5088
FAX (617) 449-5958

IW245. This large Victorian home has two pleasant third-floor guest rooms with shared bath and a master suite with private bath. Fully restored and beautifully furnished, this family home is on a quiet street close to shops and public transit. $65-90.

Bed and Breakfast Greater Boston and Cape Cod

P.O. Box 35, Newtonville, 02160
(617) 964-1606; (800) 832-2632
FAX (617) 332-8572

The Park Lane. A large Baronial-style stucco set in a quiet residential area within walking distance of public transit, shops, and restaurants. Three rooms on two levels offer double, single with trundle, or queen-size beds. Baths, shared and private, include one Jacuzzi shower/bath. Also available are TV, air conditioning, a sitting room, and a front porch. A generous Continental breakfast is served. Other conveniences include airport pickup, room phones, and visitor T-pass tickets. No smoking. Children welcome. Open year-round. $50-100.

Host Homes of Boston

P.O. Box 117, Boston, 02168
(617) 244-1308; FAX (617) 244-5156

Park Lane. This large Baronial-style stucco (1911) on quiet street has a Victo-

rian motif. Friendly host offers two third-floor guest rooms, one with double-bed and the other with trundle bed (choice of single twins or king-size), second floor with queen-size bed, private bath Jacuzzi, air conditioning, cable TV. First floor guest parlor with fireplace. Village, public transit (Green Line-D), restaurants all within ten-minute walk. Five miles from Boston. No smoking. Children welcome. $64-85.

NORTH EASTHAM

Bed & Breakfast Inns of New England

128 South Hoop Pole Road, Guilford, CT 06437
(203) 457-0042; (800) 582-0853

MA-1051. This house, a half-Cape with saltbox addition, is decorated with quilts and collectibles. In a quiet neighborhood less than a mile from Cape Cod National Seashore Visitors Center, it is minutes from bay beaches, freshwater ponds, and two ocean beaches. Two guest rooms are available, both with shared baths. The first-floor room has a king-size bed, and the upstairs room has a double bed. No smoking. House dog; no guest pets. $50-60.

NORTH FALMOUTH (CAPE COD)

Bed and Breakfast Cape Cod

P.O. Box 341, West Hyannisport, 02672-0341
(508) 775-2772; FAX (508) 775-2884

51. Built in 1793, this Cape Cod Colonial was expanded and fully restored to its original condition and appearance some years ago. Primitive Early American decor and antiques fill this antique dealer's home. Two guest rooms each have a private bath, double canopied beds, fireplaces, and a sitting area where the hostess serves breakfast. $85.

NOTES: Credit cards accepted: A MasterCard; B Visa; C American Express; D Discover; E Diners Club; F Other; 2 Personal checks accepted; 3 Lunch available; 4 Dinner available; 5 Open all year; 6 Pets welcome;

NORTHAMPTON (FLORENCE) _____

The Knoll

230 North Main Street, 01060-1221
(413) 584-8164

The Knoll can be found on 17 acres over-looking farmland and forest. It is in town and yet in a rural setting, with an acre of lawn and a large circular driveway. This is the five-college area of western Massachusetts: Smith, Amherst, Mount Holyoke, University of Massachusetts, and Hampshire colleges.

Host: Mrs. Lee Lesko
Rooms: 3 (SB) $45-55
Full Breakfast
Credit Cards: None
Notes: 2, 5, 7, 10, 11, 12, 13

NORWELL _____

Bed and Breakfast Associates Bay Colony, Ltd.

P.O. Box 57166, Babson Park, Boston 02157-0166
(617) 449-5302; (800) 347-5088
FAX (617) 449-5958

SS330. In the pretty suburban town of Norwell, this country home was built in 1810. The house features beamed ceilings, Oriental rugs, and antiques. Three guest rooms share a bath. Full breakfast; children welcome; no smoking. $68.

NORWOOD _____

Bed and Breakfast Associates Bay Colony, Ltd.

P.O. Box 57166, Babson Park, Boston 02157-0166
(617) 449-5302; (800) 347-5088
FAX (617) 449-5958

IW560. Just 15 minutes from Boston, this four-bedroom inn was built in 1850, and is authentically furnished with antiques and reproduction pieces. Each room has a private bath, TV, and telephone. $65.

Host Homes of Boston

P.O. Box 117, Boston, 02168
(617) 244-1308; FAX (617) 244-5156

Lyman Smith House. Return to genteel times in this historic home, circa 1851, carefully restored in period decor. Enjoy the sitting room replete with memorabilia and breakfast in the tea room. Browse through the gift shop. Four large second floor guest rooms with authentic furnishings offer three double beds, one twin bed, bath, TV, and telephone in deference to modern needs. Walk to a variety of restaurants and shops. Fifteen miles southwest of Boston. Train four blocks away. Parking available. Air-conditioned. No smoking. $81.

OAK BLUFFS (MARTHA'S VINEYARD) _____

The Beach House Bed and Breakfast

Corner of Seaview and Pennacook Avenue, 02557
(508) 693-3955

A newly renovated 1890s house directly across from large, sandy swimming beach. Friendly, helpful, and relaxed atmosphere. Rooms have brass queen-size beds, ceiling fans, and TV. Close to town, shops, restaurants, ferries, shuttle bus, and tours; moped, car, bike, and boat rentals. Oak Bluffs is a magnificent town for strollers and photographers, with its many-hued gingerbread cottages. It is also home to the Flying Horses, the nation's oldest carousel.

Hosts: Pamela, Calvin, and Justin Zaiko
Rooms: 9 (PB) $60-130
Continental Breakfast
Credit Cards: A, B, C, D, E
Notes: 5, 9, 10, 11, 12

Bed and Breakfast Inns of New England

128 South Hoop Pole Road, Guilford, CT 06437
(203) 457-0042; (800) 582-0853

---

7 No smoking; 8 Children welcome; 9 Social drinking allowed; 10 Tennis nearby; 11 Swimming nearby; 12 Golf nearby; 13 Skiing nearby; 14 May be booked through a travel agent.

MA1080. This 1873 Victorian inn offers relaxing, casual accommodations across the street from the beautiful beaches of Oak Bluffs. Choose from seven guest rooms, some with private baths. Six have views of the ocean and the boats arriving at the pier. Guests may enjoy the piano nook, a living room with fireplace, a sun porch, and deck to help view the brilliant sunrise over the sound. There are band concerts around the corner in Ocean Park, bicycle races, tennis, and kite-flying contests on the green. Families welcome. $65-115.

Bed and Breakfast Nantucket/ Martha's Vineyard

P.O. Box 341, West Hyannisport, 02672-0341
(508) 775-2772; FAX (508) 775-2884

201. This 1872 Victorian cottage has seven bedrooms for bed and breakfast and is one city block from the beaches. Bedrooms with private baths and king-size or double beds are available. Continental breakfast is served from 8:00-10:00 A.M. Public tennis and public transportation to other parts of the island are two blocks away. $80-130.

206. The Victorian cottage was built 95 years ago 500 feet from the banks of the ocean on Nantucket Sound. It is a unique house that has been in the owner's family for generations. The four bedrooms share two baths. One bedroom has twin beds and three have queen-size beds. Enjoy the beach a few steps away from the house. Shops, restaurants, tennis, golf, and biking are within three-fourths mile of the house. Relax in the parlor, savoring great music in front of a fireplace. A great getaway any time of the year. No children. No smoking. $55-95.

209. Oak Bluffs is a Victorian village at the heart of the island. The ferry, buses, and the beach are steps away. The inn was built in 1989 and reflects the quaint style of the houses in the community. All rooms are air-conditioned, with private full baths, TVs, and telephones. The Continental breakfast is served in the dining area. Lovely grounds offer outdoor breakfasts and spots for lounging. Harbor views from some rooms and several suites for three to four persons are available. A great island accommodation. Bike, jeep, or car rentals available nearby. $75-155.

Dockside Inn

Circut Avenue Extension, Box 1206, 02557-1206
(800) 245-5979; FAX (508) 696-7293

Built in 1989, this inn has all the Victorian charm of the 1800s. In historic Oak Bluffs Harbor, it is just a short walk to public beaches, shops, restaurants, and ferries. All 20 rooms are tastefully decorated and include full private baths, air conditioning. cable TV, and private entrances. Efficiency suites suitable for families. Decks with water veiws. Landscaped gardens. Group rates and packages available.

Hosts: Tom and Kim Miller
Rooms: 20 (PB) $95-275
Continental Breakfast
Credit Cards: A, B, C, D
Notes: 2, 7, 8, 9, 10, 11, 12, 14

Tivoli Inn

222 Circuit Avenue, P.O. Box 1033, 02557
(508) 693-7928

A newly restored Victorian home which has the island charm and exudes a clean and friendly atmosphere. Walking distance to town shops, restaurants, nightlife, ferries, beach, and public transportation. A great place to stay with all the comforts of home. Each room is charmingly decorated with a Victorian flair. Come visit the treasured island of Martha's Vineyard. Seasonal rates available.

Hosts: Lisa and Lori Katsounakis
Rooms: 6 (3 PB; 3 SB) $50-125
Continental Breakfast
Credit Cards: A B, C
Notes: 5, 7, 8, 9, 10, 11, 12, 14

NOTES: Credit cards accepted: A MasterCard; B Visa; C American Express; D Discover; E Diners Club;
F Other; 2 Personal checks accepted; 3 Lunch available; 4 Dinner available; 5 Open all year; 6 Pets welcome;

Tucker Inn

Tucker Inn

46 Massasoit Avenue, P.O. Box 2680, 02557
(508) 693-1045

The Tucker Inn has the perfect ingredients for a great stay in Oak Bluffs, from its in-town location on a quiet park to its oversize bedrooms, veranda, and inviting living room. The inn is within walking distance of everything. Just down the street are stores, boutiques, theaters, churches, restaurants, clubs, bike and car rental agencies, and the town beach. Public transportation and boat lines are within a five-minute walk.

Innkeepers: Bill Reagan
Rooms: 8 (6 PB; 2 SB) $55-135
Continental Breakfast
Credit Cards: A, B
Notes: 2, 7, 8, 9, 10, 11, 12, 14

ORLEANS

Bed and Breakfast Cape Cod

P.O. Box 341, West Hyannisport, 02672-0341
(508) 775-2772; FAX (508) 775-2884

8. This dramatic, contemporary home is built on high ground and overlooks five acres of wooded land. The large deck is next to an in-ground pool. Interior features include a soaring cathedral ceiling, Oriental carpets, wood-burning fireplaces, and spiral staircase. Bedrooms have queen-size beds and private baths, and Nauset Beach is two miles away. A cottage is also available. Full breakfast. No smoking. Children over 11 welcome. $100.

18. This carriage house is on the banks of an ocean pond. The suite on the second floor is spacious with a king-size bed, private bath with shower, a full kitchen, and a sitting area. A pull-out is available for two extra persons. From the shaded deck overlooking the pond guests can see the host's dock where there is a canoe available for guests. The Continental breakfast is served in suite with fresh baked goods daily. A wonderful place for a honeymoon couple or for a very secluded getaway with great privacy. No children under six. No smoking. $110.

24. Built nearly 78 years ago on land that has been in the host's family for five generations, this is a marvelous house on a private estate. It has an expanded wing, with a suite which includes a king-size bed, a den with fireplace and large deck overlooking the ocean. A marvelously relaxing accommodation with complete suite privacy and a private beach 100 yards from the house. The village two and one-half miles away features some of the best restaurants on Cape Cod. Full breakfast. No children under 12. No smoking. $100.

60. In a quiet wooded section of Orleans near Skaket Beach is a home built in 1992. It offers a bedroom with twin beds and a private bath. The breakfast is Continental and served in the dining room or on the deck each morning. The village is a few miles from the house and offers fine restaurants and shops. This is a great spot for two women or a couple requiring twin beds. No smoking. No children. $70.

Bed and Breakfast Greater Boston and Cape Cod

P.O. Box 35, Newtonville 02160
(617) 964-1606; (800) 832-2632
FAX (617) 332-8572

Shady Elms. A charming small accommodation within two miles of Nauset Beach.

---

7 No smoking; 8 Children welcome; 9 Social drinking allowed; 10 Tennis nearby; 11 Swimming nearby; 12 Golf nearby; 13 Skiing nearby; 14 May be booked through a travel agent.

The guest room offers a queen-size and a twin bed, plus a roll away, with private bath, TV, and refrigerator; it is also air-conditioned. A Continental breakfast is provided in an adjoining room and may be taken to guest room or outdoors. No smoking. Children welcome. Fifteen dollars for extra person. $75.

Orleans Bed and Breakfast Associates

P.O. Box 1312, 02653
(508) 255-3824; (800) 541-6226

Arey's Pond Relais. A very special house filled with warmth, myriads of delightful details, and intriguing collections. Flower-filled patio serves as private entrance to guest rooms. Queen-size bed with white wicker headboard invites rest. Private bath, small guest refrigerator. Adjacent queen room can accommodate children or other travelers in the group. Breakfast is served on deck overlooking Arey's Pond. $70.

The 1840 House. An 1840 Greek Revival in a residential neighborhood within walking distance of town center, restaurants, galleries, and the Academy of Performing Arts. One twin room, one double room, each with private bath. Sitting room with TV. Breakfast served on fine china. Roll away bed available ($30). $65.

Gray Gables. An enormous old elm shades a secluded yard with lawn furniture set out for guests' pleasure. A private entrance leads to the guest wing of this fine old house with plenty of charm and wonderfully warm hosts. Comfortably spacious, air-conditioned guest room has queen-size and single beds, refrigerator, and TV. Adjacent bath has huge tiled shower. Continental breakfast is set out to enjoy at leisure, in-room or under the elm. Handsome English springer spaniel in residence. $75.

Hilltop. Overlooking Baker's Pond, this sparkling new Cape Cod home offers two comfortable bedrooms with connecting bath, each room freshly furnished; one with queen-size bed and the other with a double plus a single bed. Generous Continental breakfast served on sunny, spacious deck. Swim in clear, fresh water with private sandy beach. Walk to nearby Nickerson State Park's many beautiful trails and ponds. $70.

Maison de La Mer. Attractively decorated contemporary country home on Cape Cod Bay, a short, pretty walk to Skaket Beach. Spacious first-floor twin room with private bath. Second-floor bedroom has water view, queen-size bed, and private bath with whirlpool tub. Guests are encouraged to use living room with front entrance. The sunny dining area overlooks a lovely seaside garden, or enjoy an alfresco meal on the deck. $80-90.

Morgan's Way. This dramatic Cape contemporary home built on high ground overlooks five acres of lovely gardens, lawns, and woods. A massive deck is next to the heated swimming pool. Interior features are soaring cathedral ceilings, Oriental carpets, original art, and a wood-burning fireplace. Two miles to Nauset Beach and one mile to the village center. Air-conditioned bedrooms have queen-size beds and private baths. Full breakfasts are a special treat. Cat in residence. $100.

Mayflower House. Handsome reproduction bow roof house on residential dead-end road. Spacious first-floor bedroom with queen-size bed, upstairs bedroom with two double beds; each has private bath, color TV, and air conditioning. Relax or read in first-floor parlor or on secluded deck. Dog-lovers welcome, as hosts have a fat, friendly Doberman. $75.

NOTES: Credit cards accepted: A MasterCard; B Visa; C American Express; D Discover; E Diners Club; F Other; 2 Personal checks accepted; 3 Lunch available; 4 Dinner available; 5 Open all year; 6 Pets welcome;

Rive Gauche. This exciting, light-filled artist's studio offers the quintessential Cape Cod experience. Separate stairway leads to spacious room over large barn, now used for garage. King-size bed, full bath, TV, telephone, and a kitchenette stocked for breakfast. Guests can have morning coffee on balcony high over "Lonnie's Pond." Saltwater swimming and boating at doorstep; walk over to Crystal Lake or wander the trails of Kent's Point conservation area. $110.

Sweet Retreat. A delightful in-town studio. Outside stairs lead to a private deck with view of attractive garden. Enter into kitchenette area with breakfast table. A step down into bedroom with queen-size bed and private bath. Host owns a beautiful patisserie and catering business. Count on good things for breakfast. Bike to beaches and walk to village. $85.

Winterwell. Restored 19th-century Cape Cod farmhouse, a short stroll to Skaket Beach yet close to town and bike path, offers two comfortable accommodations. The main house offers a first-floor guest room with separate entrance and private bath. Main living room for occasional reading and TV. A spacious guest wing with separate entrance has bedroom with private bath, sitting room, and kitchen-dining area. All guests enjoy breakfast on enclosed porch overlooking large private yard with busy bird feeder. $75-95.

OSTERVILLE

Bed and Breakfast Cape Cod

P.O. Box 341, West Hyannisport, 02672-0341
(508) 775-2772; FAX (508) 775-2884

50. This gracious Cape-style home was built in 1974 in the village of Osterville. The house has an in-ground pool and overlooks a freshwater lake that is ideal for fishing or simply a restful ride. The luxuriously appointed house has three bedrooms, game room, and library for guests. One-half mile into the village and only a few miles from Hyannis and the ferry to either Nantucket or Martha's Vineyard. TV in all rooms and complete central air conditioning. This is a very quiet, relaxed, and special acommodation for the discriminating visitor. $125.

59. Imagine the quintessential New England village, and travelers have found Osterville. This ten-year-old spacious Colonial house offers three guest accommodations, two with double beds and the other with a pair of twin beds. One room has a private bath, and the other two share a bath. No smoking. $52-68.

PEABODY

The International Bed & Breakfast Club, Inc.

504 Amherst Street, Buffalo, NY 14207
(800) 723-4262; FAX (716) 873-4462

MA0191PP. Ten minutes from historic Salem, this inn offers three bedrooms, two with twin beds and adjoining bath; one with double bed and shared bath. Continental breakfast and coffee served at all times. Living room fireplace, porch, and in-ground pool and patio. $60.

PERU

American Country Collection

1353 Union Street, Schnectady, NY 12054
(518) 439-7001; FAX (518) 439-4301

069. Built in 1830 as the town parsonage, this private homestay features the original wide-plank floors and floor-to-ceiling windows that look out onto old stone walls and 13 acres of woods. Guests dine in a sunroom with bay windows and French doors that lead onto a patio. The decor is French country, and the home is furnished with antiques and colorful Waverly and Laura Ashley chintz fabrics. Three excellent cross-country centers and one downhill ski area are within an eight-mile radius. Two bedrooms with private baths and double beds. No smoking. $65.

PETERSHAM

Winterwood at Petersham

19 North Main Street, 01366
(508) 724-8885

An elegant 16-room Greek Revival mansion built in 1842, just off the common of a classic New England town. The inn boasts numerous fireplaces and several porches for relaxing. Cocktails available. On the National Register of Historic Places.

Hosts: Jean and Robert Day
Rooms: 6 (PB) $63.42-84.56
Continental Breakfast
Credit Cards: A, B, C
Notes: 2, 5, 7, 8, 9, 12, 13, 14

Winterwood at Petersham

PITTSFIELD

The Olde White Horse Inn

378 South Street, 01201
(413) 442-2512

The Olde White Horse Inn is a charming, spacious Colonial home built around the turn of the century. Centrally found in the Berkshires near Tanglewood, it has nine, cozy guest rooms, each with a private bath and air conditioner. Guest rooms are tastefully decorated with country charm, fresh flowers, and fluffy comforters on one or two double beds. Wine and cheese are served on Saturday evenings in the parlor. Open May to October.

Hosts: Ron and Paula Virgilio
Rooms: 9 (8 PB; 1 SB) $75-145
Continental Breakfast
Credit Cards: A, B, C
Notes: 2, 7, 9, 10, 11, 12, 13

PLYMOUTH

Bed and Breakfast Associates Bay Colony, Ltd.

P.O. Box 57166, Babson Park, Boston, 02157-0166
(617) 449-5302; (800) 347-5088
FAX (617) 449-5958

SS795. An easy drive from Plymouth Rock takes guests to this fabulous 1820 Cape-style country home on 40 pastoral acres. This delightful restoration is enhanced by an impressive collection of antique American and English furniture and collectibles. Two richly furnished guest rooms in separate guest wing have private baths. Full breakfast. $88.

Remembrance

265 Sandwich Street, 02360
(508) 746-5160

Remembrance is an old, cedar-shingled, Cape-style home in a lovely residential neighborhood one mile from historic Plymouth, Plimoth Plantation, and the expressway; two blocks from the ocean. It is delightfully decorated with antiques, wicker, original art, plants, and flowers. Delicious full breakfasts served at guests' convenience in the greenhouse overlooking the garden and bird feeders. Tea time. No smoking. Gentle resident pets.

Host: Beverly Bainbridge
Rooms: 2 (SB) $65

NOTES: Credit cards accepted: A MasterCard; B Visa; C American Express; D Discover; E Diners Club; F Other; 2 Personal checks accepted; 3 Lunch available; 4 Dinner available; 5 Open all year; 6 Pets welcome;

Full Breakfast
Credit Cards: None
Notes: 2, 5, 7, 9, 11

PROVINCETOWN

Bed and Breakfast Greater Boston and Cape Cod

P.O. Box 35, Newtonville, 02160
(617) 964-1606; (800) 832-2632
FAX (617) 332-8572

The East End Guest House. A lovely historic home, dating back to the 1800s, which offers both rooms and apartments. Six guest rooms are beautifully decorated; two apartments are fully equipped. A self-service Continental breakfast is available in the common room. Guests may use the microwave, sink, and refrigerator, relax watching TV, or use the VCR. (Apartments rent in-season by the week only; off-season, they rent by night with a two-night minimum.) $75-125.

Bradford Gardens Inn

178 Bradford Street, 02657
(508) 487-1616; (800) 432-2334

An 1820 Colonial country inn with rooms offering fireplaces, ceiling fans, and antiques. Fireplaced cottages set in the beautiful gardens. All units have private baths. One block from the ocean and a five-minute stroll to town center for shopping, fine dining, art galleries, and whale watching.

Hosts: Linda Harris and Carol Cimmino
Rooms: 8 (PB); 9 cottages (PB) $69-175
Full Breakfast
Credit Cards: A, B, C
Notes: 2, 5, 7, 9, 10, 11, 12, 14

The Captain's House

350A Commercial Street, 02657
(508) 487-9794; (800) 457-8885

Open year-round the house in the center of town is within walking distance to shopping, restaurants, and night life. Reasonable rates and immaculate accommodations. Continen-

tal breakfast with home-baked pastries. Private and shared baths with cable TV and a pleasant common room with VCR and music for guests' pleasure. A private patio for sun bathing is also provided. Major credit cards accepted. Off-season rates available.

Hosts: Bob Carvalho and David Brennan
Rooms: 11 (3 PB; 8 SB) $50-80
Continental Breakfast
Credit Cards: A, B, C, D
Notes: 2, 5, 9, 11

Lamplighter Inn

26 Bradford Street, 02657
(508) 487-2529; (800) 263-6574

A sea captain's home with commanding 50-mile vistas of the ocean and Cape Cod. Convenient to shopping, museums, whale watching, beaches, restaurants, shows, and tours. Clean, airy rooms and suites with private baths await guests' arrival for a memorable stay at the Lamplighter on old Cape Cod. Packages available.

Hosts: Steven Vittum and Brent Lawyer
Rooms: 9 (7 PB; 2 SB)
Continental Breakfast
Credit Cards: A, B, C
Notes: 2, 5, 7, 9, 10, 11, 12, 14

Land's End Inn

22 Commercial Street, 02657
(508) 487-0706

High atop Gull Hill, Land's End Inn overlooks Provincetown and all of Cape Cod Bay. Large, airy, comfortably furnished living rooms, a large front porch, and lovely antique-filled bedrooms provide relaxation and visual pleasure to guests.

Host: David Schoolman
Rooms: 16 (PB) $98-250
Continental Breakfast
Credit Cards: None
Notes: 2, 5, 7, 9, 10, 11, 12

Rose and Crown Guest House

158 Commercial Street, 02657
(508) 487-3332

7 No smoking; 8 Children welcome; 9 Social drinking allowed; 10 Tennis nearby; 11 Swimming nearby; 12 Golf nearby; 13 Skiing nearby; 14 May be booked through a travel agent.

Rose and Crown Guest House

The Rose and Crown is a classic Georgian "square rigger" built in the 1780s. The guest house sits behind an ornate iron fence, and a ship's figurehead greets visitors from her post above the paneled front door. During restoration, wide floorboards were uncovered and pegged posts and beams exposed. An appealing clutter of Victorian antiques and artwork fills every nook and cranny.

Host: Sam Hardee
Rooms: 8 (5 PB; 3 SB) $45-110
Continental Breakfast
Credit Cards: A, B, E
Notes: 5, 9, 11, 14

Six Webster Place

6 Webster Place, 02657
(508) 487-2266

A restored 1750s bed and breakfast on a quiet lane in the heart of Provincetown, the bed and breakfast is one block from the Town Hall and Commercial Street and 200 yards from the bay beaches. All rooms have period furnishings, most offer working fireplaces, and most have private baths. A delicious Continental breakfast is served each morning; and in the off-season, host serves tea or a glass of wine by a roaring fire in the afternoon. Open all year. Three apartments are available.

Host: Gary Reinhardt
Rooms: 11 (7 PB; 4 SB) $35-95
Continental Breakfast

Credit Cards: A, B, C, D
Notes: 2, 5, 6, 8, 9, 14

Watership Inn

7 Winthrop Street, 02657
(508) 487-0094

Rustic 1820 sea captain's home, with Colonial rooms, private baths, and spacious lobby. Open year-round, serving Continental breakfast daily. Parking is available, and a five-minute walk gets visitors to the beach or to the center of town.

Host: Jim Foss
Rooms: 15 (PB) $29-90
Continental Breakfast
Credit Cards: A, B, C, D
Notes: 5, 9, 10, 11

White Wind Inn

174 Commercial Street, 02657
(508) 487-1526

A white Victorian, circa 1845, across the street from the beach and a five-minute walk from almost everything. Continental breakfast. Write or call for brochure. Seasonal rates available. Personal checks accepted for deposit only. Must call for confirmation regarding pets.

Host: Russell Dusablon
Rooms: 11 (PB) $65-165
Continental Breakfast
Credit Cards: A, B, C
Notes: 5, 8, 9, 10, 11, 12

QUINCY

Host Homes of Boston

P.O. Box 117, Boston, 02168
(617) 244-1308; FAX (617) 244-5156

Quincy Adams Bed and Breakfast. This elegant turn-of-the-century home near the ocean has fireplaces, canopied beds, and a den with a TV and hot tub. There are three guest rooms; two have queen-size beds and the third-floor maid's quarters has a double. Near Bayside Expo Center, restaurants, and

NOTES: Credit cards accepted: A MasterCard; B Visa; C American Express; D Discover; E Diners Club;
F Other; 2 Personal checks accepted; 3 Lunch available; 4 Dinner available; 5 Open all year; 6 Pets welcome;

historic mansions. Boston is 15 minutes away, and the Red Line is one block away. $68-75.

REHOBOTH

Five Bridge Farm Bed and Breakfast

154 Pine Street, P.O. Box 462, 02769
(508) 252-3190

Five Bridge Farm is a unique property near Providence, Newport, Cape Cod, and Boston. Enjoy hiking, cross-country skiing, tennis, swimming, or quiet time in the library, gazebo, or 60 acres. Guests are treated to old-fashioned hospitality and delicious homecooked breakfasts. Horseback riding, golf, fine restaurants, beaches, and antiquing are all nearby. No smoking inside. Inquire about accommodations for children.

Hosts: Harold and Ann Messenger
Rooms: 5 (3 PB; 2 SB) $55-85
Full Breakfast
Credit Cards: A, B, C, D, E
Notes: 2, 3, 5, 6, 9, 10, 11, 12, 14

Gilbert's Tree Farm Bed and Breakfast

30 Spring Street, 02769
(508) 252-6416

A 150-year-old New England Cape home with authentic hardware, wood floors, and

Gilbert's Tree Farm

windows is on a 100-acre tree farm only 12 miles east of Providence. Guests may enjoy in-ground pool, hiking, and pony cart rides. Delicious full country breakfasts. Within one hour of Boston, Plymouth, Newport, and Mystic. An additional $15 to stable horses.

Hosts: Jeanne and Martin "Pete" Gilbert
Rooms: 3 (SB) $50
Suite: 1 (PB) $75
Full Breakfast
Credit Cards: None
Notes: 2, 5, 6, 7, 8, 9, 10, 11, 12, 14

Perryville Inn

157 Perryville Road, 02769
(508) 252-9239

This 19th-century restored Victorian on the National Register of Historic Places is on four and one-half wooded acres with a quiet brook, mill pond, stone walls, and shaded paths. Bicycles are available for guests, including a tandem. The inn overlooks an 18-hole public golf course. All rooms are furnished with antiques and accented with colorful handmade quilts. Nearby are antique stores, museums, Great Woods Performing Arts Center, fine seafood restaurants, and an old-fashioned New England clambake. Arrange for a horse-drawn hayride or a hot air balloon ride. Within one hour of Boston, Plymouth, Newport, and Mystic.

Hosts: Tom and Betsy Charnecki
Rooms: 5 (3 PB; 2 SB) $50-85
Continental Breakfast
Credit Cards: A, B, C, D
Notes: 2, 5, 8, 9, 10, 11, 12, 14

REVERE

Bed and Breakfast Marblehead and North Shore

P.O. Box 35, Newtonville, 02160
(617) 964-1606; (800) 832-2632
FAX (617) 332-8572

Oceanside Bed and Breakfast. A beautifully decorated bed and breakfast home with two guest rooms with full and queen-size beds, sharing a bath and a half. Both guest rooms have TVs, air conditioning, and ceiling fans. Guests may enjoy use of downstairs sitting room or back yard, weather permitting. A wonderful Continental breakfast is included. Points of Pines is the nicest private residential area of Revere and is very convenient to Boston by bus into the Haymarket Square-Faneuil Hall area, and only ten minutes from the airport. By prior appointment hosts will pick up or drop off at airport for a fee. Easy access to Olde Towne Marblehead by bus. Only one minute from private sandy beach. No smoking. $80.

Golden Slumber Accommodations

640 Revere Beach Boulevard, 02151
(800) 892-3231

Golden Slumber features an unrivaled array of screened accommodations on the seacoast of Massachusetts including Cape Cod, the North and South Shores, and greater Boston. From sprawling oceanfront villas to quaint, country road retreats, gracious historic residences and unique contemporary facilities offer the paramount in Yankee hospitality. Several feature incomparable water views, canopied beds, fireplaces, private entrances, and swimming pools. No reservation fee. Children welcome. Limousine and gift service. Brochure and directory available.

Owner: Leah A. Schmidt
Rooms: 150 (90 PB; 60 SB) $55-220
Full and Continental Breakfasts
Credit Cards: A, B
Notes: 2, 4, 5, 8, 9, 10, 11, 12

RICHMOND

A Bed and Breakfast in the Berkshires

1666 Dublin Road, 01254
(413) 698-2817; (800) 795-7122
FAX (413) 698-3158

A Bed and Breakfast in the Berkshires

This 1963 home with pillars and shutters on three and one-half acres with serene valley views and rolling lawns can be found on a country lane in the Berkshire Hills three and one-half miles from Tanglewood Music Festival and Hancock Shaker Village. Features three rooms with private baths, down pillows and comforters, handmade quilts, antiques, and roses. Cable TV and air conditioning. Continental breakfast with homemade breads, jams, fresh fruit, Berkshire apple pancakes, and afternoon tea or sherry. Hosted by Doane Perry and son Curt, who has lived and traveled in five countries, speaks French, German, Swahili, and Greek. Open all year-including holidays. No smoking or pets are allowed due to the birds.

Hosts: Doane Perry and Curt Perry
Rooms: 3 (PB) $60-125
Continental Breakfast
Credit Cards: A, B, C
Notes: 2, 5, 7, 8, 9, 10, 11, 12, 13, 14

ROCKPORT

Addison Choate Inn

49 Broadway, 01966-1527
(508) 546-7543; (800) 245-7543

This charming New England village inn, built in 1851, provides a traditional setting for a mix of antique and reproduction furnishings and accessories. Complimentary Addison Choate coffee and home-baked Continental buffet breakfast are served in the dining room, which was originally the kitchen of this rambling old house. There is a wraparound porch for fair-weather breakfast overlooking the perennial garden. Parking. Pool. Galleries, shops, restaurants, beaches, and train are all just a short walk away from the inn.

Hosts: Knox and Shirley Johnson
Rooms: 6 (PB) $70-118
Continental Breakfast
Credit Cards: A, B, D
Notes: 2, 5, 7, 8, 9, 10, 11, 12, 14

Addison Choate Inn

Bed & Breakfast/ Inns of New England

128 South Hoop Pole Road, Guilford, CT 06437
(203) 457-0042; (800) 582-0853

MA-1005. An intimate, welcoming guest house open year-round, only one block from Main Street and the T-Wharf, which is full of shops, galleries, and restaurants. Leave the car and walk to everything. A spacious sun deck is reserved for guests. TV, games, magazines, and books are available. Guests have use of their own refrigerator. Seven rooms are available. Children welcome. No smoking. House cat; no guest pets. $60-75.

MA-1006. A small, central inn limited to nonsmokers, this 1987 facility is within a five-minute walk from Rockport's art galleries, Headlands beach, restaurants, and

shops. Three ground-floor larger-than-average rooms with private bathrooms are available with king- or queen-size beds; all three have private bathrooms. All rooms have controlled air conditioning and heat, cable TV, refrigerators, and microwaves. No children. No smoking. No pets. $80-85.

Bed and Breakfast Marblehead and North Shore

P.O. Box 35, Newtonville, 02160
(617) 964-1606; (800) 832-2632
FAX (617) 332-8572

Rockport Guest House. This guest house is a beautiful 120-year-old home in the quiet South End. Accommodations include a queen-size bedroom with private full bath and two additional rooms which share a shower/bath. Two comfortable sitting areas and several small outside decks are also available to guests. Host prepares a wonderful breakfast every morning and offers personal tours of the area. It is within walking distance to the ocean and sandy beach, and close to the Bearskin Neck tourist area. Open year-round. No smoking. $75-95.

The Inn on Cove Hill

37 Mount Pleasant Street, 01966
(508) 546-2701

A friendly atmosphere with the option of privacy, this painstakingly restored 200-year-old Federal home is just two blocks from the harbor and shops. Meticulously appointed, cozy bedrooms are furnished with antiques, and some have canopied beds. Wake up to the delicious aroma of hot muffins, and enjoy a Continental breakfast at the umbrella tables in the Pump Garden. The fresh sea air is preserved in the non-smoking facility.

Hosts: John and Marjorie Pratt
Rooms: 11 (9 PB; 2 SB) $48-102
Continental Breakfast
Credit Cards: None
Notes: 2, 7, 9, 11, 12

7 No smoking; 8 Children welcome; 9 Social drinking allowed; 10 Tennis nearby; 11 Swimming nearby; 12 Golf nearby; 13 Skiing nearby; 14 May be booked through a travel agent.

Eden Pines Inn

48 Eden Road, 01966
(508) 546-2505

Eden Pines Inn is perched along the rocky coast, directly on the ocean, and guests are spellbound by its unique beauty. There are beaches nearby, and the inn is one and one-half mile from downtown Rockport with its shops and art galleries. Six of the seven tastefully decorated bedrooms have private decks. All have private baths in marble or tile. Buffet breakfast includes fruit, cereals, breads, cake, yogurt, and juice. The living room has a stone fireplace, sun-room/dining room is filled with lattice, bright fabrics, and white wicker. Open brick deck on the ocean for sunning and viewing lobster men and the twin lighted towers of Thacher's Island. Smoking on porches and decks. Inquire about accommodations for children.

Host: Inge Sullivan
Rooms: 7 (PB) $80-150
Continental Breakfast
Credit Cards: A, B
Notes: 2, 9, 10, 11, 12, 14

Lantana House

22 Broadway, 01966
(508) 546-3535

An in-town Victorian guest house open year-round in the historic district of Rockport, a classic, picturesque, seacoast village. A short walk takes visitors to the beaches, art galleries, restaurants, and gift shops. Rockport is an artist's haven. A nonsmoking inn. Air conditioning available. Continental plus breakfast.

Host: Cynthia Sewell
Rooms: 7 (5 PB; 2 SB) $60-75
Continental Breakfast
Credit Cards: None
Notes: 2, 5, 8, 10, 11, 12

Linden Tree Inn

26 King Street, 01966-1444
(508) 546-2494

An 1840 Victorian bed and breakfast inn with 18 bedrooms with private bathrooms, 12 with air conditioning. Short walk to beaches, galleries, restaurants, gift shops, and train to Boston. Come enjoy Dawn's made-from-scratch Continental breakfast, fresh flowers in the rooms, and lemonade and cookies in the afternoon. Spectacular view of the ocean and town from the cupola. Cannot accept pets.

Hosts: Dawn and Jon Cunningham
Rooms: 18 (PB) $85-98
Continental Breakfast
Credit Cards: A, B
Notes: 2, 7, 8, 9, 10, 11, 12, 14

Peg Leg Inn and Restaurant

2 King Street, 01966
(800) 346-2352

The original charm of five Colonial New England homes on the edge of the sea overlooking beautiful Front Beach and Rockport's picturesque shoreline. Panoramic oceanviews from the guest rooms. Each welcomes with a warm and pleasant atmosphere, including private bath and TV. Lawns, gardens, and decks for guests' pleasure and relaxation. A short stroll to the quaint village that abounds in lovely shops and art galleries. The inn's own oceanview restaurant is famous for fresh local seafood and Yankee specialities, and an original working greenhouse serves as an added dining room.

Rooms: 33 (PB) $65-125
Continental Breakfast
Credit Cards: A, B
Notes: 2, 3, 4, 8, 10, 11, 12, 14

Rocky Shores Inn and Cottages

65 Eden Road, 01966
(508) 546-2823; (800) 348-4003

Rocky Shores Inn sits on the easternmost point of Cape Ann, between the picturesque harbors of Rockport and Gloucester. The inn is a 1905 seaside mansion that overlooks the historic twin lights of Thacher

NOTES: Credit cards accepted: A MasterCard; B Visa; C American Express; D Discover; E Diners Club; F Other; 2 Personal checks accepted; 3 Lunch available; 4 Dinner available; 5 Open all year; 6 Pets welcome;

Island and the open sea. Guests enjoy the beautiful beaches, whale watching, sailing, fishing, shopping on famous Bearskin Neck, and having lobsters in harbor-front restaurants. Continental plus breakfast.

Hosts: Renate and Gunter Kostka
Rooms: 11 (PB) $76-110
Cottages: 11
Continental Breakfast
Credit Cards: A, B, C
Notes: 2, 8, 9, 10, 11, 12, 14

Seacrest Manor

131 Marmion Way, 01966
(508) 546-2211

Decidedly small, intentionally quiet. Gracious hospitality in luxurious surroundings with magnificent views overlooking woods and sea. Spacious grounds, lovely gardens, and ample parking. Famous full breakfast and afternoon tea included. No pets. Not recommended for children. Fresh flowers, cable TV, free daily paper, mints, and turndown. Mobil-rated three stars. Across the street from the nine-acre John Kieran Nature Preserve. Only an hour north of Boston by car or train. A nonsmoking inn. Closed December through March.

Hosts: Leighton Saville and Dwight MacCormack
Rooms: 8 (6 PB; 2 SB) $92-128
Full Breakfast
Credit Cards: None
Notes: 2, 7, 11, 12

Seacrest Manor

Seaward Inn and Cottages

62 Marmion Way, 01966
(508) 546-3471

Quietly tucked away on Boston's rocky North Shore, this grand old oceanfront estate offers the perfect respite for weary travelers. Elegant oceanfront dining, expansive grounds and beautiful gardens, active bird sanctuary, putting green, private cottages with fireplaces, spectacular oceanviews at every turn, and impeccable service are only the beginning. Short stroll to downtown Rockport (300-year-old fishing village and art colony), shops and boutiques, and wide sandy beaches.

Hosts: Anne and Roger Cameron
Rooms: 38 (PB) $98-138
Full Breakfast
Credit Cards: A, B
Notes: 2, 4, 8, 10, 11, 12, 14

Seven South Street—The Inn

7 South Street, 01966
(508) 546-6708

Built in 1750, the inn has a friendly, informal atmosphere in a quiet setting with gardens, deck, and pool. An ample Continental breakfast is served each morning, after which the guest is free to explore the art galleries and shops within walking distance of the inn.

Host: Aileen Lamson
Rooms: 6 (3 PB; 3 SB) $68-78
Continental Breakfast
Credit Cards: None
Notes: 2, 8, 10, 11

The Tuck Inn Bed and Breakfast

17 High Street, 01966
(508) 546-7260

A cozy 1790 Colonial home on a quiet secondary street, one block from the village center. The inn features the charm of yesterday with antiques, quilts, wide-pine floors, and living room with fireplace, coupled with modern conveniences such as

7 No smoking; 8 Children welcome; 9 Social drinking allowed; 10 Tennis nearby; 11 Swimming nearby; 12 Golf nearby; 13 Skiing nearby; 14 May be booked through a travel agent.

private baths, cable TVs, air conditioning, and a pool. Guests have remarked on the lavish home-baked buffet breakfast and are treated to good old-fashioned New England hospitality.

Hosts: Liz and Scott Wood
Rooms: 11 (PB) $47-87
Continental Breakfast
Credit Cards: A, B
Notes: 2, 5, 7, 8, 9, 10, 11, 12, 13

SAGAMORE BEACH

Bed and Breakfast Cape Cod
P.O. Box 341, West Hyannisport, 02672-0341
(508) 775-2772; FAX (508) 775-2884

19. Perched on a cliff 50 feet above Cape Cod Bay, this contemporary home built in 1987 features two suites for guests. The honeymoon suite has a Jacuzzi overlooking the ocean, private bath, king-size bed, and Laura Ashley bed coverings. The second suite has a queen-size bed and oceanview. A ground-floor basement suite offers a parlor with a fireplace, two sleeping rooms, one with a king-size bed and the other with twin beds and small kitchen. $85-125.

36. On the banks of beautiful Cape Cod Bay this two-story beach house is a modern luxurious private home with spectacular waterviews. The second-floor suite with a double bed and a twin bed has a sitting area with couch and private bath. On the ground floor is a king-size bedroom with a private bath. Breakfast is served with home-baked goods in the dining room overlooking the ocean. It is a short drive to fine restaurants and shops. No smoking. $75-95.

Widow's Walk
152 Mark Road, Box 605, 02562
(508) 888-0762

Just 200 feet from beautiful Sagamore Beach on Cape Cod Bay, this Cape-style country home gives guests that "home-coming feeling." It has two beautifully decorated bedrooms on the second floor and also has an authentic widow's walk. Hosts offer a lovely, fully equipped apartment with private entrance on the ground floor.

Rooms: 2 (SB) $80-85
Continental Breakfast
Credit Cards: F
Notes: 2, 5, 7, 9, 10, 11, 12

SALEM

Amelia Payson House
16 Winter Street, 01970
(508) 744-8304

Visitors will enjoy the grace and charm that is the tradition at a bed and breakfast, while appreciating the convenience of the downtown historic district site. A five-minute stroll from the elegantly restored 1845 Greek Revival finds the Peabody Essex Museum, the Witch Museum, Salem Maritime National Historic Site, and the House of Seven Gables. Shops, waterfront dining, and the Amtrak train to Boston are all convenient to this location. The seaside towns of Rockport and Gloucester are a short drive up the coast. Comfort amenities include private baths, TV, and air conditioning. Color brochure available. Children over 12 welcome. Continental plus breakfast.

Hosts: Ada and Donald Roberts
Rooms: 4 (PB) $75-95
Continental Breakfast
Credit Cards: A, B, C
Notes: 5, 10, 11, 12

Bed and Breakfast Associates Bay Colony, Ltd.
P.O. Box 57166, Babson Park, Boston, 02157-0166
(617) 449-5302; (800) 347-5088
FAX (617) 449-5958

CN178. These two glorious 19th-century sea captains' homes have been restored and decorated with the warmth and charm of yesterday and all the amenities and conveniences that everyone expects and enjoys today. The two inns offer a total of 30 guest rooms, suites, and family apartments, all with private baths, individual climate controls, cable color TVs, and telephones. Several rooms have Jacuzzis and fireplaces. The inn's restaurant offers two intimate dining rooms, a patio, and garden. Honeymoon suite available. $89-159.

Bed and Breakfast Marblehead and North Shore

P.O. Box 35, Newtonville, 02160
(617) 964-1606; (800) 832-2632
FAX (617) 332-8572

Essex Street Bed and Breakfast. This turn-of-the-century wood frame house is in the McIntyre historic district of Salem. The hosts have lovingly labored to restore their home to its former elegance and charm. One guest room with private bath, separate entrance, and air conditioning is available. Continental breakfast is served. No smoking. Children welcome. $75-85.

The Inn on the Green. In the heart of Salem, this inn is close to many tourist attractions, historic sites, world-famous museums, shopping, and wonderful restaurants. The inn is a Greek Revival-style built in 1846 as a private residence. It has been completely restored to its 19th-century elegance, with modern amenities added. Each of the guest rooms has a queen-size bed, private bath, and color cable TV. There is also a suite with two queen-size beds and adjacent sitting room for families or groups of four. Continental breakfast. Restricted smoking area provided. $75-95.

Suite Dreams. Perfect for a couple or a family with one child, as well as for business travelers. A large ground-level suite in host's ranch-style home has a queen-size bed, private bath and kitchen area, TV, VCR, radio, table, and chairs; a cot or roll away can also be added; the kitchen area

includes a refrigerator, microwave, coffeemaker, and toaster. For longer stays, a washer and dryer are also available. Extra fee for additional adult or child. Open April-October. No smoking. Special rates for weekly and longer stays. $85-100.

The Inn at Seven Winter Street

7 Winter Street, 01970
(508) 745-9520

Come, be a guest at The Inn at Seven Winter Street! This magnificently restored French Victorian inn is an award winner. Each room finely appointed with period antiques and furnishings. All rooms have something beautifully unique: marble fireplace, canopied bed, Jacuzzi, and sun deck. In a historic area, within a one-minute walk to the waterfront, historic sites, dining, and museums. Evening tea. Off-street parking. No smoking.

Hosts: Sally Flint, Jill and D. L. Coté
Rooms: 10 (PB) $75-140
Continental Breakfast
Credit Cards: A, B, C
Notes: 2, 5, 7, 9, 10, 11, 12, 14

The Inn at Seven Winter Street

The Salem Inn

7 Summer Street, 01970
(508) 741-0680; (800) 446-2995

Elegantly restored 1834 and 1854 Federal and Italianate townhouses, in the heart of Salem's historic district, have 31 luxuriously appointed rooms with private baths

7 No smoking; 8 Children welcome; 9 Social drinking allowed; 10 Tennis nearby; 11 Swimming nearby; 12 Golf nearby; 13 Skiing nearby; 14 May be booked through a travel agent.

and some working fireplaces. Direct-dial telephones, cable TVs, and air conditioning. Hearty Continental breakfast and lovely rose garden. Jacuzzi and canopied suites available. Limited smoking. Cross-country skiing nearby.

Hosts: Richard and Diane Pabich
Rooms: 31 (PB) $85-159
Continental Breakfast
Credit Cards: A, B, C, D, E
Notes: 2, 3, 4, 5, 6, 8, 9, 10, 11, 12, 13, 14

Stephen Daniels House

1 Daniels Street, 01970
(508) 744-5709

Built by a sea captain in 1667 and enlarged in 1756, the house is beautifully restored and furnished with antiques. Wood-burning fireplaces in the bedrooms with charming canopied beds. Continental breakfast is served before two huge fireplaces. Walk to 11 points of interest in Salem.

Host: Catherine Gill
Rooms: 5 (3 PB; 2 SB) $50-95
Continental Breakfast
Credit Cards: C
Notes: 2, 5, 6, 7, 8, 9, 10, 11, 12, 13, 14

SANDWICH

Bay Beach Bed and Breakfast

1-3 Bay Beach Lane, Box 151, 02563
(508) 888-8813

Luxury beachfront bed and breakfast with super amenities in a romantic setting overlooking Cape Cod Bay. Six spacious guest rooms with decks and oceanviews, plus two honeymoon suites with king-size bed and Jacuzzi are available for guests to choose. A two-fireplaced living room and an exercise room with a Lifecycle and Stairmaster are also for guests to enjoy. A full Continental breakfast is served each morning. All rooms have air conditioning, telephones, cable TV, refrigerators, and compact disk players. AAA Four-Diamond Inn. Four crown ABBA. No smoking. Adults only.

Hosts: Emily and Reale Lemieux
Rooms: 5 (PB) $125-195
Continental Breakfast
Credit Cards: A, B
Notes: 2, 7, 10, 11, 12, 14

Bed and Breakfast Associates Bay Colony, Ltd.

P.O. Box 57166, Babson Park, Boston, 02157-0166
(617) 449-5302; (800) 347-5088
FAX (617) 449-5958

CC250. Ten minutes to the Bridge! Private guest house set atop a pretty driveway just steps from the village center, with duck pond, famous Cape museums, and tiny cafe. Stylish country decor with cathedral ceiling, skylights, and all-new private bath. Picture-perfect honeymoon suite! $110.

CC255. In the Cape's most enchanting village, this modern home with contemporary decor provides three guest rooms with all the basic comforts and amenities for a pleasant stay, at a most attractive price. Walk to town center and museums. $50-70.

Bed and Breakfast Cape Cod

P.O. Box 341, West Hyannisport, 02672-0341
(508) 775-2772; FAX (508) 775-2884

1. This elegant Victorian-style house was built in 1849 and meticulously restored in 1987. The five guest rooms have private baths and are furnished with antiques. The first-floor common rooms for dining and reading are available for guest use. A full breakfast is served each morning in the dining room. Convenient to many fine restaurants, Heritage Plantation, Sandwich Glass Museum, and the beach. Children over 11 welcome. $75-125.

20. Overlooking a beautiful pond, across the street from the oldest house on Cape Cod, this circa 1920 home is a choice bed and

NOTES: Credit cards accepted: A MasterCard; B Visa; C American Express; D Discover; E Diners Club; F Other; 2 Personal checks accepted; 3 Lunch available; 4 Dinner available; 5 Open all year; 6 Pets welcome;

breakfast location. Nicely restored and beautifully maintained, it features a four-room second-floor suite complete with full kitchen, TV, and an air-conditioned bed-room. Convenient to local shops, historical sites, and fine restaurants, this interesting accommodation is ideal for guests with infants or older children. No children under ten. $80.

27. Built in 1741 in the heart of what is now the center of the village, this lovely restored Colonial-style home is on the National Register of Historic Places. Walk to all village sites, including the pond off the village square. Start the day with a full breakfast, or walk the village streets enjoying the picture of a community not much changed from 200 years ago. The English hosts will treat guests as special visitors, offering a meal in their authentic English tea-room with every reservation. A special place that will give guests memories to cherish. No smoking. $85-95.

31. The design of this 1699-built home reflects the charm of early America. Three bedrooms with private baths are furnished with antiques or furniture with an Early American design. Across the street from a saltwater marsh full of birds, this bed and breakfast is a short walk to many restaurants and shops. A Continental breakfast is served in a keeping room with a beehive oven. No smoking. Children over 12 welcome. $70-85.

Capt. Ezra Nye House

152 Main Street, 02563
(508) 888-6142; (800) 388-2278

Comfort and warmth amid antique-filled rooms, some with fireplaces and canopies, make any stay a treat in this 1829 Federal home. Museums, lake, and restaurants within a block. Featured in *Glamour* and

Capt. Ezra Nye House

Innsider magazines, and chosen Best Bed and Breakfast, Upper Cape, by Cape Cod Life magazine in 1993 and 1994. "Thank you for opening your hearts and your home to us....You have made our first trip to Cape Cod a memorable one!" Children over five welcome.

Hosts: Elaine and Harry Dickson
Rooms: 5 (PB) $60-95
Suite: 1(PB)
Full Breakfast
Credit Cards: A, B, C, D
Notes: 2, 5, 7, 9, 10, 11, 12, 14

The Cranberry House

50 Main Street, 02563
(508) 888-1281

The Cranberry house is a friendly place to stay on Cape Cod. A full Continental breakfast is served in the breakfast room or on the deck. Relax in the den overlooking the beautifully landscaped yard. Hosts offer cable TV and complimentary drinks. Sandwich, the Cape's oldest town, has many shops, restaurants, museums, gardens, and beaches. The Cape Cod canal has walking and biking trails. No smoking in bedrooms. Children over ten welcome. BYOB.

Hosts: John and Sara Connolly
Rooms: 2 (1 PB; 1 SB) $50-65
Continental Breakfast
Credit Cards: F
Notes: 2, 5, 10, 11, 12

7 No smoking; 8 Children welcome; 9 Social drinking allowed; 10 Tennis nearby; 11 Swimming nearby; 12 Golf nearby; 13 Skiing nearby; 14 May be booked through a travel agent.

Dillingham House

71 Main Street, 02563
(508) 833-0065

Built circa 1650, the Dillingham House is
one of the oldest in the country. It offers its
guests an interesting historical experience
while providing a quiet and comfortable,
natural environment off the beaten path.
Sandwich has many historical attractions, as
well as quiet beaches for relaxation and a
scenic waterfront nearby.

Host: Kathy Kenney
Rooms: 4 (2 PB; 2 SB) $65-75
Continental Breakfast
Credit Cards: None
Notes: 2, 9, 10, 11, 12

The Summer House

158 Main Street, 02563
(508) 888-4991

Elegant circa 1835 Greek Revival bed and
breakfast featured in *Country Living* magazine, in the heart of historic Sandwich Village, Cape Cod's oldest town (settled 1637).
Antiques, hand-stitched quilts, working
fireplaces, flowers, large sunny rooms, and
English-style gardens. Close to dining,
museums, shops, pond, and gristmill;
boardwalk to beach. Bountiful breakfast,
elegantly served. Afternoon tea in the
garden included.

Hosts: David and Kay Merrell
Rooms: 5 (1 PB; 4 SB) $55-75

The Summer House

Full Breakfast
Credit Cards: A, B, C, D
Notes: 2, 5, 7, 9, 10, 11, 12, 14

SCITUATE

The Allen House

18 Allen Place, 02066
(617) 545-8221

Sleep comfortably and quietly in a gracious,
gabled Victorian merchant's home overlooking an unspoiled New England fishing
town and harbor. Only an hour's drive south
of Boston. Then wake to classical music
and gourmet cuisine. The hosts are English,
professional caterers, and cat lovers. On
every sunny, warm day expect a full breakfast—and sometimes afternoon tea—on the
porch overlooking the harbor.

Hosts: Christine and Iain Gilmour
Rooms: 6 (4 PB; 2 SB) $79-139
Full Breakfast
Credit Cards: A, B, C, D
Notes: 2, 5, 7, 9, 11, 14

Bed and Breakfast Associates Bay Colony, Ltd.

P.O. Box 57166, Babson Park, Boston, 02157-0166
(617) 449-5302; (800) 347-5088
FAX (617) 449-5958

SS250. Just one mile from the ocean, this
pretty home affords visitors to the South
Shore the opportunity to relax and enjoy
nearby tennis, yacht club, pool, and clam
digging. The hosts are active tennis players.
Two guest rooms, one with private bath.
Full breakfast on weekends; children welcome; no smoking. Family and monthly
rates available; $50-55.

SS260. Offered by a gourmet caterer and
her husband, this circa 1905 home is a scant
two-minute walk from Scituate Harbor.
They have lovingly remodeled their fine
bed and breakfast and filled it with period
furniture, classical music, and English-
style hospitality. Guests will surely make

themselves comfortable in the cheerful parlor, indulge in the fabulous gourmet breakfast (or ask for a low-cal or "happy heart" diet), relax before the Edwardian fireplace, or gaze out at the yachts in the bustling harbor. A short stroll brings visitors to local shops and seafood restaurants. Three guest rooms, two with private baths. Full breakfast; children over 16 welcome; no smoking. $89-119.

Bed and Breakfast Cape Cod

P.O. Box 341, West Hyannisport, 02672-0341
(508) 775-2772; FAX (508) 775-2884

64. Oceanviews and English elegance characterize this 1905 Victorian-style inn. Four guest rooms feature queen-size or double beds and water views; two rooms have a private bath, and two other rooms share a bath. English hosts serve a full gourmet breakfast in the morning, and afternoon tea at 5:00 P.M. each day. Breakfast is served in the Victorian dining room or on a porch overlooking the harbor. No smoking. No children. $69-99.

SHEFFIELD

American Country Collection

1353 Union Street, Schnectady, NY 12054
(518) 439-7001; FAX (518) 439-4301

173. An authentic 1840s Colonial barn conversion of hand-hewn beams, plank floors, and stenciled walls nestled on three wooded acres below Mount Everett in the Berkshire's Taconic range. Hike from the inn on a connecting trail that runs along a racing stream to the Appalachian Trail via Mount Race Falls. Thirteen guest rooms in the main house, and three guest rooms in each of two cottages, all different, unique, and individually decorated in a cozy country motif with textured fabrics, quilts, rugs, and stenciling. Several rooms are interconnecting, offering suite arrangements for families with private outside entrances, private

baths, and rooms for children. Each cottage room also has its own private bath and entrance as well. A kitchen and laundry are available for guest use. Continental breakfast. No resident pets; well-behaved guest pets with prior arrangements. There is an additional ten percent added to the room rates on high season weekends and holidays. $65-83.

Covered Bridge

P.O. Box 447A, Norfolk, CT 06058
(203) 542-5944

1SHMA. This charming log home, commanding a sweeping view of the Berkshires, is the perfect spot for an idyllic, pastoral retreat. A horse grazes nearby, and it's a short walk across the fields to the swimming pond. A full breakfast is served in the kitchen or on the porch. The host, an actress, has traveled extensively and is also well-informed about area activities. There are two double guest rooms that share a bath. $85.

2SHMA. Bordering the Appalachian Trail, this 1830s renewed barn with hand-hewn beams, plank floor, and stenciled walls is set on three wooded acres offering a low-key retreat in a perfect setting. The twelve guest rooms are individually decorated in a cozy country motif with textured fabrics, quilts, rugs, and stenciling. Several rooms are interconnecting, offering suite arrangements with private entrances, private baths, and rooms for children. A Continental breakfast is served in the living/dining room area. $75-145.

Race Brook Lodge

864 South Undermountain Road, 01257-9641
(413) 229-2916; FAX (413) 229-6629

Berkshire mountain getaway two hours from New York City and three hours from Boston. Rustic restored historic 1790s timber-peg barn. Brookside cottages. Com-

7 No smoking; 8 Children welcome; 9 Social drinking allowed; 10 Tennis nearby; 11 Swimming nearby; 12 Golf nearby; 13 Skiing nearby; 14 May be booked through a travel agent.

fortable country-style rooms and suites. Planked floors. Beamed ceilings. Private baths. Air conditioning. Hearty Continental breakfast buffet. Cultural mecca for Tanglewood, Norman Rockwell, Shakespeare, Edith Wharton. Hiking and skiing heaven. Antiquing. Wonderful restaurants. Jazz brunch third Sunday each month. Relaxed, informal common rooms. Guest wine bar. Ideal for romantics, celebrating families, and focused work groups. Restricted smoking. Inquire about lunch and dinner.

Hosts: Ernie Couse, lodge keeper; David Rothstein,
    proprietor
Rooms: 19 (16 PB; 3 SB) $69-99
Continental Breakfast
Credit Cards: A, B, C
Notes: 2, 5, 8, 9, 10, 11, 12, 13, 14

Ramblewood Inn

Ramblewood Inn

Box 729, 01257
(413) 229-3363

This stylish country house, furnished for comfort and romance, is in a beautiful natural setting of mountains, pine forest, and serene private lake for swimming and canoeing. Private baths, fireplaces, central air, lovely gardens, and gourmet breakfasts. Convenient to all Berkshire attractions: Tanglewood, drama/dance festivals, antiques, Lime Rock Racing, skiing, and

hiking. Minimum stay requirements for weekends and holidays.

Hosts: June and Martin Ederer
Rooms: 6 (PB) $80-110
Full Breakfast
Credit Cards: A, B
Notes: 2, 5, 7, 8, 9, 10, 11, 12, 13

Stagecoach Hill Inn

Route 41, 01257
(413) 229-8585

In the heart of the Berkshires, the historic Stagecoach Hill Inn has been catering to weary travelers since 1829. This handsome red brick ediface features a cozy, dark-beamed, fireplaced tavern with its own pub menu and a more formal, candlelit dining room. Eleven guest rooms, most with private bath, have telephones and air conditioning. A large screened porch, upstairs reading library, and outdoor swimming pool are available to house guests. Close to all Berkshire Mountain scenic, sports, and cultural attractions. Full American breakfast menu available. Limited smoking.

Host: Sandra MacDougall
Rooms: 11 (9 PB; 2 SB) $50-125
Full Breakfast
Credit Cards: A, B, C
Notes: 2, 4, 5, 10, 12, 13

SHELBURNE

Orchard Hill

Colrain-Shelburne Road, 01370
(413) 625-6802

Orchard Hill is set amid 400 acres of apple orchards. Built before the American Revolution, it is one of few European Capes still in existence, and was restored and renovated after 40 years of neglect. In the western hills of Massachusetts, it is accessible to Tanglewood, famous for its music, and to Jacob's Pillow, world-renowned for dance. Within range of Vermont's ski slopes. Guest rooms share bath, but arrangements can be made for private bath. Smoking outside only.

Host: Joy A. Davenport
Rooms: 3 (SB) $55-60
Full Breakfast
Credit Cards: None
Notes: 2, 5, 8, 9, 11, 12, 13

SOMERVILLE

Greater Boston Hospitality

P.O. Box 1142, Brookline, 02146
(617) 277-5430

131. Immaculately maintained mansard
Victorian, this home offers guest rooms
with either twin beds or king-size beds with
private half-bath or shared bath and deck.
Full breakfast served on weekends, Continental plus during the week, in dining room
or on lovely patio. Minutes to Tufts Uni-
veristy. A few short stops on the Red Line
to Harvard and MIT. Air-conditioned.
Thank you for not smoking. Children welcome. Parking included. Cot available at
$15 additional. $70.

SOUTHBOROUGH

Bed and Breakfast Associates Bay Colony, Ltd.

P.O. Box 57166, Babson Park, Boston, 02157-0166
(617) 449-5302; (800) 347-5088
FAX (617) 449-5958

CW642. A 200-year-old homestead, lovingly restored with great attention to historical detail. Near Southborough Center, a
40-minute drive from downtown Boston.
Three attractive guest rooms, one with a private bath. $80.

Host Homes of Boston

P.O. Box 117, Newton, 02168
(617) 244-1308; FAX (617) 244-5156

Apple Tree. Antique charm in 200-year-old
homestead in rural setting, with orchards,
barn, and country kitchen. First-floor guest
room features queen-size bed. Second-floor

suite with double and twin beds has connecting bath. Guest parlor with fireplace. Family
has cats and Great Dane. Between Boston
and Worcester; abutting Framingham and
Westboro off Routes 9, I-90 and I-495. No
smoking. Children are welcome. $85.

SOUTH CHATHAM (CAPE COD)

Bed and Breakfast Cape Cod

P.O. Box 341, West Hyannisport, 02672-0341
(508) 775-2772; FAX (508) 775-2884

5. This house was built on Nantucket Island
in 1847 and moved to its present location
when the island lost its whaling business.
Restored five years ago, it is now an inn
with five private-bath bedrooms, all decorated in Victorian and traditional decor.
Seven-tenths of a mile away are the warm-
water beach and the waters of Nantucket
Sound. A full Continental breakfast is
served each morning in the kitchen or
dining area. Shopping, the Chatham fish
pier, and recreational activity are all nearby.
No children under eight. $65-85.

SOUTH DARTMOUTH

The Little Red House

631 Elm Street, 02748
(508) 996-4554

A charming gambrel Colonial home in the
lovely coastal village of Padanaram. A decorator's dream featuring antiques and country accents with luxuriously comfortable
four-poster or brass and iron beds. A full
homemade breakfast is a delectable treat.
The backyard gazebo overlooks a neighboring cow pasture providing peaceful
moments of relaxation. Close to beaches,
historic sites, and the ferry to Martha's
Vineyard and Cuttyhunk. A short distance
to Newport, Cape Cod, and Boston.

Host: Meryl Zwirblis
Rooms: 2 (SB) $65-75

---

7 No smoking; 8 Children welcome; 9 Social drinking allowed; 10 Tennis nearby; 11 Swimming nearby; 12
Golf nearby; 13 Skiing nearby; 14 May be booked through a travel agent.

Full Breakfast
Credit Cards: None
Notes: 2, 5, 7, 11, 12

Salt Marsh Farm

Salt Marsh Farm

322 Smith Neck Road, 02748
(508) 992-0980

A 1780 Federal farmhouse with narrow stairs, fireplaces, antiques, and an interesting library of local and natural history. On a 90-acre nature preserve with trails, stone walls, organic gardens, and laying hens. Bikes available. Scenic coastal community convenient to Martha's Vineyard ferry and day trips to Plymouth, Cape Cod, Newport, Mystic, Boston, and Nantucket. New Bedford Whaling Museum, historic waterfront, and beaches are nearby. Children over five welcome.

Hosts: Larry and Sally Brownell
Rooms: 2 (PB) $65-90
Full Breakfast
Credit Cards: A, B
Notes: 2, 5, 7, 9, 11

SOUTH DENNIS (CAPE COD)

Bed and Breakfast Cape Cod

P.O. Box 341, West Hyannisport, 02672-0341
(508) 775-2772; FAX (508) 775-2884

3. Built in 1828, with major additions in 1879, this Cape-style house was changed to Queen Anne Victorian. For many years the house was a private home before being changed to a guest house. The restoration several years ago now provides an inn with five guest rooms, four with private baths. The full breakfast served in the dining room each morning includes a variety of special house dishes. The 22-mile bike trail is one-half mile away. Some of the best shopping on Cape Cod is within a few miles of the inn. $45-75.

SOUTH ORLEANS

Bed and Breakfast Cape Cod

P.O. Box 341, West Hyannisport, 02672-0341
(508) 775-2772; FAX (508) 775-2884

37. The Atlantic Ocean is directly in front of this circa 1780 home that offers three bedrooms with private baths and choice of a king-, queen-size, or twin beds. Enjoy the full breakfast served each morning before walking out to the beach or the host's boathouse on the water. Children over five are welcome. $75-90.

80. On high ground above Pleasant Bay, this 1973 Cape Cod-style home offers three bedrooms. One is a large room with a queen-size bed and private bath, and the other two share a bath and have a double bed or a pair of twins. This lovely home is convenient to both Chatham and Orleans shops and restaurants. The deck is great for relaxing after spending the day at the beach. No smoking. $55-70.

Hillbourne House

Route 28, #654, 02662
(508) 255-0780

This charming bed and breakfast was built in 1798 and during the Civil War was part of the Underground Railroad. A circular hiding place is still in evidence beneath the trap door in the Common Room. Enjoy a magnificent view of Pleasant Bay and the great dunes of Outer Beach on the Atlantic. Convenient to all Cape activities. Private beach and dock.

NOTES: Credit cards accepted: A MasterCard; B Visa; C American Express; D Discover; E Diners Club; F Other; 2 Personal checks accepted; 3 Lunch available; 4 Dinner available; 5 Open all year; 6 Pets welcome;

Host: Barbara Hayes
Rooms: 8 (PB) $50-85
Full or Continental Breakfast
Credit Cards: None
Notes: 2, 5, 9, 11, 12

SOUTH WELLFLEET (CAPE COD)

Orleans Bed and Breakfast Associates

P.O. Box 1312, Orleans, 02653
(508) 255-3824; (800) 541-6226

Owl's Nest. Peace and quiet surround this Gothic contemporary home on six acres known as Owl Woods. Charming cathedral-ceilinged living and dining rooms, filled with antiques and collectibles to enjoy. Upstairs a skylighted sitting area separates two queen-size bedrooms which share a large bath. Continental breakfast is served inside or on the 40-foot deck overlooking perennial gardens and pine woods. Walk down a country lane to a picturesque bay beach. It's a short ride to ocean or pond swimming. $75.

The White Eagle. What a neat spot for a Cape visit! Ground-floor private entrance into large room with breakfast table and sitting area, king-size bed, full private bath, TV, and wet bar with refrigerator, stocked for breakfast. Sliders open to a pretty patio with comfortable reclining chairs to loaf in and admire the woodsy views. Walk to Bay Beach, or take a short drive to the ocean. $70.

SOUTH YARMOUTH (CAPE COD)

Bed and Breakfast Associates Bay Colony, Ltd.

P.O. Box 57166, Babson Park, Boston, 02157-0166
(617) 449-5302; (800) 347-5088
FAX (617) 449-5958

CC380. Contemporary elegance in an antique setting. Ten wonderful guest rooms in this 1845 sea captain's mansion.

Every amenity thoughtfully provided in this magnificent restoration. Seasonal rates. $100-225.

Bed and Breakfast Cape Cod

P.O. Box 341, West Hyannisport, 02672-0341
(508) 775-2772; FAX (508) 775-2884

68. This 1880 sea captain's house has a belvedere, reflecting the character of architecture in the whaling ship days. Charming restorations with Victorian decor and wide-board, highly burnished floors characterize this house. Bedrooms with private baths, queen-size beds, and a Jacuzzi are some of the features. Breakfast is a special full service treat served in the dining room. Hyannis and the ferry to either Nantucket or Martha's Vineyard are only 15 minutes away by car. This home has been featured in Fodor's travel guide. No children under 12 are allowed. No smoking is allowed. $60-100.

74. This captain's house was built in 1845. It had fallen into disrepair and then restored beautifully in 1993. Ten rooms, some with Jacuzzi's, some with king- or queen-size beds are decorated with charm and care to retain the character of the old house. It is only a few miles from Hyannis and the ferry to either Nantucket or Martha's Vineyard. The full breakfast prepared by a professionally trained chef is marvelous. Enjoy the beaches, shopping, and the history of the area in a wonderful bed and breakfast. No children under 12. No smoking. $75-225.

STOCKBRIDGE

Arbor Rose Bed and Breakfast

8 Yale Hill, 01262-0114
(413) 298-4744

Lovely old New England millhouse with pond, gardens, and mountain view. Walk to Berkshire Theatre and Stockbridge Center. Beautiful rooms, good beds, antiques,

7 No smoking; 8 Children welcome; 9 Social drinking allowed; 10 Tennis nearby; 11 Swimming nearby; 12 Golf nearby; 13 Skiing nearby; 14 May be booked through a travel agent.

paintings, and sunshine. Fireplace and TV in front parlor. Weekend getaway specials, ski packages, weekly rates, and home-baked breakfast. Full breakfast on week-ends; Continental breakfast on weekdays. No smoking.

Hosts: Christina Alsop and family
Rooms: 4 (2 PB; 2 SB) $55-150
Full and Continental Breakfast
Credit Cards: A, B, C, D
Notes: 2, 5, 7, 8, 10, 12, 13, 14

Berkshire Thistle Bed and Breakfast

P.O. Box 1227, Route 7, 01262
(413) 298-3188

This Colonial home is nestled on five acres, which offer beautiful gardens, lawns, and a spacious swimming pool. In front is a corral that is home to two thoroughbred horses. There are five rooms of which one is a suite; all are decorated with a feel of elegance, but are simply comfortable and waiting for guests to unwind and enjoy. After a night's sleep, wake up to a full country breakfast served in the dining room or on the large porch in warm weather. Near all area attrac-tions: skiing, Tanglewood, and the Norman Rockwell Museum. Feel welcomed in the heart of the Berkshires by the hosts.

Hosts: Gene and Diane Elling
Rooms: 5 (4 PB; 1 SB) $65-120

Berkshire Thistle

Full Breakfast
Credit Cards: None
Notes: 2, 5, 7, 9, 10, 11, 12, 13

Historic Merrell Inn

1565 Pleasant Street, South Lee, 01260
(413) 243-1794; (800) 243-1794

This 200-year-old brick stagecoach inn in a small New England village along the banks of the Housatonic River is listed on the National Register of Historic Places. Rooms with fireplaces, canopied beds, and antique furnishings. Full breakfast is served in the original tavern room. One mile to Norman Rockwell's beloved Stockbridge.

Hosts: Charles and Faith Reynolds; Pamela Hurst
Rooms: 9 (PB) $55-135
Full Breakfast
Credit Cards: A, B
Notes: 2, 5, 7, 9, 11, 13

The Inn at Stockbridge

Route 7 North, P.O. Box 618, 01262
(413) 298-3337; FAX (413) 298-3406

Consummate hospitality and outstanding breakfasts distinguish a visit at this turn-of-the-century Georgian Colonial estate on 12 secluded acres in the heart of the Berkshires. Close to the Norman Rockwell Museum, Tanglewood, Hancock Shaker Village, summer theaters, and four-season recreation. The inn has a gracious, English country feel-ing, with two well-appointed living rooms, a formal dining room, and a baby grand piano.

Hosts: Alice and Len Schiller
Rooms: 8 (PB) $85-235
Full Breakfast
Credit Cards: A, B, C
Notes: 2, 5, 7, 11, 12, 13

The Roeder House Bed and Breakfast

Route 183, Box 525, 01262
(413) 298-4015

A restored 1856 Federal farmhouse with flower gardens, in-ground pool, and patios. Queen-size, four-poster canopied beds, private baths, fine country antique furnishings, and Audubon prints. Full breakfast served on English china. Winter midweek rates available. Cancellation policy with service charge. Half a mile from Rockwell and Chesterwood museums. Air conditioning and paddle fans. Nonsmoking inn. Brochures available. Children over 11 welcome.

Hosts: Diane and Vernon Reuss
Rooms: 6 (PB) $95-220
Full Breakfast
Credit Cards: A, B, C, D
Notes: 2, 4, 5, 7, 9, 10, 12, 13

STOWE

Bed and Breakfast Associates Bay Colony, Ltd.

P.O. Box 57166, Babson Park, Boston, 02157-0166
(617) 449-5302; FAX (617) 449-5958

CW325. Authentic Colonial farmhouse, circa 1734, features romantic guest rooms. Honeymoon suite has a sitting room, Jacuzzi in the bath, and queen-size canopied bed. All guest rooms have handmade quilts, decorative fireplaces, and antique furnishings. $80-100.

STURBRIDGE

Bed and Breakfast Marblehead and North Shore

P.O. Box 35, Newtonville, 02160
(617) 964-1606; (800) 832-2632
FAX (617) 332-8572

The Village Bed and Breakfast. This large gambrel Colonial-style home near Old Sturbridge village offers three beautiful guest rooms and a suite. One queen-size bedroom has a private bath, while a double bed and a twin-single room share a bath. The separate-entrance guest suite features a double bed, half-bath, refrigerator, microwave, and desk. Perfect for executive

homestays or extended tourist visits. Common areas include a sitting room with TV, a screened porch, and a back yard deck. A wonderful full breakfast is served. No smoking. Multiple-night discounts. $80-95.

Colonel Ebenezer Crafts Inn

Fiske Hill Road, P.O. Box 187, 01566-0187
(508) 347-3313; (800)-PUBLICK

The Colonel Ebenezer Crafts Inn was built in 1786 by David Fiske, Esquire, on one of the highest points of land in Sturbridge, which offered him a commanding view of his cattle and farmland. The house has since been restored by the management of the Publick House. Accommodations at Crafts Inn are charming. There are two queen-size canopied beds, as well as some four-poster beds. Guests may relax by the pool or in the sunroom, take afternoon tea, or enjoy sweeping views of the countryside. Breakfast includes freshly baked muffins and sweet rolls, fresh fruit and juices, and coffee and tea. Those seeking a more hearty breakfast, lunch, or dinner can stroll down to the

Publick House just over a mile away. Cross-country skiing nearby.

Host: Mary Stocum
Rooms: 8 (PB) $69-150
Continental Breakfast
Credit Cards: A, B, C, E
Notes: 2, 8, 9, 10, 11, 12, 13, 14

Sturbridge Country Inn

530 Main Street, P.O. Box 60, 01566
(508) 347-5503; FAX (508) 347-5319

Historic 1840s inn, near old Sturbridge village. Each room features a fireplace and whirlpool tub. Complimentary breakfast and wine. Food and spirits available in the Fieldstone Tavern. Walk to antique shops, boutiques, crafts, and more. Live theater in the "Loft" June through October. Off-season discounts and packages available. Limited smoking allowed. Children over four welcome.

Host: Patricia Affenito
Rooms: 9 (PB) $59-159
Continental Breakfast
Credit Cards: A, B, C, D
Notes: 2, 3, 4, 5, 9, 10, 11, 12, 13, 14

SUDBURY

Host Homes of Boston

P.O. Box 117, Boston, 02168
(617) 244-1308; FAX (617) 244-5156

Arabian Horse Inn. Huge, gracious Victorian, circa 1890, on nine-acre Arabian horse farm with pond, woods in picturebook Sudbury Center. Double parlor with fireplace. Wraparound porch. Breakfast in dining room, country kitchen or latticed pergola. Three second floor guest rooms. King-size canopied with fireplace, TV, two-person Jacuzzi bath. King-size motionless waterbed and small double share hall bath. Near historic Concord and train and Framingham. Boston is 20 miles away. No smoking. Telephone. $68-125.

Sudbury Bed and Breakfast

3 Drum Lane, 01776
(508) 443-2860

A large Garrison Colonial home with traditional furnishings on a quiet tree-studded acre. A Continental breakfast is served with homemade muffins and rolls. Close to Boston, Lexington, and Concord. An abundance of outdoor recreation and historical sights nearby. Friendly hospitality for the New England visitor.

Hosts: Don and Nancy Somers
Rooms: 2 (S1.5B) $55-65
Continental Breakfast
Credit Cards: None
Notes: 2, 5, 8, 9, 11, 12

SWAMPSCOTT

Bed and Breakfast Associates Bay Colony, Ltd.

P.O. Box 57166, Babson Park, Boston, 02157-0166
(617) 449-5302; FAX (617) 449-5958

NS200. Just two and one-half blocks to a sandy beach. This hostess collects antiques, refinishes furniture, and enjoys quilting. As a tour escort around New England, she has a wealth of information to share with her guests. Her small Colonial home in a quiet neighborhood is neat and clean. Three guest rooms share a bath. Full breakfast; children over 12 welcome; no smoking. Family and monthly rates available; $50-60.

Bed and Breakfast Marblehead and North Shore

P.O. Box 35, Newtonville, 02160
(617) 964-1606; (800) 832-2632
FAX (617) 332-8572

Oceanview Victorian. Beautiful turn-of-the-century home offering wonderful views of the ocean. American country decor with hand-stenciled walls in three lovely guest rooms that share two baths. One room has a private half-bath. One oceanfront room has

---

NOTES: Credit cards accepted: A MasterCard; B Visa; C American Express; D Discover; E Diners Club;
F Other; 2 Personal checks accepted; 3 Lunch available; 4 Dinner available; 5 Open all year; 6 Pets welcome;

a private deck. Color cable TV and air conditioning. Guest phone and refrigerator in the hallway. In the winter months, relax by the wood stove in the sitting room. Easy access to Boston, Salem, and Marblehead. Airport pickup with prior arrangement. Children over six welcome. No smoking. Continental breakfast. Parking. $75-85.

Greater Boston Hospitality

P.O. Box 1142, Brookline, 02146
(617) 277-5430

115. Salt air, flowers, beaches, sunshine, Ping-Pong, and wonderful walks around the ocean are all here. This spacious 1940 Dutch Colonial is one block from the Atlantic Ocean. The guest room has double bed with coach that sleeps one extra person. A view of the ocean can be had from a private deck off the guest bedroom. Guests share one and one-half baths. Full breakfast. Children welcome. Parking included. Weekly rate available. $70-85.

TRURO

Bed and Breakfast Cape Cod

P.O. Box 341, West Hyannisport, 02672-0341
(508) 775-2772; FAX (508) 775-2884

9. From 1836 this Colonial-style home has been the site of a working farm and now a vineyard. Restoration was completed in 1994. Featured are wide-board floors, open-beam ceilings, and tasteful decor of the Victorian era. Bedrooms have queen-size beds and private baths, one with a Jacuzzi. Continental breakfasts are served with grace and delightful foods in the dining room or outside on the patio. It is an enchanting, comfortable, and relaxing accommodation. Beaches, a lighthouse, restaurants, golf, tennis, and Provincetown are a few miles away. Children over 12 welcome. No smoking. $65-115.

Orleans Bed and Breakfast Associates

P.O. Box 1312, Orleans, 02653
(508) 255-3824; (800) 541-6226

South Hollow Vineyards Inn. On five picturesque acres, the historic Hughes/Rich Farmstead, circa 1836, remains one of the last working farms on Cape Cod. In 1993, a French vinifera winegrape vineyard was planted on the rolling hills behind the farmhouse, the first of its kind on the Cape. This rambling Federal-style farmhouse has been carefully restored and furnished. Romantic, spacious rooms with queen-size or double poster beds and tiled baths. Sweeping views of the vineyard from the breakfast garden room and adjoining outdoor patio, or from a spacious upstairs sun deck. Sheltered and quiet, the inn is only a mile from Highland Golf Course, Cape Cod Lighthouse and the beaches, and only a short drive from Provincetown. $85-115.

Parker House

P.O. Box 1111, 02666
(508) 349-3358

The Parker House is an 1820 classic full-Cape nestled into the side of Truro Center between the Cobb Memorial Library and the Blacksmith Shop Restaurant. Clean ocean and bay beaches two miles to east or west. Many art galleries and restaurants in Provincetown and Wellfleet ten minutes away by car. Golf, tennis, sailing, and whale watches nearby. The Cape Cod National Seashore and Audubon Sanctuary offer many trails and guided walks. The Parker House offers haven to a limited number of guests who can rest and read or enjoy the many activities nearby.

Host: Stephen Williams
Rooms: 2 (SB) $55
Continental Breakfast
Credit Cards: None
Notes: 2, 5, 9, 10, 11, 12

7 No smoking; 8 Children welcome; 9 Social drinking allowed; 10 Tennis nearby; 11 Swimming nearby; 12 Golf nearby; 13 Skiing nearby; 14 May be booked through a travel agent.

TYRINGHAM

American Country Collection

1353 Union Street, Schnectady, NY 12054-1606
(518) 439-7001; FAX (518) 439-4301

202. This 250-year-old farmhouse stands on a hillside overlooking the first Shaker settlement in the Berkshires. Tanglewood, Stockbridge, and the Norman Rockwell Museum are within nine miles. One of two common rooms has couches, chairs, a TV, and a fireplace. Lodgings include one air-conditioned room on the first floor with a private porch and twin beds. Two rooms have a private half-bath and share a hall bath. Three air-conditioned rooms on the second floor have double beds, twin beds, and a shared bath. An apartment on the second floor has a double bed, an air-conditioned kitchen, a living area, and bath. A full breakfast is served from 8:00 to 10:00 A.M. in a dining room decorated with Shaker furniture. Intimate dinners are available for an additional charge on Thursdays-Saturdays in late spring, summer, and early fall. Call for information regarding children and pets. Smoking outside only. $75-100.

The Golden Goose

Main Road, Box 336, 01264
(413) 243-3008

Small, friendly, 1800 country inn nestled in Tyringham Valley in the Berkshires. Victorian antiques, sitting rooms with fireplaces, homemade breakfast fare. Within one-half hour are Tanglewood, Stockbridge, Jacob's Pillow, Hancock Shaker Village, the Norman Rockwell Museum, Berkshire Theater Festival, skiing, golf, and tennis. The inn is one mile off the Appalachian Trail. Near Butternut, Otis, Jiminy Peak, and Catamount ski slopes. Children over eight welcome.

Hosts: Lilja and Joe Rizzo
Rooms: 6 (4 PB; 2 SB) $70-120
Full Breakfast
Credit Cards: A, B, C, D
Notes: 2, 5, 7, 9, 10, 11, 12, 13, 14

The Golden Goose

VINEYARD HAVEN (MARTHA'S VINEYARD)

Bed and Breakfast/ Inns of New England

128 South Hoop Pole Road, Guilford, CT 06437
(203) 457-0042; (800) 582-0853

MA 1070 and **1075.** Two historic inns built in two historic towns (1070 in Vineyard Haven and 1075 in Edgartown), built in the 1840s as sea captains' homes, and have been meticulously restored and furnished to reflect the charm and elegance of that period. Enjoy the Continental breakfast in the elegant dining room or enchanting flower garden. The inns' romantic guest rooms conjure up memories of yesteryear. Each is uniquely different and decorated with fine furnishings. Each has a private bath. Three-night minimum stay on weekends. Two-night minimum stay for some holidays and during high season. Children are welcome. No guest pets. $75-180.

Bed and Breakfast Nantucket/ Martha's Vineyard

P.O. Box 341, West Hyannisport, 02672-0341
(508) 775-2772; FAX (508) 775-2884

202. This wonderful two-acre estate in the village of Vineyard Haven was restored in 1989. It is secluded and romantic, and offers a casual elegance. The luxurious furnishings add to the charm, creating a relaxing getaway. The seven private-bath guest rooms, some with fireplaces, are each unique and beautifully maintained. The special gourmet breakfast is served on the porch or in the dining room. Play the piano or a game of chess while enjoying the warmth of the fireplace in the winter months. This is a very special accommodation. No smoking allowed. No children under 12. $90-189.

205. This home was built nearly 100 years ago as a private home. Later it was used for 40 years as a guest house. It was restored several years ago, and the present owner uses eight rooms for bed and breakfast. Each room has a private bath, and all are clean and bright with tasteful decor. The Continental breakfast is served in a common room where guests meet and greet one another. Walk to all Vineyard Haven shops, stores, and restaurants. Bike rental available on the premises. $75-160.

208. Vineyard Haven, a popular community on the island, is the setting for this 15-room inn that features all private baths, TVs, and air-conditioned bedrooms that provide either queen-size beds or two double beds. Decks from the rooms offer sunning areas and private entrances, making this a very private yet convenient location within walking distance of the shops, restaurants, and the ferry in the village. Continental breakfast is available each morning. Many rooms have a pull-out available for a third or fourth person in the room. No smoking. $65-145.

Captain Dexter House of Vineyard Haven

100 Main Street, Box 2457, 02568
(508) 693-6564

A perfect country inn! Built in 1840, the house has been meticulously restored and exquisitely furnished to reflect the charm of that period. Be surrounded by flowers from the garden and pampered by innkeepers who believe in old-fashioned hospitality.

The inn's eight romantic guest rooms are distinctively decorated. Several rooms have working fireplaces (as does the parlor) and four-poster canopied beds. Stroll to town and harbor. Continental plus breakfast.

Hosts: Rick and Birdie
Rooms: 8 (PB) $55-160
Continental Breakfast
Credit Cards: A, B, C, E
Notes: 2, 5, 8, 9, 10, 11, 12, 14

Crocker House Inn

4 Crocker Avenue, P.O. Box 1658, 02568
(508) 693-1151; (800) 772-0206

A charming turn-of-the-century bed and breakfast nestled in the historic village of Vineyard Haven. Eight bedrooms with private baths. Just one block from the ferry, shops, restaurants, golf, tennis, and cycling. Come enjoy the serenity of Martha's Vineyard and a homemade chocolate chip cookie every afternoon on the veranda of the Crocker House Inn.

Host: Darlene Stavens
Rooms: 8 (PB) $75-155
Continental Breakfast
Credit Cards: A, B, C
Notes: 7, 9, 10, 11, 12

The Hanover House

10 Edgartown Road; P.O. Box 2107, 02568
(508) 693-1066; (800) 339-1066 (MA)
FAX (508) 696-6009

Recommended by the *New York Times,* the Hanover House is a large, old inn that has been fully renovated, offering guests modern conveniences while still retaining the quaintness and personalized hospitality of the lovely old inns of yesteryear. The guest rooms all feature private baths, color cable TV, queen-size or double beds, air conditioning, and individual heat controls. Continental breakfast is served on the sun porch year-round. The inn is within walking distance of the ferry in the town of Vineyard Haven. A nonsmoking inn.

Hosts: Kay and Ron Nelson
Rooms: 15 (PB) $55-185

7 No smoking; 8 Children welcome; 9 Social drinking allowed; 10 Tennis nearby; 11 Swimming nearby; 12 Golf nearby; 13 Skiing nearby; 14 May be booked through a travel agent.

Continental Breakfast
Credit Cards: A, B, C, D
Notes: 5, 7, 8, 9, 10, 11, 12, 14

High Haven House

P.O. Box 289, 02568
(508) 693-9204; (800) 232-9204
FAX (508) 693-7807

On the island, away from the main stream, but just a short walk to the ferry and shopping. High Haven House offers a variety of meticulously maintained accommodations that will suit any budget and need. Breakfast is served in the common room or on the patio. Relax at the pool and hot tub after a day at one of the beautiful beaches or nature trails. Small families can be accommodated in one of the housekeeping units.

Hosts: Joe and Kathleen Schreck
Rooms: 11 (6 PB; 5 SB) $85-180
Continental Breakfast
Credit Cards: A, B, D
Notes: 2, 5, 8, 9, 10, 11, 12, 14

Lambert's Cove Country Inn

Rural Route 1, Box 422, 02568
(508) 693-2298

Once a lovely country estate, Lambert's Cove Country Inn in West Tisbury offers guest rooms in three charming buildings: the original 1790 residence, a converted 18th-century barn, and a carriage house. The setting is seven and one-half acres of lawn, meadows, gardens, and woodlands,

Lambert's Cove

with towering trees, an orchard, and vine-covered stone walls. Each room has its own charm. The dining room, which is open to the public, features some of the finest meals on the island.

Host: Russ Wilson
Rooms: 15 (PB) $85-175
Continental Breakfast
Credit Cards: A, B, C
Notes: 2, 4, 5, 7, 10, 11, 12

Lothrop Merry House

Lothrop Merry House

Owen Park, Box 1939, 02568
(508) 693-1646

The Merry House, built in the 1790s, overlooks Vineyard Haven Harbor and has a flower-bordered terrace, a private beach, and an expansive lawn. Most rooms have oceanviews and a fireplace. All are furnished with antiques and fresh flowers. Complimentary canoe and Sunfish for guests' use. Sailing also available on 54-foot ketch *Laissez Faire*. Close to ferry and shops. Open year-round.

Hosts: John and Mary Clarke
Rooms: 7 (4 PB; 3 SB) $68-175
Continental Breakfast
Credit Cards: A, B
Notes: 2, 5, 8, 9, 10, 11, 12

NOTES: Credit cards accepted: A MasterCard; B Visa; C American Express; D Discover; E Diners Club;
F Other; 2 Personal checks accepted; 3 Lunch available; 4 Dinner available; 5 Open all year; 6 Pets welcome;

WALTHAM

Bed and Breakfast Associates Bay Colony, Ltd.

P.O. Box 57166, Babson Park, Boston, 02157-0166
(617) 449-5302; (800) 347-5088
FAX (617) 449-5958

IW300. This friendly hostess will welcome guests to this charming little house with a white picket fence and a screened porch. It is in a neighborhood of manicured lawns just one and one-half miles from I-95, which circles Greater Boston. Two guest rooms on the second floor share a bath. Full breakfast upon request. Children welcome. $55. Family rates available.

WARE

Mulberry Bed and Breakfast

257 High Street, 02571
(508) 295-0684

Mulberry Bed and Breakfast sits on a half-acre lot shaded by the majestic mulberry tree in the historic section of Wareham. This Cape Cod-style bed and breakfast home, built in 1847 by a blacksmith, offers three cozy guest rooms with shared baths. Furnishings and decor are in keeping with the home's vintage. Enjoy a hearty New England breakfast. Within an hour's drive are historic Plymouth, Boston, and Newport, the whaling-fishing city of New Bedford, and scenic Cape Cod. Wareham boasts 54 miles of coastline. Thus, saltwater activities of every description are available. Two cats in residence. Cross-country skiing nearby.

Hosts: Frances A. Murphy
Rooms: 3 (3 S2B) $45-60
Full Breakfast
Credit Cards: A, B, C, D
Notes: 2, 5, 7, 8, 9, 10 ,11, 12, 13, 14

The Wildwood Inn

121 Church Street, 01082
(413) 967-7798

This homey, welcoming, 1880 Victorian furnished in American primitive antiques, handmade heirloom and new quilts, and early cradles. Drive up a maple-canopied street with stately Victorian homes. Laze in the hammock, swing, or rock on the wrap-around front porch. Play croquet or sit under the fir trees to read. Try a jigsaw puzzle or board game. Wander in the 110-acre park. Canoe, bike, or ski nearby. An easy drive to the five-college area, Old Sturbridge and Old Deerfield, the Basketball Hall of Fame, and I-90. Come try the "no-lunch" breakfast! Children over six welcome.

Hosts: Fraidell Fenster and Richard Watson
Rooms: 9 (7 PB; 2SB) $60-89
Full Breakfast
Credit Cards: A, B, C
Notes: 2, 5, 7, 9, 10, 11, 12, 13, 14

WELLESLEY

Bed and Breakfast Associates Bay Colony, Ltd.

P.O. Box 57166, Babson Park, Boston, 02157-0166
(617) 449-5302; (800) 347-5088
FAX (617) 449-5958

IW500. This urbane hostess offers three guest rooms in this handsome home in Wellesley's desirable Cliff Estates. The first-floor suite features two rooms and an attached bath set apart from the main living area of the house. Those wishing designer decor with French antiques, flowered chintz, and lace can request the master guest room and bath. Driveway parking. $68-90.

7 No smoking; 8 Children welcome; 9 Social drinking allowed; 10 Tennis nearby; 11 Swimming nearby; 12 Golf nearby; 13 Skiing nearby; 14 May be booked through a travel agent.

WEST BARNSTABLE

Bed and Breakfast Cape Cod

P.O. Box 341, West Hyannisport, 02672-0341
(508) 775-2772; FAX (508) 775-2884

44. This Cape cottage-style home is in a rural setting amid the quiet historic section of Barnstable. The immaculate accommodation with a European flair offers three guest rooms with private baths, full breakfast, and a rich feeling of spacious relaxation. A place where guests can get away and enjoy a wonderful vacation setting. German and English spoken on premises. Out-of-doors in the natural gardens and inside, this is a delightful place to stay. Five miles to the Hyannis ferry to Nantucket or Martha's Vineyard. No children under seven. No smoking allowed. $60-85.

WEST DENNIS

Bed and Breakfast Cape Cod

P.O. Box 341, West Hyannisport, 02672-0341
(508) 775-2772; FAX (508) 775-2884

15. On the warm waters of Nantucket Sound is this 62-year-old beach home that has been restored into a seven-bedroom, private bath, and breakfast accommodation. From all rooms there is an ocean or pond view. The carefully maintained house has a breakfast room overlooking a deck that leads to the 100 yards of private sandy beach. A kitchen on the ground floor is available for guests to cook and eat on the beach. All equipment is available. Convenient to many shops and restaurants, only minutes away from Hyannis. $60-110.

Golden Slumber Accommodations

640 Revere Beach Boulevard, Revere, 02151
(800) 892-3231; (617) 289-1053

156. Immaculate, contemporary, waterfront mansion provides commanding views of the Swan River and nearby Atlantic Ocean. Spacious one-bedroom apartment accessible by elevator or conventional staircase is equipped with kitchenette, queen-size or twin beds, immense private bath, and large dining area with deck overlooking private residential dock. Impressive suspended catwalk leads to two impeccably appointed separate chambers featuring antique double or queen-size beds, deck and private or shared baths. Exquisite! $60-125.

WEST FALMOUTH (CAPE COD)

Bed and Breakfast Cape Cod

P.O. Box 341, West Hyannisport, 02672-0341
(508) 775-2772; FAX (508) 775-2884

70. Built in 1739 and expanded through the years, this lovely old home is now an inn with nine guest rooms. The decor is antique with each room offering special touches of charm. The grounds are divided into beautiful garden settings. A fabulous breakfast is served each morning in the dining room or on the deck. Convenient location, not far from the ferry to Martha's Vineyard. A short walk to the little village of West Falmouth. A popular and historic location. No smoking. No children under 14. $65-85.

WEST GROTON

Bed and Breakfast Associates Bay Colony, Ltd.

P.O. Box 57166, Babson Park, Boston, 02157-0166
(617) 449-5302; (800) 347-5088
FAX (617) 449-5958

CW550. Get away to this "gentleman's farm" in the country. This gracious home was recently built as a reproduction of the owner's circa 1800 farmhouse that was destroyed by fire at this site. The new home, overlooking pastures and grazing cattle, is grand in every detail and provides the finest accommodations in a country retreat: elegant furnishings, thoughtful amenities, in-ground pool gloriously set on the meadow, and nearby canoeing, cross-country skiing, biking, and renowned antiquing. Three guest rooms. Master suite has bath ensuite and working fireplace. $80-95.

WEST HARWICH

Bed and Breakfast Cape Cod

P.O. Box 341, West Hyannisport, 02672-0341
(508) 775-2772; FAX (508) 775-2884

16. This 35-year-old ranch-style home is three blocks from the warm waters of Nantucket Sound. One wing is set aside for bed and breakfast guests. The first-floor bedroom has a queen-size bed, private bath, large sitting area, color TV, Oriental carpets, and a small refrigerator for guest use. A marvelous full breakfast is served from 8:00-9:30 A.M. Convenient to shopping and restaurants. No smoking. No children. $80.

26. This six-guest-room inn was originally built as a sea captain's home in the 1820s. It features pine-board floors and an original-style "captain's stairs" leading to the second floor. A large pool for guest use is next to the main house. There are six bedrooms with private baths, and some of the suites adjacent to the pool will accommodate up to four persons. A full country breakfast is served in a dining area overlooking the pool. $60-120.

The Gingerbread House Bed and Breakfast

141 Divison Street, 02671
(508) 432-1901; (800) 788-1901

One of the most beautiful homes on Cape Cod, the Gingerbread House is a classic example of Victorian architecture. On the south side of Cape Cod with warm beautiful beaches, within walking distance to major attractions. Accommodations with private and shared baths include home-cooked breakfast with European flavor. Afternoon English tea and dinners served to the public.

Hosts: Stacia and Les Kostecki
Rooms: 5 (PB) $65-105
Full Breakfast
Credit Cards: A, B
Notes: 3, 4, 7, 8, 9, 10, 11, 12, 14

WEST STOCKBRIDGE

Card Lake Inn

29 Main Street, 01266
(413) 232-0272

This Colonial inn is in the heart of the Berkshires, minutes from Tanglewood, Jimmy Pesk, and Butternut ski areas. The atmosphere is warm, comfortable, and casual. An on-premises tavern and restaurant offers good food and drink at reasonable prices. Open year-round.

Hosts: Edward and Lisa Robbins
Rooms: 8 (4 PB; 4 SB) $45-125
Continental Breakfast
Credit Cards: A, B, C, D, E, F
Notes: 2, 3, 4, 5, 8, 9, 10, 11, 12, 13, 14

WEST TISBURY (MARTHA'S VINEYARD)

Bed and Breakfast Nantucket/ Martha's Vineyard

P.O. Box 341, West Hyannisport, 02672-0341
(508) 775-2772; FAX (508) 775-2884

207. Built in 1790 as a rural farmhouse and converted into an inn, this charming building is in a very quiet, remote section of the island and boasts a fine gourmet restaurant for evening meals only. Eighteen rooms in four buildings offer private baths and queen-size beds. Many rooms are air-conditioned though it is seldom needed. A library with fireplace and a wonderful outside deck for guest use provide a variety of spots for relaxation. This is a great place for weddings as well as for a romantic honeymoon getaway. No children under six. $75-175.

7 No smoking; 8 Children welcome; 9 Social drinking allowed; 10 Tennis nearby; 11 Swimming nearby; 12 Golf nearby; 13 Skiing nearby; 14 May be booked through a travel agent.

WESTWOOD

Bed and Breakfast Associates Bay Colony, Ltd.

P.O. Box 57166, Babson Park, Boston, 02157-0166
(617) 449-5302; (800) 347-5088
FAX (617) 449-5958

IW725. This country house and barn are graced by an inviting brick patio with a large in-ground pool. The first floor has been redesigned to provide a view of the grounds through walls of glass. Three guest rooms on the second floor share a bath. A Boston tour guide, this hostess claims there is a "friendly ghost" in the house. Children welcome. $55; family rates available.

IW726. This private hideaway is a converted schoolhouse. A party of five can enjoy the two-story apartment with two bedrooms, two full baths, a kitchen, dining area, living room, and deck. Sleeping space includes an antique double bed, two twins that can be made up as a king, and one single. Children welcome; no smoking. $150 for four adults; $120 for family of four.

WEST YARMOUTH

The Manor House

57 Maine Avenue, 02673
(508) 771-3433; (800) 9MANOR9

The Manor House is a lovely 1920s six-bedroom Dutch Colonial bed and breakfast overlooking Lewis Bay. Each room has a private bath and all are decorated differently and named after special little touches of Cape Cod such as Cranbury Bog and Picket Fence. Easy access to virtually everything the Cape has to offer. Enjoy a bountiful breakfast, afternoon tea, and friendly hospitality at the Manor House.

Hosts: Rick and Liz Latshaw
Rooms: 6 (PB) $74-88
Continental Breakfast
Credit Cards: A, B, C, D
Notes: 2, 5, 7, 9, 10, 11, 12

WEYMOUTH

Host Homes of Boston

P.O. Box 117, Boston, 02168
(617) 244-1308; FAX (617) 244-5156

Thayer's Landing. Historic 1696 Colonial on the river that has been restored by the friendly third-generation owners. Guest suite on the second floor with a queen-size and twin beds has a fireplace and a river view. The bright first-floor guest room has a queen-size bed and a river view. Breakfast is served in the dining room or on the porch by the river. Families are welcome. Near Bayside Expo Center and Plymouth. Red Line or water shuttle to Boston. No smoking. $68.

WILLIAMSTOWN

American Country Collection

1353 Union Street, Schnectady, NY 12054
(518) 439-7001; FAX (518) 439-4301

029. This 600-acre dairy farm is nestled in a valley, but energetic guests can hike up the rolling hills to the pond to swim, fish, or just feast on the beautiful three-state view. Barn cats and calves delight visiting children. Join the host family in the living room for conversation, TV, or perhaps playing the piano. The two cozy, paneled guest rooms have comfortable beds and are cool, clean, and quiet. Shared bath. Breakfast is served on antique china and may be enjoyed on the porch on nice summer days. $45.

167. This newly renovated facility on 350 acres in the Berkshires offers cozy rooms with private bath, one-, two-, and three-bedroom suites with living room and fireplace, kitchen, and bedroom with queen-size bed, and secluded cottages with one, two, or three bedrooms, each with a fireplace. Heated pool. Air-conditioned, with telephone and TV. Children under 16 are welcome and stay

NOTES: Credit cards accepted: A MasterCard; B Visa; C American Express; D Discover; E Diners Club;
F Other; 2 Personal checks accepted; 3 Lunch available; 4 Dinner available; 5 Open all year; 6 Pets welcome;

free. Pets permitted in cottages. Continental breakfast. Smoking permitted. $68-188.

Steep Acres Farm Bed and Breakfast

520 White Oaks Road, 01267
(413) 458-3774

Two miles from Williams College and the Williamstown Theatre Festival. A country home on a high knoll with spectacular views of the Berkshire Hills and Vermont's Green Mountains. Trout and swimming pond are tempting on this farm's 52 acres adjacent to the Appalachian and Long trails. Short distance to Tanglewood and Jacob's Pillow.

Hosts: Mary and Marvin Gangemi
Rooms: 4 (SB) $45-70
Full Breakfast
Credit Cards: None
Notes: 2, 5, 7, 9, 10, 11, 12, 13, 14

WINDSOR

Windfields Farm

154 Windsor Bush Road, Cummington, 01026
(413) 684-3786

Secluded 100-acre homestead on a dirt road surrounded by gardens, birds, fields, and forests, with swimming pond and

hiking trails. Guests have private entrance, book-lined living room, fireplace, piano, and dining room. Family antiques, paintings, and flowers. Organic produce, eggs, maple syrup, raspberries, and wild blueberries enrich the hearty breakfasts. Near Tanglewood, Williams and Smith colleges, and the new Norman Rockwell Museum. Closed March and April. Children over 12 are welcome.

Hosts: Carolyn and Arnold Westwood
Rooms: 2 (SB) $63-70
Full Breakfast
Credit Cards: None
Notes: 2, 9, 11, 13

The Marlborough

WOODS HOLE

The Marlborough

320 Woods Hole Road, 02543
(508) 548-6218; (800) 320-2322 (reservations);
FAX (508) 457-7519

The Marlborough is an intimate Cape Cod home with five guest rooms and cozy poolside cottage, individually decorated with antiques and collectibles, each with private bath and air conditioning. The spacious wooded grounds include a pool and paddle tennis court. One and one-half miles to the Martha's Vineyard ferry. Enjoy easy day trips to Boston, Newport, Plymouth,

7 No smoking; 8 Children welcome; 9 Social drinking allowed; 10 Tennis nearby; 11 Swimming nearby; 12 Golf nearby; 13 Skiing nearby; 14 May be booked through a travel agent.

Provincetown, and Nantucket. Delightful breakfast. AAA rated three diamonds.

Host: Diana Smith
Rooms: 5 (PB) $85-125
Full Breakfast
Credit Cards: A, B, C
Notes: 2, 5, 7, 9, 10, 11, 14

WORTHINGTON

Hill Gallery

137 East Windsor Road, 01098
(413) 238-5914

On a mountaintop in the Hampshire Hills on 25 acres. Enjoy relaxed country living in an owner-built contemporary home with art gallery, fireplaces, and swimming pool. Self-contained cottage also available. Minimum stay of two nights on holidays. Children over five welcome.

Hosts: Ellen and Walter Korzec
Rooms: 2 (PB) $60
Full Breakfast
Credit Cards: None
Notes: 2, 5, 9, 10, 11, 12, 13

YARMOUTH (BASS RIVER)

Golden Slumber Accommodations

640 Revere Beach Boulevard, Revere, 02151
(800) 892-3231; (617) 289-1053

Captain Farris House. The ambience of an 1845 sea captain's home graciously offers 1990s amenities. Although one finds antique furnishings around the king- and queen-size beds, the baths are graced with French sinks and Jacuzzi bathtubs. Most rooms offer private entrances; others boast decks and suites. Gourmet breakfasts are served under the chandelier in the dining room or in the open-air courtyard at the center of the house. Other meals are also available to guests. Full breakfast.

YARMOUTH PORT

Bed and Breakfast Cape Cod

P.O. Box 341, West Hyannisport, 02672-0341
(508) 775-2772; FAX (508) 775-2884

71. This Cape Cod-style house built in 1800 has three bedrooms with private baths, one with a queen-size bed, one with a double, and one with twin beds. A parlor with a TV is available for guests. Enjoy a nice Continental breakfast. Walk to the freshwater pond or to the beach nearby, or simply relax on the pleasant grounds. $65-85.

75. An authentic 1809 Greek Revival host home is available with two bedrooms, each with a queen-size bed and private bath. Restored by its owners several years ago, the house is on the village green in the historic district and is on the National Register of Historic Places. Walk on 1.75 miles of nature trails. Visit the village historical society headquarters next door. Sit on the patio under giant trees and recall what life may have been like here several hundred years ago. Enjoy a great daily breakfast and village convenience, including fine restaurants, shops, and points of historic interest. No smoking. No children under 15. $110.

79. Built in 1710 in the heart of the village, this Cape Cod cottage offers the charm and quaintness that is pure Cape Cod. It is a delightful home offering three private-bath bedrooms, two with doubles and one with a pair of twins. The wonderful full breakfast is served each morning in the dining room or on the terrace. Walk to nature trails, restaurants, village shops, or the ocean on Cape Cod Bay, less than a mile away. Step back into history in this home now on the National Register of Historic Places. No smoking. $85-95.

NOTES: Credit cards accepted: A MasterCard; B Visa; C American Express; D Discover; E Diners Club; F Other; 2 Personal checks accepted; 3 Lunch available; 4 Dinner available; 5 Open all year; 6 Pets welcome;

Colonial House Inn

Colonial House Inn

277 Main Street, Route 6A, 02675
(508) 362-4348; (800) 999-3416
FAX (508) 362-8034

This registered historical landmark has antique appointed guest rooms, private baths, and air conditioning. It features Old World charm and traditional New England cuisine. Full liquor license, fine wines, indoor heated swimming pool and Jacuzzi. Lovely grounds, large deck, reading room, TV room, close to nature trails, golf, tennis, antique shops, beaches, and shopping. Wedding receptions and other function space available up to 135 people.

Host: Malcolm J. Perna
Rooms: 21 (PB) $70-95
Continental Breakfast
Credit Cards: A, B, C, D
Notes: 2, 3, 4, 5, 6, 8, 9, 10, 11, 12, 13, 14

Olde Captain's Inn

101 Main Street, 02675-1709
(508) 362-4496

Charming restored captain's home, in the historic district. Fine lodgings and superb Continental breakfast. Cable TV. The inn has a truly friendly, elegant atmosphere. Walk to shops and restaurants. No smoking in the guest rooms. Continental-plus breakfast is served. Stay two nights and the third night is free. Suites are available starting at $300 per week.

Hosts: Betsy O'Connor and Sven Tilly
Rooms: 5 (3 PB; 2 SB) $50-100
Continental Breakfast
Credit Cards: None
Notes: 2, 5, 7, 9, 10, 11, 12

One Centre Street Inn

Route 6A and Old Kings Highway, 02675
(508) 362-8910

On the historic north side of Cape Cod, One Centre Street Inn is a short walk or bike ride from Gray's Beach, antique shops, bookstores, and fine restaurants. Newly redecorated in understated elegance, this inn offers guests the perfect combination of comfort and style. A sumptuous breakfast awaits guests with homemade granola, muffins, and scones, and such selections as blueberry lemon yogurt pancakes or Eggs Karina, an original creation of the inn's new owner. Children over ten welcome.

Host: Karen Iannello
Rooms: 6 (4 PB; 2 SB) $75-110
Full Breakfast
Credit Cards: A, B
Notes: 2, 5, 7, 9, 10, 11, 12, 14

The Village Inn

92 Main Street, Route 6A, P.O. Box 1, 02675
(508) 362-3182

This charming sea captain's home built in 1795 has been an inn since 1946. Noted for cordial hospitality and comfortable rooms with private baths. Public rooms,

The Village Inn

7 No smoking; 8 Children welcome; 9 Social drinking allowed; 10 Tennis nearby; 11 Swimming nearby; 12 Golf nearby; 13 Skiing nearby; 14 May be booked through a travel agent.

screened porch, and shaded lawn. The inn is within easy walking distance of Cape Cod Bay, excellent restaurants, and antique shops. No smoking.

Hosts: Mac and Esther Hickey
Rooms: 10 (8 PB; 2 SB) $40-85
Full Breakfast or Continental Breakfast
Credit Cards: A, B
Notes: 2, 5, 6, 8, 9, 10, 11, 12, 14

Wedgewood Inn
83 Main Street, 02675
(508) 362-5157

Situated in the historic area of Cape Cod, the inn is on the National Register of Historic Places and has been featured in *Country Inns of America.* Near beaches, art galleries, antique shops, golf, boating, and fine restaurants. Fireplaces and pri-

Wedgewood Inn

vate screened porches. Limited smoking. Children over ten welcome.

Hosts: Milt and Gerrie Graham
Rooms: 6 (PB) $115-160
Full Breakfast
Credit Cards: A, B, C, E
Notes: 2, 5, 9, 10, 11, 12, 14

Michigan

Bed and Breakfast on Campus

921 East Huron, 48104
(313) 994-9100

Bed and Breakfast on Campus is housed in a unique contemporary building across the street from the University of Michigan campus and five university theaters. It is within walking distance to the hospital and Ann Arbor's cosmopolitan downtown area with diverse restaurants and theaters. It has a spacious common area and five elegantly furnished guest rooms with private baths. A full gourmet breakfast is served. Covered parking is provided at the main entrance.

Host: Virginia Mikola
Rooms: 5 (PB) $55-85
Full Breakfast
Credit Cards: A, B, C
Notes: 2, 5, 9, 10, 11, 12, 13

Bed and Breakfast Reservations of Michigan

4655 Charest, Waterford, 48327
(810) 682-2665

101. Country French-style home built in 1930s. Convenient to University of Michigan and Medical Center, shopping, and many fine restaurants. Relax in front of the fireplace, play a game of cards in the library alcove, or enjoy a good book from the eclectic collection. Three guest rooms with private and shared baths. One cat in residence. No smoking. Full breakfast served. $55-75.

Woods Inn

2887 Newport Road, 48103
(313) 665-8394

Built in 1859, this large, two-story stone and wood Early American home contains four commodious guest rooms as well as an ample kitchen, dining room, parlor, and a large screened porch filled with wicker furniture. Nestled on three acres of pine and hardwoods, the inn shares its scenic setting with abundant gardens, a barn, and one of the few remaining smokehouses in Michigan. Inside, the comfortable Early American furnishings and period collections of ironstone, colored art glass, and Staffordshire figurines all create a welcoming, hospitable ambience that puts visitors at their ease, and brings them back again and again.

Host: Barbara Inwood
Rooms: 4 (2 PB; 2 SB) $50-60
Full Breakfast
Credit Cards: None
Notes: 2, 5, 7, 8, 9, 10, 11, 12, 13

Woods Inn

Michigan

ATLANTA

Bed and Breakfast Reservations of Michigan

4655 Charest, Waterford, 48327
(810) 682-2665

102. Modern redwood lodge on shore of Thunder Bay River. Five guest rooms, beautifully decorated in Victorian country. Private baths, one with Jacuzzi. Large deck with beautiful scenery. Canoes and rowboats available. Afternoon tea and full breakfast. No smoking. $50.

BATTLE CREEK

Greencrest Manor

6174 Halbert Road, 49017
(616) 962-8633

To experience Greencrest is to step back in time to a way of life that is rare today. From the moment of entrance through iron gates, guests will be mesmerized. This French Normandy mansion on the highest elevation of St. Mary's Lake is constructed of sandstone, slate, and copper. Formal gardens, fountains, and garden architecture. Chosen by Country Inns as one of the "top twelve inns" in North America for 1992. Air-conditioned.

Hosts: Kathy and Tom Van Doff
Rooms: 8 (6 PB; 2 SB) $75-170
Continental Breakfast
Credit Cards: A, B, C, E
Notes: 2, 5, 7, 8, 9, 10, 12, 13

BAY CITY

Clements Inn

1712 Center Avenue M-25, 48708
(517) 894-4600

This 1886 Queen Anne Victorian home features six fireplaces, magnificent woodwork, an oak staircase, amber-colored glass windows, working gas lamps, organ pipes, two claw foot tubs, and a third-floor ballroom. Each of the seven bedrooms includes cable television, telephone, a private bath, and air conditioning. Special features include in-room gas fireplaces, and in-room whirlpool tubs, and the 1,200-square-foot, fully furnished (including kitchen) Alfred Lord Tennyson Suite.

Hosts: Brian and Karen Hepp
Rooms: 7 (PB) $70-150
Continental Breakfast
Credit Cards: A, B, C, D, E
Notes: 2, 5, 7, 8, 9, 10, 12, 14

Stonehedge Inn Bed and Breakfast

924 Center Avenue M-25, 48708
(517) 894-4342

Built by a lumber baron, this 1889 English Tudor home is indeed an elegant journey into the past. Original features include nine fireplaces, stained-glass windows, speaking tubes, and even a warming oven. Its magnificent open foyer with its grand oak staircase leads to eight bedrooms. Ideal for small weddings, parties, and meetings. Corporate rates Sunday through Thursday. Continental plus breakfast.

Host: Ruth Koerber
Rooms: 7 (S3B) $75-85
Continental Breakfast
Credit Cards: A, B, C, D, E
Notes: 2, 5, 7, 8, 9, 10, 12, 14

BAY VIEW

Bed and Breakfast Reservations of Michigan

4655 Charest, Waterford, 48327
(810) 682-2665

103. Forty-two rooms in a historic turn-of-the-century inn in the charming village of Bay View. Two blocks from private Lake

---

NOTES: Credit cards: A MasterCard; B Visa; C American Express; D Discover; E Diners Club; F Other; 2 Personal checks accepted; 3 Lunch available; 4 Dinner available; 5 Open all year; 6 Pets welcome; 7 No smoking; 8 Children welcome; 9 Social drinking allowed; 10 Tennis nearby; 11 Swimming nearby; 12 Golf nearby; 13 Skiing nearby; 14 May be booked through a travel agent.

Michigan beach, hiking trails, and tennis courts. Summer activity and cultural programs available. In winter, sleigh rides and cross-country skiing at the doorstep. Continental breakfast included and fine dining available for dinner. All rooms have private baths and contain original period furniture. A variety of activity weekends are offered. $66-96.

The Florence

317 Park Avenue, P.O. Box 1031, 49770
(616) 348-3322

Step back in time in this 1878 summer home overlooking the heart of Bay View, a national historic landmark on the shores of Little Traverse Bay. Stroll through winding streets of a village that comes to life only a few months each year. Unwind on the flower-laden wraparound porch and in rooms filled with antiques and colorful charm. Experience an elegant gourmet breakfast and the Bay View Summer Music Festival. Open May through October.

Hosts: Paul and Elizabeth Nelson
Rooms: 8 (PB) $65-120
Full Breakfast
Credit Cards: A, B
Notes: 2, 8, 9, 10, 11, 12, 14

The Florence

BELLAIRE

Bed and Breakfast Reservations of Michigan

4655 Charest, Waterford, 48327
(810) 682-2665

104. A step back in time—a spectacular example of Queen Anne Victorian architecture, this bed and breakfast is on the National Register of Historic Places and has the honor of being featured on the cover of Kathryn Bishop Eckert's *Buildings of Michigan,* a well-known guide to the state's most notable buildings. Decorated with period antiques and wall coverings, it's easy to feel as if you've gone back to the turn of the century. A full breakfast is served in the formal dining room; freshly brewed coffee and the morning paper are brought to the hall outside guests' room. Relax on the wicker-filled, wraparound porch, or try the bicycle built for two. Four guest rooms with private baths, Victorian decor, and one room has a fireplace. No smoking. Nearby downhill ski area and championship golf course. $60-90.

BIG BAY

Bed and Breakfast Reservations of Michigan

4655 Charest, Waterford, 48327
(810) 682-2665

105. Breathtaking views of Lake Superior await guests at this bed and breakfast in a restored lighthouse. Secluded and beautifully renovated, experience history, nature, and lighthouse architecture. Tours leave daily to the many waterfalls in one of the most beautiful areas of Michigan. Explore the 40 wooded acres and two miles of trails for hiking. The 1,500-pound Third Order Fresnal Lens, the second largest ever used on the Great Lakes, is available for inspec-

NOTES: Credit cards accepted: A MasterCard; B Visa; C American Express; D Discover; E Diners Club;
F Other; 2 Personal checks accepted; 3 Lunch available; 4 Dinner available; 5 Open all year; 6 Pets welcome;

tion. Seven guest rooms, most with private baths. Full breakfast. Sauna available in the tower. Smoking outside. No pets. $85-165.

BLACK RIVER

Silver Creek Lodge Bed and Breakfast

4361 U.S. 23 South, 48721
(517) 471-2198

On 60 beautiful acres, this comfortably decorated four-bedroom home with cathedral ceilings offers lots of wildlife, hiking, cross-country skiing in winter, and down home hospitality. Just minutes from golfing, swimming, and fine restaurants; there is something for everyone. A full breakfast with homemade bread, muffins, and jams awaits guests. Children over five welcome.

Hosts: Larry and Gladys Farlow
Rooms: 4 (S2B) $55
Full Breakfast
Credit Cards: None
Notes: 2, 5, 9, 10, 11, 12

BLANEY PARK

Celibeth House Bed and Breakfast

Route 1 Box 58A, Blaney Park Road, 49836
(906) 283-3409

This lovely home is on 86 acres overlooking a small lake. The rooms are spacious and tastefully furnished with antiques. Guests may also use a large living room with fireplace, reading room, enclosed front porch, a large outside deck, and nature trails. Within an hour's drive of most of the scenic attractions in Michigan's Upper Peninsula.

Host: Elsa R. Strom
Rooms: 7 (PB) $45-75
Continental Breakfast
Credit Cards: A, B
Notes: 2, 7, 8, 9, 10, 11, 13

BROOKLYN

Bed and Breakfast Reservations of Michigan

4655 Charest, Waterford, 48327
(810) 682-2665

106. Victorian farmhouse built in 1860s sits atop a knoll overlooking beautiful Dewey Lake. Country Victorian decor. A glass-enclosed porch overlooking the lake provides a pleasant place to relax. Eighteen acres to explore a picnic area by the lakeshore. Five guest rooms, each with private baths. Accommodations for children. Continental plus breakfast. No smoking. $50-65.

The Chicago Street Inn

219 Chicago Street, 49230
(517) 592-3888

An 1880s Queen Anne Victorian, in the heart of the Irish Hills. Furnished with family and area antiques. Antiquing, hiking, biking, swimming, shops, museums, and more are available. Area of quaint villages. Three Jacuzzi suites available.

Hosts: Karen and Bill Kerr
Rooms: 6 (PB) $65-150
Full Breakfast
Continental Breakfast
Credit Cards: A, B
Notes: 2, 5, 11, 12

CALUMET

Calumet House

1159 Calumet Avenue, P.O. Box 126, 49913
(906) 337-1936

The Calumet House is on the scenic, historic Keweenaw Peninsula. The house was built by the Calumet and Hecla Mining Company, circa 1895. It features original woodwork and antique furniture. Breakfast is served in the formal dining room, which has the original butler's pantry. Near

Michigan Technological University and Suomi College.

Hosts: George and Rose Chivses
Rooms: 2 (SB) $25-30
Full Breakfast
Credit Cards: None
Notes: 2, 5, 7, 9, 10, 11, 12, 13

Willow Brook Inn

CANTON

Willow Brook Inn Bed and Breakfast

44255 Warren Road, 48187
(313) 454-0019

Willow Brook Inn sits on a wooded acre through which Willow Brook winds and wanders. This semi-Arts-and-Crafts-style bungalow offers a quiet retreat graced with country antiques, local hand crafts, pastel quilts, and childhood keepsakes. Breakfast is served in the dining room, on the covered breezeway, or in guest's room. Area attractions include Henry Ford museum, East Greenfield village, the Detroit Zoo, antique shops, art galleries, and gift stores.

Hosts: Michael and Bernadette Van Lenten
Rooms: 4 (2 PB; 2 SB) $75-95
Full Breakfast
Credit Cards: A, B
Notes: 2, 3, 4, 5, 7, 8, 9, 10, 11, 12

CHAMPION

Michigamme Lake Lodge

US 41 West, P.O. Box 97, 49814
(906) 339-4400; (800) 358-0058

A historic landmark, this two-story grand lodge is on the shores of Lake Michigamme. Log construction built in 1934, the lodge is surrounded by birch trees, flower gardens, and the Peshekee River. Large room for gatherings also has a two and one-half story fireplace. Large screened porch facing south over lake. All antique-decorated rooms have down quilts. Gifts and antiques on property. Thirty miles west of Marquette. Sandy beach, swimming, fishing, canoeing, and hiking trails. Guided lodge tours daily.

Hosts: Linda and Frank Stabile
Rooms: 9 (3 PB; 6 SB) $59-125
Full Breakfast
Credit Cards: A, B
Notes: 7, 8, 9, 10, 11, 12, 14

CLIO

Chandelier Guest House

1567 Morgan Road, 48420
(810) 687-6061

Relax in this country home underneath a beautiful crystal chandelier in the dining room. Full country breakfast, served in bed or in the dining room. Full or queen-size beds. Nine miles from Frankenmuth. Minutes from Birch Runs, manufacturer's marketplace outlet center, Chesaning showboat, and Flint's Crossroads village. Pleasant view from the enclosed sun porch. Flint and Genesee County owner/operator hospitality award winner. Senior discount.

Hosts: Alfred and Clara Bielert
Rooms: 2 (SB) $49.95-54.95
Full Breakfast
Credit Cards: None
Notes: 2, 5, 7, 8, 9, 11, 12, 14

COLDWATER

Batavia Inn

1824 West Chicago Road, US 12, 49036
(517) 278-5146

This 1872 Italianate country inn with original massive woodwork and high ceilings offers a restful charm. Seasonal decorations are a speciality, and an in-ground pool and mini-golf are available for guests to enjoy in the summer. Guests are pampered with evening turndown and gourmet breakfast. Antique and discount shopping nearby. Recreation and acres of wildlife trails nearby.

Host: E. Fred Marquardt
Rooms: 5 (PB) $59-99
Full Breakfast
Credit Cards: A, B
Notes: 2, 5, 7, 11, 12, 13

Chicago Pike Inn

215 East Chicago Street, 49036
(517) 279-8744

Turn-of-the-century renovated Colonial mansion adorned with antiques from the Victorian era. Eight guest rooms with private baths, two with Jacuzzi, individually decorated for pleasure and comfort. Formal dining room, library, and reception room featuring sweeping cherry staircase, parquet floors, and stained-glass window. Full country breakfast and seasonal refreshments served. Come and enjoy the restfulness of the inn.

Host: Rebecca Schultz
Rooms: 8 (PB) $80-165
Full Breakfast
Credit Cards: A, B, C
Notes: 2, 5, 10, 12, 13

ChicagoPike Inn

DETROIT

Bed and Breakfast Reservations of Michigan

4655 Charest, Waterford, 48327
(810) 682-2665

107. Towering porch pillars and ten-foot entrance doors of etched glass are impressive as guests approach this mansion built in 1905. Only one-half block from the Detroit River, close to Detroit's beloved Belle Isle. The interior features elegant plastering, oak woodwork and floors, antique furnishings, and state-of-the-art amenities. Breakfast of fresh fruit and home-baked goods. Eight bedrooms in Victorian decor all with private baths. A third-floor suite exudes romance with artistic murals and spacious hot tub. $60-115.

The Blanche House Inn

506 Parkview, 48214
(313) 822-7090

The Blanche House Inn was built at the turn of the century and has been lovingly restored to its former elegance. It is decorated with post-Victorian antiques, and each room has its own style. All guest rooms are equipped with cable TV, telephone, and bath or shower; three rooms have hot tubs. Just three and one-half miles from downtown Detroit and close to shopping in the suburbs. Many packages available.

Hosts: Mary-Jean and Sean Shannon
Rooms: 8 (PB) $65-115
Full Breakfast
Credit Cards: A, B, C, D
Notes: 2, 5, 7, 8, 9

DIMONDALE

Bannick's Bed and Breakfast

4608 Michigan Road, 48821
(517) 646-0224

This large ranch-style home features attractive decor with stained-glass entrances.

7 No smoking; 8 Children welcome; 9 Social drinking allowed; 10 Tennis nearby; 11 Swimming nearby; 12 Golf nearby; 13 Skiing nearby; 14 May be booked through a travel agent.

Almost three rural acres offer a quiet escape from the fast pace of the workaday world. On a main highway (M99) five miles from Lansing and close neighbor to Michigan State University.

Hosts: Pat and Jim Bannick
Rooms: 2 (SB) $25-35
Full Breakfast
Credit Cards: None
Notes: 5, 8, 11, 12, 13

DOUGLAS (SAUGATUCK) _____

Bed and Breakfast Reservations of Michigan
4655 Charest, Waterford, 48327
(810) 682-2665

108. This renovated Victorian home, circa 1890, lies in a quiet village within three minutes of Saugatuck. Quaint shops, charter fishing, marinas, art galleries, beaches, and a wide range of dining experience await you in this bustling resort area. A peaceful alternative to the hustle and bustle of Saugatuck. All guest rooms have private baths and are furnished in Victorian splendor with lace, antiques, and Laura Ashley prints. Air-conditioned throughout with electronic air filter for allergy sufferers and soundproofing to ensure a restful sleep. Breakfasts free on weekends. Special rates midweek and winter. $70-90.

Goshorn House Inn Bed and Breakfast
89 South Washington, 49406
(616) 857-1326

Enjoy a weekend of romantic luxury in this beautifully renovated Victorian home. Antiques, original woodwork and fireplace, wraparound porch, and a screened deck await guests. Four guest rooms, all with private baths. Full breakfast served on weekends and a Continental plus breakfast served Monday through Friday. In a quiet

neighborhood, shops, restaurants, cruises, and golf are within one mile. Owners are delighted to assist in recommendations and reservations. Central air conditioning. Smoking on decks and porches only.

Rooms: 4 (PB) $60-105
Continental Breakfast
Credit Cards: A, B
Notes: 2, 5, 9, 10, 11, 12, 13, 14

EATON RAPIDS _____

Bed and Breakfast Reservations of Michigan
4655 Charest, Waterford, 48327
(810) 682-2665

109. Elegant Tudor mansion built in 1927 by Irving J. Reuter, President of Oldsmobile. Six guest rooms each with private bath, telephone, and cable TV. Two cottages, one with original marble fireplace, offer scenic views of meadows and the Grand River and gardens. Enjoy fine dining at the inn's gourmet restaurant or your favorite beverage at the English-style pub. Eighteen miles south of state capitol. Many cultural and sports events are nearby. Full breakfast. No smoking. $75-155.

FENNVILLE _____

Bed and Breakfast Reservations of Michigan
4655 Charest, Waterford, 48327
(810) 682-2665

110. Victorian farmhouse on four acres in the country is 110 years old. Spacious and comfortable with large yard, including croquet and volleyball court. Guests may enjoy the hot tub or an ice cream social every Saturday night. Four guest rooms with private bath and one guest room with shared bath. Great for children with yard games, porches and swings.

NOTES: Credit cards accepted: A MasterCard; B Visa; C American Express; D Discover; E Diners Club; F Other; 2 Personal checks accepted; 3 Lunch available; 4 Dinner available; 5 Open all year; 6 Pets welcome;

111. Beautiful Victorian built in 1886 features a tower, lovely open staircase, and Italian marble fireplace. Decorated with antique furnishings and Victorian prints and lace. Seven guest rooms, all with private baths. The honeymoon suite in the tower offers a romantic setting with fireplace and whirlpool. Full breakfast. No smoking. $50-125.

The Crane House

The Crane House

6051 124th Avenue M-89, 49408
(616) 561-6931

Take a step back in time at the Crane House. A time of simplicity, relaxation, and grandma's feather beds. This 1870 family farmhouse is elegantly primitive with hand-stenciling, handmade quilts, and antique furnishings. The house sits on a 300-acre family-run fruit farm and is just minutes from Saugatuck, Holland, and South Haven. Come visit and relax in an atmosphere of yesteryear. Featured in *Country Living,* August 1992.

Hosts: Nancy Crane McFarland and Lue Crane
Rooms: 5 (3 PB; 2 SB) $65-95
Full Breakfast
Credit Cards: A, B, C, D
Notes: 2, 3, 5, 7, 9, 11, 12, 13, 14

Heritage Manor Inn

2253 Blue Star Highway, 49408
(616) 543-4384; FAX (616) 543-4711

Country hospitality is served daily in this lovely English manor. Enjoy homemade country breakfast, Jacuzzis, fireplace suites, indoor pool and whirlpool, volleyball, and basketball. Hiking and horseback riding nearby. Four townhouses, two with sunken Jacuzzis and elegant, white marble fireplaces. Near Saugatuck and Lake Michigan. Ideal for family reunions and holiday retreats. Specializing in honeymoons and anniversaries.

Hosts: Ione Rahrig
Rooms: 14 (PB) $65-145
Townhouses: 4 (PB)
Full Breakfast
Credit Cards: A, B, C, D
Notes: 5, 8, 9, 10, 11, 12, 13, 14

Hidden Pond Bed and Breakfast

5975 128th Avenue, P.O. Box 461, 49408
(616) 561-2491

Hidden Pond Bed and Breakfast is a quiet retreat set on 28 acres. Full gourmet breakfast included. Sunny breakfast porch, fireplace, library, and 60-foot deck for guests' exclusive use. Behind the house is a ravine with a pond, the perfect spot to relax and watch the wildlife. This lovely retreat is near the beaches of Lake Michigan, the boutiques of Saugatuck, and the winery and cider mill in Fennville.

Hosts: Larry and Priscilla Fuerst
Rooms: 2 (PB) $64-110
Full Breakfast
Credit Cards: None
Notes: 2, 5, 9, 10, 11, 12, 13, 14

The Kingsley House

626 West Main Street, 49408
(616) 561-6425

An elegant Victorian inn on the edge of Fennville, near Saugatuck, Holland, and South Haven. The guest rooms are decorated in Victorian elegance. Honeymoon suite with Jacuzzi and fireplace. Beaches, shopping, fine dining, and a playhouse theater nearby. The Allegan State Forest, with miles of nature trails, is enjoyable to explore. Bicycle rides to the lake or winery available. Country lover's delight. Featured

7 No smoking; 8 Children welcome; 9 Social drinking allowed; 10 Tennis nearby; 11 Swimming nearby; 12 Golf nearby; 13 Skiing nearby; 14 May be booked through a travel agent.

The Kingsley House

in *Innsider* magazine, *Great Lakes Getaway.* Chosen one of the top 50 inns in America by *Inn Times.* Limited bookings through travel agents.

Hosts: Gary and Kari King
Rooms: 7 (PB) $50-125
Full Breakfast
Credit Cards: A, B, C, D
Notes: 2, 5, 7, 9, 10, 11, 12, 13, 14

FLINT

Avon House Bed and Breakfast

518 Avon Street, 48503
(810) 232-6861

Built in the 1890s, Avon House is an enchanting Victorian home with spacious rooms, beautiful warm woodwork, and antiques. A comfortable, homey setting for business persons, tourists, and out-of-town guests with a delicious homemade breakfast served every morning of guests' stays. Within walking distance of downtown, the University of Michigan-Flint, and Flint's Cultural Center, which includes Alfred P. Sloan Museum, Flint Institute of Arts, Flint Institute of Music, Flint Public Library, Whiting Auditorium, Bower Theatre, Longway Planetarium, and Sarvis Center. Other points of interest within short driving distance.

Host: Arletta E. Minore
Rooms: 3 (SB) $40

Full Breakfast
Credit Cards: F
Notes: 2, 5, 7, 8, 9, 10, 12

FRANKENMUTH

Bed and Breakfast at The Pines

327 Ardussi Street, 48734
(517) 652-9019

"Come as a stranger—leave as a friend." Frankenmuth, a Bavarian village, is Michigan's number-one tourist attraction. This ranch-style home is within walking distance of tourist areas and famous restaurants. Bedrooms tastefully decorated with heirloom quilts, antique accents, and ceiling fans. Enjoy homemade breads and rolls as part of the modified-full breakfast. Recipes shared. No smoking please.

Hosts: Richard and Donna Hodge
Rooms: 3 (1 PB; 2 SB) $35-50
Full Breakfast
Credit Cards: None
Notes: 2, 5, 7

Bed and Breakfast Reservations of Michigan

4655 Charest, Waterford, 48327
(810) 682-2665

112. Traditional home built in 1963 is set in quaint Bavarian Village nationally known for Bavarian restaurants, the world's largest Christmas store, and outlet shopping nearby. Four guest rooms with private and shared baths. Continental plus breakfast. No smoking. $55-65.

FRUITPORT

Bed and Breakfast Reservations of Michigan

4655 Charest, Waterford, 48327
(810) 682-2665

113. Quaint 1873 home across from park and lake, with tennis and boat launching available. Six guest rooms with private baths. The perfect place to relax and renew. Guests may choose a Wellness Weekend, which includes two nights' lodging, healthy breakfasts, therapeutic massage, programs on the art of massage and stress management, and the use of exercise room, sauna and outdoor hot tub. No smoking. $50-75.

GLEN ARBOR

Sylvan Inn

6680 Western Avenue, 49636
(616) 334-4333

The Sylvan Inn is a beautifully decorated historic landmark building in the heart of the Sleeping Bear Dunes National Lakeshore. Its easy access to Lake Michigan and other inland lakes makes a stay at the Sylvan Inn a unique experience. Closed March, April, and November. Children over seven welcome.

Hosts: Jenny and Bill Olson
Rooms: 14 (7 PB; 7 SB) $60-120
Continental Breakfast
Credit Cards: A, B
Notes: 2, 10, 11, 12, 13, 14

Sylvan Inn

GRAND HAVEN

Bed and Breakfast Reservations of Michigan

4655 Charest, Waterford, 48327
(810) 682-2665

114. Late 19th-century Queen Anne Victorian within walking distance of downtown Grand Haven. Seven rooms all have private baths, two with Jacuzzi tubs, two with gas fireplace. Each room has a unique decor of its own, including crocheted canopies, antique four-poster bed, European artwork, and Southwestern influences. Kitchenette and common area on second floor offer convenience and social interaction. Full breakfast served in the sunny dining room by gracious hosts who bring a European touch, each coming from the Netherlands. Smoking is restricted. $75-120.

Boyden House Inn Bed and Breakfast

301 South Fifth Street, 49417
(616) 846-3538

Built in 1874, this Victorian-style inn is in the heart of Grand Haven, within walking distance of shopping, restaurants, beach, and the boardwalk. Some rooms have fireplaces and balconies. Two rooms have two-person whirlpool baths. Central air conditioning. Great kitchen and two common rooms are available for guest use. Full homemade breakfast served in the beautiful dining room.

Hosts: Corrie and Berend Snoeyer
Rooms: 5 (PB) $65.75-85
Suites: 2 (PB) $95-110
Full Breakfast
Credit Cards: A, B, C, D
Notes: 2, 5, 7, 8, 9, 10, 11, 12, 13, 14

Harbor House Inn

114 South Harbor Drive, 49417
(800) 841-0610

Built in 1987, this luxurious Victorian-style inn overlooks Grand Haven's historic Lake Michigan harbor. Seventeen rooms, all offering private bath and air conditioning. Many rooms have fireplaces and whirlpool tubs. Two common rooms are ideal for meetings. The beach, shops, and

7 No smoking; 8 Children welcome; 9 Social drinking allowed; 10 Tennis nearby; 11 Swimming nearby; 12 Golf nearby; 13 Skiing nearby; 14 May be booked through a travel agent.

restaurants are only a short walk away. Homemade breakfast buffet. A separate cottage is also available.

Hosts: Emily Ehlert, Innkeeper;
   Tiiu Arrak, Assistant Innkeeper
Rooms: 17 (PB) $90-180
Continental Breakfast
Credit Cards: A, B
Notes: 2, 5, 7, 9, 11, 12, 13

Village Park Bed and Breakfast

60 West Park Street, Fruitport, 49415-9668
(616) 865-6289

Overlooking the welcoming waters of Spring Lake and Village Park where guests can picnic, play tennis, or use the pedestrian bike path and boat launch. Spring Lake has access to Lake Michigan. Relaxing common area with fireplace; guests may also relax on the decks and in hot tub. Historic setting of mineral springs health resort. Tradition continues with "Wellness Weekend" special package including complimentary massage, use of exercise facility, programs on stress management, and creative visualization. Serving the Grand Haven and Muskegon areas. Close to Hoffmaster Park and Gillette Sand Dune Nature Center. Great Romantics Weekend and Bed and Breakfast Vacation Week packages are also available.

Village Park

Hosts: John and Virginia Hewett
Rooms: 6 (PB) $60-90
Full and Continental Breakfast
Credit Cards: A, B
Notes: 2, 5, 7, 10, 11, 12, 13, 14

GRAND RAPIDS

Empire House Bed and Breakfast

11015 LaCore, South, P.O. Box 203, 49630-0203
(616) 326-5524

This 19th-century farmhouse, on picturesque acreage, is in the beautiful Sleeping Bear Dunes Lakeshore area. Four rooms with outside entrances are available for guests. A large screened porch is also available. There is a separate two-bedroom apartment for weekly or daily use. A quiet, homey atmosphere, fresh-ground coffee, and a wonderful Continental plus breakfast. Close to the beaches of Lake Michigan, golf, tennis, hiking trails in the summer and skiing trails in the winter. Inquire about accommodations for pets.

Hosts: Rosemary and Harry Friend
Rooms: 4 (1 PB; 3 SB) $47.70-53
Apartment: $55-60
Continental Breakfast
Credit Cards: None
Notes: 2, 5, 10, 11, 12, 13

HARRISON

Carriage House Inn

1515 Grant Avenue, 48625
(517) 539-1300; FAX (517) 539-5661

The Carriage House Inn is nestled in a 127-acre pine plantation, overlooking Budd Lake, offering guests intimate accommodations. The seven guest rooms are furnished with country classics and antiques. All rooms have private baths, most having whirlpool tubs, color TV/VCR, telephone, coffee maker, refrigerator, and air conditioning. Executive retreat accommodations, private retreats, and reception and training facilities are also available. Amenities and

NOTES: Credit cards accepted: A MasterCard; B Visa; C American Express; D Discover; E Diners Club; F Other; 2 Personal checks accepted; 3 Lunch available; 4 Dinner available; 5 Open all year; 6 Pets welcome;

attention make the Carriage House Inn a perfect place to spend an "Escape to the North" in any season. AAA rated.

Hosts: John and Connie Mlinarcik
Rooms: 7 (PB) $75-125
Continental Breakfast
Credit Cards: A, B
Notes: 2, 5, 7, 8, 10, 11, 12, 13, 14

HILLSDALE

Bed and Breakfast Reservations of Michigan

4655 Charest, Waterford, 48327
(810) 682-2665

115. A Gothic Victorian home built in 1863, this bed and breakfast is in the historic district and is only five blocks from Hillsdale College. Nearby lakes, beaches, golfing, and hiking. Each room has a different decor. Many antiques and unique architectural features, including a Victorian iron fireplace in the parlor. Two guest rooms with private baths; three with shared bath. Continental plus breakfast. $58-68.

HOLLAND

Bed and Breakfast Reservations of Michigan

4655 Charest, Waterford, 48327
(810) 682-2665

116. Traditional 1920s home on two acres of beautiful lakefront property with woods and gardens. Complimentary boat ride in the afternoon. Full breakfast on a screened porch in warm weather. Three rooms with private and shared baths. No smoking. Children over 12 welcome. $70-95.

Dutch Colonial Inn

560 Central Avenue, 49423
(616) 396-3664; FAX (616) 396-0461

An award-winning Dutch Colonial Inn built in 1928 features elegant decor with

Dutch Colonial Inn

1930s furnishings and lovely heirloom antiques. All guest rooms have tiled private baths, some with whirlpool tub for two. Honeymoon suites available for that "special getaway." Attractions include excellent shopping, Hope College, bike paths, ski trails, and Michigan's finest beaches. Business people welcome; corporate rates available. Air conditioning. Open year-round with special Christmas touches. Dutch hospitality at its finest.

Hosts: Bob and Pat Elenbaas; Ellen Moes
Rooms: 5 (PB) $60-150
Full Breakfast
Credit Cards: A, B, C, D
Notes: 2, 5, 7, 10, 11, 12, 13

HUDSON

Sutton Weed Farm Bed and Breakfast

18736 Quaker Road, 49247
(517) 547-6302; (800) VAN FARM

Visiting this seven-gable Victorian farmhouse, built in 1873, is like going back to grandma's. Filled with family antiques on 180 acres of woods, trails, wildlife, and birds. Ancient maple trees are still tapped for syrup to be enjoyed at the breakfast table. Good restaurants nearby.

Hosts: Jack and Barb Sutton
Rooms: 4 (SB) $70
Full Breakfast
Credit Cards: A, B
Notes: 2, 5, 7, 9, 12

7 No smoking; 8 Children welcome; 9 Social drinking allowed; 10 Tennis nearby; 11 Swimming nearby; 12 Golf nearby; 13 Skiing nearby; 14 May be booked through a travel agent.

INTERLOCHEN

Bed and Breakfast Reservations of Michigan
4655 Charest, Waterford, 48327
(810) 682-2665

117. Cape Cod design built in 1980 on shore of secluded 1,000-acre Lake Dubonnet, only 15 minutes from Traverse City. Interlochen Arts Academy offers classical concerts and top recording artists. Two guest rooms with private baths, one with fireplace and Jacuzzi. One room has shared bath. Gourmet breakfast. $69-230.

IONIA

Union Hill Inn Bed and Breakfast
306 Union Street, 44846
(616) 527-0955

Enjoy a peaceful and romantic getaway among pre-Victorian splendor. Elegant, historic 1868 Italianate home noted for its expansive veranda and panoramic view. Only two blocks from downtown. Rooms tastefully decorated with antiques. Each room has a TV and clock radio. Central air.

Hosts: Tom and Mary Kay Moular
Rooms: 5 (SB) $50-65
Full Breakfast
Credit Cards: None
Notes: 2, 5, 7, 8, 11, 12, 13

JONES

Bed and Breakfast Reservations of Michigan
4655 Charest, Waterford, 48327
(810) 682-2665

118. Luxury in seclusion. Pamper yourself in a beautifully appointed Jacuzzi suite located on 93 wooded acres. Queen-size beds, full bath, private Jacuzzi and fireplace, service bar with refrigerator, and private balcony for each guest room. Uniquely decorated to bring nature indoors, with murals and canopies of tree branches. Common areas provide panoramic views of woods and wildlife. In-ground swimming pool available May through September. Close to wineries, Amish settlements, antique shops, canoeing, fishing, and golf. Conference facilities for meetings, parties, and retreats. Special packages available. $179.

KALAMAZOO

Hall House
106 Thompson Street, 49006
(616) 343-2500; FAX (616) 373-5706

Hall House is adjacent to the lovely hillside campus at Kalamazoo College, five blocks from the city. This 1923 Georgian Revival home awaits guests' arrival. Exceptional craftsmanship, warmth, and elegance abound. Spacious rooms with private baths, TV, telephones, robes, and full breakfast weekends. Inquire about special wedding and anniversary packages.

Hosts: Liz and Bob Costello and Sharon Josephson
Rooms: 5 (PB) $75-95
Continental and Full Breakfast
Credit Cards: A, B, C, D
Notes: 2, 5, 7, 9, 10, 11, 12, 13

LAKE CITY

Bed and Breakfast Reservations of Michigan
4655 Charest, Waterford, 48327
(810) 682-2665

119. A quaint chalet nestled among the pines on Sapphire Lake. Fireplace in common area. Handicap room. Swimming, hiking, fishing, boating, and cross-country skiing. Comfortable cottage decor. Two guest rooms, one with private bath and one with shared bath. Full breakfast. No smoking. $55-60.

LAURIUM

Bed and Breakfast Reservations of Michigan

4655 Charest, Waterford, 48327
(810) 682-2665

120. Built in 1908 by a wealthy copper mine owner, this 13,000-square-foot mansion will take you back to an elegant era. Silver-leaf covered ceilings in the music parlor, embossed and gilded elephant-hide wall coverings and stained glass in the dining room, and grand staircases of hand-carved oak are some of the unique and elegant features. Ten rooms with private baths. Full breakfast.

Laurium Manor

Laurium Manor Inn and Victorian Hall

320 Tamarack Street, 49913-2141
(906) 337-2549

Opulent 1908 mansion in the middle of the Keweenaw Peninsula with 42 rooms in 13,000 square feet of accommodations. Some unique features include hand-painted murals; embossed and gilded elephant hide and leather wall coverings; hand-carved oak fireplaces and staircases; built-in wall-size oak, tile, and marble ice box; gilded tile and marble fireplaces; and 1,000 square feet of tiled porch. Activities and attractions nearby include skiing, snowmobiling, scuba diving, cycling, antiques, autumn colors, and ghost towns. Guided tours daily 12:00 to 3:00 P.M., May through November, three dollars.

Hosts: Julie and Dave Sprenger
Rooms: 18 (12 PB; 6 SB) $49-109
Full Breakfast
Credit Cards; A, B, D
Notes: 2, 5, 8, 9, 10, 12, 13, 14

LEROY

Bed and Breakfast Reservations of Michigan

4655 Charest, Waterford, 48327
(810) 682-2665

121. For adventurous nature lovers, hunters, mountain bikers, and cross-country skiers. Rustic, primitive cabin in wooded seclusion or bunkstyle accommodations for skiers. Some primitive campsites available. Wooded acreage and lake on property. Groomed cross-country ski trails. Full breakfast. Open December through March. $20-35.

LEXINGTON

Governor's Inn

7277 Simons Street, P.O. Box 471, 48450
(810) 359-5770

One block from Lake Huron, this charming 1859 Victorian home is listed on the National Register of Historic Places. The

Governor's Inn

---

7 No smoking; 8 Children welcome; 9 Social drinking allowed; 10 Tennis nearby; 11 Swimming nearby; 12 Golf nearby; 13 Skiing nearby; 14 May be booked through a travel agent.

inn is comfortably furnished with antiques in sunny, spacious rooms. Walk to the beach, marina, restaurants, and shopping district of historic Lexington. Spend relaxing evenings passing time on the old-fashioned wraparound veranda. Continental plus breakfast. Smoking on porches only. Cross-country skiing.

Hosts: Marlene and Jim Boyda
Rooms: 3 (PB) $45-55
Continental Breakfast
Credit Cards: A, B
Notes: 2, 5, 8, 9, 10, 11, 12, 13

LOWELL

McGee Homestead Bed and Breakfast
2534 Alden Nash N.E., 49331
(616) 897-8142

Surrounded by orchards, this 1880s brick farmhouse stands on five acres and has a barn filled with petting animals. The guest area of the bed and breakfast has its own entrance, living room with fireplace, parlor, and small kitchen. Four spacious guest rooms are individually decorated with antiques and all have private baths. A big country breakfast is served. A golf course is next door and Grand Rapids is 20 minutes away. The largest antique mall in Michigan is five miles away.

Hosts: Bill and Ardie Barber
Rooms: 4 (PB) $38-58
Full Breakfast
Credit Cards: A, B
Notes: 2, 6, 7, 8, 9, 10, 11,12, 13, 14

LUDINGTON

Bed and Breakfast Reservations of Michigan
4655 Charest, Waterford, 48327
(810) 682-2665

122. Elegant accommodations in an 1889 Queen Anne Victorian mansion appointed with treasured antiques and cherished collectibles. Six guest rooms, including two with fireplaces. All have private baths. Early morning coffee and muffins served in parlor, followed by a full breakfast in the dining room. Smoking restricted. $55-85.

123. Victorian home built in late 1800s as a home and office for a local doctor. Includes interesting architectural nuances. Decor is a mix of antiques and contemporary with European and American artwork. All four guest rooms have private baths, color TV, and phone. One room features a Jacuzzi. Beautiful decor and special amenities guarantee each guest a memorable experience. Full breakfast served in the dining room or on the terrace. Innkeepers fluent in German. $65-95.

The Inn at Ludington
701 East Ludington Avenue, 49431
(616) 845-7055

This bed and breakfast might look like Queen Victoria's mansion, but it feels like home. Enjoy comfort and elegance in rooms filled with treasured antiques and cherished collectibles. "On the avenue" close to shopping, fine dining, and miles of Lake Michigan's sandy beaches. Early morning coffee and homemade muffins in the parlor are followed by a sumptuous breakfast in the dining room. Murder mysteries, sweetheart weekend, and a Dickens Christmas weekend.

Host: Diane Shields
Rooms: 6 (PB) $60-85
Full Breakfast
Credit Cards: A, B, C
Notes: 2, 3, 5, 8, 9, 10, 11, 12, 13, 14

The Lamplighter
602 East Ludington Avenue, 49431
(616) 843-9792; FAX (616) 845-6070

Unique centennial home in town is only minutes from beautiful, sandy Lake

Michigan beaches, the car ferry to Wisconsin, and one of Michigan's most beautiful state parks. Fine antiques, original paintings and lithographs, queen-size beds, and private baths create a unique ambience of elegance, comfort, and convenience. A whirlpool for two is the ideal setting for a romantic getaway. Gourmet breakfasts are served in the formal dining room or gazebo. Smoke-free.

Hosts: Judy and Heinz Bertram
Rooms: 4 (PB) $65-105
Full Breakfast
Credit Cards: A, B, C, D
Notes: 2, 5, 7, 9, 11, 12, 14

MACKINAC ISLAND

Cloghaun

P.O. Box 203, 49757
(906) 847-3885

Cloghaun, a large Victorian home built in 1884, is close to shops, restaurants, and ferry lines. The name *Cloghaun* is Gaelic and means "land of little stones." Built by Thomas and Bridgett Donnelly to house their large Irish family, the Cloghaun represents the elegance and ambience of a bygone era. The house is still owned by their descendants and has undergone recent renovations to bring it back to its original elegance.

Host: James Bond
Rooms: 10 (8 PB; 2 SB) $70-110
Continental Breakfast
Credit Cards: None
Notes: 2, 8, 9, 10, 11, 12

Haan's 1830 Inn

P.O. Box 123, 49757
3418 Oakwood Avenue,
Island Lake, IL 60042 (winter address)
(906) 847-6244; (847) 526-2662 (winter)

Lovely restored Greek Revival home furnished with antiques and decorated from the period. In a quiet neighborhood three blocks from historic fort and 1900s downtown. Dining room has 12-foot harvest table for breakfast of home-baked cakes and muffins, plus cereals and fruit. A short ferry ride brings guests to this historic and beautiful island. Sightseeing, bicycling, horseback riding, fine dining, golf, tennis, and shopping nearby. Or sit on one of the three porches and watch the horse-drawn carriages go by.

Hosts: Nicholas and Nancy Haan
Rooms: 7 (5 PB; 2 SB) $80-128
Continental Breakfast
Credit Cards: None
Notes: 2, 8, 9, 10, 11, 12, 14

MANISTEE

Inn Wick-A-Te-Wah

3813 Lakeshore Drive, 49660
(616) 889-4396

Enjoy Lake Michigan sunsets and a panoramic view of Portage Lake in a quiet, relaxing setting. Lakeside living with swimming, sailing, and fishing. This 1912 bungalow offers bright, airy bedrooms with unusual period furnishings and comfortable beds. Wicker-filled porch, cozy living room, and sunroom with wood stove ensure guests' comfort. Guests applaud the special gourmet country breakfast. Open April 15 through January 1.

Hosts: Len and Marge Carlson
Rooms: 4 (1 PB; 3 SB) $65-75
Full Breakfast
Credit Cards: None
Notes: 2, 7, 9, 11, 14

1879 E. E. Douville House

111 Pine Street, 49660
(616) 723-8654

This Victorian home, completed with lumber from nearby forests, features ornate pine woodwork hand-carved by area craftsman. Interior wooden shutters on windows, a soaring staircase, and elaborate archways with pocket doors are also original to the house. Antiques and collectibles fill the home. Ceiling fans in every room. Manistee Victorian Village, Riverwalk to Lake Michigan, and historic buildings are nearby.

Hosts: Barbara and Bill Johnson
Rooms: 3 (SB) $50-55
Continental Breakfast
Credit Cards: None
Notes: 2, 5, 7, 9, 10, 11, 12, 13

MENDON

Bed and Breakfast Reservations of Michigan

4655 Charest, Waterford, 48327
(810) 682-2665

124. Originally built in 1943 as an inn and rebuilt in 1873, this house has a history of many uses. Now, an inn once again, it has been lovingly restored to provide modern conveniences and beautiful country decor. Continental breakfast. Bicycle built for two. Outdoor barbecue and picnic area for guests. Great for retreats, business meetings, and banquets. Eleven guest rooms with private and shared baths. Jacuzzi suites available. Special canoe and golf packages available. $65-150.

Mendon Country Inn

440 West Main Street, P.O. Box 98, 49072
(616) 496-8132

The historic Wakeman House, now known as the Mendon Country Inn, was originally built in 1843 and rebuilt out of brick in 1873 by Adams Wakeman. Eight-foot windows, high ceilings, and spacious rooms complement the walnut spiral staircase in the lobby. There are numerous antique shops, a local Amish settlement, flea markets, golf, and wineries nearby. There is also canoeing at the inn. Hosts endeavor to provide guests with the comforts of home, the friendliness of small-town life, a great Continental plus breakfast, nine Jacuzzi suites with fireplaces, and a truly enjoyable stay.

Hosts: Dick and Dolly Buerkle
Rooms: 18 (PB) $50-150
Continental Breakfast
Credit Cards: A, B, C, D
Notes: 2, 5, 7, 8, 9, 10, 11, 12, 13, 14

MICHIGAMME

Bed and Breakfast Reservations of Michigan

4655 Charest, Waterford, 48327
(810) 682-2665

125. Watch sunsets over beautiful Lake Michigamme from this historic lodge. Explore 1,700 feet of private shoreline with sandy beaches, swimming, boating, fishing, and hiking trails. Canoes are available for guests to use. Excellent winter sports area for cross-country skiing, snowmobiling, and snowshoeing. Nine guest rooms with private and shared bath, antiques, and spectacular views. Full breakfasts, featuring gourmet coffee, hot cinnamon waffles, and nut bread. The grand room provides a place to relax and gather in front of the massive stone fireplace. The sun porch faces south, overlooking the lake with antiques and Adirondack furniture. A perfect spot for small business meetings and retreats. $59-119.

MOUNT PLEASANT

Country Chalet Bed and Breakfast

723 South Meridian Road, 48858
(517) 772-9259

The Country Chalet is a comfortable Bavarian-style home atop a hill surrounded by rolling wooded farmland, 25 acres of pastures, and woods and ponds that are playgrounds to wild animals and birds. Guests in the three upper level bedrooms share a living/dining room with fireplace, and all guests are welcome to enjoy the chalet's sauna, game room, and fireplace in the lounge. For those who love to watch

NOTES: Credit cards accepted: A MasterCard; B Visa; C American Express; D Discover; E Diners Club; F Other; 2 Personal checks accepted; 3 Lunch available; 4 Dinner available; 5 Open all year; 6 Pets welcome;

good college competition, Central Michigan University is less than a ten-minute drive from the chalet.

Hosts: Ron and Carolyn Lutz
Rooms: 3 (SB) $49-59
Full Breakfast
Credit Cards: None
Notes: 2, 5, 7, 8, 9, 10, 11, 12

MUSKEGON

Bed and Breakfast Reservations of Michigan

4655 Charest, Waterford, 48327
(810) 682-2665

126. This two-story house built in 1857 lies in the historic Heritage Village in downtown Muskegon. Country- and Victorian-style furnishings. Beveled stained glass windows in parlor. Cozy library and wrap-around porch. Cherry County Playhouse close by. Take a trolley ride to sandy Lake Michigan beaches. Four rooms with private baths. $60.

NILES

Yesterdays Inn Bed and Breakfast

518 North 4th, 49120
(616) 683-6079

Brick Italianate built in 1875 has 12-foot ceilings and lace-covered nine-foot windows. Furnished in antiques from early 1800s to 1930s. Comfy beds and quiet rooms promise a good night's sleep. Candlelight, soft music, and home-baked breakfast on old china will start the day (low fat/sugar on request). Close to Notre Dame University and Fernwood Botanical Gardens.

Hosts: Elizabeth Baker
Rooms: 4 (PB) $60-75
Full Breakfast
Credit Cards: A, B, D
Notes: 2, 5, 7, 8, 9, 10, 11, 12, 13, 14

ONEKAMA

Lake Breeze House

5089 Main Street, 49675-0301
(616) 889-4969

Two-story frame house overlooking Portage Lake, where guests share the family bath, living room, and breakfast room. Each room has its own special charm of family antiques. Come relax and enjoy the back porch and the sounds of the babbling creek with a full breakfast. Reservations and deposit required.

Hosts: Bill and Donna Erickson
Rooms: 3 (1 PB; 2SB) $55-65
Full Breakfast
Credit Cards: None
Notes: 2, 7, 8, 10, 11, 12, 13

OSSINEKE

Bed and Breakfast Reservations of Michigan

4655 Charest, Waterford, 48327
(810) 682-2665

127. This bed and breakfast originally built as a tea room in 1932 and now recently renovated lies on the sandy shore of Thunder Bay on beautiful Lake Huron. Two rooms decorated with antiques and stenciled walls. Semi-private bath. Fieldstone fireplace and old-fashioned sun porch add to the cozy, vacation home atmosphere. Paddle boat available. Full breakfast. No smoking. $45-55.

OWOSSO

R&R Farm-Ranch

308 East Hibbard Road, 48867
(517) 723-3232; (517) 723-2553

A newly remodeled farmhouse from the early 1900s, the Rossmans' ranch sits on 150 acres overlooking the Maple River Valley. Rossman's large concrete circular

7 No smoking; 8 Children welcome; 9 Social drinking allowed; 10 Tennis nearby; 11 Swimming nearby; 12 Golf nearby; 13 Skiing nearby; 14 May be booked through a travel agent.

drive and white board fences lead to stables of horses and cattle. Guests may use the family parlor, game room, and fireplace or stroll about the gardens and pastures along the river. Breakfast is served in the dining room or outside on the deck. Central air conditioning. Cross-country skiing nearby.

Hosts: Carl and Jeanne Rossman
Rooms: 2 (SB) $45-55
Continental Breakfast
Credit Cards: None
Notes: 2, 5, 6, 7, 8, 10, 12, 13

PAW PAW

Carrington Country House

43799 60th Avenue, 49079
(616) 657-5321

Carrington Country House is a 150-year-old farmhouse built in the center of fruit and grape vineyards near I-94. Just down the street is a public access to spring fed Lake Cora. It is a short walking distance from the house. The picturesque country road leading to the house is lined with large, old sugar maples that form a canopy of gold and green throughout the year. Each of the three guest rooms is uniquely decorated and filled with antiques that are family heirlooms. The guest rooms are spacious, and the glassed-in year-round front porch, where breakfast is served, looks out over a cherry orchard and a grape vineyard. Spring and fall are especially beautiful seasons to enjoy.

Host: William H. Carrington III
Rooms: 3 (SB) $35-55
Full Breakfast
Credit Cards: F
Notes: 5, 6, 7, 8, 9, 11, 12

PENTWATER

Historic Nickerson Inn

262 West Lowell, Box 986, 49449
(616) 869-6731

Since 1914, historic Nickerson Inn and Restaurant has been a place of charm and

hospitality. Completely renovated in 1991. Ten guest rooms, all with private baths and air conditioning, plus two Jacuzzi suites with gas log fireplaces and balconies overlooking Lake Michigan, which is one block away. A quaint village of small shops, four marinas, and beautiful white sandy beaches. Dinner is served every Friday and Saturday evening. Breakfast and lunch served weekends. Open all summer every day for meals. Cross-country skiing nearby.

Hosts: Harry and Gretchen Shiparski
Rooms: 12 (PB) $80-175
Full Breakfast
Credit Cards: A, B
Notes: 2, 5, 7, 9, 10, 11, 12, 13, 14

Pentwater Inn

180 East Lowell, Box 98, 49449
(616) 869-5909

Lovely 1868 Victorian Inn with English and American antiques in beautifully appointed rooms. Charter boats, marinas, international shopping, the beach on Lake Michigan, and good food and drink all within a few minutes' walk. At the inn, enjoy complimentary drinks and snacks each evening at 6:00 P.M. and a breakfast to remember. Use the hot tub, bikes, or cable TV, or relax on one of the decks. Fishing, cross-country skiing, and golf are close by. Limited smoking permitted.

Hosts: Donna and Quintus Renshaw
Rooms: 5 (PB and SB) $60-75
Full Breakfast
Credit Cards: A, B
Notes: 2, 5, 8, 9, 10, 11, 12, 13

Pentwater Inn

PETOSKEY

Benson House
Bed and Breakfast

618 East Lake Street, 49770
(616) 347-1338

Northwest Michigan: home to Mackinac
Island and the Mighty Mac (the longest
suspension bridge in North America),
Sleeping Bear Dunes, Sault St. Marie and
her seaway locks, hills and vales, pic-
turesque little towns, glistening lakes and
sandy beaches, and the 117-year-old
Benson House Bed and Breakfast. Benson
House is a magnificently preserved
Victorian home sitting on a hillside in
Petoskey, overlooking Lake Michigan's
Little Traverse Bay. Close to shops, galleries and all vacation activities, Benson
House features four large, comfortable
rooms, private baths, a full country breakfast, and afternoon wine and snacks. The
nostalgic atmosphere makes it seem like
Norman Rockwell lives right around the
corner.

Hosts: Rod and Carol Benson
Rooms: 4 (PB) $85-120
Full Breakfast
Credit Cards: A, B
Notes: 2, 5, 7, 9, 10, 11, 12, 13, 14

PLAINWELL

The 1882 John Crispe
House Bed and Breakfast

404 East Bridge Street, 49080
(616) 685-1293

Museum-quality Victorian elegance, elaborate original gaslight fixtures, and beautiful
plaster moldings complement this home's
fine Victorian furnishings. Between
Kalamazoo and Grand Rapids, the inn is
within walking distance of some of
Michigan's finest gourmet dining and
antique districts. The two-and-one-half-
acre parklike grounds on the banks of the

Kalamazoo River offer a relaxing atmosphere for guests to enjoy.

Host: Nancy E.. Lefever
Rooms: 5 (3 PB; 2 SB) $55-95
Full Breakfast
Credit Cards: A, B
Notes: 2, 5, 7, 12, 13

PORT AUSTIN

Lake Street Manor
Bed and Breakfast

8569 Lake Street, 48467
(517) 738-7720

Large bays, high-peaked roof, and gingerbread trim set off this brick Victorian
manor house. Continental breakfast served
in the gaslight room, or guests may have
breakfast in bed. The kitchen is open for
guests' use. Hot tub for relaxing, fenced
yard for picnics, and bikes for a trip to the
beach. Color TV and VCRs in all rooms, as
well as a selection of movies. Sitting room
to socialize and play cards.

Host: Carolyn Greenwood
Rooms: 5 (3 PB; 2 SB) $50-60
Continental Breakfast
Credit Cards: F
Notes: 2, 7, 9, 10, 11, 12

PORT HOPE

Stafford House

4489 Main Street, 48468
(517) 428-4554

In 1886, William R. Stafford built a lovely
Victorian home as a wedding gift for his
daughter. The home is on the National
Register of Historic Places and is furnished
with authentic antiques. The house retains
many of its original features. Guests are
invited to experience the charm of an era
gone by. Each elegant yet comfortable
room has it's own private bath. Guests
might decide to walk on the beach, enjoy
the local fishing, cross-country ski, or sit

7 No smoking; 8 Children welcome; 9 Social drinking allowed; 10 Tennis nearby; 11 Swimming nearby;
12 Golf nearby; 13 Skiing nearby; 14 May be booked through a travel agent.

by the fire in the cozy parlor. A full country breakfast is served.

Hosts: John and Patricia Baran
Rooms: 4 (PB) $50-75
Full Breakfast
Credit Cards: None
Notes: 2, 5, 7, 9, 10, 11, 12, 13

RAPID RIVER

Bed and Breakfast Reservations of Michigan

4655 Charest, Waterford, 48327
(810) 682-2665

128. Contemporary bed and breakfast in the Hiawatha Forest. Secluded two-and-one-half-mile driveway. Two private, stocked lakes. Drive your own dog sled team or enjoy cross-country skiing and the hiking trails on the premises. Full breakfast. Lunch and dinner available during dog sled season. Outside kennel for pets. Restricted smoking. Three rooms with shared bath. $69.

ROCHESTER HILLS

Paint Creek Bed and Breakfast

971 Dutton Road, 48306
(313) 651-6785

A casual, rambling five-bedroom ranch in a quiet country setting on three and one-half wooded acres. Birds and squirrels abound in the trees surrounding the mostly glass family room overlooking a pond and a trout stream 25 feet below. Convenient to the Palace at Auburn Hills, the Pontiac Silverdome, and the Meadowbrook Music Festival. Excellent shopping and local restaurants.

Hosts: Rea and Loren Siffring
Rooms: 3 (SB) $40-45
Full Breakfast
Credit Cards: None
Notes: 2, 5, 6, 8, 9, 11, 12, 13, 14

ROMULUS

Bed and Breakfast Reservations of Michigan

4655 Charest, Waterford, 48327
(810) 682-2665

129. Modern furniture on 20-acre pumpkin farm with wooded trails and picnic area. Pick your own fruits and berries for a snack. Full country breakfast. Twenty minutes to Detroit, Ann Arbor, Greenfield Village, and Windsor. Two rooms with shared baths. $45.

SAGINAW

Brockway House Bed and Breakfast

1631 Brockway Street, 48602
(517) 792-0746

Brockway House has been completely restored, using a mixture of primitive antiques, reproduction wallpaper, and Victorian touches. Explore Michigan from Saginaw's national historic bed and breakfast. Mackinac Island, Lelaneau Peninsula, and Traverse City are about two and one-half hours away. Twenty-five minutes from Frankenmuth's October Fest, Birch Run's Outlet Mall with over 150 stores, and Bay City, offering Saginaw Bay's great fishing and boating. Never more than 85 miles from a great lake.

Hosts: Richard A. Zuehlke and Zoe
Rooms: 4 (PB) $95-175
Full Breakfast
Credit Cards: A, B
Notes: 2, 5, 7, 8, 9, 10, 11, 12, 13, 14

ST. IGNACE

Bed and Breakfast Reservations of Michigan

4655 Charest, Waterford, 48327
(810) 682-2665

NOTES: Credit cards accepted: A MasterCard; B Visa; C American Express; D Discover; E Diners Club;
F Other; 2 Personal checks accepted; 3 Lunch available; 4 Dinner available; 5 Open all year; 6 Pets welcome;

130. Victorian-style home overlooking the Mackinac Straits. Eight guest rooms furnished in Victorian decor. In traditional European bed and breakfast styles, the inn utilizes shared baths. Full breakfast. Open May through October. Smoking restricted. Directly across the street from the lakeside boardwalk and a ferry line to Mackinac Island. $69.

ST. JOSEPH

Bed and Breakfast Reservations of Michigan

4655 Charest, Waterford, 48327
(810) 682-2665

131. English country-style inn built in 1917 overlooks Lake Michigan. Within walking distance to downtown St. Joseph and shopping. Close to beaches and local marinas. Six guest rooms, all with private bath, decorated with traditional and antique furnishings. Many rooms with views of Lake Michigan. One room with whirlpool tub. Continental breakfast. Smoking restricted. $70-110.

South Cliff Inn Bed and Breakfast

1900 Lakeshore Drive, 49085
(616) 983-4881

South Cliff Inn is an English cottage bed and breakfast overlooking Lake Michigan. Guests will experience a soothing relaxation within the luxurious accommodations. Each room has been individually decorated with imported fabrics, and all furnishings were designed and tailored specifically for that room. Partake in a homemade breakfast in the lakeside sunroom. Walk to beautiful downtown St. Joseph for an enjoyable morning of shopping. Choose lunch from the wide variety of restaurants, both fun and fancy, that adorn St. Joseph. Spend the afternoon at the beach or explore many of the fascinating attractions in the southwestern Michigan area. Simply enjoy the stay. Voted best bed and breakfast in southwestern Michigan and was awarded 1994 Readers' Choice Award.

Host: Bill Swisher
Rooms: 7 (PB) $60-115
Continental Breakfast
Credit Cards: A, B, C, D
Notes: 5, 9, 10, 11, 12, 13, 14

SAUGATUCK

Maplewood Hotel

428 Butler Street, P.O. Box 1059, 49453
(616) 857-1771

The Maplewood Hotel architecture is unmistakably Greek Revival. Some rooms have fireplaces and double Jacuzzis. Other areas include a library, dining room, lounge, sunroom, screened porch, and lap pool. An elegant brunch is served on Sundays. In downtown Saugatuck, within walking distance to all shops and restaurants.

Hosts: Catherine L. Simon and Sam Burnell
Rooms: 15 (PB) $65-155
Full Breakfast
Credit Cards: A, B, C
Notes: 2, 5, 7, 8, 9, 10, 11, 12, 13, 14

The Newnham SunCatcher Inn

131 Griffith, P.O. Box 1106, 49453
(616) 857-4249

Inside this inn, built near the turn of the century with a wraparound veranda, guests will find beautiful oak floors graced with

The Newnham SunCatcher Inn

---

7 No smoking; 8 Children welcome; 9 Social drinking allowed; 10 Tennis nearby; 11 Swimming nearby; 12 Golf nearby; 13 Skiing nearby; 14 May be booked through a travel agent.

oval braided rugs and family antiques. Sun deck, whirlpool spa, and heated swimming pool. One block from business district. Full breakfast. Private and shared baths. Air conditioning. Suites with fireplaces.

Hosts: Barb and Nancy
Rooms: 7 (5 PB; 2 SB) $75-120
Full Breakfast
Credit Cards: A, B
Notes: 2, 5, 7, 9, 10, 11, 12, 13, 14

"The Porches" Bed and Breakfast

2297 Lakeshore Drive, Fennville, 49408
(616) 543-4162

Built in 1897, "The Porches" offers five guest rooms each with private bath. Only three miles south of Saugatuck, we have a private beach and hiking trails. Large common room has TV. Inn overlooks Lake Michigan. Beautiful sunsets from the front porch. Open May 1 through November 1. Full breakfast on Sunday. Continental plus breakfast Monday through Saturday.

Hosts: Bob and Ellen Johnson
Rooms: 5 (PB) $69-79
Full and Continental Breakfast
Credit Cards: A, B
Notes: 2, 9, 10, 11, 12, 14

The Red Dog Bed and Breakfast

132 Mason Street, 49453
(616) 857-8851

At this comfortable place in the heart of Saugatuck, guests are steps away from shopping, restaurants, art galleries, marinas, and all the year-round activities that have made this harbor village the "Cape Cod of the Midwest." Built in 1879, the Red Dog features a mix of contemporary and antique furnishings. No minimum stay requirement on weekends.

Hosts: Daniel Indurante, Kristine Richter, Gary Kott
Rooms: 7 (5 PB; 2 SB) $60-100
Full Breakfast
Credit Cards: A, B, C, D, E
Notes: 2, 5, 8, 9, 10, 11, 12, 13, 14

Rosemont Inn

83 Lakeshore Drive, P.O. Box 214, 49453
(616) 857-2637

This country inn, selected as "one of the Midwest's top ten romantic retreats" in 1994 by the *Chicago Sun-Times,* offers 14 delightful rooms, each with private bath and air conditioning. Lakeview rooms with gas fireplaces. Outdoor heated pool with large indoor spa and sauna. Public beach on Lake Michigan across the street. Cross-country skiing at doorstep. Complimentary bicycles. Complete buffet breakfast each morning. Large common areas to hold business or social meetings.

Hosts: The Sajdak family
Rooms: 14 (PB) $70-165
Full Breakfast
Credit Cards: A, B, C, D
Notes: 2, 5, 9, 10, 11, 12, 13, 14

Sherwood Forest Bed and Breakfast

938 Center Street, P.O. Box 315, 49453
(800) 838-1246

This beautiful Victorian-style house is surrounded by woods. The guest rooms are decorated with antiques and traditional furnishings. One guest room has a Jacuzzi, and another has a mural painted in the entire room along with a fireplace. Central air conditioning, heated swimming pool, and wraparound porch. The eastern shore of Lake Michigan and a public beach are a half-block away, and the charming shops of Saugatuck are just two miles away.

Hosts: Keith and Susan Charak
Rooms: 4 (PB) $60-140
Continental Breakfast
Credit Cards: A, B, D
Notes: 2, 5, 7, 9, 10, 11, 12, 13, 14

Twin Oaks Inn

227 Griffith Street, P.O. Box 867, 49453
(616) 857-1600

Built in 1860, this totally renovated inn offers old English warmth and charm along

---

NOTES: Credit cards accepted: A MasterCard; B Visa; C American Express; D Discover; E Diners Club; F Other; 2 Personal checks accepted; 3 Lunch available; 4 Dinner available; 5 Open all year; 6 Pets welcome;

with all modern amenities. Queen- or king-size beds, and private baths. Air conditioning along with cable TV, VCRs, and a library of more than 700 films, assures a wonderful stay no matter what the weather. Common areas with fireplace and outdoor hot tub along with antiques throughout guarantee a memorable escape. Homemade breakfast. Cottage with sleeping loft and private hot tub.

Hosts: Nancy and Jerry Horney
Rooms: 6 (PB) $65-115
Cottage: 1
Full and Continental Breakfast
Credit Cards: A, B, D
Notes: 2, 5, 7, 8, 9, 10, 11, 12, 13, 14

SOUTH HAVEN

Arundel House—An English Bed and Breakfast

56 North Shore Drive, 49090
(616) 637-4790

This turn-of-the-century resort has been restored to its former elegance and is registered with the Michigan Historical Society. Guest rooms are individually decorated with antiques. Afternoon tea is available to guests. Walking distance to restaurants, shops, marina, and Lake Michigan Beach. Midweek and off-season rates available. Limited smoking allowed.

Hosts: Patricia and Tom Zapal
Rooms: 7 (PB) $55-100
Continental Breakfast
Credit Cards: A, B, C, D
Notes: 2, 5, 10, 11, 12, 13

A Country Place

79 North Shore Drive North, 49090
(616) 637-5523

This traditional bed and breakfast is an 1860s Greek Revival on five and one-half acres of woodland, two miles from the center of town and one-half block to the beach. The English country theme throughout is created by the use of pretty prints, floral arrangements, and antique furnishings. The

A Country Place

cozy common area features a fireplace and entertainment center. Warm days are enjoyed on the spacious deck or gazebo. Leisurely breakfasts feature home-baked goodies and lots of fresh fruit.

Hosts: Art and Lee Niffenegger
Rooms: 5 (PB) $70-85
Full Breakfast
Credit Cards: A, B, C, D
Notes: 2, 5, 7, 9, 10, 11, 12, 13, 14

Ross House

229 Michigan Avenue, 49090
(616) 637-2256

The historic Ross house was built in 1886 by lumber tycoon Volney Ross. it sits on a quiet, tree-lined street on the south side of the black River. Lake Michigan public beaches, downtown shopping area, Kal-Haven Trail, and many fine restaurants are only blocks away. Cross-country skiing nearby.

Hosts: Cathy Hormann and Brad Wilcox
Rooms: 7 (1 PB; 6 S3B) $45-55
Full Breakfast (weekends)
Credit Cards: None
Notes: 2, 5, 7, 9, 10, 11, 12, 13

Seymour House Bed and Breakfast

1248 Blue Star Highway, 60690
(616) 277-3918

On 11 acres of beautiful Michigan countryside, one-half mile from Lake Michigan and halfway between the popular resort towns of Saugatuck and South Haven, the Seymour House is a brick Italianate-style Victorian built by William H. Seymour in 1862 and recently restored. Enjoy swimming pool, one-acre stocked pond, and trails through woods. Close to sandy beaches, wineries, golf, antique shops, and fine restaurants. Five tastefully decorated guest rooms have private baths with showers and air conditioning.

Hosts: Tom and Gwen Paton
Rooms: 5 (PB) $82-142
Full Breakfast
Credit Cards: A, B
Notes: 2, 5, 7, 9, 11, 12, 13,1 4

Yelton Manor Bed and Breakfast

140 North Shore Drive, 49090
(616) 637-5220

Elegant, gracious Victorian mansions on the sunset shore of Lake Michigan. Seventeen gorgeous rooms, all with private bath, some with Jacuzzi and fireplace. Panoramic lake views, plentiful common area, two salons with fireplaces, cozy wing chairs, floral carpets, four-poster beds, and a pampering staff set the tone for relaxation and romance. Enjoy wonderful breakfasts, day-long treats, and evening hor d'oeuvres. Guests will never want to leave.

Hosts: Elaine and Rob
Rooms: 17 (PB) $95-195
Full Breakfast
Credit Cards: A, B, C
Notes: 2, 5, 7, 9, 10, 11, 12, 13

STEPHENSON

Top of the Hill

South 310 Center Street, 49887-9306
(906) 753-4757

A comfortable bilevel home in a small town in the Upper Peninsula of Michigan has lower guest room with access to large family room, full kitchen, and bath with shower. Upper guest room has shared bath with hosts. Cross-country skiing.

Hosts: Art and Phyllis Strohl
Rooms: 2 (1PB; 1SB) $35
Continental Breakfast
Credit Cards: None
Notes: 2, 5, 7, 8, 9, 10, 12, 13

TRAVERSE CITY

Bed and Breakfast Reservations of Michigan

4655 Charest, Waterford, 48327
(810) 682-2665

132. Victorian farmhouse, circa 1892, set on ten acres with lovely pond. Two rooms with shared bath. Country Victorian decor. Guests may enjoy a gourmet breakfast fireside as they view the pond and countryside. The Enchanted Cottage, a renovated grainery, is the perfect romantic getaway. Private bath, two double beds, refrigerator, cable TV, and phone. Breakfast served in cottage or the breakfast room. Hot tub outdoors for all to enjoy. $55-85.

Bowers Harbor Bed and Breakfast

13972 Peninsula Drive, 49686
(616) 223-7869

Private sandy beach, West Bay sunsets, and all the fun of Traverse City are found at this bed and breakfast on Old Mission Peninsula. Three lovely bedrooms, all with private baths and brass beds. Enjoy the beautiful sunsets from the wraparound stone front porch or from the beach. Close to restaurants and wineries. Includes a full breakfast. No smoking inside.

Hosts: Gary and Mary Ann Verbanic
Rooms: 3 (PB) $90-120
Full Breakfast
Credit Cards: None
Notes: 2, 5, 9, 10, 11, 12, 13

Victoriana 1898

622 Washington Street, 49686
(616) 929-1009

Touch a bit of history and take home a memory to be long remembered when staying at this Victorian treasure. Magnificently crafted with tiled fireplaces, oak staircase, gazebo, and carriage house. The home is furnished with antiques and family heirlooms. In a quiet, historic district close to West Bay and downtown. Very special breakfast served.

Hosts: Flo and Bob Schermerhorn
Rooms: 3 (PB) $60-80
Full Breakfast
Credit Cards: A, B
Notes: 2, 5, 7, 9, 10, 11, 12, 13, 14

UNION PIER

Bed and Breakfast Reservations of Michigan

4655 Charest, Waterford, 48327
(810) 682-2665

133. Vintage 1925 house in the heart of Michigan's beautiful harbor country. Close to wineries, Lake Michigan, and sand dunes. Four guest rooms, all with private baths, are uniquely decorated in garden themes that are both cozy and elegant. Spectacular rooms with choice of Jacuzzi, fireplace, or private balcony. Amenities include outdoor hot tub, massage therapy, social hour, bicycles, and fireplace in the common area. No smoking. $90-140.

The Inn at Union Pier

9708 Berrien Street, P.O. Box 222, 49129
(616) 469-4700

Only 90 minutes from Chicago and 200 steps to the beach, the inn caters to both weekend getaways and weekday corporate retreats. Choose from 16 guest rooms, many featuring Swedish fireplaces and porches or balconies, and two luxurious whirlpool suites. Unwind in the outdoor hot tub or sauna, or enjoy Michigan wines and popcorn in the Great Room. "Harbor Country" offers diverse dining, antiquing, and wineries, and year-round outdoor activities from biking to cross-country skiing.

The Inn at Union Pier

Hosts: Joyce Erickson Pitts and Mark Pitts
Rooms: 16 (PB) $105-180
Full Breakfast
Credit Cards: A, B, D
Notes: 2, 5, 7, 9, 10, 11, 12, 13

Pine Garth Inn and Cottages

15790 Lakeshore Road, P.O. Box 347, 49129
(616) 469-1642

The Pine Garth Inn and Cottages are nestled on the shores of Lake Michigan in a heavily wooded area of summer houses within the village of Union Pier. Steps and spacious decks lead to 200 feet of private sugar-sand beach. The inn is completely renovated and designer-decorated with walls of windows overlooking the lake. Also available are five cottages with kitchens, fireplaces, hot tubs, and a private walkway and decks to the beach. Children welcome in the cottages only.

Hosts: Russ and Paula Bulin
Rooms: 7 (PB) $80-145
Full Breakfast
Credit Cards: A, B, C, D
Notes: 2, 5, 9, 10, 11, 12, 13, 14

WATERFORD

Bed and Breakfast Reservations of Michigan

4655 Charest, Waterford, 48327
(810) 682-2665

---

7 No smoking; 8 Children welcome; 9 Social drinking allowed; 10 Tennis nearby; 11 Swimming nearby; 12 Golf nearby; 13 Skiing nearby; 14 May be booked through a travel agent.

Bed and Breakfast Reservations of Michigan offers reservation services for over 60 bed and breakfast homes and inns throughout Michigan. All bed and breakfasts are fully inspected to assure guests of cleanliness, location, decor, and ambience. Accommodations are available to suit personal tastes and needs from simple to elegant, country to urban, and economical to luxurious. Unique settings for anniversaries, weddings, business meetings, romantic getaways, and other special events are offered. Experience four seasons of beauty in Michigan. Enjoy hundreds of scenic lakes, miles of forests, countless cultural activities and sporting events, and hospitality that is unmatched. No fee or service charge for this reservation service.

Rooms: 300 (200 PB; 100 SB) $40-200
Full and Continental Breakfast
Credit Cards: A, B
Notes: 2, 3, 4, 5, 6, 8, 9, 10, 11, 12, 13

WILLIAMSBURG

Bed and Breakfast Reservations of Michigan
4655 Charest, Waterford, 48327
(810) 682-2665

134. A 1930s home recently renovated to a Bavarian-style bed and breakfast. Surrounded by beautiful acreage with orchards and wildflowers. Guests may catch a glimpse of deer, grouse, and other wildlife. Within two miles of beautiful golf courses. One mile to boat launch and near to Traverse City. Three rooms with private baths. Antique furnishings with a German theme, two cozy sitting rooms, a smoking room, and a summer deck with hot tub. A full German breakfast is served by the delightful German innkeeper. $75-95.

WILLIAMSTON

Bed and Breakfast Reservations of Michigan
4655 Charest, Waterford, 48327
(810) 682-2665

135. This spacious, comfortable, contemporary home rests on 20 acres. Seven bedrooms with five full baths and two half baths. The library provides a quiet place to read. The bar serves as a smoking lounge and a place to relax with a favorite beverage. The library and living room both have fireplaces. Indoor pool, sauna, hot tub, and exercise rooms available for relaxation and enjoyment. Full breakfast. $55-110.

YPSILANTI

Bed and Breakfast Reservations of Michigan
4655 Charest, Waterford, 48327
(810) 682-2665

136. Built in 1893, this Victorian home was originally a parsonage for a local church. Restored in 1987 and moved to its current address, it is now close to downtown Ypsilanti, the historic Depot Town, and EMU. The nine guest rooms, two parlors, and breakfast room are decorated with Victorian colors and wallpapers and are furnished with the finest period antiques. Each guest room has a private bath, cable TV, and telephone. Full breakfast. Fireplace in parlor. One room with Jacuzzi. $65-105.

NOTES: Credit cards accepted: A MasterCard; B Visa; C American Express; D Discover; E Diners Club;
F Other; 2 Personal checks accepted; 3 Lunch available; 4 Dinner available; 5 Open all year; 6 Pets welcome;

Minnesota

The Thayer Inn

60 West Elm and Highway 55, 55302
(612) 274-8222; (800) 944-6595

Experience the romance of a bygone era in this charming Victorian inn. Built in 1895 and listed on the National Register of Historic Places, the Thayer Inn offers guests the graciousness of yesterday with all the conveniences of today. Each of the 13 themed, air-conditioned rooms is lovingly furnished with authentic antiques and handmade quilts, plus a private bath with claw-foot tub. A stay is further complemented with a sumptuous *petite déjeuner* served bedside. Minutes from the Twin Cities in the heart of the lakes region. No matter the season, activity abounds. Mystery weekends, packages, and group and corporate rates available. Limited smoking allowed. Inquire about accommodations for children and pets.

Hosts: Sharon and Warren Gammell
Rooms: 13 (PB) $69.95-125
Credit Cards: A, B, C, D
Notes: 2, 3, 4, 5, 9, 10, 11, 12, 13, 14

CHATFIELD

Lunds' Guest House

218 Southeast Winona Street, 55923
(507) 867-4003

Two charming houses furnished with 1920s and 1930s furniture. Quaint kitchens, dining rooms, living rooms, one with fireplace, TV, and electric organ or piano. Eight bedrooms and seven and one-half baths available. Large screened front porches and small screened back porches. Central air conditioning. Reasonable rates. Inquire about accommodations for children.

Hosts: Shelby and Marion Lund
Rooms: 8 (7-1/2 PB) $55-65
Continental Breakfast
Credit Cards: None
Notes: 2, 5, 7, 10, 11, 12, 13

CROOKSTON

Elm Street Inn

422 Elm Street, 56716
(218) 281-2343; (800) 568-4476

Lovingly restored 1910 home with antiques, hardwood floors, stained- and beveled-glass windows, and fireplace. Private bath. Wicker-filled sun porch. Old-fashioned beds with quilts, terry robes, and fresh flowers. Memorable candlelight breakfast. Intimate dinners, wine service, and bicycles available. Limo to casino. Indoor community pool next door. Excellent birding. Near the University of Minnesota campus. No pets. No smoking.

Hosts: John and Sheryl Winters
Rooms: 4 (PB) $55-65
Full Breakfast
Credit Cards: A, B, C
Notes: 2, 4, 5, 7, 9, 10, 11, 12, 14

FERGUS FALLS

Bakketopp Hus

Rural Route 2, Box 187 A (Long Lake), 56537
(218) 739-2915; (800) 739-2915

This chalet lake home is nestled in the woods with decks overlooking a scenic

Minnesota

Bakketopp Hus

lake where guests can hear loons calling to each other. It is decorated with antiques, handmade quilts, down comforters, and fine linens. One suite has a private spa, another a draped canopy bed, and the other a fireplace. Ten minutes from I-94 at Exit 50, guests are in the wooded hills and valleys of lake country. The home is near a state park with nature, ski, snowmobile, and hiking trails and other recreation. Scenic villages, antique shops, restaurants, and golf courses are nearby. Enjoy this relaxed, romantic getaway with breakfast served overlooking the lake.

Hosts: Judy and Dennis Nims
Rooms: 3 (PB) $60-95
Full Breakfast
Credit Cards: A, B, D
Notes: 2, 5, 7, 9, 10, 11, 12, 13

HIBBING

Adams House

201 East 23rd Street, 55746
(218) 263-9742

The Adams House is a quiet, smoke-free accommodation in the center of the city and its attractions. A brief distance to lakes, woods, golf, and skiing. The English Tudor-style house features antique- and chintz-decorated bedrooms, a guest lounge with a kitchenette, and a charming flower

garden. Continental breakfast served in the sunny dining room includes Swedish coffee and warm conversation.

Hosts: Marlene and Merrill Widmark
Rooms: 5 (1 PB; 4 SB) $43-48
Continental Breakfast
Credit Cards: None
Notes: 2, 5, 7, 8, 9, 10, 12

LAKE KABETOGAMA

Bunt's Bed and Breakfast Inns

12497 Burma Road, 56669
(218) 875-2691; FAX (218) 875-3008

Three bed and breakfasts one-half mile apart. One inn is on the shores of Lake Kabetogama and Voyageurs National Park. Another on 300 secluded acres. The third is in a converted school and church building. Private baths, full kitchens, fireplaces, whirlpool, Jacuzzis, saunas, many decks, beach, dock, satellite, color TVs, VCRs, and washers and dryers. Truly three touches of class in the midst of the wilderness.

Host: Bob Buntrock
Rooms: 10 (6 PB; 4 SB) $65-130
Continental Breakfast
Credit Cards: A, B, C, D
Notes: 2, 3, 4, 5, 8, 9, 10, 11, 12, 13, 14

LUTSEN

Lindgren's Bed and Breakfast

County Road 35, P.O. Box 56, 55612-0056
(218) 663-7450

A 1920s log home in Superior National Forest on walkable shoreline of Lake Superior. Knotty cedar interior decorated with trophies of bear, moose, timber wolf, wild turkey, and fox. Massive stone fireplaces, Finnish sauna, whirlpool, baby grand piano, TVs, VCR, and CD player. A hearty Northwoods breakfast is served. In

NOTES: Credit cards: A MasterCard; B Visa; C American Express; D Discover; E Diners Club; F Other;
2 Personal checks accepted; 3 Lunch available; 4 Dinner available; 5 Open all year; 6 Pets welcome;
7 No smoking; 8 Children welcome; 9 Social drinking allowed; 10 Tennis nearby; 11 Swimming nearby;
12 Golf nearby; 13 Skiing nearby; 14 May be booked through a travel agent.

center of area known for skiing, golf, stream and lake fishing, skyride, mountain biking, snowmobiling, horseback riding, alpine slide, kayaking, fall colors, Superior Hiking Trail, Boundary Waters Canoe Area entry point, and state parks. Spacious manicured grounds. One-half mile off Highway 61 on the Lake Superior Circle Tour.

Host: Shirley Lindgren
Rooms: 4 (PB) $85-125
Full Breakfast
Credit Cards: A, B
Notes: 2, 5, 7, 9, 10, 11, 12, 13, 14

MARINE ON ST. CROIX

Asa Parker House

17500 St. Croix Trail North, 55047
(612) 433-5248

The Asa Parker House is a restored lumberman's home, sitting high on a hill overlooking the beautiful St. Croix Valley and the historic village of Marine on St. Croix. four charming flower-filled bedrooms, all of which have private baths, period antiques, and English fabrics and wallpapers, are available for guests. A wicker-filled porch, gazebo, tennis court, and marina with canoes are available for guests to enjoy. Cross-country skiing and bike trails are in the adjacent state park. Scrumptious breakfast awarded four stars. Midweek rates available.

Host: Marjorie Bush
Rooms: 5 (PB) $99-135
Full Breakfast
Credit Cards: A, B, D
Notes: 2, 5, 7, 9, 10, 13, 14

MINNEAPOLIS

Evelo's Bed and Breakfast

2301 Bryant Avenue South, 55405
(612) 374-9656

This 1897 house is in the Lowry Hill East neighborhood and has a well-preserved Victorian interior. The three guest rooms are on the third floor, each furnished in period furniture. The entire first floor is done in original dark oak millwork. A small refrigerator, coffee maker, telephone, and TV are available for guest use. The bed and breakfast is within walking distance of downtown, Lake of the Isles, Upton shopping area, Walker Art Center, Guthrie Theatre, and the Minneapolis Art Institute. Established in 1979, it was featured in *Innsider* magazine (June 1989). Cross-country skiing nearby.

Hosts: David and Sheryl Evelo
Rooms: 3 (SB) $50
Continental Breakfast
Credit Cards: A, B, C
Notes: 2, 5, 7, 8, 9, 10, 11, 12, 13, 14

Nan's Bed and Breakfast

2304 Fremont Avenue South, 55405
(612) 377-5118; (800) 214-5118

Comfortable urban 1890s Victorian family home offering guest rooms furnished with antiques. Friendly, outgoing hosts will help guests find their way around town. Near downtown, lakes, theaters, galleries, restaurants, and shopping. One block from buses.

Hosts: Nan and Jim Zosel
Rooms: 3 (SB) $45-50
Full Breakfast
Credit Cards: A, B, C
Notes: 2, 5, 6, 7, 8, 10, 11, 12

MORRIS

The American House

410 East Third Street, 56267
(612) 589-4054

Victorian home decorated with antiques and country charm. Ride the tandem bike on scenic trails. Within walking distance of area restaurants and shops. One block from the University of Minnesota-Morris campus.

Host: Karen Berget
Rooms: 3 (SB) $35-50
Full Breakfast
Credit Cards: A, B
Notes: 2, 5, 8, 9, 10, 11, 12, 14

NOTES: Credit cards accepted: A MasterCard; B Visa; C American Express; D Discover; E Diners Club; F Other; 2 Personal checks accepted; 3 Lunch available; 4 Dinner available; 5 Open all year; 6 Pets welcome;

OWATONNA

The Northrop-Oftedahl House Bed and Breakfast

358 East Main Street, 55060
(507) 451-4040

This three-story home is one of 12 historic homes in Owatonna. Built in 1898, it was the home of the late Dr. Harson A. Northrop, candidate for U.S. Senate and governor, and Tessie Oftedahl Northrop, humanitarian. The home features oak woodwork, stained-glass windows, and original family furnishings. Continental breakfasts feature fresh garden fruit. Business rate available. Lunch and dinner available by reservations. Pets welcome by prior arrangement. Smoking permitted on porches.

Rooms: 5 (2-1/2SB) $39.95-59
Continental Breakfast
Credit Cards: None
Notes: 2, 5, 8, 10, 11, 12, 13, 14

PARK RAPIDS

Dickson Viking Huss Bed and Breakfast

202 East Fourth Street, 56470
(218) 732-8089

"Aunt Helen" invites guests to this charming contemporary home with vaulted ceiling and fireplace in the living room that features a watercolor exhibit. Big Continental breakfast. Bicycle or snowmobile the Heartland Trail. Visit Itasca Park and the source of the Mississippi or cross-country ski. Unique shop and restaurant attractions. State inspected.

Host: Helen K. Dickson
Rooms: 3 (1 PB; 2 SB) $26.50-46.50
Continental Breakfast
Credit Cards: A, B
Notes: 2, 5, 7, 8, 9, 10, 11, 12, 13, 14

ST. PAUL

The Garden Gate Bed and Breakfast

925 Goodrich Avenue, 55105
(612) 227-8430; (800) 967-2703

A large 1906 Victorian duplex in St. Paul's lovely Crocus Hill neighborhood. Newly decorated rooms with individual air conditioning. Therapeutic massages available to guests along with soft cotton sheets and fresh flowers. Two blocks to bus and Grand Avenue's fine restaurants and shops. Easy access to downtown, colleges, airport, and Mall of America. Transportation available.

Hosts: Mary and Miles Conway
Rooms: 4 (SB) $65-85
Full Breakfast
Credit Cards: None
Notes: 2, 5, 8, 9, 10, 11, 12, 13

The Rose Bed and Breakfast

2129 Larpenteur Avenue West, 55113
(612) 642-9417

This 1925 English Tudor is in a large, wooded area between a historic farm museum and a golf course in the center of the Twin Cities metro area. Beside the University of Minnesota-St. Paul campus. Fresh flowers, private tennis court, cross-country skiing, art, books, and privacy or conversation. Full, wonderful breakfasts accommodating any personal dietary preferences or requirements.

Hosts: Carol Kindschi and Larry Greenberg
Suites: 2 (PB) $75-85
Full Breakfast
Credit Cards: None
Notes: 2, 5, 7, 9, 10, 11, 12, 13

SHERBURN

Four Columns Inn

Route 2, Box 75, 56171
(507) 764-8861

Built in 1884 as a stagecoach stop, this lovingly remodeled Greek Revival inn welcomes travelers. Four antique-filled guest-bedrooms, claw-foot tubs, and working fireplaces welcome guests. A library, circular stairway, living room with a grand piano, and a solarium with Jacuzzi make a stay here memorable. A hideaway bridal suite with access to a roof deck with a super view of the countryside is perfect for honeymooners. Full breakfast is served in the formal dining room, on the balcony, in the gazebo, or in the kitchen by the fireplace. Near lakes, antiques, amusement park, and live theater. Two miles north of I-90, between Chicago and the Black Hills. Call to inquire about pets and children being welcome. Limited amount of social drinking allowed.

Hosts: Norman and Pennie Kittleson
Rooms: 4 (3 PB; 1 SB) $50-70
Full Breakfast
Credit Cards: None
Notes: 2, 5, 7, 11, 12, 13, 14

SILVER BAY

The Inn at Palisade Bed and Breakfast

384 Highway 61 East, 55614
(218) 226-3505; FAX (218) 226-4648

This cozy, Cape Cod-style with bay window on Lake Superior has four guest rooms and one suite with a kitchen and fireplace. Accommodations are decorated in checks and ginghams. A full breakfast is served in the dining room. Easy access to beach and Tettegouche State Park. Open Wednesday through Sunday, including holidays, June through mid-October.

Hosts: Mary and Bob Barnett
Rooms: 5 (PB) $80-95
Full Breakfast
Credit Cards: A, B, D
Notes: 2, 7, 9, 10, 12

SPRING VALLEY

Chase's

508 North Huron Avenue, 55975
(507) 346-2850

It's life in the slow lane at this Second Empire mansion. It's flowers, birds, stars, and exploring this unglaciated area. Step back in time with a tour: Amish, Laura Ingalls Wilder, or caves. Enjoy the trails, trout streams, and bike trail. Closed December through February.

Hosts: Bob and Jeannine Chase
Rooms: 5 (PB) $60-75
Full Breakfast
Credit Cards: A, B, D
Notes: 2, 7, 8, 9, 10, 11, 12

STILLWATER

Rivertown Inn/ Cover Park Manor

306 West Olive Street, 55082
(612) 430-2955; FAX (612) 430-0034

This three-story Victorian, circa 1882, was built by prominent lumber baron John O'Brien. Framed by an iron fence, the home has a screened wraparound veranda. Each guest room has been decorated with antiques, as well as the parlors and sitting areas on each floor. Double whirlpool and fireplace suites available. Homemade pastries, breads, delectable entrées, fresh fruits, and juices overflow the dining room buffet each morning. The St. Croix River is just a short walk away.

Hosts: Chuck and Judy Dougherty
Rooms: 12 (PB) $69-159
Full Breakfast
Credit Cards: A, B, C, D
Notes: 2, 5, 7, 9, 10, 11, 12, 13

TAYLORS FALLS

The Old Jail Company

349 Government Road, Box 203, 55084
(612) 465-3112

The historic Taylors Falls Jail Guesthouse and the Cave and Playhouse suites in the Schottmuller Saloon building next door overlook the St. Croix River Valley. Just a few yards from Interstate Park with its

NOTES: Credit cards accepted: A MasterCard; B Visa; C American Express; D Discover; E Diners Club; F Other; 2 Personal checks accepted; 3 Lunch available; 4 Dinner available; 5 Open all year; 6 Pets welcome;

ancient glacial potholes and dramatic black rock cliffs. Enjoy swimming, fishing, canoeing, hiking, riverboat cruises, antiques, potteries, and much more.

Hosts: Julie and Al Kunz
Rooms: 3 (PB) $90-110
Full Breakfast
Credit Cards: None
Notes: 2, 5, 7, 9, 10, 11, 12, 13

WINONA

Carriage House Bed and Breakfast

420 Main Street, 55987
(507) 452-8256

Carriage House

Guests can indulge themselves at Winona's Carriage House Bed and Breakfast. Stay in one of the beautifully decorated rooms, each with its own special charm. Built in 1870, the Carriage House is near the Mississippi River. Enjoy a wonderful breakfast, free tandem bikes, and old-fashioned river town hospitality.

Hosts: Deb and Don Salyards
Rooms: 4 (PB) $70-90
Continental Breakfast
Credit Cards: A, B
Notes: 2, 5, 7, 9, 10, 11, 12, 13, 14

7 No smoking; 8 Children welcome; 9 Social drinking allowed; 10 Tennis nearby; 11 Swimming nearby; 12 Golf nearby; 13 Skiing nearby; 14 May be booked through a travel agent.

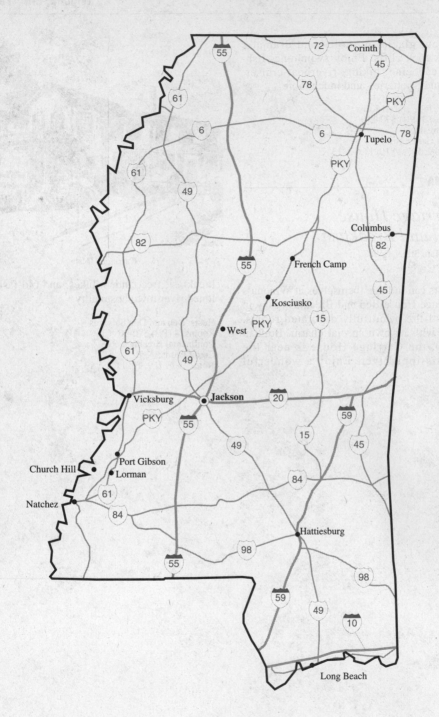

Mississippi

Mississippi

CHURCH HILL

Natchez Trace Bed and Breakfast Reservation Service

P.O. Box 193, Hampshire, TN 38461
(615) 285-2777; (800) 377-2770

CHU01. Just north of Mount Locust, only six miles from the Trace, overlooking 176 acres of wooded landscape, accented with beautiful moss-draped trees and ponds, this magnificent plantation home was previously owned by actor George Hamilton. There's a classic Greek Revival front section with a double gallery and white columns. A gracious Southern plantation breakfast is served. Large bedrooms, one with a fireplace, and a third-floor suite with fireplace and Jacuzzi are available. $135-175.

COLUMBUS

White Arches Bed and Breakfast

122 7th Avenue South, 39701
(601) 328-4568; (601) 328-7576

Standing among the magnolias in the historic district, White Arches offers gracious accommodations including original period furnishings, sumptuous Southern breakfasts, and a comprehensive tour of the house. Each bedroom is beautifully decorated with private balconies and baths. Built in 1857 and carefully restored to its former elegance, White Arches is listed on the National Register of Historic Places.

Shop in restored downtown or leisurely stroll through the historic neighborhood.

Hosts: Ned and Sarah Hardin
Rooms: 5 (PB) $85-125
Full Breakfast
Credit Cards: A, B, C
Notes: 2, 5

CORINTH

The Generals' Quarters Bed and Breakfast

924 Fillmore Street, 38834
(601) 286-3325

Circa 1870, this fabulous restored home is in the historic district of the old Civil War village of Corinth. It is close to Battery Robinette and a pleasant country ride from the famous Civil War battle area of Shiloh National Military Park. All rooms are fully furnished in period antiques, yet with modern conveniences. There are plenty of shopkeepers offering antiques and flea markets. Beautiful surrounding area for joggers and walkers. Pickwick recreational area is only 15 minutes away. Four rooms and one suite feature private baths. A full Southern breakfast is included. Just a short trip from Memphis or Jackson, Tennessee, while en route to perhaps Nashville, Tennessee, or while traveling the Natchez Trace Parkway.

Hosts: Charlotte Brandt and Luke Doehner
Rooms: 4 (PB) $75
Suite: (PB) $85
Full Breakfast
Credit Cards: A, B, D
Notes: 2, 5, 7, 8, 10, 11, 12

NOTES: Credit cards: A MasterCard; B Visa; C American Express; D Discover; E Diners Club; F Other; 2 Personal checks accepted; 3 Lunch available; 4 Dinner available; 5 Open all year; 6 Pets welcome; 7 No smoking; 8 Children welcome; 9 Social drinking allowed; 10 Tennis nearby; 11 Swimming nearby; 12 Golf nearby; 13 Skiing nearby; 14 May be booked through a travel agent.

Natchez Trace Bed and Breakfast Reservation Service

P.O. Box 193, Hampshire, TN 38461
(615) 285-2777; (800) 377-2770

COR-01. Milepost 320. Built circa 1870s. In the historic district of the old Civil War village of Corinth, near Battery Robinette and the site of Fort Williams. Only 22 miles from Shiloh National Military Park; host will be happy to tell guests all about he history of the area. Five rooms with pri-/ate baths. Full Southern breakfast is served. $75-85.

COR-02. Milepost 270, 320, or 320-A. This Southern Colonial-style home, circa 1870, is on two acres of oak trees, dogwoods, boxwoods, and azaleas in historic Corinth. Guests can enjoy a delicious breakfast on the back porch, relaxing in antique wicker furniture with veranda ceiling fans. Complimentary afternoon tea and refreshments are served on arrival. Convenient to Shiloh and Pickwick Lake and State Park. $70.

FRENCH CAMP

Natchez Trace Bed and Breakfast Reservation Service

P.O. Box 193, Hampshire, TN 38461
(615) 285-2777; (800) 377-2770

FRC-01. Milepost 181. Two blocks from the Trace, a rustic inn constructed from two century-old log cabins. Known as French Camp, this area is steeped in early Trace history. Enjoy a breakfast of sorghum-soaked biscuits, creamy grits, fresh eggs, crispy bacon, and homemade jams and jellies. Hosts will share the tale of the origin of this historic two-story log cabin and their collection of quilts, antique books, and linens. $60.

HATTIESBURG

Tally House

402 Rebecca Avenue, 39401
(601) 582-3467

Tally House, a 1907 mansion with 13,000 square feet of floor space in a large National Register district, has been restored to its original grandeur. The Tally House sits on large grounds with formal gardens, fountains, and statuary. Tally House is furnished throughout with antiques. Hosts are avid collectors; therefore Tally House has something to interest everyone. Antiques, shopping malls, the zoo, three golf courses, the university, and nice restaurants within five minutes.

Rooms: 4 (PB) $60-75
Full Breakfast
Credit Cards: A, B
Notes: 2, 5, 7, 9, 10, 12, 14

JACKSON

Natchez Trace Bed and Breakfast Reservation Service

P.O. Box 193, Hampshire, TN 38461
(615) 285-2777; (800) 377-2770

MAD-01. Milepost 110. Just six and a half miles from the Trace, near Madison, and convenient to Jackson, this elegant home features heart-pine floors, antique furnishings, ten-foot ceilings, Oriental carpets and porcelains, and expansive grounds. It is a modern home, yet deep Southern authenticity is readily apparent, from its columnar facade to its spacious interior. Rooms with private bath. $85.

KOSCIUSKO

Natchez Trace Bed and Breakfast Reservation Service

P.O. Box 193, Hampshire, TN 38461
(615) 285-2777; (800) 377-2770

KOS-01. Milepost 160. Stately two-story structure built in 1884, one of Kosciusko's finest examples of Queen Anne architecture, with a distinctive Victorian multicolor scheme, a three-story octagonal corner tower, and fishscale shingles. Houses a tea room as well, which serves lunch Monday through Friday, dinner Saturday evening from 6:30 P.M. until 9:00 P.M. Only two miles from the Trace. $75-100.

Redbud Inn

121 North Wells Street, 39090
(601) 289-5086; (800) 379-5086

The Redbud Inn is listed in the National Register of Historic Places. A two-story Queen Anne-style house that travelers have been using as a bed and breakfast since the 1890s. Restaurant and antique shop on premises. Mile marker 160, Natchez Trace Parkway.

Hosts: Maggie Garrett and Rose Mary Burge
Rooms: 5 (4 PB; 1 SB) $75-100
Full Breakfast
Credit Cards: A, B
Notes: 2, 3, 4, 5, 7, 8, 10, 11, 12, 14

LONG BEACH

Red Creek Colonial Inn

7416 Red Creek Road, 39560
(601) 452-3080 (information)
(800) 729-9670 (reservations)

This three-story, raised French cottage is on 11 acres of live oaks and magnolias. The 64-foot porch and six fireplaces add to the relaxing atmosphere of this circa 1899 brick-and-cypress home. English, French, Victorian, and country antiques and working wooden radios and a Victrola are for guests' use. Golf packages available, and casinos are nearby. The inn is just one and one-half miles south of I-10 off exit 28 and about five miles from Beach Highway 90, via Menge Avenue in Pass Christian to Red Creek Road. Biloxi is about 20 minutes, and New Orleans is about an hour away.

Hosts: Karl and Toni Mertz
Rooms: 7 (5 PB; 2 SB) $49-89
Continental Breakfast
Credit Cards: None
Notes: 2, 5, 7, 8, 9, 10, 11, 12, 14

LORMAN

Natchez Trace Bed and Breakfast Reservation Service

P.O. Box 193, Hampshire, TN 38461
(615) 285-2777; (800) 377-2770

LOR-01. Milepost 30. Completed in 1857 by an architect of Windsor, whose awesome ruins stand nearby. Classic Greek Revival with 14 rooms, 14-foot ceilings, columned galleries, winding stairway, and original slave quarters. Visitors may read in the diary of an early owner of the house about plantation life before and during the Civil War. Even a resident ghost! Rooms are upstairs; canopied beds, private baths, TV, movies, and telephones. Refreshments on arrival, full breakfast, heated pool, and spa. AAA approved. $99-125.

Rosswood Plantation

Route 552, 39096
(601) 437-4215; (800) 533-5889
FAX (601) 437-6888

Authentic antebellum mansion, close to Natchez and Vicksburg, offering luxury,

Rosswood Plantation

comfort, charm, and hospitality on a serene country estate. Once a cotton plantation, Rosswood now grows Christmas trees. Ideal for honeymoons. A Mississippi landmark; National Register; AAA rated three diamonds. Closed during the months of January and February.

Hosts: Jean and Walt Hylander
Rooms: 4 (PB) $95-125
Full Breakfast
Credit Cards: A, B, C, D
Notes: 2, 7, 8, 9, 11, 14

NATCHEZ

Bed and Breakfast Mansions of Natchez

P.O. Box 347, Canal Street Depot, 39121
(601) 446-6631; (800) 647-6742
FAX (601) 446-8687

The Briars. Elegant Southern plantation architecture, circa 1814, on 19 acres of lush and beautiful gardens overlooking the Mississippi River. Amenities include 13 antique-filled bedrooms with telephone and TV, and 24-hour use of living areas of house, gardens, and pool. Delicious four-course seated breakfast served in Riverview Pavilion. AAA rated four diamonds. Smoking in designated areas.

The Burn. Historic elegance, circa 1834, combines the traditions of the antebellum South with present-day comfort. Exquisite antiques and canopied beds in seven warm, inviting rooms. Nightly turndown with sweets and wine. Guests feast on a full seated hot Southern breakfast. Pool. TV in room. Designated smoking areas.

Camellia Gardens. Elegant Queen Anne Victorian house, circa 1897, in downtown Garden District. Recently restored to exhibit the richness of late Victorian interiors with period decoration. Rare old camellias and swimming pool in the garden. Evening

dessert tray, full Southern breakfast. Antique car collection. No smoking.

Dunleith. Picturesque Greek Revival mansion, circa 1856, on a 40-acre landscaped park near downtown Natchez, is a national historic landmark. Eleven rooms; three in the main house and eight in the courtyard wing. All rooms have working fireplaces and TVs. Full Southern breakfast. No children.

Elgin. Guests enjoy a plantation experience in the 1853 Guest House. Bedrooms with antique furnishings open onto a private gallery. Downstairs are sitting room, kitchen, and dining room where seated breakfast is served. Ten minutes from city center. Featured in *Gourmet,* April 1993. Designated smoking areas.

Glen Auburn. A rare French Second Empire, circa 1875, offers overnight guests a taste of Victorian elegance in the center of Natchez. Recent restoration enhanced original features while adding modern luxuries. Four spacious rooms in the main house. Eclectic carriage house. Nightly turndown refreshments. Jacuzzis. Pool. Telephone and TV in rooms. Designated smoking areas.

Glenburnie. Circa 1833. Escape to the charm of history and ambience of country gardens in a quaint three-room cottage on grounds of Glenburnie. Standing near the heart of downtown Natchez, cottage features beautifully appointed rooms and caters to the demands of today's traveler with kitchen, washer, and dryer. No smoking. Continental breakfast.

Glenfield. Charming English Gothic house, circa 1812 and 1845, in a country setting, yet only a short distance from downtown Natchez. House is furnished with period antiques. Five generations of the owner's family have lived at Glenfield. Enjoy the hospitality of descendants of early Natchez families. Designated smoking area.

The Governor Holmes House. Circa 1794. One of the oldest and most historic houses in the Old Spanish Quarter. It was the home of the last governor of the Mississippi Territory and the first governor of Mississippi when it became a state in 1817. The house is decorated with period furnishings and paintings. AAA rated three diamonds. TV in room. There are designated smoking areas.

Highpoint. Victorian "country manor" residence, circa 1890, in lovely Historic District with rare camellias and antique roses. One block from the bluffs and panoramic view of the river. Spacious bedrooms furnished with antiques and period reproductions. Complimentary beverage and snack upon arrival. No smoking.

Hope Farm. This home, circa 1775-89, served the Spanish governor in 1789. Four bedrooms furnished in authentic antiques include distinctive four-poster beds with draped testers. Breakfast served in formal dining room. Surrounded by 20 acres of old-fashioned gardens, a short distance from the Natchez city park. Designated smoking areas.

Lansdowne. Hidden within 100 parklike acres just three miles from downtown Natchez and still occupied by direct descendants of the builder, it is one of the most authentic houses in the area. Spacious rooms in 1853 dependency are furnished with antiques. Breakfast served in dining room of main house. TV in guest room. Designated smoking areas.

Linden. An imposing Federal plantation home, circa 1800, in a parklike setting, its front doorway was copied for *Gone with the Wind*. Seven bedrooms furnished with exquisite heirlooms and canopied beds from six generations. Delectable Southern breakfast served in the formal banquet room. AAA three-diamond rated. Designated smoking areas.

Monmouth. On 27 landscaped acres, Monmouth, circa 1818, is a National Historic Landmark. Nineteen rooms and suites. Four-diamond rated; member Small Luxury Hotels of the World. Candlelight dinner served Tuesday through Saturday. Pond, fishing, croquet course, and nature walks. Groups and corporate retreats welcome. TV in room.

Ravenna. Elegant family home, circa 1835, secluded in three acres of an old-fashioned garden a few blocks from downtown Natchez. Known for its three-story elliptical stairway. Three large antique-filled bedrooms in main house; one-bedroom guest house by swimming pool. Seated breakfast served in formal dining room.

Shields Town House. Circa 1860. Exclusive bed and breakfast suites in beautiful private setting feature modern amenities, antique charm, and individual landscaped courtyards. Garage parking adjacent to each suite. Main house courtyard features a large three-tier fountain and splendid gardens. Telephone and TV in room. Continental breakfast.

Texada. First brick house, circa 1792, in the Mississippi Territory. Elegant townhouse in Spanish Quarter. English and American period antiques with four-poster beds. Four large bedrooms and central sitting room with private entrance. Guest House with sitting room accommodates

7 No smoking; 8 Children welcome; 9 Social drinking allowed; 10 Tennis nearby; 11 Swimming nearby; 12 Golf nearby; 13 Skiing nearby; 14 May be booked through a travel agent.

four. Enclosed landscaped courtyard. Designated smoking areas.

Weymouth Hall. A magnificent Greek Revival mansion, circa 1855, stands alone on the bluffs with a beautiful panoramic view of the Mississippi River. Furnished with period antiques and fine porcelains. Guests may relax on the recessed gallery or in the gazebo. Southern breakfast served in main dining room. Designated smoking areas.

The Burn

The Burn

712 North Union Street, 39120
(601) 442-1344; (800) 654-8859

Circa 1834, three-story mansion especially noted for its semispiral stairway, unique gardens, and exquisite collection of antiques. Overnight guests are pampered with a seated plantation breakfast, tour of the home, and use of the swimming pool. Member of the Independent Innkeepers Association.

Host: Ann White
Owners: Larry and Deborah Christensen
Rooms: 7 (PB) $90-125
Full Breakfast
Credit Cards: A, B, C, D
Notes: 2, 5, 7, 10, 11, 12

Dunleith

84 Homochitto, 39120
(601) 446-8500; (800) 433-2445

A National Historic Landmark, circa 1856, this picturesque Greek Revival mansion is on a 40-acre landscaped park near downtown Natchez. There are 11 guest rooms: three in the main house, eight in the courtyard wing. All rooms have working fireplaces. Full Southern breakfast is served in the Poultry House.

Host: Nancy Gibbs
Rooms: 11 (PB) $85-130
Full Breakfast
Credit Cards: A, B, C, D
Notes: None

Glen Auburn

300 South Commerce Street, 39120
(601) 442-4099; (800) 833-0170

A French Second Empire rarity, recently restored, in the center of antebellum Natchez, offers overnight guests a taste of Victorian elegance. Five deluxe suites, Jacuzzis, all luxury amenities. Evening refreshments. Southern breakfast. Pool. A special place to make memories or to just get away.

Hosts: Carolyn and Richard Boyer
Suites: 5 (PB) $125-175
Full Breakfast
Credit Cards: A, B
Notes: 2, 5, 9, 10, 11, 12, 14

The Governor Holmes House

207 South Wall Street, 39120
(601) 442-2366; FAX (601) 442-0166

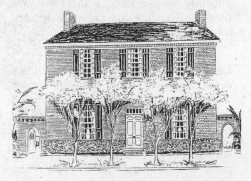

The Governor Holmes House

The Governor Holmes House was built in 1794, one of the oldest and most historic homes in the Old Spanish Quarter. It was the home of the last governor of the Mississippi Territory and the first governor of the state of Mississippi when it became a state in 1817. The home was also in the painting of Natchez that Audubon painted in 1823 and is on the National Register of Historic Places.

Host: Robert Pully, Owner/Manager
Rooms: 4 (PB) $85-115
Full Breakfast
Credit Cards: A, B, C, D
Notes: 2, 5, 7, 9, 10, 11, 12, 14

The Guest House Historic Hotel

201 North Pearl, 39120
(601) 442-1054; (800) 442-1054
FAX (601) 442-1374

This hotel, circa 1840, has 16 luxurious oversized rooms filled with some of the finest antiques. Each room is furnished with private bath, refrigerator, coffee maker, and cable TV with remote control. Guests are in the heart of the historic district and within walking distance to antique row, gift shops, excellent restaurants, the Mississippi River, and the trolley stop.

Rooms: 16 (PB) $59-99
Continental Breakfast
Credit Cards: A, B, C, D, E
Notes: 2, 4, 5, 6, 8, 9, 10, 11, 12, 14

Linden

1 Linden Place, 39120
(601) 445-5472

Linden sits on seven landscaped acres and has been in the present owner's family for six generations. It is a Federal-style house furnished in antiques and many heirlooms. All seven bedrooms have four-poster beds and other antiques of the Federal period. The front doorway was copied in *Gone with the Wind.* Early morning coffee, a full Southern plantation breakfast, and a tour of the house are included in the price of a room. Linden is on the famous spring and fall pilgrimages, quality rated by Mobil Guide, and three-diamond rated by AAA. The owner welcomes her guests and gives the tour of the home herself. Limited smoking allowed. Children over ten welcome.

Host: Jeanette S. Feltus
Rooms: 7 (PB) $90
Full Breakfast
Credit Cards: None
Notes: 2, 5, 9, 10, 11, 12, 14

Natchez Trace Bed and Breakfast Reservation Service

P.O. Box 193, Hampshire, TN 38461
(615) 285-2777; (800) 377-2770

NAT-01. Milepost 8. This 1880 Victorian mansion in the historic district is furnished with antiques. A full breakfast is served in the formal dining room; afternoon wine, cheese, and tea is offered in the parlors. Within walking distance of several antebellum homes and other historic sites. No children under 14. Suites with private bath, $110; two-bedroom suite, $160. Inquire about special summer and holiday rates.

NAT-02. Milepost 8. Built in 1794, this is one of the oldest and most historic homes in Natchez, having been the home of the last governor of the Mississippi Territory and first governor of Mississippi. Listed in the National Register of Historic Places, it is beautifully decorated with period furnishings, porcelain paintings, and Oriental carpets. It features suites with private, modern baths. A delicious plantation breakfast is served in the formal dining room or the quaint breakfast room. No small children. Governor's Suite $115; other rooms $85.

NAT-03. Milepost 8. This Natchez home, built between 1774 and 1789, is listed in the National Register of Historic Places and was owned by the first Spanish governor of the territory. It features exquisite antique furniture from the early 18th century. Each guest room is furnished with a distinctive four-poster bed with draped testers. Private baths. No small children. A large Southern-style breakfast and tour of the home is included. $80-90 double; $20 each additional person.

Oakland Plantation

1124 Lower Woodville Road, 39120
(601) 445-5101; (800) 824-0355

This charming retreat is about eight miles south of Natchez, with 360 acres of pastures, nature trails, fishing ponds, and a tennis court. The guest house dates back to 1785, and guests to the estate include Andrew Jackson and his wife, Rachel. Come for the peace and quiet and relax in an 18th-century atmosphere.

Hosts: Andy and Jeanie Peabody
Rooms: 3 (2 PB; 1 SB) $65-75
Full Breakfast
Credit Cards: A, B
Notes: 2, 5, 8, 9, 10, 12, 14

Weymouth Hall Inn

1 Cemetery Road, 39120
(601) 445-2304

On the bluff overlooking the mighty Mississippi River, Weymouth Hall stands alone, with its unequaled scenic view. Guests can relax on recessed porches in the

Weymouth Hall Inn

late afternoon while delighting in the panoramic view of the river. The outstanding home is furnished completely with an impressive collection of period antiques. Closed January. No smoking in rooms.

Host: Gene Weber
Rooms: 5 (PB) $80-85
Full Breakfast
Credit Cards: A, B
Notes: 2, 14

PORT GIBSON

Natchez Trace Bed and Breakfast Reservation Service

P.O. Box 193, Hampshire, TN 38461
(615) 285-2777; (800) 377-2770

POR-01. Enjoy the small-town charm of Port Gibson, referred to by General Grant as "too beautiful to burn"; only two miles from the Trace. Named one of the ten best bed and breakfasts in Mississippi, this historic late Federal/early Greek Revival mansion was built in 1830 and is known for its spiral staircase that extends two and one-half stories. All rooms furnished with period antiques and tester beds; the suite features a private wicker sun porch. Full breakfast. $75-120.

POR-02. This home in Port Gibson is two miles from the Trace. The grounds of this 1850 mansion contain three guest houses with twelve rooms for guests, each with a massive four-poster canopied bed and other antique furnishings. A tour of the full house and grounds is conducted every evening for overnight guests. A full Southern breakfast, complete with grits and biscuits, is served each morning. $85.

Oak Square Plantation

1207 Church Street, 39150
(601) 437-4350; (800) 729-0240

Oak Square, circa 1850, is Port Gibson's largest and most palatial Greek Revival antebellum mansion. Visitors experience a quiet retreat into the past. Family heirloom antiques, canopied beds, full Southern breakfast, and a tour of the mansion and grounds. In the National Register of Historic Places and AAA four-diamond rated. Port Gibson is the third oldest town in Mississippi referred to by Gen. U. S. Grant as "the town too beautiful to burn." Area attractions include antebellum homes, churches, a military state park, Civil War battlefields, and museums. Home to the 1800s Spring Festival during the last weekend in March.

Hosts: Mr. and Mrs. William D. Lum
Rooms: 12 (PB) $75-95
Full Breakfast
Credit Cards: A, B, C, D
Notes: 2, 5, 8, 9

TUPELO

The Mockingbird Inn Bed and Breakfast

305 North Gloster, 38801
(601) 841-0286

Discover the romance of a different place and time in an enchanting getaway in the heart of Tupelo. Each guest room of this 70-year-old home represents the decor from a different area of the world. Cable TV, telephones, and truly comfortable queen-size beds. Evening refreshments, soft drinks, juice, coffee, and tea are complimentary. Two Civil War battlefields are close by; five minutes to Elvis's birthplace and across the street from the school where he attended both sixth and seventh grades. Just off the Natchez Trace Parkway, halfway between Nashville and Natchez. Eight blocks from the Coliseum. Across the street from two of Tupelo's most popular restaurants in lovely old homes. Rated in the top ten bed and breakfasts in Mississippi. Handicapped accessible. Children over 13 welcome. Lunch and dinner available across the street.

Hosts: Jim and Sandy Gilmer
Rooms: 7 (PB) $65-110
Full Breakfast
Credit Cards: A, B, C, D
Note: 2, 5, 6, 7, 9, 10, 11, 12, 14

Annabelle

VICKSBURG

Annabelle

501 Speed Street, 39180
(601) 638-2000; (800) 791-2000

Overnight memories are taken from this historic 1868 two-story Victorian home in Riverview, Vicksburg's historic garden district. Elegantly, but comfortably, furnished in beautiful period antiques, Annabelle offers king- and queen-size beds, some with canopies, 12-foot-high ceilings, in-room cable TV, air conditioning, and a beautiful Vieux Carré courtyard surrounded by crepe myrtles and pecan and magnolia trees. A delicious Southern breakfast is served in the formal dining room. AAA three-diamond rated.

Hosts: Carolyn and George Mayer
Rooms: 5 (PB) $80-100
Suites: 2 (PB) $125-145
Full Breakfast
Credit Cards: A, B, C, D, E
Notes: 2, 5, 7, 9, 10, 12, 14

Cedar Grove Mansion–Inn

2200 Oak Street, 39180
(601) 636-1000; (800) 862-1300
FAX (601) 634-6126

7 No smoking; 8 Children welcome; 9 Social drinking allowed; 10 Tennis nearby; 11 Swimming nearby; 12 Golf nearby; 13 Skiing nearby; 14 May be booked through a travel agent.

Cedar Grove Mansion

Largest antebellum Greek Revival mansion in Vicksburg. Used as a Civil War hospital and has a cannonball still lodged in the parlor wall. The home was built as a wedding gift for General Sherman's cousin. Opulent gas-lit chandeliers, towering gold-leaf mirrors, and one of the largest collections of antiques and oil paintings in the South! Garden room restaurant and piano bar inside the mansion. Roof garden with Mississippi River view, swimming pool, and tennis.

Rooms: 29 (PB) $90-165
Full Breakfast
Credit Cards: A, B, C, D, E
Notes: 4, 5, 7, 9, 10, 11, 12, 14

The Corners Mansion

601 Klein Street, 39180
(800) 444-7421

Step back to 1873 in this beautiful Southern residence with its high ceilings, period antique furnishings, 65-foot verandas overlooking the Mississippi, and fragrant gardens filled with blossoms throughout the summer. The hosts introduce their guests to the traditional Southern lifestyle by encouraging them to relax throughout the home. A full plantation breakfast is served in the formal dining room and is followed by an enjoyable tour and historical narrative of the mansion and the original parterre gardens.

Hosts: Cliff and Bettye Whitney
Rooms: 11 (PB) $85-105
Full Breakfast
Credit Cards: A, B, C, D, E
Notes: 2, 5, 6, 7, 8, 9, 12, 14

Natchez Trace Bed and Breakfast Reservation Service

P.O. Box 193, Hampshire, TN 38461
(615) 285-2777; (800) 377-2770

VIC-01. Milepost 60 or 67. In historic Vicksburg, 15 miles from the Trace, this circa 1873 mansion, built as a wedding present to a daughter, is listed in the National Register of Historic Places. All rooms are furnished with antiques and include TV; some have working fireplaces. There is a 68-foot gallery with a spectacular view of the Mississippi River. Full plantation breakfast is included. $85-105.

WEST

The Alexander House

210 Green Street, P.O. Box 187, 39192
(601) 967-2266; (800) 350-8034

Step inside the front door of the Alexander House Bed and Breakfast and return to a more leisurely and gracious way of life. The Alexander House represents Victorian decor at its prettiest and country hospitality at its best. Captain Alexander, Dr. Joe, Ulrich, Annie, and Miss Bealle are the names of the rooms waiting to cast a spell over those who visit. Day trips to historic or recreational areas may be charted or chartered.

Hosts: Ruth Ray and Woody Dinstel
Rooms: 5 (3 PB; 2 SB) $65
Full Breakfast
Credit Cards: A, B, C, D
Notes: 2, 3, 4, 5, 7, 9, 14

NOTES: Credit cards accepted: A MasterCard; B Visa; C American Express; D Discover; E Diners Club; F Other; 2 Personal checks accepted; 3 Lunch available; 4 Dinner available; 5 Open all year; 6 Pets welcome;

Missouri

ARROW ROCK

Borgman's Bed and Breakfast

706 Van Buren, 65320
(816) 837-3350

The hosts invite guests to experience the historic town of Arrow Rock in the warmth of the century-old home. Choose one of four spacious guest rooms that share three baths, and relax in the sitting room or on the porch. Wind up the old Victrola for a song, choose a game or puzzle, browse through a book, or just sit for a spell, and listen to the sounds of Arrow Rock. In the morning guests will enjoy a family-style breakfast of freshly baked bread, juice or fruit, coffee, and tea.

Hosts: Kathy and Helen Borgman
Rooms: 4 (1 PB; 3 SB) $45-50
Continental Breakfast
Credit Cards: None
Notes: 2, 5, 7, 8

ASH GROVE

Ozark Mountain Country Bed and Breakfast

P.O. Box 295, Branson, 65616
(417) 334-4720; (800) 695-1546

OMC 249. This "shopkeeper's" apartment is ten miles from Springfield airport avoiding city traffic. Built in the early 1800s, it was originally a hotel and later a townhouse. Amenities include two bedrooms; each has a double bed. Decorated with antiques. Parlor, music room, kitchen, bath with claw-foot tub. Full breakfast. Extra meals can be arranged. No children. $40.

BONNEVILLE

Ozark Mountain Country Bed and Breakfast

P.O. Box 295, Branson, 65616
(417) 334-4720; (800) 695-1546

OMC 273. This 1883 Queen Anne mansion overlooks the Missouri River on the famous Katy Trail. Decorated with antiques. Four guest rooms have king-, queen-size, or double beds, and private and semiprivate baths. Therapeutic massage available at an extra charge. Full breakfast. Smoking outdoors only. Children over ten welcome. $60-90.

BRANSON

The Barger House Bed and Breakfast

621 Lakeshore Drive, 65616
(417) 335-2134

Casual country elegance on Lake Taneycomo in the beautiful Ozark Hills, the Barger House is a charming version of an 18th-century Colonial home furnished with French and Victorian antiques and collectibles. A deck with a hot tub and large pool provides a beautiful view of the lake and downtown Branson. Trout fishing off a private boat dock. Delicious multicourse breakfast served in the dining room or on the deck.

Hosts: Ralph and Cathy
Rooms: 3 (PB) $65-85
Full Breakfast
Credit Cards: None
Notes: 2, 5, 8, 9, 10, 11, 12, 14

7 No smoking; 8 Children welcome; 9 Social drinking allowed; 10 Tennis nearby; 11 Swimming nearby; 12 Golf nearby; 13 Skiing nearby; 14 May be booked through a travel agent.

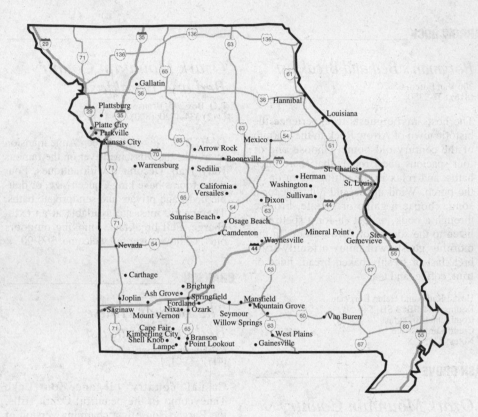

Missouri

The Branson Hotel Bed and Breakfast Inn

214 West Main, 65616
(417) 335-6104

"Branson's Best Lodging," according to *Southern Living* (April 1994), and winner of AAA four-diamond awards in 1994 and 1995. History, romance, and elegance await guests at this historical inn that has provided memories to visitors since 1903. Premier location in downtown Branson. Cable TV and in-room phones. Two large verandas overlook downtown. Full breakfast served in the glass-enclosed dining room. Children over 12 welcome.

Hosts: Teri Murguia and Susan Jones
Rooms: 9 (PB) $85-105
Full Breakfast
Notes: 2, 9, 10, 11, 12, 14

The Branson House Bed and Breakfast Inn

120 Fourth Street, 65616
(417) 334-0959

Surrounded by rock walls of native fieldstone, old oak trees, and country flower gardens, the Branson House sits on a hillside of downtown Branson overlooking the town and the bluffs of Lake Taneycomo. Built in the early 1920s, this spacious home is unique to the area and remains Branson's grandest old home. The English country ambience offers serenity for visitors after a busy day in Branson. Air-conditioned. Open March through mid-December. AAA and Mobil Guide recommended. Children over 12 welcome.

Host: Opal Kelly
Rooms: 7 (PB) $65-85
Full Breakfast
Credit Cards: None
Notes: 2, 9, 10, 11, 12, 14

Josie's Peaceful Getaway

Indian Point Road, HCR. 1, Box 1104, 65616
(417) 338-2978; (800) 289-4125

A pristine, gorgeous lakefront view awaits guests at Josie's on famous Table Rock Lake. Sunsets and moonlit nights lace the sky. Contemporary design with cathedral ceilings and a 15-foot-high stone fireplace. Victorian touches include stained glass, china dishes, crystal goblets, candlelight, and fresh flowers. Experience cozy wood-burning fireplaces, lavish Jacuzzi spas, or a secluded picnic lunch in the gazebo. Celebrate special occasions in style. Five minutes to marina and Silver Dollar City. Eight miles to the shows in Branson. Air-conditioned.

Hosts: Bill and JoAnne Coats
Rooms: 2 (PB) $55-95
Suite: 1
Full Breakfast
Credit Cards: A, B, C
Notes: 2, 5, 7, 8, 9, 11, 12, 14

Ozark Mountain Country Bed and Breakfast

P.O. Box 295, Branson, 65616
(417) 334-4720; (800) 695-1546

Annie's Place. Private A-frame cottage features a spectacular view and hot tub. The guest room has two queen-size beds and a private bath. Open year-round. Children over eight welcome. Continental breakfast. $85.

Aunt Sadie's Garden Glade. Contemporary with country Victorian decor has two guest areas in the main house and two private cottages with private entrances, fireplaces, king- and queen-size beds, and private baths. Whirlpool and hot tub available outside. Children welcome. Full breakfast. $70-89.

Bayside Inn. New contemporary home with lakeside has four guest rooms that have private baths and king- and queen-size beds. Enjoy the view while having a full

NOTES: Credit cards: A MasterCard; B Visa; C American Express; D Discover; E Diners Club; F Other;
2 Personal checks accepted; 3 Lunch available; 4 Dinner available; 5 Open all year; 6 Pets welcome;
7 No smoking; 8 Children welcome; 9 Social drinking allowed; 10 Tennis nearby; 11 Swimming nearby;
12 Golf nearby; 13 Skiing nearby; 14 May be booked through a travel agent.

Ozark Mountain Country Bed and Breakfast (continued)

breakfast. Children over six welcome. No smoking. $70-75.

Bird's Eye View. Private suite overlooks Branson's skyline and Lake Taneycomo with kitchen and whirlpool for two, plus hot tub on deck. King-size bed, private bath, and private entrance. Full breakfast. No smoking. $95.

Branson House. This elegant 1920s inn is furnished with antiques in Branson's historic district. There are seven guest rooms with king- and queen-size beds and private baths. Full breakfast. Children over 12 welcome. No smoking. $65-85.

Brass Swan. Elegant contemporary home with easy access to attractions has two private hot tubs. Four guest rooms have king- and queen-size beds and private baths. One suite has whirlpool and fireplace. No smoking. Full breakfast. No children. $70-85.

Cameron's Crag. Contemporary on bluff overlooks Lake Taneycomo and valley. Two luxurious suites with king-size beds have private baths and private entrances. One hot tub inside and another outside. Full breakfast. Children over six welcome. No smoking. $75-95.

Country Lane. Contemporary home uphill from Table Rock Lake features a two-room suite with wood stove. There are three guest areas with private baths. Children welcome. No smoking. Continental breakfast. $40-55.

Country Welcome. Contemporary home with private guest area overlooks wooded valley. One guest room with private bath. Children welcome. No smoking. Full breakfast. $45.

Emory Creek Inn. Charming new Victorian inn filled with 18th-century antiques features landscaped grounds and hiking trails. Seven guest rooms have king- or queen-size beds and private baths with whirlpool tubs. No smoking. Full breakfast. $75-95.

Fall Creek Bed and Breakfast. Two-story Victorian reproduction has pool and whirlpool for guests. Eighteen guest rooms have king- and queen-size beds and private baths. Children welcome. No smoking. Buffet breakfast. $55-85.

Fox Haven. Contemporary home features a guest room with king-size mirrored canopied waterbed and private bath. Deck overlooking the Ozarks has a hot tub. Children welcome. No smoking. Full breakfast. $65.

Gaines Landing. Charming contemporary features a pool and private outdoor hot tub. Three guest suites with king- or queen-size beds, private baths, and private entrances. Children welcome. No smoking. Full breakfast. $75-95.

Historic Kite Home. Charming turn-of-the-century home furnished with antiques features nook with play area for children. Two guest rooms with private baths. Children welcome. No smoking. Full breakfast. $55-75.

Inn at Fall Creek. Country-style home with country and antique furnishings has easy access to Branson shows. Five guest rooms have king- or queen-size beds, private baths, and one guest room has a pri-

NOTES: Credit cards accepted: A MasterCard; B Visa; C American Express; D Discover; E Diners Club; F Other; 2 Personal checks accepted; 3 Lunch available; 4 Dinner available; 5 Open all year; 6 Pets welcome;

vate entrance. Whirlpool and hot tub available. No smoking. Full breakfast. $70-95.

Lakes Loft. Private upstairs apartment features panoramic view of lakes, dam, and valley from the deck. King-size bed, private bath, and private entrance. No smoking. Full breakfast. $70.

The Light in the Window. Comfortable raised ranch home has a "light in the window" for guests. Two guest rooms have a queen-size beds and two twin-size. Private baths. Children welcome. No smoking. Full breakfast. $50.

Lodge at We Lamb Farm. The 8,000-square-foot lodge on farm features pool, hiking, fishing in two ponds, and animals to watch. Four guest rooms. Children welcome. Full breakfast. $85.

Lonesome Dove. Private log cabin near Hollister has wood fireplace, whirlpool for two, sitting area, and kitchen. King-size bed, private bath, and private entrance. Children welcome. No smoking. $95.

Lost Loft. Contemporary suite has bedroom, living room, dining area, full kitchen, and extra guest area in home. Queen-size beds, private baths, and a private entrance. Children over ten welcome. No smoking. Continental breakfast. $55-75.

Red Bud Cove. Seven suites on Table Rock Lake have bedrooms each with king- or queen-size beds, living room, kitchenette, private baths, and private entrances. Boat access with dock. Three whirlpools available. Children welcome. No smoking. Full breakfast. $70-90.

Rene's Retreat. Contemporary has private entrance and king-size bed or spacious two-room suite including living room and kitchen. Private bath. No smoking. Full breakfast. $65-80.

Schroll's Lakefront. New rustic cedar home overlooking Lake Taneycomo features country Victorian decor. Five guest rooms with queen-size beds, private baths, and private entrances. Whirlpool and hot tub. Children welcome. No smoking. Full breakfast. $60-85.

Thurman House. Country home has private living area, kitchenette, and two bedrooms with two queen-size beds and one double bed. Private hot tub on patio. Children welcome. No smoking. Full breakfast. $85.

Wildwood Terrace. Two-bedroom condo with whirlpool and fireplace is within walking distance to shows. King- or queen-size beds, private bath, and private entrance. No smoking. $95.

Red Bud Cove Bed and Breakfast Suites

162 Lakewood Drive (Lake Road 65-48, County Road 65-180), Hollister, 65672
(800) 677-5525

Red Bud Cove

On Table Rock Lake, nine miles south of Branson. Spend the evening in comfort in a spacious suite with lakefront patio and deck. Seven suites with private entrances have living room (some with fireplace), bedroom with king- or queen-size bed, bathroom (some with spa), fully equipped kitchenette and dining area, air conditioning, TV, and phones. Full breakfast is served in the main dining room. Outdoor hot tub, rental boats, and dock space are available for guests' added enjoyment.

Hosts: Rick and Carol Carpenter
Rooms: 7 (PB) $70-90
Full Breakfast
Credit Cards: A, B, C, D
Notes: 2, 5, 7, 12, 14

BRIGHTON

Ozark Mountain Country Bed and Breakfast

P.O. Box 295, Branson, 65616
(417) 334-4720; (800) 695-1546

OMC 204. Private guest cottage is 15 miles from Springfield. Hot tub on deck. Wildlife sanctuary. Working fireplace. Handmade hickory bedstead (double). Kitchenette. Stocked pond is open to guests for fishing. Hike. Pet animals. Relax. $95.

CALIFORNIA

Memory Lane Bed and Breakfast

102 South Oak, 65018
(314) 796-4233

Memory Lane is an 1894 home that has been renovated carefully to retain its Victorian character. Guest bedrooms feature antique furnishings while the remainder of the house is decorated with a blend of antique and modern furniture. Antique lovers can enjoy the nostalgia of using an authentic crank telephone or listening to a

Memory Lane

Thomas Edison crank phonograph. There are more than 50 antique shops within a 35-mile radius of California.

Hosts: Joe and Mary Ellen Laprise
Rooms: 3 (3 SB) $38
Full breakfast
Credit Cards: None
Notes: 2, 5, 7, 10, 11, 12

Ozark Mountain Country Bed and Breakfast

P.O. Box 295, Branson, 65616
(417) 334-4720; (800) 695-1546

OMC 222. This 1896 Victorian is decorated with antiques and is next door to an antique shop. Three guest rooms with double and twin beds and a shared hall bath. Smoking on porches only. Resident dog and cats. $30-35.

CAMDENTON

Ozark Mountain Country Bed and Breakfast

P.O. Box 295, Branson, 65616
(417) 334-4720; (800) 695-1546

OMC 207. Peaceful getaway in parklike setting close to HaHa Tonka State Park and Bridal Cave. Full, hearty breakfast in dining room or on the shady deck. TV/VCR. Air-conditioned. Victorian and traditional decor.

Three guest rooms have queen-size beds and share two hall baths. Guest sitting area. Children over five welcome. No pets. No smoking. $50-85.

Ramblewood Bed and Breakfast

402 Panoramic Drive, 65020
(314) 346-3410 after 5:00 P.M.

This inviting cottage nestles in a grove of oak and dogwood trees. The decor is traditional, touched with Victorian. Guests are welcomed with tea or lemonade and homemade goodies. Breakfast is special, beginning with a beautiful fruit plate, followed by tempting dishes and breads. Minutes from the lake, state park, fine restaurants, music shows, and shops.

Host: Mary E. Massey
Rooms: 3 (SB) $50
Full Breakfast
Credit Cards: None
Notes: 2, 5, 7, 9, 12

CAPE FAIR

Ozark Mountain Country Bed and Breakfast

P.O. Box 295, Branson, 65616
(417) 334-4720; (800) 695-1546

OMC 168. Ranch-style home on Table Rock Lake is decorated with antiques. Three guest rooms have queen-size and vibrating twin beds and private baths. Living room for guests. Full breakfast. Three resident poodles. Smoking permitted in common areas only. Sunroom overlooks lake. Two miles from boat launch. Children welcome. $55.

CARTHAGE

Ozark Mountain Country Bed and Breakfast

P.O. Box 295, Branson, 65616
(417) 334-4720; (800) 695-1546

OMC 209. This 676-acre farm is eight miles northeast of Carthage. The 22-room, four-story mansion built in 1900-1904 is decorated with family heirloom antiques. Four second-floor guest rooms with two baths. Continental breakfast. Available year-round. Pool table and Ping-Pong table. Rate includes a tour of the home and grounds. $55.

OMC 227. Return to the Victorian era in this 1890s mansion decorated with antiques. There are five elegant guest rooms with private baths available for guests. New central air conditioning. Lap pool. Unique furnishings throughout. Hearty breakfast served. Three nights' stay includes a candlelight dinner. $65-85.

OMC 261. This 1901 Victorian Carthage stone house is decorated with antiques, stained glass, and lace curtains. Central air conditioning and heat. Mosaic-tiled solarium with marble fountain. Fine crafted woodwork. Three floors of elegance. Elevator. Both private and shared baths are available. $55.

DIXON

Ozark Mountain Country Bed and Breakfast

P.O. Box 295, Branson, 65616
(417) 334-4720; (800) 695-1546

OMC 254. Spectacular view of Gasconade River. Three-bedroom cottage for up to six people. Children and pets welcome. Self-serve breakfast. Smoking only on decks. The entire upstairs in the home is also available: two bedrooms, private bath, sitting room. Full breakfast. Not suitable for children and pets. Open year-round. Extra meals can be arranged. Discounts available December through March and four-night stays. $48-97.

7 No smoking; 8 Children welcome; 9 Social drinking allowed; 10 Tennis nearby; 11 Swimming nearby; 12 Golf nearby; 13 Skiing nearby; 14 May be booked through a travel agent.

FORDLAND

Red Oak Inn

Route 1, Box 166 A, 65652
(417) 767-2444

A true country bed and breakfast, this 1940s barn has been converted into a three-story country inn with several sitting rooms, side porches, and balcony. Four guest rooms, each with private bath. Breakfast served in a lovely sunroom. Fireplace. Air-conditioned. Inn sits on 66 acres.

Hosts: Carol and Larry Alberty
Rooms: 4 (PB) $55-65
Full Breakfast
Credit Cards: None
Notes: 2, 5, 7, 8, 12

GAINESVILLE

Ozark Mountain Country Bed and Breakfast

P.O. Box 295, Branson, 65616
(417) 334-4720; (800) 695-1546

OMC 225. Overlooking a private lake, this 10,000-square-foot Colonial-style mansion offers four guest rooms with king- or queen-size beds. Two private baths and two shared hall baths. A game room has a pool table and a Ping-Pong table. TV. Indoor pool. Hot tub. Paddle boat. No smoking, alcohol, children, or pets. $60-65.

GALLATIN

Ray Home Bed

212 West Van Buren, 64640
(800) 301-STAY

Ray Home was built in 1896 by Anderson Taylor Ray. The home is a Queen Anne-style and was placed on the National Register of Historic Place in 1980. The home features six fireplaces with carved mantels, front and rear staircases, stained-

lead crystal-etched and carved windows, ornate woodwork, and pocket doors and is furnished with period antiques. Guests may use the sitting room, parlor, library, and two lemonade balconies (weather permitting). On winter evenings guests may enjoy hot chocolate by a cozy fire. Rates include dessert and drink in the evening. Wake up with coffee or a beverage of your choice. Full breakfast. Tours available by appointment. Inquire about accommodations for pets. Smoking in designated areas. Children over 13 welcome.

Hosts: Bill and Jane Due
Rooms: 3 (1/2 PB; 2 SB) $75
Full Breakfast
Credit Cards: A, B
Notes: 2, 5, 10, 11, 12

HANNIBAL

Garth Woodside Mansion

Rural Route 1, Box 304, 63401
(314) 221-2789

Stay at this award-winning 1871 Victorian country estate for the ultimate experience. Original furnishings span more than 150 years with potpourri-scented air, canopied beds, and nightshirts. Spacious bedchambers are a careful selection of lace, fabrics, and textures chosen to blend with an eye toward every detail and comfort. Stroll on

Garth Woodside Mansion

39 magnificent wooded acres or rock and relax on the veranda. Judged one of the Midwest's "Ten Best Inns." Two-night minimum stay requried during holidays. Limited smoking allowed. Children over 12 are welcome.

Hosts: Irv and Diane Feinberg
Rooms: 8 (PB) $65-105
Full Breakfast
Credit Cards: A, B
Notes: 2, 5, 9, 10, 12

Die Gillig Heimat

HERMAN

Die Gillig Heimat

HCR 62 Box 30, 65041
(314) 943-6942

A warm, inviting country home with beautiful views in every direction. A hearty breakfast is served in the large country kitchen. Historic Hermann is nearby. Come enjoy a relaxing stay.

Hosts: Ann and Armin Gillig
Rooms: 2 (PB) $55-65
Full Breakfast
Credit Cards: None
Notes: 2, 5, 7, 8, 10, 11, 12, 14

JOPLIN

Visages

327 North Jackson, 64801
(800) 896-1397

Visages, built in 1898, is named for the faces on the exterior masonry walls and the family portraits inside the house. Its beauty is achieved through artistry and ingenuity, not money. Marge and Bill, retired teachers, find guests fascinating and enjoy serving a delicious typical mid-American breakfast.

Hosts: Bill and Marge Meeker
Rooms: 3 (1 PB; 2 SB) $40-60
Full Breakfast
Credit Cards: C, D
Notes: 2, 5, 8, 9, 10, 11, 12, 14

KANSAS CITY

Hotel Savoy

219 West 9th Street, 64105
(816) 842-3575

Hotel Savoy is one of the finest European bed and breakfast hotels in the United States. Built in 1888, it offers the opportunity to drift back in time in suites filled with antiques and Victorian decor. Breakfast consists of more than 32 items, such as lobster bisque, salmon and caviar, medallions of beef, or even oysters Rockefeller. In the heart of Kansas City's historic garment district. A very romantic getaway.

Host: Larry Green
Rooms: 110 (PB) $79-120
Full Breakfast
Credit Cards: A, B, C, D, E, F
Notes: 2, 3, 4, 5, 7, 8, 9, 14

Hotel Savoy

7 No smoking; 8 Children welcome; 9 Social drinking allowed; 10 Tennis nearby; 11 Swimming nearby; 12 Golf nearby; 13 Skiing nearby; 14 May be booked through a travel agent.

Pridewell

600 West 50th Street, 64112
(816) 931-1642

A fine Tudor residence in a residential area on the site of the Civil War battle of Westport. Near the Nelson Art Gallery, University of Missouri-Kansas City, Missouri Repertory Theatre, and Rockhurst College. Adjacent to Country Club Plaza shopping district, including several four-star restaurants, public transportation, public tennis courts, and park.

Hosts: Edwin and Louann White
Rooms: 2 (1 PB; 1 SB) $65-70
Full Breakfast
Credit Cards: None
Notes: 2, 5, 8, 9, 14

Southmoreland on the Plaza

116 East 46th Street, 64112
(816) 531-7979

A two-time winner of the American Bed and Breakfast Association's Four Crown Award, recognized for Outstanding Achievement in Preservation by the Association of American Historic Inns, and named Most Romantic New Urban Inn by *Romantic Hideaways* newsletter, this classic New England Colonial between Country Club Plaza and the Nelson-Atkins Museum of Art presents an elegant bed and breakfast atmosphere with small hotel amenities.

Southmoreland on the Plaza

Rooms offer private decks, fireplaces, or Jacuzzi baths. Special services designed for business travelers. Sport and dining privileges at a nearby historic private club. Mobil Travel Guide four-star winner since 1993.

Hosts: Penni Johnson and Susan Moehl
Rooms: 12 (PB) $100-145
Full Breakfast
Credit Cards: A, B, C
Notes: 2, 5, 9, 10, 11, 14

KIMBERLING CITY _____

Ozark Mountain Country Bed and Breakfast

P.O. Box 295, Branson, 65616
(417) 334-4720; (800) 695-1546

Anderson House. Contemporary home with Victorian furnishings and antiques. Has two-room suite with sitting area, queen-size bed, private bath, and private entrance. Children welcome. No smoking. Full breakfast. $60.

Cajun Hospitality. Contemporary home great for couple or small group. Suite includes kitchen and parlor. Four guest areas, three of which have private entrances, queen-size beds, and private baths. Children over 12 welcome. No smoking. Full breakfast. Lake access for boats. $50-75.

Cinnamon Hill. Contemporary home is near golf course with special breakfast and features large rooms with private entrances. Three guest areas with queen-size beds and private baths. Children welcome. No smoking. Full breakfast. $55-65.

Lakehouse Bed and Breakfast. Three lakeview suites have a sitting area, fireplace, queen-size beds, and private baths. One suite has whirlpool. Children welcome. No smoking. Full breakfast. $75-95.

NOTES: Credit cards accepted: A MasterCard; B Visa; C American Express; D Discover; E Diners Club; F Other; 2 Personal checks accepted; 3 Lunch available; 4 Dinner available; 5 Open all year; 6 Pets welcome;

Victoria's Parlor. Stately two-story home overlooking Table Rock Lake has heated pool and hot tub, four guest areas, two of which have private entrances, king- or queen-size beds, and private baths. Children welcome. No smoking. Full breakfast. $69-99.

LAMPE

Ozark Mountain Country Bed and Breakfast

P.O. Box 295, Branson, 65616
(417) 334-4720; (800) 695-1546

Grandpa's Farm. Turn-of-the-century farm home features two-level suite with hot tub, private baths, and king-size beds. Country breakfast. Children welcome. No smoking allowed. Private entrance for guests. $65-85.

Hillside Hide-a-Way. Rustic retreat is next to Grandpa's Farm. Each suite sleeps four adults and two children. Kitchen or whirlpool available. King-size beds. Private entrance. Private bath. Children are welcome. No smoking allowed. Full breakfast. Wood stove. $75.

Just Like Grandma's. Two-story Victorian reproduction with antiques, features a hot tub. Uphill from Table Rock Lake. Four guest areas, two of which have private entrances, queen-size or twin beds, and private baths. Children over six welcome. No smoking allowed. Full breakfast served. $65-75.

Vitalaire Lodge. A log cabin at a vegetarian health retreat offers four bedrooms, telephones, chemical-free environment, hot tub, and sauna. Private entrance. Private bath. Children welcome. No smoking. Double beds. $85.

Williams Mountain. Contemporary three-level home featuring three lakeview guest rooms includes atrium, pool table, and whirlpool. Queen-size beds. Private baths. Private entrances. Children over six welcome. Full breakfast. $55-75.

LOUISIANA

The International Bed & Breakfast Club, Inc.

504 Amherst Street, Buffalo, NY 14207
(800) 723-4262; FAX (716) 873-4462

MO4067PP. This Victorian home with its beautiful stained-glass windows is old enough to be unique, yet modern enough for comfort. It offers two rooms, one with a queen-size bed and the other with a double bed, which share a bath. Amenities include a private patio with a large spa. Continental breakfast and coffee are served. Dinners for guests and small groups are available by appointment. $55-75.

Louisiana Guest House Bed and Breakfast

1311 Georgia Street, 63353
(314) 754-6366

The town of Louisiana is on the Mississippi River 25 minutes south of Mark Twain's boyhood home at Hannibal and a little over an hour's drive north of St. Louis. Antique shops, "Old World" Amish settlement, golf, hiking, biking, and special holiday events await guests year-round. The romance of the Louisiana Guest House is captured in its Victorian antique-filled rooms, a charming wicker-filled porch overlooking gardens, snacks and beverages upon arrival, chats by the fire, and clawfoot tubs. Children over 12 welcome.

Hosts: Betty and Mett Bryant
Rooms: 2 (PB) $60-75
Full Breakfast
Notes: 2, 5, 9, 10, 11, 12, 14

7 No smoking; 8 Children welcome; 9 Social drinking allowed; 10 Tennis nearby; 11 Swimming nearby; 12 Golf nearby; 13 Skiing nearby; 14 May be booked through a travel agent.

MANSFIELD

Ozark Mountain Country Bed and Breakfast

P.O. Box 295, Branson, 65616
(417) 334-4720; (800) 695-1546

OMC 234. Contemporary-style bed and breakfast is "a stone's throw" from Laura Ingalls Wilder's home. Explore *Little House*'s Shapla's Cave. Enjoy great room, fireplace, and TV. Two guest rooms have one king-size and one double bed and share a hall bath with tub/shower. Full bedroom with private bath. Delicious breakfast served. $75.

OMC 253. Stately three-story turn-of-the-century Colonial Revival mansion with antiques has four guest rooms, two queen-size and two double beds, and private baths. Two rooms share a screened balcony. No children under 12 or pets allowed. Full breakfast served. Smoking allowed in the smoking room or on the porches only. $45-70.

MARIONVILLE

Ozark Mountain Country Bed and Breakfast

P.O. Box 295, Branson, 65616
(417) 334-4720; (800) 695-1546

OMC 210. Restored 1896 Victorian mansion with antiques has six guest rooms and a separate cottage. Parquet floors, stained glass, and hearty country breakfast. Private and shared baths. Watch for rare white squirrels. Special rates available for groups, winter guests, and weddings and honeymoon combinations. Open year-round. Children over ten welcome. Cigarette smoking is limited to the common areas. Resident dog. $45-75.

Hylas House

MEXICO

Hylas House Inn

811 South Jefferson, 65265
(314) 581-2011

A gracious and elegant bed and breakfast experience. Italianate architecture, magnificent staircase, molded scroll work on staircase, windows with leaded glass, white carpeting, and deep cherry wood. Three bedrooms. One shared bathroom. Suite with parlor and lounging balcony with chairs. Cable-remote TV in all rooms with telephones. Rooms redecorated. Gourmet full breakfast includes freshly ground coffee, eggs olé, waffles, and mixed fresh fruits. Museums and antique stores within a ten-minute walk. Spacious lawns and flower beds. Smoking allowed but limited.

Hosts: Tom and Linda Hylas
Rooms: 3 (2 PB; 1 SB) $85-95
Full Breakfast
Credit Cards: A, B,
Notes: 2, 5, 9, 12, 14

MINERAL POINT

Green Acres Farm Family Bed and Breakfast

Route 1, Box 575, 63660
(314) 749-3435

NOTES: Credit cards accepted: A MasterCard; B Visa; C American Express; D Discover; E Diners Club; F Other; 2 Personal checks accepted; 3 Lunch available; 4 Dinner available; 5 Open all year; 6 Pets welcome;

Green Acres Farm is a small, active family farm on the Big River, 65 miles south of St. Louis. A portion of the 100-plus farm pets live in Noah's Ark Barn. Guests can milk a cow, feed a goat, gather eggs, and do many other farm activities. Visiting Green Acres is like visiting Grandma's. No antiques here except Grandpa. A real country breakfast with the farm's own pork sausage, fresh country eggs, biscuits and gravy.

Host: Virginia Dickinson
Rooms: 4 (PB) $39
Full Breakfast
Credit Cards: None
Notes: 2, 3, 4, 7, 8

MOUNTAIN GROVE

Ozark Mountain Country Bed and Breakfast

P.O. Box 295, Branson, 65616
(417) 334-4720; (800) 695-1546

OMC 237. Rambling country home with parklike grounds is near Big Spring region, near streams, springs, and national forest. Relax in the garden gazebo. Sun deck with hot tub and pool. Antiques. Both private and detached baths are available. Full gourmet breakfast served. Five guest areas with double, queen-, and king-size beds. Carriage House suite with wood-burning fireplace. There is a special guest parlor. TV/VCR and video library. Smoking allowed only on the main floor. A perfect year-round getaway for the romantically inclined. $60-85.

OMC 250. Elegant farm home built in 1926. Hearty country breakfast served in spacious dining room. Lunch and dinner can be arranged in advance for an extra charge. Two main-level guest rooms each have double beds and share a bath. Upstairs guest room with private bath. Children welcome. $55-95.

MOUNT VERNON

Ozark Mountain Country Bed and Breakfast

P.O. Box 295, Branson, 65616
(417) 334-4720; (800) 695-1546

OMC 231. Charming Victorian reproduction home with two upstairs guest rooms. Queen-size bed and private bath in each. Not suitable for children. Smoking only on patio. Glass sunroom. TV. No pets or alcoholic beverages. Hearty homemade breakfast. Open year-round. $55.

NEVADA

Ozark Mountain Country Bed and Breakfast

P.O. Box 295, Branson, 65616
(417) 334-4720; (800) 695-1546

OMC 264. Charming 1906 stately Colonial with antiques. Main-level room has double bed, private bath, and handicapped access. Four upstairs guest rooms with queen-size beds, whirlpool, and private baths. Three rooms have double, twin, or queen-size beds and share a hall bath. Large front veranda and deck in back. Wicker furnishings. Full breakfast. No smoking. Children under 16 stay free. $35-55.

NIXA

Ozark Mountain Country Bed and Breakfast

P.O. Box 295, Branson, 65616
(417) 334-4720; (800) 695-1546

OMC 248. Exclusive use of restored rock cabin filled with family heirlooms and country memories. Surrounded by Ozark beauty. Eight miles southwest of Nixa. Complete kitchen, living room with sleeper-sofa, bath with tub and shower, bedroom

7 No smoking; 8 Children welcome; 9 Social drinking allowed; 10 Tennis nearby; 11 Swimming nearby; 12 Golf nearby; 13 Skiing nearby; 14 May be booked through a travel agent.

with double bed, and sleeping loft with double and two single beds. Not suitable for small children. No smoking allowed inside. $55-65.

OMC 211. Charming country home with antiques. Four miles south of Springfield. Open year-round. Full country breakfast served on antique china. Two guest accommodations. One has a queen-size canopied bed, bath with tub/shower, sitting room, and day bed. The other has a day bed or double bed and shares a hall bath. Whirlpool. Resident dogs and cats. No smoking or pre-teens. Air-conditioned. $45-100.

OSAGE BEACH

Ozark Mountain Country Bed and Breakfast

P.O. Box 295, Branson, 65616
(417) 334-4720; (800) 695-1546

OMC 228. Contemporary two-level lakeside home between Osage Beach and Camdenton. Lower-level guest accommodation has queen-size bed and private hall bath with shower. Main level has two guest rooms, each with double beds and hall bath. Sitting area on each level for guests' use. Dock for swimming and fishing. Hearty breakfast served. No smoking allowed. $60.

OMC 208. Private suite overlooks Lake of the Ozarks. Boat dock. Private entrance. Only one guest party at a time. Lakeview suite. Sitting area with TV. Microwave and refrigerator. Continental breakfast in suite. The guest bedroom has queen-size bed and two twin beds. Private patio. The sitting and dining area overlooks the lake. Smoking is permitted. Open March through November. $55.

OZARK

Ozark Mountain Country Bed and Breakfast

P.O. Box 295, Branson, 65616
(417) 334-4720; (800) 695-1546

OMC 255. Charming rustic cabin near Ozark is private and secluded. Amenities include pine floors, antique four-poster bed, air conditioning, refrigerator, coffee pot, casual country decor, handmade quilts, and a whirlpool for two. Hearty breakfast is delivered to the cabin. Antique wood-parlor stove. Not designed for children or pets. Smoke-free environment. Discounts for weekdays and after third night's stay. $85.

OMC 236. Rustic home built by Amish craftsmen, ten miles from Ozark and 25 miles from Springfield in wooded area overlooking Mark Twain National Forest near a creek. Only one guest party at a time. Suite choices include living room with fireplace on either main level or in the loft; each has a double bed. Private bath with shower. Hot tub on deck. Resident cat and dogs. No smoking. Bountiful breakfast. Open year-round. $75.

OMC 309. This 1887 Victorian home near the Arkansas River is just one block from the town square. Four large guest rooms have either queen-size or double beds. The honeymoon suite has a fireplace and double canopied bed. Dinner and evening dessert available. Central heat and air. Full gourmet breakfast. No pets, alcohol, or smoking. Children over 12 welcome. $50-75.

OMC 310. This contemporary, rustic three-room cottage overlooks the Arkansas River. Amenities include fully equipped kitchen, living room, Hide-a-Bed, central heat and air, full bed, and private bath.

Open year-round. Continental breakfast served. $60.

PARKVILLE

Ozark Mountain Country Bed and Breakfast

P.O. Box 295, Branson, 65616
(417) 334-4720; (800) 695-1546

OMC 245. Earth-sheltered home with indoor heated pool on farm near Kansas City airport. Great room has fireplace and piano. Guest entrance and parking. Four guest rooms available with double or twin beds and private baths. Decorated with quilts and antiques. Fish in farm pond. Children welcome. Smoking outdoors only. Full breakfast. $75.

PLATTE CITY

Basswood Country Inn Bed and Breakfast

15880 Interurban Road, 64079-9185
(816) 431-5556

Country at the city's doorstep. Most beautiful secluded, wooded, private lakefront accommodations in Kansas City area. Try the Truman, Bing Crosby, or Rudy Vallee suites, the 1935 mother-in-law cottage, or country French suites.

Hosts: Don and Betty Soper
Rooms: 7 (PB) $66-128
Cottage: 1 (PB) $96
Continental Breakfast
Credit Cards: A, B, D
Notes: 2, 5, 8, 9, 11, 12, 13, 14

PLATTSBURG

Charlotte's Apple Blossom Inn

200 West Broadway, 64477
(813) 539-3243

A renovated 1910 home, within 30 miles of Kansas City and St. Joseph, in rural mid-America. After a day of sightseeing in the Jesses James, Pony Express, Amish areas, or a day on the lake at Smithville, relax on the wraparound porch with an apple dessert. Then stroll the quiet streets enjoying the Victorian homes. After breakfast with freshly ground coffee served on china and crystal, browse the antique and specialty shops. Smoking permitted on porch and patio.

Hosts: Darrell and Charlotte Apple
Rooms: 3 (PB) $50
Full Breakfast
Credit Cards: None
Notes: 2, 5, 12

POINT LOOKOUT

Cameron's Crag

P.O. Box 526, 65726
(800) 933-8529

Perched high on a bluff overlooking Lake Taneycomo and Branson, Cameron's Crag offers three guest suites featuring spectacular scenery, a hearty breakfast, and easy access to area attractions. All suites have private entrances, king-size beds, hot tubs, private baths, and cable TV/VCR.

Hosts: Kay and Glen Cameron
Rooms: 3 (PB) $75-95
Full Breakfast
Credit Cards: A, B, C, D
Notes: 2, 5, 7, 11, 12, 13, 14

SAGINAW

Lakeside Cottages and Aviary

P.O. Box 99, 64864
(417) 781-9230

A special place where guests can enjoy the ultimate in romance, luxury, and seclusion, yet just three miles from Joplin, Missouri. Contemporary cottage overlooks a stocked five-acre lake for fishing or canoeing.

7 No smoking; 8 Children welcome; 9 Social drinking allowed; 10 Tennis nearby; 11 Swimming nearby;
12 Golf nearby; 13 Skiing nearby; 14 May be booked through a travel agent.

Cottage has a fully equipped kitchenette stocked with breakfast foods, fireplace, TV, VCR, stereo, queen-sized canopied feather bed, and a large Jacuzzi tub for two. Owners breed and raise macaws, parrots, and cockatoos. No smoking inside.

Hosts: Roberta and Clyde Jeffries
Room: 2 (PB) $95-119
Continental Breakfast
Credit Cards: A, B
Notes: 2, 5, 9, 11, 12

ST. CHARLES

Boone's Lick Trail Inn

1000 South Main Street, 63301
(314) 947-7000

In the 1840s this Federal-style building rose where Main Street met Boone's Lick Road. Herb and rose gardens scent the morning, while folk art, regional antiques—including a duck decoy collection—and traditional breakfast invite guests to linger peacefully. But exploration is traditional for guests of the inn. The state's largest historic district, Missouri River waterfront, Katy Trail, *Goldenrod* showboat, casino, antique and craft shops, wineries, and restaurants all beckon visitors to stroll the bricked streets and walkways.

Hosts: Vietta Anne and Paul Mydler
Rooms: 5 (PB) $85-135
Full Breakfast
Credit Cards: A, B, D, E
Notes: 2, 5, 7, 8, 9, 10, 11, 12, 14

Boone's Lick Trail Inn

STE. GENEVIEVE

Inn St. Gemme Beauvais

78 North Main, 63670
(314) 883-5744

This magnificent structure has been redecorated and updated recently. It boasts of being the oldest continuously operating inn in Missouri and is in the historic district. Each room has a unique theme and most are two-room suites. A three-course breakfast is served in the elegant Victorian living room, and all historic buildings are within walking distance. Lunch, high tea, and hors d'oeuvres are served daily. Dinner is served by special arrangement.

Host: Janet Joggerst
Rooms: 7 (PB) $69-125
Full Breakfast
Credit Cards: A, B
Notes: 2, 3, 5, 7, 8, 9, 10, 11, 12

Ozark Mountain Country Bed and Breakfast

P.O. Box 295, Branson, 65616
(417) 334-4720; (800) 695-1546

OMC 267. Elegant inn with antiques and whirlpool suite. Eight upstairs guest rooms have double beds. Whirlpool suite has a queen-size bed. No smoking. Children welcome. Resident dog. $55-95.

ST. LOUIS

Lafayette House Bed and Breakfast

2156 Lafayette Avenue, 63104-2543
(314) 772-4429

Guests are in the center of things to do in St. Louis in an 1876 historically significant brick Queen Anne mansion overlooking Lafayette Park. Third-floor suite has its own kitchen. Extensive book collections, mostly cookbooks. Resident cats. Limited smoking permitted.

Hosts: Sarah and Jack Milligan
Rooms: 5 (2 PB; 3 SB) $50-75
Full Breakfast
Credit Cards: A, B
Notes: 2, 5, 8, 9, 10, 11, 12, 13, 14

Napolean's Retreat

Napoleon's Retreat Bed and Breakfast

1815 Lafayette Avenue, 63104
(314) 772-6979

Elegantly restored Second Empire Victorian townhouse in historic Lafayette Square. Three spacious guest rooms furnished with period antiques. Each room has a private bath, while one room, a full suite, has a wet bar, refrigerator, and a view of downtown St. Louis and the Gateway Arch. Telephone and TV in each room. Beautiful secluded garden and patio. Minutes to downtown, riverfront, Gateway Arch, St. Louis Union Station, Busch Stadium, and Missouri Botanical Garden. Full gourmet breakfast.

Hosts: Michael Lance and Jeff Archuleta
Rooms: 3 (PB) $65-80
Full Breakfast
Credit Cards: A, B
Notes: 2, 5, 7

Ozark Mountain Country Bed and Breakfast

P.O. Box 295, Branson, 65616
(417) 334-4720; (800) 695-1546

OMC 240. This 1876 Queen Anne mansion overlooks Lafayette Park and is decorated with antiques. Four guest areas have private and shared baths. A suite includes a small kitchen. Sitting area for guests' use has TV/VCR. Smoking is allowed outdoors and in the lounge. Resident cats. Full breakfast. Children welcome. $45-65.

OMC 241. Large two-story suburban home decorated with antiques. Two guest accommodations on the second floor have double beds and private baths with shower. Cable TV in main-floor sitting room. Patio for guests' use. Full breakfast of homemade goodies. Add $30 for an extra guest. $55.

OMC 242. This restored French Colonial home was built in 1790. It has a spacious solarium and a dining room with working fireplace. Decorated with antiques and quilts. Three guest rooms offer private and shared baths, and one room has a fireplace. Resident cats. Children welcome. A hearty breakfast features homemade breads. $60.

OMC 243. This 1840 inn is in the historic district and is decorated with 1800s antiques. There are six guest rooms, four with private showers and entrances, and two rooms share a bath (claw-foot tub and shower). Furnished with old quilts. Resident dog. Children over ten welcome. No smoking. Hearty breakfast. $65-105.

OMC 258. This three-story Victorian was built in 1850. A Queen Anne suite on the second floor has two bedrooms and is decorated with antiques. The Soulard Suite on the third floor has two bedrooms and a casual country decor. Sitting area and bath,

7 No smoking; 8 Children welcome; 9 Social drinking allowed; 10 Tennis nearby; 11 Swimming nearby; 12 Golf nearby; 13 Skiing nearby; 14 May be booked through a travel agent.

featuring claw-foot tubs, can be found on each floor. Queen-size beds. Children over ten welcome. Smoking permitted in kitchen or on porches. $68-95.

OMC 403. This elegant 1876 mansion is decorated with antiques. Guests have full use of parlors, fireplace, and TV/VCR. The second floor has a two-bedroom suite with a king-size four-poster bed, a double bed, and a cozy sitting room with TV/VCR. Two third-floor rooms have either a king-size waterbed or a double and a twin bed, private baths, and share a sitting area. Children welcome. No smoking. Full breakfast in formal dining room on first floor. $65.

Somewhere!! A Bed and Breakfast Guesthouse

2049 Sidney Street, 63104-2828
(314) 644-4PAM (726)

The first and only minority-owned-and-operated bed and breakfast in the city of St. Louis. This three-story Victorian brick boasts many original 1881 architectural features, including six marble fireplaces, pocket doors, and a Victorian garden. The three guest rooms are on the third floor and feature queen-size beds, Jacuzzi baths, crystal chandeliers, cable TV, VCRs, and complimentary "welcome home" snacks. A full country breakfast buffet is served and features the owner's homemade yeast rolls and cinnamon rolls "from scratch," gourmet coffee, and teas. Candlelight dinners, transportation services, and other special amenities are available. Just five minutes south of downtown St. Louis, within walking distance of Soulard Market, Sidney Street Cafe, and the Anheuser Busch Brewery, and 30 minutes from Lambert Airport.

Host: Pam Pullman
Rooms: 3 (PB) $125
Full Breakfast
Credit Cards: A, B, C, D, E
Notes: 2, 3, 4, 5, 9

The Winter House

3522 Arsenal Street, 63118
(314) 664-4399

Nine-room Victorian built in 1897 features pressed-tin ceiling in lower bedroom, a suite with balcony, and decorative fireplace on second floor. The Continental plus breakfast is served in the dining room using crystal and antique Wedgwood china and always includes freshly squeezed orange juice. Tea and piano music are available by reservation, with live piano music by Prof. J. Epstein complimentary at breakfast with advance notice. Fruit, candy, and fresh flowers are provided in bedrooms. Nearby attractions include a Victorian walking park on the national register and the Missouri Botanical Garden. Within four miles are the Arch, Busch Baseball Stadium, the new Science Center, zoo, symphony, and Union Station. Walk to fine dining. Reservations required. Additional fee of $15 for one-night stays.

Hosts: Kendall Winter
Rooms: 2 (PB) $70-80
Suite: 1 (PB) $85-95
Continental Breakfast
Credit Cards: A, B, C, D, E, F
Notes: 2, 7, 8, 9, 10, 11, 14

The Winter House

SEDILIA

Ozark Mountain Country Bed and Breakfast

P.O. Box 295, Branson, 65616
(417) 334-4720; (800) 695-1546

OMC 244. This turn-of-the-century Colonial home on a farm is decorated with antiques. Four guest rooms feature a queen-size, double, or twin beds. One room has a private bath and the other three share a hall bath. Guest parlor available. Hearty breakfast. Resident dogs. Guest pets welcome. $48-65.

SEYMOUR

Ozark Mountain Country Bed and Breakfast

P.O. Box 295, Branson, 65616
(417) 334-4720; (800) 695-1546

OMC 268. Private farm home on working dairy farm 18 miles from Mansfield. Only books one guest party at a time. Amenities include living room, two bedrooms with either queen-size or double beds, and an equipped kitchen. Generous Continental breakfast. Children welcome. No alcohol. No pets. No smoking. $60.

SHELL KNOB

Ozark Mountain Country Bed and Breakfast

P.O. Box 295, Branson, 65616
(417) 334-4720; (800) 695-1546

Home Sweet Home. Three-bedroom suite on Table Rock with living room and full kitchen. Hot tub on deck with playground area for kids. No smoking. Full breakfast. Queen-size and twin beds. $85.

Shore Hollow. Contemporary home featuring lakeview suite with hot tub and pool on deck plus fishing boat. Three guest areas and one private bath. King- and queen-size beds. Children welcome. No smoking. Full breakfast. $40-70.

SILVER DOLLAR CITY

Ozark Mountain Country Bed and Breakfast

P.O. Box 295, Branson, 65616
(417) 334-4720; (800) 695-1546

Haus Waldesruh. A contemporary hillside home overlooking Table Rock Lake. Guest suite with fireplace, king-size bed, lakeview, and private entrance. Children welcome. Full breakfast. $60-70.

Hummingbird's Nest. Indian Point close to Silver Dollar City. Features suite with indoor hot tub in atrium and king-size waterbed. Children over four welcome. No smoking. Full breakfast. $55-80.

Josie's, The Peaceful Getaway. Contemporary home on Table Rock Lake. Features lakeview suite with whirlpool. Children welcome. No smoking. King- and queen-size beds. Fireplace. Full breakfast. $55-95.

Journey's End. Private cabin built in 1920s and furnished with antiques. Double bed. No children. No smoking. Continental breakfast. $65.

Lakeshore Bed and Breakfast. Contemporary home with boat dock on Table Rock Lake. Three guest areas, two of which have private entrances, queen-size beds, and private baths. Children welcome. No smoking. Full breakfast. $65-75.

7 No smoking; 8 Children welcome; 9 Social drinking allowed; 10 Tennis nearby; 11 Swimming nearby; 12 Golf nearby; 13 Skiing nearby; 14 May be booked through a travel agent.

Pine Lodge at Journey's End. Private log cabin with hot tub and real wood-burning fireplace. No smoking. Queen-size bed. $95.

SPRINGFIELD

Mansion at Elfindale

1701 South Fort, 65807
(417) 831-5400

The Mansion, built in the 1800s, features ornate fireplaces, stained-glass windows, and unique architecturally designed rooms. It offers 13 suites, all with private baths, and a full breakfast served in the dining room and prepared by an English chef. Weddings, banquets, or even small business meetings can be accommodated at the Mansion. Come relive the past in Missouri's largest bed and breakfast.

Host: Jef Wells
Rooms: 13 (PB) $70-125
Full Breakfast
Credit Cards: A, B, C, D, E
Notes: 2, 5, 7, 11, 12, 14

Ozark Mountain Country Bed and Breakfast

P.O. Box 295, Branson, 65616
(417) 334-4720; (800) 695-1546

OMC 206. This 1894 Queen Anne Victorian mansion is in the historic district. Eleven distinctive rooms with European antiques, feather beds, four-poster beds, air conditioning, skylights, claw-foot tubs; suites with fireplaces and Jacuzzis. All rooms have private baths. Walk to restaurants, theaters, and shops. No smoking. Open year-round. Full breakfast. $75-145.

OMC 262. Stately two-story farmhouse built in 1906 and comfortably furnished with antiques and collectibles. Hearty breakfast served in dining room on Virginia Rose dishes. One main-level room with queen-size bed and claw-foot tub. Three upstairs rooms with two queen-size beds, one double bed, and private baths. Smoking permitted on porches. Children welcome. $50-60.

Virginia Rose Bed and Breakfast

317 East Glenwood, 65807
(417) 883-0693

This two-story farmhouse built in 1906 offers a country atmosphere and hospitality right in town. On a tree-covered acre, the home is complete with red barn, rockers on the porch, lovely period furnishings, and quilts on queen-size beds. Guests can relax in the parlor with a glass of iced tea or snickerdoodle coffee as they read or watch TV. Hearty homemade breakfasts are served with freshly baked muffins or biscuits on Virginia Rose dishes that have been lovingly collected for years.

Hosts: Jackie and Virginia Buck
Rooms: 5 (PB) $50-100
Full Breakfast
Credit Cards: A, B
Notes: 2, 5, 7, 8, 11, 12, 14

Walnut Street Inn

900 East Walnut, 65806
(417) 864-6346; (800) 593-6346

This award-winning 1894 Queen Anne Victorian inn, in the historic district, invites

Walnut Street Inn

guests to escape. Friendly innkeepers, flickering fireplaces, European antiques, four-poster beds, feather comforters, thick Turkish bathrobes, Jacuzzis, skylights, and Victorian flower gardens abound. Walk to performing arts centers, theaters, cafes, boutiques, and antique shops. Near Bass Pro shops, Branson music shows, with the glorious Ozark Mountains at the backdoor.

Hosts: Karol and Nancy Brown
Rooms: 14 (PB) $75-150
Full Breakfast
Credit Cards: A, B, C, D, E, F
Notes: 2, 5, 7, 8, 9, 10, 11, 12, 13, 14

SULLIVAN

Ozark Mountain Country Bed and Breakfast

P.O. Box 295, Branson, 65616
(417) 334-4720; (800) 695-1546

OMC 271. This two-story Victorian is decorated with antiques and stained glass. Three suites available with king-size beds and private bath with double wide tub. Two smaller rooms are also available with double beds and a shared bath. $47-67.

SUNRISE BEACH

Ozark Mountain Country Bed and Breakfast

P.O. Box 295, Branson, 65616
(417) 334-4720; (800) 695-1546

OMC 235. Private carriage house apartment on lake in quiet country setting with landscaped gardens and trails. King-size bed, kitchenette, bath (shower), and TV. Open year-round. Gourmet breakfast served in owner's home with great lakeview. Continental breakfast may be delivered to suite. Dock privileges for swimming and fishing. Special candlelight dinners can be arranged in advance. $75.

OMC 259. Private suite on lake with a fireplace. Access to lake for swimming and fishing. Fully equipped kitchen. Full breakfast delivered to suite. Two bedrooms with double beds in each. Books only one guest party at a time. Not suitable for small children. Smoking permitted on deck or breezeway. $95.

VAN BUREN

Ozark Mountain Country Bed and Breakfast

P.O. Box 295, Branson, 65616
(417) 334-4720; (800) 695-1546

OMC 256. Dine in the sky and wake up above the clouds in this charming country inn. View of the Current River, the valley, and mountains. Comfortable suites each with waterbed, private entrance, bath, and wood-burning stove. Hearty breakfast and other meals available. Inquire about accommodations for children and pets. $50-75.

OMC 257. Two-bedroom secluded cottage by private lake has fully equipped kitchen with microwave. TV and VCR. King-size and double beds. Full bath. Continental breakfast. $85.

VERSALES

Ozark Mountain Country Bed and Breakfast

P.O. Box 295, Branson, 65616
(417) 334-4720; (800) 695-1546

OMC 266. This 1877 Victorian home is ten miles from the Lake of the Ozarks. Four rooms with private baths. A two-room suite with queen-size beds and sitting area with TV. Children over five welcome. Full breakfast. Air-conditioned. $55-95.

Cedarcroft Farm

WARRENSBURG

Cedarcroft Farm

431 Southeast "Y" Highway, 64093
(816) 747-5728; (800) 368-4944

Cedarcroft Farm offers old-fashioned country hospitality, country quiet, and more-than-you-can-eat country cooking on an 1867 family farm on the national register. Guests may explore the 80 acres of secluded woods, meadows, and streams, and savor a full country breakfast. Civil War reenactor hosts demonstrate 1860s soldiers' life. Home of Old Star Fertilizer, as featured on CNN. Limited smoking allowed.

Hosts: Sandra and Bill Wayne
Suite: 1 (PB) $65
Full Breakfast
Credit Cards: A, B, C, D
Notes: 2, 4, 5, 8, 9, 11, 12, 14

Ozark Mountain Country Bed and Breakfast

P.O. Box 295, Branson, 65616
(417) 334-4720; (800) 695-1546

OMC 216. This 1867 farmhouse books only one guest party at a time. Two-bedroom suite contains three double beds and one three-quarter bed, parlor, and downstairs bath. Open year-round. Resident dog. Smoking only on porch. Hearty country breakfast. $65.

WASHINGTON

Washington House Bed and Breakfast

3 Lafayette Street, 63090
(314) 239-2417; (314) 239-9834

Washington House, built circa 1837, is in a national historic district. This authentically restored inn on the Missouri River features riverviews, canopied beds, antiques, and full breakfast. Washington House is in the heart of Missouri's wine country, only 45 minutes west of St. Louis.

Hosts: Chuck and Kathy Davis
Rooms: 3 (PB) $55-75
Full Breakfast
Credit Cards: None
Notes: 2, 5, 8, 9, 10, 11, 12

WAYNESVILLE

Ozark Mountain Country Bed and Breakfast

P.O. Box 295, Branson, 65616
(417) 334-4720; (800) 695-1546

OMC 263. Quaint stone home with two unique guest rooms decorated with antiques and country charm. Children welcome. Full breakfast served in dining room. Guests in the master bedroom may enjoy breakfast in room. $45-55.

WEST PLAINS

Ozark Mountain Country Bed and Breakfast

P.O. Box 295, Branson, 65616
(417) 334-4720; (800) 695-1546

OMC 212. Relax on a 20-acre farm where only one guest party is booked at a time. Ranch-style home accessorized with antiques and doll collection. Outdoor pets welcome. Guest room has double bed, TV, and private hall bath. Children welcome on weekends. No smoking. Resident cat. $38.

OMC 219. Colonial-style 1887 home with antiques. Three upstairs guest rooms, two with queen-size beds, and one with twin bed, hall bath upstairs and downstairs. Full gourmet breakfast. Children welcome. $25-50.

OMC 274. Health resort lodge on 100 wooded acres at a private lake, circa 1924. Completely refurbished and redecorated. Seven guest rooms have twin, king- or queen-size beds and private baths. A two-bedroom suite is also available. No smok-

ing. Children welcome. Full breakfast. Resident cat. $55-110.

WILLOW SPRINGS

Ozark Mountain Country Bed and Breakfast

P.O. Box 295, Branson, 65616
(417) 334-4720; (800) 695-1546

OMC 272. Rustic two-room bunkhouse with antiques on an Ozark farm. Only one guest party booked at a time. Sleeps four (two bunk beds), bath with shower, sitting area has TV and air conditioning. Children welcome. Country breakfast. $40.

7 No smoking; 8 Children welcome; 9 Social drinking allowed; 10 Tennis nearby; 11 Swimming nearby; 12 Golf nearby; 13 Skiing nearby; 14 May be booked through a travel agent.

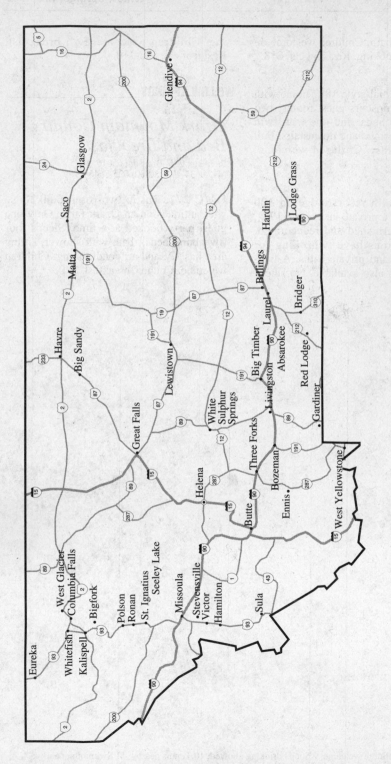

Montana

Montana

ABSAROKEE

Bed and Breakfast Western Adventure

P.O. Box 4308, Bozeman, 59772
(406) 585-0557; FAX (406) 585-2869

145. Serenity on the Stillwater River describes the setting for this handsome and comfortable log lodge. Guests can observe the tranquil beauty from the porch swing or walk in the large yard that surrounds the home. Some of Montana's best hiking, fishing, white-water rafting, and horseback riding are minutes away. One large guest room decorated with antiques on the second floor, with private bath on the first level, has views of the Beartooth Mountain Range. A sitting room houses a well-stocked library and a small sofa bed and leads to a small deck. Dinner and pack lunches available with prior notice. Full breakfast. No smoking. No pets. Children over 12 welcome. $75.

BIGFORK

Burggraf's Countrylane Bed 'n' Breakfast on Swan Lake

Rainbow Drive, 59911
(406) 837-4608; (800) 525-3344
FAX (406) 837-2468

Log home on seven acres beside Swan Lake with panoramic view, only 45 minutes from Glacier National Park. All-you-can-eat breakfast. Complimentary bottle of wine with fruit and cheese tray upon arrival. Guest refrigerator and Jacuzzi/whirlpool tub. All rooms with TVs.

Hosts: Natalie and R. J. Burggraf
Rooms: 5 (PB) $80-90
Full Breakfast
Credit Cards: A, B
Notes: 2, 3, 7, 8, 9, 10, 11, 12, 13, 14

O'Duachain Country Inn

675 Ferndale Drive, 59911
(406) 837-6851; (800) 837-7460

Luxurious log lodging with full gourmet breakfast. Five acres of landscaped solitude. Walking trails, ponds, and wildlife. One-day junkets include Glacier National Park, Flathead and Swan lakes and valleys, Jewel Basin hiking, and National Bison Range. Golf, swimming, boating, and skiing areas abound. Pets welcome by prior arrangement.

Hosts: Margot and Tom Doohan
Rooms: 3 (PB) $125
Full Breakfast
Credit Cards: A, B, C
Notes: 2, 5, 7, 8, 9, 10, 11, 12, 13, 14

BIG SANDY

Bed and Breakfast Western Adventure

P.O. Box 4308, Bozeman, 59772
(406) 585-0557; FAX (406) 585-2869

253. This working cattle ranch is in the heart of the Plains Indian country surrounded by cowboys, buffalo, and the giant stone sentinels of the Missouri Breaks.

NOTES: Credit cards: A MasterCard; B Visa; C American Express; D Discover; E Diners Club; F Other; 2 Personal checks accepted; 3 Lunch available; 4 Dinner available; 5 Open all year; 6 Pets welcome; 7 No smoking; 8 Children welcome; 9 Social drinking allowed; 10 Tennis nearby; 11 Swimming nearby; 12 Golf nearby; 13 Skiing nearby; 14 May be booked through a travel agent.

Participate in ranch life: groom horses, gather eggs, feed chickens, or view resident wildlife. The ranch house has four bedrooms that share two baths. Two cabins that can accommodate four each are also available two miles north of Big Sandy. Amenities include ranch tours, horseback riding, and arranged picnic lunches. Historical Virgelle Mercantile, with antiques and canoe rentals, is 15 miles south of Big Sandy. No smoking. Continental plus breakfast served. $60.

BIG TIMBER

Bed and Breakfast Western Adventure

P.O. Box 4308, Bozeman, 59772
(406) 585-0557; FAX (406) 585-2869

226. This grand old hotel, built in 1890, has recently been restored to its original splendor and is listed on the National Register of Historic Places. Big Timber has the Yellowstone River to the north, Boulder River to the west, and Yellowstone National Park 90 miles south. The hotel offers seven rooms appointed with their Victorian best: high ceilings and period furnishings. Ideal for a getaway weekend or as a base for fall hunting. Six rooms share a suite of bathrooms made up of two full baths, two lavatories, two showers, and a sauna. There are three bedroom suites with private baths and two honeymoon suites, one with two bedrooms. The staff is well informed. Fishing and hunting guides and outfitters nearby. Crib and roll aways available. Dining and full bar. Sunday brunch. No smoking. Pets restricted. Full breakfast. $55-85.

312. This handsome, rustic, dark cedar-sided home boasts a spectacular panoramic view of the Yellowstone River and the Crazy Mountains from a wide expanse of surrounding decks. The river affords easy fishing access and bird watching. Two attractively decorated rooms share a bath. Children and pets welcome. Private entrance, arrangements for golf or horseback riding. Horse boarding also available. Tours and guided fishing on jet or drift boats. Bird hunting arranged in season. Playhouse and swing set for children. Laundry facilities available with longer stays. No smoking. Full breakfast. $60.

BILLINGS

Bed and Breakfast Western Adventure

P.O. Box 4308, Bozeman, 59772
(406) 585-0557; FAX (406) 585-2869

123. This charming 1915 two-story clapboard historic home was once known as Mrs. Potter's Women's Boarding House. Within walking distance of downtown Billings with theater performances, fine dining, museums, and art centers. A large wraparound porch encourages lounging and people-watching. Guests can relax in the sitting room and other common areas on the main floor. Five guest rooms have double or queen beds. Two rooms share a bath; the others are private. Minutes from the airport, Metra Park, medical facilities, and historic attractions. One hour to skiing or Custer battlefield. Public golf courses are nearby. River trips and dinner reservations can be arranged. No smoking. No pets. Children over 12 welcome. Full breakfast. $62-75.

129. This modest blue split-level home in a quiet east Billings neighborhood opens onto a lovely redwood deck that overlooks a beautifully landscaped back yard with rock gardens and peaceful lounging areas. Guest quarters occupy the main upper level with two bedrooms that share a bath. Ideal for two couples or a three- to five-member family who would enjoy fishing and char-

---

NOTES: Credit cards accepted: A MasterCard; B Visa; C American Express; D Discover; E Diners Club; F Other; 2 Personal checks accepted; 3 Lunch available; 4 Dinner available; 5 Open all year; 6 Pets welcome;

tered tours of Bighorn Lake and other nearby waters. Both hosts are Coast Guard licensed and offer tours of area waters. They can also arrange guided fishing trips and tours to the Little Bighorn battlefield. Airport pickup and dog kennel available. Fax, copier, word processing available for business travelers. Smoking restricted. Cat in resident. Full breakfast. $55.

297. Gingerbread trim denotes the turn-of-the-century construction of this renovated farmhouse, which is set on five acres and is home to about twenty sheep in spring and winter. Hardwood floors, flowered wallpaper, and antiques grace this pretty little home. Three light and airy bedrooms. Private shower baths. The rooms are decorated with fluffy curtains, quilts, and sheepskin rugs. Close to Billings, the largest city in Montana. One and one-half hours from Custer battlefield. Lambing in the spring. Visit the little black-faced critters. No smoking. No pets. Full breakfast. $50-55.

BOZEMAN

Bed and Breakfast Western Adventure

P.O. Box 4308, Bozeman, 59772
(406) 585-0557; FAX (406) 585-2869

187. A pretty little white stucco home tucked at the base of the Bridger Mountains with surrounding views that are breathtaking. Mountain and wildlife views surround this home by day, and the Bozeman city lights can be seen at night. Ideal for an active couple or family who enjoys hiking. Two large rooms with queen-size beds and a smaller room with a twin bed share a bath. The daylight level suite has its own entrance, living room, and fireplace. Host is owner of a western clothing store in Bozeman, and hostess is a potter. Ski at Bridger Bowl and Big Sky. One and one-half hours to Yellowstone National Park.

Hiking trails are nearby, and host can conduct tour. No smoking. No pets. Children over eight welcome. Cat in resident. Full breakfast. $65.

202. This attractive 1906 clapboard Colonial Revival home in the historic district has a large front porch and swing. Comfortably furnished with turn-of-the-century antiques and interesting collectibles from hosts' travels. Three rooms on the second floor; two with queen-size beds and private bath, and one with king-size bed and private bath. A remodeled carriage house with kitchenette, bath, bedroom, loft, and sitting room sleeps up to six people (a queen-size bed on the main floor, a queen-size and twin beds upstairs). Short walk to Montana State University, museums, and downtown. Ski Bridger Bowl is 15 miles distant. Big Sky Resort, 45 miles. Yellowstone Park, 90 miles. No smoking. No pets. Cat in residence. Full breakfast. $75-85.

235. This attractive bungalow is in the Cooper Park historic district close to downtown Bozeman. The lovely interior decor and little extras give guests a pampered experience at this bed and breakfast. Breakfast is served on Danish china in the dining room. Two tastefully appointed rooms, one with a king-size bed and one with twins (or king), share a bath. Rooms can be reserved as a suite with private bath. Guests can use kitchen for evening meals. Outdoor hot tub. Airport pickup can be arranged. Close to Bridger Bowl Ski Area, Museum of the Rockies, and Montana State University. No smoking. No pets. Full and Continental breakfast. $50-60.

335. This large, handsome, cedar-sided home is nestled on thirty acres at the foot of the Bridger Mountain Range. The view of the evening city lights is impressive. Just minutes from Montana State University,

7 No smoking; 8 Children welcome; 9 Social drinking allowed; 10 Tennis nearby; 11 Swimming nearby; 12 Golf nearby; 13 Skiing nearby; 14 May be booked through a travel agent.

the Museum of the Rockies, fine dining, and many art galleries. In the summer, activities abound in the city. Outdoor activities like rock climbing, fly fishing, whitewater rafting, horseback riding, or hiking are close by. Guests may choose from tastefully decorated rooms and a suite, each with private bath, that opens onto one of the beautifully landscaped gardens and a large outdoor hot tub. Ten miles from Bridger ski area and airport. Just minutes from blue ribbon fishing streams. Two miles from Bozeman's museums, restaurants, shopping. No smoking. No pets allowed. Children over 12 are welcome. Dog in residence. Full breakfast served. $80-100.

366. A handsome, little, cedar-sided cabin sits a short distance from the wooded banks of a meandering creek. It shares the scene with the main house. The rustic two-story, two-bedroom guest house sleeps five and has one and one-half baths, a fully furnished kitchen, living/dining area, and a gas-burning fireplace. A large deck provides a relaxed opportunity to feel the serenity and observe the wildlife. Only minutes from Montana State University and Museum of the Rockies. Excellent restaurants, galleries, and shopping are all within a short distance. Hot springs nearby. No smoking allowed. No pets allowed. No host. $95.

Fox Hollow Bed and Breakfast at Baxter Creek

545 Mary Road, 59715
(406) 582-8440; (800) 431-5010

A country setting in the heart of the Gallatin River Valley. Enjoy panoramic views of majestic mountain ranges from the wraparound deck or hot tub spa. This 1993 country-style home offers spacious guest rooms with plush queen-size beds and private baths. Wake to full country breakfasts every morning. Montana is a traveler's par-

adise. Choose from world-famous fly fishing, hiking, mountain biking, or alpine and cross-country skiing. Yellowstone National Park is only 90 minutes away.

Hosts: Michael and Nancy Dawson
Rooms: 3 (PB) $100-120
Full Breakfast
Credit Cards: A, B
Notes: 2, 5, 7, 9, 10, 11, 12, 13, 14

The Lindley House

202 Lindley Place, 59715
(406) 587-8403; (800) 787-8404
FAX (406) 582-8112

The Joseph M. Lindly House was built in 1889 by one of Bozeman's early pioneers. It is a charming and distinctive Victorian manor house listed on the National Register of Historic Places and close to the downtown area. Guest rooms have private baths. A full gourmet breakfast is served every morning. Elegant wallcoverings, light fixtures, and antiques adorn the newly remodeled rooms. Lindley House offers beautiful and luxurious accommodations to the discriminating traveler desiring comfort and quality. Lunch and dinner are available upon prior arrangement. Children over ten are welcome.

Host: Stephanie Volz
Rooms: 5 (PB) $110-250
Full Breakfast
Credit Cards: A, B
Notes: 2, 5, 7, 8, 10, 11, 12, 13, 14

Torch and Toes Bed and Breakfast

309 South Third Avenue, 59715
(406) 586-7285; (800) 446-2138

Set back from the street, it looks much as it did when it was built in 1906. A tall, trim brick-and-frame house in the Colonial Revival style. Just enough lace curtains and turn-of-the-century furniture to remind guests that this is a house with a past. Smells of blueberry muffins, coddled eggs, and fresh fruit will entice guests to breakfast in the oak-paneled dining room with the wood-burning fireplace.

Hosts: Ronald and Judy Hess
Rooms: 4 (PB) $60-85
Full Breakfast
Credit Cards: A, B
Notes: 2, 5, 7, 8, 9, 10, 11, 12, 13, 14

Voss Inn

Voss Inn Bed and Breakfast

319 South Wilson, 59715
(406) 587-0982

Magnificently restored Victorian inn in the historic district with elegant guest rooms and private baths. A delightful gourmet breakfast is served in the privacy of guests' rooms. Bozeman is 90 miles north of Yellowstone Park, near skiing, fishing, hiking, and snowmobiling. Guided day trips are conducted into Yellowstone and the surrounding area by the hosts. Full afternoon tea. Airport transportation available. Children over five welcome.

Hosts: Bruce and Frankee Muller
Rooms: 6 (PB) $80-90
Full Breakfast
Credit Cards: A, B, C
Notes: 2, 5, 7, 9, 10, 11, 12, 13, 14

BRIDGER

Bed and Breakfast Western Adventure

P.O. Box 4308, Bozeman, 59772
(406) 585-0557; FAX (406) 585-2869

185. This handsome horse ranch is on 24-acres in the beautiful Clark's Fork Valley overlooking the Beartooth Range. The home borders Sand Creek and is surrounded by large cottonwood trees. The slate blue split-level home has three guest rooms. Close to Pryor Mountains, home to more than 100 free-roaming mustangs. Two hours from Yellowstone Park; one hour from Red Lodge Ski Area, Big Horn Canyon National Recreation, Pryor Mountains and Cody, Wyoming, home of the Buffalo Bill Historical Center, the world's finest Western history museum. Horse boarding available with large corral and loafing shed. No smoking. No pets. Three dogs in residence. Full breakfast. $40-50.

317. If guests are looking for a true Western experience, a stay at this ranch may be just the place. The main house is a handsome redwood two-story that sits in the middle of the Beartooth and Pryor Mountain ranges. This breathtaking view is seen from the large decks surrounding the house. Two rooms on the lower daylight level share a bath. Families who want a more rustic setting can stay in small cabins. Shower and restroom facilities are nearby. Tepees are set up on a ridge overlooking the Clark's Fork Valley. Experience a working cattle ranch. Ride horseback in the beautiful countryside. Family-style dining and ranch entertainment. No smoking. No pets. Dog in residence. Full breakfast. Cabin $125 per person. $65.

BUTTE

Bed and Breakfast Western Adventure

P.O. Box 4308, Bozeman, 59772
(406) 585-0557; FAX (406) 585-2869

182. This three-story historical 1897 brick home in the Uptown Butte Historic District

---

7 No smoking; 8 Children welcome; 9 Social drinking allowed; 10 Tennis nearby; 11 Swimming nearby; 12 Golf nearby; 13 Skiing nearby; 14 May be booked through a travel agent.

was used as a boarding house for copper miners at the turn of the century. Butte, the only intact turn-of-the-century industrial city remaining in the United States, is a must for history buffs. The home has been completely renovated and landscaped. Comfortable amenities have been added for today's traveler. Seven rooms, each with queen-size beds and private shower baths, are available to guests. There is also a large shared bathroom in period decor. Skiing, fishing, and horseback riding are about 45 minutes away; golf at a municipal course is ten minutes away. National Museum of Mining and the trolley tour of Historic Butte and Berkeley Mining Pit are nearby. No smoking. No pets. Full breakfast. $55-60.

COLUMBIA FALLS

Bad Rock Country Bed and Breakfast

480 Bad Rock Drive, 59912
(800) 422-3666

A special place to stay, for the visitor to Glacier National Park. This elegant country home is on 30 beautiful acres. There are four luxurious rooms available with fireplaces in new log cottages with Montana handmade log furniture; three guest rooms in the home, all with private baths. Beautiful Old West antiques. Secluded hot tub with time reserved for each guest. Experience the quiet of the country and the magnificence of front-yard mountains. Enjoy fantastic breakfasts and the very best in superb hospitality. For nonsmoking guests. Inspected and approved by AAA, ABBA, MBBA. Children over nine are welcome.

Hosts: Jon and Susie Alper
Rooms: 7 (PB) $95-135
Full Breakfast
Credit Cards: A, B, C, D, E
Notes: 2, 5, 7, 9, 12, 13, 14

ENNIS

Bed and Breakfast Western Adventure

P.O. Box 4308, Bozeman, 59772
(406) 585-0557; FAX (406) 585-2869

164. The Madison River, renowned for its trout fishing, is high in the northern Rockies. This lovely two-story ranch house sits on the river bank in a beautiful valley and overlooks the Madison Mountain range. Family antiques and collectibles grace this attractive ranch home. Three gracious and cozy guest rooms share a living room and fireplace. Guided fishing. Use of drift boats and rafts can be arranged. Box lunches and sumptuous dinners by prior arrangement. Horseback riding nearby. Fly fishing for rainbow and brown trout. Yellowstone River is 60 miles away. Abundant wildlife. RV hookup available. VISA and MasterCard accepted. Host is a licensed fly-fishing guide. No smoking or pets. Dog in residence. Full breakfast served. $55-80.

321. This elegant cedar-sided hillside home is nestled at the base of a hill with a spectacular view of Fan Mountain and the Spanish peaks of the Madison Range. This lovely inn is a haven for fishermen and sightseers. An expansive living room with stone fireplace provides a quiet corner to curl up with a good book and another for evening conversation. Three bedrooms are available, one with king-size bed and private bath on the upper level. A two-room suite on the lower level with queen-size and twin beds shares a bath and has a sitting area and coffee niche that opens onto a patio with hot tub and a view of the mountains. Hot tub and pool. Fishing guides can be arranged. Fish hatchery and Virginia City nearby, cross-country skiing and snowmobiling in winter. Within walking distance of boutiques and restaurants of Ennis. No smoking. No pets. Children over

NOTES: Credit cards accepted: A MasterCard; B Visa; C American Express; D Discover; E Diners Club; F Other; 2 Personal checks accepted; 3 Lunch available; 4 Dinner available; 5 Open all year; 6 Pets welcome;

12 are welcome. Two dogs in residence. Full breakfast. $80-85.

EUREKA

Huckleberry Hannah's Montana Bed and Breakfast

3100 Sophie Lake Road, 59917
(406) 889-3381 (for reservations and free brochure)

Nearly 5,000 square feet of old-fashioned charm. Fifty wooded acres, fabulous trout-filled lake, glorious views of the Rockies. This bed and breakfast depicts a quieter time in history, when the true pleasures of life represented a walk in the woods or a moonlight swim, not to mention comfortable, sunny rooms and wonderful food. Owned and operated by the author of one of the Northwest's best-selling cookbooks, *Huckleberry Hannah's Country Cooking Sampler.* Questions cheerfully answered. Ask about kids and pets. Limited smoking permitted. Senior discounts.

Hosts: Jack and Deanna Doying
Rooms: 5 (PB) $40-75
Cottage: 1 (PB)
Full Breakfast
Credit Cards: A, B, D
Notes: 2, 3, 4, 10, 11, 13, 14

GARDINER

Bed and Breakfast Western Adventure

P.O. Box 4308, Bozeman, 59772
(406) 585-0557; FAX (406) 585-2869

173. The historic town of Gardiner was the original entrance to Yellowstone that was dedicated by Teddy Roosevelt in 1903. The inn is at the crossroads of the Yellowstone River and the park entrance lies a handsomely restored, historic inn, offering a relaxed and comfortable atmosphere in two turn-of-the-century stone houses. There are cozy parlors, fireplaces, and attentive personnel. Several accommodations, all attractively furnished, are available: a stone cottage, a suite, or seven rooms—three with private baths and four that share. Depending upon the time of year, park tours, fishing guides, horseback riding, pack trips, white-water rafting, snowmobiling, and cross-country skiing, wildlife photo excursions, and other activities can be arranged through the inn. No smoking. No pets. Full breakfast. $64-94.

286. This 1903 home made of river stone, a short distance from the historic Roosevelt Arch at the north entrance to Yellowstone Park, is decorated to reflect turn-of-the-century Victorian charm. Breakfast is served in the common area on the second floor where guests can enjoy the TV and music center. Off the common area is a hot tub and deck surrounded by the quiet and beauty of the gardens interspersed throughout the yard. There are two guest rooms on the third floor that can be used as a suite or a room with a private bath. The third room on the second floor, with queen-size bed, shares the bath on the first floor. Enjoy the backyard hot tub and deck or fish in the Yellowstone River at the end of the street. Galleries, shops, and restaurants are nearby. No smoking. No pets. Children over 15 welcome. Continental plus breakfast served. $60-85.

GLASGOW

Bed and Breakfast Western Adventure

P.O. Box 4308, Bozeman, 59772
(406) 585-0557; FAX (406) 585-2869

139. This three-story cedar home with vaulted ceilings sits on 240 acres in northern Montana. Five guest rooms are decorated in Western decor, one with queen-size bed and one with two doubles, share a bath. An open balcony and abundant windows surround the home to provide a sweeping view of the Milk River, wheat fields, and prairie grasses. A butcher block stairwell is decorated to harmonize with surrounding landscape. There is a separate bunkhouse with three bedrooms. Swimming pool, hot tub, pool table, large-screen TV, and fax. Other structured or unstructured activities include branding, fishing, and water sports. Zortman mine nearby. Dinner by reservation. No guest pets allowed. Pet llama, dog, cat, and bird in residence. Full breakfast served. $50.

GLENDIVE

Bed and Breakfast Western Adventure

P.O. Box 4308, Bozeman, 59772
(406) 585-0557; FAX (406) 585-2869

162. A charming 1912 two-story home sits on a quiet street in Glendive near the Yellowstone River. Two guest rooms, decorated with country crafts, antiques, and handmade quilts, share a full bath. Guests may relax in the hot tub and enjoy the sitting room, sun porch, and deck. Close to downtown and Dawson Community College. Golf, swimming, fishing, hunting, cross-country skiing, tennis, waterslide nearby. Hiking at Makoshika State Park. No smoking allowed. No pets allowed. Young people over 16 are welcome. Full breakfast served. $45-50.

The Hostetler House Bed and Breakfast

113 North Douglas Street, 59330
(406) 365-4505; FAX (406) 365-8456

Two blocks from downtown shopping and restaurants, the Hostetler House is a charming 1912 historic home with two comfortable guest rooms, sitting room, sun porch, deck, gazebo, and hot tub. Full gourmet breakfast is served on Grandma's china. On

I-94 and the Yellowstone River, close to parks, swimming pool, tennis courts, golf course, antique shops, and churches.

Hosts: Craig and Dea Hostetler
Rooms: 2 (SB) $50
Full Breakfast
Credit Cards: A, B, D
Notes: 2, 5, 7, 9, 10, 11, 12, 14

GREAT FALLS

Bed and Breakfast Western Adventure

P.O. Box 4308, Bozeman, 59772
(406) 585-0557; FAX (406) 585-2869

197. Charming restored Victorian home, built in 1904, is in the historic section of downtown. The room on the third floor has a Scottish theme, queen-size bed, and a private bath with a six-foot tin tub. Three rooms on the second floor have twin, double, or queen-size beds and share a bath. The main floor has a room with private bath and queen-size bed. Lots of antiques grace the home that also has secluded porches and an intimate book-lined library. A shaded garden with gazebo and fountain offers another peaceful retreat. The home has the general theme of a Welsh Country Inn. A shaded garden with gazebo and fountain offers a peaceful retreat. No smoking. No pets. Full breakfast. $50-75.

HAMILTON

Bed and Breakfast Western Adventure

P.O. Box 4308, Bozeman, 59772
(406) 585-0557; FAX (406) 585-2869

326. Enjoy the beauty of the Bitterroot Valley from one of the decks of this handsome two-story Western home. Guests are invited to join in the daily ranch activities such as gathering eggs or feeding livestock. Four accommodations are available. Two of these are spacious suites (one with its own double Jacuzzi tub and the other with panoramic views and private balcony). Or stay in the bunkhouse that comfortably accommodates five. Fish, swim, or raft in nearby lakes, rivers, and streams. Hike national forests. Horseback riding and fly-fishing guides can be arranged. Ask about local rodeos, county fair, powwow, music festival, and golf. Horse boarding available. Dinner by arrangement. No smoking. No pets. Full breakfast. $65-90.

HARDIN

Bed and Breakfast Western Adventure

P.O. Box 4308, Bozeman, 59772
(406) 585-0557; FAX (406) 585-2869

304. "The Madison Avenue of Hardin," this handsome 1915 brick inn was rescued in 1988 by the present innkeepers and has been lovingly restored. On the National Register of Historic Places, the inn has a library and parlor for guests. Smoking is permitted on the first- and second-floor verandas. Seven guest rooms, each with a private sink, are furnished with period antiques. Two rooms on the main floor share a bath; five rooms on the second floor share a bath. Air-conditioned. Big Horn County Museum and Custer battlefield are nearby. Home of Custer reenactment on third weekend of June and the Crow Fair the third weekend of August. Fish the Big Horn River; a guide can be arranged. No pets. Children over 12 welcome. Cat in residence. Full breakfast. $65.

Kendrick House Inn Bed and Breakfast

206 North Custer Avenue, 59034
(406) 665-3035

The Kendrick House Inn was built in 1914 by Elizabeth Kendrick to serve as a boarding house. In 1943 it became the area hos-

pital, serving the Hardin community until 1945, and later it was made into private residences. In 1988, the boarding house was restored, and now the seven guest rooms are filled with antique furniture and period memorabilia. Unique features include two glassed-in verandas, a library, and some common areas for relaxing. Each room has a sink; baths are shared. Sometimes closed during the winter months, so call in advance. Smoking is permitted on the second-floor veranda.

Hosts: Steve and Marcie Smith
Rooms: 7 (S2B) $65
Full Breakfast
Credit Cards: A, B
Notes: 2, 5, 6, 8, 9, 10, 11, 12, 14

HAVRE

Bed and Breakfast Western Adventure

P.O. Box 4308, Bozeman, 59772
(406) 585-0557; FAX (406) 585-2869

306. This attractive two-tone blue two-story bed and breakfast home is on northern Montana's Highway 2 "highline." Enjoy a superb view of the rugged Bear Paw Mountains from the dining room or the rustic deck, where guests can also enjoy morning or afternoon coffee. Two attractively decorated rooms with queen-size beds share a bath. Children welcome. Walking distance to golf and minutes to fishing. Tour Havre's fascinating historic "Underground." Be sure to inquire about a variety of nearby Native American powwows and celebrations. No smoking. No pets. Pets in residence. Full breakfast. $60.

HELENA

Bed and Breakfast Western Adventure

P.O. Box 4308, Bozeman, 59772
(406) 585-0557; FAX (406) 585-2869

7 No smoking; 8 Children welcome; 9 Social drinking allowed; 10 Tennis nearby; 11 Swimming nearby; 12 Golf nearby; 13 Skiing nearby; 14 May be booked through a travel agent.

Bed and Breakfast Western Adventure (continued)

208. This Victorian home, steeped in Helena's historic past, offers elegant accommodations. Built in 1875 by Harriet and Wilbur Sanders and restored 112 years later, it combines the spirit of times past with the comfort of today. Seven richly detailed and elaborately furnished guest rooms have private baths, touch-tone phones, and TVs. On the National Register of Historic Places. Gourmet breakfasts. Large parlor and sitting room with fireplace. Short walking distance from historic downtown and St. Helena's Cathedral. Off-street parking. Air conditioning. Fax available. Credit cards accepted. No smoking. No pets. Dog in residence. Full breakfast. $80-105.

310. An elegant 1874 Victorian three-story mansion adjacent to the magnificent St. Helena Cathedral is within walking distance of downtown, fine restaurants, shops, and galleries. A handsome porch and large yard invite relaxing afternoon or morning strolls. Five guest rooms on the second floor are exquisitely decorated, all have private baths and feature queen-size turn-of-the-century replica beds. The first-floor common area features a formal dining room and piano in the parlor. The enclosed sun porch has ice cream tables. The library, game room, room with computer and office equipment are for guests' use. Airport shuttle. Evening refreshments. No smoking. Children over ten welcome. Dog in residence. Full breakfast. $80.

313. This beautifully restored 1890 three-story Victorian home is surrounded by a large porch and the seasonal changes of a colorful garden. The first floor of the inn is a common area with two sitting rooms, dining room, and kitchen, where guests are welcome to refreshments. Handsomely refinished antiques can be found throughout the home, especially in the six guest rooms. Four rooms on the second floor have private baths; two rooms on the third floor share a bath and kitchen. Can accommodate executive meetings and small receptions. Walking trails nearby; minutes from golf courses and historic Last Chance Gulch. Inquire about the many activities and museums in Montana's capital city. Seasonal or weekly rates available. No smoking. Children over 12 welcome. Dog in residence. Full breakfast. $65-85.

315. Enjoy the solitude of nature in the mountains. This handsome cedar-log lodge was the summer home of pioneer entrepreneur C. B. Power. The massive native stone fireplace in the living room invites relaxation and conversation. Guests are welcome to sit on the large porch and observe an ever-present variety of wildlife. Four light and airy rooms, one with private bath, are furnished with antiques, two with the original furniture chosen by Marshall Field. Savor breakfast in the formal dining room or the adjoining sun porch; other meals by arrangement. Children welcome. Nearby recreation areas offer fishing and floating on the Dearborn and Missouri Rivers and Holter Lake; 20 minutes to Gates of the Mountains. Horse boarding can be arranged. No smoking. No pets. Full breakfast served. $70-85.

337. This 1915 farmhouse offers lovely views of the Capitol building, St. Helena Cathedral, and nearby mountains. The exterior is brick with white trim and window boxes. Relax under the ancient crab apple trees in the front yard or in the pocket garden tucked away behind the garage. The gardens are small but provide a welcoming touch for the traveler ready to get away and renew. The interior is furnished simply with country antiques, quilts, simple prints, and

NOTES: Credit cards accepted: A MasterCard; B Visa; C American Express; D Discover; E Diners Club; F Other; 2 Personal checks accepted; 3 Lunch available; 4 Dinner available; 5 Open all year; 6 Pets welcome;

original art. Two rooms share a bath; one with double bed and view of St. Helena Cathedral and the other has a three-quarter rope feather bed with an enticing view of downtown Helena and mountains. Within walking distance of Reeders Alley, historic Westside walking tour, historic Last Chance Gulch, Grand Street Theatre, and fine restaurants. Games, coffee, and tea available. Full buffet breakfast on Saturday and Sunday. Continental plus breakfast weekdays. No smoking or pets. Children over 16 welcome. Cats in residence. $60-75.

The Sanders

328 North Ewing, 59601
(406) 442-3309

This 1875 Victorian mansion offers elegant accommodations steeped in Helena's historic past. Appointed with original furnishings, each spacious guest room has a private bath, TV, and telephone. Brass beds, high ceilings, and ornately framed paintings radiate the quiet charm of days past. In the heart of Helena and listed on the National Register, the Sanders combines friendly hospitality with grand turn-of-the-century living.

Hosts: Rock Ringling and Bobbi Uecker
Rooms: 7 (PB) $80-98
Full Breakfast
Credit Cards: A, B, D
Notes: 2, 5, 7, 8, 9, 10, 11, 12, 13

KALISPELL

Bed and Breakfast Western Adventure

P.O. Box 4308, Bozeman, 59772
(406) 585-0557; FAX (406) 585-2869

195. Panoramic views from every window distinguish this contemporary home that smacks of rustic elegance. Conveniently between Kalispell and Whitefish, it sits on a ridge amid 36 acres of wheat. Hand-picked river rock trims the exterior, while traditional and Victorian accents warm the interior. A luxurious master suite is decorated in rich fabrics with a four-poster bed adjacent to a lavish marble bath, complete with dual shower and windowed Jacuzzi. One room has two queen-size beds and private bath; two rooms, both with queen-size beds, share a large bath. An open tile kitchen and formal dining room welcome guests for breakfast. Hot tub, flower-topped steam hut, man-made pond. Sound system throughout, large tropical aquariums, three decks. Ski Big Mountain or enjoy Flathead Lake, both within 20 minutes. Glacier Park is only 25 minutes away. Off-season rates are available. No smoking allowed. No guest pets allowed. Children over 12 are welcome. Dog in residence. Full breakfast served. $80-150.

212. This beautifully furnished Victorian house is in the northwestern town of Kalispell near Glacier Park. Enjoy tea or coffee in the common area that has been lovingly decorated to create turn-of-the-century charm. The four guest rooms, three with queen-size beds, one with twin beds, are furnished with Victorian laces, quilts, and antiques and coordinated with the other rooms. Two rooms have private baths; two share a bath. Near historic Conrad mansion, Woodland Park, and shopping within walking distance. Downhill and cross-country skiing, fishing, hunting, boating, hiking, and rafting are only minutes away. No smoking allowed. No guest pets allowed. Children over 15 are welcome. Full breakfast served. $70-85.

Creston Country Willows

70 Creston Road, 59901
(406) 755-7517; (800) 257-7517

Quiet charm and rural serenity are waiting at this delightful two-story farmhouse with mountain and valley views. The inn's

7 No smoking; 8 Children welcome; 9 Social drinking allowed; 10 Tennis nearby; 11 Swimming nearby; 12 Golf nearby; 13 Skiing nearby; 14 May be booked through a travel agent.

Creston Country Willows

rooms are furnished in old-country style and offer the finest in overnight accommodations. A hearty Montana breakfast is served featuring a colorful fresh fruit plate and never-ending pancakes. Minutes away from Glacier National Park, Flathead Lake, golf, skiing, white-water rafting, antiquing, and theater.

Hosts: Marlene and Tom Brunaugh
Rooms: 4 (PB) $75-85
Full Breakfast
Credit Cards: A, B
Notes: 2, 5, 7, 8, 9, 11, 12, 13, 14

LAUREL

Bed and Breakfast Western Adventure

P.O. Box 4308, Bozeman, 59772
(406) 585-0557; FAX (406) 585-2869

127. This handsome newly remodeled home is in a large forested country setting on the shores of the Yellowstone River. This is truly a getaway haven that inspires tranquility whether guests want to sit on the shore and watch the world go by or try a few casts. The two guest rooms on their own main floor wing have private baths; one is across the hall. Outdoor screened-in hot tub. Fly-fishing out the back door, nature walk on island, golf nearby, downhill and cross-country skiing at Red Lodge, 15 minutes from Billings' shopping. No smoking. Children of ten welcome. Cat in residence. Full breakfast. $60.

LEWISTOWN

Bed and Breakfast Western Adventure

P.O. Box 4308, Bozeman, 59772
(406) 585-0557; FAX (406) 585-2869

331. This 1909 stately native sandstone three-story home has been restored and is in the historic Silk Stocking District of Lewistown. The large rambling porch extends a warm invitation to relax with morning coffee. The carved woodwork and stained-glass windows of the interior speak of the artisans who were prevalent in the early 1900s. Three bedrooms are beautifully decorated with quilts, lace, and antiques. All rooms have sinks and share a large bath; one has a toilet. One room has a queen-size bed; two have double beds. Within walking distance of downtown shopping and art museum. Excellent fishing and fish hatchery nearby. Three ghost towns are 15 minutes away. No smoking. No pets. Children over 12 welcome. Full breakfast. $50-70.

LIVINGSTON

Bed and Breakfast Western Adventure

P.O. Box 4308, Bozeman, 59772
(406) 585-0557; FAX (406) 585-2869

131. This cedar-sided home is in spectacular Paradise Valley and offers panoramic views of the Yellowstone River from the three guest rooms. Two spacious rooms have queen-size beds and private baths decorated with antiques, handmade quilts, and down comforters. The third room has twin beds. Two decks with native floral landscaping act as a natural bird refuge. Spacious parlor with view, books, TV, and VCR. Excellent blue-ribbon fishing and rafting nearby. Mountain trails to hike. Arrangements can be made for horseback

NOTES: Credit cards accepted: A MasterCard; B Visa; C American Express; D Discover; E Diners Club; F Other; 2 Personal checks accepted; 3 Lunch available; 4 Dinner available; 5 Open all year; 6 Pets welcome;

riding. Fine dining and hot mineral pools nearby. No smoking. No pets. Young people over 16 welcome. A full breakfast is served. $85-95.

LODGE GRASS

Bed and Breakfast Western Adventure

P.O. Box 4308, Bozeman, 59772
(406) 585-0557; FAX (406) 585-2869

199. Nestled in the heart of the Crow Indian Reservation on the banks of the Bighorn River is a truly authentic pioneer homesite, just eighteen miles from the Bighorn battlefield. Guests are welcome to roam the scenic beauty of this newly renovated 1900s ranch. A cabin bunkhouse is decorated with a French country flavor, accommodates four, with private bath and view of Bighorn River. A little more rustic but very comfortable is the large, upscale tepee on the lake shore with two pole beds and sitting area. A bath is a short walk down a lighted path. Fish or hike along the lake or seven miles of river flowing through the ranch. A blue-ribbon trout stream is one hour from ranch with guides available. Hot tub and barbecue may be used by guests until 10 P.M. No smoking. Dog in residence. Full breakfast. $60-95.

MALTA

Bed and Breakfast Western Adventure

P.O. Box 4308, Bozeman, 59772
(406) 585-0557; FAX (406) 585-2869

178. The past comes to life in this 1898 clapboard turn-of-the-century farmhouse. It is designated a historic home by the Phillips County Historical Society. An interesting array of antiques and collectibles were used to decorate the home. A large back yard with mature trees is next to the Milk River. Five attractively decorated guest rooms are available with a variety of bed combinations and two shared baths. Three of the five rooms have walkout porches adorned with gingerbread trim. Smoking is allowed. Special five-day rates available to hunters and travelers. Lunches and dinners can be arranged with host. Laundry services available. Pets must be leashed. Full breakfast. $57.

MISSOULA

Bed and Breakfast Western Adventure

P.O. Box 4308, Bozeman, 59772
(406) 585-0557; FAX (406) 585-2869

147. This beautiful two-story Newport blue home is secluded on acres of spacious lawn and graced with a variety of mature trees. Take a leisurely stroll to the expansive back yard that centers around a gazebo and hot tub. The exquisite woodwork on the front door, wainscot paneling, and banister are from the Marcus Daly Hotel. Two attractively furnished rooms, one with a queen-size bed and marble fireplace and the other with a double bed, have a private baths. There is room for a roll away. Five minutes from airport. One hour from Bob Marshall Wilderness and Flathead Lake. Two hours from Glacier National Park; 20 minutes to fishing and downhill skiing. An art gallery of fine crafts and works from regional artists is adjacent to the bed and breakfast. No smoking. Pets restricted. Young people over 16 welcome. Cat in residence. Full breakfast. $75-85.

239. This attractive two-story Colonial home is surrounded by 25 acres of woods and meadows. It provides a relaxing, elegant country atmosphere while being only minutes from downtown Missoula, one of Montana's major cities and home to the University of Montana. Two spacious guest bedrooms, furnished with period pieces, share a large bath. An adjacent private sitting room has library, TV, and fireplace. A third room is available. Missoula and the university are ten minutes away. Rafting and fishing on Clark Fork River are within minutes. Marshall Ski area is ten minutes away, and Snow Bowl is 30 minutes away. No smoking allowed. No guest pets allowed. Young people over 16 are welcome. Full breakfast served. $65.

260. This 1911 stately brick home was built for a president of the University of Montana. Moved to its present site, it now overlooks the majestic Clark Fork River. There are four suites, each with a queen-size bed, private bath, balcony, and sitting room. Three more rooms have queen-size beds and private baths; two have fireplaces. The living area is relaxed but elegant with comfortable chairs, fireplace, and library. Walking distance to downtown businesses, restaurants, theaters, and the University of Montana. Off-street parking. Receptions and small weddings can be arranged. Honeymoon suite with soaking tub available. Smoking is restricted. No guest pets allowed. Continental plus breakfast served. $89-129.

Goldsmith's Inn

809 East Front Street, 59801
(406) 721-6732

This beautiful 1911 brick home is on the banks of the Clark Fork River, four blocks from downtown Missoula. Guests can enjoy breakfast in a dining room that provides an unparalleled view of the Bitterfoot Mountain and the sparkles of the Clark Fork River glistening in the morning sun. Formerly the home for several University of Montana presidents.

Hosts: Jean and Richard Goldsmith
Rooms: 7 (PB) $65-95
Full Breakfast
Credit Cards: A, B, C, E
Notes: 2, 3, 4, 5, 8, 9, 10, 11, 12, 13, 14

POLSON

Bed and Breakfast Western Adventure

P.O. Box 4308, Bozeman, 59772
(406) 585-0557; FAX (406) 585-2869

299. This attractive English Tudor home was built in 1929 by a local attorney in Polson. The home boasts of seven gables and sits on a quiet shady street just blocks from the shores of Flathead Lake and downtown shopping. It has been lovingly furnished with family heirlooms. The four guest rooms are graced by antiques and warmed with flowered quilts and lacy curtains. They share two baths. Within walking distance of golf, white-water rafting, scenic boat trips on Flathead Lake. An hour from Glacier National Park and Bigfork Summer Playhouse. No smoking. No pets. Children over four welcome. Full breakfast. $50-55.

Ruth's Bed and Breakfast

802 Seventh Avenue West, 59860
(406) 883-2460

A cottage with two guest rooms and portable bathroom facilities. Bath and shower are shared. One room has a double bed, while the other has a queen-size bed and daveno. Both have TVs and are heated.

Host: Ruth Hunter
Rooms: 2 (SB) $28
Full Breakfast
Credit Cards: None
Notes: 2, 5, 7, 8, 9, 10, 11, 12

RED LODGE

Bed and Breakfast Western Adventure

P.O. Box 4308, Bozeman, 59772
(406) 585-0557; FAX (406) 585-2869

269. This lovely 1903 Queen Anne Victorian home sits in the middle of the

---

NOTES: Credit cards accepted: A MasterCard; B Visa; C American Express; D Discover; E Diners Club; F Other; 2 Personal checks accepted; 3 Lunch available; 4 Dinner available; 5 Open all year; 6 Pets welcome;

quaint mining town of Red Lodge. The living room is appointed with bright flowered pillows, polished carved woodwork, overstuffed sofas, and interesting pictures. Leaded-glass windows allow a view of the mountains and large pines. Colorful quilts, lace pillows, and delicate antiques accent the five guest rooms. Both private and shared baths. Two guest cottages with kitchen facilities sleep five or six. Breakfast not included with the cottages. One block from antique shops, museums, and restaurants. Fish in Rock Creek just behind the inn or ski at Red Lodge Mountain. Highway 212 to the Beartooth Pass and to Yellowstone Park is a national scenic highway. No smoking. No pets. Children over 10 welcome. Continental plus breakfast. $50-70.

324. This cedar ranch-style home nestled on the wooded banks of Rock Creek is home to elk, fox, bald eagle, and other wonders of nature. The pastoral setting offers quiet and solitude just minutes from Red Lodge, a historic mining community that today is a year-round resort town. Just off Highway 22, which leads to scenic Beartooth Pass and takes visitors to the northeast entrance to Yellowstone Park. Two guest rooms, one with queen-size bed and sleeper-sofa, the other with twin beds, share a bath. Guests have private sitting room and entrance from a massive wooden deck that overlooks Rock Creek. This is a great getaway. Skiing, fishing, and golfing are nearby. Horseback riding available nearby. No smoking. No pets. Children over ten welcome. Dog in residence. Full breakfast. $70.

Willows Inn

224 South Platt Avenue P.O. Box 886, 59068
(406) 446-3913

Spectacular mountain scenery surrounds this delightful turn-of-the-century inn. Flanked by giant evergreens and colorful flower beds, it is reminiscent of a bygone era, complete with white picket fence, gingerbread trim, and a porch swing. Five individually decorated guest rooms have brass-and-iron four-poster beds. Delicious home-baked pastries and afternoon refreshments are served. Close to hiking, fishing, and Yellowstone Park. Video movies, books, games, and a large sun deck are available. Two storybook cottages are ideal for families. They have two bedrooms, laundry facilities, and a kitchen and are decorated in cheerful country decor. Children over ten welcome.

Hosts: Kerry, Carolyn, and Evelen Boggio
Rooms: 5 (3 PB; 2 SB) $50–75
Continental Plus Breakfast
Credit Cards: A, B, D
Notes: 2, 5, 7, 9, 10, 11, 12, 13, 14

RONAN

The Timbers Bed and Breakfast

1184 Timberlane Road, 59864
(406) 676-4373; (800) 775-4373

Private lodging on 21 acres with a magnificent view of the Mission Mountains. Cathedral ceilings, hand-hewn beams, barn wood dining area, and furnishings that hosts have collected give this home a sophisticated yet warm country feel. Elegant two-room suite with private bath can sleep four people. A full country breakfast and use of barbecue are included.

The Timbers

7 No smoking; 8 Children welcome; 9 Social drinking allowed; 10 Tennis nearby; 11 Swimming nearby; 12 Golf nearby; 13 Skiing nearby; 14 May be booked through a travel agent.

Nearby attractions include Flathead Lake, National Bison Range, Glacier National Park, whitewater rafting, horseback riding, art galleries, fishing, local rodeos, and powwows. Additional adult in suite: $35; child over ten years old in suite: $20.

Hosts: Doris and Leonard McCravey
Rooms and Suite: 2 (1 PB; 2 SB) $95-115
Full Breakfast
Credit Cards: A, B
Notes: 2, 5, 7, 9, 10, 11, 12, 13, 14

SACO

Bed and Breakfast Western Adventure

P.O. Box 4308, Bozeman, 59772
(406) 585-0557; FAX (406) 585-2869

153. This handsome, historic two-story brick building was designed as a bank in 1909. It has been lovingly restored in the period style with the vault and embossed tin ceiling tiles still in the lobby. History lovers will find many original furnishings, including antique beds, furniture, and other collectibles that have been used in each of the rooms. Five guest rooms sharing two baths have been tastefully and comfortably furnished. A gourmet breakfast is served. Relax and enjoy the large comfortable lobby. Within an hour's drive of Fort Peck Reservoir and the Missouri River and five hours from Glacier National Park. Assistance offered for hunting and fishing. No smoking. No pets. Children over ten welcome. Dog in residences. $40.

ST. IGNATIUS

Bed and Breakfast Western Adventure

P.O. Box 4308, Bozeman, 59772
(406) 585-0557; FAX (406) 585-2869

281. Enjoy the beauty and seclusion of this natural wood mountain home nestled among tall pines and providing views of the Mission Mountains. This furnished house on nine acres is well suited for hiking and bird and wildlife viewing. The five bedrooms with twin and bunk beds can accommodate a large group, up to 16 people. There is a fully equipped kitchen, comfortable living room, large meeting room, wraparound deck, and flower gardens that would make this the ideal setting for a family reunion or retreat. Horseback riding is available at a nearby ranch. Fishing, historic mission church, trading post, and museum are within minutes. Flathead Lake and the People's Cultural Center nearby. Glacier Park is only 90 minutes away. No smoking allowed. No pets allowed. Children over six are welcome. No host. $35 per person.

SEELEY LAKE

Bed and Breakfast Western Adventure

P.O. Box 4308, Bozeman, 59772
(406) 585-0557; FAX (406) 585-2869

This majestic 11,000-square-foot gabled brick lodge commands a spectacular view of the sunny valley tucked between the ranges of the Rocky Mountains at the headwaters of the Columbia River. The house overlooks a private lake amid meadows, forests, and streams. Wide porches wrap around the lodge and woodland paths offer visitors the peace and tranquility of the beautiful Montana wilderness. Five guest rooms, two with private baths, are handsomely decorated with period furniture, feather duvets, fresh flowers, and fine art. A two-bedroom family suite with kitchen on the lower level and the original homestead cabin are also available. Boating, rafting, canoeing, and fishing are available at nearby Seeley Lake. Excellent wildlife and bird-watching opportunities. Fishing guide can be arranged. No smoking allowed. Full breakfast served. $85.

STEVENSVILLE

Bed and Breakfast
Western Adventure

P.O. Box 4308, Bozeman, 59772
(406) 585-0557; FAX (406) 585-2869

135. *Handsome* and *charming* are words
that come to mind for this lovingly restored
turn-of-the-century schoolhouse. The original entrance and the bell tower can still be
seen; traditional furnishings are complimented with antiques. The home sits on a beautiful prairie. The Bitterroot and Sapphire
Mountain Ranges are its backdrop, and a
meticulously pampered yard is surrounded
by neat Western fencing. One guest room
with a king-size bed has a private whirlpool
shower bath. Near the Metcalf Wildlife
Refuge. Only sixty minutes from Lost Trail
Ski Area. Guests have fishing access to the
Bitterroot River. Carriage rides with a beautiful Clydesdale horse can be arranged. No
smoking allowed. No guest pets allowed.
Dog in residence. Continental plus breakfast
served. $65.

SULA

Camp Creek Inn Bed and
Breakfast Guest Ranch

7674 Highway 93 South, 58971
(406) 821-3508; FAX (406) 821-3808

Old-fashioned Western comfort awaits
guests at this 160-acre ranch and one-time
stage stop. Accommodations include three
guest rooms in the original 1920 ranch
house and two cabins with kitchens. A delicious and hearty ranch breakfast is included
with all stays. Guided horseback rides and
stalls for guest horses are available in the
summer. More than one hundred miles of
gorgeous Bitterroot Forest trails surround
the ranch, including the breathtaking
Continental Divide trail. Ski packages are
available with Lost Trail Powder Mountain,

which is only nine miles away. Lunch is
available during the summer.

Hosts: Sandy Skorupa; Jeff and Ronda Lang
Rooms: 5 (4 PB; 1 SB) $55-65
Full Breakfast
Credit Cards: None
Notes: 2, 5, 7, 8, 9, 11, 13, 14

THREE FORKS

Bed and Breakfast
Western Adventure

P.O. Box 4308, Bozeman, 59772
(406) 585-0557; FAX (406) 585-2869

252. This stately three-story 1910 hotel was
acclaimed to be the most opulent and luxurious in Montana in the early 1900s. Brass
lamps and the warm glow of polished wood
beams are a testimony to its former elegance. A large veranda fronts the inn and
invites guests to lounge in one of the deck
chairs. The inn's 33 rooms, all with private
baths, are attractively decorated with period
antiques and modern comforts. Hot tub
available. Restaurant open year-round; ask
for reservations. Roll aways available. The
Madison, Gallatin, and Jefferson Rivers
join to form the Missouri River at Three
Forks, making this an angler's dream and a
photographer's paradise. The inn and surrounding area are steeped in Lewis and
Clark history. Small conferences can be
arranged. No smoking. Pets restricted. Dog
in residence. Continental plus breakfast.
$65-85.

VICTOR

Bed and Breakfast
Western Adventure

P.O. Box 4308, Bozeman, 59772
(406) 585-0557; FAX (406) 585-2869

193. This handsome cedar-sided guest
house, adjacent to the main house, is on
160 acres on the Bitterroot River. It is

7 No smoking; 8 Children welcome; 9 Social drinking allowed; 10 Tennis nearby; 11 Swimming nearby;
12 Golf nearby; 13 Skiing nearby; 14 May be booked through a travel agent.

beautifully appoint.ч with a large porch and breathtaking views in all directions. Two guest rooms share a bath. There is a full kitchen, living area with TV and radio, and a wood stove. In the meadows are two Norwegian fjord horses and a pond with ducks and geese. Hiking in the Bitterroot-Selway Wilderness, blue-ribbon stream fishing, horseback riding, and river rafting can be arranged. Cross-country and downhill skiing are an hour away. Two dogs in residence. Continental plus breakfast. $90.

WEST GLACIER

Mountain Timbers

P.O. Box 94, 59936
(406) 387-5830; (800) 841-3835
FAX (406) 387-5835

On 260 acres, surrounded by national forest, a magnificent log lodge hideaway provides spectacular vistas into Glacier National Park only seven miles away. Features include massive stone fireplaces in comfortable seating areas, Jacuzzi, video and game rooms, library, 15k of private cross-country skiing, hiking, and mountain biking trails. Convenient to downhill skiing, snowmobiling, rafting, fishing, hiking, horseback riding, golfing, shopping, restaurants, and water slides.

Hosts: Don Fleenor and Karen Schweitzer
Rooms: 7 (4 PB; 3 SB) $55-125
Full Breakfast
Credit Cards: A, B
Notes: 2, 5, 7, 8, 9, 12, 13, 14

WEST YELLOWSTONE

Bed and Breakfast Western Adventure

P.O. Box 4308, Bozeman, 59772
(406) 585-0557; FAX (406) 585-2869

230. This home holds lots of country and sportsman's appeal from the wraparound

porch to the mix of its style and furnishings of Colonial, farm, and rustic. Its exquisitely decorated rooms offer a haven of welcome and warmth while viewing majestic mountains and abundant wildlife from birds to moose, frequently seen in the backyard. Yellowstone National Park is eight miles away; the Madison and Gallatin Rivers and Hebgen and Henrys Lakes are within 30 minutes. Five rooms are available with private baths. Three housekeeping cabins are also available for family or group use, three-day minimum. Children are welcome in the cabins. Easy and close access to Yellowstone National Park, trout streams, lakes, and hiking trails. Cross-country skiing and snowmobiling in winter. Outdoor hot tub, terry robes. Fly-tying facilities available. No smoking. No pets. Children over 12 welcome. Three dogs in residence. Full breakfast. $85-95.

Sportsman's High

Sportsman's High Bed and Breakfast

750 Deer Street, 59758
(406) 646-7865; FAX (406) 646-9434

Charming accommodations with antique furnishings and a country decor welcome each visitor. This haven, with its spectacular mountain views, wildlife, wraparound porch, and acreage of quaking aspen and pines, is only eight miles from the west entrance to Yellowstone National Park. A stay here is further enhanced by such fine amenities as feather pillows, terry-cloth robes, outdoor hot tub, and a full, hot delicious breakfast that is worth bouncing out of bed for.

Hosts: Diana and Gary Baxter
Rooms: 5 (PB) $75-95
Full Breakfast
Credit Cards: A, B, C
Notes: 2, 5, 7, 10, 11, 12, 13

WHITEFISH

Bed and Breakfast Western Adventure

P.O. Box 4308, Bozeman, 59772
(406) 585-0557; FAX (406) 585-2869

161. This rustic ranch home sits in a lovely meadow with the Mission Mountains of Glacier Park as a backdrop. The home boasts two fireplaces, one in the recreation room that provides access to the outdoor hot tub. Three guest rooms with queen-size beds and private baths are beautifully decorated in distinctive motifs. Airport and Amtrack pickup. Minutes from groomed cross-country ski trails, Big Mountain Ski Resort, and West Glacier Park entrance. No smoking. No pets. A delicious full gourmet breakfast is served. $65-115.

Castle Bed and Breakfast

900 South Baker, 59937
(406) 862-1257

Enjoy one of three comfortable guest rooms in this home that is listed on the National Register of Historic Places. The Castle has unusual architecture and charm. Breakfasts are hearty and tempting and include delicious homemade breads and freshly ground gourmet coffee to complement the featured menu of the day. The Castle is only nine miles from the Big

Castle

Mountain Ski Resort and 25 miles from Glacier National Park.

Hosts: Jim and Pat Egan
Rooms: 3 (1 PB; 2 SB) $63-98
Full Breakfast
Credit Cards: A, B, D
Notes: 2, 7, 9, 10, 11, 12, 13

Good Medicine Lodge

537 Wisconsin Avenue, 59937
(800) 860-5488; FAX (406) 862-5489

A classic Montana getaway hewn from solid cedar timbers has nine guest rooms with private baths, direct-dial telephones, balconies, mountain views, custom-made lodgepole beds, hearty breakfasts, laundry, and ski room. Only minutes from guests' favorite outdoor activity, shopping, dining, the airport, and Amtrak. Relax in front of crackling fireplaces or unwind in the outdoor spa. AAA rated three diamonds. Handicapped accessible.

Hosts: Christopher and Susan Ridder
Rooms: 9 (PB) $75-95
Full Breakfast
Credit Cards: A, B
Notes: 2, 7, 8, 9, 10, 11, 12, 13, 14

---

7 No smoking; 8 Children welcome; 9 Social drinking allowed; 10 Tennis nearby; 11 Swimming nearby; 12 Golf nearby; 13 Skiing nearby; 14 May be booked through a travel agent.

WHITE SULPHUR SPRINGS

Bed and Breakfast Western Adventure

P.O. Box 4308, Bozeman, 59772
(406) 585-0557; FAX (406) 585-2869

248. This handsome and stately cedar-sided lodge is in a beautiful wooded area of the Little Belt Mountains, conveniently between Yellowstone and Glacier National Parks. Ideal for a serene getaway or the more stimulating activities of summer and winter sport recreation prevalent in this area. Five attractively decorated guest rooms, each with private bath, have views of the surrounding forest and mountains. Snowmobiling on 200 miles of groomed snowmobile trails, fishing in nearby Smith River. Ten miles from alpine and Nordic skiing at Showdown. Guided fishing, hunting, horseback riding, or eco/wildlife viewing tours by prior arrangement. Dinner available with advance notice. No smoking allowed. No guest pets allowed. Full breakfast served. $70.

The Columns

The Columns

19 East Wright Street, P.O. Box 611, 59645
(406) 547-3666

Recently renovated red brick 1882 private home with an eclectic blend of yesterday's charm and today's comfort in the middle of cow country. Big Sky hospitality at its best. Delicious ranch-style breakfasts. Children over six welcome.

Host: Dale N. McAfee
Rooms: 3 (1 PB; 2 SB) $35-50
Full Breakfast
Credit Cards: A, B
Notes: 2, 5, 7, 9, 10, 11, 12, 13, 14

Nebraska

BEATRICE

The Carriage House Bed and Breakfast

Rural Route 1, Box 136 B, 68310
(402) 228-0356

This beautiful 18-room Georgian mansion filled with 1800s antiques is nestled in the quiet countryside on the edge of Beatrice. Enjoy a ride through the countryside in a horse-drawn carriage; tour the shop and experience the craft of restoring carriages. View the crimson sunset from the swing on the porch or unwind with a stroll through the garden to the gazebo. Awake to the aroma of a delicious home-cooked breakfast after spending a restful night in one of the six guest rooms. Inquire about accommodations for pets. Smoking permitted on porches. Children ten and over welcome.

Hosts: Floyd and Jody Forke
Rooms: 6 (1 PB; 5 SB) $49.28-65.70
Full Breakfast
Credit Cards: A, B
Notes: 2, 10, 11, 12

BREWSTER

Sandhills Country Cabin

HC 63, Box 13, DeGroff Ranch, 68821
(308) 547-2460

Rustic cabin with a comfortable, quiet country setting has private shower and kitchen. One bedroom has queen-size bed. Old barn has three bedrooms, one with private bath and two rooms with shared tub and shower, kitchen, and living room, beautiful view. Inquire about accommodations for pets. No children under seven.

Hosts: Lee and Beverly DeGroff
Rooms: 4 (2 PB; 2 SB) $60-75
Full Breakfast
Credit Cards: None
Notes: 2, 4, 5, 7, 9

BROKEN BOW

Pine Cone Lodge

Route 2, Box 156 C, 68822
(308) 872-6407

The lodge is nestled among pine and spruce at the edge of town, providing a quiet country atmosphere. Each of the three rooms is unique in its decor. Bay windows in the dining room afford a wonderful view of the outdoors while guests enjoy a full breakfast that features homemade breads, jellies, and syrups. A peaceful respite with warm Western hospitality. Children over ten are welcome.

Host: Helen Reiber
Rooms: 3 (1 PB; 2 SB) $40-45
Full Breakfast
Credit Cards: None
Notes: 2, 5, 7, 10, 11, 12

CRETE

The Parson's House

638 Forest Avenue, 68333
(402) 826-2634

Enjoy warm hospitality in a restored four-square home built at the turn of the century in a quiet neighborhood near Doane College and its beautiful campus.

7 No smoking; 8 Children welcome; 9 Social drinking allowed; 10 Tennis nearby; 11 Swimming nearby; 12 Golf nearby; 13 Skiing nearby; 14 May be booked through a travel agent.

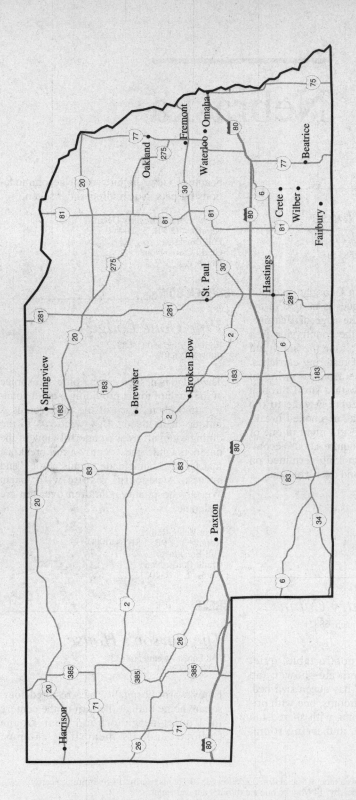

Nebraska

Furnished with much antique furniture and a modern whirlpool bathtub. A full breakfast is served in the formal dining room.

Host: Sandy Richardson
Rooms: 2 (SB) $35
Full Breakfast
Credit Cards: None
Notes: 2, 5, 7, 10, 11, 12

FAIRBURY

Personett House Bed and Breakfast Inn

615 Sixth Street, 68352-2406
(402) 729-2902

Built sometime before 1904, the Personett House was formerly a boarding house run by Susie Personett from 1916 to 1941. During World War II the Jefferson County Chapter of the Red Cross acquired the house and used it for various war-related purposes. Clothing and first aid articles were assembled for shipment to England, and training courses in first aid were also offered. The Personett House is one block from downtown and offers seven lovely guest rooms with individual air conditioners and shared baths. Smoking is allowed downstairs on the porch.

Host: Jean Paneitz
Rooms: 7 (SB) $35
Continental Breakfast
Credit Cards: None
Notes: 2, 5, 8, 9, 10, 11, 12

FREMONT

Bed and Breakfast of Fremont

1624 East 25th Street, Rural Route 4, 68025
(402) 727-9534

The Bed and Breakfast of Fremont is a two-story Colonial home on four and one-half acres. Guest facilities include five private bedrooms, sitting room, upper balcony, and lower-level Garden Room.

Guests may enjoy breakfast in the formal dining room or garden room, depending on the season.

Hosts: Dr. Paul and Linda Von Behren
Rooms: 5 (1 PB; 4 SB) $49-69
Full Breakfast
Credit Cards: None
Notes: 2, 5, 7, 8, 10, 11, 12, 14

HARRISON

Sowbelly Bed and Breakfast Hideaway

407 Sowbelly Road, P.O. Box 292, 69346
(308) 668-2537

A beautiful, secluded, partially earth-sheltered home is in Sowbelly Canyon in northwestern Nebraska, the Pineridge area five miles northeast of Harrison. Two bedrooms, queen-size beds, and two baths. Watch nature from inside the huge glassed doors or sit on the patio in the quietness of country living. No smoking indoors. Big country breakfast. Golf is 20 miles away.

Hosts: Morris and Alda Engebretsen
Rooms: 2 (PB) $35
Full Breakfast
Credit Cards: None
Notes: 2, 3, 4, 5, 8, 9, 11

HASTINGS

Grandma's Victorian Inn Bed and Breakfast

1826 West 3rd Street, 68901
(402) 462-2013

Built circa 1886, this Victorian home has an open staircase and outstanding woodwork. For guests' comfort, each room has a private bath. Antique furniture is exhibited in the home with an accent on rocking chairs and queen-size beds within each room. Enjoy a lemonade on the beautiful balcony or relax in the front porch swings. Breakfast is served in the dining room; breakfast in

NOTES: Credit cards: A MasterCard; B Visa; C American Express; D Discover; E Diners Club; F Other; 2 Personal checks accepted; 3 Lunch available; 4 Dinner available; 5 Open all year; 6 Pets welcome; 7 No smoking; 8 Children welcome; 9 Social drinking allowed; 10 Tennis nearby; 11 Swimming nearby; 12 Golf nearby; 13 Skiing nearby; 14 May be booked through a travel agent.

bed can be arranged at additional charge. Return to the memories of yore and "whispers of yesterday." Children over 12 are welcome.

Manager/Innkeeper: Marilyn DiMartino
Rooms: 5 (PB) $60
Full Breakfast
Credit Cards: A, B, D
Notes: 2, 5, 10, 11, 12

OAKLAND

Benson Bed and Breakfast

402 North Oakland Avenue, 68045
(402) 685-6051

Built as a rooming house in 1905, the Benson was always a flurry of activity. On the main level is a craft and gift shop and also a beauty salon. Upstairs there are 16 rooms, softly decorated and furnished in a traditional antique motif. Family room has a large collection of soft drink collectibles. Breakfast served at a time to please the traveling guests in a beautiful, large dining room. The large bathroom has a whirlpool tub for two and color TV on the wall. A relaxing time awaits guests at Benson Bed and Breakfast, three blocks west of Highway 77. One more thing—the coffee pot is always brewing. Children over 12 are welcome.

Hosts: Stan and Norma Anderson
Rooms: 3 (SB) $45-55
Full Breakfast
Credit Cards: None
Notes: 2, 5, 7, 10, 11, 12, 14

OMAHA

The Jones's

1617 South 90th Street, 68124
(402) 397-0721

Large private residence with deck and gazebo in the back. Fresh homemade cinnamon rolls are served for breakfast. Horse racing nearby in summer as well as several golf courses and Boys Town.

Hosts: Don and Theo Jones
Rooms: 3 (1 PB; 2 SB) $25
Continental Breakfast
Credit Cards: None
Notes: 2, 5, 6, 8, 9, 10, 12

The Offutt House

140 North 39th Street, 68131
(402) 553-0951

This comfortable mansion, built in 1894, is in the section of large homes built around the same time by Omaha's most wealthy residents. Rooms are comfortably spacious and furnished with antiques. Some feature fireplaces. The house is near downtown Omaha and the historic Old Market area, which offers many beautiful shops and excellent restaurants. Full breakfast on Sundays. Reservations required.

Host: Jeannie K. Swoboda
Rooms: 7 (PB) $45-85
Full or Continental Breakfast
Credit Cards: A, B, C
Notes: 2, 5, 8, 9, 10, 11, 12, 14

The Offutt House

PAXTON

Gingerbread Inn

212 South Oak, P.O. Box 247, 69155
(308) 239-4265

Guests are invited to enjoy warm hospitality and relax in the atmosphere of a bygone era. Take a leisurely stroll through the yard, featuring flower gardens, trees, a beautiful gazebo, and picnic grounds, or sit and relax on the porch swing. Among the special touches are gingerbread boys or girls greeting guests at the breakfast table. For guests' added comfort a garden room and gift shop were added in 1995. Continental breakfast is served before 7 A.M.

Host: Gwen Meyer
Rooms: 5 (2 PB; 3 SB) $40-55
Full and Continental Breakfast
Credit Cards: A, B
Notes: 2, 5, 7, 10, 11

ST. PAUL

Miss Lizzie's Boardin' House

1023 Kendall Street, 68873
(308) 754-4137

Built in 1890, this history-rich home formerly served as a boarding house. Recently renovated, Miss Lizzie's is tastefully decorated with heirlooms, antiques, and Victorian accents throughout. Upon arrival, guests immediately feel welcome in this unique family home. Guests may choose to curl up with a good book and relax in the parlor or perhaps indulge with a bubble bath in the antique claw-foot tub. Enjoy delicious evening desserts and bountiful breakfasts served on antique china.

Host: Elizabeth King
Rooms: 2 (SB) $50
Full Breakfast
Credit Cards: None
Notes: 2, 5, 8, 9, 11, 12

SIDNEY

Snuggle Inn

1516 Jackson, 69162
(308) 254-0500; FAX (308) 254-7813

Comfortable elegance in the peaceful serenity of the plains is what guests will find as they visit this bed and breakfast right off I-80. Cabel's retail store's wildlife display, Fort Sidney's museum, and Colonel's home are just examples of the

nearby attractions. A full breakfast includes fresh breads, potatoes, eggs, breakfast meats, fresh fruit, and beverages. AAA three-diamond rating.

Hosts: Scott and Angelyn Nienhuser
Rooms: 4 (PB) $60-65
Full Breakfast
Credit Cards: A, B, D
Notes: 2, 3, 4, 5, 7, 9

SPALDING

Esch Haus

Rural Route 1, Box 140, 68665
(308) 497-2628

The Esch Haus is a new home, built in 1986, and has all the advantages of modern living. An A-frame construction permits a beautiful view from the loft that consists of three bedrooms, a central living area, and bath. One bedroom is on the first floor. A deck surrounds the house and is used for breakfast and relaxing when weather permits. Breakfast is renowned for cinnamon rolls baked fresh each morning. Birthdays and anniversaries are celebrated with a bottle of wine and balloons.

Host: Cora Esch
Rooms: 5 (SB) $35
Full Breakfast
Credit Cards: None
Notes: 2, 5, 7, 8, 9, 10, 11, 12

SPRINGVIEW

Big Canyon Inn

HC 82, Box 107, 68778
(402) 497-3160; (800) 437-6023

Big Canyon Inn sets atop the Niobrara River Canyons. The Niobrara River area is the largest canoeing spot in Nebraska. The Big Canyon Inn is there to serve guests for one night of quiet rest or an exciting weekend of canoeing, sightseeing, hiking, and hunting. Four rooms in a lovely remodeled ranch-style home in the country for guests' enjoyment. Inquire about facilities for pets.

7 No smoking; 8 Children welcome; 9 Social drinking allowed; 10 Tennis nearby; 11 Swimming nearby; 12 Golf nearby; 13 Skiing nearby; 14 May be booked through a travel agent.

Hosts: Roger and Edith Wentworth
Rooms: 4 (SB) $36-50
Full Breakfast
Credit Cards: None
Notes: 2, 5, 7, 8, 12, 13

WATERLOO

The J. C. Robinson House

102 East Lincoln Avenue, 68069-0190
(402) 779-2704; (800) 779-2705

Just a 12-mile drive from Omaha, the J. C.
Robinson House is an elegant 21-room
Greek Revival home boasting Ionic
columns and a front balcony. The inn, surrounded by 100-year-old trees, is on the
National Register of Historic Places.
Antiques, collectibles from all over the
world, and a stunning clock collection dating back to 1735 set off the attractive interior. Fishing, bicycling, and canoeing are
within a stone's throw, or guests may stroll
the historic villages, its famous restaurants,
and antique shops. Inquire about accommodations for pets. Children over 12 welcome.

Hosts: Linda and Bill Clark
Rooms: 4 (1 PB; 3 SB) $50-75
Full and Continental Breakfast
Credit Cards: None
Notes: 2, 4, 5, 7, 9, 12, 14

WILBER

Hotel Wilber
Bed and Breakfast Inn

Second and Wilson Streets, P.O. Box 641, 68465
(402) 821-2020; (800) 609-4663

Escape to tranquility at this 1895 hotel, now
a bed and breakfast in nostalgic Wilber,
Nebraska, Czech capital of the United
States. Just 40 minutes from Lincoln, and
90 minutes from Omaha. Soothing country-
and Victorian-style antique-furnished rooms
await, each with cable TV and individually
controlled air and heating. Relax in the
charming pub, garden, lobby, or dining
room where sumptuous breakfasts are
served each morning. Traditional Czech and
American cuisines are offered weekends
and by appointment. Baths are all shared
with separate his and her shower, plus
rooms and two separate commodes. Inquire
about pets. Restricted smoking.

Host: Frances Erb
Rooms: 10 (SB) $42-65
Full Breakfast
Credit Cards: A, B
Notes: 2, 5, 8, 9, 10, 11, 12, 14

NOTES: Credit cards accepted: A MasterCard; B Visa; C American Express; D Discover; E Diners Club;
F Other; 2 Personal checks accepted; 3 Lunch available; 4 Dinner available; 5 Open all year; 6 Pets welcome;

Nevada

Deer Run Ranch

CARSON CITY (WASHOE VALLEY)_____

Deer Run Ranch Bed and Breakfast

5440 Eastlake Boulevard, 89704
(702) 882-3643

Western ambience in a unique architect-designed ranch house on spacious grounds, between Reno and Carson City. Just minutes from Lake Tahoe and Virginia City. Pond with a boat for summer, skating in winter. Above-ground pool and lots of privacy on 200 acres.

Hosts: David and Muffy Vhay
Rooms: 2 (PB) $80-95
Full Breakfast
Credit Cards: A, B, C
Notes: 2, 5, 7, 9, 11, 12, 13

EAST ELY _____

Steptoe Valley Inn

P.O. Box 151110, 220 East 11th Street, 89315-1110
(702) 289-8687 (June-September)
(702) 435-1196 (October-May)

Elegantly reconstructed in 1990 from the Ely City Grocery of 1907, this inn is one-half block from the Nevada Northern Railway Museum with its weekend train excursions, and 70 miles from the Great Basin National Park. Its individually decorated guest rooms are on the second floor and have private balconies with views of the mountains and valley or the gazebo and rose garden. Guests have use of the veranda, Victorian living/dining room, and library. Jeep rental available. Open June through September.

Hosts: Jane and Norman Lindley
Rooms: 5 (PB) $79-85
Full Breakfast
Credit Cards: A, B, C
Notes: 2, 7, 12, 14

Steptoe Valley Inn

GENOA _____

The Genoa House Inn Bed and Breakfast

180 Nixon Street, P.O. Box 141, 89411
(702) 782-7075

The Genoa House Inn is an authentic Victorian home listed on the National Register of Historic Places. The house has been restored to the charm and tranquility

7 No smoking; 8 Children welcome; 9 Social drinking allowed; 10 Tennis nearby; 11 Swimming nearby;
12 Golf nearby; 13 Skiing nearby; 14 May be booked through a travel agent.

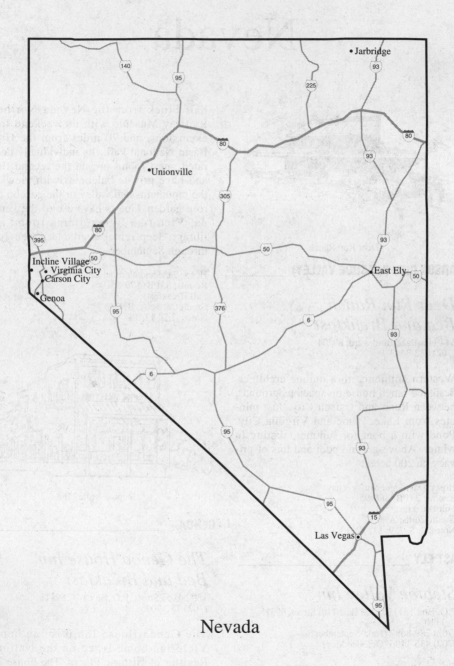

- Jarbridge
- Unionville
- Incline Village
- Virginia City
- Carson City
- Genoa
- East Ely
- Las Vegas

Nevada

of an earlier time. Take a romantic step into the past, and enjoy the gracious accommodations accented by antiques and collectibles. Wine in the afternoon, a coffee tray delivered to room, followed by a full breakfast, and the use of Walley's Hot Springs spa are all included.

Hosts: Bob and Linda Sanfilippo
Rooms: 3 (PB) $99-130
Full Breakfast
Credit Cards: A, B, C
Notes: 2, 5, 7, 9, 10, 11, 12, 13

Wild Rose Inn

P.O. Box 256, 2332 Main Street, 89411
(702) 782-5697

A Queen Anne Victorian set on the eastern foothills of the Sierra Nevada Mountains overlooking the Carson Valley. Guests enjoy comfortable, spacious rooms with lovely views, complimentary use of nearby mineral hot springs, and delicious buffet breakfasts.

Hosts: Joe and Sandi Antonucci
Rooms: 5 (PB) $95-115
Full Breakfast
Credit Cards: A, B, C
Notes: 2, 5, 9, 10, 11, 12, 13

INCLINE VILLAGE

Haus Bavaria

P.O. Box 3308, 89450
(702) 831-6122; (800) 731-6222
FAX (702) 831-1238

Haus Bavaria is a European-style guest house, built in 1980. Each of the five upstairs guest rooms opens onto a balcony, offering a view of the surrounding mountains, while the living room, with its rustic wood paneling and collection of German bric-a-brac, retains an alpine charm. Breakfast is served in the cozy dining room downstairs and includes freshly baked goods, seasonal fruits and juices, freshly ground coffee, and a selection of teas.

Host: Bick Hewitt
Rooms: 5 (PB) $90-150
Full Breakfast
Credit Cards: A, B, C, D
Notes: 2, 5, 7, 9, 10, 11, 12, 13, 14

JARBRIDGE

Tsawhawbitts Ranch Bed and Breakfast

P.O. Box 260090, 89826
(702) 488-2338

In the beautiful Jarbridge Canyon of the Humboldt National Forest Wilderness area, Tsawhawbitts Ranch is 100 miles from Twin Falls, Idaho, and Elko, Nevada. It is one of the last untouched Western ghost towns of the Old West, and the site of the last horse-drawn stagecoach robbery in the United States. Guided horse and hunting trips available. Lunch and dinner available on request.

Hosts: Krinn and Chuck McCoy
Rooms: 9 (2 PB; 7 SB) $65-100
Full Breakfast
Credit Cards: A, B
Notes: 2, 5, 7, 8, 9, 11, 13

LAS VEGAS

Mi Casa Su Casa

P.O. Box 950, Tempe, Arizona 85280-0950
(602) 990-0682; (800) 456-0682

334. This large 1950 home with a Southwestern-style exterior is in an established quiet neighborhood within two miles of the Strip. Hostess is an interior designer. Antiques are blended with other lovely furnishings throughout this bed and breakfast. Two guest rooms with two hall baths are available. Bicycles are also on hand for guests to use if they desire. Prefer two-night minimum stay on weekends. Full breakfast served. Smoking is permitted outside only. $50-55.

NOTES: Credit cards: A MasterCard; B Visa; C American Express; D Discover; E Diners Club; F Other; 2 Personal checks accepted; 3 Lunch available; 4 Dinner available; 5 Open all year; 6 Pets welcome; 7 No smoking; 8 Children welcome; 9 Social drinking allowed; 10 Tennis nearby; 11 Swimming nearby; 12 Golf nearby; 13 Skiing nearby; 14 May be booked through a travel agent.

UNIONVILLE

Old Pioneer Garden Country Inn

79 Main Street, 89418
(702) 538-7585

The main house includes three guest rooms, and across the field, the Hadley House guest cottage provides six additional bedrooms and a shared library, farm kitchen, and spacious sitting room. The emphasis is on country with all the right touches: brass, iron, and oak beds; fireplaces; old trunks; and window sills filled with baskets of dried flowers. Full breakfast is served at the eight-foot-long wooden table in the large kitchen that is warmed by an old-fashioned wood stove. Lots of farm animals. Call regarding children and pets. Closed January and February.

Hosts: Lew and Mitzi Jones
Rooms: 9 (3 PB; 6 SB) $65-75
Full Breakfast
Credit Cards: None
Notes: 2, 3, 4, 6, 8, 9, 12, 14

VIRGINIA CITY

Gold Hill Hotel

Highway 342, P.O. Box 710, 89440
(702) 847-0111

The Gold Hill Hotel is Nevada's oldest hotel, circa 1859. This country inn is a wonderful combination of luxury and rustic charm, placed in a setting that is fascinating for its history, beauty, and personalities. Guests enjoy a range of accommodations: some share an antique claw-foot tub, some have spacious rooms with fireplaces. All rooms are decorated with period antiques. Fabulous dinners accented with a choice of over 160 wines create a memorable escape.

Hosts: Doug and Carol McQuide
Rooms: 13 (11 PB; 2 SB) $35-135
Continental Breakfast
Credit Cards: A, B
Notes: 2, 4, 5, 8, 12, 13, 14

NOTES: Credit cards accepted: A MasterCard; B Visa; C American Express; D Discover; E Diners Club;
F Other; 2 Personal checks accepted; 3 Lunch available; 4 Dinner available; 5 Open all year; 6 Pets welcome;

New Hampshire

ALEXANDRIA

Stone Rest Bed and Breakfast

652 Fowler River Road, 03222
(603) 744-6066

Contemporary home in a rural setting on 14 acres with 200 feet on a mountain stream with swimming hole. Close to Newfound Lake, Mount Cardigan, Ragged Mountain, shopping, and other major tourist attractions. Adjacent cottage and studio units also available. Hearty country breakfasts. Barbecue grills, picnic tables, horseshoes, and volleyball on grounds. Videos, library, and much more. Individual heat.

Hosts: Dick and Peg Clarke
Rooms: 7 (5 PB; 2 SB) $38-60
Full Breakfast
Credit Cards: None
Notes: 2, 5, 7, 8, 9, 10, 11, 12, 13

ANDOVER

The English House

Main Street, P.O. Box 162, 03216-0162
(603) 735-5987

The English House

The goal of the hosts is to combine Old England (Del is an "English gentleman") with New England hospitality (Karen is a Yankee). This atmosphere is created in the seven-bedroom inn offering traditional furnishings, hand-crafted quilts and afghans, plus a breakfast featuring daily hot specialties from hosts' favorite Old World cookbooks. All this is found in an idyllic New Hampshire setting. Children over ten welcome.

Hosts: Karen and Del Newman
Rooms: 7 (PB) $85
Full Breakfast
Notes: 2, 5, 7, 9, 11, 12, 13

ANTRIM

The Steele Homestead Inn

125 Keene Road, 03440
(603) 588-2215

Enjoy warm, personal hospitality in this beautifully restored 1810 home. Lovely decor throughout, and the home is filled with antiques. Three spacious guest rooms with private baths are available, two with fireplace. Friendly, relaxed, smoke-free atmosphere. Healthy gourmet breakfast.

Hosts: Barbara and Carl Beehner
Rooms: 3 (PB) $60-68
Full Breakfast
Credit Cards: A, B
Notes: 2, 5, 8, 9, 11, 12, 13, 14

ASHLAND

Glynn House Victorian Inn

P.O. Box 719, 43 Highland Street, 03217
(603) 968-3775; (800) 637-9599

7 No smoking; 8 Children welcome; 9 Social drinking allowed; 10 Tennis nearby; 11 Swimming nearby; 12 Golf nearby; 13 Skiing nearby; 14 May be booked through a travel agent.

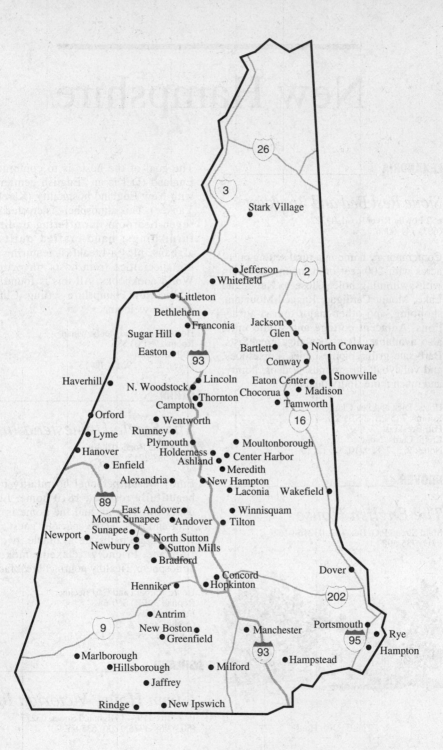

3

Stark Village

Jefferson

Whitefield

2

Littleton

Bethlehem

Franconia

Jackson

Sugar Hill

Glen

Easton

Bartlett

North Conway

93

Conway

Lincoln

Eaton Center

Snowville

Haverhill

N. Woodstock

Thornton

Chocorua

Madison

Campton

Tamworth

Orford

Wentworth

16

Lyme

Rumney

Hanover

Plymouth

Moultonborough

Holderness

Center Harbor

Enfield

Ashland

Meredith

Alexandria

New Hampton

Laconia

Wakefield

89

East Andover

Winnisquam

Mount Sunapee

Andover

Tilton

Newport

Sunapee

North Sutton

Newbury

Sutton Mills

Bradford

Dover

Concord

Henniker

Hopkinton

202

Antrim

9

New Boston

Manchester

Portsmouth

Greenfield

95

Rye

Marlborough

93

Hampstead

Hampton

Hillsborough

Milford

Jaffrey

Rindge

New Ipswich

New Hampshire

Step back in time to Victorian yesteryear. A romantic escape in the heart of the White Mountains and *On Golden Pond* Lakes Region of New Hampshire. Come enjoy the local colors of each season. Seven gracious bedrooms with private baths. Jacuzzi and fireplace amenities. Gourmet breakfast is served. Waterville Valley and Loon Mountain close by. Just two hours from Boston; I-94, exit 24.

Hosts: Karol and Betsy Paterman
Rooms: 5 (PB) $75-135
Full Breakfast
Credit Cards: A, B, E
Notes: 2, 5, 7, 9, 10, 11, 12, 13, 14

The Notchland Inn

Hosts: Les Schoof and Ed Butler
Rooms: 11 (PB) $120-200
Full Breakfast
Credit Cards: A, B, C, D
Notes: 2, 4, 5, 7, 9, 10, 11, 12, 13, 14

BETHLEHEM

Adair Country Inn

Old Littleton Road, 03574
(603) 444-2600; (800) 441-2606
FAX (603) 444-4823

Adair Country Inn is of classic Georgian Colonial Revival design and offers extensive gardens and landscaping originally designed by the Olmsted Brothers of Boston's Emerald Neckland and New York's Central Park fame. There are dramatic views of the Presidential and Dalton Mountain ranges in addition to terrific breakfasts, an all-weather tennis court, and strolling paths. Golf, skiing, hiking, and fine shops are nearby. Evening dining is available in season. Adair is a recipient of the prestigious AAA four-diamond award.

Hosts: Pat, Hardy, and Nancy Banfield
Rooms: 8 (PB) $105-175
Full Breakfast
Credit Cards: A, B, C
Notes: 2, 5, 7, 9, 11, 12, 13, 14

Glynn House Victorian Inn

BARTLETT

The Notchland Inn

Hart's Location, 03812
(603) 374-6131; (800) 866-6131

A traditional country inn where hospitality has not been forgotten. There are eleven guest rooms, all with working fireplaces and private baths. Delicious gourmet dining, spectacular mountain views, hiking, cross-country skiing, and swimming are some of the many recreations offered at this secluded mountain estate.

NOTES: Credit cards: A MasterCard; B Visa; C American Express; D Discover; E Diners Club; F Other; 2 Personal checks accepted; 3 Lunch available; 4 Dinner available; 5 Open all year; 6 Pets welcome; 7 No smoking; 8 Children welcome; 9 Social drinking allowed; 10 Tennis nearby; 11 Swimming nearby; 12 Golf nearby; 13 Skiing nearby; 14 May be booked through a travel agent.

The Mulburn Inn

Main Street, Route 302, 03574
(603) 869-3389; (800) 457-9440

Charming inn on historic Woolworth
estate. Spacious warm and comfortable surroundings. Seven elegant rooms, private
baths. Four-season attractions including
hiking, biking, fishing, Storyland, and
Santa's Village for Children. Minutes from
the scenic beauty of Franconia Notch,
Mount Washington, and skiing at Cannon
Mountain and Bretton Woods. Members of
Ski-93. AAA and Mobil approved.

Rooms: 7 (PB) $55-80
Full Breakfast
Credit Cards: A, B, C, D
Notes: 2, 5, 7, 8, 9, 10, 11, 12, 13, 14

New Hampshire Bed and Breakfast

128 South Hoop Pole Road, Guilford, CT 06437
(203) 457-0042; (800) 582-0853

NH135. Built circa 1892, this Victorian "cottage" is a wonderful example of Victorian
ingenuity. Trimmed like a pagoda with bells
and dragons. Complete with veranda and
comfortable rocking chairs, this inn has been
cited by many home and travel magazines.
Guest rooms have overstuffed chairs, touches
of lace and wicker, firm mattresses, and soft,
fluffy towels. Throughout the house, family
heirlooms and memorabilia mix with pleasing surprises. Relax with morning coffee and
enjoy a full breakfast. Seasonal beverages,
sherry, and afternoon tea are always available. Four guest rooms with private baths.
Two suites and one guest cottage. $50-70.

BRADFORD

The Bradford Inn

Main Street, 03221
(603) 938-5309; (800) 669-5309

The Bradford Inn, a restored 1898 small
country hotel, features comfortable lodging
and J. Albert's Restaurant, which serves

Continental-style dining. Fireplaces, large
parlors, wide halls with antiques and personal mementos. Four-season activity area.

Hosts: Connie and Tom Mazol
Rooms: 12 (PB) $59-79
Full Breakfast
Credit Cards: A, B, C, D, E
Notes: 2, 4, 5, 6, 8, 9, 10, 11, 12, 13, 14

Candlelite Inn

Candlelite Inn Bed and Breakfast

Route 114, 5 Greenhouse Lane, 03221
(603) 938-5571

An 1897 country Victorian inn nestled on
three acres in the Lake Sunapee region. A
candlelit breakfast is served in the lovely
dining room or in the sunroom overlooking
a babbling brook and pond. A gazebo porch
is available for lazy summer days, and on
chilly winter evenings, guests can sit by the
cozy fire in the parlor. The inn is nonsmoking. Come and enjoy the relaxed and
friendly atmosphere of the Candlelite Inn.

Hosts: Les and Marilyn Gordon
Rooms: 6 (PB) $65-75
Full Breakfast
Credit Cards: A, B, D
Notes: 2, 5, 8, 9, 10, 11, 12, 13, 14

CAMPTON

Campton Inn

Rural Route 2, Box 12, 03223
(603) 726-4449

In 1836, the Campton Inn was built on
Main Street, the same year Campton

NOTES: Credit cards accepted: A MasterCard; B Visa; C American Express; D Discover; E Diners Club;
F Other; 2 Personal checks accepted; 3 Lunch available; 4 Dinner available; 5 Open all year; 6 Pets welcome;

Village was built. A boarding house and inn since 1880, this classic farmhouse still has its original pine floors, screened porch, large cozy common room with wood stove, and the finest in New England hospitality. A full country breakfast is served. In the heart of the White Mountains with skiing, swimming, biking, hiking, and other recreations found at every corner, or guests can just sit back and relax.

Hosts: Robbin and Peter Adams
Rooms: 6 (1 PB; 5 SB) $50-70
Full Breakfast
Credit Cards: None
Notes: 2, 5, 7, 8, 9, 10, 11, 12, 13, 14

Mountain-Fare Inn

Mad River Road, P.O. Box 553, 03223
(603) 726-4283

Lovely 1840s village home full of the antiques, fabrics, and feel of country cottage living. Flowers and gardens in summer, and foliage in fall; a true skier's lodge in the winter. Accessible, peaceful, warm, friendly, and affordable. Featuring White Peaks Room for honeymoons or special occasions. Hearty breakfasts. Great local dining. Unspoiled beauty from Franconia Notch to Squam Lake. Wonderful four-season sports, music, theater, and wandering in the "Whites."

Hosts: Susan and Nick Preston
Rooms: 10 (7 PB; 3 SB) $50-90
Full Breakfast
Credit Cards: A, D, E
Notes: 2, 5, 8, 9, 10, 11, 12, 13, 14

New Hampshire Bed and Breakfast

128 South Hoop Pole Road, Guilford, CT 06437
(203) 457-0042; (800) 582-0853

NH116. Just minutes from I-93, the Waterville Valley four-season resort area, the Franconia Notch State Park, and Plymouth. This large white clapboard farmhouse has gables, a farmer's porch, and a warm hearth. Guests can enjoy the recreational activities in the White Mountains: hiking the marked Appalachian Mountain Club trails, bicycling, snowmobiling, swimming, picnicking, and an excellent selection of alpine and cross-country skiing. The large lawns feature volleyball and croquet sets. Guests are welcome to use the large country living room with fireplace, color cable TV with VCR, games, puzzles, and books. Enjoy a full breakfast and generous seasonal snacks. Ten guest rooms with private baths, three with shared bath. Children welcome. No smoking. $75-105.

Osgood Inn

P.O. Box 419, 03223
(603) 726-3543

The hosts welcome visitors year-round to this warm and gracious village home with four spacious rooms featuring handmade quilts and lovely views. Close to skiing, hiking, golf, shopping, and tourist attractions. Full country breakfast is served in the morning, and afternoon tea is served every day. Charming common room with fireplace, serene gardens, and back porch are available for guests to enjoy. Housekeeping two-bedroom suite available in the Annex. Minutes from I-93.

Hosts: Dexter and Pat Osgood
Rooms: 4 (SB) $50-55
Full Breakfast
Credit Cards: None
Notes: 2, 5, 7, 8, 9, 12, 13

Osgood Inn

7 No smoking; 8 Children welcome; 9 Social drinking allowed; 10 Tennis nearby; 11 Swimming nearby; 12 Golf nearby; 13 Skiing nearby; 14 May be booked through a travel agent.

CENTER HARBOR

New Hampshire Bed and Breakfast

128 South Hoop Pole Road, Guilford, CT 06437
(203) 457-0042; (800) 582-0853

NH215. On 75 beautiful acres on Long Island in the center of Lake Winnipesaukee (connected by bridge). The house was built in the 1830s and was established as an inn in 1874. It is now run by a descendant of the original family. Guests enjoy the 75 acres of lawns, fields, and woods that run to the water's edge, either of two private beaches, the lakeside picnic area, and the large living room with fieldstone fireplace. A hearty country breakfast is served in the dining room. Children welcome. No smoking; no pets. Open from the end of June through September. $60-70.

NH218. Just five minutes from the center of a pleasant village, visitors can enjoy the amenities of this contemporary ranch-style home, yet be surrounded by tall pine trees, singing birds, and a peaceful, wooded setting. Sunbathe or swim at the town beach, take a breakfast cruise on Lake Winnipesaukee, or visit any of the fine craft, antique, and retail shops, including the region's most expansive quilt shop. Enjoy the large screened porch, the living room with fieldstone fireplace, or the den with ample books, magazines, and TV. Continental breakfast. No smoking. No pets. Children welcome. $55-60.

CHOCORUA

New Hampshire Bed and Breakfast

128 South Hoop Pole Road, Guilford, CT 06437
(203) 457-0042; (800) 582-0853

NH107. This spacious hilltop Colonial is on 22 acres of woodlands with majestic views of Mount Chocorua and Ossipee Lake. Relax beside the fire in the living room with a good book, play board games, watch TV, or strike up a tune on the piano. Screened porch; tennis court. Hearty country breakfast. Horseshoes, badminton, croquet, and nature walks. Enjoy hiking, boating, swimming, antiquing, auctions, summer theater, and restaurants. Three guest rooms; shared baths. Rooms have spectacular mountain views, hand-stenciled walls, and antique furnishings. A private guest house with fireplace, deck, kitchen, and wood-burning stove for four guests is also available. Open May-October. $50-75.

CONCORD

New Hampshire Bed and Breakfast

128 South Hoop Pole Road, Guilford, CT 06437
(203) 457-0042; (800) 582-0853

NH610. This large Colonial farmhouse enjoys a hilltop setting and scenic mountain views. The peaceful site out of downtown Concord allows for rest and relaxation, yet guests are only five minutes from the state capitol, outlet shops, restaurants, and nearby colleges and private secondary schools. Three guest rooms, one with a private bath. A den with a TV and wood stove. A large country kitchen, where the home-baked, full breakfast is served. No smoking. Resident cat and dog. Guest pets are welcome. $50-60.

CONWAY

Darby Field Inn

Bald Hill Road, 03818
(603) 447-2181; (800) 426-4147

A charming, out-of-the-way country inn that offers excellent dining, a cozy atmosphere, and spectacular mountain views. An outdoor pool, cross-country ski trails, and a staff that is both friendly and courteous.

Reservations recommended. Rate includes breakfast, tax, and gratuity. Midweek and off-season packages. Minimum stay on weekends is two nights and on holidays is two to three nights. Inquire about accommodations for children.

Hosts: Marc and Maria Donaldson
Rooms: 16 (12 PB; 4 SB) $108-168
Full Breakfast
Credit Cards: A, B, C, E
Notes: 2, 4, 5, 7, 9, 10, 11, 12, 13, 14

Merrill Farm Resort

428 White Mountain Highway, P.O. Box 1340, 03860
(603) 447-3866; (800) 445-1017

Cozy rooms in the main house, all with private baths. Efficiency cottages and spacious loft units with fireplaces. Some non-smoking rooms. Outdoor pool, canoes on the river, in-room whirlpools, conference facilities. All rooms have cable TV and telephones. Relaxed, informal setting (age 17 and under free). Tax-free outlet shopping in a summer and winter recreation area. Three-diamond AAA rating.

Hosts: Lee and Christine Gregory
Rooms: 60 (PB) $39-139
Continental Breakfast
Credit Cards: A, B, C, D, E
Notes: 5, 7, 8, 9, 10, 11, 12, 13, 14

DOVER

New Hampshire Bed and Breakfast

128 South Hoop Pole Road, Guilford, CT 06437
(203) 457-0042; (800) 582-0853

NH410. The charming 100-year-old Queen Anne Victorian offers a special experience for a traveler who wants more than the ordinary. A turned oak staircase and fretwork welcome guests to the turn-of-the-century era. Relax on the tree-shaded porch or enjoy the living room in all seasons. In the seacoast area, convenient to UNH, Portsmouth, Durham, and Maine. Two guest rooms furnished with antiques and a double bed share a full bath. Children over four welcome. No smoking. $45-50.

NH412. A large Victorian country home dating from the mid-19th century, this farm offers comfortable, spacious guest rooms in a unique rural setting. The inn is set among rolling fields with nature trails along the Cacheco River. Guests are welcome to use the antique-filled formal parlor and library. There are horseshoe pits and a volleyball net. Swimming, cross-country skiing, golf, and snowmobiling are available nearby. A full, home-cooked breakfast is complemented by fresh fruits and juices, home-made muffins, breads, scones, and freshly brewed coffee, all served with a touch of Scottish hospitality. Near the seacoast and mountains, near Spaulding Turnpike. Downtown Dover is two miles away and Portsmouth is 15 minutes away. Five guest rooms share two antique baths and are furnished with antiques. No smoking. Children welcome. $70-87.

Silver Street Inn

103 Silver Street, 03820
(603) 743-3000

The inn was once the private home of the Frank B. Williams family of Dover, who decorated it with beautiful imported materials including Spanish mahogany, Austrian

Silver Street Inn

crystal doorknobs, Italian slate, and French Caen stone fireplaces. Host has installed fire alarm and sprinkler systems. Full breakfast. Rooms have private baths, cable TV, and telephones. Open year-round.

Host: Lorene L. Cook
Rooms: 10 (9 PB; 1 SB) $69-89
Full Breakfast
Credit Cards: A, B, C, D, E
Notes: 2, 5, 12

EAST ANDOVER

Bed and Breakfast Marblehead and North Shore

P.O. Box 35, Newtonville, MA 02160
(617) 964-1606; (800) 832-2632
FAX (617) 332-8572

The Lakeside Inn. A Colonial farmhouse dating back to 1800 is in a four-season vacation area. Seasonal activities include fall-foliage hikes, snowmobiling, cross-country skiing, ice skating and fishing, boating, fishing, swimming, and golf. Guest rooms include twin, queen- and king-size beds, all with private baths. Several rooms have fireplaces. The inn is only 23 miles northwest of Concord and easy to reach from Routes 89, 91, or 93. A full breakfast is included. No smoking. Children over eight welcome. Third person in room is $20 additional. $85-100.

EASTON (FRANCONIA)

New Hampshire Bed and Breakfast

128 South Hoop Pole Road, Guilford, CT 06437
(203) 457-0042; (800) 582-0853

NH105. In a beautiful meadow setting, only ten minutes from Franconia Notch, an unadorned, restored Victorian farmhouse. Built in 1887, it was considered haunted by some in the 1940s. Guests will appreciate the decorative painting, stenciling, and glazing. A full breakfast is served in the common room. Minutes from hiking and cross-country skiing on the Appalachian Trail. A day's trip to the attractions of the White Mountains, the Connecticut River Valley, and Vermont. Four guest rooms have shared baths. One room has a private bath. Children are welcome. No smoking allowed. Dog in residence. No guest pets permitted. $65-90.

The Inn at Crystal Lake

EATON CENTER

The Inn at Crystal Lake

Route 153, P.O. Box 12, 03832
(603) 447-2120; (800) 343-7336
FAX (603) 447-3599

Unwind in a restored 1884 country Victorian inn, in a quiet scenic corner of the Mount Washington Valley. Eleven guest rooms are furnished with antiques and have private baths. Relax in the living room with fireplace and large-screen TV or retreat to the antique parlor or library. Swim, fish, sail, canoe, ski, skate, or outlet shop. Limited smoking permitted.

Hosts: Richard and Janice Octeau
Rooms: 11 (PB) $60-130
Full Breakfast
Credit Cards: A, B, C, D, E
Notes: 2, 5, 8, 9, 10, 11, 12, 13, 14

NOTES: Credit cards accepted: A MasterCard; B Visa; C American Express; D Discover; E Diners Club; F Other; 2 Personal checks accepted; 3 Lunch available; 4 Dinner available; 5 Open all year; 6 Pets welcome;

ENFIELD

Boulder Cottage on Crystal Lake

Rural Route 1, Box 257, 03748
(603) 632-7355

A turn-of-the-century Victorian cottage owned by the hosts' family for 70 years. The inn faces beautiful Crystal Lake in the Dartmouth-Sunapee region. Open April through October.

Hosts: Barbara and Harry Reed
Rooms: 3 (2 PB; 1 SB) $45-60
Full Breakfast
Credit Cards: None
Notes: 2, 7, 9, 10, 11, 12

FRANCONIA

Bed and Breakfast Marblehead and North Shore

P.O. Box 35, Newtonville, MA 02160
(617) 964-1606; (800) 832-2632
FAX (617) 332-8572

This English Tudor-style bed and breakfast inn offers gracious hospitality and country casualness year-round. Built in 1890, the historic 18-room inn is at the top of Franconia Notch in the White Mountains, offering breathtaking views of the surrounding mountains and valley landscape. Guests may relax on the covered porch, in the sun-filled solarium, the Alpine Room, or the living room. Most rooms have private baths, and king- or queen-size beds. A three-room suite on the third floor can be taken with a private bath or as three separate rooms with a shared bath. Early morning coffee is provided before breakfast for those who want to walk the trails around the property. A full gourmet breakfast is served. Year-round activities include golf, hiking, swimming, fishing, tennis, boating, horseback riding, alpine skiing, and cycling. Guests can also ski free at the Franconia Touring Center, Bretton Woods, or Loon Mountain. Discount tickets are available for Cannon and Bretton Woods. Children over 11 welcome. Cat in residence. No smoking. $80-95.

Blanche's Bed and Breakfast

351 Easton Valley Road, 03580
(603) 823-7061

Named for the family dog, Blanche's is a sunny, century-old farmhouse restored to a former glory it probably never had. Quiet, pastoral setting with views of the Kinsman Ridge. In the English bed and breakfast tradition, offering cotton linens, down comforters, comfortable beds, and a great breakfast which might include fresh fruit salad, spinach omelet, or blueberry pancakes (with pure maple syrup) and homemade muffins. Decorative painting throughout; working studio featuring unusual handmade floorcloths. Close to all outdoor activities. Dinner available for groups.

Hosts: Brenda Shannon and John Vail
Rooms: 5 (1 PB; 4 SB) $40-85
Full Breakfast
Credit Cards: A, B, C
Notes: 2, 5, 7, 8, 9, 10, 11, 12, 13, 14

Bungay Jar Bed and Breakfast

P.O. Box 15, Easton Valley Road, 03580
(603) 823-7775

Secluded woodlands with spectacular mountain views, brook, and gardens make memorable; this home built from an 18th-

Bungay Jar

7 No smoking; 8 Children welcome; 9 Social drinking allowed; 10 Tennis nearby; 11 Swimming nearby; 12 Golf nearby; 13 Skiing nearby; 14 May be booked through a travel agent.

century barn. King or queen suites, private balconies, skylights, six-foot soaking tub, sauna, canopied bed. Two-story common area with fireplace for reading, music, and talk. Mountain-gaze in the morning sun while breakfasting outside in summer. Small in scale; intimate. Owners are a landscape architect, a patent attorney, and their young son. New cottage with fireplace and Jacuzzi, private setting in the woods, screened porch. Higher rates during foliage season. School-age children welcome.

Owners: Kate Kerivan and Lee Strimbeck
Innkeeper: Janet Engle
Rooms: 6 (4 PB; 2 SB) $65-130
Full Breakfast
Credit Cards: A, B, C, D
Notes: 2, 5, 7, 9, 10, 11, 12, 13

Franconia Inn

Franconia Inn

Easton Road, 03580
(603) 823-5542; (800) 473-5299
FAX (603) 823-8078

A charming inn on 107 acres in the Easton valley, affording breathtaking views of the White Mountains. The inn's 34 rooms are decorated simply, yet beautifully. Elegant American cuisine highlights the inn's quiet country sophistication. Children are welcome. On Route 116. Closed April 1 through May 15.

Hosts: The Morris Family
Rooms: 34 (30 PB; 4 SB) $75-110
Full Breakfast
Credit Cards: A, B, C
Notes: 3, 4, 8, 9, 10, 11, 12, 13, 14

The Hilltop Inn

Route 117, Sugar Hill, 03585
(603) 823-5695; (800) 770-5695
FAX (603) 823-5578

A charming Victorian country inn, circa 1895. Antique furnishings throughout make each of the six guest rooms unique and the common rooms cozy and inviting. All guest rooms include immaculate private baths, English flannel sheets, and handmade quilts. Lovely sunset views from the deck. Strolls along quiet country lanes to spectacular mountain views. Watch the many native birds flock to feeders and perennial flower beds. A wide assortment of games is also available. Friendly conversation by a wood-burning fireplace. During the fall, indulge in fine dining and spirits in the intimate candlelit dining room. A large country breakfast each morning. Pets are welcome if they can get along with the resident dog and cats. Rated three diamonds by AAA.

Hosts: Meri and Mike Hern
Rooms: 6 (PB) $70-130
Full Breakfast
Credit Cards: A, B, D
Notes: 2, 3, 5, 6, 7, 8, 9, 10, 11, 12, 13

The Horse and Hound Inn

205 Wells Road, 03580
(603) 823-5501; (800) 450-5501

A beautiful inn on a quiet country road is close to all activities. Full breakfast served every morning. In the evening, enjoy a quiet cocktail in our lounge and candlelight dining. Main living room offers a quiet place to read by the fire. Close to hiking, biking, swimming, skating, glider rides, horseback riding. Large covered patio and lawn offer the perfect place for weddings, receptions, and other parties. Closed April 1 through May 10 and October 28 through November 30.

Hosts: Bill Steele and Jim Cantlon
Rooms: 10 (8 PB; 2 SB) $79.95
Full Breakfast
Credit Cards: A, B, C, D, E
Notes: 2, 4, 6, 8, 10, 11, 12, 13, 14

The Inn at Forest Hills

P.O. Box 783, Route 142, 03580
(603) 823-9550; (800) 280-9550 (reservations)

NOTES: Credit cards accepted: A MasterCard; B Visa; C American Express; D Discover; E Diners Club; F Other; 2 Personal checks accepted; 3 Lunch available; 4 Dinner available; 5 Open all year; 6 Pets welcome;

The Inn at Forest Hills

This charming, historic 18-room, over-100-year-old Tudor manor house beguiles guests to enjoy the majestic scenery and year-round attractions of the White Mountains of New Hampshire. Enjoy gracious hospitality in eight comfortable guest rooms, most with private baths. Relax in country casualness in the sun-filled solarium or by the fireplaces in the living room and alpine room. Savor a gourmet New England breakfast by the fireplace in a fine old country inn!

Hosts: Joanne and Gordon Haym
Rooms: 8 (5 PB; 3 SB) $65-95
Full Breakfast
Credit Cards: A, B
Notes: 2, 5, 7, 9, 10, 11, 12, 13

Lovett's Inn

Route 18, 03580
(603) 823-7761; (800) 356-3802

Built in 1784 and listed on the National Register of Historic Places, Lovett's Inn offers a variety of accommodations in either the historic inn or the intimate cottages, most with fireplaces and all with private baths. Enjoy a drink at the Blue Heron Pub with its exquisite marble bar or curl up with a book by the fire in the living room with its hand-hewn beams. Breathtaking mountain views and lush forests surround the inn. Candlelit dinners and sunlit breakfasts are

only a part of why many have fallen in love with Lovett's. Bed and breakfast and MAP rates available. Inquire about availability of lunch. Closed April.

Innkeepers: JoAnna and Lee Wogulis
Full Breakfast
Credit Cards: A, B, C, D
Notes: 2, 4, 6, 7, 8, 9, 10, 11, 12, 13, 14

GLEN

The Bernerhof Inn

P.O. Box 240, 03838
(603) 383-4414; (800) 548-8007

Elegant small hotel in the foothills of the White Mountains. Victorian inn featuring nine nonsmoking rooms (two suites, one with sauna), most with two-person spas and brass beds, all with private baths and color cable TV. European-style pub and restaurant featuring European classics and creative Continental dishes. Host of A Taste of the Mountains Cooking School.

Hosts: Ted and Sharon Wroblewski
Rooms: 9 (PB) $69-139
Suites: 2
Full Breakfast
Credit Cards: A, B, C
Notes: 2, 3, 4, 5, 7, 8, 9, 10, 11, 12, 13

GREENFIELD

Greenfield Bed and Breakfast Inn

Box 400, Junction Routes 136 and 31, 03047
(603) 547-6327

A romantic Victorian mansion on three acres of lawn in Greenfield, a mountain valley village between Keene and Manchester just 90 minutes from Boston. Enjoy the relaxing mountain view from the spacious veranda. A full hot breakfast is served with crystal, china, and Mozart. Very close to skiing, swimming, hiking, tennis, golf, biking, and bargain antique shopping. A favorite of Mr. and Mrs. Bob

7 No smoking; 8 Children welcome; 9 Social drinking allowed; 10 Tennis nearby; 11 Swimming nearby; 12 Golf nearby; 13 Skiing nearby; 14 May be booked through a travel agent.

Hope and honeymooners of all ages. Senior citizen discount. Vacation suites and sleep-six cottage also available.

Hosts: Vic and Barbara Mangini
Rooms: 12 (8 PB; 4 SB) $49-99
Full Breakfast
Credit Cards: A, B
Notes: 2, 5, 8, 9, 10, 11, 12, 13, 14

HAMPSTEAD

New Hampshire Bed and Breakfast

128 South Hoop Pole Road, Guilford, CT 06437
(203) 457-0042; (800) 582-0853

NH605. Built by the Ordway family in 1850, this Greek Renaissance Italianate rests on gentle acreage on Main Street in Hampstead. Three stairways, five chimneys, hardwood floors with Oriental rugs, working wood stoves, and fireplaces. An expanded Continental breakfast is served on weekdays, and a full, hot, hearty breakfast is served in the formal dining room on weekends. Complimentary wine greets guests upon arrival, and the cookie jar is always full. Five minutes to Sunset Lake, and one-half hour from both Manchester and Nashua. Four sets of accommodations are available. Children welcome. No smoking. $60-90.

Stillmeadow Bed and Breakfast at Hampstead

545 Main Street, P.O. Box 565, 03841
(603) 329-8381

Southern New Hampshire's premier bed and breakfast, Stillmeadow is an 1850 Greek Renaissance Italianate Colonial house accessible to both the mountains and the seacoast. Four rooms with private bath and refrigerator are available, including one family suite with crib, changing table, and "secret stairs" that lead to a children's playroom and playyard. Attractions nearby include the Robert

Stillmeadow

Frost Farm, America's Stonehenge, Kingston State Park, and Rockingham Race Track. Between Manchester and Boston. Antique hardwood floors.

Hosts: Lori and Randy Offord
Rooms: 4 (PB) $65-90
Continental Breakfast
Credit Cards: A, B, C
Notes: 2, 5, 7, 8, 9, 10, 11, 12, 13

HAMPTON

New Hampshire Bed and Breakfast

128 South Hoop Pole Road, Guilford, CT 06437
(203) 457-0042; (800) 582-0853

NH421. This restored custom Cape is on five country acres, just over the Exeter line. The large sunny rooms are furnished with many antiques and lovely reproductions that are crafted by a descendant of Darby Field. Enjoy fresh fruit in the air-conditioned guest room and comfortable cozy living room, or enjoy the breeze on the porch. A full country breakfast is served each morning. Three quiet rooms, two of which have private baths, and one of which shares a bath, are air-conditioned and furnished with antiques. Limited smoking. No small children. $65.

The Oceanside

365 Ocean Boulevard, 03842
(603) 926-3542

The Oceanside overlooks the Atlantic Ocean and its beautiful sandy beaches.

NOTES: Credit cards accepted: A MasterCard; B Visa; C American Express; D Discover; E Diners Club;
F Other; 2 Personal checks accepted; 3 Lunch available; 4 Dinner available; 5 Open all year; 6 Pets welcome;

Each of the ten rooms is tastefully and individually decorated, many with period antiques. Private baths. The intimate café is open for breakfast during July and August and features homemade bread and pastries. Complimentary Continental breakfast is available. This gracious inn is in a less congested part of Hampton Beach within easy walking distance of restaurants, shops, and other attractions. Closed mid-October through mid-May. Inquire about accommodations for children.

Hosts: Skip and Debbie Windemiller
Rooms: 10 (PB) $90-125
Continental Breakfast
Credit Cards: A, B, C, D
Notes: 9, 10, 11, 12

HANOVER

New Hampshire Bed and Breakfast

128 South Hoop Pole Road, Guilford, CT 06437
(203) 457-0042; (800) 582-0853

NH320. This 180-year-old residence is on two acres with handsome red barns and lovely old trees. A former dairy farm, it belonged to a prominent local citizen who entertained President and Mrs. Coolidge and Amelia Earhart. A large formal living room, with beamed ceilings and curved oak staircase, has a wood-burning stove to ward off the chill on winter nights. Lovely private stone terrace. Elaborate Continental breakfast. A variety of rooms with private and shared baths. Children welcome; smoking limited. Two resident dogs, but no guest pets allowed. $90-100.

HAVERHILL

Haverhill Inn

Route 10, 03765
(603) 989-5961

This gracious 1810 Colonial home is in the Haverhill Corner historic district. Enjoy hikes in the nearby White Mountains, take walks along country lanes, converse in the parlor, or choose a book and settle in by the fire. Four rooms, all of which have private baths and working fireplaces, are available.

Hosts: Stephen Campbell and Anne Baird
Rooms: 4 (PB) $85
Full Breakfast
Credit Cards: None
Notes: 2, 7, 9, 10, 13

Haverhill Inn

HENNIKER

Henniker House Bed and Breakfast

2 Ramsdell Road, Box 191, 03242
(603) 428-3198

Henniker House, a 19th-century Victorian home with wraparound porches, is bracketed by huge pine trees. The solarium/breakfast room overlooks the Contoocook River; the 50-foot deck overhangs the water. Henniker is the site of New England College, is in the heart of antiquing, and hosts a fiber studio, arts and crafts, quilting, summer music festivals, theater, and symphony. Camping, fishing, skiing, boating, canoeing, kayaking, hiking, mountain biking, golf, windsurfing, and sailing are all available, or just relax in this little village.

Hosts: Cam and Julie Williams
Rooms: 4 (2 PB; 2 SB) $55-65
Full Breakfast
Credit Cards: A, B
Notes: 2, 5, 7, 8, 9, 10, 11, 12, 13, 14

7 No smoking; 8 Children welcome; 9 Social drinking allowed; 10 Tennis nearby; 11 Swimming nearby; 12 Golf nearby; 13 Skiing nearby; 14 May be booked through a travel agent.

Meeting House Inn

Meeting House Inn

35 Flanders Road, 03242
(603) 428-3228

The Meeting House Inn is family owned and operated. It is a renovated country farmstead (established 1982). A relaxed and cozy atmosphere where special attention is paid to individual comfort. A nonsmoking inn. The restaurant serves a delicious selection of individually prepared entrées. Rooms are filled with family furnishings and antiques, and all have private baths. Breakfast is brought to the room in a country basket. Air-conditioned. AAA approved. Private hot tub and sauna are available.

Rooms: 6 (PB) $65-98
Full Breakfast
Credit Cards: A, B, C, D
Notes: 4, 5, 7, 9, 10, 11, 12, 13, 14

HILLSBOROUGH

The Inn at Maplewood Farm

447 Center Road, P.O. Box 1478, 03244
(603) 464-4242; (800) 644-6695

The simple charm of New England with the elegance of a European country inn. An all-suites bed and breakfast. Guest rooms are filled with American and European antiques, an inviting bed, and unique amenities. A four-seasons getaway, the inn is a great starting point for a retreat of skiing, hiking, swimming, or golfing. In the heart of antique country and on 14 acres of foliage trees. Homemade breakfast every day.

Hosts: Laura and Jayme Simoes
Rooms: 4 (PB) $65-75
Full Breakfast
Credit Cards: A, B, C, D
Notes: 2, 5, 7, 8, 9, 10, 11, 12, 13, 14

New Hampshire Bed and Breakfast

128 South Hoop Pole Road, Guilford, CT 06437
(203) 457-0042; (800) 582-0853

NH511. This home is a passive-solar Cape with open concept downstairs. Full southern exposure allows year-round enjoyment of the all-glass breakfast room and patio, which features scenic views of fields, woods, and birds. A full breakfast of bacon and eggs, or waffles, sausage, muffins, and fruits is served. Walk to Gleason Falls and the stone arch bridge, or enjoy the brook and swimming hole nearby. Resident cat. No children. Smoking permitted. $60-70.

Stonebridge Inn

365 West Main Street, 03244
(603) 464-3155

The inn was a mid-1800s Colonial farmhouse, lovingly restored and redecorated, much by the hosts' own hands, to create the kind of small country inn guests have always hoped to find. There are four air-conditioned guest rooms, each uniquely decorated and with its own private bath. While at the inn, there's no lack of things to do and see whatever the season. Open May 1 through January 1.

Hosts: Clara and George Adame
Rooms: 4 (PB) $45-49
Continental Breakfast
Credit Cards: A, B
Notes: 2, 8, 9, 10, 11, 12

HOLDERNESS

The Inn on Golden Pond

Route 3, P.O. Box 680, 03245
(603) 968-7269

An 1879 Colonial home on 50 wooded acres. Bright and cheerful setting, breakfast, and game rooms. Close to major ski areas. Nearby is Squam Lake, the setting for the film *On Golden Pond*. Minimum stay on holidays. Children over 12 welcome.

Hosts: Bill and Bonnie Webb
Rooms: 9 (PB) $90-135
Full Breakfast
Credit Cards: A, B, C
Notes: 2, 5, 7, 9, 10, 11, 12, 13, 14

The Manor on Golden Pond

Route 3, Box T, 03245
(603) 968-3348; FAX (603) 968-2116

This turn-of-the-century English country manor house is on 14 acres on Squam Lake. Elegant rooms, most with wood-burning fireplaces and some with whirlpools for two. Three dining rooms and the Three Cocks Pub for guests to enjoy on premises. Rated three stars. Pool, tennis, croquet, horseshoes, canoes, and paddle boat in the boathouse at the lake. Golf, horseback riding, and skiing nearby. Snowshoeing and cross-country skiing can be reached under two hours from Boston. Rates include afternoon tea, four-course dinner, turndown service, and breakfast. Children welcome in cottages.

Hosts: David and Bambi Arnold
Rooms: 27 (PB) $180-325
Full Breakfast
Credit Cards: A, B, C
Notes: 2, 4, 5, 7, 9, 10, 11, 12, 13, 14

HOPKINTON

New Hampshire Bed and Breakfast

128 South Hoop Pole Road, Guilford, CT 06437
(203) 457-0042; (800) 582-0853

NH611. This 18th-century Colonial reproduction features wide pine floors, a Fumford fireplaced keeping room, a living room, and a family room. Three guest rooms have private baths and ceiling fans.

The home is set on 15 acres of lawns, pastures, and woodlands. Guests will enjoy the spectacular view of distant mountain ranges from the cupola high atop the barn. Rest in rockers on the wraparound porch or take a dip in the pool. Nearby guests can visit the Shaker Village in Canterbury, or all of the offices, restaurants, shops, and museums in the state capitol area of Concord. No smoking. No guest pets, please. $65-75.

Windyledge Bed and Breakfast

1264 Hatfield Road, 03229
(603) 746-4054

This elegant hilltop Colonial is surrounded by nine acres of fields and woods. Bordered by picturesque hills and the White Mountains beyond. The hosts' delicious gourmet apricot-glazed French toast, ricotta soufflé, or honey-and-spice blueberry pancakes are served on the airy sun porch or outside on the deck or in the country dining room. Lakes, golf, skiing, craft shops, and numerous restaurants nearby. After a full day's activities, return "home" to a dip in the pool, wine by the fireside, or good conversation. Come and recapture the romance!

Hosts: Dick and Susan Vogt (pronounced "Vote")
Rooms: 3 (1 PB; 2 SB) $55-85
Full Breakfast
Credit Cards: A, B
Notes: 2, 5, 8, 9, 10, 11, 12, 13, 14

Windyledge

7 No smoking; 8 Children welcome; 9 Social drinking allowed; 10 Tennis nearby; 11 Swimming nearby; 12 Golf nearby; 13 Skiing nearby; 14 May be booked through a travel agent.

JACKSON

Dana Place Inn

Box L, Pinkham Notch, 03846
(603) 383-6822; (800) 537-9276

Century-old inn at the base of Mount Washington on 300 acres along the Ellis River. Dana Place features cozy rooms, fine dining, indoor heated pool, river swimming, Jacuzzi, tennis, hiking, walking trails, fishing, and cross-country skiing on the premises. Golf, outlet shopping, and downhill skiing nearby. Seasonal escape packages available.

Hosts: Harris and Mary Lou Levine
Rooms: 33 (29 PB; 4 SB) $85-125
Full Breakfast
Credit Cards: A, B, C, D, E
Notes: 2, 3, 4, 5, 6, 7, 8, 9, 10, 11, 12, 13, 14

Ellis River House

Route 16, P.O. Box 656, 03846
(603) 383-9339; (800) 233-8309
FAX (603) 383-4142

Sample true New England hospitality at this enchanting small hotel just a short stroll from the village. There are 18 comfortable, king- and queen-size guest rooms decorated with Laura Ashley prints, some with fireplaces and two-person Jacuzzis, cable TV, scenic balconies, and period antiques and all with individually controlled heat and air conditioning. Two-room and family suites, riverfront cottage, hot tub, sauna, heated pool, sitting and game rooms, and delightful

Ellis River House

sun deck overlooking the pristine Ellis River. Enjoy a full country breakfast with homemade breads, or a delicious trout dinner. Afterwards relax with libations and billiards in the pub. Seasonal rates available.

Hosts: Barry and Barbara Lubao
Rooms: 18 (15 PB; 3 SB) $69-229
Full Breakfast
Credit Cards: A, B, C, D, E
Notes: 2, 4, 5, 6, 7, 8, 9, 11, 12, 13

Nestlenook Farm

Nestlenook Farm Resort

Dinsmore Road, Box Q, 03846
(603) 383-9443

Escape into a Victorian past on a 65-acre estate. Seven elegant guest rooms, all of which have two-person Jacuzzis and some of which have parlor stoves, canopied beds, and fireplaces, charming guest kitchen, antiques, and fireplaced gazebo. Horse-drawn sleighs, horseback riding, mountain bikes, rowboats, fishing, and Victorian pool. Savor the romance and step back in time at a gingerbread country inn.

Hosts: Robert and Nancy Cyr
Rooms: 7 (PB) $125-270
Full Breakfast
Credit Cards: A, B
Notes: 5, 7, 10, 11, 12, 13

New Hampshire Bed and Breakfast

128 South Hoop Pole Road, Guilford, CT 06437
(203) 457-0042; (800) 582-0853

NH109. On a birch-covered hill looking towards Mount Washington, this brand-

NOTES: Credit cards accepted: A MasterCard; B Visa; C American Express; D Discover; E Diners Club;
F Other; 2 Personal checks accepted; 3 Lunch available; 4 Dinner available; 5 Open all year; 6 Pets welcome;

new house has opened recently as a bed and breakfast to rave reviews. The home offers 18th-century antiques, textiles, folk art, handmade quilts, designer sheets, fresh flowers, fruit baskets, and terrycloth robes. The full gourmet breakfast served on English bone china features sticky buns, shortbread, and fudge. Afternoon tea is served. The living room has a fireplace, TV, and VCR. The deck, hammock, and flower gardens provide splendid mountain views. Three guest rooms with private baths. One room has a private Jacuzzi tub and private deck looking towards Mount Washington. No smoking allowed; no guest pets allowed. Children over ten are welcome. $65-95.

The Village House

P.O. Box 359, Route 16A, 03846
(603) 383-6666

Just over the covered bridge is this charming Colonial inn with wraparound porch facing the mountains. In summer, enjoy tennis, swimming, and Jacuzzi on premises; riding, golf, hiking, canoeing, and fine dining nearby. In winter visitors ski from the door of the house onto the 157 kilometers of cross-country trails. Downhill skiing is available at four major nearby mountains. Sleigh rides, ice skating, and snowshoeing are also available. Kitchenettes and family suites available.

Host: Robin Crocker
Rooms: 15 (13 PB; 2 SB) $40-125
Continental Breakfast; Full Breakfast in ski season
Credit Cards: A, B, D, E
Notes: 2, 5, 7, 8, 9, 10, 11, 12, 13, 14

Whitneys' Inn

P.O. Box 822, Route 16B, 03846-0822
(603) 383-8916; (800) 677-5737

A classic country inn nestled in a lovely pastoral setting in the heart of the White Mountains. Spacious, comfortable rooms grace this restored New England farmhouse, circa 1842. Adjacent to the main inn are cozy fireplace cottages and family suites. The dining room, featuring delicious full country breakfasts and country gourmet dinners, is open to the public. Seasonal on-site activities range from tennis, swimming, and hiking in the summer, to cross-country and downhill skiing during the winter.

Rooms: 29 (PB) $64-124
Full Breakfast
Credit Cards: A, B, C, D
Notes: 2, 4, 5, 6, 8, 9, 10, 11, 12, 13, 14

JAFFREY

Benjamin Prescott Inn

Route 124 East, 03452
(603) 532-6637

Come discover the charm of the past and the comforts of the present within a classic Greek Revival home furnished with antiques. Ten charming guest rooms, each of which has its own private bath, are available for guests, and a full breakfast of hearty country fare is served each morning. Relax and enjoy the surrounding dairy farm, walk the stonewall-lined lane, shop, climb Mount Monadnock, visit local artisans, and eat in excellent restaurants. Children ten and over welcome.

Hosts: Jan and Barry Miller
Rooms: 10 (PB) $65-130
Full Breakfast
Credit Cards: A, B, C
Notes: 2, 5, 7, 9, 11, 12, 13, 14

Benjamin Prescott Inn

The Galway House Bed and Breakfast

247 Old Peterborough Road, 03452
(603) 532-8083

A traditional bed and breakfast operated like those in the Old Country. A great way to get to know the area and its people. Set on a quiet woodland road in the heart of the Monadnock region, the Currier and Ives corner of New Hampshire, this inn makes an excellent point from which to enjoy the many attractions of this four-season area. Closed July. Smoking restricted.

Hosts: Joe and Marie Manning
Rooms: 2 (SB) $50
Full Breakfast
Credit Cards: None
Notes: 2, 8, 9, 10, 11, 12, 13

New Hampshire Bed and Breakfast

128 South Hoop Pole Road, Guilford, CT 06437
(203) 457-0042; (800) 582-0853

NH520. This country setting affords plenty of opportunities for recreation and enjoyment of the natural beauty of Monadnock Region. Set on 200 acres of beautiful countryside, guests can enjoy a lake with sandy beaches, swimming, boating, fishing, golf, hiking, cross-country skiing, ice skating, bicycling, and lawn games. The Cathedral of the Pines, the Friendly Farm petting zoo, antique shops, boutiques, and covered bridges all nearby. Private baths. Full or Continental breakfast. Relax in the fireplaced living rooms or the game room. No smoking. $75-100.

JEFFERSON

Applebrook Bed and Breakfast

Route 115A, 03583-0178
(603) 586-7713; (800) 545-6504

Taste the midsummer raspberries while enjoying spectacular mountain views from

Applebrook Bed and Breakfast

this old Victorian farmhouse. Bike, hike, fish, ski, go antiquing, or just relax in the sitting room by the goldfish pool. Near Santa's Village and Six Gun City. Dormitory rooms available in addition to private guest rooms. Brochure available. Try the hot tub under the stars!

Hosts: Sandra J. Conley and Martin M. Kelly
Rooms: 10 (4 PB; 6 SB) $40-60
Dorm Rooms: $20 per person
Full Breakfast
Credit Cards: A, B
Notes: 2, 5, 6, 7, 8, 9, 10, 11, 12, 13, 14

The Jefferson Inn

Route 2, RFD 1, Box 68A, 03583
(603) 586-7998; (800) 729-7908

Among the White Mountains National Forest, the Jefferson Inn offers a 360-degree mountain view. Each room is furnished uniquely along a Shaker, Victorian, or New England theme. With Mount Washington nearby, the inn is an ideal

The Jefferson Inn

NOTES: Credit cards accepted: A MasterCard; B Visa; C American Express; D Discover; E Diners Club;
F Other; 2 Personal checks accepted; 3 Lunch available; 4 Dinner available; 5 Open all year; 6 Pets welcome;

location for hiking and cross-country and downhill skiing. Six golf courses nearby. Afternoon tea is provided. Swimming pond. Two-family suites are available. Two-night minimum stay during foliage weekends and holidays. Closed November and April.

Hosts: Marla Mason and Don Garretson
Rooms: 11 (PB) $62-120
Full Breakfast
Credit Cards: A, B, C, D
Notes: 2, 7, 8, 9, 10, 11, 12, 13

New Hampshire Bed and Breakfast

128 South Hoop Pole Road, Guilford, CT 06437
(203) 457-0042; (800) 582-0853

NH125. Built in 1896, this charming Victorian is nestled among the White Mountain National Forest and enjoys 360-degree mountain views. Look across the Jefferson Meadows to Franconia Notch, Mount Washington, and the northern Presidential Range. See Mount Star King and Waumbek in back of the inn. Each room is furnished with period antiques and has a character of its own, such as the Victorian and Shaker rooms. Daily afternoon tea is served in the common room. Ideal for hiking, golf, biking, fishing, canoeing, swimming, antiquing, alpine and Nordic skiing, skating, and snowshoeing. Right in town are Santa's Village and Six Gun City attractions. Ten guest rooms, five with private baths. A two-room suite with private bath accommodates families. Children welcome. No smoking; no pets. $55-85.

LACONIA

New Hampshire Bed and Breakfast

128 South Hoop Pole Road, Guilford, CT 06437
(203) 457-0042; (800) 582-0853

NH235. Four blocks from downtown Laconia, this large Victorian home, built in 1903, offers guests a formal living room with fireplace and piano; a den with books, games, and TV; a carpeted front porch with comfortable wicker and cane rockers; and a magnificent two-story solar greenhouse addition with wood-burning stove and tables for board games and puzzles. A delicious full breakfast is served in the formal dining room and there are tea and beverages for afternoon snacks. Two guest rooms with a shared bath. Children ages three to sixteen are welcome. No smoking allowed in the bedrooms; no pets allowed. $45-50.

NH238. In the local Native American tongue, *Winnisquam* means "smiling water." Guests cannot help but smile at this beautiful setting. The serenity of the lake, mountains, and surrounding woodlands lifts the spirit. This recently built contemporary was expertly designed and finished by the host. All of the wood finish is native oak and pine milled from trees where the house now stands. There is a two-story solarium greenhouse overlooking the lake that serves as a wonderful place to read or have a snack. Two sitting rooms have TVs, books, and board games; guests are welcome to use the canoe or sunfish sailboat. Breakfast is an expanded Continental, and three freshly decorated guest rooms are available. Resident dog, but no guest pets. Children are welcome. No smoking allowed. $60-85.

LINCOLN

Red Sleigh Inn

Pollard Road, P.O. Box 562, 03251
(603) 745-8517

Family-run inn with mountain views. Just off the scenic Kancamagus Highway. One mile to Loon Mountains. Waterville, Cannon, and Bretton Woods nearby. Many summer attractions and superb fall foliage. Shopping, dining, and theater are minutes away. Hiking, swimming, golf, and train rides are available.

Hosts: Bill and Loretta
Rooms: 6 (3 PB; 3 SB) $65-85
Full Breakfast
Credit Cards: A, B
Notes: 2, 5, 11, 12, 13, 14

LITTLETON

The Beal House Inn

2 West Main Street, 03561
(603) 444-2661

For the perfect blend of relaxation and adventure, guests are welcomed to this cheerful 1833 in-village inn! In the heart of the White Mountains, the Beal House offers thoughtful lodging with antique-filled guest rooms, down comforters, and special touches. Fireside breakfast gatherings get guests off to a great start, and the delicious gourmet evening dining features New England-style cuisine with a flair. Country picnic baskets prepared to guests' specifications with one-day notice. Afternoon refreshments are provided.

Hosts: Barbara and Ted Snell; Heidi and Vincent Hurley
Rooms: 13 (9 PB; 4 SB) $55-80
Full Breakfast
Credit Cards: A, B
Notes: 2, 4, 5, 8, 9, 10, 11, 12, 13, 14

LYME

Loch Lyme Lodge

RFD 278, Route 10, 03768
(800) 423-2141; FAX (603) 795-2141

Loch Lyme Lodge has been hosting guests since 1924. From Memorial Day to Labor Day the 24 cabins and four rooms in the main lodge are open for the enjoyment of summer vacationers. During the fall and winter, three rooms in the main lodge, a farmhouse built in 1784, are open for bed and breakfast guests. Children are welcome during any season and the emphasis is

Loch Lyme Lodge

always on comfortable, informal hospitality. The lakeside location is only 11 miles north of Dartmouth College-Hanover and provides many vacation possibilities, including outdoor recreation, fall foliage, seasonal attractions, shopping, antiquing, theater, and relaxation.

Hosts: Paul and Judy Barker
Rooms: 4 (SB) $48-88
Summer Cabins: 24
Full Breakfast
Credit Cards: None
Notes: 2, 3, 4, 5, 7, 8, 9, 10, 11, 12, 13

MADISON

New Hampshire Bed and Breakfast

128 South Hoop Pole Road, Guilford, CT 06437
(203) 457-0042; (800) 582-0853

NH110. On 80 acres of fields and woods, in a peaceful farm and ranch town, this comfortable farmhouse bed and breakfast is only 15 minutes from the Conways and the Scenic Kancamagus Highway. Guests may enjoy the country kitchen with fireplace and the guest parlor, furnished with antiques. The spacious grounds offer scenic trails for walking, cross-country skiing, and wagon or sleigh rides. A full breakfast is served in the dining room. Children welcome. No smoking in bedrooms. No pets. $60-70.

NOTES: Credit cards accepted: A MasterCard; B Visa; C American Express; D Discover; E Diners Club; F Other; 2 Personal checks accepted; 3 Lunch available; 4 Dinner available; 5 Open all year; 6 Pets welcome;

MANCHESTER

New Hampshire Bed and Breakfast

128 South Hoop Pole Road, Guilford, CT 06437
(203) 457-0042; (800) 582-0853

NH612. A Victorian gazebo near the outdoor pool offers guests the choice of restful moments or refreshing dips, even during moonlit swims. Three guest rooms with private or shared baths, an enclosed sun porch, and a formal dining room where a full course breakfast is served. Near offices, the airport, five colleges, the Corner Gallery of Art, live theaters, restaurants, and shopping. Smoking allowed. Pets accepted with prior approval. $50-60.

MARLBOROUGH

Peep-Willow Farm

51 Bixby Street, 03455
(603) 876-3807

Peep-Willow Farm is a working thoroughbred horse farm that also caters to humans. On 20 acres with a view all the way to the Connecticut River valley. Guests are welcome to help with chores or watch the young horses frolic in the fields, but there is no riding. Flexibility and serenity are the key ingredients to enjoying the stay. Call to see what type of pets welcome. Cross-country skiing.

Host: Noel Aderer
Rooms: 3 (SB) $25-45
Full Breakfast
Credit Cards: None
Notes: 2, 5, 7, 8, 9, 10, 11, 12, 13, 14

MEREDITH

New Hampshire Bed and Breakfast

128 South Hoop Pole Road, Guilford, CT 06437
(203) 457-0042; (800) 582-0853

NH211. On the shore of Lake Winnipesaukee, four miles from the center of town, sits this beautiful turn-of-the-century home. Enjoy swimming, boating, canoeing, and badminton. Relax on the screened porch or in front of the fireplace in the living room, overlooking the Ossipee Mountains and Lake Winnipesaukee. Shops, galleries, antiques, and restaurants all nearby. In the Lakes Region, enjoy such attractions as scenic train and boat rides, amusement centers, golf, tennis, and boat rentals. Full breakfast is served on the porch or on the 80-foot deck. Three guest rooms with shared bath. Children welcome; smoking outdoors; pets accepted. Open May, June, September, and October. $55.

NH212. The closest bed and breakfast to Meredith Bay village. Just a short stroll to the Marketplace of shops, galleries, restaurants, and Lake Winnipesaukee. On a quiet residential lane, it guarantees peaceful days and nights, yet is central to all activities of the Lakes Region. Minutes away from Winnipesaukee Scenic Railroad, the M.S. Mount Washington cruise ship, Analee's Dolls Gift Shop and Museum, and Weirs Beach. Enjoy an Early American ambience of fluffy quilts, hand-stenciled walls and floors, antique furnishings, and a romantic brick fireplace in the parlor. Continental breakfast served in the dining room. Seasonal beverages and freshly baked delights in the evening. Five guest rooms, two with private baths. Children welcome. No smoking. Small pets permitted. $50-65.

MILFORD (NASHUA)

New Hampshire Bed and Breakfast

128 South Hoop Pole Road, Guilford, CT 06437
(203) 457-0042; (800) 582-0853

NH614. This alpine pension replica, affords a unique European flavor throughout. The

7 No smoking; 8 Children welcome; 9 Social drinking allowed; 10 Tennis nearby; 11 Swimming nearby;
12 Golf nearby; 13 Skiing nearby; 14 May be booked through a travel agent.

guests enjoy the Stube (common room) for its recreational use and for time to visit with new-found friends. Its coziness is enhanced by the alpine tile stove (a kachelofen). Eight guest rooms with private baths feature special, comfortable beds. Continental plus breakfast is served each morning. No smoking. $55-65.

MOULTONBOROUGH

Olde Orchard Inn

Route 1, Box 256, 03254
(603) 476-5004; (800) 598-5845

This bed and breakfast features five guest rooms, with private baths, in a beautifully restored farmhouse. The inn is on 13 acres with a mountain brook and pond. Hosts offer guests a large country breakfast with home-baked goods and all the fixings. Only one mile away from the beautiful Lake Winnipesaukee, and only minutes away from many lakes, regional attractions, and activities. Within one hour's drive, guests will find five major ski areas, or guests may decide to take a cross-country ski tour from the inn's front door. The foliage is stunning in the autumn, but anytime is a delightful time to stay here. Call to inquire about facilities for pets.

Hosts: The Senner Family
Rooms: 5 (PB) $70-80
Full Breakfast
Credit Cards: B,
Notes: 2, 5, 7, 8, 9, 10, 11, 13, 14

Olde Orchard Inn

MOUNT SUNAPEE

Blue Goose Inn

24 Route 103B, P.O. Box 2117, 03255
(603) 763-5519

This well-restored, early 19th-century Colonial farmhouse stands on three and one-half acres along Lake Sunapee, at the base of Mount Sunapee. The cozy, comfortable guest rooms are furnished in a quaint, country style. Guests can make themselves at home in any of the common areas. The living room has a fireplace, TV, VCR, and book and video library; the card and game room has plenty of diversions; there's refrigerator space in the kitchen; and the porch, weather permitting, is ideal for breakfast and snacks. Kids will have fun in the summer playhouse. The Mount Sunapee area is a miniresort for vacationers of all ages, offering boating, swimming, hiking, downhill and cross-country skiing, snowmobiling, crafts fairs, antiquing, and much more.

Hosts: Meryl and Ronald Caldwell
Rooms: 5 (4 PB; 1 SB) $55
Full Breakfast
Credit Cards: A, B
Notes: 2, 5, 7, 8, 9, 10, 11, 12, 13, 14

NEW BOSTON

Colburn Homestead Bed and Breakfast

280 West Colburn Road (off Route 136), 03070
(603) 487-5250

This Colonial farmhouse in a country setting is 70 miles from Boston, 20 miles from Manchester, and near many shopping and recreational facilities. Swimming pool available in season. TVs in all the rooms. Christmas shop with gifts and crafts open year-round.

Hosts: Olive and Robert Colburn
Rooms: 3 (SB) $50-65
Full Breakfast
Credit Cards: A, B
Notes: 2, 5, 8, 11, 12, 13

NOTES: Credit cards accepted: A MasterCard; B Visa; C American Express; D Discover; E Diners Club; F Other; 2 Personal checks accepted; 3 Lunch available; 4 Dinner available; 5 Open all year; 6 Pets welcome;

NEWBURY

The 1806 House

Route 103 Traffic Circle, P.O. Box 54, 03255
(603) 763-4969

In the unspoiled New Hampshire countryside, the 1806 House has beamed ceilings,
wide plank floors, and a charming living
room complete with candlelight, cozy
couches, wing chairs, and a wood-burning
stove. Every guest room has been tastefully
and individually decorated with period furnishings and modern conveniences. A special breakfast is served every morning,
complete with fine china, candlelight, and a
Pavarotti aria. A perfect getaway. Mount
Sunapee is close by. There are many nearby
restaurants to choose from. Skiing, hiking,
boating, and swimming are also just across
the road.

Hosts: Lane and Gene Bellman
Rooms: 4 (PB) $79
Full Breakfast
Credit Cards: A, B
Notes: 2, 5, 7, 9, 11, 12, 13

NEW HAMPTON

New Hampshire Bed and Breakfast

128 South Hoop Pole Road, Guilford, CT 06437
(203) 457-0042; (800) 582-0853

NH240. This 150-year-old antique-filled
home with a converted barn is in the heart
of the Lakes Region. Common rooms
include the living room with a fireplace,
den with TV and Nordic Track, and a pool
room with pool table, piano, and stereo system. A hearty full breakfast is served, wine
will be offered, candy will be in the room,
and fruit is always on the table. New
Hampton, home to the co-ed prep school by
the same name, is an easy stroll from the
inn. Four guest rooms are available. No
smoking allowed. Children are welcome.
$50-65.

NEW IPSWICH

The Inn at New Ipswich

Porter Hill Road, P.O. Box 208, 03071
(603) 878-3711

Relax a while in a graceful 1790 home amid
fruit trees and stone walls. Cozy fireplaces,
front-porch rockers, and large, comfortable
guest rooms furnished country style. One
family suite sleeps four. Refreshments
offered upon arrival. Enjoy scrumptious
hearthside breakfasts. In the Monadnock
region of New Hampshire. Hiking, band
concerts, antique auctions, unsurpassed
autumn color, cross-country and downhill
skiing are all available. Children over eight
are welcome.

Hosts: Ginny and Steve Bankuti
Rooms: 5 (PB) $65
Suite: 1 (PB) $85
Full Breakfast
Credit Cards: A, B
Notes: 2, 5, 7, 9, 12, 13, 14

NEWPORT

The Eagle Inn at Coit Mountain

523 North Main Street, 03773
(603) 863-3583; (800) 367-2364

All four seasons provide nature's backdrop
to this gracious, historic Georgian-Federal
estate summer residence that was built for
an aristocratic French family with unlimited
income and a lifestyle to match. Enjoy a
hearty full country breakfast. In the evening
a nightcap and dessert are delivered to
guests' rooms. Dinner is available in the
Greene Room Restaurant. There are many
outdoor activities year-round in the Lake
Sunapee region. Numerous shops, parks,
historic sites, and museums to enjoy in the
surrounding area.

Hosts: Jim and Courtney Forman; Georgia Hopkins
Rooms: 6 (3 PB; 3 SB) $79-129
Full Breakfast
Credit Cards: A, B, C
Notes: 2, 3, 4, 5, 6, 8, 9, 10, 11, 12, 13, 14

7 No smoking; 8 Children welcome; 9 Social drinking allowed; 10 Tennis nearby; 11 Swimming nearby;
12 Golf nearby; 13 Skiing nearby; 14 May be booked through a travel agent.

The Buttonwood Inn

NORTH CONWAY

The Buttonwood Inn

Mount Surprise Road, P.O. Box 1817, 03860
(603) 356-2625; (800) 258-2625 U.S. and Canada
FAX (603) 356-3140

Tucked away on Mount Surprise, the inn is an 1820s Cape. Quiet and secluded, yet only two miles to the village, excellent dining, and tax-free shopping. Nine uniquely appointed guest rooms, pool, and extensive gardens. Enjoy 65 kilometers of groomed cross-country ski trails right from the back door. Full breakfast. Dinners served on Saturdays during foliage season and in January and February. Perfect romantic getaway for families, groups, reunions, or weddings.

Hosts: Claudia and Peter Needham
Rooms: 9 (PB and SB) $60-150
Full Breakfast
Credit Cards: A, B, C
Notes: 2, 4, 5, 7, 8, 9, 10, 11, 12, 13, 14

Cabernet Inn

Route 16, 03860
(800) 866-4704

Nestled in a grove of towering pines, this 1842 Victorian cottage was refurbished and enhanced into an elegant nonsmoking inn. Deluxe rooms have either Jacuzzis or fireplaces, queen-size beds, and air conditioning. Two guest living rooms with fire-

places open to shaded outdoor patios and provide relaxing ambience. Period lighting and furnishings reflect the innkeepers' passion for antiquing, and when guests step into the large gourmet kitchen, the secrets behind the delicious, bountiful breakfasts are all revealed.

Hosts: Chris and Bob Wyner
Rooms: 10 (PB) $69-169
Full Breakfast
Credit Cards: A, B, C
Notes: 2, 5, 9, 10, 11, 12, 13, 14

The Center Chimney-1787

P.O. Box 1220, River Road, 03860
(603) 356-6788

One of the earliest houses in North Conway is now a cozy, affordable bed and breakfast. Just off Main Street and the Saco River (swim, fish, and canoe). Walk to shops, restaurants, summer theater, free ice skating, and cross-country skiing. Rock and ice climbing on nearby Cathedral Ledge.

Host: Farley Ames Whitley
Rooms: 4 (SB) $44-55
Continental Breakfast
Credit Cards: None
Notes: 2, 5, 8, 9, 10, 11, 12, 13

The Center Chimney-1787

The Farm by the River

2555 West Side Road, 03860
(603) 356-2694

Since the 1780s, this bed and breakfast has been not just an inn but a tradition. A land grant from the king of England, the Farm has been passed down in one family for over 200 years. An award-winning home for sensitive historic preservation, it radiates country charm and hospitality. The ten guest rooms are decorated with family heirlooms. In the winter months enjoy a fireside breakfast, in summer the panoramic views of the mountains while having breakfast on the patio. Relax in the historic and pastoral setting on 65 acres of forest, river, and pastureland. Sleigh rides, cross-country skiing, hay rides, fly fishing, canoeing, and swimming on site.

Hosts: Rick Davis and Charlene Browne-Davis
Rooms: 10 (4 PB; 6 SB) $55-110
Full Breakfast
Credit Cards: A, B
Notes: 2, 5, 7, 8, 9, 10, 11, 12, 13, 14

New Hampshire Bed and Breakfast

128 South Hoop Pole Road, Guilford, CT 06437
(203) 457-0042; (800) 582-0853

NH108. This elegant country Victorian inn offers both mountain and river views and is on the banks of the Saco River in the heart of the Mount Washington Valley. Four guest rooms, all with private baths, a living room with fireplace, and a full gourmet breakfast await guests. Walk to hundreds of famous outlet shops, restaurants, galleries, skiing, entertainment, and attractions. Minutes away, guests will find even more ski areas and exciting White Mountain attractions. No smoking. One resident cat. No guest pets, please. Children over 12 are welcome. $65-90.

Nereledge Inn

River Road (off Main Street, Route 16)
P.O. Box 547, 03860
(603) 356-2831

Come and enjoy the charm, warm hospitality, and relaxation of this 1787 traditional bed and breakfast with eleven comfortable guest rooms and views of Cathedral Ledge. Relax by the wood stove in the sitting room, enjoy a game of darts in the English-style pub room, or daydream in a rocking chair on the front porch. A friendly and informal nonsmoking atmosphere awaits guests. A delicious country breakfast includes warm apple crumble with ice cream. Close to hiking trails, rock climbing, skiing, and ice climbing. Walk to the village for shopping, dining, and theater; walk to the river for swimming, canoeing, or fishing.

Hosts: Valerie and Dave Halpin
Rooms: 11 (6 PB; 5 SB) $60-100
Full Breakfast
Credit Cards: A, B, C
Notes: 2, 5, 8, 9, 10, 11, 12, 13

Scottish Lion Inn and Restaurant

Route 16, Main Street, 03860-1527
(603) 356-6381

At the Scottish Lion guests will find country inn atmosphere with splendid cuisine and comfortable accommodations. All eight rooms have private baths. Five have clan names with corresponding decor. The pride of the Lion is its unique and varied menu of international and Scottish favorites. The inn has the largest selection of single malts and Scotches in New Hampshire, and it is the only inn in New England to serve 100 percent Kona coffee.

Hosts: Chef Michael and Janet Procopio
Rooms: 8 (PB) $49.95-99
Full Breakfast
Credit Cards: A, B, C, D, E
Notes: 3, 4, 5, 7, 8, 9, 10, 11, 12, 13, 14

The 1785 Inn and Restaurant

3582 White Mountain Highway
P.O. Box 1785, 03860-1785
(603) 356-9025; (800) 421-1785 (reservations)
FAX (603) 356-6081

The 1785 Inn has a famous view of Mount Washington popularized by the White Mountain School of Art in the 1800s. The inn was completely refurbished by the current owners and offers romantic accommodations where guests can relax and savor

7 No smoking; 8 Children welcome; 9 Social drinking allowed; 10 Tennis nearby; 11 Swimming nearby;
12 Golf nearby; 13 Skiing nearby; 14 May be booked through a travel agent.

the view while being pampered with fine dining and friendly service. On six pristine acres with swimming pool, skiing, nature trails, 210-year-old fireplaces, hiking, biking, fishing, etc. Free color brochure.

Hosts: Becky and Charlie Mallar
Rooms: 17 (12 PB; 5 SB) $69-159
Full Breakfast
Credit Cards: A, B, C, D, E
Notes: 2, 4, 5, 7, 8, 9, 10, 11, 12, 13, 14

Sunny Side Inn

Seavey Street, P.O. Box 557, 03860
(603) 356-6239; (800) 600-6239

Sit back, relax, and daydream on the sun-filled, flower-trimmed porches. The comfortable 1850 farmhouse is in a quiet residential setting. Just a five-minute walk to North Conway village with its many fine shops and restaurants to explore. A homey refuge in which to relax and recharge.

Hosts: Peter and Diane Watson
Rooms: 9 (PB) $53-107
Full Breakfast
Credit Cards: A, B, C, E, F
Notes: 2, 5, 7, 8, 9, 10, 11, 12, 13, 14

The Victorian Harvest Inn

28 Locust Lane, Box 1763, 03860
(603) 356-3548; (800) 642-0749
FAX (603) 356-3548

Nonsmokers will delight in this 1850s multigabled Victorian find. The inn is on a

The Victorian Harvest Inn

quiet side street, yet is within walking distance to quaint North Conway Village shops and eateries. All rooms have antiques with modern bed and bath comforts in mind. Start a romantic adventure with a full country breakfast and hospitality of New England as it was meant to be. Fireplace, in-ground pool, and air-conditioned. American Bed and Breakfast three-crown rated (A). AAA three-diamond award. Dinner available for groups. Children over six welcome. Fully nonsmoking inn.

Hosts: Robert and Linda Dahlberg
Rooms: 6 (4 PB; 2 SB) $65-105
Full Breakfast
Credit Cards: A, B, C, D
Notes: 2, 5, 7, 9, 10, 11, 12, 13, 14

Wildflowers Inn

Route 16, 03860
(603) 356-2224

Return to the simplicity and elegance of yesteryear. With an ideal location and gracefully decorated rooms, this small 1878 Victorian inn specializes in comfort and convenience for the modern-day traveler. From the cheery dining room with fireplace to the porch rockers overlooking the award-winning gardens, Wildflowers will be a welcoming respite on any journey. Closed November through April.

Hosts: Dean Franke and Eileen Davies
Rooms: 6 (2 PB; 4 SB) $54-99.36
Continental Breakfast
Credit Cards: A, B
Notes: 2, 7, 8, 9, 10, 11, 12, 13

Wyatt House Country Inn

Main Street, Route 16, P.O. Box 777, 03860
(603) 356-7977; (800) 527-7978

Experience the charm of an elegant country Victorian inn with panoramic mountain and river views. Six guest rooms are uniquely decorated and furnished with antiques. A candlelit gourmet multi-entrée breakfast is served on English Wedgwood and Irish lace. Stroll from the back yard to the Saco River for swimming or fishing. Early morn-

NOTES: Credit cards accepted: A MasterCard; B Visa; C American Express; D Discover; E Diners Club; F Other; 2 Personal checks accepted; 3 Lunch available; 4 Dinner available; 5 Open all year; 6 Pets welcome;

ing coffee and muffins are served in the handsome study, as well as afternoon tea and cakes. Village location, and minutes to downhill and cross-country skiing. Tax-free outlet shopping. Smoking limited to Victorian wraparound porch and grounds. Fresh flowers, fruits, and cookie baskets. AAA rated.

Hosts: Bill and Arlene Strickland
Rooms: 6 (4 PB; 2 SB) $65-95
Full Breakfast
Credit Cards: A, B, C, D
Notes: 3, 5, 7, 9, 10, 11, 12, 13, 14

Follansbee Inn

NORTH SUTTON

Follansbee Inn

P.O. Box 92, 03260
(603) 927-4221; (800) 626-4221

An authentic 1840 New England inn with white clapboard and green trim. On peaceful Kezar Lake, with an old-fashioned porch, comfortable sitting rooms with fireplaces, and charming antique furnishings. Nestled in a small country village but convenient to all area activities (four miles south of New London and 95 miles north of Boston). Midway between Montreal and Cape Cod. Private pier with rowboat, canoe, paddle boat, and windsurfer for guests. Beautiful walk around the lake during all seasons. Beer and wine license. Healthy nonsmoking inn. Closed parts of November and April. Children over ten welcome.

Hosts: Dick and Sandy Reilein
Rooms: 23 (11 PB; 12 SB) $75-95
Full Breakfast
Credit Cards: A, B
Notes: 2, 4, 7, 9, 10, 11, 12, 13

NORTH WOODSTOCK

New Hampshire Bed and Breakfast

128 South Hoop Pole Road, Guilford, CT 06437
(203) 457-0042; (800) 582-0853

NH117. This 80-year-old inn offers seven personally decorated guest rooms and family suites, each with views of the gardens, Mooselake River, or the south ridge of Loon Mountain. The living room has a fireplace, TV, and games. The spacious front porch is a favorite among guests. Breakfast in the dining room includes apple or cranberry-walnut pancakes with pure New England maple syrup and jugs of freshly ground café au lait. Guests may also choose a Continental breakfast in bed. Close to many parks and resort areas. Children welcome. Smoking limited; no pets. $40-95.

Wilderness Inn Bed and Breakfast

Routes 3 and 112, RFD Box 69, 03262
(603) 745-3890; (800) 200-WILD-200

Built in 1912, the Wilderness Inn is decorated with antiques and turn-of-the-century photographs. Guest rooms have views of Lost River or the mountains. Avid skiers, canoers, and hikers themselves, the owners are delighted to help guests explore the area. Breakfasts include fresh fruit and juice, home-baked muffins, a choice of apple- or cranberry-walnut pancakes, crêpes with sour cream and homemade applesauce, or vegetable omelets.

Hosts: Michael and Rosanna Yarnell
Rooms: 8 (6 PB; 2 SB) $40-90
Full Breakfast
Credit Cards: A, B, C
Notes: 2, 5, 8, 9, 10, 11, 12, 13, 14

7 No smoking; 8 Children welcome; 9 Social drinking allowed; 10 Tennis nearby; 11 Swimming nearby; 12 Golf nearby; 13 Skiing nearby; 14 May be booked through a travel agent.

ORFORD

The American Country Collection

4 Greenwood Lane, Delmar, NY 12054
(518) 439-7001

178. This is a large country home surrounded by 125 acres of open fields/acres of woods and wonderful views. It has a living room with fireplace, cozy sitting room with wood stove, and a screened veranda. A second-floor sitting room has TV/VCR. Bedrooms have individually controlled heating and are comfortably furnished with carpets or area rugs, reading lamps, sitting areas, and down pillows and comforters. Children are welcome; 14 and under stay free in the same room as parents, and half-price for children under 18 staying in separate room. No resident pets. Smoking permitted outside. Continental breakfast served. $55-95.

PLYMOUTH

Colonel Spencer Inn

Rural Route 1, Box 206, 03264
(603) 536-3438; (603) 536-1944

The inn is a tastefully restored 1764 Colonial home featuring hewn post and beam construction, wainscoting, paneling,

Colonel Spencer Inn

gunstock corners, Indian shutters, and wide pine floors. Seven antique-appointed bedrooms with private baths welcome guests with New England warmth and hospitality. A full country breakfast is served in a fire-placed dining room within view of the White Mountains and the Pemigewasset River. Convenient to lake and mountain attractions, at Exit 27, off I-93, one-half mile south on Route 3.

Hosts: Carolyn and Alan Hill
Rooms: 7 (PB) $45-65
Credit Cards: None
Notes: 2, 5, 7, 8, 9, 10, 11, 12, 13, 14

Crab Apple Inn

Rural Route 4, Box 188, 03264
(603) 536-4476

Nestled at the foothills of the White Mountains, this 1835 brick Federal-style inn offers comfort in its antique-appointed guest rooms. A cheery breakfast room and spacious parlor provide ample room to enjoy a gourmet breakfast or the challenge of finishing the ever-present jigsaw puzzle. Spacious grounds and gardens complement this beautiful country inn. Children over 12 welcome.

Host: Christine De Camp
Rooms: 5 (3 PB; 2 SB) $60-85
Full Breakfast
Credit Cards: A, B
Notes: 2, 5, 7, 9, 10, 11, 12, 13

PORTSMOUTH

Bed and Breakfast Marblehead and North Shore

P.O. Box 35, Newtonville, MA 02160
(617) 964-1606; (800) 832-2632
FAX (617) 332-8572

Great Islander Bed and Breakfast. A short drive from the downtown area of Portsmouth transports guests to the wonderful island experience of New Castle. Enjoy New Castle's peace and tranquility and lovely beach/park, before heading back

NOTES: Credit cards accepted: A MasterCard; B Visa; C American Express; D Discover; E Diners Club; F Other; 2 Personal checks accepted; 3 Lunch available; 4 Dinner available; 5 Open all year; 6 Pets welcome;

to the mainland. This cozy bed and breakfast offers the comforts of home in a two-story traditional Colonial built in the 1700s and fully restored with modern amenities. Two guest rooms share a full bath. Guests may relax and unwind in the TV/sitting room. Continental breakfast served. No smoking allowed. Open May through October. $75-100.

The Riverfront Inn. A 19th-century brick building on the Piscataqua River. Ten rooms include queen-size brass beds, reading chairs and full private baths; one extra-large room has an additional queen-size pullout sofa and small refrigerator. An expanded complimentary breakfast is served in the sunny breakfast room. fax service is available on-site. Open year-round. No smoking. $89-195.

The Bow Street Inn

121 Bow Street, 03801
(603) 431-7760

An attractive alternative for any seacoast tourist, the Bow Street Inn is also irresistible lodging for the traveling professional and visitor. On the Piscataqua River, in downtown Portsmouth, the inn's newly decorated and furnished rooms offer spectacular river views, rooftop views of Portsmouth, telephone, full bath, and color TV. Guests can also enjoy a complimentary Continental breakfast in the breakfast room. The Bow Street Theatre is on the premises. Guests can take a walk across the city's classic liftbridge into Maine or enjoy the flower gardens at Prescott Park, which is just two blocks away. Other local attractions include 25 restaurants within three blocks and easy access to waterfront decks and the marina.

Host: Liz Hurley
Rooms: 10 (PB)
Continental Breakfast
Credit Cards: A, B, C, D
Notes: 2, 5, 7, 9, 11, 12

Governor's House Bed and Breakfast

32 Miller Avenue, 03801
(603) 431-6546

A welcoming warmth is immediately felt as Nancy and John greet guests in this stately Georgian Colonial. A bottomless cookie jar reigns in the dining room with afternoon tea. Each air-conditioned bedroom has a different motif with unique private baths that enhance the elegant antique decor. A ten-minute stroll brings guests to the harbor cruises, historic mansions, shops, and fine restaurants. A hidden treasure in Portsmouth. Children over 14 welcome.

Hosts: Nancy and John Grossman
Rooms: 4 (PB) $75-140
Full Breakfast
Credit Cards: A, B, C
Notes: 2, 5, 7, 9, 10, 11, 12, 14

Cathedral House

RINDGE

Cathedral House

63 Cathedral Entrance, 03461
(603) 899-6790

The Cathedral House is on the grounds of the internationally renowned Cathedral of the Pines. Here guests and their families can enjoy the comforts of a tasteful 1850s farmhouse surrounded by meadows and mountain ranges. Marked trails lead to a grassy pond for fishing and canoeing or to the cathedral gardens and chapels where outdoor weddings, christenings, and ser-

---

7 No smoking; 8 Children welcome; 9 Social drinking allowed; 10 Tennis nearby; 11 Swimming nearby; 12 Golf nearby; 13 Skiing nearby; 14 May be booked through a travel agent.

vices for all faiths are conducted. Bring the family and step back to a time when traveling meant being welcomed into a stranger's house only to find a home away from home.

Hosts: Donald and Shirley Mahoney
Rooms: 5 (SB) $50-75
Full Breakfast
Credit Cards: A, B
Notes: 2, 5, 7, 8, 11, 12, 13

RUMNEY

New Hampshire Bed and Breakfast

128 South Hoop Pole Road, Guilford, CT 06437
(203) 457-0042; (800) 582-0853

NH248. This 1790 Early American farmhouse and attached ell sit on 125 acres of beautiful fields and woodland, with views of the White Mountains. Gardens, a real sugar house, and a barn all add to the peaceful country setting. Guests will enjoy private sitting areas, games, books, and the full country breakfast in the dining room of the main house. Hiking, walking, or cross-country ski trails are available throughout the property. The sugar house is in operation during March and April of every year. Three guest rooms available. Resident dog. Children welcome. No smoking. $55-75.

RYE

Rock Ledge Manor Bed and Breakfast

1413 Ocean Boulevard, Route 1A, 03870
(603) 431-1413

Gracious traditional seaside manor home (1840-80) with wraparound porch. All rooms have oceanview. Six minutes to historic Portsmouth; 20 minutes to University of New Hampshire; 15 minutes to Hampton; 30 minutes to southern Maine's seacoast attractions. Children over 15 welcome.

Hosts: Norman and Janice Marineau
Rooms: 4 (2 PB; 2 SB) $75-90
Full Breakfast
Credit Cards: None
Notes: 2, 5, 7, 9, 10, 11, 12

SNOWVILLE

Snowvillage Inn

Stuart Road, P.O. Box 68, 03832
(603) 447-2818

On a New Hampshire hillside with a sweeping view of the White Mountains, Snowvillage Inn is an ideal romantic getaway. This 18-room inn is a classic New England country inn. All rooms have private baths, some have mountain views and fireplaces. The many unique features of this inn from llama hikes to cross-country skiing from the front door make it a very special place. Enjoy elegant country dining in the restaurant that is also open to the public. Four-course candlelit dinner. Children over seven welcome.

Hosts: Barbara and Kevin Flynn
Rooms: 18 (PB) $59-125
Full Breakfast
Credit Cards: A, B, C, D, E
Notes: 2, 4, 5, 7, 9, 10, 11, 12, 13, 14

STARK VILLAGE

New Hampshire Bed and Breakfast

128 South Hoop Pole Road, Guilford, CT 06437
(203) 457-0042; (800) 582-0853

NH130. In historic Stark Village on the banks of the Upper Ammonoosuc River, this large, rambling white farmhouse has been restored and updated to offer guests a large living room with TV and fireplace, a country kitchen with antique wood stove, and a dining room where wonderful breakfasts are served. The inn borders the White Mountains National Forest and is three miles from the Nash Stream Valley Wilderness Area known for some of the best hunting and fishing in New Hampshire. Hiking, swimming, canoeing, bicycling, picnicking, hunting, fishing, cross-country skiing, snowmobiling, and skating are all available. Three guest rooms with private baths. Children welcome. No pets; no smoking. $45-55.

SUGAR HILL

New Hampshire Bed and Breakfast

128 South Hoop Pole Road, Guilford, CT 06437
(203) 457-0042; (800) 582-0853

NH133. On the eastern slope of Sugar Hill overlooking Franconia Notch, Mount Washington, and the Presidential Range. Relax on the porch in a comfortable rocker and enjoy views of expansive fields with a backdrop of Mount Washington's snow-capped peak. The surrounding White Mountains region offers year-round recreation and activities, and an on-site tennis court and nearby golf course are available for guests to use. A full country breakfast is served each morning, and three guest rooms, all of which offer private baths, are available. Within a short drive to Franconia Notch State Park, the Robert Frost Farm, Cannon Mountain Ski Area, and the New England Ski Museum. Resident dog. Children welcome. No smoking. $65-80.

SUNAPEE

New Hampshire Bed and Breakfast

128 South Hoop Pole Road, Guilford, CT 06437
(203) 457-0042; (800) 582-0853

NH302. In the heart of New Hampshire's Lake Sunapee region, this 18th-century farmhouse sits on six country acres. This bed and breakfast prides itself on warm hospitality, cleanliness, and a hearty home-made breakfast served in a room that overlooks the pond. Fun awaits in the game room where guests will find a pool table, a variety of board games, or a good book or movie. During the winter months, savor the comfort of a crackling fire with a complimentary cup of hot soup or stew. Four guest rooms share two baths. Smoking is allowed downstairs only. Resident dog. Children over six are welcome. $40-50.

SUTTON MILLS

Bed and Breakfast Marblehead and North Shore

P.O. Box 35, Newtonville, MA 02160
(617) 964-1606; (800) 832-2632 outside MA

The Quilt House. This is one of the prettiest bed and breakfasts in the area. It is a 130-year-old Victorian country house overlooking a quaint village. The hostess runs workshops on quilting, and there are many fine quilts throughout the house. Three guest rooms on the second floor share two baths. Ten minutes away from summer theater, excellent restaurants, fine shopping, and antiquing. Delicious full breakfast. Children welcome. No smoking. $50-65.

TAMWORTH

New Hampshire Bed and Breakfast

128 South Hoop Pole Road, Guilford, CT 06437
(203) 457-0042; (800) 582-0853

NH100. In the center of historic Tamworth Village, this 18th-century Colonial dates back to 1785 and is furnished with period antiques. Exposed beams, wainscoting, stenciled floors, gunstock posts, and fireplaces exude the charm one hopes to find in a country inn. The inn is only a stone's throw from the Swift River for trout fishing; a stroll to summer theater; minutes from AMC hiking trails; and a short drive to North Conway and Mount Washington Valley areas. Breakfast is a hearty affair served on antique china in the dining room. Four guest rooms, one with private bath. Children 12 and older welcome. Smoking permitted. No pets. $50-85.

THORNTON

Amber Lights Inn Bed and Breakfast

Route 3, 03223
(603) 726-4077

Lovingly restored 1815 Colonial offering a sumptuous six-course breakfast, homemade bread, and muffins like Grandma made. Queen-size country beds with handmade quilts and meticulously clean guest rooms. Private and semiprivate baths, Hannah Adams dining room with fireplace, guest library, and garden rooms. Hors d'oeuvres served nightly. Between Loon Mountain and Waterville Valley. Close to all White Mountains attractions. Take a stroll through five acres to a private brook. No pets. Murder mystery weekends available. Children over seven welcome.

Hosts: Paul Sears and Carola Warnsman
Rooms: 5 (1 PB; 4 SB) $60-75
Full Breakfast
Credit Cards: A, B, C, D
Notes: 2, 5, 7, 9, 10, 11, 12, 13, 14

TILTON

Black Swan Inn

308 West Main Street, 03276
(603) 286-4524; FAX (603) 286-8260

An 1880 restored Victorian in the Lakes Region on four acres overlooking the Winnipesaukee River. Mahogany and oak woodwork and stained-glass windows, two screened porches, and formal gardens. Refrigerator and sodas available. One mile from I-93 and two miles from Lakes Region Outlet Mall. Three-diamond-rated by AAA.

Closed March. No smoking on first floor. Children ten and over welcome.

Hosts: Janet and Bob Foster
Rooms: 9 (5 PB; 4 SB) $65-100
Full Breakfast
Credit Cards: A, B, C, D, E
Notes: 2, 9, 10, 11, 12, 13

Tilton Manor

28 Chestnut Street, 03276
(603) 286-3457

Tilton Manor is a 16-room turn-of-the-century mansion nestled in a tranquil three and one-half-acre setting. Furnished only with antiques and handmade afghans. A full country breakfast is served daily. Awaken to the aroma of home cooking and freshly baked muffins. Dinner is served upon request only. Reservations are requested. Travelers checks are accepted. Outlet shopping minutes away.

Hosts: Diane and Chip
Rooms: 4 (2 PB; 2 SB) $55-65
Full Breakfast
Credit Cards: A, B, C, D
Notes: 2, 4, 5, 6, 7, 8, 9, 10, 11, 12, 13

WAKEFIELD

Jon Gilman Homestead Bed and Breakfast

Governor's Road, 03872
(603) 522-3102

More than 200 years old, this home belonged to one of the town's first settlers. Atmosphere is warm and restful. Accommodations are homey and welcoming, allowing guests to take a step back in time. Easy day trips to the lakes, Mount Washington, Portsmouth, and New Hampshire tax-free shopping. Summer fun and winter sports are near or just restful countryside. Ten dollars per extra person per room.

Rooms: 5 (SB) $40
Continental Breakfast
Credit Cards: None
Notes: 2, 5, 7, 8, 11, 12, 13

NOTES: Credit cards accepted: A MasterCard; B Visa; C American Express; D Discover; E Diners Club; F Other; 2 Personal checks accepted; 3 Lunch available; 4 Dinner available; 5 Open all year; 6 Pets welcome;

WENTWORTH

Hilltop Acres

East Side and Buffalo Road, 03282
(603) 764-5896

Guests can treat themselves to this peaceful country retreat; large pine-paneled recreation room with fireplace, piano, games, and cable TV. Spacious grounds surrounded by pine forest with natural brook; lawn games; peaceful atmosphere. Rooms with private baths; housekeeping cottages. Near White Mountains and Lakes Region attractions. Open May through October. Inquire about accommodations for pets.

Host: Marie A. Kauk
Rooms: 4 (PB) $65
Cottages: 2 (PB) $80
Continental Breakfast
Credit Cards: A, B, C, D
Notes: 2, 8, 9, 11, 12, 13, 14

New Hampshire Bed and Breakfast

128 South Hoop Pole Road, Guilford, CT 06437
(203) 457-0042; (800) 582-0853

NH120. This charming home, built in the early 1880s, is within an easy drive of both the Lakes Region and Franconia Notch, where guests can enjoy outdoor sports, shops, crafts and art galleries, theater, and fine restaurants. Wentworth offers three natural swimming holes, many hiking trails, fishing streams, and antique shops. The home itself is furnished with antiques. The pine-paneled recreation room is complete with an antique piano, games, an extensive library, and cable TV. Continental breakfast and afternoon teas are served. Six guest rooms, four with private bath. Two housekeeping cottages with kitchen unit, private living room with fireplace, and screened porch available. Children welcome. No smoking; no pets. $65-80.

WHITEFIELD

The Spalding Inn

Mountain View Road, 03598
(603) 837-2572; (800) 368-VIEW

Travel down a winding country road lined with stone walls to find this historic inn. On 200 acres with glorious mountain views, warm hospitality awaits guests. This lovely inn has many amenities including four clay tennis courts, a nine-hole golf course, and a heated swimming pool. The inn has large common rooms and an extensive library. A variety of accommodations are available in the main house, the romantic carriage house, or family cottage. A full country breakfast is served. Dinner is also included in room rates.

Hosts: Dione Cockwell and Michael Flinder
Rooms: 36 (PB) $79-89
Full Breakfast
Credit Cards: A, B
Notes: 2, 3, 4, 6, 7, 8, 9, 10, 11, 12, 14

WINNISQUAM

Tall Pines Inn

752 State Route 3, P.O. Box 327, 03284-0327
(603) 528-3632; (800) 722-6870
FAX (603) 528-8550

Tall Pines Inn is a homestay bed and breakfast country inn in the heart of New Hampshire's Lakes Region. The inn is on the south shore of Lake Winnisquam and features an outstanding view of the lake and White Mountains to the north. There are three lovely, comfortable rooms, one with private bath and two that share a bath. Room rental includes full all-you-can-eat country breakfast.

Hosts: Kent and Kate Kern
Rooms: 3 (1 PB; 2 SB) $55-75
Full Breakfast
Credit Cards: A, B, D
Notes: 2, 4, 5, 9, 10, 11, 12, 13, 14

7 No smoking; 8 Children welcome; 9 Social drinking allowed; 10 Tennis nearby; 11 Swimming nearby; 12 Golf nearby; 13 Skiing nearby; 14 May be booked through a travel agent.

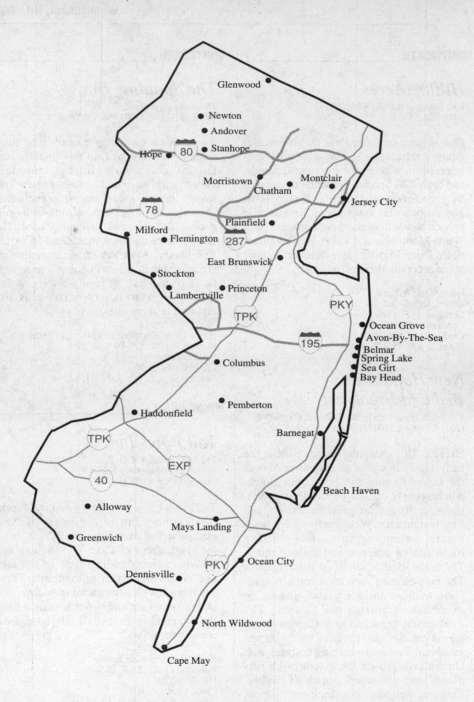

New Jersey

New Jersey

ALLOWAY

Guesthouse, Inc.

P.O. Box 2137, Westchester, PA 19380
(215) 692-4575

873. In 1836, three brothers built three imposing Greek Revival manor houses in a line across from their shipyard. The first house borders the creek and has massive double chimneys and a free-standing spiral staircase. The house is open to the public during historic and house-and-garden tours.The present owners have completely restored the building to its former grandeur and have added hospitable touches such as indoor plumbing (with Old World charm) and central air conditioning. There are three bedrooms with fireplaces, two bedrooms with baths ensuite, one of which has a fireplace and a bathroom the size of a bedroom. All rooms are romantically decorated and furnished with period antiques. The main floor public rooms are large and graciously furnished. A full breakfast is served in the formal dining room or on the terrace, where classical music is played, adding to the genteel ambience of the lovely gardens. The property has been cleared to provide a path to the adjoining 112-acre lake where guests will find a rowboat and paddles purely for exercise and amusement or for bass fishing. Other activities include antiquing at nearby Mullica Hill. Golf outings can be arranged, including lunch and greens fee for less than $20 per person. $100-200.

ANDOVER

Crossed Keys Bed and Breakfast

289 Pequest Road, 07821
(201) 786-6661; FAX (201) 786-6320

In an 1800 setting on 12 beautiful acres with stream pond reflecting pools, the Crossed Keys is decorated with fine antiques, reproduction furnishings, elegant linens, and five fireplaces. Separate artist studio with pool table, player piano, shuffle board, and comfortable sofas for relaxing. The stone cottage with a two-person Jacuzzi is decorated with a touch of France. A full country breakfast is served on fine china, crystal, and silver in a 1700 dining room. Near Waterloo Village, Skylands Ball Park, Delaware recreation area, Great Gorge, Action Park, hiking, skiing, and antiquing.

Hosts: Pat Toye and Peter Belder
Rooms: 5 (3 PB; 2 SB) $90-125
Full Breakfast
Credit Cards: A, B, C
Notes: 5, 7, 9, 10, 11, 12, 13, 14

AVON-BY-THE-SEA

The Avon Manor Inn

109 Sylvania Avenue, 07717-1338
(908) 774-0110

Pass through the columned portico and be greeted by a friendly and informal atmosphere in this Colonial Revival home. Furnished with antiques and wicker, the Avon Manor Inn was built in 1907 only

---

NOTES: Credit cards: A MasterCard; B Visa; C American Express; D Discover; E Diners Club; F Other; 2 Personal checks accepted; 3 Lunch available; 4 Dinner available; 5 Open all year; 6 Pets welcome; 7 No smoking; 8 Children welcome; 9 Social drinking allowed; 10 Tennis nearby; 11 Swimming nearby; 12 Golf nearby; 13 Skiing nearby; 14 May be booked through a travel agent.

The Avon Manor

one block from the ocean. Enjoy breakfast in the sunny dining room, ocean breezes on the full wraparound veranda, and the charm of this small seaside town. A full breakfast is served. The large living room has a fireplace for cozy winter nights. Rediscover romance at this charming seaside inn. Personal checks accepted for deposit only.

Hosts: Jim and Kathleen Curley
Rooms: 8 (6 PB; 2 SB) $80-110
Full Breakfast
Credit Cards: A, B, C
Notes: 5, 7, 8, 9, 10, 11, 12, 14

Cashelmara Inn

22 Lakeside Avenue, 07717
(908) 776-8727; (800) 821-2976

Oceanside/lakefront Victorian inn allows guests to enjoy views of the Atlantic from bed. Rooms decorated in beautiful Victorian antiques and a wicker-filled veranda overlooking the ocean make stays here memorable. A suite with a fireplace is also available. Only 55 minutes from New York City and one hour from Philadelphia. Singles $10 less. Minimum stay summer weekends: three nights; summer holidays: four nights.

Host: Mary E. Wiernasz
Owner: Martin J. Mulligan
Rooms: 12 (PB) $75-165
Suite: 1 (PB)
Full Breakfast
Credit Cards: A, B, C, D
Notes: 2, 5, 8, 9, 10, 11, 12

The Sands Bed and Breakfast Inn

42 Sylvania Avenue, 07717
(908) 776-8386

The Sands is in a small Victorian town just seven houses from the nicest beach on the Jersey shore. The inn radiates warmth and hospitality. Each of the nine rooms has a paddle fan, and many have sinks and refrigerators. Spend an afternoon on the beautiful white sandy beach or walk on the new boardwalk. A lovely breakfast is served each morning in the family dining room or on the porch. A stay at the inn will make guests feel relaxed and refreshed.

Host: Ann Suchecki
Rooms: 9 (SB) $55-75
Full Breakfast
Credit Cards: C
Notes: 2, 7, 9, 10, 11, 12

BARNEGAT

The Dynasty

Pebble Beach, 248 Edison Road, 08005
(609) 698-1566

A quiet, bayside, air-conditioned home on a peninsula with dock space. Breakfast is served around an award-winning pool amid

The Dynasty

beautiful foliage. Enjoy a picturesque view of the sunset and wildlife reserve, the warmth of a designer's fireplace, and the ultimate in antiques collected from around the world. Just minutes to the world's largest playground, Atlantic City. Closed October 16 through May 5

Host: Stanley Finkelstein
Rooms: 3 (1 PB; 2 SB) $66-125
Full Breakfast
Credit Cards: None
Notes: 2, 8, 9, 10, 11, 12, 13, 14

BAY HEAD

Conover's Bay Head Inn

646 Main Avenue, 08742
(908) 892-4664

The 12 romantic, antique-filled bedrooms have views of the ocean, bay, marina, or gardens. The aroma of inn-baked biscuits, muffins, or coffeecake awakens guests each morning. The full breakfast may feature a savory egg casserole, French toast, or a special blueberry pancake. Enjoy a large collection of original art or swim at the private ocean beaches. Collect seashells and sea glass. Walk to Twilight Lake and feed the ducks or relax in the garden.

Hosts: Carl and Beverly Conover
Rooms: 12 (PB) $90-195
Full Breakfast
Credit Cards: A, B, C
Notes: 2, 5, 9, 10, 11, 12

BEACH HAVEN

The Bayberry Barque

117 Centre Street, 08008
(609) 492-5216

The Bayberry Barque is a beautifully restored Victorian home in Beach Haven's historic district, a half block from the beach. A Continental plus breakfast features home-baked specialties and is highlighted by the morning sun shining through a unique 4- x 8-feet stained glass window.

Rooms are large, comfortable, and decorated with period pieces. Relax to the sound of surf on the wraparound porch. Walk to Surflight Playhouse, movies, restaurants, and Atlantic City Cruise ship. Children over 12 welcome.

Hosts: Tom and Barbara DeSanto
Rooms: 8 (5 PB; 3 SB) $65-135
Continental Breakfast
Credit Cards: A, B, C
Notes: 2, 9, 10, 11

Bed and Breakfast Adventures

Suite 132, 2310 Central Ave., N. Wildwood, 08260
(606) 522-4000; (800) 992-2632

482. This charming authentic Victorian bed and breakfast, circa 1876, on the beach corner, offers guests nine antique-filled rooms complete with stained glass windows and all the comforts of home. The Old World charm and atmosphere are a reflection of the host's style. Guests are offered a sumptuous breakfast, afternoon tea, Saturday evening wine and cheese, sunsets, Sunday brunch, espresso and cappuccino served with biscotti, and warm ocean breezes on the wraparound veranda. Guests can enjoy the large yard with a gazebo and fountain. The beach is one block away, and shopping and a summer theater are nearby, as are fishing, other water sports, and fine restaurants. Take the cruise ship to Atlantic City. In the winter, the fireplace offers a perfect spot to relax and enjoy a book. Mid-week specials and minimum stays may apply. The inn is also smoke-free and does not accept pets. Open year-round. $50-150.

BELMAR

Down the Shore Bed and Breakfast

201 Seventh Avenue, 07719
(908) 681-9023

Off exit 98 on Garden State Parkway, this newly constructed home offers three guest rooms with private or shared baths. Guest parlor with TV, refrigerator, and microwave. Shaded porch for guests to enjoy. Just one block to beach and boardwalk. Midweek special rates.

Hosts: Annette and Al Bergins
Rooms: 3 (1 PB; 2 SB) $50-80
Full Breakfast
Credit Cards: None
Notes: 2, 5, 7, 8, 9, 11, 12, 14

The Inn at the Shore

301 Fourth Avenue, 07719
(908) 681-3762; FAX (201) 945-2944

Enjoy the inn's casual Victorian ambience on the expansive wraparound porch, where a rocking chair takes one back to the seashore of days gone by. Relax in the spacious common areas, including a café-style brick patio ready for barbecues or refreshing beverages after a day at the beach. The large living room with its lovely stone fireplace and state-of-the-art entertainment center, the grand dining room, and the library are perfect for reading, writing, or just unwinding. The beach is only a short walk away, as is Silver Lake, home of the first flock of swans bred in America.

Hosts: Rosemary and Tom Volker
Rooms: 12 (3 PB: 9 SB) $55-95
Continental Breakfast
Credit Cards: A, B, C, D, E
Notes: 2, 5, 7, 8, 9, 10, 11, 12, 14

The Inn at the Shore

The Seaflower Bed and Breakfast Inn

110 Ninth Avenue, 07719-2302
(908) 681-6006

A comfortable Dutch Colonial inn a half-block from the beach and boardwalk. Guest rooms feature the sound of the ocean and the scent of flowers. Wallpapers set off an eclectic mixture of antiques, four-poster canopy beds, and an abundance of paintings. Enjoy the view from the porch's teak Adirondack chairs. One of the East Coast's major deep-sea fishing ports is nearby. Children over nine welcome.

Hosts: Knute Iwaszko and Pat O'Keefe
Rooms: 6 (4PB; 2 SB) $75-100
Full Breakfast
Credit Cards: C
Notes: 2, 5, 7, 9, 10, 11, 12

CAPE MAY

The Abbey

34 Columbia Avenue and Gurney Street, 08204
(609) 884-4506

The Abbey consists of two restored Victorian buildings in the heart of Cape May's historic district. Originally owned by the family of Philadelphia coal baron John B. McCreary. Line drawings of the main house are on file in the Library of Congress. The cottage is a delightful example of Second Empire Mansard Revival style. All rooms are furnished with period Victorian antiques and have private baths and small refrigerators. Most have air conditioning in season. Some on-site parking; beach chairs and tags included. Afternoon tea. Three-night minimum stay from June 15 through September 30, major holidays, and most weekends. Closed mid-December to March. Personal checks for deposit only. Children 12 and over welcome.

Hosts: Jay and Marianne Schatz
Rooms: 14 (PB) $95-200
Full Breakfast
Credit Cards: A, B, D
Notes: 7, 9, 10, 11, 12

NOTES: Credit cards accepted: A MasterCard; B Visa; C American Express; D Discover; E Diners Club; F Other; 2 Personal checks accepted; 3 Lunch available; 4 Dinner available; 5 Open all year; 6 Pets welcome;

The Albert Stevens Inn

The Albert Stevens Inn

127 Myrtle Avenue, 08204
(609) 884-4717

Built in 1889 by Dr. Albert G. Stevens for his bride, Bessie, this Queen Anne Victorian home offers its guests a warm, restful visit. Just three blocks from the beach and shopping. A three-course hot breakfast is served each morning with a relaxing tea in the afternoon. Dinner is available in the off-season. Soak in the 102-degree hot tub before strolling through the unusual Cat's Garden.

Hosts: Curt and Diane Diviney Rangen
Rooms: 9 (PB) $65-155
Full Breakfast
Credit Cards: A, B, C, D
Notes: 2, 5, 7, 9, 10, 11, 12, 14

Amanda's Bed and Breakfast

21 South Woodland Avenue, East Brunswick, 08816
(908) 249-4944

168. Built in 1840 and enlarged in 1900, this Victorian mansion retains the ambience and grandeur of the era. Enjoy elegance and comfort, period reproduction wallpapers, and the original furnishings of the Wilbraham family. Heated swimming pool available to guests. Four blocks from the beach, and beach passes are available. Seven accommodations, all with private baths. Full breakfast. $95-185.

Angel of the Sea

5-7 Trenton Avenue, 08204
(800) 848-3369

Just off the beach, Angel of the Sea is a national award-winning Victorian mansion. All 27 guest rooms are uniquely furnished and decorated, and all have private baths. Porches and verandas offer guests a panoramic view of the Atlantic Ocean. All rates include a full-service gourmet breakfast, afternoon tea and sweets, wine and cheese, bicycles, all beach equipment, and private off-street parking.

Hosts: John and Barbara Girton
Rooms: 27 (PB) $135-250
Full Breakfast
Credit Cards: A, B
Notes: 2, 5, 7, 9, 10, 11, 12

Association of Bed and Breakfasts in Philadelphia, Valley Forge, Brandywine

P.O. Box 562, Valley Forge, PA 19481-0562
(610) 783-7838; (800) 344-0132
FAX (610) 783-7783

0905. This comfortable and tastefully decorated second-floor condo is six-blocks from the ocean. Guest quarters consist of two bedrooms—one has a double bed and the other has twin beds—a living room and dining area, and full kitchen. A two-night minimum stay is required on weekends. $75-100.

Barnard-Good House

238 Perry Street, 08204
(609) 884-5381

The Barnard-Good House is known for its breakfasts, which were selected as number one by *New Jersey Monthly* magazine. The hosts continue to make them even better.

7 No smoking; 8 Children welcome; 9 Social drinking allowed; 10 Tennis nearby; 11 Swimming nearby;
12 Golf nearby; 13 Skiing nearby; 14 May be booked through a travel agent.

Breakfast consists of four courses, all gourmet and homemade. This purple house caters to happiness and comfort. All rooms have private baths and air conditioning. Three-day minimum stay required in season; four nights required for holidays in season. Closed November 1 to April 1. Children over 14 welcome.

Hosts: Nan and Tom Hawkins
Rooms: 5 (PB) $90-128
Full Breakfast
Credit Cards: A, B
Notes: 2, 7, 9, 10, 11, 12

Bed and Breakfast Adventures
Suite 132, 2310 Central Ave., N. Wildwood, 08260
(606) 522-4000; (800) 992-2632

NJ488. An 1877 Victorian home lovingly restored to its original elegance, this inn is a short walk to Washington Street Mall, the ocean promenade and beach, and the area's fine restaurants. All rooms and suites have private baths and in-room refrigerators, and are cooled by ocean breezes and fans or air conditioning. A full buffet breakfast is served each morning. Well-behaved children over ten are welcome. Open year-round. Smoking permitted only on the veranda. $85-150.

NJ594. This 120-year-old carpenter Gothic-style inn in the historic district is two blocks from the ocean. Personal touches are everywhere, including family heirlooms, old photos of relatives, and an upright 1895 piano. A portion of the wicker-furnished veranda is screened in summer and glass-enclosed and heated in winter. The inn has eight guest rooms, which have either king-size or double beds. Four rooms have private baths, two have private hall baths, and two third-floor rooms share a bath with robes provided. Every room has polished period brass beds, restored armoires, marble-topped tables, washstands, dressers, air conditioners, and ceiling fans. A full breakfast is served in the morning, and afternoon tea, lemonade, or cider is avail-

able after a long day at the beach or sightseeing. Outside shower, beach passes, bicycle rack, and dressing room are also available. The inn is open year-round and has a two- or three-night minimum stay on weekends, depending on season. No pets or smoking permitted. $65-150.

NJ612. Restored in 1985, this 24-room Victorian carpenter Gothic inn offers a vacation living experience typical of the Gay Nineties. Accommodations include private and shared baths and a two-room suite with a private sitting room. Guests may also enjoy the large pillared living room with fireplace, formal dining room, and library. A delicious breakfast is prepared daily. The inn is within a block of Washington Street Mall, beaches, and restaurants. No smoking. Children over 12 welcome. $95-170.

NJ627. This Colonial Revival bed and breakfast inn is in a quieter area of Cape May yet is only two blocks from the ocean and within walking distance of the Victorian Mall. A three-story home with Victorian charm inside and outside. Visitors will find a large living room with a fireplace and French doors leading to a side patio. The dining room, with relaxed formality, has a tree in the corner that is decorated for a particular holiday season of the year. Guest rooms consist of king-, queen-size, or twin beds with private baths. A full breakfast of homemade delicacies is offered each morning. Plenty of off-street parking is available. Guests have use of beach tags and sand chairs. Open February through December. $85-115.

Captain Mey's Inn
202 Ocean Street, 08204
(609) 884-7793

The Dutch heritage is evident from the Persian rugs on table tops to Delft blue china to European antiques. Guests will

Captain Mey's Inn

marvel at the Eastlake paneling in the dining room, leaded-glass bay window, and the restored fireplace. All guest rooms are air-conditioned. A full country breakfast is served accompanied by homemade breads, juice, meats, fresh fruit, and jellies. The meal is served by candlelight with classical music in the formal dining room, and in the summer guests may enjoy breakfast on the lovely wraparound veranda, with antique wicker and hanging ferns. Cape May offers beaches, shops, fine restaurants, a lighthouse, walking and trolley tours, bird watching, boating, fishing, and gaslit streets. Children over eight are welcome.

Hosts: George and Kathleen Blinn
Rooms: 8 (PB) $75-210
Full Breakfast
Credit Cards: A, B, C
Notes: 2, 5, 7, 9, 10, 11, 12, 14

Chalfonte Hotel

301 Howard Street, 08204
(609) 884-8409; FAX (609) 884-4588

The Chalfonte is a rambling, old-fashioned summer hotel that has preserved the best of the Victorian lifestyle. Both dinner and breakfast are included in the room rates, and guests are encouraged to sit at family tables seating up to ten people. Families are welcome. Children six and under dine in a supervised dining room. Smoking is not allowed in the rooms.

Hosts: Anne LeDuc and Judy Bartella
Rooms: 77 (11 PB; 66 SB) $81-165

Full Breakfast
Credit Cards: A, B
Notes: 2, 4, 8, 9, 10, 11, 12, 14

Cliveden Inn

709 Columbia Avenue, 08204
(609) 884-4516

Fine Victorian accommodations, delicious, hearty homemade buffet breakfast, and afternoon tea with treats. Two blocks to the beach and within easy walking distance of the Victorian Mall, tours, and fine restaurants. Closed November through mid-April. Cozy Victorian cottages available year-round.

Hosts: Sue and Al De Rosa
Rooms: 10 (PB) $90-135
Continental Breakfast
Credit Cards: A, B, C
Notes: 2, 8, 9, 10, 11, 12

Colvmns by the Sea

1513 Beach Drive, 08204
(609) 884-2228; (800) 691-6030
FAX (609) 884-4789

This elegant turn-of-the-century mansion on the ocean in a landmark Victorian village has large, airy rooms decorated with antiques and featuring breathtaking oceanviews. Watch the dolphins at play from the magnificent seaside veranda. Gourmet

Colvmns by the Sea

7 No smoking; 8 Children welcome; 9 Social drinking allowed; 10 Tennis nearby; 11 Swimming nearby;
12 Golf nearby; 13 Skiing nearby; 14 May be booked through a travel agent.

breakfast, high tea, evening snacks. Complimentary bikes and beach badges. Great for history buffs, bird watching, or just relaxing. Limited smoking. Inquire about accommodations for children.

Host: Bernadette Brennan Kaschner
Rooms: 11 (PB) $135-210
Full Breakfast
Credit Cards: A, B, F
Notes: 2, 3, 5, 9, 10, 11, 12, 14

Duke of Windsor Bed and Breakfast Inn

817 Washington Street, 08204
(609) 884-1355

Queen Anne Victorian house with 45-foot tower, built in 1890 and restored with period furnishings. Foyer has three-story, carved-oak staircase, and fireplace. Sitting room, parlor with fireplace, library, and dining room. Beach tags, hot and cold outdoor showers, and off-street parking available. Air conditioning. Smoking on the veranda only. Children over 12 welcome.

Hosts: Bruce and Fran Prichard
Rooms: 10 (8 PB; 2 SB) $75-185
Full Breakfast
Credit Cards: A, B
Notes: 2, 9, 10, 11, 12

Duke of Windsor Inn

Gingerbread House

28 Gurney Street, 08204
(609) 884-0211

The Gingerbread House is a meticulously and elegantly restored 1869 Victorian seaside cottage in the historic district, one-half block from the beach. Period antiques, original Cape May watercolor paintings, classical music, Fred's photographs, and exquisite woodwork combine with friendly service and attention to detail. Breakfast, afternoon tea and goodies, beach passes, fireplace, and guest veranda overlooking the quaint garden.

Hosts: Fred and Joan Echevarria
Rooms: 6 (3 PB; 3 SB) $95-165
Full Breakfast
Credit Cards: A, B
Notes: 2, 5, 7, 8, 9, 10, 11, 12

The Humphrey Hughes House

29 Ocean Street, 08204
(609) 884-4428; (800) 582-3634

Nestled in the heart of Cape May's historic section is one of its most authentically restored inns—perhaps the most spacious and gracious of them all. Until 1980 it was the Hughes family's home. While the house is filled with magnificent antiques, it still feels more like a home than a museum.

Hosts: Lorraine and Terry Schmidt
Rooms: 10 (PB) $85-210
Full Breakfast
Credit Cards: A, B
Notes: 2, 5, 7, 10, 11, 12

The Inn on Ocean

25 Ocean Street, 08204
(800) 304-4477

An intimate, elegant Victorian inn. Fanciful Second Empire style with an exuberant personality. Beautifully restored. King- and queen-size beds. Private baths. Centrally air-conditioned. Full breakfast. Wicker-filled oceanview porches. Billiard room.

NOTES: Credit cards accepted: A MasterCard; B Visa; C American Express; D Discover; E Diners Club; F Other; 2 Personal checks accepted; 3 Lunch available; 4 Dinner available; 5 Open all year; 6 Pets welcome;

Open year-round. Free on-site parking. Seasonal rates.

Rooms: 5 (PB) $99-275
Full Breakfast
Credit Cards: A, B, C, E
Notes: 2, 5, 7, 9, 10, 11, 12, 14

The Inn on Ocean

Leith Hall—Historic Seashore Inn

22 Ocean Street, 08204
(609) 884-1934

Elegantly restored 1880s home in the heart of the historic district. Only one-half block from the beach and three blocks from the mall. The inn features period antiques and wallpapers, oceanviews, full gourmet breakfasts, and afternoon English tea. Open year-round. Free parking.

Hosts: Elan and Susan Zingman-Leith
Rooms: 7 (PB) $75-150
Full Breakfast
Credit Cards: A, B
Notes: 2, 5, 9, 10, 11, 12

Mainstay Inn

635 Columbia Avenue, 08204
(609) 884-8690

Selected one of the "Five Top Inns for Quality and Value in 1993" by *Zagat Survey*. Spacious rooms and suites with fine antiques, some with fireplaces and private porches. All private baths, some with whirlpool tubs. Luscious breakfasts and afternoon teas.

Hosts: Tom and Sue Carroll
Rooms: 16 (PB) $95-250
Full and Continental Breakfast
Credit Cards: None
Notes: 2, 5, 7, 9, 10, 11, 12

The Manse Bed and Breakfast

510 Hughes Street, 08204
(609) 884-0116

The Manse is an elegant turn-of-the century home in the heart of Cape May's historic district. It boasts spacious rooms, natural floors, Persian rugs, lace curtains, antiques, and two generations offering unsurpassed hospitality. Breakfast is a special occasion with homemade delights served in a formal dining room or on the veranda. One block from the Victorian Mall and less than two blocks from the ocean.

Hosts: Karsten and Anita Dierk
Rooms: 6 (4 PB; 2 SB) $75-150
Full Breakfast
Credit Cards: None
Notes: 2, 5, 7, 8, 10, 11, 12

The Mason Cottage

625 Columbia Avenue, 08204
(609) 884-3358; (800) 716-2766 (reservations)

The Mason Cottage was built in 1871 as the summer residence for a Philadelphia entrepreneur and his family. In the historic district, the inn is Second Empire with a concave mansard roof. Within the inn, guests discover elegance, meticulous restoration, and warm hospitality. Guest room accommodations include four air-conditioned suites. Nearby attractions, house tours, antique shops, beaches, and Victorian shopping mall. The inn is one block from the beach and within walking distance of most of Cape May's finest restaurants.

Hosts: Joan and Dave Mason
Rooms: 9 (PB) $95-265
Full Breakfast
Credit Cards: A, B, C
Notes: 2, 7, 9, 10, 11, 12, 14

7 No smoking; 8 Children welcome; 9 Social drinking allowed; 10 Tennis nearby; 11 Swimming nearby; 12 Golf nearby; 13 Skiing nearby; 14 May be booked through a travel agent.

The Mooring

801 Stockton Avenue, 08204
(609) 884-5425; FAX (609) 884-1357

Built in 1882, one of Cape May's original guest houses. Comfortable elegance in a classic Second Empire inn, with grand entrance hall and wide spiral staircase leading to spacious guest rooms; each with private bath, ceiling fan, and period furnishings; most with air conditioning. Enjoy breakfast and afternoon tea in the dining room or on the front veranda. One block from the beach. Open April 1 through New Year's Day. Children over six welcome.

Host: Leslie Valenza
Rooms: 12 (PB) $75-150
Full Breakfast
Credit Cards: A, B
Notes: 2, 7, 9, 10, 11, 12, 14

Perry Street Inn

29 Perry Street, 08204
(609) 884-4590

Built as a beach house for a Victorian family at the turn of the century. Original family atmosphere endures. Antique decor throughout. Morning starts with fragrant home-baked breads. Breakfast served in sunlit dining room or open front porch with sea breezes and oceanview. Several guest rooms have oceanviews. Adjacent motel has one-bedroom suites with kitchen and TV. Prime historic district, a half-block to beach, mall. On-site parking. Packages include murder mystery weekends, wildlife sightseeing, and Christmas tours.

Hosts: John and Cynthia Curtis
Rooms: 10 (7 PB; 3 SB) $45-110
Full Breakfast
Credit Cards: A, B, C
Notes: 2, 3, 5, 7, 9, 10, 11, 12, 14

The Primrose

1102 Lafayette Street, 08204
(609) 884-8288; (800) 606-8288

A delightful blend of yesterday's charm and hospitality with today's comforts and conveniences in this completely restored 1850s home. Full breakfast includes home-baked goodies. Refreshments in the afternoon. A relaxing getaway year-round. On-site parking. Guests will fall in love with romantic, historic Cape May.

Hosts: Buddy and Jan Wood
Rooms: 4 (PB) $80-150
Full Breakfast
Credit Cards: A, B
Notes: 2, 5, 7, 9, 10, 11, 12, 14

The Queen Victoria

102 Ocean Street, 08204
(609) 884-8702

The Wells family welcomes guests as friends and treats them royally with unpretentious service and attention to detail. Three restored buildings furnished with antiques are in the center of the historic district. Nationally recognized for its special Christmas.

Hosts: Dane and Joan Wells
Rooms: 16 (PB) $85-250
Suites: 7 (PB)
Full Breakfast
Credit Cards: A, B
Notes: 2, 5, 8, 9, 10, 11, 12

The Queen Victoria

White Dove Cottage

619 Hughes Street, 08204
(609) 884-0613; (800) 321-3683

This elegant little bed and breakfast, circa 1866, is in the center of the historic district

NOTES: Credit cards accepted: A MasterCard; B Visa; C American Express; D Discover; E Diners Club;
F Other; 2 Personal checks accepted; 3 Lunch available; 4 Dinner available; 5 Open all year; 6 Pets welcome;

on a quiet, tree-lined, gaslit street. Four rooms plus two suites offer cheerful accommodations for guests. Bicycle rental, golf course, ocean, and beach are all nearby. Tea and snacks are served every afternoon, and a full breakfast starts the day. AAA, PAII, and NJBBA approved. Children over ten welcome.

Hosts: Frank and Sue Smith
Rooms: 6 (PB) $75-190
Full Breakfast
Credit Cards: None
Notes: 2, 5, 7, 9, 10, 11, 12, 14

Windward House

Wilbraham Mansion

133 Myrtle Avenue, 08204
(609) 884-2046

Antique-furnished Victorian mansion with period wallpaper and five magnificent gilded mirrors. A warm, hospitable staff presides over a delicious breakfast and refreshing afternoon tea. Bicycles, beach tags, ten air-conditioned bedrooms, and, best of all, an indoor heated swimming pool. A glassed-front porch abounds with plants and flowers year-round. Limited smoking permitted.

Rooms: 10 (PB) $95-185
Full Breakfast
Credit Cards: A, B
Notes: 2, 5, 10, 11, 12

Windward House

24 Jackson Street, 08204
(609) 884-3368

All three stories of this gracious Edwardian-style seaside inn contain antique-filled rooms. Beveled and stained glass cast rainbows of flickering light from the windows and French doors, while gleaming chestnut and oak paneling set off the museum-quality furnishings and collectibles. Spacious guest rooms have queen-size beds, private baths, air conditioning, and TV. Enjoy spectacular summer porches and wintertime coziness fireside. Prime historic district. A half-block to beach, shopping, mall, and restaurants.

Bicycles available. Limited smoking permitted. Children over eight welcome.

Hosts: Sandy and Owen Miller
Rooms: 8 (PB) $80-145
Full Breakfast
Credit Cards: A, B
Notes: 2, 5, 9, 10, 11, 12

The Wooden Rabbit

609 Hughes Street, 08204
(609) 884-7293

On one of the prettiest streets in Cape May, the Wooden Rabbit is nestled in the heart of the historic district, surrounded by Victorian cottages, shady trees, and brick walkways. Two blocks from beautiful sandy beaches. One block from Cape May's quaint shopping mall and within easy walking distance of fine restaurants. All guest rooms and suites are air-conditioned with private baths and TVs. The rooms sleep two to four persons comfortably. The hosts of the Wooden Rabbit are comfortable, casual folks who look forward to sharing their inn with guests. The decor is country and relaxed. A delicious, big breakfast is served year-round. Family atmosphere complete with owner's pet felines.

Hosts: Greg and Debby Burow
Rooms: 3 (PB) $85-195
Full Breakfast
Credit Cards: A, B, D
Notes: 2, 5, 7, 8, 9, 10, 11, 12, 14

7 No smoking; 8 Children welcome; 9 Social drinking allowed; 10 Tennis nearby; 11 Swimming nearby; 12 Golf nearby; 13 Skiing nearby; 14 May be booked through a travel agent.

Woodleigh House

808 Washington Street, 08204
(609) 884-7123; (800) 399-7123

Victorian, but informal, with off-street parking, beach bikes, comfortable parlor, courtyard, and gardens. Full breakfast and afternoon refreshments. Walk to everything: marvelous restaurants, sights galore, nearby nature preserve, dinner theater, and craft and antique shows. Queen-size beds, private baths. Call regarding facilities for children.

Hosts: Jan and Buddy Wood
Rooms: 4 (PB) $80-150
Full Breakfast
Credit Cards: A, B
Notes: 2, 5, 7, 10, 11, 12, 14

CHATHAM

Parrot Mill Inn at Chatham

47 Main Street, 07928
(201) 635-7722

Built in 1790 as a mill house. Today the inn hosts weddings, rehearsal dinners, small parties, receptions, and business meetings. English country decor. Private baths, TVs, and phones. Continental breakfast includes homemade breads or muffins, freshly squeezed juice, and hot coffee or tea. Outstanding restaurants, shopping, antiquing, and points of historical interest nearby. New York is 40 minutes away, and the Newark airport is within 12 minutes.

Host: Betsy Kennedy
Rooms: 11 (10 PB; 1SB) $95
Continental Breakfast
Credit Cards: A, B, C
Notes: 2, 5, 7, 8, 9, 10, 11, 12, 14

COLUMBUS (MOUNT HOLLY)

Bed and Breakfast Adventures

Suite 132, 2310 Central Ave. N. Wildwood, 08260
(606) 522-4000; (800) 992-2632

NJ463. This Federal-style home, circa 1845, has been featured in many country magazines. All guest rooms are air-conditioned and furnished with period antiques and country decor; one has a queen-size bed and working fireplace. Private bath. Occupancy limited to one couple at a time, or two traveling together. A full breakfast is served in the formal dining room or the country kitchen. Racetracks, canoeing, antiquing, or nature-walking nearby. A variety of resident pets. $85-100.

DENNISVILLE

Henry Ludlam Inn

Cape May Country, 1336 Route 47, Woodbine, 08270
(609) 861-5847

This circa 1760 home, voted Best of the Shore 1991, offers enchanting rooms, scrumptious gourmet breakfasts, bedroom fireplaces, and fireside picnic baskets. Guests invest in memories here. Mecca for birdwatchers. Children over 12 welcome.

Hosts: Ann and Marty Thurlow
Rooms: 5 (PB) $85-125
Full Breakfast
Credit Cards: A, B, C, D
Notes: 2, 3, 5, 9, 10, 11, 12, 14

EAST BRUNSWICK

Amanda's Bed and Breakfast

21 South Woodland Avenue, 08816
(908) 249-4944

273. Enjoy a charming and comfortable bed and breakfast experience in this spacious Cape Cod-style home nestled in the privacy of the East Brunswick suburbs. Sumptuous breakfasts served on the screened-in patio. Three guest rooms; shared baths. $60.

FLEMINGTON

Jerica Hill—A Bed and Breakfast Inn

96 Broad Street, 08822
(908) 782-8234

NOTES: Credit cards accepted: A MasterCard; B Visa; C American Express; D Discover; E Diners Club; F Other; 2 Personal checks accepted; 3 Lunch available; 4 Dinner available; 5 Open all year; 6 Pets welcome;

Jerica Hill

Be warmly welcomed at this gracious country inn in the historic town of Flemington. Spacious, sunny guest rooms, all with private bath and air conditioning, living room with a fireplace, and a wicker-filled screened porch invite guests to relax. A guests' pantry offering beverages and snacks is available 24-hours a day. Champagne hot-air balloon flights are arranged, as well as country picnics and winery tours. A delightful Continental plus breakfast is served. Corporate and midweek rates available. AAA rated three diamonds. Featured in *Country Inns Bed and Breakfast* and *Mid-Atlantic Country*.

Host: Judith S. Studer
Rooms: 5 (PB) $90-105
Continental Breakfast
Credit Cards: A, B, C
Notes: 2, 5, 7, 9, 10, 11, 12, 14

GLENWOOD

Apple Valley Inn Bed and Breakfast

Corner Routes 517 and 565, P.O. Box 302, 07418
(201) 764-3735

A Colonial mansion built in 1831 allows guests to relax in the sunroom, porches, formal parlor, or the extensive gardens and in-ground pool. Stroll through the apple orchard or fish the trout stream. Select an antique from the on-premises shop. This picturesque inn is four miles from Action Park and exclusive ski slopes. The inn is on the fall foliage tour. The Appalachian Trail is one mile away. The New Jersey Botanical Gardens, Waterloo Village, and Skylands are a short drive away. West Point and the Hudson Valley make for a wonderful day. Guests start the day with a full country breakfast. Picnic lunches are available. Children over 13 welcome.

Hosts: Mitzi and John Durham
Rooms: 6 (1 PB; 5 SB) $60-75
Full Breakfast
Credit Cards: None
Notes: 2, 9, 10, 11, 12, 13, 14

GREENWICH

Bed and Breakfast Adventures

Suite 132, 2310 Central Ave., N. Wildwood, 08260
(606) 522-4000; (800) 992-2632

NJ533. More than two centuries of history and style grace the main house of this Colonial bed and breakfast, which reflects the building styles of 1783, 1930, and 1957. Four guest rooms are furnished in a decor depicting each era of the home's history. Bedrooms have either shared or private baths. The pool has its own cabana with kitchen, bar, and two changing rooms with baths. $75-100.

HADDONFIELD

The Queen Anne Inn

44 West End Avenue, 08033
(609) 428-2195

The only accommodation in South Jersey within walking distance to the high-speed line (17 minutes to Philadelphia, less to the Aquarium or Rutgers Camden). No car required. Walk to shops and restaurants. Stay in this fully restored Victorian (on the National Register) in an elegant residential neighborhood in historic Haddonfield.

Relax on the beautiful porch or in the common rooms. Free local phone calls and free parking. Continental plus breakfast.

Hosts: Nancy Lynn and Fred Chorpita
Rooms: 5 (PB) $65-15
Continental Breakfast
Credit Cards: A, B, C, D
Notes: 5, 7, 8, 9, 10, 11, 12, 14

HOPE

The Inn at Millrace Pond

Route 519, P.O. Box 359, 07844
(908) 459-4884

A gracious country inn restored to Colonial grandeur along Beaver Brook in historic Hope. Seventeen individually decorated guest rooms, each with private bath and modern amenities. Scenic location offers hiking, canoeing, tennis, riding, golf, Waterloo Village, craft fairs, wineries, and antique shows. Grist Mill Dining Room open daily for dinner and Sunday from noon until 8:00 P.M. for lunch and dinner. Three stars from Mobil guide. Three diamonds from AAA. Four-crown award from the ABBA. May be booked through a travel agent, except on corporate rate.

Hosts: Cordie and Charles Puttkammer
Rooms: 17 (PB) $85-165
Continental Breakfast
Credit Cards: A, B, C, E
Notes: 2, 4, 5, 7, 8, 9, 10, 12, 13

JERSEY CITY

Bed and Breakfast Adventures

Suite 132, 2310 Central Ave., N. Wildwood, 08260
(606) 522-4000; (800) 992-2632

NJ611. In the heart of the Van Horst Park Historic District, this early-19th-century house supports a garden apartment and a triplex. Accommodations include double beds, period furniture, air conditioning, TV, and a shared bath. Guests have access to the parlor and dining room. Breakfast is a variety of fresh fruits, juices and homemade breads, with an assortment of jellies and jams. Well-behaved children and nonsmokers are welcome, as are midweek corporate travelers. $55-75.

LAMBERTVILLE

Bed and Breakfast Adventures

Suite 132, 2310 Central Ave., N. Wildwood, 08260
(606) 522-4000; (800) 992-2632

444. This gracious country inn began as a small farmhouse in 1820. The impressive stone and frame Colonial complex is on ten rolling acres of lush greenery with a formal garden and a maze of boxwoods. The interior of the main house is graced with raised paneling, wide plank floors, and three stairwells leading to guest rooms. Original works of art by local artists throughout. The guest rooms are furnished in antiques and period reproductions. Most rooms have sitting areas. Private baths, king- or queen-size beds, and air conditioning. A Continental plus breakfast is served in the dining room or in the garden. A guest pantry is stocked with soft drinks, snacks, and ice. Freshly brewed coffee and teas are always available. Discover the charming town of Lambertville or cross the Delaware River and explore the village of New Hope and Bucks County, Pennsylvania. Midweek corporate rates available. $85-150.

MAYS LANDING

Bed and Breakfast Adventures

Suite 132, 2310 Central Ave., N. Wildwood, 08260
(606) 522-4000; (800) 992-2632

NJ595. Just minutes away from the glitter and excitement of the casinos of Atlantic City, this lovely 1860s Victorian mansion offers guests a quiet respite. The three guest rooms and one two-room suite have queen-size beds, private baths (two with whirlpool tubs), antique furnishings, and a quiet atmosphere. The Victorian parlor provides a pleasant setting for games, reading, and conversation. During the summer, tea is served in the English manner on Saturdays and selected weekdays. It is a leisurely stroll to beautiful Lake Lenape, shops, and parks. A short drive to wineries, beaches, and other attractions. Nonsmokers, couples, and well-behaved children over ten are welcome. $75-125.

MILFORD

Bed and Breakfast Adventures
Suite 132, 2310 Central Ave., N. Wildwood, 08260
(606) 522-4000; (800) 992-2632

NJ610. This 200-year-old stone inn is in a quaint village on the Delaware River. Renovated in 1949, this host-home offers a quiet respite for all seasons. Two upstairs bedrooms have double beds and shared bath. Guests enjoy a swimming pool, library, fireplace, TV, and stereo. A Continental plus breakfast is provided. The area has antique shops, wineries, and hot-air ballooning. Only 30 minutes from New Hope, Pennsylvania. Nonsmokers and children are welcome. $85 and up.

MONTCLAIR

Bed and Breakfast Adventures
Suite 132, 2310 Central Ave., N. Wildwood, 08260
(606) 522-4000; (800) 992-2632

NJ617. A country setting awaits guests in this two-story Colonial home in the heart of Montclair's estate section. There are two guest rooms, each with adjoining private bath. The beds are full size, and each room has its own sitting area. A full breakfast is served each morning, with the hostess's special recipes. It is convenient to many tourist attractions, including the Meadowlands and the Thomas Edison home; guests are within minutes of I-280. Nonsmokers and corporate travelers are welcome. $75-85.

MORRISTOWN

Bed and Breakfast Adventures
Suite 132, 2310 Central Ave., N. Wildwood, 08260
(606) 522-4000; (800) 992-2632

NJ450. This 22-room estate manor house is in the country club area two miles from the city center. Four tastefully decorated rooms are available; amenities include a queen-size bed, sitting area, TV, air conditioning, and a small bar with refrigerator. One room becomes a suite with library and fireplace at an additional charge. Private bath also available. A Continental breakfast is served daily. Couples, corporate and nonsmoking travelers welcome. $60-100.

NEWTON

The Wooden Duck
140 Goodale Road, 07860
(201) 300-0395; FAX (201) 300-0141

This custom-built Colonial home is 15 years old, furnished with antiques and reproductions, and set on a secluded 17-acre miniestate about an hour's drive from New York City. It is close to antiques, golf, the Delaware Water Gap, Waterloo Village, and winter sports. The rooms are spacious with private baths, TV, VCR, telephone, and desks. Central air conditioning. Visitors will enjoy the in-ground pool, game room, and living room with see-through fireplaces. Biking and hiking are at the doorstep with a 1,000-acre state park across the street and a "Rails to Trails" running behind the property. There are always homemade cookies in the dining room and cold or hot beverages in the self-service kitchen area.

Hosts: Bob and Barbara Hadden
Rooms: 5 (3 PB; 2 SB) $85-100
Full Breakfast
Credit Cards: A, B, C
Notes: 2, 5, 7, 9, 10, 11, 12, 13

7 No smoking; 8 Children welcome; 9 Social drinking allowed; 10 Tennis nearby; 11 Swimming nearby; 12 Golf nearby; 13 Skiing nearby; 14 May be booked through a travel agent.

NORTH WILDWOOD

Candlelight Inn

2310 Central Avenue, 08260
(609) 522-6200

"There is a quaint haven for those in a vintage romantic mood," wrote the *Philadelphia Inquirer* (July 1988). The Candlelight Inn is a beautifully restored bed and breakfast built at the turn of the century by Leaming Rice. This Queen Anne Victorian structure served as the family home for many years until it was purchased by its present innkeepers in 1985. Within minutes of Cape May and Atlantic City. Special touches and personalized service abound.

Hosts: Paul DiFilippo and Diane Buscham
Rooms: 8 (PB) $85-250
Suites: 2
Full Breakfast
Credit Cards: A, B, C, D
Notes: 2, 5, 7, 9, 10, 11, 12, 14

OCEAN CITY

Beach End Inn
Bed and Breakfast

815 Plymouth Place, 08226
(609) 398-1016

Nestled on a quiet beach-block street in the heart of town, guests are steps from the

Beach End Inn

ocean and boardwalk. Six distinctly decorated and themed guest rooms feature Victorian antiques. Common areas include the parlor room with fireplace, game room, dining room, and front porch. Guests receive complimentary beach tags during the summer. Nightly turndown service. Monthly murder mystery affairs. Minutes from Atlantic City. Bicycling, fishing, water sports, and historical attractions are at hand.

Host: Len Cipkins
Rooms: 6 (3 PB; 3 SB) $65-120
Full Breakfast
Credit Cards: A, B
Notes: 2, 5, 7, 9, 10, 11, 12

Delancey Manor

869 Delancey Place, 08226
(609) 398-9831

A turn-of-the-century summer house is just 100 yards to a great beach and the boardwalk. Summer fun for families and friends. Two breezy porches with oceanviews. Walk to restaurants, boardwalk fun, and the Tabernacle with its renowned speakers. In a residential neighborhood in a dry town. Near Atlantic City and Cape May. Larger family rooms available. Continental plus breakfast optional for a small charge. Advance reservations recommended.

Hosts: Stewart and Pam Heisler
Rooms: 7 (3 PB; 4 SB) $40-70
Continental Breakfast
Credit Cards: None
Notes: 2, 8, 10, 11, 12

New Brighton Inn

519 Fifth Street, 08226
(609) 399-2829

Magnificently restored 1800s seaside Queen Anne Victorian. Premises comfortably furnished with antiques throughout. Breakfast on sun porch. A romantic, relaxing, charming hideaway close to the beach, boardwalk, tennis courts, restaurants, and fine shops. Children over 10 welcome.

NOTES: Credit cards accepted: A MasterCard; B Visa; C American Express; D Discover; E Diners Club; F Other; 2 Personal checks accepted; 3 Lunch available; 4 Dinner available; 5 Open all year; 6 Pets welcome;

Hosts: Daniel and Donna Hand
Rooms: 5 (PB) $80-90
Full Breakfast
Credit Cards: A, B, C, D
Notes: 2 , 5, 7, 10, 11, 12

Ocean City Guest and Apartment House Association Referral Service

P.O. Box 356, 08226
(609) 399-8894 (9 A.M. to 9 P.M. only)

An association of 30 owners helps guests find lodgings in the city. A wide range of accommodations includes apartments, bed and breakfasts, and guest homes throughout Ocean City. "American's greatest family resort," from the beach to the bay to the boardwalk. Call or write for information.

Pine Tree Inn

10 Main Avenue, 07756
(908) 775-3264

A small Victorian Inn offers a quiet interlude for visitors to the Jersey Shore. Stroll along the tree-lined main avenue of quaint shops, restaurants, and other specialty stores. The innkeeper is a lifelong resident of this beautiful area and will share her home and knowledge with guests. Ocean Grove is also a historic landmark and is listed in the National Register of Historic Places. Continental plus breakfast is served. Children over 12 welcome.

Host: Karen Mason
Rooms: 12 (4 PB; 8 SB) $45-100
Continental Breakfast
Credit Cards: A, B
Notes: 2, 5, 7, 9, 10, 11, 12

OCEAN GROVE

Cordova

26 Webb Avenue, 07756
(908) 774-3084 (in season); (212) 751-9577 (winter)
FAX (212) 207-4720

This delightful century-old Victorian inn in historic Ocean Grove has a friendly atmos-

Cordova

phere exuding Old World charm. Visitors are made to feel like members of an extended family. The inn was recently listed in *Jersey* magazine as one of the seven best places to stay on the Jersey coast. There are 15 guest rooms and two cottages that sleep four to eight people. Less than a 90-minute bus or train ride to Manhattan, Philadelphia, and Atlantic City. The weekly rate gives guests seven nights for the price of five. Continental plus breakfast. Open Memorial Day to Labor Day.

Host: Doris Chernick
Rooms: 15 (5 PB; 10 SB) $45-80
Cottages: 2 (PB) $105-150
Continental Breakfast
Credit Cards: None
Notes: 2, 7, 8, 9, 10, 11, 14

PEMBERTON

Bed and Breakfast Adventures

Suite 132, 2310 Central Ave., N. Wildwood, 08260
(606) 522-4000; (800) 992-2632

NJ613. Built in the mid-1800s, this home underwent high-style Victorian conversion soon after its construction. The inn offers charming and comfortable guest rooms, each with private bath and queen-size bed. There is also a suite with a garden tub in the bath and a sitting area. Breakfast is served each morning. Hosts also offer murder mystery weekends. Well-behaved children over ten and nonsmokers are welcome. Discounted rate available for military families and Deborah Hospital visitors. $65-125.

7 No smoking; 8 Children welcome; 9 Social drinking allowed; 10 Tennis nearby; 11 Swimming nearby;
12 Golf nearby; 13 Skiing nearby; 14 May be booked through a travel agent.

PLAINFIELD

The Pillars

922 Central Avenue, 07060-2311
(908) 753-0922; (800) 372-REST

Guests may make themselves at home in this restored 1880s mansion. In a secluded acre of trees, the Pillars offers an easygoing, yet elegant ambience. Enjoy the music room, with organ, stereo, and wood fire. Relax in the living room, with library and TV. Use the laundry or raid the refrigerator. A stained-glass skylight illuminates the circular staircase. Close to the shore, with easy access to Newark Airport and New York City. All rooms are air-conditioned and feature private baths. An expanded Continental Swedish breakfast is served. Dogs welcome. Children under two and over 12 welcome.

Hosts: Tom and Chuck Hale
Rooms: 3 (PB) $65-105
Continental Breakfast
Credit Cards: A, B, D
Notes: 2, 5, 7, 9, 10, 11, 12, 14

The Pillars

PRINCETON

Bed and Breakfast of Princeton

P.O. Box 571, 08542
(609) 924-3189; FAX (609) 921-6271
Internet: 71035.757@compuserve.com

Bed and Breakfast of Princeton offers homestay accommodations in several local homes and two self-catering apartments. Some accommodations are within walking distance of the town center while others are minutes away by automobile or public transportation. Some homes are nonsmoking. Princeton is the site of many business, research, and academic institutions. Midway between New York and Philadelphia, it offers a variety of recreational, historical, cultural, and sightseeing opportunities. $50.

The Peacock Inn

20 Bayard Lane, 08540
(609) 924-1707; FAX (609) 924-0788

The Peacock Inn was built in 1775 and opened its doors to the public in 1912. The staff is committed to friendly, courteous service and will be happy to guide lodgers to various shopping and dining sites in Princeton. One block from the university and home of Le Plumet Royal, an award-winning French restaurant. Guests are invited to dine at the restaurant with a *prix fixe* menu. Acknowledged as the "best dining in Princeton."

Rooms: 15 (13 PB; 2 SB) $90-125
Full and Continental Breakfast
Credit Cards: A, B, C
Notes: 2, 3, 4, 5, 6, 8, 9, 14

SEA GIRT

Holly Harbor Guest House

112 Baltimore Boulevard, 08750
(908) 449-9731; (800) 348-6999 (outside NJ)

Sea Girt is a quiet, residential town 60 miles south of New York City on the Jersey shore. Gracious cedar-shingled house is bordered by holly trees and has a spacious front porch. Only one block from the beach.

Hosts: Bill and Kim Walsh
Rooms: 12 (SB) $75-125
Full Breakfast
Credit Cards: A, B, C
Notes: 2, 5, 8, 9, 10, 11, 12

NOTES: Credit cards accepted: A MasterCard; B Visa; C American Express; D Discover; E Diners Club; F Other; 2 Personal checks accepted; 3 Lunch available; 4 Dinner available; 5 Open all year; 6 Pets welcome;

SPRING LAKE

Ashling Cottage

106 Sussex Avenue, 07762
(908) 449-3553; (800) 237-1877

Under sentinel sycamores since 1877 in a storybook setting, Ashling Cottage, a Victorian seaside inn, has long served as a portal to an earlier time. A block from the ocean and just one-half block from a fresh-water lake. Closed January through March.

Hosts: Goodi and Jack Stewart
Rooms: 10 (8 PB; 2 SB) $70-150
Full Breakfast
Credit Cards: None
Notes: 2, 7, 9, 10, 11, 12, 14

The Chateau

500 Warren Avenue, 07762
(908) 974-2000

The house may be 108 years old, but it is brand new inside: air conditioning, private baths, ceiling fans, refrigerator, color cable TVs, VCRs, radios, and two telephones. Most suites and parlors have marble bathrooms with soaking tubs for two, wood-burning fireplaces, sofas, and wet bars. Some rooms with private porches and balconies overlooking Spring Lake Park.

Host: Scott Smith
Rooms: (PB) $65-180
Suites: (PB) $79-205
Continental Breakfast
Credit Cards: A, B, C, D, E
Notes: 2, 5, 7, 8, 9, 10, 11, 12, 14

Hamilton House Inn

15 Mercer Avenue, 07762
(908) 449-8282

The Hamilton House Inn is a newly renovated bed and breakfast. The rooms are spacious, comfortable, and exquisitely decorated. All have king- or queen-size beds and each has an individual theme. The in-ground pool is crystal clear and always inviting on a warm day in the summer. Winter and spring offer quiet seasons that beckon guests to a vacation with an unhurried pace. Wonderful full breakfasts. Hospitality in the Old World tradition.

Hosts: Anne and Bud Benz
Rooms: 8 (PB) $95-225
Full Breakfast
Credit Cards: A, B, C
Notes: 2, 5, 7, 9, 10, 11, 12

Normandy Inn

Normandy Inn

21 Tuttle Avenue, 07762
(908) 449-7172

Less than a block from the ocean, this 1888 Italianate villa has been authentically restored inside and out. Antique-filled guest rooms and parlors invite guests to step back in time to 19th-century elegance. The wide front porch with wicker furniture invites quiet conversation and cool breezes at sunset. A hearty country breakfast awaits visitors in the morning. Explore the wide, tree-lined streets, turn-of-the-century estates, quaint shops, and boutiques. Golf, tennis, horseback riding, and historic villages are nearby. Minimum-stay requirements for March through November weekends, July and August during mid-week, and holidays.

Hosts: Michael and Susan Ingino
Rooms: 15 (PB) $86-161
Suites: (PB) $200-250
Full Breakfast
Credit Cards: A, B, C, D, E
Notes: 2, 5, 8, 9, 10, 11, 12, 14

7 No smoking; 8 Children welcome; 9 Social drinking allowed; 10 Tennis nearby; 11 Swimming nearby; 12 Golf nearby; 13 Skiing nearby; 14 May be booked through a travel agent.

Sea Crest by the Sea

19 Tuttle Avenue, 07762
(908) 449-9031; (800) 803-9031

A lovingly restored 1885 Victorian specializing in pampering guests. Enjoy relaxation
and romance. Convenient to both New
York City and Philadelphia. Each guest
room offers a different fantasy. Choose
from the Victorian Rose, the Pussy Willow,
the Washington, or the Casablanca. Seven
rooms have fireplaces. The ocean and
beach are just one-half block away. There
is a stable of bikes for riding. The library
has books and games, and the porch is a
convenient place for developing new
friendships. Full breakfast begins at 9:00
A.M. with freshly baked scones and
muffins, fruit, and Sea Crest granola served
on family china, silver, and crystal.

Hosts: John and Carol Kirby
Rooms: 10 (PB) $110-179
Suite: 1 (PB) $195-239
Full Breakfast
Credit Cards: A, B, C
Notes: 2, 5, 9, 10, 11, 12

Victoria House

214 Monmouth Avenue, 07762
(908) 974-1882

The Victoria House provides the perfect
retreat from today's hustle and bustle.
This Eastlake-style residence exhibits
typical Victorian appeal with its gingerbread accents, stained-glass windows, and
Gothic shingles. Come and relax on the
spacious wraparound porch and enjoy the
cool ocean breezes. Stroll a few steps to
the lake or beach or browse through the
quaint shops in the village. Spring Lake is
easily accessible by car, bus, or train from
both New York and Philadelphia.
Featured on 1995 Historical Society tour.
Children over ten welcome.

Hosts: Louise and Robert Goodall
Rooms: 9 (7 PB; 2 SB) $95-165
Full Breakfast
Credit Cards: A, B, C, D
Notes: 2, 5, 7, 9, 10, 11, 12

Villa Park House

417 Ocean Road, 07762
(908) 449-3642

This bed and breakfast home has a wonderful wraparound front porch with comfortable wicker furniture. Breakfast is fresh
and hearty. The Atlantic Ocean is less than
five blocks away. The hosts' aim is to provide a squeaky clean and comfortable
accommodation. Decorated in country and
pleasant Victorian. Many handmade furniture pieces from the host's workshop. Each
room has a TV and small refrigerator.
Bikes and beach passes also available.

Hosts: Alice and David Bramhall
Rooms: 5 (4 PB; 1 SB) $75-100
Full Breakfast
Credit Cards: None
Notes: 2, 5, 7, 8, 10, 11, 12

STANHOPE

Whistling Swan Inn

110 Main Street, 07874
(201) 347-6369; FAX (201) 347-3391

A turn-of-the-century Queen Anne
Victorian home renovated by the owners.
The house features tiger-oak woodwork,
fireplaces downstairs, and a huge sitting
porch. Near Waterloo Village, International
Trade Zone, skiing, wineries, antiques,
museums, shops, and restaurants. Near to
historic Morristown and just six miles north
of Chester. This is a four-season region of
New Jersey.

Hosts: Joe Mulay and Paula Williams
Rooms: 10 (PB) $75-110
Full Breakfast
Credit Cards: A, B, C, D
Notes: 2, 5, 7, 10, 11, 12, 13, 14

STOCKTON

Woolverton Inn

6 Woolverton Road, 08559
(609) 397-0802

An elegant stone manor in a pastoral setting, the Woolverton Inn offers the best of

past times and the amenities of present comforts. Sitting majestically above the Delaware, the inn features a classic country setting, rooms with fireplaces, Jacuzzi, family antiques, terry cloth robes, afternoon refreshments, full country breakfast, fireplaced living and dining room, wicker rocking chairs on the porch, horseshoes, croquet, resident sheep, air conditioning. Whether on business, pleasure, or celebrating a wedding, come as a guest, but expect to be treated more like a family friend.

Woolverton Inn

Hosts: Elizabeth and Michael Palmer
Rooms: 11 (PB) $75-150
Suites: 3
Full Breakfast
Credit Cards: A, B, C
Notes: 2, 5, 7, 9

7 No smoking; 8 Children welcome; 9 Social drinking allowed; 10 Tennis nearby; 11 Swimming nearby; 12 Golf nearby; 13 Skiing nearby; 14 May be booked through a travel agent.

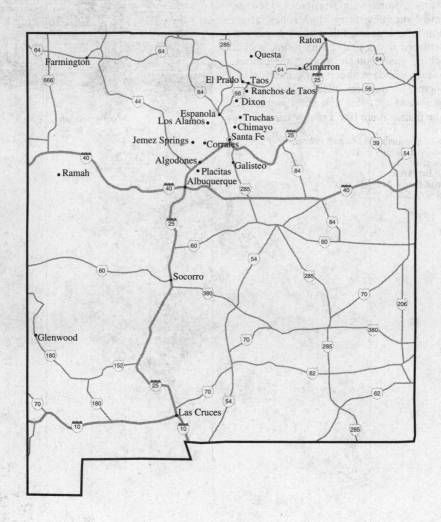

New Mexico

New Mexico

Las Palomas Inn

2303 Candelaria Road Northwest, 87107
(505) 345-7228; (800) 909-DOVE
FAX (505) 345-7328
Internet: laspalomas@aol.com

One of Albuquerque's most beautiful historic adobe estates, this lovely inn occupies three glorious acres of lawns, gardens, and orchards near Old Town. Outdoor hot tub, tennis court, croquet, and bike trails complement the uniquely furnished suites. All rooms have king- or queen-size beds, antique furnishings, private bathrooms and lounges, and splendid views. A full breakfast is served in the lovely dining room or on the lawns. Limited smoking permitted.

Hosts: Meg and Rick Stone
Rooms: 7 (PB) $85-125
Full Breakfast
Credit Cards: A, B
Notes: 2, 5, 8, 9, 10, 11, 12, 13, 14

Las Palomas Inn

Mi Casa Su Casa

P.O. Box 950, Tempe, AZ 85280-0950
(602) 990-0682; (800) 456-0682

1800. Just 20 minutes from downtown Albuquerque, this Southwestern-style home is in a quiet, residential neighborhood, decorated in a delightful mix of antiques, handmade collectibles, and family mementos. Surrounded by fruit trees with a large vegetable garden in the corner side yard, this bed and breakfast brings a taste of the country to a convenient city location. Three sets of accommodations are available. Dog in residence. Smoking restricted. Full breakfast is served. $35-55.

1810. The only bed and breakfast accommodation in Old Town proper, this spacious mansion with shaded grass and garden courtyard is visible from the Plaza. On the National Register of Historic Places, the 1912 Victorian Mansion was built in "four-square style" and is unusual when compared to most of the Old Town's architecture. The decor, food, and hospitality reflect the Indian, Spanish, and Anglo cultures of the area. Seven sets of accommodations are available. Full breakfast. No pets. Smoking restricted. Minimum two-night stay on weekends. Credit cards accepted. $79-109.

Old Town Bed and Breakfast

707 Seventeenth Street Northwest, 87104
(505) 764-9144

Old Town Bed and Breakfast is an adobe home on a beautiful, quiet street just two

NOTES: Credit cards: A MasterCard; B Visa; C American Express; D Discover; E Diners Club; F Other;
2 Personal checks accepted; 3 Lunch available; 4 Dinner available; 5 Open all year; 6 Pets welcome;
7 No smoking; 8 Children welcome; 9 Social drinking allowed; 10 Tennis nearby; 11 Swimming nearby;
12 Golf nearby; 13 Skiing nearby; 14 May be booked through a travel agent.

Old Town Bed and Breakfast

blocks from historic Old Town Plaza, the museums, and a lovely park. The second-floor guest room has a queen-size bed, private bath, private entrance, and provides views of the mountains and tree-lined neighborhood streets. The spacious first-floor guest room has a king-size bed, kiva fireplace, private entrance, and Jacuzzi bath, shared with owner only. Single beds provided upon request. Additional sleeping accommodations in adjacent sitting room. A secluded garden setting for guests' enjoyment. Continental plus breakfast.

Host: Nancy Hoffman
Rooms: 2 (1 PB; 1 SB) $60-75
Continental Breakfast
Credit Cards: None
Notes: 2, 5, 7, 8, 9, 10, 12, 13, 14

ALGODONES

B&B of New Mexico

P.O. Box 2805, Santa Fe, 87504
(505) 982-3332

410. This hacienda just 30 miles south of Santa Fe offers the grace and elegance of historic New Mexico. It is decorated with antique furniture. Each room has its own handmade kiva fireplace. The tranquility offered there complements the peace and serenity found in the hacienda courtyard and garden. The largest room is the Wagner Room with Jacuzzi bathtub, fireplace, sitting area, and queen-size bed. The Peña Room has a queen-size bed. Both the Piñon and Pueblo Rooms have full-size beds and private baths. $79-109.

Mi Casa Su Casa

P.O. Box 950, Tempe, AZ 85280-0950
(602) 990-0682; (800) 456-0682

1809. A gracious, warm host couple welcome guests to a delightful 200-year-old spacious hacienda. The Hacienda Vargas is full of light, has polished tile floors, Southwestern art, Indian arts and crafts, and a nice mix of antiques. Guests are welcome in the living room or library. The chef presents special full breakfasts. Four guest rooms each have kiva fireplaces, private baths, and private entrances to courtyard or hot tub. The large Wagner Room has a whirlpool tub and a queen-size bed. The Peña Room and the Pueblo Room have queen-size beds. The Piñon Room has a double bed. No resident pets. Smoking allowed outside. Roll away available. $69-129.

CHIMAYO

La Posada de Chimayó

P.O. Box 463, 87522
(505) 351-4605

A cozy, comfortable adobe inn in a traditional northern New Mexico village famous for its tradition of fine Spanish weaving and its beautiful old church, El Santuario. Off the beaten path, La Posada offers guests a taste of real northern New Mexico. National forests, archaeological sites, and several

Indian pueblos are within a half-hour's drive. Thirty miles north of Santa Fe on the high road to Taos. Minimum stay during holidays of two to four nights. Pets welcome with prior approval. Smoking is permitted outside only. Children over 12 are welcome.

Host: Sue Farrington
Rooms: 4 (PB) $80-100
Full Breakfast
Credit Cards: A, B
Notes: 2, 9

CIMARRON

Casa del Gavilan

P.O. Box 518, 87714
(505) 376-2246

A remote, turn-of-the-century adobe home perched between the Sangre de Christo Mountains and the open plains of eastern New Mexico. Enjoy tranquility and elegant service in a magnificent setting. Full breakfast served. Four guest rooms with private baths plus a two-room suite.

Hosts: Gina and Woody Crumbo
Rooms: 6 (4 PB; 2 SB) $65-100
Full Breakfast
Credit Cards: A, B, C, D
Notes: 2, 5, 7, 8, 9

CORRALES

Casa la Resolana

7887 Corrales Road, 87048
(505) 898-0203; (800) 884-0203

This Southwestern adobe occupies more than four acres in historic Corrales. Kiva fireplaces enhance the warmth and flavor of New Mexico in this beautiful and spacious country hacienda. Spectacular mountain

Casa la Resolana

views, orchards, covered portal with swing, courtyard with spa, and rave-review breakfasts. Close to Indian ruins. Golf packages available. King- and queen-size beds.

Hosts: Nancy and Jerry Thomas
Rooms: 3 (PB) $85-95
Full Breakfast
Credit Cards: A, B, C
Notes: 2, 5, 7, 9, 12, 13, 14

DIXON

Casa Lucita

P.O. Box 430, 87527
(800) 484-6923 ext. 4300

This bed and breakfast is a retreat in the center of a charming art community offering a private suite with private balcony and bath or rooms with shared bath. Besides breakfast, hosts provide guests with massage therapy to make the stay a luxurious experience.

Rooms: 3 (1 PB; 2 SB) $49-69
Continental Breakfast
Credit Cards: None
Notes: 2, 5, 7, 8, 10, 12, 13

EL PRADO

Little Tree Bed and Breakfast

P.O. Box 960, 87529
(505) 776-8467; (800) 334-8467

Pueblo-style adobe hacienda on a quiet country road just 14 miles from Taos Ski Valley and ten miles from Taos Plaza. Fireplaces, private entrances off rambling porches, and adobe-walled courtyard. Stunning panoramic views. "Paradisical and affordable"–*New York Daily News,* "Best bed and breakfast...too good to keep a secret"–*Houston Chronicle.* Continental plus breakfast served.

Hosts: Charles and Kay Giddens
Rooms: 4 (PB) $65-95
Continental Breakfast
Credit Cards: A, B, D
Notes: 2, 5, 7, 8, 9, 10, 12, 13, 14

---

7 No smoking; 8 Children welcome; 9 Social drinking allowed; 10 Tennis nearby; 11 Swimming nearby; 12 Golf nearby; 13 Skiing nearby; 14 May be booked through a travel agent.

ESPAÑOLA

Bed and Breakfast Inn Arizona
8900 East Via Linda, Suite 101, Scottsdale, AZ 85258
(602) 860-9338 (phone and FAX)

NM124. Enjoy breathtaking views from the hot tub at this pueblo-style bed and breakfast. All main rooms have ceilings of Viga and Latia construction; there are arched pueblo-styled doorways; and Mexican tile is used throughout. Twenty-three minutes to Santa Fe, 45 minutes to Taos, minutes to all eight Northern Pueblos make this a perfect getaway.

B&B of New Mexico
P.O. Box 2805, Santa Fe, 87504
(505) 982-3332

260. This simple, elegant adobe casita is nestled in the pine cliffs of northern New Mexico. It is filled with local handmade crafts and furniture. High-beamed ceiling, Talavera tile, pine floors, and a fireplace in the bedroom. The sleeping arrangements can be either a king-size bed or two twin beds. Near Española, halfway between Santa Fe and Taos. It is a short walk from the Chama River. The casita is detached from the main house to afford privacy. Full breakfast. $95.

261. This home, between Santa Fe and Taos, has a wonderful Southwest atmosphere, magnificent mountain views, king- and queen-size beds, and private baths. Also a lap pool, so bring a bathing suit and a favorite beach towel. Full breakfast and afternoon refreshments. The host has two dogs. $80.

Mi Casa Su Casa
P.O. Box 950, Tempe, AZ 85280-0950
(602) 990-0682; (800) 456-0682

1811. Host couple welcome guests to a handsome, new, New Mexico-style home, an easy drive to many places of interest, such as Santa Fe, Taos, Los Alamos, and Bandelier National Monument. Two guest rooms, each with private bath and TV, are available. One has a queen-size bed, the other a king-size bed. Guests are welcome in the large living room with a fireplace, ceramic tiled floors, and log-beamed ceilings. Afternoon refreshments. Seasonal lap pool. Full breakfast offers New Mexican specialities. Smoking allowed outside. No children, please. Two-night minimum. $80.

FARMINGTON

B&B of New Mexico
P.O. Box 2805, Santa Fe, 87504
(505) 982-3332

601. A traditional northern New Mexico adobe on the cliffside confluence of the San Juan and La Plata Rivers on the outskirts of Farmington. This newly constructed bed and breakfast suite includes bedroom with queen-size bed, living room/dining room with two twin day beds, bathroom with Mexican tile shower, kitchen, and hot tub. $65-80.

GALISTEO

The Galisteo Inn
HC 75, Box 4, 87540
(505) 466-4000

The Galisteo Inn

Visit this 240-year-old adobe hacienda in the beautiful countryside of northern New Mexico, 23 miles southeast of Santa Fe. Enjoy the hot tub, sauna, pool, bicycles, horseback riding, and massage. The dinners feature creative Southwestern cuisine nightly, except Monday and Tuesday. Reservations required for accommodations and dining. A buffet breakfast is offered. Limited smoking allowed.

Hosts: Joanna Kaufman and Wayne Aarniokoski
Rooms: 12 (8 PB; 4 SB) $100-175
Continental Breakfast
Credit Cards: A, B, D
Notes: 2, 3, 4, 9, 10, 11, 13, 14

GLENWOOD

Los Olmos Guest Ranch

US 180 and Catwalk Road, P.O. Box 127, 88039
(505) 539-2311

A quiet country inn in a narrow valley amidst a bulky mountain range. Situated in a popular outdoor recreation area; hiking, bird watching, and fishing abound. Guest recreation room is in the main building, and guest accommodations are in individual stone cottages with private baths. A swimming pool, spa, bicycles, and horseback riding are all available. Please inquire about pets.

Hosts: Jerry and Tiffany Hagemeier
Rooms: 13 (PB) $65-80
Full Breakfast
Credit Cards: A, B, C, D
Notes: 2, 4, 7, 8, 9, 11

JEMEZ SPRINGS

Jemez River Bed and Breakfast Inn

16445 Highway 4, 87025
(505) 829-3262 (telephone and FAX)
(800) 809-3262

Native American-style inn with six rooms, all decorated and named after an Indian

Jemez River Inn

tribe's artifacts. The entire inn is as close to being a museum as anything else. Big country breakfast, huge views of the mountains and mesas surrounding the property. Jemez River runs right through our back yard. On three and one-half acres with plenty to do. Designated hummingbird sanctuary. Literally thousands and thousands of birds right outside each bedroom door in an open air plaza. Inquire about children being welcome.

Hosts: Larry and Rose Ann Clutter
Rooms: 6 (PB) $79-119
Full Breakfast
Credit Cards: A, B, C, D, E, F
Notes: 2, 3, 4, 5, 7, 8, 9,13, 14

LAS CRUCES

Bed and Breakfast Inn Arizona

8900 East Via Linda, Suite 101, Scottsdale, AZ 85258
(602) 860-9338 (phone and FAX)

LC101. Classic adobe architecture and magnificent paintings surround guests in this combination art gallery and bed and breakfast inn in Las Cruces. There are a sparkling fountain and historic antique furniture in the main gallery. The 14 rooms are named after the artist whose work is featured in them, and all have private baths. A lavish Continental breakfast is put out in the morning. Children are welcome. Deluxe to superior rates.

7 No smoking; 8 Children welcome; 9 Social drinking allowed; 10 Tennis nearby; 11 Swimming nearby; 12 Golf nearby; 13 Skiing nearby; 14 May be booked through a travel agent.

B&B of New Mexico

P.O. Box 2805, Santa Fe, 87504
(505) 982-3332

506. Just 11 miles from Las Cruces at the foot of the Organ Mountains. Surrounded by U.S. government land, the area is quiet and beautiful. Horse boarding is available and guests can take their horses for a ride in the mountains. Owners speak German, French, Greek, Spanish, Arabic, and understand Italian. The home has a pool for guests. Two guest rooms are available: one has two twin beds and a private bath; the other has an atrium door that opens onto the deck surrounding the pool, double bed, private bath, and kitchenette. $50-60.

T. R. H. Smith Mansion Bed and Breakfast

909 North Alameda Boulevard, 88005
(505) 525-2525; (800) 526-1914
FAX (505) 524-8227

This stately 1914 mansion was built by bank president T. R. H. Smith and designed by Henry Trost, a Frank Lloyd Wright contemporary, in the heart of the fertile Mesilla Valley. Four distinctive bedrooms are named for the owners' favorite vacation areas: European, Southwestern, Polynesian, and Latin America. Formal dining and living rooms, sun porch, and basement game/TV room offer relaxing respites alone or to enjoy with other guests. Full breakfast features fresh fruits or fruit drinks.

Hosts: Marlene and Jay Tebo
Rooms: 4 (2 PB; 2 SB) $60
Full Breakfast
Credit Cards: A, B
Notes: 7, 9, 10, 11, 12, 14

LOS ALAMOS

Casa del Rey

305 Rover Street, 87544
(505) 672-9401

Quiet residential area, friendly atmosphere.

In White Rock, minutes from Los Alamos and 40 minutes from Santa Fe. Excellent recreational facilities and restaurants nearby. The area is rich in Indian and Spanish history. Breakfast features homemade granola and breads served on the sun porch overlooking flower gardens, with views of the mountains. Children over eight welcome.

Host: Virginia King
Rooms: 2 (SB) $45
Continental Breakfast
Credit Cards: None
Notes: 2, 5, 7, 10, 11, 12, 13

PLACITAS

B&B of New Mexico

P.O. Box 2805, Santa Fe, 87504
(505) 982-3332

415. Guests awaken each morning to the sound of the trickling fountain in the tree-shaded patio. This quiet, peaceful spot affords spectacular views of the Sandia Mountains and of the sunsets over the western mesas. The cheery interior of this casita is furnished in Southwestern decor with the owners' original art (both are retired museum directors). The tiled bath opens off a central entryway, providing privacy for both the bedroom and living room. The efficient little kitchen is equipped with all that's needed for light housekeeping. The sofa is a sleeper; the bedroom has a queen-size bed. No smoking. $80 double, $100 for three or four persons.

QUESTA

B&B of New Mexico

P.O. Box 2805, Santa Fe, 87504
(505) 982-3332

210. Large, cozy, rustic log home is waiting for travelers at the base of the Sangre de Cristo Mountains with three bedrooms, two baths, hot tub, and sauna. Area is quiet and restful with close access to Rio Grande. Wild river hiking, wilderness area, three

NOTES: Credit cards accepted: A MasterCard; B Visa; C American Express; D Discover; E Diners Club; F Other; 2 Personal checks accepted; 3 Lunch available; 4 Dinner available; 5 Open all year; 6 Pets welcome;

major ski resorts, wildlife, and shopping in Taos are all at guests' disposal. Continental breakfast, Southwestern style. Rent whole house at $250 per day. Can accommodate eight adults and three children. $40-70.

RAMAH

Mi Casa Su Casa

P.O. Box 950, Tempe, AZ 85280-0950
(602) 990-0682; (800) 456-0682

1805. Enjoy warm-hearted hospitality on this working cattle ranch owned by a descendant of rancher and writer Evon Vogt. Built in 1915 of rocks from the nearby Anasazi Indian ruins, this old farmhouse has wood floors, Navajo rugs, large enclosed gardens, and big elm trees. Two bedrooms, both of which have Navajo rugs and original artworks, lead off from the large central living room. There is also a separate guest house. No smoking. No pets. Full breakfast. $50-65.

The Vogt Ranch Bed and Breakfast

P.O. Box 716, 87321
(505) 783-4362

Feel the history of New Mexico's frontier with Navajo rugs, artifacts, and a Southwestern book collection. Crisp, sunny mornings are greeted by a crackling cedar fire in the Kalamazoo cook stove, the aroma of freshly brewed coffee, and (very likely) blue-corn pancakes. This historic home is nestled among the piñon trees between the Navajo and Zuni Indian Reservations near the Arizona border. Great exploring at Indian ruins and pueblos, petroglyphs, volcanos, and two national parks.

Hosts: Anita Davis and Scott Clifford
Rooms: 2 (PB) $65-75
Full Breakfast
Credit Cards: None
Notes: 2, 7, 9

RANCHOS DE TAOS

Mi Casa Su Casa

P.O. Box 950, Tempe, AZ 85280-0950
(602) 990-0682; (800) 456-0682

1812. This 160-year-old adobe home is on four acres of pines, fruit trees, and pasture on the tranquil outskirts of Taos. The Grand Portal of 80 feet stretches the length of the main entry, an inviting place to sit and enjoy the sunrise or sunset. There is a stream with an old stone bridge. Views of the ever-changing colors on Taos Mountain. Fifteen minutes to the Rio Grande Gorge and 25 minutes to Taos Ski Valley. Nearby 1,100-year-old Taos Pueblo, the oldest living Indian pueblo in the country. Four guest rooms in the main house. Guest cottage available. Dog in residence. Minimum two-night stay on weekends. Smoking restricted. No pets. Children over 12 welcome. Credit cards accepted. Full gourmet breakfast. An additional $20 for third person in room. $95-125.

1813. This bed and breakfast is a real find for guests, especially those who enjoy experiencing the old Southwest. Across the street from the 400-year-old St. Francis Church in Ranchos Plaza, this beautifully refurbished 250-year-old adobe home has the traditional blue trim on the windows and the front door. Guests enter the walled front yard through imposing mesquite gates. A guest cottage is available. A five-night minimum stay is required. Continental plus breakfast. Smoking restricted. No pets. No children. $110.

RATON

The Red Violet Inn

344 North Second Street, 87740
(505) 445-9778

Follow the Santa Fe Trail and step back into the past at this appealing 1902 red-brick

7 No smoking; 8 Children welcome; 9 Social drinking allowed; 10 Tennis nearby; 11 Swimming nearby; 12 Golf nearby; 13 Skiing nearby; 14 May be booked through a travel agent.

Victorian home three blocks from Raton's historic downtown. Guests have use of the parlor, dining room, porches, and flower-filled yard. Repeat visitors arrange to be on hand for the classical music and social hour from 5:30 to 6:30 P.M. Full breakfast is served in the formal dining room, accompanied by friendly conversation. A theater and gallery are within a few blocks, and hiking and fishing facilities (Surarite State Park) are just ten miles away. Other area attractions include a golf course, several antique shops, and a museum. Capulin Volcano National Monument is only 30 minutes away. Member of the New Mexico Bed and Breakfast Association.

Hosts: Ruth and John Hanrahan
Rooms: 4 (2 PB; 2 SB) $50-65
Full Breakfast
Credit Cards: A, B, C
Notes: 2, 3, 4, 7, 8, 9, 10, 11, 12, 14

SANTA FE

Adobe Abode

202 Chapelle, 87501
(505) 983-3133; FAX (505) 986-0972

Just three blocks from the Plaza, this is a historic adobe home restored into an inviting and intimate European-style bed and breakfast inn. Decorated with flair and authentic Southwest charm, the inn has private baths, phones, and TVs in all guest rooms. There are two guest rooms and a two-room suite in the main house, plus three detached casitas with fireplaces, private entrances, and landscaped patios, all in pure Santa Fe style. Complimentary sherry, cookies, and morning newspaper are all offered in the stylish guest living room with fireplace. A full gourmet breakfast is served.

Host: Pat Harbour
Rooms: 6 (PB) $95-155
Full Breakfast
Credit Cards: A, B, D
Notes: 2, 5, 7, 8, 9, 12, 13, 14

Alexander's Inn

Alexander's Inn

529 East Palace, 87501
(505) 986-1431

For a cozy, romantic stay in Santa Fe, come to a bed and breakfast featuring the best of American country charm. In a lovely residential neighborhood on the town's historic east side, the inn is within walking distance of the downtown Plaza and Canyon Road. Afternoon tea, homemade cookies, and a Continental plus breakfast are served.

Hosts: Carolyn Delecluse and Mary Jo Schneider
Rooms: 7 (4 PB; 3 SB) $75-150
Continental Breakfast
Credit Cards: A, B
Notes: 2, 5, 6, 7, 8, 9, 10, 11, 12, 13, 14

B&B of New Mexico

P.O. Box 2805, 87504
(505) 982-3332

105. Beautiful two-story home less than one mile from the Plaza. Large downstairs bedroom with queen-size bed, refrigerator, lots of closet space, and a private bath and shower. Upstairs room has twin beds, walls covered with watercolors, and private three-quarter bath. Breakfast upstairs in dining room with view of hills filled with piñon trees. Living room has views of Sangre de Cristo Mountains, beamed ceilings, and kiva fireplace. Spanish tile in kitchen and hallways. No smoking. $50-75.

107. Pure Santa Fe! This new adobe-style home has high-beam and rough-sawn ceilings throughout, with 12-inch-thick walls, saltillo tile floors, Mexican tile in baths and kitchen, kiva fireplace, and vigas in the living room. One-half block to historic Canyon Road, one mile to the Plaza. Both rooms are on the second floor and have private baths. One room has its own private portal, $85. The other has its own private sitting room with twin bed. No smoking. $95 for two; $130 for three in suite.

108. Small, cozy adobe home two blocks from Canyon Road and five blocks from downtown Plaza. Kiva fireplace in living room, enclosed courtyard in front. Door from guest room opens onto back garden area. Host very knowledgeable about activities in Santa Fe. Private full bath down the hall and king-size bed. No smoking. $75.

110. Beautiful pueblo-style home in the foothills of the Sangre de Cristo Mountains. Gorgeous sunsets and views of the city lights at night. Jogging trails behind the house. Very quiet except for the sounds of nature. Only 15 minutes to ski basin, ten minutes to the Plaza. Patio for sunning; living room and dining room have high-beamed ceiling and fireplace. Master bedroom has king-size bed, dressing area, walk-in closet, private bath, and views of the foothills. Smaller bedroom has twin beds, large closet, and private bath. Cat in residence. No smoking. $65-80.

115. New Santa Fe pueblo-style home with 15-foot coved ceilings with large vigas and large open rooms. Sunny and cozy half-moon banco breakfast nook in which guests can sit and relax. Shepard's fireplace in living room, saltillo tile floors throughout, and carpeted bedrooms. Master suite has king-size canopied bed, kiva fireplace, TV, huge tiled double-head shower room, and step-into tiled whirlpool tub with garden window. Attached but private sitting room with twin bed and TV is available at an additional cost. Cozy room with Santa Fe queen-size bed, TV, and private bath. $80-95.

117. This home has wonderful views of the mountains, city, and sunsets. There is a secluded patio accessible from the living room. Tall entrance hall contains a gallery with dozens of paintings. This home offers three guest rooms: one with two twin beds and adjoining queen-size sleeper (same party only and both rooms share a bath), and the third room has queen-size bed, private bath, and private entrance to flagstone patio. $75-80.

119. From 1867 to 1890 this lovely old adobe was the Santa Fe Meat and Livestock Headquarters. In the heart of the historic district five blocks from the Plaza and one block south of Canyon Road. Parts of the home are believed to date prior to 1846. All of the outside and some of the inside walls are made of adobe, in some cases 30 inches thick; the ceiling of the living room has six inches of dirt on top in spite of the pitched roof. There is a parlor grand piano in the home that guests can use. The bunkhouse can sleep four in two queen-size beds sharing a bath (same party). Queen-size bed, private bath, and private library in the main house. No smoking allowed. $80.

125. Enjoy the graceful privacy of this Santa Fe location only a five-minute drive from the Plaza. This quiet residence has a completely equipped kitchen, TV, telephone, private patio, bath, and a large living room/dining room, all furnished with tasteful elegance, including antiques and artwork. King-size bed. $80-100.

128. This is a delightful home on the east side, one-half block to Canyon Road and within walking distance of town. It has hardwood floors and some antiques. Enjoy breakfast on the cheerful sun porch. Cable TV is available. There are two rooms to choose from. One is a master bedroom with a private bath and queen-size bed; the other

7 No smoking; 8 Children welcome; 9 Social drinking allowed; 10 Tennis nearby; 11 Swimming nearby; 12 Golf nearby; 13 Skiing nearby; 14 May be booked through a travel agent.

B&B of New Mexico (continued)

guest room has a full-size bed with private three-quarter bath. $80.

139. This home begins with the hostess's music space and ends with the host's painting area. The bedroom corridor gives a warm welcome to visitors. The queen-size bedroom is a comfortable size and overlooks the garden; the single bedroom, though smaller, enjoys the spaciousness of a mountain view and a wall of books to tempt a guest tired from tourist activities. Cat and dog are also on the premises. Both rooms share same bath. $50-65.

142. Romantic guest suite in the heart of Santa Fe's historic east side. This adobe residence is at the end of a narrow lane, secluded and quiet, surrounded by rock walls, coyote fence, and adobe walls, yet minutes to Canyon Road, galleries, shops, and restaurants. Features include sun-filled bedroom, queen-size four-poster bed, kiva fireplace, vigas, and clerestory windows so guests can watch the stars. Also available are a cozy sitting room and cable TV, with both rooms opening onto patio. $90.

146. Simply elegant, this restored 100-year-old spacious adobe features fireplace, hardwood floors, plastered walls, full furnishings, custom kitchen cabinets, washer and dryer, CD, and cable TV. Eight blocks from the Plaza. Queen-size four-poster bed $150 for two persons; queen-size pull-out beds. $175 for four persons; $225 for five persons.

Canyon Road Casitas

652 Canyon Road, 87501
(505) 988-5888; (800) 279-0755

In the historic district behind a walled private courtyard garden on Santa Fe's famous Canyon Road. Built around 1887, the accommodations include a suite with dining room, kitchen, and two separate beds. Fine amenities include duvets, down pillows, imported linens, custom toiletries, pima cotton towels, guest robes, French-roast coffee, and wine and cheese upon check-in. The finest in Southwestern decor, including kiva fireplace, hand-carved beds, vigas, latillas, original art, and hand-tiled private baths. An award-winning inn.

Host: Trisha Ambrose
Rooms: 2 (PB) $85-169
Continental Breakfast
Credit Cards: A, B, C, D, E
Notes: 2, 5, 8, 9, 14

Casa de la Cuma

105 Paseo de la Cuma, 87501
(505) 983-1717

Casa de la Cuma is a beautiful bed and breakfast inn just four blocks from the Santa Fe Plaza, the historic and artistic center of the city. The living room and each of the three bedrooms are richly decorated with Navajo textiles, Mexican antiques, and original art. Friendly, Southwestern hospitality offers afternoon snacks in front of the fireplace or on the guest patio. Vacation rentals (with kitchens) are also available near the Plaza.

Hosts: Art and Donna Bailey
Rooms: 3 (1 PB; 2 SB) $75-115
Continental Breakfast
Credit Cards: A, B, C
Notes: 2, 5, 7, 9, 10, 11, 12, 13, 14

Don Gaspar Compound

623 Don Gaspar Compound, 87501
(505) 986-8664; FAX (505) 986-0696

Built in 1912 in Santa Fe's Don Gaspar Historic District, the compound is a classic example of Mission and Adobe architecture. Six private suites enjoy a secluded adobe-walled garden courtyard. The soothing sound of falling water from the courtyard's fountain invites guests to wander among the brilliant heirloom flowers or just relax. A pleasant walk from the Plaza, Canyon Road, art galleries, museums, and fine restaurants. No smoking.

Hosts: The Alfords
Rooms: 6 (PB) $95
Continental Breakfast
Credit Cards: A, B, C
Notes: 2, 5, 7, 8, 9, 10, 11, 12, 13, 14

Dunshee's

986 Acequia Madre, 87501
(505) 982-0988

A romantic adobe getaway in the historic east side, about a mile from the Plaza. Guests can choose either a two-room suite or a two-bedroom guest house with kitchen. Both units have kiva fireplaces, antiques, folk art, fresh flowers, homemade cookies, phone, TV, pretty linens, private bath, patio, and a great Continental plus breakfast. Two-night minimum stay weekends and holidays.

Host: Susan Dunshee
Rooms: 2 (PB) $110-120
Continental Breakfast
Credit Cards: A, B
Notes: 2, 5, 7, 8, 9, 13

Four Kachinas Inn

512 Webber Street, 87501
(505) 982-2550; (800) 397-2564

Four Kachinas Inn, a short walk from Santa Fe's historic Plaza, offers four rooms with private baths and entrances. The rooms are furnished with Navajo rugs, Hopi kachina dolls, and handcrafted wooden furniture. Three ground-floor rooms have individual garden patios, while the upstairs room offers a view of the Sangre de Cristo Mountains. A Continental plus breakfast including award-winning baked goods is served in the room. The old adobe guest lounge features afternoon tea and cookies.

Hosts: John Daw and Andrew Beckerman
Rooms: 4 (PB) $85-115
Continental Breakfast
Credit Cards: A, B, D
Notes: 7, 10, 11, 12, 13

Grant Corner Inn

Grant Corner Inn

122 Grant Avenue, 87501
(505) 983-6678

An exquisite Colonial manor home in downtown Santa Fe. Just two blocks from the historic Plaza, the inn is nestled among intriguing shops, restaurants, and galleries. Each room is individually appointed with antiques and treasures from around the world: quilts, brass and four-poster beds, armoires, and art. Private telephones, cable TV, and ceiling fans. Complimentary wine is served in the evening.

Hosts: Louise Stewart and Pat Walter
Rooms: 12 (10 PB; 2 SB) $70-140
Full Breakfast
Credit Cards: A, B
Notes: 2, 3, 5, 7, 9, 10, 11, 12, 13, 14

Hacienda Vargas

P.O. Box 307, Algondones, 87001
(505) 867-9115; (800) 261-0006

Romantic, secluded, and historic. Elegantly renovated. Amid the majestic New Mexico mesas, beside the Rio Grande, and lined by cottonwood trees. Six rooms with fireplaces, private baths, and private entrances. Two suites with two-person Jacuzzi. Barbecue and open-air hot tub area. Thirty minutes south of Santa Fe and north of Albuquerque. Romance packages available.

7 No smoking; 8 Children welcome; 9 Social drinking allowed; 10 Tennis nearby; 11 Swimming nearby; 12 Golf nearby; 13 Skiing nearby; 14 May be booked through a travel agent.

A place of enchantment in the land of enchantment. Children over 12 welcome.

Hosts: Pablo and Julia De Vargas
Rooms: 6 (PB) $69-129
Full Breakfast
Credit Cards: A, B
Notes: 5, 7, 9, 12, 13, 14

Mi Casa Su Casa

P.O. Box 950, Tempe, AZ 85280-0950
(602) 990-0682; (800) 456-0682

1801. Santa Fe Territory-style accommodations in the Canyon Road Historic District, a mixed zoning area of shops, restaurants, and residences. Guests can choose from two separate accommodations sharing a courtyard behind a shop. The suite consists of a bedroom with a queen-size bed, a sitting room with futon and fireplace, full bath, and kitchenette. The compact casita has a queen-size bed, kitchenette, and bath. Santa Fe furnishings, quality linens and toiletries, original art, and Mexican tile floors. Self-catering Continental breakfast. Higher rates during holidays and special area events. $85-169.

1814. Secluded and quiet, this more than 70-year-old adobe home is on a narrow lane in the heart of the historic east side of Santa Fe. Surrounded by rock walls, a coyote fence, and old gates, it is minutes from Canyon Road art galleries, shops, restaurants, the Plaza, and museums. The host is a retired writer for a major newspaper, and the guest wing is a lovely L-shaped accommodation with a kiva fireplace, private bath, minirefrigerator, coffee maker, telephone, and daily maid service. Minimum stay is two nights. No children. Continental plus breakfast. $85.

1816. Host couple welcomes guests to a large, contemporary adobe-style house built in 1990 in a quiet country setting on six acres in beautiful Sunlit Hills just ten minutes' driving time from the Plaza. Beautiful mountain views and sunsets.

Guest house is separate from the main house. Continental plus breakfast. Minimum two-night stay. Dog and cat in residence. No smoking. No pets. Children over ten welcome. Weekly and monthly rates available. $100.

1817. This historic inn is owned by a friendly hostess from England. An adobe house, built in 1906, has a patio and garden. Air-conditioned. There are five guest accommodations. Dinner is available with prior arrangements. Credit cards accepted. Smoking restricted. No pets. Children over 12 welcome. Full breakfast. Seasonal rates available. $85-148.

1818. Constructed in 1948, this small, two-bedroom, New Mexico Territorial-style house is in a residential historic neighborhood in an excellent location. The attractive front yard and patio have a high adobe wall for privacy. There is one guest room available. Near public transportation. Two-night minimum stay weekends. Handicapped accessible. Full breakfast. Smoking outside. An infant or small child welcome. Upon request, hostess will arrange for a crib. Pets welcome with prior arrangement. Seasonal and weekly rates available. $65-75.

1819. Friendly couple welcome guests to a two-story Santa Fe adobe-style house with natural landscaping. It is one mile from the Plaza. The Continental plus breakfast is served in the dining area on the second floor with a lovely view of the Sangres Mountains. There are two guest accommodations. Smoking restricted. No pets. No children. $50-75.

El Paradero

220 West Manhattan, 87501
(505) 988-1177

Just a short walk from the busy Plaza, this 200-year-old Spanish farmhouse was

---

El Paradaro

restored as a charming Southwestern inn. Enjoy a full gourmet breakfast, caring service, and a relaxed, friendly atmosphere. The inn offers lots of common space and a patio for afternoon tea and snacks. Pets welcome by prior arrangements.

Hosts: Thom Allen and Ouida MacGregor
Rooms: 14 (10 PB; 4 SB) $50-130
Full Breakfast
Credit Cards: A, B
Notes: 2, 5, 7, 8, 9, 10, 11, 12, 13, 14

Pueblo Bonito Bed and Breakfast Inn

138 West Manhattan Avenue, 87501
(505) 984-8001; FAX (505) 984-3155

Historic adobe estate can be found in downtown Santa Fe, three blocks south of the Plaza. Choose from 18 guest rooms, each with private bath, unique corner fireplace, and 12-inch-thick adobe walls and window sills. While there are a variety of sizes, decors, and amenities throughout the rooms, each has been furnished with native antiques, Indian rugs, sand paintings, and works of local artists. Area attractions include historic downtown sites, museums, Indian pueblos, and speciality shops. Continental "create your own" breakfast

buffet offers a variety of fresh fruits, danish muffins, and croissants.

Rooms: 18 (PB) $65-130
Continental Breakfast
Credit Cards: A, B
Notes: 2, 5, 8, 9, 10, 11, 12, 13, 14

Temple of Light

2407 Camino Capitan, 87505
(505) 471-4053

Simple and affordable. Peaceful and loving. Private home just a few minutes from Plaza. Car recommended. No smoking.

Host: Jean Gosse
Rooms: 1 (SB) $40
Continental Breakfast
Credit Cards: None
Notes: 2, 5, 7, 11, 12, 13

Water Street Inn

427 West Water Street, 87501
(505) 984-1193

Part of an award-winning adobe restoration two blocks from the Plaza. Surrounded by fine restaurants, shops, and galleries. Next door to a premier piano bar and opposite Old Santa Fe Music Hall. Spacious rooms, kiva and antique fireplaces, wood stoves, cable TV, and telephones with private message service. Beautifully appointed rooms. Excellent breakfast, morning paper, and happy hour of hors d'oeuvres and wine.

Host: Tom Getgood
Rooms: 8 (PB) $90-155
Continental Breakfast
Credit Cards: A, B, C
Notes: 2, 5, 7, 8, 9, 11, 12, 13, 14

SOCORRO

The Eaton House Bed and Breakfast Inn

403 Eaton Avenue, 87801
(505) 835-1067

Thick walls and high ceilings combine comfort with a sense of history in this 1881

7 No smoking; 8 Children welcome; 9 Social drinking allowed; 10 Tennis nearby; 11 Swimming nearby; 12 Golf nearby; 13 Skiing nearby; 14 May be booked through a travel agent.

adobe. In the formal dining room guests are pampered with a full breakfast of home-made specialties. Rooms open onto a wide brick portal. Relax and enjoy the antics of dozens of hummingbirds. A breakfast basket enhances morning explorations of the Bosque del Apache Wildlife refuge.

Hosts: Anna Appleby and Tom Harper
Rooms: 5 (PB) $75-120
Full Breakfast
Credit Cards: B, C
Notes: 2, 3, 5, 7, 9, 12

American Artists Gallery House

TAOS _____

American Artists Gallery House

P.O. Box 584, 87571
(505) 758-4446; (800) 532-2041

Charming Southwestern hacienda filled with artwork by American artists. Gourmet breakfasts, adobe fireplaces, private baths, outdoor hot tub, and gardens. Magnificent view of mountains. Minutes from art galleries, museums, restaurants, St. Francis Assisi Church, and ski valley.

Hosts: LeAn and Charles Clamurro
Rooms: 7 (PB) $75-140
Full Breakfast
Credit Cards: A, B
Notes: 2, 5, 7, 9, 10, 11, 12, 13

The Brooks Street Inn

119 Brooks Street, P.O. Box 4954, 87571
(505) 758-1489

Selected as one of the ten best inns of North America for 1988 by *Country Inns*

magazine. Atmosphere is casual and fun. Just a short walk from the Plaza. The rambling main house and charming guest house feature fireplaces, reading nooks, skylights, and private baths. Full espresso bar.

Host: Carol Frank
Rooms: 6 (PB) $81.58-104.97
Full Breakfast
Credit Cards: A, B, C
Notes: 2, 5, 7, 8, 9, 10, 11, 12, 13, 14

Cañon Bed and Breakfast

1014 Witt Road, P.O. Box 3005, 87571
(505) 758-0207

A European-style bed and breakfast in an old adobe home on a quiet street in the Cañon area of Taos. The hosts are both artists. The house is two and one-half miles from the center of Taos with its abundance of art galleries and museums. Near the Kit Carson National Forest's hiking trails. Other sporting facilities are nearby.

Hosts: Marilynn and Peter Nicholson
Rooms: 1 (PB) $65
Full or Continental Breakfast
Credit Cards: None
Notes: 5, 7, 8, 9, 10, 11, 12, 13

Casa Encantada

416 Liebert Street, P.O. Box 6460, 87571
(505) 758-7477; (800) 223-TAOS

A few short blocks from the Taos Plaza—in a world of its own—experience Casa Encantada. Peace, beauty, and warm hospitality abound. The ten rooms have private entrances and baths. Each room and suite is designed for charm and comfort, portraying the diversity of the area. Healthy breakfasts include fruit cereals, home-baked goodies, and Southwest delights and are served in a sunny, plant-filled atrium. Information to enhance the Taos experience is generously provided. Inquire about pets and children.

Host: Sharon Nicholson
Rooms: 10 (PB) $75-155
Full Breakfast
Credit Cards: A, B, C
Notes: 2, 5, 10, 12, 13, 14

NOTES: Credit cards accepted: A MasterCard; B Visa; C American Express; D Discover; E Diners Club; F Other; 2 Personal checks accepted; 3 Lunch available; 4 Dinner available; 5 Open all year; 6 Pets welcome;

Hacienda del Sol

P.O. Box 177, 87571
(505) 758-0287

A 190-year-old historic, charming, quiet adobe with fireplaces, viga ceilings, and surrounded by century-old trees. Guest rooms have down comforters, carefully selected furnishings, and fine art. Enjoy an unobstructed view of the Taos mountains from the deck of the outdoor hot tub. Generous breakfasts are served by a crackling fire in the winter, or on the patio in the summer. Chosen by *USA Weekend* as one of America's ten most romantic inns. One mile north of Taos Plaza.

Hosts: John and Marcine Landon
Rooms: 9 (PB) $65-120
Full Breakfast
Credit Cards: None
Notes: 2, 5, 7, 8, 9, 10, 11, 12, 13

Orinda

461 Valverde, 87571
(800) 847-1837

A beautiful 50-year-old adobe estate that combines spectacular views with country privacy and is still within walking distance of Taos Plaza. Three bedrooms are available with private baths and entrances. A delicious and hearty breakfast is served each morning.

Hosts: Cary and George Pratt
Rooms: 3 (PB) $70-90
Continental Breakfast
Credit Cards: A, B, D
Notes: 2, 5, 7, 8, 9, 10, 11, 12, 13

Orinda

El Rincon Bed and Breakfast

114 Kit Carson, 87571
(505) 758-4874

A special bed and breakfast in a historic adobe home, conveniently nestled in the heart of Taos. It boasts a fine art collection distributed throughout the house. In the summer, breakfast is served on a flower-filled patio. In the winter, it is served near a blazing adobe fireplace. Breakfast is available early, for those who are headed for Taos's fine ski areas. Most rooms have fireplaces, some have refrigerators and VCRs. Hot tub or Jacuzzi available. A lovely blend of old and new. Inquire about accommodations available for pets.

Hosts: Nina C. Meyers and Paul C. Castillo
Rooms: 12 (PB) $49-109
Continental Breakfast
Credit Cards: A, B, C
Notes: 2, 8, 9, 10, 11, 12, 13, 14

Salsa del Salto Bed and Breakfast

P.O. Box 1468, El Prado, 87529
(505) 776-2422; (800) 530-3097

Designed by world-renowned architect Antoine Predock, this beautiful home offers eight guest rooms, each reflecting Southwestern earth tones and pastel colors. All are decorated to tend to the guests' every need, with king-size beds, down comforters, furniture specially designed by local artisans for Salsa del Salto, and original paintings by Taos artists. As an added treat, all rooms have spectacular views of the mountains and mesas. Breakfast is a delicious gourmet's delight. Hot tub, heated pool, and private tennis court are available on the premises. Children over six are welcome.

Hosts: Dadou Mayer and Mary Hockett
Rooms: 8 (PB) $85-160
Full Breakfast
Credit Cards: A, B
Notes: 2, 5, 7, 9, 10, 11, 12, 13, 14

7 No smoking; 8 Children welcome; 9 Social drinking allowed; 10 Tennis nearby; 11 Swimming nearby; 12 Golf nearby; 13 Skiing nearby; 14 May be booked through a travel agent.

Touchstone Bed and Breakfast Inn

110 Marbel Dodge Lane, P.O. Box 2896, 87571
(505) 758-0192; (800) 758-0192
FAX (505) 758-3498

On two lush acres bordering Pueblo lands and Rio Pueblo, Touchstone offers a quiet ambience one mile from the Plaza. Intimate gourmet breakfasts; kiva fireplaces, viga ceilings, fine art, Oriental rugs, down pillows, comforters, cable TV, VCR, telephones, and tape decks complete the most luxurious of room accommodations; custom designed private baths, some with Jacuzzi tub. Hot tub. Historical adobe.

Host: Bren Price
Rooms: 6 (PB) $75-150
Full Breakfast
Credit Cards: A, B, C
Notes: 2, 5, 7, 9, 10, 11, 12, 13,1 4

The Willows Inn

Corner of Kit Carson Road and Dolan Streets
NDCBU 4558, 87571
(505) 758-2558; FAX (505) 758-5445

The Willows Inn is a small bed and breakfast establishment on a secluded acre lot in the heart of Taos. The atmosphere within the adobe-walled buildings and grounds is one of elegance, refinement, and restful contemplation. Each of the inn's five guest rooms has a private entrance and private bath plus a welcoming Kiva fireplace, which is set daily. The rooms are decorated in a variety of themes highlighting the cultures unique to the Taos area. Listed on the national and state historic registries, the property and buildings were once the home and studio of the late E. Martin Hennings. Two-night minimum stay on holiday weekends.

Hosts: Janet and Doug Camp
Rooms: 5 (PB) $95-130
Full Breakfast
Credit Cards: A, B
Notes: 8, 9, 10, 11, 12, 13, 14

TRUCHAS

Rancho Arriba

P.O. Box 338, 87578
(505) 689-2374

A European-style bed and breakfast with an informal and tranquil atmosphere, this traditional adobe hacienda is on a historic Spanish land grant. Spectacular mountain view in every direction, amid Colonial villages featuring traditional arts and architecture. Adobe churches, hand weaving, wood carving, and quilting. Limited smoking permitted.

Host: Curtiss Frank
Rooms: 4 (SB) $45-60
Full Breakfast
Credit Cards: A, B, E, F (Mesa Grande, C&B)
Notes: 2, 4, 5, 8, 9, 13

New York

ALBANY

American Country Collection

1353 Union Street, Schenectady, 12054
(518) 439-7001; FAX (518) 439-4301

097. This elegant turn-of-the-century Victorian home is on the bus route and just a few minutes' drive from all of the major area colleges, state buildings, and attractions. Six guest rooms are available; two rooms have private baths, and four rooms have shared baths. All rooms have telephones and air conditioning. Children over 12 are welcome. Continental breakfast served. Guests are welcome to use the TV in the living room. Off-street parking is provided. $49-79.

110. City convenience combined with quiet residential living makes this suburban ranch home an ideal location. Just one block from the bus line. In summer months, a hearty Continental breakfast is served on the screened porch. There's a redwood deck for sunning and a living room with a fireplace. One guest bedroom with shared bath. Double sofa bed also available. Children welcome. $55; $70 for two persons taking both rooms.

111. Once a residence for Albany's earliest extended families, this Victorian bed and breakfast also served as a tavern and grocery store. In the shadow of the Empire State Plaza. Twelve guest rooms with private baths, air conditioning, color cable TV, and telephone. Children are welcome. Smoking permitted. Cat resides in owner's apartment. $95-145.

142. Restored in 1991 as a private bed and breakfast inn, this in-town brownstone is registered as a historic landmark with the Historic Albany Foundation. Completed in 1881, it represents one of the earliest examples of a private building in Albany built in the neoclassical style of architecture. Twelve rooms on the second and third floors offer double and single beds, and one suite with two double beds features a working fireplace. Six guest rooms have private baths, and six have one double bed and share three hall baths. Breakfast includes bread and muffins, seasonal fresh fruit, cereal, juices, and beverages, including gourmet tea and coffee. No pets. Children welcome. Smoking permitted. $49-110.

The International Bed and Breakfast Club, Inc.

504 Amherst Street, Buffalo, 14207
(800) 723-4262; FAX (716) 873-4462

NY1574PP. This century-old Victorian home is in the heart of Pine Hills. Within a 30-minute drive of Saratoga Springs and the Adirondack and Catskill Mountains. Four rooms on the second floor have iron beds with feather mattresses and either shared or private baths. Continental breakfast is served in the large dining room. Off-street parking available. Smoking permitted on the front or back porch. $49-79.

Mansion Hill Inn

115 Philip Street at Park, 12202
(518) 465-2038

An urban inn, around the corner from the New York State Governor's Mansion and

---

7 No smoking; 8 Children welcome; 9 Social drinking allowed; 10 Tennis nearby; 11 Swimming nearby;
12 Golf nearby; 13 Skiing nearby; 14 May be booked through a travel agent.

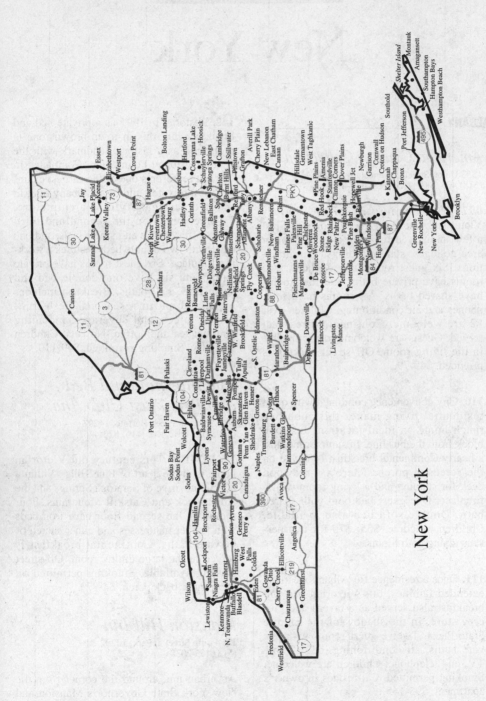

New York

Mansion Hill Inn

Empire State Plaza in a quiet residential neighborhood. The inn is comprised of a complex of Victorian-era buildings centered around a landscaped courtyard. The inn boasts a four-star restaurant, which serves dinner, lunch, and guests' breakfast. All rooms feature individually controlled air conditioning, telephones, color TV, desks, and off-street parking. 1994 Chamber of Commerce Small Business of the Year, and the Blue Chip 1995 Enter Prize Initiative.

Hosts: Maryellen, Elizabeth, and Steve Stofelano Jr.
Rooms: 8 (PB) $105-145
Full Breakfast
Credit Cards: A, B, C, D, E, F
Notes: 2, 3, 4, 5, 6, 7, 8, 9, 10, 11, 12, 13, 14

ALTAMONT

American Country Collection

1353 Union Street, Schenectady, 12054
(518) 439-7001; FAX (518) 439-4301

020. A renovation in 1910 added the large front pillars on the veranda to give the house its Southern Colonial flavor, but this impressive home on the site of the first town meeting of Guilderland was actually built in 1765. It first served as a tavern and is now on the state and national historic registers. It is at the base of the Helderburg Mountains on six acres of grounds. Four guest rooms with shared baths. Pets in residence. Children welcome. Crib available. Smoking in common rooms on first floor. There is an additional charge for the use of in-room fireplaces. Seasonal rates are also available. $55-65.

045. This 75-year-old refurbished Colonial is just 20 miles from the state capital. It is on 15 acres of well-groomed lawns, old shade trees, a swimming pool, barns, patio, and orchards. Business travelers find this location offers convenient access to both Albany and Schenectady. One third-floor suite has two bedrooms, living room, and private bath. One single room and two other rooms—one with a king-size bed combination and one with a double sofa bed on the second floor—share the bath with the owner. Pets in residence. Children welcome. Smoking outdoors only. $40-60.

AMAGANSETT

Mill-Garth Country Inn

23 Windmill Lane, P.O. Box 700, 11930
(516) 267-3757

The Mill-Garth Country Inn is a charming 153-year-old main building that is loosely surrounded by even more wonderful small cottages and a lovely expanse of lawns. The suites and studios have been furnished to create a restful atmosphere. The picturesque village of Amagansett is within walking distance, as is the beautiful ocean beach.

Hosts: Tommie Alegre and Jean Romolo
Rooms: 12 (PB) $125-260
Continental Breakfast
Credit Cards: A, B
Notes: 2, 5, 8, 10, 11, 12, 14

AMENIA

Covered Bridge

P.O. Box 447 A, Norfolk, CT 06058
(203) 542-5944

2AMNY. Contemporary home set on three acres has been tastefully decorated with

NOTES: Credit cards: A MasterCard; B Visa; C American Express; D Discover; E Diners Club; F Other;
2 Personal checks accepted; 3 Lunch available; 4 Dinner available; 5 Open all year; 6 Pets welcome;
7 No smoking; 8 Children welcome; 9 Social drinking allowed; 10 Tennis nearby; 11 Swimming nearby;
12 Golf nearby; 13 Skiing nearby; 14 May be booked through a travel agent.

lovely antiques and paintings from the owner's gallery. A delicious full breakfast is served in the dining room. The house has central air conditioning. There are four guest rooms, two of which share a bath. Double, twin, queen-, and king-size beds are available. House is available by the week also. $75-95.

Nutmeg Bed and Breakfast Agency

P.O. Box 1117, West Hartford, CT 06107
(203) 236-6698

343. This contemporary home in a 400-acre community offers a room with both a double and a twin bed and a shared bath. There is also a third-floor loft with a king-size bed and private bath. Close to prep schools and Lime Rock. Continental breakfast served; children over eight are welcome. Two resident cats.

Troutbeck

Leedsville Road, 12501
(914) 373-9681; FAX (914) 373-7080

This English country house is on 442 gentle acres and was once a gathering place for the literati and liberals of an earlier period. Nowadays, Troutbeck caters to corporate business groups during the week, and inngoers and wedding and restaurant guests on the weekends. Just two hours from Midtown Manhattan, Troutbeck has been nationally acclaimed for both its cuisine and ambience. Guests also enjoy year-round swimming, tennis, beautiful gardens, and handsome furnishings. Rates are for two nights and include six meals and an open bar. Smoking is allowed in the dining room only. Children under 1 and over 12 are welcome.

Owner and Innkeeper: Jim Flaherty
Rooms: 42 (37 PB; 5 SB) $600-825
Full and Continental Breakfast
Credit Cards: A, B, C
Notes: 2, 3, 4, 5, 9, 10, 11, 12, 13, 14

AMHERST

The International Bed and Breakfast Club, Inc.

504 Amherst Street, Buffalo, 14207
(800) 723-4262; FAX (716) 873-4462

NY4357PP. This center-entrance Colonial, convenient to downtown Buffalo and minutes from Niagara Falls, is a cozy and comfortable family home in one of Buffalo's most admired areas. Relax on the patio or in the library of this quality inn, minutes from the airport and college campus activities. Five rooms, shared bath. Continental breakfast plus coffee. $50.

AMSTERDAM

American Country Collection

1353 Union Street, Schenectady, 12054
(518) 439-7001; FAX (518) 439-4301

118. The guest rooms in this brick Federal Colonial have wide-plank floors, fireplaces, and are decorated with a mix of antiques, country furniture, and treasures found in the home. The history of the house is preserved in photos and mementos displayed throughout the home. Guests are treated to afternoon tea served in the English tradition with light pastries and sweet cakes. Three guest rooms with shared bath. Parakeet in residence. Children welcome. Crib available. No smoking. $35.

ANGELICA

The International Bed and Breakfast Club, Inc.

504 Amherst Street, Buffalo, 14207
(800) 723-4262; FAX (716) 873-4462

NY3295PP. Guests can relax in this elegant mansion built in 1886. Five rooms with private baths are available. Stained-glass windows, crystal chandeliers, lofty ceilings, parquet floors, and oak staircase. Full breakfast is available. Three-diamond rating from AAA of Western New York. $60-70.

APULIA

Elaine's Bed and Breakfast Selections

4987 Kingston Road, Elbridge, 13060
(315) 689-2082

This comfortable old white farmhouse has three guest rooms. Two have queen-size beds, and one has twin beds. Shared bath. The house is updated for convenience and safety and has a wonderful, quiet country setting, yet it's just five minutes from I-81. Full homemade breakfasts on weekends in the kitchen-family room, where guests can play the piano, enjoy the view of the distant hills, relax on the sofa, and stay warm by the wood stove. Close to three Central New York ski areas: Toggenburg, Laborador, and Song Mountain. Thirty minutes south of Syracuse and about 20 minutes north of Cortland. $55.

ATTICA

The International Bed and Breakfast Club, Inc.

504 Amherst Street, Buffalo, 14207
(800) 723-4262; FAX (716) 873-4462

NY1573PP. Warm, friendly hospitality in a country setting. This turn-of-the-century home is atop the rolling hills of Wyoming County. Three rooms, shared bath. Spectacular scenery, lovely landscaped grounds, gorgeous fall foliage viewing. Porch, patio, and fireplace. No smoking. Children welcome. Thirty-five miles east of Buffalo, 20 miles from Letchworth State Park. $45.

AUBURN

Elaine's Bed and Breakfast Selections

4987 Kingston Road, Elbridge, 13060
(315) 689-2082

On Owasco Lake, this 1910 Adirondack cottage-lodge features two spacious rooms, excellent craftsmanship, and solid wood paneling. In each room, picture windows overlook the lake and double French doors open onto a large screened porch. Each room has a private half-bath and shares a full bath. The living room has a large field-stone fireplace and a view of the entire lake. Breakfasts vary, with homemade hot casseroles, muffins, fruit, juice, coffee, and cold cereal. No smoking. No children under 12. No pets. No credit cards. $85.

The Irish Rose Bed and Breakfast

102 South Street, 13021
(315) 255-0196 (phone and FAX)

This 1870s Victorian mansion offers five rooms, one suite, private and semiprivate baths. Full gourmet candlelight breakfast, guest refrigeration, complimentary sparkling waters, homemade candies, and free video movies. Walk to historic homes, museums, and Harriet Tubman Homestead. Has been a bed and breakfast since 1990. Pets under 20 pounds welcome. No smoking in rooms.

Rooms: 5 (3 PB; 2 SB) $55-95
Full Breakfast
Credit Cards: A, B, C, D
Notes: 2, 5, 8, 9, 10, 11, 12, 13, 14

AVERILL PARK

Ananas Hus Bed and Breakfast

148 South Road, 12018
(518) 766-5035

The Tomlinsons' hillside ranch home, in West Stephentown on 30 acres, offers a

7 No smoking; 8 Children welcome; 9 Social drinking allowed; 10 Tennis nearby; 11 Swimming nearby; 12 Golf nearby; 13 Skiing nearby; 14 May be booked through a travel agent.

panoramic view of the Hudson River Valley with its natural beauty and tranquility. Patio dining in summer and the warmth of a fireplace in winter. Skiing and culture abound in nearby western Massachusetts and the capital district of New York State. Closed on Christmas Day. Children over 12 are welcome.

Hosts: Thelma and Clyde Tomlinson
Rooms: 3 (SB) $60
Full Breakfast
Credit Cards: C
Notes: 2, 5, 7, 9, 11, 12, 13, 14

The Gregory House Country Inn and Restaurant

P.O. Box 401, 12018
(518) 674-3774; FAX (518) 674-8916

Built in 1830, the Gregory House provides gracious dining and hospitality year-round. Guest rooms, all with private baths, are decorated in classic Victorian style. Guests can enjoy the inn's grounds, nearby lakes, golflinks, and downhill and cross-country skiing. An excellent location for parents and students who are visiting the local colleges of Albany, Troy, and New York State's capital district.

Rooms: 12 (PB) $80
Continental Breakfast
Credit Cards: A, B, C, D, E
Notes: 4, 5, 9, 10, 11, 12, 13, 14

The Gregory House

AVOCA

Patchwork Peace Bed and Breakfast

4279 Waterbury Hill, 14809
(607) 566-2443

Enjoy the sights, sounds, and smells of a real farm. Visit dairy cows and calves. Observe the patchwork of fields in different hues of greens and golds. Take a delightful walk. This 1920 farmhouse with natural floors and woodwork and light, airy bedrooms affords a gentle night's sleep nestled in sun-dried linens. Heirloom quilts throughout. Incredibly quiet. Country breakfast with hosts. Spend a night or a week. Special weekly rates.

Hosts: Bill and Betty Mitchell
Rooms: 3 (1 PB; 2 SB) $40-65
Full Breakfast
Credit Cards: None
Notes: 2, 5, 7, 9

AVON

The International Bed and Breakfast Club, Inc.

504 Amherst Street, Buffalo, 14207
(800) 723-4262; FAX (716) 873-4462

NY2838PP. This 30-room mansion, built in 1894, is a private estate on a winding, tree-lined drive. Nestled among 400 acres of Genessee Valley farmland, it features seven rooms, some with private baths. Complimentary cheese and fruit each evening on the veranda or in front of a crackling fire in the library. It's also a perfect setting for special occasions, celebrations, anniversaries, weddings and receptions, retreats, seminars or meetings, showers, rehearsal dinners, or family reunions. In-ground swimming pool. Children welcome. Smoking is limited to porches and living room. $65-125.

Berry Hill Gardens

BAINBRIDGE

Berry Hill Gardens Bed and Breakfast

Rural Delivery 1, Box 128, 13733
(607) 967-8745; (800) 497-8745

A friendly, informal atmosphere. Sunrises, sunsets, stargazing, fresh air, views. Restored 1820s farmhouse on a hilltop surrounded by vegetable, flower, and herb gardens. On its 180 acres guests can hike, swim, bird watch, pick berries, skate, cross-country ski, or just sit on the wraparound porch and watch the nature parade. The rooms are furnished with comfortable antiques, and a scrumptious country breakfast is served. A 10-minute drive takes visitors to restaurants, golf, tennis, auctions, and antique centers.

Hosts: Jean Fowler and Cecilio Rios
Rooms: 4 (SB) $60-70
Full Breakfast
Credit Cards: A, B, C
Notes: 2, 5, 7, 8, 9, 10, 11, 12, 13, 14

BALDWINSVILLE

Elaine's Bed and Breakfast Selections

4987 Kingston Road, Elbridge, 13060
(315) 689-2082

Spacious, historic Colonial in the village. The home was built around 1845 and, in keeping with its character, is decorated with many antiques and collectibles. Four guest rooms available, some with private bath and one with working fireplace. The house is on two acres high on a hill, a short walk to stores and the picturesque Seneca River. $50-85.

BALLSTON SPA

American Country Collection

1353 Union Street, Schenectady, 12054
(518) 439-7001; FAX (518) 439-4301

009. This renovated Second Empire Victorian is the focal point of the historic district of this tiny village. The home is divided into two segments. The rear bed and breakfast section has a private entrance, guest living room with fireplace, dining room, kitchen, and porch for afternoon refreshments. The second floor has two guest rooms, each with a private bath and queen-size bed. Rooms in this section are ideal for family gatherings and groups of four traveling together. There are three additional rooms in the front section, each with a queen-size bed and private bath. Smoking outdoors only. No pets. Children over 11 welcome. Younger children permitted when entire bed and breakfast section is rented to one party. $85-125.

119. This working farm and girls' summer riding academy is on 100 acres of rolling meadows and scenic farmland. Riding lessons are available in the indoor riding arena. A heated swimming pool on the premises is available for guests to use. The two guest bedrooms, one with private bath, have air conditioning. No smoking allowed. Children are welcome. Crib available, but guests should bring their own crib linens. Dogs and cats indoors; horses, ducks, geese, goats outside on the farm. $65-95.

7 No smoking; 8 Children welcome; 9 Social drinking allowed; 10 Tennis nearby; 11 Swimming nearby; 12 Golf nearby; 13 Skiing nearby; 14 May be booked through a travel agent.

BALMVILLE

The Red Caboose

476 River Road, 12550
(914) 561-1715

An authentic restored New York Central Railroad caboose. It features built-in twin berths with an additional berth over the bathroom, air conditioning, TV, kitchenette, and sitting room with wood-burning stove. Beautiful landscaping overlooking the majestic Hudson River with in-ground pool and cabana. Only 13 miles to West Point, 40 minutes to Hyde Park, and 60 minutes to New York City. Private entrance, unique accommodations, and Continental breakfast. Pets in residence.

Hosts: Doris and Kenneth Sheeleigh
Room: 1 (PB) $70-80
Continental Breakfast
Credit Cards: None
Notes: 2, 6, 8, 10, 11, 12, 14

BARNEVELD

Bed and Breakfast Leatherstocking

P.O. Box 53, Herkimer, 13350
(315) 733-0040; (800) 941-BEDS (2337)

001. Grand scale farmhouse from the Victorian era, graciously remodeled and restored with large entrance hall, formal living room, dining room, and informal family rooms and fireplaces. Short ride from Utica. Close to area colleges and ski centers. A private family suite and a king-size bed suite, both with private baths. Two singles with shared baths. Gourmet breakfasts and fresh flowers daily. $45-115.

BOLTON LANDING

American Country Collection

1353 Union Street, Schenectady, 12054
(518) 439-7001; FAX (518) 439-4301

056. This 11-room farmhouse was built in 1926 as the caretaker's cottage for a large estate on Millionaire's Row along the west side of Lake George. Two second-floor rooms have a shared bath. A third second-floor room has its own private bath. Children over four are welcome. Pets in residence. Swimming, fishing and ice fishing, skating, parasailing, and boating are all available. Just 20-25 miles to Fort Ticonderoga and Great Escape Amusement Park. $50-60.

BROCKPORT

The International Bed and Breakfast Club, Inc.

504 Amherst Street, Buffalo, 14207
(800) 723-4262; FAX (716) 873-4462

NY0220PP. This historic Greek Revival landmark includes three porches, massive columns, pediments, and a cupola. This 1850 mansion, with three guest rooms and shared bath, is nestled among sycamore, maple, and blue spruce trees. Surprisingly detailed Victorian Continental breakfast served, along with Kettledrum (afternoon tea). Three fireplaces, antiques, chocolates, music-box melodies, and aromatherapy to pamper and exhilarate the spirit. Near colleges, parks, golf courses, lake, antique stores, and shops. Smoking in permitted areas only. No pets. $45-50.

BRONX

Le Refuge Inn Bed and Breakfast

620 City Island Avenue, 10464
(718) 885-2478; FAX (212) 737-0384

Le Refuge Inn Bed and Breakfast, a 100-year-old Victorian, offers six rooms with queen-size beds and shared bath and one suite with a private bath. There is also one room that has twin beds. In the country,

NOTES: Credit cards accepted: A MasterCard; B Visa; C American Express; D Discover; E Diners Club; F Other; 2 Personal checks accepted; 3 Lunch available; 4 Dinner available; 5 Open all year; 6 Pets welcome;

just 20 minutes from Manhattan. Dinner served nightly.

Hosts: Pierre and Emmanuelle Saint-Denis
Rooms: 8 (1 PB; 7 SB) $75-125
Continental Breakfast
Credit Cards: C
Notes: 2, 4, 5, 8, 9, 10, 11, 12, 14

BROOKFIELD

Gates Hill Homestead

P.O. Box 96, Dugway Road, 13314
(315) 899-5837

A quiet, secluded pioneer-type farmstead, cleared, designed, and built by owners. Unusual saltbox open-beamed construction with massive central fireplace, wide-plank flooring, stenciling, candle chandeliers. Air-conditioned. Full breakfast. Selected in 1987 by *Frommer's Guide to Bed & Breakfasts in North America* as one of the 100 best. Optional entertainment: 70-minute, four-horse stagecoach tour of *The Eternal Hills* (1973), followed by an elegant country dinner, all home-cooking, by reservation.

Hosts: Charlie and Donna Tanney
Rooms: 3 (2 PB; 1 SB) $59-79
Full Breakfast
Credit Cards: A, B
Notes: 2, 4, 5, 6, 7, 8, 13

BROOKLYN

Bed and Breakfast on the Park

113 Prospect Park West, 11215
(718) 499-6115

This opulent 1892 limestone Victorian four-story mansion is fully renovated and decorated in period antiques, Oriental rugs, stained-glass windows, and original paintings. Guests enjoy the ambience of gracious living from the turn of the century. Original mantels and woodwork with modern amenities. In Brooklyn just two miles from Manhattan; one-half mile from the Brooklyn Museum and Botanic Gardens;

two blocks from shopping and restaurants. Guests keep coming back to this charming Big Apple inn.

Host: Liana Paolella
Rooms: 7 (5 PB; 2 SB) $100-250
Full Breakfast
Credit Cards: A, B
Notes: 2, 5, 7, 8, 9, 10

BUFFALO

Bryant House

236 Bryant Street, 14222
(716) 885-1540

Stay in a charming Victorian house, a pleasant and reasonable alternative to commercial accommodations. Five minutes to downtown and the Canadian border. Convenient to theaters, boutiques, excellent restaurants, and Niagara Falls. A delicious Continental breakfast is served in the formal dining room or on the multilevel deck, weather permitting. Brochure on request. Personal checks accepted for deposit only.

Host: John C. Nolan
Rooms: 3 (PB) $50-60
Continental Breakfast
Credit Cards: None
Notes: 5, 8, 9, 14

Bryant House

7 No smoking; 8 Children welcome; 9 Social drinking allowed; 10 Tennis nearby; 11 Swimming nearby; 12 Golf nearby; 13 Skiing nearby; 14 May be booked through a travel agent.

The International Bed and Breakfast Club, Inc.

504 Amherst Street, 14207
(800) 723-4262; FAX (716) 873-4462

NY0770PP. Find charming accommodations in this Westside Buffalo inn, circa 1870, with an Oriental flavor. It can accommodate up to three persons in its double room and adjoining but separate single room, each with twin beds. Shared bath with tub and shower. Full gourmet breakfast served daily, under skylight in dining area or on the lovely deck overlooking the yard, pool, and garden. Conveniently minutes from the Peace Bridge to Canada, downtown Buffalo, and historic Allentown. Off-street parking available. Pets considered. $50-60.

NY1428PP. This 1910 Victorian home, designed by well-known architect E. B. Green, features one bright, air-conditioned suite with sauna, porch, and private entrance. It can accommodate up to five adults and includes a double bed, roll away, pull-out sofa bed, and crib, with private bath. TV, refrigerator, and microwave in room. Continental and full breakfasts are served. Blocks from restaurants, shops, colleges, museums, and park. Five minutes to downtown Buffalo. Ten minutes to Canada. Smoking accepted. Children welcome. Extended-stay discount available. $60-65.

NY1540PP. Stay in a charming Victorian house, a pleasant and reasonable alternative to more commercial accommodations. Offering three rooms with private baths, this lovely house also has antiques, a fireplace, and a patio. Convenient to theaters, boutiques, excellent restaurants, and Niagara Falls; five minutes to downtown Buffalo and Canada. A delicious Continental breakfast is served in the formal dining room or on the multilevel deck. $50-60.

Warnick's Village Bed and Breakfast

328 Wardman Road, 14217
(716) 875-5860

The hosts welcome guests to this three-story wood-frame home on a residential tree-lined street just north of the city of Buffalo. The air-conditioned bedrooms are furnished with beautiful antiques, and fluffy robes are provided for guests' comfort. The home is just minutes from historical Allentown, antique shops, Albright-Knox Art Gallery, the Buffalo waterfront, and many fine restaurants. Wake up to the aroma of freshly ground coffee, locally made sausage, delicious homemade muffins, and fresh fruit. Limited smoking is permitted.

Hosts: Connie and Fred Warnick
Rooms: 2 (SB) $50
Full Breakfast
Credit Cards: None
Notes: 5, 8, 9, 10, 12

BURDETT

The Red House Country Inn

4586 Picnic Area Road, 14818-9716
(607) 546-8566

The Red House Country Inn is within the beautiful Finger Lakes National Forest. Twenty-eight miles of maintained hiking and cross-country ski trails. In-ground pool. Six wineries ten minutes from the inn. Completely restored 1840s farmstead. Five acres of groomed lawns and flower gardens. Beautifully appointed rooms. Large country breakfast. Fully equipped guest kitchen. Dinner is available November through April. Children over 12 are welcome.

Hosts: Sandy Schmanke and Joan Martin
Rooms: 5 (SB) $60-85
Full Breakfast
Credit Cards: A, B, C, D
Notes: 2, 5, 7, 9, 10, 11, 12, 13, 14

NOTES: Credit cards accepted: A MasterCard; B Visa; C American Express; D Discover; E Diners Club; F Other; 2 Personal checks accepted; 3 Lunch available; 4 Dinner available; 5 Open all year; 6 Pets welcome;

BURNT HILLS

American Country Collection

1353 Union Street, Schenectady, 12054
(518) 439-7001; FAX (518) 439-4301

114. The oldest part of this home was built in 1796. The main house, a brick Center Hall Colonial, was completed about 150 years ago. The home is surrounded by trees and old-fashioned flower gardens that abut a 12-acre apple orchard. Two guest rooms with private baths. One guest room opens onto a third room to form a suite. Smoking limited to sitting room and outdoors. Children school-age and over welcome. No pets in residence but may accept guest pet (charge $10). $65-85.

CAMBRIDGE

American Country Collection

1353 Union Street, Schenectady, 12054
(518) 439-7001; FAX (518) 439-4301

010. The main house dates from 1896-1903 and features stained-glass windows, ceiling murals, and an Otis brass cage elevator. The carriage house offers a variety of eight suites, each with one to three bedrooms, living room, refrigerator, color TV, and private bath. Smoking permitted. Children welcome. Playpen available; no crib. No pets. $65-75.

CAMILLUS (SYRACUSE)

American Country Collection

1353 Union Street, Schenectady, 12054
(518) 439-7001; FAX (518) 439-4301

168. Italianate Colonial inn in a suburban/rural area, completely furnished with antiques and period pieces. Fully restored in 1980. There is also an attached full-service restaurant and pub serving lunch and dinner. Six rooms, all with private bath, air conditioning, and TV. Two of the rooms have a Jacuzzi. Continental breakfast. Children welcome. $60-99.

CANAAN

Shaker Mill Inn

Cherry Lane, Route 22, 12029
(518) 794-9345; FAX (518) 794-9344

The beamed sunroom of this 1824 Shaker-built stone grist mill offers a lovely view of the millstream splashing down the adjacent hillside from a picturesque waterfall. The inn offers a quiet retreat for rest and reflection. Grounds include a pond, lawns, gardens, and outdoor dining. Shaker Mill is a popular base for hiking, biking, and outdoor adventure as well as numerous cultural destinations, including nearby Tanglewood and the Hancock Shaker Village. Inquire about accommodations for pets. Smoking restricted.

Hosts: Ingram Paperny and Jean and Sean Cowhig
Rooms: 20 (PB) $50-120
Full Breakfast
Credit Cards: A, B
Notes: 2, 4, 5, 8, 9, 10, 11, 13

CANANDAIGUA

The Acorn Inn

4508 Route 64 South, Bristol Center, 14424
(716) 229-2834; (716) 394-5260
FAX (716) 229-5046

The Acorn Inn

---

7 No smoking; 8 Children welcome; 9 Social drinking allowed; 10 Tennis nearby; 11 Swimming nearby; 12 Golf nearby; 13 Skiing nearby; 14 May be booked through a travel agent.

Warm hospitality awaits guests at this 1795 stagecoach inn where rooms are charmingly furnished with period antiques, comfortable canopied beds, and luxury linens. Select a book from the 5,000-volume library and relax before a cheery fire in the quaint common room or in the hammock in the secluded gardens. Wonderful country breakfasts are served in the dining room where Windsor arm chairs encourage guests to linger and enjoy the tranquility of yester-year. Air-conditioned.

Hosts: Joan and Louis Clark
Rooms: 4 (PB) $75-140
Full Breakfast
Credit Cards: A, B, D
Notes: 2, 5, 7, 9, 11, 12, 13, 14

The International Bed and Breakfast Club, Inc.

504 Amherst Street, Buffalo, 14207
(800) 723-4262; FAX (716) 873-4462

NY0375PP. Choose from a selection of four beautifully appointed accommoda-tions, each with private bath, sumptuous fluffy towels, and firm, luxurious bedding. The hosts invite guests to arrive as strangers and depart as friends. In the beau-tiful Finger Lakes area this bed and break-fast offers so much. Convenient to antique shops, boating, Bristol Mountain skiing, Sonnenberg Gardens and Mansion, winery tours, and the Finger Lakes Performing Arts concerts, and summer home of the Rochester Philharmonic Orchestra. Full breakfast. $75-135.

NY1793PP. Convenient to Canandaigua Lake, this three-bedroom Victorian home offers the plentiful activities of the region, in addition to private amenities. The inn is beautifully decorated with Victorian period antiques and is a pleasant place for tourists, weekend getaways, and business travelers. Nearby attractions include Finger Lakes Race Track, Bristol Mountain Ski Resort, Finger Lakes Performing Arts Center,

Naples Vineyards, Captain Grey's Boat Tours, Canandaigua Lady Dinner Excursions, Bristol Valley Playhouse, Cobblestone Performing Arts Center, and many fine dining establishments, both on the lake and in the city. Just 30 minutes from Rochester. Hosts invite guests to join them for an experience of elegance. Full breakfast. $50-100.

Oliver Phelps Country Inn

252 North Main Street, 14424
(716) 396-1650

A historic Federal-style home decorated in country charm. Each guest room is hand stenciled and has a private bath. A full coun-try breakfast is served by a warm fire.

Hosts: John and Joanne Sciarratta
Rooms: 4 (PB) $75-110
Full Breakfast
Credit Cards: A, B, C
Notes: 2, 5, 7, 8, 10, 11, 12, 13, 14

Thendara Inn and Restaurant

4356 East Lake Road, 14424
(716) 394-4868; FAX (716) 396-0804

Elegant 1900s Victorian home built on the shores of Canandaigua Lake. Thendara offers fine cuisine for any occasion. View spectacular sunsets or stay overnight in the lakeview guest rooms, one with a skylight Jacuzzi. Thendara is a great location for dinners, receptions, conferences, retreats, or any special occasion. Truly the most beautiful setting in the Finger Lakes region. Lunch available during the summer.

Hosts: Rick and Joy Schwartz
Rooms: 5 (PB) $65-165
Continental Breakfast
Credit Cards: A, B, C
Notes: 2, 4, 5, 8, 9, 10, 11, 12, 13, 14

CANTON

American Country Collection

1353 Union Street, Schenectady, 12054
(518) 439-7001; FAX (518) 439-4301

200. This lovingly restored 1850s rural farmhouse sits on 165 acres of rolling farmland, meadows, fields, and forest, and is decorated with antiques, Oriental rugs, and deep, dark wood moldings and trim. Two guest rooms with private bath, TV/VCR, telephone, individually controlled heating, and sitting area. One room has air conditioning, a jet tub for two, and a marble floored bath; the other is larger, and has a ceiling fan and an excellent view. Enjoy lake swimming, canoeing, skiing, a sandy beach, volleyball court, fishing equipment, and outdoor hot tub. Guests are invited to use the cottage. Two roll aways available as well as one "overflow" room with a double bed and shared bath. Children welcome. Crib available. Dog in residence. Please inquire about pets. Full breakfast. Smoking outside only. $60-65.

CAZENOVIA

American Country Collection

1353 Union Street, Schenectady, 12054
(518) 439-7001; FAX (518) 439-4301

162. Peaceful, quiet retreat directly on the shore of Cazenovia Lake. Unique, modern home furnished with antiques and collectibles from owner's world travels. Large living room with fireplace. Swimming at lake shore and rowboat available. First-floor room with queen-size bed, private deck and bath. Second floor has four rooms, two with queen-size beds and two with twin beds, that share two baths. Continental breakfast served in the dining room or on the outside patio. Smoking permitted. Handicapped accessible. Children welcome. Dog in residence. $60-90.

Brae Loch Inn

5 Albany Street, US Route 20, 13035
(315) 655-3431

The 15 quiet rooms in this inn are on the second floor of the Brae Loch. They feature the old-time charm of antiques, the classic luxury of Stickley furniture, and the modern comfort of some king-size beds in selected rooms. All rooms have private baths, and these rooms are so handsome and so reasonably priced that guests will want to visit over and over again.

Hosts: Jim and Val Barr
Rooms: 15 (13 PB; 2 SB) $55-125
Continental Breakfast
Credit Cards: A, B, C, D
Notes: 4, 5, 8, 9, 10, 11, 12, 13, 14

The Brewster Inn

6 Ledyard Avenue, P.O. Box 507, 13035
(315) 655-9232

Built in 1890 on the shore of Cazenovia Lake, the Brewster Inn is an elegant country inn known for fine dining, gracious hospitality, and comfortable lodging. Three attractive dining rooms provide a relaxed atmosphere for superb American cuisine and an award-winning wine list. Seventeen hotel rooms offer variety in decor. Each room has a private bath, television, air conditioning, and telephone. Four rooms have Jacuzzis. Cazenovia offers quaint shops, swimming, hiking, golfing, cross-country and downhill skiing, and the impressive Chittenango Falls.

Hosts: Richard and Catherine Hubbard
Rooms: 17 (PB) $70-160
Penthouse: 3 rooms $225
Continental Breakfast
Credit Cards: A, B, E
Notes: 4, 5, 8, 9, 10, 11, 12, 13, 14

CHAPPAQUA

Crabtree's Kittle House

11 Kittle Road, 10514
(914) 666-8044

Built in 1790, Crabtree's Kittle House maintains a distinctive blend of country style and comfort. Only 20 miles from New York City, the inn is also a comfortable base from which to explore Van Cortlandt

7 No smoking; 8 Children welcome; 9 Social drinking allowed; 10 Tennis nearby; 11 Swimming nearby; 12 Golf nearby; 13 Skiing nearby; 14 May be booked through a travel agent.

and Philipsburg manors, Sunnyside, and Pocantico Hills. Dinner specialties include Dijon herb-crusted loin of free-range lamb and magret of Hudson Valley moulard duck with apricot Armagnac sauce. A "grand award" winning wine list. Live jazz and dancing Thursday through Saturday.

Hosts: John and Dick Crabtree
Rooms: 11, $79-89
Continental Breakfast
Credit Cards: A, B, C, D, E, F
Notes: 2, 3, 4, 5, 7, 8, 9, 12

CHARLTON

American Country Collection

1353 Union Street, Schenectady, 12054
(518) 439-7001; FAX (518) 439-4301

087. A sense of history prevails throughout this pre-Revolutionary War estate set on 100 acres just a few miles west of Saratoga. One guest room has wide-plank pine walls, built-in bookcases, cannonball bed, and comfortable sitting area. The master suite has a canopied bed and adjacent nursery, and, if needed, a third connecting room with double bed. Private baths. Children welcome. Smoking permitted. $65-85.

CHAUTAUQUA

The International Bed and Breakfast Club, Inc.

504 Amherst Street, Buffalo, 14207
(800) 723-4262; FAX (716) 873-4462

NY2070PP. Casually elegant and elegantly casual, Oriental carpets and fine furniture create a lovely background to this charming air-conditioned home. Guest rooms have private baths and overlook Chautauqua Lake. Relax around the secluded swimming pool, tie up a boat at the Spindlers' dock, or enjoy the Amish quilt shops, antique stores, wineries, art galleries, or seasonal sports. Famed Chautauqua Institution is nearby. Continental plus breakfast. $55-70.

Plumbush

Rural Route 33, P.O. Box 864, 14722
(716) 789-5309

Newly restored, circa 1865, Italian villa on a hilltop surrounded by 125 acres. Just one mile from Chautauqua Institute. Bluebirds and wildlife abound. Bicycles available; cross-country ski trail. Sunny rooms, wicker, antiques, and a touch of elegant charm. As seen in *Victorian Homes* (Summer 1991), *Innsider* magazine (May-June 1990), and *Victoria* magazine (August 1989).

Hosts: George and Sandy Green
Rooms: 5 (PB) $85-100
Full Breakfast
Credit Cards: A, B, D
Notes: 2, 5, 7, 9, 10, 11, 12, 13, 14

CHERRY CREEK

The International Bed and Breakfast Club, Inc.

504 Amherst Street, Buffalo, 14207
(800) 723-4262; FAX (716) 873-4462

NY8957PP. Every effort has been made to provide an environment of 19th-century grace, beauty, and comfort in this Italianate inn on 60 acres, with a four-acre stocked pond. Arched windows, multiple roofs, and antiques abound. Five guest rooms are available with private baths. A gourmet breakfast is served daily. Cockaigne Ski Resort is a five-minute drive, and fine cuisine may always be found at the Grainery restaurant. $65-85.

CHERRY PLAIN

Covered Bridge

P.O. Box 447 A, Norfolk, CT 06058
(203) 542-5944

1CPNY. This 1790 Colonial, nestled in the New York Berkshires, is secluded yet minutes from Tanglewood and summer theaters. Hiking trails, cross-country skiing, and a pond for fishing and skating are available on the grounds. Enjoy a full breakfast and dinner, both made with natural foods. The four guest rooms, two with antique canopied beds, have private baths. The rate includes dinner. $110.

CHESTERTOWN

Friends Lake Inn

Friends Lake Road, 12817
(518) 494-4751

In the Adirondacks overlooking Friends Lake, this fully restored 19th-century inn is 20 minutes north of Lake George, with Gore Mountain Ski Center only 15 minutes away. Breakfast and gourmet dinner are served daily accompanied by an award-winning wine list. Canoeing, biking, swimming, hiking, and cross-country skiing facilities are on the grounds.

Hosts: Sharon and Greg Taylor
Rooms: 14 (PB) $120-190
Full Breakfast
Credit Cards: A, B, C
Notes: 2, 4, 5, 7, 8, 9, 10, 11, 12, 13, 14

CHICHESTER

Maplewood Bed and Breakfast

6 Park Road, 12416
(914) 688-5433

A lovely Colonial home in the heart of the Catskill Mountains, 12 miles from Hunter or Belleayre Mountain for skiing; close to fishing, tubing, antiquing, and hiking; 20 minutes to Woodstock. Single, double canopied, queen, and king bedrooms share two bathrooms. Each room has a different view of the mountains. Beautiful porch, gardens, and in-ground pool. A full breakfast is served.

Hosts: Nancy and Albert Parsons
Rooms: 4 (SB) $65
Full Breakfast
Credit Cards: None
Notes: 2, 5, 7, 8, 9, 10, 11, 12, 13

CLEVELAND

Bed and Breakfast Leatherstocking

P.O. Box 53, Herkimer, 13350
(315) 733-0040; (800) 941-BEDS (2337)

002. This spacious Victorian is on the north shore of the beautiful Oneida Lake, close to Syracuse, Oswego, Utica, Rome, and other central New York locales. Relax by the in-ground swimming pool. Host offers four double guest rooms with working fireplaces and private baths. The single unit beach house built over the lake boasts dramatic sunrises and moonlit nights with a Jacuzzi, kitchenette, two bedrooms, two baths, sun deck, and a small bar. Extended stays are welcomed. $50-170.

Elaine's Bed and Breakfast Selections

4987 Kingston Road, Elbridge, 13060
(315) 689-2082

On the north shore of Oneida Lake, guests will find this circa 1820 white Colonial built by an early industrial baron. It has 6,000 square feet of living space. An open porch welcomes guests with antique wicker and a hammock. From the wide center hall, there is a large playroom with billiard table, jukebox, many musical instruments, and the owner's collection of prizes from showing his many antique automobiles. The family room features a large TV, stereo, and beautiful stained-glass leaded window behind the bar. All rooms are large and have working fireplaces and private baths. There is a formal living room full of antiques, a large cheery dining room with a player piano and more than 1,000 rolls. As this is a musical inn, there is an organ and a nickelodeon. A contemporary furnished beach house is also available for $170. Perfect for small conferences. No pets. No smoking. No children under 16. $50-75.

7 No smoking; 8 Children welcome; 9 Social drinking allowed; 10 Tennis nearby; 11 Swimming nearby; 12 Golf nearby; 13 Skiing nearby; 14 May be booked through a travel agent.

CLINTON CORNERS

American Country Collection
1353 Union Street, Schenectady, 12054
(518) 439-7001; FAX (518) 439-4301

181. This modern, air-conditioned, luxurious Greek Revival home is only 90 minutes away from the buzz of Manhattan. Guests enter a large living room with cathedral ceiling, spectacular floor-to-ceiling windows, and a beautiful grand piano. Next comes a dining room decorated in floral patterns, connected to a delightful Blue Stone patio where a delicious full or Continental breakfast is served, if the weather cooperates. The two master bedrooms have king-size beds and full marble bath with bidet and large Jacuzzi. Leading from the landing on the second floor are the other two spacious guest rooms, each with queen-size bed and private bath. Rhinebeck, the Aerodrome, FDR home, Vanderbilt mansion, Clermont State Historic Site, and other area attractions are only 10-15 miles away. $95-125.

195. Guests can relax in a charming country cottage surrounded by colorful flower gardens and a winding brick path, bordering on a pristine lake for swimming, boating, fishing, ice skating, or cross-country skiing. This contemporary lakefront home has a common room with cathedral ceiling, Colonial fireplace, and deck overlooking gardens and lake. One guest room is lakeside, with a sitting room, TV, skylight, full private bath, and lakeview balcony and another room has a double bed, fireplace, lakeview balcony, and private bath. Furnishings are a mixture of Colonial and handcrafted Van Hoen furniture. Only 15 miles from Rhinebeck, Millbrook, Culinary Institute, Vanderbilt mansion, Roosevelt home and library, Hyde Park, and other attractions. $110.

COLDEN

The International Bed and Breakfast Club, Inc.
504 Amherst Street, Buffalo, 14207
(800) 723-4262; FAX (716) 873-4462

NY6789PP. Guests will enjoy this scenic rural valley about 25 minutes southeast of Buffalo. The suite has double bed, private bath, living room with queen-size sofa bed, and a small kitchen. Continental breakfast includes home-baked breads and is served in the living area, on the deck, or on the garden table. $65.

CONSTANTIA

Elaine's Bed and Breakfast Selections
4987 Kingston Road, Elbridge, 13060
(315) 689-2082

Large, cozy, and warm farmhouse overlooks Oneida Lake. Three guest rooms and bath upstairs, and two rooms with private baths downstairs. Next to restaurant. All freshly remodeled and cheery. $50-65.

The International Bed and Breakfast Club, Inc.
504 Amherst Street, Buffalo, 14207
(800) 723-4262; FAX (716) 873-4462

NY9559PP. This spacious turn-of-the-century farmhouse, recently restored, is on Oneida Lake, 24 miles northeast of Syracuse. It features one queen-size bedroom on the main floor, with private bath and a deck overlooking the pool; on the second floor, two full-size rooms with lakeviews and one twin room all share a bath. A full breakfast is served in the cheerful dining room overlooking the lake, while Continental breakfast is served at poolside.

NOTES: Credit cards accepted: A MasterCard; B Visa; C American Express; D Discover; E Diners Club; F Other; 2 Personal checks accepted; 3 Lunch available; 4 Dinner available; 5 Open all year; 6 Pets welcome;

There are several fine restaurants nearby, as well as antique shops, golf courses, a fish hatchery, beaches, cross-country skiing, and shopping centers. $40-65.

COOPERSTOWN

American Country Collection

1353 Union Street, Schenectady, 12054
(518) 439-7001; FAX (518) 439-4301

128. Enjoy this rural farmhouse on 7.5 acres just outside historic Cooperstown. Surrounded by a pond, sugar bush, hills, and meadows, this inn offers travelers a parlor room for relaxing or reading, an air-conditioned breakfast room, and an adjoining room with TV. Three bedrooms are available for guests. One room has two double beds and a private bath, and the other two rooms, with twin and double beds, share a full hall bath. Smoking outdoors only. Full country breakfast. Children are welcome. $55-70.

Angelholm

14 Elm Street, Box 705, 13326
(607) 547-2483; FAX (607) 547-2309

On a quiet residential street within easy walking distance of the Baseball Hall of Fame, museums, shops, restaurants, and other attractions. Angelholm is a gracious

Angelholm

1805 Federal-period home with comfortably elegant furnishings. Five rooms, all with private baths. A full breakfast is served in the formal dining room. Afternoon tea and lemonade are served on the veranda or in the living room. Off-street parking available.

Hosts: Jan and Fred Reynolds
Rooms: 5 (PB) $80-95
Full Breakfast
Credit Cards: A, B
Notes: 2, 5, 7, 9, 10, 11, 12, 14

Bed and Breakfast Leatherstocking

P.O. Box 53, Herkimer, 13350
(315) 733-0040; (800) 941-BEDS (2337)

038. In the heart of Cooperstown, just a few short blocks from the Baseball Hall of Fame, this 100-year-old Victorian offers respite and quiet elegance in three guest rooms: a four-poster king-size bed, a queen-size bed with private bath, or a wicker double with private or shared bath. Enjoy an old-fashioned tradition of porch sitting, or beautiful Otsego Lake and famous museums. All rooms are air-conditioned and have remote-controlled cable color TV with HBO. A full country breakfast is served in the dining room each morning. Smoking restricted. $65-85.

Creekside Bed and Breakfast

Rural Delivery 1, Box 206, 13326
(607) 547-8203

"A personal favorite," wrote American Express's *Travel & Leisure.* This nationally renowned bed and breakfast, also featured in *Country Inns* magazine, offers beautiful surroundings in an elegant atmosphere. Its elegant Colonial features, bridal suite, honeymoon cottage, and penthouse suite are ideal for honeymooners, reunions, or romantic escapes. Hosts are founders of and performers with Glimmerglass Opera. Five guest rooms all have king- or queen-size beds, private bath, and TV/HBO. Five

7 No smoking; 8 Children welcome; 9 Social drinking allowed; 10 Tennis nearby; 11 Swimming nearby; 12 Golf nearby; 13 Skiing nearby; 14 May be booked through a travel agent.

minutes to Baseball Hall of Fame. Twenty minutes from opera house.

Hosts: Gwen and Fred Ermlich
Rooms: 5 (PB) $80-150
Full Breakfast
Credit Cards: A, B, C
Notes: 2, 5, 7, 8, 9, 10, 11, 12, 14

The Inn at Cooperstown

The Inn at Cooperstown

16 Chestnut Street, 13326
(607) 547-5756

The Inn at Cooperstown, built in 1874, continues to provide genuine hospitality within walking distance of all of Cooperstown's attractions. The 17 guest rooms, each with private bath, are simply decorated with the guests' well-being in mind. Enjoy the comfortable beds and the large, thirsty towels. Relax in a rocking chair on the sweeping veranda shaded by 100-year-old maples or in front of the cozy fireplace in the sitting room. Off-street parking is available behind this award-winning inn. Smoking restricted.

Host: Michael Jerome
Rooms: 17 (PB) $88-95
Continental Breakfast
Credit Cards: A, B, C, D
Notes: 2, 5, 8, 9, 10, 11, 12, 13, 14

Serendipity Bed and Breakfast

Rural Route 2, Box 1050, 13326
(607) 547-2106

Serendipity is a contemporary home, designed by a student of Frank Lloyd Wright, that offers a friendly, casual atmosphere and panoramic views of Otsego Lake in a quiet, serene setting with guests' own private entrance and deck. Rates include queen-size bed and a low-cholesterol breakfast. Enjoy the romantic, natural beauty of the surrounding woods and lake.

Host: Vera A. Talevi
Room: 1 (PB) $75-95
Full Breakfast
Credit Cards: None
Notes: 2, 7, 9, 11, 12

CORINTH

American Country Collection

1353 Union Street, Schenectady, 12054
(518) 439-7001; FAX (518) 439-4301

151. Travelers are invited to share a most unusual country inn at the gateway to the Adirondacks, only minutes from the villages of Saratoga Springs, Lake George, and Lake Luzerne. Five rooms, all with private baths. Access ramp for handicapped guests is available. Saratoga, the racetracks, Skidmore College, and SPAC all within an easy drive. Breakfast features a fresh fruit platter, juice selection, muffins with jam, Belgian waffles with cinnamon apples or strawberry blend, coffee, and tea. $60-125.

CORNING

DeLevan House

188 DeLevan Avenue, 14830
(607) 962-2347

Southern Colonial with homelike hospitality. Overlooking Corning. Quiet surroundings, outstanding accommodations, complimentary cool drink served on the beautiful screened porch. Free pickup from and delivery to the airport. Member of the International Bed and Breakfast Club. Children over 12 welcome.

Host: Mary M. DePumpo
Rooms: 3 (1 PB; 2 SB) $55-85
Full Breakfast
Credit Cards: F
Notes: 2, 5, 9, 10, 11, 12, 13

NOTES: Credit cards accepted: A MasterCard; B Visa; C American Express; D Discover; E Diners Club;
F Other; 2 Personal checks accepted; 3 Lunch available; 4 Dinner available; 5 Open all year; 6 Pets welcome;

1865 White Birch Bed and Breakfast

69 East First Street, 14830
(607) 962-6355

Imagine a friendly, warm atmosphere in an 1865 Victorian setting. Cozy rooms await guests; both private and shared baths. Awake to the tantalizing aromas of a full home-baked breakfast. Walk to museums, historic Market Street, and the Corning Glass Center. Experience it all here.

Hosts: Kathy and Joe Donahue
Rooms: 4 (2 PB; 2 SB) $50-85
Full Breakfast
Credit Cards: A, B, C
Notes: 2, 5, 7, 8, 9, 10, 11, 12, 13

The International Bed and Breakfast Club, Inc.

504 Amherst Street, Buffalo, 14207
(800) 723-4262; FAX (716) 873-4462

NY2347PP. This brick Colonial is in a quiet, residential neighborhood overlooking the city, one mile from Routes 15 and 17. It features three guest rooms, one with private bath. There are antiques and a small glass museum in the dining room. Full breakfast is served. Airport pickup available. Private parking in drive. Close to Corning Glass Center, Rockwell Museum, Taylor Wine Company, and Watkins Glen Racetrack. Smoking restricted. Adults preferred; no pets. $55-85.

CORNWALL

American Country Collection

1353 Union Street, Schenectady, 12054
(518) 439-7001; FAX (518) 439-4301

184. Historic country estate built in traditional manor style with elegant Greek Revival front, set on seven acres of woodlands and gardens. Guests can step back in time and be surrounded with history and elegance. Play croquet, visit the neighboring farm's craft and gift shop, relax by the goldfish pond, walk through the formal gardens, or explore the rolling hills and mountains. Stay in one of nine sumptuously appointed, color-coordinated rooms or suites, all containing sitting-reading areas, private baths, and air conditioning. Breakfast is served in the breakfast room or the back veranda. It is only one mile to the Storm King Art Center and Black Rock Forest hiking trails, five miles to West Point and Brotherhood Winery, and 11 miles to Bear Mountain for swimming and hiking. $105-250.

Cromwell Manor Inn

Angola Road, 12518
(914) 534-7136

An 1820 formal antebellum mansion set on a seven-acre, country-style estate offering 13 rooms with private baths. The inn is furnished with antiques and with canopied and poster beds. A wonderful weekend retreat with romance awaits guests at the manor. One hour north of New York City and five miles north of historic West Point. Cromwell Manor sits in the Hudson Highland overlooking a 4,000-acre forest preserve with seven mountain lakes. A wonderful place to hike and picnic. Air-conditioned. Open year-round. Two or three-bedroom cottages are available with early booking; please inquire.

Hosts: Dale and Barbara Ohara
Rooms: 13 (12 PB; 1 SB) $95-250
Full Breakfast
Credit Cards: A, B
Notes: 2, 5, 7, 9, 10, 11, 12, 13, 14

COSSAYUNA LAKE

American Country Collection

1353 Union Street, Schenectady, 12054
(518) 439-7001; FAX (518) 439-4301

187. Designed and built by the host, this contemporary trilevel home sits on a hillside surrounded by pines on the shore of

7 No smoking; 8 Children welcome; 9 Social drinking allowed; 10 Tennis nearby; 11 Swimming nearby;
12 Golf nearby; 13 Skiing nearby; 14 May be booked through a travel agent.

Cossayuna Lake. Inside, the cathedral ceiling, large rooms with sliding glass doors, and lots of space give the common room a light and airy openness. There is a huge rear deck for relaxing and dining; also for guest use are three fireplaces, a pool table, two TV viewing areas, and a 10-person Jacuzzi. Guests may swim in the adjacent lake fed by hot springs. Breakfast is served either in the kitchen or on the rear deck. Saratoga and Manchester, Vermont, are only 25 miles away, Willard Ski area is 18 miles away; cross-country skiing and snowmobiling can be arranged locally. Deposit. $45-50.

CROTON-ON-HUDSON

Alexander Hamilton House

49 Van Wyck Street, 10520
(914) 271-6737

The Alexander Hamilton House, circa 1889, is a sprawling Victorian home on a cliff overlooking the Hudson. Grounds include a miniorchard and in-ground pool. The home has many period antiques and collections. Guest accommodations include a suite with a queen-size bed and a fireplaced sitting room, a suite with double-size beds and a fireplace and small sitting room, two large rooms with queen-size beds, and a bridal chamber with king-size bed, Jacuzzi, entertainment center, pink marble fireplace, and lots of skylights. There is also a new master suite with a view of the river. Nearby attractions include West Point, the Sleepy Hollow restorations, Lyndhurst, Boscobel, the Rockefeller mansion, hiking, biking, sailing, and New York City just an hour away. No smoking or pets. Children welcome. Off-street parking.

Host: Barbara Notarius
Rooms: 7 (3 PB; 4 SB) $75-250
Full Breakfast
Credit Cards: A, B, C, D
Notes: 2, 5, 7, 8, 9, 11, 12, 14

American Country Collection

1353 Union Street, Schenectady, 12054
(518) 439-7001; FAX (518) 439-4301

157. Perfect for vacations, business travel, and romantic getaways, this stately Victorian home, circa 1889, is nestled on a cliff above the Hudson River, only a short walk from the picturesque village of Croton-on-Hudson. Luxurious without being ornate, this bed and breakfast offers three suites, each with a private bath and fireplace, three rooms on the second floor with private baths, and two third-floor suites, each with a king-size bed, fireplace, and full Jacuzzi. Breakfast offers juice, deep-dish pancakes, stuffed French toast or eggs, coffee, or tea. Smoking outside only. Train station is close. Children welcome. $95-250.

CROWN POINT

American Country Collection

1353 Union Street, Schenectady, 12054
(518) 439-7001; FAX (518) 439-4301

095. It took three years for a team of Italian craftsmen to complete this 18-room Victorian mansion, circa 1887, on five and one-half acres in the center of this small town. Carved woodwork, doors, and stair railing from oak, cherry, mahogany, and walnut grace the home. All five guest rooms have private baths. In winter, breakfast is served in front of the fireplace in the dining room. Fort Ticonderoga and Fort Crown Point are nearby. Children are welcome. $50-95.

Crown Point Bed and Breakfast

Main Street, Route 9N, 12928
(518) 597-3651 (phone and FAX)

The Wyman House (named after its banker-owner) is an elegant "Painted Lady" Victorian manor house on five and one-half acres. Its gracious interior is filled with period antiques. Each bedchamber is distinctly decorated and has a private bath. The house glows with woodwork panels and stained glass. Continental plus breakfast is served in an oak paneled dining room or on one of the three porches. Blooming gardens and a fountain grace the property. Picnic lunch is available at an extra cost. Inquire about accommodations for children.

Hosts: Hugh and Sandy Johnson
Rooms: 5 (PB) $50-65
Continental Breakfast
Credit Cards: A, B
Notes: 2, 5, 7, 9, 10, 11, 12, 13, 14

DE BRUCE

De Bruce Country Inn on the Willowemoc

De Bruce Road, 12758
(914) 439-3900

In a spectacular 1,000-acre natural setting within the Catskill Forest Preserve and overlooking the Willowemoc trout stream, the inn offers turn-of-the-century charm and hospitality. Terrace dining, wooded trails, wildlife, pool, sauna, outdoor activities in all seasons, fresh air, and mountain water. Fireside lounge, the best food two hours from New York City. Celebrating tenth year in business. Personal checks accepted for deposits. Inquire when open for the season. Inquire about accommodations for pets.

Hosts: Ron and Marilyn
Rooms: 15 (PB) from $75/person
Full Breakfast
Credit Cards: None
Notes: 4, 8, 9, 10, 11, 12, 13

DEPOSIT

American Country Collection

1353 Union Street, Schenectady, 12054
(518) 439-7001; FAX (518) 439-4301

194. Federal Greek Revival-style mansion built in 1820 is furnished with museum-quality antiques, Persian carpets, and hand-carved highboard beds. All rooms have private baths, special linens, air conditioning, TV, and bath amenities. Full breakfast served. King-size, double, and twin beds available. Gourmet dinners are a specialty. $85-135.

Chestnut Inn at Oquaga Lake

498 Oquaga Lake Road, 13754
(607) 467-2500; (800) 467-7676
FAX (607) 467-5911

Built in 1928, the Chestnut Inn at Oquaga Lake is a classic example of architecture and building construction at its best. The inn is almost totally constructed of the now extinct North American chestnut. Enjoy the many amenities of a lakeside resort. Guests may also enjoy the ultimate dining experience in relaxed elegance in the main dining room, or casual dining in the lakeside sunroom, or out on the lovely waterfront terrace. Enjoy a pleasurable boating experience aboard *Pickles,* a replica of the inn's launch that once graced the waters of the Oquaga Lake.

Hosts: James Gross (general manager) and
   Joe Laskaris (assistant manager)
Rooms: 30 (10 PB; 20 SB) $69-199
Credit Cards: A, B, C, D, E
Notes: 2, 3, 4, 5, 7, 8, 9, 10, 11, 12, 13, 14

DEWITT

Elaine's Bed and Breakfast Selections

4987 Kingston Road, Elbridge, 13060
(315) 689-2082

Near Shoppington, this fine, older Colonial is warmly furnished with some antiques. A large front guest room has an antique double bed, and a den with a sofa bed is available for families. $55.

7 No smoking; 8 Children welcome; 9 Social drinking allowed; 10 Tennis nearby; 11 Swimming nearby;
12 Golf nearby; 13 Skiing nearby; 14 May be booked through a travel agent.

DOLGEVILLE

Adrianna Bed and Breakfast

44 Stewart Street, 13329
(315) 429-3249; (800) 335-4233

Adrianna is just off the New York Thruway at exit 29A amid glorious views of the Adirondack foothills. Just a short ride to Cooperstown, Saratoga, Syracuse, and Utica areas. A most cozy and hospitable bed and breakfast. Minimum stay weekends and holidays is two nights.

Host: Adrianna Naizby
Rooms: 3 (1 PB; 2 SB) $50-65
Full Breakfast
Credit Cards: A, B
Notes: 2, 5, 11, 12, 13

Adrianna

Bed and Breakfast Leatherstocking

P.O. Box 53, Herkimer, 13350
(315) 733-0040; (800) 941-BEDS (2337)

031. Just off the New York Thruway (I-90) at exit 29A, is this lovely bed and breakfast, with central air conditioning, three guest rooms, one with a private bath, all decorated and furnished with personal comfort in mind. Bath amenities and bathrobes are provided for guests. Enjoy a full breakfast by candlelight in the dining room. Convenient to Cooperstown, Utica, Saratoga, and Albany. VISA and MasterCard accepted. Smoking restricted. $40-65.

DOVER PLAINS

Covered Bridge

P.O. Box 447 A, Norfolk, CT 06058
(203) 542-5944

1DPNY. Genuine old farmhouse with a large sitting porch on which to relax and admire the views of the Connecticut hills. Enjoy a full farm breakfast in the sunny dining room or on the porch. Four beautifully appointed guest rooms, one with private bath, are decorated with the owner's collection of antique linens. There are three doubles and one room with twin beds. There is also a pool for guests to enjoy. $65-95.

Nutmeg Bed and Breakfast Agency

P.O. Box 1117, West Hartford, CT 06107
(203) 236-6698

311. Tucked just over the border from Kent, Connecticut, is this charming "Eyebrow" Colonial built in 1850. Guests can use the living room with TV, warm up by the wood-burning stove, lounge on the large front porch complete with wicker furniture, and enjoy the pool. All four guest rooms are on the second floor. Three rooms share a bath. The room with a private bath has a handsome double sleigh bed. All rooms have spectacular views of the surrounding countryside, a foliage lover's delight. Full breakfast. Children are welcome. Pets in residence.

DOWNSVILLE

Adams' Elegant Farmhouse Bed and Breakfast

Upper Main Street, P.O. Box 18, 13755
(607) 363-2757

Be pampered in this beautiful old farmhouse full of antiques, surrounded by majestic

Catskill Mountains, nestled in a small, friendly town full of good things to do—canoeing, swimming, horseback riding, hiking, antiquing, golfing, and more—or just sitting on the front porch. Enjoy a breakfast fit for a country lady and gent. A feast of afternoon sweets awaits. Near Binghamton, Cooperstown, and Oneonta.

Hosts: Nancy and Harry Adams
Rooms: 3 (1 PB; 2 SB) $35-50
Full Breakfast
Credit Cards: None
Notes: 2, 7, 8, 9, 10, 11, 12, 14

The International Bed and Breakfast Club, Inc.

504 Amherst Street, Buffalo, 14207
(800) 723-4262; FAX (716) 873-4462

NY2757. Beautiful old farmhouse full of antiques on Main Street. Surrounded by maple trees, babbling brook, lots of flowers and grass. Wicker-furnished porch is great for leisure time; many activities nearby. Three guest rooms, one with private bath, full gourmet breakfast, afternoon tea, and evening refreshments. Antiques, gardens, picnic tables, and grill. No smoking, please. No pets, please. Senior citizen discount. $50.

DRYDEN

The Candlelight Inn

49 West Main Street, P.O. Box 1109, 13053
(607) 844-4321; (800) 579-4629

Guests are personally welcomed by owners Doris and Sam. On the National Register of Historic Places, this antique-furnished circa 1828 Federal-style homestead is subtly elegant yet unpretentious. Enjoy deluxe rooms and suites, air conditioning, fireplace, porches, library, TV, VCR, herb and flower gardens, afternoon tea, beds, and breakfasts to make guests sigh. At edge of the village. Convenient to Cortland, Ithaca, Cornell, wineries, and Finger Lakes.

Hosts: Doris and Sam Nitsios
Rooms: 4 (PB) $55-120
Suites: 2 (PB)
Full Breakfast
Credit Cards: A, B, C, D, E
Notes: 2, 5, 8, 9, 10, 11, 12, 13, 14

The Candlelight Inn

DURHAMVILLE

American Country Collection

1353 Union Street, Schenectady, 12054
(518) 439-7001; FAX (518) 439-4301

166. Completely restored 1800s farmhouse and barn on three tree-shaded acres. Decorated in a country motif and furnished with solid cherry furnishings. Four rooms with queen-size, double, or single beds and shared baths. Full breakfast; children welcome. Resident barn cat. Smoking in common rooms. $40-50.

Bed and Breakfast Leatherstocking

P.O. Box 53, Herkimer, 13350
(315) 733-0040; (800) 941-BEDS (2337)

030. Beautifully renovated and refurbished, this old farmhouse is just a short distance from Turning Stone Casino, Colgate University, Hamilton College, Vernon Downs raceway, Verona Beach, and SUNY Morrisville. It's ideally between Utica and

7 No smoking; 8 Children welcome; 9 Social drinking allowed; 10 Tennis nearby; 11 Swimming nearby;
12 Golf nearby; 13 Skiing nearby; 14 May be booked through a travel agent.

Syracuse, offering quick access to the best of both urban areas, yet retaining its rural unspoiled charm. VISA and MasterCard accepted. This immaculate home has four guest rooms sharing two bathrooms. Children under five stay free. Full breakfasts. Extended stays welcome and discounted. $50-60.

Elaine's Bed and Breakfast Selections

4987 Kingston Road, Elbridge, 13060
(315) 689-2082

This stately old farm Colonial sits on its own quiet three acres in the country yet has easy access to all activities in the Oneida Valley: Sylvan Beach, Verona Beach, fishing, boating, Vernon Downs, antique shops on Route 20, historic Fort Stanwix in Rome, and several nearby colleges. The interior is brand-new and carpeted throughout. Four guest rooms share two full baths and have individual heat control. TV/VCR in living room. MasterCard and VISA. Children under five free. $45-75.

EAST CHATHAM

American Country Collection

1353 Union Street, Schenectady, 12054
(518) 439-7001; FAX (518) 439-4301

206. This authentic 1790s Center Hall Colonial farmhouse is in Shaker country, nestled on eight acres and overlooking a wetlands reserve. Inside, there is a Shaker-plain look and touch of the Far East with Asian art interspersed with American country quilts and antiques. There are wide board floors, beamed wooden ceilings, a fireplace in the living room, and a keeping room with a wood stove. Guests may use an outdoor grill and picnic table or request a catered picnic. Two rooms on the second floor, king- and queen-size beds, and private baths. One has a two-person whirlpool tub. Near three Shaker museums, within 20

minutes of Massachusetts Berkshire attractions, and five ski areas are within 30 minutes and cross-country skiing is readily available with rentals in town. Smoking permitted in keeping room and outside. Children welcome. Small pets welcome. Full breakfast. Seasonal rates available. $60-65.

EDEN

Eden Inn Bed and Breakfast

8362 North Main Street, 14057
(716) 992-4814

The Eden Inn was built in 1904 and is the largest home in Eden, New York. Seventeen miles southwest of Buffalo, just one hour from Niagara Falls, the inn is near tourist trains, wineries, Buffalo Raceway, and Erie County Fairgrounds. Each room at the Eden Inn is tastefully appointed with a theme in mind, including the Rose Suite with private whirlpool tub, the Garden Room, the Train Room, the Vineyard, and the Bluhmen Suite (whirlpool bath). Child and cats in residence. Continental breakfast on weekdays. Full breakfast on weekends.

Hosts: Betsy and Chris Walits
Rooms: 5 (3 PB; 2 SB) $50-95
Continental and Full Breakfast
Credit Cards: C
Notes: 5, 7, 8, 9, 12, 13, 14

The International Bed and Breakfast Club, Inc.

504 Amherst Street, Buffalo, 14207
(800) 723-4262; FAX (716) 873-4462

NY4814PP. In the Garden Spot of western New York, approximately 17 miles southwest of Buffalo, one-half hour from skiing at Kissing Bridge, and one hour from Ellicottville. Within an hour's drive of Merritt, Woodbury, and Johnson wineries, the New York and Lake Erie Railroad, state parks, and Niagara Falls. Beautifully appointed rooms. Breakfast served daily in the solarium, which has a working fireplace. Wine and cheese receptions on weekends. Four guest rooms with private baths are tastefully appointed with a theme in mind. Specializing in accommodating wedding guests. Book the house for that special weekend. Groups and corporate business welcomed. Reduced package prices and relocation discounts. Variety of special packages, including honeymoon, holiday, spa, and others, in addition to suggestions for activities to enhance guests' stay. Continental breakfast served during the week and full breakfast on the weekends. No smoking is allowed in the facility. Parking available behind the home. $45-70.

EDMESTON

Elaine's Bed and Breakfast Selections

4987 Kingston Road, Elbridge, 13060
(315) 689-2082

Six varied guest rooms, two baths, above a fine restaurant. Great location in a tiny village near Cooperstown, Baseball Hall of Fame, Farmers Museum, Otsego Lake, cruises, golf, good restaurants, art galleries, and Glimmerglass Opera.

ELBRIDGE

American Country Collection

1353 Union Street, Schenectady, 12054
(518) 439-7001; FAX (518) 439-4301

222. This large century-old country home is surrounded by woods on a quiet rural road in the Finger Lakes region, with Skaneateles Lake only five miles away. Trails provide hiking in summer and cross-country skiing on groomed trails in winter. Three guest rooms, one private bath. No smoking. Full traditional-style breakfast served in large country kitchen with fireplace. Children over six welcome. $40-65.

Elaine's Bed and Breakfast Selections

4987 Kingston Road, 13060
(315) 689-2082

A freshly remodeled and decorated modest ranch-style home in the country on five acres, just 20 minutes west of Syracuse, seven minutes from downtown Skaneateles, and 12 minutes from Auburn. There are two guest rooms with good firm double beds sharing one and one-half baths. Quiet, peaceful, cozy, and comfortable. Smoke-free. Resident cat. Continental plus breakfast, more if required. Open year-round. Hostess runs Elaine's Bed and Breakfast Selections and buys and sells small antiques. Off Route 321 between Routes 5 and 20. From the west on Route 90, use Weedsport exit, from the east take 690 over Syracuse. Syracuse is the nearest large city. $45-50.

Fox Ridge Farm Bed and Breakfast

4786 Foster Road, 13060
(315) 673-4881

A large farmhouse in a picturesque setting with expansive lawns and flower gardens, on a quiet rural road. Hiking and cross-country ski trails wander through 120 acres of forests and meadows with sparkling streams and abundant wildlife. Guests may enjoy the large family room with a grand piano, wood-burning stove, TV, and numerous books. The guests' bedrooms are all individually decorated with floral wallpaper and lovely handmade quilts. A delicious, hearty full breakfast is served in the large country kitchen that has a unique stone fireplace.

Hosts: Marge and Bob Sykes
Rooms: 3 (1 PB; 2 SB) $55-65
Full Breakfast
Credit Cards: A, B
Notes: 2, 7, 8, 9, 10, 11, 12, 13

---

7 No smoking; 8 Children welcome; 9 Social drinking allowed; 10 Tennis nearby; 11 Swimming nearby;
12 Golf nearby; 13 Skiing nearby; 14 May be booked through a travel agent.

ELIZABETHTOWN

American Country Collection
1353 Union Street, Schenectady, 12054
(518) 439-7001; FAX (518) 439-4301

072. This bed and breakfast, circa 1775, was a sawmill, a "dine and dance," a resident summer art school and home of Wayman Adams, and since 1972 a summer residence for student classical musicians. It is on two and one-half acres bordered on two sides by the Bouquet River, a favorite fishing and swimming hole for the locals. Five guest rooms available, four with private bath. In summer, breakfast is served on the covered stone patio that overlooks the grounds. Children welcome. Resident pets. $66-78.

Stony Water Bed and Breakfast
Rural Route 1, Box 69, 12932
(518) 873-9125; (800) 995-7295

On 87 wooded acres tucked in a quiet valley between two running brooks, Stony Water provides a perfect refuge from the complexities of today's world. Two hours from Montreal and Albany, a half-hour from Lake Placid, and minutes from major Adirondack High Peaks' trailheads. This historic, restored Italianate house has strong ties to its literary and artistic past: Robert Frost, Louis Untermeyer, and Rockwell Kent. Four guest rooms, each with private baths, have views of the extensive perennial gardens and surrounding countryside. One room opens onto the in-ground swimming pool and woodlands beyond; one is a small cottage in the back garden. Dinner available except during July and August. Rated excellent by the ABBA.

Hosts: Winifred Thomas and Sandra Murphy
Rooms: 4 (PB) $75-85
Cottage: 1
Full Breakfast
Credit Cards: A, B, C
Notes: 2, 3, 5, 7, 8, 9, 10, 11, 12, 13

ELLICOTTVILLE

Ilex Inn
P.O. Box 1585, 14731
(716) 699-2002; (800) 496-6307
FAX (716) 699-5539

A turn-of-the-century Victorian farmhouse furnished with antiques and period decor. Each guest room has a private bath. Guests may enjoy the hot tub or heated in-ground pool and are offered terry robes and Turkish towels. The elegant yet comfortable living room features a fireplace, cable TV, and video library. The upstairs sitting room and library-gallery have morning coffee, parlor games, and a lovely view. The innkeepers' double-smoked ham or freshly squeezed orange juice may accompany the pumpkin-ginger pancakes or fresh fruit fritters as samples of the plentiful daily fare. Golf or ski packages, canoe excursions, mountain bikes, feather beds, and other amenities, such as flannel bed sheets, are available upon request.

Host: Bill Brown
Rooms: 5 (PB) $75-160
Full Breakfast
Credit Cards: A, B
Notes: 5, 7, 8, 9, 10, 11, 12, 13

ESSEX

American Country Collection
1353 Union Street, Schenectady, 12054
(518) 439-7001; FAX (518) 439-4301

183. Sitting atop a slight rise and well back from the road, this completely renovated 1836 Greek Revival home boasts spectacular views of Lake Champlain and the surrounding mountains. House is on the National Register of Historic Places. Guests can savor the solitude just by walking down to the lake through heirloom gardens. Furnishings are a mix of antiques and modern pieces. Each of the two guest rooms has a queen-size bed, ceiling fan, sit-

---

NOTES: Credit cards accepted: A MasterCard; B Visa; C American Express; D Discover; E Diners Club;
F Other; 2 Personal checks accepted; 3 Lunch available; 4 Dinner available; 5 Open all year; 6 Pets welcome;

ting area, and private bath. Continental breakfast is served on the rear deck or in the breakfast room. Essex Ferry to Vermont is a quarter of a mile away. Ausable Chasm, horseback riding, and Elizabeth Museum are all only ten miles; Westport Summer Theater is 12 miles away. $95.

189. Overlooking Lake Champlain, this charming, fully restored farmhouse dates back to the mid-1800s. The original buildings, surrounded by rolling fields and large locust trees, are on the National Register of Historic Places. Guests entering the home find themselves first in the common room, which contains comfortable chairs, sectional couch, and TV. Next comes the kitchen with its authentic working wood-burning stove. Beyond the kitchen is the formal dining room, where either a full country or Continental breakfast (guest's choice) is served. Adjacent to the dining room is the living room, containing piano, entertainment center, and large fieldstone fireplace. Four guest rooms boast hardwood floors, Oriental rugs, antique furnishings throughout, and lake or mountain views. Historic Essex and Essex Ferry to Vermont are only two miles away, while Westport Summer Theater and horseback riding are only eight miles farther. $65-75.

FAIR HAVEN

Brown's Village Inn Bed and Breakfast

Stafford Street, P.O. Box 378, 13064
(315) 947-5817

Traveling the Seaway Trail? For a warm welcome and old-fashioned hospitality, stop by and enjoy quality accommodations in a quiet and relaxing atmosphere. Minutes to shops, restaurants, and the beach. Guest cottage and antique shop on premises.

Host: Sally Brown
Rooms: 5 (1 PB; 4 SB) $50-65
Continental Breakfast
Credit Cards: A, B, D
Notes: 2, 5, 7, 8, 9, 10, 11, 12, 13

FAIRPORT

Woods-Edge

151 Bluhm Road, 14450
(716) 223-8877

Woods-Edge is in a quiet area surrounded with trees and wildlife. Near exit 45 (NYS I-90) and only 20 minutes from downtown Rochester. The home is artistically decorated with barn beams and antique pine furnishings. Home has two guest rooms with private baths. The on-premises guest house is fully equipped, including large fireplace, for a private, hideaway weekend. Delicious home-cooked breakfasts. Reservations requested.

Hosts: Bill and Betty Kinsman
Rooms: 3 (PB) $65-95
Full Breakfast
Credit Cards: None
Notes: 2, 5, 7, 8, 9, 10, 12, 13, 14

FAYETTEVILLE

Bed and Breakfast Leatherstocking

P.O. Box 53, Herkimer, 13350
(315) 733-0040; (800) 941-BEDS (2337)

003. In the old, historic section of this pretty suburban town stands this authentic antebellum home filled with period antiques. Only a few short minutes from Syracuse University, the airport, Lemoyne College, and Green Lake State Park. Thirty minutes from Clinton's Hamilton College. Walking distance to Fayetteville Mall. Four baths provide optional private bath possibilities to five air-conditioned bedrooms, one with whirlpool. Full breakfast on weekends. Continental breakfast on weekdays. $45-95.

7 No smoking; 8 Children welcome; 9 Social drinking allowed; 10 Tennis nearby; 11 Swimming nearby; 12 Golf nearby; 13 Skiing nearby; 14 May be booked through a travel agent.

Elaine's Bed and Breakfast Selections

4987 Kingston Road, Elbridge, 13060
(315) 689-2082

Italianate brick built in 1830 and 1854. Many antiques, wide plank floors upstairs, main living room with original pier mirror, walnut valances, fireplace, light fixtures. First floor room has double futon, private bath, and sitting room. Second floor has three guest rooms; two rooms have antique double beds, another has two double beds. One bath upstairs at present, new bath being built soon. About five miles east of Syracuse on Route 5. In the historic preservation area. Walk to restaurants and stores. $55-75.

FLEISCHMANNS

American Country Collection

1353 Union Street, Schenectady, 12054
(518) 439-7001; FAX (518) 439-4301

161. This 1867 classic Victorian summer retreat is at the entrance to the high peaks of the Catskill Mountains. A spacious late Victorian village cottage, its guest and common rooms are attractively furnished with select antiques, wicker, brass, and country chintz. Trout streams and well-marked hiking trails are all nearby. Skiing only five minutes away. Ten rooms, six with private baths, four with shared bath, and one efficiency apartment with private bath. Apartment is handicapped accessible. Smoking permitted in apartment only, not in the bed and breakfast. Children are welcome. Resident dog. $60-95.

FLY CREEK

Bed and Breakfast Leatherstocking

P.O. Box 53, Herkimer, 13350
(315) 733-0040; (800) 941-BEDS (2337)

004. Just four miles from Cooperstown, this old country farmhouse is thoroughly inviting and updated. Unpretentious, homey, and clean. Thirty minutes from SUNY-Oneonta and Hartwick College. Offers a rustic charm and low rates. Families are welcome. Single and double beds in three rooms. Shared bath. Crib available. Sits on 95 acres of rolling fields, wetlands, and woods. A Christian family endeavor, it welcomes all. Hearty country breakfast. $40.

FOSTERDALE

Fosterdale Heights House

205 Mueller Road, 12726
(914) 482-3369

Historic 1840 bed and breakfast on a Catskill mountaintop overlooks the scenic Delaware River Valley. A Victorian parlor with grand piano, billiards, library, 20 acres of grounds, a pond, and a Christmas tree farm, surrounded by woodland. Canoeing and horseback riding are nearby, and a bountiful country breakfast is served each morning. Make new friends, or just relax alone together. A cool mountain breeze in the summer, exquisite fall foliage, warm and cozy by the stove in winter, and the mountain mist in the spring truly makes this a bed and breakfast for all seasons.

Host: Roy Singer
Rooms: 11 (5 PB; 6 SB) $58-117
Full Breakfast
Credit Cards: A, B, C
Notes: 2, 4, 5, 9, 10, 11, 12, 13, 14

FREDONIA

The White Inn

52 East Main Street, 14063
(716) 672-2103

Circa 1868. Built on the home site of the county's first physician, this elegant mansion features a 100-foot-long veranda where refreshments are served. Period antiques and reproductions are found in

NOTES: Credit cards accepted: A MasterCard; B Visa; C American Express; D Discover; E Diners Club; F Other; 2 Personal checks accepted; 3 Lunch available; 4 Dinner available; 5 Open all year; 6 Pets welcome;

The White Inn

every bedroom. Guests and the public may enjoy gourmet meals at the inn, a charter member of the Duncan Hines "Family of Fine Restaurants." Antique shops, wineries, and the Chautauqua Institution are nearby.

Hosts: Robert Contiguglia and Kathleen Dennison
Rooms: 23 (PB) $59-159
Full Breakfast
Credit Cards: A, B, C, D, E
Notes: 2, 3, 4, 5, 8, 9, 12, 13, 14

FULTON

Battle Island Inn

Rural Route 1, Box 176, 13069
(315) 593-3699

Battle Island Inn is an 1840s farm estate overlooking the Oswego River, with a golf course across the road, on four acres of lawn and gardens. Each guest room is furnished with period antiques, private bath, telephone, and TV. Guests enjoy a full breakfast in the Empire dining room and are often found relaxing on one of the porches. There are two sitting rooms and a formal parlor with fireplaces where guests can feel at home with a book, playing the piano, or watching a movie on the VCR.

Hosts: Richard and Joyce Rice
Rooms: 6 (PB)
Full Breakfast
Credit Cards: A, B, C, D
Notes: 2, 5, 7, 8, 9, 12, 13, 14

GALWAY

American Country Collection

1353 Union Street, Schenectady, 12054
(518) 439-7001; FAX (518) 439-4301

049. This was a stagecoach stop and tavern run by Gen. E. Stimpson in the late 1700s. Local tradition indicates it was a stopover for George Washington and Lafayette. In the 1960s, it housed famous and wealthy visitors. On three acres of tree-shaded lawns. The three guest rooms have private baths and Colonial decor, including some four-poster beds, comfortable chairs, and fresh flowers. Guests may use the in-ground pool. Smoking permitted in common areas only. Well-behaved children welcome. Pets in residence. A fully furnished cottage with bed loft, TV, wood-burning stove, and kitchen is available for weekly and monthly rental. $65-105.

GARRISON

The Bird and Bottle Inn

Route 9, Old Albany Post Road, 10524
(914) 424-3000

Originally known as Warren's Tavern in 1761, this building was a stagecoach stop along the Albany Post Road. It is a perfect spot to stay overnight in one of the three rooms in the main building, each with a private bath, working fireplace, air conditioning, and canopied bed. A cottage steps away from the main building offers the same appointments. Near West Point, Boscobel restoration, antiquing, and hiking. Price includes gourmet dinner and full breakfast Wednesday through Sunday. On Mondays and Tuesdays, a Continental breakfast is served. Member Independent Innkeepers Association.

Host: Ira Boyar
Rooms: 4 (PB) $210-240
Full Breakfast
Credit Cards: A, B, C, E
Notes: 5, 9, 10, 11, 12, 13, 14

7 No smoking; 8 Children welcome; 9 Social drinking allowed; 10 Tennis nearby; 11 Swimming nearby; 12 Golf nearby; 13 Skiing nearby; 14 May be booked through a travel agent.

Conesus Lake

GENESEO

Conesus Lake
Bed and Breakfast

2388 East Lake Road, 14435
(716) 346-6526; (800) 724-4841

On beautiful Conesus Lake near Route 390. Unique European styling with private balconies and flower boxes. Relaxing resort atmosphere includes large private dock, picnic pavilion, boat rentals, and overnight boat docking with mooring whips. Each attractive bedroom has queen-size bed and cable TV. Private bathroom and double whirlpool tub are available. Near excellent restaurants. Reservations suggested.

Hosts: Dale and Virginia Esse
Rooms: 3 (1 PB; 2 SB) $60-85
Full Breakfast
Credit Cards: A, B, D
Notes: 2, 5, 9, 11, 12, 13

GENEVA

Elaine's Bed and
Breakfast Selections

4987 Kingston Road, Elbridge, 13060
(315) 689-2082

A. A freshly decorated, comfortable, clean, and convenient brick Federalist house offers first-floor room with private bath and double bed. Upstairs there are two additional guest rooms, one with a queen-size bed and the other with a double. These rooms share a bath. Near historic Main Street, colleges, Cornell Experimental Agriculture Center, state park on Seneca Lake. $50-75.

B. A rambling white brick mansion built in 1865 on two plus acres in the heart of historic Geneva. All the rooms are filled with antiques and treasures. The grounds are parklike with croquet set up on the lawn in the summer. Guests may enjoy the covered stone patio in the garden and use the barbecue. Four guest rooms with three double beds and one single bed, and shared and private baths. A suite, on the third floor, with its own living room is also available. Breakfast is guests' choice when planned ahead. Children over 12 welcome. No smoking. Guests may have light kitchen use. $45-75.

Geneva on the Lake

1001 Lochland Road, P.O. Box 929, 14456
(315) 789-7190; (800) 3GENEVA

Geneva on the Lake is an elegant, small resort on Seneca Lake in the Finger Lakes wine district. An Italian Renaissance villa offering luxurious suites overlooking a furnished terrace, formal gardens, pool, and lake. "The food is extraordinarily good," writes *Bon Appétit*. Friendly, attentive staff. Awarded AAA four diamonds for the 13th consecutive year. Suite rates include Continental breakfast; complimentary wine, fresh fruit, and flowers on arrival; a wine and cheese party on Friday evenings; and a daily copy of the *New York Times* is provided. Lunch available July and August. Dinner available weekends only.

Host: William J. Schickel
Suites: 29 (PB) $119-462
Continental and Full Breakfast
Credit Cards: A, B, C, D
Notes: 2, 3 , 4 , 5, 7, 8, 9, 10, 11, 12, 13, 14

NOTES: Credit cards accepted: A MasterCard; B Visa; C American Express; D Discover; E Diners Club; F Other; 2 Personal checks accepted; 3 Lunch available; 4 Dinner available; 5 Open all year; 6 Pets welcome;

99 William Street

99 William Street, 14456
(315) 789-1273

99 William Street is a pre-Civil War home that lends itself to gracious hospitality in these modern hectic times. In Geneva, New York, in the heart of the Finger Lakes region. Deep in history and rich with natural beauty, the inn is within a day's drive to wineries, state parks, and lakes, as well as Rochester, Ithaca, and Syracuse. Offered are two bedrooms with private baths and the privacy that guests expect and require. Reservations requested.

Hosts: Christopher M. Lang and David B. Gallipeau
Rooms: 2 (PB) $65
Continental or Full Breakfast
Credit Cards: None
Notes: 2, 5, 9, 10, 11, 12, 13

Virginia Deane's Bed and Breakfast

168 Hamilton Street, Routes 5 and 20, 14456
(315) 789-6152

Enjoy a little history in this antique-filled Colonial home in the 200-year-old city of Geneva. Next to Hobart and William Smith Colleges. Choose from five rooms, each offering a different kind of charm. Minnie's Room is a combination bedroom and sitting room with a double bed, sofa,

Virginia Deane's

chairs, TV, and private bath. The Victorian Room has a separate entrance, private bath, TV, Victorian decor including a four-poster bed, and a marble-top vanity and dresser. Dolly's Bedroom is large and bright with rock maple beds and dresser, TV, and shared bath. The Brass Room has an antique brass bed surrounded by brass accessories, TV, and shared bath. The Little Penthouse has a living room, private bath, TV, and air conditioning.

Host: Deane V. Cunningham
Rooms: 5 (2 PB; 3 SB) $50-80
Continental Breakfast
Credit Cards: None
Notes: 2, 5, 7, 8, 9, 10, 11, 12, 13

GERMANTOWN

American Country Collection

1353 Union Street, Schenectady, 12054
(518) 439-7001; FAX (518) 439-4301

102. Built by Peter Rockefeller around 1807, this Center Hall Colonial was a roadside tavern and dance hall, then a fox farm until World War II. It features post-and-beam construction, oak-pinned rafters, hand-hewn timbers, and poured-glass windows. Four guest rooms, all with private baths, have air conditioning. Children over nine welcome. Smoking permitted on the first floor only. No pets. Full country breakfast. $75.

113. Wonderful views of the Catskill Mountains and the Hudson Valley can be had from this 18-year-old home. The guest quarters include two bedrooms and a private bath. There is a family room with fireplace, piano, and TV. Breakfast is served on the porch or in the dining room. Guests are welcome to use the in-ground swimming pool. Smoking outdoors only. Children welcome. Crib available. No pets allowed. Full breakfast served on weekends; Continental breakfast served Tuesday through Thursday. $60-65.

7 No smoking; 8 Children welcome; 9 Social drinking allowed; 10 Tennis nearby; 11 Swimming nearby; 12 Golf nearby; 13 Skiing nearby; 14 May be booked through a travel agent.

GHENT

American Country Collection

1353 Union Street, Schenectady, 12054
(518) 439-7001; FAX (518) 439-4301

082. This early 19th-century farmhouse on ten scenic acres of open fields is perfect for walking and picnicking. There is also a private one-acre pond for fishing and paddle-boating and a miniature horse farm. The guest rooms on the second floor are air-conditioned and have a TV and private bath. The two-room suite on the third floor is air-conditioned and has a TV. Smoking outdoors only. Children welcome. $65-70.

GLEN HAVEN

Elaine's Bed and Breakfast Selections

4987 Kingston Road, Elbridge, 13060
(315) 689-2082

Ranch-style house has four bedrooms with individual heat, two bathrooms, living room, family room, dining room, and fully equipped kitchen. Deck and hot tub outside. Entire house or by the room as bed and breakfast. Three rooms in owner's house also available. On 28 acres with a fishing pond. Two boat launches nearby. Restaurants and golf courses an easy drive. Close to Homer, SUNY at Courtland, Ithaca, Syracuse, Skaneateles, and the Finger Lakes area. VISA and MasterCard accepted. Well-behaved children welcome. Full breakfast. At south end of Skaneateles Lake. Between Routes 41 and 41A. Not on most road maps. $45-200.

GORHAM

Elaine's Bed and Breakfast Selections

4987 Kingston Road, Elbridge, 13060
(315) 689-2082

This 14-room country Colonial-style farmhouse was built before the turn of the century and is decorated with many family treasures and special "finds." Take the opportunity to walk the five acres, enjoying the many wildflowers, fruit trees, berry bushes, and the owner's herb garden, or relax on one of the three porches. Choice of double or queen-size beds. The master bedroom suite has a king-size waterbed, sitting room, spacious private bath, whirlpool, and a wicker settee. Full breakfast on weekends and Continental breakfast weekdays. Two children over ten welcome. No pets, but there is a boarding kennel nearby. $60-65.

GOWANDA

The Teepee

14396 Four Mile Level Road, 14070-9796
(716) 532-2168

This bed and breakfast is operated by Seneca Indians on the Cattaraugus Indian Reservation near Gowanda. Tours of the reservation and the Amish community nearby are available.

Hosts: Maxwell and Phyllis Lay
Rooms: 3 (SB) $45
Full Breakfast
Credit Cards: None
Notes: 2, 5, 6, 7, 8, 9, 10, 11, 12

GRAFTON

American Country Collection

1353 Union Street, Schenectady, 12054
(518) 439-7001; FAX (518) 439-4301

145. Step back in time into this quaint country inn in eastern Rensselaer County where the Green Mountains, the Berkshires, and the Taconic Valley come together. Relax and unwind in the common room furnished with period antiques, paintings, and prints, or sit by the warm double-sided fireplace. The five bedrooms offer oak furnishings, braided rugs, antiques, and a collection of period pieces, along with

NOTES: Credit cards accepted: A MasterCard; B Visa; C American Express; D Discover; E Diners Club; F Other; 2 Personal checks accepted; 3 Lunch available; 4 Dinner available; 5 Open all year; 6 Pets welcome;

mints on the pillow each evening. Guests share two baths. Skiing, fishing, and hiking are nearby. Full breakfast. Open April 15 through January 15. Children are welcome. Smoking on the first floor only. $45-55.

GRANDVIEW

American Country Collection

1353 Union Street, Schenectady, 12054
(518) 439-7001; FAX (518) 439-4301

218. This is a historic Colonial, circa 1835, that is on and overlooks the Hudson River. In back is a large garden with swimming pool and pool house as well as a breakfast patio and sunken barbecue. Accommodations include two rooms and one studio that has a private entrance and kitchenette. Each is decorated with Laura Ashley or Ralph Lauren bedding and furnished with antiques and color TV. Bathrobes, hair dryer, and laundry facilities are available. Breakfast is an informal affair in that guests may have it prepared or simply help themselves if they decide to arise later than expected. Smoking is permitted in the kitchen or outside. Children are welcome. There are two cats in residence. $80-90.

GREENFIELD

American Country Collection

1353 Union Street, Schenectady, 12054
(518) 439-7001; FAX (518) 439-4301

112. It was an inn for British officers during the War of 1812, then a stagecoach stop in the 1820s before serving as part of the Underground Railroad before the Civil War. A rich sense of history is enhanced by Oriental rugs and fine antiques from Europe and the Middle and Far East. Four guest rooms, all with private baths. One room has a jet tub. Smoking outdoors and on the patio. Children over 11 welcome. Pets outside. $75-135.

GREENHURST

Spindletop Bed and Breakfast on Chautauqua Lake

Polo Drive off East Avenue, 14742
(716) 484-2070

Enjoy the days and nights in this casually elegant yet elegantly casual home with lakefront docking and secluded in-ground pool. Full breakfast and a bottle of wine are available each day. Visit famed Chautauqua Institution and prowl the antique shops, galleries, and Amish areas for a treasure. Come and be pampered.

Hosts: Lee and Don Spindler
Rooms: 4 (PB) $65-75
Full Breakfast
Credit Cards: A, B, C, D
Notes: 2, 5, 7, 8, 9, 10, 11, 12, 13, 14

GREENVILLE

Greenville Arms

P.O. Box 659, 12083
(518) 966-5219

A historic Victorian inn in the Hudson River Valley, featuring 14 unique guest rooms, six acres of lush lawns, gardens, shade trees, and a 50-foot pool. Golf and tennis nearby. Catskill Mountain sightseeing and hiking. Original art, antiques, and

Greenville Arms

fireplaces add warmth and grace to the dining rooms where guests enjoy famous country breakfasts. Elegant country dining in the Vanderbilt Room on weekends.

Hosts: Eliot and Letitia Dalton
Rooms: 14 (PB) $110-125
Full Breakfast
Credit Cards: A, B, D
Notes: 2, 3, 4, 5, 9, 10, 12, 13, 14

GROTON

Elaine's Bed and Breakfast Selections

4987 Kingston Road, Elbridge, 13060
(315) 689-2082

This charming 1867 Victorian in the country has three guest rooms plus a single-size pull-out bed in the TV den upstairs. All guest rooms are large, bright, and individually decorated. Rear room has an authentic antique three-quarter-size bed, heirloom quilt on the wall, and other family antique decorations. There are two sunny front rooms: one has a double bed, the other has two twin beds. Full country breakfast on weekends and Continental on weekdays. Family room with TV and wood-burning stove. Children over five years old are welcome. $35-55.

GUILFORD

Bed and Breakfast Leatherstocking

P.O. Box 53, Herkimer, 13350
(315) 733-0040; (800) 941-BEDS (2337)

039. Four bedrooms, all elegantly furnished and decorated, are the essential grace of this 150-year-old country bed and breakfast. Guest rooms have queen-size beds, many antiques, fine fabrics, and original art works. A full breakfast is served in the dining room each morning. It is only minutes away from Colgate, Hartwick, and SUNY Oneonta. Horse farms and dairy farms abound. Or, enjoy nearby swimming, boating, golfing, antiquing, crafts, live Little Theater, and fine restaurants. Only a short drive to Cooperstown Baseball Hall of Fame and Oneonta's Soccer Hall of Fame. No smoking. Children welcome. $50-75.

HADLEY

American Country Collection

1353 Union Street, Schenectady, 12054
(518) 439-7001; FAX (518) 439-4301

135. Built in the late 1800s and purchased in 1988 by the present owners, this restored Victorian country inn is in the southern Adirondacks within easy driving distance to Saratoga, Glens Falls, and Lake George. Five distinctive guest rooms, all with private baths, are individually decorated and named and offer their own special amenities; two have Jacuzzis and one has a fireplace. Private dinners and breakfasts can be arranged in the three larger rooms. A gourmet breakfast served each morning may include Grand Marnier French toast or eggs Anthony, home-baked muffins, juice, coffee, or tea. Packages available. $80-145.

HAGUE

American Country Collection

1353 Union Street, Schenectady, 12054
(518) 439-7001; FAX (518) 439-4301

198. Perched on a ledge above Lake George, this luxurious fieldstone home, circa 1900, boasts a panoramic view of the lake and the surrounding Adirondack Mountains. A full breakfast is served in the dining room with a 180-degree view of the lake or on the front porch facing the lake. Living room includes Oriental rugs, marble chess and backgammon set, grand piano, and a small library. Four guest rooms with private baths take up the whole second floor, all furnished with antiques and carpets. Spacious bathrooms convey an aura of Victorian grace and elegance. There are hiking trails, a swimming beach, boat launch, and horseback riding within five miles of the house. Lake George Village is 22 miles away. $90-125.

HAINES FALLS

The Huckleberry Hill Inn

Route 23A, Box 398, 12436
(518) 589-5799; (800) 804-5799
FAX (518) 589-5934

The Huckleberry Hill Inn was built in the early 1800s as a summer resort. The name is derived from the train, whose tracks bordered the property. The train had to climb such a steep incline that it went slowly enough for the passengers to pick huckleberries, which grew along the tracks. Fireplace and cable TV. At the Bar and Grill guests can have a bite to eat or sign up for snowmobiling and (ATV) rentals on the mountain trails.

Hosts: Tim and Colleen Legg
Rooms: 16 (9 PB; 7 SB) $55-80
Full Breakfast
Credit Cards: A, B, C
Notes: 2, 3, 4, 5, 6, 8, 9, 10, 11, 12, 13, 14

HAMBURG

The International Bed and Breakfast Club, Inc.

504 Amherst Street, Buffalo, 14207
(800) 723-4262; FAX (716) 873-4462

NY8989PP. This quaint bed and breakfast offers homespun hospitality. It features three bedrooms with shared bath and is an ideal setting for families. Close to Rich Stadium, the Buffalo Raceway, Erie County Fairgrounds, and other attractions. A delicious Continental breakfast is served daily. $40.

HAMLIN

The International Bed and Breakfast Club, Inc.

504 Amherst Street, Buffalo, 14207
(800) 723-4262; FAX (716) 873-4462

NY7528PP. This 1910 English Tudor amid six wooded acres and perennial gardens features natural woodwork, stained-glass windows, feather pillows, and Amish quilts. Three guest rooms with two shared baths are available. Full breakfasts include fresh fruit and homemade breads. It is a short stroll to Sandy Creek, and Hamlin Beach is just minutes away. Rochester is within 30 minutes, and Niagara Falls less than a 90-minute drive. Smoking in permitted areas only. No pets. $40-50.

Sandy Creek Manor House

1960 Redman Road, 14464-9635
(716) 964-7528; (800) 594-0400

Capture peace and solitude at this 1910 Tudor home on six wooded acres. Salmon fishing in the backyard, more than 25 perennial gardens. Antique player piano, feather pillows, and front porch take guests back to quieter times. Less than five miles to Hamlin Beach, seven miles to SUNY Brockport. Take the Seaway Trail to Niagara Falls in about 70 minutes. TV and air conditioning.

Rooms: 4 (1 PB; 3 SB) $55-70
Full Breakfast
Credit Cards: A, B, C, D
Notes: 2, 5, 6, 7, 8, 9, 10, 11, 12, 13, 14

HAMMONDSPORT

Blushing Rosé Bed and Breakfast

11 William Street, 14840
(607) 569-3402; (607) 569-3483

The Blushing Rosé has served as a pleasant hideaway for honeymooners, anniversary

---

7 No smoking; 8 Children welcome; 9 Social drinking allowed; 10 Tennis nearby; 11 Swimming nearby; 12 Golf nearby; 13 Skiing nearby; 14 May be booked through a travel agent.

Blushing Rosé

celebraters, and romantic trysters alike. Whether spending the day driving, hiking, biking, or just relaxing, this is the ideal haven in which to end the day and a great place to start the day with a copious specialty breakfast. The village has shopping, dining, and great walking. Keuka Lake is just a few doors away; wineries are nearby, as is the Corning Glass Center and Watkins Glen.

Hosts: The Laufersweilers
Rooms: 4 (PB) $65-85
Full or Continental Breakfast
Credit Cards: F
Notes: 2, 9, 10, 11, 12, 13

Gone with the Wind on Keuka Lake

453 West Lake Road, Branchport, 14418
(607) 868-4603

The name paints the picture of this 1887 stone Victorian. Fourteen acres on a slight rise overlook a quiet lake cove adorned by an inviting gazebo. Feel the magic of total relaxation and peace of mind, enjoying the solarium hot tub, nature trails, three fireplaces, and delectable breakfasts. Private beach and dock.

Hosts: Linda and Robert Lewis
Rooms: 5 (SB) $65-95
Full Breakfast
Credit Cards: None
Notes: 2, 5, 7, 10, 11, 12, 13

HAMPTON BAYS

House on the Water

P.O. Box 106, 11946
(516) 728-3560

Ranch house with two acres of garden on Shinnecock Bay. Quiet location. One mile to village, train, and bus. Seven miles to Southampton and Westhampton. Two miles to ocean beaches. Bicycles, windsurfers, pedal boat, barbecue, beach lounges, and umbrellas. German, Spanish, and French spoken. Kitchen facilities available. Closed November 1 through May 1. Limited smoking permitted.

Host: Mrs. Ute
Rooms: 2 (PB) $75-95
Full Breakfast
Credit Cards: F
Notes: 2, 9, 10, 11, 12, 14

HANCOCK

The Cranberry Inn Bed and Breakfast

38 West Main Street, P.O. Box 574, 13783
(607) 637-2788

"Where you come as a guest, you leave as a friend." Built in 1894, this stately, turn-of-the-century Victorian is enveloped by the glorious Upper Catskill Mountains, the famous Delaware River, and a great front

The Cranberry Inn

porch. Inside, enjoy a romantic fireplace, antique and Art Deco design, fine woodwork, and old-style architecture. The inn offers warmth, charm, and hospitality. Come fish and canoe the rivers, bicycle and hike the miles of country roads, or shop for antiques. Seasonal packages are also available.

Hosts: Lorene and George Bang
Rooms: 4 (2 PB; 2 SB) $65-85
Full Breakfast
Credit Cards: A, B, D
Notes: 2, 3, 4, 5, 8, 9, 11, 12, 13

HARTFORD

American Country Collection

1353 Union Street, Schenectady, 12054
(518) 439-7001; FAX (518) 439-4301

160. Within a short drive of both Saratoga Springs and Lake George, this historic Colonial tavern offers a relaxed country atmosphere in a quiet, rural setting. A history buff's delight, this restored home was built in 1802 and "remodeled" in 1878. Three second-floor rooms and one first-floor room are available for guests and offer both private and shared baths. A bountiful, full breakfast is served each morning in the dining room and includes juices and cereals, homemade rolls, breads, and muffins, eggs, bacon or sausage, coffee, and tea. $45-60.

HIGH FALLS

Captain Schoonmaker's Bed and Breakfast

913 State Route 213, 12440
(914) 687-7946

Capture the past in this pre-Revolutionary War home. This Dutch 1760 stone house is decorated with quilts, baskets, coverlets, and oil portraits that set an ambience of earlier times. A trout stream and waterfall enhance the setting of the restored barn that

now serves as an additional guest house complete with canopied feather beds and private porches with a woodland view. Breakfast is a seven-course event. Soufflés, strudels, poached raspberry pears, apricot walnut danishes, and many other delicacies delight the appetite. Wines, cheese, soft drinks, and snacks are served at six in the solarium by a fire.

Hosts: Sam and Julia Krieg
Rooms: 14 (3 PB; 11 SB) $80-90
Full Breakfast
Credit Cards: None
Notes: 2, 5, 8, 9, 10, 11, 12, 13, 14

HILLSDALE

American Country Collection

1353 Union Street, Schenectady, 12054
(518) 439-7001; FAX (518) 439-4301

199. Built in 1850, this historic Colonial cottage with gingerbread trim sits on a half-acre on the main street of Hillsdale. Just eight miles from the Massachusetts border, it is convenient to restaurants, shopping, and all the cultural attractions of Columbia County and the Berkshires: Lenox, Tanglewood, Stockbridge, and Great Barrington. Entrance to guest room is private, and there is a color TV and air conditioning. Outside the rear door is a garden and an outside deck. Ski Catamount (four miles away) or Butternut (ten miles). Norman Rockwell Museum in Stockbridge is a 25-minute drive, and the Shaker Museum and Mac-Hyden Theater are each 15 miles. $75.

HOBART

Breezy Acres Farm Bed and Breakfast

Rural Delivery 1, Box 191, 13788
(607) 538-9338

For a respite from a busy, stressful lifestyle, visit Breezy Acres. Offering cozy

7 No smoking; 8 Children welcome; 9 Social drinking allowed; 10 Tennis nearby; 11 Swimming nearby; 12 Golf nearby; 13 Skiing nearby; 14 May be booked through a travel agent.

accommodations with private baths in the 1830s farmhouse. Awake refreshed to wonderful aromas from the kitchen. A full, homemade breakfast is provided. Guests can spend a week leisurely exploring the museums, Howe Caverns, and Baseball Hall of Fame, leaving some time each day to roam the 300 acres or to sit in a wicker swing on the old-fashioned pillared porch, soaking in the view of meadows, pastures, and rolling hills. Or make use of nearby golfing, tennis, fishing, and skiing.

Hosts: Joyce and David Barber
Rooms: 3 (PB) $60-75
Full Breakfast
Credit Cards: A, B, C
Notes: 2, 5, 9, 10, 11, 12, 13

HOMER

Elaine's Bed and Breakfast Selections

4987 Kingston Road, Elbridge, 13060
(315) 689-2082

Built in 1834, this village home was the first brick house in the quaint, picturesque village of Homer. Guests may use both living rooms and piano. Breakfast served in dining room. Four guest rooms. Children welcome. Furnished with antiques and wide plank floors. Easy to find and guests can walk to Main Street. Homer is just north of Courtland and about halfway between Ithaca and Syracuse. Close to I-81. A lovely scenic drive along Skaneateles Lake to the village of Skaneateles takes about 30 minutes. The view from the lake road is breathtaking. No smoking. $60-70.

The International Bed and Breakfast Club, Inc.

504 Amherst Street, Buffalo, 14207
(800) 723-4262; FAX (716) 873-4462

NY4354PP. Built in 1827, this Federal-style home is listed on the National Register of Historic Places. Abraham Lincoln's presidential secretary, William Stoddard, lived in this house and it was once part of the Underground Railroad. It was the first brick house in Homer and was the site of many notable firsts for the village. Many activities are nearby for all-season enjoyment. Ski areas, Cornell University, and Ithaca College, local festivals, and state parks are close by. Three guest accommodations with shared bath. Full breakfast. $50-80.

HOOSICK

Hoosick Bed and Breakfast

P.O. Box 145, 12089
(518) 686-8575

On scenic Route 7, eight miles from historic Bennington (Vermont), 15 miles from Williamstown (Massachusetts), 40 miles from Saratoga Springs, and minutes away from antique centers. This recently restored 1840s Greek Revival farmhouse has tastefully decorated rooms and is surrounded by flower gardens and breathtaking views. Enjoy a home-cooked breakfast, evening tea, and the use of a full kitchen. Also, barnyard animals for all to enjoy.

Hosts: John and Maria Recco
Rooms: 3 (SB) $39-49
Full Breakfast
Credit Cards: None
Notes: 2, 5, 6, 7, 8, 9, 10, 11, 12, 13, 14

HOPEWELL JUNCTION

Covered Bridge

P.O. Box 447 A, Norfolk, CT 06058
(203) 542-5944

1HJNY. This 1841 Georgian Colonial built for a prominent Dutch silversmith is set on six acres that include lovely perennial gardens and a pool. The house has six fireplaces with double living rooms that are adorned with large imported crystal chandeliers and a fabulous sunroom that overlooks the grounds. The common rooms and

NOTES: Credit cards accepted: A MasterCard; B Visa; C American Express; D Discover; E Diners Club; F Other; 2 Personal checks accepted; 3 Lunch available; 4 Dinner available; 5 Open all year; 6 Pets welcome;

the four guest rooms are beautifully decorated with antiques. A full country breakfast is served by the hostess, who attended the Culinary Institute of America. $95-140.

Nutmeg Bed and Breakfast Agency

P.O. Box 1117, West Hartford, CT 06107
(203) 236-6698

342. This 14-room Georgian Colonial was built in 1841. There are six fireplaces, a formal dining room, and a sunroom overlooking two acres of lawn, a perennial flower garden, and swimming pool. The guest rooms feature queen-size beds, private baths, and each offers a Jacuzzi or working fireplace. Full gourmet breakfast. No children. No smoking.

ILION

Bed and Breakfast Leatherstocking

P.O. Box 53, Herkimer, 13350
(315) 733-0040; (800) 941-BEDS (2337)

005. Here is that fabled Victorian mansion with 14-foot ceilings and a wheeled ladder in the library, authentic furnishings, huge chandeliers and staircase, hangings, objets d'art, and other period artifacts. Four guest rooms on the second floor with private and shared baths. Canopied beds, sleigh beds, a feather bed, and fireplaces. $30-55.

ITHACA

The Federal House

P.O. Box 4914, 14852-4914
(607) 533-7362; (800) 533-7362

A gracious circa 1815 inn featuring spacious rooms, exquisitely furnished with antiques and hand-carved mantels in the parlor and Seward Suite. The inn is in the heart of the Finger Lakes, just 15 minutes

from Cornell and Ithaca Colleges, downtown, wineries, state parks, and less than two miles from Cayuga Lake. The landscaped grounds, with gardens and gazebo, border the Salmon Creek and Falls, a wonderful, relaxing fishing and biking area. Full breakfast served. AAA approved.

Host: Diane Carroll
Rooms: 4 (PB) $55-150
Full Breakfast
Credit Cards: A, B, C, D
Notes: 2, 5, 7, 9, 10, 11, 12, 13, 14

Hanshaw House Bed and Breakfast

15 Sapsucker Woods Road, 14850
(607) 257-1437; (800) 257-1437

Framed by a white picket fence, this 1830s farmhouse is comfortable and elegant. Overlooking a pond and woods. Rooms are furnished with antiques and colorful chintzes in an English country decor. Birds and wildlife complete the view. Scrumptious breakfasts are served in an elegant new dining room added on in the style of the house. Enjoy the gardens and patio in warm weather. Private baths, goose-down comforters and pillows, and air conditioning. Near colleges, state parks, skiing, fine restaurants, and vineyards.

Host: Helen Scoones
Rooms: 4 (PB) $68-110
Full Breakfast
Credit Cards: A, B, C
Notes: 2, 5, 7, 8, 9, 10, 11, 12, 13

Hanshaw House

7 No smoking; 8 Children welcome; 9 Social drinking allowed; 10 Tennis nearby; 11 Swimming nearby; 12 Golf nearby; 13 Skiing nearby; 14 May be booked through a travel agent.

The International Bed and Breakfast Club, Inc.

504 Amherst Street, Buffalo, 14207
(800) 723-4262; FAX (716) 873-4462

NY4455PP. An elegantly restored 1809 farmhouse on three picturesque acres of manicured lawns and gardens. Four charming guest rooms furnished with antiques and handcrafted rugs, with shared baths. The farmhouse also has a fireplace, patio, whirlpool, and private entrance. Full breakfast. $60-80.

Log Country Inn

Box 581, 14851
(607) 589-4771; (800) 274-4771

Enjoy the rustic charm of a log house at the edge of a 7,000-acre state forest. Modern accommodation in the spirit of international hospitality. European country breakfast, afternoon tea. Hiking, skiing, and sauna available. Convenient to Ithaca College, Cornell, Corning Glass, wineries, and antique shopping.

Host: Wanda Grunberg
Rooms: 3 (1 PB; 2 SB) $45-65
Full Breakfast
Credit Cards: A, B
Notes: 2, 5, 6, 8, 13, 14

Peregrine House Victorian Inn

140 College Avenue, 14850
(607) 272-0919

An 1874 brick home with sloping lawns and pretty gardens, just three blocks from Cornell University. Down pillows, fine linens, and air-conditioned bedrooms with Victorian decor. In the center of Ithaca, one mile from Cayuga Lake, with its boating, swimming, summer theater, and wineries. Wonderful breakfasts, free snacks.

Host: Nancy Falconer
Rooms: 8 (PB) $69-109
Full Breakfast
Credit Cards: A, B, D
Notes: 2, 7, 9, 10, 11, 12, 13

Rose Inn

Route 34 North, Box 6576, 14851-6576
(607) 533-7905; FAX (607) 533-7908

An elegant 1840s Italianate mansion on 20 landscaped acres. Fabulous circular staircase of Honduran mahogany. *Prix fixe* dinner served with advance reservations. Close to Cornell University. Twice selected by Uncle Ben's as one of the Ten Best Inns in America. Mobil four-star rated; AAA, four diamonds. Children over ten welcome.

Hosts: Sherry and Charles Rosemann
Rooms: 15 (PB) $100-160
Suites: $185-250
Full Breakfast
Credit Cards: A, B
Notes: 2, 4, 5, 7, 9, 10, 11, 12, 13, 14

A Slice of Home

178 North Main, Spencer, 14883
(607) 589-6073

A 150-year old farmhouse with four bedrooms and a full, hearty country breakfast designed so guests won't need lunch. A Slice of Home is just 20 minutes from Ithaca and Watkins Glen and in the center of Finger Lakes. Hiking, winery tours, biking (day or overnight bicycle tours planned), picnic tables, tenting, and outside grill. Cross-country skiing on site.

Host: Bea Brownell
Rooms: 4 (2 PB; 2 SB) $35-110
Full Breakfast
Credit Cards: None
Notes: 2, 5, 7, 8, 9, 13, 14

La Tourelle

La Tourelle

1150 Danby Road, 96 B, 14850
(607) 273-2734; FAX (607) 273-4821
(800) 765-1492 Reservations

Rated highly by AAA and Mobil travel guides, La Tourelle is the perfect blend of Old World charm and contemporary comfort. Next to John Thomas Steakhouse. The beautifully appointed guest rooms are reminiscent of the delightful country hotels of Europe, each with private bath, air conditioning, TV, and telephone. Choose one of the king- or queen-size bedrooms or indulge in the Fireplace Suite or romantically exciting Tower Room.

Host: Leslie Leonard
Rooms: 35 (PB) $87-135
Continental Breakfast
Credit Cards: A, B, C
Notes: 4, 5, 6, 7, 8, 9, 10, 11, 12, 13, 14

JAMESVILLE

Elaine's Bed and Breakfast Selections

4987 Kingston Road, Elbridge, 13060
(315) 689-2082

Country atmosphere. High on a hill, with a view for 35 miles, including three lakes, this owner-designed contemporary home offers the ultimate in peace and quiet, though only 15 minutes from downtown Syracuse or the university. Unique solari-um full of plants and casual seating; rear deck with picnic table offers marvelous view. Guest room has private bath and queen-size bed. Resident cat. $60.

JAY

The Book and Blanket Bed and Breakfast

P.O. Box 164, Route 9N, 12941-9998
(518) 946-8323

This charming, 100-year-old Greek Revival is nestled in the quaint hamlet of Jay, just seven miles from Whiteface Mountain and less than 20 minutes from Lake Placid. View of the covered bridge, and fishing and swimming in the Ausable River. The living room features a large fireplace, and an extra large porch is available for guests to enjoy. A booklover's dream, three guest rooms honor Jane Austen, F. Scott Fitzgerald, and Jack London, with their works well represented. Borrowers and browsers welcome. Full breakfast.

Hosts: Kathy, Fred, Samuel, and Daisy
  the Basset Hound
Rooms: 3 (1 PB; 2 SB) $45-65
Full Breakfast
Credit Cards: C
Notes: 2, 5, 9, 11, 13

JEFFERSONVILLE

The Griffin House

Rural Delivery 1, Box 178, Maple Avenue, 12748
(914) 482-3371

Victorian elegance, architectural excellence; all in this exquisite home where FDR was a welcomed guest. Nearby Delaware River, golf, tennis, horseback riding, and fine dining. New York *Newsday*'s "Inn of the Week."

Hosts: Irene and Paul Griffin
Rooms: 4 (2 PB; 2 SB) $75-95
Full Breakfast
Credit Cards: None
Notes: 2, 3, 4, 5, 7, 9, 10, 11, 12, 13, 14

7 No smoking; 8 Children welcome; 9 Social drinking allowed; 10 Tennis nearby; 11 Swimming nearby; 12 Golf nearby; 13 Skiing nearby; 14 May be booked through a travel agent.

JOHNSTOWN

American Country Collection

1353 Union Street, Schenectady, 12054
(518) 439-7001; FAX (518) 439-4301

099. This 100-year-old in-town home is on one-half acre of manicured lawns and vegetable and flower gardens, with an above-ground swimming pool. Two guest rooms, one bath shared with owners. Rooms are normally rented to one party traveling together. The bedrooms have lots of natural light and cross ventilation. TV in the living room and den. No smoking in bedrooms. No pets. Children over two are welcome. $40.

KATONAH

American Country Collection

1353 Union Street, Schenectady, 12054
(518) 439-7001; FAX (518) 439-4301

155. Dream away in this 16th-century Dutch Colonial farmhouse on four acres of woods, gardens, and maple sugar bush. A short climb up four steps brings guests to the master bedroom, which has a brass bed, free-standing fireplace, and private, hand-painted Portuguese tile bath. A small study with a desk and library connects to the bedroom and a common room. The third floor has two more bedrooms that share a bath. Across the street is a lovely pond for trout fishing or swimming. A full breakfast is served each morning. No smoking. $60-80.

KEENE

The Bark Eater Inn

Alstead Hill Road, Box 139, 12942
(518) 576-2221; FAX (518) 576-2071

Originally a stagecoach stopover, the inn is on an old farm nestled in the famous Adirondack Mountains minutes from the Olympic village of Lake Placid. The inn is filled with antiques and all rooms are graciously appointed. Famous for its food, the inn's style is refreshing country gourmet. The inn has an extensive horseback riding program including polo, and offers wonderful cross-country skiing in winter. In addition to spectacular views and great sightseeing in the Olympic area, summer and winter sports activities abound for both the participant and the viewer.

Host: Joe-Pete Wilson
Rooms: 11 (6 PB; 5 SB) $90-110
Full Breakfast
Credit Cards: A, B, C
Notes: 2, 3, 4, 5, 7, 8, 9, 10, 11, 12, 13, 14

KEENE VALLEY

High Peaks Inn

Route 73, P.O. Box 701, 12943
(518) 576-2003

A 1910 Adirondack lodge with wraparound porch with swing, living room with granite fireplace and piano, TV parlor, lots of books and board games, pool table, and grill on patio; all surrounded by mountain views. The inn offers small-town charm and tranquility, but it is still close to Lake Placid/Olympic region attractions including cross-country and downhill skiing at Whiteface Mountain, rock and ice climbing, hiking, and fishing and canoeing the Ausable River. Afternoon snacks provided.

Hosts: Jerry and Linda Limpert
Rooms: 8 (3 PB; 5 SB) $65-80
Full Breakfast
Credit Cards: A, B
Notes: 2, 3, 5, 7, 8, 9, 12, 13

KENMORE

The International Bed and Breakfast Club, Inc.

504 Amherst Street, Buffalo, 14207
(800) 723-4262; FAX (716) 873-4462

NY5860PP. Casual country ambience awaits the traveler in this nicely appointed inn. Two rooms with shared bath in hall are available. Hosts are well versed regarding golf and entertainment in the Buffalo area. Full breakfast. $45-50.

LAKE PLACID

Blackberry Inn

59 Sentinel Road, 12946
(518) 523-3419

This Colonial home, built in 1915, is one mile from the center of the village on Route 73. Four guest rooms offer country flair. Convenient to all major Olympic sites; surrounded by the Adirondack parks. Nearby recreation includes skiing, skating, hiking, golf, and fishing. Delicious home-baked breakfasts.

Hosts: Bill and Gail Billerman
Rooms: 4 (PB) $50-70
Full Breakfast
Credit Cards: None
Notes: 2, 5, 7, 8, 9, 10, 11, 12, 13

Highland House Inn

3 Highland Place, 12946
(518) 523-2377

Peaceful, central location in the village of Lake Placid. Lovely Adirondack decor throughout. Year-round dining in the glass-enclosed garden dining room. Full break-fast including blueberry pancakes, always! All rooms have TVs and ceiling fans. Hot tub spa on the deck amidst the trees and always at peak temperature throughout the year. Fully efficient cottage with fireplace available, next to the inn.

Hosts: Teddy and Cathy Blazer
Rooms: 7 (PB) $65-75
Cottage: $80-105
Full Breakfast
Credit Cards: A, B
Notes: 2, 5, 7, 8, 9, 10, 11, 12, 13, 14

South Meadow Farm Lodge

HCR 1, Box 44, Cascade Road, 12946
(800) 523-9369

Small farm on 75 acres, bordered by state land in the heart of the Adirondack high peaks. Ski out the back door onto 50 kilometers of Olympic cross-country trails. Family-style lodging with full, hearty meals. Come any time of the year and share the lodge, the view, and the Adirondack hospitality.

Hosts: Tony and Nancy Corwin
Rooms: 5 (SB) $70-90
Full Breakfast
Credit Cards: A, B
Notes: 2, 3, 4, 5, 7, 8, 9, 10, 11, 12, 13, 14

Spruce Lodge Bed and Breakfast

31 Sentinel Road, 12946
(800) 258-9350

Spruce Lodge has been in the Wescott family since 1949. The buildings were erected in the early 1900s. Large lawns extend down to a pond where guests can picnic or fish. Inside Lake Placid and close to all area activities. There is a view of the Sentinel Range and Whiteface from the back of the property.

Rooms: 7 (2 PB; 5 SB) $45-99
Cottage: 1
Continental Breakfast
Credit Cards: A, B
Notes: 2, 5, 7, 8, 9, 10, 11, 12, 13

Highland House Inn

---

7 No smoking; 8 Children welcome; 9 Social drinking allowed; 10 Tennis nearby; 11 Swimming nearby; 12 Golf nearby; 13 Skiing nearby; 14 May be booked through a travel agent.

Stagecoach Inn

370 Old Military Road, 12946
(518) 523-9474

An Adirondack experience since 1833. Quiet, convenient location, close to winter and summer recreation, restaurants, sight-seeing, and shopping. Rooms lovingly decorated with quilts, Indian art, and antiques. Outstanding great room and a front porch with rockers and a swing. Two-room family suites available. Fireplaces.

Host: Peter Moreau
Rooms: 9 (5 PB; 4 SB) $55-85
Full Breakfast
Credit Cards: A, B
Notes: 2, 5, 9, 10, 11, 12, 13, 14

LEWISTON

The International Bed and Breakfast Club, Inc.

504 Amherst Street, Buffalo, 14207
(800) 723-4262; FAX (716) 873-4462

NY4869. Built in 1975 this inn is a unique, circular, elegant modern air-conditioned home. Featuring three spacious lovely guest rooms, two with queen-size beds, one with a double bed. All three rooms feature private ensuite baths. Lovely large sitting room with pool table, TV, and wood-burning fireplace, opens onto a covered patio. Ample off-street parking. Full or Continental breakfast served in an elegant dining room or on the deck overlooking the golf course. Close to many fine restaurants, wineries, and golf courses. Ninety minutes to Toronto. Thirty-five minutes from Buffalo International Airport, nine miles north of Niagara Falls, and convenient to bridges to Canada. $70-90.

NY8598PP. This renovated 1850s Colonial home is in a quiet residential area on the east bank of the Niagara River. It is only a few minutes from Fort Niagara and Niagara Falls. Four rooms are available: the master suite with queen-size bed, color TV with cable, ensuite bath, and dressing room; a four-poster bed and private ensuite bath; a queen-size bed; and a two-bedroom loft suite with double and twin beds. An extra single roll away is also available. Baths include three private and one shared facility. A full breakfast is served. No smoking except in designated area. $60-85.

NY9114PP. The hosts take pride in the restoration of this 1906 Victorian-style farmhouse. On eight acres of the Niagara escarpment, this restored home features three beautifully decorated bedrooms, each with its own individual magnificent view. Private baths are tastefully blended into the decor and furnishings of each room to maintain the original charm while providing modern amenities to make your stay pleasant and comfortable. Guests are invited to stroll the grounds, enjoy games in the separate recreational building or simply make themselves comfortable in the warm and cozy ambience of the home. All guest rooms are equipped with air conditioning, ceiling fans, and private baths. Full country breakfast. Smoking allowed in the game room, but not in the home. $50-65.

LITTLE FALLS

Bed and Breakfast Leatherstocking

P.O. Box 53, Herkimer, 13350
(315) 733-0040; (800) 941-BEDS (2337)

006. White wooden Ionic columns decorate this 17-room wood-frame Victorian inside and out. Two grand pianos are in the music salon, and original art hangs in the art salon. Breakfast in the solarium, on the huge wraparound porch, or on the rear sun deck. Bookstore and art studio on the premises. Rail lift available on the main staircase. Three rooms with private and shared baths. Full breakfast. $50-65.

034. For every romantic heart, here is the epitome of the perfect getaway: an 18-room, four-story limestone Victorian, with switchboard telephone service, fine dining, and cocktail lounge on the premises. All newly opened. At present only five rooms are offered, one with private bath, the others sandwich two shared baths. All rooms professionally tailored and coordinated with drapery, down-filled comforters, huge pillows; working fireplaces in three of the rooms, one of these rooms also has a rooftop solarium. Exquisite interior trims of rare woods, parquet floors, lots of interesting history, plenty of acreage for long woodsy walking trails. Area is near everything and off exit 29A. $120-175.

LIVERPOOL

Elaine's Bed and Breakfast Selections

4987 Kingston Road, Elbridge, 13060
(315) 689-2082

Victorian house filled with country charm and antiques. A 100-year-old, three-story house overlooking the Yacht Club on Onondaga Lake. Conveniently next to antique and craft center. Walk everywhere: restaurants, shops, library, prize-winning Johnson Park, grocery, just one-half block to Onondaga Lake Park. Only five minutes from NYS Thruway (I-90), exit 38, and only five minutes to downtown Syracuse. One large guest room with a four-poster bed and bay window alcove with table and chairs for private morning coffee before going downstairs to a full country breakfast. The room is fresh, bright, and beautifully decorated. Another guest room features a maple and pine antique bed with matching chests and collections of powder boxes and dresser jars. These rooms share a lovely modern tub and shower bath. Smoking in designated areas. Ideal for a party of four. $45-65.

LIVINGSTON MANOR

Clarkes' Place in the Country

811 Shandelee Road, 12758
(914) 439-5442

A unique, contemporary rustic home on three acres in the heart of the Catskills. White pine interior throughout with great room that features a 20-foot cathedral ceiling and wood stove. Deep-water, spring-fed stocked pond for year-round recreation, and a hot spring spa has been added for under-the-stars tubbing! Minutes from downhill and cross-country skiing and some of the finest golfing. Certified executive chef serves a gourmet breakfast in the solarium. Fine food, live entertainment, terrific antiques, and auctions only moments away. The world's best trout fishing. Ask about the weekend gourmet cooking class!

Hosts: Bob, Nan, and Josh Clarke
Rooms: 3 (PB) $65-85
Full Breakfast
Credit Cards: A, B
Notes: 2, 5, 7, 8, 10, 11, 12, 13

LOCKPORT

Hambleton House

130 Pine Street, 14094
(716) 439-9507; (716) 634-3650

Charm and hospitality in this historic Lockport home, circa 1850. Each room has

Hambleton House

7 No smoking; 8 Children welcome; 9 Social drinking allowed; 10 Tennis nearby; 11 Swimming nearby;
12 Golf nearby; 13 Skiing nearby; 14 May be booked through a travel agent.

a delicate blending of past and present. A grand staircase leads to two guest rooms and a guest parlor and dining room. The third and largest guest room is on the first floor. Air-conditioned. Walking distance to historic Erie Barge Canal Locks. Short driving trips to many other attractions, including Niagara Falls and Old Fort Niagara.

Hosts: The Hambleton Family
Rooms: 3 (PB) $55-75
Continental Breakfast
Credit Cards: A, B
Notes: 2, 5, 7, 9, 14

The International Bed and Breakfast Club, Inc.

504 Amherst Street, Buffalo, 14207
(800) 723-4262; FAX (716) 873-4462

NY3502PP. This former produce farm is in historic Niagara County. Four large guest rooms on the second floor include a four-poster queen-size, a full-size sleigh bed and twin beds, and another full-size bed and twin bed for a child. There are two shared baths. A family-style breakfast is served with varying menus. Guests may dine in a formal dining room, country kitchen, or breakfast room. $55

NY9507PP. This historic home is within walking distance of historic Erie Barge Canal and the city's main street. Five rooms are available with private and semi-private baths. The largest bedroom has a double bed, a day bed that sleeps two, and a private bath. A Continental plus breakfast is served. $55-75.

LYONS

Elaine's Bed and Breakfast Selections

4987 Kingston Road, Elbridge, 13060
(315) 689-2082

Convenient to the popular Finger Lakes region, halfway between Rochester and

Syracuse and Lake Ontario and Seneca Lake, this charming brick Greek Revival was built in the mid-1840s. It was remodeled in the 1880s with Victorian touches. Three guest rooms share two and a half baths and are named for roses, some of which can be found on the rose lawn or in the garden behind the house. Sweet Briar has skylights and stenciled walls and is furnished in golden oak that dates from the early 1900s. Garden Party has a skylight and is furnished with an antique iron and brass bed and wicker chairs. Rubaiyat has an antique mahogany bed, damask wallpaper, and lace curtains. $50-60.

The International Bed and Breakfast Club, Inc.

504 Amherst Street, Buffalo, 14207
(800) 723-4262; FAX (716) 873-4462

NY4218PP. This mid-1840s Greek Revival home was remodeled during the 1880s with Victorian touches. Each of the three guest rooms (which share a bath) is named for a type of rose; their namesakes may be found on the rose lawn or back garden, where Jackson and Perkins roses in the preliminary marketing stage are grown. Full gourmet breakfast served on weekends, Continental on weekdays; served in the garden or on the porch, weather permitting. Music room with organ, a fireplace and an upstairs sitting room. Only a one-hour drive to Rochester to the west or Syracuse to the east; 20 minutes to Seneca Lake or Lake Ontario. Smoking is restricted. $60.

MARATHON

Elaine's Bed and Breakfast Selections

4987 Kingston Road, Elbridge, 13060
(315) 689-2082

This accommodation consists of a main house with master guest room having a queen-size bed, private bath, ceiling fan, and complete carpeting. Also in the main house there is a guest room with a double bed and shared bath. The main feature, however, is the small rustic guest cottage in this quiet pleasant country setting. It has a bedroom with queen-size bed; a living room sleeper-sofa can sleep two, and a chairbed can take a small child. There is cable color TV, stocked counter-top refrigerator, and a coffee maker. This is a smoke-free environment. Just 25 minutes from Binghamton, 35 minutes to Ithaca, and 45 minutes to Syracuse. A good, healthy Continental breakfast served in the main house. $60-75.

MARCELLUS _____

The Debevic Homested
2527 West Seneca Turnpike, 13108
(315) 673-9447

This old house has a wooded area for guests to stroll through. Rooms furnished in antiques, antique shop in house, and artist in residence. Close to great fishing, state fairgrounds, Finger Lakes attractions, Cooperstown, New York State wineries, colleges, and cultural events in Skaneateles and Syracuse. Basket lunches provided at an additional cost. Artist weekends with workshops may be arranged.

Hosts: Frank and Jan Debevic
Rooms: 2 (SB) $40-55
Continental Breakfast
Credit Cards: None
Notes: 2, 7, 8, 9, 10, 11, 12

MARGARETVILLE _____

American Country Collection
1353 Union Street, Schenectady, 12054
(518) 439-7001; FAX (518) 439-4301

220. A Queen Anne Victorian that is sure to delight all. Built in 1886 and set overlooking Catskill Mountain State Park, this bed and breakfast is furnished throughout with period Victorian furniture, area rugs, and family pictures. There is a formal parlor, TV/VCR room, and lots of toys for children of all ages. A wraparound porch provides the perfect setting for a bountiful morning breakfast as well as a place to read and relax in one of the many white wicker chairs or hammock. Guest rooms all have lace curtains and/or drapes, bath amenities, sitting areas, and views. The inn is surrounded by mountains and hillside, all making for an excellent opportunity for hiking, country walking, and winter skiing at Bellaeyre, which is only eight miles away. Smoking permitted outside. Children welcome. One dog in residence. Small guest.pets welcome with prior arrangement. Full breakfast. $60-85.

MONTAUK _____

Shepherds Neck Inn
Second House Road, P.O. Box 639, 11954
(516) 668-2105

Guests will enjoy the friendly ambience at Shepherds Neck Inn, where one will feel relaxed and at home. The guest rooms are spacious and comfortable, attractively decorated in the charming style of a country inn. All rooms have private baths, color cable TV, telephones, and air conditioning. The inn offers both bed and breakfast and Modified American Plan.

Hosts: Marie and George Hammer
Rooms: 70 (PB) $69-149
Full and Continental Breakfast
Credit Cards: A, B, D
Notes: 2, 3, 4, 5, 7, 8, 10, 11, 12, 14

MONTGOMERY _____

American Country Collection
1353 Union Street, Schenectady, 12054
(518) 439-7001; FAX (518) 439-4301

182. This Center Hall Colonial inn was built in stages beginning around 1790.

7 No smoking; 8 Children welcome; 9 Social drinking allowed; 10 Tennis nearby; 11 Swimming nearby; 12 Golf nearby; 13 Skiing nearby; 14 May be booked through a travel agent.

Recently completely renovated, it has the original wide board oak floors, now covered discreetly with Oriental rugs. Decor is French Country, and furnishings are a mix of contemporary and antique. The common room has couches, fireplace, and piano, while the dining room, also with fireplace, is dominated by a gigantic antique French armoire. The six guest rooms are all large, with private bath, sitting area, TV, and air conditioning. Continental or full breakfast (guest's choice) is served in the room, on the rear deck, or in the main dining room. Three miles to horseback riding, four to hiking, tennis, boating, swimming, and golf, and 10 to 15 to wineries and SUNY at New Paltz. $90.

206. This country farmhouse, circa 1930, is surrounded by 265 acres of farmland. All guest areas are on one level, making for excellent handicapped accessibility as well as a safe and convenient place for children. TV/VCR room, dining room where breakfast is served, and living room with a wood pellet stove for cozy winter evenings. Connected to the family area is a five-room apartment/suite. It is fully carpeted with a Victorian flair, a living room with sleigh day bed and sofa, TV, dining area, fully equipped kitchen, bedroom with attached room with crib for traveling baby/infant, full private bath, and private entrance. Exercise/playroom with TV/VCR and six- to eight-person Jacuzzi. Guest room has a double bed and private bath. The home and suite are fully air-conditioned. Smoking permitted in common areas and outside. Children welcome. Dog in residence. Full breakfast. $65-125.

NAPLES

Elaine's Bed and Breakfast Selections

4987 Kingston Road, Elbridge, 13060
(315) 689-2082

This big, rambling 1830s house in a country setting has a spectacular view of Canandaigua Lake. Enjoy a congenial Bavarian atmosphere, full breakfast, complimentary candy, outdoor recreations, spacious picnic grounds, gazebo, and patios. Quiet library, TV, and VCR. Marble fireplace. Separate smoking room. Accessible to the physically challenged. Just 13 miles from antique centers, the Finger Lakes Performing Arts Center, Finger Lakes Raceway, and Sonnenberg Gardens. Even closer to Bristol Mountain ski area, Bristol Valley Playhouse, wineries, fishing, swimming, and boating. Golf nearby. Discounts for private groups, seniors, or extended stays. Open year-round. $60.

The International Bed and Breakfast Club, Inc.

504 Amherst Street, Buffalo, 14207
(800) 723-4262; FAX (716) 873-4462

NY6271PP. This inn offers escape and serenity on a mountain in upstate New York. Several rooms are available. Guests may choose a suite with private deck and porch, king-size bed, two sitting areas, TV/VCR, and a private bath with Jacuzzi. Another suite has a queen-size bed, fireplace, sitting area, and private bath with hot tub. A third room has a king-size bed, dining table, small refrigerator, microwave, stone fireplace, private bath, and hot tub spa. A full gourmet breakfast is served. $80-175.

NELLISTON

Bed and Breakfast Leatherstocking

P.O. Box 53, Herkimer, 13350
(315) 733-0040; (800) 941-BEDS (2337)

009. A lovingly restored limestone from the 1850s Federalist period, on the National Register of Historic Places. Fifty-foot sun deck at the rear overlooks the shores of the Mohawk and farmlands. Parking and turn-around available. Near Cooperstown and Howe Caves. Just a stone's throw to the capital district. Three rooms available to guests. All shared baths. $40-55.

NEW BALTIMORE

American Country Collection

1353 Union Street, Schenectady, 12054
(518) 439-7001; FAX (518) 439-4301

089. Originally a farmhouse in the early 1800s, this Victorian home was enlarged during the 1860s in Italianate style. Three guest rooms with private baths. One room has a working fireplace and air conditioning. The suite is air-conditioned. The living room has a piano and fireplace; the library has a TV and Victorian gas stove. Breakfast is served in front of the fire in the kitchen, in the dining room, or on the porch or terrace. It's an easy walk to the historic hamlet with its marina, old mill stream, and early cemetery. Smoking permitted. Inquire about accommodations for children. $80.

NEWBURGH

American Country Collection

1353 Union Street, Schenectady, 12054
(518) 439-7001; FAX (518) 439-4301

156. Fully restored Queen Anne Victorian mansion, listed on the National Register of Historic Places, in the heart of the historic district. Enjoy a full breakfast served either in front of a 12-foot grand parlor fireplace with a crackling fire, or on a cabanalike sun porch with panoramic views of the majestic Hudson River and mountains. Both guest rooms are on the second floor and are furnished with antiques. One has a fireplace, air conditioning, and semiprivate bath, and the other has a shared bath. Two apartments for daily, long-, or short-term rental also available. $65-120.

213. The house, a contemporary two-story peaked Colonial-Cape, sits well off a rambling, almost country road, yet only minutes from I-84, the New York Thruway, and a variety of fine restaurants and shops. A candlelight full breakfast is served on the deck or in the dining room. The living room, private for guest use, has a large Oriental rug, a piano, and a sizeable collection of books and music. Upstairs are two carpeted guest bedrooms, each with its own sitting area. The bath is private to either room or private to a party of four. Smoking permitted outside. Two cats in residence outside. Dinner available with prior arrangement. $75.

The International Bed and Breakfast Club, Inc.

504 Amherst Street, Buffalo, 14207
(800) 723-4262; FAX (716) 873-4462

NY1715PP. This fully restored New York Central Railroad caboose features a magnificent Hudson River view. It has a living room with fireplace and a complete galley; private twin platform beds and an upper cupola bunk provide sleeping space for up to three guests. Private shower, TV, full heat and air conditioning. Pool privileges. Continental breakfast. Ideal for West Point and Hudson Valley lovers. $85.

NEW LEBANON

American Country Collection

1353 Union Street, Schenectady, 12054
(518) 439-7001; FAX (518) 439-4301

132. This historic Colonial was built in 1797 for a preacher and his family. Nestled on 18 acres just outside of town, this country inn is convenient to Lenox, the Berkshires, the capital district, and major ski areas. There is a suite on the first floor with a feather mattress, day bed with a trundle, and a private bath; and four bedrooms on the second floor: two with private baths; the other two form a suite with a

7 No smoking; 8 Children welcome; 9 Social drinking allowed; 10 Tennis nearby; 11 Swimming nearby; 12 Golf nearby; 13 Skiing nearby; 14 May be booked through a travel agent.

common sitting room and bath. Rooms are light and airy with homemade quilts and period Colonial furniture. A full country breakfast is served on weekends and a Continental breakfast is served on weekdays. Smoking outside only. $60-90.

Covered Bridge

P.O. Box 447, Norfolk, CT 06058
(203) 542-5944

This 1797 Colonial farmhouse set on 18 acres offers a quiet country retreat but is close to all of the activities offered in the Berkshires. Guests may relax beside the fireplace in the living room, or enjoy the beautiful front porch with a view of the Taconic Hills. A full country breakfast is served in the dining room. There is a first-floor suite with a private bath, two guest rooms on the second floor that share a bath, and a two-bedroom suite with a private bath. $75-100.

Elaine's Bed and Breakfast Selections

4987 Kingston Road, Elbridge, 13060
(315) 689-2082

A. A cozy home filled with antiques, this rambling farmhouse on 50 acres lies in the heart of Shaker country. It has wide-plank floors, five delightful guest rooms, and three baths. The original house dates back to 1836. Share the relaxed country atmosphere with other interesting guests, a dog, and the cat family. Children and pets are welcome. A spacious new three-room contemporary apartment in an adjacent building is available. Moderate rates.

B. A fully remodeled creamery adds sleeping facilities for 25 and catering for all guests' special get-togethers, whether for family reunions or business meetings. There is a meeting space with adjacent miniconference rooms, as well as a dining area, lounge, and complete kitchen. Enjoy

being surrounded by Shaker antiques, four generations of furniture, and an unusual art collection. Outside the meadows, gardens, and birds beckon guests to a leisurely stroll or a cross-country ski outing.

NEW PALTZ

American Country Collection

1353 Union Street, Schenectady, 12054
(518) 439-7001; FAX (518) 439-4301

116. Rejuvenating one's mind and body can be as simple as strolling through the apple, pear, and quince orchards on a warm summer day, or as fascinating as a session on stress management and holistic health offered by the host. Four guest rooms, two private baths, two shared baths. One room has a double Murphy bed, working fireplace, air conditioning, and private bath. All rooms have air conditioning. A healthful gourmet breakfast is served in the light and airy country kitchen. Smoking in guest rooms and outdoors. Children under seven stay for free. No pets. $78-95.

117. Plan the day from the rambling lemonade porch of this immaculate Queen Anne Victorian in this tiny village near the Shawangunk Mountains. Three guest rooms, all with queen-size beds and private baths. Guests in the master bedroom have a view of the solarium and the gardens from their indoor balcony. Smoking is allowed outdoors only. Children over ten are welcome. There are two cats in residence. $85-95.

NEWPORT

Bed and Breakfast Leatherstocking

P.O. Box 53, Herkimer, 13350
(315) 733-0040; (800) 941-BEDS (2337)

010. This huge Georgian four-square limestone built around 1812 sits far back and high up on a groomed lawn in this pretty little village. All modern conveniences, networked security system, common rooms, and fireplaces; all rooms lovingly decorated. Two rooms: one double, one twin, both with private baths. Full breakfast is served. $40-55.

NEW ROCHELLE

Rose Hill Guest House

44 Rose Hill Avenue, 10804
(914) 632-6464

The hostess at this beautiful, intimate French Normandy home is a real estate agent and bridge Life Master. Weather permitting, enjoy breakfast on the flower patio or in the chandeliered library/dining room. Thirty minutes to Manhattan by train or car. Safe parking behind house. Two-night minimum stay required for holidays.

Host: Marilou Mayetta
Rooms: 2 (SB) $55-68 plus tax
Continental Breakfast
Credit Cards: C
Notes: 2, 5, 6, 8, 9, 10, 12, 14

NEW WINDSOR

American Country Collection

1353 Union Street, Schenectady, 12054
(518) 439-7001; FAX (518) 439-4301

197. A nice combination of country, romance, and coziness awaits guests at the contemporary trilevel home. It sits on a slight rise, surrounded by 165 acres of lawn, fields, and woods where guests are free to wander. Furnishings are a mixture of traditional pieces and family antiques, each with its own history. Common living room, screened side porch, and TV room with wood-burning stove. The three guest rooms are decorated in country-Victorian ambience. Continental breakfast is served during the week, full breakfast on weekends. West Point, cross-country skiing, and Sugar Loaf Craft Village and Museum are each only 12

to 15 miles away. Even closer are the Brotherhood Winery and Crestview Lake for swimming and fishing. $60-85.

NEW YORK

Aaah! Bed and Breakfast #1, Ltd.

342 West 46th Street, 10036
(212) 246-4000

Hosted apartments include all areas in Manhattan. Brownstones, high-rises, all good areas, convenient to all transportation, safe neighborhoods, owner personally inspected apartments. Unhosted studio, one-, two-, and three-bedroom apartments. Full kitchens. $80-100.

At Home in New York

P.O. Box 407, 10185
(212) 956-3125
(800) 692-4262 (reservations only, M-F, 9A.M.-5P.M.)
FAX (212) 247-3291

At Home in New York offers more than 300 well-placed, carefully screened bed and breakfasts and private flats in Manhattan, including luxury high-rises, private brownstones, artists' lofts, and modest flats. Gracious hospitality, cheerful, immaculate accommodations. Affordable rates. Free brochure and sampling. Personal checks accepted for deposit or if received 14 days ahead of arrival date. Some accommodations are no smoking. Children welcome in some accommodations.

Hosts: more than 300
Rooms: 150 (75 PB; 75 SB) $75-125
Continental Breakfast
Credit Cards: None
Notes: 5, 9, 14

Bed and Breakfast (& Books)

35 West 92nd Street, 10025
(212) 865-8740

Sample listings: Beautifully renovated townhouse on quiet tree-lined street near Central Park offers one double-bed room

7 No smoking; 8 Children welcome; 9 Social drinking allowed; 10 Tennis nearby; 11 Swimming nearby; 12 Golf nearby; 13 Skiing nearby; 14 May be booked through a travel agent.

with private bath. Convenient to museums, theaters, shopping, and all transportation. Children welcome in loft areas. $80. Working artist's loft in the heart of Soho has comfortable twin-bed room, sitting area, and bath ensuite. Convenient to Soho galleries, shops, and restaurants. Sofa opens to sleep two. $92.50.

Host: Judith Goldberg
Rooms: 50 (45 PB; 5 SB) $70-90
Continental Breakfast
Credit Cards: None
Notes: 5, 14

Bed and Breakfast Network of New York

134 West 32nd Street, Suite 602, 10001
(212) 645-8134; (800) 900-8134

A reservation service for New York City, mostly Manhattan. Accommodations are in some of the most exciting parts of town: Greenwich Village, Midtown, Upper East and West sides, etc. Ranging from modest to luxurious, from townhouse to lofts to million-dollar high-rise condos. Weekly and monthly rates available. Also represents unhosted furnished apartments and studios ranging from $80-300. Personal checks accepted for deposit. Inquire about accommodations for pets and children.

Rooms: 300 (100 PB; 200 SB) $80-90
Continental Breakfast
Credit Cards: None
Notes: 5, 14

The New York Bed and Breakfast Reservation Center

P.O. Box 2646, Southampton, 11969-2646
(212) 577-3512

Wide range of bed and breakfasts in New York City, some within a few blocks of major Midtown hotels. Hosted and unhosted accommodations available. The majority of accommodations are in doormen security buildings, others are in townhouses. Unhosted accommodations can house up to nine people. Checks accepted

for deposit only. Inquire about pets. Some bed and breakfasts are smoke free. Apartments by the month also available.

Rates: $80-90 (hosted); $90 and up (unhosted)
Continental Breakfast
Credit Cards: C
Notes: 5, 10, 11, 14

Urban Ventures, Inc.

38 West 32, #1412, 10001
(212) 594-5650; FAX (212) 947-9320

Established in 1979, Urban Ventures has about 600 accommodations. Each has been inspected by Urban Ventures. A range of fifth-floor walk-ups to a three-bedroom house in center city. This service can provide unhosted apartments and bed and breakfasts in every area of the city. Guests need only express their needs and they will find them met. In peak seasons, book at least three weeks prior to arrival. Brochure is free. The capable staff has been with this service for years.

Rooms: 300 (PB and SB) $65-95
Continental Breakfast
Credit Cards: A, B, C, D, E
Notes: 2, 5, 8, 9, 14

NIAGARA FALLS

An's House

745 Fourth Street, 14301
(716) 285-7907

An's House is a gracious, yet intimate, bed and breakfast in the heart of downtown in historic Niagara Falls. Each season brings its own delights to one of the seven wonders of the world. Restored and refurnished to 1925 with 1950s nostalgia and game room. Experience the ultimate in bed and breakfasts. Smoking allowed in designated areas only.

Hosts: Ann and Jack Slote
Rooms: 4 (2PB; 2SB) $50-80
Full Breakfast
Credit Cards: A, B, C, D
Notes: 5, 9, 12, 13

NOTES: Credit cards accepted: A MasterCard; B Visa; C American Express; D Discover; E Diners Club; F Other; 2 Personal checks accepted; 3 Lunch available; 4 Dinner available; 5 Open all year; 6 Pets welcome;

The Cameo Inn

The Cameo Inn

4710 Lower River Road, Route 18F, Lewiston, 14092
(716) 745-3034

This stately Queen Anne Victorian commands a majestic view of the lower Niagara River and Canadian shoreline. Lovingly furnished with period antiques and family heirlooms, the Cameo will charm guests with its quiet elegance. Here one can enjoy the ambience of days past in a peaceful setting far from the bustle of everyday life. Three guest rooms with private or shared baths are available, as well as a three-room private suite that overlooks the river.

Hosts: Greg and Carolyn Fisher
Rooms: 4 (2 PB; 2 SB) $65-115
Full Breakfast
Credit Cards: A, B, D
Notes: 5, 9, 10, 11, 12, 13, 14

The International Bed and Breakfast Club, Inc.

504 Amherst Street, Buffalo, 14207
(800) 723-4262; FAX (716) 873-4462

NY2144PP. Spend some quality time in this tastefully restored inn, small enough to guarantee that guests don't get lost in the crowd. The personal attention guests deserve at a price that makes sense. Enjoy old-fashioned hospitality in a convenient setting. Four guest rooms, some with private baths, some shared. Full breakfast is served. Plenty of off-street parking. Within walking distance of many Niagara Falls sights and sounds. $70.

NY3070PP. This beautiful property is right on the Niagara River. The two guest rooms have a view of the river and access to the available sandy beach. The guest quarters have a separate entrance and a large living room for relaxing in front of the fireplace. The gardens and dock area offer a delightful spot to enjoy the outdoor scenery. The short drive to Niagara Falls takes guests past one of the largest Factory Outlet malls and also the area's prime shopping mall for fashion and department stores. $65.

NY4626PP. A beautifully restored turn-of-the-century home with outstanding architectural detailing. Queen-size, double, and twin beds in four guest rooms, with both private and shared baths. Full breakfast and afternoon tea served. Within walking distance of the falls and many popular tourist attractions. $50-75.

NY7907PP. A gracious yet intimate bed and breakfast in the heart of downtown in historic Niagara Falls. Constructed in 1925 and painstakingly restored to its original beauty and character, preserving the authentic wood trim, leaded-glass windows, and nostalgic atmosphere. Furnished with antiques. The area abounds with interesting and excellent sightseeing. A short walk to the aquarium, fine restaurants, and, of course, Niagara Falls. Enjoy a leisurely breakfast, a pleasurable walk in the colorful fall season, bargain hunting for Christmas gifts, or a spring drive through the fabulous New York countryside. Play the organ or enjoy the library. The home can accommodate up to ten guests in four guest rooms with shared baths. The hosts are also happy to assist in organizing any special occasion, from small business seminars to shopping

7 No smoking; 8 Children welcome; 9 Social drinking allowed; 10 Tennis nearby; 11 Swimming nearby;
12 Golf nearby; 13 Skiing nearby; 14 May be booked through a travel agent.

sprees, even second honeymoons. Full breakfast. Air-conditioned. Ample parking in well-lit setting. Open year-round. $60-65.

NORTH RIVER

Garnet Hill Lodge

13th Lake Road, 12856
(518) 251-2444; FAX (518) 251-3089

Garnet Hill Lodge, a four-season destination resort, is nestled in the heart of New York's Adirondack Mountains. Guests are greeted by the spaciousness of a great hotel, the warmth of a rustic mountain lodge, and the friendly charm of a country inn. The front windows offer a magnificent lake and mountain view. Warm-season guests enjoy swimming, boating, and fishing from the clear waters of Thirteenth Lake, hiking trails, and tennis. In winter, Garnet Hill is a complete cross-country ski center with more than 50K of groomed ski trails and miles of back country ski routes. The chefs create a variety of delicious meals, from simple breakfasts to full-course dinners and home-baked bread and desserts. Menu choices include low-fat cuisine and vegetarian entrées. Special programs include guided naturalist hikes, bird watching, fly fishing workshops, or working in the maple syrup sugarhouse. Nonsmoking rooms available.

Hosts: George and Mary Heim
Rooms: 27 (PB) $85-125
Full Breakfast
Credit Cards: A, B
Notes: 2, 3, 4, 5, 8, 9, 10, 11, 12, 13, 14

Highwinds Inn

Barton Mines Road, P.O. Box 70, 12856
(518) 251-3760

At an elevation of 2,500 feet on 1,600 acres of land in the middle of a garnet mine. All guest rooms and the dining area have a spectacular view to the west. On the property there is mountain biking, canoeing, hiking to several peaks and ponds, garnet mine tours, gardens, cross-country ski tour-

ing, tennis, swimming, and guided summer and winter midweek trips available. Nearby spring rafting on the Hudson; Lake George; Octoberfest. Picnic lunches can be arranged for guests. Closed April through June and November through Christmas. Children over 12 welcome.

Host: Kim Repscha
Rooms: 4 (PB) $100
Full Breakfast
Credit Cards: A, B
Notes: 2, 3, 4, 6, 7, 9, 10, 11, 12, 13

NORTH TONAWANDA

The International Bed and Breakfast Club, Inc.

504 Amherst Street, Buffalo, 14207
(800) 723-4262; FAX (716) 873-4462

NY6119PP. Relax and enjoy the view from the veranda of this countryside setting overlooking the historic canal. One king-size room with private bath, warmly decorated with family antiques and a lovely view of the gardens. Continental plus breakfast served. Minutes to entertainment, restaurants, shopping, and biking/hiking paths. Friendly, hospitable hosts invite guests to enjoy the Niagara Frontier from Buffalo to Niagara Falls. $60.

NORTHVILLE

American Country Collection

1353 Union Street, Schenectady, 12054
(518) 439-7001; FAX (518) 439-4301

175. In the foothills of the Adirondacks, on the shores of the Great Sacandaga Lake, lies this charming lakefront Victorian inn where visitors can relax in the timely elegance of years gone by. There is a large common room with mahogany staircase, cable TV, comfortable sofa, chairs, and fireplace. Breakfast is available each morning in an adjacent dining room with guest refrigerator. Complimentary refreshments are served in the afternoon. Dinner is available in the evening at an additional cost. Boat docking space is free in season. Arrangements can be made for small private parties, weddings, and business meetings. Six rooms, five on the second floor and one on the first floor, all with private baths. Smoking outside only. Well-behaved children are welcome; children under 12 must room with their parents. $65-75.

OLCOTT

Bayside Guest House

1572 Lockport Olcott Road
(State Road 78), 14126-0034
(716) 778-7767; (800) 438-2192

Overlooking the harbor and marina, near Lake Ontario, this country-style Victorian home offers fishermen and travelers a comfortable, relaxed stay. Antiques and collectibles furnish this guest house. Great fishing, a county park, and many shops within walking distance. Plenty of restaurants. One-half hour from Niagara Falls, one hour from Buffalo. Smoke free. Friendly cats will make you feel right at home!

Host: Jane M. Voelpel
Rooms: 5 (SB) $30
Continental Breakfast
Credit Cards: D
Notes: 2, 5, 6, 7, 8, 9, 10, 12

Bayside Guest House

OLIVEREA

Slide Mountain Forest House

805 Oliverea Road, 12410
(914) 254-5365; (914) 254-4269

Nestled in the Catskill Mountains State Park, this inn offers the flavor and charm of the Old Country. Enjoy the beautiful country setting, superb lodging, fine dining, and chalet rentals. Having run this bed and breakfast for more than 60 years, the hosts strive to give guests a pleasant and enjoyable stay. German and Continental cuisine, a bar and lounge, pool, tennis, hiking, fishing, antiquing, and more are available for guests' pleasure. Chalets open year-round.

Hosts: Ursula and Ralph Combe
Rooms: 21 (17 PB; 4 SB) $50-70
Full Breakfast
Credit Cards: A, B, D
Notes: 2, 3, 4, 7, 8, 9, 10, 11, 12, 13

ONEIDA CASTLE

Bed and Breakfast Leatherstocking

P.O. Box 53, Herkimer, 13350
(315) 733-0040; (800) 941-BEDS (2337)

035. What a marvelous place to come to, to get away from the mundane! The house carries guests back 180 years to a time when political history was being made here and this house was being built. Its 15 rooms, complete with garret and widow's watch were the standard of the wealthy of its day. Now four large rooms with private baths (one is a suite with its own sitting room) command the public's attention as a new bed and breakfast for this area. All rooms have color cable TV with remote and HBO, telephones, custom-tailored fabrics, and ensembles. Full breakfasts; high-tech security system installed. Central air conditioning being installed. Major credit cards accepted. $65-115.

7 No smoking; 8 Children welcome; 9 Social drinking allowed; 10 Tennis nearby; 11 Swimming nearby; 12 Golf nearby; 13 Skiing nearby; 14 May be booked through a travel agent.

OTTO

The International Bed and Breakfast Club, Inc.

504 Amherst Street, Buffalo, 14207
(800) 723-4262; FAX (716) 873-4462

NY5140PP. This charming turn-of-the-century farmhouse is nestled among the old willow trees overlooking Cattaraugus Creek. Five rooms are available with shared baths. Guests may enjoy the spa on the terrace and a variety of seasonal activities: rafting, fishing, swimming, hiking, horseback riding, cross-country skiing, snowmobiling, ice skating, and tobogganing. New York's finest downhill skiing is nearby. A full breakfast is served, as well as other meals, featuring natural foods. $65.

PALENVILLE

American Country Collection

1353 Union Street, Schenectady, 12054
(518) 439-7001; FAX (518) 439-4301

031. This large old Victorian with wraparound porch is nestled along the creek by the scenic mountain road that leads to Tannersville. Leaf peepers, creek swimmers, waterfall seekers, hikers, and nature lovers will find this area exciting. Four second-floor rooms share two baths. The living room has a fireplace, TV, and piano. Smoking limited. Children welcome. Pets in residence. Full breakfast served. $40-50.

The Kenmore Country Bed and Breakfast

Malden Avenue, 12463
(518) 678-3494

This quaint country home was built in the late 1800s and is nestled at the bottom of Hunter Mountain. Spend the night in one of

The Kenmore

the three cozy bedrooms. Enjoy the day relaxing in the large living room or screened porch. Close to many attractions. Cottage rental also available, but breakfast is not included. Inquire about accommodations for pets. Limited smoking permitted.

Hosts: John and Lauren Hanzl
Rooms: 3 (1 PB; 2 SB) $50-60
Full Breakfast
Credit Cards: A, B, D
Notes: 5, 9, 11, 12, 13

PENN YAN

Finton's Landing

661 East Lake Road, 14527
(315) 536-3146

A secluded lakeside lawn leads to Finton's Landing where steamboats loaded grapes at harvest along 165 feet of private beach. A scrumptious breakfast is relished in the sunny dining area or on the romantic porch. The parlor and living room, with fireplace, are filled with warmth and memories of a home more than 100 years old. Join the hosts and escape to countryside, fine waterfront restaurants, antique shops, and vineyard wine tastings.

Hosts: Doug and Arianne Tepper
Rooms: 4 (PB) $79
Full Breakfast
Credit Cards: A, B
Notes: 2, 5, 7, 10, 11, 12, 13

NOTES: Credit cards accepted: A MasterCard; B Visa; C American Express; D Discover; E Diners Club;
F Other; 2 Personal checks accepted; 3 Lunch available; 4 Dinner available; 5 Open all year; 6 Pets welcome;

The Fox Inn

158 Main Street, 14527
(315) 536-3101; FAX (315) 536-7612

This 1820 pillared Classic Revival home, decorated with antiques and Orientals, can be found surrounded by manicured lawns and rose gardens. Gourmet breakfast in the formal dining room. Private baths available. Handicap ramp and bedroom. Comfortable elegance in fine home. Near Keuka and Seneca Lakes of the Finger Lakes. Proximate to many of the region's small estate wineries. The Fox Inn can be found in the village of Penn Yan, one of the nation's 100 best small towns. The inn was named one of the Top Fifty Inns in America by *The Inn Times* for 1991. United States personal checks accepted.

Hosts: Myron, Matt, and Reed White
Rooms: 6 (5 PB; 1 SB) $75-85
Full Breakfast
Credit Cards: A, B
Notes: 2, 5, 7, 8, 9, 10, 11, 12, 13

The Wagener Estate Bed and Breakfast

351 Elm Street, 14527
(315) 536-4591

This bed and breakfast is a historic 1796 home furnished with antiques and nestled on four acres in the Finger Lakes area.

The Wagener Estate

Hospitality, country charm, comfort, and an elegant breakfast await.

Hosts: Norm and Evie Worth
Rooms: 5 (3 PB; 2 SB) $60-70
Full Breakfast
Credit Cards: A, B, C
Notes: 2, 5, 7, 9, 10, 11, 12, 13

PERRY

Eastwood House

45 South Main Street, 14427
(716) 493-2335

Older, comfortable home offering economy accommodation. Continental breakfast served. Near Letchworth State Park, known as "the Grand Canyon of the East." Along Gorge of Genesee River. Close to golfing, swimming, and boating. Approximately one and one-half hours from Finger Lakes wineries, Corning Glass, and Niagara Falls.

Host: Joan Ballinger
Rooms: 2 (SB) $30-32
Continental Breakfast
Credit Cards: None
Notes: 2, 8, 10, 11, 12, 13

PINE BUSH

American Country Collection

1353 Union Street, Schenectady, 12054
(518) 439-7001; FAX (518) 439-4301

205. Guests are invited to relax in front of the four working fireplaces in the common rooms, sit or swing in a rocker on the wrap-around porch, or stroll through the garden with its sitting areas and constantly running stream. Inside is a vintage billiard room stocked with board games and cards as well as a turn-of-the-century pool table and an adjacent "Great Hall" and library. Accommodations include one king-size suite on the first floor and five rooms on the second floor, all with private bath and furnished with antiques, area rugs, and matching bed comforters. Breakfast is served in the dining room at individual

7 No smoking; 8 Children welcome; 9 Social drinking allowed; 10 Tennis nearby; 11 Swimming nearby; 12 Golf nearby; 13 Skiing nearby; 14 May be booked through a travel agent.

tables or with other guests at the dining room table or, as weather permits, on the porch or streamside. For skiing enthusiasts, Belleayre is only a half-mile away with jitney pickup and return service available. Hiking, swimming, tubing, fishing, and horseback riding are within a five- to ten-minute drive. Smoking permitted in common rooms only. Children welcome. One dog in residence. Full breakfast. $75-150.

209. Guests will find a little bit of English countryside tucked away in the foothills of the Shawangunk Mountains. A cedar shingled cottage built in the late 1700s is set on 22 acres of mostly wooded land. Throughout are antiques, and decorative painting—on floors, walls, and furniture. In back is a more modern addition, a spacious living room/dining room with cathedral ceiling and a fireplace overlooking a small field, woods, and seasonal stream. A TV/VCR room features the original exposed oak beams and a pegged oak floor. Hiking and swimming are available. There are two guest accommodations. One has a double bed and private bath, and the other has twin beds and a shared bath. Smoking permitted outside. One indoor dog and several cats in residence. Inquire about accommodations for guest pets. Children welcome. Full breakfast. $40-60.

PINE PLAINS

Nutmeg Bed and Breakfast Agency

P.O. Box 1117, West Hartford, CT 06127-1117
(203) 236-6698; (800) 727-7592

Beautifully restored 23-room Victorian mansion with six antique-furnished guest rooms, some with private baths. One suite with sitting room and lovely view. Four porches for relaxing. Continental breakfast. Children over 12 are welcome. Smoking is permitted.

PITTSTOWN

Maggie Towne's Bed and Breakfast

Rural Delivery 2, Box 82, Valley Falls, 12185
(518) 663-8369; (518) 686-7331

An old Colonial amid beautiful lawns and trees, 14 miles east of Troy on NY Route 7. Enjoy tea or wine before the fireplace in the family room. Use the music room or read on the screened porch. The hostess will prepare lunch for guests to take on tour or enjoy at the house. It's 20 miles to historic Bennington, Vermont, and 30 to Saratoga Springs.

Host: Maggie Towne
Rooms: 3 (SB) $35-45
Full Breakfast
Credit Cards: None
Notes: 2, 3, 5, 8, 9, 10, 11, 12, 13, 14

POMPEY

Elaine's Bed and Breakfast Selections

4987 Kingston Road, Elbridge, 13060
(315) 689-2082

Charming, well-furnished, sparkling ranch on two acres with a view of a sculpture garden. Guests may have the entire main floor. Two double bedrooms. Master bedroom opens to another room with a sleeper-sofa for a family suite. One and one-half baths. Southeast of Syracuse in the country. Just north of Route 20. Less than 30 minutes from Syracuse. Moderate rates.

PORT JEFFERSON

Compass Rose Bed and Breakfast

P.O. Box 511, 11777
(516) 928-8087

Dating from the 1820s, this home and barn of a ship's captain are above the busy harbor of Port Jefferson with its ferry to Connecticut. Beautiful Port Jefferson is a restored whaling village with unique shops and fine restaurants. Although modernized with new baths and central air conditioning, the home is decorated with antiques and country furnishings. Breakfast specialties of homemade breads, jams, freshly ground coffee, teas, and cereals are served each morning in the Rose Parlor.

Host: Kathleen Burk
Rooms: 4 (2 PB; 2 SB) $58-125
Continental Breakfast
Credit Cards: A, B, C, D
Notes: 2, 5, 8, 9, 10, 11, 12, 14

PORT ONTARIO

Elaine's Bed and Breakfast Selections

4987 Kingston Road, Elbridge, 13060
(315) 689-2082

An authentic stone lighthouse built in 1838 to help guide shipping on Lake Ontario is now completely furnished for nightly or weekly rental. First floor has large kitchen complete with kitchenwares for cooking, living room with fireplace, two bedrooms, and a bath. Second floor has two bedrooms and sitting room or third bedroom. There is a glassed-in cupola that may be accessed by a steel ladder. There are also three housekeeping cabins with three bedrooms each on this six-acre property. They have color cable TV and new rustic furniture. Two twin beds in each bedroom. There is also a marina. Port Ontario is just three miles west of Pulaski and I-81. $100-700.

POUGHKEEPSIE

Inn at the Falls

50 Red Oaks Mill Road, 12603
(914) 462-5770; (800) 344-1466

Inn at the Falls in Dutchess County combines the most luxurious elements of a

modern hotel with the ambience and personal attention of a country home. Continental breakfast is delivered to guest rooms each morning. Twenty-two hotel rooms and 14 suites are all individually decorated for those who demand the finest in overnight accommodations.

Host: Arnold Sheer
Rooms: 22 (PB) $110-150
Suites: 14
Continental Breakfast
Credit Cards: A, B, C, D, E
Notes: 5, 8, 9, 10, 11, 12, 13, 14

PULASKI

Elaine's Bed and Breakfast Selections

4987 Kingston Road, Elbridge, 13060
(315) 689-2082

A. On the banks of Salmon River is this executive-type house that is now a bed and breakfast and fisherman's lodge. On the first floor, with a separate entrance, there is a guest room with a double bed and two twins. The second-floor guest rooms can accommodate three, four, and five people. The basement has a large lounge with billiard table, a tackle shop, mud room, and full bath. Continental plus breakfast is served. Well-behaved children over five are welcome. Pets are welcome. Full meal plans and boxed lunches are available for a moderate price. $20-31 per person.

B. A great stopping-off place on I-80 between Syracuse and Watertown, this original large brick Victorian sits back splendidly from the main street. Recently purchased by new owners, it has been refurbished where necessary yet reflects its origins via its great front porch and tall, mature trees in the front yard. There is a study where guests may watch cable TV or play table games. Elegantly furnished with antiques, the main house has four spacious guest rooms individually decorated, with

7 No smoking; 8 Children welcome; 9 Social drinking allowed; 10 Tennis nearby; 11 Swimming nearby; 12 Golf nearby; 13 Skiing nearby; 14 May be booked through a travel agent.

private baths, and two rear rooms share a bath. The gracious dining room has a fireplace with a lovely gilded mirror above it. The living room decor is Victorian. In addition to the main house, there are several efficiency cabins available on the property. MasterCard, VISA, and Discover Cards accepted. Moderate rates.

QUEENSBURY

American Country Collection

1353 Union Street, Schenectady, 12054
(518) 439-7001; FAX (518) 439-4301

126. Original gingerbread accents this 100-year-old farmhouse on a working berry farm. There's a comfortable country feeling here with family furnishings and mementos, patchwork quilts, and oak furnishings. Two guest rooms with queen-size beds and private baths. One room has a whirlpool tub. Excellent location for outlet shopping, hot air balloon festival, Great Escape Amusement Park, and Lake George. Smoking is permitted outdoors only. Children over six are welcome. Cat in residence. $60-70.

Crislip's Bed and Breakfast

693 Ridge Road, 12804
(518) 793-6869

Just minutes from Saratoga Springs and Lake George, this landmark Federal home provides spacious accommodations, complete with period antiques, four-poster beds, and down comforters. The delicious country breakfast menu features buttermilk pancakes, scrambled eggs, and sausages. The hosts invite guests to relax on the porches and enjoy the beautiful mountain view of Vermont.

Hosts: Ned and Joyce Crislip
Rooms: 3 (PB) $55-75
Full Breakfast
Credit Cards: A, B
Notes: 2, 5, 7, 8, 9, 10, 11, 12, 13

RED HOOK

American Country Collection

1353 Union Street, Schenectady, 12054
(518) 439-7001; FAX (518) 439-4301

115. This Federal-style home, built in 1821 and restored in 1988, offers a ground-level suite with private entrance and bath, non-working fireplace, antique table and chairs, microwave, coffee maker, and small refrigerator. Smoking outdoors only. Children welcome. Port-a-crib available. No pets. Bréakfast, made with only the freshest organic ingredients, is served at the table in front of the two deep-silled windows that look out to two acres of trees and vegetable and flower gardens. Add $10 for one-night stays. $95.

REMSEN

Bed and Breakfast Leatherstocking

P.O. Box 53, Herkimer, 13350
(315) 733-0040; (800) 941-BEDS (2337)

013. A rare Welsh Barngarten greets the traveler, inviting the guest to sit among its array of blossoming plants, while the house, an old Victorian farmhouse with Welsh motif throughout, provides a secluded shelter in the foothills of the Adirondacks. The Victorian sitting room, with harmonium and old lithographs, is prologue to the three comfortably furnished rooms upstairs. Full breakfast. $55-60.

RENSSELAER

Tibbitts House Inn

Routes 9 and 20, 100 Columbia Turnpike, 12144
(518) 472-1348

A 136-year-old farmhouse acquainted with country living. The old house has an 84-foot

Tibbitts House Inn

windowed porch on which breakfast is served in season. Rooms are papered in cheerful patterns with braided and rag rugs on polished fir floors. Handmade quilts top crisp bed linens. Antiques abound. Two miles from Albany and the state capitol, museums, convention center, the new Knickerbocker Arena, and Hudson River boat launch.

Host: Claire E. Rufleth
Rooms: 5 (1 PB; 4 SB) $48-55
Full and Continental Breakfast
Credit Cards: None
Notes: 2, 5, 7, 8, 10, 11, 12

REXFORD

American Country Collection
1353 Union Street, Schenectady, 12054
(518) 439-7001; FAX (518) 439-4301

042. This Queen Anne Victorian manor house had a humble beginning in 1763 as a cabin, grew to a farmhouse in the early 19th century, and in 1883 took on its present elegant form. Air-conditioned. One suite on the second floor has two bedrooms, a sitting room with TV, and a private bath. Two first-floor rooms with TV and private entrances. An English country buffet breakfast is served in the dining room or on the terrace. The Mohawk River, a yacht club, two golf courses, and a bicycle path are within walking distance. Smoking permitted with consideration for other guests. Children welcome. Two dogs in residence. $85-130.

123. An idyllic landscape of rolling hills, grassy fields, woodlands, and flowers surround this private suite set 800 feet back from a cul-de-sac on seven country acres. The suite includes a private bath, kitchenette, and separate entrance. No smoking. Children school age and over welcome. No pets. Arrangements for guest dog may be made occasionally. Fixings for breakfast provided in kitchenette for leisurely breakfast at guests' convenience. Weekly and monthly rates available. $75-95.

RHINEBECK

American Country Collection
1353 Union Street, Schenectady, 12054
(518) 439-7001; FAX (518) 439-4301

060. Skilled local craftsmen have painstakingly restored this 1860 Victorian in the heart of a historic village filled with antique and specialty shops, art galleries, and fine restaurants. The Aerodrome and Roosevelt and Vanderbilt mansions are just a short drive away. A gourmet breakfast is served at small tables in the fireplaced oak dining room. Five guest rooms with private baths. One room has a working fireplace. Guests may choose from brass, canopied, or carved Victorian beds. Smoking limited to parlor. Children over 16 welcome. No pets. $175-275.

192. A rambling contemporary home filled with light from large windows and sliding glass doors, overlooking 15 acres of rolling private countryside. House is furnished with an interesting combination of contemporary, antique, and modern pieces. Dining/breakfast room has an antique Spanish oak table, which seats ten, and an ornate crystal chandelier. Full gourmet breakfast. All guest rooms are air-conditioned, and all baths have a skylight. Cross-country skiing, horseback riding, golf, tennis, and sailing, and the town of Rhineback are all less than six miles away. $65-175.

7 No smoking; 8 Children welcome; 9 Social drinking allowed; 10 Tennis nearby; 11 Swimming nearby;
12 Golf nearby; 13 Skiing nearby; 14 May be booked through a travel agent.

210. A 140-year-old historic Colonial near the Bard College campus. Breakfast is enjoyed in the kitchen or around a circular table whenever one wishes; no set time or time schedule in this bed and breakfast. The home is cozy, furnished with many antiques and nary a room in the home is not filled with books. Each of the four guest rooms is well lighted, has a desk and chair, and is fully air-conditioned. Private and shared baths. TV/VCR. Smoking permitted outside. Children welcome. Two cats (not allowed in bedrooms) in residence. $85-120.

RICHFIELD SPRINGS

Bed and Breakfast Leatherstocking

P.O. Box 53, Herkimer, 13350
(315) 733-0040; (800) 941-BEDS (2337)

014. There is no pretension here with glorifying antiques. Instead, an invitingly clean, comfortable, homey atmosphere suitable for large family gatherings awaits the traveler. A 14-room former railroad hotel and general store has been converted to a fine family dwelling with modern sun deck and turn-around, a family suite, or three immaculate guest rooms, with private and shared baths offered. Children welcome. $35-80.

029. Stately charm describes this 19-room Queen Anne Victorian with portico as it stands on a small but commanding knoll overlooking the main thoroughfare of this quaint old village. Full breakfasts are served as well as prearranged picnic baskets and formal dining. Washer and dryer available to guests. Five guest rooms are offered, most with private baths. Only short minutes from Glimmerglass opera, Cooperstown, and Glimmerglass State Park. VISA and MasterCard are accepted. $60-75.

Country Spread Bed and Breakfast

23 Prospect Street, P.O. Box 1863, 13439
(315) 858-1870

Built in 1893 within the village limits, directly on New York State Route 28. Enjoy the many central Leatherstocking attractions including antiquing, Glimmerglass opera, Cooperstown (the home of baseball), swimming, and boating. Guest rooms have a country-decorated flair. Breakfast offers many delicious choices from Karen's kitchen. Families welcome. The hosts have two well-behaved children. The perfect place for a casual respite with genuine and sincere hospitality. Rated and approved by the ABBA.

Hosts: Karen and Bruce Watson
Rooms: 2 (PB) $50-75
Full Breakfast
Credit Cards: A, B
Notes: 2, 5, 7, 8, 9, 10, 11, 12, 14

RICHLAND SPRINGS

Jonathan House

39 East Main Street, P.O. Box 9, 13439
(315) 858-2870

Jonathan House is a towering 1880s Victorian richly furnished with English, French, and American antiques, Persian rugs, and works of art. Here guests will be able to step back a full 100 years to an opulent, more gracious time for a memorable vacation experience. All rooms have queen-size beds. A full breakfast is grandly served in the very elegant dining room. Minutes from Cooperstown and the Glimmerglass Opera.

Host: Peter Bickford
Rooms: 4 (2 PB; 2 SB) $55-75
Full Breakfast
Credit Cards: A, B, C
Notes: 2, 5, 7, 9, 10, 11, 12, 13, 14

NOTES: Credit cards accepted: A MasterCard; B Visa; C American Express; D Discover; E Diners Club; F Other; 2 Personal checks accepted; 3 Lunch available; 4 Dinner available; 5 Open all year; 6 Pets welcome;

RICHMONDVILLE

American Country Collection

1353 Union Street, Schenectady, 12054
(518) 439-7001; FAX (518) 439-4301

125. This renovated Federal-style home is on 23 acres of scenic pastures and pines. Three guest rooms have private baths and shared baths. In addition, there is a studio apartment suite and two cottages. There is a large living room with fireplace, light and airy dining room, and a deck. Special treats include fresh fruit at night and gifts at breakfast table on holidays. Smoking permitted. Resident dog. Guest pets accepted with $15 deposit. Children welcome. Crib available. $60-135.

ROCHESTER

Dartmouth House Bed and Breakfast

215 Dartmouth Street, 14607
(716) 271-7872

Enjoy 1905 Edwardian charm, antiques, cozy window seats, grand piano, and fireplace. Stroll through this quiet, architecturally fascinating neighborhood to the George Eastman Mansion and International Museum of Photography. Just a mile from downtown, in the heart of the Cultural Park/East Avenue area, it's an easy walk to Rochester's largest collection of antique shops, bookstores, and trendy or formal restaurants. Breakfast? Full gourmet and served by candlelight, using owners' Depression glass collection. Dress code? Be comfy! Phones in rooms and air conditioning. Smoking outside.

Hosts: Ellie and Bill Klein
Rooms: 4 (2 PB; 2 SB) $50-110
Full Breakfast
Credit Cards: A, B, C
Notes: 2, 5, 7, 9, 10, 11, 12, 14

The International Bed and Breakfast Club, Inc.

504 Amherst Street, Buffalo, 14207
(800) 723-4262; FAX (716) 873-4462

NY0758PP. Built in the 1920s, this ten-room white frame house is just two minutes from the expressway serving Rochester's downtown and cultural district. The second-floor wing has two guest bedrooms that share a common sitting room and full bath. A delicious breakfast is served in the dining room or on the patio, weather permitting. Resident dog and cat. No smoking allowed. $70.

Strawberry Castle

1883 Penfield Road, Penfield, 14526
(716) 385-3266

In suburban Rochester, this 1875 landmark Victorian Italianate villa combines the historic charm of yesteryear with the pleasures of a private luxury pool and patio on three acres of grounds. Brass or Empire beds in large, air-conditioned rooms. Fine restaurants and golf courses nearby. A visit to this gracious inn will turn any trip into a special memory.

Hosts: Anne Felker and Robert Houle
Rooms: 3 (PB) $60-115
Full Breakfast
Credit Cards: A, B, C
Notes: 2, 5, 9, 10, 11, 12, 14

ROME

Bed and Breakfast Leatherstocking

P.O. Box 53, Herkimer, 13350
(315) 733-0040; (800) 941-BEDS (2337)

028. Beautifully modern split-level, fully air-conditioned, smoke-free home in historic northwest Rome. Accommodations include three rooms, one with private bath,

7 No smoking; 8 Children welcome; 9 Social drinking allowed; 10 Tennis nearby; 11 Swimming nearby; 12 Golf nearby; 13 Skiing nearby; 14 May be booked through a travel agent.

a common family room, and a spacious deck. Full breakfast specialties are served in a sunny dining room. Winter and summer sports available. Near casino, raceway, Hamilton College, fine dining, and urban shopping malls. $45-65.

Elaine's Bed and Breakfast Selections

4987 Kingston Road, Elbridge, 13060
(315) 689-2082

A. On six acres near state thruway, this 1840 Cape saltbox is warmly furnished with many antiques and crafts made by the hostess. Full country breakfast of guests' choice. Suite features double bed, sitting area, and private bath. Two other rooms with one double bed each share main bath. Cot available. Perfect stop-off from Route 90 about halfway between Boston and Toronto. $45-60.

B. This brick Victorian farmhouse built in 1857 features complete antique furnishings. Three guest rooms are upstairs; one room offers a double and single bed. Near Griffiss Air Force Base. Pool, 40 acres, gardens, hiking trails, cross-country skiing. Near downhill skiing area. Resident dog and cat.

The Little Schoolhouse

6905 Dix Road, 13440
(315) 336-4474

A warm and welcoming 1840 Colonial saltbox on six private, quiet acres. Furnished in Early American with handcrafts throughout. Quick access to I-90, airport, and recreational facilities. Near Hamilton College. Enjoy breakfast in the summer kitchen or cozy dining room with homemade pastries and jellies always on the menu. Then take a tour of the Little Schoolhouse in the back yard, authentically furnished for the period 1900-1920.

Host: Beverly Zingerline
Rooms: 3 (1 PB; 2 SB) $50-60
Full Breakfast
Credit Cards: None
Notes: 2, 5, 8, 12, 13, 14

ROSCOE

Huff House

100 Lake Anawanda Road, 12776
(800) 358-5012

A beautiful New England-style inn, only two hours from New York City in the renowned trout-fishing capital of the East. Undiscovered on a mountaintop with 80-mile views and 188 acres laced with trails. Fly fishing pond featuring Ovis Fly Fishing School. Executive golf course with golf school throughout the summer. Heated pool, tennis. Exceptional cuisine and wine cellars. Warm hospitality. Antiquing and sightseeing. Closed December through March. Inquire about accommodations for pets.

Hosts: Joseph and Joanne Forness
Rooms: 45 (PB) $105-150
Full Breakfast
Credit Cards: A, B, C
Notes: 2, 3, 4, 7, 8, 9, 10, 11, 12, 14

ST. JOHNSVILLE

Bed and Breakfast Leatherstocking

P.O. Box 53, Herkimer, 13350
(315) 733-0040; (800) 941-BEDS (2337)

037. Through innovative and artistic creative skills, this 1835 historic mill, in a tranquil parklike setting, with cascading waterfalls, herb, flower, and water gardens, offers three richly decorated guest rooms, all with private baths. A family suite containing two rooms that share a bath is also available. These are in the century-old miller's home that also includes a stocked modern kitchen, a sitting room, and a game parlor. A sumptuous gourmet breakfast is served in the dining room of the grist mill

NOTES: Credit cards accepted: A MasterCard; B Visa; C American Express; D Discover; E Diners Club;
F Other; 2 Personal checks accepted; 3 Lunch available; 4 Dinner available; 5 Open all year; 6 Pets welcome;

itself. Guests may browse the museum in its emporium-like atmosphere filled with gifts, herbs, and floral arrangements. No smoking is permitted. Credit cards are accepted. Children over ten are welcome. $65-85.

SANBORN

The International Bed and Breakfast Club, Inc.
504 Amherst Street, Buffalo, 14207
(800) 723-4262; FAX (716) 873-4462

NY3693PP. This chalet-style home is quietly nestled in an apple orchard, set back from the road in the country, yet convenient to shopping and the historic sites of Niagara County. Historic Pekin United Methodist Church and the regionally renowned Schimschack's Restaurant, where Joe DiMaggio once dined with Marilyn Monroe, are both nearby. Guests will also enjoy the area hiking. Two rooms with shared bath are available. A full country breakfast may be enjoyed either on the deck or in the dining room. $50.

SARANAC LAKE

Fogarty's Bed and Breakfast
37 Riverside Drive, 12983
(518) 891-3755; (800) 525-3755

Fogarty's is high on a hill overlooking Lake Flower and Mounts Baker, McKenzie, and Pisgah, but is still only three minutes from the center of town. The bed and breakfast's porches, wide doors, and call buttons attest to its delightful past as a cure cottage. The living room and dining room are uniquely decorated with handsome woodwork, and the bathrooms have the original 1910 fixtures. Swimmers and boaters are welcome to use Fogarty's dock, and cross-country skiers will find trails within a mile. More ambitious athletes

should take a brief drive to Lake Placid's Olympic course or to the slopes of Whiteface.

Hosts: Jack and Emily Fogarty
Rooms: 5 (SB) $45
Full Breakfast
Credit Cards: None
Notes: 2, 5, 7, 8, 9, 10, 11, 12, 13

SARATOGA SPRINGS

Adelphi Hotel
365 Broadway, 12866
(518) 587-4688

Charming Victorian hotel built in 1877 in historic downtown Saratoga Springs. The Adelphi has 37 guest rooms lavishly decorated with period artwork, antiques, and wall coverings. These spacious rooms are air-conditioned, have private baths, cable TV, and direct-dial phones. A delightful complimentary Continental breakfast is served in the morning to the guest's room, parlor, or piazza overlooking Broadway. A beautifully landscaped outdoor pool is available to guests. The Adelphi Cafe offers a full bar, desserts, and special coffees throughout the entire season; dinner served in July and August only.

Hosts: Sheila Parkert and Gregg Siefker
Rooms: 37 (PB) $90-295
Continental Breakfast
Credit Cards: A, B, C
Notes: 2, 8, 9, 11, 12, 14

American Country Collection
1353 Union Street, Schenectady, 12054
(518) 439-7001; FAX (518) 439-4301

105. The friendly atmosphere of this working organic farm is a delight for children and adults. The Victorian farmhouse and barns have been restored to offer seven air-conditioned guest rooms, all with private baths. Seven rooms available with private bath and double or queen- or king-size beds. One room has two double beds, private bath, TV, wood-burning stove, and

7 No smoking; 8 Children welcome; 9 Social drinking allowed; 10 Tennis nearby; 11 Swimming nearby; 12 Golf nearby; 13 Skiing nearby; 14 May be booked through a travel agent.

American Country Collection (continued)

private deck. A gourmet breakfast is served in the Florida room amid flowering plants and the hot tub/Jacuzzi. The Saratoga Performing Arts Center and racetrack are two miles away. Smoking permitted. Children welcome. $100-115.

107. This cozy, restored Victorian cottage with gingerbread millwork was probably the caretaker's home for one of the nearby mansions on North Broadway. It is within walking distance of the downtown shops and Skidmore College. Two guest rooms share one bath with the owner. Rooms are comfortable and immaculately clean. No smoking allowed. Cat in residence. Children are welcome. $55-95.

136. This minisuite in a 140-year-old historic Federal-period brick home in town offers two private apartments/suites that include a sitting room, refrigerator, microwave, coffee maker, porch, color TV, kitchenette, and antique furnishings. Its spacious front porch with wicker furniture and flower boxes invites guests to sit and enjoy the beauty of an evening sunset or a refreshing glass of lemonade. A Continental plus breakfast and a daily newspaper are delivered to the door each morning, and two ten-speed bikes are available to guests. $80-125.

139. This in-town historic home is only three blocks from the Saratoga Racetrack. Built in 1868 by a Civil War captain, it offers a front porch with white wicker furniture and a porch rocker and a side lawn with a patio, a picnic table, and an outdoor grill. Antiques, floral print wallpaper, lace curtains, and fresh and dried arrangements. One first-floor room with a double bed and shared bath, one-second floor room with

queen-size, double, and single beds and a private bath, two second-floor rooms with double beds and shared bath, and one second-floor room with a double bed, private side porch, and a shared bath. An apartment with full kitchen, microwave, cable TV, air conditioning, a double bed, and private bath. Full breakfast. $65-135.

141. Capture the peace and charm of Saratoga in this warm and inviting 100-year-old Queen Anne-style home restored to its original elegance by its owners. Across the street from the Saratoga Racetrack, this bed and breakfast is minutes from the harness track and the Saratoga Performing Arts Center. Three rooms share one large bath with a double sink and vanity; two rooms have double beds; and a third room has two single beds. Bedrooms are light and airy, and all three rooms are air-conditioned in the summer. Full breakfast. $65-110.

180. This Colonial-style cobblestone home is just minutes from Victorian Round Lake and Saratoga. Guests are welcomed with gracious hospitality and casual elegance. There are four guest rooms on the second floor all with luxury linens, firm mattresses, ceiling fans, fresh flowers, and private or shared baths. Breakfast is served fireside in the spacious dining room, or in the summer months on the deck surrounded by fragrant flowers. Wake-up coffee is available for early risers, and refreshments are served in the afternoons. Smoking on the deck or porch only. No children. $70-115.

Apple Tree Bed and Breakfast

49 West High Street, 12020
(518) 885-1113

Victorian and romantic ambience in the historic district only two miles from Saratoga Performing Arts Center. A delightful full breakfast is served each morning. Rooms offer gracious antique furnishings with all the comforts of home away from home. Private baths with whirlpool. Air-conditioned. Twenty-five miles north of Albany and only four miles to beautiful Saratoga and its year-round attractions.

Hosts: Dolores and Jim Taisey
Rooms: 4 (PB) $75-100
Full Breakfast
Credit Cards: A, B, C
Notes: 5, 7, 9, 10, 11, 12, 13, 14

The Clarion Inn at Saratoga

231 Broadway, 12866
(518) 583-1890

A turn-of-the-century, fully restored historic inn in the heart of Saratoga, offering delightful atmosphere and cozy surroundings. Enjoy the intimate cocktail lounge and sample a special selection offered nightly in the Victorian-appointed dining room, complete with a fireplace. Oversized rooms echo the Victorian era, and many overlook an English garden. Nearby are several quaint shops and boutiques, as well as outlet malls. Near the world-famous Saratoga thoroughbred track and historic mineral baths.

Rooms: 38 (PB) $39-300
Continental Breakfast
Credit Cards: A, B, C, D, E
Notes: 2, 4, 5, 7, 8, 9, 10, 11, 12, 13, 14

The Inn on Bacon Hill

P.O. Box 1462, 12866
(518) 695-3693

A peaceful alternative where guests come as strangers and leave as friends, just ten minutes east of Saratoga Springs. This 1862 Victorian is in a quiet, pastoral setting with four air-conditioned bedrooms. Enjoy beautiful gardens and gazebo, explore country lanes, or relax in comfortable guest parlor with an extensive library. Baby grand piano adorns a Victorian parlor suite. Innkeeping

The Inn on Bacon Hill

courses offered. Full country breakfasts included. Smoking permitted outside.

Host: Andrea Collins-Breslin
Rooms: 4 (PB) $65-135
Full Breakfast
Credit Cards: A, B
Notes: 2, 5, 9, 10, 11, 12, 13, 14

Lombardi Farm Bed and Breakfast

41 Locust Grove Road, 12866
(518) 587-2074

A restored Victorian farm, two miles from the center of historic Saratoga Springs. Air-conditioned, private baths, and gourmet breakfast served in the Florida room. Hot tub/Jacuzzi. A peaceful country setting within two miles of the National Museum of Dance, National Museum of Racing, thoroughbred racetrack, harness track, polo club, Skidmore College, Yaddo Artists Retreat and Gardens, and famous Saratoga Mineral Baths. Open year-round. Member of Bed and Breakfast Association of Saratoga, Lake George, and Gore Mountain, and listed in AAA tour guidebook. Rates are different during the flat track racing season.

Hosts: Vincent and Kathleen Lombardi
Rooms: 4 (PB) $100
Full Breakfast
Credit Cards: None
Notes: 2, 5, 9, 10, 11, 12, 13, 14

Saratoga Bed and Breakfast

434 Church Street, 12866
(800) 584-0920; FAX (518) 584-4500

7 No smoking; 8 Children welcome; 9 Social drinking allowed; 10 Tennis nearby; 11 Swimming nearby; 12 Golf nearby; 13 Skiing nearby; 14 May be booked through a travel agent.

Saratoga

Circa 1850. Beautifully restored rooms with fireplaces in a historic Victorian city 30 miles north of Albany in the foothills of the Adirondack Mountains. Horse racing, championship golf, opera, ballet, symphonies, museums, skiing, mineral spas, and architecture spanning two centuries. Acres of lawns and pine trees. Kings, queens, private baths, air conditioning, TV and telephone in rooms, and delicious Irish breakfasts! Open all year. Recommended by the *New York Times*. Rates during the racing season are higher.

Hosts: Noel and Kathleen Smith
Rooms: 8 (PB) $65-135
Full Breakfast
Credit Cards: A, B, C, D
Notes: 2, 5, 7, 9, 10, 11, 12, 13, 14

Six Sisters Bed and Breakfast

149 Union Avenue, 12866
(518) 583-1173; FAX (518) 587-2470

This beautifully appointed 1880 Victorian is on a historic, flower-laden boulevard in the heart of Saratoga Springs. Luxurious, immaculate rooms and suites offer king-size beds, private baths, and air conditioning. Antiques, Oriental carpets, hardwood floors, and Italian marble create a resplendent

decor. The inn is close to Skidmore College, convention center, the racetracks, SPAC, downtown, museums, spa, antiques, and restaurants. SPAC discounts. The owner is a native of Saratoga eager to share local information. Recommended by *Country Folk Art, Gourmet, McCall's,* and the *New York Times.* Children over ten welcome.

Hosts: Kate Benton and Steve Ramirez
Rooms: 4 (PB) $60-125
Full Breakfast
Credit Cards: A, B, C
Notes: 2, 5, 7, 9, 10, 11, 12, 13, 14

The Westchester House

102 Lincoln Avenue, Box 944, 12866
(518) 587-7613

This gracious 1885 award-winning Queen Anne Victorian inn features elaborate chestnut moldings, antique furnishings, and up-to-date comforts. Elegantly appointed bedrooms have king- and queen-size beds, tiled baths, and air conditioning. Enjoy the extensive library or play the baby grand piano. The charm and excitement, museums and racetracks, boutiques and restaurants of historic Saratoga are an easy walk from the Westchester House. After a busy day sampling the delights of Saratoga, relax on the wraparound porch, in the old-fashioned gardens, or in the double Victorian parlors and enjoy a refreshing glass of lemonade. Rates higher during racing season. Two-night

Westchester House

minimum stay is required for weekends and holidays. AAA three-diamond rating. Children over 12 welcome.

Hosts: Bob and Stephanie Melvin
Rooms: 7 (PB) $70-125
Continental Breakfast
Credit Cards: A, B, C
Notes: 2, 5, 9, 10, 11, 12, 13, 14

SCHENECTADY

American Country Collection

1353 Union Street, Schenectady, 12054
(518) 439-7001; FAX (518) 439-4301

043. This bed and breakfast, formerly a tavern, is in the heart of the city's historic Stockade district. The entire house can be rented for overnight lodging, weddings, or long-term stays. Three second-floor guest rooms, each with a TV, share one and one-half baths. One has a working fireplace, and two are air-conditioned. The luxurious bath has a Jacuzzi and a separate shower. All are air-conditioned. Breakfast is served in the dining room or in the breakfast room that looks out into the gardens and terrace. Within walking distance to theaters, shopping, restaurants, bike trail, train station, and Union College. Smoking limited. Children welcome. No pets. $95.

172. Set in the heart of historic Schenectady, this late Victorian-style home has been meticulously restored to its former charm and grace. Maple, cherry, and walnut antiques. All hardwood floors. There are two guest rooms, one with a double bed and the other with a queen-size bed; both are air-conditioned. A separate guest sitting room overlooks the garden. It has a TV, ceiling fan, and rattan rocking chairs. There is a half-bath on the first floor and full bath with extra-large tub on the second floor. Before retiring, guests fill out an individual menu request card for breakfast. Wake-up coffee available. Smoking in garden only. Children are welcome; no provisions for infants. Resident cat. $50-55.

SCHOHARIE

American Country Collection

1353 Union Street, Schenectady, 12054
(518) 439-7001; FAX (518) 439-4301

219. Built in 1800 and later Victorianized around 1860, this bed and breakfast home offers truly quaint country rooms and the most genuine of personal attention and hospitality. Decorated with an eclectic mix of Colonial-primitive to Victorian pieces and leaded, stained-glass windows. The upstairs guest rooms have queen-size beds and share a bath. The common room has a couch, chair, and TV/VCR. Smoking permitted outside. Children five years and older welcome. Two cats in residence. Full breakfast. $60.

SCHUYLERVILLE (SARATOGA SPRINGS)

American Country Collection

1353 Union Street, Schenectady, 12054
(518) 439-7001; FAX (518) 439-4301

124. Built in 1770, this home is in the midst of an apple orchard on an elevation overlooking the Hudson River. The mantel holds cannonballs that American troops fired at the house when it served as a hospital for British and Hessian troops during the Revolutionary War. In the main house, there are three guest rooms with shared bath and a two-room suite with a double bed and private bath. The Apple Cottage offers one bedroom, one and one-half baths, living room with fireplace, kitchen, and sitting area with fireplace. The Island Cottage offers two bedrooms, bath, loft, living room/kitchen with fireplace, and screened porch. Smoking in common areas only. Children welcome in the Island Cottage. They are welcome at the main house and Apple Cottage when the pool is not open. Pets in residence. Full and Continental breakfast offered. $65-175.

7 No smoking; 8 Children welcome; 9 Social drinking allowed; 10 Tennis nearby; 11 Swimming nearby; 12 Golf nearby; 13 Skiing nearby; 14 May be booked through a travel agent.

SHELDRAKE

Elaine's Bed and Breakfast Selections

4987 Kingston Road, Elbridge, 13060
(315) 689-2082

This 145-year-old Queen Anne house on Cayuga Lake is a destination in itself. Completely renovated in 1993, including new private baths. Two rooms have Jacuzzis and fireplaces, and two have private balconies. Four of the guest rooms have queen-size beds. A fifth guest room has two twin beds and a shared bath. There are ceiling fans in all rooms. There is private lake frontage for guests who enjoy swimming and boating. Complimentary rowboats and bikes for guests. Hiking and cycling opportunities abound. Golf and wineries are nearby. Gourmet breakfast served. Infants and children over 12 are welcome. $99-125.

SHELTER ISLAND

The Bayberry Bed and Breakfast

36 South Menantic Road, P.O. Box 538, 11964
(516) 749-3375

Experience an island accessible only by ferry with a simple, peaceful lifestyle, and a third of it is a nature conservancy. Activities include hiking, bird watching, biking, beaching, boating, fishing, winery tours, and antiquing. This home is in a setting abounding with wildlife, furnished with antiques, has an exceptionally large king-size bedroom, hammocks, swimming pool, and a cozy living room with a fireplace and a piano. Off-season rates are available. Children over 14 welcome.

Hosts: Suzanne and Richard Boland
Rooms: 2 (PB) $105-125
Credit Cards: None
Notes: 2, 7, 9, 10, 11, 12

SKANEATELES

Elaine's Bed and Breakfast Selections

4987 Kingston Road, Elbridge, 13060
(315) 689-2082

A. This beautiful new, custom-designed country ranch-style home has a gorgeous view of drumlins. Two guest bedrooms are available, each with a separate entrance and double bed. Full country breakfast served. Several fine restaurants, boutiques, gift and antique shops, and art galleries in the nearby village of Skaneateles, as well as an old-fashioned "five and dime." Also convenient to the Schweinfuth Art Center and Cayuga Museum of History, Seward House, and Harriet Tubman House (a few minutes away in Auburn). Seasonal or Sunday scheduling of antique shows, the Syracuse Symphony, the Merry-Go-Round Playhouse, polo matches, and the Skaneateles Music Festival. $65.

B. Nestled against a wooded hillside on a picturesque quiet country road, this remodeled farmhouse offers three freshly decorated guest rooms and two modern baths. One room has a double and single bed; one has two twins; and one has a double bed. A roll away bed and a chair bed are also available if they are needed. A large family room with grand piano, large color TV, VCR, and stereo is also available for guests' use on the same level. A delicious Continental breakfast featuring homemade breads, muffins, and jams is served in the roomy country kitchen with a custom-built stone fireplace. A larger hot breakfast is available for a nominal fee. There are hiking and cross-country ski trails on the 100-acre property. Children over ten are preferred. This is a smoke-free house. Only five miles north of Skaneateles Village, and 14 miles west of Syracuse. $55-65.

NOTES: Credit cards accepted: A MasterCard; B Visa; C American Express; D Discover; E Diners Club; F Other; 2 Personal checks accepted; 3 Lunch available; 4 Dinner available; 5 Open all year; 6 Pets welcome;

C. A beautifully remodeled executive ranch nicely furnished with good traditional furniture, Oriental pieces, and antiques. Offers a guest room with a new queen-size antique iron bed with good firm bedding, new wallpaper and matching carpet, antique chest, and sparkling new private bath. No smoking allowed. A Hide-a-Bed is available in the den if it is necessary for other people in the same guest party. Delicious full breakfast served. Hostess is active in Skaneateles Art Guild. Needlepoint, handmade quilts, and art decorate this lovely home. Resident cat. $75.

D. Cute, clean, comfortable, convenient, cozy, congenial, casual country atmosphere in a newly remodeled modest ranch on five acres. Adults preferred. Two modest guest rooms, each with a firm double bed, share a new bathroom. The hostess can direct guests to almost any place in Onondaga County including Syracuse (12 miles), Auburn (nine miles), Skaneateles Village (four miles). No smoking. Resident cat. $40-50.

SODUS

The International Bed and Breakfast Club, Inc.

504 Amherst Street, Buffalo, 14207
(800) 723-4262; FAX (716) 873-4462

NY4765PP. This is a lakefront bed and breakfast on two and one-half acres on Lake Ontario. Guests enjoy the peacefulness, the panoramic view of the lake, the breakfast fare, and the opportunity to wander freely, bonfires on the beach, and the community of Sodus Point offering Bi-Centennial Renaissance Faire, Hill Cumorah Pageant, Eslow Fishing Derby, and the Apple Blossom Fest. Three guest accommodations with private and shared baths. Gourmet breakfast. $65-75.

SODUS BAY

Elaine's Bed and Breakfast Selections

4987 Kingston Road, Elbridge, 13060
(315) 689-2082

This turn-of-the-century waterfront home with expansive lawns and mature trees is on the east side of Sodus Bay. Three large guest rooms, each with private bath, TV, radio, and king- or queen-size beds, occupy the main house. A suite overlooking the bay has a full kitchen, living-dining room, king-size bed, private bath, TV, radio, and cassette player. Two guest cottages are also available: Guests may choose the Summer House with queen-size and double beds, private baths, a balcony, and porch; or the Caretaker's House, with living room, TV sleeper-sofa, full kitchen, dining area, bath, and two bedrooms with two double or queen-size beds. A roll away bed is also available. Parking area also accommodates boat and trailer. Full gourmet breakfast is served. Smoking allowed outside only. Resident cat. $65-110.

SODUS POINT

Carriage House Inn

8375 Wickham Boulevard, 14555
(315) 483-2100; (800) 292-2990

Voted one of the top 50 inns in America. Also featured in Rand McNally's *Best Bed and Breakfast and Country Inns in the Northeast* and *American Historic Inns*. All rooms have private baths and include a full breakfast. This Victorian house, built in 1870, and the stone carriage house sit on four acres in a quiet residential area overlooking the historic lighthouse and Lake Ontario, with beach access.

Rooms: 8 (PB) $65-90
Full Breakfast
Credit Cards: A, B, C
Notes: 5, 8, 9, 10, 11, 12, 13

---

7 No smoking; 8 Children welcome; 9 Social drinking allowed; 10 Tennis nearby; 11 Swimming nearby; 12 Golf nearby; 13 Skiing nearby; 14 May be booked through a travel agent.

SOUTHAMPTON

The Old Post House Inn

136 Main Street, 11968
(516) 283-1717

The Old Post House, a small, charming country inn, was built in 1684 and is listed on the National Register of Historic Places. All rooms have private baths and air conditioning. Continental breakfast is included in the rates. Close to many boutiques and Saks Fifth Avenue. Children over 12 are welcome.

Hosts: Cecile and Ed Courville
Rooms: 7 (PB) $80-170
Continental Breakfast
Credit Cards: A, B, C
Notes: 3, 4, 5, 9, 10, 11, 12

Village Latch Inn Resort

101 Hill Street, 11968
(516) 283-2160

Village Latch Inn is known internationally for its charming ambience. A 40-room Gatsby mansion on five acres, yet in town and near the beach. Antiques to modern duplexes. Number-one choice in 50 inn books from Frommer's to Fodor's. Also, the mansion is available for special celebrations, corporate outings, and romantic weddings. The minimum stay on weekends is two nights.

Hosts: Marta and Martin White
Rooms: 70 (PB) $85-195
Continental Breakfast
Credit Cards: A, B, C, D
Notes: 5, 6, 8, 10, 11, 12, 14

SOUTHOLD

Goose Creek Guesthouse

1475 Waterview Drive, 11971
(516) 765-3356

This Civil War-era bed and breakfast home is nestled in the woods on the south side of Goose Creek, a quiet, serene setting. A full country breakfast is served, featuring all homemade foods: granola, whole wheat or cornmeal pancakes, jams, jellies, freshly baked bread, and the house specialty, apple rings. Close to the ferry to New London (Connecticut) and Montauk Point via the Shelter Islands ferries. Personal checks accepted for deposit only.

Host: Mary J. Mooney-Getoff
Rooms: 3 (SB) $60-75
Full Breakfast
Credit Cards: None
Notes: 5, 7, 8, 9, 10, 11, 12, 14

SOUTH OTSELIC

Bed and Breakfast Leatherstocking

P.O. Box 53, Herkimer, 13350
(315) 733-0040; (800) 941-BEDS (2337)

018. Surrounded by a picket fence, bordering state-owned hunting and fishing tracts with stocked trout streams, here is the ideal getaway for hiking, fishing, hunting, and skiing. Twenty-five minutes from SUNY Cortland and 30 minutes from Colgate. Huge kitchen with potbelly stove completes the country setting. Two guest rooms with shared baths. Full country breakfasts served year-round. $40-60.

SPENCER

Elaine's Bed and Breakfast Selections

4987 Kingston Road, Elbridge, 13060
(315) 689-2082

This large updated farmhouse is just 20 minutes south of Ithaca and also convenient to Binghamton, Endicott, Elmira, and Watkins Glen. Across the road are five acres next to a quiet stream where the hostess allows tenting and picnics. She also arranges bike tours with or without lunch. There are hiking trails and cross-country skiing. Children over 12 are welcome.

NOTES: Credit cards accepted: A MasterCard; B Visa; C American Express; D Discover; E Diners Club; F Other; 2 Personal checks accepted; 3 Lunch available; 4 Dinner available; 5 Open all year; 6 Pets welcome;

There are outside kennels for roving with Rover. No pets inside. A full, hearty country breakfast is served, including delicious homemade breads and muffins and jams. This is a smoke-free bed and breakfast. Open year-round.

STANFORDVILLE

Lakehouse Inn on Golden Pond

Shelley Hill Road, 12581
(914) 266-8093

The most enchanting lakefront sanctuary in the Hudson River Valley, this inn offers swimming, fishing, boating, suites with private Jacuzzi for two, wood-burning fireplaces, private decks, and stunning views of the lake and woods. Gourmet breakfasts and afternoon appetizers. A unique private inn where guests are free to enjoy a special time in splendid circumstances. Just 90 minutes from Manhattan.

Hosts: Judy and Rich Kohler
Rooms: 8 (PB) $175-450
Full Breakfast
Credit Cards: A, B
Notes: 5, 7, 8, 10, 11, 12, 13

STILLWATER

American Country Collection

1353 Union Street, Schenectady, 12054
(518) 439-7001; FAX (518) 439-4301

005. This is a quiet retreat on 100 acres of rolling countryside, complete with mountain vistas. The circa 1800 barn has been transformed into an exquisite home. It is conveniently between Saratoga Lake and Saratoga National Historical Park. Two rooms and two second-floor suites with king- and queen-size bed, each with private bath and air conditioning. Breakfast is served in the dining room or on the deck overlooking the countryside. Smoking outdoors only. Children over nine welcome.

Dog in residence. $10-charge for one-night stays. $85-135.

STONE RIDGE

The Inn at Stone Ridge/ Hasbrouck House

Route 209, 12484
(914) 687-0736

This 18th-century Dutch Colonial mansion is set on 40 acres of lawns, gardens, and untouched woods with a beautiful lake. The guest rooms are furnished in period antiques. A guest parlor with a full-size antique billiard table, sitting room, and library. Milliway's, a fine dining restaurant, is on the first floor of the mansion. The Hudson River to the east, Woodstock to the north, and the Catskill Mountains all around, only 95 miles from Midtown Manhattan.

Hosts: Daniel and Suzanne Hauspurg
Rooms: 11 (2 PB; 9 SB) $60-145
Full Breakfast
Credit Cards: A, B, C, D
Notes: 2, 4, 5, 6, 8, 9, 10, 11, 12, 13

SYRACUSE

Bed and Breakfast Wellington

707 Danforth Street, 13208
(315) 471-2433; (800) 724-5006
FAX (315) 474-2557

Salt City's finest. Historic 1914 brick and stucco Tudor-style home designed by the prolific arts-and-crafts architect Ward Wellington Ward. Contains rich wood interiors, ample interior glass, tiled fireplaces, and cozy porches. Antiques abound. Central to downtown, medical centers, the Carousel Center, and universities. Short drive to Finger Lakes Outlet Center. Spacious suites and private rooms available. Gift certificates available. Professional bed and breakfast consulting services/classes. Full gourmet breakfast is

7 No smoking; 8 Children welcome; 9 Social drinking allowed; 10 Tennis nearby; 11 Swimming nearby; 12 Golf nearby; 13 Skiing nearby; 14 May be booked through a travel agent.

served on weekends; a Continental plus breakfast is served on weekdays. Lunch and dinner available upon request. Children over six welcome.

Hosts: Wendy Wilber and Ray Borg
Rooms: 5 (PB) $65-105
Full and Continental Breakfasts
Credit Cards: A, B, C
Notes: 2, 5, 9

Elaine's Bed and Breakfast Selections

4987 Kingston Road, Elbridge, 13060
(315) 689-2082

A. Convenient to Syracuse University and LeMoyne College, this delightful knotty pine basement apartment can sleep two and has a completely furnished eat-in kitchen and attractive shower-bath with many built-ins. The living room/bedroom includes color TV, desk, easy chairs, game table, and much more. Patio and yard. Quiet dead-end street with a great view. Use of laundry for long-term guests. Long-term rates available. $65-75.

C. In the Eastside area near LeMoyne College and Syracuse University, this cute, customized Cape Cod has a newly redecorated first-floor guest room with a double bed, handmade chest, rocker, window seat, and private bath. An adjacent TV den can be a second guest room with a sofa bed or part of this as a suite. Both rooms are in a separate, rear wing of the house. $75.

6. On the western edge of the city, this three-year-young contemporary Cape is set on three acres. The guest room has a double bed and private bath. The property is a designated wildlife habitat. Peaceful, quiet setting, yet quite handy to shopping, state fair, zoo, restaurants, Onondaga Community College, highways, and Syracuse University. $50-60.

Pandora's Getaway

83 Oswego Street, Baldwinsville, 13027
(315) 635-9571

This beautifully restored Greek Revival home with sloping lawns is listed on the National Register of Historic Places and is only 20 minutes away from Syracuse. Guests will find that they have easy access to the thruway, NYS fairgrounds, Syracuse University, and Oswego. Relax on the front porch or in front of a fire in the living room. Various decors and amenities throughout the house.

Host: Sandy Wheeler
Rooms: 4 (2 PB; 2 SB) $50-80
Full Breakfast
Credit Cards: A, B
Notes: 2, 5, 7, 8, 9, 10, 11, 12, 13, 14

THENDARA

Moose River House Bed and Breakfast

12 Birch Street, P.O. Box 184, 13472
(315) 369-3104

During the 19th century, Moose River House was accessible only by the *Fawn,* a tiny side-wheeler that steamed upstream from Minnehaha, where New York's only wooden train rails terminated. Today, there are several routes to this northern Adirondack inn. However guests choose to arrive, they will not want to leave. From cross-country and downhill skiing in the winter, to hiking, horseback riding, and canoeing in the summer, the recreational options are almost unlimited. The adjacent town of Old Forge has a wealth of shops, restaurants, and recreational fun. Children over 12 are welcome.

Hosts: Kate and Bill Labbate
Rooms: 4 (2 PB; 2 SB) $65-85
Full Breakfast
Credit Cards: A, B
Notes: 2, 5, 7, 9, 10, 11, 12, 13

NOTES: Credit cards accepted: A MasterCard; B Visa; C American Express; D Discover; E Diners Club; F Other; 2 Personal checks accepted; 3 Lunch available; 4 Dinner available; 5 Open all year; 6 Pets welcome;

TOMKINS COVE

American Country Collection

1353 Union Street, Schenectady, 12054
(518) 439-7001; FAX (518) 439-4301

217. This contemporary, air-conditioned home sits upon a hillside about 200 feet above the Hudson River. Accommodations include a living room with cathedral ceiling, solarium, and air conditioning. Two guest rooms have double beds and share a bath. The third room has a queen-size bed and private bath. Smoking permitted outside. Children ten and older are welcome. Continental breakfast during the week; full breakfast on weekends. $65-80.

TROY

American Country Collection

1353 Union Street, Schenectady, 12054
(518) 439-7001; FAX (518) 439-4301

158. This unique Victorian farmhouse, circa 1849, is above Troy and set back 300 feet from the road with a long circular drive. It is near Rensselaer Polytechnical Institute, the Emma Willard School, Russell Sage College, and the Hudson Valley Community College. Four second-floor guest rooms share two full baths and a first-floor half-bath, and full country breakfast is served each morning. Smoking is allowed in designated areas only. $40-50.

TRUMANSBURG

The Archway Bed and Breakfast

7020 Searsburg Road, 14886
(607) 387-6175; (800) 387-6175

Charming 1861 Greek Revival home abounds with delight and comfort inside and out. Take a catnap in the porch hammock or stargaze in the hammock between the trees. Meander through old-fashioned gardens or play golf at the bordering public course. Full "light gourmet" breakfast provides a healthy choice for hearty appetites. Convenient to both Cayuga and Seneca Lakes, Ithaca, Watkins Glen, Taughannock Falls State Park, and area wine trails.

Hosts: Meredith Pollard and Joe Prevost
Rooms: 3 (1 PB; 2 SB) $60-80
Full Breakfast
Credit Cards: None
Notes: 2, 5, 7, 8, 9, 10, 11, 12, 13

TULLY-VESPER

Elaine's Bed and Breakfast Selections

4987 Kingston Road, Elbridge, 13060
(315) 689-2082

Just four scenic miles from Route 81, on Route 80, this custom-built raised ranch offers two double bedrooms with a shared bath and a master bedroom with private bath. Well furnished and in a very quiet location at the rear of the home. Full country breakfast included. Very close to Song Mountain downhill ski area and a short drive to Labrador and Toggenburg ski areas. After skiing, guests may relax in front of the Pennsylvania bluestone fireplace. Take a pretty country drive to Cazenovia and Bouckville on Route 20 for the annual antique show and sale held in August. Open year-round. $55-65.

UTICA

Bed and Breakfast Leatherstocking

P.O. Box 53, Herkimer, 13350
(315) 733-0040; (800) 941-BEDS (2337)

019. Elegant brick Federalist-period home built around 1826 and on the National Register of Historic Places. Prearranged private dining and picnic lunches available.

7 No smoking; 8 Children welcome; 9 Social drinking allowed; 10 Tennis nearby; 11 Swimming nearby;
12 Golf nearby; 13 Skiing nearby; 14 May be booked through a travel agent.

There are five guest rooms in the house with queen-size or single beds. Private and shared baths. Full breakfast served daily. Lots of history on a quiet street in a busy city in the center of New York State. $45-75.

020. Country charm in the city. Relax in this antique-filled, stenciled home year-round, enjoying breakfast on the porch in summer with herbs and vegetables fresh from the garden. A glass of mulled cider and a roaring fire greet guests in the fall and winter months. In an ideal location in south Utica. Just minutes from museums, shops, theaters, colleges, and restaurants. Single, double, and family suite available. $50-75.

The Iris Stonehouse Bed and Breakfast

16 Derbyshire Place, 13501-4706
(315) 732-6720; (800) 446-1456

In town, close to everything, this stately stone house with leaded-glass windows, listed on the local register of historic places. A separate guest sitting room, and guest rooms with private and shared baths. Full breakfast from the daily menu, central air, three miles from I-90, exit 31 (NYS Thruway), one block off Genesee Street, three blocks from the North-South arterial and Routes 5, 8, and 12. No smoking.

Hosts: Shirley and Roy Kilgore
Rooms: 4 (2 PB; 2 SB) $45-75
Full Breakfast
Credit Cards: A, B, C
Notes: 2, 5, 7, 9, 12, 13, 14

VERNON

Bed and Breakfast Leatherstocking

P.O. Box 53, Herkimer, 13350
(315) 733-0040; (800) 941-BEDS (2337)

021. Steeped in history, this 18th-century inn has been lovingly restored, providing a clean, charming bed and breakfast close to cultural centers, antique centers, and universities. Two queen-size private rooms are available and include a delicious full breakfast. Also available are dried flower arrangements, quilts, crafts, and weavings, all of which are homemade on the premises by the owners. $75-90.

Elaine's Bed and Breakfast Selections

4987 Kingston Road, Elbridge, 13060
(315) 689-2082

A marvelous sprawling Victorian-Italianate manor house atop a knoll on seven acres. Filled with antiques, this home has been featured in several local history books and is a must-see for architectural and history buffs. There are five guest rooms. Children and well-behaved pets welcome. Full breakfast. No smoking allowed in the bedrooms. $60-70.

VERONA

Bed and Breakfast Leatherstocking

P.O. Box 53, Herkimer, 13350
(315) 733-0040; (800) 941-BEDS (2337)

036. Pure country! This 14-room restored 1876 farmhouse, only five miles from exit 33 (I-90) on the New York Thruway, is close to casino, Vernon Downs raceway, colleges, and greater Utica-Rome attractions. A private air-conditioned suite consisting of two bedrooms, private bath, and fully equipped kitchenette is available. Continental breakfast served. Common room on the first floor has game-dining table, easy chairs, and a large, cozy fireplace, plenty of room to relax in a quiet rural area. $55-85.

Golden Rule

VICTOR

Golden Rule Bed and Breakfast

6934 Rice Road, 14564
(716) 924-0610

This completely renovated and enlarged 1865 country schoolhouse is at the gateway to the Finger Lakes region of New York State. Two beautifully decorated large bedrooms containing antiques and offering panoramic views of the beautiful Bristol Hills. A complete gourmet breakfast is included in addition to afternoon tea.

Hosts: Karen and Dick de Mauriac
Rooms: 2 (SB) $60-80
Full Breakfast
Credit Cards: None
Notes: 2, 5, 9, 11, 12, 13

WALDEN

American Country Collection

1353 Union Street, Schenectady, 12054
(518) 439-7001; FAX (518) 439-4301

212. Early 19th-century replica saltbox home on 21 acres of fields, woodlands, flowers everywhere, and a serene pond. Three guest accommodations with either a double or queen-size bed and shared bath. One suite has a fireplace, queen-size waterbed, and private bath. Air-conditioned.

A robe is provided for guests that share a bath. Smoking permitted outside. Children welcome. One dog and two cats in residence. Guest pets are welcome with prior arrangement. Full breakfast. $65-95.

WARRENSBURG

American Country Collection

1353 Union Street, Schenectady, 12054
(518) 439-7001; FAX (518) 439-4301

067. This 1850 Greek Revival inn has a new guest house featuring ten rooms and a Jacuzzi in a plant-filled solarium. In the center of an old-fashioned Adirondack village that features bandstand concerts in the summer. The inn itself has a public restaurant, a cozy fireplace tavern, and a common room with TV. Ten rooms and one family suite with private baths, air conditioning, fireplace, queen-, king-size, or two twin beds. Handicapped access. Smoking permitted with consideration for nonsmokers. No pets. Children over 11 welcome. Minimum stay of two nights on holiday weekends and on July and August weekends. $95-160.

207. A 14-room country farmhouse, where parts of the original building date back to the late 1700s. Four guest rooms have double or queen-size beds and shared baths. Also available is a guest suite with queen-size and single beds, kitchenette, TV, and private bath. All bedrooms have air-conditioners and telephones. Nonsmoking establishment. Children welcome by prior arrangements. Full breakfast. $85-109.

Country Road Lodge

HCR 1, Box 227, Hickory Hill Road, 12885
(518) 623-2207

With a view of the Adirondack Mountains and the Hudson River and minutes from Lake George, the lodge has offered its

Country Road Lodge

seclusion and casual comfort since 1974. Homemade bread, hiking, skiing, horse-shoes, badminton, books, board games. Fine restaurants and antiquing nearby.

Hosts: Steve and Sandi Parisi
Rooms: 4 (2 PB; 2 SB) $52-65
Full Breakfast
Credit Cards: None
Notes: 2, 5, 7, 9, 10, 11, 12, 13, 14

The Merrill Magee House

2 Hudson Street, 12885
(518) 623-2449

From the inviting wicker chairs on the porch to the elegant candlelit dining rooms, this inn offers the romance of a visit to a country estate. Guest rooms abound with 19th-century charm and 20th-century com-forts. Guests can relax in the inn's secluded gardens, enjoy the outdoor pool, or shop for antiques in the village. In the Adirondack Park, all outdoor activities are minutes away. Smoking restricted. Inquire about accommodations for children.

Hosts: Ken and Florence Carrington
Rooms: 10 (PB) $85-105
Suite: 1
Full Breakfast
Credit Cards: A, B, C, D
Notes: 2, 3, 4, 5, 9, 10, 11, 12, 13, 14

White House Lodge

53 Main Street, 12885
(518) 623-3640

An 1847 Victorian in the heart of the Adirondacks. The home is furnished with

many antiques. Only five minutes to Lake George Village, historic Fort William Henry, and Great Escape Amusement Park. Walk to restaurants, antique shops, and shopping areas. Enjoy the comfort of the air-conditioned TV lounge or rock on the front porch. Only 20 minutes to Gore Mountain Ski Lodge and the Adirondack Balloon Festival. Smoking allowed in TV lounge only.

Hosts: James and Ruth Gibson
Rooms: 3 (SB) $85
Continental Breakfast
Credit Cards: A, B
Notes: 5, 11, 12, 13

WATERLOO

Elaine's Bed and Breakfast Selections

4987 Kingston Road, Elbridge, 13060
(315) 689-2082

A wonderful Federal brick Colonial built in 1833. The house is furnished with antiques that guests are welcome to purchase. There is also an antique shop on the first floor. This great old home is delightful with its fire-warmed dining room with wide plank floors and so much more to see! Full American breakfasts of choice. Restaurants, shops, and historic homes are within walking distance. Children over ten are welcome. Well-behaved dogs are also welcome; resident Shih Tzu. $50-75.

WATERVILLE

Bed and Breakfast Leatherstocking

P.O. Box 53, Herkimer, 13350
(315) 733-0040; (800) 941-BEDS (2337)

022. Consummate privacy and convenience are embodied here in a newly renovated modern suite that features a fully equipped kitchen, queen suite, private bath, living room with queen-size sofa bed, TV, stereo,

NOTES: Credit cards accepted: A MasterCard; B Visa; C American Express; D Discover; E Diners Club; F Other; 2 Personal checks accepted; 3 Lunch available; 4 Dinner available; 5 Open all year; 6 Pets welcome;

and solarium. Only minutes from Utica, Colgate, Hamilton, Bouckville, golf courses, fishing, hiking, riding, shopping, and fine dining. Easy parking. No pets. Continental breakfast. Can accommodate up to four adults; children 12 and older. $75-125.

Bed and Breakfast of Waterville

211 White Street, 13480
(315) 841-8295

This Victorian home in a historic area is close to Utica, Hamilton College, Colgate University, antique shops. One block from Route 12, and one mile from Route 20. Accommodations include a triple with private bath, triple and double rooms with shared bath. Experienced, enthusiastic hosts are a retired utility manager and an avid quiltmaker.

Hosts: Carol and Stanley Sambora
Rooms: 3 (1 PB; 2 SB) $35-65
Full Breakfast
Credit Cards: A, B
Notes: 2, 5, 7, 8, 9, 10, 12, 13, 14

WATKINS GLEN

Clarke House Bed and Breakfast

102 Durland Place, 14891
(607) 535-7965

Charming English Tudor home, circa 1920, in the lovely village of Watkins Glen. Walk to the famous gorge, restaurants, and activities at Seneca Lake. Short drive to Watkins Glen International Raceway, famous wineries, and Corning Glass. Immaculate bedrooms feature antique decor and twin, double, or queen-size beds. Hearty breakfast graciously served in the formal dining room, with high tea served at 4:00 P.M. Central air conditioning. Private baths.

Hosts: Jack and Carolyn Clarke
Rooms: 4 (PB) $55-65
Full Breakfast
Credit Cards: B
Notes: 2, 5, 7, 9, 10, 11, 12, 14

Reading House Bed and Breakfast

P.O. Box 321, 14891
(607) 535-9785

A restored 1820 home with spacious grounds, two ponds, and exceptional views of Seneca Lake five miles north of Watkins Glen. The perfect place for guests if they like old houses, antiques, comfortable beds, private baths, delicious full breakfasts, good company, good books, and warm relaxation. And it is an ideal center point from which to tour Keuka, Seneca, and Cayuga Lakes, Ithaca, Corning, and Hammondsport. Children over ten are welcome. Cross-country skiing is available nearby.

Hosts: Rita and Bill Newell
Rooms: 4 (PB) $55-65
Full Breakfast
Credit Cards: None
Notes: 2, 5, 7, 9, 10, 11, 12, 13

WEST AMHERST

The International Bed and Breakfast Club, Inc.

504 Amherst Street, Buffalo, 14207
(800) 723-4262; FAX (716) 873-4462

NY8394PP. The quality of the Victorian era in the setting of a newly built home adds to the unique ambience of this bed and breakfast. Guests enjoy three beautifully decorated bedrooms, including a private Master Suite complete with ensuite whirlpool that is an ideal setting for special anniversaries and wedding couples. The best of both worlds, with the blending of family antiques and new construction, adds an unusual and distinctive aspect to the bed and breakfast experience. Complemented by a delicious full country breakfast, the Victorian flavor of this bed and breakfast, combined with friendly, warm hosts, keeps guests wanting to return to Niagara again and again. $65-85.

7 No smoking; 8 Children welcome; 9 Social drinking allowed; 10 Tennis nearby; 11 Swimming nearby; 12 Golf nearby; 13 Skiing nearby; 14 May be booked through a travel agent.

WEST FALLS

Pipe Creek Farm, Inc.

9303 Falls Road, 14170
(716) 652-4868

Featuring three charming bedrooms, one with double bed, one with queen-size bed, and one with twin beds. Two full bathrooms are shared and a half bath for convenience. Hosts welcome guests to their home with afternoon tea by the fireplace or swimming pool. Large TV with VCR, board games, and library. Pipe Creek is a working equine farm, where they train and teach the horse and rider. Escorted trail riding is available on 200 acres of land. During the winter, cross-county and downhill skiing, six miles away, are available. In the summer horseback riding and swimming are available.

Hosts: Phil and Kathy Crone
Rooms: 3 (SB) $50-70
Full Breakfast
Credit Cards: None
Notes: 2, 5, 6, 7, 8, 10, 11, 12, 13, 14

WESTFIELD

Westfield House

East Main Road, Route 20, 14787
(716) 326-6262

The Westfield House is an 1840 Gothic Revival historic European bed and breakfast inn. It has beautiful common rooms, huge Gothic windows, a sweeping staircase, and fireplaces. The seven guest rooms and suites all have private baths. Shops and a carriage barn. Excellent location, just two miles from I-90, and midway between Erie and Buffalo.

Host: Betty P. Wilson
Rooms: 7 (PB) $65-95
Full Breakfast
Credit Cards: A, B
Notes: 2, 7, 8, 9, 10, 12, 13, 14

WESTHAMPTON BEACH

1880 House

2 Seafield Lane, 11978
(800) 346-3290

This 100-year-old country retreat is only 90 minutes from Manhattan on Westhampton Beach's exclusive Seafield Lane. A swimming pool and tennis court are on the premises, and it's only a short walk to the beach. The Hamptons offer numerous outstanding restaurants and shops. Indoor tennis is available locally, as is a health spa at Montauk Point. Minimum stay is two nights. ABBA excellent rating.

Host: Elsie Pardee Collins
Rooms: 2 (PB) $100-200
Full Breakfast
Credit Cards: A, B, C
Notes: 4, 5, 7, 8, 9, 10, 11, 12, 14

Pear Tree Farm

P.O. Box 268, Remsenburg 11960
(516) 325-1443

Circa 1795, this charming farmhouse nestled among many historic homes offers a romantic getaway. Surrounded by beautiful flower and herb gardens and filled with antiques and country charm. Alfred Hitchcock summered here. There is a pool, outdoor sauna, and two private guest cottages. The historic feeling of the old house has been maintained with original wood-burning fireplaces in two parlors with wide plank floors. A walk to Moriches Bay, a short drive to the ocean. The Hamptons, Montauk Point, numerous antique shops, old burial grounds, Gurney's Spa, and the Tanger Outlet Mall are some of the nearby attractions. Full breakfast is available.

Hosts: Barbara and Victor Genco
Rooms: 4 (PB) $95-165
Continental Breakfast
Credit Cards: None
Notes: 2, 3, 5, 6, 7, 8, 9, 11, 12

NOTES: Credit cards accepted: A MasterCard; B Visa; C American Express; D Discover; E Diners Club;
F Other; 2 Personal checks accepted; 3 Lunch available; 4 Dinner available; 5 Open all year; 6 Pets welcome;

All Tucked Inn

WESTPORT

All Tucked Inn

53 South Main Street, P.O. Box 324, 12993
(518) 962-4400

All Tucked Inn, on Lake Champlain in the historic hamlet of Westport, is a magical, whimsical place where troubles flee and peace presides. Within walking distance to shops, beaches, golf course, and a scenic drive to Adirondack Mountains hiking and skiing, this four-season inn offers lovely bedrooms, five with lakeview, three with fireplace. TV/VCR in fireplaced living room. For beauty, history, and serenity, guests owe it to themselves to discover All Tucked Inn.

Hosts: Claudia Ryan and Tom Haley
Rooms: 9 (PB) $55-95
Full Breakfast
Credit Cards: None
Notes: 2, 4, 5, 7, 9, 10, 11, 12, 13, 14

The Inn on the Library Lawn

1 Washington Street, 12993
(518) 962-8666

Restored 1875 Victorian inn overlooks Lake Champlain, nestled between the Green Mountains of Vermont and the Adirondack Mountains of New York. Walk to marina, beach, yacht club, 18-hole golf course and country club, summer concerts, and theater. Spacious rooms with private baths, air conditioning, and lake views. Full breakfast served on the outside deck or in the lakeview dining room. Local crafts and art featured. Browse the resident antique shop and art gallery or the other fine shops and visit historical sites in the area.

Hosts: Don and Susann Thompson
Rooms: 10 (PB) $70-99
Full Breakfast
Credit Cards: A, B, C
Notes: 2, 5, 7, 9, 10, 11, 12, 13

WEST TAGHKANIC

American Country Collection

1353 Union Street, Schenectady, 12054
(518) 439-7001; FAX (518) 439-4301

211. In what used to be a general store, now resides a special farmhouse bed and breakfast and antique shop. Each of the guest rooms has its own private bath and is air-conditioned. The living room has beautiful wide-board floors, a Victorian-era sofa, a TV/VCR, and is graciously furnished with antiques and a Persian rug. Smoking permitted outside. Children are welcome. No guest pets allowed. A delicious full American breakfast is served. $65-90.

WEST WINFIELD

Bed and Breakfast Leatherstocking

P.O. Box 53, Herkimer, 13350
(315) 733-0040; (800) 941-BEDS (2337)

023. Here is an antique and stencil-laden Victorian frame house with deep front porch, great for getaways. Gracious hospitality and service await guests in this beautifully furnished home, resplendent with craft items made on the premises. Near Bouckville, Hamilton, and Cooperstown.

7 No smoking; 8 Children welcome; 9 Social drinking allowed; 10 Tennis nearby; 11 Swimming nearby; 12 Golf nearby; 13 Skiing nearby; 14 May be booked through a travel agent.

Three bridal suites are available, each with its own private bath and Jacuzzi; central air conditioning, and color TV. Common rooms. A delicious full breakfast is served. $65-145.

WILLET

Woven Waters

6624 Route 41, Cincinnatus Lake, 13863
(607) 656-8672

A beautifully renovated 100-year-old barn on the shores of a lovely private lake in south central New York. The beautiful interior is accented with unique antiques and gorgeous imported laces. Relax in the large, comfortable living room with beamed cathedral ceiling and massive stone fireplace, or on one of the porches overlooking the lake (one porch is open, one is enclosed).

Hosts: Erika and John
Rooms: 4 (SB) $58
Full Breakfast
Credit Cards: A, B, D
Notes: 5, 9, 13, 14

WILSON

The International Bed and Breakfast Club, Inc.

504 Amherst Street, Buffalo, 14207
(800) 723-4262; FAX (716) 873-4462

NY6906PP. Enjoy spectacular Lake Ontario sunsets at this lakeside inn, in a casual countryside family-like atmosphere with friendly hosts. Four beautifully appointed rooms, some with private baths, along with a private sitting room exclusively for guests. Full breakfast served. Near Niagara Falls, Canada, and the Seaway Trail of New York State. $55-60.

WINDHAM (HENSONVILLE)

American Country Collection

1353 Union Street, Schenectady, 12054
(518) 439-7001; FAX (518) 439-4301

214. Nestled in the heart of New York's northern Catskill Mountains and just two minutes from Ski Windham, village shops, and restaurants sits this 110-year-old Victorian bed and breakfast with white clapboards and wraparound porch. Within is a dining room-common room with an unusual wainscoted ceiling, a wood stove, and either large table seating or a small table surrounded by an elegant window seat. Guests are invited to serve themselves coffee, fruit, and pastry and relax in the dining room before being served a full country breakfast. Guest "family area" with raised-hearth wood-burning fireplace, sofa, chairs, and cable TV. Four guest rooms, each with its own special accents and charm. Smoking permitted outside. Children welcome. One friendly dog in residence. $60-85.

WOLCOTT

The International Bed and Breakfast Club, Inc.

504 Amherst Street, Buffalo, 14207
(800) 723-4262; FAX (716) 873-4462

NY2273PP. The perfect setting to enjoy complete relaxation for vacationers, special occasions, or business travelers amidst expansive lawns and trees in a turn-of-the-century setting overlooking the east side of Great Sodus Bay. Accommodations in the main house include a suite overlooking the bay, large guest room with wainscoting and a cathedral ceiling. A charming caretaker's cottage with two large bedrooms, a living room, dining room, and full bath is also available. An additional guest house offers three additional rooms with queen-size beds and private baths. $65-110

WOODSTOCK

Bed by the Stream

9 George Sickle Road, Saugerties, 12477
(914) 246-2979

Five-acre farm on streamside property. In-ground pool. Breakfast served on sun porch overlooking stream. Seven miles from Woodstock, three miles from exit 20 on the New York Thruway. All rooms are air-conditioned. Hiking and biking nearby.

Hosts: Odette and Bill Reinhardt
Rooms: 3 (PB) $60-75
Full Breakfast
Credit Cards: None
Notes: 2, 5, 7, 8, 9, 10, 11, 12, 13

Mount Tremper Inn

Route 212 and Wittenberg Road
Box 51, Mount Tremper, 12457
(914) 688-5329

Victorian hospitality and elegant antiques await guests in this 23-room mansion built in 1850 in the Catskill Mountains. Large parlor with fireplace, library-game room, classical music at breakfast. Outdoor dining in season. Near Woodstock, all ski slopes, historic Kingston, and Rhinebeck. Limited smoking permitted.

Host: Lou Caselli
Rooms: 12 (2 PB; 10 SB) $65-98
Full Breakfast
Credit Cards: A, B
Notes: 5, 9, 10, 11, 12, 13

YOUNGSTOWN

The International Bed and Breakfast Club, Inc.

504 Amherst Street, Buffalo, 14207
(800) 723-4262; FAX (716) 873-4462

NY4085PP. Large, comfortable country home built in 1880 offers three charming guest rooms with double beds and shared bath. Continental breakfast served in the Wagner Dining Room or on the covered porch in season. Only minutes away: historic Fort Niagara, sailing and sport fishing on Lake Ontario, and the lower Niagara. Also convenient to Niagara Falls, the beautiful nature trails of the Niagara River Gorge, and the nearby bridges to Canada, Niagara on the Lake and the Shaw festival. Smoking not permitted in the house. Open year-round. $55.

NY7052PP. This country home inn features three rooms, two with double beds and one with a single, sharing one bath. Guests enjoy the player-piano and traditional Irish guitar music. A 5:00 A.M. breakfast for fishermen or for those attending mass at the world-famous Lady of Fatima Shrine, one mile away. Special breakfast for children; full breakfast served daily. Convenient to Niagara Falls, Lewiston, and Youngstown. Artpark, Lewiston Art Festival, Fort Niagara, and the fishing derby are among the nearby attractions. $40-60.

7 No smoking; 8 Children welcome; 9 Social drinking allowed; 10 Tennis nearby; 11 Swimming nearby; 12 Golf nearby; 13 Skiing nearby; 14 May be booked through a travel agent.

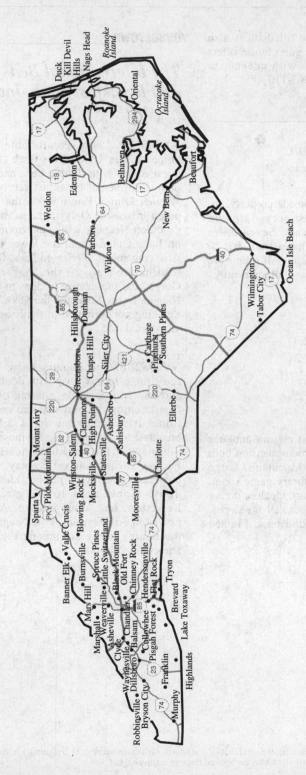

North Carolina

North Carolina

The Doctor's Inn

ASHEBORO

The Doctor's Inn

716 South Park Street, 27203
(910) 625-4916; (910) 625-4822

The Doctor's Inn is a home filled with antiques. It offers its guests the utmost in personal accommodations. Amenities include a gourmet breakfast served on fine china and silver, fresh flowers, terry-cloth robes and slippers, homemade "goodies," and a refrigerator stocked with soft drinks, juices, and ice cream parfaits. Nearby are 60 potteries and the North Carolina Zoo.

Hosts: Marion and Beth Griffin
Rooms: 2 (1 PB; 1 SB) $50-75
Full Breakfast
Credit Cards: None
Notes: 2, 5, 7, 9, 10, 12

ASHEVILLE

Acorn Cottage

25 Saint Dunstans Circle, 28803
(704) 253-0609; (800) 699-0609
FAX (704) 253-0866

An English country cottage in the heart of Asheville. The four guest rooms feature queen-size beds, fine linens, air conditioning, TVs, and private baths. Come relax in this 1925 architecturally designed home built of North Carolina granite, maple hardwood floors, and a beautiful stone fireplace. Acorn Cottage is in a natural woodland setting, yet in the heart of Asheville, only one-quarter mile from the Biltmore Estate.

Host: Connie Stahl
Rooms: 4 (PB) $80-95
Full Breakfast
Credit Cards: A, B, D
Notes: 2, 5, 7, 8, 9, 10, 11, 12, 13, 14

Albemarle Inn

86 Edgemont Road, 28801-1544
(704) 255-0027

Unmatched hospitality in a distinguished Greek Revival mansion with exquisite carved oak staircase, balcony, paneling, and high ceilings. In a beautiful residential area. On the National Register of Historic Places.

Albemarle Inn

NOTES: Credit cards: A MasterCard; B Visa; C American Express; D Discover; E Diners Club; F Other;
2 Personal checks accepted; 3 Lunch available; 4 Dinner available; 5 Open all year; 6 Pets welcome;
7 No smoking; 8 Children welcome; 9 Social drinking allowed; 10 Tennis nearby; 11 Swimming nearby;
12 Golf nearby; 13 Skiing nearby; 14 May be booked through a travel agent.

Eleven spacious and tastefully decorated guest rooms with TV, telephones, air conditioning, and private baths with claw-foot tubs and showers. Delicious breakfast served in the dining room and sun porch. Swimming pool. Children over 13 welcome.

Hosts: Dick and Kathy Hemes
Rooms: 11 (PB) $85-140
Full Breakfast
Credit Cards: A, B, D
Notes: 2, 5, 7, 9, 10, 11, 12, 14

Applewood Manor

Applewood Manor

62 Cumberland Circle, 28801
(704) 254-2244

A fine, turn-of-the-century Colonial Revival manor set on two acres of rolling lawn and woods in Asheville's historic Montford District. Within 15 minutes of the finest restaurants, antique shops, and area attractions, including the Biltmore Estate. Amenities include private baths, queen-size beds, fireplaces, balconies, full gourmet breakfasts, and afternoon tea. Bikes, badminton, croquet, and complimentary fitness club passes are available.

Hosts: Maryanne Young and Susan Poole
Rooms: 4 (PB) $90-135
Cottage: 1
Full Breakfast
Credit Cards: A, B
Notes: 2, 5, 7, 9, 10, 12, 14

Asheville Accommodations Reservations Service

P.O. Box 16936, 28816
(704) 251-9055; (800) 770-9055

A reservations service for bed and breakfasts and country inns in Asheville and throughout western North Carolina. The service is able to assist travelers wishing to visit the Biltmore Estate with comfortable accommodations at in-town sites. Many of the bed and breakfasts are in historic homes elegantly furnished with antiques. The service is also able to find lodging for those who want to explore the mountains of the region. Offering lakeside lodges or hilltop retreats close to the Blue Ridge Parkway. Also the service is able to arrange for activities including golf, tennis, boating, skiing, and horseback riding.

Rates: $45-195
Full Breakfast
Credit Cards: None
Notes: 2, 3, 4, 5, 7, 8, 9, 10, 11, 12, 13

Beaufort House Victorian Bed and Breakfast

61 North Liberty Street, 28801
(704) 254-8334

Built in 1894, Beaufort House stands today as an eloquent testimony to the gentle style of living prevalent at the turn of the century. Encompassing romance, history, and elegance, Beaufort House offers guests the comforts of modern luxuries such as central air conditioning, TVs, VCRs, telephones, Jacuzzis, fitness facility, and bicycles. The Beaufort House is listed on the National Register of Historic Places and was previously featured in *National Geographic Traveler* magazine.

Hosts: Robert and Jacqueline Glasgow
Rooms: 6 (PB) $85-195
Full Breakfast
Credit Cards: A, B
Notes: 2, 5, 7, 8, 9, 10, 11, 12, 13, 14

Cairn Brae

217 Patton Mountain Road, 28804
(704) 252-9219

Cairn Brae is in the mountains above Asheville. Very private, on three acres of woods, but only 12 minutes from downtown. Private guest entrance to living room with fireplace. Complimentary snacks on the terrace overlooking Beaverdam Valley. Beautiful views. Woodsy trails. Quiet and secluded. Closed December through March. Children over ten welcome.

Hosts: Milli and Ed Adams
Rooms: 3 (PB) $90-105
Full Breakfast
Credit Cards: A, B, D
Notes: 2, 7, 9, 10, 11, 12, 14

Carolina Bed and Breakfast

177 Cumberland Avenue, 28801
(704) 254-3608

Comfortable turn-of-the-century home on an acre of beautiful gardens in the historic Montford district. Charming guest rooms, four with fireplaces, have antiques and collectibles, as well as private baths. Convenient to downtown shopping, galleries, restaurants, and the Biltmore Estate. A quiet, relaxing getaway in the heart of the city. Limited smoking permitted. Children over 12 welcome.

Hosts: Sam and Karin Fain
Rooms: 5 (PB) $80-90
Full Breakfast
Credit Cards: A, B, D
Notes: 2, 5, 9, 10, 12, 14

Cedar Crest Victorian Inn

674 Biltmore Avenue, 28803
(704) 252-1389

An 1890 Queen Anne mansion listed on the National Register of Historic Places. Features carved oak paneling, ornate glasswork, authentic Victorian decor with period antiques, and romantic guest rooms. Croquet court, fireplaces, and English gardens. One-quarter mile from the entrance to the Biltmore Estate and four miles from the Blue Ridge Parkway. Children over 12 welcome.

Hosts: Jack and Barbara McEwan
Rooms: 9 (PB) $115-150
Suites: 2
Continental Breakfast
Credit Cards: A, B, C, D, E
Notes: 2, 5, 7, 9, 10, 12, 14

The Colby House

230 Pearson Drive, 28801
(704) 253-5644; (800) 982-2118

This elegant and charming Dutch-Tudor house in the Montford historic district is known as "a special place." There are beautiful gardens, an outdoor porch, and inviting fireplaces. The home has four guest rooms, each with individual decor, queen-size beds, and private baths. A full breakfast is varied daily. Southern hospitality abounds in the hosts' personal attention to every guest's needs.

Hosts: Everett and Ann Colby
Rooms: 4 (PB) $80-110
Full Breakfast
Credit Cards: A, B, C
Notes: 2, 7, 9, 10, 11, 12, 13

Corner Oak Manor

53 Saint Dunstans Road, 28803
(704) 253-3525

This lovely English Tudor home is just minutes away from the famed Biltmore Estate and Gardens. Antiques, handmade wreaths, weavings, and stitchery complement the restored elegance of this home. Breakfast specialties include orange French toast, blueberry-ricotta pancakes, or four-cheese herb quiche. A living room

Corner Oak Manor

---

7 No smoking; 8 Children welcome; 9 Social drinking allowed; 10 Tennis nearby; 11 Swimming nearby; 12 Golf nearby; 13 Skiing nearby; 14 May be booked through a travel agent.

with fireplace and baby grand piano, and outdoor deck with Jacuzzi are among the gracious amenities.

Hosts: Karen and Andy Spradley
Rooms: 4 (PB) $90-140
Full Breakfast
Credit Cards: A, B, C, D
Notes: 2, 3, 5, 7, 9, 10, 11, 12

Flint Street Inns

100 and 116 Flint Street, 28801
(704) 253-6723

Two lovely old homes on an acre lot with century-old trees. Comfortable walking distance to town. Guest rooms, furnished with antiques and collectibles, have air conditioning, and some have fireplaces. The inns provide complimentary beverages and restaurant menus. Breakfast is full Southern-style, featuring home-baked breads and iron-skillet biscuits. Smoking in designated areas only.

Hosts: Rick, Lynne, and Marion Vogel
Rooms: 8 (PB) $90
Full Breakfast
Credit Cards: A, B, C, D
Notes: 2, 5, 9, 12, 14

The Inn on Montford

296 Montford Avenue, 28801
(704) 254-9569

A turn-of-the-century Arts and Crafts home by Asheville's most famous architect. Filled with light, it is a perfect setting for the owners' fine collection of antiques, porcelains, and Oriental rugs. Fireplaces in all rooms, whirlpools in several, a wide front porch, boxwood garden with an arbor behind the house. The inn is in the Montford historic district, close to downtown and a ten-minute drive from the Biltmore Estate.

Hosts: Alexa Royden and Lynn Royden
Rooms: 4 (PB) $100-130
Full Breakfast
Credit Cards: A, B, C, D
Notes: 2, 5, 7, 10, 12, 13, 14

Mountain Springs Cabins/Chalets

P.O. Box 2, Candler, 28715
(704) 665-1004

Rustic yet modern country cabins/chalets situated on 30 unspoiled, landscaped acres overlooking mountain stream–near Blue Ridge Parkway and famous Biltmore Estate. All cabins have fireplaces, grills, rockers, and swings on porches. They are furnished with antiques, oil lamps, and lace curtains. Flowers bloom in window boxes. Guests can relax in a hammock, hike or picnic in the woods, go fishing or tubing in the stream, or take a short drive up into the clouds and dine at a mountaintop inn. Waterfalls, horseback riding, and balloon rides nearby. Three-diamond AAA rating. Come and refresh your spirit. There is magic at Mountain Springs! Inquire about children being welcome.

Hosts: Sara and John Peltier
Rooms: 12 (PB) $80-125
Credit Cards: A, B
Notes: 5, 9, 10, 11, 12, 13

The Old Reynolds Mansion

The Old Reynolds Mansion

100 Reynolds Heights, 28804
(704) 254-0496

Bed and breakfast in an antebellum mansion listed on the National Register of Historic Places. Beautifully restored with furnishings from a bygone era. Country setting with acres of trees and mountain views from all rooms. Wood-burning fireplaces, two-story verandas, and pool. Two-night minimum weekends and holidays. Open weekends only January through March.

Hosts: Fred and Helen Faber
Rooms: 10 (8 PB; 2 SB) $55-100
Cottage: $120
Continental Breakfast
Credit Cards: None
Notes: 2, 5, 9, 10, 11, 12, 13

Reed House

119 Dodge Street, 28803
(704) 274-1604

Come stay in this comfortable Victorian home built in 1892. Near Biltmore Estate. Breakfast, featuring homemade low-sodium muffins, is served on the wraparound porch. Relaxing rocking chairs everywhere. Furnished in period decor. On the National Register of Historic Places and a local historic property. Closed November 1 through May 1.

Host: Marge Turcot
Rooms: 3 (1 PB; 2 SB) $50-70
Cottage: $95
Continental Breakfast
Credit Cards: A, B
Notes: 2, 8, 9, 10, 11, 12

Richmond Hill Inn

87 Richmond Hill Drive, 28806
(800) 545-9238; FAX (704) 252-8726

Historic Victorian mansion built in 1889 overlooking the Blue Ridge Mountains and the Asheville skyline. Listed on the National Register of Historic Places.

Richmond Hill Inn

Magnificently restored mansion elegantly furnished with antiques, this AAA four-diamond inn features 36 guest rooms, all with private bath and many with a fireplace. Fine dining in the AAA four-diamond gourmet restaurant with mountain view. Croquet lawn and extensive library. Close to the Blue Ridge Parkway and Biltmore Estate.

Host: Susan Michel
Rooms: 36 (PB) $130-350
Full Breakfast
Credit Cards: A, B, C
Notes: 2, 3, 4, 5, 7, 8, 9, 14

The Wright Inn and Carriage House

235 Pearson Drive, 28801
(704) 251-0789; (800) 552-5724
FAX (704) 251-0929

The Wright Inn and Carriage House, circa 1899-1900, is on the National Register of Historic Places. Guests may choose from eight sleeping rooms and a suite, all with central air conditioning, private baths, cable TVs, and telephones. The Coleman parlor has period furniture and handmade oak trim. Afternoon tea and cookies served in the gazebo or in front of an inviting fire in the Willows drawing room. A scrumptious full breakfast is served in the formal dining room or in the gazebo for inn guests only. Inquire about bringing children.

Hosts: Carol and Art Wenczel
Rooms: 8 (PB) $80-95
Suite: 1 (PB) $110
Carriage House: 3 (S2B) $175
Full Breakfast
Credit Cards: A, B
Notes: 2, 5, 7, 9, 10, 11, 12

BALSAM

Balsam Lodge Bed and Breakfast

Valley Road, Box 279, 28707
(704) 456-6528; (800) 699-6528

The Balsam Lodge has four efficiency units housed in a renovated 1908 train depot. The

---

7 No smoking; 8 Children welcome; 9 Social drinking allowed; 10 Tennis nearby; 11 Swimming nearby; 12 Golf nearby; 13 Skiing nearby; 14 May be booked through a travel agent.

Depot is the original structure used by the Southern Railway during the earliest years in Balsam. It was moved to its current location in 1959. From the porch you can enjoy a breathtaking view of the Balsam Mountains. Enjoy the many nearby attractions and activities or simply relax. Full breakfast is served each morning in the main house. Open year-round.

Host: Marti S. Shaver
Rooms: 4 (PB) $60
Full Breakfast
Credit Cards: A, B, C, D
Notes: 2, 3, 5, 6, 7, 8, 9, 10, 11, 12, 13, 14

Balsam Mountain Inn

P.O. Box 40, 28707
(704) 456-9498

Nestled among lofty peaks in the Great Smoky Mountains and just off the Blue Ridge Parkway, this historic inn was built in 1908 to serve the highest railroad depot in the east. The inn was restored in 1991, and now offers 34 cheerful rooms, two 100-foot porches with rockers and a view, a 2,000-volume library, and gracious dining. Plump pillows and soft comforters inspire pleasant dreams! Hiking, biking, relaxing, rafting, rail excursions, and shopping abound. Lunch is available June–October. Box lunches all year. Inquire about the age of children welcome.

Host: Merrily Teasley
Rooms: 34 (PB) $88-150
Full Breakfast
Credit Cards: A, B, D
Notes: 2, 3, 4, 5, 9, 10, 11, 12, 13, 14

BANNER ELK

Archers Mountain Inn

Route 2, Box 56 A, 28604
(704) 898-9004

Archers Mountain Inn is nestled on Beech Mountain at nearly 5,000 feet above sea level among evergreens, beechs, and flowers. Archers Mountain Inn plays backyard to two of the highest ski slopes in the eastern United States. Guests are treated to breathtaking views of Sugar and Grandfather Mountains while enjoying a congenial atmosphere unparalleled in mountain retreats costing twice as much. Each day begins with crystal clean mountain air and a hearty country breakfast served up by the innkeepers. Activities abound for each season, and at the end of the day guests can relax in front of their private fireplace watching the color fade softly in the sky as the lights of the Elk River Valley twinkle below. Archers is a cozy grouping of three beamed-ceiling structures. Every room features private bath, fireplace, and one with Jacuzzi.

Hosts: Candi and Tony Catoe
Rooms: 14 (PB) $60-125
Full Breakfast
Credit Cards: A, B, D
Notes: 2, 4, 5, 7, 8, 9, 10, 11, 12, 13, 14

The Banner Elk Inn Bed and Breakfast

Highway 194 North (Main Street), Route 3, Box 1134, 28604
(704) 898-6223

The Banner Elk Inn Bed and Breakfast is a charmingly restored cozy little inn in town, population approximately 800, close to fine restaurants and the major attractions of Grandfather Mountains, Valle Crucis, Sugar and Beech Mountain ski resorts, and the nearby towns of Boone and Blowing Rock.

The Banner Elk Inn

There are four guest rooms, two with private large baths and two sharing baths for a four-person suite. Furnished with antiques and paintings collected from around the world. There is a wonderful great room, cable TV, stereo, and fireplace with a long walnut breakfast table set elegantly with fine china. Gourmet full breakfasts. English garden overlooking a restored splashing fountain. Inquire about accommodations for pets. Children over five welcome.

Host: Beverly Lait
Rooms: 4 (2 PB; 2 SB) $75-100
Full Breakfast
Credit Cards: A, B
Notes: 2, 7, 9, 10, 12, 13, 14

Rainbow Inn

317 Old Turnpike Road, 28604
(704) 898-5611

The beautiful Blue Ridge Mountains set the scene for the Rainbow Inn's picturesque setting at the base of ever-popular Beech Mountain with neighboring Sugar and Grandfather Mountains close by. Beneath the red tin roof of this wonderful 110-year-old truly American farmhouse lives the warmth of braided rugs, authentic antique furniture, patchwork quilts, wicker baskets, home-canned goods, roaring fires. Guests will enjoy all the comforts they love to come home to. Open year-round.

Hosts: Tammy and Steve Rondinaro
Rooms: 4 (2 PB; 2 SB) $65-90
Full Breakfast
Credit Cards: A, B
Notes: 2, 5, 7, 9, 10, 11, 12, 13, 14

BEAUFORT

The Cedars Inn

305 Front Street, 28516
(919) 728-7036; (800) 732-7036

This recently restored 18th-century inn offers 14 elegantly appointed rooms with private baths and fireplaces. The dining room offers the finest breakfasts on the Carolina coast. Daily tours of historic Beaufort and the Outer Banks are available in season. Special weekly rate for Sunday night through Friday morning, including breakfast. Minimum stay on in-season weekends is two nights; holidays is three nights.

Rooms: 14 (PB) $85-175
Full Breakfast
Credit Cards: A, B
Notes: 2, 5, 7, 9, 11, 12, 14

Delamar Inn

Delamar Inn

217 Turner Street, 28516
(919) 728-4300

Enjoy the Scottish hospitality of this Civil War home in the heart of Beaufort's historic district. The inn offers three guest rooms with antique furnishings and private bath. After a delightful breakfast, enjoy a stroll to the waterfront, specialty shops, or historic sites. Borrow the hosts' bicycles or beach chairs, and upon return, guests will find soft drinks, cookies, and a smile waiting. The hosts are pleased to have been selected for Beaufort's 1991–95 historic homes tour.

Hosts: Mabel and Tom Steepy
Rooms: 3 (PB) $58-88
Continental Breakfast
Credit Cards: A, B
Notes: 2, 5, 7, 12, 14

7 No smoking; 8 Children welcome; 9 Social drinking allowed; 10 Tennis nearby; 11 Swimming nearby; 12 Golf nearby; 13 Skiing nearby; 14 May be booked through a travel agent.

Pecan Tree Inn

116 Queen Street, 28516
(919) 728-6733

A gracious 1866 Victorian home filled with antiques, one-half block from the waterfront in Beaufort's historic district. Relax on one of the three porches or stroll through the large English garden. There are seven air-conditioned rooms, all with private baths. The bridal suite features a Jacuzzi tub for two and a king-size canopied bed. Guests will enjoy the delicious breakfast with freshly baked homemade muffins, breakfast cakes, and breads, along with a choice of fruit, cereal, and beverages for breakfast. Only a few blocks from wonderful restaurants and quaint shops.

Hosts: Susan and Joe Johnson
Rooms: 7 (PB) $65-120
Continental Breakfast
Credit Cards: A, B, D
Notes: 2, 5, 7, 9, 10, 11, 12, 14

BELHAVEN

River Forest Manor and Marina

600 East Main Street, 27810
(919) 943-2151; (800) 346-2151

River Forest Manor is an ornately decorated Victorian mansion with all private baths. The inn is appropriately furnished with period furniture. Other amenities include a delicious Continental breakfast, tennis court, swimming pool, hot tub Jacuzzi, bar lounge, and marina. A buffet dinner each night includes Southern-style cooking from oyster fritters and seafood casserole to homemade lemon pie. Lunch is available on Sundays.

Hosts: Melba G. Smith and Ayson Smith
Rooms: 9 (PB) $50-85
Continental Breakfast
Credit Cards: A, B
Notes: 4, 5, 9, 10, 11, 12

BLACK MOUNTAIN

Black Mountain Inn

718 West Old Highway 70, 28711
(704) 669-6528

Discover a peaceful retreat for body and soul. Built 150 years ago, this lovingly restored inn is cloaked in a long and colorful history. Once a studio and haven for artists, this small and intimate inn embraces its guests with long-forgotten hospitality and charm. There are seven comfortable guest rooms, each with private bath and decorated with casual country decor.

Host: June Bergern Colbert
Rooms: 7 (PB) $65-75
Full Breakfast
Credit Cards: C
Notes: 2, 7, 9, 10, 11, 12, 14

BLOWING ROCK

Maple Lodge

Box 1236, Sunset Drive, 28605
(704) 295-3331

Elegant furnishings reflect the simplicity and charm of an earlier time. Guest rooms, filled with antiques, goosedown comforters, lace, and handmade quilts, have private baths, and king- or queen-size beds; some are canopied. A short stroll to craft shops, art galleries, professional summer theater, and fine restaurants. Grandfather Mountain, Linville Falls, the Blue Ridge Parkway, hiking, golf, and white-water rafting nearby.

Hosts: Marilyn and David Bateman
Rooms: 9 (PB) $65-111
Full Breakfast
Credit Cards: A, B, D
Notes: 2, 5, 7, 9, 10, 11, 12, 13, 14

BREVARD

The Inn at Brevard

410 East Main Street, 28712
(704) 884-2105

NOTES: Credit cards accepted: A MasterCard; B Visa; C American Express; D Discover; E Diners Club; F Other; 2 Personal checks accepted; 3 Lunch available; 4 Dinner available; 5 Open all year; 6 Pets welcome;

Listed on the National Register of Historic Places, this inn hosted a reunion dinner for Stonewall Jackson's troops in 1911. Beautifully restored in 1984 with a European flavor throughout. Just a few minutes from Brevard Music Center, Blue Ridge Parkway, and Pisgah National Forest. Dinner is available on Friday, Saturday, and Sunday. Inquire ahead about the age of children welcome. Smoking is restricted.

Hosts: Eileen and Bertrand Bourget
Rooms: 15 (14 PB; 1 SB) $69-125
Full Breakfast
Credit Cards: A, B
Notes: 2, 9, 10, 11, 12

The Red House Inn

412 West Probart Street, 28712
(704) 884-9349

The Red House was built in 1851 in the Blue Ridge Mountains and has been lovingly restored and beautifully furnished in gorgeous turn-of-the-century period antiques. Enjoy the wonderful Brevard Music Center performances every night during the summer and breathtaking mountain colors in the fall. Come sit and relax on the porch. Closed November 30 through April 1.

Hosts: Lynne Ong and Mary MacGillycuddy
Rooms: 6 (PB and SB) $45-79
Full Breakfast
Credit Cards: A, B
Notes: 2, 7, 9, 10, 11, 12, 14

Womble Inn

301 West Main, P.O. Box 1441, 28712
(704) 884-4770

Two blocks from the center of Brevard, the Womble Inn invites guests to relax in a welcoming, comfortable atmosphere. Each of the six guest rooms is especially furnished in antiques. All of the guest rooms have private baths and air conditioning. After a sound sleep, guests will be served breakfast on a silver tray, or guests may prefer to be seated in the dining room. Full breakfast is an option.

Hosts: Steve and Beth Womble
Rooms: 6 (PB) $48-58
Continental Breakfast
Credit Cards: A, B
Notes: 2, 5, 8, 9, 10, 11, 12

BRYSON CITY

Fryemont Inn

P.O. Box 459, 28713
(704) 488-2159; (800) 845-4879

This inn overlooks the Great Smoky Mountains National Park. All rooms have private bath. Dinner and breakfast are included in the daily rate, and the inn is on the National Register of Historic Places. Featured in *Bon Appétit*. Guest rooms closed November through mid-April. Cottage suites open year-round. Smoking restricted.

Hosts: Sue and George Brown
Rooms: 39 (PB) $67-169
Full Breakfast
Credit Cards: A, B, D
Notes: 2, 3, 4, 5, 8, 9, 10, 11, 12

BURNSVILLE

Hamrick Inn
Bed and Breakfast

7787 Highway 80 South, 28714
(704) 675-5251

This charming three-story Colonial-style stone inn is nestled at the foot of Mount

Hamrick Inn

7 No smoking; 8 Children welcome; 9 Social drinking allowed; 10 Tennis nearby; 11 Swimming nearby; 12 Golf nearby; 13 Skiing nearby; 14 May be booked through a travel agent.

Mitchell, highest mountain east of the Mississippi. Much of the lovely furniture was built by the hosts. There is a private porch off each guest room, where the view and cool mountain breezes may be enjoyed. Golf, hiking, fishing, rock hounding, and craft shopping are local activities. Near the Blue Ridge Parkway. Open April 1 through October 31.

Hosts: Neal and June Jerome
Rooms: 4 (PB) $60-70
Full Breakfast
Credit Cards: A, B
Notes: 2, 8, 10, 11, 12, 13

Nu-Wray Inn

Town Square, P.O. Box 156, 28714
(704) 682-2329; (800) 3NUWRAY

This historic country inn was built in 1833. Nestled in the Blue Ridge Mountains in a quaint town square setting. Thirty miles northeast of Asheville. Close to Blue Ridge Parkway, Mount Mitchell, Grandfather Mountain, golf, antiques, crafts, hiking, fishing, or just relax on the porch. Room rates include hearty country sideboard breakfast and afternoon refreshments. Famous family-style dinners.

Hosts: Chris and Pam Strickland
Rooms: 26 (PB) $70-110
Full Breakfast
Credit Cards: A, B, C
Notes: 2, 4, 5, 7, 8, 10, 11, 12, 13, 14

CANDLER

Owl's Nest Inn at Engadine

2630 Smoky Park Highway, 28715
(704) 665-8325; (800) 665-8868
FAX (704) 667-2539

In the mountains on more than four acres just outside of Asheville, Owl's Nest Inn was built in 1885 and has been restored and decorated to maintain its Victorian character. There are wraparound porches and benches in the meadow to enjoy the breathtaking mountain views. Full breakfast is

served by the fireplace in the formal paneled dining room. All of the guest rooms are spacious, air-conditioned, and have private baths.

Hosts: Mary and Jim Melaugh
Rooms: 4 (PB) $90-120
Full Breakfast
Credit Cards: A, B
Notes: 2, 5, 7, 9, 12, 13, 14

CARTHAGE

The Blacksmith Inn

703 McReynolds Street, P.O. Box 1480, 28327
(910) 947-1692; (800) 284-4515

This beautiful example of 1870 Southern architecture has been lovingly restored and is the former home of the blacksmith for the Tyson and Jones Buggy Factory. Four spacious, tastefully decorated rooms are available, with a fireplace in each room. Just 12 minutes from Pinehurst (the golf capital of the world), 20 minutes from Seagrove (the pottery center of North Carolina), and Cameron and Aberdeen's antique shops and historic districts. On the National Register of Historic Places. No smoking inside.

Hosts: Gary and Shawna Smith
Rooms: 4 (2 PB; 2 SB) $50
Full Breakfast
Credit Cards: None
Notes: 2, 5, 8, 12, 14

CHAPEL HILL

The Fearrington House Inn

2000 Fearrington Village Center, Pittsboro, 27312
(919) 542-2121

In a cluster of low, attractive buildings grouped around a courtyard and surrounded by gardens and rolling countryside, this elegant inn offers luxurious quarters in a country setting. A member of Relais et Châteaux. The restaurant's sophisticated regional cuisine prepared in the classical techniques has received national acclaim, including AAA's five-diamond award.

Hosts: Jenny and R. B. Fitch
Rooms: 24 (PB) $150-275
Full Breakfast
Credit Cards: A, B, C
Notes: 2, 3, 4, 5, 9, 10, 11, 12, 14

The Inn at Bingham School

P.O. Box 267, 27514
(919) 563-5583; (800) 566-5583
FAX (919) 563-9826

The Inn is an award-winning restoration of a National Trust Property. A unique combination of Greek Revival and Federal styles. Listed in the historic registry. Stroll the surrounding woodlands or curl up by the fire. Welcome the day over an elaborate Southern breakfast. Just 11 miles west of Chapel Hill, which offers a charming combination of peace and history close to gourmet dining, shopping, and UNC. Dinner available with three-day notice.

Hosts: François and Christina Deprez
Rooms: 5 (PB) $75-110
Full Breakfast
Credit Cards: A, B, C
Notes: 2, 5, 7, 8, 9, 10, 12, 14

The Inn at Bingham School

CHARLOTTE

The Elizabeth Bed and Breakfast

2145 East Fifth Street, 28204
(704) 358-1368

This 1927 lavender "lady" is in historic Elizabeth, Charlotte's second-oldest neighborhood. European country-style rooms are beautifully appointed with antiques, ceiling fans, decorator linens, and unique collections. A guest cottage offers a private retreat in elegant Southwestern style. All rooms have central air and private baths; some have television and telephones. Enjoy a generous breakfast, then relax in the garden courtyard, complete with charming gazebo, or stroll beneath giant oaks trees to convenient restaurants and shopping.

Host: Joan Mastny
Rooms: 3 (PB) $58-88
Cottage: 1 (PB)
Continental and Full Breakfast
Credit Cards: A, B
Notes: 2, 5, 7, 9, 11, 14

The Homeplace

5901 Sardis Road, 28270
(704) 365-1936

Restored 1902 Country Victorian with wraparound porch and tin roof, nestled amid two and one-half wooded acres. Secluded "cottage-style" gardens with a gazebo, brick walkways, and a 1930s log barn further enhance this nostalgic oasis in southeast Charlotte. Experienced innkeepers offer three guest rooms, a full breakfast, and a Victorian garden room for small meetings and special occasions. Opened in 1984, the Homeplace is "a reflection of the true bed and breakfast experience." Children over 12 welcome.

Hosts: Peggy and Frank Dearien
Rooms: 3 (2 PB; 1 SB) $98
Suite: 1 (PB) $115
Full Breakfast
Credit Cards: A, B, C
Notes: 2, 5, 7, 14

7 No smoking; 8 Children welcome; 9 Social drinking allowed; 10 Tennis nearby; 11 Swimming nearby; 12 Golf nearby; 13 Skiing nearby; 14 May be booked through a travel agent.

The Inn Uptown

The Inn Uptown

129 North Poplar Street, 28202
(704) 342-2800; (800) 959-1990

Constructed in 1890 and historically listed as
the Bagley-Mullen House, this chateau-esque
home has been restored into "an elegant alternative in uptown hospitality." Convenient for
both corporate and leisure travelers. Each of
the six beautifully appointed rooms features a
private bath, complimentary wine, remote
control cable TV, telephone, and nightly turndown service. A complimentary full breakfast
features specialties from the inn's kitchen and
is served in the dining room. Approved for
three-diamond AAA rating. Corporate rates
are available.

Host: Elizabeth J. Rich
Rooms: 6 (PB) $89-149
Full Breakfast
Credit Cards: A, B, C, D, E
Notes: 2, 5, 9, 14

McElhinney House

10533 Fairway Ridge Road, 28277
(704) 846-0783 (phone and FAX)

In a quiet area of southeast Charlotte, close
to I-77, I-85, and the new Charlotte outer-
belt. Six golf courses, including PiperGlen
and Charlotte Golf Links, are just minutes
away. Close to many Charlotte attractions
and northern South Carolina. The host
speaks French, Italian, and German.

Lounge area, TV, hot tub, and telephone
are all available for guests' use.

Hosts: Mary and Jim McElhinney
Rooms: 2 (PB) $55-65
Continental Breakfast
Credit Cards: A, B
Notes: 2, 5, 8, 9, 12

Still Waters

6221 Amos Smith Road, 28214
(704) 399-6299

A log resort home on two wooded acres
overlooking the Catawba River at the upper
end of Lake Wylie; within 15 minutes of
downtown Charlotte. Full breakfast is
served on glassed-in porch overlooking the
lake. Enjoy the sportcourt, the garden,
swimming, boating, fishing, or sitting in
the lakeside gazebo. Convenient to I-85,
airport, and Billy Graham Parkway.

Hosts: Janet and Rob Dyer
Rooms: 3 (PB) $55-85
Full Breakfast
Credit Cards: A, B, E
Notes: 2, 5, 7, 8, 9, 10, 11, 12, 14

CHIMNEY ROCK

Esmeralda Inn and Restaurant

P.O. Box 57, Highway 74A, 28720
(704) 625-9105

Built in 1890, this three-story inn is surrounded by tall trees and within sight of the
Chimney Rock Park. A great getaway, just
22 miles from Asheville. Come relax or
dine on the open-air porches or in the dining room. Dinner served nightly; lunch is
available six days a week. Thirteen bedrooms are available. Open mid-March to
mid-December. Smoking in designated
area only.

Hosts: Ackie and Joanne Okpych
Rooms: 13 (7 PB; 6 SB) $45-70
Continental Breakfast
Credit Cards: A, B, C, D
Notes : 3, 4, 8, 9, 10, 11, 12

NOTES: Credit cards accepted: A MasterCard; B Visa; C American Express; D Discover; E Diners Club;
F Other; 2 Personal checks accepted; 3 Lunch available; 4 Dinner available; 5 Open all year; 6 Pets welcome;

CHIMNEY ROCK VILLAGE

The Dogwood Inn

P.O. Box 159, Highway 64-74, 28720
(704) 625-4403

A charming, white, two-story European-style bed and breakfast. Come enjoy the five porches that grace this wonderful early 1900s inn on the banks of the peaceful Rocky Broad River. Massive Chimney Rock Mountain can be seen from any of the porches. A full buffet breakfast is served each morning. Children over 12 are welcome. Come rest a while. The river is calling.

Hosts: Marsha and Mark Reynolds
Rooms: 10 (6 PB; 4 SB) $70-90
Full Breakfast
Credit Cards: A, B, C, D
Notes: 2, 9, 10, 11, 12, 14

CLEMMONS

Tanglewood Manor House Bed and Breakfast Inn

Highway 158 West, 27012
(910) 766-0591; FAX (910) 766-1571

Renovated to reflect the traditional style of its former proprietors, William Neal and Kate B. Reynolds, the Tanglewood Manor House Bed and Breakfast Inn exudes Southern hospitality and charm. Surrounded by over 1300 acres of lush forest, landscaped grounds, award-winning rose gardens, and first-class recreational facilities, guests will feel they have stepped back in time to an area of gentility the South is famous for. Tanglewood Manor House is directly off Interstate 40 just 12 miles west of Winston-Salem.

Host: Angela Schultz (Accommodations Manager)
Rooms: 10 (PB) $77-107
Continental Breakfast
Credit Cards: A, B, C, E
Notes: 2, 5, 8, 9, 10, 11, 12, 14

CLYDE

Mountain Sunset Inn

10 Mountain Sunset Drive, 28721
(704) 627-1400

Situated on 15 mountaintop acres at an elevation of 4,765 feet in the Blue Ridge Mountains. A contemporary lapboard country inn with stone fireplace, patio, large wraparound porch, beautiful walking trails on the property, and a hearty country breakfast served in an atmosphere of country splendor. A secluded inn thoughtfully decorated for your comfort and pleasure with magnificent view of the mountains from every room.

Hosts: Jo Ann and Ralph Johnson
Rooms: 3 (PB) $90
Full Breakfast
Credit Cards: None
Notes: 2, 5, 7, 9, 10, 11, 12, 13

Windsong: A Mountain Inn

120 Ferguson Ridge, 28721
(704) 627-6111

Enjoy a secluded, romantic interlude at this contemporary log inn high in the breathtaking Smoky Mountains. Though the inn is small and intimate, the rooms are large

Windsong

---

7 No smoking; 8 Children welcome; 9 Social drinking allowed; 10 Tennis nearby; 11 Swimming nearby;
12 Golf nearby; 13 Skiing nearby; 14 May be booked through a travel agent.

and bright, with high-beamed ceilings, pine log walls, and Mexican tile floors. Each room has a fireplace, oversize tub, separate shower, and private deck or patio. Guest lounge with billiards and wet bar. Full breakfast included. On 25 acres, with pool, tennis, hiking, and lovable llamas. Newly added is the Pond House, a separate two-bedroom log guest house with full kitchen. Near Maggie Valley. Llama trekking in national forest available. Open year-round.

Hosts: Donna and Gale Livengood
Rooms: 5 (PB) $90-130
Full Breakfast
Credit Cards: A, B, D
Notes: 2, 5, 7, 9, 10, 11, 12, 14

CULLOWHEE

Cullowhee Bed and Breakfast

150 Ledbetter Road, 28723
(704) 293-5447

On a hillside among pines, oaks, and maples, this bed and breakfast offers the relaxing atmosphere of an immaculate country home and a beautiful view of the mountains. All bedrooms are comfortably furnished with queen- or king-size beds. Three bedrooms have private porch. The coffee pot starts at dawn for early risers, and a special treat awaits at breakfast with full country fare and hot muffins.

Hosts: Charles and Janet Moore
Rooms: 4 (PB) $55-65
Full Breakfast
Credit Cards: None
Notes: 2, 5, 7, 12, 13

DILLSBORO

Applegate Inn

163 Hemlock Street, P.O. Box 567, 28725
(704) 586-2397

The gateway to country charm, relaxation, and Southern hospitality at its best. In the village of Dillsboro, Applegate is on Scott's

Creek, a footbridge from the Great Smoky Mountain Railway Depot and Dillsboro's 50 unique shops. Within a few miles drive of western North Carolina's many attractions. A quaint country home, families and seniors appreciate the easy access in this one-level establishment. Private baths and queen-size beds. Full country breakfasts include apple pancakes, one of the inn's many specialties.

Hosts: Judy and Emil Milkey
Rooms: 6 (5 PB; 1 SB) $55-75
Full Breakfast
Credit Cards: A, B, D
Notes: 2, 5, 7, 8, 9, 14

Olde Towne Inn Bed and Breakfast

300 Haywood Road, P.O. Box 485, 28725-0485
(704) 586-3461

Enjoy mountain views and breezes while rocking on the front porch of this 1878 home in Dillsboro, the "town of magic." Walk to all gift shops, galleries, restaurants, and the Great Smoky Mountains Railroad excursions. Go hiking, rafting, tubing, fishing, panning for rubies and gold, or visit Cherokee Indian Reservation. Three guest rooms upstairs with air conditioning, ceiling fans, and decorated in country decor with antiques. Children over ten welcome.

Hosts: Gretchen and Dave Dilks
Rooms: 3 (PB) 60-75
Full Breakfast
Credit Cards: A, B
Notes: 2, 5, 7, 11, 12, 13

DUCK

Advice 5¢: A Bed and Breakfast

111 Scarborough Lane, P.O. Box 8278, 27949
(919) 255-1050; (800) ADVICE5 (238-4235)

Advice 5¢ is a casual place, the kind the ocean invites. In the heart of Duck on the Outer Banks, just a short walk from Duck's shops and restaurants. All guest rooms have private decks to enjoy the view. The suite includes a sitting area, cable television, and a Jacuzzi-style bathtub. Outdoor showers, beach chairs, beach towels, and afternoon tea provided. Seasonal rates available.

Hosts: Nancy Caviness and Donna Black
Rooms: 5 (PB) $110-140
Continental Breakfast
Credit Cards: A, B
Notes: 2, 5, 7, 9, 10, 11, 12

The Sanderling Inn Resort

1461 Duck Road, 27949
(919) 261-4111; (800) 701-4111

Year-round oceanfront resort (1985) only five miles from town—all rooms with bath, color cable TV, and private porch. Some with kitchen, wet bar, and refrigerator. Wheelchair accessible. Restaurant and bar and meeting rooms for 100 people. Health club with sauna, pools, hot tub, and tennis courts. Private beach. Nonsmoking rooms, massage therapy, private conference center, and off-season packages available.

Manager: Christine Berger
Rooms: 88 (PB) $110-350
Continental Breakfast
Credit Cards: A, B, C, D
Notes: 2, 3, 4, 5, 8, 9, 10, 11, 12, 14

DURHAM

Arrowhead Inn

106 Mason Road, 27712
(919) 477-8430; (800) 528-2207

Arrowhead Inn

This restored 1775 manor house on four rural acres offers homey hospitality in an atmosphere that evokes Colonial Carolina. But along with 18th-century architecture, decor, and furnishings, the inn features contemporary comfort, sparkling housekeeping, and bounteous home-cooked breakfasts. Open year-round. Mentioned in *Food and Wine*, *USA Today*, and many metro newspapers. Celebrating 11 years in business.

Hosts: Jerry, Barbara, and Cathy Ryan
Rooms: 8 (6 PB; 2 SB) $88.80-183.15
Full Breakfast
Credit Cards: A, B, C, D, E
Notes: 2, 5, 8, 9, 10, 11, 12, 14

EDENTON

The Lords Proprietors' Inn

300 North Broad Street, 27932
(919) 482-3641

Establishing a reputation for the finest accommodations in North Carolina, the inn offers 20 elegantly appointed rooms with private baths and spacious parlors for gathering for afternoon tea by the fire. A four-course dinner is served Tuesday through Saturday by reservation. MAP rates Tuesday to Saturday.

Hosts: Arch and Jane Edwards
Rooms: 20 (PB) $105-215
Full Breakfast
Credit Cards: None
Notes: 2, 5, 8, 9, 10, 11, 12, 14

ELLERBE

Ellerbe Springs Inn

2537 North Highway 220, 28338
(919) 652-5600; (800) 248-6467

Ellerbe Springs Inn is a beautiful, historic country inn nestled in nearly 50 acres of rolling hills and lush greenery. Established in 1857, the pre-Civil War manor has been completely renovated and redecorated as of 1988. Each of the 14 charming guest rooms features antique furniture, Oriental carpets, private bathrooms, and color cable TV. Just

7 No smoking; 8 Children welcome; 9 Social drinking allowed; 10 Tennis nearby; 11 Swimming nearby; 12 Golf nearby; 13 Skiing nearby; 14 May be booked through a travel agent.

opened! A historic honeymoon cottage overlooking the lake. Two suites. Enjoy delectable Southern cooking in the gracious first-floor dining room, open seven days serving breakfast, lunch, and dinner. It's an easy drive from Charlotte, Greensboro, Raleigh, and Myrtle Beach. Family owned and operated. Listed in the National Register of Historic Places.

Host: Beth Cadieu-Diaz
Rooms: 16 (PB) $54-94
Full Breakfast
Credit Cards: A, B, C, D
Notes: 2, 3, 4, 5, 7, 8, 9, 10, 12, 14

Ellerbe Springs Inn

FLAT ROCK

Flat Rock Inn

2810 Greenville Highway, 28731
(800) 266-3996

Victorian elegance in a country setting offering four theme-decorated guest rooms, each furnished to take guests back to a by-gone era. Breakfast is served family style. The menu is a blend of gourmet and country styles. Conveniently on US 25 south, one-half mile south of Carl Sandburg's home and the Flat Rock Playhouse. Seasonal rates available. Smoking on porch only. Children over 10 welcome.

Hosts: Dennis and Sandi Page
Rooms: 4 (PB) $85-95
Full Breakfast
Credit Cards: A, B
Notes: 2, 5, 9, 10, 12, 14

FRANKLIN

Buttonwood Inn

190 Georgia Road, 28734
(704) 369-8985

A quaint, small mountain inn awaits those who prefer a cozy country atmosphere. Before hiking, golf, gem mining, or horse-back riding, enjoy a breakfast of puffy scrambled eggs and apple sausage ring or eggs Benedict, Dutch babies, blintz soufflé, strawberry omelet, or stuffed French toast. Closed December through March. Smoking restricted. Children over 10 welcome.

Host: Liz Oehser
Rooms: 4 (2 PB; 2 SB) $54.50-65.40
Full Breakfast
Credit Cards: None
Notes: 2, 9, 10, 11, 12, 14

The Franklin Terrace

67 Harrison Avenue, 28734
(704) 524-7907; (800) 633-2431

The Franklin Terrace, built as a school in 1887, is listed in the National Register of Historic Places. Wide porches and large guest rooms filled with period antiques will carry guests to a time gone by, when Southern hospitality was at its best. Antiques, crafts, and gifts are for sale on the main floor. Within walking distance of Franklin's famous gem shops, clothing boutiques, and fine restaurants. Air conditioning. Private baths in all rooms. Open April 1 through November 15. Cable TV in all rooms.

Hosts: Ed and Helen Henson
Rooms: 9 (PB) $52-65
Full Breakfast
Credit Cards: A, B, C, D
Notes: 10, 11, 12, 14

GREENSBORO

Greenwood

205 North Park Drive, 27401
(910) 274-6350

NOTES: Credit cards accepted: A MasterCard; B Visa; C American Express; D Discover; E Diners Club;
F Other; 2 Personal checks accepted; 3 Lunch available; 4 Dinner available; 5 Open all year; 6 Pets welcome;

Greenwood

Enjoy the warm hospitality of this 1905 home in the park in the historic district of Greensboro. Fine Western art, collectibles, and antiques adorn the house. Air conditioning, two fireplaces in living rooms, swimming pool, TV room, and guest kitchen. Minutes from fine dining, shops, and sites.

Host: Mike and Vanda Terrell
Rooms: 5 (PB) $80-120
Full Breakfast
Credit Cards: A, B, C, D
Notes: 2, 5, 7, 8, 9, 10, 12, 14

HENDERSONVILLE

Apple Inn

1005 White Pine Drive, 28739-3951
(704) 693-0107; (800) 615-6611

Come and relax in this beautiful turn-of-the-century romantic Revival home. The peaceful country setting features three and one-half acres just five minutes from downtown shopping and dining. Convenient to Carl Sandburg's home and Flat Rock Playhouse. Thirty minutes to Biltmore Estate, Pisgah Forest, and the Lake Lure/Chimney Rock area. Delicious homemade breakfast, fresh flowers, turndown, and other amenities make this a memorable stay. Ten percent discount for AARP. Ten dollars off December through March.

Hosts: Bob and Pam Hedstrom
Rooms: 5 (PB) $75-140
Cottage: 1 (PB)

Full Breakfast
Credit Cards: A, B
Notes: 2, 5, 7, 9, 10, 11, 12, 13, 14

Claddagh Inn

755 North Main Street, 28792
(704) 697-7778; (800) 225-4700

The Claddagh Inn is in downtown Hendersonville, just two blocks from the beautiful Main Street Shopping Promenade. The inn has undergone extensive remodeling. The guest rooms have private bath, telephone, and air conditioning. TV available. Guests awaken to a delicious full country breakfast. AAA approved. Listed on the National Register of Historic Places.

Hosts: Vickie and Dennis Pacilio
Rooms: 14 (PB) $69-99
Full Breakfast
Credit Cards: A, B, C, D
Notes: 2, 5, 7, 8, 9, 10, 11, 12, 14

Mountain Home Bed and Breakfast

10 Courtland Boulevard, P.O. Box 234, 28758
(704) 697-9090; (800) 396-0077

Between Asheville and Hendersonville, near airport. Antiques and Oriental rugs grace this quiet, beautiful English-style inn. Tennessee pink marble porch and rocking chairs to relax the day or night away. Cable TV and telephones in all rooms. Some rooms with private entrance. Full candlelight breakfast. Convenient to Biltmore Estate (on their preferred lodging list), Flat Rock Playhouse, Chimney Rock, Pisgah National Forest, Carl Sandburg's home, and more.

Hosts: Bob and Donna Marriott
Rooms: 8 (6 PB; 2SB) $75-125
Full Breakfast
Credit Cards: A, B
Notes: 2, 5, 6, 9, 10, 12, 13, 14

The Waverly Inn

783 North Main Street, 28792
(704) 693-9193; (800) 537-8195
FAX (704) 692-1010
email JSHEIRY @aol.com

7 No smoking; 8 Children welcome; 9 Social drinking allowed; 10 Tennis nearby; 11 Swimming nearby; 12 Golf nearby; 13 Skiing nearby; 14 May be booked through a travel agent.

The Waverly Inn

Listed in the National Register of Historic Places, The Waverly Inn is the oldest inn in Hendersonville. The recently renovated inn has something for everyone, including claw-foot tubs and king- and queen-size canopied beds. Convenient to restaurants, shopping, Biltmore Estate, Carl Sandburg home, Blue Ridge Parkway, and Flat Rock Playhouse. Member of NCBBI and IIA.

Hosts: John and Diane Sheiry
Rooms: 15 (PB) $89-139
Full Breakfast
Credit Cards: A, B, C, D
Notes: 2, 5, 8, 9, 10, 11, 12, 14

HIGHLANDS

Colonial Pines Inn

Route 1, Box 22B, 28741
(704) 526-2060

A quiet country guest house with lovely mountain view. Comfortably furnished with antiques and many fine accessories. One-half mile from Highlands' fine dining and shopping area. Full breakfast includes egg dishes, homemade breads, fresh fruit, coffee, and juice. Three separate guest houses with kitchens and fireplaces are great for families. Children welcome in cottages only.

Hosts: Chris and Donna Alley
Rooms: 6 (PB) $65-95
Guest House: $85-200
Full Breakfast
Credit Cards: A, B
Notes: 2, 5, 7, 10, 11, 12, 13

The Laurels: Freda's Bed and Breakfast

Route 2, Box 102, 28741
(704) 526-2091

The Laurels, a unique bed and breakfast, is in historic Horse Cove, two and one-half miles outside of Highlands. It is on seven acres. Come in the afternoon and have an English tea. Two cozy fireplaces warm the cool evenings. The large English country breakfast features fresh fruit, bacon, ham, and eggs any way guests want them. The hosts grind their own whole-wheat flour and make crunchy toast, "from scratch" pancakes, homemade jams, and a lemon curd specialty. Fish the half-acre pond stocked with rainbow trout. No smoking.

Hosts: Warren and Freda Lorenz
Rooms: 5 (PB) $60-70
Full Breakfast
Credit Cards: None
Notes: 2, 8, 9, 11, 12

Long House Bed and Breakfast

Highway 64E, P.O. Box 2078, 28741
(704) 526-4394; (800) 833-0020

Long House Bed and Breakfast offers a comfortable retreat in the scenic mountains of western North Carolina. Any time of the year guests can enjoy the beauty and charm

Long House

NOTES: Credit cards accepted: A MasterCard; B Visa; C American Express; D Discover; E Diners Club; F Other; 2 Personal checks accepted; 3 Lunch available; 4 Dinner available; 5 Open all year; 6 Pets welcome;

of this quaint town and the scenic wonders of the Nantahala National Forest. The rustic mountain bed and breakfast offers country charm and warm hospitality. A hearty breakfast is served family style and is usually the highlight of everyone's visit.

Hosts: Lynn and Valerie Long
Rooms: 4 (PB) $55-95
Full Breakfast
Credit Cards: A, B
Notes: 2, 5, 8, 9

Ye Olde Stone House Bed and Breakfast

Route 2, Box 7, 28741
(704) 526-5911

This house built of stone is a mile from town. Rooms are bright, cheerful, and comfortably furnished. Perfect places for relaxing include a sunroom, porch, 30-foot deck, and attached year-round gazebo, all with view. Two fireplaces provide gathering spots. After a restful night's sleep, rise to the smell of freshly brewed coffee and a full country breakfast. Separate, completely furnished chalet and log cabin with fireplaces and meadow views.

Hosts: Jim and Rene Ramsdell
Rooms: 4 (PB) $50-85
Full Breakfast
Credit Cards: A, B
Notes: 2, 5, 8, 9, 10, 11, 12, 13

HIGH POINT

The Bouldin House Bed and Breakfast

4332 Archdale Road, 27263
(910) 431-4909; (800) 739-1816

This finely crafted, historic four-square sits on three acres of a former tobacco farm. Country atmosphere; relaxed and casual, yet elegant. Warmly decorated rooms combine old and new, each with spacious, modern, private bathrooms. America's largest concentration of furniture showrooms is

only minutes away. Awaken to early morning coffee/tea service. Follow the aroma of the generous, home-cooked breakfast to the oak-paneled dining room.

Hosts: Larry and Ann Miller
Rooms: 4 (PB) $70-95
Full Breakfast
Credit Cards: A, B
Notes: 2, 5, 7, 9, 10, 12, 14

The Colonial Inn

HILLSBOROUGH

The Colonial Inn

153 West King Street, 27278
(919) 732-2461

A charming old country inn in historic Hillsborough, the Colonial Inn has served guests continuously since 1759, among them Lord Cornwallis and Aaron Burr. A short distance from Chapel Hill, Durham, and Duke University. Convenient to I-85 and I-40. Famous for Southern cooking and homelike comfort. Great antique shopping nearby.

Hosts: Carlton and Sara McKee
Rooms: 8 (6 PB; 2 SB) $55-65
Full Breakfast
Credit Cards: A, B
Notes: 2, 3, 4, 5, 8, 9, 14

KILL DEVIL HILLS

Cherokee Inn

500 North Virginia Dare Trail, 27948
(919) 441-6127; (800) 554-2764

This large beach house with cypress-wood interior is five hundred feet from ocean

7 No smoking; 8 Children welcome; 9 Social drinking allowed; 10 Tennis nearby; 11 Swimming nearby; 12 Golf nearby; 13 Skiing nearby; 14 May be booked through a travel agent.

Cherokee Inn

beach. Quiet and restful. Ideal for relaxing and romance. Close to fine restaurants, golf, hang gliding, kayaking, scuba diving, wind surfing, deep-sea fishing, shopping, and other attractions. Three-night minimum stay required for holidays. Closed November through March.

Hosts: Bob and Kaye Combs
Rooms: 6 (PB) $60-95
Continental Breakfast
Credit Cards: A, B, C
Notes: 2, 7, 9, 10, 11, 12, 14

LAKE TOXAWAY

Greystone Inn

Greystone Lane, 28747
(704) 966-4700; (800) 824-5766

Located on a spectacular mountain lake, the Greystone Inn is a charming destination resort. Included with the daily tariff are a six-course gourmet dinner and a high country breakfast as well as afternoon tea and evening hors d'oeuvres. A wide array of complimentary activities including hiking, water skiing, boating, and tennis are available on property. Championship golf is available just steps away. The staff's "commitment to excellence" combined with an exceptional array of amenities will make any getaway memorable.

Host: Tim Lovelance (owner/innkeeper)
Rooms: 33 (PB) $260-345
Full Breakfast
Credit Cards: A, B, C
Notes: 2, 3, 4, 7, 8, 9, 10, 11, 12, 13, 14

LITTLE SWITZERLAND

Alpine Inn

Highway 226 A, P.O. Box 477, 28749
(704) 765-5380

Alpine Inn is a small, quaint establishment with rustic mountain charm. An excellent view, from all rooms, of mountain ranges and valleys. One mile from the Blue Ridge Parkway. Guest rooms are cozy and comfortable with a homelike atmosphere. There is a variety of accommodations from a one bedroom to a full apartment. Breakfasts, which are optional, are hearty and healthy, and range from $1 to $5. Full vegetarian breakfast available. Breakfast is served on the main balcony. Commune with nature's sunrises!

Hosts: Sharon E. Smith and William M. Cox
Rooms: 14 (PB) $36-60
Full and Continental Breakfast
Credit Cards: A, B
Notes: 2, 8, 9, 12, 13

MARSHALL

Marshall House Bed and Breakfast Inn

5 Hill Street, P.O. Box 865, 28753
(704) 649-9205; FAX (704) 649-2999

Truly in the mountains, overlooking the quaint town of Marshall, the French Broad River, and the mountains, this 1903 house is decorated with fancy chandeliers, mirrors, and lots of antiques. Resident cats add extra charm, and the porch is for rocking in this very relaxed atmosphere. Listed on the National Register of Historic Places, the house welcomes all in an atmosphere of bygone days. Continental plus breakfast is served.

Hosts: Ruth and Jim Boylan
Rooms: 9 (2 PB; 7 SB) $39-75
Continental Breakfast
Credit Cards: A, B, C, D, E
Notes: 5, 6, 8, 11, 13, 14

NOTES: Credit cards accepted: A MasterCard; B Visa; C American Express; D Discover; E Diners Club; F Other; 2 Personal checks accepted; 3 Lunch available; 4 Dinner available; 5 Open all year; 6 Pets welcome;

MARS HILL

Baird House, Ltd.

41 South Main Street, 28754
(704) 689-5722

Five guest rooms—two with a working
fireplace, two with private bath—are featured in an old brick, antique-filled bed and
breakfast inn that once was the grandest
house in this pastoral corner of the western
North Carolina mountains. Eighteen miles
north of Asheville. Closed December.

Host: Yvette Wessel
Rooms: 5 (2 PB; 3 SB) $42.40-53
Full Breakfast
Credit Cards: C
Notes: 2, 7, 8, 9, 10, 11, 12, 13

MOCKSVILLE

Boxwood Lodge

Highway 601 at 132 Becktown Road, 27028
(704) 284-2031

Boxwood Lodge, a Colonial Revival 25-
room country mansion by Delano, is on 51
acres of beautifully wooded land at the corner
of Highway 601 and 132 Becktown Road.
Convenient to I-85 or I-40 travelers. Enjoy a
nearby game of golf, leisure walk, fishing,
game of billiards, afternoon tea, reading by
the fireside in the library, or just browsing
around looking at Edmund Osthaus paintings.
BYOB social drinking allowed.

Host: Martha Hoffner
Rooms: 8 (5 PB; 3 SB) 55-95
Full Breakfast
Credit Cards: A, B
Notes: 2, 5, 7, 12

MOORESVILLE

Oak Ridge Farm Bed and Breakfast

1108 Oak Ridge Farm Highway, 28115
(704) 663-7085

Enjoy traditional Southern hospitality in this
charming 1871 home, shaded by giant oak
trees. Comfortable rockers on a spacious
wraparound porch help create a relaxed
atmosphere to enjoy real country living. Full
country breakfast, Southern-style.
Accommodations available with double or
twin beds, air conditioning, private bath, and
private sitting area. Children welcome.
Please—no smoking, no pets, no alcohol.

Hosts: Harold and Rustina Hansen
Rooms: 2 (PB) $85
Full Breakfast
Credit Cards: None
Notes: 2, 5, 7, 10, 11, 12

MOUNT AIRY

Pine Ridge Inn

2893 West Pine Street, 27030
(919) 789-5034

Built in 1948, this Southern mansion offers
private bedroom suites, swimming pool with
sun deck, horseback riding, and golf nearby.
Smoking limited.

Hosts: Ellen and Manford Haxton
Rooms: 6 (PB) $60-100
Full or Continental Breakfast
Credit Cards: A, B, C
Notes: 2, 5, 8, 9, 10, 11, 12, 14

MURPHY

Huntington Hall Bed and Breakfast

500 Valley River Avenue, 28906
(704) 837-9567; (800) 824-6189
FAX (704) 837-2527

Ginger-peach crepes, English ivy, and low
stone walls await. Five guest rooms with
private baths. Wonderful breakfasts served
on the sun porch overlooked by 100-year-
old maple trees. This former mayor's home
is warm and comfortable. Circa 1881. Here
in the mountains of western North Carolina,
guests can hike, white-water raft, ride the
Great Smoky Mountains Railway, visit the

---

7 No smoking; 8 Children welcome; 9 Social drinking allowed; 10 Tennis nearby; 11 Swimming nearby;
12 Golf nearby; 13 Skiing nearby; 14 May be booked through a travel agent.

John C. Campbell Folk School, or just relax on the porch and smell the mountain breeze. Murder mystery weekends available.

Hosts: Bob and Katie DeLong
Rooms: 5 (PB) $49-85
Full Breakfast
Credit Cards: A, B, C, D, E
Notes: 2, 5, 7, 8, 9, 10, 11, 12, 14

NAGS HEAD

First Colony Inn

6720 South Virginia Dare Trail, 27959
(919) 441-2343; (800) 368-9390 reservations
FAX (919) 441-9234

Enjoy Southern hospitality at the Outer Banks' only historic bed and breakfast inn (National Register). Private beach access, pool, continuous wraparound verandas with rockers, elegant library, antique-filled rooms with private tiled bath, heated towel bars, Jacuzzis, wet bars with microwave ovens or kitchenettes, and remote-controlled heat pumps. Enjoy the complimentary Continental breakfast buffet and afternoon tea in the sunny breakfast room. See The Lost Colony and Wright Brothers Memorial, fish, windsurf, hang glide, or stroll the beach. Honeymoons, anniversaries, weddings, and small conferences are specialties. Personal checks accepted for deposit 30 days in advance only.

Hosts: The Lawrences
Rooms: 26 (PB) $75-225 seasonal
Continental Breakfast
Credit Cards: A, B, D
Notes: 5, 7, 8, 9, 10, 11, 12, 14

NEW BERN

King's Arms Inn

212 Pollock Street, 28560
(919) 638-4409; (800) 872-9306

The King's Arms Inn, named for an old New Bern tavern said to have hosted members of the First Continental Congress, upholds a heritage of hospitality as New Bern's winner of the "Best of the Best"

award for bed and breakfast accommodations. Spacious rooms with comfortable four-poster canopied or brass beds, all modern amenities, and elegant decor harbor travelers who want to escape the present and steep themselves in Colonial history. Home-baked breakfasts feature piping hot specialty ham and cheese and seasonal fruit muffins from the owner's exclusive recipe, fresh fruit, juice, and coffee or tea are delivered to the guests' room along with the morning paper. The inviting third-floor Mansard Suite offers a view of the Neuse River and features unique open gables and the tongue-and-groove paneling added to this 1848 Greek Revival during the last part of the 19th century.

Hosts: Richard and Pat Gulley
Rooms: 10 (8 PB; 2 SB) $85
Suite: $125
Continental Breakfast
Credit Cards: A, B, C
Notes: 2, 5, 7, 8, 9, 10, 12, 14

New Berne House Inn

709 Broad Street, 28560
(800) 842-7688

Listed on the National Register of Historic Places and one block from Tryon Palace, New Berne House offers the charm and ambience of English country house decor. Guest rooms all have private baths, some with claw-foot tubs and pedestal sinks. Antique beds piled with pillows; crisp eyelet sheets; fireplaces in some rooms. The inn is noted for its fine breakfasts, includ-

New Berne House

ing Southern specialties such as pralines 'n' cream waffles and peach French toast. Special packages and rates, including mystery weekends, are available.

Hosts: Marcia Drum and Howard Bronson
Rooms: 7 (PB) $60-80
Full Breakfast
Credit Cards: A, B, C
Notes: 2, 5, 7, 9, 10, 11, 12, 14

OCEAN ISLE BEACH

The Winds-Clarion Carriage House Inn

310 East First Street, 28469
(800) 334-3581 (US and Canada);
FAX (910) 579-2884

This delightful inn, surrounded by palm trees and lush subtropical landscaping, is on the oceanfront on an island beach just 20 minutes from North Myrtle Beach, South Carolina. The Winds features oceanfront two- and three-room suites and studios with full kitchens or kitchenettes and seaside balconies. Amenities include daily housekeeping, a heated pool (enclosed in winter), whirlpool, sauna, beach volleyball, fitness room, rental bicycles, sailboats, golf on 80 courses, and free tennis on the island. Complimentary Continental breakfast buffet. Free summer golf. There are several restaurants on the island and nearby Myrtle Beach offers many more.

Hosts: Miller and Helen Pope
Rooms: 73 (PB) $53-186
Continental Breakfast
Credit Cards: A, B, C, D, E
Notes: 5, 7, 8, 9, 10, 11, 12, 14

OLD FORT

The Inn at Old Fort and Gardens

116 West Main Street, 28762
(704) 668-9384; (800) 471-0637 PIN 1709

The Inn at Old Fort is a restored two-story Victorian country home built in 1880. The

Inn, decorated with antiques, is set on over three and one-half acres. The grounds are shaded by more than 100-year-old walnut and hemlock trees. The terraced lawn includes a variety of gardens. Along with a front porch for rocking and large, comfortable bedrooms, a parlor and a library are for guests' use.

Hosts: Chuck and Debbie Aldridge
Rooms: 4 (PB) $45-65
Continental Breakfast
Credit Cards: None
Notes: 2, 5, 7, 8, 9, 10, 11, 12, 14

ORIENTAL

The Tar Heel Inn

P.O. Box 176, 205 Church Street, 28571
(919) 249-1078

This circa 1890 inn has been restored to capture the feeling of an old English country inn. The garden and patio are for the guests to enjoy. Bikes are available for guests to pedal around town. Oriental is a quiet fishing village on the Neuse River and Pamlico Sound. It is known as the sailing capital of the Carolinas. Excellent restaurants and shops, sailing, golf, tennis, and fishing are within walking or biking distance.

Hosts: Shawna and Robert Hyde.
Rooms: 8 (PB) $60-85
Full Breakfast
Credit Cards: A, B
Notes: 2, 5. 7, 8, 9, 10, 11, 12

PILOT MOUNTAIN

Scenic Overlook Bed and Breakfast

Scenic Overlook Lane, 27043
(910) 368-9591 (phone and FAX)

If the feeling of peace and tranquility tops guests' priority list along with breathtaking sunrises and sunsets and lavishly appointed rooms, then this is the place to be. Enjoy a beautiful lakeside view of Mount Pilot as guests relax in one of the large, luxurious

7 No smoking; 8 Children welcome; 9 Social drinking allowed; 10 Tennis nearby; 11 Swimming nearby; 12 Golf nearby; 13 Skiing nearby; 14 May be booked through a travel agent.

suites. Amenities include whirlpools, fireplaces, 37 acres of land, six acres of lake, gazebo, paddleboats, row boats, refrigerator, microwave, coffee maker, TV, VCR, hair dryers, robes, and free movies.

Hosts: Al and Gayle Steinbicker
Rooms: 4 (PB) $95-115
Full Breakfast
Credit Cards: A, B
Notes: 2, 5, 7, 9, 11, 12, 14

PINEHURST

The Magnolia Inn

65 Magnolia Street, P.O. Box 818, 28374
(910) 295-6900; FAX (910) 215-0858

In the village center, this small, quaint inn has 12 rooms, all with private baths and three with working fireplaces. In the rear of the inn, an English pub leads out to the pool and patio. An elegant dining room serves breakfast, lunch, and dinner. Privileges to all areas, public and private, Pinehurt Country Club courses, as well as tennis, and carriage rides through the village.

Rooms: 12 (PB) $80-130
Full Breakfast
Credit Cards: A, B, C
Notes: 2, 3, 4, 5, 10, 12

PISGAH FOREST

The Pines Country Inn

719 Hart Road, 28768
(704) 877-3131

The Pines Country Inn is in the Blue Ridge Mountains overlooking a beautiful valley. Truly a country inn, where guests are treated like family at Grandma's house. Available by day, week, or month. Between Brevard and Hendersonville.

Hosts: Tom and Mary McEntire
Rooms: 18 (16 PB; 2 SB) $55-65
Full Breakfast
Credit Cards: None
Notes: 2, 7, 8, 11, 12

ROBBINSVILLE

Blue Boar Lodge

200 Santeetlah Road, 28771
(704) 479-8126

Secluded mountain retreat cooled by mountain breezes. Hiking, fishing, hunting, bird watching, and canoeing are all very close by. Rustic but modern house. Meals served family-style on the lazy-susan table. Away from all city traffic, ten miles northwest of Robbinsville. Quiet and peaceful. Rate includes breakfast and dinner. Open April 1 through mid-October.

Hosts: Roy and Kathy Wilson
Rooms: 7 (PB) $90
Full Breakfast
Credit Cards: A, B
Notes: 2, 4, 5, 8, 11

SALISBURY

Rowan Oak House

208 South Fulton Street, 28144
(704) 633-2086; (800) 786-0437

"Romantic" and "lavish" describes this Queen Anne Victorian mansion: wraparound porch, rocking chairs, elaborate woodwork, stained glass, and original fixtures. Bedrooms are enormous with air conditioning, English and American antiques, fruit, and flowers. One room has Jacuzzi and gas log fireplace. A full gourmet breakfast will

Rowan Oak House

be served with silver, crystal, and Queen Louise china. In the heart of the historic district, one mile from I-85, exit 76B.

Hosts: Barbara and Les Coombs
Rooms: 4 (2 PB; 2 SB) $75-110
Full Breakfast
Credit Cards: A, B
Notes: 2, 5, 9, 10, 11, 12, 14

SILER CITY

Bed and Breakfast at Laurel Ridge

3188 Siler City-Snow Camp Road, 27344
(919) 742-6049; (800) 742-6049

In the heart of North Carolina, Laurel Ridge is a 12-year-old post and beam country home with an eclectic collection of antique and traditional furniture. The house sits on a ridge, overlooking the Rocky River surrounded by one of the largest natural stands of mountain laurel east of the mountains. The setting is captivating, with English country gardens, nature trails, and wildlife. The innkeeper is one of the area's most respected chefs.

Hosts: David J. Simmons and Lisa Reynolds
Rooms: 3 (1 PB; 2 SB) $55-95
Full Breakfast
Credit Cards: A, B, C
Notes: 2, 5, 7, 9, 10, 11, 12, 14

SOUTHERN PINES

Knollwood House

1495 West Connecticut Avenue, 28387
(919) 692-9390

A luxurious English manor house appointed with 18th-century antiques and contemporary comforts. On three acres of long leaf pines, dogwoods, magnolias, holly trees, and hundreds of flowering shrubs. Less than 100 feet to the 15th fairway of a championship golf course. And there are more than 30 courses just minutes away. Tennis, swimming, and riding too! Suites and guest rooms, all with private baths. Meeting

Knollwood House

rooms, wedding facilities, and catering are available. Smoking restricted.

Hosts: Mimi and Dick Beatty
Rooms: 5 (PB) $80-130
Full Breakfast
Credit Cards: A, B
Notes: 2, 5, 9, 10, 11, 12, 14

SPARTA

Turby-villa

Highway 18 North, Star Route 1, Box 48, 28675
(910) 372-8490

The Turby-villa is on 20 acres of beautiful mountain farmland. Breakfast is selected from a menu and served on a glassed-in porch with a beautiful view of the mountains. The bed and breakfast is ten miles from the Blue Ridge Parkway, which is maintained by the National Park Service, on Highway 18, two miles from Sparta. Dinner available by prior arrangement.

Host: Maybelline Turbiville
Rooms: 3 (PB) $53
Full Breakfast
Credit Cards: None
Notes: 2, 5, 8, 9, 10, 12

SPRUCE PINE

Ansley/Richmond Inn

101 Pine Avenue, 28777
(704) 765-6993

This lovely half-century-old elegant country inn, specializing in pampering guests, is

7 No smoking; 8 Children welcome; 9 Social drinking allowed; 10 Tennis nearby; 11 Swimming nearby; 12 Golf nearby; 13 Skiing nearby; 14 May be booked through a travel agent.

nestled into the hills overlooking the town of Spruce Pine and the Blue Ridge Parkway just four miles to the south. Ideal for hiking, crafts, skiing, golf, and gem mining, the inn has seven luxurious rooms, all with private baths, and serves a full breakfast each morning and a complimentary glass of wine in the evening.

Hosts: Bill Ansley and Lenore Boucher
Rooms: 7 (PB) $55-75
Full Breakfast
Credit Cards: A, B
Notes: 2, 5, 7, 8, 9, 10, 11, 12, 13, 14

The Fairway Inn Bed and Breakfast

110 Henry Lane, 28777
(704) 765-4917; (904) 725-7379 (off season)

A lovely country home overlooking a public 18-hole golf course with a lovely view of the mountains. The inn is just three miles north of the Blue Ridge Parkway and in the center of everything. Great for day trips in either direction. The large, comfortable rooms are eclectic in decor. The inn specializes in warmth and relaxation. Smoking restricted.

Hosts: Margaret and John P. Stevens
Rooms: 5 (PB) $70-120
Full Breakfast
Credit Cards: A, B
Notes: 2, 8, 9, 10, 11, 12

STATESVILLE

Cedar Hill Farm Bed and Breakfast

778 Elmwood Road, 28677
(704) 873-4332; (800) 484-8457 ext. 1254

An 1840 farmhouse and private cottage on a 32-acre sheep farm in the rolling hills of North Carolina. Antique furnishings, air conditioning, color cable TV, and telephones in rooms. After a full country breakfast, swim, play badminton, or relax in a porch rocker or hammock. For a busier day, visit two lovely towns with historic districts, Old Salem, or two large cities in a

45-mile radius. Convenient to restaurants, shopping, and three interstate highways. Smoking in designated areas only.

Hosts: Jim and Brenda Vernon
Rooms: 2 (PB) $60-75
Full Breakfast
Credit Cards: A, B
Notes: 2, 5, 8, 9, 11, 12, 14

Madelyn's Bed and Breakfast

514 Carroll Street, 28677
(704) 872-3973; (800) 948-4473
FAX (704) 881-0713

Fresh flowers and homemade cookies await guests' arrival at Statesville's first bed and breakfast. It is a charming 1940s brick home filled with unique collections of family antiques, Raggedy Anns, iron dogs, and bottles. There are three lovely bedrooms with private baths. Each has a different size bed to suit any traveler's needs. A full gourmet breakfast includes a choice of juice, fresh or baked fruit, bread, and entrée. The house has central air conditioning. No smoking.

Hosts: Madelyn and John Hill
Rooms: 3 (PB) $65-75
Full Breakfast
Credit Cards: A, B
Notes: 2, 3, 5, 7, 9, 10, 11, 12, 13, 14

Madelyn's

TABOR CITY

Four Rooster Inn

403 Pireway Road, 28463
(910) 653-3878

Experience the gracious hospitality of the Old South in the charm of a small town setting. This family home has been restored to a comfortable elegance with antiques, china and crystal, beautiful fabrics, and fine linens. Afternoon tea awaits guests' arrival. Turndown service is accented with chocolates at bedtime. Awaken to a tray of coffee or tea and the morning news at the door. A full Southern gourmet breakfast is served in the dining room. Myrtle Beach golf courses begin four miles from the inn.

Hosts: Gloria and Bob Rogers
Rooms: 4 (2 PB; 2 SB) $50-75
Full Breakfast
Credit Cards: A, B
Notes: 2, 5, 7, 9, 10, 12, 14

TARBORO

Little Warren

304 East Park Avenue, 27886
(919) 823-1314; (800) 309-1314

Established in 1984, Little Warren is a large, gracious Edwardian family home, renovated and modernized, in a quiet neighborhood in the historic district. Furnished with family English and American antiques and collectibles, the house has a fireplaced common room and a deeply set wraparound front porch that overlooks the Town Common, one of two originally chartered commons remaining in the United States. Member North Carolina Bed and Breakfast Association. Children over six welcome.

Hosts: Patsy and Tom Miller
Rooms: 3 (PB) $68.90
Continental and Full Breakfasts
Credit Cards: A, B, C, D
Notes: 2, 5, 9, 10, 14

TRYON

Pine Crest Inn

200 Pine Crest Lane, 28782
(704) 859-9135; (800) 633-3001

The four-diamond Pine Crest Inn is nestled in the foothills of the Blue Ridge Mount-

Pine Crest Inn

ains. Listed on the National Register of Historic Places, the inn has 30 private rooms, suites, or cottages from which to choose. The gourmet restaurant, fireplaces, wide porches, and beautiful grounds complement each other and combine to create a casual elegance and a relaxing atmosphere. Nearby attractions include the Blue Ridge Parkway and the famous Biltmore Estate and Gardens.

Hosts: Jeremy and Jennifer Wainwright
Rooms: 30 (PB) $125-165
Continental Breakfast
Credit Cards: A, B, C, D
Notes: 2, 4, 5, 7, 8, 9, 10, 11, 12, 14

Stone Hedge Inn

P.O. Box 366, 28782
(704) 859-9114

A beautiful grand old estate on 28 acres at the base of Tryon Mountain. Lodging is available in the main building, cottage, and guest house. Amenities include private baths, TV, antiques, and wonderful views. Some rooms have kitchens and some have fireplaces. A delicious full breakfast is served in the dining room by the picture windows. The restaurant features fine Continental cuisine. Children over six are welcome.

Hosts: Ray and Anneliese Weingartner
Rooms: 6 (PB) $75-95
Full Breakfast
Credit Cards: A, B
Notes: 2, 4, 5, 7, 8, 9, 10, 11, 12, 14

7 No smoking; 8 Children welcome; 9 Social drinking allowed; 10 Tennis nearby; 11 Swimming nearby; 12 Golf nearby; 13 Skiing nearby; 14 May be booked through a travel agent.

Mast Farm Inn

VALLE CRUCIS

Mast Farm Inn

P.O. Box 704, 28691
(704) 963-5857

Restored mountain inn on the National
Register of Historic Places. Vegetables and
berries for the dining room are grown on
the 18-acre farm in North Carolina's High
Country near the Blue Ridge Parkway.
Country cooking with a gourmet touch.
Golf, hiking, swimming, fishing, and skiing
are nearby. Breakfast and dinner are
included. Rates quoted are Modified
American Plan rates. Open mid-January to
early-March; mid-April to mid-December;
December 27 to New Years.

Hosts: Sibyl and Francis Pressly
Rooms: 13 (11 PB; 2 SB) $90-165
Continental Breakfast
Credit Cards: A, B, D
Notes: 2, 4, 7, 9, 10, 11, 12, 13, 14

WAYNESVILLE

Grandview Lodge

809 Valley View Circle Road, 28786
(704) 456-5212; (800) 255-7826

A country inn in the western North
Carolina mountains; open all year.
Southern home cooking, with breakfast fea-
turing homemade breads, jams, and jellies.
Dinner includes fresh vegetables, freshly
baked breads, and desserts. Meals, served

family style, are included in the rates.
Private bath and cable TV. Reservations
required.

Hosts: Stan and Linda Arnold
Rooms: 11 (PB) $100-110
Full Breakfast
Credit Cards: None
Notes: 2, 4, 5, 7, 8, 9, 10, 11, 12, 13, 14

Haywood House
Bed and Breakfast

409 South Haywood Street, 28786
(704) 456-9831

Built at the turn of the century, this historic
home is graced with antique furnishings,
beautiful oak paneling, cabinets, and mantels.
Enjoy the cozy library for books and games,
or great conversation in the parlor. A large
veranda with rockers offers a panoramic view
of the mountains. Walk to Main Street's
shops and restaurants. Four charming guest
rooms. Home-baked breakfast is served in the
lovely dining room. A perfect home for small
groups of family or friends.

Hosts: Lynn and Chris Sylvester
Rooms: 4 (2 PB; 2 SB) $55-75
Full Breakfast
Credit Cards: None
Notes: 2, 5, 7, 9, 12, 13

Heath Lodge Mountain Inn

900 Dolan Road, 28786
(704) 456-3333; (800) 432-8499

Heath Lodge

NOTES: Credit cards accepted: A MasterCard; B Visa; C American Express; D Discover; E Diners Club;
F Other; 2 Personal checks accepted; 3 Lunch available; 4 Dinner available; 5 Open all year; 6 Pets welcome;

Shaded by majestic oaks, this mountain inn is a rustic, secluded getaway 3,200 feet up in the North Carolina Smokies. The rustic mountain atmosphere belies the comfortably furnished and renovated 18 guest rooms and four suites, all with private baths and color cable TV. A massive stone fireplace dominates the picturesque dining room where the inn's famous bountiful mountain breakfasts and country American dinners are served. Two guest lounges, with over 400 feet of porches with rockers, aid in an exceptional mountain inn experience. Close to horseback riding, whitewater rafting, spectacular golf courses, mountain trails, and other attractions, and within walking distance of the many charming shops of Waynesville.

Hosts: Robert and Cindy Zinser
Rooms: 18 (PB) $75-120
Suites: 4 (PB)
Full Breakfast
Credit Cards: A, B, D
Notes: 2, 4, 5, 8, 9, 10, 11, 12, 13

WEAVERVILLE

Weaverville Featherbed and Breakfast

3 Le Perrion Drive, 28787
(704) 645-7594; FAX (704) 658-3905

This Romantic Revival mountaintop home was built at the turn of the century in an era when true comfort was the mark of excellence. Enjoy the awesome mountain view from every room. Majestic sunsets and fluffy feather beds ensure the ultimate peaceful night's rest. Wake to crisp mountain air and a full mountain-size breakfast. Just seven miles north of Asheville and all of its attractions. A honeymoon suite is available.

Hosts: Sharon Ballas and Shelly Burtt
Rooms: 6 (PB) $85-195
Full Breakfast
Credit Cards: A, B
Notes: 2, 5, 7, 8, 9, 10, 11, 12, 13, 14

Weldon Place Inn

WELDON

Weldon Place Inn

500 Washington Avenue, 27890
(919) 536-4582; (800) 831-4470

This home-away-from-home is only two miles off I-95, exit 173. Sleep in a canopied bed, wake to singing sparrows, stroll through the cozy historic hometown, and savor a gourmet breakfast. At the Weldon Place Inn the guest's peace of mind begins with antiques and country elegance. Personal attention is provided to ensure the guest the ultimate in solitude and relaxation. Local attractions include state historic site, early canal system, and railroad.

Hosts: Angel and Andy Whitby
Rooms: 4 (PB) $60-85
Full Breakfast
Credit Cards: A, B, C
Notes: 5, 7, 10, 14

WILMINGTON

Anderson Guest House

520 Orange Street, 28401
(910) 343-8128

An 1851 Italianate townhouse with separate guest quarters overlooking the private garden. Furnished with antiques, ceiling fans, and working fireplaces. Drinks on arrival. A

7 No smoking; 8 Children welcome; 9 Social drinking allowed; 10 Tennis nearby; 11 Swimming nearby; 12 Golf nearby; 13 Skiing nearby; 14 May be booked through a travel agent.

delightful gourmet breakfast is served. Limited smoking permitted.

Hosts: Landon and Connie Anderson
Rooms: 2 (PB) $60-75
Full Breakfast
Credit Cards: None
Notes: 2, 5, 6, 8, 9, 10, 11, 12

Anderson Guest House

Catherine's Inn

410 South Front Street, 28401
(910) 251-0863; (800) 476-0723

Experience the gracious atmosphere of this restored 1883 classic Italianate home featuring wrought-iron fence and gate, a Colonial Revival wraparound front porch, and two-story screened rear porch. The 300-foot private lawn overlooks the Cape Fear River. The only bed and breakfast on the river in Wilmington, Catherine's Inn offers deluxe and personal services; choice of charming rooms, each with private bath; central air conditioning and ceiling fans; cozy library with cable TV and VCR; horseshoes, croquet, and bicycles at guests' disposal. Complimentary refreshments. Off-street parking and wraparound porches for guests' enjoyment. Corporate rates available. Smoking restricted. Children over ten welcome.

Host: Catherine-Warren Ackiss
Rooms: 4 (PB) $80-85
Full Breakfast
Credit Cards: A, B
Notes: 2, 5, 9, 10, 11, 12, 14

Graystone Inn

100 South Third Street, 28801
(910) 763-2000; FAX (910) 763-5555

Graystone Inn, a European-style bed and breakfast establishment housed in the stately Bridgers Mansion, is in the heart of the Wilmington historic district. Each of the guest bedrooms has been designed to offer guests both Old World charm and luxury combined with all the modern-day conveniences.

Rooms: 7 (PB) $85-150
Continental Breakfast
Credit Cards: A, B, C
Notes: 5, 7, 8, 9, 10, 11, 12, 14

The Inn on Orange

410 Orange Street, 28401
(910) 815-0035; (800) 381-4666

The Inn on Orange offers bedrooms with private baths, a comfortable living room and dining room (both with fireplaces), as well as a lovely bricked courtyard with a small swimming pool. A full breakfast is served each morning and guests may dine on the front porch, around the pool, or in the dining room. Complimentary coffee and cold beverages are always available. In the historic district and just a short walk to the Cape Fear River and Wilmington's better restaurants and night spots. Special rates can be arranged for extended stays by business people and the film industry.

Hosts: Paul Marston and Thomas Renner
Rooms: 4 (PB) $55-95
Full Breakfast
Credit Cards: A, B
Notes: 2, 5, 7, 9, 10, 11, 12, 14

James Place Bed and Breakfast

9 South Fourth Street, 28401
(910) 251-0999; (800) 303-9444

This bed and breakfast is within Wilmington's historic district, minutes from some of Carolina's finest beaches. A carefully restored turn-of-the-century four-square-style home with large front porch for rocking and reminiscing. The Renewal Room has a special quality of intimacy with a Jacuzzi bathroom, queen-size bed, and personal balcony. The Nesting Suite has a queen-size canopied nesting bed, sitting area, and private bath. The Sharker Room has a queen-size bed, twin bed, and private bath.

Hosts: Maureen and Tony Spataro
Rooms: 3 (PB) $60-95
Full and Continental Breakfast
Credit Cards: A, B
Notes: 2, 5, 7, 8, 9, 10, 11, 12, 14

Market Street Bed and Breakfast

1704 Market Street, 28403
(910) 763-5442; (800) 242-5442

Built in 1917, this elegant Georgian-style brick house is listed on the National Register of Historic Places but has modern conveniences, including central air conditioning and paved off-street parking. Furnished with antiques and reproductions with a piano for guests' use. On US Highways 17 and 74, with beaches, restaurants, and shopping all nearby.

Hosts: Jo Anne and Bob Jarrett
Rooms: 4 (PB) $75-85
Full Breakfast
Credit Cards: A, B
Notes: 2, 5, 7, 9, 10, 11, 12

Market Street

Taylor House Inn

14 North Seventh Street, 28401
(910) 763-7581; (800) 382-9982 (reservations)

The Taylor House Inn is a romantic turn-of-the-century house in the historic district of downtown Wilmington. The antique furnishings and Oriental rugs accentuate the drama of high ceilings, carved oak staircase, parquet floors, and golden oak fireplaces. Enjoy a full gourmet breakfast, antiquing, shopping, sightseeing, and a walk to the beautiful riverfront. Enjoy rocking and swinging on the front porch. Air-conditioned. Children over 12 welcome.

Innkeeper: Glenda Moreadith
Rooms: 4 (PB) $85-100
Full Breakfast
Credit Cards: A, B, C
Notes: 2, 5, 7, 9, 10, 11, 12, 14

The Worth House

412 South Third Street, 28401
(919) 762-8562

Romantic Queen Anne Victorian inn in historic district, short walk to riverfront, restaurants, and shopping. Antiques, period furniture, and art in parlor, library, and formal dining room. Seven guest rooms all with private bath and sitting areas, some with fireplaces and enclosed porches. Full breakfast, free soft drinks and snacks. Large screen TV, room telephones, FAX available.

Hosts: Francie and John Miller
Rooms: 7 (PB) $90-105
Full Breakfast
Credit Cards: A, B
Notes: 2, 5, 7, 9, 10, 11, 12, 14

WILSON

Miss Betty's Bed and Breakfast Inn

600 West Nash Street, 27893-3045
(919) 243-4447; (800) 258-2058 reservations only

Selected as one of the "Best Places to Stay in the South," Miss Betty's is comprised of

7 No smoking; 8 Children welcome; 9 Social drinking allowed; 10 Tennis nearby; 11 Swimming nearby; 12 Golf nearby; 13 Skiing nearby; 14 May be booked through a travel agent.

four beautifully restored historic homes. In a gracious setting in the downtown historic section, where quiet Victorian elegance and charm abound in an atmosphere of all modern-day conveniences. Guests may browse for antiques at Miss Betty's or in any of the numerous antique shops that have given Wilson the title of "Antique Capital of North Carolina." A quiet eastern North Carolina town also known for its famous eastern Carolina barbecue, Wilson features four beautiful golf courses, numerous tennis courts, and Olympic-size pool. Midway between Maine and Florida, along the main North-South Route I-95.

Hosts: Betty and Fred Spitz
Rooms: 10 (PB) $60-75
Full Breakfast
Credit Cards: A, B, C, D, E, F
Notes: 2, 5, 7, 9, 10, 11, 12

WINSTON-SALEM

Colonel Ludlow Inn

434 Summit at West Fifth, 27101
(910) 777-1887; (800) 301-1887
FAX (910) 777-1890

Two adjacent houses from the late 1800s listed on the National Register of Historic Places have been converted into a luxurious inn. The unique guest rooms (each with private deluxe bath and most with two-person whirlpool tubs) are furnished with beautiful period antiques. All rooms have telephones, stereo and tapes, cable TV and VCR with free movies, minirefrigerators, and coffee/tea makers. Fireplaces and king-size

Colonel Ludlow Inn

beds available. Gourmet restaurants, cafes, shops, and parks are within easy walking distance.

Host: Ken Land
Rooms: 13 (PB) $89-189
Full Breakfast
Credit Cards: A, B, C, D
Notes: 2, 3, 4, 5, 9, 10, 11, 12, 14

Hylehurst Bed and Breakfast Inn

224 South Cherry Street, 27101
(910) 722-7873; (800) 731-7873

Built in 1884, Hylehurst has been said to be "the finest standing example of high Victorian architecture in Winston-Salem." The house features handsome woodwork of curly maple, cherry, birch, oak, and pine. Upstairs are four guest rooms arranged around a balcony overlooking the living hall and grand staircase. A guest refrigerator is stocked with soft drinks. Full breakfast includes Belgian waffles. In downtown within walking distance of Old Salem, convention center, Hawthorne Conference Center, and fine restaurants.

Host: Janice Tuttle
Rooms: 4 (3 PB; 1 SB) $60-125
Full Breakfast
Credit Cards: A, B
Notes: 2, 5, 7, 9, 10, 11, 12, 14

Lady Anne's Victorian Bed and Breakfast

612 Summit Street, 27101
(919) 724-1074

Warm Southern hospitality surrounds guests in this 1890 historic Victorian. An aura of romance touches every suite and room, all of which are individually decorated with period antiques and treasures, while skillfully including modern luxuries, such as private baths, whirlpools, balconies, porches, cable TV with HBO, stereo with music and tapes, telephones, room refrigerators, coffee maker, and microwave. An evening dessert/tea tray and a delicious full breakfast are served on fine china and lace. Near downtown attractions, performances, restaurants, and shops. Near Old Salem Historic Village.

Host: Shelley Kirley
Rooms/Suites: 5 (PB) $55-145
Full Breakfast
Credit Cards: A, B, C
Notes: 5, 7, 9, 10, 11, 12, 14

MeadowHaven

MeadowHaven Bed and Breakfast

NC Highway 8, P.O. Box 222, Germantown, 27019
(910) 593-3996

A contemporary retreat on 25 country acres along Sauratown Mountain. Sixteen miles north of Winston-Salem and ten minutes from Hanging Rock State Park and the Dan River. Heated indoor pool, hot tub, game room, guest pantry, fishing pond, fireplaces, TV/VCR and movies. "Luv Tubs" for two and sauna available. Hiking, canoeing, horseback riding, golf, winery, art gallery, fresco, dining nearby. Plan a "lovebirds' retreat" to MeadowHaven.

Hosts: Samuel and Darlene Fain
Rooms: 3 (PB) $65-95
Luxury Cabin: $125-175
Full Breakfast
Credit Cards: A, B, C, D
Notes: 2, 5, 7, 10, 11, 12, 14

Mickle House Bed and Breakfast

927 West Fifth Street, 27101
(919) 722-9045

Step back in time to a quaint 1892 Victorian cottage. A gracious welcome, lovely antiques, restful canopied and poster beds, and a delicious breakfast served in the spacious dining room or on the brick patio. The old-fashioned rocking chairs and swing on the porch and the boxwood gardens offer guests a respite from all cares. In the picturesque National Historic District of West End, it is only five minutes from Old Salem, the Medical Center, and the downtown/convention center. Walk to fine restaurants, parks, shops, the YMCA, churches, and library. Golf, tennis, and swimming nearby.

Host: Barbara Garrison
Rooms: 2 (PB) $65-75
Full Breakfast
Credit Cards: A, B
Notes: 2, 5, 9, 10, 11, 12, 14

Wachovia Bed and Breakfast, Inc.

513 Wachovia Street, 27101
(919) 777-0332

Lovely rose and white Victorian cottage on a quiet street, within walking distance of city center, Old Salem, antique shops, and gourmet restaurants are nearby. A European-style bed and breakfast, with flexible check-in/check-out. No rigid breakfast schedule. Expanded breakfast. Complimentary wine. No smoking.

Host: Susan Pfaff
Rooms: 5 (2 PB; 3 SB) $55-65
Full Breakfast
Credit Cards: A, B
Notes: 2, 5, 7, 8, 9, 10, 12

7 No smoking; 8 Children welcome; 9 Social drinking allowed; 10 Tennis nearby; 11 Swimming nearby;
12 Golf nearby; 13 Skiing nearby; 14 May be booked through a travel agent.

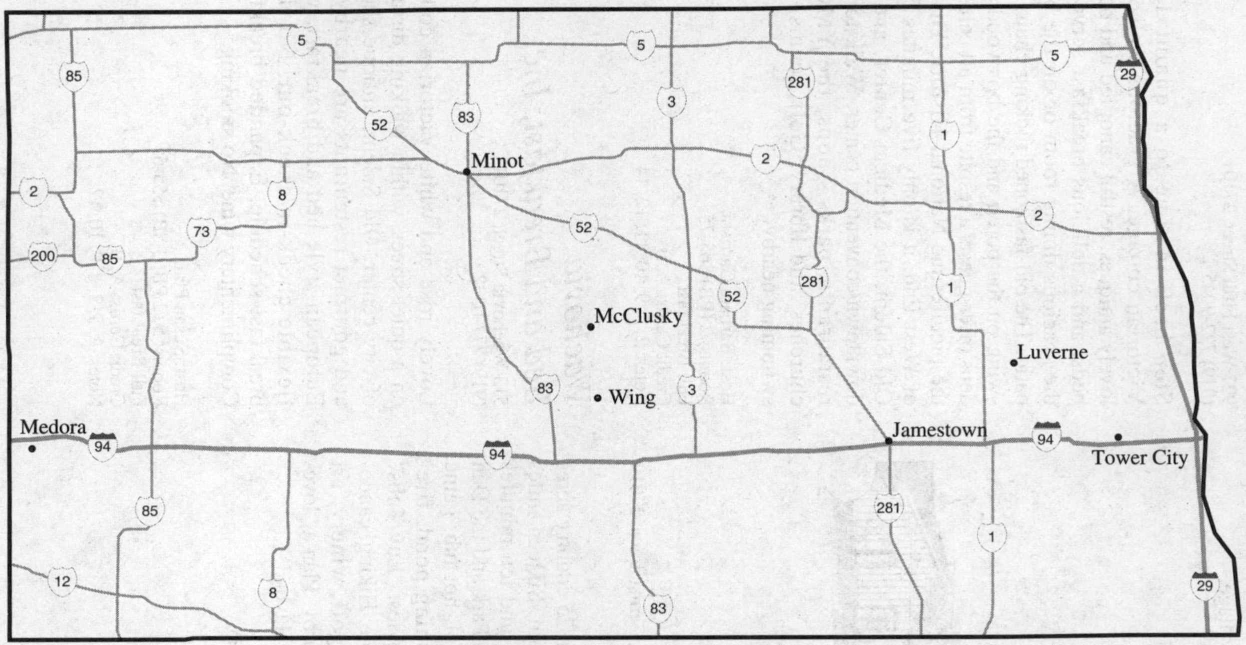
Minot
McClusky
Wing
Medora
Jamestown
Luverne
Tower City
5
85
52
83
2
8
73
200
94
3
281
1
29
12

North Dakota

North Dakota

JAMESTOWN

Country Charm Bed and Breakfast

7717 35th Street, SE, 58401-9050
(701) 251-1372

Whether it's a special occasion or a quiet getaway, this bed and breakfast offers peaceful ambience everyone needs from time to time. An 1897 farmhouse on 12 parklike acres one and one-half miles off Interstate 94. Centrally air-conditioned for summer, toasty warm in winter. Decorated with antiques and collectibles.

Hosts: Tom and Ethel Oxtoby
Rooms: 4 (4 SB) $40-80
Full Breakfast
Credit Cards: None
Notes: 2, 3, 4, 5, 10, 11, 12, 13, 14

LUVERNE

Volden Farm Bed and Breakfast

Rural Route 2, Box 50, 58056
(701) 769-2275

A retreat in the most real sense of the word. Peace, quiet, beauty, good books, art,

Volden Farm

nature, and animals join with home comforts, good food, great coffee, and conversation for an ideal stay on the Volden farm. Four guest rooms available with shared and private baths. Separate house available for privacy with deck, feather bed, and more. Outdoor smoking permitted.

Hosts: Jim and JoAnne Wold
Rooms: 4 (1 PB; 3 SB) $50-95
Full Breakfast
Credit Cards: None
Notes: 2, 3, 4, 5, 8, 9, 10, 11, 12, 13, 14

MCCLUSKY

Midstate Bed and Breakfast

Route 3, P.O. Box 28, 58463
(701) 363-2520

Country "peace and quiet" prevail at this easy-to-find location alongside Highway 200. This newer home is on a working grain and livestock farm. The house features a private entrance to the guests' lower level, which includes a bedroom, private bath, large TV lounge with fireplace, and a kitchenette. Upper level bedrooms share a bath. Guests may breakfast in a choice of locations, including the plant-filled atrium. For hunting enthusiasts, over 4,500 acres are reserved for guests to experience excellent hunting of upland game, water fowl, and deer. Hunting parties qualify for special rates.

Hosts: Grace and Allen Faul
Rooms: 4 (1 PB; 3 SB) $30
Full Breakfast
Credit Cards: None
Notes: 2, 4, 5, 6, 7, 8, 9, 10, 11

NOTES: Credit cards: A MasterCard; B Visa; C American Express; D Discover; E Diners Club; F Other;
2 Personal checks accepted; 3 Lunch available; 4 Dinner available; 5 Open all year; 6 Pets welcome;
7 No smoking; 8 Children welcome; 9 Social drinking allowed; 10 Tennis nearby; 11 Swimming nearby;
12 Golf nearby; 13 Skiing nearby; 14 May be booked through a travel agent.

MEDORA

Rough Riders Hotel Bed and Breakfast

58645
(701) 623-4444; FAX (701) 623-4494

Boardwalks, "gas-lit" street lanterns, and the unique charm and history of the Rough Riders will help one see why President Theodore Roosevelt fell in love with the savagely beautiful Badlands of North Dakota. The peace and serenity of the Theodore Roosevelt National Park are within walking distance of guests' room. Enjoy breakfast in bed or in the dining room. On Friday and Saturdays, gourmet dinners are served in the dining room. Even in the active summer season, the pace in Medora is a step slower—enjoy the relaxed atmosphere. Closed October 1 through May 1.

Host: Bill Campbell
Rooms: 9 (PB) $50
Full Breakfast
Credit Cards: A, B, C
Notes: 2, 8, 9

MINOT

Lois and Stans' Bed and Breakfast

1007 Eleventh Avenue, NW, 58703
(701) 838-2244

Home away from home. It's more like staying at Grandma's. "We'll even nag you if you're homesick."

Rooms: 3 (3 SB) $35
Full Breakfast
Credit Cards: D
Notes: 2, 5, 9, 10, 11, 12

TOWER CITY

Tower City Inn Bed and Breakfast

502 Church Street, 58071
(701) 749-2660

Tower City Inn Bed and Breakfast is a beautiful three-story house built in 1904. All restored in French country. Just off I-94 for easy access.

Hosts: Joanne and Duane Wetch
Rooms: 3 (3 SB) $60.90
Full Breakfast
Credit Cards: A, B, D
Notes: 5, 7, 8

WING

Eva's Bed and Breakfast

27250 331st Avenue, NE, 58494-9710
(701) 943-2461

The hosts are retired farmers who built a new house in 1983. Two bedrooms for guests share a bath, large family room, fireplace, and library. A full breakfast is served, and a tour of the farm is available upon request. Good hiking to Haystack Butte one mile away. Mitchel Lake recreation is four miles away, and a toy museum with handmade pieced quilts and stuffed toys is within five miles. Open year-round.

Hosts: Harold and Eva Williams
Rooms: 2 (2 SB) $25
Full Breakfast
Credit Cards: None
Notes: 2, 3, 4, 5, 7, 8

NOTES: Credit cards accepted: A MasterCard; B Visa; C American Express; D Discover; E Diners Club; F Other; 2 Personal checks accepted; 3 Lunch available; 4 Dinner available; 5 Open all year; 6 Pets welcome;

Ohio

ASHTABULA

Michael Cahill Bed and Breakfast

1106 Walnut Boulevard, 44004
(216) 964-8449

The Cahill bed and breakfast is on Lake Erie in the center of Ashtabula Harbor. The Cahill home was built in 1887 in the Victorian stick style. The whole nine-room house is used for the bed and breakfast. There are four guest rooms; two have private baths; two share one and one-half baths. Guest rooms are air-conditioned. There is a convenience kitchen for guests' use. A large, open porch surrounds the front of the house. It is a short walk to Walnut Beach, marine museum, charter boat fishing, and restored shops and restaurants on Bridge Street.

Hosts: Paul and Pat Goode
Rooms: 4 (2 PB; 2 SB) $45-55
Full Breakfast
Credit Cards: None
Notes: 2, 5, 8, 9, 10, 11, 12, 14

BELLVILLE

The Frederick Fitting House

72 Fitting Avenue, 44813
(419) 886-2863

An 1863 Victorian home in a quaint country village between Columbus and Cleveland. Near Mohican and Malabar Farm State Parks, downhill and cross-country skiing, canoeing, and Kenyon and Wooster Colleges. Gourmet breakfast served in hand-stenciled dining room, garden gazebo, or country kitchen. Closed Thanksgiving and Christmas.

Hosts: Ramon and Suzanne Wilson
Rooms: 3 (PB) $48-72
Full Breakfast
Credit Cards: None
Notes: 2, 3, 4, 7, 8 , 9, 10, 11, 12, 13

CENTERVILLE

Yesterday Bed and Breakfast

39 South Main Street, 45458
(513) 433-0785; (800) 225-0485

Ten miles south of the center of Dayton, in the heart of the Centerville historic district, this house adjoins a group of fine antique shops. The Lavender and Old Lace Shop features fine bath products and vintage linens. The house was built in 1882 and is tastefully furnished with antiques. Near restaurants and two museums. Within easy driving distance of the Air Force Museum in Dayton, Kings Island Amusement Park, and historic Lebanon and Waynesville,

Yesterday

7 No smoking; 8 Children welcome; 9 Social drinking allowed; 10 Tennis nearby; 11 Swimming nearby; 12 Golf nearby; 13 Skiing nearby; 14 May be booked through a travel agent.

Ohio

both major antique centers. The University of Dayton and Wright State University are 15 to 20 minutes away. Discount for stay of three or more nights. Continental plus breakfast is served. Children over 12 welcome. May be booked through travel agent for stay on weekdays.

Host: Barbara
Rooms: 3 (PB) $70-75
Continental Breakfast
Credit Cards: None
Notes: 2, 9, 12

CHILLICOTHE _____

The Greenhouse Bed and Breakfast

47 East Fifth Street, 45601
(614) 775-5313

A Queen Anne-style home built in 1894 and listed on the National Register of Historic Places. Leaded-glass doors and windows, parquet floors, and cherry beamed ceilings. The guest rooms are large, quiet, comfortable, and furnished with antiques. A full breakfast is served in the formal cherry dining room. In the historic district close to museums, antique and specialty shops, restaurants, and the Majestic Theatre in downtown Chillicothe. No smoking in the bedrooms.

Hosts: Tom and Dee Shoemaker
Rooms: 4 (PB)
Full Breakfast
Credit Cards: A, B, C
Notes: 2, 8, 9, 10, 11, 12

CINCINNATI _____

Prospect Hill Bed and Breakfast

408 Boal Street, 45210
(513) 421-4408

Nestled into a wooded hillside, this Italianate Victorian townhouse was built in 1867 on Prospect Hill, Cincinnati's first suburb and now a national historic district. The bed and breakfast has been restored, keeping original woodwork, doors, hardware, and light fixtures. Each room is furnished with period antiques and offers fireplaces, skeleton keys, and spectacular views. A Continental plus buffet breakfast is served. Hot tub. Ample free parking. The only bed and breakfast downtown. Sixteen blocks to Convention Center.

Host: Gary Hackney
Rooms: 4 (2 PB; 2 SB) $79-109
Continental Breakfast
Credit Cards: A, B, D
Notes: 2, 5, 7, 9

The Victoria Inn of Hyde Park

3567 Shaw Avenue, 45208
(513) 321-3567; FAX (513) 321-3147

The Victoria Inn of Hyde Park is an elegant and comfortable bed and breakfast in the heart of Cincinnati's most charming neighborhoods. The inn received a *Better Homes & Gardens* award for outstanding renovation. Perfect for a unique business or romantic getaway. Fifteen minutes from downtown, Riverfront Stadium, the zoo, and numerous local universities. The only bed and breakfast in the area that supplies private phones, a fax, copier, and in-ground

The Victoria Inn

swimming pool. Voted "Best B&B," *Cincinnati Magazine,* October 1993.

Hosts: Tom Possert and Debra Moore
Rooms: 4 (PB) $69-129
Full Breakfast
Credit Cards: A, B, C
Notes: 5, 7, 10, 11, 12

The Baricelli Inn

CLEVELAND

The Baricelli Inn

2203 Cornell Road, 44106-3805
(216) 791-6500; FAX (216) 791-9131

The turn-of-the-century brownstone is on the corner of Murray Hill and Cornell Roads in the historic Little Italy area of Cleveland. By staying at the inn, guests are within walking distance of Case Western, university hospitals, and world-class museums. The seven European-styled guest rooms are comfortably furnished, and each features a private bath. Morning begins with a Continental breakfast featuring fresh fruits and sumptuous homemade pastries.

Host: Paul Minnillo
Rooms: 7 (PB) $100-130
Continental Breakfast
Credit Cards: A, B, C, E
Notes: 4, 5, 9, 14

Private Lodgings, Inc. A-1

P.O. Box 18590, 44118
(216) 321-3213

A variety of accommodations including bed and breakfast lodgings, homeshare for longer stays, or short-term rentals in houses and apartments in the greater Cleveland area. Near the Cleveland Clinic, Case Western Reserve University, major museums and galleries, metro park system, downtown Cleveland business district, and Lake Erie. No credit cards. $45-125.

CLEVELAND HEIGHTS

Notre Maison Inc.

2557 North Park Boulevard, 44106
(216) 932-8769; (800) 216-8769;
FAX (216) 932-8769

This French manor on two acres, surrounded by pine, oak, and maple trees, has a vast patio with balustrade and parking facility on premises. The home is full of antiques and Persian rugs. Near museums, Cleveland orchestra, universities, hospitals, and shopping. A Continental breakfast includes croissants, coffeecake, jam, jellies, juice, coffee, tea, cereals, and milk. A fax, copier, and telephones are available. Peaceful, safe, and immaculate. Airport pickup. The inn has been run by Renée, with the help of a complete staff, for eight years. Renée is a French chef and has been a cooking class instructor and a singer. A world traveler, Renée speaks seven languages. A coach house for a family of four is also available but inquire about the rate.

Hosts: Renée Van Cauwenberghe Lewis
Rooms: 3 (PB) $55-75
Continental Breakfast
Credit Cards: None
Notes: 2, 5, 7, 8, 10, 11, 12, 13

COLUMBUS

The House of the Seven Goebels

4975 Hayden Run Road, 43221
(614) 761-9595

From the pineapple hospitality sign above the front walk to the warmth of the keeping room, the House of the Seven Goebels beckons to those who enjoy and appreciate the past. On two acres along a stream, convenient to Dublin, Hilliard, and Columbus. A reproduction of a 1780 Connecticut River Valley farmhouse. Two bedrooms with wood-burning fireplaces.

Hosts: Pat and Frank Goebel
Rooms: 2 (PB) $65
Full Breakfast
Credit Cards: A, B
Notes: 2, 5, 7

Lansing Street Bed and Breakfast

180 Lansing Street, 43206
(614) 444-8488; (800) 383-7839

Lansing Street Bed and Breakfast is in the heart of German Village, a popular historic area near downtown. The village is famous for restored homes, slate roofs, wrought iron gates, enclosed courtyards, quaint shops, great restaurants, and cobblestone streets. This comfortable home is tastefully furnished and carefully decorated with select artwork. The great room has a brick fireplace that overlooks a courtyard with a fountain and wind chimes. Two spacious suites have all the desired amenities and private baths. A creative gourmet breakfast is served each morning by a hostess who loves to cook. Inquire about pets.

Host: Marcia A. Barck
Rooms: 2 (PB) $70
Full Breakfast
Credit Cards: None
Notes: 2, 5, 7, 8, 9, 10, 11

Shamrock Bed and Breakfast

5657 Sunbury Road, Gahanna, 43230-1147
(614) 337-9849

The Shamrock is a brick split-level ranch on over an acre of professionally landscaped grounds with perennial beds, roses, grape arbor, and flowering bushes. Guests enjoy the entire first floor, fireplace, Florida room, and patio with gas grill. All

rooms are furnished with original art and antiques. Large library. CDs and videos are available. Easy freeway access to most attractions and close to airport. Large traditional Irish breakfast. Generally handicapped accessible. Smoking restricted.

Host: Tom McLaughlin
Rooms: 2 (PB) $50-55
Full Breakfast
Credit Cards: None
Notes: 2, 3, 5, 8, 10, 11, 12, 13

DANVILLE

The White Oak Inn

29683 Walhonding Road, 43014
(614) 599-6107

This turn-of-the-century farmhouse in a rolling wooded countryside features antiques and hand-stitched quilts. Guests read, play board games, or socialize in the common room with a fireplace, or relax on the 50-foot-long front porch. An outdoor enthusiast's haven. Three rooms have fireplaces. Near the world's largest Amish population and historic Roscoe Village.

Hosts: Yvonne and Ian Martin
Rooms: 10 (PB) $70-140
Full Breakfast
Credit Cards: A, B, D
Notes: 2, 4, 5, 7, 9, 10, 11, 12, 13, 14

DE GRAFF

Rollicking Hills

2 Rollicking Hills Lane, 43318
(513) 585-5161

This is a 160-acre farm in scenic hills. The homestead began as an Indian trading post in the late 1700s on a path that became the county stagecoach road. Remodeling in 1825 and an eight-room addition by the host's grandfather in 1865 are part of the home's five-generation history. Hiking, horseback riding, a natural peat bog left by a glacier, and farm animals including llamas. Lake well stocked with blue gill and

7 No smoking; 8 Children welcome; 9 Social drinking allowed; 10 Tennis nearby; 11 Swimming nearby; 12 Golf nearby; 13 Skiing nearby; 14 May be booked through a travel agent.

large-mouth bass. Canoe to a bullfrog chorus. Spartan in-ground pool, cross-country skiing, beech-maple climax woods. No smoking. No alcohol or drugs. No pets.

Hosts: Susanne and Robert Smithers and Family
Rooms: 4 (1 PB; 3 SB) $32-60
Full Breakfast
Credit Cards: None
Notes: 2, 3, 4, 5, 7, 8

Whispering Pines

DELLROY

Whispering Pines Bed and Breakfast

P.O. Box 340, 44620
(216) 735-2824

Come to this 1880 Victorian home overlooking Atwood Lake. Filled with elegant antiques of the period, each guest room has a breathtaking view of the lake and a private bath. One room has a wood-burning fireplace. The Honeymoon Suite features a two-person Jacuzzi, balcony, king-size bed, and wood-burning fireplace. Central air. A scrumptious breakfast served on the enclosed porch makes this a perfect romantic getaway. Pontoon with deluxe seating is available for rental. Golf, boating, and private candlelight dinners available.

Hosts: Bill and Linda Horn
Rooms: 5 (PB) $95-125
Honeymoon Suite: $160-175
Full Breakfast
Credit Cards: A, B
Notes: 2, 4, 5, 7, 9, 10, 11, 12, 13, 14

EAST FULTONHAM

Hill View Acres

7320 Old Town Road, 43735
(614) 849-2728

Ten miles southwest of Zanesville off US 22 West. Spacious home on 21 acres with pond. Enjoy the pool, year-round spa, or relax in the family room by the fireplace. Country cooking is a specialty. The area is popular for antiquing, pottery, and outdoor activities.

Hosts: Jim and Dawn Graham
Rooms: 2 (SB) $40-45
Full Breakfast
Credit Cards: A, B, C
Notes: 2, 3, 4, 5, 8, 9, 10, 11, 12

FREDERICKTOWN

Heartland Country Resort

2994 Township Road 190, 43019
(800) 230-7030

The Heartland Country Resort is a beautifully remodeled, spacious 1878 farmhouse with scenic views of rolling fields, pastures, and woods. There are a variety of things to do, including horseback riding on wooded trails with streams and hills or riding in one of the arenas. Guests can go swimming in the heated pool in the summer, go skiing in the winter, play pool in the large recreation room, or just relax on the comfortable screened porch or deck. Continental plus breakfast served. Lunch

Heartland Country Resort

NOTES: Credit cards accepted: A MasterCard; B Visa; C American Express; D Discover; E Diners Club; F Other; 2 Personal checks accepted; 3 Lunch available; 4 Dinner available; 5 Open all year; 6 Pets welcome;

and dinner available by prior arrangement. Inquire about pets. Smoking permitted only on the porch.

Host: Dorene Henschen
Rooms: 4 (PB) $85-125
Continental Breakfast
Credit Cards: A, B, D
Notes: 2, 5, 8, 9, 11, 12, 13, 14

GENEVA-ON-THE-LAKE

The Otto Court Bed and Breakfast

5653 Lake Road, 44041
(216) 466-8668

Hotel and cottage complex overlooking Lake Erie. Within walking distance of the famous Geneva-on-the-Lake amusement center, Geneva State Park and Marina, and the Old Firehouse Winery. Near the historic Ashtabula Harbor area and 13 covered bridges. Two-night minimum stay required for weekends and holidays.

Host: C. Joyce Otto
Rooms: 12 (8 PB; 4 SB) $48-65
Full Breakfast
Credit Cards: A, B, D, F
Notes: 2, 4, 5, 8, 9, 10, 11, 12, 13, 14

GEORGETOWN

Bailey House Bed and Breakfast

112 North Water Street, 45121-1332
(513) 378-3087; (513) 378-6237

The Bailey House is a Greek Revival brick home built in 1830. The spacious rooms have Federal-style mantels, woodwork, and original ash flooring. Guests have antique beds, chests of drawers, and washstands. Bailey House offers small-town friendliness, a restful setting in a historic area, and a full breakfast to start the day. Museums, U. S. Grant home, art gallery, and antique shops are within walking distance. Boating, fishing, hiking are available nearby. No smoking in the guest rooms.

Hosts: Nancy Purdy and Jane Sininger
Rooms: 2 (SB) $55
Full Breakfast
Credit Cards: None
Notes: 2, 5, 9, 10, 12

Buxton Inn

GRANVILLE

Buxton Inn

313 East Broadway, 43023
(614) 587-0001; FAX (614) 587-1460

Ohio's oldest continuously operating inn in its original building. A complex of five buildings has 25 period guest rooms, 7 dining rooms (seating up to 250 people), meeting rooms that can accommodate up to 30, a tavern, and wine cellar. Formal gardens, brick walls, and sparkling fountains provide an elegant setting for a leisurely stay.

Hosts: Orville and Audrey Orr
Rooms: 25 (PB) $70-85
Full and Continental Breakfast
Credit Cards: A, B, C, D, E
Notes: 2, 3, 4, 5, 7, 8, 9, 10, 11, 12

The Follett Wright House

403 East Broadway, 43023
(614) 587-0941

Built in 1860 and listed on the National Register of Historic Places, this gracious bed and breakfast overlooks the historic village of Granville. Within walking distance of Dennison University, shopping, and restaurants. Breakfast consists of homemade danish rolls and other delicious specialties.

Hosts: Kirsten and Jurgen Pape
Rooms: 2 (PB) $60
Full Breakfast
Credit Cards: None
Notes: 2, 5, 6, 7, 8, 9, 10, 11, 12

7 No smoking; 8 Children welcome; 9 Social drinking allowed; 10 Tennis nearby; 11 Swimming nearby; 12 Golf nearby; 13 Skiing nearby; 14 May be booked through a travel agent.

HANOVERTON

The Spread Eagle Tavern

10150 Plymouth Street, P.O. Box 277, 44423
(216) 223-1583

The Spread Eagle Tavern is an artfully
restored Federal-style three-story historic
brick inn that features a gourmet restaurant,
a unique rathskeller, seven dining rooms,
and six guest rooms for overnight lodging.
All rooms are tastefully decorated with
antiques that give insight into Ohio's canal
period history. Listed on the National
Register of Historic Places. Quiet, romantic, and unique.

Hosts: Peter and Jean Johnson
Rooms: 6 (4 PB; 2 SB) $75-125
Continental Breakfast
Credit Cards: A, B, D
Notes: 3, 4, 5, 7, 8, 9, 12

HIRAM

The Lily Ponds

6720 Route 82, 44234
(216) 569-3222; (800) 325-5087

This spacious, lovely home in a quiet country setting is surrounded by woods and
ponds. Five-minute walk to Hiram College
campus; 15-minute drive to SeaWorld,
Geauga Lake, and Aurora Farms; 45 minutes to Cleveland, Akron, and Youngstown.
Charming guest rooms with private baths.
Central air conditioning. The owner is a
world traveler.

Host: Marilane Spencer
Rooms: 3 (PB) $55-75
Full Breakfast
Credit Cards: None
Notes: 2, 5, 7, 8, 9, 10, 11, 12, 13, 14

HURON

Captain Montague's Bed and Breakfast

229 Center Street, 44839
(419) 433-4756; (800) 276-4756

Captain Montague's

The Captain's is that perfect romantic
retreat in a stately Southern Colonial manor
that radiates Victorian charm. Experience a
bygone era of lace, luster, and love. Nestled
in the heart of vacationland on the shores of
Lake Erie, The Captain's is within minutes
of golf courses, estuaries, boating, and
shopping. Cedar Point and the Lake Erie
islands are nearby. Enjoy the in-ground
swimming pool and impeccable gardens.
The Captain's is truly in the "heart" of
Ohio. Minimum weekend stay is two
nights, Memorial Day through Labor Day.
Expanded Continental breakfast. Cross-
country skiing nearby.

Hosts: Judy and Mike Tann
Rooms: 7 (PB) $68-105
Continental Breakfast
Credit Cards: None
Notes: 2, 5, 7, 9, 10, 11, 12, 14

JACKSON

The Maples

14701 State Route 93, 45640
(614) 286-6067

Maple trees surround this 1907 farmhouse
on two acres. The house boasts five fireplaces, massive oak pocket doors, and
leaded-glass windows. Guest rooms are furnished in antiques and handmade quilts, and
the house is fully air-conditioned for year-
round comfort. A hearty full breakfast is

served in the dining room, but guests may wish to dine on the screened porch or the patio in the rose garden. Enjoy gracious hospitality and country comfort at the Maples.

Hosts: Maria and Tony De Castro
Rooms: 4 (2 PB; 2 SB) $45-55
Full Breakfast
Credit Cards: A, B, C, D
Notes: 2, 5, 8, 12, 14

LEXINGTON

White Fence Inn

8842 Denman Road, 44904
(419) 884-2356

A breathtaking country retreat on 73 acres, with gardens, apple orchard, grapevines, fishing pond, and fields. Breakfast is delectable and includes homemade granola, homemade jams, grape juice, pastries, and farm-fresh eggs. Dine in the large country dining room or out on the porch. Two large sitting rooms with fireplaces, games, TV, and spectacular views from every window. Special wedding or anniversary baskets available, and dessert bar Saturday nights for all guests, in season. The largest guest room boasts a king-size four-poster bed, cathedral wood ceiling, sunken tub, fireplace, and private deck.

Hosts: Bill and Ellen Hiser
Rooms: 7 (5 PB; 2 SB) $60-105
Full Breakfast
Credit Cards: None
Notes: 2, 5, 6, 8, 9, 10, 12, 13

MARION

Olde Towne Manor

245 St. James Street, 43302
(614) 382-2402; (800) 341-6163

This elegant stone home is on a beautiful acre of land on a quiet street in Marion's historic district. Enjoy a quiet setting in the gazebo, or relax while reading from more than 1,000 books available in the library. A leisurely stroll will take guests to the home of President Warren G. Harding and the Harding Memorial. A quiet, relaxed, and elegant atmosphere for a stay. Awarded the 1990 Marion Beautification Award for Most Attractive Building. Limited smoking permitted. Children over 12 welcome.

Host: Mary Louisa Rimbach
Rooms: 4 (PB) $55-65
Full Breakfast
Credit Cards: A, B, C
Notes: 2, 5, 10, 12

MARTIN'S FERRY

Mulberry Inn
Bed and Breakfast

53 North Fourth Street, 43935
(614) 633-6058

This Victorian house built in 1868 by Dr. Ong features three period rooms with antiques, paintings, and quilts. Relax in the beautiful parlor and enjoy a full breakfast in the private dining room. Visit the oldest organized settlement in Ohio and Walnut Grove Cemetery (in which lies Betty Zane, who saved Fort Henry in the last battle of the Revolutionary War). Within walking distance of the Ohio River, museums, and

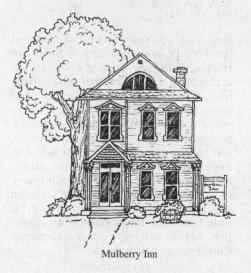

Mulberry Inn

shops. Wheeling, West Virginia, is five minutes away, where guests can visit Oglebay Park, Festival of Lights, Jamboree USA, dog races, many golf courses, and ice skating rinks. The inn is air-conditioned in the summer and has a beautiful wood-burning fireplace in the parlor. Smoking is restricted.

Hosts: Shirley and Charlie Probst
Rooms: 3 (1 PB; 2 SB) $35-45
Full Breakfast
Credit Cards: A, B, D
Notes: 2, 5, 8, 9, 10, 11, 12, 13

Ravenwood Castle

NEW PLYMOUTH

Ravenwood Castle

Route 1, Box 52-B, 45654
(800) 477-1541

Step back 800 years to a bit of medieval England in southeast Ohio's beautiful Hocking Hills area. Cresting a forested 50-acre hilltop and back a half-mile private road, Ravenwood Castle evokes an air of romance and mystery. All rooms or suites (some with whirlpools) have gas fireplaces, balconies or decks, stained-glass windows, and antique furnishings. A great hall with huge stone fireplace and Gothic dining tables and chairs, an english pub (game room), a library, hiking trails, and seclusion highlight every stay. Nearby are caves, waterfalls, rock formations, riding, canoeing, scenic railway, and much more. Children over eight welcome.

Hosts: Jim and Sue Maxwell
Rooms: 4 (PB) $85-150
Full Breakfast
Credit Cards: A, B, C
Notes: 2, 3, 4, 5, 7, 9, 11, 12, 14

ORRVILLE

Grandma's House Bed and Breakfast

5598 Chippewa Road, 44667
(216) 682-5112

Peace and quiet prevail on this 1860s farm home with comfortable beds, antiques, and handmade quilts. In the heart of Wayne County's rolling farmland, planted in alternating strips of corn, soybeans, and wheat. Several hiking trails meander through the large woods on the hill. Hickory rockers grace the front porch for relaxing. Just a few minutes from Amish country.

Hosts: Marilyn and Dave Farver
Rooms: 5 (3 PB; 2 SB) $55-90
Continental Breakfast
Credit Cards: None
Notes: 2, 5, 7, 8, 9, 11, 12

OXFORD

The Duck Pond

6391 Morning Sun Road
State Road 732 North, 45056
(513) 523-8914

An 1863 Civil War farmhouse on five and one-half acres. Furnished in country antiques and collectibles. Full country-style breakfast, including such specialties as Hawaiian French toast, German pancakes, and cheese blintzes. Three miles north of Miami University, two miles south of Hueston Woods State Park with golf, nature trails, boating, swimming, and fishing. Enjoy antiquing in Fairhaven on weekends, seven miles north, and in several other nearby towns during the week. Cat in residence. Ten-dollar charge for extra person in room. Closed Christmas. Certified and approved by Ohio Bed and Breakfast Association.

NOTES: Credit cards accepted: A MasterCard; B Visa; C American Express; D Discover; E Diners Club;
F Other; 2 Personal checks accepted; 3 Lunch available; 4 Dinner available; 5 Open all year; 6 Pets welcome;

Hosts: Don and Toni Kohlstedt
Rooms: 4 (1 PB; 3 SB) $50-70
Full Breakfast
Credit Cards: None
Notes: 2, 5, 7, 9, 10, 11, 12

POLAND

Inn at the Green

500 South Main Street, 44514
(216) 757-4688

A classically proportioned Victorian town-house on the south end of the green in pre-served Connecticut Western Reserve Village. Featuring beautiful large moldings, 12-foot ceilings, five lovely working Italian marble fireplaces, interior-shuttered win-dows, the original poplar floors, and a relaxing patio garden. Children over seven are welcome.

Hosts: Ginny and Steve Meloy
Rooms: 4 (PB) $55-60
Continental Breakfast
Credit Cards: A, B
Notes: 2, 5, 9, 10, 11, 12, 14

RIPLEY

The Signal House

234 North Front Street, 45167
(513) 392-1640

Share historic charm and hospitality while visiting this 1830s home on the scenic Ohio River. View spectacular sunsets from three porches or elegant parlors. Enjoy spacious rooms furnished with family antiques. The area offers antiques and craft shops, restaurants, winery, herb farms, covered bridges, history (early pioneers and the Underground Railroad), and lots of friendly people. River nearby for swim-ming and water skiing.

Hosts: Vic and Betsy Billingsley
Rooms: 2 (SB) $65-75
Full Breakfast
Credit Cards: A, B, D
Notes: 2, 5, 9, 10, 11, 12, 13, 14

1890 Queen Anne

SANDUSKY

1890 Queen Anne Bed and Breakfast

714 Wayne Street, 44870-3507
(419) 626-0391

A family home for 33 years. The hosts have enjoyed sharing this home and community with guests. Three bedrooms furnished with family antiques and a lovely porch over-looking gardens and patio for breakfast in the warm months make a stay here unfor-gettable. Close to ferries for Cedar Point and Lake Erie Islands. Air conditioning. Continental plus breakfast is served.

Hosts: Joan and Robert Kromer
Rooms: 3 (PB) $70-80
Continental Breakfast
Credit Cards: A, B, D
Notes: 5, 7

The Red Gables Bed and Breakfast

421 Wayne Street, 44870
(419) 625-1189

A lovely old Tudor Revival home finished in 1907, the Red Gables is in the historic Old Plat District. Guests are welcomed into the great room, which features a massive fireplace and a large bay window where breakfast is served. The home features

7 No smoking; 8 Children welcome; 9 Social drinking allowed; 10 Tennis nearby; 11 Swimming nearby; 12 Golf nearby; 13 Skiing nearby; 14 May be booked through a travel agent.

The Red Gables

many interesting architectural details, including plenty of beautiful oak woodwork. The Red Gables is decorated in an eclectic style, from Oriental artifacts in the great room to flowered chintz in the bedrooms. The rooms are filled with handmade slipcovers, curtains, and comforters made by the innkeeper, a semiretired costumemaker. The guest rooms are light and airy and have access to a wicker-filled sitting area, refrigerator, coffee maker, and tea kettle. Guests have said, "It's like going to Grandma's house!" Air-conditioned. Inquire about accommodations available for children.

Host: Jo Ellen Cuthbertson
Rooms: 4 (2 PB; 2 SB) $50-90
Continental Breakfast
Credit Cards: A, B
Notes: 2, 5, 7, 9, 10, 11, 12

Wagner's 1844 Inn

230 East Washington Street, 44870
(419) 626-1726

Elegantly restored, antique-filled Victorian home. Built in 1844 and listed on the National Register of Historic Places. Features a Victorian parlor with antique Steinway piano, living room with wood-burning fireplace, billiard room, screened porch, and enclosed courtyard. Air-conditioning. In downtown Sandusky within walking distance of parks, historic buildings, antique

shops, museums, and ferries to Cedar Point and Lake Erie islands.

Hosts: Walt and Barb Wagner
Rooms: 3 (PB) $50-90
Continental Breakfast
Credit Cards: A, B, D
Notes: 5, 9, 10, 11, 12

SHARON CENTER

Hart and Mather Guest House

1343 Sharon Copley Road, P.O. Box 93, 44274
(216) 239-2801; (800) 352-2584

This 1840s home and the Sharon Center Circle where it sits are both on the National Register of Historic Places. Furnished with both traditional antiques and reproductions, Hart and Mather offers three guest rooms with private baths, one suite with an adjoining room, fireplace, and private bath. All rooms have color TV with VCR and cable. Common living room with fireplace is available for guests' use, and a delicious breakfast comes from the in-house kitchen. Conference rooms available. Gift shop open to the public.

Hosts: Thomas and Sally Thompson
Rooms: 4 (PB) $69-119
Continental Breakfast
Credit Cards: A, B, C, D
Notes: 2, 5, 9, 12, 13, 14

SMITHVILLE

The Smithville Bed and Breakfast

171 West Main Street, P.O. Box 142, 44677
(216) 669-3333; (800) 869-6425

Turn-of-the-century simple elegance. Enjoy breakfast in a solid cherry dining room. Breakfast features homegrown blueberry specialties. An ideal stopping place while visiting the College of Wooster or Amish country. Three-room cottage suites available. Special rates for weekly, monthly, and yearly options. Visit our Cat's Meow gift shop. F. J. Design factory nearby. Famous

---

NOTES: Credit cards accepted: A MasterCard; B Visa; C American Express; D Discover; E Diners Club;
F Other; 2 Personal checks accepted; 3 Lunch available; 4 Dinner available; 5 Open all year; 6 Pets welcome;

restaurants are nearby, as well as gift, craft, and antique shops. On State Road 585 just five miles northeast of Wooster.

Hosts: Jim and Lori Kubik
Rooms: 5 (PB) $52-62
Full Breakfast
Credit Cards: A, B, D
Notes: 2, 5, 7, 8, 10, 11, 12

SOMERSET

Somer Tea Bed and Breakfast

200 South Columbus Street, P.O. Box 308, 43783
(614) 743-2909

Somer Tea Bed and Breakfast was named for a collection of more than 350 small teapots and the small village of Somerset. The hosts invite guests to their two-story brick home, circa 1850, to enjoy yesterday's charm with today's conveniences. There is antiquing around this historic area. Tea is available at all times, and guests can use any teapot they wish.

Hosts: Richard L. and Mary Lou Murray
Rooms: 2 (SB) $45
Full Breakfast
Credit Cards: None
Notes: 2, 5, 6, 7, 8, 9

SOUTH BLOOMINGVILLE

Steep Woods

24830 State Route 56, 43152
(614) 332-6084; (800) 900-2954

This new log home on a wooded hillside is in the beautiful Hocking Hills, 60 miles southeast of Columbus. Nearby is the Hocking State Park with its famous recessed caves, waterfalls, and unusual rock formations. Available in the area are hiking, swimming, canoeing, fishing, horseback riding, and the Hocking Valley Scenic Railroad.

Hosts: Barbara and Brad Holt
Rooms: 2 (SB) $40
Full Breakfast
Credit Cards: None
Notes: 2, 5, 7, 8, 9

TIPP CITY

Willow Tree Inn

1900 West Street, Route 571, 45371
(513) 667-2957

This restored 1830 Federal manor home has four fireplaces. There are a pond, ducks, and the original 1830 barn on the premises, as well as a working springhouse and smokehouse, and beautiful gardens to stroll in. Just minutes north of Dayton in a quiet location complete with attentive personal service.

Hosts: Chuck and Jolene Sell
Rooms: 4 (1 PB; 3 SB) $48-68
Full Breakfast
Credit Cards: A, B
Notes: 2, 5, 7, 8, 9, 10, 11, 12, 14

TROY

Allen Villa Bed and Breakfast

434 South Market Street, 45373
(513) 335-1181

This bed and breakfast has seven fireplaces and is decorated in Victorian antiques. Each room has a private bath, TV, telephone, and central air conditioning. Both king- and queen-size beds are available. A self-serve snack bar is for guests' evening pleasure, and a bountiful breakfast is served on the 15-foot antique dining room table that seats 12 guests. Two furnished kitchenettes are

Allen Villa

7 No smoking; 8 Children welcome; 9 Social drinking allowed; 10 Tennis nearby; 11 Swimming nearby; 12 Golf nearby; 13 Skiing nearby; 14 May be booked through a travel agent.

available monthly. Walking distance to three fine restaurants and hometown theater.

Hosts: Robert and June Smith
Rooms: 4 (PB) $54-74
Full Breakfast
Credit Cards: A, B, C, D
Notes: 2, 5, 7, 9, 10, 11, 12

WAVERLY

Governor's Lodge

171 Gregg Road, 45690
(614) 947-2266

Governor's Lodge is a place like no other. Imagine a beautiful, shimmering lake, an iridescent sunset, and a quiet calm. A friendly atmosphere in an eight-room bed and breakfast that is open year-round and in the Lake White area. Magnificent views can be enjoyed from every room. An affiliate of Bristol Village Retirement Community, it offers a meeting room and group rates for gatherings using the whole lodge.

Hosts: David and Jeannie James
Rooms: 8 (PB) $53.70-68.20
Continental Breakfast
Credit Cards: A, B, C, D, E
Notes: 2, 5, 8, 10, 11, 12

WEST ALEXANDRIA

Twin Creek Country Bed and Breakfast

5353 Enterprise Road, 45381
(513) 787-3990; (513) 787-4264; (513) 787-3279

This 1830s farmhouse has been remodeled to offer a quiet getaway for families and couples. The entire house, upper or lower level, or individual rooms are available. There are three bedrooms, two bathrooms, a furnished kitchen, and a living room. The owners live 100 yards away. Guests can roam the 170 acres, which include 50 acres of woods. Restaurants, deli foods, and antique shops are only a short distance away. Local catering available. Suitable

for two families at once. Close to the I-70/I-75 interchange.

Hosts: Dr. Mark and Carolyn Ulrich
Rooms: 3 (1 PB; 2 SB) $69-89
Full Breakfast
Credit Cards: A, B, C
Notes: 2, 5, 7, 8, 11, 12

Twin Creek Towne House

Twin Creek Towne House Bed and Breakfast

19 East Dayton Street, 45381
(513) 787-3990; (513) 787-4264
(513) 787-3279

This Italianate Victorian home, built in 1875, offers two guest rooms on the upper level, furnished in antiques, with TV and air conditioning. The home has beautiful butternut woodwork. The Twin Creek Towne House Tea Room is on the lower level and is open for lunch on Wednesday, Thursday, and Friday from 11:00 A.M. to 2:00 P.M. Roll away beds are available, and a sitting parlor gives guests extra room to relax. Easily accessible from I-70. Close to I-70/I-75 interchange.

Hosts: Dr. Mark and Carolyn Ulrich
Rooms: 2 (PB) $69
Full Breakfast
Credit Cards: A, B, C
Notes: 2, 5, 7, 8, 11, 12

NOTES: Credit cards accepted: A MasterCard; B Visa; C American Express; D Discover; E Diners Club;
F Other; 2 Personal checks accepted; 3 Lunch available; 4 Dinner available; 5 Open all year; 6 Pets welcome;

WESTERVILLE

Priscilla's Bed and Breakfast

5 South West Street, 43081
(614) 882-3910

Priscilla's 1854 home is surrounded by one-half acre of white picket fence. Lovely perennial gardens, bird feeders, and bird-baths accompany the one-time log cabin in the historic setting adjacent to Otterbein College. Borrow bicycles, cook on the patio, and enjoy the water garden and adjoining Alum Creek Park. Leisurely browse through 35 shops. At the rear of the house, Priscilla operates a miniature dollhouse shop. Robes are provided. Two miles north of Columbus. Free airport pickup is available.

Host: Priscilla H. Curtiss
Rooms: 3 (1 PB; 2 SB) $45-60
Continental Breakfast
Credit Cards: None
Notes: 2, 5, 7, 8, 9, 10, 11, 12

WORTHINGTON

The Worthington Inn

649 High Street, 43085
(614) 885-2600

Historic inn, built in 1831 and refurbished in 1983 and 1990. Ohio's second oldest inn. Four-star Mobil rating. Has 26 exquisitely appointed hotel suites furnished with stunning period antiques. Highly acclaimed restaurant featuring regional American cuisine. Banquet facilities accommodate 150 guests. Stay includes full breakfast and champagne turndown. Details large and small taken care of professionally and personally. One mile south of I-270 at the corner of High and New England.

Hosts: Stephen and Susan Hanson
Rooms: 26 (PB) $140-215
Full Breakfast
Credit Cards: A, B, C, D, E
Notes: 2, 3, 4, 5, 7, 8, 9, 10, 11, 12, 13, 14

ZOAR

The Cider Mill Bed and Breakfast

198 East 2nd Street, P.O. Box 438, 44697
(216) 874-3240; FAX (216) 339-7505

The Cider Mill was originally a barn used by the community of Separatists to make and store cider. It has been converted to living quarters featuring a three-floor spiral staircase. Furnished with antiques and decorated country style. Built in 1863, it has received a historic marker and is listed on the national register. Rooms are available with shared or private baths. Reservations encouraged. Central to outdoor dramas, the Pro Football Hall of Fame, Ohio's largest antique mall, several historic sites, three golf courses, canoe livery, horse academy, making it easy and quick to travel to entertainment. Rates are based on guests' requirements.

Hosts: Vernon and Dorothy Furbay
Rooms: 2 (PB or SB) $60-75
Full Breakfast
Credit Cards: None
Notes: 2, 5, 7, 10, 11, 12, 13

7 No smoking; 8 Children welcome; 9 Social drinking allowed; 10 Tennis nearby; 11 Swimming nearby; 12 Golf nearby; 13 Skiing nearby; 14 May be booked through a travel agent.

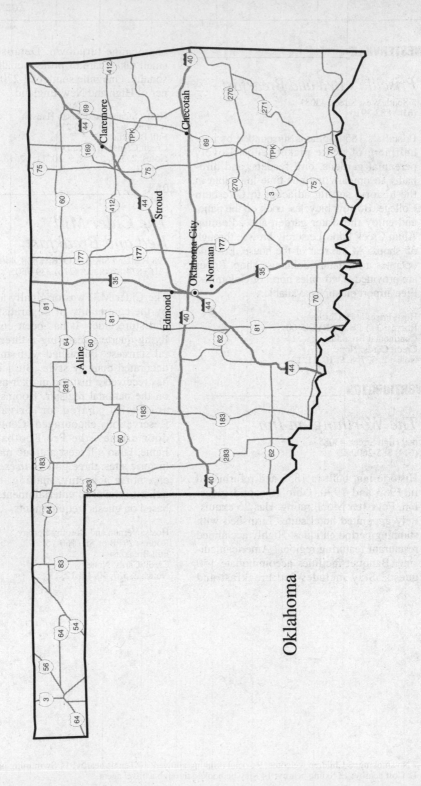

Oklahoma

Oklahoma

ALINE

Heritage Manor

Rural Route 3, Box 33, 73716
(405) 463-2563; (405) 463-2566

Heritage Manor is a country getaway on 80 acres that was settled in the Land Run of 1893 in northwest Oklahoma. Two prestatehood homes have been joined together and restored by the innkeepers using a Victorian theme. Beautiful sunrises, sunsets, and stargazing from the rooftop deck. Guests can relax in the hot tub or read a book from the 5,000-volume library. Ostriches, donkeys, and Scotch Highland cattle roam a fenced area. Close to Homesteaders 1894 Sod House, selenite crystal digging area, and several other attractions. Lunch and dinner available by reservation. Water skiing in the area. Pets welcome by prior arrangement. Smoking restricted. Inquire about accommodations for children.

Hosts: A. J. and Carolyn Rexroat
Rooms: 4 (SB) $50
Full Breakfast
Credit Cards: None
Notes: 2, 5, 10, 11

CHECOTAH

Sharpe House

301 Northwest Second, 74426
(918) 473-2832

Sharpe House is in a one-stoplight town in eastern Oklahoma just eight miles north or Lake Efaula. The house was built in 1911 and is filled with antiques and family heir-looms. Each room has a paddle fan and air conditioning. Breakfast is served in the formal dining room or on the huge screened porch. Enjoy a few days of peace and quiet and Southern hospitality. Inquire about accommodations for pets.

Host: Kay Kindt
Rooms: 3 (PB) $50
Full Breakfast
Credit Cards: None
Notes: 2, 5, 7, 8, 9, 10, 11, 12

CLAREMORE

Country Inn Bed and Breakfast

Route 3, Box 1925, 74017
(918) 342-1894

Leland and Kay invite guests to this country retreat. Stay in the charming barn-style guest quarters, separate from the main house. Enjoy the swimming pool, horse shoes, country walks, and bicycles or just relax country style. Guests may want to

Country Inn

visit the numerous antique shops or take in the history of the J. M. Davis Gun Museum and Will Rogers Memorial.

Hosts: Leland and Kay Jenkins
Rooms: 2 (PB) $52
Suite: 1 (PB) $65
Full Breakfast
Credit Cards: None
Notes: 2, 5, 7, 9, 11, 12

EDMOND

The Arcadian Inn Bed and Breakfast

328 East First Street, 73034
(405) 348-6347; (800) 299-6347

Grand wraparound front porch beckons to an old-fashioned intimate retreat. Luxurious Victorian bed and breakfast offers romantic packages, corporate accommodations, and family getaways. Special guest rooms fulfill dreams of yesterday. Private Jacuzzis and garden spa available. Enjoy Edmond's antique tours, tea rooms, and fine restaurants as well as Oklahoma City and Guthrie attractions. Dinner available by reservation.

Hosts: Martha and Gary Hall
Rooms: 6 (PB) $85-195
Full Breakfast
Credit Cards: A, B, C, D
Notes: 2, 5, 10, 11, 12, 14

NORMAN

Holmberg House Bed and Breakfast

766 DeBarr, 73069
(405) 321-6221 (phone and FAX); (800) 646-6221

In Norman's national register historic district across the street from the University of Oklahoma campus, this handsome 1914 Craftsman house was built by Professor Fredrik Holmberg and his wife, Signy. Each of the four guest rooms is individually decorated with antiques and has color cable TV and a private bath with a claw-

foot tub. A parlor with a fireplace, porches with rockers, and gardens are for guest's pleasure. A full breakfast is served in the formal dining room.

Hosts: Jo Meacham and Richard Divelbiss
Rooms: 4 (PB) $65-85
Full Breakfast
Credit Cards: A, B, C, D
Notes: 2, 5, 7, 9

Country House

OKLAHOMA CITY

Country House Bed and Breakfast

10101 Oakview Road, 73165
(405) 794-4008

A romantic, quiet country getaway on five acres is perfect for a weekend or longer. Some of the furnishings in the home include 19th-century antiques, heirloom quilts, an 1817 grandfather clock, and country collectibles. One mile from water sports and riding stables at Lake Draper. Start the day with a full, homemade breakfast served on antique Spode china in the dining room, or on the balcony. Spacious rooms and bathrooms. TVs in rooms upon request. Guests are pampered with fresh fruit, Godiva chocolates, and sparkling drinks in their rooms. Ask about the Honeymoon Suite that features a red, heart-shaped whirlpool. Pets are kept outside only. Smoking in designated areas. Water skiing is available nearby.

NOTES: Credit cards accepted: A MasterCard; B Visa; C American Express; D Discover; E Diners Club; F Other; 2 Personal checks accepted; 3 Lunch available; 4 Dinner available; 5 Open all year; 6 Pets welcome;

Hosts: Dee and Nancy Ann Curnutt
Rooms: 2 (PB) $60-85
Full Breakfast
Credit Cards: None
Notes: 2, 5, 8, 9, 10, 11, 12

Flora's Bed and Breakfast

2312 Northwest Forty-sixth, 73112
(405) 840-3157

In a quiet neighborhood, this home is furnished with antiques and collectibles, and includes an elevator. Guests may relax in front of the large wood-burning fireplace, or enjoy the outdoors on a 1,500-square-foot balcony with a large spa. There is covered parking, and the hosts enjoy square dancing. Easy access to Cowboy Hall of Fame, Remington Park Race Track, Omniplex, and other points of interest. Many good eating places in the vicinity. Children over 11 welcome.

Hosts: Newton W. and Joann Flora
Rooms: 2 (PB) $50-55
Continental Breakfast
Credit Cards: None
Notes: 2, 5, 7, 8, 9, 10, 12, 14

The Grandison Inn

1841 Northwest Fifteenth, 73106
(405) 521-0011

This country Victorian, circa 1896, has all of its original stained glass and brass lighting fixtures. The private suite with fireplace and Jacuzzi covers the entire third floor. Honeymoon and anniversary packages are available, as well as breakfast in bed and other room services. Enjoy the beautiful gazebo among fruit trees and gardens, relax on the rocker-lined front porch, or just spend time in the Victorian parlor. Convenient to downtown and I-35 and I-40. Smoking in designated areas only.

Hosts: Claudia and Bob Wright
Rooms: 5 (PB) $55-125
Full Breakfast
Credit Cards: A, B, C, D
Notes: 2, 3, 4, 5, 6, 9, 14

Willow Way

27 Oakwood Drive, 73121-5410
(405) 427-2133; FAX (405) 427-8907

Willow Way is a wooded town retreat in English Tudor style with antique decor and genuine charm. The den, with lofty beamed ceiling, fireplace, and picture window, is the guests' favorite place for bird watching and breakfast. Comfortable and safe, with off-street parking. Quiet, near the race track, Cowboy Hall of Fame, and many other area attractions. One easy mile east of I-35. Five minutes to downtown. Business rates are available.

Hosts: Johnita and Lionel Turner
Rooms: 3 (2 PB; 1 SB) $50-80
Full Breakfast
Credit Cards: A, B, D
Notes: 2, 5, 7, 8, 9, 12, 14

STROUD

The International Bed and Breakfast

504 Amherst Street, Buffalo, NY 14207
(800) 723-4262; FAX (716) 873-4462

Midway between Tulsa and Oklahoma City, Stroud is the home of Tanger Mall, the region's largest factory outlet fashion mall. Just two miles from the mall and one block off Stroud's main street, the bed and breakfast is listed on the National Register of Historic Places and is the ancestral home of the town founder. Built in 1900, this two-story Victorian beauty retains its turn-of-the-century charm with the added comforts of modern life. Fresh flowers, green plants, decorator linens and window treatments, fresh fruit, bottled water, and its own famous cookies are a few of the many amenities available. Gourmet breakfast served. $60-75.

7 No smoking; 8 Children welcome; 9 Social drinking allowed; 10 Tennis nearby; 11 Swimming nearby; 12 Golf nearby; 13 Skiing nearby; 14 May be booked through a travel agent.

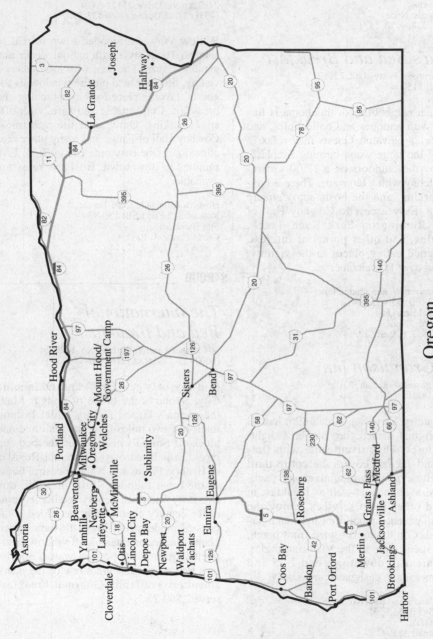

Oregon

Joseph
Halfway
La Grande
84
82
3
11
82
84
Hood River
97
Portland
Beaverton
Milwaukee
Oregon City
Welches
Mount Hood/
Government Camp
Yamhill
Newberg
Lafayette
McMinnville
Otis
Lincoln City
Depoe Bay
Newport
Waldport
Yachats
Cloverdale
Sublimity
Elmira
Eugene
Sisters
Bend
Coos Bay
Bandon
Port Orford
Roseburg
Grants Pass
Merlin
Jacksonville
Medford
Ashland
Brookings
Harbor
Astoria
30
26
101
18
20
126
101
5
5
5
42
138
230
58
62
62
66
140
97
97
31
20
20
126
126
197
26
26
395
395
395
140
97
78
20
26
95
95

Oregon

Adams Cottage

ASHLAND

Adams Cottage Bed and Breakfast

737 Siskiyou Boulevard, 97520
(503) 488-5405; (800) 345-2570

Adams Cottage, built in 1900, offers picket-fence country charm with beautiful grounds surrounding the two-story house and secluded carriage house. Queen-size and twin beds, private bath, air conditioning, antiques, in-room fireplace, and gourmet breakfast. Short walk to shops, theater, SOSC, and museum of natural history. ABBN member.

Host: Jeff von Hauf
Rooms: 4 (PB) $59-110
Full Breakfast
Credit Cards: None
Notes: 2, 5, 8, 9, 10, 11, 12, 13, 14

Ashland's Victory House

271 Beach Street, 97520
(503) 488-4428

Celebrate the 1940s in this charming Tudor with eclectic furnishings that can accommodate couples or a group of 12 comfort-ably. Enjoy the USO den with a jukebox, piano, classical movies, and memorabilia. Soak in FDR's Hot Springs Spa on the deck. Full, nutritious vegetarian breakfasts provided. Ashland offers Oregon Shakespeare Festival, art, music, and museum of natural history. Rogue River, Crater Lake, and Mount Ashland provide nearby rafting, hiking, fishing, and skiing. Limited smoking permitted. Inquire about children.

Host: Dale Swire
Rooms: 5 (PB) $59-95
Full Breakfast
Credit Cards: None
Notes: 2, 5, 9, 10, 11, 12, 13, 14

Country Willows Bed and Breakfast Inn

1313 Clay Street, 97520
(503) 488-1590; (800) WILLOWS
FAX (503) 488-1611

Combine Ashland's theatrical attractions with a peaceful rural setting at this restored 1896 farmhouse on five acres. Guest rooms have views of the surrounding Siskiyou and Cascade Mountains. Hiking trails are accessible from the grounds. Guests can relax in the Jacuzzi, the heated swimming pool, or on the inn porches, where the country quiet is disturbed only by the occasional honks of ducks and geese. Rooms are in the main house, a separate cottage, and the barn. Private baths and air conditioning. Bicycles are available. Full gourmet breakfast.

Host: Dan Durant
Suite: 1 (PB) $90-165
Full Breakfast
Credit Cards: A, B
Notes: 2, 5, 7, 9, 10, 11, 12, 13, 14

NOTES: Credit cards: A MasterCard; B Visa; C American Express; D Discover; E Diners Club; F Other;
2 Personal checks accepted; 3 Lunch available; 4 Dinner available; 5 Open all year; 6 Pets welcome;
7 No smoking; 8 Children welcome; 9 Social drinking allowed; 10 Tennis nearby; 11 Swimming nearby;
12 Golf nearby; 13 Skiing nearby; 14 May be booked through a travel agent.

Cowslip's Belle Bed and Breakfast

159 North Main Street, 97520
(503) 488-2901; (800) 888-6819

Teddy bears, chocolate truffles, sweet dreams, and scrumptious breakfasts can be enjoyed here. Just three blocks to the heart of town. Beautiful 1913 Craftsman bungalow and carriage house. Four queen/twin rooms with private baths and entrances. Featured in *Weekends for Two in the Pacific Northwest—50 Romantic Getaways, Best Places to Kiss in the Northwest,* and *Northwest Best Places.*

Hosts: Jon and Carmen Reinhardt
Rooms: 4 (PB) $75-115
Full Breakfast
Credit Cards: A, B
Notes: 2, 5, 7, 9, 10, 11, 12, 13, 14

Daniel's Roost

1920 East Main Street, 97520
(503) 482-0121; (800) 215-9031
FAX (503) 482-7493

Daniel's Roost, with breathtaking views in all directions, offers a private, parklike setting nestled on two acres with two creeks and a pond. Custom-built designer home elegantly furnished in antiques. Air-conditioned bedroom or suite with queen-size beds. Fresh flowers daily and a superb breakfast. A mere four-minute drive to the theaters. Inquire about accommodations for children.

Hosts: Michele Martin and Daniel Fischer
Rooms: 2 (1 PB; 1 SB) $60-100
Full Breakfast
Credit Cards: None
Notes: 2, 5, 7, 9, 10, 11, 12, 13, 14

Hersey House

451 North Main Street, 97520
(503) 482-4563

Gracious living in an elegantly restored Victorian with a colorful English country garden. Also, a separate bungalow for families or groups that sleeps two to six.

Hersey House

Sumptuous breakfasts. Central air conditioning. Walk to plaza and three Shakespeare theaters. Nearby, guests will find white-water rafting on the Rogue and Klamath Rivers, Crater Lake National Park, Britt Music Festival, Jacksonville National Historic District, and Oregon wineries. Children over 12 welcome.

Hosts: Gail Orell and Lynn Savage
Rooms: 4 (PB) $99-115
Bungalow: 1 (PB) $120-180
Full Breakfast
Credit Cards: A, B
Notes: 2, 7, 9, 10, 11, 12, 13, 14

The Iris Inn

59 Manzanita Street, 97520
(503) 488-2286; (800) 460-7650

A 1905 Victorian furnished with antiques. Elegant breakfasts feature eggs Benedict and cheese-baked eggs. Mountain views, quiet neighborhood. Near the Oregon Shakespeare Theater and the Rogue River for rafting. Cross-country and downhill skiing is also nearby. The Oregon Cabaret Theater operates year-round, and the Britt Music Festival is enjoyed during the summer. Children over seven welcome.

Host: Vicki Lamb
Rooms: 5 (PB) $98
Full Breakfast
Credit Cards: A, B
Notes: 2, 5, 7, 10, 11, 12, 13

NOTES: Credit cards accepted: A MasterCard; B Visa; C American Express; D Discover; E Diners Club; F Other; 2 Personal checks accepted; 3 Lunch available; 4 Dinner available; 5 Open all year; 6 Pets welcome;

The Morical House

668 North Main Street, 97520
(503) 482-2254; (800) 208-0960

On one and one-half acres of beautifully
landscaped grounds, this superbly restored
1880s farmhouse offers 18th-century hospitality with 20th-century comfort. The
Morical House features seven gracious, air-
conditioned guest rooms, a bountiful breakfast menu that changes daily, afternoon
refreshments, extensive gardens with ponds
and deck, and an unobstructed view of the
Rouge Valley and Cascade Mountains. No
smoking inside. Children over 12 welcome.

Hosts: Gary and Sandye Moore
Rooms: 7 (PB) $85-145
Full Breakfast
Credit Cards: A, B, D
Notes: 2, 5, 9, 11, 12, 13, 14

Mount Ashland Inn

550 Mount Ashland Road, 97520
(503) 482-8707; (800) 830-8707

Enjoy mountain serenity and spectacular
views from this beautifully handcrafted log
inn 16 miles from Ashland. Relax in comfortable, welcoming surroundings accented

Mount Ashland Inn

by the sunny deck, rock fireplace, stained
glass, hand carvings, Oriental rugs, and
antiques. Hike and cross-country ski from
the door; closest lodging to downhill ski
area. AAA and Mobil recommended.
Member of the Oregon Bed and Breakfast
Guild and the Professional Association of
Innkeepers International. Children over
nine welcome.

Hosts: Jerry and Elaine Shanafelt
Rooms: 5 (PB) $85-130
Full Breakfast
Credit Cards: A, B, D
Notes: 2, 5, 9, 10, 12, 13, 14

Oak Hill Country Bed and Breakfast

2190 Siskiyou Boulevard, 97520
(503) 482-1554; (800) 888-7434

This 1910 farmhouse, minutes from the
Oregon Shakespeare Festival, offers the
convenience of the city with the ambience
and tranquility of the country. An old-
fashioned veranda, spacious living room,
gardens, and deck provide variety for
guests' relaxation. Each of the inn's five
air-conditioned bedrooms has a queen-size
bed and a private bath. The family-style,
gourmet breakfast is truly the "main
event" at Oak Hill. All of the inn's guests
eat together in the spacious, sunny dining
room. Children over eight welcome.

Rooms: 5 (PB) $60-90
Full Breakfast
Credit Cards: A, B
Notes: 2, 5, 7, 9, 10, 11, 12, 13, 14

Pinehurst Inn at Jenny Creek

17250 Highway 66, 97520
(503) 488-1002

Constructed in 1923 with logs harvested
from the property, the lodge accommodated
travelers on the new State Highway 66
built to replace the old southern Oregon
wagon road. The inn is on the west bank of
Jenny Creek, where the Cascade and
Siskiyou Mountains meet, 23 miles east of

7 No smoking; 8 Children welcome; 9 Social drinking allowed; 10 Tennis nearby; 11 Swimming nearby;
12 Golf nearby; 13 Skiing nearby; 14 May be booked through a travel agent.

Ashland and 39 miles west of Klamath Falls. The restaurant serves breakfast, lunch, and dinner to both our guests and the public.

Hosts: Mike and Mary Jo Moloney
Rooms: 4 (PB) $75-95
Suites: 2 (PB)
Full Breakfast
Credit Cards: A, B, D
Notes: 2, 3, 4, 5, 7, 9, 12, 13

The Queen Anne Bed and Breakfast

125 North Main Street, 97520
(503) 482-0220; (800) 460-6818

This elegant 1880 Victorian home is furnished with antiques and vintage quilts. Splendid rose gardens and an exquisite English flower garden with a waterfall, gazebo, and spacious deck to enjoy. Two blocks away from the Shakespeare theaters and downtown. Full country breakfasts served in the morning. Seasonal rates.

Host: Elaine Martens
Rooms: 4 (PB) $75-130
Full Breakfast
Credit Cards: None
Notes: 2, 5, 7, 10, 12, 13

Romeo Inn

295 Idaho Street, 97520
(503) 488-0884

Mobil gives this inn a three-star rating. A quiet, elegant, lovely Cape Cod amid pines with a valley view. Four spacious rooms with central air conditioning. Some rooms

Romeo Inn

have fireplaces. Two luxurious suites with fireplaces; one has a whirlpool tub. Other amenities include a spa and pool, beautiful gardens, and gourmet breakfasts. Walk to the Oregon Shakespeare theaters and town. Member of the Oregon Bed and Breakfast Guild; AAA-rated three diamonds.

Hosts: Margaret and Bruce Halverson
Rooms: 6 (PB) $105-175
Full Breakfast
Credit Cards: A, B
Notes: 2, 5, 9, 10, 11, 12, 13, 14

The Wood's House Bed and Breakfast Inn

333 North Main Street, 97520
(503) 488-1598; (800) 435-8260

In the historic district of Ashland, four blocks from the Shakespeare theaters, 100-acre Lithia Park, restaurants, and shops, this 1908 Craftsman-style home offers six sunny and spacious guest rooms. Simple furnishings of warm woods, antique furniture, fine linens, watercolors, Oriental carpets, lace, leather books, and private-label amenities invite guests to relax in this comfortable yet elegant home. The one-half-acre terraced English gardens provide many areas for guests to relax, read, and socialize. Golf, swimming, hiking, biking, rafting, and hot-air ballooning nearby.

Hosts: Françoise and Lester Roddy
Rooms: 6 (PB) $65-112
Full Breakfast
Credit Cards: A, B
Notes: 2, 5, 7, 8, 9, 10, 11, 12, 13, 14

ASTORIA

Astoria Inn Bed and Breakfast

3391 Irving Avenue, 97103
(503) 325-8153

Relax and be pampered in the comfort of an 1890s Victorian. Magnificent views of the Columbia River. Hiking trails in the forest behind the inn. Beautifully decorated guest rooms with private baths. Full breakfast and daily snacks in rooms. Beautiful, quiet residential neighborhood just three minutes from shopping and restaurants.

Host: Mickey Cox
Rooms: 3 (PB) $60-85
Full Breakfast
Credit Cards: A, B, D
Notes: 2, 5, 7, 9, 12, 14

Columbia River Inn Bed and Breakfast

1681 Franklin Avenue, 97103
(503) 325-5044; (800) 953-5044

A five-star Victorian charmer. Guests note an elegant "Painted Lady" when they enter the Columbia River Inn Bed and Breakfast, built in the late 1870s. Nearby, guests will find the Columbia River Maritime Museum and Captain George Flavel House. The ocean is five miles away. Full breakfast, and a gift shop on the premises; riverview; off-street parking. Enjoy the new Stairway to the Stars, a unique terraced garden view of the celebrated Columbia River. Gazebo available for outdoor weddings and parties; write and ask for details and prices. During the summer and holidays, a minimum two-night stay is required. Closed Thanksgiving and Christmas day. Seasonal rates are also available.

Host: Karen N. Nelson
Rooms: 4 (PB) $75-125
Full Breakfast
Credit Cards: A, B, D
Notes: 2, 5, 7, 8, 12

Franklin Street Station Bed and Breakfast

1140 Franklin Street, 97103
(503) 325-4314; (800) 448-1098

This Victorian home is rated one of the finest bed and breakfast establishments in many publications. Six rooms, all with private baths (three suites), and three rooms with views of the Columbia River. Try the Captain's Quarters, with a fabulous view,

wet bar, fireplace, TV, VCR, stereo, and luxurious bath. Full breakfast. Close to downtown and within walking distance of museums. Make reservations in advance, if possible.

Host: Renee Caldwell
Rooms: 6 (PB) $63-115
Full Breakfast
Credit Cards: A, B
Notes: 2, 5, 8, 9, 10, 11, 12, 14

Grandview Bed and Breakfast

1574 Grand Avenue, 97103
(503) 325-5555; (800) 488-3250

Wonderful views of the Columbia River; close to the best maritime museum on the West Coast and other museums, churches, and Victorian homes. Domestic and foreign ships in port. Light, airy three-story Victorian with hardwood floors. Guest rooms and two-bedroom suites available.

Host: Charleen Maxwell
Rooms: 3 (PB) $39-92
Suites: 3 (2 bedrooms, PB) $86-140
Full Breakfast
Credit Cards: A, B, D
Notes: 2, 5, 7, 8, 10, 11, 12, 14

Windover House Bed and Breakfast

550 West Lexington Avenue, 97103
(503) 325-8093; (800) 990-9330

Windover House is in the historic town of Astoria, the first settlement west of the Mississippi in 1844. Enjoy the panoramic view of the mouth of the Columbia River and the Port of Astoria. The rooms are decorated with some family antiques, and a large Danish porcelain collection is displayed. A Danish breakfast is one of the breakfasts served. Limited smoking allowed. Children over seven welcome.

Host: Coralie F. Smith
Rooms: 3 (PB) $65-75
Full Breakfast
Credit Cards: A, B, E
Notes: 2, 12, 14

7 No smoking; 8 Children welcome; 9 Social drinking allowed; 10 Tennis nearby; 11 Swimming nearby; 12 Golf nearby; 13 Skiing nearby; 14 May be booked through a travel agent.

BANDON

Lighthouse Bed and Breakfast

650 Jetty Road, P.O. Box 24, 97411
(503) 347-9316

The gateway of the Pacific Ocean meets the mouth of the Coquille River with the Bandon Historical Lighthouse illuminating the scene. Walking distance to historical old downtown Bandon or the beach and surf. Unsurpassed views. Four guest rooms. One king-size room with Jacuzzi and fireplace. Continental plus breakfast. Children over 12 welcome.

Host: Shirley Chalupa
Rooms: 4 (PB) $90-115
Continental Breakfast
Credit Cards: A, B
Notes: 2, 5, 7, 9, 11, 12

Sea Star Guesthouse

370 First Street, 97411
(503) 347-9632

This guest house is a comfortable, romantic coastal getaway with European ambience. It is on the harbor and provides harbor-, river-, and ocean views. The shops, galleries, theater, and other sights of Old Town are just a step away. The newly decorated rooms offer a warm, private retreat. Some rooms have skylights and open-beam ceilings; all have decks. Breakfast discount vouchers may be purchased for use in the charming bistro. Full breakfast available.

Hosts: Eileen Sexton and Robert O'Neal
Rooms: 4 (PB) $35-85
Full Breakfast
Credit Cards: A, B
Notes: 3, 4, 5, 7, 8, 9, 11, 12

BEAVERTON

The Yankee Tinker Bed and Breakfast

5480 Southwest 183rd Avenue, 97007
(503) 649-0932; (800) 846-5372

Suburban convenience close to Washington County wineries, farms, and orchards, as well as high-tech Sunset Corridor. Ten miles west of Portland, midway between the coast and the mountains. Windsurf, fish, boat, or canoe on Hagg Lake, or canoe the lazy Tualatin River. Canoe available. Private yard with gardens and deck. Local Oregon wines offered from 4:00-6:00 P.M. Comfortable rooms are furnished with family heirlooms, antiques, cozy quilts, and garden flowers. The acclaimed breakfast often includes the Yankee tradition of pie.

Hosts: Jan and Ralph Wadleigh
Rooms: 3 (2 PB; 1 SB) $60-70
Full Breakfast
Credit Cards: A, B, C, D, E
Notes: 2, 5, 9, 10, 11, 12, 14

BEND

Farewell Bend Bed and Breakfast

29 Northwest Greeley, 97701
(503) 382-4374

Restored 70-year-old Dutch Colonial house. Four blocks from downtown shopping, restaurants, and Drake Park on the Deschutes River. In winter, ski Mount Bachelor. In summer, golf, white-water raft, fish, and hike. Complimentary wine or

Farewell Bend

sherry. King-size beds, down comforters, handmade quilts, and terry-cloth robes.

Host: M. Lorene Bateman
Rooms: 3 (PB) $70-75
Full Breakfast
Credit Cards: C
Notes: 2, 5, 7, 9, 10, 11, 12, 13, 14

Juniper Acres

65220 Smokey Ridge Road, 97701
(541) 389-2193

This bed and breakfast is a lodge-style log home nestled among the trees. The home overlooks seven mountain peaks and is seven minutes from town. Each bedroom has a private bath. A full breakfast is served. This home has been featured in three magazines.

Hosts: Della and Vern Bjerk
Rooms: 2 (PB) $65
Full Breakfast
Credit Cards: None
Notes: 2, 5, 7, 12, 13, 14

Lara House Bed and Breakfast

640 Northwest Congress, 97701
(503) 388-4064

A magnificent historic home overlooking Drake Park and Mirror Pond. Cozy living room with fireplace, cable TV, reading/game sitting area. Sunroom with view of park and sprawling manicured grounds. Five suites uniquely decorated with sitting areas and private baths. One two-bedroom suite with private bath. Hot tub. Homemade breakfast. Close to skiing, fishing, hiking, rafting, and cycling. Two blocks from downtown shops and restaurants.

Hosts: Doug and Bobbye Boger
Rooms: 6 (PB) $65-85
Full Breakfast
Credit Cards: A, B, D
Notes: 2, 5, 7, 8, 9, 10, 11, 12, 13

The Sather House Bed and Breakfast

7 Northwest Tumalo Avenue, 97701
(503) 388-1065

Historic Victorian home. Step back in time to a serene, elegant era. Period furnishings define the four spacious guest rooms. Wicker furniture graces the veranda. Walk to Deschutes River, Drake Park, and downtown. The Cascade Mountains and beautiful lakes provide year-round recreation. Enjoy a tour by a horse-drawn carriage. Fireside tea served on cool days. Cold drinks and homemade treats served on the veranda on warm days and evenings.

Host: Robbie Giamboi
Rooms: 4 (2 PB; 2 SB) $75-85
Full Breakfast
Credit Cards: A, B, D
Notes: 5, 7, 10, 11, 12, 13

BROOKINGS

Chetco River Inn

21202 High Prairie Road, 97415
(503) 469-8128 (radiophone)
(800) 327-2688 Pelican Bay Travel

Relax in the peaceful seclusion of 35 forested acres. Near the seacoast town of Brookings. The inn is small, so guest numbers are limited. Surrounded on three sides by the lovely Chetco River, the inn uses alternative energy, but it will offer guests all modern amenities. Delicious big meals. River fishing, swimming, hiking, bird watching, mushrooming, and just plain relaxing. Smoking in designated areas. Swimming is available in the river. May book through a travel agent if called direct.

Host: Sandra Brugger
Rooms: 4 (3 PB; 1 SB) $85
Full Breakfast
Credit Cards: A, B
Notes: 2, 4, 5, 8, 9

Holmes Sea Cove Bed and Breakfast

17350 Holmes Drive, 97415
(503) 469-3025

A delightful seacoast hideaway with a spectacular oceanview, a trail to the beach,

7 No smoking; 8 Children welcome; 9 Social drinking allowed; 10 Tennis nearby; 11 Swimming nearby; 12 Golf nearby; 13 Skiing nearby; 14 May be booked through a travel agent.

private guest entrances, and a tasty, expanded Continental breakfast served in the guest rooms. Enjoy beachcombing and whale watching.

Hosts: Jack and Lorene Holmes
Rooms: 3 (PB) $80-95
Continental Breakfast
Credit Cards: A, B
Notes: 2, 5, 7, 10, 11, 14

The South Coast Inn

516 Redwood Street, 97415
(503) 469-5557; (800) 525-9273
FAX (503) 469-6615

A 1917 vintage home designed in the Craftsman style by Bernard Maybeck. Restored and furnished with antiques and treasures, this home has a happy, warm feeling. Large parlor, indoor hot tub/sauna, spacious bedrooms upstairs. Oceanview. Just a few blocks from the river and harbor. Gourmet breakfast includes Norwegian waffles. A private garden cottage is also available. Fully licensed. Children over 12 are welcome.

Hosts: Ken and Keith
Rooms: 4 (PB) $74-94
Full Breakfast
Credit Cards: A, B, C, D
Notes: 2, 5, 9, 10, 11, 12, 14

CLOVERDALE (PACIFIC CITY)

Sandlake Country Inn

8505 Galloway Road, 97112
(503) 965-6745

Sshhh…it's a secret hideaway on the awesome Oregon coast—a private, peaceful place for making marriage memories. This 1894 shipwreck-timbered farmhouse on the Oregon historic register is tucked into a bower of old roses. Hummingbirds, Mozart, cookies at midnight, marble fireplaces, whirlpools for two, bikes, honeymoon cottage, breakfast ensuite, vintage movies, "green" rooms, no smoking,

wheelchair accessible, closed-caption TV. Togetherness Baskets available.

Hosts: Margo and Charles Underwood
Rooms: 4 (PB) $80-125
Full Breakfast
Credit Cards: A, B, D
Notes: 2, 3, 4, 5, 7, 12, 14

Blackberry Inn Bed and Breakfast

COOS BAY

Blackberry Inn Bed and Breakfast

843 Central, 97420
(503) 267-6951

On the southern Oregon coast, this charming bed and breakfast offers the elegant atmosphere of an old Victorian home. Since the inn is separate from the hosts' residence, guests can enjoy the hospitality and have privacy, too. A quick walk to several restaurants, stores, a theater, an art museum, and the city park, with its lovely Japanese gardens, tennis courts, and picnic areas.

Hosts: John and Louise Duncan
Rooms: 4 (3 PB; 1 SB) $35-50
Continental Breakfast
Credit Cards: A, B
Notes: 2, 5, 8, 9, 10, 11, 12

DEPOE BAY

The Channel House Inn, Inc.

35 Ellingson, P.O. Box 56, 97341
(503) 765-2140; (800) 477-2140
FAX (503) 765-2191

The Channel House Inn is dramatically perched on the ocean at the entrance to Oregon's Depoe Bay. Watch ocean storms and spouting whales from one of 12 ocean-front rooms or from the privacy of a whirlpool tub. Deep-sea fishing, fireplaces, and lots of sea air.

Host: Vicki Mix
Rooms: 15 (PB) $60-200
Continental Breakfast
Credit Cards: A, B, D
Notes: 2, 5, 7, 12, 14

ELMIRA

McGillivray's Log Home Bed and Breakfast

88680 Evers Road, 97437
(503) 935-3564

West of Eugene, guests will find the best of yesterday with the comforts of today. Set on five wooded acres, this air-conditioned home has wheelchair access. The hearty breakfasts are often prepared on an antique wood-burning cook stove.

Host: Evelyn R. McGillivray
Rooms: 2 (PB) $50-70
Full Breakfast
Credit Cards: A, B
Notes: 2, 5, 7, 9

EUGENE

Atherton Place Bed and Breakfast

690 West Broadway, 97402
(503) 683-2674

Close to downtown and University of Oregon on a tree-lined residential street is a quiet 1928 Dutch Colonial home featuring ceiling fans, antiques, French doors, and original crown molding. Each guest room has a firm queen-size bed; one room has a twin bed also. A three-course breakfast is creatively prepared and served. Amenities include upstairs sitting room with cable

TV, early morning freshly ground coffee, and sweet dreams tea at bedtime.

Host: Marne Krozek
Rooms: 3 (1 PB; 2 SB) $50-80
Full Breakfast
Credit Cards: None
Notes: 2, 5, 7, 10, 11, 12, 13, 14

Kjaer's House in the Woods

814 Lorane Highway, 97405
(503) 343-3234

A 1910 Craftsman-style home in a peaceful setting on a quiet, countrylike road ideal for walking, jogging, hiking, or deer and bird watching. Antiques, Oriental carpets, and square grand piano available. Member of the Oregon Bed and Breakfast Guild. "Urban convenience/suburban tranquility." Inquire about accommodations for children.

Hosts: George and Eunice Kjaer
Rooms: 2 (PB) $40-75
Full Breakfast
Credit Cards: None
Notes: 2, 5, 7, 9, 10, 11, 12, 13, 14

Kjaer's House in the Woods

The Oval Door

988 Lawrence at Tenth, 97401
(503) 683-3160; FAX (503) 485-5339

Newly built as a bed and breakfast inn, this 1920s farmhouse-style home in the heart of Eugene has a wraparound porch and an inviting front door with an oval glass. Guest rooms are spacious and comfortable, each with large private bathroom. The Tub Room with Jacuzzi for two is a relaxing haven with bubbles, candle, and music. Hearty breakfast with homemade specialities. Guests love the porch swing and cozy library.

Hosts: Judith McLane and Dianne Feist
Rooms: 4 (PB) $65-90
Full Breakfast
Credit Cards: A, B, C
Notes: 2, 5, 8, 9, 12, 13, 14

Pookie's Bed 'n' Breakfast on College Hill

2013 Charnelton Street, 97405
(503) 343-0383; (800) 558-0383
FAX (503) 343-0383
internet: URL www.travelassist.com

This restored Craftsman home built in 1918 offers distinctive rooms with many antiques. The two rooms with queen-size bed and twin beds are upstairs and share a cozy sitting room. In a quiet, older neighborhood close to the University of Oregon, downtown, shopping, and fine restaurants. The hosts pamper their guests with a full breakfast served in the formal dining room at guests' convenience. Beautiful grounds with rose garden and wonderful yard where guests can relax. This is a nonsmoking facility, but smoking is permitted outside.

Hosts: Pookie and Doug Walling
Rooms: 2 (1 PB; 1 SB) $65-80
Full Breakfast
Credit Cards: None
Notes: 2, 5, 7, 8, 9, 10, 11, 12, 13

GRANTS PASS

AHLF House Inn Bed and Breakfast

762 Northwest Sixth Street, 97526
(800) 863-1374

"The Jewel" of Grants Pass, this 1902 Queen Anne Victorian is the town's largest historic residence. Completely remodeled, this beautifully appointed home offers trav-

elers pleasing accommodations. Featured on the walking tour of national historic buildings. A full breakfast and evening dessert and beverage are served. Rooms are spacious and comfortable with private baths; Jacuzzi available.

Hosts: Kenneth and Cathy Neuschafer
Rooms: $65-85
Full Breakfast
Credit Cards: A, B, C
Notes: 2, 5, 7, 8, 9, 12, 14

Lawnridge House

1304 Northwest Lawnridge, 97526
(503) 476-8518

Restored, antique-furnished 1909 Craftsman, shaded by 200-year-old oaks. Beamed ceilings, fireplace, and a VCR in guest living room. One suite features queen-size canopy bed, balcony, closeted refrigerator full of goodies, TV, air conditioning, telephone, sitting room, and bath. A second contains handmade canopied king-size bed, bay windows, TV, air conditioning, telephone, and private bath. A third room offers a queen-size bed, bay windows, and TV. Dark wood floors, Oriental rugs, and full Northwest regional breakfasts.

Host: Barbara Head
Rooms: 3 (2 PB; 1 SB) $45-70
Full Breakfast
Credit Cards: None
Notes: 2, 5, 8, 9, 11, 12, 14

Pine Meadow Inn

1000 Crow Road, Merlin, 97532
(503) 471-6277 (phone/FAX); (800) 554-0806

A distinctive country retreat on nine acres of meadow and woods at the gateway to the wild and scenic area of the Rogue River. Enjoy nearby white-water rafting, Shakespeare Festival, historic Jacksonville, and California redwoods. Wraparound porch with wicker furniture, English cutting and herb gardens, a hot tub under the pines, Koi pond. All guest rooms are sunny and well lit for reading, with queen-size, pillow-top mattresses, private baths, window seats, and sitting area. Turn-of-the-century antiques. Delicious, healthy breakfasts. Central air. Children over eight are welcome.

Hosts: Maloy and Nancy Murdock
Rooms: 3 (PB) $65-110
Full Breakfast
Credit Cards: None
Notes: 2, 5, 7, 9, 12

Pine Meadow Inn

HALFWAY

Birch Leaf Farm Bed and Breakfast

Rural Route 1, Box 91, 97834
(503) 742-2990

This 42-acre farm is at the foot of the Wallowa Mountains in eastern Oregon, near the Oregon Trail Interpretive Center. Close to Hells Canyon National Recreation Area and the Eagle Cap Wilderness, two of the most rugged and beautiful places in the western U.S. The home is a turn-of-the-century farmhouse wrapped by large verandas. Each guest room has a wonderful view of the surrounding valley. Breakfast is served family-style in the dining alcove, but during the summer guests frequently take it to the deck. The area provides fishing, boating, horseback riding, hiking, and cross-country skiing. MasterCard and Visa accepted during the summer. Inquire about accommodations for pets.

Rooms: 5 (3 PB; 2 SB) $65-75
Full Breakfast
Credit Cards: None
Notes: 2, 3, 4, 5, 7, 8, 9, 11, 13, 14

HARBOR

Oceancrest House

15510 Pedrioli Drive, 97415
(503) 469-9200; (800) 769-9200

Escape from the ordinary! Oceancrest House, on the Oregon coast three and one-half miles north of the California border, offers a private place to relax, a panoramic view of the bay, and stairs to a beautiful secluded beach. Hosts pamper guests with luxurious furnishings and delicious baked goodies. Breakfast is served in guests' room for privacy and maximum relaxation. Enjoy watching the whales and pelicans, walking on the beach, or visiting the nearby redwood forests.

Hosts: Georgine Paulin and Ronya Robinson
Rooms: 2 (PB) $79-89
Continental Breakfast
Credit Cards: A, B, D
Notes: 2, 5, 9, 10, 12, 14

HOOD RIVER

Brown's Bed and Breakfast

3000 Reed Road, 97031
(503) 386-1545

This house is a functioning farmhouse built in the early 1930s and remodeled in 1985. It has a modern kitchen where the large farm-style breakfasts are prepared and a new bathroom that is shared by the two bedrooms. One bedroom has twin beds and overlooks beautiful Mount Hood, the other bedroom has a double bed and overlooks the orchard. Nestled in the forest and at the end of the road; the only noise to be heard is that of birds chirping. There are nature trails for either hiking or jogging.

Hosts: Al and Marian Brown
Rooms: 2 (SB) $60
Full Breakfast
Credit Cards: A, B
Notes: 2, 5, 7, 8, 10, 11, 12, 13

State Street Inn Bed and Breakfast

1005 State Street, 97031
(503) 386-1899

Circa 1932. This traditionally styled English house with gabled roof and leaded-glass windows overlooks the Columbia River and Mount Adams. Each of the four air-conditioned guest rooms is decorated in a different style: Colorado Old West, Massachusetts Colonial, California Sunshine, and Southern Maryland. Guests may sample wines at nearby wineries, try the local brew pub, or take a scenic train ride through local orchards.

Hosts: Mac and Amy Lee
Rooms: 4 (SB) $60-80
Full Breakfast
Credit Cards: A, B
Notes: 2, 5, 9, 10, 11, 12, 13, 14

JACKSONVILLE

Jacksonville Inn

175 East California Street, P.O. Box 359, 97530
(503) 899-1900; (800) 321-9344

Jacksonville Inn's eight air-conditioned rooms are furnished with restored antiques. A historic honeymoon cottage is furnished with everything imaginable. A lovely breakfast is provided. An award-winning dinner house featuring gourmet dining and more than 1,000 wines is in the 1861 vintage building.

Hosts: Jerry and Linda Evans
Rooms: 9 (PB) $80-175
Full Breakfast
Credit Cards: A, B, C, D, E
Notes: 2, 3, 4, 5, 7, 8, 9, 10, 11, 12, 13, 14

Orth House

Orth House Bed and Breakfast Inn

105 West Main Street, P.O. Box 1437, 97530
(503) 899-8665

In the historic corridor of Jacksonville, built in 1880, and listed on the National Register of Historic Places. Featured on TV and in magazines for its unique restoration with hidden electronic wizardry and memorabilia museum room. One block from Britt Music Pavilion. Senior discount rates.

Hosts: The Jays
Rooms: 3 (PB) $95-175
Full Breakfast
Credit Cards: A, B, C, D
Notes: 2, 3, 4, 5, 7, 9, 10, 11, 12, 13, 14

Reames House 1868

540 East California Street, P.O. Box 128, 97530
(503) 899-1868

Built by one of Jacksonville's early sheriffs and prosperous merchants, this inn is on the National Register of Historic Places. Victorian elegance—lace, climbing roses, and potpourri. Surrounded by spacious lawns and beautiful perennial gardens. Four guest rooms with period decor, two with private bath, share a bright sitting room furnished with white wicker, plants, and twining rose stenciling. Breakfast dishes include Oregon's bounty of fruits, berries,

NOTES: Credit cards accepted: A MasterCard; B Visa; C American Express; D Discover; E Diners Club; F Other; 2 Personal checks accepted; 3 Lunch available; 4 Dinner available; 5 Open all year; 6 Pets welcome;

and home-baked goods. Three blocks from the center of town.

Hosts: George and Charlotte Harrington-Winsley
Rooms: 4 (2 PB; 2 SB) $80-90
Full Breakfast
Credit Cards: None
Notes: 2, 5, 7, 9, 11, 12, 13, 14

JOSEPH

Chandlers' Bed, Bread and Trail Inn

700 Main Street, P.O. Box 639, 97846
(503) 432-9765; (800) 452-3781

The Chandlers' post-and-beam inn offers warm hospitality. At the base of the Wallowa Mountains, it provides a home base as guests explore the Eagle Cap Wilderness, visit bronze casting foundries, galleries, or swim and fish at nearby Wallowa Lake. In the winter, Nordic skiing and snowmobiling are popular activities.

Hosts: Ethel and Jim Chandler
Rooms: 5 (SB) $60
Full Breakfast
Credit Cards: A, B
Notes: 2, 7, 9, 10, 11, 12, 13

Chandlers'

LAFAYETTE

Kelty Estate Bed and Breakfast

675 Third Street, P.O. Box 817, 97127
(503) 864-3740

Built in 1872 in historic Lafayette, this early Colonial-style home is listed on the National Register of Historic Places. In the heart of Oregon wine country, Kelty Estate is perfect for visiting the entire Willamette Valley. After a breakfast that features Oregon-grown products, stroll across the street to browse at the antique mall or visit the county museum or one of the many nearby wineries. Less than an hour's drive to the state capital, Salem, or the many attractions of Portland. Within two hours' drive of scenic Mount Hood, the Columbia River Gorge, or the colorful Oregon coast.

Hosts: Ron and JoAnn Ross
Rooms: 2 (PB) $55-65
Full Breakfast
Credit Cards: None
Notes: 2, 5, 7, 8, 9, 12

LA GRANDE

Pitcher Inn Bed and Breakfast

608 "N" Avenue, 97850
(503) 963-9152

The host and hostess lay out the welcome mat for guests at this recently remodeled Georgian home. The Pitchers have redecorated this 1925 home to give it its original feel. The homey dining room with oak floor and table welcomes guests in the morning for a full breakfast. Four guest rooms are available, and each room mingles a touch of romance with a different color theme and accents of roses, bows, and pitchers. Guests are welcome to enjoy the privacy of their room or join others downstairs in the living room. No smoking. Children over 12 allowed. Closed January 2 through 15.

Hosts: Carl and Deanna Pitcher
Rooms: 4 (1 PB; 3 SB) $55-95
Full Breakfast
Credit Cards: A, B
Notes: 2, 7, 10, 12, 13, 14

Stang Manor Inn

1612 Walnut Street, 97850
(503) 963-2400

Open the doors of this elegant old mansion and be surrounded by warm hospitality and the graciousness of the 1920s. Built by lumber baron August Stange, this Georgian Colonial home is in the beautiful Grande Ronde Valley of northeastern Oregon on the Oregon Trail, one mile from I-84. Afternoon tea and a sumptuous breakfast are served.

Hosts: Pat and Marjorie McClure
Rooms: 5 (PB) $70-90
Full Breakfast
Credit Cards: A, B
Notes: 2, 5, 7, 9, 10, 11, 12, 13

LINCOLN CITY

Brey House Ocean View Bed and Breakfast Inn

3725 Northwest Keel Avenue, 97367
(503) 994-7123

This three-story Cape Cod-style house has a nautical theme that shows throughout the home. Across the street from the ocean, it is a short walk to shops and restaurants. Queen-size beds are in all the rooms, and guests can use the hot tub under the stars. Close to sea lion caves and the world's smallest harbor. Lincoln City is also the kite capital of the world. Enjoy watching the ocean while eating a fantastic breakfast served by the hosts.

Hosts: Milt and Shirley Brey
Rooms: 4 (PB) $65-125
Full Breakfast
Credit Cards: A, B, D
Notes: 5, 7, 9, 10, 11, 12, 14

McMINNVILLE

Steiger Haus

360 Wilson Street, 97128
(503) 472-0821; (503) 472-0238

An architecturally delightful classic inn with Old World character and a lovely wooded garden setting. Within walking distance to Linfield College, downtown restaurants, and shops. Regional wine trips and northwest Oregon day trips inspire

countless return visits. Named the number-two inn in America in 1991 by *The Inn Times*. Recommended by *Northwest Best Places*, Frommer's, and Fodor's. Children over ten welcome.

Hosts: Doris and Lynn Steiger
Rooms: 5 (PB) $70-100
Full Breakfast
Credit Cards: A, B
Notes: 2, 5, 7, 14

Waverly Cottage

MEDFORD

Waverly Cottage and Associated Bed and Breakfast

305 North Grape, 97501
(503) 772-1841

The state historic preservation officer describes Waverly Cottage as the most ornate Queen Anne-style cottage still standing in South Oregon. Fifteen years of authentic restoration by innkeeper. Guests may reserve the whole cottage for one low price. Three other adjacent historic properties. Full kitchens and private baths and entrances. Firm queen- and king-size beds available. Award-winning roses. Central air conditioning, fireplaces, and Jacuzzi. Color cable TV, VCR, and private cordless phones. Within walking distance of a dozen restaurants. "We hug visitors."

Host: David Fisse
Rooms: 11 (PB) $35-125
Continental Breakfast
Credit Cards: A, B, C, E, F
Notes: 2, 5, 6, 8, 9, 10, 11, 12, 13, 14

NOTES: Credit cards accepted: A MasterCard; B Visa; C American Express; D Discover; E Diners Club; F Other; 2 Personal checks accepted; 3 Lunch available; 4 Dinner available; 5 Open all year; 6 Pets welcome;

MERLIN

Morrison's Rogue River Lodge

8500 Galice Road, 97532
(503) 476-3825; (800) 826-1963
FAX (503) 476-4953

Morrison's Rogue River Lodge is in southern Oregon on the famous Rogue River. It was built in the 1940s and has grown from a fishing lodge to a full service destination resort catering to romantics as well as families, outdoorsmen, rafting enthusiasts, and fishermen. First-class accommodations in cozy riverview cabins with fireplaces or country decor lodge rooms. Well known for its fabulous cuisine. Overnight accommodations include a four-course gourmet dinner and a bountiful country breakfast. Whether fishing, white-water rafting, hiking, mountain biking, playing tennis, or simply relaxing, Morrison's offers unequaled beauty in a fabulous wilderness setting.

Host: Michelle Hanten
Rooms: 13 (PB) $160-240
Full Breakfast
Credit Cards: A, B
Notes: 2, 3, 4, 8, 9, 10, 11, 12, 14

MILWAUKIE

Historic Broetje House

3101 Southeast Courtney, 97222
(503) 659-8860

An 1890 Queen Anne estate with 40-foot water tower nestled in quiet residential area 15 minutes from downtown Portland. Approximately two acres of lovely gardens, gazebo, and 100-year-old redwood trees. House and grounds used for weddings and receptions. Antique-filled rooms and country decor lend a warm, cozy atmosphere. Close to shopping and restaurants.

Hosts: Lorraine Hubbard and Lois Bain
Rooms: 3 (1 PB; 2 SB) $45-85
Full Breakfast
Credit Cards: A, B, C
Notes: 2, 5, 7, 8, 9, 10, 11, 12, 13, 14

MOUNT HOOD AREA

Falcon's Crest Inn

87287 Government Camp Loop Highway
P.O. Box 185, 97028
(503) 272-3403; (800) 624-7384
FAX (503) 272-3454

Elegance "Mount Hood-style" features three rooms and two suites with private baths. Individually decorated with family heirlooms, in-room telephones, bed turn-down service, morning refreshment tray. A full breakfast is served in the morning. In the heart of a year-round recreation area. Skiing, hiking, fishing, and horseback riding are all nearby. Corporate, private, and mystery parties. Holiday and ski packages are a specialty. Fine evening dining and spirits available.

Hosts: Melody and Bob Johnson
Rooms: 5 (PB) $85-169
Full Breakfast
Credit Cards: A, B, C, D
Notes: 2, 4, 5, 7, 9, 11, 12, 13, 14

NEWBERG

Secluded Bed and Breakfast

19719 Northeast Williamson Road, 97132
(503) 538-2635

Beautiful country home on ten acres. The ideal retreat in the woods for hiking, country walks, and observing wildlife. Ten minutes' drive to several wineries; about one hour to the coast. Breakfast is a special occasion. Many antiques in the home. Near George Fox College and Linfield College.

Hosts: Durell and Del Belanger
Rooms: 2 (1 PB; 1 SB) $50-60.50
Full Breakfast
Credit Cards: None
Notes: 2, 5, 7, 8, 10, 11, 12, 14

Spring Creek Llama Ranch Bed and Breakfast

14700 Northeast Spring Creek Lane, 97132
(503) 538-5717 (phone/FAX)

7 No smoking; 8 Children welcome; 9 Social drinking allowed; 10 Tennis nearby; 11 Swimming nearby; 12 Golf nearby; 13 Skiing nearby; 14 May be booked through a travel agent.

"Quiet, peaceful, relaxing, beautiful setting, lovely home, wonderful hospitality." That's how guests describe their stay at the llama ranch. Spacious and immaculate inside, this enormous home is nestled in the midst of 24 acres of rolling pasture and forest. Artifacts and llamas accent the rooms. Friendly llamas and contented barn cats love visitors. Spring is baby time. In the wine country of Yamhill County, Oregon, just 25 minutes from downtown Portland. Air-conditioned.

Hosts: Dave and Melinda Van Bossuyt
Rooms: 2 (PB) $60-75
Full Breakfast
Credit Cards: None
Notes: 2, 5, 7, 8, 10, 11, 12, 14

NEWPORT

Oar House

520 Southwest Second Street, 97365
(503) 265-9571

Oar House, a Lincoln County historic landmark in the picturesque Nye Beach area of Newport, has offered comfort and conviviality to guests since the early 1900s. Originally a boarding house, later a bordello, and now a bed and breakfast, Oar House continues to attract visitors to its history, mystery, ghost, nautical theme, and hospitality. Each guest room has a

queen-size bed, new furnishings, and a view of the ocean. The lighthouse tower provides 360-degree views from Yaquina Head to Yaquina Bay.

Host: Jan LeBrun
Rooms: 4 (PB) $90-120
Full Breakfast
Credit Cards: A, B, D
Notes: 5, 7, 9, 10, 11, 12

Ocean House Bed and Breakfast

4920 Northwest Woody Way, 97365
(503) 265-6158; (800) 56 B-AND-B

Ocean House at beautiful Agate Beach has guest rooms that overlook gardens and the surf. A private trail leads to beach and tidal pools. Nearby attractions include the lighthouse, aquarium, marine science center, and bay front, with restaurants and galleries. Storm and whale watching lure winter guests, and the spacious great room is just the place to gather. Morning coffee for early birds is followed by breakfast in the sunroom. Special winter rates and gift certificates are available.

Host: Bob Garrard
Rooms: 4 (PB) $70-115
Full Breakfast
Credit Cards: A, B
Notes: 2, 5, 7, 9, 10, 11, 12

Sylvia Beach Hotel

267 Northwest Cliff, 97365
(503) 265-5428

Oceanfront bed and breakfast for book lovers. Each room is named after a different author and decorated individually. Some have fireplaces. Hot spiced wine is served in the library at 10:00 P.M. Dinner served nightly. The inn is not suitable for young children.

Hosts: Goody Cable and Sally Ford
Rooms: 20 (PB) $61-135
Full Breakfast
Credit Cards: A, B, C
Notes: 2, 4, 5, 7, 9, 10, 11, 12

OREGON CITY

Inn of the Oregon Trail

416 South McLoughlin, 97045
(503) 656-2089

Enjoy Gothic Revitalization! Our Gothic Revival-style home built in 1867 by E. B. Fellow has three tastefully appointed guest rooms on the third floor overlooking landscaped gardens. An additional room on the bottom floor offers a private entrance, bath, fireplace, and wet bar. The main floor houses the Fellows House Restaurant, open to the public weekdays, 11:00 A.M. to 3:00 P.M. Private dinners for inn guests are available with prior notice. Discover historic Oregon City, the end of the Oregon Trail. Just nine miles east of Portland on 99 East.

Hosts: Mary and Tom DeHaven
Rooms: 4 (PB) $55-85
Full Breakfast
Credit Cards: A, B
Notes: 2, 3, 4, 5, 9, 12, 13

OTIS

Salmon River Bed and Breakfast

5622 Salmon River Highway (Highway 18), 97368
(503) 994-2639

Rooms have TV and VCR. Rooms with private baths are off a main sitting room with fireplace and private entry. Decks and a covered patio with chairs provide places for smokers. One room has twin beds. This and one other room can accommodate a cot or crib, which hosts can provide at an additional charge of $15. Lady guests can choose a craft from the greeter's basket. Emphasis on hospitality and low rates. Eight miles from Lincoln City and coast. Hosts have traveled all 50 states, plus Canada, Mexico, Japan, Australia, and the "Kiwi" land.

Hosts: Marvin and Pawnee Pegg
Rooms: 4 (2 PB; 2 SB) $50-60
Full Breakfast
Credit Cards: A, B, D
Notes: 2, 5, 7, 8, 10, 11, 12, 14

General Hooker's

PORTLAND

General Hooker's Bed and Breakfast

125 Southwest Hooker, 97201
(503) 222-4435; (800) 745-4135
FAX (503) 295-6410
e-mail: 74627.414 @ compuserve.com

In a quiet historic district and within walking distance of downtown, General Hooker's is a casually elegant Victorian townhouse that combines the best of two centuries: the mellow charm of family heirlooms from the 19th century and the comfort and convenience of the 20th century. Eclectic in ambience, the house features a restrained use of Victorian detail, an interesting collection of Northwest art (some done by artists in the host's family), comfortable, tasteful furniture, and the music of Bach and Vivaldi playing throughout. Knowledgeable host is a fourth-generation Portlander and a charter member of Oregon's Bed and Breakfast Guild. Sociable Abyssinian cat in residence. Wine and beer sold on premises. Two-night minimum stay required for holidays and some weekends. Personal checks accepted with bankcard. May be booked through travel agent with two-night minimum stay.

Host: Lori Hall
Rooms: 4 (2 PB; 2 SB) $70-115
Continental Breakfast
Credit Cards: A, B, C
Notes: 5, 7, 9, 10, 11, 12

7 No smoking; 8 Children welcome; 9 Social drinking allowed; 10 Tennis nearby; 11 Swimming nearby; 12 Golf nearby; 13 Skiing nearby; 14 May be booked through a travel agent.

Georgian House Bed and Breakfast

1828 Northeast Siskiyou, 97212
(503) 281-2250; FAX (503) 281-3301

Step back in time to charming "Olde England" at this restored handsome brick Georgian Colonial featured in *Better Homes and Gardens* magazine. Relax on the sun deck or in the gazebo. Stroll through the colorful rose garden or the quiet historic Irvington neighborhood. Close to shopping, restaurants, theaters, easy freeway access to I-5, I-205, and I-84. Close to convention center, coliseum, Lloyd Center Mall, downtown, and MAX Light Rail. Winding staircase to second floor, hardwood floors, and antiques.

Host: Willie Ackley
Rooms: 4 (1 PB: 3 SB) $60-85
Continental Breakfast
Credit Cards: A, B
Notes: 2, 5, 7, 10, 11, 12, 13

Portland Guest House

John Palmer House

4314 North Mississippi Avenue, 97217
(503) 284-5893

Just 45 minutes from Columbia Gorge, Mount Hood, and wine country. One hour from the Pacific Ocean. This beautiful, historic Victorian can be guests' home away from home. Award-winning decor. Gourmet chef. The dinner-for-two is a not-to-be-missed experience. Kitchen units available for families. Daily, weekly, and monthly rates available.

Hosts: Mary and Richard Sauter
Rooms: 7 (2 PB; 5 SB) $45-125
Full Breakfast
Credit Cards: A, B, C, D
Notes: 2, 4, 5, 7, 8, 9, 10, 11, 14

Portland Guest House

1720 Northeast Fifteenth Street, 97212
(503) 282-1402

This 1890 Victorian is in the historic Irvington neighborhood. All rooms have telephones, antiques, vintage linens, and great beds. Luscious breakfasts. Family suite with three beds, two rooms with two beds, and five rooms with private baths. Herb, vegetable, and flower gardens. Closest bed and breakfast to convention center. Convenient transit to downtown. Walk to restaurants, delis, coffee shops, and boutiques. Central air-conditioning.

Host: Susan Gisvold
Rooms: 7 (5 PB; 2 SB) $55-85
Full Breakfast
Credit Cards: A, B, C, D
Notes: 2, 5, 7, 8, 9, 10, 11, 12, 13

PORT ORFORD

Home by the Sea Bed and Breakfast

44 Jackson Street, P.O. Box 606, 97465-0606
(503) 332-2855
email: 72672.1072 @ compuserve.com

The hosts built this contemporary wood home on a spit of land overlooking a stretch of Oregon coast that takes one's breath away. Queen-size Oregon myrtle wood beds are featured in both accommodations; ideal quarters for two couples traveling together. A short walk to restaurants, public beaches, historic Battle Rock Park, and the harbor. Amenities include a dramatic oceanview, direct beach access, smoke-free environment, full breakfast, laundry privileges, cable TV, and telephone jacks in the rooms. No pets. No children. Brochure available. Macintosh spoken.

Hosts: Alan and Brenda Mitchell
Rooms: 2 (PB) $75-85
Full Breakfast
Credit Cards: A, B
Notes: 2, 5, 7, 8, 9

ROSEBURG

The Umpqua House

7338 Oak Hill Drive, 97470
(503) 459-4700

A contemporary two-story house on six wooded acres with a picturesque view of the beautiful Umpqua Valley. In addition to warm hospitality and a charming setting, guests enjoy comfortably furnished rooms, separate entrance, and lounging area. Near wineries and Wildlife Safari with golf, tennis, and fishing area. Two rooms with shared full bath. Full breakfast includes freshly squeezed orange juice, fresh fruit, entrée, and home-baked goodies. Able to cater to dietary needs. Inquire about pets.

Hosts: Allen and Rhoda Mozorsky
Rooms: 2 (SB) $60
Full Breakfast
Credit Cards: None
Notes: 2, 7, 8, 9, 10, 11, 12, 14

SISTERS

Cascade Country Inn

15870 Barclay Drive, P.O. Box 834, 97759
(503) 549-4666; (800) 316-0089

Built in 1994, Cascade Country Inn is elegant yet homey with a romantic country

theme. Antiques, stained glass, and quilts invite guests to relax and enjoy the fabulous Cascade Range outside the windows. Soak in the outdoor spa, sit on the porch swing and gaze at a spectacular sunset, or ride to town on mountain bikes. Fly in or drive. On the grounds of Sisters Eagle Air, a small community airport.

Hosts: Judy Tolonen and Victoria Tolonen
Rooms: 6 (PB)
Full Breakfast
Credit Cards: None
Notes: 2, 5, 7, 8, 9, 10, 12, 13, 14

SUBLIMITY

Silver Mountain Bed and Breakfast

4672 Drift Creek Road SE, 97385
(503) 769-7127

Visit a working farm in the Cascade foothills near Salem. Stay in the modernized "barn" with hot tub, sauna, pool table, Ping-Pong, TV/VCR, fireplace, and kitchen. Join in the farm chores or relax by the swimming pool. Five minutes to Silver Falls State Park for biking, hiking, and picnicking. Fishing, hiking, whitewater rafting, and float trips available on the nearby Santiam River. One hour from the ocean, mountains, or Portland. Open March through October.

Hosts: Jim and Shirley Heater
Rooms: 2 (PB) $60-75
Full Breakfast
Credit Cards: None
Notes: 2, 6, 7, 8, 10, 11, 12

WALDPORT

Cliff House

1450 Adahi Street-Yaquina John Point
Box 436, 97394
(503) 563-2506

"Pampered elegance by the sea." Each room is uniquely decorated with antiques, chandeliers, carpeting, remote control color TV; all have private cedar baths and balconies. Elegant lodging coupled with magnificent panoramic oceanview. Deep-sea fishing, river fishing, crabbing, golf club (one-half mile), and croquet. Close to horseback riding. Massage by appointment. New sauna-steam room. Minimum-stay requirements for weekends and holidays. The inn is closed from October 15 through March 31.

Host: Gabrielle Duvall
Rooms: 5 (PB) $95-225
Full Breakfast
Credit Cards: A, B
Notes: 2, 7, 9, 11, 12

WELCHES

Old Welches Inn
Bed and Breakfast

26401 East Welches Road, 97067
(503) 622-3754

Since the 19th century travelers have spent their vacations at the Old Welches Inn, the oldest building on Mount Hood. The inn is traditionally styled, reminiscent of the fine old homes of the South. Light-filled rooms with large French windows let the surrounding vistas of rivers and mountains greet guests daily. A variety of outdoor activities, including skiing, hiking, fishing, golf, etc., is only minutes away. A two-bedroom cottage that sleeps five is also available on the grounds. Call ahead to make arrangements for pets. Children over 12 are welcome.

Hosts: Judith and Ted Mondun
Rooms: 3 (SB) $74.50-100
Full Breakfast
Credit Cards: A, B, C, D
Notes: 2, 5, 7, 9, 10, 11, 12, 13, 14

YACHATS

The Sanderling
Bed and Breakfast

7304 Southwest Pacific Coast Highway,
Milepost 160, 97498
(503) 563-4752

Large guest rooms, dining, and viewing room are all oceanfront. Private baths, two-person Jacuzzi, and showers. Feather mattress and comforters. Full breakfast and special treats are often offered in evening. Early morning beverage of choice outside room. Miles of easy-walking sandy beach. Inside lockup for cycles. Books, games, puzzles, and kites. The uncrowded Oregon beach provides beauty year-round. Breathtaking sunsets and dramatic winter storms.

Hosts: Ernie and Pat Swinn
Rooms: 4 (PB) $100-130
Full Breakfast
Credit Cards: A, B, D
Notes: 2, 5, 7, 9, 12

YAMHILL

Flying M Ranch

23029 Northwest Flying M Road, 97148
(503) 662-3222; FAX (503) 662-3202

The bounty of Yamhill County's wine country joins with the coastal mountains to harbor the Flying M's spectacular log lodge. Delectable cuisine, year-round horseback riding, and limitless outdoor activities. Full-service restaurant, lounge, airstrip, gift shop, primitive camping, fishing, and dancing on Friday and Saturday evenings.

Hosts: Bryce and Barbara Mitchell
Rooms: 35 (PB) $50-150
Full Breakfast
Credit Cards: A, B, C, D, E
Notes: 2, 3, 4, 5, 6, 8, 9, 10, 11, 14

NOTES: Credit cards accepted: A MasterCard; B Visa; C American Express; D Discover; E Diners Club; F Other; 2 Personal checks accepted; 3 Lunch available; 4 Dinner available; 5 Open all year; 6 Pets welcome;

Pennsylvania

Adamstown Inn

ADAMSTOWN

Adamstown Inn

62 West Main Street, P.O. Box 938, 19501
(717) 484-0800; (800) 594-4808

Experience the simple elegance of the Adamstown Inn, a Victorian bed and breakfast resplendent with leaded-glass windows and doors, magnificent chestnut woodwork, and Oriental rugs. All four guest rooms are decorated with family heirlooms, handmade quilts, lace curtains, fresh flowers, and many distinctive touches that make any stay special. The accommodations range from antique to king-size beds. All rooms have private baths (two rooms feature two-person Jacuzzis). In the heart of the antique district, only minutes from the Reading outlet centers and Lancaster. Experience the magic of yesteryear.

Hosts: Tom and Wanda Berman
Rooms: 4 (PB) $65-105
Continental Breakfast
Credit Cards: A, B
Notes: 2, 5, 7, 9, 10, 11, 12, 14

ADAMSTOWN (REINHOLDS)

Bed and Breakfast Adventures

Suite 132, 2310 Central Avenue
North Wildwood, NJ 08260
(606) 522-4000; (800) 992-2632

PA703. Springwoods is a Civil War-era frame farmhouse that has been added to and tastefully restored. Accommodations include three guest rooms: one has a double bed and a private bath ensuite; another features brass twin beds, a queen-size sofa bed, sitting area, and detached bath; the third room with its double bed shares the bath when guests are traveling together. All rooms share a guest parlor with TV. Guests may swim in the pool, hike through the hillside, use the nearby public golf course, or shop at the Reading outlets. Lancaster Amish country and the Adamstown antique emporiums are both also nearby. Nonsmokers and children are welcome. $75.

AIRVILLE

Spring House

1264 Muddy Creek Forks Road, 17302
(717) 927-6906

Built in 1798 of fieldstone, the house is named for the pure spring it protects in the tranquil pre-Revolutionary War river valley village. The village and house are on the National Register of Historic Places. Lovingly restored to stenciled whitewashed walls, furnished with antiques and art, the inn offers full breakfast of local specialties, wine by the fire or on the front porch,

7 No smoking; 8 Children welcome; 9 Social drinking allowed; 10 Tennis nearby; 11 Swimming nearby; 12 Golf nearby; 13 Skiing nearby; 14 May be booked through a travel agent.

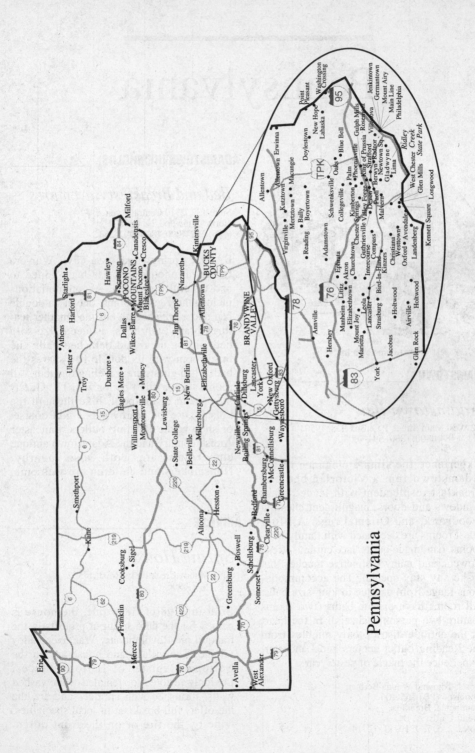

Pennsylvania

Spring House

Amish-made cheese, and caring hospitality. Horseback riding, scenic railroad, wineries, hiking, and trout fishing in immediate area. Near Amish community. Minimum stay weekends and holidays: two nights.

Host: Ray Constance Hearne
Rooms: 5 (3 PB; 2 SB) $52-85
Full Breakfast
Credit Cards: None
Notes: 2, 5, 8, 9, 11, 12, 14

AKRON (LANCASTER COUNTY)

Boxwood Inn

Corner Diamond Street and Tobacco Road
P.O. Box 203, 17501
(800) 238-3466

Relax in the comfort of a newly renovated and professionally decorated 1768 stone farmhouse filled with quiet country charm. Hosts offer large common rooms and spacious grounds. Afternoon tea is served in the garden room. In addition to the guest rooms in the main house, there is a separate carriage house with fireplace, Jacuzzi, and balcony. Enjoy biking, walking, or driving through Amish farm country. Visit the gift shop. Rated three diamonds by AAA. Closed January.

Hosts: June and Dick Klemm
Rooms: 5 (PB) $75-135
Full Breakfast
Credit Cards: A, B
Notes: 2, 7, 9, 14

ALLENTOWN

Association of Bed and Breakfasts in Philadelphia, Valley Forge, Brandywine

P.O. Box 562, Valley Forge, 19481-0562
(610) 783-7838; (800) 344-0123
FAX (610) 783-7783

1201. Circa 1835 Stone Farmhouse. Set amid nine huge sycamore trees. The inn is decorated in antiques. Guests are welcome to sit by the fire in the parlor, play games or cards, or watch the cable TV or VCR. There are five guest rooms. The Gentlemen's Room sports a male look; however, female guests love it as well. It features an oak bed and writing desk. The Oak Room features an oak antique bed with matching washstand. The Ashley Room is decorated in Victorian and features a queen-size bed with an antique Victorian headboard and gorgeous late 1800s settee. The Victorian Room is decorated fully Victorian with an iron and brass queen-size bed and comfortable fainting couch. The Primitive Room is decorated with primitive country antiques. This room features a private outhouse bath. $70-80.

ALTOONA

Hoenstine's Bed and Breakfast

418 Montgomery Street, Hollidaysburg, 16648
(814) 695-0632

This inn is any antique lover's dream, in an elegant 1839 townhouse in downtown registered historic Hollidaysburg. Right next door to a private historical and genealogical library. The hearty breakfast is the whim of the host's fancy and the area's seasonal ingredients. Inquire about accommodations for children and pets. Only three miles to Altoona, and near many antique shops and local parks in a beautiful residential section

NOTES: Credit cards: A MasterCard; B Visa; C American Express; D Discover; E Diners Club; F Other; 2 Personal checks accepted; 3 Lunch available; 4 Dinner available; 5 Open all year; 6 Pets welcome; 7 No smoking; 8 Children welcome; 9 Social drinking allowed; 10 Tennis nearby; 11 Swimming nearby; 12 Golf nearby; 13 Skiing nearby; 14 May be booked through a travel agent.

of Pennsylvania. Protected by attack cats and a standard poodle.

Host: Barbara Hoenstine
Rooms: 3 (1 PB; 2 SB) $50-60
Full Breakfast
Credit Cards: A, B
Notes: 2, 5, 7, 9, 10, 11, 12, 13

Swatara Creek Inn

ANNVILLE

Swatara Creek Inn

Rural Delivery 2, Box 692, 17003
(717) 865-3259

An 1860 Victorian mansion in a country setting near Hershey and featuring ten rooms with private baths, air conditioning, queen-size canopied beds, and a delicious full breakfast served in the dining room. There are a sitting room and a gift shop on the first floor. Restaurant within walking distance. Near Amish, Hershey, outlet shops, and Renaissance Faire at Mount Hope Winery. Handicapped accessible; AAA approved. No guest pets permitted. No smoking allowed.

Rooms: 10 (PB) $50-70
Full Breakfast
Credit Cards: A, B, C, D, E
Notes: 2, 5, 7, 8, 9, 10, 11, 12, 14

ATHENS

Fáilte Inn

Rural Route 2, Box 323, 18810
(717) 358-3899

Fáilte Inn is nestled in the Susquehanna Valley surrounded by the beautiful Endless Mountains of rural Pennsylvania. Enjoy the unhurried lifestyle of yesterday's Victorian elegance by browsing the inn's library. Visit the restored speakeasy dating from the days of Prohibition. In winter, relax by the cozy fire, or in summer rest under the lazy breezes of the paddle fans. Breakfast is served in the elegantly appointed dining room or on the wide screened verandas overlooking three acres of beautiful grounds and gardens. Closed December 10 through December 29. Children over 12 welcome. Smoking and nonsmoking rooms available. Two-night minimum stay on holidays. Hunting and fishing abound.

Hosts: Jim and Sarah True
Rooms: 5 (PB) $55-65
Full Breakfast
Credit Cards: A, B
Notes: 2, 9, 10, 12, 13

AVELLA

Weatherbury Farm

1061 Sugar Camp Run Road, 15312
(412) 587-3763

One hundred acres of meadows, gardens, fields, and valleys create a tranquil setting at this Tudor bed and breakfast, the perfect getaway from everyday pressures. Guests' rooms at this 1860s farmhouse are lovingly furnished with old-fashioned country charm. Guests' awaken to a bountiful farm breakfast. Later, guests may wish to get acquainted with the farm's sheep, cattle, and chickens. Opportunities for golfing, fishing, boating, hiking, bicycling, and antiquing abound in the local area. Visit historic Meadowcroft Village, Starlake Amphitheater, and panhandle West

Virginia. Convenient to Pittsburgh. Picnic lunches are available from a local source.

Hosts: Dale, Marcy, and Nigel Tudor
Rooms: 4 (PB) $60
Full Breakfast
Credit Cards: A, B
Notes: 2, 5, 7, 8, 9, 10, 11, 12, 14

AVONDALE

Association of Bed and Breakfasts in Philadelphia, Valley Forge, Brandywine

P.O. Box 562, Valley Forge, 19481-0562
(610) 783-7838; (800) 344-0123
FAX (610) 783-7783

0500. The Hepburn Farm. Now reduced to three acres, was built in 1890 and occupied by Katharine Hepburn's grandparents. It has been totally renovated and centrally air-conditioned. Guests have a choice of two rooms or two suites. Each has a queen-size bed and a private bath. Breakfasts are full and hearty. Within the common room, guests will find a fireplace, TV, VCR, and a stationary bike (which will get the rider nowhere). Walk or jog down a quiet road, ride a ten-speed bike, pitch horse shoes, or just relax on the veranda. All of the Brandywine Valley attractions are within a 20-minute drive. No pets. No children under 12 years. $80-90.

The International Bed and Breakfast Club, Inc.

504 Amherst Street, Buffalo, NY 14207
(800) 723-4262; FAX (716) 873-4462

PA3703PP. This 1844 mill house overlooks horses grazing in a meadow in the heart of the Brandywine Valley, midpoint between historic Philadelphia and quaint Lancaster County. Three rooms are offered including a canopied double bed, a Victorian wicker single, and a wing with twin beds. Guests enjoy a hot tub and TV.

A delicious full breakfast with homemade breads is included in the rate. Rooms share a bath. $75.

BALLY

Guesthouses, Inc.

P.O. Box 2137, West Chester, 19380
(610) 692-4575

006. A two-story Cotswold cottage charmingly furnished with antiques and handmade pieces. Meant to be the perfect getaway just for two. Downstairs there is a living room with antique wood-burning stove and an efficiency kitchen. The bedroom with full-size bed and bath is upstairs. The kitchen can be stocked for breakfast or guests may have breakfast served to them in the nearby Woodcutter's House before an open fire or alfresco, depending on the season. $80.

BEDFORD

Bedford's Covered Bridge Inn

Rural Delivery 2, Box 196, 15559
(814) 733-4093

Delightful countryside accommodations in a historic home near a covered bridge afford guests scrumptious full breakfasts and private baths amid a picture book setting. Hiking, biking, antiquing, fly fishing, bird watching, and cross-country skiing are all available just outside the door. Old Bedford Village, Blue Knob ski resort, Shawnee State Park, Coral Caverns, and many covered bridges are nearby. Only eight miles from exit 11, I-76. There is also a cottage available, which is perfect for families.

Rooms: 6 (PB) $65-85
Full Breakfast
Credit Cards: A, B, C, D
Notes: 2, 5, 7, 9, 10, 11, 12, 13, 14

---

7 No smoking; 8 Children welcome; 9 Social drinking allowed; 10 Tennis nearby; 11 Swimming nearby; 12 Golf nearby; 13 Skiing nearby; 14 May be booked through a travel agent.

BELLEVILLE

Hickory Grove Bed and Breakfast

Rural Delivery 1, Box 281, 17004
(717) 935-5289

Charming country style bed and breakfast in the heart of Amish country, only 30 minutes from Penn State University. Other nearby attractions include state parks, the Big Valley Auction and Flea Market, crafts, antiques, gift and quilt shops, plus a craft shop on the premises. Enjoy the flower and vegetable gardens, swing under the grape arbor, picnic on the patio. Homemade muffins and fruit cobbler made from fresh berries raised at Hickory Grove grace the breakfast table. Private entrance, fireplace, and family room.

Hosts: Caleb and Bertha Peachey
Rooms: 5 (1 PB; 4 SB) $40-45
Continental Breakfast
Credit Cards: None
Notes: 2, 5, 7, 8

BERWYN

Association of Bed and Breakfasts in Philadelphia, Valley Forge, Brandywine

P.O. Box 562, Valley Forge, 19481-0562
(610) 783-7838; (800) 344-0123
FAX (610) 783-7783

0501. Circa 1770 Country Farmhouse. This farmhouse features beamed ceilings, hand-stenciled walls, antique country furnishings, samplers, and local quilts. The oldest part is a restored 1770 tenant house. Set on five acres, there are pastoral views from every room. Guest rooms may have a canopied bed and fireplace or a private stairway to the cozy den with fireplace. A country breakfast is served in a brick-floored sunroom overlooking the gardens. Minutes from tennis and swimming. Resident Pomeranian. Two guest rooms with private bath. $87.50-118.

1912. Hilltop Privacy. This home is in a quiet wooded area. The guest quarters occupy the entire downstairs and include two bedrooms, family room with fireplace, hot tub solarium, and bar area with private entrance off the gardens. Other amenities include cable TV, refrigerator, telephone, air conditioning, laundry facilities, use of the kitchen, and a breathtaking setting. Ingredients for breakfast are provided; self-serve at guests' leisure. Basic French and Dutch spoken. Weekly and monthly rates upon request.

The Village Inn

BIRD-IN-HAND

The Village Inn of Bird-in-Hand

2695 Old Philadelphia Pike, P.O. Box 253, 17505
(717) 293-8369

The historic Village Inn of Bird-in-Hand was originally built in 1734. It is listed on the National Register of Historic Places. The innkeepers reside in the inn and provide guests with the finest hospitality. It is in the heart of the Pennsylvania Dutch country. Each morning a Continental plus breakfast including fresh fruits, pastries, and cereals is served. All guests enjoy free use of the indoor and outdoor swimming pools and tennis courts within walking distance. A complimentary tour of the surrounding Amish farmlands is offered daily, except Sunday.

Hosts: Richmond and Janice Young
Rooms: 11 (PB) $79-144

NOTES: Credit cards accepted: A MasterCard; B Visa; C American Express; D Discover; E Diners Club;
F Other; 2 Personal checks accepted; 3 Lunch available; 4 Dinner available; 5 Open all year; 6 Pets welcome;

Continental Breakfast
Credit Cards: A, B, C, D
Notes: 2, 5, 8, 10 ,11, 14

BLAKESLEE

The International Bed and Breakfast Club, Inc.

504 Amherst Street, Buffalo, NY 14207
(800) 723-4262; FAX (716) 873-4462

PA7144PP. Nestled among lush mountains, streams, lakes, and ponds on hundreds of acres with glacial wetlands with rare plants and peatlands, this charming bed and breakfast inn is truly unique. Guests will discover a modern building constructed in 1994 filled with all the charm of yesteryear. There are six well-appointed rooms with modern baths and each offers a spectacular view of nature. There is a game room, outside spa, whirlpool, and a great room with a beautiful stone fireplace. Horseback riding, white-water rafting, auto racing, and outlet shopping are all nearby. Full breakfast. $85-110.

BLUE BELL

Association of Bed and Breakfasts in Philadelphia, Valley Forge, Brandywine

P.O. Box 562, Valley Forge, 19481-0562
(610) 783-7838; (800) 344-0123
FAX (610) 783-7783

1106. Blue Heron. Picture this 19th-century farmhouse with original broad-beamed pine floors, thick stone walls with traditional curved windows, a cozy fireplace stove, and varied views of landscape and wildlife. This home is open to guests in the tradition of country hospitality, offering a home away from home in the privacy of two large, beautiful double rooms with private baths. Both rooms are furnished with antiques and traditional and contemporary

artwork. Each room has a telephone. Breakfast is served. $65-75.

0307. Carriage House at Stoney Creek. Enjoy a stay on this lovely estate with the main house dating back to 1764. Originally the site of a grist mill from which soldiers were fed at Valley Forge. Sadly, the mill no longer exists but the manor house does and so do the 15 acres of meadow, woodland, creek, black walnut grove, and garden setting around the swimming pool. The carriage house dates back to 1776. The 1991 renovation on the carriage house consists of two kitchens, laundry room, three bedrooms, three baths, and a huge living room. The original stone of the carriage house is evident throughout. Weekly and monthly rates upon request. Inquire about accommodations for children. Fifteen dollars for extra person. $80-125.

BOILING SPRINGS

The Garmanhaus

217 Front Street, Box 307, 17007
(717) 258-3980

By the lake in the historic village of Boiling Springs, this gracious Victorian house has four guest rooms of double occupancy. Sitting room, where breakfast is served, overlooks lake. For the fisherman, world famous for its fly fishing is Yellow

The Garmanhaus

Breeches—a five-minute walk. Antique shops in nearby Carlisle. Excellent gourmet restaurant with an impressive wine list is a two-minute walk. The hosts promise a warm and charming time for all who stay. Children over five welcome.

Hosts: John and Molly Garman
Rooms: 4 (SB) $50
Continental Breakfast
Credit Cards: None
Notes: 2, 5, 7, 9, 10, 11, 12, 13

Yellow Breeches House

213 Front Street, P.O. Box 221, 17007
(717) 258-8344; (800) 258-1639
FAX (717) 258-9882

The Yellow Breeches House is a three-story circa 1870 Federal home with exposed wood beams and wood floors. The lodge is eclectically furnished for comfort with many fly fishing antiques and memorabilia. The public rooms include a cozy dining room with a view of the lake, a huge third-floor library, den area, and kitchen. During the summer, spring, and fall, enjoy the 35-foot sun porch. Within walking distance to the famous Catch and Release area of Yellow Breeches fly fishing stream. Learn fly fishing. Programs and guiding available. Orvis-endorsed. Lunch and dinner available one block away.

Hosts: Matt and Nicole Zito
Rooms: 3 (1 PB; 2 SB) $85-119
Full Breakfast
Credit Cards: A, B, C
Notes: 5, 7, 8, 9, 10, 11, 12, 13, 14

BOSWELL

The Picket Fence

Ligonier Highlands, Rural Delivery 2, 15531
(412) 238-5818

Lovely countryside home atop Laurel Mountain, nine miles east of Ligonier, set amongst scenic woodlands, wild ferns, perennial blooms, and herb and fragrance gardens. Primitive antiques and whimsical

collectibles throughout the home lend charm to a beamed cathedral ceiling bedroom and sitting area for two. Relaxing view of woods, gardens, bird feeders from room, sun deck, or garden benches. Hosts' culinary and gardening pursuits enhance breakfast served on enclosed sun porch overlooking gardens and water statuary or in the cozy family room by the glowing wood-burning stove. Small wonder in the woods.

Hosts: Carole and William P. McCray
Rooms: 1 (PB) $80
Full Breakfast
Credit Cards: None
Notes: 2, 5, 7, 9, 10, 11, 12, 13, 14

BOYERTOWN

The Enchanted Cottage

22 Deer Run Road, 19512
(610) 845-8845

Be the only guests in this rustic, romantic, one and one-half story Cotswold-style stone cottage nestled among rolling, wooded acres. Gourmet breakfasts are served in the main house beside the garden or before a blazing fire. Fine restaurant within walking distance. Close to historic sites, country auctions, Amish area, antiques, retail outlets, and flea markets. With fresh flowers and complimentary wine and cheese, this wonderful bed and breakfast offers an infor-

The Enchanted Cottage

mal but gracious lifestyle in a storybook atmosphere.

Hosts: Peg and Richard Groff
Room: 1 (PB) $90
Full Breakfast
Credit Cards: None
Notes: 2, 3, 5, 7, 9, 10, 12, 13, 14

BRANDYWINE

Bed & Breakfast Connection/ Bed & Breakfast of Philadelphia

P.O. Box 21, Devon, 19333
(610) 687-3565; (800) 448-3619 (outside PA)
FAX (610) 995-9524

G-03. Enjoy a peaceful visit at this beautifully restored, three-story farmhouse, built around 1850, on 32 acres along the Brandywine Creek, just two and one-half miles north of Chadds Ford and four miles from Longwood Gardens. Partake in a game of pool or relax by the fireplace in the newly renovated Carriage House addition. A hot tub on the back deck allows guests to enjoy the rolling hills of Brandywine scenery. Two guest rooms with private, attached bathrooms are available in the Carriage House. There is a guest room with private bath and a two-room suite with hall bath available in the house. Breakfast is a hearty, full meal. $70-85.

G-04. Discover this tucked-away, quietly elegant manor house near the heart of the Brandywine Valley. With 36 acres, historic buildings, gardens, paths, and trails, each season is special at this bed and breakfast. Well-appointed rooms offer canopied king-size beds, queen-size, doubles, twins, suites, and five large country baths with showers. All rooms have TV, and most have private baths. A full country breakfast with homemade breads, muffins, croissants, and other goodies is served each morning. Concierge services are offered, and arrangements can be made for local activities. $90-120.

G-05. Step back in time at this 1850 Italian Federal Victorian mansion. High ceilings, Oriental rugs, fireplaces, teal paneling, and handcrafted grand staircase decorate the inside of this home. Seven guest rooms decorated in a unique Victorian theme. All share hall bathrooms, except the Darlington Room that, in addition to a private bathroom, offers a working fireplace for evening ambience. Full breakfast served. $80-110.

Hamanassett

BRANDYWINE VALLEY

Hamanassett

P.O. Box 129, Lima, 19037
(610) 459-3000

Enjoy an elegantly quiet getaway at this private estate and magnificent 19th-century country mansion with 48 secluded acres of woodlands, gardens, fields, and trails. Near beautiful Brandywine Valley attractions, including Longwood Gardens, Winterthur, Nemours, Hagley, and much more. Excellent local dining. Rooms have king-size, queen-size, double, and twin beds; large, full private baths; TV; and other amenities. Brochure available.

Host: Evelene Dohan
Rooms: 8 (7 PB; 1 SB)
Full Breakfast
Credit Cards: None
Notes: 2, 5, 7, 9, 10, 12, 14

7 No smoking; 8 Children welcome; 9 Social drinking allowed; 10 Tennis nearby; 11 Swimming nearby; 12 Golf nearby; 13 Skiing nearby; 14 May be booked through a travel agent.

BUCKS COUNTY

Association of Bed and Breakfasts in Philadelphia, Valley Forge, Brandywine

P.O. Box 562, Valley Forge, 19481-0562
(610) 783-7838; (800) 344-0123
FAX (610) 783-7783

1804. The Mill Manor. A small Federal-style inn of the early 1800s on four landscaped acres. Four tastefully appointed guest rooms, all with private baths. A full gourmet breakfast is served and in pleasant weather may be served on the outdoor patio. Enjoy the in-ground pool. Nearby tourist sights include a winery, lake with sailboats, the Pearl Buck estate, Michener Art Museum, Mercer Museum, Peddler's Village, New Hope, etc. Excellent restaurants in the area. $75-110.

1901. Oak Farm Bed and Breakfast. This traditional 18th-century farmhouse is in the heart of Bucks County on ten wooded acres. Open-beamed ceilings and Persian carpets throughout the 14 rooms contribute to its rustic charm and elegance. After a full day, relax in the redwood hot tub or on cool days by the fire. Five guest rooms with queen-size bed and private or shared baths. The delightful breakfast can be enjoyed in the dining room or on the lovely sun porch. $95-125.

Bed & Breakfast Connection/ Bed & Breakfast of Philadelphia

P.O. Box 21, Devon, 19333
(610) 687-3565; (800) 448-3619 (outside PA)
FAX (610) 995-9524

C-06. Nestled in beautiful central Bucks County, this inn offers comfortable lodging on more than four handsomely landscaped acres. Thoughtful improvements by each successive owner have enhanced the property to its present state. Each room is taste-fully furnished with period pieces reflecting a warm and relaxing atmosphere. There is a cozy fireplace to enjoy in the winter, and a patio and swimming pool to enjoy in the summer. Sleep in the luxury of an elegant queen-size spindle post bed, or choose the cozy twin-bed room. Private and semi-private baths available. A delicious full gourmet breakfast is served in the dining room. $75-95.

C-07. In early 1720, a small stone house and a flour mill were built on the bank of Neshaminy Creek. That simple stone cabin survived almost 300 years and today is incorporated into the large house, constructed in 1840. The dining room, where a full breakfast is served, features a magnificent working walk-in fireplace. Nine charming guest rooms and suites are available as guest accommodations, each furnished with period furniture of the 1800s, with hand-sewn quilts and country antiques. All rooms have private baths and air conditioning. Many attractions are found near the inn. Beautiful Lake Galena offers sailing or canoeing, fishing, and swimming. New Hope is a lovely 20-minute drive through Bucks County farmland. Philadelphia is only about 45 minutes by car. $115-200.

CANADENSIS

Brookview Manor Bed and Breakfast Inn

Rural Route 1, Box 365, 18325
(717) 595-2451

On four picturesque acres in the Pocono Mountains, Brookview Manor offers eight guest rooms and suites uniquely appointed with country and antique furnishings. Enjoy the wraparound porch, hiking trails, fishing, and nearby skiing, golf, tennis, boating, and antiquing. A delicious full breakfast, afternoon refreshments, and warm hospitality are all included. Children over 12 are welcome.

Hosts: Patty and David DeMaria
Rooms: 8 (6 PB; 2 SB) $70-145
Full Breakfast
Credit Cards: A, B, C, D, E
Notes: 2, 5, 9, 10, 11, 12, 13, 14

Dreamy Acres

Box 7, 18325
(717) 595-7115

Dreamy Acres is in the heart of the beautiful Pocono Mountains vacationland on three acres of land with a stream flowing into a small pond. The house is 500 feet back from the highway, giving a pleasing, quiet atmosphere. Minimum stay on weekends is two nights; on holidays, three nights. Closed Christmas. Children over 12 are welcome.

Hosts: Esther and Bill Pickett
Rooms: 6 (4 PB; 2 SB) $38-50
Continental Breakfast (May-October)
Credit Cards: None
Notes: 2, 5, 7, 9, 10, 11, 12, 13

The Pine Knob Inn

Route 447, P.O. Box 295, 18325
(717) 595-2532

Step back into yesteryear. Experience the atmosphere of years gone by in this 1840s inn abounding with antiques and art on six and one-half acres. Enjoy gourmet dining. Wine and spirits are available. Guests may gather on the veranda for relaxing summer evenings or by the fireplace after a day on the slopes. Fireplace rooms are available. Come enjoy the area hiking, biking, fishing, fall foliage, and many other attractions. The daily rate includes a delicious breakfast and dinner. The perfect place for a romantic wedding.

Hosts: Dick and Charlotte Dornich
Rooms: 27 (21 PB; 6 SB) $70-125
Full Breakfast
Credit Cards: A, B
Notes: 2, 4, 5, 7, 8, 9, 10, 11, 12, 13, 14

Line Limousin Farmhouse

CARLISLE

Line Limousin Farmhouse Bed and Breakfast

2070 Ritner Highway, 17013
(717) 243-1281

This 110-acre homestead has an 11-room brick-and-stone home. It is only one and one-half miles from exit 12 of I-81 and within close proximity to Dickinson College and many fine restaurants. Carlisle Fairgrounds, home of many fine automobile shows, is nearby. Furnishings inside the inn include antiques and a player piano that guests will enjoy pumping. Hosts raise Limousin beef cattle, and guests may play croquet, bocce , or drive golf balls on farm or two of the golf courses that border the farm. No smoking.

Hosts: Robert and Joan Line
Rooms: 4 (2 PB; 2 SB) $50-75
Full Breakfast
Credit Cards: None
Notes: 2, 5, 7, 9, 12

CHAMBERSBURG

Amanda's Bed and Breakfast

1428 Park Avenue, Baltimore, MD 21217-4230
(410) 225-0001; (800) 899-7533
FAX (410) 728-8957

308. A special, spacious residence that was once the summer home of a railroad executive. Original woodwork throughout emphasizes the grandeur of a past era. Eight rooms each with private bath, some with Jacuzzi and/or a fireplace. Full breakfast is served on weekends. The Victorian era is highlighted every day with a Christmas theme. $89-150.

Falling Spring Inn

1838 Falling Spring Road, 17201
(717) 267-3654

Enjoy country life in a mid-19th-century Pennsylvania stone farmhouse. Falling Spring Inn is two miles south of exit 6 off I-81 and Route 30 in Chambersburg. The inn takes its name from the Falling Spring, a nationally renowned freshwater trout stream that moves slowly through inn property. The stream, a large pond, lawns, meadows, and wooded areas make for a pleasant overnight stay.

Hosts: Adin and Janet L. Frey
Rooms: 5 (PB) $49-69
Full Breakfast
Credit Cards: A, B, D
Notes: 2, 5, 7, 8, 10, 11, 12, 13, 14

Shultz Victorian Mansion Bed and Breakfast

756 Philadelphia Avenue, 17201
(717) 263-3371

This charming 1880 Victorian-styled brick home is along Route 11, just north of Route 30, and one mile from I-81. Intricate wood carving is found throughout the house, from the corner turret to the elaborately designed and crafted foyer, hearth, and open staircase. A family collection of antiques enhances the richness of the home. Guests enjoy porches, balcony, gardens, or relax in the common rooms by the fire. Rooms are large, pleasant, and air-conditioned.

Rooms: 8 (6 PB; 2 SB) $59-78
Full Breakfast
Credit Cards: A, B
Notes: 2, 5, 7, 9, 10, 11, 12, 13

CHESTER SPRINGS

Association of Bed and Breakfasts in Philadelphia, Valley Forge, Brandywine

P.O. Box 562, Valley Forge, 19481-0562
(610) 783-7838; (800) 344-0123
FAX (610) 783-7783

0604. Hunt Country Inn. This Colonial stone inn in fox-hunt country is in a national register historic district 20 minutes west of Valley Forge National Historic Park. There is also a full-service restaurant. For guests planning a day in the country or Valley Forge Park, a stocked picnic basket for two can be prepared for an additional cost. Reception, business meetings, luncheons, and special occasions are welcome. There are stalls that will hold three guest horses. Each guest room has a different theme—nautical, safari, Jessica, and French suite. $55-125.

1302. Springdale Farm. A circa 1840 farmhouse on ten acres of lawns and woods perfect for biking, jogging, hiking, or just appreciating. Good location for Longwood Gardens and Brandywine area. An expanded Continental breakfast is served in the formal dining room, with random-width flooring, fireplace, and beehive oven. Guests may choose to stay in the Blue Room, with a reading corner and windows on three sides, or in Grandmother's Room, with Early American pine furniture and rope bed. Enjoy fireplaces, porches, barbecue, patio, and chairs by the stream. $65.

Bed & Breakfast Connection/ Bed & Breakfast of Philadelphia

P.O. Box 21, Devon, 19333
(610) 687-3565; (800) 448-3619 (outside PA)
FAX (610) 995-9524

F-08. Complimentary wine or sparkling water await guests upon arrival at this

---

NOTES: Credit cards accepted: A MasterCard; B Visa; C American Express; D Discover; E Diners Club; F Other; 2 Personal checks accepted; 3 Lunch available; 4 Dinner available; 5 Open all year; 6 Pets welcome;

lovely 1830s farmhouse with classic mid-century features. Two spacious guest rooms share a hall bath. While visiting, guests are invited to jog or walk a meandering trail or relax by the stream on this quiet ten-acre country retreat. A Continental plus breakfast is served in the dining room in front of the original fireplace and beehive oven. No smoking. Resident cat. $75.

CHESTNUT HILL

Bed & Breakfast Connection/ Bed & Breakfast of Philadelphia

P.O. Box 21, Devon, 19333
(610) 687-3565; (800) 448-3619 (outside PA)
FAX (610) 995-9524

D-02. This spacious suburban home is set high above the street in a lovely garden. A three-minute walk from commuter rail and bus. Queen-size bed with a private bath, a pair of twins with a shared bath, and a double bed with a shared bath. $60.

D-06. This historically certified townhouse was built circa 1900 and is furnished in Victorian style with many antiques. On the third floor there is a room with a double bed and shared bath, and on the fourth floor there is a double bed with a shared bath, and a room with a pair of twins and a shared bath. $60-65.

CHRISTIANA

The Georgetown

1222 Georgetown Road, 17509
(717) 786-4570

Once a miller's home, the original structure was converted to a bed and breakfast for the enjoyment of guests in a relaxing home away from home. Entrance to the house is by a brick walkway. The herb garden on the left lets guests smell the lavender and mint that are just two of the herbs used to garnish morning breakfasts. There is a choice of three bedrooms decorated with antiques and collectibles. Lancaster County Amish, a unique group of people who travel in horse-drawn carriages, pass in front of the Georgetown. Visit the local Strasburg Train Museum.

Host: Doris W. Woerth
Rooms: 3 (1 PB; 2 SB) $40
Full Breakfast
Credit Cards: None
Notes: 2, 5, 7, 11, 12

CHURCHTOWN

The Inn at Twin Linden

2029 Main Street, Narvon, 17555
(717) 445-7619

This bed and breakfast is a perfect getaway in Pennsylvania Dutch country. Elegant restored historic estate with six guest rooms and one deluxe suite, private baths, queen-size canopied beds, air conditioning, unsurpassed gourmet breakfast, and outdoor Jacuzzi. On two acres of beautifully landscaped grounds and Amish farm views. A renowned candlelight dinner is served on the weekends. Intimate romantic setting with wicker-filled porches and private gardens.

The Inn at Twin Linden

Afternoon tea and sherry included. Dinner available on weekends.

Hosts: Bob and Donna Leahy
Rooms: 6 (PB) $90-132
Suite: 1 (PB) $212
Full Breakfast
Credit Cards: A, B, C, D
Notes: 2, 5, 7, 9

Conifer Ridge Farm

CLEARVILLE (BEDFORD)

Conifer Ridge Farm

Rural Route 2, Box 202A, 15535
(814) 784-3342

A beautiful, contemporary, passive solar home with a rustic exterior and an interior of exceptional design beauty. The 125-acre farm features a wading stream, a lake for swimming, fishing, boating, woodlands and mountains for hiking, Christmas trees, and grazing cattle. The Granary is a cabin that sleeps four. Day trips to Bedford Village, Raystown Lake, country auctions, and historic Bedford.

Rooms: 2 (PB) $55
Cabin: 1 (PB) $30
Full Breakfast
Credit Cards: None
Notes: 2, 4, 5, 7, 8, 9, 12, 13, 14

COLLEGEVILLE

Association of Bed and Breakfasts in Philadelphia, Valley Forge, Brandywine

P.O. Box 562, Valley Forge, 19481-0562
(610) 783-7838; (800) 344-0123
FAX (610) 783-7783

1305. Fircroft. Near Ursinas College. In 1838, this spacious Federal-style home with wraparound porch was built around the original 1769 homestead. The quaint country kitchen has striking beamed ceiling and stained glass. A delicious and hearty full country breakfast is served in the large formal dining room. Guest quarters are private and appealing. The bath has a flowered pedestal sink with gold fixtures and a claw-foot tub. $65.

1904. Victorian Elegance. Skilled European and American craftsmen fashioned this 22-room Victorian mansion in 1897. Stained glass and fireplaces abound. A three-story winding chestnut staircase leads to the air-conditioned guest rooms, which offer such touches as marble lavatory, ornate medicine cabinet, and built-in armoire of exotic woods. A full breakfast is served in the dining room. This elegant mansion is renowned for year-round house tours, weddings both in the mansion and in the gardens, small corporate meetings, dinners in the dining room, and the perfect setting for wedding pictures. Seven guest rooms are available for guests, each with private bath. $75-85.

COMPASS

Guesthouses, Inc.

P.O. Box 2137, West Chester, 19380
(610) 692-4575

775. This circa 1960 Victorian manor house is in the heart of Amish country. The downstairs common rooms are decorated in period furniture and include a large living room with fireplace, formal dining room where breakfast is served, and a light and sunny small conservatory where a welcoming refreshment is served. There are four large corner bedrooms available for guests. A delicious full country breakfast is served. $95-125.

NOTES: Credit cards accepted: A MasterCard; B Visa; C American Express; D Discover; E Diners Club; F Other; 2 Personal checks accepted; 3 Lunch available; 4 Dinner available; 5 Open all year; 6 Pets welcome;

COOKSBURG

Gateway Lodge and Cabins

Route 36, Box 125, 16217
(814) 744-8017

Experience gracious hospitality in an authentic, rustic log cabin country inn that has been chosen as one of *Money* magazine's 1994 travel destinations. In William Penn's forest primeval, it offers cozy cottages with fireplaces and an antique-filled lodge that are open year-round. Indoor heated pool, sauna, teatime, and planned activities available for lodge and cottage guests. On-premise gift shop, restaurant, and meeting facility. Activities abound. Call or write for a free brochure. Lunch available May through October. Call regarding accommodations for children.

Hosts: Joe and Linda Burney
Rooms: 16 (11 PB; 5 SB) $105-148
Full Breakfast
Credit Cards: A, B, C, D
Notes: 2, 4, 5, 9, 10, 11, 12, 13

CRESCO

LaAnna Guest House

Rural Delivery 2, Box 1051, 18326
(717) 676-4225

Built in the 1870s, this Victorian home welcomes guests with large rooms that are furnished in Empire and Victorian antiques.

LaAnna Guest House

In a quiet mountain village with waterfalls, mountain views, and outdoor activities.

Host: Kay Swingle
Rooms: 2 (SB) $25-30
Continental Breakfast
Credit Cards: None
Notes: 2, 5, 7, 9, 10, 11, 12, 13

DALLAS

The International Bed and Breakfast Club, Inc.

504 Amherst Street, Buffalo, NY 14207
(800) 723-4262; FAX (716) 873-4462

PA3245PP. This inn is in the scenic Endless Mountains of northeast Pennsylvania. Each room has a private bath. Guest rooms include twin, double, king-size, and bunk beds. Suites are available, and the entire home is available to guests. Outdoor activities include canoeing, swimming, volleyball, cross-country skiing, ice skating, and tobogganing. A hearty farm breakfast is served. Children are welcome. No smoking in the inn or other buildings on the farm. $55-75.

Ponda-Rowland Bed and Breakfast Inn and Farm Vacations

Rural Route 1, Box 349, 18612
(717) 639-3245; (800) 854-3286
FAX (717) 639-5531

Large, scenic farm in the mountains. Farm animals. Includes a 30-acre wildlife refuge offering ponds, hiking, canoeing, swimming, pony rides, cross-country skiing, and ice skating. State park, game land, fishing, horseback riding, antiquing, restaurants, skiing, and county fairs nearby. Museum-quality country antiques. Large stone fireplace. Circa 1850 timberframe (post and beam) double-plank construction. Rooms with king-size beds and fireplaces. Satellite TV. Awarded Gold Seal of Approval by Bed and Breakfast Worldwide. Featured in

7 No smoking; 8 Children welcome; 9 Social drinking allowed; 10 Tennis nearby; 11 Swimming nearby; 12 Golf nearby; 13 Skiing nearby; 14 May be booked through a travel agent.

B&B/Unique Inns of Pennsylvania. Member of ABBA and PAII. AAA approved. Inquire about accommodations for pets

Hosts: Jeanette and Clifford Rowland
Rooms: 5 (PB) $65-95
Full Breakfast
Credit Cards: A, B, C, D
Notes: 2, 5, 7, 8, 9, 11, 12, 13, 14

DEVON

Bed & Breakfast Connection/ Bed & Breakfast of Philadelphia

P.O. Box 21, 19333
(610) 687-3565; (800) 448-3619 (outside PA)
FAX (610) 995-9524

From elegant townhouses in history-filled Center City to a manor house in scenic Bucks County; from an elegant home-within-a-barn in the suburbs to charming Victorian inns in York, Bed and Breakfast Connection /Bed and Breakfast of Philadelphia offers a wide variety of styles and locations in its scores of inspected homes, guesthouses, and inns. Choose from accommodations just three blocks from "America's most historic square mile," Independence National Historical Park, within easy distance of Valley Forge Park, or in the heart of the Brandywine Valley area with its magnificent historic estates and museums. Stay on a working farm in the Amish country of Lancaster County. Cover seven counties in the southeastern corner of Pennsylvania offering houses with one guest room and inns with many rooms. Credit cards accepted. Full and Continental breakfasts available. $30-200.

DILLSBURG

Guesthouses, Inc.

P.O. Box 2137, West Chester, 19380
(610) 692-4575

163. A lovely historic manor house. All rooms and outbuildings are furnished with antiques. There are two bedrooms with fireplaces and one full bath for parties or families traveling together; downstairs there is a one-bedroom suite, guest-house-type facility with kitchen, bath, sitting room with fireplace, and bedroom with fireplace. There is also the Wash House that has a kitchen and sitting room downstairs, bedroom, and bath with shower on second floor. Have a full country breakfast in the main house or have the kitchen stocked for an extensive Continental breakfast. $100-135.

DILWORTHTOWN

Guesthouses, Inc.

P.O. Box 2137, West Chester, 19380
(610) 692-4575

168. Charming early 19th-century house surrounded by open fields where wildlife is appreciated. The English antique-furnished guest rooms are on the second floor, with a cozy downstairs common room with fireplace in the original section of the house. Central air conditioning assisted by fans in the bedrooms. A full country breakfast is served with homemade biscuits and lemon curd. $85.

DOYLESTOWN

Association of Bed and Breakfasts in Philadelphia, Valley Forge, Brandywine

P.O. Box 562 Valley Forge, 19481-0562
(610) 783-7838; (800) 344-0123
FAX (610) 783-7783

1906. The Butler's House. The original owners came to the unsettled wilderness of Bucks County in 1720 and built a stone dwelling to which a main formal house was added in 1840. A magnificent walk-in fireplace greets arriving guests. After a full day, guests can relax next to a fire in the

NOTES: Credit cards accepted: A MasterCard; B Visa; C American Express; D Discover; E Diners Club;
F Other; 2 Personal checks accepted; 3 Lunch available; 4 Dinner available; 5 Open all year; 6 Pets welcome;

living room or library. The country kitchen has rustic stone walls, beehive oven, and hand-hewn beams. Seven guest rooms, all with private baths. $95.

The Inn at Fordhook Farm

105 New Britain Road, 18901
(215) 345-1766

For more than 100 years Fordhook Farm has been the private home of W. Atlee Burpee, founder of the Burpee Seed Company, and his family. Nine major historic buildings constitute Fordhook Farm. Three of these are used for the inn: the main house, which began as a typical mid-18th-century Pennsylvania fieldstone farmhouse; the two-story carriage house, built in 1868 and converted into a private library in 1915 (it features a Gothic-style great room with exposed beams and rafters and chestnut paneling); and the converted Bucks County-style barn. Guest rooms and common areas are filled with family antiques, furnishings, and mementos. There are 60 acres of meadows, woodlands, gardens, and seed-development trial grounds to explore. Children over 12 welcome. Cross-country skiing on 60 acres.

Hosts: Elizabeth Romanella and
   Blanche Burpee Dohan
Rooms: 7 (4 PB; 3 SB) $93-175
Full Breakfast
Credit Cards: A, B, C
Notes: 2, 5, 7, 9, 14

Sign of the Sorrel Horse

4424 Old Easton Road, 18901
(215) 230-9999; (800) BUCK-CTY
FAX (215) 230-8053

Built in 1714 as a gristmill in the historic village of Dyerstown near New Hope in the heart of Bucks County, the old mill supplied flour to Washington's troops and provided lodging for Lafayette and his officers during the Revolution. Converted into one of the most gracious inns and awarded "Best Inn Dining of the Year" for 1993-94 by *Country*

Inns Bed and Breakfast magazine, DiRoNA Award 1993-94, AAA three-star rated. Fine gourmet dining in the Escoffier Room, and New American/Continental cuisine in the New York-Paris Cafe. Garden weddings are the specialty of this inn.

Hosts: Monique Gaumont-Lanvin and Jon Atkin
Rooms: 5 (PB) $85-175
Continental Breakfast
Credit Cards: A, B, C, E
Notes: 2, 4, 5, 7, 9, 10, 11, 12, 13

Cherry Mills Lodge

DUSHORE

Cherry Mills Lodge

Rural Route 1, Route 87 South, 18614
(717) 928-8978

This historic inn, circa 1865, is in the scenic Endless Mountains near two beautiful state parks, covered bridges, and many waterfalls. Furnished with antiques, the lodge welcomes guests year-round. Relax with reading, fishing at the creek, and taking country walks in the beautiful valley, once an 1800s logging village. There is mountain biking, hiking, nearby cross-country skiing, tobogganing, hunting, swimming, canoeing, golf, and antiquing. Visit the Victorian town of Eagles Mere.

Hosts: Florence and Julio
Rooms: 8 (1 PB; 7 SB) $55-75
Full Breakfast
Credit Cards: None
Notes: 2, 5, 8, 9, 11, 12, 13, 14

7 No smoking; 8 Children welcome; 9 Social drinking allowed; 10 Tennis nearby; 11 Swimming nearby; 12 Golf nearby; 13 Skiing nearby; 14 May be booked through a travel agent.

EAGLES MERE

Crestmont Inn

Crestmont Drive, P.O. Box 371, 17731
(717) 525-3519; (800) 522-8767

Perched high in the Endless Mountains of
Sullivan County, Pennsylvania, is this vintage 1920s resort country inn. Each season
provides an array of outdoor recreational
activities in the refreshing and nostalgic setting of beautiful Eagles Mere—"The town
that time forgot." Wonderful hiking and
cross-country ski trails abound directly off
the inn's grounds. The inn is surrounded by
nature conservancy and is a short walk to
the pristine Eagles Mere Lake. It promises
comfortable lodging, fine dining, and warm
hospitality. Thirty-three miles northeast of
Williamsport. Smoking allowed in lounge
and restaurant only.

Hosts: Kathleen and Robert Oliver
Rooms: 18 (PB) $89-138
Apartment: $750 weekly (European Plan)
Full Breakfast
Credit Cards: A, B
Notes: 2, 4, 5, 8, 9, 10, 11, 12, 13, 14

ELIZABETHTOWN

West Ridge Guest House

1285 West Ridge Road, 17022
(717) 367-7783

Tucked midway between Harrisburg and
Lancaster, this European-type manor can
be found four miles off Route 283 at the
Rheems-Elizabethtown exit. Nine guest
rooms, four in the main house and five in a
separate guest house that offers complete
privacy. Three rooms with fireplace, three
with Jacuzzi, four rooms feature decks, and
all rooms have a telephone, TV, and VCR.
Private baths. Each room decorated to
reflect a different historical style. Exercise
room with hot tub, large social room, and
dining area with country estate setting. Fish
in one of two ponds, or travel 20 to 40 min-

utes to local attractions, such as Hershey
Park, Lancaster County Amish farms, outlet shopping, Masonic homes, or
Gettysburg. A delicious full breakfast is
served. No smoking allowed. Handicapped
accessible.

Host: Alice P. Heisey
Rooms: 9 (PB) $60-100
Full Breakfast
Credit Cards: A, B, C, D
Notes: 2, 7, 10, 12, 14

Inn at Elizabethville

ELIZABETHVILLE

Inn at Elizabethville

30 West Main Street, 17023
(717) 362-3476

In the heart of central Pennsylvania, the Inn
at Elizabethville serves business and leisure
travelers to northern Dauphin County. Built
in 1883 and furnished in Mission Oak/Arts
and Crafts style, the inn has seven guest
rooms with private baths. Convenient to
superb hiking, fishing, hunting, golf, and
country auctions. A conference room, fax,
telephone, and copy service cater to business clients.

Host: Jim Facinelli
Rooms: 7 (PB)
Continental Breakfast
Credit Cards: A, B
Notes: 2, 5, 7, 8, 9, 11, 12, 14

EPHRATA

Clearview Farm Bed and Breakfast

355 Clearview Road, 17522
(717) 733-6333

A beautiful limestone farmhouse built in 1814, this bed and breakfast overlooks a large pond with a pair of swans. Beautifully restored and lovingly redecorated, it is surrounded by a well-kept lawn on 200 acres of peaceful farmland. A touch of elegance in Pennsylvania Dutch country, it was featured in *Country Decorating Ideas*. Rated four diamonds by AAA.

Hosts: Glenn and Mildred Wissler
Rooms: 5 (PB) $95-115
Full Breakfast
Credit Cards: A, B, D
Notes: 2, 5, 9, 10, 11, 12

Hackman's Country Inn Bed and Breakfast

140 Hackman Road, 17522
(717) 733-3498

Hackman's Country Inn is an 1857 farmhouse on a 90-acre working farm in Lancaster County. Shaded lawns and a porch provide a peaceful retreat on hot summer days. The house features four spacious, air-conditioned rooms with bubble-glass windows and patchwork quilts. Breakfast is served in the keeping room by the walk-in fireplace. Shop the nearby antique malls and outlets. Tour beautiful Amish country.

Host: Kathryn H. Hackman
Rooms: 4 (2 PB; 2 SB) $60-70
Full Breakfast
Credit Cards: A, B
Notes: 2, 5, 8, 9, 11, 12

The Historic Smithton Inn

900 West Main Street, 17522
(717) 733-6094

A romantic 1763 stone inn with fireplaces in every room, canopied beds, easy chairs,

The Historic Smithton Inn

quilts, candles, down pillows, nightshirts, flowers, chamber music, and feather beds. Parlor, library, and Smithton's dahlia gardens are all open for guests to enjoy. Lancaster County is an antique and crafts area settled by the Pennsylvania Dutch, Mennonite, and Amish.

Host: Dorothy Graybill
Rooms: 8 (PB) $65-135
Full Breakfast
Credit Cards: A, B, C
Notes: 2, 5, 6, 7, 8, 9, 10, 11, 12

The Inns at Doneckers

318-324 North State Street, 17522
(717) 738-9502

Experience Doneckers' warm hospitality in the picturesque setting of historic Lancaster County. Four inn properties surround the Doneckers community, each within walking distance of Doneckers Fashion Stores for the family and home, and a gourmet restaurant. Artworks complex of more than 30 studios and galleries of fine art, quilts and designer crafts, and farmers' market. Each of the 40 rooms is appointed in fine antiques, hand-stenciled walls, some suites with fireplace and Jacuzzi. Choose from the Guesthouse, Historic 1777 House, Homestead, and Gerhart House. Closed Christmas Day.

Host: H. William Donecker
Rooms: 40 (38 PB; 2 SB) $59-185
Continental Breakfast
Credit Cards: A, B, C, D, E, F
Notes: 2, 3, 4, 5, 8, 10, 11, 12, 14

---

7 No smoking; 8 Children welcome; 9 Social drinking allowed; 10 Tennis nearby; 11 Swimming nearby; 12 Golf nearby; 13 Skiing nearby; 14 May be booked through a travel agent.

ERIE

Grape Arbor Inn

51 East Main Street, North East, 16428
(814) 725-5522; FAX (814) 725-8471

Restored 1832 Federal-style brick mansion
just east of Erie in the historic village of
North East. Once a stagecoach tavern and a
station on the Underground Railroad, this
home now serves as a luxurious bed and
breakfast in the heart of Pennsylvania wine
country with local wineries offering daily
tours and tasting. Enjoy a variety of activities including antiquing, biking, skiing, or
visits to nearby Chautauqua Institution,
Presque Isle State Park, and Peek 'n Peak
Ski Resort. Children over 10 welcome.

Hosts: Debra and Michael Ducato and Joy Northup
Rooms: 5 (PB) $75-125
Full Breakfast
Credit Cards: A, B, C
Notes: 2, 5, 7, 9, 10, 11, 12, 13, 14

Historic Zion's Hill

8951 Miller Road, Cranesville, 16410
(814) 774-2971

Built in 1830, this Colonial home welcomes guests with five cozy rooms furnished with beautiful antiques. On a knoll
surrounded by 100 acres of scenic hiking
trails and a bird sanctuary, it was once the
home and winter quarters of Dan Rice,

Historic Zion's Hill

model for America's Uncle Sam (1868).
Convenient to beaches, Presque Isle State
Park, fishing, and skiing.

Hosts: John and Kathy Byrne
Rooms: 5 (3 PB; 2 SB) $55-75
Continental Breakfast
Credit Cards: None
Notes: 2, 5, 7, 8, 9, 10, 11, 12, 13, 14

ERWINNA

Evermay-on-the-Delaware

River Road, P.O. Box 60, 18920
(610) 294-9100

Lodging is available in manor house and
carriage house. Liquor license. Parlor with
fireplace. A significant, distinguished country retreat on 25 acres of gardens, woodland paths, and pastures between the
Delaware River and canal. Dinner served
Friday, Saturday, Sunday, and holidays.
Minimum stay weekends: two nights.
Closed Christmas Eve.

Hosts: Ron Strouse and Fred Cresson
Rooms: 16 (PB) $90-170
Continental Breakfast
Credit Cards: A, B
Notes: 2, 5, 7, 8, 9, 10, 11, 12, 14

Golden Pheasant Inn

River Road, 18920
(215) 294-9595

This 1857 fieldstone inn is between the
Delaware River and the Pennsylvania
Canal. Six intimate guest rooms feature
four-poster, queen-size canopied beds.
Three romantic dining rooms, including a
candlelit greenhouse overlooking the canal.
Masterful classical French cuisine by chef-
owner Michel Faure. Extensive wine selections. Dinner served Tuesday through
Sunday. Sunday brunch is from 11:00 A.M.
to 3:00 P.M. Minimum stay weekends: two
nights; holidays: three nights.

Hosts: Michel and Barbara Faure
Rooms: 6 (PB) $95-135
Continental Breakfast
Credit Cards: A, B, C, E
Notes: 2, 5, 6, 7, 8, 9, 11, 14

NOTES: Credit cards accepted: A MasterCard; B Visa; C American Express; D Discover; E Diners Club;
F Other; 2 Personal checks accepted; 3 Lunch available; 4 Dinner available; 5 Open all year; 6 Pets welcome;

Quo Vadis

FRANKLIN

Quo Vadis Bed and Breakfast

1501 Liberty Street, 16323
(814) 432-4208; (800) 360-6598

"Whither Goest Thou?" A stately brick home, accented with terra cotta tile, Quo Vadis is an eclectic Queen Anne structure built in 1867. Spacious rooms with high ceilings, parquet floors, detailed woodworking, moldings, and friezes are hallmarks of Victorian elegance. The furnishings are heirloom antiques from four generations of the same family. The quilts and embroidery are the handiwork of two beloved ladies. Quo Vadis is in an architecturally prominent historic district listed in the national register with a walking tour in the beautiful Allegheny River Valley. Quo Vadis is on Pennsylvania Route 8 and US 62 near the junction of US 322. From I-80, exit 3, 14 miles north on Pennsylvania Route 8. Call to inquire about accommodations for children.

Hosts: Erin and Jerry Cassady
Rooms: 6 (PB) $60-80
Full Breakfast
Credit Cards: A, B, C
Notes: 2, 5, 7, 9, 14

GETTYSBURG

Amanda's Bed and Breakfast

1428 Park Avenue, Baltimore, MD 21217-4230
(410) 225-0001; (800) 899-7533
FAX (410) 728-8957

125. On Oak Ridge, this restored Colonial offers a splendid view of the town. Enjoy the charm of a bygone era with the comforts of home-cooked breakfasts, cozy quilts, and country antiques. Rooms are decorated with Civil War accents. Nine rooms have both private and shared baths. $75-110.

345. A quiet, off-the-beaten-path, woodsy setting. The oldest part of the house served as a field hospital during the War Between the States. New additions enhance the former residence. Each room has a private bath. Several new rooms with fireplaces. Small conference facilities available. Full country breakfast. $68-89.

Baladerry Inn at Gettysburg

40 Hospital Road, 17325
(717) 337-1342

On four secluded acres at the edge of the Gettysburg battlefield. The brick Federal-style home, circa 1812, served as a hospital during the War Between the States. A two-story great room dominated by a massive brick fireplace serves as both a dining and gathering area. A brick terrace provides an outdoor area for socializing, while a gazebo affords a private place of tranquility. Guest rooms in the carriage house, newly renovated in 1994, have fireplaces or a private brick patio plus a common area with fireplace, sunroom, and brick patio. Horseback riding nearby. Suitable for small business meetings and retreats. Rated three diamonds by AAA.

Hosts: Tom and Caryl O'Gara
Rooms: 8 (PB) $75-95
Full Breakfast
Credit Cards: A, B, C, E
Notes: 2, 5, 9, 10, 11, 12, 13, 14

Beechmont Inn

315 Broadway, Hanover, 17331
(800) 553-7009

An elegant 1834 Federal-period inn with seven guest rooms, private baths, fireplaces,

7 No smoking; 8 Children welcome; 9 Social drinking allowed; 10 Tennis nearby; 11 Swimming nearby;
12 Golf nearby; 13 Skiing nearby; 14 May be booked through a travel agent.

Beechmont Inn

air conditioning, afternoon refreshments, and gourmet breakfast. One large suite has a private whirlpool tub, canopied bed, and fireplace. Gettysburg battlefield, Lake Marburg, golf, and great antiquing nearby. Convenient location for visits to Hershey, York, or Lancaster. Weekend packages and romantic honeymoon or anniversary packages offered. Picnic baskets available. Great area for biking and hiking. AAA and Mobil approved. Children over 13 welcome.

Hosts: Susan and William Day
Rooms: 7 (PB) $80-135
Full Breakfast
Credit Cards: A, B, C
Notes: 2, 5, 7, 9, 10, 11, 12, 13, 14

The Brafferton Inn

44 York Street, 17325
(717) 337-3423

Enjoy the grace and charm of the oldest house in historic downtown Gettysburg. This 1786 fieldstone home, recently updated, is listed on the National Register of Historic Places. Antiques and stenciling throughout. Featured in the February 1988 issue of *Country Living* magazine. Children over eight welcome.

Hosts: Jane and Sam Back
Rooms: 10 (PB) $70-110
Suites: 2 (PB) $100-125
Full Breakfast
Credit Cards: A, B
Notes: 2, 5, 7, 9, 10, 12, 13, 14

Hickory Bridge Farm

96 Hickory Bridge Road, 17353
(717) 642-5261

At the edge of the mountains just eight miles west of Gettysburg. Country cottages in a quiet, wooded area by a pure mountain stream. Dinners are offered Friday, Saturday, and Sunday in a restored barn furnished with fine antiques. Family-owned and operated for 15 years. Reservations appreciated.

Hosts: Dr. and Mrs. James Hammett and
    Mary Lynn and Robert Martin
Rooms: 4 (PB) $45-85
Full Breakfast
Credit Cards: A, B
Notes: 2, 4, 5, 7, 8, 9, 11, 12, 13

Keystone Inn

231 Hanover Street, 17325
(717) 337-3888

Keystone Inn is a large late-Victorian brick house filled with lots of natural woodwork. The guest rooms are bright, cheerful, and air-conditioned. The soft pastels and ruffles give guests a warm welcome. Each room has a reading nook and writing desk. Relax with a book in Aunt Weasie's Library. Choose a breakfast from the full menu.

Hosts: Wilmer and Doris Martin
Rooms: 4 (2 PB; 2 SB) $59-75
Full Breakfast
Credit Cards: A, B
Notes: 2, 5, 7, 8, 10, 11, 12, 13

Keystone Inn

NOTES: Credit cards accepted: A MasterCard; B Visa; C American Express; D Discover; E Diners Club; F Other; 2 Personal checks accepted; 3 Lunch available; 4 Dinner available; 5 Open all year; 6 Pets welcome;

The Old Appleford Inn

218 Carlisle Street, 17325
(717) 337-1711; (800) APLEFRD

This elegant three-story Victorian mansion, built in 1867, has 12 antique-filled guest rooms, each with private bath and air conditioning. The living room features high ceilings, baby grand piano, and complimentary sherry. The Lincoln Library features many unique collections, books, and solitude. There's a plant-filled sunroom with white wicker and afternoon beverages. The apple-stenciled dining room is where the sumptuous breakfasts are served. Surrounded by history, this inn is on the Historic Pathway. Antiquing and sports nearby. Gettysburg College within walking distance. The carriage house offers special accommodations for honeymooners. AAA rated three diamonds. Children over 14 are welcome.

Hosts: Maribeth and Frank Skradski
Rooms: 12 (PB) $93-138
Full Breakfast
Credit Cards: A, B, C, D
Notes: 2, 5, 7, 9, 10, 12, 13, 14

GETTYSBURG BATTLEFIELD

The Doubleday Inn

104 Doubleday Avenue, 17325
(717) 334-9119

Directly on the Gettysburg battlefield, this Colonial inn is beautifully restored with Civil War accents, comfortable antiques, and central air conditioning. Enjoy daily afternoon tea and a delicious candlelight country breakfast in the morning. Roam the lovely grounds and enjoy the splendid views. The inn is overlooking historic Gettysburg and the National Military Park. On selected evenings, participate in a discussion with a Civil War historian who brings the battle back to life with fascinating stories, accurate accounts, authentic memorabilia, and weaponry. Children over eight are welcome.

Hosts: Charles and Ruth Anne Wilcox
Rooms: 9 (5 PB; 4 SB) $83-105
Full Breakfast
Credit Cards: A, B, D
Notes: 2, 5, 7, 9, 10, 11, 12, 13, 14

The Doubleday Inn

GLADWYNE

Association of Bed and Breakfasts in Philadelphia, Valley Forge, Brandywine

P.O. Box 562, Valley Forge, 19481-0562
(610) 783-7838; (800) 344-0123
FAX (610) 783-7783

0202. Glad Haven. This spacious, air-conditioned Cape Cod Colonial home stands on a large wooded lot. Fine furnishings, collectibles, art, and expanses of windows all contribute to the sunlit, cheerful atmosphere. The gourmet country breakfasts are served in the formal dining room or in the sunroom with its wicker and foliage. The adjoining terrace, gardens, lawn, reflecting pool, and fountain enhance the feeling of privacy and rest. Private baths. $55.

0602. Gladwyne Bed and Breakfast. In one of the prettiest rural areas on the Main Line, yet only 20 minutes from Philadelphia or King of Prussia and Route 202 on a beautiful acre opposite a golf course. Pre-World War II stone Colonial is built in Pennsylvania Dutch farmhouse style.

7 No smoking; 8 Children welcome; 9 Social drinking allowed; 10 Tennis nearby; 11 Swimming nearby; 12 Golf nearby; 13 Skiing nearby; 14 May be booked through a travel agent.

Second-floor double bedroom has privacy and the option of an additional single room should a two-room suite be required. The private bath adjoins the suite. The third-floor accommodation consists of one double bedroom and a private bath. Guests are welcome to use the grounds, living room, kitchen, and eat-in screened porch. $75.

Bed & Breakfast Connection/ Bed & Breakfast of Philadelphia

P.O. Box 21, Devon, 19333
(610) 687-3565; (800) 448-3619 (outside PA)
FAX (610) 995-9524

E-02. This comfortable ranch-style suburban home with relaxing sun porch and beautiful gardens offers a room with a double bed and private bath, and a room with a single bed and a shared bath. The host and hostess are widely traveled medical professionals. $60.

GLEN MILLS

Guesthouses, Inc.

P.O. Box 2137, West Chester, 19380
(610) 692-4575

838. Surrounded by 55 acres of fields and woods, Sweetwater Farm, circa 1734, is the quintessential American bed and breakfast. The four corner bedrooms of the main house all contain working fireplaces, four-poster or canopied queen-size beds, high ceilings, beautifully carved woodwork, and tall windows overlooking two sides of the countryside. Three of these rooms share a large hall bath. The Lafayette Room has a new private bath. Two rooms with queen-size beds, and another with two beds, all with private adjoining baths, in the tavern wing of the main house. There are also five guest houses with one or two bedrooms. Full, hearty farm breakfast served. Swimming pool. Children and pets are welcome. $175-225.

GLEN ROCK

Dogwood House at Spoutwood Herb and Flower Farm

Rural Delivery 3, Box 66, 17327
(717) 235-6610

This antique-furnished private cottage sits on a peaceful 19th-century Pennsylvania German farm among rolling hills and streams. Fifteen percent guest discount on classes in gardening, cooking, healing with herbs, and dried flower design (call for schedule). Enjoy the gardens and the hot tub in season. Well-equipped kitchen. Close to hiking, swimming, boating, antiquing, Gettysburg, Lancaster, and Baltimore. Added fee for more than double occupancy.

Hosts: Rob and Lucy Wood
Cottage: 1 (PB) $70
Full Breakfast
Credit Cards: A, B
Notes: 2, 5, 7, 8, 12, 14

Glen Rock Mill Inn

Glen Rock Mill Inn

50 Water Street, P.O. Box 236, 17327
(717) 235-5918

An old mill built in 1837 has been transformed into an inn that offers cozy rooms furnished with comfortable antiques. The inn also operates as a restaurant featuring casual and fine dining. American breakfast and Sunday brunch are served. The restaurant has a waterfall in one dining room. The Mill Inn is in the gentle rolling green hills of southern York County, close to antique shops, wineries, golf, and within an easy drive of both Baltimore and Washington, D.C.

Hosts: Tom and Bette Ranc
Rooms: 14 (PB) $55-155
American Breakfast
Credit Cards: A, B, C
Notes: 2, 3, 4, 5, 8, 9, 12, 13, 14

GREENCASTLE

Welsh Run Inn Bed and Breakfast

11299 Welsh Run Road, 17225
(717) 328-9506

Stately turn-of-the-century farmhouse in the historic village of Welsh Run in a rural setting. Friendly, casual atmosphere. A wonderful full-course breakfast is served by candlelight in the formal dining room. Lovely hand-stenciled bedrooms. Antiquers will enjoy the many shops and malls the area has to offer. Only minutes from I-81, Whitetail Ski area, Greencastle Greens Golf Course, historic Mercersburg, and Hagerstown, Maryland. One hour to Gettysburg and Harpers Ferry. Ninety minutes to Washington, D.C., Baltimore, or Harrisburg.

Hosts: Bob and Ellie Neff
Rooms: 3 (1 PB; 2 SB) $55-65
Full Breakfast
Credit Cards: A, B, C
Notes: 2, 5, 8, 9, 11, 12, 13, 14

GREENSBURG

Huntland Farm Bed and Breakfast

Rural Delivery 9, Box 21, 15601
(412) 834-8483

The 100-acre Huntland Farm is three miles northeast of Greensburg, a convenient halfway stop between the East Coast and the Midwest. From Pennsylvania Turnpike, exit at New Stanton (east) or Monroeville (west).

Circa 1848 house in scenic, historical Laurel Highlands of western Pennsylvania. Four corner bedrooms, two shared baths. Living areas furnished with antiques. Good restaurants and antique shops nearby. Full country breakfast. Children over 12 welcome.

Hosts: Robert and Elizabeth Weidlein
Rooms: 4 (SB) $50-75
Full Breakfast
Credit Cards: C
Notes: 2, 5, 7, 9, 12, 13, 14

GULPH MILLS

Association of Bed and Breakfasts in Philadelphia, Valley Forge, Brandywine

P.O. Box 562, Valley Forge, 19481-0562
(610) 783-7838; (800) 344-0123
FAX (610) 783-7783

0306. The Barn at Rebel Hill. A home made from a barn, this fabulous luxury barn offers an atmosphere of quiet taste to highlight any visit to this historic area. All guest rooms are off the spacious entrance hall. A full breakfast is served in the parlor or in the great room with a fireplace and antiques. In warm weather, lounge or dine on the upper deck overlooking the enclosed stone paddock, the rolling green hills, and pond. Close to Valley Forge and Philadelphia. An easy drive to Brandywine and Amish areas. Three guest rooms, each with a private bath. $85-95.

GUTHRIESVILLE

Association of Bed and Breakfasts in Philadelphia, Valley Forge, Brandywine

P.O. Box 562, Valley Forge, 19481-0562
(610) 783-7838; (800) 344-0123
FAX (610) 783-7783

1503. Circa 1805 Pennsylvania Farmhouse. Hosts invite guests to share the special

7 No smoking; 8 Children welcome; 9 Social drinking allowed; 10 Tennis nearby; 11 Swimming nearby; 12 Golf nearby; 13 Skiing nearby; 14 May be booked through a travel agent.

warmth and serenity of this lovely example of an early 19th-century Pennsylvania farmhouse and experience the seclusion and relaxation offered. Enjoy the antiques throughout the bed and breakfast, the private porch and lawn area with lovely view of the surrounding countryside. Walk about eight acres of hills, meadow, and hedgerow. View the amazing abundance of plant and wildlife that live in the small marshland. Accommodations include two rooms, each with private bath, double bed, telephone, TV, and air conditioning. A third room is suitable for children and has a double bed and single bed. $55-75.

HARFORD

Bed and Breakfast Adventures

Suite 132, 2310 Central Avenue
North Wildwood, NJ 08260
(606) 522-4000; (800) 992-2632

PA715. This country bed and breakfast is named after the settlement of nine pioneers who lived here more than 200 years ago. Its symmetrical floor plan and Colonial façade with nine narrow windows recalls the 18th-century Massachusetts homes those pioneers left behind. There are double, queen-, and twin-size bedrooms, each with a private bath and fireplace. Continental plus breakfast featuring a hot entrée served daily. Skiing, hiking, cycling, antique shops, and historic exhibits nearby. $85.

HAWLEY

Academy Street Bed and Breakfast

528 Academy Street, 18428
(717) 226-3430; (609) 395-8590 (winter)

Outstanding historic 1863 Italianate Victorian built by a Civil War hero, the first sheriff of Wayne County. Near the largest and most beautiful recreational lake in the state, with all activities. Convenient to I-84.

Lovely furnished inn; full gourmet breakfast and afternoon tea. Air-conditioned rooms. Cable TV. Closed November through April.

Host: Judith Lazan
Rooms: 7 (3 PB; 4 SB) $65-80
Full Breakfast
Credit Cards: A, B
Notes: 7, 9, 10, 11, 12

HERSHEY

Pinehurst Inn Bed and Breakfast

50 Northeast Drive, 17033
(717) 533-2603

Spacious brick home surrounded by lawns. Warm, welcoming, many-windowed living room. Large porch with an old-fashioned porch swing. Within walking distance of all Hershey's attractions: Hershey Museum and Rose Gardens, Hershey Park, Chocolate World, fitness/nature trail, and many golf courses. Less than one hour's drive to Lancaster and Gettysburg. Each room has a queen-size bed with a Hershey Kiss on each pillow.

Hosts: Roger and Phyllis Ingold
Rooms: 15 (2 PB; 13 SB) $45-72
Full Breakfast
Credit Cards: A, B
Notes: 2, 5, 7, 8, 9, 10, 11, 12, 14

HESSTON

Aunt Susie's Country Vacations

Rural Delivery 1, Box 225, 16647
(814) 658-3638

Experience country living in a warm, friendly renovated country store and post office. All rooms furnished with antiques and oil paintings. Raystown Lake is nearby; boating, swimming, and fishing are within three miles. Bring the family to the country.

Host: Paul Bonfiglio
Rooms: 5 (1 PB; 4 SB) $50-55
Continental Breakfast
Credit Cards: None
Notes: 2, 5, 7, 8, 9, 10, 11, 12, 13

HOLTWOOD

Bed and Breakfast Adventures

Suite 132, 2310 Central Avenue
North Wildwood, NJ 08260
(606) 522-4000; (800) 992-2632

PA705. This unique country cottage, all one floor, features two bedrooms: one is entered through the bathroom with shower and has a double bed; the other room is glass-enclosed and has a queen-size bed. Guests have access to a TV and VCR in the living room and a complete kitchen is available off of the dining room. A Continental breakfast is delivered to the cottage each morning. The air-conditioned cottage can hold up to ten people and is ideal for families or groups traveling together. Couples, children, and pets are welcome. $100.

HUNTINGDON VALLEY

Bed & Breakfast Connection/ Bed & Breakfast of Philadelphia

P.O. Box 21, Devon, 19333
(610) 687-3565; (800) 448-3619 (outside PA)
FAX (610) 995-9524

C-03. Tucked away in a corner of this large, forest-rimmed back lawn of a comfortable suburban home is a small cottage with an attached greenhouse. The room includes a queen-size bed. The room's private bath is the greenhouse, walled and curtained with white boards and ruffled green calico for privacy, but open to the sun and moon and treetop vistas. Firewood is provided for the wood-burning stove, and a generous breakfast basket filled with a delicious Continental assortment is left at the guests' doorstep for them to enjoy at their leisure. Children are welcome. Smoking is allowed. $85.

INTERCOURSE (LANCASTER COUNTY)

Carriage Corner Bed and Breakfast

3705 East Newport Road, P.O. Box 371, 17534-0371
(717) 768-3059

With tasteful, handcrafted touches of folk art, this inn offers a relaxing country atmosphere. A five-minute walk takes visitors to Intercourse, which is a bustling village from yesteryear with Amish buggies converging. The inn overlooks the Stoltzfus Farm and accompanying family restaurant. In town, Kitchen Kettle Village lures all visitors to its unique shops. The surrounding area, in the heart of Amish farmlands, has myriad attractions and historic sites. Amish dinners arranged.

Hosts: The Schuit family
Rooms: 4 (2 PB; 2 SB) $55-68
Full Breakfast
Credit Cards: A, B
Notes: 2, 5, 8, 12

JACOBUS

Past Purr-fect

216 North Main Street, 17407
(717) 428-1634

This 100-plus-year-old Victorian home features beautiful handcrafted oak floors and trim. Cat theme offers a variety of collectibles. Begin the day with a complete breakfast in the formal dining room. Air-conditioned bedrooms. Off-street parking. Biking and water activities minutes away. Convenient to Gettysburg, Hershey, Lancaster, Harrisburg, Baltimore, and Washington, D.C. Easy access to Route 30 and I-83. Inquire about facilities for pets.

Hosts: John and Susan Trevaskis
Rooms: 4 (1 PB; 3 SB) $60-75
Full Breakfast
Credit Cards: A, B, C
Notes: 2, 5, 7, 8, 9, 10, 11, 12, 14

7 No smoking; 8 Children welcome; 9 Social drinking allowed; 10 Tennis nearby; 11 Swimming nearby; 12 Golf nearby; 13 Skiing nearby; 14 May be booked through a travel agent.

JENKINTOWN

Bed & Breakfast Connection/ Bed & Breakfast of Philadelphia

P.O. Box 21, Devon, 19333
(610) 687-3565; (800) 448-3619 (outside PA)
FAX (610) 995-9524

C-02. Just off Jenkintown's main thorough-fare on a quiet street sits this statuesque stone Victorian home. From the large porch, guests walk through double ruby-glass doors into a large foyer with a stair-case to the second-floor bedroom, which has a double bed, recliner/rocker, TV/AM radio, private bath, sitting room with two sofas, comfortable chairs, and reading lamps. Children over six are welcome. No smoking allowed. $50.

JIM THORPE

The Harry Packer Mansion

Packer Hill, P.O. Box 458, 18229
(717) 325-8566

This 1874 Second Empire mansion features original appointments and Victorian decor. Completely restored for bed and breakfast, fabulous mystery weekends, and a host of other activities. The adjoining carriage house is decorated in a hunt motif. Guest

The Harry Packer Mansion

rooms are elegant but comfortable and fea-ture period antiques.

Hosts: Bob and Patricia Handwerk
Rooms: 13 (9 PB; 4 SB) $85-135
Full Breakfast
Credit Cards: A, B
Notes: 2, 5, 9, 10, 11, 12, 13

KANE

Kane Manor Bed and Breakfast

230 Clay Street, 16735
(814) 837-6522; FAX (814) 837-6664

One of the Allegheny's best kept secrets. Come and experience the feeling of being surrounded by the Allegheny National Forest. The 250 acres of property afford guests four or five miles of blazed cross-country ski trails that double as hiking trails during the warmer months. Kane Manor boasts ten guest rooms, each with its own personal charm and decor. To com-plete the package, hosts offer Saturday night dining, a weekend cellar pub, and gift shop. Boating, swimming, fishing, golf, and tennis available within the immediate area. Breakfast is chef's choice on week-ends.

Hosts: Dusty Byham and Helen Johnson
Rooms: 10 (6 PB; 4 SB) $65-89
Continental Breakfast
Credit Cards: A, B, C, D
Notes: 2, 5, 8, 9, 10, 11, 12, 13, 14

KENNETT SQUARE

Association of Bed and Breakfasts in Philadelphia, Valley Forge, Brandywine

P.O. Box 562, Valley Forge, 19481-0562
(610) 783-7838; (800) 344-0123
FAX (610) 783-7783

0302. Circa 1704 Stone Farmhouse. This Chester County fieldstone farmhouse sits on 20 acres of rolling farmland. Special amenities include pool, hot tub, and two rooms with a fireplace. The six guest rooms are furnished for guests' comfort and can accommodate up to six people in the suite. There is an array of beds such as a spool bed, rope bed, and crocheted canopied four-poster. A full breakfast is served. Near Valley Forge, Lancaster, Philadelphia, and Wilmington. Small conference meetings, weddings, and rental of entire house welcome (rates upon request). $95-168.50.

0601. The Mill at Longwood. This bed and breakfast was built prior to the Civil War, the barn being attached to the house. A double bedroom and a twin bedroom share a full bath. The breakfasts are full, hot, and hearty. The common room includes a fireplace, color cable TV, refrigerator, microwave, and a stove. All facilities are handicapped accessible. Ideal for visiting the Brandywine Valley, five minutes from Longwood Gardens, ten minutes from the Brandywine River Museum, and fifteen minutes from Winterthur. Two horses reside as well as a dog and cat. Guests welcome to bring their horses. $70.

2001. Brandywine Guest Suite. A full suite with private entrance adjoins this brick ranch home in the Brandywine Valley. Queen-size bedroom, TV, private bath, kitchen, deck, grill, and private entrance are surrounded by magnificent landscaping. In the main house hosts offer a twin bedroom with private bath. A full, hot, and hearty breakfast. Winterthur, Longwood Gardens, Brandywine River Museum, Kennett Square, and Wilmington within minutes. Central air conditioning. $70-75.

Bed and Breakfast at Walnut Hill

541 Chandler's Mill Road, Avondale, 19311
(610) 444-3703

This 1840 antique-filled mill house with warm country charm is on a crooked coun-

Bed and Breakfast at Walnut Hill

try road facing a horse-filled meadow and stream. Walnut Hill is only minutes from Longwood Gardens, Winterthur, and the Brandywine River Museum. The hosts enjoy discussing local lore, mapping out tours and points of interest, and making reservations. A gourmet country breakfast will start guests on their way. Guests may enjoy the hot tub for relaxing moments. Canoeing nearby. Guests say they came as strangers, left as friends.

Hosts: Tom and Sandy Mills
Rooms: 2 (SB) $80
Full Breakfast
Credit Cards: None
Notes: 2, 5, 7, 8, 9, 10, 11, 12, 14

Meadow Spring Farm

201 East Street Road (Route 926), 19348
(610) 444-3903

The hosts of this 1836 farmhouse on a working farm with animals invite guests to participate in gathering eggs for breakfast. The house is filled with family antiques, Amish quilts, fine linens, and a doll collection, including Santas and cows. The hosts will prepare a gourmet breakfast for guests before they start their day touring the area. Guests are welcome to enjoy the pool, hot tub, game room, and solarium. This bed and breakfast has been featured in *Country Inns,* the *New York Times,* and Washington's Channel 7 television. In the heart of Brandywine

7 No smoking; 8 Children welcome; 9 Social drinking allowed; 10 Tennis nearby; 11 Swimming nearby; 12 Golf nearby; 13 Skiing nearby; 14 May be booked through a travel agent.

Valley, minutes from Longwood Gardens, Brandywine River Museum, and Winterthur.

Hosts: Anne Hicks and Debbie Axelrod
Rooms: 7 (4 PB; 3 SB) $65-85
Full Breakfast
Credit Cards: None
Notes: 2, 5, 7, 8, 9, 10, 11, 12

KIMBERTON

Association of Bed and Breakfasts in Philadelphia, Valley Forge, Brandywine

P.O. Box 562, Valley Forge, 19481-0562
(610) 783-7838; (800) 344-0123
FAX (610) 783-7783

0705. Sycamore Springs Farm. Guests are invited to take a walk, pat the horses, or sit and relax on the veranda and enjoy the gorgeous view at this circa 1780 eight-acre farm. There is a private-entrance guest cottage that has a full kitchen, fireplace, bedroom, and bath. Fresh pastries are left in the kitchen along with fruit, juice, and coffee each morning. Enjoy a leisurely morning and a late breakfast. $100.

KING OF PRUSSIA

Association of Bed and Breakfasts in Philadelphia, Valley Forge, Brandywine

P.O. Box 562, Valley Forge, 19481-0562
(610) 783-7838; (800) 344-0123
FAX (610) 783-7783

0201. Tranquil Haven. This home is set in a peaceful, heavily wooded neighborhood and is decorated with both antique and modern furnishings. Sitting room with fireplace and color cable TV, laundry facilities, and in-ground pool. Gourmet breakfasts are served in the dining room or on the spacious screened porch overlooking the garden. Some French spoken. Two cats in residence. Three guest rooms with private baths. $45-55.

KINTNERSVILLE

The Bucksville House

Route 412 and Buck Drive
4501 Durham Road, 18930-1610
(610) 847-8948

Country charm and a friendly atmosphere await guests at this 1795 Bucks County registered historic landmark. Offering beautifully decorated rooms with many quilts, baskets, antiques, and handmade reproductions. Enjoy the seven fireplaces, air conditioning, gazebo, pond, herb garden, and brick courtyard. Near New Hope, Peddler's Village, and Nockamixon State Park.

Hosts: Barbara and Joe Szollosi
Rooms: 5 (PB) $100-130
Full Breakfast
Credit Cards: A, B, C, D
Notes: 2, 5, 7, 9, 10, 11

The Bucksville House

KINZERS

Sycamore Haven Farm

35 South Kinzer Road, 17535
(717) 442-4901

This dairy farm is 15 miles east of Lancaster, right in Pennsylvania Dutch country. The rooms are newly papered and painted, and there is a porch in the back of the house with a lovely swing. There is also a balcony with lounge chairs. Forty dairy cows are milked morning and evening. The children will really enjoy the numerous kittens, who like a lot of attention, and the lawn, perfect for play.

Hosts: Charles and Janet Groff
Rooms: 3 (SB) $30
Continental Breakfast
Credit Cards: None
Notes: 2, 5, 6, 7, 8, 10, 11, 12

KUTZTOWN

Around the World Bed and Breakfast

30 South Whiteoak Street, 19530
(610) 683-8885; FAX (610) 298-8414

This is a truly unique bed and breakfast decorated with artifacts from various regions of the world. There are two spacious private rooms and two lovely suites; all have their own private baths, luxurious queen-size beds, and are fully air-conditioned. A delicious country-style breakfast is served daily. Guests will find the conveniences of a hotel with the personality, comfort, and ambience of visiting an old friend. Fifteen minutes from Reading, Pennsylvania, the outlet shopping capital of the world.

Host: Jean F. Billig
Rooms: 2 (PB) $59-79
Suites: 2 (PB) $95-125
Full Breakfast
Credit Cards: A, B, D
Notes: 2, 5, 10, 11, 12, 13, 14

LAHASKA

The Inn at Lahaska

5775 Route 202, 18931

The Inn at Lahaska is in historic Bucks County adjacent to the shops at Peddler's Village and Penn's Purchase outlet stores. The inn radiates warmth and hospitality. Each of the six air-conditioned rooms has a private bath. Spend the day shopping for antiques, browsing for knickknacks, or relaxing at one of the many restaurants within walking distance. A Continental

breakfast is served daily as well as afternoon and evening refreshments.

Host: Kathy Myers
Rooms: 6 (PB) $80-115
Continental Breakfast
Credit Cards: None
Notes: 2, 5, 7, 9

LANCASTER

Association of Bed and Breakfasts in Philadelphia, Valley Forge, Brandywine

P.O. Box 562, Valley Forge, 19481-0562
(610) 783-7838; (800) 344-0123
FAX (610) 783-7783

0207. The Village Inn. The inn, circa 1734, is on the old road, that, in those days, was the gateway to the West. In the heart of Amish country and convenient to all of the most popular attractions. There are 11 rooms and/or suites with private baths for guests to choose from, all furnished for comfort, relaxation, and enjoyment. Tennis courts and both indoor and outdoor swimming pools nearby. Continental breakfast is served each morning. Children under three stay free, four and over $10 additional in the same room on a roll away. There is a two-night minimum on some rooms and rates will vary from season to season. $59-139.

0303. A circa 1735 inn in the heart of Pennsylvania Dutch country. An intimate inn for all seasons. Historic, affordable, and highly recommended. The inn is a splendid fieldstone mansion overlooking picture-postcard fields and farms, and just minutes from all the attractions of Lancaster County. The inn features a full breakfast, lovely Victorian parlors, nine elegant but cozy bedrooms, six private and two shared baths, queen-size and single beds, air conditioning, TV, carriage rides, barbecues, mystery weekends, dinner at an Amish home, and holiday packages. $54-140.

7 No smoking; 8 Children welcome; 9 Social drinking allowed; 10 Tennis nearby; 11 Swimming nearby; 12 Golf nearby; 13 Skiing nearby; 14 May be booked through a travel agent.

0704. The Mansion. A restored 1845 country home surrounded by farmland and in the rolling hills of Pennsylvania that combines Old World charms with all modern conveniences. Guest rooms are beautifully appointed in a setting that includes genuine friendliness and hospitality. A full country breakfast is a delightful repast, including home-baked breads, rolls, and muffins. Breakfast is served in the cheerful dining room or on the front porch. Maps for bike tours are available. $70-100.

1307. Jackie's Bed and Breakfast. This bed and breakfast was completed in 1919. The focal point is an elaborate leaded-glass doorway. The bed and breakfast has been kept in its original state throughout and has been furnished and decorated with antiques, Amish quilts, and crafts. $60.

The Australian Walkabout Inn

837 Village Road, Lampeter, 17537
(717) 464-0707

The Walkabout Inn is an authentic Australian-style bed and breakfast in the heart of Amish country, convenient to all major attractions. The house is a 22-room brick 1925 Mennonite farmhouse with wraparound porches. The grounds feature a fountain and wildflower gardens and outdoor Jacuzzi. Australian-born Richard and his wife, Maggie, serve a full five-course candlelight breakfast. Guest rooms have private baths, canopied and/or queen-size beds, antiques, and cable TV, fireplaces, and whirlpools. Ask about the $199 one-night dinner tour. Anniversary and honeymoon specials available. Rated three diamonds by AAA. Smoking in designated areas only. Children over 12 welcome.

Hosts: Richard and Margaret Mason
Rooms: 5 (PB) $79-99
Suites: 2 (PB) $149
Full Breakfast
Credit Cards: A, B, C
Notes: 2, 4, 5, 9, 11, 12, 14

Bed & Breakfast Connection/ Bed & Breakfast of Philadelphia

P.O. Box 21, Devon, 19333
(610) 687-3565; (800) 448-3619 (outside PA)
FAX (610) 995-9524

H-01. This historic 18th-century house, once a stagecoach stop, is on a working dairy farm surrounded by Amish farms. The three-story home is a showcase for Colonial period furniture and local crafts, including salt-glazed Bennington pottery, hand-dipped scented candles with handmade tin holders, stenciled walls, and dried flower arrangements. There are three large comfortable guest bedrooms on the second floor that share a bath. All bedrooms are air-conditioned and a color TV is available. A full, country breakfast, served in the sunny, antique-filled sitting room/dining room, may include homemade breads, muffins, or sticky buns. Being a working farm, there are cows, dogs, and cats. Twenty minutes to Amish country, 25 minutes to the Brandywine River area. A Scottish golf course is within a few miles and, if given advance notice, the hostess will arrange for horseback riding or horse-drawn buggy rides. $60-75.

H-02. This is a simple, cozy farm owned by two remarkable, likable people who go out of their way to make their guests feel at home. Hannah's farm breakfasts are enormous, and what guests say about their visits here indicates that it is a very special place. Two second-floor guest rooms, one of which has a double bed and the other a twin bed, share a bath with a tub and shower. Children welcome. No smoking. $55.

H-03. This country home is in a peaceful setting surrounded by Amish farms. A comfortable ranch house with a large sunroom to enjoy a full breakfast. There are two guest rooms on the ground level that share a bath. The location is ideal for tour-

---

NOTES: Credit cards accepted: A MasterCard; B Visa; C American Express; D Discover; E Diners Club; F Other; 2 Personal checks accepted; 3 Lunch available; 4 Dinner available; 5 Open all year; 6 Pets welcome;

ing Pennsylvania Dutch country, 20 minutes from Lancaster, and 12 minutes from Longwood Gardens and Winterthur. A special attraction for golf enthusiasts is the 18-hole golf course at Moccasin Run only a mile away. $55.

H-06. The Davis Farm, as it is know by the local folks of Lancaster County, has an idyllic farmland setting; nestled in a hillside, beside a creek with a mill dam, under ancient shade trees and gardens with beautiful views of the tranquil surrounding farmland from each of the five guest rooms with private or shared baths. Only fifteen minutes west of Lancaster City, it is convenient to all attractions of the Pennsylvania Dutch. Full breakfast. $65.

Bed and Breakfast: The Manor Inn

830 Village Road, Route 741
P.O. Box 416, Lampeter, 17537
(717) 464-9564

This cozy farmhouse is just minutes away from historic sights and attractions. Guests delight in Mary Lou's delicious breakfasts, featuring gourmet treats such as eggs Mornay, crepes or strata, apple cobbler, and homemade jams and breads. A swim in the pool or a nap under one of the many shade trees is the perfect way to cap a day of touring. Amish dinners can be arranged. Groups welcome.

Hosts: Mary Lou Paolini and Jackie Curtis
Rooms: 6 (4 PB; 2 SB) $75-99
Full Breakfast
Credit Cards: A, B
Notes: 2, 5, 7, 8, 10, 11, 12

Cedar Hill Farm

305 Longenecker Road, Mount Joy, 17552
(717) 653-4655

This 1817 stone farmhouse sits in a quiet area overlooking a stream. The charming

bedrooms have private baths and central air-conditioning. This working farm is near Amish farms and Hershey. Other attractions include the nearby farmers' markets, quaint antique shopping, and interesting country villages.

Hosts: Russel and Gladys Swarr
Rooms: 5 (PB) $65-75
Continental Breakfast
Credit Cards: A, B, C, D
Notes: 2, 5, 7, 8, 9, 10, 11, 12

The Columbian

The Columbian

360 Chestnut Street, 17512
(717) 684-5869; (800) 422-5869 (reservations)

This restored turn-of-the-century mansion is a splendid example of Colonial Revival architecture, complete with unique wraparound sun porches, ornate stained-glass window, and magnificent tiered staircase. Uniquely decorated with antiques in Victorian and country style, the spacious air-conditioned rooms offer queen-size beds and private baths. The delicious and hearty country breakfast consists of a variety of fresh fruit, hot main dishes, and homemade breads.

Hosts: Becky and Chris Will
Rooms: 6 (PB) $70-85
Full Breakfast
Credit Cards: A, B
Notes: 2, 5, 7, 8, 9, 10, 11, 12, 13

Gardens of Eden
Bed and Breakfast

1894 Eden Road, 17601
(717) 393-5179

Victorian ironmaster's home built circa 1860 on the banks of the Conestoga River is three miles northeast of Lancaster. Antiques and family collections of quilts and coverlets fill the three guest rooms, all with private baths. The adjoining guest cottage (restored summer kitchen) features a walk-in fireplace, bedroom, and bath on second floor. Marilyn's floral designs and friends' crafts are for sale. The three acres of gardens feature herbs, perennials, and wildflowers among the woodsy trails. Local attractions are personalized by a tour guide service and dinner in a young Amish couple's home. Canoe and rowboat available. Two bike trails pass the house. Children welcome in guest house.

Hosts: Marilyn and Bill Ebel
Rooms: 4 (2 PB; 2 SB) $65-110
Full Breakfast
Credit Cards: A, B
Notes: 2, 5, 7, 9, 10, 11, 12, 14

Hollinger House
Bed and Breakfast

2336 Hollinger Road, 17602-4728
(717) 464-3050

Natural, friendly, romantic, comfortable— Hollinger House. A three-story Adams-period brick home built in 1870 on more than five and one-half acres with woodland

Hollinger House

stream and grazing sheep. Original hardwood floors, fireplaces, high ceilings, and large wraparound porch. The rooms have king- or queen-size beds, private baths, and air conditioning. Welcoming snacks are served. Minutes from downtown Lancaster, shopping outlets, historic attractions, farmers' markets, and Amish country. Children over ten welcome.

Hosts: Gina and Jeff Trost
Rooms: 7 (5 PB; 2 SB) $90-100
Full Breakfast
Credit Cards: None
Notes: 2, 3, 4, 5, 7, 9, 10, 11, 12, 13

Homestead Lodging

184 East Brook Road, Smoketown, 17576
(717) 393-6927

Come to this beautiful Lancaster County setting, where guests hear the clippity-clop of Amish buggies going by and can experience the sights and freshness of the farmlands. The clean country rooms provide a homey atmosphere, and an Amish farm is adjacent to the property. There is a large grassy area and a creek to enjoy. Within walking distance of restaurants and within minutes of farmers' markets, quilts, antiques and craft shops, outlets, auctions, and museums. Personal checks accepted for deposit only.

Hosts: Robert and Lori Kepiro
Rooms: 5 (PB) $34-56
Continental Breakfast
Credit Cards: A, B
Notes: 5, 8, 9, 10, 11, 12

The King's Cottage
A Bed and Breakfast Inn

1049 East King Street, 17602
(800) 747-8717

Traditionally styled elegance, modern comfort, and warm hospitality in Amish country. King- and queen-size beds, gourmet breakfasts, and personal service create a friendly atmosphere at this award-winning Spanish-style mansion. Relax by the fire

The King's Cottage

and enjoy afternoon tea in the library while chatting with innkeepers about directions to restaurants and attractions. Special Amish dinners or personal tours arranged. Near farmers' markets, Gettysburg, and Hershey. Listed on the National Register of Historic Places. AAA- and Mobil-listed excellent. Honeymoon Cottage in the Carriage House is handicapped accessible.

Hosts: Karen and Jim Owens
Rooms: 9 (PB) $80-175
Full Breakfast
Credit Cards: A, B, D
Notes: 2, 5, 7, 9, 10, 11, 12, 14

Lincoln Haus Inn Bed and Breakfast

1687 Lincoln Highway East, 17602
(717) 392-9412

A suburban home, built in 1915, with distinctive hip roofs in Lancaster County. Front porch for sitting and double lawn swings for relaxing. Inside are natural oak woodwork and gleaming hardwood floors. Antique furniture and rugs are throughout the house. Mary, a member of the Old Order Amish church, serves a full breakfast family-style in her shining, homey dining room. Her specialty is to be a great hostess. Dinner can be made available with prior notice.

Host: Mary K. Zook
Rooms: 5 (PB) $48-75
Apartment: (PB)
Full Breakfast
Credit Cards: None
Notes: 2, 5, 7, 8, 10, 11, 12, 14

Meadowview Guest House

2169 New Holland Pike, Route 23, 17601
(717) 299-4017

In the heart of the Pennsylvania Dutch area, close to historic sites, antiques, farmers' and flea markets, and excellent restaurants. Large air-conditioned rooms, and guest kitchen with coffee and tea. To help guests enjoy the beautiful county, personalized maps are provided. Children over six welcome.

Hosts: Ed and Sheila Christie
Rooms: 3 (1 PB; 2 SB) $30-50
Continental Breakfast
Credit Cards: None
Notes: 2, 5, 9, 10, 11, 12

Patchwork Inn

2319 Old Philadelphia Pike, 17602
(717) 293-9078; (800) 584-5776

Patchwork Inn is a 19th-century farmhouse furnished throughout with antique oak. The inn is decorated with more than 70 new and antique quilts from all parts of the United States. The queen-size beds are covered with handmade quilts, and other private collections include 25 old telephones and an extensive Delft china collection. Reading material abounds, and bike storage and routes are available. Patchwork Inn is east of Lancaster, across the street from a working Amish farm.

Hosts: Lee and Anne Martin
Rooms: 4 (2 PB; 2 SB) $65-85
Full Breakfast
Credit Cards: A, B, D
Notes: 2, 5, 7, 9, 12

Witmer's Tavern Historic 1725 Inn

2014 Old Philadelphia Pike, 17602
(717) 299-5305

Lancaster's oldest, only pre-Revolutionary War inn still lodging travelers. Reflects rural and historic flavor of the area. Restored to the simple, authentic, pioneer

7 No smoking; 8 Children welcome; 9 Social drinking allowed; 10 Tennis nearby; 11 Swimming nearby; 12 Golf nearby; 13 Skiing nearby; 14 May be booked through a travel agent.

Witmer's Tavern

style that was familiar to European immigrants who joined the Conestoga wagon trains being provisioned at the inn for the western and southern treks into the wilderness areas. Fresh flowers, working fireplaces, antique quilts, and antiques in all the romantic rooms. Pandora's Antique Shop is on the premises. Bird-in-Hand and Intercourse villages, other antique shops, and auctions just beyond. Valley Forge, Hershey, Gettysburg, Winterthur, Chadds Ford, and New Hope all within a 90-minute drive. On the National Register of Historic Places and a national landmark. Beautiful park across the street. Inquire about accommodations for children.

Host: Brant Hartung
Rooms: 7 (2 PB; 5 SB) $60-90
Continental Breakfast
Credit Cards: None
Notes: 2, 5, 9, 10, 11, 12, 13, 14

Ye Olde Bank Bed and Breakfast

29 North Prince Street, 17603
(717) 393-7774

In the heart of downtown Lancaster within walking distance of the farmers' markets, the Fulton Theatre, and a variety of shops and restaurants. Enjoy the delightful Continental plus breakfast, downy robes, and relaxing in a private bath.

Host: Nina Balgar
Rooms: 2 (PB) $75-105
Continental Breakfast
Credit Cards: None
Notes: 2, 5, 7, 8, 9

LANDENBERG

Cornerstone Bed and Breakfast

Rural Delivery 1, Box 155, 19350
(215) 274-2143

To understand history is to live it. Charming 18th-century country inn with canopied beds, fireplaces in bedrooms, private baths, and antiques galore. Just minutes from Brandywine Valley museums and gardens: Longwood, Winterthur, and Hagley.

Hosts: Linda and Marty
Rooms: 5 (PB) $85-125
Full Breakfast
Credit Cards: A, B, C, D
Notes: 2, 7, 8, 9, 10, 11, 12, 14

Guesthouses, Inc.

P.O. Box 2137, West Chester, 19380
(610) 692-4575

019. Choose either a king-size or two twin-size beds at this owner-hosted "Top Suite" residence. A full breakfast is served at the baronial dining table or on the terrace. Also available are two suites and a guest house with complete laundry facilities, telephones, color TVs, and either fireplaces or wood stoves. Can be rented by the month. Call for rates. Winterthur, White Clay Creek nature conservancy, fine dining, hiking, cross-country skiing, trout-fishing, and golf are nearby. Two-night minimum stay on weekends; three-night minimum stay on holiday weekends. $125.

LEOLA

Turtle Hill Road Bed and Breakfast

111 Turtle Hill Road, 17540
(717) 656-6163

Split-level home one mile off routes 272 and 222, between Ephrata and Lancaster in Lancaster County. Rural area overlooks the

Conestoga River, near an old mill and waterfall. Very scenic, quiet, and peaceful. A photographer's paradise!

Host: Jean W. Parmer
Rooms: 2 (SB) $55
Full Breakfast
Credit Cards: None
Notes: 2, 8, 10, 11, 12

LEWISBURG

Blue Ridge Bed and Breakfast

Route 2, Box 3895, 22611
(703) 955-1246; (800) 296-1246

Beautifully restored German stone home of the Federal period built in 1810. Thirty-three acres of rolling countryside in the tranquil Susquehanna Valley. Five bedrooms, all with private baths. Walking and cross-country skiing on premises; golfing and all water sports arranged by owners. Dinner is available by prior reservation. $65-75.

LIMA

Amanda's Bed and Breakfast

1428 Park Avenue, Baltimore, MD 21217-4230
(410) 225-0001; (800) 899-7533
FAX (410) 728-8957

279. This bed and breakfast is a large 19th-century country manor house. Built in 1856, it has been on the National Register of Historic Places since 1971. More than three-fourths of the land is covered with luxuriant growth. Eight guest rooms, all with private baths, are available. $85-125.

LITITZ

Alden House

62 East Main Street, 17543
(717) 627-3363; (800) 584-0753

Fully restored 1850 brick Victorian in the heart of the town's historic district. All local attractions are within walking distance. Relax at the end of the day on one of three spacious porches and watch Amish buggies or experience a whiff of fresh chocolate from the local candy factory. Home of the nation's oldest pretzel bakery. Family suites, off-street parking, and bicycle storage available. Antiques abound in this area as well as local handmade quilts. Enjoy old-fashioned hospitality. Children over six welcome.

Hosts: Fletcher and Joy Coleman
Rooms: 6 (PB) $75-105
Full Breakfast
Credit Cards: A, B
Notes: 2, 5, 9, 12, 14

Alden House

Spahr's Century Farm Bed and Breakfast

192 Green Acre Road, 17543-8759
(717) 627-2185

This Lancaster County farm has been in the Spahr family since 1855. Antique shops and candy and pretzel factories are in nearby Lititz. Biking, walking, and peace and quiet surround this charming bed and breakfast.

Host: Naomi Spahr
Rooms: 3 (1 PB; 2 SB) $47.50-63.50
Continental Breakfast
Credit Cards: None
Notes: 2

7 No smoking; 8 Children welcome; 9 Social drinking allowed; 10 Tennis nearby; 11 Swimming nearby; 12 Golf nearby; 13 Skiing nearby; 14 May be booked through a travel agent.

LONGWOOD

Guesthouses, Inc.

P.O. Box 2137, West Chester, 19380
(610) 692-4575

721. The guest entrance into the lofty guest living room with fieldstone fireplace is by way of a flagstone terrace enclosed by a screened porch. There are two bedrooms, one with queen-size bed, the other with twin beds, opposite a bath for both rooms. At the end of the great room is a kitchenette where guests may store cold drinks and such. Full country breakfast. $85-135.

MACUNGIE

Sycamore Inn
Bed and Breakfast

165 East Main Street, Route 100, 18062
(215) 966-5177

Kick-off-shoes comfort, hearty breakfast, personable hosts, and plenty of hospitality are what guests will find at this bed and breakfast. Look for a circa 1835 stone farmhouse with two houses in one. The quiet back house is the very cozy inn. Offering guest rooms furnished with antique theme, common room with walk-in fireplace, and enclosed porch surrounded by windows. There is also a "live-in" antique shop for guests' enjoyment. Easy to find; lots to do. Children over 12 welcome.

Hosts: Mark and Randie Levisky
Rooms: 5 (3 PB; 2 SB) $70-80
Full Breakfast
Credit Cards: A, B
Notes: 2, 5, 7, 9, 10, 11, 12, 13

MAIN LINE

Bed & Breakfast Connection/
Bed & Breakfast of Philadelphia

P.O. Box 21, Devon, 19333
(610) 687-3565; (800) 448-3619
FAX (610) 995-9524

E-07. This Colonial-style home in a pleasant suburban neighborhood offers the advantages of quiet neighborhood living and proximity to Main Line universities. It is also within walking distance of a nature center well known in the area for bird watching. The third-floor accommodations (just two short flights up) are attractively decorated. The beds can be made up as one king-size or two twin-size beds. The private attached bath has a stall shower. For those guests needing to catch up on paperwork, there is a small desk. Or relax in a comfortable wing chair to enjoy TV. The hostess serves a hearty Continental breakfast on the deck, weather permitting, or in the large formal dining room. $70.

Guesthouses, Inc.

P.O. Box 2137, West Chester, 19380
(610) 692-4575

706. The house has been built entirely within a grand old bank barn. The guest floor is on the level of the main entrance and consists of a large open hall with entrance doors to the guest rooms. The suite consists of an oversized bedroom with sitting area and bar, furnished with antiques and a king-size or twin beds, and attached private bath. The other two guest rooms each have attached private baths, are generously furnished with creature comforts, and have queen- and king-size or twin beds. The guest level has its own elegant living room, complete with concert grand piano. A full country breakfast is served by candlelight in the large formal dining room. Fully air-conditioned. $95-110.

MALVERN

Association of Bed and
Breakfasts in Philadelphia,
Valley Forge, Brandywine

P.O. Box 562, Valley Forge, 19481-0562
(610) 783-7838; (800) 344-0123
FAX (610) 783-7783

NOTES: Credit cards accepted: A MasterCard; B Visa; C American Express; D Discover; E Diners Club; F Other; 2 Personal checks accepted; 3 Lunch available; 4 Dinner available; 5 Open all year; 6 Pets welcome;

0702. Eaglesmere. This 21-sided contemporary home is nestled on a wooded cul-de-sac. It boasts three cathedral ceilings, exposed beams, and walls of windows overlooking Great Valley and Valley Forge Mountain. A gourmet breakfast is served in the dining room or on one of four decks. The enormous lower level contains the guest quarters. Preheated beds, bath gels, bathroom toe warmers, and thick terry-cloth robes are provided for guests' pleasure. Two guest rooms with private bath. $75.

1202. Pickering Bend Bed and Breakfast. Bank house, circa 1790, offers the most bucolic atmosphere in Valley Forge country. This bed and breakfast is in the historic village of Charlestown; about six miles from the Valley Forge National Historic Park. Guests are invited to walk the grounds and enjoy the gazebo. The private entrance guest suite consists of patio, two bedrooms—one single bed and one queen-size bed—full kitchen, private bath, and bar area. The guest quarters have a phone, A/C, color TV, VCR, fireplace, sofa, and desk. Breakfast foods are self-service and provided in the guest's kitchen. Decor is country comfortable. $85-$100.

MANHEIM

Herr Farmhouse Inn

2256 Huber Drive, 17545
(717) 653-9852

Lancaster County, Pennsylvania (Amish). Completely restored 1750 stone plantation home on eleven and one-half scenic acres. Inn includes all original woodwork, flooring, and cabinets. Take a step into yesteryear amidst antiques and reproductions of Colonial furnishings. The farm is intact with all outbuildings but is nonworking with the exception of one piece of livestock, a house cat named Clyde. Enjoy the six working fireplaces as well as Amish

dining and other fine restaurants, indoor bicycle storage, central air, antiques, and historic attractions nearby. Children over 12 are welcome.

Host: Barry A. Herr
Rooms: 4 (2 PB; 2 SB) $75-90
Suite: $100
Full Breakfast
Credit Cards: A, B
Notes: 2, 5, 7, 9, 10, 11, 12, 13

Herr Farmhouse Inn

MARIETTA

The River Inn

258 West Front Street, 17547
(717) 426-2290

Restored home, circa 1790, in national historic district of Marietta. Along Susquehanna River, near Lancaster, York, and Hershey attractions. Decorated with antiques and reproductions, this home offers three cozy guest rooms. When weather permits, breakfast is served on the screened porch. In the winter, warm the body with the six fireplaces throughout the home. Enjoy the herb and flower gardens. Owner can provide guided boat fishing on river. Air conditioning; cable TV.

Hosts: Joyce and Bob Heiserman
Rooms: 3 (PB) $60-70
Full Breakfast
Credit Cards: A, B, D, E
Notes: 2, 5, 9, 14

---

7 No smoking; 8 Children welcome; 9 Social drinking allowed; 10 Tennis nearby; 11 Swimming nearby; 12 Golf nearby; 13 Skiing nearby; 14 May be booked through a travel agent.

Vogt Farm Bed and Breakfast

1225 Colebrook Road, 17547
(717) 653-4810; (800) 854-0399

Vogt Farm guests are treated like friends by the hosts of this bed and breakfast. The guest rooms are decorated with antiques and other family treasures. Guests are welcome to enjoy the fireplace in the family room, cozy porches, and air conditioning. Breakfast is served at 8:30 A.M. weekdays and 8:00 A.M. on Sunday in the large farm kitchen. Air-conditioned, spacious yard, three porches, and animals. Terry-cloth robes.

Rooms: 3 (1 PB; 2 SB) $55-80
Full Breakfast
Credit Cards: A, B, C, D, E
Notes: 2, 5, 7, 8, 10, 11, 12

McCONNELLSBURG

Market Street Inn

131 West Market Street, 17233
(717) 485-5495

In the Green Mountains 90 miles north of Washington, D.C., Market Street Inn offers canopied beds, toasty rooms, and private baths in a McConnellsburg historic district neighborhood along the Lincoln Highway. Gourmet breakfasts feature Burnt Cabins Grist Mill pancakes, locally smoked sausages, and seasonally stirred apple butter. Weekend antique and estate sales common. Minutes from Whitetail Ski Resort, Cowans Gap State Park (lake swimming and picnicking), Buchanan State Forest (mountain biking, cross-country skiing, and hiking), and great fishing holes. Inquire about the 1996 Victorian Christmas dinners. Air-conditioned. Close to Interstates 70 and 81 and exit 13 of the Pennsylvania Turnpike.

Hosts: Margaret and Timothy Taylor
Rooms: 3 (PB) $60
Full Breakfast
Credit Cards: A, B
Notes: 2, 5, 7, 8, 9, 10, 11, 12, 13, 14

MERCER

Magoffin Inn

129 South Pitt Street, 16137
(412) 662-4611; (800) 841-0824

An experience in affordable luxury with the quiet elegance of an era past. The Magoffin Inn, circa 1884, features Victorian antique furnishings, five gracious bedrooms with private baths, and three dining rooms for breakfast, lunch, and dinner. Guest rooms have cable TV, fireplaces, and private sitting areas. Next door is the Historical Museum, and one of the country's most impressive courthouses is across the street. Only minutes from the crossroads of I-79 and I-80, and within seven miles of the Grove City factory shops.

Rooms: 10 (8 PB; 2 SB) $55-105
Full Breakfast
Credit Cards: A, B, C
Notes: 2, 5, 7, 8, 9, 10, 11, 12, 14

Magoffin Inn

MERCERSBURG

The Mercersburg Inn

405 South Main Street, 17236
(717) 328-5231; FAX (717) 328-3403

The Mercersburg Inn is a magnificently restored 20,000-square-foot mansion built in 1909 as the private estate of Harry and Ione Byron. Fifteen elegantly appointed guest rooms feature down comforters, canopied beds, balconies, views of the Tuscarora Mountains, and working fireplaces. A six-course dinner is served Friday and Saturday evenings.

Host: Chuck Guy
Rooms: 15 (PB) $110-180
Full Breakfast
Credit Cards: A, B, D
Notes: 2, 5, 7, 8, 10, 12, 13, 14

MERTZTOWN

Longswamp Bed and Breakfast

1605 State Street, 19539
(215) 682-6197

This 200-year-old home, furnished with antiques and every comfort, is set in gorgeous countryside, yet is close to Reading, Kutztown, Allentown, and Amish country. Delicious, bountiful breakfasts draw raves from guests.

Hosts: Elsa and Dean Dimick
Rooms: 10 (6 PB; 4 SB) $63-79.50
Full Breakfast
Credit Cards: A, B, C
Notes: 2, 5, 7, 8, 9, 10, 11, 12, 13

MILFORD

Black Walnut Bed and Breakfast Inn

Rural Delivery 2, Box 9285, 18337
(717) 296-6322

Tudor-style stone house with historic marble fireplace and 12 charming guest rooms plus one suite with antiques and brass beds. A 160-acre estate, it is quiet and peaceful and convenient to horseback riding, antiquing, golf, skiing, rafting, and canoeing on the Delaware River. Serving the finest cuisine and cocktails in a beautiful country setting overlooking a five-acre lake just outside of Milford.

Hosts: Robert Bateman and Cheryl Anderson
Rooms: 12 (8 PB; 4 SB) $60-150
Full Breakfast
Credit Cards: A, B, C
Notes: 2, 4, 5, 9, 11, 12, 13

Cliff Park Inn

Cliff Park Inn and Golf Course

Rural Route 4, Box 7200, 18337-9708
(717) 296-6491; (800) 225-6535

Historic country inn surrounded by long-established golf course with cliffs overlooking the Delaware River. Inn and restaurant rated three stars by Mobil. Fine dining. Rooms with fireplaces available. Modified American Plan or bed and breakfast plan available. Golf school. Inn/golf packages. Cross-country skiing in winter. Golf and ski equipment rentals. Conferences. Country weddings. Ninety minutes from New York City. Brochures by fax.

Hosts: The Buchanan Family
Rooms: 18 (PB) $93-155
Full Breakfast
Credit Cards: A, B, C, D, E
Notes: 2, 3, 4, 5, 8, 9, 10, 11, 12, 13, 14

MILLERSBURG

Victorian Manor Inn

312 Market Street, 17061
(717) 692-3511

Victorian Manor Inn is on Route 147 between Harrisburg and Sunbury, only one block from the picturesque Susquehanna River and historic Millersburg Ferry. This elegantly restored Second Empire home is furnished with period antiques and collectibles. Guests will enjoy wicker-filled porches, gazebo, and courtyard, or relax

7 No smoking; 8 Children welcome; 9 Social drinking allowed; 10 Tennis nearby; 11 Swimming nearby; 12 Golf nearby; 13 Skiing nearby; 14 May be booked through a travel agent.

in the spacious parlor. Whether visiting during the holiday season amid the exquisite Christmas decorations or in the summer with the quaint gardens in bloom, breakfast is always a treat.

Hosts: Skip and Sue Wingard
Rooms: 4 (2 PB; 2 SB) $ 50-75
Full Breakfast
Credit Cards: A, B, C
Notes: 2, 5, 7, 8, 9, 10, 11, 12

MONTOURSVILLE

The Carriage House at Stonegate

Rural Delivery 1, Box 11 A, 17754
(717) 433-4340

Nestled in the lower Loyalsock Creek Valley on one of the oldest farms in the valley, the Carriage House offers its guests a unique concept in the bed and breakfast world. President Herbert Hoover was a descendant of the original settlers of the farm. The converted carriage house provides visitors with total privacy and 1,400-square feet of space on two floors. The Carriage House is furnished in antiques and period reproductions. There are two bedrooms and a bath upstairs, with a fully equipped kitchen, half-bath, and living-dining area downstairs.

Hosts: Harold and Dena Mesaris
Rooms: 2 (SB) $50
Continental Breakfast
Credit Cards: None
Notes: 2, 5, 6, 8, 9, 10, 11, 12, 13, 14

MOUNT JOY

The International Bed and Breakfast Club, Inc.

504 Amherst Street, Buffalo, NY 14207
(800) 723-4262; FAX (716) 873-4462

PA4781PP. The Pennsylvania Dutch countryside of Lancaster County beckons guests to explore this former dairy farm built in 1866. The two-and-a-half-story brick farmhouse is in the middle of the largest section of open land in the township. Five large air-conditioned guest rooms, some with private baths, invite guests to "come home to the farm," unwind, and stay the night in a peaceful, rural setting. A delicious and hearty full breakfast is served each morning. $60-75.

MOUNT POCONO

Farmhouse Bed and Breakfast

HCR 1, Box 6 B, 18344
(717) 839-0796

An 1850 homestead on six manicured acres. Separate cottage and four suites, all with fireplace. Farm-style breakfast complete with original country recipes prepared by the host, a professional chef. Enjoy bedtime snacks that are freshly baked each day. Antiques adorn each room, with cleanliness being the order of the day. All accommodations have private baths, queen-size beds, TV, telephones, VCR, and air conditioning. Nonsmokers only.

Hosts: Jack and Donna Asure
Rooms: 5 (PB) $85-105
Full Breakfast
Credit Cards: A, B, D
Notes: 5, 7, 9, 10, 11, 12, 13

Farmhouse

MUNCY

The Bodine House

307 South Main Street, 17756
(717) 546-8949

Built in 1805 and in the national historic district of Muncy, the Bodine House offers guests the opportunity to enjoy the atmosphere of an earlier age. The comfortable rooms are individually furnished with antiques, and candlelight is used in the living room by the fireplace, where guests can socialize and enjoy refreshments. Three blocks from town center, movies, restaurants, library, and shops. Children over six are welcome.

Hosts: David and Marie Louise Smith
Rooms: 4 (PB) $50-75
Full Breakfast
Credit Cards: A, B, C
Notes: 2, 5, 7, 9, 10, 11, 12, 13, 14

NAZARETH

Classic Victorian Bed and Breakfast

35 North New Street, 18064
(610) 759-8276

Come to the historic district of the quaint Moravian settlement of Nazareth, established in 1740, and enjoy the feeling of being relaxed and pampered in this classic Victorian bed and breakfast. This turn-of-the-century Colonial Revival is a wonderful mix of Victorian and 18th-century traditional furnishings accented with lace, Oriental rugs, stained glass, and chestnut woodwork. Evening turndown and afternoon tea. A full candlelight breakfast complemented with Wedgewood and fine flatware and linens may be served in the formal dining room, sweeping front veranda, or second-floor balcony. The classic Victorian is 12 minutes from Bethlehem, 15 minutes away from the Bach Festival in May, skiing, major colleges, universities,

and music festival in August. Five minutes from world-renowned Martin Guitar Factory.

Hosts: Irene and Dan Sokolowski
Rooms: 3 (1 PB; 2 SB) $65-95
Full Breakfast
Credit Cards: A, B, C
Notes: 2, 5, 7, 8, 9, 12, 13, 14

Classic Victorian

NEW BERLIN

The Inn at Olde New Berlin

321 Market Street, 17855-0390
(717) 966-0321; FAX (717) 966-9557

This elegantly appointed Victorian inn is the perfect setting for capturing quiet pleasures. Memories are made from the inviting front porch swing to the baby grand piano in the step-down living room to the herb garden where the restaurant's seasonings and garnishes are selected. Superb dining opportunities at Gabriel's Restaurant, coupled with antique-laden guest rooms, provide luxury and romance. Discover upscale pampering in a rural setting. Depart feeling nurtured, relaxed, inspired, and ready to return.

Hosts: John and Nancy Showers
Rooms: 5 (PB)
Full Breakfast
Credit Cards: A, B
Notes: 2, 3, 4, 5, 7, 8, 9, 10, 12

7 No smoking; 8 Children welcome; 9 Social drinking allowed; 10 Tennis nearby; 11 Swimming nearby; 12 Golf nearby; 13 Skiing nearby; 14 May be booked through a travel agent.

NEW HOPE (BUCKS COUNTY) _____

Association of Bed and Breakfasts in Philadelphia, Valley Forge, Brandywine

P.O. Box 562, Valley Forge, 19481-0562
(610) 783-7838; (800) 344-0123
FAX (610) 783-7783

0706. The Cottage on the Delaware. The cottage is a reproduction 18th-century dwelling that was inspired by the Josias Moody house in Williamsburg. It occupies three and one-half acres on the banks of the Delaware River about 15 minutes from New Hope. The original house, occupied by the owners, is a restored circa 1790 farmhouse and offers all the amenities of a complete house with a queen-size bedroom and room for one more in the dining room. The living room boasts a working fireplace for comfort during the winter months. In the summer, it is air-conditioned. Breakfast is self-service in a well-stocked kitchen. Less than 20 minutes from all of the attractions in the New Hope area and adjacent New Jersey. Center City Philadelphia is only 40 minutes away. Twenty-five dollars additional for third person. $125-150.

1003. Cubbyhole Cottage. This Colonial cottage set on three acres among perennial and rose gardens is buffered on three sides by large pine trees and open farmland. The cottage is professionally decorated with antiques and reproductions by a master craftsman and has been featured in *Better Homes and Gardens*. Amenities include a fireplace, TV, VCR, full kitchen with microwave, and telephone. Peddler's Village, New Hope, and Newtown are within four miles of the cottage. The main floor consists of living room with fireplace, Williamsburg kitchen; the second floor, a canopied four-poster bed and bath. Air-conditioned. $125.

The Inn at Phillips Mill

2590 North River Road, 18938
(215) 862-2984

Country French cuisine in a renovated 18th-century stone barn. Candlelit dining by the fire in winters and on the flower-filled patio in summers. Five cozy guest rooms decorated with antiques, each with private bath. Closed January. Children over 10 welcome.

Hosts: Brooks and Joyce Kaufman
Rooms: 5 (PB) $75-85
Continental Breakfast
Credit Cards: None
Notes: 2, 4, 9, 11

Tattersall Inn

Tattersall Inn

Box 569, Point Pleasant, 18950
(215) 297-8233

Overlooking a river village, this Bucks County manor house dates to the 18th century and features broad porches for relaxation and a walk-in fireplace for cool evenings. Continental plus breakfast in the dining room, in the guests' room, or on the veranda. Enjoy the antique-furnished rooms and collection of vintage phonographs. Close to New Hope. AAA three diamonds, Mobil two-star rated. Limited smoking permitted. Cross-country skiing nearby.

Hosts: Gerry and Herb Moss
Rooms: 6 (PB) $70-109
Continental Breakfast
Credit Cards: A, B, C, D
Notes: 2, 5, 8, 9, 10, 11, 14

NOTES: Credit cards accepted: A MasterCard; B Visa; C American Express; D Discover; E Diners Club;
F Other; 2 Personal checks accepted; 3 Lunch available; 4 Dinner available; 5 Open all year; 6 Pets welcome;

Wedgwood Inn of New Hope

111 West Bridge Street, 18938-1401
(215) 862-2570; FAX (215) 862-2570

This charming inn was voted Inn of the Year by the readers of inn guidebooks. The historic inn is on two acres of landscaped grounds and is only steps from the village center. Antiques, fresh flowers, and Wedgwood china are the rule at the inn, where guests are treated like royalty. AAA three diamonds. Innkeeping seminars are offered.

Hosts: Carl A. Glassman and Nadine Silnutzer
Rooms: 12 (PB) $70-190
Continental Breakfast
Credit Cards: A, B, C
Notes: 2, 5, 7, 8, 9, 10, 11, 12, 13, 14

NEW HOPE (WASHINGTON CROSSING) ___

Inn to the Woods

150 Glenwood Drive, 18977
(215) 493-1974; (800) 982-7619

Come enjoy secluded elegance in historic Bucks County. This European-style bed and breakfast inn will enchant guests with its ten acres of forest crisscrossed with deer paths and hiking trails. Deluxe accommodations include private bath, individually controlled heat and air conditioning, cable TV, hair dryer, and numerous other amenities. Guests will enjoy the owner's worldwide collection of art and antiques, including a morning quiz on Victoriana during a gourmet breakfast and champagne brunch on Sundays. Continental breakfast is served weekdays. Afternoon tea is served with hors d'oeuvres, and in the evening, sit back and sip sherry. Relax in the great room with raised hearth fireplace, atrium, and indoor fishpond. Just minutes from New Hope, and one mile from I-95.

Hosts: Barry and Rosemary Rein
Rooms: 7 (PB) $85-145
Full and Continental Breakfast
Credit Cards: A, B, C
Notes: 2, 5, 7, 9, 13, 14

NEW HOPE (WRIGHTSTOWN) ___

Backstreet Inn of New Hope

144 Old York Road, 18938
(215) 862-9571

The Backstreet Inn of New Hope offers the comfort and serenity of a small inn in the town of New Hope, Bucks County. It is in a quiet, tucked-away street, yet within walking distance of the center of town. Minimum-stay requirements for weekends and holidays.

Hosts: Bob Puccio and John Hein
Rooms: 7 (PB) $78-120
Full Breakfast
Credit Cards: B, C·
Notes: 2, 5, 7, 8, 10, 11, 12, 13, 14

Hollileif Bed and Breakfast Establishment

677 Durham Road (Route 413), Wrightstown, 18940
(215) 598-3100

An 18th-century farmhouse on five and one-half acres of Bucks County countryside with romantic ambience, gourmet breakfasts, fireplaces, central air conditioning, and private baths. Gracious service is combined with attention to detail. Each guest room is beautifully appointed with antiques and country furnishings. Enjoy afternoon refreshments by the fireside or on

Hollileif

the arbor-covered patio. Relax in a hammock in the meadow overlooking a peaceful stream. View a vibrant sunset and wildlife. Close to New Hope. AAA and Mobil rated.

Hosts: Ellen and Richard Butkus
Rooms: 5 (PB) $85-130
Full Breakfast
Credit Cards: A, B, C, D
Notes: 2, 5, 7, 10, 11, 12, 13, 14

NEW OXFORD

Guesthouses, Inc.

P.O. Box 2137, West Chester, 19380
(610) 692-4575

164. The main house, furnished with antiques, offers three accommodations for guests on the two upper floors. The guest house, a reconstruction of the carriage house, has a living room, dining room, kitchen, laundry, and large bath on the first floor, and two bedrooms and lavatory sink on the second floor. There is more than one-half mile of river frontage. Guests are welcome to use the row boat or ice-skate in season. Available for long term. $95-225.

NEWVILLE

The Quaint Occasion

1209 Doubling Gap Road, 17241
(717) 776-6575

The Quaint Occasion is a cedar contemporary home nestled in the foothills of the Tuscarora Forest. Wooded trails, wildlife, a stocked pond, shade trees, and a cool mountain stream are favorites on the 50-acre estate. Colonel Denning State Park also nearby. Indoors, a cathedral ceiling accentuates the brick fireplace. Relax in the cozy library, or from the sunroom take in a fabulous view of the woodlands and countryside, including the sunset. A hearty breakfast always served. Personal checks accepted in advance. Children over 12 are welcome.

Hosts: Lauri and Bob Crochunis
Rooms: 3 (PB) $75-145
Full Breakfast
Credit Cards: A, B
Notes: 3, 7, 9, 11, 12

OAKS

Association of Bed and Breakfasts in Philadelphia, Valley Forge, Brandywine

P.O. Box 562, Valley Forge, 19481-0562
(610) 783-7838; (800) 344-0123
FAX (610) 783-7783

0605. At the Herb Garden. This is an ongoing restoration of a Federal-style, pointed-stone farmhouse built in 1833. Highlights include five fireplaces, some of which work, original woodwork, stenciling, and antique furnishings. Breakfast is served in the keeping room in front of a working walk-in fireplace. Fragrances from the herb garden are an aromatic delight in spring and summer. The farmhouse is in a small suburb close to Valley Forge and Amish country, and an easy drive to the Brandywine area. Two guest rooms are available. $65-75.

ODESSA

Guesthouses, Inc.

P.O. Box 2137, West Chester, 19380
(610) 692-4575

794. Just south of Wilmington and New Castle in the restored village of Odessa, this quaint early 1800s worker's house seems part of another place and time. Decorated in period furnishings appropriate to the age and scale of this prosperous workingman's house-in-town. The guest rooms are on the second and third floors and share the second-floor bath. A queen-size bed and new bath with Jacuzzi are on the third floor. Breakfast is served in the dining room. The rooms are air-conditioned in summer, and fires are lighted for winter ambience. The town's brick sidewalks make a pleasant place to stroll. Featured in *Mid-Atlantic Country* magazine. $75-95

OLEY

Guesthouses, Inc.

P.O. Box 2137, West Chester, 19380
(610) 692-4575

007. A charming 18th-century reconstructed stone cottage sits on a lovely historic farm. This is a fine place for young, adventurous couples to visit. Children over five can be accommodated as well and will especially enjoy the complimentary surrey ride in good weather. Dine in front of the open hearth. The bath is on the first floor. The living room is up narrow, winding stairs on the middle level with wide floor boards, beamed ceiling, and fireplace. The bedroom with double bed is above. The antique furnishings and decorations have been carefully chosen to complement the plain historic character of the farm. The bedroom is air-conditioned in the summer months. Breakfast is brought to the guesthouse each morning. Some local attractions include French Creek State Park, Ephrata Cloisters, Hopewell (iron) Village, antique and craft markets of Kutztown and Adamstown, the outlet stores of Reading, and the nature enthusiast's Hawk Mountain. Monthly rates available. $70.

OXFORD

Association of Bed and Breakfasts in Philadelphia, Valley Forge, Brandywine

P.O. Box 562, Valley Forge, 19481-0562
(610) 783-7838; (800) 344-0123
FAX (610) 783-7783

0802. Oxford Bed and Breakfast. This modern log house is in a quiet wooded area away from all traffic noises. Families with children are welcome. One guest

room is handicapped accessible. Complimentary beverages and snacks are offered, and each morning a full hot breakfast is served. The decor is comfortable, well-lighted, relaxing, and livable. $50.

Guesthouses, Inc.

P.O. Box 2137, West Chester, 19380
(610) 692-4575

789. This fine old Federal-style brick building, circa 1790, is part of a working farm. The house is cheerful with country antiques and collectibles worthy of its feature in *Country Magazine.* Guests are welcomed at the Williamsburg Raleigh Tavern-style caged bar. The air-conditioned bedrooms are on the second floor and consist of a large corner room with full-size bed and a single bed with a new shower-only bath ensuite. Two other corner rooms can share the full bath in the hall between them. An old-fashioned farm-style breakfast is served in the breakfast room. Near the Delaware and Maryland border, easily accessible from I-95 or US Route 1 or US Route 40, and is within a half-hour of Wilmington, Chadds Ford, or Lancaster. $60-75.

PALM

Summer Brook Farm

974 Gravel Pike Chapel, 18070
(215) 679-0773

Built in 1796, this historic stone home and once former inn is once again welcoming guests. At present there are two bedrooms and a private bath if only one room is occupied. Cooked breakfast served in the former tavern room. Private sitting area, completely air-conditioned. Coffee, tea, and cold drinks served any time.

Hosts: Joan and Bob Bergey
Rooms: 2 (SB) $65
Full Breakfast
Credit Cards: None
Notes: 2, 5, 7, 11, 12, 13

---

7 No smoking; 8 Children welcome; 9 Social drinking allowed; 10 Tennis nearby; 11 Swimming nearby; 12 Golf nearby; 13 Skiing nearby; 14 May be booked through a travel agent.

PAOLI

Association of Bed and Breakfasts in Philadelphia, Valley Forge, Brandywine

P.O. Box 562, Valley Forge, 19481-0562
(610) 783-7838; (800) 344-0123
FAX (610) 783-7783

0701. The General's Inn. This inn has been in service since 1745. It is authentically restored and furnished; air-conditioned. Eight complete suites, three with fireplaces and one with Jacuzzi. The first floor is an upscale restaurant and lounge open to the public for lunch and dinner. A Continental breakfast is served in the dining room. No pets; no children under 12. $85-135.

0203. The Houseman House. On four acres, this 15-room stone farmhouse, built in 1692, is the second oldest in the state. It is one of the 100 oldest in the country. The original flooring, exposed beams, hand-wrought hinges, and fireplaces add to the charm. An English breakfast is served in front of the walk-in fireplace in the kitchen. Each of the three guest rooms is hand-stenciled, accented with handmade quilts, air-conditioned, furnished with antiques, TV, and radio. Refrigerator, coffee pot, and microwave are provided for guests. Swimming pool. $70-80.

Guesthouses, Inc.

P.O. Box 2137, West Chester, 19380
(610) 692-4575

557. Large three-story stucco-over-stone house built before the 18th century. Guest rooms on the third floor are air-conditioned and comfortably decorated with antiques. There is a room with queen-size bed and single bed, with bath, and a room with queen-size bed with a semiprivate hall bath. On the second floor there is a large guest room with double bed and sitting area with either a private or semiprivate bath. A full hearty breakfast is served in the old kitchen with its walk-in fireplace and open hearth fires. Guests are invited to enjoy the pool in season. $75-110.

PHILADELPHIA

Association of Bed and Breakfasts in Philadelphia, Valley Forge, Brandywine

P.O. Box 562, Valley Forge, 19481-0562
(610) 783-7838; (800) 344-0123
FAX (610) 783-7783

0101. Trade Winds Bed and Breakfast. This historically certified townhouse was built in 1790. Two third-floor guest rooms are elegantly appointed with collectibles and Old World antiques. Each room has color cable TV, telephone, and central air conditioning. The twin room has a refrigerator. A full breakfast is served on the French Empire table in the dining area. For special occasions, guests may consider a very large second-floor guest room with antique brass bed, fireplace, cable TV, telephone, private bath, and air conditioning. On the Washington Square-Society Hill border. Six blocks to Independence Hall and one block to South Street. Public tennis courts across the street. $65-90.

0104. Society Hill Bed and Breakfast. This townhouse was built about 1805 and renovated in the Federal style during the post-Civil War era. Four guest rooms with individual thermostat control for heat and air conditioning, and TV. Full breakfast. During warm weather, breakfast may be served on the patio. One and one-half blocks to Independence Hall. If guests stay over a Saturday night, there is a two-night minimum. $80.

NOTES: Credit cards accepted: A MasterCard; B Visa; C American Express; D Discover; E Diners Club; F Other; 2 Personal checks accepted; 3 Lunch available; 4 Dinner available; 5 Open all year; 6 Pets welcome;

0205. Spruce Garden Bed and Breakfast. Guest quarters are a private first-floor suite in an 1840 townhouse in Center City Philadelphia. A full breakfast is served in the second-floor dining area. The guest suite consists of two bedrooms, two bathrooms, and a sitting room for reading, TV, cards, or sipping sherry. If both rooms are rented at the same time, the occupants must be relatives or good friends, as one must pass through one bedroom to get out or enter the other. $60.

0206. Country Inn the City. This 12-room country inn in the historic area of Philadelphia is a restored circa 1769 guest house within Independence National Historic Park. All rooms are individually decorated and have private baths, telephones, TV, and period furniture. An enclosed parking garage is next door. Continental breakfast is served weekdays, and a full breakfast on weekends. Walk to restaurants and the major historic sites in Philadelphia. $90-160.

0300. Teneleven. This circa 1836 Federal period townhouse is in Center City Philadelphia and is recognized by the Historical Society of Philadelphia. Very upscale with quality linens, beautifully decorated with a mix of period antiques, fireplace, kitchen, all private entrances, and private baths. Air-conditioned by window units. Two guest accommodations. $90-125.

0402. Mount Vernon House. This is a recently renovated, three-story, brick historic dwelling that is large and spacious with balconies and an atrium. The living room serves as a common room for the guest's use. A full, hot, hearty breakfast is served. There are several good restaurants within walking distance. The Art Museum, Boathouse Row, Fels Planetarium, Academy of Science, and the old Eastern State Penitentiary (now a historical landmark) are all within reasonable walking distance. Two bedrooms, one with a queen-size bed and the other with twins, share a bath when both are occupied. $60-70.

0403. Circa 1860 Victorian Townhouse. This 1860 Federalist townhouse was purchased and lovingly restored in 1974. The beautifully restored plaster molding, ceiling medallion, and the magnificent gold leaf chandelier imported from Ireland in 1989 serve as elegant backdrops for the Victorian furnishings. Private bath. Full breakfast. $65.

0801. The Spite House. This historically certified home is associated with the Museum Council of Philadelphia and Delaware Valley and the Historical Society of Pennsylvania. This is one of the "spite houses," so-called because it was built, according to legend, with its back to its neighbors. Full breakfast served. The first floor houses the kitchen, with its Victorian oak oval table and washstand. The second level features the parlor with grand piano, dining room, and butler's pantry, with original soapstone sink and dumbwaiter. In Mount Airy amid the Lutheran Seminary, Spring Garden College, and the Coombs College of Music. Near train station. $60-65.

1308. Logan Square Bed and Breakfast. Guests are offered bed and breakfast in this cozy 150-year-old row house with hospitality that is memorable. The two third-floor rooms share a shower and bath, and one room has a private roof deck. Air conditioning in the double room. Breakfast is full, hot, and hearty and is served in the airy breakfast room. Nearby parking lots and street parking. Close to the Art Museum, Please Touch Museum, Rodin Museum, Franklin Institute, and the Academy of Natural Sciences. No smoking. $35-45.

7 No smoking; 8 Children welcome; 9 Social drinking allowed; 10 Tennis nearby; 11 Swimming nearby; 12 Golf nearby; 13 Skiing nearby; 14 May be booked through a travel agent.

1401. Marietta's. This turn-of-the-century elegant townhouse has high ceilings and is furnished throughout with antiques and artwork. Easy access to Center City, Rittenhouse Square, and an elegant shopping area. Good restaurants abound. $75.

1905. Mrs. Ritz's Rooms. These guest accommodations consist of a spacious entire second floor that includes a bedroom with four-poster double bed, a private bath, and an adjoining sitting room with color cable TV. Hospitality, charm, and a delicious breakfast are offered. $70-75.

1907. Chestnut Hill. This home is a lovely, renovated stone schoolhouse. The atmosphere exudes the warmth and welcome of a cozy fire on a cold day. Its location in the historic area of Chestnut Hill in Philadelphia reminds one of the early days of this great nation. $70-75.

2203. Historic Philadelphia Bed and Breakfast. This circa 1811 certified historic home is near Society Hill. Guests have access to the city while also enjoying a historic atmosphere. Two guest rooms with private bath. Very comfortable. $65.

2101. Trinity Bed and Breakfast. This home is one of four in a small court in the lovely and quiet Rittenhouse Square section within the bustle of the city. Guests have access to all the attractions of the city and can still enjoy a private retreat after a day of sightseeing. $75.

Bed & Breakfast Connection/ Bed & Breakfast of Philadelphia

P.O. Box 21, Devon, 19333
(610) 687-3565; (800) 448-3619
FAX (610) 995-9524

A-01. Built between 1805 and 1810 and redone after the Civil War in Federalist style, this charming Society Hill townhouse saw further renovation when its current owners bought it as a shell some 20 years ago. This creative host has done much of the renovation himself, finding unusual artifacts in old churches and homes in the city that have created a unique and inviting atmosphere. The second-floor bedroom offers a color TV, telephone jack, and individual thermostat with a private hall bath. On the third floor there are two more rooms, one with a trundle bed and a queen-size bed and the other with a double bed. All rooms have an individual thermostat, TV, and private bath. Continental breakfast is served in the pleasant kitchen in the winter or on the patio in the warm months. Two-night minimum stay. $80.

A-05. This historic 1811 Philadelphia brick townhouse was transformed from a dilapidated shell into a comfortable, attractive home with a modern interior. The two air-conditioned bedrooms on the second floor are simply furnished with a double bed in each room, private baths, and TV. There is a working fireplace on the third floor for guests' enjoyment. A full breakfast is served to guests willing to rise early on weekdays and at a more leisurely hour on weekends. $65.

A-07. On the very edge of the South Street excitement, Colonial Gardens offers a respite from the hustle and bustle. Three charming Colonial houses have been combined to make a unique inn with a country feeling that has the modern conveniences, such as air conditioning, private baths, and telephones in all rooms. The buildings have been left as intact as possible, lending each of the nine guest rooms a distinct character. $75-105.

A-10. This cozy 1820 Federal townhouse is at 12th and Lombard, convenient to anywhere in Center City. The convention center is within walking distance as is Independence Mall. A bus that stops in front of the door will take guests to the University of Pennsylvania. A few blocks away is Antique Row, home to many antique shops. A circular staircase leads to the guest rooms on the second floor. The main room has twin beds, a desk, and a dresser. TV and radio are also available. The bath is shared with the adjoining room that can be used as a sitting room or the sofa bed can be opened to accommodate two people. The house is centrally air-conditioned. $45.

A-11. Just two blocks from the Italian Market and two blocks from Antique Row, this home offers private third-floor accommodations. The double-bedded guest room furnished with antiques and collectibles has a sitting room and a private attached bath. A large collection of books is available for guests to enjoy during their stay, and the hosts are fluent in Portuguese and French and have a deep interest in music. Breakfast is a hearty Continental with delicious pastries, fresh fruit, coffees, and teas from nearby bakeries and markets. No smoking. $60.

A-13. On a tree-lined residential street, this 1840s townhouse is convenient, comfortable, and charming. At the end of the street, there is a tiny park. Antique Row, convention center, and Independence Park are all nearby. On the ground level, there is a living room with a working fireplace, queen-size sofa bed, love seat, and TV, and a separate four-poster queen-size bedroom and bath. The second floor has a brass queen-size bed and a private bath. $90-125.

B-05. This townhouse is near the Franklin Institute, Museum of Natural History, and the Moore College of Art. The third-floor bedrooms share the bathroom and its old-fashioned claw-foot tub with the hosts. One room offers a double bed and air conditioning for the summer nights. The other has a single bed and is fan-cooled. $30-45.

B-07. This 1850 Victorian townhouse on Architect's Row is in the art museum section of the city. The guest quarters on the air-conditioned third floor are a self-contained suite with private bath. It is furnished in the Queen Anne style with matching walnut twin beds and dressers. A writing desk is provided for those addicted to sending postcards to the folks back home. The full English breakfast may be served in the sunny kitchen greenhouse or in the city garden. $65.

B-09. Victorian Inn. This 16-room mid-Victorian home offers a quiet retreat and the elegance of a Queen Anne Victorian home. Surrounded by the original iron fence and tall hedge, the 1889 home is sheltered by mature species gardens that create a natural seclusion from the bustle. The eight magnificently appointed second- and third-floor guest rooms are furnished in period antiques. Most rooms have private baths and some have working fireplaces. Fifteen- to twenty-minute drive to Center City Philadelphia. $60-80.

B-11. This historic registered row home provides generous third-floor guest quarters and is close to the University of Pennsylvania, Drexel University, the Civic Center, and Children's Hospital. At one end of the third floor, guests will find a bedroom that can accommodate a family with its two twin beds and a double. The sitting room is at the opposite end of the hall and is perfect for relaxing in front of the TV or curling up with a book. Private bath. Laundry facilities and refrigerator space are available. $55.

Bed and Breakfast, Ltd.
P.O. Box 216, New Haven, CT 06513
(203) 469-3260

23. An 1850s row house with green shutters. One double room with four-poster

---

7 No smoking; 8 Children welcome; 9 Social drinking allowed; 10 Tennis nearby; 11 Swimming nearby; 12 Golf nearby; 13 Skiing nearby; 14 May be booked through a travel agent.

cherry double bed and Edison phonograph. Ten minutes to everything. French and Portuguese spoken. Great breakfast. $65-85.

Germantown Bed and Breakfast

5925 Wayne Avenue, 19144
(215) 848-1375

This cozy 1900s oak bedroom in a 100-year-old house has cable TV and a private tiled bath. This is a homestay with a family with four children. Twenty minutes to Independence Hall; walk to other historic sites, restaurants, and conveniences. Call for a detailed brochure. Five-dollar service charge for one-night stays.

Hosts: Molly and Jeff Smith
Room: 1 (PB) $45
Continental Breakfast
Credit Cards: None
Notes: 2, 5, 8, 9, 12, 14

Guesthouses, Inc.

P.O. Box 2137, West Chester, 19380
(610) 692-4575

106. The house is listed on the National Register of Historic Places. Historic Head House Square, Independence National Historic Park, and the Delaware River Penn's Landing Park are within a five-minute walk. Three spacious guest rooms are elegantly appointed with period textiles and furnishings, all feature working fireplaces (for use in season), luxurious baths ensuite, TVs, and central air conditioning. Package holiday weekends are offered throughout the year, coordinating with Philadelphia's civic festivities. $125-175.

502. This beautiful historic property, listed on the Philadelphia Register of Historic Places, is set amid flowering gardens and an arboretum of magnificent trees. The 1781 Georgian frame central block was constructed by the same craftsmen who created Carpenter's Hall. The building was expanded in the 1830s and again in the

1900s. The air-conditioned guest quarters have a separate entrance with a grand staircase that leads to two suites with a king- or queen-size bed, private hall and bath, queen-size sofa bed, cable TV, and telephone. Continental plus breakfast is served weekdays, and a full breakfast is served on the weekends. Guests are welcome to use the butler's kitchen. The large formal first-floor rooms are available for weddings and parties. Two-night minimum stay on weekends. $125-150.

The International Bed and Breakfast Club, Inc.

504 Amherst Street, Buffalo, NY 14207
(800) 723-4262; FAX (716) 873-4462

PA7349PP. Built in the 1830s and lovingly renovated in the 1970s, this bed and breakfast is not just a home, but an experience. A medium red brick townhouse, set on the side of a narrow stone street, it is filled with the silent stories of the lady who once lived there. Just a block away is Washington Square Park, set aside by William Penn, who believed each citizen should have a patch of grass to call his own. Two rooms, shared bath. Full breakfast. $65.

PHOENIXVILLE

Association of Bed and Breakfasts in Philadelphia, Valley Forge, Brandywine

P.O. Box 562, Valley Forge, 19481-0562
(610) 783-7838; (800) 344-0123
FAX (610) 783-7783

0201. Tinker Hill. This contemporary house on two and one-half acres is in a private, wooded area. Two-story glass-walled living room. Guest rooms are separated from the suite and overlook the woods. Hot tub on the deck; swimming pool. Full breakfast. $60.

0301. Manor House. Built in 1928 by a British executive, this English Tudor home stands on a lovely sycamore-lined street. It boasts a massive slate roof and original red oak flooring and stairway. The spacious living room and cozy den both have fireplaces. Gourmet breakfasts are served in the formal dining room or on the brick-floored screened porch overlooking the garden. Complimentary bedtime beverage and snack in the room. Five guest rooms with private bath. $45-70.

1910. Federal House Bed and Breakfast. This three-story brick Italianate home was built in 1867 on land purchased from the Phoenix Iron Company in historic Chester County. From the stars on the ceiling to the faux marbled foyer, the interior of this home is decorated with period pieces from the 1800s to the 1930s, pulled together with an artistic 1990s flair. Enjoy the large living room, formal dining room, privately enclosed patio, and use of the Jacuzzi, which is open all year and is large enough to comfortably seat eight adults. Full breakfast including fruit, juices, hot beverage, and a choice of breakfast entrées. The guest rooms have queen-size beds, private bath, TV, and air conditioning. $65-75.

Bed & Breakfast Connection/ Bed & Breakfast of Philadelphia
P.O. Box 21, Devon, 19333
(610) 687-3565; (800) 448-3619
FAX (610) 995-9524

F-01. Dating back to the 1860s, this former general store has been converted to a charming bed and breakfast with touches of the Netherlands. Three European-style guest rooms are on the second floor. The first is a large room with platform queen-size bed, private bath, and private deck. The other two rooms have queen-size or twin beds (which could be made into a king-size bed) and attached sitting rooms. These two rooms share a bath. Breakfast includes choice of American or, house special, Dutch West Indies. No smoking. Cat and dog in owner's quarters only. $75.

POCONO MOUNTAINS

Bed & Breakfast Connection/ Bed & Breakfast of Philadelphia
P.O. Box 21, Devon, 19333
(610) 687-3565; (800) 448-3619
FAX (610) 995-9524

XC-3. A large, attractively appointed first-floor guest room offers a queen-size bed, sitting area, and private bath suite with oversized tub and stall shower. Sliding glass doors lead to the deck and commanding views of the mountains beyond. Two other comfortably appointed double-bed guest rooms are on the ground floor. In addition to providing a delightful full gourmet breakfast, the hosts will do everything possible to ensure a stay in the Pocono area is pleasant and memorable. Within 30 minutes of five major ski areas and just a short drive from the many attractions of the popular four-season area. $60-85.

XC-4. A historic Civil War-period inn, set in the heart of the Poconos, preserves the traditions of yesteryear. Eighteen rooms with private baths are decorated with antiques. Two guest houses and a cottage allow the inn to accommodate up to 50 people. An oversized pool, tennis court, horseshoes, badminton, shuffleboard, and other lawn games are available for exercise. For quieter moments there are books and board games. Fishing and golf are nearby. In the winter, skiers are only five minutes from Alpine Mountain or 20 minutes from Camelback, Shawnee, or Jack Frost Ski Areas. For cross-country skiing, Promiseland State Park is nearby. The real pride of the inn is the food. Choose bed and breakfast accommodations with a full breakfast or the MAP that includes a five-course gourmet dinner. $70-110.

7 No smoking; 8 Children welcome; 9 Social drinking allowed; 10 Tennis nearby; 11 Swimming nearby; 12 Golf nearby; 13 Skiing nearby; 14 May be booked through a travel agent.

Guesthouses, Inc.
P.O. Box 2137, West Chester, 19380
(205) 692-4575

751. This white farmhouse and gazebo was built in the 1800s beside a mountain wall. Enter by way of a broad deck with hot tub into the kitchen where delicious hearty breakfasts are prepared. The apartment with separate entrance is on the floor below. A queen-size bedroom with bath is available on the main floor, and a spacious two-room suite on the floor above has sufficient seating for a full-size bed (if needed) in addition to a brass queen-size bed. The other accommodation on this level is a twin-bedded room. In the summer there is plenty of scenery to view while hiking. Convenient to winter ski resorts, with night skiing available. Call for weekly rates on the apartment. $75-105.

Nearbrook Bed and Breakfast
Rural Delivery 1, Box 630, Canadensis, 18325
(717) 595-3152

Meander through rock garden paths and enjoy the roses, woods, and stream at Nearbrook. A hearty breakfast is served on the outdoor porch, weather permitting. The hosts will join guests at breakfast, map out the best hiking trails, and describe the many activities available. A contagious informality encourages guests to play the

Nearbrook

upright piano and enjoy the trunk full of games. Restaurant menus are available.

Hosts: Barbara and Dick Robinson
Rooms: 3 (1 PB; 2 SB) $45
Full Breakfast
Credit Cards: None
Notes: 2, 5, 7, 8, 10, 11, 12, 13, 14

RADNOR

Association of Bed and Breakfasts in Philadelphia, Valley Forge, Brandywine
P.O. Box 562, Valley Forge, 19481-0562
(610) 783-7838; (800) 344-0123
FAX (610) 783-7783

2601. Main Line Estate. This expansive English Tudor, built in 1969, is surrounded by three and one-half acres of original grounds belonging to two estates owned by brothers who made a local German beer. The spacious guest rooms can be reached privately by a back staircase. A full breakfast is served in the country French kitchen. Greenhouse, swimming pool, cabana, and tennis court. Washer/dryer, baby equipment, and cable TV available. $75.

RIDLEY CREEK STATE PARK

Guesthouses, Inc.
P.O. Box 2137, West Chester, 19380
(610) 692-4575

125. The main house was built in the mid-1800s, and all the rooms are decorated with antique furnishings and decorative objects appropriate to the house. The guest wing is newly built and is separate from the rest of the house. The bedroom is large and sunny with a king-size bed and sitting area; the large bath is luxuriously appointed. Breakfast is served in the new garden room and kitchen. When the weather is mild, guests can take a swim and have breakfast served by the formal garden swimming pool. Fully air-conditioned. $125.

NOTES: Credit cards accepted: A MasterCard; B Visa; C American Express; D Discover; E Diners Club; F Other; 2 Personal checks accepted; 3 Lunch available; 4 Dinner available; 5 Open all year; 6 Pets welcome;

SCHELLSBURG (BEDFORD AREA)

Amanda's Bed and Breakfast

1428 Park Avenue, Baltimore, MD, 21217-4230
(410) 225-001; (800) 899-7533
FAX (410) 728-8957

130. A farmhouse with historic credentials, now a lovely bed and breakfast with modern touches. A trout stream and covered bridge, state park, plus other historic, scenic attractions. One hour to Falling Water, designed by Frank Lloyd Wright. Roast marshmallows by the open fireplace in the smokehouse. Full breakfast. $75.

SCRANTON

The Weeping Willow Inn

Rural Delivery 7, Box 254, Tunkhannock, 18657
(717) 836-5877

This comfortable Colonial home, circa 1840, has been lovingly restored. Experience its warmth and rich history. Three graciously appointed rooms furnished with a mixture of family treasures and antiques. A hearty country breakfast is served by candlelight. The hosts promise that a visit here will be one guests will never forget. Tunkhannock abounds in scenic views, beautiful farmland, lovely lakes, and sleepy villages. Within 25 minutes of Wilkes Barre and Scranton. Relax, enjoy, and experience yesterday today.

Hosts: Patty and Randy Ehrengeller
Rooms: 3 (PB) $60-70
Credit Cards: None
Notes: 2, 5, 7, 8, 10, 11, 12, 13

SIGEL

Discoveries Bed and Breakfast

Rural Delivery 1, Box 42, 15860
(814) 752-2632

This Victorian house has four bedrooms and three baths. It has an ambience of country elegance—bedrooms are beautifully decorated and furnished in antiques. Breakfast is served on the enclosed front porch, with home-cured meats and home-baked breads. Adjacent to the house is a finished crafts and antique shop with fine Victorian furniture and handcrafted items. Six miles from Cook Forest State Park and three miles from Clear Creek State Park. Nine miles north of interstate exit 13. Route 80 on Pennsylvania Route 36.

Hosts: Pat and Bruce MacBeth
Rooms: 4 (1 PB; 3 SB) $50-60
Full Breakfast
Credit Cards: None
Notes: 2, 7, 9, 11, 12

SMETHPORT

Blackberry Inn
Bed and Breakfast

820 West Main Street
(US 6 and Highway 59) 16749-1039
(814) 887-7777

A Victorian home built in 1881 and restored in 1988-89. Guest parlor with TV. Guest telephone. Two large open porches. Breakfast is served at time guest desires. Friendly small-town atmosphere. Near Kinzua Bridge State Park and Allegheny National Forest. Wonderful area for hiking, biking, fishing, fall foliage tours, festivals, skiing, or just relaxing.

Hosts: Mert and Jan Wilson
Rooms: 5 (SB) $45-65
Full Breakfast
Credit Cards: A, B, C, D
Notes: 2, 5, 6, 7, 8, 10, 11, 12, 13, 14

SOMERSET

Bayberry Inn
Bed and Breakfast

611 North Center Avenue, Route 601, 15501
(814) 445-8471

A romantic, friendly, comfortable inn that pays attention to detail, offering all non-

---

7 No smoking; 8 Children welcome; 9 Social drinking allowed; 10 Tennis nearby; 11 Swimming nearby; 12 Golf nearby; 13 Skiing nearby; 14 May be booked through a travel agent.

smoking rooms with private baths. Homemade baked goods served at a table for two. Near exit 10 of the Pennsylvania Turnpike. Close to Seven Springs and Hidden Valley resorts, Frank Lloyd Wright's Falling Water, Ohiopyle white-water rafting, state parks, antique shops, and outlet malls. Children over 11 welcome.

Hosts: Marilyn and Robert Lohr
Rooms: 11 (PB) $45-55
Continental Breakfast
Credit Cards: A, B, C, D
Notes: 2, 5, 7, 9, 10, 11, 12, 13, 14

H.B.'s Cottage

231 West Church Street, 15501-1941
(814) 443-1204; FAX (814) 443-4313

Exclusive and elegant bed and breakfast in a stone-and-frame 1920s cottage with oversize fireplace in the living room. Furnished in traditional manner with accent pieces from overseas travels by the innkeepers, and collectible teddy bears from the hostess's collection. Guest room romantically decorated, with a private porch. Downhill and cross-country skiing, biking, and tennis are specialties of hosts. Close to Seven Springs, Falling Water, biking and hiking trails, and white water.

Hosts: Hank and Phillis Vogt
Room: 2 (PB) $65
Full Breakfast
Credit Cards: A, B
Notes: 2, 5, 7, 9, 10, 11, 12, 13

SPLIT ROCK

Guesthouses, Inc.

P.O. Box 2137, West Chester, 19380
(610) 692-4575

031. This large, privately owned lodge is within an exclusive luxury resort on a large lake with every imaginable recreational facility available, including some of the area's finest skiing. The lodge is on two levels with decks all around on both levels: top floor has living, dining area, kitchen,

bedroom, and bath. The lower floor has living-dining area, two bedrooms, and bath. There are fireplaces for seasonal use.

STARLIGHT

The Inn at Starlight Lake

Box 27, 18461
(717) 798-2519; (800) 248-2519
FAX (717) 798-2672

A classic country inn since 1909 on a clear lake in the rolling hills of northeast Pennsylvania, with activities for all seasons from swimming to cross-country skiing. Near the Delaware River for canoeing and fly fishing. Excellent food and spirits, convivial atmosphere. Modified American Plan. Limited smoking allowed.

Hosts: Jack and Judy McMahon
Rooms: 26 (20 PB; 6 SB) $110-154
Suite: $170-200
Full Breakfast
Credit Cards: A, B
Notes: 2, 3, 4, 5, 8, 9, 10, 11, 12, 13, 14

STATE COLLEGE

The International Bed and Breakfast Club, Inc.

504 Amherst Street, Buffalo, NY 14207
(800) 723-4262; FAX (716) 873-4462

PA2424PP. Overlooking the 17th green of Toftrees golf course in State College, visitors to central Pennsylvania can partake of a special legacy of hospitality. Discover the delights of another place and time. Sunny window seats invite guests to curl up with a book. Rockers on long porches beckon guests outside with their breakfast coffee. Settle into a deep library chair for a post-golf libation and pleasant conversation. The 22 individually appointed rooms and suites are interspersed with antique-filled spaces that tempt guests to linger. All guest rooms have private baths. Continental plus breakfast served. $150.

STRASBURG (LANCASTER COUNTY)

The Decoy Bed and Breakfast
958 Eisenberger Road, 17579
(717) 687-8585; (800) 726-2287

The Decoy is in a quiet rural location with a spectacular view. A former Amish home, it has five rooms with private baths. Double, queen-, and king-size beds are available. Breakfasts are an adventure, with wonderful recipes gleaned from the large collection of cookbooks. The hostess is an avid quilter. Bicyclists are welcome, and hosts can help guests in planning their tours. Two resident cats also make guests feel welcome.

Hosts: Debby and Hap Joy
Rooms: 5 (PB) $53-74.20
Full Breakfast
Credit Cards: None
Notes: 2, 5, 8, 9, 12

SUSQUEHANNA RIVER VALLEY

Bed & Breakfast Connection/ Bed & Breakfast of Philadelphia
P.O. Box 21, Devon, 19333
(610) 687-3565; (800) 448-3619
FAX (610) 995-9524

H-11. Lovingly restored, this late 1800s six-room guest house is nestled in the woods beside a meandering stream. Relax on the screen porch and take in the beauty and serenity of this magnificent Susquehanna River estate, once the home of Benjamin Franklin's grandson. Fish in the stream, swim in the old-fashioned swimming hole, bike or jog on the country roads, or wander through the grist mill that is being restored. Fine restaurants and a winery nearby. Lancaster County attractions within an easy drive. An ideal spot for business meetings. Telephone and fax. $95.

H-12. A converted antique carriage house offers two large bedrooms, a fully appli-anced kitchen, screened porch, two baths, fireplaced dining and sitting room along with a library on the lower level. Comfortably decorated with antiques, the guest house has a telephone and TV with VCR. The hostess personally oversees customized guest services such as riding, tennis, skiing, fishing, antiquing, shopping, or curling up by the fireplace with a great book. Or in warm weather enjoy the flower-laden swimming pool complete with pool house and wet bar. Even stabling is available for guest horses. This bed and breakfast is in a secluded, idyllic area in southern Pennsylvania's pristine agricultural and recreational country near the famous Renninger's. Gettysburg, Hershey, Lancaster, Chester County, Baltimore, and Washington, D.C. are perfect day trips. A full breakfast is brought to the carriage house at guests' convenience. $95.

TROY

Golden Oak Inn Bed and Breakfast
196 Canton Street, 16947
(717) 297-4315; (800) 326-9834

Golden Oak Inn is in the heart of the Endless Mountains. The elegant 90-year-old house features charming oak woodwork and Victorian decor with Civil War accents. Antiquing, fishing, hunting, hiking, and golf nearby. Corning Glass, Mount Piscah State Park, Pennsylvania's Grand Canyon, Watkins Glen, Mansfield University, and the Finger Lakes are within commuting distance. Rich, a graduate of the Culinary Institute of America, serves delicious gourmet breakfasts each morning. Complimentary wine is served in the evening. Handcrafted gifts for sale.

Hosts: Rich and Sharon Frank
Rooms: 4 (SB) $50-60
Full Breakfast
Credit Cards: A, B
Notes: 2, 5, 7, 9, 10, 11, 12, 13

7 No smoking; 8 Children welcome; 9 Social drinking allowed; 10 Tennis nearby; 11 Swimming nearby; 12 Golf nearby; 13 Skiing nearby; 14 May be booked through a travel agent.

ULSTER

Misty Meadow Farm

Rural Route 2, Box 226, 18850
(717) 596-4077

Misty Meadow Farm Bed and Breakfast is a
lovely old restored farm and house in East
Smithfield that sits on 60 breathtaking
acres. Each season brings its own charm,
beauty, and excitement. A country breakfast
is served in the Keeping Room by candlelight and fine music. The fire burns in the
wood stove when weather calls for it.
Relax, read a book, play the piano, take a
nature walk, or do some bird and wildlife
watching. Bring a camera. Stay for a day, or
stay for a week. Children over 12 welcome.

Hosts: Jack and Patricia Ardolina
Suites: 2 (PB) $69
Full Breakfast
Credit Cards: None
Notes: 2, 5, 7, 9, 10, 11, 12, 13

VALLEY FORGE

Association of Bed and Breakfasts in Philadelphia, Valley Forge, Brandywine

P.O. Box 562, Valley Forge, 19481-0562
(610) 783-7838; (800) 344-0123
FAX (610) 783-7783

0804. Deep Well Farm. This 18th-century
fieldstone farmhouse has 16-inch-thick
walls and exposed beams overhead.
Originally it was part of Gen. Anthony
Wayne's estate. The two and one-half acres
accommodate a horse barn and a pond
where geese gather. The bedrooms are spacious and comfortable, cooled by ceiling
fans. A full breakfast is served in the country dining room or kitchen. A parrot and
two horses reside. One mile to Valley
Forge Park; one-half mile to Valley Forge
Music Fair. $60-65.

1400. Treetops Bed and Breakfast. Private,
cozy guest cottage accommodating up to
four people consists of a living room with
TV and queen-size sofa bed, full kitchen
stocked with goodies, private bath, deck,
and queen-size bedroom. Close to Valley
Forge National Historic Park, hiking and
biking trails, tennis, golf, skiing, horseback
riding, live theater, antiquing, shopping
malls, and great restaurants. $90-115.

2302. Valley Forge Mountain Bed and
Breakfast. This French Colonial home is in
a peaceful wooded setting. Just 200 yards
from the Valley Forge Park border, guests
can walk along the bridle path and into the
park. Hosts offer a California king-size bedroom and a Victorian furnished double bedroom. Hosts assure guests comfort with all
the amenities, including a stocked refrigerator, in-room telephones, central air conditioning, sitting room with TV or join the
hosts in the Florida room or common room
for cable TV, VCR, and fireplace. Full, hot,
hearty breakfasts are the norm. The cheerful
solarium is a favorite place to observe the
deer eating the garden. $50-60.

Bed & Breakfast Connection/ Bed & Breakfast of Philadelphia

P.O. Box 21, Devon, 19333
(610) 687-3565; (800) 448-3619
FAX (610) 995-9524

E-13. This home within a barn offers private
quarters that provide more than a refreshing
night's sleep and a delicious breakfast. The
two-story entrance hall and stairway welcome guests to this 19th-century bank barn.
There are three guest rooms with private
baths. The first is a large king-size bedded
room with a table and four chairs. For
guests preferring a queen-size bed, there is
a large sunny corner room. Both rooms
have a small refrigerator. The third room
offers twin or king-size sleigh bed accommodations, whichever guests prefer, and a
sitting area. Breakfast is served either in
guest room or in the two-story great room
with a fireplace or, in warm weather, on the
upper deck. $90-110.

NOTES: Credit cards accepted: A MasterCard; B Visa; C American Express; D Discover; E Diners Club;
F Other; 2 Personal checks accepted; 3 Lunch available; 4 Dinner available; 5 Open all year; 6 Pets welcome;

F-03. Lush greenery greets the eyes if guests arrive in spring or summer. This two-story Colonial-style house is nestled on a hillside bordered by flowering shrubs and trees. The hostess is a college professor and knowledgeable about many cultural and human service organizations. Breakfast is guests' preference. Three rooms, one with a pair of twin beds and a private bath, another with a pair of twin beds and shared bath, and a third with one single bed and shared bath. Children welcome. No smoking allowed. $55-65.

F-04. Enjoy the charm of this historic home convenient to the Valley Forge area. The original part of the house was built sometime before 1700, and two additions, each more than 200 years old, were constructed in the traditional Colonial style. Two third-floor rooms offer guests spacious privacy and the convenience of a small refrigerator, microwave oven, and telephone on the landing. A large, inviting second-floor room has an antique double bed and a sitting area with a camelback chair and queen-size sofa bed. All rooms have private or semiprivate baths. A full English-style breakfast is served in the oldest part of the house in front of the fireplace with its huge mantle and eight-foot-wide hearth. Resident dog and smoker. $70-80.

The Great Valley House of Valley Forge

110 Swedesford Road, Rural Delivery 3
Malvern, 19355
(215) 644-6759

This historic 1690 stone farmhouse has rooms filled with antiques, lovely hand-stenciled walls, and quilts throughout. On four acres with swimming pool and walking trails for guests, this old farmhouse is ideal for a quiet getaway. A full breakfast is served in the pre-Revolutionary kitchen in front of a 14-foot walk-in fireplace. Just a short drive from Philadelphia, Lancaster, and Brandywine Valley. The Great Valley House has been featured in the *Philadelphia Inquirer* and the *Washington Post.*

Rooms: 3 (2PB; 1SB) $70-85
Full Breakfast
Credit Cards: None
Notes: 2, 3, 5, 7, 8, 9, 11, 12, 14

Valley Forge Mountain Bed and Breakfast

Box 562, 19481
(610) 783-7838; (800) 344-0123
FAX (610) 783-7783

George Washington had headquarters here. Between Philadelphia, Lancaster County, Reading outlets, and Brandywine Valley. French Colonial on three wooded acres adjacent to Valley Forge Park. Air conditioning, complimentary breakfast, guest room telephone, TV, VCR, computer, printer, fax, two fireplaces. Bridle and hiking trail. Fine shopping, antiquing, restaurants, cross-country skiing, horseback riding, and golf within minutes. California king-size bed with private bath. Victorian decor double bed with private bath. Jacuzzi on outdoor deck. Smoking allowed on porch and deck.

Host: Carolyn Williams
Rooms: 2 (PB) $45-65
Full Breakfast
Credit Cards: A, B, C, E
Notes: 2, 5, 7, 8, 9, 10, 11, 12, 14

VILLANOVA

Association of Bed and Breakfasts in Philadelphia, Valley Forge, Brandywine

P.O. Box 562, Valley Forge, 19481-0562
(610) 783-7838; (800) 344-0123
FAX (610) 783-7783

1903. English Regency. This home, featured on house tours, is on one and one-half acres in an elegant, quiet, wooded area. It is furnished with lovely antiques, art, and Oriental rugs. The guest room is beautifully appointed and includes a graceful canopied bed and leather wing chair. On weekdays, breakfast is self-serve Continental. On weekends, a delicious full breakfast is served. Central air conditioning. $75.

Bed & Breakfast Connection/ Bed & Breakfast of Philadelphia

P.O. Box 21, Devon, 19333
(610) 687-3565; (800) 448-3619
FAX (610) 995-9524

E-12. Elegant accommodations in this gracious 40-year-old English Regency-style home. Traditional and antique furniture grace the two second-floor guest rooms. Both provide double-bed accommodations and are attractively decorated with floral wallpaper reminiscent of the French countryside. Each room has a private bath. A delicious full breakfast is served in the conservatory overlooking the English gardens and tennis court, weather permitting, or in the formal dining room in the winter months. Feel free to relax with a book in the conservatory or in the first-floor library. There are two resident dogs. No smoking allowed. $70.

VIRGINVILLE (KUTZTOWN)

Bed and Breakfast Adventures

Suite 132, 2310 Central Avenue
North Wildwood, NJ 08260
(606) 522-4000; (800) 992-2632

PA701. Nestled in the rolling hills of Berks County, this country cottage is separate from the main house. The bathroom with shower is on the first floor; the large upstairs bedroom includes a swooning couch. The hostess delivers breakfast to the cottage daily. Close to Kutztown State University, antique shopping, and the Reading outlets. Nonsmokers and children are welcome. $85.

WAYNE

Association of Bed and Breakfasts in Philadelphia, Valley Forge, Brandywine

P.O. Box 562, Valley Forge, 19481-0562
(610) 783-7838; (800) 344-0123
FAX (610) 783-7783

0904. Fox Knoll. Completely private accommodations in this 12-room old stone Colonial filled with antiques and country comfort. The guest entrance leads from the terrace to a spacious room with areas for eating, sitting, and sleeping. The kitchenette is fully equipped and stocked for breakfast, or join the hosts in the country dining room. The stone terrace with grill and umbrella are for guest use. Other amenities include a large stone fireplace, TV, and stereo. A cheerful bedroom with sitting room in the main house is also available. $65-90.

1309. Woodwinds. Newly remodeled home on two acres on a quiet, wooded street, surrounded by gardens, lawns, and trees. The light, comfortable guest room is up a short, private flight of stairs separated from the hosts' quarters. Continental breakfast served in the formal dining room or on the terrace. One-half block from the Main Line train station and the Paoli local to Philadelphia. $65-70.

WAYNESBORO

Guesthouse, Inc.

P.O. Box 2137, West Chester, 19380
(610) 692-4575

562. A lovely circa 1780 Pennsylvania stone farmhouse with 19th- and 20th-century additions is in a peaceful rural scene. The house features a beamed keeping room with cooking fireplace where guests may relax in the evening. The guest rooms on the second floor are furnished with antiques and country quilts. Two rooms have private baths and a third room has a shared bath. A full country breakfast is served in the breakfast area. Close to the working Colonial Plantation at Ridley Creek State Park, Waynesboro, the Wharton Escherick Museum, the vast expanses of hills, fields, and valleys, and Valley Forge. Year-round swimming is available nearby by arrangement. Convenient to major roads. Fifteen minutes from Valley Forge, Bryn Mawr, West Chester, or Swarthmore. $85-120.

Saint's Rest

WEST ALEXANDER

Saint's Rest Bed and Breakfast

77 Main Street, P.O. Box 15, 15376
(412) 484-7950

Earl and Myrna invite guests to visit this beautiful gingerbread-style Victorian home one minute from Interstate 70 east or west. Fifteen minutes from Oglebay Park, Jamboree USA, and Wheeling Downs dog track. Saint's Rest stands on Old National Road. Fresh flowers, homemade muffins, a welcome-in drink, and good beds are just some of the guests' comments about this friendly home away from home.

Hosts: Myrna and Earl Lewis
Rooms: 2 (PB) $60
Full Breakfast
Credit Cards: None
Notes: 2, 5, 8, 9

WEST CHESTER

Association of Bed and Breakfasts in Philadelphia, Valley Forge, Brandywine

P.O. Box 562, Valley Forge, 19481-0562
(610) 783-7838; (800) 344-0123
FAX (610) 783-7783

0800. West Chester Farm. Circa 1755 historic farm bed and breakfast that has been recognized by the local historic society. Standing on wooded acres, surrounded by meadowland, pastureland, hunt country, and dirt roads. Children are welcome! Enjoy TV, VCR, games, and cards, and the wood-burning stove in the parlor. Fish, hike, or throw horseshoes outdoors. Continental breakfast served. $60-65.

1802. Essex Bed and Breakfast. This house, built in 1890, is on the National Register of Historic Places and is nestled among eight wooded acres. There are 17 rooms plus three full baths and two powder rooms. Much of the house, including three bedrooms, three baths, and one powder room, has been restored for guests. Restoration of two additional bedrooms and baths is in progress. Guests may enjoy walking the trails or simply observing beautiful sunsets, fall foliage, snowdrifts, and animals. $65-75.

The Bankhouse Bed and Breakfast

875 Hillsdale Road, 19382
(610) 344-7388

An 18th-century "bankhouse" nestled in a quiet country setting with view of pond and horse farm. Rooms are charmingly decorated with country antiques and stenciling. Offers a great deal of privacy, including private entrance, porch, sitting room-library, and air conditioning. Near Longwood Gardens, Brandywine River Museum, and Winterthur. Easy drive to

The Bankhouse

Valley Forge, Lancaster, and Philadelphia. Canoeing, horseback riding, biking, and walking/jogging trails offered in the area. Also, luscious country breakfast and afternoon snacks.

Hosts: Diana and Michael Bove
Rooms: 2 (1 PB; 1 SB) $65-85
Full Breakfast
Credit Cards: None
Notes: 2, 5, 9, 12, 13

The Crooked Windsor

409 South Church Street, 19382
(215) 692-4896

Charming Victorian home in West Chester, completely furnished with fine antiques. Full breakfast served, along with teatime and refreshments for those who so desire. Also, pool and garden in season. Points of interest are within easy driving distance.

Host: Winifred Rupp
Rooms: 4 (SB) $65
Full Breakfast
Credit Cards: None
Notes: 2, 5, 7, 9, 11, 12

Guesthouses, Inc.

P.O. Box 2137, 19380
(610) 692-4575

105. The guest house, a former carriage house, has been newly reconstructed and air-conditioned. There are two separate sections: one a first-floor apartment with fireplace, the other, on the up side of the building, has a living room with a clear view and a night telescope. There is a dining area and a kitchen that is stocked with breakfast treats. Bedroom is furnished with either twins or king-size bed with a festoon of dried spring flowers. $150.

627. The house is lovingly furnished with old Pennsylvanian family antiques and treasures. A quaint common room with modern entertainment is for guest use. The guest bedrooms are two to a floor in the front wing of the house: all large corner rooms, with tall ceilings and cross ventilation, and all furnished with antique canopied high-post double-size beds. Country breakfast is served in the breakfast room or formal dining room. There is an outdoor swimming pool with spa. $75-120.

701. In 1889 the respected Philadelphia architect Frank Miles Day was hired to create a spacious and airy retreat in the small summer colony of Bradford Hills. The house is now on the National Register due to its distinguished creator's reputation. Although this was built as a summer house, it is now used year-round by the family that has been here for a quarter century. The cheerful guest bedrooms are on the second floor (family quarters are on the third floor by way of two separate, hidden circular staircases). The three guest rooms are comfortably furnished with an antique double bed, a queen-size bed, and a king-size (in a whimsical tower room) that can be made into two separate beds. All have their own bath, but only the queen has the bath ensuite. There is a comfortable common room with easy chairs, sofa, desk, and TV for guests on this floor. A Continental plus breakfast is served in a breakfast area of the first-floor great room. $75-85

707. The Valentine is newly restored and furnished to its original grandeur. The public rooms on the first floor are very elegant with high ceilings, carved woodwork, plas-

NOTES: Credit cards accepted: A MasterCard; B Visa; C American Express; D Discover; E Diners Club; F Other; 2 Personal checks accepted; 3 Lunch available; 4 Dinner available; 5 Open all year; 6 Pets welcome;

ter ornamentation, gleaming hardwood floors, and tall Jefferson windows that open out to the loggia. Guest rooms are on the second and third floors. All are furnished in the Victorian Romantic-style and all have antique full-size beds. There are two additional bedrooms on the second floor that share a large hall bath. The top floor has four bedrooms that share a large hall bath. A full breakfast is served in the formal dining room. $75-110.

WESTTOWN

Guesthouses, Inc.

P.O. Box 2137, West Chester, 19380
(610) 692-4575

110. On the outskirts of the rolling hills of Westtown, the beautifully preserved historic three-and-one-half-story stone farmhouse has been featured on *Chester County Day*. The interior is warm and inviting, generously furnished with antiques of the period and decorated with colors, fabrics, and objects of historical integrity. There is a choice of two lovely second-floor, air-conditioned guest rooms; one with a full-size bed and one with twin beds. A country breakfast is served by the fire in the kitchen or in the sunroom, depending on season. $85.

WILKES BARRE

The Weeping Willow Inn

Rural Delivery 7, Box 254, Tunkhannoch, 18657
(717) 836-5877

This comfortable Colonial home, circa 1840, has been lovingly restored, and the hosts cordially invite guests to experience its warmth and rich history. Three graciously appointed rooms furnished with a mixture of family treasures and antiques. A hearty country breakfast is served by candlelight. The hosts promise that a visit here will be one guests will never forget.

Tunkhannoch abounds in scenic views, beautiful farmland, lovely lakes, and sleepy villages. Within 25 minutes of Wilkes Barre and Scranton. Come relax, enjoy, and experience yesterday today.

Hosts: Patty and Randy Ehrengeller
Rooms: 3 (PB) $60-70
Credit Cards: None
Notes: 2, 5, 7, 8, 10, 11, 12, 13

YORK

Amanda's Bed and Breakfast

1428 Park Avenue, Baltimore, MD 21217-4230
(410) 225-0001; (800) 899-7533
FAX (410) 728-8957

105. This 1836 restored brick Colonial is on three acres of manicured lawns with trees, shrubs, and flowers. This farmhouse with a fireplace has an antique shop on the premises. Three guest rooms with two shared baths. Just 20 minutes from Lancaster and a little more than an hour from Baltimore. $65.

Bed & Breakfast Connection/ Bed & Breakfast of Philadelphia

P.O. Box 21, Devon, 19333
(610) 687-3565; (800) 448-3619
FAX (610) 995-9524

H-09. After enjoying the attractions of York County, retreat to the quiet elegance of this lovely 1836 Colonial home appointed with a blend of antiques and authentic reproductions. On arrival, chat with the host in the comfortable living room to learn the history of the house, and then discover three tastefully decorated second-floor rooms, each with its own unique charm and decor. These three rooms share two full baths. A full gourmet breakfast, including dessert, is served in the large country dining room. The host will gladly help plan trips in the area, whether guests choose to go to York County, Amish country, Baltimore's inner harbor, or Gettysburg. Resident cat and smoker. $60.

7 No smoking; 8 Children welcome; 9 Social drinking allowed; 10 Tennis nearby; 11 Swimming nearby; 12 Golf nearby; 13 Skiing nearby; 14 May be booked through a travel agent.

Smyser-Bair House Bed and Breakfast

30 South Beaver Street, 17401
(717) 854-3411

A magnificent 12-room Italianate townhouse in the historic district, this home is rich in architectural detail and contains stained-glass windows, pier mirrors, and ceiling medallions. There are three antique-filled guest rooms and a two-room suite. Enjoy the warm hospitality, walk to the farmers' markets, historic sites, and antique shops. Eight blocks to the York Fairgrounds; near Lancaster and Gettysburg.

Hosts: The King Family
Rooms: 4 (1 PB; 3 SB) $60-80
Full Breakfast
Credit Cards: A, B
Notes: 2, 5, 7, 8, 9, 12, 13, 14

Rhode Island

_____

The Atlantic Inn

High Street, P.O. Box 188, 02807
(401) 466-5883; (401) 466-2005
FAX (401) 466-5678

An elegant Victorian inn, built and first opened in 1876, occupies six acres of gently rolling slopes overlooking the Atlantic Ocean and Old Harbor Village. Contains 21 rooms, each individually decorated with antiques and period furnishings. All private baths. A gourmet restaurant for up to 85 guests is in the inn and caters to individuals, couples, and families. Activities include a formal croquet court, two full-size tennis courts, a horseshoe pit, and landscaped gardens and paths. The unique location, extraordinary views, expansive grounds and gardens, conference facilities, and recreation options all come together with Victorian ambience and charm to make the Atlantic Inn truly a unique property to Block Island and Rhode Island itself.

Hosts: Anne and Brad Marthens
Rooms: 21 (PB) $99-195
Suite: $210
Continental Breakfast
Credit Cards: A, B, C
Notes: 2, 4, 7, 8, 9, 10, 11, 14

Hotel Manisses

Spring Street, 02807
(401) 466-2421; (401) 466-2063

Step into 19th-century yesteryear at this romantic Victorian hotel with 17 meticulously appointed rooms. Private baths and authentic Victorian furniture. Some rooms have Jacuzzis. The award-winning dining room serves lunch and dinner. Sample delicious selections from the widely varied menu as featured in *Gourmet* magazine. Tableside flaming coffees, after-dinner drinks, and desserts served nightly in the upstairs parlors. The petting zoo has llamas, Sicilian donkeys, Nubian, Pygmy, and fainting goats, and other wonderful animals. Children over ten welcome.

Hosts: The Abrams Family
Rooms: 17 (PB) $65-300
Full Breakfast
Credit Cards: A, B, C
Notes: 2, 4, 5, 7, 9, 10, 11, 14

Old Town Inn

P.O. Box 351, 02807
(401) 466-5958

The Old Town Inn is at the junction of Old Town Road and Center Road, about one mile from the ferry landing. Ten guest rooms, four in the old section featuring antique furniture and six in the new east wing featuring queen-size beds, full bath, refrigerator, etc. Breakfasts, served in the 19th-century dining rooms, are the best on the island. On about four acres of landscaped area.

Hosts: Ralph, Monica, and David Gunter
Rooms: 10 (8 PB; 2 SB) $80-120
Full Breakfast
Credit Cards: A, B
Notes: 2, 7, 9, 14

Rose Farm Inn

Roslyn Road, Box 3, 02807
(401) 466-2021

Experience the romance of the Victorian era. Guests can treat themselves to a romantic

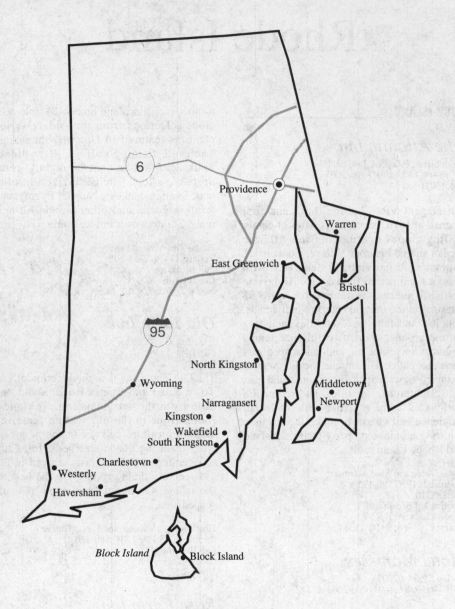

6

Providence

Warren

East Greenwich

Bristol

95

North Kingston

Middletown

Narragansett

Newport

Kingston

Wakefield

South Kingston

Charlestown

Westerly

Haversham

Block Island

Block Island

Rhode Island

room beautifully furnished with antiques and king-size canopied bed or queen-size bed. Enjoy the peaceful tranquility of the farm from shaded decks cooled by gentle ocean breezes. Gaze at the ocean from the guest room window or share a whirlpool bath for two. Awaken to a light buffet breakfast served in the charming porch dining room with an ocean view. Bicycle rentals available. Closed November through March. Children over 12 welcome.

Hosts: Robert and Judith Rose
Rooms: 19 (17 PB; 2 SB) $90-175
Continental Breakfast
Credit Cards: A, B, C, D
Notes: 2, 7, 9, 10, 11, 14

The Sheffield House Bed and Breakfast

High Street, P.O. Box C-2, 02807
(401) 466-2494; FAX (401) 466-5067

The Sheffield House, an 1888 Queen Anne Victorian, is set amidst perennial gardens, a five-minute walk from beaches, shops, and restaurants. The seven guest rooms are individually decorated with antiques and family pieces for the comfort of the guests. Rocking chairs on the porch, a country kitchen, and quiet private garden ensure a tranquil getaway.

Hosts: Steve and Claire McQueeny and Family
Rooms: 7 (5 PB; 2 SB) $50-150
Continental Breakfast
Credit Cards: A, B, C
Notes: 2, 5, 7, 9, 10, 11, 14

The 1661 Inn and Guest House and the Nicholas Ball Cottage

Spring Street, 02807
(401) 466-2421; (401) 466-2063

Enjoy the spectacular oceanviews and authentic New England decor of the 1661 Inn. Most rooms feature an oceanview, private deck, and Jacuzzi. Some rooms feature fireplaces. Marvel at the spectacular views

of the Atlantic Ocean from the canopy-covered deck while enjoying a full buffet breakfast. The Nicholas Ball Cottage has three luxurious rooms with fireplaces and Jacuzzis. Guest house open all year. There is a petting zoo with llamas, Sicilian donkeys, Nubian, Pygmy, and fainting goats, plus other wonderful animals.

Hosts: Joan and Justin Abrams; Steve and Rita Draper
Rooms: 19 (14 PB; 5 SB) $65-300
Full Breakfast
Credit Cards: A, B, C
Notes: 2, 3, 4, 5, 7, 8, 9, 10, 11, 14

The White House

Spring Street, 02807
(401) 466-2653

Large island manor house with two bedrooms sharing two baths and opening onto balconies overlooking the ocean. French Provincial antique furnishings. Notable collection of presidential autographs and documents. Full breakfast. All kinds of in-house services and amenities. Inquire about accommodations for pets and children.

Host: J. V. Connolly
Rooms: 2 (SB) $100-120
Full Breakfast
Credit Cards: A, B, C
Notes: 2, 5, 9, 10, 11

BRISTOL

Anna's Victorian Connection

5 Fowler Avenue, Newport, 02840
(401) 849-2489

0007. One of the oldest wooden houses still standing in the United States, this three-story mansion built in 1698 has a center hall, double parlors, and double chimneys. The Marquis de Lafayette, George Washington, and Thomas Jefferson were among its notable guests. Later, it was a haven for escaping slaves on the pre-Civil War Underground Railroad. Hosts love sharing their home's history over breakfast

NOTES: Credit cards: A MasterCard; B Visa; C American Express; D Discover; E Diners Club; F Other;
2 Personal checks accepted; 3 Lunch available; 4 Dinner available; 5 Open all year; 6 Pets welcome;
7 No smoking; 8 Children welcome; 9 Social drinking allowed; 10 Tennis nearby; 11 Swimming nearby;
12 Golf nearby; 13 Skiing nearby; 14 May be booked through a travel agent.

in the dining room. (Rumor has it that there may be a ghost or two still lurking around.) Shared baths. Twenty minutes from Newport and Providence. $40-95.

William's Grant Inn

154 High Street, 02809
(401) 253-4222; (800) 596-4222

Just two blocks from Bristol's harbor is William's Grant Inn, circa 1808. The home of a sea captain, this five-bay, high-style Federal house is now a gracious inn for guests to enjoy. It is a showcase for traditional and whimsical artwork throughout. The eclectic full breakfasts are always a treat with chefs Mary and Mike! A central location to Boston, Providence, and Newport. Seven museums and a 30-mile bike path within two miles of the inn. Children over 12 welcome.

Hosts: Mary and Mike Rose
Rooms: 5 (3 PB; 2 SB) $65-95
Full Breakfast
Credit Cards: A, B, C, E, F
Notes: 2, 5, 7, 9, 10, 11, 12, 14

CHARLESTOWN

Bed and Breakfast Referrals of South Coast Rhode Island

P.O. Box 562, 02813-0562
(800) 853-7479

A referral service of eighteen bed and breakfasts along the south coast of Rhode Island, between Wickford and Westerly, and including two bed and breakfasts in Richmond and two close to the University of Rhode Island. This group is aware of vacancies, rates, and general information.

One Willow by the Sea

1 Willow Road, 02813
(401) 364-0802

Enjoy hospitality year-round in a peaceful, rural home. South County shoreline commu-

nity, where guest comfort is a priority. Wake to birds, sunshine, and sea breezes. Delicious gourmet breakfast is served in summer on the sun deck. Explore the miles of beautiful sandy beaches, salt ponds, and wildlife refuges. A birder's paradise! Restaurants, theaters, live music, antique shows, craft fairs, historic New England and Narragansett Indian landmarks nearby. Providence, Newport, Block Island, and Mystic are short drives away. Host speaks French. Inquire about children.

Host: Denise Dillon Fuge
Rooms: 4 (SB) $65-75
Full Breakfast
Credit Cards: None
Notes: 2, 5, 7, 9, 10, 11, 12, 14

A Place Called "Hathaways" Bed and Breakfast

4470 Old Post Road, 02813
(401) 364-6665

Offering an alternative to contemporary lodging. Private cottages nestled in a peaceful country location. Whether guests are swimming, antiquing, or just relaxing. The Victorian dining room in the main house is a great place to meet with friends over breakfast. Guests come from all over the globe, so breakfast can be a real international event. Air-conditioned, color TV, rest and relaxation.

Hosts: The deRochambeau Family
Cottages: 6 (PB) $69-95
Continental Breakfast
Credit Cards: A, B, C
Notes: 8, 10, 11, 12

EAST GREENWICH

Anna's Victorian Connection

5 Fowler Avenue, Newport, 02840
(401) 849-2489

0017. The host, a retired executive and town councilman, welcomes travelers to his home with every comfort he ever wished for in his own years of travel. His quiet

NOTES: Credit cards accepted: A MasterCard; B Visa; C American Express; D Discover; E Diners Club;
F Other; 2 Personal checks accepted; 3 Lunch available; 4 Dinner available; 5 Open all year; 6 Pets welcome;

home in East Greenwich has been designed with guests' privacy in mind. Both guest rooms have king-size beds, convertible to twin, and private baths. Shoot pool in the pool room or relax on the deck overlooking a former cranberry bog. $55-95.

HAVERSHAM

Covered Bridge

P.O. Box 447A, Norfolk, CT 06058
(203) 542-5944

1HR1. Early 1900s beach home the artist/architect owner has redone to create a spectacular home in a secluded setting overlooking a saltwater pond with a view of the ocean. There are two guest rooms in the main house, one with a balcony, which are decorated with antiques and paintings done by the owner. There are also two cottages on the grounds. A Continental plus breakfast is served in the dining room or on the terrace overlooking the water. $95-150.

MIDDLETOWN

Anna's Victorian Connection

5 Fowler Avenue, Newport, 02840
(401) 849-2489

0004. This small Victorian farmhouse has been completely restored by its owner to an airy country decor. Two twin rooms and a double room share two bathrooms—one is a "country bath," reminiscent of Saturday nights in a big steaming tub; the other is a modern bath with shower. Only two miles from Newport, this charming home offers easy access to beaches, a bird sanctuary, and St. George's School. $65–75.

Bed and Breakfast Inns of New England

128 South Hoop Pole Road, Guilford, CT 06437
(203) 457-0042; (800) 582-0853

RI905. Away from the hustle of downtown Newport, enjoy the serenity of this small bed and breakfast home in a peaceful residential area. One-half mile to the beaches and the Newport line, one mile to Bellevue Avenue, famous Cliff Walk and mansions, Ocean Drive and boutique shops. Guests can also enjoy the wildlife refuge, the bird sanctuary, museums, yachting, tennis, art galleries, and historical names. Choose from four guest rooms, two with private bath, a common room, large deck and yard. Full breakfast is included. No smoking. No pets. $70-85.

The Briar Patch

42 Briarwood Avenue, 02842
(401) 841-5824

The Briar Patch is a small homestay inn featuring personal attention, bright, flowery decor, and ocean views. Only a four-minute walk from Newport Beach and the famous Cliff Walk, with restaurants and clubs also within walking distance. Tennis, swimming, and golf are all nearby. Special off-season discounts are available. Children over 12 are welcome.

Host: Maureen McCracken
Rooms: 2 (2 PB) $75-95
Full Breakfast
Credit Cards: None
Notes: 2, 5, 7, 9, 10, 11, 12

Finnegan's Inn at Shadow Lawn

120 Miantonomi Avenue, 02842
(401) 849-1298; (800) 828-0000
FAX (401) 849-1306

Finnegan's Inn at Shadow Lawn, one of Newport County's finest bed and breakfast inns, is on two acres of beautifully landscaped lawns and gardens. This 1850s Victorian mansion, with its crystal chandeliers and stained-glass windows, has eight large bedrooms, each with private bath, television, refrigerator, and air conditioning. Five rooms also have attached kitchens and working fireplaces. Enjoy a

7 No smoking; 8 Children welcome; 9 Social drinking allowed; 10 Tennis nearby; 11 Swimming nearby;
12 Golf nearby; 13 Skiing nearby; 14 May be booked through a travel agent.

complimentary bottle of wine and join the hosts daily for a glass of sherry.

Hosts: Randy and Selma Fabricant
Rooms: 8 (PB) $65-130
Continental Breakfast
Credit Cards: A, B, F
Notes: 5, 7, 8, 9, 10, 11, 12

Lindsey's Guest House

6 James Street, 02840
(401) 846-9386

One mile to Newport's famous mansions, Cliff Walk, and the Tennis Hall of Fame. Lindsey's is a split-level home with a large yard, deck, Continental plus breakfast, and off-street parking. Ten-minute walk to beaches and Norman Bird Sanctuary.

Host: Anne
Rooms: 3 (PB) $50-90
Continental Breakfast
Credit Cards: A, B, C
Notes: 2, 5, 7, 8, 9, 10, 11, 12, 14

NARRAGANSETT

Bed and Breakfast Inns of New England

128 South Hoop Pole Road, Guilford, CT 06437
(800) 582-0853; (203) 457-0042

RI903. Enjoy the elegance of a circa 1884 oceanfront Victorian summer estate on the National Register of Historic Places. Overlooking the ocean and set on two acres. Explore the grounds, play croquet, sunbathe, swim in the ocean, and relax on the sun porch or patio. The eight guest rooms have a variety of bed sizes and are furnished with antiques and collectibles. Many have ocean views, and all rooms have private baths. Children over ten are welcome. Resident dog, but no guest pets. No smoking. $60-125.

Four Gables

12 South Pier Road, 02882
(401) 789-6948

Built by an architect in 1898, this charming home has many interesting features. It is furnished with antiques and unique hand-crafted items and offers an extensive library, especially in needlework and gardening. Fishing equipment and advice available. Breakfast is served in the dining room overlooking the ocean, or guests may choose to enjoy the veranda with its spectacular views. Within walking distance of the beach, restaurants, and shops, and within a short drive to many attractions. Children over 12 welcome.

Hosts: Terry and Barbara Higgins
Rooms: 2 (SB) $60-90
Full Breakfast
Credit Cards: A, B
Notes: 2, 5, 9, 10, 11, 12, 14

Ilverthorpe Cottage

41 Robinson Street, 02882
(401) 789-2392

A 100-year-old Victorian just a few blocks from the beach and the open ocean. Pleasantly decorated rooms and common areas with all the lacy frills of the period. Rooms are comfortable and clean with the special touches of the house. Knowledgeable hosts can suggest activities to fill one's days and evenings.

Hosts: Chris and John Webb
Rooms: 4 (2 PB; 2 SB) $60-80
Full Breakfast
Credit Cards: None
Notes: 2, 9, 10, 11, 12

1900 House

59 Kingstown Road, 02882
(401) 789-7971

Restored Victorian, circa 1900, with antique furniture, quiet street, lavender front door, and pretty gardens. Each room is unique, but all include country antiques, wooden bed frames, canopied beds, thick Oriental rugs, and small special touches, such as the original owners' marriage certificate. Beach is a five-minute walk.

NOTES: Credit cards accepted: A MasterCard; B Visa; C American Express; D Discover; E Diners Club; F Other; 2 Personal checks accepted; 3 Lunch available; 4 Dinner available; 5 Open all year; 6 Pets welcome;

Guests have use of a porch, which has cool sea breezes. Full gourmet breakfast served.

Hosts: Bill and Sandra Panzeri
Rooms: 3 (1 PB; 2 SB) $55-75
Full Breakfast
Credit Cards: None
Notes: 2, 5, 10, 11, 12

The Old Clerk House

49 Narrangansett Avenue, 02882
(401) 783-8008

Enjoy English country comfort in this Victorian home. Twin, queen-, and king-size beds with private baths, color cable TV, VCR, and air conditioning. Full, home-cooked breakfast, all made from scratch—no mixes—is served in the plant-filled sunroom. Only one block from beautiful beach and fine restaurants. Kayaking, fishing, whale watching, bay cruises, water sports, Block Island ferry, and URI nearby. Eighteen miles from Newport. Foxwoods Casino is a half-hour drive. Off-street parking.

Host: Patricia Watkins
Rooms: 2 (PB) $65-85
Full Breakfast
Credit Cards: None
Notes: 2, 5, 7, 9, 10, 11, 12, 14

Pleasant Cottage

104 Robinson Street, 02882
(401) 783-6895

This charming cottage is on a half-acre of woods and gardens. A quiet, serene atmosphere awaits guests just blocks from lovely Narragansett Beach. Enclosed outdoor shower. Relax on large screened porch. Bedrooms with shared bath, or private bath and private entrance. Full breakfast served, including a treat for coffee lovers. Reservations and advance deposit required.

Hosts: Fred and Terry Sepp
Rooms: 2 (1 PB; 1 SB) $55-65
Full Breakfast
Credit Cards: None
Notes: 2, 9, 10, 11, 12

The Richards

144 Gibson Avenue, 02882
(401) 789-7746

These gracious and elegant accommodations are in an 1884 historic manse. Relax by the crackling fire in the library or in the guest room with a fireplace. Enjoy a leisurely and delicious full breakfast, complete with homemade muffins, strudels, and blintzes. The hostess's special touches will spoil anyone—down comforters, canopied beds, and flowers fresh from the gardens. There are minimum-stay requirements for weekends and holidays. Special suite rates are available for couples who are traveling together.

Hosts: Steven and Nancy Richards
Rooms: 4 (2 PB; 2 SB) $60-85
Suite: (PB) $100-160
Full Breakfast
Credit Cards: None
Notes: 2, 5, 7, 9, 10, 11, 12

White Rose

22 Cedar Street, 02882
(401) 789-0181

The White Rose is a classic Victorian in Narragansett-by-the-Sea, just a half-block from the beach. The upbeat atmosphere is simple and elegant. Sip a complimentary cocktail in the shade of the front porch or soak up the sun on the rear porch smothered by roses (our namesake). During the colder months cuddle by the hearth or play your favorite tunes on the baby grand. The attractively decorated rooms are bright, cheery, furnished with antiques, and offer twin, double, or king-size beds. Walk to the beach, shops, and restaurants or drive (30 minutes) to Newport, Mystic, and Foxwoods Casino. Bicycles, fishing gear, diving gear, croquet, horseshoes, darts, and more are available or arrange a private charter aboard the sailing sloop *White Rose*. A sumptuous, hearty breakfast buffet is served daily. Your hosts are athletic and health-oriented, so smoking is not allowed

7 No smoking; 8 Children welcome; 9 Social drinking allowed; 10 Tennis nearby; 11 Swimming nearby; 12 Golf nearby; 13 Skiing nearby; 14 May be booked through a travel agent.

inside the house. A pleasant fun-filled stay is guaranteed.

Hosts: Pat and Sylvan Vaicaitis
Rooms: 4 (SB) $50-75
Full Breakfast
Credit Cards: None
Notes: 2, 5, 7, 8, 9, 10, 11, 12, 14

NEWPORT

Admiral Farragut Inn

31 Clarke Street, 02840
(401) 846-4256; (800) 343-2863
FAX (401) 846-4289

The Admiral Farragut Inn, circa 1702, is a classic American Colonial. Exclusive and charming on a quiet gas lamp-lit street. Living history in authentic period antiques and handmade pencil-post beds with comfortable duvets. Ideal for a winter getaway. Close to America's first synagogue, First Free Black Church, First Baptist Church, and First Unitarian Church. Also near 1638 Trinity Church, the first Quaker meeting house, and the Friends Museum. A true experience. Sailing nearby. Full breakfast is served each morning. Private baths and telephones in all guest rooms. Air-conditioned.

Host: Mary Ann Brett
Rooms: 10 (PB) $55-165
Full Breakfast
Credit Cards: A, B, C, D, E, F
Notes: 5, 7, 9, 10, 11, 12, 14

The Admiral Fitzroy Inn

398 Thames Street, 02840
(401) 848-8000; (800) 343-2863
FAX (401) 846-4289

This inn is in the heart of Newport's yachting district, central to all that Newport has to offer. The inn is decorated in its own distinctive style, artfully conceived, and a showcase for fine craftsmanship. Sleigh and brass beds, lace linens, and plush duvets are part of each room's individual decor, and each room has glazed finished walls, hand-painted with pleasing designs and crisp motifs. Hidden away within the

handmade Swedish cupboards are a TV with cable, a small refrigerator, electric tea kettle, and fixings. Each room also has a telephone, heat and cool controls, private bath with a tub, and a hair dryer. Full breakfast can be enjoyed downstairs, in the guest room, or on the deck overlooking Newport Harbor. Sailing is nearby.

Host: Holly Eastman
Rooms: 18 (PB) $85-225
Full and Continental Breakfasts
Credit Cards: A, B, C, D, E
Notes: 5, 7, 8, 9, 10, 11, 12, 14

Anna's Victorian Connection

5 Fowler Avenue, 02840
(401) 849-2489

0001. A beautiful 1883 Dutch Colonial Revival house with terrific views of Newport's Easton Beach in winter. Now retired, the hosts have two very graciously appointed suites, for two to four guests each, with private baths, telephone, and TV. Children of all ages welcome. Breakfast is served in the dining room, and in warmer months on a sun porch with water view. Smoking is permitted. A cat is in residence. $75-175.

0002. Husband and wife psychologists have turned the third floor of their Victorian home into a comfortable bed and breakfast. The Blue Room has a pop-up trundle bed, which becomes a double bed for couples or a pair of twins for others; the Yellow Room has a king-size bed and room for a third person or child; the Peach Room also has a day bed with a pop-up trundle. All are air-conditioned and share a bath. There is also a Toy Room, where children are welcome to play. Close to downtown Newport. Off-street parking. Easy walk from restaurants and shopping. Dog and cat in residence. $50-95.

0003. An elegant Greek Revival "cottage" in a quiet, downtown Newport neighborhood, this private home offers truly exquisite decor, with a crackling fire in the living room in winter, and a screened porch furnished with wicker in the summer. Antiques and beautiful collections abound throughout. The guest rooms have canopied beds in both double- and king-size rooms; there are also two guest sitting rooms. $95-150.

0006. Escape via launch from Newport or guests can bring their own boats to this classic 1869 lighthouse on a one-and-a-half-acre island in Narragansett Bay. A museum and two guest rooms share the first floor; the lighthouse keeper's apartment is on the second. The rooms feature authentic period furnishings, and the view of the water and sky is unbeatable! No smoking. $50-140.

0008. This exquisite Empire Victorian house, built in 1873, is in the historic Point section of Newport. Luxury accommodations are available in rooms furnished with antiques, cable TV, air conditioning, and private baths. Many have spectacular views of Newport Harbor and the city. Full breakfast is served in the dining room, on the front porch, or in the garden, depending on the season. Off-street parking is available so guests may walk into downtown Newport and its attractions. $85-195.

0010. Built around the turn of the century on the grounds of Newport's famous Ocean House, a favored resort of 19th-century society, this charming Victorian has been restored to its former elegance with a delightful mix of antiques and Shaker-style furniture. Each guest room features a queen-size bed, hand-stenciled walls, private bath, air conditioning, and TV. Full breakfast is served in the dining room or on the porch overlooking the garden. No smoking allowed. Children over six are welcome. $55-125.

0013. When this villa, designed by William Ralph Emerson, was built in 1869, the *Boston Journal* said, "The most elegantly finished house ever built in Newport is that of Mr. M. H. Sanford, just completed." This magnificent home, the last remaining example of its style, has been in the hosts' family since 1895, and they take pride in offering extraordinary accommodations. Sit on the waterfront porch and watch the boats sail by, enjoy the pool and spa (by arrangement), or stroll into downtown Newport. $65-295.

0016. This elegant and historic Newport inn was built in 1760 for Col. Francis Malbone, a wealthy shipping merchant. Seized by the British during the Revolutionary War, it was used to store gold, giving it the nickname, Treasure House. Painstakingly restored and proudly listed on the National Register of Historic Places, the inn offers period charm and comfort in guest rooms and suites with private baths, elegant sitting and dining rooms, and beautifully landscaped gardens. Children over 12 welcome. $95-295.

Beech Tree Inn

34 Rhode Island Avenue, 02840
(401) 847-9794; (800) 748-6565
FAX (401) 847-6824

The Beech Tree Inn is a bed and breakfast offering the largest breakfast with the greatest variety of entrées in Newport. The inn was completely renovated in 1994, and all guest rooms are large with new bathrooms. Some rooms have fireplaces and Jacuzzis. Some have outside decks. A casual and relaxed atmosphere with charming Colonial decor. No smoking in guest rooms.

Hosts: Ed and Kathy Wudyka
Rooms: 8 (PB)
Full Breakfast A, B, C, D
Notes: 2, 5, 8, 9, 10, 11, 12, 14

7 No smoking; 8 Children welcome; 9 Social drinking allowed; 10 Tennis nearby; 11 Swimming nearby; 12 Golf nearby; 13 Skiing nearby; 14 May be booked through a travel agent.

Bellevue House

14 Catherine Street, 02840
(401) 847-1828; (800) 820-1828

Built in 1774, Bellevue House was converted into the first summer hotel in Newport in 1828. On top of Historic Hill, off the famous Bellevue Avenue, three blocks from the harbor. The house retains a combination of ideal location, Colonial history, nautical atmosphere, and Victorian charm. All guest rooms have air conditioning and are nonsmoking. Children over 12 welcome.

Hosts: Joan and Vic Farmer
Rooms: 8 (6 PB; 2 SB) $70-115
Continental Breakfast
Credit Cards: A, B
Notes: 2, 7, 9, 10, 11, 12, 14

Brinley Victorian Inn

23 Brinley Street, 02840
(401) 849-7645

Romantic year-round, the inn becomes a Victorian Christmas dream come true. Comfortable antiques and fresh flowers fill every room. Friendly, unpretentious service and attention to detail will make this inn a traveler's haven in Newport. Park and walk everywhere. AAA approved. Minimum stay on weekends is two nights and on holidays is three nights. Children over 12 welcome.

Hosts: John and Jennifer Sweetman
Rooms: 17 (13 PB; 4 SB) $55-149
Continental Breakfast
Credit Cards: A, B
Notes: 2, 5, 7, 9, 10, 11, 12, 14

Cliffside Inn

2 Seaview Avenue, 02840
(401) 845-1811

An elegant Victorian Inn near the beginning of Newport's famous Cliff Walk and the beach. Built in 1880 by Governor Thomas Swann of Maryland as a summer residence, the house became the first location of St. George's School in 1897 and was later owned by Newport artist Beatrice Turner. In addition to a full breakfast, host serves appetizers. Guest rooms have private baths, some with whirlpool or steam baths. Some rooms have fireplaces. Air conditioning, cable TV, and telephones. Conference facilities are also available. "One of Newport's best kept secrets"—*Bed and Breakfast in New England.*

Host: Stephan Nicolas
Rooms: 12 (PB) $135-325
Full Breakfast
Credit Cards: A, B, C, D
Notes: 2, 5, 7, 9, 10, 11, 12, 14

Cliff View Guest House

4 Cliff Terrace, 02840
(401) 846-0885

A two-story 1870 Victorian on a quiet dead-end street leading to the beautiful Cliff Walk, a three-mile path bordering the ocean. Five-minute walk to beach; 15-minute walk to downtown harbor area. Ten-room house with four guest bedrooms; two share a bath and have view of ocean; two have private baths, but no oceanview. Two rooms have air conditioning. The hostess's French-speaking grandson is on the premises during school summer vacation.

Host: Pauline Shea
Rooms: 4 (2 PB; 2 SB) $55-75
Continental Breakfast
Credit Cards: A, B
Notes: 2, 9, 10, 11, 12, 14

The 1855 Marshall Slocum Guest House

29 Kay Street, 02840
(401) 841-5120

The house is comfortably furnished with a mixture of antiques, collectibles, and family treasures. Guests enjoy the floor-to-ceiling mirrored foyer leading upstairs to the five bedrooms; two with private half-baths, and three full baths. Hosts share the parlor, TV/reading room, and dining room where a full breakfast is served each morning. The spacious back yard and deck and the front porch with rockers are lovely places to breakfast, plan the day's activities, or take some sun and relax.

Host: Joan Wilson
Rooms: 5 (2 PB; 3 SB) $70-120
Full Breakfast
Credit Cards: A, B, C, D, E
Notes: 2, 3, 4, 5, 9, 10, 11, 12, 14

The Francis Malbone House

392 Thames Street, 02840
(401) 846-0392

This historic inn was built in 1760 for Col. Francis Malbone, who made his fortune as a shipping merchant. The design of the house is attributed to Peter Harrison, the architect responsible for Touro Synagogue and the Redwood Library. Guests will enjoy the comfortable elegance of the Francis Malbone House, which is proudly listed on the National Register of Historic Places. The inn offers a downtown harbor location, private baths, full breakfast, fireplaces, corporate packages, and gracious rooms and gardens for elegant entertaining.

Host: Will Dewey
Rooms: 9 (PB) $105-295
Full Breakfast
Credit Cards: A, B, C
Notes: 2, 5, 7, 11, 14

The Inn at Old Beach

19 Old Beach Road, 02840
(401) 849-3479; FAX (401) 847-1236

Elegant Victorian bed and breakfast in one of Newport's most prestigious areas. Built in 1879, this inn was once the home of an affluent physician and commodore and is now listed on the Rhode Island historic register. The fabled mansions, Cliff Walk, the beach, and historic harbor front are only a short walk away. Each of the romantic guest rooms has a private bath, and several have fireplaces. Continental plus breakfast. Seasonal rates. Children over 12 welcome.

Hosts: Luke and Cynthia Murray
Rooms: 7 (PB) $75-145
Continental Breakfast
Credit Cards: A, B, C
Notes: 2, 5, 7, 9, 10, 11, 12, 14

The Inntowne Inn

6 Mary Street, 02840
(401) 846-9200; (800) 457-7803
FAX (401) 846-1534

An elegant traditional inn in the heart of downtown Newport offers some four-poster beds with canopies and a rooftop deck. Use of health club and pool within walking distance. Afternoon tea and Continental breakfast served daily. One mile from the Newport mansions. Take harbor cruises, shop for antiques, or just enjoy the bustle of the harbor.

Host: Carmella L. Gardner
Rooms: 25 (PB) $110-250
Continental Breakfast
Credit Cards: A, B, C
Notes: 2, 5, 8, 11, 12

Jenkins Guest House

206 South Rhode Island Avenue, 02840
(401) 847-6801

The hosts built this Cape Cod when they were married. Since their eight children who were raised in this house are now grown and on their own, the hosts have been using the extra rooms for guests since 1978. Having lived in Newport all their lives, they have interesting stories to tell from a local viewpoint and can provide helpful information about restaurants and places to visit. On a quiet little street just a three-minute walk from the beach or a ten-minute walk to the mansions or the harbor, with plenty of parking on the grounds. Enjoy the homemade muffins for breakfast

Jenkins Guest House

in a country-in-the-city atmosphere. Air-conditioned.

Hosts: David and Sally Jenkins
Rooms: 3 (1 PB; 2SB) $65
Continental Breakfast
Credit Cards: None
Notes: 2, 8, 9, 10, 11

La Forge Cottage

96 Pelham Street, 02840
(401) 847-4400

A Victorian bed and breakfast in the heart of Newport's Historic Hill area. Close to beaches and downtown. All rooms have private baths, TVs, telephones, air conditioning, refrigerators, and full breakfast room service. French, Spanish, and German spoken. Reservations suggested. Minimum stay on weekends is two nights and on holidays is three nights.

Hosts: Louis and Margot Droual
Rooms: 6 (PB) $56-145.60
Suites: 4 (PB) $78.40-173.60
Full Breakfast
Credit Cards: A, B, C, D
Notes: 2, 5, 7, 8, 9, 10, 11, 12

The Melville House

39 Clark Street, 02840
(401) 847-0640

Step back into the past and stay at a Colonial inn, built circa 1750, "where the past is present." The Melville House is on the National Register of Historic Places and is in the heart of Newport's beautiful historic district. Walk around the corner to the Brick Market and the wharves. Enjoy a leisurely homemade breakfast in the morning, and join the hosts for complimentary tea and sherry before dinner. Off-street parking.

Hosts: Vince DeRico and David Horan
Rooms: 7 (5 PB; 2 SB) $60-125
Suite: $150
Full Breakfast
Credit Cards: A, B, C, D
Notes: 2, 3, 5, 7, 9, 10, 11, 12, 14

Mill Street Inn

Mill Street Inn

75 Mill Street, 02840
(800) 392-1316; FAX (401) 848-5131

Luxury all-suite hotel, award-winning contemporary interior in a renovated national historic mill. Townhouses have spectacular views from private decks. Parking available. One block to harbor, mansions, restaurants, and shops. Continental breakfast buffet each morning. Breakfast served on the rooftop deck overlooking the harbor. Dinner packages available. Gift certificates.

Hosts: Bob and Paula Briskin
Rooms: 23 (PB) $75-285
Continental Breakfast
Credit Cards: A, B, C, E
Notes: 5, 7, 8, 9, 10, 11, 12

Pilgrim House Inn

123 Spring Street, 02840
(401) 846-0040; (800) 525-8373

This Victorian inn, with its comforts and elegance, is two blocks from the harbor in the midst of the historic district. A living room with fireplace, immaculate rooms, and wonderful atmosphere await. Breakfast is on the deck overlooking Newport's harbor. Just outside the door are the mansions, shops, and restaurants. Closed January. AAA approved. Children over 12 welcome. Call regarding a special offer available from October 15 through April 30.

Hosts: Pam and Bruce Bayuk
Rooms: 10 (8 PB; 2 SB) $45-165
Continental Breakfast
Credit Cards: A, B
Notes: 2, 7, 10, 11, 12

NOTES: Credit cards accepted: A MasterCard; B Visa; C American Express; D Discover; E Diners Club; F Other; 2 Personal checks accepted; 3 Lunch available; 4 Dinner available; 5 Open all year; 6 Pets welcome;

Polly's Place

349 Valley Road, Route 214, 02842
(401) 847-2160

A quiet retreat one mile from Newport's harbor, historic homes, and sandy beaches. Polly is a long-time Newport resident willing to give helpful advice to travelers interested in the area. Rooms are large, clean, and very attractive. Breakfast is served in the dining room with a lovely view of wildlife and birds of the area. The hostess also offers a one-bedroom apartment that is available by the week and completely equipped. This bed and breakfast has been inspected and approved for cleanliness and quality. Children over 12 welcome.

Host: Polly Canning
Rooms: 4 (1 PB; 4 SB) $80
Apartment: 1
Full Breakfast
Credit Cards: None
Notes: 2, 7, 9, 10, 11, 12, 14

Rhode Island House

77 Rhode Island Avenue, 02840
(401) 848-7787; FAX (401) 849-3104

Spacious, elegant, grand 1881 Victorian residence featuring unsurpassed sun-filled rooms, personalized decor, and relaxed ambience. Each bedroom has a private bath, fine linens, queen-sized beds, and air conditioning. Fireplaces, Jacuzzis, and private deck available. Easy walk to restaurants, shopping, beach, and tourism sites. A full gourmet breakfast is prepared by a renowned chef to the Newport summer colony.

Hosts: Michael Dupre and John Rich
Rooms: 5 (PB) $95-195
Full Breakfast
Credit Cards: A, B, C
Notes: 2, 5, 7, 9, 10, 11, 12, 14

Stella Maris Inn

91 Washington Street, 02840
(401) 849-2862

Elegant, romantic 1861 Victorian mansion completely restored in 1990. Some rooms with water view and fireplaces, all tastefully furnished with antiques. Large wraparound front porch with water view. Spacious gardens and tennis court. Hearty Continental breakfast featuring homemade muffins and breads. Walking distance to town. Parking on premises.

Hosts: Dorothy and Ed Madden
Rooms: 8 (PB) $65-150
Continental Breakfast
Credit Cards: None
Notes: 2, 5, 7, 10, 11, 12

Villa Liberté

22 Liberty Street, 02840
(401) 846-7444; (800) 392-3717

Neatly tucked away off historic Bellevue Avenue, the Villa Liberté offers the charm and romance of the City by the Sea. From warm cherrywood furnishings to lush imported bedding, the villa offers uniquely appointed queen-size rooms, elegant master suites, and comfortable apartment suites; each with private bath, air conditioning, telephone, TV, and private parking. Dramatic black and white tile baths feature pedestal sinks and arched alcoves. Enjoy buffet Continental breakfast in the tea room or on the terrace sun deck. Walk to the mansions, Newport's beautiful beaches, Brick Marketplace, and the wharf area.

Host: Leigh Anne Mosco
Rooms: 15 (PB) $59-175
Continental Breakfast
Credit Cards: A, B, C
Notes: 7, 8, 10, 11, 12

The Willows of Newport, "The Romantic Inn"

8 and 10 Willow Street, Historic Point, 02840
(401) 846-5486

In the historic section of Newport, the Willows pampers guests with Secret Gardens, solid brass canopied beds, fresh flowers, mints on pillows, champagne glasses and silver ice bucket, and the lights on dim. Breakfast in bed on bone china and

7 No smoking; 8 Children welcome; 9 Social drinking allowed; 10 Tennis nearby; 11 Swimming nearby; 12 Golf nearby; 13 Skiing nearby; 14 May be booked through a travel agent.

silver service. Three blocks from downtown and the waterfront. Parking and air conditioning. Open April 1 through November; closed December through March. Mobil three-star award.

Host: Patricia Murphy
Rooms: 5 (PB) $88-185
Continental Breakfast
Credit Cards: None
Notes: 2, 7, 9, 10, 11, 12, 14

NORTH KINGSTOWN

The John Updike House

19 Pleasant Street, Wickford Village, 02852-5019
(401) 294-4905; FAX (401) 295-2825

Built in 1745, this elegant Georgian has retained its beauty and charm for nearly two and one-half centuries. It continues to be the only bed and breakfast on the west passage of Narragansett Bay, overlooking the bay and Wickford Harbor, and can be used as a travel base, since it is an easy day trip to Newport, Block Island, South Shore beaches, Providence, and Cape Cod. A private, sandy beach is available for guests' pleasure. Accommodations vary depending on individual needs: two rooms with common room; a suite of two bedrooms and common room; an apartment that includes suite and full private kitchen.

Hosts: Mary Anne and Bill Sabo
Rooms: Variable $90-180
Continental Breakfast
Credit Cards: None
Notes: 2, 5, 7, 8, 9, 10, 11, 12, 14

PROVIDENCE

Anna's Victorian Connection

5 Fowler Avenue, Newport, 02840
(401) 849-2489

0009. This restored Federalist-style house, built in the heart of Providence in 1890, has the comfort and charm of a bed and breakfast, plus the privacy of a hotel. Ten guest rooms, each with private bath, pamper guests with canopied beds and fireplaces,

air conditioning and TV, and a full breakfast. Close to the Rhode Island state capitol and government buildings, the inn is just a five-minute walk from the Amtrak station, while historic Benefit Street is only ten minutes away. No smoking. Children welcome. $69-109.

0011. Built in 1905 by a prosperous lumber dealer, this shingled Victorian house is listed by the Rhode Island Historic Preservation Commission. Its Art Nouveau stained-glass window is glorious! The college-professor host welcomes guests with comfortable beds, fireplace, and rocking chairs. This quiet home on Providence's East Side is close to Brown University and Rhode Island School of Design, yet within an hour of Newport, Cape Cod, Mystic Seaport, and Boston. No smoking. Children welcome. $45-75.

Old Court Bed and Breakfast

144 Benefit Street, 02903
(401) 751-2002

In the heart of Providence's historic Benefit Street area, guests will find the Old Court, where tradition is combined with contemporary standards of luxury. The Old Court was built in 1863 and reflects early Victorian styles. In rooms that overlook downtown Providence and Brown University, visitors feel as if they have entered a more gracious era. Lunch and dinner available by special request. Limited smoking. Inquire about accommodations for children.

Host: Christine Nation
Rooms: 11 (PB) $95-250
Full Breakfast
Credit Cards: A, B, D
Notes: 2, 5, 10, 11, 12, 14

State House Inn

43 Jewett Street, 02908
(401) 351-6111

In the center of a quiet and quaint neighborhood, the State House Inn is a

NOTES: Credit cards accepted: A MasterCard; B Visa; C American Express; D Discover; E Diners Club;
F Other; 2 Personal checks accepted; 3 Lunch available; 4 Dinner available; 5 Open all year; 6 Pets welcome;

100-year-old building newly restored and renovated into a country bed and breakfast. Minutes from downtown Providence and the many local colleges and universities. Brings country living to the big city.

Hosts: Frank and Monica Hopton
Rooms: 10 (PB) $79-109
Full Breakfast
Credit Cards: A, B, C
Notes: 5, 7, 8, 9, 14

SOUTH COUNTY

Anna's Victorian Connection

5 Fowler Avenue, Newport, 02840
(401) 849-2489

0005. Dating from 1732, the living room of this ten-room, red-shingled farmhouse was once a plantation blacksmith's shop. The fireplace, granite walls, original wood ceiling, and hand-hewn beams provide authentic Colonial atmosphere. The Yellow and Peach Rooms share a bath, but each has a private lavatory. One has a queen-size bed; the other, twin four-posters. The Green Room sleeps four in king-size and double beds, with private bath. There is also a swimming pool. No smoking. Children over five welcome. $50-95.

SOUTH KINGSTOWN

Bed and Breakfast Inns of New England

128 South Hoop Pole Road, Guilford, CT 06437
(800) 582-0853; (203) 457-0042

910. The past comes alive in this 1898 Victorian that has been lovingly restored and furnished with antiques in the Victorian style. Only one block from an ocean beach. A Continental breakfast is served at the family-style table in a large dining room complete with a charming tiled fireplace. Guest rooms are as varied as they are appealing. Each room is furnished in a different representative period. Some

have a view of the ocean and others are tucked among the caves. All have a warmth and charm to please almost everyone. Supervised children over ten are welcome. Limited smoking. Resident dogs and cats; no guest pets. $60-125.

Hamilton's Garret Bed and Breakfast

182 North Road, 02883-2105
(401) 789-5438

One mile from downtown Wakefield, in the village of Peace Dale, this bed and breakfast is convenient to the University of Rhode Island, museums, libraries, antique shops, art galleries, and many fine restaurants. There are seven municipal and state saltwater beaches within minutes, plus numerous fishing facilities and private beaches. Day trips to Mystic Seaport and Aquarium, Plymouth, Cape Cod, Newport festivals and mansions, and Block Island. Thirty minutes away from the state capitol, civic center, convention center, Roger Williams Park and Zoo, Brown University, RISD School and Museum. History abounds. Lady Emma's Garden has a queen-size bed, and Sir William's Conservatory has a double and can be booked individually with a shared bath or as a suite with a private bath, kitchenette, and dining-sitting area. Grill available for barbecuing.

Hosts: Robert and Joyce Butcher
Rooms: 2 (SB)
Full Breakfast
Credit Cards: None
Notes: 2, 3, 4, 5, 7, 8, 9, 10, 11, 12

Larchwood Inn

521 Main Street, Wakefield, 02879
(401) 783-5454; (800) 275-5450
FAX (401) 783-1800

The Larchwood Inn is a family-run country inn that has kept pace with the 20th century without sacrificing its rural beauty. Holly House, across the front lawn from the main inn, offers additional lodging. Most rooms

7 No smoking; 8 Children welcome; 9 Social drinking allowed; 10 Tennis nearby; 11 Swimming nearby; 12 Golf nearby; 13 Skiing nearby; 14 May be booked through a travel agent.

have private baths, and all guests are encouraged to use the services of the main inn, which includes three restaurants (all of which serve three meals daily) and a cocktail lounge (with lunch and happy hour daily, and live music on the weekends). Near beaches, boating, hiking, horseback and bike riding, and skiing. Breakfast not included in rates.

Host: Francis and Diann Browning
Rooms: 20 (12 PB; 8 SB) $40-100
Credit Cards: A, B, C, D, E
Notes: 2, 3, 4, 5, 6, 7, 8, 9, 10, 11, 12, 13, 14

WAKEFIELD

Green Shadows Bed and Breakfast

803 Green Hill Beach Road, 02879-6228
(401) 783-9752

This new home is in the beautiful Green Hill area of South Coast Rhode Island. Set on a wooded acre, the ocean and the beach are a ten-minute walk away. Light-filled bedrooms with king-size beds and private baths, quiet lounge with cable TV, VCR, screened porch for breakfast and relaxing with views of Green Hill Pond. First-floor accommodations, full breakfast. Within easy drive of Mystic Seaport, Foxwoods Casino, wildlife preserves, flea markets, antique shops, summer theater, and Newport.

Hosts: Don and Mercedes Kratz
Rooms: 2 (PB) $75-85
Full Breakfast
Credit Cards: None
Notes: 2, 7, 11, 12

WARREN

Nathaniel Porter Inn

125 Water Street, 02885
(401) 245-6622

Carefully restored 1750/1795 sea captain's home on the National Register of Historic Places in the historic section one block from harbor. Antique furnishings through-

out building including two canopied beds. Fireplaces in each of the nine rooms. Antique shopping and a bike path nearby. Three-star award-winning restaurant for dinner, plus Sunday champagne buffet brunch. Featured in *Colonial Home* and *Country Living* magazines. Dinner for two available for additional cost of $29.

Hosts: Robert and Viola Lynch
Rooms: 3 (PB) $70
Continental Breakfast
Credit Cards: A, B, C, D
Notes: 2, 4, 5, 9, 11

WESTERLY

Anna's Victorian Connection

5 Fowler Avenue, Newport, 02840
(401) 849-2489

0015. Minutes from Rhode Island's lovely ocean beaches, this deluxe European-style bed and breakfast offers seven uniquely decorated units in a private, relaxing atmosphere. The lovely gardens and grounds include a Mediterranean pool and Jacuzzi on a private terrace. An ideal setting for weddings, honeymoons, or rekindling romance! $75-175.

Bed and Breakfast Inns of New England

128 South Hoop Pole Road, Guilford, CT 06437
(203) 457-0042; (800) 582-0853

RI912. This stately, turn-of-the-century hilltop home offers splendid oceanviews. Eleven guest rooms, with private or shared baths, a wraparound stone porch, spacious grounds, common TV room with VCR, table games, player piano, and books await guests. The hearty Continental breakfast is served on the sun porch. Watch Hill and Westerly beaches are nearby. Walk to tennis or golf. No smoking. $75-85.

RI915. On a hilltop and surrounded by 20 acres of rolling fields and gardens, this

NOTES: Credit cards accepted: A MasterCard; B Visa; C American Express; D Discover; E Diners Club; F Other; 2 Personal checks accepted; 3 Lunch available; 4 Dinner available; 5 Open all year; 6 Pets welcome;

Colonial reproduction is filled with antiques, handmade quilts, and wide board floors. Guests may chose from three guest rooms with private bath, enjoy the library, living, and keeping rooms with fireplaces, rock on the porch or enjoy the 40-inch in-ground pool. Full breakfast is included. The Westerly and Watch Hill beaches are nearby. All the excitement and fun of Newport or Mystic, Connecticut, are each 30 minutes away. No smoking inside. Two resident cats. No guest pets. $60-105.

Grandview Bed and Breakfast

212 Shore Road, 02891
(401) 596-6384; (800) 447-6384

Stately turn-of-the-century home with splendid ocean view. Hearty Continental breakfast served on cheery breakfast porch. Large comfortable living room with stone fireplace. Walk to tennis and golf. A short drive to beaches, Mystic Seaport, Newport mansions, Watch Hill shopping, and the Foxwoods Casino. Fax available.

Host: Pat Grande
Rooms: 11 (4 PB; 7 SB) $75-95
Continental Breakfast
Credit Cards: A, B, C
Notes: 2, 5, 7, 8, 10, 11, 12, 14

Nutmeg Bed and Breakfast Agency

P.O. Box 1117, West Hartford, CT 06107
(203) 236-6698

504. Savor the splendid views from the wraparound stone porch of this turn-of-the-century bed and breakfast. There are 12 guest rooms, two with private baths. The home has a large family room equipped with a player piano, cable TV, games, and variety of reading material. Pick-up available from local train station or airport. If guests love the beach, this home is a perfect base for enjoying the five Rhode Island beaches nearby. Only minutes from Mystic, Connecticut. Continental breakfast. Limited smoking. Children welcome. Pets in residence.

507. Five minutes from the beach, this renovated 1920 summer home is by a saltwater pond that looks out to the ocean. Originally a working farm, it provides the perfect quiet getaway. One guest room has two double beds, many windows, and a private bath with shower. The second guest room has a canopied double bed, private deck with a view of the water, and a private bath with a tub. For the family getaway, there are also two summer cottages available, one with three bedrooms and the other with six. Continental breakfast. No smoking. Children welcome. Pets in residence.

Shelter Harbor Inn

10 Wagner Road, 02891
(401) 322-8883

Originally a farm established in the early 1800s, the property is now a comfortable, unpretentious country inn. Numerous decks and terraces overlook beautiful fields and gardens bordered by stone walls. The inn is just a short drive from the gorgeous private beach and includes a hot tub overlooking Block Island, two paddle tennis courts, and a professional croquet court. Open daily, year-round for breakfast, lunch, and dinner.

Hosts: Jim and Debbye Dey
Rooms: 23 (PB) $86-122
Full Breakfast
Credit Cards: A, B, C, D, E
Notes: 2, 3, 4, 5, 7, 8, 9, 10, 11, 12, 14

The Villa

190 Shore Road, 02891
(401) 596-1054; (800) 722-9240

Escape to this hideaway of flower gardens, Italian porticoes, and verandas. Open year-round, The Villa is the ideal setting for honeymoons and rekindling romances. Imagine being in a private suite in the winter, gazing at the hypnotic flames of a sensuous crackling fire. Summers here are warm and golden with cool ocean breezes. Some suites offer fireplaces or Jacuzzis, and all have color cable television and air

7 No smoking; 8 Children welcome; 9 Social drinking allowed; 10 Tennis nearby; 11 Swimming nearby; 12 Golf nearby; 13 Skiing nearby; 14 May be booked through a travel agent.

conditioning. Enjoy the Mediterranean-accented pool and patio with hot tub. A pleasing, complimentary buffet breakfast is served in the dining room, poolside, or in private room. The romance of Italy awaits. Smoking restricted.

Host: Jerry Maiorano
Rooms: 7 (PB) $75-175
Credit Cards: A, B, C
Notes: 2, 5, 6, 9, 10, 11, 12, 14

Woody Hill

Woody Hill Bed and Breakfast

149 South Woody Hill Road, 02891
(401) 322-0452

The hostess, a high school English teacher, invites guests to share this reproduction Colonial home with antiques and gardens. Snuggle under quilts, relax on the porch swing, visit nearby Newport and Mystic, and swim in the pool or at beautiful ocean beaches. Westerly has it all! Closed one week in February.

Host: Dr. Ellen L. Madison
Rooms: 4 (3 PB or SB) $60-105
Full Breakfast
Credit Cards: None
Notes: 2, 5, 7, 8, 9, 10, 11, 12, 14

WYOMING

The Cookie Jar Bed and Breakfast

64 Kingstown Road (Exit 3A, Just off I-95), 02898
(401) 539-2680; (800) 767-4262

The heart of this home, the living room, was built in 1732 as a blacksmith's shop. The original ceiling, hand-hewn beams, and granite walls remain today. Each bedroom has a color TV and is air-conditioned. The country property includes a barn, a swimming pool, 60 fruit trees, grapevines, a flower garden, and an acre of grass. The hosts offer friendly homestyle living just a short drive from the beaches, Newport, the University of Rhode Island, Foxwoods Casino, Mystic, and Providence.

Hosts: Dick and Madelein Sohl
Rooms: 3 (PB) $75
Full Breakfast
Credit Cards: None
Notes: 2, 5, 7, 8, 9, 10, 11, 12, 14

South Carolina

AIKEN

New Berry Inn

240 Newberry Street Southwest, 29801
(803) 649-2935

The New Berry Inn is a two-story Dutch Colonial home, furnished with antiques, in a parklike surrounding. Guests start their day with a full breakfast, visit the antique shops or the historical district of Old Aiken, golf, horseback ride, and finish the evening with dinner at one of the fine restaurants near the inn.

Hosts: Mary Ann and Hal Mackey
Rooms: 5 (PB) $45-60
Full Breakfast
Credit Cards: A, B, C, D, E
Notes: 5, 7, 8, 9, 10, 12, 14

ANDERSON

River Inn

612 East River Street, 29624
(803) 226-1431

Constructed of heart-pine, inn was completed in 1914 by Dr. Archer LeRoy Smethers, founder of one of Anderson's first hospitals. It is in the first established residential area in Anderson and features ten-foot ceilings and the warmth of beautiful walnut-stained woodwork. Each bedroom has a private bath and working fireplace. A full breakfast is served. There is a large side porch with swing and rockers for guests' enjoyment and a hot tub in the spacious backyard for relaxation. Dinner available by reservation. Water skiing nearby.

Hosts: Pat Clark and Wayne Hollingsworth
Rooms: 3 (PB) $50-75
Full Breakfast
Credit Cards: A, B, C
Notes: 2, 5, 9, 10, 11, 12, 14

BEAUFORT

TwoSuns Inn Bed and Breakfast

1705 Bay Street, 29902
(803) 522-1122; (800) 532-4244
FAX (803) 522-1122

Small, resident-host bed and breakfast overlooking the bay in a remarkably beautiful historic district midway between Charleston and Savannah. Panoramic bayview veranda, individually appointed king- or queen-size guest rooms, an informal afternoon "tea and toddy hour," and a sumptuous breakfast to begin the day. The setting is idyllic, the atmosphere casually elegant. The inn features collectibles and antiques in a restored 1917 grand home with modern personal, business, and handicap amenities. Children over 12 welcome. Smoking outside only. Rated by AAA, Mobil. Charter member of SCBBA.

Hosts: Carrol and Ron Kay
Rooms: 5 (PB) $105-129
Full Breakfast
Credit Cards: A, B, C
Notes: 2, 5, 7, 9, 10, 11, 12, 14

BENNETTSVILLE

The Breeden Inn and Carriage House

404 East Main Street, 29512
(803) 479-3665

Built in 1886, the romantic Breeden Inn is a beautifully restored Southern mansion.

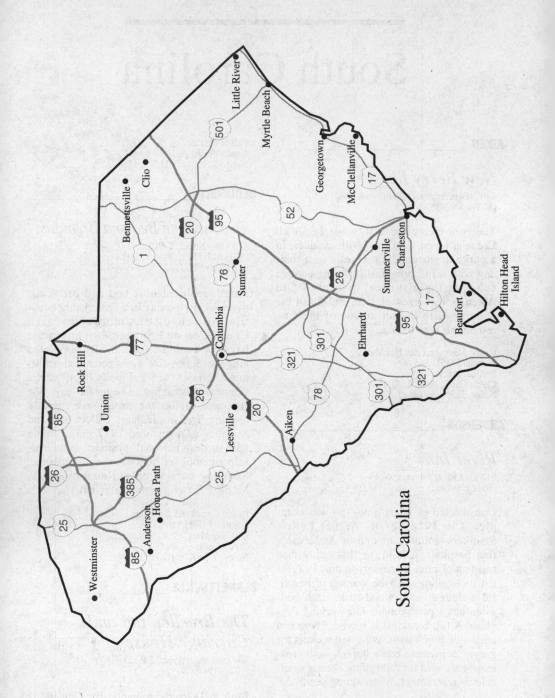

South Carolina

On two acres in the historic district, well-preserved architectural delights highlight the interior. Provides very comfortable and livable surroundings that capture interest and inspire imagination. Listed on the National Register of Historic Places, the inn is 20 minutes off I-95. A great halfway point between Florida and New York. The gathering room in the Carriage House and the great country kitchen, verandas, porticos and grounds—truly a Southern tradition—can be enjoyed at both houses. Beautiful antique decor, pool, cable TV in each room, phone in most rooms. A haven for antique lovers, runners, and walkers.

Hosts: Wesley and Bonnie Park
Rooms: 7 (PB) $65
Full Breakfast
Credit Cards: A, B, D
Notes: 2, 5, 7, 8, 10, 11, 12, 14

CHARLESTON

Ann Harper's Bed and Breakfast

56 Smith Street, 29401
(803) 723-3947

This circa 1870 home is in Charleston's historic district. Two rooms with connecting bath and sitting area with TV. The owner is a retired medical technologist and enjoys serving a full breakfast. Two-night minimum stay requested. Extra charge for single night. Smoking limited. Children over ten welcome.

Host: Ann D. Harper
Rooms: 2 (PB) $60-75
Full Breakfast
Credit Cards: None
Notes: 2, 5, 9, 10, 11, 12

Ashley Inn Bed and Breakfast

201 Ashley Avenue, 29403
(803) 723-1848

This circa 1832 historic home offers seven bedrooms, beautifully decorated with antique four-poster canopied beds. A place to be pampered and sleep in until the aroma of sizzling sausage and home-baked biscuits announces a full breakfast on the columned piazza overlooking the garden and fountain. Tour nearby historic sites on complimentary bicycles and return to more pampering with afternoon tea, sherry, and sumptuous home-baked goods. Private baths, color TV, off-street parking, and very special Southern hospitality. Rated three diamonds by AAA. Carolopous award 1995. Smoking on piazzas only. Children over 12 welcome.

Hosts: Bud and Sally Allen
Rooms: 7 (PB) $69-135
Full Breakfast
Credit Cards: A, B, C, D
Notes: 2, 5, 9, 10, 11, 12, 14

The Barksdale House Inn

27 George Street, 29401
(803) 577-4800

One of Charleston's most luxurious inns. A 215-year-old home featuring 14 individually designed rooms, five with whirlpool tubs and fireplaces. Flowers, daily newspaper, wine, champagne, tea, sherry, fountain in the courtyard, and off-street parking. Guests can enjoy a Continental breakfast served on silver in the privacy of their rooms or in the courtyard.

Hosts: George and Peggy Sloan
Rooms: 14 (PB) $80-160
Continental Breakfast
Credit Cards: A, B
Notes: 2, 5, 10, 11, 12, 14

The Battery Carriage House Inn (1843)

20 South Battery, 29401
(800) 775-5575

Stay in the carriage house of this landmark antebellum mansion at White Point Gardens (on the waterfront), the most elegant residential district of old and historic

Charleston. Eleven rooms. Ample street parking. Silver tray Continental breakfast in room or garden. Fluffy robes and towels. Turndown service. Afternoon refreshments. Quiet garden. Cable TV and HBO. Private steambaths. Whirlpool tubs. Friendly, professional staff. Described as "Simply the best," "European," "Romantic," and "An unforgettable Charleston experience." Highly recommended.

Host: Katharine Hastie
Rooms: 11 (PB) $79-199
Continental Breakfast
Credit Cards: A, B, C, D
Notes: 2, 5, 7, 9, 10, 11, 12, 14

Brasington House

The Belvedere

40 Rutledge Avenue, 29401
(803) 722-0973

A Colonial Revival mansion built in 1900 with an exquisite Adamesque interior taken from the circa 1800 Belvedere Plantation house. In the downtown historic district, on Colonial Lake, within walking distance of historical points of interest, restaurants, and shopping. Guests are welcome to use the public areas and piazzas in this romantic, beautifully restored and refurbished mansion. Closed December 1 to February 10.

Hosts: David S. Spell and Rick Zender
Rooms: 3 (PB) $110
Continental Breakfast
Credit Cards: None
Notes: 2, 7, 9, 10, 11, 12, 14

Brasington House Bed and Breakfast

328 East Bay Street, 29401
(803) 722-1274

Elegant accommodations in a splendidly restored Greek Revival Charleston single house, furnished with antiques, in Charleston's beautiful historic district. Four lovely, well-appointed guest rooms with central heat and air conditioning include private baths, telephones, cable TV, and tea-making services. King-, queen-, and twin-size beds available. Included is a bountiful family-style breakfast, wine and cheese served in the living room, liqueurs and chocolates available in the evening. Off-street parking.

Hosts: Dalton K. and Judy Brasington
Rooms: 4 (PB) $89-115
Full Breakfast
Credit Cards: A, B
Notes: 2, 5, 7, 9, 10, 11, 12

Cannonboro Inn Bed and Breakfast

184 Ashley Avenue, 29403
(803) 723-8572

Imagine sleeping in until the aroma of home-baked biscuits and freshly brewed coffee fills the air. Enjoy a savory sausage soufflé with fluffy zucchini cheddar biscuits overlooking a beautiful Low Country garden. Tour nearby historic sites on bicycles, then return in time for afternoon tea, coffee, and sherry with sumptuous baked goods. Enjoy warm Southern hospitality at Charleston's most special gourmet breakfast place. Smoking permitted on the piazza only. Children over 12 welcome.

Hosts: Bud and Sally Allen
Rooms: 6 (PB) $69-150
Full Breakfast
Credit Cards: A, B, C, D
Notes: 2, 5, 9, 10, 11, 12, 14

NOTES: Credit cards accepted: A MasterCard; B Visa; C American Express; D Discover; E Diners Club; F Other; 2 Personal checks accepted; 3 Lunch available; 4 Dinner available; 5 Open all year; 6 Pets welcome;

Country Victorian Bed and Breakfast

105 Tradd Street, 29401-2422
(803) 577-0682

Rooms have private entrances and contain antique iron and brass beds, old quilts, oak and wicker antique furniture, and braided rugs over the heart-of-pine floors. Homemade cookies will be waiting. The house, built in 1820, is within easy walking distance of restaurants, antique shops, churches, art galleries, museums, and all points of historical interest. Parking and bicycles are available for guests. Many extras are provided. Children over ten are welcome.

Host: Diane Deardurff Weed
Rooms: 2 (PB) $70-95
Continental Breakfast
Credit Cards: None
Notes: 2, 5, 7, 9, 10, 11, 12

1837 Bed and Breakfast and Tea Room

126 Wentworth Street, 29401
(803) 723-7166

These delightful accommodations are in a wealthy cotton planter's home and brick carriage house, now owned by two artists. In the center of the historic district, within walking distance of boat tours, old market, antique shops, restaurants, and main attractions. Full gourmet breakfast is served in the formal dining room or on the outside piazzas. Visit with others while enjoying such specialties as sausage pie, eggs Benedict, ham omelets, and home-baked breads (lemon, apple spice, banana, and cinnamon swirl). Afternoon tea is served. Canopied poster rice beds, verandas, rockers, and Southern hospitality. Limited smoking allowed.

Hosts: Sherri Weaver and Richard Dunn
Rooms: 8 (PB) $59-115
Full Breakfast
Credit Cards: A, B, C
Notes: 2, 5, 9, 10

Fulton Lane Inn

202 King Street, 29401
(803) 720-2600; (800) 720-2688

Set off King Street on a quiet pedestrian lane in the heart of the antique and historic district. Many rooms have cathedral ceilings or fireplaces, canopied beds, and large whirlpool baths to give a special romantic feeling of a bygone era. The gracious Southern hospitality includes a silver-service breakfast, wine and sherry, turndown with chocolates, and a newspaper. AAA four diamonds. Free parking. No smoking.

Host: Randall Felkel
Rooms: 27 (PB) $105-180
Continental Breakfast
Credit Cards: A, B
Notes: 2, 5, 7, 8, 9, 10, 11, 12, 14

Historic Charleston Bed and Breakfast

60 Broad Street, 29401
(803) 722-6606; (800) 743-3583

Representing more than 50 bed and breakfast properties in and around Charleston's historic district. Accommodations include private homes and carriage houses. Call for details.

John Rutledge House Inn

116 Broad Street, 29401
(803) 723-7999; (800) 476-9741

This national landmark was built in 1763 by John Rutledge, a framer and signer of the U.S. Constitution. Large rooms and suites in the main and carriage houses offer the ambience of historic Charleston. Rates include wine and sherry upon arrival, turndown service with brandy and chocolate, and breakfast with newspaper delivered to guests' room. Free parking. AAA-rated four diamonds. Historic Hotels of America.

Rooms: 19 (PB) $140-210
Continental Breakfast
Credit Cards: A, B, C
Notes: 2, 5, 7, 8, 9, 10, 11, 12, 14

7 No smoking; 8 Children welcome; 9 Social drinking allowed; 10 Tennis nearby; 11 Swimming nearby; 12 Golf nearby; 13 Skiing nearby; 14 May be booked through a travel agent.

King George IV Inn and Guests

32 George Street, 29401
(803) 723-9339

A Federal-style house in the historic district, four-stories tall with three levels of lovely Charleston porches. All rooms have fireplaces, either Federal or plain Gothic Revival, 10- or 12-foot ceilings, seven-foot windows, original lovely wide-planked hardwood floors, original eight-foot oak doors, architectural moldings and details, and antiques. Includes parking, air conditioning, private baths, refrigerators, and Continental breakfast. Smoking permitted outside only. Inquire about accommodations for pets. May be booked through a travel agent June through March.

Hosts: B.J., Mike, and Deb
Rooms: 8 (PB) $70-110
Continental Breakfast
Credit Cards: A, B
Notes: 2, 5, 7, 8, 9, 10, 11, 12, 13

Kings Courtyard Inn

198 King Street, 29401
(803) 723-7000; (800) 845-6119

Kings Courtyard Inn, circa 1853, is in the heart of the antique and historic district. Convenient to attractions, shops, and restaurants. Rate includes Continental breakfast and newspaper, and wine and sherry served in the lobby. Turndown service with chocolate and brandy. Free parking. AAA four diamonds. Historic Hotels of America. Double, king-, and queen-size beds and suites are available.

Host: Laura Howard
Rooms: 44 (PB) $110-180
Continental Breakfast
Credit Cards: A, B, C
Notes: 2, 5, 7, 8, 9, 10, 11, 12, 14

King's Inn

136 Tradd Street, 29401
(803) 577-3683

This private home in the historic district includes two bed and breakfast units with separate entrances. One has a full kitchen. The waterfront, antique shops, and house museums are minutes away. The entire historic area can be covered on foot. Enjoy blooming gardens and magnificent house tours in April, the international arts festival—Spoleto—in May, and warm beaches in June. The hostess is a registered tour guide for Charleston.

Host: Hazel King
Rooms: 2 (PB) $90-100
Continental Breakfast
Credit Cards: None
Notes: 2, 5, 7, 8, 9

The Kitchen House (Circa 1732)

126 Tradd Street, 29401
(803) 577-6362

Nestled in the heart of the historic district, the Kitchen House is a completely restored 18th-century dwelling. Southern hospitality and a decanter of sherry await guests' arrival. The refrigerator and pantry are stocked for breakfast. Absolute privacy, cozy fireplaces, antiques, patio, and Colonial herb gardens. This pre-Revolutionary home was featured in

The Kitchen House

NOTES: Credit cards accepted: A MasterCard; B Visa; C American Express; D Discover; E Diners Club; F Other; 2 Personal checks accepted; 3 Lunch available; 4 Dinner available; 5 Open all year; 6 Pets welcome;

Colonial Homes magazine and the *New York Times.* Complete concierge services.

Host: Lois Evans
Rooms: 3 (1 PB; 2 SB) $100-195
Full Breakfast
Credit Cards: A, B
Notes: 2, 5, 7, 8, 9, 10, 11, 12, 14

Maison DuPré

317 East Bay Street, 29401
(803) 723-8691; (800) 844-INNS

Three restored Charleston "single houses" and two carriage houses constitute Maison DuPré, originally built in 1804. The inn features period furniture and antiques and is in the historic Ansonborough district. Complimentary Continental breakfast and a Low Country tea party are served. "Maison DuPré, with its faded stucco, pink brick, and gray shutters is one of the city's best-looking small inns"—*New York Times.*

Hosts: Lucille, Bob, and Mark Mulholland
Rooms: 15 (PB) $98-200
Continental Breakfast
Credit Cards: A, B, C
Notes: 2, 5, 8, 9, 10, 11, 12, 14

Nineteen King Street Bed and Breakfast

19 King Street, 29401
(803) 723-3212

This pre-Revolutionary home is in the historic district just off the Battery. It offers two exquisite bedrooms with private baths that accommodate up to eight persons. French doors from each room lead to the piazza that offers harbor views. Both rooms are elegantly furnished with antiques and reproductions and are air-conditioned with fireplaces, cable TV, and telephones. Continental breakfast is served in the dining room. Daily and seasonal rates.

Hosts: Marie and Emerson B. Read
Rooms: 2 (PB) $95-115
Continental Breakfast
Notes: 2, 5, 8, 9, 10, 11, 12

133 Broad Street Bed and Breakfast

133 Broad Street, 29401
(803) 577-5965

The house, circa 1870, is in the heart of Charleston's historic district and within walking distance to everything. Three guest suites are tastefully furnished in Victorian period decor and antiques. All suites have bedroom, sitting room, small kitchen, and private bath. Guests have full use of piazzas and walled garden. All suites are fully air-conditioned and have TVs. Elevator in the house, and off-street parking provided.

Hosts: Doll and Jim Ward
Suites: 3 (PB) $100-120
Continental Breakfast
Credit Cards: None
Notes: 5, 7, 9, 10, 11, 12

The Planters Inn

112 North Market Street, 29401
(803) 722-2345; (800) 845-7082

The Planters Inn is in the center of Charleston's 800-acre historic district, steps away from landmark houses, gardens, and the waterfront park. The newly renovated inn has 41 spacious rooms and suites featuring high ceilings, oversized private baths, and large closets. Guests are treated to a silver-service breakfast, refreshments each afternoon in the lobby, and turndown service every night.

Host: Larry Spelts
Rooms: 41 (PB) $90-175
Continental Breakfast
Credit Cards: A, B, C, D, E
Notes: 3, 4, 5, 8, 9, 10, 11, 12, 14

R.S.V.P. Savannah: Bed and Breakfast Reservation Service

9489 Whitfield Avenue
Box 49, Savannah, GA 31406
(912) 232-7789; (800) 729-7787

All accommodations are in historic homes or old cotton warehouses within walking distance to major museums, parks, shops, churches, restaurants, and waterfront areas in Georgia (Savannah, Tybee Island, and Brunswick) and South Carolina (Charleston and Beaufort). The agent has been in every room in each inn and will help with accommodations and provide maps and information on tours, restaurants, etc. Included are 15 hosted private homes, 20 bed and breakfast inns, and 8 unhosted accommodations. Discounts vary for children under twelve. Many provide sleeper-sofas or cots. Discount for seven days or more. $60-285.

Rutledge Victorian Inn and Guest House

114 Rutledge Avenue, 29401
(803) 722-7551

Elegant old Charleston house in the downtown historic district. This century-old house with decorative Italianate architecture was originally the Brodie-Pinkussohn House. All rooms have fireplaces, 12-foot ceilings, hardwood floors, 10-foot doors and windows, and antiques. Lovely round porch overlooks the park and Roman columns, the remains of the Confederate Soldiers Reunion Hall. Relaxed atmosphere, air conditioning, private baths, parking, TVs, and formal dining room with refreshments and Continental plus breakfast. A five- to twenty-minute walk to all historic sights. Inquire about accommodations for pets. Smoking permitted on porches only. Water skiing nearby.

Hosts: Linda, Lynn, B.J., and Mike
Rooms: 10 (7 PB; 3 SB) $55-110
Continental Breakfast
Credit Cards: A, B
Notes: 2, 5, 8, 9, 10, 11, 12, 14

Thirty-Six Meeting Street

36 Meeting Street, 29401
(803) 722-1034; FAX (803) 723-0068

Built in 1740, this pre-Revolutionary War single house offers three elegant suites in the heart of the historic district a block and a half from the Battery. Each suite is elegantly furnished with rice beds, kitchenette, and private bath. Guests can enjoy the private walled garden for breakfast or after a day of sightseeing. Continental breakfast and bicycles available for guests.

Host: Anne Brandt
Rooms: 3 (PB) $75-125
Continental Breakfast
Credit Cards: A, B
Notes: 2, 5, 7, 8, 9, 10, 11, 12

Two Meeting Street Inn

2 Meeting Street, 29401
(803) 723-7322

"The Belle of Charleston's bed and breakfasts." This Queen Anne Victorian mansion, circa 1890-92, has welcomed guests for more than 50 years. In the historic district overlooking the Battery, the inn charms its visitors with exquisite Tiffany windows, canopied beds, Oriental rugs, and English antiques. The day starts with freshly baked muffins served in the oak-covered dining room or courtyard, and ends with evening sherry on the wraparound piazza. The epitome of Southern hospitality and turn-of-the-century luxury. Two-night minimum stay requested for weekends and holidays. Water skiing nearby.

Hosts: The Spell Family
Rooms: 9 (PB) $120-225
Continental Breakfast
Credit Cards: None
Notes: 7, 10, 11, 12

Two Meeting Street

Victoria House Inn

208 King Street, 29401
(803) 720-2944; (800) 933-5464

Built in 1889, this Romanesque-style building has 16 elegantly renovated guest rooms. Modern amenities are provided in every room, including a stocked refrigerator. Guests receive evening turndown service, and wine and sherry is served in the lobby. Continental breakfast and newspaper delivered to the room each morning. Free on-site parking is available. AAA four diamonds.

Host: Randall Felkel
Rooms: 16 (PB) $125-160
Continental Breakfast
Credit Cards: A, B
Notes: 5, 6, 7, 8, 9, 10, 11, 12, 14

Villa de la Fontaine Bed and Breakfast

138 Wentworth Street, 29401
(803) 577-7709

Villa de la Fontaine is a columned Greek Revival mansion in the heart of the historic district. It was built in 1838 and boasts a three-quarter-acre garden with fountain and terraces. Restored to impeccable condition, it is furnished with museum-quality furniture and accessories. The hosts are retired ASID interior designers and have decorated the rooms with 18th-century American antiques. Several of the rooms feature canopied beds. Breakfast is prepared by a master chef who prides himself on serving a different menu every day. Off-street parking. Minimum-stay requirements for weekends and holidays. The inn offers guests a choice among its four rooms and two suites. Inquire about rates for four guests or family.

Hosts: William Fontaine and Aubrey Hancock
Rooms: 6 (PB) $100-120
Full Breakfast
Credit Cards:None
Notes: 2, 5, 7, 9, 10, 11, 12

CLIO

The Henry Bennett House

301 Red Bluff Street, 29525
(803) 586-2701

A turn-of-the-century Queen Anne Victorian in the historic district. Enormous wraparound veranda where guests can sit and enjoy a cool summer breeze or go to the back yard and enjoy a swim. Gracious entrance foyer with a two-landing stairway with detailed and decorative woodwork dowels, spindles, and paneling. Working fireplace in each guest room. The countryside is rural, quiet, and peaceful.

Rooms: 3 (SB) $50
Full Breakfast
Credit Cards: A, B
Notes: 2, 4, 5, 6, 8, 9, 11, 12

COLUMBIA

Claussen's Inn

2003 Greene Street, 29205
(803) 765-0440; (800) 622-3382

Restored bakery, circa 1928, listed on the National Register of Historic Places and within walking distance of shopping, restaurants, and entertainment. Luxurious rooms with private baths, outdoor Jacuzzi, and four-poster beds. Rates include a Continental breakfast delivered to the room, complimentary wine and sherry, turndown service with chocolates and brandy, and a newspaper.

Host: Dan O. Vance
Rooms: 29 (PB) $105-120
Continental Breakfast
Credit Cards: A, B, C
Notes: 5, 7, 8, 9, 10, 12, 14

EHRHARDT

Ehrhardt Hall Inn

South Broadway, P.O. Box 246, 29081
(803) 267-2020

A stay at the Ehrhardt Hall is a return to the elegance of yesterday. The inn has been

7 No smoking; 8 Children welcome; 9 Social drinking allowed; 10 Tennis nearby; 11 Swimming nearby;
12 Golf nearby; 13 Skiing nearby; 14 May be booked through a travel agent.

restored to its original grandeur. It is reminiscent of an era when graciousness and thoughtfulness were a way of life. All rooms are oversized with ceiling fans, armoires, sitting areas, private baths, color TV, fireplaces, and central heat and air conditioning. Indoor pool, large spa, gym, and dry sauna. Tennis and golf nearby.

Host: Gwen Varn
Rooms: 6 (PB) $50-90
Continental Breakfast
Credit Cards: A, B, C
Notes: 5, 7, 10, 11, 12, 14

GEORGETOWN

The International Bed and Breakfast Club, Inc.

504 Amherst Street, Buffalo, NY 14207
(800) 723-4262; FAX (716) 873-4462

SC4821PP. This West Indies-style home was built in 1790 in the historic district of Georgetown. Quality craftsmanship and elegant furnishings. Public rooms include a large drawing room with fireplace, a parlor/game room, a beautiful dining room, and a wraparound veranda facing gardens and historic homes. All guest rooms feature early Colonial furnishings and private baths. Cottage with Jacuzzi. Available for meetings and social gatherings. Gourmet breakfast. Evening refreshments served. Smoking on veranda and patio. Special rates and discounts available. $70-115.

1790 House

630 Highmarket Street, 29440
(803) 546-4821

Meticulously restored, this 200-year-old Colonial plantation-style inn is in the heart of historic Georgetown. Spacious, luxurious rooms with sitting areas and central heat and air. Stay in the Rice Planters Room, the beautiful romantic cottage with Jacuzzi tub, or in one of the other lovely rooms. Gourmet breakfasts. Walk to shops, restau-

rants, and historic sights. Just a short drive to Brookgreen Gardens, Myrtle Beach, and Grand Strand—a golfer's paradise. One hour to Charleston. Rated excellent by ABBA, three diamonds by AAA and Mobil.

Hosts: John and Patricia Wiley
Rooms: 6 (PB) $75-115
Full Breakfast
Credit Cards: A, B, C, D
Notes: 2, 5, 7, 8, 9, 10, 12, 14

The Shaw House

The Shaw House

613 Cypress Court, 29440
(803) 546-9663

Lovely view overlooking Willowbank Marsh; wonderful bird watching. Many antiques throughout the house; rocking chairs on porch. Within walking distance of the historic district and many wonderful restaurants. Fresh fruits and Southern breakfast. One-hour drive to Myrtle Beach or Charleston.

Hosts: Mary and Joe Shaw
Rooms: 3 (PB) $60
Full Breakfast
Credit Cards: C
Notes: 2, 5, 8, 9, 10, 11, 12, 14

"ShipWright's"

609 Cypress Court, 29440
(803) 527-4475

Serving tourists or boaters. Transportation from intracoastal waterways provided.

Quiet, spacious with a tasteful decor of heirlooms and antiques. Experience the breathtaking view of the Avenue of Live Oaks and the Alive Marshes of the Black River while rocking on the large porch or gazing out the parlor window. Taste Grandma Eicher's pancakes, freshly ground coffee, and fresh fruit. Guests say, "I feel like I just visited my best friend." AAA approved.

Host: Leatrice Wright
Rooms: 2 (PB) $55
Full Breakfast
Credit Cards: None
Notes: 2, 5, 7, 8, 9, 10, 11, 12

HILTON HEAD ISLAND

Ambiance

8 Wren Drive, 29928
(803) 671-4981

Marny welcomes guests to sunny Hilton Head Island. This cypress home, nestled in subtropical surroundings, is in Sea Pines Plantation. Ambiance reflects the hostess's interior decorating business by the same name. All the amenities of Hilton Head are offered in a contemporary, congenial atmosphere. The climate is favorable year-round for all sports. Ambiance is across the street from a beautiful beach and the Atlantic Ocean. Smoking outside only.

Host: Marny Kridel Daubenspeck
Rooms: 2 (PB) $70-75
Continental Breakfast
Credit Cards: None
Notes: 2, 5, 7, 9, 10, 11, 12, 14

HONEA PATH

Sugarfoot Castle's Bed and Breakfast

211 South Main Street, 29654
(803) 369-6565

Enormous trees umbrella this circa 1880 brick Victorian home. Fresh flowers grace the 14-inch-thick walled rooms furnished

Sugarfoot Castle

with family heirlooms. Enjoy the living room's interesting collection or the library's comfy chairs, TV, VCR, books, fireplace, desk, and game table. Upon rising, guests will find coffee outside their doors, followed by a breakfast of fresh fruit, cereal, hot breads, and beverages served in the dining room by candlelight. Rock away the world's cares on the screened porch overlooking peaceful gardens. Children over ten welcome.

Hosts: Cecil and Gale Evans
Rooms: 3 (SB) $48-51
Continental Breakfast
Credit Cards: A, B
Notes: 2, 5, 7, 9, 10, 11, 12

LEESVILLE

Able House Inn

244 East Columbia Avenue, 29072
(803) 532-2763

Chateau estate, ten miles from I-20 on Route 1, 30 minutes from Columbia. Choose from five guest rooms, each with private bath. Living room, sunroom, swimming pool, and patio are available to guests. Fresh popcorn and soft drinks each evening. Smoking restricted.

Hosts: Annabelle and Jack Wright
Rooms: 5 (PB) $55-60
Continental Breakfast
Credit Cards: A, B
Notes: 2, 5, 9, 11, 12

7 No smoking; 8 Children welcome; 9 Social drinking allowed; 10 Tennis nearby; 11 Swimming nearby; 12 Golf nearby; 13 Skiing nearby; 14 May be booked through a travel agent.

LITTLE RIVER _____

Stella's Guest Home

P.O. Box 564, Highway 17, 29566
(803) 249-1871

Sometimes something different can be best, and when planning a trip to South Carolina's Grand Strand, guests are invited to stay with Stella. All of the guest rooms and suites are charmingly, tastefully, and luxuriously decorated and offer private baths, entrances, and color cable TV. Guests will find Stella's Guest Home to be genuinely convivial and welcoming. The hosts consider each guest a visiting friend and take a personal interest in their enjoyment.

Hosts: Mr. and Mrs. Lamb
Suites: 3 (PB) $30-50
No Breakfast
Credit Cards: None
Notes: 2, 5, 12

McCLELLANVILLE _____

Laurel Hill Plantation

8913 North Highway 17, P.O. Box 190, 29458
(803) 887-3708

Laurel Hill faces the Intracoastal Waterway and the Atlantic Ocean. Porches provide a scenic view of marshes and creeks. The house is furnished in charming country and primitive antiques that reflect the Low

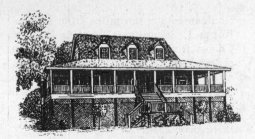

Laurel Hill Plantation

Country lifestyle. Thirty miles north of Charleston, and only 60 miles south of Myrtle Beach. Smoking is allowed in restricted areas only.

Hosts: Jackie and Lee Morrison
Rooms: 4 (PB) $65-95
Full Breakfast
Credit Cards: A, B
Notes: 2, 5, 9, 10, 11, 12, 14

MYRTLE BEACH _____

Serendipity

407 71st Avenue North, 29572
(803) 449-5268; (800) 762-3229

Award-winning Spanish-style inn. Unique, elegant, and secluded. Only 300 yards from 60 miles of white sand beaches. Amenities include an outdoor hot tub, heated pool, shuffle board, Ping-Pong table, and gas grill. Choice of five queen-size, two master doubles, seven studios, or two suites. Air conditioning, TVs, refrigerators, and private baths in all rooms. Close to all of the country theaters, more than 70 golf courses, tennis, deep-sea fishing, and great shopping.

Hosts: Terry and Sheila Johnson
Rooms: 14 (PB) $45-110
Continental Breakfast
Credit Cards: A, B, C
Notes: 5, 8, 9, 10, 11, 12, 14

ROCK HILL _____

East Main Guest House

600 East Main Street, 29730
(803) 366-1161

In the downtown historic district, this Craftsman-style bungalow has been completely renovated and has been beautifully decorated. Guest rooms include private baths, cable TV, telephones, fireplaces, and queen-size beds. The Honeymoon Suite has a canopied bed and a whirlpool tub. A TV/sitting/game room is provided, and breakfast is served in the beautifully appointed dining room or under the patio pergola. AAA three-diamond rated.

Hosts: Jerry and Melba Peterson
Rooms: 3 (PB) $59-79
Continental Breakfast
Credit Cards: A, B
Notes: 2, 5, 7, 9, 10, 11, 12, 14

SUMMERVILLE

Bed and Breakfast of Summerville

304 South Hampton Street, 29483
(803) 871-5275

Sleep in the slave quarters of an 1862 house in a quiet historic district. Near restaurants and antique and speciality shops. Queen-size bed, telephone, TV, kitchenette, bath with shower, bikes, and pool. Short drive to Charleston, Middleton and Magnolia Gardens. Winter breakfast is self-prepared from the stocked refrigerator. For the rest of the year, breakfast in the greenhouse is an option. Advance reservation, please. Winter monthly rental is also available.

Hosts: Dusty and Emmagene Rhodes
Room: 1 (PB) $45-50
Continental Breakfast
Credit Cards: None
Notes: 2, 5, 9, 10, 11, 12

SUMTER

Bed and Breakfast of Sumter

6 Park Avenue, 29150
(803) 773-2903

Featured in the *New York Times* and *Sandlapper* magazine, this restored 1896 Prairie-style home sits in the heart of Sumter's historic district across from Memorial Park. Large front porch with swings and rocking chairs. Gracious guest rooms with antiques, fireplaces, all private baths. Formal Victorian parlor and TV sitting room. Cable. Fax. Gourmet breakfast

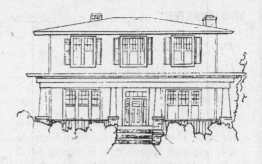

Bed and Breakfast of Sumter

(fruit, entrée, home-baked breads). Antique shops, Swan Lake, and golf courses are all close by. The inn is rated three diamonds by AAA. Smoking is permitted on the porch only.

Hosts: Jess and Suzanne Begley
Rooms: 5 (PB) $55-70
Full Breakfast
Credit Cards: A, B
Notes: 2, 5, 9, 10, 12, 14

UNION

The Inn at Merridun

100 Merridun Place, 29379
(803) 427-7052 (phone and FAX)

This 1855 Greek Revival mansion has many interesting architectural details and is on nine wooded acres, yet it is only a five-minute walk to downtown. Don't miss the opportunity to exercise the rockers on the marble verandas and have a picture taken on the curved stairway with or without J.D., the inn cat. Evening desserts and beverages and a full country gourmet breakfast are all included in the rates; dinners are available by prior appointment at an additional charge. The inn is also available for weddings, private meetings, and catered functions.

Hosts: Jim and Peggy Waller
Rooms: 5 (PB) $75-100
Full Breakfast
Credit Cards: None
Notes: 2, 3, 4, 5, 7, 9, 10, 12, 14

7 No smoking; 8 Children welcome; 9 Social drinking allowed; 10 Tennis nearby; 11 Swimming nearby; 12 Golf nearby; 13 Skiing nearby; 14 May be booked through a travel agent.

WESTMINSTER

Fieldstone Farm Bed and Breakfast

640 Fieldstone Farm Road, 29693
(803) 882-5651

Fieldstone Farm is an 1870s plantation-style home on 85 acres, nine miles from Clemson and one mile from scenic Highway 11. It offers cozy bedrooms with fireplaces, private baths, and complimentary wine. A full gourmet breakfast is served in the room or in the parlor. Enjoy the outdoor hot tub, fishing on the pond, walking trails, cattle, and horses. Nearby state parks, antiques, white-water rafting, and Clemson University athletics. Children over 12 are welcome.

Rooms: 2 (PB) $95
Full Breakfast
Credit Cards: None
Notes: 2, 5, 9, 10, 12

South Dakota

BRUCE

The International Bed and Breakfast

504 Amherst Street, Buffalo, NY 14207
(800) 723-4262; FAX (716) 873-4462

SD9200PP. Quiet country atmosphere. Built in 1908 in rural Brookings County in east central South Dakota. A home away from home for travelers, hunters, and fishermen. Four comfortable rooms, shared baths, and complete breakfasts provided. The inn also features a TV/game room and on-site laundry facilities. Convenient to the Laura Ingalls Wilder Museum and Pageant, the Summer Arts Festival at Brookings, and South Dakota State University. In addition to the full breakfast included in the room rate, other meals are available. Children are welcome. $35.

CANOVA

Skoglund Farm

Route 1, Box 45, 57321
(605) 247-3445

Enjoy the prairie: cattle, fowl, peacocks, a home-cooked evening meal, and full breakfast. Visit nearby attractions: Little House on the Prairie, Corn Palace, Doll House, and Prairie Village. Relax, hike, and enjoy a family farm. Rate includes evening meal and breakfast: $30 for adults; $20 for teens; $15 for children; children five and under free.

Hosts: Alden and Delores Skoglund
Rooms: 5 (SB) $30
Full Breakfast
Credit Cards: None
Notes: 2, 3, 4, 5, 6, 8, 9, 10, 11, 12, 14

CHAMBERLAIN

Riverview Ridge

HC69 Box 82A, 57325
(605) 734-6084

Contemporary home built on a bluff overlooking a scenic bend in the Missouri River. King- and queen-size beds, full breakfast, and secluded country peace and quiet are all available. Just three and one-half miles north of downtown Chamberlain on Highway 50. Enjoy outdoor recreation; visit museums, Indian reservations, and casinos; or just make this a special home away from home.

Hosts: Frank and Alta Cable
Rooms: 3 (1 PB; 2 SB) $50-60
Full Breakfast
Credit Cards: None
Notes: 2, 5, 7, 8, 9, 11, 12

CROOKS

Janet's Country Homestead

47016 256 Street, 57020
(605) 543-5232

Old-fashioned family farm home in the rolling countryside. Close to South Dakota's largest city. Enjoy a walk in the fresh, clean air or sit on the patio and absorb the peace and quiet. Many attractions nearby. Guests will find a friendly and gracious welcome plus good conversation. Hosts offer down-home hospitality at its best.

Hosts: Leonard and Janet Johnson
Rooms: 2 (SB) $45-50
Full Breakfast
Credit Cards: None
Notes: 2, 5, 6, 7, 8, 10, 11, 12

7 No smoking; 8 Children welcome; 9 Social drinking allowed; 10 Tennis nearby; 11 Swimming nearby; 12 Golf nearby; 13 Skiing nearby; 14 May be booked through a travel agent.

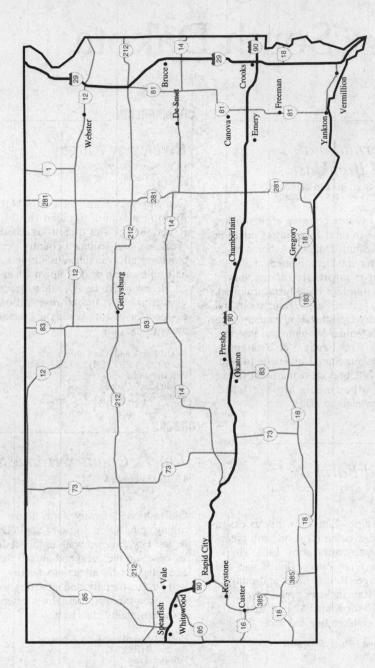

South Dakota

Custer Mansion

CUSTER

Custer Mansion Bed and Breakfast

35 Centennial Drive, 57730
(605) 673-3333

Historic 1891 Victorian Gothic home listed on the National Register of Historic Places. Features a blend of Victorian elegance and country charm with Western hospitality. Clean, quiet accommodations and delicious home-cooked breakfasts. Central to all of the Black Hills attractions, such as Mount Rushmore, Custer State Park, and Crazy Horse Memorial. Recommended by *Bon Appétit*, and Mobil travel guide.

Hosts: Mill and Carole Seaman
Rooms: 6 (4 PB; 1 SB) $50-90
Full Breakfast
Credit Cards: None
Notes: 2, 5, 7, 8, 10, 11, 12, 13, 14

DE SMET

The Prairie House Manor

Rural Route 2, Box 61A, 57231
(605) 854-9131; (800) 297-2416

This bed and breakfast is in the hometown of Laura Ingalls Wilder and welcomes many international guests. The rooms have private baths, TV, and air conditioning. Two doors away from Laura Ingalls Wilder attractions. The Rose Garden and Americana Medley are family rooms with two or more beds. Chantilly Lace and Here's My Heart give couples an inexpensive evening. Full hot, hearty breakfast. The summer tea room is open from June through August. Pies and light lunches served daily except Sundays. Homey atmosphere.

Hosts: Larry and Connie Cheney
Rooms: 4 (PB) $35-60
Full Breakfast
Credit Cards: None
Notes: 2, 3, 6, 7, 8, 9, 10, 11, 12, 14

EMERY

The Emery House Bed and Breakfast

301 North Seventh Street, 57332
(605) 449-4855

Relive the charm of an era gone by in this turn-of-the-century home in America's Heartland. Enjoy coffee on the balcony that overlooks the sloping hills of southeastern South Dakota. Soak in the huge claw-foot bathtub after a day of scenic tours or shopping in the region's finest shopping center, only minutes away. A formal parlor and dining room lend a touch of elegance to the prairie. Lunch and dinner available.

Hosts: Colonel and Greta Echols
Rooms: 3 (1 PB; 2 SB) $40-55
Full Breakfast
Credit Cards: None
Notes: 2, 5, 7, 8, 9, 10, 11, 12, 13

FREEMAN

Farmers Inn

Route 2, Box 39-W, 57029
(605) 925-7580

The Farmers Inn is in a rural setting along US 81. It is a Midwestern four-square built

NOTES: Credit cards: A MasterCard; B Visa; C American Express; D Discover; E Diners Club; F Other;
2 Personal checks accepted; 3 Lunch available; 4 Dinner available; 5 Open all year; 6 Pets welcome;
7 No smoking; 8 Children welcome; 9 Social drinking allowed; 10 Tennis nearby; 11 Swimming nearby;
12 Golf nearby; 13 Skiing nearby; 14 May be booked through a travel agent.

in 1914 furnished with antiques that have been collected over 35 years. Features a fitness center, sauna, and crafts. Accommodations include a three-room Victorian suite with refrigerator, the Country Room with two single beds, the Native American Room with double bed and private balcony, and an attic hideaway with double whirlpool tub. The rooms are furnished with telephones, TV, and private baths and are air-conditioned. Inquire about accommodations for children.

Hosts: MarJean and Russell Waltner
Rooms: 4 (PB) $40-65
Full Breakfast
Credit Cards: None
Notes: 2, 3, 4, 5, 7, 9, 10, 11, 12

Golden Robin Nest

1210 East 4th Street, 57029
(605) 925-4410

Enjoy a quiet Christian atmosphere, hosted by a mature couple in a small town. Enter via family room, play games and the piano, or watch TV. Steps from this room lead to guest rooms. Freeman is 35 miles north of Yankton (Gavin's Point Dam), 45 miles from Sioux Falls (winter skiing), and Mitchell (balloon races, Doll Museum, Corn Palace) is 55 miles away. Inquire about accommodations for pets.

Hosts: Goldie and Bob Boese
Rooms: 2 (SB) $30
Full Breakfast
Credit Cards: None
Notes: 2, 5, 7, 8, 10, 11, 12, 13

GETTYSBURG

Harer Lodge
Bed and Breakfast

Rural Route 1, Box 87A, 57442
(605) 765-2167; (800) 283-3356

Set in a prairie where buffalo once roamed, this modern cedar lodge has a miniature golf course, miniature horses, farm ani-

mals, and five lovely guest rooms, all with private baths. Enjoy the recreation room, reading room, fresh flowers in every room, and coffee and cookies when guests arrive. An authentic Native American tepee is available for campers, and a separate honeymoon cottage, done in romantic wispy white with an oversized Jacuzzi set in the floor, is available for newlyweds and anniversaries. The honeymoon suite has sliding glass doors leading from the bathroom to a small private garden, complete with a porch swing and lots of privacy. Lunch and beverage served by candlelight, and breakfast is served in the cottage. Country store with South Dakota crafts, antiques, and a sweet shop is in a cream station/store restored on premises.

Hosts: Norma and Don Harer
Rooms: 5 (PB) $45-65
Cottage: 1 (PB) $75
Full Breakfast
Credit Cards: A, B
Notes: 2, 3, 4, 5, 8, 9, 11, 12, 14

GREGORY

Gray House Inn
Bed 'n' Breakfast

Rural Route 2, East Highway 18, 57533
(605) 835-8479

Hosts encourage guests to enjoy their stay in this spacious eight-bedroom inn, six of which have private baths. Four of the bedrooms are on the main floor and four are on the second floor; both have decks to walk out on so that guests can enjoy the clean air of South Dakota. Conveniently along Highway 18, just 25 miles from the Missouri River and in the heart of pheasant country, this inn is known for its comfort and South Dakota hospitality.

Hosts: Bruce and Alice Shaffer
Rooms: 8 (6 PB; 2 SB) $47
Full Breakfast
Credit Cards: A, B
Notes: 2, 5, 7, 8, 9, 11, 12, 14

KEYSTONE

Bed and Breakfast Inn

208 First Street, 57751
(605) 666-4490

This historic home can be found just three miles from Mount Rushmore in Old Keystone. Two bedroom units available, cable TV, air conditioning, and king- or queen-size beds. AAA-rated and member of BBISD. Off season rates available from September 10 through May 25. Families welcome. Pets welcome at an extra charge. Call for rates.

Hosts: Delbert and Wanda Wilhelms
Rooms: 7 (PB)
Continental Breakfast
Credit Cards: A, B, D
Notes: 5, 7, 8, 9

OKATON

Prairie Rose

HC 74, Box 16, 57562
(800) 705-1165

Relax away from it all in the bunkhouse on a working ranch. Seven miles from I-90. Children and pets welcome. Minutes away from world-famous Pioneer Auto Museum. Between Corn Palace at Mitchell and the Black Hills. Tennis, swimming, and golf are 17 miles away.

Hosts: Mel and Clarice Roghair
Rooms: 2 (SB) $50
Full Breakfast
Credit Cards: None
Notes: 2, 3, 4, 5, 6, 8

PRESHO

Sweeney's Bed and Breakfast

132 Main Avenue, P.O. Box 340, 57568-0340
(605) 895-2586

This bed and breakfast is halfway between Sioux Falls and Rapid City on I-90 in central South Dakota. Newly redecorated 1900s home. Very homey and comfortable. Pheasant hunting is a top priority in Lyman County. Hunters welcome. Dogs may be kept outside.

Hosts: Paul and Wanda Sweeney
Rooms: 2 (SB) $50
Full Breakfast
Credit Cards: None
Notes: 2, 5, 7, 8, 9, 10, 11, 12

RAPID CITY

Abend Haus Cottage and Audrie's Cranbury Corner Bed and Breakfast

23029 Thunderhead Falls Road, 57702-8524
(605) 342-7788

The Black Hills "inn place." Ultimate in charm and Old World hospitality, this country home and five-acre estate is surrounded by thousands of acres of national forest. Thirty miles from Mount Rushmore and seven miles from Rapid City. Each quiet, comfortable suite and cottage has a private entrance, private bath, hot tub, patio, cable TV, and refrigerator. Free trout fishing, biking, and hiking on site.

Hosts: Hank and Audry Kuhnhauser
Rooms: 6 (PB) $85
Full Breakfast
Credit Cards: None
Notes: 2, 5, 9, 10, 11, 12, 13

Abend Haus

---

7 No smoking; 8 Children welcome; 9 Social drinking allowed; 10 Tennis nearby; 11 Swimming nearby; 12 Golf nearby; 13 Skiing nearby; 14 May be booked through a travel agent.

Anemarie's Country Bed and Breakfast

10430 Big Piney Road, 57702
(605) 343-9234

Escape to tranquility. Anemarie's combines the essence of European style with contemporary convenience. The inn lies nestled against the Black Hills forest off Highway 44. Spacious suites have private deck entrances, individual hot tubs, TV, VCR, refrigerator, and memorable breakfasts served to suite. A haven for recreational and business travelers alike. Smoking is limited to decks.

Hosts: Cathy and Randy Blaseg
Rooms: 4 (PB) $65-90
Full Breakfast
Credit Cards: None
Notes: 2, 5, 8, 9, 10, 11, 12, 13, 14

Bed and Breakfast Western Adventure

P.O. Box 4308, Bozeman, MT 59772
(406) 585-0057; FAX (406) 585-2869

403. This beautiful, large log country inn sits at the back of an expansive lawn with mature trees and is visible from the highway. There are several cozy sitting areas around the massive stone fireplace. Six tastefully decorated rooms have a variety of sleeping arrangements, all with private baths. Wildlife can be spotted by a leisurely walk around the grounds. Thirty minutes from Mount Rushmore, Custer State Park, gambling in the city of Deadwood, and downhill skiing. Outdoor hot tub. Conference facilities. Special honeymoon suite with private indoor hot tub. Full breakfast. No smoking. Cat on premises. $65-99.

Hotel Alex Johnson

523 Sixth Street, P.O. Box 20, 57701
(800) 888-2539

Visit the Hotel Alex Johnson and stay at a historic landmark. There are 141 newly restored guest rooms. Old World charm combined with award-winning hospitality, this legend offers a piece of Old West history in the heart of downtown Rapid City. Listed on the National Register of Historic Places. Nonsmoking rooms available.

Rooms: 141 (PB) $58-88
Full Breakfast
Credit Cards: A, B, C, D, E
Notes: 2, 3, 4, 5, 8, 9, 10, 12, 13, 14

Willow Springs Cabins

11515 Sheridan Lake Road, 57702
(605) 342-3665

Private one-room log cabins in the beautiful Black Hills National Forest. This secluded setting offers privacy like no other retreat. Each cabin is charmingly decorated with many antique treasures and extras. Breakfast is wonderful, featuring freshly ground coffee, juices, baked goods, and egg dishes served in the privacy of the cabin. Hiking, swimming, private hot tub, and fishing abound. Featured in *Country Living* magazine, October 1993.

Hosts: Joyce and Russell Payton
Cabins: 2 (PB) $90-100
Full Breakfast
Credit Cards: A, B
Notes: 2, 5, 7, 8, 9, 10, 11, 12, 13, 14

SPEARFISH

Eighth Street Inn Bed and Breakfast

735 Eighth Street, 57783
(605) 642-9812; (800) 642-9812

This Queen Anne-style home, circa 1900, is conveniently off I-90. Listed on the National Register of Historic Places, the home is filled with family heirlooms that possess not only beauty but character as well. Nestled among large shade trees, the front wraparound porch is the perfect spot to sip iced tea and relax in the shade. Guests will find a main floor bedroom with private bath or three second-floor rooms that share two baths. Each room has special features such as bay windows, brass beds, and cozy comforters, and the entire inn is flooded with sunlight during the day. Within walking distance to the downtown shopping district, restaurants, antiques shops, parks, and the historic fish hatchery.

Hosts: Brad and Sandy Young
Rooms: 5 (2 PB: 3 SB) $55-85
Full Breakfast
Credit Cards: A, B
Notes: 2, 5, 7, 8, 9, 10, 11, 12, 13, 14

WEBSTER

Lakeside Farm Bed and Breakfast

Rural Route 2, Box 52, 57274
(605) 486-4430

Guests are invited to sample a bit of country life at Lakeside Farm. Feel free to explore the grove, barns, and pastures, or just relax with a cup of tea in the farmhouse. Accommodations for four to five guests on the second floor. The second-floor bathroom and shower serve both guest rooms. Children welcome. In northeastern South Dakota with museums featuring pioneer and Native American culture. Fort Sisseton nearby. No smoking or alcoholic beverages.

Hosts: Glenn and Joy Hagen
Rooms: 2 (SB) $40
Full Breakfast
Credit Cards: None
Notes: 2, 5, 7, 8, 12, 14

VALE

Dakota Shepherd Bed and Breakfast

Route 3, Box 25C 57788
(605) 456-2836

Experience country life at its best on an authentic South Dakota sheep farm/ranch. Twenty miles north of Sturgis, along Highway 79. Modern ranch house with four guest rooms, 1940s furnishings, family heirlooms, and country charm. Near historic Bismarck Trail and Bear Butte State Park. Perfect for artists and photographers.

Hosts: Robert and Sheryl Trohkimoinen
Rooms: 4 (2 PB; 2 SB) $65-100
Full Breakfast
Credit Cards: A, B
Notes: 2, 4, 5, 7, 8, 12, 13, 14

VERMILLION

The Goebel House Bed and Breakfast

102 Franklin, 57069
(605) 624-6691

A friendly old home built in 1916 and furnished with antiques and collectibles. Vermillion is home of the nationally known Shrine to Music Museum and the University of South Dakota. Four bedrooms grace the upper chambers and have both private and shared baths. Each room is individually decorated with furniture and mementos of the past.

Hosts: Don and Pat Goebel
Rooms: 4 (2 PB; 2 SB) $45-50
Full Breakfast
Credit Cards: None
Notes: 2, 5, 9, 10, 11, 12

WHITEWOOD

Rocking Horse

Rural Route 1, Box 133, 57793
(605) 269-2625

Quiet one and one-half story adorable modern country cottage for honeymoon privacy or families in beautiful rolling foothills of the rustic Black Hills. Deer often graze nearby and wild turkeys strut across the valley. Coyotes are heard in the evenings. A rooster's crow awakens guests. Enjoy nature walks or visit the horses. Pony rides available for the kids. Near historic Deadwood, world-renowned Passion play, scenic route Spearfish Canyon, and one hour from

7 No smoking; 8 Children welcome; 9 Social drinking allowed; 10 Tennis nearby; 11 Swimming nearby; 12 Golf nearby; 13 Skiing nearby; 14 May be booked through a travel agent.

Mount Rushmore. Full country breakfast includes fresh fruits (in season), homemade breads, special egg and cheese dishes, and more. Open May through September.

Hosts: Gerald and Sharleen Bergum
Rooms: 3 (1 PB; 2 SB) $65
Full Breakfast
Credit Cards: A, B
Notes: 2, 7, 8, 11, 12, 13, 14

YANKTON

Mulberry Inn

512 Mulberry Street, 57078
(605) 665-7116

This beautiful inn was built in 1873 and offers the ultimate in comfortable lodging with historic charm. Included in the National Register of Historic Places. Features parquet floors, six guest rooms furnished with antiques, two parlors with marble fireplaces, and a large porch for

Mulberry Inn

evening relaxation. In a quiet residential area and within walking distance to the Missouri River, downtown, and fine restaurants. Only minutes from the beautiful Lewis and Clark Lake and Gavins Point Dam. Full breakfast at additional cost.

Hosts: Millie and Garrald Cameron
Rooms: 6 (2 PB; 4 SB) $35-51
Continental Breakfast
Credit Cards: A, B, C
Notes: 2, 5, 7, 8, 9, 10, 11, 12, 13

Tennessee

Bird Song Country Inn Bed and Breakfast

Sycamore Mill, 1306 Highway 49 East, 37015
(615) 792-4005; FAX (615) 792-4005

Built in 1910 by the Cheek family of Maxwell House Coffee fame, this cedar lodge is listed on the National Register of Historic Places. An extensive collection of original art and period antiques brings the rooms to life. Natural surroundings provide beautiful ways to relax. Stroll in the woods along Sycamore Creek; soak in the heated spa on the flagstone patio; enjoy a good book, a nap, or relax in the hammocks under stately trees. Trail rides and spa services available by advance reservations. Near Nashville Zoo, Beach Haven Winery, antiques shops, and fish restaurants on the river. Nashville is 20 minutes away.

Hosts: Anne and Brooks Parker
Rooms: 3 (PB) $85-90

Bird Song Country Inn

Suite: 2 (PB) $150
Full Breakfast
Credit Cards: A, B, C
Notes: 2, 4, 5, 6, 7, 8, 9, 10, 11, 12, 14

ATHENS

Woodlawn

110 Keith Lane, 37303
(615) 745-8211; (615) 745-6029

Woodlawn is an elegant and charming bed and breakfast in historic downtown Athens. The antebellum Greek Revival mansion is filled with family antiques and gorgeous Oriental rugs. Built in 1858 by Alexander Keith, it was a Union hospital during the Civil War. Listed on the National Register of Historic Places. Thirteen-foot ceilings, large bedrooms with private baths. True Southern hospitality awaits guests. The innkeepers try to make guests feel right at home in this classic bed and breakfast halfway between Chattanooga and Knoxville off I-75.

Hosts: Barry and Susan Willis
Rooms: 4 (PB) $75-90
Full Breakfast
Credit Cards: A, B
Notes: 2, 4, 5, 7, 8, 9, 10, 12, 14

BELL BUCKLE

Bed and Breakfast About Tennessee

P.O. Box 110227, Nashville, 37222-0027
(615) 331-5244; FAX (615) 833-7701

Three double rooms, one room with two double beds, one room with a double and single. $50.

7 No smoking; 8 Children welcome; 9 Social drinking allowed; 10 Tennis nearby; 11 Swimming nearby; 12 Golf nearby; 13 Skiing nearby; 14 May be booked through a travel agent.

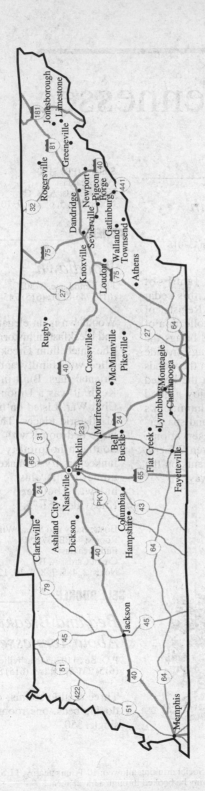

Tennessee

Adams Hilborne

CHATTANOOGA

Adams Hilborne

801 Vine Street, 37403
(615) 265-5000; FAX (615) 265-5555

Cornerstone to the Fort Wood historic district, this majestic Romanesque Victorian mansion is built in castle-like proportions of native mountain stone. The Adams Hilborne pampers guests with fine antiques, original artwork, and exquisite fabrics in all the oversized guest suites. The 1995 Designer Showhouse for the city of Chattanooga. The five reception rooms are resplendent in heavily carved moldings, coffered ceilings, 16-foot-tall arched poulett doors and silver-plated hinges. Fine dining in the banquet hall is available by advance arrangements. Private parties of up to 250 or large seated dinners in the Fort Wood Ballroom available. Minutes from the Tennessee Aquarium and other attractions.

Hosts: Wendy and Dave Adams
Rooms: 9 (PB) $100-295
Continental Breakfast
Credit Cards: A, B, C
Notes: 2, 4, 5, 7, 9, 10, 11, 12, 14

Bed and Breakfast About Tennessee

P.O. Box 110227, Nashville, TN 37222-0227
(615) 331-5244: FAX (615) 833-7701

The Charlet House. A quiet retreat on Signal Mountain, large trees, sidewalks, and 20 minutes from Chattanooga's riverfront attractions and restaurants. Two luxury suites with king-size beds and kitchenettes. Master suite has Jacuzzi and balcony. Large screened porch, deck area with grill overlooking pool. $85-95.

Near Ocoee River and Deer Park. Hunting and fishing nearby. One double and one single room, private/shared bath, one single room with bath, one single room with shared bath. $26-40.

Rambling Tudor House. On Signal Mountain. Nine miles to downtown and convenient to tourist attractions. King-size room with private bath. Twin room with shared bath. $60-85.

Restored Museum House. Fifteen minutes from Chattanooga near Chickamauga Battlefield Park. This antebellum plantation house features four rooms and three baths and a two-bedroom suite with bath and kitchen. A guest house is also available. $55-125.

View of Lake. Near public access to lake for boating and fishing, public swimming, and picnic area. Food is provided, guests prepare own breakfast. Private twin suite with living room and kitchen. Near attractions, Lookout Mountain, Interstates 24 and 75. $60.

Tennessee Aquarium. Visitors to the new aquarium will want to see this nearby suite; queen-size bedroom with private bath, sitting room, and small kitchen. Swimming pool on premises. Three miles from University of Tennessee-Chattanooga; eight miles from airport. Children welcome. $85-100.

Bluff View Inn

412 East Second Street, 37403
(615) 265-5033; FAX (615) 265-3684

NOTES: Credit cards: A MasterCard; B Visa; C American Express; D Discover; E Diners Club; F Other;
2 Personal checks accepted; 3 Lunch available; 4 Dinner available; 5 Open all year; 6 Pets welcome;
7 No smoking; 8 Children welcome; 9 Social drinking allowed; 10 Tennis nearby; 11 Swimming nearby;
12 Golf nearby; 13 Skiing nearby; 14 May be booked through a travel agent.

Bluff View Inn

In the Bluff View art district, Bluff View Inn encompasses two early 1900s buildings, the C. G. Martin House and the T. C. Thompson House. Both recently restored houses provide guests with modern luxuries while preserving their original elegance. Each room is furnished with antiques and original artwork. Guests can enjoy unique dining at one of the four restaurants. River Gallery and River Gallery Sculpture Garden provide a haven for art and nature lovers.

Host: Sue Crockett, innkeeper
Rooms: 9 (PB) $95-225
Full Breakfast
Credit Cards: A, B, D
Notes: 2, 3, 4, 5, 7, 8, 9

Chanticleer Inn

1300 Mockingbird Lane
Lookout Mountain, GA 37350
(706) 820-2015

Unique mountain stone buildings offer king- and queen-size, double, and twin rooms, some of which have antiques and fireplaces. Suites, cable TV, and a pool are all available in a quiet atmosphere. Great for honeymoons, families, reunions, or weekends. Only one block from Rock City Gardens and 15 minutes from the Tennessee Aquarium. AAA-approved. Senior discounts. No pets.

Host: Gloria Horton
Rooms: 16 (PB) $40-86
Continental Breakfast
Credit Cards: A, B, C
Notes: 5, 8, 9, 11

The Milton House Bed and Breakfast

508 Fort Wood Place, 37403
(615) 265-2800

This beautifully restored Southern mansion promises the perfect lodging experience for a wonderful stay in Chattanooga. Relive the past, yet still enjoy the luxuries and amenities of today in one of these elegant rooms furnished with period antiques. A sampling of the amenities includes a Jacuzzi, fireplaces, balcony, day room, telephones, cable TV, and claw-foot tubs. Listed on the national and local historic registers. In the downtown historic district of Fort Wood. A full home-cooked breakfast awaits guests each morning.

Host: Susan Mehlen
Rooms: 4 (3 PB; 1 SB) $65-175
Full Breakfast
Credit Cards: A, B, C, D
Notes: 2, 5, 7, 8, 9, 10, 11, 12, 14

CLARKSVILLE

Bed and Breakfast About Tennessee

P.O. Box 110227, Nashville, TN 37222-0227
(615) 331-5244; FAX (615) 833-7701

Beautiful property with wedding chapel on site and dining room supervised by internationally known chef. Excellent for weddings, family reunions, and anniversaries. Three log guest houses, circa 1790, accommodate from two to four couples. Meals available in nationally known dining room adjoining guest houses. Meals served at extra cost. $65.

COLUMBIA

Locust Hill Bed and Breakfast

1185 Mooresville Pike, 38401
(615) 388-8531; (800) 577-8264

NOTES: Credit cards accepted: A MasterCard; B Visa; C American Express; D Discover; E Diners Club; F Other; 2 Personal checks accepted; 3 Lunch available; 4 Dinner available; 5 Open all year; 6 Pets welcome;

Locust Hill is a beautifully restored 1840 home decorated with family antiques, hand-made quilts, and embroidered linens. Guests are pampered with morning coffee in their rooms and evening refreshments at the fireside. Delicious gourmet breakfasts feature country ham, featherlight biscuits, and homemade jams enjoyed in the dining room or sunroom. Enjoy the fireplaces and relax in the library, flower gardens, or on one of the three porches. French and German are spoken.

Hosts: Bill and Beverly Beard
Rooms: 3 (PB) $80-100
Full Breakfast
Credit Cards: A, B
Notes: 2, 3, 4, 5, 7, 10, 11, 12, 14

COLUMBIA

Natchez Trace Bed and Breakfast Reservation Service

P.O. Box 193, Hampshire, 38461
(615) 285-2777; (800) 377-2770

CUL-01 Milepost 409. Thirteen miles from Columbia and just five miles from Interstate 65, this 1901 farmhouse has been newly restored to elegant perfection. Double wraparound porch provides view of the Middle Tennessee countryside. The Columbia area is the antebellum home capital of Tennessee. A gourmet breakfast is served on fine linens and china. $80-95.

COL-01 Milepost 409. Thirteen miles from the Natchez Trace, near Columbia, Tennessee, this log cabin inn was built in the early 1800s and boasts a kitchen and living room, as well as claw-foot bathtubs, fireplaces, and a balcony that offers a panoramic view of the countryside. Pieces of the hosts' artwork are in the inn. Rates include access to the grounds and tennis court. Luxury suite in main house. Cabin available. $85-130.

CORDOVA

The Bridgewater House

7015 Raleigh La Grange Road, 38018
(901) 384-0080

A Greek Revival home converted from a school house that is over 100 years old. A lovely, elegant dwelling filled with remembrances of travels, antiques, family heirlooms, and Oriental rugs. The Bridgewater House has original hardwood floors cut from trees on the property, enormous rooms, high ceilings, leaded-glass windows, and deep, hand-marbleized moldings. There are two very spacious bedrooms with private baths. A certified chef and a food and beverage director serve a full gourmet breakfast.

Hosts: Steve and Katherine Mistilis
Rooms: 2 (PB) $75-100
Full Breakfast
Credit Cards: A, B, D
Notes: 2, 5, 7

CROSSVILLE

An-Jen Inn Bed and Breakfast

Route 1, Box 594, 38555
(615) 456-6515; (615) 456-2155

Two-story, white Southern Colonial home on 25 acres on highest point on the Cumberland Plateau. Peaceful, slow-paced, laid-back atmosphere. Privacy or area for groups. Popcorn and Kool-Aid for a snack before bed. Full country breakfast and dinner served by reservation only. Wedding chapel on grounds. Honeymoon suite and reception available in bed and breakfast. Murder Mystery dinner parties and Kidnapping weekends available.

Host: Sandra D. Monk
Rooms: 6 (PB) $60
Honeymoon Suite: $125
Full Breakfast
Credit Cards: None
Notes: 2, 3, 4, 5, 7, 10, 11, 12, 14

Betty's Bed and Breakfast

Rural Route 7, Box 359E, 38555-9807
(615) 484-8827

Just down the road from the nationally acclaimed Fairfield Glade Resort, Betty's Bed and Breakfast provides a warm and friendly atmosphere for that special getaway. Sit on the wraparound porch and enjoy the beauty of the Cumberland Plateau. Wake up to the smell of a delicious full breakfast, served in Aunt Hattie's dining room. Nearby are the Cumberland County Playhouse and the Cumberland State Park. Fully air-conditioned and open year-round. Lunch is also available with reservation.

Host: Betty Bryan
Rooms: 4 (PB) $55
Full Breakfast
Credit Cards: A, B, D
Notes: 2, 7, 8, 9, 10, 11, 12

DANDRIDGE

Sugar Fork Bed and Breakfast

743 Garrett Road, 37725
(615) 397-7327; (800) 487-5634

Guests will appreciate the tranquil setting of Sugar Fork Bed and Breakfast on Douglas Lake in the foothills of the Great Smoky Mountains. Private access and floating dock. Enjoy warm-weather water

Sugar Fork

sports and fishing year-round. Fireplace in common room, guest kitchenette, wraparound deck, swings, and park bench by the lake. A hearty breakfast is served family-style in the dining room or on the deck.

Hosts: Mary and Sam Price
Rooms: 3 (2 PB; 1 SB) $55-65
Full Breakfast
Credit Cards: A, B
Notes: 2, 5, 7, 8, 9, 10, 11, 12, 13

Sweet Basil and Thyme

P.O. Box 1132, 102 West Meeting Street, 37725
(800) 227-7128

This historically registered Victorian home, circa 1830, is surrounded by gorgeous rose gardens and furnished with antiques while reflecting the ambience of the past. A full gourmet breakfast is served, possibly in the garden, weather permitting. Dinner is available with advance reservations. Relax in the parlor or library, or simply stroll among the gardens. Within easy driving distance of Gatlinburg, Dollywood, Great Smoky Mountains National Park, and the University of Tennessee. Smoking is not allowed in the guest rooms.

Hosts: Dolores and Bill Pudifin
Rooms: 3 (1 PB; 2 SB) $50-65
Full Breakfast
Credit Cards: None
Notes: 5, 9, 12, 13

NOTES: Credit cards accepted: A MasterCard; B Visa; C American Express; D Discover; E Diners Club; F Other; 2 Personal checks accepted; 3 Lunch available; 4 Dinner available; 5 Open all year; 6 Pets welcome;

DICKSON

Bed and Breakfast About Tennessee

P.O. Box 110227, Nashville, TN 37222-0227
(615) 331-5244: FAX (615) 833-7701

Beautiful home filled with antiques. Experience the traditions, food, and customs of a contemporary Tennessee family in a small town near two state parks. Two rooms available with canopied bed or king-size waterbed. $45-55.

East Hills Bed and Breakfast Inn

100 East Hill Terrace, 37055
(615) 441-9428

This fully restored traditional home with Southern charm was built in the late forties by the current owner's father. It has 4,000 square feet of living area, built on four acres in a residential area on Highway 70 East. The house is near Luther Lake (excellent for walking and feeding the ducks) and is only six miles from Montgomery Bell State Park; convenient to shopping, hospital, restaurants, and downtown area. Large living room, and library/den with fireplaces and TV for guests to enjoy. Furnished throughout with period antiques. The long front porch has rocking chairs and a swing. Enjoy the big front yard with lots of trees.

Hosts: John and Anita Luther
Rooms: 4 (PB) $50-75
Full and Continental Breakfast
Credit Cards: A, B
Notes: 2, 5, 7, 10, 11, 12

FAYETTEVILLE

The Heritage House

315 East College Street, 37334
(615) 433-9238

Visit this charming, antebellum brick Colonial-style home with high ceilings, thick walls, and pocket doors. Relax in comfort-ably furnished rooms with cable TV, refrigerator, and antiques. Guests are welcome to enjoy the swing on the balcony or wicker chairs on the long front porch. Within walking distance of churches, movie theater, restaurants, historical district, museum, and gift and antique shops. Other points of interest include Tims Ford Lake, Space and Rocket Center, and the Jack Daniel's Distillery.

Hosts: Nina and Ken May
Rooms: 2 (PB) $50-100
Continental Breakfast
Credit Cards: None
Notes: 2, 5, 8, 9

FLAT CREEK (SHELBYVILLE)

Bottle Hollow Lodge

111 Gobbler Ridge Road, P.O. Box 92, 37160
(615) 695-5253

Nestled high in the rolling hills of Middle Tennessee, Bottle Hollow Lodge occupies 68 acres of beautiful countryside and magnificent views. The ultimate in peace, quiet, and solitude, this inn is just minutes from Lynchburg's Jack Daniel's Distillery and the site of the Tennessee Walking Horse National Celebration in Shelbyville. Bottle Hollow Lodge, with its inviting rockers on the front porch and plush sofas in front of the large stone fireplace, will add to the enjoyment of activities in the area. Lunch and dinner available by reservation.

Host: Pat Whiteside
Rooms: 5 (PB) $85-150
Full Breakfast
Credit Cards: A, B
Notes: 2, 5, 7, 9, 12, 14

FRANKLIN

Lyric Springs Country Inn

7306 South Harpeth Road, 37064
(615) 329-3385; (800) 621-7824
FAX (615) 329-3381

AAA antique-filled inn featured in the May 1993 *Better Homes & Gardens* and August

7 No smoking; 8 Children welcome; 9 Social drinking allowed; 10 Tennis nearby; 11 Swimming nearby;
12 Golf nearby; 13 Skiing nearby; 14 May be booked through a travel agent.

1993 *Country Inns* magazines. Haven for romance and retreat with gourmet food. Spa services with reservation. Enjoy billiards, fishing, hiking, swimming, biking, and music. Partake in sports of a cerebral nature—chess, backgammon, and clever after dinner conversation.

Hosts: Patsy Bruce and Michelle Clymer
Rooms: 4 (PB) $100-115
Full and Continental Breakfast
Credit Cards: A, B, C
Notes: 4, 5, 7, 9, 11, 12, 14

Natchez Trace Bed and Breakfast Reservation Service

P.O. Box 193, Hampshire, 38461
(615) 285-2777; (800) 377-2770

LEI-01 Milepost 436. Set in the lovely Leipers Creek valley near the village of Leiper's Fork, this country home is only two and one-half miles from the Natchez Trace. There are facilities for horses; the trail along the Trace is just minutes away. Large guest rooms with private baths. Enjoy a full breakfast and look out over the peaceful setting. Swimming pool and exercise room available. $65-85.

GATLINBURG

Bed and Breakfast About Tennessee

P.O. Box 110227, Nashville, TN 37222-0227
(615) 331-5244: FAX (615) 833-7701

A. Browse through an art gallery filled with original works of art and works of local craftsmen. Take in the expansive view of the Smoky Mountains or take the Arts and Crafts Tour Road. Near Cades Cove and Dollywood. One mile from Pigeon Forge and all the sights. One queen-size room with brass bed and private bath. One room with two double beds and private bath. $60-70.

Grandma's House. Two doubles with private bath; or suite of rooms featuring two bedrooms. Featuring Mystery Weekends. $55-75.

1865 Antebellum Plantation. Home has grand entrance, nine working fireplaces, listed with National Registry of Historic Places, and overlooking the Tennessee River. Beautiful swimming pool, gazebo, and arbor. Five bedrooms with private baths. Generous candlelight breakfast. $150.

B. High on a hilltop above Gatlinburg. Hiking, skiing, horseback riding, ice skating all nearby. Antiques, cable TV, four rooms with private baths. View Mount LeConte from deck. $100.

Buckhorn Inn

2140 Tudor Mountain Road, 37738
(615) 436-4668

A unique country inn offering peaceful seclusion with the feeling and tradition of early Gatlinburg. Established in 1938, Buckhorn Inn is on a hillside facing magnificent views of Mount LeConte. There are 35 acres of woodland, meadows, and quiet walkways, including a self-guiding nature trail. Six miles northeast of Gatlinburg near the Greenbriar entrance to the Great Smoky Mountains National Park. Closed over Christmas.

Hosts: John and Connie Burns
Rooms: 12 (PB) $105-250
Full Breakfast
Credit Cards: A, B
Notes: 2, 4, 5, 7, 9, 10, 11, 12, 13

Butcher House in the Mountains

1520 Garrett Lane, 37738
(615) 436-9457

Just 2,800 feet above the main street of Gatlinburg and the main entrance to the Great Smoky Mountains National Park, Butcher House in the Mountains offers seclusion as well as convenience. The spacious home is graced by Victorian, French, Queen Anne, and American country furniture. Antiques are tastefully placed throughout the house, and a downstairs kitchen is available for a before-bed dessert. The color coordination throughout is a delight to the senses with navy, blue, rose, and creams being the predominant hues.

Hosts: Hugh and Gloria Butcher
Rooms: 5 (PB) $79-119
Full Breakfast
Credit Cards: A, B, C
Notes: 2, 5, 7, 9, 10, 11, 12, 13, 14

Eight Gables

Eight Gables

219 North Mountain Trail, 37738
(615) 430-3344; (800) 279-5716

Guests of this new bed and breakfast are welcomed by a peaceful mountain setting. Near the trolley stop, it features a unique design and decor. Comfort is assured in the spacious guest rooms, each decorated with an individual theme and style. Each first-floor guest room has a private entrance, and all of the second-floor guest rooms are graced with cathedral ceilings and arched windows. There are a "gathering room" for relaxing and a lounge for viewing TV. Full sit-down breakfast. Dramatic surroundings inside and out. Everything a guest might need marks this tribute to Southern hospitality. AAA four-diamond-rated.

Host: Don and Kim Cason
Rooms: 10 (PB) $95-115
Full Breakfast
Credit Cards: A, B, C, D
Notes: 2, 3, 5, 7, 10, 11, 12, 13, 14

GREENEVILLE

Bed and Breakfast About Tennessee

P.O. Box 110227, Nashville, TN 37222-0227
(615) 331-5244; FAX (615) 833-7701

Restored Victorian. In historic district. Porches, stained-glass windows. Grand entrance hall. Five guest rooms, four baths. Dinner available by appointment only. Full breakfast. $65-85.

Hilltop House

6 Sanford Circle, 37743
(615) 639-8202

Experience the serenity of a 1920s manor house overlooking the Nolichucky River Valley with the Appalachian Mountains in the background. All three guest rooms have private baths and spectacular mountain views, two have their own verandas. Enjoy afternoon tea at 4 P.M. each day. Nearby golf, mountain hiking, trout fishing, white-water rafting, mountain biking, or antiquing. The house is beautifully furnished with Oriental rugs, English antiques, and reproduction pieces. Children over three welcome.

Host: Denise M. Ashworth
Rooms: 3 (PB) $70-75
Full Breakfast
Credit Cards: A, B, C
Notes: 2, 3, 4, 5, 7, 9, 11, 12, 14

Oak Hill Farm Bed and Breakfast

3035 Lonesome Pine Trail, 37745
(615) 639-5253; FAX (615) 639-7158

Only three miles from historic Greeneville, quiet, peaceful, on highest hill in area. Overlooks 200 miles of Appalachian Mountains. Close to several historic sites; camping, hiking, and bicycle trails available. Close to several TVA lakes; smallmouth bass fishing on the Nolichucky River. Within one-hour drive to two of the finest trout streams in the country. Guided trips available.

Hosts: Bill and Marie Guinn
Rooms: 3 (PB) $75-150
Full Breakfast
Credit Cards: A, B, C
Notes: 3, 4, 5, 7, 8, 9, 11, 12

HAMPSHIRE

Natchez Trace Bed and Breakfast Reservation Service

P.O. Box 193, 38461
(615) 285-2777; (800) 377-2770

HAM-01 Milepost 392. Contemporary cedar home furnished with antiques, set on 170 acres of wooded hills near the village of Hampshire, between Columbia and Hohenwald. Picture windows look out over the woods; have coffee on the spacious deck. Clear streams, a waterfall, birds, and wildflowers. Near Meriwether Lewis Park, Metal Ford, and Jackson Falls on the Trace. The hosts are experts on local wildflowers. Full breakfast served. There is one guest room in the home. Private cottage is also available for up to four people. $65-80.

JACKSON

Bed and Breakfast About Tennessee

P.O. Box 110227, Nashville, TN 37222-0227
(615) 331-5244: FAX (615) 833-7701

A stately home of distinct charm, offering comfortable accommodations and Southern hospitality. Full breakfast served. One double bed with antiques and private bath. Room with two double beds, antiques, and shared bath. $50-60.

JONESBOROUGH

Jonesborough Bed and Breakfast

100 Woodrow Avenue, P.O. Box 722, 37659
(615) 753-9223

This beautifully restored home was built in 1848 and is in Jonesborough's historic district. All restaurants and shops are within easy walking distance. To make a visit memorable, guests will find robes, high beds, antique furnishings, fireplaces, large porch with rocking chairs, secluded terrace, air conditioning, and a big breakfast. Private baths upon request. Seasonal rates.

Host: Tobie Bledsoe
Rooms: 5 (PB/SB) $54-99
Full Breakfast
Credit Cards: None
Notes: 2, 5, 7, 8, 9, 11, 12

KNOXVILLE

Bed and Breakfast About Tennessee

P.O. Box 110227, Nashville, TN 37222-0227
(615) 331-5244: FAX (615) 833-7701

Maryville. Two rooms with shared bath. Restaurant on-site. $45-50.

Restored 1900s Home. In quiet neighborhood, has antiques and beautiful decor. Four miles from University of Tennessee and near Smoky Mountain sites. Breakfast served, other meals by appointment with host. Twin room and double room with shared bath. $45-60.

Mitchell's

1031 West Park Drive, 37909
(615) 690-1488

This bed and breakfast offers a comfortable room in a private home in a pleasant tree-shaded neighborhood near fine shops and restaurants. Parking at a private entrance, double bed, TV, refrigerator, and microwave; rollaway bed and crib available. It is 45 minutes to the Smoky Mountains, 25 minutes to Oak Ridge, one and one-half miles to I-75/I-40, and eight miles to downtown Knoxville.

Host: Mary M. Mitchell
Room: 1 (PB) $40
Continental Breakfast
Credit Cards: None
Notes: 2, 5, 6, 8, 9

LIMESTONE

Snapp Inn
Bed and Breakfast

1990 Davy Crockett Park Road, 37681
(423) 257-2482

These hosts will welcome guests into this gracious 1815 Federal home furnished with antiques and set in farm country. Enjoy the mountain view from the full back porch or play a game of pool or horseshoes. Close to Davy Crockett Birthplace Park; 15-minute drive to historic Jonesborough or Greeneville. Third person in room at no extra charge. Only one child at a time allowed.

Hosts: Dan and Ruth Dorgan
Rooms: 2 (PB) $50
Full Breakfast
Credit Cards: None
Notes: 2, 5, 6, 7, 9, 11, 12, 14

LOUDON (KNOXVILLE)

The Mason Place
Bed and Breakfast

600 Commerce Street, 37774
(615) 458-3921

The Mason Place can be found in a quaint little Civil War town. Impeccably restored, this antebellum plantation home is tastefully decorated throughout with quality antiques, original chandeliers, delightful feather beds, and ten working fireplaces. Candlelight breakfast served in the dining room. Three acres of lawn, gardens, swimming pool, gazebo, and wiste-

ria-covered arbor for guests' enjoyment. Near Knoxville, the Smoky Mountains, I-75, and I-40. North of Chattanooga.

Hosts: Bob and Donna Siewert
Rooms: 5 (PB) $96-120
Full Breakfast
Credit Cards: None
Notes: 2, 5, 9, 10, 11, 12, 13, 14

LYNCHBURG

"Lynchburg Bed and Breakfast," built 1877

Lynchburg

Lynchburg
Bed and Breakfast

P.O. Box 34, 37352
(615) 759-7158

This 19th-century home is within walking distance of the Jack Daniel's Distillery. Each spacious room features carefully selected antiques. Formerly the home of the first Moore County sheriff (1877).

Host: Virginia Tipps
Rooms: 2 (PB) $50-55
Continental Breakfast
Credit Cards: A, B
Notes: 5, 10, 11, 12

Mulberry House
Bed and Breakfast

8 Old Lynchburg Highway, Mulberry, 37359
(615) 433-8461

7 No smoking; 8 Children welcome; 9 Social drinking allowed; 10 Tennis nearby; 11 Swimming nearby; 12 Golf nearby; 13 Skiing nearby; 14 May be booked through a travel agent.

Mulberry House

This 110-year-old home in Mulberry, where Davy Crockett spent a winter, is nestled in the hills of Middle Tennessee, only seven miles from Lynchburg, the home of Jack Daniel's Tennessee whiskey. Only 45 minutes from Huntsville, Alabama. There are numerous craft and antique shops to visit.

Host: Candy Richard
Rooms: 2 (PB) $45
Continental Breakfast
Credit Cards: A, B
Notes: 2, 5, 7, 8, 9

McMINNVILLE

Falcon Manor
Bed and Breakfast

2645 Faulkner Springs Road, 37110
(615) 668-4444

Escape to the peaceful romance of the 1890s in one of the South's finest Victorian mansions. Rock on gingerbread verandas shaded by giant trees. Indulge in the luxury of museum-quality antiques. Enjoy stories about the mansion's history and the innkeepers' adventures in restoring it. An ideal base for a Tennessee vacation, Falcon Manor is near the center of the Nashville-Chattanooga-Knoxville triangle. Easy access from I-24 and I-40. A country setting just minutes from town. Children over 12 are welcome.

Hosts: George and Charlien McGlothin
Rooms: 5 (1 PB; 4 SB) $75-85
Full Breakfast
Credit Cards: A, B
Notes: 2, 5, 9, 10, 11, 12, 14

MEMPHIS

Bed and Breakfast
About Tennessee

P.O. Box 110227, Nashville, TN 37222-0227
(615) 331-5244: FAX (615) 833-7701

Guest House. With twin beds, kitchenette, Hide-a-Bed. Breakfast served at guest's leisure. $45-55.

Overton Park Area. Beautiful restored home furnished in antiques with swimming pool on site. Pool house available. Twin room with antique Eastlake furnishings; Queen-size room with canopied bed and antiques; four-poster canopied bed with private bath. $90-100.

Twenty-five Minutes from Downtown. Three rooms with private baths, beautifully appointed, generous breakfast, genial hosts, picturesque surroundings. The surprise is the enormous enclosed room with a heated pool, waterfalls, sprays, flora, and large hot tub. Breakfast can be served in this surrounding if desired. $90.

Bed and Breakfast
in Memphis

P.O. Box 41621, 38174-1621
(901) 726-5920; (800) 336-2087
FAX (901) 725-0194

D-0302. Gracious Southern living on the mighty Mississippi epitomizes this open and airy garden condo beautifully decorated with antiques and Oriental rugs. Two guest rooms, each with its own private bath, Continental breakfast served in full view of the river, and a thoroughly engaging Southern hostess all take guests back to a more gentle time of grace and elegance. The Wonders Series world-class exhibitions are within walking distance; great jazz and blues on famous Beale Street. Smoking outside only. $100.

NOTES: Credit cards accepted: A MasterCard; B Visa; C American Express; D Discover; E Diners Club;
F Other; 2 Personal checks accepted; 3 Lunch available; 4 Dinner available; 5 Open all year; 6 Pets welcome;

D-0306. This bed and breakfast on the river has a guest suite available. Two bedrooms with twin and queen-size beds. Living room and more. $100.

D-0310. Private suite on the river. Professionally designed and decorated guest apartment overlooks pool and lush gardens; enjoy wraparound porch and much more. The epitome of bed and breakfast for the business or pleasure traveler. A lovely basket of fresh breakfast surprises delivered to guests' doors each morning. Weekly stays are encouraged at excellent rate. Queen-size-bed sleeping area, living area, deck, galley kitchen, washer and dryer, cable TV, VCR on request, and local telephone line. Warm hospitality, comfort, charm, and convenience. One and one-fourth mile to convention center, Pyramid, and trolley. Nonsmoking. $135.

D-7369. Southern living at its best. Arkansas working farm and Southern mansion just 30 minutes from downtown Memphis. Tour the farm and cotton gins and enjoy complimentary tea on the veranda each evening and country breakfast each morning. Poke around antique shops, and eat some of the best catfish ever caught in nearby smaller towns. Take a jaunt into Memphis for nightlife or bring a book and just relax. Three handsome guest rooms and two guest baths in the upstairs wing; TV in rooms. Resident dog. $85.

E-1706. Leave cares behind and retreat to this beautiful private suite in elegant east location. Bright and cheery library opens to guest bedroom with four-poster double bed and private bath with Jacuzzi. Hosted. Dogs in residence. $85.

G-1900. This friendly host couple travels extensively in bed and breakfasts. Guests will enjoy breakfast on the screened porch in fashionable Germantown. Spacious guest room with antique pineapple twin beds, private bath, and use of office area for business travelers. Privacy, comfort, and congeniality for only $65.

G-3801. Elegant estate in fashionable Germantown nestled in beautifully manicured gardens, stables, and a horse or two. Two guest rooms with private bath and charming, fully decorated and equipped guest house featuring kitchen, living room, spacious bath, and one bedroom. Resident dog. Smoking outside only. $90-100.

M-0405. Say good-bye to expensive hotel rates and living out of a suitcase. For anyone forced to be away from loved ones, this is the next best thing. Charming one-bedroom apartment in award-winning midtown high-rise offers large living room with Stearnes and Foster queen-size sleeper, dining and work area, full bath with shower, fully equipped kitchen with microwave, and ample closet space. Cable TV, VCR, and one complimentary video. Fax and secretarial services available. Unhosted. Minimums may apply. Weekly and monthly rates available. $125.

M-1200. Lovely gardens, lush trees, and scampering squirrels are all right in the heart of the city. Professionally decorated host home in the historic Hein Park near Rhodes College and the zoo. Choice of upstairs suite (double and single beds) with shower and wet bar, or downstairs guest room with king-size bed, cable TV, VCR, and private bath. Popular hostess teaches English at a local college and travels extensively. $75.

SE-1500. Habla Espanol? Delightful hostess teaches Spanish, travels extensively, and looks forward to welcoming business women and couples to her attractive garden condo in bustling southeast area. Pool. Guest room with double brass bed and private bath. $45.

7 No smoking; 8 Children welcome; 9 Social drinking allowed; 10 Tennis nearby; 11 Swimming nearby; 12 Golf nearby; 13 Skiing nearby; 14 May be booked through a travel agent.

Lowenstein-Long House

217 North Waldran, 38105
(901) 527-7174

This beautifully restored Victorian mansion near downtown is listed on the National Register of Historic Places. Convenient to major attractions, such as the Mississippi River, Graceland, Beale Street, the Memphis Zoo, Brooks Museum, and the Victorian Village. Free off-street parking.

Hosts: Col. Charles and Margaret Long
Rooms: 4 (PB) $50-80
Full Breakfast
Credit Cards: None
Notes: 2, 5, 7, 8, 9

Adams Edgeworth Inn

MONTEAGLE

Adams Edgeworth Inn

Monteagle Assembly, 37356
(423) 924-4000; FAX (423) 924-3236

A showcase for fine antiques, original paintings, handmade quilts, and sculptures; nestled among prize-winning roses on top of Monteagle Mountain. Two hundred feet of verandas supply ample space for rocking away the day. Fine dining by candlelight available every evening. In a 115-year-old Chautauqua village; abundant hiking, views, vistas, and natural activities in the area. Also proximity to Jack Daniel's, University of the South, Sewanee, and Arnold Engineering Center with the largest wind tunnel in the world.

May be booked through a travel agent, but rates will include the 10 percent commission.

Hosts: Wendy and Dave Adams
Rooms: 12 (PB) $75-150
Continental Breakfast
Credit Cards: A, B, C
Notes: 2, 4, 5, 7, 9, 10, 11, 12

North Gate Inn

Monteagle Assembly 103, 37356
(615) 924-2799

The bright blue awning of this former 1890s boarding house welcomes guests to warm hospitality and sumptuous breakfasts. Attractive common areas include one large room for meetings and parties and two inviting porches, one with a blue enamel wood stove for winter use. Original iron beds, custom mattresses, antique quilts, and ceiling fans in each charming guest room. Two-bedroom cottage also available. Close to hiking trails, waterfalls, caves, mountain vistas, antiques, and crafts. Explore the grounds of the historic Chautauqua of the South, Monteagle Assembly, or rock a while on the porch.

Hosts: Nancy and Henry Crais
Rooms: 7 (PB) $65-80
Cottage: $100-150
Full Breakfast
Credit Cards: None
Notes: 2, 5, 7, 8, 9, 10, 11, 12, 14

MURFREESBORO

Bed and Breakfast About Tennessee

P.O. Box 110227, Nashville, 37222-0027
(615) 331-5244; FAX (615) 833-7701

Beautiful View. Spacious new inn with large pretty rooms, private baths. Master suite sleeps four, vaulted ceiling, with stove fireplace, sitting area with recliners. Ten miles from Shelbyville, Lynchburg, Tullahoma, and 15 miles from Fayetteville. Children over 12 accepted. Smoking outside only. Dinner by reservation. $75-150.

NOTES: Credit cards accepted: A MasterCard; B Visa; C American Express; D Discover; E Diners Club; F Other; 2 Personal checks accepted; 3 Lunch available; 4 Dinner available; 5 Open all year; 6 Pets welcome;

Historic Log House. One large room, private bath. Good kitchen facilities with food provided for breakfast. Room has private balcony overlooking the pool. $55.

Clardy's Guest House

Clardy's Guest House

435 East Main Street, 37130
(615) 893-6030

In the historic district, this 20-room Victorian Romanesque home is filled with antiques and features ornate woodwork and fireplaces. An eight-by-eight-foot stained-glass window overlooks the magnificent staircase. The area has much to offer history buffs and antique shoppers. Thirty miles from Nashville, just two miles off I-24.

Hosts: Robert and Barbara Deaton
Rooms: 3 (2 PB; 1 SB) $38-48
Continental Breakfast
Credit Cards: None
Notes: 2, 5, 7, 8, 9, 10, 11, 12, 14

NASHVILLE

Bed and Breakfast About Tennessee

P.O. Box 110227, Nashville, TN 37222-0227
(615) 331-5244: FAX (615) 833-7701

Belle Meade Area. Private suite, including queen-size bed, living room with fireplace, kitchenette, full bath, hot tub, and TV. No children. No pets. No smoking. $100.

Blue "Old Saltbox" House. Surrounded by wooded hills just 20 minutes from downtown Nashville. House is decorated with woodcrafts by hosts. Breakfast, accompanied by homemade jam, is served in the sunny kitchen. Guests are welcome to tea in the Japanese garden or on the patio. One child on folding cot. No pets. No smoking. $45-60.

Built in Mid-1800s. On the site of Indian camping grounds is this beautiful Greek Revival with Victorian decorative elements. Served as a hospital during the Civil War. This home is 15 minutes from Nashville. Log guest house and main house are furnished in antiques. $75-85.

Congenial Hosts/Contemporary Home. Two rooms, one twin, one double, private/shared baths. $45-50.

1800s Restored Stagecoach Inn. Ten miles from interstate near Brentwood. Resplendent with antiques. Downstairs has one double room with canopied bed, private bath, fireplace, and garden view. Upstairs features two double rooms with canopied beds, private/shared bath, antique vanities in each room. Creekside gingerbread cottage also available. Twenty minutes from Nashville. $65-75.

English-Style Cottage. Including living room, fireplace, kitchen loft, and master bedroom. One block from bus. $75-85.

Guest House. Three-room guest house with swimming pool. Large rooms, bath, kitchen. French doors open onto pool. $100.

Historic District of Nashville. This restored Victorian was built in 1902 by then-mayor of Nashville. Recently restored by an interior designer, the bedroom is furnished with

7 No smoking; 8 Children welcome; 9 Social drinking allowed; 10 Tennis nearby; 11 Swimming nearby;
12 Golf nearby; 13 Skiing nearby; 14 May be booked through a travel agent.

Bed and Breakfast
About Tennessee
(continued)

antiques and features a huge adjoining bath. Across the street is a 100-year-old Catholic church. $55.

Insurance Broker and nurse have one double and one twin room near major interstates and convenient to area colleges. $45-50.

Large Rural Estate. Very scenic and private. Ten rooms, each with double and single, half-bath, rustic decor. Large baths in hall. Thirteen miles from Nashville. Perfect for corporate retreats, family reunions, and large groups. Parklike setting with picnic area, three swimming pools, on beautiful creek, near lake. $55.

Log Lodge. Near Opryland. Home features antiques, comfortable sitting area, and TV. Double room with private bath. Swimming pool in summer. No children. No pets. $75.

Music Row. All suite property with limited access door. Full suites, beautifully furnished. There is a swimming pool on the property. $90-125.

Near Downtown. Beautiful older home has collections displayed throughout the house. Grand staircase to bed and breakfast rooms. One double with private bath; two doubles with shared bath; suite with small kitchen, and sitting room. $80-100.

Near I-65 South. One king-size room, one queen-size room, one double room with private/shared bath. Host is a teacher who loves music. Prefers no smoking. $45-55.

Near Maryland Farms. Side entrance, deck, queen-size room with antiques, and private bath. Two single rooms upstairs with shared bath. $40-55.

Near Vanderbilt. Restored 1900s house has two suites. Suite one has double bed and adjoining Florida room with lots of windows and private bath. Suite two has double bed, private bath, and fireplace. Near interstates, downtown, antiques mall, and universities. $75-90.

Oldest House in Downtown. Built in 1859, this home features 12-foot ceilings and fireplaces. First floor is tea room where guests have breakfast. One block from Nashville Convention Center; fifteen minutes from Opryland. Rooms furnished in antiques. Private/shared baths. $55-75.

One block from Lipscomb University. This home has two double rooms and private baths. Recording artist and counselor enjoy people and are interested in country music. $45-50.

Overlooking the Cumberland River. Professionally decorated log house with fireplace, screened porch, and full kitchen. Two bedroom, two baths, and cable TV. Professional chef available. $95-150.

Pleasant Home on Wooded Lot. Three bedrooms, two baths, near major thoroughfares and airport. Host smokes. Children welcome. $45-50.

Quiet, Secluded Poolside Guest House. With twin beds and private bath. Close to I-40. Eight miles to downtown Nashville. Near good fishing. Adjoins 24-foot above-ground pool. $45-60.

NOTES: Credit cards accepted: A MasterCard; B Visa; C American Express; D Discover; E Diners Club; F Other; 2 Personal checks accepted; 3 Lunch available; 4 Dinner available; 5 Open all year; 6 Pets welcome;

Relax in Peace. Privacy and comfort at a cedar log lodge in the beautiful Tennessee hills, just 20 minutes from Nashville. Built in 1910 by the Cheek family of Maxwell House Coffee fame and listed on the National Register. Bird Song offers lazy hammocks and woodsy creekside beauty; lovely gardens and fascinating art. Three bedrooms with private baths; suite available. Deluxe Continental breakfast served. $85-100.

Terrawin. Rock on the front porch, watch the cows, or lie in the hammock and enjoy the parklike grounds. Minutes from Opryland, the largest shopping district in Nashville, downtown, I-65 and I-40. Upstairs large room with queen-size bed, another large room with twin bed, and bath. Large suite with twin beds, and sleeper sofas. Room for sleeping bags. Fireplace and pool table available. Continental breakfast served. $50-55.

Vanderbilt Area. Double room with beautiful antique bed, comfortable mattress, sitting room with desk, and private bath. Lovely antiques throughout the house. $60.

Bed and Breakfast Adventures

P.O. Box 150586, 37215
(615) 383-6611; (800) 947-7404

Bed and Breakfast Adventures is a reservation service representing homestays and inns personally visited and approved by this establishment. Choose from historic or contemporary homes, romantic inns, condominiums, guest houses, log cabins, lake or mountain retreats, or working farms. Convenience, reason for visit, interests, etc., are carefully considered, then several hosts are selected for guests to choose from, so the stay will be a truly memorable and pleasant experience. $50-195.

Monthaven

1154 Main Street West, Hendersonville, 37075
(615) 824-6319

On the National Register of Historic Places, Monthaven offers both a heritage of nearly 200 years and a 75-acre estate for the enjoyment of visitors to Nashville and Middle Tennessee. The main house served as a field hospital during the Civil War. Log cabin, built in 1938 from 200-year-old timber, is available.

Hosts: Hugh Waddell, Donna West,
    and Alan Waddell
Rooms: 3 (PB) $75
Log Cabin: (PB) $85
Continental Breakfast
Credit Cards: A, B, C
Notes: 2, 5, 6, 9, 10, 11, 12, 14

Natchez Trace Bed and Breakfast Reservation Service

P.O. Box 193, Hampshire, 38461
(615) 285-2777; (800) 377-2770

ASH-01 Milepost 450. Built in 1920 by the Cheek family of Maxwell House Coffee fame, this cedar log lodge is listed on the National Register of Historic Places. Extensive collection of art and antiques, large sunny guest room, masterful yet cozy great room, screened porch, and heated spa. Stroll along the creek or enjoy a nap in a hammock under stately trees; tennis and swimming nearby. A pleasant 20-minute drive to Nashville. Hosts have borrowed the best ideas from country inns on several continents to make this a unique and wonderful place. $85-95.

FAI-01. Milepost 438. Ten miles from the Trace, this contemporary country home features a swimming pool and a hot tub. Guests can rent horses and bicycles from hosts, and they are convenient to both the bridle trail along the Trace and to Fairview

7 No smoking; 8 Children welcome; 9 Social drinking allowed; 10 Tennis nearby; 11 Swimming nearby; 12 Golf nearby; 13 Skiing nearby; 14 May be booked through a travel agent.

Nature Park's riding trails. Guests can even get a personal fitness workout for an extra charge. $50.

LEI-02. Milepost 438 or 429. This home, with seven surrounding acres, is a very private place and only six miles from the Trace. Guests will enjoy the deck and the view of the countryside. The host is a professional artist and craftsperson, and her works decorate the home and are available for guests to purchase. Room with private bath. $55.

Woodshire Bed and Breakfast

600 Woodshire Drive, Goodlettsville, 37072
(615) 859-7369

Family antiques, homemade preserves, and Southern hospitality—all just 15 to 20 minutes from Nashville's universities, museums, Parthenon, Opryland, and many country music attractions. Private entrance, use of screened porch, and Continental breakfast. Country atmosphere with urban conveniences. Also a private telephone is available for guests and cable TV is in two rooms. A mid-1800s reconstructed log cabin is also available.

Hosts: John and Beverly Grayson
Rooms: 2 (PB) $40-50
Log Cabin: $60-70
Continental Breakfast
Credit Cards: None
Notes: 2, 7, 8, 10, 11, 12, 14

NEWPORT

Christopher Place Country Inn

1500 Pinnacles Way, 37821
(423) 623-6555

Surrounded by expansive mountain views, this premier Southern estate includes over 200 acres to explore, a pool, tennis court,

Christopher Place Country Inn

and sauna. Relax by the marble fireplace in the library, retreat to the game room, or enjoy a hearty mountain meal in the dining room. Romantic rooms are available with a hot tub or fireplace. Off I-40 at Exit 435, just 32 scenic miles from Gatlinburg and Pigeon Forge. Handicapped accessible. AAA rated four diamonds.

Host: Drew Ogle
Rooms: 10 (PB) $75-175
Full Breakfast
Credit Cards: A, B
Notes: 2, 4, 5, 9, 10, 11, 12, 14

PIGEON FORGE

Hilton's Bluff Bed and Breakfast

2654 Valley Heights Drive, 37863
(615) 428-9765

Romantic hilltop hideaway. Beautiful two-story cedar inn with covered decks, oak rockers, and nature's ever-changing mountain views. Decorated with country quilts and lace. Ten guest rooms, executive, deluxe, and honeymoon, feature king-size beds, waterbeds, and heart-shaped Jacuzzis. Den with stone fireplace and game room/meeting room. Southern gourmet breakfast. Elegant country living, minutes from the heart of Pigeon Forge and the Great Smoky Mountains National Park. Personal checks accepted in advance. Lunch and dinner available for groups renting the entire inn. Smoking restricted. Inquire about accommodations for children.

Hosts: Jack, Norma, Jay, and Cathy Hilton
Rooms: 10 (PB)$79-119
Full Breakfast
Credit Cards: A, B, C
Notes: 5, 9, 10, 11, 12, 13, 14

NOTES: Credit cards accepted: A MasterCard; B Visa; C American Express; D Discover; E Diners Club;
F Other; 2 Personal checks accepted; 3 Lunch available; 4 Dinner available; 5 Open all year; 6 Pets welcome;

PIKEVILLE

Fall Creek Falls Bed and Breakfast

Route 3, Box 298B, 37367
(615) 881-5494

Enjoy the relaxing atmosphere of a country manor home on 40 acres of rolling hillside one mile from the nationally acclaimed Fall Creek Falls Resort Park. Beautiful accommodations have a common sitting area with TV. Lodging includes a full breakfast served in a cozy country kitchen, an elegant dining room, or a sunny Florida room with a magnificent view. Assistance with touring, dining, and shopping information. Off-season rates. AAA rated.

Hosts: Doug and Rita Pruett
Rooms: 8 (PB) $65-140
Full Breakfast
Credit Cards: A, B
Notes: 2, 3, 4, 7, 9, 10, 11, 12, 14

ROGERSVILLE

Hale Springs Inn

110 West Main Street, 37857
(423) 272-5171

This elegant, three-story Federal brick building, built in 1824, is the oldest continuously run inn in Tennessee. Beautifully

Hale Springs Inn

furnished with antiques from the period. Some of the rooms feature four-poster canopied beds, and all rooms have working fireplaces. Air conditioning. Guests may bring their own wine. Candlelight dining.

Host: Ed Pace
Rooms: 9 (PB) $45-75
Continental Breakfast
Credit Cards: A, B, C
Notes: 3, 4, 5, 7, 8, 9, 10, 11, 12

RUGBY

Grey Gables Bed 'n' Breakfast Inn

Highway 52, P.O. Box 52, 37733
(423) 628-5252

Nestled on the outskirts of the 1880s English village of Rugby, Grey Gables offers the best of the Victorian English and Tennessee country heritage, creatively blending Victorian and country antiques. Fare includes lodging, evening meal, and country breakfast. Visit the beautiful Cumberland Plateau, historic Rugby, and Grey Gables. In the tradition of the forebears, guests will receive a hearty welcome, a restful bed, and a full table. Reservations required. Lunch available by reservation. Smoking restricted.

Hosts: Bill and Linda Brooks Jones
Rooms: 8 (4 PB; 4 SB) $95
Full Breakfast
Credit Cards: A, B
Notes: 2, 4, 5, 9, 11, 12, 14

Newbury House at Historic Rugby

P.O. Box 8, Highway 52, 37733
(423) 628-2441; (423) 628-2430

Newbury House was the Rugby colony's first boarding house, established in 1880. Sash and pulley cords on the windows reveal an 1879 patent date. Board and batten siding, a lovely front porch, mansard roof, and dormer windows are all hallmarks of this beautifully restored, Victorian-furnished

7 No smoking; 8 Children welcome; 9 Social drinking allowed; 10 Tennis nearby; 11 Swimming nearby;
12 Golf nearby; 13 Skiing nearby; 14 May be booked through a travel agent.

bed and breakfast. Newbury House lodged both visitors and incoming settlers, as well as British author Thomas Hughes's utopian colony. In a nationally registered village with historic building tours, museum stores, specialty restaurant, and river gorge hiking trails. Victorian cottages also available.

Host: Historic Rugby
Rooms: 5 (3 PB; 2 SB) $60-70
Full Breakfast
Credit Cards: A, B
Notes: 2, 3, 4, 5, 9, 11, 12

SEVIERVILLE

Blue Mountain Mist Country Inn and Cottages

1811 Pullen Road, 37862
(423) 428-2335; (800) 497-2335

Experience the silent beauty of mountain scenery while rocking on the big wrap-around porch of this Victorian-style farmhouse. Common rooms filled with antiques lead to 12 individually decorated guest rooms. Enjoy many special touches, such as old-fashioned claw-foot tubs, high antique headboards, quilts, and Jacuzzis. Nestled in the woods behind the inn are five country cottages designed for romantic getaways. The Great Smoky Mountains National Park and Gatlinburg are only 20 minutes away.

Hosts: Norman and Sarah Ball
Rooms: 12 (PB) $79-125
Cottages: 5
Full Breakfast
Credit Cards: A, B
Notes: 2, 5, 7, 8, 9, 12, 13, 14

Calico Inn

757 Ranch Way, 37862
(423) 428-3833; (800) 235-1054

The Calico Inn is an authentic log inn with touches of elegance. It is decorated with antiques, collectibles, and country charm. It has a spectacular mountain view and is on a hilltop with 25 acres surrounding it. Each guest room has its own private bath. Guests

Calico Inn

will be served a full delicious breakfast daily. Only minutes away from the Great Smoky Mountains National Park, Dollywood, Gatlinburg, hiking, fishing, golfing, and all the attractions, yet completely secluded. Children ten and older welcome.

Hosts: Lill and Jim Katzbeck
Rooms: 3 (PB) $85-95
Full Breakfast
Credit Cards: A, B
Notes: 2, 5, 7, 9, 10, 11, 12, 13, 14

Huckleberry Inn

1754 Sandstone Way, 37876
(423) 428-2475

Huckleberry Inn is an authentic mountain log home on 25 acres, just behind Dollywood and surrounded by Pigeon Forge, Gatlinburg, and Sevierville. There are four guest rooms, all with private whirlpool baths, two with fireplaces. Enjoy a full country breakfast on the screened porch or eat in the kitchen by the stone fireplace. Relax on the high back porch, and enjoy beautiful mountain views. Take a walk down to the spring or hike up the mountain. It's all here. Smoking restricted.

Hosts: Rich and Barb Thomas
Rooms: 4 (PB) $79-89
Full Breakfast
Credit Cards: A, B
Notes: 2, 4, 5, 8, 9, 12, 13, 14

Little Greenbrier Lodge

3685 Lyon Springs Road, 37862
(423) 429-2500; (800) 277-8100

One of the oldest rustic lodges from yesteryear nestled in the trees overlooking Wears

Valley. The inn offers guests today's modern comforts, yet recaptures yesterday's charm with antique Victorian decor. The view of the valley provides a perfect backdrop for the country breakfast, and the lodge provides peace, quiet, and privacy.

Host: Barbara J. Matthews
Rooms: 11 (8 PB; 3 SB) $65-110
Full Breakfast
Credit Cards: A, B, C, D
Notes: 7, 9, 12

Persephone's Retreat

2279 Hodges Ferry Road, 37876
(423) 428-3904; FAX (423) 453-7089

A peaceful rural estate nestled in a grove of huge shade trees overlooking pastures and a beautiful river, yet within minutes of exciting Sevier and Knox Counties' tourist attractions. An elegant two-story home offers three extremely comfortable bedrooms with private baths and large porches. Enjoy spacious grounds, hiking, yard games, farm animals, miniature horses, fruit trees, shiitake mushrooms, and two-hole practice golf course. Smoking restricted.

Hosts: Bob Gonia and Victoria Nicholson
Rooms: 3 (PB) $75-95
Continental Breakfast
Credit Cards: A, B
Notes: 2, 7, 8, 9

Place of the Blue Smoke

3760 Cove Mountain Road, 37862
(423) 453-6355

Place of the Blue Smoke is on Cove Mountain on 90 wooded acres. The inn has large

Place of the Blue Smoke

porches and decks that open out from each room. Enjoy relaxing in the rockers or take a hike down to the waterfall. Near the Great Smoky Mountains National Park and Dollywood, outlet malls, and Cades Cove.

Hosts: Charlie and Nonnie Knight
Rooms: 4 (PB) $95-105
Full Breakfast
Credit Cards: A, B
Notes: 2, 5, 7, 13, 14

Von-Bryan Inn

2402 Hatcher Mountain Road, 37862
(423) 453-9832; (800) 633-1459

The Von-Bryan Inn is a magnificent log home with beautiful views from every window and every relaxing spot on the grounds. The inn is on top of a 2,100-foot mountain, and the views are almost breathtaking. No wonder most of the guests find it hard to break away long enough to take in the amusement parks and outlet malls. Jacuzzi, hot tub, pool, and a hearty Tennessee breakfast are offered. The two-bedroom log cabin is great for families. Picnic basket lunch and dinner available.

Hosts: Joann and D. J. Vaughn and sons Patrick
  and David
Rooms: 10 (PB) $80-125
Full Breakfast
Credit Cards: A, B, C, D
Notes: 2, 5, 7, 8, 9, 11, 12, 13, 14

TOWNSEND

Richmont Inn

220 Winterberry Lane, 37882
(615) 448-6751

This lovely inn can be found on the "peaceful side of the Smokies." This Appalachian barn is beautifully furnished with 18th-century English antiques and French paintings in both the living and dining rooms. Enjoy the breathtaking mountain views. Graciously appointed rooms with sitting areas, king-size beds, wood-burning fireplaces, spa tubs for two, and private balconies. French and

Swiss cuisines are served at breakfast. Flavored coffees and special gourmet desserts by evening candlelight. Featured as one of *Country Inns* magazine's top inns of 1994 and awarded grand prize for dessert by *Gourmet* magazine. Ten minutes away from the Great Smoky Mountains. Arts and craft shops and historic Cades Cove are nearby.

Hosts: Susan and Jim Hind
Rooms: 10 (PB) $90-140
Full Breakfast
Credit Cards: None
Notes: 2, 5, 7, 9, 12, 14

WALLAND

The Inn at Blackberry Farm
1471 West Millers Cove Road, 37886
(615) 984-8166

The Inn at Blackberry Farm is an elegant country house hotel and mountain estate conveniently located 20 minutes from the Knoxville airport, yet peaceful and secluded on 1,100 acres in the foothills of the Great Smoky Mountains. The inn is a AAA four-diamond property and a member of the prestigious association of Relais and Chateaux. *Andrew Harpers Hideaway Report*, a connoisseur's guide to peaceful and unspoiled places, has named the Inn at Blackberry Farm as a Country House Hotel of the Year. This full service property is ideal for relaxing weekend getaways, corporate retreats, small meetings, and traditional holidays.

Rooms: 29 (PB) $375-495
Full Breakfast
Credit Cards: A, B, C
Notes: 2, 3, 4, 5, 7, 9, 10, 11, 12, 13, 14

NOTES: Credit cards accepted: A MasterCard; B Visa; C American Express; D Discover; E Diners Club; F Other; 2 Personal checks accepted; 3 Lunch available; 4 Dinner available; 5 Open all year; 6 Pets welcome;

Texas

ABILENE

Bolin's Prairie House Bed and Breakfast

508 Mulberry, 79601
(915) 675-5855

Nestled in the heart of Abilene is a 1902 home furnished with antiques and modern luxuries combined to create a warm, home-like atmosphere. Downstairs, there are high ceilings, hardwood floors, and a wood-burning stove. Upstairs are four unique bedrooms (Love, Joy, Peace, and Patience), each beautifully decorated. Breakfast of special baked-egg dishes, fruit, and home-made bread is served in the dining room that is decorated with a collection of cobalt glass and blue and white china.

Hosts: Sam and Ginny Bolin
Rooms: 4 (2 PB; 2 SB) $50-65
Full Breakfast
Credit Cards: A, B, C
Notes: 2, 5, 7

AMARILLO

Parkview House Bed and Breakfast

1311 South Jefferson, 79101
(806) 373-9464

This 1908 Prairie Victorian in the heart of the Texas panhandle has been lovingly restored by the present owners to capture its original charm. It is furnished with antiques and comfortably updated. Guests may relax, read, or engage in friendly conversation on the wicker-filled front porch; browse through the garden; or soak leisurely in the romantic hot tub under stars. Convenient to biking, jogging, tennis, hiking, and the award-winning musical drama *Texas* in Palo Duro State Park. Old Route 66, antique shops, restaurants, various museums, and West Texas A&M University are nearby. Continental plus breakfast. Smoking restricted. Inquire about accommodations for children.

Hosts: Nabil and Carol Dia
Rooms: 5 (3 PB; 2 SB) $65-85
Continental Breakfast
Credit Cards: A, B, C
Notes: 2, 5, 9, 10, 11, 12, 13, 14

ATHENS

Bed and Breakfast Texas Style

4224 West Red Bird Lane, Dallas, 75237
(214) 298-8586

New York Texas Cheesecake. This wonderful two-story farmhouse overlooks about 25 acres of a peaceful meadow and a well-stocked bass lake. The new inn has four upstairs guest bedrooms; two bedrooms have private baths, and two bedrooms share a hall bath. The host is famous for New York Texas cheesecake, which is offered to all who come through the door. The inn provides a library, formal dining room, wonderful veranda with big rocking chairs, and rooms filled with antiques that are for sale. Breakfast will be a bonanza of ham or sausage, buttered new potatoes, and eggs with mushroom-and-onion sauce. Children and pets are welcome. Smokers are welcome to smoke on the porch. $79.

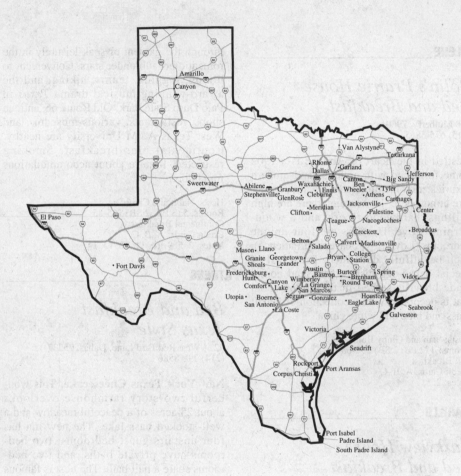

Texas

AUSTIN

Austin's Wildflower Inn

1200 West 22 1/2 Street, 78705
(512) 477-9639

Austin's Wildflower Inn is a carefully restored New England country-style bed and breakfast. Each room is furnished with antiques; all windows are filled with lace or embroidered curtains; antiques and hand-made quilts fill an antique captain's chest. A hearty full breakfast is served in the dining room or on the beautiful bilevel deck in the back garden. Tennis and trails for hiking and biking are nearby. Business rates available.

Host: Kay Jackson
Rooms: 4 (2 PB; 2 SB) $59-75
Full Breakfast
Credit Cards: A, B, C
Notes: 2, 5, 7, 9, 10, 11, 12

Bed and Breakfast Texas Style

4224 West Red Bird Lane, Dallas, 75237
(214) 298-8586

Cliffside Guesthouse. The beautiful view and the large greenbelt area keep folks coming back to this cozy guest house with kitchenette. High above Barton Springs Creek, there is a queen-size Hide-a-Bed and private bath. Breakfast goodies are placed in the small refrigerator for guests to prepare at their leisure. Smoking is permitted outside only. Two-night minimum stay. $65.

Tarrytown. This private residence in an older, affluent area of the city is perfect for business men and women who need to be near the heart of the city. The guest bedroom has a double bed and private bath. The home has many lovely antiques as well as contemporary furnishings. Breakfast will be Continental, served in the cozy breakfast nook. No smoking. Cat in residence. $60-75.

The Brook House

The Brook House Bed and Breakfast

609 West 33rd Street, 78705
(512) 459-0534

The Brook House was built in 1922 and restored to its present country charm. It is located seven blocks from the University of Texas with easy access to local restaurants and live music. Enjoy one of five guest rooms, each of which has a private bath and telephone. A full breakfast is served daily in the dining room which has a fireplace or, weather permitting, outside on the veranda. No smoking in rooms.

Host: Barbara Love
Rooms: 5 (PB) $55-79
Full Breakfast
Credit Cards: A, B, C, D, E
Notes: 2, 5

Carrington's Bluff Bed and Breakfast

1900 David Street, 78705
(512) 479-0638

Carrington's Bluff is in the heart of Austin on one acre of tree-covered bluff. Choose from an 1877 farmhouse, an 1897 Neoclassical Victorian, or an 1910 country

NOTES: Credit cards: A MasterCard; B Visa; C American Express; D Discover; E Diners Club; F Other; 2 Personal checks accepted; 3 Lunch available; 4 Dinner available; 5 Open all year; 6 Pets welcome; 7 No smoking; 8 Children welcome; 9 Social drinking allowed; 10 Tennis nearby; 11 Swimming nearby; 12 Golf nearby; 13 Skiing nearby; 14 May be booked through a travel agent.

Carrington's Bluff

cottage. A collection of historic houses in the downtown area, just blocks from the University of Texas and state capitol grounds. Each has been transformed into an inviting bed and breakfast in the English country tradition. Antique-filled rooms and the sweet smell of potpourri await. Breakfast begins with gourmet coffee, fresh fruit, and homemade granola served on fine English china. Homemade muffins, breads, and a house specialty ensure guests won't go away hungry. Children over ten welcome.

Hosts: Gwen and David Fullbrook
Rooms: 16 (14 PB; 2 SB) $60-99
Full Breakfast
Credit Cards: A, B, C, D, E, F
Notes: 2, 5, 7, 9, 10, 11, 12, 14

Fairview—A Bed and Breakfast Establishment

1304 Newning Avenue, 78704
(512) 444-4746; (800) 310-4746

Surrounded by huge live oak trees on an acre of landscaped grounds, this turn-of-the-century Colonial Revival Austin historic landmark offers gracious accommodations. Carefully selected antique furnishings give each room its own unique style and romance. Fairview's six rooms range from luxury suites to elegant retreats. The gardens are a wonderful place to relax after a busy day. "Fairview is probably the grandest bed and breakfast in Austin (and

one of the top two or three in the state)"—*Texas Monthly*, August 1993.

Hosts: Duke and Nancy Waggoner
Rooms: 6 (PB) $89-129
Full Breakfast
Credit Cards: A, B, C, E
Notes: 2, 5, 7, 9, 10, 11, 12, 14

The McCallum House

613 West 32nd Street, 78705
(512) 451-6744 (phone and FAX)

The historic McCallum House, an Austin landmark with a Texas historical marker, is six blocks north of the University of Texas-Austin and 20 blocks north of the Texas capitol and downtown. All rooms and suites have private baths, period Victorian furnishings, private telephones, kitchen facilities, sitting areas, color TVs, and private porches, as well as many other amenities. Owner-occupant innkeepers are the hosts. Easy access to state capitol, LBJ Library, Highland Lakes, Zilker Park, Mount Bonnell, and lots more. A $15 per night discount Sunday to Thursday with two nights or more. Two-night minimum stay on weekends. Smoking outside only.

Hosts: Nancy and Roger Danley
Rooms: 5 (PB) $85-105
Full Breakfast
Credit Cards: A, B
Notes: 2, 5, 9, 10, 11, 12

The McCallum House

Southard House

908 Blanco, 78703
(512) 474-4731

Centrally downtown off West Sixth Street are
two beautifully restored homes—one is an
1890s Greek Revival and the other is a 1910
bungalow. A two-block stroll will take guests
to the wonderful West End area, full of restaurants and shopping. All of the antique-decorated rooms and suites have private baths and
telephones. Some of the rooms have features
such as claw-foot tubs, fireplaces, coffee makers, TVs, and small refrigerators. Continental
buffet is served on weekdays; full breakfast is
served on weekends.

Hosts: Jerry and Rejina Southard
Rooms: 11 (PB) $59-129
Full and Continental Breakfast
Credit Cards: A, B, C, D, E
Notes: 2, 5, 7, 8

Woodburn House
Bed and Breakfast

4401 Avenue D, 78751
(512) 458-4335

This lovely 1909 Victorian landmark with
double wrap porches is nestled among 100-
year-old trees in the historic Hyde Park
neighborhood, a national register district.
Four spacious rooms are available. Full formal breakfasts, antique furnishings, and
luxurious linens provide the right environment for a truly pleasant stay. A mile and
one-half north of the University of Texas.
Discounts for singles and longer stays.
Children over 10 welcome.

Hosts: Herb and Sandra Dickson
Rooms: 4 (PB) $75-82
Full Breakfast
Cards: A, B, C
Notes: 2, 5, 7, 9, 10, 11, 12, 14

BASTROP

The Historic Pfeiffer House

1802 Main Street, 78602
(512) 321-2100

The Historic Pfeiffer House

The Pfeiffer House is one of Bastrop's 25
Texas Historic Homes and is listed on the
National Register of Historic Places. Each
room is tastefully decorated with
antiques, offering guests relaxation free
from TV and telephone. A full breakfast
is served formally in the dining room. The
three upstairs bedrooms are charmingly
decorated to give each room a warm, welcome feeling. Two porches invite guests
to "sit a spell" and relax.

Hosts: Charles and Marilyn C. Whites
Rooms: 3 (SB) $66
Full Breakfast
Credit Cards: None
Notes: 2, 5, 10, 11, 12

BELTON

Bed and Breakfast
Texas Style

4224 West Red Bird Lane, Dallas, 75237
(214) 298-8586

The Belle of Belton. A beautiful antebellum home right in town with four bedrooms to charm and pamper guests. The
rooms are named after the four seasons:
Spring, with twin four-poster beds and
claw-foot tub across the hall; Summer,

7 No smoking; 8 Children welcome; 9 Social drinking allowed; 10 Tennis nearby; 11 Swimming nearby;
12 Golf nearby; 13 Skiing nearby; 14 May be booked through a travel agent.

with king-size bed, white wicker furniture, and shared bath; Fall, with brass bed, rocking chairs in the triple window, and private bath with shower; Winter, with a corner cupola where poinsettias are displayed, queen-size bed, and private bath. Continental breakfast includes quiche or croissants, fresh fruit, and specially blended coffees or teas. $75.

BEN WHEELER

Bed and Breakfast Texas Style

4224 West Red Bird Lane, Dallas, 75237
(214) 298-8586

The Arc Ridge Guest Ranch. This 600-acre ranch in East Texas near Canton and Tyler has its own lake. Three guest houses have two bedrooms, living room, complete kitchen, and shower. Fishing and paddleboats are available. No hunters allowed in this environmentally protected area. Breakfast will be left in the refrigerator for guests to prepare themselves. Family rates will be considered. Two-night minimum stay. $75.

BIG SANDY

Annie's Bed and Breakfast

106 North Tyler, 75755
(903) 636-4355

Come capture a special moment in time at Annie's Bed and Breakfast, a place to savor the charm of bygone days...back to a time when a stay away from home was an experience worth remembering. This elegant Victorian country inn offers gracious accommodations with all the romance and charm of the turn of the century. Each room is individually decorated with soft floral wallpapers, antique furnishings, elegant appointments, and a small old-fashioned refrigerator. Some rooms feature balconies,

many have private baths, and three even have lofts—perfect for kids. Room rate includes full breakfast for two. Add $15 each for additional persons (space permitting, breakfast is included). No charge for children under five. All rooms are subject to sales tax. Come enjoy old-fashioned hospitality and let the hosts turn back the hands of time.

Hosts: Clifton and Kathy Shaw
Rooms: 12 (10 PB; 2 SB) $50-115
Full Breakfast
Credit Cards: A, B, C, D
Notes: 2, 3, 4, 5, 7, 8, 9, 14

Bed and Breakfast Texas Style

4224 West Red Bird Lane, Dallas, 75237
(214) 298-8586

Annie's Bed and Breakfast. Take a step back in time at this fascinating inn that has 12 bedrooms, each with small refrigerator for soft drinks and fruit. Breakfast is served in Annie's Tea Room, a historical home that has been converted into a charming restaurant. Tyler is only 10-15 minutes away; Jefferson is 90 minutes away. Call early since rooms are booked far in advance. No smoking. $50-115.

BOERNE

Borgman's Sunday House Bed and Breakfast Inn

911 South Main, 78006
(210) 249-9563; (800) 633-7339

In a quaint and appealing setting in the beautiful Texas Hill Country. Each room is unique and most are furnished with antiques. All guest rooms are delightfully decorated, cozy, and immaculate. A bountiful breakfast is served in the restored German Sunday House. Close to antique and craft shops. Twenty-five miles from San Antonio and Sea World. Fifteen miles from Fiesta Texas theme park. Smoking

NOTES: Credit cards accepted: A MasterCard; B Visa; C American Express; D Discover; E Diners Club;
F Other; 2 Personal checks accepted; 3 Lunch available; 4 Dinner available; 5 Open all year; 6 Pets welcome;

restricted. Inquire about accommodations for children.

Hosts: Mike and Mary Jewell
Owners: Lou and Mary Lou Borgman
Rooms: 13 (PB) $45-70
Full Breakfast
Credit Cards: A, B, C, D, E
Notes: 2, 5, 11, 12, 14

BRENHAM

Captain Clay Home

Route 5, P.O. Box 149, 77833
(409) 836-1916

This early Texas home, circa 1852, is on a hilltop overlooking beautiful rolling countryside. Enjoy the peaceful porches, watching miniature horses frolic in the pastures, a walk to the creek, or a visit to the nearby Antique Rose Emporium. Air conditioning for summer and a big, cozy fireplace for winter make this a place to stay for all seasons. A private spa is available for year-round pleasure. Smoking restricted.

Host: Thelma Zwiener
Rooms: 5 (3 PB; 2 SB) $50-75
Full Breakfast
Credit Cards: None
Notes: 2, 5, 8, 9, 11, 12, 14

BROADDUS

Sam Rayburn Bed and Breakfast: The Cole House

Woodvillage Addition, Route 1,
    P.O. Box 258, 75929
(409) 872-3666

In the piney woods of the Angelina National Forest is a peaceful little getaway on Sam Rayburn Lake. Not a traditional bed and breakfast, this is a cozy little guest house that will sleep nine adults. The setting would delight Thoreau himself, with the peaceful waters of the lake and tall, shady oak and pine trees, and absolute seclusion. Thirty years of antique collecting fill this five-room

cottage on the lake. Fully central air conditioning. All-electric kitchen. Everything is furnished for a peaceful, relaxing stay.

Hosts: Gene and Jean Cole
Cottage: 2 (SB) $55
Continental Breakfast
Credit Cards: None
Notes: 2, 5, 7, 9, 11, 13, 14

BRYAN

Bed and Breakfast Texas Style

4224 West Red Bird Lane, Dallas, 75237
(214) 298-8586

Creekway. A contemporary home right in the middle of town, just ten minutes from Texas A&M University. Three guest rooms share two baths. Continental breakfast consists of sausage kolaches (Czech), fresh fruit platter, cereal assortment, and coffee or tea. Cats in residence. Smoking permitted outside only. $60-70.

BURTON

Knittel Homestead Inn

520 Main Street, 77835
(409) 289-5102

This fully restored Queen Anne Victorian home resembles a Mississippi steamboat with wraparound porches. Beautifully furnished with antiques and country furniture, the home features three spacious bedrooms each with a private bath. Guests are treated to a delicious, all-you-can-eat country breakfast, and complimentary sodas, juices, and snacks. The home is listed on the National Register of Historic Places, and numerous local historic sites are within walking distance. Children over 12 welcome.

Hosts: Steve and Cynthia Miller
Rooms: 3 (PB) $75-100
Full Breakfast
Credit Cards: None
Notes: 2, 5, 7, 9

7 No smoking; 8 Children welcome; 9 Social drinking allowed; 10 Tennis nearby; 11 Swimming nearby; 12 Golf nearby; 13 Skiing nearby; 14 May be booked through a travel agent.

CALVERT

Bed and Breakfast Texas Style

4224 West Red Bird Lane, Dallas, 75237
(214) 298-8586

Our House. The town of Calvert is a gem, with almost all its buildings on the National Register of Historic Places. This home offers five guest rooms and two baths in the hall. Breakfast is a gourmet treat, with Belgian waffles, ham and cheese omelets, fresh fruit, and beverage. Children welcome. The location is convenient to Bryan-College Station and all Aggie events. No smoking allowed. $75.

CANTON

Heavenly Acres Bed and Breakfast Guest Ranch

Route 3, Box 470, Mabank, 75147
(800) 283-0341; FAX (903) 887-6108

Heavenly Acres, 12 miles southwest of Canton, offers separate and private guest houses with a total guest capacity of 50 people. Each accommodation has TV/VCR with video library. All houses provide full kitchens with microwaves and coffee makers and are stocked with country breakfast grocery items and a variety of gourmet coffees, teas, and creamers. Snack baskets are provided. Guests can meet and dine in the large fellowship hall. There are hookups for RVs available. There are two private lakes with small fishing boats and paddle boats. Petting zoo with barnyard animals, trails, gazebo, and picnic areas. Children welcome. Pets allowed with prior approval. Smoking outside only. No minimum night stay required. Additional person $15 extra.

Host: Vickie J. Ragle
Houses: 4 (PB) $85
Full or Continental Breakfast
Credit Cards: A, B, C, D
Notes: 2, 3, 4, 5, 9, 10, 11, 12, 14

CANYON

Hudspeth House

1905 Fourth Avenue, 79015
(806) 655-9800; (800) 655-9809
FAX (806) 655-7457

This historic bed and breakfast is on the road to and only 20 minutes from Palo Duro Canyon, home of the famous *Texas* musical drama. The facilities offer beautiful accommodations, good ol' American breakfasts. Take a stroll to the Panhandle Plains Museum or just relax and enjoy the warm hospitality. Lunch and dinner available with reservations.

Hosts: Mark and Mary Clark
Rooms: 8 (PB) $55-85
Full Breakfast
Credit Cards: A, B, C, D
Notes: 2, 5, 7, 8, 9, 10, 11, 12, 14

CARTHAGE

Bed and Breakfast Texas Style

4224 West Red Bird Lane, Dallas, 75237
(214) 298-8586

Best Little Horse House. Completely renovated, this carriage house was originally a stable that the host had moved to a beautiful spot surrounded by tall pines. Collectibles and fine antiques are attractively displayed in this getaway cottage. Breakfast may be delivered to the cottage in the morning or guests are invited into the main home for an exquisite meal. $75.

CENTER

Pine Colony Inn

500 Shelbyville Street, 75935
(409) 598-7700

In a quiet East Texas town, this inn sits just west of the Sabine River, which runs between Texas and Louisiana. Only a few

NOTES: Credit cards accepted: A MasterCard; B Visa; C American Express; D Discover; E Diners Club; F Other; 2 Personal checks accepted; 3 Lunch available; 4 Dinner available; 5 Open all year; 6 Pets welcome;

Pine Colony Inn

miles from Toledo Bend, it is a popular spot for bass fishing. Group gatherings and meetings are welcome.

Hosts: Regina Wright and Marcille Hughes
Rooms: 12 (8 PB; 4 SB) $27-55
Full Breakfast
Credit Cards: None
Notes: 2, 5, 7, 8, 9, 12, 14

CLEBURNE

Bed and Breakfast Texas Style

4224 West Red Bird Lane, Dallas, 75237
(214) 298-8586

Anglin Queen Anne. Fine architecture, a magnificent collection of antiques, and genuine hospitality make a stay in this inn a memorable experience. There are four guest rooms, three with private baths. The bridal suite upstairs has two rooms. The bedroom has a double bed with matched bird's eye maple furniture including armoire and washstand. Three other rooms available. A full breakfast is served in the formal dining room or the big kitchen. The inn may be reserved for corporate meetings, weddings, teas, and other social events. Handicapped accessible. No smoking allowed. No pets allowed. $70-125.

CLIFTON

Bed and Breakfast Texas Style

4224 West Red Bird Lane, Dallas, 75237
(214) 298-8586

The Sweetheart Cottage. A historical home, once damaged in a tornado, now restored for a perfect weekend getaway. A loft room has a queen-size bed, and a pull-out sofa is available downstairs. Country breakfast fare is left in the complete kitchen for the guests to prepare. No smoking. Two-night minimum stay required. $70.

COLLEGE STATION

Bed and Breakfast Texas Style

4224 West Red Bird Lane, Dallas, 75237
(214) 298-8586

Country Gardens. A sense of peace and tranquility will descend on guests as they enter this little country hideaway on four acres. Stroll through the wooded glen, fruit orchard, grapevines, and berry patches and enjoy the birds and wildflowers. The hosts will prepare a delicious breakfast of wheat pancakes or homemade bread; coffee, tea, or milk; and fruit in season. $60-65.

COMFORT

The Comfort Common

818 High Street, P.O. Box 539, 78013
(512) 995-3030

Historic limestone hotel, circa 1880, listed on the National Register of Historic Places. Rooms and suites are furnished with antiques. The downstairs of the hotel features numerous shops filled with American antiques. A stay at the Comfort Common

7 No smoking; 8 Children welcome; 9 Social drinking allowed; 10 Tennis nearby; 11 Swimming nearby; 12 Golf nearby; 13 Skiing nearby; 14 May be booked through a travel agent.

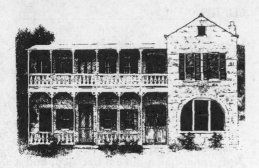

The Comfort Common

will put guests in the heart of the Texas Hill Country with Fredericksburg, Kerrville, Boerne, Bandera, and San Antonio all a brief 15-30 minutes away. Fiesta Texas theme park is only 20 minutes away.

Hosts: Jim Lord and Bobby Dent
Rooms: 6 (PB) $55-90
Full Breakfast
Credit Cards: A, B, C, D
Notes: 2, 5, 9, 12

CORPUS CHRISTI

Sand Dollar Hospitality

3605 Mendenhall Drive, 78415
(512) 853-1222

Bay Breeze. Within view of the sparkling bay waters, this fine older home reflects the "elegance of yesteryear" and offers four accommodations, all with private baths. Guests are invited to enjoy the large sunroom, shoot pool on the 1930s billiard table, listen to music, watch TV, or just relax and chat with the hosts who are lifelong residents of the community. A cat and dog are on premises. It's less than a five-minute drive to the business district and city marinas where guests can enjoy fine dining and recreation or purchase shrimp direct from the net. Guests are only a short stroll to the city's finest bayfront park and fishing pier. Full breakfast. Smoking outside only, please. $60-85.

Bay Haven. This 60-year-old brick home is in one of the city's finest older neighborhoods just two blocks from the bay waters and about five minutes' driving time from downtown. There is one guest room. The hosts offer a collection of games and videos that guests are invited to enjoy. The spacious plant-filled deck leads to an outdoor Jacuzzi, a popular attraction after a day of sightseeing. Full breakfast. $75.

Cape Comfort. A spacious Colonial-style brick home close to Corpus Christi Bay. This home has two guest bedrooms with private baths. A full breakfast is served in the sunny breakfast room or on the back patio. The hostess is a school teacher, so occupancy is limited to weekends during the school year. $60.

Linda's Downtown Bed and Breakfast. This newly remodeled two-story frame house has preserved the ambience of an earlier time and features a large bedroom and bath on the first floor and two smaller bedrooms with a shared bath upstairs. An alcove off the living room accommodates a single day bed. The fully equipped kitchen is complete with microwave and the cozy living room includes a recliner and TV. Convenient to downtown and only three blocks from the bay, this home has covered off-street parking and laundry facilities. Full breakfast. $125 family rate. $75.

La Maison Du Soleil. Within a quiet walled community, reminiscent of the medieval cities of Provence. This secure home offers a guest room with private bath, a heated pool, and access to nearby tennis courts. On a direct route to the city's main thoroughfare and midway between downtown and the gulf beaches. Driving time is 25 minutes in either direction. Full breakfast. Smoking outside only, please. $75.

Parkview. A well-landscaped and attractively furnished one-story brick home near a shady, well-maintained park. Guests are assured of privacy and quiet in either of the two guest bedrooms. Both rooms have ceiling fans and share a bath. There is cable TV in the living room, and magazines and books are available. The hostess is a nurse whose working hours vary. In the event that she is unavailable, a Continental breakfast will be prepared for dining outside on the patio or in the sunny breakfast room. A dog and two cats in residence. Full or Continental breakfast. Smoking is permitted. $100 family rate. $60.

The Pelican. This 20-year-old brick home is on the city's south side, convenient to major shopping malls and about 15 minutes from downtown. The Hans Suter Wildlife Park and a public golf course are close by. Guest quarters consist of a two-room suite with a double bed, a sitting room, and private bath. Full breakfast. Available Thursdays through Saturdays. $54.

Primrose Cottage. A beguiling blend of antiques, decorator whimsy, and down-home comfort contribute to the charm of this two-room guest cottage with private bath. The cottage is separate from the owner's residence, so guest are assured of complete privacy. The hosts are a young military couple with two small, well-behaved children. A full breakfast can be delivered to the cottage each morning, or it can be served on the spacious deck adjoining the main house. $66.

The Seagull. New England antiques collected by the hosts, a retired navy couple, add to the charm and ambience of this lovely home. Only one block from Corpus Christi Bay, this 50-year-old home is in a quiet neighborhood just a five-minute walk from the city's largest bayside park. Guests are invited to relax in the enclosed patio/den with TV, wet bar, and cozy surroundings. Two bedrooms with private baths are available. Older children are welcome. Full breakfast. Smoking outside only, please. $45 for children. $60.

The White House. Country French furnishings and family heirlooms give this distinctive home an air of warm and informal hospitality. The attractive guest bedroom has a private bath as well as a small refrigerator stocked with fruit juices and bottled water. Also provided are a coffee maker and cable TV that includes two movie channels. The plant-filled back yard and partially covered patio provide an enjoyable outdoor area for dining and relaxing. The patio features an African grey parrot that's a real people pleaser. The White family, their pre-teenage daughter, and their Yorkshire terrier are the hosts of the appropriately named White House. Full breakfast. Smoking outside only, please. $75.

The Wimberly. Midway between downtown and the beach and adjoining a private 18-hole country club golf course nestled among large oaks, this stately, vine-covered home reflects traditional European country elegance. The luxurious master suite has a canopied king-size bed, sunken tub and spa, an entertainment center, a fireplace, its own secluded patio, and a private bath. Upstairs are three spacious and beautifully appointed guest rooms with private baths as well as a sitting room with stereo and TV. Wine and cheese may be served on the patio in the evening. Full breakfast. Smoking outside only, please. $90-200.

Wood Duck. This attractive two-story brick home is in one of the city's newer neighborhoods and is convenient to downtown and the gulf beaches. The home has two guest rooms upstairs with a shared bath. There is also an upstairs sitting room with cable TV. The well-landscaped back yard

7 No smoking; 8 Children welcome; 9 Social drinking allowed; 10 Tennis nearby; 11 Swimming nearby; 12 Golf nearby; 13 Skiing nearby; 14 May be booked through a travel agent.

includes a swimming pool with a diving board and an adjacent deck with an umbrella table and chairs, where late afternoon refreshments are served. Pipi, an adopted greyhound with a gentle disposition, is kept in the hostess's quarters at night and put outside at all mealtimes. The hostess prefers only family members or parties traveling together. Children over 12 welcome. Full breakfast. Smoking outside only, please. $37.50 for children. $75.

CROCKETT

Bed and Breakfast Texas Style

4224 West Red Bird Lane, Dallas, 75237
(214) 298-8586

The Arledge House. This wonderful historic two-story home built in 1895 is on a spacious corner lot and is surrounded by large pecan trees. The bedrooms have king-size beds and private baths, TVs, and collectible items from the hosts' family. For breakfast the hosts will prepare a Mexican buffet or homemade cinnamon rolls with fresh fruit and coffee. $85.

DALLAS

The American Dream Bed and Breakfast

P.O. Box 670275, 75367
(214) 357-6536; (800) 373-2690
FAX (214) 357-9034

Share the meaning of the American Dream with these multilingual hosts, who especially welcome foreign and business guests. Modern home features contemporary art. Choose the bedroom/library suite with private bath (can sleep four) or the master suite with luxury bath. Superior northwest Dallas location minutes from the city's major shopping malls, restaurants, entertainment,

and corporate offices. Convenient to Dallas/Fort Worth Airport and minutes from Love Field. Easy access to area attractions. Off-street parking. Full breakfast served on weekends; Continental breakfast served weekdays.

Hosts: Pat and André Biczynski
Rooms: 3 (2 PB; 1 SB) $69-75
Full and Continental Breakfast
Credit Cards: A, B
Notes: 5, 7, 9, 10, 11, 12, 14

Bed and Breakfast Texas Style

4224 West Red Bird Lane, 75237
(214) 298-8586

Artist's Haven. This private home offers two upstairs guest rooms with lovely amenities and shared bath. One room has twin beds, and the other room has a king-size bed. Breakfast is Continental plus, with fruit, pastries, and beverages. Cat in residence. No smoking. Children are welcome. $70.

The Cloisters. This lovely home is one block from White Rock Lake in a secluded area of Dallas. There are two guest rooms, each with a private bath. Both rooms have double beds, one with an antique Mexican headboard that is a conversation piece. Breakfast will be lots of protein, eggs, and/or blueberry pancakes. A bicycle is available for riding around the lake. No smoking. $75.

Fan Room. The antique fan displayed in this lovely twin bedroom is the focal point and was the start of a large collection of fans. The home is near Prestonwood, Marshall Fields, and the Galleria Mall. Southfork Ranch is a 15-minute drive north. A full country breakfast includes jalapeño muffins for first-time Texas visitors. Second bedroom near the kitchen with a double bed and private bath. $60.

NOTES: Credit cards accepted: A MasterCard; B Visa; C American Express; D Discover; E Diners Club;
F Other; 2 Personal checks accepted; 3 Lunch available; 4 Dinner available; 5 Open all year; 6 Pets welcome;

The Rose. This historical home was built in 1901 and has four guest bedrooms, each with a private bath. Guests are treated to special breakfasts on the weekends, Continental during the week. Children over 12 are welcome. Smoking is permitted. $60-85.

Tudor Mansion. Built in 1933 in an exclusive neighborhood in the shadow of downtown, this Tudor-style mansion offers queen-size bed and private bath. A full gourmet breakfast of cheddar on toast, Texas-style creamed eggs with jalapeño, or fresh vegetable omelet is served. The bus line is three blocks away. Spanish and French are spoken. Three miles from downtown. Close to a public golf course. $80.

EAGLE LAKE

Bed and Breakfast Texas Style

4224 West Red Bird Lane, Dallas, 75237
(214) 298-8586

Eagle Hill Retreat. A historical mansion, circa 1936, and adjoining estate, 75 minutes from Houston and 90 minutes from San Antonio, offers an Olympic-size pool, wet and dry saunas, lighted tennis courts, two guest houses, and six bedrooms upstairs in the main home. Most rooms have two double beds and private baths, but the bridal suite has a four-poster king-size bed and fireplace. The guest houses have three bedrooms each and shared baths. A full Texas-style breakfast is served in the large dining room. The nearby national wildlife refuge protects the Attwater's prairie chicken, which has been on the endangered species list. Children are welcome. Smoking is restricted. Visitors may choose the guest house or the main house. $65-150.

EL PASO

Sunset Heights Bed and Breakfast Inn

717 West Yandell Avenue, 79902
(915) 544-1743; (800) 767-8513
FAX (915) 544-5119

National historic home offers restored Victorian elegance. Built in 1905, architectural details feature Tiffany doors, windows, chandeliers, and stained-glass windows. Elegance surrounds guests inside and out. Palm trees, pool with Jacuzzi. All rooms have an individual motif. Marble baths and balcony baths. Antiques. Security. Mature adults will appreciate gourmet French and Continental foods. Breakfast is three to eight courses. Dinner is six to twelve courses. Reservations required for dinner party of six or more. Reservations required.

Hosts: R. Barnett and R. Martinez
Rooms: 6 (PB) $70-165
Full Breakfast
Credit Cards: A, B, C, D
Notes: 2, 3, 5, 7, 9, 10, 11, 12, 14

ENNIS

Raphael House

500 West Ennis Avenue, 75119
(214) 875-1555

These six exquisite bedrooms with private baths are set in a beautifully restored 1906

Raphael House

7 No smoking; 8 Children welcome; 9 Social drinking allowed; 10 Tennis nearby; 11 Swimming nearby; 12 Golf nearby; 13 Skiing nearby; 14 May be booked through a travel agent.

Neoclassical mansion appointed with original antiques, rich wall coverings, and luxurious fabrics. Amenities include oversize beds with down comforters and pillows, claw-foot tubs with imported toiletries, afternoon refreshments, and turndown service. A full breakfast is served on the weekends, and a Continental breakfast on weekdays. In a national register historic district just 35 minutes from Dallas and 15 minutes from Waxahachie. Antiques, shopping, museums.

Host: Danna Cody Wolf
Rooms: 6 (PB) $65-100
Full and Continental Breakfasts
Credit Cards: A, B, C, D, E
Notes: 2, 5, 7, 9, 10, 11, 12, 14

FORT DAVIS

The Veranda Country Inn

210 Court Avenue, P.O. Box 1238, 79734
(915) 426-2233

This unique adobe building, with two-foot-thick walls and 12-foot ceilings, has eight large rooms and suites furnished with antiques and collectibles. Its walled gardens and quiet courtyards provide weary professionals and exploring travelers with a change of pace and lifestyle in mile-high Fort Davis. A large, separate carriage house has two bedrooms, a bath, living room, and kitchen. The Veranda is within 20 minutes of renowned sites for astronomy, historical forts and buildings, hiking, and bird watching.

Hosts Paul and Kathie Woods
Rooms: 9 (PB) $67.50-99
Full Breakfast
Credit Cards: A, B, D
Notes: 2, 5, 7, 9, 10, 11

FREDERICKSBURG

Country Cottage Inn— Nimitz Birthplace

249 East Main Street, 78624
(210) 997-8549

Country Cottage Inn

Fredericksburg's two most historic homes (the Chester Nimitz Birthplace and Kiehne House) form this inn. Thick limestone walls, hand-cut beams and woodwork, and mellow stone fireplaces are in both homes. Both are on the National Register of Historic Places. Enjoy complimentary wine, Laura Ashley linens, king-size beds, old ceiling fans, room refrigerators, microwaves, bathrobes, giant whirlpool tubs, tubside candles, and fireplaces. Common room with fireplace, sitting area, and large dining table. Courtyard with fountain. Outdoor porch swing gliders. Shopping in all directions. New this year is a lovely courtyard house built from native limestone and 100-year-old long leaf yellow pine.

Host: Jeffrey Ann Webb
Rooms: 11 (PB) $80-120
Full Breakfast
Credit Cards: A, B
Notes: 2, 5, 7, 8, 9, 10, 11, 12, 14

Das College Haus

106 West College, 78624
(210) 997-9047; (800) 654-2802

Visit historic Fredericksburg and stay at Das College Haus, just three blocks from downtown. Spacious rooms with private baths; all have access to the porches and balcony with porch swing and wicker rockers, where guests can relax and visit. Das College Haus is beautifully appointed with comfortable period furniture and original art and a wonderful "at home" atmosphere. Enjoy a full breakfast served in the old-fashioned dining room. Central heat and air, cable TV, VCR, and a collection of movies.

Hosts: Myrna Dennis
Rooms: 4 (PB) $70-85
Full Breakfast
Credit Cards: None
Notes: 2, 5, 8, 9, 10, 11, 12, 14

Haus Wilhelmina

409 North Cora Street, 78624
(210) 997-3827; FAX (210) 997-6398

Television-featured, historic turn-of-the-century German kindergarten preserved and restored into one of Texas's first bed and breakfasts. German-speaking hostess enjoys serving hearty breakfasts in chandelier dining room or pecan-tree-covered garden patio. Many videos, CDs, and family room just for guests. Hostess lives adjoining. Three blocks from main street shopping paradise.

Rooms: 2 (1 PB; 1 SB) $75
Full Breakfast
Credit Cards: None
Notes: 2, 5, 7, 8, 10, 11, 12

Magnolia House

101 East Hackberry, 78624
(210) 997-0306

Built circa 1923 and restored in 1991, this inn exudes Southern hospitality in a grand and gracious manner. Outside, magnolias and a bubbling fishpond and waterfall set a soothing mood. Inside, beautiful living room and formal dining room provide areas for guests to mingle. Four romantic rooms and two beautiful suites have been thoughtfully planned, decorated with antiques. Southern-style breakfast and complimentary wine cap a memorable experience.

Hosts: Joyce and Patrick Kennard
Rooms: 6 (4 PB; 2 SB) $80-110
Full Breakfast
Credit Cards: A, B, C
Notes: 2, 5, 10, 11, 12

GALVESTON

The 1887 Coppersmith Inn

1914 Avenue M, 77550
(409) 763-7004; (713) 965-7273

Beautiful and historical Queen Anne Victorian is complete with gingerbread trim, double veranda, and turret corners with bay windows. An elaborate staircase, built-in china cabinet, and ornate woodwork are among the outstanding features. The home was renovated using many interesting faux painting art forms and is filled with period antiques. Beach, Strand Historical District, live theater, fine restaurants, and mansion tour nearby. Breakfast catered to guests' schedule. Children over six welcome.

Host: Lisa Hering
Rooms: 4 (1 PB; 3 SB) $85-135
Full or Continental Breakfast
Credit Cards: A, B, C
Notes: 2, 5, 7, 9, 11, 12, 14

Hazlewood House

1127 Church Street, P.O. Box 1326, 77553
(409) 762-1668

Romantic Victorian home with three rooms to choose from with private baths. Jacuzzi in room or Jacuzzi suite available. Antique furnishings, Oriental carpets, and fine tapestries throughout. Wine and cheese on arrival; morning coffee and a hearty Continental breakfast are served on fine china, crystal, and silver. Ten blocks to the beach; near historical tours, musicals, museums, and trolley.

Host: Pat Hazlewood
Rooms: 3 (PB) $55-125
Continental Breakfast
Credit Cards: A, B
Notes: 2, 5, 9, 10, 11, 12, 13, 14

Madame Dyer's Bed and Breakfast

1720 Postoffice Street, 77550
(409) 765-5692

7 No smoking; 8 Children welcome; 9 Social drinking allowed; 10 Tennis nearby; 11 Swimming nearby; 12 Golf nearby; 13 Skiing nearby; 14 May be booked through a travel agent.

From the moment guests enter this carefully restored turn-of-the-century Victorian home built in 1889, they will be entranced by such period details as wraparound porches, high airy ceilings, wooden floors, and lace curtains. Each room is furnished with delightful antiques that bring back memories of days gone by. In the morning, on an antique buffet sideboard located on the second floor, guests will find teas and freshly brewed coffee provided for the early riser. Breakfast is a special treat, served abundantly in the dining room. Come as a guest to Madame Dyer's and leave as a friend. Stay here and experience the splendor of the Victorian era on historic Galveston Island. Limited smoking allowed. Children over 12 are welcome.

Hosts: Linda and Larry Bonnin
Rooms: 3 (PB) $100-125
Full Breakfast
Credit Cards: A, B
Notes: 2, 5, 9, 11, 12, 13, 14

Madame Dyer's

The Queen Anne Bed and Breakfast

1915 Sealy Avenue, 77550-2312
(409) 763-7088; (800) 472-0930

This home is a four-story Queen Anne Victorian built in 1905. Stained-glass windows, beautiful floors, large rooms, pocket doors, and 12-foot ceilings with transom doors; beautifully redecorated in 1991. Walk to the historic shopping district, restaurants, 1886 opera house, museums, and the historic homes district. A short drive to the beach. A visit to Queen Anne is to be anticipated, relished, and long-remembered.

Hosts: John McWilliams and Earl French
Rooms: 4 (SB) $85-125
Full Breakfast
Credit Cards: A, B, C
Notes: 2, 5, 7, 9, 10, 11, 12, 13, 14

Trube Castle Inn

1627 Sealy Avenue, 77550
(800) 662-9647

This remarkable castle, built in 1890, has been completely restored and is listed on the National Register of Historic Places. Offering just two exclusive suites, this 27-room mansion is furnished throughout with period antiques. Accommodations include private baths, private living rooms, porches, stereo systems, TV, VCR, and in-room refrigerators. Within walking distance of historic Strand and beaches, "Texas's most fantastic Victorian home" replicates the Danish royal castle of the period and offers a unique opportunity to sample 1890s wealth and extravagance. Smoking is restricted.

Host: Nonette O'Donnell
Suites: 2 (PB) $125-195
Full Breakfast
Credit Cards: A, B, C, D
Notes: 2, 5, 9, 10, 11, 12, 14

The Victorian Inn

511 Seventeenth Street, 77550
(409) 762-3235

Massive Italian villa built in 1899. Spacious guest rooms are romantically decorated with king-size beds and antiques. The four rooms on the second floor have balconies. Third-floor suite has a private bath and two bedrooms. The inn is within walking dis-

The Victorian Inn

tance of historic Strand: restaurants, shops, and boats. Less than one mile to the beach.

Host: Marcy Hanson
Rooms: 6 (2 PB; 4 SB) $85-175
Continental Breakfast
Credit Cards: A, B, C
Notes: 5, 11

GARLAND

Bed and Breakfast Texas Style

4224 West Red Bird Lane, Dallas, 75237
(214) 298-8586

Catnip Creek. Right on Spring Creek, the hot tub on the deck overlooks a wooded creek. The guest room has a queen-size bed, private bath, and private entrance. Breakfast has granola and cinnamon-raisin biscuits or other homemade muffins and breads. Weekend guests are treated to a healthy quiche or pancakes. Herbal teas and special blended coffees are offered. Bicycles are provided. Just 30 minutes from downtown Dallas and very near Hypermart, the newest tourist attraction of the metroplex. Also near Southfork Ranch. $38.

GEORGETOWN

Bed and Breakfast Texas Style

4224 West Red Bird Lane, Dallas, 75237
(214) 298-8586

Page House. This Queen Anne-style house, perched on top of a grassy knoll overlooking the banks of the South San Gabriel River, was built in 1903. Guests have a choice of four bedrooms, three upstairs and one downstairs, all with private baths. Lovely family treasures and antiques are throughout the home. Many items in the rooms may be purchased. The Tea Room, known for its delicious lunches, will be used for breakfast by guests. Dinner theater in the barn at the back of the property. Smoking outdoors only. $85.

Claibourne House

912 Forest, 78626
(512) 930-3934; (512) 867-6928 (voice mail)

Claibourne House is three blocks west of the historic courthouse square in the heart of "old Georgetown." Built in 1896, this spacious Victorian residence was restored in 1987-88 and adapted as a bed and breakfast inn. Guests are graciously accommodated in four bedrooms, each with private bath. An intimate upstairs sitting room and downstairs grand hall and parlor and wraparound porch are available for guests. The guest rooms are handsomely furnished with treasured family furniture, antiques, and distinctive fine art.

Host: Clare Easley
Rooms: 4 (PB) $85-95
Continental Breakfast
Credit Cards: A, B
Notes: None

GLEN ROSE

Bussey's Something Special

202 Hereford Street, P.O. Box 1425, 76043
(817) 897-4843

Relax in a private guest cottage in downtown Glen Rose historic district. King-size and full beds with crib upstairs. Lie back in the hand-crafted lounges to read or meditate. Enjoy the artwork, books, games, toys, and recliners or just sit outside on the front porch swing. Full kitchen includes all regular appliances plus microwave, toaster, and coffee pot. Breakfast items are furnished for a self-served meal. Feast on a variety of cereals, pastries, juices, coffee, tea, eggs, bread, and more. Seashell and oak bathroom with shower (no tub). Tours and fossil hunts available.

Hosts: Susan and Morris Bussey
Cottage: 1 (PB) $80
Continental Breakfast
Credit Cards: None
Notes: 2, 5, 7, 8, 10, 11, 12, 14

The Lodge at Fossil Rim

P.O. Box 2189, Route 1, Box 210, 76043
(817) 897-7452

In a secluded area, this Austin stone-and-cedar lodge offers luxurious accommodations surrounded by beautiful vistas and the abundant wildlife of Fossil Rim Wildlife Center. Pamper yourself with a choice of five spacious and uniquely furnished guest bedrooms, including private fireplaces, Jacuzzis, patios, and a delicious and generous multicourse breakfast prepared to taste. Fill the day with sunbathing by a spring-fed pool, relaxing while enjoying the stunning view from the marvelous wraparound deck, or discovering some of the world's most endangered wildlife. Only 75 miles southwest of Dallas.

Rooms: 5 (3 PB; 2 SB) $125-225
Full Breakfast
Credit Cards: A, B, C, D
Notes: 2, 5, 8, 9, 11, 12

GONZALES

St. James Inn

723 St. James, 78629
(210) 672-7066

A former cattle baron's mansion. This bed and breakfast is a welcome respite from the busy life. Furnished with antiques, colorful collections, and warm hospitality. The rural area offers a fun opportunity for hiking,

biking, antiquing, and roaming. The inn has cold lemonade on the front porch or spiced tea in front of a fire.

Hosts: Ann and J. R. Covert
Rooms: 5 (4 PB; 1 SB) $65-150
Full Breakfast
Credit Cards: A, B, C
Notes: 2, 3, 4, 5, 7, 9, 10, 11, 12

GRANBURY

Pearl Street Inn Bed and Breakfast

319 West Pearl Street, 76048
(817) 279-PINK

Relax and reminisce in the stately, stylish comfort of a 1912 Prairie-style home. Three blocks from Granbury's historic square, this tastefully restored historical home features antique furnishings, two porches, cast-iron tubs, pocket doors, and scrumptious breakfasts. Indulge in live theater, state parks, drive-in movies, antique shopping, or festivals in a charming country setting, 30 miles south of the Dallas/Fort Worth metroplex. Guests may also simply stay in and enjoy a delightful home where days move gently in all seasons.

Host: Danette D. Hebda
Rooms: 4 (PB) $59-98
Full Breakfast
Credit Cards: None
Notes: 2, 5, 9, 10, 11, 12, 14

GRANITE SHOALS

La Casita Bed and Breakfast

1908 Redwood Drive, 78654
(210) 598-6443; (800) 798-6443

Nestled 50 feet behind the main house, this private cottage is rustic and Texan on the outside, yet thoroughly modern inside with a queen-size bed. Native Texan hosts can suggest Highland Lakes parks, wineries, and river cruises. However, relaxing and bird watching in a country setting are the main attractions here. Guests choose an entrée with a full breakfast. Ideal location for small weddings, anniversaries, and birthdays. Arbor and garden are available for relaxing. Children welcome. Brochure available.

Hosts: Joanne and Roger Scarborough
Cottage: 1 (PB) $65-70
Full Breakfast
Credit Cards: None
Notes: 2, 5, 7, 8, 9, 11, 12

HOUSTON

The Highlander

607 Highland Avenue, 77009
(713) 861-6110; (800) 807-6110

This romantic 1922 four-square sits in a tranquil wildlife garden, yet is only five minutes from downtown. Between I-10W and I-45N and one block to Metro line, the location is convenient to everything. As longtime residents of Houston, hosts can help in planning itineraries. Amenities include fresh flowers, robes, telephones, turndown service, bedside snacks, and lovely full breakfast, along with Southern charm and Christian hospitality. Ask about Enchanted Evenings. Fax service available. Amtrak pickup free.

Hosts: Arlen and Georgie McIrvin
Rooms: 4 (2 PB; 2 SB) $75
Full Breakfast
Credit Cards: A, B, C, D
Notes: 2, 5, 7, 10, 11, 12, 14

Patrician
Bed and Breakfast Inn

1200 Southmore Avenue, 77004-5826
(713) 523-1114; (800) 553-5797
FAX (713) 523-0790

There will always be fresh flowers and a full breakfast at this 1919 three-story Colonial Revival mansion. Queen-size beds and private baths. Several rooms have adjoining sitting rooms, and some baths have claw-foot tubs and shower contrap-

Patrician

tions. Between downtown Houston and the Texas Medical Center. Walk to Houston Zoological Gardens, Hermann Park, and the Museum of Fine Arts. Excellent dining is available nearby.

Host: Pat Thomas
Rooms: 5 (PB) $75-95
Full Breakfast
Credit Cards: A, B, C, D, E
Notes: 2, 5, 7, 9, 10, 12, 14

Robin's Nest

4104 Greeley, 77006
(713) 528-5821; (800) 622-8343

Historic, circa 1897, two-story wooden Queen Anne. Feather beds atop fine mattresses, convenience of central location, and taste (buds) make the stay worthwhile. The rooms are spacious, furnished in eclectic Victorian with custom-made drapes, bed covers, etc. Robin's Nest is decoratively painted in concert with her sister "Painted Ladies." In the museum and arts District, surrounded by museums, art galleries, downtown, excellent restaurants, and the theater district. Inquire about accommodations for pets.

Host: Robin Smith
Rooms: 4 (PB) $65-110
Full Breakfast
Credit Cards: A, B, C, D
Notes: 2, 5, 7, 8, 9, 11, 12, 14

7 No smoking; 8 Children welcome; 9 Social drinking allowed; 10 Tennis nearby; 11 Swimming nearby; 12 Golf nearby; 13 Skiing nearby; 14 May be booked through a travel agent.

Sara's Bed and Breakfast Inn

941 Heights Boulevard, 77008
(713) 868-1130; (800) 593-1130

This Queen Anne Victorian is in Houston Heights, a neighborhood of historic homes, many of which are on the National Register of Historic Places. Each bedroom is uniquely furnished, having either single, double, queen-, or king-size beds. The balcony suite consists of two bedrooms, two baths, kitchen, living area, and balcony. The sights and sounds of downtown are only four miles away.

Hosts: Donna and Tillman Arledge
Rooms: 14 (12 PB; 2 SB) $55-150
Continental Breakfast
Credit Cards: A, B, C, D, E, F
Notes: 2, 5, 8, 9, 10, 11, 14

Sara's

Webber House Bed and Breakfast

1011 Heights Boulevard, 77008
(713) 864-9472

Built in 1907 by brickmason Samuel Webber, this red brick Queen Anne home is on the National Register of Historic Places. It features leaded and stained glass, curved oriel windows, beautiful cypress woodwork, and venetian glass chandeliers. Accommodations range from a tall

mahogany rice bed to an antique iron bed, all king- or queen-size. Private baths, one with Jacuzzi. The Webber House is in the middle of Historic Heights with antique shopping and dining nearby.

Host: Jo Ann Jackson
Rooms: 4 (PB) $75-110
Full Breakfast
Credit Cards: A, B, C, D
Notes: 2, 5, 7, 9, 14

HUNT

River Bend Bed and Breakfast

Route 1, Box 114, FM 1340, 78024
(210) 238-4681; (800) 472-3933

"A peaceful and relaxing retreat." Nestled in the Texas Hill Country along the beautiful Guadalupe River. Enjoy canoeing, swimming, tubing, and fishing. Hike over 55 acres of fossil-lined paths. Wake to the smell of freshly brewed coffee; feast on a gourmet breakfast. Relax in quaint, Victorian rooms with antique furnishings, wrought iron beds, lace curtains, and footed bathtubs. Only a short distance to antiquing, art galleries, museums, and fine dining.

Hosts: Becky Key; Conrad and Terri Pyle
Rooms: 16 (PB) $85-175
Full Breakfast
Credit Cards: A, B, C, D
Notes: 2, 5, 7, 8, 9, 10, 11, 12, 14

JACKSONVILLE

The English Manor

540 El Paso Street, 75766
(800) 866-0946; FAX (903) 589-0753

Built in 1932 and completely renovated in 1994-95, this three-story Tudor home offers its guests rooms filled with lively colors, shelves full of books, sturdy and comfortable antique furnishings, feather beds, bedside reading lamps, and luxurious amenities. Guest rooms are uniquely furnished and decorated. All have a large, private bath. Breakfast may include sour cream coffee cake, one of the hosts' special egg dishes, or buttermilk blueberry pancakes, and fresh coffee.

Hosts: Linda and Dwight Holley
Rooms: 5 (PB) $65-85
Full Breakfast
Credit Cards: A, B
Notes: 2, 5, 7, 9, 12, 14

JEFFERSON

McKay House
Bed and Breakfast Inn

306 East Delta Street, 75657
(903) 665-7322; (214) 348-1929 (Dallas)

Jefferson is a riverport town from the frontier days of the Republic of Texas. It has historical mule-drawn tours, 30 antique shops, boat rides on the Big Canyon Bayou, and a narrow-gauge train. The McKay House, an 1851 Greek Revival cottage, offers period furnishings, cool lemonade, porch swings, and fireplaces. Seven rooms that vary from the Keeping Room to the Garden Suite with two antique footed tubs. A full gentleman's breakfast is served in the Garden Observatory. Victorian nightclothes are provided. VIP guests have included Lady Bird Johnson and Alex Haley. Mobil travel guide.

Owner: Peggy Taylor
Innkeeper: Alma Anne Parker
Rooms: 7 (PB) $75-125
Full Breakfast
Credit Cards: A, B, C
Notes: 2, 5, 7, 8, 12, 14

McKay House

Pride House

409 Broadway, 75657
(903) 665-2675; (800) 894-3526

The first bed and breakfast in the state of Texas, Pride House offers ten rooms, all with private baths and inherited family Victorian antiques. Porches with rockers and swings, footed tubs, showers for two, and fireplaces. Large, sunny breakfast room that is used for small business conferences is where a full breakfast, made from Ruthmary's famous recipes, is served. Luxurious amenities and luscious interiors. The morning sun shines through original stained-glass windows of this 1888 Victorian mansion. King- and queen-size beds. Telephones and TVs are available by request.

Hosts: Carol and Lois
Rooms: 10 (PB) $65-100
Full Breakfast
Credit Cards: A, B
Notes: 2, 5, 7, 8, 9, 12, 14

Urquhart House of
Eleven Gables

301 East Walker Street, 75657
(903) 665-8442

Allen Urquhart, grandson and namesake of the co-founder of Jefferson, moved his wife, Mattie Rogers (daughter of Capt. Thomas Rogers of the Captain's Castle), and young daughter into this Victorian Queen Anne home on the corner of Frious and Walker Streets. Envision the first outdoor tennis courts in Jefferson that once stood where now stand beautiful spacious twin pecan trees. This stately and elegant home is undergoing complete restoration with many added amenities.

Host: Joyce Jackson
Rooms: 4 (PB) $75-125
Full Breakfast
Credit Cards: None
Notes: 2, 5, 7, 12, 14

7 No smoking; 8 Children welcome; 9 Social drinking allowed; 10 Tennis nearby; 11 Swimming nearby;
12 Golf nearby; 13 Skiing nearby; 14 May be booked through a travel agent.

LA COSTE

Bed and Breakfast Texas Style

4224 West Red Bird Lane, Dallas, 75237
(214) 298-8586

Swan and Railway Inn. At one time this inn was known as the City Hotel and it had only three guest bedrooms. It has now increased to five rooms, three with private baths. There is a new pool for guests to enjoy. Breakfast may be yogurt and granola or bran muffins, fruit, and herb teas. About 18 to 20 minutes from San Antonio and ten minutes from Sea World. La Coste was a French settlement, and nearby Castroville has German roots. $65-75.

LA GRANGE

Meerscheidt Haus

(La Grange Bed and Breakfast)
458 North Monroe Street, 78945
(409) 968-9569

Built in the 1880s, this gracious Victorian home offers four guest bedrooms, each with its own private bath. All rooms are furnished with period antiques that are available for guests to purchase. The living room features games, puzzles, and relaxing music, for resting or socializing. The porch swing invites sunset watching. The delicious breakfast in the formal dining room features German and Czech pastries, homemade breads and granola, and seasonal fruits. Meerscheidt Haus offers a special retreat from the everyday. Come experience a return to the grace and elegance of yesteryear! In the Austin/Houston/San Antonio triangle.

Hosts: Elva and Royce Keilers
Rooms: 4 (PB) $45-105
Full Breakfast
Credit Cards: A, B
Notes: 2, 7, 10, 11, 12, 14

LEANDER

Trails End Bed and Breakfast

12223 Trails End Road, 7, 78641
(512) 267-2901

Trails End Bed and Breakfast is a six-acre scenic, restful, romantic setting in the Texas Hill Country close to Austin and Lake Travis. The main house is a two-story Colonial-type with fireplace, two wraparound porches, and observation deck with a panoramic view of the Hill Country and Lake Travis. The main house has architectural fixtures from 1920s through 1950s with mahogany furniture throughout. Full breakfast served in the dining room. Gift shop for guests, swimming pool, gazebo, bicycles, gardens and benches to enjoy the outdoors. Guest house sleeps up to six and has decks and patios to enjoy.

Hosts: JoAnn and Tom Patty
Rooms: 2 (PB) $65-95
Full Breakfast
Credit Cards: A, B, C
Notes: 2, 4, 5, 7, 8, 9, 11, 12, 13, 14

Trails End

LLANO

Bed and Breakfast Texas Style

4224 West Red Bird Lane, Dallas, 75237
(214) 298-8586

Fraser House. Enjoy the four upstairs guest bedrooms of this 1900 solid granite house in the middle of town. The bedrooms have private baths with claw-foot tubs, a sleigh bed, a Jenny Lind bed, and iron beds. A ham and quiche breakfast along with complimentary mimosas will be served. $85.

MADISONVILLE

Bed and Breakfast Texas Style

4224 West Red Bird Lane, Dallas, 75237
(214) 298-8586

Ranch 102. This charming log home was built by the hosts as a getaway home about eight years ago. Heated by a Ben Franklin stove that produces ample heat for the loft and three rooms downstairs. The full, well-stocked kitchen includes a microwave. TV, VCR, and lots of movies are provided for guests. Guests are invited to fish in the seven-acre lake and to walk around the farm. The hosts serve a full breakfast. $95.

MASON

Hasse House

1221 Ischar, P.O. Box 58, 76856
(915) 347-6463

The Hasse House, circa 1883, is where country quality lives in historic architecture laced with modern conveniences. Complete with period furniture, microwave, dishwasher, washer-dryer, central air, two bedrooms, two baths, living room, and complete kitchen. Guests may explore the 320-acre ranch with two-mile hiking path

Hasse House

and abundant wildlife. Only one party in the house at a time. "Let us invite you to the complete peace of rural living."

Host: Laverne Lee
Rooms: 2 (PB) $85
Continental Breakfast
Credit Cards: A, B
Notes: 2, 5, 8, 9, 12

MERIDIAN

Bed and Breakfast Texas Style

4224 West Red Bird Lane, Dallas, 75237
(214) 298-8586

The Hastings House. This charming older home is on a farm near Meridian, just south of Fort Worth and Dallas. Close to Lake Whitney. The farmhouse is about 60 years old and has a large front porch, three bedrooms, living room, breakfast nook, and kitchen. There is a large bath. Breakfast is left in the refrigerator for guests to prepare. Local attractions include the Safari in nearby Clifton, the Dinosaur Tracks Park in Glenrose, and the pageant *The Promise* in Glenrose on weekends. $65.

NACOGDOCHES

Hardeman Guest House

316 North Church Street, 75961
(409) 569-1947

This beautiful late-Victorian house listed on the National Register of Historic Places is

7 No smoking; 8 Children welcome; 9 Social drinking allowed; 10 Tennis nearby; 11 Swimming nearby;
12 Golf nearby; 13 Skiing nearby; 14 May be booked through a travel agent.

in the heart of the oldest town in Texas. English, Oriental, French, and American rooms, furnished with antiques, quilts, original art, and owner's collections of American art pottery and Oriental porcelain. Home-baked breakfast breads and homemade jams and jellies highlight delicious breakfasts served on fine china, crystal, and silver. Furniture, paintings, collectibles, and crafts available. Special weekday business travel rates.

Host: Lea Smith
Rooms: 4 (PB) $65-80
Full Breakfast
Credit Cards: A, B
Notes: 2, 5, 6, 7, 8, 9

PineCreek Lodge Bed and Breakfast Country Inn

Route 3, Box 1238, 75964
(409) 560-6282

On a peaceful 140-acre wooded property near a flowing creek. Acres of beautiful grounds and flowers. Miles of surrounding country roads for driving and hiking enjoyment. Special features include large decks with swings and rocking chairs, hammock, pool, spa, fishing pond, and hiking trail. Each room has a private bath and deck with swing, air conditioning, ceiling fans, TV/VCR, refrigerator, phone, monogrammed robes, and fresh flowers. Refreshments at check-in. Smoking restricted.

Hosts: The Pitts Family
Rooms: 7 (PB) $45-65
Full Breakfast
Credit Cards: A, B, C
Notes: 2, 3, 4, 5, 7, 8, 11, 12, 13

PADRE ISLES

Sand Dollar Hospitality

35 Mendenhall Drive, Corpus Christi, 78415
(512) 853-1222

Kathy's Condo. This handsome townhouse is on one of the major canals at North Padre

Island and features two bedrooms upstairs, each with king-size bed and private bath. Downstairs there is a queen-size sofa bed and TV in the living room. Sliding glass doors open from the living/dining room to the deck. The kitchen is fully equipped, including a microwave and dishwasher, and nearby is a washer, dryer, and powder room. The owner does not live on the premises but will greet guests upon their arrival with needed breakfast supplies. Group and weekly rates available. $135.

La Mansion. This hideaway on Texas's North Padre Island is cradled between Laguna Madre Bay and the Gulf of Mexico. This is a unique bed and breakfast inn in a complex of ten condominiums. Each unit has a living room with cable TV, a bedroom with queen-size bed, a fully equipped kitchen with microwave, and a washer and dryer. There is also an outside grill available for cooking. The three-story, red-tiled roofed structure is at the intersection of five canals on the bay side of the island. The main canal leads to the fabulous fishing grounds of the Laguna Madre just a short distance away by boat. Continental plus breakfast. Smoking outside only, please. Weekly and monthly rates available. $96.

PALESTINE

Bed and Breakfast Texas Style

4224 West Red Bird Lane, Dallas, 75237
(214) 298-8586

Grandma's House. Nestled in the heart of East Texas is a country Christmas tree farm with a guest house furnished with twin beds and private bath. Relax on the front porch, stroll among the Christmas trees, or ride a paddleboat around the pond. Hearty breakfast of homemade bread, jellies, fresh farm eggs, quail, and gravy. Convenient to

NOTES: Credit cards accepted: A MasterCard; B Visa; C American Express; D Discover; E Diners Club; F Other; 2 Personal checks accepted; 3 Lunch available; 4 Dinner available; 5 Open all year; 6 Pets welcome;

antique shopping, historical sites, spring dogwood trails, and fall foliage. Just 30 minutes to the Texas State Railroad steam train ride at Palestine or Rusk, Canton's First Monday Trade Day, and Athens's Black-eyed Pea Jamboree. $70.

The Sunday House. A charming duplex with two bedrooms, large parlor, full kitchen, and shared hall bath is a classic brick residence near downtown. Near the historic Texas State Railroad steam train and the dogwood trails in spring, Palestine is a quaint town filled with many historic homes. A Continental breakfast is left in the kitchen for guests to prepare, or they may drive to the Christmas tree farm about 12 miles away and partake of the full Texas country breakfast. $70.

PORT ARANSAS

Sand Dollar Hospitality

3605 Mendenhall Drive, Corpus Christi, 78415
(512) 853-1222

Harbor View. This three-story Mediterranean-style home on the Port Aransas Municipal Harbor offers four large bedrooms, one with private bath. The inn is within convenient walking distance of restaurants, shops, charter boats, and fishing operations. On-site mooring facilities are available for craft up to 50 feet in length. Bikes are available at no charge. Full breakfast. Cots for children are available at $15 per child. $75-90.

Sea Song. A two-story, year-round beach home on the shores of the Gulf of Mexico on Mustang Island. This unique and beautiful home has an outstanding view and radiates a special ambience. The comfortably furnished living room has a TV and wet bar. There are three bedrooms that share one full bath. Sliding doors open from the living room to a deck that offers an oppor-

tunity for maximum relaxation. Because of the limited bathroom facilities, the hostess prefers only family members or parties traveling together. Older children are welcome. Smoking outside only, please. Full breakfast. $45 for children. $90.

PORT ISABEL

Yacht Club Hotel and Restaurant

700 Yturria Street, P.O. Box 4114, 78578
(512) 943-1301

Since 1926, the Yacht Club Hotel and Restaurant has provided its guests with fine dining in the casual atmosphere of the 1920s and 1930s. There are 24 cozy rooms that overlook the harbor. Come fish, beachcomb, visit Mexico, or relax and sip margaritas on the veranda. The award-winning restaurant serves fresh seafood, steaks, and pasta. Continental breakfast included in rates.

Host: Lynn Speter
Rooms: 24 (PB) $40-99
Continental Breakfast
Credit Cards: A, B, C, E
Notes: 4, 5, 8, 9, 10, 11, 12, 14

RHOME

Chisholm Trail Ranch

P.O. Box 649, 76078
(817) 638-2410; (800) 216-8865
FAX (817) 636-2411

This beautiful 2,200-acre guest ranch on the original Chisholm Cattle Trail is a true and authentic working cattle ranch with 5,000-square-foot bed and breakfast lodge, secluded cottage, historic home built in the 1800s, diverse landscape for camping, mystic rolling hills, 12 stocked fishing lakes, 100-foot cliffs, and beautiful meadows with 200-year-old oaks. Activities on the rustic, romantic, and relaxing ranch include horseback riding, historic tours, hayrides, dances, fishing, horseshoes, volleyball, hiking, bik-

7 No smoking; 8 Children welcome; 9 Social drinking allowed; 10 Tennis nearby; 11 Swimming nearby; 12 Golf nearby; 13 Skiing nearby; 14 May be booked through a travel agent.

ing, and jogging. The bed and breakfast specializes in family reunions, company/private picnics, barn dances, corporate team building, church retreats, school field trips, Western weddings, and meeting facilities.

Rooms: 7 (3 PB; 4 SB) $85-125
Cottages: 2-$195
Full and Continental Breakfast
Credit Cards: A, B, C
Notes: 2, 3, 4, 5, 8, 9, 14

nished with selected European and American antiques. Comfortable, well-appointed rooms and baths. Suppers and picnic lunches may be booked in advance. Antiques and decorative arts gallery on the premises.

Hosts: Julia and Bill Bishop
Rooms: 4 (PB) $90-110
Full Breakfast
Credit Cards: None
Notes: 2, 3, 4, 5, 9, 10, 12

ROCKPORT

Sand Dollar Hospitality

35 Mendenhall Drive, Corpus Christi, 78415
(512) 853-1222

Anthony's By the Sea. Innkeepers offer four guest bedrooms in the main house plus two guest cottages. All units throughout the inn include a refrigerator, cable TV, and VCR. A spacious plant-filled patio connects the main house and the two guest cottages. There is ample outdoor seating and a barbecue grill for guest use. Off to the side is a swimming pool and hot tub. A full breakfast is served in a large, open dining area with a picture window that overlooks an enormous live oak tree. The Aransas Wild Life Refuge is less than an hour's drive away. Group, weekly, and monthly rates available. $66-95.

ROUND TOP

Broomfields

419 North Nassau Road, 78954
(409) 249-3706; FAX (409) 249-3706

Country retreat five miles from Round Top on 40 acres of meadowland with wooded tracts and stocked pond. Historic restorations, classical music, and semiannual antique shows nearby. Spectacular displays of wildflowers in spring and foliage in fall. An 1800s Texas-vernacular modern home built with 100-year-old barn beams and fur-

SALADO

The Rose Mansion and The Inn at Salado

P.O. Box 500, 76571
(817) 947-8200

The Inn at Salado. Salado's first bed and breakfast is in the heart of the historic district. Restored to its original 1872 splendor, the inn was once the home of early Texas statesman Col. James Norton. Within walking distance of Salado's finest shops and restaurants. The inn offers nine rooms, all with private baths and most with fireplaces. Its decor and ambience is enhanced with numerous antiques and six covered porches that beckon guests to relax and linger awhile. Inquire about availability of dinner.

The Rose Mansion. Nestled among towering oaks, elms, and persimmon trees, this traditional Greek Revival-style mansion and additional complimentary cottages are on four acres of landscaping and are surrounded by a white picket fence. The main home, built in 1870 by Maj. A. J. Rose, has four bedrooms (three with fireplaces), a grand parlor, an elegant dining room, and a cozy country kitchen. There are two beautifully restored log cabins, a summer kitchen cottage, and a larger Greek Revival cottage. The mansion contains Rose family memorabilia and authentic antiques. There are a windmill with a cypress storage tank, a

NOTES: Credit cards accepted: A MasterCard; B Visa; C American Express; D Discover; E Diners Club; F Other; 2 Personal checks accepted; 3 Lunch available; 4 Dinner available; 5 Open all year; 6 Pets welcome;

rock smokehouse, and an old wagon to act as nostalgic reminders of a simpler past. A total of ten rooms are available for guests to use.

Hosts: Mansion—Lori Long; Inn—Suzanne Petro
Rooms: Mansion—10; Inn—9
Full Breakfast
Credit Cards: A, B, C, D
Notes: 2, 5, 8, 10, 11, 12

SAN ANTONIO

Adams House Bed and Breakfast and Guest House

231 Adams Street, 78210
(210) 224-4791; (800) 666-4810
FAX (210) 223-5125

Adams House is a turn-of-the-century two-story house in the King William historic district. All rooms have queen-size beds and private baths. The Guest House is in the Southtown historic district. It has queen-size beds, and private and shared baths. Both are decorated with antiques. A large, cooked breakfast is served for both houses at the Adams House.

Hosts: Betty Lancaster and Scott Lancaster
Rooms: 12 (8 PB; 4 SB) $45-130
Full Breakfast
Credit Cards: A, B, C, D
Notes: 2, 5, 7, 8, 9, 14

Adelynne's Summit Haus and Summit Haus II

427 West Summit, 78212
(210) 736-6272; (800) 972-7266

Two elegant 1920s residences in the heart of San Antonio, five minutes from downtown and Riverwalk. The main house is furnished with rare Biedermeier antiques. The cottage is furnished with 18th- and 19th-century French and English antiques. It is ideal for those who prefer an entire house to themselves. All rooms have TV, telephone, and refrigerator with complimentary beverages. Central heat and air, fireplaces, tree-shaded decks, and off-street parking. Personal service from people who care.

Host: Adelynne H. Whitaker
Rooms: 5 (3 PB; 2 SB) $75-95
Full Breakfast
Credit Cards: A, B, C
Notes: 2, 5, 7, 8, 9, 10, 11, 12, 14

Beckmann Inn and Carriage House

222 East Guenther Street, 78204
(210) 229-1449

This elegant Victorian inn is in the heart of San Antonio in the King William historic district. The beautiful wraparound porch welcomes guests to this beautiful home. All rooms are colorfully decorated, featuring ornately carved Victorian queen-size beds, antiques, and private baths. Ride the trolley or take the Riverwalk to the Alamo, restaurants, shops, Mexican market, and much more. Guests receive gracious and warm hospitality during their stay. Gourmet breakfast with a breakfast dessert. Children over 12 welcome. May be booked through travel agent for midweek stays only based on availability—no special events or holiday bookings through travel agent.

Hosts: Betty Jo and Don Schwartz
Rooms: 5 (PB) $80-130
Full Breakfast
Credit Cards: A, B, C, E
Notes: 2, 5, 7, 9, 12

Beckmann Inn

7 No smoking; 8 Children welcome; 9 Social drinking allowed; 10 Tennis nearby; 11 Swimming nearby; 12 Golf nearby; 13 Skiing nearby; 14 May be booked through a travel agent.

Bed and Breakfast Texas Style

4224 West Red Bird Lane, Dallas, 75237
(214) 298-8586

Romantic Hideaway. In a secluded area just 20-30 minutes west of San Antonio in the Hill Country lies this separate apartment that is perfect for a getaway from the city. There are two single beds, one double bed, and a private bath. Breakfast fixings are left in the refrigerator in the well-stocked kitchen. Inquire about accommodations for pets. Children are welcome. Smoking restricted. Nightly and weekly rates. $60-250.

The Belle of Monte Vista

505 Belknap Place, 78212
(210) 732-4006

J. Riely Gordon designed this Queen Anne-style Victorian as a model house. Built in 1890 with limestone, the house has been beautifully restored and is in the elegant Monte Vista historic district. Inside, guests will find eight fireplaces, stained-glass windows, a hand-carved oak staircase, and Victorian furnishings. Hosts serve a full Southern breakfast and will help guests plan the day. There is a two-night minimum stay on weekends.

Hosts: JoAnn and David Bell
Rooms: 6 (4S2B) $40-75
Full Breakfast
Credit Cards: A, B, C
Notes: 2, 5, 7, 8, 10, 12

The Columns on Alamo

1037 South Alamo, 78210
(800) 233-3364

Resident innkeepers welcome guests to their gracious 1892 Greek Revival home and guest house in the historic King William area. Blocks from the Riverwalk, restaurants, shopping, convention center, and Alamo; short drive to Sea World and Fiesta Texas. Furnished with comfortable antiques and period reproductions, queen- and king-size beds, telephones, TVs, large common areas and verandas, and off-street parking. Full breakfast is served in the main house. The inn is smoke-free except for verandas and outdoors. Two-night minimum stay on Saturday.

Hosts: Ellenor and Art Link
Rooms: 11 (PB) $85-135
Continental Breakfast
Credit Cards: A, B, C
Notes: 5, 7, 9, 14

Falling Pines Inn

Falling Pines Inn

300 West French Place, 78212
(210) 733-1998

Falling Pines is in the Monte Vista historic district one mile north of downtown. Construction of the home began in 1911 under the direction of famed architect Atlee Ayres. Pine trees, not native to San Antonio, tower over the mansion on a one-acre parklike setting. Brick and limestone construction, a green tiled roof, and shuttered windows enhance a magnificent limestone archway entry and veranda on the front facade. The guest rooms are on the second level. The entire third floor is the Persian Suite and commands a grand view of downtown San Antonio. Fully restored, the mansion is furnished with traditional and antique furniture. Children over ten welcome.

Hosts: Grace and Bob Daubert
Rooms: 4 (PB) $100-150
Full Breakfast
Credit Cards: A, B, C
Notes: 2, 5, 9, 10, 12, 14

NOTES: Credit cards accepted: A MasterCard; B Visa; C American Express; D Discover; E Diners Club; F Other; 2 Personal checks accepted; 3 Lunch available; 4 Dinner available; 5 Open all year; 6 Pets welcome;

Norton Brackenridge House

230 Madison, 78204
(210) 271-3442; (800) 221-1412

This is a 90-year-old fully restored home in the King William historic district, the oldest historic district in Texas. It is a two-story house with Corinthian columns and verandas on the front and back. Decorated with Victorian antiques, it has private entrances and baths, central air and heat, and fans in all rooms. A delicious breakfast is served on the veranda or in the dining room. Pets and children welcome at guest house only.

Owners and Innkeepers: Bonnie and Sue Blansett
Rooms: 5 (PB) $89-125
Guest house: 2 (PB)
Full Breakfast
Credit Cards: A, B, C, D
Notes: 2, 5, 7, 9, 10, 11, 12, 14

The Ogé House on the Riverwalk

209 Washington Street, 78204
(800) 242-2770; FAX (210) 226-5812

Step back to an era of elegance and romance in this historic antebellum mansion shaded by massive pecans and oaks, on one and one-half landscaped acres along the banks of the famous San Antonio Riverwalk. The inn, beautifully decorated with antiques, has large verandas and a grand foyer. All rooms have either queen- or king-size beds, private baths, air conditioning, telephones, and TVs. Dining, entertainment, convention centers, trolley, and the Alamo are steps away. Smoking restricted.

Hosts: Patrick and Sharrie Magatagan
Rooms: 10 (PB) $135-195
Continental Breakfast
Credit Cards: A, B, C, D, E
Notes: 2, 5, 9, 10, 12

Riverwalk Inn

329 Old Gailbeau Road, 78204
(210) 212-8300; (800) 254-4440
FAX (210) 229-9422

The Riverwalk Inn is comprised of five two-story log homes, circa 1840, that have been restored on the San Antonio Riverwalk and are tastefully decorated in period antiques. Amenities include fireplaces, refrigerators, private baths, telephones, balconies, 80-foot porch, and conference area. Continental plus breakfasts and desserts served. Swimming nearby. Smoking permitted outside only. No children.

Hosts: Johnny Halpenny; Jan and Tracy Hammer
Rooms: 11 (PB) $89-135
Continental Breakfast
Credit Cards: A, B, C, D
Notes: 2, 5, 10, 11, 12, 14

San Antonio Yellow Rose

229 Madison, 78204
(210) 229-9903; (800) 950-9903

The 1879 home built by Charles Mueller, a German immigrant, is a brick Victorian with a mansard roof and large porches. The home has five bedrooms distinctively decorated with antiques, each with a private bathroom and television. A large living and dining room with 18th-century furnishings provide space to get comfortable. The bed and breakfast offers a full breakfast and off-street parking. In the King William historic district, just two blocks from the Riverwalk.

Hosts: Jennifer and Cliff Tice
Rooms: 5 (PB) $85-120
Full Breakfast
Credit Cards: A, B, C, D
Notes: 2, 5, 7, 8, 9, 10, 12, 14

The Victorian Lady Inn

421 Howard Street, 78212
(210) 224-2524; (800) 879-7116

Experience the ultimate in Victorian elegance. This 1898 historic mansion offers spacious guest rooms furnished with period antiques. High back beds, claw-foot tubs, fireplaces, and verandas complete guests' pampered retreat. Savor a fabulous full breakfast each morning. Enjoy the book exchange or try a bicycle for a scenic ride. The Alamo, Riverwalk, convention center,

7 No smoking; 8 Children welcome; 9 Social drinking allowed; 10 Tennis nearby; 11 Swimming nearby;
12 Golf nearby; 13 Skiing nearby; 14 May be booked through a travel agent.

and 25¢ trolley are just blocks away. Rediscover the genteel ambience of 100 years ago at the Victorian Lady Inn. Children over 12 welcome.

Hosts: Joe and Kathleen Bowski
Rooms: 7 (PB) $70-160
Full Breakfast
Credit Cards: A, B, C, D
Notes: 2, 5, 7, 9, 10, 11, 12, 14

SAN MARCOS

Crystal River Inn

326 West Hopkins, 78666
(512) 396-3739

Romantic, luxurious Victorian mansion that captures all the fun and flavor of the Texas Hill Country. Close to headwaters of crystal-clear San Marcos River. Antiques, fireplaces, and fresh flowers adorn the rooms. Wicker-strewn veranda, gardens, and fountains offer hours of peaceful rest and relaxation. Enjoy sumptuous brunches including gourmet items such as stuffed French toast and bananas Foster crêpes. Mystery weekends, river trips, and romantic getaways are the hosts' speciality.

Hosts: Mike and Cathy Dillon
Rooms: 12 (10 PB; 2 SB) $55-110
Full Breakfast
Credit Cards: A, B, C, D, E, F
Notes: 2, 5, 7, 9, 10, 11, 12, 14

SEABROOK

Bed and Breakfast Texas Style

4224 West Red Bird Lane, Dallas, 75237
(214) 298-8586

High Tide. Right on Galveston Bay at the channel where shrimp boats and ocean liners go in and out, this Cape Cod-style cottage is available for families or romantic getaways. It will sleep seven to nine people with two bedrooms downstairs, each with a private bath. A loft room upstairs with two double beds and a twin bed has a half-bath.

A large deck with chairs is perfect for sunning and watching birds and boats. Continental breakfast. $65.

The Pelican House Bed and Breakfast Inn

1302 First Street, 77586
(713) 474-5295; FAX (713) 474-7840

This 90-year-old home can be found on the "Back Bay" just down the street from Galveston Bay and is in the Old Seabrook Art and Antique Colony. The Pelican House is the closest bed and breakfast to the Space Center Houston and less than five minutes to the 19 Clear Lake area marinas. The Pelican House is decorated whimsically with pelicans and fish. Relax in rocking chairs on the front porch or on the back deck where water bird viewing is at its best. Children over 10 welcome.

Host: Suzanne Silven
Rooms: 4 (PB) $60-70
Full Breakfast
Credit Cards: A, B, C, D
Notes: 2, 5, 7, 9, 10, 11, 12, 14

SEADRIFT

Hotel Lafitte

302 Bay Avenue, 77983
(512) 785-2319

A unique bed and breakfast on San Antonio Bay. Built in 1909 and fully restored in 1988. Furnished in antique Victorian style. In Seadrift, Texas, 30 miles south of Victoria on Highway 185.

Hosts: Frances and Weyman Harding
Rooms: 10 (4 PB; 6 SB) $60-115
Full Breakfast
Credit Cards: A, B, C
Notes: 2, 5, 9, 11

SOUTH PADRE ISLAND

Brown Pelican Inn

207 West Aries, P.O. Box 2667, 78597
(210) 761-2722

NOTES: Credit cards accepted: A MasterCard; B Visa; C American Express; D Discover; E Diners Club; F Other; 2 Personal checks accepted; 3 Lunch available; 4 Dinner available; 5 Open all year; 6 Pets welcome;

The Brown Pelican Inn is a place to relax, make oneself at home, and enjoy personalized service. The porches are a great spot to sit and watch the sun set over the bay. The inn is comfortably furnished with European and American antiques; all guest rooms have private baths, and most rooms have spectacular bayviews. Breakfast in the parlor includes freshly baked breakfast, fresh fruit, cereal, juice, and gourmet coffee or tea. Smoking restricted. Children over 12 welcome.

Hosts: Vicky and Ken Conway
Rooms: 8 (PB) $70-150
Continental Breakfast
Credit Cards: A, B
Notes: 2, 5, 9, 11

The Oxford House

SPRING

McLachlan Farm Bed and Breakfast

P.O. Box 538, 24907 Hardy Road, 77383
(713) 350-2400; (800) 382-3988

The McLachlan family homestead, built in 1911, was restored and enlarged in 1989 by the great-granddaughter, and her husband, of the original McLachlan family who settled the land in 1862. Set back among huge sycamore and pecan trees, it is a quiet oasis that returns guests to a time when life was simpler. Visitors may swing on the porches, walk in the woods, or visit Old Town Spring where there are more than 150 shops to enjoy. Call for brochure.

Hosts: Jim and Joycelyn (McLachlan) Clairmonte
Rooms: 4 (2 PB; 2 SB) $65-75
Full Breakfast
Credit Cards: A, B, C, D
Notes: 2, 5, 7, 12, 14

STEPHENVILLE

The Oxford House

563 North Graham Street, 76401
(817) 965-6885

Stephenville is in the northern tip of the beautiful Texas Hill Country. Situated on Highway 67 west of Lake Granbury and east of Proctor Lake. Tarleton State University is in town. Only 30 minutes from Fossil Rim Wildlife Preserve and Dinosaur Valley. The Oxford House was built in 1898 by Judge W. J. Oxford, Sr., and the completely restored, two-story Victorian, presently owned by the grandson of the judge, has antique furnishings. Enjoy a quiet atmosphere and country breakfast. Shopping within walking distance. Smoking restricted. Children over ten are welcome.

Hosts: Bill and Paula Oxford
Rooms: 5 (4 PB; 1 SB) $65-75
Full Breakfast
Credit Cards: A, B
Notes: 2, 4, 5, 9, 10, 11, 12, 14

TEAGUE

Hubbard House Inn Bed and Breakfast

621 Cedar Street, 75860-1617
(817) 739-2629; (817) 562-2496

Having served as the Hubbard House Hotel for railroad employees during part of its history, this red brick and white frame Georgian home is furnished mostly with Early American antiques. There is a second-floor balcony porch with swings that offers guests a place to relax. A country breakfast is served in the large formal dining room on a glass-topped antique pool table. Reservations should be made at least 48 hours before arrival. Inquire about accommodations for children. May be booked through a travel agent if stay is for two or more nights.

Host: John W. Duke
Rooms: 6 (SB) $64.95
Full Breakfast
Credit Cards: A, B, C, E
Notes: 2, 5, 7, 12

TEXARKANA

Mansion on Main

802 Main Street, 75501
(903) 792-1835

"Twice As Nice," the motto of Texarkana (Texas and Arkansas) USA, is standard practice at the Mansion on Main. The 1895 Neoclassical Colonial, surrounded by 14 tall columns, was recently restored by the owners of the McKay House, a popular bed and breakfast in nearby Jefferson. Six bed chambers vary from the Governor's Suite to the Butler's Garret. Business and leisure guests enjoy Southern hospitality, period furnishings, and a full gentleman's breakfast. Telephone system and decks for convenience of business travelers. Ross Perot's home and Perot Theater are within a few blocks. Just 30 miles from the town of Hope, the birthplace of President Bill Clinton. Rated by AAA.

Host: Javeta Hawthorne
Owners: Peggy and Tom Taylor
Rooms: 6 (PB) $60-110
Full Breakfast
Credit Cards: A, B, C
Notes: 2, 5, 7, 12, 14

TYLER

Bed and Breakfast Texas Style

4224 West Red Bird Lane, Dallas, 75237
(214) 298-8586

Vintage Farm Home. This newly renovated, circa 1836-1864, home, once an original dogtrot plantation home, sits in the piney woods of East Texas. Catch the morning sun or evening breeze on the large veranda where rocking chairs and a swing invite relaxation. Take a stroll through the trails during dogwood season or fall foliage. The guest room has a king-size bed and private bath. Breakfast is served downstairs in the cozy nook. $85.

Mary's Attic Bed and Breakfast

413 South College, 75702
(903) 592-5181; FAX (903) 592-3846

A two-bedroom, two-bath 1920 bungalow restored and furnished with English and American antiques on the brick streets in the historic part of Tyler. The Continental breakfast features homemade sweet rolls and breads. Refrigerator stocked with complimentary cold drinks, juice, and fresh fruit tray. Additional annex apartment, which sleeps five, has three bedrooms, one bath, and full kitchen. Children welcome in apartment only. Breakfast is an extra charge in the apartment, $60 for one person and $15 for each additional person. No smoking. No pets.

Rooms: 2 (PB) $75
Continental Breakfast
Credit Cards: A, B, D
Notes: 2, 5, 9, 10, 11, 12

Rosevine Inn Bed and Breakfast

415 South Vine, 75702
(903) 592-2221

Rosevine Inn is in the historic Brick Street Shoppes area of Tyler. There are several shops within walking distance and a lovely courtyard with fountain and fireplace. There is also an outdoor hot tub and game room complete with billiards for guests' enjoyment. There are now two suites available. A full gourmet breakfast is served.

NOTES: Credit cards accepted: A MasterCard; B Visa; C American Express; D Discover; E Diners Club; F Other; 2 Personal checks accepted; 3 Lunch available; 4 Dinner available; 5 Open all year; 6 Pets welcome;

The hosts look forward to meeting guests and welcoming them to the Rose Capital of the World.

Hosts: Bert and Rebecca Powell
Rooms: 7 (PB) $75-150
Full Breakfast
Credit Cards: A, B, C, D, E
Notes: 2, 5, 7, 8, 9, 10, 11, 12, 14

The Woldert-Spence Manor

611 West Woldert Street, 75702-7149
(903) 533-9057; (800) WOLDERT

This beautifully restored, two-story Queen Anne home is in the historic Brick Street district of Tyler. It has a historical designation, with roots that go back to the 1850s. The original hardwood floors and stained-glass windows have been restored, and the home is decorated in antiques and collectibles. Rooms available with fireplace, private balcony or screened porch, and baths with restored claw-foot tubs. Covered spa available under the large shade trees in the rear garden, which also has a fish bowl with fountain and covered wishing well. An all-you-can-eat hearty breakfast is served on antique china with crystal in the formal dining room downstairs. A great place for that special getaway or for business. Walking distance to antique shops and minutes from Tyler Rose Garden, museums, lakes, and Caldwell Zoo. No minimum stay required. Smoking restricted. Inquire about accommodations for children.

Hosts: Richard and Patricia Heaton
Rooms: 5 (PB) $75-95
Full Breakfast
Credit Cards: A, B, C, D
Notes: 2, 5, 9, 10, 11, 12

UTOPIA

Bed and Breakfast Texas Style

4224 West Red Bird Lane, Dallas, 75237
(214) 298-8586

Bluebird Hill Ranch. A private cabin on a creek in a secluded corner of this 260-acre ranch home is now available for guests. Breakfast will be left in the refrigerator in the complete kitchen. The cabin will accommodate six people. Near Garner State Park and the Frio River, one hour to San Antonio. Two-night minimum stay. Smoking outside. $75.

VAN ALYSTYNE

Bed and Breakfast Texas Style

4224 West Red Bird Lane, Dallas, 75237
(214) 298-8586

The Durning House. Historic home that was an antique shop in the past and is now a bed and breakfast with one guest room. The owners welcome guests, then leave them with complete privacy. Breakfast is homemade cinnamon rolls, juice, and coffee. The downstairs room has an antique headboard almost to the ceiling and a double bed. Comfortable parlor and dining area downstairs. $85.

VICTORIA

Friendly Oaks Bed and Breakfast

210 East Juan Linn Street, 77901
(512) 575-0000

In the shelter of ancient live oaks, history comes alive at the Friendly Oaks Bed and Breakfast in a preservation area of 80 restored Victorian homes. Each of the four rentable rooms has a private bath, its own brand of individualized decor, and reflects the preservation efforts of Victoria, Texas. The scrumptious gourmet breakfasts feature local produce. Whether guests are looking for a getaway weekend, a calm retreat for off-duty interim business time, or a honeymoon suite, the Friendly Oaks Bed and

7 No smoking; 8 Children welcome; 9 Social drinking allowed; 10 Tennis nearby; 11 Swimming nearby; 12 Golf nearby; 13 Skiing nearby; 14 May be booked through a travel agent.

Breakfast can fill all their hospitality needs. In addition, a conference room provides a quiet setting for retreats, meetings, seminars, parties, showers, and small weddings. Children over ten welcome.

Hosts: Bill and Cee Bee McLeod
Rooms: 4 (PB) $55-75
Full Breakfast
Credit Cards: A, B, C
Notes: 2, 5, 7, 9, 10, 11, 12

VIDOR

Bed and Breakfast Texas Style

4224 West Red Bird Lane, Dallas, 75237
(214) 298-8586

Poppa Bear's House. A warm and loving home near the Louisiana border and Beaumont. Teddy bears are displayed throughout the home. There is a pool for summer fun, fireplace for cozy visiting in winter. Breakfast will be Czech kolaches, homemade cinnamon rolls, juice or fruit, and coffee or tea. Visit the downs in Louisiana or the beach just south of Beaumont. Two rooms have queen-size beds, one with private bath. There is one room with a double. No smoking. Children welcome. $55.

WAXAHACHIE

Bed and Breakfast Texas Style

4224 West Red Bird Lane, Dallas, 75237
(214) 298-8586

Millie's Victorian. This beautiful Queen Anne-style mansion filled with antiques has a guest bedroom downstairs with private entrance and private bath with a claw-foot tub. Enjoy a full breakfast in the dining room. Another guest area is a private gingerbread cottage behind the main home. Breakfast will be left in the kitchen of the private cottage. Nonsmokers. $75-150.

BonnyNook Inn

414 West Main, 75165
(214) 938-7207; (800) 486-5936

This bed and breakfast is in the historic district of the picturesque town of Waxahachie. There are four bedrooms upstairs with private baths. All rooms have antique double beds. One room has a lovely sleigh bed set. Jacuzzis available in two rooms. A Pennsylvania Dutch breakfast including shoofly pie and crêpes will be served in the formal dining room. Lunch and dinner are available at an extra charge. Scarborough Fair is popular in the spring.

Hosts: Bonnie and Vaughn Franks
Rooms: 4 (PB) $70-95
Full Breakfast
Credit Cards: A, B, C, D, E
Notes: 2, 5, 8, 9, 12, 14

WIMBERLEY

Blair House

1 Spoke Hill, Route 1, Box 122, 78676
(512) 847-8828

Created to provide guests the ultimate inn experience, is nestled on 85 acres of beautiful Texas Hill Country, 45 minutes from Austin and San Antonio. Rooms have Jacuzzi tubs and are gracefully decorated to provide every comfort. Each room has a CD player, fresh flowers, and chocolates. The library has CDs, books, periodicals, TV, and movies. Three dining rooms, a large living room with fireplace, sauna, massage room, rocking chairs, hammocks, and swings. Fine cuisine; all breads, pastries, and desserts are made in the kitchen daily. Full gourmet breakfasts start the day; it ends with irresistible desserts. Saturday evening dining is unforgettable. Special events, weddings, seminars, and business retreats are tailored to fit guests' needs.

Host: Jonnie Stansbury
Rooms: 6 (PB) $135
Full Breakfast
Credit Cards: A, B, D
Notes: 2, 4, 5, 7, 9, 10, 11, 12, 14

NOTES: Credit cards accepted: A MasterCard; B Visa; C American Express; D Discover; E Diners Club; F Other; 2 Personal checks accepted; 3 Lunch available; 4 Dinner available; 5 Open all year; 6 Pets welcome;

Rancho Cama

Rancho Cama
Bed and Breakfast

2595 Flite Acres Road, 78676-9707
(512) 847-2596; (800) 594-4501

Pampered privacy in romantic guest house—queen-size bed, sitting area, electric organ, and private bath. Bunk House comfortably sleeps six, featuring extra-long twin beds, double beds, and bunk beds with a shared bath. Both houses have color cable TV, refrigerator, and coffee maker. Homemade breakfast. Pool, hot tub, and river access. On a miniature horse and donkey ranch with Nigerian dwarf goats—foals, kids, and puppies galore! Live oak setting with 360-degree view of Hill Country and abundant wildlife. Town hosts shops, galleries, restaurants, and Lion's Market Day.

Hosts: Curtis and Nell Cadenhead
Rooms: 3 (1 PB; 2 SB) $60-85
Full Breakfast
Credit Cards: None
Notes: 2, 5, 7, 9, 10, 11, 12, 14

Southwind
Bed and Breakfast

2701 FM 3237, 78676
(512) 847-5277; (800) 508-5277

Southwind is five minutes from the quaint village of Wimberley and one hour from Austin or San Antonio. Rocking chairs on the porches are good places to view hills and valleys, wildlife, and sunsets, and the hot tub is grand for star gazing. Fireplaces, queen- and king-size beds, and antique and reproduction furniture. No smoking. Children over 12 welcome. No pets at all.

Host: Carrie Watson
Rooms: 3 (PB) $70-80
Full Breakfast
Credit Cards: A, B, D
Notes: 2, 5, 9, 10, 11, 12, 14

7 No smoking; 8 Children welcome; 9 Social drinking allowed; 10 Tennis nearby; 11 Swimming nearby; 12 Golf nearby; 13 Skiing nearby; 14 May be booked through a travel agent.

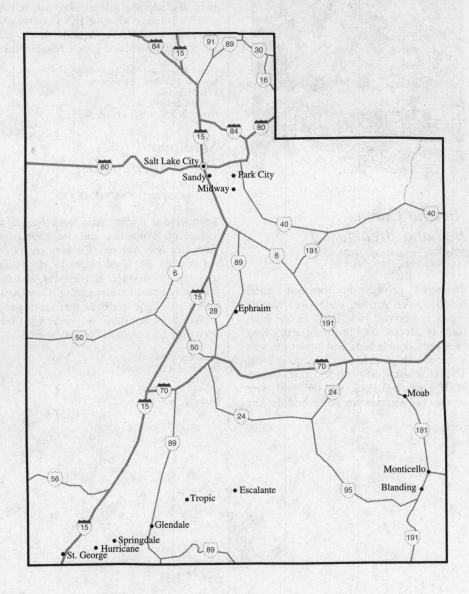

Utah

Utah

BLANDING

Grayson Country Inn
Bed and Breakfast

118 East 300 South (86-6), 84511
(801) 678-2388

Grayson Country Inn sits in the heart of
San Juan County, known for Lake Powell,
Monument Valley, Anasazi ruins, and
canyonlands. Close to Arches National
Monument, Rainbow Bridges, and the
Natural Bridges. The inn sits one block off
Main Street and is near a pottery factory,
Nations of the Four Corners Cultural
Center, and gift shops. Some of the best
hiking spots in the world are in the back
country. Grayson has eight guest rooms,
each with private bath, TV, and air condi-
tioning. Welcome all singles, couples, fam-
ilies, and friends.

Hosts: Dennis and Lurlene Gutke
Rooms: 8 (PB) $42-52
Full Breakfast
Credit Cards: A, B, C
Notes: 5, 7, 8, 11, 14

Ephraim Homestead

surrounded by old-fashioned gardens under
a canopy of trees. Breakfast is cooked on a
century-old Monarch stove and served privately to guests in the cabin; others are
served in the hosts' dining room or outdoors. A delicious nighttime treat is also
provided. Truly a unique and memorable
experience. Cross-country skiing nearby.

Hosts: Sherron and McKay Andreasen
Log Cabin: 1 (PB) $75
Barn: 2 (SB) $45-55
Full Breakfast
Credit Cards: None
Notes: 2, 5, 8, 10, 11, 12, 13

EPHRAIM

Ephraim Homestead
Bed and Breakfast

135 West 100 North (43-2), 84627
(801) 283-6367

Ephraim Homestead offers lodging in a pioneer log cabin or a rustic barn. The hosts'
Victorian cottage is also occasionally available. All are furnished with antiques and

ESCALANTE

Rainbox Country
Bed and Breakfast

P.O. Box 333, 84726
(801) 826-4567 (phone and FAX); (800) 252-UTAH

Spacious bed and breakfast on Utah's scenic
Byway 12, one hour from Bryce Canyon.
Scenic views and hot tub, recreation room

NOTES: Credit cards: A MasterCard; B Visa; C American Express; D Discover; E Diners Club; F Other;
2 Personal checks accepted; 3 Lunch available; 4 Dinner available; 5 Open all year; 6 Pets welcome;
7 No smoking; 8 Children welcome; 9 Social drinking allowed; 10 Tennis nearby; 11 Swimming nearby;
12 Golf nearby; 13 Skiing nearby; 14 May be booked through a travel agent.

with pool table and large-screen TV. Full country breakfast. Jeep and hiking tours in red-rock canyons and alpine forest. Area activities include horseback riding, cross-country skiing, fishing, boating, and the national parks. Use this bed and breakfast as a home base for exploring the hidden wilderness country. Brochure available.

Hosts: Gene Windle and Bruce Hailey
Rooms: 4 (2 PB; 2 SB) $40-60
Full Breakfast
Credit Cards: A, B
Notes: 3, 4, 5, 6, 7, 8, 9, 11, 14

GLENDALE

Eagle's Nest Bed and Breakfast

500 Lydia's Canyon Road, P.O. Box 160, 84729
(801) 648-2200; FAX (801) 648-2221

Enjoy the tranquility of Lydia's Canyon in the heart of colorful southwest Utah off US Highway 89. Zion Canyon, Bryce Canyon, Cedar Breaks, and Grand Canyon National Parks are easily accessible. Every room is detailed to provide a relaxed and romantic setting with unique furnishings from around the world. Enjoy a country gourmet breakfast in the sunlit, antique-filled dining room. Soak carelessly in the spa. All rooms have private baths, two with fireplaces. Inquire about accommodations for children.

Hosts: Shanoan and Dearborn Clark
Rooms: 4 (PB) $69-107
Full Breakfast
Credit Cards: A, B
Notes: 3, 4, 5, 7, 9, 11, 12, 13, 14

Smith Hotel

Highway 89, P.O. Box 106, 84729
(801) 648-2156

This historic hotel-boarding house was built in 1927 by Mormon settlers. Enjoy Western charm. Screened porch overlooking the hills of southern Utah's beautiful Long Valley. Close to the scenic wonders of Zion, Bryce, and Grand Canyon National Parks and the recreational facilities of Lake Powell. All

rooms have private baths. Late 1800s private family cemetery on property. Continental plus breakfast served in family dining room. Meet other guests from all over the world.

Host: Shirley Phelan
Rooms: 7 (PB) $40-60
Continental Breakfast
Credit Cards: A, B
Notes: 7, 9, 12

HURRICANE

Pah Tempe Hot Springs Bed and Breakfast

825 North 800 East (35-4), 84737
(801) 635-2879

Set in a beautiful southern Utah canyon, Pah Tempe Hot Springs was originally a sacred Paiute healing center. Today, Pah Tempe welcomes visitors from all over the world who enjoy the natural hot mineral pools along the Virgin River. Six bed and breakfast rooms, a group center, camping, and day-use passes are available. Close to Zion, Bryce, and the Grand Canyon National Parks. Reservations required.

Hosts: The Anderson family
Rooms: 6 (2 PB; 4 SB) $55-75
Full Breakfast
Credit Cards: A, B
Notes: 2, 5, 7, 8, 11, 12, 13, 14

MIDWAY

Schneitter Family Hotel at the Homestead Resort

700 North Homestead Drive, 84049
(801) 654-1102; (800) 327-7220

The original Schneitter Family Hotel at the historic Homestead Resort. Eight Victorian rooms individually appointed with antiques, linens, and special amenities. Adjacent solarium and whirlpool. This AAA four-diamond resort offers golf, swimming, horseback riding, tennis, elegant dining, sleigh rides, cross-country skiing, snowmobiling, and complete meeting facilities. Restricted smoking.

Host: Britt Mathwich
Rooms: 8 (PB) $89-105
Continental Breakfast
Credit Cards: A, B, C, D, E
Notes: 2, 3, 4, 5, 9, 10, 11, 12, 13, 14

MOAB

Castle Valley Inn

424 Amber Lane, CVSR Box 2602, 84532
(801) 259-6012

Castle Valley Inn offers guests sophisticated comfort in the rugged canyonlands of southeast Utah. Its 11 acres of orchards, lawns, and fields feature 360-degree red-rock-to-mountaintop views. Visitors enjoy the outdoor Grandview hot tub. The inn offers full meal service to registered guests, with a complete gourmet breakfast included in room rates. No TV. VCRs and film library available. Close to Arches and Canyonlands National Parks. Five minutes to Colorado River Canyon.

Hosts: Eric and Lynn Thomson
Rooms: 8 (PB) $85-145
Full Breakfast
Credit Cards: A, B
Notes: 2, 3, 4, 7, 12

Mi Casa Su Casa Bed and Breakfast

P.O. Box 950, Tempe, AZ 85280-0950
(602) 990-0682; (800) 456-0682

1101. The casual atmosphere of a ranch-style home nestled between the snow-capped La Sal Mountains and the red-rock canyons of the Colorado River. Mountain biking, white-water challenging, and downhill or cross-country skiing are nearby. This home is a perfect place to relax at the end of the day. Four rooms with queen-size beds have private baths. One room with twin beds shares a bath. Hot tub. Maximum 14 guests. Full breakfast.

Resident cats. No smoking. Children six and older are welcome. Roll away beds are available. $59-87.

1107. A rugged old cattleman settled down and built a sturdy adobe home about 100 years ago. The host couple has renovated the original farmhouse and added a cozy country cottage. Combines country charm with comfort. Guests will discover quaint antiques, fanciful stenciling, and luxurious beds with colorful linens. Air-conditioned. Private baths. Outdoor hot tub, lush gardens, patios, barbecue, and adventure library. Outstanding breakfast buffet. No smoking or pets. Children welcome by prior arrangement. $55-95.

Westwood Guest House

81 East 100 South, 84532
(801) 259-7283

Seven uniquely decorated condos with a kitchen, living room, and private bath. Hot tub in private back yard with decks and patios. Each unit will sleep three to eight people comfortably. All have telephones and color TV. The seventh day of stay is free. The visitors center, museum, ball park, tennis courts, shopping, and several restaurants are one to two blocks away. Golf course is four miles away. Due to mild winters, biking, hiking, cross-country skiing are 30 to 40 minutes from Moab. Kitchens are stocked with do-it-yourself breakfast items of milk, coffee, tea, juice, bagels, eggs, and hot cakes.

Host: Betty Beck
Rooms: 7 (PB) $59
Continental Breakfast
Credit Cards: A, B, C, D
Notes: 2, 5, 8, 9, 10, 12, 13

MONTICELLO

Mi Casa Su Casa Bed and Breakfast

P.O. Box 950, Tempe, AZ 85280-0950
(602) 990-0682; (800) 456-0682

---

7 No smoking; 8 Children welcome; 9 Social drinking allowed; 10 Tennis nearby; 11 Swimming nearby; 12 Golf nearby; 13 Skiing nearby; 14 May be booked through a travel agent.

1100. This "salt-box" structure was built in 1933 at the foot of the Blue Mountains. Standing at an elevation of 7,000 feet, the three-story building was originally known as the Old Monticello Flour Mill. Today the original one-cylinder diesel engine and pulley shaft still poke out of nooks and crannies. The bran sacker sits in the dining room and the flour sacker stands in the lobby. Six beautiful suites, all with private baths, are decorated with antiques and collectibles. Several attractions are within driving distance, including the Four Corners area, Lake Powell, Natural Bridges National Monument, Canyonlands and Arches National Parks, and Monument Valley. Guests are welcome to enjoy the sitting room with fireplace, the library with a view of the Blue Mountains, the TV room, the deck, or the whirlpool. There is a local golf course. No smoking. No pets. Inquire about bringing children. $52.

PARK CITY

The Blue Church Lodge

424 Park Avenue, P.O. Box 1720, 84060
(801) 649-8009; (800) 626-5467
FAX (801) 649-0686

Listed on both the Utah and National Registers of Historic Places, the church was originally built in 1897. It was structurally rebuilt and remodeled in 1983, then redecorated in 1994. A unique Victorian era church on the outside, inside the lodge houses seven charmingly quaint and cozy, distinctively different, condominiums, ranging from a room with a private bath up to a four-bedroom suite. Amenities include indoor spa, game room, laundry, private phones, cable TV, private parking, ski lockers, maid service, gas-burning fireplaces, and Continental breakfast.

Host: Nancy Schmidt
Rooms: 7 (PB) $90-275
Continental Breakfast
Credit Cards: A, B, D
Notes: 2, 7, 8, 9, 13, 14

The Old Miners' Lodge

615 Woodside Avenue, Box 2639, 84060
(801) 645-8068; (800) 648-8068
FAX (801) 645-7420

A restored 1889 miners' boarding house in the national historic district of Park City, with ten individually decorated rooms filled with antiques and older pieces. Close to historic Main Street, with the Park City ski area in its back yard, the lodge is "more like staying with friends than at a hotel!" A nonsmoking inn. Minimum-stay requirements Christmas and some special events.

Hosts: Hugh Daniels and Susan Wynne
Rooms: 10 (PB) $50-195
Full Breakfast
Credit Cards: A, B, C, D
Notes: 2, 5, 7, 8, 9, 10, 11, 12, 13, 14

Washington School Inn

P.O. Box 536, 84060
(801) 649-3800; (800) 824-1672

Historic restoration of an old schoolhouse, decorated with modified Victorian furnishings. Hot tub and sauna on the property. Full breakfast and afternoon tea service included in rates. In downtown historic Park City, close to Salt Lake area airport (45 minutes) and some of the best skiing in the world.

Hosts: Nancy Beaufait and Delphine Covington
Rooms: 15 (PB) $75-225
Full Breakfast
Credit Cards: A, B, C, D, E
Notes: 5, 7, 9, 10, 11, 12, 13, 14

NOTES: Credit cards accepted: A MasterCard; B Visa; C American Express; D Discover; E Diners Club; F Other; 2 Personal checks accepted; 3 Lunch available; 4 Dinner available; 5 Open all year; 6 Pets welcome;

ST. GEORGE

Aunt Annie's Inn

139 North 100 West, 84770
(801) 673-5504; (800) 257-5504 (UT)

Aunt Annie's Inn is established in a quaint two-story 1890s adobe home nestled in the heart of historic St. George. It has a spacious parlor and dining area available to guests. The guest rooms are decorated with colorful wallpaper, antique furniture, and homemade quilts. Each room has a private bath, most of which have unique old-fashioned fixtures. Many shops and restaurants are within walking distance of the inn. National parks, golf, and skiing are only a few miles away.

Hosts: Bob and Claudia Tribe
Rooms: 5 (PB) $45-75
Full Breakfast
Credit Cards: A, B, C, D
Notes: 2, 5, 7, 8, 10, 11, 12, 13, 14

Greene Gate Village

76 West Tabernacle Street, 84770
(801) 628-6999; (800) 350-6999
FAX (801) 628-6989

Step back in time behind the green gates, where nine beautifully restored homes provide modern comfort in pioneer elegance. Try the Bentley House and its elegant Victorian decor, or the quaint Tolley House. The Grainery has rooms where early settlers loaded supplies for their trek to California. The Orson Pratt home, built by another early Mormon leader, is on the National Register of Historic Places. Green Hedge, with one of the village's five bridal suites, was originally built in another part of town but was moved here in 1991. The Greenehouse, built in 1872, has all the conveniences of a full kitchen, swimming pool, and tennis court.

Hosts: John and Barbara Greene
Rooms: 18 (PB) $50-110
Full Breakfast
Credit Cards: A, B, C, D
Notes: 2, 4, 5, 8, 10, 11, 12, 13, 14

An Olde Penny Farthing Inn

278 North 100 West, 84770
(801) 673-7755

Built in the 1870s, this traditional pioneer Victorian was built with 12-inch adobe handmade brick and a lava foundation. In the historical district on a quiet residential street. Five theme-decorated rooms done in antiques, collectibles, and handmade quilts. Honeymoon suite with queen-size brass bed done in whites, mauve, and lace, pull-chain water closet, and whirlpool. The Sir Winston has the typical English motif, pull-chain water closet, and claw-foot tub. The Betsy Ross's decor is in Americana motif with complete bath. The Sego Lily has pioneer style and complete bath. The Morning Dove has a Southwest theme. Handicapped accessible.

Hosts: Alan, Jacquie, and the "Madam"
Rooms: 5 (PB) $55-110
Full Breakfast
Credit Cards: A, B, D
Notes: 2, 5, 7, 10, 11, 12, 13, 14

Seven Wives Inn

217 North 100 West, 84770
(801) 628-3737; (800) 600-3737

The inn consists of two adjacent pioneer adobe homes with massive hand-grained moldings, framing windows, and doors. Bedrooms are furnished with period antiques and handmade quilts. Some rooms have fireplaces; two have whirlpool tubs. Swimming pool on premises.

Hosts: Donna and Jay Curtis; Alison and Jon Bowcutt
Rooms: 12 (PB) $65-125
Full Breakfast
Credit Cards: A, B, C, D, E
Notes: 2, 5, 7, 8, 9, 10, 12, 14

SALT LAKE CITY

The Anton Boxrud Bed and Breakfast Inn

57 South 600 East, 84102
(801) 363-8035; (800) 524-5511
FAX (801) 596-1316

7 No smoking; 8 Children welcome; 9 Social drinking allowed; 10 Tennis nearby; 11 Swimming nearby;
12 Golf nearby; 13 Skiing nearby; 14 May be booked through a travel agent.

This "Grand Old Home" is a half-block from the governor's mansion and six blocks from Temple Square and City Center. The Anton Boxrud Bed and Breakfast Inn is within walking distance to many restaurants and the ski bus. Truly Salt Lake City's most conveniently located bed and breakfast. Whether enjoying a cozy fire, a soothing soak in the hot tub after a great day of skiing, or simply relaxing on a cool summer evening on the front porch after a day of sightseeing, life at the Anton Boxrud is truly uncomplicated—an invitation to relax and unwind.

Hosts: Mark A. Brown and Keith Lewis
Rooms: 6 (3 PB; 3 SB) $55-119
Full Breakfast
Credit Cards: A, B, C, D
Notes: 2, 5, 7, 8, 9, 10, 11, 12, 13, 14

Mi Casa Su Casa Bed and Breakfast

P.O. Box 950, Tempe, AZ 85280-0950
(602) 990-0682; (800) 456-0682

1095. The Salt Lake City Historic Society has recognized this two-and-one-half-story brick house as one of Salt Lake's "Grand Old Homes." The beveled-glass windows and beautiful woodwork have been carefully restored according to the original 1901 plans. Rooms are furnished with antiques, including a hand-carved German dining table where a full breakfast is served. Close to the governor's mansion, downtown, University of Utah, and Temple Square. Five guest rooms on the second floor have queen-size or double beds, private and shared baths. Hot tub. Smoking allowed outside. Full breakfast. $45-109.

Saltair Bed and Breakfast

164 South 900 East, 84102
(801) 533-8184; (800) 733-8184

Antiques and charm complement queen-size brass beds, Amish quilts, and period lamps. A full breakfast featuring house juice and wake-up favorites such as pumpkin-walnut waffles and saltair muffins greet each guest. Hospitality offered by innkeepers includes snacks and use of parlor, dining room, TV, and phone. Close to the University of Utah, historic downtown, skiing, canyons, and seasonal recreation.

Hosts: Jan Bartlett and Nancy Saxton
Rooms: 7 (4 PB; 3 SB) $55-139
Full Breakfast
Credit Cards: A, B, C, E
Notes: 2, 5, 7, 8, 9, 10, 11, 12, 13, 14

Wildflowers, A Bed and Breakfast

936 East 1700 South, 84105
(801) 466-0600

Wildflowers is an 1891 Victorian home surrounded by quaking aspen, blue spruce, and an abundance of wildflowers. Listed on the National Register of Historic Places, it sits amid homes of old Salt Lake. Five minutes from downtown, and 30 minutes from skiing (seven areas to choose from). In their careful restoration, the owners have kept the delights of the past and added the comforts of the present, including air conditioning. Hand-carved staircases, stained-glass windows, claw-foot bathtubs, original chandeliers, Oriental rugs, antiques, private baths, a deck, and a reading room make up the present Wildflowers. Guests will be warmly welcomed by owners and hosts who serve a gourmet breakfast. Suite available with balcony and view of mountains.

Hosts: Cill Sparks and Jeri Parker
Rooms: 5 (PB) $68-125
Full Breakfast
Credit Cards: A, B, C
Notes: 2, 5, 7, 8, 9, 10, 11, 12, 13, 14

SANDY/SALT LAKE CITY

Mountain Hollow Inn Bed and Breakfast

10209 South Dimple Dell Road, 84092
(801) 942-3428

Mountain Hollow is nestled at the base of Little Cottonwood Canyon, close to major ski resorts, mountain biking areas, and the metropolitan night life of Salt Lake City. Twenty-five miles from Salt Lake International Airport. On a two-acre estate with trees, a creek, and a restful atmosphere. Each guest room is decorated with antique Victorian or country furniture. Complimentary beverages and treats available all the time. Come to relax and unwind in this country atmosphere.

Hosts: Doug and Kathy Larson
Rooms: 10 (1 PB; 9 SB) $62-150
Continental Breakfast
Credit Cards: A, B, C, D
Notes: 2, 5, 7, 10, 11, 12, 13, 14

Mountain Hollow Inn

SPRINGDALE

Mi Casa Su Casa Bed and Breakfast

P.O. Box 950, Tempe, AZ 85280-0950
(602) 990-0682; (800) 456-0682

1098. Built in 1988 in a contemporary pioneer ranch style, this two-story inn is on a quiet dead-end street less than one mile from the south entrance to Zion National Park. Comfortable, clean, and bright with a contemporary interior, original artwork, and collectibles. One room is on the first floor with queen-size bed and private bath. Three rooms on the second floor all have queen-size beds and private baths. Children

are welcome by prior arrangement. No smoking. Complimentary beverages. Breakfast is a culinary event! Hot tub. Visa and MasterCard are accepted. $75-90.

1108. Completed in 1977, this two-story inn was originally built for the Madsen family and their nine children. The rooms are large with a cathedral-ceiling living room and full-length windows to take advantage of the fabulous views. The Southwest-style construction has a Spanish flair with an exterior of wood, stucco, natural sandstone walkways, patios, and planters. It is surrounded with spacious lawns and gardens, including fruit, nut, and large pine trees. The brilliantly colored mountains of Zion National Park can be seen from the 35-foot balcony. The entire upstairs is devoted to bed and breakfast guests, including the large balcony, a family room with TV and VCR, a game room with pool table, a special reading room, and library. There are three bedrooms with private baths. Smoking restricted. No pets. $60-70.

TROPIC

Mi Casa Su Casa Bed and Breakfast

P.O. Box 950, Tempe, AZ 85280-0950
(602) 990-0682; (800) 456-0682

1099. In tiny picturesque Tropic, this bed and breakfast is within walking distance of Bryce Canyon National Park's western boundary. The house was built in the early 1930s and a two-story addition was built in 1990. Come and go without entering the common rooms, or guests are welcome to share the living room with other guests. There are wraparound decks with spectacular views where guests can watch the sunset play upon the hoodoos of Bryce Canyon, as they turn from orange to pink to lavender. Five spacious guest rooms, each with queen-size bed, private bath, and picture windows. Children are welcome. Full breakfast. No smoking. A ten dollar-charge for additional person in room. $65.

1105. This bed and breakfast is a modern log home with flower gardens on a ten-acre working farm that produces grain and hay. The host couple is knowledgeable about area activities and sights. The three rooms all have private baths. Room one is on the first floor. Room two has a queen-size, a double bed, and TV. Room three has a queen-size bed and TV. Children are welcome. Full breakfast. Smoking allowed outside. Roll away beds available. Handicapped possible. $65.

Vermont

ALBURG

Auberge Alburg

Rural Delivery 1, Box 3, 05440
(802) 796-3169

The Auberge—meaning *inn* in French—is a cozy, cosmopolitan, and multilingual bed and breakfast overlooking Lake Champlain. The ambience includes music, books, good conversation, espresso on the porch, and freshly baked croissants for breakfast. There are guest rooms in both the main house and the renovated barn, which also has dormitory space for bikers and others. On the Vermont-New York-Québec border, one hour from Montréal. Swimming and golf nearby. Pets welcome. Children welcome.

Hosts: Gabrielle Tyrnauer and Charles Stastny
Rooms: 5 (1 PB; 4 SB) $50-75
Continental Breakfast
Credit Cards: None
Notes: 2, 3, 4, 6, 7, 8, 9, 11, 12

Thomas Mott

lawn games, and canoes. Complimentary Ben and Jerry's ice cream. Rest and relaxation. On the information highway, access Prodigy or Internet. Approved AAA, ABBA, *Yankee* magazine, *Vermont Life,* Mobil, and more than 30 bed and breakfast books. Children over six welcome.

Host: Patrick J. Schallert Sr.
Rooms: 5 (PB) $59-79
Full Breakfast
Credit Cards: A, B, C, D, E, F
Notes: 2, 4, 5, 7, 9, 10, 11, 12, 13, 14

Thomas Mott Bed and Breakfast

Blue Rock Road, Route 2, Box 149B, 05440-9620
(802) 796-3736; (800) 348-0843 (out of state)

Open all year and hosted by Patrick J. Schallert Sr., a prominent importer and distributor of fine wines, retired, this 1838 farmhouse offers five rooms overlooking Lake Champlain, all with private baths. Across the lake, a full view of the Green Mountains or the Adirondacks can be enjoyed from all rooms in this beautifully restored bed and breakfast. Less than one hour to Burlington or the Island of Montréal. All-season lake activities. Cross-country skiing, game room with bumper pool and darts,

ANDOVER

Inn at HighView

Rural Route 1, Box 201A, 05143
(802) 875-2724

Vermont the way guests always dreamed it would be, but the way they've never found it. Secluded and relaxed elegance; breathtaking views of countryside from overlook gazebo and screened porch. Classically restored 18th-century farmhouse comfortably furnished. Warm conversation by a blazing fire, hearty breakfasts, and gourmet dinners. All rooms with private baths. Cross-country skiing-hiking trails on 72 acres. Rock garden, swimming pool, and sauna. Ten minutes from Okemo Mountain,

7 No smoking; 8 Children welcome; 9 Social drinking allowed; 10 Tennis nearby; 11 Swimming nearby; 12 Golf nearby; 13 Skiing nearby; 14 May be booked through a travel agent.

Vermont

Weston, and Chester. Conference facilities and planning services available. Inquire about accommodations for pets.

Hosts: Greg Bohan and Sal Massaro
Rooms: 8 (PB) $80-125
Full Breakfast
Credit Cards: A, B
Notes: 2, 3, 4, 5, 8, 9, 10, 11, 12, 13, 14

ARLINGTON

The Arlington Inn

Historic Route 7A, 05250
(800) 443-9442

A stately Greek Revival mansion set on lushly landscaped lawns offers elegantly appointed rooms filled with antiques and amenities. All rooms have private baths, air conditioning, and include breakfast. Between Bennington and Manchester. Antique shops, boutiques, museums, skiing, hiking, biking, canoeing, fly fishing, golfing, and many other outdoor activities are nearby. Tennis on the private court. Outstanding cuisine is served by romantic candlelight in the fireplaced, award-winning dining room with superb service. AAA three-diamond rating, and Mobil three-stars rating.

Hosts: Deborah and Mark Gagnon
Rooms: 13 (PB) $65-175
Full Breakfast
Credit Cards: A, B, C, D, E
Notes: 4, 5, 7, 8, 9, 10, 11, 12, 13, 14

The Arlington Inn

The Evergreen Inn

The Evergreen Inn

Sandgate Road, Box 2480, 05250
(802) 375-2272

Country inn, family owned and operated since 1934. In a beautiful mountain valley by a stream. Friendly informal atmosphere. Home cooking and baking. Close to art centers, concerts, summer theaters, antiques, auctions, fairs, golf courses, and discount stores. Hiking, cycling, canoeing, and swimming. Dinner available by reservation. Closed October 30 to May 1. Send for brochure.

Hosts: Mathilda and Kathleen Kenny
Rooms: 19 (PB and SB) $50-70
Full Breakfast
Credit Cards: None
Notes: 2, 3, 4, 6, 7, 8, 9, 10, 11, 12

Hill Farm Inn

Rural Route 2, Box 2015, 05250
(802) 375-2269; (800) 882-2545

Visit one of Vermont's original farmsteads that has been an inn since 1905. Stay in a 1790 or 1830 farmhouse and enjoy hearty home cooking and mountain views. Nestled at the foot of Mount Equinox and surrounded by 50 acres of farmland with the Battenkill River bordering the lower pasture. Two-day minimum stay required

NOTES: Credit cards: A MasterCard; B Visa; C American Express; D Discover; E Diners Club; F Other; 2 Personal checks accepted; 3 Lunch available; 4 Dinner available; 5 Open all year; 6 Pets welcome; 7 No smoking; 8 Children welcome; 9 Social drinking allowed; 10 Tennis nearby; 11 Swimming nearby; 12 Golf nearby; 13 Skiing nearby; 14 May be booked through a travel agent.

Hill Farm Inn

for weekends, three nights for holidays. Inquire about accommodations for pets.

Hosts: George and Joanne Hardy
Rooms: 13 (8 PB; 5 SB) $50-110
Full Breakfast
Credit Cards: A, B, C, D
Notes: 2, 4, 5, 7, 8, 9, 10, 11, 12, 13, 14

Ira Allen House

Rural Delivery 2, Box 2485, 05250
(802) 362-2284

Vermont State Historic Site, home of Ira Allen (brother of Ethan, who lived here with him). Norman Rockwell Museum, Robert Todd Lincoln's Hildene, hiking, canoeing, biking, skiing, and antiques. Enjoy the unique experience of a relaxing stay at this historic inn on the Battenkill River along with a bountiful home-cooked breakfast. Dinner is available on Saturday evenings during the winter. Children over ten are welcome.

Hosts: Rowland and Sally Bryant
Rooms: 9 (4 PB; 5 SB) $55-70
Full Breakfast
Credit Cards: A, B, C
Notes: 2, 7, 9, 10, 11, 12, 13, 14

Shenandoah Farm

Battenkill Road, Route 313, 05250
(802) 375-6372

This Colonial home near the Battenkill River is five miles from Route 7A on Route 313. Close to Norman Rockwell Museum and recreational activities. Five antique-

filled guest rooms are offered with private or shared baths.

Host: Woody Masterson
Rooms: 5 (4 PB; 1 SB) $70
Full Breakfast
Credit Cards: A, B
Notes: 2, 5, 7, 8, 9, 10, 11, 12, 13, 14

BELLOWS FALLS

Blue Haven Christian Bed and Breakfast

227 Westminster Road, 05101
(802) 463-9008; (800) 228-9008

This 1830 schoolhouse offers warm, cheery ambience. Far from the hustle-and-bustle world, tucked securely into a lush mountainside, Blue Haven is peaceful and protected. Canopy beds amid hand-painted vintage furnishings make this a retreat back to gentler times. Colorful antique glassware and crisp linens set the tone in the large farm kitchen, heady with irresistible aromas. The common room's ancient rocking chairs flank an old stone fireplace. Guests will have the feeling of visiting an old friend. Full breakfast offered on weekends; Continental on weekdays. French spoken.

Host: Helene A. Champagne
Rooms: 6 (5 PB; 1 SB) $55-85
Full and Continental Breakfast
Credit Cards: A, B, C
Notes: 2, 5, 7, 8, 9, 10, 11, 12, 13, 14

BELMONT

The Leslie Place

P.O. Box 62, 05730
(802) 259-2903; (800) 352-7439

A recipe for the perfect getaway: a secluded 100-acre setting near Weston, wonderful mountain views, spectacular fall foliage, walking trails and gardens, combined with spacious rooms, private baths, hearty breakfasts, and a warm fire. Close to summer theater, the Long Trail, fine restaurants, and shops, as well as many of Vermont's famous antique and craft shows. Brochure available.

Host: Mary K. Gorman
Rooms: 3 (PB) $65-85
Full Breakfast
Credit Cards: A, B
Notes: 2, 5, 7, 8, 9, 10, 11, 12, 13

The Leslie Place

BENNINGTON

American Country Collection

1353 Union Street, Schenectady, NY 12054
(518) 439-7001; FAX (518) 439-4301

041. This carefully landscaped Victorian has a stream on the back property and a large front porch for rocking. There's a wood-burning stove on the brick hearth in the first-floor common room. Braided rugs cover wide-plank pine floors. Six guest rooms, two with private baths, and one cottage with king-size bed and private bath with Jacuzzi. Full gourmet breakfast includes pancakes, French toast, eggs, Belgian waffles, blintzes, or quiche. Smoking outdoors only. Children over 11 welcome. Ten percent gratuity. $65-140.

Four Chimneys Inn

21 West Road, 05201
(802) 447-3500; FAX (802) 447-3692

The parklike setting of this beautiful Georgian estate and food preparation under the supervision of Master Chef Alex Koks create a dining experience in elegance. "Join us for a meal, a drink or a night if you prefer the finer things in life!" Rated three diamonds by AAA, and three stars by Mobil.

Hosts: James and Mary Fabian
Rooms: 11 (PB) $125-175
Continental Breakfast
Credit Cards: A, B, C, E
Notes: 3, 4, 5, 6, 8, 9, 10, 11, 12, 13, 14

Molly Stark Inn

1067 East Main Street, 05201
(800) 356-3076

A true country inn with an intimate atmosphere, this 1890 Victorian home is on the main road through a historic town in southwestern Vermont and welcomes visitors year-round. Decorated and tastefully furnished with antiques, country collectibles, braided rugs on gleaming hardwood floors, and patchwork quilts on the beds. Private guest cottage with king-size brass bed, Jacuzzi, and woodstove. Guests are invited to use the wraparound front porch with rocking chairs, and the den and parlor with wood-burning stoves are most inviting on those cool Vermont nights. Clean, affordable. Champagne dinner packages available.

Hosts: Cammi and Reed Fendler
Rooms: 7 (2 PB; 5 SB) $65-85
Cottage: $125
Full Breakfast
Credit Cards: A, B, C, D
Notes: 2, 4, 5, 7, 8, 9, 14

BETHEL

Greenhurst Inn

Rural Route 2, Box 60, River Street, 05032-9404
(802) 234-9474

Queen Anne Victorian mansion listed on the National Register of Historic Places. In central Vermont near I-89, halfway between Boston and Montréal. Mints on the pillows and a library of 3,000 volumes. The inn was featured in the *New York*

7 No smoking; 8 Children welcome; 9 Social drinking allowed; 10 Tennis nearby; 11 Swimming nearby;
12 Golf nearby; 13 Skiing nearby; 14 May be booked through a travel agent.

Times on March 3, 1991. Inquire about accommodations for pets.

Host: Lyle Wolf
Rooms: 13 (7 PB; 6 SB) $50-100
Continental Breakfast
Credit Cards: A, B, D
Notes: 2, 5, 8, 9, 11, 12, 13, 14

Greenhurst Inn

Poplar Manor
Bed and Breakfast

Rural Delivery 2, Box 136
Combined Routes 107 and 12, 05032
(802) 234-5426

In a beautiful setting in central Vermont, this 1810 Federal home offers friendly hospitality and quiet comfort. The rooms are decorated with antiques and homey collectibles. Guests are welcome to all indoor and outdoor areas. Many attractions are nearby. Continental plus breakfast.

Host: Carmen E. Jaynes
Rooms: 3 (SB) $38-40
Continental Breakfast
Credit Cards: None
Notes: 2, 5, 6, 8, 9, 10, 11, 12, 13, 14

BRANDON

American Country Collection

1353 Union Street, Schenectady, NY 12054
(518) 439-7001; FAX (518) 439-4301

177. This restored 1860s three-story manor offers travelers a truly Victorian experience. The owners painstakingly gathered authentic Victorian furnishings that make the intimacy of the inn more than just a notion. The elegant breakfast and common room are comfortably arranged for socializ-

ing or just relaxing before the fireplace with a good book. Guests may enjoy the wicker rockers on the porch, or stroll through the gardens and enjoy the hummingbirds and butterflies. Four guest rooms with private and shared baths are on the second floor; two with queen-size beds, one with twin, and one with double. Two additional guest rooms with private baths are on the third floor; one with twin bed and one with queen-size bed. Full breakfast is served. Children 12 and over welcome. Smoking permitted outside only. $65-85.

Churchill House Inn

Rural Route 3, Box 3115, 05733
(802) 247-3078; FAX (802) 247-6851

A century-old inn at the edge of the Green Mountain National Forest is a center for outdoor activities with extensive hiking, biking, and cross-country skiing available. Outdoor pool and rental bikes. The inn's casual atmosphere, award-winning cuisine, and comfortable, antique-appointed accommodations complement an active day. All eight rooms have a private bath, some with a Jacuzzi. The sky-lit porch and two sitting rooms provide a homey setting. A candle-lit, four-course dinner served around an antique oak table completes the house-party atmosphere. Picnic lunches available.

Hosts: The Jackson Family
Rooms: 8 (PB)
Full Breakfast
Credit Cards: A, B
Notes: 2, 4, 7, 8, 9, 10, 12, 13

Hivue Bed and
Breakfast Tree Farm

Rural Route 1, Box 1023
High Pond Road, 05733-9704
(802) 247-3042

A smoke-free, rural, peaceful bed and breakfast on 76 acres. Enjoy panoramic views of Pico and Killington from the deck and large windows. The raised ranch is just three and one-half miles from the center of

Brandon and many fine restaurants. A nature lover's paradise with trout stream, wildlife habitats, miniature horses and ponies, plus a one and one-half-mile interpretive trail. TVs, and VCRs. Box lunches are available, and dinner is available by reservation. Additional charge for additional persons. Call about pets.

Hosts: Wini and Bill Reuschle
Rooms: 3 (PB) $50
Full Breakfast
Credit Cards: None
Notes: 2, 5, 7, 8, 9, 10, 11, 12, 13

BRANDON (MIDDLEBURY)

Rosebelle's Victorian Inn

P.O. Box 370, Route 7, 05733-0370
(802) 247-0098; (800) 556-7673

Charming 1839 Victorian mansard listed on National Register of Historic Places. Antiques, full gourmet breakfast, and afternoon tea. Hiking, biking, golf, and spectacular foliage. Swimming is available at the state park 15 minutes from the inn. Nordic and alpine skiing nearby. Visit museums and antique shops, or read a good book. Only minutes from Middlebury College. Special packages and gift certificates available. French spoken. Brochure available. Children over 12 are welcome.

Hosts: Ginette and Norm Milot
Rooms: 6 (2 PB; 4 SB) $65-85
Full Breakfast
Credit Cards: A, B
Notes: 2, 5, 7, 9, 10, 11, 12, 13, 14

Rosebelle's Victorian Inn

BRATTLEBORO

The Tudor

76 Western Avenue, 05301
(802) 257-4983; FAX (802) 258-2632

Enjoy luxurious comfort and personalized service. The Tudor is an elegantly furnished English-brick mansion with striking formal gardens and a beautiful gallery of international crafts and works by area artists. All rooms have cable TV and air conditioning; three have fireplaces. Savor a "ginormous" Vermont breakfast, featuring home-baked goods and fresh juice. Convenient to four seasons' recreation, tourist destinations, fine restaurants, and shopping.

Hosts: John Penford and Joy Wallens-Penford
Rooms: 4 (3 PB; 1 SB) $85-110
Full Breakfast
Credit Cards: A, B
Notes: 2, 5, 7, 8, 9, 10, 11, 12, 13, 14

BROOKFIELD

Green Trails Inn

By the Floating Bridge, 05036
(802) 276-3412; (800) 243-3412

Comfortably elegant, 17-acre 1840s country estate—relax and be pampered! Separate 18th-century guest house; one corner room has the original wall stenciling. There is a wonderful antique clock collection throughout the inn. Ice skating, sledding, and horse-drawn sleigh rides are available in the winter, and fishing, swimming, canoeing, and biking can be enjoyed in the summer; 30K of cross-country skiing in the winter and hiking in the summer and fall—or just put your feet up and relax! Bed and breakfast year round; MAP available by request in the winter.

Hosts: Sue and Mark Erwin
Rooms: 13 (9 PB; 4 SB) $68-80
Credit Cards: A, B
Notes: 2, 4, 7, 9, 11, 12, 13, 14

7 No smoking; 8 Children welcome; 9 Social drinking allowed; 10 Tennis nearby; 11 Swimming nearby; 12 Golf nearby; 13 Skiing nearby; 14 May be booked through a travel agent.

CABOT

Creamery Inn Bed and Breakfast

P.O. Box 187, 05647
(802) 563-2819

This spacious and comfortable home, circa 1835, is picturesquely set only a mile from the Cabot Creamery. Guests may walk the country roads, enjoy ponds and waterfalls, drive to Burke Mountain or Stowe for skiing, or just relax. Enjoy the full, homemade breakfast, featuring Finnish pancakes, muffins, and more. Special rates for stays of more than two nights. Candlelight dinners by advance reservation.

Host: Dan Lloyd
Rooms: 4 (2 PB; 2 SB) $50-70
Full Breakfast
Credit Cards: None
Notes: 2, 5, 7, 8, 9, 11, 13, 14

CHELSEA

Shire Inn

8 Main Street, 05038
(802) 685-3031

An 1832 historic brick Federal, "Very Vermont" inn. Enjoy 18th-century accommodations with 20th-century bathrooms. Small and intimate; some rooms have working fireplaces. Chef-owned and operated, with five-course dining available. Just

Shire Inn

30 miles north of Woodstock and Quechee; 34 miles to Hanover and Dartmouth; 30 miles south of Montpelier. Two-night minimum stay required for weekends and holidays. Children over six are welcome.

Hosts: Jay and Karen Keller
Rooms: 6 (PB) $90-194
Full Breakfast
Credit Cards: A, B, C, D
Notes: 2, 4, 5, 9, 10, 11, 12, 13

CHESTER

Bed and Breakfast Inns of New England

128 South Hoop Pole Road, Guilford, CT 06437
(203) 457-0042; (800) 582-0853

VT702. This lovely 1890 Victorian home features gorgeous antiques and striking Oriental rugs throughout. Come enjoy the beautiful views of the town green. There are two semiprivate-bath guest rooms, each with antique beds. There is a large living room for relaxing, a tea room, and a delightful Victorian-style gift shop, too. Close to horseback riding, swimming, and cross-country and alpine skiing. Walk a half-block to the shops around the green. $75-85.

Greenleaf Inn

Depot Street, Box 188, 05143
(802) 875-3171

This lovely 1860s Victorian is now an elegant village inn facing an expansive lawn. Five charming rooms, each with a private bath. Walk to antique shopping and village green attractions. A delicious and hearty Vermont breakfast is served in the sunny dining room. Afternoon refreshments are served also.

Hosts: Jerry and Robin Szawerda
Rooms: 5 (PB) $70-95
Full Breakfast
Credit Cards: A, B, C, D
Notes: 2, 5, 7, 9, 10, 11, 12, 13

NOTES: Credit cards accepted: A MasterCard; B Visa; C American Express; D Discover; E Diners Club; F Other; 2 Personal checks accepted; 3 Lunch available; 4 Dinner available; 5 Open all year; 6 Pets welcome;

Henry Farm Inn

Henry Farm Inn

P.O. Box 646, Green Mountain Turnpike, 05143
(802) 875-2674

The Henry Farm Inn provides the beauty of Vermont with old-time simplicity. Nestled on 50 acres of rolling hills and meadows, assuring peace and quiet. Spacious rooms, private baths, country sitting rooms, kitchen, and sunny dining room guarantee a feeling of home. Come visit for a day or more.

Host: B. M. Bowman
Rooms: 7 (PB) $50-90
Full Breakfast
Credit Cards: A, B, C
Notes: 2, 5, 7, 8, 9, 11, 12, 13, 14

The Hugging Bear Inn and Shoppe

Main Street, P.O. Box 32, 05143
(802) 875-2412; (800) 325-0519

Bed, breakfast, and bears. Charming Victorian home on the village green. The shop has more than 4,000 teddy bears, and guests may "adopt" a bear for the night as long as he is back to work in the shop by 9:00 A.M. Puppet show often performed at breakfast; breakfast music provided by an 1890 music box. Two lovable cats in residence. A magical place to visit! Two-night minimum stay required for holidays and high season weekends.

Hosts: The Thomases
Rooms: 6 (PB) $75-95
Full Breakfast
Credit Cards: A, B, C, D
Notes: 2, 5, 7, 8, 9, 10, 11, 12, 13

The Inn at Long Last

Main Street, P.O. Box 589, 05143
(802) 875-2444

A warm and welcoming inn where all the rooms have individual themes, where the decor is highly personal, and where the staff hospitality is exceptional. Gardens, tennis courts, food, and theme weekends draw raves. Modified American Plan meals.

Host: Jack Coleman
Rooms: 30 (25 PB; 5 SB) $160
Full Breakfast
Credit Cards: A, B
Notes: 2, 4, 7, 8, 9, 10, 12, 13, 14

Night with a Native Bed and Breakfast

P.O. Box 327, 05143-0327
(802) 875-2616

Feel at home at this bed and breakfast. Enjoy the warm ambience of hand-stenciled rooms, family-made rugs, antiques, collectibles, and wood stoves. TV in living room. The host, a sixth-generation Vermonter, offers true Vermont hospitality. Complimentary refreshments. The unforgettable breakfast includes homemade maple syrup. Walking distance to restaurants.

Host: Doris Hastings
Rooms: 2 (SB) $55-65
Full Breakfast
Credit Cards: None
Notes: 2, 5, 7, 9, 10, 11, 12, 13

Old Town Farm Inn

Rural Route 4, 05143
(802) 875-2346

Built in 1861, the inn has 11 acres with a spring-fed pond for swimming and ice-skating. Ten minutes from Okemo Mountain ski area and 30 minutes from Killington ski area. Cross-country skiing is also available. Foliage season, with its beautiful colors and crisp New England air, beckons people from all over the world. Rent a bike and see the countryside.

7 No smoking; 8 Children welcome; 9 Social drinking allowed; 10 Tennis nearby; 11 Swimming nearby; 12 Golf nearby; 13 Skiing nearby; 14 May be booked through a travel agent.

Country Inn Spring Water, which was started in 1984, is served and distributed exclusively from the inn. Children over six welcome.

Hosts: Fred and Jan Baldwin
Rooms: 11 (3 PB; 8 SB) $58-68
Full Breakfast
Credit Cards: A, B
Notes: 2, 5, 7, 9, 10, 11, 12, 13

Finchingfield Farm

CRAFTSBURY

Finchingfield Farm Bed and Breakfast

Rural Route 1, Box 1195
East Craftsbury Road, 05826
(802) 586-7763

This elegant, turn-of-the-century country house is set in the tranquil, picturesque village of East Craftsbury. Guest facilities include a library, cozy sitting room, four large, bright bedrooms (two with private baths), down comforters, and English antique furniture. The decor and service are distinctively British.

Hosts: Janet and Bob Meyer
Rooms: 4 (2 PB; 2 SB) $60-80
Full Breakfast
Credit Cards: A, B
Notes: 2, 5, 8, 11, 12, 13

CUTTINGSVILLE (SHREWSBURY)

Buckmaster Inn

Rural Route 1, Box 118, Lincoln Hill Road
Shrewsbury, 05738
(802) 492-3485

This historic country inn was originally a stagecoach stop and stands on a knoll overlooking a typical red-barn scene and picturesque valley. The charm of a center hall, grand staircase, and wide-pine floors show off family antiques. The wood-burning fireplaces, library, huge porches, dining room, and country kitchen with wood-burning stove are always special favorites of guests. Hiking trails and ski areas are close by. Eight miles southeast of Rutland near Cuttingsville.

Hosts: Sam and Grace Husselman
Rooms: 4 (2 PB; 2 SB) $50-65
Full Breakfast
Credit Cards: F
Notes: 2, 5, 7, 8, 9, 10, 11, 12, 13

Maple Crest Farm

Lincoln Hill Road, Box 120, 05738
(802) 492-3367

High in the Green Mountains, ten miles south of Rutland and 12 miles north of Ludlow, this 1808 27-room beautiful historic home has been lovingly preserved for five generations. Cross-country skiing and hiking are offered on the farm. Close to many major ski areas, Rutland, and places of historic interest. A real taste of old Vermont hospitality. Maple syrup made on the premises. This year marks 25 years in business.

Hosts: William and Donna Smith
Rooms: 6 (1 PB; 5 SB) $54-75
Full Breakfast
Credit Cards: None
Notes: 2, 5, 8, 9, 10, 11, 12, 13, 14

DANBY

Quails Nest Bed and Breakfast Inn

Box 221, 05739
(802) 293-5099

Nestled in a quiet mountain village, the inn offers its guests friendly conversation around the fireplace, rooms filled with cozy quilts and antiques, tips about local attractions, and a hearty home-cooked

NOTES: Credit cards accepted: A MasterCard; B Visa; C American Express; D Discover; E Diners Club; F Other; 2 Personal checks accepted; 3 Lunch available; 4 Dinner available; 5 Open all year; 6 Pets welcome;

breakfast in the morning. Children over eight welcome.

Hosts: Nancy and Greg Diaz
Rooms: 6 (4 PB; 2 SB) $60-85
Full Breakfast
Credit Cards: A, B, C
Notes: 2, 5, 7, 9, 10, 11, 12, 13, 14

Silas Griffith Inn

South Main Street, Rural Route 1, Box 66 F, 05739
(802) 293-5567

Built in 1891 by Vermont's first million-aire, now a lovingly restored Victorian mansion and carriage house. Relax in antique-filled guest rooms with spectacular Green Mountain views. Two-night mini-mum stay required over holidays.

Hosts: Paul and Lois Dansereau
Rooms: 17 (14 PB; 3 SB) $70-88
Full Breakfast
Credit Cards: A, B
Notes: 2, 3, 4, 7, 8, 9, 10, 11, 12, 13, 14

DERBY LINE

The Birchwood Bed and Breakfast

48 Main Street, P.O. Box 550, 05830
(802) 873-9104

A 1920 lovingly restored home in a charming village in the Northeast Kingdom at the Canadian border. Three individually decorated, antique-filled bedrooms include pri-

The Birchwood

vate bathrooms. A full breakfast is served each morning in the sunlit dining room. The region offers miles of unspoiled scenery. Enjoy the beauty of the area as well as the comfort and spaciousness of this home. A warm welcome awaits guests at the Birchwood Bed and Breakfast.

Hosts: Betty and Dick Fletcher
Rooms: 3 (PB) $60-65
Full Breakfast
Credit Cards: None
Notes: 2, 5, 9, 10, 11, 12, 13

Derby Village Inn

46 Main Street, 05830
(802) 873-3604

A restored old Victorian mansion in the quiet village of Derby Line. Five charming rooms, each with private bath. Nestled within walking distance of the Canadian border and the world's only international library and opera house. The nearby countryside offers year-round recreation: downhill and cross-country skiing, water sports, cycling, fishing, hiking, golf, snowmobiling, sleigh rides, antiquing, and most of all, peace and tranquility. No smoking.

Hosts: Tom and Phyllis Moreau
Rooms: 5 (PB) $55-65
Full Breakfast
Credit Cards: A, B, D
Notes: 2, 5, 7, 8, 9, 10, 11, 12, 13

DORSET

Barrows House

Route 30, 05251
(802) 867-4455; (800) 639-1620 (out of state)

The Barrows House is a collection of white clapboard buildings on 11 acres in the heart of a small picture-book Vermont town. Guests have a choice of 28 accommodations in eight different buildings (21 rooms and 7 suites), all with a history and style of their own. Dining is an informal and delicious adventure in American regional cuisine (offering a four-course

7 No smoking; 8 Children welcome; 9 Social drinking allowed; 10 Tennis nearby; 11 Swimming nearby; 12 Golf nearby; 13 Skiing nearby; 14 May be booked through a travel agent.

Barrows House

country dinner with an elegant flair), which is included in the rate. The complex offers tennis courts, outdoor heated pool, bicycles, sauna, and cross-country ski shop. Children welcome. Modified American Plan.

Hosts: Linda and Jim McGinnis
Rooms: 28 (PB) $140-190
Full Breakfast
Credit Cards: A, B, C, D, E
Notes: 2, 4, 5, 6, 8, 10, 11, 12, 13, 14

The Little Lodge at Dorset

Route 30, Box 673, 05251
(802) 867-4040; (800) 378-7505

This delightful old house sits on a hillside overlooking a pond and mountains beyond and is surrounded by wildflowers, white birch, and pines. Quilts, stenciling, wide floorboards, and antiques add to this appealing inn. Barnboard den with fireplace, wet bar, refrigerator, TV, games, puzzles, and books. Screened porch. Continental plus breakfast of unusual toasted homemade breads, Vermont cheese, and crackers offered. Coffee, tea, and hot chocolate always available. Hiking, fishing, biking, boating, summer theater, antiquing, swimming, tennis, golf, and skiing are nearby. Some rooms are air-conditioned. Very pleasant ambience.

Hosts: Allan and Nancy Norris
Rooms: 5 (PB) $85-105
Continental Breakfast
Credit Cards: C, D
Notes: 2, 8, 9, 10, 11, 12, 13, 14

Marble West Inn

Dorset West Road, 05251
(800) 453-7629

Find peace and serenity in a restored 1840 Greek Revival country home in an informal elegant atmosphere that is graced with polished dark hardwood floors, Oriental rugs, a grand piano, library, and fireplaces. Two acres of land contain herb and flower gardens and trout ponds, providing stunning views of Dorset mountains. Afternoon tea and cookies are served. Special packages are available.

Hosts: June and Wayne Erla
Rooms: 8 (PB) $90-135
Full Breakfast
Credit Cards: A, B, C, E
Notes: 2, 5, 7, 9, 10, 11, 12, 13, 14

EAST DOVER

Cooper Hill Inn

Cooper Hill Road, Box 146, 05341
(802) 348-6333

Informal and cozy hilltop inn with "one of the most spectacular mountain panoramas in all New England." Quiet country road location. Hearty home-cooked meals are a tradition here. Seven double rooms and three family suites all feature private baths. Closed for one week in April and November.

Hosts: Pat and Marilyn Hunt
Rooms: 10 (PB) $76-110
Full Breakfast
Credit Cards: A, B, D
Notes: 2, 4, 7, 8, 9, 10, 11, 12, 13, 14

EAST MIDDLEBURY

Waybury Inn

Route 125, 05753
(802) 388-4015; (800) 348-1810

Built in 1810 the Waybury Inn has 14 individually appointed guest rooms, all with private baths. Known to many as the inn featured on *The Bob Newhart Show*, the inn offers dinner daily and Sunday brunch. The Pub opens at 4:00 P.M. No smoking.

Hosts: Marty and Marcia Schuppert
Rooms: 14 (PB) $80-115
Full Breakfast
Credit Cards: A, B, D
Notes: 2, 4, 5, 7, 8, 10, 11, 12, 13, 14

Berkson Farms

ENOSBURG FALLS

Berkson Farms

Rural Delivery 1, Route 108, 05450
(802) 933-2522

Despite its being on a 600-acre working farm, this century-old restored farmhouse presents a homey, relaxed atmosphere. Surrounded by a large variety of animals and all the simple, wonderful joys of nature and life itself. Warm hospitality and country home cooking.

Hosts: Bob and Connie Fletcher
Rooms: 4 (1 PB; 3 SB) $58.85-69.55
Full Breakfast
Credit Cards: None
Notes: 2, 3, 4, 5, 8, 9, 10, 11, 12, 13

ESSEX (BURLINGTON)

The Inn at Essex

70 Essex Way, 05452
(802) 878-1100; (800) 727-4295 (reservations)
FAX (802) 878-0063

A beautiful 97-room Colonial-style inn, no two rooms alike, 30 with wood-burning fireplaces. Enjoy the library, the art gallery, or watching the chefs in the pastry shop. The most outstanding feature is the food service, which is operated by the acclaimed New England Culinary Institute. There are more than 100 student chefs and 18 chef instructors. Two restaurants offer country, casual, or more formal dining experiences. Enjoy the patio, the outdoor pool, and the gardens. Hiking, snowshoeing. Nearby upscale shopping at Essex Outlet Fair. Ten minutes from Burlington International Airport via complimentary shuttle service. Just minutes from Lake Champlain, Vermont Teddy Bear Company, Ben & Jerry's Ice Cream Factory, Shelburne Museum, and the University of Vermont.

Hosts: Jim and Judi Lamberti
Rooms: 97 (PB) $89-190
Continental Breakfast
Credit Cards: A, B, C, D, E
Notes: 2, 3, 4, 5, 8, 9, 10, 11, 12, 13, 14

ESSEX JUNCTION

Country Comfort Bed and Breakfast

36 Old Stage Road, 05452
(802) 878-2589

Country charm near city sights, on a grassy plateau with distant mountain views creating a feeling of peace and space. Each room decorated with its name in mind

Country Comfort

7 No smoking; 8 Children welcome; 9 Social drinking allowed; 10 Tennis nearby; 11 Swimming nearby; 12 Golf nearby; 13 Skiing nearby; 14 May be booked through a travel agent.

(Country, Jenny Lind, Victorian, New England) with hand-picked antiques and collectibles. Guest living room with fireplace and TV. Full Vermont breakfast served in guest dining room. Grazing sheep and clucking hens complete the tranquil theme. "Guests arrive as strangers and depart as friends." Only nine miles from Burlington.

Hosts: Ed and Eva Blake
Rooms: 4 (2 PB; 2 SB) $55-65
Full Breakfast
Credit Cards: A, B
Notes: 2, 5, 7, 9, 10, 11, 12, 13, 14

FAIRFAX

American Country Collection

1353 Union Street, Schenectady, NY 12054
(518) 439-7001; FAX (518) 439-4301

149. Imagine being in a completely renovated New England carriage house in the year 1790, and begin the journey through this inn with original exposed beams and wood-burning stove. Four rooms are available for guests. Two rooms on the second floor share a bath, and two rooms on the first floor share another bath and a whirlpool tub. Snacks, wine, beer, and soft drinks are available to guests, and a fax machine, Macintosh computer, copier, and antique and gift shop are on premises. In the spring, enjoy watching maple syrup being made. Breakfast is served from 8:00-9:00 A.M. $48-78.

The Inn at Buck Hollow Farm

Rural Route 1, Box 680, 05454
(802) 849-2400

The Inn at Buck Hollow Farm is a small country inn on 400 spectacular acres. It features canopied beds, beamed ceilings, sunroom with fireplace, and antique decor. The guests enjoy a heated pool, hot tub/spa, Jacuzzi, cross-country skiing, and an antique shop. With Burlington's famed marketplace and major ski resorts only

minutes away, the Inn at Buck Hollow Farm is truly a four-season retreat.

Hosts: Dody Young and Brad Schwartz
Rooms: 4 (SB) $55-75
Full Breakfast
Credit Cards: A, B, C, D
Notes: 2, 5, 8, 9, 11, 13, 14

The Inn at Buck Hollow Farm

FAIR HAVEN

American Country Collection

1353 Union Street, Schenectady, NY 12054
(518) 439-7001; FAX (518) 439-4301

077. This circa 1843 Greek Revival home is on three and one-half acres of lawn and gardens and features beautiful moldings and wide-plank pine and maple parquet floors. The five guest rooms, with private baths, have picture-perfect farm and mountain views and are individually decorated in period styles; four have a fireplace. Each room has extra pillows and blankets, quilts, extra thick towels, reading lamps, TV, telephone (if requested), candies, and wine glasses. Suites have decanter of sherry. Either mix with other guests or find a quiet corner to curl up with a book. The keeping room has a fireplace and TV. There is also a BYOB tavern. Bike rentals available. Full breakfast. Restricted smoking. $70-105.

Maplewood Inn

Route 22A South, 05743
(802) 265-8039
(800) 253-7729 (reservations only)

Romantic, historic 1843 Greek Revival inn offering exquisitely appointed guest rooms and suites with private baths, antiques, working fireplaces, in-room color cable TV, radio, telephones, and air conditioning. Common rooms include keeping room with fireplace, gathering room/library, BYOB tavern, and parlor with games and complimentary cordial bar. Bikes and canoe are available on-site. Near lakes, skiing, restaurants, and many other attractions. Three-star Mobil, three-diamond AAA, three Ovations-INNovations. Hearty Continental breakfast is served. Call for information regarding accommodations available for children.

Hosts: Cindy and Doug Baird
Rooms: 5 (PB) $70-105
Continental Breakfast
Credit Cards: A, B, D, E, F
Notes: 2, 5, 9, 10, 11, 12, 13, 14

FAIRLEE

The Lake Morey Inn Resort and Country Club

Lake Morey Road, P.O. Box 48, 05045
(802) 333-4311

A four-season resort in the heart of the Green Mountains. Conveniently off I-91, exit 15. The resort features an 18-hole championship golf course (home of the Vermont Open), a 600-plus-acre lake, water sports, boating, bicycle and hiking tours, tennis, full health club, conference facilities, lakeside dining, family packages, supervised children's activities, and more. Miles of groomed and tracked trails on the golf course for cross-country skiing. Package deals are available with $15 downhill lift tickets at local mountains. Rates quoted below are MAP with breakfast and dinner and include recreational amenities, such as golf.

Hosts: Caroline White and Bob Ferlazo
Rooms: 164 (PB) $68-102 per person
Full Breakfast
Credit Cards: A, B
Notes: 2, 3, 4, 5, 8, 9, 10, 11, 12, 13, 14

Silver Maple Lodge and Cottages

Route 5, 05045
(802) 333-4326; (800) 666-1946

Historic bed and breakfast country inn. Cozy rooms with antiques or knotty pine cottages, some with fireplaces. Enjoy the beach, boating, fishing, and swimming at Lake Morey, one mile away. Golf, tennis, skiing, and hot-air balloon rides nearby. Dartmouth College is 17 miles away. Walk to restaurants. Two-night minimum stay required for holidays. Closed Christmas Eve.

Hosts: Scott and Sharon Wright
Rooms: 16 (14 PB; 2 SB) $50-74
Continental Breakfast
Credit Cards: A, B, C, D
Notes: 2, 5, 6, 8, 9, 10, 11, 12, 13, 14

Silver Maple Lodge

GAYSVILLE

The Cobble House Inn

P.O. Box 49, 05746
(802) 234-5458

A lovely 1864 Victorian inn sitting on a mountaintop with the White River bordering the property. Each room features a queen-size bed, sitting area, and private bath. Charming country quilts and antiques throughout. Dining room and great room with fireplaces. Wonderful full hot breakfast and afternoon hors d'oeuvres. Dinner by reservation. Chef owned. Lots of great skiing, hiking, and swimming available in the area. Personal checks can be accepted for deposit only. Children over eight are welcome.

Rooms: 4 (PB) $100
Full Breakfast
Credit Cards: A, B, C
Notes: 4, 5, 7, 9, 10, 11, 12, 13

GRAFTON

The Old Tavern at Grafton
Main Street, 05146
(802) 843-2231; (800) 843-1801
FAX (802) 843-2245

Centerpiece of picturesque and historic Grafton village since 1801, this elegant inn offers 66 antique-furnished guest rooms, most with four-poster canopied beds, all with private bath. Six beautifully appointed guest cottages with four to seven rooms, a honeymoon cottage, secluded on a hilltop meadow. A stable with six stalls is also on the grounds. All rates include buffet breakfast and afternoon tea. Award-winning dining and live country and jazz music in Phelps Barn Pub, a unique, fully renovated, air-conditioned barn. Freshwater swimming pond, 30K cross-country ski area, tennis, bicycles, and hiking are all available on property. Member of Historic Hotels of American. Smoking is allowed only in the dining room.

Host: Tom List
Rooms: 66 (PB) $95-165
Full Breakfast
Credit Cards: A, B
Notes: 2, 3, 4, 5, 8, 9, 10, 11, 12, 13, 14

GREENSBORO

Highland Lodge
Rural Route 1, Box 1290, Craftsbury Road, 05841
(802) 533-2647; FAX (802) 533-7494

Highland Lodge is a family-owned country inn and complete resort in a turn-of-the-

Highland Lodge

century summer community on Caspian Lake. The lodge has a clay tennis court, lawn games, and a private beach for swimming and boating. Dirt roads for biking and hiking lead through farm country and a nature preserve. Golf is nearby in the village. Children love the play program. The delicious food is complimented by all. Admire the breathtaking vistas at fall foliage time and from the lodge's own cross-country ski trails. Dinner and breakfast are both included in the rates per person per night.

Hosts: David and Wilhelmina Smith
Rooms: 11 (PB) $87.50-107.50
Cottages: 10
Full breakfast
Credit Cards: A, B, D
Notes: 2, 3, 4, 5, 8, 10, 11, 12, 13, 14

HARDWICK

American Country Collection
1353 Union Street, Schenectady, NY 12054
(518) 439-7001; FAX (518) 439-4301

215. Victorian home, circa 1899, with porch, large lawn, and perennial gardens. Heirloom and antique furniture. Four rooms share two full baths. Queen-size and twin beds. Smoking outside. Full breakfast. Children welcome. No pets. $65.

Somerset House Bed and Breakfast

24 Highland Avenue, 05843
(802) 472-5484

Four pretty bedrooms are offered in this comfortable, circa 1880, house where a gracious and elegant setting combines with a relaxing, friendly atmosphere. On a quiet maple-lined street near the village center. Start the day with a good breakfast featuring quality homemade dishes, then explore the hidden perennial garden, the village, and the unspoiled countryside beyond.

Hosts: Ruth and David Gaillard
Rooms: 4 (SB) $65-75
Full Breakfast
Credit Cards: A, B
Notes: 2, 5, 8, 9, 10, 11, 12, 13

HARTLAND

American Country Collection

1353 Union Street, Schenectady, NY 12054
(518) 439-7001; FAX (518) 439-4301

163. Modern home in a rural farm setting. Guests have the privacy of the entire first floor, including private entrance, if desired. Mostly new and modern furnishings. Continental breakfast. Two rooms, one with twin beds and one with a double bed; each has a private bath. Resident cat. Children welcome. No smoking. $60-70.

HYDE PARK

Bed and Breakfast Inns of New England

128 South Hoop Pole Road, Guilford, CT 06437
(203) 457-0042; (800) 582-0853

VT725. In the lovely Lamoille River Valley on a hill overlooking the magnificent Green Mountains, this inn, circa 1794, offers a special opportunity to enjoy a true Vermont experience. Set on four acres of woodland and central to Vermont's all-season vacation country, guests can choose from any number of activities: skiing, fishing, hiking, biking, canoeing, tennis, golf, auctions, and antique shopping. The inn is only ten minutes from Stowe, one hour from Burlington Airport, and two hours from Montréal. A full gourmet breakfast is included, and dinners are available. Five tastefully decorated guest rooms, a Colonial dining room, a Federalist-style living room, and a comfortable library full of videotapes and books are available to guests. Private and shared baths. Children over nine welcome. No smoking. $59-95.

JACKSONVILLE

American Country Collection

1353 Union Street, Schenectady, NY 12054
(518) 439-7001; FAX (518) 439-4301

165. Victorian country home built in 1840. Queen Anne Colonial furnishings and in-ground pool. Dining room with fireplace, living room, and sitting room with TV. Three guest rooms with private and shared baths. Twenty minutes from Mount Snow. Full breakfast. Children welcome. Smoking outside. $45-65.

JAMAICA

Three Mountain Inn

P.O. Box 180 A, 05343
(802) 874-4140

Small, romantic 1780s authentic country inn. Fine food and comfortable rooms. Many original details can be found, including three wood-burning fireplaces on the main floor, and several guest rooms also boast original fireplaces. In a historic village, just four blocks to hiking in the state park and cross-country skiing. Swimming

7 No smoking; 8 Children welcome; 9 Social drinking allowed; 10 Tennis nearby; 11 Swimming nearby;
12 Golf nearby; 13 Skiing nearby; 14 May be booked through a travel agent.

pool on premises. Ten minutes to Stratton. The innkeepers plan special day trips with detailed local maps of the area. Special midweek rates. Honeymoon suites available. Small weddings, reunions, meetings. Bed and Breakfast and Modified American Plan available.

Hosts: Charles and Elaine Murray
Rooms: 16 (14 PB; 2 SB) $75-180
Full Breakfast
Credit Cards: A, B, C, D
Notes: 2, 4, 8, 9, 10, 11, 12, 13, 14

JEFFERSONVILLE

Jefferson House Bed and Breakfast

Main Street, P.O. Box 288, 05464
(802) 644-2030

Enjoy the picturesque beauty of this turn-of-the-century Victorian home in historic Jeffersonville. It features a large wrap-around porch; a warm, friendly atmosphere; attractive, comfortable rooms; and a hearty, home-cooked breakfast. In spring and summer bike the country roads, hike the Long Trail or Mount Mansfield. Autumn's foliage is a sight to behold. In the winter, nearby Smuggler's Notch offers great skiing while other activities are only minutes away.

Hosts: Dick and Joan Walker
Rooms: 3 (SB) $40-50
Full Breakfast
Credit Cards: None
Notes: 2, 5, 7, 8, 12, 13

Mannsview Inn

Rural Route 2, Box 4319, Route 108 South, 05464
(802) 644-8321; (800) 937-6266 (reservations)

Mannsview Inn, circa 1875, is a Colonial-style home with a Victorian flair. Completely restored, it offers queen-size high-poster beds, a library, parlor, fireplace, cable TV, and home-cooked breads and muffins with a full breakfast. At the base of Mount Mansfield in the heart of Vermont's number-

one resort area, guests are surrounded by breathtaking mountain views, pastures, and trout streams. On the premises guests will also find a 10,000-square-foot antique center, canoe touring, skiing, hiking, and canoeing packages available. Canadian 20 percent. Box lunches available.

Hosts: Bette and Kelley Mann
Rooms: 6 (2 PB; 4 SB) $50-70
Full Breakfast
Credit Cards: A, B, C
Notes: 2, 7, 10, 11, 12, 13, 14

Sterling Ridge Inn and Cabins

Rural Route 2, Box 5780, 05464
(802) 644-8265; (800) 347-8266

On a scenic back road surrounded by mountains and meadows, overlooking Vermont's tallest peak, Mount Mansfield. Eight comfortable guest rooms in Laura Ashley-style and three individual log cabins with two bedrooms each and full kitchens. All modern amenities. At the inn enjoy outdoor hot tub, heated swimming pool, cross-country trails, three miles to Smugglers Notch, and 15 miles to Stowe.

Hosts: Susan and Scott Peterson
Rooms: 11 (7 PB; 4 SB) $48-114
Full Breakfast
Credit Cards: A, B
Notes: 2, 5, 7, 8, 9, 10, 11, 12, 13, 14

Windridge Inn

Main Street, P.O. Box 426, 05464
(802) 644-5556

Early American-style inn with antique furniture, old wood or slate floors, solid wide pine boards, and stenciled walls. This rusticity is balanced by the comfort of the king-size beds and silent air conditioning. The inn is renowned for its restaurant, Le Cheval d'Or, which features Vermont or New England products prepared in the French manner. Dinner is served by candlelight. There is a full bar and an excellent wine cellar. The inn and most of the village are on the National Register of Historic

Places. Breakfast is not available at the inn but is served next door.

Host: Yves Labbé
Rooms: 4 (PB) $49-75
Credit Cards: A, B, C
Notes: 3, 4, 5, 9, 10, 11, 13, 14

Henry M. Field House

JERICHO

Henry M. Field House Bed and Breakfast

Rural Route 2, Box 395, 05465
(802) 899-3984

Henry M. Field House is near skiing, cycling, hiking, swimming, and golf. The house is convenient to Burlington area colleges and shops. The Italianate Victorian was built in 1875 and features tall ceilings, wood floors, etched glass, and period decor including antique furniture and lighting. Vegetable crêpes with a mushroom sauce, banana French toast, and a variety of home-baked items are specialties of the house. Children are welcome but must be in another rented room.

Hosts: Mary Beth and Terrence Horan
Rooms: 3 (PB) $65-85
Full Breakfast
Credit Cards: A, B
Notes: 2, 5, 7, 9, 10, 11, 12, 13

Homeplace

Rural Route 2, Box 367, 05465
(802) 899-4694

A quiet spot in a hundred wood. The spacious house is filled with European and American antiques. The living room has a large fireplace and looks out on Mount Mansfield. The house is surrounded by perennial gardens, and there are many wooded trails on the property. Friendly house and barn animals complete the picture.

Hosts: Hans and Mariot Huessy
Rooms: 3 (1 PB; 2 SB) $55-65
Full Breakfast
Credit Cards: None
Notes: 2, 5, 8, 10, 11, 12, 13, 14

JOHNSON

The Homestead Bed and Breakfast

Rural Route 2, Box 623, 05656
(802) 635-7354

The quiet beauty of Vermont's countryside surrounds this circa 1830 brick Colonial farmhouse. A hearty breakfast starts guests on the way to enjoying the many activities offered in the area: canoeing, hiking, fishing, biking, antiquing, and skiing.

Hosts: Erwin and Ella May Speer
Rooms: 4 (SB) $45-55
Full Breakfast
Credit Cards: A, B
Notes: 2, 3, 4, 5, 7, 8, 10, 11, 12, 13

KILLINGTON

Bed and Breakfast Inns of New England

128 South Hoop Pole Road, Guilford, CT 06437
(203) 457-0042; (800) 582-0853

VT711. Having been a working farm for more than a century, this country farmhouse and big red barn, originally built in the 1850s, have been converted and decorated

7 No smoking; 8 Children welcome; 9 Social drinking allowed; 10 Tennis nearby; 11 Swimming nearby; 12 Golf nearby; 13 Skiing nearby; 14 May be booked through a travel agent.

with comfortable, up-to-date guest accommodations. Sturdy beams, barnboard, and big fieldstone fireplaces accompany the guest rooms, all with private bath. A game room, TV room, and a large living room with fireplace and picture-window views across the lake and into the mountains. In the winter, enjoy all of Killington and Pico's alpine and cross-country ski areas. During summer and fall, enjoy boating, fishing, and swimming in the lake. There is also an outdoor in-ground pool. If hiking, biking, theater, concerts, mountaintop chairlift rides, Alpine slide rides, golf, tennis, antiquing, and shopping aren't enough—wait for the fall foliage. $78-95.

Cortina Inn

HC 34, Box 33, Route 4, 05751
(802) 773-3333; (800) 451-6108
FAX (802) 775-6948

This inn has 97 individually decorated rooms with cable TVs, telephones, private baths, some with Jacuzzi and fireplace. Enjoy fresh flowers, complimentary afternoon tea with cookies, room service, courtesy shuttle to the slopes, two restaurants, indoor pool, whirlpool, saunas, exercise room, game room, library, art gallery, tennis, hiking, mountain biking trails with bike rentals. Sleigh rides, ice skating, and snowmobiling in the winter. The hospitality of a country inn, the amenities of a resort. Restricted smoking.

Hosts: Bob and Breda Harnish
Rooms: 97 (PB) $149-199
Full Breakfast
Credit Cards: A, B, C, D, E, F
Notes: 2, 4, 5, 6, 8, 9, 10, 11, 12, 13, 14

Red Clover Inn

Woodward Road, Rural Route 2
Box 7450, Mendon, 05701
(802) 775-2290; (800) 752-0571

Down a winding country road, amid 13 acres, Red Clover Inn offers guests warmth, pampering, and exceptional gourmet fare.

From enticing rooms with handmade quilts, antiques, some whirlpools, and cozy fires to sumptuous breakfasts and candlelit dining with soft music, the atmosphere is relaxed and peaceful. An added treat is Gruffy, a carrot-loving pony, and Minnie, his lovable miniature horse companion. Pool on premises. A stay at this inn turns guests into friends who cannot wait to return. Closed in mid-April and re-opening for Memorial Day weekend. Call before bringing pets. Children over eight welcome.

Hosts: Sue and Harris Zuckerman
Rooms: 12 (PB) $100-200
Full Breakfast
Credit Cards: A, B
Notes: 2, 4, 7, 9, 10, 11, 12, 13, 14

LONDONDERRY

The Blue Gentian Lodge

Magic Mountain Road, Rural Route 1
Box 29, 05148
(802) 824-5908 (phone and FAX)

The Blue Gentian Lodge in south central Vermont has a splendid view of Magic Mountain. The 13 rooms are comfortable, each with a private bath and cable TV. One is completely handicapped accessible, as is the dining area and the lounge. Outdoor pool on the premises. Numerous attractions in the area for hiking, museums, skiing, summer theater, and shopping.

Hosts: Dorothy and Paul Alberti
Rooms: 13 (PB) $50-80
Full Breakfast
Credit Cards: None
Notes: 2, 5, 7, 8, 9, 10, 11, 12, 13

The Highland House

Route 100, 05148
(802) 824-3019

This 1842 inn, with swimming pool and tennis court, is set on 32 acres and offers 17 rooms, 15 with private bath. Classic candlelight dining with homemade soups, breads, and desserts. Within minutes of skiing, hiking, horseback riding, golf, shopping, and points of interest. Two-day, two-night minimum stay required on weekends and three-night stay on holidays. Closed one week in November and three weeks in April and May.

Hosts: Mike and Laurie Gayda
Rooms: 17 (15 PB; 2 SB) $75-103
Full Breakfast
Credit Cards: A, B, C
Notes: 2, 4, 7, 10, 11, 12, 13

Swiss Inn

Route 11, Rural Route 1, Box 140, 05148
(802) 824-3442; (800) 847-9477

The Swiss Inn is in the heart of the Green Mountains with spectacular views of the surrounding area. These cozy, comfortable rooms all feature cable TV, telephones, and private baths. Full Vermont breakfast is served daily. Two fireside sitting rooms, game room, and library are available. Restaurant on premises features Swiss specialties. Both downhill and cross-country skiing nearby in the winter. Shopping, antiques, golf, summer theater, and fall foliage at its best.

Hosts: Joe and Pat Donahue
Rooms: 18 (PB) $50-89
Full Breakfast
Credit Cards: A, B
Notes: 2, 4, 5, 8, 9, 10, 11, 12, 13

LUDLOW

The Andrie Rose Inn

13 Pleasant Street, 05149
(802) 228-4846; (800) 223-4846

At the base of Okemo Mountain discover this stylish 1829 village inn, selected as one of the top inns in America and the best bed and breakfast at Okemo. AAA rated four diamonds. Beautiful antique-filled guest rooms, designer linens, skylights, and whirlpool tubs. Unforgettable country breakfast by candlelight. Magnificent luxury suites with oversized whirlpool tubs in front of a fireplace,

The Andrie Rose Inn

the ultimate in accommodations. Family suites with fireplaces, whirlpools, and gourmet kitchens. Use inn bikes to tour back roads. Minutes from lakes, theaters, golf, tennis, hiking, and downhill and cross-country skiing. Full breakfast for those staying in the main lodge, and breakfast baskets for guests in the luxury suites.

Hosts: Jack and Ellen Fisher
Rooms: 19 (PB) $70-250
Full Breakfast
Credit Cards: A, B, C
Notes: 2, 4, 5, 7, 8, 10, 11, 12, 13, 14

Black River Inn

100 Main Street, 05149
(802) 228-5585

Rated "outstanding," a charming 1835 country inn on the bank of the Black River at the base of Okemo Mountain. Ten guest rooms furnished with antiques, eight with private baths. A variety of antique beds with down comforters and feather pillows, including a 1794 walnut four-poster in which Abraham Lincoln once slept. Full country breakfast, fireside cocktails, dinners available. Near downhill and cross-country skiing, bicycle rentals, golf, hiking, swimming, and fishing. Children over 12 welcome.

Hosts: Rick and Cheryl DelMastro
Rooms: 10 (8 PB; 2 SB) $75-120
Full Breakfast
Credit Cards: A, B, C, D
Notes: 2, 4, 5, 9, 10, 11, 12, 13, 14

7 No smoking; 8 Children welcome; 9 Social drinking allowed; 10 Tennis nearby; 11 Swimming nearby; 12 Golf nearby; 13 Skiing nearby; 14 May be booked through a travel agent.

The Combes Family Inn

Rural Free Delivery 1, Box 275, 05149
(802) 228-8799

Bring the family to the Combes Family Inn
in Vermont. The inn, a century-old farmhouse on a country backroad, offers a quiet
respite from the hustle and bustle of today's
hectic lifestyle! Relax and socialize (BYOB)
in the Vermont Barnboard "keeping room,"
furnished with turn-of-the-century oak.
Sample Bill's country breakfasts and Ruth's
delicious home cooking. Lush Green
Mountains invite a relaxing, casual vacation.
Eleven cozy, country-inspired guest rooms—
all with private baths. Minimum-stay
requirements for fall and winter weekends
and for holidays. Closed April 15 through
May 15.

Hosts: Ruth and Bill Combes
Rooms: 11 (PB) $78-90
Full Breakfast
Credit Cards: A, B, C, D
Notes: 2, 3, 4, 6, 8, 9, 10, 11, 12, 13, 14

Echo Lake Inn

P.O. Box 154, 05149
(800) 356-6844

Year-round country inn and resort built in
1840. One of six inns in Vermont originally
built as an inn. In beautiful lakes region,
minutes to ski areas and golf. Tennis, pool,
boating, fishing. Full breakfast and dinner,
porch dining. Cocktail lounge, tavern,

Echo Lake Inn

game room, steam bath, and Jacuzzi.
Homemade desserts by the hostess. Lunch
is seasonal. Dinner included in the rates.
Menu according to season: homemade
pasta, venison, and other game dishes,
always fresh fish. Close to many points of
interest, such as the birthplace of President
Calvin Coolidge and the cheese factory. On
Route 100, five miles north of Ludlow.
Closed April. Modified American Plan
available. Smoking restricted. Children
over five welcome.

Hosts: John and Yvonne Pardieu and Chip Connelly
Rooms: 26 (12 PB; 14 SB) $84-178
Full Breakfast
Credit Cards: A, B, C, D
Notes: 2, 4, 9, 10, 11, 12, 13, 14

The Governor's Inn

86 Main Street, 05149
(802) 228-8830; (800) GOVERNOR

It is pure pleasure to be a guest at the
Governor's Inn. The Marbles have made
innkeeping an art form. They love what
they do and guests will too. Both graduated
from French cooking school (Roger Verge)
and present their famous cuisine on museum-quality antique china. In fact, they
share all of their collections with guests:
precious knife rests, Waterford crystal,
magnificent chocolate pots, polished silver,
and whimsical breakfast bells. A Mobil
four-star inn. Picnic lunches available.

Hosts: Charlie and Deedy Marble
Rooms: 8 (PB) $95-160
Full Breakfast
Credit Cards: A, B
Notes: 2, 4, 5, 7, 9, 10, 11, 12, 13, 14

LYNDON

*Branch Brook
Bed and Breakfast*

South Wheelock Road, P.O. Box 143, 05849
(802) 626-8316; (800) 572-7712

This restored 1850 house in northeast
Vermont has an attractive living room, din-

Branch Brook

ing room, and library all available for guests' use. Five guest rooms, three with private baths. One-half mile off I-91 at exit 23. Burke Mountain ski area is eight miles away and provides both downhill and cross-country skiing. Hiking, biking, and swimming available. A complete breakfast prepared on an English AGA cooker is served in the dining room. AAA.

Hosts: Ted and Ann Tolman
Rooms: 5 (3 PB; 2 SB) $55-70
Full Breakfast
Credit Cards: A, B
Notes: 2, 5, 7, 8, 9, 10, 11, 12, 13

LYNDONVILLE

The Wildflower Inn

Darling Hill Road, 05851
(800) 627-8310

A perfect spot for a family getaway. The innkeepers and their warmhearted staff invite guests to enjoy each season's offering: nature trails, tennis court, spectacular heated pool, and delightful gardens in summer; wildflowers and fishing in spring; excellent alpine and cross-country skiing in winter. Breathtaking views, great meals, teddy bear pancakes, petting barn, and much more all year-round. Known as Vermont's best family inn. Rates include

breakfast and snack. Off-season discount rates available.

Hosts: Jim and Mary O'Reilly
Rooms: 22 (20 PB; 2 SB) $89-145
Full Breakfast
Credit Cards: A, B
Notes: 2, 4, 5, 7, 8, 9, 10, 11, 12, 13, 14

MANCHESTER

American Country Collection

1353 Union Street, Schenectady, NY 12054
(518) 439-7001; FAX (518) 439-4301

080. Guests will find tranquility in this 1890 tenant farmer's house on a five-acre plot at the foot of the Green Mountains. Two cozy guest rooms are decorated in country pastels and prints. Each room has a magnificent view and private bath. Guests may enjoy tea on the deck by the brook, by the wood-burning stove in the dining room, or by the fireplace in the living room. Continental breakfast can be served in the dining room or on the deck. Smoking permitted, but not in the guest rooms. Children over 12 welcome. Dog in residence. $60.

Bed and Breakfast Inns of New England

128 South Hoop Pole Road, Guilford, CT 06437
(203) 457-0042; (800) 582-0853

VT704. This lovely Queen Anne Victorian inn sits on a hilltop overlooking the town. It enjoys beautiful views of Mount Equinox. All guest rooms are furnished with country antiques, feather beds, down comforters, lace curtains, and private baths. Numerous common rooms include a game room, two TV rooms, and a living room. Large outdoor pool. People love Manchester for its wide variety of recreational offerings such as hiking, soaring, skiing, swimming, museums, and numerous brand-name outlet and specialty shops. No smoking. $105-125.

1811 House

Box 39, 05254
(802) 362-1811

This classic Vermont inn offers guests the warmth and comfort of their own home. Built in the 1770s, the house has operated as an inn since 1811 except for one brief period when it was the residence of Abraham Lincoln's granddaughter. All guest rooms have private baths; some have fireplaces, Oriental rugs, fine paintings, and canopied beds. More than three acres of lawn contain flower gardens and a pond and offer an exceptional view of the Green Mountains. Walk to golf and tennis, near skiing, fishing, canoeing, and all sports. Young people over 16 welcome.

Hosts: Marnie and Bruce Duff
Rooms: 14 (PB) $110-200
Full Breakfast
Credit Cards: A, B, C, D
Notes: 2, 5, 7, 9, 10, 11, 12, 13, 14

The Inn at Manchester

Historic Route 7A, Box 41, 05254-0041
(802) 362-1793

Beautifully restored turn-of-the-century Victorian set on four acres in the picture-book village of Manchester. Elegant rooms with bay windows, brass beds, antiques, and an extensive art collection. Luscious full country breakfast. Secluded pool, skiing, shops, and theater in

the area. Come for peace, pancakes, and pampering. Guests can choose between 14 rooms and 4 suites. Smoking restricted. Children over eight welcome.

Hosts: Stan and Harriet Rosenberg
Rooms: 18 (PB) $95-130
Full Breakfast
Credit Cards: A, B, C, D
Notes: 2, 5, 9, 10, 11, 12, 13, 14

Manchester Highlands Inn

Box 1754 AD, Highland Avenue, 05255
(802) 362-4565

Discover Manchester's first painted lady, a graceful Queen Anne Victorian inn on a hilltop overlooking town. Front porch with rocking chairs, large outdoor pool, game room, and pub with stone fireplace. Rooms individually decorated with feather beds, down comforters, and lace curtains. Gourmet country breakfasts and afternoon snacks are served.

Hosts: Robert and Patricia Eichorn
Rooms: 15 (PB) $85-125
Full Breakfast
Credit Cards: A, B, C
Notes: 2, 5, 7, 8, 9, 10, 11, 12, 13, 14

MANCHESTER CENTER

Brook-n-Hearth Inn

State Route 11 and 30, Box 508, 05255
(802) 362-3604

Homey Colonial-style inn one mile east of US 7 on Routes 11 and 30. Features full breakfast, cozy rooms with air conditioning, private baths, family suite, cable TV, lounge, BYOB, recreation rooms, outdoor heated swimming pool, and walking trails near a brook. Two-night minimum stay required over holidays. Closed mid-April to mid-May and early November to November 16.

Hosts: Larry and Terry Greene
Rooms: 3 (PB) $54-80
Full Breakfast
Credit Cards: A, B, C, D
Notes: 2, 7, 8, 9, 10, 11, 12, 13

NOTES: Credit cards accepted: A MasterCard; B Visa; C American Express; D Discover; E Diners Club;
F Other; 2 Personal checks accepted; 3 Lunch available; 4 Dinner available; 5 Open all year; 6 Pets welcome;

The Inn at Ormsby Hill

Historic Route 7A, Rural Route 2
P.O. Box 3264, 05255
(802) 362-1163

This splendid restored manor house is on two
and one-half acres overlooking the Green
Mountains. Listed on Vermont's Register of
Historic Places, the inn offers six guest
rooms, all with private baths, four with fireplaces and whirlpools. Rates include a full
breakfast. There are many excellent places
for lunch and dinner nearby. Manchester is a
four-season resort community with a full
assortment of sports and cultural activities.

Hosts: Nancy and Don Burd
Rooms: 6 (PB) $95-170
Full Breakfast
Credit Cards: A, B, C
Notes: 2, 7, 9, 10, 11, 12, 13, 14

River Meadow Farm

P.O. Box 822, 05255
(802) 362-1602

Secluded farm at the end of a country lane
with beautiful views of the surrounding
countryside. The remodeled farmhouse was
built just prior to 1800. Five guest bedrooms sharing two and one-half baths,
large country kitchen with a fireplace and
adjoining screened-in, glassed-in porch,
pleasant dining room, living room with
baby grand piano, and den with TV.
Seventy acres to hike or cross-country ski,
bordered by the famous Battenkill River.
Swimming is available ten miles away.

Host: Patricia J. Dupree
Rooms: 5 (SB) $25/person
Full Breakfast
Credit Cards: None
Notes: 2, 7, 8, 9, 10, 12, 13

MANCHESTER VILLAGE

The Battenkill Inn

P.O. Box 948, 05254
(802) 362-4213; (800) 441-1628

Guests are invited to share the hospitable
warmth of a bygone era in an exquisite

Victorian setting. Fine antiques and heavenly breakfasts are enjoyed amid the
painterly beauty of the Battenkill River
Valley. Play afternoon croquet on sweeping lawns and delight in evening hors
d'oeuvres by a marble-mantled fire. Alpine
and cross-country skiing, antiquing, golfing, canoeing, and discount shopping are
nearby. Air-conditioned rooms with private baths, some with fireplaces.

Hosts: Ramsay and Mary Jo Gourd
Rooms: 10 (PB) $75-165
Full Breakfast
Credit Cards: A, B, C
Notes: 5, 7, 8, 9, 10, 11, 12, 13, 14

The Reluctant Panther Inn and Restaurant

West Road, P.O. Box 678, 05254-0678
(800) 822-2331

Relax and forget the world in quiet, individually decorated guest rooms or suites.
All rooms have private baths, telephones,
air conditioning, and cable TVs. Some have
wood-burning fireplaces and Jacuzzis.
Enjoy the Panther Bar or the tree-shaded
patio, and experience an extraordinary candlelight dinner at the award-winning
restaurant. House guests enjoy priority at
the fireplace or solarium tables. Modified
American Plan available.

Hosts: Maye and Robert Bachofen
Rooms: 16 (PB) $160-300
Full Breakfast
Credit Cards: A, B, C
Notes: 2, 4, 5, 9, 10, 11, 12, 13, 14

MIDDLEBURY

The Annex

Route 125, 05740
(802) 388-3233

This 1830 Greek Revival home was originally built as an annex to the Bob Newhart
"Stratford Inn." The annex features six
rooms decorated in a blend of country,
antiques, and homemade quilts. The nearby

7 No smoking; 8 Children welcome; 9 Social drinking allowed; 10 Tennis nearby; 11 Swimming nearby;
12 Golf nearby; 13 Skiing nearby; 14 May be booked through a travel agent.

national forest provides hiking, skiing, and biking trails. Visit the UVM Morgan Horse Farm and the Shelburne Museum while in the area. Please inquire about accommodations for children.

Host: T. D. Hutchins
Rooms: 6 (4 PB; 2 SB) $50-75
Continental Breakfast
Credit Cards: None
Notes: 2, 5, 9, 10, 11, 12, 13

Bed and Breakfast Marblehead and North Shore

P.O. Box 35, Newtonville, MA 02160
(617) 964-1606; (800) 832-2632
FAX (617) 332-8572

19th-Century Farmhouse. Built in 1879, this beautiful country farmhouse is off a quiet country road on 20 acres of meadowland, surrounded by spacious lawns and lovely gardens. There are four beautifully decorated guest rooms and a two-bedroom suite that sleeps up to four with a private entrance, living room with cable TV, wood stove, dining area, and kitchen. All rooms have private baths. Full country breakfast in the morning, and complimentary wine and cheese in the evenings. Close to Middlebury College, many wonderful tourist attractions, and downhill and cross-country skiing areas. A cat and dog are resident pets. No smoking. Children over eight are welcome. Open year-round. Two-night minimum stay. $100-165.

The Middlebury Inn

Courthouse Square, P.O. Box 631, 05753
(802) 388-4961; (800) 842-4666

Elegantly restored 1827 village inn in the historic district of a lovely college town. Guest rooms have private baths, telephones, and TVs. Formal or informal dining; afternoon tea served daily. Museums, unique shops, and historic sites to explore. Swimming, golf, hiking, boating, downhill and cross-country skiing are nearby. Special packages are available. Call before

The Middlebury Inn

bringing pets. Smoking restricted. Full breakfast can be added for $6 per person.

Hosts: Frank and Jane Emanuel
Rooms: 75 (PB) $86-206
Full Breakfast
Credit Cards: A, B, C, D, E
Notes: 2, 3, 4, 5, 8, 9, 10, 11, 12, 13, 14

A Point of View

Rural Delivery 3, Box 2675, 05753
(802) 388-7205

This country bed and breakfast, with fantastic views of the valley and Green Mountains, offers excellent beds in comfortable air-conditioned rooms. The living room has a large cable TV. The game room includes a pool table. This is a warm, friendly atmosphere where each guest is treated specially. Hostess prides herself on serving a Vermont-style breakfast featuring seasonal fruits and generous entrées. Area attractions include the Morgan Horse Farm, museums, and crafts center. Smoking restricted.

Host: Marie Highter
Rooms: 2 (1 PB; 1 SB) $50
Full Breakfast
Credit Cards: None
Notes: 2, 5, 8, 9, 10, 11, 12, 13

MIDDLETOWN SPRINGS

American Country Collection

1353 Union Street, Schenectady, NY 12054
(518) 439-7001; FAX (518) 439-4301

147. There is a treat waiting for guests as they step back 100 years in time to an age of elegance in this rural New England village. Listed on the National Register of Historic Places, this historic home is filled with antiques and a large music box collection. Near Lake St. Catherine for boating and picnicking. Fishermen will love the trout that can be caught in a stream bordering the property. Six guest rooms are available, all with private baths, and a full breakfast. Dinner available nightly. $55-75.

MONTGOMERY CENTER

The Inn on Trout River

P.O. Box 76, The Main Street, 05471
(802) 326-4391; (800) 338-7049

Surrounded by magnificent mountain ranges in a quaint Currier and Ives-style village, this 100-year-old country Victorian inn features private baths, queen-size beds, down comforters, feather pillows, flannel sheets, cozy fireplaces, antiques, gourmet restaurant, a pub, and game room. Close to summer and winter sports, covered bridges, and shopping. A full menu at breakfast is always included. AAA three-diamond Historic Country Inn and AAA two-diamond restaurant.

Hosts: Michael and Lee Forman
Rooms: 10 (PB) $86-103
Full Breakfast
Credit Cards: A, B, C, D
Notes: 2, 4, 5, 7, 8, 9, 10, 11, 12, 13, 14

Phineas Swann Bed and Breakfast

Main Street, Box 43, 05471
(802) 326-4306

A charming Victorian home with a country flavor, Phineas Swann has an enclosed porch and lots of gingerbread trim. Four large, cozy guest rooms. The nearby Green Mountains and Jay Peak provide plenty of hiking, skiing, and biking. Within walking distance of shops and restaurants. Awake to a hearty candlelight breakfast.

Hosts: Glen Bartolomeo and Michael Bindler
Rooms: 4 (1 PB; 3 SB) $55-70
Full Breakfast
Credit Cards: A, B, D
Notes: 2, 5, 7, 8, 9, 11, 12, 13, 14

Phineas Swann

MONTPELIER

Betsy's Bed and Breakfast

74 East State Street, 05602
(802) 229-0466; FAX (802) 229-5412

Betsy's Bed and Breakfast is a warm and inviting Queen Anne home in the nation's smallest capital. The rooms are lavishly furnished with period antiques. Guests are invited to linger over a cup of coffee in the sun-filled dining room, chat with the owners by a crackling fire in the formal parlor, lift weights or cycle in the exercise room, rock on the front porch, hot tub under the stars, or hide away in their room and enjoy the peace and quiet.

Hosts: Jon and Betsy Anderson
Rooms: 8 (PB) $50-115
Full Breakfast
Credit Cards: A, B
Notes: 2, 3, 5, 7, 8, 9, 10, 11, 12, 13, 14

7 No smoking; 8 Children welcome; 9 Social drinking allowed; 10 Tennis nearby; 11 Swimming nearby; 12 Golf nearby; 13 Skiing nearby; 14 May be booked through a travel agent.

MORGAN

Hunts Hideaway

Rural Route 1, Box 570, West Charleston, 05872
(802) 895-4432; (802) 334-8322

Contemporary split-level on 100 acres: brook, pond, and a 44-foot in-ground pool. In Morgan, six miles from I-91, near the Canadian border. Guests may use kitchen and laundry facilities. Lake Seymour is two miles away; 18-hole golf courses at Newport and Orleans; bicycling, jogging, skiing at Jay Peak and Burke Mountain, antiquing, bird watching, and fishing.

Host: Pat Hunt
Rooms: 3 (SB) $35
Full Breakfast
Credit Cards: B
Notes: 2, 5, 8, 9, 10, 11, 12, 13

MOUNT SNOW

The Inn at Quail Run

HCR 63, P.O. Box 28, Smith Road
Wilmington, 05363
(802) 464-3362; (800) 34 ESCAPE

Enjoy pristine mountain views, comfortable large rooms, a full country breakfast, and après ski snacks. On a quiet country road away from traffic, the entire inn is nonsmoking. In winter, enjoy cross-country trails, and in summer, enjoy the heated pool. Large sauna, TV room, library, exercise room, game room, and antique store. A charming and romantic getaway.

Hosts: Tom, Marie, and Molly Martin
Rooms: 15 (14 PB; 1 SB) $80-125
Full Breakfast
Credit Cards: A, B, C, D
Notes: 2, 5, 7, 8, 9, 10, 11, 12, 13, 14

NEWBURY

A Century Past

Box 186, Route 5, 05051
(802) 866-3358

A charming, historic house dating back to 1790 and nestled in the tranquility of a quaint Vermont village. A cozy sitting room with fireplace; chat with newfound friends or curl up with a good book. Wake up to freshly baked muffins, hot coffee or tea, great French toast—all served in a comfortable dining room. Activities include walking, biking, and canoeing. Children over 12 welcome. The inn is open May 1 through December 1 and by reservation at any other time.

Host: Patricia Smith
Rooms: 4 (SB) $60
Full Breakfast
Credit Cards: A, B
Notes: 2, 7, 9, 10, 11, 12, 13

NEWFANE

Bed and Breakfast Inns of New England

128 South Hoop Pole Road, Guilford, CT 06437
(203) 457-0042; (800) 582-0853

VT705. On 30 acres of lovely Vermont countryside, this country farmhouse is surrounded by mountains and bordered by the West River. Explore the wooded hills, the quiet streams, and wildlife by horseback, canoe, hiking, or cycling. Numerous music festivals, summer theaters, fairs, craft festivals, antique shops, flea markets, and historic sites are within easy reach. Eight guest rooms with private or shared baths and comfortable antiques in the fireplaced living room with piano, a traditional pine-paneled dining room, and relaxing porches. No smoking indoors. Resident cat and dog. No guest pets, please. $70-80.

NORTHFIELD

Northfield Inn

27 Highland Avenue, 05663
(802) 485-8558

This turn-of-the-century mansion, restored to its original elegance, sits on a hillside with magnificent panoramic views of the Green Mountains and the Northfield Valley

NOTES: Credit cards accepted: A MasterCard; B Visa; C American Express; D Discover; E Diners Club;
F Other; 2 Personal checks accepted; 3 Lunch available; 4 Dinner available; 5 Open all year; 6 Pets welcome;

below. Graceful porches and gardens, gentle breezes and golden sunsets add to the natural beauty of this romantic getaway. Antiques, Oriental art, European feather bedding, private baths, lovely decor, and ambience of the Victorian era of comfort. Lunch available for groups by arrangement.

Host: Aglaia Stalb
Rooms: 8 (PB) $85-130
Full Breakfast
Credit Cards: A, B
Notes: 2, 4, 5, 7, 9, 10, 11, 12, 13, 14

NORTH HERO ISLAND

Charlie's Northland Lodge

Rural Route 1, Box 88, US Route 2, 05474
(802) 372-8822

Early 1800s guest house in a quiet village setting on North Hero Island on Lake Champlain. Three guest rooms furnished with country antiques share a modern bath, private entrance, and living room. A place to fish, sail, canoe, bike, or just plain relax. In winter, guests may ice fish and cross-country ski.

Hosts: Dorice and Charlie Clark
Rooms: 3 (SB) $50-55
Continental Breakfast
Credit Cards: A, B, D
Notes: 2, 5, 7, 9, 10, 11, 12, 13

NORTH THETFORD

Stone House Inn

Route 5, P.O. Box 47, 05054
(802) 333-9124

An 1835 stone farmhouse on the banks of the Connecticut River in central Vermont. Enclosed porches and a sitting room with fireplace. Central location and proximity to Dartmouth College make the inn a good base for touring. Nearby lakes and trails for boating and hiking. Smoking restricted.

Hosts: Art and Dianne Sharkey
Rooms: 6 (SB) $50
Continental Breakfast
Credit Cards: A, B
Notes: 2, 5, 9, 10, 11, 12, 13

NORTH TROY

American Country Collection

1353 Union Street, Schenectady, NY 12054
(518) 439-7001; FAX (518) 439-4301

193. Rural farmhouse on 52 acres with fields, woods, and panoramic view of Canadian mountains. A farm homestay that is very restful and quiet. Common room with parlor stove, TV, and piano. Three guest rooms: one double bed with private bath, and two rooms with double and single beds in each with a shared bath. Full breakfast. Children over six welcome. No smoking allowed. $35-60.

Bed and Breakfast Inns of New England

128 South Hoop Pole Road, Guilford, CT 06437
(203) 457-0042; (800) 582-0853

VT740. Enjoy this bed and breakfast farm with 52 acres of fields and woods and panoramic views of the Canadian Sutton Range and Jay Peak. There is nearby fishing, tennis, and golf; however, guests are welcome to stay around the farm and relax. Breakfast is full in the winter and Continental in the summer. Three guest rooms: one with a double bed and private bath; one with double bed and shared bath with bedroom with twin bed. Children over 12 are welcome. No smoking. There are a resident dog and cat; no guest pets allowed. Additional adults, $20. Additional children, $15. $50-60.

Bed and Breakfast Marblehead and North Shore

P.O. Box 35, Newtonville, MA 02160
(617) 964-1606; (800) 832-2632
FAX (617) 332-8572

Canadian Border Guesthouse. In northern Vermont, close to the Canadian border, this wonderful old farmhouse sits on 52 acres and offers panoramic views of the

Sutton Range and Jay Peak. Acres of woodlands and fields provide outdoor enthusiasts with options for hiking, cross-country or downhill skiing, snowshoeing, fishing, and horseback riding. Guest accommodations include two rooms with shared bath, one room with private bath, a cozy living room with a parlor stove, TV, and piano. A delicious full and hearty country breakfast is included. No smoking. $45-100.

ORWELL

Historic Brookside Farms— A Four Season Country Inn

Route 22A, 05760
(802) 948-2727; FAX (802) 948-2015

This 1789-1843 historic register Greek Revival mansion is on 300 acres. All rooms are furnished in period antiques. Enjoy a full country breakfast, afternoon tea, and romantic candlelit gourmet dinner. Cross-country ski on miles of trails through 78 acres of magnificent forest. Hiking, lawn games, boating, and fishing on a 20-acre lake. There is a lovely antique shop on the premises. Family owned and operated. Limited smoking allowed.

Rooms: 7 (4 PB; 3 SB) $85-150
Full Breakfast
Credit Cards: None
Notes: 2, 3, 4, 5, 8, 9, 10, 11, 12, 13, 14

PITTSFIELD

Swiss Farm Lodge

Route 100, 05762
(802) 746-8341; (800) 245-5126

A homey, comfortable, and attractive lodge nestled in a beautiful valley surrounded by mountains. Delight in the ambience of a working farm, producing the hosts' own polled Hereford beef. Maple syrup is made from the trees on the farm. Convenient to

major downhill and cross-country ski areas. Anything guests may desire is nearby. All meals are homecooked and served in a large, pleasant dining room.

Hosts: Mark and Sandy Begin and family
Rooms: 17 (14 PB; 3 SB) $40-50
Full Breakfast
Credit Cards: A, B
Notes: 5, 7, 8, 9, 10, 11, 12, 13

POULTNEY

Bed and Breakfast Inns of New England

128 S. Hoop Pole Road, Guilford, CT 06437
(203) 457-0042; (800) 582-0853

VT712. This bed and breakfast is a 100-year-old beautifully restored Queen Anne Victorian. A wraparound porch and tower make this inn distinctive. Three guest rooms welcome guests with brass beds, antique oak, stenciling, and gorgeous views. An expanded Continental breakfast is served each morning, and all guests receive a loaf of "parting bread" when they leave. Lake St. Catherine is only three miles away, and five ski areas are within 20 miles. Private and shared baths. Children over eight are welcome. Smoking permitted. Resident dog and cats, but no guest pets, please. $55-60.

Lake Saint Catherine Inn

Cones Point Road, 05764
(802) 287-9347; (800) 626-LSCI (reservations)

Rural country resort on crystal-clear Lake Saint Catherine. Relaxation and wholesome dining. Families welcome. AAA approved. Rates include use of aluminum boats, canoes, paddleboats, and sailboats. Breakfast, dinner, and all gratuities are included in the daily rate. One housekeeping cottage sleeps six and is available with weekly rates. Many specials available throughout the season. Modified American

---

NOTES: Credit cards accepted: A MasterCard; B Visa; C American Express; D Discover; E Diners Club; F Other; 2 Personal checks accepted; 3 Lunch available; 4 Dinner available; 5 Open all year; 6 Pets welcome;

Plan is available. Open mid-May through mid-October.

Hosts: Patricia and Raymond Endlich
Rooms: 35 (PB) $128-168
Full Breakfast
Credit Cards: None
Notes: 2, 4, 8, 9, 10, 11, 12, 14

Stonebridge Inn

3 Beaman Street, Route 30, 05764
(802) 287-9849

The Stonebridge Inn is in the village of Poultney, which dates back to 1761. Green Mountain College, a small, private four-year college, is within walking distance. The inn occupies one of Poultney's most opulent buildings, sitting on a knoll overlooking Main Street. Stonebridge Inn is ideal for year-round activities. In winter, ski Killington and Pico. At other times, enjoy swimming, fishing, and boating in one of the nearby lakes. Golf is minutes away, and hiking trips for all ability levels can be arranged at the inn.

Rooms: 6 (3 PB; 3 SB) $64-84
Credit Cards: A, B, C
Notes: 2, 4, 5, 8, 9, 10, 11, 12, 13

PUTNEY

American Country Collection

1353 Union Street, Schenectady, NY 12054
(518) 439-7001; FAX (518) 439-4301

176. Just imagine ten acres of rolling hills, fields, and meadows mingled with a view that invites lingering and relaxation from a rear, three-tiered deck with gazebo. A very private setting in a rural farm area, yet only 15 minutes' driving time from Brattleboro. A contemporary center-chimney Cape, with hardwood floors, Oriental rugs, wing-back chairs, and wonderful views all around. There are a living room and dining room, where a full breakfast is served each morning. Each bedroom has a full private bath, ceiling fan, large closet, antique furni-

ture and fixtures, eyelet sheets, and colorful coverlets and quilts. Children are welcome. Smoking is permitted outside only. There are five resident cats, which are not allowed in the guest rooms, and two outside dogs. $55-75.

Bed and Breakfast Inns of New England

128 South Hoop Pole Road, Guilford, CT 06437
(203) 457-0042; (800) 582-0853

VT701. This charming center-chimney Cape overlooks a beautiful section of the Connecticut River Valley. Ten acres of rolling hills and meadows are filled with wildflowers, apple trees, old stone walls, a gazebo, and herb gardens. Three guest rooms with private baths, a common room with a cozy fireplace, games, and books. Antiques decorate the house with wide yellow pine floors. Enjoy a full country breakfast in the dining room with fireplace or enjoy the views of a busy hummingbird right outside the window. Resident cats and dogs. No smoking. $65-85.

Bed and Breakfast Marblehead and North Shore

P.O. Box 35, Newtonville, MA 02160
(617) 964-1606; (800) 832-2632
FAX (617) 332-8572

Cozy Meadows Bed and Breakfast. In the scenic countryside of Vermont's Connecticut River Valley, this charming center-chimney Cape overlooks rolling hills and meadows filled with wildflowers and apple trees. Guests are invited to stroll out back and relax on the deck or in the gazebo. Ten acres of land offer the opportunity for enjoying great exercise and nature at its best. The landscaped grounds and perennial gardens are a spring and summer treat. The fall foliage is spectacular. Winter snow provides a crisp white blanket as guests relax in front of a cozy fire. Three beautifully furnished bedrooms, all with private baths, feature wonderful views from bath and bedroom alike. Awaken to the aroma of fresh coffee and a delicious full country breakfast, featuring homemade muffins and jams. Local attractions include antiquing, canoeing, cycling, fishing, hiking, swimming, river excursions, and downhill and cross-country skiing. No smoking. $65-95.

Holland Hill Bed and Breakfast

Holland Hill Road, 05346
(802) 387-4234; FAX (802) 398-4224

Even before guests step through the door, they will know they are at a very special place. A sunny and spacious country home with panoramic views set on 60 acres of gardens, meadows, and woods, inviting exploration of its unexpected spaces and handcrafted details. Sip coffee in the solarium and be treated to an elegant breakfast. Meander along tranquil country roads, through quaint villages. Enjoy the swimming pond. Ski cross-country trails and alpine slopes.

Host: Kate Bayer
Rooms: 3 (2 PB; 1 SB) $75
Full Breakfast
Credit Cards: A, B
Notes: 2, 6, 7, 8, 9, 10, 11, 12, 13

The Putney Inn

Depot Road, P.O. Box 181, 05346
(802) 387-5517; (800) 653-5517
FAX (802) 387-5211

The inn began its varied history in 1790 as a farming homestead. Hand-hewn beams, central hearth, antiques, and lush plants create the warmth of the main building.

National award-winning chef Ann Cooper offers New England specialties and traditional favorites. Overnight accommodations in adjacent building radiate charm with modern amenities. Walk to the river or the center of town. The bucolic glory of pastoral mountains abounds.

Host: Randi Ziter
Rooms: 25 (PB) $58-93
Full Breakfast
Credit Cards: A, B, C, D
Notes: 2, 3, 4, 5, 6, 8, 9, 10, 11, 12, 13, 14

RIPTON

The Chipman Inn

Route 125, 05766
(802) 388-2390; (800) 890-2390

A traditional Vermont inn built in 1828 in the Green Mountain National Forest. Fine food, wine, and spirits for guests. Nine rooms, all with private bath. Fully licensed bar and large fireplace. Closed November 15 to December 26 and April 1 to May 15. Children over 12 welcome.

Hosts: Joyce Henderson and Bill Pierce
Rooms: 9 (PB) $80-110
Full Breakfast
Credit Cards: A, B, C
Notes: 2, 4, 9, 11, 12, 13

ROCHESTER

Liberty Hill Farm

Rural Route 1, Box 158, 05767
(802) 767-3926

Liberty Hill Farm is a family dairy farm where guests can relax and enjoy the coun-

The Putney Inn

NOTES: Credit cards accepted: A MasterCard; B Visa; C American Express; D Discover; E Diners Club; F Other; 2 Personal checks accepted; 3 Lunch available; 4 Dinner available; 5 Open all year; 6 Pets welcome;

tryside and help with farm chores, if they desire. Meals—breakfast and dinner—are served family style. There are seven guest rooms and four shared baths. Plenty of recreational activity nearby including tennis, swimming, golf, and skiing. Children welcome. Modified American Plan.

Hosts: Bob and Beth Kennett
Rooms: 7 (SB) $120
Full Breakfast
Credit Cards: None
Notes: 2, 3, 4, 5, 7, 8, 10, 11, 12, 13

ROYALTON

Fox Stand Inn

Route 14, 05068
(802) 763-8437

Built in 1818 as a stagecoach stop. On the banks of the White River, the dining room and tavern are open to the public and offer international creations. The inn's second floor has five comfortably furnished guest rooms. In the center of one of Vermont's acclaimed recreation regions. Swimming, canoeing, tubing, bicycling, hiking, and fishing are readily at hand. Antique shops, auctions, flea markets, and horse shows are found throughout the countryside.

Hosts: Jean and Gary Curley
Rooms: 5 (SB) $50-60
Full Breakfast
Credit Cards: A, B
Notes: 2, 4, 5, 7, 9, 10, 11, 12, 13

RUTLAND

The Inn at Rutland

70 North Main Street, Route 7, 05701
(802) 773-0575

The Inn at Rutland is an 1890s Victorian mansion restored to its original condition. Guest rooms have been tastefully decorated to recreate the past while maintaining modern comforts. All rooms have private bathrooms, telephones, and cable TV. A large, gourmet breakfast is served. The common rooms offer a comfortable atmosphere for

The Inn at Rutland

conversation, reading by the fireplace, watching movies, or just relaxing. Carriage house for ski or bike storage, with some mountain bikes available for guests. Children over six welcome.

Hosts: Bob and Tanya Liberman
Rooms: 10 (PB) $59-149
Full Breakfast
Credit Cards: A, B, D, E
Notes: 5, 7, 9, 10, 11, 12, 13, 14

ST. JOHNSBURY

The Looking Glass Inn

Rural Free Delivery 3, Box 199, 05819
(802) 748-3052

The Looking Glass Inn welcomes guests to a relaxed world of warmth and comfort. Each of the six individually decorated rooms is furnished with an antique double bed. There are four large baths. Each morning a hearty country breakfast is served in the dining room at guests' leisure. Relax in the afternoon with tea or a warming glass of sherry. A candlelight dinner, by special request, adds a romantic touch to an evening. Curl up by the parlor stove with a good book or good friends. Vermont has it all, whether guests seek the advantages of the great outdoors or desire pure serenity. The entire inn is available for special occasions. Inquire about dinner availability.

Hosts: Barbara and Perry Viles
Rooms: 6 (2 PB; 4 SB) $60-80
Full Breakfast
Credit Cards: A, B
Notes: 2, 5, 7, 9, 10, 11, 12, 13, 14

7 No smoking; 8 Children welcome; 9 Social drinking allowed; 10 Tennis nearby; 11 Swimming nearby; 12 Golf nearby; 13 Skiing nearby; 14 May be booked through a travel agent.

SHAFTSBURG

Covered Bridge

P.O. Box 447A, Norfolk, CT 06058
(203) 542-5944

1SHUT. An 1890 Colonial in a charming village setting close to Williamstown, Massachusetts, and Bennington, Vermont. The three guest rooms, all decorated with antiques, share a bath. A full gourmet breakfast is served. $50-65.

SOUTH HERO

American Country Collection

1353 Union Street, Schenectady, NY 12054
(518) 439-7001; FAX (518) 439-4301

179. A quiet, secluded retreat on more than ten acres with panoramic views of the Green Mountains and Lake Champlain. On a hill overlooking the surrounding countryside is a three-room studio suite with private entrance, patio, and landscaped garden. Furnished with modern pieces, it is a complete living unit. Included is a bedroom with a double bed, kitchen, large bath, washer and dryer, and a living room with TV, VCR, sofa, easy chairs, and wood stove. Sliding glass doors off the living room provide access to the outdoor patio. Smoking outside only. Extra fee for each extra adult and child over three. $60-80.

SOUTH LONDONDERRY

The Londonderry Inn

P.O. Box 301-70, 05155-0301
(802) 824-5226; FAX (802) 824-3146

An 1826 homestead that has been welcoming guests for 50 years. Overlooks the West River and the quiet village of South Londonderry in the Green Mountains of southern Vermont. Special family accommo-

dations. Living room with huge fireplace, billiards, and Ping-Pong rooms. Dinner available on weekends and holidays.

Hosts: Jean and Jim Cavanagh
Rooms: 25 (20 PB; 5 SB) $33-87
Full Breakfast
Credit Cards: None
Notes: 2, 5, 8, 9, 10, 11, 12, 13, 14

The Londonderry Inn

SPRINGFIELD

Hartness House Inn

30 Orchard Street, 05156
(802) 885-2115; (800) 732-4789

This beautiful 1903 inn is listed on the National Register of Historic Places. Once the home of Gov. James Hartness, this inn invites guests to step back in time to a setting of gracious living, with carved beams, majestic fireplaces, and a grand staircase leading up to 11 beautifully decorated rooms. Guests may also choose from 29 modern rooms in the annex. Enjoy swimming, tennis, gracious dining, and a unique feature: a 1910 tracking telescope and a small underground museum reached via a 240-foot tunnel. Smoking restricted.

Host: Eileen Gennette-Coughlin
Rooms: 40 (PB) $80-130
Full Breakfast
Credit Cards: A, B, C
Notes: 2, 3, 4, 5, 8, 9, 10, 11, 12, 13

NOTES: Credit cards accepted: A MasterCard; B Visa; C American Express; D Discover; E Diners Club;
F Other; 2 Personal checks accepted; 3 Lunch available; 4 Dinner available; 5 Open all year; 6 Pets welcome;

STOWE

American Country Collection

1353 Union Street, Schenectady, NY 12054
(518) 439-7001; FAX (518) 439-4301

074. Drive over the wooden bridge that crosses the brook and up the long drive to the white Colonial set amid tall pine trees. The inn operates as a bed and breakfast from spring until the end of autumn. For the remainder of the year, the Modified American Plan is honored. The five guest rooms are large and sleep three or four people. Four rooms have private baths. Guests may use the living room/lounge with stone fireplace, game room, and workshop, where guests repair and sharpen skis. Easy access to antiquing, biking, hiking, canoeing, and leaf peeking. Smoking permitted. Full breakfast is offered. $63-113.

091. Contemporary alpine-style private home on the side of the Worcester Mountain Range, just six miles from Stowe. The second floor is entirely for guests' use. The one guest room has a private bath. There is an additional room with a private half-bath for use by larger groups. Breakfast is served in the elegant country kitchen in front of the wood-burning stove. No smoking. Couples only. Two-night minimum stay in foliage season. $65-95.

190. Set on a knoll above a two-acre pond stocked with trout and on 21 acres of rolling meadows and forest is this cozy eight-year-old Colonial-style farmhouse. Upstairs are two guest rooms, each with private bath and sitting area. One room with double bed and one room with queen-size bed and up to two additional single beds. First-floor bath has full Jacuzzi. Breakfast served at guest's request. Children and pets welcome. Outside smoking only. $60-80.

Andersen Lodge
An Austrian Inn

3430 Mountain Road, 05672
(802) 253-7336; (800) 336-7336

A small, friendly Tyrolean inn in a quiet setting. Heated swimming pool, tennis court, living rooms with fireplaces, TV, and air conditioning. Near a major ski area, 18-hole golf course, riding, hiking, and fishing. Recreational path close by. Sauna and Jacuzzi. Closed April 10 to June 1 and October 25 to December 10. Smoking allowed in certain areas.

Hosts: Dietmar and Trude Heiss
Rooms: 78 (PB) $78-98
Full Breakfast
Credit Cards: A, B, C, D
Notes: 2, 4, 6, 8, 9, 10, 11, 12, 13, 14

Bed and Breakfast
Inns of New England

128 S. Hoop Pole Road, Guilford, CT 06437
(203) 457-0042; (800) 582-0853

720. An old-fashioned inn on 28 acres, with a big fieldstone fireplace, knotty pine walls, and a Ping-Pong table. In 1991, this inn celebrated its 50th anniversary as Stowe's very first ski lodge. A Continental breakfast is served each morning in summer months. Ten large rooms on two floors, each with a double and a single bed. Some rooms have private full baths. Children over five are welcome. Guest pets are sometimes allowed. Smoking allowed. Fifteen dollars per additional adult. $50-85.

Brass Lantern Inn

717 Maple Street, 05672
(802) 253-2229; (800) 729-2980

A traditional Vermont bed and breakfast inn in the heart of Stowe. Award-winning restoration of an 1810 farmhouse and carriage barn overlooking Mount Mansfield, Vermont's most prominent mountain. The

7 No smoking; 8 Children welcome; 9 Social drinking allowed; 10 Tennis nearby; 11 Swimming nearby;
12 Golf nearby; 13 Skiing nearby; 14 May be booked through a travel agent.

inn features period antiques, air conditioning, handmade quilts, and planked floors.
Some rooms have whirlpools or fireplaces
and most have views. Award-winning
breakfast. An intimate spot for house
guests only. AAA three-diamond inn.
Special packages include honeymoon,
adventure, skiing, golf, air travel, sleigh
and surrey rides, and more.

Host: Andy Aldrich
Rooms: 9 (PB) $70-150
Full Breakfast
Credit Cards: A, B, C
Notes: 2, 5, 7, 9, 10, 11, 12, 13, 14

Butternut Inn at Stowe

2309 Mountain Road, 05672
(800) 3 BUTTER

Award-winning inn on eight acres of beautifully landscaped grounds alongside a
mountain stream. Cottage gardens, pool,
antiques, afternoon tea, and collectibles.
All rooms have private baths. Close to
sleigh rides, downhill and cross-country
skiing, summer hiking, golf, tennis, horseback riding. Highlighted as one of the "best
bed and breakfasts in the northeast" by
Skiing magazine. Honeymoon and anniversary packages available. Enjoy real
"Texas" hospitality in Vermont.

Hosts: Jim and Deborah Wimberly
Rooms: 18 (PB) $90-140
Full Breakfast
Credit Cards: A, B, D
Notes: 2, 7, 9, 10, 11, 12, 13, 14

Fitch Hill Inn

Rural Free Delivery 1, Box 1879
Fitch Hill Road, Hyde Park, 05655
(802) 888-3834; (800) 639-2903

Friendly affordable elegance on a hilltop
overlooking Vermont's highest mountains
in the beautiful Lamoille River Valley. Ten
miles north of Stowe, the historic Fitch Hill
Inn, circa 1794, offers four tastefully
antique-decorated rooms, all of which have
views, and a two-bedroom suite. There are
three common living room areas and more

than 300 video movies for guests to enjoy.
Three porches offer spectacular views; rest
and relax in our beautiful gardens. A full
gourmet breakfast is served, and candlelight four-course dinners are available by
reservation. Bedrooms include double and
twin beds. Packages available.

Host: Richard A. Pugliese
Rooms: 4 (SB) $69-125
Full Breakfast
Credit Cards: A, B, C
Notes: 2, 3, 4, 5, 7, 8, 9, 10, 11, 12, 13, 14

The Gables Inn

1457 Mountain Road, 05672
(802) 253-7730; (800) GABLES-1

A classic Vermont country inn with 19
beautifully appointed rooms in an 1860s
inn. Romantic carriage house and riverview
suites have queen- or king-size beds, fireplaces, Jacuzzis, and TVs. Outdoor hot tub
and pool, sitting room, and den. Hearty
country breakfasts, summer garden lunch,
and candlelight dinners during the winter.
Minutes from seasonal attractions and
Stowe Village. No smoking.

Hosts: Sol and Lynn Baumrind
Rooms: 19 (PB) $60-200
Full Breakfast
Credit Cards: A, B, C, D
Notes: 2, 3, 4, 5, 7, 8, 9, 10, 11, 12, 13, 14

Guest House Christel Horman

4583 Mountain Road, 05672
(802) 253-4846; (800) 821-7891

Small, cozy bed and breakfast offers eight
large double rooms with full private baths.
Guest living room with color TV, VCR,
hearthstone fireplace, and many books and
magazines. Rates include choice menu
breakfast. One and one-half miles to downhill and cross-country skiing. Ski week rate
available. Children over ten welcome.

Hosts: Christel and Jim Horman
Rooms: 8 (PB) $60-80
Full Breakfast
Credit Cards: A, B
Notes: 2, 5, 7, 9, 10, 11, 12, 13, 14

NOTES: Credit cards accepted: A MasterCard; B Visa; C American Express; D Discover; E Diners Club;
F Other; 2 Personal checks accepted; 3 Lunch available; 4 Dinner available; 5 Open all year; 6 Pets welcome;

The Siebeness

The Siebeness

3681 Mountain Road, 05672
(802) 253-8942; (800) 426-9001

A warm welcome awaits guests at this charming country inn. Antiques, private baths, homemade quilts, and air conditioning. Fireplace lounge, BYOB bar, hot tub, pool with beautiful mountain views. Famous for outstanding food. Dinner available in fall and winter. Adjacent to Stowe's famous recreation path. Honeymoon, golf, and ski packages available.

Hosts: Nils and Sue Andersen
Rooms: 10 (PB) $60-95
Full Breakfast
Credit Cards: A, B, C, D
Notes: 2, 4, 5, 7, 8, 9, 10, 11, 12, 13, 14

Ski Inn

Route 108, 05672-4822
(802) 253-4050

This comfortable inn, noted for good food and good conversation, is a great gathering place for interesting people. Guests enjoy themselves and others. Nearest lodge to all Stowe ski lifts, with miles of cross-country trails at the door. Cool and quiet in the summer. Rooms are large and colorful, each with a double and single bed. Evening meal available during ski season. A minimum two-day, three-night stay is required over holidays.

Host: Harriet Heyer
Rooms: 10 (5 PB; 5 SB) $40-60
Full and Continental Breakfast
Credit Cards: C
Notes: 2, 4, 5, 7, 8, 9, 10, 11, 12, 13, 14

Stowe-Bound Lodge

673 South Main Street, 05672
(802) 253-4515

A small guest house on a sheep farm in the beautiful Green Mountains. Downhill and cross-country skiing in the winter. Hiking and biking in summer. Meals are plentiful. Anyone desiring to exchange the fast pace of city life for some relaxation and slower pace of country life will find Stowe, sometimes called the Ski Capital of the East, a refreshing change. Why not be Stowe-Bound?

Hosts: Dick and Erika Brackenbury
Rooms: 12 (4 PB; 8 SB) $40-80
Full Breakfast
Credit Cards: None
Notes: 2, 4, 5, 6, 8, 10, 11, 12, 13

Timberholm Inn

452 Cottage Club Road, 05672
(802) 253-7603; (800) 753-7603
FAX (802) 253-8559

7 No smoking; 8 Children welcome; 9 Social drinking allowed; 10 Tennis nearby; 11 Swimming nearby; 12 Golf nearby; 13 Skiing nearby; 14 May be booked through a travel agent.

Timberholm Inn

Nestled in the woods, this ten-room bed and breakfast is friendly, romantic, and comfortable. The large, airy common room has a striking fieldstone fireplace. Enjoy beautiful mountain views from the deck. Guests are also invited to relax and enjoy the outdoor hot tub. The two-bedroom suites are ideal for families. Near skiing, golf, hiking, tennis, and bike trails. Feast on a Vermont country buffet breakfast. Game room.

Hosts: Louise and Pete Hunter
Rooms: 10 (PB) $70-130
Full Breakfast
Credit Cards: A, B
Notes: 2, 5, 7, 8, 9, 10, 11, 12, 13, 14

WalkAbout Creek Lodge

199 Edson Hill Road, 05672
(802) 253-7354; (800) 426-6697

Rustic mountain lodge offers 20 guest rooms and one fully equipped chalet. Spacious living room with a massive fieldstone fireplace, TV room, Billabong Pub and game room, outdoor swimming pool, and tennis. Set on five wooded acres beside a flowing creek. Australian hospitality at its truly best.

Hosts: Joni and Hutch
Rooms: 20 (14 PB; 6 SB) $70-150
Full Breakfast
Credit Cards: A, B
Notes: 2, 4, 5, 6, 7, 8, 9, 10, 11, 12, 13, 14

TOWNSHEND

Boardman House Bed and Breakfast

Box 112, 05353
(802) 365-4086

A 19th-century farmhouse set on the village green next to the most photographed church in Vermont. This is a prime foliage and antiquing area. Direct access to state routes 30 and 35 allows guests to pursue other interests from cross-country and downhill skiing to canoeing on the West River. Guests may choose between five rooms and one suite. Gourmet breakfasts feature pear pancakes, individual soufflés, hot fruit compotes, homemade muffins, and more. Inquire about restrictions concerning pets and smoking.

Hosts: Sarah Mesenger and Paul Weber
Rooms: 6 (5 PB; 1 SB) $65-85
Full Breakfast
Credit Cards: None
Notes: 2, 5, 8, 11, 12, 13

UNDERHILL

Sinclair Inn Bed and Breakfast

Rural Route 2, Box 35, 05489
(802) 899-2234; (800) 433-4658

A showcase of builder Edward Sinclair's craftsmanship and fully restored in 1989, this 1890 Queen Anne Victorian has been

Sinclair Inn

described as "a study in architectural styles, incorporating features such as towers, gables, turrets, colored glass, and an intricately carved fretwork valance across the living room and stairway." Halfway between Burlington and Smuggler's Notch. Enjoy the nearby hiking, boating, sailing, biking, festivals, and shows. Discount ski lift tickets available. One room with fireplace. Handicapped accessible bathroom. Children over 12 welcome.

Hosts: Jeanne and Andy Buchanan
Rooms: 6 (PB) $65-95
Full Breakfast
Credit Cards: A, B
Notes: 2, 5, 7, 10, 11, 12, 13

VERGENNES

Emerson's Bed and Breakfast

82 Main Street, 05491
(802) 877-3293

Experience fine Vermont hospitality in this 1850 Victorian home surrounded by spacious lawns and flowers. Relax in the gracious living quarters or on the porch. Enjoy a full breakfast, which includes homemade breads and muffins. Visit nearby Shelburne Museum, Morgan Horse Farm, and Kennedy Brothers Marketplace. Area recreation includes fishing, boating, canoeing, hiking, and bicycling. Walk to fine nearby restaurants.

Hosts: Jeannette and Donald Michalets
Rooms: 6 (2 PB; 4 SB) $50-80
Full Breakfast
Credit Cards: A, B
Notes: 2, 5, 7, 9, 10, 12, 13

WAITSFIELD

Bed and Breakfast Inns of New England

128 South Hoop Pole Road, Guilford, CT 06437
(203) 457-0042; (800) 582-0853

716. This inn, tucked alongside picturesque Route 100, is remarkable for not just one,

but three, reasons. The first is the wonderful full gourmet breakfast. The second is the inn itself, which is a piece of Vermont history. The third is the variety of attractions and activities its convenient location affords. All six bedrooms have private baths. Two-night minimum stay required during the fall and on weekends. Children over six are welcome. No smoking, please. Resident dog and horses. $75-115. Twenty dollars for third person.

1824 House Inn

Route 100, Box 159, 05673
(802) 496-7555

Enjoy relaxed elegance in a perfect country setting. Seven beautiful guest rooms, all with their own private baths. Enjoy classical music, Oriental rugs, fireplaces, and a sun porch. The gourmet breakfast includes breakfast soufflés and freshly squeezed orange juice. Stroll on 52 acres on the Mad River. Even a private swimming hole! Featured in the *Los Angeles Times, Glamour* magazine, and *Travel & Leisure.* Rated three diamonds by AAA and two stars by Mobil. Seasonal rates. Children over six are welcome.

Hosts: Lawrence and Susan McKay
Rooms: 7 (PB) $85-130
Full Breakfast
Credit Cards: A, B, C, D
Notes: 2, 3, 4, 5, 7, 9, 10, 11, 12, 13, 14

Hyde Away Inn

Route 17, Rural Route 1, Box 65, 05673
(802) 496-2322; (800) 777-HYDE

A comfortable and casual, circa 1820 inn, less than five minutes from Sugarbush and Mad River Glen Ski areas, hiking and biking trails, and historic Waitsfield Village. Fourteen rooms (private and semiprivate baths), common area with TV, and children's toy area. Public restaurant with delicious and affordable American cuisine: steaks, fresh seafood, and pastas. Rustic tavern with tavern menu. Package and

7 No smoking; 8 Children welcome; 9 Social drinking allowed; 10 Tennis nearby; 11 Swimming nearby; 12 Golf nearby; 13 Skiing nearby; 14 May be booked through a travel agent.

group rates available. Ideal for groups and family gatherings. Please call ahead before bringing pets.

Hosts: Bruce and Margaret
Rooms: 14 (4 PB; 10 SB) $49-80
Continental Breakfast
Credit Cards: A, B, C
Notes: 4, 5, 8, 9, 10, 11, 12, 13, 14

The Inn at Round Barn Farm

East Warren Road, Rural Route 1, Box 247, 05673
(802) 496-2276; FAX (802) 496-8832

This is the inn that lives on in everyone's imagination. A place that is rich in history, elegant, luxurious, and charming, without the least bit of pretension. Enjoy dreamlike guest rooms with roaring fireplaces, relaxing steam showers, Jacuzzi tubs, and canopied beds. A scrumptious breakfast of blueberry Belgium waffles and cinnamon coffee. In winter, ski the 30K of groomed trails. Rosignol equipment rentals, snowshoes, and instruction available. In summer, stroll the 85 acres of lush gardens, meadows, ponds, and woodlands. AAA rated three diamonds, Mobil three stars, featured in the *New York Times, Snow Country* magazine, and *Country Living* magazine.

Hosts: Jack, Doreen, and AnneMarie Simko
Rooms: 11 (PB) $100-185
Full Breakfast
Credit Cards: A, B, C
Notes: 2, 4, 7, 9, 10, 11, 12, 13, 14

Knoll Farm Guest House

Bragg Hill Road, 05673
(802) 496-3527; (802) 496-3939

This unique combination of inn and farm sits beautifully high in Green Mountains with spectacular views, rural setting, Scotch Highland cattle, and horses. Organic gardens and abundant farm-fresh meals. Comfortable 1800s farmhouse with sunny bedrooms and family heirloom furniture. Expansive lawn, hammocks, swings, and nature paths. A special place since 1950s for rest, peaceful atmosphere,

simple country living, beauty, and spiritual renewal. Guests have returned for more than 35 years.

Host: Ann Day
Rooms: 4 (SB) $70-90
Full Breakfast
Credit Cards: None
Notes: 2, 4, 7, 9, 10, 11, 12

Lareau Farm Country Inn

Box 563, Route 100, 05673
(802) 496-4949

In an open meadow near the Mad River, this 1832 Greek Revival farmhouse is only minutes from skiing, shopping, dining, soaring, and golf. Sleigh rides, cross-country skiing, and swimming on the premises. When guests come, they feel at home and relaxed. Hospitality is the inn's specialty. "One of the top 50 inns in America"—*Inn Times*.

Hosts: Dan and Susan Easley
Rooms: 13 (11 PB; 2 SB) $60-125
Full Breakfast
Credit Cards: A, B
Notes: 2, 5, 8, 10, 11, 12, 13, 14

The Mad River Inn Bed and Breakfast

Tremblay Road, P.O. Box 75, 05673
(802) 496-7900; (800) TEA-TART

A romantic 1860s country Victorian inn nestled alongside the Mad River with picturesque mountain views. Nine unique guest rooms with feather beds and private baths. Gourmet breakfast and afternoon tea included daily. Porches, gardens, gazebo, Jacuzzi, and swimming hole. Fireplace, library, BYOB lounge. Catered weddings. Midweek specials. Families and groups welcome.

Host: Luc Maranda
Rooms: 9 (PB) $59-125
Full Breakfast
Credit Cards: A, B, C
Notes: 2, 5, 8, 9, 10, 11, 12, 13, 14

NOTES: Credit cards accepted: A MasterCard; B Visa; C American Express; D Discover; E Diners Club; F Other; 2 Personal checks accepted; 3 Lunch available; 4 Dinner available; 5 Open all year; 6 Pets welcome;

Millbrook Inn

Route 17, Rural Free Delivery, Box 62, 05673
(802) 496-2405; (800) 477-2809 (reservations)

Relax in the friendly, unhurried atmosphere
of this cozy 1850s inn. Seven guest rooms
are decorated with hand stenciling, antique
bedsteads, and handmade quilts. Breakfast
and dinner included in the daily rate. Dine
in the romantic, small restaurant that features hand-rolled pasta, fresh fish, veal,
shrimp, and homemade desserts from a varied menu. Full breakfast is available during
the summer only; Modified American Plan
during winter and fall. Two-day minimum
stay required for weekends, three-nights for
holidays. Closed from April 5 to June 10
and October 25 to Thanksgiving. Call
before taking pets. Children over six are
welcome.

Hosts: Joan and Thom Gorman
Rooms: 7 (4 PB; 3 SB) $50-140
Credit Cards: A, B, C
Notes: 2, 4, 7, 9, 10, 11, 12, 13

Mountain View Inn

Rural Free Delivery, Box 69, Route 17, 05673
(802) 496-2426

This small country inn (circa 1826) has
seven guest rooms, each with private bath,
accommodating two people. The rooms are
decorated with stenciling, quilts, braided
rugs, and antique furniture. Meals are
served family style around an antique har-

Mountain View Inn

vest table. Good fellowship is enjoyed
around the wood-burning fireplace in the
living room. Two-night minimum stay
required on weekends.

Hosts: Fred and Susan Spencer
Rooms: 7 (PB) $37.80-70.20
Full Breakfast
Credit Cards: None
Notes: 2, 4, 5, 7, 8, 9, 10, 11, 12, 13, 14

The Valley Inn

Rural Route 1, Box 8, 05673
(802) 496-3450; (800) 638-8466

An extraordinary country inn set in the historic village of Waitsfield in a quiet corner
of the Mad River Valley. Traditional
accommodations with private baths and
decorated with hand-stenciling and New
England country oak furnishings. Families
and groups welcome year-round. Enjoy the
best of sports, including hiking, biking,
soaring, and skiing. Close to everything,
yet light years from everyday cares.

Hosts: Bill and Millie Stinson
Rooms: 20 (PB) $49-89
Full Breakfast
Credit Cards: A, B, C
Notes: 5, 7, 8, 9, 10, 11, 12, 13, 14

The Waitsfield Inn

Route 100, Box 969, 05673
(802) 496-3979

This gracious 1820s restored Colonial inn
is in the heart of the beautiful Mad River
Valley. The inn, just minutes from
Sugarbush, is convenient to spectacular skiing and wonderful hiking, shopping,
antiquing, and much more. Relax in one of
the 14 rooms, all of which are beautifully
appointed with antiques, quilts, and private
baths. Enjoy a delicious full breakfast and
let the "innspired" hosts make every stay a
memorable one.

Hosts: Steve and Ruth Lacey
Rooms: 14 (PB) $69-119
Full Breakfast
Credit Cards: A, B, C, D
Notes: 2, 5, 7, 8, 9, 10, 11, 12, 13, 14

7 No smoking; 8 Children welcome; 9 Social drinking allowed; 10 Tennis nearby; 11 Swimming nearby;
12 Golf nearby; 13 Skiing nearby; 14 May be booked through a travel agent.

WALLINGFORD

American Country Collection

1353 Union Street, Schenectady, NY 12054
(518) 439-7001; FAX (518) 439-4301

055. This restored 1840 Colonial farmhouse, listed on the National Register of Historic Places, is on 20 acres of pasture and woods. The Gothic-style barn, a Vermont landmark, is often painted by artists. Swimming, fishing, and canoeing on the premises; golf, tennis, and horseback riding nearby. Four guest rooms, all with private baths. No smoking. Children over ten welcome. Pets in residence. Also, one fully equipped cottage with king-size bed and jet tub. Breakfast is $10 extra for cottage guests. Rates slightly higher during foliage season. Two-night minimum stay during foliage season. $70-140.

White Rocks Inn

Rural Route 1, Box 297, 05773
(802) 446-2077

Circa 1840s farmhouse inn, listed on the National Register of Historic Places, beautifully furnished with antiques, Oriental rugs, and canopied beds. All five rooms have private baths. Charming cottage with slate roof and cupola is also available.

White Rocks Inn

Cathedral ceiling in living area, loft bedroom, whirlpool bath, kitchenette, and deck overlooking pastures. Close to four major ski areas, hiking, horseback riding, canoeing, summer theater, and good restaurants. Minimum-stay requirements for weekends and holidays. Closed November. Personal checks accepted for deposit only. Children over ten welcome. European Plan for cottage rental.

Hosts: June and Alfred Matthews
Rooms: 5 (PB) $60-95
Cottage: 1 (PB) $130
Full Breakfast
Credit Cards: A, B, C
Notes: 7, 9, 10, 11, 12, 13

WARREN

Beaver Pond Farm Inn

Rural Delivery Box 306, Golf Course Road, 05674
(802) 583-2861; FAX (802) 583-2860

Beaver Pond Farm is an elegantly restored Vermont farmhouse on a quiet country meadow with spectacular views of the nearby Green Mountains. It is adjacent to the Sugarbush Golf Course and 40K of groomed cross-country ski trails. One mile from downhill trails of Sugarbush. Hearty breakfasts, snacks, hors d'oeuvres, and setups. *Prix fixe* dinners are available Tuesday, Thursday, and Saturday during winter season. Package plans are available, including skiing in winter and golf in summer. Closed April 15 to May 25. Children over seven welcome. Rates are based per person.

Hosts: Bob and Betty Hansen
Rooms: 6 (4 PB; 2 SB) $32-65
Full Breakfast
Credit Cards: A, B
Notes: 2, 7, 9, 10, 11, 12, 13, 14

Bed and Breakfast Inns of New England

128 South Hoop Pole Road, Guilford, CT 06437
(203) 457-0042; (800) 582-0853

VT713. This small, elegant restored Vermont farmhouse sits on a quiet country meadow with spectacular mountain views. The inn is in the midst of cross-country ski trails and is close to Sugarbush Valley's fine alpine runs. Golfers walk next door to a Robert Trent Jones-designed 18-hole course. Six guest rooms are available, most with private baths, and are complemented by a sitting room with TV and VCR and a dining room where a full Vermont breakfast is served. This central location, on one of Vermont's most scenic routes (Route 100), affords the option of traveling north to the exciting Waterbury-Stowe region or south toward Weston-Manchester. Smoking allowed in the guest living room only. One resident cat. No guest pets, please. Children seven and older welcome. $72-96.

Sugartree Inn

Rural Route 1, Box 38
Sugarbush Access Road, 05674
(802) 583-3211; (800) 666-8907
FAX (802) 583-3203; email: sgrtree@aol.com

An intimate mountainside inn at Sugarbush. Nine guest rooms furnished with antiques, brass or canopied beds, and one fireplaced suite. In summer, flowers abound. Relax in the gingerbread gazebo. Golf, tennis, hiking, and swimming holes nearby. Winter brings cross-country and downhill skiing just a quarter-mile away. Warm up with hot cider by the parlor fireplace. Hearty country breakfasts. Picnic lunches available. Dinner is available for groups.

Hosts: Frank and Kathy Partsch
Rooms: 9 (PB) 80-135
Full Breakfast
Credit Cards: A, B, C, D
Notes: 2, 5, 7, 9, 10, 11, 12, 13, 14

West Hill House
Bed and Breakfast

West Hill Road, Rural Route 1, Box 292, 05674
(802) 496-7162 (phone and FAX); (800) 898-1427

West Hill House

Up a quiet country lane on nine acres, this 1860s farmhouse features gardens, pond, apple orchard, and fantastic views. One mile from Sugarbush Ski Resort, adjacent to championship golf course and cross-country ski trails. Extraordinary hiking, cycling, canoeing, and fishing. Near fine restaurants, covered bridges, quaint villages, and shops. Enjoy the comfortable front porch, fireplace, eclectic library, Oriental rugs, original art, and antiques. Bedrooms feature premium linens, down comforters, and good reading lights. Guest pantry with BYOB wet bar. Memorable breakfasts, afternoon and bedtime snacks. Dinner available by reservation with six-guest minimum.

Hosts: Dotty Kyle and Eric Brattstrom
Rooms: 5 (PB) $85-115
Full Breakfast
Credit Cards: A, B, C
Notes: 2, 5, 7, 8, 9, 10, 11, 12, 13, 14

WATERBURY

American Country Collection

1353 Union Street, Schenectady, NY 12054
(518) 439-7001; FAX (518) 439-4301

039. This 1790 Cape Cod was once a stagecoach stop and is now a haven for modern-day travelers seeking country comfort and hospitality. The six guest rooms are filled with country antiques. One room has a working fireplace. Four have private baths. The inn has a library, living room, dining room, large porch, and country kitchen, where a full breakfast is served at the long trestle table next to the brick hearth overlooking the Green Mountains. Smoking in common areas only. Children over six are welcome. Three-night minimum stay over holiday weekends. $65-125.

Bed and Breakfast Inns of New England

128 South Hoop Pole Road, Guilford, CT 06437
(203) 457-0042; (800) 582-0853

VT717. Come enjoy the wonderful comfort of this restored 1832 farmhouse. The front porch, furnished with wicker chairs and flowers, is an inviting spot to relax, watch the sun go down, or enjoy a glass of wine. The sunny common rooms are large but cozy. Each of the six guest rooms has a private bath and individually controlled heat and air conditioning. A full breakfast of homemade sweetbreads, muffins, raspberry and blueberry pancakes, eggs, juices, and coffee is served each morning. The neighborhood offers downhill and cross-country skiing, snowmobile rides, and the inn's big screen TV and VCR. Children over six are welcome. No guest pets, please. No smoking. $65-105.

VT718. This three-story Austrian chalet is a classic example of Tyrolean architecture, complete with intricately carved balconies. The stenciled booths in the BYOB pub are perfect for a game of backgammon or checkers, and the adjacent Austrian dining room is set for memorable musical breakfasts. Ten second-floor guest rooms overflow with antiques, comforters, and quilts. Each room opens to a balcony that surrounds the bed and breakfast and provides relaxing views of the Green Mountains. Private and shared baths. Children of all ages welcome. Two resident cats, but no guest pets, please. No smoking. Seasonal rates available. $55-125.

Grünberg Haus

Grünberg Haus Bed and Breakfast

Rural Route 2, Box 1595 AD, Route 100 S, 05676
(802) 244-7726; (800) 800-7760

Romantic Austrian chalet on a quiet mountainside, hand-built of native timber and fieldstone. Gorgeous guest rooms, secluded cabins, and spectacular carriage house. Warm-weather Jacuzzi, cold-weather sauna, ski center and walking trails, tennis court, year-round fireplace, and BYOB pub. Savor our memorable breakfast feasts. In Ben & Jerry's hometown, between Stowe and Sugarbush ski resorts. "Home of hospitable innkeepers, chickens, and teddy bears." Central to Stowe, Burlington, Montpelier, covered bridges, and waterfalls.

Hosts: Christopher Sellers and Mark Frohman
Rooms: 15 (10 PB; 5 SB) $55-125
Full Breakfast
Credit Cards: A, B, C, D
Notes: 2, 5, 7, 8, 9, 10, 11, 12, 13, 14

Inn at Blush Hill

Blush Hill Road, Box 1266, 05676
(802) 244-7529; (800) 736-7522

Waterbury's oldest inn, a circa 1790 restored Cape on five acres with beautiful mountain views. The inn has four fireplaces, a large sitting room, fireplaced guest room, canopied bed, down comforters, and lots of antiques. Across from a golf course, and all summer sports are nearby. Enjoy skiing at Stowe, Sugarbush, and Bolton Valley. Back to back to Ben and Jerry's factory. Packages available. AAA and Mobil rated. Children over six welcome.

Hosts: Gary and Pam Gosselin
Rooms: 5 (PB) $75-125
Full Breakfast
Credit Cards: A, B, C, D
Notes: 2, 5, 7, 9, 10, 11, 12, 13, 14

WATERBURY CENTER

The Black Locust Inn

Rural Route 1, Box 715, 05677
(800) 366-5592; FAX (802) 244-7490

Circa 1832 farmhouse set on a hill graced with black locust trees and looking to the Green Mountains and Camel's Hump. Antiques, old beds, lace curtains, Laura Ashley wallpapers, and Oriental rugs on polished hardwood floors. In the large living room there are movies, books, music, games, and magazines. Wine and cheese served in the afternoon. Comfort, wonderful breakfasts, and a relaxed atmosphere are the inn's number one amenities. AAA three-diamond award and three-crown rating by ABBA.

Hosts: Anita and George Gajdos
Rooms: 6 (PB) $65-110
Full Breakfast
Credit Cards: A, B, C, D
Notes: 2, 5, 7, 9, 10, 11, 12, 13, 14

WEATHERSFIELD

American Country Collection

1353 Union Street, Schenectady, NY 12054
(518) 439-7001; FAX (518) 439-4301

076. This gracious inn was once a farmhouse that served as a stagecoach stop, part of the Underground Railroad, and a summer estate. Ten guest rooms and two suites, all with private baths. Most rooms have working fireplaces. Handicapped accessible. Guests can relax in the conservatory or

work out in the exercise room complete with Finnish sauna and pool table. A four-course breakfast begins the day. English high tea is served each afternoon, and a gourmet dinner is prepared each evening. Smoking in designated areas. Well-behaved children over eight welcome. Rates include breakfast, tea, and dinner. Two-night minimum stay on weekends; three nights on holidays. $201.25-235.75.

WEST DOVER

Deerhill Inn and Restaurant

P.O. Box 136, Valleyview Road, 05356-0136
(802) 464-3100; (800) 99-DEER-9

A friendly English-style country house with mountain views, candlelight dining, superb cuisine, spacious sitting rooms, fine antiques, art gallery, a licensed lounge, private baths, some rooms with fireplaces, lovely grounds, swimming pool, and tennis court. In Mount Snow area. Alpine and Nordic skiing, mountain biking, two championship golf courses, golf school, walking, fishing, boating, antiquing, shopping, craft fairs, Marlboro Music Festival, and just plain relaxing. Weddings a specialty. Children over eight welcome.

Hosts: Michael and Linda Anelli
Rooms: 17 (PB) $99-130
Full Breakfast
Credit Cards: A, B, C
Notes: 2, 4, 5, 10, 11, 12, 13

Deerhill Inn

Shield Inn

Route 100, P.O. Box 366, 05356
(802) 464-3984; FAX (802) 464-5322
e-mail: shieldinn@aol.com

Romantic, quiet, trilevel, nonsmoking country inn set back from Route 100 on a three-acre wooded lot. Relax in one of 12 beautifully decorated rooms, each with private bath and TV. Half have Jacuzzis and wood-burning fireplaces. Full breakfast served each morning and dinner during ski season. A Steinway grand piano enhances the living room. Chamber music and jazz series, planned and impromptu. Near Mount Snow Haystack and Marlboro Music Festival. Children ten and older welcome. Bed and breakfast and MAP rates available.

Hosts: Phyllis and Lou Isaacson
Rooms: 12 (PB) $90-239
Full Breakfast
Credit Cards: A, B
Notes: 2, 5, 7, 9, 10, 11, 12, 13, 14

West Dover Inn

Route 100, P.O. Box 506, 05356
(802) 464-5207

This historic old inn, circa 1846, in the foothills of the Green Mountains features elegant rooms, all with private baths, and luxurious fireplace suites with whirlpool tubs. Elegant dining in the Capstone Restaurant, featuring tableside cooking and an extensive wine list. Full bar and lounge. Minutes to golf, skiing, tennis, and swimming. AAA three-diamond rated. Children over eight welcome.

Hosts: Don and Madeline Mitchell
Rooms: 12 (PB) $80-195
Full Breakfast
Credit Cards: A, B, C
Notes: 2, 4, 9, 10, 11, 12, 13, 14

WESTON

Bed and Breakfast Inns of New England

128 South Hoop Pole Road, Guilford, CT 06437
(203) 457-0042; (800) 582-0853

700. "Vermont's favorite breakfast," said the *Yankee Travel Guide* about this Early American, circa 1790, Colonial-style bed and breakfast. The hosts hope that beginning the day with a hearty old-fashioned breakfast will set the proper tone for a very enjoyable day in Vermont. Guests can enjoy the large common room with woodstove, books, board games, TV, and large solar sunroom area. Each room is decorated with antique furnishings and heavy quilts and comforters. There are eight guest rooms available with double or twin beds and shared baths. Six larger rooms have private baths and TV. Children are welcome. No smoking, please. No guest pets. $55-85.

Inn at Weston

P.O. Box 56, 05161
(802) 824-6789; (800) 754-5804

Enjoy beautifully appointed guest rooms and Continental cuisine served in gracious style in this historic country inn. Set on the Green Mountains in the heart of the picture-book village of Weston, the inn was recently featured in *Gourmet* magazine. A pleasant walk to the Weston Playhouse, shops, and galleries. Dining rooms open to the public for dinner. Golf, tennis, downhill and cross-country skiing, and other activities close by.

Hosts: Bob and Jeanne Wilder
Rooms: 19 (12 PB; 7 SB) $66-111
Full Breakfast
Credit Cards: A, B, C, D
Notes: 2, 4, 5, 9, 10, 11, 12, 13

The Wilder Homestead Inn and 1827 Craft Shoppe

25 Lawrence Hill Road, 05161
(802) 824-8172

An 1827 brick home listed on the National Register of Historic Places. Walk to shops, museums, and summer theater. Crackling fires in common rooms, canopied beds, and down comforters. Rooms have original

The Wilder Homestead Inn

Moses Eaton stenciling and are furnished with antiques and reproductions. Weston Priory nearby. Minimum-stay requirements August through October, during winter, and for holidays. Children over six welcome.

Hosts: Peggy and Roy Varner
Rooms: 7 (5 PB; 2 SB) $65-100
Full Breakfast
Credit Cards: A, B
Notes: 2, 5, 9, 10, 11, 12, 13

WILMINGTON

Misty Mountain Lodge

326 Stowe Hill Road, Box 114, 05363
(802) 464-3961

A circa 1803 farmhouse inn on 150 acres. All rooms have a beautiful view of the Green Mountains. Two guest rooms with private bath and TV, two deluxe rooms with private bath and TV (one with whirlpool tub), and four rooms with shared baths. Home-cooked meals (dinner by reservation) are prepared by owners. Cozy living room with fireplace for reading, visiting, or joining in a sing-along with hosts. Close to skiing, hiking, boating, golf, and Marlboro Music Festival.

Hosts: Buzz and Elizabeth Cole
Rooms: 8 (4 PB; 4 SB) $45-105
Full Breakfast
Credit Cards: A, B, D
Notes: 2, 5, 7, 8, 9, 10, 11, 12, 13, 14

Nordic Hills Lodge

179 Coldbrook Road, 05363
(800) 326-5130

Become spoiled at Nordic Hills, where one of the family members will serve a choice-of-menu breakfast to start the day. This lodge offers the nostalgia of a country inn, with the relaxing qualities of modern amenities including a Jacuzzi, sauna, outdoor pool, game room, and in-room TV. For the more active, skiing, championship golf, tennis, and horseback riding are within minutes. Dinner available December 26 through March 16. Three-diamond AAA rating.

Hosts: George and Sandy Molner and
    Marianne Coppola
Rooms: 27 (PB) $70-130
Full Breakfast
Credit Cards: A, B, C, D, E
Notes: 2, 4, 7, 8, 9, 10, 11, 12, 13, 14

Nutmeg Inn

Route 9 West, Molly Stark Trail, 05363
(802) 464-3351

Beautifully restored 1770s farmhouse. Just as guests have always imagined a New England country inn to be. Beautifully appointed bedrooms with private baths, all king- or queen-size beds (four-posters, brass, and wrought iron). Most rooms are complete with fireplace and TV. Also, luxurious suites with living rooms, fireplaces, TVs, and VCRs. Menu country breakfast served daily. All guest rooms have air conditioning and in-room telephones. Living

Nutmeg Inn

7 No smoking; 8 Children welcome; 9 Social drinking allowed; 10 Tennis nearby; 11 Swimming nearby; 12 Golf nearby; 13 Skiing nearby; 14 May be booked through a travel agent.

room with fireplaces and BYOB. Complimentary hot chocolate, tea, coffee, and lemonade.

Hosts: Del and Charlotte Lawrence
Rooms: 13 (PB) $78-210
Full Breakfast
Credit Cards: A, B, C, D
Notes: 2, 5, 7, 8, 9, 10, 11, 12, 13

The Red Shutter Inn

Route 9 West, Box 636, 05363
(802) 464-3768; (800) 845-7548

This 1894 nine-room Colonial inn with fireplace suites sits on a hillside within walking distance of the town of Wilmington. Tucked behind the inn is the renovated carriage house with four rooms, one a two-room fireplace suite with a two-person whirlpool bath. A renowned restaurant with candlelight dining (alfresco dining on an awning-covered porch in the summertime). Championship golf (golf packages), skiing at Mount Snow and Haystack, cross-country skiing, hiking, boating, and antiquing are minutes away. Experience the congenial atmosphere of country inn life. Closed April. Inquire about availability of dinner. No smoking in dining room.

Hosts: Max and Carolyn Hopkins
Rooms: 9 (PB) $90-165
Full Breakfast
Credit Cards: A, B, C, D
Notes: 2, 9, 10, 11, 12, 13

Shearer Mill Farm Bed and Breakfast

P.O. Box 1453, 05301
(802) 464-3253; (800) 437-3104

Pristine farm setting on country road, five miles from center of Wilmington. Large rooms with private baths. Delicious Vermont breakfast. Near downhill skiing, groomed cross-country skiing trails on property, swimming, hiking, boating, shop-

ping, Marlboro Music Festival, horseback riding, and many fine restaurants.

Hosts: Bill and Patti Pusey
Rooms: 6 (PB) $80
Full Breakfast
Credit Cards: A, B, C, D
Notes: 2, 5, 7, 9, 10, 11, 12, 13, 14

Trail's End—A Country Inn

Smith Road, 05363
(802) 464-2727; (800) 859-2585

A unique country inn tucked away on ten acres with flower gardens, a clay tennis court, heated outdoor pool, and a stocked pond. Described as "irresistibly romantic" by the author of *Best Place to Kiss in New England.* Picture-perfect rooms, including fireplace rooms and fireplace suites with canopy beds and whirlpool tubs. Full breakfast menu and afternoon tea. Warm hospitality and attention to detail are the hosts' specialties. Inspected and approved by ABBA three-crown, A-plus Excellent. Ski and golf packages available as well as dining discounts. Closed mid-April through mid-May.

Hosts: Bill and Mary Kilburn
Rooms: 15 (PB) $90-150
Suites: $140-180
Full Breakfast
Credit Cards: A, B, C
Notes: 2, 8, 9, 10, 11, 12, 13

The White House of Wilmington

Route 9, P.O. Box 757, 05363
(802) 464-2135; (800) 541-2135
FAX (802) 464-5222

Set on the crest of a high, rolling hill overlooking the Deerfield Valley, the White House of Wilmington is southern Vermont's premier landmark. Built in 1915 as a private summer home, the Victorian mansion now offers romantic accommodations amidst casual surroundings. It's easy to see why the inn was voted "one of the ten most romantic inns" by both the *New*

York Times and *Boston Herald*. Sixteen guest rooms, 13 fireplaces, indoor and outdoor pools, whirlpool and sauna. Ski Touring Center.

Host: Robert Grinold
Rooms: 16 (PB) $128-195
Full Breakfast
Credit Cards: A, B, C, E
Notes: 2, 4, 5, 10, 11, 12, 13, 14

WINDSOR

Juniper Hill Inn

Rural Route 1, Box 79, 05089
(802) 674-5273; (800) 359-2541

This elegant but informal inn allows guests to pamper themselves. Antique-furnished guest rooms, many with working fireplaces. Marvelous views. Sumptuous candlelight dinners and hearty breakfasts. Cool off in the pool, canoe, bike, hike, or visit antique and craft shops, covered bridges, and museums. Twenty minutes from Woodstock and Quechee, and Hanover, New Hampshire. A perfectly romantic inn. Mobil and AAA rated. Closed April.

Hosts: Rob and Susanne Pearl
Rooms: 16 (PB) $85-140
Full Breakfast
Credit Cards: A, B
Notes: 2, 4, 7, 9, 10, 11, 12, 13, 14

WOLCOTT

American Country Collection

1353 Union Street, Schenectady, NY 12054
(518) 439-7001; FAX (518) 439-4301

130. Twelve miles north of Stowe, this Greek Revival-style three-bedroom inn is bordered by the LaMoille River and has authentically appointed rooms and spacious bedchambers. The three guest rooms are decorated according to themes. Full breakfast. Smoking outdoors only. Children 12 and older welcome. $59-74.

WOODSTOCK

Bed and Breakfast Inns of New England

128 South Hoop Pole Road, Guilford, CT 06437
(203) 457-0042; (800) 582-0853

VT710. This 1810 Greek Revival mansion is registered with the National Register of Historic Places. In Vermont's premier village it's okay to park the car and walk to all local attractions. Trendy restaurants, exciting shops and boutiques, galleries, golf, tennis, skiing, museums, and a lovely covered bridge are all a short stroll away. Seven guest rooms, all with private baths, are decorated with period antiques and Oriental rugs. A fireplace warms the guest living room. Enjoy a full Vermont country breakfast and an evening snack. No smoking. No guest pets, please. Children over nine welcome. $110-135.

Canterbury House

43 Pleasant Street, 05091
(802) 457-3077

A 115-year-old village townhome just east of the village green. This bed and breakfast, furnished with authentic Victorian antiques, has eight rooms with private baths. Living room with TV and stereo. Within walking distance of shops, the historic district, and restaurants. A full gourmet breakfast is served in the dining room. Guest rooms have air conditioning and fresh flowers. Bicycles provided summer and fall. Described as elegant but comfortable. Lunch and dinner available with prior reservations. Children over eight welcome.

Hosts: The Holdens
Rooms: 7 (PB) $85-140
Full Breakfast
Credit Cards: A, B, C
Notes: 2, 3, 4, 5, 7, 9, 10, 11, 12, 13, 14

The Charleston House

21 Pleasant Street, 05091
(802) 457-3843

This circa 1835 Greek Revival home has been authentically restored. Listed on the National Register of Historic Places, it is furnished with antiques, combined with a hospitality reminiscent of a family home-coming. In the picturesque village of Woodstock, "one of the most beautiful villages in America."

Hosts: Barb and Bill Hough
Rooms: 7 (PB) $90-150
Full Breakfast
Credit Cards: A, B, C
Notes: 2, 5, 7, 9, 10, 11, 12, 13, 14

The Woodstocker
Bed and Breakfast

Route 4, 61 River Street, 05091
(802) 457-3896

At the foot of Mount Tom in the picturesque village of Woodstock, this romantic 1830s inn offers nine large, elegantly decorated, air-conditioned rooms with private baths. Bed chambers are appointed with queen-size or full beds as well as FM/cassette/CD stereos. A sumptuous gourmet breakfast begins every day. Afternoon refreshments are served. A short stroll over a covered bridge brings you to fine dining and shopping.

Hosts: Jerry and JaNoel Lowe
Rooms: 9 (PB) $95-125
Full Breakfast
Credit Cards: A, B
Notes: 2, 5, 7, 9, 10, 11, 12, 13, 14

Woodstock House
Bed and Breakfast

Route 106, P.O. Box 361, 05091
(802) 457-1758

Renovated old farmhouse with exposed hand-hewn beams and lovely mellow old floors. Three miles south of Woodstock on Route 106. Open May through December.

Host: Mary Fraser
Rooms: 5 (3 PB; 2 SB) $60-75
Full Breakfast
Credit Cards: None
Notes: 2, 7, 9, 10, 11, 12, 13

Woodstock House

Virginia

Inn on Town Creek

P.O. Box 1745, 445 East Valley Street, 24212-1745
(703) 628-4560; FAX (703) 628-9611

A historic creek is the theme of this bed and breakfast on four acres of beautifully landscaped property. Multilevel brick patios and rock gardens provide tranquil privacy; air-conditioned, antique-filled rooms, and the cordiality of the innkeepers offer a peaceful getaway to the discerning guest. Near fine dining, entertainment. Ample parking. Smoking restricted.

Hosts: Dr. and Mrs. Roger D. Neal
Rooms: 6 (5 PB; 1 SB) $85-165
Full Breakfast
Credit Cards: A, B
Notes: 2, 4, 5, 9, 10, 11, 12, 14

Litchfield Hall

247 East Valley Street, 24210
(703) 676-2971

The character of Litchfield Hall has been preserved and a relaxing atmosphere created with antiques, collectibles, and mementos from the host's family's extended living and traveling throughout the world. Recently renovated. Living room, dining room, porch, patio, and garden room available for guests. Gas fireplaces in living and dining rooms. Spanish spoken. Off-street parking. Catered dinners with prior notice. Children over 12 welcome.

Host: Lena C. McNicholas
Rooms: 3 (PB) $65-80
Full Breakfast
Credit Cards: None
Notes: 2, 5, 7, 9, 10, 11

River Garden Bed and Breakfast

19080 North Fork River Road, 24210-4560
(703) 676-0335; (800) 952-4296

River Garden is nestled in the foothills of the Clinch Mountains, on the bank of the north fork of the Holston River outside historic Abingdon. Furnished with traditional, antique, and period furniture, each room has its own riverside deck overlooking the gentle rapids. Private exterior entrance, full, queen-, or king-size bed, full bath, and central heat and air. Guests are also granted kitchen privileges. Common areas include living room, den, dining room, and recreation room.

Hosts: Carol and Bill Crump
Rooms: 4 (PB) $60-65
Full Breakfast
Credit Cards: None
Notes: 2, 5, 7, 9, 11, 12, 13, 14

Summerfield Inn

101 West Valley Street, 24210
(703) 628-5905

Summerfield Inn is in the Abingdon historic district, just two blocks from the

Summerfield Inn

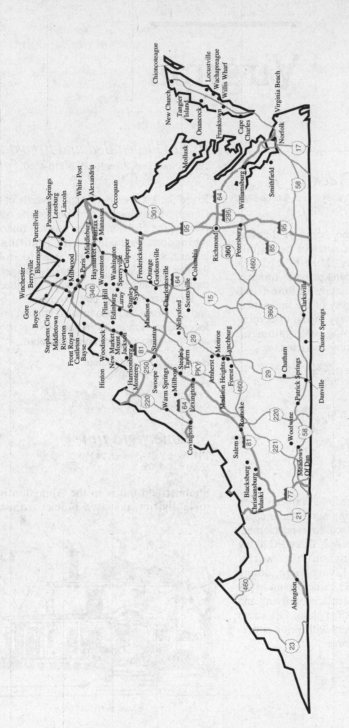

Virginia

world-famous Barter Theatre. Near the Appalachian Trail, Mount Rogers National Recreation Area, South Holston Lake, the Blue Ridge Parkway, Virginia Creeper Trail, excellent restaurants, and marvelous shops. Just off I-81 at exit 17. New cottage addition with Jacuzzi and in-room TV and telephone. Bikes available. Smoking restricted. Children over six welcome.

Hosts: Champe and Don Hyatt
Rooms: $70-125
Full Breakfast
Credit Cards: A, B, C, D
Notes: 2, 9, 10, 12, 14

ALEXANDRIA

Morrison House

116 South Alfred Street, 22314
(703) 838-8000

Centrally in Old Town Alexandria, Morrison House is a stroll from historic landmarks, quaint boutiques, and international dining. Downtown Washington, D.C., is less than ten minutes away, Washington National Airport is only three miles. Built in the style of an 18th-century manor house, Morrison House offers 45 elegantly appointed guest rooms, including three suites. All guest rooms are enhanced by fine Federal-period reproductions including mahogany four-poster beds, brass chandeliers, decorative fireplaces, and Italian marble baths. Services offered include 24-hour butler, concierge and room service, indoor valet parking, specialized laundry and valet services, shoe shine and newspaper available each morning, nightly turndown service with chocolates, and health club privileges. Complementary morning coffee in the parlor; afternoon tea is served daily from 3:00-5:00 P.M. in the parlor.

Hosts: Mr. and Mrs. Robert E. Morrison
Rooms: 45 (PB) $165-295
Credit Cards: A, B, C, E
Notes: 2, 3, 4, 5, 7, 8, 9, 10, 11, 12, 13, 14

Princely Bed and Breakfast, Ltd.

819 Prince Street, 22314
(703) 683-2159

Thirty historic (1770-1875) homes in Old Town Alexandria. Most are furnished with antiques, many of which are museum quality. Breakfasts are Continental plus. Walk to all restaurants, shops, and monuments. Metro subway is a fast 15 minutes to the White House. Ten major universities within ten miles. Mount Vernon is seven miles away. Continental plus breakfast. Call 10:00 A.M. to 6:00 P.M., Monday through Friday. $75-100.

Host: E. T. Mansmann
Homes: 30 (PB) From $75
Continental Breakfast
Credit Cards: None
Notes: 2, 5, 7, 8, 9, 10, 12

AMHERST

Dulwich Manor Bed and Breakfast

Route 5, Box 173 A, 24521
(804) 946-7207

Gracious country lodging in an elegant English-style manor house with views of the Blue Ridge Mountains. Six beautifully appointed bed chambers with fireplaces; window seats or whirlpool tub; canopied, brass, and antique beds. Enjoy the hot tub in the Victorian gazebo. Surrounded by 85 acres of natural beauty at the end of a country lane. This perfect romantic getaway is convenient to Richmond, Charlottesville, Lynchburg, and Washington, D.C. A sumptuous country breakfast is served. Mobil three-star rating. Smoking restricted. Swimming 40 minutes away. Skiing 30 minutes away.

Hosts: Bob and Judy Reilly
Rooms: 6 (4 PB; 2 SB) $69-89
Full Breakfast
Credit Cards: None
Notes: 2, 5, 8, 9, 10, 12, 14

NOTES: Credit cards: A MasterCard; B Visa; C American Express; D Discover; E Diners Club; F Other; 2 Personal checks accepted; 3 Lunch available; 4 Dinner available; 5 Open all year; 6 Pets welcome; 7 No smoking; 8 Children welcome; 9 Social drinking allowed; 10 Tennis nearby; 11 Swimming nearby; 12 Golf nearby; 13 Skiing nearby; 14 May be booked through a travel agent.

Sky Chalet Country Inn

BASYE

Sky Chalet Country Inn and Alpine View Restaurant

P.O. Box 300, 22810
(703) 856-2147

A romantic hideaway with spectacular, breathtaking, panoramic mountain and valley views. Accommodations are simple but comfortable. Individual rooms with private baths. Also the Treetop Cabin with private baths and living rooms with fireplaces. "The mountain lovers' paradise." Mountaintop dining near the open stone fireplace, specializing in northern European cuisine, homemade breads, pastries, and desserts. Old English-style pub with largest selection of draught beers in the area, serving wine and spirits also. For restaurant reservations, call (703) 856-2555.

Hosts: Ken and Mona Seay
Rooms: 10 (PB) $49-79
Continental Breakfast
Credit Cards: A, B, D, E
Notes: 2, 3, 4, 5, 6, 8, 9, 10,11, 12, 13, 14

BERRYVILLE

Blue Ridge Bed and Breakfast

Route 2, Box 3895, 22611
(703) 955-1246; (800) 296-1246

A. Colonial Williamsburg reproduction furnished with lovely antiques; near the Shenandoah River on 11 acres complete with Christmas trees. Perfect getaway; ideal for weekend bikers and hikers. Only 90 minutes from Washington, D.C. $55-95.

BLACKSBURG

L'Arche Bed and Breakfast

301 Wall Street, 24060
(703) 951-1808

An oasis of tranquility just one block from the Virginia Tech campus, L'Arche Bed and Breakfast is an elegant turn-of-the-century Federal Revival home situated among terraced gardens in downtown Blacksburg. Spacious rooms have traditional antiques, family heirlooms, handmade quilts, and private baths. Delicious full breakfasts feature homemade breads, cakes, jams, and jellies.

Host: Vera G. Good
Rooms: 5 (PB) $80
Full Breakfast
Credit Cards: A, B
Notes: 2, 5, 10, 12, 13

L'Arche

Per Diem

Per Diem Bed and Breakfast

401 Clay Street SW, 24060
(703) 953-2604

A unique cluster of three houses in downtown Blacksburg, Per Diem is one block from Virginia Tech and the Huckleberry Trail. The main house, built in 1929, reflects traditional and Southwestern styles. The guest houses have complete kitchens and living areas and are connected by wooden decks to the main house; covered patio and heated swimming pool. All houses have cable TV and telephones.

Host: Joanne Anderson
Rooms: 3 (PB); Suites: 4 (PB) $75-85
Full Breakfast
Credit Cards: A, B, C
Notes: 2, 5, 7, 9, 10, 11, 12

Sycamore Tree Bed and Breakfast Inn

P.O. Box 10937, 24062-0937
(703) 381-1597

A romantic, luxurious vacation on a picturesque mountain meadow, in a custom-built bed and breakfast where guests are pampered, enjoy wildlife from the porches, sip tea by the fire, or hike over 126 acres. The six guest rooms have private baths and central heat and air. Nearby are excellent restaurants, antique shops, golf courses, swimming, and university activities. Come be a part of the magic of the mountains.

Buffet breakfast is served. Children over 12 welcome.

Hosts: Charles and Gilda Caines
Rooms: 6 (PB) $85-110
Continental Breakfast
Credit Cards: A, B
Notes: 2, 5, 7, 10, 11, 12

BLUEMONT

Blue Ridge Bed and Breakfast

Route 2, Box 3895, Berryville, 22611
(703) 955-1246; (800) 296-1246

A. Perfect for hiking the Appalachian Trail or biking. This retreat on the Shenandoah River 50 miles west of Washington, D.C., is a restful stopover for a bed and meals. From $30.

BOYCE

Blue Ridge Bed and Breakfast

Route 2, Box 3895, Berryville, 22611
(703) 955-1246; (800) 296-1246

A. In the heart of fox hunt country. Lovely modern stone and clapboard house has a true Western ranch house feel. Complete fox hunting arrangements available seven days a week for experienced riders, including complete care for horse and tack. Groom quarters available. Indoor ring. In the middle of 60 acres with beautiful views of mountains, a swimming pool, stable house, and kennel. $75-100.

B. Historic estate built in 1748 is graced by a lovely English hostess. On the National Register of Historic Places and featured in major books and the *Washington Post*. Over 1,000 spring bulbs, wicker-filled porch, acreage to hike, in-ground pool, and two lakes on property. George Washington really did sleep here, as well as Col. John S. Mosby. $90.

7 No smoking; 8 Children welcome; 9 Social drinking allowed; 10 Tennis nearby; 11 Swimming nearby; 12 Golf nearby; 13 Skiing nearby; 14 May be booked through a travel agent.

C. Beautiful view of the Blue Ridge to enjoy. Guests might even get a ride in a horse and buggy in this farm country. Less than two hours from the nation's capital. $55.

CAPE CHARLES

Amanda's Bed and Breakfast

1428 Park Avenue, Baltimore, MD 21217-4230
(410) 225-0001; (800) 899-7533
FAX (410) 728-8957

122. Lovely, quiet, rural setting along the Chesapeake Bay featuring unspoiled land, abundant wildlife, game birds, miles of private beach, and nature's most fabulous sunsets. This two-story brick home has a great view of the bay and is decorated with antiques, reproductions, and collectibles. Three rooms with private baths. Full breakfast. $85.

138. Restored 1910 Colonial Revival. Just steps from a public beach on the bay. Relax on one of the porches, sample the cool breezes off the bay, or bike through the historic town. Guests set their own pace and explore. Four guest rooms and one cottage. Full breakfast. $89-129.

Nottingham Ridge Bed and Breakfast

28184 Nottingham Ridge Lane, 23310
(804) 331-1010

This lovely home reflects the beauty and charm of Virginia's historical Eastern Shore. Private secluded beach on the Chesapeake Bay bordered by tall trees and sandy dunes. Abundant wildlife. Breakfast on the porch while watching boats and birds play along the bay. Cooler times are spent in the den by a crackling fire. Biking, fishing, tennis, golfing, running, bird watching, crabbing, swimming, and sightseeing are among guests' favorite pastimes. Visitors to Nottingham Ridge can look forward to an informed and relaxed atmosphere with emphasis on the small details that create a memorable stay. Spectacular sunsets! Children over seven welcome.

Hosts: Bonnie Nottingham and Scotty Scott
Rooms: 4 (PB) $80-100
Full Breakfast
Credit Cards: None
Notes: 2, 5, 7, 9, 10, 12, 14

Pickett's Harbor

Pickett's Harbor

P.O. Box 97AA, 23310
(804) 331-2212

Guests, seagulls, pelicans, and herons all love this secluded, marvelous, and wide beach nestled in pines and dogwoods on 27 acres. A Colonial home (big house, little house, and kitchen) with cupboards, doors, and floors made from old barn rafters. Fireplaces, antiques, and reproductions. All rooms and the porch face the Chesapeake Bay. Country breakfast served overlooking the bay. Complimentary late afternoon beverage. Central air.

Hosts: Sara and Cooke Goffigon
Rooms: 6 (2 PB; 4 SB) $65-125
Full Breakfast
Credit Cards: None
Notes: 2, 5, 7, 10, 11, 12

Sea Gate Bed and Breakfast

9 Tazewell Avenue, 23310
(804) 331-2206

In the sleepy town of Cape Charles, just steps from Chesapeake Bay on Virginia's

NOTES: Credit cards accepted: A MasterCard; B Visa; C American Express; D Discover; E Diners Club; F Other; 2 Personal checks accepted; 3 Lunch available; 4 Dinner available; 5 Open all year; 6 Pets welcome;

undiscovered Eastern Shore. The day begins with a country breakfast followed by leisure, hiking, bird watching, bathing, or exploring the historic area. Tea prepares guests for the glorious sunsets over the bay. Sea Gate is the perfect place to rest, relax, and recharge—away from the crush of modern America. Winter special available. Smoking restricted. Children seven and older welcome.

Hosts: Chris Bannon
Rooms: 4 (2 PB; 2 SB) $70-80
Full Breakfast
Credit Cards: None
Notes: 2, 5, 9, 10, 11, 12, 14

CASTLETON

Blue Knoll Farm

110 Gore Road, 22716
(703) 937-5234

This lovingly restored 19th-century farmhouse is in the foothills of the Blue Ridge Mountains. The original house was built before the Civil War. Four guest rooms with private baths are open to guests. Blue Knoll provides a charming, rural retreat minutes from a renowned five-star restaurant, the Inn at Little Washington, and other fine dining. Near Shenandoah National Park and Skyline Drive. Smoking restricted.

Hosts: Gil and Mary Carlson
Rooms: 4 (PB) $95-125
Full Breakfast
Credit Cards: A, B
Notes: 2, 5, 9

Blue Ridge Bed and Breakfast

Route 2, Box 3895, 22611
(703) 955-1246; (800) 296-1246

A. Fabulous pre-Civil War house built in 1850, in a lovely country setting in the middle of five and one-half acres with small pond. Close to Thornton River, Inn at Little Washington, and Skyline Drive. Lovely mountain views. Two bedrooms and a suite with Jacuzzi are available. $95-125.

CHARLOTTESVILLE

Clifton—The Country Inn

Route 13, Box 26, 22901
(804) 971-1800

A Virginia historic landmark, Clifton is among the few remaining large plantation properties in Albemarle County. On 40 secluded acres with walking trails, private lake, spring-fed pool with waterfall, heated spa, tennis courts, and croquet pitch. Guest rooms feature wood-burning fireplaces, private baths, sitting areas, and canopied or four-poster beds. Award-winning wine list and gourmet dining. Only five miles to Charlottesville and Monticello.

Hosts: Craig and Donna Hartman
Rooms: 14 (PB) $165-225
Full Breakfast
Credit Cards: A, B, C, E
Notes: 2, 4, 5, 7, 8, 9, 10, 11, 12, 13, 14

Guesthouses Bed and Breakfast

P.O. Box 5737, 22905
(804) 979-7264; FAX (804) 293-7791

Afton House. A mountain retreat with panoramic views east to valleys and hills, this spacious home is on the old road up the mountain pass. There are four bedrooms, mostly furnished with antiques. One has a private adjoining bath, and three share two hall baths. Full breakfast is served. Antique shop on the premises and others in the village. $75-80.

Alderman House. This large, formal Georgian home is authentic in style and elegant in decor. It was built by the widow of the first president of the University of Virginia in the early 1900s and is about one mile from the university. Breakfast is served with true Southern hospitality. Guests may choose a room with a four-poster bed or one with twin beds, each with adjoining private bath. Air conditioning. No smoking in the house. $80-86.

7 No smoking; 8 Children welcome; 9 Social drinking allowed; 10 Tennis nearby; 11 Swimming nearby; 12 Golf nearby; 13 Skiing nearby; 14 May be booked through a travel agent.

Guesthouses Bed and Breakfast (continued)

Ammonette Farm. This 110-year-old restored farmhouse is on a small farm with a pastoral setting and beautiful views. The guest room has three large windows, bright cheery colors, and private bath. Go hiking, enjoy the scenery, or just sit! Only 20 minutes to Charlottesville; 30 to Wintergreen. This farmhouse is ideal for families, as additional bedrooms are usually available for children. $68-80.

Auburn Hill. An antebellum cottage on a scenic farm that was part of the original Jefferson plantation. The main house was built by Jefferson for one of his overseers. It is convenient to Monticello and Ash Lawn, just six miles east of the city. The cottage has a sitting room with fireplace, bedroom with four-poster queen-size bed, and connecting bath and shower. Guests may use the pool in summer. Scenic trails, walks, and views. Air conditioning. No smoking. Supplies provided for guests to prepare breakfast. Weekly rates available. $100-125.

Balla Machree. A deluxe separate suite in a contemporary home, this superb lakefront location offers complete privacy for guests. The suite is ten miles west of Charlottesville and overlooks a 250-acre lake with excellent fishing. The cozy quarters have a private entrance, large brick fireplace, and comfortable bedroom with iron frame double bed and private adjoining bath. Tennis is available on new courts, but please bring proper shoes. Golf, riding, hiking, fishing, and canoeing are nearby. Continental breakfast supplies left in the suite for guests to prepare. Air conditioning. $100-125.

Belleview. This contemporary frame guest cottage offering complete privacy to guests five miles west of Charlottesville, in the Farmington hunt country. These lovely quarters include living room with fireplace, Pullman kitchen, two bedrooms (one with twin beds, one with double tester bed), and full bath. A flagstone terrace off the living room offers privacy and mountain views. Air conditioning. Supplies provided for guests to prepare breakfast. $125-200.

Bollingwood. A lovely home in a convenient neighborhood with a private "city" garden featured on the spring 1988 Friendly Garden Tour, this guest house is within walking distance of the University of Virginia, restaurants, and shops. One guest room with twin canopied beds has a hall bath. The second room has a double canopied bed, a three-quarter bed, and an adjacent bath. Air conditioning. $68-88.

Boxberry Cottage. In an English country setting just a few miles west of Charlottesville, this cozy one-room cottage has a queen-size bed and full bath. The sitting area with sliding glass doors opens onto a small deck overlooking fields and woods where deer graze. Continental breakfast supplies are left for guests in the refrigerator in the Pullman kitchen. Air-conditioned. No smoking inside. Two-night minimum stay.

Buck's Elbow Mountain Cottage. Mountain top retreat with 360-degree views. Buck's Elbow Mountain is the highest point in Albemarle County and looks down on the Skyline Drive and Appalachian Trail, which runs adjacent to the farm. Wake up in the king-size bed and see the Valley of Virginia without getting out of bed. The cottage is contemporary with lots of glass, a cathedral ceiling in the living room, full kitchen, two bedrooms, and one and one-half baths, one with a Jacuzzi with views. Two-night minimum stay. Air-conditioned. $200.

NOTES: Credit cards accepted: A MasterCard; B Visa; C American Express; D Discover; E Diners Club; F Other; 2 Personal checks accepted; 3 Lunch available; 4 Dinner available; 5 Open all year; 6 Pets welcome;

Carrsbrook. Peter Carr built this estate home in 1798 using many of the architectural innovations of his uncle and guardian, Thomas Jefferson, including 15-foot ceilings and Jefferson's characteristic way of hiding stairways. Private entrance to the suite is from a large patio overlooking a formal boxwood garden with the deepest hand-dug well in Albemarle County. Downstairs is the sitting room with a pull-out sofa, adjacent bath, and small refrigerator. Upstairs is a bedroom with a king-size bed. Listed on the National Register of Historic Places. Air conditioning. No smoking. $100-125.

Christmas Cottage at Harris Mountain Farm. A carefully restored log house, tastefully furnished with country antiques. There is a cozy living room with an old-fashioned porch, bedroom with double bed, and full bath downstairs; two attractive additional bedrooms upstairs with double and single beds. There is a new addition with great room, kitchen, and comfortable sitting area with adjacent deck overlooking a pond. Thirty minutes from Charlottesville. No smoking. Air-conditioned. $150-200.

The Claim House. Built around 1725 and homesteaded on a land grant from the king this log cabin has spectacular views of the Blue Ridge Mountains. The root cellar has been converted into a kitchen-dining area and bath, exposing the original stone foundation. The main floor has a large fireplace in the sitting room; there is a fascinating Dutch coal stove in the adjoining sitting room. Upstairs there are two bedrooms; one room has a fireplace and double bed and the other room has two double beds. Air-conditioned. TV and VCR.

Clover Green Farm. This farm is in beautiful rolling country in the foothills of the Blue Ridge Mountains. Guests are welcome to sit by the fire in the living room or enjoy the spectacular views from the sunroom. The first-floor guest room with double bed is a large, sunny room furnished with Victorian family pieces. It has an adjoining bath with a shower stall. Smokers welcome. $72-80.

Coleman Cottage. A late 19th-century servant's house on Seven Oaks Farm, an antebellum estate 15 miles west of Charlottesville. Sitting below Afton Mountain, it offers guests splendid mountain views and spacious grounds. The cottage has three bedrooms (two with double, one with twin), living and dining rooms, kitchen, bath, and two porches. Convenient to Wintergreen ski resort 20 miles away. Air conditioning. Supplies provided for guests to prepare breakfast. $150-200.

La Colina. In complete harmony with the surrounding hardwoods, this mountaintop guest cottage affords a private retreat just 15 minutes from downtown Charlottesville. A large living room overlooking a wooded natural area is furnished with antiques. Also a queen-size sofa bed and a wood-burning fireplace. The bedroom has a double bed. There is a full bath and a kitchen area where supplies for a full breakfast are left for one to four guests. The busy hosts own one of Charlottesville's most popular restaurants. There are a patio and a pool for warm weather use. Air-conditioned. Smoking outside only.

Copps Hill Farm. This ranch home is set on a small horse farm seven miles northwest of Charlottesville. Guests may enter through private lower-level entrance, where they have the seclusion of their own suite, a family room with TV and sofa bed, and two bedrooms with adjoining bath. A full farm-style breakfast is served in the dining room or on the sun porch overlooking rolling pastures. Air conditioning. $68-80.

7 No smoking; 8 Children welcome; 9 Social drinking allowed; 10 Tennis nearby; 11 Swimming nearby; 12 Golf nearby; 13 Skiing nearby; 14 May be booked through a travel agent.

Guesthouses Bed and Breakfast (continued)

Cross Creek. A spectacular wood, stone, and glass "cottage" on a hilltop nine miles west of Charlottesville, Cross Creek is a perennial favorite. The living room, dining room, half-bath, and kitchen are built around a massive central stone fireplace. A deck provides a wonderful wooded view. Two bedrooms (one double, one king) are on the lower level with a full bath across the hall. Air conditioning. Supplies provided for guests to prepare breakfast. $125-200.

Foxbrook. This lovely home just blocks north of the bypass is convenient to either downtown or the university area. Guest quarters consist of a sitting room overlooking a lovely garden, a bedroom with a queen-size bed, and a large bath with separate shower and sunken tub. Full breakfast. Air-conditioned. No smoking. $80-100.

Fox Lane Farm. Lovely new home in the Victorian style built in beautiful Keswick hunt country. The guest quarters offer complete privacy in a large room with cathedral ceiling and many Victorian pieces. An old quilt hangs behind the brass double bed. There is a private entrance from a lovely deck overlooking the woods and garden. There is an adjoining full bath and a Pullman kitchen where breakfast supplies will be left for guests. No smoking. Air conditioning. $80-100.

Indian Springs. This new cottage with a rustic feel is in a lovely wooded setting on a private lake. The lake is stocked and has a small dock for fishing, basking in the sun, or swimming at guests' own risk. There is a large main room with a king-size bed, a sitting area with a queen-size sofa bed, dining area, kitchen, and bath. This cottage has complete privacy. TV and air conditioning.

Supplies are provided for guests to prepare breakfast. $125-200.

Ingleside. A farm that has been in the same family for several generations, Ingleside lies on 1,250 acres of rolling pasture backed by steep, wooded mountains. The house was built around 1840 of bricks made from the farm's red clay. Accommodations consist of a large antique-furnished room with double bed, fireplace, and adjacent bath. A tennis court is available for guest use. Air conditioning. $72-80.

Ingwood. In a lovely villa on six wooded acres in one of Charlottesville's most prestigious neighborhoods, Ingwood is an elegant, separate-level suite with its own drive and private entrance. The bedroom is appointed with antiques, queen-size bed, and adjoining bath. The sitting room includes a fireplace, Pullman kitchen, and sofa for an extra person. A second bedroom with twin beds and private bath is also available. Sliding glass doors open to a secluded terrace with a view of the woods. Air conditioning. Breakfast supplies are left in the suite for guests to prepare. $80-100.

The Inn at the Crossroads. Built as a tavern in 1820 to serve travelers on the Staunton-James River Turnpike, the inn is a four-story brick structure with timber framing and an English kitchen on the lower level. The house features a long front porch and simple Federal-style details. An easy 15-minute drive from Charlottesville, this country inn is on spacious, pleasant grounds with boxwood, well, and outbuildings. Each of the five newly renovated bedrooms has a different theme carried out by books and decorations. Choose from three rooms with double beds and two with king-size beds. Each room has a ceiling fan and a wooden washstand. The rooms share two baths. Stroll the grounds, relax on the porch

NOTES: Credit cards accepted: A MasterCard; B Visa; C American Express; D Discover; E Diners Club; F Other; 2 Personal checks accepted; 3 Lunch available; 4 Dinner available; 5 Open all year; 6 Pets welcome;

or deck overlooking rolling vistas, or meet other guests in the common room. Listed on the Virginia Landmark. A hearty breakfast is served in the keeping room. No smoking indoors. Children eight and older welcome. Air-conditioned. $75-80.

Ivy Rose Cottage. An original cypress cottage, handmade by the host, is surrounded by gardens and offers mountain views. The ground floor has a double drawing room, separated by a screen, with a sitting area and a hand-wrought-iron queen-size bed. There is a rainforest sunroom with adjoining kitchen and bath with shower. Upstairs is creatively furnished with stained glass and lace curtains. It has heart pine floors, an antique double bed, and a half-bath. The host is a potter and the cottage showcases her work and that of her father, photographer Stan Jorstad. Full breakfast. Gas log stove. Air-conditioned. Smoking outside only. $150-200.

Lenox Farm. In historic Keene, just 20 minutes south of Charlottesville. The earliest part of the house is log and was built in 1795 with interesting additions over the years. The last major renovation was in 1960. The present owners, having had a bed and breakfast in England, welcome guests English-style and include a lovely full breakfast of homemade items. There are two guest rooms, each with a queen-size bed and private adjoining bath. One room is on the ground floor and the other is tucked under the eaves. There is a log slave quarters close by. Air-conditioned. Smoking outside on the lovely terrace. $100.

Log House. A fascinating house made by joining two log cabins, this home is in the woods conveniently one long block off the US 250 bypass with easy access to downtown as well as the university area. Imaginatively furnished with antiques, this house offers a guest suite with a private

entrance, twin bedroom, sitting room, and bath. Air-conditioned. No smoking. $80.

Luke's Cottage. Built in 1930s, one of the first homes in this city neighborhood, this attractive cottage has been the home of several families with University of Virginia connections. The affable hostess offers a first floor single bed with a private adjoining bath. Upstairs is a double bedroom with a shared bath. A full breakfast is served. No air conditioning. Ceiling fans. $60-68.

Maho-Nayama. Attention to detail is evident in the landscaping and furnishings of this beautiful Japanese-style home. The large master bedroom has a king-size bed with custom furnishings. The master bath has a sunken tub. Two rooms with double beds share a connecting bath. A private tennis court is available with advance notice and a service fee. Maho-Nayama is in a rural wooded area six miles northeast of town. Air conditioning. $80-100.

Meadow Run. Enjoy relaxed rural living in this new Contemporary/Classical home six miles west of Charlottesville. Guest rooms have either a double bed or twin beds and share a bath. Guests are welcome to browse in the boat lover's library, play the grand piano, or lounge in the living room. Many windows offer bucolic vistas of the southwest range. Fireplaces in the kitchen and living room add to the homey, friendly feel. Air conditioning. $68-80.

Millington House. Overlooking the winding Moorman's River, this charming early 19th-century cottage was the home of the miller whose business stood nearby. Recently restored and furnished with antiques and appropriate reproductions, the cottage is surrounded by pastureland and gardens. The guest room, with a sitting area, has a double canopied bed and private

Guesthouses Bed and Breakfast (continued)

hall bath. Continental plus breakfast. No smoking. No air conditioning. $80.

Millstream. A lovely, large house about 20 minutes north of Charlottesville up a long driveway lined with old box bushes. The house, with a brick English basement, was built before the Civil War and enlarged in 1866. There are two guest rooms, each with private bath. Guests may enjoy the fireplace in the library or the mountain views from the living room. A full breakfast is served in the kitchen, which has hand-hewn exposed beams. No smoking. Air conditioning. $80-100.

Nicola Log Cabin. This is a romantic, 200-year-old log cabin on a 150-acre farm in historic Ivy eight miles west of Charlottesville, with spectacular views of the Blue Ridge Mountains. The one-room cabin has a double bed, sleeper sofa, a new bath with shower, microwave oven, refrigerator, and wood-burning stove. Children's playset and tennis court available. Supplies provided for guests to prepare breakfast. $100-150.

Northfields. This gracious home is on the northern edge of Charlottesville. The guest room is furnished with twin beds and has a TV, private bath, and air conditioning. There is another bedroom available with a double four-poster bed and private hall bath. A full gourmet breakfast is served. No smoking. $60-68.

Northwood. This 1920s city house is convenient to the historic downtown area of Charlottesville, only a few blocks from Thomas Jefferson's courthouse and the attractive pedestrian mall with many shops and restaurants. The guest quarters have a double bed and private adjoining bath. Many of the furnishings are antique, and next to the bedroom there is a small, comfortable sitting room with TV. Window air conditioning.

Park Street Victorian. This late Victorian mansion is one of the largest homes in the downtown historical district. Surrounded by a large lawn and gardens, this accommodation offers a two-room suite with fireplace. Antique furnishings feature a stately highback double bed. Private bath with shower adjoins the guest room. A Continental breakfast is served in a beautiful formal dining room. Air conditioning. $100-120.

Pocahontas. A large white clapboard house built in the 1920s as a summer retreat in the countryside near Ivy, west of Charlottesville. The large porch and beautiful gardens provide a wonderful place to stop and enjoy life passing by. A large guest room, furnished in Victorian pieces, greets guests with a bright and sunny warmth and offers a queen-size bed and private adjoining bath with shower. Other rooms are available for larger groups or families on special weekends. No air conditioning but the house stays cool through the use of attic fans and large, high-ceilinged rooms. $68-80.

Polaris Farm. In the middle of rolling farm land dotted with horses and cattle, this architect-designed brick home offers guests an atmosphere of casual elegance. The accommodations consist of a ground-floor room with twin beds and adjoining bath, and two upstairs rooms with twin beds and shared bath. There are gardens and terraces where one can view the Blue Ridge Mountains; a spring-fed pond for swimming, boating, and fishing; miles of trails for walking or horseback riding (mounts available at nearby stables). Air conditioning. $68-100.

Recoletta. An older Mediterranean-style house built with flair and imagination. The red tile roof, walled gardens with fountain, and artistic design create the impression of a secluded Italian villa within walking distance of the University of Virginia, shopping, and restaurants. Many of the beautiful antique furnishings are from Central America and Europe. The charming guest room has a beautiful brass double bed and a private hall bath with shower. Air conditioning. $72-80.

The Rectory. This charming home in a small village five miles west of Charlottesville was a church rectory. It is furnished with lovely antiques and has an English garden in the back. The guest room overlooking the formal rose garden has its own entrance, twin beds, and adjoining full bath. Air conditioning. No smoking allowed. $72-80.

Rolling Acres Farm. A lovely brick Colonial home in a wooded setting on a small farm, this guest house has two bedrooms with a hall bath upstairs. One room has a double bed and the other has twin beds. The house is furnished with many Victorian pieces. No smoking. Air conditioning. $68-72.

The Rutledge Place. These hosts are only the third family to own this elegant Virginia farmhouse built around 1840 with magnificent mountain views. The original brick structure has been left intact, adding only a bathroom wing. The guest accommodations are light and airy in the English basement and offer a large twin bedroom, a sitting room, and a full bath. The home is furnished with antiques from the hosts' family homes in the Valley of Virginia. The suite opens to a brick terrace and gardens facing the mountains. Full breakfast is offered. Air-conditioned. No smoking allowed. $100-150.

Shelterwood Farm. This contemporary home with a traditional feel is surrounded by carefully tended gardens. The guest suite, attractively furnished, offers views of the Blue Ridge Mountains, woods, and fields. The hostess raises bees and her guests will be able to enjoy the homegrown honey with the Continental breakfast left in the kitchen area. There is a large sitting room with TV and VCR, comfortable twin beds in the bedroom, and private bath and entrance. Air-conditioned. No smoking. $80.

Upstairs Slave Quarters. A fascinating place to stay if guests want interesting decor with the privacy of their own entrance. There is a harmonious mixture of antiques and art objects. The guest suite consists of a sitting room with a fireplace and two bedrooms (king and single) with bath (tub only). A couch in the sitting room opens to a double bed for extra guests. Adjacent to the University of Virginia and fraternity row, it is especially convenient for university guests. Air conditioning. $80-130.

Valentine House. This house was built in 1911 for the only previous owner. This young doctor and his family have filled the house with Art Deco and Art Nouveau furnishings. In a convenient downtown location, it is withing walking distance of the historic district and restaurants. There is a double bedroom with private entrance and bath with shower. A Continental breakfast is served in the main part of the house. No smoking.

Westbury. Built around 1820, this antebellum plantation home is a beautiful reminder of what country living and Southern hospitality are all about. Once a carriage stop between the James River and the Shenandoah Valley, Westbury now returns to the old tradition of welcoming travelers. In Batesville, a tiny community southwest

7 No smoking; 8 Children welcome; 9 Social drinking allowed; 10 Tennis nearby; 11 Swimming nearby; 12 Golf nearby; 13 Skiing nearby; 14 May be booked through a travel agent.

of Charlottesville with a genuine country store, Westbury is only 20 minutes from Skyline Drive and the Appalachian Trail. A comfortable double four-poster bed awaits in the guest room. Private hall bath. No air conditioning. $68-72.

Windrows Farm. This 200-year-old restored chestnut log cabin surrounded by large oak trees overlooks extensive vegetable and flower gardens, a pond, and lovely fields to stroll through. The cottage consists of one large room with a double bed, a comfortable sitting area in front of the fireplace, a kitchen including a refrigerator, and a four-burner stove with an oven and a broiler, and a bathroom. There is a porch for rocking and picnicking. Breakfast supplies are left for guests. Window air conditioning. No smoking. No pets. $125-150.

Winston. This quaint Cape Cod brick home is on a quiet side street in an academic neighborhood near the University of Virginia. The private upstairs guest room offers twin beds and an adjoining bath. A home-style breakfast is served. Air conditioning. $52-60.

Winton on Pantops. A brick Colonial east of town on Pantops Mountain overlooking the city of Charlottesville. The home offers two double bedrooms. One room also has a single bed, and both rooms share a hall bath. Full breakfast is served. There are resident cats. No air conditioning. $52-60.

High Meadows—Virginia's Vineyard Inn

Highmeadows Lane, Scottsville, 24590
(804) 286-2218; (800) 232-1832

Enchanting 19th-century European-style auberge with tastefully appointed, spacious guest rooms, private baths, and period antiques. Two-room suites available.

Several common rooms, fireplaces, and tranquility. Pastoral setting on 50 acres. Privacy, relaxing walks, and gourmet picnics. Virginia wine tasting and romantic candlelight dining nightly. Virginia Architectural Landmark. National Register of Historic Places. Two-night minimum stay on weekends and holidays. Closed December 24-25.

Hosts: Peter, Sushka, and Mary Jae Abbitt
Rooms: 12 (PB) $90.52-172.42
Full Breakfast
Credit Cards: A, B
Notes: 2, 4, 6, 7, 8, 9, 10, 11, 13, 14

The Inn at the Crossroads

Route 2, Box 6, North Garden, 22959
(804) 979-6452

Built in 1820 as a tavern on the historic James River Turnpike, the inn continues its long tradition, offering a quiet respite for the weary traveler. A four-story brick building with a long front porch. It is on five acres overlooking pastures and the foothills of the Blue Ridge Mountains, and is convenient to Monticello and Charlottesville, as well as the James River and Skyline Drive.

Hosts: John and Maureen Deis
Rooms: 5 (SB) $65-75
Full Breakfast
Credit Cards: A, B
Notes: 2, 5, 9, 10, 11, 12, 13, 14

The Inn at the Crossroads

Mountain Meadows Bed and Breakfast

P.O. Box 4, Ivy, 22945
(804) 977-6855 day; (804) 296-2934 evenings
(800) 395-5074

A charming bedroom suite with a private entrance and bath built in a converted creamery. In a peaceful country setting with spectacular views of the Blue Ridge Mountains. A short drive to Charlottesville, the University of Virginia, Monticello, Ash Lawn, vineyards, and Wintergreen ski resort. Go to sleep to the sound of the soft bleating of the sheep and wake to a breakfast of farm eggs, laid by the happy hens.

Host: Sarah Churchill
Room: 1 (PB) $50-65
Full and Continental Breakfast
Credit Cards: A, B
Notes: 2, 5, 10, 12, 13

Palmer Country Manor

Route 2, Box 1390, 22963
(800) 253-4306; FAX (804) 589-1300

A gracious 1830 estate on 180 secluded acres. Palmer Country Manor is only minutes from historic Charlottesville; Monticello, Thomas Jefferson's beloved home; Ash Llawn, home of James Monroe; Michie Tavern, one of Virginia's oldest homesteads; and some of Virginia's finest wineries. Come and enjoy one of ten private cottages. Each features a living area with fireplace, color TV, private bath, and a deck. On the grounds, enjoy the swimming pool, five miles of trails, and the fishing pond; use one of the bikes; or take a hot air balloon ride. Golf is available nearby.

Hosts: Gregory and Kathleen Palmer
Rooms: 12 (10 PB: 2 SB) $85-140
Full Breakfast
Credit Cards: A, B, C, D, E
Notes: 2, 3, 4, 5, 8, 9, 11, 12, 14

Silver Thatch Inn

3001 Hollymead Drive, 22901
(804) 978-4686

Silver Thatch Inn is a rambling white clapboard home that dates from 1780. With three dining rooms and seven guest rooms, it is a sophisticated retreat on the outskirts of Charlottesville. Silver Thatch's modern American cuisine uses the freshest of ingredients, and all sauces are prepared with fruits and vegetables. The menu features grilled meats, poultry, game in season, and there are always vegetarian selections. The inn provides a wonderful respite for the sophisticated traveler who enjoys fine food and a quiet, caring atmosphere.

Hosts: Vince and Rita Scoffone
Rooms: 7 (PB) $110-150
Continental Breakfast
Credit Cards: A, B, C, E
Notes: 2, 4, 5, 7, 8, 9, 10, 11, 12, 14

Eldon

CHATHAM

Eldon—The Inn at Chatham

Route 1, Box 254B, State Road 685, 24531
(804) 432-0935

Classically restored 1835 historic plantation manor home. One-half mile from Chatham, "Virginia's prettiest town." Five guest rooms, private baths, and full gourmet country breakfast. Formal garden, wooded country setting with original dependencies (smokehouse, ice house, stable, and servants' cottage). Intimate gourmet restaurant with a Culinary Institute of America graduate as chef and CHIC graduate as pastry chef. Former home of Virginia's governor and U. S. secretary of

7 No smoking; 8 Children welcome; 9 Social drinking allowed; 10 Tennis nearby; 11 Swimming nearby; 12 Golf nearby; 13 Skiing nearby; 14 May be booked through a travel agent.

the Navy, Claude A. Swanson. Member BBAV. Smoking restricted.

Hosts: Joy and Bob Lemm
Rooms: 6 (4 PB; 2 SB) $55-120
Full Breakfast
Credit Cards: A, B
Notes: 2, 4, 5, 8, 9, 10, 12

House of Laird
Bed and Breakfast

335 South Main Street, P.O. Box 1131, 24531
(804) 432-2523; (800) 201-7355

Built in 1880, this Greek Revival house has been totally, lovingly restored and professionally decorated. The house sits in a garden surrounded by 200-year-old oaks. Famous for its Library Suite, two working fireplaces, antiques, Oriental rugs, Irish-estate canopied bed, roses, chocolates, bath with heated towels, cable TV, and gourmet breakfast in front of fire. Luxurious and private. This quiet setting is a short distance from historical houses and battlefields, vineyards, seasonal festivals, antique auctions, fine dining, scenic mountain drives, horseback riding, hiking, and boating.

Hosts: Mr. and Mrs. Ed Laird
Rooms: 4 (PB) $75-135
Full Breakfast
Credit Cards: A, B, C
Notes: 2, 7, 9, 12, 14

CHINCOTEAGUE

The Garden and the Sea Inn

Virginia Eastern Shore, Route 710
P. O. Box 275, New Church, 23415
(804) 824-0672

Elegant European-style country inn with French-style gourmet dining. Near beautiful beach and Chincoteague Wildlife Refuge. Large, luxurious rooms, beautifully designed with custom canopied beds, designer fabrics, Victorian detail, stained glass, Oriental rugs, bay windows, and skylights. Spacious private baths with whirlpool tubs. Hearty Continental breakfast. Gourmet dining on premises, candlelight. Romantic escape package available. Beach, wildlife refuge, boating, tennis, and golf are nearby. Mobil three-star and AAA three-diamond ratings. Smoking restricted.

Hosts: Tom and Sara Baker
Rooms: 5 (PB) $85-155
Continental Breakfast
Credit Cards: A, B, C
Notes: 2, 4, 6, 8, 9, 10, 11, 12, 14

Island Manor House

4160 Main Street, 23336
(804) 336-5436; (800) 852-1505 (reservations)

Gracious and romantic, this beautifully furnished antebellum home is filled with Federal-style antiques. A garden sitting room with a fireplace opening onto a private brick courtyard with a fountain and rose garden is inviting to sit in, and all rooms are air-conditioned. Delicious homemade breakfast and afternoon tea specialties. Four minutes from Chincoteague Wildlife Refuge (with over 300 species), and a beautiful ocean beach. Bicycling, hiking, swimming, antiquing, and canoeing nearby. Ideal for small weddings, parties, and meetings. Free bicycles. Smoking restricted. May book through travel agent off season.

Hosts: Charles D. Kalmykow and Carol W. Rogers
Rooms: 8 (6 PB; 2 SB) $65-120
Full Breakfast
Credit Cards: A, B
Notes: 2, 5, 9, 10, 11, 12

Island Manor House

The Watson House

The Watson House

4240 North Main Street, 23336
(804) 336-1564; (800) 336-6787 (reservations)

The Watson House has been tastefully restored with Victorian charm. Nestled in the heart of Chincoteague, the house is within walking distance of shops and restaurants. Each room has been comfortably decorated, including air conditioning, private baths, and antiques. A full, hearty breakfast and afternoon tea are served in the dining room or on the veranda. Enjoy free use of bicycles to tour the island. Chincoteague National Wildlife Refuge and its beach are two minutes away, offering nature trails, surf, and Chincoteague's famous wild ponies. AAA rated three diamonds. Smoking restricted. Inquire about accomodations for children.

Hosts: David and Jo Anne Snead and
 Tom and Jacque Derrickson
Rooms: 6 (PB) $65-105
Full Breakfast
Credit Cards: A, B
Notes: 2, 9, 10, 11, 12, 14

CHRISTIANSBURG

Evergreen: The Bell-Capozzi House

201 East Main Street, 24073
(703) 382-7372

An inn for all seasons in the mountains of southwest Virginia. Fireplaces, central air conditioning, in-ground heated pool, wraparound porch with rockers, arbor with swings, and gazebo on property. Gallery of local artists and library nearby. Within minutes of Randford University, Virginia Tech, Blue Ridge Parkway, New River Bike Trail, Route 76 Bike Trail, Claytor Lake, and Smith Mountain Lake. On I-81, in historic area of 200-year-old county seat for Montgomery County.

Hosts: Rocco and Barbara Bell-Capozzi
Rooms: 5 (PB) $75-105
Full Breakfast
Credit Cards: A, B, C
Notes: 2, 5, 7, 11, 12

CLARKSVILLE

Needmoor Inn

801 Virginia Avenue, P.O. Box 629, 23927
(804) 374-2866

Needmoor Inn, circa 1875, a Victorian bed and breakfast in the heart of beautiful Kerr Lake. The inn stands amid one and one-fourth acres of stately shade and fruit trees and a large herb garden. Enjoy comfortable antiques, private baths, gourmet breakfasts, complimentary bicycles, and a therapeutic massage. Activities in the area include water sports, excellent bass fishing, Occoneechee State Park, and Prestwould Plantation.

Hosts: Lucy and Buddy Hairston
Rooms: 3 (PB) $50-70
Full Breakfast
Credit Cards: None
Notes: 2, 5, 7, 8, 9, 10, 11, 12

CLUSTER SPRINGS

Oak Grove Plantation

1245 Cluster Springs Road, P.O. Box 45, 24535
(804) 575-7137

Operated from May to September, by descendants of the family who built the house in 1820. Full country breakfast in the Victorian dining room. Hiking, biking, bird watching, and wildflower walks on 400 acres of grounds. Near Buggs Island for swimming, boating, and fishing; Danville to tour the last capital of the Confederacy; and Appomattox. One hour north of Raleigh-Durham.

Host: Pickett Craddock
Rooms: 3 (SB) $60
Full Breakfast
Credit Cards: None
Notes: 2, 4, 8, 9, 10, 11, 12, 14

COLUMBIA

Upper Byrd Farm Bed and Breakfast

6452 River Road West, 23038
(804) 842-2240

A turn-of-the-century farmhouse nestled in the Virginia countryside on 26 acres overlooking the James River. Enjoy fishing or tubing. Canoe rentals available. Visit Ash Lawn and Monticello plantations. See the state's capitol, or simply relax by the fire surrounded by antiques and original art from around the world. Breakfast is special. Children 12 and older welcome. Open on weekends only in winter. Winter Green skiing area is one hour away.

Hosts: Ivona Kaz-Jespen and Maya Laurinaitis
Rooms: 4 (SB) $70
Full Breakfast
Credit Cards: None
Notes: 2, 11, 14

COVINGTON

Milton Hall Bed and Breakfast Inn

207 Thorny Lane, 24426
(703) 965-0196

Milton Hall Bed and Breakfast Inn is a Virginia Historic Landmark, listed on the National Register of Historic Places. This country manor house, built by English nobility in 1874, is on 44 acres adjoining the

George Washington National Forest and one mile from I-64, exit 10. The spacious rooms are decorated in the style of the period and furnished with a combination of antiques, period reproductions, and unique pieces collected from various locations across the United States and overseas. Guest rooms feature queen-size beds, private baths, and sitting areas. All guest rooms, as well as common rooms, have fireplaces for guests' enjoyment.

Hosts: John and Vera Eckert
Rooms: 6 (PB) $75-140
Full Breakfast
Credit Cards: A, B
Notes: 2, 3, 5, 6, 7, 8, 9, 10, 11, 12, 13, 14

Fountain Hall

CULPEPER

Fountain Hall Bed and Breakfast

609 South East Street, 22701-3222
(703) 825-8200; (800) 29-VISIT

Built in 1859, this grand bed and breakfast is within walking distance of historic downtown Culpeper. The inn is highlighted with beautiful antiques and extends a warm welcome to both business and leisure travelers. Five guest rooms are offered, each with private bath. Breakfast is Continental plus. Area activities and attractions include wineries, historic battlefields, antique shops, Skyline Drive, Montpelier, and restaurants. Convenient to major airports. Golf packages offered. No smoking. AAA, Mobil, and BBAV inspections.

Hosts: Steve, Kathi, and Leah-Marie Walker
Rooms: 5 (PB) $75-150
Continental Breakfast
Credit Cards: A, B, C, D, E, F
Notes: 2, 5, 7, 8, 9, 10, 11, 12, 13, 14

DANVILLE

Broad Street Manor Bed and Breakfast and Executive Rental

124 Broad Street, 24541
(804) 792-0324

Gracious hospitality in a stately Victorian home. Gourmet breakfast. Single room or full suites. Available daily or on a special rate weekly basis.

Rooms: 3 (PB) $50-75
Full Breakfast
Credit Cards: B
Notes: 9, 10, 11, 12

EDINBURG

Edinburg Inn Bed and Breakfast, Ltd.

218 South Main Street, 22824
(540) 984-8286

This Victorian inn is in the heart of the Shenandoah Valley on the edge of town

Edinburg Inn Bed and Breakfast, Ltd.

next to Stoney Creek and the Edinburg Mill Restaurant. The inn is reminiscent of Grandma's country home, with a full breakfast. Walk to nearby restaurant and antique and craft shops.

Hosts: Judy and Clyde Beachy
Rooms: 3 (PB) $75
Full Breakfast
Credit Cards: None
Notes: 2, 5, 7, 8, 9, 10, 11, 12, 13

FAIRFAX

The Bailiwick Inn

4023 Chain Bridge Road, 22030
(703) 691-2266; (800) 366-7666

In the heart of the historic city of Fairfax, 15 miles west of the nation's capital. George Mason University is just down the street, and Mount Vernon and Civil War battlefields are nearby. On the National Register of Historic Places. Fourteen rooms with queen-size feather beds and private baths, fireplaces, Jacuzzis, and bridal suite. Afternoon tea. Candlelight dinner served by reservation. Small meetings and weddings. Social drinking allowed in rooms.

Hosts: Annette and Bob Bradley
Rooms: 14 (PB) $130-275
Full Breakfast
Credit Cards: A, B, C
Notes: 2, 4, 5, 7, 8, 10, 11, 12, 14

FLINT HILL

Blue Ridge Bed and Breakfast

Route 2, Box 3895, Berryville, 22611
(703) 955-1246; (800) 296-1246

A. Lovely stone home built in 1812 with working fireplaces in bedrooms; a working cattle farm adjacent to Shenandoah National Park. With Virginia's Blue Ridge Mountains in the background, this inn offers guests a beautiful setting. Scenic pasture lands are surrounded by stone fences. Close to Inn at Little Washington

7 No smoking; 8 Children welcome; 9 Social drinking allowed; 10 Tennis nearby; 11 Swimming nearby; 12 Golf nearby; 13 Skiing nearby; 14 May be booked through a travel agent.

and Old Rag Mountain. Private dining by appointment. $70-100.

B. Charming old schoolhouse completely renovated into a lovely restaurant and inn. Bedrooms are very spacious with queen-size beds and private baths. Lovely area with great hiking. Close to northern entrance to Skyline Drive. $125.

FOREST

The Summer Kitchen at West Manor

Route 4, Box 538, 24551
(804) 525-0923

Come enjoy a romantic English country cottage on a beautiful working dairy farm. This private, restored summer kitchen, circa 1840, sleeps four with fireplace, loft, sunroom, and Jacuzzi. Enjoy a full country breakfast while overlooking 600 acres of rolling cropland, pastures, cattle, and mountains. Afternoon tea and strolls through the gardens complete each day. Come escape to this country haven. Area interests include Thomas Jefferson's Poplar Forest, antique shops, and Blue Ridge Mountains.

Hosts: Sharon and Greg Lester
Cottage: 1 (PB) $115
Full Breakfast
Credit Cards: None
Notes: 2, 5, 7, 8, 12

FRANKTOWN

Amanda's Bed and Breakfast

1428 Park Avenue, Baltimore, MD 21217-4230
(410) 225-0001; (800) 899-7533
FAX (410) 728-8957

150. This charming 1895 Victorian home is in a setting of old maples, loblolly, white pines, dogwood, magnolia, and azaleas. The library is filled with volumes of books, many of them historical. Guests may also use the

piano. Afternoon tea is served. Two rooms with private baths. Full breakfast. $75-85.

FREDERICKSBURG

Fredericksburg Colonial Inn

1707 Princess Anne Street, 22401
(703) 371-5666

A restored country inn in the historic district, 32 antique-appointed lodging rooms with private baths, telephones, TV, refrigerators, and Civil War motif. Over 200 antique dealers, 20 major tourist attractions, and battlefields. Continental breakfast. Less than one hour from Washington, D.C., and Richmond. A great getaway. Suites and family rooms available. Wonderful restaurants within walking distance. AARP welcomed. Group rates upon request.

Host: Mr. Jim Crisp
Rooms: 32 (PB) $45-65
Continental Breakfast
Credit Cards: A, B, C
Notes: 2, 5, 8, 12

Kenmore Inn

1200 Princess Anne Street, 22401
(540) 371-7622

Elegant inn built in the late 1700s. On the historical walking tour, near shops and the river. Grand dining and a relaxing pub for enjoyment. Serving lunch and dinner six days.

Host: Alice Rawlings
Rooms: 13 (PB) $85-150
Continental Breakfast
Credit Cards: A, B, C, E
Notes: 2, 3, 4, 5, 7, 8, 9, 12, 14

The Spooner House Bed and Breakfast

1300 Caroline Street, 22401-3704
(540) 371-1267

A lovely two-room suite with private bath and private entrance in a 1794 Federal-style

The Spooner House

home in the town's national historic district. Full breakfast brought with a morning newspaper at the guests' convenience to their private quarters. Complimentary tour of the Rising Sun Tavern next door to the Spooner House. Within walking distance of attractions, museums, restaurants, Amtrak, and shopping.

Hosts: Peggy and John Roethel
Room: 1 suite (PB) $95
Full Breakfast
Credit Cards: None
Notes: 2, 5, 7, 8, 9

La Vista Plantation

4420 Guinea Station Road, 22408
(540) 898-8444; (800) 529-2823

This lovely 1838 Classical Revival home is just outside historic Fredericksburg. On ten quiet acres, the grounds present a fine balance of mature trees, flowers, shrubs, and farm fields. The pond is stocked with bass. Choose from a spacious apartment that sleeps six with a kitchen and a fireplace, or a formal room with a king-size mahogany rice-carved four-poster bed, fireplace, and Empire furniture. Homemade jams and farm-fresh eggs for breakfast.

Hosts: Michele and Edward Schiesser
Rooms: 1 (PB) $95
Apartment: 1
Full Breakfast
Credit Cards: A, B
Notes: 2, 5, 7, 8, 9, 10, 12, 14

Blue Ridge Bed and Breakfast

Route 2, Box 3895, Berryville, 22611
(703) 955-1246; (800) 296-1246

A. Gorgeous Georgian mansion in the heart of scenic Front Royal. Furnished with fabulous antiques. Close to Skyline Caverns and Skyline Drive. Many antique shops nearby. $70-95.

Chester House

43 Chester Street, 22630
(540) 635-3937; (800) 621-0441

A stately Georgian mansion with extensive formal gardens on two acres in Front Royal's historic district. Quiet, relaxed atmosphere in elegant surroundings, often described as an oasis in the heart of town. Easy walking distance to antique and gift shops and historic attractions; a short drive to Skyline Caverns, Skyline Drive, Shenandoah River, golf, tennis, hiking, skiing, horseback riding, fine wineries, and excellent restaurants.

Hosts: Bill and Ann Wilson
Rooms: 6 (4 PB; 2 SB) $65-110
Continental Breakfast
Credit Cards: A, B, C
Notes: 2, 5, 9, 10, 11, 12, 13, 14

Killahevlin

1401 North Royal Avenue, 22630
(703) 636-7335; (800) 847-6132
FAX (703) 636-8694

Historic Edwardian mansion with spectacular views. Spacious bedrooms, professionally designed and restored with working fireplaces, private baths, and whirlpool tubs. Private Irish pub for guests. Complimentary beer and wine. Close to Skyline Drive, Shenandoah National Park, hiking, golf, tennis, canoeing, horseback riding, antiquing, fine dining, wineries, and live theater. Property was built in 1905 for William E. Carson, father of Skyline Drive.

7 No smoking; 8 Children welcome; 9 Social drinking allowed; 10 Tennis nearby; 11 Swimming nearby; 12 Golf nearby; 13 Skiing nearby; 14 May be booked through a travel agent.

Killahevlin

National Register of Historic Places and Virginia Landmarks Register.

Hosts: Susan and John Lang
Rooms: 6 (PB) $95-160
Full Breakfast
Credit Cards: A, B, C, D
Notes: 2, 5, 7, 9, 10, 11, 12, 13, 14

GORDONSVILLE

Sleepy Hollow Farm Bed and Breakfast

16280 Blue Ridge Turnpike, 22942
(800) 215-4804; FAX (703) 832-2515

Sleepy Hollow Farm lies on historic Route 231 in the heartland of American history, where evidence of Indians and the Revolutionary and Civil War periods still exists. An 18th-century farmhouse and restored slave cottage offer six bedrooms, all with private baths, some with fireplaces and whirlpool tubs. Established since 1984. Near Montpelier, Monticello, Skyline Drive, wineries, battlefields, museums, art galleries, and fine dining. Ninety minutes from Washington, D.C., and 60 minutes from Richmond.

Hosts: Beverley Allison and Dorsey Allison Comer
Rooms: 6 (PB) $65-95
Full Breakfast
Credit Cards: A, B
Notes: 2, 4, 5, 6, 8, 9, 11, 12, 13, 14

GORE

Blue Ridge Bed and Breakfast

Route 2, box 3895, Berryville, 22611
(703) 955-1246; (800) 296-1246

A. Breathtaking view of Blue Ridge Mountains on top of Timber Ridge. Great North Mountain. Twenty acres for cross-country skiing; close to Skyline Drive and Capon Bridge. Stocked trout fishing. $50.

HARRISONBURG

Kingsway Bed and Breakfast

3581 Singers Glen Road, 22801
(540) 867-9696

Enjoy the warm hospitality, carpentry, and home-making skills of your hosts who make guests' comfort their priority. This scrupulously clean ranch-style home is in a rural area of the beautiful Shenandoah Valley, just four and one-half miles from downtown. On the mountains to the east drive the beautiful Skyline Drive, visit caverns, historic Monticello, New Market battlefield, Natural Bridge, antique shops, flea markets and Valley Mall. Continental plus breakfast is served. Pets welcome outdoors only.

Hosts: Chester and Verna Leaman
Rooms: 2 (PB) $50-55
Continental Breakfast
Credit Cards: None
Notes: 2, 5, 7, 8, 11, 12, 13, 14

HAYMARKET

Blue Ridge Bed and Breakfast

Route 2, Box 3895, Berryville, 22611
(703) 955-1246; (800) 296-1246

A. Lovely home in middle of one and one-fourth acres. Fabulous views of Bull Run Mountain. Ten minutes from Manassas battleground. In-ground pool, handmade quilts. The hostess has worked for U.S. presidents. $55-65.

HINTON

Boxwood

Route 1, Box 130, 22831
(703) 867-5772; FAX (703) 867-5701

Shenandoah Valley bed and breakfast is beside a trout stream in a spacious private home of river rock and wood and is wonderfully integrated with its setting. Swimming and fishing are available in the nearby river.

Rooms: 3 (1 PB; 2 SB) $60
Full Breakfast
Credit Cards: None
Notes: 2, 5, 7, 8, 9, 11

LEESBURG

Fleetwood Farm Bed and Breakfast

Route 1, Box 306-A, 22075
(800) 808-5988; FAX (703) 327-4325

Beautiful 1745 plantation manor house in the hunt country, a Virginia Historic Landmark. On the National Register of Historic Places. Fireplaces, air conditioning, private baths (one with large Jacuzzi), full country breakfast, cookout facilities, horseshoes, croquet, canoe, and fishing equipment. Riding stables nearby. Lovely gardens. Working sheep farm with sheep and herb products. Near Middleburg, Manassas battlefield, Harpers Ferry, and Wolftrap; 40 miles to Washington, D.C. Member of PAII and BBAV; AAA rated three diamonds. Smoking outside only. Children over 12 are welcome.

Hosts: Bill and Carol Chamberlain
Rooms: 2 (PB) $110-135
Full Breakfast
Credit Cards: None
Notes: 2, 5, 9, 10, 11, 12, 14

Leesburg Colonial Inn

19 South King Street, 22075
(703) 777-5000; (703) 478-8503; (800) 392-1332

The Leesburg Colonial Inn has well-appointed rooms, all in the 18th-century decor, but with all the modern amenities (cable TV, telephone, private bath). A true gourmet breakfast is served as part of the package while staying at the inn. Some of the rooms have fireplace as well as whirlpool; all rooms have grand period pieces such as rustic farm dresser, fine Persian and Oriental rugs, and queen-size poster bed. The inn is conveniently in the center of historic Leesburg, among many antique shops, where guests can find the charm of early Virginia. The chef can delight the most discriminating palate with his award-winning cuisine. Conference rooms available. Can cater for two as well as 100 persons. Surrounded by Virginia's hunt country, yet only 30 minutes from Washington, D.C., and 15 minutes from Dulles International Airport.

Hosts: Mr. Fabian E. Saeidi
Rooms: 10 (PB) $58-150
Full Breakfast
Credit Cards: A, B, C, D, E
Notes: 2, 3, 4, 5, 6, 7, 8, 9, 10, 11, 12, 13, 14

The Norris House Inn

108 Loudoun Street, SW, 22075
(703) 777-1806; (800) 644-1806
FAX (703) 771-8051

Elegant accommodations in the heart of historic Leesburg. The six charming guest rooms are all furnished with antiques, and three of the rooms have working fireplaces. Full country breakfasts served by candlelight and evening libations served. Convenient in-town location with several restaurants nearby. Only one hour's drive to Washington, D.C. In the heart of the Virginia hunt country, rich in Colonial and Civil War history. Lots of antiquing and wineries. The perfect place for special romantic getaways, small meetings, and

7 No smoking; 8 Children welcome; 9 Social drinking allowed; 10 Tennis nearby; 11 Swimming nearby; 12 Golf nearby; 13 Skiing nearby; 14 May be booked through a travel agent.

The Norris House

weddings. The inn is open daily by reservation. Children over 12 are welcome.

Hosts: Pam and Don McMurray
Rooms: 6 (SB) $80-140
Full Breakfast
Credit Cards: A, B, C, D, E
Notes: 2, 5, 7, 9, 10, 11, 12, 14

LEXINGTON

The Hummingbird Inn

Wood Lane, P.O.Box 147, Goshen, 24439
(800) 397-3214; (703) 997-9065

On a tranquil acre of landscaped grounds, the Hummingbird Inn, a unique Carpenter Gothic villa, offers accommodations in an early Victorian setting. Comfortable rooms are furnished with antiques and combine an old-fashioned ambience with modern convenience. Architectural features include wraparound verandas on the first and second floors, original pine floors of varying widths, a charming rustic den dating from the early 1800s, and a solarium. A wide trout stream defines one of the property lines, and the old red barn was once the town livery. Full breakfasts include country bacon, ham, or sausage, homemade bread, and unique area recipes.

Hosts: Diana and Jerry Robinson
Rooms: 4 (PB) $70-95
Full Breakfast
Credit Cards: A, B, C
Notes: 2, 4, 5, 9, 13, 14

Llewellyn Lodge at Lexington

603 South Main Street, 24450
(540) 463-3235; (800) 882-1145
FAX (540) 464-3122

A warm and friendly atmosphere awaits guests at this lovely brick Colonial. Upon arrival, receive a welcome with refreshments. A hearty gourmet breakfast is served that includes omelets, Belgian waffles, sausage, bacon, and homemade muffins. The decor combines traditional and antique furnishings. Within walking distance of the Lee Chapel, Stonewall Jackson House, Washington and Lee University, and Virginia Military Institute.

Hosts: Ellen and John Roberts
Rooms: 6 (PB) $70-85
Full Breakfast
Credit Cards: A, B, C
Notes: 2, 5, 7, 9, 10, 11, 12, 14

Oak Spring Farm and Vineyard

Route 2, Box 356, Raphine 24472
(703) 377-2398

Recently restored 1826 plantation house on 40-acre working farm with vineyard. Modern conveniences, rural setting, antiques, peaceful, quiet, home atmosphere, and historic. Near historical towns of Lexington and Staunton. Excellent Continental plus breakfast included with good nearby restaurants. Three rooms all with private baths and air-conditioned. Easy access to I-81 and 63. Lots to see and do in the area.

Hosts: Pat and Jim Tichenor
Rooms: 3 (PB) $63-73
Continental Breakfast
Credit Cards: None
Notes: 2, 5, 7, 9, 11

LINCOLN

Springdale Country Inn

22078
(703) 338-1832; (800) 388-1832

Restored historic landmark 45 miles west of Washington, D.C., on six acres of secluded

NOTES: Credit cards accepted: A MasterCard; B Visa; C American Express; D Discover; E Diners Club;
F Other; 2 Personal checks accepted; 3 Lunch available; 4 Dinner available; 5 Open all year; 6 Pets welcome;

terrain with babbling brooks, foot bridges, and terraced gardens. Meal service for groups; breakfast included in room price. Fully air-conditioned. New heating system and seven fireplaces.

Host: Nancy Fones
Rooms: 9 (3 PB; 6 SB) $95-125
Full Breakfast
Credit Cards: A, B, D
Notes: 2, 4, 5, 7, 8, 14

LOCUSTVILLE

Amanda's Bed and Breakfast

1428 Park Avenue, Baltimore, MD 21217-4230
(410) 225-0001; (800) 899-7533
FAX (410) 728-8957

143. This 18th-century Colonial is near Wachapreague and just one mile from the ocean. Quiet and comfortable. Water sports nearby. One room with double bed and private bath. Continental breakfast. $75.

LURAY

Blue Ridge Bed and Breakfast

Route 2, Box 3895, Berryville, 22611
(703) 955-1246; (800) 296-1246

A. Fabulous mansion built in 1739. Eighteen acres with ponds, in-ground pool, great mountain views, and antique furnishings. Two separate cottages are also available. $85-150.

B. Large Victorian house with each room providing a private bath and fireplace. Jacuzzi. Bikes and canoes provided. Complete with resident ghost. Full country breakfast and afternoon buffet provided for guests. Mystery weekends available.

C. Built in 1931, this grand old inn rests on 14 acres of lawn and formal gardens. Delights its guests with a Colonial dining room offering traditional menu. A gallery features the art of P. Buckley Moss who is often a guest at the inn. The Gilded Cage specializing in antiques and fine art restoration, is on the lower level. Single, double, and family units available. Also suites with private parlors. This inn boasts a banquet room that will accommodate up to 200 people. A solarium and terrace overlook the formal gardens. Eleanor Roosevelt was an honored guest at this inn. Jacuzzi available. $45-99.

The Woodruff House Bed and Breakfast

330 Mechanic Street, 22835
(540) 743-1494

This 1882 fairy-tale Victorian is beautifully appointed with period antiques, hallmarked silver, and fine china. Each room includes working fireplace and private bathroom. Escape from reality, come into this fairy-tale where the ambience never ends! Awaken to a choice of freshly brewed coffees (22 blends) delivered to guests' room door; a gourmet candlelit breakfast follows. Sumptuous candlelit high tea buffet dinner included. Relax in the fireside candlelit garden spa. Complimentary canoes and bicycles. Inquire about accommodations for children.

Hosts: Lucas and Deborah Woodruff
Rooms: 3 (PB) $85-145
Full Breakfast
Credit Cards: A, B, D
Notes: 2, 3, 4, 5, 9, 10, 11, 12, 13, 14

LYNCHBURG

Blue Ridge Bed and Breakfast

Route 2, Box 3895, Berryville, 22611
(703) 955-1246; (800) 296-1246

A. Built in 1874, this fabulous Victorian home is on the National Register of Historic Places, and has received the Merit Award from the Lynchburg Historic Association for outstanding exterior renovation. Near Blue Ridge Parkway and Appomattox battleground. $65-70.

7 No smoking; 8 Children welcome; 9 Social drinking allowed; 10 Tennis nearby; 11 Swimming nearby; 12 Golf nearby; 13 Skiing nearby; 14 May be booked through a travel agent.

Lynchburg Mansion

Lynchburg Mansion Inn Bed and Breakfast

405 Madison Street, 24504
(804) 528-5400; (800) 352-1199

Luxury accommodations in a 9,000-square-foot Spanish Georgian mansion in a residential downtown historic district. On the National Register of Historic Places. The street is still paved in turn-of-the-century brick. Known for attention to detail and quality of service. Remarkable interior cherry columns and wainscoting. Amenities include king- and queen-size beds, private ensuite bathrooms, fireplaces, TV with HBO, 200-thread-count sheets, turndown with chocolates, and hot tub. Full sumptuous breakfast is served in the formal dining room on antique china with fine silver and crystal. Two of the rooms are suites. Well-supervised children welcome. Skiing one hour away.

Hosts: Bob and Mauranna Sherman
Rooms: 4 (PB) $89-119
Full Breakfast
Credit Cards: A, B, C, E
Notes: 2, 5, 8, 10, 11, 12, 14

The Madison House Bed and Breakfast

413 Madison Street, 24504
(804) 528-1503; (800) 828-6422

Lynchburg's finest Victorian bed and breakfast, circa 1880, boasts a magnificent, authentic interior decor. Civil War library. Spacious, elegantly appointed guest rooms graced with antiques, private baths, plush robes, and linens. Full breakfast served on antique Limoges and Wedgwood china; afternoon tea included. Central air, in-room telephones and TV, and off-street parking available. Near colleges, Appomattox, Thomas Jefferson's Poplar Forest, and fine restaurants. Free Civil War tour packets for guests.

Hosts: Irene and Dale Smith
Rooms: 3 (PB) $79-109
Suite: 1 (PB)
Full Breakfast
Credit Cards: A, B, C
Notes: 2, 5, 7, 9, 10, 11, 12, 14

MADISON

Guesthouses Bed and Breakfast

P.O. Box 5737, Charlottesville, 22905
(804) 979-7264

Laurel Run. A recently built cottage in the woods of Madison County, 30 miles north of Charlottesville. This private cabin offers a great room, kitchen, dining area, and two bedrooms on the first floor. The loft has a double bed and cot. The broad, screened porch offers views of a stream, fields, and woods. Hiking, fishing, and riding are available in nearby Shenandoah National Park. Breakfast supplies are included for the first morning of guests' stay. $100-200.

Shenandoah Springs Country Inn

P.O. Box 770, 22727
(703) 923-4300

Relax on 1,000 acres of forest land, meadows, shady lanes, bridle trails, and scenic views. Try our majestic Shenandoah Springs Lake for fishing, canoeing, and ice skating in the winter, also cross-country skiing on our trails. Cottages available.

Inquire to see if lunch and dinner are available. Children over six welcome.

Hosts: Anne and Douglas Farmer
Rooms: 4 (PB) $75-120
Full Breakfast
Credit Cards: None
Notes: 2, 5, 7, 11, 12, 13

MADISON HEIGHTS

Blue Ridge Bed and Breakfast

Route 2, Box 3895, Berryville, 22611
(703) 955-1246; (800) 296-1246

A. This 80-year-old grand Southern Colonial mansion is in the middle of 14 acres with fabulous views of Blue Ridge Mountains. Just minutes from Blue Ridge Parkway. Fishing on the James River. Near Appomattox battleground. $49-59.

Winridge

Route 1, Box 362, 24572
(804) 384-7220

Enjoy wonderful mountain views while relaxing on the large porches of this grand Southern Colonial home. Swing under the shade trees and stroll through the gardens, where guests can admire the beauty of flowers, birds, and butterflies. Relax in the warm, casual atmosphere with the Pfister pfamily. Garden shop featuring perennials, unusual annuals, and container gardening. The Blue Ridge Parkway, Appomattox

Winridge

Court House, Poplar Forest, and much more are close by for guests' diversion.

Hosts: LoisAnn and Ed Pfister and Pfamily
Rooms: 3 (1 PB; 2 SB) $65-79
Full Breakfast
Credit Cards: None
Notes: 2, 5, 8, 10, 11, 12, 13, 14

MANASSAS

Blue Ridge Bed and Breakfast

Route 2, Box 3895, Berryville, 22611
(703) 955-1246; (800) 296-1246

A. In Manassas battlefields, this beautiful restored farmhouse was built upon General McDowell's campsite. Just five miles from I-66 and 35 minutes from Washington, D.C. Antiques, fireplaces, stone walls, barn and livestock, and old gas lamps throughout make this a special treat. $65.

MEADOWS OF DAN

Spangler's Bed and Breakfast

Route 2, Box 108, 24120
(703) 952-2454

On Country Road 602 within view of the Blue Ridge Parkway at milepost 180, four miles from Mabry Mill, this 1904 farmhouse has a kitchen with fireplace, piano, and four porches. There is also an 1826 private log cabin perfect for one couple. An additional 1987 log cabin has two bedrooms, complete kitchen, and wraparound porch. Fishing in the lake, swimming, three boats, bikes, horseshoes, and volleyball.

Hosts: Harold and Trudy Spangler
Rooms: 7 (2 PB; 5 SB) $50-60
Full Breakfast
Credit Cards: None
Notes: 2, 5, 8, 9, 10, 11, 12

MIDDLEBURG

Blue Ridge Bed and Breakfast

Route 2, Box 3895, Berryville, 22611
(703) 955-1246; (800) 296-1246

7 No smoking; 8 Children welcome; 9 Social drinking allowed; 10 Tennis nearby; 11 Swimming nearby; 12 Golf nearby; 13 Skiing nearby; 14 May be booked through a travel agent.

A. Two-hundred-year-old cozy commercial inn in the heart of Middleburg with working fireplaces in all bedrooms. Complete facilities for dinner. Accessible to quaint shops and eateries. $95.

Middleburg Inn and Guest Suites

105 West Washington Street, P.O. Box 984, 22117
(703) 687-3115; (800) 432-6125

In the heart of hunt country, elegantly furnished living quarters for short- or long-term stays. Each centrally air-conditioned suite has a canopied bed, private bath, telephone, and color TV. Fresh cut flowers, cotton bathrobes, and a complimentary Continental breakfast at the Red Fox are a few of the extra touches that make a visit memorable.

Host: Marilyn Moya, Manager
Room: 5 (PB) $130-195
Continental Breakfast
Credit Cards: A, B
Notes: 2, 5, 8, 9, 11

Welbourne

22117
(703) 687-3201

A seven-generation, antebellum plantation home in the middle of Virginia's fox-hunting country. On a 600-acre working farm. Full Southern breakfasts, working fireplaces, and cottages. "Faded elegance." On the National Register of Historic Places.

Hosts: Nat and Sherry Morison
Rooms: 10 (PB) $64-96
Full Breakfast
Credit Cards: None
Notes: 2, 5, 6, 8, 9

MIDDLETOWN

Blue Ridge Bed and Breakfast

Route 2, Box 3895, Berryville, 22611
(703) 955-1246; (800) 296-1246

A. Historic Victorian home on Main Street close to famous restaurant and theater. All period furniture. Minutes from many antique shops, Passion play, and small lake with beach. $65.

MILLBORO

Fort Lewis Lodge

HCR 3, Box 21A, 24460
(703) 925-2314

At the heart of a 3,200-acre mountain plantation is a truly unique country inn. The main lodge features wildlife art and locally handcrafted Shaker-style furnishings. A silo with 3 bedrooms "in the round" and two historic hand-hewn log cabins with stone fireplaces are ideal for a romantic getaway. A vibrant mix of fresh tastes and interesting menus are served nightly in the historic Lewis Mill dining room.

Hosts: John and Caryl Cowden
Rooms: 13 (PB) $130-180 Modified American Plan
Cabins: 2 (PB)
Full Breakfast
Credit Cards: A, B
Notes: 2, 3, 4, 8, 9, 11, 12

MILLWOOD

Blue Ridge Bed and Breakfast

Route 2, Box 3895, Berryville, 22611
(703) 955-1246; (800) 296-1246
A. Guests in the 1780s section of this stone mansion can enjoy huge fireplaces in every room. There is easy access through a separate entrance to the Shenandoah River. Easy drive to and from Washington, D.C., which is just an hour away. $70-108.

MOLLUSK

Guesthouses on the Water at Greenvale

Route 354, Box 70, 22517
(804) 462-5995

Two separate and private guesthouses on 13 acres on the Rappahannock River and

NOTES: Credit cards accepted: A MasterCard; B Visa; C American Express; D Discover; E Diners Club; F Other; 2 Personal checks accepted; 3 Lunch available; 4 Dinner available; 5 Open all year; 6 Pets welcome;

Greenvale Creek. Pool, dock, private beach, and bicycles. Each house is furnished with antiques and reproductions, and has two bedrooms, two baths, living room, kitchen, and deck. Air-conditioned. Enjoy sweeping water views, breathtaking sunsets, and relaxing and peaceful tranquility. Weekly rates available.

Hosts: Pam and Walt Smith
Guest houses: 2 (PB) $85-125
Continental Breakfast
Credit Cards: A, B
Notes: 2, 5, 9, 10, 11, 12

MONROE

Blue Ridge Bed and Breakfast

Route 2, Box 3895, Berryville, 22611
(703) 955-1246; (800) 296-1246

A. A unique retreat with 200-year-old chestnut beams, vaulted ceilings, and colorful antiques. Sitting on 300 historic acres with a creek, lake, pond, and fields, the inn comes complete with splendid views of High Peak Mountains. Just minutes off of the Blue Ridge Parkway and Appomattox battleground. Hosts are a retired educator and World War II British war bride who offer scrumptuous breakfasts on English china and linens. $55.

MONTEREY

Highland Inn

Main Street, P.O. Box 40, 24465
(703) 468-2143

Classic Victorian inn listed on the National Register of Historic Places. Tranquil location in the picturesque village of Monterey, nestled in the foothills of the Allegheny Mountains. There are 17 individually decorated rooms furnished with antiques and collectibles, each with private bath. Full-service dining room offers Continental cuisine for dinner Wednesday through Saturday and

Highland Inn

Sunday brunch. Antiquing, hiking, fishing, golf, and mineral baths are nearby.

Hosts: Michael Strand and Cynthia Peel
Rooms: 17 (PB) $49-79
Continental Breakfast
Credit Cards: A, B
Notes: 2, 4, 5, 8, 9, 11, 12, 14

MOUNT JACKSON

Amanda's Bed and Breakfast

1428 Park Avenue, Baltimore, MD 21217-4230
(410) 225-0001; (800) 899-7533
FAX (410) 728-8957

181. An 1830 Colonial homestead on seven acres overlooking the George Washington Mountains. Some bedrooms have wood-burning fireplaces, and the antique furniture is for sale. Pool on premises. Area activities include craft fairs, hiking, fishing, tennis, and horseback riding. Five rooms with private baths. Two guest cottages. Full breakfast. $65-85.

Blue Ridge Bed and Breakfast

Route 2, Box 3895, Berryville, 22611
(703) 955-1246; (800) 296-1246

A. This 1830 stately Colonial is near George Washington Parkway, ten miles from Bryce. Six bedrooms with working fireplaces. There is also a cozy two and one-half room cottage separate from the main house. Pool and full breakfast. $65-90.

7 No smoking; 8 Children welcome; 9 Social drinking allowed; 10 Tennis nearby; 11 Swimming nearby; 12 Golf nearby; 13 Skiing nearby; 14 May be booked through a travel agent.

The Widow Kip's Country Inn

355 Orchard Drive, 22842
(703) 477-2400

A stately 1830 Colonial on seven rural acres in the Shenandoah Valley overlooking the mountains. Friendly rooms filled with family photographs, bric-a-brac, and antiques. Each bedroom has a working fireplace and canopied, sleigh, or Lincoln bed. Two cozy cottages are also available. Pool on premises; nearby battlefields to explore, caverns, canoeing, hiking, or downhill skiing. Bicycles, picnics, and grill are available for guests to use. Holiday stay is a minimum of two nights.

Host: Betty Luse
Rooms: 7 (PB) $65-85
Full Breakfast
Credit Cards: A, B
Notes: 2, 3, 5, 6, 7, 8, 10, 11, 12, 13, 14

NELLYSFORD

Acorn Inn, Inc.

P.O. Box 431, 22958
(804) 361-9357

European-style inn with Dutch cyclist and American artist as hosts. Ten cozy guest rooms in a renovated horse stable that features a center lounge with Finnish soapstone fireplace, striking photographs, and woodcut prints. The atmosphere is artistic, friendly, and contemporary. There is also a charming cottage available. Delicious homemade breads and fruit cobbler are provided for guests' enjoyment. Close to Wintergreen ski/golf resort, Blue Ridge Parkway, Appalachian Trail, and beautiful scenic waterfalls. Continental plus breakfast served.

Hosts: Kathy and Martin Versluys
Rooms: 10 (SB) $47
Cottage: 1 (PB) $95
Continental Breakfast
Credit Cards: A, B
Notes: 2, 5, 8, 10, 12, 13

Guesthouses Bed and Breakfast

P.O. Box 5737, Charlottesville 22905
(804) 979-7264; FAX (804) 293-7791

Meander Inn. A 75-year-old Victorian farmhouse on 50 acres of pasture and woods skirted by hiking trails and traversed by the Rockfish River. The inn offers five twin or queen-size bedrooms, some with private bath. A delicious full country breakfast is served each morning. Guests may enjoy the hot tub, wood-burning stove, player piano, deck, or front porch. Wintergreen Resort and Stoney Creek golf and tennis facilities are available to guests. Smoking is permitted outdoors only. Air conditioning. $60-90.

Looking Glass. In the Rockfish Valley directly under the Blue Ridge Mountains and close to Wintergreen Resort, this Victorian farmhouse is deceptive on the outside. Inside guests will find the comfort and elegance of an English country home. Vintage linens, down duvets, tasteful hangings, and clever wall treatment belie the relaxed comfort to be found here. Four guest rooms with private baths. Full breakfast. Air-conditioned. Smoking outside on comfortable porches. Children welcome. $90-100.

The Mark Addy. Near Nellysford in the Rockfish Valley near the foot of Wintergreen, this inn has magnificent mountain views. Relax on one of the porches or in the library or parlor, or stroll around the beautiful grounds. This inn offers eight guest rooms or suites furnished with lovely antiques and collectibles, each with a private bath. Two rooms have Jacuzzis. A bountiful breakfast is served. Smoking outdoors on the porches only. Not suitable for children under 12. Air-conditioned. $90-125.

NOTES: Credit cards accepted: A MasterCard; B Visa; C American Express; D Discover; E Diners Club;
F Other; 2 Personal checks accepted; 3 Lunch available; 4 Dinner available; 5 Open all year; 6 Pets welcome;

NEW CHURCH

Amanda's Bed and Breakfast

1428 Park Avenue, Baltimore, MD 21217-4230
(410) 225-0001; (800) 899-7533
FAX (410) 728-8957

210. Twenty minutes from the most beautiful beaches on the East Coast and a star-rated restaurant. Elegant lodging with gourmet candlelight dining. Five rooms, some complete with Jacuzzi and canopied beds. Breakfast served in pleasant dining room. $85-135.

NEW MARKET

Blue Ridge Bed and Breakfast

Route 2, Box 3895, Berryville, 22611
(703) 955-1246; (800) 296-1246

A. Beautiful Colonial house built in 1790 on 20 acres with fabulous view of Massanetta Mountains, and a fishing creek. Franklin D. Roosevelt slept here in 1936. Ski resort is only 15 miles away. $55-65.

B. Beautiful carriage house built in 1873 offers two rooms in the main house. There is a cottage on the premises that offers two rooms decorated with lovely country decor and many oak and wicker antiques. In the heart of a busy Civil War town within easy walking distance of many quaint country shops and restaurants. $60-65.

A Touch of Country

9329 Congress Street, 22844
(540) 740-8030

Come relax at this restored 1870s home where a warm, friendly atmosphere awaits. Daydream on the porch swings or stroll through town, with its antique shops, gift shops, and restaurants. Rest in one of six bedrooms decorated with a country flavor.

In the morning enjoy a down-home country breakfast. Near caverns and battlefields.

Hosts: Jean Schoellig and Dawn Kason
Rooms: 6 (PB) $60-75
Full Breakfast
Credit Cards: A, B, D
Notes: 2, 5, 7, 8, 9, 10, 11, 12, 13, 14

NORFOLK

Page House Inn

323 Fairfax Avenue, 23507
(804) 625-5033

The restoration of the Page House Inn is a work of art, and a stay here is an experience not to be missed. This three-story Georgian Revival in-town mansion, made of brick laid in a Flemish bond pattern, underwent an award-winning rehabilitation, completed in 1991. The award was given by the city of Norfolk to the present owners for the quality of the workmanship and the attention paid to historic detail. The interior is picture perfect and has been featured in *Country Inns* magazine, April 1993, and chosen one of that publication's "Best Inns" for 1993 (February 1994). Rated four diamonds by AAA and highly rated by Mobil and Frommer's, as well as by several other well-known guides. A stay at the Page House is like a step back in time to a place where guests are warmly received and well fed—almost like going to

Page House Inn

Grandma's! Walk to all of the best cultural and tourist attractions as well as to the area's finest restaurants from the inn's central location in the Ghent historic district. Afternoon refreshments served 4:00-6:00 P.M. on request. Complimentary beverages and snacks (self-serve). Children over 12 welcome.

Hosts: Stephanie and Ezio DiBelardino
Rooms: 4 (PB) $80-120
Suites: 2 (PB) $130-145
Continental Breakfast
Credit Cards: A, B
Notes: 2, 5, 7, 9, 11, 12, 14

OCCOQUAN

Rockledge Mansion

410 Mill Street, 22125
(703) 690-3377

National historic landmark built in 1758, this stone house is less than a mile from I-95 and is 30 minutes from Washington, D.C. Working fireplaces, antiques, oversized Jacuzzis, and kitchenettes in accessory buildings. Walk to the river, shops, art galleries, restaurants. Very quiet and private on two acres in the center of town.

Hosts: Joy and Ron Houghton
Suites: 4 (PB) $75-120
Continental Breakfast
Credit Cards: None
Notes: 2, 5, 8, 9, 10, 11, 12, 14

ONANCOCK

The Spinning Wheel Bed and Breakfast

31 North Street, 23417
(804) 787-7311

An 1890s Folk Victorian home with antiques and spinning wheels throughout. Waterfront town listed on the National Register of Historic Places. Calm Eastern Shore getaway from D.C., Virginia, Maryland, Delaware, and New Jersey. Full breakfast. All rooms with private bath, queen-size bed, and air

conditioning. Walk to restaurants, shops, and deep-water harbor. Golf and tennis available at private club. Near beach, bay, and ocean. Bicycles, antiques, museums, festivals, fishing, wildlife refuge, and Tangier Island cruise. Open May through October. AAA approved.

Hosts: Karen and David Tweedie
Rooms: 5 (PB) $85-95
Full Breakfast
Credit Cards: A, B
Notes: 2, 7, 9, 10, 11, 12, 14

ORANGE

Hidden Inn

249 Caroline Street, 22960
(703) 672-3625; (800) 841-1253

A romantic Victorian featuring ten guest rooms, each with private bath. Jacuzzis, working fireplaces, and private verandas are available. Wicker and rocking chairs on the wraparound verandas; handmade quilts and canopied beds enhance the Victorian flavor. Full country breakfast, afternoon tea, and gourmet dinners are served. Minutes from Monticello, Montpelier, and Virginia wineries.

Hosts: Ray and Barbara Lonick
Rooms: 10 (PB) $79-159
Full Breakfast
Credit Cards: A, B, C
Notes: 2, 4, 5, 7, 8, 9, 10, 12, 14

The Holladay House

155 West Main Street, 22960
(703) 672-4893

The Holladay House, circa 1830, is a restored Federal-style home that has been in the Holladay family since 1899. The large, comfortable rooms are furnished with family pieces and each one features its own sitting area. Breakfast is normally served to guests in their own rooms. Surrounded by a residential neighborhood on three sides, the Holladay House is two blocks from the center of the historic town of Orange and just 90 minutes from Richmond or Washington, D.C.

Hosts: Pete and Phebe Holladay
Rooms: 6 (4 PB; 2 SB) $95-185
Full Breakfast
Credit Cards: A, B, D
Notes: 2, 5, 7, 8, 9, 10, 12, 13, 14

PACONIAN SPRINGS

Cornerstone Bed and Breakfast

Route 1, Box 82-C, 22129
(703) 882-3722

Two lovely rooms with private baths, air conditioning, queen-size beds, and antique furnishings. Amenities include bicycles, porch swings, exquisite gardens, swimming, and an evening deer watch. Country breakfast is served in the Victorian dining room. Just four miles from Waterford and Leesburg, convenient to Oatlands, Morven Park, Hedgelands Equestrian Center, the W&OD Bike Trail, and western Loudoun's history and happenings. Easy drive to Shenandoah River, Harpers Ferry, Charles Town, West Virginia, and the Appalachian Trail.

Hosts: Molly and Dick Cunningham
Rooms: 2 (PB) $75-90
Full Breakfast
Credit Cards: None
Notes: 2, 7, 8, 9, 10, 11, 12

PARIS

The Ashby Inn and Restaurant

Route 1, Box 2A, 22130
(703) 592-3900

In the quiet 18th-century village of Paris, just 12 miles west of Middleburg. Selected by the *Washington Post* in 1993 as one of "North America's 20 Most Romantic Hideaways." Stunning views of the Blue Ridge. Ten guest rooms, five with fireplaces, reflect their early 19th-century origins. A first-rate restaurant, whose daily menu is guided more by tradition than

The Ashby Inn

trend. Midweek conferences. Antiquing, vineyards, riding, and golf. Sunday brunch.

Hosts: John and Roma Sherman
Rooms: 10 (8 PB; 2 SB) $90-175
Full Breakfast
Credit Cards: A, B
Notes: 2, 3, 4, 5, 7, 9, 10, 11, 12

PATRICK SPRINGS

Maple Springs Inn

Route 1, Box 327-B, 24133
(540) 629-2954

Maple Springs Inn is near the Blue Ridge Parkway and within a 20-mile radius of Smith Mountain Lake, Phillpot Lake, and Fairystone State Park. The main lodge is the hosts' home, a three-story log dwelling with large dining room and living room with sky lights. There is also a honeymoon cottage that is private. Bedrooms are decorated to feature years gone by. Beautiful trails with different trees, springs, and wildlife. Breakfast is Continental plus. Afternoon snack with beverage at no additional charge. TV and telephone available in main lodge. Bedrooms are air-conditioned. Dinner available upon request. Smoking outside only. Children over 12 welcome. Swimming, golf, and skiing within a 20-mile radius.

Hosts: Lloyd J. and Virginia Barker
Rooms: 4 (2 PB; 2 SB) $50-60
Continental Breakfast
Credit Cards: None
Notes: 2, 5

7 No smoking; 8 Children welcome; 9 Social drinking allowed; 10 Tennis nearby; 11 Swimming nearby; 12 Golf nearby; 13 Skiing nearby; 14 May be booked through a travel agent.

PETERSBURG

Mayfield Inn

3348 West Washington Street, 23804
(804) 733-0866; (804) 861-6775

Mayfield Inn is a 1750 manor house listed on the National Register of Historic Places. It was authentically restored and won the Virginia APVA Award in 1987. Guest accommodations are luxuriously appointed with Oriental carpets, pine floors, antiques, period reproductions, and private baths. Situated on four acres of grounds, with a 40-foot outdoor swimming pool. Large herb garden and gazebo.

Hosts: Jamie and Dot Caudle, and Cherry Turner
Rooms: 4 (PB) $69-95
Full Breakfast
Credit Cards: A, B
Notes: 2, 5, 8, 9, 11, 12, 14

PULASKI

The Count Pulaski Bed and Breakfast and Gardens

821 North Jefferson Avenue, 24301
(703) 980-1163

In a mountain village in southwest Virginia at the major north-south artery I-81. Comfortable, spacious 80-year-old house furnished with family antiques, the owner's paintings, and items collected from living

The Count Pulaski

and traveling around the world. It is softly carpeted, with king- or queen-size beds, private baths, dimmer lights, ceiling fans, air conditioning, and three fireplaces. Gourmet breakfast is served elegantly by candlelight on a 150-year-old table. Nearby are antique shops, a variety of restaurants, hiking/biking trails, and water sports on the New River and Claytor Lake. A restful, relaxing getaway or travel stopover.

Host: Flo Stevenson
Rooms: 3 (PB) $75
Full Breakfast
Credit Cards: A, B
Notes: 2, 5, 7, 9

PURCELLVILLE

Blue Ridge Bed and Breakfast

Route 2, Box 3895, Berryville, 22611
(703) 955-1246; (800) 296-1246

A. Lovely Victorian cottage, circa 1850, one hour from the nation's capital. Authentically furnished in period antiques, down to rope beds. Extensive gardens with lovely view of the Blue Ridge Mountains. $80.

RICHMOND

The Emmanuel Hutzler House

2036 Monument Avenue, 23220
(804) 355-4885; (804) 353-6900

This large Italian Renaissance-style inn has been totally renovated in the past three years and offers leaded-glass windows, coffered ceilings, and natural mahogany raised paneling throughout the downstairs, as well as a large living room with marble fireplace for guests' enjoyment. There are four guest rooms on the second floor, each with private bath. One suite has a four-poster queen-size bed, love seat, and wing chair. The two queen-size rooms have a sitting area and private baths. The largest suite has a marble fireplace, four-poster mahogany bed, antique sofa, dresser, and a private bath with shower and Jacuzzi. Full breakfast on weekends, Continental plus weekdays. Children over 12 welcome.

Hosts: Lyn M. Benson and John E. Richardson
Rooms: 4 (PB) $89-135
Continental and Full Breakfasts
Credit Cards: A, B, C, D
Notes: 2, 5, 7, 9, 10, 11, 12, 14

West-Bocock House

West-Bocock House

1107 Grove Avenue, 23220
(804) 358-6174

Circa 1817 historic house in the heart of Richmond offers elegant guest rooms with private baths, French linens, fresh flowers, full breakfast, and off-street parking. Convenient to museums, historic sites, restaurants, shopping, and Capitol Square. The Wests invite visitors to sample true Southern hospitality. Smoking in designated areas only.

Host: Billie Rees West
Rooms: 3 (PB) $65-75
Full Breakfast
Credit Cards: None
Notes: 2, 5, 9, 12, 14

The William Catlin House

2304 East Broad Street, 23223
(804) 780-3746

Antiques, family heirlooms, and working fireplaces await at the William Catlin House, Richmond's first and oldest bed and breakfast. In the historic district of Church Hill, the house was built in 1845. The luxury of bedroom fireplaces, goose down pillows, and evening sherry promises a restful night. Each morning a delicious full breakfast and endless pots of steaming hot coffee or tea await guests in the elegant dining room. While in the area, be sure to visit some of the numerous nearby historic sites. As seen in *Colonial Homes, Southern Living,* and *Mid-Atlantic* magazines.

Hosts: Robert and Josephine Martin
Rooms: 5 (3 PB; 2 SB) $70-95
Full Breakfast
Credit Cards: A, B, D
Notes: 2, 5, 7, 8, 9, 10, 12, 14

ROANOKE

The Manor at Taylor's Store

Route 1, Box 533, Smith Mountain Lake, 24184
(703) 721-3951; (800) 248-6267
FAX (703) 721-5243

Explore this secluded, historic 120-acre estate convenient to Smith Mountain Lake, Roanoke, and the Blue Ridge Parkway. The manor has six guest suites with extraordinary antiques and Oriental rugs. Guests enjoy all luxury amenities, including central air conditioning, hot tub, fireplaces, private porches, billiard room, exercise room, guest kitchen, movies, and six private, spring-fed ponds for swimming, fishing, and canoeing. A lovely gazebo overlooks the ponds for picnics. A full heart healthy gourmet breakfast is served in the dining room with breathtaking panoramic views of the countryside. The cottage sleeps up to six people. No smoking allowed in the house. Children are welcome in the cottage only.

Hosts: Lee and Mary Lynn Tucker
Rooms: 6 (4 PB; 2 SB) $80-125
Cottage: 1 (PB) $90-190
Full Breakfast
Credit Cards: A, B
Notes: 2, 3, 5, 9, 10, 11, 12, 13, 14

7 No smoking; 8 Children welcome; 9 Social drinking allowed; 10 Tennis nearby; 11 Swimming nearby; 12 Golf nearby; 13 Skiing nearby; 14 May be booked through a travel agent.

The Mary Bladon House

The Mary Bladon House

381 Washington Avenue Southwest, 24016
(540) 344-5361

A lovely 1890s Victorian house in the historic Old Southwest neighborhood. Spacious rooms, tastefully decorated with crafts and period antiques to capture the charm of a time when elegant comfort was a way of life. A step back in time for the young and the young at heart.

Hosts: Bill and Sheri Bestpitch
Rooms: 3 (PB) $80
Full Breakfast
Credit Cards: A, B
Notes: 2, 5, 7, 8, 9, 10, 11, 12, 14

SALEM

The Old Manse

530 East Main Street, 24153
(703) 389-3921

The Old Manse was built on land once owned by Andrew Lewis, famed Indian fighter, leader at the battle of Point Pleasant ,and Revolutionary War general. The house was built in 1847 and is furnished with antiques. The Old Manse is listed on the National Register of Historic Places. It is open year-round and offers a sitting room and parlor for visiting or TV watching.

Porches and a patio are also available for lounging and relaxing. The Peaks of Otter, farmers' markets (both Salem and Roanoke), tennis courts, Longwood Park for walking and exercise trails, Roanoke College, Hollins College, I-81, and Confederate battlefield and cemetery are all nearby.

Host: Charlotte Griffith
Rooms: 2 (PB) $50
Full Breakfast
Credit Cards: None
Notes: 2, 5, 7, 8, 10, 12

SCOTTSVILLE

Guesthouses Bed and Breakfast

P.O. Box 5737, 22905
(804) 979-7264

Chester. This charming, large country home in Scottsville, 25 minutes south of Charlottesville, was built 1825 through 1875; lots of history and beautiful trees are on the grounds. Five guest rooms make this a great retreat for a large group, or come with a smaller group and meet fellow guests. Accommodations have bed sizes from a twin to a queen, and the house is furnished with an interesting and eclectic collection of pieces from the owner's travels. Several porches provide a pleasant place to sit at night. Full breakfast is served in the morning, and dinner is available by reservation. $80-120.

The Prodigal. On the site of an old summer kitchen, this cottage sits behind a farmhouse built around 1830. It features a large fireplace, sleeper-sofa, Pullman kitchen, full bath downstairs, and a room with a double bed upstairs. Fish in the pond, swim nearby in the Hardware River swimming hole, or rent a tube or canoe on the James River. Guests can even bring their horses. There are extra stalls and wooded trails. Air conditioning. Supplies provided for guests to prepare breakfast. $80-125.

NOTES: Credit cards accepted: A MasterCard; B Visa; C American Express; D Discover; E Diners Club;
F Other; 2 Personal checks accepted; 3 Lunch available; 4 Dinner available; 5 Open all year; 6 Pets welcome;

SMITHFIELD

Isle of Wight Inn

1607 South Church Street, 23430
(804) 357-3176

This luxurious Colonial bed and breakfast inn is found in a delightful historic river-port town. Several suites with fireplaces and Jacuzzis. Antique shop featuring tall-case clocks and period furniture. More than 60 old homes in town dating from 1750. Just 30 minutes and a ferry ride from Williamsburg and Jamestown; less than an hour from James River plantations, Norfolk, Hampton, and Virginia Beach. No smoking allowed in the rooms and common areas.

Hosts: The Harts and the Earls
Rooms: 10 (PB) $53-99
Full Breakfast
Credit Cards: A, B, C, D
Notes: 2, 5, 8, 9, 10, 11, 12, 14

SPERRYVILLE

The Conyers House Inn and Stable

3131 Slate Mills Road, 22740
(703) 987-8025; FAX (703) 987-8709

Nestled in the foothills of the Blue Ridge Mountains, the Conyers House is the first and oldest country inn in historic Rappahannock County, Virginia. Amidst Virginia's most beautiful hunt country, the guests enjoy cross-country trail rides in the company of the host's Jack Russell terriers. Known for elegant seven-course dinners. All rooms have private bathrooms, fireplaces, and porches. Smoking permitted outside. Inquire about accommodations available for children.

Hosts: Sandra and Norman Cartwright-Brown
Rooms: 8 (PB) $100-200
Full Breakfast
Credit Cards: A, B, D
Notes: 2, 4, 5, 6, 9, 10, 12, 13, 14

STANLEY

Jordan Hollow Farm Inn

Route 2, Box 375, 22851
(703) 778-2285; FAX (703) 778-1759

A restored Colonial horse farm featuring 21 rooms with private baths, several with fireplaces and whirlpool baths. Full-service restaurant and pub. Horseback riding, English and western. In the Shenandoah Valley just ten miles from Skyline Drive and six miles from Luray Caverns. Box lunches available. Full dinner provided in addition to a full breakfast under the Modified American Plan. Member IIA.

Hosts: Jetze and Marley Beers
Rooms: 21 (PB) $140-180
Full Breakfast
Credit Cards: A, B, D, E
Notes: 2, 5, 8, 9, 10, 11, 12, 13, 14

Jordon Hollow Farm

STAUNTON

Ashton Country House

1205 Middlebrook Avenue, 24401
(540) 885-7819; (800) 296-7819

Ashton Country House, circa 1860, is a Greek Revival brick home on 25 peaceful acres on the outskirts of Staunton in the Shenandoah Valley, yet only a five-minute drive into town. Each of the five spacious guest rooms features a private bath and a queen-size bed and air conditioning. Three

7 No smoking; 8 Children welcome; 9 Social drinking allowed; 10 Tennis nearby; 11 Swimming nearby; 12 Golf nearby; 13 Skiing nearby; 14 May be booked through a travel agent.

rooms with romantic wood-burning fireplaces. Mornings begin with a hearty breakfast. Convenient to historic attractions, fine restaurants, and area colleges.

Hosts: Dorie and Vince Distefano
Rooms: 5 (PB) $85-105
Full Breakfast
Credit Cards: A, B, C, D, E
Notes: 5, 7, 9, 10, 11, 12, 13, 14

Frederick House

28 North New Street, P.O. Box 1387, 24402-1387
(800) 334-5575

A small hotel, Chumley's tearoom, and McCormicks restaurant in the European tradition. Large, comfortable rooms or suites. Amenities include private baths, air conditioning, TV, telephones, robes, private entrances, and antique furnishings. Some balconies or fireplaces. Gourmet breakfast, and delicious dining at McCormicks. Award-winning restoration and gardens. Listed in the National Register of Historic Places. Across from Mary Baldwin College. Near shops, restaurants, and the Woodrow Wilson Birthplace. In Central Shenandoah Valley near Skyline Drive and Blue Ridge Parkway.

Hosts: Joe and Evy Harman
Rooms: 14 (PB) $65-95
Full Breakfast
Credit Cards: A, B, C, D, E
Notes: 2, 3, 5, 7, 8, 9, 10, 11, 12, 13, 14

Kenwood

235 East Beverley Street, 24401
(540) 886-0524

Spacious, restored 1910 Colonial Revival brick home adjacent to Woodrow Wilson Birthplace and Museum. Filled with period furniture and antiques, Kenwood offers comfortable accommodations in a relaxed atmosphere. Two miles west of the I-81 and I-64 intersections, near the Museum of American Frontier Culture, Skyline Drive, Blue Ridge Parkway, Statler Brothers Museum, and Monticello. Four guest

rooms with queen-size beds, private baths, air conditioning, and full breakfast.

Hosts: Liz and Ed Kennedy
Rooms: 4 (PB) $70
Full Breakfast
Credit Cards: A, B
Notes: 2, 5, 7, 8, 9, 10, 11, 12

The Sampson Eagon Inn

The Sampson Eagon Inn

238 East Beverley Street, 24401
(540) 886-8200; (800) 597-9722

In the Virginia historic landmark district of Gospel Hill, this gracious, circa 1840, town residence has been thoughtfully restored and transformed into a unique inn offering affordable luxury and personal service in an intimate, inviting atmosphere. Each elegant, spacious, air-conditioned room and suite features private bath, sitting area, canopied queen-size bed, and antique furnishings. Adjacent to the Woodrow Wilson Birthplace and Mary Baldwin College, the inn is within two blocks of downtown dining and attractions.

Hosts: Laura and Frank Mattingly
Rooms: 5 (PB) $85-99
Full Breakfast
Credit Cards: None
Notes: 2, 5, 7, 9, 10, 11, 12, 13, 14

Thornrose House at Gypsy Hill

531 Thornrose Avenue, 24401
(540) 885-7026

A wraparound veranda and Greek colonnades distinguish this turn-of-the-century

Georgian residence. Family antiques, a grand piano, and fireplaces create an elegant, restful atmosphere. Breakfast specialties served in a formal dining room energize guests for sightseeing in the beautiful Shenandoah Valley. Beside a 300-acre park with golf, tennis, swimming, and trails. Other attractions include the Woodrow Wilson Birthplace, the Museum of American Frontier Culture, and the nearby Skyline Drive and Blue Ridge Parkway.

Hosts: Suzanne and Otis Huston
Rooms: 5 (PB) $55-75
Full Breakfast
Credit Cards: None
Notes: 2, 5, 7, 8, 9, 10, 11, 12, 13

STEELE'S TAVERN

Amanda's Bed and Breakfast

1428 Park Avenue, Baltimore, MD, 21217-4230
(410) 225-0001; (800) 899-7533
FAX (410) 728-8957

340. Explore historic towns of Virginia including Lexington, Charlottesville, Appomattox, and Monticello, or explore along the back roads. Enjoy Goshen Pass, Natural Bridge, antique shops, and crafts. Enjoy the sunsets in the mountains. Eleven rooms, each with private bath and wood-burning fireplaces. Full breakfast. $85-110.

Sugar Tree Inn

Highway 56, 24476
(540) 377-2197 (information and FAX)
(800) 377-2197 (reservations)

Sugar Tree, Virginia's mountain inn, is nestled into a mountainside less than a mile from the Blue Ridge Parkway. Guests find romantic seclusion here in rustically elegant surroundings. Each spacious room or suite offers a private wood-burning fireplace and beautiful, comfortable furnishings. There are 40-mile views from the front porch rockers with spectacular sunsets and busy hummingbirds. Hike Sugar Tree trails, explore historic Virginia, shop,

or simply relax. Here spring wildflowers, brilliant summer days with cool nights, and dazzling falls await. Open April 1 through December 1. Great hiking, antiquing, scenery, and historic attractions nearby.

Rooms: 11 (PB) $90-120
Full Breakfast
Credit Cards: A, B
Notes: 2, 4, 7, 9, 14

STEPHENS CITY

Blue Ridge Bed and Breakfast

Route 2, Box 3895, Berryville, 22611
(703) 955-1246; (800) 296-1246

A. Lovely brick home built in 1819. Served as a tavern for 100 years. In a beautiful historic district. Decor includes lovely antiques, Oriental rugs, and beautiful old woodwork. Only minutes away from Belle Grove Plantation, Wayside Theater, and Skyline Drive. $55-65.

SWOOPE

Lambsgate Bed and Breakfast

Route 1, Box 63, 24479
(540) 337-6929

Six miles west of Staunton on Routes 254 and 833. Restored 1816 farmhouse and

Lambsgate

working sheep farm in the historic Shenandoah Valley. Relaxing country setting with hiking and biking nearby. Central for visiting historic sites, national park, and forests. Minimum stay over July 4 holiday is two nights.

Hosts: Dan and Elizabeth Fannon
Rooms: 3 (SB) $52.55
Full Breakfast
Credit Cards: None
Notes: 2, 5, 7, 8, 9

SYRIA

Graves' Mountain Lodge

Route 670, 22743
(703) 923-4231; FAX (703) 923-4312

This peaceful lodge is on a large cattle and fruit farm in the shadow of the Blue Ridge Mountains next to the Shenandoah National Park. Guests enjoy three meals a day on the American Plan while getting rest and relaxation during their visit. Rooms, cabins, and cottages to choose from. Trout stream and farm ponds are available for fishing. Hiking trails and horseback riding are also available for guests' enjoyment. Open mid-March through November. Seasonal rates available. Both smoking and nonsmoking rooms available.

Hosts: Rachel and Jim Graves
Rooms: 45 (38 PB; 7 SB) $60-92.50
Cottages: 9 (PB) $51-88
Full Breakfast
Credit Cards: A, B, D
Notes: 2, 3, 4, 6, 8, 9, 10, 11

TANGIER ISLAND

Sunset Inn

Box 156, 23440
(804) 891-2535

The soft crab capital of the nation, Tangier is a romantic destination for those who would see a largely unspoiled fishing village with quaint, narrow streets. The inn

offers 11 rooms. All have air conditioning and private baths. There is a deck and cable TV. Guests enjoy a wonderful view of the bay. One half-block from the beach. Continental breakfast is served.

Hosts: Grace and Jim Brown
Rooms: 11 (10 PB; 1 SB) $60
Continental Breakfast
Credit Cards: None
Notes: 2, 5, 7, 8, 9, 11

VIRGINIA BEACH

Angie's Guest Cottage

302 24th Street, 23451
(804) 428-4690

Angie's Guest Cottage is in the heart of the resort area, just one block from the ocean. Early-20th-century beach house that former guests describe as "cute, cozy, quiet, and extra clean with fresh flowers everywhere!" All rooms are air-conditioned; some have small refrigerators and private entrances. A Continental plus breakfast is served on the front porch, and there are also a sun deck, barbecue pit, and picnic tables. International atmosphere. Closed October 1 through March 31. Two-night minimum stay in season.

Host: Barbara Yates
Rooms: 6 (1 PB; 5 SB) $52-79.20
Continental Breakfast
Credit Cards: None
Notes: 7, 8, 9, 10, 11, 12

Barclay Cottage

400 16th Street, 23451
(804) 422-1956

Enjoy casual sophistication in a warm, historic, innlike atmosphere. Two blocks from the beach and in the heart of the Virginia Beach recreational area, the Barclay Cottage has been decorated in turn-of-the-century-style with antique furniture. The hosts welcome guests to the Barclay Cottage where their theme is, "We go where our dreams take us." Open May through October.

Barclay Cottage

Hosts: Peter and Claire
Rooms: 6 (3 PB; 3 SB) $65-80
Full Breakfast
Credit Cards: A, B, C
Notes: 7, 10, 11, 12, 14

The Picket Fence

209 43rd Street, 23451
(804) 428-8861

The furnishings in this comfortable Colonial home glow with the patina of loving care. The beach is just one block away, and beach chairs and umbrellas are provided for comfort. Near the new Marine Science Museum. One room and a suite are available year-round. A guest cottage is open May through October.

Host: Kathleen J. Hall
Room: 1 (SB) $50-85
Suite: 1 (PB)
Cottage: 1 (PB)
Full Breakfast
Credit Cards: None
Notes: 2, 5, 9, 10, 11, 12

WACHAPREAGUE

Amanda's Bed and Breakfast

1428 Park Avenue, Baltimore, MD 21217-4230
(410) 225-0001; (800) 899-7533
FAX (410) 728-8957

267. Lovely Victorian, circa 1875, in a quaint fishing village. Four bedrooms, two full baths, contemporary kitchen, living room, dining room, fireplace, central heat and air, cable TV, and stereo. Self-catered breakfast. Whole house rental. $500/week.

The Burton House

11 Brooklyn Street, 23480
(804) 787-4560

The Burton House is composed of two side-by-side Victorian houses in a seaside fishing village. Air conditioning when needed. Guests can enjoy biking, bird watching, and boating. Bikes are provided and rental boats are available. Generous country breakfast and afternoon tea or coffee. Quiet, affordable elegance. Cottages are also available. Marina is very close; guests should feel free to bring their own boats. Smoking outside only. Children over 12 welcome.

Hosts: Pat and Tom Hart
Rooms: 10 (PB) $65-85
Cabins: 4 (PB) $40-50
Full Breakfast
Credit Cards: A, B
Notes: 2, 5, 10, 11, 12, 14

WARM SPRINGS

Blue Ridge Bed and Breakfast

Route 2, Box 3895, Berryville, 22611
(703) 955-1246; (800) 296-1246

A. This rambling old house was originally an 18th-century tavern and is within ten minutes of the famous Homestead Ski Resort, and five minutes from George Washington National Forest in the Allegheny Mountains. The home has gorgeous antiques, and suites and rooms (one with private fireplace). Only a few doors away from famous warm pools bubbling up at 98° F. $55-90.

Meadow Lane Lodge

Star Route A, Box 110, 24484
(703) 839-5959

A little jewel of a country inn, set in meadows and mountains on a 1,600-acre estate. Surrounded by bountiful resources for tennis, golf, swimming, riding, trout fishing, bird watching, botanizing, hiking, walking,

7 No smoking; 8 Children welcome; 9 Social drinking allowed; 10 Tennis nearby; 11 Swimming nearby; 12 Golf nearby; 13 Skiing nearby; 14 May be booked through a travel agent.

and creative loafing. Wake to the sounds of roosters crowing in the barn and the smells of what will be a memorable breakfast.

Hosts: Cheryl and Steve Hooley
Rooms: 11 (PB) $105-145
Full Breakfast
Credit Cards: A, B, C
Notes: 2, 3, 4, 5, 7, 8, 9, 10, 11, 12, 13

WARRENTON

The Black Horse Inn

Route 3, Box 240, 22186
(703) 349-4020

The Black Horse Inn is a beautiful Southern Colonial estate just one and one-half miles from historic Warrenton in the heart of some of Virginia's finest horse country. The original part of this lovely old home was built prior to the Civil War; the remainder was constructed approximately at the turn of the century. Legend has it that the Black Horse Inn was used as a hospital during the Civil War and was once used as a courthouse for Fauquier County. The Black Horse Inn is a gracious, comfortable country home with rooms of generous proportions. Fox hunting is available; hunter stable can accommodate equine guests. Wine tours. Golf nearby. Only 45 minutes from Washington, D.C.

Hosts: Lynn A. Pirozzoli and Franklin P. Williams
Rooms: 9 (PB) $85-125
Credit Cards: A, B C
Notes: 2, 5, 8, 9, 12

WASHINGTON

Blue Ridge Bed and Breakfast

Route 2, Box 3895, Berryville, 22611
(703) 955-1246; (800) 296-1246

A. Lovely 1850s house on quiet street with great views of mountains. Easy walk to Inn at Little Washington and local theater. House has lovely antiques including Rose Kennedy chaise lounge and working fireplace in bedroom. $80-125.

B. In quaint village close to world-renowned cuisine and many charming antique shops. Turn-of-the-century home offers lovely garden, two bedrooms, and one full suite. Children welcome. Close to Old Rag Mountain and Little and Big Devil's Staircase, hiking trails, as well as trout fishing. $85-125.

Caledonia Farm—1812

Route 1, Box 2080, Flint Hill, 22627
(703) 675-3693; (800) BNB-1812

Beautifully restored 1812 stone home and romantic guest house on a farm adjacent to Shenandoah National Park. This landmark, listed on the National Register of Historic Places, offers splendor for all seasons in Virginia's Blue Ridge Mountains. Skyline Drive, wineries, caves, historic sites, and superb dining. Fireplaces, air conditioning, and bicycles. Only 68 miles to Washington, D.C. AAA-rated three diamonds. Children over 12 welcome.

Host: Phil Irwin
Rooms: 2 plus suite (1 PB; 2 SB) $80-140
Full Breakfast
Credit Cards: A, B, D
Notes: 2, 5, 7, 9, 10, 11, 12, 13, 14

Caledonia Farm

The Foster-Harris House

Main Street, Box 333, 22747
(703) 675-3757

A turn-of-the-century home in a historic village nestled in the foothills of the Blue Ridge Mountains, with country antiques, fresh

NOTES: Credit cards accepted: A MasterCard; B Visa; C American Express; D Discover; E Diners Club; F Other; 2 Personal checks accepted; 3 Lunch available; 4 Dinner available; 5 Open all year; 6 Pets welcome;

flowers, and outstanding mountain views. Near Shenandoah National Park. Five-star restaurant in town. All rooms feature private baths and central air conditioning.

Host: Phyllis Marriott
Rooms: 4 (PB) $95-135
Full Breakfast
Credit Cards: A, B, C, D
Notes: 2, 5, 7, 9, 10, 11, 12, 14

Heritage House

Heritage House

P.O. Box 427, 22747
(703) 675-3207

This 1837 manor house is in Little Washington, a picturesque village originally surveyed by George Washington. Guests are invited to enjoy heirloom antiques, international collectibles, gourmet breakfasts, and gorgeous panoramic views. Central to fine dining, antiquing, hiking, horseback riding, historic attractions, wineries, and the joys of Skyline Drive and the Shenandoah National Park. AAA three-diamond approved.

Hosts: Jean and Frank Scott
Rooms: 4 (PB) $100-125
Full Breakfast
Credit Cards: A, B
Notes: 2, 5, 7, 9, 10, 12, 14

WHITE POST

L'Auberge Provençale

P.O. Box 119, 22663
(703) 837-1375; FAX (703) 837-2004

Elegant overnight accommodations, with romantic dining and the breakfast of one's dreams. L'Auberge Provençale offers the perfect getaway for pleasure or business. Superb French cuisine moderne is created by Master Chef Alain. Chosen by the James Beard Foundation Great Country Inn Series; four-diamond rating. L'Auberge Provençale has recreated an inn of the South of France. Country charm, city sophistication—"Where great expectations are quietly met."

Hosts: Alain and Celeste Borel
Rooms: 10 (PB) $145-205
Full Breakfast
Credit Cards: A, B, C, D, E
Notes: 2, 4, 7, 9, 10, 11, 12, 14

WILLIAMSBURG

Amanda's Bed and Breakfast

1428 Park Avenue, Baltimore, MD 21217-4230
(410) 225-0001; (800) 899-7533
FAX (410) 728-8957

253. This Flemish-bond brick home was one of the first homes built on Richmond Road after the restoration of Colonial Williamsburg began in the late 1920s. The house features 18th-century decor, and the owner's apple collection is evident throughout. Four rooms with private baths. Continental plus breakfast. $70-110.

262. Three blocks from historic area and across from the College of William and Mary's Alumni House and Zable Stadium. Recent renovations have restored the house to its original charm when built in 1926. Antique furnishings throughout. Five guest rooms each with private bath. $90-105.

Applewood Colonial

605 Richmond Road, 23185
(804) 229-0205; (800) 899-2753

Circa 1921, this Flemish-bond brick home was built during the restoration of Colonial Williamsburg. The inn's parlor is decorated Colonial style and features dentil crown molding. A crystal chandelier hangs above the dining table where breakfast is served. The Colonel Vaughn Suite boasts private entrance, fireplace, and queen-size canopied bed.

Host: Fred Strout
Rooms: 4 (PB) $75-120
Full Breakfast
Credit Cards: A, B
Notes: 2, 5, 7, 8, 9, 10, 12, 14

Candlewick Bed and Breakfast

706 Richmond Road, 23185
(804) 253-8693; (800) 418-4949

This wonderful country home looks as though it jumped off the pages of *Country Living* magazine. A charming blend of 18th century, country, elegant bedrooms with canopied beds, and private baths. One bedroom can sleep three. Within walking distance of historic area and William and Mary College. Complimentary bicycles. Children over ten welcome.

Host: Mary Peters
Rooms: 4 (PB) $85-95
full Breakfast
Credit Cards: A,B
Notes: 2, 5, 7, 8, 9, 10, 11, 12, 14

The Cedars

616 Jamestown Road, 23185
(804) 229-3591; (800) 296-3591

Across the street from the College of William and Mary and a 10-minute walk to Colonial Williamsburg, the Cedars offers traditional Colonial elegance, comfort, and hospitality. The three-story brick Georgian is the oldest and largest bed and breakfast in Williamsburg. Scrumptious full breakfasts are served by candlelight from a handhewn huntboard on the tavern porch. In the evening, the porch serves as a meeting place for cards, chess, or other diversions. On cool evenings, the fireplace in the sitting room invites relaxation and conversation. Each guest room has a unique personality. Four-poster and canopied beds abound. Cottage has two fireplace suites. Off-street parking.

Hosts: Carol, Jim, and Brona Malecha
Rooms: 8 (PB) $95-135
Cottage: 2 (PB) $150
Full Breakfast
Credit Cards: A, B
Notes: 2, 5, 7, 8, 9, 12, 14

Colonial Capital Bed and Breakfast

501 Richmond Road, 23185
(804) 229-0233; (800) 776-0570
FAX (804) 253-7667

Only three blocks from the historic area, this charming Colonial Revival home, circa 1926, and its gracious hosts welcome guests. Enjoy spring gardens, summer festivities, autumn colors, and Colonial Christmastide. Antique furnishings blend charm and elegance from the large parlor with wood-burning fireplace to the airy guest rooms, each with canopied bed and private bath. Full breakfast with a gourmet touch and afternoon tea and wine. ABC licensed, bikes, and free off-street parking. Gift certificates available. fax can receive 24 hours a day. Special rates available January through March. Smoking permitted outside. Children over six welcome.

Hosts: Barbara and Phil Craig
Rooms: 5 (PB) $95-125
Full Breakfast
Credit Cards: A, B, C, D
Notes: 2, 5, 9, 10, 12, 14

Colonial Capital

Colonial Gardens
Bed and Breakfast

1109 Jamestown Road, 23185
(804) 220-8087; (800) 886-9715

The Colonial Gardens Bed and Breakfast offers the perfect escape in a quiet woodland setting. The charming interior is beautifully decorated with heirloom antiques and original art. Enjoy breakfast in the cheerful sunroom overlooking the beautifully landscaped yard. In the evening, relax with other guests in the large living room around the game table and cozy sitting areas. Convenient to the College of William and Mary and Colonial Williamsburg. Enjoy the attentive service and gracious hospitality at this beautiful bed and breakfast.

Hosts: Scottie and Wilmot Phillips
Rooms: 3 (PB) $85-125
Full Breakfast
Credit Cards: A, B
Notes: 2, 5, 7

For Cant Hill Guest Home

4 Canterbury Lane, 23185
(804) 229-6623

This home is only a few blocks from the restored area of Williamsburg, yet very secluded and quiet in a lovely wooded setting overlooking a lake that joins the College of William and Mary campus. The rooms are beautifully decorated, and the hosts are happy to make dinner reservations for guests and provide helpful information on the many area attractions. Large Continental breakfast served in the guests' room. Children over ten welcome.

Hosts: Martha and Hugh Easler
Rooms: 2 (PB) $65-75
Continental Breakfast
Credit Cards: None
Notes: 2, 5, 9, 10, 11, 12, 14

Fox and Grape
Bed and Breakfast

701 Monumental Avenue, 23185
(804) 229-6914; (800) 292-3699

Fox and Grape

Genteel accommodations just five blocks north of Virginia's restored Colonial capitol. Furnishings in this lovely two-story Colonial with a large wraparound porch include antiques, counted cross-stitch, duck decoys, and a cup plate collection. Four guest rooms with private baths.

Hosts: Pat and Bob Orendorff
Rooms: 4 (PB) $78-84
Continental Breakfast
Credit Cards: A, B, D
Notes: 5, 7, 8, 9, 14

Goswick-Whittaker Guest Home

102 Thomas Nelson Lane, 23185
(804) 229-3920

One room on the first floor in a quiet, nice neighborhood. Within walking distance to very nice restaurant and also fast food if preferred. Off-street parking available.

Host: Ann C. Whittaker
Rooms: 1 (1 1/2 PB) $50
Continental Breakfast
Credit Cards: None
Notes: 2, 7, 12

Governor's Trace

303 Capitol Landing Road, 23185
(804) 229-7552; (800) 303-7552

"Closest inn to the historic district...vies for the most romantic [in Williamsburg]"— *Washington Post*. Starting their tenth year in business as a bed and breakfast, Sue and Dick hold Williamsburg's record for longevity and are pioneers of the industry in town. Enjoy the special ambience created

7 No smoking; 8 Children welcome; 9 Social drinking allowed; 10 Tennis nearby; 11 Swimming nearby; 12 Golf nearby; 13 Skiing nearby; 14 May be booked through a travel agent.

Governor's Trace

by these longtime innkeepers: candlelit breakfasts served in the privacy of guest room, king- and queen-size beds, and spacious antique-filled rooms; one has a real wood-burning fireplace, another a private screened-in porch. Come to Governer's Trace any season and for any reason.

Hosts: Sue and Dick Lake
Room: 3 (PB) $95-115
Continental Breakfast
Credit Cards: A, B
Notes: 2, 5, 9, 10, 11, 12, 14

The Homestay Bed and Breakfast

517 Richmond Road, 23185
(804) 229-7468 information
(800) 836-7468 reservations

Cozy and convenient. Enjoy the comfort of a lovely Colonial Revival home, furnished with turn-of-the-century family antiques and country charm. It is only four blocks to Colonial Williamsburg, and just minutes away from Jamestown, Yorktown, and other local attractions. Adjacent to the College of William and Mary. A full break-

fast featuring homemade breads and a delicious hot dish is served in the formal dining room. Complimentary bicycles available. Children ten and older welcome.

Hosts: Barbara and Jim Thomassen
Rooms: 3 (PB) $75-85
Full Breakfast
Credit Cards: A, B
Notes: 2, 5, 7, 9, 12, 14

Hughes Guest Home Bed and Breakfast

106 Newport Avenue, 23185-4212
(804) 229-3493

Directly opposite the Williamsburg Lodge on Newport Avenue, the Hughes Guest Home has been in operation since 1947. A lovely two-minute stroll to Colonial Williamsburg's restored district, golfing facilities, and numerous dining facilities including the Colonial taverns. The College of William and Mary, Merchant's Square, and several Civil War museums are also within easy walking distance. The house is decorated lavishly with family antiques and the gardens may be appreciated from the screened porch or patio. Do come and enjoy the Southern hospitality.

Rooms: 3 (1 PB; 2 SB) $60
Continental Breakfast
Credit Cards: None
Notes: 2, 5, 7, 8, 12

Indian Springs Bed and Breakfast

330 Indian Springs Road, 23185
(800) 262-9165

In a quiet, wooded setting downtown, Indian Springs offers a delightful retreat for guests after a day of sightseeing. Charming suites include king-size feather beds, private baths, and private entrances. Veranda overlooking shady ravine is bird watchers' heaven. A hearty breakfast is always on the menu. Cottage with fireplace available. AAA rated three diamond.

NOTES: Credit cards accepted: A MasterCard; B Visa; C American Express; D Discover; E Diners Club; F Other; 2 Personal checks accepted; 3 Lunch available; 4 Dinner available; 5 Open all year; 6 Pets welcome;

Hosts: Kelly and Paul Supplee
Rooms: 4 (PB) $75-125
Full Breakfast
Credit Cards: A, B
Notes: 2, 5, 7, 8, 9, 10, 11, 12, 14

Newport House

710 South Henry Street, 23185-4113
(804) 229-1775

Newport House was designed in 1756 by Peter Harrison. It is furnished totally in the period, including four-poster canopy beds. Each room has a private bathroom. The full breakfast includes authentic Colonial-period recipes. Only five-minutes from the historic area (as close as one can get). The host is a former museum director and author of many books on Colonial history. Enjoy Colonial dancing in the ballroom every Tuesday evening.

Hosts: John and Cathy Millar
Rooms: 2 (PB) $105-120
Full Breakfast
Credit Cards: None
Notes: 2, 5, 8, 10, 12, 14

Newport House

Piney Grove at Southall's Plantation

P.O. Box 1359, 23187-1359
(804) 829-2480

Piney Grove is only 20 miles west of Williamsburg in the James River plantation country, among working farms, country stores, and historic churches. The elegant accommodations at this National Register of Historic Places property are in two restored antebellum homes (1800 and 1857). Guests are welcome to enjoy the parlor-library, pool, nature trail, farm animals, or a game of croquet or badminton. Upon arrival, guests are served mint juleps and Virginia wine. Restaurants nearby.

Hosts: Brian, Cindy, Joan, and Joseph Gordineer
Rooms: 5 (PB) $125-150
Full Breakfast
Credit Cards: None
Notes: 2, 5, 7, 8, 9, 11, 12, 14

War Hill Inn

4560 Long Hill Road, 23188
(804) 565-0248; (800) 743-0248

This replica of an 18th-century home sits on a 32-acre farm three miles off Route 60. Close to the College of William and Mary, Colonial Williamsburg, Busch Gardens, and shopping outlets. Seven antique-furnished guest rooms with private baths. Cable TV. Country breakfast.

Hosts: Shirley, Bill, Cherie, and Will Lee
Rooms: 7 (PB) $70-95
Suites: 2
Cottage: 1 (PB) $110
Full Breakfast
Credit Cards: A, B
Notes: 2, 5, 7, 8, 9, 10, 11, 12, 14

Williamsburg Manor Bed and Breakfast

600 Richmond Road, 23185
(804) 220-8011; (800) 422-8011

This 1927 Georgian home was built during the reconstruction of historic Colonial Williamsburg. Recently restored to its original elegance and furnished with exquisite pieces including antiques and collectibles. Five well-appointed guest rooms with private bath, TV, and central air conditioning. Guests are treated to a lavish fireside breakfast prepared by the executive chef. Home is available for weddings, private

7 No smoking; 8 Children welcome; 9 Social drinking allowed; 10 Tennis nearby; 11 Swimming nearby;
12 Golf nearby; 13 Skiing nearby; 14 May be booked through a travel agent.

parties, dinners, and meetings. Ideal location within walking distance of the historic area. On-site parking. Off season rates available.

Host: Laura Macknight
Rooms: 5 (PB) $90-150
Full Breakfast
Credit Cards: None
Notes: 2, 4, 5, 9, 10, 11, 12, 14

Williamsburg Manor

Williamsburg Sampler Bed and Breakfast

922 Jamestown Road, 23185
(804) 253-0398; (800) 722-1169

This elegant plantation-style six-bedroom brick Colonial is richly furnished with antiques, pewter, and samplers. Lovely rooms and suites with four-poster king- and queen-size beds, plus fireplaces, wet bar, and private baths. "Skip-lunch" breakfast. Internationally known as a favorite for honeymoons, anniversaries, or romantic getaways. The hosts return guests to an era when hospitality was a matter of pride and fine living was an art. Close to all major attractions. AAA-rated three diamonds. Voted 1995 Inn of the Year. Appeared on *CBS This Morning*.

Hosts: Helen and Ike Sisane
Rooms: 4 (PB) $90-130
Suites: 2 (PB)
Full Breakfast
Credit Cards: A, B
Notes: 2, 5, 7, 9, 10, 11, 12, 14

WILLIS WHARF

Amanda's Bed and Breakfast

1428 Park Avenue, Baltimore, MD 21217-4230
(410) 225-0001; (800) 899-7533
FAX (410) 728-8957

145. Eighty-year-old country farmhouse with wraparound porch and gazebo by a stream. Near freshwater pond, bird watching, photographic scenes, and guided tours. Amenities include outside swings, hammock, play gym, and bicycles. Relaxed family atmosphere. Four rooms with shared and private baths. Full breakfast. $60-75.

WINCHESTER

Blue Ridge Bed and Breakfast

Route 2, Box 3895, Berryville, 22611
(703) 955-1246; (800) 296-1246

A. In urban Winchester, this lovely Dutch Colonial reproduction filled with Oriental antiques from all over the world is just seconds from I-81 and Shenandoah University. Easy drive to northern entrance of Skyline Drive. Outstanding cuisine and unique antique shops. Noted for delicious country breakfasts. Less than an acre of land is lushly decorated with gorgeous gardens. $75.

WOODSTOCK

Azalea House

551 South Main Street, 22664
(703) 459-3500

The Azalea House dates back 100 years when it was built in the Victorian tradition and used as a church manse. The guest rooms are pleasing and comfortable, with antique furnishings and mountain views. Situated in the rolling hills of the Shenandoah Valley near fine restaurants, vineyards, shops, caverns, Civil War sites, hiking, and fishing. A great place to relax!

NOTES: Credit cards accepted: A MasterCard; B Visa; C American Express; D Discover; E Diners Club; F Other; 2 Personal checks accepted; 3 Lunch available; 4 Dinner available; 5 Open all year; 6 Pets welcome;

Hosts: Margaret and Price McDonald
Rooms: 3 (PB) $50-70
Full Breakfast
Credit Cards: A, B, C
Notes: 2, 5, 9, 10, 11, 12, 13

Azalea House

Blue Ridge Bed and Breakfast

Route 2, Box 3895, Berryville, 22611
(703) 955-1246; (800) 296-1246

A. Quaint turn-of-the-century house built in 1885 offers casual country hospitality, many games, hiking, cycling, and antiquing. Close to military academy, Skyline Drive, and skiing. $45-60.

B. Lovely home in quaint town is on the National Register of Historic Places. Built in 1840, log house was the toll gate house. Has 21 boxwoods and over 1,000 spring bulbs. Furnished with New England antiques. $45-55.

C. Gorgeous mansion built in 1892 filled with antiques and hand-stenciled rooms. Hundreds of azaleas. In-ground swimming pool. $45-65

D. Beautiful farmhouse on 17 acres built in the 1880s. Completely refurbished and has huge deck overlooking Blue Ridge Mountains. Hosts welcome guests to share traditional Jewish Sabbath meals and customs. $40-55.

The Inn at Narrow Passage

US 11 South, P.O. Box 608, 22664
(703) 459-8000

Historic log inn with five acres on the Shenandoah River. Colonial-style rooms, most with private baths and working fireplaces. Once the site of Indian attacks and Stonewall Jackson's headquarters, it is now a cozy spot in winter with large fireplaces in the common living and dining rooms. In spring and summer, fishing and rafting are at the back door. Fall brings the foliage festivals and hiking in the national forest a few miles away. Nearby are vineyards, caverns, historic sites, and fine restaurants. Washington, D.C., is 90 miles away.

Hosts: Ellen and Ed Markel
Rooms: 12 (10 PB; 2 SB) $85-110
Full Breakfast
Credit Cards: A, B
Notes: 2, 5, 8, 9, 10, 11, 12, 13, 14

WOOLWINE

Mountain Rose Bed and Breakfast

Route 1, Box 280, 24185
(703) 930-1057

This turn-of-the-century Victorian inn can be found in the shadow of the Blue Ridge Mountains. Five guest rooms offering private baths, air conditioning, and antique manteled fireplaces. Just miles from the Blue Ridge Parkway, the inn sits on 100 acres of forested hills, is fronted by a stocked trout stream, and offers a swimming pool and six porches.

Hosts: Hermien and Maarten Ankersmit
Rooms: 5 (PB) $65-70
Full Breakfast
Credit Cards: A, B
Notes: 2, 5, 8, 9, 11, 12, 14

7 No smoking; 8 Children welcome; 9 Social drinking allowed; 10 Tennis nearby; 11 Swimming nearby; 12 Golf nearby; 13 Skiing nearby; 14 May be booked through a travel agent.

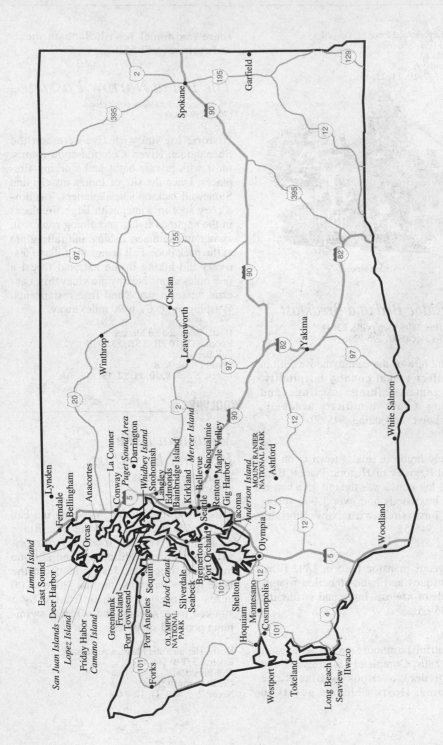

Washington

Washington

ANACORTES

Albatross Bed and Breakfast

5708 Kingsway West, 98221
(360) 293-0677; (800) 622-8864

Across from the Skyline Marina, this 1927 Cape Cod-style home features delicious full breakfasts, king- and queen-size beds, private baths, fine art, antiques, and island views. The marina offers charter boats, a deli, and fine dining. Nearby are the Washington Park and ferries to the San Juan Islands and Victoria, British Columbia. Sightseeing cruises aboard host's 46-foot sailboat are available. AAA approved.

Hosts: Barbie and Ken
Rooms: 4 (PB) $75-95
Full Breakfast
Credit Cards: A, B, C
Notes: 2, 5, 7, 9, 10, 11, 12, 13, 14

Channel House Bed and Breakfast

2902 Oakes Avenue, 98221
(360) 293-9382; (800) 238-4353

A classic island home built in 1902, the Channel House offers large, comfortable rooms, two with fireplaces, and lovely water and island views. The outdoor hot tub is a treat after a busy day of hiking or biking on the islands. Pat's oatmeal-raisin cookies are baked fresh every day. Anacortes is the beginning of the San Juan Islands and

Channel House

Sydney, British Columbia, ferry routes, and a center for chartering sail- and power boats for wonderful vacation trips.

Hosts: Dennis and Patricia McIntyre
Rooms: 6 (PB) $69-95
Full Breakfast
Credit Cards: A, B, C, D
Notes: 2, 5, 7, 9, 12, 14

Hasty Pudding House Bed and Breakfast

1312 Eighth Street, 98221
(360) 293-5773; (800) 368-5588

Celebrate romance in this delightful 1913 heritage home. A wonderful example of Craftsman-style architecture, this home is filled with Victorian antiques, fresh flowers, window seats, and wonderful private rooms, all with turn-of-the-century charm and comfort guests will enjoy. Snuggle in king-size, queen-size, and twin top-of-the-line beds that Grandmother would envy. Melinda's luscious breakfasts and table setting will begin this Anacortes adventure each day of guests' stay.

Hosts: Mikel and Melinda Hasty
Rooms: 4 (2 PB; 2 SB) $65-85
Full Breakfast
Credit Cards: A, B, C, D
Notes: 2, 5, 9, 10, 11, 12, 13, 14

A Pacific Reservation Service

701 Northwest 60th Street, Seattle, 98107
(206) 784-0539

Anacortes. This restored Victorian turn-of-the-century home features fine antiques, Oriental carpets, a library, colorful flower gardens, three fireplaces, and an outdoor hot tub. Wonderful views of Puget Sound can be seen from two of the guest rooms and the shared bathrooms. Intimate in size with warm hospitality. $69-125.

Sunset Beach Bed and Breakfast

100 Sunset Beach, 98221
(360) 293-5428; (800) 359-3448

On the exciting Rosario Strait overlooking seven San Juan iIslands, this bed and breakfast invites guests to enjoy the water scenery that includes water birds, deer, fishing boats, and more. Take a stroll and enjoy the scenic view of the Olympic Mountains, or amble down the beach. Close to the ferry, marina, and excellent restaurants, and adjacent to Washington Park. Full breakfasts, queen-size beds, and private bath. Hot tub on request.

Hosts: Joann and Hal Harker
Rooms: 3 (1 PB; 2 SB) $69-79
Full Breakfast
Credit Cards: A, B, D
Notes: 2, 5, 7, 9, 10, 11, 12, 13, 14

ANDERSON ISLAND

The Inn at Burg's Landing

8808 Villa Beach Road, 98303
(206) 884-9185; (206) 488-8682

Catch the ferry from Steilacoom to stay at this contemporary log homestead built in 1987. It offers spectacular views of Mount Rainier, Puget Sound, and Cascade Mountains and is ten miles south of Tacoma off I-5. Choose from three guest rooms, including the master bedroom with a queen-size "log" bed with skylight above and private whirlpool bath. The inn has a private beach. Collect seashells and agates, swim in one of the two freshwater lakes nearby, or enjoy a game of tennis or golf. Tour the scenic island by bicycle or on foot and watch for sailboats and deer. Relax in the hot tub. Families are welcome.

Hosts: Ken and Annie Burg
Rooms: 3 (2 PB; 1 SB) $65-90
Full Breakfast
Credit Cards: A, B
Notes: 2, 5, 7, 8, 9, 10, 11, 12, 13

ASHFORD

Growly Bear Bed and Breakfast

37311 State Road 706, P.O. Box 103, 98304
(800) 700-2339

Experience a bit of history and enjoy a mountain stay at a rustic homestead house built in 1890. Hike in nearby Mount Rainier National Park. Dine at unique restaurants within walking distance of guests' room. Be lulled to sleep by the whispering sounds of Goat Creek just outside the window. Awake in the morning to the sight of tall evergreen trees and the early morning melodies of the

Growly Bear

mountain birds. Indulge in a basket of warm scrumptuous pastries from nearby Sweet Peaks Bakery.

Host: Susan Jenny
Rooms: 2 (1 PB; 1 SB) $70-110
Full Breakfast
Credit Cards: A, B, C
Notes: 2, 5, 9, 13, 14

Mount Meadows Inn Bed and Breakfast

28912 State Road 706 East, 98304
(360) 569-2788

Gracious hospitality, unique, quiet country atmosphere. This restored 1910 sawmill superintendent house is a museum for an extensive model railroad collection and logging memorabilia. Relax on ten acres, enjoying nature trails, evening campfires, s'mores, and Big Foot stories. All rooms are private bath. Full country breakfast is cooked on an 1889 cook stove. Furnished with antiques and a player piano for guests' use, VCR and movies in the living room by the fireplace. Mount Rainier National Park and Mount Rainier Scenic Railroad are only six miles away offering all-season recreation. Just two hours' drive to Seattle. Two-night minimum stay during holidays. Inquire about accommodations for pets. Inquire about the age of children welcome.

Host: Chad Darrah
Rooms: 5 (PB) $65-95
Full Breakfast
Credit Cards: A, B
Notes: 2, 5, 7, 9, 11, 12, 13, 14

BAINBRIDGE ISLAND

Bombay House

8490 Beck Road, 98110
(206) 842-3926; (800) 598-3926

The Bombay House is a spectacular 35-minute ferry ride from downtown Seattle. The house was built in 1907 and sits high on a hillside in the country overlooking Rich Passage. Widow's walk; rustic, rough-cedar

Bombay House

gazebo; masses of gardens exploding with seasonal color. Watch the ferry pass and see the lights of Bremerton in the distance. Just a few blocks from the beach, a country theater, and fine dining. A great spot for the Seattle business traveler or vacationer.

Hosts: Bunny Cameron and Roger Kanchuk
Rooms: 5 (3 PB; 2 SB) $55-125
Continental Breakfast
Credit Cards: A, B, C
Notes: 2, 5, 7, 9, 10, 11, 12, 14

A Pacific Reservation Service

701 Northwest 60th Street, Seattle, 98107
(206) 784-0539

Bainbridge Island-1. This special country inn invites guests to sit on the wraparound porch, enjoy the beautiful flower gardens, the gazebo, or snuggle up by the crackling fire in the fireplace. A stay here will renew and refresh spirits. Built for a ship's captain, this lovely bed and breakfast offers nice views over the water, three bedrooms with private baths, and two bedrooms that share a bath. Legendary country breakfast. $65-95.

Bainbridge Island-2. This Bainbridge accommodation is on a beautifully landscaped acre enclosed by a forest on both sides. Guests can relax on comfortable wicker furniture and look out at the rose garden after a day of sightseeing or exploration.

7 No smoking; 8 Children welcome; 9 Social drinking allowed; 10 Tennis nearby; 11 Swimming nearby; 12 Golf nearby; 13 Skiing nearby; 14 May be booked through a travel agent.

Perfect for honeymooners and couples. The cookie jar here is always deep, a new snack is served on the table next to the sofa every day, and the bedroom has a queen-size bed with a wonderful new mattress and a private bath. $85.

BELLEVUE

Petersen Bed and Breakfast

10228 Southeast Eighth, 98004
(206) 454-9334

Petersen Bed and Breakfast is in a well-established neighborhood five minutes from the Bellevue Shopping Square and 20 minutes from Seattle. It offers two rooms, one with a queen-size waterbed, and a spa on the deck off the atrium kitchen. Home-style breakfast.

Hosts: Eunice and Carl Petersen
Rooms: 2 (SB) $50-55
Full Breakfast
Credit Cards: None
Notes: 5, 8

BELLINGHAM

Bed and Breakfast Guild of Whatcom County

2610 Eldridge Avenue, 98225
(206) 676-4560

1. This elegant 1897 Queen Anne has a breathtaking sweeping view of the bay and islands. Near the university. Ten guest rooms. Enjoy a sumptuous breakfast each morning. $55-79.

2. This charming home, surrounded by giant trees, overlooks sparkling Lake Whatcom. Guest rooms are spacious, comfortable, and gaily decorated. Homemade breakfasts are an adventure. Smoking porch, RV parking, private baths, and

queen-size feather beds. Home away from home. $90-110.

4. Charming, elegant, turn-of-the-century home with magnificent sunset views overlooking Bellingham Bay. Central location on two and one-half acres of mature gardens. Rose Room suite and Blue Room double are romantically decorated. Both rooms have private baths. Deliciously generous breakfasts. Hosts, Susan and Ernie, welcome guests. $50-130.

6. Victorian home in historic neighborhood overlooking bay and islands. Friendly hosts, Van and Barbara, offer local insights and a game of pool in the parlor. Guest rooms feature private baths and family heirlooms. Breakfast will help guests start the day with a smile. $45-70.

11. Nestled on 65 beautiful secluded acres. Enjoy wilderness trails, full breakfast, six luxurious guest rooms, and conference space. Llama breeding ranch and weekend retreat center. A central location for snow skiing, shopping, dining, bicycling, hiking, and boating activities. Visa and MasterCard accepted. $75-125.

13. This modern A-frame has two suites plus a honeymoon cottage set amid tall evergreens overlooking Lake Whatcom. All the amenities: hot tub, Jacuzzi, tennis courts, and gourmet breakfast. $100-170.

North Garden Inn

1014 North Garden, 98225
(800) 922-6414 (U.S.); (800) 367-1676 (Canada)

North Garden Inn is a Queen Anne Victorian on the National Register of Historic Places. Several of the guest rooms have splendid views of Bellingham Bay. The inn boasts two grand pianos for the enjoyment

North Garden Inn

of the guests. The inn is within walking distance to fine dining, shopping, and Western Washington University.

Hosts: Barb and Frank De Freytas
Rooms: 10 (8 PB; 2 SB) $54-79
Full Breakfast
Credit Cards: A, B, D
Notes: 2, 5, 7, 8, 9, 10, 11, 12, 13, 14

A Pacific Reservation Service

701 Northwest 60th Street, Seattle, 98107
(206) 784-0539

Bellingham. Decorated with stained glass and etchings crafted by the hostess, this restored Victorian overlooking the bay is a great spot for a special getaway. The two guest rooms have private baths. The hosts will be more than happy to give advice to sightseers if needed. Guests are assured a warm, friendly welcome at this bed and breakfast. $79.

Schnauzer Crossing

4421 Lakeway Drive, 98226
(360) 733-0055; (800) 562-2808;
FAX (360) 734-2808

Schnauzer Crossing is a luxury bed and breakfast between Seattle and Vancouver, British Columbia. Enjoy this destination bed and breakfast, with its lakeside ambience, outdoor

hot tub, and its master suite with fireplace and Jacuzzi. There is also a new cottage available for guests to stay in. Sail in the beautiful San Juan Islands or climb 10,000-foot Mount Baker. Experience the many wonders of Washington State!

Hosts: Vermont and Donna McAllister
Rooms: 3 (PB) $110-180
Full Breakfast
Credit Cards: A, B, D
Notes: 2, 5, 7, 8, 9, 10, 11, 12, 13

BREMERTON

Willcox House

2390 Tekiu Road, Northwest, 98312
(360) 830-4492

Overlooking Hood Canal and the Olympic Mountains is a special place where time stands still. Life is paced by the slow, steady hand of nature. It is quiet enough to hear the birds sing. Deer amble through the gardens. Saltwater beaches and good books wait for quiet companions. Willcox House is an elegant 10,000-square-foot mansion built in 1936 with landscaped grounds, private pier, and beach. There are five guest rooms, all with private baths and magnificent views of Hood Canal and Olympic Mountains.

Hosts: Cecilia and Phillip Hughes
Rooms: 5 (PB) $115-175
Full Breakfast
Credit Cards: A, B
Notes: 2, 3, 4, 5, 7, 9, 14

Willcox House

---

7 No smoking; 8 Children welcome; 9 Social drinking allowed; 10 Tennis nearby; 11 Swimming nearby; 12 Golf nearby; 13 Skiing nearby; 14 May be booked through a travel agent.

CAMANO ISLAND

Willcox House Bed and Breakfast

1462 Larkspur Lane, 98292
(206) 629-4746

Built in 1985, this two-story house with a wraparound covered porch is furnished with family antiques and named for an early 1900s children's illustrator, Jessie Willcox Smith. The rooms overlook the Puget Sound where snow geese and trumpet swans migrate each fall. Mount Baker looms in the distance. Gourmet breakfasts are served in a peaceful country setting. The house is on an island one hour north of Seattle connected by bridge to the mainland, close to picturesque towns and Canada.

Host: Sharon Boulanger
Rooms: 4 (PB) $65-75
Full Breakfast
Credit Cards: A, B, D
Notes: 2, 5, 8, 9, 10, 11, 12, 13

CHELAN

The Brick House Inn

304 Wapato Avenue, 98816
(509) 682-2233; (800) 799-2332

Built in 1910, this three-story Victorian home boasts casual elegance, blending the old with the new. Stress-free relaxation in the heart of the city entices both the young and the young-at-heart! The wraparound porch and ample lawn invite outdoor comfort all year round. Group rates available. The house is completely nonsmoking inside. Whether a party of two or twelve, the hosts go out of their way to make guests' stay one of a kind!

Hosts: Mike, Debbie, and Amy Mack
Rooms: 6 (1 PB; 5 SB) $63-80
Continental Breakfast
Credit Cards: A, B, D
Notes: 2, 5, 7, 9, 10, 11, 12, 13, 14

Cooney Mansion

COSMOPOLIS

Cooney Mansion

1705 Fifth Street, 98537
(360) 533-0602

This historically registered Arts and Crafts-style lumber baron's retreat features original furniture and private baths. Relax in the Jacuzzi, exercise room, or sauna. Play golf, tennis, or curl up with a book from the extensive library. Sit in the rose garden or amble through Mill Creek Park with its bridges and waterfalls. The Cooney Mansion exudes an old-fashioned warmth and relaxed atmosphere. Two minutes' drive from Aberdeen and Hoquiam. The ballroom is perfect for retreats and weddings. Close to beaches, museums, antique shops, and historic seaport. Swedish massage available by reservation.

Hosts: Judi and Jim Lohr
Rooms: 8 (5 PB; 3 SB) $55-115
Full Breakfast
Credit Cards: A, B, C, D, E
Notes: 5, 7, 9, 10, 12

DARRINGTON

Hemlock Hills Bed and Breakfast

612 Stillaguamish, P.O. Box 491, 98241
(360) 436-1274; (800) 520-1584

Hemlock Hills is a place to share warmth, comfort, and friendship. The hosts' home is in Darrington with views of the surrounding mountains. This is a place to enjoy country living. Hemlock Hills has inviting rooms filled with antiques, country furnishings, and quilts. Relax in the parlor or spend time in the game room. Hosts offer two double occupancies with shared bath and serve a full country breakfast. Close to hiking, bicycling, and mountain car tours. Restaurants within walking distance. Golf is 20 miles away.

Hosts: Dale and Elaine Hamlin
Rooms: 2 (SB) $50
Full Breakfast
Credit Cards: None
Notes: 2, 5, 7, 8, 9, 10, 13, 14

DEER HARBOR (ORCAS ISLAND)

Palmer's Chart House

Box 51, 98243
(360) 376-4231

The first bed and breakfast on Orcas Island (since 1975) with a magnificent water view. The 33-foot private yacht *Amante* is available for a minimal fee with Skipper Don. Low-key, private, personal attention makes this bed and breakfast unique and attractive. Well-traveled hosts speak Spanish. Children over ten welcome.

Hosts: Majean and Donald Palmer
Rooms: 2 (PB) $45-60
Full Breakfast
Credit Cards: None
Notes: 2, 5, 9, 10, 11, 12, 14

Palmer's Chart House

EASTSOUND (ORCAS ISLAND)

Kangaroo House

Box 334, 98245
(360) 376-2175

A 1907 Craftsman-style home on Orcas Island, gem of the San Juans. Period furnishings, large guest sitting room with stone fireplace, extensive lawns, flower gardens, and hot tub. Smashing gourmet breakfasts. Walk to village shops, galleries, and restaurants. Panoramic view of the islands from Moran State Park. Special winter rates.

Hosts: Jan and Mike Russillo
Rooms: 5 (2 PB; 3 SB) $70-110
Full Breakfast
Credit Cards: A, B
Notes: 2, 5, 7, 8, 9, 10, 11, 12, 14

Turtleback Farm Inn

Route 1, Box 650 (Crow Valley Road), 98243
(206) 376-4914

This meticulously restored farmhouse has been described as a "marvel of bed and breakfastmanship decorated with country finesse and a sophisticated sense of the right antiques." Seven bedrooms with private baths. Award-winning breakfasts. Inquire about accommodations for children.

Hosts: William and Susan Fletcher
Rooms: 7 (PB) $80-160
Full Breakfast
Credit Cards: A, B
Notes: 2, 5, 7, 9, 10, 11, 12, 14

EDMONDS

Harrison House

210 Sunset Avenue, 98020
(206) 776-4748

New waterfront home with sweeping view of Puget Sound and the Olympic Mountains. Many fine restaurants within walking distance. Spacious rooms have private bath, private deck, TV, wet bar, telephone, and king-size bed. University of Washington is nearby.

Hosts: Jody and Harve Harrison
Rooms: 2 (PB) $45-65
Continental Breakfast
Credit Cards: None
Notes: 2, 5, 7, 9, 10, 11, 12, 13

FERNDALE

Bed and Breakfast Guild of Whatcom County

2610 Eldridge Avenue, Bellingham 98225
(206) 676-4560

2. Completely restored Victorian close to golfing, mountains, water, and shopping. Only 12 miles to Canadian border. Four lovely rooms with private baths. $60-85.

FORKS

Miller Tree Inn

654 East Division Street, P.O. Box 953, 98331
(360) 374-6806

Wonderful 1917 country homestead on three acres. Twelve miles from Pacific beaches, hot rain forest, and five fish-filled rivers. Breakfast is served 7:30-9:00 AM, consisting of fresh fruit, cereal, and pastry bar followed by cooked-to-order entrée. Two living rooms, hot tub, and reasonable rates. For the fisherman: guide referrals, trailer shuttles, pre-dawn breakfasts (October through May), secure off-road parking, and river reports. AAA diamond, eight years "best places." Pets welcome, but must be leashed. Children over eight welcome.

Hosts: Ted and Prue Miller
Rooms: 6 (3 PB; 3 SB) $55-75
Full Breakfast
Credit Cards: A, B
Notes: 2, 5, 7, 9, 10, 14

FREELAND

Cliff House

5440 Windmill Road, 98249
(360) 331-1566

On Whidbey Island, a setting so unique there is nothing anywhere quite like Cliff House. In a private world of luxury, this stunning home is the guests' alone. Secluded in a forest on the edge of Puget Sound, the views are breathtaking. Stone fireplace, spa, and miles of driftwood beach. King-size feather bed and gourmet kitchen. Also the snug and enchanting Seacliff Cottage. Two-night minimum stay required.

Hosts: Peggy Moore and Walter O'Toole
Rooms: 2 (PB) $155-310
Continental Breakfast
Credit Cards: none
Notes: 2, 5, 7, 9, 11, 12

FRIDAY HARBOR

Hillside House Bed and Breakfast

365 Carter Avenue, 98250
(206) 378-4730; (800) 232-4730

Hillside House is a large contemporary home set among fir and pine trees on the side of a hill overlooking pastures, the harbor entrance, and Mount Baker, less than a half-mile from the center of town. The hosts offer seven distinctive guest rooms with private baths, cozy window seats, and a variety of sleeping arrangements. Homemade cookies, coffee, teas, and juices are always within easy reach. Seasonal rates. Smoking permitted outside only. Children over ten welcome.

Hosts: Dick and Cathy Robinson
Rooms: 7 (PB) $80-155
Full Breakfast
Credit Cards: A, B, C, D
Notes: 2, 5, 10, 11, 12, 14

Tower House Bed and Breakfast

1230 Little Road, 98250
(360) 378-5464

This Queen Anne-style home on ten acres overlooks the San Juan Valley. Two suites offer a blend of Victorian spirit and contemporary comfort. Retreat to the library with the sunroom or watch sunsets through stained glass from the window seat of the Tower Room. Cherished old linens, china, and crystal recall the ceremony of the past as guests enjoy breakfast. Play the piano or view a movie by the fire in the paneled parlor. Vegan breakfast (no animal products) available with advance notice.

Host: Chris and Joe Luma
Rooms: 2 (PB) $90-110
Full Breakfast
Credit Cards: A, B, C, D
Notes: 2, 5, 7, 9, 10, 11, 12, 14

Tucker House Bed and Breakfast with Cottages

260 B Street, 98250
(206) 378-2783; (800) 965-0123
FAX (206) 378-6437

A Victorian home, circa 1898, with two upstairs bedrooms, queen-size beds, TV/VCR units, and a shared bath. The property is surrounded with flowers, stately trees, and a white picket fence. The outside hot tub is available to all guests. There are three cottages on the property, each having a queen-size bed, private bath, woodstove, TV, and kitchenette, with room for additional guests. Two blocks from the ferry terminal and the heart of picturesque Friday Harbor. Tennis, swimming, and golf nearby. Small dogs welcome. Children welcome in the cottages.

Hosts: Skip and Annette Metzger
Rooms: 5 (3 PB; 2 SB) $75-135
Full Breakfast
Credit Cards: A, B, C, D
Notes: 2, 5, 7, 9, 10, 11, 12, 14

Wharfside Bed and Breakfast on Board the Jacquelyn

P.O. Box 1212, 98250
(206) 378-5661

A romantic winter retreat or challenging summer adventure—aboard the *Jacquelyn,* the West Coast's original floating bed and breakfast. This elegantly restored 60-foot traditional sailing vessel offers two spacious, private guest staterooms with private half-baths, a main salon replete with antiques, art, and artifacts, as well as a wood-burning stove for cozy evenings. Bask on deck while enjoying a sumptuous and hearty breakfast. Take a spin in the rowing gig.

Hosts: Clyde and Bette Rice
Rooms: 2 (SB) $80-85
Full Breakfast
Credit Cards: A, B
Notes: 2, 5, 6, 8, 9, 10, 11, 12, 14

GARFIELD

A Pacific Reservation Service

701 Northwest 60th Street, Seattle, 98107
(206) 784-0539

Garfield. This beautiful guest home was built as a Classical Revival house in 1898 and offers two comfortable guest rooms, one with a double bed and the other with two twin beds. There is a large shared bathroom with a huge claw-foot soaking tub. The delicious and hearty full breakfast might include fresh juices, flapjacks prepared with local organic red wheat, homemade jams, real maple syrup, home-baked breads, and other delights that are prepared on a cozy old-fashioned wood-burning stove. $75.

---

7 No smoking; 8 Children welcome; 9 Social drinking allowed; 10 Tennis nearby; 11 Swimming nearby; 12 Golf nearby; 13 Skiing nearby; 14 May be booked through a travel agent.

GIG HARBOR

A Pacific Reservation Service

701 Northwest 60th Street, Seattle, 98107
(206) 784-0539

Orchard. This lovely bed and breakfast was built in 1984 on three acres of rural land between Gig Harbor and Bremerton, 90 minutes from Seattle. The large guest room features a double bed and a private bath, and welcomes guests to relax in the two-person whirlpool tub. Views of Mount Rainier can be seen from the living and dining rooms. What a perfect spot for a quiet country getaway! $75.

Guest House Cottages

GREENBANK

Guest House Cottages

3366 South Highway 525, Whidbey Island, 98253
(360) 678-3115

A couple's romantic retreat, this AAA four-diamond-rated bed and breakfast hideaway offers six storybook cottages and one log mansion in cozy settings on 25 acres. Fireplaces, VCRs, more than 400 complimentary movies, in-room Jacuzzis, kitchens, feather beds, country antiques, and wildlife pond are all amenities guests can enjoy. Continental plus breakfast. Pool and spa. Privacy, peace, and pampering. Voted

Best Place to Kiss in the Northwest. Near winery. Special midweek rates October 31 through March 15. Minimum-stay requirements for weekends and holidays.

Hosts: Don and Mary Jane Creger
Rooms: 6 (PB) $140-285
Continental Breakfast
Credit Cards: A, B, C, D
Notes: 2, 5, 9, 11, 12, 14

HOOD CANAL

A Pacific Reservation Service

701 Northwest 60th Street, Seattle, 98107
(206) 784-0539

Hood Canal Waterfront Victorian. This bed and breakfast offers three guest rooms, a charming atmosphere of genteel living, and sloping grounds leading to the beach. Enjoy a home-cooked breakfast and a relaxed, friendly environment just right for getaways. $65.

Waterfront Mansion Hood Canal. Experience the grandeur of a bygone time and the opulence of the rich and famous in the 1930s at this premier bed and breakfast inn. Built in 1936, this inn is on several acres of waterfront property and features a combination of Art Deco and the architecture of northern China, seasoned with Northwestern flair. There are five guest rooms with private baths, towel warmers, clothes steamers, down comforters, and hair dryers. $105-165.

HOQUIAM

A Pacific Reservation Service

701 Northwest 60th Street, Seattle, 98107
(206) 784-0539

HO-1. A historic 20-room mansion is offered to guests on the southern tip of the

Olympic Peninsula and only two hours from Seattle and minutes to the Pacific Ocean. The mansion is filled with a fascinating array of antiques. The five guest bedrooms each have queen-size beds and they share three baths. A full and delicious breakfast is served in the large, formal dining room. Recommended by the *Los Angeles Times*. $85.

ILWACO

Chick-a-Dee Inn at Ilwaco

120 Williams Street NE, 98624-0922
(360) 642-8686 (phone and FAX)

The inn, a 1928 New England/Georgian-style church lovingly transformed into a gracious bed and breakfast with a 120-seat wedding chapel. Cozy guest rooms nestled under eaves and dormers. Generous and informal parlor with library. Eclectically furnished, some old, some new, some antiques, and country touches. Occupies hillside site overlooking historic port town where the Columbia River meets the ocean. Nearby are 28 miles of sandy beach, working lighthouses, museums, and nationally acclaimed restaurants.

Host: Chick and Delaine Hinkle
Rooms: 10 (8 PB; 2 SB) $55-150
Full Breakfast
Credit Cards: A, B
Notes: 2, 3, 4, 5, 7, 8, 9, 10, 11, 12, 14

KIRKLAND

Shumway Mansion

11410 99th Place Northeast, 98033
(206) 823-2303

Overlook Lake Washington from this award-winning 23-room mansion dating from 1909. Eight individually decorated guest rooms with private baths. Variety-filled breakfast. Complimentary use of athletic club. Short distance to all forms of shopping; 20 minutes to downtown Seattle.

Water and snow recreation close at hand. Children over 12 welcome.

Hosts: Richard and Salli Harris
Rooms: 8 (PB) $65-95
Full Breakfast
Credit Cards: A, B, C
Notes: 2, 5, 7, 9, 10, 11, 12, 13, 14

LA CONNER

Benson Farmstead

1009 Avon-Allen Road, Bow, 98232
(206) 757-0578

The Benson Farmstead is a 1914 restored 17-room farmhouse filled with antiques, quilts, and a cozy decor. It is surrounded by flower gardens and farmland and is just off I-5 near La Conner, Burlington, Chuckanut Drive, and the tulip fields. Third-generation Skagit Valley farmers, Jerry and Sharon are friendly hosts who serve a full country breakfast every morning and dessert and coffee in the evening.

Hosts: Jerry and Sharon Benson
Rooms: 4 (2 PB; 2 SB) $65-75
Full Breakfast
Credit Cards: A, B
Notes: 2, 5, 7, 8, 9, 10, 11, 12, 13, 14

A Pacific Reservation Service

701 Northwest 60th Street, Seattle, 98107
(206) 784-0539

LA-2. Guests can relax and enjoy themselves in this beautiful Victorian-style country inn. The hosts offer ten guest rooms with private baths, telephone, TV, and some with fireplaces and wonderful views. The honeymoon suite features a Jacuzzi. Guests are invited to enjoy the outdoor hot tub. $80.

Ridgeway Farm Bed and Breakfast

1292 McLean Road, P.O. Box 475, 98257
(360) 428-8068; (800) 428-8068

7 No smoking; 8 Children welcome; 9 Social drinking allowed; 10 Tennis nearby; 11 Swimming nearby; 12 Golf nearby; 13 Skiing nearby; 14 May be booked through a travel agent.

Ridgeway Farm Bed and Breakfast

The perfect getaway in the heart of the Skagit Valley tulip fields. Come enjoy the unique feeling of this 1928 brick Dutch Colonial farmhouse on a "ridgeway" out of the historic waterfront town of La Conner. Large windows offer an open, airy feeling, with views of the mountains and farms. Homemade desserts served by the fireplace in the evenings. Wake up to coffee, tea, or hot chocolate to sharpen the appetite for a hearty breakfast. Recently opened 1934 two-bedroom cottage for special privacy with three bathrooms. Lilacs, rhododendrons, azaleas, roses, and thousands of tulips and daffodils. Flat terrain will delight bicycle fans. The hosts can fly guests on a scenic flight to the San Juan Islands. Balloon flights can also be arranged.

Hosts: Louise and John Kelly
Rooms: 7 (4 PB; 3 SB) $75-125
Full Breakfast
Credit Cards: A, B, C, D
Notes: 2, 5, 7, 8, 9, 11, 12, 13, 14

The White Swan Guest House

1388 Moore Road, Mount Vernon, 98273
(360) 445-6805

The White Swan is a "storybook" farmhouse only six miles from the historic waterfront town of La Conner. Fine restaurants, great antiquing, and interesting shops are all available in Washington's favorite artist community. Just an hour north of Seattle and 90 miles south of Vancouver. Separate honeymoon cottage available.

Gardens seen in *Country Home* magazine. Two stars in *Northwest Best Places*.

Host: Peter Goldfarb
Rooms: 4 (1 PB; 3 SB) $65-75; Cottage: $125
Continental Breakfast
Credit Cards: A, B
Notes: 2, 5, 7, 9, 12, 14

LANGLEY

Eagles Nest Inn

3236 East Saratoga, 98260
(360) 221-5331

The inn's rural setting on Whidbey Island offers a sweeping view of Saratoga Passage and Mount Baker. Casual elegance and natural splendor abound. Relax and enjoy the large rooms, spa, library, and bottomless chocolate chip cookie jar. Write or call for brochure. Two-night minimum stay requirement for holiday weekends. Children over 12 welcome.

Hosts: Joanne and Jerry Lechner
Rooms: 4 (PB) $95-115
Full Breakfast
Credit Cards: A, B, D
Notes: 5, 10, 11, 12

Eagles Nest Inn

Log Castle

3273 East Saratoga Road, 98260
(360) 221-5483

On Whidbey Island, 30 miles north of Seattle. Log lodge on secluded beach. Big stone fireplace, turret bedrooms, panoramic views of Puget Sound and the Cascade Mountains. Norma's breakfast is a legend. Watch for bald eagles and orca whales from the widow's walk. Two-night minimum stay required for holidays.

Hosts: Senator Jack and Norma Metcalf
Rooms: 4 (PB) $80-105
Full Breakfast
Credit Cards: A, B, D
Notes: 2, 5, 7, 10, 11, 12, 14

Lone Lake Cottages and Breakfast

5206 South Bayview Road, 98260
(206) 321-5325

Whidbey's Shangri-la. Enjoy privacy in the waterfront cottages or in a sternwheel houseboat. All are decorated with touches of the Orient. View, fireplace, kitchen, TV/VCR, Jacuzzi, canoes, fishing, and bicycles.

Host: Dolores Meeks
Rooms: 3 (PB) $110
Continental Breakfast
Credit Cards: None
Notes: 2, 5, 7, 9, 10, 11, 12, 14

The Whidbey Inn

106 First Street, P.O. Box 156, 98260
(360) 221-7115

Perched on a bluff, this bed and breakfast offers a dramatic view of the Saratoga Passage waterway, the Cascade Mountains, and Camano Island from each room. When guests arrive, the host will greet them warmly and encourage them to take a moment and relax over a glass of sherry and an appetizer. Each of the rooms is decorated with antiques and offers a private bath with English amenities and Swiss chocolates on the pillows. The Whidbey Inn is a perfect setting for romance.

Host: Gretchen Bower
Rooms: 6 (PB) $95-150
Full Breakfast
Credit Cards: A, B, C
Notes: 2, 5, 7, 10

All Seasons River Inn

LEAVENWORTH

All Seasons River Inn Bed and Breakfast

P.O. Box 788, 8751 Icicle Road, 98826
(509) 548-1425; (800) 254-0555

A magical and enchanting place, the All Seasons River Inn is unique in that it was built as a bed and breakfast but offers each guest the comfortable and warm hospitality of home. Nestled in the evergreens overlooking the Wenatchee River, all of the guest rooms are spacious with antique decor, private baths, and riverfront decks. Some rooms are available with Jacuzzis and fireplaces. The hosts invite guests to enjoy an evening in the guest living room, game room, and TV room, or listen to the relaxing sounds of the water below the decks. Guests will awaken to a delicious hearty breakfast that will last them through the day. Hiking, biking, rafting, fishing, or cross-country skiing are all less than a mile from the door. Once guests have visited All Seasons River Inn, they want to return again and again!

Hosts: Kathy and Jeff Falconer
Rooms: 5 (PB) $95-125
Full Breakfast
Credit Cards: A, B
Notes: 2, 5, 9, 10, 11, 12, 13, 14

7 No smoking; 8 Children welcome; 9 Social drinking allowed; 10 Tennis nearby; 11 Swimming nearby; 12 Golf nearby; 13 Skiing nearby; 14 May be booked through a travel agent.

A Pacific Reservation Service

701 Northwest 60th Street, Seattle, 98107
(206) 784-0539

This peaceful country inn is in a town that has taken on a Bavarian atmosphere with German stores, shops, restaurants, and flowers everywhere. Enjoy the wonderful views, hot tub, pool, and the Continental breakfast. Some rooms have private baths. $65.

Pine River Ranch

19668 Highway 207, 98826
(509) 763-3959; (800) 669-3877

An area landmark since 1941, with its huge block barn and silo, the Pine River Ranch serenely sits in a beautiful valley against a backdrop of mountains and towering pines. The guest rooms and suites emphasize comfort and seclusion. Amenities include Jacuzzis, fireplaces, wet bars equipped with refrigerators, microwaves, and an espresso maker. Two outdoor hot tubs to assure privacy. One mile from golfing and water sports. Hike, stream fish, or cross-country ski on premises. Shop in the Bavarian village of Leavenworth or ski downhill at Stevens Pass.

Hosts: Michael and Mary Ann Zenk
Rooms: 6 (4 PB; 2 SB) $74-125
Full Breakfast
Credit Cards: A, B
Notes: 2, 5, 7, 9, 10, 11, 12, 13, 14

Pine River Ranch

Run of the River Bed and Breakfast

9308 East Leavenworth Road, P.O. Box 285, 98826
(509) 548-7171; (800) 288-6491

Imagine the quintessential Northwest log bed and breakfast inn. Spacious rooms feature private baths, hand-hewn log beds, and fluffy down comforters. Celebrate in a suite with your own heartwarming wood stove, jetted Jacuzzi surrounded by river rock, and a bird's eye loft to laze about with a favorite book. From the guests' rooms' log porch swing, view the Icicle River, surrounding bird refuge, and the Cascade peaks, appropriately named the Enchantments. To explore the Icicle Valley, get off the beaten path with hiking, biking, and driving guides written just for guests by the innkeepers, avid bikers and hikers. Take a spin on complimentary mountain bikes. A delicious hearty Northwest breakfast sets the day in motion! The inn is an ideal base for side trips to Winthrop, Lake Chelan, and Grand Coulee. Very quiet, relaxing, and smoke-free. The perfect spot for a special Northwest adventure.

Hosts: Monty and Karen Turner
Rooms: 5 (PB) $90-140
Full Breakfast
Credit Cards: A, B, C, D
Notes: 2, 5, 7, 9, 10, 11, 12, 13, 14

LONG BEACH

Boreas Bed and Breakfast

607 North Boulevard, P.O. Box 1344, 98631
(360) 642-8069

This 1920s beach house, remodeled in eclectic style, skillfully combines art and antiques with comfort and casualness. Oceanview bedrooms and spacious living rooms with stereo, musical instruments, and marble fireplace. The enclosed sun deck has a relaxing hot tub. Delicious full breakfast is served. Walk or bike to the boardwalk, shopping, and restaurants. Ten minutes to

NOTES: Credit cards accepted: A MasterCard; B Visa; C American Express; D Discover; E Diners Club; F Other; 2 Personal checks accepted; 3 Lunch available; 4 Dinner available; 5 Open all year; 6 Pets welcome;

beautiful state parks for hiking, kayaking, and the many other outdoor activities Washington has to offer.

Hosts: Sally Davis and Coleman White
Rooms: 4 (2 PB: 2 SB) $75-95
Full Breakfast
Credit Cards: A, B
Notes: 2, 5, 7, 8, 9, 10, 12, 14

A Pacific Reservation Service

701 Northwest 60th Street, Seattle, 98107
(206) 784-0539

LB-1. A three- to four-hour drive will take guests to this lovely but often undiscovered spot of the state where the Columbia River meets the Pacific Ocean. The best possible beachcombing, clam digging, salmon fishing, and relaxation can be found here. This historic inn offers 12 guest rooms that are furnished in antiques as a reminder of a gentler time. Five of the rooms have private baths. $85.

LOPEZ ISLAND

Aleck Bay Inn

Route 1, Box 1920, 98261
(360) 468-3535

The inn has seven acres bounded by the beaches and off-shore islands at the south end of Lopez Island. Enjoy a sun deck with hot tub overlooking the Strait of San Juan de Fuca. An absolute artist paradise. Full breakfast is served in the solarium beside the bay. All rooms have their own private bath, queen-size bed, Victorian canopies, floral linens, etc. Two rooms have a Jacuzzi tub. Guests may enjoy the TV/VCR, table tennis, billiards, piano, violin, and all kinds of games. Bike rental is available for guests.

Hosts: David and May
Rooms: 3 (PB) $85-139
Credit Cards: A, B, C, D, E
Notes: 2, 4, 5, 7, 9, 10, 12

Edenwild Inn

Box 271, 98261
(360) 468-3238

This elegant country inn in Lopez Village, within walking distance of shops and restaurants, offers eight large, comfortable guest rooms, each of which has its own private bath, some with fireplaces, and some with water or garden views. There are facilities for children and a room designed for the handicapped. Included with the room is a delicious full family-style breakfast served in the dining room or in the guests' room upon request, and an afternoon apéritif. If guests have any allergies or diet restrictions, just let the hosts know in advance, as they hope to make every stay a pleasant one. For the comfort of the guests, this is a nonsmoking establishment. Ferry landing, sea plane, or airport pickup is available.

Host: Sue Aran
Rooms: 8 (PB) $85-140
Full Breakfast
Credit Cards: A, B
Notes: 2, 3, 4, 5, 8, 9, 12, 14

Inn at Swifts Bay

Route 2, Box 3402, 98261
(360) 468-3636; FAX (360) 468-3637

On beautiful Lopez Island, in the San Juans of Washington State, the Inn at Swifts Bay occupies three wooded acres. There are five guest rooms available, three with their own private baths and fireplaces. There are also fireplaces to be enjoyed in the common areas, a soothing hot tub to soak in on the deck, a private beach for quiet walks, and delicious award-winning breakfasts. A designated three-star Northwest Best Place, Mobil, and WBBG.

Hosts: Robert Herrmann and Christopher
   Brandmeir
Rooms: 5 (3 PB; 2 SB) $75-155
Full Breakfast
Credit Cards: A, B, C, D
Notes: 2, 5, 7, 12, 14

7 No smoking; 8 Children welcome; 9 Social drinking allowed; 10 Tennis nearby; 11 Swimming nearby; 12 Golf nearby; 13 Skiing nearby; 14 May be booked through a travel agent.

MacKaye Harbor Inn

Route 1, Box 1940, 98261
(360) 468-2253

The ideal beachfront getaway. Lopez's only bed and breakfast on a low-bank sandy beach. Kayak and mountain bike rentals and/or instruction. This 1927 Victorian home has been painstakingly restored. Guests are pampered in comfortable elegance. Eagles, deer, seals, and otters frequent this Cape Cod of the Northwest. Commendations from *Sunset*, *Pacific Northwest* magazine, the *Los Angeles Times*, and *Northwest Best Places*.

Hosts: Brooks and Sharon Broberg
Rooms: 5 (3 PB; 2 SB) $69-139
Full Breakfast
Credit Cards: A, B
Notes: 2, 5, 7, 9, 12, 14

A Pacific Reservation Service

701 Northwest 60th Street, Seattle, 98107
(206) 784-0539

LI-1. At the first stop by the ferry, relax at this Victorian waterfront inn with lovely antiques, a restaurant on the premises, and all the charm of a tranquil setting. Grand sunsets, sandy beaches, tidal pools, and beachcombing. Watching the eagles and other wildlife will keep guests busy. Bring a kayak, bicycles, windsurfing, or fishing gear. Five guest rooms, one with private bath. $75-125.

LUMMI ISLAND

Bed and Breakfast Guild of Whatcom County

2610 Eldridge Avenue, Bellingham 98225
(206) 676-4560

1. Only 17 minutes from Bellingham to the ferry, then a five-minute ferry ride. Loganita, a lovely white villa, commands a breathtaking 180-degree marine view.

Magnificent sandy beach! Beautiful sunsets. Luxurious suites, rooms, cottage (weekly), spa, and fireplaces. Visa and MasterCard accepted. No smoking. $95-225.

West Shore Farm Bed and Breakfast

2781 West Shore Drive, 98262
(206) 758-2600

Unique, octagonal owner-built home with 180-degree view of islands, passing boats, sunsets, eagles, seals, and Canadian mountains on the northern horizon. The quiet natural beach, garden, orchard with resident poultry, stock of books, maps, bicycles, and natural gourmet food are rejuvenating. Lunch and dinner available at an extra charge. Inquire about pets.

Hosts: Carl and Polly Hanson
Rooms: 2 (PB) $90
Full Breakfast
Credit Cards: A, B
Notes: 2, 5, 8, 9, 13

The Willows Inn

2579 West Shore Drive, 98262
(360) 758- 2620

Established in 1911 by Victoria's grandparents, the Willows is an island landmark. On the sunset side of the island, it boasts a private beach and a spectacular view of the San Juan Islands. Noted for its fine dining

The Willows Inn

NOTES: Credit cards accepted: A MasterCard; B Visa; C American Express; D Discover; E Diners Club; F Other; 2 Personal checks accepted; 3 Lunch available; 4 Dinner available; 5 Open all year; 6 Pets welcome;

and award-winning gardens, The Willows is a most peaceful and romantic destination. Ten minutes from I-5 near Bellingham and a seven-minute ferry ride brings guests to this quiet little island.

Hosts: Victoria and Gary
Rooms: 7 (PB) $95-135
Full Breakfast
Credit Cards: A, B
Notes: 2, 4, 9, 11

LYNDEN

Bed and Breakfast Guild of Whatcom County

2610 Eldridge Avenue, Bellingham 98225
(206) 676-4560

10. Come feel the quiet, peaceful, Victorian elegance of this beautifully restored century-old home. At the edge of Lynden, a quaint Dutch village. Enjoy the third-floor Century Tower Suite or second-floor garden-view rooms. Breakfast is the specialty here. Come and enjoy. $60-85.

Dutch Village Inn

655 Front Street, 98264
(206) 354-4440

This is a unique hotel built in a windmill in the charming Dutch community. Each room is individually decorated with antiques and is representative of a Dutch province. Continental breakfast served on Sundays. Full breakfast served weekdays.

Hosts: Elaine and Deena
Rooms: 6 (PB) $65-95
Full and Continental Breakfast
Credit Cards: A, B
Notes: 2, 3, 4, 5, 7, 8, 9, 10, 11, 12, 13, 14

MAPLE VALLEY

Maple Valley Bed and Breakfast

20020 Southeast 228, 98038
(206) 432-1409

Maple Valley

Welcome to this warm cedar home in the wooded Northwest. Spacious grounds, wildlife pond, and fine feathered friends. Experience the "Good Morning" rooster, hootenanny pancakes, "hot babies," and gracious family hospitality. Crest Airpark is just minutes away. Be special. Be a guest at Maple Valley.

Hosts: Jayne and Clarke Hurlbut
Rooms: 2 (SB) $59-69
Full Breakfast
Credit Cards: None
Notes: 2, 3, 5, 7, 8, 9, 10, 11, 12, 13, 14

MERCER ISLAND

A Travellers Bed and Breakfast Reservation Service

P.O. Box 492, 98040
(206) 232-2345

This reservation service represents guest homes, inns, private residences, and cottages. More than 200 accommodations in the Pacific Northwest, including Vancouver and Victoria, British Columbia and Oregon coast. Assists in personal itineraries including ferries and car rental. All lodgings personally inspected and meet this company's high standards. In business since 1981. For reservations call Monday through Friday from 9:00 A.M. through 5:00 P.M. $65-175.

7 No smoking; 8 Children welcome; 9 Social drinking allowed; 10 Tennis nearby; 11 Swimming nearby; 12 Golf nearby; 13 Skiing nearby; 14 May be booked through a travel agent.

MONTESANO

Sylvan Haus—Murphy Bed and Breakfast

417 Wilder Hill Drive
P.O. Box 416, 98563
(360) 249-3453

A gracious, three-story family home surrounded by towering evergreens at the top of Wilder Hill Drive. Watch the changing seasons while breakfasting at the old round oak dining table. Grays Harbor, Sea-Tac Airport, Olympic Peninsula, and Lake Quinalt Rain Forest are easily accessible; only 30 minutes to beautiful ocean beaches. Children over 14 are welcome.

Hosts: Mike and JoAnne Murphy
Rooms: 3 (1 PB; 2 SB) $65
Full Breakfast
Credit Cards: None
Notes: 2, 5, 7, 11, 12

MOUNT RAINIER

Jasmers Bed and Breakfast and Cabins

30005 State Road 706 East, Ashford, 98304
(360) 569-2682

A perfect balance of pampering and privacy! A love nest! Two rooms apart from the main house, private baths with showers for two, queen-size beds, refrigerator and microwave, TV/VCR, and one room with a fireplace. All of this on a gorgeous three-acre farm with a hot tub. Our "cabin on Big Creek" has a complete kitchen, bath, two bedrooms, wood stove, deck with hot tub, and a picture perfect wooded setting on the creek. Come! See! Smell! Relax amid the splendors of nature! Children over ten are welcome.

Hosts: Luke and Tanna Osterhaus
Rooms: 6 (PB) $75-125
Continental Breakfast
Credit Cards: A, B
Notes: 2, 5, 7, 9, 11, 13, 14

MOUNT RAINIER AREA

A Pacific Reservation Service

701 Northwest 60th Street, Seattle, 98107
(206) 784-0539

Country Inn. Originally built in 1912, this inn was restored in 1984 and features 11 guest rooms with queen-size beds. The handmade quilts, antiques, Tiffany lamps, and stained-glass windows all add to the comfort of this bed and breakfast. There is also a critically acclaimed restaurant that serves delicious food in a relaxed, genteel fashion by a big stone fireplace. $75.

OLYMPIA

The Cinnamon Rabbit

1304 Seventh Avenue Southwest, 98502
(360) 357-5520

This is an older home (1935) in a quiet neighborhood, just a 20-minute walk from downtown Olympia, Capitol Lake, and Budd Bay Inlet. There are a big front porch with wicker chairs and a real "cinnamon" rabbit. Guests enjoy a queen-size bed, the run of the living/TV/music room, and the hot tub. Hosts are professional bakers so breakfast is always good! Hosts offer discounts for cash payment.

Hosts: Penny and Bob Williams-Young
Room: 1 (PB) $55-65
Full Breakfast
Credit Cards: A, B
Notes: 2, 5, 7, 8, 9, 10, 11

Harbinger Inn

1136 East Bay Drive, 98506
(360) 754-0389

Completely restored national historic landmark. View of East Bay marina, the capitol, and Olympic Mountains. Ideal setting for boating, bicycling, jogging, fine

---

NOTES: Credit cards accepted: A MasterCard; B Visa; C American Express; D Discover; E Diners Club; F Other; 2 Personal checks accepted; 3 Lunch available; 4 Dinner available; 5 Open all year; 6 Pets welcome;

dining, and business ventures. Hiking in an old-growth forest with trails. A Northwest Best Place.

Hosts: Marisa and Terrell Williams
Rooms: 4 (3 PB; 1 SB) $60-100
Continental Breakfast
Credit Cards: A, B, C
Notes: 2, 5, 7, 9, 12

Puget View Guest House

7924 61st Avenue Northeast, 98516
(360) 459-1676

Classic Puget Sound. This quaint waterfront guest cottage suite sleeps four and is on the shore of Puget Sound next to the hosts' log home. Gorgeous and expansive marine-mountain view is breathtaking. Breakfast is served privately in the cottage. Great for a special honeymoon or romantic retreat. Near Tolmie State Park, only five minutes off of I-5, just north of downtown Olympia.

Hosts: The Yunkers
Cottage: 1 (PB) $89
Continental Breakfast
Credit Cards: A, B
Notes: 2, 5, 6, 7, 8, 9, 11

OLYMPIC

A Pacific Reservation Service

701 Northwest 60th Street, Seattle, 98107
(206) 784-0539

Olympic-1. With an unobstructed view over the water, this private two-bedroom cottage with double and twin beds invites guests to linger. Adjacent to a state park, one can rent a boat and enjoy the lovely water, or relax in the privacy of the cottage, which is nicely furnished and decorated in country style. The delicious breakfast is served in the morning on a tray, to eat outside or in, depending on the weather. Minimum stay of two nights required on the weekends. $85.

OLYMPIC PENINSULA

A Pacific Reservation Service

701 Northwest 60th Street, Seattle, 98107
(206) 784-0539

Olympic Peninsula-1. A splendid historic lodge. In a picturesque setting with the finest views ever offered from a lodge, the gravel lobby of this home with its imposing stone fireplaces offers the quiet elegance and charm of yesteryear. Cocktails by the fire, an elegant dinner in the restaurant, and a refreshing dip in an indoor pool add up to a great vacation experience. European-style bath in the lodge. Two-night minimum stay on weekends. $85.

ORCAS

A Pacific Reservation Service

701 Northwest 60th Street, Seattle, 98107
(206) 784-0539

OI-1. A large two-story log inn welcomes guests with seven bedrooms, all with private baths. Most of the rooms have views of the water. Rustic and comfortable, this inn is newly built and has a restaurant on the premises. Breakfast will be delivered in a basket to enjoy in the privacy of guests' own room. Seasonal rates. $89.

PORT ANGELES

Domaine Madeleine

146 Wildflower Lane, 98362
(360) 457-4174; fax (360) 457-3037

Secluded, elegant, five-acre waterfront estate with water and mountain views. Three rooms with Jacuzzis. All rooms have fireplaces. Monet garden replica. Lawn games; whale, eagle, and deer watching; golf and skiing nearby. Breakfast so good that the inn pays if guests have lunch before 2:00 P.M. Practice languages or cooking with the hostess.

Hosts: Madeleine and John Chambers
Rooms: 4 (PB) $95-165
Full Breakfast
Credit Cards: A, B, C, D
Notes: 2, 5, 7, 9, 10, 11, 12, 13, 14

Tudor Inn

Tudor Inn

1108 South Oak, 98362
(360) 452-3138

Between the mountains and the sea, this half-timbered Tudor home was built by an Englishman in 1910 and has been tastefully restored and furnished with European antiques and an English garden. Two-night minimum stay required for weekends in July through September and for holidays. Children over 12 welcome.

Hosts: Jane and Jerry Glass
Rooms: 5 (PB) $85-110
Full Breakfast
Credit Cards: A, B, D
Notes: 2, 5, 7, 9, 10, 11, 12, 13

PORT ORCHARD

Reflections— A Bed and Breakfast Inn

3878 Reflection Lane, East, 98366
(206) 871-5582

Reflections is a Colonial home filled with New England antiques. Four rooms, each

with a gorgeous view of Puget Sound. Relax in the hot tub, or enjoy the view from the gazebo on two and one-half acres of landscaped grounds. Gateway to the Olympic Peninsula; scenic ferry ride to Seattle. Full gourmet breakfast is served. Antique shopping in Port Orchard. Quality golf courses nearby.

Hosts: Jim and Cathy Hall
Rooms: 4 (2 PB; 2 SB) $55-90
Full Breakfast
Credit Cards: A, B
Notes: 2, 5, 7, 9, 12

PORT TOWNSEND

Ann Starrett Mansion Bed and Breakfast Inn

744 Clay Street, 98368
(360) 385-3205; (800) 321-0644

Victorian mansion, circa 1889, epitomizes the heart and soul of this Victorian seaport community. Internationally renowned for its classical architecture, antiques, and excellent service and food. In a quiet residential area within walking distance to town, theater, restaurants, beach, and ferry. Tennis, swimming, golf, and skiing nearby. Jacuzzi and fireplace. Full breakfast served. No children. Ten-day cancellation policy.

Hosts: Edel and Bob Sokol
Rooms: 11 (PB) $75-225
Full Breakfast
Credit Cards: A, B, C, D
Notes: 2, 5, 7, 9, 10, 11, 12, 13, 14

The English Inn

718 F Street, 98368
(360) 385-5302

This 1885 Italianate-style Victorian house has five large, sunny bedrooms. Two of the guest rooms have views of the nearby Olympic Mountains. Full, delectable breakfast! The large garden offers a gazebo to linger in and a hot tub where guests can relax. Fifty miles from Seattle, Port Townsend is a Victorian seaport providing

NOTES: Credit cards accepted: A MasterCard; B Visa; C American Express; D Discover; E Diners Club;
F Other; 2 Personal checks accepted; 3 Lunch available; 4 Dinner available; 5 Open all year; 6 Pets welcome;

visitors with quaint shops, fine restaurants, and cultural events.

Hosts: Nancy Borino
Rooms: 5 (PB) $65-95
Full Breakfast
Credit Cards: A, B, C, D
Notes: 2, 5, 7, 8, 9, 10, 11, 12, 14

Holly Hill House Bed and Breakfast

611 Polk, 98368
(360) 385-5619; (800) 435-1454

Charming 1872 Victorian home located in the heart of the historic district of Port Townsend. Five graciously furnished bedrooms, all with private baths. Enjoy views of Admiralty Inlet, Cascade Mountains, lovely rose gardens, the towering holly trees, and the "upside down" Camperdown elm. Relax in the cozy library, wander the exquisite gardens, or sip tea or wine in front of the parlor fireplace. Full sumptuous breakfast served in the formal dining room.

Host: Lynne Sterling
Rooms: 5 (PB) $76-130
Full Breakfast
Credit Cards: A, B
Notes: 2, 5, 7, 9, 10, 11, 12

The James House

1238 Washington Street, 98368
(360) 385-1238; (800) 385-1238

The first bed and breakfast in the Northwest, the James House is on the bluff overlooking this charming Victorian seaport town. With unobstructed views of Puget Sound, Mount Rainier, the Olympic and Cascade mountain ranges, the James House offers 12 rooms, including a cottage, master/bridal suite, and lovely two-bedroom suites. A full breakfast, afternoon sherry, homemade cookies, and lovely gardens are just a few of the amenities at this beautiful inn.

Hosts: Carol McGough and Anne Tiernan
Rooms: 12 (10 PB; 2 SB) $65-150
Full Breakfast
Credit Cards: A, B, C
Notes: 2, 5, 7, 9, 10, 12, 13

Lizzie's Victorian Bed and Breakfast

731 Pierce Street, 98368
(206) 385-4168

An 1888 Victorian mansion within walking distance of shops and restaurants. The inn is decorated in antiques and some original wallpaper. Parlors are comfortable retreats for reading or conversation. Gateway to the Olympic Mountains, San Juan Islands, and Victoria. Wonderful breakfasts! Children over ten welcome.

Hosts: Bill and Patti Wickline
Rooms: 7 (PB) $70-135
Full Breakfast
Credit Cards: A, B, D
Notes: 2, 5, 7, 9, 10, 12

Lizzie's Victorian

Manresa Castle

Seventh and Sheridan, P.O. Box 564, 98368
(206) 385-5750; (800) 732-1281 (WA only)

This historic landmark, listed on the National Register of Historic Places, now houses 40 Victorian-style guest rooms, an elegant dining room, and an Edwardian-style lounge. Set atop Castle Hill, almost all rooms, including the dining room and lounge, have spectacular views of the town, harbor, marina, and/or Olympic Mountains. The guest rooms offer private baths, direct dial telephones, TV, and Continental breakfast.

Hosts: Lena and Vernon Humber
Rooms: 40 (PB) $65-175
Continental Breakfast
Credit Cards: A, B, D
Notes: 2, 4, 5, 8, 9, 10, 11, 12, 14

7 No smoking; 8 Children welcome; 9 Social drinking allowed; 10 Tennis nearby; 11 Swimming nearby; 12 Golf nearby; 13 Skiing nearby; 14 May be booked through a travel agent.

A Pacific Reservation Service

701 Northwest 60th Street, Seattle, 98107
(206) 784-0539

1892 Castle. The castle sits on a hill with commanding marina views. It features rooms with private baths and Victorian decor, and lovely gardens. The landmark mansion is on the National Register of Historic Places and was totally restored in 1973. Enjoy splendid luxury while in Port Townsend. Continental breakfast. $75-150.

The Grand Dame. The most photographed house in Port Townsend, this great Victorian was built in 1889 by a wealthy contractor for his wife as a wedding present. It features a spiral freestanding staircase that is one of the finest in existence. Special frescoes in the dome will delight guests. Most of the rooms on the second floor have a wonderful view of the water and the mountains. Five bedrooms on the second floor, and four bedrooms on the carriage level. Both shared and private bath. Healthy breakfast is served on fine china. $75.

Sequim Victorian. A fine bed and breakfast inn, one-half mile from the beach, on Dungeness Spit, a quiet, peaceful area, yet only minutes from Port Townsend, Port Angeles, or the Victoria ferry. Remember that this area is the "Banana Belt" of the region, with less rainfall. Guests' favorite beverage and morning paper are delivered to their doors in the morning. A full breakfast is served downstairs. Four bedrooms, two that share a bath, and two that offer private baths, are available. $85.

The Palace Hotel

1004 Water Street, 98368
(206) 385-0773; (800) 962-0741 (WA only)

The Palace Hotel on Water Street is a beautifully restored Victorian hotel in the heart of Port Townsend's historic district. Close to galleries and shops, it offers convenient off-street parking and is within blocks of ferry and bus services. Accommodations range from Continental-style bedrooms with a shared bath to multiroom suites with kitchens and luxurious private baths. Any stay at the Palace includes a complimentary Continental breakfast. All rooms have cable TV, coffee, and tea. Many nonsmoking rooms are available, and children are welcome. Off-season discounts offered during the winter.

Rooms: 15 (12 PB; 3 SB) $65-119
Continental Breakfast
Credit Cards: A, B, C, D
Notes: 2, 3, 4, 5, 7, 8, 14

Quimper Inn

1306 Franklin Street, 98368
(206) 385-1060; (800) 557-1060

This 1886 mansion in the historic uptown district offers lovely water and mountain views. Four comfortable bedrooms, plus a two-room suite with a sitting room and bath. Antique period furniture, lots of books, and two porches for relaxation. A short walk to historic downtown with its many shops and restaurants. A wonderful breakfast is served. Off-season rates October through May.

Hosts: Ron and Sue Ramage
Rooms: 5 (3 PB; 2 SB) $70-140
Full Breakfast
Credit Cards: A, B
Notes: 2, 5, 7, 9, 10, 11, 12, 13

Quimper Inn

NOTES: Credit cards accepted: A MasterCard; B Visa; C American Express; D Discover; E Diners Club; F Other; 2 Personal checks accepted; 3 Lunch available; 4 Dinner available; 5 Open all year; 6 Pets welcome;

Water Street Hotel

635 Water Street, 98368
(360) 385-5467; (800) 735-9810

Built in 1889 and completely renovated in 1990 the Water Street Hotel is in a secluded waterfront community. It combines the Old World charm of historic downtown Port Townsend with a panoramic view of Puget Sound and the majestic Olympic Mountains. It's within walking distance of downtown shops, restaurants, and the Keystone ferry. A Continental breakfast is served across the street at the bakery. Pets welcome at an additional charge.

Hosts: Mary Hewitt and Dawn Pfeiffer
Rooms: 16 (11 PB; 5 SB) $45-125
Continental Breakfast
Credit Cards: A, B, C
Notes: 5, 7, 8, 10, 11, 12

PUGET SOUND INLET

A Pacific Reservation Service

701 Northwest 60th Street, Seattle, 98107
(206) 784-0539

Puget Sound Inlet-1. On the water, this bed and breakfast offers a delightful Victorian farmhouse with a rolling lawn down to the water's edge. Furnished with antiques and three bedrooms to choose from, this is a favorite of weekenders. A great breakfast is served in the morning. Shared bath. $80.

RENTON

Holly Hedge House

908 Grant Avenue South, 98055
(206) 226-2555

Experience the ultimate in pampering and privacy in this meticulously restored 1900 scenic hilltop retreat. This unique lodging facility reserves the entire house to one couple to indulge in the beauty and affordable luxury. Landscaped grounds, wood deck with hot tub, swimming pool, well-stocked gourmet kitchen, whirlpool tub, CD, video, reading library, fireplace, and glassed-in veranda. Ten minutes from Sea-Tac International Airport, 20 minutes from Seattle, and five minutes from Lake Washington. A vacation, honeymoon, or corporate travel getaway. Ask about the Spirit Package.

Hosts: Lynn and Marian Thrasher
House: 1 (PB) $110
Full Breakfast
Credit Cards: A, B
Notes: 2, 5, 7, 9, 10, 11, 12, 13

SAN JUAN ISLANDS

A Pacific Reservation Service

701 Northwest 60th Street, Seattle, 98107
(206) 784-0539

Friday Harbor. A floating inn designed from a restored 60-foot wooden sailboat offers guests two staterooms, one with a queen-size bed and private bath, the other with a double bed, two bunk beds, and shared bath. The hosts will provide a full seaman's breakfast that might be served on the deck in fair weather or in front of a roaring fire in the parlor. Have a totally different experience here! $95.

Orcas Island Country Inn. This is a beautiful country inn nestled in a valley with fine views of meadows and mountains. The inn offers eight guest rooms, all with private baths with claw-foot tubs, and antique furnishings. Guests can enjoy a gourmet breakfast in a charming, elegant atmosphere. $105.

Waterfront Country Inn. Built before 1888, this inn has been used as a town meeting hall, a barber shop, a general store, a post office, and a jail. Now as a popular getaway, it offers guest rooms with and without private baths,

---

7 No smoking; 8 Children welcome; 9 Social drinking allowed; 10 Tennis nearby; 11 Swimming nearby; 12 Golf nearby; 13 Skiing nearby; 14 May be booked through a travel agent.

hand-carved beds, marble-topped dressers, and a collection of period memorabilia. No pets, please. $80.

SEABECK

The Walton House Bed and Breakfast Establishment

12340 Seabeck Highway, NW, 98380
(206) 830-4498

There is a feeling of Grandma's house in this three-story 1904 home filled with family antiques and operated by the third generation of Waltons. Old-fashioned double beds in two guest rooms with private baths. A fabulous view of the Olympic Mountains and Hood Canal with 350 feet of beach to explore. Movie theaters, restaurants, antique shops, and a shopping mall are six miles away.

Host: Shirley Walton
Rooms: 2 (PB) $63-72
Full Breakfast
Credit Cards: None
Notes: 2, 5, 7, 9, 12

SEATTLE

Alexis Hotel

1007 First Avenue at Madison, 98104
(206) 624-4844; (800) 426-7033 (reservations)

The elegant Alexis Hotel is snuggled in the heart of downtown Seattle, between colorful Pike Place Market and historic Pioneer Square. Just a block from the waterfront and financial district, the Alexis is the ideal spot for business and leisure travelers. Many superior luxury amenities are offered, including complimentary Continental breakfast, evening turndown, welcome sherry, morning newspaper, overnight shoe shine service, 24-hour room service and concierge, and use of the private steamroom. The hotel has a strict no-tipping policy for the staff. Enjoy the three restaurants. For those who prefer more

room, ask about the condominium-style rooms, the Arlington Suites.

Host: Stan Kott
Rooms: 54 (PB) $185-350
Continental Breakfast
Credit Cards: A, B, C, D, E, F
Notes: 2, 3, 4, 5, 6, 8, 9, 14

Bacon Mansion

Bacon Mansion

959 Broadway East, 98102
(206) 329-1864; (800) 240-1864
FAX (206) 860-9025

This is one of Seattle's most gracious mansions, within two blocks of the Broadway shopping district. The Bacon Mansion is in the Harvard-Belmont historic district. Most of the rooms have their own private baths. There are a beautiful grand staircase and a turn-of-the-century library in the house; breakfast is served in the formal dining room.

Hosts: Daryl King and Tim Stiles
Rooms: 9 (7 PB; 2 SB) $65-125
Continental Breakfast
Credit Cards: A, B, C, D
Notes: 2, 5, 7, 8, 9, 10

NOTES: Credit cards accepted: A MasterCard; B Visa; C American Express; D Discover; E Diners Club; F Other; 2 Personal checks accepted; 3 Lunch available; 4 Dinner available; 5 Open all year; 6 Pets welcome;

Bellevue Place
Bed and Breakfast
on Capitol Hill in Seattle

1111 Bellevue Place East, 98102
(206) 325-9253; (800) 325-9253
FAX (206) 455-0785

Bellevue Place is in the Landmark District of Capitol Hill. This 1905 storybook house with leaded glass and Victorian charm is close to Broadway restaurants and stores, Volunteer Park, and a 20 to 25-minute walk to downtown Seattle. Pressed cotton sheets and queen-size beds.

Hosts: Gunner Johnson and Joseph C. Pruett
Rooms: 3 (SB) $75-85
Full Breakfast
Credit Cards: A, B, C, D
Notes: 5, 10, 13, 14

B. Williams House
Bed and Breakfast

1505 Fourth Avenue North, 98109
(206) 285-0810; (800) 880-0810
FAX (206) 285-8526

A family bed and breakfast in an Edwardian home with much of the original woodwork and original gaslight fixtures. Decorated with antiques, most guest rooms have views of Seattle, the mountains, or the water. A sunny enclosed porch is shared by all. Beautiful gardens! Close to downtown, the Space Needle, and public market. Public transportation available. Limited smoking allowed. Call to inquire about children.

Hosts: The Williams Family
Rooms: 5 (2 PB; 3 SB) $70-99
Full Breakfast
Credit Cards: A, B, C
Notes: 2, 5, 10, 11, 12

Capitol Hill House
Bed and Breakfast

2215 East Prospect Street, 98112
(206) 322-1752; FAX (206) 527-4680

Beautifully furnished, traditional brick home built in 1923 on a tree-lined street in an exclusive, residential neighborhood. Near Broadway, one of the more exciting and diverse shopping areas in the city. Within walking distance to the Seattle Asian Art Museum and University of Washington and ten to fifteen minutes from downtown Seattle, theaters, shopping, and the Washington State Convention and Trade Center. Three-hour drive to Vancouver and Victoria, British Columbia. Peaceful surroundings, which include antiques, marble-top tables, and Persian rugs. Guests are encouraged to use the main floor living room and to enjoy the fireplace in the winter. A covered terrace and beautiful garden provide guests with a place to relax out-of-doors. Each room is equipped with its own TV and telephone. Credit cards are accepted only to hold the reserved room while the hostess is waiting on the guests' check for deposit on the room. Smoking on first floor only. No smoking allowed in the rooms.

Host: Mary A. Wolf
Rooms: 3 (1 PB; 2 SB) $55-70
Full and Continental Breakfast
Credit Cards: None
Notes: 2, 5, 8, 9, 10, 11, 12, 13, 14

Chambered Nautilus

5005 22nd Avenue Northeast, 98105
(206) 522-2536

Seattle's finest, a gracious 1915 Georgian Colonial nestled high on a hill. This famous hospitable inn is furnished with a mixture of

Chambered Nautilus

American and English antiques and reproductions, Persian rugs, a grand piano, and a 2,000-plus volume library. It offers national award-winning breakfasts, plus excellent access to Seattle's fine restaurants, theaters, shopping, public transportation, bike and jogging trails, tennis, golf, and the nearby University of Washington campus.

Hosts: Bunny and Bill Hagemeyer
Rooms: 6 (4 PB; 2 SB) $79-105
Full Breakfast
Credit Cards: A, B, C, E, F
Notes: 2, 5, 7, 9, 10, 11, 12, 13, 14

Chelsea Station
Bed and Breakfast Inn

4915 Linden Avenue North, 98103
(206) 547-6077; (800) 400-6077
FAX (206) 632-5107

Nestled between the Fremont neighborhood and Woodland Park, Chelsea Station is minutes north of downtown Seattle. Largely decorated in Mission style, the inn features antiques throughout. The beds invite guests with soft down comforters. Awake to the aroma of brewing coffee followed by a hearty breakfast. Freshly baked cookies are always available. Take time for a stroll to the zoo or rose garden. Enjoy the warm and casual mood of Chelsea Station: a place to refresh one's spirit. Children 12 and over welcome.

Hosts: John Griffin and Karen Carbonneau
Rooms: 6 (PB) $69-104
Full Breakfast
Credit Cards: A, B, C, D, E
Notes: 2, 5, 7, 9, 10, 11, 12, 13, 14

Chelsea Station

Gaslight Inn

1727 15th Avenue, 98122
(206) 325-3654

This beautifully restored turn-of-the-century home is on Capitol Hill in downtown Seattle. Oak paneling, fireplaces, decks, and a heated in-ground pool make the Gaslight a very special place for the guests, whether they are visiting for pleasure or business. Guests may choose between nine rooms and five suites.

Hosts: Steve Bennett and Trevor Logan
Rooms: 14 (11 PB; 3 SB) $68-98
Continental Breakfast
Credit Cards: A, B, C
Notes: 2, 5, 7

Green Gables Guesthouse

1503 Second Avenue West, 98119
(206) 282-6863; FAX (206) 284-3124

A tranquil, in-city retreat on historic Queen Anne Hill, just three blocks from Kerry Park, offers a commanding view of Seattle. Walk to many restaurants, shops, the Space Needle, and performing arts. Built in 1904, this home is filled with antiques, costumes, and family heirlooms. Spectacular box-beam ceilings and leaded-glass windows make for a truly vintage setting. A private garden leads to Mercer House which is designed for longer stays. Guests are served generous farm-style breakfasts. Skiing one hour away.

Hosts: David and Lila Chapman
Rooms: 5 (3 PB; 2 SB) $75-125
House: 3 (2 PB; 1 SB)
Full Breakfast
Credit Cards: A, B, C, D
Notes: 2, 5, 7, 8, 10, 11, 12

Mildred's Bed and Breakfast

1202 15th Avenue East, 98112
(206) 325-6072

A traditional 1890 Victorian gem in an elegant style. Old-fashioned hospitality awaits. Red carpets, lace curtains, fireplace, grand piano, and wraparound porch. Across

Mildred's

the street is the Seattle Art Museum, flower conservatory, and historic 44-acre Volunteer Park. Electric trolley at the front door. Minutes to city center, freeways, and all points of interest.

Host: Mildred Sarver
Rooms: 3 (PB) $75-85
Full Breakfast
Credit Cards: A, B, C, D, E
Notes: 2, 5, 8, 9, 10, 11, 12, 14

A Pacific Reservation Service

701 Northwest 60th Street, 98107
(206) 784-0539

The Downtown Hotel. Built in 1928 and recently remodeled, this lovely European-style hotel offers guests comfortable rooms with double or twin beds. Walk to the waterfront, scores of fine restaurants, Pike Place Market, the Kingdome, Amtrak station, and the convention center. Many of the original fixtures, such as the mahogany door and tiling, were left. Personal service, friendly staff, and professional help is at guests' beck and call. Continental breakfast. Parking available. $70.

BA-1. Here is the private apartment with everything: private entrance, living room with TV, telephone, private bath, queen-size bed, and equipped kitchen. Maid service, chocolates on the pillow, fresh flowers, and a warm welcome. One block to bus lines and a 15-minute ride to downtown. Close to the University of Washington area. $50.

BA-2. All the comforts of home can be found in this two-bedroom cottage in a quiet neighborhood. One bedroom features a 1925 antique bedroom set, and the second room offers twin beds. The cottage sleeps up to four, and is comfortably furnished with brass and oak accents. Close to Greenlake, the university, parks, the zoo, beaches, marinas, shops, and restaurants. Children welcome. No smoking. Monthly rates available. $95.

BA-4. A brand new home, Northwest-style, offers a private suite of two rooms with sliding glass doors leading to a private patio. Private bath and queen-size bed. There is a kitchenette with breakfast supplies provided. Occasionally breakfast is served upstairs in the dining room. Close to Greenlake and restaurants. $65.

BA-5. For families or business groups, nothing compares to the comfort of one's own house. Guests may take over the entire house or rent just one room, but will always receive a great value staying here. Close to Greenlake, shops, restaurants, and only minutes from downtown via the freeway. Two bedrooms are available, but sleeping accommodations can be made for up to ten guests. No smoking. No pets. Free off-street parking. $65.

Bellevue-1. This wonderful contemporary home offers a private suite with two bedrooms, a living room, one full bath, and a private entrance. Have a full breakfast served upstairs in the dining room. Guests are also welcome to use the hot tub in the

7 No smoking; 8 Children welcome; 9 Social drinking allowed; 10 Tennis nearby; 11 Swimming nearby; 12 Golf nearby; 13 Skiing nearby; 14 May be booked through a travel agent.

A Pacific Reservation Service (continued)

back. An urban oasis at its finest. One mile from the center of Bellevue, this guest home will be a comfortable retreat after a day of sightseeing or business. $55.

Bellevue-2. Hospitable retired hosts offer guests two bedrooms, with a living room, private bath, kitchenette, private entrance, and a tasty breakfast. Handy location. Fine views of the lake. $65.

CH-2. Here is a true Victorian built in 1890 with stained-glass windows, fine period furniture, original woodwork, and an ambience that is unequaled. The hostess makes everyone feel right at home. All the little touches that provide that special bed and breakfast experience are here. Breakfasts are legendary. $85.

CH-4. An elegantly furnished traditional brick house with a lovely garden and covered patio is on a tree-lined street in an exclusive residential neighborhood. Within a few minutes from the University of Washington, downtown, theaters, shopping, and the convention center. On the bus lines. Breakfast is served in the formal dining room. Children welcome.

CH-5. A large turn-of-the-century home that looks like a castle has been lovingly restored. The location is handy to everything in the city, only 12 blocks from downtown. The guest rooms are on the first floor and have private baths. The library with a wonderful window seat is available to lounge, read, watch TV, or sit and plan the day's activities. $65.

CH-6. A spacious Victorian greets its visitors with warm hospitality. From the second floor guests will have a great view of the

city, the Space Needle, Puget Sound, and the Olympic Mountains. Walk to restaurants, shops, action on Broadway, and art museum. Two guest rooms share a bath. Home-cooked breakfast served in dining room by an experienced hostess. Some Spanish, Norwegian, and Indonesian spoken. $75-125.

CH-12. Private entrance, private bath, hot tub, and double bedroom, all in this wonderful brick home. Guests may have as much privacy as they want. Self-catered breakfast is in the refrigerator. Visiting relatives love this spot, because of its convenience to the city, 15 minutes to downtown, or the bus lines. The hosts are young professionals, most interested in making guests' stay as pleasant as possible. So close to the University of Washington, one could even walk there. A fine garden is available for guests to enjoy. $65.

MAG-2. Two miles northwest of downtown, this bed and breakfast offers a quiet street and a private bedroom with a double bed, a single bed, and a private bath. Full breakfast is served, and guests have a lovely view of Seattle from the patio where breakfast is served. $65.

MI-4. A private, cozy, two-bedroom cottage on Lake Washington. Completely furnished in a country decor. Awake to a beautiful sunrise. Conveniently between Seattle and Bellevue. Close to Snoqualmie Pass for summer hiking and winter skiing. A relaxed, peaceful setting. Maid service. No pets. Smoking permitted outside the cottage only. Continental breakfast. $95.

QA-1. A beautiful professional facility in an impressively restored building with a comfortable, relaxed atmosphere. Guests wish they could stay longer to enjoy the proximity to downtown, the fine antiques, the window seat, the wicker furniture, and

NOTES: Credit cards accepted: A MasterCard; B Visa; C American Express; D Discover; E Diners Club; F Other; 2 Personal checks accepted; 3 Lunch available; 4 Dinner available; 5 Open all year; 6 Pets welcome;

great breakfasts that are served in the formal dining room. Four bedrooms, some with private baths. $75.

QA-6. On lower Queen Anne, only two blocks from the Seattle Center and all the restaurants and shops there, this bed and breakfast offers a delightful alternative to motels. Stay in these fine studio apartments, with queen-size beds, TV, telephones, and kitchenettes. $70.

QA-12. If there ever was the ultimate lodging for travelers, this must be it. The setting is Queen Anne Hill, the most desirable location in the city. Private suite with private bath, a European kitchen, private entrance, TV, telephone, queen-size bed, and security system. The large deck lets one drink in the great view of Puget Sound and the Olympic Mountains. Ideal for honeymooners, business travelers, and visiting relatives. $75.

UD-3. A greenbelt with a creek through the adjacent property sets the tone for this stunning, architecturally designed, traditional home. Skylights, bright and airy, a sun deck, two double bedrooms, each of which is individually decorated, one of which has a full bath, and a private living room all add up to a great bed and breakfast experience. Add a breakfast home-cooked with great flair, and guests will never want to leave. $60-75.

Wallingford. Private suite with a queen-size bed, private entrance, living room, and kitchen in a private home, which is on the bus line. Guests are only a short three miles from the downtown core of the city and conveniently near the University of Washington and the people-oriented university district. This home is ideal for longer stays for the person who is looking for comfortable private lodgings. $60.

WE-1. In a quiet neighborhood, yet two blocks away from the bus line and 15 minutes from downtown. Within walking distance to one of the premier bakeries and restaurants. Suite with a bay window and window seat, a large sitting area with couch, tables, and a very comfortable queen-size bed. $75.

Prince of Wales Bed and Breakfast

133 13th Avenue East, 98102
(206) 325-9692; (800) 327-9692; FAX (206) 322-6402

Convenient to the business and convention traveler. Within walking distance of or a short bus ride to downtown Seattle and the Washington State Convention and Trade Center. A charming turn-of-the-century bed and breakfast on scenic Capitol Hill. Rooms include a romantic attic hideaway with private deck and panoramic view of the city skyline, Puget Sound, and Olympic Mountains. Restaurants and shops nearby. Great breakfasts! Seasonal rates. May be booked through a travel agent October through April only.

Host: Carol Norton
Rooms: 4 (PB) $75-110
Full Breakfast
Credit Cards: A, B, C, D
Notes: 2, 5, 7, 8, 9, 10, 11, 12

Prince of Wales

7 No smoking; 8 Children welcome; 9 Social drinking allowed; 10 Tennis nearby; 11 Swimming nearby; 12 Golf nearby; 13 Skiing nearby; 14 May be booked through a travel agent.

Queen Anne Hill Bed and Breakfast

1835 Seventh Avenue West, 98119
(206) 284-9779

Picturesque view of the Olympic Mountains and Puget Sound. Beautiful art, unique collectibles, and antiques are accented by hardwood floors and Oriental carpets. Close to the Seattle Center, downtown, and historic Pike Place Market. Breakfast includes home-baked goods, fresh fruit, and made-to-order items.

Hosts: Mary and Chuck McGrew
Rooms: 5 (2 PB; 3 SB) $55-85
Full Breakfast
Credit Cards: A, B, D
Notes: 5, 7, 8, 9, 10, 11, 12, 14

Salisbury House

750 16th Avenue East, 98112
(206) 328-8682

An elegant turn-of-the-century home on Capitol Hill, just minutes from Seattle's cultural and business activities. Gracious guest rooms with private baths. A well-stocked library and wraparound porch invite relaxation. In a historic neighbor-

Salisbury House

hood with parks, shops, and restaurants. Two friendly cats in residence. Recommended by Frommer's and Fodor's.

Hosts: Mary and Cathryn Wiese
Rooms: 4 (PB) $70-105
Full Breakfast
Credit Cards: A, B, C, E
Notes: 2, 5, 7, 9, 10, 11, 12, 13

Shafer-Baillie Mansion Bed and Breakfast

907 14th Avenue East, 98112
(206) 322-4654; (800) 922-4654
FAX (206) 329-4654

A quiet and livable atmosphere, Shafer-Baillie Mansion is the largest estate on historic Millionaire's Row on Seattle's Capitol Hill. This bed and breakfast has recently undergone a facelift, and guests will enjoy new luxury services and surroundings that are second to none. Explore 15,000 square feet of mystery, romance, and elegance. Entirely smokeless, but smoking is allowed on porches and balconies. A TV and refrigerator are in every room, and a gourmet Continental breakfast is served between 8:30 and 9:30 A.M. with the morning newspaper. Offering 13 suites, most with private baths. Telephone in most rooms.

Host: Erv Olssen
Rooms: 13 (10 PB; 3 SB) $69-115
Continental Breakfast
Credit Cards: C, D
Notes: 2, 5, 7, 8, 9, 10, 11, 13, 14

Three Tree Point Bed and Breakfast

17026 33rd Avenue, SW, 98166
(206) 669-7646; FAX (206) 242-7844

An enchanting private suite in a new home with a 280-degree view of Mount Rainier, Puget Sound, and the Olympic Mountains. Enjoy beach walks, Indian trails, windsurfing, and ship watching. Breakfast in guests' kitchen. Other features include: barbecue, patio dining, laundry facility, in-room TV,

NOTES: Credit cards accepted: A MasterCard; B Visa; C American Express; D Discover; E Diners Club;
F Other; 2 Personal checks accepted; 3 Lunch available; 4 Dinner available; 5 Open all year; 6 Pets welcome;

and telephone. fax available. Guest membership at a local fitness gym with an indoor swimming pool. Ten minutes from SeaTac Airport.

Hosts: Penny, Doug, and Braly Whisler
Rooms: 1 (PB) $95-135
Full Breakfast
Credit Cards: A, B
Notes: 2, 5, 7, 8, 11

Tugboat Challenger

1001 Fairview Avenue North, 98109
(206) 340-1201

Restored 1944 tugboat downtown. Carpeted, granite fireplace, and laundry. Refrigerators, TV, telephone, VCR, sinks, and sprinkler system, and private entrance for each room. Restaurants, bars, classic and modern sailboats, power boats, rowboats, and kayak rentals. Featured in *Travel & Leisure*, *Cosmopolitan*, and many major papers. Two-night minimum stay on weekends from June 1 through September 1.

Hosts: Jerry and Buff Brown
Full Breakfast
Credit Cards: A, B, C, D, E
Notes: 2, 5, 7, 8, 9, 11, 14

SEAVIEW

Gumm's Bed and Breakfast

3310 Highway 101 and 33 Avenue, P.O. Box 447, 98644
(360) 642-8887

This fine old house was built in 1900. Features a large living room with a great stone fireplace. A sun porch offers a warm spot for conversation or reading. Four inviting guest rooms are all uniquely decorated with special thoughts to the comfort of the guest. Two rooms have queen-size beds and private bath. Two rooms have double beds and share a bath. TV in each room. Hot tub.

Host: Mickey Slack
Rooms: 4 (2 PB; 2 SB) $65-80
Full Breakfast
Credit Cards: A, B
Notes: 2, 5, 7, 8, 9, 10, 11, 12, 14

SEQUIM

Granny Sandy's Orchard Bed and Breakfast

405 West Spruce, 98382
(360) 683-5748

Like visiting Grandma's, Granny Sandy serves a selection of breakfasts family style. All rooms are beautifully decorated, clean, homelike, and have excellent beds. Well-behaved children of all ages are welcome. Near everything and easy to find, Granny Sandy's promotes a be-at-home atmosphere. Happy guests from five continents and many nations are represented in the hostess's books for more than ten years.

Host: Sandy Ross
Rooms: 5 (2 PB; 3 SB) $35-75
Full Breakfast
Credit Cards: A, B
Notes: 2, 5, 7, 8, 10, 11, 12, 13

Greywolf Inn

Greywolf Inn

395 Keeler Road, 98382
(360) 683-5889; FAX (360) 683-1487

Enjoy a scenic drive from Seattle to Greywolf Inn, a five-acre country estate at the edge of nature's playground; the ideal starting point for light adventure on the Olympic Peninsula. Enjoy nearby bird watching, boating, or golfing, or head for the woods. Choices include Olympic National Park, Hurricane Ridge, the Hoh Rain Forest, and Sequim's own Dungeness

Spit and Wildlife Refuge. A steaming hot tub, a good night's sleep, and plenty of pampering. Join the hosts for fine food and good cheer at their splendid country inn. Picnic lunch available.

Hosts: Peggy and Bill Melang
Rooms: 5 (PB) $65-125
Full Breakfast
Credit Cards: A, B, C
Notes: 2, 5, 7, 9, 10, 11, 12, 13, 14

SHELTON

Twin River Ranch Bed and Breakfast

5730 Highway 3, 98584
(360) 426-1023

Rural 1918 manor house is on the Olympic Peninsula. Stone fireplace, antiques, and granny rooms tucked under the eaves overlooking the garden and stream. Black Angus cattle graze on 140 acres of pasture surrounded by old-growth trees. Puget Sound laps the marsh, and gulls, blue heron, and eagles circle overhead in season. By reservation only. No smoking upstairs.

Hosts: Phlorence and Ted Rohde
Rooms: 2 (SB) $59
Full Breakfast
Credit Cards: A, B
Notes: 2, 12

SILVERDALE

Seabreeze Beach Cottage

16609 Olympic View Road Northwest, 98383
(206) 692-4648

Challenged by lapping waves at high tide, this private retreat will awaken the five senses with the smell of salty air, a taste of fresh oysters and clams, views of the Olympic Mountains, the exhilaration of sun, surf, and sand. Spa at water's edge.

Host: Dennis Fulton
Rooms: 2 (PB) $119-149
Continental Breakfast
Credit Cards: A, B
Notes: 2, 5, 6, 7, 8, 9, 11, 12, 14

Countryman

SNOHOMISH

Countryman Bed and Breakfast

119 Cedar Street, 98290
(206) 568-9622

A beautiful 1896 landmark Queen Anne Victorian with all the extras. Near 250 antique shops. Fireplace, jetted Greek tub, art gallery. Complimentary tour of the historic district. Private parking and private airport nearby.

Hosts: Larry and Sandy Countryman
Rooms: 3 (PB) $65
Full Breakfast
Credit Cards: A, B, D
Notes: 2, 5, 6, 7, 8, 9, 10, 11, 12, 13, 14

Eddy's Bed and Breakfast

425 Ninth Street, 98290
(360) 568-7081

An 1884 Queen Anne-style Victorian country home surrounded by a white picket fence and beautifully landscaped gardens. There is an in-ground heated pool for guests to enjoy. King- and queen-size canopied guest rooms with private baths, furnished with antiques, Grandma's handmade quilts, and resident teddy bears. A full breakfast is served in the dining room. Swimming, fishing, hiking, biking, skiing, and antique

NOTES: Credit cards accepted: A MasterCard; B Visa; C American Express; D Discover; E Diners Club; F Other; 2 Personal checks accepted; 3 Lunch available; 4 Dinner available; 5 Open all year; 6 Pets welcome;

shopping are just minutes away. Snohomish, Antique Capital of the Northwest is only 25 miles northeast of Seattle on Highway 2 East.

Hosts: Ted and Marlene Bosworth
Rooms: 3 (2 PB; 1 SB) $65-85
Full Breakfast
Credit Cards: A, B
Notes: 2, 5, 7, 8, 9, 10, 11, 12, 13, 14

A Pacific Reservation Service

701 Northwest 60th Street, Seattle, 98107
(206) 784-0539

SNO-1. This beautifully restored Victorian country estate was built in 1884. Crowning the crest of a hill overlooking Snohomish, with a panoramic view of the Cascades, Mount Rainier, and the Olympics, the accommodation offers guests quiet serenity and a relaxed atmosphere. Guests are encouraged to linger in the sun-filled parlors, stroll the beautiful gardens, or just relax and swim in the heated pool. Guest rooms are tastefully decorated with antiques, handmade quilts, and unique beds. $65.

SNOQUALMIE

A Pacific Reservation Service

701 Northwest 60th Street, Seattle, 98107
(206) 784-0539

At the side of the spectacular Snoqualmie Falls, this new inn offers guests unequaled comfort, privacy, and style in each of the 90-plus rooms. Curl up in front of the wood-burning fireplace or relax in a personal spa. Each room has its own private bath. A library, country store, and fine restaurant are available for guests' enjoyment. Hiking, biking, skiing, golf, wineries, fishing, and many other attractions are all close by. $175-600.

SPOKANE

The Fotheringham House

2128 West Second Avenue, 99204
(509) 838-1891; FAX (509) 838-1807

This 1891 Victorian home of the city's first mayor features beautiful hand-carved woodwork, tin ceilings, and an open, curved staircase. The recent award-winning restoration of the exterior and grounds returns this inn to its rightful place as one of the finest homes in historic Browne's Addition. Period furniture, wraparound porch, library, player piano, afternoon and evening tea, and nearby antique shops will delight all guests.

Hosts: Jackie and Graham Johnson
Rooms: 3 (1 PB; 2 SB) $70-85
Full Breakfast
Credit Cards: A, B
Notes: 2, 5, 7, 9, 10, 12, 13, 14

The Fotheringham House

Hillside House

1729 East 18th, 99203
(509) 535-1893 (day); (509) 534-1426 (night)

This is a charming guest house that was built in the 1930s and enlarged through several additions over the years. The inn offers country decor and exquisite hospitality. On a quiet residential street on a hillside overlooking the city and mountains.

7 No smoking; 8 Children welcome; 9 Social drinking allowed; 10 Tennis nearby; 11 Swimming nearby; 12 Golf nearby; 13 Skiing nearby; 14 May be booked through a travel agent.

Hosts love to cook and share their knowledge of the community.

Hosts: Jo Ann and Bud
Rooms: 2 (SB) $50-55
Full Breakfast
Credit Cards: A, B
Notes: 2, 5, 7, 10, 11, 12, 13, 14

Marianna Stoltz House

East 427 Indiana, 99207
(509) 483-4316; (800) 978-6587

American four-square classic historic home is five minutes from downtown Spokane. Furnished with antiques, old quilts, and lace, the hosts offer a wraparound veranda, sitting room, and parlor, which provide relaxation and privacy. King-size, queen-size, or single beds, with private or semiprivate baths, air conditioning, and cable TV. A tantalizing, unique, and hearty breakfast is prepared fresh every day. Close to the opera house, convention center, and Riverfront Park. Children over 12 welcome.

Host: Phyllis Magune
Rooms: 4 (2 PB; 2 SB) $65-75
Full Breakfast
Credit Cards: A, B, C, D, E
Notes: 2, 5, 7, 9, 12, 14

TACOMA

Commencement Bay Bed and Breakfast

3312 North Union Avenue, 98407
(206) 752-8175; FAX (206) 759-4025
EMAIL: GREATVIEWS@aol.com

From its elevated perch above the scenic waterfront, this stately Colonial home affords breathtaking views of Mount Rainier, Commencement Bay, and the Cascades. Three elegantly appointed guest rooms with private baths. A variety of common areas offer a fireplace, hot tub, game room, and outdoor deck An office area with fax and modem hookup awaits business travelers. Full and Continental breakfasts

provided with gourmet coffees daily. Tennis, swimming, hiking, fishing, and golf nearby. Bikes available for guest use. The hosts are knowledgeable of the historical, cultural, and natural aspects of the Tacoma area. Special rates for summer and winter. AAA approved. Children over 12 welcome. Skiing one hour away.

Hosts: Bill and Sharon Kaufmann
Rooms: 3 (PB) $75-105
Full Breakfast
Credit Cards: A, B, C, D
Notes: 2, 5, 7, 9, 10, 11, 12, 14

A Pacific Reservation Service

701 Northwest 60th Street, Seattle, 98107
(206) 784-0539

Cottage in the Woods. Standing on 15 forested acres, this hidden cottage will be equally suitable for long or short stays, honeymoons, anniversaries, or getaways. Overlooking a salmon stream and next to a golf course, it affords guests total privacy. Hosts live on the property and are available to assist guests with sightseeing plans, but will honor the privacy guests seek. One room has a freestanding fireplace on a hearth, brass bed, and kitchenette where breakfast is self-catered. $85.

Tacoma Tudor. This cozy bed and breakfast is next door to the Victorian Guesthouse. Enjoy friendly hospitality and comfort in this home with country-style decor. Guests should allow themselves to be pampered here. $45-55.

Victorian Guesthouse. This lovely guesthouse is near the university on a tree-lined street, away from the busyness of downtown. Mount Rainier and Commencement Bay are nearby. While relaxing in the parlor, the innkeeper can help guests with sightseeing plans. The Guesthouse offers clean, comfortable guest rooms furnished with country antiques. $40-50.

TOKELAND

Tokeland Hotel

100 Hotel Road, 98590
(206) 267-7006

A national historic landmark, the Tokeland
Hotel is on a peninsula bordering
Washington's Willapa Bay and the Pacific
Ocean. No smoking in rooms.

Host: Erin Radke
Rooms: 18 (SB) $43.50-95
Full Breakfast
Credit Cards: A, B, D
Notes: 2, 3, 4, 5, 8, 9, 11, 12, 14

Tokeland Hotel

WESTPORT

A Pacific Reservation Service

701 Northwest 60th Street, Seattle, 98107
(206) 784-0539

WE-1. A small, lovely town on the ocean
where the salmon fishing is the greatest. If
guests are not into fishing, there are many
other activities to enjoy. This historic mansion occupies eight acres, two blocks from
the ocean, and possesses the peacefulness
one desires. Choose from five bedrooms,
all with private baths, with lace curtains,
antiques, and fine period furnishings. Don't
forget to take a long soak in the large hot

tub on the grand cedar deck under the gazebo. Also enjoy the barbecue and picnic
areas, badminton, volleyball, and horseshoes. $75.

WHIDBEY ISLAND

A Pacific Reservation Service

701 Northwest 60th Street, Seattle, 98107
(206) 784-0539

Oak Harbor. At this bed and breakfast
guests can enjoy a fresh, complete
Northwest breakfast, including salmon or
mussels prepared in the hostess's sunlit
kitchen. Spend the day searching out the
treasures of Whidbey Island, and spend the
evening refreshing in the hot tub while
enjoying the outside view. The hosts offer
three wonderful, cozy rooms to guests
when they are ready to retire for the
evening. $65-95.

Whidbey-3. On a quiet cove along wooded
shores, this turn-of-the-century country inn
offers guests the charm and comfort of
rooms and cottages. Some guest rooms are
furnished with antiques. The cottages with
kitchenettes are suitable for family getaways. Guests are invited to enjoy the
charm of the big stone fireplace in the parlor and the breathtaking views over the
water. $85-150.

Whidbey-4. This new and splendidly built
waterfront inn offers a great getaway location. All rooms have lanais, queen-size
beds, whirlpool bath for two, wood-burning
fireplaces, and are beautifully decorated.
Restaurant with award-winning cuisine is
on the premises. $185.

Whidbey-5. This bed and breakfast is a
spacious, modern beach home decorated
with comfortable, homey antiques, including a beautiful diamond-tufted leather love

seat with matching wing-backed chairs. Sit back, enjoy a warm, crackling fire, watch the 52-inch TV, or enjoy a game of pool. The breathtaking view of the Olympic Mountains, Puget Sound, and the San Juan Islands encourages visitors to linger with a cup of freshly ground coffee. $65-95.

WHITE SALMON

The Inn of the White Salmon

172 West Jewett, P.O. Box 1549, 98672
(800) 972-5226

The inn, built as a small hotel in 1937, is now a bed and breakfast providing both privacy and an intimate atmosphere. Explore the Columbia River Gorge. The inn is just 65 miles east of Portland, Oregon. Enjoy elegant antiques, a cozy parlor, room or suite with private bath, a soak in the hot tub. Indulge in a lavish breakfast of more than 20 pastries and breads, and choose from among six breakfast entrées.

Rooms: 16 (PB) $89-115
Full Breakfast
Credit Cards: A, B, C, E
Notes: 2, 5, 6, 8, 9, 12, 13, 14

Llama Ranch Bed and Breakfast

1980 Highway 141, 98672
(509) 395-2786; (800) 800-LAMA

This inn stands between two snow-capped mountains. The hosts offer hands-on experience with llamas, including guided llama walks through the woods. Get better acquainted with these beautiful, intelligent animals. The bedrooms have queen-size beds and spectacular views. Nearby are refreshing waterfalls and natural lava bridges. Other activities in the area include white-water rafting, golf, plane trips over

Mount St. Helens, fishing, hunting, hiking, cave exploration, and huckleberry picking. Cross-country skiing and snowmobiling in the winter. Close to nice restaurants.

Hosts: Jerry and Rebeka Stone
Rooms: 7 (2 PB; 5 SB) $55-75
Full Breakfast
Credit Cards: A, B, D
Notes: 2, 5, 7, 8, 9, 12, 13, 14

WINTHROP

Dammann's Bed and Breakfast

716 Highway 20, 98862
(509) 996-2484; (800) 423-0040

These antique-filled guest rooms are on the banks of the Methow River. Hosts offer a recreation room and piano. The valley is a recreation paradise for photography, seasonal hunting, fishing, hiking, camping, and skiing. Eight lakes within six to eight miles; right at the foot of the Cascade Mountains.

Hosts: Hank and Jean Dammann
Rooms: 2 (1 PB; 1 SB) $55
Continental Breakfast
Credit Cards: None
Notes: 2, 5, 7, 9, 10, 11, 12, 13

WOODLAND

Grandma's House

4551 Lewis River Road, 98674-9305
(360) 225-7002

Bed and breakfast featuring country charm in a three-bedroom 1917 farmhouse on 35 secluded acres overlooking the north fork of the Lewis River. Relax on the deck and view the river and occasional deer and eagles. Private boat launch. Good salmon and steelhead fishing. Eight miles east of Woodland and I-5 and 20 miles west of Cougar on Highway 503, scenic route to Mount St.

NOTES: Credit cards accepted: A MasterCard; B Visa; C American Express; D Discover; E Diners Club; F Other; 2 Personal checks accepted; 3 Lunch available; 4 Dinner available; 5 Open all year; 6 Pets welcome;

Helens National Volcanic Monument. Full country breakfast. AAA approved.

Hosts: Warren and Louise Moir
Rooms: 2 (SB) $55-64
Full Breakfast
Credit Cards: A, B
Notes: 2, 5, 8, 9, 11, 12

YAKIMA

Birchfield Manor Country Inn

2018 Birchfield Road, 98901
(509) 452-1960; (800) 375-3420

Romantic country inn near Washington wine country. European-trained chef/owner. Award-winning restaurant featuring local items and a large wine cellar with many local wines. Some rooms have fireplaces, two-person tubs, and decks. Flower-filled grounds and swimming pool (in season). Hosts will be happy to help guests plan their tour of the valley's great wineries.

Hosts: The Masset Family–Wil, Sandy, Brad, and Greg
Rooms: 11 (PB) $80-195
Full Breakfast
Credit Cards: A, B, C, E
Notes: 2, 4, 5, 7, 9, 11, 12, 14

'37 House

4002 Englewood Avenue, 98908
(509) 965-5537

'37 House is a lovely 7,500-square-foot mansion built in the 1930s. There are five guest rooms with shuttered window panes, window seats under the eaves, and fully tiled private baths. The main floor offers a knotty-wood pine-paneled library with fireplace and TV for reading, relaxing, or socializing; and an elegant dining room with a fireplace. A lower-level recreation room is more informal and offers a pool table and fireplace with informal furnishings. The grounds have the feeling of an oasis in the middle of the city. Area attractions include Yakima wineries, the Sundome, and much more. A delicious full breakfast is included with all room rates. A function room is available for private dinners, meetings, and weddings.

Hosts: Penny Burrows and Vickie Hissong
Rooms: 5 (PB) $70-140
Full Breakfast
Credit Cards: A, B, C
Notes: 2, 3, 5, 7, 8, 9, 12, 13

7 No smoking; 8 Children welcome; 9 Social drinking allowed; 10 Tennis nearby; 11 Swimming nearby; 12 Golf nearby; 13 Skiing nearby; 14 May be booked through a travel agent.

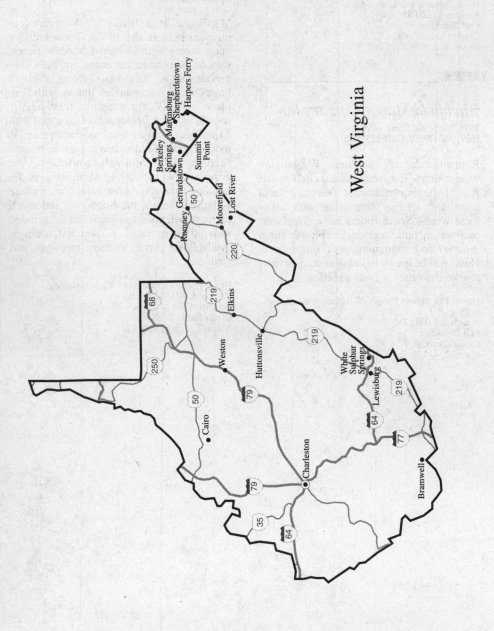

West Virginia

Harpers Ferry
Shepherdstown
Martinsburg
Berkeley
Springs
Gerrardstown
Romney
Summit
Point
50
Moorefield
Lost River
220
68
219
Elkins
Weston
Huttonsville
219
White
Sulphur
Springs
Lewisburg
219
250
64
50
79
77
Cairo
Charleston
Bramwell
79
35
64

West Virginia

Amanda's
Bed and Breakfast

1428 Park Avenue, Baltimore, MD 21217-4230
(410) 225-0001; (800) 899-7533
FAX (410) 728-8957

336. A four-season resort with mountains, lakes, pool, tennis, hiking, fishing, cross-country skiing, sauna, and spa. Chalets. Surrounded by natural beauty. Get pampered. Wood-burning fire stoves.

Blue Ridge
Bed and Breakfast

Route 2, Box 3895, Berryville, VA 22611
(703) 955-1246; (800) 296-1246

A. Two houses; eight rooms completely redone. Near mineral waters, castle, Roman bath and massage, fish ponds, health resort, golf, and horseback riding. $50-65.

B. Lovely Second Empire Victorian home built 110 years ago. On the National Register of Historic Places. Close to antique shops, horseback riding, swimming, fishing, boating, and tennis. $85-120.

Folkestone
Bed and Breakfast

Route 2, Box 404, 25411
(304) 258-3743

This English Tudor-style house was built in 1929, just two miles east of the nation's first health spa. The eight-room residence and surrounding wooded grounds reflect the best of its English heritage and its natural country setting, rich with dogwood, azalea, oak, forsythia, and rhododendron.

Host: Hettie Hawvermale
Rooms: 2 (PB) $60-90
Full Breakfast
Credit Cards: None
Notes: 2, 5, 9, 10, 11, 12, 13

The Glens Country Estate

Route 2, Box 83, 25411
(304) 258-4536; (800) 984-5367
FAX (304) 258-3881

Premiere country inn provides eight beautiful guest rooms. Nestled in the private and quiet Shenandoah valley countryside just three miles from the historic spa-town of Berkeley Springs. Two on-site massage therapists; Jacuzzis; estate gardens; full breakfast; and candlelit, 5-course evening meals served on Lenox/Cherrywood crystal. Healthy cuisine. Wine list. Weekend dinner packages. Midweek spa packages.

Rooms: 8 (PB) $235-265
Full Breakfast
Credit Cards: A, B, C, D, E, F
Notes: 2, 3, 4, 5, 7, 9, 10, 11, 12, 13, 14

Three Oaks and a Quilt

P.O. Box 84, 24715
(304) 248-8316

The oaks—to keep guests cool…the quilts—to keep guests warm. Grandfather

---

NOTES: Credit cards: A MasterCard; B Visa; C American Express; D Discover; E Diners Club; F Other;
2 Personal checks accepted; 3 Lunch available; 4 Dinner available; 5 Open all year; 6 Pets welcome;
7 No smoking; 8 Children welcome; 9 Social drinking allowed; 10 Tennis nearby; 11 Swimming nearby;
12 Golf nearby; 13 Skiing nearby; 14 May be booked through a travel agent.

bought the home in 1904 and it has remained in the family ever since. It was restored in 1985 and 1986, using and reusing everything possible. Most people come to Bramwell to see the coal operators' mansions, which give the the feeling of a town having stood still since the early 1900s. (The bed and breakfast does have modern conveniences.) One is quickly renewed in the restful, relaxing atmosphere. A Whig Rose appliqued quilt hangs on the front porch wall; it is one of three dozen at the inn. Children over 12 welcome.

Host: B. J. Kahle
Rooms: 3 (1 PB; 2 SB) $58.30
Full Breakfast
Credit Cards: None
Notes: 2, 5, 7, 9, 10, 11, 12, 13

CAIRO

Blue Ridge
Bed and Breakfast

Route 2, Box 3895, Berryville, VA 22611
(703) 955-1246; (800) 296-1246

Spectacular log guest house built in the early 1800s offers total privacy. In the middle of 430 acres this property includes two ponds for swimming or fishing and three creeks. Outstanding hiking and walking trails. Home of the American oil business—oil and gas wells on premises. Close to North Bend State Park, as well as glass, marble, and clothing outlets. $48-54.

CHARLESTON

Blue Ridge
Bed and Breakfast

Route 2, Box 3895, Berryville, VA 22611
(703) 955-1246; (800) 296-1246

Seventeen acres of formal and wild gardens. This 1923-1927 Tudor manor house is full of pure luxury and antiques, rare art, history, and gourmet cooking. Feather beds and down comforters. Private dining by appointment. Over 2,100 panes of glass in the house. Working fireplaces. $190 per person.

Brass Pineapple

Brass Pineapple
Bed and Breakfast

1611 Virginia Street East, 25311
(304) 344-0748; (800) CALL WVA

This cozy but elegant 1910 brick home is in Charleston's historic district. The house has been carefully restored to its original grandeur, with antiques throughout, lots of stained glass, and original oak woodwork. Guest rooms are furnished in elegant style with private baths, phones, and cable TV. Catering to business travelers, this bed and breakfast has two business-plan rooms offering phones with data jacks to accommodate laptop PCs, computer tables, and unlimited coffee, tea, and sodas. A small copier and fax are on the first floor. Mints on pillows, fluffy robes, and turndown service add that special touch. Candlelight breakfast is accented with crystal and silver, and may be had alfresco in the petite rose garden in season. Smoking outside only. Children over eight welcome.

Host: Sue Pepper
Rooms: 6 (PB) $80-100
Continental and Full Breakfasts
Credit Cards: A, B, C, E
Notes: 2, 5, 9, 10, 11, 12, 14

NOTES: Credit cards accepted: A MasterCard; B Visa; C American Express; D Discover; E Diners Club; F Other; 2 Personal checks accepted; 3 Lunch available; 4 Dinner available; 5 Open all year; 6 Pets welcome;

Cottonwood Inn

Route 2, Box 61-S
Kabletown Road and Mill Lane, 25414
(304) 725-3371

The Cottonwood Inn offers bed and breakfast accommodations in a restored farmhouse. The inn is on Bullskin Run in the historic Shenandoah Valley near Harpers Ferry and Charles Town and is furnished with antiques and period reproductions. Fireplaces in the dining room, parlor/library, and one guest room. Guests are invited to enjoy the inn's memorable breakfast, warm hospitality, and peaceful, secluded acres surrounded by farmlands.

Hosts: Joe and Barbara Sobol
Rooms: 7 (PB) $75-105
Full Breakfast
Credit Cards: A, B, C, D
Notes: 2, 5, 7, 12, 14

Gilbert House Bed and Breakfast

P.O. Box 1104, 25414
(304) 725-0637

Near Harpers Ferry and Antietam Battlefield. A touch of class in the country. Magnificent stone house, circa 1760, listed on the National Register of Historic Places and the Historic American Building Survey (1938). Spacious and romantic rooms with wood-burning fireplaces and air conditioning. Bridal Suite has curtains around the bed and a claw-foot tub. Many European treasures, some from royal families. In the Middleway historic district. The village is one of the first European settlements in the Shenandoah Valley and is on the original settlers' trail. Colonial-era mill sites, theater at the Old Opera House, horse and auto races, shooting clubs, rafting, and outlet shopping. Village ghost.

Host: Bernie Heiler
Rooms: 3 (PB) $80-140
Full Breakfast
Credit Cards: A, B, C
Notes: 2, 5, 7, 9, 12, 14

ELKINS

Tunnel Mountain Bed and Breakfast

Route 1, Box 59-1, 26241
(304) 636-1684

This charming, three-story fieldstone home is nestled on the side of Cheat Mountain on five private, wooded acres, surrounded by scenic mountains, lush forests, and sparkling rivers. The interior is finished in pine and rare wormy chestnut woodwork. Tastefully decorated throughout with antiques, collectibles, and crafts, it extends a warm and friendly atmosphere to guests.

Hosts: Anne and Paul Beardslee
Rooms: 3 (PB) $65-75
Full Breakfast
Credit Cards: None
Notes: 2, 5, 7, 9, 10, 11, 12, 13

Tunnel Mountain

GERRARDSTOWN

Gerrardstown's Prospect Hill Farm

Box 135, 25420
(304) 229-3346

Gerrardstown's Prospect Hill is a Georgian mansion set on 225 acres and listed on the National Register of Historic Places. Once a well-to-do gentleman's home, it has a permanent Franklin fireplace, antiques, and a hall mural depicting life in the early republic. Guests may choose one of the

Prospect Hill Farm

beautifully appointed rooms in the main house or the former slave quarters, where rooms are complete with country kitchen and fireplace. There is much to do on this working farm near Harpers Ferry, Martinsburg, and Winchester. Children are welcome in the cottage.

Hosts: Charles and Hazel Hudock
Rooms and Cottage: (PB) $85-95
Full Breakfast
Credit Cards: A, B
Notes: 2, 5, 7, 9, 10, 11, 12

HARPERS FERRY

Fillmore Street Bed and Breakfast

Fillmore Street, 25425
(304) 535-2619; (410) 321-5634

With a clear mountain view, this antique-furnished Victorian home is known for its hospitality, service, and gourmet breakfast. Private accommodations and baths, TVs, air conditioning, complimentary sherry and tea, and a blazing fire on cool mornings. Closed Thanksgiving, Christmas, and New Year's Day. Smoking is permitted outside on the porch only. Children over 12 are welcome.

Hosts: Alden and James Addy
Rooms: 2 (PB) $70-75
Full Breakfast
Credit Cards: None
Notes: 2, 5, 9

HUTTONSVILLE

Hutton House

General Delivery, P.O. Box 88, 26273
(304) 335-6701

Enjoy the relaxed atmosphere of this historically registered and antique-filled Queen Anne Victorian. Guest rooms are individually styled, and each guest has his/her own personal favorite. Breakfast varies from gourmet to hearty. Sometimes it is served at a specific time, while at other times it is served at guests' leisure. Children can play games on the lawn. Guests can lose themselves in the beauty of the Laurel Mountains as they lounge on the wraparound porch.

Hosts: Dean Ahren and Loretta Murray
Rooms: 6 (PB) $60-70
Full Breakfast
Credit Cards: A, B
Notes: 2, 5, 7, 8, 9, 12, 13, 14

LEWISBURG

General Lewis Inn

301 East Washington Street, 24901
(304) 645-2600; (800) 628-4454

The General Lewis Inn is one of 54 historic buildings in the National Historic District of Lewisburg. It was created in 1929 by adding to an 1834 home. All rooms are furnished with antiques. The dining room serves a delicious selection of meals. A pond and garden, a living room with books, puzzles, and fireplace, and a wide veranda for rocking encourage relaxing. Two blocks away are shops for antiques, gifts, and clothing. Full breakfast is available at an extra cost.

Hosts: Mary Noel Hock Morgan and Jim Morgan
Rooms: 25 (PB) $60-88
Full Breakfast
Credit Cards: A, B, C
Notes: 2, 3, 4, 5, 6, 7, 8, 9, 10, 11, 12, 14

LOST RIVER

Blue Ridge
Bed and Breakfast

Route 2, Box 3895, Berryville, VA 22611
(703) 955-1246; (800) 296-1246

This outstanding log house comes complete
with conference rooms, hot tub room, swimming pool, washer-dryer, Jacuzzi, six guest
bedrooms with cable TV, and private baths.
Fabulous view of Allegheny Mountains.
Land borders George Washington National
Forest. $82.

MARTINSBURG

Amanda's
Bed and Breakfast

1428 Park Avenue, Baltimore, MD 21217-4230
(410) 225-0001; (800) 899-7533
FAX (410) 728-8957

341. Historic area near Harpers Ferry,
Antietam, C&O Canal, and Potomac River.
Ten beautiful acres of large trees and boxwoods. A long lane lined with maple trees
frames the large stone manor house, circa
1812. There are six guest rooms; most have
their own private bath; one room has a fireplace. $100-125.

Aspen Hall Inn

405 Boyd Avenue, 25401
(304) 263-4385

This majestic 18th-century limestone mansion is surrounded by several beautiful
acres of lawn and woods. An evening stroll
will lead to a footbridge crossing the
Tuscarora Creek. Stop by the gazebo to
enjoy a cool drink and watch the ducks.
Then explore the recently restored 1757
private fort. There are five lovely antique-
furnished queen-size guest rooms with air
conditioning. Fireplace and extra beds

available. After a delicious country breakfast, there is outlet shopping and Harpers
Ferry nearby.

Hosts: Gordon and LouAnne Claucherty
Rooms: 5 (PB) $95-110
Full Breakfast
Credit Cards: A, B
Notes: 2, 7, 9, 10, 11, 12, 13, 14

Boydville, The Inn
at Martinsburg

601 South Queen Street, 25401
(304) 263-1448

This 1812 stone plantation mansion is on a
ten-acre park with 100-year-old trees and
boxwood. Originally part of a Lord Fairfax
grant. The land, once part of a large plantation, was purchased by General Elisha
Boyd in the 1790s and was a retreat for
Stonewall Jackson and Henry Clay. Enjoy
beautiful craftmanship from a past era,
including woodwork, window glass, French
chandeliers, and foyer wallpaper hand-
painted in England in 1812. Great porch
with rockers. Continental plus breakfast.
On the National Register of Historic
Places. Just off of I-81, one and one-half
hours from Washington, D.C., in the heart
of Civil War country. Closed during the
month of August.

Hosts: LaRue Frye, Bob Boege, Carolyn Snyder,
and Pete Bailey
Rooms: 6 (4 PB; 2 SB) $100-125
Continental Breakfast
Credit Cards: A, B
Notes: 2, 7, 9, 10, 12, 13, 14

Pulpit & Palette Inn

516 West John Street, 25401
(304) 263-7012

Oriental ambience in a Victorian home.
Two bedrooms sharing bath. Morning cof-
fee/tea with shortbread and newspaper
served in bed. Full breakfast, afternoon
tea, evening drinks and hors d'oeuvres.
Fifty-store outlet one block away. Other

attractions and golf nearby. No children allowed. No smoking allowed.

Hosts: Bill and Janet Starr
Rooms: 2 (SB) $75
Full Breakfast
Credit Cards: A, B, D
Notes: 2, 7, 9, 12

MIDDLEWAY

Blue Ridge
Bed and Breakfast

Route 2, Box 3895, Berryville, VA 22611
(703) 955-1246; (800) 296-1246

Beautiful stone mansion built in 1760 in an 18th-century village. Close to Harpers Ferry. Romantic rooms and suite. Working fireplaces in bedrooms. Great hospitality. Walking tours and lectures given. On the National Register of Historic Places. $90-150.

MOOREFIELD

McMechen House Inn
Bed and Breakfast

109 North Main Street, 26836
(304) 538-7173; (800) 2 WVA INN (reservations)

Return to the mid-1800s and imagine a time of delicate antebellum grace backdropped by roaring political activity. This Greek Revival home, circa 1853, is in historic Moorefield, and served as Civil War headquarters to both Union and Confederate forces as military control of this lovely valley changed hands many times. Here guests will find excellent food, spacious rooms, friendship, and generous hospitality. Hiking, golfing, train excursions, and wineries nearby. Lunch available six days a week (closed Mondays), March through December. Dinner available Friday, Saturday, and Sunday evenings, March through December. Listed on National Register of Historic Places.

Licensed to serve West Virginia wines. Smoking is restricted.

Hosts: Linda, Bob, and Larry Curtis
Rooms: 7 (4 PB; 3 SB) $60-85
Full Breakfast
Credit Cards: A, B, C, E
Notes: 2, 5, 8, 9, 10, 11, 12, 13

PENCE SPRINGS

Pence Springs Hotel
Country Inn

Route 3/12 Pence Springs, P.O. Box 90, 24962
(304) 445-2606

One of the famous old mineral spas of the Virginias and a roaring 1920s resort. Then the state prison for women (1946-1985), it is now on the National Register of Historic Places, particularly restored as a family-run country inn on 400 acres. Its gardens supply the hotel's country-style meals and the gourmet fare of the nearby Riverside Inn. Pets welcome with special arrangement. Mentioned in *Southern Living*, May 1995.

Innkeepers: O. Ashby Berkley, Rosa Lee Berkley-Miller
Rooms: 15 (PB) $59.50-125
Full Breakfast
Credit Cards: A, B, C, D, E
Notes: 2, 4, 7, 8, 9, 12, 14

ROMNEY

Hampshire House 1884

165 North Grafton Street, 26757
(304) 822-7171

Completely renovated 1884 brick home. Period furniture, fireplaces, and air conditioning; quiet. Private baths and garden. The charm of the 1880s with the comforts of today in a sleepy small town on the beautiful south branch of the Potomac River. Therapeutic massage available.

Hosts: Jane and Scott Simmons
Rooms: 5 (PB) $65-85
Full Breakfast
Credit Cards: A, B, C, D, E
Notes: 2, 5, 7, 9, 10

NOTES: Credit cards accepted: A MasterCard; B Visa; C American Express; D Discover; E Diners Club; F Other; 2 Personal checks accepted; 3 Lunch available; 4 Dinner available; 5 Open all year; 6 Pets welcome;

SHEPHERDSTOWN

Stonebrake Cottage

Shepherd Grade Road, P.O. Box 1612, 25443
(304) 876-6607

Stonebrake Cottage offers a private getaway
near historic Shepherdstown on a 145-acre
farm. The Victorian cottage, furnished with
antiques, has a fully equipped kitchen, two
bathrooms, three bedrooms, and central air.
It is within minutes of the C&O Canal tow
path, Harpers Ferry, Antietam Battlefields,
Blue Ridge outlet center, and the Charles
Town race track. Golf and horseback riding
nearby. Discount for one-week stays.

Host: Anne Small
Rooms: 3 (2 PB; 1 SB) $80-90
Full Breakfast
Credit Cards: A, B
Notes: 2, 5, 7, 8, 9, 10, 11, 12, 13, 14

Thomas Shepherd Inn

Box 1162, 25443
(304) 876-3715

Small, charming inn in a quaint, historic Civil
War town that offers that special hospitality
of the past. Guests find fresh flowers at their
bedsides, fluffy towels and special soaps in
their baths, complimentary beverage by the
fireside, memorable breakfasts. Picnics available. Children over eight welcome.

Host: Margaret Perry
Rooms: 7 (PB) $55-125
Full Breakfast
Credit Cards: A, B, C, D
Notes: 2, 5, 7, 12, 13

Thomas Shepherd Inn

SUMMIT POINT

Blue Ridge Bed and Breakfast

Route 2, Box 3895, Berryville, VA 22611
(703) 955-1246; (800) 296-1246

Small bed and breakfast inn between
Harpers Ferry and Winchester, Virginia.
Tucked away on a lovely tree-lined side
street in quaint rural village. Decorated
with a charming mixture of old and new
collectibles, baskets, and quilts. Old-fashioned hospitality welcomes the crowd-
weary traveler. $60.

VALLEY CHAPEL/WESTON

Ingeberg Acres Bed and Breakfast

Millstone Road, P.O. Box 199, 26446
(304) 269-2834

Guests can have a unique experience at
this scenic 450-acre horse and cattle farm
seven miles from Weston. The three air-
conditioned guest rooms have shared bath.
Enjoy patio, deck, and pool. Casual
atmosphere, private pond for fishing, seasonal hunting, hiking, and bird watching.
Full breakfast. No smoking.

Hosts: Inge and John Mann
Rooms: 3 (SB) $59
Full Breakfast
Credit Cards: None
Notes: 2, 5, 7, 8, 9, 11, 12

WHITE SULPHUR SPRINGS

Blue Ridge Bed and Breakfast

Route 2, Box 3895, Berryville, VA 22611
(703) 955-1246; (800) 296-1246

Mansion built in 1819 just three blocks from
famous Greenbrier resort and spa. Outside
Greenbrier State Forest. Close to National

7 No smoking; 8 Children welcome; 9 Social drinking allowed; 10 Tennis nearby; 11 Swimming nearby;
12 Golf nearby; 13 Skiing nearby; 14 May be booked through a travel agent.

Fish Hatchery. Trout-stocked rivers. Skiing and white-water rafting. $65-90.

The James Wylie House Bed and Breakfast

208 East Main Street, 24986
(304) 536-9444; (800) 870-1613

A beautiful, circa 1819, Georgian Colonial house, this bed and breakfast is in a lovely small-town setting, only ten blocks from the Greenbrier resort and nine miles from historic Lewisburg. Large, spacious rooms offer visitors comfortable luxury in a gracious historic home. A family suite and a log cabin guest house are available accommodations as well. The Wylie House has been given excellent reviews in a national golf magazine, *Mid-Atlantic*

James Wylie House

Country magazine, and many statewide newspapers.

Hosts: Cheryl and Joe Griffith
Rooms: 4 (PB) $65-120
Full Breakfast
Credit Cards: A, B, C
Notes: 2, 5, 7, 8, 9, 10, 11, 12, 13

Wisconsin

ALBANY

Albany Guest House

405 South Mill Street, 53502
(608) 862-3636

Enjoy a restored, spacious block house in the heart of south central Wisconsin's Swiss communities. The refinished wood floors support Oriental carpets, king- and queen-size beds, antiques, and interesting pieces. Swing or rock among the flowers on the front porch, or stroll the two acres of lawn and gardens. Light the master bedroom fireplace or bike the Sugar River Trail.

Hosts: Bob and Sally Braem
Rooms: 4 (PB) $55-68
Full Breakfast
Credit Cards: None
Notes: 2, 5, 7, 8, 9, 12, 13

ALGOMA

Amberwood Beach Inn

N7136 Highway 42 Lakeshore Drive, 54201
(414) 487-3471

Lake Michigan beachfront. Private wooded acreage on the shores of Lake Michigan, less than ten miles from Door County. Large luxury suites, each with private bath and double French doors with private decks opening to the beach. Whirlpool tub, wet bars, refrigerators, Finnish sauna, and hot tub. Sleep to the sound of the waves; awaken to a sunrise over the water.

Hosts: Jan and George
Rooms: 5 (PB) $65-85
Full Breakfast
Credit Cards: A, B
Notes: 2, 7, 9, 11, 12

ALMA

Laue House Inn

P.O. Box 176, 54610
(608) 685-4923

The Laue House Inn is the best remaining example of domestic Italianate architecture in Buffalo County. Placed on the National Register of Historic Places in 1979. Step back in time and enjoy the moderately priced rooms of one of Alma's oldest and most elegant houses. There are six guest rooms with TV, air conditioning, and coffee. Fish cleaning facilities, gas grill for a picnic, canoe rental, and public beach with tennis courts are also available. Basketball, hiking trails, and golf course are nearby.

Rooms: 6 (SB) $25-38
Continental Breakfast
Credit Cards: None
Notes: 2, 6, 7, 9, 10, 11, 12

BARABOO

Gollmar Mansion Inn

422 Third Street, 53913
(608) 356-9432

Elegant, 1889 Victorian circus mansion. Original furniture, antiques, chandeliers, handpainted murals, and beveled glass. Oak and maple wood floors. Untouched beaded oak woodwork, charming guest parlor library. Romantic guest rooms, queen-size beds, and private baths. Full outdoor patio, picnic areas, and gardens on grounds. Central air conditioning. Four blocks from downtown Baraboo and Circus World Museum, five minutes from the Crane

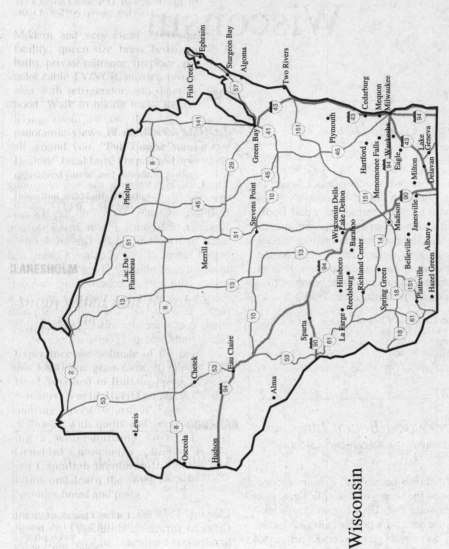

Wisconsin

Foundation and Devils Lake State Park, and ten minutes from the Delton-Dells area. Rates are subject to change. Children over six welcome.

Hosts: Tom and Linda Luck
Rooms: 3 (PB) $75
Full Breakfast
Credit Cards: A, B
Notes: 2, 5, 7, 9, 10, 11, 12, 13

Pinehaven Bed and Breakfast

E13083 Highway 33, 53913
(608) 356-3489

This chalet-style inn overlooks a scenic valley and small private lake. Each distinctly different guest room has a queen-size bed or twin beds; some have wicker furniture or antiques. The common room has a fireplace, TV/VCR, game table, and baby grand piano. Take a stroll in this inviting setting. Ask about the private guest house. Area activities include Devils Lake State Park, Circus World Museum, Wisconsin Dells International Crane Foundation, and ski resorts. Excellent restaurants nearby.

Hosts: Lyle and Marge Getschman
Rooms: 4 (PB) $65-95
Full Breakfast
Credit Cards: A, B
Notes: 2, 5, 7, 8, 9, 10, 11, 12, 13

BELLEVILLE

Abendruh Bed and Breakfast Swiss Style

7019 Gehin Road, 53508
(608) 424-3808

Experience bed and breakfast Swiss-style. This highly acclaimed Wisconsin bed and breakfast offers true Swiss charm and hospitality. The serenity of this peaceful retreat is one of many treasures that keep guests coming back. Spacious guest rooms adorned with beautiful family heirlooms. Sitting room with high cathedral ceiling

and cozy fireplace. An Abendruh breakfast is a perfect way to start a new day or end a peaceful stay.

Host: Mathilde Jaggi
Rooms: 2 (PB) $45-65
Full Breakfast
Credit Cards: A, B
Notes: 2, 5, 7, 10, 11, 12, 13

CEDARBURG

Stagecoach Inn

West 61 North 520, Washington Avenue, 53012
(414) 375-0208; FAX (414) 375-6170

The Stagecoach Inn is a historic, restored 1853 stone building of Greek Revival style. Its 12 cozy rooms feature stenciled walls and Laura Ashley comforters, central air conditioning, and private baths. Six suites with large whirlpool baths are available. In the heart of historic Cedarburg, the inn also features an on-premises pub with a 100-year-old bar and a chocolate shop. Restaurants, antique shops, and winery within walking distance.

Hosts: Liz and Brook Brown
Rooms: 12 (PB) $70-105
Continental Breakfast
Credit Cards: A, B, C, D
Notes: 2, 5, 7, 9, 10, 11, 12, 13, 14

CHETEK

Canoe Bay Inn and Cottages

W16065 Hogback Road, 54728
(800) 568-1995

Wisconsin's ultimate getaway destination. Share the seclusion of this special hideaway with guests who want the very best! The inn is built in the grand tradition of northern lodges with a huge fieldstone fireplace and soaring cedar ceilings. Suites have oversized whirlpools. The lodge sits on the shore of a 50-acre crystal-clear, spring-fed private lake. Cottages are ultra-luxurious

NOTES: Credit cards: A MasterCard; B Visa; C American Express; D Discover; E Diners Club; F Other; 2 Personal checks accepted; 3 Lunch available; 4 Dinner available; 5 Open all year; 6 Pets welcome; 7 No smoking; 8 Children welcome; 9 Social drinking allowed; 10 Tennis nearby; 11 Swimming nearby; 12 Golf nearby; 13 Skiing nearby; 14 May be booked through a travel agent.

with fireplaces and private decks! The grounds include a 280-acre private forest of aspen, oak, and maple. Falls are brilliant with color. Winter sports of every type are available. Simply the best!

Hosts: Dan and Lisa Dobrowolski
Rooms: 4 (PB) $95-195
Cottages: 4 (PB)
Full Breakfast
Credit Cards: A, B, D
Notes: 2, 4, 5, 7, 10, 11, 12, 13

Eagle Centre House

DELAVAN

EAGLE

Allyn Mansion Inn

511 East Walworth Avenue, 53115
(414) 728-9090

This meticulously restored 1885 National Register mansion in Wisconsin's Southern Gateways region offers an authentic Victorian setting. Guests are encouraged to enjoy the entire house with its spacious rooms and fine antique furnishings. Read by one of the ten marble fireplaces, play the grand piano, peruse the collections of Victoriana, have a good soak in a copper bathtub, or swap stories with the hosts on restoration or antiquing.

Hosts: Joe Johnson and Ron Markwell
Rooms: 8 (S6B) $80-90
Full Breakfast
Credit Cards: A, B
Notes: 2, 5, 7, 9, 10, 11, 12, 13, 14

Eagle Centre House

W370 S9590 Highway 67, 53119
(414) 363-4700

A replicated 1846 Greek Revival stage-coach inn decorated with authentic antiques on 20 secluded acres in the Southern Kettle Moraine Forest. Five large chambers with private baths, two with whirlpools. Near Old World Wisconsin, the state of Wisconsin's outdoor living history museum. Ski, bike, hike, shop, golf, swim, fish, or go horseback riding.

Hosts: Riene Wells (Herriges) and Dean Herriges
Rooms: 5 (PB) $85-145
Full Breakfast
Credit Cards: A, B, C
Notes: 2, 5, 7, 9, 11, 12, 13, 14

EAST TROY

Greystone Farms Bed and Breakfast

N9391 Adam's Road, 53120
(414) 495-8485

Tucked away on a hill above a quiet back road, this 115-year-old gentleman farmer's home welcomes guests to a true bed and breakfast experience. Just 19 miles north of Lake Geneva and only a few miles away from the Southern Kettle Moraine State Forest offering hiking, biking, and cross-country skiing. Visit Old World Wisconsin, a living outdoor museum covering almost 600 acres. The philosophy at Greystone

Allyn Mansion

Farm is to provide guests with clean, comfortable lodging; great food; and, of course, old-fashioned hospitality.

Rooms: 4 (S2B) $55-75
Full Breakfast
Credit Cards: A, B, C
Notes: 2, 5, 8, 9, 11, 12, 13, 14

EAU CLAIRE

The Atrium Bed and Breakfast

5572 Priu Road, 54701
(715) 833-9045

Named for its most unique feature, this contemporary home is built around a 20-x 20-foot garden room where a palm tree and bougainvillea vines stretch toward the glassed ceiling. The home is nestled on 15 wooded acres on Otter Creek, beckoning the explorer. Bicycling, cross-country skiing, antiquing, and an Amish community nearby. The best of both worlds: relaxed seclusion only minutes from restaurants, shopping, and the University of Wisconsin, Eau Claire. Full breakfast on weekends; Continental Monday through Friday. Children over 12 welcome.

Host: Celia and Dick Stoltz
Rooms: 3 (1 PB; 2 SB) $50-75
Full and Continental Breakfast
Credit Cards: A, B
Notes: 2, 5, 7, 9, 11, 12, 13

Maple Manor Motel

2507 South Hastings Way, 54701
(800) 624-3763; (715) 834-1148

Rooms are tastefully decorated to reflect the charm and traditions of the Chippewa Valley. River's End, Rose Memories, Yesterday's Forest, porches, parlors, apple harvest, country charm, tales of the North, dreamcatcher, autumn leaves, and more.

Host: Mike Stangel
Rooms: 17 (PB) $39.95-59.95
Full Breakfast
Credit Cards: A, B, C, D, E
Notes: 2, 3, 5, 6, 7, 8, 9, 12

Otter Creek Inn

2536 Highway 12, 54701
(715) 832-2945

Enjoy romantic double whirlpools, breakfast in bed, warm hospitality, and a crackling fire in the great room. Spacious three-story inn with country Victorian decor on one wooded acre. Relax amid the magnificent ambience of area antiques, and watch the deer and other wildlife saunter by on their way to the creek. Imagine all this country charm less than three minutes from numerous restaurants, shops, and museums.

Hosts: Randy and Shelley Hansen
Rooms: 5 (PB) $79-139
Continental Breakfast
Credit Cards: A, B, C, D, E, F
Notes: 2, 5, 7, 9, 10, 11, 12, 13

Otter Creek Inn

EPHRAIM

Eagle Harbor Inn

9914 Water Street, P.O. Box 588, 54211
(414) 854-2121

Nestled in the heart of historic Ephraim in Door County, Eagle Harbor is a gracious, antique-filled country inn. This bed and breakfast is across from the lake and close to the boat ramp, golf course, park, beach, and cross-country ski trails. Children over ten welcome.

Hosts: Nedd and Natalie Neddersen
Rooms: 9 (PB) $79-139
Full Breakfast
Credit Cards: A, B, C
Notes: 2, 5, 7, 9, 10, 11, 12, 13, 14

7 No smoking; 8 Children welcome; 9 Social drinking allowed; 10 Tennis nearby; 11 Swimming nearby; 12 Golf nearby; 13 Skiing nearby; 14 May be booked through a travel agent.

Hillside Hotel

9980 Highway 42, P.O. Box 17, 54211
(414) 854-2417; (800) 423-7023

This beautifully restored 1890s country-Victorian inn overlooks Eagle Harbor on Green Bay. Special to this inn are the full, delightful breakfasts and afternoon teas; feather beds; a spectacular view from the 100-foot veranda and most guest rooms; antique furnishings; and a large, private beach. The hosts also have two deluxe housekeeping cottages available for guests. Near galleries, shops, water sports, and cultural events for visitors to enjoy. Hillside is listed on the National Register of Historic Places.

Rooms: 12 (SB) $68-89
Full Breakfast
Credit Cards: A, B, D
Notes: 2, 5, 7, 8, 10, 11, 12, 13, 14

FISH CREEK (DOOR COUNTY)

Settlement Courtyard Inn

9126 Highway 42, P.O. Box 729, 54212
(414) 868-3524

Seattle into cozy, spacious rooms and suites with white plastered walls, and light oak moldings and furniture, all with individual fireplaces and kitchenettes. Meet others in the lounge by the big stone fireplace or start up a game of chess. Take any of the trails ready for walking, mountain-biking, or cross-country skiing beside stone fences, through quiet woods, and along limestone bluffs overlooking Fish Creek Valley. Browse in the adjacent courtyard shops and galleries or play a lazy game of horseshoes. Seasonal rates are available. Nonsmoking rooms are available.

Hosts: Marise Redmann and John Redmann
  (brother-sister team)
Rooms: 32 (PB) $59-150
Continental Breakfast
Credit Cards: A, B, C, D
Notes: 2, 5, 8, 9, 10, 11, 12, 13

GREEN BAY

The Astor House

637 South Monroe Avenue, 54301
(414) 432-3585

Rooms in five decorative motifs indulge guests: restful Victorian London Room; country French Marseilles Garden; expansive third-floor Hong Kong retreat; the contemporary surprise of New York loft; and desert-palette of Laredo. Private baths, whirlpools, fireplaces, refrigerators, cable TV, telephone, stereos, videos, and CDs all provide first-class comfort. Outstanding bakery, fruit, and gourmet coffee greet the guests each morning. The ideal choice for a business or vacation trip. Museums, performing arts center, casino, restaurants, shopping, sports, and the Green Bay Packers.

Hosts: Doug Landwehr
Rooms: 5 (PB) $79-129
Continental Breakfast
Credit Cards: A, B, C
Notes: 2, 5, 7, 8, 9, 12, 14

HARTFORD

Jordan House

81 South Main Street, 53027
(414) 673-5643

This warm and comfortable Victorian home, furnished with beautiful period antiques, is only forty miles from Milwaukee. Near the attractions of Majestic Holy Hill Shrine, Horicon Wildlife Refuge, and Pike Lake State Park. Walk to the state's largest antique auto museum, which features Kissel automobiles, or browse through antique shops and do some downtown shopping.

Rooms: 4 (1 PB; 3 SB) $55-65
Full Breakfast
Credit Cards: A, B
Notes: 2, 5, 8, 10, 11, 12, 13

NOTES: Credit cards accepted: A MasterCard; B Visa; C American Express; D Discover; E Diners Club;
F Other; 2 Personal checks accepted; 3 Lunch available; 4 Dinner available; 5 Open all year; 6 Pets welcome;

HAZEL GREEN

DeWinters of Hazel Green

2225 Main Street, P.O. Box 384, 53811
(608) 854-2768

DeWinters of Hazel Green is housed in a Federal and Greek Revival-style building, built of brick 145 years ago for John Faherty's home and store. By the end of the century, the building was a hotel hosting up to 45 people a night. Purchased by Edward Simison in 1946; his son, Don, started renovation of DeWinters in 1984. The store and house are furnished with heirlooms from the Simison family. Enjoy a quiet mining town, close to Galena, Illinois, and Dubuque, Iowa, the Point of Beginning, and the cutest little gal in southwest Wisconsin. Inquire about children.

Hosts: Don and Cari Simison
Rooms: 3 (1 PB; 2 SB) $45-75
Full Breakfast
Credit Cards: None
Notes: 2, 5, 11, 12, 13

HILLSBORO

Mascione's Hidden Valley Villas

Rural Route 2, Box 74, 54634
(608) 489-3443

Among 80 acres are five of the most beautiful villas guests could possibly find. Beautifully furnished, very private in the Hidden Valleys area. All have fireplaces, private baths, and a full breakfast is served in a separate dining room. Large villas accommodate up to four people in two bedrooms with living room and fully equipped kitchen. Small villas have large loft bedroom, living room with fireplace, and private bath. Come to relax and find peace by the ponds. Children over 12 welcome.

Host: Mary Ann Mascione
Villas: 7 (PB) $90-190
Full Breakfast
Credit Cards: F
Notes: 2, 7, 9, 10, 11, 12, 14

Jefferson-Day House

HUDSON

Jefferson-Day House

1109 Third Street, 54016
(715) 386-7111

This 1857 home offers antique collections, air-conditioned rooms, double whirlpools, gas fireplaces, and three-course fireside breakfasts. The pleasing decor and friendly atmosphere will relax guests, while the nearby St. Croix River, Octagon House Museum, and Phipps Theatre for the Arts will bring enjoyment. Thirty minutes from Minneapolis, St. Paul, and the Mall of America. Children over nine welcome.

Hosts: Sharon and Wally Miller
Rooms: 4 (PB) $99-169
Full Breakfast
Credit Cards: A, B
Notes: 2, 5, 7, 9, 10, 11, 12, 13, 14

JANESVILLE

Jackson Street Inn Bed and Breakfast

210 South Jackson Street, 53545
(608) 754-7250

This 1900 air-conditioned home with oak intricate paneling, coffered ceilings, and cut-glass windows provides Old World charm. Spacious rooms with queen-size and twin beds. Sitting room with telephone, refrigerator, and books. Lovely parks, botanical gardens, bike and hiking trails,

7 No smoking; 8 Children welcome; 9 Social drinking allowed; 10 Tennis nearby; 11 Swimming nearby;
12 Golf nearby; 13 Skiing nearby; 14 May be booked through a travel agent.

Jackson Street Inn

Olympic pool, beach, and dream playground. Rated excellent by ABBA and two stars by Mobil. Ninety minutes to O'Hare Airport on Highway 11 near I-90.

Rooms: 4 (2 PB; 2 SB) $50-75
Full Breakfast
Credit Cards: A, B
Notes: 2, 5, 7, 8, 9, 10, 11, 12, 13, 14

LAC DU FLAMBEAU

Ty-Bach

3104 Simpson Lane, 54538
(715) 588-7851

For a relaxing getaway anytime of the year, share this modern home on the shore of a tranquil northwoods lake with 80 acres of woods to explore. Guest quarters include a large living area and a deck overlooking Golden Pond. Visit the area attractions: the cranberry marshes, the Native American Museum, pow-wows, professional theater, wilderness cruises, and more. Golf is 12 miles away. Guests are pampered with delicious country breakfasts served at flexible times. Closed March and April. Inquire about pets being welcome.

Hosts: Kermit and Janet Bekkum
Rooms: 2 (PB) $50-60
Full Breakfast
Credit Cards: None
Notes: 2, 7, 9, 10, 11, 12, 13

LA FARGE

Trillium

Route 2, Box 121, 54639
(608) 625-4492

One's own private cottage on this farm amid 85 acres of fields and woods near a tree-lined brook. Experience Wisconsin in a thriving Amish farm community just 35 miles southeast of La Crosse. Children under 12 stay free.

Host: Rosanne Boyett
Cottage: 1 (PB) $65-70
Full Breakfast
Credit Cards: None
Notes: 2, 5, 7, 8, 9, 10, 11, 12, 13

LAKE DELTON

The Swallow's Nest Bed and Breakfast

141 Sarrington, P.O. Box 418, 53940
(608) 254-6900

The unique decor is English in taste with period collectibles. New home with cathedral windows and ceiling. Offers seclusion among the trees and bird's-eye view of the lake. Relax in the library or by the fireplace. Fine restaurants nearby. Close to Wisconsin Dells, Devils Head, two state parks, and Circus World Museum. Gift certificates available.

Hosts: Rod and Mary Ann Stemo
Rooms: 4 (PB) $65-70
Full Breakfast
Credit Cards: A, B
Notes: 2, 5, 7, 11, 12, 13

LAKE GENEVA

Eleven Gables Inn on the Lakes

493 Wrigley Drive, 53147
(414) 248-8393

Nestled in evergreen amid giant oaks in the Edgewater historic district, this quaint lakeside Carpenter's Gothic inn offers privacy in a prime area. The romantic bedrooms, bridal chamber, and unique country cottages all have fireplaces, down comforters, baths, TVs, and wet bars or cocktail refrigerators. Some of the accommodations have charming lattice courtyards, balconies, and private entrances. A private pier provides exclusive water activities for guests. Bike rentals are available. This charming "Newport of the Midwest" community provides visitors with fine dining, boutiques, and entertainment year-round. Call about rates and special packages.

Host: A. Milliette
Rooms: 12 (PB)
Full Breakfast weekends
Continental Breakfast midweek
Credit Cards: A, B, C, E
Notes: 5, 8, 9, 10, 11, 12, 13, 14

T. C. Smith Inn Historic Bed and Breakfast

865 Main Street, 53147
(414) 248-1097; (800) 423-0233

Experience classic elegance and recapture the majesty of 19th-century ambience. The downtown lakeview inn is complete with Oriental carpets, fine period antiques, and European paintings. The decor is traditional to the grand Victorian era. The inn offers eight spacious guest chambers with private baths, several of which have whirlpools and fireplaces. A delicious buffet breakfast is served in the grand parlor under a crystal chandelier before a marble fireplace. A garden, a fountain, and Neoclassical statues grace the large courtyard surrounding the 1845 historical mansion. Gift certificates are available. Call for a brochure.

Hosts: The Marks Family
Rooms: 8 (PB) $75-275
Full Breakfast
Credit Cards: A, B, C, D, E
Notes: 2, 5, 6, 8, 9, 10, 11, 12, 13, 14

LEWIS

Seven Pines Lodge

P.O. Box 137, 54851
(715) 653-2323; FAX (715) 653-2236

A grand, 1903 fly-fishing lodge with many of its original Mission-style furnishings tucked away in a virgin white pine forest. On the National Register of Historic Places. Dine on spectacular year-round porches overlooking the private trout stream. Twelve charming bed and breakfast rooms. Wooded trails and fly fishing on property. Gourmet dinners served with advance reservations. Business conferences, retreats, and weddings planned with attention to detail.

Rooms: 9 (3 PB; 6 SB) $84-170
Continental Breakfast
Credit Cards: A, B
Notes: 2, 5, 7, 8, 9, 10, 11, 12, 13

MADISON

Annie's Bed and Breakfast

2117 Sheridan Drive, 53704
(608) 244-2224; fax (608) 242-9611

Since 1985, when guests want the world to go away, they come to Annie's Bed and Breakfast. This quiet little inn on Warner Park offers a beautiful view and deluxe accommodations. Enjoy the romantic gazebo surrounded by butterfly gardens or

Annie's

the lily pond by the terrace for morning coffee, followed by a sumptuous breakfast. The two-room suites are cozy with antiques, gorgeous quilts, and down comforters. Double Jacuzzi is available. Convenient to everything. Children over twelve welcome.

Hosts: Anne and Larry Stuart
Suites: 2 (PB) $94-114
Full Breakfast
Credit Cards: A, B, C
Notes: 2, 5, 7, 8, 9, 10, 11, 12, 13

Arbor House
An Environmental Inn

3402 Monroe Street, 53711
(608) 238-2981

The inn is across the street from the UW Arboretum with its 1,200 acres ideal for biking, walking, and bird watching. While preserving the charm of this nationally registered historic home, the inn is evolving into a model for urban ecology. The original wood floors, natural stone fireplaces, and sunny breakfast room are admired by visitors. There are whirlpools and TVs in some guest rooms. A delicious full gourmet breakfast is served on weekends. Weekdays, breakfast is Continental plus. Guests are treated to a Gehl's Iced Cappuccino welcome beverage upon arrival, as well as a canoeing pass and Aveda and the Body Shop personal care products. A corporate lodging rate and meeting space are available. A great place for a business retreat or a unique family reunion.

Hosts: John and Cathie Imes
Rooms: 5 (PB) $69-115
Credit Cards: A, B, C
Notes: 2, 5, 7, 8, 9, 10, 11, 12, 13

Canterbury Inn

315 West Gorham, 53703
(608) 283-2541; (800) 838-3850
FAX (608) 283-2541

Canterbury Inn is a literary bed and breakfast directly above what has become a Madison classic, Canterbury Booksellers Coffeehouse. Each of the inn's six rooms is decorated with murals depicting an individual story from Chaucer's *Canterbury Tales*. The rooms also hold bookshelves brimming with old and new titles for guests to enjoy, and a complimentary book and breakfast are provided with each stay. An intimate environment of another age, along with the most contemporary amenities including valet parking, whirlpools, VCRs, microwave ovens, and afternoon wine and cheese. The inn also has in-room fax machine access, a conference room, and a corporate discount plan that, along with its central location in downtown Madison, make it the ideal accommodations for all travelers.

Hosts: Trudy and Harvey Barash
Rooms: 6 (PB) $100-250
Continental Breakfast
Credit Cards: A, B, C
Notes: 2, 3, 4, 5, 7, 8, 9, 10, 11, 12, 13

Collins House
Bed and Breakfast

704 East Gorham, 53703
(608) 255-4230

The Collins House captures the essence of Madison, from its restored Prairie School architecture to its lakefront location and capitol-university proximity. Experience this Midwestern, down-to-earth ambience while enjoying a host of indulgences: famous full breakfasts (oatmeal pancakes with brown sugar pecan sauce and sautéed apples or creamy scrambled eggs with asparagus and shiitake mushrooms), fresh homemade pastries and signature chocolate truffles from the bakery, whirlpools, and lake sunset. The staff are eager to share their love of Madison and make every stay memorable. Pets restricted.

Hosts: Barb and Mike Pratzel
Rooms: 5 (PB) $80-140
Full Breakfast

NOTES: Credit cards accepted: A MasterCard; B Visa; C American Express; D Discover; E Diners Club;
F Other; 2 Personal checks accepted; 3 Lunch available; 4 Dinner available; 5 Open all year; 6 Pets welcome;

Credit Cards: A, B
Notes: 2, 5, 7, 8, 9, 10, 11, 13

Mansion Hill Inn

424 North Pinckney Street, 53703
(608) 255-3999; (800) 798-9070
FAX (608) 255-2217

Eleven luxurious guest rooms, each with a sumptuous bath. Whirlpool tubs, stereo with headphones, hand-carved marble fireplaces, minibars, and elegant Victorian furnishings help to make this restored mansion Madison's only four-diamond inn. Private wine cellar, VCRs, and access to private dining and an athletic club are available upon request. Turndown service. Evening refreshments are available in the parlor. The ideal spot for a perfect honeymoon. Listed on the National Register of Historic Places.

Host: Janna Wojtal
Rooms: 11 (PB) $100-270
Continental Breakfast
Credit Cards: A, B, C
Notes: 2, 5, 7, 9, 11, 14

MEQUON

Port Zedler Motel

10036 North Port Washington Road, 53092
(414) 241-5850 (phone and fax)

Convenient to downtown, casino, and excellent restaurants (only 12 minutes north of downtown Milwaukee). In-room telephones. Full private bath with shower. Winter plug-ins. In-room refrigerator and microwave oven are available upon request. Rate includes cable TV (HBO and Showtime), parking, and ice. AAA approved. Air-conditioned. No charge for children under 12. Senior, AARP, and AAA discounts available. German spoken. Nonsmoking rooms available.

Host: Sheila
Rooms; 16 (PB) $34.95-59.95
Continental Breakfast
Credit Cards: A, B, C, D
Notes: 5, 6, 8, 9, 10, 11, 12, 13, 14

MENOMONEE FALLS

Dorshel's Bed and Breakfast Guest House

W140 N7616 Lilly Road, 53051
(414) 255-7866

Contemporary home decorated with beautiful antiques and in a lovely wooded residential area. Enjoy breakfast on a screened porch or in the formal dining room. Play a game of pool or watch the wildlife feast at special feeders. Two fireplaces offer cozy warmth. Only 20 minutes from Milwaukee. Full Continental breakfast always includes Wisconsin's finest cheese, fresh fruits of the season, and special breads and pastries.

Hosts: Dorothy and Sheldon Waggoner
Rooms: 3 (2 PB; 1 SB) $45-60
Continental Breakfast
Credit Cards: None
Notes: 2, 5, 11, 12, 13

MERRILL

Candlewick Inn

700 West Main Street, 54452
(715) 536-7744; (800) 382-4376

Warm, romantic, and elegant. This 1883 lumber baron's mansion welcomes guests. Fully restored to its original beauty and appointed with fine antiques and period furnishings. Spacious, wicker-filled screened porch, fireplaces, and gift shop.

Host: Dan Staniak
Rooms: 5 (3 PB: 2 SB) $55-110
Full Breakfast
Credit Cards: A, B
Notes: 2, 5, 7, 9, 10, 11, 12, 13,1 4

MILWAUKEE

Marie's Bed and Breakfast

346 East Wilson Street, 53207
(414) 483-1512

Handsome 1896 Victorian home in historic Bay View district. Six minutes from

7 No smoking; 8 Children welcome; 9 Social drinking allowed; 10 Tennis nearby; 11 Swimming nearby; 12 Golf nearby; 13 Skiing nearby; 14 May be booked through a travel agent.

downtown and seven minutes from airport. Furnished with heirlooms, collectibles, and original artwork. Full breakfast served in the Fan Room or the garden. Off-street parking. Central air conditioning. Please write or call for a brochure.

Host: Marie M. Mahan
Rooms: 4 (S2B) $58-70
Full Breakfast
Credit Cards: A, B
Notes: 2, 5, 7, 8, 9, 10, 11, 12

MILTON

The Heritage Bed and Breakfast Registry

758 Wacker Drive, Suite 3600, Chicago, IL 60601
(312) 857-0800; FAX (312) 857-0805

H500. The house sits on a ten-acre farm, affording beautiful sunsets and country walks. The interior has a country flavor, punctuated with architectural pieces from churches. There are a variety of guest rooms available, one with a private bath. The most deluxe of these boasts a skylight. Within blocks of highway. Parking available. Other languages spoken. Pets on premises. Fireplace. No smoking. Full breakfast. $40-50.

OSCEOLA

St. Croix River Inn

305 River Street, 54020
(715) 294-4248; (800) 645-8820

A meticulously restored 80-year-old stone home nestled in one of the region's finest recreational areas. Ski at Wild Mountain or Trollhaugen. Canoe or fish in the lovely St. Croix River. Then relax in a suite, some with fireplaces, all with Jacuzzi whirlpool baths. Breakfast served in room.

Host: Bev Johnson
Rooms: 7 (PB) $85-200
Full Breakfast
Credit Cards: A, B, C
Notes: 9, 10

PHELPS

Limberlost Inn

2483 Highway 17, 54554
(715) 545-2685

Modern log home with rustic northwoods charm surrounded by acres of national forest and lakes. Relax on the porch swing, in the hammock, or in the sauna before retiring to the comfort of down pillows and handmade quilts. Enjoy the screened porch, decks, or VCR and movie collection in the living room. Full breakfast is served in front of the fieldstone fireplace in the dining room.

Hosts: Bill and Phoebe McElroy
Rooms: 2 (SB) $55
Full Breakfast
Credit Cards: None
Notes: 2, 5, 7, 9, 10, 11, 12, 13

PLATTEVILLE

Cunningham House

110 Market Street, 53818
(608) 348-5532

Built in 1906 by Dr. Cunningham, the Cunningham House can be found on the park in the heart of historic downtown Platteville. Gleaming floors, lace curtains, and old-fashioned wallpaper have been restored to this historic home. Original fixtures, beautiful leaded glass, and a corner fireplace in the par-

Cunningham House

lor all add to the charm and grace that was then and is now the Cunningham House.

Hosts: Arletta and Jud Giese
Rooms: 3 (PB) $50-60
Full Breakfast
Credit Cards: None
Notes: 2, 5, 8, 9, 10, 11, 12

PLYMOUTH

52 Stafford
An Irish Guest House

52 Stafford Street, 53073
(414) 893-0552; (800) 421-4667

Listed on the National Register of Historic Places, this inn has 19 rooms, 17 of which have whirlpool baths and cable TV, and 13 of which are nonsmoking. 52 Stafford features one of the most beautiful pubs in America, serves lunch daily and dinner seven nights a week. Also features a full-time pastry chef. There are 35,000 acres of public recreation land nearby; cross-country skiing, hiking, biking, sports fishing, boating, swimming, and golf. Crystal-clear lakes and beautiful fall colors. Continental breakfast served weekdays. Full breakfast served weekends.

Hosts: Rip and Christine O'Dwanny
Rooms: 19 (PB) $69-99
Full Breakfast and Continental Breakfast
Credit Cards: A, B, C, D, E
Notes: 2, 3, 4, 5, 6, 8, 9, 10, 11, 12, 13, 14

REEDSBURG

Parkview Bed and Breakfast

211 North Park Street, 53959
(608) 524-4333

In Reedsburg's historic district, this 1895 Queen Anne Victorian home has fish ponds, a windmill, and playhouse enhancing the grounds. Across from City Park and one block from downtown. Discover the original woodwork and hardware, tray ceilings, suitor's window, and built-in buffet inside

Parkview

this cozy home. Wisconsin Dells, Baraboo, Spring Green, and bike trails are nearby. Inquire about accommodations for children.

Hosts: Tom and Donna Hofmann
Rooms: 4 (2 PB; 2 SB) $60-75
Full Breakfast
Credit Cards: A, B, C
Notes: 2, 5, 7, 9, 10, 11, 12, 13

RICHLAND CENTER

The Mansion

323 South Central, 53581
(608) 647-2808

This 19-room brick mansion was built in the early 1900s by a lumberman and is just around the corner from the Frank Lloyd Wright Warehouse-Museum in the city of Wright's birth. Quarter-sawn oak woodwork and parquet floors of oak, walnut, and maple. Quietly elegant, but affordable. Air-conditioned, but no TV. Call regarding pets. Children over 12 welcome. Continental plus breakfast is served.

Hosts: Beth Caulkins and Harvey Glanzer
Rooms: 5 (S2B) $45-55
Continental Breakfast
Credit Cards: None
Notes: 2, 5, 10, 11, 12, 13

7 No smoking; 8 Children welcome; 9 Social drinking allowed; 10 Tennis nearby; 11 Swimming nearby; 12 Golf nearby; 13 Skiing nearby; 14 May be booked through a travel agent.

SPARTA

The Franklin Victorian Bed and Breakfast

220 East Franklin Street, 54656
(608) 269-3894; (800) 845-8767

This turn-of-the-century home welcomes guests to bygone elegance with small town quiet and comfort. The four spacious bedrooms, two with a shared bath and two with private baths, provide a perfect setting for ultimate relaxation. Enjoy a full home-cooked breakfast served before starting the day of hiking, biking, skiing, canoeing, antiquing, or exploring this beautiful area. Canoe rental and shuttle service for bikers and canoeists available. Children over eight welcome.

Hosts: Lloyd and Jane Larson
Rooms: 4 (2 PB; 2 SB) $70-92
Full Breakfast
Credit Cards: A, B
Notes: 2, 5, 7, 9, 10, 11, 12, 13, 14

Just-n-Trails Bed and Breakfast Farm Vacation

Route 1, Box 274, 54656
(608) 269-4522; (800) 488-4521

A bed and breakfast specializing in recreation, relaxation, and romance. Separate buildings: Paul Bunyan log cabin, with two bedrooms, whirlpool in the atrium, and a fireplace; the Granary and Little House on the Prairie log cabins, each with whirlpool and fireplace; and the Carriage House for families and groups. Five rooms in 1920 farmhouse on active dairy farm. Laura Ashley linens. Four-course breakfasts. Near famous Elroy-Sparta Bike Trail. Skiing on premises.

Hosts: Donna and Don Justin
Rooms: 8 (7 PB; 1 SB) $65-195
Full Breakfast
Credit Cards: A, B, C, D
Notes: 2, 5, 6, 7, 8, 9, 12, 13, 14

SPRING GREEN

Bettinger House Bed and Breakfast

Highway 23, Plain, 53577
(608) 546-2951

This 1904 brick home, once owned by the host's midwife grandmother, is near the world famous House on a Rock, Frank Lloyd Wright's Taliesin, and the American Players Theatre. A home-cooked full breakfast is served every morning.

Hosts: Marie and Jim Neider
Rooms: 6 (2 PB; 4 SB) $50-65
Full Breakfast
Credit Cards: A, B
Notes: 2, 5, 7, 9, 10, 11, 12, 13, 14

STEVENS POINT

Dreams of Yesteryear Bed and Breakfast

1100 Brawley Street, 54481
(715) 341-4525

Designed by J. H. Jeffers, this bed and breakfast was built in 1901 and is lavish in Victorian detail. Period furniture is evident throughout. The hosts love to visit with guests and talk about this cozy home and its furnishings. The home is listed on the

Dreams of Yesteryear

National Register of Historic Places, and its restoration was featured in *Victorian Homes* magazine. Children over 12 welcome.

Hosts: Bonnie and Bill Maher
Rooms: 5 (PB) $55-125
Full Breakfast
Credit Cards: A, B, C
Notes: 2, 5, 7, 9, 10, 11, 12, 13, 14

STURGEON BAY

The Gray Goose Bed and Breakfast

4258 Bay Shore Drive, 54235
(414) 743-9100

One of Door County's special places. An intimate bed and breakfast on a quiet, wooded site near the city. Wonderful woods, water, and sunset views. Warm hospitality in a Civil War home. Authentic country antique furnishings. Four large, cheerful guest rooms. Guest sitting room with games, books, cable TV, and piano. Outstanding gourmet breakfasts in a beautiful dining room. Complimentary snacks and beverages. Full porch with wicker and swing. Brochure. Gift certificates. Charter member of Wisconsin Bed and Breakfast Association.

Hosts: Jack and Jessie Burkhardt
Rooms: 4 (S2B) $65-80
Full Breakfast
Credit Cards: A, B, C
Notes: 2, 5, 9, 10, 11, 12, 13, 14

Inn at Cedar Crossing

336 Louisiana Street, 54235
(414) 743-4200

Warm hospitality, elegant antique-filled guest rooms, and creative regional cuisine are a tradition at this most intimate Door County inn, listed on the National Register of Historic Places. Luxurious whirlpool tubs, cozy fireplaces, and evening refreshments await pampered travelers. Exquisite dining (breakfast, lunch, and dinner) features fresh regional ingredients, scratch

bakery, fine wines, and libations. Set in the beauty and culture of Wisconsin's Door Peninsula. Inquire about accommodations for children.

Host: Terry Wulf
Rooms: 9 (PB) $79-138
Continental Breakfast
Credit Cards: A, B, D
Notes: 2, 3, 4, 5, 7, 9, 10, 11, 12, 13

The Scofield House Bed and Breakfast

908 Michigan Street, P.O. Box 761, 54235
(414) 743-7727

Described as "Door County's most elegant bed and breakfast." Authentic bed and breakfast in turn-of-the-century restored Victorian Queen Anne house, circa 1902. Prominent home of Sturgeon Bay Mayor Bert Scofield. Very ornate interior with inlaid floors and ornamented woodwork. Six guest rooms, each with private bath, most with double whirlpool, fireplaces, cable TV, VCR, and stereo. Free movie library. High Victorian decor throughout with fine antiques. Air-conditioned. Full gourmet breakfast and afternoon complimentary sweet treats and teas. Call or write for brochure. Mobil Three-Star. Featured in *Chicago Tribune, Country Inns,* and *Midwest Living.* Listed number 10 in top 25 inns and bed and breakfasts in the U. S. and American Historic inns.

Hosts: Bill and Fran Cecil
Rooms: 6 (PB) $89-190
Full Breakfast
Credit Cards: None
Notes: 2, 5, 7, 9, 10, 11, 12, 13

White Lace Inn

16 North Fifth Avenue, 54235
(414) 743-1105

The White Lace Inn is a romantic getaway featuring three restored turn-of-the-century homes surrounding lovely gardens and a gazebo. The 15 wonderfully inviting guest rooms are furnished with antiques,

White Lace Inn

four-poster and Victorian beds, in-room fireplaces in some rooms, and double whirlpool tubs in others.

Hosts: Bonnie and Dennis Statz
Rooms: 15 (PB) $49-168
Continental Breakfast
Credit Cards: A, B, C, D
Notes: 2, 5, 7, 9, 10, 11, 12, 13

TWO RIVERS

Red Forest Bed and Breakfast

1421 25th Street, 54241
(414) 793-1794

The Red Forest Bed and Breakfast is on Wisconsin's east coast. Minutes from Manitowoc, Wisconsin's port city of the Lake Michigan car ferry. Also midway from Chicago and the Door County Peninsula. The hosts invite guests to step back in time to 1907 and enjoy the gracious three-story, shingle-style home. Highlighted with stained-glass windows and heirloom antiques. Inquire about accommodations for children.

Hosts: Kay and Alan Rodewald
Rooms: 4 (2 PB; 2 SB) $60-80
Full Breakfast
Credit Cards: A, B, C, D
Notes: 2, 5, 7, 9, 10, 11, 12, 13, 14

WAUKESHA

Mill Creek Farm Bed and Breakfast

S47 W22099 Lawnsdale Road, 53186
(414) 542-4311; FAX (414) 542-8579

Amid gently rolling hills of eastern Waukesha County lies Mill Creek Farm Bed and Breakfast with 160 acres of forest, pond, lawns, and trails. Just 30 minutes west of Milwaukee and two hours north of Chicago's Loop is this area's loveliest private wooded estate. Seasonal indoor and outdoor activities available. Two beautifully decorated rooms. Shared bath. Tantalizing cooked breakfast. Telephone, fax, and copy machine available. Cross-country skiing on property.

Hosts: Vern and Kathryn Herman
Rooms: 2 (SB) $65-75
Full Breakfast
Credit Cards: None
Notes: 2, 5, 7, 8, 11, 12, 13, 14

WISCONSIN DELLS

Thunder Valley Inn

W15344 Waubeek Road, 53965
(608) 254-4145

Scandinavian hospitality in a country setting. Homemade breads, rolls, and jams will delight the guests. Real old-fashioned comfort. Stroll the farmstead, pet the animals, or relax with a good book and cider or Norsk coffee. Near famous Dells. Rated one of ten Midwest best.

Hosts: Anita, Kari, and Sigrid Nelson
Rooms: 6 (PB) $45-80
Full Breakfast
Credit Cards: A, B
Notes: 2, 5, 7, 8, 9, 10, 11, 12, 13

NOTES: Credit cards accepted: A MasterCard; B Visa; C American Express; D Discover; E Diners Club; F Other; 2 Personal checks accepted; 3 Lunch available; 4 Dinner available; 5 Open all year; 6 Pets welcome;

Wyoming

BIG HORN

Spahn's Bighorn Mountain Bed and Breakfast

Box 579, 82833
(307) 674-8150

Towering log home and secluded guest cabins on the mountainside in whispering pines. Borders one million acres of public forest with deer and moose. Gracious mountain breakfast served on the deck with binoculars to enjoy the 100-mile view. Owner was a Yellowstone ranger. Just 15 minutes from Sheridan and I-90.

Hosts: Ron and Bobbie Spahn
Rooms: 4 (PB) $65-100
Full Breakfast
Credit Cards: A, B
Notes: 4, 5, 7, 8, 9, 13

BUFFALO

Bed and Breakfast Western Adventure

P.O. Box 4308, Bozeman, MT 59772
(406) 585-0557; FAX (406) 585-2869

121. Built by a wealthy rancher as his "in town" house, this bright, gracious, turn-of-the-century bungalow-styled home has always been the focal point of the Buffalo community. Guests can enjoy one of the five spacious bedrooms, attractively decorated with interesting antiques, three with private baths. Guests are also invited to relax in front of a fossil rock fireplace, soak in the Jacuzzi, or unwind on the porch or balcony that overlooks the big yard; bird watching is encouraged. Hot tub. A golf course and Olympic-size municipal pool are two blocks away. Horseback riding, cycling, fishing, boating, and hiking are nearby; Buffalo is the entrance to the Big Horn Mountains at Highway 16. Full breakfast. No smoking. No pets. $55-75.

Cloud Peak Inn

Cloud Peak Inn

590 North Burrit Avenue, 82834
(307) 684-5794

The Cloud Peak Inn, circa 1906, features five guest bedrooms which exhibit unique personalities ranging from romantic to nostalgic. The Cloud Peak Room features a hand-painted floral garland on the ceiling and a private balcony with a view. The remaining rooms are comfortable with twin, double, or queen-sized beds. Three of the guest rooms have private baths. Guests can relax in the cozy den in front of fossil rock fireplace or enjoy the sunroom and Jacuzzi.

Hosts: Rick and Kathy Brus
Rooms: 5 (3PB; 2SB) $40-75
Full Breakfast
Credit Cards: A, B, C
Notes: 2, 5, 7, 8, 9, 10, 11, 12, 13, 14

---

7 No smoking; 8 Children welcome; 9 Social drinking allowed; 10 Tennis nearby; 11 Swimming nearby; 12 Golf nearby; 13 Skiing nearby; 14 May be booked through a travel agent.

Wyoming

212 · Newcastle · 85 · Devils Tower · 90 · 16 · 14 · 59 · 25

Cheyenne · 85 · Wheatland · 26 · 25 · 80 · Laramie · 287 · 230

Casper · 487 · Saratoga · 287

Big Horn · Buffalo · 14 · 90 · 25 · 16 · 20 · 220 · 287 · 80 · 789

Cody · 14 · 20 · 310 · 20 · Riverton · 287 · 26 · 789 · Lander · 28

Dubois · 26 · Pinedale · 191 · Jackson/Jackson Hole · 189

Wilson · 89 · 212 · 191 · 89 · 30 · 80 · 189 · 30 · 191

CASPER

Bed and Breakfast Western Adventure

P.O. Box 4308, Bozeman, MT 59772
(406) 585-0557; FAX (406) 585-2869

72. Built in 1917, this attractive two-story home is conveniently near downtown Casper. One bedroom has a queen-size bed and private bath. Four large bedrooms, one offering a fireplace, share three baths. A huge living room with a fireplace and bookcases and a large dining room, where family-style meals are served, are common areas available to guests. A small conference room is available for meetings. A cement deck and patio off the living room for relaxing in the fresh air. Within walking distance of downtown shops, planetarium, and museums. Ski areas 20-60 minutes away. Lakes nearby for boating, sailing, or fishing. Lunch or dinner by prior arrangement. No pets. Smoking restricted. Children over 14 welcome. Full breakfast. $55-70.

CHEYENNE

A. Drummond's Ranch Bed and Breakfast

399 Happy Jack Road, State Highway 210, 82007
(307) 634-6042 (phone and FAX)

Quiet, gracious retreat on 120 acres; 20 minutes to Cheyenne or Laramie, through Medicine Bow National Forest on the scenic bypass for I-80. Near state park. Mountain biking, hiking, rock climbing, cross-country skiing, and fishing. Bring own horse and train at 7,500 feet. Boarding for horses and pets in transit. Soft "adventure at your pace" packages available. Outdoor hot tubs. Private suite with fireplace, steam sauna, and private deck. Featured in *Country Inns* and *Country Extra* magazines. Terry-cloth robes for guests dur-

ing stay. Beverages, fresh fruit, and homemade snacks always available. AAA and Mobil approved. Reservations required.

Host: Taydie Drummond
Rooms: 4 (2 PB; 2 SB) $65-150
Full Breakfast
Credit Cards: A, B
Notes: 2, 3, 4, 5, 7, 8, 9, 12, 13, 14

Bed and Breakfast Western Adventure

P.O. Box 4308, Bozeman, MT 59772
(406) 585-0557; FAX (406) 585-2869

65. This handsome, Southwestern ranch-style home is on 100 acres of pasture and prairie that invite guests to observe the spectacular sunrises and sunsets. The house is surrounded by an adobe fence. An abundance of flowering bushes enhances the rambling porches. Wildlife is usually within view, grazing in pastures beside farm animals that reside at the ranch. Four guest rooms, each with queen-size bed and private bath, have their own unique decor. Connecting rooms can be used as a suite for four people. A library with fireplace and TV is a common area for all guests. Videos, games, and traveling materials available. Dinner by reservation, refreshments served upon arrival; a large yard invites games of croquet and horseshoe. Kennels are available for pets. Children welcome; cribs available. No smoking. Full breakfast. $60-70.

75. A quiet, gracious, 120-acre retreat is in the Laramie Range near Medicine Bow National Forest and Curt Gowdy State Park. Enjoy the glorious night sky and relax in the surrounding serenity. Comfortable rooms, tastefully decorated with quilts, antiques and collectibles, and private art collection await each guest. Two rooms on the second floor, one with sink, share a bath. On the first floor, a room with queen-size bed and private bath has an outdoor hot tub on a private deck. A private carriage house suite with queen-size bed, private bath with steam shower, outdoor hot tub, kitchen, gas fireplace, and private entrance is available. Fresh flowers, terry-cloth robes, outdoor hot tub, and afternoon refreshments always available. Dinner and lunch with advance reservations. Dietary restrictions accommodated. Dog and horse boarding on premises. AAA and Mobil approved. No smoking. Dog in home. Full breakfast. $75-100.

242. This secluded ranch home, on ten country acres, has a view of mountains of the west. A big Wyoming welcome awaits guests in this rural western atmosphere. There are three guest rooms; upper level has queen-size bed and private bath; on lower level, two rooms, one with queen-size bed, one with twin beds, share a bath and sitting room with pool table and TV. Old West Museum, state capitol, Frontier Days nearby, also the "Daddy of 'Em All" rodeos at Frontier Park. Terry Buffalo Ranch. Big game hunting and fishing. Pets in home include cat, dog, and others. Full breakfast. $50.

The Howdy Pardner

1920 Tranquility Road, 82009
(307) 634-6493

A big Wyoming welcome awaits guests in a relaxed country setting. This very Western but modern, secluded ranch home on ten country acres is perched high on a hill, with views all around that invite walkabouts, yet is only ten minutes from Frontier Park, the airport, I-25, and I-80. Area attractions include the Old West Museum, Terry Bison Ranch, Laramie-Fox Park Excursion Trainride, Old Fort Laramie, Oregon Trail Wagon Ruts, Signature Cliff, and Frontier Days "Daddy of 'Em All" rodeos, and night shows during the last full week of July.

Host: Jan Peterson
Rooms: 3 (1 PB; 2 SB) $50-65
Full Breakfast
Credit Cards: A, B
Notes: 2, 5, 6, 7, 8, 9, 10, 11, 12, 13, 14

Porch Swing

Porch Swing
Bed and Breakfast

712 East 20th Street, 82001
(307) 778-7182 (phone and FAX)

Long ago is not far away in this charming, authentically restored 1907 two-story cottage filled with antiques. Handmade quilts on every bed. Summer gardens are fragrant with flowers and herbs. Edible flowers at breakfast. Breakfast by the fire in winter and on the back porch in summer. Vegetarian and vegan breakfasts on request. Walk to downtown, museums, and restaurants. Not far from mountain parks for hiking, bicycling, and cross-country or downhill skiing. Afternoon snacks. Guided tours available. Pets with prior approval. Inquire about for children.

Hosts: Tom and Carole Eppler
Rooms: 3 (1 PB; 2 SB) $43-66
Full Breakfast
Credit Cards: A, B
Notes: 2, 4, 5, 7, 9. 10, 11, 12, 14

CODY

Bed and Breakfast
Western Adventure

P.O. Box 4308, Bozeman, MT 59772
(406) 585-0557; FAX (406) 585-2869

116. This log-style home is part of a small ranch just east of Cody that is home to a

NOTES: Credit cards accepted: A MasterCard; B Visa; C American Express; D Discover; E Diners Club;
F Other; 2 Personal checks accepted; 3 Lunch available; 4 Dinner available; 5 Open all year; 6 Pets welcome;

group of horses that can be seen prancing in nearby pastures. From the front porch look across the valley to see the Heart Mountains with the Beartooths peeking on the side. Relax on the red-tiled patio in the back and see the Carter Mountain range and on a clear day, the Bighorn Mountains. The large, petrified wood fireplace forms the focal point of the guests' common area in the dining and living rooms. The musically adventurous can take a turn at the piano. Two comfortably decorated guest rooms, each with a double bed, share a bath. In Cody there are nightly rodeos, the Buffalo Bill Historical Center, and Old Trail Town. Fish or raft in nearby Shoshone River. Airport pickup, horse boarding, and horseback riding can be arranged. No smoking. No pets. Children over five welcome. Cats on premises. Full breakfast. $75.

246. This attractive, well kept, white mansion was built near the turn of the century by Buffalo Bill Cody and was the family home of his daughter, Irma. Guests get a feeling of the country when taking a relaxing walk around the lovely grounds and seeing the large country garden filled with vegetables and beautiful flowers. Four guest rooms, each with private bath and double beds (two are extra long), are handsomely appointed with antique furnishings, quilts, and period decor. Yellowstone National Park is an hour away. Buffalo Bill Historical Center (Winchester Arms Museum and some of the world's finest Western art), Old Trail Town, and Indian battle grounds are nearby. Buffalo Bill Dam, Reservoir, and Visitor Center are six miles. Rodeos occur nightly during the summer. No smoking. No pets. Full breakfast. $70-80.

Hunter Peak Ranch

Box 1731, Painter Route, 82414
(307) 587-3711; (307) 754-5878 (winter)

Hunter Peak Ranch, at 6,700-foot elevation, is in the Shoshone National Forest, with access to North Absaroka and Beartooth Wilderness Areas and Yellowstone National Park. Come enjoy the area's photographic opportunities, hiking, fishing, and horseback riding. Open May through December. Minimum stay of three nights. Personal checks accepted for deposit only. Smoking restricted.

Hosts: Louis and Shelley Cary
Rooms: 8 (PB) $87
Full Breakfast
Credit Cards: None
Notes: 3, 4, 8, 9, 11, 14

The Lockhart Inn Bed and Breakfast

109 West Yellowstone Avenue, 82414
(307) 587-6074; (800) 377-7255
FAX (307) 584-8644

The historic home of famous Cody author Caroline Lockhart. Built in the 1890s and refurbished from 1985 to 1994. Seven guest rooms, all with private baths, are decorated in turn-of-the-century style with modern conveniences. Enjoy breakfast in the dining area where coffee, tea, cider, and brandy are always available. Wood-burning stove in parlor with piano. Within walking distance of Buffalo Bill Historical Center, Cody Nite Rodeo, Old Trail Town, and river rafting.

Host: Cindy Baldwin
Rooms: 7 (PB) $72-95
Full Breakfast
Credit Cards: A, B, D
Notes: 2, 3, 5, 7, 8, 9, 10, 11, 12, 13, 14

Trout Creek Inn

Yellowstone Highway 14, 16, 20, West, 82414
(307) 587-6288

Imagine basking in the morning sunshine, a sumptuous "all you can eat" breakfast on a lawn table, and scenic mountains all around (unless guests would prefer to be served in their rooms). This bed and breakfast is in the valley Theodore Roosevelt called the "world's most scenic." Private pond and stream trout fishing, swimming, horseback riding, and picture taking. Four kitchenettes

7 No smoking; 8 Children welcome; 9 Social drinking allowed; 10 Tennis nearby; 11 Swimming nearby; 12 Golf nearby; 13 Skiing nearby; 14 May be booked through a travel agent.

available; accessible to the handicapped. Lunch and dinner nearby. Tennis and golf are 15 miles away. Children's playground and petting zoo.

Hosts: Bert and Norma Sowerwine
Rooms: 21 (PB) $35-78
Full Breakfast
Credit Cards: A, B, C, D, F
Notes: 2, 5, 6, 7, 8, 9, 10, 11, 12, 13

DEVILS TOWER

Bed and Breakfast Western Adventure

P.O. Box 4308, Bozeman, MT 59772
(406) 585-0557; FAX (406) 585-2869

241. This elegant and relaxed country home has a large yard, often visited by wildlife, with a spectacular view of Devils Tower. A handsomely decorated bedroom with king-size bed, lush quilts, and private shower has its own redwood deck. A beautiful and interesting place to relax on a cross-country tour of the West. In summer, walking distance of ranger-guided nature walk, visitors center, and evening campfire programs at Devils Tower. Cross-country skiing and hunting. No smoking. No pets. Continental plus breakfast. $60.

DUBOIS

Bed and Breakfast Western Adventure

P.O. Box 4308, Bozeman, MT 59772
(406) 585-0557; FAX (406) 585-2869

91. This handsome rustic home sits high on a hillside its many windows providing breathtaking views of the homestead, the Wind River Mountains to the south, and the Badlands to the north. An expansive yard with large trees and meandering creek has the original, nearly century-old, sod-covered buildings. Two tastefully decorated guest rooms share a bathroom with Jacuzzi

and separate sauna. Fishing on property. See knives custom-made by host and lovely gardens in the yard. No smoking. No pets. Full breakfast. $65.

Jakey's Fork Homestead

Fish Hatchery Road, P.O. Box 635, 82513
(307) 455-2769

Jakey's Fork Homestead nestles in the shadow of the wild and majestic Wind River Mountains. The main house overlooks the original, century-old, sod-covered buildings and an unspoiled front stream. Its two guest bedrooms are light and airy with spectacular views from every window. The large bathroom has a Jacuzzi and a sauna. Down on the creek is the bunkhouse, rustic but cozy, with a wood cookstove. Nearby is the cowboy town of Dubois, a gateway to Yellowstone and Teton Parks.

Hosts: Irene and Justin Bridges
Rooms: 3 (SB) $40-65
Full Breakfast
Credit Cards: A, B
Notes: 2, 3, 4, 5, 7, 8, 9, 10, 12, 13, 14

JACKSON

Bed and Breakfast Western Adventure

P.O. Box 4308, Bozeman, MT 59772
(406) 585-0557; FAX (406) 585-2869

60. This lovely ranch-style home, built with Colorado flagstone, is in downtown Jackson. The interior has a European design that is highlighted with antique furnishings. The present owner represents the third generation. There are three bedrooms on the main floor, each with private bath. One bedroom has a queen-size bed; the other two rooms have two double beds. A downstairs recreation room with pool and Ping-Pong tables. Afternoon tea served. No smoking. Children over ten welcome. Cat in residence. Full breakfast. $90.

NOTES: Credit cards accepted: A MasterCard; B Visa; C American Express; D Discover; E Diners Club; F Other; 2 Personal checks accepted; 3 Lunch available; 4 Dinner available; 5 Open all year; 6 Pets welcome;

110. This beautiful, newly built inn has the warmth and comfort of western country and the elegance of hand-stenciled hardwood floors and Mission-style headglass windows. Antiques can be found throughout the home and gracing the five guest rooms, each with private bath. Bedrooms overlook Snow King Mountain or the National Elk Refuge. Handicapped accessible and within walking distance of the downtown Jackson boutiques, museums, restaurants, etc. All mountain and water sports areas available, from fishing and rafting, to hiking, snowmobiling, and Nordic and alpine skiing. No smoking. No pets. Full breakfast. $135-155.

The Wildflower Inn

P.O. Box 3724, 83001
(307) 733-4710

A lovely log home with five sunny guest rooms, this bed and breakfast is on three acres of land only five minutes from the Jackson Hole ski area, 10 minutes from the town of Jackson, and 30 minutes from Grand Teton.

Hosts: Ken and Sherrie Jern
Rooms: 5 (PB) $120-140
Full Breakfast
Credit Cards: A, B
Notes: 2, 5, 8, 9, 10, 11, 12, 13, 14

The Wildflower Inn

JACKSON HOLE

The Alpine House

285 North Glenwood, P.O. Box 20245, 83001
(307) 739-1570; (800) 753-1421

A bright and sunny timber frame lodge on a quiet street two blocks from the town square and all its restaurants and shops. All seven rooms have a private bath, private balcony, country antiques, heated floors, and down comforters. A full homemade breakfast and wine and cheese are served. The hosts are former Olympic skiers and invite guests to come experience life in the mountains.

Hosts: Hans and Nancy Johnstone
Rooms: 7 (PB) $65-110
Full Breakfast
Credit Cards: A, B
Notes: 2, 5, 7, 8, 9, 10, 11, 12, 13,14

Bed and Breakfast Western Adventure

P.O. Box 4308, Bozeman, MT 59772
(406) 585-0557; FAX (406) 585-2869

50. A hike up 95 timbered steps to a snug, dramatic home with spectacular views of the Jackson Hole Valley below. This four-story, beautifully furnished, rustic home has a two-story living/dining room with fireplace where guests are always welcome. Six rooms with private showers have king- and queen-size and twin beds. There is a dog that lives outside. An ideal home for active people who want to experience nature first hand. All outdoor activities are nearby. Appears in Frommer's *Best Bed and Breakfasts*. No pets. Continental plus and full breakfasts. $95-145.

89. This rustically elegant and spacious log home sits in a quiet field nestled in the foothills of the Grand Teton Mountains. It grants the serenity of the country while being minutes away from the art galleries, shopping, crafts, and famous restaurants of Jackson. It is perfect for the romantic interlude or a family vacation. All summer and winter activities abound in the area. Five guest rooms, each with private bath and view of the Tetons, have their own unique charm. Full gourmet breakfast and afternoon tea are included. Twenty minutes from

7 No smoking; 8 Children welcome; 9 Social drinking allowed; 10 Tennis nearby; 11 Swimming nearby; 12 Golf nearby; 13 Skiing nearby; 14 May be booked through a travel agent.

Jackson Airport and Teton National Park. Fly fish in Snake River. Golf and Nordic ski across the road. Golf, downhill or cross-country skiing, camera hunts, Elk Refuge sleigh rides, and more can be arranged by hostess. Large hot tub. No smoking. Full breakfast. $99-129.

257. This large, elegant lodge sits on three aspen-covered acres adorned with wildflowers in summer and a blanket of snow in winter. The inn has five sunny guest rooms with views of mountains and woodland. Down comforters, pine furniture, and interesting art collectibles embellish each room. All have private baths; four have private redwood decks. Skiing, tennis, golf, fishing, climbing, and hiking are within minutes. Birds and wildlife always in view. Solarium and hot tub. Climbing in the Tetons and Wild River Canyons can be arranged with host. No smoking. Children over four welcome. Cat and dog in residence. Full breakfast. $130-140.

tions include South Pass City Historic Site, Wind River Indian Reservation, Indian petroglyphs, Red Desert, and Oregon Trail. Hiking, fishing, snowmobiling, mountain biking, and wildlife viewing are nearby. No smoking allowed. No pets allowed. Full breakfast served. $90.

Annie Moore's Guest House

LANDER

Bed and Breakfast Western Adventure

P.O. Box 4308, Bozeman, MT 59772
(406) 585-0557; FAX (406) 585-2869

112. Hideaway like the outlaws of old on one of the area's largest working cattle ranches. This cabin was built of standing dead lodgepole pine trees harvested from the mountain forests on the ranch. Furnished with handcrafted log furnishings and cozy quilts. Enjoy spectacular sunrises or evening stargazing from the front porch or just sit back and enjoy the quiet of country life. A small cabin for guests includes a bedroom with queen-size bed and a loft with two twin beds. There is a refrigerator and microwave in the living and dining area warmed by a wood stove. Area attrac-

LARAMIE

Annie Moore's Guest House

819 University Avenue, 82070
(307) 721-4177; (800) 552-8992

Restored Queen Anne home with six individually decorated guest rooms, four with sinks. Large, sunny, common living rooms, second-story sun deck. Across the street from the University of Wyoming; two blocks from the Laramie Plains Museum; six blocks from downtown shops, galleries, and restaurants. Just 15 minutes from skiing, camping, biking, and fishing in uncrowded wilderness areas.

Hosts: Ann Acuff and Joe Bundy
Rooms: 6 (SB) $55-65
Continental Breakfast
Credit Cards: A, B, C, D
Notes: 2, 5, 7, 9, 12, 13

NEWCASTLE

4W Ranch Recreation

1162 Lynch Road, 82701
(307) 746-2815

Looking for the unbeaten path? Spend a few days on this working cattle ranch with 20,000 acres of diversified rangeland to explore at leisure. Rates include three meals a day.

Hosts: Bob and Jean Harshbarger
Rooms: 2 (SB) $60-100 (American Plan)
Full Breakfast
Credit Cards: None
Notes: 2, 3, 4, 8, 9, 11

PINEDALE

Window on the Winds

10151 Highway 191, Box 135, 82941
(307) 367-2600

The McKays invite guests to this rustic home. The hosts offer lodgepole pine queen-size beds, a large common room, all decorated in Western and Plains Indian decor. Enjoy the breathtaking view of the Winds or relax in the hot tub. Only minutes from year-round mountain adventures such as hiking, fishing, skiing, and snowmobiling, and less than two hours from Jackson and Yellowstone. The perfect base for a western Wyoming vacation.

Hosts: Leanne McClain and Doug McKay
Rooms: 4 (SB) $52-68
Full Breakfast
Credit Cards: A, B
Notes: 2, 3, 4, 5, 6, 7, 8, 9, 11, 12, 13, 14

RIVERTON

Bed and Breakfast Western Adventure

P.O. Box 4308, Bozeman, MT 59772
(406) 585-0557; FAX (406) 585-2869

218. This working Western ranch is surrounded by the Wind River Reservation, home of the Shoshone and Arapahoe tribes. A real Western ranch experience awaits guests. There are three rooms on the second floor that share a bath. Crib available. A chance to experience life on a Western ranch with talented and hospitable hosts. Hunting, snowmobiling, and excellent fishing nearby. No smoking. Full breakfast. $50-55.

SARATOGA

Brooksong Bed and Breakfast Home

Star Route Box 9L Ryan Park, 82331
(307) 326-8744

Brooksong Bed and Breakfast home is in the beautiful Snowy Range, off Highway 130 in historic Ryan Park. It offers a lovely forested panoramic view, crystal trout stream, and hearty breakfasts. The cozy upstairs guest rooms are decorated with a blend of antique and modern country furnishings. The guests are pampered with many amenities. Easy access to summer mountain biking, fishing, hiking, and more. Winter cross-country skiing, snowmobiling, etc. Beautiful mountains, wildlife, wildflowers, and magic memories.

Host: Donna Beach
Rooms: 3 (2 PB; 1 SB) $49-59
Full Breakfast
Credit Cards: None
Notes: 2, 3, 7, 8, 9, 13

Hotel Wolf

P.O. Box 1298, 82331
(307) 326-5525

The historic Hotel Wolf, built in 1893, served as a stagecoach stop. During its early years, the hotel was the hub of the community and noted for its fine food and convivial atmosphere. The same holds true

7 No smoking; 8 Children welcome; 9 Social drinking allowed; 10 Tennis nearby; 11 Swimming nearby; 12 Golf nearby; 13 Skiing nearby; 14 May be booked through a travel agent.

today. The dining room is acclaimed as one of the finest in the region. AAA-rated restaurant. Nearby is a mineral hot springs and excellent fishing.

Hosts: Doug and Kathleen Campbell
Rooms: 6 (PB) $24-35
Suites: 3 (PB) $55-75
Credit Cards: A, B, C, E
Notes: 2, 3, 4, 5, 8, 9, 10, 11, 12, 14

The Blackbird Inn

WHEATLAND

The Blackbird Inn

1101 Eleventh, 82201
(307) 322-4540

This elegant three-story brick home has four bedrooms and one suite sharing three baths. Each bedroom has a different decorating theme. The Blackbird Inn is noted for its wonderful front porch, complete with swing, wicker furniture, and lemonade in the summer. On chilly days, sit by the fireplace and sip a cup of herbal tea or hot chocolate. Great biking, fishing, and bird watching nearby. Thirty minutes from the mountains and the Oregon Trail.

Host: Dan Brecht
Rooms: 5 (SB) $35-50
Full Breakfast
Credit Cards: None
Notes: 2, 5, 6, 7, 8, 9, 10, 11, 12, 14

WILSON

Moose Meadows Bed and Breakfast

1225 Green Lane, P.O. Box 371, 83014
(307) 733-9510; (800) 652-9510
FAX (307) 739-3053

On five acres facing the Tetons, near the Snake River, six miles west of Jackson, Moose Meadows has four comfortable guest rooms, large living room, deck, hot tub, and family animals to make guests feel at home. Juli, American, owns Antiques of Jackson Hole and has furnished the home with family antiques and artworks. Alan, British, prepares full breakfasts combining Wyoming and English cuisines (Elk sausage with Bubble and Squeak, for example).

Hosts: Juli and Alan Blackburn
Rooms: 4 (2 PB; 2 SB) $65-135
Full Breakfast
Credit Cards: A, B, D
Notes: 2, 5, 7, 8, 9, 12, 13, 14

WILSON (JACKSON HOLE)

Teton Tree House

Box 550, 83014
(307) 733-3233

This secluded but convenient mountain lodge is a classic bed and breakfast inn with

Teton Tree House

NOTES: Credit cards accepted: A MasterCard; B Visa; C American Express; D Discover; E Diners Club; F Other; 2 Personal checks accepted; 3 Lunch available; 4 Dinner available; 5 Open all year; 6 Pets welcome;

warm, on-premises hosts. All rooms have private baths, excellent beds, and most have decks and wonderful views. The great room has a fireplace, piano, and walls of books. Breakfast is a low-cholesterol feast featuring huckleberry pancakes, coffee cakes, yeast breads, and other homemade treats. It is only eight miles from Grand Teton National Park, mountain climbing, and the rodeo. The hosts are 30-year locals who delight in sharing information about the area with guests.

Hosts: Chris and Denny Becker
Rooms: 6 (PB) $95-135
Full Breakfast
Credit Cards: A, B
Notes: 2, 5, 7, 8, 9, 10, 11, 12, 13

Teton View
Bed and Breakfast

2136 Coyote Loop, Box 652, 83014
(307) 733-7954

Rooms all have mountain views, cozy country decor, orthopedic mattresses, private entrance, private deck overlooking Teton Mountain range, and comfortable lounge area with books and refrigerator. Convenient location to Yellowstone and Grand Teton national parks.

Hosts: John and Jo Engelhart
Rooms: 3 (1 PB; 2 SB) $60-90
Full Breakfast
Credit Cards: A, B
Notes: 2, 6, 7, 8, 9, 10, 11, 12, 13, 14

7 No smoking; 8 Children welcome; 9 Social drinking allowed; 10 Tennis nearby; 11 Swimming nearby; 12 Golf nearby; 13 Skiing nearby; 14 May be booked through a travel agent.

Canada
Puerto Rico
Virgin Islands

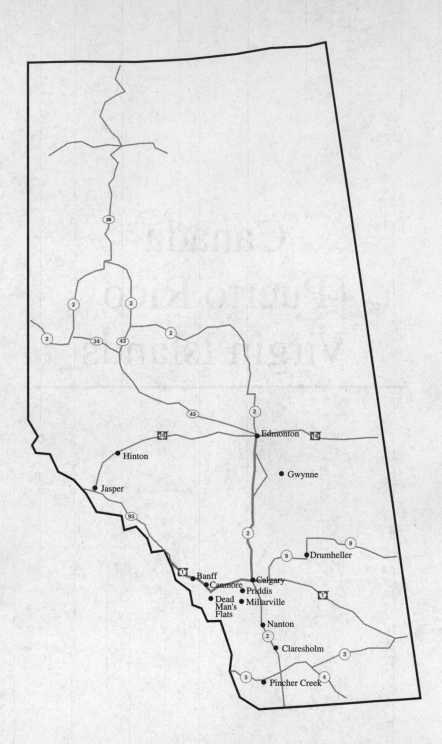

Alberta

Alberta

Alberta and Pacific Bed and Breakfast

P.O. Box 15477, MPO, Vancouver, BC V6B 5B2
(604) 944-1793

The finest guest house in Banff offers four guest rooms: two with queen-size beds and two with extra-long twin beds, each with a private bath. There is a parlor with a fireplace for the use of guests. Visit unforgettable Lake Louise or Banff Centre within walking distance and see the beauty of the Canadian Rocky Mountains.

Blue Mountain Lodge

Box 2763, T0L 0C0
(403) 762-5134; FAX (403) 762-8081

One block from Banff Avenue, minutes from shopping, restaurants, and hiking trails. Rooms and cabins are unique and feature spectacular mountain views and period decor, with private or shared bath. Kitchen facilities, full Continental breakfast, complimentary tea and coffee, sun decks with barbecue. Tennis, swimming, golf, and skiing nearby. No smoking.

Hosts: Hugh and Irene Simpson
Rooms: 12 (7 PB; 5 SB) $59-89
Continental Breakfast
Credit Cards: A, B
Notes: 5, 8, 9, 10, 11, 12, 13

Brewster's Kananaskis Guest Ranch

Box 964, T0L 0C0
(403) 673-3737; FAX (403) 762-3953

The original Brewster Homestead offers cabin and chalet accommodations featuring antique furnishings, cedar interiors, and private shower baths. On the shores of the Bow River, the guest ranch also has a licensed dining room and cocktail lounge, whirlpool, trail riding, and western barbecues. Golf, white-water rafting, hiking, and mountain biking opportunities are also available. Just 45 minutes west of Calgary; 30 minutes east of Banff.

Hosts: The Brewster Family
Rooms: 33 (PB) $95
Full Breakfast
Credit Cards: A, B
Notes: 3, 4, 8, 9, 11, 12, 14

Eleanor's House

125 Kootenay Avenue, P.O. Box 1553, T0L 0C0
(403) 760-2457; FAX (403) 762-3852

Banff's finest guest home reflects mid-century elegance for the discerning traveler. Newly renovated and enlarged with private entrance. Spacious superior bedrooms have private full bathrooms. Mountain views from all windows, and each bedroom has views in two directions. In a quiet, prestigious neighborhood, walking distance from the town center or the famous Banff Springs Hotel. The hosts provide guests with an individual daily itinerary to make the best of their days in the area. Together they have over fifty years' experience in mountain hospitality and national park management.

Hosts: Eleanor House and Rick Kunelius
Rooms: 2 (PB) $65-105 Canadian
Continental Breakfast
Credit Cards: B
Notes: 2, 5, 9, 10, 11, 12, 13

NOTES: Credit cards: A MasterCard; B Visa; C American Express; D Discover; E Diners Club; F Other;
2 Personal checks accepted; 3 Lunch available; 4 Dinner available; 5 Open all year; 6 Pets welcome;
7 No smoking; 8 Children welcome; 9 Social drinking allowed; 10 Tennis nearby; 11 Swimming nearby;
12 Golf nearby; 13 Skiing nearby; 14 May be booked through a travel agent.

CALGARY

Alberta and Pacific Bed and Breakfast

P.O. Box 15477, MPO, Vancouver, BC V6B5B2
(604) 944-1793

Modern, older home, pre-1919, has three upstairs spacious guest rooms; one "honeymoon" room with queen-size bed and en suite bath; one with twin beds plus a single for king-size bed and en suite private bath; one with double bed and en suite private bath.

Barb's Bed and Breakfast

1308 Carlyle Road SW, T2V 2T8
(403) 255-6596

A quiet, spacious home in a well-treed residential area, close to Heritage Park, and minutes from downtown and transit. An easy 80-minute drive to Banff. Small kitchen, TV, sitting area, and private entrance. Full Continental breakfast at the guest's leisure. Queen-size and double rooms. Tennis, golf, and skiing nearby. Smoking restricted.

Host: Barbara I. Cook
Rooms: 2 (SB) $60
Continental Breakfast
Credit Cards: None
Notes: 5, 9, 10, 12, 13

Bed and Breakfast at Harrison's

6016 Thornburn Drive NW, T2K 3P7
(403) 274-7281; FAX (403) 531-0069

Harrison's is a cozy bungalow in a well-treed, quiet residential area of Calgary, where birds and squirrels are regular visitors. Guests share the comfortable living room and sheltered patio. Breakfast is served overlooking the front garden. Swimming nearby.

Host: Susan Harrison
Rooms: 2 (SB) $50
Full Breakfast
Credit Cards: None
Notes: 2, 5, 9, 11, 13, 14

Homeplace Guest Ranch and Trail Rides

Site 2, Box 6, Rural Route 1, Priddis, T0L 1W0
(403) 931-3245 (phone and FAX)

The Homeplace is a year-round working ranch in the Rocky Mountains foothills 25 miles southwest of Calgary. Bordered by ranches and the Kananaskis Forest Reserve, it offers an abundance of wildlife. Guests will be comfortable at the home lodge in their own private room with bath. Evenings are often spent casually around an outdoor fire. On those cold nights, a woodburning stove and a fireplace in the living room offer warm memories. Enjoy privacy or join the ranch members. Pack trips into Rocky Mountains or Kananaskis areas are available. In winter, these areas can be reached by cross-country skis. Rates include all meals, accommodations, and riding.

Rooms: 7 (PB) $75-120
Credit Cards: None
Notes: 2, 3, 4, 5, 7, 8, 9, 10, 11, 12, 13, 14

Paradise Acres Bed and Breakfast

Box 20, Site 2, Rural Route 6
(403) 248-4748 (phone and FAX)

On Paradise Road just minutes away from the Calgary International Airport. Guests can enjoy a beautiful lake, golf course, shopping, and recreation nearby. Hosts have several rooms fitted with queen-size or double beds. There are private and shared baths. Relax next to a luxurious marble fireplace or enjoy the city or mountain view. Inquire about accomodations for children.

Hosts: Brian and Char Bates
Rooms: 3 (1 PB; 2SB) $55-65 Canadian
Full and Continental Breakfast
Credit Cards: None
Notes: 2, 5, 7, 10, 11, 12, 13, 14

The Robin's Nest

Box 2, Site 7, Rural Route 8, T2J 2T9
(403) 931-3514

NOTES: Credit cards accepted: A MasterCard; B Visa; C American Express; D Discover; E Diners Club; F Other; 2 Personal checks accepted; 3 Lunch available; 4 Dinner available; 5 Open all year; 6 Pets welcome;

Guests are treated to new, luxurious cedar cabins with panoramic mountain views. Succulent rainbow trout, freshly milled whole-grain breads, and Saskatoon berries from the farm orchard grace the breakfast table. Sheep, Highland cattle, and fjord ponies graze the hillside pastures. Walk the interpretive nature trails through the private wildlife sanctuary. Twenty minutes southwest of Calgary. Experience the serenity and romance of yesteryear on this century-old Jackson family homestead.

Hosts: Bill and Dorothy Jackson
Rooms: 3 (2 PB; 1 SB) $60-85
Full Breakfast
Credit Cards: None
Notes: 5, 7, 8, 9, 10, 11, 12, 13, 14

Scenic Waters Bed and Breakfast

Box 33, Site 20, Rural Route 2, T2P 2G5
(403) 286-4348

This bed and breakfast is set in a beautiful valley siding the Bow River on 15 acres. The home is a cedar country home with rustic fireplaces and large floor-to-ceiling windows overlooking the river valley. The birds and wildlife are abundant in this area. Thirty-minute drive will take guests to the Rocky Mountains, 40 minutes to Kananaskis country, 60 minutes to Banff and Lake Louise, 15 minutes to Calgary Olympic Park, and 25 minutes to City Centre.

Hosts: Martha and Irvin Proppe
Rooms: 3 (1PB; 2 SB) $50-60
Full Breakfast
Credit Cards: B, C
Notes: 5, 7, 8, 9, 13, 14

CANMORE

Alberta and Pacific Bed and Breakfast

P.O. Box 15477, MPO, Vancouver, BC V6B 5B2
(604) 944-1793

Hosts will welcome the guests to their lovely new home 22 kilometers from Banff National Park. The Canmore Nordic Center, site of the 1988 Winter Olympics Nordic events, is minutes away. Breakfast is homemade and features European and Canadian cuisine. On the second floor one guest room with queen-size bed, one with twin bed. Both rooms have mountain views and full en suite baths. On the main floor one guest room with handicapped facilities, double beds and shared bath.

Cougar Creek Inn

P.O. Box 1162, T0L 0M0
(403) 678-4751

Quiet, rustic cedar chalet with mountain views in every direction. Grounds border on Cougar Creek. Land reserve with hiking trails borders property. Hostess is an outdoor enthusiast with a strong love for mountains and can assist guests' plans for local hiking, skiing, canoeing, mountain biking, and backpacking. Bonfire pit, private entrance, fireplace, sitting room with TV, games, private dining, serving area, and sauna. Personal checks accepted for deposit.

Host: Patricia Doucette
Rooms: 4 (S2B) $55-60
Full Breakfast
Credit Cards: None
Notes: 3, 5, 8, 9, 10, 11, 12, 13

The Georgetown Inn

1101 Bow Valley Trail; P.O. Box 3327, T0L 0M0
(403) 678-3439; FAX (403) 678-3630

At the gateway to Banff National Park, the Georgetown Inn offers all the comforts of a bed and breakfast and the privacy of an old-fashioned inn. The inn is furnished with antiques. All 14 rooms are individually decorated, have down duvets, and antique dressers. Small English pub serves home-cooked meals by the fireplace. Full breakfast is provided in the Three Sisters dining room. Smoking only in pub.

Hosts: Barry and Doreen Jones and Family
Rooms: 14 (PB) $75-95
Full Breakfast
Credit Cards: A, B, C
Notes: 2, 4, 5, 8, 9, 10, 11, 12, 13, 14

7 No smoking; 8 Children welcome; 9 Social drinking allowed; 10 Tennis nearby; 11 Swimming nearby; 12 Golf nearby; 13 Skiing nearby; 14 May be booked through a travel agent.

Monarch Bed and Breakfast

317 Canyon Close, P.O. Box 2679, T0L 0M0
(403) 678-2566 (phone and FAX)

Modern and very clean 3,000-square-foot facility, queen-size brass beds, four-piece baths, private entrance, fireplace, pool table, color cable TV/VCR, movies, private eating area with refrigerator, and quiet neighborhood. Walk to hiking trails. Relax in your living room or on the deck enjoying panoramic views of the Rocky Mountains all around you. "Full Course" and "Heart Healthy" breakfasts. Owned and operated by registered nurse and mounted policeman.

Hosts: Jim and Marilyn Bradley
Rooms: 3 (1 PB; 2 SB) $60-85
Full Breakfast
Credit Cards: A, B
Notes: 4, 5, 7, 8, 9, 10, 11, 12, 13

CLARESHOLM

Anola's Bed and Breakfast

Box 340, T0L 0T0
(403) 625-4389

Experience the solitude of the prairies on this 3,800-acre grain farm, 30 minutes from Head Smashed in Buffalo Jump, a United Nations World Heritage site. Tea and muffins served on arrival. Private cottage decorated with quilts and antiques including a wood-burning stove. Explore Granddad's museum, a collection of western Canadian memorabilia, or tour the farms and learn the story of how wheat becomes bread and pasta.

Hosts: Anola and Gordon Laing
Rooms: 3 (1 PB; 2 SB) $50-95
Full Breakfast
Credit Cards: None
Notes: 2, 10, 11, 12

DEAD MAN'S FLAT

Alberta and Pacific Bed and Breakfast

P.O. Box 15477, MPO, Vancouver, BC V6B 5B2
(604) 944-1793

Twenty miles from Banff, 20 minutes to Kananaskis Village, this large room offers three spacious, beautifully appointed and decorated guest rooms, each with queen-size bed and seating area, each with private bath.

DRUMHELLER

The Victorian House

541 Riverside Drive West, T0J 0Y3
(403) 823-3535

Enjoy a quiet, scenic location overlooking the river; close to shopping, restaurants, swimming pool, water park, seniors' center, and walking and cycling path. Three bedrooms with shared bathroom with jet tub. Evening tea and cookies. Ski package deals available.

Hosts: Jack and Florence Barnes
Rooms: 3 (S1B) $50
Full Breakfast
Credit Cards: B
Notes: 2, 5, 7, 8, 9, 10, 11, 12, 13

EDMONTON

Alberta and Pacific Bed and Breakfast

P.O. Box 15477, MPO, Vancouver, BC V6B 5B2
(604) 944-1793

This home is a short drive to famous West Edmonton Mall, largest entertainment and shopping mall ever built. Two guest rooms are offered, one queen-size, one twin, and one guest bath. A full English breakfast is served or join the hosts for a weight-control breakfast.

Alberta Setting Sun Bed and Breakfast

7911-98th Avenue, T6A 0B5
(403) 468-3217

Relax in own private apartment suite that includes a kitchen, living/dining room, bedroom, and private bath. Enjoy the lovely yard surrounded by towering spruce trees. Full Canadian breakfast served. Centrally near city center, convention centre, Northland Coliseum, legislature/government centre, University of Alberta, Old Strathcona, the beautiful River Valley parks, and West Edmonton Mall. The inn is within easy access of bus routes.

Hosts: Paul and Peggy Martel and Babykins (resident cat)
Rooms: 2 (1 PB; 1 SB) $50
Full or Continental Breakfast
Credit Cards: None
Notes: 3, 5, 7, 8, 9, 10, 11, 12, 13, 14

Chez Suzanne Bed and Breakfast

18603-68 Avenue, T5T 2M8
(403) 483-1845

Relax and enjoy the privacy of one entire level of hosts' home. Unwind by the fireplace with books, color TV, VCR movies, or games. There are a refrigerator and beverage station for guests' convenience where they can help themselves to complimentary coffee, tea, hot chocolate, or soup. There are three well-appointed bedrooms. Laundry facilities available. Neighborhood restaurants are a five-minute stroll away, ideal after a long day's drive.

Hosts: Suzanne and Paul Croteau
Rooms: 3 (1 PB; 2 SB) $55
Full Breakfast
Credit Cards: B, F
Notes: 4, 5, 7, 8, 9, 11, 12, 13

GWYNNE

Gwynalta Farm

T0C 1L0
(403) 352-3587

Gwynalta is a lovely 400-acre farm in central Alberta. The farm has a natural valley and a mile of rugged lakeshore, with areas for bird watching, walking, and biking. Home-cooked meals and plenty of coffee and chatter. Experience the quiet serenity

of a rural setting and the warm, friendly atmosphere of a farm home.

Host: Mabel Glaser
Rooms: 2 (SB) $30-60
Full Breakfast
Credit Cards: None
Notes: 3, 5, 7, 8, 10, 11, 12, 13

HINTON

Black Cat Guest Ranch

Box 6267, T7V 1X6
(403) 865-3084; FAX (403) 865-1924

Historic Albertan guest ranch celebrates its 60th anniversary in 1995. Guests are offered guided trail rides, hiking, rafting in the summer, and cross-country skiing in the winter. Relaxation year-round. Home-style meals and sociable surroundings in a beautiful mountain setting one hour's drive from Jasper townsite.

Hosts: Amber and Perry Hayward
Rooms: 16 (PB) $107-154 Canadian
Full Breakfast
Credit Cards: A, B
Notes: 2, 3, 4, 5, 9, 10, 11, 12, 13, 14

Black Cat Guest Ranch

JASPER

Alberta and Pacific Bed and Breakfast

P.O. Box 15477, MPO, Vancouver, BC V6B 5B2
(604) 944-1793

A private entrance to a newly furnished and beautifully decorated suite: living room with queen-size Hide-a-Bed and cable TV, bedroom with queen-size bed, kitchenette with microwave and refrigerator, and private bath. A separate small bedroom is also available in the same area with double bed, TV, and private bath.

MILLARVILLE

Hilltop Bed and Breakfast

Rural Route 1, T0L 1K0
(403) 931-3356

Enjoy the magnificent view of the Rockies just west of Millarville. Quiet, relaxing atmosphere. Three attractive guest rooms on the main floor, one with bath en suite and two with shared bath. Choice of breakfast including home baking, homemade preserves, and hosts' own honey. Children ten and over welcome.

Hosts: Bob and Lill Tedrick
Rooms: 3 (1 PB; 2SB) $55-70
Full Breakfast
Credit Cards: None
Notes: 2, 5, 7, 12, 13

NANTON

Broadway Farm Bed and Breakfast

Box 294, T0L 1R0
(403) 646-5502

In the beautiful and spacious prairies of south Alberta with a panoramic view of the Rocky Mountains and lovely sunsets. Full breakfast served in the atrium with beautiful plants. Three guest rooms with shared bath. Families welcome. Restricted smoking. Hosts offer pig roasts for group functions.

Hosts: Bill and Mary Gelden
Rooms: 3 (SB) $50
Full Breakfast
Credit Cards: None
Notes: 3, 4, 5, 7, 8, 9, 10, 11, 12

Timber Ridge Homestead

P.O. Box 94, T0L 1R0
(403) 646-5683; (403) 646-2480 (winter)

Timber Ridge Homestead is a rustic establishment in the beautiful foothills of ranching country, lying about 70 miles southwest of Calgary. There are good, quiet horses to help guests explore the abundant wildflowers, wildlife, and wonderful views of the Rockies. Good, plain cooking.

Hosts: Bridget Jones and Family
Rooms: 3 (SB) $25-50
Full Breakfast
Credit Cards: None
Notes: 2, 3, 4, 8, 9

PINCHER CREEK

Allison House

1108 Hewetson Avenue; Box 1351, T0M 1W0
(403) 627-3739

Allison House is an Alberta-registered Heritage house in beautiful southwestern Alberta. Built in 1911 by early pioneers, it maintains the original floor plan and features stained-glass art designed by the owner. Easy access to Waterton National Park, Head Smashed in Buffalo Jump, World Heritage Site, and fishing in the Crowsnest Pass. Sporting facilities are on the nearby Oldman River Dam. Home to the Annual Cowboy Poetry and Western Art Show in June.

Hosts: Suzanne and Csaba Lorinczl
Rooms: 2 (1 PB; 1 SB) $35-55, Cash Only.
Full Breakfast
Credit Cards: None
Notes: 10, 11, 12, 13

PRIDDIS

Dwelling Place

Box 27, Site 4, Rural Route 1, T0L 1W0
(403) 931-2639; (403) 931-2649

Nestled quietly in the Alberta foothills, west of Calgary, experience tranquility on this ten-acre hillside forest. Enjoy restful sleeps under country duvets, deep blue skies, and majestic trees. Hearty home-cooked meals. Nearby, enjoy Kananskis country, filming sites, Calgary Stampede, Banff, equestrian facilities, fishing, hiking, cycling, and many other attractions. There are on-site private guest quarters with a private exit, security, office workspace, laundry, organ, astronomical observing, campfires, animals, and nature walking trails. Eat delicious Alberta beef. Enquire about manor expansion and wheelchair access. One-half kilometers south of Highway 22 North. Be divinely touched. Pets are welcome with prior arrangements.

Dwelling Place

Hosts: Grace and Roger Nelson
Rooms: 5 (3 PB; 2 SB) $50-65
Full Breakfast
Credit Cards: None
Notes: 3, 4, 5, 7, 8, 9, 12, 13, 14

Sointula

Quadra Island

Denman Island

Gibsons

Campbell River
Courtenay
Qualicum Beach
Parksville

North Vancouver

Whistler

Salmon Arm

Kamloops

Vernon

Nanoose Bay
Gabriola Island
Cobble Hill
Tofino
Ucluelet
Port Alberni
Mill Bay
Ladysmith
Shawnigan Lake
Chemainus
Duncan

Coquitlam

Vancouver

West Vancouver

Kelowna

Fort Steele

Penticton

Nelson

New Westminster

Westbank

Osoyoos

Burnaby

White Rock

N-Delta

Lander

Mayne Island

Saturna Island

Victoria

Pender Island

Sooke

Sidney

Metchosin

Salt Spring
Island

British Columbia

British Columbia

A B and C Bed and Breakfast of Vancouver

4390 Frances Street, V5C 2R3
(604) 298-8815; (800) 488-1941
FAX (604) 298-5917

Single to king-size beds, private and shared baths, suites, cabins to mansions, Jacuzzis, pools, and full to gourmet breakfasts included. This service covers North and West Vancouver, Vancouver, Victoria, Parksville, Whistler, Richmond, Surrey, White Rock, and many others. Car rentals and sightseeing tours can be arranged. Weekly and off-season rates are available. $75-150.

Born Free Bed and Breakfast of British Columbia, Ltd.

4390 Frances Street, V5C 2R3
(604) 298-8815; (800) 488-1941
FAX (604) 298-5917

This reservation service will help the guest find a splendid home away from home in a clean, comfortable house with especially friendly hosts and hostesses. From modest to average to luxurious accommodations, all guests' needs are considered. There are also accommodations available for film crews, students, and those with long-stay and special requirements. Covering Vancouver, Victoria, and throughout British Columbia.

April Point Lodge

P.O. Box 1, V9W 4Z9
(604) 285-2222; FAX (604) 285-2411

The Peterson family, who has owned and operated April Point for 50 years, welcomes families, corporate groups, vacationing couples, and singles from around the world. The area is famous for salmon fishing—from early spring to late fall, guests fish for coho, chinook, tyee, chum, and northern coho salmon. The guide staff at April Point is the most experienced in the area and ensures a quality fishing experience. Alternative activities include cycling and walking as well as a nearby Native Indian museum, tennis courts, and horseback riding.

Hosts: The Peterson Family
Rooms: 38 (35 PB; 3 SB) $99-229
Continental Breakfast
Credit Cards: A, B, C, D, E, F
Notes: 2, 3, 4, 6, 8, 9, 10, 11, 12, 13, 14

Campbell River Lodge and Fishing Resort

1760 Island Highway, V9W 2E7
(604) 287-7446

Small, intimate fishing lodge on the banks of the famous Campbell River. Originally constructed of logs in 1948, the lodge is the oldest and most unique in the area. Offers Old World charm and modern conveniences. Dine in the gourmet dining room or English-style pub. Relaxing outdoor hot

NOTES: Credit cards: A MasterCard; B Visa; C American Express; D Discover; E Diners Club; F Other; 2 Personal checks accepted; 3 Lunch available; 4 Dinner available; 5 Open all year; 6 Pets welcome; 7 No smoking; 8 Children welcome; 9 Social drinking allowed; 10 Tennis nearby; 11 Swimming nearby; 12 Golf nearby; 13 Skiing nearby; 14 May be booked through a travel agent.

Campbell River Lodge

tub overlooking Campbell River. Light Continental breakfast served daily.

Host: Brian Clarkson
Rooms: 28 (PB) $49-93
Continental Breakfast
Credit Cards: A, B
Notes: 3, 4, 5, 6, 7, 8, 9, 10, 11, 12, 14

Haida Inn

1342 Island Highway, V9W 2E1
(604) 287-7402

Full-service hotel in downtown Campbell River overlooks scenic Discovery Passage. This facility includes 75 guest rooms, a coffee shop, lounge with entertainment on weekends, JJ's Pub, a cold beer and wine Store, and a selection of banquet meeting rooms for groups up to 120 people. Nonsmoking rooms available.

Rooms: 75 (PB) $63-73
Full Breakfast
Credit Cards: A, B, C, E
Notes: 3, 4, 5, 8, 9, 10, 11, 12, 13, 14

CHEMAINUS

All Seasons Bed and Breakfast Agency

P.O. Box 5511, Station B, Victoria, V8R 6S4
(604) 655-7173

Hummingbird House. Oceanview, large suites with queen-size beds, and private baths. Magnificent view, extensive gardens, fresh baking, and full breakfast. Boat

charters, scenic cruises, and fishing. Children welcome. No smoking or pets. Wheelchair accessible.

Garden City Bed and Breakfast Reservation Service

660 Jones Terrace, Victoria, V82 2L7
(604) 479-1986; FAX (604) 479-9999

K-12. Warm hospitality awaits at this modern, cozy home on a quiet road. Five-minute walk to beach. There are lovely sunsets, golf courses, restaurants, village, and marina. Fishing trips can be arranged. Walk to bus for skiing at Mount Washington. Guest room with queen-size bed and private bath overlooks the English garden. Freshly ground coffee and delicious breakfast served inside or on patio. From $65.

K-29. Beautiful, self-contained rooms in the heart of Chemainus. Walking distance to the theater, sea, famous murals, and all the shops. Private entrance. Queen-size and double rooms beautifully decorated. From $65.

Little Inn on Willow

9849 Willow Street, Box 958, V0R 1K0
(604) 246-4987

Little Inn on Willow

Imagine booking an entire luxury hotel for an evening! The entire property consists of one tiny fairy cottage, carefully crafted by local artisans to capture the romance that this seaside village is famous for. Features a fireplace, jet tub for two, TV/VCR, chilled champagne, and orange juice. Guests can also book a private steam and massage for an extra cost. Tennis, swimming, and golf nearby. The Continental breakfast is a Belgium waffle and coffee at Billy's Delight. Newsletter by request.

Hosts: Dave and Sonia Haberman
Room: 1 (PB) $150
Continental Breakfast
Credit Cards: A
Notes: 5, 9, 10, 11, 12

Pacific Shores All-Suite Inn

9847 Willow Street, Box 958, V0R 1K0
(604) 246-4987

Quaint European-style inn blended with all the amenities of a North American all-suite hotel. Three tastefully decorated suites with handmade feather duvets, kitchens, cable TV, and VCR. The King Suite is a spacious one bedroom with a queen-size bed and double foldout bed in the living room. The Duchess is done with antiques, including a very comfortable turn-of-the-century queen-size bed and private library. The Princess is a bright, cheery suite with the early morning sun shining through its corner turret. Tennis, swimming, and golf nearby. The Continental breakfast is a Belgium waffle and coffee at Billy's Delight. Newsletter by request.

Hosts: Dave and Sonia Haberman
Rooms: 3 (PB) $75-95
Continental Breakfast
Credit Cards: A
Notes: 5, 8, 9, 10, 11, 12

Sea-Breeze Tourist Home

2912 Esplanade Street, P.O. Box 1362, V0R 1K0
(604) 246-4593 (phone and FAX)

Turn-of-the-century home just steps from the beach and boat ramp in picturesque

Chemainus. Play park and picnic area at the beach. Beautiful views from every room. Lighthouse and island view. Full breakfast is served on linen with silver and candles. English and German spoken. Smoking in designated areas only.

Hosts: John and Christa Stegemann
Rooms: 4 (2 PB; 2 SB) $45-55
Full Breakfast
Credit Cards: None
Notes: 5, 8, 10, 11, 12

COBBLE HILL (VANCOUVER ISLAND)

Garden City Bed and Breakfast Reservation Service

660 Jones Terrace, Victoria, V8Z 2L7
(604) 479-1986; FAX (604) 479-9999

K-28. Welcome to this brand new home, nestled in a peaceful 40-acre forest. Choose between spacious queen-size or twin beds, each with en suite bath. A creek murmurs in the distance and deer may wander past the windows. The host, a former executive chef, prepares the incredible breakfast. From $60.

COQUITLAM

Green Gables Bed and Breakfast

2242 Park Crescent, V3J 6T2
(604) 469-7105

Lovely home 30 minutes from Vancouver in a very quiet location with a creek flowing through the natural garden property. Private suite with comfortable king-size bed, private bathroom, guest lounge with queen-size sofa bed, and gas fireplace. Gourmet breakfast served. English and German spoken.

Host: Gabriela Butz
Room: 1 (PB) $70
Full Breakfast
Credit Cards: None
Notes: 5, 7, 8, 9, 10, 11, 12, 14

7 No smoking; 8 Children welcome; 9 Social drinking allowed; 10 Tennis nearby; 11 Swimming nearby;
12 Golf nearby; 13 Skiing nearby; 14 May be booked through a travel agent.

COURTENAY

Greystone Manor

4014 Haas Road, Rural Route 6, Site 684-C2
V9N 8H9
(604) 338-1422

A lovely view across Comox Bay to the mainland British Columbian coast mountains. One and a half acres of beautiful English gardens are the setting for Greystone Manor. Built in 1918, the manor is one of the oldest homes in the area. The guest sitting room has a wood fireplace and baby grand piano. The hosts are originally from Bath, England. Children over 12 are welcome.

Hosts: Mike and Maureen Shipton
Rooms: 4 (SB) $60-70
Full Breakfast
Credit Cards: A, B
Notes: 5, 7, 11, 12, 13

DENMAN ISLAND

Denman Island Guest House

3806 Denman Road, V0R 1T0
(206) 335-2688

Enjoy bed and breakfast accommodations in a turn-of-the-century farmhouse on Denman Island. The small farm has a beautiful mountain view with glimmers of the Strait of Georgia. Great location near the ocean and beaches. There are all the attractions of shore and water to enjoy. Hiking, cycling, and beachcombing are popular activities on the island as well as exploring the many craft stores. The fully licensed dining facilities feature hearty, country breakfasts and delectable seafood dinners. Antique furniture complements the traditional farmhouse.

Host: Bob Okrainec
Rooms: 5 (SB) $50
Full Breakfast
Credit Cards: None
Notes: 4, 5, 7, 8, 9, 10, 11, 14

DUNCAN

Country Gardens Bed and Breakfast

1665 Grant Road, V9L 4T6
(604) 748-5865

Enjoy quiet country charm in a lovely cedar log home on a private acreage overlooking beautiful Quamichan Lake. A delicious home-cooked breakfast is served on the patio overlooking the lake or the tranquil garden with lily ponds. Resident briard dog. Dutch spoken.

Host: Marjorie Gunnlaugson
Rooms: 2 (PB) $50-60
Full Breakfast
Credit Cards: None
Notes: 2, 5, 7, 12

Grove Hall Estate Bed and Breakfast

6159 Lakes Road, V9L 4J6
(604) 746-6152

Take a scenic drive 36 miles north of Victoria and discover this historic Edwardian Tudor mansion, hidden away on 17 tranquil lakefront acres. Magnificent antiques throughout. Exotic and romantic theme rooms highlighted by ornate Chinese wedding bed in the Singapore Room; Balinese art and batiks in the Indonesian Suite; flavors of Bangkok enhancing the Siamese Room. There is also a one-bedroom cottage available. Relax on the veranda while sipping tea and watching the graceful swans on the lake. Enjoy tennis or billiards. Close to the attractions of Chemainus, sailing, golfing, and hiking. Two-night minimum stay required.

Host: Judy Oliver
Rooms: 3 (SB) $120-145 Canadian
Cottage: $135 Canadian
Full Breakfast
Credit Cards: None
Notes: 2, 5, 9, 10, 11, 12, 14

NOTES: Credit cards accepted: A MasterCard; B Visa; C American Express; D Discover; E Diners Club; F Other; 2 Personal checks accepted; 3 Lunch available; 4 Dinner available; 5 Open all year; 6 Pets welcome;

FORT STEELE

Alberta and Pacific Bed and Breakfast Agency

P.O. Box 15477, MPO, Vancouver, V6B 5B2
(604) 944-1793

Wild Horse Farm is a spacious two-story, 12-room manor that was built in the early 1900s by William Astor Drayton of New York. Many of the original fixtures are still in use. Guests are invited to enjoy the living room with its antiques, player piano, and games table. An upstairs guest room has a queen-size canopied bed and private bath; a suite on the main floor has a private entrance, a corner guest room with king-size bed, large picture windows that face the mountains, and private bath; a two-level, self-contained apartment with upstairs queen-size bed, main floor single bed and Hide-a-Bed, kitchenette, and private bath ideal for family use.

Wild Horse Farm

Box 7, V0B 1N0
(604) 426-6000

A log-faced, two-story manor house built in 1929 by a nephew of John Jacob Astor IV. It is set against a Canadian Rockies backdrop, surrounded by 80 acres of meadows, woodlands, pastures, and gardens. Highland cows and assorted fowl keep an eye on guests playing croquet, lawn bowling, or relaxing on the grounds and screened veranda. Furnishings range from Tiffany lamps to bearskin rugs. Memorable breakfasts incorporate farm produce in vegetable fritattas, puffy oven pancakes, and fruit muffins served with homemade jams and fruit syrups. Smoking restricted. May be booked through a travel agent, but guests must pay the 10 percent commission.

Hosts: Bob and Orma Termuende
Rooms: 3 (2 PB; 1 SB) $58-93
Full Breakfast
Credit Cards: B
Notes: 2, 5, 8, 9, 10, 11, 12, 13

GABRIOLA ISLAND

Surf Lodge

885 Berry Point Road, Rural Route 1, Site 1
V0R 1X0
(604) 247-9231; FAX (604) 247-8336

On ten acres on the northwest shore of Gariola Island, facing the Georgia Strait and Vancouver Island and mainland mountains, Surf Lodge offers a relaxed atmosphere in a quiet setting. There are nine rooms in the main lodge and nine cabins, all with private paths, some with kitchenettes. Sunset watching from the dining room, deck, or licensed lounge. Seawater pool and other outdoor recreation. Golf, tennis, scuba, and fishing charters nearby.

Host: Rae Beckman
Rooms: 9 (PB) $55-78
Cabins: 9 (PB)
Continental Breakfast
Credit Cards: A, B
Notes: 2, 4, 5, 6, 8, 9, 10, 11, 12, 14

GALIANO ISLAND

Garden City Bed and Breakfast Reservation Service

660 Jones Terrace, Victoria, V8Z 2L7
(604) 479-1986; FAX (604) 479-9999

K-20. On over five acres of natural forest, this home offers queen-size or twin beds, hot tub, sauna, and bicycles. Watch deer wander and eagles soar while enjoying a delicious breakfast or while exploring the scenic Gulf islands and beaches. Bordering Bluff Park, guests are close to golf courses, shops, and pubs. From $65.

GIBSONS

Ocean-View Cottage Bed and Breakfast

Rural Route 2, S46-C10, 1927 Grandview Road
V0N 1V0
(604) 886-7943

---

7 No smoking; 8 Children welcome; 9 Social drinking allowed; 10 Tennis nearby; 11 Swimming nearby; 12 Golf nearby; 13 Skiing nearby; 14 May be booked through a travel agent.

A short cruise from Vancouver to this home and spacious self-contained cottage overlooking the Strait of Georgia and Vancouver Island. Queen-size and twin bedrooms with en suite bath, private entrances, and sun deck. Hearty breakfast served. Close to shops, attractions, and fine dining. Self-contained cottage with one bedroom, sleeper-sofa, cot, and futon is also available. Sleeps six.

Hosts: Dianne and Bert Verzyl
Rooms: 3 (PB) $55-80
Full Breakfast
Credit Cards: A, B
Notes: 2, 5, 8, 9, 10, 11, 12, 13

HORNBY ISLAND

Sea Breeze Lodge

V0R 1Z0
(604) 335-2321

Comfortable waterfront accommodations with spectacular view of beach, ocean, mountains, and glorious summer sunsets. American plan (three meals/day inclusive) from June 15 through September 15. Fully licensed dining facilities. Kitchenette units available off-season. Hot tub, grass tennis court, and fireplaces. Catered weddings, seminars, and winter retreats.

Rooms: 12 (PB) $64-188
Full Breakfast
Credit Cards: A, B
Notes: 2, 3, 4, 5, 7, 8, 9, 10, 11

KAMLOOPS

Alberta and Pacific Bed and Breakfast Agency

P.O. Box 15477, MPO, Vancouver, V6B 5B2
(604) 944-1793

9. Lakefront property with beautiful view of Paul Lake and the mountains. There is a private dock for swimming, fishing, and windsurfing, as well as hiking, walking, and biking trails. Three guest rooms, one with queen-size bed, TV, and full private bath;

one with double bed and private bath; one with single bed and shared bath.

Park Place Bed and Breakfast

720 Yates Road, V2B 6C9
(604) 554-2179

Delightful riverfront home on two acres with large swimming pool and breakfast solarium with a view. Full or Continental breakfast. Air-conditioned. Hosts' motto: "Come as a guest, leave as a friend."

Hosts: Lynn and Trevor Bentz
Rooms: 3 (1 PB; 2 SB) $50-60
Full Breakfast
Credit Cards: None
Notes: 2, 5, 7, 9, 10, 11, 12, 13

KELOWNA

Alberta and Pacific Bed and Breakfast Agency

P.O. Box 15477, MPO, Vancouver, V6B 5B2
(604) 944-1793

Hosts give charm, warmth, and comfort when they welcome guests to their home in the Okanagan that is decorated with antiques and has a view of the Okanagan Lake, mountains, and orchards. There are three guest rooms available; one with double and single bed, seating area with fireplace, and private bath; one with queen-size bed and en suite private bath. Weather permitting, breakfast is served on the covered patio overlooking the garden and view. This home is close to the beach.

The Gables Country Inn

Box 1153, 2405 Bering Road, V1Y 7P8
(604) 768-4468

Discover the elegance and romance of yesteryear at the Okanagan's only Heritage award-winning bed and breakfast. Lovely antique furnishings grace each unique upstairs bedroom. Linger through a delicious breakfast of freshly baked scones and muffins, homemade jams, and freshly ground coffee on the old-fashioned covered veranda. Enjoy a crackling fire in the spacious sitting room or a dip in the swimming pool set in the secluded sunken garden. Near orchards and wineries.

Hosts: Brenda and Kim Clark
Rooms: 4 (SB) $55-65
Full Breakfast
Credit Cards: None
Notes: 2, 5, 7, 8, 9, 10, 11, 12, 13, 14

LADNER

Primrose Hill Guest House

4919 48th Avenue, V4K 1V4
(604) 940-8867

A 1913 Craftsman-style home that has been lovingly restored to reflect the look and feel of the Edwardian period. In the center of Ladner, a quaint farming and fishing village. Breakfast is served in the spacious dining room and includes fresh fruit, juices, homemade muffins, breads, and egg dishes. Bike or walk to Fraser River dikes or visit the Reifil Bird Sanctuary. Off-street parking. Ten minutes to Tsawwassen ferry terminal, sailings to Victoria, Nanaimo, and Gulf Islands; 25 minutes to Vancouver International Airport; 35 minutes to downtown Vancouver; 25 minutes to U. S. border.

Hosts: Christine Friedrich and James Price
Rooms: 6 (4 PB; 2 SB) $65-125
Full Breakfast
Credit Cards: B
Notes: 5, 7, 10, 11, 12, 13

LADYSMITH

Mañana Lodge and Marina

4760 Brenton Page Road, Rural Route 1, V0R 2E0
(604) 245-2312; FAX (604) 245-7546

Approximately six miles from downtown Ladysmith, this rustic lodge on the beautiful Ladysmith Harbour was built in the 1940s. Guests may enjoy a relaxing evening in the licensed restaurant overlooking the water and mountains. View the wildlife and tidal pools. All rooms include a full breakfast and the complimentary use of canoe, rowboat, and bikes.

Hosts: James and Ruth Bangay and
Don and Gail Kanelakos
Rooms: 7 (PB) $65-129
Full Breakfast
Credit Cards: A, B
Notes: 12, 14

LANGFORD

Garden City Bed and Breakfast Reservation Service

660 Jones Terrace, Victoria, V8Z 2L7
(604) 479-1986; FAX (604) 479-9999

L-21. Cozy, rustic log home with loft, stone fireplace, and Jacuzzi bathtub. Full country breakfast enjoyed either in the dining room or the old-fashioned porch overlooking coastal rain forest surrounding this home. Trails and a trout stream in the backyard. From $70.

MADRONA POINT

Garden City Bed and Breakfast Reservation Service

660 Jones Terrace, Victoria, V8Z 2L7
(604) 479-1986; FAX (604) 479-9999

K-2. A touch of luxury and romance in a spectacular natural setting. Hot tub under the stars. Walk the miles of easy access beach. Breakfast in a room overlooking the ocean or on the oceanfront deck. Honeymoon in privacy with a fireplace by the bed. From $60.

MAYNE ISLAND

Garden City Bed and Breakfast Reservation Service

660 Jones Terrace, Victoria, V8Z 2L7
(604) 479-1986; FAX (604) 479-9999

7 No smoking; 8 Children welcome; 9 Social drinking allowed; 10 Tennis nearby; 11 Swimming nearby; 12 Golf nearby; 13 Skiing nearby; 14 May be booked through a travel agent.

K-25. Near Miner's Bay and village, this delightful retreat is one of the most colorful and whimsical buildings on the island. Wonderful gardens of edible and medicinal herbs, flowers, and fruit trees, spacious decks, and magnificent views await guests' perusal. Guests can bicycle, drive, ramble through idyllic landscapes and marine scenery, or spend recreation time on the water. Groups and families are welcome. From $60.

Oceanwood Country Inn

630 Dinner Bay Road, V0N 2J0
(604) 539-5074; FAX (604) 539-3002

Overlooking the water, Oceanwood has 12 charming guest rooms, most with fireplaces and soaking tubs, plus a comfortable living room, well-stocked library, and cozy game room. The intimate 30-seat waterfront restaurant, open for dinner every day, serves Pacific Northwest cuisine. The extensive wine list features the best from British Columbia, Washington, Oregon, and California. There are a large hot tub and a sauna. Breakfast and afternoon tea provided. Closed December to February. Limited smoking allowed. Golf available on the adjacent island.

Hosts: Marilyn and Jonathan Chilvers
Rooms: 8 (PB) $120-200
Full Breakfast
Credit Cards: A, B
Notes: 4, 9, 10, 11, 14

Oceanwood Country Inn

METCHOSIN (VANCOUVER ISLAND)

Garden City Bed and Breakfast Reservation Service

660 Jones Terrace, Victoria, V8Z 2L7
(604) 479-1986; FAX (604) 479-9999

L-8. Enjoy this log home and unique country charm on over three acres of forest. Complete privacy including private hot tub. Queen-size bed, cozy down duvets, and en suite bath. Close to city center, Sooke, and lower Vancouver Island. Parks, trails, beaches, fishing, golf, plus a touch of wilderness. From $85.

MILL BAY (VANCOUVER ISLAND)

Garden City Bed and Breakfast Reservation Service

660 Jones Terrace, Victoria, V8Z 2L7
(604) 479-1986; FAX (604) 479-9999

K-3. A waterfront home 35 minutes from Victoria and 55 minutes from Nanaimo. Sweeping views of Saltspring Island, ocean, etc. Beach offers shell, driftwood, and rock collecting, swimming, canoeing, walking, and sunning. Golf courses, fishing charters, hiking, craft and art shows year-round, and a country music festival at the end of May. A fishing derby is in mid-August. Children welcome. Wheelchair accessible. Weekly rates available. From $55.

Pine Lodge Farm Bed and Breakfast

3191 Mutter Road, V0R 2P0
(604) 743-4083

A charming pine lodge built on a 30-acre farm overlooking ocean and islands. Walking trails, farm animals, deer, and magnificent arbutus trees in a paradise-like setting. Antique-filled lodge with stained-glass windows features cozy bedrooms with private baths, furnished with beautiful antiques. Enjoy a full breakfast with homemade jams, and then browse through a spectacular collection of antiques. Featured in *Country Living* and on CBS-TV.

Hosts: Cliff and Barbara Clarke
Rooms: 8 (PB) $75-95
Full Breakfast
Credit Cards: A, B
Notes: 2, 7, 9, 12, 14

NANAIMO

Garden City Bed and Breakfast Reservation Service

660 Jones Terrace, Victoria, V8Z 2L7
(604) 479-1986; FAX (604) 479-9999

K-31. Bed and breakfast in royal style. Majestic, panoramic view of Georgia Strait and snowcapped mountains with bonus of fantastic sunsets. Simmons Beautyrest king- or queen-size beds. Families welcome. Very quiet area but close to shopping. Congenial hosts look forward to providing incredible hospitality. From $55.

NANOOSE BAY

All Seasons Bed and Breakfast Agency

Box 5511, Station B, Victoria, V8R 6S4
(604) 655-7173

The Garden Patch. Bright, spacious contemporary home in Departure Bay close to ferry and beach. Home reflects the eclectic tastes of the owners. Queen-size bed with shared bath. Full breakfasts with organic produce from their garden. Enjoy sitting by a fish pond in the Japanese garden. Private entrance and large lounge provided for guests. No smoking. No pets. $60.

Madrona Point. Unrivaled West Coast beauty. Walk-on beach. Unwind and relax; this is paradise. Only minutes from Parksville and Rathtrevor Beach. Join over

90 percent of the guests who rate it a ten out of ten. Great swimming and some of British Columbia's best scuba diving year-round. Large suite with fireplace, private bath, private entrance, and hot tub outside the door— very romantic. Another guest room has a private bath, private entrance, and deck. Breakfast is served in room or on the patio. $75-95.

Somerville's by the Sea. Beautiful contemporary home on the Strait of Georgia. Explore the tidal pools below the separate suite that contains a queen-size bedroom, sitting room with TV, private bath, deck, and entrance. Two single sofa beds complete the scene. Another suite is also available. There is a wood-burning fireplace where guests can cook up a steak or a salmon. Horseback riding nearby, as are Fairwinds Golf Course and Schooner Cove Marina. Enjoy a melt-in-your-mouth breakfast. $75-85.

The Brown House

3020 Dolphin Drive, V0R 2R0
(604) 468-7804

Self-contained suite with private entrance, living room with TV and fireplace, bathroom with shower, Colonial bedroom with double bed. Peek-a-boo view of the Strait of Georgia. Four golf courses, three marinas, Rath Trevor Beach, horseback riding, nature trails, and many types of restaurants in the area. Fifteen miles north of Nanaimo, five miles south of Parksville, and a two-hour drive to Tofino.

Hosts: Edith and Ern Deadman
Room: 1 (PB) $50
Full Breakfast
Credit Cards: None
Notes: 2, 5, 9, 10, 11, 12, 13

Garden City Bed and Breakfast Reservation Service

660 Jones Terrace, Victoria, V8Z 2L7
(604) 479-1986; FAX (604) 479-9999

K-1. Two acres of quiet paradise conveniently 20 minutes from Nanaimo's Departure Bay ferry. Unique setting with mountain- and oceanviews; resident deer and eagles abound; only minutes to golf, marina, and nature trails. Beautifully appointed rooms and sun decks with oceanview. From $75.

The Lookout at Schooner Cove

3381 Dolphin Drive, V0R 2R0
(604) 468-9796 (phone and FAX)

Halfway between Victoria and Tofino, this cedar home is set in tall evergreens, with a 180-degree view of the Georgia Strait and the majestic mountains beyond. Relax on the wraparound deck in this little bit of heaven and enjoy the passing boats, Alaskan cruise ships, eagles, and whales. Fairwinds Golf Course and Schooner Cove Marina and Resort are within one-half mile. Hearty breakfast is served on the deck or in dining room at guests' convenience.

Hosts: Marj and Herb Wilkie
Rooms: 3 (2 PB; 1 SB) $55-75
Full Breakfast
Credit Cards: None
Notes: 2, 7, 9, 10, 11, 12, 13, 14

Schooner Cove Oceanside Bed and Breakfast and Vacation Suite

3161 Dolphin Drive, Rural Route 2, Box 26
Blueback, V0R 2R0
(604) 468-9241

Rural waterfront with sandy beach. Secluded among tall evergreens; spectacular views of ocean, islands, and mountains from dining room. King-size en suite with oceanview and deck. Queen-size with garden view. Oceanview suite with king-size bed, bathroom, kitchen, family room, pull-out sofa, TV, fireplace, and deck. Three twin-size beds adjacent to suite. Nearby is waterfront dining, marina, nature trails, riding stables, waterfront parks, ancient forests, arts and craft shops, and minigolf. Charter fishing with host.

Hosts: Mr. Lee Chapman and
Mrs. Leone Chapman
Rooms: 4 (2 PB; 2 SB) $55-85 Canadian
Full Breakfast
Credit Cards: None
Notes: 7, 8, 9, 10, 11, 12, 14

N-DELTA

Sunshine Hills

11200 Bond Boulevard, V4E 1M7
(604) 596-6496; FAX (604) 596-2560

A bed and breakfast in quiet surroundings, across from the park, with tennis courts. Close to good bus connections, 30 minutes to downtown Vancouver, and 20 minutes to the airport, U.S. border, and ferries to Vancouver Island. Private entrance to the guest rooms, each with double bed or twin beds, a sitting area, and TV and kitchenette in hallway. A full breakfast is served in the dining room, with view of the park. Dutch and German spoken. Many Dutch antiques in the house.

Hosts: Putzi and Wim Honing
Rooms: 2 (SB) $50 Canadian
Full Breakfast
Credit Cards: F
Notes: 7, 8, 9, 10, 11, 12

NELSON

Alberta and Pacific Bed and Breakfast Agency

P.O. Box 15477, MPO, Vancouver, V6B 5B2
(604) 944-1793

12. This British Columbia city has turn-of-the-century architecture with Victorian homes. A 1926 character home in the downtown area. Decorated with antiques. Four guest rooms. Ground-level guest rooms with queen-size and twin beds with view of lake share one guest bath. Upstairs

---

NOTES: Credit cards accepted: A MasterCard; B Visa; C American Express; D Discover; E Diners Club;
F Other; 2 Personal checks accepted; 3 Lunch available; 4 Dinner available; 5 Open all year; 6 Pets welcome;

guest rooms each have queen-size beds, one with double Hide-a-Bed, and seating area, each with private bath. Host is a chef from Vancouver and offers a full gourmet breakfast as well as vegetarian or low-sodium breakfasts if requested. A 10 percent discount is offered to seniors.

NEW WESTMINSTER

"Welcome" Bed and Breakfast

325 Pine Street, V3L 2T1
(604) 526-0978

A warm welcome awaits guests in the hosts' home in a distinctive residential area of the city. The bed and breakfast is within walking distance to stores, parks, and restaurants. Two blocks from a bus link to a 30-minute skytrain ride into downtown Vancouver. The accommodations include twin and queen-size beds, shared guest bathroom, and a guest sitting room. Experience the many exciting sites of Vancouver while enjoying morning and evening quiet amidst Heritage homes in charming New Westminster.

Hosts: Alice and Gerry VanKessel
Rooms: 3 (SB) $45
Full Breakfast
Credit Cards: None
Notes: 2, 3, 5, 8, 9, 10, 11, 13, 14

NORTH VANCOUVER

Helen's Bed and Breakfast

302 East Fifth Street, V7L 1L9
(604) 985-4869

Welcome to this old Victorian home, its charm and comfort enhanced by antiques, wonderful views, and color cable TV in each room. Five blocks to the Pacific; 20 minutes to the Horseshoe Bay ferries to Victoria; minutes to Grouse Mountain Sky Ride, Whistler Ski Resort, restaurants, and shopping. Gourmet breakfast served in the elegant dining room. Ten percent senior dis-

Helen's

count; 10 percent discount from November through April. Member of the North Vancouver Chamber of Commerce. No GST.

Host: Helen Boire
Rooms: 3 (1 PB; 2 SB) $65 plus
Full Breakfast
Credit Cards: B
Closed Christmas
Notes: 2, 5, 7, 9, 11, 12, 13

Laburnum Cottage Bed and Breakfast

1388 Terrace Avenue, V7R 1B4
(604) 988-4877

Set on one-half acre of award-winning English garden, nestled against a forest, yet only 15 minutes from downtown. Each of the guest rooms in the main house has its own decor, featuring delicate wallpapers, stunning antiques, and invitingly warm colors complemented by magnificent garden views. All rooms have private baths. Also two cottages in the garden. Breakfasts are jolly occasions in the big country house-style kitchen near the cozy Aga cooker or in the breakfast room, where all can enjoy a full three- or four-course meal. May be booked through a travel agent, but not encouraged.

Hosts: Delphine and Margot Masterton-Segers
Rooms: 4 (PB) $115-150 Canadian
Cottages: 2
Full Breakfast
Credit Cards: A, B
Notes: 2, 5, 7, 8, 9, 10, 11, 12, 13

---

7 No smoking; 8 Children welcome; 9 Social drinking allowed; 10 Tennis nearby; 11 Swimming nearby; 12 Golf nearby; 13 Skiing nearby; 14 May be booked through a travel agent.

Norgate Park House Bed and Breakfast

1226 Silverwood Crescent V7P 1J3
(604) 986-5069; FAX (604) 986-8810

This cedar-sided rancher has had an architect's hand in its renovations. Its intriguing nooks and crannies are filled with statues, wall hangings, and interesting knick-knacks from around the world. Two of the guest rooms open onto an unexpected large West Coast garden that includes more than 1,000 square feet of patio decking. The third room has its own private patio tucked off in a corner of the yard. The garden is both lush and green with ferns and rhododendrons. While sitting on the patio in the morning and having breakfast in the heart of this verdant retreat, it is hard to imagine it is only a 12-minute drive to the center of downtown Vancouver.

Hosts: Vicki Tyndall and Bill Girard
Rooms: 3 (SB) $70-80
Full Breakfast
Credit Cards: A, B
Notes: 5, 7, 10, 11, 12, 13, 14

Old English Bed and Breakfast Registry

1226 Silverwood Crescent, V7P 1J3
(604) 986-5069; FAX (604) 986-8810

1. Lie back and enjoy tranquility at the end of the day in this elegant bed and breakfast. The lovely guest rooms are built into the rocky evergreen slopes and look out through tall cedar and fir to the Pacific, sailing ships, and tiny islands. Suites are lovingly decorated with an assortment of finery that reflects both Canada and the Orient. Just 20 minutes from downtown Vancouver. Two rooms available; one is a queen-bed sitting room with private bath, fireplace, and, of course, a private patio deck to enjoy the view. The second room has a very large king-size bed, sitting room with a private bath, and private patio deck as well. $115-125.

2. Jane pampers guests year-round in their own private garden suite in North Vancouver. Tastefully decorated with fine antiques, the suite is very cozy and romantic. It is complete in every detail, including fireplace, TV, stereo, and private patio. Prepare for the memorable gourmet breakfast that awaits each morning in this first-class accommodation. Close to beaches and mountains and only 20 minutes to downtown Vancouver. Children are welcome. $95.

3. Guests will receive the royal treatment at Giselle's Bed and Breakfast in North Vancouver. This bed and breakfast is nestled on a very large lot that has a natural, park-like setting. Accommodations consist of three rooms. One room with a queen-size bed is tucked off to the side and has a private bath with a Jacuzzi for two. One of the upstairs rooms has a queen-size bed and its own patio deck. The other room is huge, with a sitting area, a king-size bed, and its own deck. Each room is equipped with its own TV and telephone. Giselle will bring coffee and the morning paper to start the day before breakfast is served. Near public transportation and 20 minutes from downtown. $75-85.

Sue's Victorian Guest House—Circa 1904

152 East Third, V7L 1E6
(604) 985-1523

This lovely, restored 1904 nonsmoking home is just four blocks from the harbor, seabus terminal, and Quay market. Close to restaurants, shops, and transportation. The decor is ideal for those who appreciate that loving-hand touch and Victorian soaker baths (no showers) and who are happy to remove outdoor shoes at the door to help maintain cleanliness. Each room is individually keyed and offers a TV, a short local-call phone, fan, and video player.

NOTES: Credit cards accepted: A MasterCard; B Visa; C American Express; D Discover; E Diners Club; F Other; 2 Personal checks accepted; 3 Lunch available; 4 Dinner available; 5 Open all year; 6 Pets welcome;

Sue's Victorian Guest House

Minimum stay is three nights during busy seasons; long-term stays encouraged. Cats in residence. Third person is $25 extra. Visa accepted for deposit only.

Host: Sue Chalmers
Rooms: 3 (1 PB; 2 SB) $50-60
No Breakfast
Credit Cards: None
Notes: 5, 7

OSOYOOS

Haynes Point Lakeside Guest House

3619 87th Street, V0H 1V0
(604) 495-7443

This bed and breakfast, overlooking Osoyoos Lake, has three bedrooms: Honeymoon, Oriental, and one with antique decors. Guests may use living room, spacious deck, hammock, and large outdoor campfire. A marvelous breakfast is served on fine china as guests relax in air-conditioned comfort. Enjoy a walk around Haynes Point Provincial Park. Golf at six courses; all water sports, tennis, biking, horseback riding, and winery tours are available. Hosts enjoy pampering so their visitors have an unforgettable

Okanagan holiday. Children 12 and older are welcome.

Hosts: John and June Wallace
Rooms: 3 (1 PB; 2 SB) $60-75
Full Breakfast
Credit Cards: None
Notes: 5, 7, 9, 10, 11, 12, 13

PARKSVILLE

All Seasons Bed and Breakfast Agency

P.O. Box 5511, Station B, Victoria, V8R 6S4
(604) 655-7173

Loon Watch. A gracious welcome awaits on Columbia Beach, close to Parksville or Qualicum. Fishermen will delight in local salmon fishing. Beachcomb or visit the many local artists and craftspeople. Cathedral Grove, with its 500-year-old trees, is a treat. Watch ships going up the Inside Passage to Alaska while lying in bed or relaxing on a private deck. Full breakfast. $45-75.

PENDER ISLAND

Corbett House Heritage Bed and Breakfast

4309 Corbett Road, Rural Route 1, V0N 2M0
(604) 629-6305

This quiet Heritage farmhouse with pastoral valley views, a pond, and sheep is only one mile from the ferry. Featuring period rooms with private baths and deck, a honeymoon suite, living room/music room/ library, fireplace, and local art. Gourmet breakfast and complimentary refreshments. Near the ocean, historic village, restaurants, and shopping. Open March through October. No pets, smoking, or children.

Hosts: Linda Wolfe and John Eckfeldt
Rooms: 3 (PB) $85-95
Full Breakfast
Credit Cards: A, B
Notes: 7, 9, 10, 11, 12

7 No smoking; 8 Children welcome; 9 Social drinking allowed; 10 Tennis nearby; 11 Swimming nearby; 12 Golf nearby; 13 Skiing nearby; 14 May be booked through a travel agent.

Hummingbird Hollow
Bed and Breakfast

Rural Route 1, 36125 Galleon Way, V0N 2M0
(604) 629-6392

In the beautiful Gulf Islands near Victoria, British Columbia, Hummingbird Hollow is a tranquil lakeside retreat. Share the natural surroundings and eclectic garden with many species of birds, ducks, and deer. Spend leisurely days exploring the many beaches and hidden coves around the island. Spacious suites have refrigerators, queen-size beds, and private sunrooms. Canoe and rowboat available. No smoking allowed inside the building.

Hosts: Doreen Ball and Chuck Harris
Rooms: 3 (PB) $70-90
Full Breakfast
Credit Cards: F
Notes 2, 5, 9, 10, 11, 12

Lakewoods

PENTICTON

Paradise Cove
Bed and Breakfast

Box 699 Penticton, 3129 Hayman Road, Naramata V3A 6P1
(604) 496-5896

Deluxe adult-oriented accommodations in this modern home in rolling orchard country overlooking Lake Okanagan. Panoramic lake, orchard, and beach views. Clean, very quiet, friendly, and comfortable. One full suite with kitchen, laundry, full bath, hot tub room, fireplace. Three queen-size rooms, two with private baths and lakeview decks. All rooms have their own phones and cable TV. There is complimentary beverage service in each room. No pets are allowed.

Hostess: Ruth Buchanan
Rooms: 4 (3 PB; 1 SB) $70-95
Full Breakfast
Credit Cards: A, B
Notes: 2, 5, 7, 9, 11, 12, 13

PORT ALBERNI

Lakewoods Bed and Breakfast

9778 Stirling Arm Circle, Site 339 C5, Rural Route 3 V9Y 7L7
(604) 723-2310

This bed and breakfast overlooks beautiful Sproat Lake and welcomes adult travelers to a peaceful waterfront home in a garden setting. Have a swim before turning in or before the hosts serve a homemade breakfast. The hosts enjoy having coffee with their guests in the evenings. Dutch as well as English is spoken.

Hosts: Dick and Jane Visee
Rooms: 3 (1 PB; 2 SB) $55-70
Full Breakfast
Credit Cards: None
Notes: 2, 5, 9, 10, 11, 12, 13

QUADA ISLAND

All Seasons Bed and
Breakfast Agency

Box 5511, Station B, Victoria, V8R 6S4
(604) 655-7173

Joha's Eagleview. A 12-minute ferry ride from Campbell River to Quathiaski Cove

NOTES: Credit cards accepted: A MasterCard; B Visa; C American Express; D Discover; E Diners Club; F Other; 2 Personal checks accepted; 3 Lunch available; 4 Dinner available; 5 Open all year; 6 Pets welcome;

on Quadra Island. Beautiful contemporary home with deck overlooking the Inside Passage to Alaska. Kayaking in saltwater or freshwater, shore diving possible from dock at Eagleview. Garden suite with oceanview suits two to four people. Three-day minimum. Rooms with ocean or garden view. Children over 11. No pets. No smoking. $60-75.

QUALICUM

Garden City Bed and Breakfast Reservation Service

660 Jones Terrace, Victoria, V8Z 2L7
(604) 479-1986; FAX (604) 479-9999

K-21. Panoramic oceanview—400-year-old trees on six and one-half acres with wildlife that includes deer, birds, sea lions, seals, and eagles. Privacy is a key word in this home where each bedroom has en suite bathroom. Enjoy meeting other guests in the game room or dining room, with ocean view. Multilanguage, multicultural host and hostess give guests the utmost in hospitality and comfort. From $70.

QUALICUM BEACH (VANCOUVER ISLAND)

All Seasons Bed and Breakfast Agency

Box 5511, Station B, Victoria, V8R 6S4
(604) 655-7173

Bahari. Rest and repast above the oyster-strewn beach where seals and sea lions bask. Cliffside overlooking the Strait of Georgia on sever acres of parkland in quiet surroundings. Easy access beach to explore or try badminton, horseshoes, or bols. All rooms en suite. Full breakfast. No smoking. No pets. Separate large self-catering suite with two bedrooms to accommodate two to six people. $85-150.

Blue Willow. Established English country charm. Tudor-style home with leaded-glass windows and beamed ceiling surround a delightful garden. Breakfasts served on the patio, weather permitting, or in cozy dining room on Blue Willow china, of course. Three guest accommodations. No smoking. No pets. Children over 12 welcome. French and German spoken. $75-85.

Garden City Bed and Breakfast Reservation Service

660 Jones Terrace, Victoria, V8Z 2L7
(604) 479-1986; FAX (604) 479-9999

K-24. Rest and relax while visiting this bed and breakfast on seven acres overlooking the Georgia Strait and the northern Gulf Islands. Watch sea lions and seals bask, shuck oysters on beach, or walk the philosopher's path. All attractions are a day trip or less away. Eiderdowns on king-, queen-size, double, or twin beds; all en suite baths. A two-bedroom, fully equipped suite with oceanview is also available. From $75.

SAANICH PENINSULA

All Seasons Bed and Breakfast Agency

Box 5511, Station B, Victoria, V8R 6S4
(604) 655-7173

Brambley Hedge. Delightful country home close to Butchart Gardens, golfing, and fishing. Outdoor fireplace, extensive garden railroad. Have coffee or tea on the pondside patio. Delicious breakfasts. Wonderful for families with children. The friendly hosts serve possibly the world's best gingersnaps. No smoking. No pets. $70-85.

Driftwood Shores. Gracious ranch-style home with antique touches and wonderful view of the water. Enjoy the low bank beach

7 No smoking; 8 Children welcome; 9 Social drinking allowed; 10 Tennis nearby; 11 Swimming nearby; 12 Golf nearby; 13 Skiing nearby; 14 May be booked through a travel agent.

All Seasons Bed and Breakfast Agency (continued)

or play tennis on an exceptional hard sur-face court. Delicious homemade breakfasts served in the elegant dining room. Minutes to Washington State and British Columbia ferries, Sidney, Butchart Gardens. No smoking. No pets. Children 12 and older welcome. $75-85.

Ease Mate. Welcoming contemporary home with extensive grounds. Antique pine furnishings, comfortable beds, and hosts who are keenly interested in the visual arts. Minutes to British Columbia ferries and Sidney. Full breakfasts. Children welcome and sometimes pets. $65-75.

Honoured Guests. Spectacular. Oriental gardens lead guests to this waterside home where they can stroll along the beach or indulge themselves with a herbal bath, curl up with a good book in the guest lounge, or relax in the hot tub. Morning greets guests with incredible sunrises. Gourmet break-fasts. Honeymoons are special. No smok-ing. No pets. No children. Close to Sidney, Washington State ferry, and airport. $125.

O'Connor Manor House. Gracious Tudor-style home in rural setting close to Butchart Gardens, golf course, ferries, etc. Beauti-fully appointed rooms with private baths. Honeymoon suite available. Breakfasts ele-gantly served. No smoking. No pets. No children. $85-95.

Orchard House. Original farmhouse owned by the family who gave the land to Sidney to develop the town. Built in 1914, it retains many original features while offer-ing total comfort. A five-minute walk from the Anacortes ferry, walking distance to beach, tennis, shops, and restaurants. A

favorite with those traveling by bicycle. Full breakfast served in the paneled dining room. Open year-round. Shared bathrooms. No smoking. No pets. $59-69.

Wind in the Willows. Quiet country charm in a West Coast-style home artfully hidden in Deep Cove with water views of the Saanich Inlet from the deck. Close to Ana-cortes and British Columbia ferries, airport, and Sidney. Sink into beds with comfy duvets, private baths. Full American break-fast supplied by a gourmet cook. No credit cards. Check in 4:00 to 6:00 P.M. No smok-ing. No pets. No children. $85.

Wintercott. A traditional country house of great charm, lovely gardens. All rooms have four-poster beds, private baths, TVs. Decorated in Laura Ashley style. Indoor hot tub. English cooked breakfasts. Tea served in the atrium or on the deck. No bet-ter place to come home to...close to Butchart Gardens. Beautiful at Christmas, too. No smoking. Occasional pets. Wheel-chair accessible. $95.

SALMON ARM

Alberta and Pacific Bed and Breakfast Agency

P.O. Box 15477, MPO, Vancouver, V6B 5B2
(604) 944-1793

11. Enjoy the uniqueness of a log home in country tradition, overlooking a wild bird sanctuary on picturesque Shuswap Lake. A ten-minute walk to beautiful Margaret Falls and Herald Park, and 15 minutes by car from Salmon Arm. This home offers a pri-vate entrance to ground-level walk-out, spacious self-contained guest suite with French doors overlooking garden and lake view, double bed, seating area, dining area, kitchen, and private bath. On the main floor are two guest rooms, each with a double bed and one guest bath.

The Silvercreek Guesthouse

6820-30th Avenue SW, V1E 4M1
(604) 832-8870

This log house is on an acreage in a picturesque setting with a view of the surrounding mountains and the Salmon River Valley. Shuswap Lake, with 1,000 kilometers of shoreline, provides a variety of water-related activities. Salmon Arm is at the north end of the Okanagan Valley, which is famous for its fruit orchards and vineyards. The Silvercreek serves a full country breakfast with farm-fresh eggs and homemade jams.

Hostess: Gisela Bodnar
Rooms: 4 (1 PB; 3 SB) $40-45
Full Breakfast
Credit Cards: None
Notes: 5, 8, 9, 10, 11, 12, 13

The Silvercreek Guesthouse

SALT SPRING ISLAND

All Seasons Bed and Breakfast Agency

Box 5511, Station B, Victoria, V8R 6S4
(604) 655-7173

Captain's Passage. Hospitality and comfort in a seaview setting tucked away in a quiet corner of the island. Relax in the spacious rooms with private baths and wonderful oceanview of the other islands and marine traffic. Guests are close enough to hear the

water. Fresh produce and home-baking provide the substantial breakfasts to start the day. The combination of hospitality and privacy make this unique bed and breakfast an ideal getaway. Check-in 4:00 to 6:00 P.M. No smoking. No children. No pets. $70.

The Ocean Roundhouse. The entire house is the guests' alone, a romantic retreat featuring two bedrooms, kitchen, living room with fireplace, and full bath. Pursue crab or dig clams on the sandy beach or go diving. Self-catering breakfast on the patio is a good place to enjoy the nature show. June to September try ocean kayaking, especially on Sundays, and spend a day learning about the fabulous sport. No smoking. No pets. Children over 12 welcome. $100.

Armand Heights Bed and Breakfast

221 Armand Way, V8K 2B6
(604) 653-9989 (phone and FAX)

Welcome to six peaceful acres almost one thousand feet up on the slopes of Mount Maxwell, where eagles soar at eye level. Glorious ocean, island, and snow-capped mainland mountain views. Spectacular sunrises and sunsets. Luxurious king- or queen-size beds and both bedrooms have full en suite bathrooms, private entrance, and deck. Delicious breakfasts with home baking. Vegetarians welcome. Adult oriented.

Hosts: Maureen and Michael Garvey
Rooms: 2 (PB) $75-85
Full Breakfast
Credit Cards: A, B
Notes: 2, 5, 7, 10, 11, 12, 14

Captain's Passage

1510 Beddis Road, V8K 2E3
(604) 537-9469

Hospitality, comfort, and privacy in a seaview setting. Five-minute walk to beach, ten-minute drive to town. First-class rooms with wonderful oceanview of other

7 No smoking; 8 Children welcome; 9 Social drinking allowed; 10 Tennis nearby; 11 Swimming nearby; 12 Golf nearby; 13 Skiing nearby; 14 May be booked through a travel agent.

Captain's Passage

islands and marine traffic. Delicious full breakfasts complete with fresh produce and home baking.

Hosts: Bob and Lauretta Wilson
Rooms: 2 (PB) $75
Full Breakfast
Credit Cards: A, B, C
Notes: 2, 5, 9, 10, 11, 12, 14

Cranberry Ridge Bed and Breakfast

269 Don Ore Drive, V8K 2H5
(604) 537-4854

New home especially designed for bed and breakfast. Two kilometers south of Ganges, the main village on the island, on the route to Mount Maxwell Park. Fantastic view of the Gulf Islands and Georgia Strait from the Sunshine Coast of British Columbia to Mount Vernon in Washington State. Three bed and breakfast rooms with private entrances to each room. The Twig Room has a fireplace. Two rooms have Jaccuzi baths and showers. Large hot tub on the deck overlooking the view. All rooms face the view. "The Best of the Best on Salt Spring." Two-night minimum stay.

Hosts: Gloria and Rodger Lutz
Rooms: 3 (PB) $101.65-139.10
Full Breakfast
Credit Cards: A, B
Notes: 5, 7, 9, 10, 11, 12, 14

Hastings House

160 Upper Ganges Road, P.O. Box 111, V8K 2E2
(604) 537-2362

In a uniquely pastoral setting, Hastings House is a tranquil retreat for the discriminating guest who seeks and appreciates a tasteful difference in resort destinations. Enjoy a five-course dinner in the dining room prepared by Hastings House's award-winning chef. Nearby activities such as golf, sea-kayaking, bird watching, and fishing round out a perfect vacation. If coming to the island only for the day, be sure to stop by the Hastings House for Sunday brunch served from 11:00 A.M. to 1:00 P.M. for $18.95 per person; advance reservations are recommended.

Hosts: Patricia Gibson and Ian Cowley
Rooms: 12 (PB) $230-440
Full and Continental Breakfast
Credit Cards: A, B, C
Notes: 4, 7, 10, 12, 14

Weston Lake Inn Bed and Breakfast

813 Beaver Point Road, V8K 1X9
(604) 653-4311

Nestled on a knoll of flowering trees and shrubs overlooking beautiful Weston Lake, this exquisite country bed and breakfast is a serene adult getaway. Down quilts, fresh bouquets, a fireside lounge, hot tub, wonderful breakfasts, and warm hospitality. Recommended in Northwest Best Places, the *Vancouver Sun*, and the *Seattle Times*. Salt Spring Island, near Victoria, has a mild climate, exceptional beauty, and a large population of artists and artisans. Hosts also offer skippered sailing charters in the beautiful waters of the Gulf Islands on a 36-foot boat.

Hosts: Susan Evans and Ted Harrison
Rooms: 3 (PB) $95-115
Full Breakfast
Credit Cards: A, B, C
Notes: 2, 5, 7, 9, 10, 11, 12, 14

NOTES: Credit cards accepted: A MasterCard; B Visa; C American Express; D Discover; E Diners Club; F Other; 2 Personal checks accepted; 3 Lunch available; 4 Dinner available; 5 Open all year; 6 Pets welcome;

SATURNA ISLAND

Garden City Bed and Breakfast Reservation Service

660 Jones Terrace, Victoria, V8Z 2L7
(604) 479-1986; FAX (604) 479-9999

K-8. Peaceful surroundings overlooking Lyall Harbour. Private suite with two bedrooms, bath, fireplace. From $65.

K-9. Recapture tranquillity of bygone ages in 80-year-old restored farmhouse on two and one-half acres over Boot Cove. Walking distance from ferry. Spacious rooms feature antiques, garden, and oceanviews. private and shared bathrooms, separate entrance. From wraparound porch watch boats, birds in the orchard, or relax with a good book. From $60.

SHAWNIGAN LAKE (VANCOUVER ISLAND)

Garden City Bed and Breakfast Reservation Service

660 Jones Terrace, Victoria, V8Z 2L7
(604) 479-1986; FAX (604) 479-9999

K-30. Peaceful country acreage. Just five minutes to beach, 45 minutes to Victoria, and near water sports, hiking, fishing, and golf. Enjoy home-cooked waffles, omelets, fresh fruit, etc. Queen-size, double, twin beds, en suite and shared baths. From $55.

SIDNEY

Garden City Bed and Breakfast Reservation Service

660 Jones Terrace, Victoria, V8Z 2L7
(604) 479-1986; FAX (604) 479-9999

A-5. A value-priced, bright, sunny home surrounded by one-half acre of gardens. A four-course breakfast awaits guests in the morning after a most relaxing sleep in rooms with queen-size or twin beds. Comfort and friendliness in a warm atmosphere. Twenty minutes to town and five minutes to Butchart Gardens. From $55.

A-12. Gracious country home, minutes from Butchart Gardens. Delicious homemade breakfasts served in country kitchen or pond terrace. Private suite with fireplace or queen-size or single room with shared bath. Delightful garden railway. Children welcome. Resident dog, cat, and fish. From $65.

A-15. Unique home on sandy beach with incredible views of Haro Strait and San Juan Islands. Sleep to the lull of lapping waves and waken to breathtaking seascape. Breakfast served in oceanview dining room. Restaurants, shopping, golfing, tennis, hiking, parks, whale watching, diving, and fishing. From $85.

B-3. This is different! Begin and end the day with Wholistic REIKE, or massage (by appointment). Breakfast includes fresh, home-baked bread with preserves or delicious waffles. Enjoy the view of the bay. Queen-size beds. Near Butchart Gardens, Brentwood Bay, and Swartz Bay ferries. From $60.

SOINTULA

Wayward Wind Bed and Breakfast

Box 300, V0N 3E0
(604) 973-6307

There are three suites in log buildings. Two suites directly look out over the ocean. There is an eagle perch between the ocean and the suites. Specialize in orca (killer whale) trips on a 28-foot sailboat. On these trips from late June through mid-October one can expect to

7 No smoking; 8 Children welcome; 9 Social drinking allowed; 10 Tennis nearby; 11 Swimming nearby; 12 Golf nearby; 13 Skiing nearby; 14 May be booked through a travel agent.

see a great variety of wildlife, such as seals and dolphins, in addition to the whales. A lunch is served on board, and the trip is seven to eight hours long. At times the trip also includes fishing, depending on the charter.

Rooms: 3 (1 PB; 2 SB) $70-75
Continental Breakfast
Credit Cards: None
Notes: 2, 3, 4, 6, 8, 9, 10, 11, 12, 14

SOOKE (VANCOUVER ISLAND)

All Seasons Bed and Breakfast Agency

Box 5511, Station B, Victoria, V8R 6S4
(604) 655-7173

Eagle Cove. The Pacific at the doorstep. Complete privacy in two-room self-contained oceanfront suite. Listen to the crashing breakers from the sitting room or view the Strait of Juan de Fuca against the magnificent scenic backdrop of the Olympic Mountains. No smoking. No pets. No children. Full breakfast. $100.

Gracefield. Restored plantation Colonial home midway between Victoria and Sooke. Eleven acres with breathtaking views of Olympic Mountains and the sea. Endless opportunities for hikers, beachcombers, photographers, naturalists, and artists. Built by the Grace family of Chicago, builders of New York's Grand Central and Winnipeg's CN Stations. Antique furnishings. Full breakfast. No smoking, pets, or children. $60-100.

Markham House. A Tudor-style country house whose peace and tranquility are guaranteed to clear the mind and refresh the soul. Ten acres of landscaped gardens and wooded trails. Relax beside the pond, watch the birds, take a picture, or even paint one. Guest lounge with fireplace. All rooms have private baths and garden views. Perfect for weddings. No smoking. No pets. No children. $90-105.

Thistledown. Cottage on the beach. Sleeps five. Magnificent view. Children and pets welcome. Weekly. $950.

French Beach Retreats

983 Seaside Drive, Rural Route 2, V0S 1N0
(604) 646-2154; FAX (604) 646-2002

Embrace a private ocean home of one's own—the Retreat, a complete home with Jacuzzi, sauna, and fireplace, is an escape for a couple or a group of six to eight in one party. The Ocean Treehouse for two, oceanfront, is a secluded hideaway. Both 20 minutes from Sooke Harbour House for fantastic dinners. Romance at French Beach Retreats is one hour west of Victoria on Vancouver Island's southwest coast.

Host: Mel Coxey
Rooms: 4 (3 PB; 1 SB) $180-300 Canadian
Continental Breakfast
Credit Cards: None
Notes: 2, 5, 6, 8, 9, 11, 12

Garden City Bed and Breakfast Reservation Service

660 Jones Terrace, Victoria, V8Z 2L7
(604) 479-1986; FAX (604) 479-9999

L-1. Beautiful country-style home with wraparound porch. Three wooded acres with rooms overlooking the forest. Art by Carey Newman, TV, VCR, and library. Activities include Galloping Goose Trail for hiking or biking; fishing charters can be arranged; a chance sighting of wildlife on property. From $50.

L-17. Two acres of incredible waterfront property overlooking a large estuary that attracts swans, geese, eagles, herons, etc. Watch the sunset or beachcomb. Private en suite bath has a sauna, a six-foot Jacuzzi tub, separate shower, etc. Four-poster queen-size bed. Full breakfast served. Friendly dog in residence, so no guest pets. Ask about the new, beautiful family suite. From $95.

Ocean Wilderness

Ocean Wilderness

109 West Coast Road, Rural Route 2, V0S 1N0
(604) 646-2116; (800) 323-2116

Ocean Wilderness offers five peaceful forested acres with beach; a natural haven for romantics. Watch for whales and eagles from the hot tub tucked in the Japanese gazebo. The large, luxurious rooms with private entrances are furnished with antiques and canopied beds. Plant a "memory tree" after a multicourse breakfast served in the rustic log dining room. The beach party seafood buffet is so popular! Enjoy fresh seafood eaten on the beach around the log fire. Pets welcome by prior arrangements.

Host: Marion Rolston
Rooms: 7 (PB) $75-175 Canadian
Full Breakfast
Credit Cards: A, B
Notes: 2, 3, 5, 7, 8, 9, 10, 11, 12, 14

Sooke Harbour House

1528 Whiffen Spit Road, Rural Route 4, V0S 1N0
(604) 642-3421; FAX (604) 642-6988

Thirteen romantic guest rooms have fireplaces and breathtaking water views, some offering Jacuzzi tubs for two or hot tubs on private decks. Internationally renowned restaurant offers fresh local fish and shellfish, organic vegetables, salad greens, and edible flowers that are grown in the gardens, grown on nearby organic farms, or harvested

in the wilds around Sooke. This romantic inn is right on the water, 45 minutes southwest of Victoria, on Vancouver Island. During full season and weekends, in-house guests are offered a complimentary lunch.

Hosts: Sinclair and Frederique Philip
Rooms: 13 (PB) $155-275
Full Breakfast
Credit Cards: A, B, C
Notes: 2, 4, 5, 6, 7, 8, 9, 10, 11, 12, 14

TOFINO

All Seasons Bed and Breakfast Agency

P.O. Box 5511, Station B, Victoria, V8R 6S4
(604) 655-7173

Westwind. Self-contained cottage on two acres of wooded privacy. Enjoy West Coast ambience and the beauty of the West Coast rain forest. A five-minute walk to Chesterman Beach and pounding surf of the Pacific. Enjoy the comfort of feather beds and goose down duvets. Fruit basket and Continental breakfast provided. Full kitchen and sitting room, two bedrooms. No smoking. No pets. $15 for additional person. $95.

Silver Cloud

Box 188, V0R 2Z0
(604) 725-3998

Large waterfront property nestled in the quiet privacy of woods, with two acres of spectacular gardens encircling the house and along the water. Bald eagles, otters, seals; excellent bird watching. Romantic, tasteful queen-size rooms and private baths with view. Continental breakfast served on fine china in solarium overlooking water. Lower deck with ramp to beach. Gas barbecue. Full apartment galley and bath also available; sleeps two to four. Limited social drinking.

Host: Olivia Mae
Rooms: 3 (PB) $80-150
Continental Breakfast
Credit Cards: None
Notes: 5, 7, 10, 11, 12

7 No smoking; 8 Children welcome; 9 Social drinking allowed; 10 Tennis nearby; 11 Swimming nearby; 12 Golf nearby; 13 Skiing nearby; 14 May be booked through a travel agent.

Wilp Gybuu (Wolf House) Bed and Breakfast

311 Leighton Way, P.O. Box 396, V0R 2Z0
(604) 725-2330

Adult guests warmly welcomed to this contemporary West Coast cedar home. Watch boats travel through beautiful Duffin Passage while enjoying a delicious full breakfast. Walk to Tonquin Beach, galleries, and restaurants. Golf, Pacific Rim National Park's beaches, and rain forest are minutes away by car. Tastefully decorated guest rooms with twin or queen-size beds have private en suite bathrooms. Cat in residence. Airport/bus pickup.

Hosts: Wendy and Ralph Burgess
Rooms: 2 (PB) $70-75 Canadian
Full Breakfast
Credit Cards: None
Notes: 5, 7, 9, 12

UCLUELET

All Seasons Bed and Breakfast Agency

P.O. Box 5511, Station B, Victoria, V8R 6S4
(604) 655-7173

Sheila's Bed and Breakfast. Quiet, friendly country setting off the Pacific Rim Highway a few minutes from Wikininsh and Long Beach. Visit Hot Springs Cove, go fishing, or go whale watching. Tofino is home to the Longhouse Gallery of Canadian artist Roy Vickers. Comfortable rooms and cheery breakfast. No smoking. No children. No pets. $66.

Burley's

1078 Helen Road, P.O. Box 550, V0R 3A0
(604) 726-4444

A waterfront home on a small drive-to island at the harbor mouth, offering single, double, and queen-size water- and regular beds, and TV in friendly Ucluelet. Enjoy the open ocean, sandy beaches, lighthouse lookout, nature walks, charter fishing, diving, fisherman's wharves, whale watching and sightseeing cruises, or later, the exhilarating winter storms. A view from every window. No pets; no smoking. Adult oriented. French spoken.

Hosts: Ron and Micheline Burley
Rooms: 6 (SB) $40-65
Full Breakfast
Credit Cards: A, B
Notes: 7, 10, 11, 12

Burley's

VANCOUVER

Alberta and Pacific Bed and Breakfast Agency

P.O. Box 15477, MPO, V6B 5B2
(604) 944-1793

There is a private entrance to this main floor apartment with living room, one bedroom with queen-size bed, one bedroom with twin beds, fully equipped kitchen, and private bath. There are also an en suite laundry, TV, VCR, and telephone. It is a short walk to the skytrain to downtown, adjacent to a recreation and fitness center, and across from scenic Trout Lake Park.

NOTES: Credit cards accepted: A MasterCard; B Visa; C American Express; D Discover; E Diners Club;
F Other; 2 Personal checks accepted; 3 Lunch available; 4 Dinner available; 5 Open all year; 6 Pets welcome;

Albion Guest House Bed and Breakfast

592 West 19th Avenue, V5Z-1W6
(604) 873-2287

This restored 1906 character home is on a quiet, tree-lined residential street in the city. Within walking distance of restaurants, speciality coffee shops, delicatessens, parks, theaters, shopping, a gambling casino, beaches, boating, parasailing, and windsurfing activities. Free bicycle rentals. Hot tub. The four guest rooms have thick feather mattresses, fine cotton linens, and down-filled duvets. The guests enjoy complimentary apéritifs, refreshments, and a gourmet breakfast. Nonsmoking establishment. Reservations recommended. AAA-approved. Listed in Best Places to Stay in the Pacific Northwest.

Hosts: Bill and Howard
Rooms: 4 (2 PB; 2 SB) $75-155
Full Gourmet Breakfast
Credit Cards: A, B
Notes: 5, 7, 9, 10, 11, 12, 13, 14

All Seasons Bed and Breakfast Agency

Box 5511, Station B, Victoria, V8R 6S4
(604) 655-7173

Jane's Gourmet Bed and Breakfast. Private suite with queen-size bed, private bath, fireplace, TV, stereo, and antiques. Unwind and relax in a quiet residential area of North Vancouver, only 20 minutes from downtown. Close to the beach, mountains, and Horseshoe Bay ferry. Memorable full breakfasts. $85.

Laburnum Cottage. This charming home with beautifully appointed rooms is set on one-half acre of award-winning English country gardens. Featured in *Country Inns* magazine June 1992. All private bathrooms and queen-size beds. Superb full breakfasts. Check-in flexible. No smoking. No pets. $125.

Beautiful

Beautiful Bed and Breakfast

428 West 40th Avenue, V5Y 2R4
(604) 327-1102

Relax in this elegant, clean, new Colonial home with antiques, fresh flowers, views, and quiet. Five minutes from downtown. Walk to tennis, golf, Queen Elizabeth Park, Van Dusen Gardens, YMCA/YWCA, three cinemas, shopping center, and fine restaurants. Three-quarters of a block from bus to downtown, airport, ferries, and UBC. Breakfast in formal dining room with linens, silver, and fresh flowers. Friendly hosts will assist with travel plans. Children over 14 welcome.

Hosts: Ian and Corinne Sanderson
Rooms: 6 (2 PB; 4 SB) $70-150 U. S.
Full Breakfast
Credit Cards: None
Notes: 7, 9, 11, 10, 12, 13, 14

Bed and Breakfast, Ltd.

P.O. Box 216, New Haven, CT 06513
(203) 469-3260

25. This 1926 cottage with two glorious bed and breakfast rooms is comfortable, cozy, and quaint. Flower-filled deck. Crib available. Children welcome. Near University of British Columbia and Jericho Beach. $75-85.

An English Garden Bed and Breakfast

4390 Frances Street, V5C 2R3
(604) 298-8815; Message (800) 488-1941
FAX (604) 298-5917

---

7 No smoking; 8 Children welcome; 9 Social drinking allowed; 10 Tennis nearby; 11 Swimming nearby; 12 Golf nearby; 13 Skiing nearby; 14 May be booked through a travel agent.

White-stucco bungalow ten minutes from the top of Burnaby Mountain with its view of Vancouver, Grouse and Seymour Mountains, and Burrard Inlet. Two guest rooms, each with TV; one room has a view of the mountains. Advance notice is appreciated.

Host: Norma McCurrach
Rooms: 2 (1 PB; 1 SB) $45-75
Full Breakfast
Credit Cards: A, B
Notes: 7, 10, 11, 12, 13, 14

Green Gables Downtown Bed and Breakfast

628 Union Street, V6A 2B9
(604) 253-6230

Receive a warm welcome and friendly hospitality at Green Gables. This recently renovated 1898 Heritage Home is only one block from public transport or ten minutes' walk to downtown. The twin rooms are bright and comfortable, and guests are encouraged to feel at home in the dining and living areas, as well as the back sun deck overlooking the colorful garden. Over a delicious breakfast, plans are made for the day, and the well-traveled hosts are glad to help with tourist information.

Hosts: Carl and Mariko Shepherd
Rooms: 7 (SB) $40-59
Full Breakfast
Credit Cards: B
Notes: 5, 8, 9, 10, 13

The International Bed and Breakfast

504 Amherst Street, Buffalo, NY 14207
(800) 723-4262; FAX (716) 873-4462

BC2855PP. Luxury home with free pickup from the airport, free parking, ten rooms, four living rooms, three kitchens, one- and two-bedroom apartments, TV, public telephones, beautiful mountain view, Jacuzzi, and patio. Just ten minutes from Vancouver International Airport and ferry to Victoria; 15 minutes from downtown Vancouver. Full breakfast. $60-65.

Johnson House

Johnson House Bed and Breakfast

2278 West 34th Avenue, V6M 1G6
(604) 266-4175

Wonderful, restored Craftsman-style home is furnished with Canadian antique furniture, carousel horses, and comfy brass and iron beds. Full breakfasts including a main course, fresh fruit, and homemade muffins and jams. The friendly hosts invite guests to stay in one of Vancouver's finest and safest city neighborhoods. The house is a six-minute drive to downtown or the university and is close to fine restaurants, services, and tourist attractions. Fifteen minutes from the airport.

Hosts: Sandy and Ron Johnson
Rooms: 3 (2 PB; 1 SB) $65-120 Canadian
Full Breakfast
Credit Cards: None
Notes: 2, 5, 7, 9, 10, 11, 12, 13, 14

Kenya Court Ocean Front Guest House

2230 Cornwall Avenue, V6K 1B5
(604) 738-7085

Oceanview suites on the waterfront in a gracious Heritage building minutes from downtown Vancouver. Across the street are tennis courts, a large heated saltwater pool, and walking and jogging paths along the water's edge. It is an easy walk to Granville Island, the planetarium, and interesting shops and restaurants. All of the guest suites are spacious and tastefully furnished. The delicious full breakfast is served in a glass solarium with a spectacular view of English Bay. Children over eight are welcome.

Host: D. M. Williams
Suites: 4 (PB) From $85
Full Breakfast
Credit Cards: F
Notes: 2, 5, 7, 9, 10, 11, 13

The Manor Guest House

345 West 13th Avenue, V5Y 1W2
(604) 876-5703

The Manor Guest House, an Edwardian Heritage mansion, is one of Vancouver's finest bed and breakfasts. Choose from nine spacious, high-ceilinged rooms, most with king-size or twin beds and private bath. The self-contained penthouse suite has a loft, kitchen, and private deck, which offers a spectacular, unobstructed view of the city. The manor is in the heart of the city, a block from city hall and close to every activity available for guests to do in

The Manor Guest House

Vancouver. A generous and delicious healthful breakfast is served, featuring fresh daily baking.

Host: Brenda Yablon
Rooms: 10 (6 PB; 4 SB) $55-115
Full Breakfast
Credit Cards: A, B
Notes: 5, 7, 8, 9, 10, 11, 12, 13, 14

Nelson House

977 Broughton Street, V6G 2A4
(604) 684-9793

Nelson House is a large, 1907 Edwardian on a quiet residential street, only a few minutes walk from downtown, Stanley Park, and the beaches. Glowing fireplaces and a happy springer spaniel assure a warm welcome. The hosts are travelers, too, and each guest room suggests a different itinerary, i.e., Vienna, the Klondike. Four rooms, which share two baths, each have a private washbasin. The Studio, however, has it all—fireplace, kitchen, deck, Jacuzzi, and romantic Asian ambience. Smoking restricted.

Hosts: David Ritchie and O'Neal Williamson
Rooms: 4 (S2B) $68-140
Full Breakfast
Credit Cards: A, B
Notes: 5, 9, 10, 11, 13, 14

Olde English Bed and Breakfast

1226 Silver Crescent, North Vancouver, V7P 1J3
(604) 986-5069; FAX (604) 986-8810

5. This Edwardian-style, three-story Vancouver home is a jewel sitting in the middle of the city. It is beautifully decorated with fine furniture and antiques. The bed and breakfast rooms are on the second floor of the home. They have a view of the North Shore Mountains. Three rooms share one full bathroom plus one-half bathroom. Each room is equipped with a small refrigerator, coffee maker, and toaster oven plus supplies for a Continental breakfast. The rooms have a king-size bed that

Olde English Bed and Breakfast (continued)

can be made into twin beds. Public transportation is close by. $70.

6. The Cliffridge is a one-level home decorated with a mixture of elegance and rattan. The guest area is a very private wing consisting of two bedrooms, a full shared bath, a living room with fireplace, and a dining area. The queen-size bedroom opens onto a sunny garden; the other has a double bed, used only for family or traveling companions. Close to Grouse Mountain, Capilano Canyon Suspension Bridge, Cleveland Dam, hiking trails, and bus transportation to the city. $95.

7. The Roberts' Bed and Breakfast is high on the hill overlooking Horseshoe Bay, where many ferries come and go. Guests have a very private king-size bedroom with private bath and shower. The sitting room includes TV, stereo, and fireplace and opens onto a patio. Downtown Vancouver is 30 minutes away; Whistler only 75 minutes. No smoking. Not suitable for small children. No pets. $95.

8. This homey Kitsilano bed and breakfast is just a few blocks away from the lively West Broadway area. Close to the university area and only 12 minutes to downtown Vancouver. The three guest rooms are decorated with quilts, some early Canadian maple, plus some pine pieces mixed with wicker. The guest room on the main floor, with its own bathroom next door, opens out onto a beautiful, terraced backyard and a sunny patio. One of the upstairs rooms has an expansive view of the North Shore Mountains and the city. The other upstairs room overlooks the garden. Both of these rooms have en suite bath. $95.

9. This elegant 1912 Edwardian home is decorated with a blend of eclectic Old World put together with a character of its own. Central to West Side, close to shops, public transport, tennis, and the Granville Island Market. The accommodation consists of a tastefully appointed, self-contained bed- and sitting room with a lovely mountain view. The sleeping arrangement is a comfortable queen-size sofa bed. The kitchen is fully equipped. The private bathroom is complete with an old-fashioned tub, shower, and a unique sun porch for two. A Continental breakfast is left in the suite to have at leisure. The accommodation is complete with telephone and TV. $95.

10. Mousehole is the ideal getaway weekend for two. The accommodation is a one-bedroom suite, complete with en suite shower, a sitting room comfortably furnished, and a color TV. French doors open onto the waterfront patio. Deep Cover offers guests peace, tranquility, beautiful scenery, salmon fishing, canoeing, kayaking, hiking, and fine dining. Yet only 20 minutes to downtown Vancouver. Adult-oriented. No smoking. $125.

Town and Country Bed and Breakfast in British Columbia

P.O. Box 74542
2803 West Fourth Avenue V6K 1K2
(604) 731-5942

Offering bed and breakfast homes in residential areas of Vancouver and Victoria, and the listings include some small inns. A few of the listings have waterfront or special views. Private and shared baths available. Some have from one to three guest rooms. Some character homes, some West Coast-style homes or townhouse accommodations. Usually within 15-20 minutes to city center.

NOTES: Credit cards accepted: A MasterCard; B Visa; C American Express; D Discover; E Diners Club; F Other; 2 Personal checks accepted; 3 Lunch available; 4 Dinner available; 5 Open all year; 6 Pets welcome;

1. This comfortable, newly decorated home is in a quiet, central neighborhood. The hospitable hosts speak French and Ukrainian and enjoy sharing helpful information on the city. Close to restaurants, shops, parks, and major bus lines. Two guest rooms. Full breakfast. From $65.

2. Rest and relax in this home away from home. Guests have a choice of three lock-and-key bedrooms, each with a unique character. Antiques and collectibles from around the world are found throughout the house. A hearty breakfast featuring pancakes, eggs cooked any style, cereals, fresh fruits and juices, muffins, and wild oat porridge topped with fruit, nuts, sunflower seeds, and brown sugar. In the City Hall Heritage area. $75-135.

3. This lovely contemporary townhouse has one guest room with private bath, queen-size bed, and patio on the ground level. Excellent location for walking to Kitsilano beach and park, Granville Island with its market, shops, galleries, restaurants, and live theater all on the waterfront. Bus within one block. Downtown five minutes. $85-95.

4. North Vancouver. Restful, peaceful seclusion. This charming home, with a Victorian air and antiques, is set on a half-acre of beautifully kept, award-winning English garden and surrounded by virgin forest. Only 15 minutes from downtown Vancouver and Horseshoe Bay; five minutes from Grouse Mountain and other North Shore attractions. Delphine and family offer beautifully appointed guest rooms, a choice of single, twin, or queen-sized beds. The Summer Cottage in the garden is a perfect honeymoon hideaway! Relax on the patio or in the cool of the garden with its little meandering creek. Everyone enjoys Delphine's great breakfasts with homemade jams, muffins, and blueberry pancakes made on the Aga stove. Only two blocks from major bus

routes, lots of parking. German and French are spoken here. No smoking. $125-155.

5. Not the usual bed and breakfast, this is a private suite one block from bus line, terrific view of mountains, sea, city. Fifteen minutes to downtown. Bedroom with queen-size bed, sitting room with queen-size sofa bed, TV, also kitchen facilities. Suitable for three or four traveling together. No children. Twenty-five dollars for additional persons. $95.

6. North Vancouver. A contemporary home with a view of the West Coast. King-size or twin beds. Nutritious and delicious breakfast. Mountain view spa. Families welcome, but children should be over eight years old. Walk to Grouse Mountain Skyride. Fifteen minutes to downtown and Stanley Park. No smoking. Seasonal rates. $65-120

The Wedgewood Hotel

845 Hornby Street, V6Z 1V1
(604) 689-7777; (800) 663-0666

In the heart of downtown Vancouver across from the courthouse, art gallery, and Robson Square, this four-star boutique hotel offers 93 luxurious guest rooms and suites, a fine Italian restaurant with dancing to live entertainment, a popular piano lounge, coffee shop, health club, meeting and banquet facilities, valet parking, and more.

Hosts: Eleni Skalbania and Joanna Tsaparas
Rooms: 93 (PB) $190-460
Full or Continental Breakfast
Credit Cards: A, B, C, D, E, F
Notes: 3, 4, 5, 7, 8, 9, 14

The West End Guest House

1362 Hard Street, V6E 1G2
(604) 681-2889; FAX (604) 688-8812

Built in 1906 for the Edwards family, the West End Guest House is constructed

7 No smoking; 8 Children welcome; 9 Social drinking allowed; 10 Tennis nearby; 11 Swimming nearby; 12 Golf nearby; 13 Skiing nearby; 14 May be booked through a travel agent.

The West End Guest House

contained guest room with adjoining family room. Twin beds and double beds. Private entrance, private bath. Single and double rooms with private bath. The guest rooms have their own VCR, cable TV, and big refrigerator. Large patio for relaxing while watching the cattle and miniature goats on green pastures against a mountain backdrop. Plenty of room; bring the children. Winter skiing, sandy beaches, excellent golf courses, trail riding, water slide, mountain chair lift, and more in the area. Canada's Playland.

Hosts: Fred and Helen Schroth
Rooms: 2 (PB) $45-55
Full Breakfast
Credit Cards: None
Notes: 5, 8, 9, 10, 11, 12, 13

entirely of straight grain cedar (meaning it has no knots). The young Edwards men operated the first photography shop in Vancouver, and many of their pictures hang in the inn. In 1985 it was restored as a bed and breakfast, complete with a "Painted Lady" pink and white exterior. It's new owner has furnished the rooms with Victorian antiques and reproductions, keeping the style elegant and interesting with memorabilia. Rooms include bathroom, TV, phone, bathrobes and slippers, and sun deck with wicker furniture where, on a hot summer day, iced tea is served. Sherry served year-round by the fireplace.

Rooms: 7 (PB) $100-195
Full Breakfast
Credit Cards: A, B, C, D
Notes: 2, 5, 7, 9, 10, 11, 12, 13, 14

VERNON

The Schroth Farm

3282 East Vernon Road, Site 6 C25, Rural Route 8
V1T 8L6
(604) 545-0010

Enjoy the farm. Only one mile from Vernon. This cozy, clean, vintage home offers a self-

VICTORIA

Alberta and Pacific Bed and Breakfast Agency

P.O. Box 15477, MPO, Vancouver, V6B 5B2
(604) 944-1793

8. Chalet, German-style home is opposite Swan Lake and within walking distance of Swan Lake Nature Sanctuary, restaurants, and a pub. Buses to the university, downtown, and Butchart Gardens. Spacious guest room has two double beds, seating area with TV, sliding glass doors to upper deck with panoramic view, and en suite bath. Second guest room is Victorian style with queen-size bed and en suite bath. Third guest room is on the main floor with double bed and shared bath and a Jacuzzi. Fourth guest room has twin beds, shared bath, Jacuzzi, available August only.

All Seasons Bed and Breakfast Agency

P.O. Box 5511, Station B, V8R 6S4
(604) 655-7173

Arundel Manor. Gracious Heritage Home on one-half acre of lawns and gardens, a short drive from city center. The property slopes to an inlet. Superb sunset views. Full breakfast served in the handsome dining room or on the veranda. All rooms have private baths. Two rooms have balconies overlooking the water. Special gatherings or small weddings can be arranged. Honeymoons are special. $95-110.

Bowden House. Built in 1913, this quiet, comfortable character home has been personally restored by the owners. It has high ceilings and the relaxed charm and ambience of the traditional bed and breakfast. Wake up to the aroma of fresh coffee and a hearty English breakfast. Stroll through Banfield Park overlooking the Seilerk Water. Shared bathrooms. $45-65.

Camelot. A true Victorian built in 1901 by James McLure. The spacious rooms are nostalgically and charmingly decorated in abundance. Expansive gardens ideal for weddings. The Honeymoon Suite features a queen-size canopied Viennese bed and full bath with slipper tub reminiscent of Lillian Russell. Morning tea or coffee delivered to guests' room. Gourmet breakfasts. Wonderful at Christmas. No smoking. No pets. Inquire about accommodations for children. $95-145.

Chez Raymonde. Congenial modern home in excellent location, within walking distance of University of Victoria. Fantastic breakfast. Shared bath. Children welcome. Lovely garden. No pets. $65.

Circles. Modern home facing Swan Lake, Christmas Hill Nature Sanctuary. Nature path around the park and lake for exercise. Bird watching tours every Wednesday and Sunday in season. Scrumptious breakfasts. $60-85.

Grahams Cedar House. Spectacular West Coast home in a woodsy setting where it is possible to listen to the peace and quiet. The town of Sidney is seven minutes away.

Close to the Stone House Pub and the ferry terminal. The romantic master suite looks out on the deck and garden. The two-bedroom suite with full kitchen, bath, private entrance, and patio accommodates up to six people. Full and healthy breakfasts and delicious baked goods often served on the sunny deck. It is a treat. No smoking. No pets. Air conditioning. $75-85.

Heathergate. Elegance and comfort tucked into the historic James Bay area close to the Inner Harbour. A relaxed and modern home furnished with great taste. Rooms have down comforters, bathrobes, telephones, and Casablanca fans. Easy walk to Parliament buildings, Conference Centre, museums, and Fisherman's Wharf. Private guest lounge with fireplace. Full breakfasts. No smoking. No pets. No children. $85-95.

Hillside House. Enjoy morning coffee or afternoon tea on the porch of this gracious 1919 character home, overlooking the city, with ocean and mountain views. Two large, cheery rooms, shared bath. The peacefulness and space provide a perfect retreat from city noise. Ten minutes from University of Victoria and all major attractions. Great breakfasts. Children welcome. No credit cards. Check in is 4:00 to 6:00 P.M. $85.

Mulberry Manor. A jewel of the post-Victorian era, one of the last great houses designed by the renowned architect Samuel Maclure. Close to Oak Bay and surrounded by delightful landscaped gardens. Most rooms have balconies. This elegant home is superbly decorated, and was featured in the *House and Gardens* tour of Victoria in May 1993. All private baths. Truly special. Check-in by arrangement. $95-150.

Myllford Haven House. Enjoy this cottage-style, early 1900s bungalow where visitors to Victoria may enjoy Canadian hospitality.

7 No smoking; 8 Children welcome; 9 Social drinking allowed; 10 Tennis nearby; 11 Swimming nearby; 12 Golf nearby; 13 Skiing nearby; 14 May be booked through a travel agent.

Begin the day with a hearty breakfast served in the bright and cheerful dining room, and finish the day by relaxing in the cozy parlor or garden. Queen-size beds and private baths. No children. No smoking. No pets. $65-85.

Pitcairn House. This Victorian Heritage Home was built in 1901 by prominent Victoria architect John Tiarks for the Australian-born John Elford. Elford arrived via the California gold fields with his family on the famous ship *Bounty,* having been christened on Pitcairn Island in the Pacific. Central to Antique Row, art gallery, and Craigdarroch Castle. Nice small garden. Full breakfasts. No smoking. No pets. No children. $80-90.

Prior House. Elegant English mansion built in 1912 for the king's representative in British Columbia. Enjoy the relaxed ambience of days gone by. Canopied beds, down comforters, private baths, and working fireplaces in every room. Breakfast is served in the paneled dining room overlooking the large garden terrace. Afternoon tea in the parlor. $110-190.

Thoti (The House on the Inlet). Romantic and relaxed accommodation on the water's edge. Relax on the spacious deck, watch the gorgeous sunsets and marine life, or walk down the shore. Contemporary home furnished with family heirlooms, antiques, and art. Splendid breakfasts served in the solarium overlooking the water. No smoking. No pets. One-night stays on Friday, Saturday, or holidays subject to extra surcharge. $100-120.

Ambleside Bed and Breakfast

1121 Faithful Street, V8V 2R5
(604) 383-9948; FAX (604) 383-3647

Ambleside offers traditional bed and breakfast hospitality in a freshly decorated 1920

Ambleside

Craftsman home in one of downtown Victoria's most scenic, walkable, and tranquil Heritage neighborhoods. Delightful easy stroll to Inner Harbour through Beacon Hill Park or along panoramic oceanside pathways. Guest rooms feature Edwardian antique beds with eiderdown comforters and excellent mattresses. King-, queen-size, and twin beds available. A full home-cooked breakfast is served in the sunny dining room and always includes fresh fruit and a special hot entrée. Children over 14 welcome.

Hosts: Marilyn and Gordon Banta-Jessen
Rooms: 3 (1 PB; 2 SB) $65-90
Full Breakfast
Credit Cards: A, B
Notes: 2, 5, 10, 11, 12, 14

AnnaLea's

856 Wollaston Street, V9A 5A8
(604) 381-1195 (phone and FAX)

Nestled in beautiful, historic old Esquimalt, AnnaLea's Guest House is an adventure through time—back to the graciousness, romance, and innocence of the Victoria era. Warm and elegant Old World hospitality, beautiful gardens, and nearby golf, tennis, and boating facilities. Hosts can also arrange for deep-sea salmon fishing charters. The house, built in 1906, offers spacious rooms furnished with era antiques, art, brass beds, lace, and fresh flowers. The two top rooms on the third floor have sitting alcoves and private baths, while the second-

NOTES: Credit cards accepted: A MasterCard; B Visa; C American Express; D Discover; E Diners Club; F Other; 2 Personal checks accepted; 3 Lunch available; 4 Dinner available; 5 Open all year; 6 Pets welcome;

floor room occupants share full bathroom facilities with the hosts.

Rooms: 3 (2 PB; 1 SB) $65-95
Full Breakfast
Credit Cards: B
Notes: 2, 5, 7, 10, 11, 12, 13, 14

Beaconsfield Inn

998 Humboldt Street, V8V 2Z8
(604) 384-4044

Heritage 1905 English manor with award-winning restoration, nine guest rooms and suites with private bathrooms, antiques, mahogany floors, fireplaces, Jacuzzis, stained glass, and down comforters. Gourmet breakfast, tea, and sherry. Guest library, sunroom, dining room. Three blocks to downtown and the waterfront. Quiet. Adult-oriented. No pets. No smoking. Cottage garden. Complimentary parking. Highly rated by *Best Places to Kiss in the Northwest,* Fodor's, AAA, *Special Places,* and *Northwest Best Places.*

Hosts: Con and Judi Sollid
Rooms: 6 (PB) $130-225 ($175-300 Canadian)
Suites: 3 (PB)
Full Breakfast
Credit Cards: A, B, C
Notes: 7, 10, 11, 12

Beaconsfield

Blenkinsop Bed and Breakfast

4049 Century Road, V8X 2E5
(604) 477-5195

Tastefully decorated new bungalow overlooking the pastoral Blenkinsop Valley.

Gourmet and heart-smart breakfasts. Warm and congenial hosts serve complimentary afternoon sherry and evening tea and snack. Large family room has TV and VCR. Quiet cul-de-sac offers peaceful hours on the deck to enjoy the valley scenes. Hosts are "travel wise." Close to University of Victoria. Three miles to downtown. Hosts are knowledgeable and helpful of what Victoria and the island have to offer.

Hosts: Charlie and Diana Shnider
Rooms: 3 (1 PB; 2 SB) $75 Canadian
Full Breakfast
Credit Cards: F
Notes: 5, 7, 9, 10, 11, 12, 14

Camelot Bed and Breakfast

Box 5038, Station B, V8R 6N3
(604) 592-8589 (phone and FAX)

A turn-of-the-century Maclure house on an acre of oak and fir trees and country gardens. Four blocks from the village of Oak Bay and seven minutes' drive from downtown Victoria. Three guest rooms have antique beds, period furnishings, and collectibles. One guest room has a brass bed; another has a wood-burning fireplace. A sitting room has a fireplace, a baby grand piano, books, and a TV. Morning paper, coffee, and tea are brought to guest rooms. Breakfast is prepared by one of the hosts, who is a professional chef, and is served in a dining room that has a chandelier and a fireplace. Breakfast choices include eggs Benedict, blueberry crêpes, smoked Canadian bacon, homemade sausages, fresh fruit in season, and home-baked coffee cakes, biscuits, and breads. Coffee and tea service on request. Outdoor hot tub. fax/telephone/message service. Laundry service. Limousine pickup by arrangement. In the hosts' own words: "Enjoy a refreshing taste of Old World charm and old-fashioned hospitality."

Hosts: Rozanne Shuey and Sonja Maans
Rooms: 3 (2PB; 1 PB) $95-145 Canadian
Full Breakfast
Credit Cards: None
Notes: 2, 5, 7, 9, 10, 11, 12, 14

7 No smoking; 8 Children welcome; 9 Social drinking allowed; 10 Tennis nearby; 11 Swimming nearby; 12 Golf nearby; 13 Skiing nearby; 14 May be booked through a travel agent.

The Captain's Palace

309 Belleville Street, V8V 1X2
(604) 388-9191; (800) 563-9656

Unique accommodations in three Heritage mansions overlooking Victoria's Inner Harbour. A five-minute walk to parks, shopping, galleries, and entertainment, yet peacefully quiet for a good night's sleep in true-to-the-period (1897) four-poster beds, canopied beds, and wicker. A welcoming libation, coffee in guests' room, a full Canadian breakfast of choice, and free parking are included in the accommodation rate. Seasonal rates.

Rooms: 20 (PB) $65-225
Full Breakfast
Credit Cards: A, B, C, E
Notes: 3, 4, 5, 6, 7, 8, 9, 10, 11, 12, 13, 14

Cherry Bank Hotel

825 Burdett Avenue, V8W 1B3
(604) 385-5380

First established in 1897, the Cherry Bank Hotel offers an Old World atmosphere in a quiet residential area two blocks from the center of town, Beacon Hill Park, the Royal British Columbia Museum, and much more. No TVs or telephones in the rooms—just old-fashioned, honest value. Enjoy comfort and charm at a reasonable price. Our rates include a full English breakfast served in the original guest dining room which houses the now-famous Spare Rib House.

Rooms: 26 (19 PB; 7 SB) $51-71
Full Breakfast
Credit Cards: A, B, C
Notes: 3, 4, 5, 8, 9, 10, 11

Crow's Nest

71 Linden Avenue, V8V 4C9
(604) 383-4492; FAX (604) 383-3140

This 1911 Heritage Home with large, bright rooms is a 20-minute walk to downtown. Bus stop at corner. Close to Beacon Hill Park and moments to the ocean with unrestricted views of the Olympic Mountains. Three blocks to "the Village" with neighborhood pub, tearooms, and interesting restaurants and shops.

Hosts: Kit and Dene Mainguy
Rooms: 3 (1 PB; 2 SB) $70-90
Full Breakfast
Credit Cards: A, B
Notes: 2, 5, 8, 9, 10, 14

Dashwood Seaside Manor

One Cook Street, V8V 3W6
(800) 667-5517

Victoria's Edwardian inn by the sea welcomes guests warmly. This 1912 Heritage mansion has 14 elegant suites. Close to town, next to lovely Beacon Hill Park, on Victoria's enchanting Marine Drive. Breathtaking views, Old World charm. Some fireplaces, balconies, Jacuzzis.

Hosts: Derek Dashwood, Family, and Staff
Rooms: 14 (PB) $63-218
Full Breakfast
Credit Cards: A, B, C, E
Notes: 2, 5, 7, 8, 9, 10, 11, 12, 14

Elk Lake Lodge Bed and Breakfast

5259 Pat Bay Highway (Route 17), V8Y 1S8
(604) 658-8879; FAX (604) 658-8879

Originally built in 1910 as a country chapel, Elk Lake Lodge has been beautifully restored, offering guests four comfortable rooms, a magnificent lounge, outdoor hot tub and patio, and delicious full breakfasts including home-baked goods and local produce. Just steps to lovely Elk Lake for swimming, picnicking, fishing, sailing, and windsurfing. Minutes from Butchart Gardens and golf courses. Minimum two-night stay during summer months. Children over 12 welcome.

Hosts: Marty and Ivan Musar
Rooms: 4 (2 PB; 2 SB) $70-90
Full Breakfast
Credit Cards: A, B, C
Notes: 9, 10, 11, 12, 14

NOTES: Credit cards accepted: A MasterCard; B Visa; C American Express; D Discover; E Diners Club;
F Other; 2 Personal checks accepted; 3 Lunch available; 4 Dinner available; 5 Open all year; 6 Pets welcome;

Garden City Bed and Breakfast Reservation Service

660 Jones Terrace, V8Z 2L7
(604) 479-1986; FAX (604) 479-9999

F-3. Come stay with a gracious hostess in her lovely updated 1912 home. Within walking distance of downtown and Royal Jubilee Hospital as well as bus routes, swimming pool, and park. Enjoy the very comfortable bedrooms with luxurious beds and then a delicious breakfast in guest dining room. From $60.

F-4. Enter this charming home through a courtyard bordered by exotic shrubs. Near art gallery, Craigdarroch Castle, the gardens of the lieutenant governor's home, and Antique Row. Twenty minutes to Inner Harbor. Queen-size brass or antique twin rooms with private deck where guests will enjoy the early morning coffee before a full gourmet breakfast. From $95.

F-5. The front porch of this charming 1919 Heritage Home overlooks the city, with ocean and mountain views. Total comfort in spacious, cheerful rooms. A perfect retreat from the city and close to all attractions. Gracious hospitality with wonderful breakfasts including free-range eggs, homemade jams, muffins, fruit salad, and more. From $70.

F-7. The historic neighborhood of Rockland, nestled among Heritage Homes, Craigdarroch Castle, and Government House Gardens. Hosts offer information and a hearty breakfast to make stays enjoyable. English and Japanese spoken. En suite baths. From $60.

F-10. Quietly elegant home built in 1915. Impressive open staircase, stained-glass windows, beautiful antiques, and friendly atmosphere. Bright and cheerful dining room. Informed hosts assist with itineraries, local sightseeing, etc. Excellent bus service is available, or walk to downtown. From $75.

I-1. This 1912 Heritage Home on one-half acre of ocean inlet is just a ten-minute drive from city center and the Inner Harbour. Large rooms, with king- or queen-size beds, reflect the charm of the old with handsome antiques and collectibles, but also the new, with the comforts being so important. Each room has private en suite bath. French doors in king-size rooms open to balconies overlooking the bird sanctuary and superb sunsets. From $85.

I-2. A lovingly restored 1913 home, especially for the bed and breakfast guest. Choose queen-size, double, twin, or single beds; each two guest rooms shares a bath. Delightfully and personally furnished. Complimentary tea and freshly baked goodies greet guests on arrival, and breakfast is guests' choice from a great menu. It is a five-minute drive to downtown, or take the bus from the corner. Overlooking a small park, only a few steps from an ocean inlet. From $50.

I-4. Large character home on excellent bus route. Ten-minute drive to downtown. Above ocean level, guests have a wonderful panoramic view, plus the sound of waves, or a two-minute walk to enjoy this spectacular setting. From $70.

J-1. Casual luxury with tasteful European and Canadian antiques. Walking distance of Parliment buildings, Inner Harbour, Empress Hotel, convention centre, etc. Beautifully decorated rooms each with down duvets, bathrobes, Casablanca fan, en suite or shared bathrooms. Charming guests' lounge with fireplace to rest, read, or play games. From $80.

7 No smoking; 8 Children welcome; 9 Social drinking allowed; 10 Tennis nearby; 11 Swimming nearby; 12 Golf nearby; 13 Skiing nearby; 14 May be booked through a travel agent.

Garden City Bed and Breakfast Reservation Service (continued)

J-2. This 1908 character home in a quiet neighborhood is within walking distance of city center, Inner Harbour, museum, etc. Warm, friendly atmosphere. Delicious breakfast. Near ocean with views of Olympic Mountains. Enjoy feeding ducks at Beacon Hill Park or explore many fine shops and restaurants. Double and queen-size beds, en suite baths, and cable TV. No resident pet. From $60.

J-3. Charming South James Bay home across the street from park with panoramic views of mountains and ocean. An early morning stroll on the beach, before breakfast? And only ten minutes to walk to downtown—the convention centre, Eaton's Centre, Inner Harbour, etc. Children welcome. Host has very friendly dogs. From $80.

J-4. Built in 1908, this charming home welcomes guests and has room for children. Waterfront is only five minutes away, and an easy walk to downtown. Spacious bedrooms, shared bathrooms, and deluxe en suite with advance notice. From $75.

S-2. This bed and breakfast offers three cozy guest rooms with double beds and shared baths. Great breakfast and friendly hosts. Between Butchart Gardens and Empress Hotel on good bus line. Children welcome. From $55.

S-3. Walk to nearby nature sanctuary, restaurants, pubs, and excellent transit system to town and university. Room with shared bath, or large quiet room with queen-size bed and en suite bath, or the deluxe room with TV, en suite bath and two double beds. Upper deck has panoramic views of city and mountains. From $60.

S-5. The guests that have stayed at this bed and breakfast have said it best: "We had a wonderful time in your lovely home high on the hill in the clouds." "Thank you so much for your outstanding, gracious hospitality and assistance." "I felt at home and comfortable immediately after I arrived." From $60.

S-6. Gracious and spacious. A private suite with bathroom, bedroom, and balcony overlooking Swan Lake Nature Sanctuary plus a bed- and sitting room with TV, stereo, and futon. Main floor and a twin-bedded room. Nature path, two kilometers, around sanctuary for bird watching or gentle exercises. Spectacular views of sunsets and Sooke Mountains. From $75.

S-7. Only 20 minutes from town, this establishment has an oversize guest room, with en suite bath, offers private balcony overlooking forest and meadow. Active sheep and horse farm offers trail and carriage rides. Hiking and biking access in parks nearby. Peace and quiet in this very distinctive area. From $95.

S-23. A cozy bungalow with gorgeous gardens. After a good night's sleep, guests will enjoy a wonderful breakfast in the antique-furnished dining room. Guests may enjoy that last cup of coffee out on the patio where they can enjoy the flowers, shrubs, and trees. From $55.

U-1. Immaculate six-bedroom home: two rooms with en suite bath, four with shared. Excellent for large groups. Walk to Mount Douglas Park, University of Victoria, excellent mall. Butchart Gardens is a 20-minute drive and downtown is a ten-minute drive. Excellent bus route. Breakfast in the solarium. From $55.

U-2. Executive-style home on the ocean all en suite bathrooms. Exclusive. From $130.

NOTES: Credit cards accepted: A MasterCard; B Visa; C American Express; D Discover; E Diners Club; F Other; 2 Personal checks accepted; 3 Lunch available; 4 Dinner available; 5 Open all year; 6 Pets welcome;

Gracefield Manor

Gracefield Manor

3816 Duke Road, Rural Route 4, V9B 5T8
(604) 478-2459

This commanding home and captivating landmark on a large acreage has recently been fully restored, recapturing the plantation-inspired feel of the Old South. Walk into the past and enjoy peaceful ambience, antique furnishings, and the charm of an era of elegant living. Retreat to the serenity of the countryside with water and mountain views and sheep in the pasture. Abundance of fresh air, beaches, parks, and golf courses. Only 20 minutes to Victoria.

Host: Shirley Wilde
Rooms: 3 (PB) $85-100
Full Breakfast
Credit Cards: B
Notes: 2, 5, 7, 12

Graham's Cedar House Bed and Breakfast

1825 Lands End Road, Sidney, V8L 5J2
(604) 655-3699; FAX (604) 655-1422

Modern air-conditioned chalet-style home in a secluded six-acre country estate next to the ocean, where tall Douglas firs sprinkle sunlight over lush fern beds. Spacious, graciously appointed four-room suite with king-size bed and private, romantic Jacuzzi room (Jacuzzi for two). Bedroom, living room, and private patio deck all overlook natural strolling gardens. Explore our forest, walk to beach, marinas, or British-style pub. Breakfast is served at guests' conve-nience. Close to Victoria, Butchart Gardens, USA/Canadian ferries.

Hosts: Dennis and Kay Graham
Suites: 1 (PB) $95-159 Canadian
Full Breakfast
Credit Cards: A, B
Notes: 2, 5, 9, 10, 11, 12, 14

Gregory's Guest House

5373 Patricia Bay Highway, V8Y 1S9
(604) 658-8404; FAX (604) 658-4604

Early 1900s farmstead overlooking Elk Lake. Enjoy the farm animals, gardens, and country setting. Only ten kilometers (six miles) from downtown. Bountiful complimentary breakfast, cozy parlor with fireplace and antique furnishings. Convenient to ferries, airport, and Butchart Gardens, nonsmoking.

Hosts: Paul and Elizabeth Gregory
Rooms: 3 (PB) $60-85
Full Breakfast
Credit Cards: A
Notes: 2, 5, 7, 8, 9, 10, 11, 12, 14

Heritage House Bed and Breakfast

3808 Heritage Lane, V8Z 7A7
(604) 479-0892

Beautiful 1910 character home on three-quarters of an acre in a country setting. Quiet and secluded with a lounging veranda. Large rooms, guest parlor with fireplace, and library-den. Private parking. Convenient to ferries, downtown, and all highways. Reservations suggested. Two-day minimum stay. No pets. Inquire about accommodations for children.

Hosts: Larry and Sandra Gray
Rooms: 4 (SB) $75-95
Full Breakfast
Credit Cards: A, B, F
Notes: 5, 7, 9, 10, 11, 12

Holland House Inn

595 Michigan Street, V8V 1S7
(604) 384-6644; FAX (604) 384-6117

7 No smoking; 8 Children welcome; 9 Social drinking allowed; 10 Tennis nearby; 11 Swimming nearby; 12 Golf nearby; 13 Skiing nearby; 14 May be booked through a travel agent.

The Holland House Inn is a unique small hotel where fine art and unequaled comfort are combined to create an atmosphere of casual elegance for guests' enjoyment. Only two blocks from Victoria's Inner Harbour and the Seattle and Port Angeles ferry terminals. Walking or jogging in the beauty of Beacon Hill Park are just minutes away. Downtown shopping, Parliament buildings, and the British Columbia Provincial Museum are all within easy walking distance. The bright and lovely accommodations—some with fireplaces, all with private baths—have queen-size beds, goose-down duvets, antique furnishings, and delightful small balconies. A full gourmet breakfast is included and may be taken in either the guest room or in the lounge.

Hosts: Robin Birsner and Lance Olsen
Rooms: 10 (PB) $90-225 Canadian
Full Breakfast
Credit Cards: A, B, C, E
Notes: 2, 5, 7, 8, 9, 10, 11, 12, 14

Maridou House Bed and Breakfast

116 Eberts Street, V8S 3H7
(604) 360-0747

Gracious Edwardian home one-half block from seafront. Sightings of orca whales not uncommon. Large home with three bedrooms available. One room has en suite bathroom with Jacuzzi tub and canopied beds. Rooms named after family Scottish clan

Maridou House

names. On direct bus route. Ten minutes from heart of downtown. Full breakfast served. Quiet residential area. Off-street parking available. No pets. Children over 12 are welcome.

Hosts: Marilyn and Douglas Allison
Rooms: $45-95
Full Breakfast
Credit Cards: A, B
Notes: 5, 7, 10, 11, 12, 14

Markham House Bed and Breakfast

1853 Connie Road, Rural Route 2, V9B 5B4
(604) 642-7542; FAX (604) 642-7538

Stroll the gardens and dream; sink into the feather beds and sleep till tomorrow; sip tea on the lawns and dine by the pond. It's another life and another time. Twenty-five minutes west of Victoria on the way to the spectacular West Coast beaches. Thirty-five-mile bike trail and 3,500-acre hiking park nearby. Feather beds, duvets, private baths, lounge, fireplace, and library. Elegant breakfast overlooking Trout Pond. Packages available. Member of Tourism Victoria.

Rooms: 4 (PB) $90-105 Canadian
Full Breakfast
Credit Cards: A, B
Notes: 2, 5, 7, 9, 10, 11, 12, 14

Maryla's Bed and Breakfast

3774 Savannah Avenue, V8X 1T2

This bed and breakfast is nestled in a quiet Victorian neighborhood. Ten minutes from downtown and close to the ferry and airport. Open year-round. Close to shopping and restaurants. Guest accommodations include one-bedroom apartment, one room with private baths, color TV, modern kitchen, and double, single, or king-size beds.

Host: M. Literoiz
Rooms: 2 (PB) $65-80
Continental Breakfast
Credit Cards: A
Notes: 7, 8, 10, 11, 12

NOTES: Credit cards accepted: A MasterCard; B Visa; C American Express; D Discover; E Diners Club; F Other; 2 Personal checks accepted; 3 Lunch available; 4 Dinner available; 5 Open all year; 6 Pets welcome;

Mulberry Manor

Mulberry Manor

611 Foul Bay Road, V8S 1H2
(604) 370-1918

In almost an acre of beautiful landscaped gardens, Mulberry Manor was the last mansion designed by Samuel Maclure. The ambience of each room is enhanced by elegant decor and complemented by luxurious furnishings to create the idyllic retreat for the discerning traveler. Sumptuous breakfasts served in the formal dining room provide the perfect start for a day's sightseeing around the provincial capital.

Host: Susan Temple
Rooms: 4 (PB) $90-150
Full Breakfast
Credit Cards: A, B
Notes: 2, 5, 7, 9, 10, 11, 12, 14

Mylfford Haven House

1239 Pandora Avenue, V8V 3R3
(604) 383-0699

Mylfford Haven House is a Heritage (restored) Home built in 1915 where the guests may enjoy legendary Canadian hospitality. A hearty breakfast is served in the bright and cheerful dining room after a quiet and restful night in one of the period bedrooms with queen-size beds. Then visit the many interesting historic and tourist sites that are within walking distance or a short drive. Bus service is also convenient. Afterward relax in the cozy parlor or private garden.

Hosts: Harold and Elizabeth Thomas
Rooms: 2 (PB) $75-85
Full Breakfast
Credit Cards: A, B
Notes: 5, 7, 10, 11, 12, 14

Our Home on the Hill Bed and Breakfast

546 Delora Drive, V9C 3R8
(604) 474-4507

A warm welcome, as well as peace and quiet, awaits guests just 20 minutes from downtown Victoria. Enjoy the seclusion of the yard, relax amid the yesteryear charm of the antique-accented home, stroll along the ocean just moments away, or take a dip in the sheltered hot tub. A guest sitting room is available. A hearty breakfast includes special homemade jams, fresh muffins, and a hot entrée. May be booked through travel agent, but must pay 10 percent commission.

Hosts: Grace and Arnie Holman
Rooms: 3 (1 PB; 2 SB) $60-65
Full Breakfast
Credit Cards: None
Notes: 2, 5, 7, 8, 9, 10, 11, 12

Pension Lakeview Bed and Breakfast

5187 Patricia Bay Highway, No. 17, V8Y 1S8
(604) 658-1517 (phone and FAX)

New country residence with superb view over Eld Lake; friendly homey atmosphere, and twin, double, and king-size beds with down duvets. Full breakfast included. Lounge with giant TV, games room, sun deck, ten kilometer trail around the lake, swimming, and boating; convenient to Butchart Gardens, downtown, ferries, and airport.

Hosts: Monique and Ray
Rooms: 7 (3 PB; 4 SB) $45-65
Full Breakfast
Credit Cards: None
Notes: 4, 5, 7, 8, 9, 10, 11, 12

Portage Inlet House, Bed and Breakfast

993 Portage Road, V8Z 1K9
(604) 479-4594; FAX (604) 479-4548

A delightful waterfront home ten minutes from downtown Victoria. Guests are wel-

7 No smoking; 8 Children welcome; 9 Social drinking allowed; 10 Tennis nearby; 11 Swimming nearby; 12 Golf nearby; 13 Skiing nearby; 14 May be booked through a travel agent.

come to stroll the "Acre of Paradise" overlooking beautiful Portage Inlet and observe the eagles, herons, swans, and ducks; in the autumn, see the coho salmon run. Some guests have their own bathrooms, entrances, TVs, and off-street parking spaces. The hosts raise much of the food themselves and purchase the balance from local farmers who are also "organically minded."

Hosts: Jim and Pat Baillie
Rooms: 4 (3 PB; 1 SB) $75-115
Full Breakfast
Credit Cards: A, B
Notes: 5, 8, 9

Prior House
Bed and Breakfast Inn

620 St. Charles Street, V8S 3N7
(604) 592-8847

Formerly a private residence of the English Crown, this grand bed and breakfast inn has all the amenities of the finest European inn, featuring rooms with fireplaces, onyx marble whirlpool tubs, ocean and mountain views, sumptuous breakfasts, and delicious afternoon teas. Heritage in a large garden setting. Rated outstanding by Northwest, Best Places, and AAA. Special private suite available for families. Inquire about accomodations for children.

Host: Candis Cooperrider
Rooms: 7 (PB) $100-260
Full Breakfast
Credit Cards: A, B
Notes: 5, 7, 10, 11, 12

Rockland House

1570 Rockland Avenue, V8S 1W5
(604) 592-3440; FAX (604) 592-7273

English Tudor residence. Close to Government House. Twenty-minute walk to downtown and Inner Harbour. Forty-inch TV in breakfast room. Suitable for busy executives and golfers. Realty information and fax service available. Quiet, relaxed atmosphere.

Host: Audrey Grimshaw
Rooms: 3 (1 PB: 2 SB) $55-110
Full Breakfast
Credit Cards: None
Notes: 5, 7, 8, 9, 10, 11, 12

Rose Cottage Bed and Breakfast

3059 Washington Avenue, V9A 1P7
(604) 381-5985; FAX (604) 592-5221

Rose Cottage is a 1912 traditional Victorian home carefully restored to retain all the Heritage features of turn-of-the-century Victoria. Rose Cottage has large, high-ceilinged rooms, period furniture, guest parlor in a nautical theme, a large dining room with library, and quiet, well-appointed bedrooms. Rose Cottage sits on a quiet street close to downtown and a few blocks from the beautiful Gorge Park Waterway. Full course breakfast including fresh fruit and muffins. The hosts, Robert and Shelley, have traveled extensively before settling in Victoria and work hard to create a welcome and fun environment.

Hosts: Robert and Shelley Bishop
Rooms: 3 (2 PB; 1 SB) $75-80 Canadian
Full Breakfast
Credit Cards: A, B
Notes: 2, 7, 8, 9, 11, 12, 14

The Sea Rose

1250 Dallas Road, V8V 1C4
(604) 381-7932

The Sea Rose is an oceanfront 1921-Victorian character home that was completely renovated in 1987 and redecorated in 1994. It is on Victoria's famous seafront

The Sea Rose

and enjoys uninterrupted sea and mountain views. Just steps from Beacon Hill Park, bus routes, and the beach, The Sea Rose is in a perfect position to access all of the attractions for which Victoria is famous. All suites have their own en suite bathrooms and are tastefully furnished; most have oceanviews. Guests are served a hot, full breakfast in the original 1921 dining room with its stunning views of ocean, park, and mountains, as well as occasional glimpses of the famous orca whales from the breakfast table. Nonsmoking building. No pets. Check in between 4:00 and 6:00 P.M. or call. Check out by 11:00 A.M.

Hosts: Gail and Herman Hamhuis
Rooms: 4 (PB) $89-139 Canadian
Full Breakfast
Credit Cards: A, B, C
Notes: 2, 5, 7, 8, 9, 10, 12, 14

Sonia's Bed and Breakfast by the Sea

175 Bushby Street, V8S 1B5
(604) 385-2700; (800) 667-4489

Walk along the ocean to the Inner Harbor. Guest rooms have king- and queen-size beds. A penthouse has a large private sun deck overlooking the Straits of Juan de Fuca and will accommodate five people comfortably. The hosts were both born in Victoria and like to lay a map out to show their guests what to see and do. They have owned and operated Sonia's Bed and Breakfast for ten years. Large hot breakfast.

Hosts: Sonia and Brian McMillan
Rooms: 3 (PB) $55-75 U.S.
Suite: $100-150 U.S.
Full Breakfast
Credit Cards: None
Notes: 2, 9, 10, 11, 12

Sunnymeade House Inn

1002 Fenn Avenue, V8Y 1P3
(604) 658-1414

Take scenic route into Victoria to discover this custom-designed, beautifully decorated,

English-style country inn in a village setting by the sea. Steps to beach, shopping, golf, and tennis courts. Pub and restaurants. New special occasion suite with view, whirlpool bath, private dining and sitting room. Lovely English garden. Delicious breakfasts.

Hosts: Jack and Nancy Thompson
Rooms: 6 (4 PB, 2 SB) $89-169
Full and Continental Breakfast
Credit Cards: None
Notes: 2, 5, 7, 9, 10, 11, 12, 14

Swallow Hill Farm

Swallow Hill Farm Bed and Breakfast

4910 William Head Road, Rural Route 1
V9B 5T7
(604) 474-4042 (phone and FAX)

Small working farm near Victoria in peaceful country setting with pasture, pond, and orchard. Spectacular mountain and sea views. Abundant wildlife: deer, eagles, seals, otters, birds. Two comfortable suites, one with separate entrance. Queen-size and single beds, private baths, decks. Delicious breakfasts and friendly conversation. Enjoy favorite outdoor activities, see the sights, curl up with a book, or just sit and watch nature unfolding. Sauna and massage now available. Whale watching, hiking, swimming, fishing, diving. So peaceful guests never want to leave.

Hosts: Gini and Peter Walsh
Rooms: 2 (PB) $65-85 Canadian
Full and Continental Breakfast
Credit Cards: A, B, C
Notes: 5, 7, 11, 12

7 No smoking; 8 Children welcome; 9 Social drinking allowed; 10 Tennis nearby; 11 Swimming nearby; 12 Golf nearby; 13 Skiing nearby; 14 May be booked through a travel agent.

Town and Country Bed and Breakfast in British Columbia

P.O. Box 74542
2803 West Fourth Avenue V6K 1K2
(604) 731-5942

1. Beautiful Edwardian home one block to waterfront road, ten-minute drive to city center. Three rooms, one with private bath, and two that share a bathroom. Furnished with antiques and other special touches. Some sea views. $75-115.

2. A delightful waterfront home overlooking Portage Inlet, with an acre of garden. Each guest has a comfortable king-size bed or twin bed, and each room has a private entrance, TV, and bathroom. Only ten minutes from downtown Victoria and its many attractions. Within easy access to all the ferries that service Victoria. An abundance of wildlife resides on or visits the property, such as swans, Canada geese, pheasants, eagles, and ducks. Guests are welcome to enjoy the acre of "paradise." Breakfast specializes in organic home-grown food: home-grown fruit and juices, homemade jams, jellies, and ketchup. This inn grinds flour from wheat to make bread, scones, and pancakes. Heated with wood in the winter and utilizes solar panels for hot water in summer. No pets. $95-125.

3. The guests are special at Arundel Manor, a 1912 Heritage Home on a half-acre of land sloping to Portage Inlet, a bird sanctuary with stunning sunset views. The four large bedrooms, decorated with an eclectic mix of antiques, collectibles, and family heirlooms, have private en suite bathrooms, and two have spacious balconies overlooking the water. The fifth room has twin beds and a private bathroom. A full home-cooked breakfast is served in the elegant dining room. A cheerful, welcoming lounge with fireplace awaits the guests. Check in between 2:00 and 4:00 P.M.; check out 11:00 A.M. No smoking. Not suitable for pets. $115-125.

4. New and unique, this lovely home with a Dutch atmosphere is in a truly beautiful scenic setting. Views of farmland, the Gulf Islands, and Mount Baker are there to enjoy. Only five minutes from sandy ocean beaches, ten minutes from Butchart Gardens, and 25 minutes from the city center. Share the living areas. Pickup from ferry or airport available. Dutch and German are second languages. No pets, please. Full breakfast is served from 7 to 10 A.M. $75-95.

Wellington Bed and Breakfast

66 Wellington Avenue, V8V 4H5
(604) 383-5976; FAX (604) 385-0477

Just one-half block from the scenic Pacific Ocean, bordered by a panoramic walkway, three blocks from beautiful Beacon Hill Park, this 1912 inn offers guests a taste of true Victorian hospitality. All rooms have private baths, walk-in closets, large windows, king- or queen-size beds, and are wonderfully appointed. The quiet, tree-lined street allows for the most restful sleep, and the breakfasts are a delight. Children over 12 welcome.

Host: Inge Ranzinger
Rooms: 3 (PB) $55-75
Full Breakfast
Credit Cards: A
Notes: 2, 5, 7, 9, 10, 11, 12, 14

Wooded Acres Bed and Breakfast

4907 Rocky Point Road, Rural Route 2, V9B 5B4
(604) 474-8959: (604) 478-8172

Country-style hospitality welcomes the guest to more than three acres of forest in the Victoria countryside. Bedrooms are decorated with antiques, queen-size beds, and cozy down-filled duvets. Special touches everywhere. Enjoy old-fashioned candlelight and soaking in the private hot tub spa. Full breakfast is a feast of specialties baked fresh every day and served at the guest's convenience. Special diets prepared on request. Brochure available. Two private suites. Smoking restricted.

Hosts: Elva and Skip Kennedy
Rooms: 2 (PB) $110
Full Breakfast
Credit Cards: None
Notes: 2, 5, 9, 10, 11, 12, 14

WESTBANK

Lakeview Mansion

3858 Harding Road, V4T 2J9
(604) 768-2205

Guests are welcomed to warm German hospitality in super large elegant home on spacious, parklike grounds just above Okanagan Lake. Comfortable, large, beautiful rooms with direct access to two hundred square feet of open and covered sun decks. Air conditioning. Breathtaking, panoramic view of lake. Relax in chlorine-free Jacuzzi. Cozy guest library with TV/VCR/movies. Delicious gourmet breakfast with fruit. Close to downtown Kelowna. Five-minute walk to beaches.

Rooms: 3 (2 PB; 1 SB) $60-70
Full Breakfast
Credit Cards: None
Notes: 2, 5, 7, 8, 9, 10, 11, 12, 13, 14

WEST VANCOUVER

Beachside Bed and Breakfast

4208 Evergreen Avenue, V7V 1H1
(604) 922-7773; (800) 563-3311
FAX (604) 926-8073

Stay in a quiet, beautiful waterfront home in one of the finest areas in Vancouver. A lovely beach is at the doorstep. Minutes from downtown, Stanley Park, Horseshoe Bay ferries, and North Shore attractions. Its southern exposure affords a panoramic view of the city, harbor, and Alaska cruise

ships. A hearty home-baked breakfast is served in the seaside dining room. Close to fishing, sailing, wilderness hiking, skiing, antiques, shopping, and great restaurants.

Hosts: Gordon and Joan Gibbs
Rooms: 3 (PB) $95-150 Canadian
Full Breakfast
Credit Cards: A, B
Notes: 2, 5, 7, 8, 9, 10, 11, 12, 13, 14

Creekside Bed and Breakfast

1515 Palmerston Avenue, V7V 4S9
(604) 926-1861; (604) 328-9400 (cellular)
FAX (604) 926-7545

Quiet, romantic parklike casual setting with a creek flowing through this natural garden property. All-you-can-eat home-baked breakfast. Luxurious en suite bath with two-person Jacuzzi in a glass-roofed bathroom. The second bath also has a Jacuzzi tub and skylights. In-room TVs with remotes, stocked mini-refrigerator, and coffee makers. Complimentary wines, beverages, snacks, toiletries, and robes. Ideal honeymoon setting. Commissionable. Fifty percent deposit required. Half-price coupons available for entertainment and dining. Two-day minimum stay. Pets welcome by prior arrangements. Smoking not permitted.

Hosts: John Boden and Donna Hawrelko
Rooms: 2 (PB) $100-135
Full Breakfast
Credit Cards: A, B
Notes: 5, 9, 10, 11, 12, 13, 14

WHISTLER

Alberta and Pacific Bed and Breakfast Agency

P.O. Box 15477, MPO, Vancouver, V6B 5B2
(604) 944-1793

13. European hospitality is offered at this chalet by French and German hosts. Enjoy the guest sitting room with wood stove, sun deck with view of Whistler and Blackcomb Mountains. Wake to a delicious Continental breakfast and the aroma of home-baked

7 No smoking; 8 Children welcome; 9 Social drinking allowed; 10 Tennis nearby; 11 Swimming nearby; 12 Golf nearby; 13 Skiing nearby; 14 May be booked through a travel agent.

croissants and rolls. Whistler is building a reputation as a year-round resort area. In summer there is hiking, horseback riding, swimming, biking, golf, tennis, canoeing, fishing, and windsurfing available in the nearby area. In winter take in two of the most superb ski areas in North America, Whistler and Blackcomb Mountains. There is ski storage and a sauna for guests to use. Winter ski packages are available. Six guest rooms, each with private bath.

Golden Dreams Bed and Breakfast

6412 Easy Street, V0N 1B6
(604) 932-2667; (800) 668-7055
FAX (604) 932-7055

Maximize a holiday and stay with locals! Uniquely decorated theme rooms feature sherry decanter and cozy duvets. Relax in a luxurious private Jacuzzi and awaken to a nutritious and delicious vegetarian breakfast. A large sun deck is available for relaxing and enjoying great views. Excellent trailside location takes guests to lake sports, village shops and restaurants, mountain biking, alpine hiking, horseback riding, rollerblading, and more! Golden Dreams is the inside edge at Whistler. Families are welcome!

Hosts: Ann and Terry Spence
Rooms: 3 (1 PB; 2 SB) $65-105
Full Breakfast
Credit Cards: A, B
Notes: 2, 5, 7, 8, 9, 10, 11, 12, 13

WHITE ROCK

Alberta and Pacific Bed and Breakfast Agency

P.O. Box 15477, MPO, Vancouver, V6B 5B2
(604) 944-1793

10. A traditional-style residence, this very large home offers comfortable rooms, a private lounge with log-burning fireplace, TV, stereo, piano, library, refrigerator, and hearty breakfasts. Three minutes from the U.S. border, 40 minutes from downtown Vancouver, 30 minutes from the international airport, and 20 minutes from the Victoria ferries. The finest of sailing, fishing, riding, and championship golf courses. Three guest rooms; private and shared baths.

Dorrington Bed and Breakfast

13851 19A Avenue, V4A 9M2
(604) 535-4408; FAX (604) 535-4409

Dorrington is a magnificent brick-and-stone estate set on a one-half acre featuring themed rooms with private bathrooms, outdoor hot tub, tennis court, pond, and gardens. A four-poster double bed graces the Victorian Room, and a unique queen-size bed hewn from maple branches themes the St. Andrews Room. Full breakfast is served in the Hunt Salon or on the patio overlooking the peaceful gardens. Dorrington is close to the border or ferry terminal to Victoria and 45 minutes from Vancouver.

Rooms: 2 (PB) $75-90 Canadian
Full Breakfast
Credit Cards: A, B
Notes: 2, 5, 7, 9, 10, 11, 12, 13, 14

NOTES: Credit cards accepted: A MasterCard; B Visa; C American Express; D Discover; E Diners Club;
F Other; 2 Personal checks accepted; 3 Lunch available; 4 Dinner available; 5 Open all year; 6 Pets welcome;

Manitoba

BOISSEVAIN

Dueck's Cedar Chalet

Box 362, R0K 0E0
(204) 534-6019

One mile east and three-fourths of a mile north of the town of Boissevain, Cedar Chalet offers accommodations with complete privacy, including Jacuzzi, TV, refrigerator, and coffee percolator. Also offered is a motor home, which is air-conditioned, fully equipped to sleep six, and allows guests to sightsee in the area for $50 plus 12 cents a mile. Car rental is also available. Extra meals by prearrangement. English and German spoken. Boissevain is the home of the Canadian Turtle Derby. The chalet is near the golf course and offers a heated outdoor swimming pool, playground, Turtle Mountain Provincial Park, lake fishing, nature trails, horseback riding, and the International Peace Gardens.

Hosts: Hilda and Henry Dueck
Rooms: 4 (SB) $40-50
Full Breakfast
Credit Cards: None
Notes: 2, 3, 4, 5, 6, 7, 8, 10, 11, 12, 13, 14

BRANDON

Bed and Breakfast of Manitoba

434 Roberta Avenue, Winnipeg, R2K 0K6
(204) 661-0300

Casa Maley. For a unique, comfortable family atmosphere and a display of genuine hospitality, come and stay at the Casa Maley! This European-style three-story Tudor house, built in 1912 with red brick exterior, has a fairy-tale, gingerbread house appearance. For breakfast guests have a choice of the host's specialties: exquisite and mouth-watering French toast, super delicious omelet, sizzling bacon and eggs, big fluffy pancakes, an exotic fruit salad; and the blended oatmeal porridge is a dream come true. No smoking. $40.

White House Bed and Breakfast. This bed and breakfast is on the north side of the Trans-Canada Highway next to Chalet Motel and Restaurant. Private parking. Greens on premises and a nine-hole golf course next door. Airport and bus pickup free. $50.

GIMLI

Bed and Breakfast of Manitoba

434 Roberta Avenue, Winnipeg, R2K 0K6
(204) 661-0300

Öndvik. Owned and operated by descendants of original Icelandic and Ukrainian settlers. This unique four-bedroom bed and breakfast is on a three-quarter-acre lot four kilometers south of Gimli in the heart of the interlake. The rustic country home features handcrafted cedar doors with iron latches, a wood-burning stove, and antique furnishings. Enjoy the scenic view from the gazebo overlooking Öndvik ("Duck Bay" in Icelandic) or soothe the soul in the indoor four-person hot tub. Enjoy campfires, canoeing, golfing, fishing, hiking, wildlife viewing, cross-country skiing, snowmobiling, swimming, or sunbathing on the private beach. $55.

7 No smoking; 8 Children welcome; 9 Social drinking allowed; 10 Tennis nearby; 11 Swimming nearby; 12 Golf nearby; 13 Skiing nearby; 14 May be booked through a travel agent.

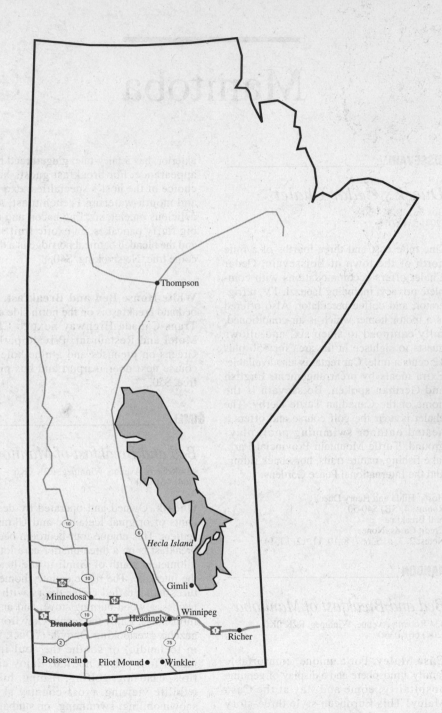

Thompson

Hecla Island

Gimli

Minnedosa

Brandon   Headingly   Winnipeg

Richer

Boissevain   Pilot Mound   Winkler

Manitoba

Willow House Bed and Breakfast. Enjoy country-style hospitality and quiet relaxation in rustic, casual surroundings on two and one-half wooded acres overlooking Willow Creek, with boating access to the lake. Five minutes from Gimli and beaches. Many summer events include Icelandic Festival, canoeing, and fishing. Winter activizes include cross-country skiing, snowshoeing, and ice fishing. Will pick-up guests at the airport and train station. Shared baths. No smoking. No pets. $40.

HEADINGLY

Bed and Breakfast of Manitoba

434 Roberta Avenue, Winnipeg, R2K 0K6
(204) 661-0300

Quiet country home ten miles west of Winnipeg, just off Trans-Canada Highway. Open year-round. English and French spoken. No Pets. Private bath. Fireplace. $45.

HECLA ISLAND

Solmundson Gesta Hus

Box 76, Hecla Provincial Park, R0C 2R0
(204) 279-2088

The guest house is within Hecla Provincial Park on 43 acres of private property. Enjoy luxurious European-style hospitality in a newly renovated and completely modern, comfortable home in an original Icelandic settlement. Relax on the veranda and enjoy the beautiful view of Lake Winnipeg. Enjoy the tranquil and peaceful atmosphere while petting the dogs and cats or feeding the ducks. The host is a commercial fisherman, so feast on the catch of the day along with garden fresh vegetables.

Hosts: Dave and Sharon Holtz
Rooms: 4 (1 PB; 3 SB) $45-75
Full Breakfast
Credit Cards: A, B
Notes: 2, 4, 5, 6, 8, 9, 10, 11, 12, 13, 14

MINNEDOSA

Bed and Breakfast of Manitoba

434 Roberta Avenue, Winnipeg, R2K 0K6
(204) 661-0300

The Castle. Restored two-turret 1901 Queen Anne two-and-one-half-story Heritage site on river. Lovely in-town location, but still a very quiet retreat. Near a lake resort, golf, skiing, and many other activities. A private, spacious honeymoon suite is available for guests, complete with a soaking tub and balcony. Beautiful leaded glass. The music room has a fireplace, antiques, Oriental carpets, and a conservatory. Bicycles are available for guests' use. The perfect location for group retreats and workshops in one of the most beautiful towns in Manitoba. The inn is open year-round. No smoking permitted. Private bath. $60-90.

The Castle Bed and Breakfast

149 Second Avenue SW, P.O. Box 1705, R0J 1E0
(204) 864-2830 (phone and FAX)

The only bed and breakfast in a castle on the Yellowhead Highway. A prime example of Queen Anne style, the castle has been restored and was designated a municipal Heritage site. The castle has 6,000 square feet of living space and a small home neatly attached by a tunnel passageway. It was built in 1901 for Judge Myers. Stay in a charming town in a completely modernized landmark house having a river flowing past the three- to four-acre grounds. Features large honeymoon suite, contemporary art collection, antiques, Oriental carpets, and conservatory. Hosts are both artists.

Hosts: Richard Yates and Mary Joyce
Rooms: 4 (PB) $55-90
Full Breakfast
Credit Cards: A
Notes: 2, 5, 6, 8, 9, 10, 11, 12, 13, 14

NOTES: Credit cards: A MasterCard; B Visa; C American Express; D Discover; E Diners Club; F Other; 2 Personal checks accepted; 3 Lunch available; 4 Dinner available; 5 Open all year; 6 Pets welcome; 7 No smoking; 8 Children welcome; 9 Social drinking allowed; 10 Tennis nearby; 11 Swimming nearby; 12 Golf nearby; 13 Skiing nearby; 14 May be booked through a travel agent.

PILOT MOUND

Bed and Breakfast of Manitoba

434 Roberta Avenue, Winnipeg, R2K 0K6
(204) 661-0300

Hillshade Farm. New country home two hours from Winnipeg in heart of Pembina Valley area. Near lakes, golf courses, tennis, swimming, boating, fishing, and downhill and cross-country skiing at Holiday Mountain. Private bath. No smoking. $45.

RICHER

Bed and Breakfast of Manitoba

434 Roberta Avenue, Winnipeg, R2K 0K6
(204) 661-0300

Geppetto's. Hosts offer country-style hospitality in an attractive and modern home. Complimentary homemade wine. Visit the 1200-square-foot gift-craft shop where Geppetto makes wooden toys! Bird watching, horseshoe pits, and six golf courses within 20 minutes. Sandy's Snack Shop on site features great homemade French fries. No smoking. No pets. Shared bath. $45.

Geppetto's

Box 2A, Rural Route 1, R0E 1S0
(807) 422-8809

Country-style hospitality in an attractive modern home, 40 minutes east of Winnipeg on Highway 1. Complimentary homemade beer and wine. Visit the 1200-square-foot craft shop where Geppetto makes wooden toys. Outdoor activities include bird watching, pitching horseshoes, cross-country skiing, snowmobiling, and hiking. Two golf courses within five minutes; four more within 20 minutes. Three rooms with shared bath.

Hosts: John and Sandy Cotie
Rooms: 3 (SB) $45
Full Breakfast
Credit Cards: B
Notes: 2, 3, 4, 5, 7, 8, 9, 12, 13

THOMPSON

Bed and Breakfast of Manitoba

434 Roberta Avenue, Winnipeg, R2K 0K6
(204) 661-0300

Anna's Bed and Breakfast. Open year-round. Anna and Robert invite guests to share this comfortable home and warm Dutch hospitality. Pickup at airport and train station. Completely private quarters and private bath. Come and enjoy the heart of the north! $30-45.

WEST ST. PAUL

Helga and Steve Hawchuk's Bed and Breakfast

22 Everette Place, R2V 4E8
(204) 339-7005

Helga and Steve Hawchuk, an artist and a riverboat captain, respectively, have created a "home away from home" in their sprawling Tudor-style house on the Red River. Silk flowers, paintings, and other handiwork brighten every room. Floor-to-ceiling windows look out over flower gardens. A scrumptious home-cooked breakfast offers a variety of homemade breads, waffles, jams, jellies, and eggs Benedict.

Hosts: Helga and Steve Hawchuk
Rooms: 4 (2 PB; 2 SB) $69 Canadian
Full and Continental Breakfast
Credit Cards: A, B
Notes: 2, 3, 4, 5, 7, 9, 10, 11, 12

WINKLER

Bed and Breakfast of Manitoba

434 Roberta Avenue, Winnipeg, R2K 0K6
(204) 661-0300

This attractive home has its own private bowling greens in a quiet and relaxing retreat area. English and German are spoken here. No smoking allowed. No pets allowed. $40.

WINNIPEG

Bed and Breakfast of Manitoba

434 Roberta Avenue, Winnipeg, R2K 0K6
(204) 661-0300

Andrews. River property in older, treed neighborhood. Close to downtown, restaurants, and attractions. Guest suite with private TV room. Relax by the fire in the family room. In summer, cruise the river in a canoe, enjoy the flowers, or relax in the gazebo. Bikes and exercise equipment available. Home-baked breakfast, tea, coffee, and snacks anytime. Close to airport, bus depot, railway, Trans-Canada Highway city route. $45.

Bannerman East. Enjoy this lovely Georgian home, evening tea, and quiet walks in St. Johns Park or along the Red River. Close to Seven Oaks Museum, the planetarium, concert hall, and Rainbow Stage. $40.

Belanger. Relaxing atmosphere in a special home built in 1900. Sitting room adjacent to guest bedroom. Can accommodate a family of four. $40.

Bright Oakes. Spacious home on one-half acre of parklike grounds near the Red River. Close to St. Vital Park, University of Manitoba, good restaurants, and St. Vital Shopping Center. Easy access to the Mint, St. Boniface, and downtown. English, French, and Polish spoken. $40.

Cozy Cove. Complete privacy in lower level with a spacious and attractive sitting lounge. Excellent transit service and public library. Cedar deck and gazebo in back yard. Quick access to the Mint, The Forks, downtown, Osborne Village, and St. Boniface Hospital. Pets welcome. $45.

Drenker. Quiet, neat home in old St. Boniface within walking distance of The Forks, the St. Boniface Hospital, and downtown. Near museum, Manitoba Theatre Centre, concert hall, and paddlewheel boats. $45.

The Ellies. Stay in the historic Armstrongs Point area. Old elm trees line and arch the streets. A peaceful and picturesque cul-de-sac in the heart of Winnipeg. Hosts are well traveled and love to cook. Superb omelets are a favorite, also home-baked bread, scones, muffins, and cinnamon buns. Savor the homemade jams and jellies. Near good bus service, Miscericordia Hospital, and all major attractions. Will pickup guests for additional charge at airport, bus, or train stations. $50.

Franz. Enjoy the atmosphere of yesteryear. Choice of breakfast in dining room, veranda, or sun deck. Wide selection of movies and books. Close to downtown, legislative buildings, and The Forks. Access to major bus routes, airport, and Polo Park. English and Low and High German spoken. Family rates negotiable. $40-45.

Goertzen. Enjoy home-baked breakfast, tea, coffee, and snacks anytime in living room or patio overlooking beautifully treed yard. Quiet surroundings for bird watching, reading, or relaxing. Close to University of Manitoba, The Forks, golf course, and Fort Whyte Nature Centre. English, German, and Spanish spoken. Near Pembina Highway. $45.

Hawchuk. On the banks of the Red River, this beautiful Tudor home has English gardens and a riverbank walkway. Top off the day with a paddlewheel dinner cruise. English, German, and French spoken. Full-course dinner is available for an additional charge. $69.

---

7 No smoking; 8 Children welcome; 9 Social drinking allowed; 10 Tennis nearby; 11 Swimming nearby;
12 Golf nearby; 13 Skiing nearby; 14 May be booked through a travel agent.

Bed and Breakfast of Manitoba (continued)

Hillman. Cozy private sitting room and a full breakfast. Downtown, close to bus route, airport, Polo Park, planetarium, concert hall, and theater center. $45.

Mary Jane's Place. Enjoy a relaxed atmosphere in this unique three-story home with beautiful oak interior. Excellent transit service, near downtown, will pick up at the airport. Quick access to The Forks Market, zoo, hospital, and Dainavert Museum. $40.

McCormack. Come for a relaxing stay in this quiet, quaint, cozy home. Guests enjoy use of living room and TV. In Fort Garry near Pembina Highway. Quick access to excellent city transit service to downtown and University of Manitoba. Near golf course, Crescent Park, and Fort Whyte Nature Centre. $45.

Mitchell's Bed and Breakfast. Lovely old Winnipeg home on a quiet tree-lined street. Air-conditioned. Close to public transportation, shopping, theaters, museums, and city center. Access to Assinboine Downs. $45.

Neufeld. Enjoy the seclusion of a pleasant back yard, hot tub, and swimming pool in season. Easy access from Perimeter. Off Pembina Highway, near University of Manitoba, parks, shopping mall, and restaurants. Easy access anywhere in city. $45.

Rand. Convenient to public transit. Close to golf, parks, shopping, and downtown. Finest accommodations with truly knowledgeable, warm, friendly hospitality. The best brownie cake anywhere! $50.

River's Bend. Nestled peaceful against the Assinboine River and sheltered in stands of elms and evergreens, River's Bend is a unique bed and breakfast experience. Enjoy breakfast in the morning sun on the cedar deck overlooking the river or bid farewell to the evening sun from the outdoor hot tub. Minutes from zoo, racetrack, and airport in tranquil Charleswood neighborhood. Pickup at airport for additional fee. $45.

Selci. Very private facilities in this private home can accommodate a family of four. Spacious back yard overlooking golf course. A warm welcome to guests, and quick access to the Trans-Canada Highway. $40.

Southern Rose Guest House. Experience the charm of decades past with a touch of Southern hospitality. Enjoy morning breakfast in the formal dining room or on the wraparound cedar sun deck. Getaway to yesterday! Red brick exterior, warm woods, burnished brass trimmed leaded glass, flickering fireplace, and live greenery. The yard provides a retreat to read, converse, or enjoy the afternoon sun. Play horseshoes, volleyball, or relax in redwood hot tub. Close to Polo Park shopping mall, The Forks, casino, good restaurants, zoo, airport, Winnipeg Convention Centre, and bicycle route. Just off express bus route. $45.

Bright Oakes Bed and Breakfast

137 Woodlawn Avenue, R2M 2P5
(204) 256-9789

Guests can relax in comfortable, spacious bedrooms, play a tune on the grand piano, or swing in a hammock in the back yard. The four-level split home with many antique furnishings is on a half-acre of landscaped grounds near the river, the university, and many restaurants, with quick and easy access to St. Boniface and downtown attractions. A full breakfast can be enjoyed on the patio overlooking the gardens.

Hosts: Francis and Anya Lobreau
Rooms: 3 (1 PB; 2 SB) $40-45
Full Breakfast
Credit Cards: None
Notes: 5, 8, 10, 11, 12

NOTES: Credit cards accepted: A MasterCard; B Visa; C American Express; D Discover; E Diners Club;
F Other; 2 Personal checks accepted; 3 Lunch available; 4 Dinner available; 5 Open all year; 6 Pets welcome;

Casa Antigua

209 Chestnut Street, R3G 1R8
(204) 775-9708

Casa Antigua is in a quiet, tree-lined neighborhood close to the heart of downtown Winnipeg. This home, built in 1906, is lovingly furnished with beautiful antiques. There are many nearby biking paths and walking trails for guests to enjoy. A full, delicious homemade breakfast is served each morning. Spanish and English are spoken. Four guest rooms are available, with shared baths. Smoking allowed in designated areas only. Easy access to cross-country skiing.

Hosts: Marcial Hinojosa and Elvera Watson
Rooms: 4 (SB) $50
Full Breakfast
Credit Cards: A
Notes: 5, 9, 10, 11

Cozy Cove Bed & Breakfast

13 Nichol Avenue, R2M 1V6
(204) 256-4430

Only fifteen minutes from downtown Winnipeg. Complete privacy in the lower level featuring an attractive sitting lounge. Air-conditioned. Can accommodate a family of five. Bikes and cross-country skis are available for guests to use. A delicious breakfast is served each morning in the sunny dining room.

Hosts: Larry and Delann Preweda
Rooms: 2 (1 PB; 1 SB) $45
Full Breakfast
Credit Cards: A, B
Notes: 2, 3, 4, 5, 6, 7, 8, 9, 10, 11, 12

Ellie's Bed and Breakfast

77 Middle Gate, R3C 2C5
(204) 772-5832; (204) 783-1462

Enjoy a stay in historic Armstrong's Point in the heart of Winnipeg. Nicely treed and peaceful. Hosts are well traveled and love to cook. Known for their superb omelet, home-baked bread, scones, and muffins.

Jams and jellies made in their own kitchen. Airport and train pickup are available for an additional charge.

Hosts: Peter and Eugenia Ellie
Rooms: 3 (1 PB; 2 SB) $50-52
Full Breakfast
Credit Cards: None
Notes: 3, 4, 5, 8, 9

Mary Jane's Place

144 Yale Avenue, R3M 0L7
(204) 453-8104

This unique, three-story Georgian-style home has a beautiful oak interior and is nestled in the historic Crescentwood area of Winnipeg. The inn is nearby many cultural and historic locations, the airport, and local highways. Dutch and English are spoken. Four guest rooms are available for guests with private and shared baths. Full or Continental breakfast is served each morning.

Hosts: Jack and Mary Jane
Rooms: 4 (1 PB; 3 SB) $40-42
Full and Continental Breakfast
Credit Cards: A, B
Notes: 2, 5, 8, 9, 11, 12

Prairie Charm
Bed and Breakfast

190 Greenview Road,
Box 124, St. Germain, R0G 2A0
(204) 253-3636

Prairie Charm offers gracious country living on a small acreage within the city's limits. The home is on private, parklike grounds. Antiques and family heirlooms add to the charm of this modern, split-level home. Three guest rooms are available with either private or shared baths. Easy access to the inn from the south Winnipeg bypass (Route 100).

Hosts: Ray and Ann Ingalls
Rooms: 3 (1 PB; 2 SB) $40
Continental Breakfast
Credit Cards: None
Notes: 2, 5, 6, 7, 8, 11, 12

7 No smoking; 8 Children welcome; 9 Social drinking allowed; 10 Tennis nearby; 11 Swimming nearby; 12 Golf nearby; 13 Skiing nearby; 14 May be booked through a travel agent.

Riverview

291 Oakwood Avenue, R3L 1E8
(204) 475-1291

Older home in a lovely, heavily treed residential area, near main highway and close to downtown Winnipeg. Bus service is excellent. Main bedroom has an adjoining sitting room. Single room also available with shared bath. Full, varied breakfast served featuring blueberry or strawberry waffles. Six restaurants within two blocks for lunch and dinner.

Hosts: Dennis and Colleen Belanger
Room: 1 (PB) $40
Full Breakfast
Credit Cards: None
Notes: 2, 5, 9, 10, 11, 12

West Gate Manor

71 West Gate, R3C 2C9
(204) 772-9788

In picturesque, historic Armstrong Point area of Winnipeg. Large living room is decorated in Victorian era splendor. Each bedroom reflects its own period and theme. One room has its own private sitting room. Sunroom with TV off the dining and living rooms. Guests receive discounts at local restaurants. Walking distance to downtown, restaurants, shopping, and cultural facilities. Children over ten welcome.

Hosts: John and Louise Clark
Rooms: 6 (SB) $50-55
Full Breakfast
Credit Cards: A, B
Notes: 2, 5, 14

NOTES: Credit cards accepted: A MasterCard; B Visa; C American Express; D Discover; E Diners Club;
F Other; 2 Personal checks accepted; 3 Lunch available; 4 Dinner available; 5 Open all year; 6 Pets welcome;

New Brunswick

ACADIAN PENINSULA

Northern New Brunswick Referrals

P.O. Box 21, New Carlisle, Quebec, G0C 1Z0
(418) 752-2725; (418) 752-6718

A wide variety of accommodations scattered along the charming and picturesque Acadian Peninsula on the coastline of the Bay des Chaleurs and Gulf of St. Lawrence of northern New Brunswick and the refreshing and ruggedly beautiful Gaspé Peninsula of Quebec on the opposite side of the bay. Choose from Victorians, contemporaries, cottages, waterfront houses, and private suites with full kitchens. Most are near villages or towns, all are near beaches, golf courses, museums, ski hills, historic sites, and universities. Some offer laundry service and guided tours. Directory describing more than 50 accommodations available for $5.

Coordinator: Helen Sawyer
Rooms: 250; $35-75
Full and Continental Breakfast
Notes: 5, 10, 11, 12, 13

BATHURST

Ingle-Neuk Bed and Breakfast

1330 Youghal Drive, E2A 4Y3
(506) 546-5758

From this friendly bed and breakfast it is only a two-minute walk to the uncrowded, safe, sandy, saltwater Youghall Beach on Chaleur Bay. The marina and a beautiful 18-hole golf course are nearby. To find the Ingle-Neuk Bed and Breakfast, take Vanier exit on Route 11 at Bathurst, left on 134, right on Youghall Drive, four kilometers to the end-1330. The family has operated a "tourist home" for four generations. Enjoy breakfast, including delicious muffins, in the sunroom. Relax in the living room in the *ingle neuk,* the "cozy corner" by the fire. No smoking allowed in rooms.

Hosts: Ken and Jean Babin
Rooms: 4 (SB) $40-45
Full Breakfast
Credit Cards: None
Notes: 9, 11, 12

CARAQUET

La Maison Touristique Dugas

683 boul St. Pierre ouest, E1W 1A1
(506) 727-3195

Feel the charms of yesteryear at La Maison Touristique Dugas in the heart of Acadia. Discover the Acadian people and the many attractions of the Acadian Peninsul while staying in a Heritage home dating to 1926.

Hosts: Martina Dugas-Landry and Camillien Landry
Rooms: 13 (2 PB; 11 SB) $46.19-71.14
Full Breakfast
Credit Cards: A, B
Notes: 5, 7, 8, 10, 11, 12, 13

GRAND MANAN ISLAND

Compass Rose

North Head, E0G 2M0
(506) 662-8570

Two small turn-of-the-century houses overlooking the Fisherman's Wharf at North Head. The ferry docks at adjoining wharf. Bedrooms are furnished simply, mostly

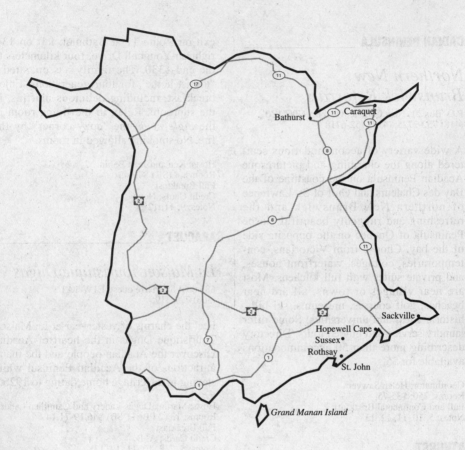

New Brunswick

with pine. The dining room—serving breakfast, lunch, afternoon tea, and dinner—opens to a long deck that is an excellent vantage point for watching harbor activities and bird watching. Evening conversations and early morning plans are made in the sitting rooms around Franklin stoves.

Hosts: Nora and Ed Parker
Rooms: 9 (SB) $58
Full Breakfast
Credit Cards: A, B
Notes: 2, 3, 4, 7, 8, 9, 10, 11, 12

HOPEWELL CAPE _____

Dutch Treat Farm

Rural Route 1, Hopewell Cape (Shepody), E0A 1Y0
(506) 882-2569

Century-old country farmhouse overlooking Grindstone Island on Shepody Bay. Hosts look forward to sharing their home with those who want to discover the legacy, history, and beauty of Albert County. All-purpose trails lead from the farm to the hills, and to the Salt Marsh with its remnants of 18th-century Acadian agriculture. Close to Fundy National Park, the Rocks Provincial Park, Mary's Point, and the Shepody National Wildlife Area. A haven for bird watchers and nature lovers. Special breakfast of blueberry pancakes and maple syrup designed to ready guests for a day of exploring. Limited smoking allowed.

Hosts: Glenn and Pat Treat
Rooms: 3 (SB) $30-35
Full Breakfast
Credit Cards: None
Notes: 2, 6, 8, 9, 10, 11, 12

ROTHESAY _____

Shadow Lawn Inn

3180 Rothesay Road, E2E 5A3
(506) 847-7539; FAX (506) 849-9238

Shadow Lawn, a four-star inn, is an ideal setting to host a variety of events, from a wedding reception, garden party, business luncheon, to a romantic dinner for two. In the typical countryside town of Rothesay, with many recreational facilities nearby, including an 18-hole golf course, tennis courts, and mooring facilities at the Rothesay Yacht Club. Shadow Lawn has nine guest rooms and two executive suites that have been richly decorated and lovingly restored. Dinner is served by reservation. Smoking in designated areas only.

Hosts: Mr. and Mrs. Patrick Gallagher
Rooms: 9 (PB) $69-125
Continental Breakfast
Credit Cards: A, B, C, D, E, F
Notes: 2, 3, 4, 5, 8, 9, 10, 11, 12, 13, 14

SACKVILLE _____

The Different Drummer

P.O. Box 188, 82 West Main Street, E0A 3C0
(506) 536-1291

Welcome to the Different Drummer Bed and Breakfast. Here guests can enjoy the comforts and conveniences of modern living in a restful and homey atmosphere. Attractive bedrooms are furnished much as they would have been at the turn of the century, and they all have private baths. In the large parlor and adjacent sunroom guests can chat, browse through a well-stocked

The Different Drummer

NOTES: Credit cards: A MasterCard; B Visa; C American Express; D Discover; E Diners Club; F Other;
2 Personal checks accepted; 3 Lunch available; 4 Dinner available; 5 Open all year; 6 Pets welcome;
7 No smoking; 8 Children welcome; 9 Social drinking allowed; 10 Tennis nearby; 11 Swimming nearby;
12 Golf nearby; 13 Skiing nearby; 14 May be booked through a travel agent.

library, watch TV, or just relax. Breakfast is served each morning. Enjoy home-baked bread, muffins, local honey, freshly ground coffee, and fresh berries in season.

Hosts: Georgette and Richard Hanrahan
Rooms: 8 (PB) $45-52
Continental Breakfast
Credit Cards: A, B
Notes: 5, 7, 8, 9, 10, 11, 12

Marshlands Inn

59 Bridge Street, P.O. Box 1440, E0A 3C0
(506) 536-0170; FAX (506) 536-0721

Inviting 1850 Victorian inn, formerly a private residence. Comfortably appointed guest rooms with antique furnishings and cozy living rooms with fireplaces. More than an inn, Marshlands is two stately manors plus a coach house with names like Hanson House, Stonehaven, and, of course, Marshlands. Offering 12 rooms in the main inn and 9 in Stonehaven, all feature magnificent oak floors and polished antiques. Private or shared bath facilities, parlors, a licensed dining room, gardens, and lawns.

Hosts: Peter and Diane Weedon
Rooms: 21 (17 PB; 4 SB) $60-100
Full Breakfast
Credit Cards: A, B, C, E
Notes: 3, 4, 5, 7, 9, 10, 11, 12, 13, 14

ST. JOHN

Five Chimneys Bed and Breakfast

238 Charlotte Street West, E2M 1Y3
(506) 635-1888; FAX (506) 635-8402

In Canada's oldest incorporated city, this 1855 Greek Revival home is near Reversing Falls and the Digby ferry. Three guest rooms with private and shared baths are available. Full breakfast includes whole-wheat and oatmeal pancakes, a cheesy egg dish, and oatmeal porridge, as well as homemade bread and jam. A warm welcome awaits all guests.

Host: Linda Gates
Rooms: 3 (1 PB; 2 SB) $55-65
Full Breakfast
Credit Cards: A, B
Notes: 2, 5, 7, 8, 9, 10, 11, 12

Parkerhouse Inn

71 Sydney Street, E2L 2L5
(506) 652-5054; FAX (506) 636-8076

Built in 1891, this wonderful Victorian inn offers nine bedrooms, all with private baths. The bedrooms are warm and cozy, decorated with antiques, plush linens, plants, and treasures. A careful restoration has preserved the original woodwork, stained-glass windows, a curved staircase, fireplaces, six-inch brass hinges on the doors, and a circular solarium. Wake up each morning to the aroma of freshly brewed coffee and homemade breads and muffins with freezer jams. Fresh fruit, bacon, sausage, eggs, and home fries are a welcome start to the day. The solarium is perfect for relaxing with a second cup of coffee and the morning paper.

Host: Pam Vincent
Rooms: 9 (PB) $79-95
Full Breakfast
Credit Cards: A, B, C, E
Notes: 4, 5, 7, 9, 11, 12, 14

SUSSEX

Anderson's Holiday Farm

Rural Route 2, Kings County, E0E 1P0
(506) 433-3786

Take exit 416 on the Trans-Canada Highway near Sussex, proceed on Route 890 on Smith's Creek Road to Newtown, only eight miles. There are sheep and beef cattle, pheasants, peacocks, swans, ducks in a pond, a donkey, goats, and a friendly dog. Nature trails and a five-minute walk to a covered bridge.

Rooms: 3 (SB) $40
Full Breakfast
Credit Cards: None
Notes: 5, 8, 10, 11, 12

NOTES: Credit cards accepted: A MasterCard; B Visa; C American Express; D Discover; E Diners Club; F Other; 2 Personal checks accepted; 3 Lunch available; 4 Dinner available; 5 Open all year; 6 Pets welcome;

Newfoundland

Thorndyke Bed and Breakfast

33 Water Street, A0E 1W0
(709) 832-0820; (709) 279-3384

The Thorndyke was built in 1917 by a Grand Banks schooner captain, John Thornhill. It was named for one of his schooners, the *Thorndyke,* last known date 1931. The house features many unique aspects: widow's walk, blown-glass windows, colored glass panels, and some historical artifacts, including captains' signatures and boats on walls dating back to 1919-21. Seasoned operation. On the Atlantic Coast, just feet from the water.

Hosts: Neil and Lynn Edwards
Rooms: 4 (1 PB; 3 SB) $45
Full Breakfast
Credit Cards: B
Notes: 8, 12

7 No smoking; 8 Children welcome; 9 Social drinking allowed; 10 Tennis nearby; 11 Swimming nearby; 12 Golf nearby; 13 Skiing nearby; 14 May be booked through a travel agent.

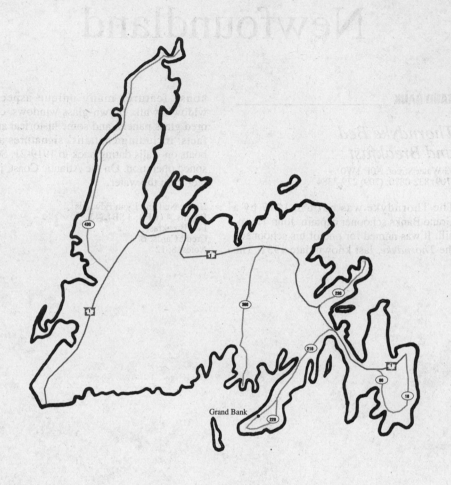

Grand Bank

Newfoundland

Nova Scotia

ANNAPOLIS ROYAL

Garrison House Inn

350 St. George Street, B0S 1A0
(902) 532-5750; FAX (902) 532-5501

The Garrison House Inn is a restored Heritage property directly across from historic Fort Anne. The hosts offer Old World ambience with modern day efficiency featuring seven bedrooms, most with private bath. The licensed restaurant serves the finest and freshest that the fertile Annapolis Valley and Bay of Fundy have to offer. It has been featured in many publications and is open to the public as well as the guests. The inn is a short stroll from the Historic Gardens, museums, theater, shops, and the Tidal Generating Station. Savor the tranquil surroundings complemented by the inn's friendly, courteous hospitality.

Host: Patrick Redgrave
Rooms: 7 (5 PB: 2 SB) $58-72
Credit Cards: A, B, C
Notes: 4, 8, 9, 10, 11, 12, 14

Hillsdale House

519 St. George Street, P.O. Box 148, B0S 1A0
(902) 532-2345; FAX (902) 532-7850

Built in 1849, the inn has been host to two kings of England, many of Canada's governors general, and leading politicians. Guests will find their rooms impressive, and the private bath en suite a welcome relief from the wearies of travel. The inn, set on a 15-acre estate, has a bird sanctuary for nature lovers. Next door are the Historic Gardens with more than a mile of meandering pathways. Within walking distance is historic Fort

Hillsdale House

Anne, museums, art galleries, fine restaurants, and many other places of interest.

Host: Leslie J. Langille
Rooms: 10 (PB) $60-85
Full Breakfast
Credit Cards: A, B
Notes: 7, 8, 9, 10, 11, 12

The King George Inn

548 Upper St. George Street, B0S 1A0
(902) 532-5286

Grand Victorian sea captain's home, furnished completely in period antiques. In historic Annapolis Royal (Canada's oldest settlement). A short walk from all major attractions. Inn features large, bright rooms with tall ceilings, cove moldings, leaded glass, rare carved woods, fireplaces, parquet floors, and legendary Nova Scotian hospitality. Family and honeymoon suites available.

Hosts: Michael and Donna Susnick
Rooms: 6 (2 PB; 4 SB) $45-52
Full Breakfast
Credit Cards: A, B
Notes: 6, 8, 9, 10, 11, 12, 14

7 No smoking; 8 Children welcome; 9 Social drinking allowed; 10 Tennis nearby; 11 Swimming nearby; 12 Golf nearby; 13 Skiing nearby; 14 May be booked through a travel agent.

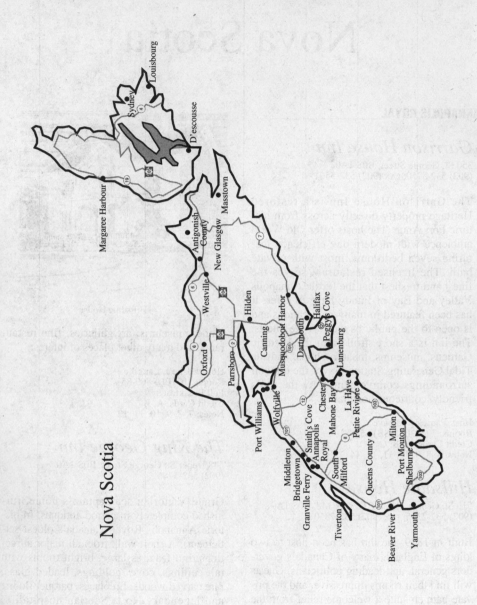

Nova Scotia

Louisbourg

Sydney

D'escousse

Margaree Harbour

19

Masstown

Antigonish County

New Glasgow

7

Westville

Hilden

Halifax

Musquodoboit Harbor

Dartmouth

Peggy's Cove

6

Canning

Lunenburg

Oxford

Parrsboro

2

Wolfville

Chester

La Have

Mahone Bay

32

Petite Rivière

103

Port Williams

Smith's Cove

Annapolis Royal

Milton

8

Middleton

Bridgetown

South Milford

Port Mouton

Granville Ferry

Queens County

Shelburne

103

Tiverton

Beaver River

101

Yarmouth

The Poplars Bed and Breakfast

124 Victorian Street, Box 277, B0S 1A0
(902) 532-7936

This restored Victorian home is in the heart of Canada's oldest permanent European settlement. A Registered Heritage site, it is shaded by huge 300-year-old poplars. Color cable TV in the family room, evening coffee and conversation. Two blocks from other amenities. Eight dollars each additional person.

Host: Iris Williams
Rooms: 9 (6 PB; 3 SB) $35-55
Continental Breakfast
Credit Cards: B
Notes: 5, 7, 8, 9

Queen Anne Inn

494 St. George Street, P.O. Box 218, B0S 1A0
(902) 532-7850 (phone and FAX)

The Queen Anne Inn was built in 1865 in the Second Empire style as a wedding gift at the unheard of cost of $13,000. Among the many features of the house is the large entrance hall with grand staircase. The fine interior woodwork of oak, ash, and mahogany is complete throughout in the best Victorian style. The house became St. Andrew's private boys' school from the

Queen Anne Inn

later part of the 1890s until 1907. In 1921 it became the Queen Hotel.

Host: Leslie J. Langille
Rooms: 10 (PB) $50-90
Full Breakfast
Credit Cards: A, B
Notes: 5, 7, 8, 9, 10, 11, 12

ANTIGONISH

Chestnut Corner Bed and Breakfast

Rural Route 1, Afton, B0H 1A0
(902) 386-2403; Canada (800) 565-0000
USA (800) 341-6096

Chestnut Corner is a relaxing country environment on Highway 4, 12.4 miles east of Antigonish town and 20 miles west of Cape Breton Island. Three tastefully decorated rooms provide single, twin, and queen-size accommodations. Clock radio and fan in each room. TV, VCR, and piano in lounges. Hiking trail on property. Nearby sandy beaches.

Hosts: Gordon and Joan Randall
Rooms: 3 (SB) $35-40
Full Breakfast
Credit Cards: None
Notes: 3, 6, 7, 8, 9, 10, 11

Green Haven Bed and Breakfast

27 Greening Drive, B2G 1R1
(902) 863-2884; (902) 867-5059

Split-level residence with patio. Quiet wooded area within walking distance of university, live theater. Homemade breakfast featuring jams and oven-fresh muffins. Well-traveled hosts speak Polish, Russian, German, Spanish, English, and French. Den with cable TV, lots of books, and fireplace. Call to inquire about availability of lunch and dinner.

Hosts: Martha and Al Balawyder
Rooms: 3 (1 PB; 2 SB) $38.85-55.50
Full Breakfast
Credit Cards: None
Notes: 2, 5, 8, 9, 10, 11, 12, 13

NOTES: Credit cards: A MasterCard; B Visa; C American Express; D Discover; E Diners Club; F Other;
2 Personal checks accepted; 3 Lunch available; 4 Dinner available; 5 Open all year; 6 Pets welcome;
7 No smoking; 8 Children welcome; 9 Social drinking allowed; 10 Tennis nearby; 11 Swimming nearby;
12 Golf nearby; 13 Skiing nearby; 14 May be booked through a travel agent.

LaBelle's

Frankville, B0H 1K0
(902) 234-2322

LaBelle's is a large, beautiful country home on acres of farmland and in view of the ocean. Quiet, homey atmosphere. Fresh toasted homemade bread and muffins are served as part of a Continental breakfast. Three guest rooms with shared bath.

Hosts: Isabel and Elmer Fougere
Rooms: 3 (SB) $30-40
Continental Breakfast
Credit Cards: None
Notes: 8, 11, 12

Lochiel Lake Bed and Breakfast

Lochiel Lake, Rural Route 5, B2G 2L3
(902) 783-2309; (902) 863-7913 (mobile)

Just 15 minutes from historic Sherbrooke Village on Route 7 (25 minutes from Antigonish town) and a few minutes from St. Mary's River, which is well known for its salmon fishing. Private dock available. Enjoy swimming, fishing, boating, skiing, and hunting (in season). Hunting guide available. Near Keppoch Mountain Ski Resort, Fish Hatchery, Black Brook Falls, a game farm and a provincial park.

Hosts: Lainie and Maggie Jo Landry
Rooms: 3 (1 PB; 2 SB) $45-55
Full Breakfast
Credit Cards: None
Notes: 5, 7, 9, 10, 11, 12, 13, 14

Old Manse Inn

5 Tigo Park, B2G 2M6
(902) 863-5696; (902) 863-5259 (off-season)

This elegant Victorian mansion was originally constructed as a Presbyterian Manse in 1874 at the cost of $2,000—a pricey sum in those days. Recently it has been completely renovated to provide modern comforts while retaining its original structure to yield a unique style and atmosphere. The Old Manse has five spacious guest bedrooms, four bathrooms, a self-contained

two-bedroom suite, living room, kitchen, and veranda. Three bedrooms contain twin beds and the other two have double beds. Cots are also available. The house is on a three-quarter hilltop lot in a quiet residential subdivision, only a stone's throw from the center of town. Open from June 1 through September 3.

Host: Barbara Pluta
Rooms: 7 (3 PB: 4 SB) $36-50 Canadian
Full Breakfast
Credit Cards: None
Notes: 7, 9, 10, 11, 12, 13, 14

BEAVER RIVER

Duck Pond Inn

Rural Route 1, Box 2495
Yarmouth County, B5A 4A5
(902) 649-2249; FAX (902) 649-2421

Elegantly restored and appointed sea captain's home. New queen-size four-poster beds, sparkling oversized bath, private lounge with TV. Full gourmet breakfast and complimentary tour of unique space museum operated by host. Beautiful rural setting yet convenient to Yarmouth and Digby ferries. Fine beach within short walk. Inn has won several awards. Reservations required.

Hosts: Tina and Harry Taylor
Rooms: 3 (1 PB; 2 SB) $80-90
Full Breakfast
Credit Cards: None
Notes: 2, 7, 11

BRIDGETOWN

Chesley House
Bed and Breakfast

304 Granville Street, B0S 1C0
(902) 665-2904

Welcome to Chesley House, a stately and spacious Queen Anne home built at the turn of the century. Offering warm hospitality, comfortable rooms, a reading area, deck, and a full breakfast including home-baked goods. Stay a while and enjoy the historic sites in Annapolis Royal, hike along the Fundy Shore, rock hound on the beach, canoe on the Annapolis River, or stroll Bridgetown's streets and take in all of the historic homes in this lovely Annapolis Valley town.

Hosts: David Shepherd and Lorelei Robins
Rooms: 3 (SB) $38-40
Full Breakfast
Credit Cards: None
Notes: 5, 7, 8, 9, 10, 11, 12

CANNING

The Farmhouse Inn

1057 Main Street, P.O. Box 38, B0P 1H0
(800) 928-4346; FAX (902) 582-7900

Charming 200-year-old farmhouse in historic shipbuilding village. Quaint decor; noted for its full breakfasts. Close to live theater, fine dining, excellent hiking, and bird watching (bald eagles). In the Annapolis Valley, famous for the Apple Blossom Festival in late May. Canopied beds, private baths. Afternoon tea included. Bicycles and fitness equipment available. Recommended by AAA and Canada Select (three and one-half stars). Owners are members of Professional Association of Innkeepers International. Smoking allowed outside only.

Hosts: Doug and Ellen Bray
Rooms: 7 (5 PB; 2 SB) $58-96 Canadian
Full Breakfast
Credit Cards: A, B
Notes: 5, 8, 9, 12, 14

CHESTER

Haddon Hall Inn

67 Haddon Hill Road, B0J 1J0
(902) 275-3577; (902) 275-3578; FAX (902) 275-5159

Haddon Hall, one of Chester's renowned summer estates, was built in 1905 by Vernon Woolrich. On top of Haddon Hill,

the residence offers a spectacular view of Mahone Bay and the town of Chester. This elegant country inn offers ten beautiful guest rooms furnished in period furnishings, private baths, TV, and telephones. Guests are invited to swim in the indoor pool or relax on the broad veranda. In the evening sit in front of a warm cracking fire in the Moose Room prior to dining in the elegant restaurant.

Host: Cynthia O'Connell
Rooms: 10 (PB) $125 and up
Continental Breakfast
Credit Cards: A, B, C
Notes: 3, 4, 5, 7, 10, 11, 12, 14

Mecklenburgh Inn

Mecklenburgh Inn

78 Queen Street, B0J 1J0
(902) 275-4638

A welcoming bed and breakfast in the heart of Chester, renowned seaside village-resort area. Rooms are spacious and comfortably appointed. Gourmet breakfasts are served around the big dining table before a crackling wood fire. The perfect home base from which to explore the area, browse the shops, or relax after a sail on the bay or a round of golf.

Host: Sue Fraser
Rooms: 4 (SB) $50-59
Full Breakfast
Credit Cards: B
Notes: 3, 8, 9, 10, 11, 12, 14

7 No smoking; 8 Children welcome; 9 Social drinking allowed; 10 Tennis nearby; 11 Swimming nearby; 12 Golf nearby; 13 Skiing nearby; 14 May be booked through a travel agent.

Stoney Brook Bed and Breakfast

Box 716, B0J 1J0
(902) 275-2342

This charming 1860s home on sprawling, landscaped property is a welcoming haven to visitors. A veranda offers comfortable chairs for relaxing and socializing. The back yard flower gardens and babbling brook offer a peaceful place for reading and enjoying nature. Five guest rooms are available, some with shared baths.

Hosts: Ned and Jeanne Nash
Rooms: 5 (3 PB; 2 SB) $50-53
Full Breakfast
Credit Cards: B
Notes: 2, 11, 12

DARTMOUTH

Caroline's Bed and Breakfast

134 Victoria Road, B3A 1V6
(902) 469-4665

This charming inn is conveniently close to MacDonald Bridge, the ferry terminal, waterfront district, golf course, Sportsplex, and buses. Cable TV in the living room, radios in the guest rooms. There are two rooms with double beds, one room with twin beds or king-size bed. Two-star rating by TIANS. Open April 30 through November 30.

Hosts: Caroline and Murray McCully
Rooms: 3 (1 PB; 2 SB) $35-40
Continental Breakfast
Credit Cards: None
Notes: 7, 8, 9, 12, 14

Riverdell Estate

68 Ross Road, Rural Route 3, B2W 5N7
(902) 434-7880

Nestled among the trees, beside a babbling brook, Riverdell offers executive country surroundings within minutes of Halifax and Dartmouth. Each day begins in the huge sun room where guests can bird watch while enjoying a hearty homemade break-

fast. Browse among the collectibles, quilts, and antiques, or have a conversation with the knowledgeable, friendly hosts. Six rooms are available with private and shared baths. Suites have two-person whirlpools, fireplace, and feather bed.

Hosts: Clare and Isabel Christie
Rooms: 6 (4 PB; 2 SB) $65-140
Full Breakfast
Credit Cards: B, C
Notes: 5, 7, 9, 10, 11, 12, 14

Stern's Mansion Inn Bed and Breakfast

17 Tulip Street, B3A 2S5
(902) 465-7414; (800) 565-3885
FAX (902) 466-2152

Restored century home with antique bedroom furnishings. Five rooms, private and shared baths, two with Jacuzzi spas, cable TV, VCR, telephone, and player piano. Four-course breakfast, evening tea and sweets. Honeymoon and special packages available.

Host: Bill deMolitor
Rooms: 5 (PB) $55-110
Full Breakfast
Credit Cards: A, B
Notes: 2, 5, 7, 9, 10, 11, 12, 14

D'ESCOUSSE

D'Escousse Bed and Breakfast

Rural Route 1, Box 510, B0E 1K0
(902) 226-2936

Early 1800s home overlooking picturesque harbor. Two and one-half baths, four rooms, TV in lounge. Kitchen facilities available. Plenty of privacy (owner resides in separate dwelling). Breakfast 7:00 A.M. to 12:00 P.M. A half-minute walk to private beach. Rowboats available. In Canada's choice of seven best villages.

Hosts: Sara and Al McDonald
Rooms: 4 (SB) $42
Full Breakfast
Credit Cards: None
Notes: 7, 8, 11

NOTES: Credit cards accepted: A MasterCard; B Visa; C American Express; D Discover; E Diners Club; F Other; 2 Personal checks accepted; 3 Lunch available; 4 Dinner available; 5 Open all year; 6 Pets welcome;

Nightingale's Landing

GRANVILLE FERRY

Nightingale's Landing Bed and Breakfast

P.O. Box 30; 5305 Granville Street, B0S 1K0
(902) 532-7615

Much-photographed 1870 Victorian ginger-bread home overlooking the Annapolis River and Annapolis Royal has three comfortable bedrooms furnished in period antiques. Enjoy the collection of antiques and family heirlooms in common rooms with high ceilings, antique chandeliers, marble fireplaces, and original wood moldings. A hearty gourmet breakfast is served in the dining room overlooking the river. Relax on the veranda and enjoy the peace and quiet of elegant country living. Thirty minutes from the St. John-Digby ferry. Children over seven welcome.

Hosts: Sandy and Jim Nightingale
Rooms: 3 (1 PB; 2 SB) $45-60
Full Breakfast
Credit Cards: B
Notes: 2, 9, 10, 11, 12, 14

HALIFAX

Fresh Start Bed and Breakfast

2720 Gottingen Street, B3K 3C7
(902) 453-6616

Modest Victorian mansion with an informal atmosphere. Less than one mile from Citadel Hill, the Public Gardens, and Historic properties. Guests enjoy breakfast at their convenience, flexible check-out times, laundry service, and complimentary refreshments. On-site parking.

Hosts: Innis and Sheila MacDonald
Rooms: 6 (2 PB; 4 SB) $45-70
Full Breakfast
Credit Cards: A, B, C, E
Notes: 5, 6, 7, 8, 9, 10, 11, 14

Prospect Bed and Breakfast

Box 68, Prospect Village, B0J 2V0
(902) 852-4493; (800) SALT-SEA

Pleasant informal atmosphere in a unique, restored century-old convent. Three guest rooms with queen-size beds, and one with a double-size bed. Canoe and rowboat for guest use. Small sand beach overlooking scenic Prospect Bay. Magnificent walking trails. Near Peggy's Cove and Halifax. This bed and breakfast is at the end of the point; visitors can't go past it without getting wet.

Hosts: Helena and Stephen O'Leary
Rooms: 4 (2 PB; 2 SB) $50
Continental Breakfast
Cards: A, B
Notes: 2, 5, 8, 9, 10, 11, 12, 14

Salmon River House Country Inn

Head Jeddore, B0J 1P0
(902) 889-3353; (800) 565-3353

Circa 1855 inn is nestled in a beautiful panorama of woods, hills, and water. Thirty-five minutes from Dartmouth-Halifax Airport. Six comfortable guest rooms, all with private baths. Wheelchair accessible. Honeymoon suite features whirlpool bath. Dining room, craft shop, and deck overlooking the water. Ask for the Romantic Getaway, Canoe Adventure, or Sailboat Cruise packages.

Hosts: Norma and Adrien Blanchette
Rooms: 6 (PB) $65-95
Credit Cards: A, B, E
Notes: 4, 5, 7, 8, 9, 11, 12, 14

7 No smoking; 8 Children welcome; 9 Social drinking allowed; 10 Tennis nearby; 11 Swimming nearby; 12 Golf nearby; 13 Skiing nearby; 14 May be booked through a travel agent.

Virginia Kinfolks

1722 Robie Street, B3H 3E8
(902) 423-6687; (800) 668-STAY
FAX (902) 423-6687

A little bit of Virginia in Nova Scotia. Antique furnishings throughout including canopied beds. Full country-style breakfast. Convenient to downtown and all Halifax attractions including the waterfront. Discounts available for seniors and stay of three nights or more. Friendly atmosphere at a reasonable price.

Hosts: Dick and Lucy Russell
Rooms: 3 (1 PB; 2 SB) $45-60
Full Breakfast
Credit Cards: None
Notes: 2, 5, 6, 7, 9, 10, 11, 12, 13

HILDEN

Ann's Farmhouse Bed and Breakfast

2627 Irwin Lake Road, B0N 1C0
(902) 897-0300; (800) 603-7887

Pleasant old farmhouse surrounded by rolling pastures and woods. Lots of sheep and birds. A great place to walk or relax and yet only 15 minutes from downtown Truro with its shops and restaurants. Three guest rooms with shared bath facilities. Full breakfast and evening snacks provided. Three-star recommended by Canada Select.

Hosts: David and Ann Pullen
Rooms: 3 (SB) $40-50
Full Breakfast
Credit Cards: B
Notes: 5, 7, 8, 12, 14

LA HAVE

Goode's Landing Bed and Breakfast

Box 33, House 3384, Route 331 South, B0R 1C0
(902) 688-2161

Experience true down-home hospitality and comfort in this turn-of-the-century home

furnished with some interesting antiques and collectibles. Relax on the veranda and watch the boats of the LaHave, the Rhine of Nova Scotia. Enjoy the private sunny patio, cast for mackerel off the wharf, stroll to Fort Point (first settled in 1632), and drop in at the famous LaHave Bakery for a snack. This artists' and bird watchers' paradise, with excellent windsurfing and cycling, is also near beaches. A short ferry ride delivers guests within minutes of Lunenburg and Mahone Bay. Two charming bedrooms, each with double bed. Shared guest-only bath. Comfortable smoke-free environment. Start each day with a hearty captain's breakfast. Ici on parle français.

Hosts: Michael and Darby Goode
Rooms: 2 (SB) $40-45
Full Breakfast
Credit Cards: B
Notes: 7, 11, 12

LOUISBOURG

Greta Cross Bed and Breakfast

81 Pepperell Street, B0A 1M0
(902) 733-2833

An older home off Main Street on a hill overlooking the harbor and the Fortress of Louisbourg. In a quiet area, it offers guests kitchen privileges, laundry services, and a baby-sitting service. Home-baked breads, muffins, oatcakes, and jams are provided for breakfast, and a snack is served on

Greta Cross

arrival if desired. Rated two and one-half stars Canada Select. Small pets welcome.

Host: Greta Cross
Rooms: 3 (SB) $45
Full Breakfast
Credit Cards: C
Notes: 2, 7, 8, 9, 10, 11

Blue Rocks Road

LUNENBURG

Blue Rocks Road Bed and Breakfast

579 Blue Rocks Road, Rural Route 1, B0J 2C0
(902) 634-3426

Comfortable home with veranda overlooking Lunenburg Bay, one hour from Halifax and close to beautiful unspoiled beaches. Friendly, relaxed atmosphere and great breakfasts including farm-fresh eggs. Also home of the Lunenburg Bicycle Barn with everything for the cyclist. Quality bike rentals. Great cycling country! German and English spoken.

Hosts: Al and Merrill Heubach
Rooms: 3 (1 PB; 2 SB) $55-65
Full Breakfast
Credit Cards: A, B
Notes: 7, 8, 9, 10, 11, 12, 14

Boscawen Inn

150 Cumberland Street, P.O. Box 1343, B0J 2C0
(902) 634-3325; FAX (902) 634-9293

The Boscawen Inn, a Victorian mansion set high on a steep incline overlooking the harbor in Lunenburg's designated National Heritage District, presents an aura of peace and tranquility amidst the elegance of a bygone era. Choose from large bedrooms to smaller, cozier rooms. Adjacent, the newly restored McLachlan House (circa 1905) offers rooms, suites, and balconies with a harborview. Sample some of Nova Scotia's finest dinner specialities in the dining room by candlelight. Enjoy a hearty breakfast the next morning. Everything is homemade and prepared from local fresh ingredients. The season is from Easter to year's end; open year-round for groups. Menus tailored for small conferences, corporate dinner meetings, weddings, and family events. Breakfast is included in McLachlan House and costs an additional $3.00 to $6.50 for guests of the Boscawen Inn. Call regarding accommodations for pets.

Hosts: Michael and Ann O'Dowd
Rooms: 21 (18 PB; 3 SB) $40-110
Full Breakfast
Credit Cards: A, B, C, D, E
Notes: 4, 7, 8, 10, 11, 12, 14

Kaulbach House Historic Inn

75 Pelham Street, B0J 2C0
(902) 634-8818

In the heart of the National Historic District and overlooking the waterfront, this Registered Heritage inn, circa 1880, offers elegant accommodation in a gracious Victorian atmosphere. Each of the eight beautifully appointed guest rooms has TV, and six rooms have private baths. An elaborate three-course breakfast is served each morning. The entrée changes daily with specialities like Cheese Strata and Maple Sugar Pears or Quiche Lorraine and Strawberry Crème Brulée. Fully licensed dining offered exclusively to guests. Off-street parking.

Hosts: Karen and Enzo Padovani
Rooms: 8 (6 PB; 2 SB) $50-88
Full Breakfast
Credit Cards: A, B, C
Notes: 4, 5, 7, 9, 10, 11, 12, 14

7 No smoking; 8 Children welcome; 9 Social drinking allowed; 10 Tennis nearby; 11 Swimming nearby; 12 Golf nearby; 13 Skiing nearby; 14 May be booked through a travel agent.

South Shore Country Inn

Broad Cove, B0J 2H0
(902) 677-2042

This is a renovated, beautifully decorated century-plus-old home with all the modern conveniences. Guest rooms are uniquely individual. The licensed dining room serves homemade English and Nova Scotian fare in elegant but comfortable surroundings. Nestled in a small scenic village, this is an ideal spot for a getaway or a little rest and relaxation.

Host: Avril Betts
Rooms: 6 (2 PB; 4 SB) $60-95
Full and Continental Breakfast
Credit Cards: A, B, C, D
Notes: 3, 4, 6, 7, 9, 11, 14

MAHONE BAY

Sou'Wester Inn
Bed and Breakfast

788 Main Street; Highway 3, Box 146, B0J 2E0
(902) 624-9296

This fine Victorian seaside shipbuilder's home comes complete with friendly and gracious accommodations. Enjoy evening tea, relax on the veranda, or sit by the water overlooking the beautiful bay. There are books, parlor games, and a piano for enjoyment on lazy days. Collectors, see the fine whale sculptures that are for sale. Antique and period furnishings throughout. This bed and breakfast is on Nova Scotia's beautiful south shore. Maps are available at the inn for scenic drives or quiet shoreline walks. Exquisite dining nearby. Three-and-one-half-star recommended by Canada Select.

Hosts: Ron and Mabel Redden
Rooms: 4 (PB) $65-70
Full Breakfast
Credit Cards: A, B
Notes: 7, 9, 10, 11, 12, 14

MARGAREE HARBOUR

Harbour View Inn
Bed and Breakfast

B0E 2B0
(902) 235-2314

Started in the early 1920s, the Harbour View Inn is an older home with a fantastic view of the Margaree Highland Mountains and a long wooden bridge where the famous salmon-fishing Margaree River begins. Three beaches are just minutes away. There are a general store, whale cruises, deep-sea fishing, a large gift shop, and historic boats all close by. There is a lounge with cable TV and VCR for guests to enjoy, and a reading room for relaxing. Hosts serve delicious home-cooked meals including lobster, crab, and other seafood. Guests are allowed use of the kitchen if they choose.

Hosts: Connie and Glenn Jennex
Rooms: 3 (SB) $40-55
Full Breakfast
Credit Cards: A, B, C
Notes: 2, 3, 4, 6, 8, 9, 10, 11, 12

MASSTOWN

Shady Maple Bed and Breakfast

Rural Route 1, B0M 1G0
(902) 662-3565

Restored century-old home and operating farm. The upstairs balcony affords a view of Cobequid Bay. Full four-course breakfast is served by candlelight. Evening snacks are provided. Enjoy the heated outdoor pool and year-round spa, or sit by the fireplace in the den. Six miles from Tidal Bore look-off.

Hosts: Jim and Ellen Eisses
Rooms: 4 (SB) $40-65
Full Breakfast
Credit Cards: B
Notes: 5, 6, 7, 8, 9, 10, 11, 13, 14

MIDDLETON

Fairfield Farm Inn

10 Main Street (Route 1 West), B0S 1P0
(902) 825-6989 (phone and FAX); (800) 565-0000

This country inn has been given three stars. This 1886 Annapolis Valley farmhouse has been completely restored and furnished in period antiques to enhance its original charm. The five bedrooms feature king- or queen-size beds and have en suite private bathrooms. Bordered by the Annapolis River and Slocum Brook, the inn is on a 75-acre fruit and vegetable farm, famous for its luscious cantaloupes. A guest kitchen and laundry facilities are available. Museums, recreational facilities, boutiques, and restaurants are just a short walk from the inn.

Hosts: Richard and Shae Griffith
Rooms: 5 (PB) $50-65 Canadian
Full and Continental Breakfast
Credit Cards: A, B, C
Notes: 3, 5, 7, 9, 10, 11, 12, 13, 14

MILTON

Second Home Bed and Breakfast

380 Main Street, P.O. Box 133, B0T 1P0
(902) 354-3573

This inn is in a quiet community close to beaches, parks, and museums. The back yard is bordered by the beautiful Mersey River. Guests are welcome to stroll through the yard. Rooms can be rented as bed and breakfast rooms or as a housekeeping unit. Common room with refrigerator, microwave, and TV. Self-serve Continental breakfast. Rates for housekeeping unit negotiable.

Hosts: Sally and Stacy Kaulback
Rooms: 3 (SB) $35
Continental Breakfast
Credit Cards: None
Notes: 7, 8, 10, 11, 12

MUSQUODOBOIT HARBOUR

The International Bed and Breakfast Club, Inc.

504 Amherst Street, Buffalo, NY 14207
(800) 723-4262; FAX (716) 873-4462

NS3684PP. This quiet inn overlooks Petpeswick Inlet only half an hour from the twin cities of Halifax and Dartmouth. Three rooms are available with private baths. A luxury suite has a whirlpool bath, private living room, stereo, fireplace, TV, and VCR. Full breakfast, candlelight dinner, and a picnic basket available. $45-65.

Wayward Goose Inn Bed and Breakfast

343 West Petpeswick Road, B0J 2L0
(902) 889-3654

The Wayward Inn is a quiet inn where deer and loons visit regularly. Thirty minutes from Halifax-Dartmouth, the Wayward Goose blends the best of urban convenience with rural charm. The area offers the best of crafts, museums, and breathtaking scenery. Hike or ski the trails, swim off the dock, sail in the daysailer, paddle a canoe, row a rowboat, skate on the inlet, relax in the private living room with fireplace, stereo, cable TV, and VCR. Rooms are tastefully appointed with private baths and other features. Honeymoon suite features a whirlpool bath for two. Packages are available.

Hosts: Randy and Judy Skaling
Rooms: 3 (PB) $49-69
Full Breakfast
Credit Cards: B
Notes: 2, 5, 7, 8, 9, 11, 12, 14

NEW GLASGOW

Pinehedge Bed and Breakfast

Rural Route 1, Westville, B0K 2A0
(902) 396-5726

---

7 No smoking; 8 Children welcome; 9 Social drinking allowed; 10 Tennis nearby; 11 Swimming nearby; 12 Golf nearby; 13 Skiing nearby; 14 May be booked through a travel agent.

Three rooms with shared shower bath. Clock radio, cable TV, telephone, and hair dryers in all rooms. Cable TV in living room. Full breakfast featuring homemade bread and muffins. Close to beaches, golf, shopping, PEI ferry, and Magic Valley fun park. Air-conditioned. Available May through October; other times by request. Skiing is a 45-minute drive away.

Hosts: Theresa and John Patton
Rooms: 3 (SB) $40
Full Breakfast
Credit Cards: None
Notes: 2, 8, 9, 10, 11, 12

OXFORD

Lea Side Bed and Breakfast

177 Water Street, P.O. Box 228, B0M 1P0
(902) 447-3039

Elegant turn-of-the-century family home in a charming small-town residential area of Oxford. Three gracious bedrooms with antique decor and modern comforts. Experience a gourmet meal in the dining room, or relax in the formal living room. Ramble through the art gallery. From a comfortable veranda enjoy a magnificent sunset or relax in the privacy of the deck overlooking gardens in a parklike setting. Smoking permitted on decks only.

Hosts: Don and Jean Wallace
Rooms: 3 (SB) $45-50
Full Breakfast
Credit Cards: A, B
Notes: 3, 4, 5, 8, 9, 10, 11, 12, 13

PARRSBORO

Spencer's Island Inn

Rural Route 3, B0M 1S0
(902) 392-2721

The house of a shipbuilder of the famous mystery ship Mary Celeste in the seaside village of Spencer's Island. Comb the nearby tidal beach for odd and interesting rocks or visit the lighthouse. Open June through

August. Take Route 209 to Spencer's Island and turn off at Spencer's Beach sign.

Hosts: Margaret Griebel
Rooms: 3 (1 PB; 2 SB) $35
Full Breakfast
Credit Cards: None
Notes: 2, 8

PEGGY'S COVE

Peggy's Cove Bed and Breakfast

19 Church Road, B0J 2N0
(902) 823-2265

Overlooking beautiful Peggy's Cove. Large comfortable rooms; friendly informal atmosphere. Four rooms have patio doors opening onto large shared balconies over the cove. Fifth room has view of the mouth of the cove, St. Margaret's Bay, the church, and the Barrens. World-renowned little fishing village within easy walking distance of all cove attractions—lighthouse, fish houses, gift shops, and restaurant.

Host: Audrey O'Leary
Rooms: 3 (SB) $60
Full Breakfast
Credit Cards: A, B, C
Notes: 7, 9, 11, 12, 14

PETITE RIVIERE

Little River Bed and Breakfast

5666 Route 331, B0J 2P0
(902) 688-1339

European-style dwelling offers peace and tranquility with ample parking for car or boat. Large deck equipped with a barbecue and picnic tables. Three rooms with private and shared bath. Full gourmet breakfast served. Cable TV, VCR, music, and piano in living room. Near beaches, nature walks, artists, swimming, and golf. Honeymoon packages available.

Hosts: Joan and Tanya Patterson
Rooms: 3 (1 PB; 2 SB) $50-65
Full Breakfast
Credit Cards: B
Notes: 2, 3, 4, 5, 6, 7, 8, 9, 11, 12, 14

NOTES: Credit cards accepted: A MasterCard; B Visa; C American Express; D Discover; E Diners Club; F Other; 2 Personal checks accepted; 3 Lunch available; 4 Dinner available; 5 Open all year; 6 Pets welcome;

PORT MOUTON

Apple Pie Bed and Breakfast

P.O. Box 32, B0T 1T0
(902) 683-2217; FAX (902) 683-2216

A pleasant turn-of-the-century home with spacious sun porch for breakfast or candlelit dinners (on request). Minutes away from beautiful white sand beaches. Host is musician-cabinet maker with a woodworking shop on premises. Very comfortable two-room suite with private bath. Bright, sunny bedroom with queen-size bed, airconditioned sitting room with sofa bed and color TV, VCR, and library. Full private bath. Can accommodate up to four persons. Just one mile off exit 21 and Highway 103. Very private beautiful oceanview from porch or upstairs sitting area. An ideal retreat for all honeymooners both young and old.

Hosts: Judy and John Adams
Suite: 1 (PB) $95
Full Breakfast
Credit Cards: A, B
Notes: 4, 5, 10, 11, 12

PORT WILLIAMS

The Old Rectory Bed and Breakfast

1519 Highway 358, Rural Route 1, B0P 1T0
(902) 542-1815

Recently renovated Victorian home with gardens and orchard. (U-Pick and cider making in season.) Evening tea served. Geology field trips can be arranged. Hike to Cape Split, visit historic Prescott House and Grand Pré Park. Enjoy the many local art galleries and cultural events available in university town.

Hosts: Ron and Carol Buckley
Rooms: 3 (1 PB; 2 SB) $50-60
Full Breakfast
Credit Cards: None
Notes: 2, 8, 11, 12, 14

QUEENS COUNTY

River View Lodge

Box 129, Greenfield, B0T 1E0
(902) 685-2376; (902) 685-2423

Rustic five-bedroom lodge with a fireplace, TV, and VCR in the living room. The dining room overlooks the scenic Medway River, which is great for its spring run of trout and Atlantic salmon. Close to a shopping mall, many historical sites, and museums. Inquire about the availability of lunch or dinner.

Hosts: Suzette and Moyal Conrad
Rooms: 5 (SB) $45
Full Breakfast
Credit Cards: B
Notes: 2, 6, 8, 9, 11, 12

SHELBURNE

Ankriston Villa

Rural Route 3, B0T 1W0
(902) 637-3005 (phone and FAX)

Overlooking the River Clyde, this elegant restored brick estate house offers superior accommodations in a scenic setting just minutes from the highway on Nova Scotia's south shore. The comfortable patio area overlooks the river where sportsmen can fish for salmon. The hosts offer one double and one twin bedroom with private bath. The spacious drawing room and dining room, both with fireplaces, encourage guests to relax in comfort. Horseback riding nearby. Exit 28 Port Clyde, two miles from Highway 103.

Hosts: Starr and Don Nelson
Rooms: 2 (PB) $35-45
Full Breakfast
Credit Cards: None
Notes: 5, 7, 8, 9, 10, 11, 12

Cooper's Inn and Restaurant

Box 959, 36 Dock Street, B0T 1W0
(902) 875-4656 (phone and FAX)
e-mail: http://fox.nstn.ca/~trogers/cooper/

7 No smoking; 8 Children welcome; 9 Social drinking allowed; 10 Tennis nearby; 11 Swimming nearby; 12 Golf nearby; 13 Skiing nearby; 14 May be booked through a travel agent.

The Cooper's Inn and Restaurant, a Registered Heritage property, is on Dock Street, in the heart of the historic waterfront area of the town of Shelburne. The house was built in 1785 by the blind Loyalist merchant George Gracie. It has been carefully restored to offer quality accommodations while retaining the charm and character of an earlier time. All guest rooms have private baths and waterviews. The three-star restaurant offers full dining facilities featuring regional cuisine and fresh local produce.

Hosts: Allan and Joan Redmond
Rooms: 7 (PB) $58-80
Continental Breakfast
Credit Cards: A, B, C, E
Notes: 4, 11, 12, 14

Harbour House Bed and Breakfast

187 Water Street, Box 362, B0T 1W0
(902) 875-2074; (800) 565-0000

A 200-year-old Loyalist home, Harbour House offers a comfortable, friendly atmosphere in a scenic location overlooking the beautiful Shelburne Harbour and Island's Park. Within walking distance of historic waterfront museum, park, harbor, stores, cinema, bank, post office, restaurants, and tourist bureau. Coffee and tea offered in the evening. English and German spoken. Free parking. Cot available.

Host: Wolfgang Schricker
Rooms: 3 (SB) $45
Full Breakfast
Credit Cards: B
Notes: 2, 7, 8, 9, 10, 11, 12, 14

Millstones Country Inn 1846

Falls Lane 2, P.O. Box 758, B07 1W0
(902) 875-3958

Lovely 1846 miller's home on the Roseway River, steeped in the history of Empire Loyalists. A stroll along the serene mill race sets a relaxing mood for dinner in the hand-cut granite block wall dining room. German and international kitchen.

The inn offers three charming rooms with private baths and a large family suite with bath. There is a lounge with cable TV for guests to enjoy. No smoking allowed in the lounge.

Hosts: Julie and Gary Jeschke
Rooms: 4 (PB) $48-78 Canadian
Full Breakfast
Credit Cards: B
Notes: 4, 8, 9, 12, 14

Harborview Inn

SMITH'S COVE

Harbourview Inn

P.O. Box 39, B0S 1S0
(902) 245-5686

A turn-of-the-century village inn overlooking the tidal waters of the beautiful Annapolis Basin, this delightful inn is furnished in charming Victorian country fashion and has welcomed summer guests through its doors since the 1890s. Harbourview offers a freshwater pool, tennis court, and an ocean beach for clamming, rock hounding, and viewing the world's most dramatic tides. Delicious breakfast and dinner are served daily in a fully licensed dining room. Fresh local seafoods are a special feature of the menu.

Hosts: Mona and Phillip Webb
Rooms: 9 (PB) $55-75
Full Breakfast
Credit Cards: A, B
Notes: 2, 4, 7, 8, 9, 10, 11, 12, 14

SOUTH MILFORD _____

Milford House

Box 521 Annapolis Royal, B0S 1A0
(902) 532-2617; (902) 532-7360 (off-season)

Milford House is a rustic wilderness resort dating back to the 1860s with all accommodations in cabins dotted around the shores of two lakes. Each cabin has two to five bedrooms, bathroom, living room, veranda, and dock. No radios or TV. The main lodge features the dining room, living rooms, library, and children's game room. Tennis courts and croquet lawn available. Rates include breakfast and dinner. Packed box lunches available. No smoking in dining room. Social drinking allowed in cabins.

Host: Maggie Nickerson
Cabins: 27 (PB) $142-155
Full Breakfast and Dinner
Credit Cards: B
Notes: 2, 6, 8, 10, 11, 12, 14

SYDNEY _____

Park Place Bed and Breakfast

169 Park Street, B1P 4W7
(902) 562-3518

Victorian-style house built for the steel plant, circa 1901. Unique feature is curved walls in

Park Place

the living room and hall. Downtown and its many attractions are very close by. Enjoy close proximity to Louisbourg and the Miner's Museum.

Host: Ev McEwen
Rooms: 3 (SB) $40
Full Breakfast
Credit Cards: B
Notes: 5, 8, 9, 10, 11, 12, 13, 14

TIVERTON _____

Bed and Breakfast/ Gallery by-the-Sea

Fisherman's Wharf, P.O. Box 719, B0V 1G0
(902) 839-2417

Why not spend some time in this quaint, traditional fishing village to learn about and enjoy the sea? The bed and breakfast is operated by marine wildlife biologist Tom Goodwin, who operates his own whale-seabird cruises from the inn, along with a delightful wildlife gift gallery. Guests will enjoy lots of extras, including a nature center on site and tours to the famous balancing rock. Just off the ferry, opposite the fishing wharf. Whale watching package is available.

Host: Tom Goodwin
Rooms: 2 (SB) $40 Canadian
Full Breakfast
Credit Cards: B
Notes: 2, 3, 6, 7, 8, 9, 14

WESTVILLE _____

Stoneycombe Lodge

Rural Route 3, B0K 2A0
(902) 396-3954

This modern house comes complete with a heated outdoor pool for relaxation. Set in the heart of the province with easy access to beaches, festivals, and the airport. Take day trips to the many areas of interest and return for a late snack in the evening. The three-star rating means that

7 No smoking; 8 Children welcome; 9 Social drinking allowed; 10 Tennis nearby; 11 Swimming nearby; 12 Golf nearby; 13 Skiing nearby; 14 May be booked through a travel agent.

guests will be well looked after. Off-season rates are in effect for fall foliage days in glorious technicolor!

Hosts: Keith and Edith Selwyn-Smith
Rooms: 3 (PB) $45-55 Canadian
Full Breakfast
Credit Cards: B
Notes: 2, 5, 7, 8, 9, 11, 12, 14

WOLFVILLE

The Gingerbread House Inn Bed and Breakfast

8 Robie Tufts Drive; P.O. Box 819, B0P 1X0
(902) 542-1458

Restored 1893 carriage house has five masterfully decorated bedrooms with private baths, entrances, and TVs. A candlelight full breakfast is included. The Garden Suite boasts a 21-foot tower, in-floor spa, fireplace, wet bar, king-size bed, and 50-inch TV. Available from May 1 to November 1. Children over five welcome.

Hosts: Ron and Doreen Cook
Rooms: 5 (PB) $59-135
Full Breakfast
Credit Cards: B
Notes: 2, 7, 9, 10, 11, 12, 13, 14

Tattingstone Inn

434 Main Street, P.O. Box 98, B0P 1X0
(902) 542-7696

Enjoy fine country dining prepared by an award-winning chef. Whether guests choose to dine overlooking the garden or by the fireplace, each evening will be memorable. The inn features ten beautifully appointed rooms with private baths. Most have queen-size beds. Antiques and original art are featured throughout. All rooms and dining areas are air-conditioned and no smoking. Tennis courts and swimming pool are on-site.

Host: Betsey Harwood
Rooms: 10 (PB) $78-138
Credit Cards: A, B, C
Notes: 4, 5, 7, 10, 11, 12, 13

Churchill Mansion Country Inn

YARMOUTH

Churchill Mansion Country Inn

Rural Route 1, B5A 4A5
(902) 649-2818

A truly unique mansion on top of a hill overlooking two lakes and the Bay of Fundy. Original light fixtures and carpets. Breakfast room overlooks Darling Lake. Widow's walk on top. Miles of sandy beach nearby. Canoe available in lake. Seafood buffet available nightly.

Host: Bob Benson
Rooms: 9 (PB) $39-59
Full Breakfast
Credit Cards: A, B, D
Notes: 3, 4, 6, 7, 8, 9, 11, 12, 14

Murray Manor Bed and Breakfast

225 Main Street, B5A 1C6
(902) 742-9625

Beautiful, well-maintained three-star Heritage Home in the Gothic style was built in the 1820s by an Englishman named Bond. The house has a bell-cast roof, a five-bay facade with pointed Gothic windows. The three bedrooms are attractive and comfortable. Each have "prayer" windows (one must kneel to see out). Extensive library for guests to enjoy throughout the house. Older children are welcome. Full breakfast.

NOTES: Credit cards accepted: A MasterCard; B Visa; C American Express; D Discover; E Diners Club; F Other; 2 Personal checks accepted; 3 Lunch available; 4 Dinner available; 5 Open all year; 6 Pets welcome;

Hosts: George and Joan Semple
Rooms: 3 (SB) $55
Full Breakfast
Credit Cards: B
Notes: 5, 9, 10, 11, 12

Victorian Vogue Bed and Breakfast

109 Brunswick Street, B5A 2H2
(902) 742-6398

Historic Queen Anne Revival has all the richness and charm guests will enjoy.

Fireplaces, pocket doors, wainscoting, and stained-glass windows are just a few of the features gracing this beautiful sea captain's home. Tea, coffee, and desserts are available in the parlor each afternoon. Yarmouth is a wonderful historic seaport to explore. Magnificent home and scenic locations abound. Continental plus breakfast.

Host: Dawn-Marie Skjelmose
Rooms: 6 (1PB; 5 SB) $45-60
Continental Breakfast
Credit Cards: A, B
Notes: 2, 5, 6, 7, 8, 9, 10, 11, 12, 14

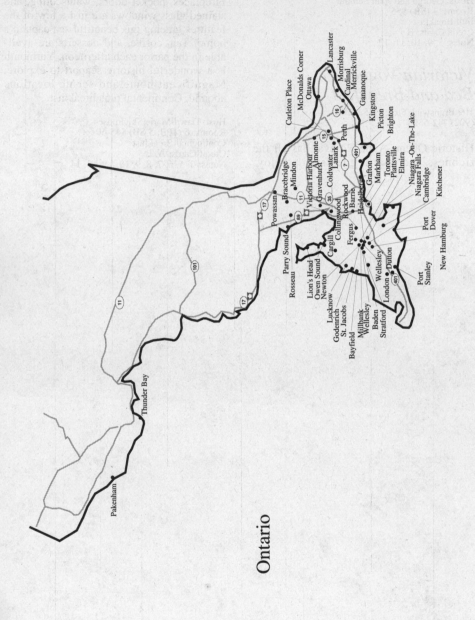

Ontario

ALMONTE

Mount Blow Farm

Rural Route 2, K0A 1A0
(613) 256-3692

Enjoy staying in this restored 150-year-old
log farm house on this sixth-generation century farm furnished with family antiques.
Country-style cooking includes homemade
bread, muffins, jams, jellies, honey, and
maple syrup. Play the piano, swim in the
pool, relax on the veranda, and walk the
fields and lanes of the 200-acre farm or ski
them in the winter. Watch for white-tailed
deer, foxes, and bluebirds. This bed and
breakfast is a 45-minute drive from Ottawa,
the nation's capital. Visit museums, antique
shops, and flea markets nearby. Lunch and
dinner available upon request.

Hosts: Eleanor and Laurie Rintoul
Rooms: 3 (SB) $45-50 Canadian
Full Breakfast
Credit Cards: None
Notes: 2, 5, 7, 8, 9, 10, 11, 12, 13

Squirrels Bed and Breakfast

P.O. Box 729, 190 Parkview Drive, K0A 1A0
(613) 256-2995

Guests will find the unique spacious home
in the style of a German chalet in beautiful
Lanark County in the Ottawa Valley. Full
breakfast, with homemade bread and marmalade served in the sunroom overlooking
the garden. Two double rooms with king-
size bed or two single beds; one single
room. Shared bath. Plenty of privacy. Hosts
are world travelers and enjoy sharing experiences with their guests. Nonsmokers only,
please. Reasonable rates.

Hosts: Pat and Ian Matheson
Rooms: 3 (SB) $45
Full Breakfast
Credit Cards: None
Notes: 2, 5, 7, 8, 9, 10, 11, 12, 13

Tackaberry's Grant

Rural Route 2, K0A 1A0
(613) 256-1481

Beautiful parklike setting in rolling farmland, 10 minutes southwest of Almonte and
40 minutes from downtown Ottawa. Two
rooms, one with queen-size bed, one with
two singles, with shared bath in a charming,
renovated 150-year-old farmhouse. Relax in
the large in-ground pool or stroll the
grounds, which include an apple orchard and
pond. Friendly family dog will be delighted
to accompany guests! Hearty full breakfast
included. Reservations recommended.

Hosts: Jack and Orchid Reid
Rooms: 2 (SB) $40
Full Breakfast
Credit Cards: None
Notes: 2, 5, 7, 8, 9, 11, 12, 13

ALTAVISTA

Ottawa Bed and Breakfast

488 Cooper Street, Ottawa, K1R 5H9
(613) 563-0161; (800) 461-7889

1. Very large, modern home. Three guest
rooms share sitting room with TV. First
bedroom en suite on ground floor with twin
beds, private bathroom. Second bedroom

NOTES: Credit cards: A MasterCard; B Visa; C American Express; D Discover; E Diners Club; F Other;
2 Personal checks accepted; 3 Lunch available; 4 Dinner available; 5 Open all year; 6 Pets welcome;
7 No smoking; 8 Children welcome; 9 Social drinking allowed; 10 Tennis nearby; 11 Swimming nearby;
12 Golf nearby; 13 Skiing nearby; 14 May be booked through a travel agent.

with twin beds and shared bath. Third bedroom with queen-size bed and shared bath. The two rooms with twin beds can be converted into a king-size bed if desired. Resident cat. No smoking.

2. Large bungalow on a wooded lot in a nice residential area of Ottawa. Choose from two guest rooms—one with double bed, the second with twin beds, shared bath. Photographs of the home have been featured in a major magazine because of the extensive restoration work hosts have done. Enjoy the lovely garden. Parliament buildings are only a few minutes' drive by car or by bus, which is available nearby. Families welcome. Hosts speak French. $55-73.

BADEN

Northridge Farm

Rural Route 2, N0B 1G0
(519) 634-8595

Enjoy the quiet, space, comfort, and hospitality on 86 acres of rolling farmland. Conveniently between Kitchener-Waterloo, St. Jacobs, and Stratford. Area is known for its Mennonites, farmers markets, shopping outlets, and Shakespeare and other festivals. Three guest rooms, one with double and single beds, one with twin beds, one with a single. Visit the horses. English riding lessons available. Children over six welcome.

Hosts: Sarah Banbury and son Michael
Rooms: 3 (SB) $55
Continental Breakfast
Credit Cards: None
Notes: 2, 4, 9

BARRIE

"Round Table" Bed and Breakfast

59 Kinzie Lane, L4M 4S8
(705) 739-0193

Homey in-town location, one hour north of Toronto, in historical Huronia cottage country house surrounded by white picket fence and English gardens. TV room, TV in each guest room, fireplace, hot tub, and bicycles. Preserves (jams and pickles) for sale. Twin and queen-size beds. Cot available. Cat and dog in residence. Reduced rates for long-term stay (one week or more). Dinner available by reservation only. Children over eight welcome.

Host: Diane C. Murray
Rooms: 2 (1 PB; 1 SB) $60
Full Breakfast
Credit Cards: None
Notes: 2, 5, 6, 9, 10, 11, 12, 13

BAYFIELD

The Little Inn of Bayfield

Main Street, P.O. Box 100, N0M 1G0
(519) 565-2611; (800) 565-1832

Originally a stagecoach stop, the inn has been welcoming guests to this picturesque lakeside village since the 1830s. This designated Heritage inn is replete with fireplaces, en suite whirlpools, sauna, games, and books. Fine dining has long been a tradition, with superb meals and imaginative menus. Guests have a perfect base from which to explore the countryside and attend the Stratford and Blyth festivals. There is much to do any time of the year.

Hosts: Patrick and Gayle Waters
Rooms: 31 (PB) $80-190
Full and Continental Breakfasts
Cards: A, B, C, E
Notes: 2, 3, 4, 5, 6, 7, 8, 9, 10, 11, 12, 13, 14

BLACKSTOCK (PORT PERRY)

Landfall Farm

3120 Highway 7A, Rural Route 1, L0B 1B0
(905) 986-5588

An 1868 stone farmhouse in south central Ontario amidst crop fields and large inviting lawns. Landfall Farm is a designated Heritage site of architectural and historic significance. Its features include air conditioning,

Landfall Farm

an antique shop, a living room with field-stone fireplace, and a screened dining patio. There is also a landscaped swimming pool and a separate enchanting and peaceful pond area. The inn is near the charming lakefront town of Port Perry, a tourist shoppers' paradise. Port Perry offers golf, tennis, fishing, boating, and canoeing, as well as the outstanding feature of an outdoor groomed ice-skating rink on Lake Scugog. Cross-country and downhill skiing are also nearby. Inquire about accommodations for pets. Smoking restricted.

Hosts: Merle and Jennifer Heintzman
Rooms: 3 (SB) $60
Full Breakfast
Credit Cards: None
Notes: 2, 5, 8, 9, 10, 11, 12, 13, 14

BRACEBRIDGE

Century House
Bed and Breakfast

155 Dill Street, P1L 1E5
(705) 645-9903

A charming, air-conditioned, restored century-old home in the province's premier recreational lake district, a two-hour drive north of Toronto. Sandy's breakfasts are creative and generous. Waffles with local maple syrup are a specialty. Century House is close to shopping, beaches, and many craft studios and gal-

leries. Enjoy the sparkling lakes, fall colors, studio tours, and winter cross-country skiing. A friendly dog is in residence. Smoking restricted.

Hosts: Norman Yan and Sandy Yudin
Rooms: 3 (SB) $55-60
Full Breakfast
Credit Cards: None
Notes: 5, 10, 11, 12, 13, 14

BRIGHTON

Sanford House
Bed and Breakfast

20 Platt Street, P.O. Box 1825, K0K 1H0
(613) 475-3930 (phone and FAX)

Stately Victorian home in the friendly town of Brighton. Large, bright, comfortable rooms, with period furniture. Off-street parking, separate guest entrance. Home-baked full breakfasts, silver service. Guests relax in large parlor, veranda, turret round room with view of Presqu'ile area, lounge with TV, VCR, and library. Walk to restaurants, shops, antiques, hiking. A 4K drive to Presqu'ile Provincial Park with sandy beaches, swimming, bird watching, guided walks, waterfowl migration viewing, marsh boardwalk, nature trails, and cycling.

Hosts: Elizabeth and Charles LeBer
Rooms: 3 (SB) $50
Full Breakfast
Credit Cards: None
Notes: 5, 7, 8, 9, 10, 11, 12, 13

BURLINGTON

Metropolitan
Bed and Breakfast
Registry of Toronto

Suite 269, 615 Mount Pleasant Road
Toronto, M4S 3C5
(416) 964-2566; FAX (416) 537-0233

Wilkie House. This large executive home in the Burlington core is just a walk away from Spencer Smith Park on the shores of

7 No smoking; 8 Children welcome; 9 Social drinking allowed; 10 Tennis nearby; 11 Swimming nearby; 12 Golf nearby; 13 Skiing nearby; 14 May be booked through a travel agent.

Lake Ontario. Close to the Joseph Brant Museum and the Burlington Art Centre. Shoppers will enjoy the boutiques of Village Square and the new Mapleview Mall. A nearby bus connects to GO Transit/Toronto. It is less than an hour's drive to Niagara, Kitchener's Mennonite country, Rockton Lion Safari, and the Mountsberg Wildlife Centre. The guest bedroom features two antique spool beds with quilts, private bath, cable TV, and VCR. Off-street parking is available. In residence is a tabby cat and a golden retriever, named Tara. Air-conditioned. Breakfast is served in the bright, formal dining room. $60.

The Yellow Door. This lovely traditional townhouse is on a quiet street overlooking a small park. The home is furnished with English antiques and is friendly and comfortable. The cheerful guest bedroom is well appointed and offers a private bath. The hosts, Pat and Terry, are originally from England and know how to make a visit a pleasant and memorable experience. Nonsmokers only. Air-conditioned. In fine weather guests may wish to enjoy breakfast in the quiet courtyard. $75.

CAMBRIDGE

Langdon Hall Country House Hotel

Rural Route 33, N3H 4R8
(519) 740-2100

This elegant and comfortable accommodation will provide guests with a home away from home. Hidden by deep woods, the country house hotel, built at the turn of the century, has 41 spacious and comfortably appointed guest rooms, most with wood-burning fireplaces. The Garden Restaurant features regional, seasonal cuisine, and E. Langdon Wilk's Bar offers a casual menu and atmosphere. The recreational facilities include billiards, tennis, croquet, a workout area, outdoor swimming pool, and extensive walking trails throughout the surrounding 200 acres. There is also the Amenity Spa, which offers indulgences such as massages, manicures, and body treatments. Enjoy the quality service and attentive courtesy of this truly unique property.

Hosts: William Bennett and Mary Beaton
Rooms: 41 (PB) $175-290
Continental Breakfast
Credit Cards: A, B, C, E
Notes: 2, 3, 4, 5, 8, 9, 10, 11, 12, 14

CARDINAL

Roduner Farm

Rural Route 1, K0E 1E0
(613) 657-4830

Experience the warmth of true country hospitality on this active dairy farm, just one and one-half miles north of Trans-Canada Highway 401. Guests may observe some of the farm activities and relax on the shaded lawn or in the comfortable house. History comes alive at Upper Canada Village and Prehistoric World near Morrisburg; huge freighters lock through at Iroquois; thrill at the Thousand Islands from the deck of a cruise boat. Ottawa with its many attractions is only a one-hour drive away. Inquire about the availability dinner. Cross-country skiing nearby.

Hosts: Walter and Margareta Roduner
Rooms: 2 (1 PB; 1 SB) $40
Full Breakfast
Credit Cards: None
Notes: 2, 5, 6, 7, 8, 9, 11, 12, 13

CARGILL (BRUCE COUNTY)

Cornerbrook Bed and Breakfast

Rural Route 2, N0G 1J0
(519) 366-2629

A warm welcome and relaxed atmosphere await in this modernized century-old brick home completely restored with two open

Cornerbrook

staircases, carpet throughout, a few hand-quilted quilts, and a smattering of antiques to add a flavor of the past. Relax on the well-shaded lawn and enjoy the flower gardens. Convenient to Walkerton, Paisley, and the beaches at Kincardine and Port Elgin. Canoe and fish on the Saugeen River. Enjoy Lake Huron sunsets. Three attractive guest rooms, one with twin beds. Good home-cooked meals. Smoking allowed on the patio.

Hosts: Elaine and John Moffatt
Rooms: 4 (2 PB; 2 SB) $45
Full Breakfast
Credit Cards: None
Notes: 3, 4, 5, 8, 10, 11, 12, 13

CARLETON PLACE _____

Graystones Inn

7 Bridge Street, K7C 2V2
(613) 253-8888; FAX (613) 253-7800

Graystones Inn is in the historic town of Carleton Place in Lanark County, half an hour's drive west of Ottawa. The town is built around the meandering Mississippi River and the Mississippi Lake and is a center for local water and other sports activities, as well as numerous cultural events throughout the year. It is also a convenient 15-minute drive from the New Palladium

Stadium, just outside Ottawa, and a healthy cycling distance from Ottawa.

Host: Barbara Wynne-Edwards
Rooms: 16 (PB) $85-100
Suite: $200
Full and Continental Breakfast
Credit Cards: A, B, C
Notes: 3, 4, 5, 7, 8, 9, 10, 11, 12, 13

Stewart's Landing Bed and Breakfast

Montgomery Park, Rural Route 1, K7C 3P1
(613) 257-1285; FAX (613) 257-5828

On Mississippi Lake, only three minutes from Carleton Place and 30 minutes from Ottawa. Enjoy comfortable smoke-free rooms with lake views. Fishing, boating, canoeing, sailing, and swimming all at the door. Relax on the deck, sip afternoon tea, listen to the loons laugh, and watch swallows dip over the lake. Several small towns and historical attractions are close by. Winter brings cross-country skiing, snowmobiling, ice fishing, and snowshoeing. In Ottawa, enjoy skating on the canal and Winterlude. A full breakfast cooked on the woodstove on cool mornings should make guests' taste buds tingle. Warm hospitality makes this spot truly "close to heaven." Lunch and dinner available upon request.

Hosts: Allen and Peggie Stewart
Rooms: 4 (1 PB; 3 SB) $48-65
Full Breakfast
Credit Cards: None
Notes: 2, 5, 7, 11, 12, 13

COLDWATER _____

Inn the Woods Bed and Breakfast

Rural Route 4, L0K 1E0
(705) 835-6193; FAX (705) 835-6916

Ninety minutes north of Toronto in the Georgian Lakelands area. Central to Barrie, Orillia, and Midland. Offering a scenic, tranquil retreat on seven wooded acres in Medonte Township. The house is a newly built, Colonial-style,

7 No smoking; 8 Children welcome; 9 Social drinking allowed; 10 Tennis nearby; 11 Swimming nearby; 12 Golf nearby; 13 Skiing nearby; 14 May be booked through a travel agent.

trilevel spacious home decorated with country charm. Guest lounge and hot tub. Three major ski resorts, three excellent 18-hole golf courses. Mountain biking and hiking five minutes away. Brochure available.

Hosts: Mary and Bob Pearson
Rooms: 4 (S21.5B) $60-90
Suite: 1 (PB)
Full Breakfast
Credit Cards: A, B
Notes: 4, 5, 7, 8, 10, 11, 12, 13

COLLINGWOOD

Beild House Country Inn

64 Third Street, L9Y 1K5
(705) 444-1522

This turn-of-the-century home has been meticulously converted into an elegant country inn. It features a five-course breakfast of guests' choice, picnic lunches, and afternoon teas, with a selection of hot and cold hors d'oeuvres offered each evening. Marvelous five-course gourmet dinners are also available. Discover the beauty of Georgian Bay and the Blue Mountains at Beild House Country Inn.

Hosts: Bill and Stephanie Barclay
Rooms: 17 (7 PB; 10 SB) $80-125
Full Breakfast
Credit Cards: A, B, C
Notes: 2, 3, 4, 5, 6, 7, 8, 9, 10, 11, 12, 13, 14

DUTTON

Dunwich Farm Bed and Breakfast

Rural Route 1, N0L 1J0
(519) 762-3006

Enjoy this 28-acre farm in scenic southwestern Ontario. This century farm home, surrounded by a variety of trees, shrubs, and gardens, is a haven in any season. Visit the farmyard, collect eggs, feed sheep, cuddle a kitten, admire the Belgian drafthorse, and play with the friendly retrievers. Enjoy a hearty country breakfast, featuring homemade preserves and baked goods. Hiking

trails, marina, beach, and shops within a short drive.

Hosts: Mike and Bonnie Rowe and Family
Rooms: 2 (SB) $45
Full Breakfast
Credit Cards: None
Notes: 2, 5, 6, 8, 9, 12

ELMIRA

Birdland Bed and Breakfast

1 Grey Owl Drive, N3B 1S2
(519) 669-1900

Come and enjoy hospitality in a chalet-style home in a quiet area of town, right in the heart of Ontario's Mennonite country. The guest rooms feature queen-size beds with private baths; one room has a private sauna. Enjoy Elmira's unique craft and gift shops, or take a drive to Elora's scenic gorge. Close to an old covered bridge, the factory outlet mall, and farmers' markets. The old-fashioned town of St. Jacobs is only minutes away. No smoking, please.

Hosts: Robert and Alice Martin
Rooms: 2 (PB) $40-50
Full Breakfast
Credit Cards: None
Notes: 2, 5, 11, 12

The Evergreens

Rural Route 1, N3B 2Z1
(519) 669-2471

Welcome to a quiet bed and breakfast nestled among the evergreens. Enjoy long walks through the forest, swimming in the pool, or cross-country skiing in winter. Two comfortable bedrooms with two guest bathrooms, and breakfast with homemade baking and preserves. In Mennonite country, with Elmira, St. Jacobs, and Elora nearby. North of Elmira, east off Regional Road 21 on Woolrich Road 3. Children welcome. No smoking in home. Open year-round.

Hosts: Rodger and Doris Milliken
Rooms: 2 (SB) $45
Full Breakfast
Credit Cards: None
Notes: 2, 5, 6, 8, 9, 11, 12, 13

NOTES: Credit cards accepted: A MasterCard; B Visa; C American Express; D Discover; E Diners Club; F Other; 2 Personal checks accepted; 3 Lunch available; 4 Dinner available; 5 Open all year; 6 Pets welcome;

Teddy Bear

Teddy Bear Bed and Breakfast Inn

Rural Route 1, N3B 2Z1
(519) 669-2379

Relax and enjoy the hospitality of this gracious and elegant inn, enhanced with Canadiana and quilts. In the Old Order Mennonite countryside close to St. Jacobs, Kitchener-Waterloo's markets, museums, Stratford, Elora, Fergus, and Guelph. Spacious deluxe bedrooms, private bathrooms, TV lounge, and craft shop. Cross-country skiing, golf, boating, hiking, tours, and more nearby. Sumptuous Continental breakfast or full breakfast on request. Seminar and private dining facilities are available.

Hosts: Vivian and Gerrie Smith
Rooms: 3 (PB) $65
Full and Continental Breakfast
Credit Cards: A, B
Notes: 4, 5, 7, 9, 12, 13

ETOBICOKE

Bed and Breakfast Homes of Toronto

P.O. Box 46093, College Park Post Office
Toronto, M5B 2L8
(416) 363-6362

Colwood. This stunningly renovated traditional home is in a prestigious area surrounded by parks and golf courses, yet it is convenient to the airport or downtown, both only 15 minutes away by car. Public transit is within walking distance. James Gardens and the Humber River with its bike trails,

picnic area, and walkways are close by. The house is bright and sunny with an outdoor swimming pool set amid a beautifully landscaped garden. Delicious full breakfasts are served in the light-filled solarium kitchen or on the deck overlooking the pool and garden. Relax in the comfort of this lovely home. Air conditioning and ceiling fans. On-site parking. Five dollars more for private bath. No smoking. Complimentary tea and coffee. Eateries close by. Discount for lengthy stays. Resident Labrador. $65-70.

FERGUS

The Breadalbane Inn

487 St. Andrew Street West, N1M 1P2
(519) 843-4770

This historic inn was built in 1860 by the founder of the town of Fergus. It boasts six tastefully decorated and comfortable bedrooms, each with en suite washroom. The inn also features four dining rooms, two main and two private, seating 75. It has been recommended by the Epicure of *Toronto Life* magazine every year since 1984. Lunch is available Tuesday through Friday. Dinner is available Tuesday through Sunday. Cross-country skiing in area. No smoking in the main dining room. A special getaway package for two featuring two nights' stay, two Continental breakfasts, a gift certificate for dinner, and a bottle of the house wine for $219.

Hosts: Jean and Phil Cardinal
Rooms: 6 (PB) $60-85
Cotinental Breakfast
Credit Cards: A, B
Notes: 2, 5, 8, 10, 11, 12

GANANOQUE

The Victoria Rose Inn

279 King Street West, K7G 2G7
(613) 382-3368

This stately mansion, with a commanding central tower, was built by the first mayor

7 No smoking; 8 Children welcome; 9 Social drinking allowed; 10 Tennis nearby; 11 Swimming nearby; 12 Golf nearby; 13 Skiing nearby; 14 May be booked through a travel agent.

in 1872. Nine elegant guest rooms with private bath and air conditioning. The honeymoon suite has a marble fireplace and Jacuzzi. Guests are welcome to enjoy the parlor, veranda, and two acres of garden. The ballroom is an ideal location for a family reunion, special party, or business meeting. The Rose Garden Tea Room is open in the summer for lunch, afternoon tea, and dinner. Close to an excellent selection of restaurants, the summer playhouse, boat tours, and interesting shopping. Cross-country skiing in area.

Hosts: Liz and Ric Austin
Rooms: 9 (PB) $85-135
Full Breakfast
Credit Cards: A, B, C, E
Notes: 3, 4, 5, 7, 10, 11, 12, 13

GLEBE

Ottawa Bed and Breakfast

488 Cooper Street, Ottawa, K1R 5H9
(613) 563-0161; (800) 461-7889

1. Cottagelike home. Double bedroom with TV and desk. Shared bath. Resident cat and dog. No smoking. Hosts speak French. $55-73.

GODERICH

La Brassine

Highway 21, Kitchigami Camp Road, N7A 3X8
(519) 524-6300

This 100-year-old farmhouse sits on 103 acres stretching from Highway 21 to Lake Huron with its own private access to the beach. Relax in the large, air-conditioned farmhouse that is decorated with European furniture and enjoy French gourmet dinners year-round.

Hosts: Tom and Nicky Blanchard-Hublet
Rooms: 5 (SB) $56 Canadian
Continental Breakfast
Credit Cards: A, B, C
Notes: 4, 5, 9, 10, 11, 12

Käthi's Guesthouse

Rural Route 4, N7A 3Y1
(519) 524-8587

This farm is set amid the rolling hills, close to Lake Huron and 12 kilometers east of Goderich. Enjoy the privacy of the Guesthouse with two bedrooms and en suite baths. A nice place for two couples traveling together or for young families with children. A crib is available. The hosts provide a full country-style breakfast. Friendly pets. English and German are spoken here. Open year-round. Reservations preferred. Deposit required. Special rates for longer stays.

Hosts: Fritz and Käthi Beyerlein
Rooms: 2 (PB) $50
Full Breakfast
Credit Cards: None
Notes: 2, 5, 8, 11

GRAFTON

Frome Farm

Rural Route 1, K0K 2G0
(905) 349-2815

This 120-year-old country house, on an active 150-acre farm, has been comfortably modernized for guests' comfort and enjoyment. The house is in the rolling Northumberland Hills, near Lake Ontario and the historic towns of Cobourg and Port Hope. Full breakfast served daily; dinner on request. Home cooking, baking, jams, and preserves.

Host: Phillippa W. Wilmer
Rooms: 2 (PB) $85
Full Breakfast
Credit Cards: None
Notes: 2, 3, 4, 5, 7, 9, 10, 11, 12

GRAVENHURST (MUSKOKA)

Amelioratvie Place: Lakefront Bed and Breakfast

590 Phillip Street, East, P1P 1M3
(705) 687-6889

A 4,000-square-foot lakefront home two hours north of Toronto, four blocks from the center of a little tourist town. Hosts offer a cathedral ceiling entrance, queen-size beds, private three-piece bathrooms, private guest living room with fireplace, and warm cedar decor. Continental breakfast with home baking and evening snacks. Swimming, canoeing, and small motor boat. Weekly and monthly rates.

Hosts: Jeff and Gail Henderson
Rooms: 2 (PB) $60-90
Continental Breakfast
Credit Cards: None
Notes: 2, 7, 9, 10, 11, 12, 13

Cunningham's

Cunningham's Bed and Breakfast

175 Clairmont Road, P1P 1H9
(705) 687-4511

Enjoy gracious living in an English garden setting in this modern home on a quiet cul-de-sac at the edge of town. Friendly family room with fireplace and TV. Enjoy home baking and preserves, afternoon tea or evening snack in the sunny Muskoka Room. It is a short walk to *Segwun* steamship tours, Bethune House, theater, restaurants, shops, and parks. Off Bay Street, five blocks west of the post office.

Hosts: Leona (Lee) and David Cunningham
Rooms: 3 (1 PB; 2 SB) $50-60
Full Breakfast
Credit Cards: None
Notes: 2, 5, 7, 8, 9, 10, 11, 12, 13

HAWKESTONE

The Verandahs

Rural Route 2, L0L 1T0
(705) 487-1910 (phone and FAX)

Victorian-style home with deep verandas on three sides on large landscaped lot close to Lake Simcoe. Bright, attractive, and comfortable interior with a welcoming ambience. Guest sitting room with fireplace, TV, books, and games. Beds are comfortable and covered with goose-down duvets. Winter season December 28 through March 31, and summer June 1 through October 15. Close to ski resorts, snowmobile trails, and ice fishing. Boat launch and beach within one-half kilometer and many attractions nearby.

Hosts: Pearl and Norm Guthrie
Rooms: 3 (1 PB; 2 SB) $55-60
Full Breakfast
Credit Cards: A, B
Notes: 2, 7, 9, 11, 12, 13

HEIDELBERG

Evergreen Lawns

64 Hilltop Court, Box 155, N0B 1Y0
(519) 699-4453

Welcome to Evergreen Lawns Bed and Breakfast in the quiet village of Heidelberg. In the hub of Mennonite country, just minutes away from the renowned farmers' markets and tourist attractions of St. Jacobs and Elmira. Close to the first outlet mall in Ontario, which opened in July 1994. Come experience another way of life in a unique country setting! Hosts are retired farmers living in a new split-level house on a large lot built mostly by themselves. They enjoy traveling and meeting people.

Hosts: Henry and Edna Shantz
Rooms: 2 (SB) $40-50
Full Breakfast
Credit Cards: None
Notes: 5, 7, 12

7 No smoking; 8 Children welcome; 9 Social drinking allowed; 10 Tennis nearby; 11 Swimming nearby; 12 Golf nearby; 13 Skiing nearby; 14 May be booked through a travel agent.

KINGSTON

Hotel Belvedere

141 King Street East, K7L 2Z9
(800) 559-0584

A delightful collection of 20 unique rooms, each freshly decorated in period style, all with their own private bathrooms. Very convenient central location. Continental breakfast can be brought to the guests' room or served on the lovely terrace. Within walking distance of the university, downtown retail shops, Lake Ontario, and the Thousand Island boat tours. Some non-smoking rooms are available.

Rooms: 20 (PB) $79-149
Continental Breakfast
Credit Cards: A, B, C, E, F
Notes: 2, 5, 8, 9, 11, 12, 14

KIRKFIELD

Metropolitan Bed and Breakfast Registry of Toronto

Suite 269, 615 Mount Pleasant Road
Toronto, Ontario M4S 3C5
(416) 964-2566; FAX (416) 537-0233

Sir William MacKenzie Inn. This grand 35-room mansion was built in 1888. On 13 acres of beautiful woods and lawns, it offers visitors the opportunity of going back to an era when leisure, grace, and beauty symbolized the good life. The inn features several comfortable lounge areas for relaxing, a homey breakfast room, a large game room, an extensive video and book library, and a separate restaurant. The six spacious guest bedrooms all have en suite bathrooms. Sit back and enjoy the fresh country air on the spacious veranda. Family-style dinners are available upon request. A delicious hot English-style gourmet breakfast is served each morning. $75-90.

KITCHENER

Austrian Home

90 Franklin Street North, N2A 1X9
(519) 893-4056

Enjoy this bed and breakfast in an Austrian-style home, 7.5 kilometers from the 401. Kitchener Transit is close by. The Austrian Home offers neat and friendly bedrooms with guest bathroom and European-style breakfast. Enjoy the garden and picnic area, as well as the many historic and cultural attractions in the area. Hosts speak English and German.

Hosts: Frank and Maria Holl
Rooms: 2 (SB) $45
Full Breakfast
Credit Cards: None
Notes: 2, 5, 7, 11, 12, 13

Roots and Wings

11 Sunbridge Crescent, N2K 1T4
(519) 743-4557; FAX (519) 743-4166

Quiet street offers country living in the city with Jacuzzi, pool, and walking trails. Choose twin, queen-size, or double beds. Full breakfast is included. From charming and unique shopping and sumptuous hearty meals to delightful country sightseeing, spend time and ride on horse-drawn trolleys to the heart of Mennonite country. Quaint villages and historic sights abound. A 30-minute drive to Stratford and Shakespearean plays, and a 90-minute drive to Niagara Falls. The host will help with sightseeing plans so as to not miss exciting new experiences.

Host: Fay Teal-Aram
Rooms: 3 (1 PB; 2 SB) $50
Full Breakfast
Credit Cards: A
Notes: 5, 6, 8, 9, 11

Why Not Bed and Breakfast

34 Amherst Drive, N2P 1C9
(519) 748-4577

Relax in this friendly, hospitable home in a quiet area, only two minutes from Highway

401 and 20 minutes from downtown. Two comfortable guest bedrooms with five-piece guest bathroom. Delicious breakfast menu. Complimentary evening beverages available. Swimming pool on property. Within a five-minute walk of beautiful forest trails, Grand River, art gallery, golf course, tennis, and indoor skating; restaurants and tourist attractions also close by. Personal checks accepted for deposit only. Inquire about accommodations for children.

Hosts: Paula and David Farmer
Rooms: 2 (SB) $50-55
Full and Continental Breakfast
Credit Cards: None
Notes: 5, 7, 9, 10, 10, 11, 12, 13

Red Eagle Guest House

LANARK

Red Eagle Guest House

Rural Route 3, K0G 1K0
(613) 259-3058

Relax and enjoy a full breakfast at this inn in Poland. For the budget-minded, guests have access to the fully equipped kitchen. Mingle in the four-bedroom guest house and hike or ski the inn's 187 acres. For a real retreat, try the log cabin in the bush; no hydro guarantees a back-to-nature vacation. Family, group, and weekly rates. Host speaks Polish, English, and French. Pets welcome.

Hosts: Donna A. and Jacques Rubacha
Rooms: 4 (SB) $45-55
Full Breakfast
Credit Cards: None
Notes: 2, 3, 4, 5, 6, 8, 9, 10, 11, 12, 13

LANCASTER

MacPine Farms

Box 51, K0C 1N0
(613) 347-2003

Welcome to MacPine Holstein Farm on the shores of the St. Lawrence River, just south of the 401, a half-mile east of the Lancaster exit, and ten miles from the Québec border. Enjoy this modernized century home with comfortable new beds. Shaded by large old pine trees. A five-minute walk to the cottage on the river, where guests can swim, paddleboat, fish for Lancaster perch, or relax and watch the ocean ships go by. Area attractions include golf, fishing, boating, and craft and antique shops. Visit Upper Canada Village or the Highland Games. Go sightseeing or shopping in Montréal, Cornwall, or Ottawa. Enjoy breakfast in the new sunroom. Smoke-free home. Children are welcome.

Hosts: Guelda and Robert MacRae
Rooms: 3 (SB) $40-45
Full Breakfast
Credit Cards: None
Notes: 2, 5, 9, 11, 12, 13

LION'S HEAD

Steinwald Bed and Breakfast

Rural Route 4, N0H 1W0
(519) 795-7894

Experience a stay at one of the Bruce Peninsula's original log homes surrounded by a nature-lover's paradise. Amiable hosts are eager to share the pleasures of their charming home and property. Full breakfast is

Steinwald

7 No smoking; 8 Children welcome; 9 Social drinking allowed; 10 Tennis nearby; 11 Swimming nearby; 12 Golf nearby; 13 Skiing nearby; 14 May be booked through a travel agent.

served in the cozy "keeping room" around the pioneer fireplace. In fine weather, guests may be served on the patio overlooking the garden sloping down to the Stokes River. Packed lunch available. Smoking restricted.

Hosts: Don and Vonnie Robinson
Rooms: 3 (SB) $50-55
Full Breakfast
Credit Cards: None
Notes: 2, 5, 9, 10, 11, 12, 13

LONDON

Clermont Place

679 Clermont Avenue, N5X 1N3
(519) 672-0767; FAX (519) 672-2449

A modern home in a parklike setting with its own heated outdoor pool. Central air conditioning, three attractive bedrooms sharing a four-piece bath. A full Canadian breakfast is served in the dining room or by the pool or gardens. Four free tennis courts behind the house; two public golf courses five minutes away. Forty minutes from the Stratford Shakespeare Festival. Close to the University of Western Ontario and University Hospital in Northeast London. Cross-country skiing in area.

Hosts: Doug and Jacki McAndless
Rooms: 3 (SB) $45-50
Full Breakfast
Credit Cards: B
Notes: 2, 3, 4, 5, 9, 10, 11, 12, 13

Hilltop

82 Compton Crescent, N6C 4G1
(519) 681-7841

Modern air-conditioned home on a quiet crescent in South London, with easy access to Highway 401 and downtown London. Offers twin and double rooms, each with private bath. Dining room overlooks city and outdoor pool, which is available to guests. Nonsmoking adults. No pets.

Hosts: Beverley and Douglas Thomson
Rooms: 2 (PB) $55
Full Breakfast
Credit Cards: None
Notes: 5, 7

Idlewyld Inn

36 Grand Avenue, N6C 1K8
(519) 433-2891

Idlewyld Inn is a Victorian mansion recently restored to a luxury inn. All 27 guest rooms are unique and beautifully decorated. Jacuzzi suites and fireplace suites. A complimentary breakfast is served each morning. Beautiful outdoor courtyard and gardens. Room service dinner is provided with 48-hour notice. Packages available.

Rooms: 27 (PB) $110-165
Continental Breakfast
Credit Cards: A, B, C, E
Notes: 2, 3, 5, 7, 8, 9, 11, 12, 13, 14

Overdale Bed and Breakfast

2 Normandy Gardens, N6H 4A9
(519) 641-0236

Overdale is a contemporary home in Northwest London. It is air-conditioned, comfortable, and quiet on a large lot with many flowers, trees, birds, and squirrels. Although almost in the country, it is just a 12-minute drive from downtown and nine minutes from the University of Western Ontario. There is a guest sitting room with TV etc. The hosts pride themselves on providing full gourmet breakfasts; special diets can also be accommodated.

Hosts: Bill and Jessica Mann
Rooms: 3 (1 PB; 2 SB) $46-55 Canadian
Full Breakfast
Credit Cards: None
Notes: 5, 8, 9, 12

The Rose House

526 Dufferin Avenue, N6B 2A2
(519) 433-9978

The Rose House is a centrally air-conditioned, 125-year-old home on a fine residential street adjacent to downtown. This area has many historically designated homes. Within 15 minutes of the University of Western Ontario, all hospitals, major malls, and recreational facilities. It is a comfortable walk to live theater, museums, art galleries, and fine restaurants. Breakfast is a full nutritional meal served family style. No small children. No federal or provincial taxes. Free parking. Reservations recommended.

Hosts: Betty and Douglas Rose
Rooms: 3 (1 PB; 2 SB) $40-55
Full Breakfast
Credit Cards: A, B
Notes: 5, 7, 9, 10, 11, 12, 13

Serena's Place

720 Headley Drive, N6H 3V6
(519) 471-6228

Air-conditioned home in prestigious residential area of West London. Three bedrooms and full bath. Sunroom for relaxation. Near Springbank Park and Thames Valley Golf Course. Skiing nearby. Fifteen minutes from Theatre London. Bus service at the door. Open year-round. Occasionally accepts personal checks.

Host: Serena Warren
Rooms: 3 (SB) $25-45
Credit Cards: None
Notes: 5, 12, 13

LUCKNOW

Perennial Pleasures Guesthome

Box 304, 558 Rose Street, N0G 2H0
(519) 528-3601

Perennial Pleasures Guesthome

A friendly welcome awaits. Three bedrooms, each attractively decorated and equipped with a comfortable double bed (two with desks). Enjoy living room, dining room, deck, and large colorful garden. One-story modern home. Enjoy walking, shopping, and antiquing in the nearby village. Lake Huron is 15 minutes away. Blythe Summer Theatre is 30 minutes. Many conservation areas offer cross-country skiing, snowmobiling, hiking, fishing, and boating.

Host: Joan Martin
Rooms: 3 (SB) $35
Full Breakfast
Credit Cards: None
Notes: 2, 3, 4, 5, 7, 8, 9, 11, 12

MARKHAM

Metropolitan Bed and Breakfast Registry of Toronto

Suite 269, 615 Mount Pleasant Road
Toronto, Ontario M4S 3C5
(416) 964-2566; FAX (416) 537-0233

Valleyview. A 1950s style home down an apple tree lane in this town just north of Toronto. The house is furnished in a traditional style and the hostess's needlepoint chairs accent the living room. Relax under the old willow tree by the babbling brook. The separate guest level has its own entrance, is roomy and inviting, and has a private bath. There is a guest refrigerator and tea-making facilities. Enjoy breakfast in the Canadian dining room or, weather permitting, on the private deck. $55.

McDONALD'S CORNERS

McDonald's Corners Bed and Breakfast

Lanark County Road 12, P.O. Box 81, K0G 1M0
(613) 278-2336

Naturalists and bird watchers will appreciate this scenic hillside-setting on the edge

7 No smoking; 8 Children welcome; 9 Social drinking allowed; 10 Tennis nearby; 11 Swimming nearby; 12 Golf nearby; 13 Skiing nearby; 14 May be booked through a travel agent.

of a hardwood forest. Quiet two bedrooms, bathroom, lounge, and breakfast area in a private guest apartment. Enjoy the exhilerating cross-country ski trail, Lady slipper orchids at Purdon Conservation Area in late June, and excellent fishing on beautiful Dalhousie Lake. Advance reservations are required.

Host: Penelope Bass
Rooms: 2 (SB) $50
Full Breakfast
Credit Cards: None
Notes: 2, 5, 7, 8, 9, 11, 12, 13

MERRICKVILLE

Gypsy Cove

Rural Route 4, K0G 1N0
(613) 269-4413

Relax in a quiet rural setting, 45 minutes south of Ottawa, north side of the Rideau Canal system. Drive three miles to historic Merrickville, with museum, art galleries, boutiques, and many fine dining establishments or just unwind in hosts' home.

Hosts: Donald and Jean Suffron
Rooms: 3 (SB) $45-50
Full Breakfast
Credit Cards: None
Notes: 5, 7, 8, 12

Millisle Bed and Breakfast

205 Mill Street, P.O. Box 341, K0G 1N0
(613) 269-3627; FAX (613) 269-4735

Circa 1850, this three-story Victorian home has been elegantly restored. The inn boasts original stained-glass windows, a wraparound veranda, and a beautiful parklike setting. Adjacent to Rideau River/Canal waterway in old Merrickville (circa 1790), a village with over 100 historic properties, shops, pubs, antiques, and more than 20 artist studios. All guest rooms have private baths. Smoke free, pet free, central heat and air. Exclusive dinner package with Baldachin Dining Room. Forty-five minutes to Ottawa, 30 minutes to highway 401 and

US-Canada border crossing. Children over eight are welcome.

Hosts: Kathy and Derry Thompson
Rooms: 5 (PB) $68
Full Breakfast
Credit Cards: A, B, C
Notes: 2, 5, 7, 9, 11, 12, 13

Sam Jakes Inn

118 Main Street East, P.O. Box 580, K0G 1N0
(613) 269-3711; (800) 567-4667
FAX (613) 269-3713

Sam Jakes Inn is an 1860s Heritage inn. Thirty guest rooms, each with private bath; an outdoor patio, a wine bar, and a full service dining room specializing in Eastern Ontario cuisine. The village is filled with various craft and antique shops, artists' studios, boutiques, pubs, and glassblowers. Nature lovers can enjoy cycling, canoeing, boating, bird watching, and fishing.

Host: Gary Clarke
Rooms: 30 (PB) $83-117 Canadian
Credit Cards: A, B, C, D, E
Notes: 3, 4, 5, 7, 9, 11, 12, 13, 14

MILLBANK

Honeybrook Farm

Rural Route 1, N0K 1L0
(519) 595-4604

Gracious guest accommodation in the heart of Ontario theater and Mennonite country. Completely restored 1866 split granite home offers spacious guest bedrooms and bathrooms with amenities of first-class accommodation. Relax in the recreation room. Enjoy refreshments on the house. Choose breakfast from a varied menu. Gourmet dinners by prearrangement. Twenty minutes' drive to the theaters of Stratford and Drayton and the markets of Kitchener-Waterloo and St. Jacobs.

Hosts: Alveretta and Jack Henderson
Rooms: 2 (1 PB; 1 SB) $45-50
Full Breakfast
Credit Cards: None
Notes: 2, 3, 5, 7, 9

NOTES: Credit cards accepted: A MasterCard; B Visa; C American Express; D Discover; E Diners Club; F Other; 2 Personal checks accepted; 3 Lunch available; 4 Dinner available; 5 Open all year; 6 Pets welcome;

MINDEN

The Stone House

Rural Route 2, K0M 2K0
(705) 286-1250

Rustic elegance in secluded, mature woods. Four styles of accommodation, each offering full privacy. The Stone House has two bedrooms, kitchen, and full bath. Large fieldstone fireplace in living room. The Roof Garden is an airy chalet-style studio with two sun decks, full bath, and kitchen. The Gingerbread Cottage has a full bath and a screened porch. The Sugar Cabin has full bath and screened porch. Laundry facilities available, and coffee and tea always on tap. Swimming, boating, and white-water rafting within one mile. Two hours from Toronto. Open May 15 to October 15. Personal checks accepted in advance. Call about pets.

Host: Phyllis Howarth
Rooms: 5 (2 PB; 3 SB) $40-75
Continental Breakfast
Credit Cards: None
Notes: 7, 9, 10, 11, 12

MORRISBURG

Upper Canada Bed and Breakfast

P.O. Box 436, K0C 1X0
(613) 543-3336

This home overlooks the St. Lawrence Seaway in the peaceful outskirts of Morrisburg. Although in the country, it is less than 15 minutes to Upper Canada Village, golf courses, the Playhouse, Queen's Gardens, nature trails, and the Seaway locks. Always lots to see and do nearby. It is only one hour to Ottawa and 90 minutes to Montréal. Down-home hospitality and good food are trademarks of this bed and breakfast.

Hosts: Nancy and George Davies
Rooms: 4 (SB) $50
Full Breakfast
Credit Cards: None
Notes: 8, 9, 11, 12

NEW HAMBURG

Glenalby Dairy Farms

Rural Route 1, N0B 2G0
(519) 625-8353

Down-on-the-farm hospitality. Scenic, award-winning, sixth-generation farm. Lassie collies, English-style flower gardens, woodland and bluebird trails. Reserve afternoon tea, country suppers of cabbage rolls, oven-fresh bread, and wild berry pie. Early Canadian brass or pine beds topped with handmade quilts. Jams, jellies, and quilts for sale. Ten minutes to Stratford Theater, Amish-Mennonite area and their farmers' market, or Shakespeare's antique shops. Children welcome. Central air.

Host: Mrs. Ruby McMillan
Rooms: 4 (1 PB; 3 SB) $50-70
Full and Continental Breakfast
Credit Cards: None
Notes: 3, 4, 8, 10 ,11, 12, 13

The Pines

124 Shade Street, N0B 2G0
(519) 662-3525

Minutes from the Stratford Shakespeare Festival and convenient to Toronto, guests are welcome to this century home in New Hamburg. Nestled beside a river, beneath towering pines, guest rooms are furnished with antiques. Double Jacuzzi also available.

Hosts: Malcolm and Winsome Aird
Rooms: 3 (1 PB; 2SB) $55-75
Full Breakfast
Credit Cards: None
Notes: 2, 5, 7, 8, 9, 10, 12, 13

The Waterlot

17 Huron Street, N0B 2G0
(519) 662-2020; FAX (519) 662-2114

The Waterlot opened in the fall of 1974 and from the outset it has been committed to quality of ambience and service. Two large and comfortably appointed rooms share a memorable marbled shower, bidet, water

7 No smoking; 8 Children welcome; 9 Social drinking allowed; 10 Tennis nearby; 11 Swimming nearby; 12 Golf nearby; 13 Skiing nearby; 14 May be booked through a travel agent.

closet, wet vanity, and sitting area. Suite has a private bath and a living area. The Waterlot is one of Ontario's finest dining establishments.

Host: Gordon Elker
Rooms: 3 (1 PB; 2 SB) $65-85 Canadian
Continental Breakfast
Credit Cards: A, B, C, E
Notes: 2, 3, 4, 5, 7, 8, 9, 10, 11, 12, 13

The Waterlot

NEWTON

Country Charm

Rural Route 1, N0K 1R0
(519) 595-8789

Come and enjoy bed and breakfast in the hosts' large country home just one kilometer south of Newton. Relax around a campfire (weather permitting) or watch the sunset near the creek. There are a sawmill and buggy shop at the crossroads. Skidoo trail bakery and cheese factory are favorite spots for guests. Jacuzzi and trampoline for guests' enjoyment. Open year-round. "Share a memory with us."

Hosts: Ezra and Marlene Streicher
Rooms: 3 (1 PB; 2 SB) $45
Full Breakfast
Credit Cards: None
Notes: 5, 7, 8, 10, 11, 12, 13

NIAGARA FALLS

Gretna Green

5077 River Road, L2E 3G7
(905) 357-2081

This tourist home offers bright, comfortable rooms with en suite bathrooms. All guest rooms are air-conditioned and have TV. Families are welcome. This is "a home away from home" where guests are treated to a full, home-cooked breakfast that includes muffins, scones, jams, and jellies. Niagara has much to offer: the falls, Skylow Tower, IMAX Theatre, the Floral Clock, the Rose Gardens, and museums. Bike rentals available. Personal checks accepted for deposit only. Smoking restricted.

Hosts: Stan and Marg Gardiner
Rooms: 4 (PB) $45-65
Full Breakfast
Credit Cards: None
Notes: 8, 9, 10, 12

The International Bed & Breakfast Club, Inc.

504 Amherst Street, Buffalo, NY 14207
(800) 723-4262; FAX (716) 873-4462

ON2803PP. Canadian villa overlooking the Niagara River in Niagara Falls, Ontario. Within walking distance to the falls. Rooms include air conditioning and cable TV. Three guest rooms include a double and two queen-size bedded rooms with en suite private shower and baths. Guests enjoy the setting and the view of the river. Ample parking. Continental breakfast. $55-65.

ON4744PP. This inn is on the Niagara's most scenic drive overlooking the river and only four blocks from the American and Canadian falls and Queen Victoria Park. The inn is distinguished by Strauss crystal chandeliers, and guests will find Old World charm and hospitality throughout. Five rooms with bath en suite are available. The George Bernard Shaw Theatre is only 20 minutes away on the scenic Niagara Parkway. Gourmet breakfast and afternoon tea are available. Guests have ample free parking on the premises. $85-129.

NIAGARA-ON-THE-LAKE

The International Bed & Breakfast Club, Inc.

504 Amherst Street, Buffalo, NY 14207
(800) 723-4262; FAX (716) 873-4462

ON6865PP. This bed and breakfast is set in the outskirts of Niagara-on-the-Lake on an acre of private lawns and mature trees. Exotic plants surround the large indoor pool, heated during the summer months. Bring own wine to enjoy at the poolside bar. Hosts have a whirlpool and sauna, and guests are welcome to picnic or sunbathe in the garden. Niagara-on-the-Lake was the original capital of Upper Canada. It has beautifully restored architecture, tree-lined avenues, exclusive boutiques, and fine restaurants. Enjoy a leisurely browse downtown for a wealth of fine quality clothing, antiques, and crafts. Niagara-on-the-Lake's most famous attraction is the Shaw Festival. From spring through October spectacular professional theater, on three stages, of plays written during the lifetime of George Bernard Shaw. Enjoy driving or cycling along the picturesque, manicured parkway following the Niagara River. Full breakfast. $75-85.

The Kiely Inn

209 Queen Street, L0S 1J0
(416) 468-4588

Elegant Georgian residence on one acre of landscaped garden overlooking golf course and Lake Ontario. Many verandas and porches. Eleven guest rooms with en suite bathrooms and telephones. Six rooms with fireplaces. Guest parlor. Inn furnished with

The Kiely Inn

antiques and decorated in period style. Sixty-seat, full-service dining room. Continental plus breakfast included in room rate. Ample on-site parking.

Hosts: Ray and Heather Pettit
Rooms: 11 (PB) $75-168
Continental Breakfast
Credit Cards: A, B, C
Notes: 3, 4, 5, 9, 10, 11, 12, 14

The Old Bankhouse

10 Front Street, P.O. Box 1708, L0S 1J0
(905) 468-7136

A gracious 19th-century inn in the heart of the old town. Stroll to theaters, fine dining, and quaint shops. Overlooking Lake Ontario. A perfect retreat for refreshing the spirit and soul. Eight tastefully decorated room/suites. Air-conditioned and on-site parking. Highly recommended by many major publications. Massages available by prior arrangements.

Host: Marjorie Ironmonger
Rooms: 8 (6 PB; 2 SB) $75-195
Full Breakfast
Credit Cards: A, B, C
Notes: 5, 7, 9, 10, 11, 12, 14

Wren House

278 Regent Street, Box 311, L0S 1J0
(905) 468-4361

Historic home, circa 1838, in the heart of historic Niagara-on-the-Lake. Quaint shops, festival theaters, dining, and historic sites within walking distance. Breakfast is an

7 No smoking; 8 Children welcome; 9 Social drinking allowed; 10 Tennis nearby; 11 Swimming nearby; 12 Golf nearby; 13 Skiing nearby; 14 May be booked through a travel agent.

assortment of special dishes and baked goods. Wineries, fruit orchards, Niagara Falls, and many other attractions are nearby. Central air-conditioning.

Hosts: Barbara and Warren Aldridge
Rooms: 3 (PB) $80-90
Full Breakfast
Credit Cards: None
Notes: 2, 5, 7, 9, 10, 12

NORTH YORK

Bed and Breakfast Homes of Toronto

P.O. Box 46093, College Park Post Office
Toronto, M5B 2L8
(416) 363-6362

Kingslake Korners. Comfort, relaxation, and hospitality await guests in a cheerful, quiet residential area of North Toronto in a family home setting, 20 to 30 minutes from downtown. Easy access to 401 and 404, and excellent public transportation. On the "doorstep" of Ford Centre for the Performing Arts. Canada's Wonderland to the north and the Metro Zoo to the east. Seneca College, York University, Ontario Science Center, Black Creek Pioneer Village, and Edward's Gardens. Relax in a clean, spacious, and tastefully decorated guest room. Children welcome. Crib and high chair are available, and playground and parks are nearby. Choice of Continental or full breakfast served in the dining room. Special diets can be accommodated. Central air. On-site parking. No smoking. Pugsley and Pokey (dog and cat) reside. No pets. $45-55.

ORILLIA

Betty and Tony's Waterside Bed and Breakfast

677 Broadview Avenue, L3V 6P1
(800) 308-2579; FAX (705) 326-2262

A modern air-conditioned house. Guests are welcomed with afternoon tea and get a full breakfast served on Wedgwood china. There are three guest rooms, a guest lounge—but guests are encouraged to visit with the hosts—also a computer room. On the 300-mile-long Trent Severn Waterway with 80 feet of dock on-site and 15-foot draught. There is ample off-road parking. Five minutes' walk to a municipal park and supervised sandy beaches. No smoking in the guest rooms.

Hosts: Betty and Tony Bridgens
Rooms: 3 (SB) $60-70
Full Breakfast
Credit Cards: None
Notes: 2, 3, 4, 5, 6, 8, 9, 10, 11, 12, 13

Pine Tree House

225 Matchedash Street, North, L3V 4V5
(705) 329-0518; (800) 375-9897

This circa 1882 Victorian home is in Orillia, a small city nestled between Lakes Simcoe and Couchiching, one hour north of Toronto. Walk to downtown shops and restaurants, the opera house, and the Port of Orillia. In winter, cross-country or downhill ski. Enjoy afternoon tea on linen-dressed trays in the parlor or on the veranda in temperate weather. Air-conditioned. Two rooms with charming, traditional surroundings reminiscent of a small inn.

Hosts: Rob Reid and Tom Ruechel
Rooms: 2 (SB) $68
Full Breakfast
Credit Cards: A, B
Notes: 5, 7, 10, 11, 12, 13

OTTAWA

Albert House

478 Albert Street, K1R 5B5
(613) 236-4479; (800) 267-1982

Gracious Victorian home built in 1875 by a noted Canadian architect. Each room is individually decorated and has private facilities, telephone, TV, and air conditioning. Guest lounge with fireplace. Famous Albert House breakfast. Parking is available, but within walking distance to most attractions. There are two large, friendly dogs in the house.

Hosts: Cathy and John Delroy
Rooms: 17 (PB) $68-90
Full Breakfast
Credit Cards: A, B, C, E
Notes: 5, 9, 14

Ambiance Bed and Breakfast

330 Nepean Street, K1R 5G6
(613) 563-0421

Ambiance is a well-kept secret in the heart of downtown Ottawa, within walking distance to the Parliament hall and many galleries and museums. The home is a lovely Victorian house mixing antiques and contemporary decorations to create a feeling of warmth. Hosts are health- and creative-conscious with food. Bike rentals. Hosts emphasize friendliness to make the guests feel welcome and comfortable.

Hosts: Steven and Laura MacDonald
Rooms: 4 (2 PB; 2 SB) $51-76
Full Breakfast
Credit Cards: A, B, C, E
Notes: 5, 7, 8, 9

Auberge McGee's Inn

185 Daly Avenue, K1N 6E8
(613) 237-6089; (800) 2MCGEES
FAX (613) 237-6201

Celebrating 11 years of award-wining hospitality. Fourteen-room historic Victorian inn, downtown on a quiet avenue. Within walking distance of excellent restaurants, museums, Parliament, Rideau Canal, and University of Ottawa. Ten guest rooms with private baths, four with shared baths. Cable TV, telephone, Jacuzzi en suites. Kitchenette facilities for longer stays. Complimentary full breakfast. Reservations recommended. Inquire about children. Limited social drinking allowed.

Hosts: Anne Schutte and Mary Unger
Rooms: 14 (10 PB; 4 SB) $58-150
Full Breakfast
Credit Cards: A, B
Notes: 5, 7, 10, 11, 12, 13

Australis Guest House

Australis Guest House

35 Marlborough Avenue, K1N 8E6
(613) 235-8461

This guest house is the oldest established and still operating bed and breakfast in Ottawa. On a quiet, tree-lined street one block from the Rideau River, with its ducks and swans, and Strathcona Park, it is a 20-minute walk to the Parliament buildings. The home boasts leaded windows, fireplaces, oak floors, and unique eight-foot stained-glass windows. The spacious rooms, including one with private bathroom, feature many collectibles from different parts of the world. The hearty, delicious breakfasts, with home-baked breads and pastries, help start the day right. Multiple winner of the Ottawa Hospitality Award and recommended by *Newsweek*.

Hosts: Brian and Carol Waters
Rooms: 3 (1 PB; 2 SB) $52-70
Full Breakfast
Credit Cards: None
Notes: 5, 7, 10, 11, 12, 13

Beatrice Lyon Guest House

479 Slater Street, K1R 5C2
(613) 236-3904

This is a beautiful old-fashioned family home surrounded by gracious large trees. The bed and breakfast is within walking

7 No smoking; 8 Children welcome; 9 Social drinking allowed; 10 Tennis nearby; 11 Swimming nearby; 12 Golf nearby; 13 Skiing nearby; 14 May be booked through a travel agent.

distance of the Parliament buildings, the Museum of Man, the National Archives, Byward Market, Rideau Canal, and Hull, Québec. Children are welcome, and baby-sitting can be arranged. The host is a member of the Downtown Bed and Breakfast Association.

Host: Beatrice Lyon
Rooms: 3 (SB) $45
Full Breakfast
Credit Cards: None
Notes: 2, 5, 8, 9, 10, 11, 12, 13

Blue Spruces

187 Glebe Avenue, K1S 2C6
(613) 236-8521

This lovely Edwardian home has been furnished with fine Victorian English and Canadian pine antiques, and is in Ottawa's downtown core. Minutes from Parliament. Delicious full breakfast, including freshly ground coffee, is served each morning in the elegant dining room.

Hosts: Patricia and John Hunter
Rooms: 3 (PB) $70
Full Breakfast
Credit Cards: A, B
Notes: 5, 7, 9, 11, 12, 13

By-the-Way

310 First Avenue, K1S 2G8
(613) 232-6840

Modern, comfortable, and elegant, By-the-Way Bed and Breakfast offers all the conveniences of modern living and is close to downtown Ottawa and many interesting attractions. A few minutes' walking distance from the Rideou Canal, fine Ottawa museums, and Carleton University. The host is happy to guide first-time visitors to Ottawa. Central air conditioning, smoke- and pollen-free.

Hosts: Krystyna, Rafal, and Adam
Rooms: 4 (2 PB; 2 SB) $50-70
Full Breakfast
Credit Cards: A, B
Notes: 7, 8, 9, 10, 11, 12, 13, 14

Gasthaus Switzerland Inn

89 Daly Avenue, K1N 6E6
(613) 237-0335; (800) 267-8788
FAX (613) 594-3327

Gasthaus Switzerland is a charming, affordable three-star inn in downtown Ottawa. All rooms feature comfortable, cozy Swiss-style beds covered with handmade duvets, smoke-free, direct-dial telephone, modem, and full cable TV. Air conditioning. Traditional Swiss hospitality in the heart of Canada's capital! Recommended by CAA, AAA, Canada Select, and Tourism of Ontario.

Hosts: Josef and Sabina Sauter
Rooms: 23 (PB) $68-108
Full Breakfast
Credit Cards: A, B, C, E, F
Notes: 5, 7, 9, 10, 11, 12, 13, 14

Haydon House

18 The Driveway, K2P 1C6
(613) 230-2697

A completely renovated and modernized Victorian-era mansion that offers rest and comfort. It is air-conditioned and has a private outdoor portico sitting area, spacious bedrooms, and modern facilities embellished with traditional Canadian pine decor. En suite, large room with double bed and two single beds, private bath. Haydon House is nestled in a tranquil residential area beside the historic and picturesque Rideau Canal and scenic parkway. All important points of interest, such as the Parliament buildings, museums, and National Art Gallery, are within a short and easy walk.

Host: Mary Haydon
Rooms: 3 (1 PB; 2 SB) $50-70
Continental Breakfast
Credit Cards: None
Notes: 2, 5, 8, 9, 10, 11, 12, 13

Ottawa Bed and Breakfast

488 Cooper Street, K1R 5H9
(613) 563-0161; (800) 461-7889

1. Large, elegant Heritage Home within walking distance of Parliament Hills and museums. Choose from three guest rooms, one with queen-size brass bed, private en suite bath, sitting area, stained-glass window, and balcony. The other two rooms, each with a double bed, share a five-piece bath. This century-old home is full of interesting furniture; the dining room chairs are antique church chairs. Resident cat. This home has been featured many times on TV and in magazine and newspaper articles. $55-73.

2. Edwardian manor-type home on a fine residential street in Ottawa's West End. Choose from two rooms with twin beds that can be converted into king-size beds if desired. Both rooms share a single bath. Enjoy the patio gardens; close to downtown Ottawa. No smoking. French spoken.

3. Contemporary brick home in the suburbs of Ottawa. Three guest rooms—large room (a triple) with double and single beds, a twin bedroom, and a single bedroom—with shared baths. Hostess has an interesting collection of artwork. Walk to a large outdoor swimming pool. Families welcome. $55-73.

Patterson Place

6327 Emerald Links Drive, Greely, K4P 1M4
(613) 822-0280

Patterson Place is a Tudor-style home overlooking the tenth fairway of a beautiful 18-hole golf course and only 20 minutes outside of Ottawa. Guests can enjoy both the attractions of the nation's capital and the serenity of the home's location in the country. Seasonal activities include skating on the canal or skiing in Gatineau Park in winter, or a round of golf, a leisurely stroll, or a bike ride in summer.

Host: Jill M. Patterson
Rooms: 4 (1 PB; 3 SB) $55-69
Full Breakfast
Credit Cards: None
Notes: 2, 5, 7, 8, 9, 12, 13

OWEN SOUND

Moses' Sunset Farms Bend and Breakfast

Rural Route 6, Twp Box S578
20th Avenue East, N4K 5N8
(519) 371-4559

Well-traveled hosts own and operate Owen Sound's longest established bed and breakfast. Forty picturesque acres just five minutes from the city's center. Ideal for day trips to Manitoulin Island, Georgian Bay, and Bruce Trail. Gorgeous during autumn. Beautiful antique furnishings. Gardens, patio, and pond for outdoor enjoyment. Host hobby is beekeeping. Hostess is gourmet cooking teacher. Special classes offered for groups. Inquire about accommodations for children.

Hosts: Bill and Cecilie Moses
Rooms: 4 (1 PB; 3 SB) $45-75
Full Breakfast
Credit Cards: None
Notes: 5, 7, 9, 10, 11, 12, 13, 14

PAKENHAM

Gillanderry Farms

3742 Dominion Springs Drive, K0A 2X0
(613) 832-2317 (phone and FAX)

Modern century farm. Spacious, treed grounds, green-shuttered stone 1858 home, delightfully decorated bedrooms and guest bathroom. On farm are computerized dairy operation and a collection of restored antique tractors. In the hosts' home enjoy fifth-generation Irish, Ottawa Valley hospitality and Maureen's raspberry muffins and homemade breads, jams, and jellies. Great base for visiting the nation's capital and surrounding attractions. Just two hours from the Canadian-American border.

Hosts: Maureen and Art Gillan
Rooms: 2 (SB) $45
Full Breakfast
Credit Cards: None
Notes: 2, 4, 5, 7, 8, 9, 11, 12, 13

7 No smoking; 8 Children welcome; 9 Social drinking allowed; 10 Tennis nearby; 11 Swimming nearby; 12 Golf nearby; 13 Skiing nearby; 14 May be booked through a travel agent.

Stalcaire Farm Bed and Breakfast

Rural Route 1, K0A 2X0
(613) 256-4980

A small Ottawa Valley sheep farm 45 minutes west of Ottawa. Offering two air-conditioned rooms in Cape Cod-style home. Enjoy the peaceful scene of sheep grazing in the pasture while sipping morning coffee in the sunroom. The large living room has a cozy fireplace for winter nights. Golf and canoeing close by in season.

Hosts: Don and Rogere Carmichael
Rooms: 2 (S1B) $50-60 Canadian
Full Breakfast
Credit Cards: None
Notes: 3, 4, 5, 8, 9, 12, 13

PARRY SOUND

Blackwater Lake Bed and Breakfast

Rural Route 1, 167 Blackwater Lake Road, P2A 2W7
(705) 389-3746; FAX (705) 389-3746

Cozy chalet-style home offers comfort and relaxation. Seven acres on the shore of Blackwater Lake just 35 minutes from Parry Sound. Enjoy fishing, swimming, boating, skiing, hiking, and hunting at the doorstep. Three guest rooms with balconies. Two full bathrooms and one powder room.

Host: Trudy Wissel
Rooms: 3 (SB) $50-85
Credit Cards: None
Notes: 2, 4, 5, 7, 10, 11, 13

Cascade 40 Bed and Breakfast

40 Cascade Street, P2A 1J9
(705) 746-8917

Wooden doorknobs, wooden deck chairs, and wooden shingles are only a few of the interesting things in this designated Heritage Home. Close to Festival of the Sound, Rainbow Theatre, 30,000 Islands cruises, town beach, and hiking trails.

Hosts offer accommodation on second floor as well as air-conditioned third-floor suite with private bath and kitchenette. No pets. Outside smoking only.

Hosts: Rick and Sally Coomber
Rooms: 4 (1 PB; 3 SB) $50
Full and Continental Breakfast
Credit Cards: None
Notes: 5, 8, 9, 10, 11, 12, 13

Evergreen

P.O. Box 223, P2A 2X3
(705) 389-3554

Elegant cedar log home. Spacious cedar decks overlooking lovely parklike grounds on the shore of Lake Manitouwabing. Comfortable guest lounge with TV and reading material. Take the spiral staircase to the billiard room with professional-size table and game table. Enjoy a hearty breakfast served on the screened summer porch. Swim at the beach or fish from the dock. Canoe available for rent.

Hosts: Shirley and Andres Wallenius
Rooms: 4 (SB) $46
Full Breakfast
Credit Cards: None
Notes: 2, 7, 8, 9, 10, 11, 12

Jantje Manor

43 Church Street, P2A 1Y6
(705) 746-5399

Beautifully restored Victorian home in the heart of Parry Sound. Entering the front door is like taking a step back in time. The front parlor entices guests to sit and visit. The library, with fireplace, invites guests to curl up with a good book. The bedrooms are tastefully decorated and furnished with antiques. In the summer, the verandas and the screened porch offer a pleasant place to sit and relax. A full breakfast is served in the dining room.

Host: Jean Weening
Rooms: 4 (1 PB; 3 SB) $50-80
Full Breakfast
Credit Cards: None
Notes: 5, 7, 10, 11, 12, 13

NOTES: Credit cards accepted: A MasterCard; B Visa; C American Express; D Discover; E Diners Club;
F Other; 2 Personal checks accepted; 3 Lunch available; 4 Dinner available; 5 Open all year; 6 Pets welcome;

Quilt Patch Bed and Breakfast

Rural Route 2, P2A 2W8
(705) 378-5279

This new home is in a quiet country setting with a cozy family room and three adjoining guest bedrooms. The parklike setting overlooks the woods. Within walking distance of the sand beach on Little Otter Lake. Good swimming. Home-cooked breakfast included. English and German spoken. No smoking or pets please. Close to Festival of the Sound, 30,000 Islands cruises, and hiking trails. Quilts on display.

Hosts: Mary and Lorne Steckley
Rooms: 3 (SB) $40-55
Full and Continental Breakfast
Credit Cards: None
Notes: 8, 11

PERTH

Drummond House

30 Drummond Street East, K7H 1E9
(613) 264-9175

Come and enjoy the heritage and elegance of a restored stone home built circa 1820. In beautiful historic Perth, one hour from Ottawa and Kingston. Drummond House sits beside the Toy River basin, which is part of the Rideau Canal system. Close to provincial parks, golf courses, skiing, lakes, antique shops, and more. The home is furnished with antiques and wicker and each room has a private bath.

Hosts: Claire and Rick Leach
Rooms: 3 (PB) $60
Full Breakfast
Credit Cards: None
Notes: 2, 5, 7, 8, 9, 11, 12, 13

House on the Corner

53 Wilson Street West, K7H 2N3
(613) 264-0901

Tastefully decorated century Victorian brick home in the heart of historic Perth. Air-conditioned, Jacuzzi, two sitting rooms, TV room with fireplace, garden deck overlooking water garden. Perth boasts many Heritage buildings, the oldest golf club in Canada, museum, antique shops, and parks. Many organized special events from the Maple Festival to theater festivals and sports tournaments. Sumptuous full breakfast served. Other meals and special picnic baskets are available by prior arrangement. Cross-country skiing in area.

Hosts: Fran and Sam Bonner
Rooms: 3 (SB) $45-60
Full Breakfast
Credit Cards: None
Notes: 2, 5, 7, 9, 11, 12, 13

Perth Manor Heritage Inn

23 Drummound Street West, K7H 2S6
(613) 264-0050; FAX (613) 264-0051

Old mansion built in 1878. Tapestry in dining room. Eight guest rooms in the main house and two in the carriage house. Private and shared baths. Solarium, bar, patio overlooking lily ponds and large perennial garden. Library, antique furniture, fireplaces, and chandeliers. Smoking in designated areas only. Inquire about accommodations for children.

Hosts: Gisela and Phil Aston
Rooms: 10 (1 PB; 9 SB) $70-135
Full Breakfast-Summer
Continental Breakfast-Winter
Credit Cards: A, B, C
Notes: 2, 3, 4, 5, 6, 9, 10, 11, 12, 13, 14

Rivendell Bed and Breakfast

Rural Route 4, Highway 7, K7H 3C6
(613) 264-2742

Comfortably restored log house, circa 1830, with view of pond and creek. Antiques, numerous wildlife prints, and a large library reflect hosts' interests. Enjoy the charm of yesteryear with the comfort of today. Separate guests' living room/library downstairs and reading area upstairs. Home-baked breakfast is served in formal dining room. Dinner and Victorian tea on request. One

7 No smoking; 8 Children welcome; 9 Social drinking allowed; 10 Tennis nearby; 11 Swimming nearby; 12 Golf nearby; 13 Skiing nearby; 14 May be booked through a travel agent.

queen-size bed with en suite, two double bed with shared bathroom.

Hosts: Marty and Tom McGuinness
Room: 3 (1 PB; 2 SB) $45-60
Full Breakfast
Credit Cards: None
Notes: 2, 5, 9

PETROLIA

Rebecca's Bed and Breakfast

4058 Petrolia Street, P.O. Box 1028, N0N 1R0
(519) 882-0118

A restored historic, three-story, 100-year-old Victorian home with Italianate influences. Furnished with some antiques, including a restored player piano. Relax and visit with other guests and the hosts on the veranda or in the parlor. The tastefully decorated guest rooms are on the third floor, where guests will find the four-piece shared bath. Enjoy a tasty Continental plus breakfast of fruit, juices, homemade muffins, and jams. Baby-sitting services available with rior notice. Twenty-five minutes from Sarnia and Port Huron, Michigan. No smoking in bedrooms.

Hosts: Rebecca and John MacLachlan
Rooms: 3 (SB) $40-45
Continental Breakfast
Credit Cards: None
Notes: 2, 5, 8, 9, 10, 11, 12, 13

PICTON

Jackson's Falls Schoolhouse (1870) Bed and Breakfast Inn

Rural Route 2, County Road 17, Milford, K0K 2P0
(613) 476-8576

This 1870 schoolhouse operated as a school until 1960. Now it serves as breakfast, dining room, and lounge for guests. The schoolroom is adjoined by four large guest rooms, all with private facilities. The inn was built in the style of an old Ontario establishment. Rooms are furnished with antiques. Close to beaches and sand dunes,

natural beauty, surrounded by Lake Ontario. Smoking is restricted.

Hosts: Pete and Nancy Fleck
Rooms: 6 (4 PB; 2 SB) $55-75
Full Breakfast
Credit Cards: None
Notes: 2, 4, 5, 9, 10, 11, 12

PLATTSVILLE

The Albion Bed and Breakfast

P.O. Box 37, N0J 1S0
(519) 684-7434

English inn atmosphere prevails in the host's home in a restored Victorian country hotel building. Enjoy the pleasure of village life—walking, biking, golfing, playing tennis, or even picnicking at the orchard (ten miles away)—all within 30 minutes of the city pleasures of Stratford with its theaters and restaurants, Kitchener's museums and Mennonite country, Cambridge with its factory outlets, and Woodstock with its gracious tree-lined streets. Home-cooking within blocks and gourmet dining is ten miles away. Antiques and craft shops in the village. Smoking restricted.

Host: Barbara Dobson
Rooms: 6 (SB) $45 Canadian
Full Breakfast
Credit Cards: None
Notes: 8, 9, 10, 12

PORT DOVER

Bed and Breakfast by the Lake

30 Elm Park, N0A 1N0
(519) 583-1010

Port Dover is a pleasant small town on the north shore of Lake Erie, a good base for exploring Long Point Bird Observatory, strolling around Port Dover Harbour's craft shops, and experiencing excellent summer theater at Lighthouse Theatre. This ranch ome is bright, open, and airy, graciously furnished with antiques and art. Attractive brick patio and garden provide lovely view of Lake Erie and easy access to sandy beach.

Hosts: Christine and Peter Ivey
Rooms: 2 (SB) $55
Full Breakfast
Credit Cards: B
Notes: 2, 5, 7, 9, 11, 12

PORT STANLEY

Great Lakes Farms Guest House

Rural Route 1, Union, N0L 2L0
(519) 782-3433; FAX (519) 633-4807

This century-old home stands amid apple trees on a 250-acre farm. Rent one room or rent the whole house for a night, a weekend, or longer. Enjoy TV, a pool table, whirlpool, Continental breakfast, and the warmth of this country retreat, just five minutes from Port Stanley.

Hosts: Bob and Marge Thomas
Rooms: 3 (SB) $45-55
House: $135
Continental Breakfast
Credit Cards: None
Notes: 2, 5, 8, 9, 11, 12, 13, 14

POWASSAN

Satis House Bed and Breakfast

Rural Route 2, P0H 1Z0
(705) 724-2187

Satis House is a large home featuring Georgian and Victorian architecture. It is approximately three and one-half hours north of Toronto between Trout Creek and Powassan. Just off Highway 11 on Concession 8 and 9 south— Himsworth Township. Gorgeous property with 100 acres providing soothing, beautiful views in all seasons. Guests return for the comfort and excellent full breakfast served. Smoking outside only.

Host: Jo-Anne Hynd
Rooms: 3 (SB) $50
Full Breakfast
Credit Cards: B
Notes: 3, 4, 5, 6, 9, 10, 11, 12, 13, 14

RIDEAU CANAL

Ottawa Bed and Breakfast

488 Cooper Street, Ottawa, K1R 5H9
(613) 563-0161; (800) 461-1889

1. A beautiful 19th-century home on Queen Elizabeth Driveway in a prestigious neighborhood facing Rideau Canal. Two guest rooms on the third floor, one with double bed, the other with twin beds, share a bath and have views of the canal or Brown's Inlet. Walk to fine restaurants and book and antique shops. No smoking. $55-73.

2. Three-story older home overlooking Rideau Canal. Host enjoys baking bread. Twin-bed guest room off the sunroom. Private bath. Resident cat. No smoking. French spoken.

ROCKWOOD

Blue Heron Bed and Breakfast

106 John Street, N0B 2K0
(519) 856-2275

In the cozy village of Rockwood, the Blue Heron has luxurious accommodations in a modern, air-conditioned home shared with a friendly St. Bernard named Friar Tuck. Sumptuous full breakfast is included. Sit and relax in the private Oriental garden. Nearby are quality golf courses, unique conservation area, antique and craft markets, and harness racing.

Hosts: Bob and Pauline Dahlke
Rooms: 2 (SB) $60
Full Breakfast
Credit Cards: None
Notes: 2, 5, 7, 9, 11, 12, 13, 14

The International Bed & Breakfast Club, Inc.

504 Amherst Street, Buffalo, NY 14207
(800) 723-4262; FAX (716) 873-4462

7 No smoking; 8 Children welcome; 9 Social drinking allowed; 10 Tennis nearby; 11 Swimming nearby; 12 Golf nearby; 13 Skiing nearby; 14 May be booked through a travel agent.

ON2275PP. A modern, comfortable home in the village of Rockwood with a unique Oriental garden for guests to relax in and enjoy. Two spacious, well-decorated rooms share a bath; the smaller bedroom has a romantic theme, the large bedroom accommodates a sitting room with a view overlooking the garden. Nearby attractions include the Rockwood Conservation Area, unique and very picturesque; Blue Springs Golf Club, home of the Canadian PGA; Radial Railway Museum of Guelph Line; Niagara Escarpment hiking. Adults only. No smoking. Full breakfast. $55.

ROSSEAU

The Giggling Otter Inn

4 Oak Street, P.O. Box 205, P0C 1J0
(705) 732-1354; FAX (705) 732-1969

Century home overlooking picturesque Lake Rosseau in Muskoka's cottage country. Large veranda, gardens, gazebo, and antiques, two living rooms, one with stone fireplace. Three bedrooms, one with balcony, with down-filled duvets and lake views. Close to summer theater and international Festival of the Sound, RMS *Segwun* and 30,000 Islands cruises, antique boat show, gallery and studio tours. Thirty minutes from Huntsville, Bracebridge, Parry Sound, and Port Carling. Cross-country and snowmobile trails at front door. Beach, boat rentals, bakery, century-old general store, gallery and crafts within walking distance. Dinner available by appointment.

Hosts: Charlene Randle and cats Toby and Ms.
Rooms: 3 (SB) $55-65
Full Breakfast
Credit Cards: None
Notes: 2, 5, 7, 10, 11, 12, 13

ST. JACOBS

Jakobstettel Guest House, Inc.

16 Isabella Street, N0B 2N0
(519) 664-2208; FAX (519) 664-1326

Jakobstettel Guest House

Turn-of-the-century renovated Victorian home has 12 individually decorated guest rooms with private baths. Library, lounge for all guests, and open kitchen all day and evening for coffee, tea, juice, and cookies. Outdoor pool, tennis court, horseshoe pits, bikes, and walking trail. Within a few blocks of more than 80 retail shops, this is a shopper's delight.

Host: Elle Burbacher
Rooms: 12 (PB) $105-150
Continental Breakfast
Credit Cards: A, B, C
Notes: 2, 5, 10, 11, 14

STRATFORD

Burnside Guest Home

139 William Street, N5A 4X9
(519) 271-7076

Burnside is an ancestral, turn-of-the-century home featuring many family antiques and heirlooms. Recently redecorated in light, airy colors. Host is a horticultural instructor and an authority on local and Canadian genealogy. Stratford Festival Theatre, Avon Theatre, and Tom Patterson Theatre only minutes away. Interesting shops and restaurants are also a short walk away. The Avon Trail, part of a network of hiking and cross-country skiing trails that can connect Tobermory, Ontario, to the Niagara

Escarpment, is nearby. Four guest rooms feature a variety of bed sizes and shared baths. Full, home-cooked breakfast served each morning . Inquire about accommodations for children.

Host: Lester (Les) J. Wilker
Rooms: 4 (SB) $55-70 Canadian
Full Breakfast
Credit Cards: A
Notes: 2, 5, 7, 9, 10, 11, 12, 13

The Stone Maiden Inn

123 Church Street, N5A 2R3
(519) 271-7129

Named after the stone maiden heads that grace the front hallway, the Stone Maiden offers quiet Victorian elegance with superior accommodations and the utmost in personal service. Handmade quilts, en suite bathrooms, and handsome antiques grace the 14 air-conditioned guest rooms. Some rooms have canopied beds, fireplaces, and whirlpool tubs. Generous breakfast and afternoon refreshments. Visit Stratford during May through October for the world-renowned Shakespearean Festival. Close to city center and three theaters. Private parking.

Hosts: Barb and Len Woodward
Rooms: 14 (PB) $85-165 Canadian
Full Breakfast
Credit Cards: A, B
Notes: 2, 7, 9, 10, 11, 12, 14

Woods Villa

62 John Street North, N5A 6K7
(519) 271-4576; FAX (519) 271-7173

Woods Villa combines Victorian elegance with modern comfort. Most of the six large bedrooms have fireplaces and all have TVs. There is a large heated pool with terrace, and ample off-street parking. Breakfast is served in the dining room. Woods Villa features a sizable collection of automatic musical instruments, player pianos, and juke boxes ready to play for guests. An easy ten-minute stroll from downtown Stratford.

Host: Ken Vinen
Rooms: 5 (SB) $85
Suite: $125
Full Breakfast
Credit Cards: A, B, D
Notes: 2, 5, 7, 9, 10, 11, 12, 13, 14

SUTTON WEST

Baldwin Mill Bed and Breakfast

24357 Highway 48, Baldwin, L0E 1R0
Rural Route 1, L0E 1R0 (Mailing Address)
(905) 722-5743; (416) 930-6891 (mobile)
FAX (905) 722-7292

Savor the sparkle of rushing water tumbling over the dam or concentrate on the best putt on the green. Only 45 minutes from downtown Toronto, this renovated 1860s grist mill is an ideal site for weddings, reunions, and any other occassions that need a special feel. Furnished largely with Canadian pine, the Mill also boasts a secluded log cabin, a favorite for honeymooners. Scrumptious breakfasts are offered fresh from the outdoor grill if the weather permits. Expansive gardens showcase the beauty of summer in Ontario. Air-conditioned. Canoeing is available; golf green on premises. Enjoy the dam and waterfall. Open May 1 through October 31.

Hosts: Ruth and Jim West
Rooms: 4 (2 PB; 2 SB) $85-115
Full Breakfast
Credit Cards: None
Notes: 2, 9, 10, 11, 12, 14

Baldwin Mill

7 No smoking; 8 Children welcome; 9 Social drinking allowed; 10 Tennis nearby; 11 Swimming nearby; 12 Golf nearby; 13 Skiing nearby; 14 May be booked through a travel agent.

THUNDER BAY

Unicorn Inn

Rural Route 1, South Gillies, P0T 2V0
(807) 475-4200

Intimate, widely acclaimed serenity of country-elegant accommodations and superb dining. Restaurant rated among top 57 in Canada by *Where to Eat in Canada 1994*. Nestled in the heart of a hidden rock valley on 640 acres of spectacular fields, forests, and mountains. Bright, cozy rooms with oak floors and handcrafted pine furniture; exquisite honeymoon cottage with bay windows and view.

Hosts: David and Arlan Nobel
Rooms: 4 (1 PB; 3 SB) $59-89
Full Breakfast
Credit Cards: A, B, E
Notes: 2, 4, 5, 8, 9, 11, 13, 14

TORONTO

Arowhon Pines

Algonquin Park, 297 Balliol Street, M4S 1C7
(705) 633-5661; (416) 483-4393 (winter)

Rates include three meals per day per person and use of all recreational facilities, such as canoes, sailboats, sailboards, hiking trails, tennis courts, sauna, swimming in pristine waters, and game room. Open June through October 9. No smoking in some cabins. BYOB.

Hosts: Eugene and Helen Kates
Rooms: 50 (PB) $120-230
Full Breakfast
Credit Cards: B
Notes: 2, 3, 4, 8, 10, 11, 12, 14

Beaconsfield Bed and Breakfast

38 Beaconsfield Avenue, M6J 3H9
(416) 535-3338 (phone and FAX)

Colorful, unpretentious 1882 Victorian home full of fun and sun, art and heart. In a quiet, downtown, multicultural neighborhood just west of the commercial core, it's a short trolley ride to major theaters and sites along West Queen Street. Choose between imaginatively decorated rooms or the very private San Miguel Mexican honeymoon suite with treetop terrace. All have top-of-the-line beds. Creative breakfasts musically served in eclectic dining room. Great location. Parking. Information galore.

Hosts: Bernie and Katya McLoughlin
Rooms: 4 (1 PB; 3 SB) $65-95
Full Breakfast
Credit Cards: None
Notes: 2, 5, 7, 8, 9

Bed and Breakfast Homes of Toronto

P.O. Box 46093, College Park Post Office
M5B 2L8
(416) 363-6362

Alcina's. A spacious Victorian brick house on a shady tree-lined, residential street. Favorite local walks can take guests to Wychwood Park, historic Spadina House, beautiful flower gardens, and the ever-popular Casa Loma. For a quicker pace, there is immediate, easy access to downtown Toronto's host of attractions (sports, shopping, theater, concerts, and dining) via the TTC (bus, subway, streetcar) or car. Casual eateries can be found locally. Guests can enjoy a generous Continental breakfast in the dining room or relax in the private little English garden. Parking available. Resident cat, Ginger. Seasonal rates. Smoking allowed in back yard seating area. $55-80.

Arsovsky's Greenwood Villa. Welcome to this casually elegant residence, just west of the popular beaches area. Repeat guests have said that they like the warm, comfortable, and cozy character of the home. Full breakfast is served in the formal dining room. This home was chosen to appear in the TV program *Hour Long* on bed and breakfasts in Toronto. Two doors away is a direct 24-hour transit system. Highway access is five minutes away. Ceiling fans.

NOTES: Credit cards accepted: A MasterCard; B Visa; C American Express; D Discover; E Diners Club; F Other; 2 Personal checks accepted; 3 Lunch available; 4 Dinner available; 5 Open all year; 6 Pets welcome;

Private or shared baths. No smoking in the house, please. English, German, and Slavic languages spoken. Free private parking. $50-80.

Butternut House. A warm, traditional home a half-minute walk from the subway in a quiet residential neighborhood. This original Tudor home with oak trim, French doors, stained glass, blazing hearth, and airy balcony invites guests to feel at home and cared for. All bedrooms are air-conditioned with color cable TV and clock radios. Continental breakfast. Special diets catered to. Parking. Nonsmoking home. Some French spoken. Pookie, gentle cat, resides. Bathroom shared by guests only. $60-75.

Feathers May and Max. A charming, spacious Victorian home in the popular "Annex," only a five-minute walk from Bathurst subway and Bloor Street. Guests are two blocks away from one of Toronto's most delightful areas of cosmopolitan restaurants and cafes, film and live theaters, bookstores and antique shops. Nineteenth-century European and Oriental furnishings, china, delicate tapestries, and an unusual collection of antique puppets lend a unique atmosphere to this interesting and beautifully restored home. Continental breakfast. Feathers is close to Casa Loma, Spadina House, Royal Ontario Museum, University of Toronto, and Mirvish Village. Convenient to the CNE and all downtown attractions. Discount offered if no breakfast desired. Central air. Color TV in guest rooms. No smoking in house, please. English, Dutch, French, and German spoken. Free parking. $58-75.

Mabel's Bed and Breakfast. A warm welcome awaits guests in this contemporary and attractive home on a quiet residential street, just a few minutes' walk from Broadview subway station and streetcar services. Guests can be downtown within ten minutes or if they prefer to explore the immediate surroundings, the bed and breakfast is right next door to Toronto's colorful and lively Greek neighborhood on the Danforth with its trendy and traditional restaurants, open-air cafes and markets, pubs, clubs, and shops. Also nearby, Riverdale Park is ideal for joggers. The home provides an ideal location from which guests can experience the many varied pleasures Toronto has to offer. A delicious, full breakfast is served in the dining room or the beautiful, bright, and airy kitchen that overlooks an attractive garden and patio. On-site parking. No smoking. Central air conditioning. TV in guest bedrooms. Easy access to major highways. Private bath add $10. $65.

Marlborough Place. This beautifully renovated Victorian townhouse furnished with antiques is within walking distance of fashionable Yorkville and Bloor Streets, the Royal Ontario Museum, the McLaughlin Planetarium, and Casa Loma. The neighborhood features tree-lined streets, historic homes, and fine restaurants. It is a five-minute stroll to the subway. The second-floor guest room has a double bed. Just outside this room is a cozy sitting area and down the hall, a large four-piece bathroom with a Jacuzzi. An open staircase leads to a tastefully furnished, spacious loft on the third floor that is "open concept." It has wooden floors and beams, its own sitting area, private bathroom, and sun deck overlooking the professionally landscaped garden. A generous Continental breakfast is served in the dining room or the kitchen. Guests are welcome to sit in the living room or on the back sun deck. Marlborough Place offers warm hospitality and a cozy yet elegant atmosphere. On-site parking. Central air. Limited smoking. $65-85.

Martyniuk. This home more than 100 years old in the Kensington Market area, is quite modest in style and decor, but at prices well below average, and is an excel-

Bed and Breakfast Homes of Toronto (continued)

lent choice for the budget traveler, especially for those without cars. The Martyniuk home is exactly one mile from the Eaton Centre, bus terminal, or Elgin and Pantages Theatres. This location is good for the CN Tower, SkyDome, Ontario Art Gallery, Chinatown, Little Italy, Canadian National Exhibition, and other downtown attractions. European-style restaurants and Toronto Western Hospital are within walking distance. The full breakfast is served in the kitchen. English, Ukrainian, Polish, and German spoken. Very limited smoking permitted. Ten percent discount from October to March if over seven days. Rooms individually air-conditioned. $45-55.

Oriole Gardens. Enjoy a warm, friendly atmosphere in this gracious family home on an upscale, tree-lined residential street. A few minutes' walk from St. Clair subway station and Yonge Street buses, and within easy reach of Toronto's major attractions. The location offers an interesting variety of restaurants, pubs, fashion stores, bakeries, bookstores, and cinemas. For the fitness conscious, the bed and breakfast is within easy jogging distance of parks and picturesque ravines. Historic Casa Loma and Spadina House are approximately 15-to-20 minutes' walking distance. Guests are encouraged to make themselves at home in the spacious, beautifully furnished sitting room. A full and healthy breakfast is served in the elegant dining room or the bright and modern kitchen that overlooks an attractive garden. On-site parking. Resident cat, Zack. $65-75.

Robin's Nest. This 1892 Heritage Home has been restored by the hosts to celebrate its great charm and character. In one of Toronto's most beautiful downtown neighborhoods, guests can enjoy tree-lined streets and parks en route to all the popular cafes, shops, and theaters. Each bedroom overlooks the gardens. One guest room includes a paneled den with fireplace and bedroom with veranda and en suite Jacuzzi bath. The other guest room has a library bedroom with bay windows, a fireplace, and separate private bathroom with shower. Guests can enjoy a relaxing, hearty breakfast in front of the fireplace in the elegant dining room or a tray of fresh fruits and home baking in the privacy of guest bedroom. Five-minute bus ride or an interesting walk to Rosedale subway on Yonge. No smoking. Free parking. Sable is our resident dog. $85-110.

Vanderkooy. This charming older, traditional home is in an excellent location on a lovely tree-lined street close to Summerhill subway, a choice of good restaurants, and fine boutiques. The house is bright and sunny, with stained-glass windows and features some original artwork. One of the bedrooms has a private two-piece bathroom and the other has a shared bath. Guests are invited to sit in the living room to watch TV or, in the warmer weather, guests may enjoy the flower-filled back yard deck. The atmosphere of this home is relaxed and casual. A full breakfast is served on a round oak table overlooking the garden. Parking. Air conditioning. Resident cat, Jazz. Very limited smoking permitted. Easy access to all downtown attractions. $60-65.

Winchester Square. Enjoy the warm hospitality offered at Winchester Square. This recently restored late 1800s three-story brick residence is in Cabbagetown, a quiet downtown Toronto neighborhood of Victorian and Edwardian homes. The guest rooms are bright, spacious, and decorated with unconventional flair by the hostess. Round-the-clock public transportation stops a block away, or guests can walk a few steps to the many charming shops and restaurants or enjoy the gardens and architecture of Heritage Homes that make up the heart of

Cabbagetown. A healthy Continental breakfast is served, followed by hot tips on what to do in the city. The guest kitchen is conveniently equipped with a dishwasher and laundry facilities for extended stays. Visiting professionals, lecturers, and families take note: Polish as a second language. Air-conditioned suite. *Phantom of the Opera* within easy reach. Smoking is allowed only on the open-air deck. Free parking. Bathroom shared by only two guest rooms and one en suite. $60-75.

The English Corner

114 Bernard Avenue, M5R 1S3
(416) 967-6474

A charming English-style home with lots of wood. Each room is different. In the heart of the city. Guests can walk or take the subway anywhere.

Hosts: Carol and Fred Hansen
Rooms: 5 (SB) $85 Canadian
Full Breakfast
Credit Cards: F
Notes: 2, 5, 7, 9, 10, 11, 12, 14

The International Bed and Breakfast

504 Amherst Street, Buffalo, NY 14207
(800) 723-4262; FAX (716) 873-4462

ON1455PP. This fully restored Heritage mansion was built in 1891. The Victorian-style private home is on a lovely tree-lined residential boulevard in Toronto's oldest historic village. The mansion is within walking distance of transportation, minutes to major downtown attractions, theaters, and museums. This "home away from home" has 14 large, bright rooms tastefully furnished with antiques. The four guest accommodations have private and shared bath arrangements. A Continental plus breakfast is served and is special when guests indulge in hot-from-the-oven homemade muffins, tea biscuits, Danish, corn bread, and the hosts' famous Sunday brunch. $50-95.

ON9464PP. This 1891 Heritage Home has been restored with care to preserve its charm and character. Guest accommodations include a suite comprised of a paneled den with fireplace adjoining a queen-size bedroom, private veranda, and en suite bath with Jacuzzi, and a library bedroom with bay windows, a sofa and chairs surrounding a fireplace, and a separate private bathroom with shower. The host has restored the gardens and, in season, guests can enjoy sitting by the fountain having afternoon tea with Sable, the family dog. A full English breakfast is served along with a substantial cold buffet of fresh fruits and home baking in the dining room at guests' leisure. On-site parking. Central air conditioning. Just a five-minute bus ride to Rosedale subway on Yonge Street. No smoking, please. $85-95.

Metropolitan Bed and Breakfast Registry of Toronto

Suite 269, 615 Mount Pleasant Road
Toronto, M4S 3C5
(416) 964-2566; FAX (416) 537-0233

Al's Place. This quiet suburban home is close to restaurants and shops in the North End of Toronto. Fairview Shopping Mall is within walking distance. Easy access to other parts of Toronto, the downtown area, and out of town. The host is a retired engineer who loves meeting people from other places. Al speaks fluent Hungarian in addition to English. Air-conditioned. No smoking. Al serves a full breakfast that includes homemade grape or other gourmet jams. $55.

Bain House. Close to the lively Greek neighborhood in Toronto's East End, this restored three-story Victorian home offers memorabilia from the fifties era that the hostess has collected. Some of the furnishings are also early fifties style. The bustling neighborhood has great shopping, sidewalk

7 No smoking; 8 Children welcome; 9 Social drinking allowed; 10 Tennis nearby; 11 Swimming nearby; 12 Golf nearby; 13 Skiing nearby; 14 May be booked through a travel agent.

Metropolitan Bed and Breakfast Registry of Toronto (continued)

fruit markets, open cafés, and all the great aromas of yummy shish kebab and other Greek specialties. After a full day of taking in the sights, guests may relax on the outside deck. Ten-minute walk to subway; easy access to all of Toronto's tourist attractions. Two guest accommodations, one with queen-size bed and one with twin bed, share a bath. Off-street parking available. Nonsmokers only. $50.

Bed and Breakfast at Bayview. This grand modern house is exquisitely decorated and furnished and has a wonderful Oriental flavor. The hosts speak Dutch, German, Indonesian, and English. The spacious lower level offers total privacy. It has a large bedroom, separate sitting room featuring a fireplace, color TV and VCR, private bath, as well as a dining area and kitchenette with a microwave oven. The pretty blue room upstairs has a queen-size bed and a full bath with Jacuzzi. The hostess, a registered nurse, caters to special dietary needs on request. Nonsmokers only. $65-80.

Bonnie's Bungalow. Enjoy birds? Watch them feed and bathe through the large living room picture window or while sitting on the spacious veranda. Make yourself at home in Bonnie's comfortable bungalow, which she shares with her dog, Rebel. The guest bedroom is well appointed with a queen-size bed and sitting area. It is on the main floor and has a shared bath. This well-kept home is fully air-conditioned and offers a Jacuzzi. $55

Brain. This friendly family is interested in music, art, and travel. In fact, interesting artifacts from all over the world decorate this very convenient home in North Toronto. They love meeting people from other parts of the world. The hostess is a very fine sculptress and has won awards for her work. The house is just a few steps to the Lawrence subway station for a fast run downtown. Walk a very short distance to Yonge Street and visit the stores, cafés, night clubs, and restaurants. There is parking and air conditioning. The dining room overlooks the garden. The two guest rooms, one with a double bed and one with a twin bed, share a bath. Nonsmokers only. Full, hot breakfast is served. $52.

Cuddle Close. On the eastern boundary of Toronto, this modern, if unusual, house backs onto Canada's largest urban park, home to much wildlife, while being convenient to Canada's largest highway. As new gardeners, the hosts are eager to discuss their developing garden and their "backs of steel—with trap doors." Allison can describe the current community theater productions—and may even be working on one—while John can discuss celestial navigation on a cloudy night with traveling sailors! Ballroom dancers will learn of the places to strut their telemarks, corta jacas, etc. Air-conditioned. Nonsmokers, please. $55-65.

Gingerbread House. This fine old house is surrounded by trees and shrubs that give it a country feeling year-round. From the outside this lovely home is more like a cottage than a house. But inside are spacious, comfortable rooms, with 1920s period furnishings and private baths. Perfect for the business traveler, downtown and airport are minutes away. Pickup at the airport available by special request. fax service available. Two blocks from the subway and GO transit. Fully air-conditioned. No smoking, please. There are two resident cats, three fireplaces, and a warm, friendly atmosphere. In summer, breakfast is sometimes served in the spectacular back yard. $60-75.

NOTES: Credit cards accepted: A MasterCard; B Visa; C American Express; D Discover; E Diners Club; F Other; 2 Personal checks accepted; 3 Lunch available; 4 Dinner available; 5 Open all year; 6 Pets welcome;

Joan's Bed and Breakfast. This neat suburban bungalow is in Toronto's East End, within walking distance of the subway for a quick trip downtown. Visitors are a short bus ride from the Metro Zoo, the Ontario Science Centre, and a major shopping mall. The pretty guest bedroom is decorated in a Canadian East Coast theme and has a shared bath. Air-conditioned. $50.

Kent House. This airy, modernized, three-story midtown home, historic in nature because of its Edwardian heritage, is in a quiet area, one and one-half blocks from Summerhill subway station. This house is furnished in eclectic style, combining the richness of tribal rugs with contemporary and antique furniture and art. Excellent restaurants and shopping are a ten-minute walk away. A short stroll toward downtown Toronto will bring guests to the internationally known Yorkville area and the Royal Ontario Museum. The cozy guest room is tastefully decorated and overlooks a quiet city garden. There is a private four-piece bath for the exclusive use of the guests. Parking is available. Fully air-conditioned. Nonsmokers only. A full English-style breakfast is served and in good weather can be enjoyed on the open-air deck. $75.

Little Italy. Enjoy the inner-city neighborhood with its cappuccino bars and cafés, gourmet pizza, Italian bakery, and authentic restaurants. The hostess lives in a Victorian row house built in 1905 and completely renovated to an open-plan look with oak floors throughout. The house is decorated with Asian art and artifacts brought back from world travels. Join the hostess in discussing theater, jazz clubs, wine tasting, and gourmet cooking. A piano and exercise bike are available. Fully air-conditioned. The two guest accommodations have double beds and a shared bath. Nonsmokers only, please. $55-60.

Midtown. This is the perfect home for visitors unfamiliar with Toronto. The well-traveled host knows her city well and enjoys advising her guests on what to see and do and how best to get there. A walk of just a block and a half along a gracious tree-lined street brings guests to a handy little bus that takes them to a subway stop and downtown in minutes. The peaceful neighborhood is one of Toronto's oldest and most distinguished. The home is tastefully appointed. The furniture is teak, and the colors are warm. The walls hold many pictures and souvenirs of the host's world travels. The comfortable guest bedroom is on the main floor and has a shared bath. Parking for one car. No smokers, please. Breakfast is served in the large formal dining room. $65.

Riverbridge. This airy, interesting home is perched high on the west bank of the Credit River west of Toronto. Once an inn, the house is set facing the river amid towering trees on half an acre of lush greenery. From the pool deck, guests can glimpse Olympic-style canoeists and scullers on the river, and excellent walks and parks are nearby. In winter, the fireplace crackles nightly. The hosts, an international photographer and a business communicator, are well traveled and speak several languages. Business facilities are available. Atmosphere is calm, relaxed, and friendly. The guest room has a queen-size bed and private bath. Air-conditioned. Ample free off-street parking. $60.

Seasons. The decor of this modern, spacious home is contemporary with a few antiques to add interest. The two guest rooms on the upper level are inviting and tastefully decorated: the Spring Room with twin beds in daffodil yellow and the Autumn Room with a king-size bed in warm shades of brown and gold. They share a bath. The host, Douglas, will be delighted to discuss amateur theater, in which he is involved, or perhaps play a selection on the

7 No smoking; 8 Children welcome; 9 Social drinking allowed; 10 Tennis nearby; 11 Swimming nearby; 12 Golf nearby; 13 Skiing nearby; 14 May be booked through a travel agent.

grand piano. Sing along or lounge on the bench in the bay window overlooking the crystal waters of the pool. Parking. Swimming. No smoking. Cat, Fluffy, in residence. Air-conditioned. A full breakfast is served in the dining room and features such delights as coddled eggs, home baking, or Linda's famous peach pancakes, with fresh fruit, juices, and cereals. $60.

Seaton Pretty. Nestled in Toronto's historic Cabbagetown stands the Edwardian home of Seaton Pretty. Charmed with interesting and unusual artifacts, this tastefully appointed home is within walking distance to the best of Toronto's attractions, shopping, theater district, and nightlife. The three guest accommodations have double or queen-size beds and share a bath. The hosts are caterers by trade. Wafting smells of fine cuisine and a unique coffee mug collection make breakfast a delightful event. Bike rentals available. $60-65.

Terrace House. Lovely residence built in 1913 is in the historic Casa Loma neighborhood of downtown Toronto. House features the original stained glass and leaded windows, and the living room has a beautiful scrolled ceiling. The dining room is rich with wood beams and oak trim. A full hot breakfast is served. The Skylight Room features a large skylight set in a sloped ceiling above the queen-size bed. The Tulip Room is blooming with tulips. It offers twin beds, a private sun porch, and a sitting room. The Peach Room is cozy with white eyelet and wicker. It has a queen-size bed and private bath with shower. All are air-conditioned. No smoking. French spoken. $65-80

Orchard View

92 Orchard View Boulevard, M4R 1C2
(416) 488-6826

Spacious 1911 home is uniquely decorated for the 1990s. Choose between the queen-sized bed with private en suite bath or the twin room with sitting area and separate entrance to the main bath. Full breakfast served. Free parking. Close to subway, shops, and restaurants.

Hosts: Donna and Ken Ketchen
Rooms: 2 (1 PB; 1 SB) $60-65
Full Breakfast
Credit Cards: None
Notes: 5, 7, 9 ,10, 11, 14

The Palmerston Inn Bed and Breakfast

322 Palmerston Boulevard, M6G 2N6
(416) 920-7842; FAX (416) 960-9529

In a charming residential neighborhood adjacent to downtown. Eight tastefully appointed rooms with washbasins, private telephones, and ceiling fans; shared baths. European-style atmosphere. Limited free parking on premises; public transportation nearby. Friendly, capable service.

Hosts: Judy and Wayne Carr
Rooms: 8 (SB) $65-85
Full Breakfast
Credit Cards: A, B
Notes: 5, 7, 8, 9, 10, 11, 12, 14

UNIONVILLE

Metropolitan Bed and Breakfast Registry of Toronto

Suite 269, 615 Mount Pleasant Road
Toronto, M4S 3C5
(416) 964-2566; FAX (416) 537-0233

River Run. This lovely modern home in the country just north of Toronto offers the best of both worlds. The village Main Street is just a short walk from the house and features many interesting shops and restaurants. Guests seeking solitude can walk from the back yard of this home through a ravine setting to a parkland area with its own pond, where they can have a picnic lunch or just enjoy the sights and sounds of nature. The hostess is an accomplished artist. Many of her interesting watercolors and glass pieces are displayed. She will be happy to describe the various works, which are available for purchase. The house is air-conditioned. Parking is provided. The guest suite has a king-size bed, large sitting room, and private bath. $60.

VICTORIA HARBOUR

Capers by the Bay Bed and Breakfast

206 Waldie Avenue, P.O. Box 456, L0K 2A0
(705) 534-7403

Relax by the waters of beautiful Georgian Bay. Two guest rooms, one large with queen-size bed, one cozy with twin beds. Enjoy full delicious breakfast. Close to Martyrs' Shrine, Ste. Marie among the Hurons, Wye Marsh Wildlife Centre, boat cruise of 30,000 Islands, Discovery Harbour, and King's Wharf Theatre.

Hosts: Jean and Norm Capes
Rooms: 2 (SB) $60-75
Full Breakfast
Credit Cards: None
Notes: 5, 6, 7, 8, 9, 11, 12, 13

WAUBAUSHENE

Bye the Water

45 Coldwater Road, P.O. Box 239, L0K 2C0
(705) 538-0987 (phone and FAX); (705) 583-2266

Waubaushene is a historic hamlet on the southeast corner of Georgian Bay at the intersection of Highways 12 and 400. The waterside accommodation is central to the many attractions of Huronia. Private entrance to sitting room with kitchenette, two bedrooms, four-piece bath, and sauna. Reduced rates for longer stays. Canadian personal checks accepted only.

Hosts: Susanne and Harry Stark
Rooms: 2 (SB) $50-65 Canadian
Continental Breakfast
Credit Cards: None
Notes: 3, 4, 5, 6, 7, 8, 9, 11, 12, 13

WELLESLEY

Firella Creek Farm

Rural Route 2, N0B 2T0
(519) 656-2974

Retreat to nature in the heart of Mennonite farming area. Full country breakfast with a view of the trout pond, stream, and orchard. Relax beside the fireplace. Hike or cross-country ski through the forest where wildlife abounds. German and Canadian meals. Local tours of the cider mill and points of interest are available upon request. On Regional Road 5 between Wellesley and Crosshill.

Hosts: Adolph and Emily Hafemann
Rooms: 3 (1 PB; 2 SB) $40-45
Full Breakfast
Credit Cards: None
Notes: 2, 3, 4, 5, 7, 8, 9, 10, 11, 12, 13

WESTPORT

Stepping Stone Bed and Breakfast Inn

Rural Route 2, Centreville Road, K0G 1X0
(613) 273-3806; FAX (613) 273-3331

This 1840s Heritage limestone inn can be found on 150 acres overlooking a spring-fed pond. Antiques, fireplaces, Jacuzzi suites, authentic period decor, Victorian porches, solarium, nature trails, horses, exotic birds, skiing, golf, and swimming. Reservations required for upscale dining and catering. Specializing in Victorian weddings and garden receptions. Small retreat.

Host: Madeleine Saunders
Rooms: 5 (3 PB; 2 SB) $70-130 Canadian
Full Breakfast
Credit Cards: A, B
Notes: 2, 3, 4, 5, 7, 8, 9, 10, 11, 12, 13

WIARTON

McIvor House

Rural Route 4, N0H 2T0
(519) 534-1769

7 No smoking; 8 Children welcome; 9 Social drinking allowed; 10 Tennis nearby; 11 Swimming nearby; 12 Golf nearby; 13 Skiing nearby; 14 May be booked through a travel agent.

This large stone farmhouse on an operating beef farm is 12 miles northeast of Wiarton. Close to Cape Crocker Indian Reserve and the Bruce Trail. Offering two double bedrooms and a suite with private entrance, as well as an in-ground pool. Breakfast is a hearty fare, including homemade jams, homemade maple syrup, breads, biscuits, and traditional bacon and eggs or pancakes. Open year-round for hikers, travelers, and skiers.

Hosts: Judy and Bill Glassford
Rooms: 3 (1 PB; 2 SB) $50
Full Breakfast
Credit Cards: None
Notes: 2, 3, 4, 5, 7, 8, 9, 11, 12, 13

WINDERMERE

Windermere House

P.O. Box 68, P0B 1P0
(800) 461-4283; FAX (705) 769-3611

Windermere House is a majestic historical landmark hotel that stands as proudly on the shores of Lake Rosseau, in the heart of the Muskoka Lakes District, as she did almost 130 years ago! On-site facilities include outdoor pool, tennis court, badminton, volleyball, shuffleboard, small watercraft rentals, boat cruises, recreation program, hiking tours, shopping, arts and crafts tours, etc. Accommodations include quaint rooms in the main lodge, two townhouse-style cottage units, which are generally priced on an

MAP package, including dinner and breakfast. Room-only rates are available upon request. Eighteen-hole championship golf course is adjacent to the hotel. Open May through October; however, the office is open year-round.

Hosts: Randy Robertson, general manager
Susan Dean, assistant manager
Rooms: 78 (PB) $50-300
Continental Breakfast
Credit Cards: A, B, C, E, F
Notes: 2, 3, 7, 8, 9, 11, 12, 14

ZEPHYR

High Fields Ranch

11570 Concession 3, Rural Route 1, L0E 1T0
(905) 473-6132; FAX (905) 473-1044

Enjoy a relaxed and informal atmosphere in a very private country setting with a peaceful panoramic view. The inn holdings include 175 acres of groomed trails for hiking, snowmobiling, cross-country skiing, and horseback riding. Aromatherapy massage and aesthetic services available on premises. Golfing, tennis, swimming, skiing very near. All meals available with advance notice. Reservation and deposit required. Credit cards accepted. Brochure is available.

Hosts: Norma and John Daniel
Rooms 3 (2 PB; 1 SB) $60-70
Full Breakfast
Credit Cards: A, B, C
Notes: 4, 5, 9, 10, 11, 12, 13, 14

NOTES: Credit cards accepted: A MasterCard; B Visa; C American Express; D Discover; E Diners Club; F Other; 2 Personal checks accepted; 3 Lunch available; 4 Dinner available; 5 Open all year; 6 Pets welcome;

Prince Edward Island

BAY FORTUNE

The Inn at Bay Fortune
Souris Rural Route 4, C0A 2B0
(902) 687-3745; (860) 296-1348 (winter)

This inn's creative contemporary cuisine is recommended by *Where to Eat in Canada* as "without question the best on the Island." Fodor's *Canada's Great Country Inns* states, "enticing…unforgettable." Former summer home of Broadway playwright Elmer Harris and most recently the late actress Colleen Dewhurst (Marilla, *Anne of Green Gables*). Eleven guest rooms, private bath (eight with fireplace sitting area). Overlooking Fortune Harbour, with the Northumberland Strait beyond. Expect a friendly welcome at the inn. The island's relaxed, casual atmosphere is reflected by the innkeeper and the staff.

Host: David Wilmer
Rooms: 11 (PB) $115-165
Full Breakfast
Credit Cards: A, B, E
Notes: 4, 8, 9, 10, 11, 12, 14

CAVENDISH

Kindred Spirits Country Inn and Cottages
Memory Lane, Route 6, C0A 1N0
(902) 963-2434 (phone and FAX)

A "decidedly country but intentionally quaint" inn that is family owned and specializes in warm hospitality. Spacious rooms and suites are beautifully furnished in country antiques and crafts. Twin, double, queen-, and king-size beds available.

Evening tea is served in the cozy parlor-lobby and complimentary breakfast is served in the dining room. Large heated pool, whirlpool. Air-conditioned. Housekeeping cottages available.

Hosts: Al and Sharon James
Rooms: 27 (PB) $60-160
Continental Breakfast
Credit Cards: A, B
Notes: 7, 8, 10, 11, 12, 14

CHARLOTTETOWN

Campbells Maple Bed and Breakfast
28 Maple Avenue, C1A 6E3
(902) 896-4488

This bed and breakfast is in suburban Charlottetown, just ten miles from the North Shore Beach and National Park. A ten-minute drive to downtown Charlottetown, and a five-minute drive to the airport. Full breakfast with fruit and muffins. Visitors will find a friendly welcome with local information provided. Living room and large garden available to guests. Open May 24 through October 31.

Rooms: 4 (SB) $45
Full Breakfast
Credit Cards: None
Notes: 2, 7, 8, 9, 10, 11, 14

Dundee Arms Management Inc.
200 Pownal Street, C1A 3W8
(902) 892-2496; FAX (902) 368-8532

This picturesque country inn is in the heart of Charlottetown just two blocks from the downtown business area. The rooms are

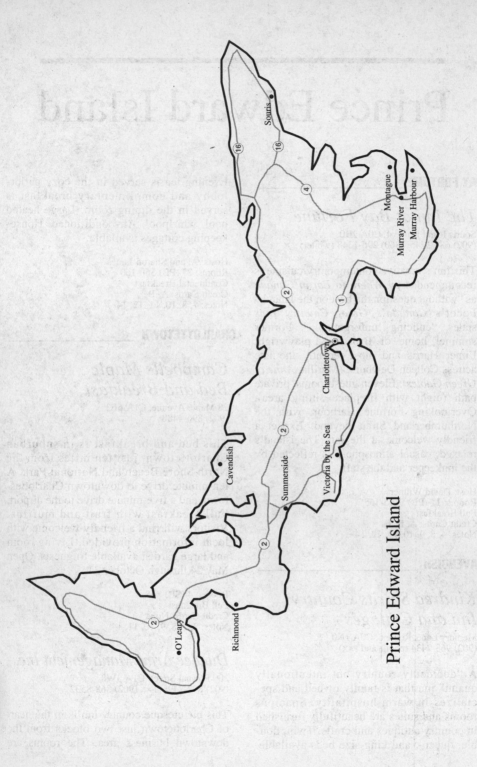

Prince Edward Island

Dundee Arms

furnished in a tasteful combination of period decor and antiques. The inn's licensed dining room and lounge were featured in *Where to Eat in Canada* magazine and have become a favorite of both tourists and local residents. The perfect place for vacationers and businesspersons alike.

Hosts: Terry and Bev Grandy
Rooms: 8 (PB) $65-138
Full and Continental Breakfast
Credit Cards: A, B, C, E
Notes: 2, 3, 4, 5, 7, 8, 9, 10, 11, 12, 14

Dunstaffnage Heights Bed and Breakfast

Rural Route 3, C1A 7J7
(902) 628-1715

Charming country Heritage home, ten kilometers from Charlottetown in Dunstaffnage, Highway 2 East. Quiet parklike setting close to beaches, golf, and other attractions. Five guest rooms, antique motif. Full bath on each floor. Reasonable rates include gourmet breakfast. Vegetarians welcome. Laundry and kitchen facilities available. Picnic and barbecue, recreation room with fireplace, TV, reading and games area, piano. Complimentary coffee, tea, wine. Separate two-bedroom, six-person cottage.

No smoking allowed in the accommodation. Ici on parle français.

Hosts: Sol and Evelyn Feldstein
Rooms: 5 (SB) $40-45
Full Breakfast
Credit Cards: None
Notes: 2, 7, 8, 9, 11, 12, 14

Wilberts Bed and Breakfast

Winsloe Rural Route 9, Harrington, C1E 1Z3
(902) 368-8145; (800) 847-8145

Pleasant, rural home landscaped with trees, shrubs, and flower and vegetable gardens. Great hiking in safe woods. Muscovy ducks and a few chickens. Central location. Five minutes north of airport, 15 minutes to Charlottetown, home of famous play *Anne of Green Gables,* 15 minutes to Brackley Beach. Close to lobster suppers, golf, trail rides, and crafts. Very friendly atmosphere. Evening social hour; tea and coffee served. Comfortable rooms. Helpful hosts.

Hosts: Vivia and Herbert
Rooms: 4 (1 PB; 3 SB) $40-44
Full Breakfast
Credit Cards: A
Notes: 7, 8, 11, 12, 14

Woodmere

Rural Route 3, C1A 7J7
(902) 628-1783; (800) 747-1783

Colonial home built with the guest in mind. Standardbred horses grazing in the fields, with fragrant roses blooming in the gardens. Each spacious room offers a view of the surrounding countryside and features private bath en suite, color TV, individually controlled heat, and attractive interiors. Close to airport, harness racing, theater, fine dining, and central to all attractions. National Park beaches and Crow Bush Golf Course just a short drive of 15 minutes.

Hosts: Doris and Wallace Wood
Rooms: 4 (PB) $55-65
Full Breakfast
Credit Cards: A, B
Notes: 2, 5, 7, 8, 9, 11, 12

NOTES: Credit cards: A MasterCard; B Visa; C American Express; D Discover; E Diners Club; F Other; 2 Personal checks accepted; 3 Lunch available; 4 Dinner available; 5 Open all year; 6 Pets welcome; 7 No smoking; 8 Children welcome; 9 Social drinking allowed; 10 Tennis nearby; 11 Swimming nearby; 12 Golf nearby; 13 Skiing nearby; 14 May be booked through a travel agent.

MONTAGUE

Lady Catherine's Bed and Breakfast

Murray Harbour North, Rural Route 4, C0A 1R0
(902) 962-3426; (800) 661-3426

Stay in a large Victorian-style home over-looking the Northumberland Strait on the scenic King's Byway. Miles of beaches for walking and swimming, two golf courses nearby, a full range of craft shops, and seal watching tours. Surrounded by quaint fishing villages. Just sit and relax on one of two verandas overlooking the water. Bicycles and fishing rods available to the guests. The Old School House Antiques and Collectibles Shop on the grounds carries homemade crafts.

Host: Catherine Currie
Rooms: 5 (SB) $40-50 Canadian
Full Breakfast
Credit Cards: A, B
Notes: 5, 9, 11, 12

Lady Catherine's

Redcliffe Farm Bed and Breakfast

Brooklyn, Rural Route 1, C0A 1R0
(902) 838-2476; (800) 663-3799 (reservations only)

Vera Bates, on Route 317, ten minutes from Wood Islands ferry. Sheep farm. Three very large bedrooms in tastefully renovated 200-year-old farmhouse. Anne Shirley Dolls studio on premises. Hand-sculptured origi-nal porcelain Anne and Matthew dolls as well as antique reproductions. Doll-making classes with six weeks advance notice. Dinner available with advance notice. Leashed pets welcome.

Rooms: 3 (SB) $40-48
Full and Continental Breakfast
Credit Cards: F
Notes: 8, 9, 10, 11, 12

MURRAY HARBOUR

The Morning Glory Bed and Breakfast

Route 18A, C0A 1V0
(902) 962-3150; (800) 881-3150

Three acres nestled among flowers and vegetable gardens in a scenic fishing village. Three rooms, one with a queen-size bed, one with a double, and one room with a double and single together. Continental breakfast and evening tea included. One and one-half bath, color TV, and VCR. Five minutes to beaches, churches, Kings Castle Park, restaurants, seal watching tours, and gift shops. Twenty minutes from Wood Islands ferry. Open June 1 through September 30.

Hosts: David and Lillian Rourke
Rooms: 3 (SB) $40
Continental Breakfast
Credit Cards: A, B
Notes: 7, 8, 9, 10, 11, 14

MURRAY RIVER

Bayberry Cliff Inn Bed and Breakfast

Rural Route 4, Little Sands, C0A 1W0
(902) 962-3395

On the edge of a 40-foot cliff, the inn consists of two converted post-and-beam barns decorated with antiques and marine art. Stairs to the shore allow for swimming, tubing, snorkeling, and beachcombing. Seal boat tours and bird watching tours nearby, as well as fine restaurants and craft shops.

NOTES: Credit cards accepted: A MasterCard; B Visa; C American Express; D Discover; E Diners Club; F Other; 2 Personal checks accepted; 3 Lunch available; 4 Dinner available; 5 Open all year; 6 Pets welcome;

Three private baths and one shared bath are available. Fully applianced, furnished apartment with two bedrooms also available at a weekly rate. Closed from October 1 to May 1.

Hosts: Nancy and Don Perkins
Rooms: 4 (3 PB; 1 SB) $60-95
Apartment: $640
Full Breakfast
Credit Cards: A, B
Notes: 7, 8, 9, 11, 12, 14

O'LEARY

Smallman's Bed and Breakfast

Knutsford, Rural Route 1, C0B 1V0
(902) 859-3469

Smallman's is on the west end of the island on Route 142 about 13 kilometers from Route 2. The bed and breakfast is a split-level home with two baths in a quiet country area. Churches, museums, swimming at the beaches, and gift shops nearby. Can watch wool being processed into yarn, blankets, and such at woolen mill. Racehorses on the premises and a track that many people use to walk, jog, or run. Deep-sea fishing can be arranged. See the beautiful red cliffs of Prince Edward Island. Also Anne of Green Gables show and museum. Smoking restricted.

Hosts: Arnold and Eileen Smallman
Rooms: 4 (SB) $32.75-44.50
Full and Continental Breakfast
Credit Cards: None
Notes: 3, 4, 5, 8, 10, 11, 12, 13, 14

Thomas Bed and Breakfast

Rural Route 3, C0B 1V0
(902) 859-3209

A friendly hospitality extended to guests in our quiet, Heritage country home near the popular Mill River Championship Golf Course. A rural setting offering uncrowded beaches, biking, and fishing. Dining facilities nearby. Four rooms on second floor share a bath, and one room with two beds and private bath on first floor. Open June 15 through September 5. Full breakfast by request.

Hosts: Harry and Grace Thomas
Rooms: 5 (1 PB; 4 SB) $30-40
Continental Breakfast
Credit Cards: None
Notes: 7, 8, 10, 11, 12, 14

RICHMOND

Mom's Bed 'n' Breakfast

C0B 1Y0
(902) 854-2419

In a quiet village in unspoiled Prince County. One hour from Charlottetown. An 1875 Heritage home, modern comfort, cherished past. Four rooms: three with double beds, one has private bath; one with two doubles and powder room. Parlor with piano. Private dining area, two verandas. Short drive to sandy beaches, Mill River Golf, village store, service station, crafts. Smoking on veranda. Reservations recommended. Bicycle storage. Open from May to October 15. Off-season rates before June 28 and after September 6. Weekly rates on request.

Hostess: Erma Gaudet-MacArthur
Rooms: 5 (1 PB; 4 SB) $35-65
Full Breakfast
Credit Cards: B
Notes: 2, 8, 9, 10, 11, 12

SOURIS

The Matthew House Inn

15 Breakwater Street, C0A 2B0
(902) 687-3461

Award-winning Victorian Heritage inn harborside near Magdalen Islands ferry. Rated four stars by Canada Select, the rooms have queen-size beds, private baths, telephones, cable TV and VCRs, period art, and antiques. Guests enjoy the library, parlor, and porches with oceanviews. Bicycles, spa, exercise room, harbor boatslip, and antique shop are available. Elegant fireside breakfasts, picnic lunches, and gourmet candlelit dining served daily, utilizing the delicious produce and herbs from hosts' own garden.

Hosts: Linda Anderson and Emma Cappelluzzo
Rooms: 6 (PB) $85-140
Full Breakfast
Credit Cards: A, B, C, E
Notes: 2, 3, 4, 7, 8, 9, 10, 11, 12, 14

SUMMERSIDE

Arbor Inn

380 MacEwen Road. C1N 4X8
(902) 436-6847; (800) 361-6847 (reservations only)

Minutes from downtown Summerside and a pleasant drive from beaches and attractions. Offering a range of accommodations from the basic cozy room, for the traveler on a budget, to the elegant royalty suite featuring a canopied bed, Jacuzzi, soft lighting, and music, a popular choice for honeymooners. Kitchen/TV room for guests' use. Cot and playpen are available. Royalty suite is open all year. The other rooms are open May through September. Special romance package rates are available.

Hosts: Ian and Joann Doughart
Rooms: 7 (4 PB; 3 SB) $35-95
Continental Breakfast
Credit Cards: A, B
Notes: 7, 8, 9, 11, 12, 14

Country at Heart Bed and Breakfast

Rural Route 3, C1N 4J9
(902) 436-9879; (800) 463-9879

Welcome to this home on Route 181, Taylor Road in North Bedeque, a 20-minute drive from Borden ferry, in a modern two-story home in the heart of scenic farmland. Quiet relaxing surroundings. Three brightly decorated rooms, each with a double bed and shared bath; also one room with an en suite. Off-season rates available September 16 to June 15. Complimentary evening snack is served.

Hosts: Carl and Vivian Wright
Rooms: 4 (1 PB; 3 SB) $34-48
Continental Breakfast
Credit Cards: None
Notes: 5, 7, 8

Silver Fox Inn

61 Granville Street, C1N 2Z3
(902) 436-4033

For more than a century, proud owners have carefully preserved the beauty of these spacious rooms with their fireplaces and fine woodwork. Combining modern comfort with the cherished past, the Silver Fox Inn offers accommodations for 12 guests. Its six bedrooms, each with private bath, feature period furnishings.

Host: Julie Simmons
Rooms: 6 (PB) $65-80
Continental Breakfast
Credit Cards: A, B, C
Notes: 5, 9, 10, 11, 12, 13, 14

The Smallmans

329 Poplar Avenue, C1N 2B7
(902) 436-5892; (902) 886-2846

Scenic, tranquil setting on spacious grounds overlooking the beautiful Stanley River. Features walking, bird watching, floating dock, boating, and swimming. Near Cavendish, trails, fishing, Green Gables, lobster suppers, beaches, crafts, golf, antiques, theater, and amusement parks. Large island stone fireplace, color TV and VCR. Also grill, boat, patios, and picnic tables. Full breakfast includes homemade jams and muffins. Complimentary evening coffee. Open early June to late September. Credit cards may be accepted for deposit only.

Hosts: Helen and George Smallman
Rooms: 3 (SB) $35-45
Full Breakfast
Credit Cards: A, B
Notes: 2, 8, 9, 10, 11, 12

NOTES: Credit cards accepted: A MasterCard; B Visa; C American Express; D Discover; E Diners Club; F Other; 2 Personal checks accepted; 3 Lunch available; 4 Dinner available; 5 Open all year; 6 Pets welcome;

VICTORIA BY THE SEA _____

The Victorian Village Inn

P.O. Box 1, C1A 5T1
(902) 658-2483

The Victoria Village Inn, circa 1886, offers quality service and elegant surroundings; a holiday haven. Nestled in Victoria-by-the-Sea, 25 minutes west of Charlottetown, the inn neighbors a theater, chocolate factory, shops, art galleries, and beaches. Sail, bicycle, or beachcomb. Laze away a summer's afternoon. Picnic lunches available.

Hosts: Pam Stevenson and Jay de Nottbeck
Rooms: 6 (3 PB; 3 SB) $60-100
Continental Breakfast
Credit Cards: B
Notes: 5, 7, 11, 12

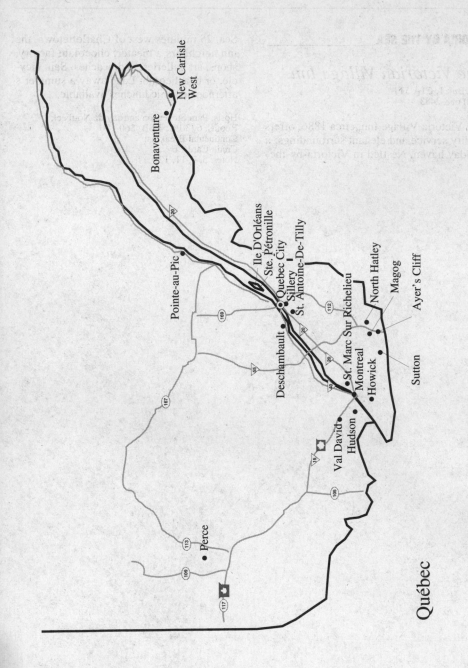

Québec

AYER'S CLIFF

Auberge Ripplecove Inn

700 Ripplecove Road, J0B 1C0
(819) 838-4296; FAX (819) 838-5541

On the shores of Lake Massawippi, Ripplecove Inn offers designer-appointed rooms and suites; many with fireplaces, whirlpool baths, and private balconies. One of only eight hotels in the province awarded AAA four-diamond classification for both food and lodging. Called a "Club Med of the North" by Fodor's, Ripplecove Inn also offers year-round recreational activities, from skiing to sailing, on-site. No smoking allowed in suites.

Hosts: Jeffrey and Debr Stafford
Rooms: 26 (PB) $126-178 (Canadian)
Full Breakfast
Credit Cards: A, B, C
Notes: 3, 4, 5, 8, 9, 10, 11, 12, 13, 14

BONAVENTURE

Bay View Manor

395, Route 132, Bonaventure East, Box 21
New Carlisle, G0C 1Z0
(418) 752-2725; (418) 752-6718

Comfortable seaside home beside 18-hole Fauvel golf course, near Bonaventure East. Lighthouse, on the ruggedly beautiful Gaspé Peninsula of eastern coastal Québec, across the Baie des Chaleurs from northern New Brunswick. Once a country store and rural post office, this home now welcomes guests from all over the world to this spectacular location. Fresh eggs, fruit, produce from the farm, freshly baked goods, homemade jams at breakfast. Hear the waves, view the sunsets, visit Acadian and United Empire Loyalist museums, fossil sites, archaeological caves, bird sanctuary, huge national parks. Play tennis, canoe, fish, hike, swim, and golf.

Host: Helen Sawyer
Rooms: 5 (1 PB; 4 SB) $35
Full Breakfast
Credit Cards: None
Notes: 5, 8, 10, 11, 12, 13

DESCHAMBAULT

Auberge Chemin Du Roy

106 St. Laurent, G0A 1S0
(418) 286-6958

Only 40 minutes from Québec, the town of Deschambault invites guests to discover its historic past by staying at this Victorian inn. The antiques evoke a feeling of serenity and romance near the fireplace. Guests can also relax with the murmuring waterfall in front of the house and the St. Lawrence River breezes.

Hosts: Francine Bouthat and Gilles Laberge
Rooms: 8 (4 PB; 4 SB) $59-74
Full Breakfast
Credit Cards: B
Notes: 4, 5, 8, 9, 10, 11, 12

GEORGEVILLE

Auberge Georgeville

71 chemin Channel, J0B 1T0
(819) 843-8683; FAX (819) 843-5045

NOTES: Credit cards: A MasterCard; B Visa; C American Express; D Discover; E Diners Club; F Other; 2 Personal checks accepted; 3 Lunch available; 4 Dinner available; 5 Open all year; 6 Pets welcome; 7 No smoking; 8 Children welcome; 9 Social drinking allowed; 10 Tennis nearby; 11 Swimming nearby; 12 Golf nearby; 13 Skiing nearby; 14 May be booked through a travel agent.

Twelve miles from Rock Island, Vermont border. Lovely Victorian mansion in immaculately preserved Loyalist village near Lake Memphremagog. Beacon to travelers since 1890, offers charm, intimacy, and character of hideaways. Exquisite, intuitive, and seasonal cuisine emphasizing local produce and regional specialties. All-season outdoor activities (local or nearby), museums, art galleries, and craft shops. Heritage sites and exhibits. Summer theaters, concert halls, sporting events, etc.

Hosts: Monique and Jacques Morissette
Rooms: 12 (8 PB; 4 SB) $88-98 Canadian
Full Breakfast
Credit Cards: A, B
Notes: 4, 9, 10, 11, 12, 13

HOWICK

Hazelbrae Farm

1650 English River Road, J0S 1G0
(514) 825-2390

Come and savor the peaceful surroundings in a spacious, comfortable fifth-generation dairy farmhouse. Homemade specialties for breakfast. Enjoy in-ground pool or visiting by back yard campfire. Less than one hour from Montréal and close to New York State border. The hosts have been welcoming guests for more than ten years.

Hosts: John and Gloria Peddie
Rooms: 4 (1 PB; 3 SB) $50
Full Breakfast
Credit Cards: None
Notes: 2, 3, 4, 5, 7, 8, 11, 12

Hazelbrae Farm

HUDSON

Riversmead Bed and Breakfast

245 Main Road, J0P 1H0
(514) 458-5053

A fine century-old Georgian brick home set on large grounds with a swimming pool. This quiet and beautiful village on the shores of the Ottawa River offers fine restaurants, antique stores, excellent shopping, bicycle routes, and easy access to Montréal or Ottawa. Riversmead was built in 1850 by host Fred Henshaw's great-grandfather, who was a riverboat ship owner and local businessman. Delicious breakfasts and warm hospitality are offered either on the sunny porch or in the Victorian dining room.

Hosts: Naomi and Fred Henshaw
Rooms: 5 (SB) $65
Full Breakfast
Credit Cards: None
Notes: 2, 5, 7, 9, 10, 11, 12, 13

ILE D'ORLÉANS

La Maison Sous les Arbres au Bord de L'eau

1415 chemin Royal, St.-Laurent, G0A 3Z0
(418) 828-9442; FAX (418) 828-9442

This home is ten minutes from Old Québec and close to the St. Lawrence River. Very quiet. Enjoy the wildlife during vacation in this home. The pool is open after 5:00 P.M. Enjoy breakfast in the Glass House, which faces the garden and river. Each room has a private entrance and gallery. No smoking. Cats in residence.

Hosts: Germaine and Louis Dumas
Rooms: 3 (1 PB; 2 SB) $60
Full Breakfast
Credit Cards: None
Notes: 5, 7, 8, 10, 11, 12, 13

Le Mas de L'Isle

155 chemin Royal, St.-Jean, G0A 3W0
(418) 829-1213

NOTES: Credit cards accepted: A MasterCard; B Visa; C American Express; D Discover; E Diners Club; F Other; 2 Personal checks accepted; 3 Lunch available; 4 Dinner available; 5 Open all year; 6 Pets welcome;

Le Mas de L'Isle is on the beautiful Île d'Orléans on a little cliff in the peaceful village of St. Jean. French and English are spoken. The breakfast is unforgettable, and the view of the St. Lawrence River is breathtaking. Guests can relax, read, or listen to music in the family room. Cat, Cannelle, on the premises. Only a 30-minute drive to Québec City and la joie de vivre of French Canada.

Hosts: Yolande and Claude Dumesnil
Rooms: 3 (SB) $55
Full Breakfast
Credit Cards: B
Notes: 5, 7, 8, 10, 11, 12, 13, 14

MAGOG

Germain's Bed and Breakfast

142 Merry Nord, J1X 2E8
(819) 847-0476

In the center of Magog, a lovely Victorian home opens its doors to welcome guests. Whether guests opt for the tranquility of the gardens or benefit from the numerous recreational tourist attractions nearby, this oasis of peace awaits. For a short or extended visit, guests are welcome to the Germain home.

Host: Darquise Pratt-Germain
Rooms: 4 $55
Continental Breakfast
Credit Cards: None
Notes: 5, 7, 8, 9, 10, 11, 12, 13, 14

MONTRÉAL

Armor Inn

151 Sherbrooke Est., H2X 1C7
(514) 285-0140

Armor Inn is a charming little European-style hotel in the heart of downtown Montréal, near Prince Arthur and St. Denis Streets. Just a 15-minute walk from Old Montréal, the Palais des Congrès, or shopping in Montréal's network of underground shopping malls. Warm family atmosphere.

Room rate includes a delicious breakfast. Parking available.

Host: Annick Morvan
Rooms: 15 (7 PB; 8 SB) $38-75
Continental Breakfast
Credit Cards: A, B
Notes: 5, 7, 8, 14

Auberge de la Fontaine

1301 East Rachel Street, H2J 2K1
(514) 597-0166; (800) 597-0597

Guests will be warmly welcomed in this charming bed and breakfast inn in front of Parc la Fontaine, an 84-acre park close to the downtown area. The 21 air-conditioned rooms and suites, some with whirlpool bath, others with terrace or balcony, are beautiful, comfortable, and will make guests feel at home. Enjoy a generous Continental buffet and free access to the kitchen for snacks. Take this opportunity to discover the exclusive shops, restaurants, and art galleries of the Plateau Mont-Royal, typical of French Montréal.

Hosts: Céline Boudreau and Jean Lamothe
Rooms: 21 (PB) $99-175
Continental Breakfast
Credit Cards: A, B, C, E, F
Notes: 5, 7, 8, 10, 11, 14

A Bed and Breakfast— A Downtown Network

3458 Laval Avenue, H2X 3C8
(514) 289-9749; (800) 267-5180
FAX (514) 287-7387

1. Downtown, turn-of-the-century home. This restored Victorian home features a marble fireplace, original hardwood floors, and a skylight. The host offers two charmingly decorated double rooms and Grandma's quilts in the winter. Guests can bird watch on the balcony or have a challenging game of Trivial Pursuit in the evening. Full breakfast. $35-55.

2. Be in the heart of everything! The big bay window of Bob's 90-year-old restored

A Bed and Breakfast—A Downtown Network (continued)

home overlooks the city's most historic park. Original woodwork and detail add to the charm of this nine-room home, where a double and triple are offered. The neighborhood is famous for excellent "bring your own wine" restaurants, and the host knows them all. Full breakfast. $35-75.

3. Downtown double off Sherbrooke Street. This antique-filled apartment on Drummond Street is tastefully decorated and only two minutes from the Museum of Fine Arts and all shopping. Mount-Royal Park is nearby, and McGill University is just two blocks away. The hosts pamper guests with a gourmet breakfast and invite them for a sherry in the evening. One double room, shared bath. $55.

4. Downtown, in the heart of the Latin Quarter. Enjoy the superb location of this restored traditional Québecoise home. The host, active in the restaurant business, offers two sunlit doubles and one triple with a bay window opening onto a typical Montréal scene. The privacy of this tastefully furnished home is perfect for first or second honeymoons. Shared bath, full breakfast. $55-75.

6. When traveling to Québec City, stop at this landmark home built in 1671 facing the beautiful St. Lawrence River. The hostess, a blue-ribbon chef, offers a memorable breakfast featuring quiche Floriane. For an unforgettable stay, guests are invited to experience the warmth and hospitality of a typical Québecoise home. Two enchanting doubles. Full breakfast. $55.

7. This Old Montréal landmark offers eight guest rooms and one suite. Decorated with

a combination of antiques and contemporary pieces, the guest rooms are spacious and air-conditioned. All have private baths in marble, some with Jacuzzi. In winter, snuggle before a crackling fire with a good book. Within strolling distance of Notre Dame church, fine restaurants, shops, and museums. Enjoy the richness of Montréal's heritage. Full gourmet breakfast. $75-95.

Bed and Breakfast à Montréal

P.O. Box 575, Snowdon Station, H3X 3T8
(514) 738-9410; (800) 738-4338
FAX (514) 735-7493

In the finest private homes and condo apartments, carefully selected for comfort, cleanliness, and location. Many are within walking distance of Old Montréal and the Convention Centre. All of the hosts are fluent in English and will enhance any visit with suggestions, outgoing personalities, and delicious breakfasts. Stay long enough to visit Old Montréal, the lively Latin Quarter, the Underground City, Botanical Gardens, Mount-Royal Park, and St. Joseph's Oratory, among others. Visits can also be arranged to Québec City. Coordinator: Marian Kahn.

Brigette's Bed and Breakfast. Brigette's love of art and antiques is obvious in this fabulous three-story townhouse. Fireplace, cozy living room, and a view of the city's most historic park all add to the charm of this home. One double with brass bed, duvet, antique pieces, and guests' own bathroom. Experience nearby "bring your own wine" restaurants. $50-70.

Jacky's Bed and Breakfast. This interior designer-hostess has created warmth and charm in this elegant downtown condo, with treasures collected from India and New Mexico. The guest room has a queen-size bed and private bathroom facilities. Sherbrooke Street, the Museum of Fine Arts, and the city's best shopping are all just two minutes away. $65-85.

NOTES: Credit cards accepted: A MasterCard; B Visa; C American Express; D Discover; E Diners Club;
F Other; 2 Personal checks accepted; 3 Lunch available; 4 Dinner available; 5 Open all year; 6 Pets welcome;

Johanna's Bed and Breakfast. This elegant hostess invites guests to this bright, airy, two-story home filled with European style. An avid gardener, she is pleased to share the joys of the garden with guests. This Westmount home is just five minutes from downtown. One double with a private bathroom is offered. $60-70.

Marian's Bed and Breakfast. Stay in this 14th-floor apartment and enjoy magnificent views of St. Joseph's Oratory and Mount-Royal Park. Guests delight in the host's special pelican collection and the textile hangings collected during international travels. One charming double room with private bath is available. Downtown is just five minutes away. $45-65.

Martha's Bed and Breakfast. Guests can walk from Martha's house to Montréal's hockey arena, the Forum, or the city's most elegant shopping complex, Westmount Square. Stenciled glass windows, original woodwork and detail, and smart period furnishings are just some of the features of this bed and breakfast. $50-70.

St. Antoine Street Bed and Breakfast. Share hosts' turn-of-the-century home featuring Victorian fireplaces, high ceilings, golden wood floors, oak paneled staircase, lovely decor, and furnishings. Three double beds each with private bathrooms available. Music and TV room exclusively for guests as well. $70-85.

Downtown Montréal Bed and Breakfast and Apartments

3523 Jeanne-Mance, H2X 2K2
(514) 845-0431

In the heart of downtown, close to all festivals, and the convention center. Color TV, radio, full breakfast. Private guest kitchen.

Limited parking available. Also, beautiful downtown apartments, all furnished for short or long rentals. Recommended by the French guide *Le Routard*, "certainly one of our best addresses."

Host: Bruno Bernard
Rooms: 7 (4 PB; 3 SB) $60-70
Full Breakfast
Credit Cards: A, B, C
Notes: 5, 14

La Maison de Grand-Pré

4660 rue de Grand-Pré, H2T 2H7
(514) 843-6458; FAX (514) 843-8691

Built in 1865, this house has maple trees out front and a small park behind. Four double rooms have fans. Guests share two large bathrooms that have showers and old-fashioned tubs. A balcony and reading-smoking room are also available. Breakfast includes hot breads and croissants fresh daily from the neighborhood bakery, fruits from the open market, homemade crêpes, French toast, omelets, and espresso. Tea, cookies, and fruit are served as a welcome snack. The Métro station is a four-minute walk from the house, and the boutiques, outdoor cafés, and restaurants of St. Denis Street are one block away. The host, a former university professor, is bilingual. Canadian personal checks accepted only.

Host: Jean-Paul Lauzon
Rooms: 4 (SB) $45-65
Full Breakfast
Credit Cards: None
Notes: 5, 7, 8, 9, 11, 14

Manoir Ambrose

3422 Stanley, H3A 1R8
(514) 288-6922; FAX (514) 288-5757

A small Victorian-style mansion. Comfortable and quiet at reasonable rates. Right in the heart of the action.

Host: Lucie Gagnon Séguin
Rooms: 22 (15 PB; 7 SB) $40-70
Continental Breakfast
Credit Cards: A, B
Notes: 5, 8, 11, 14

7 No smoking; 8 Children welcome; 9 Social drinking allowed; 10 Tennis nearby; 11 Swimming nearby; 12 Golf nearby; 13 Skiing nearby; 14 May be booked through a travel agent.

A Montréal Oasis Bed and Breakfast

3000 chemin de Breslay, H3Y 2G7
(514) 935-2312

This spacious home is in what is known as the Priest Farm District (once a holiday resort for priests). With original lead windows and slanted ceilings on the third floor. In a beautiful downtown neighborhood with large trees and pretty gardens. Swedish hostess is world traveled, loves all kinds of music and African art. Friendly blue cream Siamese cat in residence. Hostess also operates a small bed and breakfast network of homes in downtown, Old Montréal, and the Latin Quarter.

Host: Lena Blondel
Rooms: 30 (5 PB; 25 SB) $40-90
Full Breakfast
Credit Cards: None
Notes: 5, 7, 9, 13, 14

NEW CARLISLE WEST

Bay View Farm

Box 21, 337 Main Highway, Route 132, G0C 1Z0
(418) 752-2725; (418) 752-6718

Between New Carlisle and Bonaventure on the rugged and beautiful Baie des Chaleurs coastline of Québec's Gaspé Peninsula on Route 132. Seaside accommodations include five comfortable guest rooms. Full

Bay View Farm

country breakfast is made from fresh farm and garden products. Additional light meals by arrangement. Handicrafts on display. August Bay View Folk Festival, museums, historic sites, Fauvel Golf Course, beaches, lighthouse, hiking, bird watching. Breathtakingly beautiful panoramic seascapes. Tranquil and restful environment. Also available is a fully equipped seaside country house for $350 per week.

Host: Helen Sawyer
Rooms: 5 (1 PB; 4 SB) $35
Country House: $350
Full Breakfast
Credit Cards: None
Notes: 3, 4, 5, 8, 10, 11, 12, 13

Cedar Gables

NORTH HATLEY

Cedar Gables

4080 Magog Road, Box 355, J0B 2C0
(819) 842-4120

Established in 1985 as the area's premier bed and breakfast, Cedar Gables is a large, tastefully decorated home, circa 1890s, at the lakeside on Lake Massawippi in the heart of Québec's eastern townships. Easily accessible, the inn is ten minutes from the U.S./Canada I-91/Autoroute 55 northeast corridor. The five guest rooms have private baths en suite. Four rooms have king-size beds and the fifth, a canopied double. It is a five-minute walk to a unique resort village with shopping,

NOTES: Credit cards accepted: A MasterCard; B Visa; C American Express; D Discover; E Diners Club; F Other; 2 Personal checks accepted; 3 Lunch available; 4 Dinner available; 5 Open all year; 6 Pets welcome;

browsing, and a full range of dining. Detailed brochure available. Limited smoking. Children over 12 welcome.

Hosts: Ann and Don Fleischer
Rooms: 5 (PB) $80-104
Full Breakfast
Credit Cards: A, B, C
Notes: 2, 5, 6, 9, 10, 11, 12, 13, 14

PERCÉ (GASPÉ PENINSULA)

Hotel la Normandie

P.O. Box 129, G0C 2L0
(418) 782-2112; FAX (481) 782-2337

Oceanfront location facing Percé Rock. Modern units and suites with private baths. Award-winning cuisine. Meeting facilities available. Exercise room and sauna. Cordial surroundings and courteous service, all to meet guests' every need.

Host: Michel Boudreau
Rooms: 45 (PB) $79-119
Continental Breakfast
Credit Cards: A, B, C, E, F
Notes: 4, 6, 8, 10, 11, 12, 14

POINTE-AU-PIC

Auberge Donohue Inc.

145 rue Principale C.P. 211, G0T 1M0
(418) 665-4377; FAX (418) 665-3634

Right by the St. Lawrence River and walking distance from the casino. Cozy place with large rooms. Most of the rooms have a view of the river, fireplace, Jacuzzi, balcony, and queen-size beds. Wonderful place for a quiet stay. Isolated from the neighborhood by trees and gardens. Large lot with outdoor pool. Large public rooms. Furnished outdoor patio to have breakfast or just to relax. Walking distance from every important tourist attraction. Ninety miles east of Québec City.

Hosts: Monique and Orval Aumont
Rooms: 19 (PB) $60-149
Continental Breakfast
Credit Cards: A, B
Notes: 8, 9, 10, 11, 12, 13, 14

QUÉBEC CITY

Bed and Breakfast à Montréal

P.O. Box 575, Snowdon Station, H3X 3T8
(514) 738-9410; (800) 738-4338
FAX (514) 735-7493

A Québec City Choice. Delight in this restored 17th-century home in Old Québec offering three guest rooms with private bathrooms. Many special architectural features and antique furnishings. This bilingual host couple and their dog welcome guests. $55-85.

Le Chateau de Pierre

17 Avenue Sainte-Genevieve, G1R 4A8
(418) 694-0429

This old English mansion is in the heart of this historic city. Very comfortable rooms have private baths and are nicely decorated. Near all historical activities. Open year-round.

Hosts: Richard and Lily Couturier
Rooms: 16 (PB) $65-105
Continental Breakfast
Credit Cards: A, B
Notes: 2, 5, 13

Hayden's Wexford House

450 rue Champlain, G1K 4J3
(418) 524-0525

Ancestral home built in the beginning of the 18th century at the heart of the Heritage and near Old Québec City. Near many points of interest. In summer, relax in the little flower garden and in winter by the fireside. Enjoy breakfast in a warm decor and relaxed atmosphere. Spectacular river view from guest rooms. Open year-round. Apartment also available; please call for rates.

Host: Michelle Paquet Rivière
Rooms: 3 (SB) $65-70 Canadian
Full Breakfast
Credit Cards: B
Notes: 2, 5, 8, 9, 10, 11, 12, 13

7 No smoking; 8 Children welcome; 9 Social drinking allowed; 10 Tennis nearby; 11 Swimming nearby; 12 Golf nearby; 13 Skiing nearby; 14 May be booked through a travel agent.

Hôtel Marie Rollet

81 rue Sainte-Anne, G1R 3X4
(418) 694-9271

Built in 1876 by the Ursulines Order, the Marie Rollet offers the ancestral charm of a turn-of-the-century European manor. Guests will be captivated by its warm woodwork and its tranquility and serenity. All area attractions can be reached by foot. Two rooms offer a functional fireplace and most have air conditioning. A rooftop terrace with a garden view gives guests an opportunity to relax in a calm and serene environment.

Hosts: Gerald Giroux and Diane Chouinard
Rooms: 10 (PB) $55-99
No Breakfast
Credit Cards: A, B
Notes: 5, 8, 10, 11, 12, 13, 14

Hôtel Marie Rollwt

Au Petit Hotel

3 ruelle des Ursulines, G1R 3Y6
(418) 694-0965; FAX (418) 692-4320

In the heart of Old Québec, Au Petit Hotel offers quiet surroundings with a warm and hospitable atmosphere, such as the Ursulines convent, the Citadel, and Le Château Frontenac. Discriminating gour-
mets will have no trouble finding neighborhood restaurants, smart boutiques, and all kinds of entertainment.

Host: The Tim Family
Rooms: 16 (PB) $45-70
Continental Breakfast
Credit Cards: A, B, C
Notes: 5, 8, 9

Tim House

84 rue Saint-Louis, G1R 3Z5
(418) 694-0776

Built in 1900 on what is now one of Québec City's main streets, Tim House offers guests the luxury and charm of its Victorian architecture, which is complemented by its convenience to area attractions. All guests have access to the family room on the second floor of the house. Breakfast is served between 8:00 and 10:00 A.M. in a beautiful dining room, also on the second floor. All taxes are included in rates. Free parking available.

Host: Tim Supheavy
Rooms: 3 (1 PB; 2 SB) $44-70
Continental Breakfast
Credit Cards: A, B, C
Notes: 5, 8, 9, 13

ST.-ANICET

La Ferme Chez-Nous: Solange Caza Leduc

1128 chemin Rivière la Guerre, J0S 1M0
(514) 264-6533

From Montréal, take Highway 132 and Highway 236 at St. Barke and Cozaville. From Toronto, cross the river via toll bridge at Cornwall to Fort Covinton, then take Route 132 to Cozaville. La Ferme Chez-Nous is a 150-acre farm with a historic view and patio. River fishing is available on the property. Golfing, bicycling, swimming, hunting, and cross-country skiing. St.-Anicent village is only five miles away. La Ferme Chez-Nous stands on the shores of the beautiful Lac St.-François with the river running through the property. "You will feel at home in our home."

Rooms: 3 (1 PB; 2 SB) $28
Full and Continental Breakfast
Credit Cards: F
Notes: 2, 3, 4, 5, 6, 8, 9, 10, 11, 12, 13, 14

ST.-ANTOINE-DE-TILLY

Auberge Manoir de Tilly

3854 chemin de Tilly, G0S 2C0
(418) 886-2407

Manoir de Tilly dates from 1786 and is an authentic manor built by one of the king's representatives. The chef offers a highly praised cuisine, where regional farm and sea products are lovingly prepared for guests. In 1990 a 32-room pavilion was added, as well as a health center and conference facilities. The rooms are lovingly decorated and offer calm and tranquility. The manor is only a few kilometers from historic Québec City. Golf and tennis courts nearby. Call for rates.

Host: Jocelyne Gagnon
Rooms: 32 (PB)
Full Breakfast
Credit Cards: A, B, C
Notes: 4, 5, 8, 10, 12

ST.-MARC-SUR-RICHELIEU

Auberge Handfield

555 Richelieu, J0L 2E0
(514) 584-2226

This quintessentially French inn is on the Richelieu River in an ancient French-Canadian village where French is universally spoken. The somewhat rustic decor of this venerable 150-year-old mansion is complemented by antiques and locally crafted furnishings. A marina and other resort facilities, including a health club, and outstanding French cuisine make this a most enjoyable holiday experience.

Host: Conrad Handfield
Rooms: 53 (PB) $80-110
Full Breakfast

Credit Cards: A, B, C, D, E
Notes: 3, 4, 5, 7, 8, 9, 10, 11, 12, 13, 14

Hostellerie les Trois Tilleuls

290 rue Richelieu, J0L 2E0
(514) 584-2231

The Hostellerie les Trois Tilleuls is a charming inn on the banks of the Richelieu River, a short 30 minutes from Montréal. The 24 rooms with balconies overlook the river. The dining room features authentic French cuisine with an extensive wine list of exceptional vintages.

Host: Michel Aubriot
Rooms: 24 (PB) $84-145
Full Breakfast
Credit Cards: A, B, C, D, E
Notes: 3, 4, 5, 7, 8, 9, 10, 11, 12, 14

STE.-PÉTRONILLE

Auberge la Goéliche Inn

22 chemin du Quai, G0A 4C0
(418) 828-2248; FAX (418) 692-1742

Overhanging the St. Lawrence River, this castlelike inn offers a breathtaking view of Québec City, a 15-minute drive away. It is also close to famous Mont-Ste.-Anne ski center. Its 24 rooms are warmly decorated in rustic French-Canadian style. Outdoor swimming pool. English and Continental breakfasts. Guided tours of historic surroundings available.

Hosts: Janet Duplain, Andrée Marchand,
and Alain Turgeon
Rooms: 24 (PB) $80-130
Full or Continental Breakfast
Credit Cards: A, B, C, F
Notes: 3, 4, 5, 8, 9, 10, 11, 12, 13, 14

SILLERY

Fernlea

2156 rue Dickson, G1T 1C9
(418) 683-3847

Comfortable English-style home and decor, with a fireplace that is especially nice after

7 No smoking; 8 Children welcome; 9 Social drinking allowed; 10 Tennis nearby; 11 Swimming nearby; 12 Golf nearby; 13 Skiing nearby; 14 May be booked through a travel agent.

a day of skiing in the winter. In warm weather the beautiful English garden is a welcome sight, with a patio to relax on after spending a pleasant day in the city. Attractive residential neighborhood where guests may walk, bike, or jog. Québec, with hundreds of wonderful restaurants, is also a city of history. Plan to spend several days— there is so much to see and do. Tours can be arranged with pickup at the house.

Host: Joyce Butler-Coutts
Rooms: 3 (SB) $45-65
Full Breakfast
Credit Cards: None
Notes: 2, 5, 8, 9, 10, 11, 12, 13, 14

SUTTON

Auberge Schweizer

357 Schweizer, J0E 2K0
(514) 538-2129; FAX (514) 538-2129

Established by a Swiss-German family in 1938, this 130-acre estate overlooks Sutton Valley, 19 kilometers from the Vermont border. The family provides a personal atmosphere, serving garden-grown vegetables, home-baked bread, and meats from the farm. Many hiking trails, two idyllic ponds, and beautiful sunsets make guests' stay an unforgettable experience. Accommodation is double in comfortable rooms and chalets. Single rooms available at extra cost. Shared and private washrooms.

Hosts: Pauline Canzani and Heidi Schweizer
Rooms: 18 (6 PB; 12 SB) $50-125
Full Breakfast
Credit Cards: B
Notes: 2, 4, 5, 7, 8, 9, 10, 11, 12, 13, 14

VAL DAVID

Auberge Charme de Suisse

1459 rue Merette, J0T 2N0
(819) 322-3434

This inn has beautiful and quiet surroundings in the midst of various activities: golf, skiing, swimming, and an outdoor heated swimming pool on the premises. Each room has a private bath and balcony. The host is from Switzerland. Inquire for directions.

Host: Alfred Giger
Rooms: 10 (PB) $65-85
Full Breakfast
Credit Cards: A, B
Notes: 4, 5, 8, 11, 12, 13, 14

Saskatchewan

MEOTA

Lakeside Leisure Bed and Breakfast

P.O. Box 1, S0M 1X0
(306) 892-2145

From the spacious home overlooking Jackfish Lake, there is a spectacular view of the water, rolling farmland, and distant hills. Jackfish Lake is noted for fishing, sailing, and all other water sports. There are sandy beaches and swimming areas to enjoy. Enjoy a refreshing swim in the heated indoor swimming pool. Relax by the fireplace, or just sit and take in the view of Jackfish Lake and the waving grain fields. Choice of poolside rooms with private entrances or in-house rooms, some with private bathrooms. Queen and twin beds. Continental plus breakfast. Pets welcome outside.

Rooms: 6 (2 PB; 4 SB) $60-75
Full and Continental Breakfast
Credit Cards: None
Notes: 2, 7, 8, 9, 10, 11, 12, 13, 14

PARADISE HILL

Country Cottage Bed and Breakfast

P.O. Box 126, S0M 2G0
(306) 344-2137

Accommodation is a 16x32-foot guest house with kitchen (hot plate) for up to seven people. Bathroom separate. Quiet, relaxing rural setting, lots of trees, bushes, wild berries, flowers, farm animals, and birds. Lots of scenic hiking on the cattle ranch. Lakes, swimming pool, historic sites, and skiing nearby. Continental breakfast with homegrown produce on request. RVs, tenters, families with children, pets on leash. Hunters welcome (in season). No smoking in guest house. Extra $10 for each additional person and rates available for single occupancy. Children under six stay free. Different rates apply for tenters and RVs.

Hosts: Robert and Marla Rauser
Rooms: 2 (PB) $35
Continental Breakfast
Credit Cards: None
Notes: 8, 9, 10, 11, 12, 13, 14

WAWOTA

Pleasant Vista Farm

P.O. Box 194, S0G 5A0
(306) 739-2915

The view is wonderful from the 1200-acre mixed farm. This modern home is surrounded by a poplar forest and lots of wildlife, deer, elk, geese, ducks, etc. Hosts raise Aberdeen Angus cattle and beautiful Arabian horses. Close to Moose Mountain provincial park with waterslide, boating, golfing, and bike trails. Skiing in winter. Elk farm close by.

Hosts: George and Doris Husband
Rooms: 3 (SB) $40
Full Breakfast
Credit Cards: None
Notes: 2, 3, 4, 5, 6, 7, 8, 9, 10, 11, 12, 13

---

7 No smoking; 8 Children welcome; 9 Social drinking allowed; 10 Tennis nearby; 11 Swimming nearby; 12 Golf nearby; 13 Skiing nearby; 14 May be booked through a travel agent.

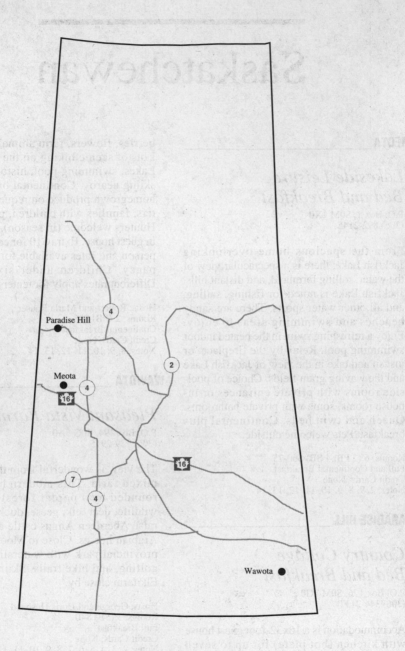

Paradise Hill

Meota

4

16

2

7

4

16

Wawota

Saskatchewan

Puerto Rico

CABO ROJO

Parador Joyuda Beach Hotel

Road 102, KM 11.7, Buzon HC-01 18410, 00623
(809) 851-5650; (800) 981-7575 (office phone)
(800) 443-0266 (U.S.); FAX (809) 255-31750

At the Parador Joyuda Beach Hotel guests are offered a family atmosphere. Enjoy swimming, snorkling, or just relaxing in the sun. The friendly staff is always ready to be of service. Guests can also view the beautiful natural beaches of the Caribbean Sea from our bar area where family and business reunions frequently take place. The hotel is also an ideal location for seminars and special activities.

Rooms: 42 (PB) $65
Continental Breakfast
Credit Cards: A, B, C, D, E, F
Notes: 2, 3, 4, 5, 7, 8, 9, 10, 11, 12, 14

Parador Perichi's

Road 102, KM 14.3, Playa Joyuda, 00623
(809) 851-3131 (0590, 0560, 0620)
FAX (809) 851-0590

Parador Perichi's Hotel, Restaurant, and Cocktail Lounge are in Joyuda, the site of Puerto Rico's famous resorts on the west. Excellence has distinguished Perichi's in its 13 years of hospitality and service. The thirty air-conditioned rooms are furnished with wall-to-wall carpeting, private baths and balconies, color TV, and telephones. Perichi's award-winning restaurant features the finest cuisine. After sunset, meet friends in the well-stocked and cozy lounge. There is live music to enjoy on the weekends at the pool area. The spacious and comfortable banquet room can accommodate up to 300 people—for those who like to combine business with pleasure.

Rooms: 30 (PB) $69.55-90.95
Full Breakfast
Credit Cards: A, B, C, D, E
Notes: 3, 4, 5, 7, 8, 9, 10, 11, 12, 13, 14

CEIBA

Ceiba Country Inn

Road 977, KM 1.2, P.O. Box 1067, 00735
(809) 885-0471; FAX (809) 885-0471

In the hills on the east coast, in a pastoral setting with a view of the sea. Quiet, serene atmosphere with a cozy cocktail lounge. Convenient for trips to El Yunque, Luquillo, San Juan, Vieques, Culebra, and St. Thomas.

Rooms: 9 (PB) $60
Continental Breakfast
Credit Cards: A, B, C, D
Notes: 5, 8, 9, 14

CULEBRA ISLAND

Casa Llave

Calle Escudero 142, P.O. Box 60, 00775-0060
(809) 742-3559

Casa Llave (Key House) is on the bay just one block from the center of town on the main thoroughfare and is ideal for both beach goers and scuba divers. The bayside yard has a picnic table and chairs for enjoying the shade. The rooms have ceiling fans, air conditioning, private entrances, and private baths.

Rooms: 2 (PB) $45-60
Full Breakfast
Credit Cards: None
Notes: 2, 5, 7, 9

7 No smoking; 8 Children welcome; 9 Social drinking allowed; 10 Tennis nearby; 11 Swimming nearby; 12 Golf nearby; 13 Skiing nearby; 14 May be booked through a travel agent.

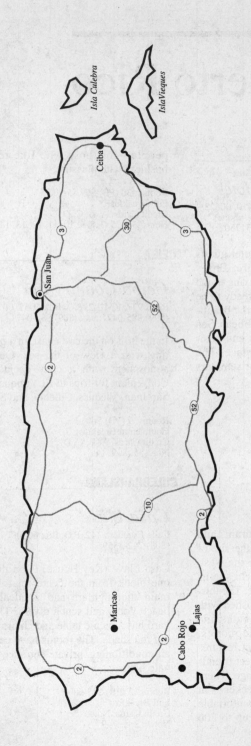

Puerto Rico

Isla Culebra

IslaVieques

Ceiba

3

30

3

San Juan

52

52

2

10

2

2

Maricao

Cabo Rojo

Lajas

2

LAJAS

Parador Posada Porlamar

P.O. Box 405, La Parguera, 00667-0405
(809) 899-4015

Parador Posada Porlamar is beside the Caribbean Sea. The facilities include air-conditioned rooms with private bath, color TV, telephone. Some rooms face the waterfront. Pool facilities will be available in June. Phosphorescent Bay trips available. Nightlife is exciting on weekends. Diving trips available from the Parador. Snorkeling, boating, water skiing, fishing, swimming, among other water activities available from the hotel.

Hosts: Ray Pancorbo and Ernesto Pancorbo
Rooms: 18 (PB) $69.55
Full Breakfast
Credit Cards: A, B, C
Notes: 3, 4, 5, 7, 8, 9, 11, 13, 14

Parador Villa Parguera

P.O. Box 273, 00667
(809) 899-7777

Parador Villa Parguera is on the southwest coast of Puerto Rico in the fishing village of La Parguera, near the famous Phosphorescent Bay. Facilities include a restaurant, bar, and saltwater swimming pool. All rooms have private baths, air conditioning, color TVs, and telephones. Trips may also be arranged for snorkeling and diving, or to the channels and the island of Mata La Gata.

Rooms: 62 (PB) $99.97
Continental Breakfast
Credit Cards: A, B, C, D, E
Notes: 3, 4, 5, 7, 8, 9, 11, 14

MARICAO

La Hacienda Juanita

Road 105, KM 23.5, Box 777, 00606
(809) 838-2550

Built 160 years ago as the main lodge of a coffee plantation, this bed and breakfast offers lush tropical vegetation and verdant views of the mountains. Caressed by the scent of orange, grapefruit, and guava, and kissed by the bright starlight of the mountain elevation. Songs of tropical birds, wide verandas with wicker furniture, and rocking chairs invite lazy siestas.

Host: Luis Rivera-Lugo
Rooms: 21 (PB) $69.55-90.95
Full Breakfast
Credit Cards: A, B, C
Notes: 2, 3, 4, 5, 7, 8, 9, 10, 11, 14

OLD SAN JUAN

The Gallery Inn

Norzagaray #204, 00901
(809) 722-1808; FAX (809) 724-7360

This 300-year-old rambling building overlooks the sea atop the north walls of fascinating Old San Juan. Walking distance to forts, museums, galleries, colorful shops, and numerous restaurants, the inn is home to well-known artist Jan D'Esopo. Although only nine guest bedrooms, visitors have access to many interesting rooms including interior courtyards, galleries, studios, porticos, music room, and rooftop gardens. D'Esopo paintings, silkscreens, sculptures, and castings are everywhere as well as in process in studios throughout the antique-filled spaces. Uneven bricks, cobblestones, and many stairs connect gardens with guest rooms. If guests enjoy watching art being created or wish to commission a portrait, guests will enjoy staying at the Gandias. Inquire about accommodations for pets. No smoking allowed in rooms.

Hosts: Jan D'Esopo and Manuco Gandia
Rooms: 9 (8 PB; 1 SB) $85-175
Continental Breakfast
Credit Cards: A, B, C
Notes: 2, 5, 8, 9, 10, 11, 12, 14

NOTES: Credit cards: A MasterCard; B Visa; C American Express; D Discover; E Diners Club; F Other; 2 Personal checks accepted; 3 Lunch available; 4 Dinner available; 5 Open all year; 6 Pets welcome; 7 No smoking; 8 Children welcome; 9 Social drinking allowed; 10 Tennis nearby; 11 Swimming nearby; 12 Golf nearby; 13 Skiing nearby; 14 May be booked through a travel agent.

SAN JUAN

At Wind Chimes Inn

53 Taft Street, Condado, 00911
(809) 727-4153; (800) 946-3244

At Wind Chimes Inn is a restored Spanish villa with 13 tropical rooms and studios cooled by ceiling fans and air conditioners. We are conveniently in the heart of Condado and Ocean Park, only four miles from the airport and historic Old San Juan. Casinos, night clubs, restaurants, pubs, and cafés are all within walking distance. Cable TV and breakfast included. Condado Beach just steps away.

Rooms: 13 (PB) $60-85
Continental Breakfast
Credit Cards: A, B, C, D
Notes: 5, 7, 8, 9, 10, 11, 12, 14

El Canario Inn

1317 Ashford Avenue, Condado, 00907
(809) 722-3861; (800) 533-2649

San Juan's most historic and unique bed and breakfast. All 25 guest rooms are air-conditioned with private bath, telephone, and cable TV. Beautiful tropical patio areas for relaxation. Only one block to beautiful Condado Beach, casinos, boutiques, and many fine restaurants. El Canario is perhaps

El Canario Inn

the best deal for the vacation dollar in the Caribbean. Higher rates apply when booked through 800-number reservation service.

Hosts: Jude and Keith Olson
Rooms: 25 (PB) $65-90
Continental Breakfast
Credit Cards: A, B, C, D, E
Notes: 5, 8, 9, 14

Green Isle Inn

Calle Uno #36, Villamar, 00979
(809) 726-6433; (800) 677-8860
FAX (809) 268-2415

Beach- and resort-area inn. Featuring the best in room accommodations and value, fully approvedthe Puerto Rico Tourism Company. Cleanliness and comfort are the main concerns. Sixty percent of the guests are repeats or referrals, truly one of the last Carribean bargains. In the heart of Isle Verde, close to the luxury hotels and casinos, famous nightlife, five minutes from the airport, and one block from Puerto Rico's most beautiful beach. TV, air conditioning, two pools, kitchenettes, and telephones.

Hosts: James Wilson and Richard Gonzales
Rooms: 46 (PB) $50-69
Continental Breakfast
Credit Cards: A, B, C
Notes: 3, 4, 5, 6, 7, 8, 9, 10, 11, 12, 13, 14

L'Habitation Beach Guest House

1957 Calle Italia Ocean Park, 00911
(809) 727-2499; FAX (809) 727-2599

L'Habitation Beach is the guest house guests have always looked for: a warm and serene but lively atmosphere. Only a few blocks from the Condado, San Juan's bustling tourist mecca, L'Habitation Beach is on a peaceful tree-lined street and has a sandy beach right at its back yard. Guests may eat or drink al fresco on the patio overlooking the sea. Chairs and beverage service are also provided in the private beach area. All rooms have private bath, air conditioning, and ceiling fan,

NOTES: Credit cards accepted: A MasterCard; B Visa; C American Express; D Discover; E Diners Club; F Other; 2 Personal checks accepted; 3 Lunch available; 4 Dinner available; 5 Open all year; 6 Pets welcome;

double or king-size beds. Remote cable color TV. From the private beach area, enjoy a well-prepared Continental breakfast. Host is ready to give a warm welcome in the lovely surroundings of L'Habitation Beach.

Host: Alain Tasca
Rooms: 9 (PB) $45-85
Continental Breakfast
Credit Cards: A, B, C, D, F
Notes: 3, 5, 6, 8, 11, 14

Ocean Walk Guest House

Atlantic Place #1, 00911
(809) 728-0855; (800) 468-0615
FAX (809) 728-6434

The largest hostelry of its kind in Puerto Rico with primarily an "alternate lifestyle" clientele. Directly on San Juan's finest beach with 44 modest but comfortable rooms and studio apartments from single to quadruple occupancy. Majority have private baths, ceiling fans, and cable TV (daily maid service, of course). The bar and grill patio, between the beach and pool, will keep guests in their chairs longer than they intended.

Rooms: 44 (38 PB; 6 SB) $45-125
Full and Continental Breakfast
Credit Cards: A, B, C, D
Notes: 3, 5, 8, 9, 10, 11, 12, 14

El Prado Inn

1350 Calle Luchetti, 00907
(809) 728-5925; (800) 468-4521

In the most elegant section of San Juan, this small, exclusive inn is perfect for a tour base in San Juan. Continental breakfast is served by the Spanish-style patio and beside the pool. A three-minute walk to major hotels, bars, discos, casinos, and restaurants. All rooms with private baths, cable TV, air conditioners, and fans.

Host: Chris Teseo
Rooms: 22 (PB) $49-89
Continental Breakfast
Credit Cards: A, B, C, D, E
Notes: 5, 6, 7, 8, 9, 10, 11, 14

Tres Palmas Guest House

2212 Park Boulevard, 00979
(809) 727-4617; FAX (809) 727-5434

This impeccably neat, gray Spanish-style house with tile roof is locked behind a wrought-iron gate. The petite hacienda beckons a small group of guests who delight in its intimacy as well as outstanding unobstructed views of the Atlantic just across the roadway. The pleasant and modest guest accommodations boast little touches such as attractive wall coverings, mirrors over the beds, and modern, private baths. All guest rooms have air conditioning, clock radios, and separate outside entrances. There are also three efficiency apartments available in the same building.

Host: Eric Torres
Rooms: 10 (9 PB; 1 SB) $55-100
Continental Breakfast
Credit Cards: A, B, C
Notes: 5, 8, 9, 10, 11, 12, 14

VIEQUES

New Dawn Caribbean Retreat and Guest House

P.O. Box 1512, 00765
(809) 741-0495

This six-room guest house was built by women for outside tropical living and is on five beautiful rural acres on the "undiscovered" island of Vieques. Only three miles from the beach. Each room can accommodate up to three people, offering queen-size beds, a loft, and a shared bath. The outside showers are under the blooming bougainvilleas and hibiscus. The perfect place for a getaway. May 15 through December 14 special low rates for family reunions and groups are available.

Host: Gail Burchard
Rooms: 6 (SB) $45
Continental Breakfast
Credit Cards: None
Notes: 2, 5, 11, 14

7 No smoking; 8 Children welcome; 9 Social drinking allowed; 10 Tennis nearby; 11 Swimming nearby; 12 Golf nearby; 13 Skiing nearby; 14 May be booked through a travel agent.

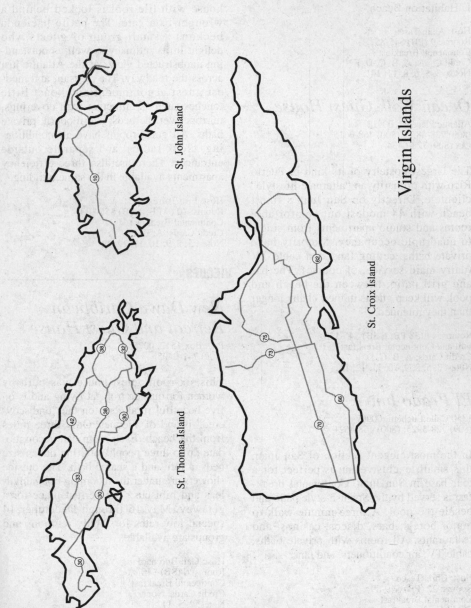

Virgin Islands

St. John Island

St. Croix Island

St. Thomas Island

private bath. A large, luxurious pool overlooks Charlotte Amalie Harbor. Continental breakfast. Gourmet restaurant serving Continental cuisine with West Indian flair is on the premises. Piano lounge with outdoor terrace for dancing. No pets. Smoking permitted. Ten percent gratuity. $95-190.

406. Overlooking Charlotte Amalie Harbor offers comfort, personal attention, hospitality, and real economy. Rooms are cozy and brightly decorated, most with private bath and air conditioning, some with TV. Jacuzzi on patio and honor bar. One cat in residence who is friendly to all. Guest pets welcome with prior arrangement. Continental breakfast. Walk to town in seven minutes. $60-95.

Danish Chalet Inn

P.O. Box 4319, 00803
(809) 774-5764; (800) 635-1531
FAX (809) 777-4886

Family-operated 13-room inn overlooking beautiful Charlotte Amalie Harbor with cool harbor and mountain breezes. Ten minutes from the airport and a five-minute walk to the center of town for duty-free shopping, fine restaurants, and waterfront activities; 15 minutes to world-famous beaches. In-room telephones, sun deck, Jacuzzi, honor bar, free beach towels, and welcoming beverage. Congenial family atmosphere.

Hosts: Frank and Mary Davis
Rooms: 13 (5 PB; 8 SB) $60-95
Continental Breakfast
Credit Cards: A, B
Notes: 5, 8, 9, 10, 11, 12

Galleon House

Box 6577, 00804
(809) 774-6952; (800) 524-2052
FAX (809) 774-6952

Lovely 14-room small hotel in a historic district one block from town. Fantastic harbor view. Warm, hospitable inn with delightful home-cooked breakfast. Freshwater pool,

easy walk to shopping and restaurants. Air-conditioned rooms with balconies, cable TV, telephones, and refrigerators. Call or write for color brochure.

Host: John Slone
Rooms: 14 (12 PB; 2 SB) $49-119
Continental Breakfast
Credit Cards: A, B, C, D
Notes: 5, 7, 8, 9, 11, 12, 14

The Heritage Manor

P.O. Box 90, 00804
(809) 774-3003; (800) 828-0757
FAX (809) 776-9585

Nineteenth-century townhouse in the downtown historic district boasts European charm and congenial atmosphere. Just steps to cafés, restaurants, duty-free shopping, and ferries to St. John and British Virgins. Eight guest rooms have air conditioning, ceiling fans, refrigerators, and some have kitchens. Cable TV available. Pool, sun deck, courtyard, and harbor views.

Host: Susan Murphy
Rooms: 8 (4 PB; 4 SB) $50-130
Continental Breakfast
Credit Cards: A, B, C
Notes: 5, 9, 10, 11, 12, 14

Island View Guest House

P.O. Box 1903, 00803
(809) 774-4270; (800) 524-2023
FAX (809) 774-6167

Island View is a relaxed, casual 15-room guest house between the airport and Charlotte Amalie, perched 545 feet above and overlooking the harbor. An affordable alternative to a costly vacation. An excellent value at moderate prices. Recommended and featured in *Fodor's Guide to the Perfect Vacation*. Full breakfast is available.

Host: Barbara Cooper
Rooms: 15 (13 PB; 2 SB) $45-99
Continental Breakfast
Credit Cards: A, B, C
Notes: 3, 5, 9, 10, 11, 14

7 No smoking; 8 Children welcome; 9 Social drinking allowed; 10 Tennis nearby; 11 Swimming nearby; 12 Golf nearby; 13 Skiing nearby; 14 May be booked through a travel agent.

Mafolie Hotel and Frigate Restaurant

Estate Mafolie #4A, 00802
(809) 774-2790; (800) 225-7035
FAX (809) 774-4091

Breathtaking, world-famous view. Ten minutes from everything. Rates include Continental breakfast and daily beach shuttle to Magens Bay. All rooms have cable TV, air conditioning, and private bath. Large pool deck, lunch and drinks served all day. Home of the Frigate Restaurant. Celebrating 31 years. Seasonal rates.

Hosts: Tony and Lyn Eden
Rooms: 23 (PB) $75-93
Continental Breakfast
Credit Cards: A, B, C
Notes: 3, 4, 5, 8, 9, 10, 11, 12, 14

Pavilions and Pools Hotel

6400 Estate Smith Bay, 00802
(809) 775-6110; (800) 524-2001

On St. Thomas's east end is this unique, small, Caribbean hotel. Romance and relaxation abound as guests enjoy the secluded garden villas and private swimming pools. Each villa has an atrium-style garden shower, floor-to-ceiling sliding glass doors opening onto private terrace and pool. Full kitchen, king-size bed, and living-dining area. Daily Continental breakfast. Complimentary use of snorkel gear and beach towels. Weekly Manager's cocktail party, and a bottle of Cruzan rum and mixers in guests' suite. Five-minute walk to Sapphire Beach.

Hosts: Tammy Waters, Mackenzie Farquhar, and Anna Lotter
Rooms: 25 (PB) $175-255
Continental Breakfast
Credit Cards: A, B, C, D
Notes: 2, 4, 5, 6, 8, 9, 10, 11, 12, 14

Villa Elaine

44 Water Island, 00802
(809) 774-0290

Experience the incredible view from the veranda and enjoy the attractively furnished two bedrooms, two baths, kitchen, living room, dining room, and family room. Enjoy a beautiful, secure, and peaceful retreat on lovely water island. Walk or hike the 500-acre island and its beaches. Swim and snorkel from the property or walk just five minutes to famous Honeymoon Beach. Take a ten-minute ferry ride to St. Thomas and all its attractions. Courtesy service to and from the ferry. Rental includes fully stocked Continental breakfast supplies. Rental is for two people, but will rent to four people if they know each other. Lunch and dinner facilities available. Golf on site.

Hosts: Elaine and James Grissom
Rooms: 2 (PB) $100
Continental Breakfast
Credit Cards: None
Notes: 2, 5, 9, 10, 11, 12